Spanish Dictionary of Business, Commerce and Finance

Diccionario Inglés de Negocios, Comercio y Finanzas

Routledge

Spanish Dictionary of Business, Commerce and Finance

Diccionario Inglés de Negocios, Comercio y Finanzas

Spanish–English/English–Spanish
Español–Inglés/Inglés–Español

Spanish terminology/Terminología española
Emilio G. Muñiz Castro
Centro Iberoamericano de Terminología (IBEROTERM)

London and New York

First published 1998
by Routledge
11 New Fetter Lane, London EC4P 4EE

Simultaneously published in the USA and Canada
by Routledge
29 West 35th Street, New York, NY 10001

© 1998 Routledge

Typeset in Monotype Times, Helvetica Neue and Bauer Bodoni
by Routledge

Printed in England by T.J. International Ltd, Padstow, Cornwall

Printed on acid-free paper

British Library Cataloguing-in-Publication Data
A catalogue record for this book is available from the British Library

Library of Congress Cataloging-in-Publication Data
Applied for

ISBN 0-415-09393-7

Spanish Dictionary of Business, Commerce and Finance
Diccionario Inglés de Negocios, Comercio y Finanzas

Project Managers/Dirección del Proyecto

Gemma Belmonte Talero   Rebecca Moy

Managing Editor/Dirección Editorial

Sinda López

Editorial/Redacción

Justine Bird   Lisa Carden
Janice McNeillie   Jessica Ramage   Robert Timms

Programme Manager/Dirección del Programa

Elizabeth White

Marketing

Vanessa Markey
Rachel Miller

Systems/Sistemas Informáticos

Omar Raman
Simon Thompson

Administration/Administración

Amanda Brindley

Production/Producción

Michelle Draycott   Nigel Marsh

Specialist Consultants/Asesores Especialistas

Professor Robert T. Moran
American Graduate School of Management

Leticia Damm de Gorostieta
Nicholas A. Gibler
Jorge Hernández Osuna
Cecilia E. Zepeda-Schwartzott
*Asociación de Traductores e Intérpretes de
Monterrey, A.C., Mexico*

Peter Bond
The Chartered Institute of Bankers

Norman Hart
The Chartered Institute of Marketing

María José Eguskiza Garai
*Consejería de Educación, Embajada de España,
London*

Suzannah Lansdell
The Environment Council

María Antonia Pires Rodrigues
Escuela Oficial de Idiomas, Badajoz

Dr Rafael Alejo González
Professor Eugenio Cortés Gómez
Dr Luis Fernando de la Macorra y Cano
*Facultad de Económicas, Universidad de
Extremadura*

Marisol Alonso Rincón
Lorenzo Elizalde Rodríguez
Carmen Lamadrid Hernández
Gabinete de Traducción Babel

Norman Bartlett
The Institute of European Trade and Technology

Dr Adán E. Pucci
*Instituto Argentino de Oceanografía y Centro
Nacional Patagónico, CONICET*

María Ofelia Cirone
Instituto Argentino de Oceanografía, CONICET

Dr Manuel de León
Instituto de Matemáticas y Física Fundamental, CSIC

Virginia Manousso
International Business Assistance, Devon

Brian Clifford
Manchester Business School

Margarita García de Cortázar Nebreda
Ministerio de Educación y Ciencia

Enric S. Dolz i Ferrer
Queen Mary and Westfield College & Universitat de València

Susan Kershaw
SK Associates

Mònica Briega Morente
Universidat Autònoma de Barcelona

Professor Pablo Coto-Millán
Professor Francisco Javier Martínez García
Dr Pablo Vázquez
Universidad de Cantabria

Dr Javier Camacho de los Ríos
Universidad de Granada

Beatriz de los Arcos
University College Galway

Professor Christopher Nobes
University of Reading

Lexicographers & Proofreaders/Lexicógrafos y Correctores de Pruebas

Michael Britton
Alison Crann
Jeremy Munday
Kathryn Phillips-Miles

Anna Reid
Jonathan Roper
Malihe Sanatian
Maggie Seaton

Keyboarders/Mecanógrafos

Emmanuelle Bels
Sara Fenby
Beatriz Fernández
Antonio Fernández Entrena
Rosa Gálvez López
Christiane Grosskopf
Ute Krebs

Ilona Lehmann
David Morgan
Roger Pena Muiño
Fabienne Rangeard
Deborah Thomas
María del Mar Villanueva Pleguezuelo
Dalia Ventura Alcalay

Acknowledgements/Agradecimientos

We also wish to acknowledge the valuable contribution of Flavia Hodges and Wendy Morris during the early stages of the project.

We are particulary indebted to the following people for their assistance during the compilation of this dictionary: Frank Abate and his team for checking American coverage; Ruperto Belmonte Monforte, María Josefa Falero García and David Galobart Mateu for their consulting services; Carlos Márquez Linares for his assistance in preparing supplementary material; and Gemma Belmonte Talero and Antonio Fernández Entrena for providing and translating specialist terminology.

Queremos agradecer la valuosa contribución de Flavia Hodges y Wendy Morris durante las tempranas etapas del proyecto

Estamos especialmente agradecidos a las siguientes personas por su ayuda durante la fase de compilación de este diccionario: Frank Abate y su equipo, por revisar la cobertura americana; Ruperto Belmonte Monforte, María Josefa Falero García y David Galobart Mateu por sus servicios de asesoramiento; Carlos Márquez Linares por su ayuda en la preparación de material suplementario; y Gemma Belmonte Talero y Antonio Fernández Entrena por proporcionar y traducir terminología especializada.

Contents/Índice de contenidos

Emilio G. Muñiz Castro MA gained his first degree, and subsequently a master's, from *L'Université Catholique*, Paris. He is founder and director of the *IBEROTERM* terminology centre and the *BIBTERM* terminology bank. He was vice president of the International Federation of Translators from 1980 to 1984, and is the author of a number of specialist dictionaries.

Emilio G. Muñiz Castro MA obtuvo una licenciatura y una maestría de *L'Université Catholique*, París. Es el fundador y director del centro de terminología *IBEROTERM* y del banco de terminología *BIBTERM*. Fue vicepresidente de la Federación Internacional de Traductores entre 1980 y 1984, y es autor de un número de diccionarios especializados.

Preface/Prólogo

The *Spanish Dictionary of Business, Commerce and Finance* is the third dictionary to be published in Routledge's programme of bilingual business dictionaries launched in December 1995 with the *French Dictionary of Business, Commerce and Finance*.

It would not have been possible to compile this dictionary within a relatively short timescale, and to the standard achieved, without the use of a highly sophisticated, custom-designed database.

The database's most significant feature is that it is designed as a relational database: term records for each language are held in separate files, with further files consisting only of link records. Links between terms in different language files represent translations, whilst links between terms within a single language file represent cross-references between abbreviations and geographical variants.

The content of the database for this dictionary was created in three principal phases. A considerable proportion of the English term list was already available following the publication of the *French Dictionary of Business, Commerce and Finance* and the *German Dictionary of Business, Commerce and Finance*. The term list was then sent to *IBERO-TERM*, who supplied Spanish and Latin American equivalents and expanded the basic term list to include the main relevant terminology for the Spanish version of this work.

The terms in each language were then vetted by native-speaker subject specialists, working at the leading edge of their respective fields, in order to ensure the currency of the terminology, the accuracy of translations and the comprehensiveness of coverage. Finally all the entries were reviewed by specialist editors to ensure coverage of geographical variants so that this information could be incorporated into the dictionary.

The creation and editing of the database of terms was, however, only the first stage in the making of the dictionary. Within the database the distinction between source and target languages is not overt, so

El *Diccionario Inglés de Negocios, Comercio y Finanzas* es el tercero de la serie de diccionarios bilingües de negocios publicados por la Editorial Routledge. La serie se inició en diciembre de 1995 con el *Diccionario Francés de Negocios, Comercio y Finanzas.*

Podemos afirmar que no habría sido posible realizar una obra de esta calidad, en un tiempo relativamente corto, si no hubiera sido por el uso de una sofisticada base de datos que se creó específicamente para nuestro programa de diccionarios.

El rasgo que distingue a esta base de datos es su estructura relacional, mediante la cual el léxico de cada lengua se almacena en un fichero y las relaciones entre los términos en otros diferentes. Las relaciones entre los términos que se encuentran en los ficheros de cada lengua funcionan como traducciones. Las relaciones entre los términos dentro de una misma lengua representan remisiones entre variantes geográficas y abreviaturas.

El contenido de la base de datos se gestó en tres fases principales. Una proporción muy considerable del vocabulario inglés ya se había elaborado para el *Diccionario Francés de Negocios, Comercio y Finanzas* y el *Diccionario Alemán de Negocios, Comercio y Finanzas*. El vocabulario se envió, acto seguido, a *IBEROTERM*. Su labor fue la de proporcionar equivalentes españoles y latino-americanos e incrementar los listados iniciales mediante la inclusión de la terminología más importante para la versión española de esta obra.

El vocabulario se sometió entonces a la verificación de diversos especialistas de cada lengua, expertos en contacto directo con los últimos avances en sus respectivas disciplinas, para asegurarse de la pertinencia de la terminología, la exactitud de las traducciones y la extensión del vocabulario. Por último, los editores revisaron todas las entradas para cerciorarse de que las variantes geográficas quedaban incluidas en el diccionario.

Con todo, la creación y edición de la base de datos léxicos fueron sólo los primeros peldaños en la

a software module was used to process the data and produce two alphabetic sequences of Spanish headwords with English translations and vice versa, each displaying the nesting of compounds, ordering of translations, style of cross-references of different types and other features according to a complex algorithm.

At this stage the formatted text was edited by a team of experienced Spanish and English lexicographers whose task it was to eliminate duplication or inconsistency; edit the entries to ensure that all relevant information was present, correct and easily interpreted; and remove terms that were on the one hand too general, or on the other, too specialized for inclusion in a business dictionary covering a broad range of areas. This phased method of working has enabled us to set very high standards of quality control throughout the compilation and editing stages of the dictionary.

The editorial team

elaboración del diccionario. En la base de datos no es pertinente la distinción entre lengua de origen y lengua de destino, así que un módulo de software se encargó de procesar y producir la información en dos series alfabéticas, una de entradas españolas con traducciones al inglés y viceversa. Cada serie muestra los cuadros de variantes de términos compuestos, el orden de las traducciones, los diferentes tipos de remisiones y demás características, todos ellos siguiendo un algoritmo complejo.

Llegados a este punto, un experimentado equipo de lexicógrafos españoles y británicos, cuya tarea consistía en eliminar redundancias e inconsistencias, revisó el texto. Dicho equipo se encargó de suprimir aquellos términos demasiado generales o demasiado especializados para ser incluidos en un diccionario de negocios que cubre una amplia gama de materias. Este método de trabajo por etapas nos ha permitido establecer altísimas cotas de control de calidad a lo largo de las fases de compilación y edición del diccionario.

El equipo editorial

Features of the dictionary/
Estructura del diccionario

The following text extracts illustrate the principal features of the dictionary. For a more detailed explanation of each of these features, and a full guide to using the dictionary, see pages xv–xvii.

Los principales rasgos del diccionario están señalados en los extractos siguientes. Para obtener una explicación más detallada de cada uno estos rasgos y una guía completa del uso del diccionario, consúltense las páginas xix–xxi.

Explanations and equivalents provide cultural information

IEF *abr* (*Instituto de Estudios Financieros*) FIN Spanish financial research institute

iglú *m* TRANSP *aviación* igloo

ignífugo *adj* COM GEN fire-resistant (*BrE*), fire-resistive (*AmE*)

Illustrative phrases are grouped together at the relevant entry after a diamond

igual[1] *adj* COM GEN equal; ◆ **a ~ delito** DER in pari delicto; **~ y opuesto** COM GEN equal and opposite; **~ para todas las categorías** COM GEN, RRHH across-the-board

igual[2] *m* MAT *signo* equal; **~ tamaño** V&M same size

iguala *f* COM GEN retainer

Genders are indicated at Spanish nouns

igualación *f* COM GEN equalization; **~ de diferencias salariales** ECON equalization of wage differentials; **~ de espacios** IND spatial equalization

igualado *adj* COM GEN matched, equalized

igualar *vt* COM GEN *precios* even out, *resultados* match

igualdad *f* COM GEN equality; **~ de derechos de voto** POL equal voting rights; **~ de oportunidad de empleo** RRHH equal employment opportunity; **~ de oportunidades** RRHH equal opportunity (*BrE*), affirmative action

British English and American English variants are given in full and labelled accordingly

(*AmE*); **~ de oportunidades aparente** DER tokenism

iguales[1]: **~ derechos a voto** *m pl* POL equal voting rights

iguales[2]: **en ~ condiciones** *fra* COM GEN, RRHH on an equal footing, on the same footing

igualitarismo *m* POL egalitarianism

igualmente *adv* COM GEN pari passu

ilegal *adj* DER unlawful, illegal

ilegalmente *adv* DER illegally, unlawfully

ilícito: ~ civil *m* DER civil wrong

ilimitado *adj* COM GEN unlimited

iliquidez *f* FIN liquidity squeeze

ilíquido *adj* BANCA illiquid

Cross-references from abbreviations to their full forms are shown

ILT *abr* (*incapacidad laboral transitoria*) PROT SOC, SEG temporary disability benefit

ilusión: ~ fiscal *f* FISC fiscal illusion; **~ inflacionaria** *f* ECON inflation illusion; **~ monetaria** *f* ECON monetary veil

Contexts give supplementary information to help locate the relevant translation

ilustración *f* MEDIOS *ejemplo, imagen* illustration

ilustraciones *f pl* COM GEN *imprenta* artwork

ilustrar *vt* COM GEN, MEDIOS illustrate

IMAC *abr* (*Instituto de Mediación, Arbitraje y Conciliación*) GES, RRHH independent concilation service, often involved in disputes between trade unions and management, ≈ ACAS (*BrE*) (*Advisory, Conciliation and Arbitration Service*)

imagen *f* COM GEN image; **~ consolidada** V&M established image; **~ corporativa** COM GEN corporate image; **~ fiel** CONT fair representation (*AmE*), true and fair view (*BrE*); **~ global** V&M global image; **~ de marca** V&M

Compound terms are listed alphabetically at the first element

brand image; **~ de pantalla** INFO soft copy; **~ del producto** V&M product image; **~ secundaria** V&M *publicidad* afterimage; **~ sobresaliente** COM GEN high image (*jarg*)

IME *abr* (*Instituto Monetario Europeo*) ECON, POL EMI (*European Monetary Institute*)

IMEF *abr AmL* (*Instituto Mexicano de Ejecutivos de Finanzas*) FIN institute of Mexican financial executives

imitaciones *f pl* IND *sector de la moda* knockoffs (*infrml*); **~ ilegales** IND *sector de la moda* counterfeit goods

Las definiciones y equivalentes ofrecen información cultural

Las frases ilustrativas se agrupan en la entrada pertinente después de un diamante

Se indican los géneros para los sustantivos españoles

Las variantes del inglés británico y americano se dan de forma completa y aparecen indicadas pertinentemente

Las remisiones entre las abreviaturas y sus formas plenas aparecen indicadas

Los contextos ofrecen información suplementaria para ayudar a elegir la traducción correspondiente

Los compuestos siguen el orden alfabético a partir de su primer elemento

file away *vt* GEN COMM archivar

filed *adj* GEN COMM archivado

filer *n* TAX declarante *mf*

Los indicadores de materia ordenados alfabéticamente muestran la traducción apropiada —— **filing** *n* GEN COMM, archivo *m*, PATENTS *of application* presentación *f*; ~ **basket** ADMIN cestilla de archivo *f*; ~ **cabinet** ADMIN archivador *m* (*Esp*), archivero *m* (*AmL*); ~ **drawer** ADMIN cajón clasificador *m*; ~ **of a return** TAX presentación *f*; ~ **statement** STOCK presentación del balance *f*; ~ **system** ADMIN sistema de archivo *m* —— *Subject area labels given in alphabetical order show appropriate translations*

fill¹: **~-in** *n* HRM, S&M cumplimentación *f*; ~ **price** *n* STOCK *options* precio de ejecución de la compraventa *m*

Las frases ilustrativas se agrupan en la entrada pertinente después de un diamante —— **fill**² *vt* GEN COMM *gap, vacancy* llenar; ◆ **~-or-kill** *AmE* (*FOK*) STOCK cancelar inmediatamente, cumplimentar inmediatamente; ~ **a position** HRM cubrir un puesto; ~ **a vacancy** HRM cubrir una vacante —— *Illustrative phrases are grouped together at the relevant entry after a diamond*

fill in *vt* GEN COMM *form* rellenar, HRM cumplimentar

filler *n* MEDIA, S&M relleno *m*; ~ **traffic** TRANSP tráfico complementario *m*

Se indican los géneros para los sustantivos españoles —— **fillers** *n pl* MEDIA *print* artículos de relleno *m pl* —— *Genders are indicated at Spanish nouns*

film *n* *BrE* (*cf motion picture AmE, cf movie AmE*) LEIS, MEDIA película *f*; ~ **advertising** *BrE* LEIS, S&M publicidad de una película *f*; ~ **festival** MEDIA festival cinematográfico *m*; ~ **industry** *BrE* (*cf motion-picture industry AmE*) ECON, LEIS, MEDIA industria cinematográfica *f*, industria del cine *f*; **~-maker** MEDIA *broadcast* productor(a) cinematográfico(-a) *m,f*; ~ **production** *Las variantes lingüísticas de España y América Latina se dan de forma completa y aparecen indicadas pertinentemente* —— **costs** *n pl* TAX costes de producción de películas *m pl* (*Esp*), costos de producción de películas *m pl* (*AmL*); ~ **rights** *n pl* LAW, MEDIA derechos cinematográficos *m pl*; ~ **rush** MEDIA primera copia de una película *f*; ~ **script** MEDIA guión cinematográfico *m*; ~ **strip** MEDIA tira de película *f*; ~ **test** MEDIA prueba cinematográfica *f* —— *Spanish and Latin American variants are given in full and labelled accordingly*

filmsetter *n* MEDIA *print* máquina de componer fotográficamente *f*

Las remisiones entre las abreviaturas y sus formas plenas aparecen tanto para los términos españoles como para los ingleses —— **filmsetting** *n* MEDIA *print* composición fotográfica *f*, fotocomposición *f* —— *Cross-references from abbreviations to their full form are shown for both the Spanish and English translation*

FILO *abbr* (*first in, last out*) ACC, GEN COMM PEUS (*primero en entrar, último en salir*)

filter *n* COMP, ECON, FIN filtro *m*

En el caso de que no existe una equivalente directa se ofrece una definición —— **filtering** *n* COMP, ECON, FIN filtración *f*; ~ **down** PROP divulgación *f* —— *Explanations are provided where no direct equivalent exists*

FIMBRA *abbr* (*Financial Intermediaries, Managers and Brokers Regulatory Association*) FIN asociación profesional de intermediarios, gestores y agentes financieros

FIME *abbr* (*Fellow of the Institute of Marine Engineers*) HRM ≈ Miembro del Instituto de Ingenieros Navales *mf*

Los homógrafos son diferenciados mediante un número superíndice —— **FIML** *abbr* (*full-information maximum likelihood*) ECON *econometrics* método de estimación de modelos econométricos con ecuaciones simultáneas —— *Superscript numbers denote homographs*

final¹: ~ **and conclusive** *adj* TAX *determination* final y concluyente

final² *n* GEN COMM, S&M final *m*; ~ **acceptance** GEN COMM *of goods* recepción definitiva *f*; ~ **accounts** *n pl* ACC cuentas finales *f pl*; ~ **assembly** GEN COMM, IND montaje final *m*; ~ **balance** ACC, BANK saldo final *m*; ~ **check-in** LEIS registro final *m*; ~ **consumption** COMP, ENVIR consumo final *m*

Using the dictionary

Range & selection of terms

This is a single-volume general business dictionary which covers a broad range of terminology drawn from all the main fields of business and commerce. As such, we have aimed to include the essential vocabulary of each subject area, as well as including more specialized references such as organizations, legal acts and financial and accounting systems. Overlap with a general bilingual dictionary has been kept to a minimum by only including terms which can be applied in a business context. The material has been checked by leading subject experts to ensure that both the English and the Spanish terms are accurate and current and that the translations are valid equivalents. Although other variant translations may sometimes be permissible in a particular subject area, we have given the terms and spellings most widely preferred by specialists in the area.

Coverage of the subject areas is weighted representatively, so that a core and wide-ranging area such as Stock Market has a count of around 4,500 terms, whereas a developing area such as Environment has fewer terms.

Placement & ordering of terms

All terms, including hyphenated compounds, are entered at their first element except where that element is an article, preposition, conjunction, pronoun or other delexicalized word. In such cases, the term is entered at the next valid element. For example:

theory^2: **in** ~ *phr* GEN COMM en teoría

When this element is itself a headword with a business-related sense of its own, compound forms follow the simple form, and the headword is replaced by a swung dash (~). If the first element has no business sense of its own, it is untranslated and a colon precedes the compounds:

kerb: ~ **market** *n* STOCK *unlisted market* bolsín *m*; ~ **weight** *n* TRANSP *motor trade* peso en orden de marcha *m*

Within nests, articles, pronouns and prepositions are ignored in determining the sequence of open compounds and phrases. For example:

economy *n* BANK, POL, WEL economía *f*; ~ **of abundance** ECON economía de la abundancia *f*; ~ **class** LEIS, TRANSP clase económica *f*; ~ **fare** LEIS tarifa económica *f*; ~ **flight** LEIS, TRANSP vuelo económico *m*; ~ **pack** GEN COMM paquete económico *m*; ~ **of size** ECON, IND economía de escala *f*, economía de tamaño *f*

In the case of very long compound nests, marginal markers have been used to make it easy to find a term more quickly. For example:

mercado:

- **~ g**   ~ **genérico** V&M generic market; ~ **de gran complejidad** BOLSA sophisticated market; ~ **gris** BOLSA gray market (*AmE*), grey market (*BrE*);
- **~ h**   ~ **hipotecario** BANCA, FIN mortgage market; ~ **homogéneo** V&M homogeneous market

Abbreviations and acronyms written in upper case appear after vocabulary words of the same form written in lower case. For example:

cap^2 *vt* GEN COMM coronar; ♦ ~ **interest rates** BANK, ECON, FIN poner tope a las tasas de interés, poner un límite a los tipos de interés
CAP^1 *abbr* (*Common Agricultural Policy*) ECON, POL PAC (*Política Agrícola Común*)

Parts of speech

Part of speech labels are given at all entries except illustrative phrases. At translations, genders are given for all Spanish nouns. In cases where nested terms have the same part of speech as the headword, parts of speech are not repeated. For a complete list of these labels and their expansions, please see page xxiii.

When terms beginning with the same element fall into two or more part-of-speech categories, the different nests are distinguished by a superscript number immediately following the headword. The sequence is: abbreviation, adjective, adverb, noun and verb, followed by less frequent parts of speech.

Illustrative phrases follow a ◆ at the end of the entry to which they refer. For example:

effect[1] *n* ECON, GEN COMM efecto *m*; ◆ **with ~ from** (*w.e.f.*) GEN COMM efectivo desde el día
effect[2] *vt* GEN COMM *settlement* efectuar

For verb entries which can have more than one part of speech, numbered sections show the relevant grammatical category. For example:

suplicar 1. *vt* COM GEN, DER petition, appeal to; **2.** *vi* COM GEN plead

Ordering of translations

Every term is accompanied by one or more subject labels indicating the area in which it is used. For a complete list of these labels and their expansions, please see pages xxiv–xxv.

Where the same term is used in more than one area, multiple labels are given as appropriate. These labels are listed in alphabetical order. Where a term has the same translation in more than one area, this translation is given after the sequence of labels. For example:

sobrevalorado *adj* BOLSA, COM GEN, ECON overvalued

When a term has different translations according to the area in which it is used, the appropriate translation is given after each subject area label or set of labels. For example:

supresión *f* COM GEN *de controles de comercio* abolition, DER *de provisiones en estatutos* deletion, ECON *de barreras* dismantling, INFO abort

Supplementary information

The gender is given for every Spanish noun term. In the case of compound terms, this is the gender of the noun head. For example:

pacto *m* COM GEN *acuerdo* agreement, pact; **~ de ayuda mutua** ECON, POL mutual aid pact

In many cases additional information is given about a term to show how it is used. Such contextual information can be:

1. the typical subject or object of a verb. For example:

flourish *vi* GEN COMM *business, competition* florecer, prosperar

2. typical nouns used with an adjective. For example:

liquid[1] *adj* BANK *funds* líquido

3. words indicating the reference of a noun. For example:

firing *n* infrml HRM *of staff* despido *m*, cese *m*

4. information which supplements the subject area label. For example:

mask *vt* S&M *advertising* ocultar

5. a paraphrase or broad equivalent. For example:

lull *n* GEN COMM *diminished activity* calma *f*

When various different translations apply in the same subject area, contextual information is also used to show which translation is appropriate in different circumstances. For example:

acquittance *n* LAW *confirmation* carta de pago *f*, *of debt* descargo *m*

Where no real equivalent of a headword exists in the target language, an explanatory translation is given and is distinguished by a change in typeface. For example:

MCSI: ~ Index *n* (*Morgan Stanley Capital International Index*) STOCK parámetros internacionales para la comparación de índices de futuros financieros

In the case of organizations and institutions, an explanatory translation is given as well as an equivalent body where it exists. For example:

Inland: ~ Revenue *n* BrE (*IR*) TAX departamento gubernamental británico para regular los impuestos, ≈ Dirección General de Tributos *f* (*Esp*)

Where the feminine form of an occupation or profession can be formed by adding **a** or **-a** to a Spanish masculine stem, the noun entry has part of speech *m,f* with the inflection indicated at the headword. For example:

director, a *m,f* COM GEN director (*dir.*), manager (*MGR*)

Cross-references

Both British and North American terms are covered, and these are differentiated by geographical labels. Coverage also includes terms from Latin America and Spain. For a complete list of these labels and their expansions, please see page xxiii.

Spelling variants are cross-referred to the preferred spelling, where full information is given. For example:

gram *n* (*g*) GEN COMM gramo *m* (*gr.*)
gramme *see gram*

In the case of geographical spelling variants, the American English form is cross-referred to the British English form. For example:

installment *AmE see instalment BrE*
instalment *n BrE* BANK, GEN COMM plazo *m*, mensualidad *f*

Geographical lexical variants are cross-referred, with full translations given at each entry:

mailbox *n AmE* (*cf postbox BrE*) COMMS buzón *m*

postbox *n BrE* (*cf mailbox AmE*) COMMS buzón *m*

Both spelling and lexical variants are given in full when they are translations:

aeroplano *m* TRANSP aeroplane (*BrE*), aircraft, airplane (*AmE*)

Abbreviations are cross-referred to their full forms

and vice versa, with the appropriate translations given at each entry. For example:

CAR *abbr* (*compound annual rate*) BANK, FIN TAC (*tasa anual compuesta*)

compound[1]: ~ **annual growth** *n* ECON, FIN crecimiento anual compuesto *m*; ~ **annual rate** *n* (*CAR*) BANK, FIN *of interest* tasa anual compuesta *f* (*TAC*)

If a source language abbreviation does not have a target language equivalent, the translation of the expanded form is given. For example:

OID *abbr* (*original issue discount*) STOCK emisión con descuento *f*

Where an abbreviation has different full forms according to subject areas, the relevant expanded forms appear after each label or set of labels:

MRP *abbr* ECON (*marginal revenue product*) ingreso del producto marginal *m*, S&M (*manufacturer's recommended price*) precio recomendado por el fabricante *m*

Consejos para la utilización de este diccionario

Selección del vocabulario

Éste es un diccionario de negocios general de un solo tomo cuyo acervo terminológico abarca desde todos los dominios principales del mundo comercial. Hemos tratado de incluir el vocabulario esencial de cada materia, así como referencias de carácter más especializado como organizaciones, procedimientos legales y sistemas financieros y contables. Hemos procurado reducir al mínimo el grado de interferencia con diccionarios generales y con vistas a ello se incluyen tan sólo aquellos términos que tienen uso en un contexto comercial. Un equipo de prominentes especialistas se ha ocupado de revisar los resultados, para asegurarnos de que tanto los términos españoles como los ingleses son precisos y actuales y de que las traducciones tienen equivalentes válidos. En aquellos casos en los que una palabra permite varias traducciones, hemos optado por los términos y las variantes ortográficas que los especialistas consultados han considerado más plausible.

La extensión concedida a cada materia es proporcional a su importancia, de modo que a un campo tan amplio como la Bolsa se le dedican 4.500 términos, mientras que al de Medio Ambiente, que aún continúa en proceso de formación, le corresponde un ámbito terminológico mucho más reducido.

Orden y colocación de las entradas

Las entradas se ordenan alfabéticamente, incluyendo los compuestos formados mediante un guión, a partir de su primer elemento. Cuando el primer elemento es un artículo, una preposición, una conjunción, un pronombre u otra palabra delexicalizada, la entrada se ordena según el próximo elemento válido. Por ejemplo:

theory[2]: **in ~** *phr* GEN COMM en teoría

Cuando varios compuestos participan de un lexema inicial común de carácter comercial o financiero, el primer elemento se reemplaza por una virgulilla (~). Si el primer elemento no tiene un significado comercial o financiero, los términos compuestos formados a partir de dicho elemento aparecen precedidos por dos puntos (:). Por ejemplo:

kerb: **~ market** *n* STOCK *unlisted market* bolsín *m*; **~ weight** *n* TRANSP *motor trade* peso en orden de marcha *m*

Los artículos, los pronombres y las preposiciones no se toman en cuenta a la hora de determinar el orden de los términos compuestos o las frases. Por ejemplo:

economy *n* BANK, POL, WEL economía *f*; **~ of abundance** ECON economía de la abundancia *f*; **~ class** LEIS, TRANSP clase económica *f*; **~ fare** LEIS tarifa económica *f*; **~ flight** LEIS, TRANSP vuelo económico *m*; **~ pack** GEN COMM paquete económico *m*; **~ of size** ECON, IND economía de escala *f*, economía de tamaño *f*

En las entradas que registran gran cantidad de acepciones se utilizan marcadores para facilitar la localización de los términos. Por ejemplo:

mercado:
~ g **~ genérico** V&M generic market; **~ de gran complejidad** BOLSA sophisticated market; **~ gris** BOLSA gray market (*AmE*), grey market (*BrE*);
~ h **~ hipotecario** BANCA, FIN mortgage market; **~ homogéneo** V&M homogeneous market

Las abreviaturas y los acrónimos escritos con mayúsculas aparecen tras términos idénticos que no están abreviados, los cuales van en minúsculas. Por ejemplo:

cap[2] *vt* GEN COMM coronar; ♦ **~ interest rates** BANK, ECON, FIN poner tope a las tasas de interés, poner un límite a los tipos de interés
CAP[1] *abbr* (*Common Agricultural Policy*) ECON, POL PAC (*Política Agrícola Común*)

Categorías gramaticales

Tras cada término, menos en las frases ilustrativas, se indica su categoría gramatical mediante abreviatura. El género aparece para cada traducción española que posea la categoría de nombre. En los casos en que un término dé origen a otros, compuestos o derivados, no se repetirá la abreviatura si la categoría no cambia. Puede consultarse una lista completa de las abreviaturas en la página xxiii.

En el caso de términos cuyo elemento inicial es idéntico pero pertenecen a diferentes categorías gramaticales, las acepciones se distinguen por la inclusion de un supraíndice tras la entrada. El orden seguido es el de abreviatura, adjetivo, adverbio, nombre y verbo, seguidos por otras categorías gramaticales de uso más restringido.

Las frases ilustrativas van precedidas por un ◆ y se encuentran a final de las entradas a las que se refieren. Por ejemplo:

effect[1] *n* ECON, GEN COMM efecto *m*; ◆ **with ~ from** (*w.e.f.*) GEN COMM efectivo desde el día
effect[2] *vt* GEN COMM *settlement* efectuar

Cuando un mismo verbo puede funcionar como transitivo, intransitivo o reflexivo, los diferentes usos se consignan en secciones numeradas dentro del mismo homógrafo. Por ejemplo:

suplicar 1. *vt* COM GEN, DER petition, appeal to; **2.** *vi* COM GEN plead

Orden de las traducciones

Cada término va acompañado de uno o más indicadores de materia que especifican el ámbito de uso. En las páginas xxiv–xxv se encuentra una lista completa de tales indicadores.

Cuando un mismo término se utiliza en varios ámbitos, se consignan alfabéticamente los indicadores pertinentes. Cuando la traducción de un término es la misma en varios ámbitos, dicha traducción va precedida por los indicadores pertinentes. Por ejemplo:

sobrevalorado *adj* BOLSA, COM GEN, ECON overvalued

Cuando un término permite diferentes traducciones según el ámbito en que se utiliza, se ofrece la traducción apropiada tras cada indicador o conjunto de indicadores de materia. Por ejemplo:

supresión *f* COM GEN *de controles de comercio* abolition, DER *de provisiones en estatutos* deletion, ECON *de barreras* dismantling, INFO abort

Información complementaria

El género aparece para cada término español que posea la categoría de nombre. Con respecto a los compuestos, éstos no llevan el género del último elemento, sino el de su radical. Por ejemplo:

pacto *m* COM GEN *acuerdo* agreement, pact; **~ de ayuda mutua** ECON, POL mutual aid pact

En muchos casos se ofrece información adicional para precisar el uso de un término. Dicha información puede consistir en:

1. El sujeto u objeto típicos de un verbo. Por ejemplo:

flourish *vi* GEN COMM *business, competition* florecer, prosperar

2. Nombres usados habitualmente con un adjetivo. Por ejemplo:

liquid[1] *adj* BANK *funds* líquido

3. Palabras que indican la referencia de un nombre. Por ejemplo:

firing *n infrml* HRM *of staff* despido *m*, cese *m*

4. Información complementaria del indicador de materia. Por ejemplo:

mask *vt* S&M *advertising* ocultar

5. Una paráfrasis o equivalente general. Por ejemplo:

lull *n* GEN COMM *diminished activity* calma *f*

En los casos en que una palabra puede traducirse de varias maneras diferentes en un mismo ámbito, se utiliza la información contextual para mostrar cuál es la traducción más apropiada en cada caso. Por ejemplo:

acquittance *n* LAW *confirmation* carta de pago *f*, *of debt* descargo *m*

Cuando no existe el equivalente real de un término en la otra lengua, se da una traducción explicativa, la cual aparece con tipografía diferente. Por ejemplo:

MCSI: ~ Index *n* (*Morgan Stanley Capital International Index*) STOCK parámetros internacionales para la comparación de índices de futuros financieros

En el caso de organizaciones e instituciones, se da una traducción explicativa así como la correspondiente institución en el otro idioma si existe. Por ejemplo:

Inland: ~ Revenue *n* BrE (*IR*) TAX departamento gubernamental británico para regular los impuestos, ≈ Dirección General de Tributos *f* (*Esp*)

Cuando el femenino de una ocupación o profesión se forma añadiendo **a** o **-a** a la raíz masculina, la entrada en cuestión tendrá como género gramatical *m,f*, y la desinencia irá indicada en la entrada principal. Por ejemplo:

director, a *m,f* COM GEN director (*dir.*), manager (*MGR*)

Remisiones

Dado que este diccionario incluye tanto los términos ingleses como los americanismos, se indica siempre su procedencia geográfica mediante indicador. La cobertura de este diccionario también incluye términos de América Latina y España. Para una lista completa de estos indicadores y de sus correspondencias, por favor consúltense la página xxiii.

 Las variantes ortográficas remiten a la forma más frecuente, donde se ofrece una información completa. Por ejemplo:

gram *n* (*g*) GEN COMM gramo *m* (*gr.*)
gramme *see gram*

Las variantes ortográficas del inglés americano remiten a las entradas respectivas en inglés británico. Por ejemplo:

installment *AmE see instalment BrE*
instalment *n BrE* BANK, GEN COMM plazo *m*, mensualidad *f*

Las variantes geográficas de carácter léxico se remiten y se ofrece traducciones completas en cada entrada. Por ejemplo:

mailbox *n AmE* (*cf postbox BrE*) COMMS buzón *m*

postbox *n BrE* (*cf mailbox AmE*) COMMS buzón *m*

Las variantes geográficas, tanto ortográficas como léxicas, se ofrecen íntegramente cuando son traducciones:

aeroplano *m* TRANSP aeroplane (*BrE*), aircraft, airplane (*AmE*)

Las abreviaturas remiten a las formas íntegras y viceversa, y las traducciones apropiadas aparecen en cada entrada. Por ejemplo:

CAR *abbr* (*compound annual rate*) BANK, FIN TAC (*tasa anual compuesta*)

compound[1]: ~ **annual growth** *n* ECON, FIN crecimiento anual compuesto *m*; ~ **annual rate** *n* (*CAR*) BANK, FIN *of interest* tasa anual compuesta *f* (*TAC*)

Cuando una abreviatura de la lengua de origen no tiene un equivalente en la lengua de destino, la traducción que se ofrece es la de la forma íntegra. Por ejemplo:

OID *abbr* (*original issue discount*) STOCK emisión con descuento *f*

Cuando una abreviatura tiene varias formas íntegras según el ámbito en que se usa, la forma íntegra se ofrece tras cada indicador o conjunto de indicadores de materia:

MRP *abbr* ECON (*marginal revenue product*) ingreso del producto marginal *m*, S&M (*manufacturer's recommended price*) precio recomendado por el fabricante *m*

Abbreviations used in this dictionary/
Abreviaturas utilizadas en este diccionario

Parts of speech/Categorías gramaticales

abbr	abbreviation	abreviatura
abr	abreviatura	abbreviation
adj	adjective	adjetivo
adv	adverb	adverbio
f	feminine	femenino
f pl	feminine plural	femenino plural
fra	frase	phrase
m	masculine	masculino
mf	masculine or feminine	masculino o femenino
m,f	masculine, feminine	masculino, femenino
m pl	masculine plural	masculino plural
n	noun	sustantivo
n pl	noun plural	sustantivo plural
phr	phrase	frase
pref	prefix	prefijo
prep	preposition	preposición
vi	intransitive verb	verbo intransitivo
v refl	verbo reflexivo	reflexive verb
vt	transitive verb	verbo transitivo

Geographic codes/Indicadores geográficos

Esp	España	Spain
AmL	América Latina	Latin America
BrE	British English	Inglés británico
AmE	American English	Inglés americano

Level codes/Registros idiomáticos

frml	formal	formal
infrml	informal	informal
jarg	jargon	jerga
obs	obsolete	obsoleto

Other abbreviations/Otras abréviaturas

sb	somebody	alguien
sth	something	algo

Subject area labels/Indicadores de materia

ACC	Accountancy	Contabilidad
ADMIN	Business Administration	Administración de Empresas
BANK	Banking	Banca
COMMS	Communications	Comunicaciones
COMP	Computing	Informática
ECON	Economics	Economía
ENVIR	Environment	Medio Ambiente
FIN	Finance	Finanzas
GEN COMM	General Commerce	Comercio General
HRM	Human Resource Management	Gestión de Recursos Humanos
IMP/EXP	Import & Export	Importación y Exportación
IND	Industry	Industria
INS	Insurance	Seguros
LAW	Law	Derecho
LEIS	Leisure & Tourism	Ocio y Turismo
MGMNT	Management	Gestión
MATHS	Mathematics	Matemáticas
MEDIA	Mass Media	Medios de Comunicación
PATENTS	Patents	Patentes
POL	Politics	Política
PROP	Property	Inmobiliarios
S&M	Sales & Marketing	Ventas y Marketing
STOCK	Stock Market	Bolsa
TAX	Taxation	Fiscalidad
TRANSP	Transport	Transporte
WEL	Welfare & Safety	Protección Social

ADMIN	Administración de Empresas	Business Administration
BANCA	Banca	Banking
BOLSA	Bolsa	Stock Market
COM GEN	Comercio General	General Commerce
COMS	Comunicaciones	Communications
CONT	Contabilidad	Accountancy
DER	Derecho	Law
ECON	Economía	Economics
FIN	Finanzas	Finance
FISC	Fiscalidad	Taxation
GES	Gestión	Management
IMP/EXP	Importación y Exportación	Import & Export
IND	Industria	Industry
INFO	Informática	Computing
INMOB	Inmobiliarios	Property
MAT	Matemáticas	Mathematics
MED AMB	Medio Ambiente	Environment
MEDIOS	Medios de Comunicación	Mass Media
OCIO	Ocio y Turismo	Leisure & Tourism
PATENT	Patentes	Patents

POL	Política	Politics
PROT SOC	Protección Social	Welfare & Safety
RRHH	Gestión de Recursos Humanos	Human Resource Management
SEG	Seguros	Insurance
TRANSP	Transporte	Transport
V&M	Ventas y Marketing	Sales & Marketing

Registered trademarks®

Every effort has been made to label terms which we believe constitute trademarks. The legal status of these, however, remains unchanged by the presence or absence of any such label.

Marcas registradas®

Hemos hecho el máximo esfuerzo para señalar los términos que estimamos protegidos por un registro de marca. Sin embargo, la ausencia o presencia de esta mención no surte efecto sobre su estado legal.

DICCIONARIO ESPAÑOL–INGLÉS

SPANISH–ENGLISH DICTIONARY

A

abajo[1]: **~ mencionado** *adj* COM GEN undermentioned

abajo[2] *adv* COM GEN *carta, documento* below; **hacia ~** COM GEN downstream, downward (*AmE*), downwards (*BrE*)

abanderizamiento *m* TRANSP *buque* flagging

abandonado *adj* COM GEN *plan* abandoned, *proposición, posibilidad* neglected

abandonar *vt* BOLSA *una opción* abandon, give up (*jarg*), COM GEN, IMP/EXP abandon, INFO quit, *programa* abort, PATENT abandon; ♦ **~ el buque** TRANSP abandon ship; **~ el puerto** TRANSP leave port

abandono *m* BOLSA *opción* abandonment, COM GEN disclaimer, abandonment; **~ de una posición** BOLSA rolling out; **~ del servicio** DER dereliction of duty

abanico *m* FISC *orden* range, IND *fila, hilera* product line, fan, V&M *surtido* product line

abaratamiento *m* BOLSA undertrading, COM GEN fall in price, FIN undertrading

abaratar *vt* BOLSA, COM GEN, FIN undertrade

abarcar *vt* COM GEN encompass, comprise

abastecer *vt* COM GEN, ECON, TRANSP supply, V&M *al mercado* serve

abastecerse: **~ de** *v refl* COM GEN take in (*infrml*)

abastecimiento *m* COM GEN *cantidad* supply, ECON victualling, TRANSP *provisiones* catering; **~ fijo** ECON fixed supply; **suficiente ~ de** COM GEN plentiful supply of

abierto *adj* BOLSA *precio* open, COM GEN open-ended, *balance* open (*AmE*), *enfoque* outward-looking, INFO open; ♦ **~ en imprenta** BOLSA open on the print

abogacía *f* BANCA, COMS, DER *ejercicio del derecho* ≈ legal profession, law practice

abogado, -a *m,f* COM GEN, DER ≈ advocate, ≈ attorney-at-law (*AmE*), ≈ attorney, ≈ barrister, ≈ solicitor, ≈ court lawyer, ≈ lawyer, ≈ brief; **~ administrativista** BANCA, COM GEN, DER ≈ public administration lawyer; **~ civilista** BANCA, COM GEN, DER civil lawyer; **≈ de empresa** BANCA, COM GEN, DER ≈ in-house lawyer; **~ especialista en derecho comunitario** BANCA, COM GEN, DER lawyer specializing in European Community law; **~ especialista en derecho internacional** BANCA, COM GEN, DER ≈ lawyer specializing in international law; **~ del Estado** DER ≈ Government lawyer; **~ jurídico(-a) militar** DER ≈ military lawyer; **~ laborista** BANCA, COM GEN, DER ≈ labor law lawyer (*AmE*), ≈ labour law lawyer (*BrE*); **~ mercantilista** BANCA, COM GEN, DER ≈ commercial lawyer, ≈ company lawyer; **~ de oficio** BANCA, COM GEN, DER ≈ court-appointed attorney; **~ penalista** BANCA, COM GEN, DER ≈ criminal lawyer; **~ tributarista** COM GEN, DER, FISC ≈ tax lawyer

abolición *f* COM GEN, DER, POL abolition

abolir *vt* COM GEN abolish, DER *mandamiento judicial* quash, IMP/EXP, POL abolish

abonado, -a *m,f* COMS, MEDIOS subscriber; **~ a prueba** MEDIOS trial subscriber; **~ telefónico(-a)** COMS telephone subscriber

abonar *vt* COM GEN, *un préstamo* credit (*cr*), *una factura* pay, CONT *en cuenta, deuda* pay

abono *m* CONT credit entry, COM GEN, TRANSP commutation ticket (*AmE*), season ticket (*BrE*); **~ a cuenta reembolsable** FISC refundable prepaid credit; **~ ferroviario** TRANSP commutation ticket (*AmE*), season ticket (*BrE*); **~ de un giro bancario** BANCA bank giro credit (*BrE*); **~ de ingresos salariales** FISC earned income allowance; **~ trimestral** COM GEN quarterly installment (*AmE*), quarterly instalment (*BrE*)

abordar *vt* COM GEN, GES approach, *problemas* tackle; ♦ **~ a alguien sobre algo** COM GEN approach sb about sth

a bordo *adv* COM GEN aboard

abrazadera: **~ a presión** *f* TRANSP *manejo de cargas* squeeze clamp

abreviar *vt* COM GEN abbreviate

abreviatura *f* COM GEN abbreviation

abrir *vt* BANCA, COM GEN, INFO open; ♦ **~ un asiento contable** CONT start an entry; **~ brecha** COM GEN break new ground; **~ brecha en** COM GEN *mercado* breach; **~ una carta de crédito** BANCA, IMP/EXP issue a letter of credit; **~ una cuenta con** BANCA open an account with; **~ un expediente** DER start proceedings; **~ el mercado a la competencia** COM GEN open up the market to competition; **~ una posición** BOLSA open a position; **~ una posición corta** BOLSA open a short position; **~ una posición larga** BOLSA open a long position; **~ las puertas a** COM GEN *oportunidad* open the door to

abrogación *f* BOLSA defeasance, DER, FISC abrogation, repeal

abrogar *vt* DER, FISC abrogate, repeal

absentismo *m* RRHH absenteeism

absentista *m* COM GEN, DER absentee

absolución *f* COM GEN, DER acquittal

absoluta: **~ o contingentemente** *adv* FISC absolutely or contingently

absolver *vt* COM GEN, DER acquit

absorber *vt* BOLSA, COM GEN, CONT *costes, beneficios* absorb, raid, ECON *una compañía a otra* take over, POL *votación* absorb; ♦ **~ una compañía de manera hostil** BOLSA raid a company; **~ un excedente** COM GEN absorb a surplus; **~ de forma insuficiente** CONT underabsorb; **~ gastos generales** CONT absorb overheads

absorbido *adj* BOLSA *títulos*, COM GEN, CONT *coste*, ECON absorbed, taken over

absorción *f* COM GEN *de una compañía* absorption, ECON takeover, POL absorption; **~ de una compañía amparada por la ley** DER statutory merger; **~ insuficiente de costes** CONT underabsorption of costs; **~ invertida** FIN reversed takeover; **~ nacional** ECON domestic absorption; **~ supranacional** FIN offshore takeover

abstención *f* ECON abstinence, POL abstention; **~ de opinión** CONT *auditoría* disclaimer of opinion

abstenerse *v refl* POL *en una elección* abstain; ♦ **~ de cobrar** BANCA, CONT *una deuda* forgo collection of

abundancia *f* COM GEN *de recursos* abundance, wealth, *de* *prosperidad* affluence; **~ de oportunidades** COM GEN wealth of opportunities

abundante *adj* COM GEN abundant, affluent

abusar *vt* COM GEN, DER, PATENT abuse

abuso *m* COM GEN, DER, PATENT abuse; **~ de autoridad** *f* DER abuse of authority; **~ de autoridad administrativa** DER abuse of administrative authority; **~ de confianza** DER *en el contrato* breach of trust, abuse of confidence, abuse of trust; **~ de derecho** DER abuse of rights; **~ de poder** DER abuse of power

acabado *m* COM GEN finishing

acabar: **~ con el déficit** *fra* FIN close the gap; **~ el trabajo** *fra* COM GEN finish work

academia: **~ de negocios** *f* RRHH business college

académico *adj* PROT SOC academic

acaparado *adj* COM GEN *mercado* monopolized, *comercialización* hoarded, cornered

acaparador[1]**,a** *m,f* COM GEN *del negocio* cornerer, *de beneficios* profiteer, *capital* monopolizer

acaparador[2] *m* COM GEN retainer; ♦ **sobre un ~** COM GEN on a retainer

acaparamiento *m* COM GEN cornering, hoarding, monopolization; **~ de bienes** COM GEN cornering of goods, hoarding of goods, monopolization of goods; **~ de bienes con fines especulativos** COM GEN speculative cornering of goods, speculative hoarding of goods, speculative monopolization of goods; **~ con fines estratégicos** COM GEN strategic stockpiling; **~ de mercancías** COM GEN cornering of goods, hoarding of goods, monopolization of goods; **~ de toda la oferta** COM GEN coemption

acaparar *vt* COM GEN *el mercado* corner, buy up, monopolize, hoard, stockpile

acarrear *vt* TRANSP carry

acarreo *m* TRANSP back haul, cartage, *ferrocarril* carriage

acatamiento *m* DER observance

acatar *vt* DER observe

acceder 1. *vt* INFO *base de datos* access; **2.** *vi* COM GEN agree, consent

accesibilidad *f* COM GEN accessibility

accesible *adj* COM GEN accessible; ♦ **~ a la llegada** TRANSP reachable on arrival; **siempre ~** TRANSP always accessible

acceso[1]: **sin ~ al mar** *adj* MED AMB *país* landlocked

acceso[2] *m* (*cf ingreso AmL*) COM GEN, INFO access, INMOB accession; **~ aleatorio** INFO random access; **~ directo** INFO direct access, immediate access; **~ a distancia** INFO remote access; **~ no restringido** COM GEN unrestricted access; **~ en paralelo** INFO parallel access; **~ portuario** TRANSP port access; **~ público** DER public access; **~ secuencial** INFO sequential access; **~ en serie** INFO serial access; **~ vertical** TRANSP vertical access; ♦ **tener ~ a la información** COM GEN have access to information

accesorio *adj* COM GEN, DER accessory, additional

accesorios: **~ e instalaciones** *m pl* COM GEN, INMOB fixtures and fittings

accidente *m* COM GEN accident; **~ durante el transporte** SEG accident to conveyance; **~ industrial** IND, RRHH industrial accident; **~ laboral** IND, RRHH industrial injury; **~ de trabajo** IND, RRHH, SEG industrial accident

accidentes: **~ en el mar** *m pl* SEG accidents at sea

acción[1]: **de ~** *adj* COM GEN action-oriented; **por ~** *adj* BOLSA per share

acción[2] *f* COM GEN stock (*stck, stk*), *titularidad pública, fracción* share (*sh, shr*), equity; **~ admitida** BOLSA approved share; **~ adquirida** BOLSA, FIN acquired share (*AmE*), acquired stock (*BrE*); **~ afirmativa** RRHH *selección de personal* affirmative action; **~ al portador** BOLSA, CONT, FIN bearer stock, *títulos valores, capital* bearer share; **~ alfa** BOLSA alpha share; **~ amigable** DER friendly suit; **~ amortizable antes del vencimiento** BOLSA, FIN retractable share; **~ asignada** BOLSA, FIN allotted share; **~ autorizada** BOLSA, FIN authorized share; **~ beta** BOLSA, FIN beta share; **~ cancelada** BOLSA, FIN canceled share (*AmE*), cancelled share (*BrE*); **~ de clase A** BOLSA, FIN category A share, class A share; **~ coercitiva** FISC enforcement action; **~ congelada** BOLSA, FIN stopped stock; **~ conjunta** DER joint action; **~ contra la cosa** DER actio in rem; **~ contra la cosa misma** DER actio in rem; **~ contra persona** DER actio in personam; **~ convertible** BOLSA, FIN convertible share; **~ sin cotización oficial** BOLSA, FIN unlisted share; **~ cotizada a menos de un dolar** BOLSA, FIN heavy share, penny share; **~ cubierta** BOLSA, FIN fully-paid share; **~ por daños y perjuicios** DER, SEG action for damages; **~ declinante** BOLSA, ECON, FIN declining share; **~ defensiva** BOLSA widow-and-orphan stock; **~ delta** BOLSA, FIN delta share; **~ con derecho de voto** BOLSA, FIN voting share; **~ sin derecho de voto** BOLSA, FIN nonvoting share; **~ diferida** BOLSA, FIN deferred share; **~ de dividendo diferido** BOLSA, FIN deferred share; **~ emitida al contado** BOLSA, FIN share issued for cash; **~ empresarial no oficial** RRHH unofficial industrial action; **~ especulativa** BOLSA, FIN hot stock (*jarg*); **~ extranjera** BOLSA, FIN foreign share; **~ ficticia** BOLSA, FIN phantom share; **~ fraccionaria** BOLSA, FIN fractional share; **~ gamma** BOLSA, FIN gamma share; **~ garantizada** BOLSA, FIN guaranteed share; **~ gratuita** BOLSA, FIN bonus share; **~ habilitante** BOLSA, FIN qualifying share; **~ ilegal** DER unlawful act; **~ impositiva** FISC assessing action; **~ in rem** DER actio in rem; **~ inconvertible** BOLSA, FIN unconverted share; **~ de índice decreciente** BOLSA, ECON, FIN declining share; **~ industrial** BOLSA industrial share, COM GEN industrial action, FIN industrial share; **~ inicial** RRHH *de huelga* primary action; **~ intercambiada** BOLSA, FIN exchanged share; **~ irredimible consolidada** BOLSA, FIN consolidated debenture stock (*BrE*); **~ laboral** RRHH job action (*jarg*); **~ legal** DER, RRHH legal action; **~ de moda** BOLSA glamor stock (*AmE*), glamour stock (*BrE*); **~ necesaria** COM GEN required action; **~ negociada públicamente** BOLSA, FIN publicly-traded share; **~ no habilitante** BOLSA, FIN nonqualifying share; **~ no oficial** RRHH unofficial action; **~ no participativa** BOLSA nonparticipating share; **~ nominativa** BOLSA, CONT registered share, personal share; **~ nueva** BOLSA, FIN new share; **~ oficial** RRHH official action; **~ ordinaria** BOLSA, CONT, FIN, FISC *títulos valores, capital* equity share, ordinary share; **~ ordinaria cubierta** BOLSA, FIN paid-up common share; **~ pagada parcialmente** BOLSA, FIN partly-paid share; **~ parcialmente liberada** BOLSA, FIN partly-paid share; **~ positiva** DER, RRHH positive action (*jarg*) (*AmE*); **~ de preferencia** BOLSA, FIN, RRHH priority share; **~ preferencial no participativa** BOLSA, FIN nonparticipating preferred stock; ~ **preferente** BOLSA, CONT, FISC *títulos valores, capital* preference share (*BrE*), preferred stock (*AmE*); ~ **preferente amortizable** BOLSA, FIN redeemable preference share; ~ **preferente convertible** BOLSA convertible preferred share; ~ **preferente de dividendo acumulable** BOLSA, FIN cumulative preference share (*BrE*), cumulative preferred stock (*AmE*); ~ **preferente con garantía prendaria** BOLSA, FISC collateralized preferred share; ~ **preferente imponible** FISC taxable preferred share; ~ **preferente con participación** BOLSA participating preference share; ~ **preferente retractable amortizable** BOLSA redeemable retractable preferred share; ~ **preferente de tipo ajustable** BOLSA adjustable rate preferred stock (*ARP*); ~ **preferente de tipo flotante** BOLSA floating-rate preferred share; ~ **preferente sin vencimiento** BOLSA perpetual preferred share; ~ **prescrita** BOLSA prescribed share; ~ **de primera clase** BOLSA golden share; ~ **privilegiada de dividendo** FIN cumulative preference share (*BrE*), cumulative preferred stock (*AmE*); ~ **privilegiada de dividendo acumulable** BOLSA cumulative preference share (*BrE*), cumulative preferred stock (*AmE*); ~ **productora de renta permanente** BOLSA permanent income bearing share (*PIBs*); ~ **recomprada** BOLSA repurchased share; ~ **de recurso** SEG action recourse; ~ **relevante** DER, RRHH *ley sindical* relevant act; ~ **segura** BOLSA safety share, safety stock; ~ **por simpatía** RRHH sympathy action; ~ **solidaria** RRHH *acción industrial* solidarity action; ~ **por solidaridad** RRHH sympathy action; ~ **subdividida** BOLSA subshare; ~ **subordinada** BOLSA junior share; ~ **sustituida** BOLSA substituted share; ~ **transferida** BOLSA transferred share; ~ **de transparencia fiscal** BOLSA flow-through share; ~ **por usurpación de funciones** DER *quo warranto;* ~ **sin valor nominal** BOLSA no-par stock, no-par-value share; ~ **con valor a la par** BOLSA par value share, full share

Acción: ~ Comunitaria *f* COM GEN *UE* Community Action

accionamiento *m* INFO drive

accionariado *m* BOLSA stockholding; ~ **mayoritario** BOLSA majority shareholding; ~ **minoritario** BOLSA minority shareholding

acciones *f pl* COM GEN *títulos valores, capital* stocks (*stcks, stks*), shares (*shs*); ~ **activas** BOLSA active shares; ~ **alfa** BOLSA alpha stock; ~ **de alto rendimiento** BOLSA gilt-edged stock, performance stock; ~ **en alza** BOLSA bullish stock; ~ **amortizables** BOLSA *títulos valores, bolsa, capital* redeemable shares; ~ **apalancadas** FIN leveraged stock; ~ **autorizadas** BOLSA shares authorized; ~ **bancarias** BANCA bank shares; ~ **de base** BOLSA base stock; ~ **beta** BOLSA beta stock; ~ **de capital** BOLSA capital shares; ~ **de capital en circulación** BOLSA outstanding capital stock; ~ **de capitalización** BOLSA capitalization shares; ~ **cíclicas** BOLSA cyclical shares, cycle stock, cyclical stock, ECON cyclical shares; ~ **en circulación** BOLSA shares outstanding; ~ **clase A** BOLSA, FIN A shares (*BrE*); ~ **clasificadas** BOLSA classified stock; ~ **de compañía de gran futuro** BOLSA growth stock; ~ **de compensación** BOLSA compensation stocks (*BrE*); ~ **comunes** BOLSA, CONT, ECON common shares (*BrE*), common stock (*AmE*); ~ **del Consejo de Administración** BOLSA directors' shares; ~ **convertibles** *f* BOLSA, FIN convertible stock;

~ **cotizables** BOLSA listed share; ~ **cotizadas oficialmente** BOLSA stock quoted officially; ~ **delta** BOLSA delta stock (*BrE*); ~ **sin demanda** BOLSA, FIN out-of-favour stock (*BrE*); ~ **depositadas en fideicomiso** BOLSA, FIN shares deposited in trust; ~ **con derecho de voto** BOLSA voting stock; ~ **sin derecho de voto** BOLSA nonvoting stock; ~ **con derechos de suscripción** BOLSA stock with subscription rights; ~ **disponibles** BOLSA, ECON tap stock; ~ **de empresas de alta tecnología** BOLSA high-tech stock; ~ **entregadas en garantía** BOLSA qualification shares; ~ **de escasa aceptación** BOLSA wallflower (*jarg*); ~ **estabilizadoras del mercado** BOLSA tap stocks (*BrE*); ~ **extranjeras** BOLSA foreign stock; ~ **de ferrocarril** BOLSA rail shares; ~ **flotantes** BOLSA floating stock; ~ **de fluctuación volátil** BOLSA yo-yo stock (*jarg*); ~ **gamma** BOLSA gamma stock (*BrE*); ~ **garantizadas** BOLSA equity-related bonds; ~ **indexadas** *m* FIN index-linked stock (*BrE*); ~ **inmovilizadas** BOLSA inactive stock; ~ **sin intereses** BOLSA noninterest-bearing securities; ~ **con intereses garantizados** BOLSA guaranteed stock; ~ **de mala calidad** BOLSA tin shares; ~ **de moda** BOLSA glamor stock (*AmE*); ~ **mojadas** BOLSA watered stock; ~ **no autorizadas** BOLSA unauthorized shares; ~ **no cotizadas en bolsa** BOLSA letter stock; ~ **no emitidas** BOLSA unissued stock, unissued capital stock; ~ **no registradas** BOLSA unregistered stock; ~ **ordinarias** BOLSA, CONT, ECON common shares (*BrE*), common shareholders' equities (*BrE*), common stock (*AmE*), common stockholders' equities (*AmE*); ~ **a la par** BOLSA par stock; ~ **pareadas** BOLSA paired shares; ~ **petrolíferas** BOLSA oil shares; ~ **de preferencia** BOLSA first preferred stock; ~ **preferentes amortizables** BOLSA callable preferred stock; ~ **preferentes convertibles** BOLSA convertible preferred stock; ~ **preferidas a otras de igual clase** BOLSA prior-preferred stock; ~ **a préstamo** BOLSA borrowed stock; ~ **de primer orden** BOLSA blue-chip stock; ~ **privilegiadas** CONT *títulos valores, capital* participating preferred stock; ~ **privilegiadas de dividendo acumulativo** BOLSA cumulative preferred stock (*AmE*), cumulative preference share (*BrE*); ~ **privilegiadas de dividendo no acumulativo** BOLSA noncumulative preferred stock; ~ **de los promotores** BOLSA, FIN founders' shares; ~ **propias readquiridas** BOLSA, CONT treasury stock (*AmE*); ~ **que se anticipan al mercado** BOLSA shares moved ahead; ~ **de rendimiento medio** BOLSA average equity; ~ **rescatables** BOLSA redeemable stock; ~ **rescatadas** BOLSA, CONT treasury stock (*AmE*); ~ **selectas** FIN blue chips; ~ **con valor inferior a un dólar** BOLSA, FIN penny stock; ~ **con valor a la par** BOLSA par value stock; ◆ **los precios de las ~ alcanzaron un máximo histórico** BOLSA stock prices reached an all time high

accionista *mf* BOLSA shareholder, stockholder, RRHH shareholder; ~ **designado(-a)** *m,f* BOLSA designated shareholder, designated stockholder; ~ **especificado (-a)** *m,f* BOLSA specified shareholder, specified stockholder; ~ **mayoritario(-a)** *m,f* BOLSA controlling shareholder, controlling stockholder, majority shareholder; ~ **minoritario(-a)** *m,f* BOLSA minority shareholder, minority stockholder; ~ **nominatario(-a)** *m,f* BOLSA nominee shareholder, nominee stockholder; ~ **nominativo(-a)** *m,f* BOLSA registered shareholder, registered stockholder; ~ **ordinario(-a)** *m,f* BOLSA common shareholder (*BrE*), common stockholder (*AmE*), equity holder, ordinary shareholder, ordinary stockholder; ~ **principal** BOLSA principal shareholder, principal stockholder; ~ **registrado(-a)** *m,f* BOLSA, RRHH shareholder of record (*AmE*), stockholder of record (*AmE*)

ACE *abr* (*Agrupación de Cooperación Europea*) ECON, POL ECG (*European Cooperation Grouping*)

aceites: ~ **de desecho** *m pl* MED AMB waste oils

aceleración *f* COM GEN acceleration

acelerado *adj* COM GEN, *cursos de formación* accelerated

acelerador *m* ECON *inversiones* accelerator; ~ **flexible** ECON flexible accelerator; ~ **de refuerzo** TRANSP *carga* booster

acelerar 1. *vt* COM GEN speed up; **2.** *vi* COM GEN accelerate, put on a spurt (*infrml*)

acento *m* COM GEN emphasis

aceptabilidad *f* COM GEN acceptability

aceptable *adj* COM GEN acceptable, eligible

aceptación *f* COM GEN acceptance, COMS *en un documento* acknowledgement, DER *de contratos*, INMOB, MEDIOS *de producto, manuscritos*, V&M *de marca* acceptance; ~ **absoluta** BANCA clean acceptance; ~ **bajo protesta** COM GEN acceptance supra protest; ~ **bancaria** BANCA *de un cheque* bank acceptance, banker's acceptance; ~ **en blanco** BANCA, FIN blank acceptance; ~ **colateral** BANCA, FIN collateral acceptance; ~ **comercial** COM GEN trade acceptance; ~ **de complacencia** COM GEN accommodation acceptance; ~ **condicionada** COM GEN qualified acceptance; ~ **condicional** BANCA, FIN conditional acceptance; ~ **del consumidor** V&M consumer acceptance; ~ **contra documentos** BANCA acceptance against documents; ~ **después del protesto** BANCA, FIN acceptance supra protest; ~ **directa** BANCA clean acceptance; ~ **de entrega** BOLSA, COM GEN acceptance of delivery; ~ **en firme** COM GEN qualified acceptance; ~ **general** BANCA, COM GEN *documento* general acceptance; ~ **de hipoteca** BANCA assumption of mortgage, mortgage assumption; ~ **por el honor de la firma** COM GEN acceptance for honour; ~ **implícita** BANCA, FIN implied acceptance, tacit acceptance; ~ **incondicional** COM GEN unconditional acceptance; ~ **por intervención** COM GEN acceptance by intervention; ~ **de marca** V&M brand acceptance; ~ **del mercado** V&M market acceptance; ~ **de pago a tanto alzado** COM GEN acceptance of lump-sum settlement; ~ **parcial** FIN partial acceptance; ~ **del pedido** BANCA, FIN order acceptance; ~ **a posteriori** BANCA, FIN after acceptance, afteracceptation; ~ **del producto** V&M product acceptance; ~ **provisional** COM GEN provisional acceptance; ~ **del riesgo** BANCA, FIN risk-taking acceptance; ~ **sin salvedades** FIN unqualified acceptance

aceptado *adj* (*accept.*) COM GEN accepted; ~ **unánimemente** COM GEN unanimously accepted

aceptante *m,f* BANCA *letra* acceptor

aceptar *vt* BANCA *tarjeta de crédito* accept, BOLSA *el beneficio que corresponde* take, COM GEN *solicitud, sugerencia, deseo* accept, admit, take up, COMS *una llamada* accept; ♦ ~ **asesoramiento jurídico** DER take legal advice; ~ **las cuentas** CONT, FIN agree the accounts; ~ **un depósito** BOLSA take a deposit; ~ **la entrega** BOLSA take delivery, COM GEN accept delivery; ~ **una garantía** FIN *préstamo, crédito* take accommodation; ~ **los libros** COM GEN agree the books; ~ **una**

llamada a cobro revertido COMS accept a collect call (*AmE*), accept a reverse-charge call (*BrE*); ~ **un margen de errores** COM GEN allow for a margin of error; **no** ~ **ninguna responsabilidad** COM GEN accept no liability; ~ **la obligación** COM GEN accept liability; ~ **una oferta** BOLSA, COM GEN accept a bid, accept a tender; ~ **en pago** BANCA, FIN accept payment; ~ **pedidos** COM GEN take orders; ~ **el porcentaje** BOLSA take the rate; ~ **referencias de alguien** RRHH take up somebody's references; ~ **a su presentación** COM GEN accept on presentation; ~ **un trabajo** RRHH take a job; ~ **trabajo extra** RRHH take in extra work

acerca: ~ **de** *fra* COMS regarding (*re.*), with reference to

acercamiento *m* COM GEN, GES approach, approximation, POL *de políticas internacionales* approximation

acería *f* IND iron and steel plant, steelworks

acero *m* IND, MED AMB steel; ~ **inoxidable** IND stainless steel

acertado *adj* COM GEN successful

acertar *vt* COM GEN succeed

acervo: ~ **hereditario neto** *m* FISC net estate (*AmE*)

achacar: ~ **algo a alguien** *fra* COM GEN refer sth back to sb

achatar *vt* MAT *curva* flatten

acíclico *adj* BOLSA noncyclical

acierto *m* COM GEN success

aclaración *f* COM GEN, GES explanation, illustration, clarification

aclarar *vt* COM GEN, GES clarify, explain, shed light on

ACNUR *abr* (*Oficina del Alto Comisionado de las Naciones Unidas para los Refugiados*) POL, PROT SOC UNHCR (*United Nations High Commission for Refugees*)

acolchado: **sobre** ~ *m* COMS Jiffy bag®

acometer *vt* COM GEN *problemas* attack, *trabajos* undertake

acomodación: ~ **continua al mercado** *f* BOLSA mark to market

acomodadizo *adj* COM GEN adaptable

acomodar *vt* COM GEN, TRANSP accommodate

acompañado: ~ **por** *fra* COM GEN accompanied by

acompañante *mf* COM GEN escort

acompañar *vt* COM GEN *escoltar* accompany, *visitante* escort

aconsejable *adj* COM GEN advisable

aconsejado: **estar bien** ~ *fra* COM GEN be well advised

aconsejar *vt* COM GEN advise, inform

acontecer *vi* COM GEN eventuate

acontecimiento: ~ **deportivo** *m* COM GEN, OCIO sports event; ~ **mediático** *m* MEDIOS media event; ~ **patrocinado** *m* V&M sponsored event; ~ **posterior al balance general** *m* CONT *contabilidad, auditoría* post balance sheet event

acopiado *adj* COM GEN accumulated

acopiar *vt* COM GEN accumulate

acopio *m* COM GEN accumulation; ~ **de efectivo** FIN cash collection

acoplado: ~ **con** *adj* INFO coupled with

acoplamiento: ~ **automático** *m* TRANSP automatic coupling; ~ **hidráulico** *m* TRANSP hydraulic coupling (*HC*)

acordado: **estar** ~ *fra* COM GEN *plan, informe* be agreed

acordar *vt* BANCA *transacciones* settle, COM GEN agree, *diferencias* resolve

acorde: ~ **con** *fra* COM GEN *expectativas* in line with

acorralar: ~ **a alguien** *fra* COM GEN push sb to the wall

acortar *vt* BOLSA, COM GEN shorten

acoso: ~ **sexual** *m* RRHH sexual harassment

acrecentamiento *m* COM GEN growth, increase; ~ **del crédito** BANCA, FIN credit enhancement

acrecimiento *m* COM GEN, CONT accretion

acreditación *f* COM GEN, PROT SOC *institución, cualificación* accreditation; ~ **de prensa** V&M press pass

acreditado *adj* COM GEN, PROT SOC accredited; ~ **para** BANCA, CONT, FIN credited to

acreditar *vt* COM GEN, PROT SOC *garantizar* accredit

acreedor, a *m,f* COM GEN creditor (*cr*); ~ **asegurado(-a)** BANCA, CONT, FIN secured creditor; ~ **beneficiario(-a)** SEG creditor beneficiary; ~ **con caución** BOLSA bond creditor; ~ **comercial** COM GEN, CONT trade creditor; ~ **garantizado(-a) por fianza** BOLSA bond creditor; ~ **hipotecario(-a)** BANCA, FIN mortgagee; ~ **de impuestos** CONT taxation creditor; ~ **judicial** FIN judgment creditor; ~ **no asegurado(-a)** CONT unsecured creditor; ~ **no garantizado(-a)** CONT unsecured creditor; ~ **ordinario(-a)** CONT general creditor; ~ **preferente** COM GEN preferential creditor; ~ **privilegiado(-a)** COM GEN preferred creditor; ~ **en segunda instancia** BANCA junior creditor; ~ **de la seguridad social** CONT social security creditor; ~ **por sentencia firme** FIN judgment creditor; ~ **en virtud de una sentencia** DER judgment creditor (*AmE*)

acta: ~ **de garantía** *f* COM GEN covering deed; ~ **notarial** *f* DER affidavit; ~ **notarial de no retención** *f* DER no-lien affidavit; ~ **oficial** *f* COM GEN official document; ~ **de proceso** *f* DER law report; ~ **de reconciliación** *f* DER reconciliation bill

Acta: ~ **Única Europea** *f* (*AUE*) DER, POL Single European Act (*SEA*)

actitud *f* COM GEN, GES, V&M attitude; ~ **del usuario** V&M user attitude

activado *adj* GES, IND, INFO activated; ~ **por el tacto** INFO touch-activated; ~ **por la voz** INFO voice-activated, voice-actuated

activador: ~ **de ajuste** *m* COM GEN adjustment trigger

activar *vt* COM GEN activate, INFO *una ventana, un campo* activate, *programas* enable

actividad[1]: **en** ~ *adj* COM GEN active

actividad[2] *f* BANCA *cuenta*, COM GEN activity; ~ **de apoyo** GES support activities; ~ **aseguradora** SEG insurance business; ~ **de auditoría** CONT audit activity; ~ **bancaria** BANCA banking activity; ~ **benéfica** FISC, PROT SOC charitable activity; ~ **clandestina** BOLSA, FIN shady dealing; ~ **comercial** COM GEN, FISC business activity, commercial activity; ~ **comercial con riesgo** COM GEN venture; ~ **de compraventa** BOLSA trading activity; ~ **diaria de consolidación** FIN day-to-day funding activity; ~ **económica** ECON economic activity; ~ **fabril** IND manufacturing activity; ~ **ficticia** COM GEN dummy activity; ~ **industrial** IND industrial activity; ~ **inversionista** ECON investment activity; ~ **no sujeta** FISC nonqualifying business; ~ **secundaria** COM GEN, ECON subactivity; ~ **de ventas** COM GEN, V&M sales activity

actividades: ~ **de apoyo** *f pl* COM GEN, INFO support activities; ~ **de la construcción** *f pl* COM GEN, INMOB construction activities; ~ **cualificadas** *f pl* FISC *manufacturación y procesamiento* qualified activities; ~ **directamente improductivas con fines lucrativos** *f pl* ECON directly unproductive profit-seeking activities (*DUP*); ~ **fiduciarias** *f pl* DER fiduciary activities; ~ **sin intereses** *f pl* FISC passive activities; ~ **primarias** *f pl* COM GEN primary activities; ~ **principales** *f pl* COM GEN primary activities; ~ **que sobrepasan sus atribuciones** *f pl* DER ultra vires activities; ~ **secundarias** *f pl* COM GEN secondary activities; ~ **secundarias e incidentales** *f pl* FISC ancillary and incidental activities; ~ **terciarias** *f pl* COM GEN tertiary activities

activista *mf* POL activist

activo[1] *adj* COM GEN active; **muy** ~ COM GEN proactive

activo[2] *m* COM GEN, BOLSA asset; ~ **acumulado** CONT accrued asset; ~ **amortizable** CONT depreciable asset; ~ **de calidad** FIN quality asset; ~ **casi líquido** CONT, COM GEN, FIN quasi-money; ~ **circulante** CONT, FIN, INMOB current asset; ~ **condicionado** CONT, FIN, INMOB contingent asset; ~ **congelado** FIN frozen asset; ~ **consumible** CONT wasting asset; ~ **contingente** CONT, FIN, INMOB contingent asset; ~ **devengado** CONT accrued asset; ~ **diferido** CONT deferred asset; ~ **disponible** BOLSA *en valores* available asset, FIN *en efectivo*, cash available; ~ **elegible** FIN eligible asset; ~ **de explotación** CONT operating asset, working asset; ~ **de la expropiación** FISC expropriation asset; ~ **exterior** COM GEN asset held abroad; ~ **exterior neto** BANCA net foreign asset; ~ **extranjero** ECON *internacional* overseas asset; ~ **fijo** COM GEN *tierras, propiedades, edificios* fixed asset, CONT noncurrent asset, ECON capital asset; ~ **financiero** FIN financial asset; ~ **flotante** CONT floating asset; ~ **fungible** FIN fungible asset; ~ **inmaterial** CONT intangible asset; ~ **inmobiliario** FIN, INMOB real asset; ~ **inmovilizado** CONT fixed asset, noncurrent asset; ~ **intangible** CONT intangible asset; ~ **interno** BANCA domestic asset; ~ **a largo plazo** BOLSA longer-term asset; ~ **líquido** CONT, FIN, INMOB *en caja* cash asset, *en efectivo* monetary asset, *de las existencias* quick asset; ~ **líquido a corto plazo** BOLSA short-term investment asset; ~ **material** COM GEN tangible asset; ~ **sin movimiento** BOLSA inactive asset; ~ **neto** CONT, FIN *balance* equity, net asset, net worth; ~ **neto circulante** CONT *balance general*, FIN net current asset; ~ **neto real** CONT effective net worth; ~ **neto realizable** CONT net quick asset; ~ **no circulante** CONT noncurrent asset; ~ **no renovable** BOLSA wasting asset; ~ **nominal** CONT nominal asset; ~ **oculto** CONT, FIN concealed asset, hidden asset; ~ **principal** CONT principal asset; ~ **protegido** CONT hedged asset; ~ **realizable** CONT, FIN, INMOB contingent asset, current asset, quick asset; ~ **de riesgo** BANCA risky asset; ~ **seguro** FIN safe asset; ~ **subordinado** CONT subordinated asset; ~ **subyacente** BOLSA underlying asset; ~ **tangible** COM GEN tangible asset

activos *m pl* COM GEN assets; **otros** ~ FIN other assets; ~ **bancarios** BANCA bank assets; ~ **de capital** CONT *en sentido económico* capital, FIN *inversiones* capital assets; ~ **en construcción** CONT assets under construction; ~ **para consumo** ECON wasting assets; ~ **contabilizados netos** CONT net recorded assets; ~ **en curso** CONT assets under construction; ~ **departamentales** CONT departmental assets; ~ **descontables** BANCA bankable assets; ~ **y devoluciones** COM GEN *economía de mercado* assets and drawbacks; ~ **difícilmente liquidables** CONT illiquid assets; ~ **difícilmente realizables** CONT illiquid assets; ~ **disponibles** BANCA, BOLSA, CONT, FIN cash assets, liquid assets; ~ **en divisas** BOLSA foreign assets; ~ **elegibles para el mercado de dinero** BANCA assets eligible for the money market; ~ **exentos** FISC exempt assets; ~ **de la explotación** CONT principal assets; ~ **en el exterior** FIN overseas assets; ~ **fijos** CONT fixed assets; ~ **fijos inmateriales** CONT intangible fixed assets; ~ **fijos intangibles** CONT intangible fixed assets; ~ **fijos tangibles** CONT tangible fixed assets; ~ **físicos** CONT, ECON, FIN physical assets; ~ **imponibles** FISC *ganancias de capital* chargeable assets; ~ **improductivos** BOLSA nonperforming assets; ~ **líquidos** BANCA cash assets, liquid assets, BOLSA cash assets, liquid assets, near-cash items, CONT, FIN cash assets, liquid assets; ~ **líquidos desgravables** FISC *de una compañía, sociedad* allowable liquid assets; ~ **líquidos y garantías gubernamentales** ECON, FIN, POL liquid assets and government securities (*LGS*); ~ **líquidos del sector personal** FIN personal sector liquid assets; ~ **materiales** CONT, ECON, FIN physical assets; ~ **monetarios** CONT monetary assets; ~ **netos subsidiarios** FIN underlying net assets; ~ **no fungibles** CONT nonfungible goods; ~ **no líquidos** CONT illiquid assets; ~ **de primera fila** BOLSA *activos en libras esterlinas* Tier One assets; ~ **principales** BOLSA chief assets; ~ **de reserva** BANCA, FIN reserve assets; ~ **de la reserva monetaria mundial** FIN world monetary reserve assets; ~ **de segunda fila** BOLSA *activos en libras esterlinas* Tier Two assets; ~ **sociales** CONT corporate assets; ~ **tangibles** BOLSA, CONT, ECON, FIN physical assets, tangibles; ~ **tangibles netos por acción** BOLSA net tangible assets per share; ~ **totales** COM GEN total assets

acto[1]: ~ **no comparado por un poder** *adj* DER ultravires

acto[2]: **en el** ~ *adv* COM GEN on the spot

acto[3] *m* COM GEN, DER, POL act; ~ **de avería gruesa** SEG *marina* general average act; ~ **de cesión** COM GEN act of cession; ~ **de daños tasados** COM GEN act of appraising damages; ~ **de garantía** BANCA, CONT covering deed; ~ **ilícito** DER legal wrong; ~ **ilícito civil** DER tort; ~ **de quiebra** BANCA, CONT act of bankruptcy, declaration of bankruptcy; ~ **de reconocimiento** DER act of acknowledgement

actos: ~ **de oposición** *m pl* PATENT opposition proceedings

actuación: ~ **judicial** *f* DER legal action; ~ **por objetivos** *f* GES, RRHH performance against objectives; ~ **subordinada** *f* RRHH secondary action

actual *adj* COM GEN current, present

actualidad: **de** ~ *fra* FIN evergreen; **en la** ~ *fra* COM GEN at the present time

actualización *f* COM GEN, INFO update, updating; ~ **de activos** CONT, FIN revaluation of assets; ~ **automática** INFO automatic updating

actualizado *adj* COM GEN, INFO up-to-date

actualizar *vt* COM GEN *representar realísticamente* actualize, update, CONT write up, INFO update

actuar 1. *vt* COM GEN *persona*, OCIO actuate; ◆ ~ **sobre** COM GEN *carta* act upon; ~ **en calidad de** COM GEN act in the capacity of; ~ **en nombre de** DER act on behalf of; **2.** *vi* COM GEN act, *espectáculo* perform; ◆ ~ **de buena fe** DER act bona fide, act in good faith

actuarial *adj* SEG actuarial

actuario, -a *m,f* SEG actuary

acudir *vi* COM GEN come; ◆ ~ **a las urnas** POL ballot, go to the polls, RRHH ballot; ~ **a votar** POL turn out to vote

acuerdo[1] *m* COM GEN *en el trato* accord, *en el precio* agreement, DER *de partes confrontadas* agreement, GES *del programa* resolution, POL *tratado* alliance;

~ a ~ **de abordo** SEG *marina* waterborne agreement; ~ **aduanero** FISC, IMP/EXP, POL, TRANSP customs arrangement, tariff agreement; ~ **de agencia exclusivo** DER exclusive agency agreement; ~ **del ámbito de una empresa** RRHH company level agreement (*BrE*); ~ **amistoso** COM GEN, DER friendly agreement; ~ **anticipado** TRANSP *navegación* advance arrangement; ~ **de anticipo** TRANSP *navegación* advance arrangement; ~ **antidumping** IND, MED AMB, POL antidumping agreement; ~ **de arbitraje** COM GEN arbitration agreement; ~ **de arrendamiento** COM GEN lease agreement, leasing agreement, rental agreement; ~ **de asegurador principal** SEG leading underwriter agreement; ~ **asegurador de responsabilidad civil y salarial del empresario** SEG workers' compensation and employers' liability agreement; ~ **de asistencia técnica** DER, PATENT know-how agreement;

~ b ~ **de las bases de un sindicato** RRHH union membership agreement (*UMA*); ~ **bilateral de carreteras** TRANSP bilateral road agreement; ~ **de Bretton Woods** ECON, POL *Fondo Monetario Internacional* Bretton Woods Agreement; ~ **de Bridlington** RRHH *sindicatos* Bridlington agreement (*BrE*);

~ c ~ **con cláusula de pago en oro** TRANSP gold clause agreement (*GCA*); ~ **de coalición** POL coalition alliance; ~ **de cobro** FISC collection agreement; ~ **comercial** ECON, POL trade agreement, V&M marketing agreement; ~ **comercial bilateral** ECON, POL bilateral trade agreement; ~ **de comercio multilateral** DER, ECON, POL multilateral trade agreement; ~ **de compensación** BANCA agreement of clearing, DER compensation settlement, ECON *comercio internacional* compensation agreement; ~ **de competencia** COM GEN knockout agreement (*infrml*); ~ **complementario** COM GEN supplementary agreement; ~ **de compraventa** BOLSA, ECON buy-and-sell agreement; ~ **conciliatorio** COM GEN compromise agreement; ~ **condicional de ventas** V&M conditional sales agreement; ~ **sin condiciones** COM GEN agreement with no strings attached; ~ **de confidencialidad** DER, PATENT confidentiality agreement; ~ **de consolidación de resultados** DER pooling arrangement; ~ **contingente** COM GEN standby agreement; ~ **de contrato** DER contract agreement; ~ **de cooperación** COM GEN, POL cooperation agreement; ~ **cuadripartito** COM GEN quadripartite agreement; ~ **de cuenta conjunta** BANCA joint account agreement;

~ d ~ **de depósito** DER deposit agreement; ~ **del diferencial futuro** BOLSA forward spread agreement (*FSA*); ~ **por distritos** RRHH district agreement; ~ **de doble fiscalidad** FISC double tax agreement; ~ **de doble imposición** FISC double taxation agreement;

~ e ~ **efectivo** DER real agreement; ~ **de eficiencia** RRHH efficiency agreement; ~ **de empresa** RRHH company agreement; ~ **entre compañías aéreas** TRANSP interline agreement; ~ **entre los concursantes** COM GEN *subastas* knockout (*infrml*); ~ **entre departamentos** DER interdepartmental settlement; ~ **entre garantes** BANCA agreement among underwriters; ~ **entre suscriptores** BANCA agreement among underwriters; ~ **de entrega de equipos** IND equipment handover agreement; ~ **por escrito** DER written agreement; ~ **estándar** COM GEN standard agreement;

~ f ~ **de fábrica** *Esp* (*cf contrato de fábrica AmL*) RRHH shop-floor agreement (*BrE*); ~ **de fideicomiso** COM GEN trust agreement; ~ **de final abierto** RRHH open-ended agreement; ~ **fiscal** ECON, FISC, POL tax treaty, tax agreement; ~ **formal** COM GEN formal agreement; ~ **de franquicia** DER franchise agreement;

~ g ~ **de garantía** BANCA guarantee agreement, guaranty agreement; ~ **general** COM GEN, RRHH blanket agreement; ~ **general de préstamos** ECON *grupo de los diez* general agreement to borrow (*GAB*); ~ **general sobre créditos** FIN general agreement to borrow (*GAB*); ~ **de gestión** GES management agreement; ~ **global** COM GEN package deal, RRHH comprehensive agreement; ~ **de grupo comprador** FIN purchase group agreement;

~ i ~ **de imposición recíproca** FISC reciprocal taxation agreement; ~ **de indemnización** DER compensation settlement; ~ **independiente** RRHH substantive agreement; ~ **informal** COM GEN informal arrangement; ~ **de interés a término** BOLSA forward rate agreement (*FRA*); ~ **de intermediario seleccionado** BOLSA selected dealer agreement; ~ **internacional** DER, POL international agreement; ~ **interno** RRHH domestic agreement (*BrE*); ~ **irrevocable** DER irrevocable settlement;

~ j ~ **de Jamaica** ECON Jamaica Agreement;

~ l ~ **laboral** RRHH labor agreement (*AmE*), labour agreement (*BrE*); ~ **legal** DER legal settlement; ~ **de licencia** DER licensing agreement; ~ **local** RRHH local agreement; ~ **de El Louvre** ECON *estabilización de tipos de cambios* Louvre Accord;

~ m ~ **marco** DER basic agreement, framework agreement; ~ **de mercado metódico** ECON orderly market agreement (*OMA*); ~ **modelo** RRHH pattern agreement; ~ **monetario** DER monetary agreement; ~ **multilateral** DER, ECON, POL multilateral agreement; ~ **multiplanta** RRHH multiplant bargaining; ~ **multisectorial** RRHH multiemployer bargaining; ~ **multisindical** RRHH multi-union bargaining (*BrE*);

~ n ~ **sin necesidad de huelga** RRHH strike-free agreement; ~ **no escrito** COM GEN, DER unwritten agreement; ~ **de no ir a la huelga** RRHH no-strike agreement, no-strike deal; ~ **de normalización** COM GEN standardization agreement; ~ **de notificación** DER *compensación de tierras* notice treaty;

~ o ~ **de ocupación limitada** DER, INMOB limited occupancy agreement; ~ **organizado** RRHH staged agreement;

~ p ~ **de pago colectivo** RRHH collective pay agreement; ~ **de participación** DER participation agreement; ~ **de planta** RRHH plant agreement; ~ **de Plaza** ECON Plaza agreement; ~ **en plica** DER escrow agreement; ~ **de precios e ingresos** RRHH prices and incomes agreement; ~ **de préstamo para la construcción** BANCA building loan agreement; ~ **de primeros aseguradores para fletes marítimos** SEG *naval* leading underwriters' agreement for marine cargo business (*LUAMC*); ~ **privado** COM GEN private arrangement; ~ **de procedimiento** RRHH procedure agreement, pro-

cedural agreement; ~ **de productividad** DER, ECON, IND, RRHH productivity agreement, productivity bargaining; ~ **provisional** COM GEN interim agreement;

~ r ~ **reajustable plurianual** FIN multiyear rescheduling agreement (*MYRA*); ~ **recíproco** DER reciprocal agreement; ~ **de recompra** ECON *comercio internacional* buy-back agreement; ~ **reestructurable plurianual** FIN multiyear rescheduling agreement (*MYRA*), multiyear restructuring agreement (*MYRA*); ~ **regional** ECON regional agreement; ~ **regulado** FIN regulated agreement; ~ **de retroventa inversa** FIN reverse repurchase agreement;

~ s ~ **y satisfacción** FIN *bono, obligación* accord and satisfaction; ~ **sectorial** RRHH *UE* industry-wide agreement; ~ **de seguridad de empleo** RRHH job security agreement; ~ **de separación** DER separation agreement; ~ **de servicio** COM GEN service agreement; ~ **sindical** RRHH union agreement; ~ **con un solo sindicato** RRHH single union agreement (*BrE*); ~ **sobre fijación de precios** DER, ECON, FIN pricing arrangement; ~ **sobre margen** BOLSA spreading agreement; ~ **sobre mercancías** COM GEN, DER, ECON commodity agreement; ~ **sobre nueva tecnología** COM GEN new technology agreement; ~ **sobre un producto básico** COM GEN, DER, ECON commodity agreement; ~ **sobre los tipos de cambio** ECON exchange rate agreement; ~ **de un solo sindicato** RRHH single union deal (*BrE*); ~ **de subordinación** COM GEN subordination agreement; ~ **de suscripción** BOLSA underwriting agreement;

~ t ~ **por tiempo establecido** RRHH fixed-term agreement, fixed-term deal; ~ **de tripulación** TRANSP crew agreement (*BrE*); ~ **de trueque** DER, ECON barter's agreement;

~ u ~ **umbral** RRHH threshold agreement; ~ **unánime** COM GEN consensus agreement; ~ **unilateral** DER, ECON, POL unilateral agreement;

~ v ~ **de venta e información** TRANSP sell and report agreement; ~ **de venta libre** TRANSP free sale agreement; ~ **verbal** COM GEN verbal agreement; ~ **vinculante** DER binding agreement; ~ **de voluntades** DER meeting of minds

acuerdo[2]: **de común** ~ *fra* COM GEN, DER by common consent, by mutual agreement, by mutual consent; **no llegar a un** ~ *fra* COM GEN fail to reach agreement; **estar de** ~ **con** *fra* COM GEN agree with, go along with, agree to; **de** ~ **con** *fra* COM GEN according to; **estar de** ~ **en** *fra* COM GEN *precio, plazos de venta* agree on; **por** ~ *fra* COM GEN by arrangement; **de** ~ **al horario** *fra* COM GEN according to schedule; **de** ~ **al programa** *fra* COM GEN according to schedule; **por** ~ **mutuo** *fra* COM GEN, DER by mutual consent; **mediante** ~ **privado** *fra* COM GEN, DER by private contract; **de** ~ **con sus instrucciones** *fra* COM GEN in accordance with your instructions; **por** ~ **tácito** *fra* COM GEN by tacit agreement

Acuerdo: ~ **de las Bermudas** *m* ECON, POL Bermuda Agreement; ~ **GATT** *m* (*Acuerdo General sobre Aranceles y Comercio*) ECON, POL GATT (*General Agreement on Tariffs and Trade*); ~ **General sobre Aranceles y Comercio** *m* (*Acuerdo GATT*) ECON, POL General Agreement on Tariffs and Trade (*GATT*); ~ **de Libre Comercio** *m* POL *entre países europeos* Free Trade Agreement (*FTA*); ~ **Multifibra** *m* ECON *comercio internacional desde 1973* Multi-Fiber Arrangement (*AmE*) (*MFA*), Multi-Fibre Arrangement (*BrE*) (*MFA*); ~ **de Schengen** *m* IMP/EXP, POL *control de* *fronteras en la UE* Schengen Agreement; **~ Voluntario de Armadores de Petroleros sobre la Responsabilidad por Contaminación de Crudos** *m* (*TOVALOP*) MED AMB, TRANSP Tanker Owners' Voluntary Agreement Concerning Liability for Oil Pollution

acuerdos: ~ bancarios *m pl* BANCA banking arrangements; **~ de disolución** *m pl* DER winding-up arrangements; **~ de fondo común** *m pl* COM GEN pooling arrangements; **~ para imprevistos** *m pl* COM GEN contingency arrangements; **~ que eximen de responsabilidad** *m pl* DER hold-harmless agreements

Acuerdos: ~ Internacionales sobre Comercio *m pl* BOLSA International Commodity Agreements (*ICA's*)

acumulable: no ~ *adj* BANCA nonaccruing, COM GEN noncumulative

acumulación *f* BANCA accumulation, COM GEN *de capital, riqueza, intereses* backlog, CONT accumulation, accrual, FIN accumulation, FISC bunching; **~ de apelaciones** FISC joinder of appeals; **~ de capital** ECON, FIN capital accumulation; **~ de existencias** COM GEN stockpiling; **~ de intereses** BANCA accrual of interest; **~ modificada** CONT modified accrual; **~ de pedidos finales** COM GEN backlog of final orders; **~ de riesgos** SEG accumulation of risk; **~ de trabajo** COM GEN backlog of work

acumulaciones *f pl* BANCA, CONT, FIN accruals

acumulado *adj* COM GEN *interés* accrued, accumulated, BOLSA gathered

acumular *vt* COM GEN *interés* accrue, *capital* accumulate, BOLSA *gradualmente* gather, *con un margen adicional* pyramid; ◆ **~ deudas** BANCA, FIN run up a debt; **~ interés** BANCA accrue interest; **~ en las pausas** BOLSA gather in the stops

acumularse *v refl* COM GEN accumulate

acumulativo *adj* BOLSA *dividendos* accumulative, COM GEN cumulative (*cum.*); **no ~** COM GEN noncumulative

acuñación *f* BANCA, ECON coinage, mintage; **~ del impuesto** ECON, FISC tax-wedge

acuñamiento: ~ de la carga *m* TRANSP blocking off

acuñar *vt* BANCA, ECON mint

acuracidad *f* MAT accuracy

acusación *f* DER *de un crimen* accusation, *de un juez* charge, *fiscal* prosecution; ◆ **la ~ no se mantuvo en el tribunal** DER the case did not stand up in court

acusador, a: ~ público(-a) *m,f* DER public prosecutor

acusar *vt* DER accuse; ◆ **~ a alguien** DER bring an accusation against sb; **~ recibo de** COM GEN *correo, bienes*, COMS *carta, cheque*, FIN acknowledge receipt of; **~ recibo por carta** COM GEN, COMS acknowledge receipt by letter

acuse: ~ de depósito de efectivo *m* FIN cash deposit acknowledgement; **~ de recepción de deuda** *m* COM GEN, FIN acknowledgement of debt; **~ de recibo** *m* COM GEN *correo certificado* acknowledgement (*Ackt.*), *justificante* acknowledgement of receipt (*Ackt.*); **~ de recibo de efectivo** *m* FIN cash acknowledgement

AD *abr* (*automatización del dibujo*) INFO DA (*design automation, drawing automation*)

ADA *abr* (*Ayuda del Automovilista*) TRANSP Spanish organization for motorists, ≈ AA (*BrE*) (*Automobile Association*), ≈ AAA (*AmE*) (*American Automobile Association*), ≈ RAC (*BrE*) (*Royal Automobile Club*)

adaptabilidad *f* COM GEN, INFO adaptability

adaptable *adj* COM GEN, INFO adaptable

adaptación *f* COM GEN *proceso* adaptation, *arreglo* tuning, adjustment, INFO adaptation, POL transposal; **~ especial** COM GEN tailoring; **~ del producto** COM GEN product adaptation

adaptado *adj* COM GEN, INFO, V&M adapted, tailored

adaptador *m* COM GEN, INFO adaptor; **~ color/gráficos** (*CGA*) INFO color/graphics adaptor (*AmE*) (*CGA*), colour/graphics adaptor (*BrE*) (*CGA*); **~ de copia** COM GEN copy-adaptor; **~ de corriente** IND, INFO current adaptor (*AmE*), mains adaptor (*BrE*); **~ de gráficos de vídeo** AmL ver *adaptador de gráficos de vídeo Esp*; **~ de gráficos de vídeo** *Esp* (*VGA*) INFO video graphics adaptor (*VGA*); **~ a la red** IND, INFO current adaptor (*AmE*), mains adaptor (*BrE*); **~ en serie** INFO serial adaptor; **~ videográfico** (*VGA*) INFO video graphics adaptor (*VGA*)

adaptar *vt* COM GEN, INFO, V&M adapt, tailor

adaptarse: ~ a *v refl* COM GEN *una situación* adjust oneself to

adecuación *f* COM GEN *a una situación* adjustment, *de tecnología, procedimientos, proyectos* adaptability

adecuadamente: ~ fundado *adj* CONT adequately funded

adecuado *adj* COM GEN proportionate, suitable, *fondos, provisiones, explicaciones* adequate; **~ para** COM GEN appropriate for

adelantado: por ~ *adv* COM GEN in advance, up front

adelantados: ~ y rezagados *m pl* BOLSA leaders and laggards

adelantamiento *m* ADMIN, COM GEN advancement

adelantar *vt* ADMIN advance, COM GEN accelerate, advance, GES *propuestas* put forward; ◆ **~ el dinero** FIN put money down; **~ el impuesto efectivo** FISC forward average; **~ el pago del impuesto** FISC forward average

adelanto[1]: **~ de** *adv* COM GEN in addition to

adelanto[2] *m* COM GEN advance; **~ de capital circulante** FIN, POL working capital advance; **~ a cuenta** BANCA, COM GEN, V&M down payment; **~ de dinero** COM GEN, CONT, FIN money up front; **~ sobre mercancías** COM GEN advance on goods

adeudar *vt* COM GEN charge against, *cuenta* debit, *un pagaré* owe

adherir *vt* COM GEN *etiqueta* affix, DER, POL comply; **~ a** COM GEN *contratos* adhere to

adhesión *f* COM GEN compliance, POL *a la UE* accession

ad hoc *adj* COM GEN ad hoc

adición *f* MAT adding, MEDIOS addendum, *corrección de textos* addition, PATENT improvement patent; ◆ **sin ~, sin corrección** COM GEN no addition, no correction

adicto, -a: ~ al trabajo *m,f* RRHH workaholic

adiestramiento *m* RRHH training

ad interim *adj* DER *juicio* ad interim

aditivos: sin ~ *adj* COM GEN free of all additives, additive-free

adj. *abr* (*adjunto*) COM GEN, COMS encl. (*enclosed*)

adjudicación *f* BOLSA allocation, COM GEN adjudication, *de contrato* award, CONT *de fondos a una reserva*, DER *de contrato* allocation, adjudication, FIN *de fondos* appropriation, *de fondos a una reserva* allocation; **~ al postor que presenta la oferta más baja** V&M allocation to the lowest tenderer; **~ de espacio para contenedores**

TRANSP container space allocation; ~ **por licitación** BOLSA allocation by tender; ~ **de préstamos** COM GEN borrowing allocation; ~ **prioritaria** BOLSA priority allocation; ~ **de quiebra** COM GEN, CONT, DER, FIN adjudication of bankruptcy order; ~ **de recursos** COM GEN resource allocation; ~ **de valores** BOLSA allotment of securities

adjudicador, a *m,f* COM GEN adjudicator

adjudicar *vt* COM GEN *subastas, contratos* adjudicate, knock down, CONT *dinero, obligaciones, contratos* allocate, DER adjudicate, award, FIN appropriate, allocate, V&M *subastas, contratos* adjudicate, knock down; ♦ ~ **importancia a** COM GEN attach importance to; ~ **una quiebra** CONT adjudicate bankruptcy

adjunta: ~ **copia de la carta** *fra* COM GEN, COMS enclosed copy of letter

adjuntar *vt* COMS, COM GEN attach, enclose

adjunto[1] *adj* (*adj.*) COMS, COM GEN enclosed (*encl.*)

adjunto[2]**,-a:** ~ **al equipo asesor** *m,f* RRHH staff assistant

administración *f* (*admón.*) ADMIN, COM GEN administration (*admin.*), management, DER back office, GES administration (*admin.*), direction, stewardship, management, INMOB *de propiedad herencia* administration, RRHH direction, management; ~ **activa** COM GEN, GES active management; ~ **de activos** CONT, FIN asset management; ~ **de activos y pasivos** CONT, FIN, GES assets and liabilities management; ~ **autoritaria** GES, RRHH authoritarian management; ~ **de la calidad** *AmL* (*cf gestión de la calidad Esp*) GES, IND, V&M quality control; ~ **del cambio** GES management of change; ~ **de carteras** COM GEN, FIN portfolio management; ~ **científica** COM GEN, GES, MAT scientific management; ~ **por contingencia** GES contingency management; ~ **por crisis** GES management by crisis; ~ **de una cuenta** BANCA account management; ~ **por cuenta ajena** DER trust; ~ **democrática** POL, RRHH democratic management; ~ **del desarrollo profesional** GES, RRHH career management; ~ **descentralizada** GES, POL decentralized management; ~ **de la deuda pública** DER, POL national debt management (*BrE*), public debt management (*AmE*); ~ **efectiva** GES, RRHH effective management; ~ **de empresas** COM GEN business administration, business management; ~ **de existencias** FIN, IND inventory management; ~ **fiduciaria** DER trusteeship; ~ **financiera** FIN financial administration, financial management; ~ **de fondos** BANCA *banca de inversión* fund management; ~ **general** GES general management; ~ **impositiva** GES, RRHH macho management; ~ **intuitiva** GES, RRHH intuitive management; ~ **de inversiones** FIN investment management; ~ **judicial** COM GEN, DER receivership; ~ **laboral** RRHH labor administration (*AmE*), labour administration (*BrE*); ~ **local** DER, POL local government; ~ **de más alto rango** GES, RRHH senior management; ~ **de materiales** TRANSP materials management; ~ **de menudeo** *AmL* (*cf gestión al por menor Esp, cf gestión minorista Esp*) IND, V&M retail management; ~ **por objetivos** GES management by objectives (*MBO*); ~ **de la pequeña empresa** COM GEN, GES small business administration (*SBA*); ~ **del personal** GES, RRHH personnel administration, personnel management, staff management; ~ **de la producción** IND production management; ~ **programada** GES programmed management; ~ **de proyectos** FIN, GES, RRHH project management; ~ **pública** DER public

administration, POL government (*govt*), public administration, Civil Service (*CS*), *ministerio* administration; ~ **racionalizada** GES rational management; ~ **de recursos humanos** GES, RRHH human resource administration, human resource management (*HRM*); ~ **del riesgo** BOLSA, FIN, GES risk management, venture management; ~ **de sueldos y salarios** RRHH wage and salary administration; ~ **superior** GES, RRHH senior management; ~ **tributaria** FISC tax administration

administrado *adj* COM GEN administered

administrador, a *m,f* ADMIN, COM GEN administrator, DER *quiebra* curator, official receiver, *de propiedad, herencia* administrator, INMOB *agrimensor, de propiedades* bailiff, *de propiedad, herencia* administrator; ~ **de activos** BOLSA asset manager; ~ **de aduanas** IMP/EXP, RRHH collector of customs; ~ **de bienes** FIN estate manager; ~ **de la cobertura** BOLSA hedge manager; ~ **del consorcio** BANCA, BOLSA, DER, INMOB trustee; ~ **de la deuda** RRHH debt manager; ~ **fiduciario(-a)** BANCA, DER, INMOB trustee; ~ **de fincas** , COM GEN, INMOB estate agent (*BrE*), realtor (*AmE*); ~ **de herencia** FIN appointed executor, appointed guardian, estate manager; ~ **judicial de una quiebra** DER *comercial* official receiver; ~ **de marketing** *Esp* (*cf administrador de mercadotecnia AmL*) RRHH marketing officer; ~ **de mercadotecnia** *AmL* (*cf administrador de marketing Esp*) RRHH marketing officer; ~ **de pasivos** BOLSA liability manager; ~ **de la propiedad** DER custodian of property; ~ **de propiedades** FIN estate manager; ~ **del sistema** INFO system administrator; ~ **único(-a)** RRHH sole director and C.E.O; ~ **de valores** COM GEN securities administrator

administrar *vt* ADMIN *personal* manage, run, COM GEN, GES *capital* administer, *personal* manage, run; ♦ ~ **mal** GES mismanage; ~ **los negocios de alguien** COM GEN, GES manage sb's affairs

administrativo[1] *adj* COM GEN administrative

administrativo[2]**,-a** *m,f* RRHH administrator, white-collar worker; ~ **superior** RRHH senior clerk

admisibilidad *f* COM GEN, DER acceptability, admissibility, ECON *de dinero* admissibility

admisible *adj* COM GEN, DER, ECON admissible

admisión *f* COM GEN, IMP/EXP, RRHH *aduanas* admission, induction, *entrada* intake; ~ **de acciones, bonos y valores** FIN admission of securities; ~ **a la cotización** BOLSA admission to quotation, admission to listing; ~ **gratuita** OCIO admission free; ~ **de tercero en juicio** DER interpleader; ~ **de un valor en bolsa** BOLSA listing; ♦ **por su propia** ~ COM GEN by his own admission

admitir *vt* COM GEN acknowledge, admit, allow, PROT SOC *asignar habitación a* accommodate, RRHH *nuevos socios en una empresa* admit, SEG *reclamación* admit, allow; ♦ ~ **en el Colegio de abogados** DER admit to the Bar

admón. *abr* (*administración*) ADMIN, COM GEN, GES, RRHH admin. (*administration*)

admonición: ~ **por mora** *f* COM GEN formal notice

adopción *f* ECON *de moneda única*, GES adoption; ~ **del sistema métrico decimal** COM GEN conversion to the metric system, metrication

adoptar *vt* COM GEN borrow, pass, *una postura* take up, *procedimientos, resoluciones* adopt; ♦ ~ **una postura conjunta** COM GEN adopt a joint stance; ~ **una postura diferente** COM GEN take a different view

adquirido *adj* COM GEN acquired, FISC *fideicomisario, beneficiario* vested

adquirir *vt* COM GEN *comprar* purchase, acquire; ◆ ~ **acciones** BOLSA take up stocks; ~ **algo a precio nominal** COM GEN take sth at face value; ~ **una opción** BOLSA acquire an option, take up an option; ~ **una participación** BOLSA take an equity stake, COM GEN acquire an interest; ~ **la residencia legal** DER take up legal residence

adquisición *f* COM GEN *compra* purchase, *de una compañía* acquisition; ~ **de acciones** BOLSA acquisition of stock, takeup of shares; ~ **de activos** CONT acquisition of assets; ~ **por compra** FIN purchase acquisition; ~ **de una empresa** INMOB capital appropriations; ~ **por fallecimiento** FISC mortality gain; ~ **fracasada** BOLSA *de empresa* bust-up acquisition; ~ **de hipoteca** BANCA mortgage assumption; ~ **mayoritaria de las acciones de una sociedad por otra** BOLSA take-over merger; ~ **de mercancías** FISC acquisition of goods; ~ **neta de activos financieros** FIN net acquisition of financial assets (*NAFA*); ~ **de una opción de compra** BOLSA call purchase; ~ **de una opción de venta** BOLSA put purchase; ~ **pagada** SEG paid-up addition; ~ **parcial** DER, INMOB partial taking; ~ **de participación en acciones** BOLSA acquisition of shareholdings

adquisiciones: ~ **apalancades** *f pl* FIN leveraged buyout; ~ **netas** *f pl* ECON, FIN net acquisitions

adscripción *f* COM GEN enrollment (*AmE*), enrolment (*BrE*)

aduana *f* COM GEN customs; ◆ **en** ~ DER, IMP/EXP, TRANSP in bond (*IB*)

aduanero, -a *m,f* FISC, IMP/EXP customs officer

aducir *vt* DER adduce

ad valórem *adj* COM GEN ad valorem (*ad val*)

adversario, -a *m,f* DER adversary

adverso *adj* COM GEN adverse

advertencia *f* COM GEN word of warning, GES word of advice, RRHH warning; ~ **escrita** GES, RRHH written warning; ~ **pública** COM GEN public warning; ~ **verbal** GES, RRHH verbal warning; ◆ **sin** ~ **previa** COM GEN without previous warning

advertencias: ~ **iterativas** *f pl* INFO iterative warnings; ~ **repetidas** *f pl* COM GEN repeated warnings

advertir *vt* COM GEN, GES, RRHH advise, warn; ◆ ~ **a uno de la situación** COM GEN acquaint sb with the situation

AEAP *abr* (*Asociación Europea de Agencias de Publicidad*) V&M EAAA (*European Association of Advertising Agencies*)

AEC *abr* (*Agencia Europea para la Cooperación*) DER, POL EAC (*European Agency for Cooperation*)

AECA *abr* (*Asociación Española de Compañías Aéreas*) TRANSP ≈ SBAC (*Society of British Aerospace Companies*)

AELC *abr* (*Asociación Europea de Libre Comercio*) ECON, POL EFTA (*European Free Trade Association*)

AENA *abr* (*Aeropuertos Españoles y Navegación Aérea*) TRANSP Spanish airports and air traffic authority, ≈ AACC (*Airport Associations Coordinating Council*)

AENOR *abr* (*Asociación Española de Normalización y Certificación*) COM GEN, PATENT ≈ BSI (*British Standards Institution*), ≈ ASA (*American Standards Association*)

AEP *abr* (*Agencia Europea para la Productividad*) ECON, POL EPA (*European Productivity Agency*)

aerobús *m* TRANSP airbus

aerodeslizador *m* TRANSP hovercraft

aeródromo *m* TRANSP *aviación* aerodrome (*BrE*), airdrome (*AmE*), airport

aeroespacial *adj* IND aerospace

aerofotogrametría *f* TRANSP aerial survey

aerofotometría *f* TRANSP aerial survey

aerograma *m* COMS aerogram

aeromoza *f* AmL (*cf azafata Esp*) OCIO, TRANSP air hostess

aeronave *f* TRANSP aeroplane (*BrE*), aircraft, airplane (*AmE*)

aeroplano *m* TRANSP aeroplane (*BrE*), aircraft, airplane (*AmE*)

aeropuerto *m* TRANSP aerodrome (*BrE*), airdrome (*AmE*), airport; ~ **de destino** TRANSP destination airport; ~ **internacional** TRANSP international airport

Aeropuertos: ~ **Españoles y Navegación Aérea** *m pl* (*AENA*) TRANSP Spanish airports and air traffic authority, ≈ Airport Associations Co-ordinating Council (*AACC*)

afecta: en lo que ~ **a** *fra* PATENT in reference to

afectación *f* ECON *de fondos para una reserva* appropriation, FIN *dinero, cargas* allocation

afectado: muy ~ *adj* COM GEN *por una pérdida* hard hit; ~ **adversamente** *adj* COM GEN adversely affected

afectar *vt* COM GEN, DER *el fallo, oferta de dinero* affect, appropriate, FIN *contrato* allocate

afianzar *vt* BANCA, FIN guarantee, secure

afiliación *f* COM GEN affiliation; ~ **sindical** RRHH trade union membership (*BrE*), trade union subscription (*BrE*), union affiliation, union membership; ~ **a un sindicato** RRHH trade union membership (*BrE*), trade union subscription (*BrE*), union affiliation, union membership

afiliado[1]: **no** ~ *adj* COM GEN unaffiliated

afiliado[2]**, -a** *m,f* COM GEN affiliate

afiliar *vt* COM GEN affiliate, join

afiliarse[1]: ~ **a** *v refl* COM GEN affiliate to

afiliarse[2]: ~ **a un sindicato** *fra* RRHH join a union

afirmación *f* COM GEN assertion; ~ **del mensaje publicitario** V&M copy claim

afirmarse *v refl* COM GEN *moneda* firm up, ECON *crecimiento económico* sustain

aflojar *vt* COM GEN stump up (*jarg*); ◆ ~ **las riendas** ECON slacken the reins

afluencia *f* ECON affluence; ~ **de capital** BOLSA, ECON capital inflow; ~ **de divisas** ECON accrual of exchange

aforamiento: ~ **del petróleo** *m* MED AMB, TRANSP oil gage (*AmE*), oil gauge (*BrE*)

aforismo *m* COM GEN aphorism

afrontar *vt* COM GEN *problemas*, GES face, tackle; ◆ ~ **los hechos** COM GEN face the facts; ~ **riesgos** BOLSA face risks

AFYDE *abr* (*Asociación para la Formación y Desarrollo Empresarial*) ECON training and business development association

agarrotarse *v refl* Esp (*cf engarrotarse AmL*) SEG bind

agencia *f* ADMIN, BANCA, COM GEN, FIN *oficina*, RRHH *departamento* agency (*agcy, agy.*); ~ **de aduanas** ECON,

FISC, IMP/EXP customs agency; **~ de alojamiento** PROT SOC accommodation agency; **~ de capacitación** *AmL* (*cf agencia de formación Esp*) RRHH training agency (*BrE*) (*TA*); **~ de cobro de deudas** FIN debt collection agency (*DCA*); **~ de colocaciones** COM GEN, RRHH employment agency, recruitment agency; **~ de creación** V&M *publicidad* hot shop (*jarg*); **~ creativa** V&M *publicidad* hot shop (*jarg*); **~ de crédito** FIN credit agency; **~ donante** PROT SOC donor agency; **~ de empleo** COM GEN, RRHH employment agency, employment bureau; **~ extranjera libre** TRANSP free foreign agency (*FFA*); **~ de formación** *Esp* (*cf agencia de capacitación AmL*) RRHH training agency (*BrE*) (*TA*); **~ implícita** COM GEN implied agency; **~ de importación** COM GEN indent house; **~ inmobiliaria** INMOB estate agency (*BrE*), real estate agency (*AmE*); **~ marítima** TRANSP shipping office; **~ de mensajería** COM GEN express agency; **~ mercantil** V&M mercantile agency; **~ multilateral** ECON, POL multilateral agency; **~ multilateral de garantía de inversión** FIN multilateral investment guarantee agency (*MIGA*), multilateral investment guaranty agency (*MIGA*); **~ de noticias** COMS, MEDIOS news agency (*BrE*), wire service (*AmE*); **~ de prensa** MEDIOS press agency; **~ privada** COM GEN private agency; **~ de publicidad** MEDIOS, V&M advertising agency; **~ de publicidad global** MEDIOS, V&M full-service agency; **~ de rating** BOLSA bond rating agency; **~ de referencias de crédito** FIN credit reference agency; **~ de relaciones públicas** MEDIOS, V&M public relations agency; **~ de servicios generales** ADMIN common service agency; **~ con servicios plenos** MEDIOS, V&M *publicidad* agency with full service; **~ de trabajo** COM GEN, RRHH employment agency, employment bureau; **~ de trabajo temporal** COM GEN, RRHH temping agency; **~ de transporte marítimo** TRANSP shipping agency; **~ de transporte urgente** COM GEN, COMS courier agency; **~ de venta de billetes** COM GEN, OCIO, TRANSP ticket agency; **~ de venta de localidades** COM GEN, OCIO, TRANSP ticket agency; **~ de ventas** V&M sales agency; **~ de viajes** OCIO travel agency, travel bureau; **~ de viajes con precios reducidos** OCIO bucket shop; **~ de voluntariado** PROT SOC voluntary agency

Agencia: **~ de Desarrollo Internacional** *f* ECON International Development Agency; **~ Espacial Europea** *f* IND, POL European Space Agency (*ESA*); **~ Europea para la Cooperación** *f* (*AEC*) DER, POL European Agency for Cooperation (*EAC*); **~ Europea para la Productividad** *f* (*AEP*) ECON, POL European Productivity Agency (*EPA*); **~ Internacional de la Energía** *f* (*AIE*) MED AMB International Energy Agency (*IEA*); **~ de las Naciones Unidas para la Ayuda a la Infancia** *f* (*UNICEF*) POL, PROT SOC United Nations Children's Fund (*UNICEF*); **~ de las Naciones Unidas para la Ayuda a los Refugiados** *f* POL, PROT SOC United Nations Relief and World Agency (*UNRWA*); **~ de Naciones Unidas para el Desarrollo Social** *f* (*ANUDS*) POL United Nations Research Institute for Social Development; **~ de Protección del Medio Ambiente** *f* MED AMB Environmental Protection Agency (*EPA*)

agencias: **~ publicitarias creativas** *f pl* V&M creative hot shops

agenda *f* COM GEN agenda, diary; **~ oculta** COM GEN, GES hidden agenda; **~ personal** ADMIN organizer;

~ provisional COM GEN tentative agenda; **~ telefónica** COMS telephone book; ◆ **estar en la ~** ADMIN, COM GEN be on the agenda

agentaria *f* BANCA Spanish national savings trust, ≈ National Savings Bank (*NSB*)

agente *mf* COM GEN agent (*agt*), SEG *de pólizas* broker, V&M agent (*agt*); **~ administrador(-a)** *m,f* GES managing agent; **~ de aduanas** IMP/EXP customs broker; **~ de agrupamiento de importaciones** RRHH import groupage operator; **~ de almacén** RRHH stockist agent; **~ asalariado(-a)** *m,f* RRHH salaried agent; **~ autorizado(-a)** *m,f* BANCA authorized dealer, COM GEN authorized agent, franchised dealer (*BrE*); **~ auxiliar de bolsa** BOLSA floor broker; **~ de cabotaje** TRANSP coasting broker; **~ de carga** IMP/EXP, TRANSP loading agent; **~ de carga y descarga en tierra** TRANSP *aviación* ground handling agent; **~ de carga fraccionada** TRANSP break bulk agent; **~ de coches de alquiler** OCIO, TRANSP car-hire operator; **~ de compensación** BANCA clearing agent; **~ comprador(a)** *m,f* COM GEN acquisition agent; **~ de compras** COM GEN procurement agent; **~ de compraventa** RRHH sale and purchase broker; **~ consignatario(-a)** *m,f* TRANSP umbrella agent; **~ del consignatario** RRHH receiver's agent; **~ de despacho de aduanas** IMP/EXP clearance agent, customs clearance agent; **~ de direcciones** COM GEN list broker; **~ económico(-a)** *m,f* ECON economic agent; **~ exclusivo(-a) de negociación** *m,f* RRHH sole bargaining agent; **~ de existencias** RRHH stockist agent; **~ expedidor(a) internacional** *m,f* TRANSP international freight forwarder; **~ de exportación** RRHH export agent; **~ de exportaciones del fabricante** IMP/EXP manufacturers' export agent; **~ exterior** COM GEN overseas agent; **~ de un fabricante** V&M manufacturer's agent; **~ financiero(-a)** *m,f* FIN financial agent; **~ de fletamento** TRANSP charter broker; **~ de fletes** TRANSP chartering agent; **~ de fletes de IATA** TRANSP IATA cargo agent; **~ de garantía** COM GEN, V&M del credere agent; **~ general** DER general agent; **~ de grupage** TRANSP groupage agent; **~ inmobiliario(-a)** *m,f* COM GEN, INMOB realtor (*AmE*), estate agent (*BrE*); **~ judicial** DER bailiff; **~ de marcas registradas** DER trade mark agent; **~ marítimo(-a)** *m,f* TRANSP shipbroker; **~ negociador(a)** *m,f* RRHH *sindicatos* bargaining agent; **~ oficial** DER authorized agent; **~ de pagos** FISC paying agent; **~ de patentes** DER, PATENT patent agent; **~ de la propiedad industrial** PATENT trade mark agent; **~ de proyecto** RRHH project agent; **~ de publicidad** MEDIOS media broker, V&M advertising agent, media broker; **~ de registros** INMOB listing agent (*AmE*), listing broker (*BrE*); **~ de seguros** SEG insurance broker; **~ de transportes** IMP/EXP, TRANSP freight forwarder, transport agent; **~ de transportes marítimos** TRANSP, RRHH shipping and forwarding agent (*S&FA*); **~ de transportes multimodal** COM GEN multimodal transport operator; **~ de ventas** COM GEN, RRHH, V&M sales agent; **~ de viajes** OCIO, RRHH, TRANSP travel agent; **~ de viajes con todo incluido** OCIO package tour operator (*BrE*)

ágil *adj* COM GEN *comercialización* brisk

agio *m* BOLSA, ECON *letras de cambio extranjeras* agio

agiotaje *m* BOLSA, ECON jobbery

agitación *f* COM GEN unrest; **~ de la actividad** BOLSA flurry of activity

agitar *vt* BANCA churn

aglomeración *f* COMS *mercado* congestion, ECON agglomeration

aglomerado *m* IND fiberboard (*AmE*), fibreboard (*BrE*)

agotado *adj* COM GEN out of stock, CONT overspent, MEDIOS *imprenta*, V&M *sin existencias* out of stock (*o.s.*)

agotamiento *m* RRHH *cansancio físico o mental* burnout; **~ de localidades** OCIO *teatro, cine* sellout (*infrml*); **~ del ozono** MED AMB ozone depletion

agotar *vt* COM GEN *existencias* draw, *recursos* exhaust; ◆ **~ una provisión** FIN terminate a fund

agradecer *vt* COM GEN thank

agradecido: estar muy ~ *fra* COM GEN be much obliged

agrario *adj* ECON, MED AMB agricultural

agravar *vt* COM GEN compound

agravio *m* DER damage, grievance, *derecho escocés* delict; **~ malicioso** DER malicious mischief

agregación: ~ de recursos *f* COM GEN resource aggregation

agregado¹ *adj* COM GEN, ECON, MAT aggregate

agregado²**,-a: ~ cultural** *m,f* RRHH cultural attaché, **~ de defensa** *m,f* RRHH *Cuerpo Diplomático* defence attaché (*BrE*) (*DA*), defense attaché (*AmE*) (*DA*); **~ militar** *m,f* RRHH defence attaché (*BrE*) (*DA*), defense attaché (*AmE*) (*DA*), military attaché; **~ de prensa** *m,f* MEDIOS, RRHH, V&M press officer

agregar *vt* COM GEN, ECON, MAT aggregate

agresivo *adj* COM GEN aggressive

agrícola *adj* ECON, MED AMB agricultural

agricultor, a *m,f* COM GEN agriculturalist, agriculturist, farmer; **pequeño(-a) ~** ECON smallholder

agricultura *f* COM GEN agriculture; **~ económica** PROT SOC villa economy; **~ a gran escala** ECON large-scale farming; **~ orgánica** MED AMB organic farming

agrimensor, a *m,f* RRHH surveyor

agroindustria *f* ECON, IND, MED AMB agribusiness, agroindustry

agronomía *f* ECON, MED AMB agriculture, agronomy

agrónomo, -a *m,f* COM GEN agriculturalist, agriculturist, agronomist

agroquímico *adj* ECON, IND, MED AMB agrochemical

agrosilvicultura *f* ECON, MED AMB agroforestry

agrupación *f* COM GEN grouping, V&M clustering; **~ por aptitud** PROT SOC *educación* ability grouping, setting; **~ en bloque** INFO blocking; **~ de empresas** BOLSA joint-venture company, joint venture (*JV*); **~ laboral** ECON job cluster; **~ de Mont Pelerin** ECON Mont Pelerin Society; **~ de países** V&M cluster of countries

Agrupación: ~ de Cooperación Europea *f* (*ACE*) ECON, POL European Cooperation Grouping (*ECG*); **~ Europea de Intereses Económicos** *f* ECON, POL European Economic Interest Grouping (*EEIG*)

agrupaciones: ~ económicas mundiales *f pl* ECON world economic groupings

agrupador, a *m,f* TRANSP consolidator

agrupamiento *m* MAT grouping, V&M bundling; **~ regional** ECON *NAFTA* regional grouping

agua: ~ dulce *f* MED AMB, TRANSP fresh water (*FW*); **~ dulce tropical** *f* MED AMB, TRANSP tropical fresh water (*TF*); **~ potable** *f* MED AMB drinking water

aguacero *m* COM GEN spate

aguas: ~ jurisdiccionales *f pl* DER, POL territorial waters; **~ territoriales** *f pl* DER, POL territorial waters

águila *f* FIN *diez dólares* eagle (*AmE*)

aguja: ~ grabadora *f* INFO stylus; **~ macho** *f* TRANSP *motor diesel* pintle

ahorra: que ~ tiempo *fra* COM GEN, GES, INFO time-saving

ahorrado: ~ todo el tiempo laborable *fra* TRANSP all working time saved

ahorrar *vt* BANCA put away, COM GEN save

ahorro *m* COM GEN saving; **~ bruto** BANCA, ECON, FIN gross savings; **~ de capital social** FIN pyramiding; **~ forzoso** BANCA, ECON, FIN forced saving, compulsory saving (*BrE*); **~ mensual** BANCA, RRHH *de empleado* monthly savings; **~ de patrimonio** BANCA, ECON, FIN life savings; **~ personal** BANCA, ECON, FIN personal saving; **~ preventivo** BANCA, ECON, FIN precautionary saving; **~ de seguridad** BANCA, ECON, FIN life savings

ahorros *m pl* COM GEN savings (*BrE*), thrift (*AmE*); **~ colectivos** BANCA, ECON, FIN corporate savings; **~ contractuales** BANCA, ECON, FIN contractual savings; **~ líquidos** BANCA, ECON, FIN liquid savings; **~ nacionales** BANCA, ECON, FIN national savings; **~ negativos** BANCA, ECON, FIN negative savings; **pequeños ~** BANCA, FIN small savings

AIE *abr* (*Agencia Internacional de la Energía*) MED AMB IEA (*International Energy Agency*)

AIF *abr* (*Asociación Internacional de Fomento*) ECON IDA (*International Development Association*)

airbus *m* TRANSP airbus

aire: en el ~ *fra* COMS, V&M on the air

airear *vt* COM GEN *opinión, observación* air

aislacionista *adj* POL isolationist

aislado *adj* BOLSA, COM GEN, ECON isolated

aislamiento: ~ del ruido *m* MED AMB noise insulation; **~ sensorial** *m* GES sensory deprivation; **~ sonoro** *m* COMS, MED AMB sound insulation

aislar *vt* BOLSA, COM GEN, ECON insulate, isolate

ajeno¹**: ~ a** *adj* COM GEN alien to, alien from

ajeno²**,-a** *m,f* GES outsider

ajetreo *m* COM GEN hustle and bustle

ajustable *adj* COM GEN *horas, tipo*, FIN *tipo hipotecario, póliza de seguros* adjustable, RRHH *pensión* index-linked

ajustado *adj* COM GEN adjusted, *descripción* accurate, FISC adjusted; ◆ **~ al valor de mercado** BOLSA *futuros* marked-to-market

ajustador, a: ~ de averías *m,f* SEG average adjuster (*AA*); **~ de déficit** *m,f* FISC gap filler; **~ independiente** *m,f* SEG independent adjuster; **~ de reclamaciones** *m,f* SEG claims adjuster

ajustar *vt* BANCA *precios, cantidad, horarios*, BOLSA make up, adjust, COM GEN settle, *déficit, componente, nivel* adjust, ECON *precios, cantidad, horarios* make up, adjust, FIN make up, IND *mecanismo, máquina, avería*, MAT *déficit, componente, nivel*, SEG adjust; ◆ **~ a** COM GEN adjust to; **~ al alza** ECON, MAT adjust upwards; **~ a la baja** ECON, MAT adjust downwards; **~ al precio del mercado** BOLSA, CONT, ECON, MAT restate, revaluate; **~ al valor del mercado** BOLSA mark to the market; **~ cuentas pendientes** COM GEN settle accounts, settle old scores (*infrml*)

ajustarse: ~ a *v refl* COM GEN *normas* conform to

ajuste *m* BOLSA fit, COM GEN *posición, velocidad*, CONT,

ECON *estadísticas, error, contabilidad acumulativa* adjustment, snugging; ~ **al coste base** *Esp* (*cf ajuste al costo base AmL*) FISC adjustment to cost base; ~ **al costo base** *AmL* (*cf ajuste al coste base Esp*) FISC adjustment to cost base; ~ **al ejercicio anterior** CONT prior period adjustment; ~ **de amortización** CONT depreciation adjustment; ~ **de la amortización** SEG amortization adjustment; ~ **del año anterior** CONT prior year adjustment; ~ **anual** FISC annual adjustment; ~ **de apalancamiento** FIN gearing adjustment (*BrE*), leverage adjustment (*AmE*); ~ **de cierre de ejercicio** CONT year-end adjustment; ~ **por combustible** TRANSP bunker adjustment factor (*BAF*); ~ **contable** CONT accounting adjustment; ~ **del coste de vida** *Esp* (*cf ajuste del costo de vida AmL*) ECON cost-of-living adjustment (*COLA*); ~ **del costo de vida** *AmL* (*cf ajuste del coste de vida Esp*) ECON cost-of-living adjustment (*COLA*); ~ **de las cuentas a cobrar** CONT adjustment of accounts receivable; ~ **de daños** SEG claims adjustment; ~ **del déficit** ECON adjustment gap; ~ **estacional** COM GEN seasonal adjustment; ~ **estructural** GES structural adjustment; ~ **impositivo** COM GEN, FISC tax adjustment; ~ **de ingresos** CONT income smoothing; ~ **de intereses** CONT yield adjustment; ~ **de Lundberg** ECON Lundberg lag; ~ **mensual del interés** BANCA monthly compounding of interest; ~ **del mercado** ECON market adjustment; ~ **obligatorio** DER *propiedad intelectual* must fit, must match; ~ **de pensión** FISC pension adjustment; ~ **por periodificación** CONT prior period adjustment, prior year adjustment; ~ **presupuestario** CONT budgetary adjustment; ~ **de prima al vencimiento** SEG adjustment premium at maturity; ~ **sin recargo** FISC nonpenalized adjustment; ~ **de rendimientos** CONT yield adjustment; ~ **retroactivo** ECON retroactive adjustment; ~ **salarial** COM GEN, RRHH wage adjustment; ~ **del sector crediticio** ECON sector adjustment lending; ~ **de la tasa de interés** BANCA interest rate adjustment; ~ **del tipo de cambio** ECON *acuerdo de Bretton Woods* adjustable peg; ~ **del tipo de interés** ECON interest rate adjustment; ~ **en la valoración de existencias** CONT *estadística*, MAT inventory valuation adjustment; ~ **de la velocidad en la tasa de producción** ECON *microeconomía* adjustment speed

ajustes: ~ **después del periodo de cierre** *m pl* CONT off-period adjustments; ~ **de fin de año por gastos acumulados** *m pl* FIN year-end adjustments for accrued expenses; ~ **referenciados a un índice** *m pl* BOLSA, CONT, ECON index-linked investments

ALALC *abr* (*Asociación Latinoamericana de Libre Comercio*) ECON, POL ≈ LAFTA (*obs*) *antes de 1981* (*Latin American Free Trade Association*), ≈ LAIA (*Latin American Integration Association*)

alargado *adj* COM GEN expanded, lengthened

alargar *vt* COM GEN expand, lengthen

alarma *f* COM GEN alarm

albacea: ~ **testamentaria** *f* DER executrix; ~ **testamentario(-a)** *m,f* DER executor (*exor., exec.*), estate executor

albarán: ~ **de entrada** *m* TRANSP receiving order (*RO*)

alborotos: ~ **populares** *m pl* POL civil riots

alcance *m* COM GEN scope, FIN *tratado* sight, PATENT *de demandas* scope, RRHH, SEG scope, V&M reach; ~ **del acuerdo** RRHH scope of agreement; ~ **acumulativo** V&M cumulative reach; ~ **de la auditoría** CONT audit coverage; ~ **bruto** V&M gross reach; ~ **de la cobertura** SEG scope of coverage; ~ **del empleo** RRHH scope of employment; ~ **y frecuencia** V&M reach and frequency; ~ **de mercado** V&M market reach; ~ **de la negociación** RRHH bargaining scope; ~ **neto** V&M net reach; ~ **del presupuesto** ECON budget incidence; ~ **publicitario** V&M advertising reach; ◆ **al ~ de** COM GEN within reach; **estar fuera de ~** COM GEN be out of range; **de gran ~** COM GEN far-reaching; **de largo ~** COM GEN *planificación* long-range

alcanzar *vt* COM GEN reach; ◆ ~ **un acuerdo** COM GEN come to an agreement; **no ~ un objetivo** ECON undershoot a target; ~ **el punto más bajo** ECON hit rock bottom; **no ~** COM GEN *expectativas, metas* fall short of; ~ **una conclusión** COM GEN bring to an end; ~ **el máximo** COM GEN, ECON peak; ~ **el punto de saturación** COM GEN reach saturation point; ~ **un total de** COM GEN reach a total of

alcismo *m* BOLSA bullishness

alcista[1] *adj* BOLSA bullish, COM GEN *tendencia* upward

alcista[2]: ~ **rezagado** *m* BOLSA stale bull

alcoholes: ~ **industriales** *m pl* IND industrial spirits

aleatoriamente *adv* COM GEN at random, randomly

aleatorio *adj* COM GEN random

aleatorización *f* COM GEN randomization

alegación *f* DER allegation, *argumentación* pleading; ~ **por deuda** DER libelling (*BrE*), libeling (*AmE*)

alegaciones *f* PATENT *de oposición, revocación* arguments, grounds

alegar *vt* DER plead; ◆ ~ **exención fiscal** FISC claim immunity from tax; ~ **ignorancia** DER plead ignorance

alegato *m* DER declaration, *en favor del acusado* pleading, *del testigo* statement, POL plea

alentador *adj* COM GEN encouraging

alentar *vt* COM GEN boost, encourage

alerta[1] *f* COM GEN alert

alerta[2]: **estar ~** *fra* COM GEN watch one's back

alevosía: **con ~** *fra* DER maliciously

alfa *adj* BOLSA alpha

alfanumérico *adj* (*A/N*) COM GEN, INFO alphanumeric (*A/N*)

alfombrilla: ~ **para ratón** *f* INFO mouse mat

álgebra: ~ **de Boole** *f* INFO, MAT Boolean algebra

algodón: ~ **en plaza** *m* SEG spot cotton

algorítmico *adj* INFO, MAT algorithmic

algoritmo *m* INFO, MAT algorithm

alianza *f* COM GEN, POL alliance; ~ **estratégica** COM GEN, GES joint venture (*JV*), strategic alliance; ~ **estratégica transfronteriza** FIN cross-border joint venture

alias[1] *adv* COM GEN alias, also known as (*a.k.a., AKA*)

alias[2] *m* COM GEN alias

alícuotas: ~ **progresivas** *f pl* MAT progressive rates

alienable *adj* COM GEN, DER, RRHH alienable

alienación *f* COM GEN, DER, RRHH alienation

alienar *vt* COM GEN, DER, RRHH alienate

alijador, a *m,f AmL* (*cf estibador Esp*) RRHH, TRANSP stevedore (*stvdr*), wharfinger, docker (*BrE*)

alijadores *m pl AmL* (*cf estibadores Esp*) COM GEN, RRHH, TRANSP stevedoring gang, dockers (*BrE*)

alimentación *f* INFO feed; ~ **por arrastre** INFO tractor feed; ~ **de cadena** INFO chain feeding; ~ **de cinta** INFO tape feed; ~ **eléctrica ininterrumpible** INFO uninterruptible power supply (*UPS*); ~ **por fricción** INFO friction feed; ~ **del papel** INFO paper feed

alimentador: ~ **automático** *m* ADMIN automatic feeder, INFO autofeeder; ~ **de hojas** *m* INFO sheet feeder; ~ **de papel** *m* INFO paper feeder; ~ **de papel manual** *m* ADMIN, INFO single-sheet feeder

alimentar *vt* COM GEN *inflación* fuel, INFO feed

alimentos: ~ **básicos** *m pl* COM GEN, IND basic foodstuffs; ~ **en conserva** *m pl* COM GEN, IND preserved foods; ~ **frescos** *m pl* COM GEN fresh food; ~ **naturales** *m pl* COM GEN, V&M health foods; ~ **sin procesar** *m pl* COM GEN, IND fresh food

alineación *f* COM GEN, DER, INFO alignment

alinear *vt* COM GEN, DER, INFO align

alistarse *v refl* COM GEN sign up

alivio: ~ **de la deuda** *m* CONT, ECON, FISC debt relief

allanamiento: ~ **de morada** *m* DER burglary

allanar: ~ **el camino para** *fra* COM GEN lay the ground for

almacén *m* COM GEN, IMP/EXP, TRANSP *existencias* storehouse, warehouse (*whse*); ~ **de consolidación** TRANSP consolidation depot; ~ **de depósito** COM GEN bond store, bonded warehouse; ~ **de exportación** IMP/EXP export shed; ~ **ferroviario interior** TRANSP inland rail depot (*IRD*); ~ **frigorífico** COM GEN, TRANSP cold store; ~ **para minoristas** V&M retail warehouse; ~ **público nacional** IMP/EXP King's warehouse (*BrE*); ~ **de rechazos** COM GEN reject bin; ~ **refrigerado** COM GEN refrigerated warehouse; ~ **de tránsito** IMP/EXP transit shed; ~ **de vino** IMP/EXP wine warehouse; ◆ **en** ~ COM GEN in stock

almacenaje *m* COM GEN storage; ~ **comercial** TRANSP commercial storage

almacenamiento *m* COM GEN storage, IND warehousing, TRANSP warehousing, *barcos* impounding; ~ **al aire libre** TRANSP open storage; ~ **de archivos** COM GEN, DER archive storage, INFO archive storage, archival storage, backing storage; ~ **de datos** INFO data storage; ~ **de gran capacidad** COM GEN bulk storage, INFO *datos* bulk storage, mass storage; ~ **intermedio** INFO buffer storage; ~ **masivo** INFO mass storage; ~ **refrigerado** COM GEN, IND, TRANSP cold storage; ~ **de trabajo** INFO working storage

almacenar *vt* IMP/EXP warehouse, INFO *datos* store, TRANSP stockpile, warehouse, *mercancías* store

almacenista *mf* COM GEN trader, RRHH storeman (*BrE*), stockman (*AmE*), warehouseman (*AmE*), trader, V&M trader

almohadilla *f* INFO *ratón* pad

almuerzo: ~ **de negocios** *m* COM GEN business lunch

alodial *adj* DER allodial

alojamiento *m* FISC, INMOB, OCIO, PROT SOC accommodation, housing; ~ **compartido** FISC, INMOB shared accommodation; ~ **exento** FISC free lodging; ~ **hotelero** OCIO hotel accommodation; ~ **de pasajeros** OCIO, TRANSP berth accommodation; ~ **residencial** INMOB, PROT SOC residential accommodation; ~ **de vacaciones** INMOB, OCIO holiday accommodation (*BrE*), vacation accommodation (*AmE*); ~ **vinculado al puesto de trabajo** INMOB, RRHH job-related accommodation

alojar *vt* COM GEN accommodate

alojarse *v refl* INFO log

alquila: **se** ~ *fra* INMOB to let (*BrE*), for rent (*AmE*)

alquilar *vt* COM GEN hire, INMOB *vivienda* hire, let, rent

alquiler *m* COM GEN equipment hire, rental, FIN leasing, INMOB lease, let, rent, PROT SOC rent; ~ **atrasado** INMOB back rent; ~ **bajo** INMOB low rent (*AmE*); ~ **básico** INMOB basic rent (*AmE*); ~ **de coches** TRANSP auto rental (*AmE*), car hire (*BrE*); ~ **comercial** INMOB commercial letting; ~ **contractual** INMOB contract rent; ~ **ejecutivo** *Esp* (*cf arrendamiento ejecutivo AmL*) GES *automóviles, negocios corporativos* executive leasing; ~ **de explotación** CONT, INMOB operating lease, TRANSP operation lease; ~ **de ida** TRANSP one-way lease; ~ **industrial** INMOB, IND industrial rent; ~ **mensual** INMOB monthly rent; ~ **de mercado** INMOB market rent; ~ **por mes de calendario** INMOB rent per calendar month (*BrE*) (*rent pcm*); ~ **de monopolio** INMOB monopoly rent; ~ **nocional** INMOB notional rent; ~ **con opción a compra** FIN leasing; ~ **con opción a compra de material** IND, INMOB equipment leasing; ~ **perpetuo** INMOB perpetual lease; ~ **de planta** COM GEN plant hire; ~ **a porcentaje** INMOB percentage lease; ~ **a precio de mercado** INMOB fair market rent; ~ **progresivo** FIN step-up lease, INMOB graduated lease; ~ **puesto en subasta** INMOB bid rent; ~ **razonable** INMOB fair rent; ~ **de referencia** INMOB index lease; ~ **semanal** INMOB weekly rent; ~ **de la tierra** INMOB ground rent, land rent; ~ **tipo venta** FIN sales type lease; ~ **de vehículo sin conductor** OCIO, TRANSP self-drive hire; ~ **de vehículos** TRANSP vehicle hire, vehicle leasing; ◆ **en** ~ INMOB for hire; **en busca de** ~ INMOB rent seeking; **en** ~ **con derecho a compra** FIN on hire purchase (*BrE*)

alrededor: ~ **de** *prep* COM GEN in the region of

alta[1]: **de** ~ **calidad** *adj* COM GEN high quality, V&M up-market; **de** ~ **mar** *adj* TRANSP *barco* ocean-going, *pesca* deepwater; **con** ~ **participación de gente** *adj* RRHH people-intensive

alta[2]: ~ **calidad** *f* COM GEN high quality, top quality; ~ **definición** *f* INFO, MEDIOS high resolution; ~ **densidad** *f* INFO high density; ~ **dirección** *f* ADMIN front office, RRHH general management; ~ **ejecutiva** *f* COM GEN, GES, RRHH senior executive, top executive; ~ **funcionaria** *f* COM GEN, RRHH top-ranking official; ~ **gerencia** *f* ADMIN front office, GES general management; ~ **tecnología** *f* COM GEN, IND high technology

altamente[1]: ~ **competitivo** *adj* COM GEN highly competitive; ~ **cualificado** *adj* RRHH highly-skilled

altamente[2] *adv* COM GEN concentrado heavily

altas: **las** ~ **finanzas** *f pl* FIN high finance

alteración *f* COM GEN alteration; ~ **de capital** COM GEN alteration of capital; ~ **falaz de un balance** BOLSA *estado de cuentas*, COM GEN, CONT *cuentas anuales* window-dressing

alterar *vt* COM GEN alter

alternar *vt* COM GEN alternate

alternativa *f* COM GEN alternative; **la mejor** ~ COM GEN the best alternative; ◆ **no hay** ~ COM GEN there is no alternative (*TINA*)

alternativo, -a *m,f* COM GEN *suplente* alternate (*AmE*), substitute (*BrE*)

alterno *adj* COM GEN *por turnos, sucesivo* alternate

Alteza: **Su** ~ **Real** *mf Esp* (*S.A.R.*) COM GEN ≈ Her Royal Highness (*BrE*) (*HRH*), ≈ His Royal Highness (*BrE*) (*HRH*)

alto[1] *adj* BOLSA high; **de** ~ **nivel** INFO, RRHH top-level; **de**

~ potencial RRHH high-caliber (*AmE*), high-calibre (*BrE*); **de ~ rendimiento** BOLSA high-return, high-yielding; **de ~ riesgo** BOLSA, FIN high-risk; **de ~ secreto** BANCA, COM GEN, DER, FISC, POL top-secret

alto[2]: **~ cargo** *m* RRHH high office; **~ coste de la vida** *m* *Esp* (*cf alto costo de vida AmL*) ECON high cost of living; **~ costo de la vida** *m* *AmL* (*cf alto coste la vida Esp*) ECON high cost of living; **~ ejecutivo** *m* COM GEN, GES, RRHH brass (*infrml*), high executive, senior executive, top executive; **~ funcionario** *m* COM GEN, RRHH top-ranking official; **~ nivel de vida** *m* PROT SOC high standard of living

alto[3]: **de ~ coeficiente de mano de obra** *fra* IND, RRHH *producción* labor-intensive (*AmE*), labour-intensive (*BrE*)

altos: **~ niveles** *m pl* COM GEN high standards

altruismo *m* COM GEN, ECON altruism

altura: **~ del agua** *f* TRANSP depth alongside; **~ cerrada** *f* TRANSP *horquilla elevadora* closed height; **~ metacéntrica** *f* COM GEN metacentric height

aluminio *m* MED AMB aluminium (*BrE*) (*alu*), aluminum (*AmE*) (*alu*)

alza[1]: **en ~** *adj* COM GEN *incremento* mounting, ECON rising

alza[2] *f* ADMIN *guía* overlay, BOLSA bull, lift, *de precios* advance, COM GEN upturn, upswing, CONT rise, ECON upswing, upturn, FIN bull; **~ de capital** *m* ECON, FIN capital appreciation; **~ extraordinaria** ECON boom; **~ de la moneda circulante** FIN currency appreciation; **~ de precios** BOLSA run-up; **~ rápida** COM GEN, ECON boom

alzada *f* COM GEN *al público* appeal

alzas: **~ y bajas** *fra* BOLSA bull and bear

a.m. *abr* (*ante merídiem*) COM GEN a.m. (*ante meridiem*)

amalgamación *f* COM GEN amalgamation

amalgamar *vt* COM GEN amalgamate

amante: **~ del riesgo** *mf* COM GEN risk lover

amarradero *m* IMP/EXP, TRANSP quay, wharf; **~ de carga general** TRANSP general cargo berth; **~ disponible** TRANSP ready berth; **~ flotante** TRANSP floating berth; **~ multiusuario** TRANSP multiuser berth; **~ principal** TRANSP lead slip; **~ de propósito general** TRANSP general purpose berth

amarrado: **~ al muelle** *m* IMP/EXP, TRANSP *navegación* quay fitting

amarrar *vt* COM GEN fasten, TRANSP moor, lay up

amarre *m* TRANSP lashing; **~ con cable** TRANSP wire lashing; **~ con cadena** TRANSP chain lashing; ♦ **único punto de ~** TRANSP single point mooring

amasar *vt* COM GEN amass

ambas: **~ fechas inclusive** *fra* COM GEN both dates inclusive (*bdi*)

ambición *f* COM GEN ambition

ambicioso *adj* COM GEN ambitious

ambientalismo *m* MED AMB environmentalism

ambiente *m* COM GEN, MED AMB atmosphere, environment; **~ fiscal** FISC tax environment; **~ laboral** RRHH working environment; **~ de trabajo agradable** RRHH pleasant working environment

ámbito[1]: **de ~ nacional** *adj* COM GEN nationwide

ámbito[2] *m* COM GEN, MAT domain, PATENT *de demandas* scope; **~ de cobertura** SEG scope of coverage;

~ financiero FIN financial field; **~ de revisión contable** CONT audit scope

ambulatorio *m* PROT SOC health center (*AmE*), health centre (*BrE*)

amenaza[1]: **~ de huelga** *f* RRHH strike threat; **~ injustificada** *f* DER unjustified threat

amenaza[2]: **bajo ~** *fra* COM GEN in terrorem

amigable *adj* COM GEN amicable

Amigos: **~ de la Tierra** *m pl* MED AMB Friends of the Earth

amnistía: **~ fiscal** *f* FISC tax break

amortiguaciones: **~ fiscales rápidas** *f pl* FISC accelerated capital cost allowance (*ACCA*)

amortiguar *vt* ECON *crecimiento* dampen

amortizable *adj* BOLSA callable, COM GEN, CONT, FIN amortizable

amortización *f* COM GEN depreciation, pay-out, repayment, write-off; **~ acelerada** COM GEN, CONT accelerated amortization, accelerated depreciation; **~ de un activo** CONT asset write-down; **~ de activos** CONT write-down of the value of assets; **~ acumulada** CONT, FIN accumulated depletion, depreciation reserve; **~ adicional del primer año** FISC additional first-year depreciation (*AmE*); **~ antes del vencimiento** FIN redemtion before due date; **~ anticipada** COM GEN *de deuda* anticipated repayment, FIN early redemption; **~ anual** SEG annual amortization; **~ anual uniforme** CONT straight-line depreciation; **~ de balance decreciente** CONT, FIN declining balance depreciation; **~ de la base impositiva** CONT, FISC tax-based depreciation; **~ constante** CONT amortization on a straight-line basis, straight-line depreciation; **~ constante durante cinco años** FISC five-year straight-line amortization; **~ del consumo de capital** ECON, FIN capital consumption allowance; **~ de cuota fija** CONT straight-line depreciation; **~ de deuda** CONT debt retirement; **~ doble de saldo decreciente** CONT double-declining balance; **~ a 2 años** COM GEN repayment over 2 years; **~ fiscal** FISC tax write-off; **~ física** CONT physical depreciation; **~ del fondo de comercio** CONT goodwill amortization; **~ en libros** CONT book depreciation; **~ lineal** CONT straight-line depreciation; **~ negativa** FIN *préstamos* negative amortization; **~ parcial** CONT partial write-off; **~ de un préstamo** FIN repayment of a loan; **~ quinquenal de variación lineal** FISC five-year straight-line amortization; **~ recuperable** CONT recapturable depreciation; **~ de los rendimientos del capital** FISC capital gains redemption; **~ del saldo de cuentas de clientes** CONT *créditos* goodwill amortization; **~ sobre la base de cuota fija** CONT amortization on a straight-line basis; **~ única** BANCA bullet (*jarg*); **~ uniforme** CONT amortization on a straight-line basis

amortizaciones: **~ netas totales** *f pl* BANCA total net redemptions

amortizado *adj* BOLSA called away; **no ~** BOLSA, CONT, FIN unamortized

amortizar **1.** *vt* BANCA amortize, COM GEN pay off, CONT, ECON, FIN *inversión* depreciate, write down, sink, *activos* amortize, INMOB depreciate; ♦ **~ un activo** CONT write down; **~ bonos por anticipado** BANCA call bonds; **~ una deuda** BANCA pay off a debt; **~ un empréstito** BANCA repay a loan; **~ la hipoteca** BANCA, FIN mortgage out; **2.** *vi* CONT amortize, FIN depreciate

amparar *vt* COM GEN shade

amparo *m* COM GEN aid, protection; ~ **fiscal** FISC tax shield; ~ **tributario** FISC tax shelter

amplia[1]: **de** ~ **base** *adj* FISC broad-based

amplia[2]: ~ **gama** *f* V&M wide range

ampliable *adj* INFO open-ended, upgradeable, *equipo, programas* expandable

ampliación *f* COM GEN enlargement, expansion; ~ **de la base** FISC base broadening; ~ **de la base impositiva** ECON, FISC broadening of tax base, tax base broadening; ~ **para los beneficios** FISC extension for returns; ~ **del capital** BOLSA *emisión de acciones* right, ECON increase in capital, capital widening; ~ **a una construcción** FISC extension to a building; ~ **de la gama** V&M line extension; ~ **de la memoria** INFO memory extension; ~ **del plazo de una garantía bancaria total** BANCA comprehensive extended term banker's guarantee (*CXBG*); ~ **de la propiedad** INMOB property development; ~ **vertical** COM GEN vertical integration

ampliaciones: ~ **fiscales** *f pl* FISC fiscal projections

ampliamente *adv* COM GEN largely; ~ **reconocido** COM GEN widely recognized

ampliar *vt* COM GEN widen, *actividades* expand, *investigación, estudio, conocimientos* extend, FISC *base fiscal* widen; ◆ ~ **la base del impuesto** COM GEN broaden the tax base; ~ **el límite de tiempo** COM GEN extend the time limit

amplitud: ~ **de banda** *f* INFO, MEDIOS, RRHH bandwidth; ~ **del ciclo** *f* COM GEN amplitude of cycle; ~ **de cobertura** *f* COM GEN extent of cover; ~ **de un derecho** *f* DER magnitude of a right; ~ **del mercado** *f* BOLSA market size; ~ **normal del mercado** *f* BOLSA normal market size (*NMS*)

A/N *abr* (*alfanumérico*) COM GEN, INFO A/N (*alphanumeric*)

análisis *m* COM GEN, GES, RRHH rationale, *cuenta, informe* analysis; ~ **de actividades** COM GEN activity analysis; ~ **año-base** ECON base year analysis; ~ **de la antigüedad de las cuentas a cobrar** CONT ageing of receivables; ~ **por aptitudes** RRHH skills analysis; ~ **de árbol de fallas** COM GEN fault tree analysis; ~ **en árbol de los fallos** COM GEN fault tree analysis; ~ **de balances** CONT financial statement analysis, statement analysis; ~ **de beneficios** CONT profit test; ~ **de beneficios y costes** *m pl Esp* (*cf análisis de beneficios y costos AmL*) CONT benefit-cost analysis; ~ **de beneficios y costos** *m pl AmL* (*cf análisis de beneficios y costes Esp*) CONT benefit-cost analysis; ~ **bidireccional de varianza** MAT two-way analysis of variance; ~ **del billete** TRANSP ticket analysis; ~ **del camino crítico** GES critical path analysis (*CPA*); ~ **de cartera** V&M portfolio analysis; ~ **por casos** MAT item analysis; ~ **de ciclo de vida** V&M life-cycle analysis; ~ **comercial** FIN commercial analysis; ~ **de competidores** V&M competitor analysis; ~ **confluente** MAT confluence analysis (*CA*); ~ **contable** CONT accounting analysis; ~ **de contribución** COM GEN, FIN contribution analysis; ~ **de corte transversal** COM GEN cross-section analysis; ~ **de coste-beneficio** *Esp* (*cf análisis de costo-beneficio AmL*) CONT, ECON cost-benefit analysis; ~ **coste-efectividad** ECON cost-effectiveness analysis; ~ **de los costes** *Esp* (*cf análisis de los costos AmL*) CONT, FIN cost analysis; ~ **de costes de distribución** *Esp* (*cf análisis de costos de distribución AmL*) V&M distribution

cost analysis; ~ **de costes por naturaleza** *Esp* (*cf análisis de costos por naturaleza AmL*) CONT analysis of costs by nature; ~ **de coste-volumen-beneficio** *Esp* (*cf análisis de costo-volumen-beneficio AmL*) FIN cost-volume-profit analysis; ~ **de costo-beneficio** *AmL* (*cf análisis de coste-beneficio Esp*) CONT, ECON cost-benefit analysis; ~ **de los costos** *AmL* (*cf análisis de los costes Esp*) CONT, FIN cost analysis; ~ **de costos de distribución** *AmL* (*cf análisis de costes de distribución Esp*) V&M distribution cost analysis; ~ **de costos por naturaleza** *AmL* (*cf análisis de costes por naturaleza Esp*) CONT analysis of costs by nature; ~ **de costo-volumen-beneficio** *AmL* (*cf análisis de coste-volumen-beneficio Esp*) FIN cost-volume-profit analysis; ~ **de crecimiento** GES incremental analysis; ~ **del crédito** BANCA, FIN credit analysis; ~ **cualitativo** IND, V&M *estudio de mercado* qualitative analysis; ~ **cuantitativo** GES, IND, V&M quantitative analysis; ~ **de cuentas** BANCA account analysis; ~ **de las cuentas a cobrar según su antigüedad** *m pl* CONT ageing of receivables; ~ **de datos transversales** COM GEN cross-section analysis; ~ **de decisión** GES decision analysis; ~ **del desfase** BANCA gap analysis; ~ **de desviaciones** *m pl* CONT variance analysis; ~ **de las desviaciones del coste** *Esp* (*cf análisis de las desviaciones del costo AmL*) CONT analysis of cost variances; ~ **de las desviaciones del costo** *AmL* (*cf análisis de las desviaciones del coste Esp*) CONT analysis of cost variances; ~ **diferencial** GES differential analysis; ~ **de la distribución del transporte** TRANSP transport distribution analysis (*TDA*); ~ **económico** ECON, FIN economic analysis; ~ **de entrada y salida** MAT input-output analysis; ~ **de entrada/salida** INFO input-output analysis; ~ **de equilibrio general** ECON *modelo teórico* general equilibrium analysis; ~ **del estado de cuentas** CONT financial statement analysis; ~ **de estados contables** CONT financial statement analysis, statement analysis; ~ **de estados financieros** CONT financial statement analysis; ~ **estratégico** POL strategic overview; ~ **del factor de beneficio** COM GEN, FIN profit-factor analysis; ~ **de factores** MAT factor analysis; ~ **de factores de las utilidades** COM GEN, FIN profit-factor analysis; ~ **factorial** MAT factor analysis; ~ **factor-producto** MAT input-output analysis; ~ **de fallos** GES failure analysis; ~ **financiero** COM GEN, FIN financial analysis, financial review; ~ **a fondo** COM GEN, GES in-depth analysis, depth analysis; ~ **de las fuerzas, debilidades, oportunidades y amenazas** V&M strengths, weaknesses, opportunities and threats analysis (*SWOT*); ~ **funcional** COM GEN functional analysis; ~ **funcional de costes** *Esp* (*cf análisis funcional de costos AmL*) CONT functional analysis of costs; ~ **funcional de costos** *AmL* (*cf análisis funcional de costes Esp*) CONT functional analysis of costs; ~ **fundamental** BOLSA, FIN *declaraciones financieras, inversiones* fundamental analysis; ~ **de grupos** V&M *estudio de mercados* cluster analysis; ~ **del horario** TRANSP timetable analysis; ~ **horizontal** CONT horizontal analysis, FIN horizon analysis; ~ **incremental** COM GEN, CONT, FISC incremental analysis; ~ **de indiferencia** MAT indifference analysis; ~ **input-output** ECON input-output analysis; ~ **de insumo/producto** FIN, IND input-output analysis; ~ **de insumos y producción** *m pl* FIN, IND input-output analysis; ~ **de inventarios** CONT inventory analysis, stock analysis; ~ **de inversiones** *f* CONT project analysis, ECON capital budgeting; ~ **marginal** CONT,

ECON, FIN marginal analysis; **~ matricial** ECON matrix analysis; **~ del medio ambiente** GES, MED AMB environmental analysis; **~ de los medios de comunicación** MEDIOS, V&M media analysis; **~ de mercado** BOLSA, V&M market analysis; **~ morfológico** FIN, MAT morphological analysis; **~ motivacional** RRHH motivational analysis; **~ multivariable** MAT multivariate analysis; **~ de necesidades** RRHH, V&M needs analysis; **~ de las necesidades de capacitación** *AmL* (*cf análisis de las necesidades de formación Esp*) COM GEN, RRHH, V&M training needs analysis; **~ de las necesidades de formación** *Esp* (*cf análisis de las necesidades de capacitación AmL*) COM GEN, RRHH, V&M training needs analysis; **~ ocupacional** RRHH occupational analysis; **~ de ocupaciones** RRHH occupational analysis; **~ operacional** IND operational analysis; **~ de las operaciones** RRHH operations analysis; **~ operativo** RRHH operational analysis; **~ parcial del equilibrio** ECON partial equilibrium analysis; **~ de Pareto** COM GEN, ECON Pareto analysis; **~ de pasajeros** OCIO passenger analysis; **~ de porcentajes** MAT percentage analysis; **~ presupuestario** CONT budget analysis; **~ del problema** GES, MAT, RRHH problem analysis; **~ de procesos** COM GEN process analysis; **~ del producto** V&M product analysis; **~ de productos básicos** BOLSA commodity analysis; **~ en profundidad** COM GEN, GES in-depth analysis; **~ de proyectos** FIN, GES, RRHH project analysis; **~ del puesto de trabajo** RRHH job analysis; **~ de puestos** RRHH job analysis; **~ del punto crítico** ECON, FIN break-even analysis; **~ del punto muerto** ECON, FIN break-even analysis; **~ de puntualidad** TRANSP punctuality analysis; **~ de ratios** MAT ratio analysis; **~ de razones** MAT ratio analysis; **~ de una red** GES, INFO network analysis; **~ de regresión** ECON, FIN, MAT regression analysis; **~ de regresión múltiple** ECON, FIN, MAT multiple regression analysis (*MRA*); **~ de las relaciones** RRHH relations analysis; **~ de la rentabilidad** CONT, FIN profitability analysis, V&M cost-effectiveness analysis; **~ de resultados** COM GEN, CONT performance review; **~ de riesgo de una cartera estándar** FIN Standard Portfolio Analysis of Risk (*SPAR*); **~ del riesgo comercial** FIN, SEG commercial risk analysis; **~ de riesgos** FIN, SEG risk analysis; **~ de la ruta** TRANSP route analysis; **~ sectorial** COM GEN sector analysis; **~ secuencial** FIN, MAT, V&M sequential analysis; **~ de sensibilidad** *f* FIN, MAT sensitivity analysis; **~ de sensibilidad del beneficio** CONT *valoración de un proyecto* profit sensitivity analysis; **~ de series temporales** COM GEN, ECON, MAT time series analysis; **~ de sistemas** COM GEN, INFO systems analysis; **~ de situación en equipo** GES, RRHH team briefing; **~ social** PROT SOC, V&M social analysis; **~ de tareas jerárquicos** GES hierarchical task analysis (*HTA*); **~ técnico** BOLSA technical analysis; **~ de tendencias** ECON trend analysis; **~ tipológico** V&M typological analysis; **~ de tráfico** TRANSP traffic analysis; **~ de transacción** COM GEN, FIN, GES transactional analysis (*TA*); **~ transaccional** COM GEN, FIN, GES transactional analysis (*TA*); **~ de la travesía** TRANSP trip analysis; **~ del uso del contenedor** TRANSP container user analysis; **~ del valor** FIN value engineering, value analysis (*VA*), V&M value analysis (*VA*); **~ de valores** FIN securities analysis; **~ de la varianza** CONT variance analysis; **~ de varianza** MAT analysis of variance (*ANOVA*); **~ de varianza de dos entradas** MAT two-way analysis of variance; **~ de**

ventas V&M sales analysis; **~ de ventas al por menor** V&M retail sales analysis; **~ vertical** CONT vertical analysis; **~ de la visita** V&M call analysis

analista *mf* BANCA, GES, RRHH analyst; **~ de bolsa** BOLSA, ECON chartist; **~ de créditos** BANCA, FIN credit analyst; **~ de inversiones bursátiles** BOLSA, ECON chartist; **~ de medios de comunicación** MEDIOS, V&M media analyst; **~ de mercados** RRHH market analyst; **~ petrolífero(-a)** *m,f* IND oil analyst; **~ de programas** INFO program analyst; **~ de riesgo marítimo** RRHH, SEG marine risk analyst; **~ de sistemas** INFO systems analyst; **~ de sistemas superior** INFO senior systems analyst; **~ de ventas** RRHH, V&M sales analyst

analítico *adj* COM GEN analytical, analytic

analizador *m* INFO analyser (*BrE*), analyzer (*AmE*)

analizar *vt* COM GEN analyse (*BrE*), analyze (*AmE*), review

analogía: por ~ *fra* DER mutatis mutandis

analógico *adj* INFO analogical; **~ a digital** INFO analog-to-digital

análogo *adj* INFO analog

anarco: ~-comunismo *m* POL anarcho-communism; **~-sindicalismo** *m* POL anarcho-syndicalism

anarquía: ~ de la producción *f* POL anarchy of production

anchura *f* GES *de pensamiento* latitude, INFO width; **~ de banda** INFO, MEDIOS, RRHH bandwidth; **~ de neumático** TRANSP tyre gauge (*BrE*), tire gage (*AmE*); **~ total** TRANSP overall width

ancla: ~ de dragado *f* TRANSP dredging anchor; **~ flotante** *f* TRANSP sea anchor

anclaje *m* COM GEN, TRANSP anchorage; **~ circular** TRANSP *aseguramiento de contenedores* bushing; **~ de esquina** TRANSP *ferrocarril* anchor bracket

andana *f* TRANSP tier

anexionar *vt* COM GEN, POL annex

anexo *m* ADMIN, COM GEN, COMS enclosed document, affixed document, *edificio, documento* annex (*AmE*), annexe (*BrE*), DER addendum, annex (*AmE*), annexe (*BrE*), MEDIOS appendix, SEG attachment, exhibit; **~ a los estados financieros** CONT notes to the financial statements

anfidromo *adj* TRANSP double-ended (*DB*)

angel: ~ caído *m* BOLSA fallen angel

ángulo *m* MAT, TRANSP angle; **~ de eslinga** TRANSP *carga y descarga* included angle; **~ de reposo** TRANSP *de material almacenado* angle of repose

anidado *adj* INFO nested

anidamiento *m* INFO nesting

anidar *vt* INFO nest

anillo: ~ de plata *m* FIN silver ring (*jarg*)

animación *f* MEDIOS animation

animales: ~ vivos a bordo *fra* TRANSP live animals on board (*LAB*)

animar *vt* COM GEN boost, encourage

animarse *v refl infrml* COM GEN *ideas, eficiencia* pick up (*infrml*)

ánimo: con ~ de lucro *fra* COM GEN profit-making, profitable; **sin ~ de lucro** *fra* COM GEN nonprofitable, nonprofit-making (*AmE*), non-profit-making (*BrE*)

aniversario *m* COM GEN anniversary

anomalía *f* COM GEN anomaly, INFO trouble

anonimato *m* COM GEN anonymity

anónimo *adj* COM GEN anonymous

anormal *adj* COM GEN abnormal

anotación: ~ **al margen** *f* COM GEN side note; ~ **del asiento de apertura** *f* CONT book of first entry; ~ **del asiento de cierre** *f* CONT book on final entry; ~ **en el libro diario** *f* CONT journal entry

anotar *vt* COM GEN jot down; ◆ ~ **una entrada** CONT post an entry; ~ **mercancías** TRANSP tally

Ansaphone® *m* COM GEN, COMS Ansaphone®

ante *prep* COM GEN ante

antecedentes *m pl* COM GEN, RRHH record, background; ~ **crediticios** BANCA, CONT, FIN client previous record, credit information; ~ **educativos** PROT SOC educational background; ~ **laborales del empleado** RRHH employee's job history; ~ **penales** DER police record; ~ **de pérdidas actuales por préstamos** BANCA actual loan loss experience

antecesor, a: ~ **legal** *m,f* DER, PATENT legal predecessor; ~ **en el título de propiedad** *m,f* PATENT predecessor in title

antecostero *adj* FIN offshore

antedatar *vt* COM GEN *cheque, contrato* backdate, *documento, cheque, situación* antedate

antefechar *vt* COM GEN foredate

antememoria *f* INFO cache buffer

ante meridiem *fra* (*a.m.*) COM GEN ante meridiem (*a.m.*)

anteplaya *f* DER foreshore

anteproyecto *m* COM GEN blueprint, preliminary project, DER blueprint, INFO draft printing, POL blueprint; ~ **de ley** DER Green Paper (*BrE*)

anterior *adj* COM GEN preceding

antesala: ~ **de salida** *f* TRANSP departure lounge

anticíclico *adj* ECON, V&M anticyclical

anticipación *f* COM GEN anticipation; ~ **del vencimiento** BANCA acceleration of maturity

anticipado *adj* COM GEN anticipated, V&M *cliente* prospective; ◆ **por** ~ COM GEN beforehand, in advance

anticipar *vt* BANCA buy down, *dinero* make an advance, COM GEN *trabajo tardío, desarrollo* expect, anticipate; ◆ ~ **un pago** BANCA make an advance payment; ~ **un préstamo** BANCA advance a loan

anticiparse: ~ **a** *vt* COM GEN second-guess

anticipo *m* BANCA, BOLSA, COM GEN advance, sum advanced, CONT *de compra* initial outlay, V&M retainer; ~ **bancario** BANCA bank advance; ~ **contable** CONT accountable advance; ~ **contra entrega de productos** COM GEN advance against goods; ~ **a corto plazo** BANCA short-term advance; ~ **en descubierto** BOLSA uncovered advance; ~ **en efectivo** COM GEN cash advance; ~ **fijo** BANCA, CONT fixed advance, standing advance; ~ **fijo para viajes** COM GEN standing travel advance; ~ **garantizado** BANCA secured advance; ~ **no oficial** MEDIOS sneak preview; ~ **pendiente** CONT outstanding advance; ~ **salarial** RRHH advance on salary; ~ **sobre el flete** TRANSP advance freight (*AF*); ~ **sobre valores** BOLSA advance on securities (*BrE*); ~ **de viaje** ECON travel advance, trip advance

anticipos *m pl* BANCA advances; ~ **a corto plazo** CONT short-term prepayments; ~ **recibidos** CONT advances received

anticomercial *adj* COM GEN unbusinesslike

anticorrosivo *adj* IND corrosion-resistant

anticuado *adj* COM GEN old-fashioned, outdated, antiquated

anticuarse *v refl* COM GEN become obsolete

antidumping *adj* MED AMB anti-dumping

antieconómico *adj* COM GEN, ECON, IND, V&M uneconomic

antiestatutario *adj* DER ultravires

antigüedad *f* RRHH seniority; ~ **de las cuentas a cobrar** CONT ageing of receivables

antiguo[1] *adj* COM GEN former, long-standing, old-established

antiguo[2]: ~ **cónyuge** *m* DER former spouse; ~ **fletamiento** *m* TRANSP old charter (*OC*)

antiinflacionista *adj* ECON, POL anti-inflationary, anti-inflationist

antimercadista *adj* COM GEN antimarket

antimonopolio *adj* DER anti-trust (*AmE*)

antimonopolista *adj* DER anti-trust (*AmE*)

antirecesión *adj* COM GEN antirecession

antitrust *adj* ADMIN anti-trust

ANU *abr* (*Asociación de las Naciones Unidas*) POL UNA (*United Nations Association*)

anual *adj* COM GEN annual, yearly, year-to-year, *descenso* year-on-year

anualidad *f* CONT, ECON, FIN annuity, FISC yearly allowance, RRHH, SEG annuity; ~ **colectiva diferida** RRHH deferred group annuity; ~ **cruzada** FIN wraparound annuity; ~ **en curso** SEG current annuity; ~ **diferida** SEG deferred-payment annuity, deferred annuity; ~ **diferida de prima única** FIN single-premium deferred annuity; ~ **fija** SEG fixed annuity; ~ **habilitante** FIN qualifying annuity; ~ **de invalidez** SEG disability annuity; ~ **mixta** SEG hybrid annuity; ~ **no habilitante** FIN nonqualifying annuity; ~ **ordinaria** SEG ordinary annuity; ~ **pagadera por anticipado** SEG annuity payable in advance; ~ **pagadera a plazo vencido** SEG annuity payable in arrears; ~ **perpetua** BOLSA, COM GEN perpetuity; ~ **protegida** FIN wraparound annuity; ~ **reversible** SEG reversible annuity, reversionary annuity; ~ **de supervivencia** SEG survivorship annuity; ~ **vencida** SEG annuity due; ~ **con vencimiento fijo** FIN fixed-term annuity

anualidades: ~ **bancarias** *f pl* BANCA bank annuities; ~ **consolidadas** *f pl* FIN consolidated annuities (*BrE*); ~ **de gobierno** *f pl* FIN government annuity; ~ **de jubilación anticipada** *f pl* FIN early retirement annuities (*jarg*)

anualizado *adj* COM GEN annualized

anualizar *vt* COM GEN annualize

anualmente *adv* COM GEN annually, yearly

anuario *m* MEDIOS yearbook, V&M annual; ~ **de datos comerciales** ECON Trade Data Elements Directory (*TDED*)

ANUDS *abr* (*Agencia de Naciones Unidas para el Desarrollo Social*) POL, PROT SOC United Nations Research Institute for Social Development

anulable *adj* COM GEN, CONT, DER, RRHH, SEG voidable

anulación *f* COM GEN *de una decisión* annulment, *contrato* avoidance, invalidation, cancellation, write-off; ~ **de la hipoteca** FIN mortgage strip; ~ **de prima** SEG cancellation of premium; ~ **en sustancia** CONT in substance defeasance

anulado *adj* COM GEN, DER annulling

anular *vt* COM GEN *factor* cancel out, *decisión* annul, CONT delete, *partida contable* write off, DER *mandamiento judicial, sentencia* quash, render null and void, annul, POL override, *decisión* overrule; ◆ ~ **una anotación** CONT reverse an entry; ~ **un asiento** CONT reverse an entry; ~ **un registro contable** CONT reverse an entry

anuncia: según se ~ *fra* COMS as reported

anunciado *adj* COM GEN advertised; **no** ~ COM GEN unadvertised; ◆ **según** ~ **en televisión** V&M as advertised on TV

anunciante *mf* V&M advertiser

anunciar *vt* COM GEN advertise, *recorte, detalles* advertise for, announce, MEDIOS advertise for, V&M advertise; ◆ ~ **un empleo** MEDIOS, RRHH advertise a job; ~ **un trabajo** MEDIOS, RRHH advertise a job

anunciarse ~ **para** *vt* COM GEN, MEDIOS, V&M advertise for

anuncio *m* COM GEN (*cf reclame*) announcement, advertisement (*ad*), MEDIOS (*cf comercial*), V&M advertisement (*ad*), commercial; ~ **de 2 x 3 metros** V&M sixteen sheet; ~ **de 75 x 100 cm** V&M quad crown; ~ **audiovisual** MEDIOS, V&M av-commercial; ~ **colectivo** V&M tie-in advertising; ~ **comercial en la radio** MEDIOS, V&M radio commercial; ~ **comercial televisivo** MEDIOS, V&M television commercial; ~ **de un cuarto de página** MEDIOS, V&M quarter page advertisement; ~ **desplegado de una plana** MEDIOS, V&M full-page advertisement; ~ **de dividendo** BOLSA dividend announcement; ~ **a doble página** MEDIOS, V&M double-spread advertising; ~ **en doble página central** MEDIOS, V&M center spread (*AmE*), centre spread (*BrE*); ~ **de emisión sindicada** BOLSA, ECON tombstone, tombstone ad; ~ **de empleo** RRHH job advertisement; ~ **en forma de noticia** MEDIOS *edición* reading notice (*jarg*); ~ **de frecuencia semanal** V&M run-of-week spot; ~ **fuera de espacio publicitario** V&M island site (*jarg*); ~ **gancho** V&M bait advertising (*AmE*); ~ **ilegal** V&M fly-posting; ~ **de página entera** MEDIOS, V&M full-page advertisement; ~ **por palabras** MEDIOS, V&M classified ad, classified advertisement; ~ **de periódico** MEDIOS, V&M newspaper advertisement; ~ **en prensa** MEDIOS, V&M press advertisement; ~ **de publicidad editorial** MEDIOS, V&M editorial advertisement; ~ **publicitario** *Esp* (*cf propaganda AmL*) COM GEN, MEDIOS, V&M advert, commercial; ~ **de radio** MEDIOS, V&M radio announcement; ~ **resaltado** MEDIOS, V&M large display advertisement; ~ **reservado de antemano a tarifa reducida** V&M pre-empt spot; ~ **sensacionalista** V&M stunt advertising; ~ **testimonial** V&M testimonial advertisement; ~ **a toda página** MEDIOS, V&M full-page advertisement; ~ **de venta** MEDIOS, V&M announcement of sale

anuncios: ~ a los lados de las escaleras mecánicas *m pl* V&M escalator cards; ~ **por palabras** *m pl* MEDIOS, V&M smalls; **pequeños** ~ *m pl* MEDIOS, V&M small ads

anverso *m* MEDIOS recto

añadido[1] *adj* BANCA, COM GEN add-on

añadido[2] *m* BANCA, COM GEN add-on

añadidura: por ~ *fra* COM GEN on the side

añadir *vt* BOLSA add, COM GEN *detalles, figuras, frases* add in, *números, resultados* add up, *documento* append (*frml*), CONT *cifras* add, INFO append

año *m* COM GEN year (*yr*); ~ **de adquisición** CONT year of acquisition; ~ **anterior** COM GEN previous year; ~ **base** ECON, FIN base year; ~ **bisiesto** COM GEN leap year; ~ **de carestía** ECON leanless year; ~ **comercial** COM GEN trading year; ~ **comercial natural** COM GEN natural business year; ~ **de la compra** CONT year of acquisition; ~ **contable** CONT, ECON, FIN accounting year; ~ **en curso** COM GEN current year; ~ **de emisión** BOLSA year of issue; ~ **fiscal** COM GEN financial year (*FY*), fiscal year (*FY*), tax year; ~ **financiero** FIN financial year (*FY*); ~ **fiscal** FISC fiscal year (*FY*), year of assessment; ~ **fiscal en curso** FISC current fiscal year; ~ **fiscal finalizado** FISC fiscal year ended; ~ **floreciente** COM GEN bumper year; ~ **insignia** COM GEN banner year; ~ **mercantil en curso** CONT current business year; ~ **natural** COM GEN calendar year; ~ **no impositivo** FISC nontaxable year; ~ **nuevo** COM GEN new year; ~ **pasado** COM GEN past year; ~ **pobre** ECON leanless year; ~ **precedente** COM GEN preceding year; ~ **del promedio** FISC year of averaging; ~ **que acaba de finalizar** FISC year then ended; ~ **de recaudación irregular** FISC short taxation year; ~ **de tributación máxima** FISC full taxation year; ◆ **por** ~ COM GEN per annum (*p.a.*), per year; **en el** ~ **de** COM GEN in the year of; **segunda parte del** ~ COM GEN second half of the year; ~ **contable finalizado** CONT accounting year then ended; **el** ~ **a examen** COM GEN the year under review; ~ **fiscal finalizado** CONT fiscal year then ended; ~ **hasta la fecha** CONT, FISC year to date

Año: ~ Europeo del Medio Ambiente *m* MED AMB European Year of the Environment

años[1]: ~ **completos** *m pl* FISC whole years

años[2]: **en los últimos** ~ *fra* COM GEN in recent years

AO *abr* (*automatización de oficinas*) ADMIN, INFO OA (*office automation*)

apaciguar *vt* BOLSA, COM GEN pacify

apagado *adj* INFO off

apagar *vt* INFO turn off

apagón *m* INFO *de energía eléctrica* blackout

apalancamiento *m* BOLSA, CONT, FIN gearing (*BrE*), leverage (*AmE*); ~ **alto** CONT high gearing (*BrE*), high leverage (*AmE*); ~ **de capital** BOLSA capital gearing (*BrE*), capital leverage (*AmE*); ~ **financiero** BOLSA financial gearing (*BrE*), financial leverage (*AmE*); ~ **inverso** CONT reverse gearing (*BrE*), reverse leverage (*AmE*); ~ **de margen** BOLSA *futuros* margin gearing (*BrE*), margin leverage (*AmE*); ~ **negativo** CONT reverse gearing (*BrE*), reverse leverage (*AmE*); ~ **operativo** CONT operating gearing (*BrE*), operating leverage (*AmE*); ~ **positivo** FIN positive gearing (*BrE*), positive leverage (*AmE*); ◆ **bajo** ~ BOLSA low-geared

apalancar *vt* BOLSA, CONT, FIN leverage up

aparato *m* COM GEN device, DER machinery, IND apparatus; ~ **administrativo** COM GEN administrative machinery; ~ **eléctrico** COM GEN electrical appliance; ~ **de fax** ADMIN, COMS, INFO fax machine; ~ **figurativo** PATENT figurative device; ~ **de transcripción** COM GEN, COMS, INFO transcriber

aparatos: ~ domésticos *m pl* COM GEN household appliances, IND durable household goods

aparcamiento *m* COM GEN, OCIO, TRANSP car parking, car park (*BrE*), parking lot (*AmE*); ~ **de corta duración** TRANSP short-term vehicle park (*STVP*)

aparcero, -a *m,f* ECON *agricultura* sharecropper (*AmE*)

aparejado *adj* DER appurtenant

aparejo *m* TRANSP *elevación de carga* tackle; ~ **a la americana** TRANSP *carga y descarga* union purchase

apartadero *m* TRANSP *ferrocarril* siding (*BrE*), side track (*AmE*); ~ **particular** TRANSP private siding (*BrE*); ◆ **ser ~** COM GEN get sidetracked

apartado[1] *adv* TRANSP *barco* aloof

apartado[2] *m* ADMIN, DER paragraph, FISC subchapter; ~ **de correos** *Esp* (*Apdo.*, *cf casilla postal AmL*) COMS Post Office Box (*POB*); ~ **de defensa** FIN defence envelope (*BrE*), defense envelope (*AmE*); ~ **de gasto directo** FIN direct spending envelope; ~ **postal** *Esp* (*cf casilla postal AmL*) ADMIN, COMS Post Office Box (*POB*); ~ **presupuestario** ECON, POL Budget Box (*BrE*)

apartamento *m AmL* (*Apt., Apto.*) (*cf piso Esp*) INMOB apartment (*AmE*), flat (*BrE*); ~ **en copropiedad** INMOB cooperative apartment

Apdo. *abr* (*apartado de correos*) COMS POB (*post office box*)

apelación *f* DER appeal

apelar *vi* COM GEN, DER appeal

apéndice *m* COM GEN appendix, DER addendum, MEDIOS appendix; ~ **de renuncia** SEG *naval* resigning addendum

apercibimiento: ~ **de mejoras** *m* RRHH *salud y seguridad* improvement notice (*BrE*); ~ **de no discriminación** *m* RRHH nondiscrimination notice; ~ **de prohibición** *m* RRHH prohibition notice

aperos: ~ **de labranza** *m pl* ECON *agricultura* farm implements

apertura *f* BOLSA *comercio*, COM GEN *de reunión* opening; ~ **al comercio** BOLSA opening up; ~ **del mercado** V&M market opening; ~ **de ofertas** COM GEN opening of tenders; ~ **de plicas** COM GEN bid opening; ◆ **a la ~** BOLSA at the opening; **de ~ total** TRANSP *contenedor* open full (*OF*)

apilable *adj* IND, TRANSP palletizable

apiladora *f* TRANSP stacker; ~ **de cierre automático** TRANSP *contenedores* lockmatic stacker; ~ **postal** TRANSP post stacker

apilamiento *m* COM GEN stacking, TRANSP stockpile, stacking; ~ **de carga** TRANSP stacking of cargo; ~ **doble** TRANSP double stacking

apilar *vt* COM GEN stack, IND palletize, TRANSP stack, stockpile, palletize; ◆ ~ **en dos niveles** TRANSP *contenedores* double stack

apisonadora *f Esp* (*cf aplanadora AmL*) IND steamroller

aplanadora *f AmL* (*cf apisonadora Esp*) IND steamroller

aplazado *adj* COM GEN deferred (*def.*), adjourned

aplazamiento *m* COM GEN adjournment, deferment, deferral, CONT deferment, installment base (*AmE*), DER adjournment, FISC deferment, deferral, GES *decisión* adjournment; ~ **ampliado** CONT extended deferment; ~ **compuesto** IMP/EXP compound deferment; ~ **del impuesto** FISC remittance of tax; ~ **del impuesto sobre la renta** FISC income tax deferral; ~ **del pago de impuestos** FISC tax deferral; ~ **simple** CONT, FIN simple deferment

aplazar *vt* COM GEN adjourn, defer; ◆ ~ **la discusión de una enmienda** DER table an amendment (*AmE*); ~ **el pago de impuestos** FISC defer tax payment, postpone tax payment

aplicable: ~ **a** *adj* COM GEN applicable to; **no ~** *adj* COM GEN not applicable (*N/A*)

aplicación *f* COM GEN *de fondos, recursos* application, CONT, ECON *de fondos a una reserva* allocation, INFO application; ~ **anterior** PATENT earlier application; ~ **caducada** CONT lapsing appropriation; ~ **de costes** *Esp* (*cf aplicación de costos AmL*) ECON cost application; ~ **de costos** *AmL* (*cf aplicación de costes Esp*) ECON cost application; ~ **de fondos** CONT application of funds; ~ **industrial** IND *de máquina*, PATENT industrial application; ~ **informática** INFO software, *programas* applications program; ~ **informática para auditoría** CONT, INFO audit software; ~ **informática para contabilidad** CONT, INFO accounting software; ~ **internacional** PATENT international application; ~ **de la ley** DER enforcement (*ENF*); ~ **de una patente** PATENT patent application; ~ **de patente europea** PATENT European patent application; ~ **personalizada para la planificación financiera** FIN, INFO personal financial planning software; ~ **práctica** RRHH practical use; ~ **prevista de un beneficio** RRHH projected benefit application; ~ **de pruebas psicométricas** MAT, RRHH, V&M psychometric testing; ~ **de recursos** IND resource industry; ~ **de software** INFO software application; ~ **de tarifa básica** BANCA basic rating; ~ **unilateral** FISC ex parte application; ◆ **en ~** FISC in applying; ~ **de buena fe de las normas contables** CONT application of accounting rules in good faith; ~ **general** COM GEN general purpose (*GP*); **con ~ intensiva de conocimientos** COM GEN knowledge-intensive

aplicaciones: ~ **de fondos** *f pl* CONT uses of funds; ~ **informáticas** *f pl* INFO applications software; ~ **informáticas para inversión** *f pl* FIN, INFO investment software

aplicado *adj* COM GEN *investigación* applied; **no ~** COM GEN, FIN unappropriated

aplicar *vt* COM GEN *principio contable* apply, CONT *costes* assign, DER *ley*, INFO *afectar, tocar* apply; ◆ ~ **contra alguien** DER *una nueva ley* bring to bear against; ~ **los costes en las cuentas apropiadas** *Esp* (*cf aplicar los costos en las cuentas apropiadas AmL*) CONT allocate costs to the appropriate accounts; ~ **los costos en las cuentas apropiadas** *AmL* (*cf aplicar los costes en las cuentas apropiadas Esp*) CONT allocate costs to the appropriate accounts; ~ **a destino indebido** DER misapply; ~ **ingresos a un periodo** CONT apply revenues to a period

aplicarse *v refl* COM GEN come into force, *norma* apply

apoderado, -a *m,f* COM GEN supervisor, BANCA official, DER attorney-in-fact (*AmE*), private attorney, *ley civil* proxyholder; ~ **en bancarrota** BANCA assignee in bankruptcy; ~ **general** DER universal agent

apoderarse *de v refl* COM GEN appropriate

apología *f AmL* (*cf disculpa Esp*) COM GEN apology

aportación: ~ **de capital** *f* FIN contribution of capital; ~ **dineraria** *f* CONT cash contribution; ~ **intangible** *f* COM GEN intangible contribution; ~ **de mano de obra** *f* ECON labour shed (*BrE*); ~ **a la seguridad social** *f* PROT SOC national insurance contribution (*BrE*) (*NIC*), social security contribution; ~ **sobre las ganancias de un trabajador por cuenta propia** *f* FISC *pensiones individualizadas* contribution payable on self-employed earnings; ~ **de tarifa** *f* CONT user charge; ~ **del usuario** *f* CONT user charge

aportaciones: ~ **de los empleados** *f pl* RRHH employee contributions; ~ **a fondos de pensión** *f pl* CONT pension charges; **~ de los sindicatos** *f pl* RRHH trade union contributions (*BrE*); **~ a sistemas complementarios de pensiones** *f pl* CONT pension charges; **~ a través del empleo** *f pl* FISC *pensiones* contributions through employment; **~ voluntarias** *f pl* FISC, PROT SOC *Seguridad Social* voluntary contributions (*BrE*)

aportar *vt* BANCA *aval* pledge, COM GEN *ingresos* bring in, *aval* pledge; ◆ **~ capital** BANCA, COM GEN provide capital; **~ una contribución** COM GEN make a contribution**~ fondos** BANCA, COM GEN provide capital; **~ una garantía** BANCA supply collateral

aporte: ~ de capital *m* FIN capital contribution; **~ posterior de dinero** *m* BOLSA billback

apoyar *vt* BANCA aid, COM GEN *moción* second, back up, support, *idea* buy into, ECON *moneda* support

apoyo *m* COM GEN, INFO support; **~ de campo** COM GEN field support; **~ de caucho** TRANSP rubber bearing (*RB*); **~ financiero** COM GEN backing, ECON financial support; **~ gerencial** RRHH management support; **~ del mercado** V&M market support; **~ oficial de créditos de exportación** FIN official supported export credits; **~ popular** POL grass-roots support; **~ de reserva** BOLSA backup support; **~ suplementario** FIN supplementary assistance; **~ técnico** INFO technical support

apreciable *adj* COM GEN appreciable

apreciación *f* BOLSA *divisas, acciones*, COM GEN, INMOB *activos, propiedades* appreciation; **~ de méritos** COM GEN, RRHH merit rating

apreciar *vt* COM GEN appreciate

apremio *m* COM GEN time pressure; **~ indebido** FISC undue hardship

aprendiz, a *m,f* RRHH apprentice, trainee (*BrE*); ◆ **estar de ~ con alguien** RRHH be apprenticed to sb

aprendizaje *m* RRHH apprenticeship; **~ asistido por computador** *AmL* ver *aprendizaje asistido por computadora AmL*; **~ asistido por computadora** *AmL* (*cf aprendizaje asistido por ordenador Esp*) INFO computer-aided learning (*CAL*); **~ asistido por ordenador** *Esp* (*cf aprendizaje asistido por computadora AmL*) INFO computer-aided learning (*CAL*); **~ común** PROT SOC common learnings; **~ de idiomas asistido por computador** *AmL* ver *aprendizaje de idiomas asistido por computadora AmL*; **~ de idiomas asistido por computadora** *AmL* (*cf aprendizaje de idiomas asistido por ordenador Esp*) INFO computer-aided language learning (*CALL*), computer-assisted language learning (*CALL*); **~ de idiomas asistido por ordenador** *Esp* (*cf aprendizaje de idiomas asistido por computadora AmL*) INFO computer-aided language learning (*CALL*), computer-assisted language learning (*CALL*); **~ juvenil** RRHH youth training (*BrE*) (*YT*); **~ programado** PROT SOC programmed learning

apresurar *vt* COM GEN expedite; ◆ **~ a los cortos** BOLSA squeeze the shorts (*jarg*)

apretado *adj* COM GEN *plan de trabajo* busy

apretarse: ~ el cinturón *fra* COM GEN scrimp and save, tighten one's belt

aprobación *f* COM GEN approval, POL enactment, V&M *producto* endorsement; **~ de cuentas** CONT approval of the accounts; **~ de una cuña radiofónica** V&M copy clearance; **~ de un préstamo** BANCA, FIN approval of a loan; **~ del proyecto** COM GEN project approval; **~ de remate** DER judicial foreclosure, judicial sale; **~ con reservas** COM GEN qualified approval

aprobado *adj* COM GEN *decisión, documento*, FISC, INFO *mecanismo, programas* approved

aprobar *vt* COM GEN pass, *acción, cuentas, decisión* approve, DER, ECON pass, FISC approve, POL enact; ◆ **sin ~** BOLSA *opciones* nonapproved; **~ una emisión** FIN subscribe to an issue

apropiación: ~ indebida *f* CONT, DER illegal seizure, misappropriation, FIN misappropriation; **~ marketing** *f* V&M marketing appropriation

apropiaciones: ~ legales *f pl* DER statutory appropriations

apropiar *vt* COM GEN adapt, apply

apropiarse *v refl* CONT, ECON, FIN *fondos* appropriate

aprovechable: totalmente ~ *adj* COM GEN *calidad* good sound merchantable (*BrE*) (*gsm*)

aprovechamiento: ~ de fondos prestados *m* BANCA draw-down

aprovechar *vt* COM GEN *oportunidad* milk (*infrml*), FIN *demanda*, V&M cash in on; ◆ **~ una oportunidad** COM GEN use a window of opportunity

aprovecharse: ~ de *v refl* COM GEN take advantage of; **~ de una oportunidad para hacer algo** *v refl* COM GEN take advantage of an opportunity to do sth

aprovisionamiento *m* COM GEN supply, TRANSP catering; **~ del Estado** ECON *UE* public procurement; **~ fijo** ECON fixed supply

aprovisionar *vt* COM GEN, ECON afford, supply

aprovisionarse: ~ de *fra* COM GEN buy in

aproximación *f* COM GEN, GES approach, POL *de políticas internacionales* approximation; **~ de coste** *Esp* (*cf aproximación de costo AmL*) FIN cost approach; **~ de costo** *AmL* (*cf aproximación de coste Esp*) FIN cost approach; **~ exponencial** MAT *técnica de predicción* exponential smoothing; **~ fiscal** FISC fiscal approximation

aproximadamente *adv* COM GEN approximately (*approx.*)

aproximar *vt* MAT approximate

Apt. *abr AmL* (*apartamento*) INMOB apartament (*AmE*), flat (*BrE*)

aptitud *f* COM GEN appropriateness, aptitude, expediency, CONT qualification, PROT SOC fitness, RRHH *de un individuo* aptitude; **~ administrativa** GES management competence; **~ física para el trabajo** COM GEN, RRHH capacity to work

aptitudes *f pl* COM GEN abilities

apto *adj* DER fit and proper; **~ para el trabajo** RRHH able to work; ◆ **ser ~ para hacer** COM GEN, RRHH be qualified to do

Apto. *abr AmL* (*apartamento*) INMOB apartament (*AmE*), flat (*BrE*)

apuesta *f* OCIO *deporte* betting

apuntalar *vt* ECON *divisa* underpin

apuntar: ~ a *vt* COM GEN target, CONT post an entry; **~ contra** COM GEN *nueva ley* bring to bear against

apunte: ~ compuesto *m* CONT compound entry; **~ contable** *m* CONT book entry; **~ fraudulento** *m* DER fraudulent entry; **~ en el libro diario** *m* CONT journal entry; **~ de opción sobre divisas indexadas** *m* BOLSA indexed currency option note (*ICON*); **~ de opción sobre rendimientos líquidos** *m* BOLSA liquid yield option note (*LYON*); **~ verbal** *m* POL oral note

apuntes: ~ de Lehman sobre oportunidades de

inversión *m pl* BOLSA Lehman Investment Opportunity Notes (*LIONs*)

apuros: estar en ~ económicos *fra* BANCA, ECON be strapped for cash

aquí: de ~ *adv* COMS hereof

aquiescencia *f* POL *del parlamento* assent

arancel *m* ECON, FISC, IMP/EXP tariff; ~ **aduanero** IMP/EXP customs authorities, customs tariff; ~ **antidumping** MED AMB retaliatory duty; ~ **común de compensación** ECON compensating common tariff (*CCT*); ~ **específico** COM GEN specific tariff; ~ **de importación** IMP/EXP import tariff; ~ **proteccionista** ECON, FISC, IMP/EXP protective tariff; ~ **de recaudación** IMP/EXP collection tariff; ~ **recíproco** IMP/EXP swinging tariff; ~ **sobre el valor** CONT, IMP/EXP, TRANSP ad valorem duty

arancelario *adj* FISC protected by tariffs

arbitraje *m* COM GEN arbitrage, arbitration; ~ **de acciones** BOLSA stock arbitrage; ~ **de agravios** RRHH grievance arbitration; ~ **de cambio** BANCA, BOLSA arbitrage, exchange arbitrage; ~ **de cartera** DER hedging, ECON, FISC, IMP/EXP charge of stocks, hedging; ~ **de divisas** BOLSA currency arbitrage; ~ **de elección simple** BANCA straight choice arbitration; ~ **espacial** COM GEN space arbitrage; ~ **fiscal** FISC tax straddle; ~ **de fusión** BOLSA merger arbitrage; ~ **industrial** RRHH industrial arbitration; ~ **nacional sobre salarios** RRHH national wage award; ~ **necesario** RRHH compulsory arbitration (*BrE*); ~ **obligatorio** RRHH compulsory arbitration (*BrE*); ~ **de la oferta final** ECON final offer arbitration; ~ **de pago al contado** BOLSA cash and carry arbitrage; ~ **pendular** RRHH pendulum arbitration; ~ **con riesgo** BOLSA risk arbitrage; ~ **salarial** RRHH wage arbitration; ~ **en el tiempo** COM GEN time arbitrage; ~ **de tipo de cambio** FIN arbitration of exchange; ~ **de última oferta** RRHH last-offer arbitration; ~ **de valores** BOLSA arbitrage in securities (*BrE*); ~ **vinculante** DER binding arbitration; ~ **voluntario** RRHH voluntary arbitration

arbitrajista *mf* BOLSA, COM GEN arbitrage dealer, arbitrageur

arbitral *adj* COM GEN arbitral

arbitrar 1. *vt* COM GEN arbitrate in; 2. *vi* COM GEN arbitrate

arbitrario *adj* COM GEN arbitrary

árbitro, -a *m,f* BOLSA, DER arbitrageur, arbiter (*arb*), arbitrator; ~ **exclusivo(-a)** RRHH single arbitrator (*BrE*); ~ **judicial** DER judicial arbitrator; ~ **de seguros marítimos** SEG average adjuster; ~ **único(-a)** SEG sole arbitrator

árbol: ~ **de correspondencia** *m* GES pertinence tree; ~ **de decisión** *m* RRHH decision tree; ~ **genealógico** *m* COM GEN, GES family tree

arbotante *m* TRANSP *contenedores* buttress

arc: ~ **sen** *m* MAT arcsin; ~ **tg** *m* MAT arctan

arcas: las ~ **del Tesoro** *f pl* FISC Treasury's purse (*BrE*)

archivado *adj* COM GEN filed

archivador[1] *m Esp* (*cf archivero AmL*) ADMIN filing cabinet

archivador[2]**,a** *m,f Esp* (*cf archivero AmL*) ADMIN, RRHH file clerk, archivist, record keeper

archivar *vt* COM GEN file, file away, archive; ◆ ~ **una declaración** FISC file a return

archivero[1] *m AmL* (*cf archivador Esp*) ADMIN filing cabinet

archivero[2]**,-a** *m,f AmL* (*cf archivador Esp*) ADMIN, RRHH file clerk, archivist, record keeper

archivista *mf* ADMIN, RRHH archivist, file clerk, record keeper

archivo *m* ADMIN, COM GEN, DER, INFO file, archive, *ocupación* filing, archiving; ~ **en anaqueles** ADMIN open-shelf filing; ~ **ASCII** INFO ASCII file; ~ **de auditoría** CONT audit file; ~ **de caracteres** INFO character file; ~ **de comandos** INFO command file; ~ **de diseño** INFO drawing file; ~ **fuente** INFO source file; ~ **gráfico** INFO graphics file; ~ **índice** COM GEN, INFO index file; ~ **por materias** ADMIN, COM GEN subject filing; ~ **negativo** BANCA negative file; ~ **numérico** COM GEN, INFO numerical filing; ~ **positivo** BANCA positive file; ~ **de programa** INFO program file; ~ **de protección** INFO backup file; ~ **de registro** INFO log file; ~ **de revisión contable** CONT audit file; ~ **de salida** INFO output file; ~ **de vencimientos** BANCA tickler file; ~ **de verificación contable** CONT audit file

Archivo: ~ **Nacional** *m* COM GEN, POL Public Record Office

archivos: ~ **policíacos** *m pl* DER, POL police files

ardid *m* COM GEN artifice, scheme, stratagem, FISC *evasión fiscal* scheme, stratagem

área *f* COM GEN, ECON, POL area; ~ **afectada** FISC impacted area; ~ **de almacenamiento** COM GEN, INFO storage area; ~ **comercial** COM GEN, V&M market place; ~ **de comercio** COM GEN trading area; ~ **de conocimientos especializados** COM GEN *de un profesional* area of expertise; ~ **de control** COM GEN span of control; ~ **de depósito** TRANSP standage area; ~ **de desarrollo** ECON development area (*BrE*); ~ **económicamente subdesarrollada** ECON, POL economically backward area; ~ **edificada** COM GEN, INMOB built-up area; ~ **de estiba** TRANSP stowage area; ~ **fuera de límites** COM GEN off-limits area; ~ **geográfica** COM GEN, IMP/EXP geographical area; ~ **industrial en declive** ECON, IND declining industrial area; ~ **industrial decreciente** ECON, IND declining industrial area; ~ **de influencia del dólar** ECON dollar area; ~ **internacional de dominio de la libra esterlina** ECON overseas sterling area (*OSA*); ~ **de libre comercio** ECON, POL free-trade area; ~ **menos favorecida** ECON *agricultura* less-favoured area (*BrE*), less-favored area (*AmE*); ~ **del mercado primario** BOLSA primary market area; ~ **metropolitana** ECON metropolitan area; ~ **de no influencia de la libra esterlina** ECON nonsterling area (*NSA*); ~ **de población mayoritariamente jubilada** ECON, OCIO grey belt (*infrml*) (*BrE*); ~ **de recepción** ADMIN, OCIO reception area; ~ **de recepción de camiones** TRANSP lorry reception area (*BrE*), truck reception area (*AmE*); ~ **de recuperación** TRANSP reclaim area; ~ **de responsabilidad** GES, RRHH area of responsibility; ~ **restringida** TRANSP restricted area; ~ **retrasada económicamente** ECON, POL economically backward area; ~ **rural** ECON, MED AMB rural area; ~ **de una superficie** ECON, MAT, PATENT, INMOB surface area; ~ **de trabajo** RRHH workspace; ~ **urbana** COM GEN urban area; ~ **vinícola** ECON, IND wine-producing area; ~ **de viraje** TRANSP turnaround (*AmE*), turnround (*BrE*), turning circle; ◆ **sobre el** ~ **de giro** TRANSP *aviación* over pivot area

Área: **~ de Desarrollo Industrial Marítimo** *f* IND Maritime Industrial Development Area; **~ Económica Europea** *f obs* ECON European Economic Area (*obs*); **~ Programática Urbana** *f* COM GEN, POL Urban Programme Area (*BrE*)

arenga *f* POL jawboning (*AmE*) (*jarg*)

argot: **~ burocrático** *m* COM GEN officialese

argumento: **~ de la industria naciente** *m* IND infant industry argument; **~ de supuesto óptimo** *m* COM GEN best-case scenario; **~ de supuesto pésimo** *m* COM GEN worst-case scenario

arma: **~ de doble filo** *m* RRHH double-edged sword (*BrE*), whipsaw (*AmE*); **~ publicitaria** *f* V&M advertising weapon

armador, a *m,f* IMP/EXP, TRANSP shipowner

armamento *m* TRANSP commissioning

armazón *m* COM GEN framework; **~ del contenedor** TRANSP container frame; **~ de unidad montacargas** TRANSP lift unit frame (*LUF*)

armella *f* TRANSP eye bolt

armonización *f* COM GEN harmonization; **~ contable** CONT accounting harmonization; **~ fiscal** ECON, FISC tax harmonization; **~ de una gama de productos** MEDIOS matching of a product line; **~ de impuestos sobre el consumo** IMP/EXP harmonization of excise duties; **~ legal** DER *EU* legal harmonization; **~ de legislaciones** POL legal harmonization; **~ mundial** CONT global harmonization

armonizar *vt* COM GEN harmonize

arquitecto, -a *m,f* INMOB architect; **~ naval** RRHH, TRANSP naval architect

arraigado: **muy ~** *adj* COM GEN long-established

arrancar *vt* COM GEN, ECON *firma, compañía* start, start up, INFO *ordenadores* boot up, *programa* set up

arranque *m* COM GEN self-starter, start, start-up, ECON start, start-up, boot-up, *máquina, periférico* start; **~ en caliente** INFO warm restart; **~ en frío** COM GEN cold start, INFO cold boot, cold start

arrastrado: **~ a cuentas anteriores** *adj* BANCA, CONT *balance* carried back; **~ por un golpe de mar** *adj* TRANSP washed overboard (*wob*)

arrastrar *vt* MEDIOS *radiodifusión* trail; ◆ **~ hacia abajo** ECON *precio* drive down; **~ una pérdida** FIN carry a loss; **~ saldos** CONT bring forward

arrastre[1] *m* TRANSP tow

arrastre[2]: **con ~ de dientes** *fra* INFO tractor-fed

arrebatar *vt* COM GEN snatch

arreglar *vt* COM GEN fix; ◆ **~ las cosas** COM GEN straighten things out; **~ cuentas** COM GEN settle the bill

arreglo *m* COM GEN *compromiso* accommodation, settlement, DER *con un acreedor* composition; **~ de aplazamiento de salario** RRHH salary deferral arrangement; **~ de disputas** RRHH settlement of disputes; **~ extrajudicial** DER out-of-court settlement; **~ financiero** BANCA, DER, FIN financial settlement; **~ global** COM GEN, DER, FIN package deal; **~ rápido** COM GEN, FIN quick fix; **~ con un solo sindicato** RRHH single union deal (*BrE*); ◆ **que no tiene ~** COM GEN beyond repair

arrendado *adj* COM GEN, INMOB leased; **no ~** INMOB untenanted

arrendador, a *m,f* COM GEN, INMOB landlord, lessor

arrendamiento *m* COM GEN *precio, acuerdo* lease, FIN leasing, INMOB leasehold, tenancy; **~ agrícola** INMOB farm tenancy; **~ al mes** DER, INMOB month-to-month tenancy; **~ por años** FIN, INMOB tenancy for years; **~ de un buque** COM GEN ship lease; **~ de capital** COM GEN capital lease agreement, CONT capital lease; **~ comercial** COM GEN commercial lease; **~compra** FIN lease-back; **~ conjunto** INMOB cotenancy; **~ de contenedores** TRANSP container leasing; **~ de deuda** INMOB leveraged lease; **~ ejecutivo** *AmL* (*cf alquiler ejecutivo Esp*) GES *automóviles, negocios corporativos* executive leasing; **~ de equipo** IND, INMOB equipment leasing; **~ de explotación** CONT, INMOB operating lease; **~ financiero** BANCA, FIN financial leasing, financial lease; **~ financiero al consumidor** BANCA consumer leasing; **~ financiero directo** ECON direct financial leasing; **~ indexado** INMOB index lease; **~ industrial** IND, INMOB industrial rent; **~ más gastos** INMOB net lease; **~ mensual** DER, INMOB month-to-month tenancy; **~ mes a mes** DER, INMOB month-to-month tenancy; **~ con opción a compra** INMOB lease with option to purchase; **~ de operación** FIN operation lease; **~ perpetuo** INMOB perpetual lease; **~ de petróleo y gas** IND oil and gas lease; **~ sin plazo fijo** DER, INMOB tenancy at will; **~ a porcentaje** INMOB percentage lease; **~ en posesión exclusiva** DER, INMOB tenancy in severalty; **~ principal** INMOB master lease; **~ progresivo** INMOB graduated lease; **~ real** FIN true lease; **~ por un subarrendatario** COM GEN, INMOB sandwich lease (*infrml*), subletting; **~ tecnológico** ECON technological rent; **~ de tierras** INMOB land lease; **~ ventajoso** FIN leverage lease (*AmE*), gearing lease (*BrE*)

arrendar *vt* COM GEN, INMOB lease

arrendatario, -a *m,f* COM GEN, INMOB holder, leaseholder, lessee, tenant; **~ agrícola** COM GEN agricultural tenant

arrepentimiento: **~ poscompra** *m* V&M post-purchase remorse

arriba[1]: **~ mencionado** *adj* COMS above-named

arriba[2] *adv* COM GEN up; ◆ **hacia ~** COM GEN upward, *movimiento* upwards; **según ~ se menciona** COMS as mentioned above

arribar *vt* COM GEN veer

arriendo *m* DER, INMOB tenancy, lease, letting, leasehold; **~ bruto** INMOB gross lease; **~ financiero de capital** COM GEN capital lease; **~ de mercado** INMOB market rent

arriesgado *adj* COM GEN risky

arriesgar *vt* COM GEN endanger, *situación* jeopardize; ◆ **~ grandes sumas** BOLSA plunge

arrojarle: **~ a alguien las normas a la cara** *fra* COM GEN throw the rule book at sb

arruinado *adj* COM GEN, FIN, RRHH *en quiebra* bankrupt

arruinar *vt* COM GEN spoil, wreck

arruinarse *v refl* COM GEN, FIN, RRHH go bankrupt, go broke (*infrml*), go to the wall (*infrml*), go toes up (*infrml*)

arte: **el ~ de lo posible** *m* POL the art of the possible; **~ de vender** *m* V&M salesmanship

artes: **~ del lenguaje** *f pl* PROT SOC language arts; **~ visuales** *m pl* MEDIOS visual arts

artesanía: **~ local** *f* RRHH local handicraft

artesano *m* RRHH craftsman

articulación: **~ de índices** *f* ECON index linking

articulado *adj* TRANSP *vehículo rodado* kneeling

artículo *m* COM GEN item, article, DER *de acta* Article; **~ de consumo** COM GEN article of consumption; **~ defectuoso** V&M faulty good; **~ equilibrado** DER balanced article; **~ explosivo** TRANSP explosive article; **~ de fondo** COM GEN, MEDIOS editorial; **~ gancho** *f* V&M bait and switch advertising (*AmE*); **~ gravable** FISC taxable article, taxable item; **~ imponible** FISC excisable good; **~ de una ley** DER legal section; **~ de lujo** COM GEN, V&M luxury good; **~ de marca** COM GEN branded good; **~ periodístico firmado** MEDIOS *imprenta* feature article; **~ de primera calidad** V&M upmarket good; **~ principal** MEDIOS lead; **~ de reclamo** V&M loss leader; **~ restringido** TRANSP restricted article (*REART*); **~ de saldo** COM GEN, V&M oddment; **~ suelto** COM GEN, V&M oddment; **~ de venta** V&M sales feature; **~ sin venta** COM GEN, V&M shelf warmer, sleeper; **~ de venta fácil** V&M fast-moving article

artículos: **~ de calidad** *m pl* COM GEN, V&M speciality goods (*BrE*), specialty goods (*AmE*); **~ de compra impulsiva** *m pl* V&M impulse goods; **~ de consumo corriente** *m pl* V&M convenience goods; **~ de consumo de primera necesidad** *m pl* COM GEN, V&M first order goods; **~ de contrabando** *m pl* FISC, IMP/EXP smuggled goods; **~ de corte y confección** *m pl* V&M dry goods; **~ cualificados** *m pl* FIN qualifying items; **~ devueltos** *m pl* COM GEN returned goods; **~ de escritorio** *m pl* COM GEN stationery; **~ especializados** *m pl* COM GEN, V&M speciality goods (*BrE*), specialty goods (*AmE*); **~ de fin de serie** *m pl* COM GEN, V&M end-of-line goods; **~ de mercería** *m pl* V&M dry goods; **~ de moda** *m pl* V&M fashion goods; **~ de mucho consumo** *m pl* COM GEN, V&M bulk goods; **~ de naufragio** *m pl* SEG stranded goods; **~ no desgravables** *m pl* FISC disallowable items (*BrE*); **~ sin marca** *m pl* COM GEN unbranded goods; **~ nuevos** *m pl* COM GEN incoming goods; **~ de papelería de la oficina** *m pl* ADMIN office stationery; **~ de primera calidad** *m pl* COM GEN upmarket goods; **~ en proceso** *m pl* COM GEN, V&M goods in process; **~ recibidos** *m pl* COMS incoming goods; **~ de relleno** *m pl* MEDIOS *imprenta* fillers; **~ suntuarios** *m pl* COM GEN, V&M prestige goods; **~ tarifados por volumen** *m pl* TRANSP measurement goods; **~ terminados** *m pl* COM GEN finished goods; **~ de una tienda** *m pl* RRHH shop's articles; **~ de tocador** *m pl* COM GEN toiletries; **~ de uso personal** *m pl* COM GEN *aduana* articles for personal use; **~ de valor** *m pl* COM GEN, V&M valuables; **~ varios** *m pl* CONT sundry articles; **~ de venta difícil** *m pl* COM GEN, V&M slow-moving goods

artificial *adj* IND man-made

artilugio *m* COM GEN gadget

asalariado, -a *m,f* RRHH salariat, salaried person, salary earner

asamblea *f* COM GEN assembly; **~ de accionistas** BOLSA, RRHH shareholders' meeting; **~ de acreedores** COM GEN, CONT, FIN, GES creditors' meeting; **~ anual** COM GEN, GES annual meeting; **~ de delegados** COM GEN, GES meeting of sub-committee; **~ electoral** COM GEN, CONT, FIN, GES election meeting; **~ de la entidad** CONT entity convention; **~ extraordinaria** COM GEN extraordinary meeting; **~ general** COM GEN general assembly (*GA*), CONT entity convention; **~ general anual** COM GEN, GES annual general meeting (*AGM*); **~ de socios** COM GEN, CONT, FIN, GES general meeting of members

ascendente *adj* COM GEN ascending, ECON, INFO upward

ascender 1. *vt* COM GEN advance, RRHH upgrade, *a un empleado* promote; ◆ **~ a** COM GEN *cuenta* amount to, come to; **~ un puesto** RRHH upgrade a post; **2.** *vi* COM GEN rise

ascendido: **ser ~** *fra* RRHH be promoted

ascensión: **~ rápida** *f* RRHH fast tracking

ascenso *m* RRHH promotion

ascensor: **~ para pasajeros** *m* COM GEN, OCIO passenger elevator (*AmE*), passenger lift (*BrE*); **~ de tijera** *m* TRANSP scissor lift

asegurabilidad *f* SEG insurability; **~ garantizada** SEG guaranteed insurability

aseguración *f* BANCA, BOLSA, FIN securitization

asegurado *adj* SEG insured, assured; **no ~** SEG uninsured, unassured; ◆ **estar ~** SEG be insured

asegurador, a *m,f* SEG underwriter (*U/W*), insurer; **~ de bienes** SEG property insurer; **~ de cascos de buques** SEG *marina* hull underwriter; **~ directo(-a)** SEG direct insurer; **~ mutualista** SEG mutual insurer; **~ registrado(-a) de bienes y accidentes** SEG chartered property and casualty underwriter; **~ de vida** SEG life insurer; **~ de vida colegiado(-a)** SEG chartered life underwriter

aseguramiento: **~ de calidad** *m* COM GEN quality assurance

asegurar *vt* BANCA securitize, BOLSA securitize, *precio* secure, FIN securitize, SEG insure; ◆ **~ contra incendios** SEG insure against fire

asentamientos: **~ de población dispersos** *m pl* PROT SOC scattersite housing (*AmE*), scattered site housing (*BrE*)

asentarse: **~ en el mercado** *fra* COM GEN get a toehold in the market

asentir *vt* COM GEN agree

asesinato: **~ con premeditación** *m* DER first degree murder (*AmE*), murder one (*infrml*) (*AmE*)

asesor, a *m,f* COM GEN, FISC, RRHH advisor, consultant; **~ administrativo(-a)** GES management consultant; **~ de crédito** FIN credit adviser, credit advisor, credit counsellor; **~ económico(-a)** ECON *de banco, gobierno*, POL economic adviser; **~ financiero(-a)** DER, FIN, SEG investment adviser; **~ fiscal** FISC tax advisor, tax consultant, tax practitioner; **~ de imagen** MEDIOS, V&M public relations consultant; **~ de informática** INFO computer consultant; **~ de inversiones** CONT, DER, FIN, SEG investment adviser; **~ jurídico(-a)** BANCA, COM GEN, DER *empresas* in-house lawyer; **~ legal** DER counsel, legal adviser; **~ de noticias** MEDIOS *relaciones públicas* news adviser; **~ privado(-a)** COM GEN aide; **~ de relaciones públicas** MEDIOS, V&M public relations consultant; **~ de seguros** CONT, DER, FIN, SEG insurance consultant; **~ de selección** RRHH recruitment consultant; **~ técnico(-a)** COM GEN, RRHH consultant engineer, technical consultant

asesoramiento *m* COM GEN advisory voice, DER counsel; **~ bancario** BANCA bank advice; **~ a los empleados** RRHH employee counseling (*AmE*), employee counselling (*BrE*); **~ financiero** FIN investment counseling (*AmE*), investment counselling (*BrE*); **~ de inversiones** FIN investment counseling (*AmE*), investment counselling (*BrE*); **~ jurídico** *f* DER legal advice; **~ legal** PROT SOC legal aid; **~ de una operación** BOLSA advice of deal

asesorar *vt* COM GEN advise, give advice, DER *a alguien* counsel

asesores: **~ no juristas** *m pl* RRHH lay members

asesoría: ~ **de empresas** *f* COM GEN, GES management consultancy; ~ **jurídica** *f* COM GEN, DER legal consultancy; ~ **de relaciones públicas** *f* COM GEN, MEDIOS, V&M public relations consultancy

así: ~ **llamado** *adj* COM GEN so-called

asiento *m* CONT entry, OCIO seat; ~ **de abono** BANCA, CONT, FIN credit entry; ~ **de actualización** CONT adjusting entry; ~ **de ajuste** CONT adjusting entry; ~ **de apertura** CONT book of first entry, opening entry; ~ **cancelado** CONT cancelling entry (*BrE*), canceling entry (*AmE*); ~ **de cargo** BANCA, CONT, FIN debit entry; ~ **de cierre** CONT book on final entry, closing entry; ~ **de cierre de ejercicio** CONT year-end closing entry; ~ **compensatorio** CONT offsetting entry; ~ **compuesto** CONT compound entry; ~ **compuesto en el diario** CONT compound journal entry; ~ **contable** CONT book entry, accounting entry; ~ **contable suplementario** CONT supplementary entry; ~ **contable en suspenso** CONT suspense entry; ~ **en el libro diario** CONT journal entry; ~ **en libros** CONT book entry; ~ **del mayor** CONT ledger entry; ~**-milla** OCIO, TRANSP seat mile; ~ **posterior** CONT *contabilidad* post-entry, IMP/EXP, TRANSP post-entry; ~ **de reclasificación** CONT reclassification entry; ~ **de suspensión** TRANSP suspension seat

asignación *f* COM GEN allocation, allotment, appropriation, settlement pattern; ~ **de activos** BOLSA asset allocation; ~ **al fondo de reserva** CONT transfer to reserve fund; ~ **de almacenamiento** INFO storage allocation; ~ **anual** CONT annual appropriation; ~ **de capital** FIN *gubernamental*, POL capital allotment; ~ **de costes** *Esp* (*cf asignación de costos AmL*) CONT allocation of costs, cost allocation; ~ **de costos** *AmL* (*cf asignación de costes Esp*) CONT allocation of costs, cost allocation; ~ **de derechos especiales de giro** BANCA allocation of special drawing rights; ~ **en divisas** FIN foreign currency allowance; ~ **eficiente** ECON efficient allocation; ~ **de empleo** COM GEN job assignment; ~ **estándar** POL standard allotment; ~ **extraordinaria** FIN nonrecurring appropriation; ~ **familiar** ECON, PROT SOC child benefit (*BrE*); ~ **para un fin concreto** COM GEN special purpose allotment; ~ **de fondos** CONT *gubernamental*, POL fund appropriation; ~ **de fondos alternativa** FIN alternative funding; ~ **de fondos en bloque** CONT *sector público*, POL block funding; ~ **para gastos imprevistos** CONT incidentals allowance; ~ **de gastos publicitarios** FIN, V&M assignment of advertising expenditure; ~ **implícita** INFO *sistema operativo* default; ~ **inadecuada** COM GEN misallocation; ~ **de ingresos** TRANSP revenue allocation; ~ **interina** COM GEN acting allowance; ~ **interna de fondos** CONT, FIN internal funding; ~ **del límite de exención** FISC allocation of exemption limit; ~ **por memoria** COM GEN memorandum allocation; ~ **no distribuida** COM GEN undistributed allotment; ~ **parlamentaria** CONT, POL parliamentary appropriation; ~ **de precio** FIN allotment price; ~ **presupuestaria** ECON, FIN, POL budgetary appropriation, budget appropriation; ~ **proporcional al patrocinio** FISC allocation in proportion to patronage; ~ **para provisiones** COM GEN provisions allocation; ~ **para publicidad** FIN advertising appropriation; ~ **de puestos** RRHH job assignment; ~ **de recursos** COM GEN resource allocation; ~ **reglamentaria** POL statutory allocation, statutory appropriation; ~ **a una reserva** CONT appropriation to a reserve; ~ **a reservas** CONT allocation to reserves; ~ **de responsabilidades** FIN, GES, RRHH allocation of responsibilities; ~ **salarial** RRHH wage assignment; ~ **de tareas** GES role set; ~ **para transporte** COM GEN travel allowance; ~ **para viajes** COM GEN travel allocation; ~ **para vivienda** PROT SOC, RRHH housing allowance, accommodation allowance; ◆ **sin** ~ FIN ex allotment

asignaciones: ~ **nacionales de defensa** *f pl* POL government defense appropriations (*AmE*), government defence appropriations (*BrE*)

asignado: **no** ~ *adj* COM GEN, FIN unappropriated, INFO unallocated

asignar *vt* COM GEN *tareas, recursos* allocate, allot, appropriate, CONT break down; ◆ ~ **los costes a las cuentas apropiadas** *Esp* (*cf asignar los costos a las cuentas apropiadas AmL*) CONT allocate costs to the appropriate accounts; ~ **los costos a las cuentas apropiadas** *AmL* (*cf asignar los costes a las cuentas apropiadas Esp*) CONT allocate costs to the appropriate accounts; ~ **fondos** FIN earmark funds

asilo *m* COM GEN, POL, PROT SOC asylum

asimetría *f* COM GEN asymmetry, MAT skewness; ~ **de la producción** ECON production asymmetry

asimilación *f* BOLSA, DER assimilation

asincrónico *adj* INFO asynchronous

asistencia *f* BANCA, ECON, INFO *ayuda* aid, assistance; ~ **financiera** ECON, POL *del gobierno* financial assistance; ~ **de jornada completa** FISC full-time attendance; ~ **jurídica** DER legal services; ~ **médica** PROT SOC medical assistance; ~ **no dedicada a proyectos específicos** ECON *ayuda al desarrollo* nonproject aid; ~ **oficial para el desarrollo** ECON *internacional* official development assistance; ~ **pública** PROT SOC public welfare; ~ **social** PROT SOC, RRHH welfare payment; ~ **técnica** IND technical assistance, technical support

asistente, -a *m,f* RRHH assistant (*asst*); ~ **de dedicación completa** FISC full-time attendant; ~ **ejecutivo(-a)** GES, RRHH assistant to manager; ~ **de línea** RRHH line assistant; ~ **personal** RRHH personal assistant (*PA*); ~ **técnico(-a)** RRHH technical assistant (*TA*)

asistentes: ~ **a una subasta** *m pl* COM GEN birdwatchers

asistido: ~ **por computador** *AmL ver asistido por computadora AmL*; ~ **por computadora** *adj AmL* (*cf asistido por ordenador Esp*) INFO computer-aided, computer-assisted; ~ **por ordenador** *adj Esp* (*cf asistido por computadora AmL*) INFO computer-aided, computer-assisted

asistir 1. *vt* BANCA *personas* aid; **2.** *vi* GES, RRHH *a una reunión, junta* attend; ◆ ~ **a una cita** COM GEN keep an appointment

asociación *f* BOLSA incorporation, COM GEN association, POL *entre países* partnership; ~ **agrícola** RRHH farmers' association; ~ **caritativa** RRHH, SEG charity; ~ **comercial** COM GEN trade association; ~ **de comercialización de préstamos a estudiantes** BANCA, FIN student loan marketing association (*SLMA*); ~ **cooperativa** RRHH, SEG cooperative association; ~ **corporativa** RRHH, SEG corporate association; ~ **de crédito cooperativo** COM GEN cooperative credit association; ~ **de crédito hipotecario** FIN mortgage credit association; ~ **de empleados** RRHH employee association, staff association; ~ **de empresas en participación** RRHH, SEG joint ventures; ~ **de fabricantes** RRHH, SEG cartel; ~ **sin fines lucrativos** COM GEN nonprofit association

(*AmE*), non-profit-making association (*BrE*); **~ sin fines de lucro** COM GEN nonprofit association; **~ internacional de puertos** IMP/EXP, TRANSP International Association of Ports and Harbours (*IAPH*); **~ de marca** V&M brand association; **~ mutua** FIN mutual association; **~ no lucrativa** COM GEN non-profit-making association (*BrE*), nonprofit association (*AmE*); **~ patronal** RRHH employers' association; **~ de préstamos y construcción** BANCA building and loan association (*AmE*); **~ de propietarios** INMOB homeowners' association; **~ para la protección e indemnización** TRANSP protection and indemnity club (*P&I club*); **~ pública de valores** BOLSA public securities association; **~ simbólica** V&M symbolic association; **~ temporal de empresas contractual** COM GEN contract joint venture; **~ de vecinos** INMOB community association

Asociación: **~ de Agentes y Corredores de Futuros** *f* BOLSA Association of Futures Brokers and Dealers (*AFBD*); **~ Española de Compañías Aéreas** *f* (*AECA*) TRANSP ≈ Society of British Aerospace Companies (*SBAC*); **~ Española de Normalización y Certificación** *f* (*AENOR*) COM GEN, PATENT ≈ British Standards Institution (*BSI*), ≈ American Standards Association (*ASA*); **~ Europea de Agencias de Publicidad** *f* (*AEAP*) V&M European Association of Advertising Agencies (*EAAA*); **~ Europea para Información de Transporte Marítimo** *f* TRANSP European Association for Shipping Information (*EASI*); **~ Europea de Libre Comercio** *f* (*AELC*) ECON, POL European Free Trade Association (*EFTA*); **~ Europea de Productores de Acero** *f* IND Association of European Steel Producers (*Euro Fer*); **~ para la Formación y Desarrollo Empresarial** *f* *Esp* (*AFYDE*) ECON training and business development association; **~ de Intermediarios Internacionales de Bonos** *f* BOLSA Association of International Bond Dealers (*AIBD*); **~ Internacional de Armadores** *f* TRANSP International Shipowners' Association (*INSA*); **~ Internacional Coordinadora de Transporte de Cargamento** *f* TRANSP International Cargo Handling Coordination Association (*ICHCA*); **~ Internacional de Coordinadoras del Medio Ambiente** *f* MED AMB International Association of Environmental Co-ordinators (*IAEC*); **~ Internacional para la Distribución de Productos Alimenticios** *f* V&M International Association for the Distribution of Food Products; **~ Internacional de Entidades del Mercado Primario de Bonos** *f* BOLSA International Primary Market Association; **~ Internacional de Fomento** *f* (*AIF*) ECON International Development Association (*IDA*); **~ Internacional de Hoteles** *f* OCIO International Hotel Association; **~ Internacional de Mercados de Emisión** *f* BOLSA International Primary Market Association (*IPMA*); **~ Internacional de Mercados de Valores** *f* BOLSA International Securities Market Association (*ISMA*); **~ Internacional de Operadores de Swap** *f* BOLSA International Swap Dealers' Association (*ISDA*); **~ Internacional para la Protección de Propiedad Industrial** *f* DER, INMOB International Association for the Protection of Industrial Property (*IAPIP*); **~ Internacional de Transporte Aéreo** *f* (*IATA*) TRANSP International Air Transport Association (*IATA*); **~ Latinoamericana de Libre Comercio** *f* (*ALALC*) ECON, POL ≈ Latin American Free Trade Association (*obs*) *antes de 1981* (*LAFTA*), ≈ Latin American Integration Association (*LAIA*); **~ de Mer-**

cados de Negociación *f* BOLSA Secondary Market Association (*SMA*); **~ de las Naciones Unidas** *f* (*ANU*) POL United Nations Association (*UNA*); **~ de Protección e Indemnización** *f* SEG *marina* Protection and Indemnity Association; **~ de Transportistas de las Comunidades Europeas** *f* TRANSP European Communities Freight Forwarders Association (*CLECAT*)

asociaciones: **~ artesanales** *f pl* RRHH craft organizations; **~ caritativas** *f pl* PROT SOC, RRHH charitable organizations

asociado[1] *adj* COM GEN associated; **~ a** COM GEN affiliated to; **no ~** COM GEN unaffiliated

asociado[2]**,-a**: **~ extranjero(-a)** *m,f* BOLSA foreign affiliate

asociado[3]: **~ con** *fra* COM GEN in association with

asociarse: **~ a** *v refl* COM GEN affiliate to; **~ con** *v refl* COM GEN associate with

aspecto *m* COM GEN aspect

aspirantes: **~ a un trabajo registrados** *m pl* COM GEN registered applicants for work (*infrml*)

astilla *f infrml* COM GEN, FIN, POL sweetener (*infrml*), V&M backhander (*infrml*); **~ muerta** TRANSP *cubierta* deadrise

astucia *f* COM GEN gamesmanship

asueto: **~ general** *m* RRHH general holiday

asumir *vt* BOLSA *riesgo* carry, COM GEN *una responsabilidad* take on, *riesgo, poder* assume; ♦ **~ un cargo** GES, RRHH, SEG come into office; **~ el control** GES take over; **~ los costes** *Esp* (*cf asumir los costos AmE*) COM GEN bear the costs; **~ los costos** *AmL* (*cf asumir los costes Esp*) COM GEN bear the costs; **~ una fecha** COM GEN bear a date; **~ una pérdida** BOLSA take a loss, COM GEN stand a loss; **~ la responsabilidad de** COM GEN assume responsibility for, take responsibility for; **~ un riesgo** COM GEN take a risk

asunción: **~ de capital** *f* CONT, FIN capital commitment

asunto *m* COM GEN issue, matter, task, *negociación* subject, *incidente, acontecimiento* affair, GES issue, matter, PATENT subject matter; **~ estratégico** GES strategic issue; **~ fiscal** DER, FISC fiscal matter; **un ~ en marcha** COM GEN an ongoing concern; **~ principal** RRHH staple matter; **~ sin resolver** COM GEN subject unsold; **~ de tercera clase** COM GEN third-class matter (*AmE*); **~ urgente** COM GEN matter of urgency; ♦ **el ~ de que se trata** COM GEN the matter in hand; **el ~ está concluido** COM GEN the matter is closed

asuntos *m pl* COM GEN affairs, issues; **~ de la agenda** COM GEN items on the agenda; **~ de la compañía** COM GEN company's affairs; **~ corporativos** V&M corporate affairs; **~ económicos** *m* ECON economic affairs; **~ europeos** COM GEN European affairs; **~ exteriores** POL foreign affairs; **~ importantes** COM GEN outstanding matters; **~ internacionales** POL foreign affairs, international affairs; **~ internos** POL domestic affairs, home affairs, national affairs; **~ judiciales** DER judicial affairs; **~ mercantiles** COM GEN mercantile affairs; **~ monetarios** COM GEN money matters; **~ pendientes** COM GEN outstanding matters; **~ políticos** POL political affairs; **~ públicos** POL public affairs

atacar *vt* COM GEN raid; ♦ **~ a una compañía** BOLSA raid a company

atadura *f* COM GEN *bono* tie; **~ del extremo de trinca** TRANSP lashing eye

ataque *m* COM GEN attack

atareado *adj* COM GEN *persona* busy

atasco *m* INFO *impresora* jam, TRANSP traffic jam

atención *f* COM GEN, V&M attention; **~ al cliente** V&M customer care; **~ y control** PROT SOC care and control; **para ~ inmediata** COM GEN for immediate attention; **~ a los pasajeros** OCIO passenger care; **~ de la salud** COM GEN health care; **~ selectiva** V&M selective attention; ◆ **a la ~ de** COM GEN for the attention of *(FAO)*; **~, interés, deseo, acción** COM GEN attention, interest, desire, action *(AIDA)*

atender *vt* BANCA *deuda* honor *(AmE)*, honour *(BrE)*, COM GEN *necesidades* meet, *cliente* serve, *a un cliente* entertain; ◆ **~ a** COM GEN cater for; **~ a un cliente** COM GEN attend to a customer; **~ al gasto público** ECON, POL cover public expenditure; **~ una letra** DER, FIN meet a draft; **~ una reclamación** COM GEN meet a claim; **~ a sus obligaciones** COM GEN meet one's obligations

atenderse: **~ a** *v refl* COM GEN *norma, decisión* abide by, *normas* keep up with, DER comply with

atenerse: **~ a** *v refl* COM GEN adhere to

atenuación *f* DER mitigation

atenuar *vt* ECON weaken, *fluctuaciones* smooth

aterrizaje: **~ forzoso** *m* TRANSP forced landing; **~ suave** *m* TRANSP soft landing

atesorar *vt* BOLSA hoard

atestar *vt* DER attest, TRANSP *contenedor* stuff *(BrE)*

atestiguar *vt* COM GEN, DER witness; ◆ **~ la firma de alguien** COM GEN, DER witness sb's signature

atmósfera *f* MED AMB atmosphere; **~ controlada** MED AMB controlled atmosphere *(CA)*

atolladero *m* COM GEN stumbling block

atracadero: **~ principal** *m* TRANSP lead slip

atracar: **~ al muelle** *vi* TRANSP dock

atracción: **~ masiva** *f* V&M *comercialización* mass appeal; **~ turística** *f* OCIO tourist attraction

atractivo[1] *adj* COM GEN *oferta* enticing, *para los inversores* attractive

atractivo[2] *m* COM GEN, V&M appeal; **~ del anuncio publicitario** *f* V&M copy appeal; **~ emocional** V&M emotional appeal; **~ personal** RRHH body-shopping; **~ de las ventas** V&M sales appeal; **~ visual** COMS visual appeal

atraer *vt* COM GEN attract, *la atención* grab; ◆ **~ la atención de alguien** COM GEN attract sb's attention; **~ nuevos negocios** COM GEN attract new business

atraque: **~ al muelle** *m* TRANSP berthing of ships; **~ de descarga** *m* TRANSP discharging berth

atrasarse: **~ en los pagos** *v refl* BANCA, FIN fall behind with payments

atrasos *m pl* BOLSA *dividendo o interés que no se ha hecho efectivo* arrears, COM GEN back payment, FIN arrearage; **~ del impuesto liquidable** FISC assessed tax arrears; ◆ **tener ~** COM GEN be in arrears

atravesar: **~ las fronteras internacionales** *fra* IMP/EXP cross international frontiers

atribución: **~ a reservas** *f* CONT allocation to reserves

atribuciones: **~ de emergencia** *f pl* RRHH emergency powers; **~ presupuestarias** *f pl* ECON, POL budgetary powers

atribuible: **~ a** *adj* COM GEN attributable to; **no ~** *adj* COM GEN nonattributable, MEDIOS *print* not for attribution *(jarg)*

atribuido: **~ a** *adj* COM GEN attributed to

atribuir: **~ algo a algo** *fra* COM GEN attribute sth to sth; **~ algo a alguien** *fra* COM GEN ascribe sth to sb, attribute sth to sb

atributo *m* COM GEN, INFO attribute

audiencia *f* COM GEN audience, DER hearing, MEDIOS, V&M audience; **~ acumulativa** V&M cumulative audience; **~ cautiva** V&M captive audience; **~ heredada** MEDIOS *radio y televisión* inherited audience *(jarg)*; **~ neta** V&M net audience; **~ a puerta cerrada** DER private hearing; **~ de radio** MEDIOS, V&M radio audience; ◆ **la ~ está abierta** DER the court is now in session

Audiencia: **~ Nacional** *f Esp* DER, POL ≈ High Court *(BrE)*, ≈ Supreme Court *(AmE)*

audioconferencia *f* COMS, INFO audio conference, audio conferencing

audiomecanografía *f* COM GEN audiotyping

audiomensajería *f* COMS, INFO voice mail

audiovisual *adj* COMS, MEDIOS, V&M audiovisual *(av)*

auditabilidad *f* CONT auditability

auditable *adj* CONT auditable

auditado[1]: **no ~** *adj* CONT unaudited

auditado[2]**,-a** *m,f* CONT auditee

auditar[1] *vt* CONT, FIN, FISC audit

auditar[2]: **sin ~** *fra* FISC nonaudit

auditor, a *m,f* CONT, FIN, FISC auditor; **~ financiero(-a) responsable** CONT senior financial auditor; **~ principal** CONT senior auditor

auditores: **~ independientes** *m pl* CONT, FIN, FISC independent auditors

auditoría *f* CONT, FIN, FISC auditing, *de declaraciones sobre la renta* audit; **~ administrativa** CONT, RRHH administrative audit, management audit; **~ de agencia** V&M agency audit, agency auditing; **~ de alcance primordial** CONT prime range audit; **~ de almacén** CONT store audit; **~ analítica** CONT analytical audit, analytical auditing; **~ basada en un sistema** CONT system-based audit; **~ basada en sistemas** CONT systems-based auditing; **~ de cierre de ejercicio** CONT year-end audit; **~ de comerciante** CONT, V&M dealer audit; **~ completa** CONT complete audit; **~ de concesionario** CONT, V&M dealer audit; **~ del consumo televisivo** V&M *investigación de mercado* television consumer audit; **~ continua** CONT continuous audit; **~ de cuentas obligatoria** CONT statutory audit; **~ de cumplimiento** COM GEN, CONT, GES performance review, compliance audit; **~ diferida de ejecución** COM GEN post-implementation audit; **~ de distribuidor** CONT, V&M dealer audit; **~ doméstica** V&M home audit; **~ de eficiencia** CONT efficiency audit; **~ de existencias** CONT store audit; **~ externa** CONT external audit, FISC field audit; **~ fiscal** FISC tax audit; **~ de gestión** CONT, RRHH management audit; **~ de imagen** V&M image audit; **~ interina** CONT interim audit; **~ de largo alcance** CONT prime* range audit; **~ legal** CONT statutory audit; **~ limitada** CONT brief audit, limited audit; **~ limpia** CONT unqualified opinion; **~ de la mano de obra** CONT, RRHH manpower audit; **~ de marketing** V&M marketing audit; **~ de minorista** V&M retail audit; **~ de muestra** CONT sample audit; **~ operacional** CONT, GES operations audit, operational audit; **~ de operaciones** CONT, GES operations audit, operational audit; **~ operativa** CONT, GES operations audit, operational audit; **~ de personal** CONT, RRHH

staff audit; ~ **de prueba** COM GEN, CONT test audit;
~ **de recursos humanos** CONT, RRHH manpower audit;
~ **secreta** CONT undercover audit; ~ **en la sede de la**
empresa COM GEN, CONT site audit; ~ **de tienda** V&M
shop audit; ~ **total** CONT complete audit

Auditoría: ~ **de Impuestos Pagados Según Ganancias**
f FISC *sección especializada de la Administración Fiscal*
Británica ≈ PAYE Audit (*BrE*)

AUE *abr* (*Acta Unica Europea*) DER, POL SEA (*Single*
European Act)

auge *m* ECON boom; ~ **económico** ECON economic
boom; ~ **de posguerra** ECON post-war boom; ~ **de**
ventas BOLSA selling climax; ♦ **estar en** ~ COM GEN,
ECON boom

aumentar *vt* BOLSA *valor* gain, COM GEN, CONT *salarios*
hike, rise, increase, ECON *desempleo* climb, *poder*
adquisitivo enhance, FIN raise, increase, hike, INFO
memoria upgrade, V&M *precios* mark up, *ventas* boost;
♦ ~ **un déficit** ECON, FIN run up a deficit; ~ **diez veces**
COM GEN increase tenfold; ~ **el doble** COM GEN increase
twofold; ~ **lentamente** ECON *precios* edge up; ~ **la**
oferta ECON increase the supply; ~ **la plantilla** RRHH
staff up; ~ **el préstamo** BANCA raise a loan; ~ **con**
rapidez COM GEN snowball; ~ **a tono con la inflación**
ECON *precio, subsidio* rise in line with inflation; ~ **de**
valor BOLSA gain value

aumento *m* BOLSA accretion, COM GEN, CONT, ECON, FIN
hike, increase, raise, rise; ~ **de actualización** RRHH
catch-up increase; ~ **de beneficios** CONT income gain;
~ **por cambio de divisas** IMP/EXP, TRANSP currency
adjustment factor (*CAF*); ~ **de capital** ECON capital
improvement; ~ **en el coste de capital** *Esp* (*cf aumento*
en el costo de capital AmL) FIN increase in cost of
capital; ~ **en el costo de capital** *AmL* (*cf aumento en el*
coste de capital Esp) FIN increase in cost of capital;
~ **del crédito** BANCA, FIN credit enhancement; ~ **de la**
cuantía de un préstamo BANCA upgrading of a loan;
~ **de devolución no imponible** FISC nontaxable repayment supplement; ~ **de la exportación** COM GEN rise in
exports; ~ **de los impuestos** ECON, FISC, POL tax
increase; ~ **de personal** COM GEN, RRHH personnel
growth; ~ **del PIB** ECON augmented gross national
product (*AGNP*); ~ **del precio** ECON price increase;
~ **de precio oculto** V&M hidden price increase; ~ **de**
precios COM GEN, V&M price increase; ~ **de producción**
debido al progreso técnico ECON capital-augmenting
technical progress; ~ **de la productividad** COM GEN,
RRHH speed-up; ~ **del producto interior bruto** ECON
augmented gross national product (*AGNP*);
~ **repentino** ECON boom; ~ **salarial** RRHH rise in wages,
wage increase; ~ **salarial diferido** RRHH deferred wage
increase; ~ **salarial por méritos** RRHH merit increase
(*BrE*), merit raise (*AmE*); ~ **salarial retroactivo** RRHH
backdated pay increase; ~ **sostenido** ECON *precio* sharp
rise; ~ **de la tasa de producción** COM GEN, RRHH
speed-up; ~ **en las utilidades** COM GEN, FIN profit
improvement; ~ **de valor** BOLSA growth in value

aunar *vt* COM GEN, ECON *recursos, capacidades* pool

A1 *adj* TRANSP *Registro de Buques de Lloyd's* A1 (*jarg*)

auricular *m* COM GEN earphone

ausencia *f* COM GEN, DER, V&M absence, lack; ~ **por**
enfermedad RRHH sick leave, *relaciones laborales* sick-
out (*jarg*); ~ **con permiso** RRHH leave of absence; ~ **sin**
permiso RRHH absence without leave; ♦ **ante la** ~ **de**

COM GEN *información* in the absence of; **en** ~ **de alguien**
COM GEN in sb's absence

ausentado, -a *m,f* COM GEN, DER absentee

ausente *adj* COM GEN, DER absent; ♦ ~ **por enfermedad**
RRHH off sick (*infrml*)

austeridad: ~ **económica** *f* ECON economic austerity;
~ **fiscal** *f* ECON fiscal austerity

autarquía *f* ECON, POL autarchy

autentificación *f* BOLSA, DER authentification

autentificado: **no** ~ *adj* BOLSA, DER unauthenticated;
~ **como copia fiel** *adj* DER certified as a true copy

auto *m* COM GEN edict, DER court order, decree,
proceeding; ~ **de casación** DER writ of error; ~ **de**
embargo DER writ of sequestration; ~ **interlocutorio**
DER interlocutory decree; ~ **de prisión** DER commitment; ~ **de procesamiento** DER commitment; ~ **de**
requerimiento DER writ of subpoena

autoabastecimiento *m* ECON self-sufficiency

autoactualización *f* GES *necesidades de Maslow*, RRHH
self-actualization

autoalmacenamiento *m* INFO autosave

autoarranque *m* INFO autoboot, autorestart, autostart,
self-start

autoayuda *f* COM GEN self-help

autobús: ~ **de dos pisos** *m* OCIO, TRANSP double-decker
bus; ~ **fluvial** *m* OCIO, TRANSP river bus; ~ **a últimas**
horas de la noche *m* TRANSP late-night bus; ~ **de un**
solo piso *m* TRANSP single-decker bus

autocargador[1] *adj* COM GEN self-loading

autocargador[2] *m* INFO autoloader

autocartera *f* BOLSA Treasury stock (*BrE*); ~ **flotante**
BOLSA floating treasury stock

autoconsumo *m* ECON home consumption

autocontrato *m* BOLSA self-dealing

autocorrelación *f* ECON autocorrelation

autodidacta *mf* PROT SOC self-taught person, autodidact

autodirección *f* GES, RRHH self-management

autodominio *m* COM GEN self-restraint

autoedición *f* INFO, MEDIOS desktop publishing (*DTP*)

autoempleo *m* FISC, RRHH self-employment

autoestable *adj* COM GEN self-supporting

autoevaluación *f* RRHH self-appraisal

autofinanciación *f* CONT, FIN internal funding, self-
financing, autofinancing; ~ **de enriquecimiento** CONT,
FIN retained earnings

autofinanciamiento *m* CONT, FIN self-financing

autofinanciar *vt* CONT, FIN self-finance

autogenerado *adj* COM GEN self-generated

autogestión *f* GES, RRHH self-management

autogobierno *m* POL self-government

autoimagen *f* RRHH, V&M self-image

autoliquidación: ~ **tributaria** *f* COM GEN self-liquidation,
FISC self-assessment

automático *adj* COM GEN, IND, INFO automatic, machine-
based

automatización *f* COM GEN, INFO, IND automation; ~ **del**
dibujo (*AD*) INFO design automation (*DA*), drawing
automation (*DA*); ~ **de oficinas** (*AO*) ADMIN, INFO
office automation (*OA*)

automatizado *adj* COM GEN, IND automated, INFO
computerized

automatizar *vt* COM GEN, IND automate, INFO computerize

automotivación *f* COM GEN, RRHH self-motivation

automóvil: **~ de la empresa** *m* COM GEN, TRANSP company car

automóviles: **~ disponibles para uso privado** *m pl* FISC cars available for private use

autonomía *f* COM GEN autonomy

autónomo *adj* COM GEN self-contained, INFO off-line, free-standing, *ordenador, sistema* stand-alone

autopista *f* TRANSP expressway, freeway (*AmE*), motorway (*BrE*) (*M*), superhighway (*AmE*), throughway (*AmE*); **~ de la información** INFO information highway; **~ de peaje** TRANSP turnpike (*AmE*), toll motorway (*BrE*)

autoregulado *adj* COM GEN self-governing

autoridad *f* COM GEN, RRHH *de directivos* authority; **~ de adquisición** INMOB *compra forzada* acquiring authority; **~ competente** POL statutory authority; **~ para comprar** COM GEN *de un tercero* authority to buy; **~ del control de gastos** ECON, POL spending authority; **~ corporativa** ADMIN, GES corporate governance; **~ discrecional** BANCA discretionary authority; **~ de la emisora** MEDIOS, V&M radio authority; **~ estimada** RRHH inferred authority; **~ expedidora** POL issuing authority; **~ de explotación** GES *liderazgo de Likert* exploitative-authoritative; **~ de explotador** GES *liderazgo de Likert* exploitative-authoritative; **~ fraccionada** GES splintered authority; **~ funcional** RRHH functional authority; **~ internacional encargada del examen preliminar** PATENT international preliminary examining authority; **~ de línea** GES, RRHH line authority; **~ lineal** GES, RRHH line authority; **~ local** POL local authority; **~ pertinente** COM GEN relevant authority; **~ portuaria** TRANSP harbour authority (*BrE*); **~ de préstamo** COM GEN borrowing authority; **~ pública** FISC, POL public authority; **~ responsable de gasto** ECON, POL spending authority; **~ sanitaria** COM GEN Health Authority (*BrE*); **~ sanitaria del puerto** TRANSP port health authority (*PHA*); **~ sobre nuevas inversiones** BOLSA New Investment Authority (*NIA*); **~ zonal de tratamiento de la exportación** IMP/EXP *Filipinas* export processing zone authority (*EPZA*); ♦ **tener ~ para** COM GEN have the power to; **tener ~ para firmar** BANCA have signing authority

Autoridad: **~ Europea de Energía Nuclear** *f* IND, POL European Nuclear Energy Authority (*ENEA*)

autoridades *f pl* BANCA, COM GEN authorities (*BrE*); **~ fiscales** FISC taxation authorities, fiscal authorities; **~ monetarias** BANCA monetary authorities; **~ reguladoras** COM GEN, DER regulatory authorities

autoritativo *adj* COM GEN authoritative

autorización *f* BANCA licence (*BrE*), license (*AmE*), COM GEN approval, DER authorization, licence (*BrE*), license (*AmE*), clearance, INMOB licence (*BrE*), license (*AmE*); **~ de comercialización** V&M *de productos farmacéuticos* marketing authorization; **~ de comercio** COM GEN trading authorization; **~ de descarga** IMP/EXP, TRANSP freight release (*F/R*); **~ para embarcar** TRANSP release for shipment; **~ expresa** COM GEN express authority; **~ del gasto** CONT authorization for expenditure; **~ general** COM GEN general authorization; **~ de importación** IMP/EXP import allowance, import permit; **~ indirecta** BANCA indirect authorization; **~ judicial**

previa FISC prior judicial authorization; **~ legal** POL warrant; **~ limitada** IMP/EXP limited authorization; **~ mancomunada** BANCA joint authorization; **~ de negociación limitada** BOLSA limited trading authorization; **~ de pago** COM GEN payment authorization; **~ de pago negociable** ECON tradeable discharge permit (*TDP*); **~ permanente** IMP/EXP standing authorization; **~ de préstamo** BANCA loan authorization; **~ para retirar fondos** BANCA withdrawal warrant; **~ en trámite** COM GEN authorization under consideration (*AC*)

autorizaciones: **~ de compra** *f pl* TRANSP authorities to purchase

autorizado *adj* COM GEN, DER permitted, PATENT licensed

autorizar *vt* COM GEN authorize, *editar* release, *dar derecho* entitle, *persona, organización, acción, cambio* allow

autorregresión: **~ vectorial** *f* MAT vector autoregression (*VAR*)

autorregulación *f* BANCA, ECON, POL self-regulation

autos: **~ de apelación** *m pl* DER appeal proceedings

autoseguro *m* SEG self-insurance

autoselección *f* V&M self-selection

autoservicio *m* COM GEN self-service; **~ sin dinero** COM GEN noncash self-service

autosostenido *adj* COM GEN *crecimiento* self-sustained

autosuficiencia *f* ECON self-sufficiency

autosuficiente *adj* COM GEN, ECON self-sufficient

auxiliar[1] *adj* COM GEN *costes* ancillary, auxiliary

auxiliar[2] *mf* RRHH *empleado* junior, TRANSP auxiliary (*aux.*); **~ administrativo(-a)** *m,f* COM GEN, RRHH office aide, assistant (*asst*), assistant administrator, administrative assistant; **~ de cuentas a pagar** CONT accounts payable clerk; **~ ejecutivo(-a)** *m,f* COM GEN executive assistant; **~ de vuelo** OCIO, TRANSP flight attendant, steward

aval *m* COM GEN guarantee, ECON collateral; **~ de la firma** BANCA guarantee of signature

avalar *vt* COM GEN *documento*, FIN guarantee; ♦ **~ a alguien** FIN bail sb out (*infrml*); **~ un préstamo** BANCA secure a loan

avalista *mf* BANCA, COM GEN guarantor

avalúo *m* AmL (*cf tasación Esp*) FIN appraisal, appraisement; **~ de gastos de capital** AmL (*cf valuación de gastos de capital Esp, cf estimación de gastos de capital Esp*) ECON, FIN capital expenditure appraisal; **~ del proyecto** AmL (*cf valoración de proyecto Esp*) COM GEN project assessment

avance *m* ADMIN, COM GEN advancement; **~ económico** COM GEN economic advancement; **~ extraordinario** COM GEN breakthrough; **~ de formato** INFO form feed (*FF*); **~ de línea** INFO line feed (*lf*); **~ de noticias** MEDIOS news flash; **~ de proyecto** TRANSP project forwarding; **~ de reconocimiento extraordinario** TRANSP advance of special survey; **~ técnico incorporado** IND embodied technical progress; **~ tecnológico** ECON, IND technological progress

avances: **~ sobre el Fondo de la Ley Agraria de los Veteranos** *m pl* POL Veteran's Land Act Fund advances

avanzado *adj* COM GEN, INFO *aplicaciones, sistemas* advanced

avanzar *vt* COM GEN, INFO advance

avenencia: ~ **sujeta a aprobación de un tribunal** *f* DER consent decree

aventajar *vt* COM GEN *sobrepasar* top

aventura: ~ **descabellada** *f* COM GEN wildcat venture

aventurarse: ~ **en** *v refl* COM GEN venture on

avería *f* COM GEN breakdown, fault, CONT average (*av.*), INFO breakdown, fault, SEG average (*av.*); ~ **común** SEG general average (*G/A*); ~ **gruesa** SEG general average (*G/A*); ~ **de máquina** COM GEN equipment failure; ~ **menor** SEG small damage (*s/d*); ~ **oculta** SEG hidden damage; ~ **pagadera** SEG payable damage; ~ **particular** SEG particular average (*P.A.*); ~ **producida por el mar** SEG, TRANSP sea damage (*SD*); ◆ **con** ~ SEG *seguros marítimos* with average (*W.A.*); **excepto** ~ **gruesa** SEG unless general average (*W.P.A*); **libre de** ~ **particular** SEG free of particular average (*f.p.a.*); **libre de** ~ **simple** SEG free of particular average (*f.p.a.*)

averiado *adj* COM GEN out of order, ailing; ◆ ~ **por el agua del mar** TRANSP *comercio granelero* sea damaged

averiarse *v refl* COM GEN, INFO fail, break down

averiguación *f* COM GEN ascertainment

averiguar *vt* COM GEN *hecho* ascertain, check

aversión: ~ **al riesgo** *f* COM GEN, ECON risk aversion

aviación: ~ **civil** *f* ECON, TRANSP civil aviation

avión *m* TRANSP aeroplane (*BrE*), aircraft, airplane (*AmE*); ~ **de carga** TRANSP cargo aircraft, air freighter, cargo plane (*infrml*), freight plane (*AmE*); ~ **carguero** TRANSP cargo aircraft, air freighter, cargo plane (*infrml*), freight plane (*AmE*); ~ **chárter** OCIO, TRANSP charter plane, chartered plane; ~ **comercial** TRANSP airliner; ~ **de fuselaje ancho** TRANSP wide-body aircraft; ~ **jumbo**) TRANSP jumbo jet (*jumbo*); ~ **de línea** TRANSP airliner; ~ **de pasajeros** TRANSP airliner, passenger aircraft; ~ **de transporte de mercancías** TRANSP freight aircraft; ◆ **por** ~ TRANSP by air

avioneta: ~ **con anuncio publicitario** *f* V&M aeroplane banner (*BrE*), airplane banner (*AmE*)

avíos: ~ **de venta** *m pl* V&M sales kit

avisar *vt* COM GEN, COMS, GES mention, advise, *telecomunicaciones* page, inform

aviso *m* COM GEN *notificación* advice, notice; ~ **de amortización** BOLSA redemption call; ~ **de anulación** BOLSA *de opción* notice of revocation; ~ **de asignación** BOLSA assignment notice; ~ **de billete de pago anticipado** OCIO, TRANSP prepaid ticket advice (*PTA*); ~ **de cambio de condiciones** TRANSP *aviación* specification change notice (*SCN*); ~ **de cancelación** BOLSA cancellation notice; ~ **de cancelación al vencimiento** SEG note of cancellation at maturity, notice of cancellation at anniversary date (*NCAD*), notice of cancellation on expiry date; ~ **de cobertura** SEG cover note (*C/N*); ~ **de cobro** BANCA advice of collection; ~ **de confirmación** COM GEN, COMS confirmation notice; ~ **de demanda** FISC notice of application; ~ **de desocupar** INMOB notice to quit; ~ **de despacho de importación** IMP/EXP import release note (*IRN*); ~ **de despido** RRHH notice, pink slip (*AmE*); ~ **de disponibilidad** TRANSP notice of readiness; ~ **de duración y/o cambio** COM GEN advice of duration and/or change (*ADC*); ~ **de embarque** TRANSP notice of shipment; ~ **de embarque normalizado** IMP/EXP, TRANSP standard shipping note; ~ **de entrega** COMS advice of delivery; ~ **escrito** RRHH written notice;

~ **especial de tráfico** TRANSP special traffic notice (*STN*); ~ **de falta de aceptación** BANCA notice of dishonour (*BrE*), notice of dishonor (*AmE*); ~ **de falta de pago** COM GEN notice of default; ~ **de huelga** COM GEN, IND, RRHH strike notice; ~ **de imposición** FISC notice of assessment, assessment notice; ~ **de imposición inicial** FISC notice of original assessment; ~ **inmediato** FIN prompt note; ~ **de intención** DER notice of intention; ~ **de llegada** COMS advice of arrival; ~ **de mora** COM GEN notice of arrears; ~ **de objeción** FISC notice of objection; ~ **de opción de compra** BOLSA call notice, notice of call; ~ **de protesto** TRANSP notice of protest; ~ **público** DER *causa civil* posting; ~ **de quiebra** BANCA, IND, RRHH bankruptcy notice; ~ **de rechazo** BANCA notice of dishonour (*BrE*), notice of dishonor (*AmE*); ~ **de recibo de mercancías** TRANSP goods received note; ~ **de reclamación** BANCA, IND, RRHH claim notice; ~ **de recurso** FISC notice of appeal; ~ **de reevaluación** FISC notice of reassessment; ~ **de remesa** COM GEN remittance slip; ~ **de retirada de fondos** BANCA, IND, RRHH withdrawal notice; ~ **de vacante** BANCA, IND, RRHH vacancy notice; ◆ **estar sobre** ~ COM GEN be on the alert; **hasta nuevo** ~ COM GEN until further notice, until further advice; **según** ~ COM GEN as per advice of; **sin** ~ COM GEN without warning, no advice (*N/A*)

avulsión *f* INMOB avulsion

axiomas: ~ **de preferencia** *m pl* ECON axioms of preference

ayuda *f* COM GEN assistance, help; ~ **administrativa** GES management aid; ~ **al desarrollo** ECON, POL development aid, development assistance; ~ **al proyecto** ECON project aid; ~ **alimentaria** ECON, POL food aid; ~ **alimenticia** ECON, POL food aid; ~ **bilateral** ECON, POL bilateral aid; ~ **bloqueada** POL blocked grant; ~ **de concesión** ECON *asistencia al desarrollo* concessional aid; ~ **condicionada** BANCA, ECON, GES, POL tied aid; ~ **sin contraprestación** ECON, POL donor aid; ~ **crediticia** BANCA, FIN *Fondo Monetario Internacional* credit tranche facility; ~ **desvinculada** BANCA, ECON, GES untied aid; ~ **a distancia** INFO remote support; ~ **económica** BANCA, ECON, GES economic aid; ~ **de emergencia** ECON, POL emergency aid; ~ **en especie** BANCA *cooperación y desarrollo* aid in kind, PROT SOC in-kind transfer; ~ **del Estado** FISC government assistance; ~ **estatal** PROT SOC state assistance; ~ **exterior** ECON, POL foreign aid, overseas aid; ~ **externa** ECON, POL foreign aid, overseas aid; ~ **federal** BANCA, ECON, GES federal aid; ~ **financiera** COM GEN bail-out, ECON, POL concessional aid, financial assistance, financial support, financial aid, capital aid; ~ **fiscal** FISC tax assistance; ~ **incondicionada** POL categorical grant; ~ **en mano de obra** RRHH manpower aid; ~ **multilateral** ECON, POL multilateral aid; ~ **no condicionada** BANCA, ECON, GES, POL untied aid; ~ **no finalista** POL nonproject aid; ~ **oficial al desarrollo** ECON, POL official development assistance; ~ **en porcentaje** PROT SOC percentage grant; ~ **a la programación** COM GEN programming aid; ~ **a la propulsión** TRANSP propulsion assistance; ~ **regional selectiva** ECON regional selective assistance; ~ **a un sector específico** ECON, POL sector-specific aid; ~ **a sectores específicos** ECON, POL sector-specific aid; ~ **técnica** POL technical assistance; ~ **técnica para exportadores** IMP/EXP technical help to exporters (*THE*); ~ **vinculada** COM GEN tied aid

Ayuda: ~ **del Automovilista** *f* (*ADA*) TRANSP Spanish organization for motorists, ≈ American Automobile Association (*AAA*) (*AmE*), ≈ Automobile Association (*AA*) (*BrE*), ≈ Royal Automobile Club (*BrE*) (*RAC*); ~ **Comunitaria** *f* ECON *UE* Community Aid; ~ **Financiera Selectiva** *f* ECON *desarrollo regional* Selective Financial Assistance (*BrE*)

ayudante, -a *m,f* COM GEN adjunct, assistant (*asst*), RRHH *enseñanza* assistant (*asst*); ~ **general** RRHH handyman; ~ **de línea** RRHH line assistant; ~ **personal** COM GEN, RRHH personal assistant (*PA*); ~ **postal** RRHH postal assistant (*PA*)

ayudar *vt* BANCA, COM GEN *financieramente* aid; ◆ ~ **a alguien con un aval** COM GEN endorse sb, go on one's note (*AmE*); ~ **con un aval** COM GEN endorse

ayudas: ~ **audiovisuales** *f pl* COMS, MEDIOS audiovisual aids; ~ **de diseño** *f pl* COM GEN design aids; ~ **para la toma de decisión** *f pl* COM GEN decision aids

Ayuntamiento *m* COM GEN, POL *competencia administrativa* borough, ≈ District Council (*BrE*), *sede de la alcaldía* town hall (*BrE*), city hall (*AmE*)

azafata *f* *Esp* (*cf aeromoza AmL*) OCIO, TRANSP air hostess

azar: **al** ~ *fra* COM GEN at random, hit-or-miss (*infrml*)

B

bache *m* COM GEN hiccup, ECON gap; ~ **inflacionista** ECON inflationary gap

baja[1]: **de ~ calidad** *adj* V&M low-grade; **de ~ categoría** *adj* RRHH menial; **de ~ gama** *adj* COM GEN, V&M *producto* down-market

baja[2] *f* COM GEN downswing, downturn, CONT writing-off, FIN *de plan de pensiones* deregistration; ~ **denominación** BANCA, FIN *billetes de banco* small denomination; ~ **densidad por una cara** INFO single-sided single density (*SSSD*); ~ **de maternidad** *infrml* RRHH maternity leave; ~ **en el mercado** COM GEN break in the market; ~ **presión** COM GEN low pressure (*LP*); ~ **repentina** COM GEN slump; ~ **en las ventas** COM GEN business slowdown; ♦ **estar a la ~** BOLSA be bearish

bajada *f* ECON *precio* roll-back (*jarg*); ~ **de precios** BOLSA break; ~ **de las ventas** V&M sales slump

bajamar *f* TRANSP *navegación* low water (*lw*); ~ **de marea de sigicia ordinaria** TRANSP low water ordinary spring tide (*LWOST*); ~ **media** TRANSP mean low water (*MLW*)

bajar 1. *vt* COM GEN take down; ♦ ~ **el promedio** BOLSA average down; **2.** *vi* BOLSA *acciones* slip, COM GEN *beneficios* dip, *cifras* fall away, fall back, *precios* decline; ♦ ~ **gradualmente** COM GEN *demanda* ease off

bajas: ~, **cancelaciones y pagos anticipados** *fra* COM GEN droppages, cancellations, and prepayments (*DCP*)

bajista[1] *adj* BOLSA bearish

bajista[2] *m* BOLSA bear

bajo *adj* BOLSA *precio de futuros* low, COM GEN low, *interés, comercio* light

bajón: ~ **en bolsa** *m* ECON *EE.UU* break

bala *f* COM GEN, IMP/EXP, TRANSP bale

balance *m* CONT, FIN balance (*bal.*), balance sheet (*B/S*), financial statement, statement; ~ **de activo y pasivo** CONT, FIN assets and liabilities statement; ~ **de apertura** BANCA, CONT opening balance; ~ **de la cartera** FIN portfolio balance; ~ **de cierre** BANCA, CONT, FIN closing balance, ending balance; ~ **de comprobación** CONT trial balance; ~ **de comprobación ajustado** CONT adjusted trial balance; ~ **de comprobación de saldos con cuentas regularizadas** CONT adjusted trial balance; ~ **de comprobación vencido** CONT aged trial balance; ~ **consolidado** CONT aggregate balance, consolidated balance sheet; ~ **de una cuenta corriente** BANCA balance on current account; ~ **a cuenta nueva** CONT balance brought down (*b/d.*); ~ **de cuentas** CONT account form; ~ **descubierto** FIN overdraft, uncovered balance; ~ **de ejercicio** CONT, FIN balance sheet (*B/S*), statement of assets and liabilities; ~ **escalonado** CONT vertical balance sheet; ~ **falso** FISC false statement; ~ **favorable** BANCA favorable balance (*AmE*), favourable balance (*BrE*); ~ **final** *f* BANCA ending balance, CONT bottom line, ending balance, FIN ending balance; ~ **para financiación oficial** CONT balance for official financing (*BOF*); ~ **en forma de cuenta** CONT horizontal balance sheet; ~ **en forma vertical** CONT vertical balance sheet; ~ **fraudulento** FISC fraudulent statement; ~ **general** CONT balance sheet (*B/S*); ~ **general**

previsto CONT projected balance sheet; ~ **global** MED AMB global balance; ~ **hipotecario** BANCA, FIN mortgage statement; ~ **horizontal** CONT horizontal balance sheet; ~ **del impacto ambiental** MED AMB environmental impact statement; ~ **de inventario** CONT second trial balance; ~ **de los libros** BOLSA book squaring; ~ **de liquidación** BANCA *en una quiebra*, COM GEN statement of affairs; ~ **llevado a cuenta nueva** CONT balance brought forward; ~ **del mayor** BANCA, CONT, FIN ledger balance; ~ **de la posición diaria** CONT daily position statement; ~ **proforma** BANCA, COM GEN, CONT pro forma balance sheet; ~ **de resultados** CONT income statement, FIN earnings report; ~ **de situación** CONT, FIN assets and liabilities statement, balance sheet (*B/S*), post-closing trial balance; ~ **de situación combinado** FIN combined balance sheet; ~ **de situación comparativo** CONT, FIN comparative statement, comparative balance sheet; ~ **de situación consolidado** CONT consolidated balance sheet; ~ **de situación mal estructurado** CONT ungeared balance sheet; ~ **social** BANCA, COM GEN, CONT social balance; ~ **de volumen** BANCA, COM GEN, CONT social balance; ~ **de volumen** BOLSA on-balance volume

balanza[1]: ~ **comercial** *f* ECON balance of trade, trade balance; ~ **comercial desfavorable** *f* ECON unfavourable balance of trade (*BrE*), unfavorable balance of trade (*AmE*); ~ **comercial favorable** *f* ECON favourable trade balance (*BrE*), favorable trade balance (*AmE*), trade surplus; ~ **comercial invisible** *f* ECON invisible trade balance; ~ **comercial negativa** *f* ECON adverse balance of trade; ~ **comercial visible** *f* ECON visible trade balance; ~ **por cuenta corriente** *f* BANCA, COM GEN current account balance; ~ **exterior** *f* ECON foreign balance; ~ **externa** *f* POL external balance; ~ **de facturación** *f* CONT balance of invoice; ~ **de financiación oficial** *f* CONT balance for official financing (*BOF*); ~ **financiera** *f* ECON financial balance; ~ **sin incluir el petróleo** *f* ECON nonoil balance; ~ **de invisibles** *f* FIN invisible balance; ~ **de pagos** *f* CONT accounting balance of payments, ECON accounting balance of payments, balance of payments (*BOP*), POL balance of payments (*BOP*); ~ **de pagos deficitaria** *f* ECON deficit balance of payments; ~ **de pagos del mercado** *f* ECON market balance of payments; ~ **de servicios** *f* ECON balance of invisible items

balanza[2]: **inclinar la ~** *fra* COM GEN tilt the balance, tip the scales

baliza: ~ **de radar** *f* COMS radar beacon, transponder

balsa: ~ **salvavidas inflable** *f* TRANSP inflatable life raft

bamboleo *m* COM GEN staggering (*infrml*)

banalización *f* TRANSP pooling system

banca *f* BANCA banking (*bkg*); ~ **libre** BANCA free banking; ~ **al por mayor** *Esp* (*cf banca al mayoreo AmL*) BANCA wholesale banking; ~ **al mayoreo** *AmL* (*cf banca al por mayor Esp, banca mayorista Esp*) BANCA wholesale banking; ~ **al por menor** BANCA retail banking; ~ **al menudeo** BANCA retail banking; ~ **automática** BANCA, INFO computerized banking; ~ **automatizada** BANCA, INFO self-service banking; ~ **de autoservicio** BANCA self-service banking;

~ comercial BANCA commercial banking; **~ computerizada** BANCA, INFO computerized banking; **~ de concentración** BANCA concentration banking; **~ corporativa** BANCA corporate banking; **~ corresponsal** BANCA correspondent bank; **~ domiciliaria electrónica** BANCA electronic home banking; **~ dual** BANCA *EE.UU.* dual banking; **~ electrónica** BANCA electronic banking; **~ estatal** BANCA state-owned bank; **~ externa** BANCA offshore banking; **~ extranjera** BANCA foreign banking; **~ fiduciaria** BANCA fiduciary banking; **~ financiera** BANCA investment banking (*AmE*), merchant banking (*BrE*); **~ internacional** BANCA international banking; **~ matriz** BANCA parent bank; **~ mayorista** *Esp* (cf *banca al por mayor Esp, banca al mayoreo AmL*) BANCA wholesale banking; **~ mercantil** BANCA investment banking (*AmE*), merchant banking (*BrE*); **~ minorista** BANCA retail banking; **~ de negocios** BANCA investment banking (*AmE*), merchant banking (*BrE*); **~ orientada al consumo** BANCA consumer banking; **~ privada** BANCA private banking; **~ de reducción de emisión** MED AMB emission reductions banking; **~ con sucursales** BANCA branch banking; **~ sin sucursales** BANCA unit banking; **~ telefónica** BANCA on-line banking, phone banking, home banking; **~ en territorio nacional** BANCA onshore banking; **~ ultramarina** BANCA offshore banking; **~ única** BANCA unit banking

bancada: ~ de bote *f* TRANSP thwartship (*Thw*)

bancario *adj* BANCA bank (*bk*), banking (*bkg*)

bancarrota *f* BANCA, COM GEN, CONT bankruptcy; **~ voluntaria** FIN voluntary bankruptcy; ◆ **al borde de la ~** COM GEN on the verge of bankrupcy; **ir a la ~** COM GEN go to the wall (*infrml*), CONT go bankrupt

banco *m* BANCA bank (*bk*); **~ de acción mancomunada** BANCA joint-stock bank; **~ por acciones** BANCA incorporated bank (*AmE*); **~ de accionistas** BANCA joint-stock bank; **~ de aceptación** BANCA acceptance house, accepting bank; **~ agente** BANCA agent bank; **~ agrícola** BANCA, ECON agricultural bank; **~ de ahorros** BANCA savings bank; **~ de ahorros en garantía** BANCA guaranty savings bank, guarantee savings bank; **~ de ahorros de la oficina de correos** BANCA post office savings bank; **~ de apertura de un crédito** opening bank; **~ autorizado** BANCA authorized bank; **~ bajo control extranjero** BANCA foreign-controlled bank; **~ central** BANCA, ECON, FIN central bank; **~ de los centros monetarios** BANCA money center bank (*AmE*), money centre bank (*BrE*); **~ de cobranzas** BANCA collecting bank; **~ de cobro** BANCA collecting agency, collection banker; **~ de coinversión** BANCA joint-venture bank; **~ comercial** BANCA business bank, deposit bank; **~ de comercio** BANCA mercantile bank; **~ de comercio exterior** BANCA foreign trade bank; **~ computerizado** BANCA computer bank; **~ de consorcio** BANCA, FIN consortium bank; **~ de conveniencia** BANCA laser banking; **~ de crédito** BANCA lending bank; **~ de crédito hipotecario** BANCA building society (*BrE*), building and loan association (*AmE*), savings and loan association (*S&L*) (*AmE*), ≈ mortgage bank, ≈ mortgage loan bank; **~ de crédito a largo plazo** BANCA long-term credit bank; **~ de datos** INFO data bank; **~ de depósitos** BANCA deposit bank; **~ de desarrollo** BANCA development bank; **~ de desarrollo multilateral** BANCA, FIN multilateral development bank; **~ de**

descuento BANCA discounting bank; **~ en dificultades** BANCA ailing bank; **~ director** BANCA lead bank; **~ electrónico** BANCA electronic bank; **~ de emisión** BANCA bank of issue, issuing bank; **~ de emisión de valores** BANCA, FIN investment bank (*AmE*), issuing house, FIN investment bank (*AmE*); **~ emisor** BANCA, ECON, FIN central bank, note-issuing bank; **~ de ensayos** COM GEN test bench; **~ de exportaciones e importaciones** IMP/EXP export-import bank (*EXIM*); **~ extranjero** BANCA foreign bank; **~ fiduciario** BANCA, FIN banker's trust company, trust banking, trust company, trust bank; **~ filial** BANCA affiliated bank, subsidiary bank; **~ financiero** BANCA investment bank (*AmE*), merchant bank (*BrE*); **~ fraudulento** BANCA bogus bank; **~ fusionado** BANCA amalgamated bank; **~ girador** BANCA advising bank; **~ hipotecario** BANCA ≈ building society (*BrE*), ≈ mortgage bank, ≈ mortgage loan bank, building and loan association (*AmE*), savings and loan association (*AmE*); **~ industrial** BANCA industrial bank; **~ interno** BANCA domestic bank, in-home banking, ECON domestic bank; **~ de inversión participado por otras entidades financieras** BANCA joint-venture investment bank (*AmE*), joint venture merchant bank (*BrE*); **~ de inversiones** BANCA, FIN investment bank (*AmE*), merchant bank (*BrE*); **~ listado** BANCA listed bank; **~ mayorista** BANCA wholesale bank; **~ de memoria** INFO memory bank; **~ de menudeo** BANCA retail bank; **~ mercantil** BANCA investment bank (*AmE*), mercantile bank, merchant bank (*BrE*); **~ mercantil participado por otras instituciones financieras** BANCA joint venture investment bank (*AmE*), joint venture merchant bank (*BrE*); **~ minorista** BANCA retail bank; **~ multinacional** BANCA multinational bank; **~ mutualista de ahorros** BANCA mutual savings bank; **~ nacional** BANCA, ECON domestic bank, national bank; **~ de negocios** BANCA, FIN investment bank (*AmE*), merchant bank (*BrE*); **~ no miembro** BANCA nonmember bank (*AmE*); **~ no residente** BANCA nonresident bank; **~ ordenante** BANCA advising bank; **~ pagador** BANCA paying bank; **~ periférico** BANCA fringe bank; **~ personal** BANCA personal bank; **~ de posición conveniente** BANCA niche bank; **~ prestatario** BANCA borrowing bank; **~ de primera mano** BANCA prime bank; **~ privado** BANCA private bank; **~ de propiedad extranjera** BANCA foreign-owned bank; **~ de pruebas** INFO *prueba de programas* bench mark; **~ receptor** BANCA receiving bank, recipient bank; **~ reembolsador** BANCA, COM GEN, FIN reimbursing bank; **~ regional** BANCA regional bank; **~ registrado** BANCA chartered bank (*AmE*); **~ representante** BANCA agency bank; **~ de reserva** BANCA reserve bank; **~ de reserva al cien por ciento** BANCA one-hundred-percent reserve banking; **~ de la Reserva Federal** ECON Federal Reserve Bank; **~ de reserva múltiple** BANCA fractional reserve banking; **~ residente** BANCA resident bank; **~ rural** BANCA land bank, MED AMB *agricultura* soil bank; **~ secundario** BANCA secondary bank; **~ de seguridad** COM GEN safety bank; **~ semiprivado** BANCA semiprivate bank; **~ de trabajo** RRHH job bank; **~ universal** BANCA universal bank

Banco: ~ Central Europeo *m* (*BCE*) BANCA, ECON, POL UE European Central Bank (*ECB*); **~ de Crédito Agrícola** *m* BANCA ≈ cooperative bank, ≈ Farm Loan Bank; **~ de España** *m Esp* BANCA national bank of Spain,

≈ Bank of England (*BE*); ~ **Europeo de Inversiones** *m* (*BEI*) BANCA, ECON *mercantil* European Investment Bank (*EIB*); ~ **Europeo para Reconstrucción y Desarrollo** *m* (*BERD*) BANCA, ECON European Bank for Reconstruction and Development (*EBRD*); ~ **Exterior de España** *m* (*BEE*) BANCA, ECON Spanish bank for international trade; ~ **Hipotecario de España** *m* (*BHE*) BANCA Spanish mortgage bank; ~ **Interamericano de Desarrollo** *m* (*BID*) BANCA, ECON Inter-American Development Bank (*IDB*); ~ **Internacional para la Cooperación Económica** *m* BANCA International Bank for Economic Cooperation (*IBEC*); ~ **Internacional para la Reconstrucción y el Desarrollo** *m* (*BIRD*) BANCA, ECON International Bank for Reconstruction and Development (*IBRD*); ~ **de Inversión Internacional** *m* BANCA International Investment Bank (*IIB*); ~ **Mundial** *m* BANCA World Bank; ~ **Nacional de Suiza** *m* BANCA, ECON, FIN Swiss National Bank; ~ **de Pagos Internacionales** *m* (*BPI*) BANCA, ECON Bank for International Settlements (*BIS*); ~ **de Pagos Internacionales** *m* (*BPI*) BANCA Bank for International Settlements (*BIS*); ~ **Unido Internacional** *m* BANCA Overseas Union Bank

bancos: ~ **AHC** *m pl* BANCA AHC Banks; ~ **importantes** *m pl* BANCA big banks

banda *f* BOLSA *mercado de futuros* range (*jarg*), ECON collar, FISC band; ~ **ancha** INFO, MEDIOS broadband; ~ **de base** INFO baseband; ~ **estrecha** ECON narrow band; ~ **fiscal** FISC tax band; ~ **de fluctuación** *tipo de cambio* band of fluctuation, fluctuation band; ~ **de fluctuación de precios** BOLSA *mercancías, valores* trading range; ~ **de goma** COM GEN rubber band; ~ **de ingresos** FIN income spread, FISC income range, income band; ~ **no publicada** ECON *Banco de Inglaterra* unpublished band; ~ **publicitaria** V&M band advertising; ~ **de sonido** COMS sound track; ~ **sonora magnética** MEDIOS, V&M magnetic soundtrack; ~ **de tipos del impuesto sobre la renta** FISC income tax rate band

bandas: ~ **de vencimiento** *f pl* ECON maturity bands

bandeja *f* COM GEN *entrada* in-tray, *salida* out-tray, IND, TRANSP *Esp* (*cf pálet AmL*) paddle, pallet; ~ **para carga** TRANSP cargo tray; ~ **de carga con alas** TRANSP winged pallet; ~ **de carga cerrada** TRANSP box pallet; ~ **de carga de dos pisos** TRANSP double-decked pallet; ~ **de carga estibadora** TRANSP master pallet; ~ **de carga reversible** TRANSP double-decked pallet; ~ **de pendientes** *Esp* (*cf charola de pendientes AmL*) COM GEN pending tray; ~ **de salida** *Esp* (*cf charola de salida AmL*) ADMIN out-tray

bandera: ~ **de conveniencia** *f* TRANSP *navegación* flag of convenience; ~ **extranjera** *f* TRANSP *navegación* foreign flag

banquero, -a *m,f* BANCA, RRHH bank employee, banker; ~ **comercial** BANCA, FIN investment banker (*AmE*), merchant banker (*BrE*)

barata *f AmL* (*cf rebaja Esp*) COM GEN *a precios reducidos* V&M sale

baratería *f* DER *fraude* barratry

baratería *f* COM GEN cheap, low-cost, low-priced

barbecho *m* ECON *agrícola* fallow

barcada *f* TRANSP *envíos* boatload

barcaza *f* TRANSP barge; ~ **de a bordo** TRANSP shipborne barge; ~ **para ganado** TRANSP cattle float; ~ **para remolque empujando** TRANSP push-tow barge

barco: ~ **de cabotaje** *m* TRANSP coaster; ~ **de carga** *m* TRANSP *navegación* cargo boat; ~ **contaminado** *m* TRANSP infected ship; ~ **inferior al promedio** *m* TRANSP substandard ship; ~ **con libertad de acción** *m* TRANSP freedom ship; ~ **mercante** *m* TRANSP *navegación* trading vessel; ~ **de pasajeros** *m* TRANSP passenger liner; ~ **de ruta variable** *m* TRANSP tramp; ~ **de transporte** *m* TRANSP *navegación* cargo boat; ~ **de vapor** *m* TRANSP steamship (*ss*), steamboat

baremo: ~ **de desgravación de los gastos de capital** *m* FISC capital cost allowance schedule; ~ **de invalidez** *m* SEG disability percentage table

barómetro *m* ECON *medición de tendencias* barometer; ~ **bursátil** BOLSA barometer stock; ~ **económico** COM GEN *índice* business barometer

barra *f* INFO, MEDIOS *tipografía* bar, slash; ~ **desmontable** TRANSP *contenedores* header bar; ~ **de espaciado** INFO space bar; ~ **espaciadora** INFO space bar; ~ **de estado** INFO status bar; ~ **inversa** INFO backslash; ~ **oblicua** INFO, MEDIOS *tipografía* slash; ~ **de trabajo** INFO tool bar

barraca *f* V&M booth

barrera *f* COM GEN barrier; ~ **aduanera** IMP/EXP customs barriers; ~ **al comercio** ECON, IMP/EXP, POL barrier to trade; ~ **arancelaria** COM GEN, ECON, POL tariff barrier, tariff wall; ~ **comercial** COM GEN trade barrier; ~ **comercial no arancelaria** COM GEN *internacional* nontariff trade barrier; ~ **de comunicación** COM GEN communication barrier; ~ **de entrada** ECON, IMP/EXP barrier to entry, entry barrier; ~ **fiscal** ECON fiscal barrier, FISC tax barrier; ~ **física** POL material barrier, physical barrier; ~ **material** POL material barrier; ~ **no arancelaria** ECON, FISC, IMP/EXP nontariff barrier (*NTB*); ~ **de salida** ECON, IMP/EXP barrier to exit, exit barrier; ~ **técnica al comercio** ECON, IND, POL technical barrier to trade

barreras: ~ **artificiales de entrada** *f pl* ECON, IMP/EXP, V&M artificial barrier to entry

barril *m* TRANSP barrel (*bbl.*); ~ **de áridos** TRANSP dry barrel

barriles *m pl* TRANSP *producción de petróleo* barrels (*b*); ~ **por día** ECON *producción de petróleo*, IND barrels per day (*b/d*)

barrio *m* COM GEN area, *fuera del centro* suburb, *en Londres* borough

barrios: ~ **exteriores** *m pl* COM GEN, POL, PROT SOC suburbs

bartear *vt* COM GEN, ECON barter

basado: ~ **en** *adj* COM GEN based on, on the basis of; ~ **en computador** *AmL ver basado en computadora AmL*; ~ **en computadora** *adj AmL* (*cf basado en ordenador Esp*) INFO computer-based; ~ **en ordenador** *adj Esp* (*cf basado en computadora AmL*) INFO computer-based; ~ **en PC** *adj* INFO *programas, equipamiento, servicio* PC-based; ~ **sobre un reparto proporcional** *adj* COM GEN on a pro rata basis

basar *vt* COM GEN base

basar en *vt* COM GEN *decisión* base on

báscula *f* TRANSP lever scale, weighing scale

basculamiento *m* TRANSP tipping

bascular *vi* INFO toggle

base *f* COM GEN basis, base; ~ **A** CONT A-base;

~ **actuarial** BANCA, CONT actuarial basis; ~ **de un acuerdo** COM GEN basis of an agreement; ~ **acumulable de contabilidad** CONT accrual basis of accounting; ~ **de acumulación** CONT accrual basis; ~ **ajustada** FISC adjusted basis; ~ **de ajuste del índice** MAT *cálculo comparativo* index basis; ~ **amortizable** *m* CONT depreciable basis; ~ **anual** MAT *estadística* annual basis; ~ **bono-año** FISC bond-year basis; ~ **de caja** BANCA, CONT cash basis; ~ **de cálculo** COM GEN, FIN base of calculation; ~ **para el cálculo de las primas** SEG basis of premium calculation; ~ **de capital** BANCA, BOLSA capital base; ~ **de capital accionario** BANCA, BOLSA equity capital base; ~ **cero** COM GEN ground zero; ~ **de cerrojo para trincaje de contenedores** TRANSP breech base; ~ **de clientes** V&M client base, customer base; ~ **comparable** CONT *de declaración* comparable basis; ~ **de conocimiento** CONT, PROT SOC *trabajo social* knowledge base; ~ **del coste** *Esp* (*cf base del costo AmL*) CONT, FISC cost base; ~ **de coste ajustada** *Esp* (*cf base de costo ajustada AmL*) CONT, FISC adjusted cost base (*ACB*), adjusted cost basis (*ACB*); ~ **de coste aplicable** *Esp* (*cf base de costo aplicable AmL*) CONT, FISC *de propiedad* relevant cost base; ~ **de coste corregida** *Esp* (*cf base de costo corregida AmL*) CONT, FISC adjusted cost base (*ACB*), adjusted cost basis (*ACB*); ~ **del coste corriente** *Esp* (*cf base del costo corriente AmL*) CONT, FISC current cost basis; ~ **del costo** *AmL* (*cf base del coste Esp*) CONT, FISC cost base; ~ **de costo ajustada** *AmL* (*cf base de coste ajustada Esp*) CONT, FISC adjusted cost base (*ACB*), adjusted cost basis (*ACB*); ~ **de costo aplicable** *AmL* (*cf base de coste aplicable Esp*) CONT, FISC *de una propiedad* relevant cost base; ~ **de costo corregida** *AmL* (*cf base de coste corregida Esp*) CONT, FISC adjusted cost base (*ACB*), adjusted cost basis (*ACB*); ~ **del costo corriente** *AmL* (*cf base del coste corriente Esp*) CONT, FISC current cost basis; ~ **de cuentas a cobrar** CONT receivable basis; ~ **de cumplimiento** CONT completion basis; ~ **de la cuota a ingresar** FISC tax-payable basis; ~ **de datos** INFO database; ~ **de datos compartida** INFO shared database; ~ **de datos corporativa** INFO corporate database; ~ **de datos distribuida** (*DDB*) INFO distributed database (*DDB*); ~ **de datos gráfica** INFO graphic database; ~ **de datos en línea** INFO on-line database; ~ **de datos relacional** (*BDR*) INFO relational database (*RDB*); ~ **de datos de tarifas** TRANSP fare database; ~ **después de impuestos** FISC after-tax basis; ~ **para la discusión** COM GEN basis for discussion; ~ **económica** ECON economic base; ~ **de efectivo** BANCA, CONT cash basis; ~ **de equilibrio** BOLSA *futuros sobre divisas* equilibrium basis; ~ **estándar** BANCA, CONT grade standard; ~ **del gasto** FISC expenditure base; ~ **gradual** FISC stepped-up basis; ~ **imponible** ECON, FISC tax base; ~ **imponible ajustada** FISC adjusted tax base; ~ **impositiva** ECON, FISC tax base; ~ **del impuesto** ECON, FISC tax base; ~ **industrial** IND industrial base, manufacturing base; ~ **de inversión** BANCA investment base; ~ **de liquidación** CONT receivable basis; ~ **del mercado** V&M market base; ~ **monetaria** ECON monetary base, deposit base; ~ **monetaria extendida** FIN wide monetary base; ~ **de necesidad de conocimiento** COM GEN, GES need-to-know basis; ~ **parcial** FIN partial basis; ~ **por porcentaje de cumplimiento del contrato** CONT percentage-of-completion basis; ~ **de provisión parcial** BOLSA, CONT *cálculo de impuestos diferidos* partial

provision basis; ~ **de recursos propios** CONT equity base; ~ **de reducción** FISC depletion base; ~ **regular y continua** FISC regular and continuous basis; ~ **de reserva** BANCA reserve base; ~ **salarial** RRHH salary base; ~ **según contrato** BOLSA *comisión de corretaje* per-contract basis; ~ **del segundo plazo** FIN, FISC second installment base (*AmE*), second instalment base (*BrE*); ~ **sistemática del coste** *Esp* (*cf base sistemática del costo AmL*) CONT systematic cost basis; ~ **sistemática del costo** *AmL* (*cf base sistemática del coste Esp*) CONT systematic cost basis; ~ **técnica** BANCA, CONT technical basis; ~ **de tipo aditivo** COM GEN add-on basis; ~ **total** CONT full basis; ~ **de transparencia fiscal** FISC flow-through basis; ◆ **sobre una ~ anual** COM GEN on an annual basis; **sobre una ~ de principal a principal** BOLSA *mercado monetario interbancario* on a principal-to-principal basis; **sobre la ~ de que** COM GEN on the premise that; **sobre una ~ sólida** COM GEN on a sound footing, on solid ground

bases: **sobre ~ consolidadas** *fra* FIN on a consolidated basis

BASIC *abr* (*código de instrucciones simbólicas de carácter general para principiantes*) INFO *lenguaje de programación* BASIC (*Beginner's All-Purpose Symbolic Instruction Code*)

básico *adj* INFO *equipo* base

bastardilla *f* MEDIOS *imprenta* bastard face, italics

bastidor *m* TRANSP *contenedores* stacking fitting; ~ **lateral** TRANSP *carga* side frame handling

basura *f* INFO garbage

batacazo *m jarg* BOLSA bath (*jarg*)

batayola: ~ **del buque** *f* TRANSP ship's rail

batería *f* INFO, SEG *automóvil* battery; ~ **de seguridad** INFO backup battery, battery-backed

batido: ~ **de las fichas para alineamiento** *m* BANCA *almacenamiento de información* jogging (*jarg*)

baudio *m* INFO baud

bazar: **gran ~** *m* POL big tent (*jarg*) (*AmE*)

BCE *abr* (*Banco Central Europeo*) BANCA, ECON, POL ECB (*European Central Bank*)

BDI *abr* (*beneficio del ejercicio después de impuestos*) BANCA, CONT profit for the year after tax

BDR *abr* (*base de datos relacional*) INFO RDB (*relational database*)

bebida: ~ **alcohólica** *f* FISC alcoholic drink

beca *f* PROT SOC grant, scholarship; ~ **de investigación** COM GEN research grant

becario, -a: ~ **de investigación** *m,f* IND, PROT SOC research student

BEE *abr* (*Banco Exterior de España*) BANCA, ECON Spanish bank for international trade

BEI *abr* (*Banco Europeo de Inversiones*) BANCA, ECON EIB (*European Investment Bank*)

beneficiar *vt* COM GEN benefit

beneficiario, -a *m,f* BOLSA allottee, COM GEN beneficiary, payee, *poder notarial* grantee; **otro(-a) ~** FIN *plan de reparto* other beneficiary; ~ **alternativo(-a)** COM GEN alternative payee; ~ **de una anualidad** COM GEN annuitant; ~ **de asistencia social** PROT SOC, RRHH social-security recipient (*BrE*), welfare recipient (*AmE*); ~ **de un aval** DER warrantee; ~ **bajo un fideicomiso** FISC beneficiary under a trust; ~ **de bienes a cargo de fiduciario** COM GEN trust beneficiary;

~ **corporativo(-a)** FISC corporate beneficiary; ~ **designado(-a)** FISC designated beneficiary; ~ **por donación** COM GEN, CONT, DER, FIN, SEG donee beneficiary; ~ **gratuito(-a)** ECON free rider (*infrml*), ghost (*AmE*) (*infrml*); ~ **no imponible** FISC nontaxable beneficiary; ~ **de una pensión** FIN pension-holder; ~ **preferente** FISC preferred beneficiary; ~ **de una renta** COM GEN annuitant; ~ **de rentas** COM GEN income receiver (*AmE*); ~ **de un subsidio** PROT SOC, RRHH recipient of an allowance (*BrE*), welfare recipient (*AmE*); ~ **sujeto(-a) a impuesto** FISC taxable beneficiary; ~ **de una transferencia** BANCA transferee

beneficiarse *v refl* COM GEN benefit

beneficiencia: ~ **pública** *f* PROT SOC public welfare

beneficio *m* COM GEN gain, profit, return, benefit, yield, *de despedida* payoff ~ **por acción** BOLSA, CONT dividend cover; ~ **de las actividades ordinarias** CONT current operating profit; ~ **acumulado** *Esp* CONT accumulated profit, earned surplus; ~ **adicional para los empleados** CONT, RRHH employee benefit, fringe benefit; ~ **al vencimiento** BOLSA maturity yield; ~ **antes de impuestos** CONT profit before taxes, pretax yield; ~ **anual después de impuestos** (*BDT*) CONT profit for the year after taxes; ~ **aparente** CONT *según libros* book profit; ~ **por automóvil** FISC automobile benefit (*AmE*); ~ **bruto** *Esp* CONT gross profit, gross earnings, trading income; ~ **bruto de explotación** CONT gross operating income; ~ **del capital después de impuestos** CONT after-tax capital gain; ~ **casual** CONT perquisite; ~ **central** ECON, FIN, GES profit center (*AmE*), profit centre (*BrE*); ~ **de cesión de acciones** CONT, ECON, FIN beneficium cedendarum actionum; ~ **complementario** CONT, RRHH *para empleados* fringe benefit; ~ **contable** CONT accounting profit, accounting return, book profit; ~ **de la contribución** CONT contribution profit; ~ **corriente de explotación** CONT current operating profit; ~ **a corto plazo** CONT short-term gain; ~ **a cuenta nueva** CONT profit carried forward; ~ **de derramamiento** CONT spillover benefit; ~ **de desbordamiento** CONT, ECON, FIN spillover benefit; ~ **designado** FISC designated benefit; ~ **después de impuestos** FISC after-tax yield, after-tax income; ~ **diferencial** CONT, ECON, FIN differential profit; ~ **distribuido** CONT allocated benefit, distributed profit; ~ **económico** ECON economic benefit, economic profit; ~ **del ejercicio** CONT accounting profit, profit for the financial year; ~ **del ejercicio después de impuestos** (*BDI*) BANCA, CONT profit for the year after tax; ~ **eventual** CONT perquisite; ~ **de explotación** *Esp* CONT operating profit; ~ **de explotación neto** CONT net operating income; ~ **extraordinario** CONT, RRHH abnormal profit, fringe benefit; ~ **fiscal** FISC tax benefit; ~ **gravable** *Esp* CONT, ECON, FISC taxable profit; ~ **del grupo** CONT group profit; ~ **ilusorio** FIN illusory profit; ~ **imponible** CONT, FISC taxable benefit; ~ **imponible equivalente** CONT, FISC equivalent taxable yield; ~ **imprevisto** CONT, ECON, FIN windfall benefit; ~ **indirecto** CONT, ECON, FIN spillover benefit; ~ **inesperado** CONT, ECON, FIN windfall benefit; ~ **justo** CONT, ECON, FIN fair return; ~ **libre de impuestos** CONT, FISC tax-free benefit; ~ **líquido** COM GEN, FISC cash benefit; ~ **marginal** ECON marginal profit; ~ **marginal privado** ECON private marginal benefit; ~ **máximo** BANCA, BOLSA maximum return, ECON profit ceiling, FIN maximum return; ~ **del**

monopolio ECON monopoly profit; ~ **mutuo** COM GEN mutual benefit; ~ **neto** COM GEN pure profit, net profit; ~ **por acción** (*BPA*) BOLSA, CONT, FIN earning per share (*EPS*); ~ **neto del año en curso** CONT net profit for the current year; ~ **neto anual** CONT annual net profit; ~ **neto consolidado** CONT consolidated net profit; ~ **neto del ejercicio** CONT net profit for the current year; ~ **neto más amortizaciones** CONT, ECON, FIN cash flow; ~ **neto de operación** *Esp* CONT net operating profit; ~ **no signado** FIN unappropriated profit; ~ **normal** CONT normal profit; ~ **de operaciones corrientes** CONT current operating profit; ~ **pecuniario** CONT, ECON, FIN pecuniary benefit; ~ **percibido** V&M perceived benefit; ~ **posible** BOLSA potential profit; ~ **por prestación de servicios** CONT service benefit; ~ **psíquico** RRHH psychic income; ~ **sin repartir** BANCA, FIN undivided profits; ~ **de restitución** COM GEN restitutio in integrum; ~ **de segmento** CONT segment profit; ~ **según libros** CONT book profit; ~ **sobre activos netos** CONT return on net assets; ~ **sobre activos netos empleados** CONT return on net assets employed; ~ **sobre el capital de acciones ordinarias** CONT return on common shareholders' equity; ~ **social** ECON social profit; ~ **suplementario** RRHH supplementary benefit; ~ **en la transacción** CONT transaction profit; ~ **de translación** ECON translation profit; ◆ **con ~ de** CONT at a profit of; **sin ~** COM GEN non-profit-making (*BrE*), nonprofit-making (*AmE*), nonprofitable; **sin ~ ni pérdida** BOLSA at-the-money (*ATM*); **sin ~ de salvamento** SEG *marítimo* without benefit of salvage (*wbs*)

beneficios[1]: ~ **por descuento** *m pl* BANCA income from discounting; ~ **diferidos** *m pl* CONT deferred revenue; ~ **en disminución** *m pl* COM GEN shrinking profits; ~ **distribuibles** *m pl* CONT distributable profit, FIN, RRHH earnings; ~ **esperados** *m pl* CONT budgeted profit; ~ **extrasalariales** *m pl* RRHH perk (*infrml*), perquisite; ~ **de fabricación** *m pl* ECON processing profits; ~ **de fabricación y procesamiento** *m pl* CONT, FISC manufacturing and processing profits; ~ **fijos** *m pl* COM GEN fixed benefits; ~ **financieros** *m pl* CONT *cuentas anuales* financial profit; ~ **frustados** *m pl* FISC abortive benefits; ~ **indirectos** *m pl* V&M spin-off; ~ **industriales** *m pl* CONT, ECON, FISC manufacturing profits; ~ **medios** *m pl* OCIO Average Revenue (*AR*); ~ **no distribuidos** *m pl* CONT, FIN retained earnings, undistributed profits; ~ **no realizados** *m pl* CONT, FIN unrealized profit; ~ **obtenidos** *m pl* COM GEN profit performance; ~ **ordinarios antes de impuestos** *m pl* CONT, FISC *cuentas anuales* ordinary profit before taxation; ~ **otorgados** *m pl* SEG vested benefits; ~ **de preadquisición** *m pl* CONT pre-acquisition profits; ~ **presupuestados** *m pl* CONT budgeted profit; ~ **primarios por acción** *m pl* BOLSA primary earnings per share; ~ **de productividad** *m pl* COM GEN productivity gains; ~ **del producto** *m pl* V&M product benefits; ~ **del productor** *m pl* OCIO producer's profits; ~ **prospectivos** *m pl* CONT budgeted profit; ~ **realizados** *m pl* CONT, FIN realized gains; ~ **repartibles** *m pl* CONT distributable profit; ~ **retenidos** *m pl* CONT, FIN retained earnings, retained profits, undistributed profits, holding gains; ~ **retenidos no asignados** *m pl* FIN unappropriated retained earnings; ~ **de la sociedad tenedora** *m pl* CONT holding gains

beneficios[2]: los ~ **superaron las previsiones en el primer trimestre** *fra* FIN profits surpassed forecasts in the first quarter

benevolente *adj* PROT SOC benevolent; ~-**autoritario** GES benevolent-authoritative

benévolo *adj* IND, POL, RRHH benevolent

BERD *abr* (*Banco Europeo para Reconstrucción y Desarrollo*) BANCA, ECON EBRD (*European Bank for Reconstruction and Development*)

best: ~ **seller** *m* MEDIOS, V&M bestseller

BHE *abr* (*Banco Hipotecario de España*) BANCA Spanish mortgage bank

biblioteca *f* INFO, PROT SOC library; ~ **de cintas** COM GEN tape library; ~ **empresarial** COM GEN *servicios públicos* business library; ~ **de programas** INFO program library

bicono: ~ **fijador** *m* TRANSP *contenedores* double stacker

BID *abr* (*Banco Interamericano de Desarrollo*) BANCA, ECON IDB (*Inter-American Development Bank*)

bidireccional *adj* INFO *impresión* duplex

bien[1]: ~ **colocado** *adj* COM GEN well-positioned; ~ **embalado** *adj* V&M well-packaged; ~ **fundado** *adj* COM GEN well-grounded; ~ **informado** *adj* COM GEN, POL well-informed; ~ **motivado** *adj* RRHH well-motivated; ~ **pagado** *adj* RRHH well-paid; ~ **preparado** *adj* RRHH well-educated; ~ **seguro** *adj* COM GEN well-tried; ~ **situado** *adj* COM GEN well-placed; ~ **surtido** *adj* COM GEN well-stocked

bien[2] *m* COM GEN asset, commodity (*cmdty*); ~ **colectivo** COM GEN, ECON collective good; ~ **compuesto** ECON composite commodity; ~ **de consumo** BOLSA, COM GEN, ECON, IND, V&M commodity (*cmdty*); ~ **deseable** ECON merit good; ~ **duradero** ECON, IND hard commodity; ~ **económico** ECON economic good; ~ **escaso** COM GEN scarce good; ~ **fungible** ECON replaceable good; ~ **gratuito** ECON free good; ~ **homogéneo** ECON homogeneous good; ~ **incorporal** INMOB incorporeal property; ~ **inducido** ECON inducement good; ~ **inmaterial** CONT, ECON intangible asset, intangible good; ~ **intangible** CONT, ECON intangible asset, intangible good; ~ **material** COM GEN tangible asset, IND material good; ~ **mixto** ECON mixed good; ~ **no básico** ECON nonbasic commodity; ~ **normal** ECON normal good; ~ **posicional** ECON positional good; ~ **de primera necesidad** ECON, V&M basic commodity, primary commodity, staple commodity; ~ **privado** ECON private good; ~ **público** ECON public good; ~ **público local** ECON local public good; ~ **semipúblico** ECON impure public good; ~ **social** ECON social good; ~ **tangible** COM GEN tangible asset, ECON tangible good; ~ **Veblen** ECON Veblen good

bienal *adj* COM GEN biennial

bienes *m pl* COM GEN goods, CONT assets; ~ **de baja calidad** COM GEN, V&M trashy goods (*infrml*), low-quality goods; ~ **de capital** COM GEN, ECON capital goods, FISC capital assets; ~ **de capital tangibles** CONT tangible capital property; ~ **comerciales** CONT business goods; ~ **en consignación** V&M goods on consignment; ~ **consumibles** MED AMB wasting assets, COM GEN expendable goods; ~ **de consumo** ECON, V&M consumption goods, consumer goods; ~ **de consumo duraderos** ECON, V&M consumer durables, consumer hardgoods, hard goods; ~ **de consumo perecederos** COM GEN, V&M soft goods; ~ **departamentales** CONT *costes* departmental assets; ~ **domésticos** COM GEN

household commodities; ~ **duraderos** V&M consumer durables, durable goods, durables; ~ **de equipo** ECON capital resources, equipment goods; ~ **fideicometidos** CONT, ECON, FIN corpus; ~ **finales** IMP/EXP end-use goods; ~ **forales** COM GEN leasehold estate; ~ **fungibles** DER fungibles; ~ **gananciales** DER community property, *derecho mercantil* after-acquired property; ~ **garantizados** COM GEN goods covered by warrant; ~ **industriales** COM GEN industrial goods; ~ **inferiores** COM GEN inferior goods; ~ **inmateriales por heredar** DER incorporeal hereditaments; ~ **inmuebles** DER, INMOB real estate, immovable estate, personal estate; ~ **inmuebles y enseres** CONT fixtures and fittings; ~ **intangibles** CONT intangible assets, intangible property; ~ **intermedios** COM GEN, IND intermediate goods; ~ **de inversión** FIN, V&M investment goods; ~ **libres de impuestos** FISC, IMP/EXP duty-free goods; ~ **de lujo** ECON luxury goods; ~ **manufacturados** ECON manufactures, IND manufactured goods; ~ **materiales por heredar** DER corporeal hereditaments; ~ **mostrencos** DER, INMOB land in abeyance; ~ **muebles** CONT movables, DER chattels, movable property, FISC, INMOB goods and chattels, personal property, INMOB chattels, movable property; ~ **muebles personales** INMOB personal chattels; ~ **no administrados** INMOB de bonis non administratis; ~ **no deseables** ECON *microeconomía* demerit goods; ~ **no duraderos** V&M *mercadotecnia* consumer nondurables, nondurable goods; ~ **no fungibles** CONT nonfungible goods; ~ **con opción de futuro** TRANSP goods called forward; ~ **perecederos** COM GEN perishable goods; ~ **personales** INMOB personal estate; ~ **primarios** IND primary commodities; ~ **de producción** CONT, ECON production goods; ~ **puestos en quiebra** INMOB bankruptcy property; ~ **raíces** INMOB real estate, landed property; ~ **raíces depreciables** INMOB depreciable real estate; ~ **para la reexportación** IMP/EXP goods for re-export; ~ **residuales** DER residuum; ~ **con reversión** INMOB estate in reversion; ~ **de segunda mano** FISC used assets; ~ **semiperecederos** COM GEN, V&M semidurable goods; ~ **y servicios** COM GEN goods and services; ~ **y servicios no solicitados** COM GEN unsolicited goods and services; ~ **sociales** CONT corporate assets; ~ **sujetos a reventa** CONT goods held for re-sale; ~ **de sustitución** V&M substitute goods; ~ **tangibles personales** INMOB tangible personal property; ~ **de uso doméstico duraderos** ECON durable household goods; ~ **de uso final** IMP/EXP end-use goods; ~ **vacantes** DER, INMOB bona vacantia; ♦ **todo tipo de ~ inmuebles** DER, INMOB land, tenements and hereditaments

bienestar *m* RRHH welfare (*infrml*); ~ **económico** ECON, POL economic well-being, PROT SOC economic welfare; ~ **mundial** ECON, POL world welfare; ~ **social** PROT SOC social welfare

bienintencionado *adj* COM GEN well-meaning

bifurcación *f* INFO branch; ~ **condicional** INFO *lenguaje de programación* conditional branch

bilateral *adj* COM GEN bilateral

bilaterales *m pl* ECON bilaterals

bilateralismo *m* ECON, POL bilateralism

billete *m* BANCA note, TRANSP ticket; ~ **abierto** OCIO open ticket; ~ **de banco** BANCA, ECON, FIN banknote (*BrE*), bank bill (*AmE*), bill (*AmE*), note (*BrE*); ~ **combinado** OCIO combined ticket; ~ **completo** COM GEN full fare;

~ **económico** OCIO economy ticket; ~ **de embarque** TRANSP mate's receipt (*MR*); ~ **de entrada** COM GEN entrance ticket; ~ **falso** BANCA, COM GEN counterfeit, forged bill (*AmE*), forged note (*BrE*); ~ **de grupo** OCIO party ticket; ~ **de ida** OCIO, TRANSP single ticket; ~ **de ida y vuelta** OCIO, TRANSP return ticket (*BrE*), round-trip ticket (*AmE*), ordinary return; ~ **en lista de espera** TRANSP standby ticket; ~ **mecanizado transitorio** TRANSP transitional automated ticket (*TAT*); ~ **nuevo** BANCA, CONT, FIN hot bill (*infrml*), sight bill; ~ **ordinario** OCIO ordinary ticket; ~ **sencillo** OCIO, TRANSP ordinary single ticket, single ticket; ~ **de temporada baja** TRANSP off-peak ticket; ~ **de transición automatizado** TRANSP transitional automated ticket (*TAT*)

bimensual *adj* COM GEN bimonthly, fortnightly

bimensualmente *adv* COM GEN fortnightly

bimetálico *adj* ECON, IND bimetallic

bimetalismo *m* ECON bimetallism

binario *adj* INFO binary

binomial *adj* ECON, MAT binomial

biocontrol *m* MED AMB biocontrol

biodegradabilidad *f* MED AMB biodegradability

bioeconomía *f* ECON bioeconomics

biotopo *m* MED AMB biotope

bióxido: ~ **de azufre** *m* MED AMB *lluvia ácida* sulphur dioxide (*BrE*), sulfur dioxide (*AmE*)

bipolar *adj* INFO bipolar

BIRD *abr* (*Banco Internacional para la Reconstrucción y el Desarrollo*) BANCA, ECON IBRD (*International Bank for Reconstruction and Development*)

bisemanal *adj* COM GEN, MEDIOS biweekly, twice a week

bit *m* INFO, MAT bit

bita *f* TRANSP bollard

bitio *m* INFO *ramación* bit; ~ **de control** INFO check bit; ~ **de datos** INFO data bit; ~ **de detención** INFO stop bit; ~ **de información** INFO information bit; ~ **de inicio** INFO start bit; ~ **de paridad** INFO parity bit

bitios: ~ **por pulgada** *fra* (*bpp*) INFO bits per inch (*bpi*); ~ **por segundo** *fra* (*bps*) INFO bits per second (*bps*)

blanca: **sin** ~ *fra infrml* COM GEN broke (*infrml*); **estar sin** ~ *fra infrml* COM GEN be on the rocks; **quedarse sin** ~ *fra infrml* COM GEN be broke

blanco¹ *adj* COM GEN blank

blanco² *m* INFO blank; ~ **de relleno** MEDIOS *edición* spacing material; ~ **de salida** MEDIOS back margin

blanqueo: ~ **de dinero** *m* BANCA, COM GEN, FIN money laundering

bloque *m* COM GEN block; ~ **del Este** POL Eastern Bloc; ~ **comercial** ECON, POL trading block; ~ **de contenedores** TRANSP container block; ~ **de control** BOLSA control block; ~ **de dividendos** BOLSA, CONT dividend gross-up; ~ **de edificios** PROT SOC tower block; ~ **mediterráneo** COM GEN Mediterranean bloc; ~ **monetario** ECON, POL monetary bloc; ~ **quinquenal promediado** FISC five-year block averaging; ~ **de viviendas construido con propósitos específicos** INMOB purpose-built block

bloqueado *adj* COM GEN blocked

bloquear *vt* COM GEN block, inhibit

bloqueo *m* COM GEN, blockade, deadlock, lockout, ECON, RRHH lockout; ~ **de cuentas** BANCA accounts close-off; ~ **de los precios** COM GEN, ECON price freeze

bobina *f* INFO spool; ~ **receptora** IND takeup reel

bobinar *vt* INFO spool

boceto: ~ **de diseño** *m* TRANSP design draft; ~ **publicitario listo para fotografiar** *m* MEDIOS *imprenta* camera-ready copy (*CRC*)

bocoy *m* TRANSP hogshead (*hhd*)

bodega *f* TRANSP *navegación* hold

BOE *abr* (*Boletín Oficial del Estado*) POL Spanish official gazette

boicot *m* COM GEN boycott

boicotear *vt* COM GEN *firma, país* boycott

boicoteo *m* RRHH boycott

bola: ~ **rodante** *f* INFO *dispositivo señalador* control ball, trackball

boleta *f* AmL (*cf vale canjeable Esp*) BOLSA dealing slip, voucher, (*cf papeleta de votación Esp*) POL, RRHH *elección sindical* ballot paper, voting paper; ~ **del banco** AmL (*cf recibo bancario Esp*) BANCA banker's ticket; ~ **de despido** AmL (*cf carta de despido Esp*) COMS, RRHH redundancy letter, pink slip (*AmL*)

boletín *m* COM GEN newsletter, report, COMS, V&M bulletin; ~ **comercial** BOLSA trade report; ~ **de cotizaciones en bolsa** *f* BOLSA stock list; ~ **de empresa** MEDIOS house journal; ~ **de prensa** COM GEN press release; ~ **de suscripción** MEDIOS registration form

Boletín: ~ **Internacional de Ayuda y Préstamo** *m* BANCA International Aid and Loan Bulletin; ~ **Oficial del Estado** *m* (*BOE*) POL Spanish official gazette

boleto: ~ **de lotería** *m* COM GEN lottery ticket

bolsa *f* BOLSA exchange, V&M *embalaje* bag; ~ **abierta las veinticuatro horas del día** BOLSA twenty-four hour trading; ~ **de cereales** BOLSA grain exchange; ~ **de comercio** BOLSA, FIN commodity exchange, securities exchange; ~ **de contratación** BOLSA, FIN commodity market, commodity exchange; ~ **de divisas** BOLSA, FIN foreign currency market; ~ **de fletes** BOLSA, FIN, TRANSP shipping exchange; ~ **de fraude** FISC fraud pocket; ~ **de inversión designada** BOLSA designated investment exchange (*BrE*); ~ **de inversión reconocida** BOLSA recognized investment exchange (*RIE*); ~ **de Nueva York** BOLSA New York Stock Exchange (*NYSE*); ~ **de pobreza** PROT SOC poverty pocket; ~ **regida por las leyes federales** BOLSA federally regulated exchange (*AmE*); ~ **regional de valores** BOLSA regional stock exchange; ~ **de trabajo** RRHH labor pool (*AmE*), labour pool (*BrE*); ~ **de valores** BOLSA securities exchange, stock exchange (*stk.*), stock market; ◆ **en la** ~ BOLSA on the stock exchange

Bolsa: ~ **de Argentina** *f* BOLSA Merval Stock Exchange; ~ **de Barcelona** *f* BOLSA Barcelona Stock Exchange; ~ **de Bilbao** *f* BOLSA Bilbao Stock Exchange; ~ **Internacional** *f* BOLSA International Stock Exchange (*ISE*); ~ **Internacional Oficial de Valores** *f* BOLSA International Stock Exchange (*ISE*), Registered International Exchange (*RIE*); ~ **de Lima** *f* BOLSA Lima Stock Exchange; ~ **de Madrid** *f* BOLSA Madrid Stock Exchange; ~ **de Méjico** *f* BOLSA Mexico Stock Exchange; ~ **de Montevideo** *f* BOLSA Montevideo Stock Exchange; ~ **Mercantil Europea** *f* BOLSA European Mercantile Exchange (*ECM*); ~ **de Santiago** *f* BOLSA Santiago Stock Exchange; ~ **de Valencia** *f* BOLSA Valencia Stock Exchange; ~ **de Valores** *f* BOLSA, COM GEN Stock Exchange; ~ **de Valores Automatizada a Tiempo Real** *f* BOLSA Automated Real-Time Investments Exchange (*Ariel*); **~ de Valores de Belfast** *f* BOLSA Belfast Stock Exchange; **~ de Valores de Birmingham** *f* BOLSA Birmingham Stock Exchange; **~ de Valores de Cincinnatti** *f* BOLSA Cincinnatti Stock Exchange; **~ de Valores de Chicago** *f* BOLSA Chicago Stock Exchange; **~ de Valores de Glasgow** *f* BOLSA Glasgow Stock Exchange; **~ de Valores de Liverpool** *f* BOLSA Liverpool Stock Exchange; **~ de Valores del Pacífico** *f* BOLSA Pacific Stock Exchange (*PSE*); **~ de Valores de Salt Lake** *f* BOLSA Salt Lake City Stock Exchange; **~ de Valores de Spokane** *f* BOLSA Spokane Stock Exchange

bolsillo *m* ECON *del consumidor* pocket

bolsín *m* BOLSA kerb market

bomba *f* MEDIOS, V&M blockbuster; **~ elevadora de presión** TRANSP *cargo movement* booster; **~ principal tipo casquete** TRANSP cap-type primer

bombear *vt* MED AMB pump; ◆ **~ fondos hacia** FIN pump funds into

bombona: **~ para ácidos** *f* TRANSP carboy, demijohn

bonanza *f* SEG *minería* bonanza

bonificable *adj* TRANSP rebateable

bonificación *f* COM GEN bonus, rebate, CONT valuation allowance; **~ compuesta** COM GEN, CONT compound bonus; **~ por contratación** COM GEN, RRHH recruitment bonus; **~ de descuento** COM GEN, CONT allowed discount; **~ diferida** ECON reversionary bonus; **~ en efectivo** COM GEN cash bonus; **~ por empleo regional** RRHH regional employment premium (*REP*); **~ por entrega como parte de pago** COM GEN trade-in allowance; **~ final** ECON *seguros*, FIN, SEG terminal bonus; **~ fiscal** COM GEN tax credit; **~ de interés** FIN interest rebate; **~ libre de impuestos** FISC tax-free allowance; **~ por maternidad** PROT SOC, RRHH maternity allowance; **~ por no tener reclamaciones** SEG no-claim bonus (*BrE*); **~ por pago anticipado** FIN *crédito al consumo* early settlement rebate; **~ por riesgo** COM GEN, CONT, FIN, FISC hazard bonus; **~ en la tasa de combustible** FISC fuel duty rebate (*BrE*); **~ de tierras** INMOB land improvement; **~ por traslado** RRHH removal allowance; **~ tributaria a la inversión** FISC investment tax credit; **~ por volumen** TRANSP volume rebate

bonificar *vt* COM GEN discount

bono *m* COM GEN voucher, ECON, FIN bond; **~ en acciones** BOLSA, FIN share bond; **~ administrativo** ECON managed bond; **~ de ahorro** BOLSA, FIN savings bond; **~ de ahorro con prima** BOLSA, FIN premium savings bond; **~ al portador** BOLSA, FIN bearer bond; **~ al portador con cupones** BOLSA, FIN coupon bond; **~ alcista y bajista** BOLSA, FIN bull-and-bear bond (*BrE*); **~ con alto descuento** BOLSA, FIN deep discount bond; **~ con alto interés y pronto vencimiento** BOLSA pickup bond; **~ amortizable antes del vencimiento** BOLSA, FIN retractable bond; **~ amortizable anticipadamente** BOLSA, FIN callable bond; **~ amortizable con los ingresos** BOLSA income bond; **~ amortizable subordinado** BOLSA, FIN subordinated redeemable bond; **~ de amortización** BOLSA, FIN redemption bond; **~ autorizado** BOLSA, FIN authorized bond; **~ de bajo rendimiento** BOLSA, FIN low-yield bond; **~ bancario** BANCA bank bond; **~ basura** BOLSA, FIN junk bond; **~ con bonificación fiscal** BOLSA, FISC special tax bond; **~ cancelado** BOLSA, FIN invalidated bond; **~ de capital** BOLSA, FIN capital bonus; **~ con**

certificado BOLSA, FIN bond with warrants; **~ sin certificado** BOLSA, FIN bond ex warrants; **~ con certificado adjunto** BOLSA, FIN bond with warrants attached; **~ en circulación** BOLSA, FIN outstanding bond; **~ clase AAA** BOLSA, FIN AAA bond, triple A bond; **~ con condiciones** BOLSA, FIN bond terms; **~ de consolidación** BOLSA, FIN funding bond; **~ consolidado** BOLSA, FIN consolidated bond; **~ de conversión** BOLSA, FIN refunding bond; **~ convertible** BOLSA, FIN convertible bond; **~ a corto plazo** BOLSA, FIN short-term bond; **~ de crecimiento garantizado con impuesto pagado** BOLSA, FIN tax-paid guaranteed growth bond; **~ sin cupón** BOLSA stripped bond; **~ de cupón cero** BANCA streaker; **~ con cupón a largo y vencimiento a corto** BOLSA, FIN super sinker bond; **~ debidamente registrado** BOLSA, FIN fully registered bond; **~ a la demanda** BANCA *mercantil* on demand bond; **~ depositario** BOLSA, FIN bail bond; **~ de desarrollo industrial** BOLSA industrial development bond; **~ para el desarrollo de la pequeña empresa** COM GEN small business development bond (*SBDB*); **~ descontado** BOLSA, FIN discount bond; **~ de descuento intensivo** BOLSA, FIN deep discount bond; **~ de deuda solidaria** BOLSA, FIN joint bond; **~ de dividendo** BOLSA, FIN dividend bond; **~ con doble garantía** BOLSA, FIN double-barreled bond (*AmE*), double-barrelled bond (*BrE*); **~ emitido a descuento** BOLSA, FIN discounted bond; **~ especial de distrito** BOLSA special district bond; **~ del Estado** BOLSA, ECON government bond (*AmE*), yearling (*BrE*); **~ del Estado a largo plazo** BOLSA long-term government bond; **~ en eurodólares** BOLSA Eurodollar bond; **~ extranjero** BOLSA, FIN foreign bond; **~ para fines privados** BOLSA private purpose bond; **~ con garantía** BOLSA, FIN bond cum warrant, mortgage bond, secured bond; **~ de garantía colateral** BOLSA, FIN, SEG collateral trust bond; **~ con garantía de compra** *f* BOLSA bond with bond-buying warrant; **~ con garantía prendaria** BOLSA, FIN, SEG collateral trust bond; **~ garantizado** BOLSA, FIN guaranteed bond; **~ del gobierno federal** BOLSA, FIN federal government bond (*AmE*); **~ con gravamen limitado** FISC limited tax bond; **~ hipotecario** BANCA, BOLSA, FIN general mortgage bond, mortgage bond, secured bond; **~ indizado** BOLSA indexed bond; **~ de interés diferido** BOLSA deferred interest bond; **~ de interés por etapas** BOLSA stepped bond; **~ de interés fijo** BOLSA fixed-interest bond; **~ de interés en mora** BOLSA, FIN defaulted bond; **~ sin intereses** BOLSA passive bond; **~ a largo plazo** BOLSA long-term bond, granny bond (*infrml*) (*BrE*), long bond; **~ matador** BOLSA killer bond; **~ a medio plazo** BANCA medium-term note (*MTN*); **~ en mora** BOLSA, FIN defaulted bond; **~ municipal imponible** FISC taxable municipal bond; **~ municipal pagadero con los ingresos** FIN utility revenue bond; **~ municipal de respaldo fiscal** BOLSA, FIN toll revenue bond; **~ negociable al portador** BOLSA, FIN bearer marketable bond; **~ no redimible** BOLSA, FIN noncallable bond; **~ nominativo con cupón** BOLSA, FIN coupon registered bond; **~ con obligación** BOLSA, FIN *hipotecario* obligation bond; **~ con opción de venta** BOLSA, FIN put bond; **~ ordinario** BOLSA straight bond; **~ pagadero** BOLSA, FIN bond payable; **~ de pago anticipado** BOLSA, FIN advance payment bond; **~ de pago en especie** BOLSA, FIN payment-in-kind bond (*PIK bond*); **~ con pago de intereses anticipado** BOLSA, FIN bond with interest paid in advance; ~ **con pago mensual de intereses** BOLSA, FIN bond with monthly-paid interest; ~ **de pago opcional** BOLSA, FIN optional payment bond; ~ **de paridad** BOLSA, FIN parity bond; ~ **de la pequeña empresa** FIN small business bond; ~ **perpetuo** BOLSA, FIN perpetual bond; ~ **perpetuo subordinado** BOLSA, FIN subordinated perpetual bond; ~ **a plazo fijo** BOLSA, FIN term bond; ~ **de premio** BOLSA, FIN prize bond; ~ **de prima** BOLSA, FIN premium bond; ~ **de primera clase** BOLSA, FIN high-grade bond; ~ **de propiedad** FIN, INMOB property bond; ~ **de recompensa** FIN prize bond; ~ **redimible antes del vencimiento** BOLSA, FIN callable bond; ~ **de regalo** COM GEN gift certificate (*AmE*), gift voucher; ~ **registrado** BOLSA, FIN registered bond; ~ **reinvertible** BOLSA, FIN bunny bond (*jarg*); ~ **de remuneración** BOLSA, FIN prize bond; ~ **de renovación** BOLSA, FIN replacement bond; ~ **de renta vitalicia** BOLSA, FIN annuity bond; ~ **con reparto de beneficios** BOLSA, FIN profit-sharing bond; ~ **con respaldo oficial** BOLSA, FIN moral obligation bond; ~ **de responsabilidad general** BOLSA general obligation bond (*AmE*) (*G-O bond*); ~ **de retención** BOLSA, FIN retention bond; ~ **retractable** BOLSA, FIN retractable bond; ~ **samurai** BOLSA, FIN samurai bond; ~ **secundario** BOLSA adjustment bond; ~ **de la serie hh** BOLSA series hh bond; ~ **sintético** BOLSA synthetic bond; ~ **social** BOLSA share certificate (*BrE*); ~ **sorteado** BOLSA drawn bond; ~ **del tesoro** BOLSA Treasury bond (*AmE*), Treasury stock (*BrE*); ~ **del Tesoro en cartera** BOLSA unissued Treasury share; ~ **de tipo de interés anual** BOLSA, FIN annual rate bond; ~ **de tipo de interés fijo** BOLSA, FIN fixed-rate bond; ~ **de trabajo** RRHH job ticket, job card; ~ **de transbordo** IMP/EXP, TRANSP transhipment bond; ~ **con valor a la par** BOLSA, FIN par bond; ~ **de vencimiento ajustable** BOLSA, FIN extendible bond; ~ **de vencimiento aplazado** BOLSA, FIN continued bond; ~ **con vencimiento elegido al azar** BOLSA, FIN serial bond; ~ **de vencimiento escalonado** BOLSA, FIN serial bond; ~ **de vencimiento fijo** BOLSA, FIN dated bond; ~ **de viaje** TRANSP travel voucher; ~ **de vivienda** BOLSA, FIN public housing authority bond, INMOB housing bond; ~ **yanqui** BOLSA, FIN Yankee bond (*AmE*)

bonos: ~ **de ahorro nacional** *m pl* BANCA, FIN National Savings Certificate (*BrE*); ~ **de arbitraje** *m pl* BOLSA arbitrage bonds (*AmE*); ~ **en bancarrota** *m pl* BOLSA default bonds; ~ **bloqueados** *m pl* FIN stopped bonds; ~ **en cartera** *m pl* BOLSA, FIN bond holding; ~ **defectuosos** *m pl* BOLSA default bonds; ~ **de depósito** *m pl* BANCA deposit bonds (*BrE*); ~ **especiales no negociables** *m pl* BOLSA special non-marketable bonds (*SGAT*); ~ **del estado** *m pl* BOLSA state bonds; ~ **del Estado del R.U.** *m pl* BOLSA UK government stocks (*BrE*); ~ **municipales sin certificado** *m pl* BOLSA certificateless municipals; ~ **de reversión** *m pl* ECON, FIN, SEG terminal bonus; ~ **reversionarios** *m pl* FIN reversionary bonus

booleano *adj* INFO Boolean

boom *m* ECON boom; ~ **de Barber** ECON Barber boom (*BrE*); ~ **económico** ECON, POL economic boom; **gran ~ económico** ECON *1940-1960* Long Boom

borderó *m* COM GEN, SEG draft, slip; ~ **de aceptación** SEG acceptance slip; ~ **de cajetines** BOLSA, SEG honeycomb slip; ~ **de casillas** FIN honeycomb slip; ~ **de línea** SEG line slip; ~ **normalizado** TRANSP *navegación* standard slip; ~ **original** SEG original slip

borrador *m* FISC *declaración* working copy, INFO draft (*dft*), POL draft (*dft*), pink paper (*jarg*) (*BrE*), V&M *publicidad* rough, scamp (*jarg*); ~ **de artículo** DER *proyecto de ley* draft clause; ~ **de cláusula** DER *bill* draft clause; ~ **de un contrato** DER draft contract; ~ **de decreto** DER *compra forzosa* draft order; ~ **de directiva** DER *UE* draft directive; ~ **de impresión** INFO print preview; ~ **de presupuesto** CONT draft budget, POL *gobierno central* supply bill; ~ **de prospecto** BOLSA draft prospectus; ~ **de riesgo** CONT exposure draft; ◆ **en ~** COM GEN in draft form; **en forma de ~** COM GEN in draft form

borrar *vt* INFO erase, blank, *limpiar, despejar* clear; ◆ ~ **algo de una cinta** COM GEN wipe sth from a tape; ~ **a alguien de una lista** COM GEN strike sb off the list

bosquejo *m* COM GEN sketch

botar *vt* TRANSP *navegación* launch

bote *m* TRANSP boat; ~ **salvavidas** TRANSP lifeboat; ~ **salvavidas hiperbárico de autopropulsión** TRANSP self-propelled hyperbaric lifeboat (*SPHL*); ~ **de servicio** TRANSP service boat

botiquín: ~ **de primeros auxilios** *m* PROT SOC first-aid kit

botón *m* INFO *de dispositivo* button; ~ **de rellamada** COMS automatic redialing (*AmE*), automatic redialling (*BrE*)

botones *m* RRHH office boy

boutique *f* COM GEN, V&M boutique

bóveda *f* BANCA vault; ~ **de seguridad** BANCA safe-deposit vault, strong room

boyante *adj* BOLSA, COM GEN *negocios* afloat, ECON buoyant

BPA *abr* (*beneficio por acción*) BOLSA, CONT, FIN EPS (*earning per share*)

BPI *abr* (*Banco de Pagos Internacionales*) BANCA, ECON BIS (*Bank for International Settlements*)

bpp *abr* (*bitios por pulgada*) INFO bpi (*bits per inch*)

bps *abr* (*bitios por segundo*) INFO bps (*bits per second*)

brainstorm *vi* GES brainstorm

brainstorming *m* GES brainstorming

brazo *m* ECON arm

brecha: ~ **deflacionaria** *f* ECON *econometría* deflationary gap; ~ **de dólares** *f* ECON dollar gap; ~ **inflacionaria** *f* ECON inflationary gap; ~ **en el mercado** *f* V&M market gap; ~ **restrictiva del ingreso nacional** *f* ECON contractionary national income gap; ~ **tecnológica** *f* ECON technological gap

Brecha: ~ **Macmillan** *f* FIN Macmillan Gap

breve[1]: **en ~** *adj* COM GEN in short

breve[2]: ~ **misiva de agradecimiento** *f* COM GEN bread-and-butter letter (*infrml*), thank-you note; ~ **resumen** *m* COM GEN brief summary

brevedad: con la mayor ~ posible *fra* COM GEN, COMS as soon as possible (*a.s.a.p.*)

briefing *m* COM GEN briefing

brigada: ~ **anticorrupción** *f* DER Serious Fraud Office (*SFO*); ~ **de producción** *f* ECON *países socialistas* production brigade (*jarg*)

brillo: sin ~ *adj* INFO *pantalla* glare-free

broker *mf* BOLSA stockbroker, FIN broker; ~ **de bolsa**

BOLSA agency broker; **~ independiente** BOLSA outsider broker; **~ de opciones registradas** BOLSA registered options broker

bromuro: **~ de metilo** *m* TRANSP methyl bromide

bruja *adj AmL infrml* (*cf sin un duro Esp*) RRHH broke (*infrml*), flat broke (*infrml*)

brusco: **~ descenso** *m* COM GEN, ECON *mercado bursátiles* sharp dive

bruto *adj* COM GEN raw, CONT, FIN gross

buceta *f* TRANSP *para provisiones* bumboat

bucle *m* POL *administración Reagan* loop (*obs*) (*AmE*); **~ de corriente** INFO *antiguos teletipos* current loop

buen[1]: **~ negocio** *m* COM GEN good bargain; **~ orden aparente de las mercancías** *m* TRANSP apparent good order of the goods; **~ promedio** *m* COM GEN good fair average (*gfa*)

buen[2]: **en ~ estado** *fra* COM GEN in good repair, in good trim (*infrml*)

buena[1]: **en ~ posición** *adj* COM GEN well off

buena[2]: **~ administración interna** *f* GES good housekeeping; **~ entrega** *f* BOLSA good delivery; **~ fe** *f* COM GEN good faith; **~ moneda** *f* ECON *Ley de Gresham* good money; **~ posición** *f* RRHH niche; **~ recaudación de taquilla** *f* OCIO *teatro, cine* good box office

buenas: **~ noticias** *f pl* COM GEN good news

buenos[1]: **~ antecedentes mercantiles** *m pl* COM GEN good business background

buenos[2]: **con los ~ oficios de** *fra* COM GEN through the agency of

bufete: **~ de abogados** *m* DER law firm

buhonero *m* V&M huckster (*infrml*)

Bundesbank *m* BANCA Bundesbank

bungalow *m* INMOB, OCIO rambler (*jarg*)

buque *m* TRANSP *navegación* vessel, ship; **~ alimentador** TRANSP feeder vessel, feeder ship; **~ de altura de transporte de pasajeros** TRANSP foreign-going passenger ship; **~ amarrado disponible** IMP/EXP *envío de mercancías* free sea carrier; **~ arribado** TRANSP arrived ship; **~ blando** TRANSP tender vessel; **~ de cabotaje de puntal bajo** TRANSP low profile coaster; **~ carbonero** TRANSP coal carrier, collier; **~ de carga** *Esp* (*cf fletero AmL*) TRANSP *navegación* cargo ship (*BrE*), cargo vessel (*BrE*), freighter (*AmE*); **~ de carga general** TRANSP *navegación* general cargo ship; **~ de carga de línea regular** TRANSP *navegación* cargo liner; **~ para cargamentos líquidos** TRANSP liquid bulk cargo ship; **~ para cargas pesadas** TRANSP heavy lift ship; **~ celoso** TRANSP stiff vessel; **~ celular de contenedores** TRANSP cellular container ship; **~ cisterna** TRANSP tanker; **~ cisterna de cabotaje** TRANSP intercoastal tanker; **~ cisterna de motor** TRANSP tanker motor vessel (*TMV*); **~ combinado** TRANSP *navegación* combi ship; **~ de comercio nacional** TRANSP home trade ship; **~ contenedor compartimentado** TRANSP fully cellular container ship (*FCC*); **~ costero** TRANSP coaster; **~ distribuidor de contenedores** TRANSP *navegación* feeder; **~ duro** TRANSP stiff vessel; **~ franco** TRANSP liberty ship; **~ frigorífico** TRANSP reefer ship; **~ gemelo** TRANSP sister ship; **~ para graneles** TRANSP bulk container ship; **~ en lastre** TRANSP light vessel (*LTV*); **~ de línea ocasional** TRANSP noncontinuous liner (*NC*); **~ de mercancía general** TRANSP general cargo ship; **~ mercante** TRANSP merchant ship, merchant

vessel; **~ mineralero** TRANSP *navegación* ore carrier; **~ de navegación de altura** TRANSP ocean-going ship; **~ de navegación marítima** TRANSP ocean-going ship; **~ nodriza** TRANSP mother ship; **~ Panamax** TRANSP Panamax vessel; **~ de pasaje** TRANSP passenger ship; **~ de pasajeros** TRANSP *navegación* liner; **~ de pasajeros con clases primera y turista** TRANSP two-class vessel; **~ perdido** TRANSP missing vessel; **~ petrolífero de línea continua** TRANSP oil-bearing continuous liner; **~ portabarcazas** TRANSP barge carrier; **~ portacontenedores** TRANSP container ship; **~ portagabarras** TRANSP lighter aboard ship (*LASH*); **~ de propulsión eléctrica por turbina de gas** TRANSP gas turbo electric ship (*GT-E*); **~ refrigerado** TRANSP refrigerated vessel, refrigerated ship; **~ registrado** TRANSP registered ship; **~ de salvamento** TRANSP *navegación* salvor; **~ para tendido de conductos submarinos** TRANSP pipe-laying ship; **~ transatlántico** TRANSP ocean-going vessel; **~ transatlántico de mercancías** TRANSP *navegación* belship; **~ para transporte de cargas rodadas** TRANSP ro/ro vessel; **~ de transporte industrial** TRANSP *navegación* industrial carrier; **~ de transporte nacional de pasajeros** TRANSP home trade passenger ship; **~ de turbina de gas** TRANSP *navegación* gas turbine ship (*GT*); **~ para uso general** TRANSP multipurpose vessel; **~ de vapor a turbinas** TRANSP turbine steamship; ♦ **el ~ está siendo reparado** TRANSP the ship is in trim

burbuja *f* BOLSA bubble (*jarg*)

burguesía *f* ECON, POL bourgeoisie

burocracia *f* POL, RRHH bureaucracy

burócrata *mf* POL, RRHH bureaucrat

burocrático *adj* POL, RRHH bureaucratic

burocratización *m* POL, RRHH bureaucratization

bursátil *adj* BOLSA stock-exchange, stock-market, COM GEN *compras* across-the-counter

bursatilidad *f* BOLSA marketability

bus *m* INFO *equipo* bus; **~ común de dirección** INFO address bus; **~ de datos** INFO data bus

busca: **~ y cambia** *fra* INFO *procesadores de textos* search and replace

buscar *vt* COM GEN search, *ayuda, empleo* seek, INFO search, RRHH *ejecutivo* headhunt; ♦ **~ averías** INFO troubleshoot; **~ clientes** COM GEN tout for custom; **~ por medios publicitarios** COM GEN, MEDIOS, V&M advertise for; **~ un mercado** BOLSA seek a market

búsqueda[1]: **~ de acción** *f* GES action research; **~ automática** *f* INFO *documento, datos* global search; **~ binaria** *f* INFO *ramación* binary search; **~ de Boole** *f* INFO Boolean search; **~ y captura** *m* COM GEN search and seizure; **~ ejecutiva** *f* GES, RRHH executive search; **~ de empleo** *f* RRHH job hunting; **~ de metas** *f* COM GEN, GES goal seeking; **~ de palabra clave** *f* INFO keyword search; **~ de puesto de trabajo** *f* RRHH job search

búsqueda[2]: **estar en la ~ de** *fra* COM GEN look out for

bustos: **~ parlantes** *m pl* MEDIOS *televisión* talking heads (*jarg*)

butacas *f pl* OCIO stalls

butano *m* MED AMB butane

buzón *m* COMS letter box (*BrE*), mailbox (*AmE*), postbox (*BrE*), INFO mailbox; **~ de sugerencias** COM GEN suggestion box

buzoneo *m AmL* COMS (*cf lista de direcciones Esp*) mailing list, INFO (*cf propaganda por correo Esp*) mailing, V&M (*cf propaganda por correo Esp*) mailing, (*cf lista de direcciones Esp*) mailing list; ~ **de propaganda** *AmL* (*cf envio publicitario Esp*) V&M mailing

byte *m* INFO byte

C

c/ *abr* (*cuenta*) BANCA a/c *account*

C *abr* (*centígrado*) COM GEN C (*centigrade*)

c/ *abr* (*calle*) COM GEN St. (*street*)

CA *abr Esp* (*Comunidad Autónoma*) POL territory governed as a unit with certain degree of autonomy, ≈ county (*BrE*)

caballaje *m AmL* (*CV*) (*cf caballo de vapor Esp*) TRANSP horsepower (*h.p.*)

caballo: **~ de vapor** *m Esp* (*CV*) (*cf caballaje AmL*) TRANSP horsepower (*h.p.*); **~ de vapor nominal** *m* TRANSP nominal horsepower (*NHP*)

cabalmente *adv* COM GEN accurately

cabecera *f* ADMIN, COM GEN header, MEDIOS *radiodifusión* header, *de periódico* news headline, *página* head

cabecilla: **~ sindical** *mf* MEDIOS, RRHH *sindicato de imprenta* mother of the chapel (*BrE*), father of the chapel (*BrE*)

cabestrillo *m* TRANSP *carga* sling

cabeza[1]: **~ de lista** *mf* POL *electoral list* front-runner, list head

cabeza[2] *f* COM GEN, CONT, INFO head; **~ de borrado** INFO erase head; **~ de carril** TRANSP railhead; **~ contable** CONT beancounter (*infrml*); **~ del contenedor** TRANSP container head; **~ de familia** FISC head of household; **~ lectora-grabadora** INFO read-write head; **~ de lectura** INFO read head; **~ de la liga** COM GEN top of the league; **~ de línea** TRANSP railhead; **~ magnética** INFO magnetic head; **~ de turco** *infrml* BOLSA fall guy (*infrml*) (*AmE*), scapegoat (*infrml*) (*BrE*); ◆ **por ~** COM GEN per capita, per head; **~ y hombros** ECON head and shoulders; **estar a la ~ de la lista** COM GEN be top of the list

cabina *f* TRANSP cabin; **~ del conductor** TRANSP driver's cab; **~ de conductores de cargas rodadas** TRANSP ro/ro drivers' cabin; **~ electoral** POL polling booth, voting booth; **~ de portazgo** TRANSP tollbooth; **~ de teléfono** *Esp* (*cf locutorio AmL*) COMS call box (*AmE*), telephone box (*BrE*); **~ para votar** POL voting booth

cable: **~ de acero de calidad especial extra** *m* TRANSP extra-special quality steel cable; **~ coaxial** *m* COMS pipeline, INFO *equipo* coaxial cable; **~ coaxil** *m AmL* (*cf cable coaxial Esp*) INFO coaxial cable; **~ de conexión a tierra** *m* INFO grounding cord; **~ de fibra óptica** *m* COMS, IND, INFO fibre-optic cable (*BrE*), fiber-optic cable (*AmE*); **~ de suspensión** *m* INFO carrying cable, running cable; **~ de sustentación** *m* INFO light cable; **~ tensor** *m* TRANSP tom

cablegrama *m* COMS cablegram

cabotaje[1]: **de ~** *adj* TRANSP intercoastal

cabotaje[2] *m* TRANSP cabotage, coasting

cabrestante *m* TRANSP capstan

cabrestantes *m pl* TRANSP winches

CAC *abr* (*compromiso de aseguramiento continuado*) BANCA, SEG RUF (*revolving underwriting facility*)

CAD *abr* IND, INFO (*diseño asistido por computador AmL, diseño asistido por computadora AmL, diseño asistido por ordenador Esp*) CAD (*computer-aided design*), POL (*Comité de Ayuda al Desarrollo*) DAC (*Development Assistance Committee*)

CADD *abr* (*diseño y dibujo asistido por computador AmL, diseño y dibujo asistido por computadora AmL, diseño y dibujo asistido por ordenador Esp*) IND, INFO CADD (*computer-aided design and drafting*)

cadena *f* COM GEN *de comercios* chain, INFO string, MEDIOS *radiodifusión* network, TRANSP *paletas* flow line, *carga y descarga* chain; **~ afiliada** V&M affiliated chain; **~ alimenticia** MED AMB food chain; **~ de bancos** BANCA bank group (*AmE*), banking group (*BrE*); **~ de bitios** INFO bit string; **~ de caracteres** INFO character string; **~ de compra y venta para manipular el mercado** BOLSA daisy chain; **~ continua de montaje** IND line production; **~ de distribución** IND chain of distribution; **~ de ensamblaje** IND, RRHH assembly line; **~ de grandes almacenes** V&M department store chain; **~ de marketing** V&M marketing chain; **~ de montaje** IND, RRHH assembly line; **~ de órdenes** GES chain of command; **~ perpetua** DER life imprisonment; **~ de producción** COM GEN flow line, assembly line, production line; **~ de suspensión** TRANSP sling; **~ de valor** FIN value chain; **~ voluntaria** COM GEN voluntary chain

cadenas: **~ de televisión** *f pl* MEDIOS television networks, webs (*AmE*)

caducado *adj* BOLSA, CONT, SEG expired, lapsed

caducar *vi* BOLSA, CONT, SEG expire, lapse

caducidad *f* BOLSA, CONT, SEG expiry, lapse, lapsing; **~ artificial** V&M artificial obsolescence; **~ programada** V&M built-in obsolescence

caer 1. *vt* BANCA *interés* run; **2.** *vi* COM GEN *precios, gobierno* fall; ◆ **~ en desuso** DER fall into abeyance; **~ en picado** BOLSA slump

cafetería: **~ para empleados** *f* RRHH work canteen

CAI *abr* (*instrucción asistida por computador AmL, instrucción asistida por computadora AmL, instrucción asistida por ordenador Esp*) INFO CAI (*computer-aided instruction*)

caída *f* COM GEN collapse, drop, ECON drop, INFO *de tensión eléctrica* brownout; **~ en desuso** V&M obsolescence; **~ en desuso artificial** V&M artificial obsolescence; **~ en desuso dinámica** V&M dynamic obsolescence; **~ en desuso funcional** V&M functional obsolescence; **~ de la divisa** ECON fall of currency; **~ fuerte de los precios** BOLSA, ECON collapse of prices, heavy fall of prices; **~ en las inversiones** BOLSA, ECON drop in investments; **~ de una moneda** BOLSA, ECON collapse of a currency; **~ en picado** BOLSA collapse, slump, COM GEN tailspin (*infrml*); **~ en picado del mercado** BOLSA market slump; **~ de la producción** IND drop in production, fall in production; **~ pronunciada** COM GEN, ECON sharp drop; **~ rápida** BOLSA, FIN *moneda* fast decline; **~ repentina** COM GEN slump; **~ de tensión** INFO power failure; **~ en los tipos bancarios** ECON fall in the bank rate; **~ de ventas** COM GEN slump in sales

caja *f* BANCA *fuerte* cash box, vault, *mesa* cash desk, COM

GEN *fuerte* vault, cash box, CONT *acumulado* cash desk, cash book, ready cash, cash box, OCIO *cine, teatro* case, V&M *supermercado* checkout; ~ **de ahorros** *Esp* BANCA savings bank (*BrE*); ~ **de Bernoulli** INFO Bernoulli box; ~ **chica** *AmL* (*cf caja pequeña Esp*) BANCA, CONT, FIN petty cash (*P/C*); ~ **para depósitos de seguridad** BANCA safety-deposit box; ~ **de diálogo** INFO dialog box (*AmE*), dialogue box (*BrE*); ~ **de Edgeworth** ECON Edgeworth Box; ~ **de fichas** ADMIN, INFO card catalog; ~ **fuerte** BANCA bank vault, safe, strongbox; ~ **jaula para materiales frágiles** TRANSP skeleton case; ~ **de madera conglomerada** V&M fiberboard case (*AmE*), fibreboard case (*BrE*); ~ **negra** INFO, TRANSP black box; ~ **pequeña** *Esp* (*cf caja chica AmL*) BANCA, CONT, FIN petty cash (*P/C*); ~ **registradora** V&M cash register; ~ **rural** BANCA ≈ agricultural credit bank; ~ **de seguridad** BANCA safe-deposit box, safety vault; ~ **de seguridad bancaria** BANCA bank vault, safe, strongbox; ~ **de una sola pieza** TRANSP one-piece box; ~ **de tracción** TRANSP pull-through box; ~ **de tres piezas** TRANSP three-piece box

Caja: ~ **Postal** *f Esp obs* BANCA ≈ National Savings Bank (*NSB*); ~ **Rural** *f* BANCA Country Bank, Land Bank

cajero[1]**,-a** *m,f* RRHH cashier, checkout clerk; ~ **adjunto(-a)** BANCA assistant cashier (*BrE*), assistant teller (*AmE*); ~ **bancario(-a)** BANCA bank teller

cajero[2]: ~ **automático** *m* BANCA automated cash dispenser (*BrE*) (*ACD*), automated teller machine (*AmE*) (*ATM*), automatic cash dispenser (*BrE*) (*ACD*), automatic teller (*AmE*), automatic telling machine (*AmE*) (*ATM*), bank teller, cash dispenser, cash-dispensing machine; ~ **bancario** *m* BANCA automated cash dispenser (*BrE*) (*ACD*), automated teller machine (*AmE*) (*ATM*), automatic cash dispenser (*BrE*) (*ACD*), automatic telling machine (*AmE*) (*ATM*)

cajón: ~ **clasificador** *m* ADMIN filing drawer

cajones *m pl* TRANSP cases (*c/s*)

caladeros *m pl* ECON fishing grounds

calado *m* TRANSP draft (*AmE*), draught (*BrE*)

calculable *adj* COM GEN, INFO, MAT calculable

calculadora *f* COM GEN, INFO calculator; ~ **de bolsillo** INFO, MAT pocket calculator; ~ **electrónica** INFO electronic calculator; ~ **mecánica** INFO hand calculator

calcular *vt* COM GEN, INFO, MAT calculate; ~ **espacio** MEDIOS cast off; ~ **el espacio tipográfico** MEDIOS, V&M cast off; ~ **espacios** V&M cast off; ~ **mal** COM GEN miscalculate

cálculo *m* COM GEN calculation, computation, reckoning; ~ **actuarial** CONT, FIN, RRHH actuary's valuation; ~ **de adecuación de la publicidad** V&M task method; ~ **anticipado** COM preliminary estimate; ~ **apriorístico** CONT, FIN, RRHH aprioristic conjecture; ~ **aproximado del impuesto** FISC walk-through assessment; ~ **complejo** CONT number crunching (*infrml*); ~ **de costes** *Esp* (*cf cálculo de costos AmL*) CONT costing; ~ **de costes de absorción** *Esp* (*cf cálculo de costos de absorción AmL*) CONT absorption costing; ~ **de costes basado en la actividad** *Esp* (*cf cálculo de costos basado en la actividad AmL*) CONT activity-based costing (*ABC*); ~ **de costes diferenciales** *Esp* (*cf cálculo de costos diferenciales AmL*) CONT marginal costing; ~ **de costes directos** *Esp* (*cf cálculo de costos directos AmL*) CONT direct costing; ~ **de costes**

funcionales *Esp* (*cf cálculo de costos funcionales AmL*) CONT functional costing; ~ **de costes de inventario** *Esp* (*cf cálculo de costos de inventario AmL*) CONT inventory costing; ~ **de costes marginales** *Esp* (*cf cálculo de costos marginales AmL*) CONT marginal costing; ~ **de costes de una misión** *Esp* (*cf cálculo de costos de una misión AmL*) V&M mission costing; ~ **de costes de proceso** *Esp* (*cf cálculo de costos de proceso AmL*) CONT, IND process costing; ~ **de costes del producto** *Esp* (*cf cálculo de costos del producto AmL*) CONT product costing; ~ **de costos** *AmL* (*cf cálculo de costes Esp*) CONT costing; ~ **de costos de absorción** *AmL* (*cf cálculo de costes de absorción Esp*) CONT absorption costing; ~ **de costos basado en la actividad** *AmL* (*cf cálculo de costes basado en la actividad Esp*) CONT activity-based costing (*BrE*) (*ABC*); ~ **de costos diferenciales** *AmL* (*cf cálculo de costes diferenciales Esp*) CONT marginal costing; ~ **de costos directos** *AmL* (*cf cálculo de costes directos Esp*) CONT direct costing; ~ **de costos funcionales** *AmL* (*cf cálculo de costes funcionales Esp*) CONT functional costing; ~ **de costos de inventario** *AmL* (*cf cálculo de costes de inventario Esp*) CONT inventory costing; ~ **de costos marginales** *AmL* (*cf cálculo de costes marginales Esp*) CONT marginal costing; ~ **de costos de una misión** *AmL* (*cf cálculo de costes de una misión Esp*) V&M mission costing; ~ **de costos de proceso** *AmL* (*cf cálculo de costes de proceso Esp*) IND process costing; ~ **de costos del producto** *AmL* (*cf cálculo de costes del producto Esp*) CONT product costing; ~ **diferencial** CONT, FIN, MAT, RRHH differential calculus; ~ **de errores** COM GEN computation of errors; ~ **exacto** COM GEN safe estimate; ~ **financiero adicional** FIN supplementary financing facility; ~ **fiscal detallado** FISC detailed tax calculation; ~ **del impuesto sobre la renta** FISC income tax assessment; ~ **infinitesimal** CONT, FIN, MAT infinitesimal calculus; ~ **integral** CONT, FIN, MAT, integral calculus; ~ **de intereses sobre saldos diarios** BANCA daily balance interest calculation; ~ **de precios** CONT, FIN, RRHH calculation of prices, pricing; ~ **de probabilidades** MAT calculus of probabilities; ~ **provisional** COM GEN tentative estimate; ~ **repartido** INFO distributed computing; ~ **de tiempo** COM GEN, CONT, FIN, RRHH timing; ~ **de tonelaje** TRANSP tonnage calculation; ~ **de ventas** V&M sales estimate

cálculos *m pl* FIN estimates; ~ **adicionales** FIN supplementary estimates; ~ **circulares** FISC circular calculations

caldera: ~ **auxiliar** *f* TRANSP auxiliary boiler; ~ **de tubos de agua de recuperación** *f* TRANSP waste heat water tube boiler

calderilla *f* COM GEN coppers, small change

calendario *m* COM GEN timescale, calendar, GES, TRANSP schedule; ~ **de acciones** GES, IND scheduling; ~ **de demanda** ECON demand schedule; ~ **de ejecución** GES, IND *producción* scheduling; ~ **fiscal** FISC tax schedule; ~ **de mantenimiento** COM GEN maintenance schedule; ~ **de pagos** BANCA schedule of repayments; ~ **de taco** COM GEN tear-off calendar

calentador *m* COM GEN heater (*htr*)

calibre *m* RRHH *del personal* caliber (*AmE*), calibre (*BrE*)

calidad *f* COM GEN quality; ~ **aceptada** BOLSA *futuros en eurodólares* contract grade; ~ **del activo** FIN asset quality; ~ **de los activos** FIN quality of assets; ~ **de**

los beneficios FIN quality of earnings; ~ **casi de impresión alta** (*NLQ*) INFO near letter quality (*NLQ*); ~ **comercial** DER, V&M merchantable quality; ~ **del crédito** BANCA credit quality; ~ **de fabricación económica** IND economic manufacturing quality; ~ **de letra** INFO, MEDIOS letter quality (*LQ*); ~ **de la mano de obra** ECON, RRHH quality of the labor force (*AmE*), quality of the labour force (*BrE*); ~ **normal** IND, RRHH basic grade; ~ **regular** COM GEN fair average quality (*f.a.q.*); ~ **total** GES, IND total quality; ~ **de vida** ECON, PROT SOC quality of life; ~ **de vida en el trabajo** ECON, PROT SOC, RRHH quality of working life (*QWL*); ♦ **de poca** ~ COM GEN third-rate; **de** ~ **aceptable** COM GEN of acceptable quality; **en** ~ **de asesor** COM GEN in an advisory capacity

calificación *f* COM GEN qualification, RRHH banding, *diploma académico o cualificación profesional* qualification; ~ **de inversión de Moody** FIN Moody's investment grade (*AmE*); ~ **de méritos** COM GEN, RRHH merit rating; ~ **mínima** RRHH *requerido en un examen* minimum grade; ~ **del personal** RRHH personnel rating; ~ **de proveedores** COM GEN vendor rating; ~ **por puntos** COM GEN points rating; ~ **del servicio** RRHH *empleo* service qualification; ~ **de solvencia** BANCA, FIN credit score; ~ **triple A** BOLSA triple-A rating

calificar *vt* COM GEN, RRHH qualify; ♦ ~ **a alguien para hacer** RRHH qualify sb to do

calificatorio *adj* COM GEN, RRHH qualifying

caligrafía *f* MEDIOS, V&M calligraphy

calle *f* (*cl*) COM GEN street (*St.*); ~ **céntrica y comercial** V&M high street (*BrE*), main street (*AmE*); ~ **comercial** COM GEN shopping street; ~ **mayor** V&M high street (*BrE*), main street (*AmE*); ~ **principal** V&M high street (*BrE*), main street (*AmE*)

callejón: ~ **sin salida** *m* COM GEN impasse, INMOB cul-de-sac

calma *f* COM GEN lull

calumnia *f* COM GEN, DER calumniation, calumny

calumniar *vi* COM GEN, DER calumniate

calumnioso *adj* DER slanderous

calzada *f* TRANSP carriageway

calzo *m* TRANSP wedge

CAM *abr* (*fabricación asistida por computador AmL, fabricación asistida por computadora AmL, fabricación asistida por ordenador Esp*) IND, INFO CAM (*computer-aided manufacturing*)

cámara *f* DER, POL *reuniones, juicios* chamber; ~ **de abogados** DER barristers' chambers (*BrE*); ~ **acorazada** BANCA bank vault, strong room; ~ **de comercio** BANCA trading room; ~ **de compensación** BANCA clearing house, BOLSA clearing house, general clearing member (*GCM*), ECON, FIN clearing house; ~ **de compensación de IATA** TRANSP IATA clearing house; ~ **de compensación internacional** BANCA international clearing house; ~ **de compensación de valores bursátiles** BOLSA stock exchange clearing house; ~ **de esclusas** TRANSP lock-chamber; ~ **lenta** BANCA slow motion safe; ~ **de movimiento ocular** V&M eye-movement camera; ~ **de observación ocular** V&M eye-observation camera; ~ **rápida** V&M accelerated motion

Cámara *f* BOLSA ≈ house (*infrml*); ~ **Alta** *Esp* POL ≈ House of Lords (*BrE*) (*HL*), ≈ The Senate (*AmE*); ~ **Baja** *Esp* POL ≈ House of Commons (*BrE*) (*HC*), ≈ House of Representatives (*AmE*); ~ **de Comercio** COM GEN, ECON, IMP/EXP Chamber of Commerce; ~ **de Comercio Americana** COM GEN, IND American Board of Trade (*ABT*), American Chamber of Commerce (*ACC*); ~ **de Comercio Anglo-Canadiense** ECON Canada-United Kingdom Chamber of Commerce (*CUKCC*); ~ **de Comercio Británico-Americana** ECON British American Chamber of Commerce; ~ **de Comercio Canadiense** ECON Canadian Chamber of Commerce (*CCC*); ~ **de Comercio Española** COM GEN Spanish Chamber of Commerce (*SCC*); ~ **de Comercio e Industria** (*CCI*) ECON, IND Chamber of Commerce and Industry (*CCI*); ~ **de Comercio Internacional** ECON International Chamber of Commerce (*ICC*); ~ **de Compensación Automatizada** BANCA, FIN Automated Clearing House (*ACH*); ~ **de Compensación Autorizada** BANCA Recognized Clearing House (*RCH*); ~ **de Compensación de Eurobonos** BOLSA Euroclear; ~ **de Compensación y Liquidación** BOLSA Spanish association for payment clearing services; ~ **de Compensación de Productos Internacionales** BOLSA International Commodities Clearing House (*ICCH*); ~ **Internacional de Comercio** COM GEN International Chamber of Commerce; ~ **Internacional de Comercio Marítimo** IND International Chamber of Shipping (*ICS*); ~ **Sindical de Agentes de Comercio** COM GEN, ECON, IMP/EXP ≈ Stock Exchange Committee; ~ **de Turismo** OCIO Tourist Board (*BrE*)

camarera *f* COM GEN, RRHH waitress

camarero *m* BOLSA waiter (*BrE*), COM GEN, RRHH waiter

camarote: ~ **para uno** *m* TRANSP single-berth cabin; ~ **para cuatro** *m* TRANSP four-berth cabin; ~ **de dos literas** *m* TRANSP two-berth cabin

cambiar 1. *vt* COM GEN change, exchange, *viejo modelo por el nuevo* trade in; ♦ ~ **materias primas por bienes manufacturados** COM GEN trade raw materials for manufactured goods; ~ **la producción** IND switch production; **2.** *vi* COM GEN change, switch, switch over; ♦ ~ **al sistema métrico** COM GEN go metric, metricate; ~ **de destinatario** TRANSP reconsign; ~ **de dueño** COM GEN, V&M change hands; ~ **de imagen** V&M re-image; ~ **a matricial** COM GEN go matrix (*jarg*); ~ **a mejor** FIN turn around; ~ **de partido** POL defect

cambiarse *vi* COM GEN change

cambio *m* BOLSA swop, amendment, COM GEN *moneda* small change, *de precio* change, shift, switchover, exchange, ECON change, FISC amendment, INFO change, POL *a izquierda o derecha* swing, RRHH *de trabajo* substitution; ~ **al contado** COM GEN spot price; ~ **base** COM GEN fixing; ~ **de categoría** RRHH grade drift; ~ **de comandante** TRANSP *aviación* master change (*MC*); ~ **completo** COM GEN turnabout; ~ **completo corporativo** COM GEN corporate turnaround; ~ **completo en la distribución** COM GEN delivery turnround; ~ **de consignatario** TRANSP rerouting; ~ **contable** CONT accounting change; ~ **de control** COM GEN control change; ~ **para descuento** ECON *internacional* discount forex; ~ **desfavorable** COM GEN unfavourable exchange (*BrE*), unfavorable exchange (*AmE*); ~ **de dirección** COMS change of address; ~ **de empleo** RRHH labor shedding (*AmE*), labour shedding (*BrE*); ~ **estacional** COM GEN seasonal swing; ~ **estructural** GES structural change; ~ **extranjero** BANCA, BOLSA, ECON, FIN foreign exchange (*forex*); ~ **favorable** BOLSA favourable

exchange (*BrE*), favorable exchange (*AmE*); ~ **fijo**
ECON, FIN fixed exchange rate, pegged exchange rate;
~ **flotante** COM GEN floating exchange; ~ **interior** COM
GEN domestic exchange; ~ **irregular** BOLSA anomaly
switch; ~ **de liquidación** COM GEN close-out price;
~ **mínimo en el precio** BOLSA minimum price change;
~ **de moneda a la par** *f* BANCA, ECON mint par of
exchange; ~ **de motor** TRANSP engine transplant;
~ **oficial** BANCA official rate; ~ **organizacional** GES
organizational change; ~ **de página** INFO page break;
~ **a la par** BOLSA par trading; ~ **a plazo** COM GEN
forward price, forward rate, ECON, FIN forward rate;
~ **político** *f* COM GEN, POL political change;
~ **porcentual** COM GEN percentage change; ~ **de
posición** FIN switching, turnaround (*AmE*), turnround
(*BrE*); ~ **de una posición** BOLSA *opciones* rolling in; ~ **a
una posición más alta** BOLSA *opciones* rolling up; ~ **a
una posición más baja** BOLSA *opciones* rolling down;
~ **de precios** BOLSA *de futuros* price change; ~ **de
propietario** ECON under new ownership; ~ **de rescate**
ECON *UE* buying-in price; ~ **en el riesgo** COM GEN
change in the risk; ~ **sobrante** COM GEN odd change;
~ **tecnológico** ECON, SEG technological change; ~ **de
tendencia** COM GEN change in the tendency; ~ **del tipo
de interés** ECON interest rate movement; ~ **de turno**
RRHH relief shift, swing shift; ~ **de venta** COM GEN
selling rate; ~ **a la vista** COM GEN demand rate; ◆ **a** ~
CONT in exchange; **a** ~ **de** COM GEN in return for; **sobre
el** ~ BOLSA *acciones*, FIN at a premium; ~ **para mejor**
COM GEN turn for the better; ~ **para peor** COM GEN turn
for the worse

cambios: ~ **cotizados después de la sesión oficial** *m pl*
BOLSA street price; ~ **de divisas** *m pl* BOLSA cambistry;
~ **fijos** *m pl* ECON, FIN *internacional* pegged rate of
exchange; ~ **flotantes** *m pl* ECON floating exchange
rate; ~ **en niveles de precios** *m pl* COM GEN price level
changes

cambista *mf* BANCA, BOLSA, FIN arbitrageur, foreign
exchange dealer; ~ **de divisas** BOLSA arbitrageur,
cambist

camino *m* COM GEN, INFO path; ~ **crítico** GES *planificación* critical path; ~ **de servicio** TRANSP
accommodation road

camión *m* TRANSP lorry (*BrE*), truck (*AmE*);
~ **basculante** TRANSP tipper; ~ **cisterna** TRANSP tank
lorry (*BrE*), tank truck (*AmE*), tanker lorry (*BrE*);
~ **cuba** TRANSP tank lorry (*BrE*), tank truck (*AmE*);
~ **para ganado** TRANSP cattle lorry (*BrE*), cattle truck
(*AmE*); ~ **gigante** TRANSP juggernaut; ~ **de mudanza**
TRANSP removal van; ~ **de plataformas** TRANSP *manejo
de cargas* pallet lorry (*BrE*), pallet truck (*AmE*);
~ **refrigerado** TRANSP refrigerated lorry (*BrE*), refrigerated truck (*AmE*); ~ **remolcador** TRANSP box trailer;
~ **de soporte de rodillos** TRANSP *camión* roller bed
lorry (*BrE*), roller bed truck (*AmE*); ~ **de tara** COM GEN
trailer unladen weight; ~ **de trinquinal** *Esp* (*cf cargador
de caballete AmL*) TRANSP straddle carrier

camionaje *m* TRANSP cartage

camionero, -a *m,f* TRANSP lorry driver (*BrE*), teamster
(*AmE*)

camisa *f* MEDIOS jacket

campaña *f* COM GEN, POL, V&M campaign; ~ **alcista**
BOLSA bull campaign; ~ **bajista** BOLSA bear campaign;
~ **en la calle principal** POL mainstreeting;
~ **corporativa** V&M corporate campaign; ~ **electoral**
POL election campaign; ~ **de limpieza** MED AMB cleanup
campaign; ~ **nacional** V&M national campaign; ~ **de
prensa** MEDIOS press campaign; ~ **preseleccionada**
V&M preselected campaign; ~ **de productividad** IND,
V&M productivity campaign, productivity drive;
~ **promocional** V&M promotional exercise;
~ **publicitaria** MEDIOS, V&M advertising campaign;
~ **publicitaria de intriga** V&M teaser campaign; ~ **de
saturación** V&M burst campaign, *publicidad* saturation
campaign; ~ **de ventas** V&M sales campaign

campesino, -a *m,f* COM GEN, RRHH farmer, farmhand

campo *m* COM GEN, IND, INFO area, field; ~ **de actividad**
COM GEN, IND, RRHH sphere of activity; ~ **de
almacenamiento** INFO storage field; ~ **comercial
nuevo** COM GEN fledgling commercial field; ~ **de
datos** INFO data field; ~ **de dirección** INFO address
field; ~ **de identificación** INFO tag; ~ **de operación**
INFO operation field; ~ **petrolífero** IND oil field; ~ **de
referencia** INFO target field; ~ **técnico** PATENT technical field; ◆ **en un** ~ **limitado** COM GEN in a limited
sphere

canal *m* COM GEN, INFO, MEDIOS channel, TRANSP canal;
~ **de acceso** TRANSP fairway; ~ **analógico** INFO analog
channel; ~ **comercial** COM GEN trade channel;
~ **comercial de televisión** MEDIOS commercial television channel; ~ **de comercialización** COM GEN, V&M
distribution channel, marketing channel; ~ **de
comunicación** COM GEN, COMS, V&M channel of
communication; ~ **de comunicaciones de marketing**
V&M marketing communications channel; ~ **de
correspondencia** ECON, FIN bus mailing; ~ **de
distribución** IMP/EXP, TRANSP, V&M channel of distribution; ~ **con esclusas** TRANSP locked canal; ~ **de
información** INFO information channel; ~ **marítimo**
TRANSP maritime canal; ~ **de pedidos** V&M channel
for orders; ~ **probabilístico** INFO random channel;
~ **publicitario** MEDIOS, V&M advertising channel; ~ **de
retorno** INFO reverse channel; ~ **selector** INFO selector
channel; ~ **único** RRHH single channel (*BrE*); ~ **de
ventas** V&M channel of sales

canales: ~ **de abreacción** *m pl* GES, RRHH abreaction
channels; ~ **de comunicación** *m pl* COMS channels of
communication; ~ **de expresión** *m pl* GES, RRHH
abreaction channels

canalizar *vt* COM GEN funnel; ◆ ~ **algo debidamente**
COM GEN put sth through the proper channels;
~ **debidamente** COM GEN go through the proper
channels; ~ **hacia** COM GEN *fondos hacia un proyecto*,
FIN channel into; ~ **a través de** COM GEN channel
through

canasta: ~ **de dinero** *f* FIN basket of rates; ~ **de
monedas** *f* FIN basket of currencies

cancelación *f* COM GEN *de pedido* cancellation, *de
contrato* annulment, CONT write-off, INFO abort; ~ **de
compromiso** CONT decommitment; ~ **de la deuda** FIN
debt forgiveness; ~ **de una deuda** COM GEN, CONT
deletion of a debt; ~ **de una hipoteca** BANCA discharge
of mortgage; ~ **de la inscripción** FISC *IVA* cancellation
of registration; ~ **de orden de saldo** BOLSA balance
order settlement; ~ **de un pagaré** BANCA redemption of
a promissory note; ~ **parcial** COM GEN, DER, PATENT
part-cancellation (*BrE*); ~ **de préstamo** BANCA loan
write-off; ~ **de tarea** COM GEN task closure; ~ **de títulos**
BOLSA securities cancellation; ~ **total** FIN write-off

Cancelación: ~ **de Fontainebleau** *f* ECON Fontainebleau abatement

cancelar *vt* COM GEN *deuda* pay off, cancel, override, annul, CONT charge off, mark off, *partida contable* write off, DER annul, ECON *agrícola* cancel, annul, FIN annul, INFO cancel, abort, TRANSP expunge; ♦ ~ **una hipoteca** BANCA pay off a mortgage; ~ **inmediatamente** BOLSA fill-or-kill (*AmE*) (*FOK*); ~ **opciones** BOLSA, COM GEN, DER, V&M call away options, cancel options

cancillería *f* DER chancery

candidato, -a *m,f* DER, POL, RRHH candidate; ~ **añadido(-a) a la lista oficial** POL write-in candidate; ~ **cautivo(-a)** POL captive candidate; ~ **propuesto(-a)** COM GEN nominee; ~ **a la vicepresidencia** POL running mate (*AmE*)

candidatos: ~ **divididos** *m pl* POL split ticket (*AmE*)

candidatura *f* DER candidature, candidacy, POL slate (*AmE*), candidature, candidacy, RRHH candidature, candidacy

canje: ~ **de activos** *m* BANCA asset swop; ~ **de bonos** *m* BOLSA bond switch; ~ **de deuda por títulos** *m* FIN debt-for-equity swop; ~ **de deuda/títulos** *m* FIN debt-equity swop

canjeabilidad *f* BANCA, FIN convertibility

canjeable *adj* BANCA, FIN cashable

canon *m* COM GEN royalty, royalties; ~ **sin gastos** BOLSA free ride (*infrml*)

cantidad *f* (*ctdad*) COM GEN quantity (*qnty, qty*), CONT volume (*vol.*), *de bienes* amount (*amt*); ~ **acumulativa imputada** FISC cumulative imputed amount; ~ **adeudada** COM GEN amount due; ~ **amortizable** CONT depreciable amount; ~ **aplazada** FISC deferred amount; ~ **apostada** COM GEN wager; ~ **asegurada** ECON assured capital, FISC amount secured, SEG assured capital; ~ **asegurada mediante una carga sobre la propiedad** FIN amount secured by a charge upon property; ~ **base** FISC base amount; ~ **básica** COM GEN basic amount; ~ **cargada** COM GEN amount charged; ~ **combinada** FISC combined amount; ~ **compensatoria monetaria negativa** FIN negative monetary compensatory amount; ~ **compensatoria monetaria positiva** FIN positive monetary compensatory amount; ~ **para cubrir gastos** IND break-even quantity; ~ **a demostrar** SEG amount to be made good; ~ **depositada en garantía** COM GEN, DER caution money; ~ **en descubierto** BANCA overdrawn amount, uncovered amount; ~ **desembolsada** CONT amount paid out; ~ **designada** FISC designated amount; ~ **detallada** COM GEN sum at length; ~ **económica por lotes** ECON economic batch quantity; ~ **de equilibrio** ECON equilibrium quantity; ~ **específica** COM GEN specific amount; ~ **estimada** COM GEN estimated amount; ~ **en exceso** COM GEN, FISC excess amount; ~ **exenta** FISC exempted sum; ~ **eximida** FISC exempted sum; ~ **exportada** COM GEN amount exported; ~ **de fabricación económica** *m* ECON, GES, IND economic manufacturing quantity; ~ **general** COM GEN blanket amount; ~ **importante de obligaciones** BOLSA active bond crowd; ~ **importante de títulos a interés fijo** BOLSA active bond crowd; ~ **inactiva** BOLSA broken amount; ~ **ingresada en una cuenta** BANCA amount credited to an account; ~ **inicial** COM GEN initial quantity; ~ **por invertir** BANCA amount to be invested; ~ **llevada a cuenta nueva** CONT amount carried forward; ~ **media** COM GEN average amount, FISC

median amount; ~ **media acumulada** FISC accumulated averaging amount; ~ **media en depósito** SEG mean amount on deposit; ~ **mínima** FISC minimum amount; ~ **mínima perceptible** FISC threshold amount; ~ **monetaria compensatoria** FIN monetary compensation amount (*MCA*); ~ **no pagada al vencimiento** BANCA, CONT amount overdue; ~ **de orden económico** ECON, MAT economic order quantity (*EOQ*); ~ **pagada** COM GEN amount paid; ~ **pagada de más** COM GEN amount overpaid; ~ **pagada de menos** BANCA, CONT, FIN amount underpaid; ~ **pagada a plazos** FISC amount paid by instalments (*BrE*), amount paid by installments (*AmE*); ~ **pagadera** FISC amount payable; ~ **a pagar** COM GEN amount due; ~ **de paridad** GES break-even quantity; ~ **de pedido** COM GEN, V&M order quantity; ~ **pendiente** BANCA, CONT, FIN amount outstanding; ~ **permitida** IMP/EXP permitted quantity; ~ **predeterminada** COM GEN denominated quantity; ~ **principal ajustada** FISC adjusted principal amount; ~ **promediada** FISC averaging amount; ~ **de punto muerto** ECON break-even quantity; ~ **real** CONT *desembolso, gasto* actual amount; ~ **reembolsable** CONT amount repayable; ~ **de trabajo** GES, RRHH workload; ~ **para vivienda** RRHH residential amount; ♦ **esta ~ no figura en las cuentas** CONT this sum does not appear in the accounts

cantidades[1]: ~ **periódicas** *f pl* FISC periodic amounts

cantidades[2]: **en grandes ~** *fra* COM GEN in large quantities

cantina: ~ **de la empresa** *f* RRHH work canteen

cantón *m* POL canton

capa *f* INFO *sistema de circuitos* layer; ~ **de ozono** MED AMB ozone layer

capacidad *f* COM GEN ability, capability, capacity, CONT qualification, ECON *producción* ability, capability, capacity, IND capacity, RRHH *del personal* caliber (*AmE*), calibre (*BrE*), *profesional* capacity; ~ **de absorción** BOLSA *mercado de valores* absorbing capacity, ECON absorptive capacity; ~ **de almacenamiento** COM GEN storage capacity; ~ **de almacenamiento de información** INFO information storage capacity; ~ **de ampliación** COM GEN extensibility; ~ **aprovechada** BANCA, ECON, FIN, IND utilized capacity; ~ **asesora** RRHH advisory capacity; ~ **de beneficio** COM GEN earning power; ~ **de cálculo** INFO computing power; ~ **de canal** BANCA, COM GEN, ECON, IND channel capacity; ~ **de carga** ECON *población* carrying capacity, TRANSP cargo capacity (*CC*), deadweight capacity (*dwc*); ~ **competitiva** COM GEN, V&M competitive power, competitiveness; ~ **contributiva** BANCA, COM GEN, ECON, FISC taxpaying ability; ~ **crediticia** BANCA, FIN creditworthiness; ~ **de crédito** BANCA lending power; ~ **de crédito comercial** BANCA commercial lending power; ~ **cúbica** COM GEN cubic capacity (*cc*); ~ **cúbica del buque** TRANSP ship's cubic capacity; ~ **distributiva** TRANSP distributive ability; ~ **económica** BANCA, COM GEN, CONT, ECON economic capacity; ~ **empresarial** COM GEN, GES entrepreneurship; ~ **de endeudamiento** COM GEN borrowing power; ~ **excedente** ECON, IND excess capacity, spare capacity, surplus capacity; ~ **exportadora** BANCA, COM GEN, ECON, IMP/EXP export capacity; ~ **de fabricación** IND manufacturing capacity; ~ **financiera** BANCA financial strength, FIN financial capacity, *of firm* financial standing; ~ **fiscal** FISC taxing capacity; ~ **de gasto discrecional** ECON *del* gobierno, POL discretionary spending power; ~ **para graneles** TRANSP bulk capacity; ~ **ideal** ECON ideal capacity; ~ **importadora** BANCA, COM GEN, ECON, IMP/EXP import capacity; ~ **impositiva** BANCA, COM GEN, ECON, FISC taxpaying ability; ~ **máxima** IND maximum capacity; ~ **máxima de carga** TRANSP deadweight cargo capacity (*dwcc*); ~ **máxima práctica** ECON maximum practical capacity; ~ **de memoria** INFO storage capacity, memory capacity; ~ **de la memoria de núcleos** INFO core size; ~ **normal** ECON, IND normal capacity; ~ **de obtención de ingresos** COM GEN earning power; ~ **ociosa** ECON, SEG idle capacity; ~ **de operar con un ordenador** INFO computer literacy; ~ **operativa** ECON operating capacity; ~ **de opinión** FIN qualification of opinion; ~ **óptima** ECON, IND optimum capacity; ~ **de pago** BANCA ability to repay, DER, FISC, RRHH ability to pay; ~ **de pasajeros** *m* TRANSP passenger tonnage; ~ **de penetración** V&M capacity of penetration; ~ **planeada** ECON, IND planned capacity; ~ **planificada** ECON, IND planned capacity; ~ **de planta** COM GEN, IND, SEG plant capacity; ~ **práctica** ECON practical capacity; ~ **de producción** IND, SEG production capacity; ~ **profesional** RRHH job skills; ~ **para el puesto** RRHH job competence; ~ **real estimada** ECON expected actual capacity; ~ **de refrigeración** TRANSP refrigerated capacity; ~ **de la ruta** TRANSP route capacity; ~ **sobrante** ECON, IND spare capacity; ~ **subutilizada** BANCA, COM GEN, ECON, IND underemployed capacity; ~ **teórica** COM GEN theoretical capacity; ~ **termoaislada** TRANSP insulated capacity; ~ **de transporte** TRANSP carrying capacity; ~ **de tributación** FISC taxation capacity; ~ **tributaria** ECON, FISC taxable capacity; ~ **única** BOLSA single capacity; ~ **utilizada** BANCA, ECON, FIN, IND utilized capacity, capacity utilization; ◆ **a plena ~** COM GEN at full capacity

capacitación *f* AmL (*cf formación Esp*) RRHH training; ~ **en análisis parcial** AmL (*cf formación en análisis parcial Esp*) COM GEN, RRHH part-analysis training; ~ **analítica** AmL (*cf formación analítica Esp*) GES, RRHH analytical training; ~ **asertiva** AmL (*cf formación asertiva Esp*) PROT SOC, RRHH assertiveness training; ~ **de capacitadores** AmL (*cf formación de formadores Esp*) RRHH training of trainers; ~ **complementaria** AmL (*cf formación complementaria Esp*) RRHH booster training; ~ **por computador** AmL *ver capacitación por computadora AmL*; ~ **por computadora** AmL (*cf formación por ordenador Esp*) RRHH computer-based training; ~ **dentro de la empresa** AmL (*cf formación dentro de la empresa Esp*) IND, RRHH in-house training, training within industry (*TWI*); ~ **ejecutiva** AmL (*cf formación ejecutiva Esp*) GES, RRHH executive training; ~ **de ejecutivos** AmL (*cf formación de ejecutivos Esp*) GES, RRHH executive training; ~ **en la empresa** AmL (*cf formación en la empresa Esp*) IND, RRHH on-the-job training; ~ **de entrenadores** AmL (*cf formación de entrenadores Esp*) RRHH training of trainers; ~ **específica** AmL (*cf formación específica Esp*) RRHH specific training; ~ **fuera del puesto de trabajo** AmL (*cf formación fuera del puesto de trabajo Esp*) IND, RRHH off-the-job training (*BrE*); ~ **general** AmL (*cf formación general Esp*) RRHH general training; ~ **gerencial** AmL (*cf formación gerencial Esp*) GES, RRHH management training; ~ **grupal** AmL (*cf formación grupal Esp*) RRHH group training; ~ **industrial** AmL (*cf formación industrial Esp*) IND, RRHH industrial training; ~ **de**

instructores AmL (*cf formación de instructores Esp*) RRHH training of trainers; ~ **interna** AmL (*cf formación interna Esp*) IND, RRHH in-company training, in-house training; ~ **de mandos** AmL (*cf formación de mandos Esp*) GES, RRHH management training; ~ **en multimedia** AmL (*cf formación en multimedia Esp*) RRHH multimedia training; ~ **ocupacional** AmL (*cf formación ocupacional Esp*) PROT SOC, RRHH employment training (*BrE*) (*ET*); ~ **de personal** AmL (*cf formación de personal Esp*) GES, RRHH staff training; ~ **de precios** AmL (*cf formación de preciosEsp*) COM GEN, ECON, V&M price determination; ~ **profesional** AmL (*cf formación profesional Esp*) PROT SOC, RRHH vocational rehabilitation, vocational training; ~ **profesional en la empresa** AmL (*cf formación profesional en la empresa Esp*) IND, RRHH on-the-job training; ~ **profesional permanente** AmL (*cf formación profesional permanente Esp*) RRHH continual professional education; ~ **en la propia fábrica** AmL (*cf formación en la propia fábrica Esp*) IND, RRHH in-plant training; ~ **en el puesto de trabajo** AmL (*cf formación en el puesto de trabajo Esp*) RRHH job training, in-service training; ~ **de sensibilidad** (*cf formación de sensibilidad Esp*) COM GEN, GES, RRHH sensitivity training; ~ **superior** AmL (*cf formación superior Esp*) RRHH advanced training; ~ **en el trabajo** AmL (*cf formación en el trabajo Esp*) IND, RRHH in-service training; ◆ **con una ~ adecuada** AmL (*cf con una formación adecuada Esp*) RRHH well-educated

capacitado *adj* BANCA eligible; ~ **para trabajar** RRHH employable

capacitador, a *m,f* AmL (*cf formador Esp*) RRHH training officer

capacitar *vt* AmL (*cf formar Esp*) RRHH train

capataz, a *m,f* INMOB, RRHH overseer, charge hand, foreman; ~ **a pie de obra** RRHH site foreman

CAPE *abr* (*compra apalancada por ejecutivos*) FIN, GES LMBO (*leveraged management buy-out*)

capear: ~ **la recesión** *vt* ECON weather the recession

capillas *f pl* MEDIOS proofs

capirón *m* TRANSP *carga* gypsy

capitación *f* ECON capitation, FISC poll tax (*obs*) (*BrE*), capitation

capital *m* COM GEN, CONT, ECON, FIN assets, stocks (*stcks, stks*), capital; ~ **accionario** COM GEN share capital; ~ **accionario autorizado** CONT, ECON, FIN authorized share capital; ~ **accionario vertical** ECON vertical equity; ~ **en acciones** *f* COM GEN share capital; ~ **en acciones diferidas** BOLSA deferred stock; ~ **de acciones emitidas** FIN issued share capital; ~ **de los accionistas** COM GEN shareholder's equity; ~ **activo** FIN active capital; ~ **adicional desembolsado** Esp (*cf capital adicional integrado AmL*) CONT additional paid-in capital (*AmE*), additional paid-up capital (*BrE*); ~ **adicional integrado** AmL (*cf capital adicional desembolsado BrE*) CONT additional paid-in capital (*AmE*), additional paid-up capital (*BrE*); ~ **ajeno a la sociedad** BANCA borrowed capital; ~ **amortizado** COM GEN, CONT, ECON, FIN amortized capital, sunk capital; ~ **aportado** BOLSA contributed capital; ~ **aportado que excede el valor nominal** BOLSA, CONT capital contributed in excess of par value; ~ **de arranque** FIN start-up capital; ~ **asegurado** ECON, SEG assured capital; ~ **autorizado** CONT, ECON, FIN authorized capital, authorized share capital; ~ **de ayuda** ECON *desarrollo*,

POL capital aid; ~ **con bajo apalancamiento** FIN low-geared capital; ~ **bancario** BANCA bank capital; ~ **base** ECON, FIN base capital; ~ **de base consolidado** COM GEN consolidated base capital; ~ **bloqueado** COM GEN, CONT, ECON, FIN frozen capital; ~ **circulante** BANCA, COM GEN, ECON, FIN circulating capital, working capital; ~ **circulante negativo** CONT negative working capital; ~ **circulante neto** CONT net working capital; ~ **constante** ECON constant capital; ~ **constituido por tierras** COM GEN natural capital; ~ **constituido por valores mobiliarios** COM GEN, CONT, ECON, FIN property capital; ~ **contable** COM GEN shareholder's equity; ~ **contable de la participación** BANCA equity value; ~ **de la contraparte** FIN counterparty capital; ~ **a corto plazo** COM GEN, CONT, ECON, FIN short-term capital; ~ **cubierto** BANCA capital cover, BOLSA, FIN paid-in capital; ~ **declarado** COM GEN stated capital; ~ **desembolsado** BOLSA, FIN paid-out capital, paid-up capital; ~ **desvalorizado** COM GEN, CONT, ECON, FIN diluted capital, watered capital; ~ **emitido** BOLSA issued capital; ~ **de empréstito** BANCA loan capital, COM GEN debt capital, CONT, ECON, FIN loan capital; ~ **errante** FIN refugee capital; ~ **de especulación** *f* BANCA, COM GEN, ECON, FIN risk-bearing capital; ~ **especulativo** ECON hot money; ~ **establecido** COM GEN stated capital; ~ **exigible** FIN due capital; ~ **de explotación** CONT, ECON, FIN operating capital, working capital; ~ **expuesto al riesgo** BOLSA position-risk capital; ~ **externo** COM GEN, CONT, ECON, FIN foreign capital; ~ **fiado** BOLSA pawned stock; ~ **ficticio** BOLSA, FIN fictitious capital, phantom capital; ~ **fijo** CONT, FIN fixed assets, fixed capital, tied-up capital; ~ **financiero** FIN financial capital; ~ **flotante** COM GEN, CONT, ECON, FIN floating capital; ~ **fugaz** COM GEN volatile capital; ~ **de garantía** COM GEN, CONT, ECON, FIN guarantee capital, guaranty capital; ~ **generador** FIN seed capital; ~ **humano** RRHH human capital; ~ **imponible** FISC taxable capital; ~ **improductivo** V&M dead stock; ~ **inactivo** COM GEN, CONT, ECON, FIN idle capital; ~ **inflado** COM GEN, CONT, ECON, FIN watered capital; ~ **para infraestructura social** FIN social overhead capital; ~ **inicial** BOLSA, FIN initial capital; ~ **inicial para lanzar un proyecto empresarial** *f* COM GEN, FIN front money; ~ **inmobiliario** COM GEN immovable capital; ~ **inmovilizado** CONT fixed capital, tied-up capital; ~ **de inversión** COM GEN, CONT, ECON, FIN investment capital; ~ **invertido** COM GEN, ECON, FIN invested capital; ~ **a largo plazo** COM GEN, CONT, ECON, FIN long-term capital; ~ **legal** COM GEN, CONT, ECON, FIN legal capital; ~ **libre de cargas** COM GEN, CONT, ECON, FIN unimpaired capital; ~ **libre de gravámenes** COM GEN, CONT, ECON, FIN unimpaired capital; ~ **libre de riesgo** FIN risk-avoiding capital; ~ **líquido** BOLSA liquid capital; ~ **maleable** COM GEN, CONT, ECON, FIN malleable capital, putty-clay, putty-putty (*infrml*); ~ **mobiliario** COM GEN freed-up capital; ~ **monopolista** BOLSA, ECON, FIN monopoly capital; ~ **de negocio** CONT business assets; ~ **neto** COM GEN, CONT, ECON, FIN capital net worth; ~ **neto de base** CONT net base capital; ~ **no desembolsado** COM GEN, CONT, ECON, FIN uncalled capital, unpaid capital; ~ **no distribuible** FIN undistributable capital; ~ **no emitido** BOLSA unissued capital; ~ **no respaldado por activo equivalente** FIN impaired capital; ~ **nominal** CONT nominal capital; ~ **nominal pagado** BOLSA nominal paid-up capital; ~ **en obligaciones** BANCA, BOLSA

debenture capital; ~ **de operación** CONT, ECON, FIN operating capital; ~ **original** FIN original capital; ~ **pagado que excede el valor nominal** CONT capital paid in excess of par value; ~ **pasivo** COM GEN, CONT, ECON, FIN capital liabilities; ~ **de un préstamo** BANCA principal; ~ **principal** ECON, FIN primary capital; ~ **privado** COM GEN, CONT, ECON, FIN private capital; ~ **productivo** ECON productive capital; ~ **del propietario** COM GEN, CONT, ECON, FIN owner's capital; ~ **propio** BOLSA, CONT net equity, capital stock (*AmE*), equity capital (*BrE*); ~ **redescontable acumulativo** FISC cumulative eligible capital; ~ **de reemplazos** FIN replacement capital; ~ **registrado** COM GEN registered capital; ~ **reinvertido** COM GEN, CONT, ECON, FIN moneyed capital; ~ **de renta fija** BOLSA bond capital; ~ **de reposiciones** FIN replacement capital; ~ **de reserva** COM GEN reserve capital; ~ **y reservas** CONT capital and reserves; ~ **retraído** COM GEN, CONT, ECON, FIN locked-in capital; ~ **de riesgo** BANCA, COM GEN, ECON, FIN risk capital, risk-bearing capital, venture capital; ~ **social** BOLSA stockholders' equity, ECON social capital; ~ **social en acciones** BOLSA, CONT capital stock (*AmE*), equity capital (*BrE*); ~ **social autorizado** BOLSA authorized capital stock; ~ **social emitido** CONT issued share capital; ~ **social exigido** CONT called-up share capital; ~ **social fijo** ECON overhead capital; ~ **suscrito** BOLSA subscribed capital; ~ **suscrito y no desembolsado** COM GEN uncalled capital; ~ **total asegurado por siniestro** SEG aggregate indemnity; ~ **totalmente desembolsado** COM GEN, CONT, ECON, FIN fully paid-up capital; ~ **de trabajo negativo** CONT negative working capital; ~ **en uso** CONT, FIN employed capital; ~ **usurario** CONT, ECON, FIN usurious capital; ~ **variable** FIN variable capital; ~ **vencido** CONT, ECON, FIN matured capital; ~ **a la vista** BANCA callable capital; ~ **volátil** COM GEN volatile capital; ◆ **~, activos, administración, ganancias, liquidez** FIN capital, assets, management, earnings, liquidity (*CAMEL*)

capitales: ~ **febriles** *m pl* BOLSA hot money

capitalismo *m* ECON, IND, POL capitalism; ~ **benevolente** ECON, IND benevolent capitalism, POL benevolent capitalism, caring capitalism; ~ **de competencia perfecta** ECON, IND, POL lemonade stand capitalism; ~ **de Estado** ECON, IND, POL state capitalism; ~ **industrial** ECON, IND, POL industrial capitalism; ~ **mercantil** ECON, IND, POL merchant capitalism; ~ **monopolista** ECON, IND, POL monopoly capitalism; ~ **periférico** ECON, IND, POL peripheral capitalism; ~ **personal** ECON, IND, POL personal capitalism; ~ **popular** ECON, IND, POL popular capitalism; ~ **puro** ECON, IND, POL pure capitalism; ~ **salvaje** ECON, IND, POL black capitalism; ~ **tardío** ECON, IND, POL black capitalism, late capitalism

capitalista[1] *adj* ECON, IND, POL capitalist, capitalistic

capitalista[2] *mf* COM GEN capitalist, contributor of capital; ~ **de riesgo** FIN venture capitalist

capitalización *f* COM GEN capital increase, capitalization; ~ **de los arrendamientos** CONT capitalization of leases; ~ **bursátil** BOLSA market capitalization; ~ **escasa** CONT thin capitalization; ~ **del impuesto** ECON, FISC tax capitalization; ~ **del interés** FIN capitalization of interest; ~ **de mercado** COM GEN market capitalization; ~ **del mercado de valores** BOLSA stock market capitalization; ~ **monetaria** BOLSA, COM GEN, CONT,

ECON, FIN money wealth capitalization; **~ de la renta** COM GEN capitalization of income; **~ total** FIN total capitalization

capitalizado *adj* COM GEN capitalized

capitalizar *vt* COM GEN capitalize, capitalize on, *interest* compound

capitán *m* RRHH, TRANSP captain, master; **~ de empresa** IND, RRHH captain of industry; **~ de puerto** RRHH harbour master (*BrE*)

capítulo *m* BANCA budget item, COM GEN *libro*, DER, MEDIOS chapter; **~ de gastos de funcionamiento** CONT *gobierno*, POL operating expenditure vote; **~ presupuestario de gastos de capital** *f* POL *gubernamental* capital expenditure vote; **~ presupuestario de gastos imprevistos del Consejo del Tesoro** POL Treasury Board contingencies vote; **~ presupuestario obligatorio** POL statutory vote

captación *f* MEDIOS pick-up, sound pick-up; **~ de capital** BANCA, FIN capital raising; **~ de datos** ECON, INFO data acquisition; **~ excesiva de fondos** BOLSA overfunding

captura: **~ de datos** *f* INFO data capture; **~ de datos en un solo país** *f* ADMIN single country data capture; **~ reguladora** *f* ECON regulatory capture; **~ total permitida** *f* MED AMB total allowable catches (*TACs*)

cara[1]**: de una ~** *adj* INFO single-sided

cara[2]**: a cara** *adv* COM GEN vis-à-vis

cara[3]**: ~ anterior desmontable** *f* TRANSP detachable front end; **~ posterior** *f* MEDIOS reverse

carácter[1]**: con ~ no consolidado** *adj* CONT on an unconsolidated basis; **sin ~ oficial** *adj* COM GEN, MEDIOS, POL off-the-record; **con ~ oficioso** *adj* COM GEN, MEDIOS, POL on-the-record

carácter[2] *m* COM GEN, INFO, V&M character; **~ alfanumérico** INFO alphanumeric character; **~ en blanco** INFO blank character; **~ de borrado** (*SUPR*) INFO delete character (*DEL*); **~ de cambio de código** INFO escape character; **~ condicional** BANCA conditionality; **~ de control** INFO check character; **~ ecológico** COM GEN, MED AMB ecological character; **~ de encuadramiento** INFO justification character, layout character; **~ gráfico** INFO graphic character; **~ ilegal** INFO illegal character; **~ en negrita** INFO bold-face character; **~ numérico** INFO, MAT numeric character; **~ de retroceso** INFO backspace character; **~ de tabulación** ADMIN, INFO tabulation character; **~ de verificación** *f* INFO control character

característica *f* INFO, PATENT distinctiveness, COM GEN feature; **~ adicional** PATENT, V&M additional feature; **~ especial** COM GEN, V&M special feature; **~ nueva** BOLSA wrinkle (*infrml*); **~ principal** COM GEN, PATENT, V&M essential feature

características: **~ del bono** *f pl* BOLSA bond features; **~ del puesto** *f pl* RRHH job characteristics

carate *m* AmL (*cf quilate Esp*) COM GEN carat

carátula *f* AmL (*cf carta de presentación Esp*) ADMIN, COM GEN, COMS covering letter

caravana *f* INMOB, OCIO caravan, mobile home

carbón *m* IND carbon, coal; **~ vegetal** IND, MED AMB charcoal

carboneras *f pl* TRANSP bunkers

carburante: **~ sin plomo** *m* MED AMB lead-free fuel

carecer *vi* COM GEN, V&M lack

carena *f* TRANSP bottom

carencia *f* COM GEN, V&M lack

careo *m* COM GEN, DER confrontation, meet

carestía *f* ECON shortage; **~ de liquidez** BANCA, CONT, FIN liquidity famine; **~ de recursos** CONT lapsing resources

carga *f* BOLSA load, COM GEN charge, encumbrance, freight (*frt*), CONT, ECON, FIN charge, FISC burden, IND charge, TRANSP cargo, freight (*frt*), loading (*ldg*), shipment; **~ adicional** CONT additional charge; **~ admisible sobre techo** TRANSP *contenedores* roof load; **~ aislada** TRANSP cargo in isolation; **~ almacenada en depósito** COM GEN, TRANSP bonded cargo; **~ de alta densidad** TRANSP high-density cargo; **~ automática** INFO autologin; **~ de baja densidad** TRANSP low density cargo; **~ por barcazas** TRANSP overside loading; **~ comercial** TRANSP commercial cargo; **~ completa** TRANSP container load; **~ concentrada** TRANSP assembly cargo; **~ convencional** TRANSP conventional cargo; **~ de cubierta** TRANSP deck cargo, deck load; **~ desarrumada** TRANSP break bulk cargo; **~ y descarga del equipaje** TRANSP baggage handling; **~ por desplazamiento** TRANSP displacement load; **~ de la deuda** ECON debt burden; **~ dispersiva** TRANSP scattershot; **~ y distribución** TRANSP loading and delivery (*ldg&dly*); **~ de entrada** IMP/EXP inward cargo; **~ explosiva** TRANSP burster; **~ extraviada** TRANSP missing cargo (*msca*); **~ familiar** FISC dependant; **~ financiera** BANCA finance charge, FIN financial burden; **~ fiscal** CONT, ECON, FISC fiscal burden, tax burden, tax charge; **~ fraccionada** TRANSP break bulk cargo; **~ general** TRANSP general merchandise; **~ a granel** TRANSP bulk cargo; **~ a granel seca** TRANSP dry bulk cargo; **~ de graneles líquidos** TRANSP wet bulk cargo; **~ heterogénea** TRANSP heterogeneous cargo; **~ homogénea** TRANSP homogeneous cargo; **~ impositiva** FISC burden of taxation; **~ incompleta del contenedor** TRANSP container partload; **~ indivisible** TRANSP indivisible load; **~ irregular indivisible** TRANSP abnormal indivisible load; **~ límite de rotura** TRANSP yield load; **~ de una máquina** IND machine load; **~ máxima** ECON peak-load pricing; **~ motorizada** TRANSP motor freight; **~ muy importante** TRANSP very important cargo (*VIC*); **~ no comercial** TRANSP noncommercial cargo; **~ no declarada** TRANSP unmanifested cargo; **~ parcial** TRANSP part load; **~ peligrosa** TRANSP dangerous cargo; **~ permanente** COM GEN dead load; **~ pesada** TRANSP heavy lift (*H/L, h/lift*); **~ de polución** MED AMB pollution charge; **~ posterior** TRANSP back load; **~ prepagada** IMP/EXP, TRANSP freight prepaid; **~ de la prueba** DER, RRHH burden of proof; **~ que sobrepasa la altura** TRANSP *en contenedores sin techo* overheight cargo; **~ real** DER, INMOB encumbrance; **~ rentable** TRANSP payload; **~ de reserva** BANCA reserve burden; **~ de retorno** TRANSP back load, return cargo (*r/c*), return load; **~ sin riesgo de trabajo** IND safe working load; **~ de rotura** TRANSP break weight; **~ seca** TRANSP dry cargo, dry freight; **~ sobre el suelo** TRANSP *barco* floor loading; **~ sujeta a derechos de aduana** IMP/EXP, TRANSP dutiable cargo; **~ a toda capacidad** IND full-capacity load; **~ de trabajo** RRHH workload; **~ unitaria** TRANSP unit load (*U*); **~ útil** TRANSP carrying capacity, payload; **~ útil real** TRANSP *peso neto* actual payload; **~ voluminosa** COM GEN bulky cargo; **♦ con ~** TRANSP under load; **libre de ~** TRANSP free in (*fi*); **exceptuando**

la ~ y descarga IMP/EXP, TRANSP exclusive of loading and unloading (*xl&ul*); **exclusivo de ~ y descarga** IMP/EXP, TRANSP exclusive of loading and unloading (*xl&ul*); **libre de ~ y descarga** IMP/EXP free in (*fi*); **la ~ de la prueba recae en la acusación** DER the burden of proof lies with the prosecution; **~ tóxica, explosiva, corrosiva, peligrosa** TRANSP toxic, explosive, corrosive, hazardous cargo (*TECH cargo*); **~ y valor declarados por el expedidor** TRANSP shipper's load and count

cargador, a *m,f* TRANSP shipper

cargador *m* TRANSP cartridge; **~ de caballete** *AmL* (*cf camión de trinquinal Esp*) TRANSP straddle carrier; **~ de cinta magnética** INFO tape cartridge; **~ elevado** TRANSP *vehículo* high loader

cargamento: **~ a granel** *m* TRANSP bulk shipment; **~ de ida** *m* IMP/EXP, TRANSP outward cargo; **~ ligero** *m* TRANSP light cargo; **~ no embarcado** *m* TRANSP shut out cargo; **~ peligroso** *m* TRANSP hazardous cargo; **~ pesado** *m* COM GEN, TRANSP deadweight cargo; **~ de peso muerto** *m* COM GEN, TRANSP deadweight cargo; **~ que no se ha podido embarcar en su totalidad** *m* TRANSP shut out cargo; **~ suelto** *m* TRANSP *carga a granel* loose cargo; **~ de vuelta** *m* TRANSP homeward cargo

cargar *vt* COM GEN *cuenta* debit, *honorarios* charge, *con deudas* burden, INFO *datos* upload, *programa* load, TRANSP load; ◆ **~ a** COM GEN *gastos* charge to; **~ un gasto a una cuenta** BANCA, FIN charge an expense to an account; **~ graneles** TRANSP laden in bulk; **~ instrucciones** INFO bootstrap; **~ interés** BANCA charge interest

cargas *f pl* CONT charges; **~ comerciales** CONT business charges; **~ extraordinarias** CONT extraordinary charges; **~ fijas** BANCA, CONT, FIN fixed charges; **~ sociales totales** CONT, POL, PROT SOC total social charges

cargo *m* COM GEN charge, fee; **~ adicional** ECON capacity charge; **~ al superávit** BANCA, CONT, FIN surplus charge; **~ al usuario** BANCA charge-back (*AmE*); **~ auxiliar** RRHH junior position; **~ del banco** BANCA bank charge; **~ binomial** ECON binomial charge; **~ por cobranza** COM GEN collection charge; **~ en concepto de intereses** FIN interest charge; **~ contingente** BANCA, CONT, FIN contingent charge; **~ por cuenta de custodia** BANCA custody account charge; **~ por custodia** BANCA custody charge; **~ por depreciación anual** CONT annual depreciation charge; **~ devengado** BANCA, CONT, FIN accrued charge; **~ por diferencia de cambios** BANCA exchange charge; **~ diferido** BANCA, CONT, FIN deferred charge; **~ directivo** GES, RRHH managerial position; **~ directo** BANCA direct debit (*DD*); **~ ejecutivo** GES, RRHH managerial position; **~ elegido** POL elected office; **~ por el empréstito** COM GEN borrowing fee; **~ por exceso de equipaje** OCIO, TRANSP excess baggage charge; **~ extraordinario** CONT extraordinary charge; **~ fijo** CONT fixed charge; **~ importante** RRHH important office; **~ de llamadas** COMS call charge; **~ de mantenimiento** BANCA maintenance fee; **~ por mantenimiento de la cuenta** BANCA account maintenance charge; **~ por el movimiento de la cuenta** BANCA account activity charge; **~ no recurrente** CONT nonrecurring charge; **~ por operaciones** BANCA, CONT, FIN operating charge; **~ por las operaciones en cuenta** BANCA account operation charge; **~ periódico** BANCA, CONT, FIN periodic charge; **~ del periodo** BANCA, CONT, FIN period charge; **~ previo** BANCA, CONT, FIN prior charge; **~ proporcionado** COM GEN *UE* commensurate charge; **~ recaudador** COM GEN collecting charge; **~ por renovación de patente** COM GEN, PATENT patent renewal fee; **~ por reservación** COM GEN reserve price; **~ del seguro** SEG insurance charge; **~ por servicio bancario** BANCA bank service charge; **~ por servicios** BANCA service charge; **~ variable** COM GEN variable charge (*VC*); **~ por ventas** BOLSA sales charge; ◆ **sin ~** COM GEN without charge (*w.c.*)

cargos *m pl* CONT charges; **~ por actividad** BANCA activity charges; **~ acumulados** BANCA accrued charges; **~ bancarios** BANCA, FIN bank charges, banking charges; **~ de la deuda** COM GEN debt charges; **~ de la deuda pública** FIN public debt charges; **~ estimados** BANCA, CONT, FIN estimated charges; **~ por flete, seguro y embarque** IMP/EXP, TRANSP freight, insurance and shipping charges (*FIS*); **~ por mantenimiento** BANCA standby charges; **~ de la PAC** ECON CAP charges; **~ por seguro de medidas preventivas** SEG sue and labor charges (*AmE*), sue and labour charges (*BrE*); **~ por tramitación** BANCA, COM GEN, CONT, FIN handling charges

carguero *m* TRANSP freighter; **~ de gas licuado de petróleo** TRANSP liquid petroleum gas carrier; **~ de graneles** TRANSP bulk carrier; **~ de mineral de fierro** *AmL* (*cf carguero de mineral de hierro Esp*) TRANSP iron ore carrier; **~ de mineral de hierro** *Esp* (*cf carguero de mineral de fierro AmL*) TRANSP iron ore carrier

carnet *m* COM GEN membership card; **~ de conducir** *Esp* (*cf licencia de conducir AmL*) ADMIN, TRANSP driver's licence (*BrE*), driver's license (*AmE*); **~ de conducir internacional** *Esp* (*cf licencia internacional AmL*) ADMIN, TRANSP international driver's licence (*BrE*), international driver's license (*AmE*), international driving permit

caro *adj* COM GEN costly, expensive, pricey (*infrml*)

carpeta *f* ADMIN folder; **~ de antecedentes** COM GEN case history

carrera: **en la ~ hacia** *f* POL *elecciones* in the run-up to; **~ de marea** *f* TRANSP tidal range

carrete[1]: **con ~ colocado** *adj* MEDIOS, V&M reel-fed

carrete[2] *m* INFO, MEDIOS, V&M reel; **~ G** V&M *publicidad* G-spool

carretera *f* TRANSP road (*Rd.*); **~ de abundante tránsito** TRANSP major road; **~ de circunvalación** TRANSP ring road; **~ nacional** (*N*) TRANSP A-road (*BrE*) (*A*), highway (*AmE*), major road, trunk road (*BrE*); **~ principal** TRANSP trunk road (*BrE*), major road, highway (*AmE*)

carretilla *f* TRANSP dolly, *ferrocarril* bogie; **~ elevadora** TRANSP pallet fork; **~ de horquilla elevadora** TRANSP fork-lift truck (*FLT*)

carretón: **~ de mano** *m* TRANSP hand barrow

carril: **~ de tránsito** *m* TRANSP traffic lane

carrito *m* TRANSP trolley; **~ de la compra** COM GEN shopping trolley

carro: **~ para equipaje** *m* OCIO, TRANSP baggage trolley; **~ de equipajes** *m* OCIO, TRANSP baggage cart (*AmE*), luggage trolley (*BrE*); **~ de equipajes para uso de los pasajeros** *m* OCIO, TRANSP self-help passenger luggage trolley

carta *f* COMS letter; **~ abierta** ADMIN, BANCA, CONT open letter; **~ de aceptación** COM GEN letter of consent; **~ de adjudicación** BOLSA, COMS letter of allotment, FISC award letter; ~ **administrativa** ADMIN, BANCA, CONT administration letter; ~ **de agradecimiento** COM GEN thank-you letter; ~ **de amonestación** ADMIN, BANCA, CONT expostulatory letter; ~ **de apoyo** BANCA, FIN comfort letter; ~ **de asignación** COM GEN *a trabajo* letter of assignment, FIN allotment letter; ~ **de autorización** COM GEN letter of authority (*L/A*); ~ **de aviso** COMS advice note, letter of advice; ~ **blanca** BANCA, COM GEN, CONT carte-blanche, free play; ~ **certificada** ADMIN, BANCA, CONT registered letter; ~ **de cesión** COM GEN *de negocio* letter of assignment; ~ **circular** COMS mail shot, mailing shot; ~ **circular de información sobre valores** BOLSA market letter; ~ **de cobranza** ADMIN, BANCA, CONT dunning letter; ~ **de cobro** ADMIN, BANCA, CONT, FIN collection letter; ~ **comercial** COM GEN, COMS business letter; ~ **de compañía** ADMIN, COMS accompanying letter; ~ **de compromiso** BANCA, CONT, DER letter of undertaking; ~ **de confirmación** ADMIN, BANCA, CONT confirming letter; ~ **de contenido** COMS letter of content; ~ **de cooperación** COM GEN, COMS letter of cooperation; ~ **por correo aéreo** COMS airmail letter; ~ **credencial** RRHH credentials; ~ **de crédito** BANCA, FIN letter of credit (*L/C, l/c*); ~ **de crédito abierta** BANCA, FIN clean letter of credit; ~ **de crédito sin condiciones** BANCA, FIN open letter of credit; ~ **de crédito confirmada** BANCA, FIN confirmed letter of credit; ~ **de crédito confirmada e irrevocable** BANCA, FIN straight letter of credit; ~ **de crédito documentaria** BANCA, FIN documentary letter of credit; ~ **de crédito garantizada** BANCA, FIN guaranteed letter of credit; ~ **de crédito ilimitada** BANCA, FIN unrestricted letter of credit; ~ **de crédito para importación** BANCA, FIN, IMP/EXP import letter of credit; ~ **de crédito irrevocable** BANCA, FIN irrevocable letter of credit (*ILOC*); ~ **de crédito no confirmada** BANCA, FIN unconfirmed letter of credit; ~ **de crédito pagada por adelantado** BANCA, FIN prepaid letter of credit; ~ **de crédito a plazo** BANCA, FIN time letter of credit; ~ **de crédito renovable** BANCA, FIN revocable letter of credit, revolving letter of credit; ~ **de crédito sin restricción** BANCA, FIN unrestricted letter of credit; ~ **de crédito restringida** BANCA, FIN restricted letter of credit; ~ **de crédito simple** BANCA, FIN clean letter of credit; ~ **de crédito a la vista** BANCA, FIN sight letter of credit; ~ **de declaración** ADMIN, BANCA, CONT representation letter; ~ **defectuosa** V&M battered letter; ~ **de deficiencias** ADMIN, BANCA, CONT deficiency letter; ~ **de delegación** BANCA, COM GEN, CONT letter of delegation; ~ **de denuncia** ADMIN, BANCA, CONT informant letter; ~ **de depósito** BANCA, CONT, FIN letter of deposit; ~ **de despido** *Esp* (*cf boleta de despido AmL*) COMS, RRHH redundancy letter, pink slip (*AmE*); ~ **de dimisión** COMS, RRHH letter of resignation; ~ **de dirección** COM GEN letter of direction; ~ **de disculpas** COMS letter of apology; ~ **de embarque** TRANSP notice of shipment; ~ **de embarque del remitente** IMP/EXP, TRANSP forwarder's bill of lading; ~ **de envío** COMS transmittal letter; ~ **estándar** V&M standard letter; ~ **de exención** ADMIN, BANCA, CONT bill of sufferance; ~ **de expedición** TRANSP dispatch note; ~ **de exportador** BANCA, CONT, IMP/EXP exporter status; ~ **fiduciaria** BANCA, CONT, DER trust letter; ~ **franqueada** ADMIN, COMS franked letter; ~ **de garantía** BOLSA guarantee letter, COM GEN letter of commitment; ~ **de gracia** BANCA, DER letter of respite; ~ **de hipoteca** BANCA,

CONT, DER letter of hypothecation; ~ **de identificación** BANCA, COM GEN, CONT letter of indication; ~ **de indemnización** BANCA, COM GEN letter of indemnity (*L/I*); ~ **de insistencia** ADMIN, COM GEN, COMS follow-up letter; ~ **de instrucción del expedidor para la emisión de cartas de rutas aéreas** IMP/EXP, TRANSP shipper's letter of instruction for issuing air waybills; ~ **de instrucciones para emisión de conocimientos aéreos** IMP/EXP, TRANSP shipper's letter of instruction for issuing air waybills; ~ **de instrucciones del expedidor** IMP/EXP *envío*, TRANSP shipper's letter of instruction; ~ **de intención** COM GEN, GES letter of intent; ~ **de intenciones** BOLSA letter of intent, DER notice of intention; ~ **de introducción** COM GEN, COMS letter of introduction; ~ **de manifestaciones** ADMIN, BANCA, CONT representation letter; ~ **de moratoria** BANCA, CONT, DER letter of respite; ~ **no reclamada** COMS unclaimed letter; ~ **de nombramiento** RRHH letter of appointment; ~ **de organización** BANCA, CONT, GES organization chart; ~ **de pago** DER *confirmación* acquittance; ~ **de pedido** ADMIN, BANCA, CONT order letter; ~ **personalizada** V&M personalized letter; ~ **de pignoración** BANCA, CONT, DER letter of hypothecation; ~ **poder** BANCA, DER letter of attorney, proxy; ~ **de poder sobre acciones** BANCA, BOLSA stock power; ~**-poder para la venta de valores** BANCA, BOLSA stock power; ~ **de porte** IMP/EXP, TRANSP bill of freight, waybill (*WB*); ~ **de porte aéreo** IMP/EXP, TRANSP air bill of lading, air consignment note; ~ **de porte por carretera** TRANSP trucking bill of lading (*AmE*); ~ **de porte por ferrocarril** TRANSP railway bill of lading (*BrE*), railroad bill of lading (*AmE*); ~ **de presentación** *Esp* (*cf carátula AmL*) ADMIN, COM GEN, COMS covering letter; ~ **de reclamación** COM GEN letter of complaint; ~ **de recomendación** BANCA, FIN comfort letter, RRHH letter of recommendation; ~ **recordatoria** ADMIN, COM GEN, COMS follow-up letter; ~ **rehusada** COMS dead letter; ~ **de remisión** DER letter of transmittal; ~ **de renuncia** BOLSA letter of renunciation; ~ **de representación** ADMIN, BANCA, CONT representation letter; ~ **de respuesta** CONT writing-back; ~ **de seguimiento** V&M follow-up letter; ~ **de seguridades** COM GEN letter of comfort; ~ **de servicios** IMP/EXP facility letter; ~ **con sobretasa** ADMIN, BANCA, CONT surcharge letter; ~ **de solicitud** COMS letter of application; ~ **de solicitud de informes** COMS letter of inquiry; ~ **de subrogación** COMS letter of subrogation, letter of subordination; ~ **de venta** V&M sales letter; ~ **verde** DER, POL, RRHH, SEG green card; ~ **por vía aérea** COMS airmail letter; ~ **de vinos** COM GEN *restaurantes* wine list

Carta: ~ **de Acuerdo del Cliente** *f* FIN Client Agreement Letter; ~ **Comunitaria de Derechos Sociales Fundamentales de los Trabajadores** *f* PROT SOC, RRHH *EU* Community Charter of Fundamental Social Rights of Workers; ~ **de Derechos del Ciudadano** *f* POL Citizen's Charter; ~ **Social** *f* COM GEN, POL *CE* Social Charter; ~ **Social Europea** *f* ECON, POL European Social Charter

cartas: ~ **al director** *f pl* MEDIOS *prensa* letters to the editor

cartel *m* ECON, RRHH cartel, V&M poster, placard; ~ **internacional** ECON *OPEP* international cartel; ~ **de productos** ECON commodity cartel; ~ **publicitario** MEDIOS bill; ~ **de la tasa de interés** BANCA interest rate cartel (*BrE*)

cartela *f* TRANSP cartouche

cartelera *f AmL* (*cf tablon de anuncios Esp*) RRHH bulletin board (*BB*), notice board (*BrE*)

cartelización *f* ADMIN cartelization

cartelón *m* V&M *hombre-anuncio* sandwich board

carteo: ~ **masivo** *m* INFO mass mailing

cárter: ~ **del motor** *m* TRANSP engine casing

cartera *f* POL *de actividad del gobierno* portfolio; ~ **de acciones** BANCA, CONT, FIN shareownership; ~ **de activos** BOLSA, FIN asset portfolio; ~ **de bonos** BANCA, CONT, FIN holding of bonds; ~ **comercial** BANCA, FIN portfolio of trade, trading portfolio; ~ **de efectos** BANCA bill portfolio; ~ **eficiente** BOLSA efficient portfolio; ~ **empresarial** ECON business portfolio; ~ **equilibrada** BOLSA, FIN balanced portfolio; ~ **de existencias** BOLSA, FIN, stock portfolio; ~ **hipotecaria** BANCA mortgage portfolio; ~ **de inversiones** BANCA, FIN investment portfolio; ~ **de inversiones a corto plazo** BOLSA, FIN short-term investment portfolio; ~ **líquida** BANCA, CONT, FIN liquidity portfolio; ~ **de marcas** BOLSA, V&M brand portfolio; ~ **de marcas comerciales** FIN brand portfolio; ~ **de negocios** BOLSA, FIN business portfolio; ~ **de operaciones que devenga interés** BOLSA interest-bearing trading portfolio; ~ **de pagos** CONT backlog of payments; ~ **de participaciones** BANCA, CONT, FIN portfolio of investments; ~ **de pedidos** BANCA, CONT, FIN orders in hand; ~ **de pedidos atrasados** BANCA, CONT, FIN backlog of orders; ~ **de préstamos** BANCA loan portfolio; ~ **de productos** BOLSA, FIN, V&M product portfolio; ~ **de tarjetas de crédito** *m* BANCA credit card portfolio; ~ **de títulos** BANCA, CONT, FIN portfolio of investments; ~ **de valores** BOLSA, COM GEN, FIN equity holdings, portfolio, stock portfolio; ~ **de valores de renta fija** BOLSA bond portfolio; ~ **de ventas** V&M sales portfolio

cartero *m* COMS postman (*BrE*), mailman (*AmE*)

cartilla: ~ **de ahorros** *f* BANCA savings book

cartón *m* COM GEN, IND, TRANSP, V&M carton, cardboard, pasteboard, strawboard; ~ **duro** IND fiberboard (*AmE*), fibreboard (*BrE*); ~ **ondulado** V&M corrugated board; ~ **ordinario** COM GEN chipboard; ~ **de pasta de madera** IND fiberboard (*AmE*), fibreboard (*BrE*)

cartoné: en ~ *adj* MEDIOS casebound

cartucho *m* TRANSP cartouche; ~ **de cinta** INFO, MEDIOS ribbon cartridge; ~ **de monedas** BANCA coin wrapper

casa *f* INMOB house; ~ **abierta al público** INMOB open house (*AmE*); ~ **de aceptaciones** BANCA, FIN accepting house; ~ **adosada** INMOB duplex (*AmE*), semidetached house (*BrE*); ~ **de arbitraje** BANCA, BOLSA, FIN arbitrage house; ~ **de banca** BANCA banking house; ~ **de cambio** BANCA exchange office; ~ **de comisiones** BOLSA commission house; ~ **compradora** V&M buying house; ~ **compradora extranjera** IMP/EXP foreign buying house; ~ **de confirmación** BANCA, ECON *comercio internacional* confirming house; ~ **construida en serie** INMOB tract house; ~ **de descuento** BOLSA bill broker; ~ **editorial** MEDIOS publishing house; ~ **emisora** BANCA issuing house; ~ **de empeño** FIN pawnshop; ~ **de expedición** TRANSP forwarding agency; ~ **exportadora** IMP/EXP export house; ~ **familiar** MEDIOS family house; ~ **filial** COM GEN affiliated firm; ~ **franca** IMP/EXP, TRANSP free house; ~ **de liquidación** BANCA, BOLSA, ECON, FIN clearing house; ~ **matriz** COM GEN, FIN head office; ~ **matriz de banco único** BANCA one-bank holding company; ~ **matriz financiera** FIN financial holding company; ~ **minorista** FIN, V&M retail house; ~ **modelo** INMOB show house; ~ **móvil** INMOB mobile home; ~ **ocupada por su propietario** FISC, INMOB owner-occupied home; ~ **prefabricada** INMOB manufactured home, prefabricated house; ~ **principal** GES head office (*H.O.*); ~ **semiseparada** INMOB duplex (*AmE*), semidetached house (*BrE*); ~ **de valores** BOLSA securities house; ◆ ~ **de** (*c/d*) COM GEN, COMS care of (*c/o*)

Casa: ~ **de la Moneda** *f* BANCA, ECON Mint, ≈ Royal Mint (*BrE*)

casa/depósito *f* IMP/EXP, TRANSP house/depot

casado *adj* DER married; ~ **legalmente** DER legally married

casar *vt* BOLSA, DER marry

cascada: en ~ *adj* FISC in cascade

casco *m* TRANSP hull; ~ **protector** IND, RRHH hard hat

caseta: ~ **de gobierno** *f* TRANSP wheelhouse; ~ **del timón** *f* TRANSP wheelhouse

casete *f* INFO, MEDIOS cassette

cash: ~-**flow** *m* CONT, ECON, FIN cash flow; ~-**flow antes de impuestos** *m* CONT before-tax cash flow; ~-**flow negativo** *m* CONT negative cash flow; ~-**flow positivo** *m* CONT positive cash flow

casi: ~ **acabado** *fra* COM GEN near completion

casilla *f* COM GEN, INFO check box (*AmE*), box (*BrE*); ~ **del código** IMP/EXP code box; ~ **de correos** *AmL* (*cf apartado de correos Esp*) ADMIN, COMS Post Office Box (*POB*); ~ **electrónica** COMS, INFO e-mail address; ~ **postal** *AmL* (*cf apartado postal Esp*) ADMIN, COMS Post Office Box (*POB*)

casillero *m* INFO rack; ~ **para fichas** INFO card bin

caso *m* DER case; ~ **cuestionable** COM GEN borderline case; ~ **dudoso** COM GEN borderline case; ~ **desequilibrado** FISC mismatch case; ~ **límite** COM GEN borderline case; ~ **de gran repercusión** FISC high impact case; ~ **de incumplimiento** BANCA, FIN event of default; ~ **modelo** COM GEN, DER textbook case; ◆ **en el** ~ **de** COMS with reference to; **en ningún** ~ COM GEN on no account

castigar *vt* DER penalize

catalizador *m* COM GEN catalyst

catalogar *vt* COM GEN catalogue (*BrE*), table (*AmE*)

catálogo *m* COM GEN, INFO catalog (*AmE*), catalogue (*BrE*); ~ **de venta por correo** V&M mail order catalog (*AmE*), mail order catalogue (*BrE*)

catastral *adj* DER, FISC, INMOB cadastral

catastro *m* DER, FISC, INMOB land register, cadastre, land registry, land registration

catedrático-a *m,f* PROT SOC, RRHH professor; ~ **adjunto(-a)** RRHH adjunct professor (*AmE*), associate professor (*BrE*)

categoría[1]**: de** ~ **superior** *adj* COM GEN, RRHH *posición en la empresa* senior (*Snr*)

categoría[2] *f* COM GEN category; ~ **aprobada** FISC approved status (*BrE*); ~ **ejecutiva** RRHH executive grade; ~ **de fideicomisario** BOLSA trustee status; ~ **fiscal** ECON, FISC tax category; ~ **impositiva** ECON, FISC tax bracket; ~ **del informe de la valoración internacional** IMP/EXP overseas status report status; ~ **de la inversión** BOLSA investment grade; ~ **profesional** RRHH professional status; ~ **del riesgo**

SEG class of risk; ~ **salarial** RRHH wage bracket; ~ **social** PROT SOC, V&M social category; ~ **socioprofesional** POL socioprofessional class; ~ **de los trabajadores** RRHH workforce rating; ~ **única** RRHH single status

Categoría: ~ **del Despacho Aduanero** *f* IMP/EXP Customs Clearance Status (*CCS*)

categorías[1]: **para todas las** ~ *adv* COM GEN across-the-board

categorías[2]: ~ **de dificultad** *f pl* PROT SOC hardship categories; ~ **genéricas de puestos de trabajo** *f pl* RRHH generic job grades (*BrE*); ~ **de tipos de construcción** *f pl* SEG categories of construction types

categórico *adj* COM GEN emphatic

categorización *f* COM GEN, DER, ECON, PATENT categorization

catering *m* OCIO catering

caución *f* COM GEN pawn, bailment

caudal: ~ **de proceso y transferencia** *m* INFO throughput, thruput (*AmE*); ~ **de transferencia de datos** *m* INFO data transfer rate

causa *f* COM GEN cause, DER lawsuit, trial; ~ **de acción** DER *reclamaciones* cause of action; ~ **de anulación de póliza** SEG cause of cancellation of policy; ~ **contractual** DER consideration; ~ **de la pérdida** COM GEN cause of loss; ~ **próxima** DER procuring cause; ◆ **por ~ de** COM GEN due to, on account of; **ver una ~ a puerta cerrada** DER hear a case in chambers

causahabiente *m* COM GEN successor

causar *vt* COM GEN cause, spark off (*infrml*); ◆ ~ **corto circuito en** IND short-circuit

causas: ~ **del desempleo** *f pl* RRHH causes of unemployment

cautelar *adj* DER cautionary

cauteloso *adj* COM GEN cautious

cautivo: ~ **de la publicidad** *adj* COM GEN *cultura, sociedad* admass

caza: ~ **de talentos** *f* RRHH *ejecutivos* headhunt

cazador,a: ~ **de gangas** *m,f* BOLSA bargain hunter

cazatalentos *mf* RRHH headhunter

cc *abr* (*centímetro cúbico*) COM GEN cc (*cubic centimeter AmE, cubic centimetre BrE*)

c/c *abr* (*cuenta corriente*) BANCA, CONT c/a (*current account BrE, checking account AmE*)

CCI *abr* (*Cámara de Comercio e Industria*) ECON, IND CCI (*Chamber of Commerce and Industry*)

c.d. *abr* (*certificado de depósito*) BANCA, FIN c.d. (*certificate of deposit*)

c/d *abr* (*casa de*) COM GEN, COMS c/o (*care of*)

CD *abr* (*certificado de depósito*) BANCA, BOLSA, FIN CD (*certificate of deposit*)

CDA *abr* (*cuenta de dividendo de capital*) BANCA, BOLSA, FISC CDA (*capital dividend account*)

CDC *abr* (*Corporación para el Desarrollo de la Commonwealth*) ECON, POL CDC (*Commonwealth Development Corporation*)

CD-I *abr* (*disco compacto interactivo*) INFO CD-I (*compact disk interactive*)

CD-ROM *abr* (*disco compacto con memoria sólo de lectura*) INFO CD-ROM (*compact disk read-only memory*)

CDTI *abr* (*Centro para el Desarrollo Tecnológico Industrial*) IND, INFO Spanish centre for industrial and technological research

CE *abr* ECON, POL (*Comunidad Europea*) EC (*obs*) (*European Community*), (*Consejo de Europa*) CE (*Council of Europe*)

CEAP *abr* (*Cooperación Económica de Asia y los Países del Pacífico*) ECON, POL APEC (*Asia Pacific Economic Cooperation*)

CECA *abr* BANCA (*Confederación Española de Cajas de Ahorro*) Spanish saving banks' association, ECON, IND (*Comunidad Europea del Carbón y el Acero*) ECSC (*European Coal and Steel Community*)

CEDEAO *abr* (*Comunidad Económica de Estados Africanos Occidentales*) ECON, POL ECOWAS (*Economic Community of West African States*)

cedente *mf* DER, PATENT, SEG assignor, cedant

ceder *vt* BOLSA assign, COM GEN abandon, *dinero en garantía, recursos* allow, DER, PATENT cede, *negociaciones* yield, *transferir* assign, POL stand down

cédula *f* DER licence (*BrE*), license (*AmE*); ~ **de caducidad** CONT *balances* lapsing schedule; ~ **de citación so pena de sanción** DER subpoena; ~ **sin cotización** BOLSA unlisted warrant; ~ **de liquidación de entrada** IMP/EXP inward clearing bill

cedulofilia *f* BOLSA scripophily

CEE *abr obs* (*Comunidad Económica Europea*) ECON, POL EEC (*obs*) (*European Economic Community*)

CEEA *abr* (*Comunidad Europea de Energía Atómica*) ECON, POL EAEC (*European Atomic Energy Community*), EURATOM (*European Atomic Energy Community*)

cel: ~**-o-tex** *m* COM GEN strawboard

celda *f* INFO, TRANSP cell; ~ **binaria** INFO bit location

celebrar *vt* COM GEN hold; ◆ ~ **una conferencia** GES hold a conference; ~ **un convenio** COM GEN enter into an agreement; ~ **una cumbre** POL hold a summit; ~ **juicio** DER sit in judgment

celsius *adj* COM GEN Celsius

CEN *abr* (*Comité Europeo para la Normalización*) ECON, IND CEN (*European Committee for Standardization*)

censo *m* COM GEN census; ~ **del comercio al por menor** ECON, V&M census of retail trade; ~ **demográfico** MAT, POL population census; ~ **electoral** COM GEN, POL electoral register, electoral roll; ~ **de empresas** ECON census of business (*AmE*); ~ **de fabricantes industriales** IND census of manufacturers (*AmE*); ~ **por muestras** V&M sample census; ~ **de población** MAT, POL *estadística* population census

censor *m* COM GEN watchdog

censura: ~ **de cuentas** *f* CONT, FIN audit, auditing

censurar *vt* COM GEN censure, CONT, FIN audit

centavo *m* BANCA cent; ◆ **estar sin un** ~ COM GEN be on the rocks

centígrado (*C*) *adj* COM GEN centigrade (*C*)

centilitro *m* (*cl*) COM GEN centilitre (*BrE*) (*cl*), centiliter (*AmE*) (*cl*)

centímetro *m* (*cm*) COM GEN centimetre (*BrE*) (*cm*), centimeter (*AmE*) (*cm*); ~ **cúbico** (*cc*) COM GEN cubic centimeter (*AmE*) (*cc*), cubic centimetre (*BrE*) (*cc*); ~**-columna** MEDIOS single column centimeter (*AmE*) (*SCC*), single column centimetre (*BrE*) (*SCC*)

centímetros: ~ **de columna** *m pl* MEDIOS column centimeters (*AmE*), column centimetres (*BrE*)

central¹ *adj* COM GEN central, INFO front-end

central²: **~ de calefacción** *f* IND heating power station; **~ eléctrica** *f* IND power station; **~ eléctrica de carga fundamental** *f* IND base-load power station; **~ de energía nuclear** *f* IND, MED AMB nuclear power station; **~ hidroeléctrica** *f* IND hydroelectric power station; **~ telefónica** *f* COMS telephone exchange; **~ termoeléctrica** *f* IND, MED AMB thermal power station

centralismo: **~ democrático** *m* POL democratic centralism

centralita *f* BOLSA phone desk, COMS *teléfono* exchange; **~ automática privada unida a la red pública** COMS *teléfono* private automatic branch exchange (*BrE*) (*PABX*)

centralizado *adj* COM GEN centralized, INFO host-driven

centralizar *vt* COM GEN centralize

centrar¹: **~ en** *vt* COM GEN focus on

centrar²: **~ la atención en** *fra* COM GEN concentrate attention on

céntrico *adj* V&M central

centro *m* COM GEN, IND center (*AmE*), centre (*BrE*); **~ de actividad** COM GEN hub of activity; **~ administrativo** ADMIN administrative center (*AmE*), administrative centre (*BrE*); **~ de adquisición** INMOB *compra forzada* acquiring authority; **~ de ajuste** PROT SOC adjustment centre (*BrE*), adjustment center (*AmE*); **~ de autorización** BANCA authorization centre (*BrE*), authorization center (*AmE*); **~ bancario** BANCA banking center (*AmE*), banking centre (*BrE*); **~ de beneficios** *m pl* COM GEN, FIN, GES profit center (*AmE*), profit centre (*BrE*); **~ de cálculo** INFO computing center (*AmE*), computing centre (*BrE*); **~ de capacitación** AmL (*cf centro de formación Esp*) RRHH training center (*AmE*), training centre (*BrE*); **~ de carga** CONT burden center (*AmE*), burden centre (*BrE*), TRANSP cargo center (*AmE*), cargo centre (*BrE*); **~ de la ciudad** ECON inner city, COM GEN city center (*AmE*), city centre (*BrE*), downtown (*AmE*), town centre (*BrE*); **~ comercial** COM GEN one-stop shopping center (*AmE*), one-stop shopping centre (*BrE*), emporium, shopping center (*AmE*), shopping centre (*BrE*), shopping mall (*AmE*), shopping precinct (*BrE*), mall (*AmE*), *ventas* mart (*infrml*) (*AmE*); **~ comercial a las afueras** COM GEN, INMOB, V&M out-of-town center (*AmE*), out-of-town centre (*BrE*); **~ comercial de cadena** COM GEN chain mall (*AmE*), chain shopping centre (*BrE*); **~ del comercio mundial** ECON World Trade Center (*AmE*), World Trade Centre (*BrE*) (*WTC*); **~ de compensación** BANCA clearing centre (*BrE*), clearing center (*AmE*); **~ de contenedores para fletes** TRANSP container freight station (*CFS*); **~ de costes** *Esp* (*cf centro de costos AmL*) BANCA, CONT cost center (*AmE*), cost centre (*BrE*), burden center (*AmE*), burden centre (*BrE*); **~ de costos** AmL (*cf centro de costes Esp*) BANCA, CONT burden centre (*AmE*), burden centre (*BrE*), cost center (*AmE*), cost centre (*BrE*); **~ cultural** COM GEN cultural centre (*BrE*), cultural center (*AmE*); **~ de datos corporativo** INFO corporate data center (*AmE*), corporate data centre (*BrE*); **~ de descarga** TRANSP break bulk center (*AmE*), break bulk centre (*BrE*); **~ de descuento** FIN discount center (*AmE*), discount centre (*BrE*); **~ de diagnosis de fallas** GES faults diagnosis clinic; **~ de distribución** TRANSP distribution center (*AmE*), dis-

tribution centre (*BrE*); **~ de distribución del estado** BANCA regional distribution center (*AmE*), regional distribution centre (*BrE*); **~ de distribución regional** BANCA regional distribution centre (*BrE*); **~ distribuidor** TRANSP distribution center (*AmE*), distribution centre (*BrE*); **~ de educación a distancia** PROT SOC, RRHH correspondence school, distance education center (*AmE*), distance education centre (*BrE*); **~ de educación técnica** PROT SOC technical college, technical education institution; **~ de evaluación** RRHH assessment center (*AmE*), assessment centre (*BrE*); **~ de exposición** COM GEN exhibition center (*AmE*), exhibition centre (*BrE*); **~ financiero** ECON, FIN financial center (*AmE*), financial centre (*BrE*), business center (*AmE*), business centre (*BrE*); **~ financiero extranjero con ventajas fiscales** BANCA offshore center (*AmE*), offshore centre (*BrE*); **~ financiero global** ECON global financial center (*AmE*), global financial centre (*BrE*); **~ financiero internacional** BANCA offshore center (*AmE*), offshore centre (*BrE*); **~ financiero mundial** ECON global financial center (*AmE*), global financial centre (*BrE*); **~ de finanzas** ECON, FIN financial center (*AmE*), financial centre (*BrE*); **~ de formación** *Esp* (*cf centro de capacitación AmL*) RRHH training center (*AmE*), training centre (*BrE*); **~ de formación profesional** *Esp* RRHH training center (*AmE*), training centre (*BrE*); **~ de gastos** CONT expense center (*AmE*), expense centre (*BrE*); **~ de gastos generales** BANCA, CONT burden center (*AmE*), burden centre (*BrE*); **~ de gravedad** TRANSP center of gravity (*AmE*), centre of gravity (*BrE*); **~ industrial** IND industrial centre (*BrE*), industrial center (*AmE*); **~ informático de empresa** INFO corporate data center (*AmE*), corporate data centre (*BrE*); **~ de ingresos** COM GEN, FISC revenue center (*AmE*), revenue centre (*BrE*); **~ de inicio de la descarga** TRANSP break bulk center (*AmE*), break bulk centre (*BrE*); **~ de innovación** IND innovation centre (*BrE*), innovation center (*AmE*); **~ de inversiones** FIN investment center (*AmE*), investment centre (*BrE*); **~ inversor** FIN investment center (*AmE*), investment centre (*BrE*); **~ de negocios** COM GEN business center (*AmE*), business centre (*BrE*); **~ neurálgico** GES nerve center (*AmE*), nerve centre (*BrE*); **~ de ocio** OCIO leisure center (*AmE*), leisure centre (*BrE*); **~ de primera responsabilidad** CONT prime responsability center (*AmE*), prime responsability centre (*BrE*); **~ de procesamiento de datos** INFO computer center (*AmE*), computer centre (*BrE*); **~ de procesamiento de texto** INFO word-processing center (*AmE*), word-processing centre (*BrE*); **~ regional** COM GEN regional center (*AmE*), regional centre (*BrE*); **~ de responsabilidad** FIN, GES responsibility center (*AmE*), responsibility centre (*BrE*); **~ de responsabilidad directa** CONT prime responsibility center (*AmE*), prime responsibility centre (*BrE*); **~ de salud** PROT SOC health center (*AmE*), health centre (*BrE*), health farm; **~ de servicios informáticos** INFO service bureau; **~ del tanque de carga** TRANSP cargo tank center (*AmE*) (*CTC*), cargo tank centre (*BrE*) (*CTC*); **~ de tanque independiente** TRANSP independent tank center (*AmE*) (*ITC*), independent tank centre (*BrE*) (*ITC*); **~ de trasbordo de graneles** TRANSP bulk transhipment centre (*BrE*), bulk transhipment center (*AmE*); **~ de tratamiento de textos** INFO word-processing center (*AmE*), word-processing centre (*BrE*); **~ de ultramar** BANCA offshore center (*AmE*), offshore centre (*BrE*); **~ urbano** COM GEN urban center (*AmE*), urban centre (*BrE*); **~ de venta al por menor** INMOB, V&M retail center (*AmE*), retail centre (*BrE*)

Centro: **~ de Comercio Internacional** *m* COM GEN International Trade Center (*AmE*), International Trade Centre (*BrE*); **~ para and el Desarrollo Tecnológico Industrial** *m* (*CDTI*) INFO Spanish Centre for industrial technology research; **~ de Estudios Internacionales** *m* ECON, PROT SOC, RRHH Centre for International Studies (*BrE*) (*CENIS*); **~ de Formación Profesional** *m Esp* PROT SOC college of further education (*CFE*); **~ de Información Económica y Social** *m* ECON, PROT SOC Centre for Economic and Social Information (*CESI*); **~ Internacional de Agricultura Tropical** *m* ECON International Centre of Tropical Agriculture; **~ Internacional de Control** *m* COM GEN International Control Centre (*ICC*); **~ Internacional para la Industria y el Medio Ambiente** *m* IND, MED AMB International Centre for Industry and the Environment (*ICIE*); **~ de Investigaciones Sociológicas** *m* (*CIS*) COM GEN Spanish insitute of social studies

CEOE *abr* (*Confederación Española de Organizaciones Empresariales*) ECON, IND Spanish association of business organizations, ≈ CBI (*Confederation of British Industry*)

CEPAL *abr* (*Comisión Económica para América Latina*) ECON, POL ≈ UN-ECLA (*United Nations Economic Commission for Latin America*)

CEPAO *abr* (*Comisión Económica para Asia Occidental*) ECON, POL ECWA (*Economic Commission for Western Asia*)

CEPE *abr* (*Comisión Económica para Europa*) ECON, POL ECE (*Economic Commission for Europe*)

CEPYME *abr Esp* (*Confederación Española de la Pequeña y Mediana Empresa*) ECON Spanish confederation of small and medium sized companies

cerca *f* BOLSA hedge

cercado: **~ de tierra** *adj* MED AMB landlocked

cercanías *f pl* COM GEN, INMOB commuter belt (*BrE*)

cerco *m* FISC ring-fence

cerrado: **~ eficazmente** *adj* TRANSP effectively closed

cerradura: **~ de seguridad** *f* INFO keylock

cerrar 1. *vt* COM GEN close, close down, seal off, CONT, INFO, V&M close; ♦ **~ un acuerdo** BOLSA close a deal; **~ un lado** BOLSA lift a leg; **~ una posición** BOLSA, FIN close a position; **~ una posición corta** BOLSA lift a short; **~ en un tipo** BOLSA *futuros* lock in a rate; **~ un trato** COM GEN make a deal; **~ una venta** INMOB complete a sale, V&M close a sale; **2.** *vi* COM GEN close down

certidumbre *f* COM GEN certainty

certificación *f* COM GEN certification; **~ del cónyuge** FISC certification by spouse; **~ de cuentas** CONT accounts certification

certificado *m* COM GEN certificate (*cert.*); **~ de acción fraccionaria** BANCA, COM GEN, ECON, FIN scrip certificate; **~ de acción ordinaria** BOLSA common share certificate (*BrE*), common stock certificate (*AmE*); **~ de acciones al portador** COM GEN share warrant to bearer; **~ de aceptación** TRANSP acceptance certificate; **~ actuarial** SEG actuarial certificate; **~ de acumulación** ECON *títulos preconvenidos* certificate of accrual (*AmE*); **~ de adeudo** COM GEN debt certificate; **~ de aduana para salir** TRANSP swing clearance; **~ de**

aeronavegabilidad TRANSP airworthiness certification; **~ de ahorro** BANCA, BOLSA savings certificate; **~ de ahorro con crecimiento** BANCA growth savings certificate; **~ de ahorros universal** BANCA all-savers certificate; **~ al portador** BOLSA bearer certificate; **~ de análisis** TRANSP certificate of analysis; **~ anual** CONT annual certificate; **~ de aptitud** COM GEN qualifying certificate; **~ de arqueo** BANCA, COM GEN, ECON, FIN measurement bill; **~ de auditoría** CONT audit certificate; **~ de la autoridad local** BOLSA local authority bill (*LAB*); **~ de autorización de gastos** BANCA, COM GEN, ECON, FIN allocatur; **~ de autorización de salida de buque** IMP/EXP, TRANSP clearance papers; **~ de avería gruesa** SEG general average certificate (*GAC*); **~ bancario** BANCA bank certificate; **~ de bono** BOLSA bond certificate; **~ de caja** FIN cash certificate; **~ de calidad** COM GEN, IMP/EXP, TRANSP quality certificate, certificate of quality; **~ de cambio monetario** BANCA, COM GEN, ECON, FIN exchange certificate; **~ de carga en cubierta** TRANSP deck cargo certificate; **~ de clasificación** TRANSP classification certificate; **~ de climatización** TRANSP certificate of conditioning; **~ de cobertura** BANCA, COM GEN, ECON, FIN covering warrant; **~ de comercio internacional** ECON international trading certificate; **~ de competencia** TRANSP certificate of competency; **~ para compra de valores** BOLSA stock purchase warrant; **~ de consignación/origen** IMP/EXP, TRANSP certificate of consignment/origin (*CC/O*); **~ de control de roedores** TRANSP rodent control certificate; **~ de copropiedad** BANCA, COM GEN, ECON, FIN participation certificate; **~ de declaración de entrada** IMP/EXP jerque note; **~ de defunción** COM GEN, DER death certificate; **~ de delegación de voto** BOLSA voting trust certificate; **~ de depósito** BANCA, BOLSA, FIN (*c.d.*, *CD*) certificate of deposit (*c.d.*, *CD*), deposit certificate, bond warrant, IMP/EXP, TRANSP warehouse receipt (*WR*); **~ de depósito en eurodólares** BANCA Eurodollar certificate of deposit; **~ de depósito de mayor cuantía** BOLSA jumbo certificate of deposit; **~ de descarga** TRANSP landing certificate; **~ de despacho** BANCA, COM GEN, ECON clearance; **~ de deuda** *f* FISC certificate of indebtedness; **~ de deuda renovable amortizada** BANCA, FIN certificate of amortized revolving debt (*BrE*) (*CARD*); **~ de dispositivo de seguridad** TRANSP safety equipment certificate; **~ de dividendo diferido** FIN scrip dividend; **~ de embalaje** TRANSP packaging certificate; **~ de embalaje del contenedor** TRANSP container packing certificate; **~ de embarque** TRANSP shipping bill; **~ de entrada pagado en exceso** IMP/EXP overpaid entry certificate (*OEC*); **~ del equipo de seguridad de buques de carga** TRANSP cargo ship safety equipment certificate; **~ de un estudio** COM GEN survey certificate; **~ de exención** FISC exemption certificate; **~ de expedición** TRANSP certificate of shipment; **~ expedido por el registro de la propiedad inmobiliaria** DER, INMOB land certificate; **~ de fabricación** SEG certificate of manufacture; **~ de fideicomiso de equipo** FIN equipment trust bond, equipment trust certification; **~ de fideicomiso tierras** DER land trust certificate; **~ de franqueo** COMS certificate of posting, postage certificate; **~ con garantía de hipoteca** BANCA guaranteed mortgage certificate; **~ con garantía hipotecaria** BANCA guaranteed mortgage certificate; **~ con garantía de prenda** BANCA, COM GEN, ECON, FIN collateral trust certificate; **~ con garantía prendaria**

BANCA, COM GEN, ECON, FIN collateral trust certificate; **~ de grano** TRANSP grain certificate; **~ de hipoteca** BANCA, FIN mortgage certificate; **~ de impedimento legal** BANCA estoppel certificate; **~ impositivo** BANCA, COM GEN, ECON, FISC tax certificate; **~ de independencia** RRHH certificate of independence; **~ de inscripción** FISC certificate of registration; **~ de inspección** TRANSP certificate of inspection, certificate of survey; **~ con intereses aplicables al pago de impuestos** FISC tax anticipation certificate, tax anticipation note (*TAN*); **~ de inventarios** CONT inventory certificate; **~ de inversión** BANCA, BOLSA, FIN investment certificate; **~ de inversión garantizado** FIN guaranteed investment certificate; **~ de inversión en mejoras** FIN mutual improvement certificate; **~ de inversión preferente** BOLSA preferred investment certificate; **~ de línea de carga** TRANSP load line certificate; **~ de llegada** BANCA, COM GEN, ECON certificate of clearing inwards; **~ médico** PROT SOC certificate of health, Bill of Health (*BH*); **~ médico negativo de que se padece una enfermedad** COM GEN, PROT SOC poor bill of health; **~ médico positivo de no padecer enfermedad** *f* COM GEN, PROT SOC clean bill of health; **~ del mercado monetario** ECON, FIN MMC (*money market certificate*), money market certificate (*MMC*); **~ de movimiento** IMP/EXP movement certificate; **~ de nacimiento** COM GEN, DER birth certificate; **~ nominativo** BANCA, COM GEN, ECON bond certificate; **~ de número de pasajeros** TRANSP passenger number certificate; **~ de ocupación** INMOB certificate of occupancy; **~ de organización de una sociedad** BANCA, COM GEN, DER certificate of incorporation; **~ de origen** FIN, IMP/EXP certificate of origin (*c/o*); **~ de origen y consignación** IMP/EXP certificate of origin and consignment (*C/OC*); **~ de pago de impuestos** FISC certificate of tax deposit (*BrE*) (*CTD*); **~ de pasajeros** TRANSP passenger certificate (*BrE*) (*PC*); **~ pasivo** BANCA, COM GEN, ECON, FIN liability certificate; **~ de patente** PATENT patent certificate; **~ de patrón** TRANSP master's certificate; **~ de peso** TRANSP certificate of weight; **~ a plazo** BOLSA, FIN term certificate; **~ de póliza de seguros marítimos** SEG marine insurance policy certificate; **~ de préstamo transferible** BANCA, FIN transferable loan certificates; **~ de préstamos** FIN loan certificate; **~ de previo pago de impuestos** FISC tax anticipation bill (*AmE*) (*TAB*); **~ de prima** BANCA, COM GEN, ECON, FIN bonus certificate; **~ de propiedad** COM GEN, DER, INMOB certificate of ownership; **~ de protección complementaria** COM GEN, PATENT Supplementary Protection Certificate (*SPC*); **~ de protesta** BANCA, COM GEN, ECON, FIN certificate of protest; **~ provisional** BOLSA interim certificate; **~ de recibo de expedición** IMP/EXP, TRANSP forwarder's certificate of receipt (*FCR*); **~ de recibo de expedición de flete** IMP/EXP, TRANSP freight forwarder's certificate of receipt (*FFCR*); **~ de recibo del expedidor** IMP/EXP, TRANSP forwarder's certificate of receipt (*FCR*); **~ de recibo del expedidor del flete** IMP/EXP, TRANSP freight forwarder's certificate of receipt (*FFCR*); **~ de registro** DER *propiedad intelectual* certificate of registration, TRANSP *navegación* certificate of registry; **~ para reintegro** BANCA, COM GEN, ECON drawback debenture; **~ respaldado por una hipoteca** FIN mortgage-backed certificate; **~ de ruta** TRANSP routeing certificate; **~ de salida** BANCA, COM GEN, ECON certificate of clearing outwards; **~ de salud** PROT SOC certificate of health; **~ con salvedades** COM GEN qualified certificate; **~ de sanidad** IMP/EXP, TRANSP certificate of pratique; **~ de seguridad de los pasajeros** OCIO, TRANSP passenger safety certificate; **~ de seguro** SEG certificate of insurance (*c/i*); **~ separable** BOLSA detachable warrant; **~ del síndico interventor** FIN receiver's certificate; **~ de solvencia** BANCA, COM GEN, ECON soundness certificate; **~ de suscripción** BOLSA subscription warrant; **~ de tierras** DER, INMOB land certificate; **~ de título** DER, INMOB certificate of title; **~ de transferencia de préstamos** BOLSA participation certificate; **~ tributario** BANCA, COM GEN, ECON, FISC tax certificate; **~ de uso** INMOB certificate of use; **~ de utilidad** PATENT utility certificate; **~ de validez de un título** INMOB opinion of title; **~ de valor** IMP/EXP certificate of value (*C/V*); **~ de valor y origen** IMP/EXP certificate of value and origin (*CVO*); **~ veterinario** IMP/EXP veterinary certificate; **~ de vida** SEG certificate of existence; **~ de vivienda móvil** BOLSA mobile home certificate (*AmE*)

Certificado: **~ de Educación Secundaria** *m* COM GEN ≈ General Certificate of Education (*obs*) (*BrE*) (*GCE*), ≈ General Certificate of Secondary Education (*BrE*) (*GCSE*); **~ de Franco a Bordo Internacional** *m* TRANSP International Load Line Certificate; **~ Nacional de Ahorro** *m* BANCA, FIN National Savings Certificate (*BrE*); **~ de la Oficina del Presupuesto** *m* IMP/EXP Budget Bureau Certificate; **~ de Promoción Industrial** *m* IND Industrial Development Certificate; **~ de Réditos sobre Letras del Tesoro** *m* BOLSA Certificate of Accrual on Treasury Securities (*AmE*) (*CATS*)

certificados: **~ de depósito acreditados** *m pl* BOLSA seasoned CD; **~ de depósito aditivos** *m pl* BOLSA add-on certificates of deposit (*BrE*) (*add-on CDs*), add-on domestic certificates of deposit (*BrE*) (*add-on CDs*); **~ nacionales de depósito aditivos** *m pl* BOLSA add-on domestic certificates of deposit (*BrE*) (*add-on CDs*)

cesación: **~ de interés** *f* BANCA cessation of interest; **~ de pago de las primas** *f* SEG cessation of payment of premiums

cesar 1. *vt* RRHH *personal* dismiss, fire (*infrml*), make redundant, sack (*infrml*); ◆ **~ a alguien** RRHH dismiss sb, give sb the sack (*infrml*) (*BrE*), give sb their cards (*infrml*) (*BrE*); **~ el trabajo** COM GEN knock off (*infrml*); **2.** *vi* COM GEN cease

cese *m* RRHH firing *infrml*, stoppage; **~ con preaviso** RRHH termination with notice (*BrE*); **~ repentino** FIN cutback

cesión *f* BOLSA assignment, COM GEN concession, transfer, CONT *cuentas y efectos a cobrar* assignment, DER assignment, *transmisión de propiedad* grant, FISC disposal, release, PATENT, SEG assignment; **~ de arriendo** DER assignment of lease; **~ de cartera** COM GEN cession of portfolio, SEG portfolio transfer; **~ conjunta** COM GEN joint assignment; **~ de derechos** SEG assignment of rights; **~ de deudas** CONT assignment of debts; **~ del excedente** FISC surplus stripping; **~ de garantía** SEG collateral assignment; **~ de ingresos** FISC assignment of income; **~ obligatoria** DER compulsory surrender; **~ de una patente** DER assignment of patent, PATENT surrender of a patent; **~ de reaseguro** COM GEN cession

cesionario, -a *m,f* BOLSA grantee, COM GEN assignee, vendee, DER, FISC, INMOB *poder notarial* grantee

cesión: **~-arrendamiento** *f* FIN lease-back

cesionista^1 *mf* FISC *derechos de sucesión* transferor (*BrE*)

cesionista^2 *m* BOLSA, CONT grantor

cesta *f* COM GEN basket; ~ **de amarre** TRANSP lashing cage; ~ **de la compra** COM GEN, ECON shopping basket, market basket; ~ **de monedas** ECON basket of currencies; ~ **de productos** ECON basket of goods, basket of products; ~ **de tipos** IND basket of rates

cestilla: ~ **de archivo** *f* ADMIN filing basket

ceteris: ~ **paribus** *fra* COM GEN ceteris paribus

CFC *abr* (*clorofluorocarbono*) MED AMB CFC (*chlorofluorocarbon*)

CFI *abr* (*Corporación de Finanzas Internacionales*) FIN IFC (*International Finance Corporation*)

CGA *abr* (*adaptador color/gráficos*) INFO CGA (*color/graphics adaptor AmE, colour/graphics adaptor BrE*)

CGPM *abr* (*Conferencia General de Pesos y Medidas*) COM GEN General Conference on Weights and Measures

chafar: ~ **un plan** *fra jarg* BOLSA pull the plug (*jarg*)

chalet *m* INMOB, OCIO rambler (*jarg*)

chanchullo *m* BOLSA price rigging, racket (*infrml*), DER graft (*infrml*) (*BrE*)

chantaje *m* COM GEN blackmail

chantajear *vt infrml* COM GEN blackmail

chantajista *mf* BOLSA, COM GEN greenmailer

chapa: ~ **de datos** *f* TRANSP *contenedores* data plate; ~ **de matrícula** *f* TRANSP license plate (*AmE*), number plate (*BrE*)

chapuzero, -a *m,f* IND cowboy *infrml*

chaquetero *adj infrml* POL turncoat (*infrml*)

charla *f* COM GEN chat, spiel (*infrml*)

charola: ~ **de pendientes** *f AmL* (*cf bandeja de pendientes Esp*) ADMIN, COM GEN pending tray; ~ **de salida** *f AmL* (*cf bandeja de salida Esp*) ADMIN, COM GEN out-tray

chárter *m* TRANSP charter

chartismo *m* BOLSA, ECON chartism

chasis: ~ **de remolque** *m* TRANSP skeletal trailer

chatarra *f* MED AMB scrap metal, COM GEN spoilage

chatarrero, -a *m,f* COM GEN scrap dealer

checar *vt AmL* (*cf fichar Esp*) IND, RRHH check in; ♦ ~ **tarjeta** *AmL a la entrada* (*cf fichar la entrada Esp*) IND, RRHH clock in, clock on (*BrE*), punch in (*AmE*), (*cf fichar la salida Esp*) *a la salida* clock off (*BrE*), clock out, punch out (*AmE*)

cheque *m* BANCA, COM GEN, FIN draft (*dft*), check (*AmE*), cheque (*BrE*); ~ **abierto** BANCA, FIN open check (*AmE*), open cheque (*BrE*); ~ **de acciones** BANCA, FIN stock check (*AmE*), stock cheque (*BrE*); ~ **de la paga** BANCA pay check (*AmE*), pay cheque (*BrE*); ~ **al portador** BANCA, FIN bearer check (*AmE*), bearer cheque (*BrE*); ~ **anulado** BANCA, FIN cancelled check (*AmE*), cancelled cheque (*BrE*); ~ **bancario** BANCA, FIN bank check (*AmE*), bank cheque (*BrE*), banker's check (*AmE*), banker's cheque (*BrE*); ~ **de banco** BANCA, FIN banker's draft, official check (*AmE*), official cheque (*BrE*); ~ **barrado** BANCA crossed check (*AmE*), crossed cheque (*BrE*); ~ **en blanco** BANCA, FIN blank check (*AmE*), blank cheque (*BrE*); ~ **bloqueado** BANCA stopped check (*AmE*), stopped cheque (*BrE*); ~ **de caja** BANCA, FIN cashier's check (*AmE*), cashier's cheque (*BrE*), officer's check (*AmE*), officer's cheque (*BrE*); ~ **cancelado** BANCA, FIN cancelled check (*AmE*), cancelled cheque (*BrE*); ~ **por la cantidad de**

BANCA, FIN check to the amount of (*AmE*), cheque to the amount of (*BrE*); ~ **certificado** BANCA, FIN certified check (*AmE*), certified cheque (*BrE*); ~ **sin cobrar** BANCA, FIN unpresented check (*AmE*), unpresented cheque (*BrE*); ~ **para cobrar en efectivo** BANCA, FIN check made to cash (*AmE*), cheque made to cash (*BrE*); ~ **compensado** BANCA, FIN cleared check (*AmE*), cleared cheque (*BrE*); ~ **confirmado** BANCA, FIN marked check (*AmE*), marked cheque (*BrE*); ~ **contra la cuenta propia** BANCA, FIN counter check (*AmE*), counter cheque (*BrE*); ~ **cruzado** BANCA crossed check (*AmE*), crossed cheque (*BrE*); ~ **sin cruzar** BANCA, FIN uncrossed check (*AmE*), uncrossed cheque (*BrE*); ~ **destinado a un determinado pago** BANCA, FIN earmarked check (*AmE*), earmarked cheque (*BrE*); ~ **devuelto** BANCA, FIN bounced check (*infrml*) (*AmE*), bounced cheque (*infrml*) (*BrE*), returned check (*AmE*), returned cheque (*BrE*); ~ **de dividendos** BANCA, FIN dividends check (*AmE*), dividends cheque (*BrE*); ~ **endosado** BANCA, FIN third-party check (*AmE*), third-party cheque (*BrE*); ~ **falsificado** BANCA, FIN forged check (*AmE*), forged cheque (*BrE*); ~ **falso** BANCA, FIN forged check (*AmE*), forged cheque (*BrE*); ~ **a favor de** BANCA, FIN check in favor of (*AmE*), cheque in favour of (*BrE*); ~ **de fecha atrasada** BANCA, FIN stale-dated check (*AmE*), stale-dated cheque (*BrE*); ~ **sin fondos** BANCA, FIN bad check (*AmE*), bad cheque (*AmE*), dud check (*infrml*) (*AmE*), dud cheque (*infrml*) (*BrE*), rubber check (*infrml*) (*AmE*), rubber cheque (*infrml*) (*BrE*), uncovered check (*AmE*), uncovered cheque (*BrE*); ~ **con fondos insuficientes** BANCA, FIN not-sufficient-funds check (*AmE*) (*N.S.F. check*), not-sufficient-funds cheque (*BrE*) (*N.S.F. cheque*); ~ **sin fondos suficientes** BANCA, FIN not-sufficient-funds check (*AmE*) (*N.S.F. check*), not-sufficient-funds cheque (*BrE*) (*N.S.F. cheque*); ~ **en garantía** BANCA, FIN memorandum check (*AmE*), memorandum cheque (*BrE*); ~ **impagado** BANCA, FIN dishonored check (*AmE*), dishonoured cheque (*BrE*), unpaid check (*AmE*), unpaid cheque (*BrE*); ~ **impagado por falta de fondos** BANCA, FIN bounced check (*AmE*), bounced cheque (*BrE*); ~ **incobrable** BANCA, FIN bad check (*AmE*), bad cheque (*BrE*); ~ **incobrable por falta de fondos** BANCA, FIN bounced check (*infrml*) (*AmE*), bounced cheque (*infrml*) (*BrE*); ~ **con intereses** BANCA, FIN interest check (*AmE*), interest cheque (*BrE*); ~ **intransferible** BANCA, FIN undeliverable check (*AmE*), undeliverable cheque (*BrE*); ~ **libre** BANCA, FIN open check (*AmE*), open cheque (*BrE*); ~ **limitado** BANCA, DER, FIN limited check (*AmE*), limited cheque (*BrE*); ~ **de mostrador** BANCA, FIN counter check (*AmE*), counter cheque (*BrE*); ~ **mutilado** BANCA, FIN mutilated check (*AmE*), mutilated cheque (*BrE*); ~ **negociable** BANCA, FIN negotiable check (*AmE*), negotiable cheque (*BrE*); ~ **no cobrado** BANCA, FIN uncashed check (*AmE*), uncashed cheque (*BrE*); ~ **no cruzado** BANCA, FIN uncrossed check (*AmE*), uncrossed cheque (*BrE*), open check (*AmE*), open cheque (*BrE*); ~ **no librable** BANCA, FIN undeliverable check (*AmE*), undeliverable cheque (*BrE*); ~ **no negociable** BANCA, FIN non-negotiable check (*AmE*), non-negotiable cheque (*BrE*); ~ **no pagado** BANCA, FIN dishonored check (*AmE*), dishonoured cheque (*BrE*), unpaid check (*AmE*), unpaid cheque (*BrE*); ~ **no presentado** BANCA, FIN unpresented check (*AmE*), unpresented cheque (*BrE*); ~ **no presentado a tiempo al cobro** BANCA, FIN stale check (*AmE*), stale cheque (*BrE*); **~ nominativo** BANCA, FIN pay self check (*AmE*), pay self cheque (*BrE*); **~ pagadero sólo por ventanilla** BANCA, FIN collection-only check (*AmE*), collection-only cheque (*BrE*); **~ en pago de dividendos** BANCA, FIN dividend warrant; **~ pendiente** BANCA, FIN outstanding check (*AmE*), outstanding cheque (*BrE*); **~ perforado** BANCA, FIN punch card check (*AmE*), punch card cheque (*BrE*); **~ personalizado** BANCA, FIN personalized check (*AmE*), personalized cheque (*BrE*); **~ posdatado** BANCA, FIN postdated check (*AmE*), postdated cheque (*BrE*); **~ posfechado** BANCA, FIN postdated check (*AmE*), postdated cheque (*BrE*); **~ postal** BANCA, FIN postal check (*AmE*), postal cheque (*BrE*); **~ preautorizado** BANCA, FIN pre-authorized check (*AmE*), pre-authorized cheque (*BrE*); **~ prescrito** BANCA, FIN stale check (*AmE*), stale cheque (*BrE*); **~ sin provisión de fondos** BANCA uncovered check (*AmE*), uncovered cheque (*BrE*); **~ sin provisión suficiente de fondos** BANCA, FIN not-sufficient-funds check (*AmE*) (*NSF check, N/S check*), not-sufficient-funds cheque (*BrE*) (*NSF cheque, N/S cheque*); **~ registrado** BANCA registered check (*AmE*), registered cheque (*BrE*); **~ rehusado** BANCA, FIN dishonored check (*AmE*), dishonoured cheque (*BrE*); **~ reservado** BANCA, FIN earmarked check (*AmE*), earmarked cheque (*BrE*); **~ de seguridad** COM GEN safety check; **~ sólo para depositar** BANCA, FIN account-only check (*AmE*), account-only cheque (*BrE*); **~ del sueldo** RRHH pay check (*AmE*), pay cheque (*BrE*); **~ de tesorería** BANCA treasurer check (*AmE*), treasurer cheque (*BrE*); **~ por valor de** BANCA, FIN check to the amount of (*AmE*), cheque to the amount of (*BrE*); **~ sin valor** BANCA, FIN worthless check (*AmE*), worthless cheque (*BrE*); **~ vencido** BANCA, FIN overdue check (*AmE*), overdue cheque (*BrE*); **~ de ventanilla** BANCA, FIN counter check (*AmE*), counter cheque (*BrE*); **~ de viajero** BANCA, FIN traveler's check (*AmE*), traveller's cheque (*BrE*); **~ a la vista** BANCA, FIN stock check (*AmE*), stock cheque (*BrE*)

chequera *f* BANCA, COM GEN, FIN check book (*AmE*), cheque book (*BrE*)

cheques: ~ **no canjeados** *m pl* BANCA float

chi: ~**-cuadrado** *m* MAT *estadística* chi square

chicharros *m pl* BOLSA drop-lock stock

chico, -a: **~ prodigio** *m,f* COM GEN whizz kid (*infrml*)

chimenea *f* IND, TRANSP smokestack, stack

chip *m* INFO chip; **~ biológico** INFO biochip; **~ de memoria** INFO memory chip; **~ de silicio** IND, INFO silicon chip

chocar *vt* TRANSP *comercio de coches* knock (*jarg*); ◆ **~ con los derechos de alguien** DER impinge on sb's rights; **~ con la ley** DER fall foul of the law

choque: **~ adverso de la oferta** *m* ECON *macroeconomía* adverse supply shock; **~ cultural** *m* COM GEN culture shock; **~ externo** *m* ECON *de la oferta* external shock; **~ de la inflación** *m* ECON inflation shock; **~ del lado de la oferta** *m* ECON supply side shock; **~ de oferta** *m* ECON supply shock; **~ de productividad** *m* ECON productivity shock

CI *abr* BOLSA (*corredor intermediario*) IDB (*BrE*) (*interdealer broker*), INFO (*circuito integrado*) IC (*integrated circuit*)

Cía *abr* (*compañía*) COM GEN Co. (*company*)

ciberespacio *m* INFO cyberspace

cibernética *f* INFO cybernetics

cíclico *adj* BOLSA, COM GEN cyclical

ciclo *m* COM GEN, ECON cycle; **~ de acceso** *Esp* (*cf ciclo de ingreso AmL*) BANCA, COM GEN, FIN, GES access cycle; **~ del activo circulante** BANCA, COM GEN, FIN, GES current asset cycle; **~ administrativo** GES management cycle; **~ amplio** COM GEN long-wave cycle; **~ de búsqueda** BANCA, COM GEN, FIN, GES search cycle; **~ de caducidad** BOLSA expiration cycle; **~ de carga** TRANSP turnaround (*AmE*), turnround (*BrE*); **~ del cerdo** ECON hog cycle; **~ comercial** COM GEN, ECON trade cycle; **~ de construcción** BANCA, COM GEN, FIN building cycle; **~ contable** CONT accounting cycle; **~ de control** BANCA, COM GEN, FIN, GES control cycle; **~ de conversión en efectivo** FIN cash conversion cycle; **~ de desarrollo del producto** IND, V&M product development cycle; **~ económico** ECON business cycle, economic cycle; **~ económico-político** ECON, POL political business cycle; **~ específico** COM GEN specific cycle; **~ de existencias** COM GEN stock cycle; **~ de facturación** COM GEN billing cycle; **~ industrial** COM GEN reference cycle; **~ de inflación de alternancias de recesión-expansión** ECON stop-go cycle of inflation; **~ de ingreso** *AmL* (*cf ciclo de acceso Esp*) BANCA, COM GEN, FIN, GES access cycle; **~ de inventario** COM GEN inventory cycle; **~ de inversión en existencias** BANCA, COM GEN, FIN, GES inventory investment cycle; **~ Juglar** ECON Juglar cycle; **~ de Kitchin** ECON Kitchin cycle; **~ de Kondratieff** ECON Kondratieff cycle; **~ Kuznets** ECON Kuznets cycle; **~ de larga duración** COM GEN long cycle, long wave cycle; **~ logístico** ECON logistic cycle; **~ menor** BANCA, COM GEN, FIN, GES minor cycle; **~ del mercado** COM GEN market cycle; **~ del mercado de valores** BOLSA stock market cycle; **~ de negocios** COM GEN business cycle; **~ de ocupación** IMP/EXP, TRANSP *vagones, buques* turnout; **~ de operación** CONT operating cycle; **~ de peritaje continuo** COM GEN continuous survey cycle (*CSC*); **~ presupuestario** BANCA, COM GEN, FIN, GES budget cycle; **~ principal** BANCA, FIN, GES major cycle; **~ del producto** ECON, IND product cycle; **~ restringido** BANCA, COM GEN, FIN, GES constrained cycle; **~ de trabajo** COM GEN, RRHH work cycle; **~ en vacío** BANCA, FIN, GES idle cycle; **~ de vencimiento** BOLSA expiration cycle; **~ de viaje** V&M journey cycle; **~ vicioso** ECON vicious cycle (*jarg*); **~ de vida** V&M *de producto* life cycle; **~ de la vida familiar** V&M family life cycle; **~ de vida de un producto** V&M product life cycle; **~ de visitas** V&M calling cycle; **~ vital de la inversión** BOLSA investment life cycle

ciencia: **~ actuarial** *f* SEG actuarial science; **~ administrativa** *f* GES management science; **~ del comportamiento** *f* GES, V&M behavioral science (*AmE*), behavioural science (*BrE*); **~ del derecho** *f* DER jurisprudence

ciencias: **~ empresariales** *f pl* GES management science

científico, -a *m,f* RRHH scientist

ciento: **por ~** *fra* (*p.c.*) COM GEN per cent (*p.c.*)

cierre *m* COM GEN, CONT closure, close, closing, *de acuerdo* conclusion; **~ del año fiscal** CONT, FISC end of the taxation year; **~ anticipado** DER *comercial* preclosing; **~ anual** BANCA, COM GEN, CONT, FIN annual closing; **~ a la baja** BOLSA bear closing; **~ bancario** COM GEN bank holiday (*BrE*), legal holiday (*AmE*); **~ de la bolsa** BOLSA, COM GEN, FIN closing of the stock exchange; ~ **central** TRANSP midlock; ~ **de la compra** BANCA, COM GEN, CONT, FIN buying end; ~ **defectuoso** TRANSP short closing; ~ **de edición** MEDIOS copy deadline; ~ **de ejercicio** CONT year-end closing; ~ **de la emisión** MEDIOS closedown; ~ **empresarial** COM GEN, ECON, RRHH lockout; ~ **de empresas** COM GEN, shut-down of plants; ~ **intermedio** BANCA, COM GEN, CONT, FIN interim closing; ~ **de libros** BANCA, COM GEN, CONT, FIN cut-off; ~ **de libros para inventario** CONT cut-off; ~ **de licitación** BOLSA bid closing; ~ **del mercado** BANCA, BOLSA, COM GEN, CONT, FIN close of the market, market close, market sealing; ~ **del negocio** BANCA, COM GEN, CONT, FIN close of business; ~ **de la operación** BANCA, COM GEN, CONT, FIN buying end; ~ **de operaciones** BANCA, COM GEN, CONT, FIN close of business; ~ **patronal** ADMIN lock-out, BOLSA shutdown; ~ **previo** BANCA, BOLSA, COM GEN, CONT, FIN previous closing; ~ **rápido** TRANSP *contenedores* quick tite®; ~ **por reforma** BANCA, COM GEN, CONT, FIN down period; ~ **de la venta de una propiedad** INMOB real estate closing; ◆ **al** ~ BOLSA at closing

ciervo *m* BOLSA stag

CI&F[1] *abr* (*coste, seguro y flete Esp, costo, seguro y flete AmL*) IMP/EXP, SEG, TRANSP CI&F (*cost, insurance and freight*)

CI&F[2]: ~ **desembarcado** *m* IMP/EXP CIF landed

cifra *f* COM GEN figure, COMS *mensaje codificado* cipher, ECON, FIN, MAT, PATENT figure; ~ **aproximada** MAT approximate range; ~ **confusa** COM GEN blind figure; ~ **de ingresos del punto muerto** CONT break-even level of income; ~ **de negocios** BANCA, COM GEN, CONT, FIN, GES, RRHH turnover; ~ **de negocios anual** COM GEN, CONT annual turnover; ~ **de ventas** COM GEN, CONT, V&M sales volume; ~ **de ventas anual** COM GEN, CONT annual turnover

cifrado *m* BANCA, COMS, INFO encryption, encoding

cifras *f pl* COM GEN figures; ~ **ajustadas a los cambios estacionales** COM GEN, FIN figures adjusted for seasonal variations; ~ **ajustadas estacionalmente** COM GEN, FIN seasonally-adjusted figures; ~ **comerciales** COM GEN trade figures; ~ **consolidadas** CONT consolidated figures; ~ **de crecimiento** COM GEN, ECON growth figures; ~ **de desempleo** POL, PROT SOC, RRHH unemployment figures; ~ **de empleo** POL, PROT SOC, RRHH employment figures; ~ **de empleo no ajustadas según los cambios estacionales** POL, PROT SOC, RRHH seasonally-unadjusted employment figures; ~ **de exportación** ECON, IMP/EXP export figures; ~ **oficiales** COM GEN official figures; ~ **reales** ECON actual figures; ~ **revisadas** COM GEN revised figures; ~ **de ventas** V&M sales data, sales figures, sales turnover; ◆ **sus** ~ **concuerdan con las nuestras** CONT your figures are in agreement with ours; **en** ~ **desajustadas** COM GEN in unadjusted figures; **en** ~ **reales** ECON in real terms; **en** ~ **redondas** FIN in round figures

cilindro *m* INFO, TRANSP cylinder (*Cy*); ~ **contrachapado en madera** *Esp* (*cf cilindro terciado en madera AmL*) TRANSP plywood drum; ~ **contrachapado en madera** *AmL* (*cf cilindro contrachapado en madera Esp*) TRANSP plywood drum

cimiento: ~ **frontal** *m* INMOB front foot (*AmE*), foundation

cimógeno *m* IND cymogene

cimómetro *m* IND cymometer

cinco: **las** ~ **grandes** *f pl* POL the Big Five

cinta *f* COM GEN, INFO, MEDIOS ribbon, tape; ~ **adhesiva para las ventanas** COM GEN window sticker; ~ **consolidada** BOLSA consolidated tape; ~ **magnética** INFO magnetic tape; ~ **para medir** COM GEN measuring tape; ~ **métrica** COM GEN tape measure; ~ **de papel** INFO paper tape; ~ **de teletipo** BOLSA ticker tape; ~ **transbordadora** COM GEN travelator; ~ **transportadora** *Esp* (*cf máquina transportadora AmL*) TRANSP conveyor belt; ~ **de video** *AmL ver cinta de vídeo Esp*; ~ **de vídeo** *Esp* COMS, INFO, MEDIOS videocassette, videotape

cinturón: ~ **ecológico** *m* MED AMB green belt; ~ **de ronda** *m* TRANSP ring road; ~ **de seguridad** *m Esp* (*cf faja de seguridad AmL*) TRANSP safety belt, seat belt; ~ **verde** *m* MED AMB green belt

circuito *m* INFO circuit; ~ **adicionador** INFO adding circuit; ~ **de alimentación** INFO feed circuit; ~ **de arranque** INFO *equipo* driver; ~ **biestable** INFO *equipo* flip-flop; ~ **cerrado** INFO closed circuit; ~ **integrado** (*CI*) INFO integrated circuit (*IC*); ~ **lógico** INFO logic circuit

circulación *f* COM GEN, ECON, MEDIOS circulation, V&M pass-along (*jarg*); ~ **por carretera** TRANSP road traffic; ~ **de cheques en descubierto** BANCA check-kiting (*AmE*), kiting (*AmE*); ~ **de cheques sin fondos** BANCA check-kiting (*AmE*), kiting (*AmE*); ~ **de la información** COM GEN, INFO information flow; ~ **limitada** TRANSP limited distribution; ~ **media colocada** COM GEN average sold circulation; ~ **vial** TRANSP road traffic

circular *f* ADMIN, COMS circular, circular letter, round robin; ~ **del director** COM GEN director's circular

círculo *m* COM GEN circle; ~ **de calidad** GES, IND, RRHH quality circle

círculos: ~ **bancarios** *m pl* BANCA banking circles; ~ **económicos** *m pl* COM GEN business circles; ~ **financieros** *m pl* FIN financial circles; ~ **informáticos** *m pl* INFO computer circles

circunflejo *m* INFO circumflex

circunstancia: ~ **material** *f* SEG material circumstance

circunstancias *f pl* COM GEN circumstances; ~ **atenuantes** DER extenuating circumstances, mitigating circumstances; ~ **especiales** COM GEN special circumstances; ~ **familiares** RRHH family circumstances; ~ **hipotéticas** COM GEN hypothetical circumstances; ◆ **en estas** ~ COM GEN under the circumstances

CIS *abr* (*Centro de Investigaciones Sociológicas*) COM GEN Spanish social studies institute

cisterna *f* TRANSP tank (*TK*)

cita *f* COM GEN appointment; ◆ **sólo con** ~ **previa** COM GEN by appointment only

citación *f* DER, PATENT citation; ~ **judicial** DER citation, judicial notice, PATENT citation

citado: **antes** ~ *adj* COMS above-mentioned, previously-mentioned

citar *vt* DER, PATENT cite; ◆ ~ **a uno** DER, RRHH take out a summons against sb

City: **la** ~ *f* BANCA, BOLSA, CONT, FIN *Londres* the City (*BrE*)

ciudad: ~ **anfitriona** *f* COM GEN host city; ~ **generatriz** *f* ECON generative city; ~ **metropolitana** *f* COM GEN metropolitan town; ~ **óptima** *f* ECON optimum city;

~ parasitaria *f* ECON parasitic city; **~ de prueba** *f* COM GEN test town; **~ satélite** *f* COM GEN satellite town

ciudadana *f* POL citizen

ciudadanía *f* POL citizenship

ciudadano *m* POL citizen; **el ~ medio** V&M the man in the street; **el ~ de a pie** V&M the man in the street; **~ de segunda clase** COM GEN second-class citizen

cl *abr* (*centilitro*) COM GEN cl (*centiliter AmE, centilitre BrE*)

clamor: ~ público *m* COM GEN public outcry

claridad *f* CONT transparency

clase *f* BOLSA *opción* class, COM GEN category, class, FISC *de las aportaciones a la Seguridad Social* class, INFO sort, PATENT category, class, POL class, RRHH grade; **~ baja** COM GEN lower classes; **~ capitalista** ECON, POL capitalist class; **~ club** OCIO, TRANSP club class; **~ de construcción** SEG class of construction; **~ dominante** COM GEN, PROT SOC ruling class; **~ económica** OCIO, TRANSP economy class; **~ ejecutiva** OCIO, TRANSP executive class; **~ de empleo** FISC class of employment; **~ mundial** COM GEN world-class; **~ de negocio** FISC class of business; **~ nocturna** PROT SOC evening class; **~ de opción** BOLSA class of option; **~ de pagos** FISC class of payments; **~ preferente** OCIO, TRANSP business class; **~ de propiedad** FISC, INMOB class of property; **~ de seguro** SEG class of insurance; **~ social** COM GEN, PROT SOC, RRHH social grade; **~ de tarifa** TRANSP rate class; **la ~ trabajadora** RRHH the working class; **~ turista** OCIO, TRANSP tourist class; **~ única** OCIO, TRANSP one class

clases: ~ de compra *f pl* V&M buy classes; **~ particulares** *f pl* PROT SOC private tuition

clasificación *f* BOLSA rating, COM GEN classification, ranking, CONT classification, INFO arrangement, sorting, MAT *estadística* grouping, RRHH ranking; **~ de acciones** BOLSA share classification, share rating; **~ de actividad** CONT activity classification; **~ por antigüedad** COM GEN ranking in order of seniority; **~ por cribadura** INFO *ramación* bubble sort, sifting sort; **~ de cuentas** CONT classification of accounts; **~ decimal** COM GEN, INFO decimal sorting; **~ industrial común** IND standard industrial classification (*SIC*); **~ industrial estándar** IND standard industrial classification (*SIC*); **~ intermedia** BOLSA mezzanine bracket; **~ laboral** RRHH work classification; **~ normalizada de mercancías de flete** TRANSP standard freight trade classification (*SFTC*); **~ numérica** INFO digital sort; **~ por objetivos** COM GEN classification by object; **~ de países del Banco Mundial** BANCA World Bank classification of countries; **~ de productos** COM GEN product classification; **~ del puesto de trabajo** RRHH job classification; **~ de responsabilidad** CONT responsibility classification; **~ retroactiva** POL retroactive classification; **~ de los riesgos** SEG classification of risks; **~ de títulos** BOLSA bond rating; **~ de valores** BOLSA security rating; **~ de White** BOLSA White's rating

Clasificación: ~ del Best *f* SEG Best's Rating (*AmE*); **~ Industrial según Normas Internacionales** *f* IND International Standards Industrial Classification (*ISIC*); **~ Internacional del Empleo** *f* ECON International Standard Classification of Occupations (*ISCO*); **~ Normativa para el Comercio Internacional** *f* COM GEN Standard International Trade Classification (*SITC*)

clasificaciones: ~ de emplazamiento de carteles *f pl* V&M poster site classifications

clasificado: no ~ *adj* COM GEN ungraded, FIN *agencias mercantiles* not rated; **~ para exposición** *adj* V&M display classified; **~ por tamaño** *adj* COM GEN graded by size

clasificador, a *m,f* COM GEN sorter

clasificadora: ~ de tarjetas *f* INFO card sorter

clasificados *m pl* MEDIOS, V&M *publicidad* smalls

clasificar¹ *vt* ADMIN classify, rank, COM GEN categorize, classify, rank, DER categorize, ECON categorize, classify, rank; ♦ **~ por fecha** CONT *cuentas* age; **~ incorrectamente** COM GEN misfile

clasificar²: **sin ~** *fra* COM GEN unsorted (*u/s*)

clasificarse *vi* COM GEN rank

claudicar *vi* IND give up

claustro *m* COM GEN staff meeting

cláusula *f* COM GEN, DER, RRHH, SEG clause; **~ de abandono** SEG *seguro marítimo* abandonment clause; **~ de abandono de mercado** BANCA, DER, SEG market out clause; **~ abrogatoria** DER *en un contrato* annulling clause, cancellation clause, cancelling clause (*BrE*), canceling clause (*AmE*); **~ de aceleración** BANCA acceleration clause; **~ de actualización de precio** DER, SEG standard of value clause; **~ adicional** DER additional clause; **~ de adquisición posterior** BANCA *contrato hipotecario* after-acquired clause; **~ al portador** BOLSA bearer clause; **~ ambos culpables de colisión** SEG *seguro marítimo* both-to-blame collision clause; **~ de arbitraje** COM GEN, DER arbitration clause; **~ de autorización** DER enabling clause; **~ de aviso de cancelación** SEG notice of cancellation clause; **~ de beneficiario** SEG beneficiary clause; **~ de beneficio del seguro** SEG benefit of insurance clause; **~ de buena fe** COM GEN bona fide clause; **~ de caducidad** SEG lapse clause, obsolescence clause; **~ de carga peligrosa** RRHH, TRANSP hot cargo clause; **~ coaseguro de daños maquinaria** SEG machinery damage co-ins clause; **~ de colisión** SEG collision clause, running down clause (*RDC*); **~ comercial** BANCA, DER, SEG commerce clause; **~ condicional** BANCA, DER, SEG contingency clause; **~ del conocimiento de embarque** BANCA, DER, SEG bill of lading clause; **~ de un contrato** BANCA, DER, SEG contract clause; **~ de conversión** BANCA, DER, SEG conversion privilege; **~ de daños de mala fe** SEG malicious damage clause; **~ de decisión** BANCA, DER, SEG action statement; **~ de depósito** TRANSP escrow clause; **~ derogatoria** BANCA, DER, SEG overriding clause; **~ de desembarco** COM GEN London clause (*LC*); **~ de desvío** SEG *marina* deviation clause (*D/C*); **~ de disponibilidad** BANCA, DER, SEG availability clause; **~ disputable** DER, SEG contestable clause; **~ de edificios en ruinas** INMOB, SEG fallen building clause; **~ de elusión** BANCA, DER, SEG escape clause; **~ de errores y omisiones** SEG errors and omissions clause; **~ de evasión** BANCA, DER, SEG escape clause; **~ de excepción** DER exceptions clause; **~ de exclusiones generales** SEG general exclusions clause; **~ exclusivamente sindical** RRHH union-only clause (*BrE*); **~ de exención** COM GEN *en contrato* exemption clause; **~ eximente de responsabilidad** DER hold-harmless clause; **~ de fin de la responsabilidad** DER, TRANSP *navegación* cesser clause; **~ de finiquito** SEG adjustment clause; **~ de franco dentro** IMP/EXP, TRANSP free in clause; **~ de franquicia** BANCA, DER, SEG franchise clause; ~ **de garantía negativa** BANCA negative pledge clause; ~ **de gestión y trabajo** DER, SEG sue and labor clause (*AmE*) (*S/LC*), sue and labour clause (*BrE*) (*S/LC*); ~ **de guerra** SEG war clause; ~ **Himalaya** TRANSP Himalaya clause; ~ **de hipoteca** BANCA, DER, SEG mortgage clause; ~ **de huelga** RRHH strike clause; ~ **de inalterabilidad** IND, INMOB *contrato de hipoteca* nondisturbance clause; ~ **de indemnización de pasajeros** BANCA, DER, SEG passenger indemnity clause; ~ **inoperante** DER inoperative clause; ~ **de insolvencia** SEG insolvency clause; ~ **de instituto** SEG institute clause; ~ **irrecusable** SEG incontestable clause; ~ **Janson** SEG *marina* Janson Clause; ~ **laboral** RRHH labor clause (*AmE*), labour clause (*BrE*); ~ **limitativa de participación en holdings** BANCA, DER, SEG grandfather clause; ~ **de límite de responsabilidad** BANCA, DER, SEG memorandum clause; ~ **de línea roja** SEG *en póliza de cargas* red-line clause; ~ **de medidas preventivas** DER, SEG sue and labor clause (*AmE*) (*S/LC*), sue and labour clause (*BrE*) (*S/LC*); ~ **de modificación parcial** BANCA, DER, SEG bisque clause; ~ **monetaria** BANCA, DER, SEG currency clause; ~ **de movilidad** RRHH mobility clause; ~ **multidivisa** BANCA, DER, SEG multicurrency option; ~ **de nación más favorecida** DER, ECON, POL most-favored nation clause (*AmE*), most-favoured nation clause (*BrE*); ~ **de negligencia** DER, SEG, TRANSP neglect clause, negligence clause; ~ **de no asegurar** SEG not to insure clause; ~ **de no contribución** SEG noncontribution clause; ~ **de no declaración de huelga** RRHH no-strike clause; ~ **de no disputa** SEG noncontestability clause; ~ **de no objeción** SEG noncontestability clause; ~ **obligatoria** SEG mandatory provision; ~ **onerosa** DER conditional clause; ~ **de otros seguros** SEG other insurance clause; ~ **pagadera a la venta** BANCA, FIN due-on-sale clause (*AmE*); ~ **de pago anticipado** FIN prepayment clause; ~ **de pagos simultáneos** FIN simultaneous payments clause; ~ **de penalización** BANCA, DER, SEG penalty clause; ~ **de pérdida sin descubrir** DER, FIN, SEG, TRANSP undiscovered loss clause; ~ **de proporcionalidad** SEG average clause; ~ **de protección** BOLSA hedge clause; ~ **de provisión para cancelaciones** SEG cancellation provision clause; ~ **puerta a puerta** SEG door-to-door clause; ~ **punitiva** BANCA, DER, SEG penalty clause; ~ **que excluye los daños por electricidad** SEG electrical damage clause; ~ **de ratificación de compromiso** SEG *marítimo* attestation clause, commitment acknowledgement clause; ~ **de reajuste** SEG escalation clause; ~ **de reanudación** RRHH reopener clause; ~ **de reconocimiento exclusivo** RRHH recognition-only clause (*BrE*); ~ **de reintegro del salto pendiente** INMOB *hipotecas* acceleration clause; ~ **de relleno** BANCA topping-up clause; ~ **de renuncia** SEG waiver clause; ~ **de reposición** SEG replacement clause; ~ **de rescisión** DER termination clause, cancellation clause, cancelling clause (*BrE*), canceling clause (*AmE*); ~ **resolutoria** DER cancellation clause, cancelling clause (*BrE*), canceling clause (*AmE*), termination clause; ~ **de responsabilidad financiera** SEG *automóviles* financial responsibility clause; ~ **de retrocompra** DER buy-back clause; ~ **de revisión** DER trigger clause; ~ **de revisión salarial automática** BANCA, DER, RRHH, SEG escalator clause; ~ **por riesgo intrínseco de explosión** SEG inherent explosion clause; ~ **roja** BANCA, FIN, IMP/EXP, TRANSP red clause; ~ **de rotación** BANCA *colocación de una emisión* rotation clause; ~ **de rotura** SEG breakage clause; ~ **de salvaguardia** BANCA, DER, SEG disaster clause, escape clause; ~ **secreta** BANCA, DER, SEG secret clause; ~ **sindical en contrato laboral** BANCA, DER, SEG union security clause; ~ **sobre actos dolosos** SEG malicious acts clause; ~ **sobre aumento de precio** BANCA, DER, SEG price escalation clause; ~ **sobre doble valoración** SEG dual valuation clause; ~ **sobre el emplazamiento** TRANSP location clause; ~ **sobre etiquetas** COM GEN label clause (*LC*); ~ **sobre paridad** SEG parity clause; ~ **sobre pedidos** BANCA, DER order clause; ~ **sobre prórroga** SEG continuation clause (*CC*), renewal clause; ~ **de status quo** RRHH status quo clause; ~ **de subrogación** DER subrogation clause; ~ **de supervivencia** SEG survivorship clause; ~ **de tasación** ECON appraisal clause; ~ **de todo o nada** BOLSA all-or-nothing clause (*BrE*) (*AON clause*); ~ **de tránsito** SEG, TRANSP *póliza de carga* transit clause; ~ **de valor convenido** SEG agreed valuation clause; ~ **de valor en mercado** INMOB, SEG market value clause; ~ **de valoración** SEG valuation clause (*VC*); ~ **de variación de precios** V&M price variation clause; ~ **de venta del buque** SEG sale of vessel clause

Cláusula: ~ **de Fletes del Instituto** *f* TRANSP Institute Cargo Clause (*ICC*); ~ **Inchmaree** *f* SEG *en pólizas de casco* Inchmaree Clause

cláusulas: ~ **comerciales internacionales** *f pl* (*INCOTERM*) ECON, IMP/EXP International Commercial Term (*INCOTERM*)

clausura *f* GES *reunión* adjournment

clausurar *vt* GES *reunión* adjourn

clave *f* INFO key, code element; ~ **de búsqueda** INFO search key, seek key; ~ **de clasificación** INFO sort key; ~ **directa** INFO hot key; ~ **de registro** INFO record key

clavo *m* BOLSA spike (*jarg*)

cliché *m* ADMIN, MEDIOS *tipografía* boilerplate

cliente *mf* BANCA, COM GEN, MEDIOS, V&M client, customer, punter (*infrml*); ~ **de auditoría** CONT audit client; ~ **corporativo(-a)** *m,f* BANCA corporate client, corporate customer; ~ **de cuenta corriente** BANCA current account customer; ~ **por derecho propio** BOLSA separate customer; ~ **extranjero(-a)** *m,f* V&M overseas customer; ~ **fijo(-a)** *m,f* COM GEN permanent customer; ~ **futuro(-a)** *m,f* COM GEN, V&M prospective customer; ~ **habitual** COM GEN regular customer; ~ **importante** COM GEN big customer; ~ **de inversión privado(-a)** *m,f* BANCA, FIN private investment client; ~ **nominativo(-a)** *m,f* DER named client; ~ **potencial** COM GEN prospect; ~ **de primer orden** COM GEN bluechip customer; ~ **principal** COM GEN principal customer; ~ **problema** COM GEN problem customer; ~ **que solicita un préstamo** BANCA, COM GEN borrowing customer; ◆ **ser** ~ **de** BOLSA be trading at

clientela *f* COM GEN custom, clientele

clientes: ~ **existentes** *m pl* V&M live customers

cliente/servidor *m* INFO client/server

clima: ~ **económico** *m* COM GEN, ECON, POL economic climate, economic weather; ~ **económico favorable** *m* ECON favourable economic climate (*BrE*), favorable economic climate (*AmE*); ~ **financiero** *m* ECON financial climate; ~ **inversor** *m* ECON investment climate; ~ **laboral sano** *m* ECON, RRHH positive labor relations (*AmE*), positive labour relations (*BrE*); ~ **político** *m*

COM GEN, POL political climate; ~ **socioeconómico** *m* ECON, PROT SOC socioeconomic climate

climatización *f* PROT SOC air conditioning

climatizado *adj* PROT SOC air-conditioned

clisé: ~ **de trazo** *m* V&M line block

clon *m* COM GEN, INFO clone

clonar *vt* COM GEN, INFO clone

clorofluorocarbono *m* (*CFC*) MED AMB chlorofluoro-carbon (*CFC*)

club: ~ **de beneficios mutuos** *m* FIN benefit club; ~ **de exportadores** *m* IMP/EXP export club; ~ **de inversión** *m* BOLSA investment club; ~ **de salud** *m* OCIO health club; ~ **de suscripción** *m* BOLSA *de intermediarios financieros* subscription club

Club: ~ **de París** *m* ECON Paris Club; ~ **de Roma** *m* ECON *a partir de 1968* Club of Rome

cm *abr* (*centímetro*) COM GEN cm (*centimeter AmE, centimetre BrE*)

CNMV *abr* (*Comisión Nacional del Mercado de Valores*) BOLSA ≈ SEC (*BrE*) (*Securities and Exchange Commission*), ≈ SIB (*BrE*) (*Securities and Investments Board*), ≈ SEC (*AmE*) (*Stock Exchange Commission*)

coacción *f* COM GEN undue influence, DER duress

coactivo *adj* COM GEN compulsory

coadyuvar *vt* DER aid and abet

coalición *f* POL coalition

coarrendatario, -a: ~ **con derecho de supervivencia** *m,f* BOLSA joint tenant with right of survivorship

coarriendo *m* DER joint tenancy

coasegurado *adj* SEG coinsured

coasegurador, a *m,f* SEG coinsurer

coaseguro *m* SEG coinsurance

coasociación *f* COM GEN joint partnership

coauditor, a *m,f* CONT joint auditor

cobertura *f* BOLSA margin, COM GEN cover (*C'vr*), coverage, hedging, margin, INFO margin, SEG cover (*C'vr*); ~ **abierta** SEG open cover (*OC*); ~ **de activos** BOLSA asset coverage; ~ **amarilla** BOLSA yellow strip; ~ **ampliada** SEG extended coverage; ~ **anticipada** BOLSA anticipatory hedge; ~ **apropiada** SEG adequacy of coverage; ~ **de aumento de coste** *Esp* (*cf cobertura de aumento de costo AmL*) SEG cost escalation cover (*BrE*); ~ **de aumento de costo** *AmL* (*cf cobertura de aumento de coste Esp*) SEG cost escalation cover (*BrE*); ~ **de averías** SEG W.A. cover; ~ **bruta** V&M gross cover; ~ **del cambio de divisas** CONT, FIN foreign exchange hedge; ~ **de cargo fijo** CONT fixed charge coverage; ~ **de colisión** SEG collision coverage; ~ **de compra** BOLSA buying hedge, purchasing hedge; ~ **de compra de una opción** BOLSA option-buying hedge; ~ **de compra con posición larga** BOLSA put buying hedge; ~ **contra cambio de precios** BOLSA hedging; ~ **contra catástrofe** SEG catastrophe cover; ~ **contra encalladura** SEG cover against stranding; ~ **contra responsabilidad del empleador** *AmL* (*cf cobertura contra responsabilidad del empresario Esp*) DER, SEG employers' liability coverage; ~ **contra responsabilidad del empresario** *Esp* (*cf cobertura contra responsabilidad del empleador AmL*) DER, SEG employers' liability coverage; ~ **contra todo riesgo** SEG all-risks cover; ~ **cruzada** BOLSA cross hedge, cross hedging; ~ **de dependientes** SEG dependent coverage; ~ **de dividendo de acciones preferentes** CONT pre-ferred dividend coverage; ~ **de dividendos** BOLSA, CONT dividend cover; ~ **eficaz** V&M *de anuncio de publicidad* effective cover; ~ **escasa** COM GEN scant coverage; ~ **fija** BOLSA fixed hedge; ~ **fiscal** *m* FISC tax umbrella; ~ **por flete, sobreestadía y defensa** SEG, TRANSP freight, demurrage and defence cover (*BrE*) (*FD&D cover*), freight, demurrage and defense cover (*AmE*) (*FD&D cover*); ~ **a futuro** BOLSA forward cover; ~ **de gastos fijos** CONT fixed charge coverage; ~ **general** V&M blanket coverage; ~ **global del precio de mercado** BOLSA overall market price coverage; ~ **de guerra y transporte marino** SEG war and marine transportation cover (*W&M cover*); ~ **informativa** MEDIOS news coverage; ~ **por insolvencia de partici-pantes en el proyecto** SEG project participants' insolvency cover; ~ **interna** V&M *publicidad* inside front; ~ **de inversión internacional** SEG overseas investment cover; ~ **local** MEDIOS *TV* spot coverage; ~ **máxima** BOLSA maximum coverage; ~ **en los medios de comunicación** MEDIOS, V&M media coverage; ~ **de mercado** V&M market coverage; ~ **neta** V&M net cover; ~ **de noticias** MEDIOS news coverage; ~ **obligatoria mínima** BOLSA minimum margin requirement; ~ **de opción** BOLSA option coverage; ~ **oro** ECON gold cover; ~ **perfecta** BOLSA perfect hedge; ~ **periodística** MEDIOS press coverage; ~ **de una posición corta** BOLSA short hedge; ~ **de posición faltante** BOLSA short covering; ~ **de una posición larga** BOLSA long hedge; ~ **publicitaria** V&M advertising coverage; ~ **repartida entre varias aseguradoras** BOLSA divided coverage; ~ **secundaria** V&M secondary coverage; ~ **del seguro** SEG insurance coverage (*AmE*), insurance cover (*BrE*); ~ **selectiva** BOLSA selective hedge; ~ **televisiva** MEDIOS television coverage; ~ **total** COM GEN *noticias*, MEDIOS *acontecimiento* full coverage, SEG full coverage, fully comprehensive cover (*fully comp*); ~ **de venta** BOLSA selling hedge; ~ **de venta de una opción** BOLSA option-selling hedge; ~ **de venta de opciones de compra** BOLSA call selling hedge; ~ **de ventas** V&M sales coverage; ♦ **de amplia ~** COM GEN wide-ranging; **sin ~** BOLSA unhedged; **de ~ total** COM GEN, DER *licencias* blanket

coberturista: ~ **de inversiones** *mf* BOLSA investment hedger

COBOL *abr* (*lenguaje común orientado a la gestión y los negocios*) INFO COBOL (*Common Business Oriented Language*)

cobrable *adj* COM GEN collectible

cobrado: **no ~** *adj* BANCA, COM GEN, FIN uncashed; ~ **y entregado** *adj* COM GEN collected and delivered (*C&D*)

cobrador, a *m,f* COM GEN, RRHH collector; ~ **de alquileres** INMOB rent collector; ~ **de deudas** FIN debt collector

cobranza *f* COM GEN collection; ~ **de primas** SEG collection of premiums

cobrar **1.** *vt* BANCA call, *cheque* cash, clear, BOLSA *prima* collect, COM GEN charge, call, FIN cash, RRHH *sueldo* earn, V&M charge; ♦ ~ **de** RRHH draw from; ~ **un cheque** BANCA cash a check (*AmE*), cash a cheque (*BrE*); ~ **una deuda** FIN collect a debt; ~ **impulso** COM GEN *tendencia* gain momentum; ~ **la jornada y media** RRHH be on time and a half; ~ **un precio excesivo** BANCA, V&M overcharge; ~ **el seguro de enfermedad** RRHH draw sickness insurance; **2.** *vi* BANCA, CONT cash up; ♦ ~ **al contado** COM GEN, RRHH accept cash payments only, be paid in cash; ~ **comisión** SEG collect commission; ~ **forma** COM GEN take shape; ~ **de más** COM GEN, V&M overcharge

cobrarse: ~ **muchas víctimas de la bancarrota** *fra* FIN take a heavy toll of bankruptcies

cobro[1]: **al** ~ *adj* BOLSA *título* for collection

cobro[2] *m* COM GEN collection, FIN, FISC collection, positive cash flow; ~ **por adelantado** TRANSP advanced charge; ~ **antes de la entrega** COM GEN, ECON, FIN cash before delivery (*CBD*); ~ **anticipado** FISC advanced collection; ~ **automático de tarifas** TRANSP automatic fare collection; ~ **de cheques** BANCA, COM GEN, ECON, FIN collection of checks (*AmE*), collection of cheques (*BrE*); ~ **coercitivo** COM GEN enforced collection; ~ **contra documentación** BANCA, COM GEN, ECON, FIN collection against documents; ~ **de cuentas** CONT collection of accounts; ~ **de una deuda** FIN debt collection; ~ **de deudas de otra persona** COM GEN factoring; ~ **en efectivo** BANCA, CONT encashment; ~ **de un efecto** BANCA, CONT collection of a bill; ~ **escalonado** FISC scale charge; ~ **excesivo** BANCA, COM GEN overcharge (*o/c*); ~ **inicial** BOLSA front-end load; ~ **de una letra de cambio** BANCA, CONT collection of a bill; ~ **en metálico** BANCA, CONT encashment; ~ **a la par** COM GEN par collection; ~ **de portes** COMS, TRANSP freight collection; ~ **de primas** SEG collection of premiums; ~ **a reembolsar** BANCA, COM GEN, ECON, FIN collection payable

cobros *m pl* CONT cash receipts, FIN monies paid in

coche: ~ **cama** *m* TRANSP sleeper, sleeping car; ~ **de la empresa** *m* COM GEN, TRANSP company car; ~ **plataforma** *m* TRANSP *ferroviario* flat car (*AmE*), flat wagon (*BrE*); ~ **restaurante** *m* OCIO, TRANSP restaurant car

cociente *m* COM GEN quotient, ratio

coconsulta *f* RRHH joint consultation

codeterminación *f* RRHH codetermination

codicilo *m* DER codicil

codicioso *adj* FIN *compañía* acquisitive

codificación *f* INFO coding, encryption; ~ **binaria** INFO binary coding; ~ **de cuentas** CONT coding of accounts

codificado *m* BANCA, COMS, INFO encoding

codificador: ~-**descodificador** *m* INFO codec

código *m* COM GEN code; ~ **de acceso** *Esp* (*cf código de ingreso AmL*) INFO access code; ~ **de actividad** CONT activity coding; ~ **de arbitraje** BOLSA code of arbitration; ~ **de área** COMS area code; ~ **de autorización** BANCA authorization code; ~ **bancario** BANCA bank code; ~ **de barras** INFO bar code (*BrE*), bar graphics (*AmE*); ~ **binario** INFO binary code; ~ **de bloques** INFO block code; ~ **bursátil** BOLSA stock symbol; ~ **de calculadora** INFO computer code; ~ **cíclico** INFO cyclic code; ~ **cifrado** INFO cipher code; ~ **civil** COM GEN, DER civil code; ~ **de comercio** COM GEN, DER commercial code; ~ **de compensación de tierras** INMOB land compensation code; ~ **de conducta** BOLSA, COM GEN rules of fair practice, DER code of practice; ~ **de conducta a bordo** TRANSP code of conduct on ships; ~ **de conferencia de buque de línea** TRANSP liner conference code; ~ **de construcción** INMOB housing code; ~ **contable** CONT account number; ~ **de control de paridad** INFO parity-check block; ~ **de cotejo** INFO collator code; ~ **de cuentas** CONT code of accounts; ~ **deontológico** COM GEN code of conduct; ~ **de**

discado COM GEN, COMS dialing code (*AmE*), dialling code (*BrE*); ~ **de divisa** BANCA currency code; ~ **del documento** INFO document code; ~ **de edificación** INMOB building code, housing code; ~ **del envase** V&M *estudio de mercado* package code; ~ **estándar** COM GEN standard code; ~ **de ética** COM GEN code of ethics; ~ **exterior** COM GEN outer code; ~ **fiscal** FISC tax code; ~ **fuente** INFO source code; ~ **hazchem** TRANSP hazchem code; ~ **impositivo** FISC tax code; ~ **de impuestos interiores** FISC internal revenue code, ~ **de instrucciones simbólicas de carácter general para principiantes** (*BASIC*) INFO Beginners's All-Purpose Symbolic Instrucction Code (*BASIC*); ~ **de ingreso** *AmL* (*cf código de acceso Esp*) INFO access code; ~ **interior** COM GEN inner code; ~ **de intervención** INFO action code; ~ **inventarial** COM GEN schedule code; ~ **legible por máquina** V&M machine readable code; ~ **de liberación** POL liberalization code; ~ **de máquina** IND machine code; ~ **objeto de la información** CONT reporting object code; ~ **de objeto normalizado** POL standard object code; ~ **de la ONU** IMP/EXP code-UN; ~ **de orden** INFO operation code, order code; ~ **de país** BANCA country code; ~ **de perforación** COM GEN punch code; ~ **postal** COM GEN, COMS postcode (*BrE*), zip code (*AmE*), postal code (*BrE*); ~ **de práctica** COM GEN code of practice; ~ **de procedimiento** BOLSA code of procedure; ~ **de procedimiento aprobado** COM GEN approved code of practice (*ACOP*); ~ **de procedimiento común** COM GEN common code of practice; ~ **de procedimiento uniforme** BOLSA uniform practice code (*AmE*); ~ **publicitario** V&M advertising code; ~ **de respuesta** ADMIN answerback code; ~ **del trabajo** DER, RRHH labor code (*AmE*), labour code (*BrE*); ~ **de transacciones aduaneras** IMP/EXP, TRANSP customs transaction code (*CT*); ~ **valor para transmitir información** BOLSA ticker symbol

Código: ~ **Adicional de Aduanas** *m* IMP/EXP Customs Additional Code (*CAC*); ~ **de Empresa** *m* DER Companies Code; ~ **Marítimo Internacional de Productos Peligrosos** *m* TRANSP International Maritime Dangerous Goods Code (*IMDGC*); ~ **Uniforme de Comercio** *m* DER Uniform Commercial Code

códigos: ~ **legales** *m pl* DER statute book

codirección *f* GES, RRHH joint management

codirector, a *m,f* BANCA, GES, RRHH co-director, co-manager, joint director

codueño, -a *m,f* COM GEN co-owner, joint owner

coeficiente[1] : **de alto** ~ **de mano de obra** *adj* RRHH labor-intensive (*AmE*), labour-intensive (*BrE*)

coeficiente[2] *m* COM GEN ratio, factor, coefficient; ~ **alfa de Pareto** ECON Pareto's alpha coefficient; ~ **de amortización** BANCA, BOLSA, ECON, FIN depreciation rate; ~ **de asociación** RRHH coefficient of association; ~ **bancario** BANCA, BOLSA, ECON, FIN banking ratio; ~ **bancario de caja** BANCA bank cash ratio; ~ **beta de regresión** BOLSA beta coefficient (*AmE*); ~ **bursátil** BANCA, BOLSA, ECON, FIN stock exchange ratio; ~ **de caja** BANCA, FIN cash ratio; ~ **de capital desembolsado** FIN capital-outlay ratio; ~ **de capitalización** FIN capitalization ratio; ~ **de carga** COM GEN, TRANSP load factor; ~ **de cobertura de deuda** CONT debt coverage ratio; ~ **de confianza** MAT confidence coefficient; ~ **contable** FIN accounting ratio; ~ **de contingencia** BANCA, BOLSA, ECON, FIN coefficient of contingency; ~ **de correlación** MAT correlation coefficient, coefficient of correlation; ~ **de correlación múltiple** MAT coefficient of multiple correlation; ~ **de deflación** MAT deflator; ~ **de desembolso de dividendos** BOLSA, CONT dividend payout ratio; ~ **de determinación** MAT coefficient of determination; ~ **de determinación múltiple** MAT coefficient of multiple determination; ~ **de discriminación del mercado** ECON market discrimination coefficient; ~ **de empréstitos** CONT borrowing ratio; ~ **de endeudamiento** FIN debt-equity ratio; ~ **de Engel** ECON Engel coefficient; ~ **de explotación** CONT working ratio; ~ **de gestión** GES management ratio; ~ **de Gini** ECON Gini coefficient; ~ **de liquidez** BANCA liquidity ratio, CONT acid test ratio, liquid ratio, liquidity ratio, FIN liquidity ratio; ~ **obligatorio de caja** BANCA fractional cash reserve; ~ **del pasivo** f BOLSA liability rate; ~ **de pérdida** BANCA, BOLSA, ECON, FIN loss coefficient; ~ **de ponderación** BANCA, BOLSA, ECON, FIN weight coefficient; ~ **de producción** BANCA, BOLSA, ECON, FIN production coefficient; ~ **de pulsaciones** ADMIN keystroke rate; ~ **de regresión** COM GEN regression coefficient; ~ **de regresión múltiple** BANCA, BOLSA, ECON multiple regression coefficient; ~ **de rendimiento** COM GEN achievement quotient; ~ **de reserva** BANCA reserve ratio; ~ **de la reserva requerida** BANCA required-reserve ratio; ~ **solicitado** BOLSA rate asked; ~ **de solvencia** CONT, FIN solvency ratio; ~ **tributario** FISC tax ratio; ~ **de utilidad bruta** CONT gross profit ratio; ~ **de variación** MAT coefficient of variation; ~ **de volumen de beneficios** FIN profit-volume ratio (P/V)

coercitivo *adj* COM GEN enforced, *poder* compulsory

cofinanciación f BANCA, ECON, FIN co-financing

cofinanciar *vt* BANCA, ECON, FIN co-finance

cogerente *mf* RRHH joint manager

cogestión f RRHH codetermination

cognición f COM GEN, GES cognition

cohacedor, a *m,f* COM GEN briber

cohacer *vt* COM GEN bribe

cohecho *m Esp* (*cf coima AmL*) COM GEN bribe, kickback (*infrml*) (*AmE*)

coherencia f COM GEN consistency

coherente *adj* COM GEN, CONT, GES, V&M consistent

cohesión f COM GEN cohesion

coima f *AmL* (*cf cohecho Esp, cf soborno Esp*) COM GEN, DER, FIN, POL, RRHH bribe, kickback (*infrml*) (*AmE*)

coincidir *vi* COM GEN, RRHH coincide

coinversión f COM GEN joint venture (*JV*); ~ **por acciones** COM GEN equity joint venture; ~ **transfronteriza** FIN cross-border joint venture

cola f BOLSA tail, COM GEN *de la lista* queue, tail, INFO queue; ~ **de espera de trabajos** INFO job queue; ◆ **hacer** ~ COM GEN queue up (*BrE*), wait in line (*AmE*)

colaboración f COM GEN, GES collaboration

colaborador[1] *adj* COM GEN, GES collaborative

colaborador[2]**,a** *m,f* COM GEN, GES collaborator, contributor

colaboradores *m pl* COM GEN, GES cooperatives

colaborar *vi* COM GEN, GES collaborate, work together

colapso *m* BOLSA, COM GEN breakdown, collapse; ~ **de circulación** COM GEN circulation breakdown; ~ **del mercado de valores** BOLSA stock market collapse; ~ **de las operaciones** COM GEN operations breakdown

colateral[1] *adj* BANCA, COM GEN, FIN, MAT collateral

colateral[2] *m* BANCA, COM GEN, FIN collateral, security

Colbertismo *m* POL Colbertism

colchón: ~ **defensivo** *m* COM GEN defensive cushion

colección: ~ **de muestras** f COM GEN show card

colectivamente *adv* COM GEN collectively

colectivización f INMOB *de tierras* communization; ~ **de la agricultura** ECON collectivization of agriculture

colectivo[1] *adj* COM GEN collective

colectivo[2]: ~ **de trabajadores** *m* RRHH workers' collective

colector, a *m,f* COM GEN collector

colegio: ~ **electoral** *m* POL electoral college (*AmE*), polling station; ~ **privado** *m* COM GEN private school

Colegio: ~ **de Abogados** *m* BANCA, COM GEN, DER ≈ Bar Association (*AmE*), ≈ Law Society (*BrE*)

colineación: ~ **múltiple** f MAT multicollinearity

colisión f TRANSP collision (*col, coll*)

collage *m* V&M collage

colocación f BOLSA *obligaciones* placement, RRHH job placement; ~ **conveniente** RRHH niche; ~ **directa** BOLSA back-to-back placement; ~ **directa a los inversores de una emisión de títulos** BANCA direct placement; ~ **de una emisión de acciones** BOLSA placing of share issue; ~ **del estado** BANCA, FIN government investment; ~ **facultativa** SEG facultative placing; ~ **internacional** BANCA, FIN offshore placement; ~ **en el mercado secundario** BOLSA secondary offering; ~ **negociada** BOLSA negotiated underwriting; ~ **del pedestal** *m* TRANSP *contenedor* pedestal fitting; ~ **privada** BANCA private placement, BOLSA *inversión, depósito* put through, FIN private placing; ~ **segura** BANCA, FIN safe investment; ~ **nueva** o **de fondos** FIN remarging

colocaciones: ~ **de dinero** f pl BOLSA money placements

colocador, a; ~ **de bonos** *m,f* BOLSA bond dealer; ~ **de paquetes** BOLSA block positioner

colocar *vt* BOLSA place, COM GEN install, INFO set; ◆ ~ **progresivamente** COM GEN, INFO phase in

colonia f POL colony

colonización f POL settlement

coloquio *m* COM GEN colloquium

color *m* INFO color (*AmE*), colour (*BrE*); ~ **del anuncio** V&M spot color (*AmE*), spot colour (*BrE*); ~ **de fondo** INFO background color (*AmE*), background colour (*BrE*)

colores: **a dos** ~ *adj* MEDIOS two-color (*AmE*), two-colour (*BrE*)

colosal *adj* COM GEN huge

columna f COM GEN, CONT, MEDIOS column (*col.*); ~ **del debe** BANCA, CONT, FIN debit column; ~ **derecha** COM GEN, CONT right column, right-hand column; ~ **editorial** MEDIOS, V&M editorial column; ~ **del haber** BANCA, FIN credit column; ~ **izquierda** COM GEN, CONT left column, left-hand column; ~ **publicitaria** V&M advertising tower; ~ **sindicada** MEDIOS syndicated column; ~ **vertebral de la economía** ECON backbone of the economy

colusión f COM GEN, DER, ECON collusion

coma: ~ **decimal** f INFO, MAT decimal point

comanditario, -a *m,f* COM GEN, RRHH limited partner

comando *m* INFO command; ~ **de control** INFO control

command; ~ **integrado** INFO embedded command; ~ **puntual** INFO dot command

comba f BOLSA bulge

combatir vt COM GEN combat

combinación f COM GEN combination (*COMB*); ~ **de activos** CONT asset mix; ~ **de barra tractora** TRANSP drawbar combination; ~ **circulante** BOLSA current blend (*CB*); ~ **de divisas** BANCA currency mix; ~ **de estrategias** V&M mix; ~ **de estrategias de comunicación** MEDIOS, V&M communication mix; ~ **de estrategias de comunicaciones de marketing** V&M marketing communications mix; ~ **de estrategias de medios de comunicación** V&M media mix; ~ **de estrategias de precios** V&M pricing mix; ~ **de estrategias de productos** V&M product mix; ~ **de estrategias de promoción** V&M promotion mix; ~ **de estrategias promocionales** V&M promotional mix; ~ **de gastos** TRANSP combination of charges; ~ **mercantil** CONT business combination; ~ **de opción de compra y venta** BOLSA straddle combination; ~ **de políticas** GES policy mix; ~ **de políticas principales y subsidiarias** m ECON catalytic policy mix; ~ **de tarifas** TRANSP combination of rates

combinaciones f pl MAT combinations

combinar vt COM GEN combine, pool, ECON *recursos* pool; ◆ ~ **con** COM GEN combine with

combustible: ~ **para calderas** m TRANSP bunker fuel oil (*BFO*); ~ **fósil** m MED AMB fossil fuel; ~ **pesado** m MED AMB heavy fuel; ~ **para turbinas de avión** m TRANSP aviation turbine fuel; ~ **de uso privado** m FISC private fuel (*BrE*); ~ **para vehículos diesel** m TRANSP Derv fuel

combustión: ~ **espontánea** f TRANSP spontaneous combustion

comentar vt COM GEN comment on, discuss

comentario m COM GEN comment, commentary, POL oral note

comentarista: ~ **de radio** mf MEDIOS radio announcer; ~ **de televisión** mf MEDIOS television announcer

comerciabilidad f COM GEN tradeability

comerciable adj COM GEN marketable, tradeable

comerciables: **no** ~ m pl BOLSA, COM GEN, ECON, V&M nontradables

comercial m AmL (*cf anuncio Esp*) COM GEN, MEDIOS *TV, radio*, V&M commercial; ~ **profesional** mf ECON professional trader

comercialidad f COM GEN commercialism

comercializable adj BOLSA, COM GEN, ECON, V&M marketable, merchantable

comercialización f BOLSA, COM GEN, ECON, V&M commercialization, merchandising; ~ **automática** V&M automatic merchandising; ~ **cruzada** V&M cross merchandising; ~ **de un estilo de vida** V&M lifestyle merchandising; ~ **de mercancías** BOLSA commodities trading; ~ **de un personaje** V&M *publicidad* character merchandising; ~ **en tiendas** V&M in-store merchandising

comercializar vt COM GEN commercialize, market

comercialmente adv COM GEN commercially; ~ **viable** COM GEN commercially viable

comerciante mf BANCA, COM GEN trader, businessman, businesswoman, merchant (*mcht*), merchandiser, dealer; ~ **activo(-a)** m,f V&M active trader; ~ **al por mayor** COM GEN, SEG, V&M wholesale merchant; ~ **al por menor** COM GEN, IND, V&M retail trader; ~ **de bienes finales** IMP/EXP end-use trader; ~ **callejero(-a)** m,f COM GEN, V&M street trader (*BrE*), street vendor (*AmE*); ~ **individual** COM GEN, CONT, IND, V&M sole trader; ~ **en lana** ECON, IND wool merchant; ~ **mayorista** COM GEN, SEG, V&M wholesale dealer; ~ **de mercancía general** TRANSP general trader; ~ **que repercute IVA** FISC VAT registered trader (*BrE*)

comerciar vi COM GEN, ECON trade; ◆ ~ **en** COM GEN traffic in; ~ **bajo nombre de** COM GEN trade under the name of; ~ **por cuenta propia** BOLSA trade on one's account

comercio m BOLSA dealing, COM GEN, ECON, V&M commerce, dealing, trade; ~ **activo** COM GEN active business; ~ **al por mayor** COM GEN, SEG, V&M wholesale business, wholesale trade; ~ **al por menor** COM GEN, SEG, V&M retail trade, retail business; ~ **al menudeo** COM GEN, IND, V&M retail trade; ~ **bilateral** ECON bilateral trade; ~ **de cabotaje** TRANSP coasting trade; ~ **cíclico** ECON cyclical trade; ~ **circular** COM GEN switch trading (*jarg*); ~ **clandestino** COM GEN black trading; ~ **combinado** COM GEN combined trade; ~ **competitivo** ECON, IND, V&M competitive trading; ~ **continental** ECON, V&M continental trade; ~ **controlado** ECON managed trade; ~ **costero** TRANSP coastal trading; ~ **desigual** ECON unequal trade; ~ **desleal** RRHH unfair shop; ~ **entre estados** COM GEN interstate commerce (*AmE*); ~ **entre industrias** IND interindustry trade; ~ **entre países extranjeros** TRANSP cross trade; ~ **equitativo** V&M *precios* fair trade; ~ **especializado** V&M speciality trade (*BrE*), specialty trade (*AmE*); ~ **especulativo** BOLSA speculative trading; ~ **de exportación indirecto** IMP/EXP indirect export trading; ~ **exterior** ECON, IMP/EXP foreign trade; ~ **floreciente** ECON brisk commerce; ~ **fronterizo** IMP/EXP border trade; ~ **histórico** TRANSP historical trade; ~ **de importación** IMP/EXP import trade; ~ **informático** ECON, INFO computer trading; ~ **intercomunitario** ECON *UE*, V&M intercommunity trade; ~ **interindustrial** IND interindustry trade; ~ **interior** COM GEN domestic trade; ~ **interior de la UE** ECON, POL intra-EU trade; ~ **internacional** ECON, GES international trade, international business; ~ **interno** COM GEN domestic trade; ~ **intracomunitario** ECON intra-Community trade; ~ **invisible** ECON invisible trade; ~ **de la lana** ECON, IND wool trade; ~ **legal** DER, ECON fair trading; ~ **marítimo** COM GEN maritime trade, shipping trade; ~ **mayorista** ECON merchant trading; ~ **mayorista de exportación** IMP/EXP direct export trading; ~ **en mercado libre** ECON open market trading; ~ **multinacional** IMP/EXP multinational trading; ~ **mundial** ECON, POL world trade; ~ **de navegación corta** TRANSP short sea trade; ~ **con paquetes de acciones** BOLSA block trades; ~ **paralelo** COM GEN parallel trading; ~ **de patentes** COM GEN, PATENT patent trading; ~ **poco escrupuloso** COM GEN wheeling and dealing (*infrml*); ~ **de productos** BOLSA commodity trading; ~ **recíproco** COM GEN, ECON reciprocal trading; ~ **textil** IND textile trade; ~ **transfronterizo** ECON cross border trading, cross-border trade; ~ **de tránsito** TRANSP transit trade; ~ **triangular** BOLSA shunting, COM GEN switch trading; ~ **de trueque** ECON barter trade; ~ **de ultramar** IMP/

EXP, TRANSP overseas trade; ~ **de ultramarinos** V&M produce trade

cometer: ~ **un error** *fra* COM GEN make an error

comida: ~ **durante el vuelo** *f* OCIO, TRANSP in-flight meal; ~ **de negocios** *f* COM GEN business lunch; ~ **preparada** *f* COM GEN, V&M ready-made meal; ~ **rápida** *f* V&M fast food

comidas: ~ **a domicilio** *f pl* PROT SOC meals on wheels

comienzo *m* COM GEN beginning, onset; ~ **del año** CONT beginning of the year; ~ **de una tarea** INFO task initiation; ◆ **al** ~ COM GEN at the outset; **cuyo** ~ **está previsto para** COM GEN scheduled to begin in

comillas *f pl* COM GEN inverted commas, quotation marks, quote (*infrml*)

comisario *m* ADMIN commissary (*AmE*), BOLSA shareholder's auditor, V&M commissary (*AmE*)

Comisarios: ~ **de Aduanas y Contribuciones Indirectas** *m pl* FISC Commissioners of Customs and Excise

comisión *f* BANCA, BOLSA commission (*comm.*), COM GEN fee, *pagos* commission (*comm.*), *junta* committee, FIN *porcentaje* factorage, GES, POL *grupo de personas* committee; ~ **de aceptación** BANCA acceptance fee, commission for acceptance, acceptance commission; ~ **de acreedores** FIN creditors' committee; ~ **ad hoc** COM GEN ad hoc committee; ~ **de administración** BANCA, BOLSA management fee; ~ **de adquisición** BOLSA, SEG acquisition fee, acquisition commission; ~ **del agente** V&M agent's commission; ~ **de agente expedidor** TRANSP forwarding agent's commission (*fac*); ~ **de agentes inmobiliarios** INMOB board of realtors (*AmE*); ~ **de apertura** BANCA commitment fee; ~ **de aplazamiento** BANCA contango; ~ **de arbitraje** BOLSA, RRHH board of arbitration; ~ **asesora** BANCA, COM GEN, FIN, POL, RRHH prudential committee (*AmE*), advisory committee (*BrE*); ~ **bancaria** BANCA bank commission, banking commission; ~ **por cancelación anticipada** BOLSA back-end load; ~ **por cobranza** COM GEN contingent fee; ~ **de compra** V&M buying commission; ~ **de compromiso** BANCA commitment fee; ~ **de confianza** ADMIN trust; ~ **contable** CONT board of accounting; ~ **del corredor de bolsa** BOLSA broker's commission; ~ **de corretaje** BOLSA brokerage fee, brokerage commission; ~ **de cuenta de custodia** BANCA custodian account fee; ~ **de custodia** BANCA custodian fee; ~ **de un delito** DER wrongdoing; ~ **de disponibilidad** BANCA commitment fee; ~ **dividida** POL split commission; ~ **ejecutiva** RRHH executive committee; ~ **especial** POL select committee (*BrE*); ~ **de expertos** RRHH paid experts; ~ **de una falta** DER wrongdoing; ~ **fija** BANCA, FIN flat fee; ~ **de garantía** BANCA, FIN underwriting fee; ~ **del gasto público** CONT, POL *parlamento* Public Accounts Committee (*BrE*); ~ **de gastos** COM GEN disbursement commission; ~ **de gestión** BANCA, COM GEN agency fee, POL management committee; ~ **gestora** POL management committee; ~ **ilícita** COM GEN, DER, FIN, POL, RRHH bribe, kickback (*infrml*) (*AmE*); ~ **de incentivo** V&M incentive commission; ~ **de indagación** RRHH commission of inquiry; ~ **inferior a lo habitual** BOLSA soft commission; ~ **inicial** COM GEN front-end fee; ~ **inmobiliaria** INMOB real estate commission; ~ **investigadora** DER investigating committee, POL committee of inquiry; ~ **de mantenimiento de cuenta** BANCA account maintenance fee; ~ **de los**

medios de comunicación MEDIOS, V&M media commission; ~ **mixta** RRHH *UE* joint committee; ~ **de operarios** RRHH *UE* Works Council; ~ **optativa** FIN option fee; ~ **parlamentaria de investigación** POL, RRHH court of inquiry (*BrE*); ~ **de participación** BANCA participation fee; ~ **permanente** POL *Parlamento Europeo* standing committee; ~ **de planificación** ECON planning commission; ~ **de prestamista** FIN procuration fee; ~ **de presupuesto** POL supply committee; ~ **por publicidad** V&M advertising commission; ~ **Randall** ECON Randall Commission (*AmE*); ~ **reguladora** DER, POL *Comisión Europea* regulatory committee; ~ **de renegociación** BANCA extension fee; ~ **por servicio bancario** BANCA bank service charge; ~ **por solicitud** IMP/EXP, TRANSP address commission; ~ **de suscripción** COM GEN spread, FIN underwriting commission; ~ **de la televisión independiente** POL, MEDIOS, V&M independent television commission; ~ **única** BOLSA single commission; ~ **de venta** V&M sale commission; ◆ **en** ~ TRANSP on consignment

Comisión: ~ **de Asociaciones de Navieros de la Comunidad Europea** *f* TRANSP Committee of Shipowners Associations of the European Community; ~ **Brady** *f* BOLSA Brady Commission (*AmE*); ~ **de las Comunidades Europeas** *f* ECON Commission of the European Communities (*CEC*); ~ **Consultiva Mixta** *f* RRHH Joint Consultative Committee; ~ **Donovan** *f* RRHH Donovan Commission (*BrE*); ~ **Económica para América Latina** *f* (*CEPAL*) ECON, POL ≈ United Nations Economic Commission for Latin America (*UN-ECLA*), ≈ Economic Commission for Latin America (*ECLA*); ~ **Económica para Asia Occidental** *f* (*CEPAO*) ECON, POL Economic Commission for Western Asia (*ECWA*); ~ **Económica para Europa** *f* (*CEPE*) ECON, POL Economic Commission for Europe (*ECE*); ~ **Ejecutiva Principal** *f* RRHH *de una reunión* Principal Executive Committee (*BrE*); ~ **de Empresas de Construcción** *f* FIN Building Societies Commission; ~ **de la Energía y el Medio Ambiente** *f* MED AMB Commission on Energy and the Environment (*CENE*); ~ **de Estudios del Mercado Monetario** *f Esp* (*CEMM*) BOLSA Spanish commission of main institutions that regulate the monetary market; ~ **Europea** *f* ECON European Commission; ~ **Forestal** *f* MED AMB Forestry Commission (*BrE*); ~ **de Medios y Arbitrios** *f* POL Committee of Ways and Means (*AmE*); ~ **Mixta Obrero-patronal** *f* RRHH Joint Consultative Committee; ~ **Nacional de Energía Atómica** *f AmL* (*CONEA*) MED AMB ≈ Atomic Energy Research Establishment (*AERE*); ~ **Nacional del Mercado de Valores** *f* (*CNMV*) BOLSA ≈ Securities and Exchange Commission (*AmE*) (*SEC*), ≈ Securities and Investments Board (*BrE*) (*SIB*), ≈ Stock Exchange Commission (*AmE*) (*SEC*); ~ **de las Naciones Unidas para el Derecho Mercantil Internacional** *f* DER, ECON, POL United Nations Commission of International Trade Law (*UNCITRAL*); ~ **para la Simplificación del Comercio Internacional** *f* ECON, POL Committee for the Simplification of International Trade Procedures (*SIPROCOM*)

comisionar *vt* ADMIN *requerir, apoderar*, COM GEN, MEDIOS, RRHH commission

comisionario, -a *m,f* RRHH commissionaire

comisiones *f pl* BANCA *sobre operaciones bancarias* charges comisionista *mf* BOLSA broker, commission broker, FIN broker, RRHH commission agent, commission merchant; ~ **en bolsa de comercio** BOLSA commission broker; ~ **bursátil** BOLSA floor broker; ~ **en colocaciones** FIN investment dealer; ~ **de exportación** RRHH export agent

comité *m* COM GEN, GES, POL board, committee; ~ **administrativo** GES management committee; ~ **de arbitraje** COM GEN arbitration committee; ~ **asesor** COM GEN advisory committee (*BrE*), prudential committee (*AmE*); ~ **de auditoría** CONT audit committee; ~ **de banca rota** COM GEN bankruptcy committee; ~ **de banqueros londinenses y escoceses** BANCA Committee of London and Scottish Bankers (*CLSB*); ~ **censor** COM GEN watchdog committee; ~ **conjunto de producción** RRHH joint production committee; ~ **conjunto del sector para la investigación de la publicidad en TV** V&M Joint Industrial Committee for Television Advertising Research (*JICTAR*); ~ **consultivo** ADMIN consultative committee; ~ **de control** POL watchdog committee; ~ **de cooperación industrial** IND Committee for Industrial Cooperation (*CIC*); ~ **directivo de cuerpo legislativo** BANCA, FIN steering committee; ~ **ejecutivo** GES, RRHH executive committee; ~ **de empleados** CONT, RRHH employees' committee; ~ **de empresa** RRHH works committee (*BrE*); ~ **estratégico para inversiones** FIN investment strategy committee; ~ **financiero de una empresa** FIN corporate financing committee; ~ **de gerencia** GES management committee; ~ **de huelga** RRHH strike committee; ~ **de inspección** DER committee of inspection; ~ **del mercado abierto** ECON open market committee; ~ **mixto** RRHH combine committee; ~ **paritario** RRHH joint committee; ~ **de patentes** CONT, PATENT Patents Advisory Committee; ~ **de planificación** COM GEN Planning Committee (*PLACO*); ~ **Plowden** ECON Plowden Committee; ~ **de trabajadores** RRHH works council (*BrE*); ~ **de usuarios de puerto** TRANSP port users' committee; ~ **de vigilancia** COM GEN, CONT, GES, RRHH supervisory board

Comité: ~ **Aeroportuario de Carga y Descarga** *m* TRANSP Airport Handling Committee (*AHC*); ~ **de Armadores de Europa** *m* TRANSP Committee of European Shipowners (*CES*); ~ **Asesor de Protección al Consumo** *m* ECON Consumer Protection Advisory Committee; ~ **de Ayuda al Desarrollo** *m* (*CAD*) ECON, POL Development Assistance Committee (*DAC*); ~ **Central de Arbitraje** *m* BOLSA Central Arbitration Committee (*CAC*); ~ **de Coordinación del Control Multilateral de las Exportaciones** *m* IMP/EXP Coordinating Committee for Multilateral Export Controls (*Cocom*); ~ **Económico y Social** *m* ECON, PROT SOC Economic and Social Committee (*ESC*); ~ **Europeo de Cooperación Jurídica** *m* DER European Committee of Legal Cooperation; ~ **Europeo para la Normalización** *m* (*CEN*) ECON, IND European Committee for Standardization (*CEN*); ~ **Europeo de Seguros** *m* SEG European Insurance Committee; ~ **Independiente de Revisión** *m* RRHH Independent Review Committee (*BrE*); ~ **Intergubernamental sobre Migraciones en Europa** *m* POL, PROT SOC Intergovernmental Committee for European Migration (*ICEM*); ~ **Internacional de Consultoría del Algodón** *m* IND International Cotton Advisory Committee (*ICAC*); ~ **Internacional de Nor-**mas **Contables** *m* CONT International Accounting Standards Committee (*IASC*); ~ **Internacional de Oriente Medio** *m* ECON Committee of Middle East Trade (*COMET*); ~ **Internacional de Prácticas de Auditoría** *m* BANCA, CONT International Auditing Practices Committee (*IAPC*); ~ **de Investigación del Gasto Público** *m* ECON Public Expenditure Survey Committee; ~ **de Litigios** *m* RRHH Disputes Committee (*BrE*); ~ **Marítimo Internacional** *m* TRANSP International Maritime Committee (*IMC*); ~ **de Procedimientos para el Tráfico de Carga** *m* TRANSP Cargo Traffic Procedures Committee (*CTPC*); ~ **Provisional de Coordinación para Convenios Comerciales Internacionales** *m* BOLSA Interim Coordinating Committee for International Commodity Arrangements; ~ **Radiomarítimo Internacional** *m* COMS International Radio-Maritime Committee; ~ **de los Representantes Permanentes de la UE** *m* ECON, POL Committee of Permanent Representatives of the EU (*COREPER*); ~ **de Sistemas y Procedimientos de Carga** *m* TRANSP Cargo Systems and Procedures Committee (*CSPC*); ~ **de los Veinte** *m* (*C-20*) COM GEN Committee of Twenty (*C-20*)

Commonwealth: nueva ~ *f* POL New Commonwealth

comodidades *f pl* INMOB *valoración* amenities

comodín *m* INFO wild card

compaginadora: ~ **de documentos** *f* INFO collator

compañero, -a *m,f* RRHH colleague, workmate; ~ **de trabajo** RRHH fellow-worker, workmate

compañía *f* (*Cía.*) COM GEN company (*Co.*); ~ **de acciones de primera clase** BOLSA blue-chip company; ~ **adquirente** COM GEN purchasing company, *toma de control* acquiring company; ~ **adquirida** COM GEN purchased company; ~ **agraria familiar** FISC family farm corporation; ~ **de agua** IND water company; ~ **apalancada** CONT leveraged company; ~ **de arrendamiento financiero** FIN leasing corporation; ~ **aseguradora** FIN, SEG insurance company; ~ **aseguradora de cascos de buques** SEG hull underwriting company; ~ **aseguradora cualificada** SEG qualified insurance corporation; ~ **aseguradora registrada de bienes y accidentes** SEG chartered property and casualty underwriting company; ~ **aseguradora de vida colegiada** SEG chartered life underwriting company; ~ **asociada** COM GEN affiliated company, associate company, associated company; ~ **asociada del extranjero** COM GEN associated company abroad; ~ **autorizada** COM GEN, FIN, RRHH admitted company; ~ **de búsqueda de ejecutivos** RRHH executive search firm; ~ **de capital abierto** FIN open-ended investment company; ~ **de capital de riesgo** BANCA venture capital corporation; ~ **de capital de riesgo reglamentaria** FIN prescribed venture capital corporation; ~ **de capitales de riesgo** FIN venture capital company; ~ **cedente** DER, PATENT, SEG ceding company; ~ **central** COM GEN parent company, core firm; ~ **cerrada** ECON closed corporation (*AmE*); ~ **cesionaria** COM GEN transferee company; ~ **de coinversión** COM GEN, ECON, GES joint-venture company; ~ **de computadoras** *AmL* (*cf compañía de ordenadores Esp*) INFO computing company; ~ **de computadores** *AmL* ver *compañía de computadoras AmL*; ~ **constituyente** BOLSA constituent company; ~ **constructora de viviendas** FISC housing corporation; ~ **de cotización oficial pública** ECON publicly listed company; ~ **desaparecida** COM GEN defunct company; ~ **designada** FISC designated corporation; ~ **disuelta** COM GEN defunct company; ~ **emisora** BOLSA issuing company; ~ **empaquetadora** IND packing company; ~ **estrechamente controlada** BOLSA, ECON closely-held corporation; ~ **excluida** FISC excluded corporation; ~ **exenta** FISC exempt corporation; ~ **extranjera** COM GEN, DER alien corporation, foreign corporation, foreign company; ~ **fiduciaria** BANCA, DER, FIN trust company; ~ **filial** COM GEN affiliated company, controlled company, subsidiary company (*BrE*), subsidiary corporation (*AmE*), subsidiary firm; ~ **financiera** FIN financial company; ~ **financiera de consumo** FIN consumer financial company; ~ **sin fines de lucro** COM GEN non-profit-making company (*BrE*), nonprofit-making company (*AmE*); ~ **fundadora** COM GEN founding company; ~ **de fusión** FIN merger company; ~ **fusionada** COM GEN, FISC amalgamated body corporate, amalgamated corporation, merged company; ~ **del gas** MED AMB gas company; ~ **de gestión de activos** FIN asset management company; ~ **de gestión de la exportación** IMP/EXP export management company; ~ **de gira** OCIO tour company; ~ **integrada** COM GEN integrated company; ~ **de interés público** ECON public interest company; ~ **con intereses públicos** ECON public interest company; ~ **de inversión** FIN investment firm; ~ **de inversión conjunta** COM GEN, ECON, GES joint-venture company; ~ **de inversiones en bienes muebles** BANCA, BOLSA, INMOB real estate investment trust (*REIT*); ~ **de inversiones en diamantes** BOLSA diamond investment trust; ~ **de inversiones inmobiliarias de vida finita** FIN finite life real estate investment trust; ~ **inversionista** BOLSA, FIN investment corporation, investment company, investment trust; ~ **inversora** BOLSA investment business; ~ **matriz** COM GEN parent company, controlling corporation, core firm; ~ **mercantil no imponible** FISC nontaxable profitable firm; ~ **mixta de seguros** SEG composite insurance company; ~ **mutua** FIN, SEG mutual company, mutual corporation; ~ **mutua de seguros** SEG mutual insurance company; ~ **de navegación** TRANSP shipping line; ~ **no bursátil** COM GEN unlisted company; ~ **no incorporada** COM GEN unincorporated company; ~ **no residente** COM GEN, DER nonresident company; ~ **de ordenadores** *Esp* (*cf compañía de computadoras AmL*) INFO computing company; ~ **petrolera** IND, MED AMB oil company; ~ **predecesora** COM GEN predecessor; ~ **prestamista** FIN loan company; ~ **privada** COM GEN private company; ~ **privatizada** ECON privatized company; ~ **promotora** FIN promotary company (*AmE*); ~ **en propiedad absoluta** BOLSA wholly-owned corporation; ~ **pública** COM GEN, ECON public company; ~ **que cotiza en la bolsa** COM GEN, ECON publicly listed company; ~ **reaseguradora** SEG reinsurance company; ~ **representante** CONT agent corporation; ~ **de seguros** *Esp* (*cf aseguradora AmL*) SEG insurance corporation, insurance company; ~ **de seguros Lloyd's** SEG Lloyd's of London (*BrE*); ~ **de seguros mutuos** SEG mutual insurance company; ~ **de seguros de vida** SEG life insurance company; ~ **de servicios** INFO *fabricante* service company; ~ **de un solo propietario** COM GEN private company, proprietary company; ~ **subsidiaria** COM GEN subsidiary, underlying company (*infrml*); ~ **sujeta a tributación** FISC taxable corporation; ~ **superviviente** COM GEN, FIN, RRHH surviving company; ~ **telefónica** COMS telephone company; ~ **tenedora** BANCA, FIN, BOLSA holding company, holding corporation; ~ **de transporte por carretera** TRANSP road haulage company; ~ **de transportes** TRANSP haulage company, transport company (*BrE*), trucking company (*AmE*); ~ **en vías de fusión** COM GEN amalgamating body corporate; ◆ **y ~** COM GEN and Co.

Compañía: ~ **de Crédito al Consumo** *f* ECON Commodity Credit Corporation (*AmE*) (*CCC*); ~ **Lloyd's** *f* SEG Lloyd's Corporation (*BrE*); ~ **Telefónica Nacional de España** *f* (*CTNE*) COMS Spanish national telecommunications network, ≈ British Telecom (*BT*)

compañías: ~ **incluidas en la consolidación** *f pl* CONT *cuentas anuales* companies included within consolidation

comparabilidad *f* RRHH comparability; ~ **de pagos** RRHH pay comparability

comparables *m pl* INMOB comparables

comparación *f* COM GEN comparison; ~ **entre empresas** COM GEN inter-firm comparison; ~ **inter-empresas** COM GEN inter-firm comparison; ~ **de rendimiento** BOLSA *bonos del Tesoro* yield comparison

comparaciones: ~ **dentro de los medios de comunicación** *f pl* V&M intramedia comparisons; ~ **entre medios de comunicación** *f pl* V&M intermedia comparisons; ~ **internacionales** *f pl* ECON international comparisons; ~ **internacionales del coste de vida** *f pl* *Esp* (*cf comparaciones internacionales del costo de vida AmL*) ECON international comparisons of the cost of living; ~ **internacionales del costo de vida** *f pl AmL* (*cf comparaciones internacionales del coste de vida Esp*) ECON international comparisons of the cost of living; ~ **por parejas** *f pl* COM GEN paired comparisons; ~ **de la utilidad interpersonales** *f pl* ECON interpersonal utility comparisons

comparar *vt* BOLSA match, COM GEN compare, V&M *éxito, calidad* match; ◆ **~ algo con algo** COM GEN compare sth to sth

comparativamente *adv* COM GEN comparatively

comparativo *adj* COM GEN comparative

comparecer *vi* DER appear; ◆ **~ ante un tribunal** DER come before a court

compartimentación *f* COM GEN *del mercado común agrícola*, GES compartmentalization

compartimentalizar *vt* COM GEN, GES compartmentalize

compartimento *m* TRANSP *ferrocarril* bay; ~ **de carga** TRANSP tote bin; ~ **individual** TRANSP *coche cama* single

compartir *vt* COM GEN, INFO share; ◆ **~ con** COM GEN go shares with; ~ **el trabajo** RRHH job share, work share

compás: ~ **de espera** *m jarg* BOLSA, COM GEN, FIN holding pattern (*jarg*), INFO timeout

compatibilidad *f* COM GEN, ECON, IND, INFO compatibility; ~ **ascendente** INFO upward compatibility; ~ **descendente** INFO downward compatibility; ~ **de equipos** INFO hardware compatibility; ~ **del PC** INFO PC-compatibility; ~ **de productos** ECON product compatibility

compatible *adj* COM GEN, ECON, INFO, IND compatible; ~ **con IBM** INFO IBM-compatible

compendio *m* DER abstract

compensación[1]: **sin ~** *adj* COM GEN *índice, cifras* unweighted

compensación[2] *f* BANCA *de cheques* set-off, clearing,

BOLSA offset, making-up, COM GEN compensation, equalization, trade-off, quid pro quo, CONT offset, *de pérdidas* making-up, ECON quid pro quo, trade-off, equalization, FIN making-up, offset, FISC equalization, quid pro quo, IMP/EXP countervailing, PROT SOC *trabajo social* take-up; **~ bancaria** BANCA bank clearing, FIN clearing; **~ de cheques** BANCA check clearing (*AmE*), cheque clearing (*BrE*); **~ de créditos** BANCA Credit Clearing (*BrE*); **~ de créditos y débitos** BANCA, FIN multilateral netting; **~ por defunción** SEG death benefit; **~ por despido** PROT SOC, RRHH severance pay, redundancy pay, redundancy payment; **~ de deudas** BANCA settlement per contra; **~ diferida** RRHH *salario* deferred compensation; **~ dinámica** FIN dynamic hedging; **~ a ejecutivos** GES *gastos de viaje* executive compensation; **~ con ejercicios anteriores** FISC carry-back; **~ equitable** INMOB just compensation; **~ especial** BANCA special clearing; **~ excesiva** RRHH overcompensation; **~ extraordinaria a un vendedor** RRHH override; **~ fiscal** FISC fiscal equalization, fiscal offset; **~ fiscal retardada** FISC tax loss carryforward; **~ fiscal retroactiva** FISC tax loss carryback; **~ de hidrocarburos** FIN petroleum compensation; **~ de ingresos y gastos** FIN equalization of revenue and expenditure; **~ en lugar de preaviso** RRHH pay in lieu of notice; **~ media** CONT average compensation; **~ por pérdida o daño** SEG compensation for loss or damage; **~ progresiva** BANCA onward clearing; **~ razonable** INMOB just compensation; **~ del riesgo** CONT risk-reward; **~ de riesgos** COM GEN balancing of portfolio; **~ de tierras** DER land compensation; **~ a los trabajadores** RRHH workers' compensation; **~ triangular** ECON triangular compensation, FIN delta hedging; **~ tributaria** FISC equalization of taxes

compensaciones: **~ en especies** *f pl* RRHH noncash rewards, nonmonetary rewards; **~ de valor elevado** *f pl* BANCA high-value clearings (*BrE*); **~ por valor justo** *f pl* CONT *de subsidiaria* fair value adjustments

compensado *adj* BANCA cleared (*Cld*), CONT balanced

compensador: **~ directo** *m* BANCA direct clearer

compensar *vt* BANCA *cheque* clear, BOLSA *precio de valores* average up, COM GEN equalize, make good, compensate, even up, CONT, FIN *pérdidas y ganancias* offset, offset against, balance out, RRHH *pagar* compensate; ♦ **~ contra** CONT *pérdidas y ganancias* offset against; **~ cuota de mercado con márgenes de beneficio** ECON trade off market share against profit margins; **~ un débito a cuenta de un crédito** BANCA, CONT, FIN set off a debit against a credit; **~ la diferencia** COM GEN make up the difference; **~ una pérdida** BOLSA offset a loss

compensatorio *adj* COM GEN compensating, compensatory

competencia *f* COM GEN, DER competence, competition, *nacional* authority, POL jurisdiction, RRHH, V&M competition, concurrency, competence; **~ abierta** DER, ECON open competition; **~ ajena a los precios** V&M nonprice competition; **~ atomizada** ECON atomistic competition; **~ sin cuartel** ECON harsh competition; **~ desleal** COM GEN predatory competition, unfair competition, dumping; **~ dura** ECON stiff competition; **~ ejecutiva** GES executive competence; **~ entre empresas del mismo ramo** ECON interindustry competition; **~ entre industrias** IND interindustry competition; **~ equitativa** COM GEN, DER, ECON, V&M fair competi-

tion; **~ imperfecta** ECON, V&M imperfect competition; **~ intensa** COM GEN cut-throat competition; **~ internacional** ECON international competitiveness; **~ justa** COM GEN, DER, ECON, V&M fair competition; **~ leal** COM GEN, DER, ECON, V&M fair competition; **~ legislativa** DER, ECON, POL law-making power; **~ monopolística** ECON monopolistic competition; **~ offshore** IMP/EXP offshore competition; **~ perfecta** ECON perfect competition, pure competition; **~ en pie de igualdad** COM GEN arm's-length competition, arm's-length transaction; **~ ruinosa** ECON destructive competition; **~ viable** ECON workable competition; ♦ **dentro de su ~** DER intra vires

competencias *f pl* DER powers

competente *adj* COM GEN *adecuado* qualified

competición: **~ abierta** *f Esp* DER, ECON open competition

competido *m* V&M *mercado* contested

competidor, a *m,f* COM GEN competitor; **~ extranjero(-a)** COM GEN foreign competitor

competir *vi* COM GEN compete; ♦ **~ contra** COM GEN compete against; **~ ventajosamente con alguien** ECON have a competitive advantage over sb

competitividad *f* COM GEN competitiveness; **~ de los precios** V&M price competitiveness

competitivo *adj* COM GEN competitive; **no ~** COM GEN anticompetitive; **sumamente ~** COM GEN *mercado* highly competitive

compilación: **~ de datos** *f* COM GEN, INFO information storage

compilador, a *m,f* COM GEN, INFO compiler

compilar *vt* COM GEN, INFO compile

complejidad *f* COM GEN complexity, sophistication; **~ financiera** FIN financial sophistication

complejo[1] *adj* COM GEN, POL complex

complejo[2]: **~ para espectáculos** *m* OCIO *cines, teatros* entertainment complex; **~ industrial** *m* IND, INMOB industrial estate (*BrE*), industrial park (*AmE*); **~ militar industrial** *m* POL military industrial complex; **~ productivo** *m* IND production complex; **~ residencial** *m* INMOB housing complex; **~ de viviendas subvencionadas** *m* PROT SOC housing estate (*BrE*), housing project (*AmE*)

complementado *adj* COM GEN supplemented

complementar *vt* COM GEN supplement

complementario *adj* COM GEN complementary, supplementary

complemento *m* COM GEN, ECON, INFO, V&M complement; **~ salarial** COM GEN, RRHH perk (*infrml*), perquisite; **~ salarial según ingresos** PROT SOC income-tested supplement

completamente *adv* COM GEN completely; ♦ **~ desmontado** TRANSP completely knocked down (*CKD*)

completar *vt* COM GEN complete

completo *adj* COM GEN *plan, informe* comprehensive, unabridged, complete, SEG comprehensive

complicación *f* COM GEN complication

complicado *adj* COM GEN sophisticated, complex, POL complex

componente[1] *adj* COM GEN, IND component

componente[2] *m* COM GEN component; **~ de capital** ECON, FIN capital component; **~ electrónico** INFO *equipo* electronic component; ~ **de un equipo** GES team player; ~ **del precio de coste** *Esp* (*cf componente del precio de costo AmL*) CONT, ECON cost factor; ~ **del precio de costo** *AmL* (*cf componente del precio de coste Esp*) CONT, ECON cost factor; ~ **tiempo** COM GEN time component; ~ **tributario** FISC tax component

componer *vt* COM GEN compose, make up; ◆ ~ **una deuda** BANCA, DER, FIN compound a debt

comportamiento *m* COM GEN, RRHH behavior (*AmE*), behaviour (*BrE*); ~ **afectivo** COM GEN affective behavior (*AmE*), affective behaviour (*BrE*); ~ **de los beneficios** RRHH earnings performance; ~ **cognitivo** V&M cognitive behavior (*AmE*), cognitive behaviour (*BrE*); ~ **de compra** V&M buying behavior (*AmE*), buying behaviour (*BrE*); ~ **del comprador** V&M buyer behavior (*AmE*), buyer behaviour (*BrE*); ~ **de las compras** V&M buying behavior (*AmE*), buying behaviour (*BrE*); ~ **del consumidor** V&M consumer behavior (*AmE*), consumer behaviour (*BrE*); ~ **del mercado** V&M market behavior (*AmE*), market behaviour (*BrE*); ~ **no profesional** RRHH nonprofessional behavior (*AmE*), nonprofessional behaviour (*BrE*); ~ **oportunista** BOLSA, ECON opportunistic behavior (*AmE*), opportunistic behaviour (*BrE*); ~ **de la organización** COM GEN, GES organization behavior (*AmE*), organization behaviour (*BrE*), organizational behavior (*AmE*), organizational behaviour (*BrE*); ~ **organizacional** COM GEN, GES organizational behavior (*AmE*), organizational behaviour (*BrE*); ~ **en las organizaciones** COM GEN, GES organizational behavior (*AmE*), organizational behaviour (*BrE*); ~ **organizativo** V&M organizational behavior (*AmE*), organizational behaviour (*BrE*); ~ **del precio** BOLSA *de opciones* price behavior (*AmE*), price behaviour (*BrE*); ~ **de la unidad familiar** ECON household behavior (*AmE*), household behaviour (*BrE*)

composición *f* COM GEN, INFO, MEDIOS composition, *imprenta* typesetting; ~ **amigable** COM GEN amicable settlement; ~ **axial** COM GEN axial composition; ~ **de la carga** TRANSP cargo mix, commodity mix; ~ **del coste** *Esp* (*cf composición del costo AmL*) COM GEN, CONT, FIN cost structure; ~ **del costo** *AmL* (*cf composición del coste Esp*) COM GEN, CONT, FIN cost structure; ~ **fotográfica** MEDIOS filmsetting; ~ **no tipográfica** ADMIN, MEDIOS cold type; ~ **orgánica del capital** ECON organic composition of capital; ~ **de página** MEDIOS, V&M page setting; ~ **del papel** V&M paper setting; ~ **tipográfica** COM GEN, INFO, MEDIOS typesetting; ~ **de tráfico** TRANSP traffic mixture

compra *f* COM GEN purchase, purchasing, *para la casa* shopping, *de una compañía* acquisition, V&M purchase, purchasing; ~ **de acciones propias** BOLSA share buy back; ~ **de acciones con sus dividendos** FIN pyramiding; ~ **de activos** COM GEN purchase of assets; ~ **agresiva a la baja** BOLSA bear raid; ~ **al alza** BOLSA long call, bull commitment; ~ **al cierre** BOLSA closing purchase; ~ **al contado** COM GEN cash purchase; ~ **al descubierto** BOLSA, COM GEN, FIN, V&M bull purchase, margin buying; ~ **al por mayor** V&M wholesale purchasing; ~ **de alcista** BOLSA bull buying, bull purchase; ~ **de alto apalancamiento** COM GEN high-leveraged takeover (*AmE*) (*HLT*); ~ **anticipada** COM GEN, ECON forward buying; ~ **apalancada** FIN, GES leveraged buyout (*LBO*); ~ **apalancada por ejecutivos** (*CAPE*) FIN, GES leveraged management buy-out (*LMBO*); ~ **bilateral** V&M reciprocal buying; ~ **por catálogo** V&M catalog buying (*AmE*), catalogue buying (*BrE*); ~ **centralizada** V&M central buying; ~ **comparativa** V&M comparison shopping; ~ **compulsiva** V&M compulsive buying; ~ **de conjunto** FIN basket purchase; ~ **de control** BOLSA buyout; ~ **corporativa** FISC, V&M corporate purchasing; ~ **a corto** BOLSA *opciones* short call; ~ **para cubrir ventas al descubierto** BOLSA bear covering; ~ **con derecho a devolución** BOLSA, FIN, V&M sale on return; ~ **directa** BOLSA, COM GEN, FIN, V&M offhand buying; ~ **de efectos a cobrar** ECON forfaiting; ~ **por ejecutivos** (*CPE*) GES *de una empresa* management buyout (*MBO*); ~ **electrónica** COM GEN, INFO electronic shopping; ~ **de la empresa por los empleados** RRHH employee buyout; ~ **escalonada de acciones** FIN *con ganancias* pyramiding; ~ **de espacios en medios de comunicación** MEDIOS, V&M media buying; ~ **de espacios publicitarios** V&M space buying; ~ **especial** V&M special purchase; ~ **especulativa** COM GEN speculative buying, forward buying; ~ **estacional** COM GEN term purchase; ~ **futura en firme** ECON outright forward purchase; ~ **sin garantía** BOLSA *opciones* naked call; ~ **global** BOLSA, COM GEN, FIN, V&M basket purchase; ~ **impulsiva** V&M impulse buy, impulse buying; ~ **de impulso** V&M impulse purchase, impulse buy; ~ **por intermediación** BOLSA *títulos* buy-in; ~ **en liquidación** BOLSA purchase for settlement; ~ **de un lote** BOLSA block purchase; ~ **de materias primas** BOLSA, COM GEN, FIN, V&M material purchase; ~ **obligatoria** COM GEN, DER, INMOB compulsory purchase; ~ **parcialmente a crédito** BOLSA margin purchase; ~ **de la parte de un socio** FIN buyout; ~ **por pedido** COM GEN, order buying; ~ **persistente** COM GEN, V&M repeat purchase; ~ **por placer** V&M pleasure shopping; ~ **a plazos** COM GEN, V&M installment purchase (*AmE*), hire purchase (*BrE*) (*HP*), never-never (*infrml*); ~ **a precio corriente** BOLSA at-the-money call; ~ **a precios escalonados** COM GEN scale buying; ~ **de previsión** BOLSA, COM GEN, FIN, V&M anticipatory purchase; ~ **de prueba** V&M trial purchase; ~ **reducida** BOLSA buy minus; ~ **repetida** V&M repeat buying; ~ **seguida de venta de los mismos títulos** BOLSA in and out trading (*jarg*); ~ **strap** BOLSA strap; ~ **strip** BOLSA strip; ~ **a tanto alzado** FIN lump-sum purchase; ~ **telefónica** FIN, V&M teleshopping; ~ **de títulos a bajo precio** BOLSA, COM GEN, FIN, V&M averaging down; ~ **total** BOLSA buy-out; ~ **por los trabajadores** FIN worker buy-out; ~ **y venta** BOLSA purchase and sale (*P&S*); ~~**venta en bloque por un especialista** BOLSA specialist block purchase and sale; ~ **y venta coincidente** BOLSA matched sale-purchase transaction; ~ **y venta del mismo valor en un día** BOLSA in and out trading (*jarg*); ~ **y venta muy próximas de un valor** BOLSA round trip trade; ~ **de vivienda** INMOB house purchase; ◆ **hacer una** ~ COM GEN make a purchase

comprador, a *m,f* BOLSA, COM GEN, ECON, V&M buyer, shopper; ~ **al contado** V&M cash buyer; ~ **anterior** V&M former buyer; ~ **de buena fe** COM GEN bona fide purchaser; ~ **de cantidad** COM GEN quantity buyer; ~ **a crédito** V&M charge buyer (*BrE*), credit buyer (*AmE*); ~ **de una cuota** BOLSA taker of a rate; ~ **por derecho de prioridad** DER pre-emptor (*AmE*); ~ **de espacio en medios audiovisuales** MEDIOS, V&M air-time buyer; ~ **de espacio publicitario** MEDIOS, V&M advertising space buyer; ~ **en firme** BOLSA firm buyer; ~ **de graneles** COM GEN bulk buyer, bulk purchaser; ~ **por**

impulso V&M impulse buyer; ~ **industrial** IND producer buyer; ~ **de medios de comunicación** MEDIOS, RRHH, V&M media buyer; ~ **múltiple** V&M multiple buyer; ~ **objetivo(-a)** V&M target buyer; ~ **de obras de arte** COM GEN art buyer; ~ **para una opción a adquirir el doble** BOLSA giver for a call of more; ~ **de una opción de compra** BOLSA call buyer; ~ **con opción de compra o venta** BOLSA straddle buyer; ~ **de opciones** BOLSA option buyer; ~ **productor(a)** IND producer buyer; ~ **de una sociedad** FISC, V&M corporate purchaser; ~ **de una sola vez** V&M one-time buyer; ~ **de tiempo** V&M time buyer

compradores *m pl* BOLSA takers-in

comprar *vt* BOLSA buy in, COM GEN, ECON, POL, V&M, purchase, buy; ◆ ~ **acciones** BOLSA take in stock, *de una compañía* buy into; ~ **acciones en el mercado abierto** BOLSA buy shares on the open market; ~ **al alza** BOLSA buy on a rise, buy for a rise, buy a bull; ~ **al cierre** BOLSA buy on close; ~ **al margen** BOLSA, FIN buy on margin; ~ **algo a condición** COM GEN buy sth on approval; ~ **algo a crédito** COM GEN buy sth on credit, buy sth on tick (*infrml*) (*BrE*); ~ **a la baja** BOLSA buy on a fall, INMOB buy down; ~ **a la baja y vender al alza** BOLSA buy low and sell high; ~ **a entrega futura** COM GEN buy for future delivery; ~ **espacio publicitario** MEDIOS *TV, radio* buy airtime; ~ **con malas noticias** BOLSA buy on the bad news; ~ **en un mercado a la baja** BOLSA buy on a falling market; ~ **en el mercado negro** ECON buy on the black market; ~ **la parte de** FIN buy out; ~ **a plazos** COM GEN buy in installments (*AmE*), buy in instalments (*BrE*), buy on hire purchase; ~ **a precio alto** BOLSA buy at the top of the market; ~ **a precio de mercado** BOLSA buy at market; ~ **a precio de oferta** BOLSA buy on bid; ~ **a precio reducido** COM GEN buy at a reduced price; ~ **a término** BOLSA buy for the account; ~ **o vender bienes más baratos que nunca** COM GEN trade down

compras: ~ **de contrapartida** *f pl* ECON counter purchase; ~ **en divisas** *f pl* CONT, FIN purchase denominated in foreign currency; ~ **fuera de la ciudad** *f pl* V&M out of town shopping; ~ **para el futuro** *f pl* BOLSA forward buying; ~ **a granel** *f pl* COM GEN bulk buying; ~ **en un mismo sitio** *f pl* V&M one-stop shopping; ~ **netas** *f pl* CONT net purchases; ~ **secundarias** *f pl* COM GEN supporting purchases; ~ **y ventas** *f pl* BOLSA calls and puts

compraventa *f* INMOB bargain and sale; ~ **de billetes bancarios** BANCA bank-note trading; ~ **a corto plazo** BOLSA round trip, round turn; ~ **de futuros** BOLSA futures trading

comprendido *adj* COM GEN including (*incl.*), inclusive (*incl.*), included (*incl.*); ◆ **todo** ~ COM GEN all-in

compresión *f* INFO compression; ~ **de datos** INFO data compression; ~ **de fichero** INFO file compression

comprimir *vt* INFO compress, *datos* pack

comprobación *f* COM GEN, INFO check; ~ **al azar** COM GEN spot check; ~ **asistida por computador** *AmL ver comprobación asistida por computadora AmL*; ~ **asistida por computadora** *AmL* (*cf comprobación asistida por ordenador Esp*) INFO computer-assisted testing (*CAT*); ~ **asistida por ordenador** *Esp* (*cf comprobación asistida por computadora AmL*) INFO computer-assisted testing (*CAT*); ~ **automática** ECON *economía de trabajo* automatic check-off, INFO automatic check, built-in check; ~ **de beneficios** CONT profit test, FISC earnings

test; ~ **de bloques** CONT block testing; ~ **en bucle** COMS message feedback; ~ **de cantidades** IND quantity surveying; ~ **del estado de la cuenta** BANCA, CONT bank reconciliation; ~ **in situ** COM GEN spot check; ~ **de los ingresos** FISC income test; ~ **interna** COM GEN internal check; ~ **de medios de vida** FISC, PROT SOC means test; ~ **de necesidades** FISC needs test; ~ **de paridad** COMS, INFO parity check; ~ **de validez** FISC validity check

comprobado *adj* SEG warranted (*Wld*)

comprobador: ~ **de código** *m* INFO code check

comprobante *m* BOLSA, COM GEN, FIN, SEG voucher, warrant; ~ **de almacén** COM GEN warehouse warrant (*WW*); ~ **de asientos contables** CONT proof of posting; ~ **de caja** CONT cash voucher; ~ **de caja chica** *AmL* (*cf comprobante de caja pequeña Esp*) CONT petty cash voucher; ~ **de caja pequeña** *Esp* (*cf comprobante de caja chica AmL*) CONT petty cash voucher; ~ **de crédito** BANCA, COM GEN credit voucher; ~ **de cuenta de crédito** BANCA credit account voucher; ~ **de depósito del impuesto** FISC certificate of tax deposit (*BrE*) (*CTD*); ~ **de deuda** FIN proof of debt (*POD*); ~ **de diario** CONT journal voucher; ~ **de dividendos** BOLSA dividend voucher; ~ **de pago** BANCA voucher, FIN, SEG satisfaction note (*jarg*); ~ **de pago de la liquidación bancaria** BANCA bank settlement voucher; ~ **de retiro** BANCA withdrawal slip; ~ **de separación** BANCA withdrawal slip; ~ **de servicios de exportación** IMP/EXP export services voucher; ~ **de transferencia de fondos** BANCA transfer of funds voucher

comprobantes *m pl* FISC vouchers

comprometer *vt* COM GEN compromise

comprometerse[1]: ~ **a** *v refl* COM GEN bind oneself to, commit oneself to, undertake

comprometerse[2]: **no** ~ *fra* COM GEN sit on the fence (*infrml*); ~ **a pagar una factura** *fra* COM GEN accept a bill, pick up the tab (*infrml*)

comprometido *adj* COM GEN committed; ◆ **estar** ~ **en** GES be engaged in

compromisario, -a *m,f* RRHH delegate

compromiso *m* COM GEN, DER, POL *contrato* undertaking, compromise, *promesa, pignoración* commitment; ~ **de aseguramiento continuado** (*CAC*) BANCA, SEG revolving underwriting facility (*RUF*); ~ **de auditoría** CONT audit engagement; ~ **de compra y reventa** BOLSA purchase and resale agreement (*PRA*); ~ **de los empleados** RRHH employees' commitment; ~ **entre el crecimiento y la rentabilidad** ECON trade-off between growth and profitability; ~ **específico** COM GEN specific commitment; ~ **de fianza** COM GEN, DER bail bond; ~ **en firme** BOLSA *suscripción de títulos* firm commitment; ~ **no librado** CONT undischarged commitment; ~ **no pagado** CONT undischarged commitment; ~ **pendiente** CONT outstanding commitment; ~ **permanente** COM GEN continuing commitment; ~ **del personal** RRHH staff commitment; ~ **potencial** COM GEN potential commitment; ~ **de préstamo** BANCA loan commitment; ~ **previo** COM GEN previous engagement; ◆ **sin** ~ COM GEN without engagement

compromisos: ~ **netos** *m pl* FIN exposure; ~ **de pago** *m pl* BANCA, FIN payment commitments

compuerta: ~ **de esclusa** *f* TRANSP hatchway; ~ **de expedición** *f* TRANSP dispatch bay

compuesto *adj* COM GEN composite; ~ **de** COM GEN composed of

computación *ver informática*

computador *AmL ver computadora AmL*

computadora *f AmL* (*cf ordenador Esp*) COM GEN, INFO computer; ~ **activa** *AmL* INFO active computer; ~ **analógica** *AmL* (*cf ordenador analógico Esp*) INFO analog computer; ~ **de bolsillo** *AmL* (*cf ordenador de bolsillo Esp*) INFO pocket computer; ~ **comercial** *AmL* (*cf ordenador comercial Esp*) INFO commercial computer, business computer; ~ **de cuarta generación** *AmL* (*cf ordenador de cuarta generación Esp*) INFO fourth-generation computer; ~ **destinataria** *AmL* (*cf ordenador destinatario Esp*) INFO target computer; ~ **doméstica** *AmL* (*cf ordenador doméstico Esp*) INFO home computer; ~ **frontal** *AmL* (*cf ordenador frontal Esp*) INFO front-end computer; ~ **fuente** *AmL* (*cf ordenador fuente Esp*) INFO source computer; ~ **híbrida** *AmL* (*cf ordenador híbrido Esp*) INFO hybrid computer; ~ **por lotes** *AmL* (*cf ordenador por lotes Esp*) INFO batch computer; ~ **de nivel superior** *AmL* (*cf ordenador de nivel superior Esp*) INFO high-end computer; ~ **periférica** *AmL* (*cf ordenador periférico Esp*) INFO peripheral computer; ~ **personal** *AmL* (*PC, cf ordenador personal Esp*) INFO personal computer (*PC*); ~ **portátil** *AmL* (*cf ordenador portátil Esp*) INFO laptop, portable computer, notebook; ~ **de primera generación** *AmL* (*cf ordenador de primera generación Esp*) INFO first-generation computer; ~ **de quinta generación** *AmL* (*cf ordenador de quinta generación Esp*) INFO fifth-generation computer; ~ **satélite** *AmL* (*cf ordenador auxiliar Esp*) INFO satellite computer; ~ **en serie** *AmL* INFO serial computer; ~ **en tándem** *AmL* (*cf ordenador en tándem Esp*) INFO duplex computer; ~ **de tercera generación** *AmL* (*cf ordenador de tercera generación Esp*) INFO third-generation computer; ~ **terminal** *AmL* (*cf ordenador terminal Esp*) INFO terminal computer; ~ **vectorial** *AmL* (*cf ordenador vectorial Esp*) INFO *en un solo paso* array processor (*AP*)

computadorizado *adj AmL* (*cf informatizado Esp*) INFO computer-based, computerized

computadorizar *vt AmL* (*cf informatizar Esp*) INFO computerize

computar *vt* COM GEN *cálculos* compute

computerizado *adj* INFO computerized

computerizar *vt* INFO computerize

cómputo *m* COM GEN reckoning; ~ **de inventario** COM GEN inventory computation

común *adj* COM GEN common

comuna *f* COM GEN, ECON, POL commune

comunal *adj* COM GEN, ECON, INMOB, POL communal

comunicación *f* COM GEN communication, call; ~ **de cobro revertido** COMS *teléfono* collect call (*AmE*), reverse-charge call (*BrE*); ~ **de datos** INFO data communication; ~ **descendente** GES downward communication; ~ **formal** COMS formal communication; ~ **horizontal** COM GEN horizontal communication; ~ **interurbana** COMS long-distance call, trunk call (*BrE*) (*obs*), toll call (*AmE*); ~ **de masas** MEDIOS mass communication; ~ **no verbal** COM GEN, GES nonverbal communication; ~ **oficial** COM GEN official statement; ~ **oficiosa** COM GEN *empresas* grapevine; ~ **persuasiva** V&M persuasive communication; ~ **verbal** COM GEN, GES verbal communication; ~ **vertical** COMS vertical communication; ~ **por vía satélite** COMS satellite communication

comunicaciones *f pl* COM GEN communications; ~ **digitales inalámbricas** COMS cordless digital telecommunications; ~ **digitales móviles** COMS cordless digital telecommunications; ~ **con los empleados** RRHH employee communications; ~ **globales** COMS global communications; ~ **internas** COMS internal communications; ~ **de marketing** V&M marketing communications

comunicado *m* COMS communiqué; ~ **de prensa** COM GEN press release; ~ **radiofónico** MEDIOS, V&M radio announcement

comunicando *adj* COMS, INFO *tono, señal* busy

comunicante *m* COMS communicator

comunicar *vt* COM GEN, COMS communicate, inform, pass on

comunidad *f* COM GEN community; ~ **agrícola** ECON, PROT SOC agricultural household; ~ **bancaria** BANCA banking community; ~ **de bienes** COM GEN community of goods; ~ **dormitorio** COM GEN, RRHH bedroom community (*AmE*), dormitory town (*BrE*); ~ **económica** ECON villa economy; ~ **de intereses** COM GEN community of interests; ~ **rural** MED AMB, ECON rural community

Comunidad: ~ **Autónoma** *f Esp* (*CA*) POL territory governed as a unit with certain degree of autonomy, ≈ county (*BrE*); ~ **Económica de Estados Africanos Occidentales** *f* (*CEDEAO*) ECON, POL Economic Community of West African States (*ECOWAS*); ~ **Económica Europea** *f obs* (*CEE*) ECON, POL European Economic Community (*obs*) (*EEC*); ~ **Europea** *f obs* (*CE, cf Unión Europea*) ECON, POL European Community (*obs*) (*EC*); ~ **Europea del Carbón y el Acero** *f* (*CECA*) ECON, IND European Coal and Steel Community (*ECSC*); ~ **Europea de Cooperativas de Consumidores** *f* ECON European Community of Consumers' Cooperatives (*Euro Co-op*); ~ **Europea de Energía Atómica** *f* (*CEEA*) ECON, POL European Atomic Energy Community (*EAEC, EURATOM*)

comunismo *m* ECON, POL communism

comunización *f* INMOB *de tierras* communization

comunizar *vt* INMOB *tierras* communize

con *prep* BOLSA cum

concatenación *f* INFO concatenation

concebido: ~ **en función del niño** *fra* PROT SOC child-centred (*BrE*), child-centered (*AmE*); ~ **para el usuario** *fra* INFO user-oriented

concedente *mf* PATENT licensor

conceder *vt* COM GEN *contrato* award, grant, DER, INMOB, PATENT *permiso* grant; ◆ ~ **un aumento salarial** RRHH award a salary increase; ~ **un crédito** BANCA extend a loan; ~ **una prórroga** COM GEN grant an extension

concejal *mf* COM GEN, POL town councillor

concentración *f* COM GEN, ECON, FIN concentration; ~ **absoluta** ECON absolute concentration; ~ **agregada** ECON aggregate concentration; ~ **de la carga** TRANSP cargo assembly; ~ **de compradores** V&M buyer concentration; ~ **del gasto al principio de un periodo** FIN front-end loading; ~ **industrial** IND industrial concentration, concentration of industry; ~ **máxima admisible** ECON maximum permissible concentration (*MPC*); ~ **del mercado** ECON market aggregation; ~ **de mercados** ECON market concentration; ~ **de metales**

pesados MED AMB heavy metal concentration; **~ relativa** MAT relative concentration; **~ de temporada** V&M seasonal concentration

concentrar: **~ en** vt COM GEN concentrate on

concepción: **~ global** f COM GEN, POL, RRHH Weltanschauung (jarg); **~ del producto** f V&M product conception

concepto m COM GEN, V&M concept; **~ de acumulación** CONT accrual concept; **~ básico** COM GEN basic concept; **~ de empresa establecida** CONT goingconcern concept; **~ de empresa en funcionamiento** CONT going-concern concept; **~ de estilo de vida** V&M lifestyle concept; **~ de marketing** V&M marketing concept; **~ publicitario** V&M advertising concept; **~ de valor** FIN value concept; ◆ **bajo ningún ~** COM GEN not on any terms

conceptos: **~ de flujo** m pl BOLSA flow concepts

concertar vt COM GEN arrange, appoint; ◆ **~ una cita** COM GEN arrange an appointment, fix an appointment, make an appointment; **~ una deuda** BANCA, DER, FIN compound a debt; **~ una entrevista** RRHH arrange an interview, set up an interview

concesión f COM GEN concession; **~ arancelaria** ECON, FISC, IMP/EXP, TRANSP tariff concession; **~ de crédito** BANCA credit granting, granting of credit; **~ de distribución** V&M distribution allowance; **~ de explotación** CONT operating grant; **~ fiscal** FISC tax concession; **~ de importación** m ECON import allowance; **~ de licencia** ECON licensing; **~ de licencia de importación** IMP/EXP import licensing; **~ de la patente** PATENT granting of patents; **~ de préstamos** BANCA lending; **~ de representación minorista** V&M retail display allowance; **~ de terrenos** INMOB land grant; **~ transferible** COM GEN marketable discharge permit, tradeable emission permit, transferable discharge permit

concesionario[1] adj COM GEN concessionary; **no ~** COM GEN nonconcessional

concesionario[2],**-a** m,f COM GEN concessionaire, licensee, V&M dealer

concesionario[3] m COM GEN franchise

concesiones: **~ económicas** f pl ECON economic grants

conciencia[1]: **~ del cliente** f V&M customer awareness; **~ fiscal** f FISC tax awareness; **~ máxima** f V&M maximal awareness; **~ tributaria** f FISC tax awareness

conciencia[2]: **con ~ ecológica** fra MED AMB consumidores green-conscious

concierto m DER, FISC covenant; **~ de voluntades** DER comercial meeting of minds

conciliación f COM GEN, DER, RRHH enfrentamientos laborales conciliation, reconciliation; **~ bancaria** BANCA, CONT bank reconciliation; **~ bancaria de cierre** BANCA cut-off bank reconciliation; **~ colectiva** RRHH collective conciliation (BrE); **~ contable** CONT reconciliation; **~ de cuentas** CONT account reconcilement, account reconciliation; **~ individual** RRHH individual conciliation

conciliador, a m,f RRHH disputas laborales conciliator, troubleshooter

conciliar vt COM GEN, DER, RRHH conciliate

concluir vt COM GEN conclude, reunión wind up, round off; ◆ **~ la emisión** MEDIOS sign off

conclusión f BANCA, COM GEN, CONT completion, de contrato conclusion, de reunión winding-up

conclusiones f pl DER findings

conclusivo adj COM GEN conclusive

Concordato: **~ Basle sobre la Supervisión Bancaria** m BANCA Basle Concordat on Banking Supervision

concretar vt COM GEN términos, detalles work out

concurrencia f COM GEN, POL en una elección turnout

concurrentes m pl FISC concurrents

concurrir vi COM GEN concur

concurso m COM GEN contest, DER tender to contract (TTC); **~ eliminatorio** COM GEN knockout competition; **~ de ventas** V&M sales contest

condena: **~ condicional** f DER suspended sentence; **~ a pagar los gastos** f DER awarding of costs

condenar vt COM GEN condemn, DER sentence

condensado adj CONT, V&M condensed

condescender: **~ con** vt COM GEN give in to

condición f COM GEN, DER condition; **~ de afiliación** COM GEN, ECON, RRHH membership; **~ de cobro** COM GEN, ECON condition of collection; **~ de comerciante** COM GEN, ECON mercantile character; **~ de contorno** MAT boundary constraint; **~ expresa** COM GEN, RRHH express condition, express term (BrE); **~ expresa del empresario** RRHH employer express term; **~ de fideicomiso** DER trusteeship; **~ implícita** COM GEN implied condition; **~ indispensable** COM GEN, DER essential condition; **~ de Marshall-Lerner** ECON Marshall-Lerner condition; **~ modificante** COM GEN qualification; **~ previa** COM GEN precondition; **~ resolutoria** DER action for cancelation (AmE), action for cancellation (BrE), condition subsequent (AmE); **~ suspensiva** DER condition precedent (AmE); ◆ **a ~ de que** COM GEN on the understanding that, on condition that; **con la ~ de que** COM GEN on the condition that

condicionado[1] adj COM GEN conditioned

condicionado[2]: **no ~ para** fra BANCA not provided for

condicionalidad: **~ ecológica** f MED AMB green conditionality

condicionante: **~ del estado de ánimo** m V&M mood conditioning

condiciones f pl COM GEN de mercado conditions, terms; **~ de aceptación** FIN terms of acceptance; **~ adversas** COM GEN, TRANSP adverse weather; **~ ambientales** MED AMB environmental conditions; **~ atractivas** COM GEN attractive terms; **~ brutas** TRANSP gross form of charter, gross terms; **~ comerciales** ECON business conditions; **~ comerciales adversas** ECON adverse trading conditions; **~ complementarias** SEG additional conditions; **~ del contrato** COM GEN, DER, TRANSP conditions of contract; **~ crediticias** f BANCA, FIN credit terms; **~ de crédito** BANCA, FIN credit conditions, credit terms; **~ de descarga** IMP/EXP, TRANSP landed terms; **~ de distribución antagónicas** POL antagonistic conditions of distribution; **~ económicas** ECON economic conditions; **~ económicas favorables** ECON favourable economic conditions (BrE), favorable economic conditions (AmE); **~ de embarque** IMP/EXP, TRANSP terms of shipment; **~ de empleo** RRHH conditions of employment, terms of employment; **~ de entrega** TRANSP delivery terms; **~ de entrega de la carga** TRANSP cargo delivery terms; **~ de entrega de la venta** IMP/EXP delivery terms of sale; **~ de funcionamiento** INFO operational environment; **~ generales del seguro** FIN guaranteed investment contract (GIC); **~ hipotéticas**

COM GEN hypothetical conditions; **~ implícitas** RRHH implied terms; **~ del intercambio** COM GEN, ECON, IMP/EXP terms of trade; **~ limitadas** SEG limited terms; **~ del mercado** COM GEN market conditions; **~ muy favorables** COM GEN concessional terms; **~ netas** TRANSP net from charter, net terms (*Nt*); **~ de la oferta** COM GEN terms of tender, conditions of tender; **~ de pago** BANCA, COM GEN payment terms, terms of payment; **~ de pago aplazado** BANCA credit facilities; **~ sobre el combustible** TRANSP fuel terms (*ft*); **~ de trabajo** RRHH working conditions; **~ del transporte** TRANSP conditions of carriage; **~ de uso** COM GEN conditions of use; **~ de venta** COM GEN, ECON, IMP/EXP, V&M conditions of sale, terms of sale, trade terms; **~ de las ventas de exportaciones** IMP/EXP terms of export sale; **~ del viaje** TRANSP voyage fixture; **~ de vida** PROT SOC living conditions; ◆ **sin ~** COM GEN no strings attached; **según las ~ de un grupo de presión** POL on lobby terms (*BrE*); **en ~ de hacer** COM GEN in a position to do; **en ~ de igualdad** CONT at arm's-length; **en ~ normales** COM GEN on usual terms; **en ~ de vuelo** TRANSP airworthy

condominio *m* COM GEN common ownership, condominium, joint ownership, cooperative (*co-op*)

condómino, -a *m,f* COM GEN co-owner, joint owner

condonar *vt* BANCA *deuda* write off

conducente: ~ a *adj* COM GEN *al crecimiento* conducive to

conducir *vt* COM GEN conduct, *persona* bring; **~ sin carga** TRANSP deadhead (*AmE*)

conducta *f* RRHH conduct; **~ afectiva** COM GEN affective behavior (*AmE*), affective behaviour (*BrE*); **~ desordenada** DER, RRHH misconduct; **~ intachable** COM GEN, DER clean hands (*jarg*); **~ poco profesional** COM GEN unprofessional conduct

conducto *m* COMS pipeline information

conductor, a *m,f* RRHH driver; **~ de camión** TRANSP lorry driver (*BrE*), teamster (*AmE*)

CONEA *abr AmL* (*Comisión Nacional de Energía Atómica*) MED AMB ≈ AERE (*Atomic Energy Research Establishment*)

conectado *adj* INFO on

conectar *vt* COM GEN, INFO connect, interface, *llamada telefónica* tap into

conexión[1]**: en ~** *adj* COM GEN on-line

conexión[2] *f* COM GEN, INFO connection, MEDIOS *radiodifusión* opt-out (*jarg*), TRANSP connection; **~ comercial** COM GEN business connection; **~ ferroviaria** TRANSP rail link; **~ en el mercado** V&M market connection; **~ de módem** INFO modem link; **~ de redes** INFO networking; **~ a tierra** TRANSP land bridge

confección *f* IND *de ropa* making, manufacture; **~ al por mayor** *Esp* (*cf confección al mayoreo AmL*) IND wholesale manufacture; **~ al mayoreo** *AmL* (*cf confección al por mayor Esp*) IND wholesale manufacture; **~ del presupuesto** CONT budgeting

confederación *f* COM GEN, POL confederation

Confederación: ~ Española de Cajas de Ahorro *f* (*CECA*) BANCA Spanish saving banks' association (*Esp*); **~ Española de Organizaciones Empresariales** *f* (*CEOE*) ECON Spanish association of business Organizations, ≈ Confederation of British Industry (*CBI*); **~ Española de la Pequeña y Mediana**

Empresa *f Esp* (*CEPYME*) ECON Spanish confederation of small and medium sized companies; **~ Internacional de Sindicatos Independientes** *f* RRHH International Confederation of Free Trade Unions (*ICFTU*); **~ de Sindicatos Europeos** *f* RRHH European Trade Union Confederation (*ETUC*)

conferencia *f* COM GEN, GES, POL conference; **~ de alto nivel** COM GEN summit conference; **~ anual de ventas** GES, V&M annual sales conference; **~ de armonización** TRANSP harmonization conference; **~ a cobro revertido** COMS collect call (*AmE*), reverse-charge call (*BrE*), transferred charge call; **~ internacional** GES international conference; **~ interurbana** COMS long-distance telephone call, toll call (*AmE*), trunk call (*BrE*) (*obs*); **~ de larga distancia** COMS long-distance telephone call, trunk call (*obs*) (*BrE*), toll call (*AmE*); **~ de líneas regulares** TRANSP liner conference; **~ de marketing** V&M marketing conference; **~ de ventas** V&M sales conference

Conferencia: ~ General de Pesos y Medidas *f* (*CGPM*) COM GEN General Conference on Weights and Measures; **~ Mundial de la Energía** *f* MED AMB World Power Conference; **~ de las Naciones Unidas sobre Comercio y Desarrollo** *f* (*UNCTAD*) ECON, POL United Nations Conference on Trade and Development (*UNCTAD*); **~ de las Naciones Unidas sobre Medio Ambiente y Desarrollo** *f* MED AMB, POL United Nations Conference on Environment and Development (*UNCED*)

conferenciante *mf Esp* (*cf conferencista AmL*) COM GEN speaker, PROT SOC, RRHH lecturer

conferencias: ~ comerciales *f pl* ECON, POL trade talks

conferencista *mf AmL* (*cf conferenciante Esp*) COM GEN speaker, PROT SOC, RRHH lecturer

conferir *vt* COM GEN, DER *derechos* confer

confesión *f* COM GEN, DER *de delito* admission, confession

confiable *adj* COM GEN reliable

confianza *f* COM GEN confidence, reliance; **~ del cliente** V&M customer confidence; **~ del mercado** V&M market confidence

confiar: ~ en *vi* COM GEN rely on

confidencial *adj* BANCA, COM GEN, DER, FISC, POL confidential, private, top-secret

confidencialidad *f* COM GEN, DER, FISC confidentiality

configuración *f* COM GEN shape, INFO configuration; **~ básica** INFO base configuration; **~ del beneficio** BOLSA *especulación* profit profile; **~ binaria** INFO bit configuration; **~ de la carga** TRANSP cargo configuration; **~ de la economía mundial** ECON shape of the world economy; **~ del equipo** INFO hardware configuration; **la ~ del futuro** COM GEN the shape of the future; **~ de salarios** RRHH wage contour; **~ en W** BOLSA W formation

configurado *adj* COM GEN shaped, tailored, COMS, INFO configured

configurar *vt* COM GEN shape up, shape, tailor, COMS, INFO configure

confirmación *f* COM GEN confirmation; **~ de pedido** COM GEN, COMS acknowledgement of order, confirmation of order; **~ positiva** CONT *auditoría* positive confirmation; **~ de renovación** SEG confirmation of renewal

confirmar *vt* COM GEN confirm, *llegada* acknowledge,

FISC *liquidación* confirm; ◆ **sin ~** COM GEN unsubstantiated

confiscación *f* COM GEN confiscation, DER forfeiture

confiscador, a *m,f* DER, FIN sequestrator

confiscar *vt* COM GEN confiscate

confitero: ~, estanquero y vendedor de periódicos *m* V&M confectioner, tobacconist and newsagent (*CTN*)

conflictivo *adj* RRHH *relaciones industriales* hot (*jarg*), troubled

conflicto *m* COM GEN conflict, *sala del consejo, laboral* dispute; **~ colectivo** ECON, POL, RRHH labor dispute (*AmE*), labour dispute (*BrE*), trade dispute, industrial dispute; **~ contable** V&M account conflict; **~ industrial** RRHH industrial conflict; **~ de intereses** COM GEN, POL conflict of interest; **~ intergremial** RRHH demarcation dispute (*BrE*); **~ laboral** ECON, POL, RRHH industrial dispute, labor dispute (*AmE*), labour dispute (*BrE*), trade dispute; **~ de leyes** DER conflict of laws

confluencia *f* COM GEN *de intereses* confluence

conforme *adj* COM GEN in agreement, *con algo o alguien* congruent, DER in agreement; ◆ **~ a** COM GEN according to, DER *requerimientos* in compliance with; **~ al auto de procesamiento** DER by indictment; **~ al plan** COM GEN according to plan; **~ al programa** COM GEN on schedule; **no ~ al reglamento** BOLSA *compraventa no coordinada* not in good delivery; **~ exige la ley** COM GEN, DER as required by law; **~ a la muestra** COM GEN true to sample; **~ a la norma** DER according to the norm; **~ a los resultados de la muestra** COM GEN up-to-sample

conformemente *adv* COM GEN consistently

conformidad[1]**: de ~** *adv* COM GEN accordingly

conformidad[2] *f* COM GEN conformity, *aceptación* approval, DER compliance; **~ con las normas contables** CONT conformity to accounting rules; ◆ **de ~ con** COM GEN, CONT *principios de contabilidad* in accordance with, in conformity with; **de ~ con el artículo** DER pursuant to article

confrontación *f* COM GEN, DER confrontation, showdown (*infrml*), SEG *naval* fronting

congelación *f* ECON, FIN *salarios, precios, crédito*, FISC freeze, freezing; **~ de alquileres** INMOB, PROT SOC rent freeze; **~ de créditos** BANCA credit freeze; **~ de empleo** RRHH job freeze; **~ de precios** COM GEN, ECON price freeze; **~ de la propiedad** FISC estate freezing; **~ salarial** RRHH wage freeze; **~ de salarios** RRHH wage standstill

congelado *adj* ECON, FIN, FISC *activos, créditos* frozen

congelamiento: ~ de depósitos *m* BANCA deposit freeze

congelar *vt* ECON, FIN *salarios, precios, crédito*, FISC freeze; ◆ **~ una cuenta** BANCA freeze an account

congestión *f* COM GEN, V&M *mercado* congestion; **~ del tráfico** TRANSP traffic congestion

conglomeración *f* ECON, FIN conglomerate; **~ financiera** FIN financial conglomerate

conglomerado *m* ECON, FIN conglomerate; **~ de empresas** ECON, FIN conglomerate

congreso[1]**: del ~** *adj* POL Congressional (*AmE*)

congreso[2] *m* COM GEN congress

Congreso: El ~ *m Esp* POL Spanish Congress, ≈ House of Commons (*BrE*) (*HC*), ≈ House of Representatives (*AmE*); **~ de los Diputados** *m Esp* POL lower house of

the Spanish parliament, ≈ House of Commons (*BrE*) (*HC*), ≈ House of Representatives (*AmE*)

congruencia *f* COM GEN congruence; **~ de objetivos** GES goal congruence

conjetura *f* DER circumstantial evidence

conjugar *vt* V&M *ventas, subastas* marry up

conjunción: en ~ con *f* COM GEN in conjunction with

conjunto[1] *adj* COM GEN *comunicado* joint

conjunto[2]**: ~ de bienes muebles** *m* FISC set of chattels; **~ de bienes públicos y privados** *m* ECON club good; **~ de bienes de una quiebra** *m* DER, FIN bankruptcy estate; **~ de caracteres** *m* INFO character array, character set; **~ de código** *m* INFO code set; **~ contable** *m* MAT countable set; **~ de contribuyentes** *m* FISC group of taxpayers; **~ de datos** *m* INFO data set; **~ finito** *m* MAT finite set; **~ de gráficos de supervideo** *AmL ver* conjunto de gráficos de supervídeo *Esp*; **~ de gráficos de supervídeo** *m Esp* (*SVGA*) INFO super video graphics array (*SVGA*); **~ de ideas irrelevantes** *m* V&M dead matter; **~ de impuestos** *m* FISC tax pool; **~ matemático** *m* INFO *datos, valores* set; **~ de medidas** *m* COM GEN set of measures; **~ de medidas económicas** *m* ECON, RRHH package deal; **~ de medidas fiscales** *m* FISC tax package; **~ de medidas sobre el impuesto sobre la renta** *m* FISC income-tax package; **~ de normas económicas** *m* ECON package deal; **~ de opciones** *m* BOLSA set of options; **~ de programas** *m* FIN, GES, INFO program package; **~ de programas de contabilidad** *m* CONT, INFO accounting package; **~ de reglas** *m* COM GEN set of rules; **~ residencial** *m* INMOB cluster housing

conmoción: ~ civil *f* SEG civil commotion (*CC*)

conmutabilidad *f* COM GEN commutability

conmutable *adj* COM GEN commutable

conmutación *f* COM GEN commutation, switching; **~ de bancos** INFO bank switching; **~ de bonos** BOLSA bond switching; **~ de mensajes** *f pl* COMS message switching

conmutador *m* INFO commuter

conmutar[1] *vt* DER *sentencia* commute

conmutar[2]**: ~ a** *fra* COM GEN switch over to

cono *m* BOLSA straddle, TRANSP *de contenedores* stacker; **~ ISO** TRANSP *de contenedores* ISO base

conocer *vt* COM GEN be acquainted with; ◆ **~ a alguien** COM GEN make sb's acquaintance

conocido[1] *adj* COM GEN known; ◆ **también ~ como** COM GEN alias, also known as (*a.k.a., AKA*); **~ por su nombre** COM GEN known by name

conocido[2]**,-a** *m,f* COM GEN acquaintance

conocimiento *m* COM GEN, GES knowledge, cognition; **~ alcanzado** ECON locked-in knowledge; **~ a bordo** IMP/EXP, TRANSP bill of lading (*B/L*), shipped bill; **~ de carga** IMP/EXP, TRANSP bill of lading (*B/L*); **~ de carga de transbordo** IMP/EXP, TRANSP transhipment bill of lading; **~ de depósito** IMP/EXP, TRANSP *navegación* dock warrant; **~ embarcado** IMP/EXP, TRANSP bill of lading (*B/L*), shipped bill; **~ de embarque** IMP/EXP, TRANSP bill of lading (*B/L*), *navegación* shipped bill of lading; **~ de embarque abreviado** IMP/EXP, TRANSP short form bill of lading; **~ de embarque aéreo** IMP/EXP, TRANSP air bill, air bill of lading, air waybill (*AWB*); **~ de embarque aéreo del capitán** IMP/EXP, TRANSP master air waybill (*MAWB*); **~ de embarque aéreo directo** IMP/EXP, TRANSP through air waybill (*TAWB*); **~ de embarque aéreo del expedidor** IMP/EXP, TRANSP forwarder air waybill (*FAWB*); **~ de embarque aéreo de IATA** TRANSP IATA air waybill; **~ de embarque aéreo local** IMP/EXP, TRANSP house air waybill (*HAWB*); **~ de embarque aéreo universal** IMP/EXP, TRANSP universal air waybill (*UAWB*); **~ de embarque del agente expedidor** IMP/EXP, TRANSP forwarding agent's bill of lading; **~ de embarque agrupado** IMP/EXP, TRANSP groupage bill of lading; **~ de embarque de agrupamiento** IMP/EXP, TRANSP groupage bill of lading; **~ de embarque al costado del buque** IMP/EXP, TRANSP alongside bill of lading; **~ de embarque bajo condiciones de la póliza de fletamento** IMP/EXP, TRANSP charter party bill of lading (*C/P b/lading*); **~ de embarque a bordo** IMP/EXP, TRANSP shipped bill; **~ de embarque caducado** IMP/EXP, TRANSP stale bill of lading; **~ de embarque con cláusula** ECON, IMP/EXP, TRANSP claused bill of lading; **~ de embarque de compañía** IMP/EXP, TRANSP house bill of lading; **~ de embarque de contenedores** IMP/EXP, TRANSP container bill of lading; **~ de embarque corrido** IMP/EXP, TRANSP through bill of lading; **~ de embarque directo** IMP/EXP, TRANSP direct bill of lading; **~ de embarque emitido a una parte determinada** IMP/EXP, TRANSP bill of lading issued to a named party; **~ de embarque en la entrada** IMP/EXP, TRANSP inward bill of lading; **~ de embarque del expedidor** IMP/EXP, TRANSP forwarder's bill of lading; **~ de embarque del expedidor para transporte combinado** IMP/EXP, TRANSP freight forwarder's combined transport bill of lading (*FCT*); **~ de embarque extraviado** IMP/EXP, TRANSP missing bill of lading (*msbl*); **~ de embarque gubernamental** IMP/EXP, TRANSP government bill of lading (*GBL*); **~ de embarque limpio** ECON, IMP/EXP, TRANSP clean bill of lading; **~ de embarque marítimo** IMP/EXP, TRANSP ocean bill of lading; **~ de embarque mínimo** IMP/EXP, TRANSP minimum bill of lading (*min B/L*); **~ de embarque negociable** IMP/EXP, TRANSP negotiable bill of lading; **~ de embarque neto** ECON, IMP/EXP, TRANSP clean bill of lading; **~ de embarque no negociable** IMP/EXP, TRANSP non-negotiable bill of lading; **~ de embarque no traspasable** IMP/EXP, TRANSP straight bill of lading; **~ de embarque nominativo** IMP/EXP, TRANSP straight bill of lading, bill of lading issued to a named party; **~ de embarque a la orden** IMP/EXP, TRANSP order bill of lading; **~ de embarque original** IMP/EXP, TRANSP original bill of lading; **~ de embarque con reservas** IMP/EXP, TRANSP dirty bill of lading, foul bill of lading; **~ de embarque sin restricciones** ECON, IMP/EXP, TRANSP clean bill of lading; **~ de embarque sobre cubierta** IMP/EXP, TRANSP on-deck bill of lading; **~ de embarque sobre el valor** IMP/EXP, TRANSP ad valorem bill of lading; **~ de embarque sucio** IMP/EXP, TRANSP foul bill of lading, claused bill of lading; **~ de embarque tardío** IMP/EXP, TRANSP stale bill of lading; **~ de embarque de transbordo** IMP/EXP, TRANSP transhipment bill of lading; **~ de embarque de transporte combinado del expedidor del flete** IMP/EXP, TRANSP freight forwarder's combined transport bill of lading (*FCT*); **~ de entrada** IMP/EXP bill of entry (*B/E*); **~ especializado** COM GEN, RRHH specialist knowledge; **~ experto** COM GEN expertise; **~ de marca** COM GEN brand awareness; **~ del mercado** V&M market awareness; **~ de mercancía recibida para embarque** IMP/EXP, TRANSP received for shipment bill of lading; **~ de muelle** IMP/EXP, TRANSP dock warrant (*D/W*); **~ del**

producto V&M product awareness, product knowledge; **~ profundo** COM GEN *de un factor particular* acute awareness; **~ con reservas** IMP/EXP, TRANSP dirty bill; **~ sucio** IMP/EXP, TRANSP dirty bill; **~ tácito** COM GEN, ECON tacit knowledge; **~ de transporte combinado** TRANSP combined transport bill of lading (*CTBL*); **~ sin trasbordos** IMP/EXP, TRANSP direct bill of lading; ◆ **tener un ~ práctico de** RRHH have a working knowledge of

conocimientos: ~ prácticos locales *m pl* RRHH local skills

consciencia: ~ del coste *f Esp* (*cf consciencia del costo AmL*) COM GEN, V&M cost consciousness; **~ del costo** *f AmL* (*cf consciencia del coste Esp*) COM GEN, V&M cost consciousness

conscienciación: ~ del coste *f Esp* (*cf conscienciación del costo AmL*) COM GEN cost awareness; **~ del costo** *f AmL* (*cf conscienciación del coste Esp*) COM GEN cost awareness

consciente *adj* COM GEN aware

consecución *f* RRHH *objetivos* accomplishment

consecuencia *f* COM GEN consequence; ◆ **como ~** COM GEN as a result

consecuencias *f pl* COM GEN implications, fallout

consecuente *adj* COM GEN, CONT, GES consistent

consecutivo *adj* COM GEN consecutive, successive

conseguir *vt* COM GEN get, *reputación* build up, *meta* realize, ECON get, RRHH accomplish, get; ◆ **~ un aumento de sueldo** RRHH get a pay rise; **~ acceso a** FIN gain entry to; **~ un buen valor por el dinero** ECON get good value for money; **~ comunicarse con alguien** COMS get through to sb; **~ un equilibrio** BOLSA find the balance; **~ nuevos pedidos** COM GEN secure new orders; **~ un gran número de telespectadores** MEDIOS score good viewer ratings; **~ una primicia informativa** MEDIOS get a first, make a scoop (*infrml*); **~ un punto de apoyo en el mercado** COM GEN get a toehold in the market; **~ resultados** RRHH get results; **~ seguridad** BOLSA obtain security; **~ un trato** COM GEN make a deal, swing the deal (*jarg*)

Consejería: ~ de Juventud y Deportes *f Esp* OCIO autonomous body in charge of promoting sports and youth programmes; ≈ Sports Council (*BrE*)

consejero, -a *m,f* COM GEN advisor, consultant, director; **~ de administración** COM GEN director (*dir.*); **~ de la defensa** RRHH difence advisor (*BrE*), defense advisor (*AmE*); **~ comercial** COM GEN, ECON, FIN commercial counsellor; **~ de crédito** FIN credit advisor; **~ delegado(-a)** GES, RRHH managing director (*MD*); **~ fiscal** FISC tax advisor; **~ impositivo(-a)** COM GEN, ECON, FIN, FISC tax agent; **~ de inversiones** COM GEN, ECON, FIN investment counsel; **~ de la Reina** DER, RRHH Queen's Counsel (*BrE*) (*QC*); **~ de salidas profesionales** RRHH careers advisor, careers officer; **~ técnico(-a)** RRHH technical advisor

consejo *m* COM GEN board, *de reunión* council, GES *información* piece of advice; **~ de administración** GES, RRHH board, executive board, directorate, board of directors, management board; **~ de administración escalonado** GES, RRHH staggered board of directors; **~ administrativo** RRHH administrative board, board of directors; **~ asesor del mercado nacional** BOLSA national market advisory board; **~ bancario** BANCA bank board; **~ de la bolsa de futuros** BOLSA futures exchange council; ~ **de control** COM GEN board of directors; ~ **de dirección** COM GEN board of management; ~ **directivo** (*cf mesa directiva AmL*) GES, RRHH board of directors, management board; ~ **de directores** CONT, GES board of directors; ~ **ejecutivo** GES executive board; ~ **de fideicomisarios** ECON, FIN, RRHH board of trustees; ~ **de inversiones** BOLSA investment counsel; ~ **de redacción** MEDIOS editorial board; ~ **de selección** RRHH screening board, selection board; ~ **de supervisión** COM GEN, CONT, GES, RRHH supervisory board

Consejo: ~ **de Asesores Económicos** *m* ECON Council of Economic Advisers (*CEA*); ~ **de Asistencia Mutua Económica** *m* ECON Council for Mutual Economic Aid (*obs*) (*CMEA, COMECON*); ~ **Comercial Europeo-ASEAN** *m* ECON, POL European/ASEAN Business Council (*EABC*); ~ **de Comercio del Este de Europa** *m* IMP/EXP East European Trade Council; ~ **para la Cooperación Económica Europea** *m* ECON, POL Council for European Economic Co-operation (*CEEC*); ~ **de la Corona** *m* COM GEN, POL Privy Council (*BrE*); ~ **Económico** *m* POL Treasury Board; ~ **Económico y Social** *m* (*ECOSOC*) ECON Economic and Social Council (*ECOSOC*); ~ **Ejecutivo del Grupo** *m* RRHH Group Executive Board; ~ **de Europa** *m* (*CE*) ECON, POL Council of Europe (*CE*); ~ **Europeo de Cargadores de Buques** *m* TRANSP European Shippers' Council; ~ **Europeo de los Ministros de Finanzas** *m* (*ECOFIN*) ECON, POL European Community Finance Ministers (*ECOFIN*); ~ **de Federaciones Industriales Europeas** *m* ECON, IND, POL Council of European Industrial Federations (*CEIF*); ~ **General del Poder Judicial** *m* POL ≈ General Council of the Judicial Power; ~ **Internacional del Estaño** *m* IND International Tin Council (*ITC*); ~ **Internacional de Operadores de Contenedores de Carga** *m* TRANSP International Council of Containership Operators (*ICCO*); ~ **Internacional del Trigo** *m* IND International Wheat Council (*BrE*) (*IWC*); ~ **de Inversiones** *m* COM GEN *Filipinas* Board of Investment (*BOI*); ~ **de Ministros** *m* ECON Council of Ministers, POL =The Cabinet; ~ **Oficial de Normas Contables** *m* CONT Governmental Accounting Standards Board (*AmE*) (*GASB*); ~ **de Productividad Nacional** *m* IND National Productivity Board; ~ **del Sindicato Nacional** *m* RRHH National Trade Union Council (*NTUC*); ~ **Superior de Investigaciones Científicas** *m* (*CSIC*) IND Spanish institute for scientific research; ~ **del Voluntariado Nacional** *m AmL* (*cf Plataforma Nacional del Voluntariado Esp*) PROT SOC organization for the coordination of voluntary associations, ≈ National Council of Voluntary Organizations (*BrE*) (*NCVO*)

consejos: ~ **de administración coincidentes** *m pl* DER interlocking directorate

consenso *m* COM GEN consensus

consensuar *vt* COM GEN agree by consensus, reach a consensus on, reach a joint agreement on

consentimiento *m* COM GEN consent; ~ **ejecutado** FISC consent executed; ◆ **por ~ mutuo** COM GEN, DER by mutual consent

consentir: ~ **a** *vt* COM GEN *aceptación* agree to

conservación *f* MED AMB conservation, *de hábitats* preservation; ~ **de cartera** COM GEN conservation of portfolio; ~ **económica** MED AMB economic conservation; ~ **de la energía** IND, MED AMB energy conservation; ~ **del margen** BOLSA margin maintenance; ~ **de la naturaleza** MED AMB nature conservation; ~ **ordinaria** COM GEN routine maintenance

conservacionista *mf* MED AMB conservationist

conservador *adj* COM GEN *gasto, estimación*, POL conservative

conservadurismo *m* COM GEN conservatism

conservantes: **sin ~** *fra* COM GEN, V&M no preservatives; **sin ~ ni aditivos** *fra* COM GEN, V&M no preservatives or additives

conservar *vt* COM GEN, MED AMB conserve, preserve

consideración: ~ **condicional** *f* COM GEN contingent consideration; ~ **parcial** *f* CONT partial consideration; ~ **para la venta** *f* COM GEN consideration for sale

considerándolo: ~ **más detenidamente** *fra* COM GEN upon further consideration

considerandos: **los ~** *m pl* DER the whereas clauses

considerar *vt* COM GEN look at; ◆ ~ **una demanda** DER sustain one's claim

consigna *f* TRANSP checkroom (*AmE*), left-luggage office (*BrE*)

consignación *f* CONT *contabilidad pública* allotment, apportionment, *de fondos* appropriation, TRANSP consignation (*consgt*); ~ **en cuanta** CONT apportionment; ~ **neta** FISC net remittance; ~ **presupuestaria** FIN, FISC allocation of funds; ◆ **en ~** TRANSP on consignment

consignador, a *m,f* TRANSP consigner

consignar *vt* CONT allocate, appropriate, allot, ECON, FIN appropriate, TRANSP *mercancías* consign; ◆ ~ **la autoridad que hace el gasto** ADMIN set forth the spending authority; ~ **fondos presupuestarios** FIN apportion budget funds

consignas: ~ **partidarias** *f pl* POL party line

consignatario, -a *m,f* CONT receiver, TRANSP shipbroker, consignee (*cnee*); ~ **de aduanas** IMP/EXP customs consignee; ~ **del buque** TRANSP ship's husband; ~ **de buques** COM GEN, TRANSP ship's agent, shipping agent; ~ **de línea marítima** RRHH liner broker; ~ **de puerto** TRANSP port agent

consistencia *f* COM GEN consistency

consistente *adj* COM GEN consistent

consolidación *f* BOLSA refunding, COM GEN *de cartera de inversiones, empresas*, CONT, FIN *de cuentas*, RRHH *del puesto de trabajo*, TRANSP consolidation; ~ **de acciones** BOLSA consolidation of shares; ~ **de balances** CONT consolidation of balances; ~ **del capital** ECON, FIN capital consolidation; ~ **de la deuda** BANCA, BOLSA, FIN debt consolidation, funding; ~ **de empresas** COM GEN merger; ~ **de flete aéreo** TRANSP air freight consolidation; ~ **de fondos** BANCA, FIN consolidation of funds; ~ **horizontal de empresas** ECON horizontal combination; ~ **de intereses** BANCA, FIN consolidation of interests; ~ **proporcional** CONT proportional consolidation

consolidado *adj* COM GEN consolidated (*consol., cons.*), well-established; **no ~** CONT nonconsolidated; **poco ~** FIN underfunded

consolidar *vt* COM GEN *posición, acuerdo* consolidate

consonancia: ~ **cognitiva** *f* ECON cognitive consonance

consorcio *m* COM GEN holding, consortium, syndicate, ECON, FIN *deuda* fund, FISC pool, RRHH consortium; ~ **de aseguradores** SEG underwriting syndicate;

~ bancario BANCA group banking, COM GEN syndicate; **~ de bancos** BANCA, FIN consortium of banks; **~ de coches** TRANSP car pool; **~ de contenedores** TRANSP container pool; **~ cualificado** RRHH qualified trust; **~ europeo de plataformas de transporte** TRANSP European pallet pool; **~ de explotación** MED AMB royalty trust; **~ de ingresos brutos** TRANSP gross receipts pool; **~ de inversiones inmobiliarias** BANCA, BOLSA, INMOB real estate investment trust (*REIT*); **~ de líneas marítimas** TRANSP liner consortium; **~ monopolístico** BANCA, ECON trust; **~ transfronterizo** FIN, IMP/EXP cross-border merger; **~ de vehículos** TRANSP pool of vehicles

consorte *mf* FISC spouse

constante *f* INFO, MAT constant; **~ de comparación** COM GEN criterion; **~ hipotecaria** BANCA mortgage constant

constantemente *adv* COM GEN steadily

constar: **~ de** *vt* COM GEN comprise

constitución *f* COM GEN incorporation, constitution, DER, POL constitution; **~ de una compañía** BOLSA formation of a corporation; **~ lesiva de hipoteca** DER injurious affection; **~ de nuevos títulos valores** BOLSA making-up; **~ de segundas hipotecas** BOLSA rehypothecation; **~ en sociedad anónima** BOLSA incorporation

constituido *adj* COM GEN incorporated, constituted, DER *fideicomiso* constituted

constituir *vt* BOLSA incorporate, COM GEN *nuevo negocio* form, *empresa* incorporate, DER incorporate; ♦ **~ una custodia en una cuenta** BANCA place a hold on an account; **~ un préstamo** BANCA, FIN take up a loan; **~ quorum** GES form a quorum; **~ una sociedad** COM GEN form a partnership

construcción *f* COM GEN construction (*constr*), manufacture, IND *de máquina* manufacture, INMOB construction (*constr*); **~ de carreteras** ECON, MED AMB, POL road building; **~ naval** IND, TRANSP shipbuilding; **~ a prueba de incendios** SEG fire-resistant construction (*BrE*), fire-resistive construction (*AmE*); **~ de red** COM GEN network building; ♦ **en ~** IND, INMOB under construction; **~ y uso** DER construction and use (*BrE*)

construcciones: **~ agrícolas** *f pl* ECON, INMOB agricultural buildings

constructor, a: **~ por encargo** *m,f* INMOB custom builder; **~ de equipos** *m,f* TRANSP gear manufacturer; **~ de naves** *m,f* TRANSP shipbuilder; **~ de propulsión eléctrica** *m,f* TRANSP electrical propulsion builder

construido: **~ de encargo** *adj* TRANSP purpose-built; **~ con propósitos específicos** *adj* INMOB purpose-built; **~ en V** *adj* TRANSP vee built (*V BLT*) (*AmE*)

construir *vt* COM GEN, INMOB build, construct

cónsul *mf* COM GEN, POL consul; **~ general** POL consul general

consulado *m* COM GEN, POL consulate

consulta *f* COM GEN consultation, enquiry, query; **~ bilateral** RRHH bilateral reference; **~ colectiva** GES joint consultation; **~ en común** GES joint consultation; **~ conjunta** GES joint consultation; **~ por despido colectivo** RRHH redundancy consultation; **~ unilateral** RRHH unilateral reference; ♦ **en ~ con** COM GEN in consultation with

consultar *vt* COM GEN, GES, INFO, RRHH, V&M consult

consulting *m* COM GEN, GES, RRHH consulting firm

consultivo *adj* COM GEN consultative, *papel* advisory; **~-democrático** GES *liderazgo de Likert* consultative-democratic

consultor, a *m,f* COM GEN, GES, INFO, RRHH consultant; **~ en administración de empresas** GES, INFO management consultant; **~ administrativo(-a)** GES management consultant; **~ financiero(-a) autorizado(-a)** FIN chartered financial consultant (*AmE*); **~ de inversiones** BOLSA investment adviser; **~ de segundo nivel** RRHH second rank consultant

consultoría *f* COM GEN, GES, RRHH consultancy, consulting firm; **~ de administración** GES management consultancy; **~ administrativa** GES management consultancy; **~ de gestión** GES management consultancy; **~ de planificación de empresa** COM GEN business plan consulting

consumado *adj* COM GEN, DER completed, consummated

consumar *vt* COM GEN, DER consummate, complete

consumible *adj* COM GEN expendable

consumibles *m pl* COM GEN supplies, INFO expendables

consumidor, a *m,f* COM GEN consumer; **~ conservador(a)** V&M laggard (*jarg*); **~ final** COM GEN end consumer, end user, V&M ultimate consumer; **~ individual** COM GEN individual consumer

consumir *vt* COM GEN consume

consumismo *m* COM GEN, ECON, V&M consumerism

consumista *mf* COM GEN, ECON, V&M consumerist

consumo *m* COM GEN, ECON consumption (C), INFO *equipo* drain, V&M consumption (C); **~ autónomo** ECON autonomous consumption; **~ de capital** ECON, FIN capital spending, capital consumption; **~ conspicuo** ECON, V&M conspicuous consumption; **~ domestico** ECON, MED AMB domestic consumption; **~ de electricidad** IND electricity consumption; **~ empresarial** ECON firm consumption; **~ externo** ECON external consumption; **~ final** INFO, MED AMB final consumption; **~ humano** MED AMB *de agua* human consumption; **~ interior** ECON, MED AMB domestic consumption; **~ intermedio** INFO, MED AMB intermediate consumption; **~ interno** ECON, MED AMB internal consumption; **~ mundial** ECON world consumption; **~ ostentoso** ECON, V&M conspicuous consumption; **~ por persona** ECON consumption per capita; **~ privado** COM GEN, ECON consumer spending, private consumption; **~ público** ECON public consumption; ♦ **no apto para el ~** COM GEN unfit for consumption

contabilidad *f* CONT accountancy (*Acc*), accounting, book-keeping; **~ del activo neto** CONT equity accounting; **~ de activos humanos** RRHH human asset accounting; **~ acumulativa** CONT accrual accounting; **~ administrativa** CONT managerial accounting; **~ de adquisiciones** CONT acquisition accounting; **~ de almacén** CONT store accounting; **~ analítica** CONT analytical accounting; **~ de la balanza de pagos** CONT, ECON accounting balance of payments; **~ bancaria** BANCA bank bookkeeping; **~ basada en el principio de prudencia** CONT conservative accounting; **~ a base de ingresos y gastos** CONT accrual accounting; **~ del beneficio obtenido por un departamento** CONT profit center accounting (*AmE*), profit centre accounting (*BrE*); **~ de caja** BANCA, CONT cash accounting, cash basis of accounting; **~ del capital social** CONT equity accounting; **~ de un centro de beneficio** CONT, FIN profit center accounting (*AmE*), profit centre accounting (*BrE*); ~ **de compras** CONT acquisition accounting; ~ **de compromisos** CONT *gubernamental* commitment accounting; ~ **por computador** *AmL ver contabilidad por computadora AmL*; ~ **por computadora** *AmL* CONT, INFO (*cf contabilidad por ordenador Esp*) computer accounting; ~ **computadorizada** *AmL* (*cf contabilidad informatizada Esp*) CONT, INFO machine accounting, electronic accounting system, computer accounting; ~ **consolidada** CONT *incluidas las divisas extranjeras* consolidated accounting; ~ **de coste de reposición** *Esp* (*cf contabilidad de costo de reposición AmL*) CONT replacement cost accounting; ~ **de costes** *Esp* (*cf contabilidad de costos AmL*) CONT cost accounting; ~ **de costes corrientes** *Esp* (*cf contabilidad de costos corrientes AmL*) CONT, ECON, FISC current cost accounting (*CCA*); ~ **de costes normalizados** *Esp* (*cf contabilidad de costos normalizados AmL*) COM GEN, CONT standard cost accounting; ~ **de costo de reposición** *AmL* (*cf contabilidad de coste de reposición Esp*) CONT replacement cost accounting; ~ **de costos** *AmL* (*cf contabilidad de costes Esp*) CONT cost accounting; ~ **de costos corrientes** *AmL* (*cf contabilidad de costes corrientes Esp*) CONT, ECON, FISC current cost accounting (*CCA*); ~ **de costos normalizados** *AmL* (*cf contabilidad de costes normalizados Esp*) COM GEN, CONT standard cost accounting; ~ **creativa** CONT creative accounting; ~ **del crecimiento** ECON *econometría* growth accounting; ~ **de créditos comprometidos** CONT *gubernamental* commitment accounting; ~ **demográfica** CONT, ECON demographic accounting; ~ **diferida** CONT accrual accounting; ~ **de dirección estratégica** CONT strategic management accounting; ~ **directiva** CONT, FIN, RRHH management accountancy, management accounting, managerial accounting; ~ **especulativa** BANCA forward accounting; ~ **ficticia** BANCA fancy accounting; ~ **fiduciaria** BANCA fiduciary accounting; ~ **financiera** CONT, FIN financial accounting; ~ **fiscal** BANCA, CONT, FISC tax accounting; ~ **del flujo de caja** BANCA, CONT, FIN cash flow accounting; ~ **del flujo de efectivo** BANCA, CONT, FIN cash flow accounting; ~ **del flujo de tesorería** BANCA, CONT, FIN cash flow accounting; ~ **de fondos** CONT fund accounting; ~ **de fusiones** CONT pooling of interests (*AmE*), merger accounting (*BrE*); ~ **de gastos corrientes** CONT, ECON, FISC current cost accounting (*CCA*); ~ **de gestión** CONT, FIN, RRHH management accountancy, management accounting, managerial accounting; ~ **de gestión estratégica** CONT strategic management accounting; ~ **gubernamental** CONT governmental accounting; ~ **del impuesto aplazado** CONT, FISC deferred tax accounting; ~ **informatizada** *Esp* (*cf contabilidad computadorizada AmL*) CONT, INFO machine accounting, computer accounting, electronic accounting system; ~ **de materiales** CONT materials accounting; ~ **mecanizada** CONT machine accounting; ~ **medioambiental** MED AMB environmental accounting, green accounting; ~ **nacional** CONT national accounting; ~ **del nivel general de precios** CONT general price level accounting (*GPLA*); ~ **del nivel de precios** CONT price level accounting; ~ **no lucrativa** CONT nonprofit accounting (*AmE*), non-profit-making accounting (*BrE*); ~ **por ordenador** *Esp* CONT (*cf contabilidad por computadora AmL*) INFO computer accounting; ~ **por partida doble** CONT, ECON double-entry accounting, double-entry book-keeping; ~ **por**

partida simple CONT, INFO single-entry book-keeping; ~ **del patrimonio neto** CONT equity accounting; ~ **previsora** CONT conservative accounting; ~ **provisional** CONT interim accounts; ~ **pública** BANCA, CONT governmental accounting, public accounting; ~ **de recursos humanos** RRHH human resource accounting; ~ **de reposición** CONT, ECON inflation accounting; ~ **de responsabilidad** CONT, FIN responsibility accounting; ~ **simplificada** ADMIN, CONT slip system bookkeeping; ~ **social** CONT social accounting; ~ **uniforme** CONT uniform accounting; ~ **en valores devengables** CONT accrual accounting; ~ **verde** MED AMB environmental accounting, green accounting

contabilización *f* CONT accounting; ~ **de cheques no pagados** BANCA booking of unpaid checks (*AmE*), booking of unpaid cheques (*BrE*); ~ **diferida y limitada** IMP/EXP limited postponed accounting; ~ **del valor actual** CONT current value accounting

contabilizar *vt* CONT book, *en el libro diario* enter in the accounts, journalize; ♦ ~ **el margen** BOLSA post margin

contable *mf Esp* (*cf contador AmL*) CONT accountant; ~ **autorizado(-a)** *m,f Esp* (*cf contador autorizado AmL*) CONT certified accountant (*BrE*) (*CA*), chartered accountant, qualified accountant; ~ **certificado(-a)** *m,f Esp* (*cf contador certificado AmL*) CONT certified accountant (*BrE*) (*CA*); ~ **colegiado(-a)** *m,f Esp* (*cf contador colegiado AmL*) CONT certified accountant (*BrE*) (*CA*), chartered accountant; ~ **cualificado(-a)** *m,f Esp* (*cf contador cualificado AmL*) CONT qualified accountant; ~ **de costes** *Esp* (*cf contador de costos AmL*) CONT cost accountant; ~ **diplomado(-a)** *m,f Esp* (*cf contador diplomado AmL*) CONT certified accountant (*BrE*) (*CA*), qualified accountant; ~ **financiero(-a)** *m,f Esp* (*cf contador financiero AmL*) COM GEN financial accountant; ~ **general autorizado(-a)** *m,f Esp* (*cf contador general autorizado AmL*) CONT certified general accountant; ~ **general certificado(-a)** *m,f Esp* (*cf contador general certificado AmL*) CONT certified general accountant; ~ **general registrado(-a)** *m,f Esp* (*cf contador general registrado AmL*) CONT certified general accountant; ~ **de gestión** *Esp* (*cf contador de gestión AmL*) CONT management accountant; ~ **habilitado(-a)** *m,f Esp* (*cf contador habilitado AmL*) CONT qualified accountant; ~ **honrado(-a)** *m,f Esp* (*cf contador honrado AmL*) BOLSA bona fide holder; ~ **independiente** *Esp* (*cf contador independiente AmL*) CONT independent accountant; ~**jefe(-a)** *m,f Esp* (*cf contador jefe AmL*) CONT chief accountant; ~ **principal** *Esp* (*cf contador principal AmL*) RRHH chief clerk, senior clerk; ~ **público(-a)** *m,f Esp* (*cf contador público AmL*) CONT certified accountant (*BrE*) (*CA*), chartered accountant; ~ **público(-a) certificado(-a)** *m,f Esp* (*cf contador público certificado AmL*) CONT Certified Public Accountant (*AmE*) (*C.P.A.*); ~ **público(-a) titulado(-a)** *m,f Esp* (*cf contador público titulado AmL*) CONT Certified Public Accountant (*AmE*) (*C.P.A.*); ~ **registrado(-a)** *m,f Esp* (*cf contador registrado AmL*) CONT certified accountant (*BrE*) (*CA*)

Contable: ~ **Colegiado(-a)** *m,f Esp* (*cf Contador Autorizado Colegiado AmL*) CONT ≈ Accredited Chartered Accountant (*ACA*)

contacto *m* BOLSA touch, COM GEN *persona* contact; ~ **directo** POL flesh pressing (*infrml*); ~ **visual** V&M *comercialización* eye contact

contado[1]: **al ~** *adj Esp* (*cf de contado AmL*) COM GEN for cash (*f.c*), across-the-counter; **de ~** *adj AmL* (*cf al contado Esp*) COM GEN for cash (*f.c.*)

contado[2] *m* COM GEN cash (*CSH*)

contador, a *m,f AmL* (*cf contable Esp*) CONT accountant; **~ autorizado(-a)** *AmL* (*cf contable autorizado Esp*) CONT certified accountant (*BrE*) (*CA*), chartered accountant, qualified accountant; **~ certificado(-a)** *AmL* (*cf contable certificado Esp*) CONT certified accountant (*BrE*) (*CA*); **~ colegiado(-a)** *AmL* (*cf contable colegiado Esp*) CONT certified accountant (*BrE*) (*CA*), chartered accountant; **~ de costos** *AmL* (*cf contable de costes Esp*) CONT cost accountant; **~ cualificado(-a)** *AmL* (*cf contable cualificado Esp*) CONT qualified accountant; **~ de dinero** COM GEN ready reckoner; **~ diplomado(-a)** *AmL* (*cf contable diplomado Esp*) CONT certified accountant (*BrE*) (*CA*); **~ financiero(-a)** *AmL* (*cf contable financiero Esp*) COM GEN financial accountant; **~ general autorizado(-a)** *AmL* (*cf contable general autorizado Esp*) CONT certified general accountant; **~ general certificado(-a)** *AmL* (*cf contable general certificado Esp*) CONT certified general accountant; **~ general registrado(-a)** *AmL* (*cf contable general registrado Esp*) CONT certified general accountant; **~ de gestión** *AmL* (*cf contable de gestión Esp*) CONT management accountant; **~ habilitado(-a)** *AmL* (*cf contable habilitado Esp*) CONT qualified accountant; **~ honrado(-a)** *AmL* (*cf contable honrado Esp*) BOLSA bona fide holder; **~ independiente** *AmL* (*cf contable independiente Esp*) CONT independent accountant; **~ jefe(-a)** *AmL* (*cf contable jefe Esp*) CONT chief accountant; **~ principal** *AmL* (*cf contable principal Esp*) RRHH *contabilidad* chief clerk, senior clerk; **~ público(-a)** *AmL* (*cf contable público Esp*) CONT certified accountant (*BrE*) (*CA*), chartered accountant; **~ público(-a) certificado(-a)** *AmL* (*cf contable público certificado Esp*) CONT Certified Public Accountant (*AmE*) (*C.P.A.*); **~ público(-a) titulado(-a)** *AmL* (*cf contable público titulado Esp*) CONT Certified Public Accountant (*AmE*) (*C.P.A.*); **~ registrado(-a)** *AmL* (*cf contable registrado Esp*) CONT certified accountant (*BrE*) (*CA*)

Contador, a: **~ Autorizado(-a) Colegiado(-a)** *m,f AmL* (*cf Contable Colegiado Esp*) CONT ≈ Accredited Chartered Accountant (*ACA*)

contaduría *f* CONT *profesión* accountancy, *de cuentas AmL* (*cf oficina de contabilidad Esp*) accounting office, (*cf departamento de contabilidad Esp*) accounting department, accounts department

contáiner *m* TRANSP container

contaminación *f* IND, MED AMB *de producto* contamination, *del medio ambiente* pollution; **~ del agua** MED AMB water pollution; **~ del aire** MED AMB air pollution; **~ de las costas** MED AMB coastal pollution; **~ por crudos** MED AMB oil pollution; **~ por lluvia ácida** MED AMB acid rain pollution; **~ por petróleo** MED AMB oil pollution; **~ por radiación** MED AMB radiation pollution; **~ de los ríos** MED AMB river pollution

contaminado *adj* IND, MED AMB contaminated, polluted

contaminante[1]: **poco ~** *adj* MED AMB *tecnología* low-polluting

contaminante[2] *f* MED AMB pollutant

contaminar *vt* MED AMB contaminate, pollute, TRANSP taint

contar *vt* MAT, POL *votos* count; ◆ **~ con** COM GEN bargain for, count on; **~ con alguien para algo** COM GEN look to sb for sth; **~ con la aprobación de** COM GEN have the approval of; **~ con los medios para** COM GEN have the means to

contención *f* ECON, POL *demanda* containment, *de política monetaria* constraint; **~ de los costes** *Esp* (*cf contención de los costos AmL*) ECON cost containment; **~ de los costos** *AmL* (*cf contención de los costes Esp*) ECON cost containment; **~ voluntaria a la exportación** IMP/EXP voluntary export restraint (*VER*);

contenedor *m* TRANSP *unidad ISO* container; **~ abatible** TRANSP collapsible container (*coltainer*); **~ de abertura lateral** TRANSP open-wall container; **~ de abertura superior** TRANSP open-topped container (*OT*); **~ abierto** TRANSP open container; **~ abierto abatible** TRANSP flat rack; **~ para cajas jaula** TRANSP cage container (*c*); **~ calorífico** TRANSP heated container; **~ de carga superior** TRANSP top loader container; **~ para cargas apiladas** TRANSP box container; **~ cerrado sin aislamiento térmico** TRANSP covered dry container; **~ de chapa ondulada** TRANSP corrugated container; **~ cisterna** TRANSP tank container; **~ completo** TRANSP full container load (*FCL*); **~ de cuba refrigerada** TRANSP insulated tank container, independent tank (IT); **~ de cubierta inferior** TRANSP lower deck container; **~ de cubierta plana** TRANSP flat container; **~ con enrejado lateral** TRANSP lattice-sided container; **~ de flete aéreo** TRANSP airfreight container (*ac*); **~ frigorífico** TRANSP insulated container, refrigerated container, reefer container; **~ para ganado** TRANSP cattle container; **~ a granel** TRANSP bulk container; **~ para graneles** TRANSP bulktainer, bulk freight container; **~ de graneles líquidos** TRANSP bulk liquid container; **~ de graneles secos** TRANSP dry bulk container (*d*); **~ IATA** TRANSP IATA container; **~ de intercambio** TRANSP interchange container; **~ intermedio** TRANSP intermediate container; **~ intermedio para graneles** TRANSP intermediate bulk container (*IBC*); **~ intermodal** TRANSP intermodal container; **~ de laterales abiertos** TRANSP open-sided container; **~ con media cubierta de lona** TRANSP half-tilt container (*ht*); **~ de mercancías** TRANSP freight container; **~ de mezcla** TRANSP alloy container; **~ de modalidad aérea** TRANSP air mode container; **~ en la panza** TRANSP belly container; **~ polivalente intermedio y masivo** TRANSP flexible intermediate and bulk container (*FIBC*); **~ de propiedad extranjera** TRANSP foreign-owned container; **~ rodante** TRANSP roll-on container; **~ sobre vagón plataforma** TRANSP container on flat car (*AmE*), container on flat wagon (*BrE*); **~ sobre vagón raso** TRANSP container on flat car (*AmE*), container on flat wagon (*BrE*); **~ de techo abierto** TRANSP soft top container; **~ de techo aislante removible** TRANSP open-topped reefer; **~ con techo removible** TRANSP open-topped container, open-top container (*OT*); **~ térmico** TRANSP thermal container; **~ terrestre** TRANSP inland container (*IC*); **~ tolva** TRANSP bin container, hopper container; **~ universal** TRANSP universal container (*U*); **~ de uso general** TRANSP general purpose freight container; **~ de ventilación mecánica** TRANSP mechanically ventilated container; **~ ventilado** TRANSP ventilated container (*VC*)

contenedorización *f* TRANSP containerization

contenedorizado *adj* TRANSP containerized

contenedorizar *vt* TRANSP containerize

contener *vt* COM GEN, ECON *demanda, inflación* contain, control; ~ **un informe** COM GEN *periódico*, MEDIOS carry a report

contenido *m* COM GEN content, contents, subject matter, tenor, FIN, INFO, PATENT subject matter, tenor; ~ **del puesto** RRHH job content; ~ **de trapo** ADMIN, MEDIOS *papel* rag content

contestación *f* COM GEN, DER answer; ~ **a la demanda** COM GEN, DER answer; ◆ **en** ~ **a** COM GEN in response to

contestador *m* COM GEN, COMS, INFO answering machine; ~ **automático** COM GEN, COMS, INFO answering machine, answerphone; ~ **telefónico** COM GEN, COMS, INFO answerphone

contestar 1. *vt* COM GEN answer, reply; ◆ ~ **a** COM GEN answer to; ~ **al teléfono** COMS answer the telephone; **2.** *vi* COM GEN answer, reply; ◆ ~ **por carta** COM GEN write back; ~ **a vuelta de correo** COMS reply by return mail

contexto *m* COM GEN, INFO context

contiene: ~ **carta de aviso** *fra* COMS advice enclosed (*ADV*)

contiguo *adj* COM GEN adjoining, INFO contiguous

continental *adj* COM GEN continental

continente: **el** ~ *m* COM GEN *Europa continental*, POL the Continent

contingencia *f* COM GEN contingency; ~ **de beneficio** CONT, FIN gain contingency; ~ **de ganancia** CONT, FIN gain contingency; ~ **de pérdidas** CONT, FIN loss contingency

contingente[1] *adj* COM GEN incidental, *responsabilidad* contingent

contingente[2]: ~ **arancelario** *m* IMP/EXP import quota, tariff quota; ~ **arancelario comunitario** *m* IMP/EXP, POL community tariff quota; ~ **comunitario** *m* IMP/EXP, POL community quota

continua *fra* COM GEN *documentos escritos* continued (*cont'd*)

continuación *f* BOLSA continuation

continuamente *adv* COM GEN around-the-clock (*AmE*), round-the-clock (*BrE*)

continuar *vi* COM GEN continue, FIN run on; ◆ ~ **con** COM GEN *desarrollos* keep up with

continuidad *f* COM GEN continuity, consistency; ~ **en la afiliación sindical** RRHH maintenance of membership; ~ **en el empleo** RRHH continuity of employment (*BrE*)

continuo *adj* COM GEN around-the-clock (*AmE*), round-the-clock (*BrE*), *interés, apoyo* continuing

contraasiento *m* BANCA contra entry, CONT contra entry, reversing entry, correcting entry

contraatacar *vi* COM GEN fight back

contrabandear *vt* FISC, IMP/EXP smuggle

contrabandista *mf* COM GEN contrabandist, FISC, IMP/EXP smuggler

contrabando *m* COM GEN contraband, FISC, IMP/EXP *actividad* smuggling

contracción *f* ECON contraction; ~ **de la demanda** *m* V&M contraction of demand, shrinkage; ~ **de la economía** COM GEN economic slowdown

contracomercio *m* ECON counter trade

contracorredor, a *m,f* BOLSA contra broker

contracorriente *f* COM GEN cross-current

contracubierta: ~ **del libro** *f* MEDIOS back cover

contradecir *vt* DER traverse

contrademanda *f* DER counterclaim, FISC cross demand

contradicción *f* DER traverse

contradictorio *adj* DER traversable

contraendosar *vt* BANCA endorse back

contraer *vt* CONT *deudas* incur, FIN *préstamo* contract

contraerse *v refl* COM GEN *crecimiento* contract, ECON shrink

contralor, a *m,f AmL* (*cf interventor Esp*) COM GEN compliance accountant, comptroller, controller, financial accountant

contramedida *f* COM GEN countermeasure

contraoferta *f* V&M counteroffer, contra-deal

contrapaquete *m* V&M counterpack

contraparte *f* BOLSA counterparty (*BrE*)

contrapartida *f* BANCA contra, CONT contra, adjusting entry, contra account, ECON balancing item, counterpart; ~ **de un contrato** DER consideration

contraportada *f* V&M fourth cover

contraprestación *f* DER consideration

contrario: **si no se especifica lo** ~ *fra* COM GEN unless otherwise specified

contrarrestar *vt* ECON counterbalance, counteract

contraseña *f* INFO password, token

contraste *m* COM GEN, INFO contrast

contratación *f* COM GEN, RRHH contract hire, engagement; ~ **de auditoría** CONT audit engagement; ~ **automática** ECON *negocios en bolsa* program deal (*AmE*), programme deal (*BrE*); ~ **automática por computador** *AmL ver* contratación automática por computador *AmL*; ~ **automática por computadora** *AmL* BOLSA program trading (*AmE*), programme trading (*BrE*); ~ **automática por ordenador** *Esp* (*cf contratación automática por computadora AmL*) BOLSA program trading (*AmE*), programme trading (*BrE*); ~ **por bloque** BOLSA block trade; ~ **y gestión del personal** RRHH staff resourcing; ~ **por incentivos** COM GEN incentive contracting; ~ **de intangibles** BOLSA sham trading; ~ **interna** RRHH internal search; ~ **del mercado laboral interno** ECON internal labor market contracting (*AmE*), internal labour market contracting (*BrE*); ~ **pública** COM GEN public engagement; ~ **y selección** RRHH recruitment and selection; ~ **por volumen** BOLSA volume trading

contratante: ~ **comprador(a)** *m,f* COM GEN bargaining party

contratar *vt* COM GEN, ECON contract, RRHH *personal* engage, hire, take on; ◆ ~ **para** COM GEN contract to; ~ **a alguien** COM GEN contract sb; ~ **y despedir** RRHH hire and fire; ~ **los servicios de alguien** COM GEN retain sb's services

contratista *mf* COM GEN, DER, IND, INMOB, RRHH contractor (*contr.*), contracts officer; ~ **de camiones** TRANSP trucking contractor; ~ **independiente** FISC independent contractor; ~ **principal** COM GEN general contractor, prime contractor; ~ **de remolques** TRANSP towage contractor; ~ **de transporte por carretera** TRANSP road haulage contractor; ~ **de transportes** TRANSP haulage contractor

contrato[1] *m* COM GEN agreement, contract, DER covenant, indenture, FISC covenant;

~ **a** ~ **abierto** BOLSA, FIN open contract, TRANSP open

charter (*OC*); ~ **de adhesión** DER adhesion contract; ~ **adjudicado** DER apportioned contract; ~ **de la administración** DER government contract; ~ **administrativo** GES management contract; ~ **de adquisición** FISC acquisition contract; ~ **al coste más honorarios** *Esp* (*cf contrato al costo más honorarios AmL*) COM GEN cost-plus contract; ~ **al costo más honorarios** *AmL* (*cf contrato al coste más honorarios Esp*) COM GEN cost-plus contract; ~ **aleatorio** SEG aleatory contract; ~ **anual por horas** RRHH annual hours contract; ~ **de anualidad** FISC annuity contract; ~ **de aparcería** COM GEN, DER metayer contract; ~ **de aprendizaje** COM GEN, DER indenture of apprenticeship; ~ **de arrendamiento principal** DER head lease;

~ b ~ **basura** RRHH employment contract for poorly paid temporary work; ~ **bilateral** DER bilateral contract; ~ **blindado** *f* FIN golden parachute (*infrml*); ~ **bursátil** BOLSA stock contract;

~ c ~ **de cambios** DER exchange contract; ~ **sin causa** COM GEN bare contract; ~ **de cobertura** BOLSA collar; ~ **colectivo** DER, IND, RRHH collective bargaining agreement; ~ **colectivo de trabajo** DER, IND, RRHH union labor contract (*AmE*), union labour contract (*BrE*); ~ **comercial** COM GEN, DER commercial contract; ~ **con el comisariado** BOLSA indenture; ~ **de compra a plazos** FIN hire purchase agreement; ~ **de compraventa de un bien inmueble** INMOB land contract; ~ **condicional** DER conditional contract; ~ **de corretaje** BOLSA, COM GEN, DER broker's note; ~ **a corto plazo** RRHH short-term contract; ~ **con coste, seguro y flete** *Esp* (*cf contrato con costo, seguro y flete AmL*) IMP/EXP, SEG, TRANSP cost, insurance and freight contract (*CIF contract*); ~ **con costo, seguro y flete** *AmL* (*cf contrato con coste, seguro y flete Esp*) IMP/EXP, SEG, TRANSP cost, insurance and freight contract (*CIF contract*);

~ d ~ **de deport** BOLSA backwardation business; ~ **diferido de compra periódica** FIN periodic purchase deferred contract; ~ **por distritos** RRHH district agreement; ~ **de divisas a plazo** BANCA forward exchange contract; ~ **doble** DER dual contract;

~ e ~ **de eficiencia** RRHH efficiency agreement; ~ **de emisión de bonos** BOLSA bond indenture; ~ **de empleo a prueba** RRHH placement test; ~ **de empresa** RRHH company agreement; ~ **de enrolamiento** TRANSP ship's articles; ~ **con entrega** TRANSP bare-boat charter; ~ **por etapas** RRHH staged agreement; ~ **de exclusividad** DER agreement for exclusiveness; ~ **explícito** DER explicit contract; ~ **expreso** DER express contract;

~ f ~ **de fábrica** *AmL* (*cf acuerdo de fábrica Esp*) RRHH shop-floor agreement (*BrE*); ~ **de fideicomiso** COM GEN, DER trust deal, trust indenture; ~ **en firme** BOLSA cash bargain; ~ **de fletamento** TRANSP charter contract; ~ **de fletamento a casco desnudo** TRANSP bareboat charter party; ~ **de fletamento de grano** TRANSP grain charter party; ~ **de fletamento no transferible** TRANSP nondemise charter party; ~ **de flete aéreo** TRANSP aircraft charter agreement; ~ **de flete a futuro** FIN freight futures contract; ~ **de fusión** BOLSA amalgamation agreement; ~ **de futuros** BOLSA futures contract; ~ **de futuros financieros** BOLSA, FIN financial futures contract; ~ **de futuros en letras del tesoro** BOLSA treasury bill futures contract; ~ **de futuros LIBOR** BOLSA LIBOR futures contract; ~ **de futuros**

sobre depósitos a plazo en eurodólares BOLSA Eurodollar time deposit futures contract; ~ **de futuros sobre renta fija** BOLSA bond futures contract; ~ **de futuros subyacente** BOLSA underlying futures contract; ~ **de futuros de tipo de interés a corto plazo** BOLSA short-term interest rate futures contract; ~ **de futuros de tipos de interés** BOLSA interest rate futures contract;

~ g ~ **de garantía** BOLSA guarantee agreement; ~ **de gas y petróleo** DER oil and gas lease; ~ **de gestión** GES management contract; ~ **a la gruesa** DER, TRANSP bottomry bond; ~ **de grupo** COM GEN group contract;

~ h ~ **honorario** COM GEN, DER honorary contract;

~ i ~ **implícito de hecho** DER implied in fact contract; ~ **incentivo** COM GEN incentive contract; ~ **de indemnización** INMOB, SEG contract of indemnity; ~ **individual** RRHH individual bargaining; ~ **de información** COM GEN information agreement; ~ **de inversión** BOLSA investment contract; ~ **de inversión garantizado** COM GEN guaranteed investment contract (*BrE*) (*GIC*);

~ l ~ **leonino** COM GEN, DER onerous contract; ~ **de licencia** COM GEN, DER licence contract (*BrE*), license contract (*AmE*); ~ **sin límites preestablecidos** DER open-end contract, open-ended contract;

~ m ~ **de mantenimiento** COM GEN, INFO service agreement; ~ **marco** COM GEN skeleton contract; ~ **a medida** DER tailor-made contract; ~ **con mención de dique** TRANSP dock charter; ~ **mixto** TRANSP *navegación* trip charter; ~ **modelo** RRHH pattern agreement; ~ **de montaje llave en mano** ECON turnkey contract; ~ **multilateral** DER, ECON, POL multilateral agreement;

~ n ~ **no ejecutable** DER unenforceable contract; ~ **nulo** COM GEN, DER void contract;

~ o ~ **de obras** COM GEN works contract; ~ **de opción** BOLSA privilege (*AmE*); ~ **con opción de futuro** IMP/EXP option forward contract; ~ **de opción sobre futuros** BOLSA futures option contract; ~ **de opciones** BOLSA option contract; ~ **de opciones de divisas** BOLSA currency options contract;

~ p ~ **de pago mínimo obligatorio** BOLSA take-or-pay contract; ~ **perfeccionado** DER executed contract; ~ **pignoraticio** COM GEN, DER pignorative contract; ~ **a plazo** BOLSA forward contract; ~ **de plazo fijo** RRHH fixed-term contract; ~ **a precio alzado** RRHH lump-sum contract; ~ **de precio fijado** V&M fixed-price contract; ~ **por precio global** RRHH lump-sum contract; ~ **prematrimonial** DER prenuptial contract; ~ **de prenda** COM GEN, DER pledge agreement; ~ **prendario** COM GEN, DER pledge agreement; ~ **prescrito** DER, COM GEN prescribed contract; ~ **de préstamo** BANCA, COM GEN, DER loan agreement; ~ **principal** DER prime contract; ~ **privado** DER private arrangement; ~ **de productos** BOLSA commodity contract; ~ **público** COM GEN *para compañías de obras públicas* public contract;

~ r ~ **de reaseguro** SEG reinsurance treaty; ~ **de relación exclusiva** ECON tying contract; ~ **de representación** DER agency agreement; ~ **de retroventa** COM GEN, DER reversion clause on bargain and sale;

~ s ~ **de salvamento** TRANSP salvage agreement; ~ **de seguros** SEG insurance contract; ~ **de seguros de adhesión** DER adhesion insurance contract; ~ **de servicio de la compañía** TRANSP company service contract; ~ **de servicio general** TRANSP general service contract (*BrE*); ~ **de servicio público** COM GEN public service contract; ~ **de servicio residencial** COM GEN, INMOB residential service contract; ~ **de servicios** COM GEN, DER, INFO, RRHH contract for services, service contract; ~ **simple** COM GEN simple contract; ~ **sinalagmático** DER bilateral contract; ~ **sindical** RRHH union agreement; ~ **sobre divisas** BOLSA currency contract; ~ **sobre futuros agrícolas** BOLSA agricultural futures contract; ~ **sobre futuros de divisas** BOLSA currency futures contract; ~ **sobre el índice bursátil** BOLSA stock index contract; ~ **sobre nueva tecnología** COM GEN new technology agreement (*BrE*); ~ **sobre tipo de interés** BOLSA interest rate contract; ~ **sobre tipos futuros** BOLSA, FIN future rate agreement; ~ **sobreentendido** COM GEN, DER implied contract; ~ **social** RRHH social contract; ~ **de sociedad** COM GEN, DER partnership agreement; ~ **de un solo sindicato de no ir a la huelga** RRHH single union no-strike agreement (*BrE*); ~ **de suministro abierto** DER, V&M open-end contract, open-ended contract;

~t ~ **tácito** COM GEN, DER implied contract; ~ **por tiempo establecido** RRHH fixed-term agreement, fixed-term deal; ~ **de trabajador autónomo** RRHH freelance contract; ~ **de trabajo** COM GEN, RRHH labor contract (*AmE*), labour contract (*BrE*), contract of employment; ~ **de trabajo a destajo** TRANSP piecework contact;

~v ~ **de venta** BANCA, DER, V&M sales agreement, sales contract; ~ **de venta en cuotas** DER installment contract (*AmE*), instalment contract (*BrE*); ~ **de venta exclusivo** INMOB exclusive right to sell listing; ~ **de venta para entrega en el futuro** COM GEN forward sales contract; ~ **para la venta de mercancías** DER, V&M contract for the sale of goods; ~ **de venta a plazos** DER installment contract (*AmE*), instalment contract (*BrE*); ~ **verbal** DER oral contract; ~ **con vigencia indefinida** RRHH open-ended agreement; ~ **vinculante** DER tying contract; ~ **por volumen del flete** (*volcoa*) TRANSP volume contract of affreightment (*volcoa*)

contrato[2]: **mediante ~ privado** *fra* COM GEN, DER by private contract; **según ~ privado** *fra* COM GEN, DER by private contract

Contrato: ~ **Social** *m* POL Social Contract

contratos: ~ **de futuros** *m pl* BOLSA nearby contracts, nearbys (*jarg*); ~ **pendientes** *m pl* BOLSA, FIN open contracts

contribución *f* COM GEN contribution, CONT, ECON, FISC tax, IMP/EXP levy; ~ **a la avería gruesa** SEG general average contribution (*G/A con*); ~ **excesiva** FISC excess contribution; ~ **indirecta** IMP/EXP excise duty; ~ **por jubilación** COM GEN superannuation contribution; ~ **marginal bruta** CONT throughput; ~ **neta** COM GEN net contribution; ~ **política** FISC political contribution; ~ **privada** ECON *con respecto a la ayuda al desarrollo* private contribution; ~ **a la seguridad social** PROT SOC national insurance contribution (*BrE*) (*NIC*), social security contribution; ~ **sobre salarios** FISC payroll tax; ~ **a tasa fija** FISC lump-sum tax; ~ **territorial** FISC real property tax, property tax, land tax; ~ **territorial urbana** FISC real property tax; ~ **tipo** ECON contribution standard; ~ **urbana** COM GEN council tax (*BrE*)

contribuir *vt* COM GEN contribute

contribuyente[1] *adj* DER contributory

contribuyente[2] *mf* ECON, FISC contributor, taxpayer; ~ **de bajos ingresos** FISC low-income taxpayer; ~ **de ingresos elevados** FISC high-income taxpayer; ~ **de ingresos medios** FISC middle-income taxpayer;

~ **moroso(-a)** *m,f* FISC delinquent taxpayer; ~ **municipal** FISC, POL ratepayer; ~ **residente** FISC resident taxpayer

control *m* COM GEN check, control, supervision; ~ **de acceso** INFO *verificación* access control; ~ **de las acciones** CONT stock control; ~ **de actuación** COM GEN performance monitoring; ~ **por adaptación** GES adaptive control; ~ **administrativo** GES managerial control; ~ **aduanero** IMP/EXP customs control; ~ **aleatorio** MAT random check; ~ **ambiental** MED AMB environmental control; ~ **de aplicación** CONT application control; ~ **de un asunto** V&M *relaciones públicas* issue management (*jarg*); ~ **automático aprobado de maquinaria no operativa** TRANSP automatic control certified for unattended engine room; ~ **automático autorizado** TRANSP automatic control certified (*ACC*); ~ **de avance** COM GEN, GES, IND progress control; ~ **de caja** CONT cash control; ~ **de calidad** IND quality control (*QC*); ~ **de calidad total** GES, IND total quality control (*TQC*); ~ **de cambios** BANCA, ECON *política del gobierno*, POL exchange control; ~ **del capital** FIN capital rationing; ~ **de cobros** CONT follow-up of invoices; ~ **de competencia y crédito** ECON Competition and Credit Control; ~ **por computador** *AmL ver control por computadora AmL*; ~ **por computadora** *AmL* (*cf control por ordenador Esp*) INFO computer control; ~ **de la configuración** INFO configuration control; ~ **de conformidad** COM GEN consistency check; ~ **del consejo** GES board control; ~ **contable** CONT accounting control; ~ **de la contaminación** IND, MED AMB, SEG pollution monitoring, pollution control; ~ **de contenedores** TRANSP container control (*CC*); ~ **de costes** *Esp* (*cf control de costos AmL*) CONT cost control; ~ **de costos** *AmL* (*cf control de costes Esp*) CONT cost control; ~ **de crédito** BANCA, ECON, FIN credit control; ~ **de cumplimiento** CONT application control; ~ **de daños** IND, TRANSP damage control; ~ **de despensa** V&M pantry check; ~ **directivo** GES managerial control; ~ **de distribución** V&M distribution check; ~ **de dividendos** BOLSA, CONT dividend control; ~ **de divisas** BANCA, ECON, POL exchange control; ~ **efectivo** COM GEN, FIN effective control, working control; ~ **de la elaboración del presupuesto** CONT budgeting control; ~ **de errores** INFO error control; ~ **estadístico** MAT statistical control; ~ **estadístico de la calidad** MAT statistical quality control (*SQC*); ~ **del Estado** ECON, POL state control; ~ **del estado de las mercancías** TRANSP condition monitoring (*CM*); ~ **estatal** ECON, POL state control; ~ **de existencias** CONT, ECON inventory control, stock control; ~ **de existencias de reserva** COM GEN reserve-stock control; ~ **a la exportación** IMP/EXP export control; ~ **financiero** FIN financial control; ~ **de flujo** INFO flow control; ~ **fronterizo** ECON, IMP/EXP border control, frontier control; ~ **de funcionamiento** COM GEN performance monitoring; ~ **del gasto público** ECON public expenditure control; ~ **de gastos** CONT expenses control; ~ **de gestión** CONT management control; ~ **ilegal del mercado** DER, ECON rigging; ~ **a la importación** IMP/EXP import control; ~ **informatizado de operaciones bursátiles** BOLSA stock watcher; ~ **de ingreso** INFO *verificación* access control; ~ **de inmigración** POL, PROT SOC immigration control; ~ **interno** CONT internal control; ~ **de inventarios** CONT inventory control (*AmE*), stock control (*Bre*); ~ **de los límites de una línea** COM GEN control of line limits; ~ **de línea** GES line control; ~ **de liquidez** COM GEN, CONT liquidity control; ~ **local de exportaciones** IMP/EXP local export control; ~ **local de las importaciones** IMP/EXP local import control (*LIC*); ~ **de lotes** SEG batch control; ~ **de mercancía** V&M merchandise control; ~ **monetario** DER, ECON rig; ~ **numérico** FIN, MAT numerical control; ~ **de obligaciones** DER commitment control; ~ **de la oferta** ECON supply control; ~ **operacional** COM GEN operational control; ~ **óptimo** ECON optimal control; ~ **por ordenador** *Esp* (*cf control por computadora Aml*) INFO computer control; ~ **del país de origen** FIN home-country control; ~ **de paridad** COMS, INFO parity check; ~ **de pasajeros** OCIO passenger control; ~ **de pasaporte** OCIO passport control; ~ **de pedidos** V&M follow-up of orders; ~ **portuario** TRANSP port control; ~ **de precios** ECON price control, price regulation; ~ **presupuestario** CONT, FIN, FISC budgetary control (*BC*) budget control; ~ **del proceso** COM GEN process control; ~ **del proceso estadístico** MAT statistical process control; ~ **de procesos** IND process control; ~ **de producción** IND manufacturing control, production control; ~ **de un programa** MEDIOS air check; ~ **de progreso** COM GEN, GES, IND progress control; ~ **provisional** COM GEN standby control; ~ **religioso** RRHH religious monitoring; ~ **del riesgo** GES risk monitoring; ~ **de rutina** COM GEN routine check; ~ **rutinario** TRANSP routine control; ~ **de salarios** RRHH wage control; ~ **de stocks** CONT, ECON inventory control (*Aml*), stock control (*BrE*); ~ **de tiempo** COM GEN, COMS time-keeping; ~ **de los trabajadores** RRHH worker control; ~ **de trabajos** RRHH job control; ~ **de tráfico** TRANSP traffic control; ~ **de tráfico aéreo** TRANSP air-traffic control (*ATC*); ~ **de tráfico portuario** TRANSP port traffic control; ~ **vegetativo** ECON vegetative control; ~ **de ventas** V&M sales control

controlado adj COM GEN administered, controlled; ~ **por computador** *AmL* ver controlado por computadora *AmL*; ~ **por computadora** *AmL* (*cf controlado por ordenador Esp*) INFO computer-controlled; ~ **a distancia** INFO remote-controlled; ~ **por ordenador** *Esp* (*cf controlado por computadora AmL*) INFO computer-controlled

controlador, a *m,f* COM GEN *cuentas del Estado* comptroller, controller; ~ **de almacén** RRHH stock controller; ~ **de existencias** RRHH stock controller; ~ **de grupo** INFO cluster controller; ~ **de inventario** COM GEN inventory controller; ~ **de tráfico aéreo** TRANSP air-traffic controller; ~ **de transporte** RRHH transport controller

Control-Alternar-Suprimir *m* INFO Control-Alternate-Delete (*CAD*)

controlar *vt* COM GEN administer, monitor, control, follow up; ◆ ~ **estrictamente** ECON hold in check; ~ **los gastos** FIN control the purse strings; ~ **un mercado** FIN control a market, V&M monitor a market

controles: ~ **administrativos y organizacionales** *m pl* CONT administrative and organizational controls; ~ **cualitativos** *m pl* BANCA qualitative controls; ~ **cuantitativos** *m pl* BANCA quantitative controls; ~ **estrictos** *m pl* DER tight controls; ~ **más estrictos** *m pl* DER tighter controls; ~ **veterinarios** *m pl* IMP/EXP veterinary controls; ~ **voluntarios** *m pl* V&M voluntary controls

controversia *f* COM GEN, MEDIOS, POL controversy, issue; ~ **dorada** BANCA Bullionist controversy (*BrE*); ~ **de oro** BANCA Bullionist controversy (*BrE*); ~ **de la productividad marginal** ECON adding-up controversy

controversias: ~ **de Cambridge** *f pl* ECON Cambridge controversies

controvertido adj COM GEN, MEDIOS, POL controversial

contumacia *f* DER nonappearance

convencer *vt* COM GEN persuade, win over, *argumento* stand up

convención *f* COM GEN, CONT, GES convention; ~ **de línea de carga** TRANSP load line convention; ~ **de negocios** COM GEN business convention; ~ **un programa-un voto** FIN one-program-to-one-vote convention (*AmE*); ~ **sobre seguridad de los contenedores** TRANSP container safety convention (*CSC*)

Convención: ~ **Europea de Derechos Humanos** *f* PROT SOC European Convention on Human Rights; ~ **Europea de Patentes** *f* DER, PATENT European Patent Convention; ~ **Internacional de Transporte de Mercancías por Ferrocarril** *f* COM GEN, TRANSP International Convention on Carriage of Goods by Rail; ~ **de Lomé** *f* ECON Lomé Convention; ~ **sobre el Contrato para el Transporte Internacional de Mercancías por Carretera** *f* COM GEN, TRANSP Convention on the Contract for the International Carriage of Goods by Road; ~ **de Varsovia** *f* TRANSP Warsaw Convention

Convenciones: ~ **de la OIT** *f pl* RRHH ILO Conventions

convenido adj COM GEN agreed; ◆ **según lo** ~ COM GEN as agreed

conveniencia: ~ **organizativa** *f* COM GEN organizational convenience

conveniente adj COM GEN, DER, GES advisable

convenio *m* COM GEN, DER, FIN agreement, arrangement, bargain, TRANSP articles of agreement; ~ **de acreedores** FIN composition of creditors; ~ **antidumping** MED AMB, POL antidumping agreement; ~ **asegurador contra incendios** SEG fire insuring agreement (*AmE*); ~ **asegurador de daños a terceros** SEG property and casualty policy insuring agreement; ~ **asegurador de responsabilidad civil** SEG liability insuring agreement; ~ **asegurador del sector del automóvil** SEG automobile policies insuring agreement; ~ **de aseguradores principales para seguro del casco del buque** SEG leading underwriters' agreement for marine hull business (*LUAMH*); ~ **bilateral** ECON bilateral agreement; ~ **colectivo** RRHH collective bargaining, collective agreement; ~ **colectivo favorable al empresario** RRHH sweetheart contract; ~ **colectivo de trabajo** DER, IND, RRHH collective labor agreement (*AmE*), collective labour agreement (*BrE*); ~ **comercial** ECON, POL trade agreement; ~ **de compensación** ECON *comercio internacional* clearing agreement; ~ **de crédito** FIN credit agreement; ~ **de crédito de fomento** BANCA, FIN development credit agreement; ~ **de doble imposición** FISC agreement on double taxation; ~ **final** FISC closing agreement (*AmE*); ~ **financiero** BANCA, DER, FIN financial settlement; ~ **fiscal** FISC tax agreement; ~ **laboral sobre esquemas** RRHH pattern bargaining; ~ **de liquidación** COM GEN clearing agreement; ~ **multimillonario de libras** FIN multimillion pound deal; ~ **de pago parcial** COM GEN partial payment agreement; ~ **de préstamo** BANCA bank agreement; ~ **de restricción del comercio** COM GEN restrictive covenant; ~ **salarial** RRHH wage agreement;

~ sindical RRHH union contract; ◆ **de ~ mutuo** COM GEN, DER by mutual agreement

convenir 1. *vt* COM GEN agree upon; **2.** *vi* DER concur

convergencia *f* COM GEN convergence

converger *vi* COM GEN converge

conversaciones: ~ de alto nivel *f pl* GES top level talks; **~ sobre salarios** *f pl* GES, RRHH pay talks; **~ sobre los sueldos** *f pl* GES, RRHH pay talks

conversión *f* COM GEN conversion; **~ acelerada** BANCA *obligaciones* accelerated conversion; **~ de la antigüedad** BOLSA senior refunding; **~ binario a decimal** INFO binary-to-decimal conversion; **~ de un buque** TRANSP ship conversion; **~ de datos** INFO data conversion; **~ de decimal a binario** INFO decimal-to-binary conversion; **~ de la deuda** FIN debt conversion; **~ del dólar con otras divisas** ECON flight from the dollar; **~ de fichero** INFO file conversion; **~ forzosa** SEG involuntary conversion (*AmE*); **~ inversa** BOLSA reverse conversion; **~ involuntaria** INMOB involuntary conversion; **~ de la moneda** ECON flight from money; **~ a una moneda extranjera** ECON foreign currency conversion; **~ de un préstamo** BANCA, FIN refunding of a loan; **~ de renta fija** BOLSA bond conversion; **~ de títulos** *m* BOLSA conversion

conversor: ~ de analógico a digital *m* INFO analog-to-digital converter (*ADC*); **~ catalítico** *m* MED AMB, TRANSP catalytic converter

convertible *adj* COM GEN convertible; **no ~** BOLSA *bono* nonconvertible; **~ en efectivo** BANCA, CONT encashable

convertido *adj* COM GEN converted; **no ~** COM GEN unconverted

convertidor: ~ catalítico *m* MED AMB, TRANSP catalytic converter; **~ de digital a analógico** *m* INFO digital-to-analog converter (*DAC*)

convertir *vt* COM GEN convert; ◆ **~ en capital** COM GEN convert into capital; **~ en dinero** COM GEN convert into cash

convocar *vt* COM GEN call for, convene, GES, RRHH *reunión, asamblea* convene

convocatoria *f* COM GEN calling

cónyuge *mf* FISC spouse; **~ divorciado(-a)** *m,f* DER divorced spouse; **~ de hecho** DER common-law spouse; **~ que no trabaja** FISC, RRHH nonworking spouse; **~separado(-a)** *m,f* DER estranged spouse; **~ superviviente** FISC surviving spouse

cooperación *f* COM GEN cooperation; **~ económica internacional** ECON international economic cooperation; **~ industrial** IND industrial cooperation; **~ monetaria europea** ECON, POL European monetary cooperation; **~ política** POL *UE* political co-operation; **~ técnica** COM GEN technical co-operation; **~ tecnológica** COM GEN technology cooperation; **~ de un tercer país** ECON, IMP/EXP, POL third country cooperation

Cooperación: ~ Económica para África *f* ECON Economic Cooperation for Africa; **~ Económica de Asia y los Países del Pacífico** *f* (*CEAP*) ECON, POL Asia Pacific Economic Cooperation (*APEC*); **~ Económica entre Países en Desarrollo** *f* ECON Economic Cooperation among Developing Countries (*ECDC*); **~ Europea en Ciencia y Tecnología** *f* (*COST*) IND, POL European Cooperation in Science and Technology (*COST*); **~ Técnica entre Países en Desarrollo** *f* ECON,

POL Technical Cooperation amongst Developing Countries (*TCDC*)

cooperador, a *m,f* IND joint operator

cooperante: ~ para el desarrollo *mf* COM GEN volunteer development worker

cooperar 1. ~ en *vt* DER aid and abet; **2.** *vi* COM GEN cooperate

cooperativa *f* COM GEN condominium, cooperative (*co-op*), res communis, social ownership; **~ agrícola** RRHH agricultural cooperative; **~ de ahorro y crédito a la construcción** INMOB building society (*BrE*), savings and loan association (*S&L*) (*AmE*); **~ de consumidores** RRHH consumer cooperative; **~ de consumo** RRHH cooperative retail society; **~ de crédito** BANCA, FIN credit union (*BrE*); **~ de inversiones** RRHH investment trust; **~ de mayoristas** RRHH wholesale cooperative; **~ de minoristas** V&M retail cooperative

coordenadas *f pl* COM GEN, RRHH *curriculum vitae* particulars

coordinación *f* COM GEN coordination; **~ negociada** ECON negotiated coordination

coordinado *adj* COM GEN coordinated

coordinador, a *m,f* COM GEN coordinator; **~ de exportación** RRHH export coordinator

coordinar *vt* COM GEN, GES, RRHH, TRANSP coordinate

coparticipación: ~ en los ingresos *f* ECON revenue sharing (*AmE*)

copia *f* COM GEN copy, INFO copy, V&M dupe (*jarg*); **~ adjunta de la carta** COMS attached copy of letter; **~ ampliada** COM GEN enlarged copy; **~ de archivo** MEDIOS air check; **~ para archivo** ADMIN file copy; **~ de la carta adjunta** COMS attached copy of letter; **~ cero** V&M answer print; **~ cero cinematográfica** V&M married print; **~ certificada** DER certified copy; **~ conformada** DER *de documento legal* conformed copy; **~ directa en papel** INFO hard copy; **~ fiel** ADMIN, DER true copy; **~ fiel y auténtica** DER certified true copy; **~ heliográfica** ADMIN blueprint; **~ maestra** COM GEN, INFO master copy; **~ mecanográfica** ADMIN, COMS carbon copy (*cc*); **~ negativa** BANCA negative file; **~ original** COM GEN top copy; **~ de la pantalla** INFO screen copy; **~ de reserva** INFO backup; **~ de respaldo** INFO security backup; **~ de seguridad** INFO backup copy, security copy; **~ de seguridad temporizada** INFO timed backup

copiadora *f* ADMIN copier

copiar *vt* COM GEN, INFO copy; ◆ **~ del original** COM GEN copy from the original

copias: ~ falsificadas *f pl* IND counterfeit copies; **~ piratas** *f pl* IND, MEDIOS pirate copies

coprocesador *m* INFO coprocessor

copropiedad *f* COM GEN joint estate, joint ownership, res communis, party to an estate, co-ownership

copropietario, -a *m,f* COM GEN co-owner, joint owner

copyright *m* DER copyright

corchetes *m pl* INFO, MEDIOS square brackets

coronar *vt* COM GEN cap

coronilla: estar hasta la ~ de trabajo *fra infrml* RRHH be up to one's neck in work (*infrml*)

corp. *abr* (*corporación*) COM GEN corp. (*corporation*)

corporación *f* (*corp.*) COM GEN corporation (*corp.*); **~ afiliada** COM GEN corporate affiliate; **~ de capital**

de riesgo BANCA venture capital corporation; **~ fusionada** BANCA, COM GEN, FISC amalgamated corporation; **~ informante** COM GEN reporting corporation; **~ intermediaria** COM GEN intermediary corporation; **~ de liquidación de opciones** BOLSA options clearing corporation (*OCC*); **~ mercantil** ECON business corporation; **~ municipal** FISC municipal body; **~ nacional** COM GEN, ECON domestic corporation; **~ no respaldada** BOLSA nonmember corporation; **~ de préstamo hipotecario** BANCA, FIN mortgage loan corporation; **~ pública matriz** COM GEN parent Crown corporation; **~ que funciona como tapadera** COM GEN shell corporation (*AmE*); **~ transnacional** (*TNC*) ECON, POL transnational corporation (*TNC*)

Corporación: **~ Canadiense de Seguro de Depósitos** *f* SEG Canada Deposit Insurance Corporation (*CDIC*); **~ de Comercialización Directa** *f* COM GEN Direct Trading Corporation (*DTC*); **~ para el Desarrollo de la Commonwealth** *f* (*CDC*) ECON, POL Commonwealth Development Corporation (*CDC*); **~ de Finanzas Industrial y Comercial** *f* IND, FIN Industrial and Commercial Finance Corporation (*ICFC*); **~ de Finanzas Internacionales** *f* (*CFI*) FIN International Finance Corporation (*IFC*); **~ Nacional de Compensación de Valores** *f* BOLSA ≈ National Securities Clearing Corporation (*AmE*)

corporativismo *m* POL corporatism

corporativo *adj* COM GEN corporate

corpóreo *m* COM GEN corporeal

corral: **~ de ganado** *m* COM GEN stockyard

correa: **~ transportadora** *f* *Esp* (*cf máquina transportadora AmL*) TRANSP conveyor belt

corrección *f* COM GEN correction, MAT *tasación* adjustment; **~ a la baja** BOLSA downward correction; **~ del mercado** BOLSA market correction; **~ monetaria** ECON indexation

correcto *adj* COM GEN correct, exact

corrector¹: **~ ortográfico** *m* INFO spellchecker

corrector²**,a** *m,f* MEDIOS copy editor; **~ de estilo** MEDIOS copy reader; **~ de pruebas** MEDIOS proofreader

corredor, a *m,f* COM GEN canvasser, runner (*jarg*); **~ de acciones en el mercado de emisión** BOLSA primary market dealer; **~ de apuestas** OCIO bookmaker; **~ del armador** TRANSP owner's broker; **~autorizado(-a) de futuros** BOLSA futures-registered broker; **~ de bolsa** BOLSA broker, stockjobber (*BrE*), trader; **~ de bolsa independiente** BOLSA floor trader; **~ de bolsa sin licencia** BOLSA unlicensed broker; **~ de bolsa con mesa** BOLSA board broker; **~ de cambios** BANCA, BOLSA, FIN bill merchant, bond broker, foreign exchange broker, money broker; **~ comercial** COM GEN business tout; **~ de comercio** BOLSA bond broker, INMOB commercial broker (*AmE*), RRHH, V&M drummer (*infrml*) (*AmE*), sales representative (*rep*), traveling salesman (*AmE*), travelling salesman (*BrE*), V&M sales representative (*rep*); **~ de despacho** BOLSA desk trader; **~ de divisas** BOLSA foreign exchange trader; **~ de espacio publicitario** V&M space broker; **~ de fincas** COM GEN, INMOB land agent; **~ fletador(a)** TRANSP chartering broker; **~ de fletes** RRHH loading broker; **~ de hipotecas** FIN mortgage broker; **~ honesto(-a)** POL honest broker; **~ independiente** BOLSA independent broker; **~ intermediario(-a)** (*CI*) BOLSA interdealer broker (*BrE*) (*IDB*), jobber (*obs*) (*BrE*);

~-intermediario(-a) de cambio y bolsa BOLSA broker-dealer; **~ jurado(-a)** BOLSA sworn broker; **~ marítimo (-a)** TRANSP shipbroker, vessel broker; **~ de mercado primario** ECON primary dealer; **~ de mercancías** BOLSA, FIN commodity broker, V&M merchandise broker; **~ de paquete pequeño** BOLSA odd-lotter; **~ de préstamos** BOLSA discount broker; **~ de productos** BOLSA, FIN commodity broker; **~ de seguros** SEG insurance broker; **~ titulado(-a)** BOLSA registered broker; **~ de valores** BOLSA security dealer

correduría: **~ de bolsa** *f* BOLSA broking house; **~ de seguros** *f* SEG insurance brokerage, insurance broking

corregido *adj* BOLSA amended, COM GEN corrected, FISC amended, MAT adjusted

corregir *vt* BOLSA amend, COM GEN *errores* correct, FISC amend, MAT *cifras, error* adjust; ♦ **sin ~** COM GEN uncorrected; **~ a la baja** COM GEN revise downward; **sin ~ los errores** INFO nondebugged; **~ pruebas de** MEDIOS proofread

correlación *f* MAT correlation; **~ exacta** MAT close correlation; **~ lineal** MAT linear correlation; **~ múltiple** MAT multiple correlation; **~ negativa** MAT negative correlation; **~ no lineal** MAT nonlinear correlation; **~ positiva** MAT positive correlation; **~ por rangos** MAT rank correlation; **~ serial** MAT serial correlation; **~ simple** MAT simple correlation

correlacionar *vt* MAT correlate

correo *m* COM GEN mail (*AmE*), mailing, post (*BrE*); **~ aéreo** COMS airmail; **~ aéreo de grandes dimensiones** COMS bulk air mail (*BAM*); **~ asegurado** SEG insured mail (*AmE*), insured post (*BrE*); **~ certificado** COMS certified mail (*AmE*), registered post (*BrE*); **~ certificado con acuso de recibo** COMS recorded delivery (*BrE*); **~ de datos** COMS data post (*BrE*); **~ de datos por pedido** COMS data post on demand (*DCD*); **~ directo** ADMIN, V&M direct mail; **~ electrónico** COMS, INFO computer mail, electronic mail (*e-mail*), post; **~ entrante** COMS incoming mail (*AmE*), incoming post (*BrE*); **~ interno** V&M house mailing; **~ sin normalizar** COMS nonstandard mail; **~ ordinario** COMS second-class mail (*AmE*), second-class post *BrE*; **~ preferencial** COMS first-class mail (*AmE*), first-class post (*BrE*); **~ de pronta expedición** COMS priority mail (*AmE*), priority post (*AmE*); **~ de respuesta comercial** COMS business reply mail (*BRM*); **~ saliente** COMS outgoing mail (*AmE*), outgoing post (*BrE*); **~ con tarifa económica** COMS third-class mail (*AmE*); **~ de tarifa reducida** COMS special fourth-class mail; ♦ **por ~** COMS by mail (*AmE*), by post (*BrE*), through the mail (*AmE*), through the post (*BrE*); **por ~ aéreo** COMS by airmail; **por ~ marítimo o terrestre** COMS by surface mail

Correos *m* COMS Spanish general post office, ≈ Post Office (*PO*)

correr *vt* COM GEN *ahorros, reservas* eat into; ♦ **~ con** BOLSA bear; **~ con el coste de** *Esp* (*cf correr con el costo de AmL*) CONT bear the cost of; **~ con el costo de** *AmL* (*cf correr con el coste de Esp*) CONT bear the cost of; **~ por cuenta de** COM GEN go to the expense of; **~ el riesgo de** COM GEN run the risk of

correspondencia *f* COM GEN, COMS *cartas* correspondence (*corr.*); **~ con franqueo impreso** COMS metered mail; **~ rápida** COMS *vía marítima o terrestre* accelerated surface post; ♦ **tener ~ con** COMS correspond

corresponder 1. *vt* ECON hit; **2.** *vi* MAT correspond; ♦ **~ a**

COM GEN pertain to, correspond to; **~ con** COM GEN, COMS *comunicar por carta* correspond with

correspondiente[1] *adj* COM GEN corresponding, ECON responsive

correspondiente[2]: **~ a** *prep* COM GEN pertaining to

corresponsal *mf* BANCA correspondent; **~ accidental** MEDIOS *prensa* stringer (*jarg*); **~ hipotecario (-a)** *m,f* FIN mortgage correspondent; **~ en el extranjero** MEDIOS foreign correspondent; **~ independiente** MEDIOS *radio y TV* freelance correspondent

corretaje *m* BOLSA brokerage, broking; **~ de bolsa** BOLSA stockbroking; **~ de descuento** BOLSA discount brokerage

corrida: **~ de producción** *f* AmL IND production run; **~ sobre un banco** *f* BANCA bank run

corriente[1] *adj* (*cte.*) instant (*inst.*); **~ y moliente** *infrml* COM GEN run-of-the-mill

corriente[2] *f* COM GEN, ECON *ascendente, rendimiento* trend; **~ de capital** BOLSA capital flow; **~ continua** COM GEN direct current; **~ empresarial** ECON business stream; **~ financiera** CONT, ECON, FIN financial flow; **~ de fondos** BOLSA, CONT, ECON, FIN funds flow

corro *m* BOLSA crowd, open outcry auction market, ring; **~ de contratación** BOLSA trading desk

corrosión *f* IND, SEG corrosion

corrupción *f* COM GEN corruption, graft (*infrml*) (*BrE*); **~ de un programa** INFO software rot

corsé *m* ECON corset (*infrml*)

corta: **de ~ duración** *adj* BOLSA, COM GEN short-run, short-term, CONT short-term

cortapisas: **sin ~** COM GEN no strings attached

cortar *vt* COM GEN, INFO cut; ◆ **~ por lo sano** COM GEN cut one's losses

corte: **~ de corriente** *m* INFO, MED AMB power failure; **~ de operaciones** *m* CONT cut-off procedures

Corte: **~ Europea** *f* DER, POL European Court; **~ Suprema** *f* DER Supreme Court (*AmE*)

Cortes: **Las ~** *f pl Esp* POL legislative assembly, ≈ Congress (*AmE*), ≈ Parliament (*BrE*); **~ Generales** *f pl Esp* POL Spanish Parliament

corto[1]: **de ~ alcance** *adj* COM GEN short-range; **~ en futuros** *adj* BOLSA short in futures; **a ~ plazo** *adj* BOLSA, COM GEN short-run, short-term, in the short term, CONT short-term

corto[2] *m* BOLSA short (*jarg*), TRANSP short; **~ circuito** SEG short-circuit; **~ plazo** COM GEN short run, short term

cos *abr* (*coseno*) MAT cos (*cosine*)

cosa: **~ juzgada** *f* DER res judicata; **~ de nadie** *f* DER, INMOB res nullius; **~ nullius** *f* DER, FISC estate in abeyance

cosecha *f* COM GEN, MED AMB crop; **~ de cereales** ECON grain crop; **~ de vid** COM GEN vine harvest; **~ vieja** ECON old crop (*OC*); **~ de vino** ECON vintage; **nueva ~** ECON new crop (*N/C*)

coseguro *m* SEG coinsurance

coseno *m* (*cos*) MAT cosine (*cos*)

COST *abr* (*Cooperación Europea en Ciencia y Tecnología*) IND, POL COST (*European Cooperation in Science and Technology*)

costa *f* TRANSP shore; **~ este de los Estados Unidos** TRANSP United States East Coast (*USEC*); **~ oeste de los Estados Unidos** TRANSP United States West Coast (*USWC*)

costado: **al ~** *prep* TRANSP atracar alongside (*a/s*)

costas: **~ judiciales** *f pl* DER, FISC legal expenses *concedidas por el tribunal* legal costs, PATENT legal expenses

coste[1]: **al ~** *adj Esp* (*cf al costo AmL*) COM GEN at cost; **~-eficiente** *adj Esp* (*cf costo-eficiente AmL*) CONT cost-efficient

coste[2] *m Esp* (*cf costo AmL*) COM GEN cost;

~ a **~ abierto** *Esp* (*cf costo abierto AmL*) COM GEN up-front cost (*infrml*); **~ absorbido** *Esp* (*cf costo absorbido AmL*) CONT absorbed cost; **~ de acatamiento** *Esp* (*cf costo de acatamiento AmL*) MED AMB cost of compliance; **~ adicional** *Esp* (*cf costo adicional AmL*) CONT additional charge; **~ administrativo** *Esp* (*cf costo administrativo AmL*) FISC administrative cost; **~ de adquisición** *Esp* (*cf costo de adquisición AmL*) CONT, FISC acquisition cost; **~ de adquisición de un alquiler** *Esp* (*cf costo de adquisición de un alquiler AmL*) FIN lease acquisition cost; **~ de ajuste social** *Esp* (*cf costo de ajuste social AmL*) RRHH social adjustment cost; **~ de la alimentación y del alojamiento** *Esp* (*cf costo de la alimentación y el alojamiento AmL*) FISC cost of meals and lodging; **~ alternativo** *Esp* (*cf costo alternativo AmL*) FIN alternative cost; **~ amortizable** *Esp* (*cf costo amortizable AmL*) CONT depreciable cost; **~ de amortización** *Esp* (*cf costo de amortización AmL*) CONT amortization expense; **~ amortizado** *Esp* (*cf costo amortizado AmL*) CONT, FISC amortized cost, depreciated cost; **~ anunciado** *Esp* (*cf costo anunciado AmL*) TRANSP published charge; **~ aplicado** *Esp* (*cf costo aplicado AmL*) CONT, ECON, FIN applied cost; **~ de arrendamiento** *Esp* (*cf costo de arrendamiento AmL*) FISC, INMOB rental cost; **~ autónomo** *Esp* (*cf costo autónomo AmL*) ECON stand alone cost (*BrE*), constrained maket pricing (*AmE*);

~ b **~ bruto** *Esp* (*cf costo bruto AmL*) FISC *de propiedad* gross cost;

~ c **~ de capital** *Esp* (*cf costo de capital AmL*) BOLSA cost of capital, ECON, FIN capital costs; **~ capitalizado** *Esp* (*cf costo capitalizado AmL*) CONT capitalized cost; **~ común** *Esp* (*cf costo común AmL*) ECON common cost; **~ conjunto** *Esp* (*cf costo conjunto AmL*) CONT joint product cost, ECON joint cost; **~ contingente** *Esp* (*cf costo contingente AmL*) CONT contingent cost; **~ continuo** *Esp* (*cf costo continuo AmL*) CONT continuing cost; **~ controlable** *Esp* (*cf costo controlable AmL*) CONT controllable cost; **~ controlado** *Esp* (*cf costo controlado AmL*) CONT, FIN managed cost; **~ corriente** *Esp* (*cf costo corriente AmL*) COM GEN, CONT, FIN current cost, replacement cost; **~ creciente** *Esp* (*cf costo creciente AmL*) ECON rising cost; **~ cubierto** *Esp* (*cf costo cubierto AmL*) BOLSA hedge cost; **~ de cumplimiento** *Esp* (*cf costo de cumplimiento AmL*) ADMIN, CONT, FISC compliance cost;

~ d **~ de depreciación** *Esp* (*cf costo de depreciación AmL*) CONT, FISC depreciable cost; **~ depreciado** *Esp* (*cf costo depreciado AmL*) CONT, FISC amortized cost, depreciated cost; **~ descargado** *Esp* (*cf costo descargado AmL*) IMP/EXP, TRANSP landed cost; **~ diferencial** *Esp* (*cf costo diferencial AmL*) CONT differential cost; **~ directo** *Esp* (*cf costo directo AmL*) ECON, V&M direct cost; **~ directo más gastos generales** *Esp* (*cf costo directo más gastos generales AmL*) CONT conversion cost; **~ directo de las ventas** *Esp* (*cf costo directo de las ventas AmL*) COM GEN direct cost of sales;

~ **discrecional** *Esp* (*cf costo discrecional AmL*) ECON discretionary cost;

■ **e** ~ **económico** *Esp* (*cf costo económico AmL*) ECON, FIN economic cost; ~ **de embalaje** *Esp* (*cf costo de embalaje AmL*) COM GEN packaging cost; ~ **de emisión** *Esp* (*cf costo de emisión AmL*) BOLSA bonding cost, FISC issuance; ~ **de un empréstito** *Esp* (*cf costo de un empréstito AmL*) BANCA, COM GEN cost of a loan, cost of borrowing; ~ **estándar** *Esp* (*cf costo estándar AmL*) COM GEN, CONT, FIN standard cost; ~ **estimado** *Esp* (*cf costo estimado AmL*) CONT estimated cost; ~ **explícito** *Esp* (*cf costo explícito AmL*) ECON explicit cost; ~ **de explotación** *Esp* (*cf costo de explotación AmL*) CONT operating cost; ~ **externo** *Esp* (*cf costo externo AmL*) CONT external cost;

■ **f** ~ **de fabricación** *Esp* (*cf costo de fabricación AmL*) COM GEN, CONT, ECON manufacturing cost; ~ **de los factores** *Esp* (*cf costo de los factores AmL*) CONT, ECON, IND factor cost; ~ **fijo** *Esp* (*cf costo fijo AmL*) COM GEN fixed cost, period cost, ECON fixed cost; ~ **fijo medio** *Esp* (*cf costo fijo medio AmL*) CONT average fixed cost; ~ **fiscal** *Esp* (*cf costo fiscal AmL*) FISC tax cost; ~ **del flete** *Esp* (*cf costo del flete AmL*) TRANSP *navegación* cost of freight; ~ **y flete** *Esp* (*c&f, cf costo y flete AmL*) IMP/EXP, TRANSP cost and freight (*c&f*); ~ **de flotación** *Esp* (*cf costo de flotación AmL*) BOLSA flotation cost; ~ **de los fondos** *Esp* (*cf costo de los fondos AmL*) FIN cost of funds; ~ **de fondos realizado** *Esp* (*cf costo de fondos realizado AmL*) BOLSA realized cost of funds;

■ **g** ~ **de gastos indirectos variables** *Esp* (*cf costo de gastos indirectos variables AmL*) FIN variable overhead cost; ~ **gravoso** *Esp* (*cf costo gravoso AmL*) FIN *construcción, propiedad inmobiliaria* hard cost;

■ **h** ~ **histórico** *Esp* (*cf costo histórico AmL*) CONT historical cost; ~ **hundido** *Esp* (*cf costo hundido AmL*) FIN sunk cost;

■ **i** ~ **identificable** *Esp* (*cf costo identificable AmL*) CONT traceable cost; ~ **implícito** *Esp* (*cf costo implícito AmL*) ECON implicit cost; ~ **imputado** *Esp* (*cf costo imputado AmL*) ECON, FIN imputed cost; ~ **incidental** *Esp* (*cf costo incidental AmL*) BOLSA carrying cost; ~ **incontrolable** *Esp* (*cf costo incontrolable AmL*) CONT noncontrollable cost; ~ **indirecto** *Esp* (*cf costo indirecto AmL*) ECON, FIN indirect cost; ~ **por información requerida** *Esp* (*cf costo por información requerida AmL*) V&M cost per inquiry; ~ **de instalación exterior** *Esp* (*cf costo de instalación exterior AmL*) INMOB *construcción* off-site cost; ~ **de insumos** *Esp* (*cf costo de insumos AmL*) CONT input cost; ~ **intangible de perforación y explotación** *Esp* (*cf costo intangible de perforación y explotación AmL*) CONT intangible drilling and development cost; ~ **de inversión** *Esp* (*cf costo de inversión AmL*) FISC capital cost; ~ **de investigación aplicada** *Esp* (*cf costo de investigación aplicada AmL*) COM GEN applied research cost; ~ **de investigación básica** *Esp* (*cf costo de investigación básica AmL*) COM GEN basic research cost;

■ **l** ~ **laboral** *Esp* (*cf costo laboral AmL*) ECON, RRHH labor cost (*AmE*), labour cost (*BrE*); ~ **en libros** *Esp* (*cf costo en libros AmL*) CONT book cost;

■ **m** ~ **de manipulación** *Esp* (*cf costo de manipulación AmL*) V&M handling charge; ~ **de la mano de obra** *Esp* (*cf costo de la mano de obra AmL*) RRHH cost of labor (*AmE*), cost of labour (*BrE*), manpower cost; ~ **marginal** *Esp* (*cf costo marginal AmL*) CONT, ECON,

FIN incremental cost, marginal cost; ~ **marginal de adquisición** *Esp* (*cf costo marginal de adquisición AmL*) CONT marginal cost of acquisition; ~ **marginal de supresión** *Esp* (*cf costo marginal de supresión AmL*) ECON marginal cost of abatement; ~ **de marketing** *Esp* (*cf costo de marketing AmL*) V&M marketing cost; ~ **medio** *Esp* (*cf costo medio AmL*) CONT average cost, mean cost; ~ **medio ponderado** *Esp* (*cf costo medio ponderado AmL*) CONT weighted average cost; ~ **medio por siniestro** *Esp* (*cf costo medio por siniestro AmL*) SEG average claim, average cost of claims; ~ **medio total** *Esp* (*cf costo medio total AmL*) CONT average total cost; ~ **de las mercancías fabricadas** *Esp* (*cf costo de las mercancías fabricadas AmL*) CONT, ECON, IND cost of goods manufactured; ~ **de las mercancías vendidas** *Esp* (*cf costo de las mercancías vendidas AmL*) CONT, ECON cost of goods sold; ~ **por mil** *Esp* (*cf costo por mil AmL*) V&M cost per thousand; ~ **mixto** *Esp* (*cf costo mixto AmL*) CONT mixed cost;

■ **n** ~ **neto** *Esp* (*cf costo neto AmL*) CONT net cost; ~ **no depreciado** *Esp* (*cf costo no depreciado AmL*) CONT undepreciated cost; ~ **no vencido** *Esp* (*cf costo no vencido AmL*) ECON unexpired cost; ~ **nominal** *Esp* (*cf costo nominal AmL*) CONT nominal cost; ~ **normalizado** *Esp* (*cf costo normalizado AmL*) COM GEN, CONT, FIN standard cost;

■ **o** ~ **de ocupación** *Esp* (*cf costo de ocupación AmL*) FISC occupancy cost; ~ **de oportunidad** *Esp* (*cf costo de oportunidad AmL*) CONT shadow price, ECON, FIN opportunity cost; ~ **de oportunidad social de las divisas** *m pl Esp* (*cf costo de oportunidad social de las divisas AmL*) BOLSA social opportunity cost of foreign exchange; ~ **por orden de trabajo** *Esp* (*cf costo por orden de trabajo AmL*) IND job order costing; ~ **de organización** *Esp* (*cf costo de organización AmL*) CONT organization cost; ~ **original** *Esp* (*cf costo original AmL*) CONT original cost;

■ **p** ~ **del pasivo** *Esp* (*cf costo del pasivo AmL*) BOLSA liability cost; ~ **de pérdida neta** *Esp* (*cf costo de pérdida neta AmL*) SEG burning cost; ~ **del periodo** *Esp* (*cf costo del periodo AmL*) CONT period cost; ~ **por peso** *Esp* (*cf costo por peso AmL*) TRANSP weight charge; ~ **del plus de fondos** *Esp* (*cf costo del plus de fondos AmL*) BANCA cost of funds plus; ~ **portuario por transporte regular** *Esp* (*cf costo portuario por transporte regular AmL*) TRANSP port liner terms charge (*PLTC*); ~ **en pozo** *Esp* (*cf costo en pozo AmL*) IND *industria petrolífera* wellhead cost; ~ **de un préstamo** *Esp* (*cf costo de un préstamo AmL*) BANCA, COM GEN *al prestamista* cost of a loan, cost of borrowing, borrowing cost; ~ **presupuestado** *Esp* (*cf costo presupuestado AmL*) CONT budgeted cost; ~ **previsto** *Esp* (*cf costo previsto AmL*) CONT anticipated cost; ~ **privado** *Esp* (*cf costo privado AmL*) ECON private cost; ~ **privado marginal** *Esp* (*cf costo privado marginal AmL*) ECON marginal private cost; ~ **del proceso** *Esp* (*cf costo del proceso AmL*) COM GEN cost of proceedings; ~ **de producción** *Esp* (*cf costo de producción AmL*) CONT, ECON, SEG cost of production, prime cost, production cost; ~ **de producción conjunta** *Esp* (*cf costo de producción conjunta AmL*) CONT joint product cost; ~ **del producto** *Esp* (*cf costo del producto AmL*) V&M product cost; ~ **promedio** *Esp* (*cf costo promedio AmL*) CONT average cost; ~ **publicitario por venta de** producto *Esp* (*cf costo publicitario por venta de producto AmL*) V&M advertising cost per product sale;

■ **r** ~ **real** *Esp* (*cf costo real AmL*) CONT, FISC actual cost, real cost; ~ **de recogida** *Esp* (*cf costo de recogida AmL*) TRANSP pick-up cost; ~ **recuperable** *Esp* (*cf costo recuperable AmL*) CONT recoverable cost; ~ **en recursos internos** *Esp* (*cf costo en recursos internos AmL*) ECON domestic resource cost (*DRC*); ~ **de reemplazo** *Esp* (*cf costo de reemplazo AmL*) CONT, SEG replacement cost; ~ **de renovación** *Esp* (*cf costo de renovación AmL*) CONT, SEG reproduction cost; ~ **de reposición** *Esp* (*cf costo de reposición AmL*) COM GEN, CONT, FIN current cost, replacement cost; ~ **de rescate** *Esp* (*cf costo de rescate AmL*) SEG surrender charge; ~ **residual** *Esp* (*cf costo residual AmL*) CONT residual cost;

■ **s** ~ **salarial** *Esp* (*cf costo salarial AmL*) ECON wage cost; ~ **de seguro** *Esp* (*cf costo de seguro AmL*) SEG insurance cost; ~ **y seguro** *Esp* (*cf costo y seguro AmL*) IMP/EXP, SEG, TRANSP cost and insurance (*C&I*); ~, **seguro y flete** *Esp* (*CI&F, cf costo, seguro y flete AmL*) IMP/EXP, SEG, TRANSP, V&M cost, insurance and freight (*CI&F*); ~, **seguro, flete y comisión** *Esp* (*cf costo, seguro, flete y comisión AmL*) IMP/EXP, SEG, TRANSP cost, insurance, freight and commission (*CIF&C*); ~, **seguro, flete, comisión y cambio** *Esp* (*cf costo, seguro, flete, comisión y cambio AmL*) IMP/EXP, SEG, TRANSP cost, insurance, freight, commission and exchange (*CIFC&E*); ~, **seguro, flete, comisión e intereses** *Esp* (*cf costo, seguro, flete, comisión e intereses AmL*) IMP/EXP, SEG, TRANSP cost, insurance, freight, commission and interest (*CIFC&I*); ~ **de seguro de flete descargado** *Esp* (*cf costo de seguro de flete descargado AmL*) TRANSP *de mercancías* landed freight insurance cost; ~, **seguro, flete e interés** *Esp* (*cf costo, seguro, flete e interés AmL*) IMP/EXP, SEG, TRANSP cost, insurance, freight and interest (*CIF&I*); ~, **seguro, flete, interés y cambio** *Esp* (*cf costo, seguro, flete, interés y cambio AmL*) IMP/EXP, SEG, TRANSP cost, insurance, freight, interest and exchange (*CIFI&E*); ~ **semifijo** *Esp* (*cf costo semifijo AmL*) CONT, V&M mixed cost, semifixed cost; ~ **semivariable** *Esp* (*cf costo semivariable AmL*) CONT mixed cost; ~ **sobre el valor** *Esp* (*cf costo sobre el valor AmL*) TRANSP value surcharge; ~ **social** *Esp* (*cf costo social AmL*) ECON social cost; ~ **social del desempleo** *Esp* (*cf costo social del desempleo AmL*) ECON, PROT SOC, RRHH social cost of unemployment; ~ **social marginal** *Esp* (*cf costo social marginal AmL*) ECON marginal social cost; ~ **social del monopolio** *Esp* (*cf costo social del monopolio AmL*) ECON social cost of monopoly; ~ **suave** *Esp* (*cf costo suave AmL*) COM GEN soft cost; ~ **suplementario** *Esp* (*cf costo suplementario AmL*) FIN supplementary cost; ~ **de sustitución** *Esp* (*cf costo de sustitución AmL*) CONT, ECON, FIN, SEG replacement costing, reproduction cost;

■ **t** ~ **de tasación** *Esp* (*cf costo de tasación AmL*) TRANSP valuation charge; ~ **total** *Esp* (*cf costo total AmL*) TRANSP through charge; ~ **total de crédito del consumidor** *Esp* (*cf costo total de crédito del consumidor AmL*) FIN total cost of credit to the consumer; ~ **del trabajo** *Esp* (*cf costo del trabajo AmL*) RRHH job costing; ~ **de transacción económica** *Esp* (*cf costo de transacción económica AmL*) ECON economics transaction cost; ~ **de las transacciones** *Esp* (*cf costo de las*

transacciones *AmL*) BANCA, BOLSA, ECON transaction cost; ~ **de transformación** *Esp* (*cf costo de transformación AmL*) CONT conversion cost; ~ **de transporte** *Esp* (*cf costo de transporte AmL*) TRANSP cost of carriage;

■ **u** ~ **unitario** *Esp* (*cf costo unitario AmL*) CONT unit cost; ~ **unitario medio** *Esp* (*cf costo unitario medio AmL*) CONT average unit cost; ~ **unitario del trabajo** *Esp* (*cf costo unitario del trabajo AmL*) IND unit labor costs (*AmE*), unit labour costs (*BrE*); ~ **de uso** *Esp* (*cf costo de uso AmL*) FIN user cost;

■ **v** ~ **por vehículo/kilómetro** *Esp* TRANSP ≈ cost per vehicle/mile; ~ **de ventas** *Esp* (*cf costo de ventas AmL*) CONT, ECON, V&M cost of sales; ~ **de viaje de ida y vuelta** *Esp* (*cf costo de viaje de ida y vuelta AmL*) TRANSP round trip cost; ~ **de la vida** *Esp* (*cf costo de la vida AmL*) COM GEN, ECON cost of living; ~ **por volumen** *Esp* (*cf costo por volumen AmL*) TRANSP volume charge

costeo: ~ **por absorción** *m AmL* CONT absorption costing; ~ **de proceso** *m AmL* SEG process costing

costes *m pl Esp* (*cf costos AmL*) COM GEN costs, expenses; ~ **de abastecimiento** *Esp* (*cf costos de abastecimiento AmL*) COM GEN procurement costs; ~ **administrados** *Esp* (*cf costos administrados AmL*) CONT, FIN managed costs; ~ **administrativos** *Esp* (*cf costos administrativos AmL*) ADMIN, COM GEN administrative costs; ~ **agregados** *Esp* (*cf costos agregados AmL*) GES add-on costs; ~ **de ampliación** *Esp* (*cf costos de ampliación AmL*) SEG extension costs; ~ **de auditoría** *Esp* (*cf costos de auditoría AmL*) CONT audit costs; ~ **básicos** *Esp* (*cf costos básicos AmL*) CONT prime costs; ~ **del capital de manufacturación y procesamiento** *Esp* (*cf costos del capital de manufacturación y procesamiento AmL*) FISC, IND cost of manufacturing and processing capital; ~ **de cierre** *Esp* (*cf costos de cierre AmL*) BANCA, FIN closing costs; ~ **de clausura** [inv pl] *Esp* (*cf costos de clausura AmL*) COM GEN closing-down costs; ~ **de compras** *Esp* (*cf costos de compras AmL*) COM GEN procurement costs, purchasing costs; ~ **contables** *Esp* (*cf costos contables AmL*) CONT accounting costs; ~ **de corretaje** *Esp* (*cf costos de corretaje AmL*) BOLSA agency cost; ~ **de demolición** *Esp* (*cf costos de demolición AmL*) COM GEN, INMOB demolition costs; ~ **directos** *Esp* (*cf costos directos AmL*) CONT, FIN direct costs, direct expenses; ~ **de distribución** *Esp* (*cf costos de distribución AmL*) CONT, TRANSP distribution costs; ~ **elevados** *Esp* (*cf costos elevados AmL*) FIN high costs; ~ **estimados de los sistemas** *Esp* (*cf costos estimados de los sistemas AmL*) FIN estimated systems costs; ~ **evitables** *Esp* (*cf costos evitables AmL*) COM GEN avoidable costs; ~ **de explotación** *Esp* (*cf costos de explotación AmL*) CONT operating costs; ~ **de fabricación** *Esp* (*cf costos de fabricación AmL*) IND factory costs; ~ **de financiación** *Esp* (*cf costos de financiación AmL*) CONT, FIN financial costs, financing charges; ~ **y gastos según factura** *Esp* (*cf costos y gastos según factura AmL*) CONT invoice cost and charges; ~ **gestionados** *Esp* (*cf costos gestionados AmL*) CONT, FIN managed costs; ~ **gravables a alguien** *Esp* (*cf costos gravables a alguien AmL*) FISC costs taxable to sb; ~ **incorporados** *Esp* (*cf costos incorporados AmL*) CONT add-on costs; ~ **incurridos** *Esp* (*cf costos incurridos AmL*) CONT, FIN incurred costs; ~ **indirectos** *Esp* (*cf costos indirectos AmL*) CONT, FIN, IND indirect costs, overheads; ~ **indirectos de**

manufactura *Esp* (*cf costos indirectos de manufactura AmL*) IND manufacturing overheads; **~ indirectos de producción** *Esp* (*cf costos indirectos de producción AmL*) IND manufacturing overheads; **~ inevitables** *Esp* (*cf costos inevitables AmL*) CONT unavoidable costs; **~ inferiores a los previstos** *Esp* (*cf costos inferiores a los previstos AmL*) CONT underrun costs; **~ laborales directos** *Esp* (*cf costos laborales directos AmL*) CONT direct labor costs (*AmE*), direct labour costs (*BrE*); **~ laborales unitarios** *Esp* (*cf costos laborales unitarios AmL*) PROT SOC unit labor costs (*AmE*), unit labour costs (*BrE*); **~ de liquidación** *Esp* (*cf costos de liquidación AmL*) COM GEN closing-down costs; **~ mancomunados del producto** *Esp* (*cf costos mancomunados del producto AmL*) CONT joint product cost; **~ de mano de obra** *Esp* (*cf costos de mano de obra AmL*) ECON labor costs (*AmE*), labour costs (*BrE*); **~ marginales** *Esp* (*cf costos marginales AmL*) CONT direct labor costs (*AmE*), direct labour costs (*BrE*), marginal costs, ECON, FIN marginal costs; **~ médicos** *Esp* (*cf costos médicos AmL*) PROT SOC, SEG medical costs; **~ mixtos** *Esp* (*cf costos mixtos AmL*) COM GEN, CONT, ECON, FIN semivariable costs; **~ de nómina** *Esp* RRHH payroll costs; **~ obligados** *Esp* (*cf costos obligados AmL*) CONT committed costs; **~ ocultos** *Esp* (*cf costos ocultos AmL*) CONT sunk costs; **~ de operación** *Esp* (*cf costos de operación AmL*) COM GEN, FIN, IND running costs; **~ de pensiones** *Esp* CONT pension costs; **~ de personal** *m Esp* (*cf costos de personal AmL*) ECON, RRHH labor costs (*AmE*), labour costs (*BrE*), staff costs; **~ de personal directos** *Esp* (*cf costos de personal directos AmL*) CONT direct labor costs (*AmE*), direct labour costs (*BrE*); **~ de personal indirectos** *Esp* (*cf costos de personal indirectos AmL*) CONT indirect labor costs (*AmE*), indirect labour costs (*BrE*); **~ presupuestarios** *Esp* (*cf costos presupuestarios AmL*) ECON, POL budgetary costs; **~ de primer establecimiento** *Esp* (*cf costos de primer establecimiento AmL*) CONT, FIN set-up costs, setting-up costs; **~ de producción de películas** *Esp* (*cf costos de producción de películas AmL*) FISC film production costs; **~ de promoción** *Esp* (*cf costos de promoción AmL*) CONT, V&M promotion cost; **~ de proveeduría** *Esp* (*cf costos de proveeduría AmL*) COM GEN procurement costs; **~ de puesta en marcha** *Esp* (*cf costos de puesta en marcha AmL*) CONT, ECON, FIN front-end costs, start-up costs; **~ realizados** *Esp* (*cf costos realizados AmL*) CONT, FIN incurred costs; **~ de recaudación** *Esp* COM GEN collection costs; **~ semifijos** *Esp* (*cf costos semifijos AmL*) COM GEN, CONT, ECON, FIN semivariable costs; **~ semivariables** *Esp* (*cf costos semivariables AmL*) COM GEN, CONT, ECON, FIN semivariable costs; **~ sumergidos** *Esp* CONT sunk costs; **~ totales** *Esp* (*cf costos totales AmL*) ECON total costs; **~ de unidad laboral** *Esp* (*cf costos de unidad laboral AmL*) CONT, ECON, RRHH unit labor costs (*AmE*), unit labour costs (*BrE*); **~ unitarios de la mano de obra** *Esp* (*cf costos unitarios de la mano de obra AmL*) CONT, ECON, RRHH unit labor costs (*AmE*), unit labour costs (*BrE*); **~ variables** *Esp* (*cf costos variables AmL*) CONT, FIN variable costs; **~ de ventas** *Esp* (*cf costos de ventas AmL*) V&M sales costs; **~ de zona europea** *Esp* (*cf costos de zona europea AmL*) TRANSP European zone charge (*EZC*)

costo[1]: **al ~** *adj AmL* (*cf al coste Esp*) COM GEN at cost; **~-eficiente** *adj AmL* (*cf coste-eficiente Esp*) CONT cost-efficient

costo[2] *m AmL* (*cf coste Esp*) COM GEN cost;

~ a **~ abierto** *AmL* (*cf coste abierto Esp*) COM GEN up-front cost (*infrml*); **~ absorbido** *AmL* (*cf coste absorbido Esp*) CONT absorbed cost; **~ de acatamiento** (*cf coste de acatamiento Esp*) MED AMB cost of compliance; **~ adicional** *AmL* (*cf coste adicional Esp*) CONT additional charge; **~ administrativo** *AmL* (*cf coste administrativo Esp*) FISC administrative cost; **~ de adquisición de un alquiler** *AmL* (*cf coste de adquisición de un alquiler Esp*) FIN lease acquisition cost; **~ de ajuste social** *AmL* (*cf coste de ajuste social Esp*) RRHH social adjustment cost; **~ de la alimentación y el alojamiento** *AmL* (*cf coste de la alimentación y del alojamiento Esp*) FISC cost of meals and lodging; **~ alternativo** *AmL* (*cf coste alternativo Esp*) FIN alternative cost; **~ amortizable** *AmL* (*cf coste amortizable Esp*) CONT depreciable cost; **~ de amortización** *AmL* (*cf coste de amortización Esp*) CONT amortization expense; **~ amortizado** *AmL* (*cf coste amortizado Esp*) CONT, FISC amortized cost, depreciated cost; **~ anunciado** *AmL* (*cf coste anunciado Esp*) TRANSP published charge; **~ aplicado** *AmL* (*cf coste aplicado Esp*) CONT, ECON, FIN applied cost; **~ de arrendamiento** *AmL* (*cf coste de arrendamiento Esp*) FISC, INMOB rental cost;

~ b **~ bruto** *AmL* (*cf coste bruto Esp*) FISC de propiedad gross cost;

~ c **~ de capital** *AmL* (*cf coste de capital Esp*) BOLSA cost of capital, ECON, FIN capital costs; **~ capitalizado** *AmL* (*cf coste capitalizado Esp*) CONT capitalized cost; **~ común** *AmL* (*cf coste común Esp*) ECON common cost; **~ conjunto** *AmL* (*cf coste conjunto Esp*) CONT joint product cost, ECON joint cost; **~ contingente** *AmL* (*cf coste contingente Esp*) CONT contingent cost; **~ continuo** *AmL* (*cf coste continuo Esp*) CONT continuing cost; **~ controlable** *AmL* (*cf coste controlable Esp*) CONT controllable cost; **~ controlado** *AmL* (*cf coste controlado Esp*) CONT, FIN managed cost; **~ corriente** *AmE* (*cf coste corriente Esp*) COM GEN, CONT, FIN current cost, replacement cost; **~ creciente** *AmL* (*cf coste creciente Esp*) ECON rising cost; **~ cubierto** *AmL* (*cf coste cubierto Esp*) BOLSA hedge cost; **~ de cumplimiento** *AmL* (*cf coste de cumplimiento Esp*) ADMIN, CONT, FISC compliance cost;

~ d **~ de depreciación** *AmL* (*cf coste de depreciación Esp*) CONT, FISC depreciable cost; **~ depreciado** *AmL* (*cf coste depreciado Esp*) CONT, FISC amortized cost, depreciated cost; **~ descargado** *AmL* (*cf coste descargado Esp*) IMP/EXP, TRANSP landed cost; **~ diferencial** *AmL* (*cf coste diferencial Esp*) CONT differential cost; **~ directo** *AmL* (*cf coste directo Esp*) ECON, V&M direct cost; **~ directo más gastos generales** *AmL* (*cf coste directo más gastos generales Esp*) CONT conversion cost; **~ directo de las ventas** *AmL* (*cf coste directo de las ventas Esp*) COM GEN direct cost of sales; **~ discrecional** *AmL* (*cf coste discrecional Esp*) ECON discretionary cost;

~ e **~ económico** *AmL* (*cf coste económico Esp*) ECON, FIN economic cost; **~ de embalaje** *AmL* (*cf coste de embalaje Esp*) COM GEN packaging cost; **~ de emisión** *AmL* (*cf coste de emisión Esp*) BOLSA bonding cost, FISC issuance; **~ de un empréstito** *AmL* (*cf coste de un empréstito Esp*) BANCA, COM GEN cost of a loan, cost of borrowing; ~ **estándar** *AmL* (*cf coste estándar Esp*) COM GEN, CONT, FIN standard cost; ~ **estimado** *AmL* (*cf coste estimado Esp*) CONT estimated cost; ~ **explícito** *AmL* (*cf coste explícito Esp*) ECON explicit cost; ~ **de explotación** *AmL* (*cf coste de explotación Esp*) CONT operating cost; ~ **externo** *AmL* (*cf coste externo Esp*) CONT external cost;

~ f ~ **de fabricación** *AmL* (*cf coste de fabricación Esp*) COM GEN, CONT, ECON manufacturing cost; ~ **de los factores** *AmL* (*cf coste de los factores Esp*) CONT, ECON, IND factor cost; ~ **fijo** *AmL* (*cf coste fijo Esp*) COM GEN fixed cost, period cost, ECON fixed cost; ~ **fijo medio** *AmL* (*cf coste fijo medio Esp*) CONT average fixed cost; ~ **fiscal** *AmL* (*cf coste fiscal Esp*) FISC tax cost; ~ **del flete** *AmL* (*cf coste del flete Esp*) TRANSP *navegación* cost of freight; ~ **y flete** *AmL* (*c&f, cf coste y flete Esp*) IMP/EXP, TRANSP cost and freight (*c&f*); ~ **de flotación** *AmL* (*cf coste de flotación Esp*) BOLSA flotation cost; ~ **de los fondos** *AmL* (*cf coste de los fondos Esp*) FIN cost of funds; ~ **de fondos realizado** *AmL* (*cf coste de fondos realizado Esp*) BOLSA realized cost of funds;

~ g ~ **de gastos indirectos variables** *AmL* (*cf coste de gastos indirectos variables Esp*) FIN variable overhead cost; ~ **gravoso** *AmL* (*cf coste gravoso Esp*) FIN *construcción, propiedad inmobiliaria* hard cost;

~ h ~ **histórico** *AmL* (*cf coste histórico Esp*) CONT historical cost; ~ **hundido** *AmL* (*cf coste hundido Esp*) FIN sunk cost;

~ i ~ **identificable** *AmL* (*cf coste identificable Esp*) CONT traceable cost; ~ **implícito** *AmL* (*cf coste implícito Esp*) ECON implicit cost; ~ **imputado** *AmL* (*cf coste imputado Esp*) ECON, FIN imputed cost; ~ **incidental** *AmL* (*cf coste incidental Esp*) BOLSA carrying cost; ~ **incontrolable** *AmL* (*cf coste incontrolable Esp*) CONT noncontrollable cost; ~ **indirecto** *AmL* (*cf coste indirecto Esp*) ECON, FIN indirect cost; ~ **por información requerida** *AmL* (*cf coste por información requerida Esp*) V&M cost per inquiry; ~ **de instalación exterior** *AmL* (*cf coste de instalación exterior Esp*) INMOB *construcción* off-site cost; ~ **de insumos** *AmL* (*cf coste de insumos Esp*) CONT input cost; ~ **intangible de perforación y explotación** *AmL* (*cf coste intangible de perforación y explotación Esp*) CONT intangible drilling and development cost; ~ **de inversión** *AmL* (*cf coste de inversión Esp*) FISC capital cost; ~ **de investigación aplicada** *AmL* (*cf coste de investigación aplicada Esp*) COM GEN applied research cost; ~ **de investigación básica** *AmL* (*cf coste de investigación básica Esp*) COM GEN basic research cost;

~ l ~ **laboral** *AmL* (*cf coste laboral Esp*) ECON, RRHH labor cost (*AmE*), labour cost (*BrE*); ~ **en libros** *AmL* (*cf coste en libros Esp*) CONT book cost;

~ m ~ **de manipulación** *AmL* (*cf coste de manipulación Esp*) V&M handling charge; ~ **de la mano de obra** *AmL* (*cf coste de la mano de obra Esp*) RRHH cost of labor (*AmE*), cost of labour (*BrE*), manpower cost; ~ **marginal** *AmL* (*cf coste marginal Esp*) CONT, ECON, FIN incremental cost, marginal cost; ~ **marginal de adquisición** *AmL* (*cf coste marginal de adquisición Esp*) CONT marginal cost of acquisition; ~ **marginal de supresión** *AmL* (*cf coste marginal de supresión Esp*) ECON marginal cost of abatement; ~ **de marketing** *AmL* (*cf coste de marketing Esp*) V&M marketing cost; ~ **medio** *AmL* (*cf coste medio Esp*) CONT average cost, mean cost; ~ **medio ponderado** *AmL* (*cf coste medio*

ponderado Esp) CONT weighted average cost; ~ **medio por siniestro** *AmL* (*cf coste medio por siniestro Esp*) SEG average claim, average cost of claims; ~ **medio total** *AmL* (*cf coste medio total Esp*) CONT average total cost; ~ **de las mercancías fabricadas** *AmL* (*cf coste de las mercancías fabricadas Esp*) CONT, ECON, IND cost of goods manufactured; ~ **de las mercancías vendidas** *AmL* (*cf coste de las mercancías vendidas Esp*) CONT, ECON cost of goods sold; ~ **por mil** *AmL* (*cf coste por mil Esp*) V&M cost per thousand; ~ **mixto** *AmL* (*cf coste mixto Esp*) CONT mixed cost;

~ n ~ **de negociación** BANCA negotiation fee; ~ **neto** *AmL* (*cf coste neto Esp*) CONT net cost; ~ **no depreciado** *AmL* (*cf coste no depreciado Esp*) CONT undepreciated cost; ~ **no vencido** *AmL* (*cf coste no vencido Esp*) ECON unexpired cost; ~ **nominal** *AmL* (*cf coste nominal Esp*) CONT nominal cost; ~ **normalizado** *AmL* (*cf coste normalizado Esp*) COM GEN, CONT, FIN standard cost;

~ o ~ **de ocupación** *AmL* (*cf coste de ocupación Esp*) FISC occupancy cost; ~ **de oportunidad** *AmL* (*cf coste de oportunidad Esp*) CONT shadow price, ECON, FIN opportunity cost; ~ **por orden de trabajo** *AmL* (*cf coste por orden de trabajo Esp*) IND job order costing; ~ **de organización** *AmL* (*cf coste de organización Esp*) CONT organization cost; ~ **original** *AmL* (*cf coste original Esp*) CONT original cost;

~ p ~ **del pasivo** *AmL* (*cf coste del pasivo Esp*) BOLSA liability cost; ~ **de pérdida neta** *AmL* (*cf coste de pérdida neta Esp*) SEG burning cost; ~ **del periodo** *AmL* (*cf coste del periodo Esp*) CONT period cost; ~ **por peso** *AmL* (*cf coste por peso Esp*) TRANSP weight charge; ~ **del plus de fondos** *AmL* (*cf coste del plus de fondos Esp*) BANCA cost of funds plus; ~ **portuario por transporte regular** *AmL* (*cf coste portuario por transporte regular Esp*) TRANSP port liner terms charge (*PLTC*); ~ **en pozo** *AmL* (*cf coste en pozo Esp*) IND *industria petrolífera* wellhead cost; ~ **de un préstamo** *AmL* (*cf coste de un préstamo Esp*) BANCA, COM GEN *al prestamista* cost of a loan, cost of borrowing, borrowing cost; ~ **presupuestado** *AmL* (*cf coste presupuestado Esp*) CONT budgeted cost; ~ **previsto** *AmL* (*cf coste previsto Esp*) CONT anticipated cost; ~ **privado** *AmL* (*cf coste privado Esp*) ECON private cost; ~ **privado marginal** *AmL* (*cf coste privado marginal Esp*) ECON marginal private cost; ~ **del proceso** *AmL* (*cf coste del proceso Esp*) COM GEN cost of proceedings; ~ **de producción** *AmL* (*cf coste de producción Esp*) CONT, ECON, SEG cost of production, prime cost, production cost; ~ **de producción conjunta** *AmL* (*cf coste de producción conjunta Esp*) CONT joint product cost; ~ **del producto** *AmL* (*cf coste del producto Esp*) V&M product cost; ~ **promedio** *AmL* (*cf coste promedio Esp*) CONT average cost; ~ **publicitario por venta de producto** *AmL* (*cf coste publicitario por venta de producto Esp*) V&M advertising cost per product sale;

~ r ~ **real** *AmL* (*cf coste real Esp*) CONT, FISC actual cost, real cost; ~ **de recogida** *AmL* (*cf coste de recogida Esp*) TRANSP pick-up cost; ~ **recuperable** *AmL* (*cf coste recuperable Esp*) CONT recoverable cost; ~ **en recursos internos** *AmL* (*cf coste en recursos internos Esp*) ECON domestic resource cost (*DRC*); ~ **de reemplazo** *AmL* (*cf coste de reemplazo Esp*) CONT, SEG replacement cost; ~ **de renovación** *AmL* (*cf coste de renovación Esp*)

CONT, SEG reproduction cost; **~ de reposición** *AmL* (*cf coste de reposición Esp*) COM GEN, CONT, FIN current cost, replacement cost; **~ de rescate** *AmL* (*cf coste de rescate Esp*) SEG surrender charge; **~ residual** *AmL* (*cf coste residual Esp*) CONT residual cost;

~ s **~ salarial** *AmL* (*cf coste salarial Esp*) ECON wage cost; **~ de seguro** *AmL* (*cf coste de seguro Esp*) SEG insurance cost; **~ y seguro** *AmL* (*cf coste y seguro Esp*) IMP/EXP, SEG, TRANSP cost and insurance (*C&I*); **~, seguro y flete** *AmL* (*CI&F, cf coste, seguro y flete Esp*) IMP/EXP, SEG, TRANSP, V&M cost, insurance and freight (*CI&F*); **~, seguro, flete y comisión** *AmL* (*cf coste, seguro, flete y comisión Esp*) IMP/EXP, SEG, TRANSP cost, insurance, freight and commission (*CIF&C*); **~, seguro, flete, comisión y cambio** *AmL* (*cf coste, seguro, flete, comisión y cambio Esp*) IMP/EXP, SEG, TRANSP cost, insurance, freight, commission and exchange (*CIFC&E*); **~, seguro, flete, comisión e intereses** *AmL* (*cf coste, seguro, flete, comisión e intereses Esp*) IMP/EXP, SEG, TRANSP cost, insurance, freight, commission and interest (*CIFC&I*); **~ de seguro de flete descargado** *AmL* (*cf coste de seguro de flete descargado Esp*) TRANSP *de mercancías* landed freight insurance cost; **~, seguro, flete e interés** *AmL* (*cf coste, seguro, flete e interés Esp*) IMP/EXP, SEG, TRANSP cost, insurance, freight and interest (*CIF&I*); **~, seguro, flete, interés y cambio** *AmL* (*cf coste, seguro, flete, interés y cambio Esp*) IMP/EXP, SEG, TRANSP cost, insurance, freight, interest and exchange (*CIFI & E*); **~ semifijo** *AmL* (*cf coste semifijo Esp*) CONT, V&M mixed cost, semifixed cost; **~ semivariable** *AmL* (*cf coste semivariable Esp*) CONT mixed cost; **~ sobre el valor** *AmL* (*cf coste sobre el valor Esp*) TRANSP value surcharge; **~ social** *AmL* (*cf coste social Esp*) ECON social cost; **~ social del desempleo** *AmL* (*cf coste social del desempleo Esp*) RRHH social cost of unemployment; **~ social marginal** *AmL* (*cf coste social marginal Esp*) ECON marginal social cost; **~ social del monopolio** *AmL* (*cf coste social del monopolio Esp*) ECON social cost of monopoly; **~ suave** *AmL* (*cf coste suave Esp*) COM GEN soft cost; **~ suplementario** *AmL* (*cf coste suplementario Esp*) FIN supplementary cost; **~ de sustitución** *AmL* (*cf coste de sustitución Esp*) CONT, ECON, FIN, SEG replacement costing, reproduction cost;

~ t **~ de tasación** *AmL* (*cf coste de tasación Esp*) TRANSP valuation charge; **~ total** *AmL* (*cf coste total Esp*) TRANSP through charge; **~ total de crédito del consumidor** *AmL* (*cf coste total de crédito del consumidor Esp*) FIN total cost of credit to the consumer; **~ del trabajo** *AmL* (*cf coste del trabajo Esp*) RRHH job costing; **~ de transacción económica** *AmL* (*cf coste de transacción económica Esp*) ECON economics transaction cost; **~ de las transacciones** *AmL* (*cf coste de las transacciones Esp*) BANCA, BOLSA, ECON transaction cost; **~ de transformación** *AmL* (*cf coste de transformación Esp*) CONT conversion cost; **~ de transporte** *AmL* (*cf coste de transporte Esp*) TRANSP cost of carriage;

~ u **~ unitario** *AmL* (*cf coste unitario Esp*) CONT unit cost; **~ unitario medio** *AmL* (*cf coste unitario medio Esp*) CONT average unit cost; **~ unitario del trabajo** *AmL* (*cf coste unitario del trabajo Esp*) IND unit labor cost (*AmE*), unit labour cost (*BrE*); **~ de uso** *AmL* (*cf coste de uso Esp*) FIN user cost;

~ v **~ por vehículo/kilómetro** *AmL* TRANSP ≈ cost per vehicle/mile; **~ de ventas** *AmL* (*cf coste de ventas Esp*) CONT, ECON, V&M cost of sales; **~ de viaje de ida y vuelta** *AmL* (*cf coste de viaje de ida y vuelta Esp*) TRANSP round trip cost; **~ de la vida** *AmL* (*cf coste de la vida Esp*) COM GEN, ECON cost of living; **~ por volumen** *AmL* (*cf coste por volumen Esp*) TRANSP volume charge

costos *m pl AmL* (*cf costes Esp*) COM GEN costs, expenses; **~ de abastecimiento** *AmL* (*cf costes de abastecimiento Esp*) COM GEN procurement costs; **~ administrados** *AmL* (*cf costes administrados Esp*) CONT, FIN managed costs; **~ administrativos** *AmL* (*cf costes administrativos Esp*) ADMIN, COM GEN administrative costs; **~ agregados** *AmL* (*cf costes agregados Esp*) GES add-on costs; **~ de ampliación** *AmL* (*cf costes de ampliación Esp*) SEG extension costs; **~ de auditoría** *AmL* (*cf costes de auditoría Esp*) CONT audit costs; **~ básicos** *AmL* (*cf costes básicos Esp*) CONT prime costs; **~ del capital de manufacturación y procesamiento** *AmL* (*cf costes del capital de manufacturación y procesamiento Esp*) FISC, IND cost of manufacturing and processing capital; **~ de cierre** *m AmL* (*cf costes de cierre Esp*) BANCA, FIN closing costs; **~ de clausura** *AmL* (*cf costes de clausura Esp*) COM GEN closing-down costs; **~ de compras** *AmL* (*cf costes de compras Esp*) COM GEN procurement costs, purchasing costs; **~ contables** *AmL* (*cf costes contables Esp*) CONT accounting costs; **~ de corretaje** *AmL* (*cf costes de corretaje Esp*) BOLSA agency cost; **~ de demolición** *AmL* (*cf costes de demolición Esp*) COM GEN, INMOB demolition costs; **~ directos** *AmL* (*cf costes directos Esp*) CONT, FIN direct costs, direct expenses; **~ de distribución** *AmL* (*cf costes de distribución Esp*) CONT, TRANSP distribution costs; **~ elevados** *AmL* (*cf costes elevados Esp*) FIN high costs; **~ estimados de los sistemas** *AmL* (*cf costes estimados de los sistemas Esp*) FIN estimated systems costs; **~ evitables** *AmL* (*cf costes evitables Esp*) COM GEN avoidable costs; **~ de explotación** *AmL* (*cf costes de explotación Esp*) CONT operating costs; **~ de fabricación** *AmL* (*cf costes de fabricación Esp*) IND factory costs; **~ de financiación** *AmL* (*cf costes de financiación Esp*) CONT, FIN financial costs, financing charges; **~ y gastos según factura** *AmL* (*cf costes y gastos según factura Esp*) CONT invoice cost and charges; **~ gestionados** *AmL* (*cf costes gestionados Esp*) CONT, FIN managed costs; **~ gravables a alguien** *AmL* (*cf costes gravables a alguien Esp*) FISC costs taxable to sb; **~ incorporados** *AmL* (*cf costes incorporados Esp*) CONT add-on costs; **~ incurridos** *AmL* (*cf costes incurridos Esp*) CONT, FIN incurred costs; **~ indirectos** *AmL* (*cf costes indirectos Esp*) CONT, FIN, IND indirect costs, overheads; **~ indirectos de manufactura** *AmL* (*cf costes indirectos de manufactura Esp*) IND manufacturing overheads; **~ indirectos de producción** *AmL* (*cf costes indirectos de producción Esp*) IND manufacturing overheads; **~ inevitables** *AmL* (*cf costes inevitables Esp*) CONT unavoidable costs; **~ inferiores a los previstos** *AmL* (*cf costes inferiores a los previstos Esp*) CONT underrun costs; **~ laborales directos** *AmL* (*cf costes laborales directos Esp*) CONT direct labor costs (*AmE*), direct labour costs (*BrE*); **~ laborales unitarios** *AmL* (*cf costes laborales unitarios Esp*) PROT SOC unit labor costs (*AmE*), unit labour costs (*BrE*); **~ de liquidación** *AmL* (*cf costes de liquidación Esp*) COM GEN closing-down costs; **~ mancomunados del producto** *AmL* (*cf costes mancomunados del producto Esp*) CONT joint product cost; **~ de mano de**

obra *AmL* (*cf costes de mano de obra Esp*) ECON labor costs (*AmE*), labour costs (*BrE*); ~ **marginales** *AmL* (*cf costes marginales Esp*) CONT direct labor costs (*AmE*), direct labour costs (*BrE*), marginal costs, ECON, FIN marginal costs; ~ **médicos** *AmL* (*cf costes médicos Esp*) PROT SOC, SEG medical costs; ~ **mixtos** *AmL* (*cf costes mixtos Esp*) COM GEN, CONT, ECON, FIN semivariable costs; ~ **de nómina** *AmL* (*cf costes de nómina Esp*) RRHH payroll costs; ~ **obligados** *AmL* (*cf costes obligados Esp*) CONT committed costs; ~ **ocultos** *AmL* (*cf costes ocultos Esp*) CONT sunk costs; ~ **de operación** *AmL* (*cf costes de operación Esp*) COM GEN, FIN, IND running costs; ~ **de pensiones** *AmL* (*cf costes de pensiones Esp*) CONT pension costs; ~ **de personal** *m AmL* (*cf costes de personal Esp*) ECON, RRHH labor costs (*AmE*), labour costs (*BrE*), staff costs; ~ **de personal directos** *AmL* (*cf costes de personal directos Esp*) CONT direct labor costs (*AmE*), direct labour costs (*BrE*); ~ **de personal indirectos** *AmL* (*cf costes de personal indirectos Esp*) CONT indirect labor costs (*AmE*), indirect labour costs (*BrE*); ~ **presupuestarios** *AmL* (*cf costes presupuestarios Esp*) ECON, POL budgetary costs; ~ **de primer establecimiento** *AmL* (*cf costes de primer establecimiento Esp*) CONT, FIN set-up costs, setting-up costs; ~ **de producción** *AmL* (*cf costes de producción Esp*) CONT, ECON, IND production costs; ~ **de producción de películas** *AmL* (*cf costes de producción de películas Esp*) FISC film production costs; ~ **de promoción** *AmL* (*cf costes de promoción Esp*) CONT, V&M promotion cost; ~ **de proveeduría** *AmL* (*cf costes de proveeduría Esp*) COM GEN procurement costs; ~ **de puesta en marcha** *AmL* (*cf costes de puesta en marcha Esp*) CONT, ECON, FIN front-end costs, start-up costs; ~ **realizados** *AmL* (*cf costes realizados Esp*) CONT, FIN incurred costs; ~ **de recaudación** *AmL* (*cf costes de recaudación Esp*) COM GEN collection costs; ~ **semifijos** *AmL* (*cf costes semifijos Esp*) COM GEN, CONT, ECON, FIN semivariable costs; ~ **semivariables** *AmL* (*cf costes semivariables Esp*) COM GEN, CONT, ECON, FIN semivariable costs; ~ **sumergidos** *AmL* (*cf costes sumergidos Esp*) CONT sunk costs; ~ **totales** *AmL* (*cf costes totales Esp*) ECON total costs; ~ **de unidad laboral** *AmL* (*cf costes de unidad laboral Esp*) CONT, ECON, RRHH unit labor costs (*AmE*), unit labour costs (*BrE*); ~ **unitarios de la mano de obra** *AmL* (*cf costes unitarios de la mano de obra Esp*) CONT, ECON, RRHH unit labor costs (*AmE*), unit labour costs (*BrE*); ~ **variables** *AmL* (*cf costes variables Esp*) CONT, FIN variable costs; ~ **de ventas** *AmL* (*cf costes de ventas Esp*) V&M sales costs; ~ **de zona europea** *AmL* (*cf costes de zona europea Esp*) TRANSP European zone charge (*EZC*)

costoso *adj* COM GEN costly

costumbre *f* COM GEN custom, FIN usance; ~ **del oficio** COM GEN trade custom; ◆ **en contra de** ~ COM GEN against policy

costumbres: ~ **y prácticas** *f pl* IND, RRHH custom and practice

cotarifas *f pl* TRANSP *fletes aéreos* co-rates

cotejado: **no** ~ *adj* COM GEN, V&M unchecked

cotejador: ~ **transitorio** *m* COM GEN suspense collator

cotejar *vt* COM GEN, V&M check, collate

cotizable *adj* BOLSA quotable

cotización *f* BOLSA quotation, quote, COM GEN quotation; ~ **de acciones** BOLSA stock quotation; ~ **automatizada**

del mercado de valores BOLSA Stock Exchange Automated Quotation (*SEAQ*); ~ **al contado** BOLSA spot price; ~ **de apertura** BOLSA opening quotation; ~ **de bonos** BOLSA bond index; ~ **de cierre** BOLSA, FIN closing price, closing quotation; ~ **diaria del oro** BANCA gold fixing; ~ **del dólar** BOLSA dollar price; ~ **dual** BOLSA dual listing; ~ **empresarial** ECON company quotation; ~ **en firme** BOLSA firm quote; ~ **inmediata** BOLSA spot quotation; ~ **sin interés** BOLSA flat quotation; ~ **mecanizada** BOLSA automated quotation; ~ **del mercado libre** BANCA, ECON open market rate; ~ **del mercado de valores** BOLSA stock exchange quotation; ~ **mínima** BOLSA minimum quote size (*MQS*); ~ **moneda de curso legal** COM GEN tender; ~ **nominal de una acción** BOLSA nominal quotation; ~ **oficial** BOLSA official list; ~ **a plazo** BOLSA forward rate; ~ **plena** BOLSA full quotation; ~ **de precio a término** BOLSA forward pricing; ~ **real** BOLSA actual quotation; ~ **de la tasa de interés** BANCA interest rate quotation; ~ **del tipo de interés** ECON interest rate quotation; ~ **de valores** BOLSA securities listing; ◆ **sin** ~ BOLSA, ECON unlisted, unquoted

Cotización: ~ **de las Letras del Tesoro** *f* BOLSA Treasury Bill Rate (*TBR*)

cotizaciones *f pl* BOLSA, CONT, ECON, FIN quotations, rates (*BrE*); ~ **máximas** BOLSA highs; ~ **oficiales** COM GEN official quotations; ~ **con prima** BOLSA *opciones* premium quotations

cotizado *adj* BOLSA, CONT, ECON, FIN quoted, listed; ~ **en la bolsa** BOLSA listed on the stock exchange

cotizar *vt* COM GEN list, *a la par* quote; ◆ ~ **al máximo** COM GEN *tipo, precio, coste* top out; ~ **en bolsa** BOLSA go public; ~ **valores en bolsa** CONT mark stock

C.O.U. *abr* (*Curso de Orientación Universitaria*) PROT SOC Spanish university entrance examination, ≈ A level (*Advanced Level General Certificate of Education*)

covarianza *f* MAT *estadísticas* covariance

coyuntura *f* COM GEN conjuncture; ~ **económica** COM GEN, ECON, POL economic conjuncture, economic situation, economic trend

CPE *abr* (*compra por ejecutivos*) COM GEN, GES MBO (*management buyout*)

crac *m* BOLSA crack, crash

creación *f* COM GEN creation, *diseño* brainchild (*infrml*); ~ **comercial** COM GEN, ECON business creation, trade creation; ~ **de empleos** RRHH job creation; ~ **de mercado** V&M market creation; ~ **de producto** V&M product creation

creador, a: ~ **de mercado** *m,f* BOLSA market maker; ~ **autorizado(-a) de mercado competitivo** *m,f* BOLSA registered competitive market maker; ~ **autorizado(-a) de mercado de valores** *m,f* BOLSA registered equity market maker; ~ **de valores innovadores** *m,f* BOLSA rocket scientist (*jarg*)

creadores: ~ **de mercado de valores de primerísima clase** *m pl* BOLSA gilt-edged market makers (*GEMM*)

crear *vt* COM GEN build up, *oportunidades, agencia* create, *subsidiaria* form, launch, ECON *demanda* create, IND *un prototipo, un modelo nuevo* develop, V&M create, make

creatividad *f* COM GEN, V&M creativity

creativo[1] *adj* COM GEN, V&M creative

creativo[2]**,-a** *m,f* COM GEN, RRHH, V&M *publicidad* art designer

creciente: ~ **ilimitado** *adj* BOLSA *beneficios máximos* unlimited on the upside

crecimiento *m* COM GEN growth, increase; ~ **anual compuesto** ECON, FIN compound annual growth; ~ **arrastrado por la demanda** COM GEN demand-led growth; ~ **del capital** BOLSA, ECON capital growth; ~ **constante** ECON steady growth; ~ **contrario** ECON antagonistic growth; ~ **corporativo** COM GEN corporate growth; ~ **del desempleo** ECON, PROT SOC, RRHH rise in unemployment; ~ **desequilibrado** ECON, FIN unbalanced growth; ~ **económico** ECON economic growth; ~ **empobrecedor** ECON immiserizing growth; ~ **equilibrado** ECON, FIN balanced growth; ~ **inducido por las exportaciones** IMP/EXP export-led growth; ~ **nominal** ECON nominal growth; ~ **orgánico** COM GEN, ECON organic growth; ~ **de la pérdida de bienestar económico** ECON immiserizing growth; ~ **personal** RRHH personal growth; ~ **rápido** ECON, IND rapid growth; ~ **real** ECON real growth; ~ **real del PIB** ECON real GDP growth; ~ **sostenible** ECON, POL sustainable growth; ~ **sostenido** ECON steady growth; ~ **sostenido no inflacionario** ECON, POL sustained noninflationary growth (*SNIG*); ◆ **sin** ~ ECON no-growth; **de** ~ **rápido** ECON fast-growing

credibilidad *f* COM GEN, V&M credibility; ~ **de la fuente** V&M source credibility; ~ **de un tercero** COM GEN *relaciones públicas* third-party credibility (*jarg*)

crédito *m* BANCA accommodation, COM GEN credit (*cr*), goodwill, loan, *reputación* standing, FIN accommodation, goodwill; ~ **abierto** COM GEN open credit; ~ **de aceptación** BANCA acceptance credit; ~ **de aceptación del exportador** BANCA exporter's acceptance credit; ~ **agrícola** COM GEN agricultural credit; ~ **ajustado** CONT accommodating credit; ~ **al consumidor** BANCA, FIN consumer loan, buyer credit; ~ **al consumo** BANCA, FIN consumer credit; ~ **al descubierto** BANCA, FIN blank credit, open credit; ~ **al gobierno** BANCA, FIN public credit; ~ **ampliado** V&M extended credit; ~ **autorizado** BANCA authorized credit; ~ **bancario** BANCA bank accommodation, bank credit; ~ **en blanco** BANCA, FIN blank credit; ~ **blando** BANCA, ECON, FIN soft credit, soft loan; ~ **de caja** COM GEN cash credit; ~ **por cheque** BANCA check credit (*AmE*), cheque credit (*BrE*); ~ **con cláusula roja** TRANSP red clause credit; ~ **combinado** BANCA credit package; ~ **comercial** COM GEN goodwill, CONT trade credit; ~ **comercial en consolidación** CONT goodwill on consolidation; ~ **para comprar** COM GEN purchase credit; ~ **confirmado** BANCA confirmed credit; ~ **congelado** *f* BANCA, FIN frozen credit; ~ **de la Corona** FISC Crown loan; ~ **corporativo** BANCA corporate credit; ~ **a corto plazo** BANCA short-term credit; ~ **cruzado** BANCA, FIN crossed loan; ~ **cubierto** BANCA, CONT, FIN secured credit; ~ **con cuenta abierta** COM GEN open account credit, open credit; ~ **descubierto** BANCA, CONT, FIN unsecured credit; ~ **de descuento** FIN discount credit; ~ **diferido** CONT deferred credit; ~ **disponible de inmediato** BANCA, FIN spot credit; ~ **disponible de spot** BANCA, FIN spot credit; ~ **de disposición inmediata** BANCA standby credit; ~ **en divisas** ECON, FIN foreign currency loan; ~ **documentario** BANCA, FIN, IMP/EXP documentary credit; ~ **documentario irrevocable** BANCA, FIN irrevocable letter of credit; ~ **documentario irrevocable no confirmado** BANCA, FIN unconfirmed irrevocable

letter of credit; ~ **económico puro** ECON pure economy credit; ~ **elevado** BANCA, FIN high credit; ~ **de empalme** BANCA, FIN bridging credit; ~ **de energía para usos domésticos** MED AMB residential energy credit; ~ **para estudios** RRHH student loan; ~ **a la exportación** IMP/EXP export credit; ~ **a la exportación multinacional** IMP/EXP multinational export credit; ~ **de exportador** BANCA, IMP/EXP exporter credit; ~ **en falta de cumplimiento** BANCA nonperforming credit; ~ **en falta de ejecución** BANCA nonperforming credit; ~ **de favor** CONT accommodating credit; ~ **de financiación** BANCA, FIN financial credit; ~ **flotante** BANCA rollover; ~ **con garantía personal** IMP/EXP accommodatory credit; ~ **garantizado** BANCA, FIN secured credit; ~ **hipotecario a interés fijo** BANCA fixed-rate mortgage; ~ **a la importación** IMP/EXP import credit; ~ **por impuestos pagados** FISC tax offset; ~ **intermedio** FIN gap loan; ~ **internacional** BANCA international credit; ~ **a la inversión** BANCA, FIN investment credit; ~ **irrevocable** BANCA irrevocable credit; ~ **irrevocable confirmado** BANCA confirmed irrevocable credit; ~ **por jubilación** FISC pension credit, pension income credit; ~ **de jubilación diferido** RRHH deferred retirement credit; ~ **justo** FISC allowable credit; ~ **a largo plazo** BANCA, FIN long-term credit; ~ **a medio plazo** BANCA, FIN intermediate credit, intermediate-term credit, medium-term credit; ~ **de mercancía** BANCA commodity credit; ~ **mercantil** COM GEN, CONT goodwill; ~ **mixto** FIN mixed credit; ~ **en mora** BANCA nonperforming credit; ~ **negociable sin condiciones** ECON, FIN freely negotiable credit; ~ **neto** BOLSA net credit; ~ **neto de la posición** BOLSA position net credit; ~ **no confirmado** BANCA unconfirmed credit; ~ **no utilizado** FISC unused credit; ~ **paquete** BANCA packaging credit; ~ **permanente** BANCA evergreen credit; ~ **personal** BANCA, FISC personal credit; ~ **a plazos** BANCA, FIN installment credit (*AmE*), instalment credit (*BrE*), usance credit; ~ **de prefinanciación** BANCA prefinancing credit; ~ **presupuestario** BANCA, FIN budget appropriation; ~ **privilegiado** BANCA, ECON, FIN soft loan; ~ **recíproco** BOLSA, BANCA, FIN swop; ~ **recíproco futuro** BOLSA, FIN forward swop; ~ **reembolsable** FISC allowable credit; ~ **refinanciable** BANCA roll-over credit; ~ **de refinanciación** BANCA refinance credit; ~ **de rehabilitación de la importación** FIN rehabilitation import credit (*RIC*); ~ **renovable** BANCA, FIN revolving credit; ~ **de reserva** BANCA standby credit; ~ **restringido** BANCA, FIN restricted credit; ~ **revocable** BANCA, FIN revocable credit; ~ **renovable** BANCA, FIN revolving credit; ~ **rotativo** BANCA, FIN revolving credit; ~ **rotatorio** BANCA roll-over loan; ~ **sindicado** BANCA, FIN participation loan, syndicated loan; ~ **social** COM GEN social credit; ~ **subsidiario** BANCA back-to-back credit; ~ **de suministrador** IMP/EXP supplier credit; ~ **transferible** BANCA, CONT assignable credit, transferable credit; ~ **en tránsito** BANCA transit credit; ~ **tributario** COM GEN, CONT, ECON, FIN, FISC tax credit; ~ **unificado** FISC unified credit; ~ **valor oro** BOLSA gold credit; ◆ **de** ~ **mejorado** BOLSA credit-enhanced

créditos *m pl* COM GEN credits; ~ **DOC** IMP/EXP DOC credits; ~ **fiscales futuros** CONT, FISC future tax credits; ~ **pendientes** BANCA, CONT credits outstanding, outstanding credits; ~ **recíprocos al descubierto** ECON *internacional* swing credits (*jarg*); **~ vigentes** BANCA, CONT credits outstanding

creer *vt* COM GEN believe, think, buy (*infrml*)

crianza: **~ de animales** *f* COM GEN stock farming, livestock farming

cribado: **~ fino** *m* V&M fine screen

crimen: **~ organizado** *m* DER organized crime

criminal *adj* DER felonious

crisis *f* COM GEN, ECON, POL crisis; **~ bancaria secundaria** BANCA fringe banking crisis, secondary banking crisis; **~ económica** ECON slump; **~ energética** IND energy crisis; **~ estructural** GES structural crisis; **~ financiera** FIN financial crisis; **~ fiscal** FISC fiscal crisis; **~ de liquidez** BANCA, COM GEN liquidity crisis; **~ manifiesta** POL *internacional* manifest crisis; **~ nerviosa** RRHH breakdown; **~ del petróleo** ECON, IND oil crisis

criterio *m* COM GEN criterion, *para medir rendimiento* yardstick; **~ de concesión de autorizaciones** MED AMB licensing standard; **~ de evaluación** CONT valuation criterion; **~ de referencia** FIN bench mark; **~ de valoración** CONT valuation criterion

criterios *m pl* COM GEN criteria; **~ económicos** ECON economic criteria; **~ de inversión** FIN investment criteria; **~ del precio de adquisición** CONT historical cost principle; **~ publicitarios** V&M advertising criteria

crítica: **~ sin posibilidad de réplica** *f* POL snipe (*jarg*)

criticar *vt* COM GEN criticize, find fault with

crítico[1] *adj* COM GEN, INFO critical

crítico[2]: **~ de salón** *m* COM GEN armchair critic (*infrml*)

crónica *f* MEDIOS *en un periódico* article, feature, report; **~ financiera** FIN financial news

cronometración: **~ del tiempo** *f* COM GEN, COMS time keeping

cronometrador, a *m,f* ADMIN timekeeper

cronometraje *m* COM GEN, FIN, RRHH timing; **~ muy exacto** COM GEN split-second timing

cronómetro *m* ADMIN timekeeper

cruce *m* BOLSA cross

crucero: **~ aéreo** *m* OCIO air cruise; **~ inaugural** *m* TRANSP inaugural cruise

crudo *m* IND, MED AMB, TRANSP crude oil

Cruz: **~ Azul** *f* SEG *plan de hospitalización* Blue Cross (*AmE*)

cruzar *vt* COM GEN, IMP/EXP cross; ♦ **~ especialmente** BANCA *cheque* cross specially; **~ una fila de manifestantes** POL, RRHH cross a picket line

CSIC *abr* (*Consejo Superior de Investigaciones Científicas*) IND Spanish institute for scientific research

cta. *abr* (*cuenta*) COM GEN a/c (*account*)

ctdad *abr* (*cantidad*) COM GEN qnty (*quantity*)

cte. *abr* (*corriente*) COM GEN inst. (*instant*)

CTNE *abr* (*Compañía Telefónica Nacional de España*) COMS Spanish national telecommunications network, ≈ BT (*British Telecom*)

cuaderna *f* TRANSP *barco* frame

cuaderno *m* ADMIN, COM GEN notebook; **~ de anotaciones** INFO scratch pad; **~ de bitácora** TRANSP logbook, log

cuadra *f* OCIO *caballos* stable

cuadrado[1] *adj* COM GEN square (*sq*)

cuadrado[2]: **~ de los libros** *m* BOLSA book squaring

cuadrar *vt* COM GEN *cuentas, libros* agree, balance, CONT redress the balance

cuadratín *m* MEDIOS em dash

cuadrícula *f* COM GEN, IND grid; **~ administrativa** GES managerial grid; **~ de la muestra** MAT sampling grid

cuadrilátero: **~ mágico** *m* ECON magic square

cuadrilla: **~ de mantenimiento** *f* IND, RRHH maintenance crew

cuadro *m* COM GEN schedule, *en un documento* table, POL cadre; **~ de amortización** BANCA, CONT amortization schedule, depreciation schedule, lapsing schedule, redemption table; **~ de amortización hipotecaria** BANCA mortgage table; **~ de conciliación** CONT reconciliation table; **~ de corrientes financieras** FIN *cuentas nacionales* flow-of-fund table; **~ de cuentas** CONT chart of accounts; **~ de depósitos especiales suplementarios** FIN supplementary special deposits scheme; **~ de depreciación** *f*, CONT depreciation schedule; **~ directivo** GES board of directors; **~ de interés** BANCA interest formula; **~ de periodificación** CONT lapsing schedule; **~ repartidor** COM GEN *electricidad y telefonía* switchboard, tagboard (*AmE*)

cuádruple: **~ expansión** *f* TRANSP quadruple expansion

cuadruplicado: **en ~** *adj* COM GEN in quadruplicate

cualificación[1]: **~ doble** *f* RRHH dual skilling; **~ múltiple** *f* RRHH multiskilling; **~ ocupacional genuina** *f* PROT SOC, RRHH genuine occupational qualification (*GOQ*); **~ del servicio** *f* RRHH service qualification

cualificación[2]: **sin ~** *fra* CONT without qualification

cualificaciones: **~ profesionales** *f pl* RRHH professional qualifications

cualificado *adj* COM GEN, RRHH qualified, skilled; **no ~** RRHH unskilled, unqualified; ♦ **estar debidamente ~ para el puesto** RRHH have the right qualifications for the job; **estar ~ para hacer** COM GEN, RRHH be qualified to do

cualitativamente *adv* COM GEN qualitatively

cualitativo *adj* COM GEN qualitative

cuantía *f* COM GEN, CONT, MAT amount (*amt*); **~ no pagada al vencimiento** BANCA, CONT, FIN amount overdue

cuantificación *f* COM GEN, CONT, MAT quantification; **~ de la indemnización** SEG measure of indemnity

cuantificar *vt* COM GEN, CONT, MAT quantify

cuantitativo *adj* COM GEN, CONT, MAT quantitative

cuanto[1] *m* COM GEN quantum

cuanto[2]: **en ~ a** *prep* COMS regarding (*re.*), with reference to, in terms of

cuarentena *f* COM GEN, IMP/EXP quarantine; **~ presupuestaria** ECON, POL Budget purdah (*BrE*)

cuarta: **~ de la rosa con rumbo al oeste** *f* TRANSP West compass point

Cuarta: **~ Directiva Europea** *f* CONT Fourth European Directive; **~ Directiva de la Ley de Sociedades Anónimas** *f* DER Fourth Company Law Directive; **~ Directiva de la Unión Europea** *f* CONT Fourth Directive of the European Union

cuartil: **~ inferior** *m* MAT lower quartile; **~ superior** *m* MAT upper quartile

cuarto *m* (*qt*) COM GEN quart (*qt*), quarter (*qtr*); **~ americano para áridos** COM GEN American dry quart; **~ americano para líquidos** COM GEN American liquid quart; **~ de galón británico** COM GEN British quart; **~ de libra** COM GEN quarter of a pound; **~ mercado** BOLSA fourth market; **~ mundo** ECON, POL Fourth World; **~ de prueba** COM GEN fitting room; **~ trimestre** COM GEN fourth quarter

cuasi[1] *adv* COM GEN quasi

cuasi[2]: **~-concavidad** *f* ECON quasi-concavity; **~ contrato** *m* BOLSA nearly contract, DER quasi contract; **~ dinero** *m* ECON near money; **~-dinero** *m* CONT, COM GEN, FIN quasi-money; **~ independencia** *f* COM GEN quasi-independence; **~ monopolio** *m* ECON quasi-monopoly; **~-renta** *f* ECON quasi-rent

cuatro: **~ libertades** *f pl* ECON four freedoms

cuba: **~ independiente** *f* TRANSP *de gas natural licuado* independent tank (*IT*)

cubicación: **~ de grano** *f* TRANSP grain cubic (*GC*)

cubicar *vt* TRANSP cube out

cúbico *adj* COM GEN cubic (*cu*)

cubierta *f* COM GEN cover (*C'vr*), wrapper, INFO hood; **~ de abrigo** TRANSP awning deck (*AWD*); **~ de abrigo abierto** TRANSP open shelter deck (*OSD*); **~ de castillo** TRANSP raised deck (*R dk*); **~ de dos carriles** TRANSP two-lane deck; **~ elevada** TRANSP raised deck (*R dk*); **~ exterior** INFO *disco* jacket; **~ de intemperie** TRANSP open deck; **~ nueva** TRANSP new deck (*ND*); **~ de popa elevada** TRANSP raised after-deck (*RAD*); **~ de toldilla** TRANSP awning deck (*AWD*); **~ de trenes** TRANSP train ferry deck; ◆ **sobre ~** TRANSP above deck (*AD*); **de una sola ~** TRANSP single deck

cubiertas: **~ de aluminio** *f pl* TRANSP aluminium covers (*BrE*), aluminum covers (*AmE*); **~ de madera** *f pl* TRANSP wooden covers

cubierto *adj* BOLSA, COM GEN covered; **~ en exceso** BOLSA oversubscribed

cubo *m* TRANSP cube, pail; **~ elevado** TRANSP high cube

cubre: **que ~ todo** *fra* GES across-the-board; **que ~ todo en general** *fra* GES across-the-board

cubridores: **~ comerciales** *m pl* BOLSA commercial hedgers

cubrir *vt* COM GEN *costes, pérdida* cover, meet; ◆ **~ un puesto** RRHH fill a position; **~ el riesgo** BOLSA hedge the risk; **~ una vacante** RRHH fill a vacancy

cuchara *f* TRANSP grab

cuello: **~ de botella** *m* COM GEN, IND bottleneck

cuenca: **~ del Mediterráneo** *f* COM GEN Mediterranean basin

cuenta[1]: **sin ~** *adj* BANCA no-account (*n/a*)

cuenta[2] *f* (*cl, cta.*) BANCA, CONT, INFO account (*a/c, acct.*), *cargos* check (*AmE*), bill (*BrE*), reckoning;

~ a ▸ **~ de abono diario de intereses** BANCA daily interest account; **~ de aceptación** BANCA acceptance account; **~ acreedora** CONT creditor account; **~ activa** BANCA, CONT active account, asset account; **~ de activo de capital** BANCA capital asset account; **~ acumulativa de ganancias de la pequeña empresa** FISC cumulative small business gains account; **~ de adelantos** BOLSA margin account; **~ adjunta** BANCA attached account; **~ de administración de fondos** BANCA, FIN cash management account (*CMA*); **~ administrada** CONT managed account; **~ de agencia** CONT agency account; **~ de agio** BOLSA, ECON agio account; **~ de ahorros** BANCA deposit account (*BrE*) (*D/A*), savings account; **~ de ahorro con interés diario** BANCA daily interest savings account; **~ de ahorro para inversión** BANCA investment savings account; **~ de ahorro de primas** BANCA bonus savings account, premium savings account; **~ de ahorro a la vista** BANCA current savings account; **~ de ahorro a la vista con interés** BANCA negotiable order of withdrawal account (*NOW account*); **~ de ajuste** CONT adjustment account; **~ alcista** BOLSA bull account; **~ de anticipos** CONT imprest account, advance account; **~ de aplicación** CONT appropriation account; **~ de arbitraje especial** BOLSA special arbitrage account; **~ del armador** TRANSP *fletes* owner's account; **~ asegurada** FIN, SEG *en una institución financiera* insured account; **~ asociada** BANCA associated account; **~ auxiliar** BANCA, CONT subsidiary account;

~ b ▸ **~ de balance** CONT balance sheet account; **~ bancaria** BANCA, FIN bank account, banking account; **~ bancaria conjunta** BANCA joint bank account; **~ bancaria departamental** BANCA, CONT *contabilidad gubernamental* departmental bank account, departmental account; **~ de beneficios en bruto** BANCA, CONT trading account; **~ de beneficios brutos** BANCA, CONT trading account; **~ bloqueada** BANCA frozen account, blocked account;

~ c ▸ **~ de caja** COM GEN, CONT cash account; **~ cancelada** BANCA, CONT, FIN closed account; **~ de capital** BANCA, CONT, ECON, FIN capital account (*C/A*); **~ de cargo** COM GEN charge account; **~ de cargo bancaria** BANCA bank postbill; **~ cedida en calidad de empeño** BANCA assigned account; **~ cerrada** BANCA, CONT, FIN closed account; **~ de cheques** BANCA checking account (*AmE*), current account (*BrE*); **~ de cliente** CONT client account, customer account; **~ de cobros y pagos** CONT receipts and payments account; **~ colateral** BOLSA collateral bill; **~ comercial** COM GEN open account, ECON trade account; **~ comercial a cobrar** CONT trade account receivable; **~ comercial estimada** FIN estimated trading account; **~ comercial a pagar** CONT trade account payable; **~ de comisión** BANCA commission account; **~ de compensación** CONT offset account, ECON *comercio entre países* clearing account, counterbalance, FIN offset account; **~ de compensación acumulativa** FISC cumulative offset account; **~ de compensación de cambios** BANCA Exchange Equalization Account (*EEA*); **~ de compensación tributaria** FISC tax equalization account; **~ conjunta** BANCA joint account (*J/A*); **~ de consignación** CONT appropriation account; **~ contable tipo T** CONT T-account; **~ de control** CONT, GES control account; **~ controlada** CONT managed account; **~ de corretaje** BOLSA brokerage account; **~ corriente** (*c/c*) BANCA, CONT, FIN checking account (*AmE*), current account (*BrE*) (*c/a*), drawing account, sight deposit account (*BrE*); **~ corriente especial** BANCA negotiable order of withdrawal account (*NOW account*); **~ corriente a la vista** BANCA charge account; **~ de costes** *Esp* (*cf cuenta de costos AmL*) COM GEN costs, CONT costs, costs account; **~ de costos** *AmL* (*cf cuenta de costes Esp*) COM GEN costs, CONT costs, costs account; **~ de crédito** BANCA, CONT, ECON, FIN credit account (*C/A*); **~ de crédito revolvente** BANCA revolving charge account; **~ con cuenta abierta** COM GEN open business account; **~ de custodia** BANCA custody account, custodianship account, custodial account;

~ d ▸ **~ de débito directo** BANCA cash account, cash in hand; **~ de deducción acumulativa** FISC cumulative deduction account; ~ **de deducciones salariales** CONT payroll deductions account; ~ **departamental** ADMIN departmental account; ~ **de depósito** BANCA, FIN deposit account (*BrE*) (*D/A*); ~ **de depósito de derechos** FISC, IMP/EXP Duty Deposit Account (*DDA*); ~ **de depósito en garantía** BANCA escrow account; ~ **de depósito del mercado monetario** BANCA, FIN money market deposit account (*MMDA*); ~ **de depósitos a la vista** BANCA checking account (*AmE*), drawing account, CONT drawing account; ~ **en descubierto** BANCA overdrawn account, short account; ~ **de desembarque** TRANSP landing account (*L/A*); ~ **deudora** CONT debit account; ~ **diferida** FISC deferred account (*AmE*); ~ **discrecional** BANCA, FIN discretionary account; ~ **de dividendo de capital** (*CDA*) BANCA, BOLSA, FISC capital dividend account (*CDA*); ~ **en divisas** BANCA foreign exchange account, FIN currency account; ~ **doble** BANCA tandem account; ~ **de dotación** CONT appropriation account;

■ **e** ~ **sin emisión de cheques** BANCA noncheckable account (*AmE*), nonchequable account (*BrE*); ~ **de empresa** BOLSA house account; ~ **de empréstitos** BANCA, BOLSA loan account; ~ **de especulaciones a la baja** BOLSA bear account; ~ **de explotación** IND operating account; ~ **con el exterior** BANCA foreign account; ~ **externa** POL external account; ~ **extranjera** BANCA foreign account;

■ **f** ~ **de fideicomiso** BANCA trust account; ~ **fiduciaria** BANCA fiduciary account; ~ **fiduciaria de ingresos** FIN revenue trust account; ~ **financiera** CONT, FIN financial account; ~ **fiscal** BANCA terminal account; ~ **del fletador** TRANSP charterer's account;

■ **g** ~ **en garantía** BANCA assigned account; ~ **con garantía prendaria** BOLSA collateral bill; ~ **de gastos** COM GEN, CONT expense account, FIN bill of costs; ~ **general** BANCA catch-all account; ~ **de gestión de activos** FIN Asset Management Account (*AMA*);

■ **h** ~ **hipotecaria** BANCA mortgage account; ~ **hipotecaria especial** BANCA negotiable order of withdrawal account (*NOW account*);

■ **i** ~ **de igualación de cambios** BANCA exchange equalization account; ~ **de igualación de tipo de cambio** BANCA Exchange Equalization Account (*EEA*); ~ **de impuestos y préstamos** BANCA, FISC tax and loan account; ~ **inactiva** BANCA, V&M dead account, dormant account, inactive account; ~ **inactiva por falta de margen** BANCA, BOLSA, CONT restricted account; ~ **incobrable** CONT uncollectable account; ~ **de indemnización de inversionistas** BANCA investors' indemnity account; ~ **de ingresos y gastos** CONT income and expenditure account; ~ **de inversión de ahorro nacional** BOLSA National Savings Investment Account (*BrE*); ~ **de inversiones** BANCA investment account;

■ **j** ~ **de jubilación individual** FISC individual retirement account (*AmE*);

■ **l** ~ **sin límite de depósito y de reembolso** BANCA super NOW account (*AmE*); ~ **de liquidación** BANCA settlement account; ~ **de liquidación de impuestos** FISC tax equalization account;

■ **m** ~ **marginal** BANCA marginal account; ~ **de mayor** CONT controlling account; ~ **del mayor** CONT ledger account; ~ **de mercaderías** CONT goods account; ~ **de metales preciosos** BANCA precious metal account; ~ **miscelánea especial** BOLSA special miscellaneous

account (*SMA*); ~ **mixta** BOLSA mixed account; ~ **morosa** CONT delinquent account; ~ **sin movimiento** BANCA, V&M dormant account, BANCA, V&M dead account;

■ **n** ~ **nacional** V&M national account; ~ **negociable** BANCA negotiable bill; ~ **de negocios** BANCA business account; ~ **no discrecional** FIN advisory account; ~ **no segregada** BOLSA nonsegregated account; ~ **nominal** BOLSA nominee account; ~ **nostra** BANCA nostro account; ~ **numerada** BANCA numbered account;

■ **o** ~ **opcional** FIN option account; ~ **de operación** BANCA operating account; ~ **en orden** CONT memorandum account; ~ **ordinaria** BANCA ordinary account;

■ **p** ~ **pagadera** CONT amount payable; ~ **de pagos** CONT disbursing account; ~ **de participación** CONT participation account; ~ **particular** CONT private account; ~ **patrimonial del propietario de una vivienda** BANCA homeowner's equity account; ~ **pendiente de aprobación** BANCA account rendered; ~ **de pérdidas y ganancias** CONT income statement, profit and loss account (*P&L account*), profit and loss statement (*P&L statement*), statement of income; ~ **de pérdidas y ganancias combinada** CONT combined statement of income; ~ **de pérdidas y ganancias en forma de lista** CONT vertical format profit and loss account; ~ **de periodo mensual** BANCA, CONT end-of-month account; ~ **permanente** CONT permanent account; ~ **a plazo** BANCA, FIN deposit account (*BrE*) (*D/A*); ~ **de posición** BOLSA position account; ~ **del préstamo** BANCA loan account; ~ **presupuestaria** CONT, FIN budget account, budgetary account; ~ **del presupuesto** CONT, FIN budget document; ~ **principal** COM GEN major account; ~ **protegida de impuestos** BANCA, FISC tax-sheltered account; ~ **de proveedores** CONT trade account payable; ~ **de provisión** CONT provision account; ~ **provisional** BANCA, CONT, FIN provisional account, suspense account;

■ **q** ~ **a la que se carga de menos** BANCA undercharged account;

■ **r** ~ **de reconciliación** BANCA, BOLSA, CONT, FIN reconciliation account; ~ **de regulación** CONT adjustment account; ~ **de remesa** BANCA, COM GEN, FISC remittance account; ~ **de reserva** BANCA reserve account; ~ **reservada** CONT earmarked account; ~ **restringida** BANCA, BOLSA, CONT restricted account; ~ **de resultados** CONT income statement, results account, P&L account, P&L statement;

■ **s** ~ **saldada** BANCA, CONT, FIN account settled, closed account; ~ **de saldo** BOLSA rest account; ~ **de seguro de desempleo** RRHH, SEG Unemployment Insurance Account; ~ **siguiente** FIN succeeding account; ~ **submarginal** BOLSA undermargined account; ~ **de subscripción de seguros** SEG underwriting account (*U/a*); ~ **subsidiaria** BANCA, CONT subsidiary account; ~ **sujeta a preaviso** BANCA notice account; ~ **de supervivencia** BANCA survivorship account; ~ **de suscripciones pagaderas** BANCA call account; ~ **de suspensión transitoria** BANCA, CONT, FIN suspense account;

■ **t** ~ **T** BANCA T-account; ~ **de trabajo** BANCA working account; ~ **de transacciones exteriores** ECON external account; ~ **de transferencia** BANCA transfer account; ~ **transitoria** BANCA, CONT, FIN suspense account;

■ **v** ~ **de valor dudoso** BANCA, CONT dubious account; ~ **de valores** BANCA securities account; ~ **vencida**

CONT aged account; **~ de ventas** BANCA, COM GEN, CONT, V&M sales account (s/a); **~ a la vista** BANCA call account, demand account

cuenta[3]: **a ~** fra RRHH in part payment; **en ~** fra COM GEN, V&M on account; **a ~ de** fra COM GEN on account of; **mi ~** fra COM GEN my account (m/a); **negociar por la ~** fra BOLSA bargain for the account; **~ de** fra COM GEN account of; **por ~ propia** fra COM GEN at one's own risk; **por ~ y riesgo del comprador** fra DER caveat emptor; **por ~ y riesgo del receptor** fra COM GEN at receiver's risk; **por ~ y riesgo del vendedor** fra DER caveat venditor; **tener en ~** fra COM GEN take into account; **tener una ~ en** fra BANCA un banco determinado bank with (BrE)

cuentas f pl COM GEN, FIN accounts; **~ anuales** CONT annual accounts; **~ auditadas de empresa individual** CONT individual company audited accounts; **~ autorizadas** CONT certified accounts; **~ certificadas** CONT certified accounts; **~ de clientes por cobrar** COM GEN, CONT trade accounts receivable, trade receivables; **~ de clientes por pagar** CONT trade accounts payable; **~ a cobrar** CONT accounts receivable, bills receivable, receivables; **~ comerciales por cobrar** COM GEN, CONT trade receivables; **~ de comercio** CONT commercial accounts; **~ consolidadas** CONT consolidated accounts; **~ consolidadas auditadas** CONT consolidated audited accounts; **~ diversas** CONT sundry accounts; **~ de la empresa** CONT company accounts; **~ de empresa individual** CONT individual company accounts; **~ empresariales** CONT company accounts; **~ enlazadas automáticamente** BANCA automatic transfer service (BrE) (ATS); **~ especiales** CONT special accounts; **~ del estado** CONT, POL government accounting; **~ estatutarias** CONT statutory accounts; **~ finales** CONT final accounts; **~ para fines específicos** CONT, POL specified purpose accounts; **~ fiscalizadas** CONT certified accounts; **~ de ganancias** CONT income accounts; **~ de gestión** CONT management accounts; **~ del grupo** CONT group accounts; **~ de ingresos** CONT income accounts; **~ interinas** CONT interim accounts; **~ intermedias** CONT interim accounts; **~ intervenidas** CONT certified accounts; **~ de jubilación** SEG superannuation accounts; **~ sin límite** BANCA unlimited accounts; **~ obligatorias** CONT statutory accounts; **~ a pagar** CONT accounts payable; **~ pendientes** BANCA, CONT credits outstanding, outstanding accounts, outstanding credits; **~ para propósitos específicos** CONT, POL specified purpose accounts; **~ publicadas** CONT published accounts; **~ públicas** CONT, POL government accounting; **~ reglamentarias** CONT statutory accounts; **~ testimoniales** ECON evidence accounts; **~ tras liquidación de impuestos** CONT, FISC tax-assessed accounts; **~ de varios** CONT sundry accounts; ◆ **en resumidas ~** COM GEN in short

cuerpo m COM GEN body, DER corpus; **~ de la demanda** DER statement of claim; **~ ejecutivo activo** RRHH active corps of executives; **~ de inspectores** PROT SOC inspectorate; **~ legislativo** POL legislative body; **~ profesional reconocido** ECON, FIN recognized professional body (RPB); **~ del texto** V&M copy body; **~ de trabajo** RRHH Job Corps (AmE); **~ de voluntarios** PROT SOC voluntary body

cuestión f COM GEN, DER issue; **~ adicional** PATENT additional matter; **~ candente** BOLSA hot issue (jarg) (AmE); **~ clave** COM GEN key issue; **~ de consumo** V&M consumer issue; **~ de derecho** DER point of law; **~ estatutaria** POL statutory item; **~ estratégica** GES strategic issue; **~ jurisdiccional** DER question of jurisdiction; **~ negociable** RRHH negotiable issue; **~ pendiente** COM GEN open question, POL pocketbook issue (infrml) (AmE); **~ política** COM GEN political issue; **~ relacionada con los ingresos básicos** POL, PROT SOC bread-and-butter issue (infrml) (BrE); **~ secundaria** COM GEN side issue; **~ técnica** DER technical point

cuestionario m COM GEN, V&M questionnaire; **~ de evaluación** COM GEN evaluation questionnaire

cuidado m COM GEN care

culminar: **~ en** vi COM GEN, POL culminate in

culpa[1]: **~ grave** f DER gross negligence

culpa[2]: **sin ~ de** fra SEG no fault of

culpabilidad f DER culpability

culpable[1] adj DER guilty, culpable

culpable[2] mf DER guilty person

culposo adj DER culpable

cultivo m COM GEN farming, ECON economía agrícola cultivation; **~ comercial** ECON cash crop; **~ extensivo** ECON, MED AMB extensive farming; **~ de huertos** ECON truck farming (AmE); **~ industrializado** ECON, MED AMB factory farming; **~ intensivo** ECON, MED AMB intensive farming; **~ no intensivo** ECON, MED AMB deintensified farming; **~ orgánico** ECON, MED AMB organic farming; **~ de subsistencia** ECON, MED AMB agricultura subsistence farming

cultivos: **~ marinos** m pl ECON seafarming; **~ de subsistencia** m pl ECON agricultura subsistence crops

culto adj RRHH educated

cultura f COM GEN culture; **~ corporativa** COM GEN corporate culture; **~ de la dependencia** PROT SOC dependency culture (jarg); **~ de organización** GES organization culture

cultural adj COM GEN cultural

cumbre f ECON, POL summit; **~ económica** ECON, POL economic summit; **~ de Maastricht** COM GEN EU Maastricht summit; **~ de Rambouillet** ECON Rambouillet summit

cumplido adj COM GEN complete

cumplimentación f RRHH, V&M suscripciones fill-in, fulfillment (AmE)

cumplimentar vt RRHH, V&M fill in; ◆ **~ inmediatamente** BOLSA fill-or-kill (AmE) (FOK)

cumplimiento m COM GEN accomplishment, de normas observance, performance, CONT de la empresa performance, DER derecho contractual compliance, performance, V&M suscripciones fulfillment (AmE), performance; **~ de contrato** DER, RRHH contract compliance; **~ forzado** DER specific performance; **~ de la ley** DER enforcement (ENF); **~ de las obligaciones fiscales** FISC tax compliance; **~ de la puntualidad** TRANSP punctuality performance; **~ tributario** FISC tax compliance; **~ voluntario** FISC voluntary compliance

cumplir 1. vt COM GEN complete, orden carry out, accomplish, fulfil (BrE), fulfill (AmE); ◆ **~ algo** COM GEN, CONT, DER, RRHH, V&M attend to; **~ un objetivo** GES meet a goal; **~ todos los requisitos para el puesto** RRHH have the right qualifications for the job; **2.** vi COM GEN comply; ◆ **~ con una cláusula** DER comply with a clause; **~ con sus obligaciones** COM GEN fulfil one's obligations (*BrE*), fulfill one's obligations (*AmE*)

cúmulo: **~ de circunstancias** *m* COM GEN conjunction of circumstances

cuña *f* TRANSP quoin; **~ publicitaria** COM GEN advertisement (*ad*), MEDIOS *emisión* commercial break, *radio* advertisement (*ad*), V&M *TV, radio* advertisement (*ad*), commercial break

cuñete *m* TRANSP keg

cuota *f* COM GEN *parte* fee, quota; **~ de aceptación** BANCA acceptance fee; **~ administrativa** BANCA management fee; **~ de afiliación** RRHH affiliation fee; **~ anual** COM GEN, CONT, FIN, SEG annual fee, annual installment (*AmE*), annual instalment (*BrE*), annuity installment (*AmE*), yearly installment (*AmE*), yearly instalment (*BrE*); **~ de cobertura** OCIO coverage fee; **~ combinada** TRANSP consolidated rate; **~ de cuenta de custodia** BANCA custodian account fee; **~ de custodia** BANCA custodian fee; **~ de desembolso** FISC disbursement quota; **~ fija** FIN fixed installment (*AmE*), fixed instalment (*BrE*); **~ de gestión** BANCA, COM GEN agency fee; **~ de importaciones** IMP/EXP import quota; **~ de incapacitados** RRHH disabled quota; **~ líquida** FISC tax liability; **~ liquidable** FISC assessing tax; **~ de mantenimiento de cuenta** BANCA account maintenance fee; **~ de marca** V&M brand share; **~ mensual** FIN monthly installment (*AmE*), monthly instalment (*BrE*); **~ de mercado** V&M market share, share of market, slice of the market; **~ de mercado relativa** V&M relative market share; **~ múltiple** TRANSP multiquota; **~ nacional** ECON national quota; **~ no reembolsable** COM GEN, V&M nonrefundable fee; **~ a pagar** FISC tax bill; **~ de participación** BANCA participation fee, FISC membership dues; **~ patronal** CONT, FISC employer's contribution; **~ del plan de producción** IND share of production plan; **~ regional** ECON regional quota; **~ de renegociación** BANCA extension fee; **~ de reserva** COM GEN booking fee; **~ de reserva para ajustes salariales** RRHH salary-adjustment reserve allotment (*SARA*); **~ sin restricciones** COM GEN unrestricted quota; **~ de la seguridad social** PROT SOC national insurance contribution (*NIC*), social security contribution; **~ sindical** RRHH check-off; **~ de suscripción** BANCA application fee; **~ de tarifa** COM GEN, IMP/EXP tariff quota; **~ de tiempo** COM GEN time slot; **~ de transporte** TRANSP transport quota; **~ tributaria final** FISC tax bill; **~ trimestral** COM GEN quarterly installment (*AmE*), quarterly instalment (*BrE*); **~ del usuario** *m* BANCA user fee; **~ vidual** DER dower; ◆ **por encima de la ~** COM GEN above quota

cuotas *f pl* RRHH dues; **~ de asistencia** RRHH attendance fees, attendance money; **~ de ingreso** FISC initiation dues, initiation fees; **~ a la Seguridad Social** FISC pension contributions; **~ sindicales** RRHH union fees, trade union dues (*BrE*); **~ voluntarias** FISC voluntary contributions (*BrE*); **~ voluntarias adicionales** FISC additional voluntary contributions (*BrE*) (*AVCs*); ◆ **en ~** BANCA in installments (*BrE*), in instalments (*BrE*); **en ~ mensuales** CONT in monthly installments (*AmE*), in monthly instalments (*BrE*)

cupo: **~ de ventas** *m* V&M sales quota

cupón[1]: **con ~** *adv* BOLSA cum coupon

cupón[2] *m* COM GEN coupon (*c., cp.*), strip; **~ al portador** FISC bearer coupon; **~ para arrancar** COM GEN tear-off coupon; **~ de un bono** BOLSA bond coupon; **~ cero** BOLSA call; **~ a corto plazo** BOLSA short coupon; **~ de dividendo** *f* BOLSA dividend coupon; **~ de intereses** FIN interest coupon; **~ a largo plazo** BOLSA long coupon; **~ de pasajero** OCIO, TRANSP passenger coupon; **~ con prima** *Esp* (*cf sello de premio AmL*) COM GEN trading stamp; **~ de respuesta pagada** COMS reply-paid card; **~ vencido** BOLSA matured coupon; **~ de vuelo** OCIO, TRANSP flight coupon; ◆ **sin ~** BOLSA ex coupon (*ex cp., xc.*)

cúpula *f* RRHH *de la organización* top

curriculum *m* COM GEN curriculum; **~ profesional** RRHH career vitae; **~ vitae** RRHH curriculum vitae (*BrE*) (*CV*), résumé (*AmE*)

cursar *vt* PATENT file

cursiva *f* INFO, MEDIOS italic

curso *m* COM GEN course; **~ de acción** GES course of action; **~ acelerado** COM GEN *cursos de formación* accelerated training course; **~ de capacitación** *AmL* (*cf curso de formación Esp*) COM GEN, RRHH training course; **~ de formación** *Esp* (*cf curso de capacitación AmL*) COM GEN, RRHH training course; **~ de introducción** RRHH, PROT SOC induction course; **~ introductorio** PROT SOC introductory course; **~ legal** FIN lawful money (*AmE*), legal tender (*BrE*); **~ monetario** ECON monetary course; **~ preliminar** PROT SOC introductory course; **~ de reactualización profesional** RRHH job retraining course; **~ de reciclaje** RRHH retraining course; **~ a tiempo completo** RRHH residential course; ◆ **en ~** COM GEN ongoing, underway; **en el ~ de** COM GEN in the course of; **ser de ~ legal** FIN be legal tender

Curso: **~ de Orientación Universitaria** *m* (*C.O.U.*) PROT SOC Spanish university entrance examination, ≈ Advanced Level General Certificate of Education (*BrE*) (*A level*), ≈ Advanced Supplementary Level General Certificate of Education (*BrE*) (*AS level*)

cursor *m* INFO cursor

curtosis *f* MAT *estadística* kurtosis

curva *f* COM GEN curve; **~ de aprendizaje** ECON, PROT SOC, RRHH learning curve; **~ de concentración** MAT concentration curve; **~ de contrato** ECON contract curve; **~ de coste marginal** *Esp* (*cf curva de costo marginal AmL*) ECON marginal cost curve; **~ de costes** *Esp* (*cf curva de costos AmL*) CONT cost curve; **~ de costo marginal** *AmL* (*cf curva de coste marginal Esp*) ECON marginal cost curve; **~ de costos** *AmL* (*cf curva de costes Esp*) CONT cost curve; **~ de crecimiento** ECON growth curve; **~ de demanda** ECON demand curve; **~ de demanda compensada** ECON compensated demand curve; **~ de demanda quebrada** ECON kinked demand curve; **~ envolvente** ECON envelope curve; **~ de evolución del buque** TRANSP turning circle; **~ de experiencia** ECON experience curve; **~ FF** ECON FF curve; **~ flexionada de la oferta de trabajo** ECON backward-bending labor supply curve (*AmE*), backward-bending labour supply curve (*BrE*); **~ en forma de campana** MAT bell-shaped curve; **~ de frecuencias** MAT frequency curve; **~ de frecuencias asimétrica** MAT skewed frequency curve; **~ de frecuencias bimodal** MAT bimodal frequency curve; **~ de frecuencias en forma de J** MAT J-shaped frequency curve; **~ de frecuencias multimodal** MAT multimodal frequency curve; **~ de frecuencias simétricas** MAT symmetrical frequency curve; **~ de gastos** ECON price consumption curve (*PCC*); **~ de Gauss** MAT Gaussian curve; ~ **de igual producción** ECON equal product curve; ~ **de indiferencia** ECON indifference curve; ~ **de ingresos** ECON, FISC revenue curve; ~ **inversa de frecuencia en forma de J** ECON reverse J-shaped frequency curve; ~ **IS** ECON IS curve; ~ **isocoste** ECON iso-cost curve, iso-outlay curve; ~ **isocuanta** ECON isoproduct curve; ~ **en J** ECON J curve; ~ **de Kuznets** ECON Kuznets curve; ~ **de Laffer** ECON Laffer curve; ~ **LM** ECON LM curve; ~ **de Lorenz** ECON Lorenz curve; ~ **de oferta** ECON supply curve; ~ **de oferta retroflexionada** ECON backward-bending supply curve; ~ **de oferta de trabajo retroflexionada** ECON backward-bending labor supply curve (*AmE*), backward-bending labour supply curve (*BrE*); ~ **de oportunidad** ECON opportunity curve; ~ **de Philips** ECON Phillips curve; ~ **de posibilidades de producción** ECON, IND product possibility curve; ~ **de progresión de sueldos** RRHH salary progression curve; ~ **de regresión** MAT regression curve; ~ **de rendimiento** BANCA, ECON yield curve; ~ **de rendimiento invertida** ECON inverted yield curve; ~ **de rendimiento negativo** ECON negative yield curve; ~ **de rendimiento positivo** ECON positive yield curve; ~ **de renta-consumo** ECON income-consumption curve (*ICC*); ~ **S** ECON S curve; ~ **de transformación** ECON transformation curve

curvas: ~ **IS-LM** *f pl* ECON IS-LM curves

custodia *f* COM GEN, DER *de niño* custody, safekeeping; ~ **de acciones** BOLSA custody of shares; ~ **de activos** BANCA safekeeping of assets; ~ **conjunta** BANCA joint custody; ~ **y control** DER *de niño* custody and control; ~ **global** FIN global custody; ~ **de haberes** BANCA safekeeping of assets; ~ **local** FIN local custody

custodio *m* BOLSA custodian; ~ **de un fondo de inversiones** BANCA mutual fund custodian

CV *abr* (*caballaje AmL, caballo de vapor Esp*) TRANSP h.p. (*horsepower*)

c&f *abr* (*coste y flete Esp, costo y flete AmL*) IMP/EXP, TRANSP c&f (*cost and freight*)

D

D/A *abr* (*digital/analógico*) INFO D/A (*digital/analog*)

dadas: ~ **las circunstancias** *fra* COM GEN given the circumstances

dado: ~ **de estampado** *m* BANCA planchette

dador, a *m,f* BOLSA giver; ~ **de capital social** BOLSA giver on stock; ~ **de la facultad de comprar el doble** BOLSA giver for a call of more; ~ **de una opción de compra** BOLSA giver for a call; ~ **de una opción de venta** BOLSA giver for a put; ~ **de una opción de venta y de compra** BOLSA giver for a put and call; ~ **de suma de opción** BOLSA giver of option money

damajuana *f* TRANSP demijohn

damnum: ~ **sine injuria** *fra* COM GEN damnum sine injuria

daña: **que no** ~ **el medio ambiente** *adj* MED AMB environmentally friendly

dañado: ~ **en tránsito** *adj* TRANSP damaged in transit

daño *m* COM GEN *a empresa, reputación* damage; ~ **por agua** COM GEN, SEG water damage; ~ **ambiental** MED AMB environmental damage; ~ **causado por extinción de incendio** SEG damage caused in extinguishing fire; ~ **causado por productos farmacéuticos** SEG damage caused by pharmaceutical products; ~ **causado por radiaciones** SEG damage caused by radiation; ~ **consecuencial** SEG, TRANSP consequential damage; ~ **por contacto** TRANSP contact damage; ~ **contra propiedad alquilada** INMOB, SEG damage to rented property; ~ **corporal** SEG bodily injury; ~ **diferido** SEG belated claim; ~ **durante carga y descarga** SEG damage whilst loading and unloading; ~ **físico** FISC physical injury; ~ **indirecto** SEG, TRANSP consequential damage; ~ **irreparable** DER irreparable damage, irreparable harm; ~ **al margen de toda otra causa** SEG injury independent of all other means; ~ **material** INMOB, SEG property damage; ~ **menor** SEG small damage (*s/d*); ~ **a mercancías en custodia** IMP/EXP, SEG, TRANSP damage to goods in custody; ~ **para la salud** SEG damage to health; ~ **a terrenos rústicos** SEG damage to rural land

daños: ~ **por corrosión** *m pl* SEG corrosion damage; ~ **nominales** *m pl* DER nominal damages; ~ **de poca consideración** *m pl* DER nominal damages; ~ **y perjuicios** *m pl* DER, RRHH damages; ~ **y perjuicios incidentales** *m pl* DER, RRHH incidental damages; ~ **punitivos** *m pl* DER, SEG punitive damages, vindictive damages

dar *vt* COM GEN give, grant; ◆ ~ **a alguien la oportunidad de** COM GEN give sb the opportunity to; ~ **a alguien un ultimátum** COM GEN give sb an ultimatum; ~ **antigüedad a las mercaderías** CONT age stocks; ~ **en arrendamiento** INMOB rent; ~ **aviso a alguien de algo** COM GEN notify sb of sth; ~ **aviso de desalojo** INMOB give notice to quit; ~ **aviso de expulsión** INMOB give notice to quit; ~ **de baja** CONT *partida contable* write off; ~ **la bienvenida a** COM GEN welcome; ~ **en el blanco** COM GEN hit the jackpot; ~ **carpetazo** *infrml* COM GEN *a un asunto* put on the back burner; ~ **una clase** PROT SOC *en universidad* deliver a lecture; ~ **cobertura en los medios de comunicación** MEDIOS give media coverage; ~ **de comer con cuchara** COM GEN *información* spoon-feed (*infrml*); ~ **a conocer** COM GEN *idea, propuesta* air; ~ **el consentimiento** COM GEN give consent; ~ **credenciales a** COM GEN *representativo, oficial* accredit; ~ **derecho** DER entitle; ~ **un día libre a los empleados** RRHH give the employees a day off; ~ **fe de algo** COM GEN attest to sth; ~ **fianza** COM GEN give bond, guarantee; ~ **en fideicomiso** DER place in trust; ~ **de lado** COM GEN overside; ~ **muy poco dinero** COM GEN short change; ~ **un nuevo destino a** RRHH redeploy; ~ **orden de no pagar un cheque** BANCA stop a check (*AmE*), stop a cheque (*BrE*); ~ **orden de suspender el pago de un cheque** BANCA stop payment on a check (*AmE*), stop payment on a cheque (*BrE*); ~ **pasos** COM GEN take steps; ~ **los pasos que se consideran necesarios** DER take such steps as are considered necessary; ~ **la pauta** COM GEN set the pace; ~ **permiso a** COM GEN license; ~ **pocos informes** COM GEN underreport; ~ **prioridad a** COM GEN, GES prioritize, give priority to; ~ **pruebas de sus aptitudes** COM GEN win one's spurs; ~**referencias** COM GEN supply references; ~ **un repaso a** *infrml* COM GEN brush up on; ~ **rienda suelta a** COM GEN give free rein to; ~ **sobornos** COM GEN give bribes; ~ **el toque final a algo** COM GEN put the final touch to sth; ~ **traslado a** DER serve; ~ **un vuelco** COM GEN take a turn

dársena *f* TRANSP basin, wet dock, *puerto* inner harbor (*AmE*), inner harbour (*BrE*); ~ **de giro** TRANSP *puerto* turning basin; ~ **de mareas** TRANSP open dock

datación *f* COM GEN dating

datáfono *m* COMS dataphone

datos *m pl* COM GEN data; ~ **de aceptación de entrada** INFO entry acceptance data; ~ **agregados** CONT aggregate data; ~ **básicos** COM GEN key data; ~ **biográficos** RRHH biographical data, curriculum vitae (*BrE*) (*CV*), résumé (*AmE*); ~ **brutos** INFO, MAT *estadística* raw data; ~ **de la carga familiar** FISC details of dependant; ~ **contables** CONT accounting data; ~ **de control** INFO control data; ~ **digitales** INFO digital data; ~ **económicos** ECON economic data; ~ **de entrada** INFO incoming data, input data; ~ **estadísticos** MAT statistical returns; ~ **de fuente** INFO source data; ~ **justificativos** MAT supporting data; ~ **mecánicos** V&M mechanical data; ~ **de muestra** INFO sample data; ~ **no procesados** MAT raw data; ~ **numéricos** PROT SOC number facts; ~ **del panel** V&M panel data; ~ **primarios** COM GEN, V&M primary data; ~ **de salida** INFO output data; ~ **secundarios** COM GEN, V&M secondary data; ~ **sobre la audiencia televisiva** MEDIOS, V&M televisual audience data; ~ **técnicos** COM GEN technical data

DCB *abr Esp* (*Diseño Curricular Base*) PROT SOC *educación* ≈ NC (*National Curriculum*) (*BrE*)

DDB *abr* (*base de datos distribuida*) INFO DDB (*distributed database*)

dealer *m* V&M dealer

debajo: **por** ~ **del cambio** *fra* BOLSA, FIN at a discount (*AAD*); **por** ~ **de la media** *fra* COM GEN below average

debate: ~ **de aplazamiento** *m* POL *Parlamento* adjournment debate (*BrE*)

debatir *vt* COM GEN debate

debe[1] *m* COM GEN debit

debe[2]: **que ~ diferirse** *fra* BOLSA one for the shelf (*jarg*)

deber: ~ **algo a** *fra* COM GEN owe

deberes: ~ **establecidos en el contrato de empleo** *m pl* RRHH duties under the employment contract; ~ **rutinarios** *m pl* COM GEN routine duties

debida: ~ **diligencia** *f* FIN, SEG due diligence

debido *adj* COM GEN due; ♦ ~ **a** COM GEN due to, on account of; **a su ~ tiempo** COM GEN in due course

débil *adj* COM GEN weak, sluggish

debilidad *f* COM GEN weakness, *de demanda* sluggishness

debilitar *vt* COM GEN soften up, weaken

débito *m* COM GEN debit, debit entry, INMOB debit; ~ **directo** BANCA direct debit (*DD*); ~ **neto** BOLSA *opciones* net debit

década *f* COM GEN decade

decadencia: **rápida ~ de la prima** *f* BOLSA *opciones* rapid premium decay

decaer *vi* COM GEN, ECON *demanda* dwindle, wane, *comercio* fall away

decaimiento: ~ **de la memoria** *m* V&M memory decay

decepcionante *adj* COM GEN disappointing

decibelio *m* COM GEN decibel (*dB*)

decidir *vt* COM GEN adjudicate, *consejo, sugerencia* act on, DER adjudicate

decimal: ~ **en código binario** *m* INFO binary-coded decimal

decir: ~ **unas palabras en favor de alguien** *fra* COM GEN put in a word for sb; ~ **unas palabras de bienvenida** *fra* COM GEN say a few words of welcome

decisión *f* COM GEN decision; ~ **de alto nivel** COM GEN high-level decision; ~ **comercial** COM GEN business decision; ~ **de compra** COM GEN purchase decision; ~ **de compromiso** COM GEN compromise decision; ~ **de fabricar o comprar** *m* COM GEN make-or-buy decision; ~ **judicial** DER judgment; ~ **mayoritaria** COM GEN majority decision; ~ **no rutinaria** COM GEN nonroutine decision; ~ **política** COM GEN policy decision; ~ **presupuestaria** ECON, FIN, POL budget resolution; ~ **racional** COM GEN rational decision; ~ **salarial nacional** RRHH national wage award; ~ **secreta** COM GEN hidden decision; ~ **de última hora** COM GEN last-minute decision

decisivo *adj* COM GEN decisive

declaración *f* COM GEN announcement, DER declaration, statement, deposition, SEG notice, TRANSP declaration; ~ **de abandono** SEG notice of abandonment; ~ **de la acusación** DER statement of prosecution; ~ **de adhesión** DER declaration of membership; ~ **adicional** IMP/EXP, TRANSP *aduanas*, post-entry; ~ **de aduana** IMP/EXP, TRANSP bill of entry (*B/E*), customs declaration (*CD*); ~ **de aduana en el transbordo** IMP/EXP, TRANSP transhipment entry; ~ **de una aeronave** TRANSP aircraft manifest; ~ **de almacenaje** COM GEN warehousing entry; ~ **de aplicación de fondos** CONT application of funds statement; ~ **arancelaria** IMP/EXP, TRANSP customs declaration (*CD*); ~ **atípica** FISC off-profile return; ~ **de bancarrota** BANCA, CONT declaration of bankruptcy; ~ **de la carga** TRANSP load sheet; ~ **de la carga fiscal** FISC announcement of a tax

burden; ~ **de la carga de importación del contenedor** IMP/EXP, TRANSP *navegación* container import cargo manifest; ~ **de cese de pago** BANCA, CONT declaration of bankruptcy; ~ **clasificada** FISC classified return; ~ **de compra y venta** BOLSA purchase and sale statement (*P&S statement*); ~ **por computador** *AmL ver declaración por computadora AmL*; ~ **por computadora** *AmL* (*cf declaración por ordenador Esp*) FISC, INFO computer return; ~ **de condiciones** RRHH statement of terms and conditions; ~ **conjunta** COM GEN, DER, POL joint statement; ~ **conjunta de interés** BANCA joint declaration of interest (*JDI*); ~ **conjunta sobre la renta** FISC joint return; ~ **del corredor de comercio** COM GEN broker's statement; ~ **defectuosa del capitán** TRANSP captain's imperfect entry (*CIE*); ~ **detallada** IMP/EXP, TRANSP *aduanas* bill of entry (*B/E*); ~ **de dividendo** BOLSA dividend declaration; ~ **del editor** MEDIOS, V&M publisher's statement; ~ **de embalaje de carga para exportación** IMP/EXP, TRANSP export cargo packing declaration (*ECPD*); ~ **del empresario** FISC employer's return; ~ **de entrada** IMP/EXP, TRANSP declaration of entry; ~ **de entrada en aduana** IMP/EXP, TRANSP customs entry; ~ **de entrada en un país** ADMIN, IMP/EXP home use entry; ~ **por escrito** DER written statement; ~ **estadística** FISC *IVA* statistical return; ~ **estimativa del impuesto** FISC declaration of estimated tax; ~ **de expedición ferroviaria** TRANSP railroad consignment note (*AmE*), railway consignment note (*BrE*); ~ **falsa** FISC false declaration, false return, false statement; ~ **falsificada** FISC dressed return; ~ **de fideicomiso** DER declaration of trust; ~ **fraudulenta** SEG fraudulent misrepresentation; ~ **de gastos de corretaje** BOLSA brokerage statement; ~ **general** COM GEN blanket statement; ~ **a hacienda** FISC income tax return, tax return; ~ **del impacto medioambiental** MED AMB environmental impact statement; ~ **impresa** FISC edited return, printed return; ~ **del impuesto sobre la renta** CONT, FISC income tax return, tax return; ~ **de impuestos sobre donativos** FISC gift tax return; ~ **incompleta** FISC *IVA* underdeclaration; ~ **incorrecta** FISC *IVA* misdeclaration; ~ **individual del impuesto sobre la renta** CONT, FISC individual income tax return; ~ **de los ingresos** FISC reporting of income; ~ **del IVA** FISC VAT return; ~ **judicial de quiebra** COM GEN adjudication of bankruptcy order; ~ **jurada por escrito** DER affidavit, sworn statement; ~ **morosa** DER delinquent return; ~ **negativa** FISC debit return; ~ **de objetivos** BOLSA, GES purposes statement, statement of objectives; ~ **por ordenador** *Esp* (*cf declaración por computadora AmL*) FISC, INFO computer return; ~ **ordinaria** COM GEN regular statement; ~ **de origen** IMP/EXP declaration of origin; ~ **de origen y aplicación de fondos** CONT, FIN source and application of funds statement; ~ **de origen certificada** IMP/EXP certified declaration of origin; ~ **de pago por partidas** RRHH itemized pay statement; ~ **de política** COM GEN policy statement; ~ **positiva** BANCA positive file; ~ **preferente** FISC prime range file; ~ **y presentación material de hechos** SEG *marina* material representation; ~ **presupuestaria** POL *gubernamental* budgetary statement; ~ **previa** COM GEN preliminary entry; ~ **de primas** BOLSA declaration of options; ~ **principal** FISC *de contribuyente* principal file; ~ **proforma** FISC pro forma return; ~ **provisional** IMP/EXP bill of sight; ~ **de quiebra** COM GEN declaration of bankruptcy; ~ **recuperada** FISC salvaged return; ~ **de**

reexportación de almacén IMP/EXP, TRANSP shipping bill; **~ de registro** BOLSA registration statement; **~ del reintegro** FISC refund return; **~ de remesas** FIN, FISC remittance return; **~ de la renta consolidada** FISC *de empresas subsidiarias* consolidated tax return; **~ de la renta separada** FISC separate tax return; **~ de salida** IMP/EXP, TRANSP entry outwards; **~ segmentada** FISC segmented return; **~ de siniestro** SEG insurance report; **~ sobre las normas de práctica contable** CONT Statement of Standard Accounting Practice (*SSAP*); **~ sobre la renta** CONT, FISC income tax return, tax return, return of income; **~ en suspenso** FISC suspense return; **~ de un testigo** DER statement of witness; **~ de tránsito** IMP/EXP, TRANSP transhipment bond; **~ veraz de los términos del préstamo** BANCA, DER, FIN truth in lending (*jarg*) (*AmE*); ◆ **sin ~ de valor** IMP/EXP no value declared (*NVD*); **no haber presentado la ~** FISC be in default in filing; **hacer una ~** DER make a statement

declaraciones: ~ ordinarias *f pl* COM GEN regular statements

declarante *mf* DER deponent, FISC filer, informant; **~ fuera de plazo** FISC late filer

declarar 1. *vt* COM GEN *cuenta* state, declare, report; ◆ **~ a alguien en bancarrota** CONT adjudicate sb bankrupt; **~ a alguien en quiebra** CONT adjudicate sb bankrupt; **~ una huelga** RRHH call a strike; **~ judicialmente fuertes daños** DER adjudge heavy damages; **~ mercancías** IMP/EXP enter goods; **2.** *vi* DER give evidence, testify; ◆ **~ bajo juramento** DER declare on oath, give evidence under oath, give evidence on oath, swear on affidavit

declararse: ~ en bancarrota *fra* CONT declare oneself bankrupt; **~ culpable** *fra* DER plead guilty; **~ ignorante** *fra* DER plead ignorance; **~ en quiebra** *fra* CONT declare oneself bankrupt

declinación: ~ de responsabilidad *f* SEG disclaimer

declinar *vt* COM GEN, ECON decline

declive *m* COM GEN declination, slope

decodificación *f* INFO decoding

decodificador *m* INFO decoder

decodificar *vt* INFO decode

decomisación *f* MED AMB, POL decommissioning

decomisar *vt* MED AMB, POL decommission

decretar *vt* DER adjudge, enact

decreto *m* COM GEN decree

Decreto: ~ de Presupuestos *m* FIN Appropriation Act (*BrE*), Appropriation Bill (*AmE*); **~ de Sociedades Mercantiles** *m* COM GEN, DER, IND Companies Act (*BrE*), Companies Bill (*AmE*)

dedicación[1]: **~ parcial** *f* RRHH *empleado* part-time work

dedicación[2]: **de plena ~** *fra* RRHH full-time

dedicado *adj* COM GEN *a fin específico*, INFO *equipo* dedicated

dedicarse: ~ a *v refl* COM GEN address oneself to

deducción *f* COM GEN allowance, FISC allowance, deduction, SEG deduction, relief, TRANSP tret; **~ por activos de crédito** FISC deduction for lending assets, business investment tax credit; **~ admisible** FISC allowable deduction; **~ por amortización** CONT allowance for depreciation; **~ por amortizaciones fiscales rápidas** FISC accelerated capital cost allowance (*ACCA*); **~ ampliada** FISC top-up deduction; **~ autorizada** CONT

allowable deduction; **~ de capital** FISC capital deduction; **~ por carga familiar** FISC dependant tax credit; **~ por cargas familiares** FISC childcare expense deduction; **~ por comidas de negocios** FISC deduction for business meals; **~ de crédito básica** FISC basic credit allowance; **~ de la cuota permitida** FISC allowable tax credit; **~ devengada sobre activos agotables** FISC earned depletion; **~ discrecional** FISC discretionary deduction; **~ por disminución mental o física** FISC credit for mental or physical impairment; **~ de dividendo** FISC dividend allowance; **~ por doble imposición** FISC double taxation relief (*DTR*); **~ por donaciones** FISC Gift Aid; **~ por empleo en ultramar** FISC overseas employment tax credit; **~ por la esposa** FISC spouse's allowance; **~ estándar** FISC standard deduction; **~ estimada** FISC estimated deduction; **~ familiar por los hijos** FISC child tax credit; **~ fiscal al fallecer un cónyuge** FISC marital deduction; **~ fiscal del empleo** FISC employment tax deduction; **~ fiscal para la energía** FISC, IND energy tax credit; **~ fiscal mínima** FISC minimum tax allowance; **~ forzosa** COM GEN compulsory deduction; **~ de gastos** FISC expense allowance; **~ por gastos de la casa matriz** FISC home office expense deduction; **~ por gastos corrientes** FISC allowance for living expenses; **~ por gastos de educación** FISC education credit; **~ por gastos de viaje** FISC allowance for traveling expenses (*AmE*), allowance for travelling expenses (*BrE*); **~ general por horas extraordinarias** FISC general holdover relief; **~ global** FISC standard deduction; **~ impositiva** FISC tax deduction; **~ de impuestos de permanencia** FISC nonresident tax deduction, nonresident withholding tax; **~ por incapacidad** FISC disability tax credit; **~ por indexación** FISC *ganancias* indexation relief; **~ del ingreso por dividendos** BOLSA, FISC dividends income deduction; **~ de los ingresos por dividendos e intereses** BOLSA, FISC interest and dividend income deduction; **~ de los ingresos por inversión** FISC investment income deduction; **~ interior por transformación** FISC inward processing relief (*IPR*); **~ por invalidez** FISC disability allowance; **~ por matrimonio** FISC marriage allowance, marriage deduction; **~ máxima permitida** FISC maximum allowable deduction; **~ por niños y cargas familiares** FISC child and dependent care credit; **~ de nivel básico** FISC *de compañía* base level deduction; **~ no utilizada** FISC unused relief; **~ en nómina** RRHH *de ingresos brutos* payroll deduction; **~ nuevo por viejo** SEG new-for-old deduction; **~ en origen** FIN deduction at source, source deduction; **~ de las pequeñas empresas** FISC small business deduction; **~ por pérdidas de créditos** FISC deduction for loan losses; **~ personal** FISC personal allowance (*BrE*), personal exemption (*AmE*); **~ por préstamos incobrables** FISC deduction for uncollectable loans; **~ progresiva** FISC *sucesión, donaciones vitalicias* taper relief; **~ por refinanciación** FISC rollover relief; **~ por regalos** FISC deduction for gifts; **~ salarial** RRHH salary deduction; **~ por separación** FISC separation allowance; **~ sobre el activo agotable** FISC depletion allowance; **~ sobre activos empresariales** FISC relief on business assets; **~ en el sobre de paga** FISC itemized deduction; **~ transferida desgravable por la carestía de la vida** FISC deduction transferred eligible for cost of living tax credit; **~ única de impuestos** FISC single tax credit; **~ por viudedad** FISC widow's bereavement allowance; ◆ **hacer una ~** FISC make a deduction

deducibilidad *f* FISC, RRHH, SEG deductibility; **no ~ de las contribuciones del empresario** RRHH nondeductibility of employer contributions; **~ de aportación patronal** FISC deductibility of employer contributions

deducible *adj* FISC, SEG deductible; ◆ **~ a efectos impositivos** FISC tax-deductible

deducir *vt* COM GEN deduce, *precio* fetch, DER recoup, FISC, MAT, SEG deduct; ◆ **~ de** BANCA net against; **antes de ~ los impuestos** FISC before tax; **después de ~ los impuestos** FISC after tax

deduplicado *m* INFO de-duped

defase *m* ECON lag

defecto[1]: **por ~** *adj* INFO by default; **sin ~** *adj* COM GEN faultless

defecto[2] *m* COM GEN flaw; **~ de alineación** COM GEN misalignment; **~ inherente** COM GEN inherent defect; **~ latente** INMOB latent defect

defectuoso *adj* COM GEN defective, faulty, flawed

defender *vt* COM GEN stand up for; ◆ **~ el propio caso** DER argue one's own case, defend oneself

defensa *f* DER answer, TRANSP *manejo de carga* skid; **~ comecocos** BOLSA, FIN *fusiones corporativas y adquisiciones* Pac-Man defense *(AmE)*, Pac-Man defence *(BrE)*; **~ del juicio contra el asegurado** SEG defence of suit against insured *(BrE)*, defense of suit against insured *(AmE)*; **~ del pleito contra el asegurado** SEG defence of suit against insured *(BrE)*, defense of suit against insured *(AmE)*; **~ de tierra abrasada** FIN, GES scorched-earth defence *(BrE)*, scorched-earth defense *(AmE)*

defensor, a: **~ del estado del bienestar** *m,f* POL welfarist

Defensor, a: **~ del Accionista** *m,f* BOLSA Ombudsman; **~ del Cliente** *m,f* BANCA Banking Ombudsman

deficiencia *f* COM GEN deficiency, shortfall; **~ de experiencia** SEG experience deficiency

deficiente[1] *adj* COM GEN deficient

deficiente[2]: **~ en desempeño** *mf* COM GEN low achiever

déficit *m* CONT shortfall, COM GEN deficiency, deficit, gap, outstanding balance, shortfall; **~ actualizado** ECON actual deficit; **~ actuarial** SEG actuarial deficit; **~ acumulado** CONT, FIN, FISC accumulated deficit; **~ de la balanza comercial** COM GEN trade gap, unfavourable balance of trade *(BrE)*, unfavorable balance of trade *(AmE)*; **~ de la balanza de pagos** ECON balance of payments deficit *(BP deficit)*; **~ de caja** BANCA teller's shortage, CONT cash deficit, cash short; **~ de cobertura** MEDIOS gap in coverage; **~ comercial** COM GEN, ECON, POL trade deficit; **~ en cuenta corriente** BANCA, CONT current account deficit; **~ deflacionario** ECON deflationary gap; **~ en una divisa** BANCA short in a currency; **~ estructural** ECON structural deficit; **~ exento** FISC exempt deficit; **~ de explotación** CONT operating deficit; **~ federal** ECON federal deficit; **~ fiscal** COM GEN fiscal deficit; **~ de fondos** ECON, FIN funding gap; **~ global** ECON overall deficit; **~ inflacionario** ECON inflationary gap; **~ inflacionario ajustado** ECON inflation-adjusted deficit; **~ déficit inflacionario decreciente** ECON narrowing inflation gap; **~ de inversión** FIN investment gap; **~ presupuestario** COM GEN budget deficit, budgetary deficit; **~ presupuestario creciente** COM GEN growing

budget deficit, increasing budget deficit, staggering budget deficit; **~ principal** ECON primary deficit; **~ de recursos** ECON resources gap; **~ del sector público** ECON public sector deficit

deficitario *adj* COM GEN deficit

definición *f* COM GEN definition; **~ de artículos** SEG definition of items; **~ básica** COM GEN basic definition; **~ esencial** COM GEN core definition; **~ del ingreso según Haigh Simons** ECON Haigh Simons definition of income; **~ de límite** SEG definition of limits

definitivo *adj* DER *mandamiento judicial, decreto* absolute

deflación *f* ECON deflation, disinflation

deflacionar *vt* ECON deflate

deflacionario *adj* ECON deflationary

deflactor: **~ implícito de precios** *m* ECON implicit price deflator

deformación *f* COM GEN deformation, distortion; **~ de la salida** BANCA, ECON, FIN, POL outlay creep *(jarg)*

deformante *adj* COM GEN distorting

deformar *vt* COM GEN deform, distort

defraudación: **~ fiscal** *f* FISC defrauded tax; **~ de seguro marítimo** *f* SEG marine insurance fraud

defraudador, a: **~ de impuestos** *m,f* FISC tax dodger *(infrml)*

defraudar *vt* COM GEN defraud, dodge *(infrml)*

DEG *abr* *(derechos especiales de giro)* BANCA, DER special drawing rights *(jarg)*

degradación *f* MED AMB *de ciudades* degradation; **~ del suelo** MED AMB soil degradation

degradar *vt* MED AMB degrade, RRHH demote

degresión *f* MAT degression

dejación *f* FISC surrender

dejar 1. *vt* COM GEN, DER leave; ◆ **~ abierto** COM GEN *el tema* leave open; **~ acumular** BANCA *deuda por sobregiro* run up; **~ algo de lado en silencio** COM GEN pass sth over in silence; **~ atrás** COM GEN outpace, leave behind; **~ claro** COM GEN make clear; **~ constancia de** COM GEN *gastos, déficit* give record of; **~ una cuenta en descubierto** BANCA overdraw an account; **~ un espacio** INFO leave a space; **~ de existir** FISC cease to be extant; **~ de lado** COM GEN put on the back burner *(infrml)*, leave aside; **~ de tener efecto** DER *contrato* cease to have effect; **~ de trabajar** RRHH *huelga* down tools; **~ en prenda** COM GEN pawn; **~ sin trabajo** RRHH stand off; **2.** *vi* COM GEN cease

dejarse: **~ sobornar** *fra* COM GEN be on the take *(infrml)*

delegación *f* COM GEN delegation *(del.)*; **~ de autorización** COM GEN delegation of authorization; **~ de firma** COM GEN delegation of signing authority; **~ local de un sindicato** RRHH local union; **~ de poderes** ECON *votos* proxy

delegado, -a *m,f* COM GEN delegate, representative *(rep.)*; **~ a una conferencia** GES, RRHH conference delegate; **~ gremial** IND, RRHH shop steward; **~ del gremio** COM GEN business agent, SEG union agent; **~ de planta** RRHH worker director; **~ sindical** RRHH trade union representative *(BrE)*

delegar *vt* COM GEN delegate; ◆ **~ la autoridad en** COM GEN delegate authority to

deletreador *m* INFO word speller

delimitación *f* COM GEN, RRHH definition, demarcation

delimitar *vt* COM GEN, RRHH define, delimit

delito *m* DER crime, criminal offence, offence; **~ econó-**

mico DER, ECON economic crime; **~ de guante blanco** DER white-collar crime; **~ menor** COM GEN misdemeanor (*AmE*), misdemeanour (*BrE*)

delta[1]: **~-neutral** *adj* BOLSA *opciones sobre futuros en eurodólares* delta-neutral

delta[2] *m* BOLSA, FIN delta; **~ neto de la posición** BOLSA *opciones* net delta position; **~ de una opción de compra** BOLSA delta call; **~ de una opción de venta** BOLSA delta put

demanda[1]: **sobre ~** *adv* FIN at call

demanda[2] *f* COM GEN *solicitud* demand, claim, *derecho penal* complaint, *judicial* suit, FIN *capital* call, FISC demand, V&M call; **~ activa** ECON active demand; **~ actual** V&M current demand; **~ acumulada** COM GEN backlog demand; **~ admisible** SEG allowable claim; **~ adquirida** ECON catch-up demand; **~ agregada** ECON, FIN aggregate demand; **~ agregada-oferta agregada** ECON *modelo macroeconómico*, ECON aggregate demand-aggregate supply (*AD-AS*); **~ alternativa** ECON option demand; **~ alternativa de aumento de remuneraciones** RRHH leapfrogging; **~ animada** COM GEN brisk demand; **~ aplazada** DER, ECON deferred demand; **~ de bienes sustitutivos** ECON, V&M alternate demand; **~ por calumnia** DER slander action; **~ cíclica** ECON cyclical demand; **~ de cobertura suplementaria** BOLSA margin call; **~ competitiva** V&M competitive demand; **~ complementaria** V&M complementary demand; **~ conjunta** ECON joint demand; **~ de los consumidores** V&M *investigación de mercado* consumer demand; **~ contenida** ECON, V&M pent-up demand; **~ creciente** ECON growing demand; **~ por daños** DER claim for damages; **~ dependiente** PATENT dependent claim; **~ derivada** ECON derived demand; **~ por difamación** DER action for libel; **~ de dinero** ECON demand for money; **~ efectiva** ECON, V&M effective demand, effectual demand; **~ elástica** ECON, V&M elastic demand; **~ estacional** ECON, V&M seasonal demand; **~ excedente** ECON, V&M excess demand; **~ exterior** ECON, V&M foreign demand; **~ final** ECON, V&M final demand; **~ financiera** CONT financial claim; **~ fiscal** FISC revenue claim; **~ global** ECON, FIN aggregate demand, overall demand; **~ de importaciones** ECON, IMP/EXP import demand; **~ industrial** IND industrial demand; **~ inelástica** ECON inelastic demand; **~ interna** ECON domestic demand; **~ de inversión** FIN investment demand; **~ laboral** ECON labor demand (*AmE*), labour demand (*BrE*); **~ latente** V&M latent demand; **~ legal** DER civil action; **~ de mala fe** DER malicious prosecution; **~ de mano de obra** ECON labor demand (*AmE*), labour demand (*BrE*); **~ máxima** ECON peak-load pricing; **~ de mercado** ECON market demand; **~ de mercancías** ECON demand for goods; **~ monetaria** ECON money demand; **~ monetaria especulativa** ECON speculative demand; **~ nacional** ECON national demand; **~ de pagar** BANCA, DER, FIN payment request; **~ perfectamente elástica** ECON perfectly elastic demand; **~ perfectamente inelástica** ECON perfectly inelastic demand; **~ persistente** COM GEN repeat demand, V&M persistent demand; **~ potencial** ECON, V&M potential demand; **~ de precaución del dinero** ECON precautionary demand for money; **~ prevista** ECON, V&M anticipated demand; **~ de reposición** ECON *de bienes de capital* replacement demand; **~ reprimida** ECON, V&M pent-up demand; **~ salarial** RRHH wage demand; **~ viscosa**

ECON viscous demand; ◆ **en ~** RRHH *trabajos* in demand; **el producto no tiene ~** COM GEN, V&M the product does not sell well; **sobre ~** BOLSA at call; **según ~** *Esp* (*cf justo a tiempo AmL*) IND just-in-time (*JIT*); **según la ~** BOLSA at the market call (*BrE*); **por ~ popular** COM GEN by popular request, by popular demand

demandado[1]: **~ y ofertado** *adj* BOLSA *precio de compra, venta* asked and bid

demandado[2],**-a** *m,f* DER defendant

demandante *mf* COM GEN, DER plaintiff, claimant

demandar *vt* COM GEN claim, DER claim, sue, lay claim to, FISC, SEG claim; ◆ **~ a alguien por libelo** DER sue for libel; **~ a alguien por violar una patente** DER, PATENT sue for infringement of patent; **~ títulos para rescate** CONT call securities for redemption

demandas: **~ de menor cuantía** *f pl* DER small claims; **~ del mismo tipo** *f pl* PATENT claims of the same category; **~ y obligaciones** *f pl* CONT claims and liabilities

demás: **sin que lo ~ se modifique** *fra* COM GEN all else being equal

democracia *f* COM GEN, POL democracy; **~ industrial** COM GEN, POL, RRHH *participación de trabajadores* industrial democracy; **~ popular** POL people's democracy; **~ social** ECON, POL social democracy

democracias: **nuevas ~** *f pl* COM GEN *política* new democracies

democráticamente *adv* COM GEN, POL democratically

democrático *adj* COM GEN, POL democratic

demografía *f* ECON, PROT SOC, V&M demography

demográfico *adj* ECON, PROT SOC, V&M demographic

demogrant *m* RRHH demogrant

demolición *m* INMOB demolition

demora *f* COM GEN delay, ECON lag, INFO delay; **~ en el pago** BOLSA arrearage

demoras: **~ de trámite** *f pl* COM GEN procedural delays

Demoscopia *m* V&M, POL Spanish market research institute, ≈ Market and Opinion Research International (*MORI*)

demostración *f* COM GEN, V&M demonstration, *de productos* show; **~ en tienda** V&M store demonstration

demostrar *vt* COM GEN *mediante tablas, gráficos*, V&M demonstrate

denegación *f* COM GEN disallowance, disclaimer, FISC disallowance, disclaimer; **~ despachada** FISC cleared reject; **~ de opinión** COM GEN denial of opinion

denegar *vt* COM GEN disallow, DER refuse, withhold, FISC disallow; ◆ **~ una fianza** DER refuse bail; **~ información** DER withhold information

denominación *f* COM GEN *para artículos* title; **~ de una cuenta** BANCA, CONT account title; **~ legal** DER *administrativo* legal name; **~ del puesto** RRHH job title

denominador *m* COM GEN denominator; **~ común** COM GEN common denominator

densidad *f* ECON, INMOB density; **~ de almacenamiento** INFO *datos* packing density; **~ en caracteres** INFO character density; **~ en dígitos binarios** INFO bit density; **~ de ocupación** TRANSP load factor; **~ de población** ECON, POL population density; **~ simple** INFO single density; **~ sindical** RRHH union density; **~ del tráfico** TRANSP traffic density

densímetro *m* MED AMB hydrometer

dentro[1]: **aquí ~** *adv* COMS herein

dentro[2] *prep* COM GEN inside; **~ de** COM GEN within; ◆ **estar ~ del alcance de** PATENT fall within the scope of

dentro[3]: **~ de los límites prescritos** *fra* DER within prescribed limits; **~ del plazo especificado** *fra* COM GEN at the specified time; **~ del plazo fijado** *fra* COM GEN within the prescribed time; **~ del precio** *fra* BOLSA in-the-money (*ITM*); **~ de una semana** *fra* COM GEN this time next week, within a week; **~ del tiempo permitido** *fra* COM GEN within the allotted time frame

denuncia *f* DER *acción civil* complaint

denunciable: no ~ *adj* BANCA, FIN uncallable

departamento *m* (*dpto.*) COM GEN department (*dept.*), INMOB *AmL* (*cf piso Esp*) apartment (*AmE*), flat (*BrE*); **~ acreedor** ADMIN creditor department; **~ actuarial** DER actuarial department; **~ de administración de bienes** GES trust department; **~ administrativo** BOLSA compliance department; **~ de análisis económico** ECON Bureau of Economic Analysis (*BEA*); **~ de atención al cliente** ADMIN, COM GEN, V&M customer service department; **~ de auditoría** CONT *de compañía* auditing department; **~ de bienestar social** PROT SOC welfare department; **~ de caja** ADMIN, COM GEN, FIN cash department, cash office, cashier's department, cashiering department; **~ de cambios** BOLSA exchange department; **~ de circulación** MEDIOS *prensa* circulation department; **~ de compras** COM GEN procurement department, purchasing department; **~ de contabilidad** *Esp* (*cf contaduría AmL*) CONT accounting department, accounts department, accounting office; **~ creativo** V&M creative department; **~ de crédito** BANCA, FIN credit department, loan department; **~ de cumplimiento** BOLSA compliance department; **~ deudor** ADMIN debtor department; **~ de envíos** TRANSP forwarding department; **~ de estiba y desestiba** TRANSP stevedoring department; **~ de expedición** TRANSP dispatch department, V&M traffic department; **~ de facturación** COM GEN billing department (*AmE*), invoicing department (*BrE*); **~ fiduciario del banco** BANCA bank trust department; **~ financiero** FIN finance department; **~ fiscal** FISC revenue department; **~ de fletes de entrada** IMP/EXP, TRANSP inward freight department; **~ de fletes de salida** IMP/EXP, TRANSP outward freight department; **~ gráfico** V&M *publicidad* art department; **~ de hipotecas** BANCA, FIN, INMOB mortgage department; **~ de impuestos** FISC tax department; **~ de información de la policía** DER police intelligence; **~ de ingeniería** COM GEN engineering department; **~ de ingeniería y diseño** COM GEN engineering and design department; **~ jurídico** DER legal department; **~ de liquidaciones** BANCA settlements department; **~ de margen** BOLSA margin department; **~ de marketing** V&M marketing department; **~ del mercado monetario** BOLSA money market department; **~ de mercancías** COM GEN goods department; **~ de nóminas** RRHH payroll department; **~ de operaciones** BOLSA *de empresa financiera*, FIN operations department; **~ de operaciones con bonos** BOLSA, FIN bond trading department; **~ de personal** COM GEN, RRHH personnel department, staff department; **~ de planificación** COM GEN, GES planning department; **~ de producción** IND manufacturing department, production department; **~ de publicidad** MEDIOS, V&M advertising department, publicity department; **~ de reclamaciones** SEG claims department;

~ del registrador BANCA registrar's department; **~ de relaciones con el inversor** BOLSA investor relations department; **~ de seguridad** BANCA safe custody department; **~ de servicio al cliente** ADMIN, COM GEN, V&M customer service department; **~ de servicios** V&M service department; **~ técnico** TRANSP operating department; **~ de ultramar** COM GEN overseas department; **~ de valores** BOLSA securities department; **~ de ventas** V&M sales department; **~ de vigilancia bursátil** BOLSA surveillance department of exchanges

Departamento: ~ de Aduanas y Tributos *m* IMP/EXP ≈ Customs & Excise Department (*BrE*) (*C&E*); **~ de Control de Prácticas Comerciales** *m* ECON ≈ Office of Fair Trading (*OFT*)

dependencia: ~ del gobierno *f* POL, RRHH government agency; **~ de los ingresos** *f* FIN revenue dependency

depender: ~ de *vi* COM GEN hinge on, *una persona* depend on, rest on, PATENT *reclamación* depend on

dependiente[1]: **totalmente ~** *adj* COM GEN wholly dependent

dependiente[2],**-a** *m,f* GES *en una fábrica o taller* shop steward, RRHH assistant (*asst*); **~ de tienda** RRHH sales clerk (*AmE*), shop assistant (*BrE*)

deposición *f* DER deposition

depositante *mf* BANCA bailer, depositor

depositar *vt* BANCA bank, deposit

depositario, -a *m,f* BANCA depository, DER bailee, FIN receiver, FISC depository; **~ y administrador(-a)** FIN receiver and manager; **~ de una apuesta** COM GEN stakeholder; **~ autorizado(-a)** BANCA approved depository; **~ de bienes embargados** DER garnishee; **~ de bienes sujetos a embargo** DER garnishee; **~ judicial** COM GEN receiver; **~ legal de documentos** FIN escrow agent

depósito[1]: **en ~** *adv* IMP/EXP in bond (*IB*)

depósito[2] *m* COM GEN repository, deposit, *edificio* depot, storeroom, DER bailment, deposit; **~ de ácido** MED AMB acid deposit; **~ de aduana** COM GEN bonded warehouse; **~ aduanero** IMP/EXP, TRANSP customs warehouse; **~ aduanero interior** IMP/EXP, TRANSP inland clearance depot (*ICD*); **~ aduanero privado** IMP/EXP, TRANSP private bonded warehouse; **~ aduanero público** IMP/EXP, TRANSP public bonded warehouse; **~ de ahorro** BANCA savings deposit; **~ al por menor** BOLSA retail deposit; **~ de avería gruesa** SEG general average deposit (*G/A dep*); **~ de averías** FIN average deposit; **~ bancario** BANCA bank deposit; **~ de buena fe** BOLSA good-faith deposit; **~ en caja de seguridad** BANCA safe deposit; **~ de carbón** MED AMB coal deposit; **~ central de abastecimiento** COM GEN central supplies depot; **~ del cliente** BANCA customer deposit; **~ de combustible parcial** TRANSP part bunker; **~ comercial** TRANSP commercial dock (*C D*); **~ de contenedores** TRANSP container park, container depot, container dock; **~ de corretaje hecho** BOLSA brokered deposit; **~ a corto plazo** BANCA short-term deposit; **~ en la cuenta corporativa** BANCA corporate account deposit; **~ y cuenta fiduciaria** BANCA deposit and trust account; **~ diario** BANCA daily deposit; **~ directo** BANCA direct deposit; **~ para distribución** TRANSP distribution depot; **~ especial** BANCA special deposit; **~ de eurodólares** BANCA Eurodollar deposit; **~ euromonetario** BANCA, ECON Euromoney deposit; **~ exigible a la vista** BANCA demand deposit; **~ fuera**

de hora BANCA night depository, night safe; **~ de garantía** BOLSA *futuros sobre divisas* margin deposit, INMOB earnest money; **~ de grupaje** TRANSP groupage depot; **~ hecho de buena fe** BOLSA good-faith deposit; **~ inicial** BANCA, COM GEN, V&M down payment; **~ interbancario** BANCA interbank deposit; **~ de interés variable** BOLSA *futuros* floating-rate deposit; **~ sin intereses** BANCA interest-free deposit; **~ con intereses diarios** BANCA daily interest deposit; **~ a largo plazo** BANCA long-term deposit; **~ en línea** BANCA deposit in transit; **~ a medio plazo** BANCA, FIN medium-term deposit; **~ de mercancías** COM GEN goods depot; **~ de muebles** COM GEN furniture depot; **~ muy alto** TRANSP super high cube (*SHC*); **~ no canjeable** BANCA nonencashable deposit (*frml*); **~ no liquidable** BANCA nonencashable deposit (*frml*); **~ no reclamado** BANCA unclaimed deposit; **~ no reembolsable** COM GEN nonrefundable deposit; **~ nocturno** BANCA night depository, night safe, overnight deposit; **~ oficial** MEDIOS *imprenta* official deposit; **~ en periodo fijo** BANCA fixed-period deposit; **~ permanente** IMP/EXP standing deposit; **~ a plazo** BANCA term deposit; **~ a plazo en eurodólares** BANCA, BOLSA Eurodollar time deposit; **~ a plazo fijo** BANCA fixed deposit, fixed-term deposit (*BrE*), time deposit (*AmE*) (*TD*); **~ a plazo con interés variable** BANCA flexible-rate term deposit; **~ que no admite cheques** BANCA nonchequable deposit (*AmE*), noncheckable deposit (*BrE*); **~ que no devenga interés** BANCA noninterest-bearing deposit; **~ receptor** TRANSP reception depot; **~ reembolsable** COM GEN, INMOB refundable deposit; **~ de reserva** ECON reserve deposit (*RD*); **~ sujeto a preaviso** BANCA notice deposit; **~ superior** TRANSP *contenedor* high cube (*HC*); **~ temporal** BANCA layoff; **~ a la vista** BANCA demand deposit, sight deposit; ◆ **en ~** COM GEN in escrow

depósitos: **~ bancarios a la vista** *m pl* BANCA bank demand deposits; **~ de clientes institucionales** *m pl* BANCA wholesale deposits; **~ de clientes particulares** *m pl* BANCA retail deposits; **~ en divisas** *m pl* BANCA, FIN currency deposits; **~ personales** *m pl* BANCA retail personal deposits; **~ a plazo fijo de tres meses en eurodólares** *m pl* BOLSA three-month Eurodollar Time Deposits; **~ que devengan interés** *m pl* BANCA interest-bearing deposits; **otros ~ por revisar** *m pl* BANCA, FIN other checkable deposits (*OCD*)

depreciación *f* BOLSA fall in value, COM GEN amortizement, depreciation, RRHH demotion, write-off; **~ acelerada** COM GEN accelerated depreciation; **~ de un activo** BOLSA, CONT write-down; **~ de los activos** BANCA, CONT write-down of the value of assets; **~ de activos fijos** BANCA depreciation of fixed assets; **~ acumulada** CONT accumulated depletion, accumulated depreciation; **~ por agotamiento** COM GEN, CONT, ECON, FISC depletion; **~ anual** CONT annual depreciation; **~ de balance decreciente** CONT, FIN declining balance depreciation; **~ de la base impositiva** CONT, FISC tax-based depreciation; **~ combinada** FIN composite depreciation; **~ compensatoria** COM GEN, CONT compensating depreciation; **~ económica** ECON *propiedad inmobiliaria*, INMOB economic depreciation; **~ física** CONT *cuentas anuales* physical depreciation; **~ irremediable** INMOB incurable depreciation; **~ libre** FIN free depreciation; **~ en libros** CONT book depreciation; **~ de la moneda circulante** ECON, FIN currency

depreciation; **~ monetaria** ECON, FIN currency depreciation; **~ planeada** ECON planned obsolescence; **~ recuperable** CONT recapturable depreciation, ECON curable depreciation; **~ de saldo decreciente** CONT, FIN declining balance depreciation

depreciado: **no ~** *adj* COM GEN undepreciated

depreciar *vt* COM GEN depreciate, write off, RRHH *trabajo* downgrade, demote

depreciarse *v refl* COM GEN fall in value, depreciate

depredador, a *m,f* V&M predator

depresión *f* ECON depression, *de curva, gráfico* trough; **~ económica** ECON slump; **~ con inflación** ECON slumpflation (*jarg*)

deprimido *adj* BOLSA, ECON *regiones* depressed; **no ~** BOLSA undepressed

depuración *f* INFO debugging, MED AMB purification; **~ del agua** MED AMB water purification; **~ de aguas residuales** *m* IND, MED AMB sewage treatment, wastewater treatment

depurar *vt* INFO debug, MED AMB depurate, purify; ◆ **~ las aguas residuales** IND, MED AMB treat sewage, treat wastewater

derecha: **nueva ~** *f* ECON *ideología*, POL New Right

derechas: **de ~** *adj* POL right-wing

derechismo *m* POL *países comunistas* rightism

derecho *m* COM GEN entitlement, *permiso* right, RRHH *carrera* law; **~ absoluto** INMOB *pertenencia* absolute title; **~ de acceso** *Esp* (*cf derecho de ingreso AmL*) DER, INFO, INMOB access right; **~ de acción** DER chose in action; **~ adjetivo** DER adjective law; **~ a administrar** GES, RRHH right to manage; **~ administrativo** DER administrative law; **~ adquirido** COM GEN vested interest; **~ de adquisición de capital social** BOLSA equity warrant; **~ de aduana ad valórem** CONT, IMP/EXP, TRANSP ad valorem duty; **~ aduanero** FISC, IMP/EXP duty; **~ al subsuelo** INMOB mineral rights; **~ al trabajo** DER, RRHH right to work; **~ de andaje o de puerto** TRANSP groundage; **~ angloamericano** DER common law; **~ antiguo** DER old law; **~ de apelación** DER right of appeal; **~ aplicable a la informática** DER, INFO computer law; **~ arancelario** FISC, IMP/EXP excise duty; **~ de arrendamiento** DER *propiedad intelectual*, INMOB, PROT SOC rental right; **~ de arrendamiento vitalicio** INMOB life tenancy; **~ del arrendatario** INMOB *compensación de tierras* tenant right; **~ de asociación** RRHH right to associate; **~ de cancelación** BANCA right of offset; **~ civil** DER civil law; **~ de cláusula de seguro** SEG duty of assured clause; **~ de combinación** DER right of combination; **~ de compensación** DER right of redress; **~ compuesto** IMP/EXP *aduanas* compound duty; **~ de conmutación** SEG commutation right; **~ constitucional** DER constitutional law; **~ a convertir** BOLSA right to convert; **~ de la corona** FISC Crown royalty; **~ de devolución** COM GEN right of return; **~ de disociación** RRHH right to dissociate; **~ a disponer** COM GEN jus disponendi; **~ a empréstito público** BANCA public lending right (*PLR*); **~ de entrada** DER right of entry; **~ escrito** COM GEN lex scripta; **~ especial de suscripción de capital** BOLSA equity warrant; **~ especificado** FISC specified right; **~ específico** FISC, IMP/EXP specific duty; **~ de establecimiento** DER right of establishment; **~ exclusivo** DER, PATENT exclusive right; **~ de expropiación** INMOB eminent domain; **~ fiscal** DER,

FISC fiscal law, tax law; ~ **general de retención** INMOB general lien; ~ **de gentes** DER ius gentium; ~ **de gestión** GES, RRHH right to manage; ~ **de ingreso** AmL (*cf derecho de acceso Esp*) DER, INFO, INMOB access right; ~ **a la huelga** RRHH right to strike; ~ **del inquilino** DER, INMOB *compensación de tierras* tenant right; ~ **internacional** DER, POL international law; ~ **internacional privado** DER conflict of laws; ~ **jurisprudencial** DER case law; ~ **laboral** DER labor law (*AmE*), labour law (*BrE*); ~ **legal** DER legal right, statutory right; ~ **legal por prescripción** DER, INMOB prescriptive right; ~ **marítimo** DER maritime law; ~ **mercantil** DER business law, commercial law, mercantile law; ~ **no reclamado** DER unclaimed right; ~ **a organizarse** RRHH right to organize; ~ **parlamentario** DER statute law; ~ **de participación en una acción** BOLSA right of interest in a share; ~ **de la patente** DER, PATENT right to a patent; ~ **preferencial** BOLSA, COM GEN, PATENT, pre-emptive right; ~ **preferente** DER *derechos civiles* pre-emption, preferential rehiring; ~ **prendario** DER lien; ~ **de prioridad** BOLSA, COM GEN, DER, PATENT pre-emption right, pre-emptive right, priority right; ~ **privado** DER private law; ~ **procesal** DER adjective law; ~ **de prohibición** DER, PATENT prohibition right; ~ **de propiedad** COM GEN, DER, INMOB ownership, proprietorship; ~ **del proyecto** DER design right; ~ **público** DER public law; ~ **de reanudación** DER right of resumption; ~ **de recuperación** DER right of recovery; ~ **de redención** FIN right of redemption; ~ **de réplica** DER right of reply; ~ **de rescate** BANCA equity of redemption; ~ **de rescisión** DER right of rescission; ~ **de residencia** POL right of residence; ~ **de retención de mercancías en tránsito** DER stoppage in transit; ~ **de retracto** FIN right of redemption; ~ **de reventa** DER, V&M right of resale; ~ **romano** DER Roman law; ~ **a saber** POL right to know; ~ **sindical** RRHH right to organize; ~ **de sociedades** COM GEN, DER company law, corporation law; ~ **de sucesión** DER, FISC death duty (*obs*) (*BrE*), inheritance tax, succession law; ~ **de supervivencia** DER right of survivorship; ~ **de suscripción** BANCA *emisión de acciones* application fee, BOLSA subscription right, stock right, application right; ~ **sustantivo** DER substantive law; ~ **de tanteo** BOLSA, COM GEN, DER, PATENT *comercial* pre-emptive right; ~ **del tanto** BOLSA, COM GEN, DER, PATENT *comercial* pre-emptive right; ~ **a trabajar** DER, RRHH right to work; ~ **del trabajo** DER labor law (*AmE*), labour law (*BrE*); ~ **a vacaciones** RRHH holiday entitlement (*BrE*), vacation entitlement (*AmE*); ~ **de voto** COM GEN voting right, right to vote; ◆ **de ~** DER de jure; **por ~** DER ex claim; **con ~ a adjudicar** DER eligible to adjudicate; **sin ~ a apelar** DER with no right of appeal; **sin ~ a dividendo** DER ex dividend (*ex div.*); **por ~ propio** COM GEN in its own right; **sin ~ de suscripción** BOLSA ex-rights; **tener ~ a** COM GEN be eligible for

derechos *m pl* COM GEN rights; ~ **y acciones** DER, PATENT rights and actions; ~ **de aceptación** BANCA acceptance duty; ~ **de admisión** COM GEN admission fee; ~ **de aduana** FISC, IMP/EXP customs duty, excise duty; ~ **aduaneros** FISC, IMP/EXP customs duties; ~ **de almacenaje** IMP/EXP warehouse charges; ~ **de anclaje** COM GEN, TRANSP anchorage charges; ~ **de antena** MEDIOS air rights; ~ **arancelarios** FISC customs duties, duty, IMP/EXP customs duties; ~ **de atraque** TRANSP dock charges; ~ **de autor** COM GEN, MEDIOS, V&M author royalties, royalties; ~ **del beneficiario en los seguros de vida** SEG creditor rights life assurance, creditor rights life insurance; ~ **de canal** TRANSP *navegación* canal dues; ~ **de la carga** TRANSP *navegación* cargo dues; ~ **de certificación** BOLSA registration fee; ~ **cinematográficos** DER, MEDIOS film rights; ~ **civiles** DER, POL, PROT SOC civil rights; ~ **de cogestión** BOLSA codetermination rights; ~ **compensatorios** IMP/EXP countervailing duties; ~ **conferidos** PATENT rights afforded; ~ **consulares** ADMIN consular fees, IMP/EXP consular fees, consulage; ~ **por contenedor** TRANSP *navegación* container dues; ~ **de conversión** BOLSA conversion rights, rights of conversion; ~ **de desarrollo de un traspaso** INMOB transfer development rights; ~ **de ejecución** DER performing rights; ~ **elevados** FISC heavy duties; ~ **de emisión** MEDIOS air rights; ~ **de entrada** COM GEN entrance fee, TRANSP customs inwards, inward charges; ~ **especiales de giro** (*DEG*) BANCA, DER special drawing rights (*jarg*); ~ **exclusivos de negociación** RRHH sole bargaining rights; ~ **de explotación de un traspaso** INMOB transfer development rights; ~ **de fabricación** DER, IND, PATENT manufacturing rights; ~ **de faro** TRANSP *navegación* light dues; ~ **fiscales sobre la importación** FISC, IMP/EXP import duty (*ID*); ~ **del hombre** DER human rights; ~ **inalienables** DER vested rights; ~ **individuales** RRHH individual rights; ~ **de interpretación** MEDIOS performing rights; ~ **mineros** DER, IND mineral rights; ~ **de muelle** TRANSP dock dues, wharf dues, wharfage dues, *tarifa* wharfage; ~ **naturales** DER natural rights; ~ **de navegación fluvial** TRANSP river tonnage dues; ~ **de negociación** BOLSA rights of exchange, trading rights; ~ **del ocupante ilegal** DER, INMOB squatter's rights; ~ **pagados de un barco de vapor** TRANSP steamer pays dues (*spd*); ~ **pagados por el fletador** TRANSP *navegación* charterer's pay dues (*cpd*); ~ **a pagar por los pasajeros** OCIO passenger dues; ~ **de patente** COM GEN patent rights, patent royalties, royalties, royalty; ~ **de pensión de jubilación** COM GEN retirement pension rights; ~ **de la propiedad** COM GEN property rights, proprietary rights; ~ **de propiedad en un seguro de vida** SEG ownership rights under life insurance; ~ **proteccionistas** FISC protective duties; ~ **de puerto** FISC, IMP/EXP, TRANSP harbor dues (*AmE*), harbour dues (*BrE*), port charges, port dues (*PD*); ~ **de remolque** TRANSP towage charges, towage dues; ~ **ribereños** DER riparian rights; ~ **sindicales** RRHH union rights; ~ **sobre la propiedad intelectual** DER, PATENT intellectual property rights; ~ **de sucesión** FISC death tax, estate duty; ~ **de tasación** BOLSA appraisal rights (*AmE*); ~ **de tonelaje** TRANSP tonnage dues; ~ **de tráfico** TRANSP traffic rights; ~ **de transferencia** DER transfer fees; ~ **de tránsito** TRANSP transit rights; ~ **de traspaso** OCIO *deporte* transfer fee; ~ **a voto** DER *de socios de empresa* equal voting rights; ~ **de vuelo** DER, TRANSP air rights; ◆ **con ~** BOLSA cum rights; **todos los ~ reservados** DER, PATENT all rights reserved, copyright

deriva[1]: **a la ~** *adj* TRANSP *navegación* adrift

deriva[2]: ~ **salarial** *f jarg* RRHH wage drift (*jarg*)

derivada *f* BOLSA derivative

derivador *m* BOLSA shunter

derivar *vt* COM GEN *llamada telefónica* tap, ECON spin off

derogación *f* COM GEN abolition, DER derogation

derogar *vt* COM GEN, DER abolish, derogate

derrama *f* COM GEN, DER apportionment

derrimido *adj* BOLSA *mercado* heavy (*jarg*)

derrumbarse *v refl* COM GEN *planes, edificios* fall down, *sistema* collapse

desacato *m* DER contempt of court

desaceleración *f* COM GEN, ECON deceleration

desacelerar *vi* COM GEN, ECON decelerate

desactivado *adj* INFO disabled

desactivar *vt* INFO lock

desacuerdo *m* COM GEN fallout (*infrml*), misalignment (*AmE*), *disputa* disagreement; ♦ **estar en ~** COM GEN be in disagreement

desaduanado: ~ sin inspección *adj* IMP/EXP cleared without examination (*CWE*)

desafiar *vt* COM GEN, RRHH challenge

desafío: ~ en el puesto *m* RRHH job challenge; **~ en el trabajo** *m* RRHH job challenge

desagregar *vt* CONT *costes* break down

desaguar *vt* IND run off

desagüe *m* IND run-off, MED AMB effluence, SEG *reaseguros* drain, TRANSP *para residuos peligrosos* outlet; **~ industrial** MED AMB industrial discharge

desahorro *m* ECON dissaving

desahuciar *vt* DER, INMOB dispossess

desahucio *m* DER, INMOB eviction; **~ efectivo** DER, INMOB actual eviction; **~ por represalia** DER, INMOB retaliatory eviction

desajustado *adj* COM GEN *números, estadísticas* unadjusted

desajuste: ~ de precios *m* BOLSA price gap

desalentar *vt* COM GEN discourage

desaliento: ~ mercantil *m* ECON slackening

desalineación *f* COM GEN misalignment, CONT mismatch

desalojar *vt* DER, INMOB evict

desalojo *m* DER, INMOB eviction; **~ constructivo** DER, INMOB constructive eviction; **~ parcial** DER, INMOB partial eviction

desanimar *vt* RRHH demotivate; ♦ **~ a alguien** RRHH take the wind out of sb's sails

desánimo *m* RRHH demotivation; **~ comercial** ECON slackening

desarmado *adj* TRANSP laid-up

desarmar *vt* TRANSP lay up

desarmonizar *vt* FIN degear

desarrollar *vt* IND *prototipo, modelo nuevo*, INFO *sistemas, programas*, TRANSP *prototipo, modelo nuevo* develop

desarrollarse *v refl* ECON spread

desarrollo¹: en ~ *adj* COM GEN developing, developmental

desarrollo² *m* COM GEN *de operaciones* development, flow; **~ administrativo** GES management development; **~ de una auditoría** CONT audit activity; **~ comercial** COM GEN, INMOB commercial development; **~ económico** ECON, POL economic development; **~ educativo** COM GEN, PROT SOC educational development; **~ de ejecutivos** COM GEN, GES executive development; **~ empresarial** COM GEN, GES business development; **~ formal de la administración** GES formal management development; **~ de marca** V&M brand development; **~ de mercado** V&M market development; **~ normal de la empresa** COM GEN normal course of business; **~ de nuevo producto** V&M new-product development; **~ por objetivos** GES, RRHH performance against objectives; **~ de la organización** GES organization development; **~ organizacional** GES organizational development; **~ del personal** GES, RRHH staff development; **~ personal** RRHH personal growth; **~ previsto de una unidad** INMOB planned unit development (*PUD*); **~ de producto** V&M product development; **~ profesional** RRHH career advancement, career development; **~ del programa** INFO program flow; **~ público** ECON public development; **~ de recursos humanos** (*DRH*) RRHH human resource development (*HRD*); **~ regional** ECON regional development; **~ del sistema** INFO system development; **~ sostenible** ECON, MED AMB, POL sustainable development; **~ por zonas** COM GEN strip development

desarrumar *vt* TRANSP break bulk

desastre *m* COM GEN *precios* collapse, **~ económico** ECON economic disaster

desatascamiento: ~ del mercado *m* ECON market clearing

desatender: ~ el pago de un cheque *fra* BANCA dishonor a check (*AmE*), dishonour a cheque (*BrE*)

desatendido *adj* INFO unattended

desbaratar *vt* COM GEN defeat

desbloquear *vt* BANCA *fondos* release, COM GEN, INFO *teclado* unblock, unlock

desbloqueo: ~ de los sueldos *m* BANCA release of pay checks (*AmE*), release of pay cheques (*BrE*)

desbordamiento *m* COM GEN spillover, V&M *mercadotecnia* overkill (*infrml*)

desbordarse *v refl* COM GEN spill over

descalificación *f* RRHH deskilling

descapitalizado *adj* COM GEN, FIN, IND undercapitalized

descarga *f* COM GEN logging, TRANSP off-loading, unloading, outlet; **~ a flote** *m* TRANSP *navegación* discharge afloat (*D/A*)

descargar *vt* COM GEN *responsabilidad, trabajo* offload, DER acquit, TRANSP offload, break bulk, unload

descargo *m* COM GEN off-loading, DER *de deuda* acquittance, *del acusado* acquittal, TRANSP off-loading, unloading

descartar *vt* COM GEN *idea, proyecto* scrap, MEDIOS *prensa* spike (*jarg*)

descendente *adj* COM GEN *tendencia* downward, INFO *dirección, posición* down, *pantalla del ordenador* downward

descendientes *m pl* DER issue

descenso *m* COM GEN, ECON downswing, downturn, fall; **~ en picado** COM GEN, ECON *mercados bursátiles* sharp dive; **~ de la población** ECON fall in population; **~ de recursos** CONT lapsing resources; **~ en la reserva de divisas** BOLSA fall in foreign exchange reserves; **~ de suministros** ECON fall in supplies

descentralización *f* COM GEN decentralization

descentralizar *vt* COM GEN decentralize

descifrado *m* COM GEN, COMS, INFO *programa* decryption

desciframiento *m* COM GEN, COMS, INFO *programa* decryption

descifrar *vt* COM GEN, COMS, INFO decrypt, unscramble

descompartimentalización *f* BOLSA decompartmentalization

descomponer *vt* POL, RRHH break down

descomposición: ~ **del trabajo en fases** *f* RRHH breakdown of tasks

desconcentración: ~ **de la carga** *f* TRANSP cargo disassembly

desconectado *adj* INFO off-line

descongelar *vt* ECON unfreeze

desconocido *adj* COM GEN unknown; ♦ ~ **en esta dirección** COMS unknown at this address

descontable *adj* COM GEN bankable, discountable; **no** ~ COM GEN indiscountable

descontado *adj* COM GEN discounted

descontar *vt* COM GEN deduct, discount (*dis, disc.*)

descontento: ~ **en el lugar de trabajo** *m* RRHH discontent in the workplace; ~ **del personal** *m* RRHH labor unrest (*AmE*), labour unrest (*BrE*)

descontratación *f* RRHH decruitment

describir *vt* COM GEN describe

descripción *f* COM GEN description; ~ **comercial** V&M *publicidad* trade description; ~ **de formato** ADMIN, INFO format; ~ **general** COM GEN overview; ~ **legal** DER legal description; ~ **de la patente** PATENT patent specification; ~ **de los productos** PATENT specification of goods; ~ **de la propiedad en venta** INMOB particulars of sale; ~ **de puesto** RRHH job description; ~ **del riesgo** BOLSA disclosure; ~ **de riesgo operativo** SEG description of operational risk; ~ **de los servicios** PATENT specification of services; ♦ **hacer una** ~ **de** COM GEN plan

descriptivo *adj* COM GEN descriptive

descuadre *m* CONT mismatch

descualificación *f* RRHH deskilling

descubierto[1]**: en** ~ *adj* BANCA overdrawn (*O/D*)

descubierto[2] *m* BANCA overdraft (*O/D*), BOLSA short (*jarg*), FISC deficiency; ~ **bancario** BANCA bank overdraft; ~ **no garantizado** BANCA unsecured overdraft

descubrimiento: ~ **importante** *m* ECON breakthrough

descuento *m* (*dto.*) COM GEN discount (*dis, disc.*), discounting, valuation allowance; ~ **por adelantado** FIN prepaid interest; ~ **bancario** BANCA bank discount, banker's discount; ~ **caducado** COM GEN lapsed discount; ~ **de cambio** BOLSA exchange discount; ~ **por cantidad** COM GEN, CONT, V&M quantity discount; ~ **con certificado** FIN warrant discounting; ~ **a clientes** COM GEN sales discount; ~ **comercial** COM GEN, CONT trade allowance, trade discount; ~ **por compra a granel** COM GEN bulk discount; ~ **de deudas** FIN debt factoring; ~ **de distribución** V&M distribution allowance; ~ **en efectivo** FIN hard discount; ~ **de efectos** CONT discounting of notes (*AmE*), discounting of bills (*BrE*); ~ **en factura** V&M invoice discount; ~ **hipotecario** BANCA, FIN, INMOB mortgage discount; ~ **de impuestos** FISC tax discounting; ~ **inmediato** TRANSP immediate rebate; ~ **de interés** FIN interest rebate; ~ **de liquidación** FIN settlement discount; ~ **de mercancías** V&M merchandise allowance; ~ **no amortizado sobre Bonos del Tesoro** BOLSA unamortized discount on Treasury bills; ~ **por pago al contado** V&M cash discount; ~ **en precios** COM GEN mark-down; ~ **de primas** FIN premium statement; ~ **promocional** V&M *publicidad* promotional allowance; ~ **con rebaja de valor** FISC writing down allowance; ~ **retrospectivo** TRANSP retrospective rebate; ~ **de series** V&M series discount; ~ **sobre acciones** BOLSA, COM GEN stock discount; ~ **sobre bonos** BOLSA bond discount; ~ **sobre bonos no amortizados** BOLSA unamortized bond discount; ~ **de temporada** V&M seasonal discount; ~ **a término** COM GEN forward discount; ~ **de transferencia** BOLSA handling allowance; ~ **de venta** BOLSA selling concession, V&M sales discount; ~ **por volumen** COM GEN volume discount; ~ **por volumen de mercancía** V&M volume merchandise allowance; ♦ **con** ~ V&M at a discount (*AAD*); **sin** ~ V&M no discount (*ND*)

descuentos: ~ **considerables** *m pl* FISC deep discounts; ~ **en nómina** *m pl* RRHH holdback pay

descuidado *adj* COM GEN in a state of neglect

descuido *m* COM GEN mistake, negligence

desdoblamiento: ~ **de dividendos** *m* FIN, FISC dividend stripping (*jarg*); ~ **de precios** *m* FIN split rating

desdoble: ~ **de acciones** *m* COM GEN stock split down

desdomiciliación *f* COM GEN, FISC dedomiciling

desechos *m pl* IND, MED AMB waste; ~ **industriales** IND, MED AMB industrial refuse; ~ **líquidos de materiales textiles** IND, MED AMB *carga peligrosa* wet textile waste; ~ **plásticos** IND, MED AMB plastic waste

deseconomía *f* ECON diseconomy; ~ **de aglomeración** ECON agglomeration diseconomy; ~ **de escala** ECON diseconomy of scale

desembarcadero *m* TRANSP landing stage, *puerto* wharf

desembarque *m* TRANSP de-planing (*AmE*), disembarkation

desembolsable *adj* CONT, ECON, FIN disbursable

desembolsar *vt* CONT, ECON, FIN disburse, pay out, *dinero* lash out (*jarg*)

desembolso *m* CONT, ECON, FIN disbursement, outgoings, outlay, expenditure; ~ **por adelantado** TRANSP advanced disbursement; ~ **bilateral** ECON *asistencia al desarrollo* bilateral disbursement; ~ **de capital** ECON, FIN capital outlay; ~ **inicial** CONT *de compra*, FIN initial outlay; ~ **multilateral** ECON *de ayuda al desarrollo* multilateral disbursement; ~ **neto** ECON *ayuda al desarrollo* net expenditure; ~ **no rentable** FIN wasteful expenditure; ~ **presupuestario** POL *gubernamental* budgetary expenditure

desembolsos: ~ **de caja** *m pl* CONT cash disbursement; ~ **exigidos sobre acciones** *m pl* CONT called-up share capital; ~ **monetarios** *m pl* ECON pecuniary returns

desempaquetado *adj* COM GEN unpacked

desempaquetar *vt* COM GEN unpack

desempeñar *vt* COM GEN play; ♦ ~ **un cometido** COM GEN play a role; ~ **un papel en** COM GEN play a part in

desempeño *m* DER acquittal; ~ **del puesto** *f* AmL (*cf ejecución del trabajo Esp*) RRHH job performance

desempleado *adj* COM GEN jobless, out of work, unemployed, workless

desempleados: los ~ *m pl* COM GEN the jobless, the unemployed; ~ **crónicos** *m pl* ECON, PROT SOC, RRHH long-term unemployed

desempleo *m* COM GEN unemployment; ~ **alimentado por migración** ECON migration-fed unemployment; ~ **cíclico** ECON, PROT SOC, RRHH cyclical unemployment; ~ **coyuntural** ECON, PROT SOC, RRHH frictional unemployment; ~ **creciente** ECON, PROT SOC, RRHH rising unemployment; ~ **crónico** ECON, PROT SOC, RRHH chronic unemployment; ~ **disfrazado** ECON, PROT SOC, RRHH disguised unemployment; ~ **encubierto** ECON, PROT SOC, RRHH concealed unemployment, hidden unemployment; ~ **estacional** ECON, PROT SOC, RRHH seasonal unemployment; ~ **estructural** ECON, PROT SOC, RRHH structural unemployment; ~ **friccional** ECON, PROT SOC, RRHH frictional unemployment; ~ **involuntario** ECON, PROT SOC, RRHH involuntary unemployment; ~ **de larga duración** ECON, PROT SOC, RRHH long-term unemployment; ~ **masivo** ECON, POL, PROT SOC, RRHH mass unemployment

deseo: ~ **de comprar** *m* COM GEN, V&M desire to purchase; ~ **del consumidor** *m* V&M consumer want

desequilibrado *adj* BOLSA unmatched

desequilibrar *vt* COM GEN wrong-foot (*infrml*)

desequilibrio *m* ECON disequilibrium, imbalance; ~ **comercial** ECON trade imbalance; ~ **económico** ECON economic disequilibrium; ~ **estructural** ECON fundamental disequilibrium; ~ **fundamental** ECON fundamental disequilibrium; ~ **de intercambios** ECON imbalance of trade; ~ **monetario** ECON financial disequilibrium; ~ **de órdenes** BOLSA imbalance of orders; ~ **de precios** ECON financial disequilibrium

desertificación *f* MED AMB desertification

desestabilizar *vt* COM GEN destabilize; ♦ ~ **una situación** COM GEN rock the boat (*infrml*)

desestacionalizado *adj* COM GEN, ECON, RRHH seasonally-adjusted

desestructurado *adj* COM GEN unstructured

desfalcador, a *m,f* COM GEN, DER, FIN embezzler

desfalcar *vt* COM GEN, DER, FIN embezzle, fiddle (*infrml*)

desfalco *m* COM GEN, DER, FIN embezzlement, fiddling (*infrml*)

desfasado: ~ **por el viaje** *adj* TRANSP *avión* jet lagged

desfase: ~ **cronológico** *m* ECON, FISC time lag; ~ **entre generaciones** *m* PROT SOC generation gap; ~ **salarial** *m* *Esp* (*cf rezago salarial AmL*) RRHH wage lag

desfavorable *adj* COM GEN unfavorable (*AmE*), unfavourable (*BrE*), adverse

desfavorecido *adj* COM GEN underprivileged

desfiguración *f* FISC misrepresentation; ♦ ~ **voluntaria de los hechos** DER wilful misrepresentation of facts

desfile: ~ **de modas** *m* COM GEN fashion parade

desforestación *f* MED AMB deforestation

desgarro: ~ **causado por ganchos** *m* TRANSP *carga y descarga* hook damage

desgaste: ~ **del mercado** *m* V&M market attrition; ~ **natural** *m* COM GEN fair wear and tear, natural wastage, natural wear and tear

desglosar *vt* BANCA, CONT *costes* break down, strip

desglose *m* BANCA, CONT unbundling, IND breakdown; ~ **de activos** CONT, ECON, FIN asset stripping; ~ **del contenido** TRANSP specification of total contents (*ETC*); ~ **de gastos** COM GEN cost trimming; ~ **de operaciones** IND operations breakdown; ~ **del trabajo** RRHH job breakdown

desgravable *adj* FISC eligible for tax relief

desgravación *f* FISC allowance, tax relief; ~ **al matrimonio** FISC married couples' allowance (*BrE*); ~ **básica** FISC basic relief; ~ **de bienes y servicios** FISC goods and services tax credit; ~ **de los combustibles** FISC fuel benefits; ~ **de los costes de inversión** *Esp* (*cf desgravación de los costos de inversión AmL*) FISC capital cost allowance (*CCA*); ~ **de los costos de inversión** *AmL* (*cf desgravación de los costes de inversión Esp*) FISC capital cost allowance (*CCA*); ~ **por devolución de**

impuestos FIN, FISC clawback; ~ **de dividendo** FISC dividend tax credit; ~ **empresarial** FISC corporate tax credit; ~ **federal de dividendos** FISC federal dividend tax credit; ~ **federal de un impuesto extranjero no mercantil** FISC federal non-business foreign tax credit; ~ **federal de impuestos pagados en el exterior** FISC federal foreign tax credit; ~ **federal de inversiones** FISC federal investment tax credit; ~ **federal reembolsable sobre ventas** FISC refundable federal sales tax credit; ~ **federal de las ventas** FISC federal sales tax credit; ~ **fiscal** FISC tax allowance, refund of tax, tax relief, tax shield; ~ **fiscal del capital de riesgo de las PYME** FISC small business venture capital tax credit; ~ **fiscal para coches de empresa** FISC tax relief for business cars; ~ **fiscal de coste de vida** *Esp* (*cf desgravación fiscal de costo de vida AmL*) FISC cost-of-living tax credit; ~ **fiscal de costo de vida** *AmL* (*cf desgravación fiscal de coste de vida Esp*) FISC cost-of-living tax credit; ~ **fiscal por disminución mental o física** FISC credit for mental or physical impairment, mental or physical impairment tax credit; ~ **fiscal del empleo** FISC employment tax credit; ~ **fiscal de los inquilinos** FISC renters' tax credit; ~ **fiscal de intereses de bonos** FISC bond interest tax allowance; ~ **fiscal mínima** FISC minimum tax credit; ~ **fiscal en origen** FISC tax relief at source (*BrE*); ~ **fiscal de la propiedad** FISC, INMOB property tax allowance, property tax credit; ~ **fiscal reembolsable** FISC refundable tax credit; ~ **de gastos de atención médica** PROT SOC, SEG medical expense credit; ~ **de gastos de exploración y explotación** FISC exploration and development expense tax credit; ~ **de gastos personales** FISC allowance for personal expenses; ~ **hipotecaria** BANCA, FIN, FISC mortgage relief; ~ **de impuestos pagados en el extranjero** FISC foreign tax credit; ~ **por indexación** FISC indexation allowance; ~ **de ingresos no empresariales gravados en el exterior** FISC nonbusiness income foreign tax credit; ~ **de los ingresos personales** FISC personal income tax credit, personal tax credit; ~ **de insumos** FISC input tax credit; ~ **de los intereses** ECON interest relief; ~ **de intereses hipotecarios en origen** BANCA, FIN, FISC mortgage interest relief at source; ~ **interior por transformación** FISC inward processing relief (*IPR*); ~ **por inventario** FISC inventory allowance; ~ **por inversión** FISC investment allowance; ~ **de la inversión empresarial** FISC business investment tax allowance, corporation investment allowance; ~ **de la investigación científica** FISC scientific research tax credit; ~ **por kilometraje** FISC motor mileage allowance (*BrE*); ~ **de pensión** FISC pension credit, pension income credit, pension tax credit; ~ **personal adicional** FISC additional personal allowance; ~ **sobre bienes de capital** CONT, FISC capital allowance; ~ **de suma redonda** FISC round sum allowance; ~ **de la venta** FISC sales tax credit; ~ **para los veteranos de guerra** FISC war veteran's allowance

desgravaciones: ~ **de suma redonda** *f pl* FISC round sum allowances

deshacerse: ~ **de algo** *fra* FISC divest oneself of sth; ~ **de las existencias** *fra* V&M dispose of stock

designación *f* COM GEN, PATENT appointment, designation; ~ **conjunta** PATENT joint designation

designado, -a *m,f* DER appointee

designar *vt* COM GEN *empleado* appoint, designate, nominate, POL *cargo* slate (*AmE*)

desigual *adj* V&M ragged

desigualdad *f* CONT mismatch, ECON, POL, RRHH inequality; ◆ **en ~ de condiciones** DER, FISC non-arm's-length

desincentivo *m* ECON disincentive

desindicalización *f* RRHH de-unionization (*BrE*)

desindustrialización *f* ECON, IND deindustrialization

desinflación *f* ECON deflation

desinformación *f* POL disinformation

desintegración *f* COM GEN, ECON, POL disintegration

desintermediación *f* BANCA, ECON, FIN disintermediation, nonintervention

desinversión *f* FIN disinvestment

desinversor, a *m,f* FIN disinvestor

desinvertir *vt* FIN disinvest

desistimiento: ~ de contrato *m* DER anticipatory breach

desistir *vi* COM GEN desist; ◆ **~ de una apelación** FISC discontinue an appeal

deslizador: ~ propulsado a reacción *m* TRANSP jet foil

desmarketing *m* V&M demarketing

desmaterialización *f* BOLSA, ECON dematerialization

desmaterializado *adj* BOLSA *certificados de depósito*, ECON dematerialized

desmonetización *f* ECON demonetization; **~ del oro** ECON gold demonetization

desmontado: ~ parcialmente *adj* TRANSP *remesa* partially knocked down (*PKD*)

desmontaje: ~ de un trust *m* COM GEN trustbusting (*infrml*)

desmontar *vt* TRANSP strip

desmoralizar *vt* RRHH demotivate, demoralize

desmotivación *f* RRHH demotivation

desmotivar *vt* RRHH demotivate

desnacionalización *f* POL denationalization

desnudo *adj* SEG bare

desobediencia *f* DER contempt of court

desocupación *f* RRHH dehiring (*AmE*), dismissal

desordenado *adj* V&M ragged

despachador, a *m,f* BANCA clearer

despachar *vt* TRANSP *tráfico* dispatch; ◆ **~ por favor** COMS please forward

despacho *m* ADMIN, COM GEN office, TRANSP *aviación* dispatching, *navegación* dispatch, shipping; **~ de abogados** DER barristers' chambers (*BrE*); **~ adelantado de carga únicamente** TRANSP dispatch loading only (*DLO*); **~ adelantado de la descarga únicamente** *f* TRANSP dispatch discharging only (*DDO*); **~ de aduanas** IMP/EXP customs clearance (*CCL*); **~ aduanero** IMP/EXP customs clearance (*CCL*); **~ de barco** IMP/EXP, TRANSP clearance of ship; **~ de billetes** OCIO, TRANSP *ferrocarril* booking office, ticket office; **~ de un buque hacia el exterior** IMP/EXP, TRANSP clearance outward of a vessel; **~ de carga por aduanas** IMP/EXP, TRANSP customs cargo clearance; **~ de carga de mercancías** IMP/EXP, TRANSP clearance of cargo goods; **~ de consultoría** RRHH consulting office; **~ en contenedores** TRANSP containerized shipping; **~ contenedorizado** TRANSP *navegación* containerized shipping; **~ de entrada** IMP/EXP, TRANSP clearance inwards; **~ privado** RRHH private office; **~ de salida** IMP/EXP, TRANSP clearance outwards

despedazar: ~ un proyecto *fra* FIN chunk a project

despedida *f* COMS letterfoot

despedido *adj* RRHH redundant, fired (*infrml*), sacked (*infrml*), ankled (*jarg*); ◆ **ser ~** RRHH get the sack (*infrml*)

despedir *vt* RRHH *personal* boot out (*infrml*), discharge, dismiss, fire (*infrml*), give sb their cards (*infrml*) (*BrE*), give sb the sack (*infrml*), dehire (*AmE*), lay off (*BrE*), make redundant, sack (*infrml*)

despedirse *v refl* GES book out, RRHH take one's leave; ◆ **~ a la francesa** COM GEN take French leave

despegar 1. *vt* COM GEN *quitar* take off; **2.** *vi* TRANSP *avión* take off

despegue *m* COM GEN, ECON, TRANSP takeoff; **~ y aterrizaje corto** TRANSP short takeoff and landing (*STOL*)

despejar *vt* COM GEN gin out (*infrml*)

desperdicio *m* MED AMB waste product, RRHH wastage (*jarg*)

desperdicios: ~ domésticos *m pl* MED AMB domestic waste

despido *m* RRHH dismissal, firing (*infrml*), redundancy; **~ por causa justa** RRHH just cause dismissal; **~ colectivo** RRHH collective dismissal, mass dismissal; **~ con una compensación en metálico** RRHH golden handshake (*infrml*); **~ constructivo** RRHH constructive dismissal; **~ disciplinario** RRHH disciplinary layoff; **~ del fideicomisario** DER discharge of the trustee; **~ improcedente** RRHH wrongful dismissal; **~ injustificado** RRHH unfair dismissal; **~ justificado** RRHH discharge for cause (*BrE*), fair dismissal; **~ masivo** RRHH mass redundancy; **~ motivado** RRHH discharge for cause (*BrE*); **~ con notificación** RRHH termination with notice (*BrE*); **~ obligatorio** RRHH compulsory redundancy; **~ de personal** RRHH lay-off; **~ sumario** COM GEN, RRHH summary dismissal; **~ voluntario** RRHH voluntary redundancy

despilfarro *m* FISC three-martini lunch (*infrml*) (*AmE*), extravagance, RRHH wastage (*jarg*)

desplazamiento: ~ de bloque *m* INFO *procesamiento de datos, textos* block move; **~ del consumo** *m* V&M shift in consumption; **~ de la demanda** *m* V&M shift in demand; **~ a la derecha** *m* INFO right shift; **~ hacia abajo** *m* INFO scrolling down; **~ hacia arriba** *m* INFO scrolling up; **~ interior** *m* IMP/EXP, TRANSP *navegación* inland haulage; **~ a la izquierda** *m* INFO left shift; **~ en lastre** *m* TRANSP *navegación* light displacement; **~ en pantalla** *m* INFO scrolling

desplazar: ~ línea a línea *fra* INFO *imagen, texto* scroll

desplegable *m* MEDIOS gatefold

desplegar *vt* COM GEN *equipo* deploy

despliegue *m* COM GEN, RRHH deployment

desplome *m* BOLSA break, crash, ECON *precio del petróleo, del comercio mundial* slump; **~ del fondo** BOLSA bottom dropped out (*BDO*)

despoblación *f* COM GEN depopulation

despojar *vt* COM GEN evict

desposeimiento *m* DER divestiture; **~ horizontal** IND horizontal divestiture (*jarg*)

despreciar *vt* COM GEN sneeze at

desprenderse: ~ de *v refl* COM GEN, RRHH *trabajadores, existencias* shed

desprovisto: ~ de *adj* COM GEN void of

desreconocimiento *m* RRHH derecognition

desregulación *f* COM GEN, ECON, POL deregulation;

~ global ECON global deregulation; **~ de precios** COM GEN price deregulation

desregular vt COM GEN, ECON, POL deregulate

destacado adj COM GEN top-ranking

destacar vt COM GEN diferencias, INFO documento procesado highlight

destajo m COM GEN task work, RRHH lump

destilación f COM GEN distilling

destinar vt CONT, ECON, FIN allocate, appropriate, earmark; ◆ **~ a la oficina** COM GEN apply at the office

destinatario, -a m,f COM GEN recipient, receiver, COMS addressee; **~ del casco desnudo** TRANSP bare-boat consignee; ◆ **si no se entrega al ~, por favor devuélvase al remitente** COMS if undelivered please return to sender

destino m INFO destination, RRHH posting, TRANSP destination; **~ de los impuestos** f FISC revenue allocation; ◆ **con ~ a** TRANSP bound for

destinos: ~ múltiples m pl TRANSP multidelivery

destituir: ~ al consejo vi GES unseat the board

destreza f RRHH manual skill

destrucción f MED AMB selvas pluviales destruction; **~ creativa** ECON creative destruction

destructora: ~ de documentos f ADMIN, INFO paper shredder

desuso: en ~ fra COM GEN in abeyance

desutilidad f ECON disutility

desvalorización f ECON devalorization; **~ del capital propio** BOLSA dilution of equity

desventaja f COM GEN, ECON, POL disadvantage, minus advantage (jarg)

desventajado adj COM GEN, ECON, POL disadvantaged

desventajoso adj COM GEN, ECON, POL disadvantageous

desviación f COM GEN discrepancy, CONT variance, DER en la ley deviation, ECON shift; **~ de corrientes comerciales** ECON, IMP/EXP, TRANSP trade diversion; **~ favorable** CONT favorable variance (AmE), favourable variance (BrE); **~ media** MAT average deviation, estadística mean deviation; **~ de la muestra** MAT estadística sampling deviation; **~ salarial** RRHH wage drift; **~ secundaria** TRANSP extension fork; **~ típica** FIN, MAT estadística standard deviation

desviar vt COM GEN turn away, recursos tap

desvío m COM GEN detour, INFO switch, TRANSP Esp (cf reencaminamiento AmL) del tráfico diversion; **~ de llamada** COMS telefonía call forwarding; **~ de la ruta** Esp (cf reencaminamiento de la ruta AmL) TRANSP del tráfico route diversion

detalle m COM GEN factura, CONT item, itemization; **~ del balance** CONT balance item; **~ de los empleados** RRHH personnel specification

detallista mf V&M retailer

detección: ~ de averías f INFO diagnostic

detención f COM GEN detention, DER, SEG marítimo arrest, TRANSP de barco, carga detention

detener vt COM GEN competición block, acciones de quiebra stop

detenido: estar ~ fra DER be on remand

detentado: no ~ adj BOLSA not held

detentar: ~ el poder fra POL hold power

deteriorado: ~ en tránsito adj TRANSP damaged in transit

deteriorar vt ECON moneda impair

deteriorarse v refl COM GEN age, deteriorate

deteriorización: ~ de precios f COM GEN, ECON price deterioration

deterioro m COM GEN deterioration, FISC impairment; **~ físico** CONT cuentas anuales physical deterioration

determinación f FISC determination; **~ del activo fijo** CONT fixed asset assessment; **~ del activo neto** CONT net worth assessment; **~ de beneficios** GES profit splitting; **~ de los costes** Esp (cf determinación de los costos AmL) BOLSA fixing of costs; **~ de costes estándar** Esp (cf determinación de costos estandard AmL) CONT, FIN standard costing; **~ de los costos** AmL (cf determinación de los costes Esp) BOLSA fixing of costs; **~ de costos estándar** AmL (cf determinación de costes estandard Esp) CONT, FIN standard costing; **~ de los hechos** DER fact-finding; **~ del impuesto** FISC tax assessment; **~ de itinerarios** COM GEN, INFO, TRANSP datos routing; **~ de objetivos** COM GEN, V&M target setting, objective-setting; **~ de precios** V&M price determination; **~ de precios del mercado** COM GEN market pricing; **~ de precios de venta con pérdida** V&M loss leader pricing; **~ del problema** INFO problem determination; **~ de una renta** DER settling of an annuity; **~ de la tara** COM GEN taring; **~ de tareas** COM GEN task setting; **~ del valor neto** CONT net worth assessment

determinadas: ~ condiciones f pl COM GEN certain conditions

determinante: ~ de precio m V&M price determinant

determinar vt COM GEN precio ascertain, determine, valor set; ◆ **~ judicialmente** COM GEN, DER demanda adjudicate; **~ una posición** BOLSA position

determinismo: ~ ambiental m MED AMB environmental determinism

detonador m TRANSP detonator

detrimento: en ~ de fra COM GEN to the detriment of

deuda f COM GEN debt, liability; **~ de acciones, bonos y valores de empresa** BANCA corporate debt securities; **~ activa** BANCA, CONT, FIN uncanceleddebt (AmE), uncancelled debt (BrE); **~ amortizable** COM GEN, CONT, FIN amortizable debt; **~ anulada** BANCA, COM GEN, CONT, FIN canceled debt (AmE), cancelled debt (BrE); **~ atrasada** BANCA, BOLSA arrears; **~ bruta** BANCA, FIN gross debt; **~ bruta federal** ECON gross Federal debt (AmE); **~ de cobro dudoso** BANCA, CONT, FIN doubtful debt; **~ conjunta** COM GEN, CONT, FIN community debt; **~ consolidada** BOLSA, CONT, FIN consolidated debt, funded debt; **~ contabilizada** CONT book debt; **~ a corto plazo** BANCA, CONT, FIN short-term debt; **~ debida a** CONT activa o pasiva debt owed to; **~ exigible** CONT solvent debt; **~ exterior** ECON, POL external debt; **~ externa** ECON, POL foreign debt; **~ fallida** CONT bad debt; **~ fiscal** FISC tax liability; **~ fiscal de una sociedad** FISC corporation tax liability; **~ flotante** FIN floating debt, unfunded debt; **~ garantizada** BANCA, FIN secured debt; **~ garantizada con bonos** BOLSA bonded debt; **~ hipotecaria** BANCA mortgage debt; **~ hipotecaria global** BANCA mortgage debt; **~ imperitiva** FISC tax liability; **~ incobrable** BANCA, COM GEN, CONT bad and doubtful debt, bad debt; **~ sin interés** CONT barren money; **~ intermedia** BOLSA mezzanine debt; **~ interna** ECON internal debt; **~ a largo plazo** BANCA, CONT, FIN long-term debt;

~ **mala y dudosa** BANCA, COM GEN, CONT bad and doubtful debt (*B&D*); ~ **nacional** ECON, POL national debt (*BrE*), public debt (*AmE*); ~ **neta** COM GEN net debt; ~ **no vencida** BOLSA unmatured debt; ~ **pasiva** COM GEN debt; ~ **pendiente** BANCA, CONT, FIN amount outstanding; ~ **pendiente de pago** BANCA, CONT, FIN outstanding debt; ~ **per capita** ECON per-capita debt; ~ **precedente** BANCA, CONT, FIN underlying debt; ~ **principal** BANCA senior debt; ~ **pública** ECON national debt (*BrE*), public debt (*AmE*); ~ **pública bruta** ECON Gross National Debt; ~ **pública total** ECON total public debt; ~ **quirografaria** BANCA, FIN unsecured debt; ~ **de recurso limitado** BANCA limited recourse debt; ~ **rentable** FIN self-supporting debt; ~ **representada por bonos** BOLSA bond debt; ~ **saldada** CONT liquidated debt; ~ **solvente** BANCA, FIN solvent debt; ~ **subordinada** BOLSA, FIN junior debt, subordinated debt; ~ **testamentaria** FISC testamentary debt; ~ **tributaria** FISC tax payable; ~ **tributaria ajustada** FISC adjusted tax payable; ~ **vencida** CONT debt due to solvent debt, FIN liquid debt, matured debt; ~ **vigente** BANCA effective debt

deudas *f pl* CONT liabilities, debts; ~ **bancarias** BANCA bank debts; ~ **comerciales** CONT trading debts; ~ **de juego** COM GEN gambling debts; ~ **a largo plazo** BANCA, CONT, FIN long-term liability; ~ **morosas** CONT bad debts

deudor, a *m,f* (*Dr*) COM GEN debtor (*Dr*); ~ **comercial** CONT trade debtor; ~ **dudoso(-a)** BANCA, CONT, FIN doubtful debtor; ~ **exterior** CONT external debtor; ~ **externo(-a)** CONT external debtor; ~ **fiscal** FISC tax debtor; ~ **hipotecario(-a)** BANCA, FIN mortgager; ~ **insolvente** COM GEN *compañía* lame duck (*jarg*); ~ **judicial** DER, FIN judgment debtor; ~ **moroso(-a)** BANCA bad debtor; ~ **principal** FIN, V&M principal debtor; ~ **por sentencia firme** DER, FIN judgment debtor; ~ **solidario(-a)** BANCA, CONT joint debtor; ~ **en virtud de una sentencia** DER, FIN judgment debtor

devaluación *f* ECON *internacional* devaluation, *moneda* debasement; ~ **monetaria** ECON *internacional*, FIN currency devaluation

devaluar *vt* ECON devalue, debase

devaluarse *v refl* ECON *moneda* devalue

devengado *adj* BANCA, CONT, FIN *intereses* accrued, accruing; **no** ~ BOLSA *cupón* unmatured

devengar *vt* BANCA, CONT, FIN accrue, bear; ◆ ~ **intereses** BANCA, CONT, FIN earn interest

devengo *m* BANCA, CONT, FIN accrual; ~ **modificado** BANCA, CONT, FIN modified accrual

devolución *f* DER, FISC refund, RRHH *comercialización* back payment, payback, TRANSP redelivery, V&M *comercialización* back payment; ~ **del alquiler** INMOB, PROT SOC rent rebate; ~ **anual** COM GEN annual repayment; ~ **de compras** V&M purchase returns; ~ **en cuotas iguales** BANCA level repayment, level payment; ~ **deducible** FISC allowable refund; ~ **de derechos** COM GEN drawback; ~ **de la deuda del sector público** ECON public sector debt repayment; ~ **económica** ECON economic devolution; ~ **por experiencia** SEG experience refund; ~ **de la fianza** COM GEN return of guarantee, return of guaranty; ~ **de las ganancias de capital** FISC capital gains refund; ~ **del impuesto** FISC tax refund; ~ **del impuesto sobre la renta** FISC income tax refund; ~ **de impuestos** FISC tax rebate; ~ **de préstamo** BANCA, FIN loan repayment; ~ **de recargo** FISC penalty return; ~ **en un solo pago** BANCA balloon repayment

devoluciones: ~ **de ventas** *f pl* CONT, FIN, V&M *estadística, ingresos* return on sales, sales returns

devolver *vt* BANCA pay back, BOLSA *futuros* bring back, COMS *paquete* return, FIN *dinero* pay back, RRHH *relaciones laborales* give back (*jarg*), V&M return; ◆ ~ **al remitente** COMS return to sender; ~ **una cantidad pagada de más** COM GEN *recaudación de impuestos*, FISC return amount overpaid; ~ **una llamada telefónica** COMS return a phone call; ~ **un préstamo** BANCA repay a loan

DG *abr* (*director general*) GES, RRHH CEO (*AmE*) (*chief executive officer*), COO (*chief operating officer*), GM (*general manager*), general director, senior manager

día *m* COM GEN day; ~ **anterior al de liquidación** BOLSA ticket day, name day; ~ **de asueto** *frml* OCIO, RRHH bank holiday (*BrE*), legal holiday (*AmE*); ~ **de aviso** TRANSP reporting day; ~ **de bancos** BANCA, CONT banking day; ~ **de calendario** COM GEN calendar day; ~ **de cesión** BOLSA *opciones* assignment day; ~ **de cierre anticipado** COM GEN early closing day; ~ **de compensación** BANCA clearing day; ~ **de cuenta** FIN account day; ~ **de descanso obligatorio** OCIO, RRHH bank holiday (*BrE*), legal holiday (*AmE*); ~ **designado** COM GEN appointed day; ~ **de elecciones** POL polling day; ~ **de embarque** TRANSP day of shipment; ~ **de entrega** BOLSA delivery day; ~ **de estudio** PROT SOC study day; ~ **de facturación** CONT billing day; ~ **feriado** COM GEN working holiday; ~ **festivo** COM GEN public holiday; ~ **hábil bancario** BANCA, CONT banking day; ~ **inhábil** DER, OCIO, RRHH bank holiday (*BrE*), legal holiday (*AmE*); ~ **laborable** COM GEN, RRHH business day, workday (*AmE*), working day (*BrE*); ~ **no laborable** COM GEN bank holiday (*BrE*), legal holiday (*AmE*), public holiday; ~ **laborable consecutivo** TRANSP *póliza de fletes* running working day; ~ **libre** RRHH day off; ~ **de liquidación en la bolsa** BOLSA settlement day; ~ **del mercado** BOLSA market day; ~ **natural** *f* DER *contrato* calendar day; ~ **de notificación** BOLSA assignment day; ~ **de oleaje** TRANSP surf day; ~ **de pago** BOLSA, COM GEN payment date, date of payment, RRHH payday; ~ **de pago de jornales** RRHH payday; ~ **previo** BOLSA preliminary day; ~ **del primer aviso** FIN first notice day; ~ **del reporte** BOLSA contango day (*BrE*); ~ **de reportes** BOLSA continuation day; ~ **reservable** BANCA reservable day; ~ **rojo** TRANSP peak day travel for trains in Spain; ~ **de temporada baja** *f* COM GEN, OCIO off-peak day; ~ **de trabajo** COM GEN, RRHH workday (*AmE*), working day (*BrE*); ~ **de trabajo de 24 horas con tiempo favorable** TRANSP *póliza de fletes* weather working day of 24 hours; ~ **de la última comunicación** FIN last notice day; ~ **de vencimiento** COM GEN term day; ◆ **efectivo desde el** ~ COM GEN with effect from (*wef*); **en el** ~ COM GEN, TRANSP same-day; **estar en el orden del** ~ ADMIN, COM GEN, GES be on the agenda; **por** ~ COM GEN per day, daily; **últimas horas del** ~ BOLSA last day hours; **a día** COM GEN day by day; **estar al** ~ **en el pago de la hipoteca** BANCA, FIN keep up payment on one's mortgage

días: ~ **laborales** *m pl* COM GEN running days; ~ **naturales** *m pl* DER running days; ~ **de plancha** *m pl* TRANSP running days (*Rd*)

diagnosis *f* COM GEN diagnosis

diagnóstico *m* COM GEN diagnostic; ~ **ambiental** GES, MED AMB environmental assessment

diagrama: ~ **de actividad** *m* GES activity chart; ~ **circular** *m* COM GEN, INFO, MAT pie chart; ~ **cruzado de Keynes** *m* ECON Keynesian cross diagram; ~ **de dispersión** *m* GES, MAT *estadística* scatter diagram, scattergram; ~ **de flujo** *m* COM GEN flowchart; ~ **de flujo de datos** *m* INFO data flow chart; ~ **de flujo de proceso** *m* GES flow process chart; ~ **de frecuencia** *m* MAT histogram; ~ **de Gantt** *m* INFO Gantt chart; ~ **de gestión** *m* ADMIN, GES management chart; ~ **de líneas verticales** *m* BOLSA vertical line charting; ~ **de procedimientos** *m* INFO process chart; ~ **de proceso** *m* MAT flow process chart; ~ **del proceso de fabricación** *m* MAT flow diagram; ~ **radial** *m* MAT bunch map; ~ **sectorial** *m* COM GEN, INFO, MAT pie chart; ~ **de sugerencias** *m* GES suggestion scheme

diagramar *vt* COM GEN *progreso* chart

diálogo *m* INFO dialog

diariamente *adv* COM GEN daily

diario[1] *adj* COM GEN day-to-day

diario[2] *m* COM GEN journal, newspaper, daybook (*db*); ~ **de caja** CONT cash journal, cash book; ~ **de caja chica** *AmL* (*cf libro de caja pequeña Esp*) CONT petty cash book; ~ **de cobros al contado** CONT cash receipts journal; ~ **en columnas** CONT columnar journal; ~ **comercial** COM GEN, MEDIOS trade journal; ~ **de compras** CONT purchases journal; ~ **de entradas en caja** CONT cash receipts journal; ~ **general** CONT general journal; ~ **de máquina** INFO computer log; ~ **de navegación** TRANSP ship's log; ~ **de operaciones** INFO log; ~ **de pagos al contado** CONT cash payments journal; ~ **de ventas** COM GEN, V&M sales journal, sold daybook

Diario: ~ **Oficial** *m* ECON Official Journal (*OJ*)

días[1]: ~ **completos** *m pl* COM GEN, TRANSP clear days; ~ **consecutivos** *m pl* COM GEN consecutive days, successive days; ~ **corridos** *m pl* COM GEN, DER running days; ~ **de espera** *m pl* COM GEN wait days; ~ **de gracia** *m pl* CONT grace days; ~ **hasta la entrega** *m pl* BOLSA days to delivery; ~ **hasta el vencimiento** *m pl* BOLSA days to maturity; ~ **de plancha** *m* TRANSP *póliza de fletes* reversible laytime; ~ **de plancha ahorrados** *m pl* TRANSP *navegación* laytime saved; ~ **de trabajo con tiempo favorable** *m pl* TRANSP *póliza de fletes* weather working days (*wwd*); ~ **de trabajo con tiempo favorable, salvo domingos y festivos** *m pl* COM GEN, TRANSP weather working days, Sundays and holidays excluded; ~ **de trabajo con tiempo favorable, salvo viernes y festivos** *m pl* COM GEN, TRANSP weather working days, Friday and holidays excluded; ~ **transcurridos desde la aceptación** *m pl* COM GEN days after acceptance (*D/A*); ~ **transcurridos desde la fecha** *m pl* COM GEN days after date (*dd*); ~ **transcurridos desde el vencimiento** *m pl* COM GEN days after date (*dd*)

días[2]: **en** ~ **alternos** *fra* COM GEN on alternate days; **en** ~ **laborables** *fra* COM GEN on weekdays; ~ **vista** *fra* TRANSP days after sight (*DS*)

dibujante *mf* COM GEN, RRHH, V&M *publicidad* art designer; ~ **publicitario(-a)** *m,f* RRHH, V&M *publicidad* commercial artist

dibujar *vt* *Esp* (*cf graficar AmL*) MAT, V&M draw, graph, plot

dibujo: ~ **lineal** *m* V&M line drawing

dicotomía: ~ **clásica** *f* ECON *literatura económica* classical dichotomy

dictamen *m* DER opinion; ~ **de auditoría** CONT auditor's certificate; ~ **jurídico** DER legal opinion; ~ **de propiedad** DER opinion of title; ~ **con salvedades** COM GEN qualified opinion

dictar *vt* ADMIN *taquigrafía*, COM GEN dictate, *leyes* lay down; ♦ ~ **un auto** DER pronounce a judicial decree, pronounce an order; ~ **un auto contra alguien** DER issue a writ against sb; ~ **un auto de prisión preventiva** DER remand in custody

diente *m* INFO *alimentador de papel* pin

diesel: ~-**eléctrico** *adj* TRANSP *maquinaria* diesel-electric (*D-E*)

dieselización *f* ECON dieselization

dieta *f* COM GEN, RRHH daily allowance, per diem allowance, subsistence allowance

dietas: ~ **por asistencia** *f pl* RRHH attendance money; ~ **de transporte** *f pl* COM GEN car allowance; ~ **de viaje** *f pl Esp* (*cf viáticos AmL*) COM GEN traveling allowance (*AmE*), travelling allowance (*BrE*), traveling expenses (*AmE*), travelling expenses (*BrE*)

difamación *f* DER defamation

difamante *adj* DER libellous (*BrE*), libelous (*AmE*)

difamatorio *adj* DER libellous (*BrE*), libelous (*AmE*)

diferencia *f* COM GEN difference, gap; ~ **a la baja** BOLSA bear spread; ~ **de cambio** CONT translation difference, ECON exchange difference; ~ **de conversión** CONT translation difference; ~ **deflacionaria** ECON deflationary gap; ~ **desfavorable** CONT unfavorable difference (*AmE*), unfavourable difference (*BrE*); ~ **entre dinero solicitado y obtenido** FIN *asignación* underrun; ~ **entre el precio de oferta y demanda** V&M spread; ~ **entre el resultado y lo previsto** COM GEN, CONT shortfall; ~ **a favor** CONT favorable difference (*AmE*), favourable difference (*BrE*); ~ **en moneda extranjera** CONT translation difference; ~ **de periodos** CONT *impuestos diferidos*, FISC timing difference; ~ **positiva de tipos de interés** ECON positive interest-rate gap; ~ **de rendimiento** BOLSA yield gap; ~ **temporal** CONT temporary difference

diferenciación *f* V&M *mercadotecnia* differentiation; ~ **de la calidad del producto** V&M product quality differentiation; ~ **de marca** V&M brand differentiation

diferencial *m* BOLSA gap, COM GEN *beneficio*, RRHH, TRANSP *transporte rodado* differential; ~ **de acceso** (*Esp*) (*cf diferencial de ingreso AmL*) ECON access differential; ~ **de ingreso** (*AmL*) (*cf diferencial de acceso AmL*) ECON access differential; ~ **al alza** BOLSA bullish spread; ~ **a la baja** BOLSA bearish spread; ~ **para compensar diferencias salariales** RRHH compensating wage differential; ~ **de demanda y oferta** BOLSA bid-offer spread; ~ **desusadamente amplio** BOLSA *sesión* wide opening; ~ **diagonal** BOLSA diagonal spread; ~ **fiscal** *f* FISC tax gap; ~ **de habilidad** RRHH skill differential; ~ **horizontal** BOLSA time spread; ~ **de inflación** COM GEN, ECON price differential; ~ **negativo del tipo de interés** BOLSA *futuros* negative interest rate gap; ~ **de opciones** BOLSA option spread; ~ **de pago** RRHH pay differential; ~ **perpendicular** BOLSA perpendicular spread; ~ **de precios** COM GEN, ECON price differential; ~ **de rendimiento** ECON yield gap; ~ **de salarios** RRHH wage differential, wage gap;

~ semántico V&M semantic differential; **~ de sueldo** RRHH earnings differential; **~ TED** BOLSA *futuros* TED spread; **~ en el tiempo** BOLSA calendar spread, horizontal spread; **~ de tipo** BOLSA *de interés* rate differential; **~ de tipos de interés** ECON interest rate differential; **~ de traducción** COM GEN translation differential; **~ de turnos** RRHH shift differential; **~ vertical** BOLSA vertical spread

diferenciar *vt* COM GEN differentiate

diferencias: ~ salariales *f pl* ECON, RRHH wage differentials

diferentes: ~ precios de un mismo artículo *m pl* ECON, V&M price-lining (*jarg*)

diferido *adj* COM GEN deferred (*def.*)

diferir 1. *vt* COM GEN defer; ♦ **~ una deuda** CONT defer a debt; **~ el pago** CONT defer payment; **~ sentencia** DER adjourn sentence; **2.** *vi* COM GEN, CONT differ

difícil: ~ de usar *adj* V&M user-unfriendly; **de ~ utilización** *adj* INFO user-unfriendly; **~ de utilizar** *adj* INFO user-unfriendly

dificultad *f* COM GEN setback; **~ imprevista** COM GEN snag (*infrml*), unforseen problem; **~ técnica** COM GEN technical hitch

dificultades: ~ crediticias *f pl* BANCA credit crunch; **~ excepcionalmente gravosas** *f pl* PROT SOC hardship; **~ laborales** *f pl* RRHH labor troubles (*AmE*), labour troubles (*BrE*)

difundido: muy ~ *adj* COM GEN widespread

difunto *adj* DER deceased

difusión *f* BOLSA spreading, COM GEN *de información* dissemination; **~ auditada** V&M audited circulation; **~ de innovación** V&M diffusion of innovation; **~ pagada neta** V&M net paid circulation; **~ de publicación que no llega al público-objetivo** V&M waste circulation; **~ salarial** ECON wage diffusion

digital *adj* COM GEN, COMS, INFO digital

digital/analógico *adj* INFO digital/analog (*D/A*)

digitalizar *vt* COM GEN, COMS, INFO digitize

dígito *m* INFO digit; **~ binario** INFO binary digit; **~ de comprobación** COM GEN, INFO check digit; **~ decimal** INFO decimal digit

dígitos: ~ borrados *m pl* BOLSA digits deleted

digno: ~ de confianza *adj* COM GEN trustworthy

dilapidación *f* INMOB dilapidation

dilema: ~ entre la confianza y el control *m* GES trust-control dilemma; **~ del prisionero** *m* ECON prisoner's dilemma

diligencia *f* DER proceeding

diligenciar *vt* TRANSP *tráfico* dispatch

diligencias: ~ de lanzamiento *f pl* DER, INMOB eviction (*BrE*), ejectment (*AmE*)

dilución *f* BOLSA, RRHH dilution; **~ del capital** BOLSA, CONT, FIN equity dilution; **~ de la mano de obra** RRHH dilution of labor (*AmE*), dilution of labour (*BrE*); **~ del trabajo** RRHH dilution of labor (*AmE*), dilution of labour (*BrE*)

dimensión: ~ nominal *f* COM GEN basic size

dimisión *f* GES, RRHH resignation; **~ sumaria** COM GEN, RRHH summary dismissal

dinámica: ~ de grupo *f* RRHH group dynamics; **~ industrial** *f* IND industrial dynamics; **~ de las máquinas** *f* IND machine dynamics; **~ de producto** *f* V&M product dynamics

dinámico *adj* COM GEN dynamic

dinamismo *m* BOLSA buoyancy, COM GEN dynamism

dinero *m* COM GEN *de curso legal* cash, money (*M*); **~ abundante** ECON easy money; **~ de alta potencia** ECON high-powered money; **~ auténtico** ECON real money (*jarg*); **~ de ayuda** BANCA aid money; **~ bancario** BANCA bank money; **~ barato** BANCA cheap money; **~ en caja** BANCA, COM GEN, ECON float, till money; **~ caliente** BOLSA hot money; **~ caro** FIN tight money; **~ centralizado** BANCA centralized money; **~ en circulación** BANCA, ECON money in circulation; **~ de compensación** COM GEN, RRHH compensation money, level money; **~ contante** BANCA specie; **~ dado como señal** COM GEN *apartamento* key money; **~ depositado en un banco** BANCA bank deposit money; **~ en depósito** BANCA deposit money; **~ desnacionalizado** BANCA, ECON denationalized money; **~ a un día** BANCA, FIN overnight money; **~ de disposición inmediata** BANCA good money; **~ en efectivo** COM GEN cash, ready money, hard cash, hard money; **~ efectivo en caja** CONT cash position; **~ exterior** ECON outside money; **~ extra** RRHH riff money (*jarg*); **~ fácil costoso** FIN expensive easy money; **~ fiduciario** BANCA, FIN fiduciary currency; **~ fresco** COM GEN new money, fresh money; **~ para gastos personales** COM GEN pin money; **~ generador** FIN seed money; **~ de gestión** COM GEN conduct money; **~ inactivo** BOLSA, ECON, FIN idle cash, idle money; **~ inicial** FIN front-end money; **~ interior** ECON inside money; **~ de mercancía** BOLSA commodity currency; **~ en metálico** COM GEN cash, ready money, hard money; **~ negro** FISC, TRANSP black money, dirty money; **~ no convertible** ECON inconvertible money; **~ nocturno** BANCA, FIN overnight money; **~ para pequeños gastos** COM GEN spending money; **~ personal** *f* BANCA, FIN personal money; **~ prestado** BANCA, FISC borrowed money; **~ productivo** FIN active money; **~ rápido** BANCA, FIN smart money; **~ recibido** FIN monies received; **~ en sentido amplio** BANCA broad money; **~ para sobornos** FIN, POL slush fund; **~ y valores** *f* SEG *empresa* money and securities; **~ a la vista** BANCA day-to-day money, demand money, ECON money at call; ♦ **estar cargado de ~** COM GEN have money to burn; **tener ~ en mano** FIN have cash in hand

dineros: ~ mal habidos *m pl* COM GEN *juego* blood money (*jarg*)

diodo *m* INFO diode; **~ electroluminiscente** INFO light-emitting diode (*LED*); **~ emisor de luz** INFO light-emitting diode (*LED*)

diploma *m* PROT SOC diploma

Diploma: ~ en Administración Pública *m* COM GEN, PROT SOC ≈ Diploma in Public Administration (*DipPA*); **~ en Comercio** *m* COM GEN, PROT SOC ≈ Diploma of Commerce (*DipCOM*); **~ en Dirección de Empresa** *m* COM GEN, PROT SOC ≈ Diploma in Industrial Management (*DIM*); **~ en Economía** *m* COM GEN, PROT SOC ≈ Diploma of Economics (*DipEcon*); **~ en Tecnología** *m* COM GEN, PROT SOC ≈ Diploma in Technology (*DipTech*)

diplomacia *f* GES diplomacy

diputado, -a *m,f* POL ≈ congressman (*AmE*), ≈ congresswoman (*AmE*), ≈ Member of Congress (*AmE*), ≈ Member of Parliament (*BrE*) (*MP*); **~ de fila** POL ≈ backbench MP (*BrE*), ≈ backbencher (*BrE*)

dique *m* TRANSP *navegación* dock, *puerto* basin; **~ de**

carenas TRANSP graving dock; ~ **cerrado** TRANSP enclosed dock; ~ **de entrega** TRANSP delivered dock; ~ **flotante** TRANSP *navegación* floating dock, *puerto* wet dock; ~ **franco** IMP/EXP, TRANSP free dock (*fd*); ~ **de mareas** TRANSP tidal dock; ~ **de presa** TRANSP cofferdam; ~ **seco** TRANSP dry docking (*DD*), *navegación* dry dock, graving dock

dirección[1]: **de una** ~ *adj* INFO one-way; **de** ~ **sur** TRANSP southbound

dirección[2] *f* COM GEN *de compañía* direction, management, COMS, INFO address (*Add*); ~ **absoluta** COMS, INFO absolute address; ~ **ascendente** GES bottom-up management; ~ **para avisos** IMP/EXP, TRANSP notify address; ~ **de base** INFO base address; ~ **de bifurcación** INFO branch address; ~ **cablegráfica** COMS cable address; ~ **de calidad** GES, IND quality management; ~ **de calidad total** GES, IND total quality management; ~ **del cambio** GES change management; ~ **de canales** GES channel management; ~ **de carteras** COM GEN portfolio management; ~ **central** IND, RRHH *de empresa* headquarters (*HQ, h.q.*); ~ **científica** COM GEN, GES, MAT scientific management; ~ **codificada** INFO code address; ~ **comercial** COM GEN business address; ~ **de las comunicaciones** GES, MEDIOS communication management; ~ **de contacto directo** GES first-line management; ~ **por contacto directo** GES management by walking around (*MBWA*); ~ **por contingencia** GES contingency management; ~ **corporativa** GES corporate management; ~ **por crisis** GES management by crisis; ~ **deficiente** GES, RRHH mismanagement; ~ **por departamentos** COM GEN, GES departmental management; ~ **de devolución** COMS return address; ~ **electrónica** COMS, INFO e-mail address; ~ **de empresas** COM GEN business administration, business management; ~ **de energía** GES, IND energy management; ~ **por excepción** GES management by exception; ~ **de fábrica** GES plant management; ~ **financiera** CONT, FIN financial management; ~ **de funciones** GES functional management; ~ **general** GES, RRHH general management; ~ **de los horarios de trabajo** GES time management; ~ **intermedia** GES, RRHH middle management; ~ **de inventario** GES inventory management; ~ **de inversiones** GES investment management; ~ **mancomunada** COM GEN, GES interlocking directorship; ~ **de máquina** INFO machine address; ~ **marítima** TRANSP shipping address; ~ **de la matriz** GES matrix management; ~ **del medio ambiente** GES, MED AMB environmental management; ~ **del mercado** V&M market management; ~ **múltiple** GES multiple management; ~ **de normalización** INFO bureau of standards; ~ **notificada** IMP/EXP, TRANSP notify address; ~ **por objetivos** GES management by objectives (*MBO*); ~ **de oficina** GES office management; ~ **de operaciones** GES operations management; ~ **operativa** GES operating management; ~ **de origen** COMS, INFO original address, source address; ~ **participativa** GES participative management; ~ **de la pequeña empresa** COM GEN, GES small business administration (*SBA*); ~ **de personal** GES, RRHH personnel management, staff management; ~ **postal** ADMIN, COMS postal address; ~ **de primera línea** GES first-line management; ~ **del producto** GES, V&M product management; ~ **profesional** COM GEN, COMS business address; ~ **programada** GES programmed

management; ~ **de proyectos** FIN, GES, RRHH project management; ~ **real** INFO actual address, real address; ~ **de recursos** COM GEN, GES resource management; ~ **de recursos humanos** GES, RRHH human resource administration, human resource management (*HRM*), manpower management; ~ **de reenvío** COMS forwarding address; ~ **del registro civil** GES vital records management; ~ **de registros** GES records management; ~ **reubicable** INFO relocatable address; ~ **de riesgos** BOLSA, FIN, GES risk management; ~ **de seguridad** GES, RRHH, SEG safety management; ~ **de sistemas** GES, INFO systems management; ~ **superior** GES, RRHH senior management; ~ **de supervisión** GES, RRHH supervisory management; ~ **de tarea** GES task management; ~ **telegráfica** COMS telegraphic address (*TA*); ~ **temporal** COMS accommodation address; ~ **de la tesorería** CONT, GES cash management; ~ **de transferencia** INFO transfer address; ~ **de ventas** GES, V&M sales management; **la** ~ **se disculpa por las molestias causadas** COM GEN the management regrets any inconvenience caused; ♦ **bajo nueva** ~ GES under new management; **la** ~ **indicada arriba** COM GEN, COMS the above address

Dirección: ~ **General de Correos y Telégrafos** *f* COMS ≈ Post Office (*PO*) (*BrE*); ~ **General de Tributos** *f* FISC Spanish tax collection department, ≈ Inland Revenue (*BrE*) (*IR*), ≈ Inland Revenue Office (*BrE*) (*IRO*), ≈ Internal Revenue Service (*AmE*) (*IRS*); ~ **de la Seguridad Social** *f* POL, PROT SOC Social Security Administration

direccionable *adj* COMS addressable

direccionamiento *m* COMS, INFO addressing; ~ **absoluto** INFO absolute addressing

directamente *adv* COM GEN directly; ♦ ~ **relacionado con** COM GEN directly related to; ~ **responsable de** COM GEN directly responsible for

directiva: ~ **común** *f* DER, POL common directive; ~ **de mercancías peligrosas** *f* COM GEN, TRANSP Dangerous Goods Board (*DGB*); ~ **de la UE** *f* DER, POL EU directive

directivo[1] *adj* GES managing

directivo[2]**,-a**: ~ **comercial** *m,f* RRHH traffic executive; ~ **de corta vida** *m,f* GES, RRHH one-minute manager; ~ **medio(-a)** *m,f* GES, RRHH middle manager; ~ **de personal** *m,f* RRHH staffer

directo *adj* RRHH straightforward, TRANSP direct (*DIR*); ♦ **en** ~ OCIO *deporte* live; ~ **o con cobertura mantenida** SEG *marina* direct or held covered

director, a *m,f* COM GEN director (*dir.*), manager (*MGR*); ~ **adjunto(-a)** BANCA, GES, RRHH assistant manager, deputy director, assistant general director, junior manager, submanager, deputy manager, associate director, associate manager, *banca internacional* co-manager; ~ **administrativo(-a)** COM GEN comptroller, controller, GES, RRHH managing director (*MD*); ~ **artístico(-a)** V&M *publicidad* artistic director; ~ **de atención al cliente** GES, RRHH, V&M consumer relations manager, customer relations manager; ~ **de banco** BANCA, GES bank manager; ~ **de centro de responsabilidad** CONT, FIN, GES, RRHH responsibility center manager (*AmE*), responsibility centre manager (*BrE*); ~ **comercial** GES, RRHH commercial director, commercial manager, merchandising director; ~ **comercial y de desarrollo** GES, RRHH commercial and development manager; ~ **de la compañía** GES, RRHH company manager; ~ **de**

compras GES, RRHH, V&M purchasing manager, head buyer; ~ **de comunicaciones de marketing** GES, V&M marketing communications manager; ~ **de contabilidad** CONT chief accounting officer; ~ **de contratos** GES, RRHH contracts manager; ~ **de cuentas** BOLSA *casa de corretaje* account executive, V&M *publicidad* account manager; ~ **de cuentas nacionales** GES, RRHH national accounts manager; ~ **de departamento** *m* GES, RRHH *compañía* department head; ~ **de desarrollo** GES, RRHH development director, development manager; ~ **de distribución** GES, RRHH, TRANSP distribution manager; ~ **de división** GES, RRHH division head, division manager; ~ **divisional** GES, RRHH division head, division manager; ~ **editorial** RRHH publishing director; ~ **ejecutivo(-a)** GES, RRHH chief executive, executive director, executive manager, executive officer (*EO*), senior manager; ~ **ejecutivo(-a) adjunto(-a)** GES, RRHH deputy chief executive, deputy managing director; ~ **de la emisión** V&M lead manager; ~ **de empresa** MEDIOS company director, RRHH business manager; ~ **del equipo auditor** CONT head of the audit group; ~ **de exportación** GES, IMP/EXP, RRHH export manager, export director; ~ **externo(-a)** GES, RRHH external director, outside director; ~ **de fábrica** GES, IND, RRHH plant manager, works manager; ~ **financiero(-a)** COM GEN *de una organización*, FIN, GES, RRHH comptroller, controller, financial director, financial officer, financial controller; ~ **de finanzas** RRHH chief financial officer (*CFO*); ~ **con firma autorizada** BANCA signing officer; ~ **de flota** RRHH, TRANSP fleet manager; ~ **de formación** *Esp* (*cf gerente de entrenamiento AmL, cf gerente de capacitación AmL*) GES, RRHH training manager; ~ **sin funciones ejecutivas** RRHH nonexecutive director; ~ **general** (*DG*) GES, RRHH chief executive officer (*AmE*) (*CEO*), chief operating officer (*COO*), general manager (*GM*), director-general, senior manager; ~ **general adjunto(-a)** GES, RRHH assistant director general (*ADG*), assistant general manager; ~ **general ejecutivo(-a)** GES, RRHH general executive manager; ~ **general de información** RRHH chief information officer (*CIO*); ~ **general de operaciones** GES, RRHH chief operating officer (*COO*); ~ **gerente** GES, RRHH managing director (*MD*); ~ **de hotel** GES, OCIO hotel manager; ~ **de importación** GES, RRHH import manager; ~ **interino(-a)** GES, RRHH acting director; ~ **de investigación** GES, RRHH research director; ~ **jurídico(-a)** DER, RRHH general counsel (*AmE*), head of legal department (*BrE*); ~ **de línea de transbordadores** RRHH, TRANSP ferry line manager; ~ **de marketing** *Esp* (*cf director de mercadotecnia AmL*) GES, RRHH, V&M marketing director, marketing manager; ~ **de marketing para la exportación** GES, RRHH, V&M export marketing manager; ~ **de mercadotecnia** *AmL* (*cf director de marketing Esp*) GES, RRHH, V&M marketing director, marketing manager; ~ **de modas** COM GEN fashion editor; ~ **de oficina** ADMIN, GES, RRHH office manager; ~ **de operaciones** GES, RRHH operations director, operations manager, operational manager; ~ **de personal** GES, RRHH head of personnel, personnel director, personnel manager; ~ **de la planta** GES, IND, RRHH works manager; ~ **de postventa** RRHH, V&M after-sales manager; ~ **de prácticas** GES, RRHH trainee manager; ~ **de préstamos** BANCA loan officer; ~ **principal** CONT, FIN, GES, RRHH senior manager; ~ **de producción** COM GEN, GES, IND, RRHH production director, production manager; ~ **provincial** GES, RRHH sectorial manager, district manager, regional manager; ~ **de proyecto** COM GEN, FIN, INFO, RRHH project leader, project manager; ~ **de publicidad** RRHH, V&M advertising director, publicity manager; ~ **de puerto** IMP/EXP, RRHH, TRANSP port director, port manager; ~ **de reclamaciones** RRHH claims manager; ~ **de recursos humanos** GES, RRHH human resources director; ~ **regional** GES, RRHH sectorial manager; ~ **registrado(-a)** GES, RRHH registered manager; ~ **de relaciones industriales** IND, RRHH industrial relations director; ~ **de relaciones laborales** RRHH director of labor relations (*AmE*), director of labour relations (*BrE*); ~ **de relaciones públicas** RRHH director of public relations (*DPR*); ~ **residente** INMOB resident manager; ~ **sectorial** GES, RRHH sectorial manager; ~ **de servicios de marketing** V&M marketing services manager; ~ **de sucursal** BANCA, GES branch manager; ~ **técnico(-a)** GES, INFO, RRHH technical manager, engineering manager, technical director; ~ **de terminal** TRANSP terminal manager; ~ **de ventas** GES, RRHH, V&M sales director, sales manager; ~ **de ventas de campo** GES, RRHH, V&M field sales manager; ~ **de ventas internas** RRHH, V&M internal sales manager

Director, a: ~ **de Certificaciones** *m,f* RRHH Certification Officer (*CO*); ~ **General de Correos** *m,f* COMS, RRHH Postmaster General (*BrE*) (*PMG*); ~ **General de la Policía** *m,f* RRHH ≈ Chief Commissioner (*BrE*); ~ **de Sanidad Ambiental** *m,f* COM GEN Environmental Health Officer (*BrE*); ~ **de la Seguridad del Estado** *m,f Esp* POL, PROT SOC head of state security

directora *f* COM GEN manageress (*MGR*)

directores: ~ **y empleados** *m pl* GES, RRHH managers and workers

directorio *m* COM GEN, INFO directory; ~ **comercial** COM GEN trade directory; ~ **de ficheros** INFO file directory; ~ **raíz** INFO root directory

directrices *f pl* COM GEN guidelines; ~ **fiscales** FISC tax guidelines; ~ **del juez** DER judge's rules (*jarg*) (*BrE*); ~ **de salarios y precios** RRHH wage-and-price guidelines

directriz: ~ **común** *f* DER, POL common directive; ~ **del diez por ciento** *f* FISC ten percent guideline; ~ **de paga igual** *f* RRHH equal pay directive; ~ **Vredeling** *f* RRHH Vredeling directive

dirigente *mf* COM GEN leader; ~ **sindical** RRHH union officer

dirigido *adj* V&M targeted; **no** ~ V&M untargeted; ~ **por computador** *AmL* ver *dirigido por computadora AmL*; ~ **por computadora** *AmL* (*cf dirigido por ordenador Esp*) INFO computer-driven; ~ **por menú** INFO menu-driven; ~ **por ordenador** *Esp* (*cf dirigido por computadora AmL*) INFO computer-driven

dirigir *vt* COM GEN run, manage, *crítica, producto, programa* direct, manage, target, aim, COMS *discurso, palabras*, DER address; ♦ ~ **la atención hacia** COM GEN turn one's attention to; ~ **críticas a alguien** COM GEN level criticism at sb; ~ **sus reclamaciones a** COM GEN address complaints to; ~ **un turno de noche** RRHH man a night-shift

dirigirse[1]: ~ **a** *v refl* COMS *referirse a alguien* address

dirigirse[2]: ~ **al librador** *fra* (*RD*) BANCA, COM GEN refer to drawer (*RD*)

discado: ~ **directo** *m* COMS direct dialing (*AmE*), direct

dialling (*BrE*); ~ **directo a distancia** *m* COMS direct distance dialing (*AmE*) (*DDD*), direct distance dialling (*BrE*) (*DDD*); ~ **internacional directo** *m* COMS international direct dialing (*AmE*), international direct dialling (*BrE*)

disciplina *f* COM GEN discipline

disciplinar *vt* COM GEN, DER, RRHH discipline

disciplinas: ~ **análogas** *f pl* PROT SOC cognate disciplines

disco *m* INFO disk; ~ **de alta densidad** INFO high-density disk; ~ **de arranque** INFO boot disk; ~ **de una cara** INFO single-sided disk (*SSD*); ~ **compacto** INFO compact disk; ~ **compacto interactivo** (*CD-I*) INFO compact disk interactive (*CD-I*); ~ **compacto con memoria sólo de lectura** (*CD-ROM*) INFO compact disc read-only memory (*CD-ROM*); ~ **de dos caras** INFO double-sided disk; ~ **duro** INFO hard disk; ~ **fijo** INFO fixed disk; ~ **flexible** INFO floppy, floppy disk; ~ **magnético** INFO magnetic disk; ~ **de origen** INFO source disk; ~ **de oro** MEDIOS *emisión* gold disc (*BrE*), gold disk (*AmE*); ~ **de platino** MEDIOS platinum disc (*BrE*), platinum disk (*AmE*); ~ **protegido contra copias** INFO copy-protected disk; ~ **de RAM** INFO RAM disk; ~ **de sistema** INFO system disk; ~ **de trabajo** INFO scratch disk

disconformidad *f* COM GEN nonconformity

discreción: ~ **limitada** *f* BOLSA limited discretion

discrecional *adj* COM GEN discretionary

discrepancia *f* COM GEN discrepancy

discreto *adj* V&M low-profile

discriminación *f* COM GEN discrimination; ~ **antes de la entrada** ECON pre-entry discrimination; ~ **directa** RRHH direct discrimination; ~ **por edad** DER, PROT SOC, RRHH age discrimination; ~ **fiscal** FISC tax loophole; ~ **horizontal** ECON horizontal discrimination; ~ **indirecta** RRHH indirect discrimination; ~ **por motivo de edad** DER, ECON, RRHH ageism; ~ **perfecta de precios** ECON perfect price discrimination; ~ **positiva** COM GEN, DER, POL, PROT SOC, RRHH positive discrimination; ~ **posentrada** ECON post-entry discrimination; ~ **de precios** COM GEN, V&M price discrimination; ~ **de precios de primer grado** COM GEN, V&M first degree price discrimination; ~ **de precios de segundo grado** COM GEN, V&M second-degree price discrimination; ~ **de precios de tercer grado** COM GEN, V&M third degree price discrimination; ~ **racial** DER, PROT SOC, RRHH race discrimination, racial discrimination; ~ **por religión** DER, PROT SOC, RRHH religious discrimination; ~ **por sexo** DER, PROT SOC, RRHH sexual discrimination; ~ **sexual** DER, PROT SOC, RRHH gender discrimination, sexual discrimination; ~ **vertical** ECON vertical discrimination

discriminar 1. ~ **a** *vt* COM GEN *desaprobación* discriminate against; **2.** *vi* COM GEN discriminate

disculpa *f* *Esp* (*cf apología AmL*) COM GEN apology

disculparse *v refl* COM GEN apologize; ♦ ~ **ante alguien por algo** COM GEN apologize to sb for sth; ~ **por** COM GEN apologize for

disculpas *f pl* COM GEN apologies; ♦ **aceptar** ~ COMS accept apologies

discurso *m* POL jawboning (*AmE*) (*jarg*)

discusión *f* COM GEN discussion; ~ **de grupo** V&M group discussion; ~ **en profundidad** COM GEN in-depth discussion; ♦ **en** ~ RRHH *con empleado* in dispute

discusiones: ~ **francas** *f pl* POL frank discussions

discutir: ~ **a fondo** *fra* COM GEN *un problema* thrash out

diseminar *vt* TRANSP *contenedores* disseminate

disentir *vi* COM GEN disagree

diseñador, a: ~ **comercial** *m,f* MEDIOS, V&M *publicidad* commercial designer; ~ **gráfico(-a)** *m,f* MEDIOS, V&M graphic designer; ~ **de modas** *m,f* COM GEN fashion designer; ~ **de motores** *m,f* IND engine designer (*ED*)

diseño[1]: **de** ~ **ergonómico** *adj* INFO *estación de trabajo* ergonomically-designed

diseño[2] *m* IND, INFO design; ~ **de alto nivel** GES high-level design; ~ **asistido por computador** *AmL* ver *diseño asistido por computadora AmL*; ~ **asistido por computadora** *AmL* (*CAD, cf diseño asistido por ordenador Esp*), computer-aided design (*CAD*); ~ **asistido por ordenador** *Esp* (*CAD, cf diseño asistido por computadora AmL*) *gráficos* computer-aided design (*CAD*); ~ **y dibujo asistido por computador** *AmL* ver *diseño y dibujo asistido por computadora AmL*; ~ **y dibujo asistido por computadora** *AmL* (*CADD, cf diseño y dibujo asistido por ordenador Esp*) INFO computer-aided design and drafting (*CADD*); ~ **y dibujo asistido por ordenador** *Esp* (*CADD, cf diseño y dibujo asistido por computadora AmL*) computer-assisted design and drafting (*CADD*); ~ **del envase** V&M package design; ~ **de la envoltura** V&M package design; ~ **gráfico** MEDIOS, V&M *publicidad* graphic design; ~ **de la muestra** MAT sample drawing; ~ **portuario** TRANSP port layout; ~ **de producto** V&M product design; ~ **de proyecto** IND project design; ~ **de un puesto de trabajo** RRHH *funciones* job design; ~ **de sistemas** INFO systems design; ~ **técnico** COM GEN engineering design; ♦ ~ **y composición** V&M *de almacén* design and layout

Diseño: ~ **Curricular Base** *m* *Esp* (*DCB*) PROT SOC *educación* ≈ National Curriculum (*BrE*) (*NC*)

disfrutar: ~ **los beneficios** *fra* BOLSA reap the benefits; ~ **las gratificaciones** *fra* BOLSA reap the rewards

disgregación: ~ **de la carga** *f* TRANSP cargo disassembly

disimulado *adj* V&M passing off

disminución *f* BANCA impairment, COM GEN abatement, FIN *en tipos de interés* decline, V&M shrinkage; ~ **de un cargo** CONT charge-off; ~ **en las cuotas de producción** FIN, IND production cut; ~ **de la demanda** V&M contraction of demand; ~ **de las existencias** COM GEN, CONT drawing down of stocks; ~ **de ingresos tributarios** FISC tax erosion; ~ **de las inversiones** CONT, FIN decline in investments; ~ **de la prima** TRANSP rate cutting; ~ **de la producción** FIN, IND production cut; ~ **del valor** COM GEN decrease in value

disminuir 1. *vt* COM GEN abate, decrease, lower, *trabajadores, negocio, demanda* diminish, lessen, slack off, ECON *activos líquidos* run down; ♦ ~ **proporcionalmente** V&M *producción* scale down; **2.** *vi* COM GEN diminish; ♦ ~ **gradualmente** ECON taper off

disolución *f* COM GEN breakup, dissolution, POL *del parlamento* dissolution; ~ **de un acuerdo mediante contrato** DER contracting out clause; ~ **de fusiones internacionales** ECON, POL cross-border demergers

disolver *vt* COM GEN *sociedad, parlamento* dissolve, *junta* break up

disolverse *v refl* COM GEN *fiesta, reunión* split up

disonancia: ~ **cognitiva** *f* ECON cognitive dissonance

disparate *m* COM GEN balderdash

disparidad f COM GEN disparity

disparo: ~ **a ciegas** m COM GEN shot in the dark

dispensa f DER dispensation

dispensador: ~ **de cambio** m BANCA change dispenser; ~ **de dinero en efectivo** m BANCA automated cash dispenser (*BrE*) (*ACD*), automated teller machine (*AmE*) (*ATM*), automatic cash dispenser (*BrE*) (*ACD*), automatic telling machine (*AmE*) (*ATM*), cash dispenser, cash-dispensing machine

dispersión: ~ **del accionista** f BOLSA stockholder diffusion; ~ **estadística** f MAT statistical spread

disponer vt BANCA arrange *un préstamo* arrange, COM GEN, RRHH deploy; ◆ ~ **de** FISC dispose of; ~ **de las existencias** V&M dispose of stock; ~ **de precios** f BOLSA price spread, FISC dispose of; ~ **de otro modo** BANCA, RRHH reploy; ~ **un préstamo** BANCA arrange a loan

disponibilidad f COM GEN, INFO, V&M availability; ~ **en efectivo** COM GEN cash holdings, CONT cash holdings, cash in hand; ~ **de fondos expeditados** BANCA, FIN Expedited Funds Availability (*AmE*) (*EFA*); ~ **de recursos** FIN resource availability

disponibilidades f pl BANCA liquid assets, BOLSA *mercancía física*, CONT, FIN actuals, liquid assets; ~ **líquidas** ECON monetary base; ~ **del mes en curso** CONT this month's actuals

disponible adj COM GEN, INFO, V&M available; **no** ~ COM GEN, INFO, V&M not available (*N/A*) unavailable; ~ **actualmente** COM GEN available on a current basis; ~ **a corto plazo** COM GEN available at short notice; ~ **en el mejor tiempo** V&M best time available; ◆ ~ **para la compra** V&M open-to-buy (*AmE*)

disposición f ADMIN layout, COM GEN regulation, CONT layout, DER provision, FISC disposal, disposition; ~ **del año en curso** FISC current year disposal; ~ **de cambio de beneficiario** SEG *de vida* change of beneficiary provision; ~ **contractual** DER contractual provision; ~ **engañosa** DER joker (*AmE*); ~ **estructural longitudinal** TRANSP *navegación* longitudinal framing; ~ **excepcional** BANCA, DER, IND grandfather clause (*jarg*); ~ **general contra la evasión legal** FISC general anti-avoidance provision, general anti-avoidance rule; ~ **legal** DER legal enactment; ~ **de la liquidez** CONT cash drawdown; ~ **de la muestra** MAT *estadística* sample drawing; ~ **portuaria** TRANSP port layout; ~ **según la función** COM GEN functional layout; ~ **de tesorería** CONT *contabilidad gubernamental* cash drawdown; ~ **testamentaria** DER, INMOB devise; ◆ **con** ~ **al riesgo** COM GEN risk-oriented

disposiciones: ~ **aduaneras** m pl IMP/EXP customs regulations; ~ **especiales** f pl FISC *aportaciones a la Seguridad Social* special provisions; ~ **sucesorias** f pl DER *testamentos*, FIN estate planning

dispositivo m COM GEN apparatus, appliance, device; ~ **de alerta** COM GEN warning device; ~ **de alimentación de documentos** INFO document feeder; ~ **de almacenamiento** INFO storage device; ~ **antirrobo** TRANSP antitheft device; ~ **automático** INFO hardware device; ~ **de carga unitaria** TRANSP unit load device (*ULD*); ~ **contabilizador de carga** TRANSP cargo accounting device; ~ **de entrada** INFO input device; ~ **de estabilización artificial de precios** ECON pegging device; ~ **externo** f INFO external device; ~ **de fijación de precios** ECON pegging device; ~ **para fijar la**

situación TRANSP position fixing device; ~ **implícito** INFO default device; ~ **lógico** f INFO logic device; ~ **de memoria masiva** INFO mass storage device; ~ **original** COM GEN original device; ~ **de paginación** INFO paging device; ~ **periférico** f INFO peripheral device; ~ **de respuesta** V&M *pedido postal* reply device; ~ **de salida** INFO output device

disputa: ~ **jurisdiccional** f RRHH jurisdiction dispute

disputar: ~ **un testamento** *fra* DER dispute a will

disputas: ~ **entre sindicatos** f pl RRHH interunion disputes (*BrE*); ~ **profesionales** f pl RRHH industrial strife

disquete m INFO diskette; ~ **flexible** INFO floppy, floppy disk; ~ **de instalación** INFO installation diskette

disquetera f INFO diskette drive

distancia[1]: ~ **al objetivo** f ECON target range; ~ **eje a eje de los asientos** f TRANSP seat pitch

distancia[2]: **a** ~ *fra* COM GEN at arm's-length, INFO remote; **a larga** ~ *fra* COMS, COM GEN long-distance

distanciamiento m COM GEN, RRHH distancing

distinción f COM GEN *cualidad destacada* distinction; ◆ **hacer una** ~ COM GEN make a distinction

distinguir: ~ **entre** *fra* COM GEN differentiate between

distintivo adj INFO, PATENT distinctive

distorsión f ECON distortion; ~ **comercial** ECON trade distortion; ~ **fiscal** FISC distortionary tax; ~ **del mercado** ECON market distortion

distorsionar vt COM GEN *cifras* distort

distribución f ADMIN layout, BOLSA dealing, COM GEN *de fondos* allocation, allotment, appropriation, dealing, distribution, RRHH, TRANSP distribution; ~ **abierta** TRANSP open distribution; ~ **del beneficio neto** CONT distribution of net profit; ~ **de los beneficios** CONT allocation of earnings, profit breakdown, RRHH allocation of earnings; ~ **de Bernoulli** MAT Bernoulli distribution; ~ **bimodal** MAT *estadística* bimodal distribution; ~ **del capital** FISC distribution of capital; ~ **de carga** TRANSP loading allocation; ~ **chi cuadrado** MAT *estadística* chi-squared distribution; ~ **comercial** V&M commercial distribution; ~ **de costes** *Esp* (*cf distribución de costos AmL*) CONT cost distribution; ~ **de costos** *AmL* (*cf distribución de costes Esp*) CONT cost distribution; ~ **de dividendos** CONT distribution of dividends; ~ **en ejercicios posteriores** CONT carryforward; ~ **eliminatoria** COM GEN, CONT *realizada por una empresa* qualifying distribution; ~ **de equipo de disposición** m IND process equipment layout; ~ **de equipo de presentación** IND process equipment layout; ~ **de equipo de procesado** IND process equipment layout; ~ **equitativa** COM GEN equitable distribution; ~ **por fases** V&M phased distribution; ~ **física** GES, TRANSP, V&M physical distribution; ~ **de frecuencias** MAT *estadística* frequency distribution; ~ **funcional del ingreso** ECON functional income distribution; ~ **de las ganancias** CONT, RRHH allocation of earnings; ~ **de gastos** COM GEN cost trimming; ~ **global** BOLSA lumpsum distribution; ~ **del ingreso excedente** FIN excess revenue allotment; ~ **de ingresos** CONT, ECON, FISC appropriation of income, income distribution; ~ **inmobiliaria** INMOB estate distribution; ~ **intergeneracional del ingreso** ECON intergenerational distribution of income; ~ **por licitación** FIN issue by tender; ~ **de muestra** MAT sampling distribution; ~ **multimodal** MAT multimodal distribution; ~ **de la**

nómina CONT payroll distribution; **~ normal** MAT *estadística* normal distribution; **~ de Pareto** ECON, MAT Pareto distribution; **~ periódica del impuesto sobre la renta** FISC interperiod income tax allocation; **~ personal del ingreso** ECON, FISC personal income distribution; **~ de planta** IND plant layout; **~ plurimodal** MAT *estadística* multimodal distribution; **~ de plusvalías** BOLSA capital gains distribution; **~ de Poisson** MAT Poisson distribution; **~ ponderada** ECON weighted distribution; **~ por porcentajes** MAT percentage distribution; **~ porcentual** MAT *estadística* percentage distribution; **~ pública de valores** BOLSA public distribution of securities; **~ de los recursos** COM GEN resource allocation; **~ de responsabilidades** FIN, GES, RRHH allocation of responsibilities; **~ de riesgos** SEG distribution of risks; **~ de la riqueza** ECON wealth distribution, distribution of wealth; **~ secundaria-primaria** BOLSA secondary-primary distribution; **~ según edad** ECON age distribution; **~ selectiva** COM GEN, CONT *realizada por empresa* qualifying distribution, selective distribution; **~ t de Student** MAT Student's t-distribution; **~ de trabajo** GES, RRHH allocation of work, job breakdown; **~ unimodal** MAT unimodal distribution; **~ por zonas** V&M zonal distribution

distribuido *adj* COM GEN distributed; **no ~** BOLSA *acciones* unallotted; **~ íntegramente** BOLSA fully distributed

distribuidor, a *m,f* IMP/EXP distributor, RRHH stockist, TRANSP distributor; **~ común** TRANSP common carrier; **~ designado(-a)** V&M appointed stockist; **~ oficial** DER franchised dealer (*BrE*)

distribuir *vt* COM GEN allot, deploy, distribute; ♦ **~ en ejercicios posteriores** CONT carry forward

distrito *m* POL district; **~ electoral marginal** POL marginal constituency; **~ financiero** COM GEN central business district (*CBD*); **~ fiscal** FISC tax district; **~ judicial** DER circuit; **~ municipal** POL municipal borough; **~ postal** COMS postal zone

disuadir *vt* COM GEN deter

divergencia *f* COM GEN, ECON divergence

divergir *vi* COM GEN *tipo de cambio*, ECON diverge

diversidad: **~ de activos** *f* CONT asset mix

diversificación *f* COM GEN diversification; **~ de activos** FIN asset diversification; **~ conglomerada** ECON, FIN conglomerate diversification; **~ de conglomerado** ECON, FIN conglomerate diversification; **~ excesiva** BOLSA overdiversification; **~ de la liquidez** BOLSA liquidity diversification; **~ mixta** BANCA *del riesgo* composite spread; **~ de los negocios** COM GEN, GES business diversification; **~ de productos** V&M product diversification

diversificar *vt* COM GEN, ECON, GES diversify; ♦ **~ riesgos** BOLSA diversify risks

diverso *adj* COM GEN diverse, CONT miscellaneous (*misc.*)

dividendo[1]: **con ~** *adv* BOLSA, FIN *todavía sin pagar* cum dividend (*cd*); **sin ~** *adv* BOLSA, FIN ex dividend (*ex div., xd.*)

dividendo[2] *m* BOLSA, FIN dividend (*div.*); **~ de una acción** BOLSA, CONT, FIN share dividend; **~ por acción** BOLSA, CONT, FIN dividend per share, earning per share (*EPS*); **~ de acción ordinaria** BOLSA, CONT, FIN common share dividend (*BrE*), common stock dividend (*AmE*); **~ en acciones** BOLSA, CONT bonus issue (*BrE*), capitalization issue (*BrE*), scrip issue (*BrE*),

stock dividend (*AmE*), stock split (*AmE*); **~ activo** BOLSA dividend (*div.*); **~ acumulado** BOLSA, CONT, FIN accrued dividend, accumulated dividend; **~ acumulativo** BOLSA, CONT, FIN cumulative dividend; **~ con adición del impuesto** BOLSA, CONT, FIN *pagado en otro país* grossed-up dividend; **~ anticipado** BOLSA, CONT, FIN interim dividend; **~ anual** COM GEN annual dividend, yearly dividend; **~ atrasado** BOLSA, CONT, FIN dividend in arrears; **~ bruto** BOLSA, CONT, FIN gross dividend; **~ de capital** BOLSA capital dividend, FIN liquidating dividend; **~ de cartera de valores** BOLSA, CONT, FIN portfolio dividend; **~ de la compañía matriz** CONT, FIN parent company dividend; **~ complementario** BOLSA, CONT, FIN year-end dividend; **~ complementario de fin de año** BOLSA, CONT, FIN year-end dividend; **~ a cuenta** BOLSA, CONT, FIN interim dividend; **~ declarado** BOLSA, CONT, FIN declared dividend; **~ después de impuestos** FISC after-tax dividend; **~ devengado** BOLSA, CONT, FIN accrued dividend; **~ diferido** BOLSA, CONT, FIN deferred dividend; **~ en efectivo** BOLSA, CONT, FIN cash dividend; **~ en especie** BOLSA, CONT, FIN dividend in kind; **~ excluido** FISC excluded dividend; **~ exento** BOLSA, CONT, FIN exempt dividend; **~ extraordinario** BOLSA extra dividend, extraordinary dividend, bonus, FIN surplus dividend; **~ extraordinario en efectivo** BOLSA *sobre bonos* cash bonus; **~ ficticio** BOLSA, CONT, FIN sham dividend; **~ final** BOLSA, CONT, FIN final dividend; **~ fiscal** FISC fiscal dividend; **~ ilegal** DER illegal dividend; **~ impagado** BOLSA, CONT, FIN passed dividend; **~ imponible** FISC taxable dividend; **~ de liquidación** BOLSA, CONT, FIN liquidation dividend; **~ neto** BOLSA, CONT, FIN dividend net, net dividend; **~ no devengado** BOLSA, CONT, FIN unearned dividend; **~ no exigido** BOLSA, CONT, FIN unrequired dividend; **~ no pagado** BOLSA, CONT, FIN unpaid dividend; **~ no repartido** BOLSA, CONT, FIN passed dividend; **~ omitido** BOLSA, CONT, FIN passed dividend, omitted dividend; **~ ordinario** BOLSA, CONT, FIN common dividend; **~ pagadero** BOLSA, CONT, FIN dividend payable; **~ pagado en bloque** BOLSA, CONT, FIN grossed-up dividend; **~ a pagar** BOLSA, CONT, FIN dividend payable, payable dividend; **~ con pagarés** BOLSA, CONT, FIN script dividend; **~ pasivo** BOLSA, CONT, FIN liability dividend; **~ de la paz** POL peace dividend; **~ de una póliza** SEG policy dividend; **~ preferente** BOLSA, CONT, FIN preferred dividend (*AmE*), preference dividend (*BrE*); **~ privilegiado** BOLSA, CONT, FIN preference dividend (*BrE*), preferred dividend (*AmE*); **~ provisional** BOLSA, CONT, FIN interim dividend; **~ de regulación** BOLSA, CONT, FIN equalizing dividend; **~ de los rendimientos del capital** FISC capital gains dividend; **~ semestral** BOLSA half-yearly dividend; **~ semianual** BOLSA, CONT, FIN semiannual dividend; **~ trimestral** BOLSA, CONT, FIN quarterly dividend

dividendos: **~ elegibles por interés** *m pl* BOLSA dividends eligible for interest; **~ de la empresa matriz** *m pl* BOLSA, CONT, FIN parent dividends; **~ de una empresa subsidiaria** *m pl* BOLSA, CONT, FIN subsidiary dividends; **~ extranjeros** *m pl* BOLSA, CONT, FIN foreign dividends

dividido: **~ por** *adj* MAT divided by

dividir *vt* COM GEN split, INFO, MAT divide; ♦ **~ arbitrariamente** POL gerrymander (*infrml*); **~ en compartimentos** COM GEN, GES compartmentalize;

~ **en dos partes** COM GEN halve; ~ **un proyecto** GES chunk a project

divisa *f* COM GEN currency (*cy.*); ~ **bajo la par** BANCA, ECON *internacional* currency at a discount; ~ **controlada** BANCA, ECON managed currency; ~ **débil** BANCA, ECON soft currency; ~ **por encima de la par** BANCA, ECON currency at a premium; ~ **exótica** BANCA, ECON exotic currency; ~ **extranjera** COM GEN foreign currency, foreign exchange (*forex*); ~ **fluctuante** BANCA, ECON, FIN fluctuating currency; ~ **no oficial** ECON parallel currency; ~ **oro** BANCA, ECON gold currency; ~ **principal** BANCA, ECON major currency; ~ **de referencia** BANCA, ECON reference currency, *internacional* key currency; ~ **única** BANCA, ECON, POL single currency

divisas: ~ **comerciales** *f pl* ECON trading currencies; ~ **a plazo** *f pl* ECON *internacional* forward exchange

divisibilidad *f* COM GEN divisibility

divisible *adj* COM GEN divisible

división *f* COM GEN division, INMOB *de tierras* severance; ~ **de cartera de valores** BOLSA, FIN portfolio split; ~ **de la comisión** CONT *de una empresa contable* fee split; ~ **en compartimentos** COM GEN, GES compartmentalization; ~ **de consultoría** RRHH consulting division; ~ **departamental** COM GEN departmentalization; ~ **inversa** FIN reverse split; ~ **operativa** COM GEN operating division; ~ **de poderes** COM GEN division of powers; ~ **del puesto de trabajo** RRHH job splitting; ~ **en tercios** COM GEN three-way split; ~ **del trabajo** ECON, RRHH division of labor (*AmE*), division of labour (*BrE*); ~ **del trabajo por sexos** ECON, RRHH sexual division of labor (*AmE*), sexual division of labour (*BrE*); ~ **por zonas** INMOB spot zoning

División: ~ **de la Comisión Económica Europea de Comercio Internacional y Tecnología** *f* ECON, POL Economic Commission for Europe for Trade and Technology Division (*ECOCOM*)

divisionalización *f* COM GEN divisionalization

divulgación *f* INMOB filtering down; ~ **completa** DER full disclosure; ~ **de información financiera** FIN financial disclosure; ~ **de nota** COM GEN note disclosure

divulgar *vt* COM GEN *opinión, observación* air, COMS *información, noticias* circulate; ◆ ~ **las propias opiniones** COM GEN air one's opinions; ~ **los propios puntos de vista** COM GEN air one's views; ~ **la noticia** MEDIOS break the news

DNI *abr* (*documento nacional de identidad*) DER, POL ID card (*national identity card*)

doblaje *m* MEDIOS, V&M dubbing

doble[1] *adj* MAT double; **de ~ acción** IND *maquinaria* double acting; **de ~ cara** INFO double-sided; **de ~ ingreso** ECON *familia, matrimonio* double-income; **de ~ precisión** INFO double precision

doble[2]: ~ **arbitraje** *m* ECON double switching; ~ **bonificación** *f* BOLSA reallowance; ~ **capacidad** *f* BOLSA *de comisionistas* dual capacity; ~ **columna** *f* MEDIOS, V&M double column; ~ **compensación** *f* BOLSA reallowance; ~ **contabilización** *f* FIN double counting; ~ **corona** *f* V&M double crown; ~ **densidad** *f* INFO double density; ~ **densidad por una cara** INFO single-sided double density (*SSDD*); ~ **depresión** *f* ECON double dip (*jarg*); ~ **distribución** *f* COM GEN double distribution; ~ **dotación de personal** *f* IND, RRHH double manning; ~ **entrada** *f* CONT, ECON double entry;

~ **espacio** *m* INFO double space; ~ **federalismo** *m* POL dual federalism; ~ **fondo** *m* TRANSP *barco* double bottom (*DB*); ~ **frontal** *f* V&M double front; ~ **fuente** *m* COM GEN dual sourcing; ~ **imposición** *f* FISC double taxation, duplicate taxation; ~ **imposición de los ahorros** *f* FISC double taxation of savings; ~ **opción** *f* BOLSA double option; ~ **pila** *f* TRANSP double stack; ~ **pulsación** *f* INFO *en procesador de textos* strikeover; ~ **reducción** *f* COM GEN double reduction; ~ **residencia** *f* FISC dual residence; ~ **responsabilidad** *f* RRHH UE dual responsibility; ~ **seguro** *m* SEG double insurance; ~ **tecleo** *m* INFO double strike

dock *m* TRANSP dock

doctor, a *m,f* PROT SOC doctor

Doctor, a *m* (*Dr*) COM GEN *título* Doctor (*Dr*) ~ **en Administración Empresarial** *m,f* COM GEN, GES Doctor of Business Management; ~ **en Comercio** *m,f* COM GEN Doctor of Commerce (*DCom*); ~ **en Derecho** *m,f* DER, RRHH Doctor of Laws (*LLD*); ~ **en Derecho Comercial** *m,f* COM GEN, DER Doctor of Commercial Law (*DComL*); ~ **en Economía** *m,f* COM GEN, ECON Doctor of Economics (*DEcon*)

doctrina: ~ **de los costes comparativos** *f Esp* (*cf doctrina de los costos comparativos AmL*) CONT doctrine of comparative costs; ~ **de los costos comparativos** *f AmL* (*cf doctrina de los costes comparativos Esp*) CONT doctrine of comparative costs; ~ **de cumplimiento sustancial** *f* DER doctrine of substantial performance; ~ **de estricta conformidad** *f* BANCA doctrine of strict compliance; ~ **fiscal** *f* FISC tax doctrine; ~ **mercantilista** *f* ECON mercantile doctrine, mercantilism; ~ **de saldos reales** *f* ECON *ley del reflujo* real bills doctrine

doctrinas: ~ **contables** *f pl* CONT accounting doctrines

documentación *f* COM GEN, INFO documentation; ~ **auxiliar contable** CONT working papers; ~ **de exportación** IMP/EXP export documentation; ~ **de viaje** OCIO travel document

documental *m* MEDIOS, V&M documentary

documento *m* COM GEN document, DER instrument, *prueba en un juicio* exhibit; ~ **de aceptación** COM GEN, DER acknowledgement; ~ **adjunto** ADMIN, COM GEN, enclosed document, COMS accompanying document, enclosed document; ~ **administrativo simple** ADMIN single administrative document (*SAD*); ~ **administrativo único** ADMIN single administrative document (*SAD*); ~ **agrícola** ECON agricultural paper; ~ **al portador** BOLSA bearer form; ~ **de antecedentes** FIN, MEDIOS background paper; ~ **por cobrar** FIN note receivable; ~ **de compromiso** DER commitment document; ~ **de contrato de compras de valores** BOLSA bought note; ~ **de crédito** BANCA, DER, FIN security; ~ **depositado en garantía** FIN escrow; ~ **de depósito** BANCA, DER memorandum of deposit; ~ **descontado** BANCA bill discounted; ~ **de enjuiciamiento reconocido** COM GEN confessed judgment note (*AmE*); ~ **externo** COM GEN external document; ~ **fuente** CONT source document; ~ **de garantía** BANCA, COM GEN accommodation paper; ~ **incobrable** BANCA bad paper (*infrml*); ~ **inseguro** FIN unsafe paper; ~ **legal** DER legal document; ~ **legal que autoriza la constitución de un banco** BANCA bank charter; ~ **de liquidación** BANCA, BOLSA, DER lidding document; ~ **maestro** INFO master document; ~ **marco de la política** BOLSA policy framework paper (*PFP*); ~ **a**

medio plazo BANCA medium-term note (*MTN*); ~ **nacional de identidad** (*DNI*) DER, POL identity card (*ID card*); ~ **no negociable** BANCA non-negotiable instrument; ~ **oficial** COM GEN official document; ~ **de origen** COM GEN original document; ~ **original** CONT source document; ~ **originario** FISC originating document; ~ **por pagar** FIN note payable; ~ **privado** INMOB private treaty; ~ **de situación** *f* POL position paper (*jarg*); ~ **de tipo renovable** BOLSA, FIN rolling-rate note; ~ **de título** BOLSA, DER, INMOB muniment; ~ **de trabajo** POL working paper; ~ **de tránsito** COM GEN transit document; ~ **de transporte** TRANSP transport document, transportation document; ~ **de transporte combinado** IMP/EXP, TRANSP combined transport document (*CTD*); ~ **de transporte internacional en ruta** IMP/EXP, TRANSP transport international routier carnet (*TIR carnet*); ~ **único de embarque** ADMIN, IMP/EXP, TRANSP *EC* single transport document

documentos: ~ **del buque** *m pl* DER, TRANSP ship's papers; ~ **del caso** *m pl* COM GEN case papers; ~ **contra aceptación** *m pl* COM GEN documents against acceptance (*D/A*); ~ **contra pago** *m pl* COM GEN documents against payment (*DAP, DP*); ~ **de embarque** *m pl* IMP/EXP, TRANSP shipping documents; ~ **justificantes** *m pl* ADMIN, CONT, DER supporting documents; ~ **justificativos** *m pl* ADMIN, CONT authoritative documents; ~ **presupuestarios** *m pl* ECON, POL *gubernamental* Budget Papers; ~ **de propiedad** *m pl* DER documents of title; ~ **de rescisión** *m pl* RRHH termination papers; ~ **temporales** *m pl* BOLSA renounceable documents; ~ **de titulación** *m pl* PROT SOC paper qualifications; ◆ **contra entrega de** ~ COM GEN against documents

dólar: ~ **al contado y a plazo** *m* FIN dollar spot and forward

dólares: ~ **actuales** *m pl* CONT, ECON current dollars; ~ **corrientes** *m pl* CONT, ECON current dollars; ~ **falsos** *m pl* ECON soft dollars; ~ **fuertes** *m pl* ECON hard dollars; ~ **de poder adquisitivo constante** *m pl* ECON constant dollars; ~ **de ultramar** *m pl* BANCA offshore dollars

dolarización *f* COM GEN, ECON *internacional* dollarization

dolo *m* COM GEN mens rea

domiciliación: ~ **bancaria** *f* BANCA, FIN automatic payment through a bank, direct debit; ~ **bancaria de pagos** *f* BANCA, FIN banker's order; ~ **fiscal** *f* DER, FISC fiscal domicile, tax domicile

domiciliado *adj* DER, INMOB domiciled

domicilio *m* DER, INMOB domicile; ~ **bancario** BANCA bank address; ~ **de entrega** TRANSP delivered domicile; ~ **fiscal** DER, FISC tax domicile; ~ **franco** IMP/EXP *carga* free domicile; ~ **legal** DER legal residence; ~ **postal** COMS mailing address; ~ **social** COM GEN principal business address, principal place of business, registered address, registered office; ~ **social fijo** COM GEN, FISC fixed place of business; ~ **telegráfico** COMS telegraphic address (*TA*)

dominación *f* COM GEN, ECON, V&M domination

dominante *adj* COM GEN, ECON, V&M dominant

dominar *vt* COM GEN, ECON *el mercado* V&M dominate; ◆ ~ **la situación** COM GEN hold center stage (*AmE*), hold centre stage (*BrE*); ~ **totalmente el mercado** COM GEN, ECON, V&M have a stranglehold on the market

dominio *m* COM GEN, MAT domain; ~ **absoluto** INMOB fee simple, fee simple absolute; ~ **del consumo** ECON, V&M consumer sovereignty; ~ **de la mecánica** IND mechanic's lien (*AmE*); ~ **del mercado** BOLSA market holding; ~ **técnico** COM GEN technical mastery; ~ **vitalicio** INMOB life estate

donación *f* DER endowment, FISC donation, gift; ~ **a un centro benéfico** FISC, PROT SOC charitable gift; ~ **determinada** FISC specified gift; ~ **en especie** FISC donation in kind; ~ **entre vivos** DER gift inter vivos; ~ **gubernamental** *f pl* FISC, POL government grant; ~ **mortis causa** DER gift causa mortis; ~ **pignorada** FISC donation pledged; ~ **política** RRHH, POL political donation; ~ **propiamente dicha** FISC outright gift; ~ **de propiedades** FISC gift of property; ~ **con retención** FISC gift with reservation; ◆ ~ **en metálico realizada sólo en una ocasión** FISC one-off cash gift

donado *adj* FISC donated

donante: ~ **de ayuda** *mf* BANCA *desarrollo* aid donor; ~ **bilateral** *m* ECON *de asistencia al desarrollo*, POL bilateral donor; ~ **multilateral** *m* ECON *de ayuda al desarrollo*, POL multilateral donor

donar *vt* FISC donate

donatario, -a *m,f* FISC donee

donativo: ~ **benéfico** *m* FISC, PROT SOC charitable donation

dongle *m* INFO dongle

dos: **de** ~ **caras** *adj* INFO two-sided; **de** ~ **direcciones** *adj* INFO two-way; **de** ~ **frentes** *adj* TRANSP *caldera* double-ended (*DB*); **de** ~ **niveles** *adj* TRANSP *de carreteras* double decker; **de** ~ **vías** *adj* TRANSP two-way

DOS *abr* (*sistema operativo de discos*) INFO DOS (*disk operating system*)

dotación *f* CONT, DER, FISC appropriation, endowment; ~ **de ayuda** ECON *ayuda al desarrollo*, POL donor aid; ~ **de capital** BOLSA, CONT, FIN capital endorsement; ~ **para contingencias** FISC appropriation for contingencies; ~ **de factores** ECON factor endowment; ~ **de personal** RRHH staffing, staffing level; ~ **presupuestaria para defensa** POL government defence appropriations (*BrE*), government defense appropriations (*AmE*); ~ **para provisiones** CONT provisions allocation; ~ **a reservas** CONT allocation to reserves

dotado *adj* PROT SOC gifted; ~ **de personal** RRHH staffed, *servicio* manned

dotar: ~ **de exceso de personal** *fra* RRHH overman; ~ **de herramientas** *fra* IND tool up; ~ **de personal** *fra* RRHH *oficina* staff

dote *f* INMOB dowry

dpto. *abr* (*departamento*) COM GEN dept. (*department*), INMOB *AmL* apartment (*AmE*), flat (*BrE*)

Dr *abr* COM GEN (*deudor*) Dr (*debtor*), (*Doctor*) Dr (*Doctor*)

drawback *m* IMP/EXP drawback

drenaje *m* ECON *de recursos* drain

DRH *abr* (*desarrollo de recursos humanos*) RRHH HRD (*human resource development*)

droga *f* COM GEN drug

dto. *abr* (*descuento*) COM GEN dis (*discount*), disc. (*discount*)

dueño, -a *m,f* COM GEN owner; ~ **de restaurante** COM GEN, RRHH restaurateur, restaurant proprietor; ~ **único(-a)** INMOB sole owner

dupdo. *abr* (*duplicado*) COM GEN copy, INFO duplicate, V&M dupe (*jarg*)

duopolio *m* ECON duopoly; **~ espacial** ECON spatial duopoly

dúplex *m* INMOB penthouse; **~ completo** INFO full-duplex (*FDX*); **~ integral** INFO full-duplex (*FDX*)

duplicación *f* COM GEN, INFO duplication; **~ de prestaciones** SEG duplication of benefits

duplicado[1] *adj* INFO backup

duplicado[2] *m* (*dupdo.*) COM GEN copy, INFO duplicate, V&M *publicidad* dupe (*jarg*); **~ del certificado de almacén** DER *comercial* warehouse warrant (*WW*)

duplicar *vt* COM GEN, INFO duplicate

duplicatorio *adj* COM GEN, INFO duplicatory

duración *f* COM GEN duration, INFO timing, POL *de cargo, del gobierno* term; **~ de la garantía** COM GEN duration of guarantee, duration of guaranty; **~ media de vida** PROT SOC, SEG average duration of life; **~ de la patente** PATENT term of patent; **~ de una patente** DER, PATENT patent life; **~ de las prestaciones** SEG duration of benefits; **~ del servicio** RRHH length of service; **~ de vida** V&M *de producto* shelf life; ♦ **de larga ~** MEDIOS long-form

duraciones: **~ de los espacios publicitarios** *f pl* MEDIOS, V&M spot lengths

durante: **~ la última década** *fra* COM GEN over the last decade

durar *vi* COM GEN last out, last

duro *adj* COM GEN *condiciones* tough, RRHH, V&M hard-boiled; **sin un ~** *Esp infrml* (*cf bruja AmL*) RRHH broke (*infrml*), flat broke (*infrml*)

E

echar *vt* COM GEN lay, RRHH *personal* boot out (*infrml*), dismiss, fire (*infrml*), give sb the sack (*infrml*) (*BrE*), give sb their cards (*infrml*) (*BrE*), make redundant, sack (*infrml*); ◆ ~ **un jarro de agua fría sobre** COM GEN put a damper on (*infrml*)

echarse: ~ **atrás** *v refl* COM GEN *plan, promesa* backtrack

ECOFIN *abr* (*Consejo Europeo de los Ministros de Finanzas*) ECON, POL ECOFIN (*European Community Finance Ministers*)

ecología *f* COM GEN, MED AMB ecology; ~ **de la producción** MED AMB production ecology

ecológico *adj* MED AMB ecological, environmentally friendly

ecologista *mf* MED AMB environmentalist

econometría *f* COM GEN, ECON econometrics

econométrico *adj* COM GEN, ECON econometric

econometrista *mf* COM GEN, ECON econometrician

economía *f* BANCA economics, economy, COM GEN, ECON, FIN *austeridad* thrift, POL economics, economy, thrift, PROT SOC economics, economy; ~ **abierta** ECON, POL open economy; ~ **de la abundancia** ECON economy of abundance; ~ **aislada** ECON enclave economy; ~ **de almacenaje** ECON warehouse economy; ~ **aplicada** ECON applied economics; ~ **de armamento permanente** ECON permanent arms economy; ~ **de asedio** ECON siege economy; ~ **austríaca** ECON Austrian Economics; ~ **autárquica** ECON self sufficient economy; ~ **de autosuficiencia** ECON auto-economy; ~ **avanzada** COM GEN advanced economy; ~ **basada en los recursos minerales** ECON mineral-based economy; ~ **basada en el trabajo en cadena** ECON networking economy; ~ **del bienestar** ECON welfare economics; ~ **budista** ECON Buddhist economics; ~ **de carácter manufacturero** ECON manufacturing-based economy; ~ **cerrada** ECON closed economy; ~ **clandestina** ECON, FIN black economy, underground economy; ~ **clásica** ECON classical economics; **la** ~ **como retórica** ECON economics as rhetoric; ~ **competitiva** ECON free enterprise economy; ~ **compleja** ECON complex economy; ~ **completa** ECON mature economy; ~ **comunal** ECON communal economy; ~ **de concentración** ECON agglomeration economy, concentration economy; ~ **constante** ECON steady state economy; ~ **de una cosecha** POL one-crop economy; ~ **débil** ECON, POL ailing economy; ~ **dependiente** ECON branch economy, dependent economy; ~ **del desarrollo** ECON, POL development economics; ~ **dinámica** ECON dynamic economics; ~ **dirigida** ECON controlled economy, command economy, managed economy, POL command economy; ~ **dormida** ECON sleeping economy; ~ **dual** ECON dual economy; ~ **de empresa** COM GEN business economics; ~ **enferma** ECON, POL ailing economy; ~ **de escala** ECON, IND economy of size; ~ **de escala interna** ECON, IND internal economy of scale; ~ **de escala pecuniaria** ECON pecuniary economy of scale; ~ **de escasez** ECON shortage economy; ~ **exterior** COM GEN external economy; ~ **externa de escala** ECON external economy of scale; ~ **externa pecuniaria** ECON pecuniary external economy; ~ **falsa** COM GEN, ECON false economy; ~ **financiera** FIN financial economy; ~ **formal** ECON formal economy; ~ **sin fundamento** POL one-crop economy; ~ **de haciendas** ECON estate economy; ~ **industrial** ECON industrial economics; ~ **inflacionista no controlada** ECON unchecked inflationary economy; ~ **informal** ECON informal economy; ~ **institucional** ECON institutional economics; ~ **interdependiente** ECON, POL interdependent economy; ~ **interna** COM GEN internal economy; ~ **sin intervención** ECON free enterprise economy; ~ **intervenida** ECON managed economy; ~ **keynesiana** ECON Keynesian economics; ~ **liberal** ECON laissez-faire economy, liberal economics; ~ **libertaria** ECON libertarian economics; ~ **madura** ECON *economía completa* mature economy; ~ **marxista** ECON Marxian economics; ~ **de mercado** ECON free enterprise economy, market economy; ~ **de mercado descentralizada** ECON decentralized market economy (*DME*); ~ **de mercado no oficial** ECON parallel market economy; ~ **de mercado pura** ECON, POL pure market economy; ~ **mixta** ECON, POL Butskellism (*BrE*), mixed economy; ~ **moderna** ECON modern economy; ~ **monetaria** ECON cash economy, monetary economics; ~ **de monocultivo** ECON one-crop economy; ~ **mundial** ECON, POL world economy; ~ **neoclásica** ECON neoclassical economics; ~ **normativa** ECON normative economics; **nueva** ~ ECON new economics; **nueva** ~ **clásica** ECON new classical economics; ~ **de oferta** ECON supply side economics; ~ **oficial** ECON blue economy (*BrE*); ~ **organizacional** ECON organizational economics; ~ **de países en vías de desarrollo** ECON, POL developmental economics; ~ **participada** BOLSA, ECON share economy; ~ **de permuta** ECON barter economy; ~ **de planificación centralizada** ECON, POL centrally planned economy (*CPE*); ~ **planificada** ECON, POL command economy; ~ **del pluriempleo** ECON moonlight economy; ~ **política** POL political economy; ~ **positiva** ECON *econometría* positive economics; ~ **principal** ECON primitive economy; ~ **y psicología** ECON, PROT SOC economics and psychology; ~ **psicológica** ECON psychological economy; ~ **pública** ECON public economics; ~ **racional** ECON rational economics; ~ **radical** ECON radical economics; ~ **real de escala** ECON real economy of scale; ~ **recalentada** ECON overheated economy; ~ **de recursos** ECON resource economics; ~ **regional** ECON regional economics; ~ **de rentas** ECON revenue economy; ~ **de la salud** ECON, PROT SOC health economics; ~ **secundaria** ECON second economy; ~ **de sitio** ECON siege economy; ~ **social de mercado** ECON social market economy; ~ **socialista** ECON, POL socialist economy; ~ **sombría** ECON shadow economy; ~ **sumergida** ECON, FIN black economy, underground economy; ~ **de tamaño** ECON, IND economy of size; ~ **de la tierra** ECON land economy; ~ **del transporte** ECON transport economics; ~ **de trueque** ECON revenge barter (*jarg*), POL dual economy; ~ **urbana** ECON urban economics; ~ **variable** ECON protean economy

economías: ~ **de escala** *f pl* ECON economies of scale

económicamente[1]: **~ sólido** *adj* COM GEN financially sound

económicamente[2] *adv* ECON, FIN, V&M economically

económico *adj* COM GEN financial, economical, ECON economic, V&M *barato* budget

economismo *m* ECON, POL economism

economista *mf* ECON, POL economist; **~ jefe(-a)** *m,f* COM GEN, ECON chief economist; **~ mercantil** COM GEN business economist

economistas: **~ vulgares** *m pl* ECON *marxismo* vulgar economists

economizador: **~ de trabajo** *adj* RRHH labor-saving (*AmE*), labour-saving (*BrE*)

economizar 1. *vt* COM GEN economize; **2.** *vi* COM GEN economize

ecosistema *m* MED AMB ecosystem

ECOSOC *abr* (*Consejo Económico y Social*) ECON ECOSOC (*Economic and Social Council*)

ecotoxicológico *adj* MED AMB ecotoxicological

ECU *abr* (*Unidad Monetaria Europea*) ECON, POL ECU (*European Currency Unit*)

ecuación *f* MAT equation; **~ del balance** CONT balance sheet equation; **~ contable** CONT accounting equation; **~ en diferencias** ECON *econometría* difference equation; **~ de Fisher** MAT Fisher equation; **~ en forma reducida** ECON reduced form equation; **~ de Slutsky** ECON Slutsky equation

ecualización: **~ espacial** *f* ECON spatial equalization

ED *abr* (*eurodólar*) ECON ED (*Eurodollar*)

edad *f* COM GEN age; **~ al vencimiento** SEG age at expiry; **~ cumplida** SEG attained age; **~ de ingreso** SEG age at entry; **~ de jubilación** RRHH pensionable age, retirement age; **~ normal de jubilación** RRHH normal retirement age; **~ de oro** ECON golden age

edades: **~ diferentes de jubilación** *f pl* RRHH multiple retirement ages

edición *f* COM GEN, INFO edition (*ed.*), MEDIOS issue; **~ ampliada** COM GEN enlarged edition; **~ atrasada** MEDIOS *de diario o revista* back issue; **~ combinada** MEDIOS *imprenta* combined issue; **~ ecológica** MED AMB green issue; **~ gráfica** INFO, MEDIOS *imprenta* graphical editing; **~ matinal** MEDIOS *prensa* bulldog edition (*AmE*); **~ de noticias de última hora de la noche** MEDIOS *radio* late night news; **~ de prensa** MEDIOS *imprenta* press edition; **~ revisada** MEDIOS *prensa* revised edition; **~ de texto** INFO, MEDIOS text editing

ediciones: **~ valoradas por libra** *f pl* V&M valued impressions per pound

edificar *vt* INMOB build

edificio *m* COM GEN, INMOB building; **~ de apartamentos** INMOB apartment building; **~ sin ascensor** INMOB walk-up (*jarg*); **~ en copropiedad** COM GEN condominium, cooperative (*co-op*); **~ multifamiliar** *AmL* (*cf edificio residencial Esp*) PROT SOC multiple unit residential building; **~ de oficinas** COM GEN, INMOB office block (*BrE*), office building; **~ residencial** *Esp* (*cf edificio multifamiliar AmL*) PROT SOC multiple unit residential building

editado *adj* COM GEN issued, published, INFO *datos, documentos, textos* edited; ◆ **no ~** COM GEN, MEDIOS unpublished

editar *vt* COM GEN *revista, periódico* issue, publish, INFO *datos, documentos, textos* edit

editor, a *m,f* COM GEN publisher, INFO *programas* editor, MEDIOS publisher, copy editor; **~ de diseño** RRHH design editor; **~ en jefe(-a) adjunto(-a)** MEDIOS *prensa* chief sub-editor (*BrE*) (*chief sub*); **~ de pantalla** INFO screen editor; **~ de textos** INFO, MEDIOS text editor

editorial *m* MEDIOS lead, editorial, leading article

editorialista *mf* COM GEN editorialist, MEDIOS leader writer

educación *f* PROT SOC education; **~ administrativa** GES management education; **~ coordinada** PROT SOC cooperative education; **~ a distancia** PROT SOC distance learning; **~ profesional permanente** CONT continual professional education; **~ sanitaria** COM GEN health education; **~ secundaria** PROT SOC secondary education; **~ superior** COM GEN, PROT SOC tertiary education, advanced education, higher education; **~ terciaria** PROT SOC tertiary education

efectivamente *adv* COM GEN effectively

efectividad: **~ del anuncio** *f* V&M advertising effectiveness

efectivo[1] *adj* COM GEN *bien tangible*, CONT *números* actual, INFO effective; ◆ **con efectivo ~** FIN cash rich; **con ~ insuficiente** FIN cash poor

efectivo[2] *m* COM GEN *fondos* cash, hard cash, ready cash; **~ de caja** CONT cash in hand; **~ en caja** BANCA till money, vault cash, COM GEN float, till money, cash holdings, CONT *existencias en caja* available cash, available cashflow, cash holdings, cash on hand; **~ disponible** BANCA till money, COM GEN cash in hand, float, till money, CONT available cash, available cash flow, cash in hand; **~ realmente desembolsado** CONT actual cash disbursement; **~ en tránsito** CONT *contabilidad nacional* cash in transit; **~ útil** FIN carrying cash; ◆ **~ en bancos** BANCA cash in bank

efectivos *m pl* BOLSA, CONT, FIN actuals

efecto[1]: **con ~ retroactivo** *adj* COM GEN backdated

efecto[2] *m* COM GEN, ECON effect, impact, FIN *pagadero, cobrable* bill; **~ de alcance** RRHH catch-up effect; **~ de alienación** V&M *publicidad* alienation effect; **~ amenazador** ECON *salarios* threat effect; **~ anticipado** FIN advance bill; **~ anuncio** POL announcement effect; **~ de aplazamiento** COM GEN holdover effect; **~ de aprendizaje** ECON, RRHH learning effect; **~ backwash** ECON backwash effect; **~ de la capacidad productiva** ECON capacity effect; **~ capitalizador de un impuesto** ECON, FISC capitalization effect of a tax; **~ colateral** COM GEN side effect; **~ como aval** BOLSA billback; **~ contable** CONT *aplicación de normas* accounting effect; **~ crowding-out** ECON crowding-out effect; **~ desincentivador** ECON disincentive effect; **~ dominó** BOLSA butterfly effect; **~ dotal** BANCA endowment effect; **~ envejecimiento de los medios de producción** ECON vintage effect; **~ de exclusión** COM GEN, ECON, FIN crowding out; **~ externo** ECON neighborhood effect (*AmE*), neighbourhood effect (*BrE*); **~ Fisher** ECON Fisher effect; **~ Gerschenkron** ECON Gerschenkron effect; **~ Giffen** V&M Giffen effect; **~ incentivador** ECON incentive effect; **~ indirecto** COM GEN spill-over effect; **~ inducido** FIN induced draft; **~ inercia** POL inertial effect; **~ de ingreso** ECON income effect; **~ inmediato** ECON impact effect; **~ inmovilizado** BOLSA locked-in effect; **~ de invernadero** MED AMB greenhouse effect; ~ **Katona** ECON Katona effect; ~ **Keynes** ECON Keynes effect; ~ **legal** FISC legal effect; ~ **Lerner** ECON Lerner effect; ~ **luxemburgo** ECON Luxemburg effect; ~ **multiplicador** ECON *econometría* multiplier effect; ~ **negociable** BOLSA trading security; ~ **no compensable** BANCA nonclearing item; ~ **a pagar** CONT bill payable; ~ **palanca** ECON ratchet effect; ~ **de los precios** ECON price effect; ~ **de propagación** ECON spread effect; ~ **de propulsión** ECON forward linkage; ~ **de rebosamiento** COM GEN spill-over effect; ~ **recíproco** COM GEN interplay; ~ **remanencia del mensaje publicitario** MEDIOS *imprenta* carry-over effect; ~ **residual** ECON ripple effect; ~ **resultante** DER consequential effect; ~ **de Ricardo** ECON Ricardo effect; ~ **riqueza** ECON wealth effect; ~ **de salarios sindicales** FIN union wage effect; ~ **de saldo real** ECON *efecto Pigou* Pigou effect; ~ **de Slutsky** ECON Slutsky effect; ~ **subsidiario** CONT, ECON, FIN spillover effect; ~ **de sustitución** ECON substitution effect; ~ **tardío** COM GEN after-effect; ~ **de un tercero** ECON third-party effect; ~ **de trinquete** ECON ratchet effect; ~ **de vencimiento a corto plazo** BANCA, FIN hot bill (*infrml*); ~ **a la vista** BANCA, CONT, FIN hot bill (*infrml*), sight bill, sight draft; ◆ **tener** ~ COM GEN inure (*frml*), take effect; **tener** ~ **legal** DER have statutory effect

efectos[1]: **a** ~ **contables** *adj* CONT for accounting purposes

efectos[2] *m pl* FIN paper (*infrml*); ~ **al portador** BOLSA bearer bill; ~ **en cartera** BOLSA, CONT securities in hand; ~ **a cobrar** CONT bills receivable; **otros** ~ **por cobrar** BANCA other receivables; ~ **a cobrar acumulados y gastos anticipados** CONT accrued receivable and pre-paid expenses; ~ **por cobrar congelados** FIN *hoja de balance* frozen receivables; ~ **comerciales en eurodivisas** BOLSA Eurocommercial paper (*ECP*); ~ **comprados bajo acuerdo de reventa** CONT *estado contable* bills purchased under resale agreement; ~ **comprados con pacto de recompra** FIN *hoja de balance* bills purchased under resale agreement; ~ **descontados** CONT bills discounted; ~ **económicos del impuesto** ECON, FISC tax consequences; ~ **especiales sonoros** MEDIOS sound effects; ~ **fiscales regionales** CONT, FISC regional tax effects; ~ **garantizados con mercancías** BOLSA commodity paper; ~ **de incentivo** ECON incentive effect; ~ **a pagar** CONT amount payable; ~ **a pagar al cierre del ejercicio** CONT payables at year-end; ~ **personales** COM GEN personal effects; ~ **públicos** POL government securities; ~ **de renta y sustitución** ECON income and substitution effects; ◆ **sin** ~ COM GEN no effects (*NE*)

efectuar *vt* COM GEN accomplish, *pago* effect, CONT *anotación, asiento, registro* pass

eficacia *f* COM GEN efficiency; ~ **administrativa** GES managerial effectiveness; ~ **organizacional** GES organizational effectiveness; ~ **publicitaria** V&M advertising effectiveness

eficaz *adj* COM GEN effective; ◆ ~ **en relación con el coste** *Esp* (*cf eficaz en relación con el costo AmL*) COM GEN, CONT cost-effective; ~ **en relación con el costo** *AmL* (*cf eficaz en relación con el coste Esp*) COM GEN, CONT cost-effective

eficiencia *f* COM GEN efficiency; ~ **bancaria** BANCA bank efficiency; ~ **de la bolsa** ECON exchange efficiency; ~ **del combustible** MED AMB fuel efficiency; ~ **económica** ECON, MED AMB economic efficiency;

~ **de la energía** IND, MED AMB energy efficiency; ~ **laboral** RRHH labor efficiency (*AmE*), labour efficiency (*BrE*); ~ **de localización** ECON, FIN allocative efficiency; ~ **marginal del capital** ECON marginal efficiency of capital; ~ **marginal de la inversión** ECON marginal efficiency of investment; ~ **de más alto nivel** ECON top-level efficiency; ~ **operativa** TRANSP operating efficiency; ~ **de Pareto** ECON Pareto efficiency; ~ **técnica** ECON technical efficiency; ~ **X** ECON X efficiency

eficiente *adj* COM GEN, INFO efficient; ◆ ~ **desde el punto de vista fiscal** FISC tax-efficient

efimeralización *f* ECON ephemeralisation (*jarg*)

efímero *adj* COM GEN shortlived

egreso *m* COM GEN expenditure

ej. *abr* (*ejemplo*) COM GEN ex. (*example*)

eje *m* MAT, TRANSP axis; ~ **de Lothar** ECON Lotharingian axis; ~ **roto** TRANSP *vehículo remolque* knock-out axle

ejecución *f* COM GEN execution, CONT *de la empresa*, DER performance; ~ **a bajo interés** BOLSA cheap execution (*BrE*); ~ **en computador** *AmL* ver *ejecución en computadora AmL*; ~ **en computadora** *AmL* (*cf ejecución en ordenador Esp*) INFO computer run; ~ **extraterritorial** DER extraterritorial enforcement; ~ **forzosa** DER specific performance; ~ **hipotecaria estatutaria** DER statutory foreclosure; ~ **hipotecaria forzosa** DER strict foreclosure; ~ **en ordenador** *Esp* (*cf ejecución en computadora AmL*) INFO computer run; ~ **de una política** POL policy execution; ~ **de una póliza** COM GEN policy execution; ~ **de prueba** COM GEN, IND, INFO, V&M *sistema, máquina* test run; ~ **rápida** DER summary application; ~ **del trabajo** *Esp* (*cf desempeño del puesto AmL*) RRHH job performance

ejecutable *adj* COM GEN exercisable, DER enforceable; ◆ **no** ~ BOLSA irredeemable

ejecutado *adj* COM GEN *cumplido o realizado en su totalidad* executed (*ex*), complete; ◆ ~ **por computador** *AmL* ver *ejecutado por computadora AmL*; ~ **por computadora** *AmL* (*cf ejecutado por ordenador Esp*) INFO computer-oriented; ~ **por ordenador** *Esp* (*cf ejecutado por computadora AmL*) INFO computer-oriented; **no** ~ COM GEN unexecuted

ejecutante *mf* ECON performer

ejecutar *vt* COM GEN execute, perform, *concesión* run, FIN *hipoteca* foreclose, GES run; ◆ ~ **una opción** BOLSA declare an option; ~ **órdenes** BOLSA execute orders; ~ **el procedimiento de entrada** INFO log in

ejecutivo[1] *adj* GES, POL executive; ◆ **no** ~ RRHH nonexecutive

ejecutivo[2]: **el** ~ *m* POL the executive

ejecutivo[3],**-a** *m,f* COM GEN executive (*exec.*), RRHH cadre, executive (*exec.*); ~ **agresivo(-a)** COM GEN aggressive executive; ~ **de la compañía** RRHH company executive; ~ **de cuentas** BOLSA *casa de corretaje* account executive, MEDIOS *publicidad*, RRHH account manager, account executive; ~ **desplazado(-a) al extranjero** COM GEN expatriate executive; ~ **de empresa** GES corporate executive; ~ **de línea** RRHH line executive; ~ **de marketing** *Esp* (*cf ejecutivo de mercadotecnia AmL*) RRHH marketing executive; ~ **de mercadotecnia** *AmL* (*cf ejecutivo de marketing Esp*) RRHH marketing executive; ~ **de reclutamiento** RRHH recruitment officer, recruiting officer; ~ **del sindicato** BANCA syndication official; ~ **de tráfico** RRHH traffic executive;

~ **de ventas** RRHH, V&M sales executive; ~ **de ventas de importación** RRHH, V&M import sales executive

ejecutorio *adj* DER enforceable, executory

ejemplar *m* COM GEN *publicidad* copy, MEDIOS issue; ~ **gratuito** MEDIOS *prensa* presentation copy; ~ **de regalo** COM GEN, MEDIOS complimentary copy; ~ **para reseña publicitaria** MEDIOS press copy

ejemplo[1]: **por** ~ *adv* (*p.ej.*) COM GEN for example (*e.g.*), exempli gratia (*e.g.*)

ejemplo[2] *m* (*ej.*) COM GEN example (*ex.*); ~ **de actividad** GES activity sampling; ~ **clásico** COM GEN classic example; ~ **típico** V&M *publicidad* case history

ejercer *vt* BOLSA *opción, derecho* exercise, COM GEN *propios derechos* enforce, practise (*BrE*), practice (*AmE*), *efecto* exert, DER exercise; ◆ ~ **influencia sobre** COM GEN have an impact on; ~ **una presión excesiva** FISC *sobre un contribuyente* cause undue hardship; ~ **presión sobre** COM GEN bring pressure to bear on

ejercicio *m* BOLSA *opción*, COM GEN *opción* exercise; ~ **de adquisición** CONT year of acquisition; ~ **anterior** CONT prior period; ~ **anual** COM GEN *empresas comerciales e industriales* business year; ~ **de un cargo** RRHH tenure; ~ **contable** CONT, FIN accounting period, financial period; ~ **de contraincendio** RRHH fire drill; ~ **en curso** ADMIN in-tray exercise (*jarg*); ~ **del derecho** DER law practice; ~ **de los derechos** BOLSA exercise of rights; ~ **económico** COM GEN financial period, financial year (*FY*), fiscal year (*FY*); ~ **económico actual** CONT current business year; ~ **económico en curso** CONT current business year; ~ **económico vigente** CONT current business year; ~ **fiscal** COM GEN financial year (*FY*), fiscal year (*FY*), tax year; ~ **financiero** COM GEN financial year (*FY*), fiscal period, fiscal year (*FY*); ~ **fiscal** BANCA, CONT, ECON, FIN, FISC financial year (*FY*), fiscal period, fiscal year (*FY*), taxable year; ~ **fiscal anterior** FISC preceding taxation year; ~ **hasta la fecha** CONT, FISC year to date; ~ **de la opción** BOLSA option exercise; ~ **de una opción** BOLSA exercise of an option; ~ **de una opción de compra** BOLSA call's strike; ~ **de una opción de venta** BOLSA put's strike; ~ **prematuro** BOLSA *opciones* early exercise; ~ **presupuestario** POL budget year; ~ **de una profesión** DER practice; ◆ ~ **contable terminado** CONT accounting year then ended; ~ **económico terminado** CONT accounting year then ended

elaboración *f* FISC, INFO processing, PATENT *de informe* drawing up; ~ **objetiva de presupuesto** V&M objective budgeting; ~ **del presupuesto** CONT budget preparation, budgeting; ~ **del presupuesto de caja** CONT, ECON cash budgeting; ~ **del presupuesto de tesorería** CONT, ECON cash budgeting; ~ **de presupuestos por programa** CONT, FIN program budgeting (*AmE*), programme budgeting (*BrE*); ~ **de tarifas** TRANSP rate construction

elaborar *vt* COM GEN manufacture, DER draw up, IND manufacture

elasticidad *f* ECON elasticity, resilience; ~ **arco** ECON arc elasticity; ~ **cruzada de la demanda** ECON, V&M cross-elasticity of demand; ~ **de la demanda** ECON, V&M elasticity of demand; ~ **de la demanda y del suministro** ECON, V&M elasticity of demand and supply; ~ **de expectativas** ECON elasticity of expectations; ~-**ingreso de la demanda** V&M income elasticity of demand; ~ **del interés de los ahorros** ECON interest elasticity of savings; ~ **negativa** ECON negative elasticity; ~ **de la oferta** ECON, V&M elasticity of supply; ~ **de la oferta y la demanda** ECON, V&M elasticity of demand and supply; ~-**precio de la demanda** ECON price elasticity of demand; ~ **precio-demanda** V&M price-demand elasticity; ~ **de la previsión** ECON elasticity of anticipation; ~ **de punto** ECON point elasticity; ~-**renta de la demanda** ECON income elasticity of demand; ~ **de la respuesta** V&M response elasticity; ~ **del suministro** ECON, V&M elasticity of supply; ~ **de sustitución** ECON elasticity of substitution; ~ **de sustitución constante** ECON constant elasticity of substitution; ~ **tributaria** ECON, FISC tax buoyancy, tax elasticity; ~ **unitaria** ECON unitary elasticity

elección *f* COM GEN choice, election, FISC, GES, POL election; ~ **del consumidor** V&M consumer choice; ~ **escalonada** POL staggered election; ~ **federal** POL federal election; ~ **parcial** POL by-election; ~ **variable** CONT, ECON choice variable

elecciones: ~ **locales** *f pl* COM GEN local election

electivo *adj* COM GEN, GES, POL elective

electorado *m* COM GEN *política* electorate

electrificación *f* TRANSP *de ferrocarriles* electrification

electrodomésticos *m pl* COM GEN household appliances, appliances, V&M brown goods, white goods

electrónica *f* IND electronics

electrostático *adj* INFO electrostatic

electrotipo *m* V&M electrotype

elegibilidad *f* FISC, POL eligibility

elegible *adj* BANCA eligible

elegido: ~ **recientemente** *adj* COM GEN newly elected

elegir *vt* POL elect; ◆ ~ **a alguien para la junta** COM GEN elect sb to the board

elemento *m* COM GEN element; ~ **de actividad** CONT activity element; ~ **de la actividad administrativa** CONT administrative activity element; ~ **del activo** BOLSA asset; ~ **auxiliar de la venta** V&M sales aid; ~ **del coste** *Esp* (*cf elemento del costo AmL*) CONT, ECON cost factor; ~ **del costo** *AmL* (*cf elemento del coste Esp*) CONT, ECON cost factor; ~ **excepcional** TRANSP exceptional item; ~ **de información** COM GEN piece of information; ~ **optativo** FIN optional item; ~ **de riesgo** COM GEN element of risk

elementos: ~ **comunes** *m pl* INMOB *de condominio* common elements; ~ **no fungibles** *m pl* CONT non-fungible goods; ~ **visuales** *m pl* COM GEN, MEDIOS, V&M *para una presentación* visuals

elevación *f* CONT, FIN raise, rise

elevado: **muy** ~ *adj* COM GEN soaring

elevador: ~ **de cangilones** *m* TRANSP *carga* bucket elevator; ~ **de carrera vertical** *m* TRANSP *carga* straight lift; ~ **de carretones** *m* TRANSP bogie lift; ~ **garantizado** *m* COM GEN bonded elevator; ~ **de grano** *m* TRANSP *de carga, descarga* grain elevator

elevar *vt* COM GEN heighten, *incremento* step up, *sanciones* lift, DER *una reclamación* file

elevarse *v refl* COM GEN *beneficios, precios* soar

eliminación *f* COM GEN removal, editing-out, CONT writing-off, INFO removal; ~ **de desperdicios** MED AMB waste disposal; ~ **de una deuda** COM GEN, CONT deletion of a debt; ~ **de las distorsiones fiscales** FISC removal of tax distortions

eliminar *vt* COM GEN eliminate, edit out, *restricciones* remove, CONT *partida contable* write off, ECON *la inflación* stamp out, INFO remove, RRHH screen out; ◆ **~ por fases** COM GEN, INFO phase out; **~ progresivamente** COM GEN, INFO *tecnología, servicio, sistema* phase out

eliminatorio *adj* COM GEN qualifying

ELIO *abr* (*estimador lineal insesgado óptimo*) ECON BLUE (*best linear unbiased estimator*)

eludir *vt* FISC avoid

elusión: ~ legal de impuestos *f* FISC tax avoidance

emancipación *f* DER, POL emancipation

embajada *f* COM GEN, POL embassy

embajador, a *m,f* COM GEN, POL ambassador

embalado: no ~ *adj* COM GEN unpacked

embalador, a *m,f* COM GEN packer; **~ de exportación** IMP/EXP export packer

embalaje *m* COM GEN, IMP/EXP, TRANSP, V&M baling, dressing, pack, packaging; **~ por contracción** COM GEN, IND, TRANSP shrink wrapping; **~ defectuoso** V&M defective packaging; **~ de exportación en la fábrica** TRANSP *carga* ex works export packing; **~ para exportación franco de fábrica** IMP/EXP *carga* ex works export packing; **~ gratuito** V&M no charges for packing; **~ impermeable** V&M waterproof packing; **~ intermodal** TRANSP intermodal packaging; **~ metálico** MED AMB metal packaging; **~ con papel de burbujas** V&M blister packaging

embalar *vt* COM GEN, IMP/EXP, TRANSP, V&M bale, pack, package

embarcación: ~ fluvial *f* TRANSP inland waterway vessel; **~ no propulsada** *f* TRANSP dumb craft; **~ del práctico** *f* TRANSP *puertos* pilot boat

embarcadero *m* TRANSP *navegación* pier; **~ al pie de la casa** TRANSP pier to house; **~ del práctico** TRANSP pilotage slip; ◆ **sobre ~** COM GEN, IMP/EXP, TRANSP ex-wharf (*x-wharf*); **~ a embarcadero** IMP/EXP *envío*, TRANSP pier to pier; **en el ~** COM GEN, IMP/EXP, TRANSP ex-wharf (*x-wharf*)

embarcado: ~ a bordo *adj* COM GEN, IMP/EXP, TRANSP shipped aboard, shipped on board

embarcador, a *m,f* COMS, IMP/EXP *transportista* forwarder (*fwdr*)

embarcar *vt* TRANSP *fletes* ship

embarcarse: ~ en *v refl* COM GEN *curso de acción* embark on

embargado *adj* DER restrained

embargador, a *m,f* DER, FIN sequestrator

embargar *vt* DER garnish, *confiscar* levy

embargo *m* DER garnishment, distraint, INMOB distraint, TRANSP embargo; **~ fiscal** FISC tax foreclosure, tax lien; **~ fiscal federal** FISC federal tax lien; **~ preventivo** DER lien; **~ de propiedad** DER, INMOB distraint of property

embargos: ~ fiscales *m pl* FISC liens for taxes, liens tax

embarque *m* TRANSP shipment, shipping, *navegación* embarkation; **~ directo** TRANSP through shipment; **~ no completo** TRANSP part shipment; **~ parcial** TRANSP short shipment; **~ volumétrico** IMP/EXP volume shipping; ◆ **~ y desembarque autopropulsado** (*ro/ro*) TRANSP *buque carguero* roll-on/roll-off (*ro/ro*)

embaucador, a *m,f* COM GEN confidence trickster

embaucar *vt* COM GEN deceive, trick

embotellado: ~ de vino *m* ECON, IND wine-bottling

embotellamiento *m* TRANSP bottleneck; **~ de tráfico** MED AMB, TRANSP traffic jam

embrague: ~ airflex *m* TRANSP airflex clutch (*AFC*); **~ en cesta** *m* TRANSP *carga y descarga* basket hitch

emergencia *f* COM GEN emergency (*emy*)

emigración *f* ECON *datos*, INFO *datos* migration

eminente *adj* RRHH *carrera* distinguished

emisario *m* MED AMB effluent

emisión *f* BOLSA issue, MED AMB *de gases* emission, MEDIOS broadcast; **~ de acciones** BOLSA stock issue; **~ de acciones al contado** BOLSA, FIN share issue for cash; **~ de acciones de una compañía** BOLSA, FIN corporate issue; **~ de acciones liberadas** BOLSA, CONT bonus issue (*BrE*), capitalization issue (*BrE*), scrip issue (*BrE*), stock dividend (*AmE*), stock split (*AmE*); **~ atractiva** BOLSA glamor issue (*jarg*) (*AmE*), glamour issue (*jarg*) (*BrE*); **~ autorizada** BOLSA authorized stock; **~ de azufre** MED AMB sulphur emission (*BrE*), sulphur emission (*AmE*); **~ bancaria** BANCA bank float (*AmE*); **~ de bonos** BOLSA bond issue, flotation; **~ de bonos subordinados** BOLSA subordinated bond issue; **~ de bonos subordinados convertibles** BOLSA subordinated convertible bond issue; **~ de carbono** IND, MED AMB carbon emission; **~ de cheques extranjeros** BANCA foreign check issue (*AmE*), foreign cheque issue (*BrE*); **~ de cheques** BANCA, COM GEN, FIN check issue (*AmE*), cheque issue (*BrE*); **~ de cheques de sueldos** BANCA release of pay checks (*AmE*), release of pay cheques (*BrE*); **~ de conversión** BOLSA conversion issue; **~ convertible** FIN conversion issue, convertible issue; **~ con derecho preferente de suscripción** BOLSA, CONT, DER rights issue; **~ de derechos** BOLSA rights issue; **~ con derechos para los accionistas** BOLSA, CONT, DER rights issue; **~ con derechos de suscripción** BOLSA, CONT rights issue; **~ con descuento** BOLSA original issue discount (*OID*); **~ con descuento original** BOLSA, FIN original issue discount bond (*OID bond*); **~ de deuda municipal a corto plazo** BOLSA revenue anticipation note (*RAN*); **~ de deuda subordinada** BOLSA junior issue (*AmE*); **~ de dióxido de carbono** *m* IND, MED AMB carbon dioxide emission; **~ en divisas** BOLSA foreign currency issue; **~ del dólar eurocanadiense** BOLSA Euro-Canadian dollar issue; **~ escalonada de obligaciones** BOLSA split offering; **~ de eurobonos** BOLSA Eurobond issue; **~ de exteriores** MEDIOS outside broadcast; **~ fiduciaria** BANCA fiduciary issue, note issue; **~ garantizada** BOLSA guaranteed issue, FIN warrant issue; **~ garantizada subordinada** BOLSA subordinated warrant issue; **~ de gases** MED AMB *vehículos automotores* exhaust emission; **~ de gases de automóviles** MED AMB car exhaust emissions; **~ a goteo** BOLSA tap issue; **~ ilimitada de cheques** BANCA unlimited checking (*AmE*), unlimited chequing (*BrE*); **~ importante** COM GEN big issue; **~ interior** BOLSA domestic issue; **~ en el mercado de eurocapitales** BOLSA, ECON Eurocapital market issue; **~ de moda** BOLSA glamor issue (*jarg*) (*AmE*), glamour issue (*jarg*) (*BrE*); **~ nacional** BOLSA domestic issue; **~ de obligaciones** BOLSA issue of debentures; **~ de opciones cubiertas** BOLSA covered option writing; **~ de papel moneda** BANCA currency issue; **~ precolocada** BOLSA bought deal; **~ primaria** BOLSA primary issue; **~ prioritaria** BOLSA senior issue; **~ privada** BOLSA private issue; **~ pública** BOLSA public issue; **~ de radio** MEDIOS *radiodifusión* radio broadcast; ~ **de rating dudoso** BOLSA salvage bond; ~ **de títulos** BOLSA equity issue; ~ **de valores** BOLSA issues of necessity; ◆ **nueva ~** BANCA *letra de cambio*, BOLSA reissue; **la ~ no fue suscrita en su totalidad** BOLSA the issue was under-subscribed

emisiones: ~ **con opción en efectivo** *f pl* BOLSA issues with currency options

emisor, a *m,f* BANCA originator, BOLSA, COM GEN issuer, writer, COMS transmitter, FIN issuer, writer; ~ **de una opción** BOLSA option writer; ~ **de una opción de compra al descubierto** BOLSA uncovered call writer; ~ **de opciones abiertas** BOLSA naked writer, uncovered writer; ~ **de opciones de compra** BOLSA call option writer, call writer; ~ **de opciones en descubierto parcial** BOLSA ratio writer; ~ **de opciones de divisas** BOLSA currency options writer; ~ **de pasivos** BOLSA liability issuer; ~ **de la tarjeta** COM GEN card issuer; ~ **de tarjetas de crédito** BANCA, FIN credit card issuer

emisora: ~ **de radio** *f* MEDIOS *radiodifusión* radio station; ~ **de radio comercial** *f* MEDIOS *radio* commercial radio station

emitido *adj* BOLSA issued; ◆ ~ **y en circulación** BOLSA issued and in circulation

emitir *vt* BOLSA *acciones* deliver, issue, *opción* write, FIN, INFO *mensaje* issue, MEDIOS *prensa, radio* broadcast; ◆ ~ **acciones al descuento** BOLSA issue shares at a discount; ~ **acciones a la par** BOLSA issue shares at par; ~ **billetes** BANCA, BOLSA issue bank notes; ~ **un cheque** BANCA make out a check (*AmE*), make out a cheque (*BrE*); ~ **un cheque a favor de alguien** BANCA make a check payable to sb (*AmE*), make a cheque payable to sb (*BrE*); ~ **un cheque pagadero a alguien** BANCA make a check payable to sb (*AmE*), make a cheque payable to sb (*BrE*); ~ **un empréstito** BANCA issue a loan, BOLSA float a loan, issue a loan; ~ **más votos que** COM GEN outvote; ~ **de nuevo** BOLSA reissue; ~ **obligaciones** BOLSA float securities; ~ **un señal sonora** INFO beep

emolumentos *m pl* COM GEN, RRHH perk, perquisites

empantanar *vt* COM GEN swamp

empantanarse *v refl* COM GEN get bogged down (*infrml*)

empaquetado[1] *adj* V&M *mercancías* prepackaged

empaquetado[2] *m* COM GEN, IMP/EXP, TRANSP, V&M packing; ~ **de cajas** TRANSP case packaging (*Cl-*); ~ **compuesto** TRANSP composite packaging; ~ **y desempaquetado** COM GEN stuffing and stripping

empaquetar *vt* COM GEN package

emparejado: ~ **con** *adj* COM GEN coupled with

emparentado: ~ **por lazos de sangre** *adj* FISC connected by blood relationship

empeñar *vt* COM GEN pawn

empeño *m* BANCA *recomendación, objeto* pledge

empeorar *vi* COM GEN worsen

empezar *vi* COM GEN begin; start; ◆ ~ **a avanzar** COM GEN *economía*, ECON gain momentum; ~ **desde cero** COM GEN start from scratch; ~ **a destacar** COM GEN come to the fore; ~ **a hacer** COM GEN set about doing

empírico[1] *adj* ECON empirical

empírico[2] *m* ECON empirics

emplazamiento *m* COM GEN site, IND site, siting, *de fábrica* location, INFO site, siting; ~ **de huelga** IND,

RRHH strike call; ~ **judicial** DER, PATENT citation; ~ **de primer orden** INMOB *propiedad minorista* prime site

emplazar: ~ **judicialmente** *fra* DER, PATENT cite

empleado[1] *adj* COM GEN employed

empleado[2],**-a** *m,f* BANCA, RRHH clerk, employee; ~ **administrativo(-a)** ADMIN, RRHH desk clerk; ~ **bancario(-a)** BANCA bank clerk, bank officer; ~ **de banco** BANCA, RRHH bank employee; ~ **de bolsa** BOLSA authorized clerk, blue button (*jarg*) (*BrE*); ~ **de confianza** COM GEN confidential clerk; ~ **de contabilidad** CONT accounting clerk; ~ **de correos** RRHH postal worker; ~ **de créditos** BANCA lending officer; ~ **de cuentas a pagar** CONT accounts payable clerk; ~ **diplomado(-a)** RRHH certifying officer; ~ **eventual** RRHH temporary (*temp.*); ~ **de exportación** IMP/EXP, RRHH, TRANSP export clerk; ~ **fantasma** RRHH dummy employee; ~ **con información confidencial** BOLSA insider; ~ **inútil** RRHH dummy employee; ~ **de oficina** RRHH *trabajador* white-collar worker; ~ **de la oficina de dirección** ADMIN front office clerk; ~ **del parquet** BOLSA floor official; ~ **postal** RRHH mail clerk (*AmE*), postal clerk (*BrE*); ~ **de primera línea** *m* RRHH front-line employee; ~ **a prueba** RRHH probationary employee; ~ **de seguridad** RRHH safety officer; ~ **sindical** RRHH union official; ~ **a sueldo** COM GEN, RRHH salaried employee; ~ **a tiempo parcial** RRHH part-time employee; ~ **en trabajos de oficina** RRHH white-collar worker

empleados *m pl* RRHH employees, personnel, staff; ~ **sin cargo** RRHH rank-and-file; ~ **eventuales** RRHH temporary staff; ~ **exentos** RRHH exempt employees (*AmE*); ~ **fijos** RRHH permanent staff; ~ **y trabajadores del más bajo nivel** RRHH rank-and-file

emplear *vt* COM GEN, RRHH *método* employ

empleo *m* COM GEN employment, MED AMB *de recursos naturales* utilization, RRHH position; ~ **civil** RRHH civilian employment; ~ **encubierto** ECON, RRHH concealed employment; ~ **involuntario** ECON involuntary employment; ~ **de media jornada** RRHH part-time work; ~ **de medio tiempo** RRHH part-time work; ~ **permanente** RRHH permanent employment; ~ **protegido** PROT SOC, RRHH sheltered employment; ~ **en el sector público** RRHH public sector employment (*PSE*); ~ **secundario** RRHH secondary employment; ~ **en el servicio público** RRHH public service employment (*PSE*); ~ **sometido a descuentos de jubilación** RRHH pensionable employment; ~ **sumergido** ECON underground employment; ~ **temporal** RRHH temporary employment; ~ **a tiempo parcial** RRHH part-time employment; ~ **vitalicio** RRHH lifetime employment; ◆ **en ~ activo** RRHH in active employment; **en el ámbito del ~** RRHH on the employment front; **pleno ~** ECON full employment

empleos: ~ **vacantes** *m pl* RRHH appointments vacant

empobrecido *adj* FIN impoverished

emprendedor *adj* COM GEN enterprising

emprender *vt* COM GEN *una tarea* undertake; ◆ ~ **acción legal** RRHH take legal action; ~ **acciones laborales** RRHH take industrial action; ~ **una campaña** POL conduct a campaign, engage in a campaign

empresa *f* COM GEN business, enterprise (*BrE*), *unión temporal* undertaking, *organización empresarial* concern; ~ **absorbente** ECON *fusión* absorbing company; ~ **administrada por los obreros** GES labor-managed firm (*AmE*), labour-managed firm (*BrE*), employee-owned firm; ~ **adquirida** ECON acquired company; ~ **afiliada** COM GEN, CONT, ECON, RRHH affiliated company; ~ **agrícola** COM GEN farming business; ~ **de alquiler de computadoras** *AmL* INFO computer leasing business; ~ **de alquiler de computadores** *AmL ver empresa de alquiler de computadoras AmL*; ~ **de alquiler de ordenadores** *Esp* (*cf empresa de alquiler de computadoras AmL*) INFO computer leasing business; ~ **de alto riesgo** COM GEN high-risk venture; ~ **aseguradora** SEG insurance carrier, underwriter (*U/W*); ~ **asociada** COM GEN associate company; ~ **avalista de las prestaciones por jubilación** RRHH pension benefit guaranty corporation, pension benefit guarantee corporation; ~ **capitalista** ECON venture capitalist; ~ **para captación de ejecutivos** RRHH executive search firm; ~ **cedente** COM GEN transferor company; ~ **comercial** COM GEN business enterprise; ~ **comercial sin cotización oficial** ECON unquoted trading company; ~ **de computadoras** *AmL* INFO computer company; ~ **de computadores** *AmL* (*ver empresa de computadoras AmL*) INFO computer company; ~ **conjunta** COM GEN, CONT joint equity venture company, joint venture (*JV*); ~ **conjunta transfronteriza** GES, IMP/EXP cross-border joint venture; ~ **constructora** COM GEN construction corporation (*CONCORP*); ~ **de consumo** COM GEN consumer company; ~ **controlada** BOLSA controlled corporation; ~ **controlada desde el exterior** COM GEN foreign-controlled enterprise; ~ **controlada por el gobierno** POL government-controlled corporation; ~ **de conveniencia** COM GEN off-the-shelf company; ~ **sin cotización en bolsa** COM GEN private company, proprietary company; ~ **de cotización plena** BOLSA fully quoted company; ~ **con cotización pública** FIN publicly listed company; ~ **cotizada en bolsa** BOLSA, ECON quoted company; ~ **departamental** ADMIN departmental corporation; ~ **derivada** COM GEN hive-off (*jarg*) (*BrE*); ~ **desleal** RRHH unfair house (*jarg*); ~ **diversificada** COM GEN, ECON, GES diversified company; ~ **dominante** ECON dominant firm; ~ **endeudada** COM GEN thin corporation; ~ **de enseñanza** PROT SOC teaching company; ~ **especializada** BOLSA pure play (*jarg*); ~ **especulativa** COM GEN business concern; ~ **estatal** ECON government enterprise, state enterprise; ~ **expedidora** IMP/EXP, TRANSP forwarding company; ~ **de explotación aurífera** MED AMB gold-mining company; ~ **extranjera** COM GEN, DER alien corporation; ~ **en fase de ampliación** ECON, POL development stage enterprise; ~ **federada** RRHH federated company; ~ **filial** COM GEN associate company; ~ **financiera** FIN finance house (*BrE*), financial enterprise; ~ **flexible** COM GEN flexible firm; ~ **en funcionamiento** COM GEN, CONT *principio contable* going concern; ~ **ganadera** COM GEN farming business; ~ **de gestión pública** BOLSA publicly traded company; ~ **de hecho** COM GEN de facto corporation; ~ **de holding bancario** COM GEN bank holding company; ~ **individual** COM GEN sole proprietorship, individual firm; ~ **inmobiliaria** COM GEN, INMOB real estate company; ~ **de intermediación** BOLSA brokerage firm; ~ **de inversión regulada** ECON, FIN regulated investment company; ~ **itinerante** RRHH runaway shop (*jarg*); ~ **manufacturera y comercializadora** COM GEN industrial and commercial company (*ICC*); ~ **en marcha** COM GEN, CONT going concern; ~ **marginal**

ECON marginal firm; ~ **matriz** BOLSA, COM GEN, CONT, ECON parent company; ~ **mayor de lo aparente** COM GEN iceberg company (*jarg*); ~ **mediadora en el mercado financiero** BOLSA stock brokerage firm; ~ **de mensajería** COM GEN, COMS courier firm; ~ **mercantil** COM GEN business corporation; ~ **multinacional** COM GEN multinational company, multinational corporation (*MNC*); ~ **nacional** COM GEN, ECON domestic corporation; ~ **nacionalizada** ECON, IND, POL nationalized enterprise; ~ **no incorporada** COM GEN unincorporated business; ~ **no lucrativa** COM GEN nonprofit enterprise (*NPE*); ~ **no residente** COM GEN, DER nonresident company; ~ **no sindicada** RRHH *relaciones industriales* non-union firm; ~ **no sindicalizada** RRHH *relaciones industriales* non-union firm; ~ **objetivo** COM GEN target company; ~ **con objetivos modestos de gestión** BOLSA lowballer (*jarg*); ~ **óptima** ECON optimum firm; ~ **de ordenadores** *Esp* (*cf empresa de computadoras AmL*) INFO computer company; ~ **paraestatal** POL government-controlled corporation; ~ **patrocinada por el gobierno** FIN government-sponsored enterprise; ~ **pequeña** COM GEN small firm; ~ **a pequeña escala** COM GEN, ECON, IND small-scale company; ~ **periférica** ECON periphery firm; ~ **con plantilla sindicada** RRHH agency shop; ~ **de préstamos hipotecarios** BANCA, FIN mortgage loan company; ~ **privada** COM GEN, ECON private enterprise, private sector company; ~ **productora de programas** INFO software house; ~ **de programación** INFO software company; ~ **proveedora** COM GEN feeder organization; ~ **de proyectos** ECON projects business; ~ **pública** COM GEN public enterprise, DER Crown corporation, ECON public enterprise, public sector company; ~ **pública creada por ley** COM GEN, DER statutory company; ~ **pública provincial** ECON provincial Crown corporation; ~ **pública de régimen especial** BOLSA qualifying utility; ~ **que cotiza en bolsa** COM GEN, ECON listed company, COM GEN public company; ~ **que funciona como tapadera** FISC shell company (*BrE*) (*jarg*); ~ **que impone la sindicación** RRHH post-entry closed shop; ~ **que no exige sindicación** RRHH open shop; ~ **que pertenece a los empleados** GES employee-owned firm, labor-managed firm (*AmE*), labour-managed firm (*BrE*); ~ **que prefiere trabajadores sindicados** RRHH *relaciones laborales* preferential shop; ~ **regulada** ECON regulated firm; ~ **relacionada** COM GEN, FISC *en relación con una donación* related business; ~ **rentable** COM GEN profit-making enterprise, CONT profitable firm; ~ **representativa** ECON representative firm; ~ **del sector privado** COM GEN, ECON private sector company; ~ **de segunda fila** COM GEN second-tier company; ~ **de seguros cautiva** SEG captive insurance company; ~ **de seguros de vida con reserva legal** SEG legal reserve life insurance company; ~ **de servicios** COM GEN service enterprise; ~ **de servicios personales** FISC personal services business; ~ **de servicios públicos** COM GEN public service corporation (*AmE*), public utility, public utility company, utility, SEG *redes europeas* common carrier; ~ **con sindicación voluntaria** RRHH open shop; ~ **situada en un área no desarrollada** RRHH greenfield site company; ~ **situada en zona verde** RRHH greenfield site company; ~ **de un solo propietario** COM GEN proprietorship; ~ **subsidiaria** COM GEN subsidiary company (*BrE*), subsidiary corporation (*AmE*), subsidiary firm; ~ **de**

tecnología de la información IND, INFO information technology company (*IT company*); ~ **tipo** ECON representative firm; ~ **de titularidad privada** BOLSA private holding corporation; ~ **transnacional** ECON, POL transnational corporation (*TNC*); ~ **de transporte aéreo** TRANSP air carrier; ~ **de transporte interior** IMP/EXP, TRANSP inland carrier; ~ **de transporte marítimo** TRANSP sea carrier; ~ **de transportes** TRANSP transport company (*BrE*), trucking company (*AmE*); ~ **de transportes por contrato** TRANSP contract carrier; ~ **vendedora** COM GEN vendor company; ~ **vertical** ECON vertical combination; ~ **en vías de consolidación** ECON, POL development stage enterprise; ~ **vinculada** COM GEN, FISC related business; ◆ esta ~ **está clasificada como triple A** BOLSA this company is rated triple-A; ~ **establecida en Tokio** COM GEN Tokyo-based company

empresaria *f* COM GEN businesswoman

empresarial *adj* COM GEN business-oriented, entrepreneurial, ECON, GES entrepreneurial, RRHH business-oriented

empresario, -a *m,f* COM GEN businessman, entrepreneur, ECON, GES entrepreneur, RRHH employer, promoter; ~ **asociado(-a)** RRHH associated employer; ~ **individual** COM GEN sole proprietor; ~ **industrial** ECON, IND industrialist; ~ **que aplica la igualdad de oportunidades** RRHH equal opportunity employer; ~ **solicitante** *m* COM GEN applicant entrepreneur; **pequeño(-a)** ~ RRHH small employer

empresas: ~ **de gran magnitud** *f pl* COM GEN big business; ~ **industriales y comerciales** *f pl* ECON industrial and commercial companies (*ICCs*); ~ **de inversión del tercer mundo reconocidas** *f pl* FIN recognized third-world investment firms; ~ **mixtas** *f pl* COM GEN joint venture (*JV*); ~ **multinacionales** *f pl* COM GEN multinational enterprises (*MNEs*); **pequeñas y medianas** ~ **industriales** *f pl* COM GEN, ECON small and medium-sized manufacturing companies

empresólogo(-a) *m,f* COM GEN business consultant

empréstito *m* BANCA, BOLSA borrowing, debenture (*db*), debenture loan, loan; ~ **calificado** BANCA, ECON, FIN qualified borrowing; ~ **consolidado** BANCA consolidated loan; ~ **de contrapartida** BANCA back-to-back loan; ~ **de conversión** FIN conversion loan; ~ **convertible** BANCA convertible loan; ~ **corporativo** BANCA corporate lending; ~ **extranjero** BANCA foreign borrowing; ~ **con garantía** BANCA collateral loan (*BrE*), Lombard loan (*AmE*), secured loan; ~ **sin garantía** BANCA uncovered loan, unsecured loan; ~ **de guerra** FIN War Loan; ~ **no consolidado** BANCA unfunded borrowing; ~ **público** FIN public loan; ~ **ultra vires** BANCA ultravires borrowing

empréstitos *m pl* BANCA, BOLSA borrowings; ~ **municipales** BANCA, BOLSA municipal bonds; ~ **netos** ECON, FIN, POL net borrowing

empuje: ~ **de ventas** *m* V&M sales push

emulación *f* INFO emulation

emulador *m* INFO emulator; ~ **de terminal** INFO terminal emulator

emular *vt* COM GEN, INFO *programa* emulate

enajenable *adj* COM GEN, DER, RRHH alienable

enajenación *f* COM GEN, DER, RRHH alienation

enajenar *vt* COM GEN, DER, RRHH alienate

encabezado: **estar ~ por** *fra* COM GEN be heading for

encabezamiento *m* COMS caption, CONT *hoja de balance* heading, INFO *tipografía* header; ~ **de columnas** CONT column heading

encaje: ~ **circulante** *m* CONT floating cash reserve; ~ **excedente** *m* BANCA, CONT cash reserve; ~ **flotante** *m* CONT floating cash reserve; ~ **legal** *m* CONT legal reserve; ~ **de primas** *m* SEG premium income

encajes: ~ **legales** *m pl* BANCA reserve requirement

encallado *adj* TRANSP aground

encallar *vi* TRANSP *barco* run aground

encaminar *vt* INFO dispatch

encanecer: ~ **a alguien** *fra* COM GEN face up to sb

encarcelamiento *m* DER imprisonment

encarcelar *vt* DER imprison, put away

encargado¹,-a *m,f Esp* GES first line manager; ~ **de facturación** COM GEN invoice clerk; ~ **de la planta** IND plant operator; ~ **de posoperaciones** RRHH post operations officer; ~ **del Registro Mercantil** RRHH registrar of companies

encargado²: **estar ~ de** *fra* COM GEN be in charge of

encargo: ~ **de auditoría** *m* CONT audit engagement

encarte *m* MEDIOS *periódicos, revistas* tip-in

encartes *m pl* MEDIOS loose inserts

encastre: ~ **en U** *m* TRANSP *contenedores* keyhole socket

encendedor *m* COM GEN, TRANSP *cargas peligrosas* igniter

encender *vt* COM GEN inflame, INFO power, turn on, *equipo* enable

encerrar *vt* BOLSA lock in

enchufar *vt* INFO plug

enchufe *f* INFO plug

enchufismo: ~ **sindical** *m* RRHH pork chop (*infrml*) (*AmE*)

encintado: ~ **al sesgo** *adj* TRANSP *cubierta neumática* bias-belted

enclavamiento *m* TRANSP *de contenedores* locking

enclavar *vt* TRANSP lock

enclave: ~ **industrial** *m* IND industrial site

encontrar *vt* COM GEN, INFO find; ◆ ~ **algo deficiente** COM GEN find sth wanting; ~ **defectos en** COM GEN fault; ~ **con** COM GEN come across, *propuesta* fall in with

encuadernación: ~ **mecánica** *f* V&M mechanical binding

encuadre *m* INFO frame

encubrimiento *m* SEG nondisclosure; ~ **corporativo** COM GEN corporate veil (*jarg*)

encuentro: ~ **de negocios** *m* COM GEN business meeting; ~ **de trabajo** *m* CONT working meeting

encuesta *f* COM GEN inquiry, survey, FISC, V&M inquiry; ~ **de campo** V&M *investigación de mercado* field survey; ~ **de consumidores** V&M consumer survey; ~ **por contacto** V&M survey by contact; ~ **de un grupo enfocado** V&M focus group survey; ~ **de inversión de la línea de valor** FIN value-line investment survey; ~ **por muestreo** V&M *investigación de mercado* sample survey; ~ **multicliente** V&M multiclient survey; ~ **por observación** V&M survey of observation; ~ **ómnibus** V&M *investigación de mercado* omnibus survey; ~ **de opinión** V&M opinion poll, opinion survey; ~ **de opiniones** V&M opinion polls; ~ **permanente** V&M continuous survey; ~ **de población activa** V&M labor free sample survey (*AmE*), labour free sample survey (*BrE*); ~ **publicada** MAT *estadística* published research

endémico *adj* COM GEN endemic

endeudado *adj* ECON, FIN indebted; ◆ **~ con** COM GEN indebted to

endeudamiento *m* ECON, FIN indebtedness; **~ externo** ECON, FIN borrowing abroad, external borrowings; **~ en el mercado del dinero** BOLSA borrowing in the money market; **~ en el mercado monetario** FIN borrowing in the money market; ◆ **sobre ~** BANCA over-indebtedness; **con índice de ~ elevado** BANCA, BOLSA, FIN highly-geared

endeudarse *v refl* ECON, FIN get into debt (*infrml*)

endogenizar: ~ lo exógeno *fra* ECON endogenizing the exogenous

endorso: ~ de ajuste por inflación *m* INMOB, SEG inflation endorsement

endosado: no ~ *adj* BANCA, COM GEN unendorsed; **~ por un banco** *adj* BANCA bank-endorsed

endosador, a *m,f* BANCA, COM GEN endonser, indorser

endosante *m* BANCA, COM GEN endorser, indorsor; **~ por aval** FIN accommodation endorser

endosar *vt* BANCA, COM GEN *certificado* endorse, guarantee, indorse

endosatario, -a *m,f* BANCA, COM GEN endorsee

endoso *m* COM GEN endorsement, security; **~ absoluto** BANCA, COM GEN absolute endorsement; **~ anterior** BANCA, COM GEN previous endorsement; **~ por aval** BANCA, COM GEN, FIN accommodation endorsement; **~ bancario** BANCA, COM GEN bank endorsement; **~ en blanco** BOLSA, COM GEN blank endorsement; **~ calificado** BANCA qualified endorsement; **~ de cobertura amplia contra actos criminales** SEG comprehensive crime endorsement; **~ condicional** FIN conditional endorsement; **~ de crédito** BANCA, COM GEN, FIN accommodation endorsement; **~ especial** BANCA special endorsement; **~ especial de garantía** BANCA, COM GEN aval; **~ de exclusión de la nómina ordinaria** SEG *empresa* ordinary payroll exclusion endorsement; **~ de extensión de cobertura** SEG extended coverage endorsement; **~ de favor** BANCA, COM GEN, FIN accommodation endorsement; **~ de garantía** BANCA, COM GEN, FIN accommodation endorsement; **~ de un pagaré** BANCA, COM GEN endorsement of a note; **~ de un tercero** V&M third-party endorsement

endurecer *vt* COM GEN, DER, ECON *normas* tighten

endurecimiento *m* COM GEN, DER, ECON *de las normas* tightening-up

energía *f* IND energy, INFO power; **~ acumulada** COM GEN pent-up energy; **~ alternativa** MED AMB alternative energy; **~ atómica** IND, MED AMB atomic energy, nuclear power; **~ ecológica** MED AMB green energy; **~ eléctrica** IND electric power; **~ hidráulica** IND, MED AMB hydraulic power, water power; **~ hidroeléctrica** IND, MED AMB hydroelectric power; **~ maremotriz** IND, MED AMB tidal power; **~ nuclear** IND, MED AMB nuclear energy; **~ solar** IND, MED AMB solar energy; **~ térmica** IND, MED AMB thermal energy

enfatizar *vt* COM GEN emphasize

enfermedad: ~ ficticia *f* RRHH malingering; **~ holandesa** *f* ECON Dutch disease; **~ laboral** *f* RRHH industrial disease; **~ profesional** *f* RRHH occupational disease, occupational illness

enfermo *adj* FISC infirm

enfiteusis *f* FIN long lease

enfoque *m* GES approach; **~ de la absorción** ECON absorption approach; **~ bayesiano para la toma de decisiones** GES Bayesian approach to decision-making; **~ de costes aplicables** *Esp* (*cf enfoque de costos aplicables AmL*) GES relevant cost approach; **~ de costos aplicables** *AmL* (*cf enfoque de costes aplicables Esp*) GES relevant cost approach; **~ cualitativo** BOLSA qualitative approach; **~ descendente de la inversión** FIN top-down approach to investing; **~ funcional** COM GEN *functional approach*; **~ invertido de la inversión** FIN bottom-up approach to investing; **~ monetario de la balanza de pagos** ECON monetary approach to the balance of payments (*MABP*); **~ previo** V&M pre-approach; **~ de productos** V&M commodity approach; **~ de sistemas** INFO systems approach; **~ de la tributación desde los beneficios** FISC benefit approach to taxation; **~ unitario** PROT SOC trabajo social unitary approach

enfriar *vt* ECON cool down

enganchar *vt* INFO, TRANSP hook

enganche *m* INFO, TRANSP hooking; **~ directo** TRANSP strapping; **~ de grúa en el contenedor** TRANSP corner casting

engañar *vt* COM GEN, DER, V&M mislead, deceive

engaño *m* COM GEN, DER, V&M deception, ramp (*infrml*) (*BrE*)

engañoso *adj* COM GEN, DER, V&M misleading, deceptive

engarrotarse *v refl AmL* (*cf pegarse Esp*) IND *maquinaria* bind

engranaje *m* TRANSP gears (*GRS*); **~ planetario** TRANSP planetary gear

enlace[1]**: ~ sindical** *mf* IND, RRHH shop steward

enlace[2] *m* COM GEN, COMS, INFO link, liaison; **~ con el cliente** COM GEN customer liaison; **~ común** TRANSP trunk (*TRK*); **~ común de datos** INFO data bus; **~ de comunicación** COM GEN communication link; **~ de datos** INFO data link; **~ rail-avión** OCIO rail-air link; **~ de transporte** TRANSP transport link

enlazar *vt* COM GEN, COMS, INFO *periféricos, conexiones* link

enmendado *adj* DER, PATENT, POL amended

enmendar *vt* DER, PATENT, POL amend

enmienda *f* DER, PATENT, POL amendment; **~ de igual valor** RRHH equal value amendment (*BrE*); **~ razonada** POL reasoned amendment

enmiendado *adj* DER, PATENT, POL amended

enmiendas: ~ al borrador *f pl* POL draft amendments; **~ de 1975 sobre las leyes de valores** *f pl* BOLSA Securities Acts amendments

enriquecimiento *m* COM GEN *trabajo, empleo* enrichment; **~ de tareas** GES, RRHH job enrichment; **~ del trabajo** GES, RRHH job enlargement

enrollamiento: ~ en espiral *m* TRANSP *carretel* convolute winding

enrollar *vt* INFO scroll up

ensacado: ~ de la carga *m* TRANSP bagging of cargo

ensamblador *m* COM GEN, INFO *lenguaje ensamblador* assembler; **~ cruzado** INFO cross assembler; **~ de referencias cruzadas** INFO cross assembler

ensamblaje *m* COM GEN, INFO assembling

ensanchamiento *m* COM GEN widening

ensayado: no ~ *adj* COM GEN untested

ensayo: ~ en banco de pruebas *m* INFO benchmark test;

~ piloto *m* COM GEN pilot run; **~ T** *m* MAT *estadística* T-test

enseres *m pl* FISC furniture and fittings; **~ domésticos** COM GEN household effects

entablar *vt* COM GEN *discusión* settle; ◆ **~ demanda contra uno** DER, RRHH take out a summons against sb; **~ una demanda por daños y perjuicios** DER file a claim for damages; **~ un pleito contra alguien** DER bring a lawsuit against sb

ente: **~ de existencia jurídica** *m* DER legal entity

entender: **~ bien algo** *fra* COM GEN get sth straight (*infrml*)

entenderse *v refl* COM GEN agree

entendido: **en el ~ de que** *fra* COM GEN provided that

entendimiento *m* COM GEN, GES cognition

entero *m* BOLSA point; **~ natural** INFO natural number

entibar *vt* ECON prop up

entidad *f* DER entity; **~ de ahorro y préstamo** BANCA savings institution (*BrE*), thrift institution (*AmE*); **~ comercial** COM GEN business concern; **~ contable** CONT accounting entity; **~ de crédito** BANCA, FIN credit association; **~ exenta** DER, FISC exempt organization; **~ sin fines de lucro** ADMIN, ECON non-profit making association; **~ privada sin fines de lucro** COM GEN, ECON, POL foundation; **~ pública** POL public body

entorno *m* INFO environment; **~ económico** ECON economic framework; **~ del mercado** V&M market environment

entrada *f* COM GEN entry, input, *de nuevos pedidos* intake, *de fondos* inflow, OCIO *recaudación* gate; **~ para almacén** IMP/EXP, TRANSP *aduanas* warehouse entry; **~ anual neta de efectivo** CONT annual net cash inflow; **~ automática al sistema** INFO autologon; **~ bruta** CONT gross revenue; **~ de capital** BOLSA, ECON capital inflow; **~ comercial** COM GEN trade entrance; **~ en compensación** BANCA clearing entry; **~ conversacional** INFO conversational entry; **~ de datos** INFO data entry; **~ de datos ordinal** INFO ordinal data entry; **~ descontrolada/salida descontrolada** (*GIGO*) INFO garbage-in/garbage-out (*jarg*) (*GIGO*); **~ sin dinero** BANCA paperless entry; **~ directa de datos** INFO direct data entry (*DDE*); **~ de divisas** *m* ECON inflow of currency; **~ en efectivo** FIN cash inflow; **~ falsa** FISC false entry; **~ fraudulenta** FISC deceptive entry; **~ gratuita** OCIO *espectáculos* free admission; **~ inmediata** PROT SOC immediate possession; **~ internacional** TRANSP *aviación* international gateway; **~ libre** OCIO *espectáculos* free admission; **~ en el mercado** V&M market entry; **~ de pedido** V&M order entry; **~ pendiente** CONT outstanding entry; **~ picada** OCIO *teatro* punched paper (*AmE*); **~ principal** CONT, IMP/EXP prime entry; **~ de proveedores** COM GEN tradesman's entrance; **~ de recursos** FISC *recursos naturales* resource income; **~ de trabajo** INFO job entry; **~ en vigor** PATENT entry into force; **~ en vigor con efecto retroactivo** COM GEN backdating

entradas *f pl* ECON revenue, INFO inputs; **~ acreditadas en el fondo** FIN receipts credited to the fund; **~ brutas** ECON revenue; **~ brutas estimadas** CONT estimated revenue; **~ de caja** CONT cash receipts; **~ de efectivo** CONT cash receipts; **~ en metálico** CONT cash receipts; **~ netas** CONT net receipts

entrada/salida *f* (*E/S*) INFO input/output (*I/O*); **~ masivas** INFO bulk input/output

entradilla *f* MEDIOS *edición* lead

entrar *vt* COM GEN enter; ◆ **~ en** COM GEN enter into; **~ de arribada** TRANSP put into port; **~ en bolsa** BOLSA go public; **~ con buen pie** COM GEN *negocios, proyecto* get off to a flying start (*infrml*); **~ en dique** TRANSP *náutica* dock; **~ en funcionamiento** DER come into operation; **~ en juego** COM GEN *factores* come into play; **~ en máquina** MEDIOS *prensa* go to press; **~ en el mercado** V&M come onto the market; **~ en el mercado de trabajo** COM GEN enter the job market (*BrE*), enter the labor market (*AmE*); **~ en negocios** COM GEN enter business; **~ en pérdidas** COM GEN run into debt; **~ en política** COM GEN, POL enter politics; **~ en recesión** ECON enter recession; **~ en vigencia** DER take effect; **~ en vigor** DER come into effect, come into force; **~ en vigor desde** COM GEN *fecha* take effect from

entrega *f* BOLSA *de acciones* delivery (*D, dely*), allotment, COM GEN remise, delivery (*D, dely*), COMS delivery (*D, dely*), TRANSP *navegación* allotment; **~ al por mayor** V&M wholesale delivery; **~ anual** COM GEN, CONT, FIN annual installment (*AmE*), annual instalment (*BrE*); **~ aplazada** BOLSA delayed delivery; **~ bruta** COM GEN gross taking; **~ de la carga a tierra** TRANSP landing storage delivery (*LSD*); **~ consolidada** TRANSP consolidated delivery; **~ contra reembolso** COM GEN cash on delivery (*COD*); **~ en el día** COM GEN, TRANSP same-day delivery; **~ directa** TRANSP direct delivery; **~ de divisas** BANCA, ECON surrender of foreign exchange; **~ a domicilio** TRANSP *por carretera* delivery on wheels (*DOW*); **~ exenta** IMP/EXP, TRANSP free delivery (*fd*); **~ fallida** BOLSA failed delivery; **~ física** BOLSA physical delivery; **~ futura** BOLSA forward delivery; **~ garantizada** BOLSA guaranteed delivery; **~ gratuita** TRANSP free issue; **~ implícita** COM GEN constructive delivery; **~ inicial** CONT *de compra* initial outlay; **~ inmediata** BOLSA spot delivery, INMOB immediate occupancy; **~ de llaves** INMOB rent-up period; **~ de mercancía incompleta** COM GEN short delivery; **~ a la par** BOLSA par delivery; **~ parcial** BOLSA partial delivery; **~ de productos almacenados al desembarque** IMP/EXP landing storage delivery (*LSD*); **~ sin trasbordos** TRANSP direct delivery; **~ por vía regular** BOLSA, COM GEN regular way delivery; **~ visible a treinta días** BOLSA thirty-day visible supply; ◆ **~ contra reembolso** BOLSA delivery versus payment, IMP/EXP cash on delivery (*COD*); **~ y devolución** TRANSP delivery and re-delivery (*dely&re-dely*); **para ~ inmediata** COM GEN for immediate delivery

entregable *adj* BOLSA *letras del Tesoro* deliverable

entregado *adj* BOLSA, COM GEN, COMS delivered (*D, dd*); ◆ **~ en buque** IMP/EXP *puerto* delivered ex ship (*DES*); **~ en dársenas** TRANSP delivered at docks (*DD*); **~ derechos pagados** FISC, IMP/EXP delivered duty paid (*DDP*); **~ en frontera** IMP/EXP *lugar convenido* delivered at frontier (*DAF*); **~ en muelle** IMP/EXP *derechos pagados* delivered ex quay (*DEQ*)

entregar *vt* BANCA *préstamo* service, BOLSA allot, COM GEN deliver, DER *una notificación* serve, FIN *préstamo* service, TRANSP allot; ◆ **más bajo por ~** BOLSA cheapest to deliver (*CTD*)

entrenamiento *m* RRHH training; **~ dentro de la industria** IND, RRHH training within industry (*TWI*); **~ específico** RRHH specific training; **~ fuera del puesto** RRHH off-the-job training (*BrE*); **~ grupal** RRHH group training; **~ práctico** RRHH hands-on training; ~ **en el puesto** RRHH on-the-job training; ~ **para el trabajo en equipo** COM GEN, GES, RRHH sensitivity training

entrenar *vt* RRHH train

entrenarse *v refl* RRHH train

entretanto *adv* COM GEN in the interim

entretenimiento: ~ **a bordo** *m* OCIO, TRANSP *barco* entertainment on board

entretenimientos: ~ **públicos** *m pl* PROT SOC public amenities

entrevista *f* MEDIOS, RRHH, V&M interview; ~ **con cuestionario prefijado** V&M patterned interview; ~ **dirigida** V&M *investigación de mercado* directed interview; ~ **estructurada** RRHH structured interview; ~ **de evaluación del comportamiento** RRHH performance appraisal interview (*PAI*); ~ **de evaluación del desempeño** RRHH performance appraisal interview (*PAI*); ~ **grupal** COM GEN group interview; ~ **informal** RRHH informal interview; ~ **no estructurada** RRHH unstructured interview; ~ **personal** V&M personal interview; ~ **en profundidad** RRHH stress interview, V&M in-depth interview, *técnica de investigación* depth interview; ~ **de salida** RRHH exit interview; ~ **de ventas** V&M sales interview

entrevistado, -a *m,f* MEDIOS respondant, RRHH interviewee, V&M *en encuesta de investigación de mercado* respondant

entrevistador, a *m,f* MEDIOS *prensa, radiodifusión, noticiarios*, RRHH, V&M interviewer

entrevistas: ~ **telefónicas** *f pl* V&M *investigación de mercado* telephone interviewing

enumeración *f* COM GEN enumeration

enumerar *vt* COM GEN enumerate

envasado: ~ **a prueba de posamiento** *m* TRANSP siftproof packaging; ~ **triple** *m* COM GEN tripack

envase¹: **en el** ~ *adj* V&M *promoción* on-pack

envase²: ~ **de burbujas** *m* V&M bubble pack; ~ **conjunto** *m* V&M *para el mismo producto* banded pack; ~ **con cupón de descuento** *m* V&M money-off pack; ~ **engañoso** *m* V&M deceptive packaging; ~ **exterior** *m* V&M outer pack; ~ **de fibra** *m* TRANSP fibreboard can (*BrE*), fiberboard can (*AmE*); ~ **gigante** *m* V&M jumbo pack; ~ **de gran tamaño** *m* COM GEN bulk package; ~ **interior** *m* V&M inner pack; ~ **no recuperable** *m* V&M nonrecuperable packing; ~ **con premio** *m* V&M bonus pack; ~ **primario** *m* COM GEN primary package; ~ **con reducción de precio en lugar destacado** *m* V&M flash pack; ~ **reutilizable** *m* COM GEN, V&M reusable pack; ~ **de segunda mano** *m* V&M second-hand case; ~ **de tamaño familiar** *m* COM GEN family-size package; ~ **unitario** *m* V&M unit pack; ~ **vacío** *m* COM GEN vacuum packaging, V&M empty; ~ **vacío devuelto** *m* MED AMB, V&M returned empty

envases: ~ **con incentivo** *m pl* V&M incentive packs; ~ **de plástico transparente** *m pl* COM GEN shrink packaging

envejecimiento: ~ **de las existencias** *m* CONT age inventories

enverdecimiento *m* MED AMB *de la opinión pública* greening (*jarg*)

envergadura *f* COM GEN *del problema* scale

enviar *vt* COMS forward (*fwd*), send, IMP/EXP forward (*fwd*), INFO *datos, información* send; ◆ ~ **por correo** ADMIN, COMS mail (*AmE*), post (*BrE*), send by post;

~ **por correo aéreo** COMS *cartas* airmail; ~ **por fax** ADMIN, COM GEN, COMS, INFO fax (*facsimile*), send by fax; ~ **con la mayor discreción** COMS send under plain cover; ~ **una orden por telegrama** COMS send an order by wire; ~ **una petición por escrito** COM GEN send a written request; ~ **por paquete postal** COMS send by parcel post (*BrE*)

envío *m* COMS *de correo* delivery (*D, dely*), TRANSP shipping, dispatch, shipment; ~ **de barcazas** TRANSP barge forwarding; ~ **en bus** INFO bus mailing; ~ **en contenedores** TRANSP containerized shipping; ~ **por correo** COMS mailing; ~ **exterior** TRANSP out shipment; ~ **incompleto** TRANSP short shipment; ~ **postal** CONT postal remittance; ~ **postal de gran volumen** COM GEN bulk mail; ~ **publicitario** *Esp* V&M mailing; ~ **de publicidad a domicilio** V&M mailing piece, mailing shot; ~ **de sellos de correos** COM GEN *método de pago* postage-stamp remittance (*AmE*); ~ **urgente** COM GEN express delivery

Envireg *f* MED AMB Envireg

envoltorio *m* COM GEN, COMS package (*pkg.*)

envolver *vt* COM GEN wrap up

epígrafe *m* *Esp* CONT *hoja de balance* heading

época: **que hizo** ~ *fra* DER *proceso* landmark

equidad *f* ECON *legalidad*, INMOB equity; ~ **entre los contribuyentes** FISC taxpayers' equity; ~ **fiscal** FISC equity taxation; ~ **impositiva** FISC tax equity; ~ **intergeneracional** ECON intergenerational equity; ~ **inter-nación** ECON inter-nation equity

equilibrado *adj* COM GEN, CONT balanced, well-balanced

equilibrar 1. *vt* COM GEN top up, CONT, ECON break even; ◆ ~ **con** COM GEN balance with; ~ **el balance** CONT redress the balance; ~ **los calados** TRANSP trim; ~ **el mercado** BOLSA clear the market; **2.** *vi* FIN, V&M break even

equilibrio *m* COM GEN equilibrium; ~ **de la balanza de pagos** ECON balance of payments equilibrium; ~ **cíclico** ECON financial roundness; **no** ~ **comercial** ECON no-trade equilibrium; ~ **del consumidor** ECON, V&M consumer equilibrium; ~ **a corto plazo** ECON short-run equilibrium; ~ **estable** ECON stable equilibrium; ~ **firme** ECON strong equilibrium; ~ **general** ECON fundamental equilibrium, general equilibrium (*GE*); ~ **inestable** ECON unstable equilibrium; ~ **interno** ECON internal balance; ~ **keynesiano** ECON Keynesian equilibrium; ~ **de Lapanov** ECON Lapanov equilibrium; ~ **a largo plazo** ECON long-run equilibrium; ~ **de Lindahl** ECON Lindahl equilibrium; ~ **del mercado** ECON market equilibrium; ~ **de mercado aislado** ECON isolated market equilibrium; ~ **meta** ECON goal equilibrium; ~ **parcial** ECON partial equilibrium; ~ **del PNB** ECON equilibrium GNP; ~ **presupuestario** CONT, ECON budget equilibrium; ~ **sostenido** ECON steady state equilibrium; ~ **temporal** ECON temporary equilibrium; ~ **volumétrico** ECON material balance; ~ **walrasiano** ECON general equilibrium

equipaje *m* OCIO, TRANSP baggage, luggage; ~ **acompañado** TRANSP accompanied baggage; ~ **admisible sin cargo** IMP/EXP, TRANSP free baggage allowance; ~ **controlado** TRANSP baggage checked; ~ **facturado** TRANSP registered luggage; ~ **no acompañado** TRANSP unaccompanied baggage; ~ **no comprobado** TRANSP unchecked baggage; ~ **permitido**

TRANSP baggage allowance; **~ personal** IMP/EXP, TRANSP personal baggage; **~ registrado** TRANSP registered baggage

equipamiento *m* COM GEN equipment

equipar *vt* COM GEN equip, fit

equiparación: ~ fiscal *f* FISC tax equalization

equipo *m* COM GEN apparel, CONT *activo fijo* plant, FIN pool, RRHH team; **~ administrativo** GES, RRHH management team; **~ agrícola** ECON farm equipment; **~ de apoyo financiero** FIN financial support staff; **~ audiovisual** V&M audiovisual equipment; **~ de auditores** CONT audit team; **~ auxiliar** INFO, RRHH auxiliary equipment; **~ de campo** V&M field force; **~ capital** GES capital equipment; **~ de carga y descarga** TRANSP *navegación* cargo handling equipment; **~ complementario** GES add-on equipment; **~ de comunicación de datos** INFO data communications equipment (*DCE*); **~ de conmutación de circuitos** INFO circuit terminating equipment; **~ encargado de un nuevo producto** V&M venture team; **~ físico** INFO hardware; **~ flexible** IND flexible plant; **~ de gestión** GES, RRHH management team; **~ de gran acometividad** POL tiger team (*jarg*) (*AmE*); **~ humano** RRHH team; **~ industrial** CONT *cuenta anual* industrial equipment; **~ de investigación** V&M *investigación de mercado* research team; **~ a largo plazo** PROT SOC *trabajo social* long-term team; **~ de manipulación mecánica** TRANSP *de carga* mechanical handling equipment (*MHE*); **~ de mantenimiento** COM GEN, IND maintenance equipment, RRHH maintenance equipment, maintenance personnel, maintenance staff; **~ de oficina** ADMIN office equipment; **~ periférico** INFO, SEG peripheral equipment; **~ de prueba** INFO test equipment; **~ radioeléctrico** MEDIOS *radiodifusión* radio set; **~ de reparación** COM GEN repair kit; **~ terminal de datos** INFO data terminal equipment (*DTE*); **~ de trabajo** RRHH team; **~ de transporte** TRANSP transportation equipment; **~ de transporte cualificado** TRANSP qualified transportation equipment; **~ de venta** V&M sales force

equipos: ~ de calidad *m pl* GES quality teams; **~ compartidos** *m pl* INFO shareware

equitativo *adj* DER equitable

equivalencia *f* COM GEN equivalence; **~ por anticipo** IMP/EXP anticipation equivalence; **~ de las cargas fiscales** FISC commensurate taxation; **~ en efectivo** V&M cash equivalence; **~ remunerativa** BOLSA yield equivalence; **~ de rendimiento** BOLSA yield equivalence

equivalente *m* COM GEN equivalent; **~ de acciones ordinarias** BOLSA common shares equivalent (*BrE*), common stock equivalent (*AmE*)

equivalentes: ~ de caja *m pl* FIN cash equivalents

equivaler: ~ a *vi* COM GEN *representar* come to

equivocación *f* COM GEN lapse

era *f* BOLSA age, COM GEN era; **~ de las computadoras** *AmL* INFO computer age; **~ de los computadores** *AmL* ver *era de las computadoras AmL*; **~ de los ordenadores** *Esp* (*cf era de las computadoras AmL*) INFO computer age

erario: el ~ *m* ECON, FIN, POL Treasury; **~ público** *m* ECON public monies, public treasury

ergofobia *f* COM GEN, RRHH ergophobia

ergonometría *f* COM GEN, RRHH ergonometrics

ergonométrico *adj* COM GEN, RRHH ergonometric

ergonomía *f* COM GEN, RRHH ergonomics; **~ cognitiva** COM GEN, RRHH cognitive ergonomics

ergonómicamente *adv* COM GEN, RRHH ergonomically

ergonómico *adj* COM GEN, RRHH ergonomic

ergonomista *mf* COM GEN, RRHH ergonomist

erosión *f* COM GEN, MED AMB *del suelo* erosion; **~ fiscal** ECON tax erosion

erosionar *vt* COM GEN, MED AMB *poder* erode

erradicar *vt* COM GEN eradicate

errar *vt* COM GEN *en una decisión* err

errata *f* COM GEN, MEDIOS *prensa* erratum, literal (*jarg*), misprint, typo (*infrml*), typographic error

erróneo *adj* COM GEN erroneous, mistaken

error *m* COM GEN error, mistake, INFO *ramación* bug; **~ absoluto** MAT absolute error; **~ aleatorio** MAT *estadística* random error; **~ de cálculo** COM GEN miscalculation, INFO computational error; **~ de codificación** INFO coding error; **~ de compensación** CONT compensating error; **~ contable** CONT accounting error; **~ de derecho** DER error of law, mistake of law; **~ grave** INFO fatal error; **~ de hecho** COM GEN factual error; **~ inherente** COM GEN inherent error; **~ judicial de envergadura** DER gross miscarriage of justice; **~ de máquina** INFO hard error; **~ mecanográfico** COM GEN typing error (*typo*); **~ de memoria** V&M memory lapse; **~ de muestreo** MAT *estadística* sampling error; **~ de observación** INFO ascertainment error; **~ de oficina** ADMIN, CONT clerical error; **~ de pase** CONT posting error; **~ permitido** COM GEN permissible error; **~ del personal de oficina** ADMIN, CONT clerical error; **~ de precios** FIN mispricing; **~ probable** MAT *estadística* probable error; **~ de programa** INFO software error; **~ del programa** INFO program bug; **~ de programación** INFO miscoding; **~ de pulsación** INFO typing error; **~ recuperable** INFO, MAT recoverable error; **~ de redondeo** MAT rounding error; **~ por redondeo** MAT round-off error; **~ de registro** CONT posting error; **~ relativo** INFO relative error; **~ residual** ECON *econometría* residual error; **~ de secuencia** INFO sequence error; **~ de sintaxis** INFO syntax error; **~ típico** MAT *estadística* standard error; **~ típico de la estimación** MAT *estadística* standard estimate error; **~ típico de la media** MAT *estadística* standard mean error; **~ tipográfico** COM GEN, INFO, MEDIOS *imprenta* typographic error, typo (*infrml*); **~ de tonelaje** TRANSP tonnage slip; **~ de transcripción** CONT posting error; **~ de trasposición** COM GEN transposition error

errores[1]**: sin ~** *adj* INFO error-free

errores[2]**: ~ y omisiones** *m pl* COM GEN errors and omissions

E/S *abr* (*entrada/salida*) INFO I/O (*input/output*)

esbozar *vt* COM GEN outline

esbozo: ~ de anuncio para TV *m* V&M *publicidad* animatic

escala *f* COM GEN scale; **~ de actitudes** V&M *investigación de mercado* attitude scale; **~ de amortización de activos** CONT, FIN, INMOB asset depreciation range (*ADR*); **~ Beaufort** COM GEN Beaufort scale; **~ de cargos** COM GEN scale of charges; **~ de la comisión** BOLSA scale of commission; **~ económica humana** ECON *filosofía económica* human scale economics; **~ de evaluación de los puestos de trabajo** RRHH job evaluation scale; **~ del impuesto sobre la renta** FISC income tax scale; **~ intermedia** TRANSP stopover; **~ de**

intervalo COM GEN interval scale; ~ **invertida** BOLSA inverted scale; ~ **de mínima eficiencia** ECON minimum efficient scale (*MES*); ~ **móvil** COM GEN, CONT sliding scale; ~ **móvil de salarios** RRHH sliding wage scale; ~ **nominal** COM GEN nominal scale; ~ **de la oferta** BOLSA offering scale; ~ **ordinal** MAT ordinal scale; ~ **porcentual** MAT ratio scale; ~ **de precios** ECON, V&M price range; ~ **progresiva** FISC progressive scale, RRHH incremental scale; ~ **de promoción** RRHH promotion ladder; ~ **regresiva** MAT regressive scale; ~ **salarial móvil** RRHH sliding wage scale; ~ **de salarios** RRHH salary scale, wage scale, wage spread; ~ **de sueldos** RRHH salary scale, wage scale, wage spread; ~ **de tipos de impuesto** FISC tax rate structure; ~ **uniforme** RRHH flat scale; ~ **de valoración** COM GEN rating scale; ♦ **a ~ internacional** COM GEN on an international scale; **a ~ mundial** COM GEN on a worldwide scale, TRANSP worldscale; **a gran ~** COM GEN *proyecto* large-scale, on a large scale; **a pequeña ~** COM GEN on a small scale

escalamiento: ~ **de categorías** m RRHH grade creep (*jarg*)

escalar vt COM GEN scale up; ♦ ~ **posiciones** RRHH scale the ladder

escalas: ~ **de pesos básica** f pl COM GEN basic weight scales

escalera: ~ **de incendios** f INMOB, RRHH, SEG fire escape; ~ **mecánica** f COM GEN *escalera móvil* escalator

escalerilla: ~ **desplazable** f TRANSP portable gangway; ~ **de doble ancho** f TRANSP double width gangway

escalón m RRHH echelon

escalonado adj COM GEN stepped

escalonamiento m COM GEN stagger; ~ **de las vacaciones** RRHH staggering of holidays (*BrE*), staggering of vacations (*AmE*)

escalonar vt COM GEN *costes* stagger, FIN *pagos* graduate

escamotear: ~ **el cambio** fra COM GEN *establecimiento comercial* short change

escándalo m COM GEN scandal

escáner m INFO scanner

escaño m POL *en el Parlamento* seat

escaparate m COM GEN, V&M shop window, window display

escaparates: mirar los ~ fra COM GEN window-shop

escape m INFO *teclado* escape key (*Esc*)

escasamente: ~ **poblado** adj ECON sparsely populated

escasas: ~ **desviaciones** f pl COM GEN trickle diversions (*jarg*)

escasear vi BOLSA run low, COM GEN, ECON be in short supply

escasez f COM GEN *liquidez, existencias* shortage, *de demanda* lack, scarcity, ECON shortage, V&M lack; ~ **absoluta** ECON absolute scarcity; ~ **de capital** BOLSA, CONT, FIN capital shortage; ~ **de dinero** ECON money scarcity; ~ **de dólares** BOLSA dollar shortage; ~ **de mano de obra** RRHH labour shortage (*BrE*), shortage of manpower, labor shortage (*AmE*); ~ **de oro** ECON gold shortage; ~ **de personal** RRHH understaffing; ~ **de petróleo** ECON oil shortage; ~ **de reservas** BANCA, CONT, FIN reserve stringency; ~ **de viviendas** INMOB housing shortage

escaso adj COM GEN in scarce supply, *recursos* scarce;

~ **de** COM GEN short of; ~ **de personal** RRHH understaffed; ~ **de plantilla** RRHH understaffed

escatimar vt COM GEN skimp on; ♦ ~ **y ahorrar** COM GEN scrimp and save

escenario m COM GEN *de negociaciones* stage; ~ **para el mejor de los casos** COM GEN best-case scenario; ~ **para el peor de los casos** COM GEN worst-case scenario

escepticismo m COM GEN scepticism (*BrE*), skepticism (*AmE*)

esclarecer vt COM GEN throw light on

escogido adj BANCA, COM GEN top-rated

escope m GES scoop

escora f TRANSP shore

escotilla f RRHH hatchway; ~ **practicable** TRANSP *póliza de fletes* workable hatch (*WH*); ♦ **por ~ y día** TRANSP per hatch per day

escotillero m RRHH, TRANSP hatchman

escribir 1. vt INFO *en memoria* write; ♦ ~ **pidiendo algo** COMS send away for sth; **2.** vi COM GEN write

escrito[1]: ~ **a máquina** adj ADMIN, PATENT typewritten

escrito[2]: ~ **de súplica** m DER petition

escrito[3]: **por ~** fra COM GEN, COMS in writing

escritor, a: ~ **freelance** m,f MEDIOS *periodismo* freelance writer; ~ **independiente** m,f MEDIOS *editoriales* freelance writer; ~ **pagado(-a) por líneas** m,f MEDIOS *imprenta* space writer

escritorio[1]: ~ **de ~** adj INFO desktop

escritorio[2] m ADMIN, INFO desk

escritura f DER, INMOB deed; ~ **del administrador** DER administrator's deed; ~ **de afianzamiento** DER bail bond; ~ **de autorización** DER *comercial* licence bond (*BrE*), license bond (*AmE*); ~ **de caución** DER bail bond; ~ **de cesión** COM GEN, DER deed of assignation; ~ **de cesión de bienes** INMOB assignment; ~ **de cesión de un derecho** INMOB quitclaim deed; ~ **de compraventa** BOLSA bought contract; ~ **de constitución** DER *de una sociedad mercantil* memorandum of association, articles of incorporation; ~ **de constitución y estatutos** DER memorandum and articles of association; ~ **de constitución de una sociedad colectiva** DER deed of partnership; ~ **de donación** DER gift deed; ~ **y estatutos** DER memorandum and articles; ~ **de extinción de derecho de redimir** DER, INMOB deed in lieu of foreclosure; ~ **de fianza** COM GEN bail bond; ~ **de fideicomiso** DER deed of trust; ~ **fiduciaria** DER trust deed, *documento* trust instrument; ~ **fundacional** DER, INMOB deed of foundation; ~ **de garantía** BANCA guarantee deed, guaranty deed, FISC deed of covenant (*BrE*); ~ **de garantía total** INMOB general warranty deed (*AmE*); ~ **de hipoteca** DER, INMOB mortgage deed; ~ **de material publicitario** COM GEN, V&M copywriting; ~ **en negrilla** INFO bold printing; ~ **privada** COM GEN, DER private contract; ~ **de propiedad** DER, INMOB evidence of title, title deed; ~ **pública** DER public instrument, deed, document, INMOB deed; ~ **de renuncia de un derecho** INMOB quitclaim deed; ~ **en sustitución de embargo de bienes hipotecados** DER, INMOB deed in lieu of foreclosure; ~ **de transmisión** COM GEN transfer deed; ~ **de traslación de dominio** DER deed of conveyance; ~ **de tutoría** INMOB guardian deed

escriturado adj DER, INMOB under article

escriturar vt DER, INMOB bind

escrutinio: ~ **en profundidad** *m* POL depth polling

escuadrón: ~ **de la verdad** *m* POL truth squad (*infrml*)

escucha: ~ **telefónica** *f* COMS wiretapping

escuchar: ~ **a la parte contraria** *fra* COM GEN audi alteram partem

escuela *f* COM GEN school; ~ **austríaca de economía** ECON Austrian School of Economics; ~ **bancaria** BANCA Banking School (*BrE*); ~ **de Cambridge** ECON Cambridge school; ~ **de Chicago** ECON Chicago School; ~ **clásica** COM GEN, ECON classic school; ~ **clásica de economía** ECON classical school of economics; ~ **del estado** COM GEN public school (*AmE*), state school (*BrE*); ~ **de Estocolmo** ECON Stockholm School; ~ **fisiocrática** ECON physiocratic school; ~ **de formación profesional** PROT SOC vocational school; ~ **Marxista** ECON Marxian school; ~ **de negocios** COM GEN business school; ~ **ortodoxa** ECON orthodox school; ~ **preescolar** PROT SOC preschool center (*AmE*), preschool centre (*BrE*); ~ **privada** COM GEN private school; ~ **pública** COM GEN public school (*AmE*), state school (*BrE*); ~ **de regulación** ECON Regulation School; ~ **superior de negocios** PROT SOC graduate school of business; ~ **vebleniana** ECON Veblenian school

Escuela: ~ **de Artes Aplicadas y Oficios Artísticos** *f* COM GEN, ECON College of Arts; ~ **de Comercio** *f* COM GEN, ECON Business School; ~ **Económica de la Utilidad Marginal** *f* ECON Marginal Utility School of Economics; ~ **Histórica** *f* ECON Historical School; ~ **Histórica alemana** *f* ECON German Historical School; ~ **de Lausana** *f* COM GEN, ECON Lausanne School; ~ **Mercantilista de Economía** *f* ECON Mercantile School of Economics; ~ **Neoclásica** *f* ECON Neoclassical School; ~ **sueca** *f* ECON Swedish School

ese: **a** ~ **respecto** *fra* COM GEN on that score

esfera *f* COM GEN sphere; ~ **de actividad** COM GEN, IND, RRHH sphere of activity; ~ **de Impresión de máquina de escribir** ADMIN typewriter ball

esferas: ~ **empresariales** *f pl* COM GEN business community

esfuerzo *m* COM GEN endeavor (*AmE*), endeavour (*BrE*); ~ **concertado** COM GEN concerted effort; ~ **fiscal** ECON, FISC tax effort; ~ **laboral óptimo** ECON optimal work effort; ~ **personal** COM GEN self-help; ~ **a toda potencia** COM GEN all-out effort; ~ **de venta** V&M sales effort

eslabonamiento *m* COM GEN linkage

eslinga *f* TRANSP sling; ~ **para automóviles** TRANSP vehicle sling; ~ **de cadena** TRANSP *manipulación de carga* chain sling; ~ **monoviaje** TRANSP *manipulación de carga* one-trip sling; ~ **SWR sinfín** TRANSP endless SWR sling

eslogan *m* MEDIOS, V&M *anuncios* slogan, tagline; ~ **publicitario** MEDIOS, V&M advertising slogan

eslora: ~ **de cubierta** *f* TRANSP *barco* deck girder

esp. *abr* (*especialmente*) COM GEN esp. (*especially*)

espaciado *m* INFO pitch; ~ **doble** ADMIN dual pitch; ~ **de letras** V&M letter spacing

espaciador *m* TRANSP spacer

espaciar *vt* FIN *devoluciones*, SEG *riesgos* spread; ~ **las devoluciones** COM GEN spread repayments

espacio *m* INFO *en textos* space, MEDIOS *prensa* slot (*jarg*) (*AmE*), space, V&M *TV, radio* spot (*jarg*); ~ **abierto** INMOB open space; ~ **adjudicado** MEDIOS, V&M appointed space; ~ **aislado** V&M solus position; ~ **amplio** IMP/EXP long room (*BrE*); ~ **aprovechable** INFO available space; ~ **para balas** TRANSP *navegación* bale space; ~ **de carga** COM GEN loading space; ~ **para carga general** TRANSP bale capacity (*B*); ~ **de carga vertical** TRANSP verticalized cargo space; ~ **designado** MEDIOS, V&M *publicidad* appointed space; ~ **del disco** INFO disk space; ~ **disponible** TRANSP spare capacity; ~ **de la eme** *f* MEDIOS *tipografía* em space; ~ **entre líneas** COMS line spacing; ~ **en estante** V&M shelf space; ~ **favorable** V&M window of opportunity; ~ **fijo** V&M *TV, radio* fixed spot; ~ **informativo** MEDIOS news bulletin; ~ **de lastre** TRANSP ballast space; ~ **muestral** MAT sample space; ~ **para oficina** COM GEN, INMOB office space; ~ **publicitario** MEDIOS *radiodifusión* airtime, station break (*AmE*), V&M station break (*AmE*); ~ **temporal** ECON *plan, proyecto* time span; ~ **de ventas** V&M selling space; ~ **vital** PROT SOC living space; ♦ **a un** ~ INFO single spacing; **a doble** ~ INFO double spacing

Espacio: ~ **Económico Europeo** *m* ECON European Economic Space

espalda: ~ **mojada** *f* COM GEN wetback (*infrml*) (*AmE*)

especial: ~ **fin de semana** *m* FIN Saturday night special (*jarg*)

especialidad *f* COM GEN speciality (*BrE*), specialty (*AmE*), RRHH skill

especialista *mf* COM GEN specialist; ~ **en bonos** BOLSA bond specialist; ~ **diplomado(-a) en subsidios laborales** *m,f* RRHH certified employee benefit specialist (*AmE*); ~ **en equipo físico** INFO hardware specialist; ~ **en informática** INFO computer scientist

especialización *f* COM GEN specialization; ~ **horizontal** GES horizontal specialization; ~ **laboral** RRHH job specialization; ~ **vertical** COM GEN vertical specialization

especializado *adj* COM GEN specialized

especializarse: ~ **en** *v refl* COM GEN specialize in

especialmente *adv* (*esp.*) COM GEN especially (*esp.*)

especie: **en** ~ *adj* COM GEN *pago* in specie, *pago, ganacias* in kind, DER in kind

especificación *f* COM GEN specification; ~ **del buque** TRANSP ship specification; ~ **del contenido** TRANSP specification of total contents; ♦ **sin** ~ **del contenido** TRANSP no specification of the total contents

especificaciones: ~ **contractuales** *f pl* DER contract specifications; ~ **de una patente** *f pl* PATENT patent specifications

especificado *adj* COM GEN specified; ♦ **no** ~ **en otro punto** COM GEN not elsewhere specified (*NES*)

específicamente: **no** ~ **dispuesto** *fra* COM GEN not specially provided for (*nspf*)

especificar *vt* COM GEN, PATENT specify

específico *adj* COM GEN specific; ~ **del país** ECON *ayuda al desarrollo* country-specific; ~ **de un dispositivo** INFO device-specific

especifidad: ~ **de activos** *f* ECON asset specificity

espécimen *m* COM GEN specimen copy

espectáculos *m pl* COM GEN, OCIO entertainment; ~ **durante el vuelo** OCIO, TRANSP in-flight entertainment

espectativa: **estar a la** ~ *fra* RRHH *en alerta* stand by (*BrE*)

especulación *f* COM GEN jobbing, speculation, agiotage;

~ **aislada** BOLSA, COM GEN, ECON, FIN adventure; ~ **alcista** BOLSA bull speculation; ~ **a la baja** BOLSA bear speculation; ~ **bursátil** BOLSA stock jobbery; ~ **eventual** BOLSA adventure, venture, COM GEN, ECON adventure, FIN adventure, venture; ~ **fuerte** BOLSA plunge; ~ **en el mercado con prima** BOLSA premium raid; ~ **mixta** BOLSA, COM GEN, ECON cross book, straddle, FIN straddle; ~ **a muy corto plazo** BOLSA scalping (*AmE*) (*infrml*); ~ **peligrosa** BOLSA flier *AmE*; ◆ **por** ~ COM GEN on speculation (*on spec*)

especulador, a *m,f* COM GEN speculator, BOLSA stag; ~ **alcista** BOLSA bull speculator; ~ **a la baja sin provisión de fondos** BOLSA uncovered bear; ~ **en bolsa** BOLSA dabbler; ~ **corporativo(-a)** BOLSA, FIN corporate raider; ~ **fuerte** BOLSA plunger; ~ **inmobiliario(-a)** INMOB, V&M property speculator; ~ **insolvente** BOLSA lame duck (*jarg*); ~**minorista** BOLSA spectail; ~ **a muy corto plazo** BOLSA scalper (*AmE*) (*infrml*); ~ **profesional** BOLSA professional speculator; **pequeño(-a)** ~ BOLSA small speculator

especular 1. *vt* BOLSA take a flier *AmE*, play the market, COM GEN speculate; ◆ ~ **en el mercado** BOLSA raid the market (*jarg*); **2.** *vi* BOLSA, COM GEN, ECON speculate; ◆ ~ **al alza** BOLSA go a bull; ~ **en contratos de futuros** BOLSA job backwards (*jarg*)

especulativo *adj* COM GEN speculative

espera[1]: **en** ~ *adj* COMS de llamadas camp-on

espera[2]: **en** ~ **de** *fra* COM GEN in expectation of

esperado *adj* COM GEN *resultado, final* expected

esperando: ~ **atraque** *fra* TRANSP waiting a berth

esperanza: ~ **matemática de vida** *f* SEG actuarial life expectation; ~ **de vida** *f* RRHH life expectancy; ~ **de vida del producto** *f* V&M product life expectancy

espigar *vi* COM GEN shoot up

espigón *m* TRANSP pier

espionaje *m* COM GEN espionage; ~ **comercial** COM GEN industrial espionage; ~ **industrial** SEG industrial espionage

espiral *f* ECON *de precios* spiral; ~ **ascendente** COM GEN *en sueldos, precios* upward spiral; ~ **descendente** COM GEN *en sueldos, precios* downward spiral; ~ **de inflación** ECON spiralling inflation; ~ **inflacionista** ECON inflationary spiral; ~ **inflacionista de salarios y precios** ECON wage-price inflation spiral; ~ **de precios-beneficios** *m* ECON profit price benefit; ~ **precios-salarios** ECON wage-price spiral

espíritu: ~ **comunitario** *m* COM GEN community spirit; ~ **de empresa** *m* COM GEN spirit of enterprise; ~ **empresarial** *m* COM GEN, GES entrepreneurial spirit; ~ **de equipo** *m* COM GEN, RRHH esprit de corps, team spirit

esponsorización *f* COM GEN sponsorship

esporádico *adj* COM GEN, TRANSP sporadic

esposa[1]: ~ **de hecho** *f* DER common-law wife

esposa[2]: **y su** ~ *fra* DER *antiguos documentos legales* et ux

esquela *f* FIN tombstone ad (*jarg*)

esquema *m* ADMIN outline, COM GEN, ECON outline, scheme; ~ **del computador** *AmL*, ~ **de la computadora** *AmL* (*cf esquema del ordenador Esp*) INFO computer map; ~ **de disposición** BANCA, CONT organization chart, GES layout chart, organigram, organization chart; ~ **del dividendo social** ECON, FISC social dividend scheme; ~ **económico** ECON economic pattern; ~ **de estabilización monetaria** ECON currency stabilization scheme; ~ **funcional** INFO block diagram; ~ **garante de la entrada en el mercado** V&M market entry guarantee scheme, market entry guaranty scheme; ~ **intervencionista en los mercados bursátiles** ECON valorization scheme; ~ **del ordenador** *Esp* (*cf esquema de la computadora AmL*) INFO computer map; ~ **de pensión contributoria** FIN, FISC, RRHH contributory pension scheme; ~ **de sugerencias** GES suggestion scheme

esquemas: ~ **de agrupación** *m pl* SEG pool schemes; ~ **de estabilización del comercio de mercancías** *m pl* ECON commodity stabilization schemes

esquemático *adj* COM GEN, ECON schematic

esquilmado: ~ **del mercado** *m* V&M market skimming

esquina *f* COM GEN corner

esquinal *m* TRANSP corner post

esquirol *mf infrml* RRHH blackleg (*infrml*) (*BrE*), scab (*infrml*), strikebreaker

esquirolismo *m infrml* RRHH strikebreaking

esquivar *vt* COM GEN sidestep

estabilidad *f* COM GEN stability; ~ **financiera** FIN financial stability; ~ **política** COM GEN, POL political stability; ~ **de precios** ECON price stability; ~ **walrasiana** ECON Walrasian stability; ◆ **tener** ~ **en el cargo** RRHH have security of tenure

estabilización *f* COM GEN stabilization; ~ **artificial de precios** ECON pegging system; ~ **de precios** ECON price stabilization, V&M price fixing; ~ **salarial** RRHH wage stabilization

estabilizador *m* ECON, FIN, POL *navegación* stabilizer; ~ **automático** ECON *gasto del gobierno*, POL automatic stabilizer; ~ **tipo tanques** TRANSP tank-type stabilizer (*TNK*)

estabilizadores: ~ **incorporados** *m pl* ECON built-in stabilizers

estabilizar *vt* COM GEN stabilize, peg

estabilizarse *v refl* COM GEN stabilize

estable *adj* COM GEN stable, steady

establecer *vt* BANCA settle, COM GEN *registro* set, *hecho, fecha* establish, *negocios* set up, *reglas* lay down, CONT ascertain, DER establish, ECON *valor* establish, set, set up; ◆ ~ **comunicación directa con** COMS establish a direct link with; ~ **un contrato con** COM GEN enter into a contract with; ~ **una diferencia entre** COM GEN draw a distinction between; ~ **los estándares** GES set the standards; ~ **la lista final** COM GEN, RRHH shortlist; ~ **las normas** DER make regulations, GES set the standards; ~ **un nuevo máximo** ECON set a new high; ~ **un orden** ADMIN, COM GEN, ECON rank; ~ **un orden del día** GES draw up an agenda; ~ **el precio de coste** CONT cost; ~ **la sede** ADMIN headquarter (*AmE*); ~ **vínculos con** COM GEN build links with

establecerse *v refl* COM GEN *trabajo, residencia, país* settle; ◆ ~ **por cuenta propia** COM GEN set up on one's own account

establecido *adj* COM GEN established (*est.*)

establecimiento *m* COM GEN, RRHH establishment; ~ **bancario** BANCA banking establishment; ~ **comercial** COM GEN business house; ~ **de comunicación** COMS, INFO handshaking; ~ **de créditos personales** BANCA, FIN consumer loan institute; ~ **docente** PROT SOC educational establishment; ~ **de metas** COM GEN, GES goal setting; ~ **de normas de contabilidad** CONT accounting standard setting; ~ **de**

objetivos COM GEN, V&M target setting; **~ de la política** GES policymaking

Establishment: **el ~** *m* COM GEN, POL the Establishment

estabilización: **~ económica** *f* ECON economic stability

estación *f* (*S*) INFO, TRANSP station (*S*); **~ de carga del acero** TRANSP steel terminal; **~ de clasificación** TRANSP railway yard (*BrE*), railyard (*AmE*); **~ emisora** COMS transmitting station; **~ de envío** TRANSP *ferrocarril* forwarding station; **~ de ferrocarril** TRANSP railway station (*BrE*), train station (*BrE*), railroad station (*AmE*); **~ fronteriza** TRANSP frontier station; **~ generadora** MED AMB generating station; **~ marítima** TRANSP harbor station (*AmE*), harbour station (*BrE*); **~ de máxima actividad** COM GEN, ECON peak season; **~ receptora** COMS, TRANSP *ferrocarril* receiving station; **~ de servicio** MED AMB gas station (*AmE*), TRANSP service station; **~ de sondeos** V&M drilling installation; **~ de trabajo** ADMIN, INFO, RRHH *espacio físico* workstation; **~ turística** ECON, OCIO tourist season

estacional *adj* COM GEN seasonal

estacionalidad: **~ de la demanda** *f* ECON seasonality of demand

estacionamiento *m* BOLSA parking, COM GEN, OCIO, TRANSP parking lot (*AmE*), car park (*BrE*); **~ automático** INFO *disco duro* autopark; **~ para remolques** TRANSP trailer park

estacionar: **~ y montar** *fra* TRANSP park and ride

estadía *f* TRANSP *navegación* lay day, reversible laytime; **~ indefinida** TRANSP indefinite laytime; **~ irreversible** TRANSP nonreversible laytime; **~ normal** TRANSP normal laytime

estadística *f* MAT statistics; **~ actuarial** MAT actuarial statistics; **~ de contraste** ECON, MAT test statistic; **~ deductiva** MAT inferential statistics; **~ demográfica** MAT *estadística* population statistics; **~ derival** MAT derival statistics; **~ descriptiva** MAT descriptive statistics; **~ de desempleo** ECON, POL, RRHH unemployment statistics; **~ inductiva** MAT inductive statistics; **~ no paramétrica** MAT *estadística* nonparametric statistics; **~ paramétrica** MAT *estadística* parametric statistics; **~ de prueba** ECON, MAT test statistic; **~ sociológica** MAT, RRHH sociological statistics

estadísticamente: **~ significativo** *adj* MAT *estadística* statistically significant

estadísticas *f pl* COM GEN statistics; **~ portuarias** TRANSP port statistics; **~ de publicidad** V&M advertising statistics; **~ de referencia** MAT benchmark statistics; **~ sobre población** POL population statistics; ◆ **las últimas ~ muestran que** MAT the latest statistics show that

estadístico[1] *adj* MAT statistical

estadístico[2],**-a** *m,f* MAT statistician

estado *m* COM GEN state (*AmE*), INFO status, state, POL state; **~ aceptable del contenedor** TRANSP *navegación* acceptable container condition (*ACC*); **~ de activos y pasivos** CONT statement of assets and liabilities; **~ de ánimo** COM GEN frame of mind; **~ anual** CONT annual statement; **~ de aplicación de fondos** CONT application of funds statement; **~ auditado** CONT audited statement; **~ autoritario** ECON authoritarian state; **~ de la balanza de pagos** ECON balance of payments (*BOP*); **~ bancario** BANCA bank statement; **~ del bienestar** ECON nanny state (*infrml*), welfare state; **~ de la cámara de compensación** BANCA clearing statement;

~ de cash flow consolidado CONT consolidated cash flow statement; **~ de cash-flow** CONT cash flow statement; **~ civil** DER, FISC marital status; **~ de conciliación** CONT reconciliation statement; **~ de conciliación de bancos** BANCA *balance* bank reconciliation statement; **~ condensado** CONT condensed statement; **~ consolidado** CONT, FIN consolidated statement; **~ consolidado del activo líquido** CONT consolidated cash flow statement; **~ de contabilidad consolidado** CONT, FIN consolidated statement of condition (*AmE*); **~ contable** CONT statement, financial statement, accounting report; **~ contable del valor de las acciones** CONT *derecho de accionistas* balance sheet value of shares; **~ corporativo** POL corporate state; **~ de cosas** COM GEN state of affairs; **~ de cuenta** COM GEN account statement, balance of account, statement of account; **~ de cuenta pormenorizado** COM GEN itemized statement; **~ de cuentas** COM GEN account statement, CONT bank balance, account form, FIN bank balance; **~ de cuentas auxiliar** CONT minor balance status; **~ de cuentas bancario** BANCA bank statement; **~ de cuentas a cobrar** CONT accounts receivable statement; **~ de cuentas de compensación** BANCA clearing balance statement; **~ de cuentas del flujo de fondos** CONT, ECON, FIN flow of funds account; **~ de cuentas global** CONT aggregate statement; **~ de la economía** ECON state of the economy; **~ de efectivo** CONT cash statement; **~ del efectivo de caja** CONT cash statement; **~ estacionario** ECON stationary state; **~ de excepción** POL state of emergency; **~ de existencias** CONT inventory sheet; **~ financiero** CONT financial statement; **~ financiero certificado** CONT certified financial statement; **~ financiero combinado** FIN combined financial statement; **~ financiero comparativo** CONT comparative financial statement; **~ financiero consolidado** CONT consolidated financial statement; **~ de flujos** CONT funds statement; **~ de flujos de caja** CONT cash flow statement; **~ de flujos de caja consolidado** CONT consolidated cash flow statement; **~ de fondos** CONT funds statement; **~ de ganancias** CONT statement of earnings; **~ general** COM GEN *cuentas* general statement; **~ de ingresos y gastos** CONT statement of income and expenses; **~ legal** DER status; **~ mayor** RRHH chief of staff; **~ mensual** BANCA, FIN *tarjeta de crédito* monthly statement; **~ miembro** POL UE member state (*MS*); **~ de origen y aplicación de fondos** CONT statement of income and expenditure; **~ de pérdidas y ganancias** CONT profit and loss statement; **~ de posición diaria** CONT daily position statement; **~ de posición financiera** CONT statement of financial position; **~ presupuestario** FIN *gubernamental* budgetary statement; **~ protector** POL buffer state; **~ de reconciliación** CONT reconciliation statement; **~ de resultados** CONT statement of income; **~ de resultados de operación** CONT operating statement; **~ resumido** COM GEN summary statement; **~ revisado** CONT audited statement; **~ de los salarios** RRHH pay statement; **~ de situación** BANCA, FIN statement of condition; **~ de situación comparativo** CONT, FIN comparative statement; **~ de la situación financiera** BANCA financial statement; **~ sólido** COM GEN solid-state; **~ temporal** DER temporary status; **~ de tesorería** CONT cash statement; **~ de tesorería consolidado** CONT consolidated cash flow statement; **~ de variación de tesorería** CONT cash flow statements; **~ verificado**

CONT audited statement; ◆ **que condiciona el ~ de ánimo** V&M *proyecto* mood-conditioning

Estado *m* POL State

estados: ~ contables anuales limitados *m pl* CONT limited annual statements; **~ financieros a costes actuales** *m pl Esp* (*cf estados financieros a costos actuales AmL*) CONT, ECON, FISC current cost accounting (*CCA*); **~ financieros a costos actuales** *m pl AmL* (*cf estados financieros a costes actuales Esp*) CONT, ECON, FISC current cost accounting (*CCA*); **~ independientes de la Commonwealth** *m pl* ECON Commonwealth of Independent States; **~ intermedios** *m pl* CONT interim statements; **~ provisionales** *m pl* CONT interim statements

estafa *f* BOLSA bubble (*jarg*), COM GEN swindle, bubble, ramp (*infrml*) (*BrE*), DER, V&M ramp (*infrml*) (*BrE*); **~ bancaria** BANCA banker's ramp (*jarg*)

estafador, a *m,f* COM GEN con artist (*infrml*), con man (*infrml*), swindler

estafeta *f* COMS courier; **~ de correos** COMS sub-post office

estagnación *f* COM GEN, ECON stagnation

estallar *vi* INFO explode

estampación *f* V&M embossing; **~ sobre metal** MEDIOS foil stamping

estampar *vt* COM GEN *firma* append, *firma, sello* affix, stamp; ◆ **~ la fecha** ADMIN *en impreso* stamp the date

estampilla *f AmL* (*cf sello de correos Esp*) COMS postage stamp

estancado *adj* COM GEN *conversaciones* stagnant, stalemated, ECON stagnant, POL deadlocked

estancamiento *f* BOLSA holding pattern (*jarg*), COM GEN stagnation, holding pattern (*jarg*), ECON stagnation, FIN holding pattern (*jarg*); **~ económico** *m* ECON economic slowdown; **~ del mercado** *m* IND economic slowdown

estancar *vt* POL deadlock

estancarse *v refl* COM GEN, ECON stagnate

estanco: ~ al agua *adj* TRANSP watertight (*WT*); **~ al petróleo** *adj* TRANSP oiltight

estándar[1] *adj* COM GEN, INFO standard

estándar[2] *m* COM GEN standard (*std*); **~ de costes** *Esp* (*cf estándar de costos AmL*) COM GEN, CONT, FIN cost standard; **~ de costos** *AmL* (*cf estándar de costes Esp*) COM GEN, CONT, FIN cost standard; **~ de emisión** MED AMB emission standard; **~ de igualdad** *m pl* POL equality standard; **~ nacional de ruido** MED AMB national noise standard; **~ presupuestario** CONT budget standard

estándares: ~ bancarios basados en riesgo *m pl* BANCA risk-based banking standards

estandarización *f* COM GEN standardization

estandarizante *adj* COM GEN standardizing

estandarizar *vt* COM GEN standardize

estandarte: ~ aéreo *m* V&M aeroplane banner (*BrE*), airplane banner (*AmE*)

estandizar *vt* MAT standardize

estanflación *f* ECON stagflation

estar: ~ en la misma onda *fra* COM GEN be on the same wavelength

estatal *adj* COM GEN *empresa* government-owned, IND state-owned

estática: ~ comparativa *f* ECON comparative statics

estático *adj* COM GEN, ECON *producción, precios* static

estatregia: ~ de tarifas *f* TRANSP rates strategy

estatus *m* COM GEN status; **~ social** PROT SOC social status

estatutario *adj* DER statutory

estatuto *m* BANCA *de banco* by-law, DER enactment, by-law (*AmE*); **~ colectivo** COM GEN blanket statute; **~ de La Habana** ECON Havana Charter; **~ personal** *f* RRHH personal statute

Estatuto: ~ de los Trabajadores *f Esp* POL ≈ National Labor Relations Act (*AmE*)

estatutos *m pl* DER articles of association; **~ sociales** DER by-law; **~ de una sociedad mercantil** DER memorandum and articles of association

esté: ~ o no atracado *fra* TRANSP whether in berth or not (*WIBON*)

estenografía *f* ADMIN, RRHH stenography

estenógrafo, -a *m,f* ADMIN, RRHH stenographer

estenotipista *mf* ADMIN, COM GEN, RRHH shorthand typist

estereotipia: ~ de los sexos *f* PROT SOC, RRHH sexual stereotyping

esterilización *f* FIN sterilization

estibador, a *m,f Esp* (*cf alijador AmL*) RRHH, TRANSP stevedore (*stvdr*), wharfinger, docker (*BrE*)

estibadores *m pl Esp* (*cf alijadores AmL*) COM GEN, RRHH, TRANSP stevedoring gang, dockers (*BrE*)

estibaje: ~ de la carga *m* TRANSP cargo stowage; **~ embandejado** *m* TRANSP palletized stowage

estibar *vt* COM GEN, RRHH, TRANSP *cargas* stow

estilete *m* INFO *mecanismo basado en una plumilla* stylus

estilista *mf* COM GEN stylist

estilizar *vt* COM GEN, GES, INFO stylize

estilo[1]**: de ~ occidental** *adj* ECON western-style

estilo[2] *m* COM GEN style; **~ administrativo** GES management style, managerial style; **~ de la casa** COM GEN, MEDIOS *imprenta* house style; **~ de gerencia** GES management style; **~ de trabajo** COM GEN work design; **~ de vida** COM GEN, V&M lifestyle; **~ de vida familiar** V&M family lifestyle

estima: tener a alguien en gran ~ *fra* COM GEN have a high regard for sb

estimación *f* COM GEN estimate, appreciation, CONT *propiedades* appreciation, INMOB assessment; **~ aproximativa** COM GEN rough estimate; **~ de la base imponible** FISC tax assessment; **~ de la base impositiva** FISC tax assessment; **~ de caja** FIN cash forecast; **~ contable** CONT accounts appraisal; **~ del coste de proceso** *Esp* (*cf estimación del costos de proceso AmL*) CONT, IND process costing; **~ de costes** *Esp* (*cf estimación de costos AmL*) COM GEN cost estimate; **~ del costo de proceso** *AmL* (*cf estimación del coste de proceso EsP*) CONT, IND process costing; **~ de costos** *AmL* (*cf estimación de costes Esp*) COM GEN cost estimate; **~ de daños y perjuicios** DER liquidated damages; **~ de empleo** RRHH job appraisal; **~ de gastos** CONT estimate of expenditure; **~ de gastos de capital** *Esp* (*cf avalúo de gastos de capital AmL*) ECON, FIN capital expenditure appraisal; **~ para ingresos devengados** FISC earned income allowance; **~ de intervalo** MAT interval estimate; **~ de la irregularidad** FISC assessment of deficiency; **~ más reciente** COM GEN latest estimate (*L/E*); **~ del mercado** COM GEN, V&M *investigación de mercado* market appraisal; ~ **objetiva** COM GEN objective evaluation; ~ **óptima** COM GEN best estimate; ~ **presupuestaria** CONT, POL budget estimate; ~ **puntual** MAT point estimate; ~ **de riesgos** FIN, GES, SEG risk assessment; ~ **de ventas** V&M sales estimate; **última** ~ COM GEN latest estimate (*L/E*)

estimaciones: ~ **complementarias regulares** *f pl* FIN regular supplementary estimates; ~ **financieras** *f pl* FIN financial forecasts; ~ **de ganancias** *f pl* FIN earnings forecasts; ~ **de sueldos** *f pl* FIN earnings forecasts; ~ **totales** *f pl* FIN total estimates; ~ **de utilidades** *f pl* FIN earnings forecasts

estimado *adj* COM GEN, FISC, MAT deemed, estimated

estimador *m* V&M estimator; ~ **eficiente** ECON *econometría* efficient estimator; ~ **insesgado** ECON *econometría* unbiased estimator; ~ **lineal insesgado óptimo** (*ELIO*) ECON best linear unbiased estimator (*BLUE*); ~ **de verosimilitud máxima** MAT maximum likelihood estimator (*MLE*)

estimar *vt* COM GEN estimate, gage (*AmE*), gauge (*BrE*), INMOB appraise; ◆ ~ **por aproximación** COM GEN guesstimate (*infrml*); ~ **necesario** COM GEN deem necessary

estime: **según se** ~ **oportuno** *fra* COM GEN at the discretion of

estimulación: ~ **de una necesidad** *f* V&M need arousal

estimulante *adj* COM GEN stimulating

estimular *vt* COM GEN stimulate, boost; ◆ ~ **un avance** ECON *mercado* fuel an advance; ~ **la inflación** ECON fuel inflation

estímulo *m* COM GEN stimulus; ~ **competitivo** ECON, V&M competitive stimulus; ◆ **ser un** ~ **para las exportaciones** IMP/EXP be a stimulus for exports

estímulos: ~ **fiscales** *m pl* FISC tax stimuli

estipulación: ~ **derogatoria** *f* DER derogatory stipulation

estipulaciones: ~ **del convenio** *f pl* TRANSP articles of agreement

estipular *vt* COM GEN stipulate; ◆ ~ **las bases para** BANCA provide the base for

esto: **a** ~ *adv* COMS hereto

estocaje *m* GES stock

estocástico *adj* COM GEN, GES, MAT stochastic

estoraje *m* GES stock

estorbo *m* COM GEN hindrance

estrangulamiento *m* COM GEN, IND bottleneck

estrategia *f* COM GEN, GES strategy; ~ **de aproximación al mínimo máximo** ECON minimax strategy; ~ **de beneficios** COM GEN, FIN profit strategy; ~ **comercial** COM GEN, ECON, GES business strategy, commercial strategy, trade strategy; ~ **competitiva** COM GEN, ECON, V&M competitive strategy; ~ **de compra y retención** BOLSA buy-and-hold strategy; ~ **de compra y suscripción** BOLSA buy-and-write strategy; ~ **de comunicación** COMS communication strategy; ~ **corporativa** COM GEN, GES corporate strategy; ~ **creativa** V&M *publicidad* creative strategy; ~ **de crecimiento** COM GEN, ECON growth strategy; ~ **defensiva** COM GEN defensive strategy; ~ **de desarrollo** GES development strategy; ~ **de diferenciación** V&M differentiation strategy; ~ **de diseño de un buque** TRANSP ship design strategy; ~ **de diversificación** V&M diversification strategy; ~ **económica** ECON, POL economic strategy; ~ **econó-**

mica alternativa ECON, POL alternative economic strategy; ~ **de la empresa** COM GEN company strategy; ~ **empresarial** ECON business strategy; ~ **de expansión** COM GEN expansion strategy; ~ **financiera** COM GEN, FIN financial strategy; ~ **financiera a medio plazo** ECON medium-term financial strategy (*MTFS*) (*BrE*); ~ **fiscal** FISC tax strategy; ~ **de fletes** TRANSP freight strategy; ~ **de la fuerza de trabajo ejecutiva** GES, RRHH executive manpower strategy; ~ **global** COM GEN global strategy; ~ **informática** INFO computer strategy; ~ **de inversión** BOLSA investment strategy, FIN capital strategy, capital investment strategy; ~ **laboral para altos cargos** GES, RRHH executive manpower strategy; ~ **de marca** FIN, V&M brand strategy; ~ **de marketing** V&M marketing strategy; ~ **de los medios de comunicación** V&M media strategy; ~ **de mensaje publicitario** V&M *publicidad* copy strategy; ~ **monetaria no oficial** ECON parallel currency strategy; ~ **multimarca** V&M multibrand stategy; ~ **de negociación** BOLSA, COM GEN, RRHH negotiation strategy; ~ **de negocios** COM GEN, ECON, GES business strategy; ~ **operativa** TRANSP operating strategy; ~ **Pac-Man** BOLSA, FIN Pac-Man strategy; ~ **de pasajeros** TRANSP passenger strategy; ~ **de personal** RRHH staff strategy; ~ **de precios** V&M pricing strategy; ~ **proactiva** COM GEN, GES proactive strategy; ~ **de producto** COM GEN, V&M product strategy; ~ **publicitaria** V&M advertising strategy; ~ **reactiva** COM GEN reactive strategy; ~ **de realización de beneficios** GES profit-taking strategy; ~ **de realización de prestaciones** GES profit-taking strategy; ~ **de realización de utilidades** *AmL* GES profit-taking strategy; ~ **sectorial** GES sectoral strategy; ~ **de segmentación** V&M segmentation strategy; ~ **de supervivencia** COM GEN, ECON survival strategy; ~ **de tira y afloja** V&M push/pull strategy; ~ **de usuario** COM GEN, V&M user strategy; ~ **de ventas** V&M sales strategy; ~ **de vuelo** TRANSP flight strategy; ◆ ~ **de cobertura contra cambios de precio** BOLSA hedging strategy

estratégico *adj* COM GEN, GES strategic

estratificación *f* V&M stratification; ~ **social** PROT SOC social stratification

estrato: ~ **de petróleo** *m* MED AMB oil deposit

estrechamiento: ~ **del crédito** *m* BANCA, FIN credit squeeze

estrechar *vt* BOLSA, COM GEN *una brecha* narrow

estrecho *adj* COM GEN *cooperación, relación* close; ◆ **en** ~ **contacto** COM GEN in close contact

estrechos *m pl* TRANSP *navegación* narrows

estrenar *vt* OCIO launch

estreno *m* OCIO *de película*, V&M *de producto* launch

estrés *m* RRHH stress; ~ **del ejecutivo** RRHH executive stress; ~ **laboral** GES, RRHH work stress

estribor *m* TRANSP starboard side (*S*)

estricta: ~ **adhesión al contrato** *f* DER strict adherence to the contract

estrictamente *adv* COM GEN stringently

estricto *adj* COM GEN *medidas, programa* stringent, *normas* hard and fast

estructura *f* COM GEN structure; ~ **administrativa** GES, RRHH management structure, managerial structure; ~ **en árbol** INFO tree structure; ~ **de autoridad** COM GEN authority structure; ~ **de capital** CONT, ECON, FIN capital structure; ~ **comercial de las existencias** ECON commodity trade structure; ~ **compleja del capital** ECON complex capital structure; ~ **conceptual** CONT *of valores* conceptual framework; ~ **del consumo** ECON, V&M consumption pattern; ~ **de control** ADMIN, V&M control structure; ~ **corporativa** COM GEN corporate structure; ~ **del coste** *Esp* (*cf estructura del costo AmL*) COM GEN, CONT, FIN cost structure; ~ **del costo** *AmL* (*cf estructura del coste Esp*) COM GEN, CONT, FIN cost structure; ~ **de datos** INFO data structure; ~ **de deribados al alza** BOLSA *opciones* long straddle; ~ **directiva** GES, RRHH management structure; ~ **económica** ECON business structure, economic structure, POL economic structure; ~ **elevadora móvil** TRANSP *contenedores* mobile lift frame; ~ **de la empresa** COM GEN company structure; ~ **de filiales nacionales** COM GEN national subsidiary structure; ~ **financiera** CONT *balance* financial structure; ~ **fiscal** ECON, FISC tax structure; ~ **del gasto** POL *contabilidad gubernamental* vote structure; ~ **geográfica comercial** ECON geographical trade structure; ~ **de la gestión** GES, RRHH management structure, managerial structure; ~ **de grupo** COM GEN group structure; ~ **histórica** INMOB historic structure; ~ **impositiva** ECON, FISC tax structure; ~ **de la inversión** FIN pattern of investment; ~ **laboral** RRHH work structuring; ~ **longitudinal** TRANSP *navegación* longitudinal framing; ~ **de matriz** COM GEN grid structure; ~ **del mercado** ECON, V&M market form, market structure, structure of the market; ~ **de negociación** RRHH bargaining structure; ~ **de la organización** COM GEN, GES organization structure; ~ **de precios** ECON, FIN, V&M price structure; ~ **del programa** COM GEN program structure (*AmE*), programme structure (*BrE*); ~ **en rejilla** FIN grid structure; ~ **salarial** ECON, RRHH salary structure; ~ **salarial de dos niveles** RRHH two-tier wage structure; ~ **de los salarios** RRHH wage structure; ~ **sindical** RRHH union structure; ~ **de tarifas** TRANSP rates structure; ~ **temporal de los tipos de interés** ECON term structure of interest rates; ~ **de los vencimientos de la deuda** BANCA, ECON maturity structure of debt; ~ **de votos** CONT vote structure

estructuración *f* COM GEN structuring; ~ **del trabajo** COM GEN work structuring

estructurado *adj* COM GEN structured

estructurar *vt* COM GEN structure

estructuras: ~ **accesorias** *f pl* SEG appurtenant structures

estruendo *m* COM GEN outcry

estuario *m* TRANSP *navegación* estuary; ~ **afectado por las mareas** TRANSP tidal river estuary

estuche *m* V&M box

estudiante *mf* PROT SOC, RRHH student; ~ **extranjero(-a)** *m,f* PROT SOC foreign student; ~ **universitario(-a)** *m,f* PROT SOC undergraduate

estudiar *vt* COM GEN review, study, spell out, PROT SOC *en la universidad* read

estudio *m* COM GEN study, studio; ~ **de actitudes** V&M *investigación de mercado* attitude survey; ~ **anual de la evolución económica** ECON Economic Trends Annual Survey (*BrE*) (*ETAS*); ~ **anual del sistema de gas inerte** MED AMB annual inert gas system survey (*AIGSS*); ~ **de casos** GES, V&M case study; ~ **de casos prácticos** GES, V&M case study; ~ **de los componentes de un artículo** CONT value engineering; ~ **de los componentes de un producto** FIN value engineering;

~ **de conjunto** COM GEN conspectus; ~ **del déficit** COM GEN, V&M gap study; ~ **de desplazamientos y tiempos** COM GEN, ECON, IND, RRHH time and motion study; ~ **de diseño** INFO, COM GEN design engineering; ~ **empírico** ECON empirical study; ~ **del excedente** ECON surplus approach; ~ **de factibilidad** COM GEN feasibility study, feasibility survey; ~ **del gasto del consumidor** COM GEN, CONT, ECON, FIN consumer expenditure survey; ~ **de gerencia** GES management survey; ~ **de impacto** V&M *comercialización* impact study; ~ **de inversiones** FIN survey on investment; ~ **laboral** RRHH job study; ~ **de medios de comunicación** MEDIOS, V&M media research; ~ **de mercado** COM GEN market study, V&M market research, market study, market survey; ~ **de métodos** COM GEN methods study; ~ **de movimientos** ECON, GES, MAT motion study; ~ **de muestra** V&M *investigación de mercado* sample study; ~ **de origen y destino** V&M *investigación de mercado* origin and destination study; ~ **piloto** COM GEN pilot study; ~ **de planes de vuelo y disponibilidad** TRANSP Airline Schedules and Interline Availability Study (*ASIAS*); ~ **de la población circulante** ECON current population survey (*CPS*); ~ **pormenorizado** COM GEN in-depth study; ~ **preliminar** COM GEN reconnaissance survey; ~ **del presupuesto temporal** ECON time budget survey; ~ **de proyección de planta** IND plant layout study; ~ **de un proyecto** COM GEN project study; ~ **de rentabilidad** FIN investment analysis; ~ **retirado** COM GEN recall study; ~ **sectorial** COM GEN sector study; ~ **de seguimiento** V&M *investigación de mercado* tracking study; ~ **sobre los ingresos** ECON New Earnings Survey; ~ **sobre el perfil de los lectores** V&M *investigación de mercado* readership survey; ~ **de sueldos y salarios** RRHH wage and salary survey; ~ **de tiempo y métodos** COM GEN time and methods study; ~ **de tiempo y movimientos** COM GEN, ECON, IND, RRHH time and motion study; ~ **de tiempos** COM GEN, MAT *estadística* time study; ~ **del trabajo** COM GEN, GES, RRHH work study; ~ **de viabilidad** COM GEN feasibility study, feasibility survey

estudios: ~ **cronometrados** *m pl* GES stopwatch studies; ~ **económicos** *m pl* ECON business studies; ~ **empresariales** *m pl* COM GEN business studies; ~ **de mercado** *m pl* [inv pl] PROT SOC business studies; ~ **sociales** *m pl* PROT SOC social studies

etapa *f* COM GEN stage; ~ **alfa** FIN alpha stage; ~ **del proceso** IND process stage; ~ **de prueba** COM GEN test stage; ~ **de transición** ECON *de mercado* stage of transition; ~ **de verificación** COM GEN, CONT verification phase; ~ **de vuelo** TRANSP flight stage; ◆ **en determinada** ~ COM GEN at some stage

etapas: por ~ *fra* COM GEN in stages

Ethernet® *m* INFO *red* Ethernet®

ética *f* COM GEN ethics, DER moral law; ~ **comercial** COM GEN business ethics; ~ **profesional** COM GEN professional ethics; ~ **del trabajo** RRHH work ethic

éticas *f pl* COM GEN *comportamiento empresarial* ethics

ético *adj* COM GEN ethical

etiqueta *f* INFO, TRANSP *identificación de carga*, V&M *mercadotecnia* label, tag; ~ **adhesiva** COMS stick-on label; ~ **de calidad** COM GEN quality label; ~ **comercial** COM GEN business etiquette; ~ **de equipaje** OCIO baggage tag; ~ **equivalente** COM GEN alias; ~ **postal** COMS address label; ~ **de precio** COM GEN, V&M price label, price tag; **~ propia** V&M own label; **~ sindical** RRHH union label

etiquetado *m* INFO, V&M labeling (*AmE*), labelling (*BrE*); **~ ecológico** MED AMB ecolabeling (*AmE*), ecolabelling (*BrE*); **~ ecologista** MED AMB ecolabeling (*AmE*), ecolabelling (*BrE*); **~ informativo** V&M informative labeling (*AmE*), informative labelling (*BrE*); **~ de origen** TRANSP cargo tag

etiquetar *vt* INFO, TRANSP, V&M label

Euro MP *abr* (*eurodiputado, -a*) POL MEP (*Member of the European Parliament*)

Eurobanco *m* BANCA Eurobank

Eurobillete: ~ a medio plazo *m* BOLSA *mercado monetario* medium-term Euronote

eurobono *m* BANCA, BOLSA Eurobond

eurocartera *f* BANCA Europortfolio

eurocéntrico *adj* COM GEN eurocentric

eurocheque *m* ECON *internacional* eurocheque

eurodinero *m* BANCA Euromoney

eurodiputado, -a *m,f* (*MEP*) POL Member of the European Parliament (*Euro MP*)

eurodivisa *f* BANCA, ECON eurocurrency

eurodólar *m* (*ED*) ECON Eurodollar (*ED*)

euroemisión *f* ECON eurocurrency issue

euroequidad *f* ECON Euroequity

euroescéptico[1] *adj* COM GEN eurosceptical

euroescéptico[2]**,-a** *m,f* COM GEN Eurosceptic

eurófilo *adj* COM GEN europhile

eurófobo *adj* COM GEN europhobic

eurofranco *m* ECON Eurofranc

euromercado *m* ECON *UE* Euromarket

euromoneda *f* BANCA Euromoney

Euronet *f* COMS Euronet

europaleta *f* COM GEN, IMP/EXP, TRANSP Europallet

europeo *adj* COM GEN European

europeseta *f* BANCA Europeseta

eurorrebelde *mf* COM GEN Eurorebel

eurotasas *f pl* BANCA Euro-rates

euroventana *f* POL Eurowindow

Eurovisión *f* MEDIOS Eurovision

evacuación: ~ de residuos *f* MED AMB refuse disposal

evadir *vt* FISC *impuestos* avoid, evade

evaloración: ~ de puestos de trabajo *m* RRHH job evaluation

evaluación *f* COM GEN assessment, evaluation, *de experto* appraisal, INMOB survey, valuation, RRHH appraisal; **~ del activo fijo** CONT fixed asset assessment; **~ de la actuación** GES performance appraisal; **~ al coste estándar** *Esp* (*cf evaluación al costo estándar AmL*) CONT valuation at standard cost; **~ al coste estimado** *Esp* (*cf evaluación al costo estimado AmL*) CONT valuation at estimated cost; **~ al coste promedio** *Esp* (*cf evaluación al costo promedio AmL*) CONT valuation at average cost; **~ de área clave** GES key-area evaluation; **~ del ciclo vital** MED AMB Life Cycle Assessment (*LCA*); **~ contable** CONT accounting evaluation; **~ continua** PROT SOC, RRHH continuous assessment; **~ al costo estándar** *AmL* (*cf evaluación al coste estándar Esp*) CONT valuation at standard cost; **~ al costo estimado** *AmL* (*cf evaluación al coste estimado Esp*) CONT valuation at estimated cost; **~ al costo medio** *AmL* (*cf evaluación al coste medio Esp*) CONT

valuation at average cost; **~ del daño** SEG appraisal of damage; **~ de la demanda** ECON demand assessment; **~ del desempeño** GES performance evaluation; **~ dinámica** COM GEN dynamic evaluation; **~ económica** ECON economic appraisal; **~ de existencias** CONT valuation of stocks; **~ financiera** FIN financial appraisal; **~ fiscal** , FISC assesment, tax assessment; **~ de ganancias** FIN earnings performance; **~ de impacto medioambiental** MED AMB environmental impact assessment; **~ interna** INMOB in-house valuation; **~ de la inversión de capital** FIN capital investment appraisal; **~ de inversiones** FIN investment appraisal; **~ de medios de comunicación** MEDIOS, V&M media evaluation; **~ del mercado** V&M market evaluation; **~ modesta** COM GEN underevaluation; **~ multidimensional por escalas** V&M multidimensional scaling; **~ del personal** GES, RRHH staff appraisal; **~ del problema** COM GEN, GES problem assessment; **~ del producto** V&M product evaluation; **~ en el propio centro educativo** PROT SOC internal school assessment; **~ de proveedores** COM GEN supplier evaluation; **~ del proyecto** COM GEN project assessment; **~ del proyecto de capital** ECON, FIN capital project evaluation; **~ de proyectos** ECON project appraisal; **~ de proyectos de capital** ECON, FIN capital project evaluation; **~ prudente** *m* COM GEN conservative estimate; **~ del puesto** RRHH job appraisal; **~ de recursos** COM GEN resource appraisal; **~ de riesgos** BOLSA, FIN, SEG risk evaluation; **~ de tareas** IND task analysis; **~ del valor neto** CONT net worth assessment; **~ de valores** BOLSA security rating

evaluado: no ~ *adj* COM GEN unassessed

evaluador, a *m,f* SEG *marítimo* assessor

evaluar *vt* COM GEN appraise, evaluate, size up (*infrml*); ◆ **~ las necesidades futuras** COM GEN make an appraisal of future needs

evasión *f* FISC evasion; **~ de divisas** ECON capital flight; **~ fiscal** ECON, FISC avoidance of tax, tax dodging, tax evasion; **~ fiscal directa e indirecta** ECON, FISC direct and indirect tax evasion; **~ de impuestos** ECON, FIN, FISC tax avoidance, tax evasion

evasivo *adj* COM GEN *respuesta, acción* evasive

evasor, a: ~ de impuestos *m,f* ECON, FISC tax evader

evento *m* INFO event

eventualidad *f* COM GEN eventuality

eventualmente *adv* COM GEN contingently

evidencia: de auditoría *f* COM GEN evidence, CONT audit evidence

evidente *adj* COM GEN evident

evitar *vt* COM GEN avoid, prevent; ◆ **~ riesgos** COM GEN play safe

evolución *f* COM GEN *precio* evolution, movement, INFO upgrading, PROT SOC *precio* movement; **~ adversa de los precios** ECON adverse price movement

evolucionar: ~ simultáneamente *fra* ECON *divisas* move together

evolutivo *adj* COM GEN, IND, INMOB, PROT SOC developmental

ex[1] *abr* (*revisado*) COM GEN ex (*examined*)

ex[2]**: ~ ante** *adj* ECON ex ante; **~ derecho** *adj* BOLSA ex-rights

ex[3]**: ~ hipótesis** *adv* COM GEN ex hypothesi

exacción: ~ de dinero *f* COM GEN shakedown (*infrml*) (*AmE*)

exacerbar *vt* COM GEN compound, exacerbate

exactitud *f* COM GEN trustworthiness, *cifras, datos* accuracy, CONT *cifras, declaración*, MAT accuracy

exacto *adj* COM GEN correct, exact

exagerar *vt* COM GEN overstretch

examen *m* COM GEN examination, GES *de sistema* overhaul, RRHH *de un candidato* examination; ~ **de aptitud** V&M aptitude test; ~ **de aptitud profesional** RRHH aptitude test; ~ **atento** COM GEN close examination; ~ **de auditoría** CONT audit examination; ~ **para la concesión de licencias** COM GEN *comercial* licensing examination; ~ **físico** COM GEN *de objeto*, PROT SOC physical examination; ~ **de ingreso** COM GEN entrance examination; ~ **de ingresos** CONT, FISC revenue test; ~ **para licencia** COM GEN licensing examination; ~ **médico** PROT SOC medical examination; ~ **de proposición** SEG examination of proposal; ~ **público** PROT SOC public examination

examinador, a *m,f* COM GEN, DER, RRHH *de un candidato* examiner; ~ **de taxistas** RRHH *policía* white coat (*jarg*)

examinar *vt* COM GEN look at, look over, *solicitud* examine, *informes* scan; ◆ ~ **en profundidad** COM GEN examine in depth

exceda: sin que ~ *fra* COM GEN not exceeding

excedente *m* CONT, ECON surplus; ~ **de acciones** BOLSA excess shares; ~ **del activo sobre el pasivo** CONT surplus of assets over liabilities; ~ **acumulado** CONT accumulated surplus; ~ **agrícola** ECON farm surplus; ~ **del ahorrador** BANCA saver's surplus; ~ **de capacidad** ECON, IND excess capacity; ~ **de capital** BOLSA, CONT, ECON, FIN capital surplus (*AmE*), share premium (*BrE*); ~ **de capital disponible** FISC capital surplus on hand; ~ **de efectivo** CONT cash surplus; ~ **de explotación** IND earned surplus; ~ **de exportación** IMP/EXP export surplus; ~ **de importación** IMP/EXP import surplus; ~ **de inversiones** FIN investment surplus; ~ **neto** COM GEN net profits; ~ **neto diario** COM GEN net daily surplus; ~ **presupuestario** FIN budgetary surplus; ~ **previsto** FISC designated surplus; ~ **de producción** IND production surplus; ~ **del productor** IND producer surplus; ~ **restringido** CONT undistributable reserve (*BrE*), restricted surplus (*AmE*); ◆ **en** ~ ECON in surplus

excedentes: ~ **alimentarios** *m pl* ECON food surplus

exceder *vt* CONT exceed, overpass, surpass

excelente *adj* COM GEN first-rate

excepción *f* COM GEN *caso* exception, RRHH odd man out; ~ **de falta de acción** DER demurrer; ◆ **con la** ~ COM GEN with the exception of; **hacer una** ~ COM GEN make an exception

excepcional *adj* COM GEN *caso, circunstancias* exceptional

excepto *prep* COM GEN excluding (*ex, excl*); ◆ ~ **que esté causado por** SEG *marítimo* unless caused by

exceptuado *adj* TRANSP excepted

excesivamente *adv* COM GEN excessively, FISC *gravado* heavily

excesivo *adj* COM GEN excessive

exceso[1]: **con** ~ **de personal** *adj* IND, RRHH overmanned

exceso[2] *m* COM GEN excess, glut, ECON glut, SEG *producción* overrun; ~ **de ahorro** BANCA oversaving; ~ **de capacidad** ECON, IND spare capacity; ~ **de carga** TRANSP load bulge, loading overside; ~ **de comercialización** ECON overtrading; ~ **de compromi-**

sos FIN overcommitment; ~ **de crédito** BANCA overstepping of appropriation; ~ **de demanda** ECON, V&M excess demand; ~ **de depósito** BANCA excess bank reserves; ~ **de desembolso** FISC *obras benéficas* disbursement excess; ~ **de edad** COM GEN overage; ~ **de efectivo** CONT excess cash; ~ **de emisión** BANCA over-issue; ~ **de empleo** RRHH overemployment; ~ **de equipaje** COM GEN, OCIO, TRANSP baggage excess; ~ **de gravamen fiscal** FISC excess burden of a tax; ~ **de inversión** *f* ECON overtrading; ~ **de liquidez** CONT excess cash; ~ **de medios** V&M *publicidad* overkill (*infrml*); ~ **de medios publicitarios** V&M advertising overkill; ~ **de mortalidad** SEG excess mortality; ~ **de oferta** BOLSA overhang, ECON, V&M excess supply; ~ **de oferta agregada** ECON slack; ~ **de pedidos** COM GEN backlog of orders; ~ **de pérdidas** SEG excess of loss; ~ **de personal** RRHH overstaffing; ~ **de peticiones de suscripción** BOLSA *acciones* oversubscription; ~ **de poder adquisitivo** ECON excess purchasing power; ~ **de rendimiento sobre la deuda** BOLSA reverse yield gap; ~ **de suministro** ECON, V&M excess supply; ~ **de tesorería** CONT *liquidez, efectivo, caja* cash-rich; ~ **de tonelaje** TRANSP over tonnaging; ~ **de trabajadores** RRHH featherbedding

excluir *vt* COM GEN bar, preclude, crowd out, exclude, rule out, ECON *prestamistas, inversores*, FIN crowd out; ◆ ~ **a alguien** COM GEN bar sb

exclusión *f* COM GEN, ECON, FIN exclusion, crowding out; ~ **del dividendo** FISC dividend exclusion (*AmE*); ~ **estatutaria** SEG statutory exclusion; ~ **general** COM GEN blanket ban; ~ **legal** SEG statutory exclusion; ~ **de riesgos comerciales** COM GEN, SEG business risk exclusion; ~ **de riesgos empresariales** COM GEN, SEG business risk exclusion; ◆ **con la** ~ **de** COM GEN to the exclusion of

exclusividad *f* V&M exclusivity

exclusivo *adj* COM GEN exclusive (*excl.*); ~ **de envío y embalaje** COM GEN exclusive of post and packing

excursión *f* TRANSP trip, junket (*infrml*) (*AmE*); ~ **en ferrocarril** OCIO, TRANSP rail tour; ~ **con gastos incluidos** *m* OCIO, TRANSP inclusive tour (*IT*); ~ **con los gastos pagados** OCIO, TRANSP package tour; ~ **con guía por ferrocarril** OCIO, TRANSP rail guided tour

ex-empleado, -a *m,f* RRHH ex-employee

exención *f* COM GEN, FISC exclusion, exemption, waiver; ~ **admisible** FISC allowable exemption; ~ **anual** FISC annual exemption; ~ **básica** FISC basic exemption; ~ **de cuota variable** FISC redemption; ~ **por edad** FISC age exemption; ~ **establecida por la ley** DER statutory exemption; ~ **fiscal** FISC tax exemption, tax loophole; ~ **fiscal para explotaciones rurales** FISC ≈ homestead tax exemption (*AmE*); ~ **de las ganancias del capital** FISC capital gains exemption; ~ **del impuesto** FISC forgiveness of tax; ~ **por matrimonio** FISC married exemption; ~ **de una obligación** FISC waiver; ~ **parcial** FISC rebate; ~ **personal** FISC personal allowance (*BrE*), personal exemption (*AmE*); ~ **personal básica** FISC basic personal exemption; ~ **personal de impuestos** FISC personal exemption from tax; ~ **por personas a cargo** FISC exemption for dependents; ~ **de prima** SEG exemption from payment of premium; ~ **de los sueldos** BANCA release of pay checks (*AmE*), release of pay cheques (*BrE*); ~ **por tener hijos al cargo** FISC exemption for dependent children; ~ **total** FISC full exemption; ~ **por vejez** FISC old age exemption; **triple ~ fiscal** FISC triple tax exempt

exenciones *f pl* RRHH exemptions, immunities (*BrE*)

exento *adj* COM GEN, FISC *de impuestos* exempt, INFO free; **no ~** FISC *impuestos* nonexempt; **~ de derechos** FISC, IMP/EXP duty-free; **~ de derechos o aranceles** FISC nondutiable; **~ de impuestos** ECON, FIN, FISC exclusive of tax, tax-exempt, tax-free; **~ de impuestos sobre la renta** FISC free of income tax (*f.i.t.*); **~ de todo impuesto** FISC free of all taxation; **~ de licencia** DER permit-free; **~ de riesgo** COM GEN riskless

exhaustivo *adj* COM GEN exhaustive

exhibición *f* DER, OCIO exhibition; **~ aérea** TRANSP air show; **~ audiovisual** V&M audiovisual display; **~ de despilfarro** COM GEN spending spree (*infrml*)

exhortar: **~ a alguien a hacer algo** *fra* COM GEN urge sb to do sth

exigencia: **~ de capital** *f* ECON, FIN capital requirement; **~ de devolución inmediata de un préstamo** *f* BANCA sharp call; **~ de dividendos** *f* BOLSA, CONT dividend requirement; **~ de impuestos** *f* FISC levying of taxes; **~ neta del capital** *f* ECON, FIN net capital requirement; **~ de preinspección** *f* BANCA pre-inspection requirement; **~ de rentabilidad** *f* FIN profitability requirement; **~ de retención** *f* FISC retention requirement

exigible: **~ sin previo aviso** *adj* COM GEN repayable on demand

exigir *vt* COM GEN demand, require; ◆ **~ algo de alguien** COM GEN require sth of sb; **~ una cantidad** FISC claim an amount; **~ un impuesto** FISC levy a tax; **~ indemnización por daños** SEG claim damages; **~ el pago** BANCA call; **~ compensación** DER seek redress

exilio: **~ fiscal** *m* FISC tax exile

eximente *adj* BANCA, DER exculpatory

eximir *vt* COM GEN exempt, DER discharge, FISC waive, RRHH *relaciones laborales* exempt (*jarg*)

existencia[1]: **~ en caja** *f* CONT cash in hand; **~ reguladora** *f* TRANSP buffer stock

existencia[2]: **en ~** *fra* COM GEN in stock

existencias *f pl* COM GEN inventory, stock, stock in hand, V&M supplies; **~ en almacén** CONT, V&M stock in; **~ en caja** COM GEN cash in hand; **~ de capital** BOLSA, CONT capital stock (*AmE*), equity capital (*BrE*); **~ para casos de emergencia** TRANSP stockpile; **~ comerciales** COM GEN commercial stocks; **~ consolidadas** FIN consolidated stock (*BrE*); **~ disponibles** COM GEN, CONT stock in hand; **~ en efectivo** BANCA cash reserve, CONT carry back, cash reserve; **~ inmovilizadas** CONT dead stock, interactive stock, junk; **~ en inventario** CONT, V&M inventory count; **~ máximas** CONT, V&M maximum stock; **~ mínimas** CONT, V&M minimum stock; **~ de productos básicos** COM GEN staple stock; **~ reales** COM GEN actual stock; **~ de seguridad** COM GEN, SEG safety stock; ◆ **sin ~** COM GEN out of stock; **mientras duren las ~** V&M while stocks last

éxito:[1] **~ crítico** *m* OCIO critical success; **~ inesperado** *m* V&M sleeper; **~ permanente** *m* COM GEN *persona, compañía, producto* continued success

éxito:[2] **tener ~** *fra* COM GEN be successful

exitoso *adj* COM GEN successful

éxodo: **~ de profesionales** *m* RRHH brain drain (*infrml*)

exoneración *f* FISC *del impuesto* remission; **~ de gastos**

FISC remission of charges; **~ de impuestos** FISC tax remission

exorbitante *adj* ECON steep

exóticas *f pl* BOLSA exotics

expansión[1]: **de triple ~** *adj* TRANSP triple expansion (*TE*)

expansión[2] *f* COM GEN expansion; **~ comercial de nuevos productos con la misma maquinaria** ECON diagonal expansion; **~ del crédito** BANCA credit expansion; **~ del crédito interior** ECON domestic credit expansion (*DCE*); **~ de la demanda** V&M expansion of demand; **~ económica** ECON, POL economic expansion; **~ industrial** SEG industrial expansion; **~ interna** ECON internal expansion; **~ de las inversiones** BOLSA, FIN investment expansion; **~ del mercado** V&M market expansion; **~ de mercado de capitales** BOLSA easing of capital market; **~ monetaria** ECON monetary expansion; **~ del negocio** COM GEN, GES business expansion; **~ del trabajo** GES job enlargement

expansionario *adj* COM GEN expanding

expansionista *adj* COM GEN *política fiscal* expansionary

expansivo *adj* COM GEN expanding, expansive

expatriado, -a *m,f* COM GEN expatriate

expectativa *f* COM GEN *algo previsto* expectation, prospect, MAT expectation; **~ de beneficio** ECON profit outlook

expectativas: **~ adaptivas** *f pl* ECON adaptive expectations; **~ del consumidor** *f pl* COM GEN consumer expectations; **~ económicas** *f pl* POL economic prospects; **~ de empleo** *f pl* RRHH job expectations; **~ exógenas** *f pl* ECON exogenous expectations; **~ extrapoladas** *f pl* ECON extrapolative expectations; **~ inflacionarias** *f pl* ECON inflationary expectations; **~ de Keynes** *f pl* ECON Keynes expectations; **~ profesionales** *f pl* RRHH career expectations; **~ racionales** *f pl* ECON rational expectations (*RE*); **~ con respecto a los precios** *f pl* COM GEN price expectations

expedición *f* BOLSA forwarding, TRANSP consignation (*consgt*), dispatch, dispatching; **~ de carga** IMP/EXP, TRANSP cargo clearance; **~ habitual** TRANSP customary despatch

expedidor, a *m,f* COMS forwarder (*fwdr*), IMP/EXP forwarder (*fwdr*), forwarding clerk, shipping officer, TRANSP consignor, dispatcher, shipper, shipping clerk, shipping officer; **~ y transportista** TRANSP shipper and carrier (*s&c*)

expediente *m* COM GEN case notes, *escrito* record; **~ académico** RRHH career record; **~ administrativo** ADMIN administrative file; **~ de antecedentes** COM GEN case history; **~ de exportación** IMP/EXP export data folder; **~ personal** RRHH personal file; **~ de reclamaciones** PATENT set of claims

expendedora: **~ automática** *f* COM GEN *para billetes* slot machine

experiencia *f* COM GEN experience, expertise, RRHH experience; **~ en agencia** V&M *publicidad* agency experience; **~ comercial** COM GEN business experience; **~ comprobada** RRHH track record; **~ en la dirección** GES management practice; **~ laboral** COM GEN, RRHH work experience; **~ práctica** RRHH hands-on experience

experimentado *adj* COM GEN, RRHH experienced, seasoned

experimentar *vt* BOLSA *una baja* record, COM GEN, RRHH *crecimiento* experience

experimento *m* COM GEN experiment; ~ **de laboratorio** PROT SOC laboratory experience (*jarg*)

experto[1] *adj* COM GEN, RRHH expert

experto[2]**,-a** *m,f* INMOB appraiser; ~ **en comercio** V&M trade expert; ~ **contable** CONT expert accountant; ~ **fiscal** FISC tax expert, tax practitioner, tax professional; ~ **en impuestos** FISC tax practitioner; ~ **independiente** RRHH independent expert; ~ **en informática** INFO computer wizard; ~ **en inversiones** BOLSA, FIN investment expert; ~ **en marketing** *Esp* (*cf experto en mercadotecnia AmL*) RRHH marketeer; ~ **en mercadotecnia** *AmL* (*cf experto en marketing Esp*) RRHH marketeer; ~ **sobre la materia** PATENT person skilled in the art; ♦ **ser un experto en** INFO be a wizard at

expiración *f* COM GEN expiration, expiry; ~ **de una patente** PATENT lapse of a patent; ~ **de una póliza** SEG expiring of a policy

expiral: ~ **del impuesto sobre los salarios** *f* ECON, FISC wage-tax spiral

expirar 1. *vt* COM GEN *un plazo* expire; **2.** *vi* FIN run out

explicación *f* CONT *notas* explanation

explicar *vt* COM GEN explain

explícito *adj* COM GEN explicit

exploración *f* COM GEN, INFO *electrónica* scanning; ~ **medioambiental** MED AMB environmental scanning; ~ **del mercado** V&M market exploration

explorador[1] *m* COM GEN scanner; ~ **medioambiental** MED AMB environmental scanner; ~ **óptico** SEG optical scanner

explorador[2]**,a** *m,f* COM GEN prospector

explorar *vt* COM GEN open up, INFO *electrónica* scan

explosión: ~ **demográfica** *f* ECON, POL population explosion; ~ **salarial** *f* RRHH wage explosion

explosivo *m* MED AMB blockbusting (*AmE*) (*jarg*); ~ **deflagrante** TRANSP *mercancías peligrosas* deflagrating explosive; ~ **detonante** TRANSP *mercancías peligrosas* detonating explosive; ~ **iniciador** TRANSP *mercancías peligrosas* initiating explosive; ~ **primario** TRANSP *mercancías peligrosas* primary explosive; ~ **secundario** TRANSP secondary explosive

explotación *f* COM GEN exploitation; ~ **del activo** BANCA asset sweating (*AmE*); ~ **agrícola** ECON agricultural unit; ~ **aurífera** IND gold mining; ~ **a cielo abierto** IND, MED AMB open cast mining (*BrE*), strip mining (*AmE*); ~ **de gas** IND gas exploitation; ~ **industrial** IND, PATENT exploitation in industry; ~ **minera a cielo abierto** IND, MED AMB open cast mining (*BrE*), strip mining (*AmE*); ~ **mutua de derechos de patente** DER, COM GEN, INFO *transferencia de tecnología* cross-licensing; ~ **de una patente** PATENT exploitation of a patent; ~ **portuaria** TRANSP port operation; ~ **de recursos petrolíferos** MED AMB tapping of oil resources; ~ **del remolque** TRANSP trailer utilization; ~ **de la tierra** MED AMB land development

explotador *m* COM GEN owner-operator

explotar *vt* COM GEN exploit, PATENT *patente* work; ♦ **sin** ~ COM GEN *recursos, mercados* untapped

exponente *m* MAT exponent

exponer *vt* BOLSA expose, COM GEN expose, discuss, *condiciones* set out, *proyecto* compromise, POL deliver; ♦ ~ **a** COM GEN *presiones* expose to; ~ **categóricamente** COM GEN state categorically; ~ **lo obvio** COM GEN state the obvious; ~ **una sugerencia**

ante un comité COM GEN put a suggestion before a committee

exportación *f* COM GEN exportation, IMP/EXP export (*exp.*), exportation; ~ **de capital** IMP/EXP capital export; ~ **directa** IMP/EXP direct exporting; ~ **indirecta** IMP/EXP indirect exporting; ~ **invisible** IMP/EXP invisible export; ~ **de materias primas** IMP/EXP staple export; ~ **postal** IMP/EXP postal export; ~ **de productos industriales** IMP/EXP export of manufactures; ~ **temporal** IMP/EXP temporary export; ~ **visible** IMP/EXP visible export

exportaciones *f pl* COM GEN export sales, exports; ~ **aún no declaradas** IMP/EXP customs pre-entry exports; ~ **de favor** IMP/EXP concessional exports; ~ **indivisibles** IMP/EXP indivisible exports; ~ **invisibles** ECON *balanza comercial* invisible exports (*jarg*); ~ **mundiales** IMP/EXP world exports; ~ **con subsidio** ECON, IMP/EXP subsidized exports; ~ **subvencionadas** ECON, IMP/EXP subsidized exports

exportado *adj* ECON, IMP/EXP exported

exportador[1] *adj* COM GEN, IMP/EXP exporting

exportador[2]**,a** *m,f* COM GEN, ECON, RRHH, V&M export merchant, exporter; ~ **a gran escala** ECON large-scale exporter

exposición *f* BOLSA, COM GEN exposition, DER representation, V&M exhibition, display, *publicidad* exposure; ~ **ambulante** V&M traveling exhibition (*AmE*), travelling exhibition (*BrE*); ~ **comercial** V&M trade exhibition, trade show; ~ **crediticia por país** ECON country exposure; ~ **en estantes** V&M shelf display; ~ **exterior** V&M display outer; ~ **máxima de la marca** V&M maximum brand exposure; ~ **en nota al pie** CONT footnote disclosure; ~ **permanente** COM GEN permanent exhibition; ~ **de pre-campaña** V&M pre-campaign exposure; ~ **racional de principio** COM GEN, GES, RRHH rationale; ~ **razonada** COM GEN, GES, RRHH rationale; ~ **al riesgo** CONT risk exposure; ~ **totalmente efectiva** V&M *publicidad* total effective exposure

expositor *m* V&M *publicidad* stand (*jarg*)

expresar *vt* ECON denominate; ~ **en** BANCA *dólares* make out in

expresión *f* INFO *lenguaje de programación* expression

expreso *adj* COM GEN *intención* express

expropiación: ~ **recíproca** *f* DER, INMOB inverse condemnation (*AmE*)

expropiar *vt* DER, INMOB expropriate

expulsar *vt* DER evict, INFO *tarjeta, disco* eject

expulsión *f* DER eviction, INFO ejection; ~ **constructiva** INMOB constructive eviction; ~ **efectiva** INMOB actual eviction; ~ **parcial** DER, INMOB partial eviction; ~ **por represalia** INMOB retaliatory eviction

extemporáneo *adj* COM GEN untimely

extender *vt* COM GEN *poder* extend, *cheque* make out, TRANSP *permiso de trasbordo* clear; ♦ ~ **un cheque** BANCA make out a check (*AmE*), make out a cheque (*BrE*), raise a check (*AmE*), raise a cheque (*BrE*), write a check (*AmE*), write a cheque (*BrE*); ~ **cheques sin fondos** BANCA issue bad checks (*AmE*), issue bad cheques (*BrE*); ~ **una factura** COM GEN make out an invoice; ~ **un pagaré** FIN make out a promissory note; ~ **una póliza** SEG issue a policy

extensión *f* INFO *nombre de fichero* extension, V&M *de tiendas* spread; ~ **del daño** SEG extent of damage; ~ **del empleo** RRHH scope of employment; ~ **de una letra** BANCA drawing of bill; ~ **de la línea de productos** IND line-stretching; ~ **de la marca** V&M brand extension; ~ **del mercado** V&M freeness of the market; ~ **del riesgo** BOLSA exposure; ~ **telefónica** *Esp* (*cf interno telefónico AmL*) COMS telephone extension (*X*); ~ **de tierras** INMOB frontage

externalidad *f* ECON externality; ~ **agotable** ECON depletable externality; ~ **contemporánea** ECON contemporaneous externality; ~ **secuencial** ECON sequential externality

externalizar *vt* ECON externalize

extinción *f* DER abatement, discharge, FISC burnout, MED AMB extinction; ~ **de una obligación o deuda** FIN forfeiture of a debt

extinguir *vt* DER abate, discharge, MED AMB extinguish

extorno: ~ **del activo** *m* CONT charge-off; ~ **por amarre** *m* SEG *marítimo* lay-up return

extorsionador, a *m* BANCA, FIN loan shark (*infrml*)

extorsionar *vt* COM GEN, FIN extort

extra[1] *adj* COM GEN extra

extra[2] *m* COM GEN extra (*ex.*)

extracción *f* COM GEN extraction; ~ **de carbón** IND, MED AMB coal mining

extracto *m* COM GEN *sumario* abstract, summary, *de un documento* extract, DER *resumen, sumario*, ECON *sumario*, FIN *resumen* abstract; ~ **de cuentas** BANCA, FIN abstract of accounts; ~ **de los debates** DER charge; ~ **del registro** PATENT extract from the register

extraer *vt* (*cf traer AmL*) COM GEN extract, bring, DER, FIN extract, INFO fetch, *datos, texto* output; ~ **de** COM GEN *recursos, mercado* tap into

extrajudicialmente *adv* DER extrajudicially

extramarginal *adj* ECON extramarginal

extranjero[1] *adj* COM GEN offshore

extranjero[2]**,-a** *m,f* DER alien, COM GEN foreigner, GES outsider; ~ **ilegal** DER illegal alien; ~ **residente** POL resident alien

extraoficial *adj* COM GEN extraofficial, unofficial; ◆ **con carácter** ~ COM GEN in an unofficial capacity

extraoficialmente *adv* COM GEN extraofficially

extrapolación *f* MAT extrapolation

extrarradio: del ~ *adj* COM GEN, IND, V&M out of town

extraterritorial *adj* COM GEN extra-territorial

extratipo *m* BANCA tip

extremado *adj* COM GEN exaggerated

extremo *m* ECON *programación lineal* extremum; ~ **alto de la banda** BOLSA high end of the range; ~ **bajo de la banda** BOLSA low end of the range; ~ **de carril** TRANSP railhead; ~ **más bajo de la gama** COM GEN, V&M bottom end of the range; ◆ **en el** ~ **superior** COM GEN *de escala* at the top end

F

F *abr* (*grados fahrenheit*) COM GEN F (*fahrenheit*)

fábrica *f* COM GEN shop factory, factory, shop floor, CONT *activo fijo* plant, IND, RRHH shop floor, shop factory, factory; **~ avanzada** IND advanced factory; **~ de componentes** IND component factory; **~ de gas** IND, MED AMB gas works; **~ de gas industrial** IND, MED AMB industrial gas works; **~ de la moneda** BANCA, ECON mint; **~ multisindical** IND, RRHH multiunion plant; **~ de papel** IND, MED AMB paper mill; **~ de productos químicos** IND chemical works; **~ de transplantes** IND, MED AMB transplant factory; ♦ **ex ~** COM GEN, IMP/EXP *lugar convenido*, TRANSP *término de expedición* ex-works (*ExW*)

fabricación *f* COM GEN making, manufacturing, manufacture; **~ asistida por computador** *AmL ver fabricación asistida por computadora AmL*; **~ asistida por computadora** *AmL* (*CAM, cf fabricación asistida por ordenador Esp*) IND, INFO computer-aided manufacturing (*CAM*); **~ asistida por ordenador** *Esp* (*CAM, cf fabricación asistida por computadora AmL*) IND, INFO computer-aided manufacturing (*CAM*); **~ en cadena** SEG flow production; **~ integrada por computador** *AmL ver fabricación integrada por computadora AmL*; **~ integrada por computadora** *AmL* (*cf fabricación integrada por ordenador Esp*) IND, INFO computer-integrated manufacture (*CIM*); **~ integrada por ordenador** *Esp* (*cf fabricación integrada por computadora AmL*) IND, INFO computer-integrated manufacture (*CIM*); **~ con licencia** IND, SEG manufacturing under licence (*BrE*), manufacturing under license (*AmE*); **~ en serie** IND mass production

fabricado *adj* COM GEN, IND manufactured (*mfd*)

fabricante *mf* COM GEN manufacturer (*mfr*), fabricator; **~ de coches** IND, RRHH, TRANSP car manufacturer; **~ de herramientas** COM GEN, IND toolmaker; **~ de lanas** ECON, IND wool textiles manufacturer, wool yarn manufacturer, woollen manufacturer

fabricar *vt* COM GEN, IND manufacture, fabricate; ♦ **~ en serie** IND mass-produce; **~ bajo licencia** IND *producción* manufacture under licence (*BrE*), manufacture under license (*AmE*)

fabril *adj* COM GEN, IND manufacturing

facción *f* RRHH faction

fachada *f* INMOB *de edificio* facade

fácil: de ~ manejo *adj* INFO user-friendly

facilidad: ~ bancaria internacional *f* BANCA international banking facility (*IBF*); **~ de crédito autorrenovable** *f* BANCA, SEG *inversión bancaria* revolving underwriting facility; **~ de manejo** *f* TRANSP ease of handling; **~ monetaria** *f* ECON, FIN monetary ease; **~ de sobregiro** *f* BANCA overdraft facility; **~ de venta** *f* V&M saleableness

Facilidad: ~ de Banco Central *f* BANCA, ECON, FIN Central Bank Facility (*BrE*)

facilidades: ~ complementarias de crédito *f* ECON additional facilities; **~ crediticias de un banco** *f pl* BANCA credit facilities at a bank; **~ de crédito** *f pl* BANCA borrowing facilities; **~ de pago** *f pl* BANCA easy payments, easy terms

facilitación *f* COM GEN, ECON facilitation; **~ comercial** ECON trade facilitation

facilitador, a *m,f* FIN arranger

facilitamiento *m* COM GEN, ECON facilitation

facilitar *vt* COM GEN, ECON *controles de crédito* ease, facilitate

facsímil *m* (*fax*) COM GEN facsimile (*fax*)

factible *adj* COM GEN achievable

fáctico *adj* COM GEN factual

factor *m* COM GEN factor; **~ de actividad** ECON activity factor; **~ de acumulación** ECON accumulation factor; **~ de agotamiento** ECON depletion allowance; **~ de ajuste del suministro de combustible** TRANSP *navegación* bunkering adjustment factor (*BAF*); **~ de alcance diario** BOLSA, FIN Daily Range Factor (*DRF*); **~ aleatorio** ECON random factor; **~ de atención** V&M *publicidad* attention factor; **~ de la banda diaria** BOLSA, FIN Daily Range Factor (*DRF*); **~ beta** BOLSA beta factor (*BrE*); **~ de capacidad** ECON capacity factor; **~ de carga** COM GEN load factor; **~ casi fijo** ECON quasi fixed factor; **~ cíclico** ECON cyclical factor; **~ común de distinción** RRHH common distinguishing factor; **~ constrictor** ECON *que limita la producción, la venta*, V&M constraining factor; **~ de consumo** COM GEN, ECON *fabricación* load factor; **~ de conversión** BOLSA, MAT conversion factor; **~ de conversión para las aportaciones del empleado** SEG *plan de pensiones* conversion factor for employee contributions; **~ del coste** *Esp* (*cf factor del costo AmL*) CONT cost factor; **~ del costo** *AmL* (*cf factor del coste Esp*) CONT cost factor; **~ delta** BOLSA delta factor (*BrE*); **~ de desgaste** V&M *publicidad* wearout factor; **~ de no discriminación** COM GEN no discrimination factor; **~ disuasorio** COM GEN deterrent; **~ endógeno** ECON endogenous factor; **~ estabilizador** ECON steadying factor; **~ estacional** COM GEN, ECON seasonal factor; **~ de estiba** COM GEN, TRANSP stowage factor; **~ de estiba alto** TRANSP high stowage factor; **~ de estibaje bajo** TRANSP low stowage factor; **~ exógeno** ECON exogenous factor; **~ fijo** ECON fixed factor; **~ impositivo** ECON, FISC factor tax; **~ de insumo** FIN input factor; **~ de lealtad** V&M loyalty factor; **~ de ocupación** COM GEN, TRANSP *aerolíneas* load factor; **~ de pensión** SEG annuity factor; **~ precio** BOLSA price factor; **~ de producción** ECON, IND factor of production; **~ de productividad** ECON, IND factor of productivity; **~ de reversión** MAT *estadística* reversionary factor; **~ de riesgo** ECON risk factor; **~ del valor presente** CONT, ECON, FIN present value method; ♦ **ser un ~ de** COM GEN be a factor in

Factor: ~ Inwood de Periodicidad Anual *m* SEG Inwood Annuity Factor

factoraje *m* FIN, MAT factoring; **~ de exportación** IMP/EXP export factoring; **~ de seguros** SEG insurance factoring

factores: ~ humanos *m pl* RRHH *psicología industrial*

human factors; ~ **M** *m pl* ECON M factors; ~ **de producción** *m pl* ECON, SEG factors of production, inputs

factoría *ver fábrica*

factorial *m* MAT factorial

factoring *m* GES factoring

factorización *f* CONT, FIN factoring

factótum *m* RRHH odd-job man

factura *f* COM GEN bill, invoice (*inv.*); ~ **de aduanas** IMP/EXP customs invoice; ~ **certificada** CONT certified invoice; ~ **a cobrar** CONT, FIN invoice receivable; ~ **comercial** CONT commercial invoice; ~ **de compra** COM GEN purchase invoice; ~ **de conciliación** FIN reconciliation bill; ~ **de conocimiento no traspasable** BANCA stale bill of lading; ~ **detallada** CONT, FIN itemized invoice; ~ **en la divisa del comprador extranjero** CONT invoice in the currency of the overseas buyer; ~ **en la divisa del vendedor extranjero** CONT invoice in the currency of the overseas seller; ~ **de embarque** IMP/EXP, TRANSP shipping bill, shipping invoice; ~ **para exportación** IMP/EXP, TRANSP export invoice; ~ **formal** COM GEN formal receipt; ~ **impagada** CONT unpaid bill; ~ **de muestra** COM GEN specimen invoice; ~ **original** COM GEN, IMP/EXP, TRANSP original bill, original invoice; ~ **a pagar** CONT, FIN invoice payable; ~ **pendiente** CONT, FIN outstanding bill; ~ **proforma** COM GEN pre-bill, pro forma invoice; ~ **provisional** COM GEN provisional invoice; ~ **de prueba** COM GEN convenience bill; ~ **rectificada** CONT, FIN corrected invoice; ~ **telefónica** COMS telephone bill; ~ **en una tercera moneda** CONT invoice in a third currency; ~ **de transporte** TRANSP shipping invoice

facturación *f* COM GEN *acción* billing, invoicing, *volumen* turnover, inventory turnover, stock rotation, stock turnover; ~ **de agencia** MEDIOS agency billing; ~ **al cliente** CONT customer billing; ~ **anticipada** CONT advance billing; ~ **anual** COM GEN, CONT annual turnover; ~ **bruta** V&M gross billing; ~ **diferida** V&M deferred billing; ~ **de exportación** IMP/EXP export turnover; ~ **extra** CONT extra-billing; ~ **de publicidad** CONT, FIN, MEDIOS, V&M advertising turnover; ~ **por tiempo** COM GEN billing for the time spent; ~ **de ventas** V&M sales revenue, sales turnover

facturador *m* COM GEN *máquina* biller

facturar 1. *vt* COM GEN *aeropuerto* check in; ◆ ~ **separadamente** COM GEN unbundle; **2.** *vi* OCIO, TRANSP *aeropuerto* check in

facturas: ~ **a cobrar** *f pl* CONT bills receivable; ~ **enviadas** *f pl* COM GEN, CONT, FIN outgoing invoices; ~ **recibidas** *f pl* COM GEN, CONT, FIN invoices inwards

facultad: ~ **de actuarios** *f* DER faculty of actuaries; ~ **para contraer compromisos** *f* FIN commitment authority; ~ **de derecho** *f* DER, PROT SOC law school; ~ **para efectuar nombramientos** *f* DER power of appointment; ~ **para ganar** *f* COM GEN ability to earn; ~ **de suscribir** *f* DER subscribing option; ~ **de vender** *f* DER, INMOB power of sale

facultativo *adj* COM GEN facultative

faja: ~ **de seguridad** *f AmL* (*cf cinturón de seguridad Esp*) TRANSP safety belt, seat belt

fajo *m* BANCA *de billetes* wad (*infrml*)

fajos: ~ **de billetes** *m pl* COM GEN banded packs

falacia *f* DER fallacy

falibilidad *f* COM GEN fallibility

falible *adj* COM GEN fallible

falla: ~ **de seguridad** *f* COM GEN security leak

fallar[1] *vi* COM GEN fail

fallar[2]: ~ **en favor de alguien** *fra* COM GEN give a ruling in favor of sb (*AmE*), give a ruling in favour of sb (*BrE*)

fallo *m* COM GEN failure, fault, DER adjudication, decree, rule, sentence, INFO failure, fault, RRHH award; ~ **de deficiencia** DER deficiency judgment; ~ **de divorcio condicional** DER decree nisi; ~ **del equipo** INFO hardware failure; ~ **de funcionamiento** COM GEN malfunction; ~ **por incomparecencia de la parte** DER default judgment; ~ **del mercado** ECON market failure; ~ **preventivo** RRHH protective award; ~ **del sistema** INFO *soporte físico* system failure

falsa: ~ **afirmación publicitaria** *f* V&M false advertising claim; ~ **alarma** *f* COM GEN false alarm; ~ **enferma** *f* RRHH malingerer; ~ **jefa** *f infrml* INMOB, RRHH straw boss (*infrml*); ~ **llamada** *f* COMS *teléfono* wrong connection; ~ **maniobra** *f* COM GEN mishandling

falseación *f infrml* CONT *de un balance* make-up

falseamiento *m* CONT, FIN *de cuentas* window-dressing; ~ **de la competencia** ECON misrepresentation of competition; ~ **de la cuenta de clientes** CONT lapping

falsear *vt* COM GEN misrepresent

falsedad: ~ **de coste sumergido** *f Esp* (*cf falsedad de costo sumergido AmL*) FIN sunk cost fallacy; ~ **de costo sumergido** *f AmL* (*cf falsedad de coste sumergido Esp*) FIN sunk cost fallacy

falsificación *f* COM GEN counterfeit, falsification, forgery; ~ **de actas** DER adulteration of proceedings; ~ **de elecciones** POL gerrymandering; ~ **de nóminas, cuentas de gastos y otros documentos contables** CONT padding

falsificar *vt* COM GEN falsify, forge, misrepresent; ◆ ~ **las cuentas** COM GEN cook the books; ~ **un memorandum** ADMIN salt a memo (*jarg*)

falso[1] *adj* COM GEN fictitious, *respuesta* wrong

falso[2]: ~ **enfermo** *m* RRHH malingerer; ~ **flete** *m* TRANSP deadfreight (*df*)

falta *f* COM GEN *en sistema* fault, ECON lack, shortage; ~ **de aceptación** COM GEN failure to accept; ~ **de capital** BOLSA want of capital; ~ **de competencia** ECON lack of competence; ~ **de consideración** COM GEN, FIN absence of consideration; ~ **de cumplimiento** DER, FISC failure to comply; ~ **de entrega** COM GEN failure to deliver; ~ **de existencias** ECON lack of inventory; ~ **de fondos** ECON insufficient funds; ~ **grave** RRHH gross misconduct; ~ **de materia prima** MED AMB lack of raw material; ~ **de pago** BANCA default of payment, dishonor (*AmE*), dishonour (*BrE*), COM GEN nonpayment, failure in payment; ~ **de pago al vencimiento** CONT, FIN dishonor at maturity (*AmE*), dishonour at maturity (*BrE*); ~ **de pago cruzado** BANCA, FIN cross default; ~ **con permiso** COM GEN leave of absence; ~ **de presentación** FISC *de declaración, formulario* nonfiling; ~ **de recursos** CONT lapsing resources; ◆ **a** ~ **de** COM GEN *noticias* in the absence of; **por** ~ **de** COM GEN for lack of; **con** ~ **de liquidez** CONT, FIN cash strapped; **a** ~ **de pruebas en contra** DER in the absence of evidence to the contrary

faltar *vi* COM GEN, V&M lack; ◆ ~ **a una cita** COM GEN miss an appointment; ~ **los fondos necesarios** FIN lack the necessary funds; ~ **a la obligación** BANCA fail

falto: ~ **de mano de obra** *adj* RRHH short-handed; ~ **de personal** *adj* RRHH short-staffed, undermanned

familia *f* COM GEN *de productos* family; ~ **de fondos de inversión** BOLSA family of funds; ~ **con ingresos reducidos** V&M *investigación de mercado* low-income household; ~ **inmediata** BOLSA immediate family; ~ **monoparental** COM GEN single-parent family; ~ **de productos** IND, V&M product family; ~ **residual** PROT SOC residual family; ~ **de tipos** INFO *tipografía*, MEDIOS font family

familiaridad *f* COM GEN, V&M familiarity

familiarización: ~ **con la informática** *f* INFO computer literacy

fanal *m* TRANSP beacon

FAO *abr* (*Organización de las Naciones Unidas para la Agricultura y Alimentación*) ECON, POL FAO (*Food and Agriculture Organization*)

fardo *m* TRANSP bundle (*bdl*)

farmacéutico *adj* COM GEN, ECON, IND pharmaceutical

fascismo *m* POL fascism

fase *f* COM GEN *instrumentación de un proyecto* phase, stage; ~ **de acabado** IND stage of completion; ~ **ascendente** COM GEN, ECON upswing, upturn; ~ **de borrador** POL draft stage; ~ **cero** POL phase zero (*jarg*); ~ **clave** COM GEN *en proceso* key stage; ~ **de crecimiento económico** ECON stage of economic growth; ~ **de depresión del mercado** BOLSA market downturn; ~ **descendente** COM GEN, ECON downswing, downturn; ~ **de ejecución** SEG production run; ~ **de expansión** COM GEN, ECON upswing, upturn, *en actividad* upsurge; ~ **expansiva del ciclo económico** ECON expansion business cycle; ~ **intermedia** FIN intermediate stage; ~ **del invento** PATENT inventive step; ~ **de lanzamiento** V&M *comercialización* introductory stage; ~ **de promoción** V&M promotional phase; ~ **de promoción bloqueada de los mandos intermedios** RRHH mid-career plateau; ~ **de recesión** ECON recessionary phase; ~ **de redacción** DER draft stage; ~ **de verificación** COM GEN, CONT verification phase; ◆ **en ~ de pruebas** MEDIOS at proof stage

fatalidad *f* PROT SOC fatality

fatiga: ~ **industrial** *f* RRHH industrial fatigue

favor: **a ~ de** *fra* COM GEN in favor of (*AmE*), in favour of (*BrE*), *estimación* on account of; **en ~ de** *fra* COM GEN on account of; **por ~, envíe su confirmación por télex** *fra* COMS please telex your confirmation; **por ~, expongan sus presupuestos** *fra* COM GEN please submit your quotations; **por ~, háganos saber qué fecha le conviene** *fra* COMS please let us know which date suits

favorabilidad *f* COM GEN favourability (*BrE*), favorability (*AmE*)

favorable *adj* COM GEN *precio, condiciones* favorable (*AmE*), favourable (*BrE*)

favorecer *vt* BANCA *a alguien con un préstamo* accommodate, *desarrollo, comprensión* aid, COM GEN *el curso de una acción* favor (*AmE*), favour (*BrE*)

favores: ~ **políticos** *m pl* POL pork (*infrml*) (*AmE*)

fax *m* (*facsímil*) COM GEN fax (*facsimile*)

FC *abr* (*ferrocarril*) TRANSP rly (*railway*)

FDA *abr* (*fin de archivo*) INFO EOF (*end of file*)

FDM *abr* (*fin de mensaje*) INFO EOM (*end of message*)

fe *f* COM GEN belief, faith; ~ **ciega** COM GEN blind faith; ◆

en ~ de lo cual DER in witness whereof; **con absoluta buena ~** DER uberrimae fides; **de buena ~** DER bona fide, in good faith; **de mala ~** DER mala fide, in bad faith, maliciously; **de total buena ~** DER uberrimae fides

febril: ~ **competitividad** *f* COM GEN rat race (*infrml*)

fecha¹: **a ~** *adj* BANCA, COM GEN as at; **sin ~** *adj* COM GEN undated; **con ~ adelantada** *adj* BANCA, COM GEN, FIN postdated (*PD*)

fecha² *f* COM GEN date; ~ **abierta** V&M open dating (*AmE*); ~ **de acumulación** CONT accrual date; ~ **de adquisición** COM GEN date of acquisition; ~ **de amortización** BOLSA redemption date; ~ **de ampliación** BANCA roll-over date; ~ **de anulación** TRANSP *navegación* canceling date (*AmE*), cancelling date (*BrE*); ~ **de apertura** COM GEN opening date; ~ **atrasada** FIN dated date; ~ **base** BOLSA *precio* base date; ~ **de caducidad** BOLSA expiration date, V&M use-by date, *alimentos* sell-by date; ~ **de cambio de interés** BANCA interest rollover date; ~ **de carga** TRANSP loading date; ~ **a ciegas** COM GEN blind date; ~ **de cierre** COM GEN, INMOB closing date; ~ **de cierre de licitación** BOLSA bid-closing date; ~ **de comunicación** COM GEN *derecho* exercise date; ~ **de concesión** BOLSA *de acciones para empleados* date of grant; ~ **de concesión de una patente** PATENT date of grant; ~ **de conservación** COM GEN retention date; ~ **de conversión** BOLSA conversion date; ~ **sin derechos** BOLSA ex-rights date; ~ **de desembolso** COM GEN pay-out date; ~ **de devengo** CONT accrual date; ~ **sin dividendos** BOLSA ex-dividend date; ~ **de efectiva** SEG *marítimo* attachment date; ~ **de ejecución** BOLSA *opciones* exercise date; ~ **de ejercicio** BOLSA *de una opción*, COM GEN *del derecho* date of exercise; ~ **de emisión** BOLSA, SEG date of issue, V&M air date, issue date; ~ **de entrada en vigor** COM GEN effective date; ~ **de entrega** BOLSA delivery date, *futuros sobre divisas* contract delivery date; ~ **esperada** COM GEN expected date; ~ **exigible** CONT recoverable date; ~ **de expiración de licencia de exportación** IMP/EXP export licence expiry date (*BrE*), export license expiry date (*AmE*); ~ **de la factura** COM GEN date of invoice; ~ **de facturación** COM GEN billing date (*AmE*), invoice date (*BrE*); ~ **fija de vencimiento** BOLSA *opciones* fixed expiration date; ~ **formal de presentación** FIN formal submission date; ~ **del interés efectivo** FISC effective interest date; ~ **de liberación** BOLSA *para acciones asignadas a empleados* release date; ~ **límite** BANCA, BOLSA, FIN cutoff date, GES cut-off time, time horizon; ~ **límite del ejercicio** BOLSA exercise deadline; ~ **límite de presentación** *m* FISC *de declaración* due date of filing; ~ **de liquidación** BOLSA *título* settlement date; ~ **de llegada** TRANSP *de remesa* arrival date; ~ **más reciente** COM GEN latest date; ~ **media de auditoría** CONT, V&M mean audit date; ~ **de negociación** BANCA float time; ~ **de oferta** BOLSA *nueva emisión* offering date; ~ **de operación** BOLSA transaction date, trade date; ~ **de pago** BOLSA, COM GEN payment date; ~ **de presentación** PATENT date of filing; ~ **prevista** COM GEN expected date; ~ **de prioridad** DER, PATENT priority date; ~ **prioritaria** DER, PATENT *propiedad intelectual* priority date; ~ **propuesta** COM GEN target date; ~ **de publicación** MEDIOS, V&M press date, publication date; ~ **de puesta a la venta** MEDIOS *imprenta* on-sale date (*AmE*); ~ **de recepción** TRANSP receiving date; ~ **de**

recepción del flete TRANSP data freight receipt (*DFR*); **~ de redacción** COM GEN copy date; **~ de registro** BOLSA *dividendos*, COM GEN record date, DER date of record, date of registration; **~ de rescate** BOLSA redemption date; **~ de retirada de la venta** MEDIOS *emisión* off-sale date; **~ de salida** TRANSP *navegación* sailing date (*S/D*); **~ de terminación** COM GEN completion date; **~ tope de la renovación** SEG due date of renewal; **~ de valor** BOLSA, FIN value date; **~ de valoración** FISC valuation day; **~ de valoración de un préstamo** BOLSA loan-pricing date; **~ de vencimiento** BANCA call date, maturity date, BOLSA, COM GEN date of maturity, deadline, expiry date, ECON maturity date; **~ de vencimiento a corto plazo** BOLSA *depósito de eurodólares* short-range maturity date; **~ de vencimiento de futuros** BOLSA futures expiry date (*AmE*); **~ de vencimiento de licencia de exportación** IMP/EXP export licence expiry date (*BrE*), export license expiry date (*AmE*); **~ de vencimiento de la prima** SEG due date of premium; ♦ **a ~** COM GEN as at; **después de ~** COM GEN after date (*A/D*); **en una ~ por determinar** COM GEN at some future date; **en ~ posterior** COM GEN at a later date, at a subsequent date **hasta la ~** COM GEN to date; **tres meses después de la ~ pago** COM GEN three months after date pay

fechado *m* COM GEN, V&M date-marking

fechar: **~ las mercaderías** *fra* CONT age stocks

FECOM *abr* (*Fondo Europeo para la Cooperación Monetaria*) ECON, POL EMCF (*European Monetary Cooperation Fund*)

FEDER *abr* (*Fondo Europeo para el Desarrollo Regional*) ECON, POL ERDF (*European Regional Development Fund*)

federación *f* POL, RRHH federation; **~ internacional de sindicatos** RRHH international union federation; **~ de mutualidades** RRHH federation of mutual societies; **~ patronal** COM GEN, RRHH employers' federation; **~ de sindicatos** RRHH federation of trade union

Federación: **~ Internacional de Asociaciones de Agentes de Transitorios** *f* TRANSP International Federation of Forwarding Agents' Associations; **~ Internacional de Asociaciones de Agentes de Transporte** *f* TRANSP International Federation of Freight Forwarders' Associations; **~ Internacional de Bolsas de Valores** *f* BOLSA International Federation of Stock Exchanges (*IFSE*); **~ Internacional de Compañías Navieras** *f* TRANSP International Shipping Federation (*ISF*); **~ Internacional de Documentación** *f* COM GEN International Federation for Documentation (*IFD*); **~ Internacional de Productores Agrícolas** *f* ECON, POL International Federation of Agricultural Producers (*IFAP*); **~ Mundial de Asociaciones de las Naciones Unidas** *f* (*FMANU*) POL World Federation of United Nations Associations (*WFUNA*); **~ Mundial de Bolsas** *f* BOLSA World Federation of Stock Exchanges

federal *adj* COM GEN, POL federal (*fed.*)

federalismo *m* COM GEN, POL federalism; **~ cooperativo** POL cooperative federalism; **~ creativo** POL creative federalism; **~ económico** ECON, POL, RRHH economic federalism; **~ fiscal** ECON, FISC top-sided-federalism, POL fiscal federalism, top-sided-federalism

federalmente: **~ regulado** *adj* FISC federally regulated

feedback *m* INFO feedback; **~ negativo** ECON, INFO negative feedback

feliz: **~ arribo** *m* AmL (*cf feliz llegada Esp*) TRANSP safe arrival (*s/a*); **~ llegada** *f* Esp (*cf feliz arribo AmL*) TRANSP safe arrival (*s/a*)

FEOGA *abr* (*Fondo Europeo de Orientación y Garantía Agrícola*) ECON, POL EAGGF (*European Agricultural Guidance and Guarantee Fund*)

feria *f* COM GEN, V&M show; **~ agrícola** ECON, V&M agricultural show; **~ de artesanía** COM GEN artisan fair; **~ comercial** COM GEN, V&M trade fair; **~ especializada** COM GEN specialized fair; **~ de la exportación** COM GEN, IMP/EXP export goods fair; **~ itinerante** TRANSP traveling fair (*AmE*), travelling fair (*BrE*); **~ de muestras** COM GEN, V&M samples fair, trade fair; **~ mundial** COM GEN world fair

ferias: **~ y seminarios de comercio internacional** *f pl* IMP/EXP overseas trade fairs and seminars

ferrocarril *m* (*FC*) TRANSP railway (*BrE*) (*rly*), rail, railroad (*AmE*); **~ transiberiano** TRANSP Trans-Siberian Railway (*TSR*); **~ subterráneo** TRANSP subway (*AmE*), tube (*BrE*), underground (*BrE*); **~ de tránsito masivo** TRANSP mass transit railway (*BrE*) (*MTR*), mass transit rairoad (*AmE*) (*MTR*)

ferrocarrilero *m* RRHH, TRANSP railman (*AmE*), railwayman (*BrE*)

ferroso *adj* IND, MED AMB ferrous

ferroviario *m* RRHH, TRANSP railman (*AmE*), railwayman (*BrE*)

fertilizante *m* MED AMB *agricultura* fertilizer; **~ nitrogenado** MED AMB nitrogen fertilizer

fertilizar *vt* MED AMB *agricultura* fertilize

festival: **~ cinematográfico** *m* MEDIOS film festival

festivo: **~ general** *m* RRHH general holiday

fetichismo: **~ de los bienes** *m* ECON, V&M commodity fetishism; **~ de la mercancía** *m* ECON *Marx*, V&M commodity fetishism

feudalismo *m* POL feudalism

fiabilidad *f* COM GEN reliability; **~ del producto** V&M product reliability

fiable *adj* COM GEN reliable

fiador[1]**,a** *m,f* BANCA *en la custodia*, COM GEN bailor, FIN sponsor

fiador[2] *m* COM GEN surety

FIAMM *abr* (*fondo de inversión en activos del mercado monetario*) BOLSA, FIN MMF (*money market fund*), MMMF (*money market mutual fund*)

fianza *f* DER bail bond, SEG fidelity bond, fidelity guarantee, fidelity guaranty, fiduciary bond; **~ de apelación** DER appeal bond; **~ de avería** SEG average bond; **~ de bonos** FIN bond guarantee, bond guaranty; **~ colectiva** SEG blanket bond; **~ comercial** COM GEN guaranty bond, guarantee bond; **~ de conservación** COM GEN, DER *comercial* maintenance bond; **~ de contratista** COM GEN contract bond; **~ de cumplimiento** COM GEN, DER maintenance bond; **~ en efectivo** DER surety in cash; **~ de embargo** DER, FIN attachment bond; **~ de entredicho** DER injunction bond; **~ de garantía** BOLSA guaranty bond, guarantee bond; **~ general** SEG blanket bond; **~ por hacer un pago inicial** BOLSA security bond for down payment; **~ de incumplimiento** BOLSA, COM GEN performance bond, FISC *declaración* fixed penalties; **~ de indemnización** SEG indemnity bond; **~ judicial** DER judicial bond; **~ de lealtad nominal** SEG *contra estafas de empleados* name schedule bond; **~ de licitación**

BOLSA, COM GEN bid bond; ~ **de la oferta** FIN bid bond; ~ **de pago** COM GEN, DER *comercial* payment bond; ~ **de puesto laboral** SEG name position bond; ~ **de puesto laboral y de lealtad nominal** SEG position schedule bond; ~ **de traslado** FIN *mercancías sujetas a derechos* removal bond

fiarse: ~ **de** *vt* COM GEN *una persona* rely on

fibra: ~ **óptica** *f* COMS, IND, INFO fiber optics (*AmE*), fibre optics (*BrE*); ~ **sintética** *f* IND man-made fibre (*BrE*), man-made fiber (*AmE*); ~ **de vidrio** *f* IND fiberglass (*AmE*), fibreglass (*BrE*)

fibroóptica *f* COMS, IND, INFO fiber optics (*AmE*), fibre optics (*BrE*)

ficha *m* FIN *propiedades, préstamos comerciales* point; ~ **de acumulación de riesgos** *f* SEG aggregate liability index; ~ **de almacén** *f* CONT stock control card; ~ **contable** *f* CONT ledger card; ~ **de control** *f* RRHH time card; ~ **de control de asistencia** *f* RRHH, SEG clock card; ~ **de cuenta** *f* CONT account card; ~ **de datos** *f* INFO data card; ~ **de existencias** *f* CONT stock card; ~ **de firmas** *f* CONT signing slip; ~ **magnética** *f* COM GEN, IND magnetic card; ~ **para muestras** *f* COM GEN sample card; ~ **de pago** *f* COM GEN credit slip; ~ **personal de trabajo** *f* RRHH gap sheet (*jarg*); ~ **de reposición** *f* SEG kanban; ~ **de salida** *f* SEG issue card

fichar *vt* (*cf checar AmL*) IND, RRHH check in; ◆ ~ **la entrada** *Esp* (*cf checar la tarjeta AmL*) IND, RRHH clock in, clock on (*BrE*), punch in (*AmE*); ~ **la salida** *Esp* (*cf checar la tarjeta AmL*) IND, RRHH clock off (*BrE*), clock out, punch out (*AmE*)

fichas: ~ **por minuto** *f pl* COM GEN cards per minute

fichero *m* ADMIN archive file, COM GEN card index, card file, archive file, file, DER, INFO archive file; ~ **activo** INFO active file; ~ **de clasificación** INFO sort file; ~ **de computador** *AmL*, ~ **de computadora** *AmL* (*cf fichero de ordenador Esp*) INFO computer file; ~ **contable** CONT accounting file; ~ **de datos** INFO data file; ~ **de direcciones** INFO address file; ~ **de edición** INFO report file; ~ **no encontrado** INFO file not found; ~ **de espera** INFO spool file; ~ **con etiqueta** INFO labeled file (*AmE*), labelled file (*BrE*); ~ **de existencias** COM GEN inventory file; ~ **de imagen** INFO image file; ~ **de impresión** INFO output file; ~ **indexado** COM GEN, INFO indexed file; ~ **informatizado** INFO computerized file; ~ **de lectura** INFO ReadMe file; ~ **maestro** COM GEN, INFO master file; ~ **de movimientos** INFO transaction file; ~ **oculto** INFO hidden file; ~ **de ordenador** *Esp* (*cf fichero de computadora AmL*) INFO computer file; ~ **padre** INFO father file; ~ **principal** INFO main file; ~ **de programa** INFO program file; ~ **de referencias** COM GEN, INFO reference file; ~ **registrado en cinta** INFO tape file; ~ **secuencial** INFO batch file; ~ **de tarjetas** ADMIN, INFO card file; ~ **transitorio** INFO scratch file

ficheros: ~ **de movimiento** *m pl* INFO change files

ficticio *adj* COM GEN artificial

fidedigno *adj* FISC creditable

fideicomisario *m,f* BANCA, BOLSA, DER, INMOB trustee

fideicomiso *m* BANCA trust, DER trusteeship, ECON *crédito sin fianza* trust; ~ **activo** DER living trust; ~ **benéfico** FISC charitable trust; ~ **de bienes** DER, INMOB land trust; ~ **de bienes raíces** DER, INMOB land trust; ~ **ciego** DER blind trust; ~ **comercial** FISC commercial trust; ~ **complejo** DER complex trust;

~ **de cuenta de ahorro** BANCA Totten trust; ~ **discrecional** BOLSA, DER discretionary trust; ~ **no discrecional** BOLSA, DER nondiscretionary trust; ~ **de empleados** FISC employee trust; ~ **entre vivos** DER inter vivos trust; ~ **extranjero** FIN offshore trust; ~ **implícito** DER involuntary trust; ~ **de inversión de bienes raíces** BANCA, BOLSA, INMOB real estate investment trust (*REIT*); ~ **irrevocable** DER irrevocable trust; ~ **pasivo** DER dry trust, passive trust; ~ **con responsabilidad fiscal del otorgante** DER, INMOB grantor trust; ~ **revocable** FIN revocable trust; ~ **testamentario** DER testamentary trust

fideicomitente *m* DER settlor (*BrE*)

fidelidad *f* COM GEN fidelity, *cliente, empleado* loyalty; ~ **a una marca** V&M brand loyalty

fiduciaría *f* BOLSA trusteeship

fiduciariamente *adv* DER fiduciarily

fiduciario[1] *adj* DER fiduciary

fiduciario[2],**a** *m,f* BANCA, BOLSA, DER, INMOB trustee

fiel *adj* COM GEN faithful

fiero *adj* COM GEN *competencia* fierce

fiesta *f* COM GEN *día festivo* holiday; ~ **de lanzamiento** MEDIOS *de libro* launch party; ~ **oficial** DER, OCIO, RRHH bank holiday (*BrE*), legal holiday (*AmE*)

figurar 1. *vt* BOLSA, COM GEN rank; ◆ ~ **por debajo de** BOLSA, COM GEN rank below; ~ **después de** BOLSA, COM GEN rank after; ~ **por encima de** COM GEN rank above; **2.** *vi* BOLSA, COM GEN rank, *artículo en catálogo* appear

fijación *f* BOLSA *precios* fixing, COM GEN fastening, CONT, ECON *precios, objetivos* targeting, fixing, RRHH *de posición* making, TRANSP locking; ~ **de acarreo de planchas** TRANSP *carga* plate lifting clamp; ~ **común de precios** *m* COM GEN, V&M common pricing; ~ **del coste** *Esp* (*cf fijación del costo AmL*) CONT cost pricing; ~ **del costo** *AmL* (*cf fijación del coste Esp*) CONT cost pricing; ~ **de cubierta** TRANSP *de container* deck socket; ~ **de cuotas** COM GEN quota fixing; ~ **de derechos de aduana** FISC, IMP/EXP assessment of duty; ~ **diferencial de precios** V&M differential pricing; ~ **estratégica de precios** V&M strategic pricing; ~ **flexible de precios** ECON flexible mark-up pricing, flexible pricing; ~ **de impuestos** COM GEN taxation; ~ **marginal de precios** CONT, ECON, FIN, V&M marginal pricing; ~ **múltiple de precios unitarios** V&M multiple unit pricing; ~ **de objetivos** GES goal setting, objective-setting, V&M target setting, targeting; ~ **del precio** V&M product costing; ~ **del precio al coste medio recargado** *Esp* (*cf fijación del precio al costo medio recargado AmL*) ECON mark-up pricing; ~ **del precio al costo medio recargado** *AmL* (*cf fijación del precio al coste medio recargado AmL*) ECON mark-up pricing; ~ **de precio alto para obtener prontos beneficios** V&M price skimming; ~ **del precio conforme al coste marginal** *Esp* (*cf fijación del precio conforme al costo marginal AmL*) CONT, ECON marginal cost pricing; ~ **del precio conforme al costo marginal** *AmL* (*cf fijación del precio conforme al coste marginal Esp*) CONT, ECON marginal cost pricing; ~ **del precio de un título** ECON pegging; ~ **del precio de transferencias** ECON transfer pricing; ~ **del precio de un valor** ECON pegging; ~ **de precios** ECON price fixing, price system, pricing; ~ **de precios agresiva** V&M aggressive pricing; ~ **de precios al punto base** ECON base point pricing; ~ **de precios anticipada** ECON anticipatory pricing;

~ de precios para cubrir los gastos V&M break-even pricing; **~ de precios depredadores** ECON predatory pricing; **~ de precios de incentivo** V&M premium pricing; **~ de precios indicativos** COM GEN, V&M target pricing; **~ de precios del inventario** CONT inventory pricing; **~ de precios marginal** V&M marginal pricing; **~ de precios más altos** V&M pricing up; **~ de precios del mercado** FIN market pricing; **~ de precios no lineal** ECON nonlinear pricing; **~ de precios no oficial** ECON, V&M parallel pricing; **~ de precios orientativos** V&M leader pricing; **~ de precios de paridad** COM GEN, ECON parity pricing; **~ de precios de prospectiva** SEG prospective rating; **~ de precios de penetración** COM GEN, V&M penetration pricing; **~ de precios de prestigio** V&M prestige pricing; **~ de precios de los productos básicos** BOLSA, V&M commodity pricing; **~ de precios psicológicos** V&M psychological pricing; **~ de precios según los costes** *Esp* (*cf fijación de precios según los costos*) CONT full-cost pricing; **~ de precios según los costos** *AmL* (*cf fijación de precios según los costes*) CONT full-cost pricing; **~ de precios táctica** V&M tactical pricing; **~ de precios por unidad** COM GEN, V&M unit pricing; **~ de precios de valor poco corriente** V&M odd-value pricing; **~ restrictiva de precios de mercado** ECON constrained market pricing (*AmE*), stand alone cot (*BrE*); **~ de tarifas** RRHH rate fixing; **~ de trinca** TRANSP *contenedores* lash end fitting; **~ de valor ante la falta de precio contractual** COM GEN quantum merit

fijador: **~ cuádruple** *m* TRANSP quadruple stacker; **~ de precios** *m* ECON, V&M *mercadotecnia* price leader

fijar *vt* BOLSA fix, settle, COM GEN *carteles* affix, focus on, focus, mail (*AmE*), post (*BrE*), ECON, FIN fix, settle, TRANSP lock; ◆ **~ el cambio** ECON peg the exchange; **~ la cifra** DER *de compensación* settle the figure; **~ contingentes** IMP/EXP fix quotas; **sin ~ fecha** COM GEN, DER sine die (*frml*); **~ la indemnización** FISC fix the claim; **~ los parámetros** INFO, MAT set parameters; **~ un precio** ECON price, set a price-point; **~ un precio excesivo para** V&M overprice; **~ un precio muy bajo** COM GEN, V&M underprice; **~ precios** FIN, V&M price; **~ precios de intervención** COM GEN trigger pricing

fijo[1] *adj* BOLSA, COM GEN, FIN flat, V&M still

fijo[2] *m* COM GEN, FIN fix; **~ disponible** COM GEN, FIN quick fix

fila *f* COM GEN *de números* row; **~ de caja** V&M checkout lane

filial[1] *adj* COM GEN subsidiary

filial[2] *f* COM GEN affiliate, affiliated company, branch office (*B.O.*); **~ bancaria** BANCA banking subsidiary; **~ consolidada** COM GEN, IND consolidated branch

filigrana *f* BANCA, ECON *papel moneda* watermark

filigranado *adj* BANCA, ECON *papel moneda* watermarked

filmación: **~ de imagen por imagen** *f* MEDIOS, V&M stop motion

filme: **~ magnético** *m* V&M magnetic film

filón *m* IND, MED AMB lead ore

filosofía *f* COM GEN philosophy; **~ del derecho** DER jurisprudence; **~ de la empresa** COM GEN company philosophy

filtración *f* ECON, FIN, INFO filtering

filtraciones *f pl* ECON, INFO, MEDIOS *en la prensa* leak

filtrar *vt* COM GEN, RRHH screen, screen out, leak (*infrml*)

filtro *m* ECON, FIN, INFO filter

FIM *abr* (*fondo de inversión mobiliario*) BOLSA real state investment fund

fin[1]: **de ~ de ejercicio** *adj* ECON year-end

fin[2] *m* COM GEN end, GES goal; **~ de año** COM GEN, CONT year end; **~ de archivo** (*FDA*) INFO end of file (*EOF*); **~ del contrato de arrendamiento** INMOB termination of tenancy; **~ de mensaje** (*FDM*) INFO end of message (*EOM*); **~ de mes** CONT end of month; **~ de programa** RRHH end of programe (*AmE*), end of programme (*BrE*); **~ del riesgo** FIN termination risk; **~ de trimestre** COM GEN, CONT quarter-end; ◆ **al ~ y al cabo** COM GEN the bottom line is

final[1]: **~ y concluyente** *adj* FISC *determinación* final and conclusive

final[2] *m* COM GEN, V&M end, final; **~ de año contable** CONT end of financial year; **~ de una cita** COM GEN termination of appointment; **~ del ejercicio contable** CONT end of financial year; **~ del empleo** RRHH termination of employment; **~ de la estación** COM GEN tail end of the season; **~ de los pedidos** TRANSP land end for orders (*LEFO*); **~ de prueba** V&M test close; **~ de la sesión** BOLSA close

finalidad *f* GES goal; **~ especulativa** FIN speculation motive

finalización *f* GES *de reunión* winding-up

finalizado *adj* COM GEN finalized

finalizar *vt* COM GEN finalize, GES wind up; ◆ **~ la comunicación** INFO log off

finalmente *adv* COM GEN eventually

financiable *adj* BANCA bankable

financiación *f* COM GEN financing, funding; **~ activa** FIN active financing; **~ de la administración local** FIN, POL local government finance; **~ de alto rendimiento** FIN high-yield financing; **~ bancaria** BANCA, FIN bank financing; **~ basada en activos** FIN asset-based financing; **~ básica** FIN core funding; **~ del capital** FIN capital financing; **~ clandestina** ECON backdoor financing; **~ coarrendataria** INMOB co-tenant finance; **~ comercial** FIN business finance; **~ del comercio** BANCA, FIN trade financing; **~ compensatoria** FIN, POL compensatory finance; **~ de compra** FIN acquisition financing; **~ en condiciones favorables** FIN, POL soft funding (*jarg*); **~ conjunta** FIN joint financing; **~ corporativa** FIN corporate financing; **~ a corto plazo** FIN short-term financing; **~ del déficit** ECON, FIN gap financing; **~ después de impuestos** FISC after-tax financing; **~ de la deuda** FIN debt financing; **~ de la exportación** FIN, IMP/EXP export financing; **~ de la exportación nacional** FIN, IMP/EXP domestic export financing; **~ externa** CONT, FIN external financing; **~ de franquicia** FIN franchise financing; **~ funcional** FIN functional financing; **~ sin garantía** FIN front-end financing; **~ industrial** FIN, IND industrial finance; **~ innovadora** FIN creative financing; **~ interna** CONT, FIN domestic financing, internal financing, internal funding; **~ del inventario** CONT inventory financing; **~ de inversiones** FIN financing of capital projects; **~ a largo plazo** BANCA long-term financing, permanent financing, FIN long-term financing; **~ con limitación de reclamaciones** BANCA, FIN limited-recourse financing, limited-recourse finance; **~ mediante cuentas a cobrar** CONT accounts receivable financing; **~ mediante déficit** ECON, FIN deficit financing; **~ mediante emisión de obligaciones** BOLSA bond financing; **~ mediante**

préstamo FIN below-the-line credit (*jarg*); ~ **a medio plazo** BANCA, FIN intermediate financing; ~ **negativa** BANCA, FIN negative financing; ~ **oficial** ECON official financing; ~ **de plan de pensiones** COM GEN pension plan funding; ~ **ponderada** FIN formula funding; ~ **sin posibilidad de recurso** FIN nonrecourse finance; ~ **de programas establecidos** FIN established programs financing; ~ **de un proyecto** FIN project financing, project finance; ~ **puente** FIN bridge financing; ~ **de la puesta en marcha** FIN front-end finance; ~ **sin recursos** FIN nonrecourse financing; ~ **retroactiva** FIN retroactive financing; ~ **secreta** FIN backdoor financing; ~ **temporal** FIN interim financing; ~ **transitoria** FIN bridge financing; ~ **por venta de participación** FIN equity financing

financiaciones *f pl* CONT capital

financiado: ~ **con dineros públicos** *fra* COM GEN publicly-funded; ~ **por un banco** *fra* BANCA bank-financed; ~ **con dineros públicos** *fra* COM GEN publicly funded; ~ **por el Estado** *fra* COM GEN government-financed; ~ **por el vendedor** *fra* FIN vendor financed

financiamiento *m* COM GEN financing, funding; ~ **intermedio** FIN mezzanine funding

financiar *vt* BANCA bankroll (*infrml*), COM GEN finance; ◆ ~ **la diferencia** ECON finance the difference; ~ **directamente** COM GEN finance directly

financiera *f* FIN finance company

financieramente: ~ **sólido** *adj* COM GEN financially sound

financiero *adj* COM GEN financial

financista *mf* FIN financier

finanza: ~ **de contrato simple** *f* FIN single contract finance; ~ **corporativa** *f* FIN corporate finance

finanzas *f pl* COM GEN finance; ~ **exteriores** FIN outside finance; ~ **federales** FIN federal finance; ~ **intermedias** FIN mezzanine finance; ~ **públicas** ECON, FIN public finance, public finances; ~ **respaldadas por activos** FIN asset-backed finance

finca *f* INMOB *tierra* property

fines: ~ **benéficos** *m pl* FISC, PROT SOC charitable purposes; ~ **fiscales** *m pl* CONT, FISC tax purposes

finiquitar *vt* RRHH pay off

finiquito *m* DER quitclaim, FISC *de jubilación* termination payment

finito *adj* MAT, MED AMB finite

finos: ~ **de popa** *m pl* TRANSP run of the ship

firma *f* COM GEN business, firm, *identification* signature; ~ **de alquiler de computadoras** *AmL* (*cf firma de alquiler de ordenadores Esp*) INFO computer leasing firm; ~ **de alquiler de computadores** *AmL ver firma de alquiler de computadoras AmL*; ~ **de alquiler de ordenadores** *Esp* (*cf firma de alquiler de computadores AmL*) INFO computer leasing firm; ~ **autentificada** BANCA, DER authenticated signature; ~ **autorizada** BANCA, DER authorized signature; ~ **en bancarrota** COM GEN bankrupt firm; ~ **en blanco** BANCA blank signature; ~ **certificada** BANCA, DER authenticated signature; ~ **clara y sin alteraciones** COM GEN clean signature; ~ **cliente** V&M client firm; ~ **de componentes electrónicos** INFO hardware firm; ~ **conjunta** BANCA joint signature; ~ **consultora** COM GEN, GES, RRHH consulting firm; ~ **contable** CONT accounting firm; ~ **de corretaje en bolsa** BOLSA brokerage house; ~ **especializada** BANCA special bracket firm;

~ **facsimilar** COM GEN facsimile signature; ~ **financiera** FIN financial firm; ~ **de ingeniería** COM GEN engineering firm; ~ **de inversión** BOLSA brokerage house; ~ **local** COM GEN local firm; ~ **no autentificada** BANCA, DER unauthenticated signature; ~ **no autorizada** BANCA, DER unauthorized signature; ~ **no reconocida** BOLSA nonmember firm; ◆ **tener** ~ **autorizada** BANCA be authorized to sign

firma/depósito *f* IMP/EXP, TRANSP house/depot

firmado *adj* COM GEN, COMS signed (*sgd*)

firmante[1] *adj* PROT SOC signing on (*BrE*)

firmante[2] *mf* COM GEN signatory, DER *contrato, tratado* signatory, *de nota* maker; ~ **del cheque** ADMIN, BANCA, FIN check signer (*AmE*), cheque signer (*BrE*); ~ **de favor** FIN accommodation party; ◆ **devuélvase al** ~ (*RD*) COM GEN refer to drawer (*RD*); **el abajo** ~, **declara que** COMS I, the undersigned, declare that

firmar[1]: **para** ~ *adj* COM GEN for signature; **sin** ~ *adj* COM GEN unsigned

firmar[2] *vt* COM GEN sign, SEG take out; ◆ ~ **conjuntamente** BANCA, DER cosign; ~ **a la entrada** GES book in; ~ **al entrar a la empresa** RRHH sign in; ~ **el registro** COM GEN book in, check in, OCIO *en un hotel* check in; ~ **a la salida** GES book out; ~ **sobre la línea de puntos** ADMIN *en formulario* sign on the dotted line

firme *adj* COM GEN *rígido* hard, DER *contratos* absolute; **en** ~ COM GEN *pedido* firm

fiscal[1] *adj* ECON, FIN, FISC, POL fiscal

fiscal[2] *mf* DER District Attorney (*AmE*) (*DA*), public prosecutor (*BrE*)

Fiscal: ~ **General del Estado** *mf Esp* (*cf Fiscal Jefe del Servicio de Acusación Pública AmL*) DER ≈ Director of Public Prosecutions (*BrE*) (*DPP*); ~ **Jefe, -a del Servicio de Acusación Pública** *m,f AmL* (*cf Fiscal General del Estado Esp*) DER ≈ Director of Public Prosecutions (*BrE*) (*DPP*)

fiscalidad: ~ **de la vivienda** *f* FISC domicile taxation

fiscalista *mf* FISC fiscalist

fiscalización: ~ **continua** *f* CONT continuous audit; ~ **directa e indirecta** *f* ECON, FISC direct and indirect taxation; ~ **de las existencias** *f* CONT, ECON, FIN inventory control

fiscalmente: ~ **opaco** *adj* FISC fiscally opaque

fisco *m* FIN ≈ Exchequer (*BrE*), Treasury (*AmE*)

físicamente *adv* COM GEN physically

fisiócratas *m pl* ECON *teoría económica* Physiocrats

fisuras: **sin** ~ *adj* COM GEN *contenedor, excusa, plan* watertight

fixing *m* BANCA fixing rate

flamante *adj* COM GEN brand-new

flecha: ~ **hacia abajo** *f* INFO *en un ordenador* down arrow; ~ **de retroceso** *f* INFO back arrow

flegmitizador *m* TRANSP *de mercancías peligrosas* phlegmitiser

fletador, a *m,f* IMP/EXP charterer, TRANSP *navegación* disponent owner, shipper, charterer

fletamento *m* DER, TRANSP affreightment, charter, chartering; ~ **de ida y vuelta** TRANSP round charter party; ~ **por tiempo y precio determinado** TRANSP time charter (*T/C*); ~ **sin tripulación** TRANSP bare-boat charter; ~ **por viaje** TRANSP voyage charter

fletamiento *m* DER, TRANSP *marítimo* affreightment,

charter, chartering; **~ de carga completa** TRANSP whole cargo charter; **~ dividido** TRANSP split charter

fletante *mf* IMP/EXP, TRANSP shipowner

fletar *vt* COM GEN, TRANSP *vehículos* charter

flete *m* COM GEN, TRANSP freight (*frt*); **~ aéreo** TRANSP air cargo, *modalidad de embarque* air freight; **~ de alta densidad** TRANSP high-density freight; **~ desembarcado y entregado** TRANSP landing and delivering cargo; **~ por distancia** TRANSP *navegacion* distance freight; **~ ferroviario** TRANSP rail freight; **~ de ida y vuelta** TRANSP round chartering; **~ listo** TRANSP spot charter; **~ marítimo** TRANSP ocean freight; **~ pagadero por entero** TRANSP lump-sum freight; **~ pagado** IMP/EXP, TRANSP carriage paid (*carr pd*), freight paid; **~ pagado por anticipado** IMP/EXP, TRANSP freight prepaid (*frt ppd*); **~ pagado por adelantado** IMP/EXP, TRANSP advance freight (*AF*); **~ a peso** TRANSP freight all kinds; **~ proporcional a la distancia** TRANSP pro-rata freight; **~ reservado por adelantado** TRANSP Advance Booking Charter (*ABC*); **~, sobrestadía y defensa** SEG, TRANSP freight, demurrage and defence (*BrE*) (*FD&D*), freight, demurrage and defense (*AmE*) (*FD&D*); **~ y sobrestadías** IMP/EXP *envío*, TRANSP freight and demurrage (*F&D*); **~ sobre el valor** TRANSP ad valorem freight; **~ por tiempo** TRANSP time freight; **~-tonelada** TRANSP freight tonne, freight ton (*F/T, frt ton*); **~ del transbordo** TRANSP transhipment freight; **~ por volumen** TRANSP measurement freight; **~ de vuelta** TRANSP back freight, return freight; ♦ **~ y seguro pagados** IMP/EXP, TRANSP carriage and insurance paid (*CIP*), freight and insurance paid

fletero *m AmL* (*cf buque de carga Esp*) TRANSP cargo ship (*BrE*), cargo vessel (*BrE*), freighter (*AmE*)

flexibilidad *f* COM GEN flexibility; **~ funcional** RRHH functional flexibility; **~ de horario** RRHH flexibility of time (*flextime*); **~ interdepartamental** RRHH interdepartmental flexibility (*IDF*); **~ numérica** RRHH numerical flexibility; **~ de precios** ECON price flexibility; **~ del puesto de trabajo** RRHH job flexibility; **~ salarial** ECON, RRHH wage flexibility; **~ en la tarea** RRHH task flexibility; **~ de tarifas** TRANSP rate flexibility

flexible *adj* COM GEN flexible

flexografía *f* MEDIOS flexography

flojo[1] *adj* COM GEN slack

flojo[2] *m* COM GEN shirker (*infrml*)

florecer *vi* COM GEN flourish

flota *f* TRANSP fleet

flotación *f* BANCA *tipo de interés, cambio*, BOLSA, FIN *de moneda* flotation, floating; **~ bancaria** BANCA bank float; **~ contracorriente** COM GEN upstream float; **~ descendente** COM GEN downstream float; **~ de deuda** BANCA debit float; **~ dirigida** ECON *internacional* dirty float; **~ limpia** ECON *internacional* clean float; **~ sucia** ECON dirty float

flotante *adj* BANCA, BOLSA, FIN floating

flotar *vt* BANCA, BOLSA, FIN float

fluctuación *f* BOLSA *precios, tipos de interés*, ECON, FIN fluctuation; **~ cíclica** BOLSA *precios de artículos*, COM GEN, ECON cyclical fluctuation; **~ de clientela** COM GEN, ECON customer flow; **~ de costes** *Esp* (*cf fluctuación de costos AmL*) CONT, ECON cost flow; **~ de costos** *AmL* (*cf fluctuación de costes Esp*) CONT, ECON cost flow; **~ económica** COM GEN, ECON economic fluctuation;

~ estacional COM GEN, ECON seasonal fluctuation; **~ financiera** CONT, ECON, FIN financial flow; **~ de inversiones** CONT, ECON flow of investments; **~ máxima del precio** BOLSA maximum price fluctuation; **~ de mercado** COM GEN, ECON market fluctuation; **~ mínima del precio** BOLSA minimum price fluctuation; **~ de precios** COM GEN, ECON price sewing; **~ del tipo de cambio** ECON, FIN exchange rate fluctuation

fluctuaciones: ~ a corto plazo *f pl* ECON short-term fluctuations

fluctuar 1. *vt* COM GEN yo-yo (*jarg*); **2.** *vi* BOLSA *precio de acciones, tipo de cambio*, ECON, FIN fluctuate

flujo *m* COM GEN flux, CONT *de fondos*, INFO *de datos*, TRANSP *tráfico de mercancías, pasajeros* flow; **~ anual de tesorería** CONT annual cash flow; **~ de bienes** COM GEN commodity flow; **~ bruto en efectivo** CONT, ECON, FIN gross cash flow; **~ de caja** CONT, ECON, FIN cash flow; **~ de caja incremental** CONT, FIN incremental cash flow; **~ de caja negativo** CONT, FIN negative cash flow; **~ de caja positivo** CONT, FIN positive cash flow; **~ circular** ECON circular flow; **~ comercial** ECON trade flow; **~ de datos** COM GEN, INFO data flow, data stream; **~ de dinero** CONT, ECON, FIN cash flow; **~ de dinero después de impuestos** FISC after-tax cash flow; **~ de efectivo en aumento** CONT, FIN incremental cash flow; **~ de efectivo descontado** BANCA, CONT, FIN discounted cash flow (*DCF*); **~ de fondos** BOLSA, CONT, ECON, FIN funds flow, flow of funds; **~ de ingresos** ECON income stream; **~ monetario** COM GEN, ECON flow of money; **~ monetario internacional** COM GEN, ECON international money flow; **~ de negocio** COM GEN business stream; **~ neto de caja** COM GEN net cash flow; **~ neto total** ECON total net flow; **~ de operaciones** INFO work flow; **~ de pasajeros** TRANSP passenger throughput; **~ de trabajo** COM GEN work flow

flujograma *m* COM GEN flowchart

flujos: ~ de capital *m pl* FIN capital flows; **~ de ganancias** *m pl* FIN earning streams

fluoruro: ~ de azufre *m* TRANSP sulfuryl fluoride (*AmE*), sulphuryl fluoride (*BrE*); **~ sulfúrico** *m* TRANSP *fumigación de contenedores* sulfuryl fluoride (*AmE*), sulphuryl fluoride (*BrE*)

FMANU *abr* (*Federación Mundial de Asociaciones de las Naciones Unidas*) POL WFUNA (*World Federation of United Nations Associations*)

FMI *abr* (*Fondo Monetario Internacional*) ECON, POL IMF (*International Monetary Fund*)

fobia: ~ informática *f* INFO computer phobia

foco: ~ industrial *m* MED AMB *de polución* industrial source; **~ de perturbaciones** *m* COM GEN trouble spot

folio *m* MEDIOS folio; **~ único de referencia** COM GEN unique reference number (*URN*)

folleto *m* COM GEN handbook, brochure, OCIO brochure, V&M handout, leaflet; **~ de emisión** BOLSA, FIN placement memorandum; **~ explicativo de una emisión** BOLSA, FIN prospectus; **~ informativo de una nueva emisión** BOLSA, FIN red herring; **~ de instrucciones** MEDIOS instruction leaflet; **~ publicitario** V&M sales folder, sales leaflet, sales literature

fomentar *vt* COM GEN promote, encourage, build up, ECON, RRHH encourage

fomento *m* COM GEN, ECON, RRHH encouragement; **~ del comercio** V&M *publicidad* trade promotion; **~ de la**

exportación IMP/EXP export promotion; ~ **del medio ambiente** MED AMB environmental development; ~ **del tiempo libre** OCIO *pensionistas* leisure development

fondeadero *m* TRANSP accommodation berth, *navegación* berth; ~ **en aguas profundas** TRANSP *navegación* deepwater berth

fondo *m* BOLSA *dinero* fund, COM GEN bottom; ~ **de acción** DER agency fund; ~ **de acciones ordinarias** BOLSA common shares fund (*BrE*), common stock fund (*AmE*); ~ **acumulativo** FISC accumulating fund; ~ **de agencia** COM GEN, MEDIOS agency fund; ~ **de alto rendimiento** BOLSA performance fund; ~ **de amortización** BOLSA, CONT, FIN amortization fund, sinking fund, depreciation reserve; ~ **de amortización de deudas** BOLSA, CONT, FIN sinking fund; ~ **para amortización de obligaciones** BOLSA, CONT, FIN bond sinking fund; ~ **de anualidad** SEG annuity fund; ~ **de ayuda a los trabajadores** CONT, PROT SOC, RRHH employees' provident fund; ~ **de beneficiencia** CONT, FIN, SEG endowment fund; ~ **de bienestar** PROT SOC welfare fund; ~ **en bloque** FISC *sector público* block funding; ~ **de bonos** BOLSA, FIN bond fund; ~ **de bonos municipales de un solo estado** BOLSA, FIN single-state municipal bond fund; ~ **buitre** FIN vulture fund; ~ **de caja chica** *AmL* (*cf fondo de caja pequeña Esp*) CONT *teneduría de libros* petty cash fund; ~ **de caja pequeña** *Esp* (*cf fondo de caja chica AmL*) CONT *teneduría de libros* petty cash fund; ~ **de cambio** BOLSA exchange fund; ~ **de capital** CONT *autoridades locales*, FIN *inversiones* capital fund; ~ **de cohesión** ECON cohesion fund; ~ **de comercio** COM GEN commercial establishment, CONT goodwill; ~ **de comercio de la consolidación** CONT goodwill on consolidation; ~ **de comercio negativo** CONT bad will; ~ **de comercio positivo** CONT goodwill; ~ **de compensación** BOLSA compensation fund, SEG equalization fund; ~ **de compras** COM GEN purchase fund; ~ **consolidado** ECON, FIN, FISC consolidated fund; ~ **de contingencia** FIN umbrella fund; ~ **contributivo para enfermedad** COM GEN, RRHH contributory sickness fund; ~ **contributivo para invalidez** COM GEN, RRHH contributory sickness fund; ~ **del corredor de comercio** COM GEN broker fund; ~ **de crecimiento** BOLSA growth fund; ~ **en custodia** BANCA, COM GEN trust fund; ~ **dedicado a la especulación en acciones** BOLSA performance fund; ~ **de dinero** BANCA money fund; ~ **de dividendo** BOLSA, CONT dividend fund; ~ **de doble finalidad** BOLSA dual purpose fund; ~ **especulativo** BOLSA speculative fund, hedge fund (*jarg*); ~ **de estabilización** FISC stabilization fund; ~ **de fideicomiso** COM GEN trust fund; ~ **fiduciario** COM GEN trust fund; ~ **fiduciario irrevocable** COM GEN irrevocable trust fund; ~ **fijo** CONT imprest fund; ~ **para la financiación de proyectos en el extranjero** ECON overseas project fund; ~ **de fluctuación** BANCA reserve for fluctuation; ~ **fundacional** BOLSA, CONT, FIN foundation fund; ~ **de garantía** BANCA guaranty fund, guarantee fund; ~ **sin gastos de gestión** BOLSA no-load fund; ~ **de huelga** RRHH strike fund; ~ **de imprevistos** FIN *presupuestos personales* contingency fund; ~ **de indemnizaciones** RRHH indemnity fund; ~ **indexado** BOLSA index fund; ~ **de inversión** BANCA, BOLSA, FIN investment fund; ~ **de inversión para acciones** BOLSA, FIN investment fund for shares; ~ **de inversión en activos del mercado monetario**

(*FIAMM*) BANCA, FIN money market fund (*MMF*), money market mutual fund (*MMMF*); ~ **de capital inversión de capital variable** FIN open-end fund; ~ **de inversión cerrado** *f* BOLSA, FIN closed-end investment fund; ~ **de inversión equilibrado** BOLSA, FIN balanced mutual fund; ~ **de inversión mobiliario** (*FIM*) BOLSA, FIN real state investment fund; ~ **de inversión no proveniente de préstamo** BOLSA no-loan fund; ~ **de inversión en propiedad hipotecaria** FIN mortgage REIT; ~ **de inversión que cobra una comisión** BOLSA load fund; ~ **de inversión de renta fija** BOLSA fixed-income fund; ~ **de inversión de renta variable** BOLSA variable yield fund; ~ **de jubilación** COM GEN superannuation fund; ~ **de jubilaciones** RRHH, SEG retirement income fund (*RRIF*); ~ **de libre disposición** FIN general fund; ~ **sin límites** FIN open-ended fund; ~ **de liquidación de siniestros** SEG claims settlement fund; ~ **de maniobra** CONT working capital; ~ **mutuo** FIN mutual fund; ~ **mutuo de interés social** FIN social consciousness mutual fund; ~ **mutuo del mercado de dinero** FIN money market mutual fund (*MMMF*); ~ **nacional de contingencia** FIN national contingency fund; ~ **con número de acciones fijo** *f* FIN closed-end fund; ~ **de operaciones negativo** CONT *balance general* negative working capital; ~ **de pensión contributivo** FIN, FISC, PROT SOC, RRHH contributory pension fund; ~ **de pensión no contributivo** FIN, FISC, PROT SOC, RRHH noncontributory pension fund; ~ **de pensiones** BOLSA, CONT mutual fund, FIN, FISC, PROT SOC, RRHH pension fund, superannuation scheme; ~ **de pensiones para enfermedad** RRHH, SEG company's sickness insurance scheme; ~ **de pensiones de ganancias máximas de capital** BOLSA maximum capital gains mutual fund; ~ **de pensiones del oro** BOLSA gold mutual fund; ~ **de pensiones de vejez** FIN, FISC, RRHH, SEG superannuation fund; ~ **político** POL, RRHH political fund; ~ **de previsión** FIN provident fund; ~ **de previsión del personal** PROT SOC, RRHH staff welfare fund, staff provident fund; ~ **que siguen la bolsa de valores** BOLSA, FIN index-tracking fund; ~ **para redención de premios** BOLSA, CONT bond redemption premium; ~ **redondo** TRANSP *de un barco* round bottom (*RDBTN*); ~ **de regulación** BOLSA, ECON buffer stock; ~ **renovable** CONT, FIN revolving fund; ~ **renovable para la producción orientada a la defensa** FIN defence production revolving fund (*BrE*), defense production revolving fund (*AmE*); ~ **renovable de provisión** ECON, FIN supply revolving fund; ~ **de reposición** CONT renewal fund; ~ **de rescate** BOLSA, CONT, FIN redemption fund; ~ **de reserva** BANCA bank reserve; ~ **de restablecimiento** SEG cleanup fund; ~ **de restablecimiento del Consejo Europeo** BANCA Council of Europe Resettlement Fund (*CERF*); ~ **de retiros** FIN retirement fund; ~ **rotatorio** CONT, FIN *contabilidad nacional* revolving fund; ~ **de salud privado** RRHH private health fund; ~ **para sobornos** FIN, POL slush fund; ~ **sobrante** BOLSA rest fund; ~ **en V** TRANSP vee bottom (*AmE*) (*V BTM*); ♦ **cualquier** ~ SEG *marino* any one bottom (*AOB*); **en el** ~ **de la cuestión** DER on its merits

Fondo: ~ **de Compensación Internacional para la Contaminación Producida por Petróleo** *m* BANCA, MED AMB International Oil Pollution Compensation Fund (*IOPC Fund*); ~ **de la Comunidad para la Cooperación Técnica** *m* ECON, POL Commonwealth Fund for Technical Cooperation (*CFTC*); ~ **para la**

Cooperación Económica Exterior *m* ECON Overseas Economic Cooperation Fund (*OECF*); **~ Consolidado de Ingresos** *m* FIN Consolidated Revenue Fund; **~ de Desarrollo para Mercados Emergentes** *m* FIN Emerging Markets Growth Fund (*EMGF*); **~ Europeo Agrícola** *m* ECON, POL European Agricultural Fund; **~ Europeo para la Cooperación Monetaria** *m* (*FECOM*) ECON, POL European Monetary Cooperation Fund (*EMCF*); **~ Europeo de Desarrollo** *m* ECON, POL European Development Fund (*EDF*); **~ Europeo para el Desarrollo Regional** *m* (*FEDER*) ECON, POL European Regional Development Fund (*ERDF*); **~ Europeo de Orientación y Garantía Agrícola** *m* (*FEOGA*) ECON, POL European Agricultural Guidance and Guarantee Fund (*EAGGF*); **~ de Inversión para Mercados Emergentes** *m* ECON, POL Emerging Markets Investment Fund (*EMIF*); **~ Monetario Europeo** *m* BANCA, ECON, POL European Monetary Fund; **~ Monetario Internacional** *m* (*FMI*) ECON, POL International Monetary Fund (*IMF*); **~ de Proyecto de Ultramar** *m* ECON Overseas Project Fund; **~ Renovable de Compensación de Hidrocarburos** *m* FIN Petroleum Compensation Revolving Fund; **~ Social Europeo** *m* (*FSE*) ECON, POL European Social Fund (*ESF*)

fondos¹: **sin ~** *adj* COM GEN no funds (*N/F*)

fondos² *m pl* COM GEN funds; **~ ajenos** BANCA, CONT, ECON, FIN loan capital; **~ asignados** CONT appropriate funds; **~ autogenerados** FIN self-generated funds; **~ de beneficencia** FISC, PROT SOC charity funds; **~ bloqueados** BANCA, CONT, FIN blocked funds; **~ caducados** CONT lapsed funds; **~ de una cámara de compensación** BANCA clearing house funds; **~ de colocación no discrecional** BOLSA advisory funds; **~ colocados en paraísos fiscales** BANCA, CONT, FIN, FISC offshore funds; **~ congelados** BANCA, CONT, FIN blocked funds; **~ a corto** BOLSA ready assets trusts (*RATs*); **~ de depósito a plazo en eurodólares** BOLSA Eurodollar time deposit funds; **~ desaprobados** FIN unapproved funds; **~ de deuda divididos** FIN times uncovered; **~ disponibles** COM GEN available funds, FIN uncommitted funds; **~ en efectivo** CONT, FIN liquid funds; **~ en efectivos** CONT, FIN liquid funds; **~ estructurales** ECON *UE* structural funds; **~ externos** FIN external funds; **~ en el extranjero** BANCA funds abroad; **~ federales** BANCA *mercado del dinero* federal funds; **~ financieros** CONT capital; **~ generados internamente** CONT internally-generated funds; **~ inmobiliarios** CONT real estate funds; **~ insuficientes** BANCA, COM GEN not sufficient funds (*N.S.F.*); **~ a interés estable** BANCA stable-rate funds; **~ de inversión en acciones** BOLSA, FIN equity investment funds; **~ de inversión en activos del mercado monetario** BOLSA, FIN money market funds; **~ líquidos** BANCA, CONT, FIN liquid funds; **~ líquidos netos** BANCA, CONT, FIN net liquid funds; **~ mixtos** BOLSA mixed funds; **~ de moneda circulante administrados** FIN managed currency funds; **~ no cobrados** BANCA uncollected funds; **~ no recaudados** BANCA uncollected funds; **~ no repartidos** CONT undistributable reserve (*BrE*), restricted surplus (*AmE*); **~ de pensiones** RRHH funded pension plan (*BrE*), *pensiones* funded retirement plan (*AmE*); **~ prestados** BANCA, FIN, POL borrowed funds; **~ de préstamo** BANCA borrow funds, loan stock, BOLSA loan stock; **~ para préstamos** BANCA lendable funds; **~ de procedencia**

desconocida PROT SOC *educación* soft money; **~ propios** BANCA, BOLSA equity, CONT net equity; **~ públicos** BOLSA gilt-edged stocks (*BrE*), CONT public funds; **~ resultantes de las operaciones** CONT funds from operations; **~ secretos** BANCA, CONT secret reserve; **~ en títulos** BOLSA, CONT equity funds; **~ totales asignados** FIN total funds provided; **~ totales solicitados** FIN total funds applied; ◆ **apartar ~** COM GEN make provision for; **con ~ adecuados** COM GEN adequately funded; **origen y aplicación de ~** CONT, FIN source and application of funds; **origen y destino de los ~** CONT, FIN source and disposition of funds

fonocaptor *m* MEDIOS pick-up, sound pick-up

fontesoro *m* BANCA, BOLSA treasury bond

forastero, -a *m,f* COM GEN outsider

forfeiting *m* COM GEN forfeiting

forma¹: **de ~ jerárquica** *adv* COM GEN top down

forma² *f* COM GEN form; **~ H** ECON H-form; **~ M** ECON M-form; **~ de negociación** RRHH bargaining form; **~ de pago** V&M payment type; **~ preferencial** BOLSA preferential form; **~ de revelar las preferencias** ECON, RRHH exit voice; **~ de solicitud** COM GEN, RRHH application form; **~ U** ECON *división de organización empresarial* U-form; **~ X** ECON X-form; ◆ **en ~ de** COM GEN in the form of; **la ~ de las cosas por venir** COM GEN the shape of things to come; **en ~ de tabla** ADMIN in tabulated form

formación *f* RRHH *Esp* (*cf capacitación AmL*) training; **~ en análisis parcial** *Esp* (*cf capacitación en análisis parcial AmL*) COM GEN, RRHH part-analysis training; **~ analítica** *Esp* (*cf capacitación analítica AmL*) GES, RRHH analytical training; **~ asertiva** *Esp* (*cf capacitación asertiva AmL*) PROT SOC, RRHH assertiveness training; **~ bruta de capital fijo** COM GEN gross fixed capital formation; **~ de capital** CONT, ECON capital formation; **~ complementaria** *Esp* (*cf capacitación complementaria AmL*) RRHH booster training; **~ condicional** *Esp* (*cf capacitación condicional AmL*) training of trainers; **~ de un consorcio** BANCA syndication; **~ dentro de la empresa** *Esp* (*cf capacitación dentro de la empresa AmL*) IND training within industry (*TWI*), RRHH in-house training, training within industry (*TWI*); **~ ejecutiva** *Esp* (*cf capacitación ejecutiva AmL*) GES, RRHH executive training; **~ de ejecutivos** *Esp* (*cf capacitación de ejecutivos AmL*) GES, RRHH executive training; **~ de una empresa** COM GEN company formation; **~ en la empresa** *Esp* (*cf capacitación en la empresa AmL*) RRHH on-the-job training; **~ de entrenadores** *Esp* (*cf capacitación de entrenadores AmL*) RRHH training of trainers; **~ de equipo** GES, INFO, RRHH team building; **~ específica** *Esp* (*cf capacitación específica AmL*) RRHH specific training; **~ de formadores** *Esp* (*cf capacitación de formadores AmL*) RRHH training of trainers; **~ fuera del puesto de trabajo** *Esp* (*cf capacitación fuera del puesto de trabajo AmL*) RRHH, IND off-the-job training; **~ general** *Esp* (*cf capacitación general AmL*) RRHH general training; **~ gerencial** *Esp* (*cf capacitación gerencial AmL*) GES, RRHH management training; **~ grupal** *Esp* (*cf capacitación grupal AmL*) RRHH group training; **~ de imágenes** INFO, V&M imaging; **~ industrial** *Esp* (*cf capacitación industrial AmL*) IND, RRHH industrial training; **~ de instructores** *Esp* (*cf capacitación de instructores AmL*) RRHH training of trainers; **~ interna** *Esp* (*cf capacitación interna AmL*) IND, RRHH in-company training, in-house training; ~ **de mandos** *Esp* (*cf capacitación de mandos AmL*) GES, RRHH management training; ~ **en multimedia** *Esp* (*cf capacitación en multimedia AmL*) MEDIOS, RRHH multimedia training; ~ **ocupacional** *Esp* (*cf capacitación ocupacional AmL*) PROT SOC, RRHH employment training (*ET*); ~ **por ordenador** *Esp* (*cf capacitación por computadora AmL*) INFO, RRHH computer-based training; ~ **de personal** *Esp* (*cf capacitación de personal AmL*) GES, RRHH staff training; ~ **de piquetes** *m* RRHH picketing; ~ **de piquetes de huelga ilegales** *m* RRHH unlawful picketing; ~ **de piquetes pacíficos** *m* RRHH *acción industrial* peaceful picketing; ~ **de precios** COM GEN, ECON, V&M price determination; ~ **profesional** *Esp* (*cf capacitación profesional AmL*) PROT SOC, RRHH vocational rehabilitation, vocational training; ~ **profesional en la empresa** *Esp* (*cf capacitación profesional en la empresa AmL*) IND, RRHH on-the-job training; ~ **profesional permanente** *Esp* (*cf capacitación profesional permanente AmL*) RRHH continual professional education; ~ **en la propia fábrica** *Esp* (*cf capacitación en la propia fábrica AmL*) IND, RRHH in-plant training; ~ **en el puesto de trabajo** *Esp* (*cf capacitación en el puesto de trabajo AmL*) RRHH job training, in-service training; ~ **de sensibilidad** *Esp* (*cf capacitación de sensibilidad AmL*) COM GEN, GES, RRHH sensitivity training; ~ **de una sociedad** BOLSA formation of a corporation; ~ **superior** *Esp* (*cf capacitación superior AmL*) RRHH advanced training; ~ **en el trabajo** *Esp* (*cf capacitación en el trabajo AmL*) IND, RRHH in-service training; ~ **vertical** COM GEN vertical formation; ◆ **con una ~ adecuada** *Esp* (*cf con una capacitación adecuada AmL*) RRHH well-educated

formador, -a *m,f Esp* (*cf capacitador AmL*) COM GEN, RRHH training officer

formal *adj* COM GEN formal

formalidad *f* COM GEN formality; ~ **aduanera** IMP/EXP customs formality

formalidades: ~ **aduaneras** *f pl* IMP/EXP customs procedure; ~ **legales** *f pl* DER legal formalities

formalización *f* COM GEN, RRHH formalization

formalizar *vt* COM GEN, RRHH formalize

formar *vt* COM GEN *plan* lay, RRHH *Esp* (*cf capacitar AmL*) train

formarse *v refl Esp* (*cf capacitar AmL*) RRHH train

formateado *m* INFO formatting

formatear *vt* INFO *disco* format; ◆ **sin ~** INFO unformatted

formato[1]: **de ~ libre** *adj* INFO free format

formato[2] *m* ADMIN, INFO, V&M *de documento* format; ~ **apaisado** ADMIN, INFO, MEDIOS, V&M *publicidad* landscape (*jarg*); ~ **de cuenta** CONT account format; ~ **horizontal** ADMIN, INFO, MEDIOS, V&M landscape (*jarg*); ~ **de informe** *Esp* (*cf formato de reporte AmL*) COM GEN report form; ~ **organizacional** COM GEN organizational shape; ~ **de registro** INFO record format; ~ **de reporte** *AmL* (*cf formato de informe Esp*) COM GEN report form; ~ **vertical** ADMIN, INFO, MEDIOS *de página*, V&M *publicidad* portrait (*jarg*); ~ **1** CONT Format 1 (*BrE*); ~ **vertical de la cuenta de pérdidas y ganancias** CONT vertical profit and loss account format

fórmula *f* COM GEN formula; ~ **de correlación por rangos de spearman** MAT spearman's rank correlation formula; ~ **de cortesía** COMS complimentary close; ~ **Du Pont** FIN Du Pont formula; ~ **de interés** BANCA interest formula; ~ **del momento producto** MAT product moment formula; ~ **de oro** RRHH golden formula (*BrE*); ~ **del promedio** BANCA averaging formula; ~ **del término medio** BANCA averaging formula; ~ **para valorar opciones** BOLSA option pricing formula

formulación *f* COM GEN, GES *de una política* formulation; ~ **de la emisión** V&M mission statement; ~ **de una estrategia** COM GEN, ECON strategy formulation; ~ **estratégica** COM GEN, ECON strategy formulation; ~ **de la misión** GES mission statement; ~ **de una política** COM GEN, GES policy formulation; ~ **de tarifas** TRANSP rates formulation

formular *vt* COM GEN draw up, file, *política* formulate, *queja* lay, GES formulate

formulario *m* COM GEN form; ~ **abreviado** IMP/EXP *certificado de embarque*, TRANSP short form; ~ **para la autorización de carga peligrosa** COM GEN, TRANSP dangerous goods authority form; ~ **en blanco** COM GEN blank form; ~ **de cheques** BANCA check form (*AmE*), cheque form (*BrE*); ~ **de conocimiento de embarque** IMP/EXP, TRANSP bill of lading form; ~ **continuo** COM GEN continuous form; ~ **copiativo** FISC sensitive form; ~ **de declaración sobre la renta** FISC tax return form; ~ **de depósito** BANCA deposit note; ~ **de encuesta** COM GEN inquiry form; ~ **extenso** IMP/EXP *certificado de embarque* long form; ~ **de Hacienda** FISC tax form; ~ **impreso** COM GEN engraved form; ~ **del impuesto sobre la renta** CONT, FISC income blank; ~ **con información salarial** FISC information return; ~ **de instrucciones de transporte** TRANSP transport instruction form; ~ **del inventario** CONT inventory sheet; ~ **de notificación de arribada** TRANSP arrival notification form (*ANF*); ~ **de notificación de buque arribado** TRANSP arrived notification form; ~ **oficial** TRANSP *contrato de fletamiento* government form (*GF*); ~ **ordinario** TRANSP *conocimiento de embarque* long form; ~ **de pedido** COM GEN, V&M order blank; ~ **de producto** TRANSP product form; ~ **de propiedad** DER, INMOB ownership form; ~ **de reclamación** SEG claim form; ~ **reglamentario** FISC *contrato de fletamiento* prescribed form; ~ **de reserva** OCIO reservation form; ~ **de solicitud** COM GEN, RRHH application form; ~ **de suscripción** BOLSA, COM GEN subscription form; ~ **de transferencia de acciones** BOLSA stock transfer form; ~ **de tránsito por la UE** TRANSP EU transit form

Formulario: ~ **de Interés Vocacional de Strong** *m* RRHH Strong Vocational Interest Blank

formularios: ~ **alineados** *m pl* ADMIN aligned forms; ~ **para ubicaciones múltiples** *m pl* SEG multiple locations forms

fornido *adj* COM GEN robust

foro *m* POL forum

forrajes *m pl* ECON *agrícola* feedstuffs

forro *m* TRANSP *navegación* skin

fortaleza: ~ **europea** *f* POL fortress Europe (*jarg*)

fortuna *f* BANCA bankroll (*AmE*); ~ **personal** FIN private means

forzar: ~ **el descenso de** *fra* ECON *tipos de interés* force down; ~ **una salida** *fra* COM GEN force an issue

fotocomposición *f* COM GEN, INFO typesetting, MEDIOS typesetting, *imprenta* filmsetting

fotocopia *f* ADMIN photocopy

fotocopiar *vt* ADMIN photocopy, Xerox®

fotograbado *m* V&M photogravure

fotografías: ~ **de prensa** *f pl* MEDIOS news pictures

fotógrafo, -a: ~ **de prensa** *m,f* MEDIOS press photographer

fotolitógrafo, -a *m,f* RRHH process worker

fotollamada *f* V&M photo call

fotostato *m* COM GEN photostat (*obs*)

fracasar *vi* COM GEN fail, *plan, negociaciones* fall apart

fracaso *m* COM GEN breakdown, flop (*infrml*), RRHH *negociaciones* breakdown

fracción *f* MAT fraction; ~ **simple** MAT simple fraction

fraccionamiento: ~ **de los honorarios** *m* CONT fee split

fraccionar *vt* MAT fractionalize; ◆ ~ **la carga** TRANSP break bulk

fractura: ~ **de cabeza** *f jarg* INFO head crash (*jarg*)

frágil *adj* TRANSP fragile

fragmentación *f* ECON *del mercado*, INFO *disco* fragmentation; ~ **de los medios de comunicación** MEDIOS, V&M media fragmentation; ~ **del mercado** ECON market fragmentation

fraguar *vt* PATENT *falsedad* make

franco[1] *adj* IMP/EXP, TRANSP franco (*fco.*), free; ◆ ~ **al costado** IMP/EXP, TRANSP free alongside (*f.a.s.*); ~ **al costado del buque** IMP/EXP, TRANSP free alongside vessel (*f.a.s.*); ~ **avión** IMP/EXP, TRANSP free on aircraft (*f.o.a.*); ~ **en barcaza** IMP/EXP, TRANSP free into barge (*f.i.b.*); ~ **por la borda** IMP/EXP, TRANSP free overboard; ~ **a bordo** IMP/EXP, TRANSP *carga* free on board (*f.o.b.*); ~ **a bordo en aeropuerto** IMP/EXP, TRANSP free on board airport; ~ **a bordo y asentado** IMP/EXP, TRANSP free on board and trimmed (*f.o.b.&t.*); ~ **a bordo y carga equilibrada** IMP/EXP, TRANSP free on board and trimmed (*f.o.b.&t.*); ~ **en buque** IMP/EXP, TRANSP free on ship (*f.o.s.*); ~ **camión** IMP/EXP, TRANSP free on truck (*f.o.t.*); ~ **de carga** TRANSP free in (*f.i.*); ~ **de carga y descarga** IMP/EXP, TRANSP free in and out (*f.i.&o.*); ~ **de carga, descarga y asentado** IMP/EXP, TRANSP free in, out and trimmed (*f.i.o.&t*); ~ **de carga, descarga y estibado** IMP/EXP, TRANSP free in, out and stowed (*f.i.o.&s.*); ~ **de carga, descarga, estibado y asentado** IMP/EXP, TRANSP free in, out, stowed and trimmed (*f.i.o.s.&t.*); ~ **de consignación** IMP/EXP, TRANSP free dispatch (*f.d.*); ~ **dentro y fuera** IMP/EXP, TRANSP free in and out (*f.i.o.*); ~ **a domicilio** IMP/EXP, TRANSP carriage paid home; ~ **fábrica** COM GEN, IMP/EXP, TRANSP exworks (*ExW*); ~ **muelle** IMP/EXP, TRANSP ex-quay (*x-quay, ExQ*), franco quay, free on quay (*f.o.q.*); ~ **de muelle a muelle** IMP/EXP, TRANSP free on quay to free on quay (*f.o.q.-f.o.q.*); ~ **en pañoles** IMP/EXP, TRANSP free into bunkers (*f.i.b.*); ~ **porteador** IMP/EXP, TRANSP free carrier (*f.c.a.*); ~ **en puerto** IMP/EXP *envío*, TRANSP free in harbor (*AmE*) (*f.i.h.*), free in harbour (*BrE*) (*f.i.h.*); ~ **de seguro y porte** IMP/EXP, TRANSP free insurance and carriage (*f.i.c.*, *FIC*); ~ **sobre vagón** IMP/EXP, TRANSP free on rail (*f.o.r.*)

franco[2]: ~ **oro** *m* ECON gold franc; ~ **porteador** *m* IMP/EXP, TRANSP free carrier (*f.c.a.*)

francobordo *m* TRANSP *navegación* freeboard (*FBD*)

franja *f* COM GEN fringe, INMOB *geográfica* strip; ~ **competitiva** ECON competitive fringe; ~ **horaria** V&M *publicidad* time segment; ~ **horaria previa o posterior a la de máxima audiencia** V&M shoulder time; ~ **horaria de primera hora de la tarde** MEDIOS *radio* early fringe; ~ **de información banda amplia** BOLSA *seguros, propiedad inmobiliaria, valores* broad tape (*AmE*)

franqueadora *f* COMS postage meter (*AmE*), postage metre (*BrE*)

franquear *vt* ADMIN frank, mail (*AmE*), post (*BrE*), COM GEN enfranchise, COMS mail (*AmE*), post (*BrE*), frank

franqueo *m* ADMIN, COMS postage; ~ **en destino** ADMIN, COMS postage-due stamp; ◆ ~ **pagado** ADMIN, COMS postage paid

franquicia *f* SEG excess, V&M franchise, franchising; ~ **de equipaje** IMP/EXP, TRANSP free baggage allowance; ~ **fiscal** FISC tax holiday

franquiciado, -a *m,f* DER, V&M franchisee

franquiciador, a *m,f* DER, V&M franchisor

frase: ~ **publicitaria** *f* COM GEN watchword

fraude *m* COM GEN, defraudación, fraud; ~ **al proveedor** COM GEN long fraud; ~ **por cambio de derrota** TRANSP *navegación* deviation fraud; ~ **en el conocimiento de embarque** IMP/EXP, TRANSP bill of lading fraud; ~ **en el contrato de fletamento** IMP/EXP, TRANSP charter party fraud; ~ **documental** COM GEN documentary fraud; ~ **fiscal** FISC tax fraud; ~ **informático** DER, INFO computer fraud; ~ **marítimo** TRANSP maritime fraud

fraudulencia *f* DER fraudulence

fraudulentamente *adv* DER fraudulently

frecuencia *f* MAT, MEDIOS frequency; ~ **absoluta** MAT absolute frequency; ~ **acumulativa** MAT cumulative frequency; ~ **de fallos** COM GEN failure rate; ~ **muy alta** (*VHF*) COMS *de radio* very high frequency (*VHF*); ~ **relativa** MAT relative frequency; ~ **de las visitas** V&M call frequency

freelance *mf* RRHH freelance

frenar *vt* ECON *inflación* pull down

frenazo: ~ **y expansión** *m* ECON stop-go

frenesí *m* GES brainstorm

frente *m* MEDIOS front (*jarg*)

frigorífico *m* TRANSP *contenedor* reefer

frontal: ~ **desmontable** *m* TRANSP *semirremolque* detachable front end

frontera *f* COM GEN, POL frontier; ~ **común** IMP/EXP mutual border; ~ **de entrega** IMP/EXP delivered frontier; ~ **exterior** COM GEN external border; ~ **interna** COM GEN internal frontier; ~ **de posibilidades de innovación** ECON innovation possibility frontier; ~ **de posibilidades de producción** ECON production possibility frontier (*PPF*); ~ **de posibilidades de utilidad** ECON utility possibility frontier

fronteras: ~ **fiscales** *f pl* ECON *UE*, POL fiscal frontiers; ~ **nacionales** *f pl* COM GEN national borders, national boundaries

frustración *f* DER frustration; ~ **de contrato** DER frustration of contract

FSE *abr* (*Fondo Social Europeo*) ECON, POL ESF (*European Social Fund*)

fuente *f* COM GEN *de fondos, información*, INFO source; ~ **de alimentación** INFO power surge; ~ **autorizada** COM GEN reliable source; ~ **de capital** BANCA, FIN source of capital; ~ **cargable por teleproceso** INFO downloadable font; ~ **de dinero** COM GEN, FIN moneymaker, money-spinner (*infrml*); ~ **y disposición de fondos** FIN, CONT source and disposition of funds; ~ **energética** COM GEN, IND, MED AMB energy source;

~ **de financiación** CONT, FIN funding source; ~ **de fondos** CONT, FIN source of funds; ~ **de ingresos** ECON cash cow (*jarg*), FISC source of income; ~ **de mensajes** V&M message source; ~ **de recursos** CONT, FIN source of funds; ~ **de tipos** INFO type font; ~ **única** COM GEN single sourcing

fuera[1]: ~ **de acta** *adj* COM GEN, MEDIOS, POL off-the-record; ~ **de almacén** *adj* ECON *existencias* out-of-stock; ~ **del balance general** *m* CONT off the balance sheet; ~ **del centro de la ciudad** *adj* COM GEN, IND, V&M out of town; ~ **de circulación** *adj* COM GEN *barco, coche* laid-up; **fuera del** ~ *m* FIN off-balance sheet (*OBS*); ~ **de cotización** *adj* BOLSA off-the-board; ~ **de funcionamiento** *adj* INFO *sistema* down; ~ **de la ley** *adj* COM GEN shady

fuera[2] *adv* COM GEN abroad; ◆ ~ **de almacén** COM GEN ex warehouse; ~ **de los días pico** *AmL* (*cf fuera de los días punta Esp*) COM GEN off-peak day; ~ **de los días punta** *Esp* (*cf fuera de los días pico AmL*) COM GEN off-peak day; ~ **de gálibo** TRANSP out of gage (*AmE*) (*OOG*), out of gauge (*BrE*) (*OOG*); ~ **de plantación** IMP/EXP *carga* ex plantation

fuerte[1] *adj* COM GEN, ECON forceful, *precio, deuda* hefty (*infrml*), *demanda* heavy, *indicio* strong

fuerte[2]: ~ **caída** *f* COM GEN, ECON sharp drop; ~ **demanda** *f* V&M heavy demand; ~ **tendencia alcista** *f* BOLSA *opciones* strong bullish play (*jarg*)

fuertemente *adv* COM GEN, CONT, ECON sharply, strongly

fuerza *f* ECON *de una moneda* strength; ~ **financiera** FIN financial muscle; ~ **laboral** RRHH *personas, trabajadores* human resources, labor (*AmE*), labor force (*AmE*), labour (*BrE*), labour force (*BrE*), work force; ~ **legal de un acuerdo colectivo** DER, RRHH legal enforceability of collective agreement; ~ **mayor** DER force majeure; ~ **del mercado** COM GEN strength of the market; ~ **motriz** COM GEN driving force; ~ **policial** DER police force; ~ **pública** DER police force, police power; ~ **de trabajo** RRHH *personas, trabajadores* human resources, labor (*AmE*), labor force (*AmE*), labour (*BrE*), labour force (*BrE*), work force; ~ **de trabajo cualificada** RRHH skilled labor force (*AmE*), skilled labour force (*BrE*); ~ **de trabajo desempleada** RRHH unemployed labor force (*AmE*), unemployed labour force (*BrE*); ~ **de trabajo de reemplazo** RRHH replacement labor force (*AmE*), replacement labour force (*BrE*); ~ **de trabajo de reserva** RRHH reserve army of labor (*AmE*), reserve army of labour (*BrE*); ~ **del viento** MED AMB wind power

fuerzas: ~ **del mercado** *f pl* ECON, V&M market forces

fuga: ~ **de cerebros** *f infrml* RRHH brain drain (*infrml*); ~ **de seguridad** *f* COM GEN security leak

fugarse *v refl* DER abscond

Fulano, -a: ~ **de Tal** *m,f* DER John Doe (*AmE*) (*infrml*), Jane Doe (*AmE*) (*infrml*)

fulcro *m* COM GEN fulcrum

fumar: **no** ~ *fra* COM GEN no smoking

función *f* COM GEN function; ~ **de ahorro** ECON savings function; ~ **asesora** RRHH advisory function; ~ **del bienestar social** ECON, PROT SOC, RRHH social welfare function; ~ **de bienestar social bergsonia** ECON, PROT SOC, RRHH Bergson social welfare function; ~ **de consumo** ECON consumption function; ~ **de costes** *Esp* (*cf función de costos AmL*) CONT cost function; ~ **de costos** *AmL* (*cf función de costes Esp*) CONT cost

function; ~ **de demanda** ECON demand function; ~ **directiva** GES managerial function; ~ **directiva y ejecutiva** COM GEN line function; ~ **de empleo** ECON employment function; ~ **exponencial** INFO *programación de ordenador*, MAT exponential function; ~ **fiscalizadora** CONT, FISC audit function; ~ **de gastos** ECON expenditure function; ~ **de inversión** FIN investment function; ~ **objetiva** MAT objective function; ~ **de oferta** ECON supply function; ~ **de oferta de lucas** ECON Lucas supply function; ~ **de pérdida** MAT loss function; ~ **de producción** ECON micro-production function, production function; ~ **de producción de Cobb-Douglas** ECON Cobb Douglas production function; ~ **programable** INFO programmable function; ~ **de pseudo-producción** ECON pseudo-production function; ~ **de reacción** ECON reaction function; ~ **de respuesta** V&M response function; ~ **sorpresa** ECON surprise function; ~ **de utilidad** ECON utility function; ◆ **como una** ~ **de** COM GEN as a function of; **en** ~ **de** COM GEN according to

funcional *adj* COM GEN functional

funcionamiento[1]: **en** ~ *adj* INFO up (*infrml*)

funcionamiento[2] *m* COM GEN *del mercado* functioning, performance, working; ~ **del circuito** TRANSP circuit working; ~ **desequilibrado** TRANSP imbalanced working; ~ **de una sucursal** COM GEN branch operation

funcionar *vt* COM GEN operate, work

funcionariado *m* POL public body

funcionario, -a *m,f* RRHH civil servant, officer, official; ~ **con antigüedad** RRHH senior civil servant; ~ **auditor(a)** CONT audit officer; ~ **de bajo nivel** RRHH petty official; ~ **de capacitación** *AmL* (*cf funcionario de formación Esp*) RRHH training officer; ~ **de la cartera de pedidos** *m* BOLSA order book officials (*OBO*); ~ **de compras** COM GEN, RRHH procurement officer, purchasing officer; ~ **de conciliación** RRHH conciliation officer (*BrE*); ~ **encargado(-a) de la ejecución de la ley** DER law enforcement official; ~ **de formación** *Esp* (*cf funcionario de capacitación AmL*) RRHH training officer; ~ **de importación** IMP/EXP, RRHH import clerk; ~ **de inmigración** IMP/EXP, RRHH immigration officer (*IO*); ~ **judicial** DER legal officer; ~ **de manifiesto** RRHH manifest clerk; ~ **no profesional** RRHH lay official; ~ **notarial** DER, RRHH commissioner of deeds; ~ **en prácticas** RRHH trainee civil servant; ~ **principal de exportación** IMP/EXP, RRHH senior export clerk; ~ **principal de importación** IMP/EXP, RRHH senior import clerk; ~ **público(-a)** RRHH civil servant; ~ **de rango superior** RRHH senior officer (*SO*); ~ **de relaciones públicas** RRHH, V&M public relations officer (*PRO*); ~ **responsable** CONT accountable officer; ~ **de tarifas** RRHH rates clerk, rates officer; ~ **a tiempo completo** RRHH full-time official (*BrE*) (*FTO*)

fundación *f* COM GEN, ECON, POL foundation; ~ **benéfica** FISC, PROT SOC charitable foundation; ~ **privada** FISC private foundation; ~ **pública** FISC public foundation; ~ **social** ECON social conscience fund

Fundación: ~ **Europea** *f* POL European Foundation (*EF*)

fundado: **estar bien** ~ *fra* COM GEN *argumento* hold water

fundador, a *m,f* FISC promoter

fundamental *adj* COM GEN fundamental

fundamentalmente *adv* COM GEN principally

fundamento *m* COM GEN groundwork; ~ **constitucional** ADMIN constitutional foundation

fundamentos *m pl* COM GEN basics

fundar *vt* COM GEN set up, launch, *una compañía* build up, establish, DER, ECON establish

fundir *vt* COM GEN *todo el dinero que se tiene* blow (*infrml*), IND smelt; ◆ ~ **sonoro** MEDIOS, V&M *radio, televisión* cross-fade

fungibilidad *f* DER fungibility

fungible *adj* DER fungible

furgón *m* TRANSP *contenedor* van; ~ **con caja frigorífica** TRANSP refrigerated box van; ~ **con caja refrigerada** TRANSP refrigerated box van; ~ **frigorífico** TRANSP insulated van; ~ **postal** COMS, TRANSP mailcar (*AmE*), mail van (*BrE*), post van (*BrE*)

furgoneta: ~ **paquetera** *f* TRANSP parcels van; ~ **para paquetes** *f* TRANSP parcels van; ~ **de socorro** *f* TRANSP breakdown van (*BrE*), tow truck (*AmE*)

fusión *f* COM GEN, fusion, *compañías* merger, amalgamation; ~ **de conglomerados** ECON, FIN *compañías, sociedades* conglomerate merger; ~ **de correo** ADMIN, INFO mailmerger; ~ **extranjera** BOLSA foreign merger; ~ **de ficheros de direcciones** ADMIN, INFO mailmerge; ~ **horizontal** COM GEN, ECON horizontal amalgamation, horizontal merger; ~ **horizontal/vertical** ADMIN, ECON horizontal-vertical amalgamation; ~ **de intereses** CONT *balance* pooling of interests (*AmE*), merger

accounting (*BrE*); ~ **inversa** ECON reverse takeover; ~ **transfronteriza** FIN, IMP/EXP cross-border merger; ~ **triangular** COM GEN triangular merger; ~ **triangular inversa** COM GEN reverse triangular merger; ~ **vertical** COM GEN vertical merger, vertical amalgamation

fusionar *vt* COM GEN amalgamate, fuse, merge

fusionarse *v refl* ADMIN *archivos* merge; ~ **a** COM GEN merge into; ~ **con** COM GEN *compañías* merge with

fusiones: ~ **y adquisiciones** *f pl* BOLSA, ECON mergers and acquisitions (*M&A*)

futuro[1] *adj* COM GEN future

futuro[2] *m* BOLSA future; ~ **financiero** BOLSA financial future; ~ **inmediato** COM GEN near future; ◆ **en el** ~ COM GEN in the future; **en un** ~ **próximo** COM GEN in the near future; **poner la mira en el** ~ COM GEN look to the future

futuros *m pl* BOLSA futures; ~ **diferidos** BOLSA, FIN deferred futures; ~ **financieros** BOLSA, FIN financial futures; ~ **relacionados con el neto patrimonial** BOLSA equity-related futures; ~ **sobre divisa** BOLSA currency futures; ~ **sobre índices** BOLSA index futures; ~ **sobre índices bursátiles** BOLSA stock index futures; ~ **sobre letras del tesoro** BOLSA treasury bill futures (*T-bill futures*); ~ **sobre productos básicos** BOLSA commodities futures; ~ **sobre tipos de interés** BOLSA, FIN interest rate futures; ~ **subyacentes** BOLSA underlying futures

G

gabarra *f* TRANSP barge, lighter; **~ de altamar** TRANSP sea-going barge

gabarraje *m* TRANSP lighterage

gabinete *m* POL cabinet

gacetilla *f* COM GEN press release

gafete: ~ de identificación *m* COM GEN name badge

gajes: ~ del oficio *m pl* COM GEN tricks of the trade (*infrml*)

galera *f* MEDIOS *prensa* galley

galería *f* COM GEN *compras* arcade

gallardete *m* BOLSA pennant

gallinero *m* OCIO gods

galón *m* COM GEN gallon (*gal*); **~ normalizado** COM GEN imperial gallon

gama[1]: **de ~ alta** *adj* COM GEN, V&M top-of-the-range, up-market

gama[2]: **~ alta del mercado** *f* V&M top end of the market; **~ baja del mercado** *m* V&M *comercialización* low end of the market; **~ media del mercado** *f* V&M middle range of the market; **~ de opciones** *f* COM GEN range of options; **~ de productos** *f* COM GEN, V&M product range, range of products, stock line; **~ superior del mercado** *f* V&M *comercialización* top end of the market

gamma *f* BOLSA gamma

ganadera: ~ experimentada *f* COM GEN top hand (*jarg*); **~ productiva** *f* COM GEN top hand (*jarg*)

ganadería: ~ intensiva *f* ECON *agricultura* intensive livestock farming

ganadero, -a *m,f* COM GEN rancher (*AmE*), stockbreeder (*BrE*)

ganador[1]**,a: ~ claro(-a)** *m,f* ECON net gainer; **~ de divisas** *m,f* COM GEN foreign exchange earner

ganador[2]**: todo para el ~** *fra* COM GEN winner takes all

ganancia *f* BOLSA *en valores de posición*, COM GEN, FISC profit, return, gain, benefit; **~ por acción** BOLSA, CONT, FIN earning per share (*EPS*); **~ acumulativa del capital neto imponible** FISC cumulative net taxable capital gain; **~ básica por acción** FIN basic earnings per share; **~ bruta** CONT, FIN gross earnings, gross profit, trading income; **~ a corto plazo** BOLSA short-term gain; **~ especulativa** FIN velvet; **~ extraordinaria** CONT extraordinary gain; **~ imponible** FISC taxable gain; **~ imponible del capital** FISC taxable capital gain; **~ inesperada** COM GEN windfall profit; **~ inmediata del capital** FISC immediate capital gain; **~ del intermediario** BOLSA turn, jobber's turn; **~ a largo plazo** FISC long-term gain; **~ neta** FIN clear profit, FISC net gain; **~ neta diaria** TRANSP net daily surplus; **~ neta imponible** FISC taxable net gain; **~ ordinaria** FISC ordinary gain

ganancias: ~ por acción totalmente diluidas *f pl* BOLSA fully diluted earnings per share; **~ en activos** *f pl* CONT earnings on assets; **~ antes de impuestos** *f pl* CONT, FISC pretax earnings; **~ anuales** *f pl* CONT annual earnings; **~ brutas** *f pl* RRHH gross earnings; **~ de capital** *f pl* BANCA, CONT, ECON, FIN capital gains; **~ de capital imponibles** *f pl* FISC chargeable capital gains; **~ de capital neto realizado por acción** *f pl* BOLSA net realized capital gains per share; **~ comerciales** *f pl* ECON gains from trade; **~ corporativas** *f pl* CONT corporate earnings; **~ corrientes** *f pl* CONT, RRHH actual earnings; **~ exentas** *f pl* FISC exempt earnings; **~ de la exportación** *f pl* IMP/EXP export earnings; **~ futuras** *f pl* FISC future gains; **~ imponibles del capital** *f pl* FISC taxable capital gains; **~ imprevistas** *f pl* ECON windfall gain; **~ sin intereses** *f pl* BANCA, BOLSA, FIN *depósito* noninterest earnings; **~ invisibles** *f pl* FIN invisible earnings; **~ netas** *f pl* COM GEN net earnings; **~ netas procedentes del empleo** *f pl* FISC net employment earnings; **~ no distribuidas** *f pl* CONT retained earnings; **~ no realizadas** *f pl* FISC unrealized gains; **~ obtenidas** *f pl* CONT, FIN realized gains; **~ por realizar** *f pl* BOLSA, CONT, FIN paper profit; **~ reconocidas** *f pl* FISC recognized gains; **~ de renta** *f pl* CONT income gains; **~ del trabajador por cuenta propia sujetas a aportación** *f pl* FISC *pensiones* contributory self-employed earnings; **~ por traspaso** *f pl* FISC gains on disposal (*BrE*)

ganar *vt* BOLSA gain, COM GEN *clientes* win, *mercado* capture, *reputación* earn; ♦ **~ dinero con algo** COM GEN raise money on sth; **~ terreno** COM GEN gain ground; **~ valor** BOLSA *divisas, acciones*, INMOB *activos, propiedades* appreciate

ganarse: ~ el favor de alguien *fra* COM GEN win sb's favor (*AmE*), win sb's favour (*BrE*); **~ la vida** *fra* ECON make a living, earn a living

gancho[1]**: sin ~** *adj* OCIO *película* legless (*jarg*)

gancho[2]**: ~ psicológico** *m* V&M psychological hook

ganga *f* COM GEN bargain

gap *m* BOLSA, ECON, V&M gap; **~ negativo del tipo de interés** BOLSA *futuros* negative interest rate gap

GAP *abr* (*gestión de activos y pasivos*) BANCA, FIN, GES ALM (*asset-liability management*)

garante *mf* BANCA guarantor, DER warranter; **~ administrador(a)** *m,f* BANCA managing underwriter; **~ de un crédito** BANCA credit guarantor

garantía[1]**: con ~** *adj* COM GEN cum warrant; **sin ~** *adj* COM GEN unsecured; **sin ~ de compra** *adj* COM GEN ex-warrant; **de doble ~** *adj* BOLSA double-barreled (*AmE*), double-barrelled (*BrE*); **sin ~ escrita** *adj* BOLSA, COM GEN clean

garantía[2]**: bajo ~** *adv* COM GEN under guarantee, under guaranty

garantía[3] *f* BOLSA *emisión de billetes* backing, COM GEN guarantee, guaranty, warrant, warranty, *préstamos* collateral, POL warrant; **~ acelerable** FIN accelerable guarantee, accelerable guaranty; **~ con activos** CONT asset coverage; **~ de actuación** BOLSA performance guarantee, performance guaranty; **~ adicional** ECON, FIN collateral security; **~ agrícola** ECON agricultural warrant; **~ de almacén** DER warehouse warrant (*WW*); **~ anticipada** BOLSA advance guarantee, advance guaranty; **~ de una aprobación** COM GEN seal of approval; **~ del arrendador** SEG homeowner warranty program (*AmE*), homeowner warranty programme (*BrE*); **~ de**

avería gruesa SEG general average guarantee, general average guaranty; **~ bancaria** BANCA bank guarantee, bank guarantee, bank security; **~ bancaria por la totalidad** BANCA comprehensive bank guarantee, comprehensive bank guaranty; **~ de los bonos del Estado** BOLSA warrant into government securities (*WINGS*); **~ de calidad** COM GEN quality assurance; **~ de comerciabilidad** COM GEN warranty of merchantability; **~ de comercio exterior** SEG external trade guarantee, external trade guaranty; **~ contra todo defecto** SEG guarantee from vice, guaranty from vice; **~ convertible** FIN convertible security; **~ de crédito** BANCA credit guarantee, credit guaranty; **~ cruzada** BANCA cross guarantee, cross guaranty; **~ cubierta** FIN covered warrant; **~ de cumplimiento** *Esp* (*cf garantía de realización AmL*) DER, INMOB completion bond; **~ del depósito** SEG deposit surety; **~ de deuda** COM GEN debt security; **~ especial** POL special warrant; **~ europea** FIN Euro-security; **~ expresa** COM GEN express warranty; **~ fiscal** FISC revenue guarantee, revenue guaranty; **~ implícita** DER implied warranty; **~ de indemnización** SEG letter of indemnity; **~ industrial** FIN industrial security; **~ de instituto** SEG institute warranty; **~ de licencia** DER permit bond; **~ de mantenimiento de la categoría** TRANSP warranted existing class maintained (*wecm*); **~ de una opción de compra** BOLSA call warrant; **~ de pago** CONT payment guarantee, payment guaranty; **~ con pago anticipado** IMP/EXP advance payment guarantee, advance payment guaranty; **~ permanente** BANCA, COM GEN, DER continuing guarantee, continuing guaranty; **~ personal** BANCA *de préstamo*, FIN personal guarantee, personal guaranty; **~ en prenda** BANCA pledged security; **~ de préstamo** BANCA, FIN loan guarantee, loan guaranty; **~ prolongada** V&M extended guarantee, extended guaranty; **~ de propiedad** COM GEN warranty of title; **~ real involuntaria** DER involuntary lien; **~ de realización** *AmL* (*cf garantía de cumplimiento Esp*) DER, INMOB completion bond; **~ de rendimiento** V&M performance guarantee, performance guaranty; **~ de servicios bancarios auxiliares** FIN auxiliary banking services undertaking; **~ solidaria** BOLSA full faith and credit (*AmE*), FIN joint guarantee, joint guaranty; **~ subsidiaria** FIN *préstamos* collateral; **~ suplementaria** SEG additional security; **~ suplementaria de los stocks** IMP/EXP supplementary stocks guarantee, supplementary stocks guaranty; **~ tácita** COM GEN implied warranty

garantías: **~ materiales** *f pl* BANCA physical collateral; **~ no transferibles** *f pl* BANCA nontransferable debentures

garantizado *adj* COM GEN guaranteed (*guar.*), warranted (*wd.*); **no ~** BANCA unendorsed, COM GEN unvouched for

garantizar *vt* COM GEN *préstamo* collateralize, grant, guarantee, warrant; ◆ **~ un abastecimiento provisional** CONT grant interim supply; **~ la ampliación de un crédito** FIN grant extended credit; **~ una deuda con una hipoteca** BANCA secure a debt by mortgage; **~ una opción** BOLSA grant an option

gas *m* COM GEN gas; **~ de escape** MED AMB *de vehículos* exhaust gas; **~ licuado de petróleo** (*LPG*) IND, TRANSP liquid petroleum gas (*LPG*); **~ del Mar del Norte** MED AMB North Sea gas; **~ natural** MED AMB natural gas; **~ nocivo** MED AMB noxious gas

gasoil: **~ para motores diesel** *m* MED AMB, TRANSP diesel oil (*DO*)

gasóleo *m* MED AMB gas oil; **~ marino** TRANSP marine diesel oil; **~ para motores diesel** MED AMB, TRANSP diesel oil (*DO*)

gasolina *f Esp* (*cf nafta AmL*) TRANSP gasoline (*AmE*), petrol (*BrE*); **~ para aviación** TRANSP aviation fuel; **~ para motores** TRANSP motor spirit; **~ sin plomo** *Esp* (*cf nafta sin plomo AmL*) TRANSP lead-free gasoline (*AmE*), lead-free petrol (*BrE*); **~ súper** *Esp* (*cf nafta súper AmL*) TRANSP four-star gasoline (*AmE*), four-star petrol (*BrE*)

gasolinera *f* COM GEN, TRANSP gas station (*AmE*), petrol station (*BrE*)

gastado: **no ~** *adj* COM GEN unexpended, unspent

gastar *vt* COM GEN spend, lay out *infrml*; ◆ **~ de menos** COM GEN, CONT underspend; **~ por debajo del presupuesto** COM GEN, CONT underspend

gasto *m* COM GEN charge, expenditure, expense, outlay; **~ actual** CONT actual expense; **~ acumulado** CONT accrued expense; **~ adicional** CONT additional charge; **~ administrativo** SEG administrative charge; **~ de agencia** TRANSP agency fee; **~ ajeno a la explotación** CONT nonoperating expense; **~ ajeno a la operación** CONT nonoperating expense; **~ de ajuste por pérdidas** SEG loss adjustment expense; **~ de almacén de la importación** IMP/EXP import depot charge; **~ autónomo** ECON autonomous expenditure; **~ de capital** COM GEN capital expenditure (*capex*), capital spending; **~ combinado** TRANSP joint charge; **~ computable** FISC eligible expense; **~ por concentración** TRANSP combination charge; **~ de consumo** ECON, V&M consumer expenditure; **~ corriente** ECON current spending; **~ corriente total** ECON total current spending; **~ por debajo del presupuesto** CONT, COM GEN underspending; **~ deducible** ECON, FIN, FISC qualified expenditure; **~ por depreciación anual** CONT annual depreciation charge; **~ de desembarque** *f* TRANSP landing charge; **~ devengado** CONT accrued expense; **~ del Estado** ECON government expenditure; **~ estatutario** ECON, POL statutory expenditure; **~ de expedición** COM GEN dispatching charge; **~ fijo** CONT fixed charge; **~ fiscal** ECON, FISC tax expenditure; **~ fiscal aumentado** FISC enriched tax expenditure; **~ fiscal negativo** FISC negative tax expenditure; **~ general del Estado** (*GGE*) ECON, POL general government expenditure (*GGE*); **~ incremental** V&M incremental spending; **~ en investigación científica** FISC *desgravaciones de capital* scientific research expenditure; **~ justificado** V&M defensive spending; **~ nacional bruto** ECON Gross National Expenditure; **~ menor de lo debido** CONT, COM GEN underspending; **~ neto de capital** ECON, FIN net capital expenditure, net capital spending; **~ no obligatorio** ECON noncompulsory expenditure; **~ no recurrente** CONT *cuentas anuales* nonrecurring charge; **~ obligatorio** ECON compulsory expenditure; **~ presupuestado** POL budget expenditure; **~ presupuestario** ECON, FIN budget expenditure; **~ previo a la producción** FISC preproduction expenditure; **~ público** ECON, POL government expenditure, public expenditure, public spending; **~ público total** ECON, POL total public expenditure, total public spending; **~ razonable** COM GEN reasonable expense; **~ regular** FIN regular expenditure; **~ de**

representación TRANSP agency fee; ~ **semivariable** COM GEN semivariable expense; ~ **de sociedad** FISC corporate spending; ~ **de transporte** TRANSP *mercancías* carrying charge; ~ **volátil de intereses** FIN interest-sensitive expenditure

gastos[1] *m pl* COM GEN expenses, charges, CONT expenses;

~ **a** ~ **de acarreo del transportista** TRANSP carrier's haulage; ~ **de acondicionamiento** INMOB *de una residencia* fixing-up expense (*infrml*); ~ **de administración** ADMIN, CONT administration costs, administration expenses; ~ **administrativos** ADMIN, CONT administrative burden, administrative expenses; ~ **de adquisición** COM GEN, CONT acquisition costs, acquisition fee; ~ **aduaneros** CONT, ECON, IMP/EXP tariff expenditures; ~ **de almacén** IMP/EXP depot charges; ~ **de almacén de la exportación** IMP/EXP export depot charges; ~ **de almacenaje** COM GEN, TRANSP storage charges, warehouse charges; ~ **de ampliación** CONT development charges; ~ **anticipados** CONT prepaid expenses, TRANSP charges prepaid; ~ **anuales de alquiler** FISC annual rental charges; ~ **de arreglo** INMOB *de una residencia* fixing-up expense (*infrml*); ~ **de atraque** TRANSP wharfage charges; ~ **autorizables** CONT allowable expenses;

~ **b** ~ **bancarios** BANCA activity charges;

~ **c** ~ **de la caja de seguridad** BANCA safety-deposit-box charges; ~ **de calle mayor** ECON high street spending (*BrE*), main street spending (*AmE*); ~ **de cancelación** COM GEN cancellation fee; ~ **de carga y descarga** TRANSP cargo handling charges (*CHC*); ~ **de cierre** INMOB *compraventa inmobiliaria* closing cost; ~ **de cobro** TRANSP collection charge; ~ **de combustible** FISC gasoline expenses (*AmE*); ~ **comerciales** COM GEN, CONT, V&M business charges, sale charges, selling expenses; ~ **de comercialización** COM GEN, CONT, V&M selling expenses; ~ **de conservación** COM GEN, FISC maintenance charges; ~ **contingentes** CONT contingent expenses; ~ **de la Corona** FISC Crown charges (*BrE*); ~ **de corretaje en operaciones a crédito** BOLSA carrying charges; ~ **corrientes y necesarios de explotación** FISC ordinary and necessary business expenses; ~ **por cuidado de menores** FISC childcare expenses;

~ **d** ~ **de debida diligencia** FIN, SEG due dilligence expenses; ~ **deducible** CONT, FISC allowable expenses; ~ **deficitarios** ECON deficit spending; ~ **del departamento del interior** FISC Home Office expenses (*BrE*); ~ **de depreciación** CONT depreciation expenses; ~ **de desarrollo** CONT development expenditures; ~ **de descuento** CONT discount charges; ~ **de la deuda** COM GEN debt charges; ~ **devengados** COM GEN accrued expenses; ~ **diferidos** CONT deferred charges; ~ **directos** COM GEN, IMP/EXP, TRANSP through rate; ~ **diversos** CONT miscellaneous expenses;

~ **e** ~ **en efectivo** COM GEN, CONT, FIN out-of-pocket costs, petty expenses; ~ **de embalaje** IND, V&M packing costs; ~ **de emisión** BOLSA flotation costs; ~ **de emisión de bonos** BOLSA, CONT bond issue expenses; ~ **de emisión de un préstamo** BANCA loan origination fee; ~ **de empleados** COM GEN employment expenses; ~ **de empleo** FISC employment expenses; ~ **de entrega** TRANSP delivery charge; ~ **de establecimiento** CONT formation expense; ~ **de estación de carga** TRANSP terminal charges; ~ **de estancia en puerto** TRANSP port disbursements; ~ **de estiba** TRANSP stowage;

~ **estimados** BANCA, CONT, FIN estimated charges; ~ **extraordinarios** CONT extraordinary charges, exceptional expenses, extraordinary expenses, extraordinary expenditure;

~ **f** ~ **de fabricación** CONT manufacturing expenses, manufacturing overheads; ~ **fijos** CONT fixed expenses; ~ **fijos proporcionales al tiempo** CONT times fixed charges; ~ **de financiación** CONT, FIN financing expenses; ~ **financieros** CONT finance charges; ~ **de formalización** INMOB *compraventa inmobiliaria* closing cost; ~ **de franqueo y empaquetado** *fra* COMS postage and packing (*p&p*); ~ **de funcionamiento** COM GEN operating expenditures; ~ **de fusión** COM GEN merger expenses;

~ **g** ~ **generales** COM GEN, CONT general expenses, overhead charges, overheads, standing expenses; ~ **generales de administración** COM GEN, FIN administrative overheads, RRHH general administrative expenses; ~ **generales aplicados** COM GEN, FIN applied overheads; ~ **generales directos** COM GEN, FIN direct overheads; ~ **generales de fábrica** CONT factory overheads; ~ **generales de fabricación** COM GEN overheads; ~ **generales de factoría** *ver gastos generales de fábrica*; ~ **generales fijos** CONT fixed overheads; ~ **generales de personal** RRHH personnel overheads; ~ **generales reales** COM GEN applied overheads; ~ **generales subutilizados** CONT underapplied overheads; ~ **de gerencia** CONT management expenses; ~ **de gestión** BANCA arrangement fee; ~ **a gran escala** FIN large exposure;

~ **h** ~ **de hospitalización** FISC hospital expenses;

~ **i** ~ **imprevistos** COM GEN *de vendedores*, CONT incidental charges, incidental expenses; ~ **incidentales** BOLSA carrying charges; ~ **incurridos** CONT, FIN incurred expenses, expenses incurred; ~ **indirectos** CONT, FIN indirect expenses; ~ **indirectos de fábrica** CONT factory overheads; ~ **indirectos de factoría** *ver gastos indirectos de fábrica*; ~ **de inhumación** SEG funeral expenses; ~ **de instalación** FIN initial expenditure; ~ **de instalación no amortizados** FIN undepreciated capital cost; ~ **de intereses** *m* CONT interest charges; ~ **por intereses de una inversión** FISC investment interest expense; ~ **de inversión** COM GEN, FISC investment expense, investment spending; ~ **de investigación y desarrollo** FISC scientific research and experimental development expenditure;

~ **j** ~ **judiciales** DER legal charges;

~ **l** ~ **de liquidación** SEG adjustment costs, claims expenses;

~ **m** ~ **de manipulación de la carga** TRANSP cargo handling charges (*CHC*); ~ **de mantenimiento** CONT, FIN operating costs, running costs, running expenses, PROT SOC living expenses, maintenance expenses; ~ **de matrícula** PROT SOC tuition fees; ~ **médicos** PROT SOC, SEG medical expenses; ~ **menores** COM GEN, CONT, FIN out-of-pocket costs, petty expenses; ~ **mensuales** COM GEN monthly expenses;

~ **n** ~ **del negocio** COM GEN business expenses; ~ **netos** CONT cash disbursement; ~ **no absorbidos o aplicados** CONT underabsorbed expenses;

~ **o** ~ **de oficina** CONT office expenses; ~ **de operación** ECON, FIN capital outlay; ~ **de operaciones** COM GEN operating expenditures; ~ **de organización** BANCA set-up costs;

~ **p** ~ **pagados** CONT prepaid charges; ~ **pagados por** anticipado CONT prepaid expenses; ~ **de peritación** COM GEN survey fees; ~ **de personal** CONT, RRHH personnel expenses; ~ **personales** FISC personal expenses; ~ **de pleito y trabajo** SEG sue and labour charges (*BrE*); ~ **preliminares** CONT preliminary expenses; ~ **prepagados** IMP/EXP charges prepaid; ~ **de préstamo** BANCA loan fee; ~ **de previsión social** COM GEN social spending; ~ **de procesamiento** BANCA processing fee; ~ **proporcionales al tiempo** CONT times fixed charges; ~ **de protesto** DER protest charges; ~ **de publicidad** FIN, V&M advertising expenditure, advertising expense; ~ **en publicidad indirecta** MEDIOS, V&M below-the-line (*jarg*); ~ **publicitarios** CONT, FIN, V&M publicity expenses, advertising expenses;

~ r ~ **reales** CONT actual expenditures; ~ **realizados** CONT incurred expenses; ~ **reglamentarios** FIN, POL statutory expenditure; ~ **por residir fuera del domicilio familiar** CONT, FISC away-from-home expenses;

~ s ~ **de salvamento** TRANSP salvage charges; ~ **de secretaría** FISC registrar fee; ~ **de seguridad social** CONT, RRHH social expenditure; ~ **sociales totales** CONT, POL, PROT SOC total social charges; ~ **de subvenciones** FIN grants expenditures; ~ **suplidos** SEG substituted expenses;

~ t ~ **del titular de la tarjeta** BANCA cardholder fee; ~ **de tramitación** BANCA negotiation fee; ~ **de transacción** BANCA transaction fee; ~ **de transferencia** COM GEN handling charges; ~ **de transformación** CONT manufacturing overheads, manufacturing expenses; ~ **de transmisión** CONT *de ganancias, pérdidas* transmission expenses; ~ **de transporte** TRANSP transportation expenses, *envíos* carriage expenses; ~ **de transporte en camión** TRANSP trucking charges; ~ **de tratamiento médico** SEG cost of medical treatment;

~ v ~ **variables** COM GEN variable expenses; ~ **varios** COM GEN sundry expenses, CONT miscellaneous expenses; ~ **de venta** COM GEN selling expenses; ~ **de viaje** RRHH travel expenses, traveling expenses (*AmE*), travelling expenses (*BrE*)

gastos[2]: **todos los ~ pagados** *fra* COM GEN all expenses paid

generación *f* COM GEN *de beneficios* generation; ~ **de electricidad** IND electricity generation (*BrE*), power generation (*AmE*); ~ **de energía** IND power generation; ~ **espontánea** COM GEN autogeny; ~ **de estados** INFO report generation; ~ **de producto** V&M product generation; **segunda ~** INFO *ordenadores* second generation (*jarg*)

generador *m* COM GEN generator; ~ **de números aleatorios** INFO, MAT *estadística* random-number generator

generales *m pl AmL* (*cf información general Esp*) RRHH personal particulars

generalista *mf* RRHH generalist

generalmente *adv* COM GEN overall

generar *vt* COM GEN *residuos, energía* generate; ◆ ~ **beneficios** BOLSA generate profits; ~ **ideas** COM GEN generate ideas; ~ **ingresos** BOLSA generate income

genérico *adj* COM GEN, V&M generic

género: ~ **trasladado** *m* V&M forward stock

géneros: ~ **a condición** *fra* COM GEN, V&M goods on approval

generoso *adj* FISC *desgravación fiscal* generous

gente: ~ **de comercio** *f* COM GEN tradespeople; ~ **selecta** *f* COM GEN smart set

geodemografía *f* V&M *investigación de mercado* geodemography

geografía: ~ **económica** *f* ECON economic geography

geográfico *adj* COM GEN geographic, geographical

geopolítico *adj* POL geopolitical

gerencia *f* GES, RRHH management; ~ **de calidad** GES quality management; ~ **de calidad total** GES total quality management; ~ **de canales** GES channel management; ~ **de carteras** COM GEN portfolio management; ~ **de las comunicaciones** GES, MEDIOS communication management; ~ **corporativa** GES corporate management; ~ **departamental** COM GEN, GES departmental management; ~ **por departamentos** COM GEN, GES departmental management; ~ **de desarrollo** COM GEN, GES development management; ~ **de la distribución física** GES, TRANSP physical distribution management (*PDM*); ~ **de energía** GES, IND, MED AMB energy management; ~ **por excepción** GES management by exception; ~ **de fábrica** GES, IND plant management; ~ **financiera** CONT, FIN financial management; ~ **de funciones** GES functional management; ~ **general** GES, RRHH general management; ~ **de los horarios de trabajo** GES time management; ~ **intermedia** GES, RRHH middle management; ~ **internacional** GES international management; ~ **de inventario** GES inventory management; ~ **de inversiones** GES investment management; ~ **de línea** GES, RRHH line management; ~ **de línea y staff** RRHH line and staff management; ~ **de la matriz** GES matrix management; ~ **del medio ambiente** GES, MED AMB environmental management; ~ **del mercado** V&M market management; ~ **múltiple** GES multiple management; ~ **de oficina** COM GEN, GES office management; ~ **de operaciones** COM GEN, GES operations management; ~ **operativa** GES operating management; ~ **participativa** GES participative management; ~ **del personal** GES, RRHH personnel management, staff management; ~ **de primera línea** GES first-line management; ~ **del producto** GES product management; ~ **de recursos** COM GEN, GES resource management; ~ **de registros** GES records management; ~ **con riesgo** COM GEN venture management; ~ **de riesgos** GES risk management; ~ **de seguridad** GES, RRHH, SEG safety management; ~ **de sistemas** GES, INFO systems management; ~ **de supervisión** GES, RRHH supervisory management; ~ **de tarea** GES task management; ~ **de la tesorería** GES cash management; ~ **de ventas** GES, V&M sales management

gerencial *adj* GES managerial

gerente *mf* (*gte.*) COM GEN manager (*MGR*), manageress (*MGR*), GES, RRHH director (*dir.*); ~ **adjunto(-a)** *m,f* GES, RRHH deputy manager, junior manager; ~ **administrativo(-a) diplomado(-a)** *m,f* RRHH certified administration manager; ~ **de área** COM GEN section manager, RRHH area manager; ~ **de capacitación** *AmL* (*cf gerente de formación Esp, cf director de formación Esp*) GES, RRHH training manager; ~ **de compras** RRHH procurement manager; ~ **de contratación** RRHH recruitment manager; ~ **de créditos corporativos** BANCA corporate credit manager; ~ **de cuentas** MEDIOS *publicidad* account manager; ~ **departamental** RRHH departmental manager; ~ **del departamento** RRHH departmental manager; ~ **de distribución** GES, RRHH,

TRANSP distribution manager; **~ de distrito** GES, RRHH district manager; **~ de división** GES, RRHH division head, division manager; **~ de entrenamiento** *AmL* (*cf gerente de formación Esp, cf director de formación Esp*) GES, RRHH training manager; **~ ejecutivo(-a)** *m,f* COM GEN, GES, RRHH executive manager; **~ de fábrica** GES, IND, RRHH works manager, plant manager; **~ de fabricación** COM GEN, GES, IND, RRHH production manager; **~ financiero(-a)** *m,f* RRHH financial manager; **~ de flotilla** RRHH *coches*, TRANSP fleet manager; **~ de formación** *Esp* (*cf gerente de entrenamiento AmL, cf gerente de capacitación AmL*) GES, RRHH training manager; **~ en funciones** RRHH de facto manager; **~ general** GES, RRHH chief executive, chief executive officer (*AmE*) (*CEO*); **~ general ejecutivo(-a)** *m,f* GES, RRHH general executive manager; **~ de ingeniería** GES, RRHH engineering manager; **~ intermedio(-a)** *m,f* GES, RRHH middle manager; **~ de línea** RRHH line manager; **~ de marcas** V&M, RRHH brand manager; **~ medio(-a)** *m,f* GES, RRHH junior manager; **~ de operaciones** GES, RRHH operational manager, operations director, operations manager; **~ de personal** GES, RRHH personnel manager, staff manager; **~ de primera línea** RRHH first line manager; **~ de producción** COM GEN, GES, IND, RRHH production manager; **~-propietario(-a)** *m* GES, RRHH owner-manager; **~ de publicidad** RRHH, V&M advertising manager; **~ regional** GES, RRHH sectorial manager, district manager; **~ de relaciones industriales** RRHH industrial relations manager; **~ de relaciones laborales** *m* RRHH labor relations manager (*AmE*), labour relations manager (*BrE*); **~ de riesgos** FIN, RRHH risk manager; **~ de sucursal** RRHH branch office manager; **~ técnico(-a)** *m,f* INFO, RRHH technical manager; **~ de territorio** GES, RRHH district manager; **~ de tráfico** RRHH traffic manager; **~ de ventas** GES, RRHH, V&M sales manager

gerentes: **~ y empleados** *m pl* GES, RRHH managers and employees

germinación *f* V&M *de idea* seed

gestión *f* ADMIN, COM GEN, GES administration (*admin*), management; **~ activa** COM GEN, GES active management; **~ de activos** CONT, FIN asset management; **~ de activos y pasivos** (*GAP*) BANCA, FIN, GES asset-liability management (*ALM*); **~ al por menor** *Esp* (*cf administración de menudeo AmL*) IND, V&M retail management; **~ de almacén** COM GEN, GES, V&M stock management; **~ de un asunto** V&M *relaciones públicas* issue management (*jarg*); **~ autoritaria** GES, RRHH authoritarian management; **~ avanzada** V&M lead management; **~ a bordo** TRANSP shipboard management; **~ de caja** CONT cash management; **~ del calendario** GES calendar management; **~ de la calidad** *Esp* (*cf administración de la calidad AmL*) GES, IND, V&M quality control; **~ del cambio** GES change management; **~ de la carrera** GES, RRHH career management; **~ de carteras** FIN portfolio management; **~ científica** COM GEN, GES, MAT scientific management; **~ por contingencia** GES contingency management; **~ de crédito** CONT, FIN credit management; **~ de crisis** GES crisis management; **~ de una cuenta** BANCA account management; **~ de datos** INFO data management; **~ deficiente** GES, RRHH mismanagement; **~ democrática** POL, RRHH democratic management; **~ por departamentos** COM GEN, GES, RRHH divisional management; **~ del desarrollo profesional** GES, RRHH career management; **~ descentralizada** GES, POL decentralized management; **~ de la deuda pública** DER, POL national debt management (*BrE*), public debt management (*AmE*); **~ del dinero** FIN money management; **~ directa** GES first-line management; **~ de la distribución física** GES, TRANSP physical distribution management (*PDM*); **~ efectiva** GES, RRHH effective management; **~ de empresas** COM GEN business administration, business management; **~ de existencias** FIN, IND inventory management; **~ de ficheros** INFO file management; **~ fiduciaria** DER trusteeship; **~ financiera** FIN financial administration, financial management; **~ financiera internacional** FIN international financial management; **~ fiscal** FISC fiscal planning; **~ de los flujos de trabajo** V&M *publicidad* traffic planning; **~ de fondos** BANCA *banca de inversión* fund management; **~ funcional** GES functional management; **~ general** GES general management; **~ impositiva** GES, RRHH macho management; **~ inmobiliaria** INMOB property management; **~ integrada de proyectos** FIN, GES integrated project management (*IPM*); **~ intuitiva** GES, RRHH intuitive management; **~ de inventarios** CONT inventory management; **~ de inversiones** FIN investment management; **~ judicial** COM GEN receivership; **~ laboral** RRHH labor administration (*AmE*), labour administration (*BrE*); **~ lineal y funcional** RRHH line and staff management; **~ de liquidez** CONT, GES cash management; **~ de la marca** V&M brand management; **~ de materiales** TRANSP materials management; **~ por matrices** MAT matrix management; **~ del mercado** V&M market management; **~ minorista** *Esp* (*cf administración de menudeo AmL*) IND, V&M retail management; **~ por objetivos** GES management by objectives (*MBO*); **~ del pasivo** BANCA liability management; **~ de la pequeña empresa** COM GEN, GES small business administration (*SBA*); **~ del personal** GES, RRHH personnel administration, personnel management, staff management; **~ portuaria** TRANSP port management; **~ presupuestaria** CONT, GES budget management; **~ de la producción** IND production management; **~ programada** GES programmed management; **~ de proyectos** COM GEN project management; **~ racionalizada** GES rational management; **~ de recursos** COM GEN, GES resource management; **~ de recursos humanos** RRHH human resource administration, human resource management (*HRM*); **~ de los recursos naturales** MED AMB natural resources management; **~ de recursos y políticas** COM GEN, GES policy and resource management; **~ de la red** BANCA networking; **~ de redes** INFO networking; **~ de los residuos** COM GEN waste management; **~ de riesgos** BOLSA, FIN, GES risk management; **~ de sistemas** GES, INFO systems management; **~ de una sociedad inversora por obligaciones** BOLSA unit trust management; **~ de sueldos y salarios** RRHH wage and salary administration; **~ de tareas** INFO task management; **~ de tesorería** CONT, GES cash management; **~ de transacciones** INFO transaction management; **~ vertical** GES top-down management

gestionado: **~ por programa** *adj* INFO software-driven

gestiones: **~ especiales** *f pl* COM GEN special arrangements

gestor, a *m,f* INFO *de programas* administrator, RRHH manager (*MGR*); **~ administrativo(-a)** ADMIN, RRHH administrative agent; ~ **de la cartera de valores** BANCA, BOLSA portfolio manager; ~ **de centro de responsabilidad** CONT, FIN, GES, RRHH responsibility center manager (*AmE*), responsibility centre manager (*BrE*); ~ **de cuentas** BANCA account manager; ~ **fiscal** FISC tax practitioner; ~ **de fondos** FIN *pensiones* fund manager; ~ **de riesgos** FIN, GES, SEG risk manager; ~ **del sindicato** BANCA *financiación corporativa* syndicate manager

gestora *f* COM GEN manageress (*MGR*)

gestoría *f* ADMIN, BANCA, COM GEN, FIN *instituciones fiduciarias* agency (*agcy, agy.*)

GGE *abr Esp* (*gasto general del Estado*) ECON, POL GGE (*general government expenditure*)

Gigante: ~ **Azul** *m* INFO *compañía IBM* Big Blue (*infrml*)

gigantomanía *f* RRHH gigantomania (*jarg*)

gigantomaníaco *adj* RRHH gigantomaniac (*jarg*)

gigaocteto *m* INFO gigabyte (*Gb*)

GIGO *abr* (*entrada descontrolada/salida descontrolada*) INFO GIGO (*garbage-in/garbage-out*)

gira *f* OCIO tour; ~ **publicitaria** V&M advertising tour; ◆ **de ~** OCIO on tour, on the road

girado, -a *m,f* ADMIN, BANCA, FIN drawee

girador, a *m,f* ADMIN, BANCA, FIN check signer (*AmE*), cheque signer (*BrE*), drawer

girar *vi* COM GEN, DER draft; ◆ ~ **contra los ahorros** FIN draw on savings

giro *m* COM GEN sight draft (*S/D*); ~ **aceptado** BANCA accepted draft; ~ **avalado** BANCA accommodation draft; ~ **bancario** BANCA bank draft (*B/D*), bank giro (*BrE*); ~ **cablegráfico** COMS cable transfer; ~ **en divisas** BANCA currency draft; ~ **documentario** BANCA, IMP/EXP, TRANSP documentary draft; ~ **de favor** COM GEN, FIN accommodation draft; ~ **de una letra** BANCA drawing of bill; ~ **monetario internacional** BANCA international money draft; ~ **del negocio** COM GEN line of business; ~ **postal** COM GEN Bank Giro (*BrE*), giro, Post Office Giro, postal money order (*AmE*), postal order (*BrE*) (*p.o.*), CONT postal remittance; ~ **postal internacional** BANCA world money order, international money order (*IMO*); ~ **renovado** BANCA redraft; ~ **telegráfico** COM GEN, COMS telegraphic money order (*TMO*), wire transfer; ~ **a la vista** BANCA demand draft (*DD*), sight draft, stock draft

girocompás *m* TRANSP gyrocompass (*GC*)

global *adj* COM GEN, aggregate, overall (*oa*), global, *respuesta* comprehensive, blanket, ECON *cantidad, pedido*, MAT aggregate

globalización *f* COM GEN globalization

globalizar *vt* COM GEN globalize, ECON, MAT aggregate

glorieta *f* COM GEN roundabout (*BrE*), traffic circle (*AmE*)

glosario *m* COM GEN glossary

Gobernador, a *m,f* POL Governor General; ~ **del Banco de España** ECON ≈ Governor of the Bank of England

gobierno[1]: **de ~ a gobierno** *adj* COM GEN government-to-government

gobierno[2] *m* DER steering, ECON, POL government (*govt*); ~ **central** COM GEN, POL central government; ~ **de coalición** POL coalition government; ~ **débil** POL unstable government; ~ **descentralizado** POL descentralized government; ~ **federal** POL federal government;

~ **inestable** POL unstable government; ~ **municipal** POL municipal government; ~ **sindical** RRHH union government

Gobierno: **the ~** *m* POL the Government

goleta *f* TRANSP schooner (*Sr*)

golpe *m* COM GEN knock; ~ **de inspiración** COM GEN flash of inspiration; ~ **rápido** FISC quick flip; ~ **sindical** RRHH union bashing (*jarg*); ~ **de suerte** *infrml* COM GEN break (*infrml*); ◆ ~ **por golpe** SEG *acuerdo* knock-for-knock (*jarg*)

góndola *f* TRANSP *ferrocarril*, V&M *supermercado* gondola (*jarg*)

gotear *vt* COM GEN *información* leak (*infrml*)

goteo *m* V&M drip

gr. *abr* (*gramo*) COM GEN g (*gram, gramme*)

grabación: ~ **en cinta** *f* COM GEN, MEDIOS tape recording; ~ **reciente** *f* BOLSA late tape; ~ **en video** *AmL ver* grabación en vídeo *Esp*; ~ **en vídeo** *f Esp* COMS video tape recording (*VTR*); ~ **en videocasete** *f* COMS, V&M videocassette recording

grabador, a: ~ **de datos** *m,f* INFO data entry operator

grabadora: ~ **de casetes** *f* INFO, MEDIOS cassette tape recorder; ~ **de cinta** *f* INFO magnetic tape recorder

grabados: **con ~** *fra* COM GEN graphically illustrated

grabar: ~ **en video** *AmL ver* grabar en vídeo *Esp*; ~ **en vídeo** *fra Esp* COMS, INFO, MEDIOS videotape; ~ **en video una entrevista** *AmL ver* grabar en vídeo una entrevista *Esp*; ~ **en vídeo una entrevista** *fra Esp* COMS, MEDIOS videotape an interview

gracias: ~ **anticipadas** *fra* COMS thanking you in advance, thanking you in anticipation; ~ **por anticipado** *fra* COMS thanking you in advance, thanking you in anticipation; ~ **por su carta** *fra* COMS thank you for your letter

grado *m* COM GEN *medida* degree, *de protección* extent; ~ **de concentración** ECON concentration ratio; ~ **de consumo** ECON level of consumption; ~ **de correlación** MAT degree of correlation; ~ **del daño** SEG degree of damage; ~ **de exactitud** COM GEN degree of accuracy; ~ **de fluctuación** BOLSA *precios futuros* degree of fluctuation; ~ **de invalidez** SEG degree of disablement; ~ **de monopolio** ECON degree of monopoly; ~ **óptimo** ECON, FIN optimal rate; ~ **óptimo de polución** MED AMB optimal rate of pollution; ~ **de rendimiento** BANCA, CONT, PROT SOC earning capacity; ~ **de riesgo** BOLSA *en el mercado*, COM GEN degree of risk; ~ **de saturación** MAT load factor; ~ **de significación** *Esp* (*cf grado de sinificancia AmL*) MAT significance level; ~ **de significancia** *AmL* (*cf grado de significación Esp*) MAT significance level; ~ **de solvencia estimado** BANCA, FIN credit rating; ~ **de utilización de la capacidad productiva** ECON, SEG capacity utilization rate; ~ **de utilización del capital** ECON capital utilization rate

graduado *m* RRHH graduate; ~ **cum laude** COM GEN honors graduate (*AmE*), honours graduate (*BrE*)

Graduado: ~ **Escolar** *m obs* COM GEN Spanish school leavers' certificate, ≈ General Certificate of Education (*obs*) (*BrE*) (*GCE*), ≈ General Certificate of Secondary Education (*BrE*) (*GCSE*)

gradual *adj* COM GEN gradual

gradualismo *m* POL gradualism

gradualmente *adv* COM GEN gradually

gráfica f COM GEN, INFO, MAT *diagrama, gráfico* chart; ~ **de utilidad** FIN profit graph

graficar vt AmL (cf *dibujar* Esp) COM GEN chart, MAT, V&M draw, graph, plot

gráficas: ~ **de gestión** f pl INFO business graphics; ~ **de Hicks** f pl ECON Hicks Charts

gráfico m COM GEN chart, graphic; ~ **de actividades múltiples** INFO multiple-activity chart; ~ **de barras** COM GEN bar chart, INFO, MAT bar chart, bar graph; ~ **de circulación** CONT flowchart; ~ **circular** COM GEN, INFO, MAT pie chart; ~ **de correspondencia** GES pertinence chart; ~ **cronológico** INFO, MAT periodgram; ~ **de punto y figura** BOLSA point-and-figure chart; ~ **de puntos** INFO, MAT dot chart; ~ **de ratios** MAT ratio chart; ~ **de sectores** COM GEN, INFO, MAT pie chart; ~ **de SIMO** ADMIN SIMO chart

gráficos m pl COM GEN graphics; ~ **comerciales** COM GEN business graphics; ~ **de gestión** COM GEN business graphics

grafista: ~ **de bolsa** mf BOLSA, ECON chartist

grafo m COM GEN chart, chart, graph

gramo m (gr.) COM GEN gram (g), gramme (g)

gran[1]: ~ **almacén** m V&M department store; ~ **cifra** f BOLSA *término del arbitrajista* big figure; ~ **disparo** m BOLSA Big Bang; ~ **despliegue publicitario** m MEDIOS hype; ~ **escala de integración** f (LSI) INFO very large scale integration (LSI); ~ **inversor, a** m,f BOLSA largest investor, FIN big investor; ~ **perceptor, a de renta** m,f COM GEN big income earner; ~ **salto hacia adelante** m ECON *agricultura* Great Leap Forward; ~ **usuario, -a industrial** m,f COM GEN big industrial user

gran[2]: **de ~ volumen** fra BOLSA high-volume; **en ~ parte** fra COM GEN to a large extent

Gran: ~ **Depresión** f ECON Great Depression

grandes: ~ **bancos** m pl BANCA big banks; ~ **masas** f pl POL broad masses; ~ **riesgos** m pl SEG large risks

granel m COM GEN, TRANSP bulk; ◆ **a ~** COM GEN in bulk

granero m TRANSP granary

granja: ~ **cooperativa** f ECON, POL cooperative farm; ~ **lechera** f Esp (cf *tambo* AmL) ECON dairy farm

grapadora f COM GEN stapler

grapón: ~ **de barril** m TRANSP *carga* barrel hook

GRASEFI abr (*Gravamen sobre los Servicios Financieros*) FIN financial services tax

gratificación f COM GEN perk (infrml), perquisite, FISC gratuity, RRHH perk (infrml), perquisite; ~ **de capital** BOLSA, SEG capital bonus; ~ **intangible** RRHH intangible reward

gratificante adj COM GEN rewarding

gratis adv COM GEN gratis, without charge (w.c.)

gratuito adj COM GEN free, *préstamo* gratuitous

gravable adj COM GEN taxable, *valor* ratable

gravado adj COM GEN taxable, *sujeto a gravamen* encumbered, taxed; ◆ **no ~** DER, INMOB free and clear (AmE); **no ~ por completo** FISC *declaración* not clean assessed; ~ **en origen** FISC taxed at source; ~ **con la tarifa vigente** FISC standard-rated

gravamen m BANCA pledge, CONT tax, DER encumbrance, lien, ECON tax, burden, FISC tax, IMP/EXP levy; ~ **bancario en prevención** BANCA bank lien; ~ **continuado** FISC floating lien; ~ **convenido** FISC conventional lien; ~ **equitativo** FISC equitable lien; ~ **estatutario** FISC statutory lien; ~ **por fallo** DER judgment lien (AmE); ~ **financiero** FIN financial encumbrance; ~ **inferior** DER junior lien; ~ **inicial** FISC **de rendimiento** initial assessment; ~ **por juicio** DER judgment lien (AmE); ~ **liquidado** FISC satisfied lien; ~ **local** TRANSP local charge; ~ **marítimo** DER maritime lien; ~ **municipal** FISC civil assessment; ~ **no liquidado** FISC unsatisfied lien; ~ **del personal** FISC staff levy; ~ **preferente** FISC preferred lien; ~ **superpuesto** FISC superimposed tax; ~ **de transportista** TRANSP carrier's lien; ~ **tributario** FISC levy

Gravamen: ~ **sobre los Servicios Financieros** m (*GRASEFI*) FIN financial services tax

gravar vt DER levy, FISC assess, levy, tax; ◆ ~ **adicionalmente** FISC charge on top; ~ **un impuesto sobre algo** FISC impose a tax on sth

gravedad: ~ **específica** f COM GEN specific gravity (SG)

gremio m RRHH craft union, guild

grillete m TRANSP *carga* shackle

grotesca f MEDIOS *tipografía* sans serif

grúa f TRANSP crane (Cr); ~ **canguro** TRANSP kangaroo crane; ~ **de descarga** TRANSP unloader crane; ~ **fija** TRANSP fixed crane; ~ **de inclinación variable** TRANSP *carga* luffing crane; ~ **de mástil para cargas pesadas** TRANSP heavy lift mast crane; ~ **móvil** TRANSP mobile crane (MC); ~ **de plataforma** TRANSP platform crane (Pc); ~ **de portal** TRANSP portainer crane; ~ **de pórtico** TRANSP *carga* gantry crane, portal crane, gantry; ~ **sobre camión** TRANSP lorry-mounted crane (BrE), truck-mounted crane (AmE)

grueso m COM GEN *de la cartera de valores* bulk

grupaje m TRANSP groupage

grupo m COM GEN group; ~ **de activos** CONT group of assets; ~ **analizado** V&M focus group; ~ **asesor** COM GEN advisory group; ~ **asociado** COM GEN affiliated group; ~ **de auditoría** CONT audit group; ~ **autónomo de trabajo** RRHH autonomous work groups; ~ **bancario** BANCA bank group (AmE), banking group (BrE), group of banks; ~ **de bancos** BANCA banking group (BrE), group of banks; ~ **de Cairn** ECON *de países exportados agrónomos* Cairn's Group; ~ **cerrado de inversores** BOLSA can crowd (infrml); ~ **de clientes conectados** COM GEN group of connected clients; ~ **de compañías** COM GEN group of companies; ~ **de compra** FIN purchase group; ~ **conservacionista** MED AMB, POL conservation camp; ~ **consultivo** ADMIN, POL consultative group; ~ **de control** V&M control group; ~ **creativo** V&M creative group; ~ **de cuentas** CONT set of accounts, V&M account group; ~ **de desgravación de los gastos de capital** FISC capital cost allowance class; ~ **de despacho** TRANSP clearance group (CG); ~ **de dirección** GES management group; ~ **de discusión** V&M discussion group; ~ **disidente** POL splinter group; ~ **de edades de consumidores** V&M consumer age group; ~ **empresarial financiero** FIN financial holding group; ~ **de empresas** COM GEN consortium, corporate group; ~ **de empresas asociadas** COM GEN group of affiliated companies; ~ **de entradas netas** CONT net receipts pool; ~ **escindido** POL splinter group; ~ **estratégico** V&M *investigación de mercado* target group; ~ **estudiado** V&M focus group; ~ **de estudios** COM GEN study group; ~ **etario** COM GEN *investigación de mercado* age group, age bracket; ~ **de expertos** COM GEN panel of experts, think-tank (infrml), RRHH brains trust; ~ **de fondos** FIN funding group; ~ **de ingresos** V&M *investigación de* *mercado* income group; ~ **de ingresos más altos** ECON higher income bracket; ~ **de ingresos más bajos** ECON lower income bracket; ~ **de ingresos medios** ECON middle-income bracket; ~ **de interés** COM GEN interest group; ~ **de inversión** FIN investor group; ~ **naviero consultivo** TRANSP consultative shipping group (*CSG*); ~ **negociador en convenios colectivos** RRHH bargaining unit; ~ **no competidor** RRHH noncompeting group; ~ **paraguas** FIN umbrella group; ~ **paritario** V&M peer group; ~ **político** POL political group; ~ **de presión** POL pressure group, lobby group; ~ **de presión de los agricultores** POL farm lobby; ~ **de presión ecologista** MED AMB, POL environmental lobby; ~ **de presión de la pequeña empresa** POL small business lobby (*jarg*); ~ **de presión verde** MED AMB, POL green lobby; ~ **prestamista** BOLSA loan crowd; ~ **de productos** V&M product group; ~ **de referencia** COM GEN reference group; ~ **relacionado** COM GEN related group; ~ **socioeconómico** ECON, PROT SOC, V&M socioeconomic groups; ~ **de tiendas** V&M store group; ~ **de toma de decisiones** ECON household decision making; ~ **de trabajo** COM GEN working party (*W/P*), POL working group; ~ **de usuarios** INFO user group; ~ **de ventas** V&M selling group; ~ **voluntario** V&M voluntary group

Grupo: ~ **del Banco Mundial** *m* BANCA, ECON, FIN World Bank Group; ~ **Consultor de Comercio Latinoamericano** *m* ECON, POL Latin American Trade Advisory Group (*LATAG*); ~ **Internacional para la Seguridad de los Petroleros y las Terminales** *m* IND International Oil Tanker and Terminal Safety Group (*IOTTSG*); ~ **de Política Económica de Cambridge** *m* ECON Cambridge Economic Policy Group; ~ **de los Siete** *m* (*G-7*) COM GEN, ECON, POL Group of Seven (*G-7*)

G-7 *abr* (*Grupo de los Siete*) COM GEN, ECON, POL G-7 (*Group of Seven*)

gte. *abr* (*gerente*) GES, RRHH, dir. (*director*)

guarda: ~ **de almacén** *mf* RRHH storeman (*BrE*), stockman (*AmE*), warehouseman (*AmE*)

guardacostas[1] *m* TRANSP *buque* cutter (*ctr*)

guardacostas[2] *mf* RRHH *persona* coastguard (*CG*)

guardamuebles *m* COM GEN furniture warehouse

guardapolvo *m* INFO dust cover

guardar *vt* BANCA *dinero en banco* put away; ◆ ~ **bajo llave** BOLSA lock away (*jarg*); ~ **en bodega** *AmL* (*cf guardar en depósito Esp*) IMP/EXP warehouse; ~ **en depósito** *Esp* (*cf guardar en bodega AmL*) IMP/EXP warehouse; ~ **en reserva** COM GEN keep in reserve

guardarropa *m* OCIO, TRANSP cloakroom (*BrE*), restroom (*AmE*)

gubernamental *adj* COM GEN, POL governmental

guerra: ~ **comercial** *f* ECON *internacional*, POL trade war; ~ **de patentes** *f* DER, PATENT patent warfare; ~ **de precios** *f* COM GEN price war, TRANSP fare war; ~ **de tarifas** *f* COM GEN rate war, tariff war

Guerra: ~ **del Golfo** *f* POL Gulf War

guía *m* COM GEN guide, GES *persona* leader, IMP/EXP *aduanas* carnet, V&M *artículo* leader; ~ **administrativa** *f* GES management guide; ~ **de aduanas** *f* COM GEN, IMP/EXP customs manifest; ~ **aproximada** *f* COM GEN rough guide; ~ **de auditoría** *f* CONT audit guide; ~ **de carrera** *f* RRHH career guidance; ~ **celular** *f* TRANSP *contenedor* cell guide; ~ **clasificada** *f* V&M classified directory; ~ **de coste** *f* *Esp* (*cf guía de costo AmL*) ECON cost leader; ~ **de costo** *f* *AmL* (*cf guía de coste Esp*) ECON cost leader; ~ **del DOS** *f* INFO DOS prompt; ~ **del entrevistador** *f* RRHH interview guide; ~ **de flete aéreo** *f* COMS, IMP/EXP, TRANSP air bill of lading; ~ **de línea aérea** *f* OCIO airline guide; ~ **oficial de aerolíneas** *f* TRANSP official airline guide (*OAG*); ~ **de plataforma de carga** *f* TRANSP pallet track; ~ **profesional** PROT SOC vocational guide; ~ **de servicios** *f* COM GEN service handbook; ~ **telefónica** *f* COMS phone book; ~ **de teléfonos** *f* COMS telephone directory; ~ **de tránsito** *f* IMP/EXP transit bond note

guión *m* COM GEN, MEDIOS scenario, *tipografía* dash, *esquema* script, V&M script; ~ **cinematográfico** MEDIOS film script; ~ **gráfico** MEDIOS, V&M *publicidad* storyboard; ~ **de rodaje** MEDIOS, V&M shooting script

guionado *m* INFO hyphenation

gusto *m* COM GEN, V&M taste

H

ha *abr* (*hectárea*) COM GEN ha (*hectare*)

habeas corpus *m* DER *penal* habeas corpus

haber *m* BANCA credit balance, FIN credit side

haberes: ~ **de impuestos diferidos** *m pl* CONT, FISC deferred tax assets; ~ **que pierden valor** *m pl* CONT, FISC wasting assets

haberse: ~ **equivocado de profesión** *fra* RRHH be in the wrong job

habilidad *f* RRHH skill; ~ **administrativa** GES, RRHH management skill; ~ **manual** RRHH manual skill

habilitación *f* FISC eligibility

habilitado: ~ **para el retiro** *fra* RRHH eligible for retirement

habitación: ~ **doble** *f* OCIO double room, twin room; ~ **individual** *f* OCIO single room

habitante *mf* COM GEN inhabitant

hábitat *m* MED AMB *de vida salvaje* habitat

hábitos: ~ **del consumidor** *m pl* V&M consumer habits; ~ **de consumo** *m pl* V&M consumer habits; ~ **de selección de programas de los telespectadores** *m pl* MEDIOS *televisión* viewing habits

habituar *vt* INMOB inure

hablar *vi* COM GEN talk; ♦ ~ **de** COM GEN discuss; ~ **de algo con alguien** COM GEN have a word with sb about; ~ **de negocios** COM GEN talk business; ~ **del oficio** COM GEN talk shop (*infrml*); ~ **del trabajo** COM GEN talk shop (*infrml*)

hacedor, a: ~ **de política** *m,f* RRHH, POL policy maker

hacendado,-a *m,f* INMOB landowner

hacer *vt* COM GEN make, do; ♦ ~ **algo muy mal** *infrml* TRANSP make a pig's ear of sth (*infrml*); ~ **arqueo** BANCA, CONT cash up; ~ **un asiento contra alguien** CONT make an entry against sb; ~ **averiguaciones** COM GEN make enquiries; ~ **bajar** COM GEN *precios, tasa de inflación* bring down; ~ **balance** CONT strike a balance, draw up a balance sheet; ~ **borrón y cuenta nueva** COM GEN wipe the slate clean; ~ **caja** BANCA, CONT cash up; ~ **una cancelación** FIN make a killing (*infrml*); ~ **caso omiso de** COM GEN dispense with; ~ **un cheque** BANCA draw a check (*AmE*), draw a cheque (*BrE*); ~ **un cliché** ADMIN stencil; ~ **una concesión** COM GEN make an allowance; ~ **constar algo** COM GEN put sth on record; ~ **una copia de seguridad** INFO back up; ~ **un cumplido** COM GEN pay lip service; ~ **cumplir** DER enforce; ~ **un depósito** BANCA, BOLSA *a plazo de eurodólares* place a deposit; ~ **desaparecer** COM GEN sink; ~ **descuento** COM GEN discount; ~ **dinero** COM GEN make money, turn into cash; ~ **efectivo** BOLSA *bonos* cash in, COM GEN *contrato* implement; ~ **una encuesta** COM GEN carry out a survey, hold a survey, POL, V&M canvass; ~ **entrega** BOLSA *de divisa* make delivery; ~ **un error tipográfico** ADMIN mistype; ~ **escala** TRANSP stop over; ~ **una evaluación de algo** COM GEN make a valuation of sth; ~ **frente a** COM GEN confront, *problemas, responsabilidades* face up to, *críticas, ataques, futuro* face; ~ **huelga** COM GEN strike; ~ **huelga por simpatía** RRHH strike in sympathy; ~ **huelga por solidaridad** RRHH strike in sympathy;

~ **incursiones** COM GEN make inroads; ~ **inventario** COM GEN take stock; ~ **la liquidación voluntaria** COM GEN go into voluntary liquidation; ~ **una lista** COM GEN make a list; ~ **la lista final** COM GEN, RRHH shortlist; ~ **a medida** COM GEN, V&M customize; ~ **mella** COM GEN diminish; ~ **una oferta** BOLSA bid, COM GEN make a bid, *proyecto* tender; ~ **una oferta en firme** BOLSA make a firm bid; ~ **un pago** BANCA, COM GEN make a down payment, make a payment; ~ **pasta rápidamente** COM GEN earn a fast buck (*infrml*); ~ **un pedido** COM GEN, V&M place an order; ~ **un plano** INMOB plan; ~ **preparativos** COM GEN plan ahead; ~ **un préstamo** BANCA make a loan; ~ **la primera jugada** COM GEN make the first move; ~ **progresos** COM GEN make headway; ~ **provisión para** COM GEN allow for; ~ **provisiones** COM GEN *situaciones excepcionales* make allowances; ~ **publicidad de** COM GEN, MEDIOS, V&M advertise for; ~ **público** COM GEN prove; ~ **rápidos progresos** COM GEN make quick progress; ~ **un recado** COM GEN run an errand; ~ **una reclamación** COM GEN lodge a complaint; ~ **responsable a alguien de algo** COM GEN hold sb responsible for sth, hold sb liable for sth; ~ **un trato** COM GEN strike a deal; ~ **un trato provechoso** COM GEN drive a hard bargain; ~ **trueques** ECON barter; ~ **una venta** BOLSA make a sale

hacerse: ~ **cargo de las deudas de alguien** *fra* COM GEN, FIN take over sb's debts; ~ **cargo de una emisión** *fra* BOLSA take over an issue; ~ **con lo mejor** *fra* COM GEN *dinero, demanda* cream off the best (*infrml*); ~ **rico** *fra* COM GEN get rich (*infrml*), strike it rich (*infrml*)

hacienda *f* INMOB homestead (*AmE*), farmstead (*BrE*); ~ **pública** FIN government finance

Hacienda: ~ **Pública** *f* ECON, FISC, POL *fiscalía, comercio, turismo* ≈ The Treasury (*BrE*), ≈ Treasury Department (*AmE*)

halagüeño *adj* COM GEN *perspectivas* rosy

hallar: ~ **el bruto** *fra* CONT gross up

halo *m* V&M *publicidad* halo (*jarg*)

hardware *m* INFO hardware

hecho[1]: ~ **para durar** *adj* COM GEN, IND made to last; ~ **de encargo** *adj* COM GEN, IND custom-made; ~ **a mano** *adj* COM GEN, IND, V&M handmade; ~ **a máquina** *adj* COM GEN, IND machine-made; ~ **a medida** *adj* COM GEN, IND, V&M customized, tailor-made, made to measure

hecho[2]: ~ **consumado** *m* COM GEN fait accompli; ~ **fortuito** *m* COM GEN, DER fortuitous event; ~ **imposible** *m* FISC taxable event; ~ **material** *m* COM GEN material fact; ~ **posterior** *m* COM GEN subsequent event; ~ **posterior al balance general** *m* CONT *auditoría* post balance sheet event; ~ **sin precedentes** *m* COM GEN unrecorded deed; ~ **verificado** *m* COM GEN ascertained fact

hecho[3]: **de** ~ *fra* DER de facto

hechos[1]: ~ **no consecutivos** *m pl* COM GEN disjoint events; ~ **y números** *m pl* COM GEN facts and figures; ~ **posteriores a la fecha de cierre** *m pl* CONT events subsequent to the closing date

hechos[2]: **de ~ posteriores** *fra* DER ex post facto

hectárea *f* (*ha*) COM GEN hectare (*ha*)

hedging *m* BANCA hedging

hegemonía *f* POL hegemony

heliestación *f* TRANSP helistop

heliográfica *f* COM GEN blueprint

helipuerto *m* TRANSP heliport

heredar *vt* DER, FISC, INMOB inherit

heredero, -a *m,f* DER, FISC, INMOB heir; **~ legítimo(-a)** DER, FISC, INMOB rightful heir

herederos: ~ y sucesores *m pl* DER *escrituras y sucesiones* heirs and assigns

herencia *f* DER, FISC, INMOB devise, inheritance

hermético *adj* COM GEN *envase, precinto* airtight

herramienta *f* COM GEN, INFO tool; **~ de marketing** V&M marketing tool; **~ de producción** COM GEN production implement; **~ de trabajo** COM GEN tool of the trade; **~ de ventas** V&M sales tool

heterogéneo *adj* COM GEN heterogeneous

heteroscedasticidad *f* MAT heteroscedasticity

heurística *f* COM GEN, GES, INFO heuristics

heurístico *adj* COM GEN, GES, INFO heuristic

híbrido *adj* INFO hybrid

hidroala *f* TRANSP hydrofoil

hidrocarburo *m* MED AMB hydrocarbon

hidroeléctrico *adj* IND, MED AMB *energía* hydroelectric (*hydro*)

hidrogenerado *adj* IND, MED AMB *electricidad* water-generated

higiene: ~ industrial *f* RRHH industrial health, industrial hygiene; **~ medioambiental** *f* MED AMB environmental hygiene; **~ en el trabajo** *f* RRHH industrial hygiene

hijo *m* COM GEN child, junior (*jnr., jr.*); **~ dependiente** FISC dependent child

hiperinflación *f* ECON hyperinflation

hiperinflacionista *mf* ECON hyperinflationist

hipermercado *m* V&M hypermarket, superstore; **~ perteneciente a una cadena** V&M chain superstore

hipoteca *f* COM GEN mortgage (*mortg.*), ECON *gasto* hypothecation; **~ abierta** BANCA, FIN, INMOB open mortgage; **~ de la administración de veteranos** BANCA, INMOB veterans' administration mortgage; **~ de amortización rápida** BANCA, FIN growing-equity mortgage (*GEM*); **~ ampliable** BANCA, FIN, INMOB open-ended mortgage; **~ anual constante** BANCA, FIN, INMOB, MAT annual mortgage constant; **~ de apertura y cierre** BANCA, INMOB open-ended mortgage; **~ autoamortizable** BANCA, INMOB self-amortizing mortgage; **~ cerrada** BANCA, INMOB closed-end mortgage; **~ colectiva** BANCA, INMOB blanket mortgage; **~ convencional** BANCA, INMOB conventional mortgage; **~ de dinero de compra** BANCA, INMOB purchase money mortgage; **~ fiduciaria** BANCA, INMOB trust mortgage; **~ fundamental** BANCA, INMOB underlying mortgage; **~ con garantía de otra hipoteca** BANCA, INMOB submortgage; **~ garantizada** BANCA, INMOB guaranteed mortgage; **~ general** BANCA, INMOB general mortgage; **~ a la gruesa** SEG *seguro marítimo* bottomry bond; **~ implícita** BANCA, INMOB underlying mortgage; **~ inversa de pago anual** BANCA, INMOB reverse annuity mortgage; **~ limitada** BANCA, INMOB closed-end mortgage; **~ a medio plazo** BANCA, INMOB rollover mortgage; **~ no residencial** BANCA, INMOB nonresiden-

tial mortgage; **~ a pagar** BANCA, FIN, INMOB mortgage payable; **~ de pago fijo** BANCA, INMOB take-out loan; **~ de pagos flexibles** BANCA, FIN flexible-payment mortgage (*FPM*); **~ de pagos proporcionales** BANCA, INMOB graduated payment mortgage; **~ de pagos variables** BANCA, FIN flexible-payment mortgage (*FPM*); **~ en paquete** BANCA, FIN, INMOB package mortgage; **~ parcial del precio de compra** BANCA, FIN, INMOB purchase money mortgage; **~ de plusvalía compartida** BANCA, INMOB shared appreciation mortgage; **~ presupuestaria** BANCA, INMOB budget mortgage; **~ de prioridad** BANCA, INMOB underlying mortgage; **~ refinanciada** BANCA, INMOB wraparound mortgage; **~ de la residencia** BANCA, INMOB home mortgage; **~ residencial** BANCA, INMOB residential mortgage; **~ de revalorización compartida** BANCA, INMOB shared appreciation mortgage; **~ en segundo grado** BANCA, INMOB junior mortgage (*AmE*), second mortgage (*BrE*); **~ sobre bienes muebles** BANCA, INMOB chattel mortgage; **~ sobre inmueble arrendado** BANCA, INMOB leasehold mortgage; **~ sobre vivienda** BANCA, INMOB house mortgage; **~ subordinada** BANCA, INMOB subordinated mortgage; **~ subyacente** BANCA, INMOB underlying mortgage; **~ de tasa ajustable** BANCA, FIN, INMOB adjustable rate mortgage (*ARM*); **~ de tasa variable** BANCA, INMOB variable rate mortgage; **~ con tipo renegociado** BANCA, INMOB renegotiated rate mortgage; **~ vinculada al capital** BOLSA equity kicker; **~ de la vivienda** BANCA, INMOB home mortgage

hipotecado: no ~ *adj* COM GEN unmortgaged

hipotecar *vt* COM GEN mortgage, DER hypothecate

hipótesis *f* COM GEN hypothesis; **~ U** ECON *distribución del ingreso* U-hypothesis; **~ de actualización tecnológica** ECON catching-up hypothesis; **~ de la aglomeración** ECON crowding hypothesis; **~ alternativa** MAT *comprobaciones estadísticas* alternative hypothesis; **~ de Bernouilli** MAT Bernouilli's hypothesis; **~ cíclica de la vida** ECON life-cycle hypothesis (*LCH*); **~ de convergencia** ECON, POL convergence hypothesis; **~ de la decisión dual** ECON dual decision hypothesis; **~ de discrepancia del valor** ECON value discrepancy hypothesis; **~ de la inversión de causa** ECON reverse causation hypothesis; **~ nula** MAT null hypothesis; **~ de la renta absoluta** ECON absolute income hypothesis; **~ de la renta permanente** ECON permanent income hypothesis; **~ de la renta relativa** ECON relative income hypothesis; **~ del salario real** ECON, RRHH real-wage hypothesis; **~ de Tiebout** ECON Tiebout hypothesis; **~ del trabajador adicional** ECON, RRHH additional worker hypothesis; **~ de trabajo** COM GEN working hypothesis; **~ de la uniformidad** ECON uniformity assumption

hipotético *adj* COM GEN hypothetical

histéresis *f* ECON hysteresis

histograma *m* MAT histogram

historia: ~ documental *f* MEDIOS *imprenta, periódico* background story; **~ de éxito** *f* V&M *publicidad* success stories; **~ financiera** *f* FIN financial history

historial *m* RRHH track record; **~ del crédito** BANCA credit history; **~ de inversión** BANCA, FIN investment history; **~ laboral** RRHH work history; **~ médico** PROT SOC health record; **~ previo** RRHH previous history; **~ probado** RRHH proven track record

históricamente *adv* COM GEN historically

histórico *adj* COM GEN historic

hito *m* TRANSP signpost

hitos: ~ **financieros** *m pl* CONT financial highlights

hogar: ~ **privado** *m* COM GEN private household

hoja *f* BANCA leaf, COM GEN sheet; ~ **de almacén** COM GEN stock sheet; ~ **de balance horizontal** CONT horizontal balance sheet; ~ **de balance del sector público** CONT, ECON public sector balance sheet; ~ **de balance vertical** CONT vertical balance sheet; ~ **base** MEDIOS base sheet; ~ **de cálculo** COM GEN spreadsheet; ~ **de costes por órdenes de trabajo** *Esp* (*cf hoja de costos por órdenes de trabajo AmL*) ECON job cost sheet; ~ **de costos por órdenes de trabajo** *AmL* (*cf hoja de costes por órdenes de trabajo Esp*) ECON job cost sheet; ~ **de cumplido** ADMIN, COMS compliments slip; ~ **de datos** V&M data sheet; ~ **de diseño de formularios** ADMIN forms design sheet; ~ **electrónica** INFO spreadsheet program; ~ **de embarque** TRANSP consignment note (*C/N*); ~ **de entrada** RRHH personal data sheet; ~ **de estilo** INFO style sheet; ~ **de jornales devengados** *Esp* (*cf hoja de tiempo AmL*) RRHH time sheet; ~ **de montaje** MEDIOS base sheet; ~ **de paga** RRHH pay sheet; ~ **de pedido** COM GEN, V&M order form; ~ **de programación** INFO work sheet, code sheet; ~ **de registro** RRHH tally sheet; ~ **de ruta aérea** IMP/EXP, TRANSP forwarder air waybill (*FAWB*); **de ~ suelta** COM GEN loose-leaf; ~ **de tiempo** *AmL* (*cf hoja de jornales devengados Esp*) RRHH time sheet; ~ **de trabajo** CONT worksheet; ~ **de transferencia de materiales** *Esp* (*cf relación de transferencia de materiales AmL*) COM GEN materials transfer note

hojas: ~ **de prueba** *f pl* MEDIOS proofs

hojear *vt* INFO *documentos* browse

holding *m* BANCA, BOLSA, FIN holding company, holding corporation

hombre: ~ **anuncio** *m* RRHH advertising man (*adman*); ~ **casado** *m* ADMIN, DER, FISC married man; ~ **con misión encomendada** *m* MEDIOS assignment man; ~ **de negocios** *m* COM GEN businessman; ~ **de la organización** *m* GES organization man; ~ **que hace de todo** *m* RRHH odd-job man; ~ **para todo** *m* RRHH handyman

homogéneo *adj* COM GEN homogeneous

homologación *f* IMP/EXP, RRHH certification mark (*AmE*), homologation

homólogo, -a *m,f* RRHH *en otra organización* opposite number

honor *m* COM GEN honor (*AmE*), honour (*BrE*)

honorario: ~ **fijo** *m* COM GEN fixed fee

honorarios *m pl* COM GEN honorarium (*frml*), CONT, PATENT fee, fee income; ~ **de administración** INMOB management fee; ~ **de los directores** RRHH directors' fees; ~ **de incentivo** V&M incentive fee; ~ **de inspección** FIN survey fee; ~ **del intermediario** COM GEN, V&M finder's fee; ~ **del letrado** DER legal fees; ~ **por mantenimiento** INMOB maintenance fee; ~ **profesionales** COM GEN professional fees; ~ **según escala** DER scale fee; ~ **de traspaso** INMOB transfer fees

honradez *f* COM GEN trustworthiness

honrar *vt* COM GEN honor (*AmE*), honour (*BrE*)

hora *f* TRANSP time; ~ **aparente en el barco** TRANSP apparent time at ship (*ATS*); ~ **de audiencia** MEDIOS *radiodifusión* listening time; ~ **de baja audiencia**

MEDIOS, V&M off-peak time; ~ **británica** COM GEN British Summer Time (*BST*); ~ **central establecida** COM GEN Central Standard Time (*CST*); ~ **centroeuropea** COM GEN Central European Time (*CET*); ~ **de comer** COM GEN lunch-hour; ~ **contada doble** RRHH double time; ~ **corriente** TRANSP *póliza de fletamento* running hour; ~ **estándar del este** COM GEN Eastern Standard Time (*EST*); ~**-hombre** GES, RRHH man-hour; ~ **de ir al mercado** COM GEN time to market; ~ **legal** COM GEN, RRHH standard time; ~ **límite de redacción** COM GEN copy deadline; ~ **local** COM GEN, MEDIOS local time; ~ **de máxima audiencia** MEDIOS, V&M *publicidad* peak time, prime time; ~ **media de Greenwich** COM GEN Greenwich Mean Time (*GMT*); ~ **de paso** TRANSP transit time; ~ **pico** *AmL* (*cf hora punta Esp*) TRANSP peak hour, rush hour; ~ **prevista** TRANSP *salida, llegada* right time; ~ **prevista de llegada** COM GEN, TRANSP estimated time of arrival (*ETA*); ~ **prevista de salida** COM GEN, TRANSP estimated time of departure (*ETD*); ~ **prevista de salida de un barco** COM GEN, TRANSP estimated time of sailing (*ETS*); ~ **punta** *Esp* (*cf hora pico AmL*) TRANSP peak hour, rush hour; ~ **de salida** COM GEN, MEDIOS *radiodifusión* station time, TRANSP departure time; ~ **universal coordinada** (*HUC*) COM GEN coordinated universal time (*UTC*); ♦ **a la ~ fijada** COM GEN at the appointed time; **a la ~ pico** *AmL* (*cf a la hora punta Esp*) COM GEN at peak time, TRANSP at rush hour; **a la ~ prevista** COM GEN on schedule; **a la ~ punta** *Esp* (*cf a la hora pico AmL*) COM GEN at peak time, TRANSP at rush hour

horario *m* COM GEN schedule, timescale, timetable (*TT*); ~ **de apertura** COM GEN opening hours; ~ **bancario** BANCA banking hours; ~ **de la bolsa** BOLSA stock exchange hours; ~ **de cierre** *f* COM GEN closing time; ~ **de contratación** BOLSA trading hours; ~ **escalonado** RRHH *relaciones laborales* spreadover (*jarg*); ~ **de Europa Oriental** COM GEN Eastern European Time (*EET*); ~ **flexible** RRHH flexible schedule, flexible time, flexitime, flexible working hours, flextime; ~ **fuera de lo normal** RRHH unsocial hours; ~ **del mercado** BOLSA market hours; ~ **móvil** RRHH flexible working hours, flexitime, flextime, gliding time (*jarg*); ~ **regresivo** GES backward scheduling; ~ **selecto** MEDIOS *radiodifusión*, V&M prime time; ~ **de trabajo** COM GEN, GES, TRANSP schedule, work schedule, working time, working timetable; ~ **de trabajo flexible** RRHH flexible working hours, flexitime, flextime, gliding time (*jarg*); ~ **de trenes** OCIO, TRANSP railway timetable (*BrE*), train timetable; ~ **de verano** *f* COM GEN daylight saving; ~ **de verano británico** COM GEN British Summer Time (*BST*)

horarios: ~ **regulares** *m pl* COM GEN regular hours; ~ **de salidas** *m pl* TRANSP *navegación* sailing schedule

horas[1]: ~ **centrales** *f pl* COM GEN core hours; ~ **de comercio** *f pl* COM GEN business hours; ~ **extra** *f pl* IND, RRHH overtime (*OT*), overtime hours; ~ **extraordinarias** *f pl* IND, RRHH overtime (*OT*), overtime hours; ~ **hábiles** *f pl* COM GEN office hours; ~ **laborables** *f pl* COM GEN office hours; ~ **de máxima audiencia** *f pl* MEDIOS, V&M prime viewing time; ~ **de oficina** *f pl* COM GEN office hours, hours of business (*h.b.*); ~ **de servicio** *f pl* COM GEN service hours

horas[2]: **antes de ~ de oficina** *fra* BOLSA before hours; **después de ~ de oficina** *fra* BOLSA after hours

horizontal *adj* COM GEN, INFO *presentación de documentos* horizontal (*hor*), landscape (*jarg*)

horizonte: ~ **de inversión** *m* FIN investment horizon; ~ **de planificación** *m* ECON *países socialistas* planning horizon

horquilla *f* TRANSP *manejo de cargas* pallet fork

hortelano, -a *m,f* ECON market gardener (*BrE*), truck farmer (*AmE*)

horticultura: ~ **comercial** *f* ECON market gardening (*BrE*), truck farming (*AmE*)

hospedaje: ~ **relacionado con el trabajo** *m* INMOB, RRHH job-related accommodation

hospedarse *v refl* INFO log

hospital: ~ **público** *m* PROT SOC public hospital

hostelería *f* OCIO catering

hotelero(a) *m,f* OCIO hotelier

HUC *abr* (*hora universal coordinada*) COM GEN UTC (*coordinated universal time*)

hueco *m* COM GEN *en un inventario* pitfall; ~ **en el mercado** V&M market gap; ~ **de oportunidad** COM GEN window of opportunity

huecograbado *m* V&M rotogravure

huelga *f* COM GEN industrial action, strike; ~ **de ausencia en el puesto de trabajo** ECON, RRHH stay-out strike; ~ **de brazos caídos** ECON, RRHH go-slow (*BrE*), sit-down strike, slowdown, stay-in strike; ~ **de celo** RRHH work-to-rule; ~ **de competencias** RRHH jurisdictional strike; ~ **ferroviaria** RRHH, TRANSP rail strike; ~ **general** IND, RRHH all-out strike, general strike; ~ **ilegal** DER, IND, RRHH illegal strike, unconstitutional strike; ~ **laboral** COM GEN, IND, RRHH walkout; ~ **legal** DER, IND, RRHH constitutional strike, official strike; ~ **no oficial** DER, IND, RRHH unofficial strike; ~ **de ocupación** RRHH sit-in; ~ **oficial** DER, IND, RRHH official strike; ~ **política** POL, RRHH political strike; ~ **sin previo aviso** IND, RRHH lightning strike; ~ **de protesta** RRHH protest strike; ~ **rápida** RRHH snap strike; ~ **relámpago** IND, RRHH hit-and-run strike, lightning strike; ~ **salvaje** IND, RRHH wildcat strike; ~ **simbólica** RRHH token strike; ~ **de solidaridad** IND, RRHH sympathy strike; ◆ **estar en** ~ RRHH on strike, stay out; **se canceló la** ~ COM GEN, RRHH the strike has been called off; **ir a la** ~ RRHH come out on strike (*BrE*), go on strike, go out on strike (*BrE*), hit the bricks (*infrml*) (*AmE*), turn out on strike

huelgas: ~ **alternativas** *f pl* RRHH *relaciones laborales* rolling strikes (*jarg*); ~, **tumultos y desórdenes** *m pl* IND, PROT SOC, RRHH strikes, riots and civil commotions (*SR&CC*)

huelguista *mf* COM GEN, IND, RRHH striker

huésped *mf* COM GEN paying guest (*PG*)

huida: ~ **de capitales** *f* ECON *internacional* flight of capital; ~ **hacia la calidad** *f* BOLSA flight to quality

hulla: ~ **blanca** *f* MED AMB white coal

humos *m pl* IND, MED AMB fumes

hundido *adj* COM GEN *empresas* collapsed, *mercado* sagging

hundimiento: ~ **del mercado** *m* BOLSA, ECON market slump

hundirse *v refl* BOLSA *precios* crash, COM GEN, V&M *precios* knock down

hurto: ~ **mayor** *m* DER grand larceny (*AmE*), serious crime (*BrE*); ~ **en tiendas** *m* DER, V&M shoplifting

husmeador, a *m,f* COM GEN muckraker

I

IA *abr* (*inteligencia artificial*) INFO AI (*artificial intelligence*)

IATA *abr* (*Asociación Internacional de Transporte Aéreo*) TRANSP IATA (*International Air Transport Association*)

ibid. *abr* (*ibidem*) COM GEN ibid. (*ibidem*)

ibidem *fra* (*ibid.*) COM GEN ibidem (*ibid.*)

ICB *abr* (*índice de capitalización bursátil*) BOLSA, ECON market capitalization index

ICO *abr* (*Instituto de Crédito Oficial*) FIN Spanish official credit institute

icono *m* COM GEN, INFO icon

íd. *abr* (*ídem*) COM GEN do. (*ditto*)

idea: ~ **genial** *f* GES brainstorm

idear *vt* COM GEN devise

ídem *adj* (*íd.*) COM GEN ditto (*do.*)

identidad: ~ **contable** *f* CONT accounting identity; ~ **corporativa** *f* V&M corporate identity

identificación *f* COm GEN, FISC *de declaraciones* identification; ~ **desde tierra** COMS ground control; ~ **de marca** V&M brand identification; ~ **de remesa de exportación** *m* IMP/EXP export consignment identifying number (*ECI*);

identificador *m* INFO identifier (*ID*); ~ **de mercado de Dun** FIN Dun's market identifier (*AmE*)

id est *fra* COM GEN id est (*i.e.*)

idoneidad *f* COM GEN eligibility, suitability

idóneo *adj* COM GEN eligible, suitable

IEF *abr* (*Instituto de Estudios Financieros*) FIN Spanish financial research institute

iglú *m* TRANSP *aviación* igloo

ignífugo *adj* COM GEN fire-resistant (*BrE*), fire-resistive (*AmE*)

igual[1] *adj* COM GEN equal; ◆ **a** ~ **delito** DER in pari delicto; ~ **y opuesto** COM GEN equal and opposite; ~ **para todas las categorías** COM GEN, RRHH across-the-board

igual[2] *m* MAT *signo* equal; ~ **tamaño** V&M same size

iguala *f* COM GEN retainer

igualación *f* COM GEN equalization; ~ **de diferencias salariales** ECON equalization of wage differentials; ~ **de espacios** IND spatial equalization

igualado *adj* COM GEN matched, equalized

igualar *vt* COM GEN *precios* even out, *resultados* match

igualdad *f* COM GEN equality; ~ **de derechos de voto** POL equal voting rights; ~ **de oportunidad de empleo** RRHH equal employment opportunity; ~ **de oportunidades** RRHH equal opportunity (*BrE*), affirmative action (*AmE*); ~ **de oportunidades aparente** DER tokenism

iguales[1]: ~ **derechos a voto** *m pl* POL equal voting rights

iguales[2]: **en** ~ **condiciones** *fra* COM GEN, RRHH on an equal footing, on the same footing

igualitarismo *m* POL egalitarianism

igualmente *adv* COM GEN pari passu

ilegal *adj* DER unlawful, illegal

ilegalmente *adv* DER illegally, unlawfully

ilícito: ~ **civil** *m* DER civil wrong

ilimitado *adj* COM GEN unlimited

iliquidez *f* FIN liquidity squeeze

ilíquido *adj* BANCA illiquid

ILT *abr* (*incapacidad laboral transitoria*) PROT SOC, SEG temporary disability benefit

ilusión: ~ **fiscal** *f* FISC fiscal illusion; ~ **inflacionaria** *f* ECON inflation illusion; ~ **monetaria** *f* ECON monetary veil

ilustración *f* MEDIOS *ejemplo, imagen* illustration

ilustraciones *f pl* COM GEN *imprenta* artwork

ilustrar *vt* COM GEN, MEDIOS illustrate

IMAC *abr* (*Instituto de Mediación, Arbitraje y Conciliación*) GES, RRHH independent concilation service, often involved in disputes between trade unions and management, ≈ ACAS (*BrE*) (*Advisory, Conciliation and Arbitration Service*)

imagen *f* COM GEN image; ~ **consolidada** V&M established image; ~ **corporativa** COM GEN corporate image; ~ **fiel** CONT fair representation (*AmE*), true and fair view (*BrE*); ~ **global** V&M global image; ~ **de marca** V&M brand image; ~ **de pantalla** INFO soft copy; ~ **del producto** V&M product image; ~ **secundaria** V&M *publicidad* afterimage; ~ **sobresaliente** COM GEN high image (*jarg*)

IME *abr* (*Instituto Monetario Europeo*) ECON, POL EMI (*European Monetary Institute*)

IMEF *abr AmL* (*Instituto Mexicano de Ejecutivos de Finanzas*) FIN institute of Mexican financial executives

imitaciones *f pl* IND *sector de la moda* knockoffs (*infrml*); ~ **ilegales** IND *sector de la moda* counterfeit goods

imitar: ~ **las marcas** *fra* BOLSA fake the marks (*infrml*)

impacto: ~ **ambiental** *m* MED AMB environmental impact; ~ **del beneficio** *m* COM GEN, FIN profit impact; ~ **multiplicador** *m* ECON impact multiplier; ~ **de una pérdida** *m* FISC impact of a loss; ~ **en las utilidades** *m* COM GEN profit impact; ~ **visual** *m* COM GEN, FIN visual impact

impagado *adj* COM GEN unpaid

impagar *vt* BANCA *cheque* bounce (*infrml*)

impago *m* COM GEN nonpayment

impar[1] *adj* COM GEN, INFO odd

impar[2] *mf* COM GEN *de par* odd one

imparcial *adj* COM GEN impartial

impedimento: ~ **legal** *m* DER estoppel

impedir *vt* COM GEN delay, prevent

imperfección: ~ **del título** *f* INMOB cloud on title (*AmE*)

imperialismo *m* POL imperialism; ~ **capitalista** ECON, POL capitalist imperialism

implantación *f* CONT layout

implantar *vt* INFO *sistema, red* install

implementación: ~ **de un artículo** *f* FIN implementation of an article; ~ **desfasada** *f* ECON implementation lag; ~ **estratégica** *f* COM GEN, GES strategy implementation; ~ **de un tratado** *f* FIN implementation of a treaty

implemento: ~ **de producción** *m* COM GEN production implement

implicación: ~ **del beneficio** *f* COM GEN, FIN profit implication; ~ **de los empleados** *f* RRHH *en actividades de organización* employee involvement (*EI*), worker involvement; ~ **financiera** *f* FIN financial involvement; ~ **del lector** *f* V&M reader involvement; ~ **de los trabajadores** *f* RRHH employee involvement (*EI*), involvement of employees, worker involvement; ~ **de las utilidades** *f* COM GEN, FIN profit implication

implicaciones: ~ **plenas** *f pl* COM GEN full implications

implicar *vt* COM GEN imply, PATENT involve

implícito *adj* COM GEN *condiciones* implied, PATENT involved

imponer *vt* COM GEN *pena* impose, *embargo* lay, *moda* set, *proyecto* steamroller, ECON *precios* command, FISC *impuesto* raise, assess, impose, lay on, GES enjoin; ◆ ~ **la moda** COM GEN set the trend

imponible *adj* FISC taxable; ◆ **no** ~ FISC nontaxable; ~ **en el consorcio** FISC taxable in the trust; ~ **en poder de** FISC taxable in the hands of

importación[1]: **de** ~ *adj* IMP/EXP imported

importación[2] *f* IMP/EXP import (*imp.*), importation (*imp.*); ~ **de capital** BOLSA, IMP/EXP capital import; ~**-exportación** INFO import-export; ~ **invisible** IMP/EXP invisible import; ~ **de oro** IMP/EXP import gold; ~ **paralela** IMP/EXP parallel import; ~ **visible** IMP/EXP visible import

importaciones: ~ **aún no declaradas** *f pl* IMP/EXP customs pre-entry imports; ~ **de la Comunidad** *f pl* IMP/EXP Community imports; ~ **estacionales** *f pl* IMP/EXP temporary importation

importado *adj* IMP/EXP imported

importador, a *m,f* IMP/EXP importer

importancia: ~ **estadística** *f* MAT *estadística* statistical significance; ~ **relativa** *f* CONT *informes contables* materiality

importante *adj* COM GEN significant

importar *vt* COM GEN, IMP/EXP *datos* import

importe *m* COM GEN *de una factura* amount; ~ **atrasado** CONT arrears; ~ **bruto** CONT gross amount; ~ **de compensación monetaria** FIN monetary compensatory amount; ~ **del coste** *Esp* (*cf importe del costo AmL*) FISC cost amount; ~ **del costo** *AmL* (*cf importe del coste Esp*) FISC cost amount; ~ **del daño** SEG amount of damage; ~ **deducible** CONT deduction; ~ **en demasía** CONT overcharge (*o/c*); ~ **efectivo** CONT *desembolso, gasto* actual amount; ~ **específico** CONT specific amount; ~ **de la factura** FIN invoice amount; ~ **neto del activo** CONT net asset amount; ~ **neto del ajuste de la reserva** CONT net reserve adjustment amount; ~ **neto de las reservas** CONT net reserve amount; ~ **no pagado al vencimiento** BANCA, CONT, FIN amount overdue; ~ **nominal** CONT nominal amount; ~ **del pago anual** FISC annual annuity amount; ~ **de un préstamo** BANCA, CONT proceeds of a loan; ~ **total** CONT full amount; ~ **total de negocios** V&M billing; ~ **unitario de la mano de obra** CONT, ECON, RRHH unit labor costs (*AmE*), unit labour costs (*BrE*); ~ **de las ventas** *m pl* CONT, V&M sales value

imposición *f* CONT, FIN, taxation, *carga, requisito* imposition, assessment; ~ **directa** FISC direct taxation; ~ **excesiva** FISC excessive taxation, overtaxation; ~ **exclusiva** FISC exclusive taxation; ~ **indirecta** FISC indirect taxation; ~ **múltiple** FISC multiple taxation; ~ **óptima** FISC optimal taxation; ~ **original** FISC original assessment; ~ **a plazo** ECON fixed term deposit (*BrE*), time deposit (*AmE*) (*TD*); ~ **regresiva** FISC regressive taxation

impositivo *adj* COM GEN, FISC tax

impresión *f* COM GEN *opinión* impression, MEDIOS *en papel* printout, printing; ~ **artística** V&M *publicidad* art print; ~ **por computador** *AmL ver impresión por computadora AmL*, ~ **por computadora** *AmL* (*cf impresión por ordenador Esp*) INFO computer print-out; ~ **del contrato** V&M contract print; ~ **de control** V&M *tirada a máquina* machine proof; ~ **inversa** INFO reverse printing; ~ **de la memoria** INFO memory print-out; ~ **por ordenador** *Esp* (*cf impresión por computadora AmL*) INFO computer print-out, ~ **de pantalla** *m* INFO print screen; ~ **sin prioridad** INFO background printing; ~ **de la segunda cara** MEDIOS *prensa* backing up; ◆ **tener una** ~ **desfavorable** COM GEN be unfavorably impressed (*AmE*), be unfavourably impressed (*BrE*)

impresionante *adj* COM GEN *aumento* impressive

impreso[1]: ~ **en negrita** *adj* MEDIOS *impresión* printed in bold type

impreso[2] *m* COM GEN printed form; ~ **al portador** BOLSA bearer form; ~ **de declaración sobre la renta** FISC tax return form; **sobre** ~ **con franqueo pagado** COMS business reply envelope; ~ **de ingreso** BANCA pay-in slip (*AmE*), paying-in slip (*BrE*); ~ **mecanográfico** COM GEN business form

impresor, a *m,f* COM GEN *persona* printer

impresora *f* COM GEN imprinter, printer, INFO *dispositivo* printer; ~ **de alta calidad** INFO letter-quality printer; ~ **de alta velocidad** INFO high-speed printer; ~ **bidireccional** INFO bidirectional printer; ~ **a chorro de tinta** INFO ink-jet printer; ~ **electrostática** INFO *equipo* electrostatic printer; ~ **de gráficos** INFO graphics printer; ~ **láser** INFO laser printer; ~ **de líneas** INFO line printer; ~ **de margarita** *Esp* (*cf impresora a rueda de mariposa AmL*) INFO daisywheel printer; ~ **matricial** INFO dot printer, matrix printer; ~ **de matriz de puntos** INFO dot-matrix printer; ~ **de percusión** INFO impact printer; ~ **de post scriptum** INFO *de página* postscript printer; ~ **por puntos** INFO *soporte físico* dot-matrix printer; ~ **de rayo láser** INFO laser printer; ~ **a rueda de mariposa** *AmL* (*cf impresora de margarita Esp*) INFO daisywheel printer; ~ **en serie** INFO serial printer; ~ **de tambor** INFO drum printer; ~ **de tarjetas de crédito** BANCA, FIN credit card imprinter

impresos *m pl* COM GEN *correos*, MEDIOS *prensa* printed matter

imprevisible *adj* COM GEN unpredictable, unforeseeable

imprevisto *adj* COM GEN unforeseen, unanticipated

imprimir *vt* COM GEN stamp, INFO output, print, print out; ◆ ~ **con plantilla** ADMIN stencil

ímprobo *adj* COM GEN dishonest

improcedente *adj* COM GEN, DER out of order

improcesable *adj* COM GEN unworkable

improductivo *adj* COM GEN nonproductive, unproductive, RRHH idle

imprudencia: ~ **temeraria** *f* DER gross negligence

impuesto *m* COM GEN levy, tax;

~ a ~ **abierto** FISC open tax; ~ **de aceptación** BANCA acceptance duty; ~ **acumulado** FISC tax accrual; ~ **acumulativo** FISC cumulative tax; ~ **acumulativo pagado en el extranjero** FISC foreign accrual tax; ~ **ad valorem** CONT, IMP/EXP ad valorem tax; ~ **adicional** FISC surtax, additional assessment, incremental tax; ~ **adicional de sociedades** FISC corporate surtax, corporation surtax; ~ **afectado** FISC earmarked tax; ~ **agrario** ECON agricultural levy; ~ **ambiental** MED AMB environmental tax; ~ **anticipado de sociedades** FISC advance corporation tax (*ACT*); ~ **aplazado** FISC deferred tax;

■ **b** ~ **básico** FISC basic tax; ~ **burocrático** FISC nuisance tax;

■ **c** ~ **de capitación** ECON, FISC capitation tax, head tax; ~ **cedular** FISC schedular tax; ~ **comercial** FISC business tax; ~ **de compensación** FISC compensation tax; ~ **complementario** FISC additional tax; ~ **por contaminación** FISC, MED AMB pollution tax; ~ **corporativo total** FISC mainstream corporation tax (*MCT*); ~ **corrector** FISC corrective tax;

■ **d** ~ **decreciente** FISC decreasing tax; ~ **degresivo** FISC degressive tax; ~ **para el desarrollo social** FISC social development tax; ~ **después de beneficios** CONT, FISC after-profits tax; ~ **diferido** FISC deferred tax; ~ **directo** FISC direct tax;

■ **e** ~ **encubierto** FISC hidden tax; ~ **escalonado** FISC graduated tax; ~ **especial** FISC special assessment; ~ **específico** FISC, IMP/EXP specific tax; ~ **estatal** FISC state tax; ~ **estimado** FISC estimated tax; ~ **en etapas múltiples** FISC multistage tax; ~ **extraordinario** FISC, POL windfall tax;

■ **f** ~ **federal neto** FISC net federal tax; ~ **federal sobre ventas** FISC federal sales tax; ~ **ficticio** FISC phantom tax; ~ **fijo** FISC fixed duty; ~ **de franquicia** FISC franchise tax (*AmE*); ~ **a la fuente** FISC source tax;

■ **g** ~ **general sobre la renta** FISC general income tax, general revenue tax; ~ **general sobre las ventas** FISC general sales tax; ~ **global** FISC lump-sum tax;

■ **i** ~ **impagado** FISC unpaid tax; ~ **impugnado** FISC disputed tax; ~ **indirecto** FISC indirect tax;

■ **l** ~ **latente** FISC latent tax; ~ **liquidable** FISC assessed tax; ~ **local** FISC, TRANSP local charge; ~ **de lujo** FISC luxury tax;

■ **m** ~ **medio** FISC average tax; ~ **minero** FISC mining tax; ~ **mínimo** FISC minimum tax; ~ **mínimo alternativo** FISC alternative minimum tax; ~ **mínimo añadido** FISC add-on minimum tax; ~ **mínimo sobre la renta** FISC minimum income tax; ~ **mínimo sobre la renta de las personas físicas** FISC minimum personal income tax; ~ **mixto sobre la renta** FISC hybrid income tax; ~ **municipal** FISC local tax, council tax (*BrE*);

■ **n** ~ **nacional** FISC national tax; ~ **nacional sobre ventas** FISC national sales tax (*AmE*); ~ **negativo sobre la renta** ECON, FISC negative income tax (*NIT*), reverse income tax; ~ **no acreditable** FISC noncreditable tax; ~ **no acumulativo** FISC noncumulative tax; ~ **de no residente** FISC nonresident tax, visitor's tax; ~ **normal** FISC normal tax; ~ **normalizado sobre la renta de las personas físicas** FISC standard individual income tax;

■ **p** ~ **pagado en el extranjero llevado al año siguiente** FISC foreign tax carryover; ~ **per cápita** FISC poll tax (*obs*) (*BrE*); ~ **político** RRHH political levy (*BrE*); ~ **por persona** ECON, FISC capitation tax;

~ **portuario** FISC, TRANSP port tax; ~ **prenatal** FISC ante-natal tax; ~ **progresivo** FISC progressive tax; ~ **progresivo sobre los ingresos del petróleo** FISC incremental oil revenue tax (*IORT*); ~ **proporcional** FISC proportional tax; ~ **proporcional sobre la renta** FISC proportional income tax;

■ **r** ~ **reducido** FISC reduced tax; ~ **reembolsable sobre insumos** *AmL* (*cf impuesto reembolsable sobre inversiones Esp*) FISC creditable input tax; ~ **reembolsable sobre inversiones** *Esp* (*cf impuesto reembolsable sobre insumos AmL*) FISC creditable input tax; ~ **de retención de tasa fija** FISC flat-rate withholding tax; ~ **retenido** FISC withholding tax; ~ **retenido a los no residentes** FISC nonresident tax deduction, nonresident withholding tax; ~ **retenido en origen** FISC tax deducted at source;

■ **s** ~ **selectivo sobre el empleo** FISC selective employment tax; ~ **sobre el automóvil** FISC car tax; ~ **sobre beneficios** CONT, FISC benefit tax, profits tax; ~ **sobre los beneficios acumulados** FISC accumulated profits tax; ~ **sobre beneficios complementarios** FISC fringe benefits tax; ~ **sobre los beneficios empresariales** FISC business income tax, corporation income tax; ~ **sobre beneficios extraordinarios** FISC excess profits tax, windfall profits tax; ~ **sobre beneficios no distribuidos** FISC undistributed profits tax; ~ **sobre bienes y servicios** FISC goods and services tax (*GST*); ~ **sobre el capital** FISC capital tax; ~ **sobre el combustible** FISC fuel tax; ~ **sobre compras** FISC purchase tax; ~ **sobre el consumo** FISC consumption tax; ~ **sobre el disponible reembolsable y desgravable** FISC allowable refundable tax on hand; ~ **sobre dividendos** FISC dividend tax; ~ **sobre donaciones** FISC gift tax; ~ **sobre el empleo** FISC employment tax; ~ **sobre explotaciones petrolíferas** FISC oil revenue tax, petroleum revenue tax (*PRT*); ~ **sobre la exportación** FISC export tax; ~ **sobre los factores de producción** FISC input tax; ~ **sobre las ganancias acumuladas** FISC accumulated earnings tax; ~ **sobre los gastos** ECON, FISC expenditure tax; ~ **sobre herencias** FISC estate duty, inheritance tax; ~ **sobre la inflación** FISC inflation tax; ~ **sobre los insumos** *AmL* (*cf impuesto sobre inversiones Esp*) FISC investment income tax; ~ **sobre los insumos de la empresa** *AmL* (*cf impuesto sobre las inversiones de la empresa Esp*) FISC business investment tax; ~ **sobre los insumos empresariales** *AmL* (*cf impuesto sobre las inversiones empresariales Esp*) FISC business input tax, tax on business inputs; ~ **sobre inversiones** *Esp* (*cf impuesto sobre los insumos AmL*) FISC investment income tax; ~ **sobre las inversiones empresariales** *Esp* (*cf impuesto sobre los insumos empresariales AmL*) FISC business investment tax; ~ **sobre mercancías** FISC commodity tax; ~ **sobre la nómina** FISC payroll tax; ~ **sobre el pago** COM GEN pay-as-paid; ~ **sobre el patrimonio** FISC wealth tax, general property tax; ~ **sobre la plusvalía** FISC betterment tax, capital gains tax (*CGT*); ~ **sobre la producción** *f* FISC production revenue tax; ~ **sobre la propiedad** FISC charge upon a property; ~ **sobre la renta** (*IRPF*) FISC ≈ Income Tax (*IT*); ~ **sobre la renta de actividades no comerciales** FISC nonbusiness income tax; ~ **sobre la renta del capital** FISC capital income tax; ~ **sobre la renta diferido** FISC deferred income tax; ~ **sobre la renta escalonado** FISC graduated income tax; ~ **sobre la**

renta de intereses y otras inversiones FISC interest and other investment income tax; **~ sobre la renta de sociedades** (*ISRS*) FISC corporate tax, corporate income tax, corporation income tax; **~ sobre retención de dividendos** FISC dividend tax withholding; **~ sobre el salario** FISC payroll tax; **~ sobre sucesiones** FISC death tax, estate duty, inheritance tax; **~ sobre la tierra** FISC charge on land; **~ sobre el tráfico de empresas** (*ITE*) FISC turnover tax; **~ sobre transacciones** FISC transaction tax; **~ sobre las transferencias de capital** FISC capital transfer tax (*CTT*); **~ sobre transmisiones patrimoniales** (*ITP*) FISC estate tax, transfer tax; **~ sobre el transporte aéreo** FISC air transportation tax (*ATT*); **~ sobre el valor añadido** (*IVA*) FISC Value Added Tax (*VAT*) (*BrE*); **~ sobre el valor de la tierra** FISC land value tax; **~ sobre valores** FISC securities tax; **~ sobre las ventas** FISC sales tax; **~ sobre las ventas al detalle** FISC retail sales tax; **~ sobre las ventas de los fabricantes** FISC manufacturers' sales tax; **~ sobre los viajeros de abono** FISC commuter tax (*AmE*); **~ sobre el volumen de ventas** FISC turnover tax; **~ de sociedades** FISC business income tax, corporation tax, corporate tax, corporate taxation, company tax; **~ superpuesto** FISC superposed tax; **~ sustitutivo** FISC replacement tax;

~ t **~ de tipo básico** FISC basic-rate tax; **~ de tipo estándar** FISC standard-rate tax; **~ de tipo fijo** FISC flat tax, proportional tax, flat-rate tax; **~ de tipo normal** FISC standard tax; **~ para turistas** FISC, OCIO tourist tax;

~ u **~ por el uso de carreteras** FISC, TRANSP road tax;

~ v **~ de visitante** FISC nonresident tax, visitor's tax

impuestos[1]: **antes de deducidos los ~** *adj* FISC before tax; **después de deducidos los ~** *adj* FISC after tax

impuestos[2]: **~ acumulados** *m pl* FISC accrued taxes; **~ aduaneros** *m pl* FISC, IMP/EXP customs duties; **~ atrasados** *m pl* FISC back taxes, tax arrears; **~ debidos** *m pl* FISC taxes due; **~ diferidos** *m pl* CONT, FISC deferred taxation; **~ incobrables** *m pl* CONT, FISC uncollectable taxes; **~ no reembolsables** *m pl* CONT, FISC nonrefundable taxes; **~ pagaderos en especies** *m pl* CONT, FISC tax otherwise payable; **~ pagados en el extranjero** *m pl* FISC foreign tax; **~ retenidos** *m pl* CONT, FISC hoja de balance taxes withheld; **~ vencidos** *m pl* CONT, FISC tax arrears, back taxes; **~ ya pagados** *m pl* FISC hoja de balance taxes actually paid

impugnar *vt* DER *testamento* contest, *reclamación* dispute

impulsado *adj* COM GEN driven; ◆ **~ por** COM GEN driven by; **~ por el mercado** V&M market-driven

impulsar *vt* IND impulsar; ◆ **~ una subida** ECON *mercado* fuel an advance

impulso *m* COM GEN impetus, *esfuerzo concertado* drive, ECON momentum, INFO pulse; **~ competitivo** ECON competitive thrust; **~ económico** ECON economy thrust

impulsor, a *m,f* RRHH thruster

imputable *adj* COM GEN, FISC chargeable; **~ a impuestos** FISC chargeable to tax

imputación *f* CONT *dinero, cargas*, ECON, FIN allocation, apportionment, imputation; **~ de costes** *Esp* (*cf imputación de costos AmL*) CONT cost allocation; **~ de costos** *AmL* (*cf imputación de costes Esp*) CONT cost allocation; **~ de fondos** FIN *organismo, proyecto gubernamental* apportionment of funds

imputar *vt* CONT *costes* assign, FIN *contrato* allocate; **~ a** CONT apply against

in personam *fra* DER in personam

inaccesibilidad *f* COM GEN, INFO unavailability

inaceptación *f* COM GEN nonacceptance

inaceptado *adj* COM GEN *factura* unaccepted

inactivo *adj* COM GEN inactive, idle

inadvertidamente *adv* COM GEN inadvertently

inalámbrico *adj* COMS cordless, wireless

inalcanzable *adj* COM GEN *objetivo inasequible* unattainable

inalienable *adj* DER unalienable

inalterado *adj* COM GEN unaltered

inanimado *adj* BOLSA lifeless

inapreciable *adj* COM GEN invaluable

inarchivado *adj* COM GEN unrecorded

inasegurable *adj* SEG uninsurable

inatacable *adj* COM GEN unassailable

inauguración *f* TRANSP launching

INB *abr* (*ingreso nacional bruto*) CONT, ECON, FIN GNI (*gross national Income*)

incambiable *adj* COM GEN unexchangeable

incapacidad *f* COM GEN incapacity, RRHH *de empleado* disability; **~ laboral transitoria** (*ILT*) PROT SOC, SEG temporary disability benefit; **~ de llegar a un acuerdo** RRHH failure to agree (*FTA*); **~ peculiar** SEG unique impairment; **~ recurrente** RRHH recurrent disability; **~ para trabajar** RRHH inability to work

incapacitado *adj* COM GEN unfit, RRHH off sick (*infrml*)

incapaz *adj* COM GEN unfit, DER incompetent

incautación *f* COM GEN confiscation, DER seizure, impounding

incautar *vt* COM GEN confiscate, DER seize, impound

incautarse: **~ de** *v refl* CONT, ECON, FIN *fondos* appropriate

incendio *m* SEG hostile fire; **~ provocado** DER, SEG arson

incentivación *f* V&M encouragement

incentivar *vt* V&M encourage

incentivo *m* COM GEN *ventas* incentive; **~ artificial** ECON *economías socialistas* synthetic incentive; **~ para el comerciante** V&M dealer incentive; **~ compatible** ECON incentive compatible; **~ económico** ECON economic incentive; **~ de empuje** V&M *publicidad* push incentive; **~ financiero** FIN financial incentive; **~ fiscal** FISC fiscal inducement, tax incentive; **~ fiscal sobre opciones** (*ISO*) BOLSA incentive stock option (*AmE*) (*ISO*); **~ de grupo** RRHH group incentive; **~ a la inversión** BANCA investment incentive; **~ monetario** FIN monetary inducement; **~ del personal** RRHH staff incentive; **~ de premio** RRHH premium bonus; **~ a la producción** RRHH production incentive; **~ por productividad** RRHH output bonus, bonus; **~ salarial** RRHH wage incentive; **~ del sector privado** RRHH private sector award; **~ de ventas** COM GEN, V&M *para el comprador o el vendedor* push money, sales incentive; **~ de viaje** V&M travel incentive

incidencia *f* FISC incidence; **~ económica** FISC economic incidence; **~ fiscal** FISC fiscal incidence, tax incidence; **~ fiscal total** FISC absolute tax incidence; **~ del impuesto diferencial** FISC differential tax incidence; **~ reglamentaria** FISC statutory incidence

incidente: **~ laboral** *m* RRHH industrial incident

incineración *f* MED AMB *de residuos* incineration

incitación *f* COM GEN prompt, DER *a violar la ley* inducement

incitar *vt* COM GEN *dar lugar a* prompt, DER induce

inclinación *f* COM GEN slant, slope

incluido *adj* COM GEN included (*incl.*), including (*incl.*); ♦ **~ en la lista negra** COM GEN, IND, RRHH blacklisted; **~ en las prestaciones** RRHH in benefit; **todo ~** COM GEN all-in, all-inclusive

incluir *vt* COM GEN include; ♦ **~ un asunto en el orden del día** GES place a question on the agenda; **~ en los ingresos** CONT take into income; **~ en el presupuesto** CONT budget for

inclusión *f* COM GEN inclusion

inclusivo *adj* COM GEN inclusive (*incl.*)

incobrable *adj* CONT, FISC uncollectable

incombustible *adj* COM GEN fireproof

incomparecencia *f* DER absence, failure to appear

incompatible *adj* COM GEN incompatible

incompetente *adj* RRHH incompetent, unqualified

incompleto *adj* COM GEN incomplete, DER inchoate

incondicional *adj* COM GEN outright, unconditional

incorporable *adj* INFO add-on

incorporación *f* RRHH joinder; **~ de reservas** BOLSA capitalization of reserves

incorporado *adj* COM GEN incorporated, INFO built-in; ♦ **~ al R.U.** DER UK-incorporated

incorporar *vt* COM GEN incorporate, DER *contrato, cláusula* build into

incorpóreo *adj* COM GEN incorporeal

incorrecto *adj* COM GEN wrong

INCOTERM *abr* (*cláusulas comerciales internacionales*) ECON, IMP/EXP INCOTERM (*International Commercial Term*)

incremental *adj* COM GEN, INFO incremental

incrementar *vt* COM GEN increase; ♦ **~ la producción** IND increase production

incrementarse *v refl* COM GEN increase

incremento *m* COM GEN increase, addition, increment; **~ por apreciación** COM GEN appraisal increment; **~ de las existencias** ADMIN, V&M addition to stock; **~ gradual de los gastos** FIN outlay creep; **~ no ganado** FIN, INMOB unearned increment; **~ de pedidos** COM GEN flow of orders; **~ del precio del petróleo** ECON, FIN, IND oil price increase; **~ salarial** RRHH salary increase; **~ vegetativo** ECON natural increase

incrementos: **~ por revalorización** *m pl* CONT appraisal increment

incumbencia *f* COM GEN term of office

incumplimiento *m* COM GEN nonfeasance, DER nonperformance, breach, nonexecution, nonfulfillment (*AmE*), nonfulfilment (*BrE*), *de la ley* noncompliance; **~ de contrato** DER, RRHH breach of contract, nonfulfillment of contract (*AmE*), nonfulfilment of contract (*BrE*); **~ del deber** DER breach of duty; **~ en la entrega de un título el día de pago** BOLSA failure to deliver a security on value date; **~ de garantía** DER breach of warranty; **~ voluntario** *f* FISC wilful default (*BrE*), willfull default (*AmE*)

incumplir *vt* DER breach; ♦ **~ la ley** DER fail to observe the law

incuria *f* DER laches

incurrir *vi* COM GEN *en gastos, deudas, costes* incur

incursión: **~ al amanecer** *f* BOLSA, FIN *venta de acciones* dawn raid (*jarg*)

indebidamente *adv* COM GEN unduly

indeciso *adj* COM GEN undecided, jumpy

indeducibilidad: **~ de las contribuciones del empresario** *f* RRHH nondeductibility of employer contributions

indefinido *adj* COM GEN indefinite

indemne *adj* COM GEN undamaged

indemnización *f* DER damages, indemnity, INMOB judgment, SEG indemnity, V&M *por mercancías dañadas o perdidas* allowance; **~ por accidente laboral** DER, PROT SOC compensation for industrial injury; **~ compensatoria** DER, PROT SOC compensatory damages; **~ por daños** SEG reparation for damage; **~ por desempleo** PROT SOC unemployment benefit (*BrE*), unemployment compensation (*AmE*); **~ por despido** RRHH dismissal wage, layoff pay, redundancy benefit, termination benefits; **~ por despido colectivo** PROT SOC, RRHH collective severance pay; **~ diaria** SEG daily allowance, daily compensation; **~ doble** DER *adjudicación* double damages; **~ en especie** COM GEN allowance in kind; **~ por fallecimento** FISC death benefit; **~ de invalidez** PROT SOC, RRHH disability benefit; **~ justa por daños y perjuicios** DER *propiedad* just compensation

indemnizaciones: **~ por cesantía** *f pl* RRHH termination benefits

indemnizar *vt* DER, SEG compensate, indemnify; ♦ **~ por daños y perjuicios** DER compensate for damage

independencia *f* COM GEN, CONT, ECON, POL independence; **~ en auditoría** CONT audit independence; ♦ **con ~ de** COM GEN independent of, irrespective of

independiente[1] *adj* COM GEN, POL independent; ♦ **~ de** COM GEN independent of; **~ de los medios de comunicación** MEDIOS, V&M media independent; **~ del tipo de dispositivo** INFO device-independent

independiente[2] *mf* RRHH freelance

independientemente[1]: **~ de** *adv* COM GEN despite, independently of

independientemente[2]: **~ de cualquier otra disposición** *fra* COM GEN, DER notwithstanding any other provision

index: **~ de Herfindahl-Hirschman** *m* ECON Herfindahl-Hirschman index

indexación *f* BOLSA, ECON indexing, RRHH indexation (*BrE*); **~ formal** FISC formal indexation

indexado[1] *adj* MAT indexed

indexado[2]: **~ de la moneda** *m* FIN currency-linked

indicación *f* INFO *guía* prompt; **~ del grupo objetivo** V&M target group index; **~ de interés** BOLSA indication of interest; **~ de precio** V&M price cue; ♦ **por ~ de** COM GEN as per advice from

indicador *m* COM GEN *tendencias* gage (*AmE*), gauge (*BrE*), ECON *econometría* indicator, INFO flag; **~ adelantado compuesto** BOLSA *estadística* composite leading indicator; **~ anticipado** ECON *econometría*, MAT *econometría* leading indicator; **~ de aviso** COM GEN warning indicator; **~ básico** ECON leading indicator; **~ de la bolsa** BOLSA stock index and average; **~ coincidente** ECON coincident indicator; **~ comercial** COM GEN, ECON business indicator; **~ de comercio**

exterior ECON, IMP/EXP external trade indicator; **~ de desempeño** COM GEN performance indicator; **~ divergente** ECON divergence indicator; **~ ecológico** COM GEN, MED AMB ecological indicator; **~ económico** ECON, POL economic indicator; **~ de empleo** ECON, POL employment figure; **~ fiscal** FISC fiscal indicator; **~ luminoso** INFO signal light; **~ del mercado** COM GEN market indicator; **~ objetivo** COM GEN objective indicator; **~ de posición en el plan** COM GEN plan position indicator; **~ de prosperidad** ECON, POL prosperity indicator; **~ relacionado con los resultados** COM GEN performance-related indicator; **~ de rendimientos** COM GEN performance indicator; **~ de resultados** COM GEN performance indicator; **~ de retardo** ECON lagging indicator; **~ de servicio de la deuda** ECON debt service indicator; **~ de tendencia** BOLSA *valores* bellwether; **~ variable** ECON indicator variable

indicar *vt* INFO flag

indicativo[1]: **~ de** *adj* COM GEN indicative of

indicativo[2] *m* MEDIOS *radiodifusión* signature tune; **~ de llamada** TRANSP *navegación* call sign

índice[1]: **de bajo ~ de operación** *adj* IND low-stream (*jarg*)

índice[2] *m* COM GEN ratio, index, V&M *de audiencia* rating; **~ de absorción** V&M absorption rate; **~ adelantado compuesto** BOLSA *estadística* composite leading index; **~ de audiencia televisiva** *f* MEDIOS television rating (*TVR*); **~ bursátil** BOLSA stock price index, stock market index; **~ bursátil del Financial Times** BOLSA Financial Times Stock Exchange Index; **~ bursátil de Standard and Poor** BOLSA Standard and Poor's 500 Stock Index (*S&P500*); **~ bursátil de valores industriales del Financial Times** BOLSA Financial Times Industrial Ordinary Share Index (*FT-30*); **~ de calidad física de vida** ECON physical quality of life index (*PQLI*); **~ de capacidad** ECON, RRHH capacity ratio; **~ de capitalización bursátil** (*ICB*) BOLSA, ECON market capitalization index; **~ de certificados de depósito del IMM** (*índice de certificados de depósito del Mercado Monetario Internacional*) BOLSA IMM CD index (*International Monetary Market certificate of deposit index*); **~ de certificados de depósito del Mercado Monetario Internacional** (*índice de certificados de depósito del IMM*) BOLSA International Monetary Market certificate of deposit index (*IMM CD index*); **~ de cobertura de deuda** CONT debt coverage ratio; **~ compuesto** ECON composite index; **~ compuesto de la Bolsa de Nueva York** BOLSA New York Stock Exchange Composite Index; **~ compuesto de fecha valor** BOLSA value-line composite index; **bajo ~ de concentración** RRHH low abstraction (*jarg*); **~ de construcción** TRANSP construction rate; **~ de conversión publicitaria** V&M advertising conversion rate; **~ del coste de la construcción** *Esp* (*cf índice del costo de la construcción AmL*) BOLSA construction cost index; **~ del coste de la vida** *Esp* (*cf índice del costo de la vida AmL*) ECON, FIN cost-of-living index; **~ del costo de la construcción** *AmL* (*cf índice del coste de la construcción Esp*) BOLSA construction cost index; **~ del costo de la vida** *AmL* (*cf índice del coste de la vida Esp*) ECON, FIN cost-of-living index; **~ de cotización de acciones en bolsa** BOLSA share index; **~ de cotización de Treinta Valores** BOLSA Thirty-Share index; **~ de cotización de valores** BOLSA stock price index; **~ de**

crecimiento BOLSA, ECON growth index, growth rate; **~ de crecimiento compuesto** ECON, FIN compound growth rate; **~ de crecimiento económico** ECON economic growth rate; **~ del Crédito Suizo** BOLSA Credit Suisse index; **~ de decadencia** BOLSA *opciones* rate of decay; **~ de decadencia del factor tiempo** BOLSA *opciones* time value rate of decay; **~ de desembolso de dividendos** BOLSA, CONT dividend payout ratio; **~ de desempleo** COM GEN unemployment rate; **~ de difusión** ECON diffusion index, IND *producción* diffusion rate; **~ de divisas** ECON Forex index; **~ de Divisia** ECON Divisia money index; **~ Dow Jones** BOLSA Dow Jones index; **~ efectivo de protección** ECON, IND effective rate of protection; **~ de eficacia** V&M strike rate (*jarg*); **~ elevado de inversión** ECON, FIN high rate of investment; **~ de escasez** ECON scarcity index; **~ del eurodólar** BOLSA Eurodollar index; **~ de éxito** V&M hit rate; **~ Footsie** BOLSA Footsie, FTSE 100 (*Financial Times-Stock Exchange 100 Share Index*); **~ Footsie Eurotrack 100** BOLSA Financial Times-Stock Exchange Eurotrack 100 Index (*FT-SE Eurotrack 100 Index*); **~ Footsie Eurotrack 200** BOLSA Financial Times-Stock Exchange Eurotrack 200 Index (*FT-SE Eurotrack 200 Index*); **~ Hang Seng** BOLSA índice Hang Seng; **~ Herfindahl-Hirschman** ECON Herfindahl-Hirschman index; **~ de indicadores adelantados** ECON index of leading indicators; **~ de indicadores anticipados** BOLSA index of leading indicators; **~ de indicadores coincidentes** FIN index of coincident indicators; **~ de indicadores retardados** ECON index of lagging indicators; **~ de indicadores muy adelantados** ECON, FIN index of longer leading indicators; **~ de indicadores poco adelantados** ECON, FIN index of shorter leading indicators; **~ de Laspeyres** ECON Laspeyre's index; **~ de lectura de la página impresa** MEDIOS, V&M page exposure; **~ de Lerner** ECON Lerner index; **~ de malestar** ECON discomfort index; **~ de materias** ADMIN subject index, COM GEN table of contents; **~ medio** CONT average rate; **~ de mercaderías** BOLSA commodities index; **~ del mercado** BOLSA market index, market rating; **~ del mercado monetario** BOLSA money market rate; **~ del mercado de valores** BOLSA stock market index, Major Market Index (*MMI*); **~ de mercancías peligrosas** COM GEN, TRANSP dangerous goods rate; **~ mixto** FIN composite index; **~ Nikkei** BOLSA *Japón* Nikkei index; **~ de Paasche** ECON Paasche index; **~ de penetración** *f* V&M penetration rate; **~ ponderado** COM GEN weighted index; **~ de popularidad** POL popularity rating; **~ de precios** CONT, ECON, FIN price index; **~ de precios al por mayor** ECON *estadística*, V&M wholesale price index; **~ de precios al por menor** ECON retail price index; **~ de precios de la Bolsa de Valores** BOLSA stock exchange price index; **~ de precios bursátiles** BOLSA stock exchange price index; **~ de precios implícitos** ECON implied price index; **~ de precios del mercado de valores** BOLSA stock market price index; **~ de precios ponderados** BOLSA price-weighted index; **~ de precios a la producción** ECON producer price index (*PPI*); **~ de producción** *f* BOLSA production rate; **~ de producción industrial** ECON index of industrial production; **~ de remanente** BOLSA carry-over rate; **~ de rendimiento** *f* CONT rate of return; **~ de reparto** V&M payout ratio; **~ de repetición** V&M repeat rate; **~ de rotación de existencias** COM GEN turnover rate; **~ salarial** RRHH salary rate; **~ de siniestralidad** BANCA,

SEG loss ratio; ~ **de solvencia** CONT, FIN solvency ratio; ~ **superior** INFO, MEDIOS *tipografía* superscript; ~ **de utilidad bruta** CONT, FIN gross profit ratio; ~ **de valor unitario** ECON unit value index (*UVI*); ~ **de valores estimados del mercado** BOLSA market value-weighted index; ~ **de volumen** COM GEN volume index

Índice: ~ **de acciones ordinarias del Financial Times** *m* (*índice Footsie*) BOLSA Financial Times Industrial Ordinary Share Index (*Footsie, FT Index*); ~ **All Ordinaries** *m* BOLSA All Ordinaries Index; ~ **BEX 35 Index** *m Esp* BOLSA BEX 35 Index; ~ **compuesto de la bolsa de Nueva York** *m* BOLSA New York stock exchange composite index; ~ **de Confianza de Barron** *m* BOLSA Barron's Confidence Index (*AmE*); ~ **de cotización de Treinta Valores** *m* BOLSA Thirty-Share Index; ~ **de descuento a tres meses del Mercado Monetario Internacional** *m* FIN International Monetary Market three-month discount index; ~ **del Financial Times** *m* (*Índice del FT*) BOLSA Financial Times Index (*FT Index*); ~ **de Fletes del Báltico** *m* TRANSP *navegación* Baltic Freight Index (*BFI*); ~ **Footsie** *m* (*índice de acciones ordinarias del Financial Times*) BOLSA Footsie (*Financial Times Industrial Ordinary Share Index*), FT Index (*Financial Times Industrial Ordinary Share Index*); ~ **Footsie 100 de cotización de acciones** *m* BOLSA FTSE 100 Share Index; ~ **del FT** *m* (*Índice del Financial Times*) BOLSA FT Index (*Financial Times Index*); ~ **Hang Seng** *m* BOLSA Hang Seng Index; ~ **Footsie Eurotrack 100** *m* BOLSA FT-SE Eurotrack 100 Index; ~ **de Letras del Tesoro del IMM** *m* (*Índice de Letras del Tesoro del Mercado Monetario*) BOLSA IMM T-bill index (*International Monetary Market Treasury bill index*); ~ **de Letras del Tesoro del Mercado Monetario** *m* (*Índice de Letras del Tesoro del IMM*) BOLSA *Internacional* International Monetary Market Treasury bill index (*IMM T-bill index*); ~ **Mundial del Capital Internacional** *m* BOLSA Capital International World Index; ~ **Nikkei 225** *m* BOLSA Nikkei 225 Index; ~ **de Precios al Consumo** *m* (*IPC*) ECON, FIN consumer expenditure survey, Consumer Price Index (*CPI*) (*BrE*); ~ **de Precios al Detalle** *m* (*IPD*) BOLSA, ECON Retail Price Index (*RPI*); ~ **de valores CBS** *m* ECON, FIN *Holanda* CBS tendency index; ~ **de Valores Value Line** *m* BOLSA Value Line Stock Index

indicio: ~ **de prueba** *m* COM GEN scrap of evidence

indicios: ~ **concretos** *m pl* DER concrete evidence; ~ **indudables** *m pl* DER conclusive evidence

indiferente *adj* BOLSA *mercado, comercio* listless

indigente: ~ **absoluto(-a)** *m,f* PROT SOC categorically needy

indirectamente *adv* COM GEN indirectly

indiscutible *adj* COM GEN unquestionable

indisponerse: ~ **con** *v refl* COM GEN fall foul of

indisponible *adj* COM GEN unavailable

individual *adj* OCIO *habitación* single

individualismo *m* RRHH individualism

individualización *f* PROT SOC individualization

individualmente *adv* COM GEN individually, singly

individuo[1] *adj* COM GEN individual

individuo[2] *m* COM GEN individual; ~ **computable** FISC eligible individual

indivisibilidad *f* ECON indivisibility

indización *f* FIN, RRHH index-linking; ~ **salarial** RRHH wage indexation

inducción: ~ **a operaciones innecesarias** *f* FIN twisting (*jarg*)

industria *f* COM GEN industry, FIN financial industry, V&M trade; ~ **del acero** ECON, IND steel industry; ~ **aeronáutica** ECON, IND aircraft industry; ~ **agrícola-alimentaria** ECON, IND agrifood industry; ~ **agropecuaria** ECON, IND, MED AMB agribusiness; ~ **en los albores** ECON, IND sunrise industry (*AmE*); ~ **alimenticia** ECON, IND food-processing industry; ~ **de alta tecnología** ECON, IND high-stream industry; ~ **con alto coeficiente de capital** ECON, IND capital-intensive industry; ~ **de la automoción** ECON, IND automotive industry (*AmE*), car industry (*BrE*), motor industry; ~ **automotriz** ECON, IND automotive industry (*AmE*), car industry (*BrE*), motor industry; ~ **bancaria** BANCA banking industry; ~ **basada en el conocimiento** ECON, IND knowledge-based industry; ~ **básica** ECON, IND basic industry; ~ **caída en desgracia** ECON, FIN, IND out-of-favor industry (*AmE*), out-of-favour industry (*BrE*); ~ **de calefacción** ECON, IND heating industry; ~ **del carbón** ECON, IND coal industry; ~ **cerrada** ECON, IND locked-in industry; ~ **de chimeneas** IND smokestack industry; ~ **cíclica** ECON, IND cyclical industry; ~ **del cine** MEDIOS, OCIO film industry (*BrE*), motion-picture industry (*AmE*); ~ **cinematográfica** MEDIOS film industry (*BrE*), motion-picture industry (*AmE*); ~ **clave** ECON, SEG key industry; ~ **consolidada** ECON, IND sunset industry; ~ **en crecimiento** ECON, IND growth industry; ~ **decadente** ECON, IND ailing industry; ~ **de demanda cíclica** ECON, IND cyclical-demand industry; ~ **en desaparición** ECON, IND declining industry; ~ **en desarrollo** ECON, IND growth industry; ~ **de la electricidad** ECON, IND electricity industry; ~ **con empleo intensivo de capital** ECON, IND capital-intensive industry; ~ **esencial** ECON, IND essential industry; ~ **de extracción** IND extractive industry; ~ **familiar** ECON, IND cottage industry; ~ **farmacéutica** ECON, IND pharmaceutical industry; ~ **financiera** ECON, FIN financial industry; ~ **forestal** ECON, IND forestry industry; ~ **del gas** ECON, IND gas industry; ~ **a gran escala** ECON, IND large-scale industry; ~ **incipiente** ECON, IND infant industry, sunrise industry (*AmE*); ~ **indumentaria** IND apparel industry; ~ **intensiva en capital** ECON, IND capital-intensive industry; ~ **de la lana** ECON, IND wool industry; ~ **ligera** ECON, IND light industry; ~ **local** ECON, IND local industry; ~ **de la logística** ECON, IND logistics industry; ~ **maderera** ECON, IND lumber industry (*AmE*), timber industry (*BrE*); ~ **manufacturera** ECON, IND manufacturing industry; ~ **minera** ECON, IND, MED AMB mineral industry, mining industry; ~ **nacional** ECON, IND domestic industry, native industry; ~ **nacionalizada** ECON, IND, POL nationalized industry; ~ **no básica** ECON, IND nonbasic industry; ~ **nuclear** IND, MED AMB nuclear industry; ~ **del ocio** OCIO leisure industry; ~ **oportunista** ECON, IND runaway industry; ~ **papelera** ECON, IND, MED AMB paper industry; ~ **patrimonial** ECON, IND patrimonial industry; ~ **pesada** ECON, IND heavy industry; ~ **pesquera** SEG fishery; ~ **petrolera** ECON, IND oil industry; ~ **primaria** ECON, IND primary industry; ~ **de procesado** ECON, IND process industry; ~ **de la publicidad** ECON, V&M advertising industry;

~ química ECON, IND chemical industry; **~ de recreación** OCIO leisure industry; **~ regulada** ECON, IND regulated industry; **~ de la ropa** IND apparel industry; **~ de servicios** ECON, IND service industry; **~ de servicios financieros** ECON, FIN financial services industry; **~ siderúrgica** ECON, IND iron and steel industry; **~ tecnológica** ECON, IND technology-based industry; **~ textil** ECON, IND textile industry; **~ de transformación** ECON, IND processing industry; **~ de tres dígitos** ECON three-digit industry; **~ turística** ECON, OCIO tourist trade; **~ con uso intensivo de mano de obra** ECON, IND, RRHH labor-intensive industry (*AmE*), labour-intensive industry (*BrE*); **~ de la ventilación** ECON, IND ventilation industry; **~ vinícola** ECON, IND wine industry; **~ vital** ECON, IND essential industry

industrial *adj* ECON, IND industrial

industrialismo *m* ECON, IND industrialism

industrialista *mf* ECON, IND industrialist

industrialización *f* ECON, IND industrialization

industrializado *adj* ECON, IND industrialized

industrializar *vt* ECON, IND industrialize

industrias: **~ afines** *f pl* IND allied industries; **~ avanzadas** *f pl* IND leading industries; **~ energéticas** *f pl* IND power industries; **~ protegidas** *f pl* IND sheltered industries; **~ de transformación** *f pl* ECON, IND manufacturing industries, transformation industries

INE *abr* ECON (*Instituto Nacional de Estadística*) ≈ CSO (*Central Statistical Office*) (*BrE*)

ineficacia *f* COM GEN *persona, máquina, organización* inefficiency

ineficiencia *f* COM GEN inefficiency

ineficiente *adj* COM GEN inefficient

inelasticidad *f* ECON inelasticity; **~ de la demanda** ECON inelasticity of demand; **~ de la oferta** ECON inelasticity of supply; **~ de los precios** ECON price inelasticity

INEM *abr* (*Instituto Nacional de Empleo*) PROT SOC, RRHH ≈ Employment Service (*BrE*)

inercia: **~ industrial** *f* IND industrial inertia

inestabilidad: **~ de los salarios** *f* RRHH earnings drift

inestable *adj* BOLSA *mercado bursátil* volatile, jumpy, ECON jumpy

inevitable *adj* COM GEN unavoidable

inevitablemente *adv* COM GEN inevitably

inexactitud *f* COM GEN inaccuracy

inexigible *adj* DER unenforceable

inexplicado *adj* COM GEN unaccounted for

infalible *adj* COM GEN unfailing

infectado: **no ~** *adj* INFO uninfected

inferencia: **~ estadística** *f* MAT *estadística* statistical inference

inferior *adj* COM GEN *producto* down-market, lower, V&M *producto* down-market; ◆ **~ al nivel medio** COM GEN substandard; **~ al precio de mercado** BOLSA, V&M below-market price; **no ~ a nadie** COM GEN second to none

infidelidad *f* DER misfeasance; **~ reincidente** RRHH double-dipping

infidencia *f* DER *acto* misfeasance

infiltración *f* COM GEN seepage

infinito[1] *adj* COM GEN infinite

infinito[2]: **al ~** *adv* COM GEN ad infinitum

inflación *f* ECON, FIN, POL inflation; **~ básica** ECON core inflation; **~ básica de los precios al consumo** ECON core consumer price inflation; **~ contenida** ECON suppressed inflation; **~ controlada** ECON administered inflation; **~ de costes** *Esp* (*cf inflación de costos AmL*) ECON cost-push inflation; **~ de costos** *AmL* (*cf inflación de costes Esp*) ECON cost-push inflation; **~ creciente** BANCA, ECON rising inflation; **~ de demanda** COM GEN demand-pull inflation, ECON demand-pull inflation, bottleneck inflation; **~ desenfrenada** ECON runaway inflation; **~ de dos cifras** ECON double-figure inflation; **~ de dos dígitos** ECON two-digit inflation, double-digit inflation; **~ estructural** ECON structural inflation; **~ galopante** ECON galloping inflation; **~ importada** ECON imported inflation; **~ inerte** ECON inertial inflation; **~ larvada** ECON hidden inflation; **~ monetaria** ECON monetary inflation; **~ mundial** ECON world inflation; **~ no acelerada por la tasa de desempleo** ECON non-accelerating inflation rate of unemployment; **~ del precio de un activo** CONT, ECON asset price inflation; **~ de precios** ECON price inflation; **~ de los precios al por mayor** ECON wholesale price inflation; **~ pura** ECON pure inflation; **~ reptante** *m* ECON creeping inflation; **~ de salarios** ECON, RRHH wage inflation, wage-push inflation (*jarg*); **~ subyacente** ECON underlying inflation, hesiflation (*jarg*)

inflacionario *adj* ECON, FIN, POL inflationary

inflacionista *adj* ECON, FIN, POL inflationist

inflar *vt* COM GEN *economía* inflate, *cuentas, fondos* swell, ECON *economía* inflate; ◆ **~ la bolsa** BOLSA churn; **~ el mercado** FIN churn

inflexible *adj* COM GEN uncompromising

influencia *f* POL leverage (*jarg*); **~ fiscal** CONT, FISC tax influence; **~ del mercado de capitales** BOLSA, CONT, FIN capital market influence; **~ personal** COM GEN personal influence

influenciar *vt* COM GEN influence

influir *vt* COM GEN *decisión* influence; **~ en** COM GEN *resultado* sway

influyente *adj* COM GEN influential

infografía *f* INFO computer graphics

infopista *f* INFO information highway

información *f* COM GEN information (*info.*); **~ actualizada** COM GEN up-to-date information; **~ para la administración** GES management information; **~ asimétrica** COM GEN asymmetric information; **~ básica** COM GEN background information; **~ confidencial** DER confidential information; **~ confidencial bursátil** BOLSA stock tips; **~ de control** COM GEN control information; **~ para la dirección** GES management information; **~ durante el vuelo** OCIO, TRANSP in-flight information; **~ equívoca** COM GEN misleading information; **~ especializada** COM GEN specialist information; **~ falsa** DER false information; **~ financiera** FIN financial reporting; **~ general** *Esp* (*cf generales AmL*) RRHH personal particulars; **~ de la gestión** GES management information; **~ de marketing** V&M marketing intelligence; **~ de navegación** TRANSP post-sailing information; **~ personal** COM GEN, RRHH particulars; **~ posvuelo** TRANSP post-flight information; **~ para la prensa** MEDIOS *imprenta* press kit; **~ de prestigio** COM GEN status information; **~ privada** COM

GEN nonpublic information; ~ **privilegiada** BOLSA, FIN inside information; ~ **publicada** COM GEN published information; ~ **registrada del mercado** BOLSA recorded market information; ~ **reglamentaria** FISC prescribed information; ~ **segmentada** COM GEN segment information; ~ **de signo pesimista** BOLSA *análisis* bearish signal information; ~ **sobre créditos** BANCA, CONT, FIN credit information; ~ **sobre el mercado** BOLSA market disclosure, V&M market intelligence; ~ **sobre el sector** CONT business segment reporting; ~ **sobre un segmento del negocio** CONT business segment reporting; ~ **del tiempo de vuelo** OCIO, TRANSP flight time information; ~ **de vuelo** OCIO, TRANSP flight information; ♦ **para más** ~ COM GEN for further details, for further information; **para su** ~ COM GEN for your information (*FYI*)

informado *adj* COM GEN *decisión, argumento* informed

informal *adj* COM GEN informal

informalidad *f* RRHH informality

informante *mf* MEDIOS *prensa* leg (*infrml*), source

informar 1. *vt* COM GEN brief, inform, COMS, GES advise; **2.** *vi* COM GEN report; ♦ ~ **a alguien de sus resultados** COM GEN report one's findings to sb; ~ **de sus conclusiones** COM GEN report one's conclusions

informática *f* INFO computer science, computing, informatics, information technology (*IT*); ~ **de alto nivel** INFO high-end computing; ~ **de gestión** INFO business computing, management computing; ~ **gráfica** INFO computer graphics; ~ **interactiva** INFO interactive computing; ~ **de usuario final** INFO end-user computing

informatización *f* INFO computerization, computing

informatizado *adj* Esp (*cf computadorizado AmL*) INFO computer-based, computerized

informatizar *vt* Esp (*cf computadorizar AmL*) INFO computerize

informe *m* Esp (*cf reporte AmL*) COM GEN briefing, report, brief, CONT statement, reporting, brief, briefing, report; ~ **de la actividad diaria** Esp (*cf reporte de la actividad diaria AmL*) COM GEN daily activity report; ~ **de aduanas** Esp (*cf reporte de aduanas AmL*) IMP/EXP customs house report; ~ **anual** Esp (*cf reporte anual AmL*) CONT annual report; ~ **del auditor** Esp (*cf reporte del auditor AmL*) CONT auditor's report; ~ **de auditoría** Esp (*cf reporte de auditoría AmL*) CONT auditor's certificate, audit report; ~ **de averías** Esp (*cf reporte de averías AmL*) SEG survey report, *marítimo* damage report; ~ **Brundtland** Esp (*cf reporte de Brundtland AmL*) ECON, POL *desarrollo sostenido* Brundtland Report; ~ **Bullock** Esp (*cf reporte Bullock AmL*) RRHH *democracia industrial* Bullock report (*BrE*); ~ **comercial** ECON trade brief; ~ **de la conferencia** Esp (*cf reporte de la conferencia AmL*) COM GEN conference report; ~ **confidencial** Esp (*cf reporte confidencial AmL*) BOLSA insider report, COM GEN tip-off, *consejo* tip, FISC tip; ~ **contable** Esp (*cf reporte contable AmL*) CONT accounting report; ~ **de contactos** Esp (*cf reporte de contactos AmL*) V&M contact report; ~ **sin correcciones** Esp (*cf reporte sin correcciones AmL*) DER clean record; ~ **crediticio** Esp (*cf reporte crediticio AmL*) COM GEN credit report; ~ **del director** Esp (*cf reporte del director AmL*) COM GEN director's report; ~ **del ejercicio** Esp (*cf reporte del ejercicio AmL*) COM GEN, GES debriefing; ~ **de entrada**

de buque Esp (*cf reporte de entrada de buque AmL*) IMP/EXP, TRANSP ship's inward report; ~ **escolar** Esp (*cf reporte escolar AmL*) COM GEN school report; ~ **de evaluación** Esp (*cf reporte de evaluaciónAmL*) COM GEN appraisal report; ~ **externo** Esp (*cf reporte externoAmL*) COM GEN external report; ~ **financiero estimado** Esp (*cf reporte financiero estimado AmL*) FIN estimated financial report; ~ **de gastos** Esp (*cf reporte de gastos AmL*) CONT expense report; ~ **de gastos del viaje** Esp (*cf reporte de gastos de viajes AmL*) TRANSP voyage account report; ~ **de la gestión financiera** Esp (*cf reporte de la gestión financiera AmL*) FIN financial management report; ~ **global financiero anual** Esp (*cf reporte global financiero anual AmL*) COM GEN, ECON, FIN, GES comprehensive annual financial report (*CAFR*); ~ **del gobierno** Esp (*cf reporte del gobierno AmL*) COM GEN, POL government report; ~ **del impacto ambiental** Esp (*cf reporte del impacto ambiental AmL*) MED AMB environmental impact statement; ~ **intermedio** Esp (*cf reporte intermedio AmL*) CONT interim report; ~ **de intervención** Esp (*cf reporte de intervención AmL*) INFO call report (*BrE*); ~ **del interventor de cuentas** Esp (*cf reporte de los inventores de cuentas AmL*) CONT auditor's report; ~ **de irregularidad** Esp (*cf reporte de irregularidad AmL*) TRANSP irregularity report; ~ **legal** Esp (*cf reporte legal AmL*) COM GEN statutory report; ~ **limpio de los datos** Esp (*cf reporte limpio de datos AmL*) TRANSP clean report of findings; ~ **de liquidación** Esp (*cf reporte de liquidación AmL*) BANCA clearing report; ~ **en lugar del folleto de emisión** Esp (*cf reporte en lugar de folleto de emisión AmL*) BOLSA statement in lieu of prospectus; ~ **meteorológico** Esp (*cf reporte meteorológico AmL*) COM GEN weather report; ~ **Pearson** Esp (*cf reporte Pearson AmL*) ECON *inversion por países en vías de desarrollo* Pearson Report; ~ **de la posición neta** Esp (*cf reporte de la posición neta AmL*) BOLSA net position report; ~ **del presidente** Esp (*cf reporte del presidente AmL*) GES chairman's brief; ~ **provisional** Esp (*cf reporte provisional AmL*) COM GEN interim statement, CONT interim report, FIN interim statement; ~ **provisional de riesgo** Esp (*cf reporte provisional de riesgo AmL*) CONT exposure draft; ~ **a punto de caducar** Esp (*cf reporte a punto de caducar AmL*) POL sunset report; ~ **Radcliffe** Esp (*cf reporte Radcliffe AmL*) ECON *sistema monetario en R.U.* Radcliffe Report (*BrE*); ~ **resumido** Esp (*cf reporte resumido AmL*) COM GEN summary report, condensed report; ~ **de saldos para transacciones** Esp (*cf reporte de saldos para transacciones AmL*) CONT transaction balance report; ~ **con salvedades** Esp (*cf reporte con salvedades AmL*) CONT qualified report; ~ **segmentado** Esp (*cf reporte segmentado AmL*) CONT segmental reporting; ~ **de la situación** Esp (*cf reporte de la situación AmL*) COM GEN situation report, GES status report; ~ **sobre el estado de la técnica** Esp (*cf reporte sobre el estado de la técnica AmL*) PATENT search report; ~ **sobre la labor realizada** Esp (*cf reporte sobre la labor realizada AmL*) COM GEN progress report, status report; ~ **sobre el mercado** Esp (*cf reporte sobre el mercado AmL*) V&M market report; ~ **tabular** Esp (*cf reporte tabular AmL*) COM GEN tabular report; ~ **del tesorero** Esp (*cf reporte del tesorero AmL*) FIN treasurer's report; ~ **Thomson** Esp (*cf reporte Thomson AmL*) ECON *política regional in UE* Thomson Report; ~ **de viabilidad** Esp (*cf reporte de viabilidad AmL*) COM GEN feasibility report; ~ **del viaje**

Esp (*cf reporte del viaje AmL*) TRANSP voyage report; ~ **de visita** *Esp* (*cf reporte de visita AmL*) V&M call report, contact report; ~ **de Werner** *Esp* (*cf reporte de Werner AmL*) ECON *unión economíca y monetaria* Werner Report

informes: ~ **económicos** *m pl* ECON economic reports; ~ **de pedidos perdidos** *m pl* V&M loose order reports

infovía *f* INFO information highway

infra- *pref* COM GEN infra-

infracapitalizado *adj* COM GEN, FIN, IND undercapitalized

infracción *f* DER unlawful trespass, infringement, PATENT infringement; ~ **fiscal** FISC tax offence; ~ **técnica** POL technical trespass (*jarg*) (*AmE*)

infractor, a *m,f* DER trespasser, PATENT infringer

infraestructura *f* COM GEN, ECON substructure, infrastructure

infraocupado *adj* RRHH underemployed

infrautilizar *vt* COM GEN underuse, *recursos* underutilize

infravaloración *f* COM GEN underestimation, undervaluation

infravalorado *adj* COM GEN undervalued

infringir *vt* DER break, violate, infringe

infructuoso *adj* COM GEN fruitless, unprofitable

infundado *adj* COM GEN groundless

ingeniería *f* IND engineering; ~ **agrícola** IND agricultural engineering; ~ **asistida por computador** *AmL ver ingeniería asistida por computadora AmL* INFO computer-aided engineering (*CAE*), computer-assisted engineering (*CAE*); ~ **asistida por computadora** *AmL* (*cf ingeniería asistida por ordenador Esp*) INFO computer-aided engineering (*CAE*), computer-assisted engineering (*CAE*); ~ **asistida por ordenador** *Esp* (*cf ingeniería asistida por computadora AmL*) INFO computer-aided engineering (*CAE*), computer-assisted engineering (*CAE*); ~ **avanzada** IND advanced engineering; ~ **biológica** IND bioengineering; ~ **de calidad** IND quality engineering; ~ **eléctrica** IND electrical engineering; ~ **estructural** IND structural engineering; ~ **financiera** FIN, IND financial engineering; ~ **genética** POL genetic engineering; ~ **industrial** COM GEN, RRHH industrial engineering; ~ **informática** INFO computer technology; ~ **invertida** COM GEN reverse engineering; ~ **ligera** IND light engineering; ~ **médica** IND medical engineering; ~ **de métodos** COM GEN methods engineering; ~ **pesada** IND heavy engineering; ~ **de precisión** IND precision engineering; ~ **de producción** GES, IND production engineering; ~ **de producto** IND, V&M product engineering; ~ **de programas** INFO software engineering; ~ **de programas asistida por computador** *AmL ver ingeniería de programas asistida por computadora AmL*; ~ **de programas asistida por computadora** *AmL* (*cf ingeniería de programas asistida por ordenador Esp*) INFO computer-assisted software engineering (*CASE*); ~ **de programas asistida por ordenador** *Esp* (*cf ingeniería de programas asistida por computadora AmL*) INFO computer-assisted software engineering (*CASE*); ~ **de sistemas** INFO systems engineering

ingeniero, -a: ~ **consultor(a)** *m,f* COM GEN, RRHH consultant engineer; ~ **de diseño** *m,f* COM GEN, RRHH design engineer; ~ **en eficiencia** *m,f* GES efficiency engineer; ~ **de funcionamiento** *m,f* COM GEN, RRHH service engineer; ~ **industrial** *m,f* COM GEN, IND, RRHH civil engineer, industrial engineer; ~ **informático(-a)** *m,f*

INFO, RRHH computer engineer; ~ **de mantenimiento** *m,f* IND, RRHH maintenance engineer; ~ **naval** *m,f* RRHH, TRANSP naval architect, marine engineer; ~ **de obra** *m,f* IND, RRHH site engineer; ~ **de producto** *m,f* IND, RRHH product engineer; ~ **de programación** *m,f* INFO, RRHH software engineer; ~ **de proyectos** *m,f* COM GEN, RRHH project engineer; ~ **de reparaciones** *m,f* IND, RRHH service engineer; ~ **de seguridad** *m,f* IND, RRHH safety engineer; ~ **de servicio** *m,f* IND, RRHH service engineer; ~ **de ventas** *m,f* RRHH, V&M sales engineer

ingeniosidad *f* COM GEN ingenuity

ingresar 1. *vt* BANCA bank; **2.** *vi* PROT SOC *en la Universidad* go up (*jarg*); ♦ ~ **al mercado del trabajo** COM GEN enter the labor market (*AmE*), enter the labour market (*BrE*)

ingreso[1]: **de bajo** ~ *adj* RRHH low-paid

ingreso[2] *m* CONT, ECON, FISC, INFO *AmL* (*cf acceso Esp*) access, V&M deposit; ~ **activo** FISC active income; ~ **acumulativo** FISC accumulating income; ~ **acumulativo del fideicomiso** FISC accumulating income of the trust; ~ **ajustado** FISC adjusted income; ~ **ajustado a la inflación** FISC inflation-adjusted income; ~ **arbitrario** FISC arbitrary income; ~ **bajo** RRHH low pay; ~ **básico** CONT, FIN basic income; ~ **bruto** FISC gross revenue, gross income; ~ **bruto ajustado** CONT, FISC adjusted gross income; ~ **calculado por capítulo presupuestario** FIN, POL vote-netting revenue; ~ **por comisión** CONT fee income; ~ **compensatorio** BOLSA compensating income (*BrE*); ~ **compuesto** FIN compound yield; ~ **contable** CONT *ganancias*, FISC accounting income; ~ **diferencial** ECON income differential; ~ **directo** BANCA, BOLSA direct yield; ~ **disponible** ECON, FISC disposable income; ~ **por dividendos** BOLSA, CONT dividend income; ~ **de los factores** ECON factor income; ~ **garantizado** FIN guaranteed income; ~ **habitual** CONT common revenue; ~ **honorario** *Esp* (*cf membresía honoraria AmL*) RRHH honorary membership; ~ **imponible ajustado** FISC adjusted taxable income; ~ **imponible sin recargo** FISC nonpenalized taxable income; ~ **imputado** CONT, ECON imputed income; ~ **libre** PROT SOC open admissions; ~ **marginal** ECON, FIN marginal revenue; ~ **marginal implícito** ECON, FIN implicit marginal income; ~ **moderado** ECON, FIN moderate income; ~ **nacional bruto** (*INB*) CONT, ECON, FIN gross national Income (*GNI*); ~ **neto** CONT, ECON clear income, net income, FIN final income; ~ **neto por comisiones** CONT net commission income; ~ **neto revisado** BANCA, CONT, FIN, FISC revised net income; ~ **nominal** ECON, FIN, FISC nominal income; ~ **obtenido por un cambio de posición** FISC rolled-up income; ~ **pendiente** CONT outstanding entry; ~ **de pensión por separación** FISC separation allowance income; ~ **percibido** FISC earned income; ~ **personal disponible** ECON personal disposable income; ~ **potencial** ECON potential income; ~ **principal** CONT prime entry; ~ **del producto marginal** ECON marginal revenue product (*MRP*); ~ **promedio** CONT, FIN average revenue (*AR*); ~ **real** RRHH real income; ~ **real disponible** ECON disposable real income (*DRY*), FISC disposable real income (*DRY*); ~ **total** CONT, ECON, FIN, FISC total revenue

ingresos *m pl* BOLSA *futuros* receipts, FISC income, revenue; **otros** ~ CONT, FISC other income; ~ **acumulados** CONT accrued income, accrued revenue;

~ agrícolas ECON farming income, farm income; **~ ajenos a la operación** CONT nonoperating revenue; **~ anuales** FISC income for the year; **~ bajo la línea** CONT below-the-line revenue; **~ en cartera** BOLSA, CONT portfolio income; **~ por concesión** FISC award incomes; **~ corrientes** CONT actual earnings, current revenues; **~ derivados de inversiones** BOLSA investment income; **~ después de impuestos** FISC tax-paid income; **~ diferidos** CONT deferred income, unearned income; **~ en efectivo** CONT, FIN cash earnings; **~ y egresos** COM GEN ingress and egress; **~ por empleo** CONT, FISC employment income; **~ estimados** CONT, FISC estimated revenue; **~ exentos de impuestos** FISC exempt income; **~ por explotación ganadera** COM GEN, ECON farming income; **~ por exportación** ECON, IMP/EXP export earnings; **~ facultativos** CONT, FISC elective income; **~ familiares** FISC family income; **~ ficticios** CONT, FISC phantom income; **~ fiscales** CONT, FISC tax receipts, tax revenue, tax take; **~ y gastos** CONT, FISC revenue and expenses; **~ gravados con un tipo más bajo** CONT, FISC income taxed at a lower rate; **~ por interés** BANCA interest income; **~ por intereses** CONT, FISC income from interest; **~ por inversiones extranjeras** CONT, FISC foreign investment income; **~ libres de impuestos** CONT, FISC nontax revenue; **~ medios** OCIO average revenue (*AR*), RRHH average earnings, average income; **~ medios por hora** COM GEN, RRHH average hourly earnings; **~ de menor cuantía** CONT, FISC small earnings; **~ monetarios** ECON money income; **~ netos** CONT, FISC net receipts; **~ netos de bienes inmobiliarios en el extranjero** FIN, INMOB net property income from abroad; **~ netos medios** CONT, FISC average net income; **~ netos pertinentes** CONT, FISC *de pensión, jubilación* net relevant earnings; **~ netos procedentes del exterior** CONT, FISC net foreign income; **~ no tributarios** CONT, FISC nontax receipts, nontax revenue; **~ opcionales** CONT, FISC elective income; **~ ordinarios** CONT, FISC ordinary income; **~ de participaciones** CONT, FISC income from participations; **~ por pensión** CONT, FISC pension income; **~ por pensión alimenticia** CONT, FISC alimony income, maintenance; **~ petrolíferos progresivos imponibles** CONT, FISC taxable incremental oil revenue; **~ presupuestados** CONT, FISC budgeted income; **~ presupuestarios** FIN, POL budgetary revenue; **~ previstos** FISC *de un fideicomiso* designated income; **~ procedentes del exterior** FISC foreign income; **~ procedentes de un fallecido** FISC income in respect of a decedent; **~ procedentes de oficios y profesiones** CONT, FISC income from trades and professions; **~ procedentes de pensiones cualificadas** CONT, FISC qualified pension income; **~ por producción** CONT, FISC production revenue; **~ profesionales** CONT, FISC professional income; **~ publicitarios** FIN, MEDIOS, V&M advertising revenue; **~ publicitarios de los medios de comunicación** FIN, MEDIOS, V&M advertising revenue by media; **~ reales** CONT, FISC actual earnings, real income, real earnings; **~ recibidos por deducción fiscal** CONT, FISC income received under deduction of tax; **~ salariales** CONT, FISC income from employment; **~ salariales sujetos a aportación** CONT, FISC contributory earnings from employment; **~ secundarios** CONT, FIN secondary income; **~ de seguros** SEG insurance proceeds; **~ de servicios** CONT income from services; **~ de la sociedad** CONT, FISC partnership income; **~ sometidos a**

descuento CONT, FISC pensionable earnings; **~ sujetos a imposición** CONT, FISC income subject to tax; **~ superiores** CONT, FISC upper income; **~ totales** CONT, ECON, FISC aggregate income, FISC total income; **~ del trabajo por cuenta propia** CONT, FISC, self-employment income; **~ de transferencia** CONT, FISC transfer earnings; **~ tributarios** CONT, FISC tax receipts, tax revenue; **~ por valores** CONT, FISC income from securities; **~ de venta** COM GEN sale proceeds; **~ por ventas** V&M sales revenue

inhóspito *adj* COM GEN inhospitable

inicia: que ~ una moda *fra* COM GEN trend-setting

iniciación: ~ del producto *f* V&M product initiation

iniciador, a *m,f* POL initiator; **~ de una moda** COM GEN trendsetter

inicial *adj* COM GEN initial

inicializar *vt* INFO *sistemas operativos* initialize, boot up

iniciar *vt* INFO *programas* initiate, V&M launch; ◆ **~ a alguien en** RRHH *empleo* start sb off as; **~ la conexión** INFO log on; **~ el despegue** COM GEN *negocios, proyecto* get off the ground (*infrml*); **~ juicio** DER bring an action

iniciarse: ~ en los negocios *fra* COM GEN start in business

iniciativa *f* COM GEN, GES initiative

inicio *m* COM GEN onset, commencement; **~ de la cobertura** SEG commencement of coverage; **~ de la descarga** TRANSP breaking load; **~ de vigencia de una póliza** SEG commencement of a policy

injuriador, a *m,f* COM GEN tort-feasor

injusticia *f* DER miscarriage of justice

inmanejable *adj* COM GEN unmanageable

INMARSAT *abr* (*Organización Internacional Marítima de Satélites*) COMS, TRANSP INMARSAT (*International Maritime Satellite Organization*)

inmigración *f* DER, ECON *internacional* immigration; **~ ilegal** POL illegal immigration

inmigrante *mf* POL, PROT SOC immigrant; **~ ilegal** POL, PROT SOC illegal immigrant

inmobiliaria *f* BANCA credit bank, Spanish mortgage bank; **~ de especulación** INMOB spec house

inmodificado *adj* COM GEN unchanged

inmovilizado: ~ inmaterial *m* CONT, FIN intangible assets; **~ material** *m* CONT, FIN tangible fixed assets

inmovilizar: ~ fondos para un cheque *fra* BANCA hold funds for a check (*AmE*), hold funds for a cheque (*BrE*)

inmueble: ~ comercial *m* INMOB trading estate

inmuebles: ~ personales *m pl* FISC, INMOB personal property

inmunidad *f* DER, FISC immunity; **~ fiscal** FISC exemption, tax immunity; **~ legal** DER, RRHH legal immunity, *sindicatos* statutory immunities; **~ tributaria** FISC immunity from taxation

inmunidades: ~ sindicales *f pl* DER, RRHH statutory immunities, trade union immunities (*BrE*)

inmunización *f* FIN, PROT SOC immunization

inmunizar *vt* FIN, PROT SOC immunize

innavegabilidad *f* TRANSP unseaworthiness

innegociable *adj* BANCA, COM GEN, FIN unnegotiable

innominado *adj* INFO *disco, archivo* unnamed

innovación *f* COM GEN, IND innovation; **~ estratégica** V&M strategic innovation; **~ tecnológica** COM GEN technological innovation

innovador[1] *adj* COM GEN, IND, V&M innovative

innovador[2]**,a** *m,f* COM GEN, IND, V&M innovator

innovar *vi* COM GEN, IND, V&M innovate

inobservancia: ~ **de las condiciones** *f* COM GEN non-observance of conditions

inocente *adj* DER innocent

input *m* ECON input; **~-output** ECON input-output

inquietud: ~ **laboral** *f* RRHH labor unrest (*AmE*), labour unrest (*BrE*)

inquilinato *m* DER lease, leasehold, INMOB tenancy

inquilino, -a *m,f* COM GEN tenant, lessee, occupier; ~ **inamovible** INMOB anchor tenant; ~ **en posesión** INMOB holdover tenant (*AmE*), sitting tenant; ~ **vitalicio(-a)** INMOB life tenant

inscribir: ~ **en el registro** *fra* PATENT *de la propiedad industrial* record in the register

inscripción *f* COM GEN enrollment (*AmE*), enrolment (*BrE*), DER *comercial* posting, PATENT registration; ~ **de un sindicato** RRHH union certification

inscrito, -a: **no** ~ *m,f* FISC nonregistrant

insensible *adj* COM GEN *mercado* unresponsive; ♦ ~ **a los fallos** INFO fault-tolerant

insertar *vt* INFO paste, insert, V&M *publicidad* insert; ♦ ~ **en su sitio** INFO slot in

insignificante *adj* COM GEN trifling, DER de minimis

insistir en *vt* COM GEN make a point of, *un precio más alto* stand out for

insoluble *adj* COM GEN insolvable

insoluto *adj* FIN *deuda* outstanding

insolvencia *f* BANCA, COM GEN, CONT insolvency, bankruptcy, bad debt

insolvente *adj* BOLSA hammered (*jarg*), COM GEN bankrupt, insolvent, shaky

inspección *f* COM GEN check, visitation, *producto* inspection, survey; ~ **aduanera** DER, IMP/EXP customs inspection; ~ **anual de controles automatizados** TRANSP *navegación* annual automated controls survey (*AAS*); ~ **del buque** TRANSP ship survey; ~ **catastral** FISC, INMOB cadastral survey; ~ **cuatrienal** FISC *de buques* quadrennial survey; ~ **de expedientes** PATENT inspection of files; ~ **extraordinaria** TRANSP *navegación* special survey (*SS*); ~ **intermedia** IND intermediate survey (*INT*); ~ **de la maquinaria** TRANSP machinery survey (*MS*); ~ **oficial de un banco** BANCA bank examination; ~ **periódica** TRANSP periodical survey; ~ **de personal** RRHH staff inspection; ~ **portuaria** TRANSP docking survey; ~ **posembarque** TRANSP post-shipment inspection; ~ **de precios** ECON price supervision; ~ **previa al embarque** TRANSP preshipment inspection; ~ **previa a la carga** TRANSP preloading inspection; ~ **previa a la entrega** TRANSP predelivery inspection; ~ **de seguridad** COM GEN safety check

Inspección: ~ **Técnica de Vehículos** *m* (*ITV*) TRANSP ≈ Ministry of Transport Test (*BrE*) (*MOT*)

inspeccionar 1. *vt* COM GEN, GES, RRHH supervise; ♦ ~ **la situación** COM GEN survey the situation; **2.** *vi* DER pass inspection

inspector, a *m,f* COM GEN comptroller, controller, INMOB surveyor, RRHH inspector; ~ **de aduanas** IMP/EXP examiner; ~ **de cantidades** IND quantity surveyor; ~ **de carga** RRHH, TRANSP cargo inspector, cargo superintendent; ~ **de fábrica** IND, RRHH factory inspec-

tor; ~ **de factoría** *ver inspector de factoría*; ~ **general** CONT Comptroller General (*AmE*); ~ **general de banca** BANCA Inspector General of Banks; ~ **de Hacienda** *m* FISC inspector of taxes (*BrE*), tax inspector; ~ **jefe(-a)** RRHH chief inspector (*CI*); ~ **oficial de bancos** BANCA bank examiner (*BrE*), commissioner of banking (*AmE*); ~ **de precios** ECON price supervisor; ~ **de quejas** RRHH claims inspector; ~ **recaudador(a)** FISC collection agent, encashing agent; **~-recaudador(a) de la Administración Fiscal** FISC Commissioner of the Inland Revenue (*BrE*); ~ **de sanidad** PROT SOC, RRHH health officer; ~ **de trabajo** PROT SOC, RRHH labor inspector (*AmE*), labour inspector (*BrE*)

instalación *f* CONT *activo fijo* plant, INFO facility, installation, INMOB fixture; ~ **de almacenamiento** COM GEN, MED AMB *para desechos tóxicos* storage facility; ~ **de apoyo** INFO backup facility; ~ **comercial** INMOB trade fixture; ~ **de crédito** BANCA borrowing facility; ~ **defectuosa** IND faulty installation; ~ **en mar abierto** TRANSP offshore installation; ~ **marítima separada de la costa** TRANSP offshore installation; ~ **recreativa** COM GEN recreational facility

instalaciones *f pl* COM GEN facilities, SEG plant (*BrE*); ~ **de atención infantil** FISC, PROT SOC childcare facilities; ~ **de intercambio normalizadas** TRANSP Standard Interchange Facilities (*SIT*); ~ **para el ocio** OCIO leisure facility; ~ **portuarias** TRANSP port facilities, harbor facilities (*AmE*), harbour facilities (*BrE*)

instalado *adj* COM GEN, INFO installed (*inst.*)

instalar *vt* COM GEN lay on, INFO *programa, periféricos* install

instancia *f* DER petition; ♦ **a** ~ **de** DER at the request of; **en esta** ~ COM GEN in this instance; **en última** ~ COM GEN as a last resort

instantánea *f* MEDIOS, V&M *publicidad, sesión fotográfica* shoot (*jarg*)

instante: **al** ~ *adj* COM GEN *información* up-to-the-minute

instar *vt* COM GEN file

instigar *vt* DER *derecho penal* counsel

instinto *m* V&M gut feeling (*infrml*), instinct; ~ **adquisitivo** COM GEN acquisitive instinct

institución *f* COM GEN, ECON institution; ~ **de ahorro y préstamo** BANCA savings institution (*BrE*), thrift institution (*AmE*); ~ **bancaria** BANCA banking institution; ~ **benéfica** COM GEN, FISC charity; ~ **benéfica registrada** FISC registered charity; ~ **Brookings** ECON Brookings Institution (*AmE*); ~ **centralizada** COM GEN centralized institution; ~ **crediticia** BANCA, FIN credit institution; ~ **de crédito** BANCA, FIN lending institution; ~ **de crédito cooperativo** BANCA, FIN cooperative credit institution; ~ **de depósito** BANCA, FIN deposit institution; ~ **económica** ECON economic institution; ~ **educativa** PROT SOC educational institution; ~ **educativa designada** PROT SOC designated educational institution; ~ **financiera** FIN financial institution; ~ **financiera especificada** FIN specified financial institution; ~ **financiera no bancaria** BOLSA, FIN nonbank financial institution; ~ **del mercado bursátil** FIN money market institution; ~ **política** POL political institution; ~ **privada** COM GEN, INMOB private institution; ~ **en quiebra** COM GEN failing institution; ~ **reconocida** FISC certified institution

instituto *m* COM GEN institute (*inst.*); ~ **de investigación aprobado** FISC approved research institute; ~ **mixto de**

enseñanza secundaria PROT SOC coeducational high school; ~ **de préstamos al consumidor** BANCA, FIN consumer loan institute

Instituto: ~ **de Asuntos Económicos** m ECON Institute of Economic Affairs (BrE) (IEA); ~ **de Banqueros** m BANCA Institute of Bankers (IOB); ~ **de Crédito Oficial** m (ICO) FIN Spanish official credit institute; ~ **de Economía Internacional** m ECON Institute for International Economics; ~ **de Educación Secundaria** m Esp PROT SOC college of further education (CFE); ~ **de Empleo** m ECON Employment Institute (BrE); ~ **de Estudios Financieros** m (IEF) FIN Spanish financial research institute; ~ **de Estudios Fiscales** m FISC, PROT SOC Institute of Fiscal Studies (IFS); ~ **Europeo de Normas de Telecomunicaciones** m COMS European Telecommunications Standards Institute (ETSI); ~ **para Finanzas Internacionales** m FIN Institute for International Finance (IIF); ~ **Internacional de Estadística** m COM GEN, MAT International Statistical Institute (ISI); ~ **Internacional de Investigación Agrícola** m IND International Agricultural Research Institute (IARA); ~ **Internacional de Prensa** m IND International Press Institute (IPI); ~ **Internacional para la Unificación del Derecho Privado** m DER International Institute for Unification of Private Law; ~ **de Mediación, Arbitraje y Conciliación** m (IMAC) GES, RRHH ≈ Advisory, Conciliation and Arbitration Service (BrE) (ACAS); ~ **Mexicano de Ejecutivos de Finanzas** m AmL (IMEF) FIN institute Mexican financial executives; ~ **Monetario Europeo** m (IME) ECON, POL European Monetary Institute (EMI); ~ **Nacional de Empleo** m (INEM) PROT SOC, RRHH bienestar governmental office for employment, ≈ Employment Service (BrE); ~ **Nacional de Estadística** m (INE) ECON ≈ Central Statistical Office (BrE) (CSO); ~ **de las Naciones Unidas para la Formación Profesional y la Investigación** m (UNITAR) POL, PROT SOC United Nations Institute for Training and Research (UNITAR); ~ **de las Naciones Unidas para la Formación Profesional y la Investigación** m (UNITAR) RRHH United Nations Institute for Training and Research (UNITAR)

instrucción f COM GEN training, DER preliminary investigation, INFO statement, programa instruction; ~ **asistida por computador** AmL ver instrucción asistida por computadora AmL; ~ **asistida por computadora** AmL (CAI, cf instrucción asistida por ordenador Esp) INFO computer-aided instruction (CAI); ~ **asistida por ordenador** Esp (CAI, cf instrucción asistida por computadora AmL) INFO computer-aided instruction (CAI); ~ **de embalaje** TRANSP packing instruction (pkg instr); ~ **de embarque** TRANSP shipping instruction; ~ **de envío** COMS forwarding instruction; ~ **de expedición de carga para exportación** IMP/EXP, TRANSP export cargo shipping instruction (ECSI); ~ **de máquina** INFO computer instruction; ~ **de pérdida limitada** BANCA, BOLSA inversión stop-loss rules; ~ **programada** COM GEN programmed instruction; ~ **real** INFO actual instruction; ~ **de reenvío** INFO breakpoint instruction; ~ **de transporte** TRANSP transport instruction

instrucciones f pl COM GEN brief; ◆ **para ~ adicionales** COM GEN for further instructions (FFI)

instructor, a m,f DER trial examiner, RRHH trainer

instruir vt COM GEN brief

instrumental adj COM GEN instrumental

instrumentalidad f COM GEN instrumentality

instrumentar vt INFO sistema implement

instrumento m COM GEN instrument, tool, DER instrument; ~ **al portador** BANCA bill to order; ~ **de cambio** FIN circulating medium; ~ **de capital** FIN capital instrument; ~ **de crédito** BOLSA futuros de tipo de interés credit instrument; ~ **de cuenta** CONT medium of account; ~ **de depósito** BANCA deposit instrument; ~ **derivado** FIN derivative instrument; ~ **derivativo de mostrador** FIN over-the-counter derivative instrument (AmE); ~ **de descuento** BOLSA discount instrument; ~ **de la deuda** COM GEN debt instrument; ~ **de deuda exento de riesgo** BOLSA letra del Tesoro risk-free debt instrument; ~ **financiero** FIN financial instrument; ~ **financiero residual** FIN residual financial instrument; ~ **fuera de la bolsa de valores** FIN off-exchange instrument; ~ **hipotecario alternativo** BANCA alternative mortgage instrument; ~ **legal** DER statutory instrument; ~ **liberado** FIN paid instrument; ~ **de licitación** COM GEN bid vehicle; ~ **a medio plazo** BOLSA medium-term instrument; ~ **del mercado de dinero a corto plazo** BOLSA hoja de balance short-term money market instrument; ~ **del mercado monetario** BOLSA money market instrument; ~ **negociable endosado por el portador** BANCA order paper; ~ **no negociable** BANCA non-negotiable instrument, nonmarketable instrument; ~ **de pago prioritario** BANCA priority payment instrument; ~ **de participación alternativa** BOLSA alternative participation instrument (API); ~ **de préstamo transferible** BANCA, FIN transferable loan instrument (TLI); ~ **primario de endeudamiento** BANCA primary instrument of indebtedness; ~ **que devenga interés** BOLSA interest-bearing instrument; ~ **de tipo de interés** BOLSA interest rate instrument; ~ **variable** ECON instrument variable

instrumentos ~ **negociables** m pl COM GEN commercial paper (CP)

insuficiencia f COM GEN, CONT, TRANSP shortfall; ~ **de tesorería** CONT liquidez, efectivo, caja cash-poor

insumos m pl DER, IND inputs; ~ **químicos** MED AMB agricultura chemical input

insurrecto, -a m,f COM GEN insurgent

integración f COM GEN integration; ~ **económica** COM GEN economic integration; ~ **empresarial vertical** COM GEN vertical business integration; ~ **de E/S** INFO spooling; ~ **horizontal** COM GEN horizontal integration, horizontal expansion; ~ **horizontal de los canales** GES horizontal channel integration; ~ **lateral** COM GEN lateral integration; ~ **progresiva** COM GEN forward integration; ~ **regresiva** COM GEN backward integration; ~ **vertical** COM GEN vertical integration, vertical expansion; ~ **vertical decreciente** COM GEN backward vertical integration; ~ **vertical progresista** COM GEN forward vertical integration

integrado adj ECON integrated, INFO built-in

integrador, a m,f IMP/EXP, TRANSP integrator

integral[1] adj TRANSP integral

integral[2] m TRANSP contenedor integral

integrar vt COM GEN integrate

integridad f COM GEN integrity, CONT datos completeness; ~ **de los datos** INFO data integrity; ~ **fiscal** FISC fiscal rectitude

íntegro adj COM GEN unabridged

inteligencia: ~ **artificial** *f* (*IA*) INFO artificial intelligence (*AI*); ~ **económica** *f* ECON economic intelligence

inteligente *adj* COM GEN knowledgeable

intempestivo *adj* COM GEN untimely

intención *f* COM GEN intention

intensidad: ~ **del uso de la tierra** *f* MED AMB land-use intensity

intensificación *f* ECON *de técnicas de cultivo* intensification; ~ **del capital** ECON capital deepening

intensificar *vt* COM GEN *esfuerzo* intensify, ECON tighten; ◆ ~ **las restricciones monetarias** ECON tighten the monetary reins

intensificarse *v refl* COM GEN intensify

intensivo *adj* BOLSA *oferta, demanda* buoyant, COM GEN intensive; ◆ ~ **en capital** IND capital-intensive; ~ **en conocimientos** COM GEN knowledge-intensive; ~ **en cuanto a gente** RRHH people-intensive; ~ **en cuanto a mano de obra** IND, RRHH labor-intensive (*AmE*), labour-intensive (*BrE*); ~ **en cuanto a personal** RRHH personnel-intensive; ~ **en trabajo** RRHH labor-intensive (*AmE*), labour-intensive (*BrE*)

intentar *vt* COM GEN attempt

intento *m* COM GEN endeavor (*AmE*), endeavour (*BrE*), *tentativa* attempt; ~ **de absorción hostil** FIN unfriendly takeover attempt, unfriendly takeover bid

interacción: ~ **tecnología-mercado** *f* COM GEN technology and market interface

interactivo *adj* COM GEN, INFO interactive

intercalación *f* INFO *con clasificación* collation

intercalado *adj* INFO collated, embedded

intercalar *vt* INFO embed

intercambiar *vt* COMS *información, puntos de vista* exchange

intercambio *m* COM GEN exchange, switch, FIN swoption; ~ **de cartas** COMS interchange of letters; ~ **de cartera** BOLSA portfolio switching; ~ **comercial** COM GEN trade, trading; ~ **de contratos** COM GEN exchange of contracts; ~ **de datos comerciales** ECON trade data interchange (*TDI*); ~ **electrónico de datos** COMS, INFO electronic data interchange (*EDI*); ~ **desigual** COM GEN unequal exchange; ~ **de la deuda** FIN debt swop; ~ **electrónico de documentos** COMS electronic document interchange (*EDI*); ~ **de favores** POL horse-trading (*infrml*); ~ **de información** COM GEN exchange of information, feedback; ~ **mercantil** BOLSA mercantile exchange; ~ **de monedas** FIN currency swop; ~ **de opciones** BOLSA options exchange; ~ **de piezas** COM GEN part exchange; ~ **portuario** TRANSP port interchange; ~ **de programa** COM GEN program trade (*AmE*), programme trade (*BrE*); ~ **rotativo** FIN roller swop; ~ **sindicado** FIN syndicated swop; ~ **de la tesorería** FIN treasury swop; ~ **de valores** BOLSA matrix trading

interceptar *vt* COM GEN shut off

interclasificadora *f* INFO collator

interconectar *vt* INFO network, interface

interconectarse *v refl* INFO attach

interconexión *f* COM GEN interconnection, INFO attachment; ~ **de sistemas abiertos** (*OSI*) INFO open systems interconnection (*OSI*)

intercontinental *adj* TRANSP intercontinental

intercostero *adj* TRANSP intercoastal

interdepartamental *adj* ADMIN, COM GEN, POL interdepartmental

interdependencia *f* ECON, POL interdependence; ~ **estratégica** COM GEN, GES strategic interdependence

interdependiente *adj* COM GEN interdependent

interdicto *m* DER garnishment, injunction, interim injunction; ~ **mandatario** DER mandatory injunction

interés[1]: **con** ~ *adj* BANCA interest-bearing

interés[2] *m* COM GEN *dinero* interest (*i, int.*); ~ **abierto** BOLSA open interest; ~ **acumulado** COM GEN accrued interest (*accrd. int., AI*), accumulated interest (*AI*); ~ **aditivo** BANCA add-on interest; ~ **anual** BANCA exact interest, CONT annual yield; ~ **de aplazamiento** FIN contango; ~ **de arrendamiento** DER leasehold interest; ~ **asegurable** SEG insurable interest; ~ **atribuido** FISC imputed interest; ~ **bancario** BANCA, CONT bank interest; ~ **en un banco** BANCA interest in a bank, stake in a bank; ~ **base** BANCA, ECON, FIN basic rate; ~ **básico sobre préstamos** BANCA base lending rate; ~, **beneficio y dividendos** ECON interest, profit and dividends (*IPD*); ~ **del bono** BOLSA bond interest; ~ **capitalizado** BOLSA capitalized interest; ~ **combinado** BANCA compound interest; ~ **comercial** COM GEN commercial interest, business interest; ~ **compuesto** BANCA compound interest; ~ **compuesto acumulado** BANCA accrued compound interest; ~ **considerable** BANCA substantial interest; ~ **corriente** BANCA running interest; ~ **creciente** BOLSA balloon interest; ~ **deudor** BANCA, CONT, FIN debit interest; ~ **devengado** BANCA interest income, earned interest, accrued interest (*accrd. int., AI*); ~ **diario** BANCA daily interest; ~ **dominante** COM GEN overriding interest; ~ **escalonado** BANCA graduated interest; ~ **exento** FISC exempt interest; ~ **extraordinario** COM GEN extra interest; ~ **por falta de pago** BANCA default interest; ~ **de fondos federales** BANCA federal funds rate (*AmE*); ~ **futuro** COM GEN *en propiedad, crédito* future interest; ~ **de garantía** BOLSA security interest; ~ **genérico** V&M generic appeal; ~ **material** BOLSA *en empresa* material interest; ~ **de la mayoría** COM GEN majority interest, majority stake; ~ **mayoritario** COM GEN majority interest, majority stake; ~ **minoritario** COM GEN minority interest, minority stake; ~ **de moratorio** BANCA interest on arrears; ~ **nacional** POL national interest; ~ **negativo** BANCA negative interest; ~ **neto devengado** BANCA net interest income; ~ **nominal** BANCA, BOLSA, FIN coupon rate, nominal interest; ~ **operativo** COM GEN operating interest; ~ **ordinario** FIN ordinary interest; ~ **a partir del vencimiento** BANCA post-maturity interest; ~ **porcentual** COM GEN *de consorcio* percentage interest; ~ **preferencial** BOLSA participating interest; ~ **preferencial a largo plazo** FIN long-term prime rate (*LTPR*); ~ **en el puesto** RRHH job interest; ~ **recibido** BANCA interest received; ~ **reducido** BANCA, BOLSA *de futuros, valores* short interest; ~ **remunerativo** BOLSA yield advantage; ~ **sin repartir** FIN undistributed interest; ~ **resultante** BANCA carried interest; ~ **simple** BANCA simple interest; ~ **sobre bonos** BOLSA interest on bonds; ~ **sobre depósitos** BANCA deposit interest; ~ **sobre préstamos bancarios** BANCA bank lending rate; ~ **sobre préstamos de un banco** BANCA bank loan rate; ~ **de subordinación** BANCA subordination interest; ~ **subordinado** BOLSA, FIN subordinated interest; ~ **a 365 días** BANCA exact interest; ~ **x** FIN x-interest; ◆ **que**

no devenga ~ BANCA, BOLSA, FIN noninterest-bearing;
~ **total admitido** TRANSP full interest admitted (*fia*);
tener un ~ **propio** BOLSA have an equity interest

interesado, -a *m,f* COM GEN, DER interested party

intereses[1]: **sin** ~ *adj* BANCA noninterest-bearing, *préstamo* interest-free

intereses[2]: ~ **acumulados por cobrar** *m pl* BANCA, CONT accrued interest receivable; ~ **acumulados por pagar** *m pl* BANCA, CONT accrued interest payable; ~ **atrasados** *m pl* BANCA, CONT interest arrears, back interest; ~ **bancarios** *m pl* BANCA, CONT bank interest; ~ **del capital** *m pl* FISC *en un fideicomiso* capital interest; ~ **no devengados** *m pl* BANCA, CONT unearned interest; ~ **opuestos** *m pl* COM GEN conflicting interest; ~ **pagados** *m pl* BANCA, CONT interest paid; ~ **patrimoniales** *m pl* DER, FISC beneficial interest; ~ **preferenciales** *m pl* BANCA prime rate (*BrE*), prime (*AmE*); ~ **recibidos** *m pl* CONT interest earned; **tener intereses en algo** *fra* COM GEN have a vested interest in sth

interestatal *adj* COM GEN *comercio* interstate (*AmE*)

interfaz *m* INFO interface; ~ **Centronics**® INFO Centronics interface®; ~ **paralelo** INFO parallel interface; ~ **de usuario** INFO user interface

interferencia *f* COM GEN, DER interference, INFO glitch, interference; ~ **con el contrato** RRHH interference with contract; ~ **del empresario** RRHH employer interference

interferencias *f pl* COM GEN, MEDIOS, TRANSP signal jamming

interfondo *m* ECON *internacional* interfund

intergrupal *adj* RRHH intergroup

intergubernamental *adj* POL intergovernmental

interino *adj* COM GEN provisional

interior: ~ **de la contraportada** *m* MEDIOS inside back cover; ~ **de la portada** *m* MEDIOS inside front cover

interiorizar: ~ **una externalidad** *fra* ECON internalize an externality

interlínea *f* MEDIOS *imprenta* line space

interlocutorio *adj* PATENT interlocutory

intermediación *f* FIN intermediation; ~ **financiera** FIN financial intermediation

intermediario[1] *adj* COM GEN intermediary

intermediario[2]**,-a** *m,f* BOLSA broker, dealer, trader, COM GEN intermediary, middleman, FIN intermediary; ~ **de arbitraje** BOLSA arbitrage trader; ~ **autorizado(-a)** BOLSA authorized dealer; ~ **de bolsa** BOLSA agency broker, stockjobber (*obs*) (*BrE*); ~ **de bolsa de entrega** BOLSA delivery broker; ~ **de bolsa minorista** BOLSA retail broker; ~ **de cambio de descuento** BOLSA discount stock broker; ~ **de efectos de descuento** BOLSA running broker; ~ **financiero(-a)** BOLSA stockbroker, FIN financial intermediary; ~ **fiscal** BOLSA fiscal agent; ~ **independiente** BOLSA outsider broker; ~ **por lotes** BOLSA block stock trader; ~ **del mercado monetario** FIN money market trader; ~ **en el mercado primario** BOLSA primary market dealer; ~ **notificador(a)** BOLSA reporting dealer; ~ **de opciones registradas** BOLSA registered options broker; ~ **de renta fija** BOLSA bond trader; ~ **en títulos** BOLSA trader in securities; ~ **de transferencias** BOLSA stock-transfer agent; ~ **en valores** BOLSA dealer in securities; ~ **de valores sin cotización** BOLSA unlisted trader; ~ **de ventas** BOLSA selling agent

intermediarios: ~ **y exportadores de derechos registrados** *m pl* IMP/EXP, TRANSP Registered Excise Dealers and Shippers (*REDS*)

intermedio *adj* COM GEN intermediate; ◆ **por** ~ **de alguien** COM GEN through sb's agency

intermitente *adj* COM GEN intermittent

intermodal *adj* TRANSP intermodal

internacional *adj* BANCA international, offshore, COM GEN international (*intl*)

internacionalismo *m* POL *terminología socialista* internationalism; ~ **proletario** ECON, POL proletarian internationalism (*jarg*)

internacionalización *f* COM GEN internationalization

internacionalizar *vt* COM GEN internationalize

internalización *f* COM GEN internalization

internalizar *vt* COM GEN internalize

Internet *m* COMS, INFO Internet, the Net, the Web

interno[1] *adj* COM GEN *organización, país* internal, *traductor* in-house, INFO *servicio, trabajador* in-house, on-board, RRHH *organización, país* internal, *traductor* in-house

interno[2]: ~ **telefónico** *m* AmL (*cf extensión telefónica Esp*) COMS telephone extension (*X*)

interoperabilidad *f* FIN, IND, INFO interoperability

interpolación *f* MAT interpolation

interponer: ~ **una acción** *fra* DER bring an action

interposición: ~ **de una apelación** *f* FISC institution of an appeal

interpretación *f* COM GEN interpretation, COMS *lenguas* interpreting

interpretador *m* INFO interpreter

interpretar *vt* COM GEN interpret; ◆ ~ **algo con flexibilidad** COM GEN give a loose interpretation of sth

intérprete *mf* COMS *lenguas* interpreter

interrelación *f* MAT *estadística* interrelation

interrogación *f* COMS polling, INFO inquiry

interrogador *m* COM GEN scanner

interrogar *vt* COM GEN query

interrogatorio *m* PATENT examination; ~ **preliminar** PATENT preliminary examination

interrogatorios *m pl* DER interrogatories

interrumpir *vt* COM GEN shut down, *misión, juicio, despegue* abort, COMS *noticias* break, INFO *programa, operación* abort; ◆ ~ **el subsidio de alguien** COM GEN stop sb's allowance

interrupción *f* COM GEN shutdown, interruption, RRHH *negociaciones* breakdown; ~ **de actividades** COM GEN business interruption; ~ **natural** V&M natural break; ~ **de las operaciones** GES operations breakdown; ~ **del pago** RRHH pay pause; ~ **del servicio** TRANSP *ferrocarril* breakdown; ~ **del trabajo** RRHH work stoppage; ~ **de los trabajos** *m* RRHH *por mobilizaciones* stoppage of work; ~ **de tránsito** V&M stoppage in transit

interruptor *m* INFO toggle, *dispositivo* switch; ~ **basculante** INFO toggle switch; ~ **de palanca** INFO toggle switch

intervalo *m* MAT range; ~ **de confianza** MAT *estadística* confidence interval; ~ **a mitad de precio de ejercicio** BOLSA *opciones* half a strike price interval; ~ **en el precio de ejecución** BOLSA *opciones* strike price interval

intervención *f* COM GEN, CONT intervention, audit; **no ~** POL nonintervention; **~ continua** CONT continuous audit; **~ estatal** ECON, POL state intervention, government intervention; **~ externa** FISC field audit; **~ fiscal** FISC tax audit; **~ interior de cuentas** CONT internal audit; **~ mínima del Estado** POL minimal state intervention; **~ monetaria** ECON intervention currency; **~ a posteriori** FISC post-audit; **~ a priori** FISC pre-audit; **~ de un teléfono** COMS telephone tapping; **~ de un tercero** RRHH third-party intervention

intervencionista *adj* POL interventionist

intervenir 1. *vt* COM GEN *llamada telefónica* tap into, DER *contrato* interfere with; **~ en** COM GEN intervene in; **2.** *vi* COM GEN intervene, step in (*infrml*)

interventor, a *m,f Esp* (*cf contralor AmL*) COM GEN compliance accountant, financial accountant, *cuentas del Estado* comptroller, controller; **~ adjunto(-a)** *Esp* (*cf contralor adjunto AmL*) RRHH *transporte marítimo* assistant controller (*AC*); **~ en caso de necesidad** *Esp* (*cf contralor en caso de necesidad AmL*) BANCA referee in case of need; **~ de cuentas** *Esp* (*cf contralor de cuentasAmL*) CONT auditor; **~ especial** *Esp* (*cf contralor especialAmL*) FISC *recursos fiscales* special commissioner (*BrE*); **~ general adjunto(-a)** *Esp* (*cf contralor general adjunto AmL*) ADMIN, RRHH deputy receiver general; **~ del naufragio** *Esp* (*cf contralor del naufragio AmL*) RRHH *de aduanas* receiver of wrecks; **~ de quiebras** COM GEN, DER Superintendent of Bankruptcy

interventores: ~ especiales *m pl* FISC Special Commissioners (*BrE*); **~ generales** *m pl* FISC General Commissioners (*BrE*)

intestado *adj* DER intestate

intimidación *f* RRHH intimidation

intradepartamental *adj* ADMIN intradepartmental

intraestatal *adj* COM GEN intrastate (*AmE*)

intramuros *m pl* FIN Chinese walls

intransferible *adj* BOLSA untransferable, not transferable, DER unassignable

introducción *f* COM GEN *libro, conferencia* introduction; **~ de datos** INFO data input; **~ de datos codificados** INFO coded data entry; **~ del producto** V&M product introduction

introducir *vt* COM GEN introduce, DER *cambios* introduce, bring in (*infrml*); ◆ **~ progresivamente** COM GEN, INFO *tecnología, servicios, sistema* phase in; **~ información en un registro** COM GEN enter information onto a register; **~ por teclado** INFO key in

introducirse[1]: **~ en** *v refl* COM GEN enter

introducirse[2]: **~ en el mercado** *fra* COM GEN enter the market

intrusión *f* DER encroachment

intrusismo: ~ laboral *m* RRHH labor piracy (*AmE*), labour piracy (*BrE*)

intruso[1] *adj* COMS, V&M intrusive

intruso[2]**,-a** *m,f* GES, RRHH *en organización* outsider

inutilizado *adj* BANCA, COM GEN *línea de crédito*, FIN nonutilized

invalidación *f* DER invalidation

invalidar *vt* COM GEN make void, *voto* invalidate

invariable *adj* COM GEN flat

invasión *f* DER trespassing; **~ de la propiedad privada** DER trespassing on private property

invención *f* ECON, IND, PATENT invention

invendible *adj* COM GEN, V&M unmarketable, unsaleable

invendido *adj* COM GEN unsold

inventar *vt* COM GEN devise, mint, IND invent

inventariado: no ~ *adj* COM GEN unstocked

inventario *m* COM GEN inventory, listing, schedule, stocktaking, CONT inventory, stock in hand; **~ actual** COM GEN actual inventory; **~ de apertura** CONT beginning inventory; **~ de artículos** COM GEN inventory item; **~ de cierre** CONT closing inventory; **~ contable** COM GEN detailed account; **~ continuo** COM GEN, CONT, ECON continuous inventory, continuous stocktaking; **~ de entrada** CONT beginning inventory; **~ de existencias** COM GEN stock inventory; **~ final** CONT closing inventory, ending inventory; **~ físico** CONT physical inventory; **~ inicial** CONT beginning inventory, opening inventory, initial inventory; **~ de intereses de Strong y Campbell** RRHH Strong-Campbell Interest Inventory; **~ en libros** BOLSA book inventory; **~ de mercancías** COM GEN merchandise inventory; **~ de producción** IND manufacturing inventory; **~ de stock** COM GEN stock inventory; **~ total de ventas** FISC aggregate sales listings (*BrE*) (*ASL*)

invento: ~ patentable *m* PATENT patentable invention

inventor, a *m,f* COM GEN inventor; **~ único(-a)** PATENT sole inventor

inversa: a la ~ *adv* COM GEN conversely

inversamente *adv* MAT inversely

inversión *f* COM GEN, IND investment, outlay, INFO case shift; **~ en acciones** BOLSA, COM GEN equity investment; **~ en acciones ordinarias** BOLSA common share investment (*BrE*), common stock investment (*AmE*); **~ en acciones de otras compañías** BOLSA, CONT share investments in other companies; **~ aceptable** BOLSA acceptable investment; **~ activa** BOLSA active investment; **~ agresiva** BOLSA aggressive investment; **~ autónoma** BOLSA autonomous investment; **~ basada en activos** BOLSA asset-based investment; **~ bruta** BOLSA gross investment; **~ de calidad** BOLSA qualified investment; **~ de capital** BOLSA capital investment; **~ en capital fijo** COM GEN capital expenditure (*capex*); **~ en capital productivo** ECON, FIN capital accumulation; **~ de cartera** BOLSA portfolio investment; **~ comercial** BOLSA trade investment; **~ cualificada** BOLSA qualified investment; **~ directa** BOLSA straight investment, direct investment; **~ en dólares constantes** BOLSA constant-dollar plan (*AmE*); **~ dominante** BOLSA, RRHH controlling interest; **~ estatal** CONT *cuentas anuales* Treasury investment (*BrE*); **~ ética** BOLSA, POL ethical investment; **~ de explotación** CONT *en edificios y equipamiento* operational investment; **~ exterior** COM GEN investment abroad; **~ extranjera** FIN foreign investment, offshore investment; **~ extranjera directa** FIN direct foreign investment; **~ extranjera neta** CONT net foreign investment; **~ fiduciaria** BANCA fiduciary investment; **~ financiera** FIN financial investment; **~ financiera a largo plazo** BANCA, CONT, FIN long-term financial investment; **~ en forma de préstamo** BANCA, FIN loan investment; **~ por fórmula** BOLSA formula investing; **~ forzosa** FIN involuntary investment; **~ garantizada** FIN guaranteed investment; **~ a interés variable** BOLSA *de futuros* floating-rate investment; **~ interna** ECON domestic investment, FIN inward investment; **~ legal** BOLSA legal investment; **~ malograda** BANCA bad investment; ~ **minoritaria** BOLSA minority investment; ~ **mixta** FIN investment mix; ~ **monetaria insegura** COM GEN *sin fondos, sin valor* blue-sky; ~ **negativa** FIN negative investment; ~ **neta interior** CONT net domestic investment; ~ **no monetaria** RRHH nonmonetary investment; ~ **no planificada** BANCA unintended investment; ~ **oportuna** BOLSA fit investment; ~ **en paquetes** FIN *sector público* block funding; ~ **privada** BANCA, FIN private investment; ~ **que genera beneficios fiscales** ECON, FIN, FISC tax-efficient investment; ~ **real** BANCA actual investment, *para hospitales, escuelas* real investment, FIN real investment; ~ **reglamentaria** FIN statutory investment; ~ **en renta fija** BOLSA fixed-income investment; ~ **de reposición** CONT, FIN replacement investment; ~ **respaldada por activos** FIN asset-backed investment; ~ **del sector privado** ECON, FIN private sector investment; ~ **segura** BANCA, FIN secure investment; ~ **en sociedades** FIN corporate investment; ~ **del Tesoro** CONT *cuentas anuales* Treasury investment (*BrE*)

inversiones *f pl* BOLSA investments

inversionista *mf* BOLSA, ECON, FIN investor

inverso *adj* MAT inverse

inversor, a *m,f* BOLSA, ECON, FIN investor; ~ **en acciones** BOLSA equity investor; ~ **acreditado(-a)** BOLSA accredited investor; ~ **activo(-a)** BOLSA active investor; ~ **contracorriente** BOLSA contrarian; ~ **corporativo(-a)** BOLSA corporate investor; ~ **con experiencia** BOLSA experienced investor; ~ **extranjero(-a)** *m* BOLSA inbound investor, foreign investor, overseas investor, inward investor; ~ **hostil** BOLSA greenmailer; ~ **individual** BOLSA individual investor; ~ **institucional** BOLSA institutional investor; ~ **minorista** BOLSA retail investor; ~ **de oportunidades** BOLSA bottom fisher; ~ **pasivo(-a)** BOLSA passive investor; ~ **potencial** BOLSA potential investor; ~ **privado(-a)** BOLSA private investor; ~ **público(-a)** BOLSA public investor; ~ **de teoría contraria** BOLSA lowballer (*jarg*)

invertible *adj* FIN investible

invertido *adj* COM GEN invested

invertir *vt* BOLSA, COM GEN invest, lay out, ECON *tendencia* reverse, *dinero* invest, INFO invert; ◆ ~ **en acciones** BOLSA invest in shares; ~ **con cobertura** COM GEN hedge one's bets; ~ **dinero en** BOLSA invest money in; ~ **en obligaciones** BOLSA invest in bonds; ~ **en propiedades** INMOB invest in property; ~ **en una renta anual** FIN invest in an annuity

invertirse *v refl* COM GEN, ECON *tendencia* turn around

investigable *adj* FISC *grupo o persona* ascertainable

investigación[1]: **con ~ intensiva** *adj* COM GEN, IND *producción* research-intensive

investigación[2] *f* COM GEN research, PATENT search; ~ **académica** PROT SOC academic research; ~ **de acción** GES action research; ~ **de antecedentes** RRHH *del solicitante* background investigation; ~ **aplicada** COM GEN applied research; ~ **básica** COM GEN basic research; ~ **de campo** V&M field research; ~ **científica** IND scientific research; ~ **de clientes** V&M customer research; ~ **comercial** COM GEN commercial research; ~ **conductista** V&M behavioral research (*AmE*), behavioural research (*BrE*); ~ **del consumidor** V&M consumer research; ~ **cualitativa** V&M qualitative research; ~ **cuantitativa** V&M quantitative research; ~ **de datos ya existentes** COM GEN desk research; ~ **y**

desarrollo (*I&D*) IND research and development (*R&D*); ~ **y desarrollo del producto** IND product research and development; ~ **económica** ECON economic research; ~ **por encuestas** V&M survey research; ~ **sin garantías** POL warrantless investigation (*jarg*); ~ **independiente** DER independent inquiry; ~ **industrial** IND, V&M industrial research; ~ **de mercado** V&M marketing research; ~ **de mercados exteriores** IMP/EXP, V&M export market research; ~ **motivacional** GES, V&M motivational research; ~ **operacional** GES, V&M operational research (*OR*); ~ **de operaciones** GES, V&M operations research (*OR*); ~ **permanente** GES, V&M continuous research; ~ **del producto** V&M product research; ~ **publicitaria** V&M advertising research; ~ **pura** RRHH blue-sky research; ~ **sin restricciones** FISC full-scale investigation; ~ **de ventas** V&M sales research

Investigación: ~ **Básica de Tecnologías Industriales para Europa** *f* IND Basic Research in Industrial Technologies for Europe (*BRITE*)

investigador, a: ~ **de campo** *m,f* V&M field investigator

investigar *vt* COM GEN *indagar*, DER *delito* investigate, look into

investir *vt* BOLSA vest; ◆ ~ **a alguien de algo** COM GEN vest sb with sth

invitación *f* COM GEN invitation, OCIO *teatro* punched paper; ~ **a emitir** INFO *redes, modem* polling; ~ **a negociar** DER invitation to treat; ~ **pública a ofertar** COM GEN public invitation to bid; ~ **para la presentación de ofertas** COM GEN *concursos, subastas* competing bid

invitar: ~ **a votar** *fra* RRHH ballot

invocar *vt* COM GEN *ley, penalización* invoke

inyección *f* ECON, FIN injection; ~ **de capital** ECON, FIN capital injection

inyectar *vt* COM GEN *fondos* inject

IPC *abr* (*Índice de Precios al Consumo*) ECON, FIN consumer expenditure survey, CPI (*consumer price index*) (*BrE*)

IPD *abr* (*Índice de Precios al Detalle*) BOLSA, ECON RPI (*Retail Price Index*)

ir *vi* TRANSP go, travel; ◆ ~ **por buen camino** COM GEN be on the right track; ~ **en contra de** BOLSA go against; ~ **en contra de la tendencia** COM GEN buck the trend (*infrml*); ~ **a contracorriente** COM GEN go against the current, go against the tide, go upstream; ~ **con la corriente** RRHH go with the flow (*infrml*); ~ **cuesta abajo** COM GEN *negocios* go downhill; ~ **directo a** COM GEN go straight to; ~ **disminuyendo** COM GEN tail away; ~ **de excursión** TRANSP junket (*AmE*); ~ **al grano** COM GEN get down to specifics; ~ **a la huelga en solidaridad con** RRHH *huelguistas* go out in sympathy with; ~ **por mal camino** COM GEN be on the wrong track; ~ **al mismo ritmo que los competidores** COM GEN keep in step with one's competitors; ~ **a pique** *infrml* COM GEN go to the wall (*infrml*); ~ **a al quiebra** COM GEN go out of business; ~ **a toda máquina** IND go full steam ahead; ~ **de vacaciones** OCIO take a holiday (*BrE*), OCIO take a vacation (*AmE*); ~ **de vacío** TRANSP *autobús, tren* run empty

IRPF *abr* (*Impuesto sobre la Renta*) FISC ≈ IT (*Income Tax*)

irrealizable *adj* COM GEN unfeasible

irrebatible *adj* TRANSP rebateable

irrecuperable *adj* INFO *datos* unrecoverable

irredimible *adj* BANCA irredeemable

irreductible *adj* COM GEN irreducible

irreemplazable *adj* COM GEN irreplaceable

irrefutable *adj* DER *indicio* irrebuttable

irregular *adj* COM GEN occasional, *tendencia* uneven, V&M ragged

irregularidad *f* COM GEN, DER irregularity

irrelevante *adj* COM GEN, DER irrelevant

irreparable *adj* COM GEN, DER *error, pérdida, daño* irreparable

irreprochable *adj* COM GEN *contrato, evidencia* unimpeachable

irrescatable *adj* BOLSA irredeemable

irreversible *adj* COM GEN *estrategia* irreversible

irrevocable *adj* COM GEN *decisión* irreversible, DER irrevocable

irrumpir *vt* COM GEN *en el mercado* break into

ISBN *abr* (*Numeración Internacional Normalizada de Libros*) MEDIOS ISBN (*International Standard Book Number*)

isla: **~ de venta** *f* ECON island

ISO *abr* BOLSA (*incentivo fiscal sobre opciones*) ISO (*incentive stock option*)

isocosto *m* ECON isocost

isocuanta *f* ECON isoquant

ISRS *abr* (*impuesto sobre la renta de sociedades*) FISC corporate tax

ITE *abr* (*impuesto sobre el tráfico de empresas*) FISC turnover tax

ítem *m* CONT item

itemizar *vt* CONT itemize

iteración *f* INFO iteration

itinerario *m* COM GEN itinerary; **~ de distribución** TRANSP multiport itinerary; **~ fijo** TRANSP fixed route

ITP *abr* (*impuesto sobre transmisiones patrimoniales*) FISC estate tax, transfer tax

ITV *abr* (*Inspección Técnica de Vehículos*) TRANSP ≈ MOT (*Ministry of Transport Test*)

IVA *abr* (*impuesto sobre el valor añadido*) ECON, FIN, FISC VAT (*Value Added Tax*) (*BrE*)

I&D *abr* (*investigación y desarrollo*) IND R&D (*research and development*)

izar: **~ algo a bordo** *fra* COM GEN, TRANSP take sth aboard

izquierda: **nueva ~** *f* POL *ideología económica* New Left

izquierdas: **de ~** *adj* POL left-wing, left

izquierdismo *m* POL leftism

izquierdista *adj* POL left-wing, left

J K

JAC abr (*Junta de Administración Cambiaria*) BANCA, POL Foreign Exchange Admiinistration Board.

japonización f ECON, FIN *comercio internacional* japanization

jaula f TRANSP cage-tainer; **~ de embalaje** TRANSP crate

jefa f COM GEN manageress (*MGR*)

jefe, -a m,f COM GEN leader, RRHH boss (*infrml*), chief, head, manager (*MGR*), senior; **~ administrativo(-a)** DER senior clerk, RRHH administration officer (*AO*); **~ de almacén** RRHH storeman (*BrE*), stockman (*AmE*), warehouseman (*AmE*); **~ de auditoría** CONT audit head; **~ auxiliar de sección** RRHH assistant head of section (*AHS*); **~ de caja** RRHH cash manager; **~ de capacitación** AmL (*cf jefe de formación Esp*) COM GEN, RRHH training officer; **~ de cobros** BANCA drawing officer; **~ comercial** GES, RRHH commercial director, commercial manager; **~ de compras** RRHH procurement manager, V&M chief buyer, head buyer; **~ de contabilidad** CONT accountant general (*A.G.*), chief accountant, accounting officer; **~ contable** CONT head accountant; **~ contable de grupo** CONT group chief accountant; **~ de contratación** RRHH recruitment officer; **~ de control de tráfico** RRHH, TRANSP chief traffic controller; **~ de créditos** FIN credit officer; **~ de cuentas** RRHH account executive; **~ de departamento** COM GEN departmental head, RRHH *universidad* head of department (*HoD*), V&M *grandes almacenes, tienda* department manager; **~ de distribución** GES, RRHH, TRANSP distribution manager; **~ de distrito** GES, RRHH district manager; **~ de división** GES, RRHH division head, division manager; **~ ejecutivo(-a)** GES, RRHH chief executive officer (*AmE*) (*CEO*); **~ de equipo** RRHH team leader; **~ de estación** TRANSP stationmaster; **~ de estado** POL head of state; **~ de estudios** PROT SOC *educación* Director of Studies (*DOS*); **~ de exportación** GES export director, export manager, IMP/EXP, RRHH export manager, export director, senior export clerk; **~ falso(-a)** m RRHH straw boss (*AmE*) (*infrml*); **~ de flota** RRHH *de máquinas*, TRANSP fleet manager; **~ de flotilla** RRHH *aviones, barcos*, TRANSP fleet manager; **~ de formación** Esp (*cf jefe de capacitación AmL*) COM GEN, RRHH training officer; **~ de grupo** RRHH group leader; **~ de importación** IMP/EXP, RRHH senior import clerk; **~ de información** RRHH chief information officer (*CIO*); **~ de inmigración** RRHH chief immigration officer (*CIO*); **~ de lista** V&M list manager; **~ de movimiento** RRHH, TRANSP traffic manager; **~ de negociado** RRHH human resources manager; **~ de obra** IND on-site manager, site manager, RRHH site manager; **~ de oficina** DER head clerk, GES, RRHH head clerk, office manager; **~ de oficina de ventas** m V&M sales office manager; **~ de parque de coches** m RRHH, TRANSP fleet manager; **~ de personal** RRHH chief of staff, personnel officer; **~ del producto** RRHH product manager; **~ de proyecto** COM GEN project leader, project manager; **~ de publicidad** RRHH, V&M advertising manager; **~ de reclamaciones** RRHH claims manager; **~ de reclutamiento** RRHH recruitment officer, recruiting officer; **~ de redacción** MEDIOS *prensa* copy chief; **~ de redacción adjunto(-a)** MEDIOS associate editor; **~ de sección** RRHH division head, head of department (*HoD*), head of section, V&M *de grandes almacenes* floor manager (*BrE*), floorwalker (*AmE*); **~ de servicio** RRHH departmental manager; **~ de taller** RRHH head foreman; **~ de unidad** RRHH head of unit; **~ de ventas** GES, RRHH, V&M sales manager; **~ de ventas de exportación** V&M export sales manager

Jefe, -a: **~ del Estado** m,f POL Head of State; **~ del Estado Mayor** m,f RRHH *milicia* Chief of Staff

jerarquía f MAT rank order, RRHH hierarchy; **~ de cuadros directivos** RRHH gorilla scale (*jarg*); **~ de efectos** V&M hierarchy of effects; **~ de necesidades** RRHH hierarchy of needs; **~ de necesidades de Maslow** GES *teoría de la motivación* Maslow's hierarchy of needs; **~ de objetivos** COM GEN hierarchy of objectives; **~ piramidal** RRHH pyramid hierarchy; **~ profesional** RRHH, V&M career ladder

jerga f COM GEN jargon; **~ de vendedor** V&M sales talk; **~ de publicidad** V&M advertising talk

jingle: **~ publicitario** m MEDIOS, V&M advertising jingle

JIT abr AmL (*justo a tiempo*) IND JIT (*just-in-time*)

jornada[1]: **de ~ completa** adj RRHH *trabajador* full-time

jornada[2]: **~ controlada** f RRHH *valoración laboral* measured daywork (*MDW*); **~ laboral** f COM GEN, RRHH workday (*AmE*), working day (*BrE*); **~ laboral partida** f RRHH split shift

jornada[3]: **tener ~ reducida** fra RRHH be on short time

jornalero, -a m,f RRHH casual worker, seasonal worker

jornales m pl RRHH wages

joven[1]: **~ y prometedor** adj COM GEN up-and-coming

joven[2]: **~ prodigio en materia de computación** mf jarg INFO computer whizz kid (*jarg*); **~ profesional con ambiciones** mf COM GEN young upwardly mobile professional (*yuppie, yumpie*); **~ promesa** mf COM GEN whizz kid (*infrml*)

joyas: **~ de la corona** f pl ECON crown jewels (*infrml*)

jubilación f COM GEN, FIN, RRHH pension, retirement, retirement income; **~ anticipada** RRHH early retirement; **~ diferida** RRHH deferred retirement; **~ forzosa** RRHH compulsory retirement (*BrE*), mandatory retirement (*AmE*); **~ normal** RRHH normal retirement; **~ obligatoria** RRHH compulsory retirement (*BrE*), mandatory retirement (*AmE*); **~ profesional** RRHH occupational pension; **~ temprana** RRHH early retirement

jubilado[1] adj COM GEN retired; **~ por edad** RRHH superannuated

jubilado[2]**,-a** m,f COM GEN, RRHH pensioner, retired person, retiree (*frml*)

jubilarse v refl RRHH retire; ◆ **~ anticipadamente** RRHH take early retirement; **~ con pensión** RRHH retire on a pension

judicatura f DER judiciary, POL *cuerpo* judicature, judiciary

judicial adj DER judicial

judicialización *f* DER, RRHH juridification

juego *m* BOLSA play, COM GEN game, gaming; **~ de la administración** GES management game; **~ de caracteres** INFO character set, *tipografía* font, MEDIOS font; **~ de documentos** IMP/EXP *de embarque*, TRANSP shipping documents; **~ de empresas** ECON, RRHH business game; **~ estable de von Neumann Morgenstern** ECON von Neumann Morgenstern stable set; **~ de facturas** FIN set of bills, set of notes; **~ limpio** COM GEN fair play; **~ marcadamente bajista** BOLSA *opciones* strong bearish play *(jarg)*; **~ de negocios** ECON, RRHH business game; **~ de suma negativa** ECON negative-sum game; **~ de suma no nula** ECON non-zero-sum game; **~ de suma positiva** ECON positive-sum game *(jarg)*

juegos: **~ de guerra** *m pl* COM GEN war games; **~ de rol** *m pl* GES *de empresa* role-playing

jueves: **~ negro** *m* BOLSA Black Thursday

juez, a *m,f* DER judge; **~ árbitro(-a)** COM GEN awarder; **~ de paz** RRHH Justice of the Peace *(BrE) (JP)*; **~ de primera instancia e instrucción** DER magistrate; **~ de turno** DER presiding judge

jugada *f* BOLSA move

jugar: **~ en bolsa** *fra* BOLSA gamble on the stock exchange

juicio *m* COM GEN, DER judgment; **~ por difamación** DER libel proceedings; **~ incidental** DER special case; **~ con jurado** DER jury trial; **~ no vinculante** COM GEN obiter dictum; **~ oral** DER trial; **~ a priori** COM GEN a priori statement; **~ de valor** COM GEN value judgment; ♦ **tener un ~ con jurado** DER have a jury trial

jumbo *m* TRANSP jumbo *(infrml)*

junta *f* COM GEN meeting; **~ de accionistas** BOLSA, RRHH shareholders' meeting; **~ anual** COM GEN, GES annual meeting; **~ anual de accionistas** BOLSA annual meeting of shareholders; **~ de arbitraje** COM GEN, RRHH board of arbitration; **~ arbitral** COM GEN, RRHH arbitration board; **~ de comercio** ECON *internacional* board of trade; **~ de conciliación** COM GEN, RRHH board of conciliation, conciliation board; **~ de conciliación y arbitraje** COM GEN, IND, RRHH board of conciliation, conciliation board; **~ de conferencias** RRHH conference board; **~ de consejo** *AmL (cf junta de la mesa directiva Esp)* COM GEN, GES board meeting; **~ del consejo de administración** COM GEN, RRHH board meeting; **~ del consejo directivo** COM GEN, RRHH board meeting; **~ constitutiva** DER statutory meeting; **~ consultiva** COM GEN, FIN, RRHH advisory board; **~ directiva** GES, RRHH management board; **~ directiva vinculada** GES interlocking directorate; **~ de directores** RRHH board of directors; **~ general de accionistas** BOLSA general meeting of shareholders; **~ general anual** COM GEN, GES annual general meeting *(AGM)*; **~ general extraordinaria** COM GEN, GES extraordinary general meeting *(EGM)*; **~ general ordinaria** BOLSA *de accionistas* ordinary general meeting; **~ de la mesa directiva** *Esp (cf junta de consejo AmL)* COM GEN, GES board meeting; **~ ordinaria** COM GEN, GES regular meeting; **~ permanente** RRHH presidium; **~ de revisión** RRHH, V&M review board; **~ de revisión de avalúos** FISC board of equalization; **~ de salarios agrarios** RRHH agricultural wages board

Junta: **~ de Asesores Económicos** *f* ECON Council of Economic Advisers *(CEA)*; **~ de Comercio** *f Esp* ECON, POL ≈ Board of Trade *(BrE) (BOT)*; **~ de Desarrollo del Comercio** *f* ECON Trade Development Board *(TDB)*; **~ Gubernamental de Normas Contables** *f* CONT Governmental Accounting Standards Board *(AmE) (GASB)*; **~ Nacional de Precios y Rentas** *f* ECON National Board for Prices and Incomes *(NBPI)*; **~ Sindical de Agentes de Cambio y Bolsa** *f* BOLSA Stock Exchange Committee

juntar: **~ dinero** *fra* COM GEN, FIN raise money

juntarse *v refl* COM GEN *empresas* join together

jurado *m* DER bar, jury; **~ de acusación** DER grand jury *(AmE)*; **~ especial** DER special jury; **~ de opinión ejecutiva** MAT *estadística* jury of executive opinion; **~ ordinario** DER trial jury

juramento *m* DER oath; **bajo ~** *adv* DER under oath

jurisdicción *f* DER *geográfica, política*, PATENT, POL authority, jurisdiction; **~ aduanera** DER customs jurisdiction; **~ fiscal** FISC tax jurisdiction; **~ del tribunal** DER competency of court

jurisprudencia *f* DER case law; **~ antigua** DER old law; **~ reciente** DER new law

jurista *mf* BANCA, COM GEN, DER jurist

justeza *f* COM GEN *juicio* accuracy

justicia: **~ rawlsiana** *f* ECON Rawlsian justice

justiciable *adj* COM GEN, DER, RRHH *reclamación* actionable

justificación *f* COM GEN *razón*, INFO *razón* justification; **~ del capítulo presupuestario** POL vote wording; **~ de título** INMOB proof of title

justificado *adj* COM GEN *razón*, INFO *derecha, izquierda* justified; ♦ **~ a la derecha** COMS, MEDIOS *documento* right-justified, flush right; **~ a la izquierda** COMS, MEDIOS *documento* left-justified, flush left

justificante *m* COM GEN receipt slip; **~ de depósito** COM GEN trust receipt; **~ fiscal** BOLSA tax voucher

justificar *vt* COM GEN *una acción* justify, COMS flush, justify; ♦ **~ a la derecha** COMS, MEDIOS right justify; **~ a la izquierda** COMS, MEDIOS left justify

justiprecio *m* COM GEN *valoración*, RRHH appraisal

justo *adj* COM GEN fair, accurate, DER fair; **~ a tiempo** *AmL (cf según demanda Esp) (JIT)* IND just-in-time *(JIT)*

juzgado *m* DER court; **~ para la bancarrota** FIN bankruptcy court; **~ de distrito** DER district court *(AmE)*; **~ de paz** DER magistrates' court

Juzgado: **~ de Letras de Menores** *m* DER children's court; **~ de lo Social** *m Esp* DER, IND, RRHH industrial tribunal *(BrE) (IT)*

keynesianismo: **~ falso** *m* ECON bastard Keynesianism

know-how *m infrml* COM GEN know-how *(infrml)*

L

laboral *adj* RRHH occupational

laboratorio *m* IND laboratory (*lab*); **~ de investigación** IND research laboratory

labores: **~ de tabaco** *f pl* COM GEN, FISC tobacco products

laborismo *m* POL, RRHH labor movement (*AmE*), labour movement (*BrE*)

labrador, a *m,f* COM GEN, RRHH farmhand

labranza *f* COM GEN farming

lacre *m* COMS sealing wax

ladeo *m* TRANSP tipping

lado: **al ~ de** *fra* COM GEN alongside; **por otro ~** COM GEN on the other hand

laissez: **~ faire** *m* ECON, POL laissez-faire

LAN *abr* (*lenguaje de alto nivel*) INFO HLL (*high-level language*)

lana *f* COM GEN wool; **~ para confección** IND apparel wool; **~ de vidrio** TRANSP glass wool

lancha *f* TRANSP launch, lighter

lanzamiento *m* BOLSA floating, INFO, V&M *programa, producto* launch, launching, release; **~ piloto** V&M pilot launch; **~ del producto** V&M product launch

lanzar *vt* COM GEN *nueva emisión* bring out, *producto* launch, FIN float, TRANSP lower; ◆ **~ una emisión de bonos** BOLSA launch a bond issue

lanzarse: **~ sobre** *v refl* COM GEN run at

lápiz: **~ óptico** *m* INFO optical wand, *fotoestilo* light pen; **~ trazador** *m* INFO plotting pen

lapso *m* COM GEN lapse; **~ ojo-mano** ADMIN hand-eye span; **~ ojo-voz** ADMIN voice-eye span; **~ de tiempo** COM GEN lapse of time

laptop *m* INFO laptop, portable computer

larga: **a la ~** *adv* COM GEN in the long run

largo[1] *m* BOLSA, COM GEN long (*jarg*); **~ cubierto** BOLSA *opciones* covered long; **~ en una divisa** ECON *comercio internacional* long in a currency; **~ en futuros** BOLSA long in futures

largo[2]: **estar ~** *fra* BOLSA go long

largometraje *m* OCIO feature film

largueros: **~ de techo** *m pl* TRANSP *contenedores* roof rail

lastre *m* TRANSP *navegación* ballast; **~ permanente** TRANSP permanent ballast

latigazo *m* BOLSA whiplash

latitud *f* COM GEN, GES *de pensamiento* latitude (*lat.*)

laudo *m* DER finding, RRHH award (*BrE*); **~ arbitral** COM GEN arbitral award

lavado: **~ de crudos** *m* TRANSP *buques cisterna* crude oil washing (*COW*); **~ de dinero** *m* BANCA, COM GEN, FIN money laundering; **~ de dividendos** *m* BOLSA dividend trading

lavar *vt* BANCA, COM GEN *dinero*, FIN launder

lazareto *m* IMP/EXP lazaretto, lazaret

lealtad *f* COM GEN loyalty; **~ del consumidor** V&M consumer loyalty; **~ a una marca** V&M brand loyalty

leasing *m* INMOB lease, leasing; **~ de material** IND, INMOB equipment leasing

lector[1]**,a** *m,f* INFO, MEDIOS, V&M *publicidad* reader

lector[2] *m* INFO *dispositivo* scanner; **~ de código de barras** INFO, V&M bar code scanner; **~ de documentos** INFO document reader; **~ de etiquetas** INFO tag reader; **~ de microfichas** ADMIN microfiche reader; **~ óptico** MEDIOS *imprenta* laser scanner; **~ óptico de caracteres** INFO optical character recognition (*OCR*); **~ óptico de código de barras** INFO bar code scanner; **~ óptico de precios** V&M price scanner; **~ en serie** INFO serial reader; **~ de tarjetas** INFO card reader

lectores: **~ múltiples** *m pl* V&M multiple readership

lector/escritor *m* INFO read/write

lectura *f* INFO read, browsing; **segunda ~** DER *decreto, directiva*, POL second reading

leer *vt* COM GEN read, *cifra* take a reading, *pruebas* correct, INFO read; ◆ **~ la cinta** BOLSA read the tape

legado *m* DER bequest, devise, legacy, INMOB devise

legajo *m* ADMIN dossier, folder

legal *adj* DER legal

legalista *adj* DER legalistic

legalización *f* DER legalization, authorization, *documento* validation

legalizar *vt* DER legalize, authorize, *documento* validate

legalmente: **~ obligado** *adj* DER legally bound; **~ vinculante** *adj* DER legally-binding

legar *vt* DER bequeath, leave

legatario, -a *m,f* DER, INMOB devisee, legatee; **~ residual** DER residuary legatee; **~ único(-a)** DER sole legatee

legible: **~ mecánicamente** *adj* INFO, V&M *código de barras* machine-readable

legislación *f* DER legislation; **~ antievasión** BOLSA, DER, FIN, FISC anti-avoidance legislation; **~ antimonopolio** DER antitrust law; **~ arancelaria** DER, FISC, IMP/EXP, POL tariff legislation; **~ concatenada** ECON, DER, POL piggyback legislation; **~ económica** DER economic law; **~ en los Estados Unidos sobre emisión y venta de valores** BOLSA, DER blue-sky law (*AmE*); **~ con fines electorales** POL pork barrel (*infrml*) (*AmE*); **~ sobre insolvencia** COM GEN insolvency legislation; **~ laboral** DER, POL, RRHH employment law; **~ nacional** DER national legislation; **~ de protección al consumidor** DER, V&M consumer-protection legislation; **~ secundaria** DER, POL secondary legislation; **~ sobre construcciones** DER, IND building regulations; **~ sobre insolvencia** DER, IND insolvency legislation; **~ social** DER, PROT SOC, RRHH welfare legislation; **~ de tarifas** DER, FISC, IMP/EXP, POL tariff legislation; ◆ **según la ~ vigente** DER as the law stands at present

legislar *vt* DER legislate

legislativo *adj* DER legislative

legislatura *f* DER legislature

legítimo *adj* COM GEN *acción* above-board

lengua: **~ franca** *f* COM GEN lingua franca

lenguaje *m* INFO, V&M *publicidad* language; **~ de alto nivel** (*LAN*) INFO high-level language (*HLL*); **~ avanzado** INFO advanced language; **~ común orien-**

tado a la gestión y los negocios (*COBOL*) INFO Common Business Oriented Language (*COBOL*); ~ **de consulta** INFO query language; ~ **corporal** GES, RRHH body language; ~ **fuente** COM GEN, INFO source language; ~ **de interrogación** INFO query language; ~ **de máquina** INFO computer language; ~ **no verbal** GES, RRHH body language; ~ **objeto** COM GEN, INFO *lingüística* target language; ~ **de orden superior** INFO high-order language; ~ **de programación** INFO program language, software language; ◆ **en ~ claro** COM GEN in plain language

lenta: ~ **disminución** *f* BOLSA *moneda* slow decline

lento[1] *adj* BOLSA, COM GEN *mercado* sluggish, ECON *recuperación económica* slow

lento[2]: ~ **aumento** *m* BOLSA *moneda* slow rise

lesión: ~ **corporal** *f* PROT SOC, RRHH *de empleado* injury; ~ **por fatiga crónica** *f* PROT SOC, RRHH repetitive strain injury (*RSI*); ~ **laboral** *f* RRHH, SEG job-related injury; ~ **personal** *f* DER personal injury

letra *f* COM GEN sight draft (*S/D*); ~ **aceptada** BANCA, COM GEN acceptance bill; ~ **al cobro** BANCA bill for collection, draft for collection; ~ **avalada** BOLSA guaranteed bill; ~ **bancaria** BANCA bank bill (*AmE*), banker's bill; ~ **de cambio** BANCA bill of exchange (*B/E*), FIN tenor bill, IMP/EXP bill of exchange (*B/E*); ~ **de cambio al doble uso** COM GEN bill at double usance; ~ **de cambio al uso** FIN usance bill; ~ **de cambio al vencimiento** BANCA, BOLSA term draft; ~ **de cambio avalada** BANCA, BOLSA backed bill of exchange; ~ **de cambio comercial** BANCA commercial bill (*AmE*); ~ **de cambio de conocimiento no traspasable** BANCA stale bill of lading; ~ **de cambio emitida** ECON drawn bill; ~ **de cambio negociable** BANCA negotiable bill of exchange; ~ **de cambio no atendida** IMP/EXP dishonored bill of exchange (*AmE*), dishonoured bill of exchange (*BrE*); ~ **de cambio de primera clase** BOLSA gilt-edged bill of exchange; ~ **de colisión** BOLSA, FIN kite (*jarg*); ~ **comercial** BANCA trade bill; ~ **de conciliación** ECON reconciliation bill (*AmE*); ~ **a corto plazo** TRANSP short bill (*SB*); ~ **descontable** BANCA bankable bill; ~ **descontada** BANCA, CONT bill discounted, discounted bill; ~ **de descuento** BANCA, CONT discount bill; ~ **documentaria** BANCA, IMP/EXP, TRANSP documentary draft; ~ **endosada** ECON made bill (*jarg*); ~ **extranjera** BANCA foreign bill; ~ **impagada** BANCA, BOLSA dishonored bill (*AmE*), dishonoured bill (*BrE*); ~ **limpia** ECON, FIN clean bill; ~ **de liquidación** BANCA settlement draft; ~ **mayúscula** INFO, MEDIOS capital letter, upper case letter; ~ **minúscula** INFO lower case letter; ~ **pagadera a la vista** BANCA, CONT bill payable at sight; ~ **de pelota** BOLSA, FIN kite (*jarg*); ~ **a plazo** BANCA, FIN time bill, usance bill; ~ **sobre el exterior** BANCA foreign bill; ~ **de tesorería** ECON treasury bond, treasury bill (*AmE*) (*T-bill*); ~ **del Tesoro** BANCA, BOLSA treasury bond, treasury bill (*AmE*) (*T-bill*); ~ **del Tesoro del Reino Unido** BOLSA gilt-edged bill of exchange (*BrE*); ~ **con varios ejemplares** FIN bills in a set; ~ **vencida** BANCA expired bill; ~ **de ventanilla** COM GEN window bill; ~ **a la vista** BANCA, CONT, FIN sight bill

letrado, -a *m,f* DER ≈ lawyer

letras *f* *pl* BANCA bills; ~ **aceptables para el redescuento** BANCA eligible bills (*BrE*); ~ **a cobrar** CONT bills receivable

levantamiento *m* COM GEN raising, *restricciones, leyes*

lifting, TRANSP *coche* lifting; ~ **de embargo** DER discharge of lien

levantar *vt* COM GEN *alarma, finanzas, restricciones* raise, lift, *barreras arancelarias* erect, *reunión* adjourn, DER *restricciones* lift, *sesión* adjourn, *acta* draw up, INMOB *hipoteca* lift

leve *adj* COM GEN slight

lex mercatoria *f* COM GEN lex mercatoria

ley *f* DER, POL *sistema, legislación* act, bill, law; ~ **de ahorro de Ramsey** ECON Ramsey saving rule; ~ **antimonopolio** DER antitrust act; ~ **bancaria** BANCA, DER banking law; ~ **bancaria internacional** BANCA, DER International Banking Act; ~ **de banderas** COM GEN, DER law of the flag; ~ **de competencia** DER, POL competition act; ~ **para la concesión de licencias** DER licence law (*BrE*), license law (*AmE*); ~ **de contabilidad** DER accounting law; ~ **contable** DER accounting law; ~ **de control** DER control law; ~ **de control monetario** DER, ECON monetary control act; ~ **de los costes** *Esp* (*cf ley de costos AmL*) ECON law of increasing costs; ~ **de costes de oportunidad crecientes** *Esp* (*cf ley de costos de oportunidad crecientes AmL*) ECON increasing opportunity costs law; ~ **de costos** *m AmL* (*cf ley de costes Esp*) ECON law of increasing costs; ~ **de costos de oportunidad crecientes** *AmL* (*cf ley de costes de oportunidad crecientes Esp*) ECON increasing opportunity costs law; ~ **de la demanda recíproca** ECON law of reciprocal demand; ~ **económica** ECON economic law; ~ **de empleo** DER, POL, RRHH employment law, job legislation; ~ **de exención de derechos** DER statute of limitations; ~ **federal del trabajo** DER, RRHH labor code (*AmE*), labour code (*BrE*); ~ **fiscal** DER, FISC law of taxation; ~ **de garantía de pensiones** DER, RRHH retirement income security act; ~ **Glass Steagall** BANCA Glass Steagall Act; ~ **de hierro de los salarios** DER, ECON iron law of wages; ~ **de inmigración** DER, POL immigration law; ~ **internacional** DER, POL international law; ~ **laboral** DER, RRHH labor law (*AmE*), labour law (*BrE*); ~ **maltusiana de la población** ECON Malthusian law of population; ~ **moral** DER moral law; ~ **nacional** DER national law; ~ **de navegación** DER, TRANSP navigation law; ~ **de la oferta y la demanda** COM GEN law of supply and demand; ~ **del pabellón** DER *comercial* law of the flag; ~ **parlamentaria** DER act, statute, POL act; ~ **de prescripción** DER statute of limitations; ~ **de prescripción de acciones** DER statute of limitation of action; ~ **productos alimenticios** DER food law; ~ **de las proporciones variables** DER, ECON law of variable proportions; ~ **de protección de la intimidad** DER privacy law; ~ **a punto de ser retirada** DER, POL sunset law; ~ **de reemplazo** DER substitution law; ~ **de reflejo** BANCA, DER law of reflux; ~ **reformada** DER amended act; ~ **de regulación del horario comercial** V&M blue laws (*AmE*); ~ **de remuneración a los trabajadores** DER, RRHH workers compensation act; ~ **de rendimientos decrecientes** ECON law of diminishing returns; ~ **de representación** DER agency law; ~ **de la saciedad de las necesidades** ECON law of satiable wants; ~ **Taft-Hartley** DER, ECON Taft-Hartley Act (*AmE*); ~ **del trabajo** DER, POL, RRHH employment law, job legislation; ~ **de transparencia** DER sunshine law (*AmE*); ~ **de transporte intermodal** DER, TRANSP intermodal transport law; ~ **del transporte multimodal** DER, TRANSP multimodal transport law; ~ **uniforme de legados a menores** DER uniform gifts to minors act; ~ **de utilidad marginal decreciente** DER, ECON law of diminishing marginal utility; ~ **del valor** DER, ECON law of value; ~ **de venta de mercancías** DER, V&M sales of goods law; ~ **de ventaja comparativa** DER, ECON *comercio internacional* law of comparative advantage; ~ **de veracidad en los préstamos** BANCA, DER, FIN truth in lending law; ~ **de Williams** DER Williams act

Ley: ~ **de Administración Fiscal** *f* DER Financial Administration Act; ~ **Agrícola** *f* DER Agriculture Act (*BrE*); ~ **Arancelaria** *f* FISC Import duty Act (*IDA*); ~ **de Asesores de Inversión** *f* DER, FIN Investment Advisers Act; ~ **de Clayton** *f* DER, ECON Clayton Act (*AmE*); ~ **de Comercio Internacional** *f* DER, ECON, POL, V&M *UE* International Trade Law; ~ **de Compra Forzosa** *f* DER Compulsory Purchase Act (*BrE*); ~ **del Congreso** *f* DER, POL ≈ Act of Congress (*AmE*), ≈ Act of the House of Commons (*BrE*); ~ **de las Cortes** *f* DER, POL ≈ Act of Congress (*AmE*), ≈ Act of the House of Commons (*BrE*); ~ **de Crédito al Consumo** *f* DER, POL, V&M Consumer Credit Act (*BrE*); ~ **de Dennison** *f* ECON Dennison's Law; ~ **de Derechos de Autor** *f* COM GEN, DER, PATENT Copyright Act; ~ **de los Derechos Civiles** *f* DER, ECON Civil Rights Act (*AmE*); ~ **de Engel** *f* ECON Engel's Law; ~ **de Finanzas** *f* DER Finance Act (*BrE*); ~ **de Goodhart** *f* DER, ECON Goodhart's law; ~ **Gramm Rudman Hollings** *f* DER, POL Gramm Rudman Hollings Act (*AmE*); ~ **de Gresham** *f* DER, ECON Gresham's Law; ~ **de Humphrey-Hawkins** *f* DER, POL Humphrey-Hawkins Act (*AmE*); ~ **del Impuesto Sobre la Renta** *f* DER, FISC Income Tax Act; ~ **de Impuestos sobre la Renta y Sociedades** *f* DER, FISC Income and Corporation Taxes Act (*BrE*); ~ **de Jubilación** *f* DER, PROT SOC ≈ Employment Retirement Income Security Act (*ERISA*); ~ **Landrum-Griffin** *f* DER, RRHH Landrum-Griffin Act (*AmE*); ~ **Lanham** *f* DER Lanham Act (*AmE*); ~ **Maloney** *f* BOLSA, DER Maloney Act; ~ **McFadden** *f* BANCA, DER McFadden Act (*AmE*); ~ **de Monnet** *f* ECON Monnet's Law; ~ **de Murphy** *f* COM GEN Murphy's Law; ~ **Norris-La Guardia** *f* DER, RRHH Norris-La Guardia Act (*AmE*); ~ **de Okun** *f* DER, ECON Okun's Law; ~ **de Pareto** *f* DER, ECON *teoría de la distribución del ingreso* Pareto's Law; ~ **de Parkinson** *f* RRHH Parkinson's Law; ~ **del Parlamento** *f* DER Act of Parliament (*BrE*); ~ **de Petty** *f* ECON Petty's Law; ~ **de Propiedades Agrícolas** *f* DER Agricultural Holdings Act (*BrE*); ~ **de Protección Ambiental de 1990** *f* DER, MED AMB Environmental Protection Act 1990 (*BrE*); ~ **de Protección de Datos** *f* DER Data Protection Act (*BrE*); ~ **de Quiebras** *f* DER, FIN Bankruptcy Act (*AmE*), Bankruptcy Law; ~ **de Reconciliación Presupuestaria** *f* DER Omnibus Budget Reconciliation Act (*OBRA*); ~ **de Reforma Fiscal** *f* FISC Tax Reform Act; ~ **de Say** *f* ECON Say's Law; ~ **Salarial** *f* DER, RRHH Wages Act; ~ **de Seguridad Social** *f* DER, RRHH Social Security Act *BrE*; ~ **de Sociedades de Inversión** *f* DER, FIN Investment Company Act ~ **de Sociedades Mercantiles** *f* COM GEN, DER, IND Companies Act (*BrE*), Companies Bill (*AmE*), Company Law, Corporate Law, Corporation Law; ~ **de Tabernas** *f* DER Dram Shop Act (*AmE*); ~ **de Transporte** *f* DER, TRANSP Transport Act (*BrE*); ~ **de Transporte Marítimo** *f* DER, TRANSP Carriage of Goods by Sea Act (*COGSA*); ~ **de Transporte de Mercancía por**

Carretera *f* DER, TRANSP Carriage of Goods by Road Act; ~ **de Valores** *f* DER, FIN Securities Act; ~ **de Verdoorn** *f* DER Verdoorn's Law; ~ **de Wagner** *f* ECON Wagner's Law; ~ **de Wagner** *f* DER, ECON *relaciones laborales* Wagner Act; ~ **de Walras** *f* ECON Walras' Law ~ **de Walsh Healey** *f* DER, ECON *trabajadores de la administración* Walsh Healey Act

leyes: ~ **antilibelo** *f pl* DER libel laws; ~ **antimonopolio** *f pl* COM GEN, DER, V&M antimonopoly laws; ~ **de granos** *f pl* ECON corn model; ~ **de Kaldor** *f pl* ECON Kaldor's laws

libelo *m* DER libel, petition

liberación: ~ **de acciones en adjudicación** *f* BOLSA, FIN payment in full on allotment; ~ **por pago de flete** *f* IMP/EXP, TRANSP freight release

liberado *adj* BOLSA *valores* freed up

liberal *adj* COM GEN liberal

liberalismo: ~ **de lujo** *m* POL limousine liberalism (*jarg*); ~ **social** *m* ECON, POL social liberalism

liberalización *f* ECON liberalization; ~ **comercial** ECON trade liberalization; ~ **del comercio** ECON *internacional* liberalization of trade

liberalizador *adj* ECON liberalizing

liberalizar *vt* ECON liberalize

liberar *vt* ECON liberalize, *dividendo* release, free; ◆ ~ **a alguien bajo fianza** DER release sb on bail; ~ **fondos** FIN unlock funds

libertad *f* DER freedom; ~ **de acción** DER freedom of action; ~ **de asociación** COM GEN, DER freedom of association; ~ **bajo fianza** DER release on bail; ~ **de competencia** COM GEN, ECON freedom of competition; ~ **económica** ECON, POL economic freedom; ~ **de elección** COM GEN, POL freedom of choice; ~ **de establecimiento** POL *UE* freedom of establishment

LIBOR: ~ **promedio** *m* BANCA *tipo interbancario de Londres* average LIBOR (*BrE*)

libra *f* COM GEN pound (*lb*); ~ **esterlina** COM GEN pound sterling; ~ **irlandesa** COM GEN punt; ~ **al contado y a plazo** ECON *cotización puntual* pound spot and forward

librado[1]: **no** ~ *adj* COM GEN, CONT, DER, FIN, TRANSP undischarged

librado[2],**-a** *m,f* ADMIN, BANCA, FIN drawee

librador, a *m,f* ADMIN, BANCA, FIN drawer; ~ **de un pagaré de favor** FIN accommodation maker

libramiento: ~ **de cheques** *m* BANCA issue of checks (*AmE*), issue of cheques (*BrE*)

libranza *f* BANCA *cheque, giro* draft, PATENT drawing

librar *vt* BANCA *cheque* draw, make out; ◆ ~ **una batalla perdida contra** COM GEN fight a losing battle against

librarse: ~ **de** *v refl* COM GEN get rid of

libras: ~ **por pulgada cuadrada** *fra* TRANSP pounds per square inch (*PSI*)

libre[1] *adj* COM GEN free, *competición* uncurbed, DER at liberty (*jarg*); ◆ **de** ~ **adquisición** PROT SOC *medicación* over-the-counter (*OTC*); ~ **de comisión por solicitud** TRANSP *navegación* free of address; ~ **de contribución** ECON, FIN, FISC tax-exempt; ~ **de deudas** COM GEN clear of debts; ~ **de gastos** COM GEN free of charge (*FOC*), TRANSP toll-free; ~ **de gravamen** INMOB unencumbered; ~ **de hipotecas** COM GEN unmortgaged; ~ **de impuestos** COM GEN, ECON, FISC, IMP/EXP tax-free, duty-free; ~ **de peaje** TRANSP toll-free; ~ **de plazo** TRANSP free of term; ~ **de riesgo** BOLSA risk-free; ~ **de**

actos de la autoridad SEG free of capture and seizure (*fc&s*); ~ **de actos de la autoridad, motines y conmoción civil** SEG free of capture, seizure and riots, and civil commotions (*fcsrcc*); ~ **para el buque la carga y estiba** TRANSP free in and stowed (*fias*); ~ **de daños** COM GEN free of damage (*fod*); ~ **de deudas** BANCA, CONT, FIN clear of debts; ~ **de disturbios y altercados civiles** SEG free of riots and civil commotions (*fr&cc*); ~ **de reclamaciones por el accidente informado** SEG free of claim for reported accident (*FCAR*); ~ **de toda avería** COM GEN free of all average (*f.a.a.*); ~ **de tumultos y desórdenes** TRANSP free of riots and civil commotions (*fr&cc*)

libre[2]: ~ **acceso y elección** *m* COM GEN free access and choice; ~ **cambio** *m* ECON *internacional*, IMP/EXP, POL free trade; ~ **circulación** *f* ECON *de bienes, servicios*, POL, TRANSP free circulation, freedom of movement; ~ **circulación de bienes y servicios** *f* DER *UE* free circulation of goods and services; ~ **circulación de mano de obra** *f* DER *UE* free movement of labor (*AmE*), free movement of labour (*BrE*); ~ **circulación de mercancías** *f* DER *UE* free movement of goods; ~ **comercio** *m* ECON, IMP/EXP, POL free trade; ~ **competencia** *f* ECON, V&M free competition; ~ **derecho de cambio** *m* BOLSA free right of exchange; ~ **economía** *f* ECON free economy; ~ **empresa** *f* ECON free enterprise

librecambismo *m* POL laissez-faire

libreta: ~ **de banco** BANCA, FIN bankbook; ~ **de ahorro** *f* BANCA savings passbook; ~ **bancaria** *f* BANCA deposit book; ~ **de calificaciones** *f* RRHH report card; ~ **de depósitos** *f* BANCA deposit passbook; ~ **de jornales** *f* RRHH time book

libro *m* BOLSA *mercado de divisas* book; ~ **de actas** COM GEN, DER minute book; ~ **de almacén** CONT inventory book, TRANSP warehouse book (*WB*); ~ **amarillo** BOLSA Yellow Book (*BrE*); ~ **de análisis** CONT analysis book; ~ **de anotaciones** BOLSA *suscripción de títulos* book; ~ **de asiento original** CONT book of original entry; ~ **auxiliar** CONT subsidiary accounting record; ~ **de balances** FIN balance book; ~ **blanco del gasto público** ECON Public Expenditure White Paper (*PEWP*) (*BrE*); ~ **de caja** CONT cash book, cash journal; ~ **de caja pequeña** *Esp* (*cf diario de caja chica AmL*) CONT petty cash book; ~ **comercial** MEDIOS trade book; ~ **de comercio** FIN trading book; ~ **de compras** CONT bought book, V&M purchase book; ~ **de contabilidad** BANCA, BOLSA, CONT book; ~ **de cuentas** CONT account book; ~ **devuelto** MEDIOS returned book; ~ **diario** CONT daybook (*db*); ~ **diario de compras** CONT bought journal, bought day book; ~ **diario especial** CONT special journal; ~ **de direcciones** COMS address book; ~ **electrónico especializado** BOLSA specialist electronic book (*SEB*); ~ **encuadernado en rústica** MEDIOS *imprenta* soft cover book; ~ **de entradas y salidas** CONT daybook (*db*); ~ **equilibrado** BOLSA matched book; ~ **de facturas** COM GEN invoice book (*IB*), CONT bill book; ~ **de inventario** CONT inventory book; ~ **de letras** CONT bill book; ~ **de letras aceptadas** CONT acceptance ledger; ~ **marrón** COM GEN, POL brown book (*jarg*) (*BrE*); ~ **mayor** CONT *teneduría de cuentas* ledger; ~ **mayor auxiliar** CONT subsidiary ledger; ~ **mayor de clientes** CONT accounts receivable ledger; ~ **mayor de compras** CONT accounts payable ledger; ~ **mayor de cuentas a cobrar** CONT accounts receivable ledger; ~ **mayor de cuentas a pagar** CONT accounts payable ledger; ~ **mayor general** CONT general ledger; ~ **mayor nominal** CONT nominal ledger; ~ **mayor del pasivo** CONT liability ledger; ~ **mayor principal** CONT general ledger; ~ **mayor privado** CONT private ledger; ~ **mayor de proveedores** CONT accounts payable ledger; ~ **mayor de ventas** COM GEN sales ledger, CONT accounts receivable ledger, sales ledger, V&M sales ledger; ~ **de normas** RRHH rule book; ~ **de normas de un sindicato** RRHH union rule book; ~ **de pasta blanda** *AmL* (*cf libro en rústica Esp*) COM GEN paperback; ~ **patrocinado** V&M sponsored book; ~ **de pedidos** COM GEN order book; ~ **registro** PATENT register, register book; ~ **de rendimiento** COM GEN yield book; ~ **en rústica** *Esp* (*cf libro de pasta blanda AmL*) COM GEN paperback; ~ **de últimas entradas** CONT book of final entry; ~ **de ventas** V&M sales book; ~ **de vuelos** TRANSP logbook

Libro: ~ **Blanco** *m* DER, POL White Paper (*BrE*); ~ **Blanco de la Comisión** *m* DER, POL Commission White Paper; ~ **Rojo** *m* FIN Red Book (*infrml*) (*AmE*); ~ **Verde** *m* DER, POL Green Discussion Paper

libros: ~ **básicos** *m pl* FIN basic books; ~ **de contabilidad** *m pl* CONT books; ~ **contables** *m pl* CONT books; ~ **legales** *m pl* DER statutory books; ~ **de pedidos acumulados** *m pl* COM GEN backlog order books; ~ **de resguardo** *m pl* V&M *publicidad* guard books (*jarg*)

licencia *f* BANCA, PATENT licence (*BrE*), license (*AmE*), RRHH *Ejército* furlough; ~ **de conducir** *AmL* (*cf carnet de conducir, permiso de conducir Esp*) ADMIN, TRANSP driver's licence (*BrE*), driver's license (*AmE*); ~ **contractual** PATENT contracting state; ~ **por contrato** IMP/EXP contract licence (*BrE*), contract license (*AmE*); ~ **exclusiva** PATENT exclusive licence (*BrE*), exclusive license (*AmE*); ~ **de exploración de gas** MED AMB gas exploration licence (*BrE*), gas exploration license (*AmE*); ~ **de exploración de petróleo** IND, MED AMB oil exploration licence (*BrE*), oil exploration license (*AmE*); ~ **de exportación** IMP/EXP export permit; ~ **general abierta** IMP/EXP open general licence (*BrE*) (*OGL*), open general license (*AmE*) (*OGL*); ~ **para graneles** IMP/EXP bulk licence (*BrE*), bulk license (*AmE*); ~ **de importación** IMP/EXP import licence (*BrE*) (*I/L*), import license (*AmE*) (*I/L*); ~ **de importación general abierta** IMP/EXP open general import licence (*BrE*) (*OGIL*), open general import license (*AmE*) (*OGIL*); ~ **individual** IMP/EXP individual licence (*BrE*), individual license (*AmE*); ~ **individual abierta** IMP/EXP open individual licence (*BrE*), open individual license (*AmE*); ~ **individual específica** IMP/EXP, TRANSP specific individual licence (*BrE*) (*SIL*), specific individual license (*AmE*) (*SIL*); ~ **individual de importación** IMP/EXP individual import licence (*BrE*), individual import license (*AmE*); ~ **de instalación** INFO site licence (*BrE*), site license (*AmE*); ~ **internacional de conducir** *AmL* (*cf carnet internacional de conducir, permiso de conducir internacional Esp*) ADMIN international driver's licence (*BrE*), international driver's license (*AmE*), international driving permit; ~ **de maternidad** *m* RRHH maternity leave; ~ **para muestras** IMP/EXP sample licence (*BrE*), sample license (*AmE*); ~ **obligatoria** DER, PATENT compulsory licence (*BrE*), compulsory license (*AmE*); ~ **de obras** DER,

INMOB planning approval (*AmE*), planning permission (*BrE*); **~ de paternidad** *m* PROT SOC, RRHH paternity leave; **~ patrón** IMP/EXP sample licence (*BrE*), sample license (*AmE*); **~ personal** IMP/EXP individual license (*BrE*), individual license (*AmE*); **~ personal de importación** IMP/EXP individual import licence (*BrE*), individual import license (*AmE*); **~ de pleno derecho del invento** PATENT title of the invention; **~ de programas de computador** *AmL ver licencia de programas de computadora AmL*; **~ de programas de computadora** *AmL* (*cf licencia de progamas de ordenador Esp*) INFO computer software licence (*BrE*), computer software license (*AmE*); **~ de programas de ordenador** *Esp* (*cf licencia de programas de computadora AmL*) INFO computer software licence (*BrE*), computer software license (*AmE*); **~ de prospección de gas** IND, MED AMB gas exploration licence (*BrE*), gas exploration license (*AmE*); **~ de prospección petrolífera** IND, MED AMB oil exploration licence (*BrE*), oil exploration license (*AmE*); **~ de urbanización** DER, INMOB planning approval (*AmE*), planning permission (*BrE*); **~ de uso** INFO site licence (*BrE*), site license (*AmE*); **~ de vigilancia** IMP/EXP surveillance licence (*BrE*) (*SL*), surveillance license (*AmE*) (*SL*); ◆ **con ~** DER, PATENT under licence (*BrE*), under license (*AmE*)

licenciado[1] *adj* DER, PATENT licensed

licenciado[2] **(-a):** **~ en Administración de Empresas** *m,f* PROT SOC, RRHH Bachelor of Science in Business Administration (*BSBA*), Bachelor of Business Administration; **~ en Ciencias** *m,f* PROT SOC, RRHH ≈ Bachelor of Science (*BSc*); **~ en Ciencias Empresariales** *m,f* PROT SOC, RRHH Bachelor of Science in Business Administration (*BSBA*); **~ en Comercio** *m,f* PROT SOC, RRHH Bachelor of Commerce (*BCom*); **~ en Derecho** *m,f* DER, RRHH ≈ Bachelor of Laws (*LLB*); **~ en Dibujo Técnico** *m,f* RRHH Bachelor of Industrial Design (*BID*); **~ en Diseño Industrial** *m,f* PROT SOC, RRHH Bachelor of Industrial Design (*BID*); **~ en Economía** *m,f* PROT SOC, RRHH Bachelor of Economics (*BEcon*); **~ en Humanidades** *m,f* PROT SOC, RRHH ≈ Bachelor of Arts (*BA*); **~ en Relaciones Laborales** *m,f* PROT SOC, RRHH Bachelor of Science in Industrial Relations (*BSIR*)

licenciar *vt* COM GEN license

licenciarse *v refl* PROT SOC, RRHH *de la Universidad* come down

licenciatario, -a *m,f* DER licensee

licitación *f* COM GEN tender to contract (*TTC*), tender, *presentación de ofertas* bidding, tendering; **~ abierta** COM GEN open bid, open tendering; **~ competitiva** COM GEN competitive tendering; **~ competitiva obligatoria** COM GEN compulsory competitive tendering (*BrE*); **~ pública** COM GEN competitive bidding

licitar *vt* COM GEN tender, *en subasta* bid

lícito *adj* COM GEN, DER lawful, legal, permissible

licuidificación *f* BOLSA liquidization (*jarg*)

líder[1] *adj* V&M *marca* leading

líder[2] *mf* GES, RRHH, V&M leader; **~ del equipo** RRHH team leader; **~ del grupo** RRHH group leader; **~ informal** RRHH informal leader; **~ del mercado** V&M market leader; **~ mundial** V&M world leader; **~ nato(-a)** *m,f* RRHH born leader; **~ de opinión** V&M *investigación de mercado* opinion leader

liderazgo *m* GES, RRHH leadership; **~ incontestable** RRHH free-rein leadership; **~ del mercado** V&M market leadership; **~ participativo** GES participative leadership

liga *f* COM GEN league

Liga: **~ Europea para la Cooperación Económica** *f* ECON European League for Economic Cooperation (*ELEC*)

ligado: **~ al ahorro** *adj* COM GEN savings-linked

light *adj* MEDIOS light

limitación *f* BANCA conditionality, POL corset; **~ al libre comercio** ECON restraint of trade; **~ de las averías** COM GEN damage limitation; **~ de los daños** COM GEN damage limitation; **~ de una escritura** DER, INMOB deed restriction; **~ de la pérdida** FIN loss limitation; **~ a la urbanización** DER, INMOB planning restriction

limitar *vt* COM GEN *riesgo* limit

límite *m* BOLSA, COM GEN limit, INMOB boundary, property line; **~ acumulativo de ganancias** FISC cumulative gains limit; **~ de ajuste** FISC adjustment limit; **~ ascendente** BOLSA ascending top; **~ asignado de exención** FISC allocated exemption limit; **~ básico de responsabilidad** SEG basic liability limit; **~ de carga** TRANSP maximum load; **~ de construcción** INMOB building line; **~ del crédito** BANCA, FIN credit limit, credit ceiling; **~ diario** BANCA, BOLSA daily limit; **~ discrecional** BANCA discretionary limit; **~ de edad** COM GEN age limit; **~ de efectivo** BANCA, ECON, RRHH cash limit; **~ del ejercicio** BOLSA exercise deadline, exercise limit; **~ de emisión** MED AMB emission limit; **~ de endeudamiento** COM GEN borrowing limit; **~ espacial del beneficio** ECON spatial benefit limitation; **~ de exención de derechos** FISC royalty exemption limit; **~ de financiación externa** FIN external financing limit (*EFL*); **~ de fluctuación** BOLSA fluctuation limit; **~ de las ganancias anuales** FISC annual gains limit; **~ del gasto** FISC expenditure limit; **~ de humedad transportable** TRANSP transportable moisture limit (*TML*); **~ ideal** ECON ideal limit; **~ de la inversión extranjera** FISC foreign investment limit; **~ de liquidez** BANCA, ECON, RRHH cash limit; **~ máximo** COM GEN ceiling; **~ máximo de hipoteca** BANCA, INMOB mortgage ceiling; **~ de navegación** TRANSP plying limit; **~ de negocio diario** BOLSA daily trading limit; **~ de posición** BOLSA position limit; **~ de precio** BOLSA price limit; **~ de propiedad** INMOB boundary, property line; **~ de reembolso del efectivo** BOLSA *futuros* cash refunding date; **~ superior** BOLSA *en valor de acciones* upper limit; **~ superior de salario** RRHH wage ceiling; **~ temporal básico** COM GEN basic time limit; **~ de tesorería** BANCA, ECON, RRHH cash limit; ◆ **no hay ~** COM GEN the sky's the limit; **sin ~** V&M *publicidad* open-end; **sin ~ al alza** BOLSA *riesgo de opciones* unlimited on upside

limpiar *vt* MED AMB clean up

limpieza: **~ de cisterna** *f* TRANSP tank cleaning

limpio *adj* ECON *comercio internacional*, MED AMB clean

linaje *m* V&M lineage

linde *f* INMOB boundary, property line

línea[1]: **en ~** *adj* INFO on-line; **de primera ~** *adj* COMS, V&M first-rate, high-profile

línea[2] *f* COM GEN, V&M line; **~ de aceptación** BANCA acceptance line; **~ aérea** TRANSP airline; **~ aérea de cabotaje** TRANSP commuter airline; **~ aérea interna** OCIO, TRANSP domestic airline; **~ aérea internacional**

TRANSP international airline; ~ **aérea principal** COMS trunk line; ~ **de apoyo** FIN backup line; ~ **de ataque** COM GEN line of attack; ~ **bancaria** BANCA bank line; ~ **base** MAT *de diagrama* baseline; ~ **de carga** TRANSP load line (*LL*); ~ **central** PROT SOC mainstreaming; ~ **central del pensamiento económico** ECON mainstream economics; ~ **de código** INFO code line; ~ **de comandos** INFO command line; ~ **compartida** COMS party line; ~ **de comportamiento** ECON behavior line (*AmE*), behaviour line (*BrE*); ~ **de compraventa de divisas** FIN swop line; ~ **de computador** *AmL ver línea de computadora AmL*; ~ **de computadora** *AmL* (*cf línea de ordenador Esp*) INFO computer line; ~ **de comunicación directa** COMS *política* hot line; ~ **de condición** INFO status line; ~ **de conducta** ECON *microeconomía* behavior line (*AmE*), behaviour line (*BrE*); ~ **de conferencia** TRANSP *navegación* conference line; ~ **de contenedores** TRANSP container line; ~ **control de la capacidad de una vía** TRANSP route capacity control airline (*RCCA*); ~ **de crédito** BANCA, FIN credit line, line of credit; ~ **de crédito de contingencia** BANCA standby line of credit; ~ **de crédito especial** BANCA special credit facility; ~ **de crédito garantizada** FIN guaranteed facility; ~ **de crédito general** FIN *multicontrato* multiple general-purpose line of credit; ~ **de crédito con interés variable** BANCA roll-over credit facility; ~ **de crédito irrevocable** BANCA irrevocable credit line; ~ **de crédito de proyección** FIN *multicontrato* multiple projected line of credit; ~ **de crédito renovable** BANCA, FIN revolving line of credit; ~ **de crédito de respaldo** BANCA backup credit line; ~ **para la dirección** V&M address line; ~ **directa de consulta** INFO support hotline; ~ **de disposición inmediata** BANCA standby facility; ~ **ecológica** MED AMB greenlining (*jarg*) (*AmE*); ~ **de enlace** TRANSP *ferrocarril* trunk line (*AmE*); ~ **especializada** INFO leased line; ~ **de impresión** INFO print line; ~ **isocuanta** ECON *mapa de indiferencias* isoproduct curve; ~ **jerárquica** GES line of command; ~ **límite de apoyo** TRANSP *navegación* interface limit line; ~ **de linotipia** ADMIN typebar, INFO print bar, typebar; ~ **marrón** COM GEN brown goods (*jarg*); ~ **de máxima carga** TRANSP Plimsoll line; ~ **de menor resistencia** COM GEN line of least resistance; ~ **del mercado de valores** BOLSA security market line; ~ **de montaje** RRHH, IND assembly line; ~ **de navegación** TRANSP shipping line; ~ **de ordenador** *Esp* (*cf línea de computadora AmL*) INFO computer line; ~ **de parcelación** INMOB lot line; ~ **de préstamo transferible** BANCA, FIN transferable loan facilities (*TLF*); ~ **principal** IND, INFO mains (*BrE*), supply network (*AmE*), TRANSP *ferrocarril* main line, V&M leading line; ~ **de prioridad** COMS *teléfono* hot line; ~ **del producto** V&M product line; ~ **punteada** COM GEN, INFO, MAT *en grafo* dotted line; ~ **de rayas** COM GEN, INFO dashed line; ~ **de referencia** INFO, MAT *de diagrama* baseline, PATENT reference line; ~ **de respaldo** BANCA backup line; ~ **secundaria de transporte** TRANSP *aviación* feeder line; ~ **y staff** *AmL* (*cf organigrama de jerarquización intermedia Esp*) RRHH line and staff; ~ **telefónica común** COMS party line; ◆ **en ~ con** COM GEN *inflación, expectativas* in line with; **sobre la ~** V&M above the line (*jarg*)

lineaje *m* MEDIOS lineage

lingote *m* COM GEN ingot

liquidación *f* COM GEN liquidation, winding-up, *de cuenta* settlement, FISC assessment, SEG *pérdida* settlement, V&M clearance sale, clearance; ~ **de activos** CONT, ECON, FIN asset stripping; ~ **anual** CONT yearly settlement; ~ **de un arbitraje** BOLSA *opciones* backspread; ~ **de averías** SEG average settlement; ~ **de balances** ECON *comercio internacional* clearing; ~ **de contratos antes del vencimiento** BOLSA *futuros* ringing out (*jarg*) (*AmE*); ~ **de daños** SEG claim settlement; ~ **de deudas** BANCA settlement of debts; ~ **diaria** BOLSA daily settlement; ~ **diaria de pérdidas y ganancias** BOLSA mark-to-the-market; ~ **de fin de año** CONT yearly settlement; ~ **forzosa** COM GEN, CONT, FIN compulsory liquidation; ~ **de una hipoteca** FIN final mortgage payment; ~ **insuficiente del impuesto** FISC under-declared tax; ~ **involuntaria** COM GEN, CONT, FIN involuntary liquidation; ~ **mediante compensación dólar por dólar** BOLSA dollar-for-dollar offset; ~ **neta continua** BOLSA continuous net settlement (*BrE*) (*CNS*); ~ **obligatoria** COM GEN, CONT, FIN compulsory liquidation; ~ **de oficio** FISC jeopardy assessment; ~ **a precios de mercado** BOLSA settlement to the market; ~ **salarial** RRHH wage settlement; ~ **del seguro** SEG insurance settlement; ~ **de siniestro** SEG claim settlement; ~ **del sueldo** ECON outsider wage-setting; ~ **de la suma asegurada** SEG settlement of sum insured; ~ **voluntaria** COM GEN voluntary winding-up

liquidado *adj* COM GEN *opciones* liquidated

liquidador, a *m,f* COM GEN liquidator; ~ **de averías** ADMIN commissioner

liquidar *vt* BANCA *fondos* clear, BOLSA *posición* liquidate, *títulos* clear, COM GEN liquidate, *deuda* pay offsell off (*BrE*), close out (*AmE*), CONT, DER liquidate, ECON, FIN *cuenta* settle; ◆ ~ **diariamente pérdidas y ganancias** BOLSA mark to the market; ~ **de forma insuficiente** CONT underassess; ~ **en metálico** BOLSA settle in cash; ~ **un negocio** COM GEN shut up shop

liquidez *f* BOLSA liquidity, COM GEN *cantidad disponible* cash, FIN liquidity; ~ **de un banco** BANCA bank liquidity; ~ **de la empresa** FIN company liquidity; ~ **internacional** ECON international liquidity; ~ **negativa** FIN negative cash flow; ~ **del sector privado** ECON private sector liquidity (*PSL*)

líquido[1] *adj* BANCA *fondos* liquid

líquido[2] *m* COM GEN *capital disponible* cash

lisamente *adv* COM GEN smoothly

lista *f* COM GEN list, RRHH *de responsabilidades del personal* roster; ~ **de alerta** BANCA warning list; ~ **aprobada** BOLSA *de inversiones* approved list; ~ **de bultos** IMP/EXP, TRANSP packing list; ~ **de candidatos** POL list of candidates (*BrE*), ticket (*jarg*) (*AmE*); ~ **de carga Lloyd's** TRANSP Lloyd's Loading List; ~ **de carga sujeta a derechos de aduana** IMP/EXP, TRANSP dutiable cargo list; ~ **de comprobación del pedido de exportación** IMP/EXP export order check list; ~ **de contribuyentes** FISC assessment roll, tax roll, INMOB assessment roll; ~ **de control** BANCA watch list, BOLSA watchlist, COM GEN checklist; ~ **cronológica** CONT ageing schedule; ~ **de cuestiones por resolver** POL laundry list (*jarg*) (*AmE*); ~ **de direcciones** *Esp* (*cf buzoneo AmL*) COMS, V&M mailing list; ~ **de direcciones de muestra** COMS sample mailing; ~ **electoral** POL slate (*AmE*); ~ **de embalaje** IMP/EXP, TRANSP packaging list, packing list; ~ **de embarque** TRANSP shipping documents; ~ **de emplazamientos disponibles** V&M

publicidad available sites list; **~ de errores** COM GEN catalog of errors (*AmE*), catalogue of errors (*BrE*), INFO error report; **~ de espera** COM GEN, OCIO, TRANSP wait list, waiting list; **~ de éxitos** V&M hit list (*infrml*); **~ de invalidaciones** BANCA hot list; **~ de Lloyd's** TRANSP Lloyd's List; **~ de los más activos** BOLSA most-active list; **~ de materiales** IND *producción* bill of materials; **~ negra** COM GEN, RRHH, SEG blacklist; **~ de obligaciones entregables** BOLSA list of deliverable bonds; **~ de pasajeros** OCIO, TRANSP passenger list, passenger return; **~ perforada** COM GEN punch list; **~ de precios** COM GEN price current, price list; **~ de precios efectivos** COM GEN price quotation list; **~ de rayas** RRHH pay sheet; **~ de remisiones** INFO cross-reference listing; **~ de seleccionados** COM GEN, RRHH shortlist; **~ de valores de alta calidad** BOLSA legal list (*AmE*); **~ de valores cotizados** BOLSA stock exchange list

Lista: **~ de Domicilios** *f* RRHH List of Addresses (*BrE*)

listado[1] *adj* COM GEN listed, tabled, INFO listed

listado[2] *m* INFO table (*jarg*), INMOB listing; **~ abierto** INMOB open listing; **~ de agencia exclusivo** INMOB *agentes* exclusive agency listing; **~ de archivos** INFO file allocation table (*FAT*); **~ múltiple** INMOB multiple listing; **~ neto** INMOB net listing

listar *vt* COM GEN list, table, INFO list

listas: **~ de aceptación de trabajo** *f pl* ECON job acceptance schedule

listero, -a *m,f* RRHH, TRANSP tally clerk

listo *adj* COM GEN ready, prepared, TRANSP *carga* prompt (*ppt*); **~ para embarcar** TRANSP ready for shipment; **~ para fotografiar** MEDIOS camera-ready

litera *f* OCIO, TRANSP couchette

litigante *mf* DER litigant

litigio[1]: **en ~** *adj* COM GEN at issue, in dispute

litigio[2] *m* DER litigation

litispendencia *f* DER lis pendens

litoral *m* TRANSP shore

llamada *f* COMS, INFO call, buzz (*infrml*); **~ de alarma** COM GEN alarm call; **~ a cobro revertido** *Esp* (*cf llamada pagadera en destino AmL*) COMS collect call (*AmE*), reverse-charge call (*BrE*); **~ directa** COMS direct call; **~ de entrada** COMS incoming call; **~ en espera** COMS call waiting; **~ internacional** COMS international call; **~ interurbana de abonado** COMS subscriber trunk dialing (*AmE*) (*STD*), subscriber trunk dialling (*BrE*) (*STD*); **~ de larga distancia** COMS long-distance call, trunk call (*BrE*) (*obs*), toll call (*AmE*); **~ libre de tasas** COMS toll-free call; **~ a licitación** COM GEN call for bids, call for tenders; **~ de negocios** COM GEN business call; **~ pagadera en destino** *AmL* (*cf llamada a cobro revertido Esp*) COMS collect call (*AmE*), reverse-charge call (*BrE*); **~ de persona a persona** COMS person-to-person call; **~ selectiva digital** COMS digital selective calling (*DSC*); **~ tridireccional** COMS three-way call, conference call

llamar 1. *vt* COMS *persona*, OCIO *teatro* call; ◆ **~ a alguien** COMS call sb, give sb a buzz (*infrml*); **~ a alguien como testigo** DER call as a witness; **~ a alguien por el intercomunicador** COMS call sb over the intercom; **~ la atención de alguien** COM GEN attract sb's attention; **~ sin pagar tasas** COMS call toll-free (*AmE*), call on a Freefone® number (*BrE*); **2.** *vi* COMS call; ◆ **~ a cobro revertido** COMS call collect (*AmE*), reverse the charges (*BrE*); **~ por teléfono** COMS call up

llamativo *adj* V&M *comercialización* eye-catching

llave: **~ en mano** *f* COM GEN *sistema, proyecto*, IMP/EXP, INFO turnkey, INMOB immediate possession

llegada *f* COM GEN, TRANSP arrival

llegar *vi* COM GEN make it (*infrml*), *bastar* be enough, *alcanzar* reach; ◆ **~ a** COM GEN *negocios* get down to; **~ a un acuerdo** COM GEN reach an agreement, strike a deal; **~ a un acuerdo amistoso** COM GEN reach an amicable settlement; **~ al límite** COM GEN *empresa* go to the wall (*infrml*); **~ al vencimiento** COM GEN come to maturity; **~ al vencimiento con beneficio potencial** BOLSA expire in-the-money; **~ al vencimiento sin valor alguno** BOLSA expire worthless; **~ a la conclusión a partir de** COM GEN conclude from; **~ a un compromiso** COM GEN reach a compromise; **~ a concretarse** COM GEN come to fruition; **~ a un entendimiento** COM GEN come to an understanding; **~ a una operación normal** IND come on stream; **~ a puerto** TRANSP make port; **~ a un punto muerto** COM GEN reach a stalemate; **~ a una solución de compromiso** COM GEN trade off; **~ a su destino** COM GEN come to hand

llenado: **~ del contenedor** *m* TRANSP container stuffing

llenar *vt* COM GEN *brecha* bridge, *vacante* fill; ◆ **~ los requisitos** COM GEN fulfill the requirements (*AmE*), fulfil the requirements (*BrE*)

llevado: **~ a cuenta nueva** *fra* BANCA, CONT *balance* brought forward (*b/f*), carried forward (*c/f*), carried over

llevar *vt* COM GEN take away, *persona* bring; ◆ **no es para ~** COM GEN not to be removed; **~ a alguien hasta el límite** COM GEN push sb to the limit; **~ a alguien a los tribunales** DER take sb to court; **~ a cabo** COM GEN carry out; **~ a cabo una conferencia** GES hold a conference; **~ a cabo una negociación** COM GEN pull off a deal; **~ un control de** COM GEN keep track of; **~ la cuenta de** COM GEN keep tally of; **~ a cuenta nueva** CONT bring forward, bring down (*b/d*); **~ la defensa** DER lead for the defence (*BrE*), lead for the defense (*AmE*); **~ información sobre** COM GEN carry information on; **~ nota** COM GEN keep a note; **~ ventaja a alguien** COM GEN have the edge over sb; **~ a visitar** COM GEN *visitante* show around, show round; **~ la voz cantante** COM GEN run the show

lluvia: **~ ácida** *f* MED AMB acid rain

local[1] *adj* COM GEN, INFO local

local[2] *m* BOLSA local (*jarg*), COM GEN premises; **~ alquilado** COM GEN, INMOB demised premises; **~ autorizado** IMP/EXP, INMOB approved premises; **~ comercial** COM GEN, INMOB business premises; **~ para oficina** COM GEN, INMOB office premises; **~ secundario** COM GEN, INMOB secondary premises; **~ sin trastienda** COM GEN, INMOB lock-up premises

localización *f* INFO *programa* localization, TRANSP allocation; **~ de averías** INFO troubleshooting; **~ de la carga** TRANSP loading allocation; **~ y corrección de fallas** *AmL* (*cf localización y corrección de fallos Esp*) COM GEN troubleshooting; **~ y corrección de fallos** *Esp* (*cf localización y corrección de fallas AmL*) COM GEN troubleshooting; **~ dinámica** COM GEN dynamic positioning (*DP*)

localizador, a *m,f* TRANSP locator; **~ de averías** INFO *depuración* troubleshooter; **~ de fallas** *AmL* (*cf localizador de fallos Esp*) COM GEN troubleshooter; **~ de**

fallos *Esp* (*cf localizador de fallas AmL*) COM GEN troubleshooter

localizar *vt* BANCA *pago*, COMS *llamada*, COM GEN, TRANSP trace, track down

locutor, a: ~ **de radio** *m,f* MEDIOS radio announcer; ~ **de televisión** *m,f* MEDIOS television announcer

locutorio *m* COMS call box (*AmE*), telephone box (*BrE*); ~ **radiofónico** COMS media studio

logical: ~ **de sistemas** *m* INFO systems software

logística *f* COM GEN, INFO, MAT logistics

logísticamente *adv* COM GEN, INFO, MAT logistically

logístico *adj* COM GEN, INFO, MAT logistical

logo: ~ **de la compañía** *m* COM GEN, V&M company logo

logóptica *f* COM GEN logoptics

logotipo *m* COM GEN, V&M logotype (*logo*); ~ **de la empresa** COM GEN, V&M company logo

lograr *vt* COM GEN *acuerdo* reach, work out, *aumento, nivel, objetivo* achieve, accomplish, pull off (*infrml*)

logro *m* COM GEN achievement, accomplishment; ~ **profesional** COM GEN professional achievement

lona *f* TRANSP tilt

longitud: ~ **de página** *f* INFO page length; ~ **de palabra** *f* INFO word length

longitudinal *adj* COM GEN longitudinal

lonja *f* ECON *comercio* exchange; ~ **de transacciones** BOLSA pit

lote *m* CONT *de facturas*, IND, INFO *de artículos* batch; ~ **de bonos** BOLSA bond crowd; ~ **completo** CONT full lot (*jarg*); ~ **desigual** COM GEN uneven lot; ~ **fraccionario** COM GEN fractional lot; ~ **suelto** BOLSA, V&M broken lot

lotería *f* COM GEN lottery

Lotería: ~ **Nacional** *f* ECON, OCIO National Lottery

LPG *abr* (*gas licuado de petróleo*) IND, TRANSP LPG (*liquid petroleum gas*)

LSI *abr* (*gran escala de integración*) INFO LSI (*large-scale integration*)

lucha *f* COM GEN conflict, struggle, fight; ~ **antiinflacionista** ECON, POL anti-inflation fight; ~ **de clases** ECON, POL class war; ~ **por la mayoría de votos** BOLSA proxy fight; ~ **por el poder** POL power struggle

luchar *vi* COM GEN fight

lucrativo *adj* COM GEN lucrative, profitable, CONT, FIN profitable; **no** ~ COM GEN nonprofitable, nonprofit-making (*AmE*), non-profit-making (*BrE*)

lucro *m* COM GEN profit; ~ **cesante** COM GEN shortfall in earnings

Luddismo *m* RRHH Luddism

Luddita *m* RRHH Luddite

lugar *m* COM GEN, IND site; ~ **de la conferencia** COM GEN, GES conference venue; ~ **contaminado** MED AMB contaminated site; ~ **de destino** COM GEN place of destination; ~ **de empleo** RRHH place of employment; ~ **de la entrega** TRANSP place of delivery (*POD*); ~ **de especial interés científico** MED AMB Site of Special Scientific Interest (*SSSI*); ~ **de inserción indeterminado** MEDIOS, V&M run-of-paper (*ROP*); ~ **de origen** TRANSP place of origin; ~ **de pago** BANCA place of payment; ~ **de popularidad** COM GEN popularity rating; ~ **de recepción** TRANSP place of acceptance (*POA*); ~ **de residencia** DER, INMOB place of abode; ~ **de trabajo** COM GEN place of work, workplace; ~ **con vallas publicitarias** V&M hoarding site; ◆ **en** ~ **de** COM GEN in lieu of

lugre *m* TRANSP *buque* lugger

lujo¹: **de** ~ *adj* MEDIOS glossy (*infrml*), V&M de luxe, luxury

lujo² *m* V&M *productos* luxury

lumpen: **el** ~ *m* FISC, RRHH *albañilería* the lump (*BrE*)

lunes: ~ **gris** *m* BOLSA grey Monday (*BrE*), gray Monday (*AmE*); ~ **negro** *m* BOLSA Black Monday

luz: ~ **verde** *f* COM GEN *autorización* green light

M

MAC *abr* (*mecanismo de ajuste de cambios*) ECON ERM (*Exchange Rate Mechanism*)

machacar: ~ **el mercado** *fra* BOLSA hammer the market; ~ **la oferta** *fra* BOLSA short the contract

macroambiente *m* COM GEN macroenvironment

macrodistribución *f* ECON macrodistribution

macroeconomía *f* ECON macroeconomics

macroeconómico *adj* ECON macroeconomic

macroempresa *f* GES macrocompany

macroinformática *f* INFO macrocomputing

macroinstrucción *f* COM GEN, INFO macro

macromarketing *m* V&M macromarketing

macroproyecto *m* GES macroproject

madera *f* IND *serrada, cortada* lumber (*AmE*), timber (*BrE*); ~ **contrachapada** *Esp* (*cf madera terciada AmL*) IND plywood; ~ **embalada** TRANSP packaged timber; ~ **terciada** *AmL* (*cf madera contrachapada Esp*) IND plywood

madre: ~ **soltera** *f* COM GEN single mother, single parent

maestra *f* TRANSP *embarcaciones* midship

magistrado, -a *m,f* DER *funcionario judicial* magistrate; ~ **autorizado(-a) para adjudicar** DER magistrate entitled to adjudicate

Magistratura: ~ **de Trabajo** *f Esp* DER, IND, RRHH industrial tribunal (*BrE*) (*IT*)

magnate *mf* COM GEN magnate, RRHH tycoon; ~ **financiero(-a)** *m,f* FIN financial magnate

magnetofón *m* INFO magnetic tape recorder

magnitud *f* MAT magnitude; ~ **del crédito** BOLSA tick size (*infrml*); ~ **organizativa** COM GEN organizational size

mago, -a: ~ **de las finanzas** *m,f* COM GEN financial wizard (*infrml*)

mailing *m* ADMIN, COM GEN mailing, COMS, V&M *publicidad* mailing list, mailshot; ♦ **hacer un** ~ COMS do a mailshot

mal[1]: ~ **pagado** *adj* RRHH low-paid; ~ **remunerado** *adj* RRHH low-paid; ~ **transportado** *adj* COM GEN wrong-shipped

mal[2]: ~ **negocio** *m* COM GEN bad bargain; ~ **nombre** *m* COM GEN bad name; ~ **pagador** *m* V&M deadbeat; **los** ~ **pagados** *m pl* RRHH the low-paid; ~ **uso del servicio** *m* COM GEN *herramienta* service abuse

mal[3]: ~ **usar** *vt* COM GEN fiddle (*infrml*); ~ **vender** *vt* COM GEN bargain away

mala: ~ **administración** *f* GES, RRHH bad management, mismanagement; ~ **compra** *f* COM GEN bad buy; ~ **cosecha** *f* ECON, MED AMB *agrícola* crop failure; ~ **entrega** *f* BOLSA bad delivery; ~ **gestión** *f* GES bad management; ~ **pagadora** *f* V&M deadbeat; ~ **salud** *f* COM GEN ill-health; ~ **voluntad** *f* COM GEN ill will, bad will

malas: ~ **noticias** *f pl* COM GEN bad news

malecón *m* TRANSP *puerto* mole

maledicencia *f* COM GEN backbiting

malentendido *m* COM GEN misunderstanding

maleta *f* OCIO suitcase; ~ **de muestra** V&M sample case

malfuncionar *vi* COM GEN break down

malgastar *vt* COM GEN fiddle (*infrml*), squander

malo *adj* COM GEN *datos, hechos* hard

maltusianismo *m* ECON Malthusianism

malvenderse *v refl* COM GEN undersell oneself

malversación *f* DER, FIN misuse; ~ **de caudales** CONT, DER, FIN misappropriation of money; ~ **de dinero** CONT, DER, FIN misappropriation of money; ~ **de fondos** CONT, DER, FIN misappropriation of funds

malversar *vt* CONT, DER, FIN misappropriate

mamparo: ~ **encerrador de escotilla** *m* TRANSP trunk (*TRK*)

management *m* RRHH management

mánager *mf* RRHH manager (*MGR*), manageress (*MGR*)

mancha *f* COM GEN, MED AMB *petróleo* slick; ~ **oleosa** COM GEN *petróleo* slick

mancheta *f* MEDIOS *en periódico* masthead, V&M earpiece

mancomunada: ~ **y solidariamente** *adv* DER *responsabilidad* jointly and severally

mancomunadamente *adv* DER, FISC jointly

mandamiento *m* DER *de los tribunales* order (*ord.*); ~ **de embargo** DER writ of attachment

mandar *vt* COM GEN, GES bid, command, order; ♦ ~ **una citación a alguien** DER, RRHH take out a summons against sb; ~ **algo mediante un representante** COM GEN send sth via an agent; ~ **a alguien a buscar algo** COM GEN send sb for sth

mandarín *m* POL *gobierno* mandarin

mandatario[1] *adj* DER mandatory

mandatario[2]**,-a** *m,f* DER proxyholder

mandato *m* COM GEN command, DER mandate, RRHH command; ~ **de pago** COM GEN warrant for payment

mando: ~ **automático** *m* INFO automatic control; ~ **intermedio** *m* GES, RRHH middle manager

mandos: ~ **intermedios** *m pl* GES, RRHH middle management

manejable *adj* COM GEN manageable

manejado: ~ **por computador** *AmL* ver *manejado por computadora AmL*, ~ **por computadora** *adj AmL* (*cf manejado por ordenador Esp*) INFO computer-operated; ~ **mediante teclado** *adj* INFO keyboard-operated; ~ **por ordenador** *adj Esp* (*cf manejado por computadora AmL*) INFO *computer-operated*

manejar *vt* COM GEN, FIN handle, GES manage, operate, INFO handle, RRHH *una máquina* man, TRANSP handle; ♦ ~ **con cuidado** COM GEN, TRANSP *inscripción en paquetes frágiles* handle with care; ~ **un déficit** ECON run a deficit; ~ **grandes sumas de dinero** FIN handle large sums of money; ~ **un superávit** ECON run a surplus

manejo *m* INFO handle, handling; ~ **del computador** *AmL* ver *manejo de la computadora AmL*; ~ **de la computadora** *AmL* (*cf manejo del ordenador Esp*) INFO computer operation; ~ **de una cuenta** BANCA account operation; ~ **de la información** COM GEN, INFO information handling; ~ **de mensajes** COMS, INFO message handling; ~ **del ordenador** *Esp* (*cf manejo de* *la computadora AmL*) INFO computer operation; ◆ **a su ~** COM GEN self-styled

manifestar *vt* COM GEN represent

manifiesto *m* IMP/EXP, TRANSP manifest; **~ del buque** TRANSP ship's manifest; **~ de carga** IMP/EXP cargo declaration, TRANSP shipping documents, cargo declaration, cargo manifest; **~ del cargamento** IMP/EXP, TRANSP transfer manifest, manifest of cargo; **~ de flete** TRANSP freight manifest; **~ de tripulación** TRANSP crew manifest

maniobra: **~ de enfrentamiento** *f* POL whipsaw (*jarg*) (*AmE*)

maniobrero *m* FIN jockey (*jarg*)

manipulación *f* BOLSA *mercado* rigging, COM GEN manipulation, FIN *precios* rigging, POL *votos* rigging, TRANSP *de mercancías* handling (*hdlg*); **~ automática modular de contenedores** TRANSP modular automated container handling (*MACH*); **~ a la baja** BOLSA bear raid, bear raiding; **~ de la carga en tierra** TRANSP *aviación* ground handling; **~ de la cobertura** BOLSA hedge management; **~ de la contabilidad** BANCA, CONT window-dressing; **~ de la contabilidad mediante operaciones** BANCA, CONT *cuentas anuales* window-dressing; **~ contable** CONT make-up; **~ de la información** POL word-engineering; **~ del mercado** BOLSA market rigging; **~ de precios** COM GEN price fixing

manipulado *adj* INFO hand-held

manipulador, -a *m,f* COM GEN manipulator; **~ de barriles** TRANSP barrel handler

manipular *vt* COM GEN *precios* manipulate, POL *votos* rig; ◆ **~ una contabilidad** CONT manipulate accounts

mano[1]: **en ~** *adj* V&M hand-held

mano[2]: **a ~** *adv* COM GEN by hand

mano[3]: **~ invisible** *f* ECON invisible hand; **~ de obra** *f* COM GEN labor (*AmE*), labor force (*AmE*), labour (*BrE*), labour force (*BrE*), manpower, work force, human resources; **~ de obra activa** *f* RRHH live labor (*AmE*), live labour (*BrE*); **~ de obra adicional** *f* RRHH additional labor (*AmE*), additional labour (*BrE*); **~ de obra común** *f* RRHH common labor (*AmE*), common labour (*BrE*); **~ de obra concreta** *f* RRHH materialized labor (*AmE*), materialized labour (*BrE*); **~ de obra contratada** *f* RRHH contract labor (*AmE*), contract labour (*BrE*); **~ de obra de coste elevado** *f* RRHH high-cost labor (*AmE*), high-cost labour (*BrE*); **~ de obra cualificada** *f* RRHH skilled labor (*AmE*), skilled labour (*BrE*); **~ de obra directa** *f* RRHH direct labor (*AmE*), direct labour (*BrE*); **~ de obra especializada** *f* RRHH skilled labor (*AmE*), skilled labour (*BrE*); **~ de obra con experiencia** *f* RRHH experienced workforce; **~ de obra explotada** *f* PROT SOC, RRHH sweated labor (*AmE*), sweated labour (*BrE*); **~ de obra de fábrica** *f* RRHH manufacturing workforce; **~ de obra ilimitada** *f* RRHH unrestricted labor (*AmE*), unrestricted labour (*BrE*); **~ de obra imprescindible** *f* RRHH core workforce; **~ de obra improductiva** *f* RRHH unproductive labor (*AmE*), unproductive labour (*BrE*); **~ de obra indirecta** *f* RRHH indirect labor (*AmE*), indirect labour (*BrE*); **~ de obra indispensable** *f* RRHH indispensable labor (*AmE*), indispensable labour (*BrE*), necessary labor (*AmE*), necessary labour (*BrE*); **~ de obra local** *f* RRHH local labor (*AmE*), local labour (*BrE*); **~ de obra migratoria** *f* RRHH migrant labor (*AmE*), migrant

labour (*BrE*); **~ de obra necesaria** *f* RRHH necessary labor (*AmE*), necessary labour (*BrE*); **~ de obra no cualificada** *f* RRHH simple labor (*AmE*), simple labour (*BrE*), unskilled labor (*AmE*), unskilled labour (*BrE*); **~ de obra no registrada** *f* RRHH unregistered labor (*AmE*), unregistered labour (*BrE*); **~ de obra no sindicada** *f* RRHH non-union labor (*AmE*), non-union labour (*BrE*); **~ de obra productiva** *f* RRHH productive labor (*AmE*), productive labour (*BrE*); **~ de obra semicualificada** *f* RRHH semiskilled labor (*AmE*), semiskilled labour (*BrE*); **~ de obra suplementaria** *f* RRHH additional labor (*AmE*), additional labour (*BrE*); **~ oculta** *f* ECON hiding hand; **~ visible de la economía** *f* ECON visible hand

manómetro: **~ de aceite** *m* MED AMB, TRANSP oil gage (*AmE*), oil gauge (*BrE*)

manos[1]: **~ limpias** *f pl* COM GEN, DER *conducta profesional* clean hands

manos[2]: **en las ~ de** *fra* COM GEN in the hands of; **estar en ~ de un liquidador** *fra* COM GEN be in the hands of a receiver; **estar en ~ de un recaudador** *fra* COM GEN be in the hands of a receiver; **estar en ~ de un síndico** *fra* COM GEN, IND be in the hands of a receiver; **en ~ de terceros** *fra* COM GEN in the hands of a third party

mantenedor, a: **~ de la familia** *m,f* PROT SOC breadwinner

mantener *vt* BANCA *fondos*, BOLSA *posición* hold, COM GEN keep, maintain, *medio ambiente, parentesco* foster, FISC *familiar dependiente* support; ◆ **~ algo en secreto** COM GEN keep sth secret, keep sth under wraps (*infrml*); **~ el archivo al día** ADMIN keep the filing up to date; **~ baja la inflación** ECON keep inflation down; **~ como garantía** BANCA, FIN, SEG hold as a security; **~ los márgenes** ECON hold margins; **~ informado a alguien** COM GEN, COMS keep sb informed; **~ los márgenes** COM GEN hold margins; **~ a raya** ECON *precios* hold in check; **~ la seguridad** BANCA stand surety

mantenerse *v refl* COM GEN *oferta, precio, puja* stand; ◆ **~ al corriente de** COM GEN *condiciones, legislaciones* keep abreast of, keep in touch with; **~ al tanto de** COM GEN keep abreast of, keep pace with; **~ en contacto con** COM GEN keep in touch with; **~ dentro de la ley** DER keep within the law; **~ un descuento** BOLSA stand at a discount; **~ firme** COM GEN stand firm, hold one's ground; **~ firme en la creencia de que** COM GEN stand firm in the belief that; **~ a flote** COM GEN *negocio* keep afloat; **~ indiferente** BOLSA stay in-the-money; **~ informado de** COM GEN keep abreast of; **~ una prima de emisión** BOLSA stand at a premium; **~ en sus trece** COM GEN stand one's ground

mantenimiento *m* COM GEN, IND, INFO maintenance; **~ al por menor** COM GEN retail price maintenance, resale price maintenance (*RPM*); **~ del contrato** COM GEN contract maintenance; **~ de corrección** COM GEN correction maintenance; **~ diferido** INMOB *tasación* deferred maintenance; **~ a distancia** INFO remote maintenance; **~ esporádico** COM GEN sporadic maintenance; **~ general** COM GEN, IND total maintenance; **~ de las instalaciones** COM GEN, IND plant maintenance; **~ mínimo** BOLSA minimum maintenance; **~ planeado** COM GEN planned maintenance; **~ del precio de reventa** COM GEN, V&M resale price maintenance (*RPM*); **~ de los precios** COM GEN price maintenance, FIN price support; **~ de los precios al por menor** COM GEN, V&M resale price maintenance

(*RPM*); ~ **preventivo** COM GEN, GES, IND preventive maintenance; ~ **productivo** IND productive maintenance; ~ **de rendimientos** BOLSA yield maintenance; ~ **y reparación** INFO servicing; ~ **total de la planta** COM GEN total plant maintenance; ♦ ~, **reparación y revisión** TRANSP maintenance, repair and overhaul (*MRO*)

manual[1] *adj* COM GEN manual

manual[2] *m* COM GEN manual; ~ **de actuación** COM GEN *de empresa* play book (*jarg*) (*AmE*); ~ **de auditoría** CONT auditing manual; ~ **de codificación** CONT coding manual; ~ **de instrucciones** COM GEN instruction manual, instruction book; ~ **de mantenimiento** COM GEN service manual; ~ **de procedimiento** COM GEN rule book; ~ **de ventas** V&M sales manual

Manual: ~ **de Carga y Descarga en Aeropuertos** *m* TRANSP Airport Handling Manual (*AHM*); ~ **de la IATA para Carga y Descarga Aeroportuaria** *m* TRANSP IATA Airport Handling Manual; ~ **de Procedimientos para Mensajes de Reservas** *m* TRANSP ATC/IATA Reservations Interline Message Procedures Manual

manualmente *adv* COM GEN manually

manufactura *f* COM GEN, IND manufacture; ~ **de planta** IND plant manufacturing

manufacturado *adj* COM GEN, IND manufactured (*mfd*)

manufacturar *vt* COM GEN, IND make, manufacture

manufacturas *f pl* IND manufactures; ~ **en depósito** IMP/EXP in-bond manufacturing

manuscrito[1] *adj* COMS handwritten

manuscrito[2] *m* MEDIOS manuscript (*MS*)

manutención *f* DER alimony

manzana *f* INMOB block; ~ **de la discordia** COM GEN bone of contention

mapa *m* INFO map

maqueta *f* MEDIOS scale model

maquiladora *f* AmL (*cf semifabricante Esp*) IND quasi-manufacturer

maquillaje *m* CONT make-up (*jarg*); ~ **de balance** *jarg* CONT make-up (*jarg*)

maquillar: ~ **los números** *fra* CONT, FIN massage the figures

máquina *f* IND machine; ~ **de autoenseñanza** PROT SOC teaching machine; ~ **calculadora** COM GEN, INFO calculating machine; ~ **de componer fotográficamente** MEDIOS *imprenta* filmsetter; ~ **destructora de documentos** ADMIN shredder; ~ **diagonal** TRANSP diagonal engine (*D*); ~ **diesel-eléctrica** TRANSP diesel-electric engine; ~ **dispensadora de dinero** BANCA cash-dispensing machine; ~ **de escribir** ADMIN, INFO typewriter; ~ **de escribir automática** ADMIN automatic typewriter; ~ **de escribir electrónica** ADMIN electronic typewriter; ~ **de escribir con memoria** ADMIN memory typewriter; ~ **estampilladora** ADMIN, COMS date-stamping machine; ~ **expendedora** COM GEN vending machine; ~ **expendedora de sellos** ADMIN, COMS vending machine; ~ **franqueadora** ADMIN, COMS franking machine; ~ **offset de bobinas** V&M web-offset; ~ **de oficina** COM GEN business machine; ~ **de sumar** COM GEN, INFO adding machine; ~ **tabuladora** ADMIN tabulating machine; ~ **transportadora** AmL (*cf cinta transportadora Esp, cf correa transportadora Esp*) TRANSP conveyor belt; ~ **de triple expansión** TRANSP triple expansion engine

maquinaria *f* COM GEN machinery (*mchy*);

~ **administrativa** POL wheels of government; ~ **sin operador** IND unmanned machinery spaces

maquinista *mf* RRHH machine operator; ~ **de guardia automático** TRANSP *navegación* automatic watch keeper

mar: **por** ~ *fra* TRANSP by sea

marca *f* BOLSA, PATENT mark, V&M *de vehículo* make, *de producto, servicio* brand; ~ **de aleación** BANCA *en oro y plata* assay mark (*AmE*), hallmark (*BrE*); ~ **de ámbito nacional** V&M national brand; ~ **de aprobación** TRANSP *vehículos* approval mark; ~ **de certificación** DER, IND, PATENT, RRHH certification mark; ~ **colectiva** PATENT collective mark; ~ **comercial** BOLSA trade ticket, COM GEN, CONT trademark, DER, IND certification mark, PATENT certification mark, trade name, trade ticket, trademark, V&M store brand; ~ **comercializable** COM GEN good marketable brand (*GMB*); ~ **conocida** COM GEN well-known mark; ~ **de consumo** V&M consumer brand; ~ **derivada** COM GEN associated mark; ~ **del distribuidor** V&M dealer brand; ~ **de los distribuidores** V&M distributors' brand; ~ **establecida** V&M established brand; ~ **exclusiva** COM GEN proprietary brand; ~ **de fábrica** COM GEN, CONT, PATENT trademark, V&M trademark, manufacturer's brand; ~ **familiar** V&M family brand; ~ **de fin de archivo** INFO end-of-file mark; ~ **genérica** V&M generic brand; ~ **de grupo** COM GEN group mark (*GM*); ~ **de identificación** DER, PATENT, IND certification mark; ~ **de identificación de servicios** DER service mark; ~ **industrial registrada** COM GEN registered trademark; ~ **del invento** PATENT device mark; ~ **líder** COM GEN, V&M brand leader; ~ **mixta** PATENT combined mark, composite mark; ~ **no registrada** COM GEN, DER, PATENT, V&M unregistered trademark; ~ **Plimsoll** TRANSP Plimsoll line; ~ **privada** V&M private brand; ~ **del productor** V&M producer's brand; ~ **propia** V&M own brand; ~ **registrada** COM GEN registered trademark; ~ **rival** V&M rival brand; ~ **de servicios** PATENT service mark; ~ **de la UE** IND *para juguetes* EU-mark; ~ **de verificación** BANCA *en el oro y la plata* certification mark; ♦ **sin** ~ TRANSP *navegación* no mark (*n/m*)

marcación *f* FIN marking

marcado *adj* COM GEN *descenso, diferencia* marked

marcaje: ~ **con código de barras** *m* INFO, V&M bar code marking

marcar *vt* COM GEN *en una lista* tick off; ♦ ~ **un hito** COM GEN score a hit; ~ **la tónica** COM GEN set a trend

marcha *f* COM GEN operation, running, work; ~ **atrás** COM GEN reversing (*REV*); ~ **del calendario de trabajo** DER, INMOB run of schedule; ~ **normal de los negocios** COM GEN ordinary course of business; ♦ **en** ~ COM GEN *proceso, máquina* at work, in operation, *negocios* up and running

marchamo: ~ **de calidad** *m* COM GEN label of quality

marco *m* COM GEN framework; ~ **conceptual** CONT *de valores* conceptual framework; ~ **jurídico** DER legal framework; ~ **del muestreo** MAT sampling frame; ~ **operativo de un plan** FIN operational plan framework; ~ **de referencia de la política** ECON policy framework paper (*PFP*); ~ **temporal** COM GEN, GES time frame; ♦ **en el** ~ **de** COM GEN in the framework of

marcos: ~ **de tonelaje** *m pl* TRANSP *navegación* tonnage mark

marea: ~ **equinoccial ordinaria** *f* TRANSP ordinary

spring tide (*ost*); ~ **menguante** *f* TRANSP ebb tide; ~ **muerta** *f* TRANSP neap tide, slack water; ~ **viva** *f* TRANSP spring tide

margen[1]: **al** ~ *adv* COM GEN marginally

margen[2] *m* COM GEN margin; ~ **adicional** BOLSA additional margin, V&M *precio al por menor* additional mark-on; ~ **del agente** BOLSA jobber's spread; ~ **alcista** BOLSA bull spread; ~ **de arbitraje** BOLSA arbitrage margin (*BrE*); ~ **bancario** BANCA spread; ~ **de beneficio** COM GEN, V&M profit margin; ~ **de beneficio bruto** CONT, FIN gross profit margin; ~ **de beneficio final** CONT, FIN bottom-line profit margin; ~ **de beneficio de la inflación** ECON mark-up inflation; ~ **de beneficio neto** COM GEN net profit margin; ~ **de beneficios del resultado final** CONT, FIN bottom-line profit margin; ~ **bruto** CONT, ECON, FIN gross margin (*GM*); ~ **bruto de autofinanciación** CONT, ECON, FIN cash flow; ~ **bruto de la emisión** BOLSA gross operating spread; ~ **de cambio al contado** BOLSA spot rate spread; ~ **del uno por ciento** BOLSA one percent spread; ~ **de cobertura** BOLSA backwardation; ~ **de cocodrilo** BOLSA *inversiones, títulos, opciones* alligator spread; ~ **comercial** BOLSA, COM GEN margin trading; ~ **de compra a la alza** BOLSA bull call spread; ~ **de compra a la baja** BOLSA bear call spread; ~ **de contribución** CONT contribution margin; ~ **del corredor de bolsa** BOLSA jobber's spread; ~ **de cotización** BOLSA quotation spread; ~ **dentro del mismo producto** BOLSA intracommodity spread; ~ **de depósito** BOLSA box spread; ~ **diferencial** ECON differential margin; ~ **entre entregas** BOLSA *futuros sobre divisas* interdelivery spread; ~ **entre oferta y demanda** BOLSA bid-ask spread; ~ **entre los precios** COM GEN, ECON, V&M price differential; ~ **entre los productos** BOLSA intercommodity spread; ~ **de error** CONT margin of error; ~ **escaso** CONT narrow margin; ~ **estadístico** MAT statistical spread; ~ **estrecho** CONT narrow margin; ~ **favorable competitivo** ECON competitive edge; ~ **de fluctuación** BOLSA variation margin; ~ **futuro** ECON forward margin; ~ **de ganancia** COM GEN, V&M profit margin; ~ **inicial** BOLSA *futuros* initial margin; ~ **de interés neto** BANCA interest margin, CONT net interest margin; ~ **de mantenimiento** BOLSA maintenance margin; ~ **de mariposa** BOLSA butterfly spread; ~ **mínimo** BOLSA minimum margin; ~ **del minorista** V&M retail margin; ~ **neto** BOLSA money spread, CONT, ECON, FIN net margin; ~ **obligatorio** BOLSA compulsory margin (*BrE*), margin requirement; ~ **operacional** COM GEN operational margin; ~ **original** BOLSA, FIN original margin; ~ **posterior** MEDIOS back margin; ~ **a ratio** BOLSA ratio spread; ~ **a ratio comprador** BOLSA ratio call spread; ~ **a ratio comprador inverso** BOLSA ratio call backspread; ~ **a ratio vendedor** BOLSA ratio put spread; ~ **a ratio vendedor inverso** BOLSA ratio put backspread; ~ **reducido** CONT narrow margin; ~ **de rescate** BOLSA call spread; ~ **de resultado de ejercicio** CONT bottom-line profit margin; ~ **de segmento** CONT segment margin; ~ **de seguridad** COM GEN margin of safety, safety margin, security margin; ~ **de solvencia** CONT, FIN solvency margin; ~ **de suscripción** BOLSA underwriting spread; ~ **de tiempo** BOLSA time spread, V&M *surtido de mercancías* lead time; ~ **de tipo a futuros** BOLSA forward rate spread; ~ **de utilidad** COM GEN, MEDIOS *prensa* mark-up; ~ **de variación** BOLSA variation margin; ~ **de venta** BOLSA put spread, spread;

~ **de venta al alza** BOLSA bull put spread; ~ **de venta a la baja** BOLSA bear put spread; ~ **vertical alcista de opción de compra** BOLSA bullish vertical call spread; ~ **vertical alcista de opción de venta** BOLSA bullish vertical put spread

márgenes *m pl* COM GEN fringes; ~ **de variación de intereses** BANCA interest spread

marginal *adj* COM GEN marginal

marginalismo *m* ECON marginalism

marginalistas *m pl* ECON Marginalists

marginalizar *vt* COM GEN marginalize

marina: ~ **mercante** *f* TRANSP merchant navy, merchant marine, merchant shipping

marino *adj* TRANSP marine

mariposa: ~ **comprada** *f* BOLSA *opciones* long butterfly; ~ **vendida** *f* BOLSA *opciones de compra y venta* short butterfly

marítimo *adj* TRANSP maritime

marketing *m* V&M marketing; ~ **agresivo** V&M aggressive marketing; ~ **blando** V&M soft marketing; ~ **boca a boca** V&M word-of-mouth marketing; ~ **de calidad total** V&M total quality marketing; ~ **de consumo** V&M consumer marketing; ~ **cooperativo** V&M cooperative marketing; ~ **creativo** V&M creative marketing; ~ **de destino** V&M destination marketing; ~ **diferenciado** V&M differentiated marketing; ~ **directo** V&M direct marketing; ~ **divergente** V&M divergent marketing; ~ **de exportación** IMP/EXP, V&M export marketing; ~ **global** V&M global marketing; ~ **industrial** V&M industrial marketing; ~ **internacional** V&M international marketing; ~ **de marca** V&M brand marketing; ~ **de masa** V&M mass marketing; ~ **negocio a negocio** V&M business-to-business marketing; ~ **no diferenciado** V&M undifferentiated marketing; ~ **de nuevo lanzamiento** V&M remarketing; ~ **de objetivos** V&M target marketing; ~ **de persuasión** V&M destination marketing; ~ **del producto** V&M product marketing; ~ **de red** V&M network marketing; ~ **de relaciones** V&M relationship marketing; ~ **de rendimiento** V&M performance marketing; ~ **de respuesta directa** V&M direct response marketing; ~ **simbiótico** V&M symbiotic marketing; ~ **sincronizado** V&M syncro marketing; ~ **de varios niveles** V&M multilevel marketing (*MLM*)

marquesina *f* COM GEN *publicidad* awning

martillo *m* COM GEN *subastador* gavel

martingala *f* MAT martingale

marxismo *m* ECON, POL Marxism

más[1]: ~ **abajo** *adj* COMS hereunder; ~ **antiguo** *adj* COM GEN, RRHH *posición en la empresa* senior (*Snr*); ~ **bajo por entregar** *adj* BOLSA cheapest to deliver (*CTD*); ~ **cerca** *adj* BOLSA *opciones* farther in; ~ **lejos** *adj* BOLSA *opciones* farther out; ~ **pobre** *adj* COM GEN worse off

más[2]: ~ **vendido** *m* MEDIOS *libro*, V&M bestseller

más[3] *prep* MAT plus

masa: ~ **de acreedores** *f* CONT body of creditors; ~ **bruta** *f* COM GEN gross mass (*G*); ~ **crítica** *f* COM GEN, ECON, V&M critical mass; ~ **de la quiebra** *f* FISC estate of bankrupt

masivo *adj* COM GEN massive

Master: ~ **de Ciencias** *m* PROT SOC Master of Science (*MSc*); ~ **de Comercio** *m* PROT SOC Master of

Commerce (*MCom*); ~ **en Dirección y Administración de Empresas** *m* (*MBA*) PROT SOC, RRHH Master of Business Administration (*MBA*); ~ **de Economía** *m* PROT SOC Master of Economics (*MEcon*)

matar: ~ **la demanda** *fra* V&M kill demand

materia *f* MED AMB material; ~ **en consideración** COM GEN subject matter; ~ **orgánica** MED AMB organic material

material[1] *adj* COM GEN substantial, material

material[2] *m* COM GEN *información* material; ~ **anticorrosión** IND, TRANSP corrosion-resistant material; ~ **de apoyo** COM GEN backup material; ~ **asignado** TRANSP allocated material; ~ **básico** ECON basic material; ~ **complementario incorporable** INFO add-on equipment; ~ **directo** ECON direct material; ~ **editorial** V&M editorial matter; ~ **a granel** COM GEN bulk material; ~ **impreso** MEDIOS print media; ~ **polimerizable** TRANSP polymerizable material; ~ **publicitario** V&M publicity material; ~ **publicitario obligatorio** V&M mandatory copy; ~ **de punto de venta** V&M point-of-sale material; ~ **recuperable** MED AMB *reciclaje* recoverable material; ~ **de referencia** COM GEN reference material; ~ **rodante** TRANSP rolling stock

materiales: ~ **auxiliares** *m pl* CONT factory supplies; ~ **de construcción** *m pl* IND, SEG building materials; ~ **de embalaje** *m pl* V&M packaging materials; ~ **de fábrica** *m pl* CONT factory supplies; ~ **de factoría** *ver* **materiales de fábrica**; ~ **de oficina** *m pl* ADMIN office supplies

materialidad *f* CONT *informes contables* materiality

materialismo *m* POL materialism

materializarse *v refl* COM GEN materialize

materias: ~ **primas** *f pl* ECON raw materials, IND raw materials, unmanufactured materials; ~ **primas agrícolas** *f pl* ECON agrifoodstuffs

matrícula *f* PROT SOC *cursos* fee; ~ **reducida** PROT SOC *cursos* concessional fee

matriculación *f* PATENT registration

matriz *f* COM GEN *matemáticas* grid, INFO *figuras, datos* array, data structure; ~ **de Boston** V&M *filial* Boston box; ~ **de cheque** BANCA check counterfoil (*AmE*), cheque counterfoil (*BrE*); ~ **de gráficos realzada** INFO *tratamiento gráfico* enhanced graphics array; ~ **interactiva** GES interaction matrix; ~ **de Leontief** ECON Leontief matrix; ~ **de medida variable** MEDIOS variable-size font; ~ **de registro** INFO record locking; ~ **de video gráfico** *AmL ver* **matriz de vídeo gráfico** *Esp*; ~ **de vídeo gráfico** *Esp* INFO video graphics array (*VGA*)

máxima: ~ **categoría jerárquica** *f* COM GEN top of the tree (*infrml*); ~ **eficiencia** *f* ECON maximum efficiency

maximización *f* COM GEN maximization; ~ **del beneficio** COM GEN revenue maximization; ~ **de beneficios** COM GEN profit maximization; ~ **de las ganancias** COM GEN profit maximization; ~ **de los ingresos** COM GEN revenue maximization; ~ **de las ventas** COM GEN sales maximization

maximizar *vt* COM GEN maximize

máximo[1] *adj* COM GEN maximum (*max.*), MAT maximal

máximo[2] *m* COM GEN maximum; ~ **histórico** BOLSA, COM GEN all-time high; ♦ **hasta un** ~ **de** COM GEN up to a maximum of

máximos: ~ **descendentes** *m pl* BOLSA descending tops

mayday *m* BOLSA *Bolsa de Nueva York* Mayday

mayor[1] *adj* COM GEN greater, major; ~ **de edad** DER adult; ♦ **al por** ~ COM GEN wholesale, by wholesale

mayor[2]: ~ **de acreedores** *m* CONT creditors' ledger; ~ **de clientes** *m* CONT customer ledger, client ledger; ~ **de compras** *m* CONT bought ledger; ~ **inversor(a)** *m,f* BOLSA largest investor; ~ **precio** *m* BOLSA highest price; ~ **privado** *m* CONT private ledger

mayoría *f* DER *de edad*, POL majority; ~ **absoluta** POL absolute majority; ~ **cualificada** POL qualified majority; ~ **precoz** V&M *de consumidores* early majority; **la** ~ **silenciosa** POL the silent majority; ~ **simple** POL simple majority; ~ **tardía** V&M late majority

mayorista *mf* COM GEN wholesaler; ~ **afiliado(-a)** *m,f* V&M affiliated wholesaler; ~ **de estanterías** MEDIOS *radiodifusión* rack jobber; ~ **de venta al contado** V&M cash and carry wholesaler

mayúscula *f* INFO, MEDIOS capital letter, upper case letter

mayúsculas *f pl* INFO, MEDIOS capital letters (*caps*), uppercase letters

Mb *abr* (*megabyte*) INFO Mb (*megabyte*)

MBA *abr* (*Master en Dirección y Administración de Empresas*) PROT SOC, RRHH ≈ MBA (*Master of Business Administration*)

MCCO *abr* (*Mercado Común del Caribe Oriental*) ECON, POL ECCM (*East Caribbean Common Market*)

mecanismo *m* COM GEN, IND mechanism; ~ **de ajuste de cambios** (*MAC*) ECON Exchange Rate Mechanism (*ERM*); ~ **de ajuste estructural** FIN Structural Adjustment Facility (*SAF*); ~ **de ajuste estructural mejorado** *f* FIN Enhanced Structural Adjustment Facility (*ESAF*); ~ **de descarga** TRANSP *en remolques* landing gear; ~ **de descuento** FIN discount mechanism; ~ **del disparador** COM GEN trigger mechanism; ~ **de emisión** FIN issuance facility; ~ **de emisión de nota** (*NIF*) FIN note issuance facility (*NIF*); ~ **financiero compensatorio** FIN compensatory financial facility (*CFF*); ~ **de flujo de especie** BANCA specie-flow mechanism; ~ **impulsor de disco** INFO disk drive; ~ **de inducción** ECON inducement mechanism; ~ **del mercado** ECON market mechanism; ~ **de negociación** RRHH *relaciones industriales* negotiating machinery; ~ **de precios** ECON price mechanism; ~ **de puesta a cero del tipo** BOLSA rate resetter (*RR*); ~ **de sistema automatizado** INFO circuit breaker mechanism; ~ **de transmisión** ECON transmission mechanism

mecanismos: ~ **de votación** *m pl* POL voting procedures

mecanización *f* IND mechanization; ~ **de la manipulación de la carga** TRANSP mechanization of cargo handling

mecanizado *adj* COM GEN, IND machine-based, mechanized

mecanizar *vt* COM GEN, IND mechanize

mecanografiado *adj* ADMIN, PATENT typewritten

mecanografiar *vt* ADMIN, INFO type, typewrite; ♦ ~ **al tacto** ADMIN, COM GEN, INFO touch-type; ~ **sin mirar al teclado** ADMIN, COM GEN, INFO touch-type

mecanógrafo, -a *m,f* ADMIN typist

media *f* COM GEN average (*av.*), MAT average (*av.*), mean; ~ **altura** TRANSP half height (*H/H*); ~ **aritmética** MAT arithmetic mean; ~ **armónica** MAT harmonic mean; ~ **bursátil del grupo Barron** BOLSA Barron's Group Stock Average (*AmE*); ~ **de ganancias** BOLSA earnings ratio; ~ **geométrica** MAT geometric mean (*GM*); ~ **incremental del coste** *Esp* (*cf media incremental del* costo *AmL*) ECON average incremental cost; ~ **incremental del costo** *AmL* (*cf media incremental del coste Esp*) ECON average incremental cost; ~ **Industrial Dow Jones** BOLSA Dow Jones Industrial Average; ~ **móvil** MAT moving average; ~ **muestral** MAT *estadística* sample mean; ~ **nacional** ECON national average; ~ **penalización por demora en el despacho** TRANSP *fletamento* despatch half demurrage (*d1/2D*); ~ **pensión** OCIO half board; ~ **tarifa** COM GEN half fare; ~ **de vida** ECON, FISC lifetime averaging; ♦ **a** ~ **jornada** COM GEN on half-time

Media: ~ **del Fondo Monetario Donoghue** *f* BOLSA Donoghue's Money Fund Average (*AmE*)

mediación *f* COM GEN mediation, agency (*agcy, agy.*), RRHH mediation; ~ **por necesidad** DER agency by necessity

mediador, a *m,f* COM GEN, RRHH mediator

mediana *f* MAT *estadística* median

medianil *m* MEDIOS *imprenta* gutter

mediar *vi* COM GEN, RRHH *entre dos o más partes* mediate

medicamento *m* COM GEN drug; ~ **de marca registrada** COM GEN proprietary drug; ~ **sin prescripción** V&M over-the-counter medicine; ~ **sin receta** V&M over-the-counter medicine

medición *f* COM GEN measurement, meterage, MAT, TRANSP *náutico* measurement (*met*); ~ **de ejecución** GES performance measurement; ~ **de líquidos** COM GEN liquid measure; ~ **de métodos para tiempos** GES methods-time measurement (*MTM*); ~ **monetaria** FIN money measurement; ~ **de la productividad** IND productivity measurement; ~ **de realización** GES performance measurement; ~ **del rendimiento** GES, RRHH performance measurement; ~ **del tonelaje** TRANSP tonnage measurement; ~ **del trabajo** COM GEN, GES, IND work measurement; ~ **del trabajo de oficina** (*MTO*) ADMIN, RRHH clerical work measurement (*CWM*)

médico *adj* COM GEN medical

medida *f* COM GEN measure; ~ **para áridos** COM GEN dry measure; ~ **de control** ECON *precios* measure of control; ~ **cuadrada** COM GEN square measure; ~ **disciplinaria** COM GEN disciplinary measure; ~ **drástica** COM GEN drastic measure; ~ **especial de empleo** RRHH special employment measure (*SEM*); ~ **estimulante** ECON stimulative measure; ~ **fiscal** FISC tax measure; ~ **en grados** MAT degree measure; ~ **de huelga** RRHH strike action; ~ **del ingreso de Hicks** ECON Hicksian income measure; ~ **de liderazgo de una empresa** ECON barometric firm leadership; ~ **de longitud** COM GEN linear measure; ~ **de presión** COM GEN industrial action; ~ **reguladora** DER regulatory measure; ~ **de represalia** COM GEN retaliatory measure; ~ **de la riqueza económica** ECON, RRHH measure of economic welfare (*MEW*); ~ **de seguridad** COM GEN security measure, safety measure, safety precaution, MED AMB safety measure; ~ **de superficie** COM GEN square measure; ~ **transitoria** FISC transitional provision; ~ **unilateral** COM GEN unilateral measure; ♦ **en cierta** ~ COM GEN to an extent; **a la** ~ **del cliente** IND customized; **como** ~ **precautoria** COM GEN as a precautionary measure; **en mayor** ~ COM GEN to a large extent; **en menor** ~ COM GEN to a lesser extent

medidas: ~ **y límites** *m pl* INMOB metes and bounds

medidor: ~ **de intervalos de tiempo** *m* ADMIN time-keeper; ~ **de neumático** *m* TRANSP tire gage (*AmE*), tyre gauge (*BrE*); ~ **de parpadeos** *m* V&M blink-meter

medio[1] *adj* INFO average

medio[2] *m* COM GEN *de comunicación* medium; ~ **de almacenamiento** COMS, INFO storage medium; ~ **ambiente** MED AMB environment; ~ **básico** MEDIOS basic medium; ~ **de cambio** ECON medium of exchange; ~ **de cambio básico** *f* ECON, FIN basic currency; ~ **comercial** COM GEN business environment; ~ **de eliminación** MED AMB *desperdicios* disposal facility; ~ **generalizado** ECON generalized medium; ~ **publicitario** MEDIOS, V&M advertising medium, advertising vehicle; ~ **de respuesta** V&M *pedidos por correo* reply vehicle; ♦ **como** ~ **de** COM GEN as a means of; **por** ~ **de** COMS via

mediodía: **antes del** ~ *fra* COM GEN ante meridiem (*a.m.*); **después del** ~ *fra* COM GEN post meridiem (*p.m.*)

medios *m pl* BOLSA *recursos* mediums, ECON means; ~ **audiovisuales** COMS, MEDIOS audiovisual aids; ~ **básicos** MEDIOS basic media; ~ **de colocación** V&M position media; ~ **de comunicación** MEDIOS media, communication media, mass media; ~ **de comunicación al público** MEDIOS mass media; ~ **electrónicos** V&M electronic media; ~ **financieros** FIN financial means; ~ **mezclados** V&M mixed media; ~ **de pago** ECON means of payment; ~ **prácticos más adecuados** COM GEN best practical means (*bpm*); ~ **publicitarios** MEDIOS, V&M advertising media; ~ **tonos** MEDIOS halftone; ~ **de transporte** COM GEN, TRANSP transport facilities; ♦ ~ **y arbitrios** ECON ways and means

medir *vt* ECON measure, INMOB survey; ♦ ~ **el desempeño de alguien** RRHH measure sb's performance

MEFF *abr* (*Mercado Español de Futuros Financieros*) BOLSA, ECON Spanish financial futures market

megabyte *m* (*Mb*) INFO megabyte (*Mb*)

megaempresa *f* COM GEN mega-corporation, megacorp (*jarg*)

mejor[1]: ~ **alternativa** *f* COM GEN best alternative; ~ **comunicante** *mf* COM GEN best profferer; ~ **después del óptimo** *f* COM GEN second best; ~ **oferta** *f* COM GEN best bid; ~ **postor(a)** *m,f* BOLSA, COM GEN highest bidder, best bidder; ~ **precio** *m* COM GEN best price; ~ **uso posible** *m* INMOB *valoración* highest and best use

mejor[2]: **al** ~ *fra* BOLSA *precio, pedido* at best

mejora *f* COM GEN improvement, INMOB *aumento de valor* betterment; ~ **de beneficios** COM GEN, FIN profit improvement; ~ **de la casa** INMOB home improvement; ~ **de inmueble arrendado** INMOB leasehold improvement; ~ **de Pareto** ECON Pareto improvement; ~ **del producto** V&M product improvement

mejorado *adj* COM GEN, V&M *calidad* upgraded

mejoramiento *m* COM GEN *sistema* improvement; ~ **de la tierra** MED AMB land improvement

mejorar *vt* COM GEN *en calidad* upgrade, look up; ♦ ~ **la oferta** BOLSA hit the bid

melodía: ~ **publicitaria** *f* MEDIOS, V&M advertising jingle

membresía: ~ **honoraria** *f* AmL (*cf ingreso honorario Esp*) RRHH honorary membership

membrete *m* COM GEN, COMS heading, letterhead

memorándum *m* COM GEN memorandum (*frml*) (*memo*); ~ **de crédito** BANCA, FIN credit memorandum; ~ **de débito** BANCA, FIN debit memorandum; ~ **de intención** COM GEN memorandum of intent; ~ **de planificación de factores** FIN planning element memorandum

memoria *f* COM GEN report, statement, CONT statement, INFO memory; ~ **de acceso aleatorio** INFO random access memory (*RAM*); ~ **adicional** INFO add-on memory; ~ **de alta velocidad** INFO high-speed memory; ~ **anual** FIN annual report; ~ **de apoyo** INFO backup memory; ~ **auxiliar** INFO auxiliary memory, *equipo* auxiliary storage; ~ **baja** INFO low memory; ~ **de burbujas** INFO bubble memory; ~ **del computador** *AmL ver memoria de la computadora AmL*; ~ **de la computadora** *AmL* (*cf memoria del ordenador Esp*) INFO computer memory; ~ **a los estados financieros** CONT notes to the financial statements; ~ **externa** INFO add-on memory; ~ **global** INFO global memory; ~ **interfaz** INFO buffer store; ~ **intermedia** INFO buffer; ~ **interna** INFO internal storage; ~ **magnética** INFO magnetic storage; ~ **de masa** INFO mass memory; ~ **de núcleos** INFO core storage, core memory; ~ **del ordenador** *Esp* (*cf memoria de la computadora AmL*) INFO computer memory; ~ **presupuestaria** ECON budgetary statement; ~ **real** INFO real storage; ~ **de sólo lectura** INFO read only memory (*ROM*); ~ **sólo de lectura programable electrónicamente** INFO electronically programmable read only memory (*EPROM*); ~ **sólo de lectura programable y que puede borrarse** INFO erasable programmable read only memory (*EPROM*); ~ **tampón** INFO buffer; ~ **temporal** INFO cache memory; ~ **de tránsito** INFO buffer store

mena *f* MED AMB *depósito* ore

mención: ~ **editorial** *f* V&M editorial mention; ~ **especial** *f* PROT SOC make a distinction

mencionado: **antes** ~ *adj* COMS aforementioned

mencionar *vt* COM GEN mention

menciones: ~ **en la prensa** *f pl* V&M press mentions

menor[1] *adj* COM GEN minor; ♦ **al por** ~ V&M retail; ~ **de edad** COM GEN minor; **de** ~ **riesgo** BOLSA no-name

menor[2] *mf* DER *edad* minor; ~ **de edad** COM GEN minor

menos[1] *adj* CONT *cuenta de pérdidas y ganancias* less, MAT minus; ♦ **poco** ~ **que perfecto** COM GEN less-than-perfect; **a** ~ **que se disponga lo contrario** DER unless otherwise provided

menos[2]: ~ **que proporcionalmente** *adv* MAT under-proportionately

menos[3] *m* MAT *símbolo* minus

menoscabo *m* FISC impairment

menospreciar *vt* COM GEN underestimate

mensaje *m* COM GEN message; ~ **básico** V&M *publicidad* basic message; ~ **de bienvenida** INFO, V&M welcome message; ~ **cifrado** COMS *por satélite* scrambled message; ~ **de diagnóstico** INFO *lenguaje de programación* diagnostic message; ~ **de entrada** INFO input message; ~ **de error** INFO error message; ~ **de intervención** INFO action message; ~ **de movimiento de aeronave** TRANSP aircraft movement message (*MVT*); ~ **publicitario** V&M advertising message, advertising copy; ~ **publicitario despectivo** V&M disparaging copy; ~ **publicitario de pre-encuesta** V&M pretesting copy; ~ **telefónico** COMS telephone message

mensajero, -a *m,f* COM GEN runner (*jarg*), COMS *en una oficina* messenger, courier, RRHH runner (*jarg*); ~ **bancario(-a)** BANCA bank messenger

mensual *adj* COM GEN monthly

mensualidad *f* COM GEN installment (*AmE*), instalment (*BrE*)

mensualmente *adv* COM GEN monthly

menú *m* INFO menu; ~ **de archivos** INFO file menu; ~ **descendente** INFO pop-down menu; ~ **de ficheros** INFO file menu; ~ **de funciones** INFO pop-up menu; ~ **principal** INFO main menu

mercaderías: ~ **futuras** *f pl* COM GEN future goods

mercado[1] *m* COM GEN market, marketplace;

~ **a** ~ **abierto** COM GEN, ECON open market; ~ **activo** BOLSA active market; ~ **de los adolescentes** V&M teenage market; ~ **altamente especializado** V&M niche market; ~ **al alza** BOLSA bull market, buoyant market; ~ **al contado** BOLSA cash market, spot market; ~ **al por mayor** COM GEN wholesale market; ~ **al por menor** COM GEN, INMOB, V&M retail outlet; ~ **alcista** BOLSA bull market, bullish market; ~ **amplio** BOLSA broad market, large market; ~ **animado** BOLSA brisk market;

~ **b** ~ **bajista** BOLSA bear market, declining market; ~ **de bienes raíces** COM GEN, INMOB real estate market; ~ **bilateral** BOLSA two-sided market; ~ **de bonos** BOLSA bond market; ~ **de los bonos yanqui** BOLSA yankee bond market (*AmE*); ~ **bursátil informal** COM GEN pink sheet market;

~ **c** ~ **de calidad** V&M quality market; ~ **de capitales** BOLSA, CONT, ECON, FIN capital market; ~ **cautivo** COM GEN niche trading, V&M captive market; ~ **de coches usados** ECON lemons market; ~ **comercial** BOLSA trading pit (*jarg*), COM GEN commercial market; ~ **de compradores** BOLSA, ECON, INMOB, V&M buyers' market; ~ **común** ECON, POL Common Market (*CM*); ~ **consolidado** V&M established market; ~ **de consumo** V&M consumer market; ~ **contable** BOLSA account market; ~ **de contangos** BOLSA contango market; ~ **de contenedores** TRANSP container market; ~ **contingente** SEG contingent market; ~ **continuo** BOLSA, COM GEN all-day trading, continuous market; ~ **a corto plazo** BOLSA short-term market, short market; ~ **sin cotización oficial** BOLSA unlisted market; ~ **crediticio** COM GEN credit market; ~ **de crédito al consumo** BANCA, FIN consumer credit market; ~ **de créditos recíprocos** BOLSA swop market;

~ **d** ~ **débil** BOLSA, ECON soft market (*jarg*), weak market; ~ **desanimado** COM GEN stale market; ~ **desarrollado** V&M developed market; ~ **de descuento** BOLSA, FIN discount market; ~ **de dinero** BANCA, BOLSA money market; ~ **de dinero doméstico** ECON, FIN domestic money market; ~ **de dinero interno** ECON, FIN domestic money market; ~ **de dinero local** ECON, FIN domestic money market; ~ **de divisas** BOLSA, ECON, FIN foreign exchange market, currency market; ~ **de divisas al contado** BOLSA, ECON spot currency market; ~ **doméstico** ECON, V&M domestic market;

~ **e** ~ **de efectos aceptados** BANCA acceptance market; ~ **eficiente** ECON *teoría* efficient market; ~ **de emisiones** BOLSA *futuros*, ECON issue market, primary market (*jarg*); ~ **equitativo** DER, ECON fair trading; ~ **con escasez de operaciones** BOLSA dull market, narrow market, thin market; ~ **escaso** BOLSA, V&M tight market; ~ **con escaso movimiento** ECON limited market; ~ **español de opciones y futuros** BOLSA Spanish options and futures stock market; ~ **estable** V&M stable market; ~ **de eurobonos** BOLSA, ECON Eurobond market; ~ **de eurodivisas** BOLSA, ECON eurocurrency market; ~ **del eurodólar** BOLSA, ECON, FIN Eurodollar market; ~ **de exportación** IMP/EXP export market; ~ **exterior** COM GEN, IMP/EXP overseas market;

~ f ~ **de factores de producción** ECON factor market; ~ **financiero** BOLSA, FIN financial market; ~ **financiero global** ECON, FIN global financial market; ~ **físico** BOLSA physical market; ~ **de fletes** BOLSA freight market; ~ **de fletes a plazo** BOLSA freight futures market; ~ **flojo** BOLSA dull market (*AmE*), narrow market, thin market (*AmE*); ~ **fluido** BOLSA liquid market; ~ **de fondos federales** BANCA federal funds market (*AmE*); ~ **fragmentado** ECON fragmented market; ~ **de futuros** BOLSA forward market, future trading, forward exchange market, futures market; ~ **de futuros en divisas** BOLSA, FIN currency futures market; ~ **de futuros financieros** BOLSA, FIN financial futures market; ~ **de futuros financieros de París** BOLSA, FIN Paris financial futures market; ~ **de futuros sobre acciones** BOLSA stock index futures market; ~ **de futuros sobre productos básicos** BOLSA commodity futures trading;

~ g ~ **genérico** V&M generic market; ~ **de gran complejidad** BOLSA sophisticated market; ~ **gris** BOLSA gray market (*AmE*), grey market (*BrE*);

~ h ~ **hipotecario** BANCA, FIN mortgage market; ~ **homogéneo** V&M homogeneous market;

~ i ~ **imperfecto** ECON, V&M imperfect market; ~ **indeciso** BOLSA, ECON disorderly market; ~ **inactivo** BOLSA quiet market; ~ **inestable** BOLSA, ECON disorderly market; ~ **inmobiliario** COM GEN, INMOB real estate market; ~ **inmovilizado** BOLSA locked market; ~ **interbancario** BANCA, ECON interbank market; ~ **de intercambio** COM GEN replacement market; ~ **interempresarial** BOLSA intercompany market; ~ **interior de títulos** BOLSA domestic securities market; ~ **internacional de capitales** BOLSA international capital market; ~ **interno** ECON internal market, domestic market; ~ **sin intervención** ECON, V&M free market; ~ **intervenido** ECON controlled market; ~ **invertido** BOLSA inverted market (*jarg*); ~ **irregular** BOLSA irregular market;

~ l ~ **laboral** ECON, RRHH job market, labor market (*AmE*), labour market (*BrE*); ~ **laboral externo** ECON external labor market (*AmE*), external labour market (*BrE*); ~ **laboral interno** ECON *de empresa* internal labor market (*AmE*), internal labour market (*BrE*); ~ **laboral local** ECON, RRHH local labor market (*AmE*), local labour market (*BrE*); ~ **laboral secundario** RRHH secondary labor market (*AmE*), secondary labour market (*BrE*); ~ **lateral** BOLSA sideways market; ~ **legalizado** ECON white market; ~ **de letras** BOLSA bill market; ~ **libre** ECON, V&M free market; ~ **libre y abierto** ECON, V&M free and open market; ~ **de libre empresa** ECON, V&M free enterprise market; ~ **de liquidación** ECON clearing market;

~ m ~ **maduro** BOLSA, V&M mature market; ~ **manipulado** BOLSA rigged market; ~ **marginal** BOLSA, V&M fringe market; ~ **de masas** V&M mass market; ~ **de metales** BOLSA metal market; ~ **monetario a corto plazo** BOLSA short-term money market; ~ **monetario restrictivo** FIN stringent money market; ~ **muerto** BOLSA graveyard market; ~ **mundial** ECON, POL, V&M world market;

~ n ~ **nacional** ECON, V&M domestic market; ~ **negro** ECON black market; ~ **no existente** ECON missing market; ~ **no intervenido** ECON, V&M free enterprise market; ~ **nominativo** FIN straights market;

~ o ~ **objetivo** V&M target market; ~ **de obligaciones**

de renta fija BOLSA bond market; ~ **oficial** ECON official market; ~ **de opciones** BOLSA options market (*OM*); ~ **de opciones europeo** BOLSA, ECON European Options Exchange (*EOE*); ~ **de opciones de París** BOLSA, FIN Paris options market; ~ **de opciones sobre bonos** BOLSA bond options market; ~ **organizado** ECON organized market; ~ **del oro** BOLSA, ECON gold market; ~ **del oro y la plata** BOLSA bullion market;

~ p ~ **de papel comercial en libras esterlinas** BANCA sterling commercial paper market (*SCP market*); ~ **de paquetería** TRANSP parcels market; ~ **de pasajeros** TRANSP passenger market; ~ **perfecto** ECON perfect market; ~ **periférico** BOLSA, V&M fringe market; ~ **a plazo** BOLSA future trading market, terminal market; ~ **poco animado** BOLSA quiet market; ~ **de préstamos** BANCA, FIN loan market; ~ **de préstamos corporativos** BANCA, FIN corporate lending market; ~ **primario** BOLSA *futuros*, ECON *emisiones* issue market, primary market (*jarg*); ~ **principal de divisas** FIN major foreign exchange market; ~ **de productos a futuro** BOLSA commodity futures market; ~ **de propiedades** INMOB, V&M property market;

~ r ~ **rápido** BOLSA fast market; ~ **regional** V&M regional market; ~ **regulado** ECON, FIN regulated market; ~ **restringido** BOLSA, ECON restricted market; ~ **retraído** COM GEN, V&M shrinking market; ~ **de reventa** V&M reseller market;

~ s ~ **saturado** COM GEN flooded market; ~ **secundario** BOLSA, ECON secondary market; ~ **de segunda mano** COM GEN second-hand market; ~ **de seguros** SEG insurance market; ~ **seminegro** ECON semiblack market; ~ **sensible** COM GEN sensitive market; ~ **sinátono** BOLSA flat market; ~ **socialista** ECON socialist market; ~ **sofisticado** BOLSA sophisticated market; ~ **sostenido** BOLSA bull market, buoyant market; ~ **de subasta** BOLSA auction market, outcry market; ~ **de subastas de viva voz** BOLSA open outcry auction market; ~ **superficial** BOLSA shallow market; ~ **de swaps** BOLSA swop market;

~ t ~ **técnico** BOLSA technical market; ~ **con tendencia a la baja** BOLSA bear market; ~ **con tendencia firme** COM GEN hardening market; ~ **de trabajo** ECON, RRHH job market, labor market (*AmE*), labour market (*BrE*); ~ **de trabajo doméstico** POL internal labor market (*AmE*), internal labour market (*BrE*); ~ **de trabajo primario** ECON primary labor market (*AmE*), primary labour market (*BrE*); ~ **de trabajo secundario** RRHH secondary labor market (*AmE*), secondary labour market (*BrE*); ~ **tranquilo** BOLSA orderly market; ~ **de tránsito** BOLSA, FIN transit market; ~ **tras el cierre** BOLSA after-hours market;

~ u ~ **único** COM GEN *de UE* Single Market; ~ **único laboral** ECON, RRHH single labor market (*AmE*), single labour market (*BrE*); ~ **único de trabajo** ECON, RRHH *de UE* single labor market (*AmE*), single labour market (*BrE*);

~ v ~ **de valores** BOLSA equity market; ~ **de valores extrabursátil** BOLSA, ECON, FIN over-the-counter market (*OTCM*); ~ **de valores de primera** BOLSA *títulos del Estado* gilt-edged market; ~ **de valores de renta fija** BOLSA fixed-income securities market; ~ **de valores de renta variable** BOLSA equity market; ~ **de vendedores** BOLSA, ECON sellers' market; ~ **de venta de la moneda al por mayor** FIN wholesale money market; ~ **vertical** V&M vertical market; ~ **de los viajes de negocios** OCIO business travel market; **~ de la vivienda** INMOB housing market

mercado[2]: **en el ~** *fra* INMOB on the market; **se ha derrumbado el ~** *fra* COM GEN the bottom has fallen out of the market; **se ha hundido el ~** *fra* COM GEN the bottom has fallen out of the market; **sin ~** *fra* BOLSA *vencimiento de operador* no market; **~ agotado** *fra* BOLSA buyers over; **el ~ de valores se consolidó** *fra* BOLSA the stock market made solid ground

Mercado: **~ Común de América Central** *m* ECON Central American Common Market (*CACM*); **~ Común Árabe** *m* ECON, POL Arab Common Market; **~ Común del Caribe Oriental** *m* (*MCCO*) ECON, POL East Caribbean Common Market (*ECCM*); **~ Europeo de Opciones** *m* BOLSA European Options Exchange; **~ Español de Futuros Financieros** *m* (*MEFF*) BOLSA, ECON Spanish financial futures market; **~ de Futuros de Chicago** *m* BOLSA Chicago Board of Trade; **~ Internacional de Acciones** *m* BOLSA International Equities Market (*IEM*); **~ Internacional de Opciones** *m* BOLSA International Options Market (*IOM*); **~ Internacional del Petróleo** *m* BOLSA International Petroleum Exchange (*IPE*); **~ Mercaderías de Liverpool** *m* BOLSA Liverpool Commodity Exchange; **~ Mercaderías de Manchester** *m* BOLSA Manchester Commodity Exchange; **~ Monetario Internacional** *m* BOLSA, ECON, POL International Monetary Market (*IMM*); **~ Nacional de Títulos** *m* BOLSA Domestic Equities Market (*DEM*); **~ Único Europeo** *m* COM GEN European Single Market; **~ de la Unión Europea** *m* COM GEN European Union Market

mercancía *f* BOLSA, COM GEN, ECON, IND commodity (*cmdty*); **~ al contado** FIN cash commodity; **~ básica** BOLSA primary commodity; **~ blanda** BOLSA soft commodity; **~ empaquetada** TRANSP, V&M packaged goods; **~ estándar** BOLSA standard commodity; **~ física** BOLSA physical commodity; **~ general** TRANSP general cargo (*GC*); **~ sobre el índice de arbitraje** *m* BOLSA stock index arbitrage

mercancías *f pl* COM GEN goods (*gds*), V&M merchandise; **~ al por mayor** COM GEN wholesale goods; **~ en almacén** TRANSP goods on hand (*GOH*); **~ en almacén de aduanas** ECON, FISC, IMP/EXP bonded goods (*b/g*); **~ ambientales** COM GEN, MED AMB environmental goods; **~ de auxilio** *f* IMP/EXP relief goods; **~ de la balanza comercial** ECON merchandise balance of trade; **~ en bruto** COM GEN crude goods; **~ comercializables** ECON *comercio internacional* commodity trades; **~ comprobadas** COM GEN ascertained goods; **~ en depósito** ECON, FISC, IMP/EXP bonded goods (*b/g*); **~ a granel** COM GEN bulk commodity; **~ imponibles** FISC dutiable goods; **~ importadas** IMP/EXP imported goods; **~ líquidas** COM GEN wet goods, wet stock; **~ no contenerizables** TRANSP uncontainerable goods (*UNCON*); **~ no vendidas** COM GEN unsold goods; **~ peligrosas** COM GEN, TRANSP dangerous goods; **~ prohibidas** COM GEN prohibited goods; **~ restituibles** COM GEN, V&M returnable goods; **~ sujetas a aranceles** FISC dutiable goods; **~ en tránsito** TRANSP cargo transit; **~ de venta fácil** V&M fast-moving consumer goods (*FMG*); **~ voluminosas** V&M bulky goods; ◆ **~ no embarcadas por falta de espacio** TRANSP cargo shut out; **las ~ todavía no se han entregado** COM GEN the goods remain undelivered

mercante *adj* RRHH merchant

mercantil *adj* ECON mercantile

mercantilismo *m* ECON *corriente económica* mercantilism

merchandising *m* V&M merchandising

Mercosur *m* ECON *comercio internacional* Mercosur

meridiano *m* COM GEN meridian

meridional *adj* COM GEN southern

mérito *m* RRHH worth, accomplishment

meritocracia *f* RRHH meritocracy

merma *f* ECON leakage, TRANSP tret, ullage; **~ en el inventario** ECON inventory shortage, inventory shrinkage; **~ natural** COM GEN, ECON, MED AMB natural wastage

mermar 1. *vt* COM GEN lessen, reduce; 2. *vi* COM GEN decrease, diminish

mermas[1]: **~ de las existencias** *f pl* COM GEN stock shortage

mermas[2]: **~ de mercancía durante el transporte** *fra* TRANSP leakage and breakage (*lkg & bkg*)

mes[1]: **~ calendario** *m* COM GEN calendar month; **~ del contrato** *m* BOLSA *futuros*, COM GEN *futuros* contract month; **~ de entrega** *m* BOLSA *futuros* delivery month, *futuros sobre divisas* contract delivery month; **~ de entrega más próximo** *m* BOLSA spot delivery month; **~ fiscal** *m* FISC fiscal month; **~ inmediato** *m* BOLSA nearest month; **~ de vencimiento** *m* BOLSA expiry month, expiration month

mes[2]: **por ~** *fra* COM GEN per calendar month (*p.c.m.*), per month (*p.m.*); **el ~ pasado** *fra* COM GEN ultimo (*ult.*)

mesa[1]: **de ~** *adj* INFO desktop

mesa[2]: **~ de cambios** *f* BANCA foreign exchange department; **~ de conferencias** *f* GES conference table; **~ directiva** *f* AmL (*cf consejo directivo Esp*) GES, RRHH board of directors, management board; **~ de negociaciones** *f* COM GEN bargaining table, GES, RRHH negotiating table; **~ redonda** *f* COM GEN round table

mesa[3]: **sobre la ~** *fra* COM GEN *propuesta* on the table

meses: **~ vencidos** *m pl* BANCA months after sight (*m/s*)

mesoeconomía *f* ECON mesoeconomy

meta *f* COM GEN, GES, IND, V&M goal, target; **~ de beneficios** CONT, FIN profit goal; **~ comercial** V&M market aim; **~ corporativa** COM GEN corporate goal; **~ de desempeño** COM GEN, GES, RRHH performance target; **~ de ejecución** COM GEN, GES, RRHH performance target; **~ de la empresa** COM GEN company goal **~ profesional** RRHH career goals; **~ de realización** COM GEN, GES, RRHH performance target; **~ de rendimiento** COM GEN, GES, RRHH performance target; **~ de ventas** FIN, V&M sales goal; ◆ **~ y cumplimiento** GES *negociaciones* carrot and stick (*infrml*)

metal: **~ fino** *m* COM GEN precious metal; **~ refinado** *m* MED AMB, SEG refined metal

metálico *m* COM GEN cash

metalista *mf* ECON *escuelas monetarias* metallist

metalúrgico[1] *adj* IND, RRHH metallurgic

metalúrgico[2]**,-a** *m,f* IND, RRHH metallurgist

metamarketing *m* V&M metamarketing

meter: **~ en máquina** *fra* MEDIOS pass for press; **~ una solicitud** *fra* AmL (*cf presentar una solicitud Esp*) RRHH put in an application

meterse: **~ en deudas** *fra* BANCA, ECON, FIN get into debt (*infrml*); **~ en mayores gastos** *fra* COM GEN go to great expense

metética *f* MAT methetics

método *m* COM GEN method; **~ ABC** CONT, GES *gestión de* *inventarios* ABC method; ~ **de abordar las ventas** V&M sales approach; ~ **aceptable** CONT receivable method; ~ **de acumulación** CONT accrual method; ~ **administrativo** GES management method; ~ **de amortización** CONT amortization method; ~ **de amortización anual uniforme** CONT straight-line method of depreciation; ~ **de amortización lineal** CONT amortization on a straight-line basis, straight-line method of depreciation; ~ **de aumento de liquidez** CONT increasing liquidity order; ~ **bayesiano** MAT Bayesian method; ~ **de caja** BANCA, CONT cash basis; ~ **del cambio de cierre** CONT *traducción a divisas* closing rate method (*BrE*), current rate method (*AmE*); ~ **del camino crítico** GES critical path method (*CPM*); ~ **a cielo abierto** IND *minería* open-cast method; ~ **del cinco por ciento** BOLSA five-percent rule; ~ **de clasificación por puntos** COM GEN points-rating method; ~ **de comparación** FIN benchmark method; ~ **de comparación de mercados** INMOB market comparison approach; ~ **de compra** CONT purchase method; ~ **de comprobación** FIN benchmark method; ~ **de consolidación** CONT *cuentas anuales* consolidation method; ~ **de contabilidad por partida doble** CONT, ECON double-entry method; ~ **de contabilidad patrimonial** CONT equity method of accounting; ~ **contable** CONT accounting method; ~ **de contrato completo** CONT completed contract method; ~ **de contrato cumplido** CONT completed contract method; ~ **de contrato ejecutado** CONT completed contract method; ~ **de contrato terminado** CONT completed contract method; ~ **de control de los tipos de cambio** ECON investment dollar pool system; ~ **de coste** *Esp* (*cf método de costo AmL*) CONT, INMOB cost method, cost approach; ~ **de coste total** *Esp* (*cf método de costo total AmL*) CONT, FIN full-cost method; ~ **de costo** *AmL* (*cf método de coste Esp*) CONT, INMOB cost method, cost approach; ~ **de costo total** *AmL* (*cf método de coste total Esp*) FIN full-cost method; ~ **de crecimiento sostenido** ECON steady-growth method; ~ **de los cuadrados mínimos en dos etapas** ECON two-stage least squares method; ~ **de los cuadrados mínimos en tres etapas** ECON three-stage least squares method; ~ **de cultivo** COM GEN farming method; ~ **de la cuota** CONT *de impuestos diferidos*, FISC liability method; ~ **de cuotas constantes** CONT *amortización* straight-line method; ~ **del deber** PROT SOC part method; ~ **de depreciación de saldos decrecientes** CONT declining balance method; ~ **de descuento directo** CONT *cuenta incobrable* direct charge-off method; ~ **de la deuda** CONT *de impuestos diferidos* liability method; ~ **económico** ECON economic method; ~ **de efectivo** BANCA, CONT cash basis; ~ **estático** CONT *pensiones* static method; ~ **de estudio de casos** GES *formulación de políticas* case-study method; ~ **de explotación ganadera** COM GEN farming method; ~ **de full-cost** CONT, FIN full-cost method; ~ **global de gastos** CONT overall expenses method; ~ **Graham y Dodd de inversión** BOLSA Graham and Dodd investment method; ~ **indagatorio** FISC *en auditorías externas* investigative approach; ~ **del índice en cadena** CONT, ECON chain-index method; ~ **de inventario periódico** CONT periodic inventory method; ~ **de licitación** COM GEN, V&M bidding technique; ~ **de la línea recta** CONT *amortización* straight-line method; ~ **lineal** CONT *amortización* straight-line method; ~ **de los mínimos cuadrados** MAT *estadística* least squares method; ~ **de**

observación aleatoria GES, MAT, V&M random observation method; ~ **de pago** COM GEN payment method, method of payment, FIN pay-back method, V&M payment method; ~ **de paridad competitiva** V&M competitive-parity method; ~ **de participación** CONT equity method; ~ **de partida doble** CONT, ECON double-entry method; ~ **de pasivo** CONT *de impuestos diferidos* liability method; ~ **de pasos** INFO steps method; ~ **de porcentaje de obra ejecutada** CONT percentage-of-completion method; ~ **de porcentaje de ventas** V&M *presupuestos de publicidad* percentage-of-sales method; ~ **de precio de compra** BOLSA purchase price method; ~ **de preparación** CONT *de cuentas* method of preparation; ~ **de rendimiento** INMOB income approach; ~ **de restituir** BANCA, FIN pay-back method; ~ **del salario real** CONT closing rate method (*BrE*), current rate method (*AmE*); ~ **de saldo decreciente** CONT diminishing-balance method; ~ **de tanteo** ECON, MAT trial-and-error method; ~ **temporal** CONT *traducción a divisas* temporal method; ~ **de transferencia de tecnología** ECON transfer of technology method; ~ **de tributación** FISC method of taxation; ~ **de unidades de producción** CONT units-of-production method; ~ **de la utilidad bruta** CONT, FIN gross profit method; ~ **válido** CONT receivable method; ~ **del valor descontado** CONT, ECON, FIN present value method; ~ **del valor presente** CONT, ECON, FIN present value method

metodología *f* GES methodology; ~ **cualitativa** V&M *investigación de mercado* qualitative methodology; ~ **cuantitativa** V&M *investigación de mercado* quantitative methodology; ~ **económica** ECON economic methodology

metraje *m* COM GEN yardage, MEDIOS footage

metro *m* TRANSP subway (*AmE*), tube (*BrE*) (*infrml*), underground (*BrE*); ~ **cúbico** COM GEN cubic metre (*BrE*) (*cbm*), cubic meter (*AmE*) (*cbm*)

metropolitano *adj* COM GEN metropolitan; **no** ~ COM GEN nonmetropolitan

metros: ~ **cúbicos para balas** *m pl* COM GEN *mercancías* bale cubic meters (*AmE*), bale cubic metres (*BrE*); ~ **cúbicos embalados** *m pl* COM GEN *mercancías* bale cubic meters (*AmE*), bale cubic metres (*BrE*)

mezcla *f* BANCA, BOLSA *valores, banca fiduciaria* commingling, COM GEN, MEDIOS *grabación* mix; ~ **de estrategias marketing** V&M marketing mix; ~ **de estrategias de productos** V&M product mix; ~ **de estrategias de ventas** V&M sales mix

mg *abr* (*miligramo*) COM GEN mg (*milligram, milligramme*)

micro *m* INFO micro

microchip *m* INFO microchip

microcomputador *AmL* ver *microcomputadora AmL*

microcomputadora *f AmL* (*cf microordenador Esp*) INFO microcomputer

microdecisión *f* ECON microdecision

microdisco *m* INFO microdisk

microeconomía *f* ECON microeconomics

microeconómico *adj* ECON microeconomic

microelectrónica *f* IND microelectronics

microelectrónico *adj* IND microelectronic

microficha *f* ADMIN microfiche

microfilme *m* ADMIN microfilm

micrófono *m* COMS microphone, mike (*infrml*)

microinformática *f* INFO microcomputing

micromarketing *m* V&M micromarketing

microordenador *m* *Esp* (*cf* *microcomputadora* *AmL*) INFO microcomputer

microplaqueta *f* INFO chip; ~ **de silicio** IND, INFO silicon chip

microprocesador *m* INFO microprocessor

microprograma *m* INFO microprogram

microprogramación *f* INFO firmware

Microsoft®: ~ **disk-operating system** *m* INFO sistema operativo de disco

miedo: ~ **a una bomba** *m* COM GEN bomb scare

miembro *mf* COM GEN, RRHH *de empresa, sindicato* member; ~ **afiliado(-a)** *m,f* COM GEN affiliate member; ~ **aliado(-a)** *m,f* BOLSA allied member; ~ **de la cámara de compensación** BOLSA, FIN *opciones sobre divisas* clearing member (*BrE*); ~ **de la cámara compensatoria** BOLSA, FIN clearing member (*BrE*); ~ **del comité** COM GEN committee member; ~ **compensador(a) directo(-a)** *m,f* BANCA direct clearing member; ~ **compensador(a) general** *m,f* BOLSA general clearing member (*GCM*); ~ **compensador(a) individual** *m,f* BOLSA individual clearing member; ~ **de conferencia** GES conference member; ~ **del consejo** RRHH member of the board; ~ **del consejo de administración** RRHH member of the board of management; ~ **del consejo de supervisión** RRHH member of the supervisory board; ~ **corporativo(-a)** *m,f* BOLSA corporate member; ~ **especificado(-a)** *m,f* FISC specified member; ~ **ex oficio** RRHH ex-officio member; ~ **fundador(a)** *m,f* COM GEN founder member; ~ **de un grupo de trabajo** RRHH team member; ~ **de la junta directiva** RRHH member of the board; ~ **no liquidador(a)** *m,f* BOLSA nonclearing member; ~ **en plantilla** RRHH staff member; ~ **de pleno derecho** COM GEN full member; ~ **que ha pagado su cuota** RRHH *sindicato* paid-up member; ~ **de un sindicato** RRHH member of a syndicate, member of a trade union

Miembro: ~ **del Congreso** *m* POL ≈ Member of Congress (*AmE*), ≈ Member of Parliament (*BrE*) (*MP*), ≈ Congressman (*AmE*), ≈ Congresswoman (*AmE*); ~ **del Instituto de Actuarios** *mf* FIN, RRHH ≈ Fellow of the Institute of Actuaries (*FIA*); ~ **del Instituto de Agentes de Seguros** *mf* SEG ≈ Fellow of the Institute of Insurance Agents; ~ **del Instituto de Banqueros** *mf* BANCA, RRHH ≈ Fellow of the Institute of Bankers (*FIB*); ~ **del Instituto de Comercio** *mf* COM GEN ≈ Fellow of the Institute of Commerce (*FIC*); ~ **del Instituto de Consignatarios Colegiados** *mf* RRHH ≈ Fellow of the Institute of Chartered Shipbrokers (*FICS*); ~ **del Instituto de Contables de Empresa** *mf* CONT, RRHH ≈ Fellow of the Institute of Company Accountants (*BrE*) (*FICA*); ~ **del Instituto de Dirección de Personal** *mf* GES, RRHH ≈ Fellow of the Institute of Personnel Management (*FIPM*); ~ **del Instituto de Exportación** *mf* IMP/EXP, RRHH ≈ Fellow of the Institute of Export (*FIEx*); ~ **del Instituto de Ingenieros Navales** *mf* RRHH ≈ Fellow of the Institute of Marine Engineers (*FIME*); ~ **del Parlamento Europeo** *m* POL Member of the European Parliament (*MEP*); ~ **de la Sociedad de Tasadores y Subastadores** *mf* COM GEN, RRHH ≈ Fellow of the Incorporated Society of Valuers and Auctioneers (*FSVA*)

miércoles: ~ **negro** *m* BOLSA Black Wednesday

migración: ~ **circular** *f* ECON circular migration

mil: ~ **millones** *m pl* BANCA, COM GEN billion (*bn*)

milésima *f* FISC *tipos fiscales* mill (*AmE*)

miligramo *m* (*mg*) COM GEN milligram (*mg*), milligramme (*mg*)

mililitro *m* (*ml*) COM GEN milliliter (*AmE*) (*ml*), millilitre (*BrE*) (*ml*)

milímetro *m* (*mm*) COM GEN millimetre (*BrE*) (*mm*), millimeter (*AmE*) (*mm*)

militante *mf* ECON activist

milla: ~ **cuadrada** *f* COM GEN square mile; ~ **marítima** *f* COM GEN, TRANSP nautical mile

millas: ~ **por galón** *f pl* TRANSP miles per gallon (*mpg*); ~ **por hora** *f pl* TRANSP miles per hour (*mph*); **~-pasajero por hora de vehículo** *f pl* TRANSP passenger miles per vehicle hour

millón *m* COM GEN million

millonaria *f* COM GEN millionairess

millonario *m* COM GEN millionaire; ~ **en el papel** COM GEN millionaire on paper

mina *f* IND mine; ~ **de carbón** IND coal mine, colliery

mineral: ~ **de arcilla** *m* IND, MED AMB clay ore; ~ **de cobre** *m* IND, MED AMB copper ore; ~ **de estaño** *m* IND, MED AMB tin ore; ~ **de fierro** *m* AmL (*cf* *mineral de hierro Esp*) MED AMB iron ore; ~ **de hierro** *m* Esp (*cf* *mineral de fierro AmL*) MED AMB iron ore; ~ **metálico** *m* MED AMB ore; ~ **metalífero** *m* MED AMB metalliferous ore; ~ **de oro** *m* MED AMB gold ore; ~ **de plata** *m* IND, MED AMB silver ore

minería *f* IND mining; ~ **del carbón** IND, MED AMB coal mining

minialmacén *m* COM GEN mini-warehouse

minicomputador *AmL ver* *minicomputadora AmL*

minicomputadora *f* AmL (*cf* *miniordenador Esp*) INFO minicomputer

minifurgoneta *f* TRANSP minivan

minimización *f* ECON minimization

minimizar *vt* COM GEN, ECON minimize

mínimo[1] *adj* COM GEN minimum (*min.*), MAT minimal, TRANSP off-peak

mínimo[2]: ~ **común denominador** *m* COM GEN lowest common denominator; ~ **de coste** Esp (*cf* *mínimo de costo AmL*) CONT *balance general* minimum cost; ~ **de costo** AmL *m* (*cf* *mínimo de coste Esp*) CONT *balance general* minimum cost; ~ **histórico** *m* BOLSA *mercado*, COM GEN all-time low; ~ **de mercado** *m* CONT lower of market

mínimos: ~ **cuadrados generalizados** *m pl* ECON generalized least squares

miniordenador *m* Esp (*cf* *minicomputador AmL, minicomputadora AmL*) INFO minicomputer

minipágina *f* V&M *publicidad* mini-page

miniserie *f* MEDIOS *radio* mini-series

Ministerio: ~ **de Economía y Hacienda** *m* ECON, FISC, POL *fiscalía, comercio* ≈ The Treasury (*BrE*), ≈ Treasury Department (*AmE*)

Ministro, -a: ~ **de Asuntos Exteriores** *m,f* POL Foreign Minister; ~ **de Economía y Hacienda** *m,f* Esp ECON, FISC, POL ≈ Chancellor of the Exchequer (*BrE*); ~ **del gobierno** *m,f* POL Cabinet Minister

minoración: ~ **de la indemnización por daños y**

perjuicios *f* DER mitigation of damages; **~ de valor** *f* CONT writing-off

minorista: **~ afiliado(-a)** *m,f* V&M affiliated retailer; **~ especializado(-a)** *m,f* V&M speciality retailer (*BrE*), specialty retailer (*AmE*); **~ independiente** *mf* V&M independent retailer; **~ de marca** *mf* V&M symbol retailer

minucias *f pl* COM GEN minutiae

minuciosamente *adv* COM GEN painstakingly

minusvalía: **~ física** *f* FISC, PROT SOC physical impairment, physical handicap; **~ mental** *f* PROT SOC mental impairment, mental handicap

minusvalías *f pl* ECON, FIN capital loss; **~ netas** ECON, FIN net capital loss

minusvaloración *f* BOLSA, COM GEN, ECON, FIN undervaluation

minuta: **~ de los costes de inflación** *f Esp* (*cf minuta de los costos de inflación AmL*) ECON menu costs of inflation; **~ de los costos de inflación** *f AmL* (*cf minuta de los costes de inflación Esp*) ECON menu costs of inflation

minutas *f pl* COM GEN *de una junta* minutes

miope *adj* POL *decisión* short-sighted

miras: **con ~ a** *fra* COM GEN with a view to

misceláneo *adj* COM GEN miscellaneous (*misc.*)

miseria: **~ absoluta** *f* ECON absolute poverty

misión *f* COM GEN, V&M mission; **~ corporativa** COM GEN, GES corporate mission; **~ diplomática** *m* POL diplomatic mission; **~ económica** ECON, GES economic mission; **~ exterior** IMP/EXP outward mission; **~ interna** V&M inwards mission; **~ de investigación** COM GEN fact-finding mission

mismo: **al ~ efecto** *fra* COM GEN ad idem; **del ~ género** *fra* COM GEN ejusdem generis; **por sí ~** *fra* COM GEN per se

mitigación *f* COM GEN alleviation

mitigar *vt* COM GEN *problemas* alleviate

mixto *adj* PROT SOC *educación* coeducational (*co-ed*)

ml *abr* (*mililitro*) COM GEN ml (*milliliter AmE, millilitre BrE*)

mm *abr* (*milímetro*) COM GEN mm (*millimeter AmE, millimetre BrE*)

MMTC *abr* (*modelo multilateral de tipos de cambio*) ECON MERM (*Multilateral Exchange Rate Model*)

mobiliario: **~ y efectos domésticos** *m pl* COM GEN household goods; **~ e instalación** *m* FISC furniture and fittings

moción *f* POL motion; **~ de censura** POL motion of censure

mod. *abr* (*modificado*) COM GEN alt. (*altered*)

moda[1]: **de ~** *adj* BOLSA attractive, COM GEN in fashion

moda[2] *f* MAT mode, V&M fashion; **última ~** COM GEN latest fashion

modalidad *f* INFO mode; **~ americana** ECON American terms; **~ aplazada** CONT installment base (*AmE*), instalment base (*BrE*); **~ byte a byte** INFO byte mode; **~ dialogada** INFO conversational mode; **~ de edición** INFO edit mode; **~ europea** ECON *comercio de divisas* European terms; **~ interactiva** INFO interactive mode; **~ normal de inversión** FIN normal investment practice; **~ en ráfagas** INFO burst mode; **~ de respuesta** INFO answer mode; **~ textual** INFO text mode

modalidades: **~ de una emisión** *f pl* BOLSA terms and conditions of an issue

modelación *f* MAT modeling (*AmE*), modelling (*BrE*); **~ estadística** MAT statistical modeling (*AmE*), statistical modelling (*BrE*)

modelado *m* COM GEN paste-up

modelo[1]: **~ de moda** *mf* COM GEN fashion model

modelo[2] *m* COM GEN model, ECON, MAT shape, model; **~ de actividad económica** ECON pattern of economic activity; **~ de administración dinámico** GES dynamic management model; **~ administrativo de la empresa** GES managerial model of the firm; **~ de ahorro de Ramsey** ECON Ramsey savings model; **~ bimetálico** MED AMB bimetallic standard; **~ de cadena de Markov** MAT Markov chain model; **~ clásico** ECON classical model; **~ de compra** V&M purchasing pattern, buying pattern; **~ de consumo** V&M consumer pattern; **~ contable** CONT, FIN accounting model; **~ de contrato** COM GEN *lenguaje normalizado* boilerplate (*jarg*); **~ corporativo** COM GEN, CONT, FIN corporate model; **~ de costes** *Esp* (*cf modelo de costos AmL*) COM GEN, CONT, FIN cost standard; **~ de costos** *AmL* (*cf modelo de costes Esp*) COM GEN, CONT, FIN cost standard; **~ de decisión** GES decision model; **~ de desarrollo de dos brechas** ECON two-gap development model; **~ duopolista de Stackelberg** ECON Stackelberg duopoly model; **~ duopolista de Bertrand** ECON Bertrand duopoly model; **~ duopolista de Cournot** ECON Cournot's duopoly model; **~ econométrico de vinculación y proyección** ECON project link; **~ económico** ECON economic model; **~ económico multipaís** ECON multi-country economic model (*MCM*); **~ de empresa** COM GEN company model; **~ de estado financiero** CONT financial reporting standard (*FRS*); **~ estático** ECON static model; **~ estructural** ECON structural model; **~ de fijación de precios de los activos de capital** (*MOFIPAC*) BOLSA, ECON, FIN capital asset pricing model (*CAPM*); **~ flexible** ECON soft modeling (*AmE*), soft modelling (*BrE*); **~ de gran escala** ECON large-scale model; **~ de gravedad** ECON gravity model; **~ de Harrod Domar** ECON Harrod Domar model; **~ de Hermes** ECON Hermes model; **~ de indicación de salida** ECON point-output model; **~ de justo a tiempo** IND just-in-time model; **~ de Lewis-Rei-Ranis** ECON Lewis-Fei-Ranis model; **~ de Mahalanobis** POL Mahalanobis model; **~ de marketing** V&M marketing model; **~ multilateral de tipos de cambio** (*MMTC*) ECON Multilateral Exchange Rate Model (*MERM*); **~ de multiplicador-acelerador** ECON multiplier-accelerator model; **~ de Mundell-Fleming** ECON Mundell-Fleming model; **~ de Muth-Mills** ECON Muth-Mills model; **~ de negociación** BOLSA trading pattern; **~ de peaje** ECON toll model; **~ de previsión** ECON linkage model; **~ de producción asiático** ECON, IND Asiatic mode of production; **~ de promedio móvil autorregresivo** MAT auto-regressive moving-average model; **~ proyectivo de investigación de inversiones** FIN value-line investment survey; **~ de simulación** ECON simulation model, simulation modelling (*BrE*), simulation modeling (*AmE*); **~ de solapación de generaciones** ECON overlapping generations model (*OLG*); **~ de tarificación de opciones Black-Scholes** BOLSA Black-Scholes option pricing model; **~ de tesorería** ECON Treasury model; **~ de Tobit** ECON Tobit model; **~ unitario** PROT soc *trabajo social* unitary model; **~ de utilidad** PATENT utility model; **~ de valoración** BOLSA pricing model; **~ Wharton** ECON Wharton model

Modelo: **~ del Mercado Común a Medio Plazo** *m* ECON Common Market Medium Term Model (*COMET*)

módem *abr* (*modulador-desmodulador*) INFO, MAT modem (*modulator/demodulator*)

moderación *f* ECON *de la política*, POL easing; **~ del ritmo** COM GEN slowdown; **~ salarial** RRHH wage restraint

moderado *adj* COM GEN *precios* low-key, subdued

moderar *vt* COM GEN moderate, soft-pedal (*infrml*), *entusiasmo* dampen

modernización *f* COM GEN modernization, ECON streamlining

modernizado *adj* INFO upgraded

modernizar *vt* COM GEN modernize, ECON streamline, INFO upgrade, V&M *imagen del producto* revamp

moderno *adj* COM GEN, V&M *equipos* modern, state-of-the-art, trendy (*infrml*) (*BrE*)

modestamente *adv* COM GEN modestly

modesto *adj* COM GEN modest

modificación *f* COM GEN *de datos*, INMOB *de edificios* modification, PATENT, POL amendment; **~ de la conducta** RRHH behavior modification (*AmE*), behaviour modification (*BrE*); **~ contable** CONT accounting change; **~ en el precio de futuros** BOLSA futures price change

modificaciones *f pl* COM GEN, INMOB *de edificios* modifications; **~ y mejoras** CONT *cuentas anuales* alterations and improvements; ♦ **con las ~ que las circunstancias requieran** COM GEN with such modifications as the circumstances require

modificado *adj* (*mod.*) COM GEN altered (*alt.*), PATENT, POL amended; ♦ **~ sobre pedido** IND customized

modificar *vt* DER *términos* vary, COM GEN modify, PATENT, POL amend; ♦ **sin ~** COM GEN unchanged; **~ sobre pedido** IND customize

modo[1]: **en ~ de bloque** *adv* INFO in block mode; **en ~ de conversación** *adv* INFO conversationally; **a ~ de porcentaje** *adv* COM GEN, MAT percentagewise; **a ~ de subvención** *adv* FIN in grant form

modo[2] *m* COM GEN method, INFO mode; **~ de ayuda** INFO help mode; **~ borrador** INFO draft mode; **~ conversación** INFO conversational mode; **~ edición** INFO edit mode; **~ de empleo** COM GEN directions for use; **~ gráfico** INFO graphics mode; **~ interactivo** INFO interactive mode; **~ manual** MEDIOS *de cálculo* manual mode; **~ de pago** COM GEN method of payment; **~ en ráfagas** INFO burst mode; **~ respuesta** INFO answer mode; **~ texto** INFO text mode; **~ de transporte** TRANSP mode of transport

modulación *f* COMS modulation; **~ de frecuencias** COMS frequency modulation

modulador: **~-desmodulador** *m* (*módem*) INFO, MAT modulator/demodulator (*modem*)

modularidad *f* COM GEN, MAT modularity

módulo: **~ de gestión** *m* INFO *programas* driver

MOFIPAC *abr* (*modelo de fijación de precios de los activos de capital*) BOLSA, ECON, FIN CAPM (*capital asset pricing model*)

mojón *m* TRANSP signpost

moldear *vt* MEDIOS, V&M *la opinión pública* mold (*AmE*), mould (*BrE*)

momento[1]: **~ concertado** *m* COM GEN appointed time

momento[2] *fra* **en algún ~ futuro** COM GEN at some time in the future

momentos *m pl* MAT moments

monádico *adj* V&M monadic

moneda *f* COM GEN coin, FIN *en que se expresa un estado financiero* reporting currency; **~ agropecuaria** ECON green currency; **~ artificial** ECON artificial currency; **~ circulante** FIN currency (*cy.*); **~ común** ECON, POL common currency; **~ convertible** BANCA, ECON, FIN convertible currency; **~ de cuenta** CONT unit of account; **~ de curso legal** ECON currency in circulation; **~ depreciada** BANCA, FIN fiat money (*AmE*), token money (*BrE*); **~ falsa** BANCA, COM GEN counterfeit; **~ fiduciaria** BANCA fiat money (*AmE*), fiduciary currency, token money (*BrE*), DER fiat standard, FIN fiat money (*AmE*), fiduciary currency, token money (*BrE*); **~ flotante** ECON, FIN *internacional* floating currency; **~ forzada** ECON, FIN forced currency; **~ forzosa** BOLSA forced currency; **~ fraccionaria** POL small change (*infrml*); **~ fuerte** ECON hard currency; **~ funcional** ECON functional currency; **~ de intervención** FIN intervention currency; **~ de inversión** FIN investment currency; **~ nacional** ECON national currency; **~ nominal** FIN fiat money (*AmE*), token money (*BrE*); **~ de oro** BANCA gold coin; **~ de oro para inversión** FIN investment gold coin; **~ de reserva** BANCA reserve currency; **~ sin respaldo estatal** ECON stateless currency; **~ sobrevalorada** ECON overvalued currency; **~ solvente** ECON sound currency; **~ subvalorada** ECON undervalued currency; **~ única** BANCA, ECON, POL single currency; **~ única europea** COM GEN single European currency; **tercera ~** COM GEN third currency

monedas: **~ combinadas** *f pl* ECON composite currency

monetario *adj* COM GEN monetary

monetarismo *m* ECON monetarism; **~ global** ECON, POL global monetarism; **~ gradual** ECON gradualist monetarism; **~ instantáneo** ECON instant monetarism

monetarista *mf* ECON monetarist

monetización *f* ECON monetization

monitor *m* COM GEN *seguridad* monitor; **~ del agua** TRANSP water monitor (*WM*); **~ analógico** INFO analog monitor; **~ visualizador** INFO display monitor

monocromo *adj* INFO *pantalla* monochrome

monoeconomía *f* ECON monoeconomics

monograma *m* COM GEN monogram

monopolio *m* BOLSA, ECON, FIN, V&M monopoly; **~ absoluto** ECON, FIN, V&M absolute monopoly; **~ bilateral** ECON bilateral monopoly; **~ capitalista del Estado** ECON state monopoly capitalism; **~ compartido** ECON shared monopoly; **~ discriminante** ECON discriminating monopoly; **~ espacial** ECON spatial monopoly; **~ exclusivo** ECON exclusive monopoly; **~ legal** ECON legal monopoly; **~ legal de patente** IND, PATENT patent monopoly; **~ local** ECON local monopoly; **~ natural** ECON natural monopoly; **~ perfecto** ECON perfect monopoly; **~ puro** ECON pure monopoly; **~ sindical** RRHH closed shop

monopolización: **~ del mercado** *f* COM GEN cornering the market

monopsónico *adj* ECON monopsonic

monopsonio *m* ECON monopsony

monorrail *m* TRANSP monorail

monóxido: ~ **de carbono** *m* IND, MED AMB carbon monoxide

montacargas: ~ **de cubetas** *m* TRANSP *carga* bucket elevator

montaje *m* V&M montage, *publicidad* paste-up *(jarg)*; ~ **final** COM GEN, IND final assembly; ~ **del negocio** V&M trade setting; ~ **de originales** MEDIOS paste-up *(jarg)*

montante *m* COM GEN amount *(amt)*; ~ **de esquina** TRANSP corner post; ~ **neto del activo** CONT net asset amount; ~ **neto del ajuste de la reserva** CONT net reserve adjustment amount; ~ **neto de las reservas** CONT net reserve inclusion amount

montar *vt* INFO *instalar* set up

monto *m* COM GEN amount *(amt)*; ~ **de la compensación monetaria** FIN *UE* monetary compensation amount *(MCA)*; ~ **global** ECON, MAT aggregate; ~ **neto de los activos** CONT net asset amount; ~ **neto del ajuste de la reserva** CONT net reserve adjustment amount; ~ **neto de la reducción de la reserva** CONT net reserve inclusion amount; ~ **de la pérdida** SEG amount of loss

montón: ~ **insoluto** *m* COM GEN amount outstanding, CONT, FIN outstanding

mora *f* COM GEN default, DER delay; ◆ **en** ~ FIN in arrears

moral *f* RRHH morale

moralidad: ~ **corporativa** *f* COM GEN corporate morality

moratoria *f* BANCA moratorium, COM GEN, FIN moratorium, standstill agreement

morir: ~ **intestado** *fra* DER die intestate

morosidad *f* CONT, DER delinquency, FIN arrears, FISC delinquency

moroso, -a *m,f* COM GEN slow payer

mortalidad: ~ **infantil** *f* PROT SOC infant mortality; ~ **prevista** *f* SEG expected mortality

mostrador *m* COM GEN *en una tienda* trade counter; ~ **de caja** COM GEN *supermercado* counter; ~ **de recepción** ADMIN front desk; ~ **de reservas** COM GEN reservation counter

mostrar *vt* CONT *pérdida, remanente* show, COM GEN show, *artículos* exhibit; ◆ ~ **claramente** CONT *auditoría* present fairly

motines: ~, **disturbios populares y huelgas** *m pl* PROT SOC riots, civil commotions and strikes *(RCCS)*

motivación *f* COM GEN motivation; ~ **del activo** ECON asset motive; ~ **extrínseca** RRHH extrinsic motivation; ~ **intrínseca** RRHH intrinsic motivation; ◆ **con** ~ **de lucro** ECON with profit in mind

motivacional *adj* COM GEN motivational

motivador, a *m,f* COM GEN motivator; ~ **de compras** *m* V&M purchasing motivator

motivar *vt* COM GEN motivate

motivo *m* COM GEN motive, *objectivo* object; ~ **de compra** V&M buying motive; ~ **de despido** RRHH grounds for dismissal; ~ **para el éxito** RRHH achievement motive; ~ **de ganancias** FIN profit motive; ~ **de salvaguarda** COM GEN precautionary motive; ◆ **ser** ~ **de interés** COM GEN, FIN excite interest

motivos: **por** ~ **de mala salud** *fra* RRHH *retiro, jubilación, permiso* on grounds of ill health

motonave *f* TRANSP motor vessel

motopetrolero *m* TRANSP motor tanker

motor *m* TRANSP engine *(ENG)*; ~ **del crecimiento** ECON engine of growth; ~ **diesel-eléctrico** TRANSP diesel-electric engine; ~ **de repuesto** COM GEN, IND replacement engine

mover: ~ **los hilos** *fra* COM GEN pull strings *(BrE)*

moverse: ~ **en serie** *fra* BOLSA move in tandem; **no** ~ *fra* COM GEN sit tight

móvil *adj* V&M mobile

movilidad *f* ECON mobility; ~ **fiscal** ECON fiscal mobility; ~ **laboral** ECON, RRHH occupational mobility, job mobility, mobility of labor *(AmE)*, mobility of labour *(BrE)*, labor mobility *(AmE)*, labour mobility *(BrE)*; ~ **laboral eficiente** ECON, RRHH efficient job mobility; ~ **de la mano de obra** ECON, RRHH occupational mobility, job mobility, mobility of labor *(AmE)*, mobility of labour *(BrE)*, labor mobility *(AmE)*, labour mobility *(BrE)*; ~ **del personal** RRHH staff mobility; ~ **de trabajo** ECON, RRHH job mobility, occupational mobility, job mobility, mobility of labor *(AmE)*, mobility of labour *(BrE)*, labor mobility *(AmE)*, labour mobility *(BrE)*; ~ **vertical** RRHH vertical mobility

movilizador: ~ **de personas** *m* TRANSP people mover

movimiento *m* COM GEN, IND, POL, PROT SOC movement; ~ **de activos** CONT, FIN asset turnover; ~ **adverso** BOLSA *precio de bonos* adverse movement; ~ **alcista** BOLSA bullish movement; ~ **alcista de los precios** BOLSA upward price movement; ~ **ascendente** COM GEN, ECON upward movement; ~ **a la baja** BOLSA bearish movement; ~ **de base popular** POL grass-roots movement; ~ **del capital de los accionistas** CONT *cuentas anuales* movement on shareholders' equity; ~ **del capital aportado** CONT *cuentas anuales* movement on shareholders' equity; ~ **crediticio** BANCA credit swing; ~ **de la cuenta** BANCA account activity, CONT account movement, account turnover; ~ **descendente** COM GEN, ECON downward movement; ~ **disciplinado** TRANSP disciplined movement; ~ **especulativo contra el dólar** COM GEN run on the dollar; ~ **de fletes** TRANSP movement of freight; ~ **de impuesto único** FISC single tax movement; ~ **libre** BOLSA free riding; ~ **de la mano de obra** ECON movement of labor *(AmE)*, movement of labour *(BrE)*; ~ **de materiales** COM GEN materials handling; ~ **obrero** POL, RRHH labor movement *(AmE)*, labour movement *(BrE)*; ~ **de precios** BOLSA price move; ~ **rápido** BOLSA *precio de opciones* sharp movement; ~ **sindical** RRHH union movement; ~ **de la tasa de interés** BANCA interest rate movement; ~ **de los valores de renta fija** BOLSA bond turnover

MS-DOS® *abr* *(Microsoft*® *disk-operating system)* INFO sistema operativo de discos

MTO *abr* *(medición del trabajo de oficina)* ADMIN, RRHH CWM *(clerical work measurement)*

mudarse: ~ **de casa** *v refl* INMOB move house; ~ **a un local más grande** *v refl* ADMIN move to larger premises

muelle *m* IMP/EXP, TRANSP *puerto* quay; ~ **para barcazas** TRANSP lighterage berth; ~ **de carga** TRANSP charging wharf, loading dock; ~ **para carga y descarga de contenedores** TRANSP container berth; ~ **de carga en rampa** TRANSP ramped cargo berth; ~ **de contenedores** TRANSP container yard *(CY)*; ~ **de desarmamento** TRANSP lay-up berth; ~ **de descarga** TRANSP discharging wharf; ~ **de exportación** TRANSP export berth; ~ **de fosfatos** TRANSP phosphate berth; ~ **franco** IMP/EXP, TRANSP free dock *(fd)*; ~ **de importaciones** TRANSP import berth; ~ **jerarquizado** TRANSP nesting berth; ~ **libre** IMP/EXP, TRANSP free dock (*fd*); ~ **multiproducto** TRANSP multi-product berth; ~ **de pórtico** TRANSP portal berth; ~ **de potasas** TRANSP potash berth; ~ **de protección** TRANSP apron wharf; ~ **seguro** TRANSP safe berth; ~ **de transbordador** TRANSP ferry berth; ~ **para transporte de cargas rodadas** TRANSP ro/ro berth; ~ **de trasvase** TRANSP shifting berth; ◆ **en el** ~ IMP/EXP, TRANSP ex-quay (*x-quay, ExQ*); **de** ~ **a muelle** IMP/EXP, TRANSP quay to quay; ~ **a puerta** IMP/EXP pier to house

muelles *m pl* IMP/EXP, TRANSP quayage

muerto[1] *adj* BOLSA lifeless, RRHH *maquinaria* idle

muerto[2]: ~ **viviente** *m* BOLSA precio bursátil que no se mueve como se esperaba, living dead

muestra *f* COM GEN sample, MAT panel; ~ **aleatoria** MAT, V&M random sample; ~ **de comparación** DER judgment sample; ~ **de firma** BANCA specimen signature; ~ **gratuita** COM GEN, V&M free sample; ~ **de probabilidad** MAT probability sample; ~ **regular** COM GEN fair sample; ~ **representativa** MAT representative sample; ~ **por segmentos** V&M cluster sample; ~ **por universos** V&M cluster sample

muestrario *m* COM GEN swatch

muestras: ~ **emparejadas** *f pl* V&M matched samples

muestreo: ~ **para aceptación** *m* V&M *control de calidad* acceptance sampling; ~ **de una actividad** *m* MAT, V&M activity sampling; ~ **al azar** *m* MAT, V&M random sampling; ~ **aleatorio** *m* V&M convenience sampling; ~ **aleatorio estratificado** *m* GES, V&M stratified random sampling; ~ **por áreas** *m* V&M area sample; ~ **de atributos** *m* CONT *auditoría*, MAT, V&M attribute sampling; ~ **en bloque** *m* CONT block sampling; ~ **característico** *m* MEDIOS attribute sampling; ~ **por cuotas** *m* COM GEN, V&M quota sampling; ~ **descubridor** *m* MAT discovery sampling; ~ **diferencial** *m* MAT, V&M differential sampling; ~ **domiciliario** *m* V&M house-to-house sampling; ~ **estadístico** *m* MAT, V&M statistical sampling; ~ **de estimación** *m* MAT, estimation sampling; ~ **estratificado** *m* MAT, V&M stratified sampling; ~ **por etapas** *m* MAT multistage sampling; ~ **multinivel** *m* MAT multistage sampling; ~ **de petróleo y gas** *m* IND oil and gas sampling; ~ **secuencial** *m* MAT sequential sampling; ~ **por segmentos** *m* V&M cluster sampling; ~ **sistemático** *m* MAT, V&M systematic sampling; ~ **del trabajo** *m* RRHH work sampling; ~ **por universos** *m* V&M cluster sampling; ~ **de variables** *m* MAT variables sampling

mujer: ~ **de negocios** *f* COM GEN businesswoman

multa *f* COM GEN, DER penalty, fine; ~ **civil** DER civil penalty; ~ **ilimitada** DER unlimited fine

multiacceso *m* COM GEN multiaccess

multianual *adj* COM GEN multiannual, multiyear

multicolinealidad *f* ECON multicollinearity

multidivisa *adj* BANCA, ECON multicurrency

multifuncional *adj* COM GEN multifunctional

multihabilidades *f pl* RRHH dual skilling

multijurisdiccional *adj* DER multijurisdictional

multilateral *adj* ECON, POL multilateral

multilateralismo *m* ECON, POL multilateralism

multilingüe *adj* COM GEN multilingual

multimedia *adj* MEDIOS, V&M *publicidad* multimedia

multimodal *adj* TRANSP multimodal

multinacional[1] *adj* COM GEN multinational

multinacional[2] *f* ECON, POL transnational corporation (*TNC*)

multinacionalmente *adv* COM GEN multinationally

múltiple *m* MAT multiple

multiplicador *m* ECON multiplier; ~ **del arrendamiento bruto** INMOB gross rent multiplier (*GRM*); ~ **del comercio exterior** ECON foreign trade multiplier; ~ **del crédito** FIN credit multiplier; ~ **de depósitos** ECON deposit multiplier; ~ **de empleo** ECON employment multiplier; ~ **fiscal** ECON, FISC fiscal multiplier; ~ **de inversión** ECON investment multiplier; ~ **de Keynes** ECON Keynesian multiplier; ~ **monetario** ECON money multiplier; ~ **de presupuesto equilibrado** ECON balanced budget multiplier; ~ **regional** ECON regional multiplier; **super** ~ ECON super multiplier

multiplicar *vt* MAT multiply

múltiplo: ~ **de capitalización de beneficios** *m* CONT price earnings multiple

multiprocesador *m* INFO multiprocessor

multiproceso *m* INFO multiprocessing

multiprogramación *f* INFO multiprogramming

multipropiedad *f* ECON timeshare, INMOB timeshare, timeshare property, time sharing; ◆ **en** ~ INMOB on a time sharing basis

multiregional *adj* COM GEN multiregional

multiruta *adj* TRANSP multiroute

multisectorial *adj* COM GEN multisector

multisindicalismo *m* RRHH multiunionism

multitarea *f* INFO multitasking, multijobbing

multiuso *adj* COM GEN multipurpose

mundial *adj* COM GEN global, worldwide

mundialización *f* COM GEN globalization

mundo *m* COM GEN world; ~ **comercial** COM GEN business world; ~ **del comercio** COM GEN commercial world; ~ **del espectáculo** COM GEN, MEDIOS show business; ~ **de las finanzas** FIN world of finance; ~ **de habla inglesa** COM GEN English-speaking world; ~ **hispanohablante** COM GEN Spanish-speaking world; ~ **de los negocios** COM GEN business world; ◆ **en todo el** ~ COM GEN all over the world

municipal *adj* COM GEN municipal

municipio *m* POL borough, municipal borough

mutualidad *f* FIN benefit society (*AmE*), friendly society (*BrE*)

mutuamente: ~ **excluyente** *adv* COM GEN mutually exclusive

mutuo[1] *adj* COM GEN mutual

mutuo[2]: ~ **acuerdo** *m* COM GEN mutual agreement, meeting of minds

N

N *abr* (*carretera nacional*) TRANSP A (*BrE*) (*A-road*)

N.A. *abr* (*nota del autor*) COM GEN author's note

nación: **~ industrializada** *f* ECON, POL industrial nation; **~ más favorecida** *f* ECON, POL most-favored nation (*AmE*) (*MFN*), most-favoured nation (*BrE*) (*MFN*)

nacional *adj* COM GEN national (*nat.*), ECON domestic, TRANSP *red* domestic; ◆ **de origen ~** COM GEN homegrown

nacionalismo *m* ECON, POL nationalism

nacionalización *f* ECON *empresa* nationalization

nacionalizar *vt* ECON, POL nationalize

nafta *f* AmL (*cf gasolina Esp*) MED AMB gasoline (*AmE*), petrol (*BrE*); **~ ecológica** *AmL* (*cf gasolina sin plomo Esp*) MED AMB lead-free gasoline (*AmE*), lead-free petrol (*BrE*); **~ sin plomo** *AmL* (*cf gasolina sin plomo Esp*) MED AMB lead-free gasoline (*AmE*), lead-free petrol (*BrE*); **~ súper** *AmL* (*cf gasolina súper Esp*) IND, MED AMB four-star gasoline (*AmE*), four-star petrol (*BrE*)

narcodólares *m pl infrml* ECON narcodollars (*infrml*)

narcotráfico *m* COM GEN drug trade

naturaleza *f* COM GEN nature; **~ de la invención** PATENT nature of the invention

naufragar *vi* COM GEN *compañía*, TRANSP *barco* go under

nave: **~ de expedición** *f* TRANSP dispatch bay; **~ industrial** *f* RRHH labor shed (*AmE*), labour shed (*BrE*)

navegabilidad *f* TRANSP seaworthiness

navegación *f* TRANSP sailing, navigation, shipping; **~ de auxilio** TRANSP relief sailing; **~ doble** TRANSP duplicate sailing; **~ fluvial** SEG *marítimo*, TRANSP inland navigation, river navigation; **~ inaugural** TRANSP inaugural sailing; **~ sin itinerario** TRANSP tramping; **~ en lastre** TRANSP ballast sailing; **~ matriz** TRANSP parent sailing; **~ Q** TRANSP Q sailing; **~ en río con corriente** TRANSP tidal river navigation; **~ de vacío** TRANSP idle shipping; **~ a vapor lenta** TRANSP slow steaming

navegar *vi* COMS, INFO *internet* surf, TRANSP navigate; ◆ **~ como el viento** COM GEN sail close to the wind

navío: **cualquier ~** *m* SEG *marino* any one vessel (*AOV*); **~ mercante motorizado** *m* TRANSP motor merchant vessel (*M/V*); **~ portabarcazas** *m* TRANSP barge-carrying vessel (*BCV*); **~ de producción a bordo** *m* TRANSP floating production vessel; **~ de producción a bordo, almacenamiento y descarga** *m* TRANSP floating production, storage and offloading vessel (*FPSO*); **~ de suministros, remolque y enmienda de anclas** *m* TRANSP anchor-handling tug supply vessel

necesidad *f* COM GEN need, requirement; **~ básica** ECON basic need; **~ de crédito** BANCA borrowing requirement; **~ de garantía inicial** BOLSA initial margin requirement

necesidades *f pl* COM GEN needs; **~ de caja** CONT cash needs; **~ de capacitación** *AmL* (*cf necesidades de formación Esp*) COM GEN, RRHH training needs; **~ del capital** COM GEN, ECON, FIN capital needs, capital requirements; **~ comerciales** BANCA needs of trade; **~ de comercio** BANCA needs of trade; **~ de contado** CONT, FIN net cash requirement (*NCR*); **~ crediticias del sector público** ECON public sector borrowing requirements (*PSBR*); **~ de efectivo** CONT cash needs; **~ de financiación** COM GEN, CONT capital requirements; **~ de financiación del gobierno central** ECON, FIN, POL central government borrowing requirements; **~ de financiación del sistema central** ECON, FIN, POL central government borrowing requirements; **~ financieras** FIN financial requirement; **~ de formación** *Esp* (*cf necesidades de capacitación AmL*) COM GEN, RRHH training needs; **~ de liquidez** CONT cash needs; **~ de memoria** INFO storage requirements; **~ preferentes** ECON merit wants; **~ de préstamo del sector público** ECON public sector borrowing requirements (*PSBR*); **~ secundarias** ECON, V&M secondary needs

negación *f* COM GEN disaffirmation, DER denial

negar *vt* COM GEN disaffirm, DER *derechos a alguien* deny

negativa *f* COM GEN, PATENT refusal

negativo *adj* COM GEN *consecuencias, influencia* adverse

negligencia *f* COM GEN negligence; **~ concurrente** DER contributory negligence; **~ en el ejercicio de un derecho** DER laches; **~ grave** DER gross negligence; **~ profesional** DER malpractice; **~ susceptible de configurar un delito** DER criminal negligence

negligente *adj* COM GEN negligent, RRHH slack

negligentemente *adv* COM GEN negligently

negociabilidad *f* COM GEN negotiability

negociable *adj* COM GEN negotiable

negociación *f* COM GEN bargaining, negotiation, *transacción* deal, RRHH bargaining; **~ activa** BOLSA active dealing, active trading, bargaining; **~ ágil** BOLSA brisk trading; **~ de asociación** RRHH association bargaining; **~ de buena fe** RRHH good-faith bargaining; **~ colectiva** COM GEN, GES joint negotiation, RRHH collective bargaining, joint negotiation; **~ comercial multilateral** ECON, POL multilateral trade negotiation (*MTN*); **~ en común** COM GEN, GES, RRHH joint negotiation; **~ conjunta** BOLSA, COM GEN, GES, RRHH joint negotiation; **~ de contrato** RRHH contract bargaining; **~ por cuenta propia** FIN self-dealing (*jarg*); **~ del día** BOLSA day trading; **~ en dos niveles** RRHH two-tier bargaining (*jarg*); **~ dura** COM GEN hard bargaining; **~ de empresa** RRHH company bargaining; **~ con un empresario individual** RRHH single-employer bargaining; **~ en la fábrica** COM GEN, DER, IND, RRHH plant bargaining, shop-floor bargaining, workshop bargaining; **~ fragmentada** RRHH fragmented bargaining; **~ ininterrumpida** BOLSA, COM GEN all day trading (*BrE*); **~ integrativa** RRHH integrative bargaining; **~ interrumpida** BOLSA suspended trading; **~ en el lugar de trabajo** RRHH workplace bargaining; **~ con múltiples empresarios** RRHH multiemployer bargaining; **~ multisectorial** RRHH multiplant bargaining; **~ multisindical** RRHH multiunion bargaining (*BrE*); **~ a nivel del establecimiento** RRHH establishment-level bargaining; **~ en un nivel único** RRHH single table bargaining; **~ del pago** BOLSA settlement bargaining;

~ **paralela** BOLSA side-by-side trading; ~ **de planta** COM GEN, IND, RRHH plant bargaining; ~ **de posiciones** BOLSA position trading; ~ **previa a la apertura** BOLSA before-hours dealing; ~ **regional de salarios** RRHH regional wage bargaining; ~ **revocable** RRHH takeback bargaining; ~ **rotativa** BOLSA switch trading; ~ **salarial** ECON wage round, RRHH wage negotiation; ~ **sobre un conjunto de valores** BOLSA basket trading; ~ **sobre la productividad** DER, IND, RRHH productivity bargaining; ~ **tras el cierre** BOLSA after-hours dealing, after-hours trading, closing trade, FIN after-hours dealing; ~ **sin valor** RRHH blue-sky bargaining (*AmE*)

negociaciones: ~ **salariales** *f* RRHH pay talks

negociado: muy ~ *adj* BOLSA heavily traded

negociador, a *m,f* COM GEN bargainer, negotiator

negociante *mf* COM GEN, RRHH, V&M *comerciante* trader; ~ **por mayor** COM GEN, V&M wholesale trader

negociar 1. *vt* COM GEN, RRHH bargain for, deal, negotiate; ◆ ~ **a la baja** COM GEN *vendedor* bargain down; ~ **por la cuenta** BOLSA *vendedor* bargain for the account; ~ **dentro de la Unión Europea** COM GEN trade within the European Union; ~ **a través de una cuenta** BOLSA bargain for account (*BrE*); **2.** *vi* COM GEN, RRHH negotiate; ◆ ~ **con alguien** COM GEN bargain with sb, negotiate with sb; ~ **con valores y bonos** BOLSA trade in stocks and bonds

negociarse *v refl* BOLSA trade at

negocio *m* COM GEN, RRHH, V&M business, trade; ~ **abierto las veinticuatro horas del día** COM GEN twenty-four hour trading; ~ **de alimentación al por menor** V&M retail food business; ~ **de aprovisionamiento** OCIO *hostelería* catering trade; ~ **básico** COM GEN, ECON core business; ~ **de bienes industriales** COM GEN, ECON, IND trade in industrial goods; ~ **comercial** COM GEN commercial concern; ~ **competitivo** COM GEN competitive business; ~ **con cuenta abierta** COM GEN open account business; ~ **de contratación preferencial** COM GEN preferential shop (*jarg*) (*AmE*); ~ **por correspondencia** V&M mail order business; ~ **cruzado** BOLSA crossed trade; ~ **familiar** COM GEN domestic business, V&M family business; ~ **granel** COM GEN bulk business; ~ **habitual** FISC *de contribuyente* ordinary business; ~ **marítimo** COM GEN maritime trade; ~ **mayorista en primas por gastos** BOLSA jobbing in contangos; ~ **a prima** BOLSA option bargain; ~ **de primer orden** COM GEN chief place of business; ~ **principal** COM GEN principal business; ~ **que se repite** COM GEN, V&M repeat business; ~ **recíproco** COM GEN, ECON reciprocal trading; ~ **de remanente** BOLSA carry-over business; ~ **sucio** COM GEN unfair trade; ~ **de vinos** IND wine trade; ◆ ~ **trasladado a** COM GEN business transferred to; **el** ~ **va bien** COM GEN business is brisk; ~ **por tramitar** COM GEN business to be transacted

negocios *m pl* COM GEN business; ~ **afines** COM GEN, IND allied trades; ~ **bancarios** BANCA banking business; ~ **interbancarios** BANCA interbank business; ~ **marítimos** COM GEN, TRANSP shipping business; ~ **no habilitantes** FISC nonqualifying business; ~ **pendientes** COM GEN pending business; ◆ **estar por** ~ COM GEN to be on business; **hacer** ~ COM GEN do business; **hacer** ~ **por teléfono** COM GEN do business over the phone

negrita *f* MEDIOS bold face, *imprenta* bold type

negro, -a *m,f jarg* V&M ghostwriter (*jarg*)

neocorporativismo *m* ECON, POL neocorporatism

neomaltusianismo *m* ECON, POL neomalthusianism

neomercantilismo *m* ECON, POL neomercantilism

nepotismo *m* RRHH nepotism

neto[1]: ~ **de** *adj* COM GEN net of

neto[2] *m* COM GEN net; ~ **patrimonial** BOLSA equity

neumático *m* TRANSP tire (*AmE*), tyre (*BrE*)

neutral *adj* COM GEN, POL neutral; ~ **a la baja** BOLSA neutral to bearish

neutralidad *f* COM GEN, POL neutrality; ~ **del dinero** ECON neutrality of money; ~ **fiscal** FISC fiscal neutrality; ~ **positiva** POL positive neutrality

neutralismo *m* COM GEN neutralism

neutralizar *vt* CONT balance out

nicho *m* V&M niche; ~ **de mercado** V&M market niche

NIF *abr* FIN (*mecanismo de emisión de nota*) NIF (*note issuance facility*), FISC (*número de identificación fiscal*) taxpayer number

ninguna:

NIT *abr* (*número de identificación tributaria*) FISC taxpayer number

nivel *m* COM GEN *de tipos de interes* level, FISC threshold, INFO level; ~ **de absentismo** *f* COM GEN, RRHH absentee rate; ~ **de actividad** *f* COM GEN activity rate; ~ **actual de desempleo** ECON, POL current level of unemployment; ~ **de apoyo** ECON support level; ~ **de aptitud** PROT SOC *trabajadores, estudiantes* ability level; ~ **arancelario** ECON, FISC, IMP/EXP, POL tariff level; ~ **de arrendamiento** INMOB rental level; ~ **de aspiración** *f* V&M aspiration level; ~ **básico** RRHH *de organización* bottom rung; ~ **de beneficios** FISC level of return; ~ **de capacidad** PROT SOC *para estudiantes* ability level; ~ **de confianza** CONT audit assurance, MAT confidence level; ~ **crítico** COM GEN critical level; ~ **elevado de endeudamiento** CONT high gearing (*BrE*), high leverage (*AmE*); ~ **de empleo de personal** RRHH staffing level; ~ **de una empresa previo a la cotización en bolsa** FIN capital de riesgo mezzanine level; ~ **de gasto** COM GEN, ECON level of expenditure; ~ **general de precios** COM GEN general price level; ~ **de importancia relativa** CONT materiality level; ~ **del índice de precios** BOLSA price index level; ~ **inferior** RRHH *de organización* bottom rung; ~ **de ingresos** FISC income threshold; ~ **de ingresos básicos** FISC basic income level (*BIL*); ~ **de los ingresos familiares** FISC family income threshold; ~ **de ingresos de punto muerto** ECON break-even level of income; ~ **de inscripción** FISC *IVA* registration threshold; ~ **de inversiones** COM GEN level of investment; ~ **del margen inicial** BOLSA initial margin level; ~ **de materialidad** CONT materiality level; ~ **máximo** BOLSA peak level; ~ **medio del mar** TRANSP *navegación* mean sea level; ~ **medio de precio** V&M pricing plateau; ~ **del mercado de valores** BOLSA market level; ~ **de negociación** RRHH bargaining level; ~ **de ocupación** INMOB occupancy level; ~ **paralelo** COM GEN parallel standard; ~ **de participación** *f* RRHH participation rate; ~ **de pedidos** V&M level of orders; ~ **de personal** RRHH manning level; ~ **de la pleamar** TRANSP high-water mark (*HWM*); ~ **de precios** ECON price level; ~ **de precios relativo** ECON relative price level; ~ **presupuestario** CONT budget level; ~ **de propiedad recíproca** FISC cross-ownership threshold; ~ **real de desempleo** ECON, POL actual level of unemployment;

~ de referencia FIN reference level; **~ de renta** FISC income range; **~ de resistencia** BOLSA resistance level; **~ del ruido** MED AMB noise level; **~ de salinidad** MED AMB salinity level; **~ de servicio** TRANSP delivery performance; **~ de significación** MAT level of significance; **~ sostenible** ECON *de demanda* sustainable level; **~ de subsistencia** COM GEN breadline (*infrml*); **~ de sueldo** RRHH salary grade, wage level; **~ de tolerancia** FIN tolerance level; **~ de tributación** FISC tax threshold; **~ de umbral** COM GEN threshold level; **~ de vida** ECON, PROT SOC standard of living; ◆ **de un solo ~** TRANSP single-plane; **a ~ internacional** COM GEN at international level; **ser del ~ requerido** COM GEN, RRHH be up to scratch (*infrml*), be up to standard

nivelación *f* FIN leveling-out (*AmE*), levelling-out (*BrE*); **~ exponencial** COM GEN exponential smoothing

nivelado: ~ de precio *m* V&M pricing plateau

nivelar *vt* COM GEN *fase de ejecución* level out, ECON level off

niveles: ~ salariales internacionales *m pl* ECON international wage levels

NLQ *abr* (*calidad casi de impresión alta*) INFO NLQ (*near letter quality*)

n.º *abr* (*número*) COM GEN no. (*number*), MEDIOS issue

nocional *adj* COM GEN notional

nocturno *adj* COM GEN overnight

nodo *m* INFO node

nombrado *adj* COM GEN, RRHH designated, appointed, posted

nombramiento *m* COM GEN *de persona*, RRHH appointment; **~ permanente** COM GEN, RRHH permanent appointment

nombrar *vt* COM GEN, RRHH appoint

nombre *m* COM GEN *de persona, empresa* name, RRHH forename; **~ y apellidos** COM GEN, RRHH full name; **~ codificado** INFO code name; **~ comercial** COM GEN, IND trading name, PATENT trading name, work mark, V&M brand name; **~ de cuenta** BANCA, CONT account name; **~ del documento** INFO document name; **~ familiar** V&M household name; **~ habitual** DER, RRHH usual first name; **~ legal** DER legal name; **~ de marca** V&M name brand; **~ del nominatario** BOLSA, COM GEN nominee name; **~ del titular** BOLSA, COM GEN nominee name; ◆ **en ~ de** COM GEN per pro (*pp*), on behalf of; **en mi ~ y representación** DER in my name and on my behalf, in my name, place and stead

nómina *f* RRHH *lista de empleados asalariados* payroll, *recibo de pago* pay slip; ◆ **estar en ~** RRHH be on the payroll

nominación *f* COM GEN nomination

nominal *adj* COM GEN nominal

nominatario, -a *m,f* COM GEN nominee

nominativo *adj* COM GEN nominal, COMS registered (*regd.*)

norma *f* COM GEN code, regulation, rule, standard (*std*); **~ aceptada** COM GEN convention; **~ ambiental** MED AMB ambient standard; **~ aplicable** FISC deemed disposition; **~ aplicada** FISC put-in-use rule; **~ de atribución** FISC attribution rule; **~ de auditoría** CONT audit standard, auditing standard; **~ básica** COM GEN ground rule; **~ de la bata blanca** V&M *publicidad* white coat rule (*jarg*); **~ de calidad** COM GEN quality standard; **~ de calidad ambiental** MED AMB environmental quality standard; **~ comercial** COM GEN trading standard; **~ de compensación** COM GEN standard of equalization; **~ de la competencia desleal** COM GEN dumping standard; **~ de contabilidad** CONT accounting standard; **~ contable** CONT accounting standard; **~ contra la evasión fiscal** FISC anti-avoidance rule; **~ de costes** *Esp* (*cf norma de costos AmL*) CONT, FIN cost standard; **~ de costos** *AmL* (*cf norma de costes Esp*) CONT, FIN cost standard; **~ de cumplimiento** CONT performance standard; **~ del derechohabiente** FISC, INMOB successor rule; **~ disciplinaria** RRHH disciplinary rule; **~ de la elegibilidad** FISC eligibility rule; **~ establecida** FISC carve-out rule; **~ de fabricación** DER product standard; **~ financiera** COM GEN, FIN financial standard; **~ fiscal** FISC tax rule; **~ general contra la evasión fiscal** FISC general anti-avoidance provision; **~ para hacer los informes** COM GEN reporting standard; **~ de higiene** PROT SOC hygiene standard; **~ industrial** ECON, IND industry standard; **~ de informes financieros** CONT financial reporting standard (*FRS*); **~ internacional** COM GEN international standard; **~ laboral** ECON labor standard (*AmE*), labour standard (*BrE*); **~ del medio año** FISC half-year rule; **~ medioambiental** MED AMB environmental standard; **~ mínima de calidad** V&M minimum quality standard; **~ de operación del auditor** CONT Auditor's Operational Standard; **~ de oro** COM GEN golden rule; **~ presupuestaria** FIN budget standard; **~ primaria** MED AMB primary standard; **~ procesal** DER court procedure; **~ de producción** COM GEN, IND production standard; **~ de producto** V&M product standard; **~ de la prudencia** BOLSA, COM GEN prudent-man rule; **~ de rendimiento** CONT, RRHH performance standard; **~ de riesgo** FISC at-risk rule; **~ sanitaria** DER health regulation, health standard; **~ de seguridad** COM GEN safety regulation, safety standard; **~ de seguridad portuaria** FISC safe harbor rule (*AmE*), safe harbour rule (*BrE*); **~ sindical** RRHH union rule; **~ técnica** IND *en la seguridad del producto* technical standard; **~ de trabajo** RRHH work rule, working pattern; **~ y uso** COM GEN standard and practice; ◆ **bajo la ~** COM GEN below the norm; **por encima de la ~** COM GEN above the norm

Norma: ~ Internacional de Auditoría *f* CONT International Auditing Standard (*IAS*); **~ Visby de la Haya** *f* TRANSP *navegación* Hague Visby Rule

normalidad *f* COM GEN normality (*BrE*), normalcy (*AmE*)

normalización *f* COM GEN standardization

normalizado *adj* COM GEN standardized

normalizar *vt* COM GEN standardize

normas[1]: **~ en caso de incendio** *f pl* DER fire regulations; **~ y reglamentos** *f pl* COM GEN, DER rules and regulations

normas[2]: **según las ~** *fra* BOLSA by the book

normativa *f* DER legislation, GES regulation; **~ comercial** COM GEN business regulations; **~ conjunta** RRHH joint regulation; **~ de construcción y explotación** TRANSP construction and use regulation (*C&U regulation*); **~ internacional sobre mercancías** IMP/EXP, TRANSP international goods regulations; **~ sobre mercancías peligrosas** IMP/EXP, TRANSP dangerous goods regulations; **~ sobre el uso del suelo** DER land-use regulation

nota *f* COM GEN note, CONT explanation; **~ de abono** BANCA, CONT, COM GEN, FIN credit note (*CN*); **~ del autor** (*N.A.*) COM GEN author's note; **~ de aviso** BANCA advised bill; **~ de cargo** COM GEN debit note (*D/N*); **~ de compromiso de avalista** BOLSA guarantor underwritten note (*GUN*); **~ de contrato** BOLSA contract note; **~ de crédito** BANCA, COM GEN, FIN credit slip, credit note (*CN*); **~ de embarque nacional normalizada** TRANSP national standard shipping note (*NSSN*); **~ de entrega** CONT, IMP/EXP, TRANSP delivery note; **~ de envío** COMS, TRANSP dispatch note; **~ de inspección** IMP/EXP jerque note; **~ marginal** ADMIN marginal note; **~ a medio plazo** BANCA medium-term note (*MTN*); **~ de mercancías peligrosas** COM GEN, TRANSP dangerous goods note (*DGN*); **~ de mercancías sujetas a derechos** IMP/EXP, TRANSP removal note; **~ no emisible** BANCA unissuable note; **~ de peso** COM GEN weight note; **~ al pie** INFO footnote; **~ a pie de página** INFO footnote; **~ de recepción** TRANSP goods received note; **~ de recepción de mercancías** TRANSP goods received note; **~ de la redacción** (*N.R.*) COM GEN editor's note (*Ed.*); **~ de reserva** TRANSP booking note; **~ del traductor** (*N.T.*) COM GEN translator's note; **~ de venta** TRANSP sold message

nota bene *fra* COM GEN nota bene (*NB*)

notación: **~ decimal** *f* INFO decimal notation; **~ exponencial** *f* MAT exponential notation; **~ polaca** *f* MAT Polish notation

notario, -a *m,f* BANCA, COM GEN, DER ≈ solicitor; **~ público(-a)** DER notary public

notas: **~ a las cuentas** *f pl* CONT notes to the accounts; **~ a los estados financieros** *f pl* CONT notes to the financial statements; **~ municipales** *f pl* BANCA municipal notes

noticia *f* COM GEN, MEDIOS news, news item

noticias: **~ de actualidad** *f* MEDIOS, POL current affairs; **~ económicas** *f pl* ECON, MEDIOS economic news; **~ manipuladas** *f pl* MEDIOS, POL managed news (*jarg*); **~ de primera plana** *f pl* MEDIOS *imprenta* front-page news

notificación *f* COM GEN notice, notification; **~ anticipada de escala** TRANSP calling forward notice; **~ de apelación** PATENT notice of appeal; **~ de cancelación** BOLSA notice of cancellation; **~ de despido** RRHH notice, pink slip (*AmE*); **~ de ejercicio** BOLSA exercise notice, notice of assignment; **~ de envío** FIN remittance advice; **~ especial de tráfico** TRANSP special traffic notice (*STN*); **~ de expiración** SEG *póliza* expiration notice; **~ interdepartamental de liquidación** FIN interdepartmental settlement advice; **~ de inversión** BOLSA investment advice; **~ legal** DER legal notice, statutory notice; **~ de liquidación** INMOB satisfaction piece (*jarg*); **~ de no discriminación** RRHH nondiscrimination notice; **~ oficial de venta** FIN official notice of sale; **~ de plaga** INMOB blight notice; **~ de prohibición** RRHH *salud y seguridad* prohibition notice; **~ de quiebra** DER bankruptcy notice; **~ de reparto** BOLSA, FIN allotment letter (*BrE*); **~ de revisión** BOLSA notice of cancellation; **~ sobreentendida** DER constructive notice (*AmE*)

notificar *vt* COM GEN inform, notify; ♦ **~ algo a alguien** COM GEN notify sb of sth; **~ a alguien una orden de detención** DER serve sb with a warrant; **~ a alguien una orden de registro** DER serve sb with a warrant; **~ un giro** BANCA advise a draft

novación *f* COM GEN *comercial* novation, CONT *de créditos, débitos* extended deferment, DER *comercial* novation

novador, a *m,f* COM GEN, IND, PATENT innovator

novedad *f* ECON fad, PATENT novelty; **~ más reciente** COM GEN *gama de productos* latest addition

N.R. *abr* (*nota de la redacción*) COM GEN editor's note (*Ed.*)

N.T. *abr* (*nota del traductor*) COM GEN translator's note

núcleo *m* COM GEN core; **~ duro** BOLSA, CONT, ECON *de accionistas* hard core; **~ de la economía** ECON core economy; **~ magnético** INFO magnetic core

nudo *m* COM GEN knot; **~ pacto** COM GEN nudum pactum

nueva: **~ división internacional del trabajo** *f* ECON, POL New International Division of Labor (*AmE*) (*NIDL*), New International Division of Labour (*BrE*) (*NIDL*); **~ edición** *f* MEDIOS new edition; **~ microeconomía** *f* ECON new microeconomics; **~ política económica** *f* ECON new economic policy (*NEP*); **~ versión** *f* MEDIOS, OCIO remake

nuevas: **~ democracias** *f pl* POL new democracies

nuevo[1]: **~ enfoque** *m* COM GEN refocusing (*AmE*), refocussing (*BrE*); **~ estado industrial** *m* ECON new industrial state; **~ federalismo** *m* POL new federalism; **~ fletamiento** *m* TRANSP new charter; **~ giro** *m* COM GEN new business; **~ informe contable** *m* BOLSA new account report; **~ keynesianismo** *m* POL new Keynesianism; **~ mecanismo económico** *m* ECON new economic mechanism; **~ orden económico internacional** *m* ECON, POL new international economic order; **~ orden mundial** *m* POL new world order; **~ paquete** *m* V&M repackage; **~ pedido** *m* V&M incoming order; **~ proteccionismo** *m* ECON new protectionism; **~ realismo** *m* RRHH new realism; **~ trato** *m* COM GEN new deal

nuevo[2]: **de ~** *fra* DER de novo

nulo: **~ y sin efecto** *fra* DER null and void

numeración[1]: **de ~ par** *adj* COM GEN even-numbered

numeración[2] *f* COM GEN numbering

Numeración *f*: **~ Internacional Normalizada de Libros** *f* (*ISBN*) MEDIOS International Standard Book Number (*ISBN*)

numerar: **~ consecutivamente** *fra* PATENT number consecutively

numerario *adj* ECON numeraire

numérico *adj* INFO, MAT numeric

número *m* (*n.º*) COM GEN number (*no.*), MEDIOS issue; **~ de acciones emitidas** BOLSA number of shares issued; **~ de acta** FIN *consejo del Tesoro* minute number; **~ de afiliación a la Seguridad Social** FISC ≈ National Insurance Number; **~ aleatorio** INFO, MAT random number; **~ atrasado** MEDIOS *diario o revista* back issue, back number; **~ de autorización** BANCA authorization number; **~ de base total** MED AMB total base number (*TBN*); **~ binario** INFO, MAT *ramación* binary number; **~ de bono** BANCA, BOLSA bond number; **~ de cifras** COM GEN figure number; **~ de coma fija** MAT fixed-point number; **~ de coma flotante** MAT floating-point number; **~ consecutivo** COM GEN running number; **~ de cotejo** INFO collator number; **~ de cuenta** BANCA, CONT, FISC account number; **~ de cuenta de remesa** BANCA, FISC remittance account number; **~ decimal** INFO decimal number; **~ de Dun** FIN Dun's Number; **~ de empleados** RRHH *hoja de balance* number of employees; **~ de etiqueta de control de la hoja de embarque** TRANSP consignment note control label number (*CCLN*); **~ exento de pago** COMS Freefone®

number (*BrE*), toll-free number (*AmE*); ~ **ID** INFO ID number; ~ **de identificación fiscal** (*NIF*) FISC taxpayer number; ~ **de identificación fiscal de la empresa** FISC employer taxation number; ~ **de identificación mediante código de barras** INFO, V&M bar-coded identification number; ~ **de identificación personal** BANCA personal identification number (*PIN*); ~ **de identificación tributaria** (*NIT*) FISC taxpayer number; ~ **índice** ECON, MAT *econometría* index number; ~ **de inscripción del IVA** FISC VAT registration number (*BrE*); ~ **de la institución benéfica** FISC charity number; ~ **interno** ADMIN intra number; ~ **de lectores** MEDIOS *de periódicos, libros*, V&M readership; ~ **de licencia de exportación** IMP/EXP, TRANSP export licence number (*BrE*), export license number (*AmE*); ~ **de líneas de un espacio publicitario** MEDIOS *imprenta* lineage; ~ **de matrícula** COM GEN, TRANSP registration number; ~ **medio de lectores de una edición** MEDIOS, V&M average issue readership; ~ **oficial** TRANSP official number (*official no., on*); ~ **ONU** TRANSP UN number; ~ **de orden** COM GEN, INFO, PATENT serial number; ~ **de página** ADMIN, COM GEN, MEDIOS page number; ~ **paralelo de lectores** MEDIOS, V&M parallel readership; ~ **de pedido** COM GEN, V&M *cumplimentación* order number; ~ **primario de lectores** MEDIOS, V&M primary readership; ~ **de puerta** TRANSP gate number; ~ **real** INFO real number; ~ **de referencia** MEDIOS *impresión* box number; ~ **registrado en aduanas** IMP/EXP customs registered number (*CRN*); ~ **de registro** COM GEN, TRANSP registration number; ~ **de secuencia** INFO, MAT sequence number; ~ **secuencial** INFO, MAT sequential number; ~ **secundario de lectores** MEDIOS, V&M secondary readership; ~ **de serie de la Norma Internacional** MEDIOS *imprenta* International Standard Serial Number (*ISSN*); ~ **de sucursal** BANCA branch number; ~ **de teléfono** COMS telephone number (*phone number, tel. no.*); ~ **terciario de lectores** MEDIOS, V&M tertiary readership; ~ **total de lectores de una edición** MEDIOS, V&M issue readership; ~ **de tren** TRANSP train number; ~ **de votantes** POL voter turnout; ~ **de vuelo** OCIO, TRANSP flight number

números: **en ~ redondos** *fra* COM GEN in round numbers; **estar en ~ rojos** *fra* COM GEN in round numbers

O

obedecer *vt* COM GEN, DER obey; ◆ **~ a** COM GEN arise from

obenque *m* TRANSP *cuerda* guy

objeción *f* COM GEN objection; **~ a una imposción** FISC objection to an assessment; ◆ **hacer una ~** COM GEN make an objection; **sin ~** COM GEN no objections; **~ denegada** DER objection overruled; **~ justificada** DER objection sustained

objetar 1. *vt* COM GEN, *argumento* put forward, present, *objeción* offer, raise; **2.** *vi* COM GEN object

objetivo *m* COM GEN objective, target; **~ de beneficios** BANCA, CONT, FIN profit target; **~ de cobertura** BOLSA hedging goal; **~ de comunicación** V&M communication objective; **~ corporativo** COM GEN corporate objective; **~ a corto plazo** COM GEN short-term objective; **~ de costes** *Esp* (*cf objetivo de costos AmL*) ECON cost objective; **~ de costos** *AmL* (*cf objetivo de costes Esp*) ECON cost objective; **~ departamental** GES departmental objective; **~ de la empresa** COM GEN company objective; **~ horario** TRANSP *navegación* hours purpose; **~ intermedio** POL intermediate target; **~ de inversiones** BANCA, CONT, FIN investment objective; **~ de investigación** COM GEN research objective; **~ a largo plazo** COM GEN long-term objective; **~ de la línea departamental** *f* ADMIN departmental line object; **~ de marketing** V&M marketing objective; **~ de mercado** V&M market objective; **~ de negocios** V&M business objective; **~ de un programa publicitario** V&M advertising programme objective (*BrE*), advertising program objective (*AmE*); **~ de ventas** COM GEN, V&M sales target, commercial target

objeto *m* COM GEN, GES *cosa* object, *meta* purpose, *tema* theme, DER exhibit; **~ de clase** COM GEN class object; **~ fuente** CONT source object; **~ del informe** COM GEN reporting object; **~ de la línea** ADMIN line object; **~ de la misión** COM GEN *de un comité* terms of reference; **~ normalizado** POL standard object; ◆ **con el único ~ de** COM GEN with the sole object of

obligación *f* BANCA debenture (*db*), debt, BOLSA, CONT debt, bond, call, debenture (*db*), DER duty, FIN bond, debenture (*db*), debt, obligation; **~ de la administración local** BOLSA local authority bond (*LAB*); **~ amortizable** BOLSA redeemable bond; **~ bancaria** BANCA, BOLSA, CONT bank debenture; **~ contingente** FISC contingent obligation; **~ contractual** DER contractual obligation; **~ convertible** BOLSA, FIN convertible bond, convertible debenture; **~ convertible de prima alta** BOLSA, FIN high-premium convertible debenture; **~ de la deuda** CONT, FISC debt obligation; **~ de deuda cualificada** FISC qualifying debt obligation; **~ directa** BANCA direct obligation; **~ de empresa** BANCA, BOLSA corporate debenture; **~ del Estado** ECON government obligation; **~ del Estado indiciada** BOLSA index-linked gilt; **~ excluida** FISC excluded obligation; **~ fuera del balance general** CONT off-balance sheet commitment; **~ sin garantía** BOLSA unsecured bond; **~ con garantía hipotecaria** BOLSA general mortgage bond; **~ con garantía preferente** BOLSA prior-lien bond; **~ con garantía privilegiada** BOLSA prior-lien bond;

~ garantizada BANCA, FIN secured debenture; **~ hipotecaria** BANCA mortgage commitment, debenture bond, BOLSA debenture bond, FIN mortgage commitment; **~ hipotecaria con garantía prendaria** BANCA, FIN collateralized mortgage obligation (*CMO*); **~ hipotecaria garantizada** BANCA, FIN collateralized mortgage obligation (*CMO*); **~ imperfecta** DER imperfect obligation; **~ implícita** COM GEN implied obligation; **~ imponible** FISC taxable obligation; **~ de interés compuesto** BANCA, BOLSA, ECON, FIN compound interest bond; **~ de interés variable** BOLSA floater, floating-rate note (*FRN*); **~ internacional** BOLSA international bond; **~ a largo plazo** BOLSA long-term security; **~ legal** DER legal obligation, statutory obligation; **~ legal de aportación de los empresarios** DER, RRHH employers' legal obligation to fund; **~ con lotes** BOLSA Premium Bond (*BrE*); **~ municipal** BANCA, BOLSA municipal bond; **~ no imponible** FISC nontaxable obligation; **~ ordinaria** BOLSA marketable bond; **~ de organismo público** BOLSA authority bond (*AmE*); **~ pagadera** CONT amount payable; **~ de pagar los gastos** PATENT awarding of costs; **~ de pago** BANCA, FIN *préstamos* payment commitment, FISC burden of payment; **~ pendiente** CONT outstanding commitment; **~ perfecta** DER perfect obligation; **~ preferente** BOLSA participating bond; **~ con prima** BOLSA premium bond; **~ de renta fija** BOLSA fixed-interest bond; **~ rescatada** BOLSA redeemed debenture; **~ sin sellar** BOLSA unstamped debenture; **~ societaria** BOLSA corporate bond (*AmE*); **~ solidaria** FISC joint obligation; **~ subordinada** BOLSA subordinated debenture; **~ del tesoro** ECON Treasury Bill Bond; **~ de tipo flotante** BOLSA floating-rate debenture; **~ de transbordo** IMP/EXP, TRANSP transhipment bond; **~ vencida** BOLSA matured bond; ◆ **sin ~** V&M without obligation; **sin ~ de compra** V&M no obligation to buy, *promoción de ventas* no purchase necessary

obligaciones *f pl* BANCA bonds, securities, liabilities, DER covenants; **~ aceptables con interés** BANCA interest-bearing eligible liabilities; **~ a corto plazo** BOLSA short-term securities, CONT short-term liabilities; **~ de impuestos diferidos** CONT, FISC deferred tax liabilities; **~ de jubilación** CONT pension liabilities; **~ que devengan intereses** CONT interest-bearing liabilities

obligacionista *mf* BANCA, BOLSA bondholder, debenture holder

obligado[1] *adj* COM GEN obliged; ◆ **no estar ~** COM GEN be under no obligation; **estar muy ~** COM GEN be much obliged; **de ~ cumplimiento** DER legally-binding; **estar ~ a hacer algo** COM GEN be under an obligation to do sth; **estar ~ legalmente a** DER be under legal obligation to

obligado[2]**,-a** *m,f* DER obligor

obligar *vt* COM GEN force, oblige, DER obligate; ◆ **~ a una jubilación anticipada** RRHH force into early retirement

obligatoriedad: ~ legal del contrato colectivo *f* DER, RRHH legal enforceability of collective agreement

obligatorio *adj* COM GEN compulsory, obligatory, DER

statutory; **no ~** COM GEN noncompulsory, nonobligatory, DER nonstatutory

obra *f* IND *de construcción* building site; **~ en carretera** TRANSP roadworks; **~ defectuosa** COM GEN bad work; **~ maestra** COM GEN *de una colección* showpiece; **~ pública** ECON public work

obrero, -a *m,f* COM GEN worker, RRHH blue-collar worker; **~ de acería** IND, RRHH steelworker; **~ de la construcción** IND, RRHH construction worker; **~ cualificado(-a)** IND, RRHH skilled worker; **~ de línea** IND, RRHH assembly line worker; **~ manual** IND, RRHH manual worker, production worker

obreros *m pl* COM GEN labour, labour force

observación *f* COM GEN observation, FISC monitoring; **~ telefónica** COMS telephone tap

observaciones *f pl* COM GEN remarks; ◆ **sin ~** CONT clean

observador, a: **~ del mercado** *m,f* COM GEN market watcher

obsolescencia *f* COM GEN obsolescence; **~ económica** ECON economic obsolescence; **~ planeada** ECON, IND built-in obsolescence; **~ planificada** V&M planned obsolescence; **~ progresiva** V&M progress obsolescence; **~ tecnológica** IND *producción* technological obsolescence

obsoleto *adj* COM GEN, V&M obsolete

obstaculizar *vt* COM GEN hinder, hamper

obstáculo *m* COM GEN hurdle, setback; **~ contractual** COM GEN contract holdback

obstante: **no ~** *prep frml* COM GEN nevertheless, notwithstanding

obstruir *vt* COM GEN obstruct, stymie (*jarg*)

obtención *f* CONT *de beneficio* making, V&M procurement; **~ de capital** BOLSA capital raising; **~ de créditos en el exterior** FIN borrowing abroad; **~ de fondos** CONT, FIN raising of funds

obtener *vt* COM GEN *meta* achieve, obtain, secure, PATENT take out; ◆ **~ algo fraudulentamente** DER obtain sth by fraud; **~ la aprobación formal de** COM GEN gain formal approval from; **~ beneficio** COM GEN make a benefit; **~ beneficios sobre algo** BOLSA make gains on sth; **~ deudas** *infrml* BANCA, ECON, FIN get into debt (*infrml*); **~ el favor de alguien** COM GEN win sb's favor (*AmE*), win sb's favour (*BrE*); **~ justicia** DER get justice; **~ permiso por escrito** COMS obtain permission in writing; **~ una respuesta** COM GEN receive an answer

O/C *abr* (*orden de compra*) COM GEN P.O. (*purchase order*)

ocasión *f* COM GEN *oportunidad* opportunity, chance, *motivo* cause

ocasionar *vt* COM GEN *gastos* involve

occidentalizado *adj* COM GEN westernized

occidentalizarse *v refl* COM GEN become westernized

OCDE *abr* (*Organización para la Cooperación y Desarrollo Económicos*) ECON, POL OECD (*Organization for Economic Cooperation and Development*)

ocio *m* OCIO leisure

ocioso *adj* OCIO at leisure, RRHH idle

octavilla *f* COM GEN pamphlet, leaflet, MEDIOS, V&M *publicidad* flyer

octeto *m* INFO byte

OCU *abr* (*Organización de Consumidores y Usuarios*) PROT SOC consumer protection advisory bureau, ≈ CAC (*AmE*) (*Consumers' Advisory Council*), ≈ CA (*BrE*) (*Consumers' Association*)

ocultación *f* DER *de información* concealment, INFO blanking; **~ de pérdidas** BOLSA, CONT concealment of losses

ocultar *vt* COM GEN hide, cover up, DER conceal, INFO blank, POL cover up, V&M *publicidad* mask

ocupación *f* DER *trabajo* occupation, INMOB occupancy, RRHH *trabajo* occupation; **~ central** RRHH central occupation; **~ comercial** INMOB commercial occupancy; **~ conjunta** FISC, INMOB joint occupancy; **~ residencial** INMOB residential occupancy; **~ vitalicia** INMOB life tenancy

ocupado *adj* COM GEN *persona* busy, COMS, INFO *señal* busy, engaged

ocupante *mf* DER, FISC, INMOB occupant

ocuparse[1]: **~ de** *v refl* COM GEN *acuerdo, crisis*, COMS deal with, look to

ocuparse[2]: **~ de las cosas diarias** *fra* COM GEN go about one's daily business

OEAC *abr* (*Organización de Estados Centroamericanos*) ECON, POL OCAS (*Organization of Central American States*)

OET *abr* (*Organización Europea de Transportes*) TRANSP ETO (*European Transport Organization*)

ofensa *f* DER offence

ofensiva: **~ comercial** *f* V&M sales offensive

oferta *f* COM GEN bid, offer, tender, V&M special offer; **~ y aceptación** DER *comercial* offer and acceptance; **~ afianzada** BOLSA hedged tender; **~ agregada** ECON aggregate supply; **~ al alza** BOLSA bidding up; **~ aniversario** V&M anniversary offer; **~ apalancada** BOLSA leveraged bid; **~ de apertura** V&M opening bid; **~ asociada** V&M banded offer; **~ atractiva** COM GEN attractive offer; **~ de autoliquidación** V&M self-liquidating offer; **~ a bajo precio** COM GEN undercutting; **~ de buena fe** COM GEN bona fide offer; **~ sin competencia** BOLSA noncompetitive bid; **~ competitiva** COM GEN, ECON, V&M competitive tendering; **~ de compra de dólares** BOLSA *opciones* dollar bid; **~ de compras** FIN buyout; **~ definitiva** COM GEN closing bid; **~ desanimada** ECON slack; **~ de dinero** ECON, FIN money supply; **~ de divisas** BOLSA exchange offer; **~ elástica** ECON, V&M elastic supply; **~ de emisión** BOLSA primary offering; **~ de empleo** RRHH employment offer, job offer; **~ por escrito** COM GEN written offer; **~ especial** V&M special offer; **~ específica** V&M specific offer; **~ excesiva** ECON oversupply; **~ en firme** BOLSA, COM GEN firm bid, firm offer; **~ fluctuante** BOLSA floating supply; **~ fraudulenta** BOLSA tailgating; **~ garantizada** BOLSA hedged tender; **~ inelástica** ECON, V&M inelastic supply; **~ invisible** COM GEN invisible supply; **~ laboral** ECON labor supply (*AmE*), labour supply (*BrE*); **~ de lanzamiento** MEDIOS, V&M *publicidad* introductory offer, launch offer; **~ de letras del tesoro** ECON Treasury bill tender; **~ más alta** COM GEN highest tender; **~ más baja** COM GEN lowest tender; **~ más elevada** BOLSA highest bid; **~ más próxima** V&M nearest offer; **~ minorista** BOLSA, V&M retail offer; **~ monetaria** BANCA, ECON, FIN money (*M*), money supply; **~ de muestras** COM GEN sampling offer; **~ original** COM GEN original bid; **~ de pago al contado** BOLSA cash tender offer; **~ en pliego**

cerrado COMS sealed tender; **~ a precio fijo** BOLSA fixed-price offering; **~ preferente** BOLSA pre-emptive bid; **~ sin presión** COM GEN soft offer; **~ primaria** BOLSA *nueva emisión* primary offering; **~ progresiva** BOLSA, FIN creeping tender; **~ de propuesta cerrada** V&M sealed-bid tendering; **~ de prueba** COM GEN, V&M trial offer; **~ pública de adquisición de una empresa** (*OPA*) BOLSA take-over bid (*TOB*), tender offer, COM GEN take-over bid (*TOB*); **~ pública de adquisición hostil** (*OPAH*) BOLSA, COM GEN hostile takeover bid; **~ pública de compra** (*OPC*) BOLSA, COM GEN takeover bid (*TOB*); **~ pública de enajenación** BOLSA, COM GEN public offering; **~ pública inicial** (*OPI*) COM GEN initial public offering (*IPO*); **~ pública de venta** (*OPV*) BOLSA, COM GEN public offering; **~ publicitada** V&M advertised bidding; **~ de reembolso total** V&M complete refund offer; **~ regresiva** ECON regressive supply; **~ secundaria autorizada** BOLSA registered secondary offering; **~ de trabajo** ECON labor supply (*AmE*), labour supply (*BrE*), RRHH job offer; **~ de venta** BOLSA offer for sale; **~ verbal** COM GEN verbal offer; **~ vinculante** COM GEN binding offer, binding tender; **~ viscosa** ECON viscous supply; ◆ **~ y demanda** COM GEN supply and demand; **en ~** INMOB *casa* under offer, V&M on offer; **u ~ más próxima** V&M *publicidad* or nearest offer (*o.n.o.*); **u ~ próxima** V&M *publicidad* or near offer; **hacer mejor ~ que** V&M outbid

ofertado *adj* BOLSA bid, COM GEN bid, offered, tendered

ofertar *vt* BOLSA bid, COM GEN offer, bid, tender, V&M sell on special offer

offset *m* MEDIOS offset

oficial[1] *adj* COM GEN official

oficial[2]**,a** *m,f* BANCA, COM GEN, RRHH officer, official; **~ de aduanas** FISC, IMP/EXP, RRHH customs officer; **~ de almacén** IMP/EXP, RRHH, TRANSP warehouse officer; **~ de capacitación** *AmL* (*cf oficial de formación Esp*) COM GEN, RRHH training officer; **~ de carga** TRANSP loadmate; **~ de control de divisas** RRHH exchange control officer; **~ de descarga** RRHH, TRANSP landing officer; **~ de desembarque** RRHH, TRANSP landing officer; **~ de distrito** RRHH district officer (*DO*); **~ de embarque** IMP/EXP, RRHH, TRANSP shipping officer; **~ de exportación** IMP/EXP, RRHH, TRANSP export clerk; **~ de formación** *Esp* (*cf oficial de capacitación AmL*) COM GEN, RRHH training officer; **~ de formación de distrito** RRHH district training officer (*DTO*); **~ de guardia** RRHH, TRANSP duty officer (*DO*); **~ médico(-a)** RRHH *ejército* medical officer of health (*MOH*); **~ de operaciones portuarias** IMP/EXP, RRHH, TRANSP Port Operations Officer (*POO*); **~ de prensa** MEDIOS, RRHH, V&M press officer; **~ de transporte motorizado** RRHH, TRANSP motor transport officer (*MTO*)

oficialmente *adv* COM GEN officially

oficina *f* ADMIN, COM GEN bureau, office; **~ de alojamiento** PROT SOC accommodation bureau; **~ de apoyo** ADMIN back office; **~ de atención a los inversores** FIN investors' service bureau; **~ bancaria extraterritorial** BANCA *de inversión* offshore banking unit (*OBU*); **~ bancaria ultramarina** BANCA *de inversión* offshore banking unit (*OBU*); **~ de bienestar social** PROT SOC, RRHH welfare agency; **~ de cambio** BANCA, OCIO foreign exchange office; **~ del catastro** ADMIN land office; **~ central** COM GEN head office (*H.O.*); **~ central de contratación de fletes** TRANSP central

freight booking office; **~ central de fletes** TRANSP central freight bureau (*CFB*); **~ central de reservas** OCIO central reservation office; **~ de colocaciones** COM GEN, RRHH employment agency, employment bureau; **~ comercial** ADMIN business office; **~ de consigna** TRANSP checkroom (*AmE*), left-luggage office (*BrE*); **~ de contabilidad** *Esp* (*cf contaduría AmL*) CONT accounting office; **~ corporativa** GES head office (*H.O.*); **~ de correos** ADMIN, COM GEN, COMS post office; **~ de crédito** BANCA, FIN credit bureau; **~ designada** PATENT designated office; **~ de distribución** TRANSP distribution office (*DO*); **~ electrónica** ADMIN, COM GEN, INFO electronic office; **~ de empleo** COM GEN, RRHH employment agency, employment bureau, recruitment agency, employment office (*BrE*); **~ de estadística laboral** MAT, RRHH Bureau of Labour Statistics; **~ de estudios** COM GEN design office; **~ de exportación** IMP/EXP, TRANSP export office; **~ del gerente** ADMIN, GES manager's office; **~ de información** ADMIN, COM GEN, OCIO information desk; **~ de información turística** OCIO tourist information office; **~ de investigaciones** COM GEN enquiry desk; **~ de licencias de exportación** IMP/EXP export licensing branch (*ELB*); **~ matriz** COM GEN head office (*H.O.*); **~ del paro** *Esp infrml* PROT SOC ≈ Unemployment Benefit Office (*BrE*); **~ de plan abierto** ADMIN open-plan office; **~ de planificación abierta** ADMIN open-plan office; **~ de planificación abierta** ADMIN open-plan office; **~ principal** COM GEN head office (*H.O.*), headquarters (*HQ, h.q.*); **~ privada** RRHH private office; **~ de proyectos** COM GEN design office; **~ de recaudación** FISC, IMP/EXP collector's office; **~ de recaudación de impuestos** FISC revenue office; **~ recaudadora** FISC, IMP/EXP collector's office; **~ de recepción** COM GEN, PATENT receiving office (*RO*); **~ de reclutamiento** RRHH recruiting office; **~ regional** COM GEN regional office; **~ de registro** ADMIN registration office; **~ del Registro Civil** ADMIN registrar's office, registry office (*BrE*); **~ de telégrafos** COMS telegraphic office (*TO*); **~ de trabajo** COM GEN, RRHH recruitment agency; **~ de ventas** V&M sales office; **~ de zona** BANCA area office

Oficina: ~ del Alto Comisionado de las Naciones Unidas para los Refugiados *f* (*ACNUR*) POL, PROT SOC United Nations High Commission for Refugees (*UNHCR*); **~ del Censo** *f* PROT SOC ≈ Office of Population Censuses and Surveys (*BrE*) (*OPCS*); **~ Central de Estadística** *f* ECON, MAT Central Bureau of Statistics; **~ de Comercio Internacional** *f* ECON, IMP/EXP Office of International Trade (*OIT*); **~ Europea para el Medio Ambiente** *f* MED AMB, POL European Environment Bureau (*EEB*); **~ General de Contabilidad** *f* *AmL* (*cf Tribunal de Cuentas Esp*) CONT ≈ General Accounting Office (*AmE*) (*GAO*); **~ Internacional de Tarifas Aduaneras** *f* IMP/EXP, TRANSP International Customs Tariffs Bureau (*BrE*) (*ICTB*); **~ de Justificación de la Difusión** *f* (*OJD*) V&M *publicidad* Audit Bureau of Circulation (*ABC*); **~ de Marcas Registradas de la Comunidad** *f* DER UE Community Trade Mark Office; **~ del Presupuesto** *f* ECON, POL Bureau of the Budget (*BB*); **~ de Protección al Consumidor** *f* COM GEN ≈ Office of Fair Trading (*BrE*); **~ Técnica de Administración Cambiaria** *f* (*OTAC*) ECON, POL Foreign Exchange Administration Technical Office; **~ de Turismo** *f* OCIO Spanish national tourism office, ≈ English Tourist Board (*ETB*)

oficinista *mf* RRHH white-collar worker, clerk

oficio[1]: **de ~** *adv* RRHH ex officio (*e.o.*)

oficio[2] *m* RRHH profession, trade

ofrecer *vt* COM GEN offer, FIN put up, RRHH *trabajo* offer; ◆ **~ acciones al público** BOLSA, FIN go public; **~ a la baja** COM GEN underbid; **~ al público** BOLSA go public; **~ dinero para saldar una deuda** DER tender money in discharge of debt; **~ por encima del valor** BOLSA overbid; **~ una magnitud considerable** COM GEN offer considerable scope; **~ más** COM GEN *contrato* bid on (*AmE*); **~ mediante contrato privado** V&M tender by private contract; **~ precios más bajos que** COM GEN undercut; **~ sus servicios** COM GEN offer one's services; **~ voluntariamente** COM GEN *información* volunteer

ofrecido *adj* BOLSA offered

ofrecimiento: **~ de bono municipal** *m* BANCA, BOLSA municipal bond offering

OIC *abr* (*Organización Internacional de Comercio*) COM GEN ITO (*International Trade Organization*)

OIML *abr* (*Organización Internacional de Metrología Legal*) COM GEN OIML (*International Organization for Legal Metrology*)

OIN *abr* (*Organización Internacional de Normalización*) COM GEN ISO (*International Standards Organization*)

OIT *abr* (*Organización Internacional de Trabajo*) POL, PROT SOC, RRHH ILO (*International Labor Organization AmE, International Labour Organization BrE*)

OJD *abr* (*Oficina de Justificación de la Difusión*) V&M ABC (*Audit Bureau of Circulation*)

ojos: **a los ~ de la ley** *fra* DER in the eyes of the law

OL *abr* (*onda larga*) MEDIOS LW (*long wave*)

oleada: **~ de compras** *f* COM GEN buying surge; **~ de gastos** *f* COM GEN spending surge

oleoducto *m* IND, MED AMB oil pipeline

oligopolio *m* ECON oligopoly; **~ colusorio** ECON collusive oligopoly; **~ espacial** ECON spatial oligopoly; **~ homogéneo** ECON homogeneous oligopoly

oligopolístico *adj* ECON oligopolistic

oligopsonio *m* ECON oligopsony

omisión *f* COM GEN omission, DER *comercial* nonfeasance; ◆ **por ~** INFO default

omitir *vt* COM GEN omit, leave out; ◆ **~ un dividendo** FIN pass a dividend (*jarg*); **~ hacer** COM GEN omit to do; **~ un pago** BANCA, FIN skip a payment (*infrml*)

OMS *abr* (*Organización Mundial de la Salud*) POL, PROT SOC WHO (*World Health Organization*)

onda *f* COM GEN wave; **~ de Kondratieff** ECON Kondratieff wave; **~ larga** (*OL*) MEDIOS long wave (*LW*)

ONG *abr* (*organización no gubernamental*) POL NGO (*nongovernmental organization*)

ONU *abr* (*Organización de las Naciones Unidas*) ECON, POL UNO (*United Nations Organization*)

ONUDI *abr* (*Organización de las Naciones Unidas para el Desarrollo Industrial*) ECON, IND, POL UNIDO (*United Nations Industrial Development Organization*)

onza *f* COM GEN ounce (*oz*); **~ fluida** COM GEN fluid ounce (*fl.oz.*); **~ de oro fino** ECON troy ounce

OPA *abr* (*oferta pública de adquisición*) BOLSA TOB (*take-over bid*), tender offer, COM GEN TOB (*take-over bid*)

opacidad: **~ bursátil** *f* BOLSA stock exchange opacity; **~ fiscal** *f* FISC fiscal opacity

OPAH *abr* (*oferta pública de adquisición hostil*) BOLSA, COM GEN hostile takeover bid

OPC *abr* (*oferta pública de compra*) BOLSA, COM GEN TOB (*take-over bid*)

opción *f* COM GEN option; **~ admitida a cotización** BOLSA listed option; **~ al contado** BOLSA cash-delivery option; **~ a la americana** BOLSA American option; **~ de arrendamiento** DER lease option; **~ de base** GES fallback option; **~ con beneficio potencial** BOLSA in-the-money option; **~ de bonos** BOLSA bond option; **~ de bonos a largo plazo** BOLSA long-term bond option; **~ caducada** BOLSA lapsed option; **~ de cambio negociada** BOLSA traded exchange option; **~ de cierre** FIN *absorción de sociedad* lock-up option; **~ de compra** BOLSA call option; **~ de compra de acciones** BOLSA share option, stock option; **~ de compra de acciones para los empleados** BOLSA, RRHH employee stock option; **~ de compra de acciones sin garantía** BOLSA naked call option; **~ de compra al portador** BOLSA bearer warrant; **~ de compra de bonos** BOLSA bond call option; **~ de compra sin cobertura** BOLSA uncovered call option, uncovered call; **~ de compra a corto sin garantía** BOLSA naked short call; **~ de compra cubierta** BOLSA covered call option; **~ de compra dentro del precio** BOLSA in-the-money call option; **~ de compra de divisas** BOLSA currency call option; **~ de compra emitida** BOLSA written call; **~ de compra indiferente** BOLSA in-the-money call; **~ de compra en junio** BOLSA June call; **~ de compra a largo plazo** BOLSA long call; **~ de compra con pérdida potencial** BOLSA out-of-the-money call; **~ de compra a precio corriente** BOLSA at-the-money call option; **~ de compra y venta** BOLSA call and put option; **~ de compra o venta divisible** BOLSA *opción sobre futuros en eurodólares* splitting spread; **~ de compra o venta no entregada del todo** BOLSA underdelivery spread; **~ del consumidor** V&M *comercialización* consumer choice; **~ cotizada** BOLSA listed option; **~ sin cubrir** BOLSA uncovered option; **~ por defecto** INFO default option; **~ doble uno a uno** BOLSA one-to-one straddle; **~ doble a corto** BOLSA short straddle; **~ doble delta-neutral** BOLSA delta-neutral straddle; **~ doble sin garantía** BOLSA naked put; **~ emitida** BOLSA written option; **~ por encima del precio de mercado** BOLSA deep-out-of-the-money option; **~ de entrada en el mercado** IMP/EXP market entry option; **~ a la europea** BOLSA European option; **~ europea americanizada** BOLSA Americanized-European option; **~ fácil** GES easy option; **~ facultativa** BOLSA optional feature; **~ ficticia sobre acciones** BOLSA, FIN phantom share option; **~ de futuro en eurodólares** BOLSA, FIN Eurodollar future; **~ con garantía** BOLSA covered option; **~ sin garantía** BOLSA naked option; **~ índice** BOLSA index option; **~ indiferente** BOLSA at-the-money option; **~ inmovilizada** BOLSA *absorciones de empresas* lock-up option; **~ intercalada** BOLSA embedded option; **~ librada al contado** BOLSA cash-delivery option; **~ de liquidación** SEG *seguro de vida* optional mode of settlement; **~ a más largo plazo** BOLSA longer-term option; **~ a menor plazo** BOLSA shorter-term option; **~ negativa** COM GEN negative option; **~ negociada** BOLSA traded option; **~ objeto de comercio** BOLSA traded option; **~ pagada al contado** BOLSA cash-settled option; **~ a plazo más corto** BOLSA shorter-term option; **~ con precio diferente al de mercado** BOLSA out-of-the-money option; **~ a precio medio de ejercicio** BOLSA middle-strike option; **~ privilegiada de compra de acciones** BOLSA qualifying stock option;

~ **de recompra** BOLSA buy-back option; ~ **de renovación** INMOB *de contrato de arrendamiento* renewal option; ~ **de reserva** GES fallback option; ~ **de ruta** TRANSP route option; ~ **sobre acciones** BOLSA, FISC share option; ~ **sobre acciones compensatorias** BOLSA compensatory stock option; ~ **sobre divisas** BOLSA currency option, forex option; ~ **sobre futuros de divisas** BOLSA option on currency futures; ~ **sobre el índice bursátil** BOLSA stock index option; ~ **sobre el neto** BOLSA equity option; ~ **sobre permuta financiera** BOLSA swop option; ~ **sobre posición mixta stellage** BOLSA stellage straddle option; ~ **strap** BOLSA strap option; ~ **de tipo europeo** BOLSA European style option; ~ **de tipo de interés** BOLSA interest-rate option; ~ **del tomador a títulos y créditos no emitidos** FIN borrower's option for notes and unwritten standby (*BONUS*); ~ **de venta** BOLSA put, put option; ~ **de venta de bonos** BOLSA bond put option; ~ **de venta sin cobertura** BOLSA uncovered put; ~ **de venta a corto sin garantía** BOLSA naked short put; ~ **de venta cubierta** BOLSA covered put; ~ **de venta dentro del precio** BOLSA in-the-money put option; ~ **de venta en descubierto** BOLSA short put; ~ **de venta de divisas** BOLSA currency put option; ~ **de venta emitida** BOLSA written put; ~ **de venta indiferente** BOLSA in-the-money put; ~ **de venta en junio** BOLSA June put; ~ **de venta con pérdida potencial** BOLSA out-of-the-money put; ~ **de venta a precio de mercado** BOLSA at-the-money put option; ~ **de venta suscrita para adquisición de acciones** BOLSA writing put to acquire stock

opcional/obligatorio *adj* IND facultative/obligatory (*factoblig*), optional/mandatory

opción: ~-bono no remunerativa *f* BOLSA nonqualifying stock option

OPEP *abr* (*Organización de los Países Exportadores de Petróleo*) IMP/EXP, POL OPEC (*Organization of Petroleum Exporting Countries*)

operación *f* BANCA, BOLSA, COM GEN, GES operation; ~ **administrativa** GES management operation; ~ **al alza** BOLSA bull operation; ~ **al cierre** BOLSA closing trade; ~ **al contado** COM GEN cash operation; ~ **alcista** BOLSA bull transaction; ~ **de arbitraje** BOLSA arbitrage dealing, arbitrage trading; ~ **arriesgada en el extranjero** COM GEN foreign venture; ~ **auxiliar** COM GEN, GES ancillary operation; ~ **a la baja** BOLSA bear operation, bear transaction; ~ **bajo cuerda** ECON backdoor operation; ~ **bancaria** BANCA banking operation; ~ **bancaria de tierras** INMOB land banking; ~ **de bolsa** BOLSA equity trading, stock exchange transaction; ~ **de bolsa bajo cuerda** BOLSA under the rule (*jarg*) (*AmE*); ~ **con bonos** BOLSA bond trading; ~ **bursátil** BOLSA stock exchange transaction; ~ **de captación de capital** BANCA, FIN capital-raising operation; ~ **con los clientes** BANCA transaction with customers; ~ **de cobertura** BOLSA hedge trading, hedging operation; ~ **de cobertura por venta a plazo** BOLSA short hedge; ~ **combinada de transporte** TRANSP combined transport operation; ~ **comercial** BANCA trading operation, ECON commercial trade; ~ **comercial del mercado intermedio** ECON middle market business; ~ **de compensación** BANCA clearing process; ~ **de compra** BOLSA buy transaction; ~ **de compra-venta extranjera** BANCA forex trading; ~ **de contado** BOLSA, COM GEN, CONT, FIN spot trading; ~ **de corrección** COM GEN corrective action; ~ **de corro**

automatizada BOLSA Automated Pit Trading; ~ **en cuenta** FIN dealing for the account; ~ **difícil** BOLSA sticky deal; ~ **discontinua** CONT discontinued operation; ~ **de dobles** COM GEN swop; ~ **con dobles primas** BOLSA put and call; ~ **de emisión de bonos** BOLSA bond issue operation; ~ **de emplazamiento** MED AMB *vertido* site operation; ~ **empresarial con riesgo** COM GEN venture; ~ **fiduciaria** BANCA fiduciary operation; ~ **furtiva** FIN backdoor operation (*BrE*); ~ **a futuros** BOLSA forward dealing; ~ **con interés de aplazamiento** BOLSA contango business (*BrE*); ~ **con intereses** CONT interest operation; ~ **interna** BOLSA in-house operation; ~ **de limpieza** MED AMB cleaning-up operation; ~ **para mantener el precio** BOLSA share support operation; ~ **con margen** BOLSA *mercado de divisas* spread trading; ~ **de la memoria** INFO memory operation; ~ **de mercado** FIN market dealing; ~ **modelo** COM GEN textbook operation; ~ **multipuerto** TRANSP multiport operation; ~ **multisegmentada** V&M multisegmented operation; ~ **no continuada** CONT discontinued operation; ~ **no válida** INFO illegal operation; ~ **normal de bolsa** BOLSA, COM GEN regular way delivery; ~ **con pizarra** BOLSA blackboard trading; ~ **a plazo** BOLSA forward operation; ~ **portuaria** TRANSP dock operation (*DO*); ~ **a precio puesto** BOLSA blackboard trading; ~ **de préstamo** BANCA lending business; ~ **programada** COM GEN program trade (*AmE*), programme trade (*BrE*); ~ **de protección cambiaria** BOLSA, FIN hedging operation; ~ **próxima al cierre del mercado** BOLSA evening trade; ~ **rápida de bolsa con idea de beneficio** BOLSA *mercado de futuros* scalp (*infrml*) (*AmE*); ~ **recíproca** BANCA counter deal; ~ **con renta fija** BOLSA contango business (*BrE*); ~ **de reporte** BOLSA contango business (*BrE*); ~ **salvavidas** BANCA lifeboat operation (*infrml*); ~ **en serie** INFO serial operation; ~ **subsidiaria** COM GEN, GES ancillary operation; ~ **a término** BOLSA *futuros* forward dealing, futures; ~ **del Tesoro e interbancaria** *m pl* BANCA *balance de cuentas* Treasury and interbank operation; ~ **triangular** ECON triangular operation; ~ **de trueque** ECON *comercio internacional* barter transaction; ~ **con valores no cotizados** BOLSA unlisted trading; ~ **a vencimiento** BOLSA forward transaction

operacional *adj* COM GEN operational

operaciones: ~ de dobles *f pl* BOLSA swop; ~ **interbancarias** *f pl* BANCA interbank transactions; ~ **de mercado abierto** *f pl* ECON, POL open market operations; ~ **con títulos** *f pl* BOLSA exchange of securities; ~ **con valores** *f pl* BOLSA securities business; ~ **de valores** *f pl* BOLSA securities dealing

operador[1]**: ~ binario** *m* INFO binary operator; ~ **de contenedores** *m,f* TRANSP container operator; ~ **terminal de communicación de precios** *m* BOLSA Price Reporting Terminal Operator (*PRTO*); ~ **de transporte combinado** *m,f* TRANSP combined transport operator (*CTO*)

operador[2]**,a** *m,f* BOLSA, COM GEN operator, RRHH driver; ~ **aéreo(-a)** RRHH, TRANSP aircraft operator; ~ **de agrupamiento** IMP/EXP, TRANSP groupage operator; ~ **alcista** BOLSA bull operator; ~ **de arbitraje** BOLSA arbitrage dealer; ~ **de la bolsa** BOLSA jobber (*jarg*), operator; ~ **de campo** COM GEN field operator; ~ **competitivo(-a) autorizado(-a)** BOLSA registered competitive trader; ~ **conjunto(-a)** IND joint operator; ~ **por cuenta propia** TRANSP own account operator;

~ **de descuento** BOLSA, RRHH value broker; ~ **de grupo** RRHH, TRANSP groupage operator; ~ **informático(-a)** INFO, RRHH computer operator; ~ **de lotes sueltos** BOLSA odd-lot dealer; ~ **de opciones autorizado(-a)** BOLSA registered options trader; ~ **de posición** BOLSA position trader; ~ **de posiciones diarias** BOLSA day trader; ~ **con salario y bonificación** TRANSP *por carretera* hire and reward operator; ~ **de teclado** INFO, RRHH keyboard operator; ~ **de teléfonos** COMS, RRHH switchboard operator; ~ **de terminal** INFO terminal operator

operando *m* MAT operand

operar *vt* BOLSA deal, broke, COM GEN *empresa* operate; ◆ ~ **con acciones a precios ficticios** BOLSA fake the marks (*infrml*)

operario, -a *m,f* COM GEN laborer (*AmE*), labourer (*BrE*), operator, worker; ~ **de fábrica** IND, RRHH factory hand; ~ **de factoría** *ver operario de fábrica*

operativo, -a *m,f* GES operative

OPI *abr* (*oferta pública inicial*) COM GEN IPO (*initial public offering*)

opinión *f* COM GEN opinion, V&M *publicidad* belief; ~ **adversa** CONT adverse opinion; ~ **del auditor** CONT auditor's opinion; ~ **clara** CONT clean opinion (*infrml*); ~ **desfavorable** CONT adverse opinion; ~ **favorable** CONT unqualified opinion, clean opinion (*infrml*); ~ **en firme** COM GEN firm belief; ~ **legal** DER legal opinion; ~ **limpia** CONT clean opinion (*infrml*); ~ **negativa** CONT adverse opinion; ~ **pública** COM GEN public opinion; ~ **de título** INMOB opinion of title; ◆ **es cuestión de** ~ COM GEN that's a matter of opinion; **tener una** ~ **pesimista de la situación** COM GEN take a gloomy view of the situation

oponerse *v refl* COM GEN object, oppose; ~ **a** COM GEN *decisión* object to, counter, oppose

oportunidad *f* COM GEN opportunity; ~ **comercial** COM GEN, GES business opportunity; ~ **de empleo** RRHH job opportunity; ~ **de inversión** BANCA, BOLSA, CONT, FIN investment opportunity; ~ **de mercado** V&M market opportunity; ~ **de negocios** COM GEN, GES business opportunity; ~ **de ventas** V&M sales opportunity

oportunismo *m* POL *marxismo* opportunism

oportunista *mf* BOLSA piker (*jarg*), quick-buck artist, COM GEN opportunist

oportuno *adj* COM GEN timely

oposición *f* COM GEN, PATENT, POL opposition

optar: ~ **por** *vt* COM GEN opt for

óptica: ~ **de fibra** *f* COMS, IND, INFO fibre optics (*BrE*), fiber optics (*AmE*)

optimalidad *f* ECON optimality; ~ **de Pareto** ECON Pareto optimality

optimismo: ~ **cauto** *m* COM GEN cautious optimism; ~ **poscontractual** *m* ECON post-contractual optimism

optimización *f* COM GEN, ECON, FIN optimization; ~ **de beneficios** COM GEN, ECON, FIN profit optimization; ~ **de las ganancias** COM GEN, ECON, FIN profit maximization; ~ **del transporte** TRANSP transport facilitation

optimizar *vt* COM GEN, ECON, FIN optimize; ◆ ~ **la función objetiva** COM GEN optimize the objective function

óptimo[1] *adj* COM GEN optimum

óptimo[2]: ~ **de Pareto** *m* ECON Pareto optimum

opulencia *f* ECON, POL, PROT SOC, RRHH, SEG affluence, wealth

OPV *abr* (*oferta pública de venta*) BOLSA, COM GEN public offering

oráculo *m* V&M oracle

orador, a *m,f* COM GEN speaker

orden *f* COM GEN, DER, RRHH order (*ord.*); ~ **de** COM GEN order of (*o/o*); ~ **abierta** BOLSA open order; ~ **administrativa** ADMIN, DER administration order; ~ **del agente de bolsa** BOLSA broker's order; ~ **al mercado** BOLSA *de compra, venta* market order; ~ **alternativa** COM GEN alternative order; ~ **de bloqueo** BOLSA stop order; ~ **de cambio de valor comercial** COM GEN commercial value movement order (*CVMO*); ~ **de cancelación** BOLSA cancel order; ~ **de cobro de deudas** FIN debt collection order (*DCO*); ~ **de compra** (*O/C*) BOLSA buy order, buying order, COM GEN indent (*BrE*), purchase order (*P.O.*); ~ **de compra abierta** COM GEN blanket order; ~ **de compra de futuros con entrega de lo disponible** BOLSA cease-trading order; ~ **de compra a largo simulada** BOLSA *opciones* synthetic long call; ~ **de compra obligatoria** DER, INMOB compulsory purchase order; ~ **de compra para un solo día** BOLSA day order, order valid only today; ~ **de compra o venta si se alcanza un precio** (*orden MIT*) BOLSA market-if-touched order (*MIT order*); ~ **de compraventa a crédito** BOLSA spread order; ~ **de compraventa vigente hasta su cancelación** (*orden GTC*) BOLSA good-till-canceled order (*AmE*) (*GTC order*), good-till-cancelled order (*BrE*) (*GTC order*); ~ **condicionada** BOLSA one-cancels-the-other order (*OCO order*); ~ **de conducción del tráfico** TRANSP routing order; ~ **de contingencia** BOLSA contingency order; ~ **decreciente** *m* INFO decreasing order; ~ **de desahucio** COM GEN, DER, INMOB eviction order; ~ **de desembarque** TRANSP *navegación* landing order; ~ **discrecional fraccionaria** BOLSA fractional discretion order; ~ **de disolución** DER winding-up order; ~ **de ejecución inmediata o cancelación** FIN immediate-or-cancel order (*IOC*); ~ **ejecutoria** COM GEN enforcement order; ~ **de entrega** TRANSP delivery order (*D/O*); ~ **de entrega del buque** TRANSP ship's delivery order; ~ **de entrega del transbordo** TRANSP transhipment delivery order; ~ **escrita de pago** CONT written order to pay; ~ **de estiba** TRANSP stowage order; ~ **de exención** FISC order of discharge; ~ **por gastos varios** TRANSP miscellaneous charges order (*MCO*); ~ **GTC** (*orden de compraventa vigente hasta su cancelación, orden vigente hasta su cancelación*) BOLSA GTC order (*good-till-cancelled order BrE, good-till-canceled order AmE*); ~ **GTD** (*orden vigente hasta su fecha*) BOLSA GTD order (*good-till-date order*); ~ **de importancia** *m* COM GEN, RRHH ranking; ~ **de liquidez decreciente** CONT decreasing liquidity order; ~ **de magnitud** *m* MAT order of magnitude; ~ **de mercado al cierre** BOLSA market order on the close (*MOC*); ~ **de mercado condicional** BOLSA *futuros* conditional market order (*BrE*); ~ **para un mes** BOLSA month order; ~ **ministerial** DER Ministerial order (*BrE*); ~ **MIT** (*orden de compra o venta si se alcanza un precio*) BOLSA MIT order (*market-if-touched order*); ~ **de moneda extranjera** BANCA foreign money order; ~ **negociable de retirada** BANCA, BOLSA, FIN negotiable order of withdrawal; ~ **de pago** BANCA order to pay, payment order, COM GEN money order (*MO*), CONT order to pay, payment order; ~ **de pago**

internacional BANCA, CONT international payment order (*IPO*); **~ de pérdida limitada** BOLSA stop-loss order; **~ permanente** BANCA standing order (*BrE*); **~ de popularidad** *m* COM GEN popularity rating; **~ de registro** DER search warrant; **~ de renovar al vencimiento** BOLSA roll-over order; **~ de reserva** COM GEN booking order; **~ de ruta** TRANSP route order, *carga* routing order (*R/O*); **~ para una semana** BOLSA week order; **~ stop con límite** BOLSA stop-limit order (*AmE*); **~ de suspensión de pagos** BANCA stop payment order; **~ tope** BOLSA resting order; **~ de trabajo** IND, RRHH job order, work order; **~ de transferencia** BANCA, FIN transfer order; **~ de transferencia de dinero** BANCA, FIN money transfer order; **~ del tribunal** DER court order; **~ de venta al precio límite** BOLSA sell-stop order; **~ de venta anticipada** BOLSA presale order; **~ de venta a un precio dado** BOLSA hit order; **~ vigente hasta su cancelación** (*orden GTC*) BOLSA good-till-canceled order (*AmE*) (*GTC order*), good-till-cancelled order (*BrE*) (*GTC order*); **~ vigente hasta su fecha** (*orden GTD*) BOLSA good-till-date order (*GTD order*); ◆ **en ~ alfabético** COM GEN in alphabetical order; **en ~ ascendente** COM GEN in ascending order; **por ~ de importancia** COM GEN in order of importance; **en ~ de prioridad** COM GEN in order of priority; **en el ~ señalado** PATENT in the order specified; **mi ~** COM GEN my order (*m/o*)

ordenación: **~ cronológica de las cuentas a cobrar** *f* CONT ageing of accounts receivable; **~ por importancia** *f* COM GEN, RRHH ranking; **~ rural** *f* COM GEN country planning

ordenador[1]: **por ~** *adj* BOLSA *certificados de depósito* paperless

ordenador[2] *m Esp* (*cf computadora AmL*) INFO computer; **~ activo** *Esp* (*cf computadora activa AmL*) INFO active computer; **~ analógico** *Esp* (*cf computadora analógica AmL*) INFO analog computer; **~ auxiliar** *Esp* (*cf computadora auxiliar AmL*) INFO satellite computer; **~ de bolsillo** *Esp* (*cf computadora de bolsillo AmL*) INFO pocket computer; **~ comercial** *Esp* (*cf computadora comercial AmL*) INFO business computer, commercial computer; **~ de cuarta generación** *Esp* (*cf computadora de cuarta generación AmL*) INFO fourth-generation computer; **~ destinatario** *Esp* (*cf computadora destinataria AmL*) INFO target computer; **~ doméstico** *Esp* (*cf computadora doméstica AmL*) INFO home computer; **~ frontal** *Esp* (*cf computadora frontal AmL*) INFO front-end computer; **~ fuente** *Esp* (*cf computadora fuente AmL*) INFO source computer; **~ híbrido** *Esp* (*cf computadora híbrida AmL*) INFO hybrid computer; **~ por lotes** *Esp* (*cf computadora por lotes AmL*) INFO batch computer; **~ de nivel superior** *Esp* (*cf computadora de nivel superior AmL*) INFO high-end computer; **~ periférico** *Esp* (*cf computadora periférica AmL*) INFO peripheral computer; **~ personal** *Esp* (*PC, cf computadora personal AmL*) INFO personal computer (*PC*); **~ portátil** *Esp* (*cf computadora portátil AmL*) INFO laptop, notebook, portable computer; **~ de primera generación** *Esp* (*cf computadora de primera generación AmL*) INFO first-generation computer; **~ de quinta generación** *Esp* (*cf computadora de quinta generación AmL*) INFO fifth-generation computer; **~ en serie** *Esp* (*cf computadora en serie AmL*) INFO serial computer; **~ en tándem** *Esp* (*cf computadora en tándem AmL*) INFO duplex computer; **~ de tercera**

generación *Esp* (*cf computadora de tercera generación AmL*) INFO third-generation computer; **~ terminal** *Esp* (*cf computadora terminal AmL*) INFO terminal computer; **~ vectorial** *Esp* (*cf computadora vectorial AmL*) INFO array processor (*AP*)

ordenanza[1] *f* DER ordinance (*AmE*); **~ comercial** ECON trade regulation

ordenanza[2] *m* RRHH office boy

ordenar *vt* COM GEN bid, GES enjoin; ◆ **~ algo** COM GEN put sth into order; **~ por antigüedad** CONT *cuentas* age; **~ por fecha** CONT *cuentas* age

órdenes[1]: **~ casadas** *f pl* BOLSA matched orders; **~ emparejadas** *f pl* BOLSA matched orders

órdenes[2]: **a ~** *fra* COM GEN for orders (*fo*)

organicidad *f* COM GEN organicity (*jarg*)

organigrama *m* COM GEN flowchart, organization chart; **~ administrativo** ADMIN, GES management chart; **~ de correspondencia** GES pertinence chart; **~ funcional** COM GEN flowchart; **~ de jerarquización intermedia** *f Esp* (*cf línea y staff AmL*) RRHH line and staff

organismo: **~ de asignación presupuestaria** *m* FIN continuing appropriation authority; **~ de clasificación** *m* BOLSA, FIN *valores* rating agency; **~ de clasificación de valores** *m* BOLSA, FIN rating agency; **~ consultivo** *m* COM GEN *comités y equipos*, GES consultative body; **~ de financiación** *m* FIN funding agency; **~ financiero ejecutivo** *m* FIN financial signing authority; **~ gubernamental** *m* FISC, POL public authority; **~ internacional** *m* COM GEN international agency; **~ legal** *m* DER statutory body; **~ de planificación** *m* MED AMB planning authority; **~ con potestad normativa** *m* COM GEN regulatory agency; **~ profesional** *m* COM GEN professional body; **~ público** *m* COM GEN public body; **~ regulador** *m* COM GEN, DER regulatory body; **~ de revisión** *m* GES, RRHH, V&M review body; **~ de revisión de los salarios más altos** *m* GES, RRHH top salaries review body; **~ del sector público** *m* COM GEN, FISC public sector body; **~ de servicio público** *m* COM GEN, FISC public service body

organización *f* COM GEN *compañía* organization (*org*); **~ sin ánimo de lucro** COM GEN, FISC nonprofit-making organization (*AmE*), non-profit-making organization (*BrE*); **~ autorregulada** BOLSA, COM GEN self-regulating organization (*SRO*); **~ autorreguladora** COM GEN self-regulatory organization (*SRO*); **~ de ayuda a la exportación** IMP/EXP export facilitation organization; **~ benéfica** FISC, PROT SOC charitable organization; **~ celular** IND *producción* cell organization; **~ comercial** COM GEN trade organization; **~ comercial multilateral** ECON, POL multilateral trade organization; **~ del consumidor** V&M consumer organization; **~ de cuadros directivos** RRHH line organization; **~ de cuadros y personal subalterno** GES, RRHH line and staff organization; **~ educativa** FISC, PROT SOC educational organization; **~ de la empresa** COM GEN business organization; **~ estricta** GES tight ship (*infrml*); **~ exterior** COM GEN field organization; **~ funcional** COM GEN, GES functional organization; **~ de la gestión** RRHH management organization; **~ horizontal** GES flat organization; **~ industrial** IND industrial organization (*IO*); **~ informal** COM GEN *sociedad*, GES informal organization; **~ de línea y personal** GES, RRHH line and staff organization; **~ lineal** COM GEN, GES line organization; **~ matricial** GES matrix organization;

~ matriz GES matrix organization; **~ y métodos** GES organization and methods (*O&M*); **~ de negocios** COM GEN business organization; **~ no gubernamental** (*ONG*) POL nongovernmental organization (*NGO*); **~ de oficinas** GES office management; **~ del personal** GES, RRHH staff organization; **~ del producto** GES, V&M product organization; **~ en el propio campo de la empresa** IMP/EXP, IND company's own field organization; **~ de un proyecto** FIN, GES project planning; **~ regional** COM GEN, GES regional organization; **~ religiosa** FISC religious organization; **~ social** POL social organization; **~ del trabajo** COM GEN, GES, RRHH work organization; **~ en tres niveles** COM GEN three-ply organization (*jarg*); **~ de ventas** V&M sales organization; **~ vertical** GES vertical organization

Organización: **~ de Aviación Civil Internacional** *f* TRANSP International Civil Aviation Organization (*ICAO*); **~ de Consumidores y Usuarios** *f* (*OCU*) PROT SOC consumer protection advisory bureau, ≈ Consumers' Advisory Council (*AmE*) (*CAC*), ≈ Consumers' Association (*BrE*) (*CA*); **~ para la Cooperación Comercial** *f* ECON Organization for Trade Co-operation (*OTC*); **~ para la Cooperación y Desarrollo Económicos** *f* (*OCDE*) ECON, POL Organization for Economic Cooperation and Development (*OECD*); **~ para la Cooperación Económica Europea** *f* ECON, POL Organization for European Economic Cooperation (*OEEC*); **~ de Estados Centroamericanos** *f* (*OEAC*) ECON, POL Organization of Central American States (*OCAS*); **~ Europea de Control de Calidad** *f* COM GEN, POL European Organization for Quality Control (*EOQC*); **~ Europea de Fomento Comercial** *f* ECON, POL European Trade Promotion Organization (*ETPO*); **~ Europea de Investigaciones Espaciales** *f* IND, POL European Space Research Organization (*ESRO*); **~ Europea de Patentes** *f* DER, PATENT European Patent Organization (*EPO*); **~ Europea de Pruebas y Certificaciones** *f* COM GEN European Organization for Testing and Certification; **~ Europea de Transportes** *f* (*OET*) TRANSP European Transport Organization (*ETO*); **~ para las Exposiciones Internacionales** *f* V&M Organization for International Exhibitions; **~ Internacional de Comercio** *f* (*OIC*) COM GEN International Trade Organization (*ITO*); **~ Internacional de Comisiones de Valores** *f* BOLSA International Organization of Securities Commissions (*IOSCO*); **~ Internacional Marítima de Satélites** *f* (*INMARSAT*) COMS, TRANSP International Maritime Satellite Organization (*INMARSAT*); **~ Internacional de Metrología Legal** *f* (*OIML*) COM GEN International Organization for Legal Metrology (*OIML*); **~ Internacional de Mineros** *f* IND International Miners' Organization (*IMO*); **~ Internacional de Normalización** *f* (*OIN*) COM GEN International Standards Organization (*ISO*); **~ Internacional Patronal** *f* RRHH International Organization of Employers (*IOE*); **~ Internacional de Puertos** *f* IMP/EXP, TRANSP International Association of Ports and Harbours (*BrE*) (*IAPH*); **~ Internacional Reguladora de Valores** *f* BOLSA International Securities Regulatory Organization (*ISRO*); **~ Internacional de Trabajo** *f* (*OIT*) POL, PROT SOC, RRHH International Labor Organization (*AmE*) (*ILO*), International Labour Organization (*BrE*) (*ILO*); **~ Marítima Internacional** *f* IND, TRANSP International Maritime Organization (*IMO*); **~ Mundial para la Propiedad Intelectual** *f* DER World Intellectual Property Organization (*WIPO*); **~ Mundial de la Salud** *f* (*OMS*) POL, PROT SOC World Health Organization (*WHO*); **~ de las Naciones Unidas** *f* (*ONU*) ECON, POL United Nations Organization (*UNO*); **~ de las Naciones Unidas para la Agricultura y Alimentación** *f* (*FAO*) ECON, POL Food and Agriculture Organization (*FAO*); **~ de las Naciones Unidas para el Desarrollo Industrial** *f* (*ONUDI*) ECON, IND, POL United Nations Industrial Development Organization (*UNIDO*); **~ de los Países Exportadores de Petróleo** *f* (*OPEP*) IMP/EXP, POL Organization of Petroleum Exporting Countries (*OPEC*); **~ del Tratado del Atlántico Norte** *f* (*OTAN*) POL North Atlantic Treaty Organization (*NATO*)

organizador[1]: **~ personal** *m* ADMIN organizer; **~ de escritorio** *m,f* ADMIN desk planner

organizador[2],**a**: **~ de una reunión** *m,f* GES, RRHH convenor; **~ de ventas** *m,f* V&M sales organizer

organizar *vt* COM GEN organize, GES *conferencia* stage; ◆ **~ una huelga** RRHH stage a strike, stage a walkout; **~ una huelga de celo** RRHH stage a go-slow (*jarg*)

órgano: **~ consultivo** *m* COM GEN *comités y consejos* advisory body

orientación[1]: **de ~ comercial** *adj* COM GEN, RRHH business-oriented; **de ~ profesional** *adj* COM GEN, RRHH career-oriented

orientación[2] *f* COM GEN, POL orientation, V&M *publicidad* line (*jarg*); **~ de los acontecimientos** COM GEN trend of events; **~ del cliente** V&M customer orientation; **~ del consumo** V&M consumer orientation; **~ interna** GES, RRHH internal orientation; **~ de marketing** V&M marketing orientation; **~ profesional** RRHH vocational guidance; **~ prudente de una cartera** COM GEN prudent portfolio approach; **~ de ventas** V&M sales orientation

orientado: **~ al cliente** *adj* COM GEN customer-oriented; **~ al consumidor** *adj* COM GEN consumer-oriented; **~ al mercado** *adj* V&M market-oriented; **~ al usuario** *adj* COM GEN, INFO, V&M user-oriented; **~ hacia los negocios** *adj* COM GEN, RRHH business-oriented; **~ a la investigación** *adj* COM GEN, IND research-oriented

orientador, a: **~ vocacional** *m,f* RRHH careers advisor, careers officer

orientar *vt* COM GEN *salida, problema* address; ◆ **~ hacia** GES gear towards

original *m* COM GEN original, MEDIOS *radiodifusión* master, original; **~ del anuncio** MEDIOS advertising copy

orilla *f* TRANSP shore

oriundo *adj* DER, POL native

oro: **~ en custodia** *m* ECON earmarked gold; **~ depositado como garantía** *m* ECON earmarked gold; **~ negro** *m* MED AMB *petróleo* black gold; **~ y plata en lingotes** *m* BANCA bullion; **~ puro** *m* MED AMB solid gold

oscilaciones *f pl* COM GEN swing; **~ estacionales** COM GEN, ECON seasonal fluctuations; **~ de los tipos de cambio** *m pl* COM GEN, ECON exchange rate movements

oscilar *vt* COM GEN *precios* fluctuate

OSI *abr* (*interconexión de sistemas abiertos*) INFO OSI (*open systems interconnection*)

ostentar *vt* COM GEN flaunt

OTAC *abr* (*Oficina Técnica de Administración Cambiaria*) ECON, POL Foreign Exchange Administration Technical Office

OTAN *abr* (*Organización del Tratado del Atlántico Norte*) POL NATO (*North Atlantic Treaty Organization*)

otorgante *mf* DER, INMOB grantor

otorgar *vt* BANCA *préstamo* provide, grant, COM GEN *proyecto, plan* agree to, PATENT *permiso* grant; ◆ **~ a alguien el derecho a** COM GEN give sb the right to; **~ ante notario** DER notarize; **~ el derecho** COM GEN confer the right; **~ importancia a** COM GEN *argumento, suposición* lend weight to

output *m* CONT, ECON output

overbooking *m* COM GEN overbooking

oxidado *adj* IND rusty

P

p *abr* (*página*) COM GEN pg. (*page*), p. (*page*)

pabellón *m* TRANSP *navegación* flag

PAC *abr* (*Política Agrícola Común*) ECON, POL CAP (*Common Agricultural Policy*)

paciente: ~ **privado(-a)** *m,f* PROT SOC private patient

pactar *vt* COM GEN agree

pacto *m* COM GEN *acuerdo* agreement, pact; ~ **de ayuda mutua** ECON, POL mutual aid pact; ~ **bancario regional** BANCA regional banking pact; ~ **de caballeros** COM GEN, DER gentleman's agreement; ~ **de no competencia** DER, V&M no-competition pact; ~ **de protección** FIN protective covenant; ~ **de recompra** (*repo*) BOLSA repurchase agreement (*repo, RP*); ~ **de retrocompra** DER *contrato* buy-back agreement

PAD *abr* (*proceso automático de datos*) INFO ADP (*automatic data processing*)

padre *m* BANCA senior, INFO parent; ~ **soltero** COM GEN single father, single parent

PAF *abr* (*porcentaje anual fijo*) BANCA, FIN FAP (*fixed annual percentage*)

pág *abr* (*página*) COM GEN pg. (*page*), p. (*page*)

paga: ~ **adicional** *f* RRHH additional pay; ~ **de antigüedad** *f* RRHH longevity pay; ~ **extra** *f* RRHH extra pay; ~ **extraordinaria de Navidad** *f* RRHH Christmas bonus; ~ **de garantía** *f* RRHH guarantee pay, guaranty pay; ~ **por horas extra** *f* RRHH overtime pay; ~ **por horas extraordinarias** *f* RRHH overtime pay; ~ **de huelga** *f* RRHH strike pay; ~ **por incentivos** *f* RRHH incentive pay scheme; ~ **por maternidad** *f* PROT SOC, RRHH maternity pay; ~ **por mérito** *f* RRHH merit pay; ~ **retrospectiva** *f* RRHH retrospective pay; ~ **de vacaciones** *f* RRHH vacation pay (*AmE*), holiday pay (*BrE*)

pagadero *adj* BOLSA mature, COM GEN payable, FIN mature; ◆ **hacer** ~ **a** BANCA make payable to; ~ **en** BANCA, COM GEN, FIN payable on; ~ **al vencimiento** BOLSA, COM GEN payable at maturity; ~ **anticipadamente** COM GEN payable in advance; ~ **después del aviso** FIN payable after notice; ~ **mensualmente a plazo vencido** BANCA, COM GEN, FIN payable monthly in arrears

pagado *adj* COM GEN *cantidades, dividendos* paid (*pd*); ◆ **no** ~ COM GEN unpaid; ~ **por adelantado** COM GEN prepaid (*p.p., Ppd*); ~ **por agente** TRANSP paid by agent (*PBA*); ~ **al contado** COM GEN cash settled; ~ **por hora** RRHH hourly paid; ~ **con los más altos salarios** RRHH top wages paid; ~ **por pieza** RRHH paid by piece rate; ~ **por unidad** RRHH paid by the piece; **totalmente** ~ COM GEN fully paid (*f.p.*)

pagador, a *m,f* FIN disburser, COM GEN payer (*BrE*), payor (*AmE*), RRHH paymaster; ~ **moroso(-a)** COM GEN, FIN slow payer

pagar 1. *vt* BANCA pay back, pay in, COM GEN pay, DER *deuda, impuesto* acquit, FIN *persona* pay back; ◆ ~ **la carga según medición** TRANSP pay for cargo by measurement; **no** ~ **un cheque** BANCA dishonor a check (*AmE*), dishonour a cheque (*BrE*); ~ **como cargamento** SEG pay as cargo; ~ **por completo** COM

GEN, FIN pay in full; ~ **la cuenta** COM GEN pay the bill; ~ **una cuota** COM GEN pay an installment (*AmE*), pay an instalment (*BrE*); ~ **una fianza a alguien** DER bail sb out (*infrml*); ~ **los gastos** COM GEN pay expenses; ~ **una letra** FIN take up a bill; ~ **mucho por algo** COM GEN pay top dollar for sth (*AmE*), pay top whack for sth (*BrE*) (*infrml*); ~ **a la orden de** BANCA pay to the order of; ~ **en origen** FISC *dividendo* exempt; ~ **un plazo** COM GEN, pay an installment (*AmE*), pay an instalment (*BrE*); ~ **totalmente** COM GEN, FIN pay in full; **2.** *vi* COM GEN pay; ◆ ~ **anualmente** COM GEN, RRHH pay yearly; ~ **al contado** *Esp* (*cf pagar de contado AmL*) COM GEN pay cash, pay in cash; ~ **de contado** *AmL* (*cf pagar al contado Esp*) COM GEN pay cash, pay in cash; ~ **en efectivo** FIN pay in ready cash; ~ **en especie** COM GEN pay in specie, COM GEN, FIN pay in kind; ~ **por giro** BANCA pay by giro; ~ **por hora** RRHH pay by the hour; ~ **en metálico** COM GEN pay cash; ~ **semanalmente** COM GEN, RRHH pay weekly; ~ **trimestralmente** COM GEN, RRHH pay quarterly

pagaré *m* BANCA bill, promissory note (*P/N, PN*), COM GEN bill, I owe you (*IOU*), promissory note (*P/N, PN*), FIN bill, promissory note (*P/N, PN*), TRANSP due bill; ~ **avalado** BANCA accommodation note; ~ **bancario** BANCA bank bill (*AmE*); ~ **deteriorado** BANCA mutilated note; ~ **especial** BANCA balloon note; ~ **de favor** BANCA accommodation bill; ~ **para financiar un proyecto** BOLSA project note; ~ **con interés variable** BANCA floating-rate note; ~ **negociable** BOLSA tradeable promissory note; ~ **con pacto de recompra** FIN *hoja de balance* note under repurchase agreement; ~ **solidario** FIN joint promissory note; ~ **del tesoro** BOLSA treasury bill (*T-bill*), treasury note; ~ **a la vista** COM GEN demand note; ~ **a la vista de tipo variable** BANCA variable-rate demand note

pagarés: ~ **del Tesoro sin deducción en origen** *m pl* BANCA, FIN national savings certificates (*BrE*)

página *f* (*p, pág.*) ADMIN, COM GEN, INFO page (*p., pg.*); ~ **asabanada** COM GEN, MEDIOS *imprenta* broadsheet; ~ **frontal** INFO home page; ~ **de portada** MEDIOS *prensa* title page; ~ **principal** INFO home page; ~ **web** INFO Web page

paginación *f* COM GEN pagination

paginar *vt* COM GEN paginate

páginas *f pl* (*págs.*) COM GEN pages (*pp.*); ~ **de negocios** COM GEN *de los periódicos* business pages

Páginas: ~ **Amarillas** *f pl* COMS, V&M Yellow Pages®

pago[1]: **sin** ~ **de alquiler** *adj* FISC, INMOB rent-free

pago[2] *m* BANCA pay-out, settlement, COM GEN payment (*PYT*), pay-out, CONT, FIN cash flow; ~ **adelantado** CONT cash in advance, money up front; ~ **adelantado del impuesto** FISC forward averaging, forward averaging tax; ~ **al buen fin** SEG *naval* no cure no pay; ~ **al contado** COM GEN cash payment, cash and carry; ~ **al hacer el pedido** COM GEN cash with order (*c.w.o.*); ~ **del alquiler** INMOB, PROT SOC rental payment; ~ **de amortización** FIN amortization payment; ~ **antes de la entrega** COM GEN, ECON, FIN cash before delivery (*CBD*); ~ **antes del vencimiento** COM GEN prepayment;

~ **anticipado** CONT advance payment; ~ **anticipado de derechos** FISC advance royalty payment; ~ **anual** COM GEN annual payment, yearly payment, FISC annuity payment; ~ **de anualidad** FISC anuity payment; ~ **de anualidad del seguro** SEG insurance annuity payment; ~ **aplazado** BANCA, FIN installment payment (*AmE*), instalment payment (*BrE*); ~ **de asistencia pública** PROT SOC, RRHH welfare payment; ~ **de asistencia social** PROT SOC social assistance payment; ~ **atrasado** BANCA, CONT, FIN outstanding payment, payment in arrears; ~ **de atrasos** RRHH back pay; ~ **por aval** FIN accommodation payment; ~ **bajo protesta** DER payment under protest; ~ **bajo reclamación** DER payment under protest; ~ **bilateral** POL bilateral disbursement; ~ **de un cheque** BANCA check payment (*AmE*), cheque payment (*BrE*); ~ **del cliente** BANCA user fee; ~ **de compensación** FISC equalization payment; ~ **compensatorio** ECON *agricultura* deficiency payment, compensation; ~ **condicionado** BANCA, CONT contingency payment; ~ **contingente** BANCA, CONT contingency payment; ~ **contra documentación** IMP/EXP cash against documents (*c.a.d.*); ~ **contra embarque** TRANSP cash on shipment (*COS*); ~ **contractual** CONT contract payment, contractual payment; ~ **en cuenta** BANCA, COM GEN payment on account; ~ **y declaración** FISC *obligaciones* pay and file; ~ **de deferencia** COM GEN accommodation payment; ~ **de una deuda** BANCA, CONT, FIN satisfaction of a debt; ~ **diferido** COM GEN deferred payment; ~ **directo** ECON *subvenciones* direct payment; ~ **de dividendos deducibles** FISC qualifying taxable dividends paid; ~ **efectivo** RRHH real pay; ~ **electrónico** BANCA, FIN electronic payment; ~ **a la entrega** TRANSP paid on delivery (*POD*); ~ **escalonado** BANCA, FIN progress payment, stage payment; ~ **especial** BANCA balloon payment; ~ **en especie** COM GEN payment in kind; ~ **específico** COM GEN specific payment; ~ **eventual** BANCA, CONT contingency payment; ~ **ex gratia** FIN ex gratia payment; ~ **en exceso** CONT overpayment; ~ **por exceso de equipaje** TRANSP excess baggage charge; ~ **externo** FIN outward payment; ~ **extraordinario** BANCA balloon payment; ~ **de facturas** BANCA settlement of account; ~ **final superior al promedio** BOLSA *obligaciones* balloon payment; ~ **fraccionario del impuesto** FISC tax installment (*AmE*), tax instalment (*BrE*); ~ **fraccionario incorrecto del impuesto** FISC deficient tax installment (*AmE*), deficient tax instalment (*BrE*); ~ **de garantía** RRHH guarantee payment, guaranty payment; ~ **global** BANCA, FIN single payment; ~ **de hipoteca** BANCA, FIN, INMOB mortgage payment; ~ **hipotecario** BANCA, FIN, INMOB mortgage payment; ~ **por horas** RRHH time rate; ~ **igual** RRHH equal pay; ~ **imponible del subsidio familiar** FISC taxable family allowance payment; ~ **de incentivo** FISC inducement payment; ~ **inicial** BANCA, COM GEN down payment, CONT *de compra* initial outlay, RRHH front-end payment; ~ **íntegro** CONT settlement in full; ~ **de interés del bono** FISC bonus interest payment; ~ **de intereses** BANCA interest payment; ~ **de intereses sobre bonos** BOLSA bond interest; ~ **internacional** ECON international payment; ~ **interno** FIN inward payment; ~ **del IVA** FISC VAT payment (*BrE*); ~ **a largo plazo del impuesto sobre la renta** FISC long-term income averaging; ~ **con letra de cambio extranjera** FIN arbitration of exchange; ~ **en nombre de otros** CONT payment on behalf of others; ~ **nominal** COM GEN,

RRHH nominal payment; ~ **nulo** BOLSA nil paid, FIN nugatory payment; ~ **parcial** CONT, FIN part payment; ~ **pendiente** CONT, FIN amount outstanding, outstanding; ~ **pendiente de ejecución** FIN back payment; ~ **de la pensión** COM GEN retirement payment, pension payment; ~ **de pensión alimenticia** DER, FISC maintenance payment; ~ **de la pensión alimenticia de los hijos** DER, FISC child maintenance payment; ~ **a plazos** BANCA installment payment (*AmE*), instalment payment (*BrE*); ~ **preautorizado** BANCA pre-authorized payment; ~ **presupuestado** ECON, POL budget payment; ~ **presupuestario** ECON, POL *ayuda al desarrollo* budget payment; ~ **de prima** BOLSA bonus payment, premium payment, RRHH premium pay; ~ **por procedimiento legal** BOLSA payment in due course; ~ **progresivo** CONT, FIN incremental payment; ~ **prorrogado** CONT, FIN extended payment; ~ **puntual** CONT, FIN prompt payment; ~ **de la reclamación** SEG claim payment; ~ **de reclamaciones** SEG claims payment; ~ **regular** COM GEN regular payment; ~ **de renta mínima** INMOB *arrendamiento de capital* minimum lease payment; ~ **de rescate** BOLSA greenmail (*AmE*); ~ **por resultados** RRHH payment by results (*PBR*); ~ **retenido** BANCA *de cheques, letras* stopped payment; ~ **secreto** COM GEN undercover payment, RRHH secret payment; ~ **según desempeño** RRHH performance-related pay (*PRP*); ~ **según resultados** RRHH payment by results (*PBR*); ~ **simple** BANCA, FIN clean payment; ~ **por subsidio familiar** FISC family allowance payment; ~ **tardío** CONT, FIN late payment; ~ **con tarjeta de crédito** COM GEN credit card payment; ~ **de transferencia** BANCA, FIN transfer payment; ~ **trimestral** COM GEN quarterly installment (*AmE*), quarterly instalment (*BrE*); ~ **del usuario** CONT user charge; ♦ **contra** ~ COM GEN against payment; **en** ~ **de** BANCA, COM GEN, FIN *deuda* in settlement of, CONT in satisfaction of; ~ **a favor de** COM GEN payment made to
pagos *m pl* FIN monies paid out
págs. *abr* (*páginas*) COM GEN pp. (*pages*)
país: ~ **sin acceso al mar** *m* MED AMB landlocked country; ~ **anfitrión** *m* COM GEN, OCIO host country; ~ **autónomo** *m* POL self-governing nation; ~ **carente de petróleo** *m* MED AMB nonoil country; ~ **desarrollado** *m* ECON, POL developed country (*DC*), advanced country (*AC*); ~ **en desarrollo** *m* ECON, POL less-developed country (*LDC*), developing country; ~ **de destino** *m* IMP/EXP country of destination; ~ **donante** *m* ECON *de ayuda internacional*, POL donor country; ~ **dotado de autogobierno** *m* POL self-governing nation; ~ **exportador de petróleo** *m* IMP/EXP oil-exporting country; ~ **sin litoral** *m* MED AMB landlocked country; ~ **de origen** *m* IMP/EXP country of origin (*COO*); ~ **prestatario** *m* ECON borrower country; ~ **productor de petróleo** *m* ECON, MED AMB, POL oil-producing country; ~ **de reciente industrialización** *m* ECON, IND newly industrialized country (*NIC*); ~ **recientemente industrializado** *m* ECON, IND newly industrialized country (*NIC*); ~ **de registro** *m* TRANSP state of registry; ~ **de residencia** *m* FISC, POL country of residence; ~ **de riesgo límite** *m* COM GEN country of ultimate risk; ~ **sin salida al mar** *m* MED AMB landlocked country; ~ **sede** *m* COM GEN, IMP/EXP home country; ~ **subdesarrollado** *m* COM GEN underdeveloped country; ~ **del tercer mundo** *m* COM GEN third world country; ~ **vecino** *m* COM GEN neighbouring

country (*BrE*), neighboring country (*AmE*); ~ **en vías de desarrollo** *m* COM GEN developing country

países: ~ **alpinos** *m pl* COM GEN Alpine countries; ~ **desarrollados** *m pl* COM GEN First World countries; ~ **de economía planificada** *m pl* COM GEN Second World countries; ~ **industrializados** *m pl* COM GEN First World countries, industrialized countries; ~ **nórdicos** *m pl* COM GEN Nordic countries; ~ **y territorios asociados de ultramar** *m pl* ECON, POL associated overseas countries and territories (*AOCTs*)

palabra *f* COM GEN, INFO word; ~ **clave** INFO keyword; ~ **de moda** COM GEN buzzword (*infrml*)

palabras: ~ **por minuto** *fra* (*ppm*) ADMIN, RRHH words per minute (*wpm*)

palanca: ~ **basculante** *f* INFO toggle; ~ **financiera** *f* BOLSA, CONT, FIN leverage; ~ **de mando** *f* INFO joystick

pálet *m AmL* (*cf paleta Esp, cf bandeja Esp*) IND, TRANSP paddle, pallet

paleta *f Esp* (*cf pálet AmL*) IND, TRANSP paddle, pallet

paletización *f* IND, TRANSP palletization

pan *m* COM GEN bread (*infrml*); ~ **comido** COM GEN walkaway (*jarg*)

pancarta: ~ **publicitaria** *f* V&M poster display

pancartas: ~ **publicitarias** *f pl* V&M poster advertising

pandilla: ~ **de los archivadores** *m pl jarg* BOLSA cabinet crowd (*jarg*)

panel: ~ **de consumidores** *m* V&M *investigación de mercado* consumer panel; ~ **de ofertas** *m* FIN tender panel (*TP*); ~ **postal** *m* V&M postal panel; ~ **publicitario** *m* V&M *estación de ferrocarril* adrail, *parada de autobús* adshel

paneuropeo *adj* COM GEN pan-European

panfleto *m* COM GEN pamphlet

pánico *m* BOLSA *entre vendedores* stampede; ~ **financiero** FIN financial panic

panorama *m* COM GEN *expectativas, perspectivas* picture; ~ **del mercado** BOLSA market view

pantalla *f* INFO screen, *ordenador* monitor; ~ **a color** INFO color display (*AmE*), colour display (*BrE*); ~ **de computador** *AmL ver* pantalla de computadora *AmL*; ~ **de computadora** *AmL* (*cf pantalla de ordenador Esp*) INFO computer screen; ~ **dividida** INFO split screen; ~ **de ordenador** *Esp* (*cf pantalla de computadora AmL*) INFO computer screen; ~ **de precios electrónica** BOLSA electronic posting board; ~ **protectora de seguridad** COM GEN protective safety screen; ~ **sensible al tacto** INFO touch-sensitive screen; ~ **de televisión** COMS television screen; ~ **terminal** INFO terminal screen; ~ **de video** *AmL*, ~ **de vídeo** *Esp* COMS video display; ◆ **a toda** ~ INFO full screen

panza *f* TRANSP belly

pañol: ~ **permanente** *m* TRANSP permanent bunker (*PB*)

papel *m* COM GEN paper, FIN 1000-peseta note; ~ **avalado** BANCA, COM GEN accommodation paper; ~ **avitelado** ADMIN wove paper; ~ **de borrador** COM GEN scrap paper; ~ **carbón** ADMIN, COMS carbon paper; ~ **comercial** COM GEN commercial paper (*CP*); ~ **comercial en esterlinas** BANCA, BOLSA, BOLSA sterling commercial paper (*SCP*); ~ **continuo** INFO continuous stationery; ~ **de copia** COM GEN manifold; ~ **para correo aéreo** COMS airmail paper; ~ **cortado** INFO cut paper; ~ **cuché mate** V&M *publicidad* art matt paper; ~ **del Estado** BOLSA gilt (*BrE*); ~ **financiero** FIN

finance paper; ~ **glaseado** MEDIOS glossy paper; ~ **moneda** BANCA, ECON, FIN paper money (*BrE*), greenback (*AmE*); ~ **oro** BANCA paper gold; ~ **de pago** COM GEN money order (*MO*); ~ **pautado** COM GEN ruled paper; ~ **de primera línea** BOLSA prime paper; ~ **a prueba de humedad** IND waterproof paper; ~ **reciclado** MED AMB recycled paper; ~ **reglado** COM GEN ruled paper; ~ **satinado** COM GEN, COMS, MEDIOS glossy paper

papeleo *m* ADMIN paperwork

papelera *f* COM GEN dump bin

papelería *m pl* ADMIN, COM GEN stationery

papelero *m* COM GEN stationer

papeles: ~ **contables** *m pl* CONT accounting papers; ~ **de trabajo** *m pl* CONT working papers; ~ **de trabajo de auditoría** *m pl* CONT audit working papers

papeleta *f* POL, RRHH *elección sindical* ballot paper, voting paper; ~ **anulada** COM GEN, POL, RRHH spoilt ballot paper; ~ **de saludos** COM GEN, COMS, V&M compliment slip; ~ **de votación** *Esp* (*cf boleta AmL*) BOLSA dealing slip, POL, RRHH *elección sindical* ballot paper, voting paper; ~ **de voto** POL, RRHH *elección sindical* ballot paper, voting paper; ~ **de voto defectuosa** COM GEN, POL spoilt voting paper

papelote *m* MED AMB waste paper

paquete *m* COM GEN, COMS packet (*pkt.*) parcel, package (*pkg.*), ECON *de reformas* package, FIN *de acciones* block, *de subvenciones, incentivos* package (*pkg.*), INFO package, OCIO *viajes* package deal, TRANSP, V&M package (*pkg.*); ~ **de acciones** BOLSA block of shares, block; ~ **de aplicaciones** INFO applications package; ~ **comercial** CONT, FIN business package; ~ **compuesto** V&M composite package; ~ **de contabilidad** INFO accounting package; ~ **contable** INFO accounting package; ~ **de decisiones** FIN, GES decision package; ~ **económico** COM GEN economy pack; ~ **de exposición** *f* V&M display pack; ~ **familiar** COM GEN family-size pack; ~ **financiero** FIN financing package; ~ **de gestión** INFO business package; ~ **del impuesto sobre la renta** FISC income-tax package; ~ **informático** INFO computer package; ~ **informativo** V&M press pack; ~ **mayoritario** BOLSA majority stake; ~ **de menos de 100 acciones** BOLSA odd-lot (*jarg*); ~ **minoritario** BOLSA minority stake; ~ **preparado para su despacho** COM GEN, COMS parcel awaiting delivery; ~ **de programas** FIN, GES, INFO software package, program package; ~ **de prueba** INFO testdeck; ~ **de reformas** POL reform package; ~ **de reivindicaciones** RRHH package deal (*BrE*); ~ **de remuneración** COM GEN, RRHH remuneration package; ~ **de riesgo** FIN risk package

par[1] *adj* INFO even

par[2] *m* COM GEN par; ◆ **a la** ~ BOLSA, COM GEN, CONT at par; **bajo la** ~ BOLSA, COM GEN, CONT below par; **sobre la** ~ BOLSA, COM GEN, CONT above par

parada *f* COM GEN *fábrica, ordenador* shutdown; ~ **de taxis** TRANSP taxi rank

paradigma: ~ **económico** *m* ECON economic paradigm

parado[1] *adj* ECON, RRHH, PROT SOC jobless, out of work, unemployed

parado[2](**-a**): ~ **de larga duración** *m,f* (*PLD*) ECON, PROT SOC, RRHH long-term unemployed (*LTU*)

paradoja: ~ **de Condorcet** *f* POL Condorcet paradox; ~ **de la frugalidad** *f* ECON thrift paradox; ~ **de Giffen** *f*

ECON Giffen paradox; ~ **de Leontief** *f* ECON Leontief paradox; ~ **de San Petersburgo** *f* ECON St Petersburg paradox; ~ **de la votación** *f* ECON voting paradox

paraíso *m* OCIO gods; ~ **fiscal** ECON, FISC tax haven; ~ **de precios** V&M price haven

paralegal *adj* DER paralegal

paralelo: en ~ con *fra* COM GEN in parallel with

paralización *f* COM GEN stalemate, *de negocios* slack

paralizado: ~ **por la huelga** *adj* RRHH strikebound

parámetro *m* COM GEN, INFO, MAT parameter; ~ **de valoración de una opción** BOLSA option-pricing parameter

parámetros *m pl* FIN bench mark

parar *vt* INFO stop

pararse *v refl* INFO stop

parásito *m* *infrml* ECON, PROT SOC, RRHH free rider (*infrml*), ghost (*infrml*) (*AmE*)

parcela *f* INMOB plot, *de tierra* parcel; ~ **y bloque** INMOB plot and block

parcelar *vt* INMOB parcel out

parcial *adj* COM GEN biased, DER contributory

parcialidad: ~ **del entrevistador** *f* MEDIOS, V&M interviewer bias

parcialmente: ~ **pagado** *adj* BOLSA *acciones* partly paid

parecer *vi* COM GEN appear; **contra su propio** ~ *fra* COM GEN against one's judgment

pared: ~ **china** *f* BANCA Chinese wall; ~ **medianera** *f* COM GEN party wall

parentesco *m* FISC relationship

paréntesis *m pl* INFO, MEDIOS *tipografía* round brackets

paridad *f* COM GEN parity; ~ **aceptada** V&M accepted pairing; ~ **adquisitiva** ECON purchasing parity; ~ **competitiva** V&M competitive parity; ~ **de conversión** BOLSA conversion parity; ~ **intrínseca** BANCA, ECON mint par; ~ **móvil** BOLSA sliding parity; ~ **oro** FIN gold parity; ~ **par** INFO even parity; ~ **de tipo de cambio** BANCA parity of exchange; ~ **de tipos** TRANSP parity of rates

parlamentario, -a: ~ **europeo(-a)** *m,f* POL European Member of Parliament (*Euro MP*)

parlamento *m* COM GEN parliament

Parlamento: ~ **Federal** *m* POL Federal Parliament

paro *m* COM GEN unemployment; ~ **conyuntural** ECON, RRHH frictional unemployment; ~ **encubierto** PROT SOC concealed unemployment; ~ **de larga duración** ECON, RRHH long-term unemployment; ~ **parcial** ECON, PROT SOC, RRHH partial unemployment; ~ **registrado** RRHH registered unemployment; ~ **voluntario** ECON, RRHH voluntary unemployment; ◆ **estar en el** ~ COM GEN, RRHH be on the dole (*infrml*), be unemployed

parpadear *vi* INFO blink, flicker

parpadeo *m* INFO *pantalla* blink, flicker

parque *m* COM GEN park, yard, estate, TRANSP *de coches de empresa* fleet; ~ **de atracciones** OCIO theme park; ~ **científico** IND science park; ~ **de desguace** COM GEN scrap yard; ~ **de empaquetado** TRANSP bundling yard; ~ **industrial** IND, INMOB industrial estate (*BrE*), industrial park (*AmE*), business park; ~ **portuario de contenedores** TRANSP dock container park; ~ **tecnológico** ECON, IND technological park; ~ **de vivienda móvil** INMOB mobile-home park (*BrE*), trailer park (*AmE*)

parqué *m* BOLSA floor, ECON ring-fence (*jarg*); ~ **de operaciones** BOLSA trading floor

párrafo *m* ADMIN, DER, MEDIOS paragraph; ~ **inicial** MEDIOS leader, lead article

parrilla *f* INFO grid; ~ **de gestión** GES managerial grid

parte *f* DER *en contrato* party, FIN *dividendo, cantidad* portion; ~ **de un acuerdo** RRHH party to an agreement; ~ **de la adquisición de valores pagadera al contado** BANCA margin requirement; ~ **agraviada** DER injured party; ~ **alcista** BOLSA long leg; ~ **alícuota** MAT aliquot part; ~ **alícuota progresiva** MAT progressive aliquot part; ~ **alta de la gama** COM GEN, V&M top end of the range; ~ **característica** PATENT characterizing portion; ~ **contratante** DER contracting party, covenantor; ~ **del contrato** DER party to a contract; ~ **convenida** FISC agreed portion; ~ **del crédito** FIN credit tranche; ~ **cualificada** DER *contrato* competent party; ~ **delantera de la tienda** COM GEN, V&M shop front; ~ **de horas trabajadas** *m* COM GEN time sheet; ~ **imponible** FISC taxable quota; ~ **integrante** COM GEN integral part; ~ **interesada** COM GEN related party; ~ **de la jurisprudencia** DER piece of legislation; ~ **del león** COM GEN lion's share; ~ **más baja de la gama** COM GEN, V&M bottom end of the range; ~ **de la negociación** BOLSA *mercado monetario* trading party; ~ **no utilizada** FISC unused part; ~ **notificante** TRANSP notifying party; ~ **ofendida** DER injured party; ~ **perjudicada** DER injured party; ~ **predominante** DER prevailing party; ~ **recortable** BANCA *de chequera* tear-off portion; ~ **de tráfico** *m* TRANSP traffic forecast; ◆ **por mi** ~ COM GEN for my part

partes: ~ **por millón** *f pl* COM GEN parts per million (*ppm*)

partición *f* INFO, INMOB partition; ~ **de acciones** BOLSA share split; ~ **de renta a efectos tributarios** FISC income splitting system

participación *f* COM GEN participation, holding; ~ **accionaria** BOLSA shareholding; ~ **en un banco** BANCA holding in a bank; ~ **en los beneficios** RRHH profit sharing; ~ **en bienes raíces** BOLSA interest in real property; ~ **en cambio de divisas** BANCA foreign exchange holding; ~ **en el capital social** BOLSA equity ownership; ~ **en una compañía** COM GEN interest in a company; ~ **controladora** BOLSA, RRHH controlling interest; ~ **diferida en beneficios** RRHH deferred profit-sharing; ~ **discrecional** BOLSA discretionary share; ~ **de los empleados** RRHH employee participation; ~ **de los empleados en los beneficios** RRHH employee profit sharing; ~ **en una empresa** COM GEN stake in a business; ~ **de Estado** FISC Crown share; ~ **en la explotación** FIN working interest; ~ **de la fuerza laboral** RRHH labor force participation (*AmE*), labour force participation (*BrE*); ~ **en las ganancias** CONT, FIN, RRHH profit sharing; ~ **horizontal** ECON horizontal equity; ~ **e implicación de los empleados** RRHH employee involvement and participation; ~ **en los ingresos tributarios federales** ECON, FISC general revenue sharing; ~ **inmobiliaria** INMOB stake in property (*BrE*), stake in real estate (*AmE*); ~ **mayoritaria** BOLSA majority holding; ~ **en el mercado** ECON, V&M market share; ~ **de la minoría en beneficios** CONT minority interests in profit; ~ **minoritaria** BOLSA, COM GEN minority holding, CONT minority participation; ~ **minoritaria en los beneficios** CONT minority interests in profit; ~ **minoritaria en una empresa** BOLSA minority stake in a business; ~ **de los obreros** RRHH shop-floor participation; ~ **permanente** CONT *balance general* permanent participation; ~ **del plan de producción** COM GEN share of production plan; ~ **en una póliza de seguro de vida** SEG interest in a life insurance policy; ~ **recíproca** BOLSA *entre empresas* cross holding; ~ **de la renta** FISC income splitting; ~ **en una sociedad** BOLSA interest in a partnership; ~ **del trabajador** RRHH employee participation; ~ **de los trabajadores en los beneficios** (*PTU*) GES, RRHH profit sharing; ~ **en una transacción** BOLSA participation in a transaction

participado *m* FIN *compañía* investee

participante *mf* BOLSA *en el mercado* participant, COM GEN *en negociaciones* player, GES *en una convención* participant

participar *vt* COM GEN participate, FIN hold a share

participativo *adj* COM GEN participating; ~**-democrático** GES *liderazgo de Likert* participative-democratic

particularidad *f* COM GEN particularity, *rasgo distintivo* special feature

partida *f* CONT item, IMP/EXP entry; ~ **de activo** CONT asset item; ~ **del balance** CONT balance sheet item; ~ **compensatoria** CONT offsetting entry; ~ **de defunción** COM GEN, DER death certificate; ~ **de desarrollo social** POL social development envelope; ~ **de la deuda pública** FIN, POL public debt envelope; ~ **extraordinaria** COM GEN extraordinary item, ECON below-the-line item; ~ **de gastos** CONT item of expenditure; ~ **inusual** COM GEN unusual item; ~ **del memorándum** CONT memo item, memorandum item; ~ **monetaria** CONT monetary item; ~ **de nacimiento** COM GEN, DER birth certificate; ~ **ordinaria de gasto** POL standard object of expenditure; ~ **ordinaria de ingresos** POL standard object of revenue; ~ **del pasivo** CONT liability item; ~ **pendiente** CONT outstanding item; ~ **plurianual de gastos** FIN multiyear spending envelope; ~ **plurianual de recursos** FIN multiyear resource envelope; ~ **de preferencia fiscal** CONT, FISC tax preference item; ~ **presupuestaria** BANCA budget item; ~ **de reserva** CONT reserve entry; ~ **en suspenso** BANCA, CONT, FIN suspense entry, suspense account

partidario, -a *m,f* COM GEN, POL supporter, follower; ~ **del Mercado Común** POL marketeer

partidas: ~ **invisibles** *f pl* COM GEN, ECON invisibles

partido: ~ **de la oposición** *m* POL opposition party; ~ **político** *m* COM GEN, POL political party; ~ **político legalizado** *m* FISC, POL registered political party; ~ **político reconocido** *m* FISC, POL recognized political party

Partido: ~ **Conservador** *m* POL Conservative Party (*BrE*); ~ **Laborista** *m* POL Labour Party (*BrE*); ~ **Laborista Socialista** *m* POL Socialist Labour Party; ~ **Verde** *m* MED AMB, POL Green Party

partir: ~ **la diferencia** *fra* COM GEN split the difference

pasada: ~ **de comprobación** *f* COM GEN trial run; ~ **en computador** *AmL* ver *pasada en computadora AmL*; ~ **en computadora** *f AmL* (*cf pasada de ordenador Esp*) INFO computer run; ~ **de máquina** *f* INFO, TRANSP machine run; ~ **de ordenador** *f Esp* (*cf pasada en computadora AmL*) INFO computer run

pasado *adj* (*pdo.*) COM GEN ultimo (*ult.*); ~ **de moda** COM GEN out of fashion

pasador: ~ **de espiga** *m* TRANSP *contenedores* pinlock

pasaje: ~ **inaugural** *m* TRANSP *navegación* inaugural voyage

pasajero, -a *m,f* OCIO, TRANSP passenger (*passr*); ~ **en tránsito** OCIO, TRANSP transit passenger; ~ **de vía aérea** OCIO, TRANSP air traveler (*AmE*), air traveller (*BrE*)

pasajeros: ~ **por milla** *m pl* TRANSP passenger mile

pasante *mf* COM GEN trainee, DER ≈ pupil, ≈ articled clerk

pasantería *f* BANCA, COM GEN traineeship, DER ≈ pupillage

pasapáginas *m* MEDIOS *imprenta* page-turner

pasaporte *m* COM GEN passport

pasar **1.** *vt* INMOB *propiedad* transfer; ♦ ~ **de contrabando** FISC, IMP/EXP smuggle; ~ **a limpio** COM GEN write a fair copy; ~ **a la prensa** MEDIOS pass for press; ~ **la prueba de fuego de la competencia** COM GEN stand the acid test of competition; ~ **las pruebas** MEDIOS pass the proofs; **2.** *vi* COM GEN pass, go; ♦ ~ **a administración judicial** DER, FIN go into receivership; ~ **apuros** ECON feel the pinch (*infrml*); ~ **por los canales debidos** COM GEN go through the proper channels; ~ **por los pelos** COM GEN scrape through; ~ **rozando** COM GEN scrape along (*infrml*)

pasarse *v refl* COM GEN *de una cosa a otra* switch; ♦ ~ **a opciones dentro del precio** BOLSA move into the money

pase: ~ **de asientos** *m* ADMIN, CONT posting; ~ **de asientos al libro mayor** *m* ADMIN, CONT ledger posting; ~ **de modelos** *m* COM GEN fashion show

paseo: ~ **aleatorio** *m* BOLSA, ECON random walk

pasillo *m* COM GEN *cines, tiendas, tren* aisle; ~ **rodante** COM GEN travelator; ♦ **en el** ~ POL below the gangway (*BrE*)

pasivo[1] *adj* V&M *publicidad* passive

pasivo[2] *m* COM GEN liability; ~ **aceptado** BANCA, CONT accepted liability; ~ **acumulado** BANCA, CONT accrued liability; ~ **asegurado** BANCA, CONT insured liability; ~ **consolidado** BANCA, CONT funded debt; ~ **contingente** BANCA, CONT contingent liability; ~ **corriente** BANCA, CONT current liability; ~ **devengado** BANCA, CONT accrued liability; ~ **por depósito** BANCA, CONT deposit liability; ~ **eventual** BANCA, CONT contingent liability; ~ **fijo consolidado** CONT, DER, FIN fixed liability; ~ **flotante** CONT floating debt; ~ **de garantía** BANCA, CONT guaranteed liability; ~ **interno** BANCA, CONT domestic liability; ~ **a largo plazo** BOLSA, FIN long-term liability; ~ **a más corto plazo** BOLSA, FIN shorter-term liability; ~ **de obligaciones** BOLSA, FIN bond liability; ~ **protegido** BANCA, CONT hedged liability; ~ **subordinado** CONT subordinated liability; ~ **total** BANCA, CONT total liability

paso[1]: ~ **a paso** *adj* COM GEN, INFO *programa, operación, rutina* step by step

paso[2]: ~ **de carácter** *m* ADMIN character pitch

pasos: **en** ~ **escalonados** *adv* COM GEN in graduated stages

pasta: ~ **gansa** *f infrml* COM GEN megabucks (*infrml*)

pata: ~ **abatible** *f* TRANSP *manipulación de carga* drop leg

patas: ~ **de eslinga** *f pl* TRANSP *manipulación de carga* dog hooks

patentabilidad *f* DER, PATENT patentability

patentable *adj* DER *propiedad intelectual*, PATENT patentable

patentado: **no ~** *adj* COM GEN, DER, PATENT unpatented

patentar *vt* DER, PATENT patent

patente *f* COM GEN, DER, PATENT patent (*pat.*); **~ dependiente** DER, PATENT dependent patent; **~ nacional** DER, PATENT national patent; **~ regional** DER, PATENT regional patent; **~ de sanidad defectuosa** COM GEN, PROT SOC unclean bill of health; **~ de sanidad limpia** COM GEN, PROT SOC clean bill of health; **~ de sanidad poco fiable** COM GEN, PROT SOC suspect bill of health; **~ de sanidad sucia** TRANSP *envíos* claused bill of health; **~ en tramitación** DER, PATENT patent pending (*pat. pend.*)

paternalismo *m* COM GEN, GES paternalism

patio *m* INMOB *construcción* yard; **~ de tanques** TRANSP tank farm

patología: **~ organizativa** *f* RRHH organizational pathology

patrimonial *adj* COM GEN proprietary, POL patrimonial

patrimonio *m* ECON wealth; **~ bruto** FISC gross estate; **~ directo** FISC direct equity; **~ de un fideicomiso** CONT, ECON, FIN corpus; **~ horizontal** FISC horizontal equity; **~ neto** CONT net equity; **~ personal** ECON personal wealth; **~ sucesorio** DER decedent's estate; **~ vertical** FISC vertical equity

patrocinado: **~ por el Estado** *adj* COM GEN *proyecto* government-sponsored

patrocinador, a: **~ de arte** *m,f* OCIO, V&M arts sponsor; **~ de un proyecto** *m,f* FIN project sponsor

patrocinar *vt* COM GEN sponsor

patrocinio *m* COM GEN sponsorship; **~ de arte** OCIO, V&M arts sponsorship; **~ de la beneficencia** PROT SOC charity sponsorship; **~ corporativo** V&M *promociones* corporate sponsorship

patrón[1] *m* COM GEN *de medida* standard (*Std*), INFO pattern; **~ de cambio del oro** ECON, FIN gold exchange standard; **~ dólar** ECON, FIN dollar standard; **~ de establecimiento** ECON settlement pattern; **~ indulgente** GES, RRHH *relaciones laborales* indulgency pattern (*jarg*); **~ lingote oro** ECON, FIN gold bullion standard; **~ monetario** BOLSA currency standard, ECON *internacional* monetary standard; **~ oro** ECON, FIN gold standard; **~ plata** ECON, FIN silver standard; **~ secundario** MED AMB secondary standard

patrón[2],**a** *m,f* COM GEN, RRHH employer; **~ asociado(-a)** RRHH associated employer; **~ determinado(-a)** FISC specified employer; **~ de remolcador** TRANSP *puerto* tugmaster

pausa *f* RRHH break; **~ para la publicidad** MEDIOS, V&M station break (*AmE*), commercial break (*BrE*)

pauta *f* COM GEN pattern, GES rule; **~ de la demanda** ECON demand pattern; **~ de gastos** COM GEN spending pattern; **~ de trabajo** RRHH work rule, working pattern

p.c. *abr* (*por ciento*) COM GEN p.c. (*per cent*)

PC *abr* (*ordenador personal Esp, computadora personal AmL, computador personal AmL*) INFO PC (*personal computer*)

PCGA *abr* (*Principios de Contabilidad Generalmente Aceptados*) ADMIN GAAP (*Generally Accepted Accounting Principles*)

P.D. *abr* (*posdata*) COM GEN, COMS P.S. (*postscript*)

pdo. *abr* (*pasado*) COM GEN ult. (*ultimo*)

peaje *m* COM GEN, TRANSP toll, *autopistas* road toll; **~ de pasajeros** TRANSP passenger toll; **~ de túnel** TRANSP tunnel toll

peatón *m* COM GEN pedestrian

peculiar *adj* COM GEN unique

peculiaridades: **~ del listado** *f pl* BOLSA listing particulars

pecuniario *adj* COM GEN pecuniary

PED *abr* (*procesamiento electrónico de datos*) INFO EDP (*electronic data processing*)

pedestal *m* TRANSP *fijación de contenedores* pedestal

pedido[1] *adj* COM GEN, V&M on order

pedido[2] *m* COM GEN, V&M order; **~ acumulado** COM GEN backlogged order; **~ al contado** COM GEN cash order (*co*); **~ anual** COM GEN, V&M annual order; **~ en blanco** COM GEN, V&M blank order; **~ del corredor de comercio** COM GEN, V&M broker's order; **~ por correo** V&M mail order (*MO*); **~ por correspondencia** COM GEN, V&M mail order (*MO*); **~ a crédito** COM GEN, V&M credit order; **~ sin entregar** COM GEN, V&M outstanding order; **~ en espera** COM GEN, V&M back order; **~ en existencia** COM GEN, V&M order on hand; **~ de exportación de bienes** IMP/EXP, TRANSP export of goods order; **~ de fabricación** COM GEN, IND, V&M manufacturing order; **~ en firme** V&M firm order; **~ futuro** COM GEN, V&M future order; **~ a granel** COM GEN, V&M bulk order; **~ importante** COM GEN, V&M large order; **~ imprevisto** BOLSA contingent order; **~ limitado** COM GEN, V&M limited order; **~ no despachado** COM GEN, V&M unfulfilled order; **~ original** COM GEN, V&M original order; **~ de prueba** COM GEN, V&M trial order; **~ retrasado** V&M back order; **~ urgente** COM GEN, V&M rush order; ◆ **mi ~** COM GEN my order (*m/o*)

pedir *vt* COM GEN ask for, order, *consejo* seek; ◆ **~ acciones en préstamo** BOLSA borrow stock; **~ adhesiones para algo** COM GEN invite subscriptions for sth; **~ algo** COMS send off for sth; **~ a alguien que haga algo** COM GEN require sb to do sth; **~ cuentas a alguien** COM GEN call sb to account; **~ dinero prestado a alguien** COM GEN borrow money from sb; **~ fondos prestados** BANCA borrow funds; **~ una opinión cualificada** COM GEN take expert advice; **~ la opinión de un experto** COM GEN seek expert opinion, seek expert advice; **~ prestado** COM GEN borrow; **~ prestado de** BANCA borrow from; **~ prestado a corto plazo** BOLSA borrow short; **~ prestado con intereses** BANCA borrow at interest; **~ prestado a largo plazo** BOLSA borrow long; **~ prestados fondos exteriores** COM GEN borrow external funds; **~ un préstamo sobre valores** BOLSA borrow on securities; **~ y recibir informe** *Esp* (*cf pedir y recibir reporte AmL*) COM GEN, GES debrief; **~ y recibir reporte** *AmL* (*cf pedir y recibir informe Esp*) COM GEN, GES debrief

pegar *vt* COM GEN *sello* affix

pegarse *v refl Esp* (*cf engarrotarse AmL*) IND *maquinaria* bind

pegatina: **~ del impuesto de circulación** *f* FISC tax disc (*BrE*)

p.ej. *abr* (*por ejemplo*) COM GEN e.g. (*exempli gratia, for example*)

pelea *f infrml* COM GEN fallout (*infrml*)

película *f* MEDIOS, OCIO film (*BrE*), motion picture (*AmE*), movie (*AmE*); **~ durante el vuelo** OCIO, TRANSP in-flight film (*BrE*), in-flight movie (*AmE*); ~ **de la serie B** OCIO B-movie; ~ **suplementaria** OCIO supporting film; ~ **taquillera** *jarg* OCIO box-office success, box-office draw

peligro *m* PROT SOC, RRHH danger; ~ **de incendio** PROT SOC, RRHH fire hazard; ~ **inminente** SEG imminent peril; ◆ **en** ~ **de** COM GEN in danger of

pelota *f* BANCA roundtripping (*infrml*)

pelotazo *m* FIN scoop

peloteo *m* BANCA roundtripping (*infrml*)

penalización *f* COM GEN, DER penalty; ~ **amortización anticipada** BANCA, BOLSA, FIN early withdrawal penalty; ~ **por falta de puntualidad** RRHH *relaciones industriales* quartering (*jarg*); ~ **por incumplimiento** DER penalty for noncompliance; ~ **por incumplimiento de contrato** DER penalty for breach of contract; ~ **en los intereses** BANCA interest penalty; ~ **por pago anticipado** BANCA prepayment penalty; ~ **por primera incidencia** FISC first occurrence penalty; ~ **por reembolso anticipado** BANCA early penalty; ~ **por retirada anticipada** BANCA, BOLSA, FIN early-withdrawal penalty; ~ **por segunda o posteriores incidencias** FISC second or further occurrence penalty

pendiente[1] *adj* COM GEN pending, *objeción, reclamación* outstanding; ◆ ~ **de amortizar** BOLSA, CONT, FIN unamortized; ~ **de aprobación** ECON, V&M subject to approval; ~ **de pago** COM GEN outstanding; ~ **de resolución judicial** DER sub judice

pendiente[2]: ~ **de concesión** *f* PATENT pending application; ~ **de renovación** *f* ECON substitution slope

pendolón *m* TRANSP king post

penetración *f* V&M *publicidad* penetration; ~ **acumulativa** V&M cumulative penetration; ~ **en el mercado** V&M market penetration; ~ **de ventas** V&M sales penetration

penetrar: ~ **en el mercado** *fra* V&M penetrate the market

peniche *m* TRANSP peniche

pensamiento *m* COM GEN *razonamiento* thinking; ~ **creativo** COM GEN, GES, V&M creative thinking; ~ **divergente** GES divergent thinking; ~ **lateral** COMS, GES lateral thinking; ~ **político** POL political thinking

pensar: ~ **lo impensable** *fra* COM GEN think the unthinkable

pensión *f* DER *al cónyuge, hijos* maintenance, PROT SOC pension; ~ **alimenticia** DER alimony, maintenance allowance, FISC alimony paid, separation allowance paid; ~ **de altos cargos** FIN top-hat pension (*infrml*); ~ **asegurada para la tercera edad** FIN, PROT SOC old-age pension; ~ **completa** OCIO full board; ~ **con desayuno incluido** OCIO bed and breakfast (*B&B*); ~ **del Estado** PROT SOC, RRHH state pension (*BrE*); ~ **de financiación interna** RRHH internally-funded pension; ~ **interina** FIN interim pension; ~ **de invalidez** FIN, PROT SOC, SEG disability pension; ~ **de jubilación** FIN, PROT SOC retirement pay, retirement pension, retiring allowance, old age pension; ~ **no consolidada** FIN, RRHH unfunded pension (*BrE*); ~ **no contributiva** FIN externally funded pension; ~ **de prejubilación** FIN preretirement pension; ~ **de retiro** COM GEN, CONT pension fund, superannuation scheme; ~ **de vejez** PROT SOC, SEG old age pension, old age security pension

pensionable *adj* FIN, PROT SOC, RRHH pensionable

pensionista: ~ **por jubilación** *mf* PROT SOC old age pensioner (*O.A.P.*)

peón *m* RRHH peon (*jarg*)

PEPS *abr* (*primero en entrar, primero en salir*) COM GEN, CONT FIFO (*first in, first out*)

pequeña: ~ **empresa** *f* COM GEN small business; ~ **empresa sujeta** *f* BOLSA, FISC qualifying small business corporation; ~ **y mediana empresa** *f* (*PYME*) ECON small and medium-size enterprise (*SME*); ~ **plataforma portátil** *f* TRANSP stillage

pequeño[1],**a**: ~ **inversionista** *m,f* FIN small investor; ~ **inversor, a** *m,f* FIN small investor

pequeño[2]: ~ **lote** *m* BOLSA odd-lot

pequeños: ~ **dragones** *m pl* ECON *países asiáticos recientemente industrializados* little dragons (*infrml*)

percentil *m* MAT percentile

percepción *f* COM GEN, GES cognition; ~ **selectiva** V&M selective perception; ~ **subjetiva** V&M subjective perception

perder *vt* COM GEN, DER *protección* lose; ◆ ~ **el empleo** RRHH lose one's job; ~ **por partida doble** BOLSA whipsaw (*jarg*) (*AmE*); ~ **terreno** COM GEN *en la competencia* lose ground

pérdida *f* BANCA loss, COM GEN loss, wastage, DER damage; ~ **actuarial** SEG actuarial loss; ~ **acumulativa de capital neto** FISC cumulative net capital loss; ~ **acumulativa de inversión neta** FIN cumulative net investment loss; ~ **de aficionado** FISC hobby loss; ~ **de agua** COM GEN *tubería* leak; ~ **al cierre** CONT terminal loss; ~ **de beneficios** *m* CONT, FIN revenue loss; ~ **de capital** COM GEN, CONT, ECON, FIN capital loss; ~ **de capital reembolsable** BOLSA allowable capital loss; ~ **de la clientela** COM GEN, V&M loss of custom; ~ **de cobertura al descubierto** BOLSA uncovered hedge loss; ~ **compensatoria** BOLSA compensating loss; ~ **consecuencial** SEG consequential loss; ~ **contable** CONT book loss; ~ **a corto plazo** BOLSA, FISC short-term loss; ~ **de credibilidad** V&M credibility gap; ~ **de crédito** BANCA, FIN credit loss; ~ **deducible en inversiones empresariales** FISC allowable business investment loss (*BrE*), deductible business investment loss (*AmE*); ~ **del derecho** DER loss of claim; ~ **económica** ECON economic loss; ~ **efectiva total** COM GEN, FIN, SEG *cláusulas de abandono* actual total loss; ~ **elemental** SEG elementary loss; ~ **de la embarcación** TRANSP craft loss (*c/l*); ~ **por evaporación** COM GEN shrinkage; ~ **del excedente** ECON deadweight loss; ~ **de la explotación** CONT operating loss; ~ **de explotación neta** CONT net operating loss; ~ **extraordinaria** CONT extraordinary loss; ~ **inesperada** ECON windfall loss; ~ **de información** INFO drop-out; ~ **inicial** CONT historical loss; ~ **a largo plazo** *f pl* FISC long-term loss; ~ **legal del derecho de un bien** DER forfeiture; ~ **líquida** FIN clear loss; ~ **de mercado** COM GEN loss of market; ~ **por mortalidad** FISC mortality loss; ~ **neta** CONT net loss; ~ **ordinaria** FISC ordinary loss; ~ **neta diaria** FIN, TRANSP *fletamento* net daily loss; ~ **parcial** SEG partial loss (*P/L*); ~ **pasiva** FISC passive loss; ~ **potencial** BOLSA paper loss; ~ **en el precio** BOLSA price loss; ~ **de prioridad** PATENT loss of priority; ~ **en la propiedad amortizable** CONT loss on depreciable property; ~ **real** CONT actual loss; ~ **de reinversión** CONT reinvestment loss; ~ **de remuneración** RRHH loss of pay; ~ **de salvamento** SEG salvage loss; ~ **según libros** CONT book loss; ~ **de sueldo** RRHH loss of earnings; ~ **superficial** COM GEN, FIN superficial loss;

~ **total** COM GEN, SEG total loss (*TL*), write-off; **sólo** ~ **total** COM GEN, SEG total loss only (*TLO*); ~ **total concertada** COM GEN, FIN, SEG arranged total loss; ~ **total constructiva** TRANSP *seguros marítimos* constructive total loss (*CTL*); ~ **total implícita** COM GEN, FIN, SEG constructive total loss (*CTL*); **sólo** ~ **total implícita** COM GEN, FIN, SEG constructive total loss only (*CTLO*); ~ **total incluida** COM GEN, FIN, SEG *seguros marítimos* comprised total loss; ~ **total parcial** SEG partial total loss (*PTL*); ~ **de traducción** ECON *comercio internacional* translation loss; ~ **en la transacción** ECON transaction loss; ~ **en tránsito** TRANSP loss in transit; ~ **traspasada al año siguiente** CONT carry-over loss; ~ **traspasada al periodo anterior** CONT carry-back of loss; ~ **de valor de los activos** BANCA, CONT, ECON, FIN loss in value of assets; ♦ **con** ~ COM GEN out of pocket; **con** ~ **por partida doble** BOLSA whipsawed (*jarg*) (*AmE*); **a toda** ~, **a todo riesgo** SEG all-loss, all-risk

pérdidas: ~ **agrarias** *f pl* FISC farm losses; ~ **de cuentas incobrables** *f pl* BANCA, CONT, ECON, FIN bad-debt losses; ~ **por débitos fallidos** *f pl* BANCA, CONT, ECON, FIN bad-debt losses; ~ **deducibles de la explotación agraria** *f pl* FISC deductible farm loss (*AmE*), allowable farm loss (*BrE*); ~ **con efecto retroactivo** *f* CONT, FISC carry-back loss; ~ **del ejercicio** *f pl* CONT trading losses; ~ **de explotación** *f pl* CONT business losses; ~ **financieras** *f pl* CONT, FIN financial losses; ~ **y ganancias** *f pl* CONT, FIN profit and loss (*P&L*); ~ **por insolvencias** *f pl* BANCA, CONT, ECON, FIN bad-debt losses; ~ **de inversión** *f pl* BOLSA investment loss; ~ **de inversión empresarial** *f pl* FISC business investment loss (*BIL*); ~ **llevadas a cuenta nueva** *f pl* CONT losses carried forward; ~ **no realizadas** *f pl* CONT, FIN unrealized losses; ~ **de préstamos** *f pl* BANCA, FIN loan loss; ~ **realizadas** *f pl* CONT, FIN realized losses; ~ **sufridas** *f pl* DER losses suffered; ~ **totales por préstamos** *f pl* BANCA actual loan loss

perdonar *vt* BANCA, CONT *una deuda* forgo collection of, COM GEN forgive

perecedero *adj* COM GEN, V&M *pescado, fruta* perishable

perecederos *m pl* COM GEN, V&M perishables

perfil[1]: **de** ~ **discreto** *adj* V&M low-profile

perfil[2] *m* COM GEN, TRANSP *navegación* profile; ~ **de adquisición** BANCA acquisition profile; ~ **del cliente** V&M customer profile; ~ **del consumidor** V&M consumer profile; ~ **discreto** V&M low profile; ~ **del empleado** RRHH employee profile; ~ **de la empresa** COM GEN company profile; ~ **de ingresos por edad** RRHH age-earnings profile; ~ **de los lectores** MEDIOS, V&M *investigación de mercado* readership profile; ~ **de marketing** V&M marketing profile; ~ **de mercado** V&M market profile; ~ **del modelo** COM GEN model profile; ~ **del producto** COM GEN, V&M product profile; ~ **del puesto** RRHH job profile, job specification, job spec (*infrml*); ~ **de recursos** COM GEN, RRHH resource profile; ~ **de riesgo** FIN, SEG risk profile; ~ **técnico** COM GEN technical profile; ~ **del usuario** V&M *mercadotecnia* user profile

perfilar: **sin** ~ *fra* POL broad-brush

perforación: ~ **costera** *f* IND offshore drilling; ~ **exploratoria** *f* IND wildcat drilling

perforadora *f* INFO *adminículo* punch; ~ **de cinta** INFO tape punch; ~ **de tarjetas** COM GEN card punch; ~ **de teclado** INFO key punch

perforista *mf* INFO keypuncher

pericia *f* DER know-how

periferia: ~ **del núcleo** *f* ECON core-periphery

periférico *adj* COM GEN peripheral

periféricos *m pl* V&M *relaciones públicas* peripherals

periódico[1] *adj* COM GEN, V&M periodic, periodical

periódico[2] *m* COM GEN, MEDIOS daily newspaper; ~ **de calidad** COM GEN, MEDIOS *imprenta* quality newspaper, broadsheet; ~ **económico** ECON, MEDIOS economic journal; ~ **de gran formato** COM GEN, MEDIOS *imprenta* broadsheet; ~ **independiente** COM GEN, MEDIOS free newspaper, freesheet; ~ **local** COM GEN, MEDIOS local newspaper; ~ **nacional** MEDIOS national newspaper

periodicucho *m infrml* MEDIOS *prensa* rag (*infrml*)

periodismo: ~ **electrónico** *m* COM GEN electronic news gathering, electronic journalism; ~ **financiero** *m* FIN financial journalism; ~ **sensacionalista** *m* MEDIOS chequebook journalism (*BrE*) (*infrml*), checkbook journalism (*AmE*) (*infrml*)

periodo *m* COM GEN *de tiempo* period, time span, term, stint; ~ **del alquiler** FISC, INMOB rental period, rental term; ~ **anterior** CONT prior period; ~ **aplicable** FISC relevant period; ~ **de aviso** RRHH notice period; ~ **base** FISC base period; ~ **de beneficios** FISC earnings period; ~ **breve de prosperidad** COM GEN, ECON boomlet; ~ **de carencia** FISC qualifying period; ~ **conflictivo** RRHH strife-ridden period; ~ **de conservación** BOLSA *acciones adjudicadas a empleados* retention period; ~ **contable** CONT, FIN accounting period; ~ **de contratación bursátil a crédito** BOLSA account period; ~ **de contratación bursátil a cuenta** BOLSA account period; ~ **de declaración** FISC reporting period; ~ **con derechos** BOLSA cum-rights period; ~ **sin derechos** BOLSA ex-rights period; ~ **de derroche** COM GEN spending spree (*infrml*); ~ **de digestión** BOLSA period of digestion; ~ **de discreción** COM GEN discretionary period; ~ **de emisión** IMP/EXP float time; ~ **de entrenamiento** RRHH traineeship; ~ **de espera** COM GEN waiting period; ~ **de espera previsto** BOLSA anticipated holding period; ~ **estimado** CONT estimated lapse; ~ **excluido** FISC excluded period; ~ **exento** CONT, ECON, FIN exempt period; ~ **financiero** CONT, ECON, FIN financial period; ~ **fiscal** COM GEN taxation period, fiscal period; ~ **flojo** COM GEN *en ventas*, IND, V&M slack period; ~ **de formación** PROT SOC qualification period; ~ **de gestación** ECON gestation period; ~ **de gracia** CONT grace period; ~ **intermedio** COM GEN intermediate term; ~ **de izada** TRANSP hook cycle; ~ **largo** ECON long period; ~ **medio de cobro** CONT average collection period; ~ **de notificación** RRHH *de despido* period of notice; ~ **obligatorio de cotización** BOLSA mandatory quote period; ~ **de ocupación gratuita** INMOB, PROT SOC rent-free period; ~ **de opción** BOLSA option period; ~ **de pago** BANCA, FIN, FISC period of payment, repayment term; ~ **de pago del impuesto** FISC averaging period; ~ **de pico máximo** MED AMB peak period; ~ **de la póliza** BANCA, FIN term policy; ~ **de posguerra** ECON postwar period; ~ **presupuestado** ECON, FIN, POL budgetary period; ~ **presupuestario** ECON, FIN, POL budgetary period; ~ **del presupuesto** ECON, FIN, POL budget period; ~ **de protección** BOLSA hedge period; ~ **de prueba** COM GEN, RRHH probation, probationary period, trial period; ~ **de recesión** COM GEN, ECON recessionary gap, recession; ~ **de recuperación** COM GEN pay-out period, CONT, RRHH payback period; ~ **de**

recuperación de la deuda BANCA, ECON, FISC debt recovery period; ~ **de reembolso** COM GEN repayment term; ~ **de reflexión** COM GEN cooling-off period; ~ **de respaldo financiero** BANCA, FIN bail-out period; ~ **de respuesta** COM GEN turnaround period (*AmE*), turn-round period (*BrE*); ~ **de rodaje** COM GEN running-in period; ~ **suplementario** FISC supplementary period; ~ **de tenencia** BOLSA holding period; ~ **de tiempo** COM GEN, GES time frame; ~ **de tiempo concreto** TRANSP time band; ~ **de transición** COM GEN transition period; ~ **transitorio** COM GEN transitional period; ~ **de vacaciones** OCIO, RRHH holiday period (*BrE*), vacation period (*AmE*); ~ **de validez de una letra de cambio** CONT currency of a bill; ~ **de valores máximos** TRANSP peak period; ♦ **durante el ~ de** COM GEN over the period of; **durante un ~ de tiempo** COM GEN over a period of time; **en el ~ subsiguiente de** COM GEN in the aftermath of; **en un ~ de** COM GEN within a period of; **para el ~ de** COM GEN for the period of

periodos: ~ **semestrales** *m pl* COM GEN six-monthly periods

peritaje *m* INMOB valuation

perito, -a: ~ **contable** *m,f* CONT expert accountant

perjudicial *adj* COM GEN prejudicial

perjuicio *m* COM GEN nuisance, *daño* prejudice

perjuicios: ~ **privados no relevantes** *m pl* ECON marginal private damage (*MPD*); ~ **sociales no relevantes** *m pl* ECON marginal social damage (*MSD*)

perjurio *m* DER perjury

permanecer *vi* COM GEN last; ♦ ~ **en un valor** BOLSA stay in the money

permaneciendo: ~ **invariable todo lo demás** *fra* COM GEN all things being equal

permanente *adj* COM GEN permanent

permisible *adj* IMP/EXP licensable

permiso[1]: **de ~** *adj* RRHH *civil* on leave

permiso[2] *m* COM GEN authorization, permit, permission, license (*AmE*), licence (*BrE*), RRHH *Ejército* furlough; ~ **aduanero general** IMP/EXP general transire; ~ **de conducir** *Esp* (cf *licencia de conducir AmL*) ADMIN, TRANSP driver's licence (*BrE*), driver's license (*AmE*); ~ **de conducir internacional** *Esp* (cf *licencia internacional de conducir AmL*) ADMIN, TRANSP international driver's licence (*BrE*), international driver's license (*AmE*), international driving permit; ~ **de construcción** DER, INMOB planning approval (*AmE*), planning permission (*BrE*); ~ **para construir** INMOB building permit (*AmE*), planning approval (*AmE*), planning permission (*BrE*); ~ **de descarga** TRANSP landing permit, release note (*RN*); ~ **ECMT** TRANSP *transporte por carretera* ECMT permit; ~ **de entrada** COM GEN, POL entry permit; ~ **de exportación** IMP/EXP export licence (*BrE*), export license (*AmE*); ~ **internacional de transporte por carretera** IMP/EXP, TRANSP international road haulage permit; ~ **multilateral** TRANSP multilateral permit; ~ **de navegación** TRANSP sea letter; ~ **pagado** RRHH paid leave; ~ **privilegiado** RRHH privilege leave; ~ **de reimportación libre** IMP/EXP bill of store; ~ **de residencia** DER, POL, RRHH residence permit; ~ **de residencia temporal** DER, POL, RRHH temporary residence permit; ~ **sindical** RRHH union leave; ~ **de trabajo** PROT SOC, RRHH working visa, work permit; ~ **de vacaciones** RRHH holiday leave (*BrE*), vacation leave (*AmE*)

permitido *adj* COM GEN, DER permissible, allowed

permitir *vt* COM GEN, DER permit; ♦ ~ **a alguien el acceso a** COM GEN give sb access to; ~ **un margen de error** COM GEN allow for a margin of error

permuta: ~ **financiera** *f* BOLSA,. FIN swop; ~ **financiera clásica** *f* BOLSA, FIN plain vanilla swop (*infrml*); ~ **financiera de tipos de interés** *f* BOLSA, FIN interest rate swop

permutación *f* MAT permutation

permutar *vt* ECON barter

perpetuidad: **a ~** *fra* COM GEN in perpetuity

perpetuo *adj* BOLSA perpetual

persecución *f* RRHH victimization

persistente *adj* ECON undamped

persona *f* COM GEN person; ~ **afiliada** COM GEN *en una sociedad* affiliated person; ~ **asociada** BOLSA associated person (*AP*); ~ **autorizada** FISC authorized person, PATENT licensee; ~ **de baja estima** GES low-flier; ~ **de bajo desempeño** COM GEN, RRHH low achiever, low-flier; ~ **de bajo rendimiento** COM GEN, RRHH low achiever, low-flier; ~ **de buen rendimiento** COM GEN, RRHH high achiever, high-flier; ~ **sin cargas familiares** ECON empty nester (*infrml*); ~ **a cargo** FISC dependant; ~ **designada** COM GEN *ejecutivo o adjunto* appointee, DER named person, appointee, FISC designated person; ~ **dinámica** RRHH self-starter; ~ **con dos empleos** RRHH double-dipper (*jarg*); ~ **de elevado desempeño** COM GEN, RRHH high achiever; ~ **de elevado rendimiento** COM GEN, RRHH high achiever; ~ **emprendedora** RRHH self-starter; ~ **especificada** FISC specified person; ~ **con éxito personal** GES, RRHH high-flier; ~ **fallecida** DER deceased person; ~ **física** COM GEN natural person; ~ **independiente** RRHH *de grupo, organización* outsider (*BrE*); ~ **jubilada** COM GEN retired person; ~ **jurídica** DER legal person, legal entity; ~ **moral** DER legal entity; ~ **mundana** POL socialite; ~ **muy destacada** COM GEN very important person (*VIP*); ~ **de nacionalidad extranjera** RRHH foreign national; ~ **no perteneciente a la UE** ADMIN, COM GEN non-EU national; ~ **en prácticas** RRHH trainee; ~ **privada** COM GEN private individual; ~ **que busca cierta posición social** COM GEN status seeker; ~ **que busca empleo** RRHH job hunter; ~ **que se hace cargo** FISC supporting person; ~ **que trabaja en Wall Street** BOLSA Wall-Streeter; ~ **sin registrar** FISC unregistered person; ~ **relacionada** FISC related person; ~ **remunerada en divisas extranjeras** COM GEN foreign exchange earner; ~ **respetuosa** FIN white knight (*infrml*); ~ **sujeta a tributación** FISC person liable to tax; ~ **de la tercera edad** FISC, PROT SOC, RRHH senior citizen; ♦ **por** ~ COM GEN per person, per head

personaje *mf* COM GEN big name; ~ **de gran éxito** MEDIOS, V&M hot property (*jarg*); ~ **taquillero** *jarg* MEDIOS, V&M hot property (*jarg*)

personal *m* COM GEN, RRHH personnel, staff; ~ **administrativo** GES management staff, RRHH administrative staff, management staff; ~ **de alta dirección** ADMIN front office personnel, GES, RRHH top management personnel; ~ **asalariado** RRHH salaried staff; ~ **de auditoría** CONT audit staff; ~ **de cabina** TRANSP cabin staff; ~ **de campo** RRHH field staff, V&M field force; ~ **a cargo** RRHH chargeable staff; ~ **directivo** GES, RRHH management staff, managerial staff; ~ **de fábrica** RRHH manufacturing workforce; ~ **del nivel más bajo** RRHH rank-and-file; ~ **obrero** IND hourly workers, work force; ~ **de oficina** ADMIN, RRHH clerical personnel, clerical staff, office staff; ~ **de la oficina de dirección** ADMIN management office staff; ~ **operativo** COM GEN operational staff; ~ **permanente** RRHH tenured staff, permanent staff; ~ **reducido** ADMIN, RRHH skeleton staff; ~ **de secretaría** RRHH secretarial staff; ~ **subalterno** RRHH down-the-line personnel; ~ **de supervisión** RRHH supervisory personnel; ~ **de tierra** COMS ground crew; ~ **de ventas** V&M sales force, sales personnel; ◆ **con alta ocupación de** ~ IND, RRHH personnel-intensive; **con exceso de** ~ RRHH over-staffed; **estar falto de** ~ RRHH be undermanned; **con menos ~ del necesario** RRHH undermanned; **con poco** ~ RRHH short-staffed; **con uso intensivo de** ~ **cualificado** RRHH skill-intensive

personalidad *f* GES personality; ~ **de marca** V&M brand personality

personalización *f* V&M *publicidad* personalization (*jarg*); ~ **por láser** V&M laser personalization

personalizado *adj* COM GEN, IND customized, INFO user-oriented, customer-driven, V&M customized

personalizar *vi* COM GEN, IND, V&M customize

personalmente: ~ **responsable** *adj* DER personally liable, *de las obligaciones* personally responsible

personas: ~ **en situación de pobreza absoluta** *f pl* ECON, PROT SOC, RRHH absolute poor

perspectiva *f* COM GEN prospect, perspective, *económica* outlook; ~ **empresarial** COM GEN business outlook; ~ **financiera** FIN financial perspective; ~ **de los sistemas mundiales** ECON world systems perspective; ◆ **en** ~ COM GEN on the horizon

perspectivas[1]: ~ **de beneficio** *f pl* COM GEN profit outlook; ~ **claves** *f pl* COM GEN key prospects; ~ **de la coyuntura económica** *f pl* ECON economic prospects; ~ **de desarrollo profesional** *f pl* RRHH career prospects; ~ **de empleo** *f pl* RRHH, SEG job prospects; ~ **laborales** *f pl* RRHH, SEG job prospects; ~ **de mercado** *f pl* V&M market forecast, market prospects; ~ **de negocio** *f pl* COM GEN business outlook; ~ **de trabajo** *f pl* RRHH work prospects; ~ **de ventas** *f pl* V&M sales prospects

perspectivas[2]: **hay ~ de mejoría** *fra* COM GEN there is scope for improvement; **tener buenas ~** *fra* COM GEN look promising

perspicacia: ~ **comercial** *f* COM GEN, GES commercial acumen; ~ **empresarial** *f* GES business acumen; ~ **en los negocios** *f* GES business acumen

perspicaz *adj* COM GEN far-sighted

persuasión *f* COM GEN *influencia* persuasion; ~ **moral** BANCA moral persuasion

persuasivo *adj* COM GEN, V&M persuasive

pertenecer: ~ **a** *vt* COM GEN pertain to

pertinente: **no** ~ *adj* COM GEN not applicable (*N/A*)

pescante: ~ **para botes** *m* TRANSP *navegación* davit; ~ **de carga** *m* TRANSP *navegación* cargo derrick

pesimismo *m* COM GEN, ECON gloom

pesimista[1] *adj* COM GEN pessimistic

pesimista[2] *mf* COM GEN pessimist

peso *m* COM GEN weight (*wgt, wt.*); ~ **bruto** COM GEN gross weight (*gr.wt.*); ~ **bruto de combinado** TRANSP *vehículo articulado* gross combination weight (*GCW*); ~ **bruto real** COM GEN actual gross weight; ~ **bruto del tren** TRANSP gross train weight (*GTW*); ~ **bruto del**

vehículo TRANSP gross vehicle weight (*GVW*); ~ **de la carga** TRANSP weight of cargo; ~ **sin cargamento** COM GEN, TRANSP unladen weight; ~ **comercial** ECON commercial weight (*CW*); ~ **completo** COM GEN full weight; ~ **comprobado** COM GEN weight ascertained; ~ **declarado por el expedidor** TRANSP shipper weight (*SW*); ~ **de descarga de automóviles** TRANSP vehicle unladen weight; ~ **descargado** TRANSP unladen weight; ~ **de la deuda** ECON debt burden; ~ **de diseño** IND design weight; ~ **del eje** COM GEN axle weight; ~ **estando vacío** COM GEN, TRANSP weight when empty; ~ **garantizado** TRANSP weight guaranteed (*wg*); ~ **de giro** TRANSP *aviación* pivot weight; ~ **máximo autorizado** COM GEN, TRANSP weight limit; ~ **del mercado** V&M market weight; ~ **muerto** COM GEN, TRANSP deadweight (*dw*); ~ **muerto del buque** TRANSP ship's deadweight; ~ **muerto total** TRANSP deadweight all told (*dwat*); ~ **neto** COM GEN, TRANSP net weight; ~ **en orden de marcha** TRANSP kerbside weight, *automotores* kerb weight; ~ **permitido sin cargas** COM GEN, TRANSP weight allowed free; ~ **de la prueba** DER, RRHH burden of proof; ~ **reducido** TRANSP reduced weight (*RW*); ~ **del revestimiento** TRANSP plated weight; ~ **en seco** TRANSP dry weight; ~ **de tara** *f* COM GEN, TRANSP tare weight; ~ **de tara bruto** COM GEN gross tare weight; ~ **de tara neto** COM GEN net tare weight; ~ **troy** COM GEN troy weight; ◆ **sobre el ~ de giro** TRANSP *aviación* over pivot weight; ◆ **y medidas** COM GEN weights and measures; **el ~ de la prueba recae en la acusación** DER the burden of proof lies with the prosecution

pesquero: ~ **de arrastre** *m* TRANSP trawler

pesticida *m* MED AMB pesticide

petición *f* FISC *de desgravación fiscal* claim, inquiry, INFO, PATENT request; ~ **de cambio** COM GEN request for change (*RFC*); ~ **de crédito** BANCA, FIN credit demand; ~ **de descarga** TRANSP request to off-load; ~ **de devolución** BANCA *préstamos* call; ~ **financiera** CONT, FIN financial claim; ~ **de fondos en la suscripción de acciones** BOLSA application money; ~ **de informes sobre créditos** BANCA, COM GEN, V&M status inquiry; ◆ **hacer una** ~ COM GEN make a request

petrobono *m* BOLSA petrobond

petrodivisa *f* COM GEN, ECON, petrocurrency

petrodólar *m* COM GEN, ECON petrodollar

petróleo *m* IND, MED AMB, TRANSP oil; ~ **bruto** IND, MED AMB, TRANSP crude petroleum; ~ **crudo** IND, MED AMB, TRANSP crude oil

petrolero *m* TRANSP tanker motor vessel (*TMV*), oil tanker

petrolífero *adj* IND, MED AMB oil-bearing

PEUS *abr* (*primero en entrar, último en salir*) COM GEN, CONT FILO (*first in, last out*)

pez: ~ **gordo** *mf infrml* COM GEN fat cat (*infrml*)

PIB[1] *abr* (*producto interior bruto, producto interno bruto*) ECON GDP (*gross domestic product*)

PIB[2]: ~ **per capita** *m* ECON GDP per capita, GDP per head

picadero *m* TRANSP *construcción naval* block

picapleitos *mf* COM GEN shyster (*infrml*)

pictograma *m* MAT pictogram

pie *m* COM GEN foot (*ft*), MEDIOS *bajo la ilustración* caption; ~ **de autor** MEDIOS by-line; ~ **de cabra** TRANSP *manejo de cargas* pinch bar; ~ **cuadrado** COM GEN square foot; **~ de elefante** TRANSP *amarra fija* elephant's foot; **~ de ilustración** MEDIOS, V&M picture caption; **~ de imprenta** MEDIOS, V&M *tipografía* imprint; ◆ **en ~ de igualdad** COM GEN on an equal footing, on the same footing, CONT, FISC at arm's-length; **al ~ de la letra** COM GEN verbatim

piedra: **~ de toque** *f* COM GEN cornerstone

pieza *f* COM GEN component; **~ legislativa** DER piece of legislation; **~ de repuesto** COM GEN, IND replacement part

pignoración *f* BANCA pledge, pledging, ECON hypothecation; **~ negativa** BANCA negative pledge

pila *f* IND *para linterna, radio* battery, INFO *datos* stack; **~ de contenedores** TRANSP container stack; **~ de discos** INFO disk pack; **~ seca** TRANSP *navegación* dry battery

piloto[1] *adj* COM GEN, TRANSP pilot

piloto[2] *m* MEDIOS *radiodifusión* pilot (*jarg*); **~ automático** TRANSP autopilot

PIN *abr* (*producto interior neto*) ECON NDP (*net domestic product*)

pinchazo *m* TRANSP puncture

pinta *f* COM GEN pint (*pt*)

piñón *m* TRANSP pinion

pionero, -a *m,f* COM GEN, IND pioneer

pipo *m jarg* BOLSA pip (*jarg*)

piquete *m* RRHH *de huelga* picket; **~ de huelga** RRHH flying picket, strike picket; **~ móvil** RRHH flying picket; **~ secundario** RRHH secondary picketing

piramidación: **~ fiscal** *f* FISC tax pyramiding

piramidal *adj* COM GEN pyramidal

pirámide: **~ financiera** *f* FIN financial pyramid; **~ de población** *f* ECON age pyramid

pirata: **~ informático** *mf* INFO hacker (*infrml*)

pirateado *adj* MEDIOS, V&M pirated

piratear *vt* INFO *sistemas* hack (*infrml*)

pirateo: **~ informático** *m* INFO hacking (*infrml*)

piratería *f* COM GEN piracy; **~ laboral** RRHH labor piracy (*AmE*), labour piracy (*BrE*); **~ marítima** TRANSP marine piracy; **~ de videos** *AmL ver piratería de vídeos Esp*; **~ de vídeos** *Esp* MEDIOS video piracy

pirómetro *m* COM GEN pyrometer

piscicultura *f* ECON *agrícola* fish farming

piscifactoría *f* ECON *agricultura* fish farm

piso *m Esp* (*cf apartamento AmL, cf departamento AmL*) INMOB apartment (*AmE*), flat (*BrE*); **~ góndola** TRANSP *contenedor* gondola flat; **~ con jardín en planta baja** INMOB garden apartment (*AmE*), garden flat (*BrE*); **~ modelo** INMOB show flat; **~ de producción** COM GEN, IND, RRHH shop floor; **~ de remates** BOLSA front office

pisos: **de varios ~** *adj* INMOB *edificio o aparcamiento* multistorey (*BrE*), multistory (*AmE*)

pista *f* COM GEN hint; **~ para el papel** INFO paper track; **~ de rodaje** TRANSP taxiway; **~ de salida** TRANSP runway

pixel *m* INFO *dibujos* pixel

placa: **~ base** *f* INFO motherboard, mothercard; **~ de características unificadas** *f* TRANSP consolidated data plate; **~ de matrícula** *f* TRANSP license plate (*AmE*), number plate (*BrE*)

plagio *m* MEDIOS *edición* pony (*jarg*) (*AmE*); **~ empresarial** COM GEN corporate plagiarism

plan[1]: **de ~ abierto** *adj* COM GEN *oficina* open-plan; **en ~ aleatorio** *adj* RRHH *solicitud de trabajo* on speculation (*on spec*)

plan[2] *m* COM GEN plan, program (*AmE*), programme (*BrE*);

▪ **a** **~ de acción** COM GEN action plan; **~ de acumulación voluntaria** FIN voluntary accumulation plan; **~ de administración de depósitos** FIN *pensiones* deposit administration plan; **~ de adquisición de acciones** BOLSA *para empleados de la compañía*, RRHH share scheme; **~ de ahorro** BANCA, FIN savings plan; **~ de ahorro para pensión** BANCA, FIN retirement savings plan; **~ de ahorros en nómina** FIN, RRHH payroll savings plan; **~ de amortización** BANCA, FIN repayment schedule, amortization schedule; **~ de amortizaciones del préstamo** BANCA, FIN repayment schedule; **~ anti-inflacionario del mercado** ECON market anti-inflation plan (*MAP*); **~ anual de auditoría** CONT annual audit plan; **~ anual de evaluación** FIN annual evaluation plan; **~ de anualidades** SEG annuity plan; **~ aprobado de participación en los beneficios** RRHH approved profit-sharing scheme; **~ de auditoría** CONT audit plan; **~ de ayuda** BANCA *desarrollo* aid scheme;

▪ **b** **~ Baker** ECON *ayuda financiera internacional* Baker Plan; **~ básico** ECON master plan; **~ de beneficios para los empleados** RRHH employee benefit plan; **~ de beneficios y rendimientos** FIN, GES profit and performance planning (*PPP*); **~ de bonificaciones** RRHH bonus scheme;

▪ **c** **~ de campaña** COM GEN, V&M campaign plan; **~ de capacitación** *AmL* (*cf plan de formación Esp*) RRHH training scheme; **~ de carga** TRANSP load plan; **~ a cinco años** BANCA five-year plan; **~ clave de las Naciones Unidas** ECON, POL United Nations layout key (*UNLK*); **~ comercial** BANCA, COM GEN, GES business plan; **~ de compensación tributaria** FISC tax equalization scheme; **~ de compensaciones diferidas** RRHH deferred compensation plan; **~ de compensaciones por enfermedad** RRHH, PROT SOC sick pay scheme (*BrE*); **~ de compra de acciones por el personal de la compañía** BOLSA employees' stock purchase plan; **~ de compra de acciones unitarias** FIN, BOLSA unit stocking plan; **~ de contabilidad** CONT accounting plan; **~ contable** CONT chart of accounts; **~ contable sectorial** CONT sectoral accounting plan; **~ de contingencia** COM GEN action plan, contingency plan, contingency planning; **~ de contribución diferida** RRHH deferred contribution plan; **~ cualificado** RRHH qualified plan;

▪ **d** **~ de deducciones en nómina** FISC *pagos* payroll deduction scheme; **~ Delors** ECON Delors Plan; **~ departamental** COM GEN, GES departmental plan; **~ de depósitos especiales suplementarios** FIN supplementary special deposits scheme; **~ diferido de participación en los beneficios** FISC deferred profit sharing plan; **~ de distribución** TRANSP distribution planning;

▪ **e** **~ de emergencia** COM GEN contingency plan; **~ de empleo compartido** RRHH job share scheme; **~ de estiba** TRANSP cargo plan, stowage plan; **~ estratégico** COM GEN, GES strategic plan; **~ de estudios** PROT SOC curriculum; **~ de etiquetado ecológico** MED AMB *de productos en venta*, V&M green labeling scheme (*AmE*), green labelling scheme (*BrE*); **~ de evaluación del programa** COM GEN program evaluation plan (*AmE*), programme evaluation plan (*BrE*); ~ **de evaluación de los puestos de trabajo** RRHH job evaluation scheme; ~ **de evaluación del trabajo** RRHH *demanda de puestos* job evaluation scheme; ~ **exhaustivo de negocios** COM GEN in-depth business plan; ~ **de explotación** TRANSP operating plan;

~ f ~ **de financiación** FIN financial package, financing plan; ~ **de financiación del capital** *f* FIN capital funding planning; ~ **fiscal actual** FISC current fiscal plan; ~ **de formación** *Esp* (*cf plan de capacitación AmL*) RRHH training scheme;

~ g ~ **de garantía de riesgo de cambio** BANCA exchange risk guarantee scheme, exchange risk guaranty scheme; ~ **general de estiba** TRANSP *barcos* general arrangement plan (*GA*); ~ **genérico de negocios** COM GEN generic business plan; ~ **de gestión múltiple** GES multiple-management plan;

~ h ~ **Halsey de primas** RRHH Halsey Premium Plan (*AmE*); ~ **de hospitalización** SEG hospitalization plan;

~ i ~ **de incentivo** RRHH incentive plan; ~ **de incentivo en fábrica** RRHH factory incentive scheme, plant incentive scheme; ~ **de incentivo en factoría** *ver plan de incentivo en fábrica*; ~ **de incentivo de grupo** RRHH group incentive scheme; ~ **de incentivo en planta** RRHH factory incentive scheme, plant incentive scheme; ~ **de incentivos salariales** RRHH incentive wage plan; ~ **indexado de inversión en valores** BOLSA indexed security investment plan; ~ **de ingresos** COM GEN revenue project;

~ j ~ **de jubilación** COM GEN pension fund, superannuation scheme, retirement plan; ~ **de jubilación con aportación** COM GEN defined contribution pension plan; ~ **de jubilación con aportación definida** COM GEN *pensiones* defined contribution pension plan; ~ **de jubilación basado en prestaciones** COM GEN benefit-based pension plan; ~ **de jubilación con prestaciones definidas** COM GEN *pensiones*, defined-benefit pension plan; ~ **de jubilación profesional** COM GEN occupational pension scheme; ~ **de jubilaciones** COM GEN retirement scheme; ~ **del juego** COM GEN game plan;

~ k ~ **Keogh** FIN *pensiones* Keogh Plan; ~ **Keynes** ECON Keynes Plan;

~ l ~ **de liquidación fiscal** FISC tax equalization scheme;

~ m ~ **maestro** GES master plan; ~ **de marketing** V&M marketing plan; ~ **de marketing y ventas** V&M marketing and sales plan; ~ **Marshall** ECON *internacional* Marshall Plan; ~ **de medios de comunicación** MEDIOS, V&M *publicidad* media plan; ~ **mensual de inversión** BOLSA, FIN monthly investment plan; ~ **de mercado** V&M market plan;

~ n ~ **nacional** POL national plan; ~ **de navegación** TRANSP ship plan; ~ **de negocios** BANCA, GES business plan; ~ **nominativo de ahorro y pensión** COM GEN registered retirement savings plan (*RRSP*);

~ o ~ **de opción de acciones** BOLSA, FISC *retribución del empleado*, RRHH share option scheme; ~ **de opción de acciones para el personal** BOLSA, RRHH employee stock option plan; ~ **de opción de compra de acciones** BOLSA stock option plan; ~ **de opción para los ejecutivos** BOLSA, GES, RRHH executive option scheme; ~ **de opción sobre acciones para ejecutivos** BOLSA, GES, RRHH executive share option scheme; ~ **de opción para todo el personal** BOLSA, RRHH all-employee option scheme; ~ **operacional plurianual**

FIN multiyear operational plan (*MYOP*); ~ **operativo del año presupuestario** CONT budget year operational plan; ~ **operativo plurianual de primavera** FIN, POL spring multi-year operational plan (*spring MYOP*); ~ **de la organización** GES organization planning; ~ **organizacional** GES organization planning;

~ p ~ **de pacientes privados** PROT SOC private patients plan (*PPP*); ~ **de pago por incentivos** RRHH payment by incentives scheme; ~ **con pago periódico** FIN periodic payment plan; ~ **de pago a plazos** BANCA installment repayment schedule (*AmE*), instalment repayment schedule (*BrE*); ~ **para pagos nivelados de la hipoteca** FIN level-payment mortgage (*AmE*); ~ **de pagos periódicos** BOLSA, FIN periodic payment plan; ~ **de participación accionaria de los empleados** BOLSA, RRHH employee shareholding scheme; ~ **de participación de acciones** BOLSA *para empleados*, FISC, RRHH share participation scheme; ~ **de participación en beneficios** CONT, FISC, RRHH profit-sharing plan, *retribución del empleado* profit-sharing scheme; ~ **de participación financiera** RRHH financial participation scheme; ~ **de pensión contributiva** FIN, RRHH, SEG contributory pension scheme; ~ **de pensión para los empleados** RRHH, SEG employee pension plan; ~ **de pensión graduado** RRHH graduated pension scheme; ~ **de pensión laboral del empresario** CONT, FISC, RRHH employer's occupational pension scheme; ~ **de pensión contributiva** FIN, FISC, RRHH contributory pension plan, contributory pension scheme; ~ **de pensión no contributivo** FIN, FISC, RRHH noncontributory pension plan, noncontributory pension scheme; ~ **de pensiones** COM GEN pension plan, pension scheme; ~ **de pensiones de beneficios definidos** FIN, RRHH defined-benefit pension plan; ~ **de pensiones dotado por adelantado** FIN advance-funded pension plan (*BrE*); ~ **de pensiones de jubilación** FIN, PROT SOC, SEG, RRHH old-age pension scheme; ~ **de pensiones no aprobado** FIN, PROT SOC, RRHH nonapproved pension scheme; ~ **de pensiones no consolidado** FIN, RRHH unfunded pension scheme; ~ **de pensiones suplementario** FIN, RRHH supplementary pension scheme; ~ **de pensiones suplementario de la compañía** FIN, RRHH supplementary company pension scheme; ~ **de pensiones suplementario de empresas del grupo** FIN supplementary intercompany pension scheme; ~ **de pensiones transitorio** FIN, RRHH bridging pension scheme; ~ **personal de jubilación** COM GEN personal pension scheme; ~ **piloto** COM GEN pilot scheme; ~ **plurianual de actuaciones** FIN multi-year operational plan (*MYOP*); ~ **principal** GES master plan; ~ **privado de seguro médico** PROT SOC, RRHH private health scheme; ~ **profesional de retiro** FIN, RRHH occupational pension plan; ~ **de propiedad de acciones de los empleados** BOLSA employee stock ownership plan (*ESOP*); ~ **provisional** COM GEN tentative plan; ~ **publicitario** *f* MEDIOS, V&M advertising schedule;

~ q ~ **quinquenal** CONT five-year plan;

~ r ~ **de recompra de acciones** BOLSA share repurchase plan; ~ **de reducción salarial** RRHH salary reduction plan; ~ **de rehabilitación** ECON recovery plan; ~ **de reinversión del dividendo de descuento** BOLSA, FIN discount dividend reinvestment plan; ~ **de reinversión de dividendos** BOLSA, CONT dividend reinvestment plan; ~ **renovable** COM GEN rolling plan;

~ de reparto de beneficios entre los empleados BOLSA, RRHH employees' profit sharing plan; **~ de reposición** CONT, FIN replacement planning; **~ de rescate de hipoteca** BANCA, INMOB mortgage rescue scheme; **~ de revisión anual** CONT annual audit plan; **~ de ruta** TRANSP route planning;

~ s **~ de sacrificio salarial** FISC salary sacrifice scheme; **~ salarial** RRHH salary scheme; **~ de saneamiento** GES *compañía* reorganization plan; **~ de seguro de gastos médicos** PROT SOC, SEG medical care insurance plan; **~ de seguro de hospitalización** PROT SOC, SEG hospital care insurance plan; **~ de seguros de enfermedad** RRHH, SEG health insurance scheme; **~ de servicios médicos privados** PROT SOC, SEG private health services plan; **~ de servicios de salud** PROT SOC, SEG health services plan; **~ simplificado de jubilación para empleados** RRHH simplified employee pension plan; **~ sistemático de reembolsos** BOLSA systematic withdrawal plan; **~ de sociedad cerrada** BOLSA *accionista fallecido* close corporation plan (*BrE*); **~ de suscripción ficticia** BOLSA phantom stock plan;

~ t **~ táctico** COM GEN tactical plan; **~ de trabajo** ADMIN, GES work plan, work schedule;

~ v **~ de venta de acciones a empleados** BOLSA, RRHH employee stock ownership plan (*ESOP*); **~ de viaje** TRANSP journey planning; **~ de vivienda** PROT SOC housing scheme

Plan: ~ de Ayuda de Servicio Internacional *m* ECON Overseas Service Aid Scheme (*OSAS*); **~ General** *m* PROT SOC *educación* National Curriculum (*BrE*); **~ Personal de Compra de Acciones** *m* BOLSA Personal Equity Plan (*BrE*) (*PEP*)

plana: ~ doble *f* MEDIOS, V&M center spread (*AmE*), centre spread (*BrE*)

plancha *f* TRANSP lay day, *navegación* laytime; **~ por avería** TRANSP *navegación* average laytime

planeación *ver planificación*

planear *vt* COM GEN plan

planes *m* COM GEN, CONT plans, V&M schemes; **~ contables coercitivos** *m pl* CONT mandatory accounting plans; **~ contables imperativos** *m pl* CONT mandatory accounting plans; **~ contables obligatorios** *m pl* CONT mandatory accounting plans; **~ contables preceptivos** *m pl* CONT mandatory accounting plans; **~ de exportación con oferta comercial especial** *m pl* V&M piggyback export schemes

planificación *f* COM GEN planning; **~ anticipada** COM GEN forward planning; **~ de los anuncios según la audiencia** V&M *publicidad* traffic planning; **~ de beneficios** COM GEN, GES profit planning; **~ de buque** TRANSP ship planning; **~ central** COM GEN, GES central planning; **~ contable** MEDIOS *publicidad*, V&M account planning; **~ de contingencia** COM GEN, GES contingency planning; **~ y control** IND planning and control; **~ y control de producción** COM GEN production planning and control; **~ de corto alcance** COM GEN, FIN short-range planning; **~ a corto plazo** COM GEN, FIN short-term planning; **~ del desarrollo** ECON *internacional*, POL development planning; **~ de dirección** GES indicative planning; **~ de la distribución** COM GEN distribution planning; **~ económica** ECON, POL economic planning; **~ de emergencia** COM GEN, GES contingency planning; **~ de la empresa** COM GEN, GES company planning, business planning; **~ empresarial** COM GEN corporate

planning; **~ de estímulo** POL *países socialistas* incitative planning (*jarg*); **~ estratégica** COM GEN, GES strategic planning; **~ estratégica corporativa** COM GEN, GES corporate strategic planning; **~ financiera** CONT, FIN, GES financial planning; **~ fiscal estratégica** ECON, FISC strategic tax planning; **~ de la flota** TRANSP fleet planning; **~ indicativa** ECON, GES indicative planning (*jarg*); **~ de las instalaciones** INFO site planning; **~ del inventario** ECON inventory planning; **~ de largo alcance** COM GEN, FIN, GES forward planning, long-range planning, long-term planning; **~ a largo plazo** COM GEN, FIN forward planning, long-range planning, long-term planning; **~ localizada** INMOB spot zoning; **~ de la mano de obra** GES, RRHH manpower planning; **~ de medios** MEDIOS *publicidad*, V&M media planning; **~ de mercado** V&M market planning; **~ de negocios** COM GEN, GES business planning; **~ de la oficina** COM GEN office planning; **~ operacional** COM GEN operational planning; **~ de la organización** COM GEN organization planning; **~ del personal** GES, RRHH staff planning; **~ del potencial humano** GES, RRHH manpower planning; **~ presupuestaria** ECON, FIN, POL budgetary planning; **~ previa** TRANSP preplanning; **~ de la producción** COM GEN, SEG production planning; **~ de los productos** GES, V&M product planning; **~ de un proyecto** *AmL* FIN, GES project planning; **~ de los recursos humanos** (*PRH*) RRHH human resource planning (*HRP*); **~ de sistemas** COM GEN, INFO systems planning; **~ táctica** COM GEN tactical planning; **~ de tierras** ECON land-use planning; **~ total** ECON planning total (*BrE*); **~ de utilidad** COM GEN, GES profit planning; **~ de utilidades** COM GEN, FIN, GES profit planning; **~ de las ventas** V&M sales planning; **~ vertical** COM GEN vertical planning; ◆ **~, programación, presupuestación** GES planning-programming-budgeting system

planificador, a *m,f* COM GEN policymaker; **~ financiero(-a)** FIN, GES financial planner; **~ financiero(-a) diplomado(-a)** BOLSA, FIN certified financial planner; **~ de medios de comunicación** MEDIOS, V&M *publicidad* media planner; **~ de viaje** TRANSP journey planner

planificar *vt* COM GEN plan

planilla *f* *AmL* RRHH *lista de empleados asalariados* payroll, *recibo de pago* pay slip; **~ de depreciación** *AmL* CONT depreciation schedule; ◆ **estar en ~** RRHH be on the payroll

plano[1] *adj* BOLSA, COM GEN flat

plano[2] *m* COM GEN *posición* plane, *arquitectura* plan, level, *de ciudad* map, MAT plane, MEDIOS, OCIO *cine, foto* shot; **~ fundamental** COM GEN ground plan; **~ de terreno** INMOB plot plan

planta[1]: **a ~ baja** *adj* INMOB ground level

planta[2] *f* CONT *activo fijo*, IND plant, INMOB floor, storey (*BrE*), story (*AmE*), RRHH *de empleados* staff, personnel; **~ armadora** *Esp* (*cf planta maquiladora AmL*) IND, RRHH assembly plant; **~ de calefacción** IND heating boiler plant; **~ de combustión** IND, MED AMB combustion plant; **~ depuradora** IND, MED AMB purification plant; **~ depuradora de aguas cloacales** IND, MED AMB sewage treatment works; **~ eléctrica de reserva** IND standby power plant; **~ de electricidad** IND power station; **~ de ensamblado** IND, RRHH assembly plant; **~ fija** IND fixed plant; **~ frigorífica** COM GEN, IND cold storage plant; **~ generadora alimentada por carbón** IND coal-fired power station; **~ de incineración** IND,

MED AMB incineration plant; ~ **de industria pesada** IND heavy industrial plant; ~ **industrial** IND industrial plant; ~ **maquiladora** *AmL* (*cf planta de ensamblado Esp*) IND, RRHH assembly plant; ~ **y maquinaria** ECON, IND plant and machinery; ~ **mezcladora** IND, MED AMB blending plant; ~ **de montaje** IND, RRHH assembly plant; ~ **nuclear** IND, MED AMB nuclear plant; ~ **paralela** IND parallel plant; ~ **piloto** IND *producción* pilot plant; ~ **de procesado** IND processing plant; ~ **de producto fijo** IND fixed plant; ~ **de producto flexible** IND flexible plant; ~ **de pruebas** IND testing plant; ~ **rentada** IND plant hire

plantación[1]: **en** ~ *adv* TRANSP *terminología de entregas* ex plantation

plantación[2] *f* ECON *agrícola* plantation

planteamiento *m* GES approach; ~ **de alta dirección** GES, RRHH top management approach

plantear *vt* COM GEN place, *cuestión* settle, *objeción* raise, GES approach

plantilla *f* IND template, INFO panel, RRHH personnel, staff, *Esp lista de empleados asalariados* payroll; ~ **de personal** ECON, COM GEN, RRHH labor force (*AmE*), labour force (*BrE*); ◆ **estar en** ~ *Esp* RRHH *salarios* be on the payroll; **estar en la** ~ RRHH be a member of the staff; **de** ~ **escasa** RRHH short-staffed

plástico: ~ **reforzado con vidrio** *m* IND, TRANSP glass-reinforced plastic

plásticos *m pl* IND plastics

plataforma *f* COM GEN platform, TRANSP flat bed, pallet; ~ **de carga** TRANSP pallet; ~ **de carga apilable** TRANSP post pallet; ~ **de carga autodesmontable** TRANSP self-demounting pallet; ~ **de carga de cuatro entradas** TRANSP four-way entry pallet, four-way pallet; ~ **de carga elevadora** TRANSP tail-lift; ~ **de carga de madera** IMP/EXP, TRANSP wooden pallet; ~ **de carga no recuperable** TRANSP expendable pallet; ~ **de carga reversible** TRANSP reversible pallet; ~ **de descarga** TRANSP unloading platform; ~ **maestra de carga** TRANSP key pallet; ~ **móvil** TRANSP yard dolly; ~ **de perforación** IND drilling platform; ~ **petrolífera** IND oil platform, oil rig, offshore oil field; ~ **promocional** V&M promotional platform; ~ **de rampa** TRANSP ramp stillage; ~ **de ventas** V&M sales platform

Plataforma: ~ **Nacional del Voluntariado** *f Esp* (*cf Consejo del Voluntariado Nacional AmL*) PROT SOC organization for the coordination of voluntary associations, ≈ National Council of Voluntary Organizations (*BrE*) (*NCVO*)

platillo *m* MAT saucer

platina *f* INFO *para cintas magnéticas* deck

platos: ~ **precocinados** *m pl* V&M convenience food

plaza *f* COM GEN job, OCIO *concierto, tren* seat, RRHH *puesto* job; ~ **bancaria** BANCA bank place; ~ **comercial** COM GEN, V&M marketplace; ~ **confirmada** ADMIN approved place; ~ **financiera** BOLSA, FIN financial marketplace; ~ **de negocios de primer orden** COM GEN chief place of business

plazo *m* BANCA installment (*AmE*), instalment (*BrE*), *tiempo* term, COM GEN time limit, term; ~ **alargado** BANCA extended term; ~ **de amortización** V&M payback period; ~ **anual** COM GEN, CONT, FIN annual installment (*AmE*), annual instalment (*BrE*); ~ **de anualidad** SEG annuity installment (*AmE*), annuity instalment (*BrE*); ~ **base** CONT installment base

(*AmE*), instalment base (*BrE*); ~ **de carencia** BOLSA waiting period; ~ **después de la vista** COM GEN time after sight; ~ **de devolución** BANCA term of payment; ~ **de entrega** COM GEN delivery time, delivery period, time of delivery, SEG, V&M lead time; ~ **de espera** COM GEN, SEG, TRANSP lead time; ~ **fijo** BANCA, FIN fixed installment (*AmE*), fixed instalment (*BrE*); ~ **final** BANCA, FIN final installment (*AmE*), final instalment (*BrE*); ~ **garantizado** BANCA guaranteed term; ~ **de gracia** COM GEN, DER period of grace; ~ **mensual** BANCA, FIN monthly installment (*AmE*), monthly instalment (*BrE*); ~ **de pago** BANCA time for payment; ~ **perentorio** COM GEN strict time limit; ~ **de recuperación** CONT, RRHH payback period; ~ **de validez** COM GEN validity period; ~ **para el vencimiento** BOLSA term to maturity; ◆ **a corto** ~ COM GEN in the short term; **a largo** ~ COM GEN long-term, in the long term; **a medio** ~ BANCA, COM GEN, FIN in the medium term; **antes del** ~ **previsto** COM GEN ahead of schedule; **a** ~ **con tipo de interés convenido** BOLSA forward-forward; **en un** ~ **de treinta días** COM GEN at thirty days' usance

plazos[1]: ~ **y condiciones** *m pl* COM GEN *de política, acuerdos*, SEG terms and conditions; ~ **especiales para el negocio** *m pl* COM GEN special terms for the trade

plazos[2]: **a** ~ *fra* COM GEN in installments (*AmE*), in instalments (*BrE*); **en** ~ **mensuales** *fra* COM GEN in monthly installments (*AmE*), in monthly instalments (*BrE*)

pleito *m* DER libel suit

plenario *adj* POL *sesión parlamentaria* plenary

pleno: ~ **empleo** *m* ECON, POL, PROT SOC, RRHH full employment; ~ **de suscripción** *m* SEG written line

pluma: ~ **estilográfica** *f* COM GEN fountain pen; ~ **fuente** *f* COM GEN fountain pen

pluralidad: ~ **de opiniones** *f* COM GEN diversity of opinions

pluralismo *m* RRHH *relaciones laborales* pluralism

pluriempleado, -a *m,f* RRHH moonlighter (*infrml*)

pluriempleo *m* RRHH dual job holding, moonlighting (*infrml*)

plus: ~ **del producto** *m* V&M product-plus

plusmarquista *mf* RRHH record breaker

plusvalía *f* COM GEN *marxismo* surplus of assets over liabilities, appreciated surplus, ECON, FIN capital gain, INMOB betterment; ~ **acumulada** CONT accumulated surplus; ~ **de capital** BOLSA, CONT, ECON, FIN capital surplus (*AmE*), share premium (*BrE*); ~ **elevada de empleo** ECON high employment surplus; ~ **restringida** CONT undistributable reserve (*BrE*), restricted surplus (*AmE*); ~ **de la tierra** FIN, INMOB unearned increment of land

plusvalías: ~ **netas** *f pl* ECON, FIN net capital gain; ~ **netas imponibles** *f pl* ECON, FIN net taxable capital gain

pmo. *abr* (*próximo*) COM GEN prox. (*proximo*)

PNB *abr* (*producto nacional bruto*) ECON GNP (*gross national product*)

PNUD *abr* (*Programa de las Naciones Unidas para el Desarrollo*) ECON, POL UNDP (*United Nations Development Programme*)

población *f* COM GEN population; ~ **abierta** ECON open population; ~ **activa** ECON, RRHH working population; ~ **activa sin empleo** ECON, POL, PROT SOC, RRHH unemployed labor force (*AmE*), unemployed labour force (*BrE*); ~ **adulta** COM GEN adult population; ~ **cerrada** ECON closed population; ~ **de derecho** ECON de jure population; ~ **que envejece** ECON ageing population; ~ **estadística** MAT statistical population; ~ **de facto** ECON de facto population; ~ **ocupada** COM GEN, ECON working population; ~ **óptima** ECON optimum population; ~ **residente** ECON resident population; ◆ **de ~ poco densa** ECON sparsely populated

poblado[1]: **densamente ~** *adj* COM GEN, ECON densely-populated; **poco ~** *adj* COM GEN, ECON underpopulated

poblado[2]: ~ **periférico** *m* COM GEN overspill town

pobre *adj* COM GEN *actuación, resultado* underperforming, ECON poor

pobres: **los ~** *m pl* ECON, PROT SOC the needy

pobreza *f* ECON, PROT SOC poverty; ~ **absoluta** ECON, PROT SOC absolute poverty

poda *f* COM GEN pruning

poder[1] *m* COM GEN *capacidad* power, DER power of attorney, POL *nacional* authority; ~ **adquisitivo** COM GEN purchasing power, buying power, spending power; ~ **adquisitivo actual** COM GEN current purchasing power (*CPP*); ~ **adquisitivo del consumidor** V&M consumer buying power; ~ **adquisitivo discrecional** V&M discretionary buying power; ~ **aparente** DER apparent authority; ~ **al portador** BOLSA bearer proxy; ~ **compensador** ECON countervailing power; **el ~ ejecutivo** POL executive power; ~ **escrito para vender acciones** BANCA, BOLSA stock power; ~ **judicial** DER, POL the judiciary; ~ **legal** DER *administrativo* power of attorney (*PA*); ~ **legislativo** DER, POL legislative power; ~ **de la mano de obra** RRHH labor power (*AmE*), labour power (*BrE*); ~ **de los medios de comunicación** MEDIOS power of the media; ~ **de mercado** ECON market power; ~ **monopolístico** ECON monopoly power; ~ **negociador** COM GEN bargaining power; ~ **obrero** RRHH labor power (*AmE*), labour power (*BrE*); ~ **para pleitos** DER power of recourse; ~ **policial** DER, POL police power; ~ **regulador** COM GEN, DER regulatory authority; ~ **de venta** DER, INMOB power of sale; ◆ **en el ~** POL *gobierno* in power; **por ~** DER by proxy, per procurationem (*p.p.*)

poder[2]: ~ **optar a** *vt* COM GEN *seguro nacional, becas, subsidios* be eligible for

Poder: ~ **General** *m* DER power of attorney (*PA*)

poderes: **los ~ fácticos** *m pl* COM GEN, POL The Establishment; ~ **indagatorios** *m pl* DER *de tribunal* investigatory powers; ~ **públicos** *m pl* POL public authorities; ~ **para solicitar préstamos** *m pl* BANCA, COM GEN borrowing powers

poderoso *adj* COM GEN powerful

polarización *f* COMS, FIN polarization

policentrismo *m* POL polycentrism

policultivo *m* ECON *agricultura* mixed farming

polígono: ~ **de descongestión** *m* IND industrial overspill area; ~ **de frecuencias** *m* MAT frequency polygon; ~ **industrial** *m* IND industrial zone

polímero: ~ **de cloruro de vinilo** *m* IND vinyl chloride monomer

polipasto *m* TRANSP *manejo de carga* hoist

polipolio *m* ECON polipoly

política *f* GES policy, POL politics; ~ **de adquisición** BOLSA acquisition policy; ~ **agraria** ECON, POL agricul-

tural policy; ~ **agrícola** ECON, POL farm policy; ~ **de ajuste monetario** ECON, POL financial adjustment policy; ~ **ambiental** MED AMB, POL environmental policy; ~ **anticíclica** ECON contracyclical policy; ~ **arancelaria** ECON, FISC, IMP/EXP, POL tariff policy; ~ **comercial** COM GEN commercial policy, V&M marketing policy; ~ **de competencia** V&M competition policy; ~ **común** COM GEN, POL common policy; ~ **de consumo** COM GEN *UE*, V&M consumer policy; ~ **contable** CONT accounting policy; ~ **contracíclica** ECON countercyclical policy; ~ **crediticia** COM GEN credit policy; ~ **demográfica** ECON, POL population policy; ~ **de desarrollo** ECON, POL development policy; ~ **de desviación** GES deviation policy; ~ **dinámicamente inconsistente** POL dynamically inconsistent policy; ~ **discrecional** POL discretionary policy; ~ **de distribución** COM GEN, TRANSP distribution policy; ~ **de dividendos** BOLSA, FIN dividend policy; ~ **de la empresa** COM GEN company policy; ~ **empresarial** COM GEN, ECON, GES business policy; ~ **de estabilización** ECON stabilization policy; ~ **estructural de ajuste** ECON structural adjustment policy; ~ **exterior del gobierno** ECON, POL external government policy; ~ **financiera** FIN financial policy; ~ **fiscal** FISC fiscal policy; ~ **fiscal activa** FISC active fiscal policy; ~ **fiscal compensatoria** ECON, FISC, POL compensatory fiscal policy; ~ **fiscal discrecional** FISC discretionary fiscal policy; ~ **fiscal restrictiva** FISC tight fiscal policy; ~ **de frenazo y expansión** ECON stop-go policy; ~ **de fuerza** POL machtpolitik (*jarg*), policy of the big stick (*infrml*), power politics; ~ **del garrote** POL policy of the big stick (*infrml*); ~ **de gastos deficitarios** CONT, ECON, POL *contabilidad gubernamental* deficit spending policy; ~ **de igualdad de oportunidades** RRHH Equal Opportunities Policy (*EOP*); ~ **industrial** SEG *producción* industrial policy; ~ **de ingresos** FIN incomes policy; ~ **de inmigración** DER, POL immigration policy; ~ **interior** ECON, POL internal policy; ~ **interior del gobierno** POL internal government policy; ~ **de inversión** FIN, POL investment policy; ~ **keynesiana** ECON Keynesian policy; ~ **legal** DER, RRHH statutory policy; ~ **ligada al mercado de acciones** BOLSA equity-linked policy; ~ **macroeconómica** ECON, POL macroeconomic policy; ~ **de marketing dirigida por el consumidor** V&M client-led marketing policy; ~ **medioambiental** MED AMB, POL environment policy; ~ **de mercado laboral** POL labor-market policy (*AmE*), labour-market policy (*BrE*); ~ **mixta** GES mixed policy; ~ **monetaria** ECON monetary policy; ~ **monetaria expansiva** ECON easy money policy; ~ **monetaria restrictiva** ECON, POL tight monetary policy, restrictive monetary policy; ~ **de no intervención** ECON, POL hands-off policy; ~ **organizativa** POL organizational politics; ~ **de pagos** COM GEN remittance policy, RRHH pay policy; ~ **de personal** GES, RRHH personnel policy; ~ **de planificación** COM GEN *desarrollo regional* planning policy; ~ **práctica** POL practical politics; ~ **de precios** COM GEN, ECON, V&M prices policy, pricing policy; ~ **de precios y rentas** ECON, POL prices and incomes policy; ~ **de presentación de informes** FIN reporting policy; ~ **de préstamos** BANCA lending policy; ~ **de préstamos de un banco** BANCA bank lending policy; ~ **presupuestaria** ECON, POL budgetary policy; ~ **de promoción** COM GEN, V&M promotional policy; ~ **prudente** COM GEN prudent policy;

~ **publicitaria** V&M advertising policy; ~ **de puertas abiertas** COM GEN, GES, POL open-door policy; ~ **real** POL Realpolitik; ~ **regional** ECON regional policy; ~ **regional de crecimiento** ECON growth pole; ~ **de rentas** COM GEN incomes policy; ~ **de rentas con base fiscal** FISC tax-based incomes policy (*TIP*); ~ **de rentas y control de precios** ECON, POL prices and incomes policy; ~ **de restricción de crédito** ECON, POL tight money policy; ~ **salarial** RRHH wage policy; ~ **salarial sindical** RRHH union wage policy; ~ **de seguir los acontecimientos** ECON wait-and-see policy; ~ **sensacionalista** POL gutter politics; ~ **sobre libre competencia** POL competition policy; ~ **social** COM GEN, RRHH, POL social policy; ~ **de una sociedad** ECON one-club policy; ~ **superficial** V&M *mercadotecnia* skimming policy; ~ **técnica** ECON, POL technical policy; ~ **de la tierra quemada** FIN, GES scorched-earth policy; ~ **de ventas** V&M sales policy

Política: ~ **Agrícola Común** *f* (*PAC*) ECON UE, POL Common Agricultural Policy (*CAP*)

políticas: ~ **de los activos fijos** *f pl* CONT fixed asset policies; ~ **de rentas** *f pl* RRHH incomes policies (*jarg*)

político[1] *adj* POL political

político[2],**a** *m,f* POL politician

politizar *vt* POL politicize

polivalencia *f* RRHH multiskilling

polivalente *adj* INFO *programa* multipurpose

póliza *f* COM GEN policy; ~ **abierta** SEG blanket policy, TRANSP open policy; ~ **al portador** FISC policy to bearer; ~ **de anualidades** SEG annuity policy; ~ **de atraque** TRANSP berth charter; ~ **de automóviles comerciales** SEG company car policy (*BrE*), business automobile policy (*AmE*); ~ **para los beneficiarios** SEG survivor policy; ~ **en blanco** SEG sample policy, unvalued policy; ~ **de carga abierta** SEG *marina* open cargo policy; ~ **de cargamento marítimo** SEG floating cargo policy; ~ **de catástrofe** SEG catastrophe policy; ~ **de cobertura de falsificaciones** SEG commercial forgery policy; ~ **colectiva** SEG *compañía* master policy (*AmE*); ~ **combinada** SEG comprehensive policy; ~ **comercial** SEG *cubrir riesgos* commercial form; ~ **comercial de seguro de enfermedad** PROT SOC, SEG commercial sickness insurance policy; ~ **de compra** BOLSA share certificate (*BrE*), stock certificate (*AmE*); ~ **conjunta** SEG block policy; ~ **constitutiva de prueba del interés asegurado** SEG policy proof of interest (*PPI*); ~ **contra pérdidas de la propiedad personal** SEG personal property floater; ~ **contra riesgo especificado** SEG named peril policy; ~ **contra robo interno** SEG interior robbery policy; ~ **cubierta** SEG *de vida* fully-paid policy; ~ **de daños materiales para empresas** SEG commercial property policy; ~ **de directores de empresa** SEG businessowners' policy; ~ **de fletamento** TRANSP charter party (*C/P*); ~ **de fletamento por tiempo y precio predeterminado** TRANSP time charter party; ~ **de fletamento de traspaso** TRANSP demise charter party; ~ **de fletamento por viaje** TRANSP voyage charter party (*voyage C/P*); ~ **de flete** SEG freight policy; ~ **flotante** SEG floating policy, *marítimo* open policy; ~ **flotante de carga** TRANSP floating cargo policy; ~ **de flotilla** SEG fleet policy; ~ **para un grupo de coches** SEG fleet policy; ~ **para los herederos** SEG survivor policy; ~ **de incendio** SEG *seguros contra incendios* standard fire policy; ~ **individual de rentas anuales** SEG individual annuity policy;

~ **de ingresos garantizados** SEG guaranteed income contract (*GIC*); ~ **con interés asegurable** SEG interest policy; ~ **de interrupción comercial** SEG business interruption policy; ~ **de jubilación** FIN *impuesto*, FISC retirement annuity policy; ~ **limitada** SEG limited policy; ~ **MAR** SEG *de carga* MAR policy; ~ **marina flotante** SEG, TRANSP floating marine policy (*FP*); ~ **marítima flotante** SEG, TRANSP floating marine policy (*FP*); ~ **de muelle** TRANSP wharf charter; ~ **nula** SEG void policy; ~ **de pagos coincidentes con los ingresos** SEG *seguro de riesgo* pay-as-paid policy; ~ **paquete de seguro de daños materiales y responsabilidad civil para empresas** SEG business property and liability insurance package; ~ **con participación en los beneficios** SEG participating policy; ~ **PPI** SEG PPI policy; ~ **provisional** SEG provisional policy; ~ **de reaseguro de excedente bruto** SEG gross excess reinsurance policy; ~ **registrada de seguro de vida** SEG registered life insurance policy; ~ **de renta familiar** SEG family income policy; ~ **con repercusión en pérdidas** SEG consequential-loss policy; ~ **de seguro** SEG insurance certificate, insurance policy; ~ **de seguro contra responsabilidad civil** SEG third-party insurance policy; ~ **de seguro para cualquier carga** SEG open cargo insurance policy (*OP*); ~ **de seguro marítimo** SEG *marítimo* marine insurance policy (*MIP*); ~ **de seguro provisional** SEG binder (*AmE*); ~ **de seguro a todo riesgo** SEG *automóvil* comprehensive insurance policy; ~ **de seguro de vida** SEG life insurance policy, life assurance policy (*BrE*); ~ **de seguro de vida universal** SEG universal life-policy; ~ **de seguros de cobertura total** SEG fully comprehensive insurance policy; ~ **de seguros global** COM GEN, SEG comprehensive insurance policy; ~ **de seguros por hipoteca** SEG mortgage insurance policy; ~ **de seguros a término** SEG term insurance policy; ~ **tarificada** SEG rated policy; ~ **de valor declarado** SEG valued policy; ~ **variable** SEG floating policy; ~ **con vencimiento fijo** SEG time policy; ~ **de viaje** SEG *marítimo* voyage policy; ~ **de vida entera** SEG whole life insurance policy; ~ **voluntaria** RRHH voluntary policy

polo: ~ **de desarrollo** *m* IND growth pole

polución: ~ **base** *f* MED AMB background pollution; ~ **marítima** *f* MED AMB marine pollution

pólvora: ~ **sin humo** *f* MED AMB, TRANSP *cargas peligrosas* smokeless powder; ~ **negra** *f* MED AMB black powder

ponderación *f* FIN, MAT, V&M weighting; ~ **de los medios de comunicación** MEDIOS, V&M *publicidad* media weight

ponderado *adj* COM GEN weighted

ponderar *vt* BOLSA *posiciones de opciones* weight

ponente *mf* COM GEN *en reunión* speaker

poner *vt* COM GEN put; ♦ ~ **el acento en** COM GEN lay the emphasis on, accentuate; ~ **al corriente** CONT write up; ~ **a uno al corriente de la situación** COM GEN acquaint sb with the situation; ~ **al día** COM GEN bring up to date, *experiencia, habilidad* brush up (*infrml*), update, INFO update; ~ **al día una cuenta** BANCA post up an account; ~ **algo al orden del día** COM GEN put sth on the agenda; ~ **algo en un almacén frigorífico** COM GEN put sth into cold storage (*infrml*); ~ **algo en el escaparate** COM GEN put sth in the window; ~ **algo por escrito** COM GEN set down sth in writing; ~ **algo en marcha** COM GEN set sth in motion, put sth into execution; **~ algo en producción** IND put sth into production; **~ algo a prueba** COM GEN put sth to the test; **~ a alguien al tanto de algo** COM GEN bring sb up to date on sth; **~ a alguien de patitas en la calle** *infrml* RRHH *personal* discharge sb, dismiss sb, fire sb (*infrml*), give sb the sack (*infrml*) (*BrE*), give sb their cards (*infrml*) (*BrE*), make sb redundant, sack sb (*infrml*); **~ un anuncio** COM GEN, MEDIOS, V&M advertise for; **~ un anuncio de empleo** MEDIOS, RRHH, V&M advertise a job; **~ en bolsa** BOLSA go public; **~ bajo control** ECON *inflación, desempleo* bring under control; **~ bajo custodia** DER place in custody; **~ bajo tutela** DER, PROT SOC place under guardianship; **~ en el buzón** COMS put in mailbox; **~ las cartas sobre la mesa** COM GEN show one's hand (*infrml*); **~ a cero** INFO *reloj, contador, datos* reset; **~ en clave** BANCA, INFO encode; **~ condiciones más estrictas** DER tighten up; **~ una conferencia a cobro revertido** COMS transfer the charges; **~ en contacto** COMS *una parte con otra* put in touch; **~ a disposición** COM GEN *dinero* make available; **~ embargo a** COM GEN place an embargo on; **~ énfasis sobre** COM GEN place emphasis on, emphasize; **~ una fecha** COM GEN set a date; **~ un impedimento a** COM GEN impede; **~ en libertad a alguien bajo fianza** DER release sb on bail; **~ un límite a los tipos de interés** BANCA, ECON, FIN cap interest rates; **~ en la lista negra** COM GEN, IND, RRHH blacklist; **~ de manifiesto** COM GEN set forth; **~ en manos de la administración judicial** DER put into receivership; **~ en marcha el papeleo** ADMIN spin red tape; **~ de moda** COM GEN bring into fashion; **~ objeciones a una imposición** FISC to object to an assessment; **~ en orden** ADMIN put in order; **~ de patitas en la calle** *infrml* RRHH *personal* boot out (*infrml*); **~ un plan en acción** COM GEN put a plan into action; **~ en práctica** COM GEN *planes* implement, *políticas* put into effect, *teoría* test out; **~ precio a** ECON price; **~ a prueba** COM GEN try out; **~ a punto** ECON, INFO *programa* fine-tune; **~ reparos a** COM GEN *propuesta* object to; **~ sobreaviso** COM GEN give the alert; **~ por los suelos** COM GEN slate; **~ sus asuntos en orden** COM GEN put one's affairs in order; **~ tope a las tasas de interés** BANCA, ECON, FIN cap interest rates; **~ en venta** INMOB put on the market; **~ en vigor** DER put into force; **~ en la red** COM GEN network

ponerse: ~ de acuerdo *fra* COM GEN agree; **~ al día** *fra* COM GEN catch up; **~ en contacto con** *fra* COM GEN make contact with; **~ al corriente de** *fra* COM GEN brush up on; **~ en evidencia** *fra* COM GEN be in evidence; **~ en marcha** *fra* TRANSP routeing; **~ a la ofensiva** *fra* COM GEN take the offensive; **~ a trabajar** *fra* COM GEN get down to work

pool *m* RRHH *de empleados* pool

pooling *m* ECON pooling

popa: ~ y castillo de proa *fra* TRANSP poop and forecastle (*PF*); **de ~ a proa** *fra* TRANSP fore and aft; **~ y puente** *fra* TRANSP poop and bridge (*PB*)

populista *mf* POL populist

porcentaje *m* COM GEN percentage; **~ de activos de reserva** BANCA, FIN reserve-assets ratio; **~ anual fijo** (*PAF*) BANCA, FIN fixed annual percentage (*FAP*); **~ apropiado** FISC appropriate percentage; **~ de beneficios pagados como dividendos** V&M *comercialización* payout ratio; **~ de capital retenido** CONT *hoja de balance* percentage of capital held; **~ de**

contribución del empresario FISC *Seguridad Social* employer rate; **~ de depreciación** TRANSP percentage of depreciation; **~ de deuda interna** ECON, POL internal debt ratio; **~ de devolución** FIN rate of return; **~ de devolución corregido** FISC amended tax return; **~ de dividendo** GES pay-out; **~ especificado** FISC specified percentage; **~ exento** FISC exempt percentage; **~ de los ingresos que se ahorran** FIN savings-to-income ratio; **~ de la muestra** COM GEN sample rate; **~ del precio del producto gastado en su promoción** V&M *publicidad* percentage of product price spent on its promotion; **~ real de devolución después de impuestos** FISC after-tax real rate of return; **~ de respuesta** V&M *mercadotecnia* response rate; **~ de sindicalismo** RRHH union rate; **~ de utilización** COM GEN utilization percent; **~ del volumen de beneficios** FIN profit-volume ratio

porcentual *adj* COM GEN, MAT percentage

porción: ~ sin utilizar *f* FISC unused portion

porqués: los ~ *m pl* COM GEN whys and wherefores

portacontenedor: ~ celular *m* TRANSP *buque* fully cellular container ship (*FCC*)

portada *f* MEDIOS, V&M front cover, cover page

portador, a *m,f* BANCA bearer; **~ de contrato** FIN contracting holder

portafolio: ~ colectivo de inversión *m* FIN collective investment undertaking; **~ colectivo de inversión abierto** *m* FIN collective investment undertaking other than of the closed-end type

portalón: ~ de doble ancho *m* TRANSP double width gangway

portátil *adj* INFO *equipo, programas* portable

portavoz *mf* COM GEN spokesperson

porte *m* TRANSP carriage; **~ suplementario** COM GEN extra postage; **~ por tren expreso** COM GEN expressage; ◆ **~ debido** IMP/EXP, TRANSP carriage forward (*carr fwd, CF*); **~ pagado** COM GEN post paid (*pp*), postage paid, postage rate; **~ y seguro pagados** IMP/EXP, TRANSP carriage and insurance paid (*CIP*), freight and insurance paid

portes[1]**: ~ del contrato de fletamento** *m pl* TRANSP charter party freight

portes[2]**: ~ debidos** *fra* COMS postage due, IMP/EXP, TRANSP carriage forward (*carr fwd, CF*), freight forward (*frt fwd*); **~ pagados** *fra* IMP/EXP, TRANSP freight prepaid (*frt ppd*)

portfolio *m* BOLSA portfolio

poscompra *adj* V&M post-purchase

poscomunista *adj* COM GEN post-Communist

posdata *f* (*P.D.*) BANCA postdate COMS postscript (*P.S.*), FIN postdate

posdatado *adj* COM GEN after date (*A/D*), postdated (*A/D*)

posdatar *vt* COM GEN postdate

poseedor, a: ~ de un abono *m,f* COM GEN, TRANSP season ticket holder (*BrE*)

poseer *vt* BOLSA, COM GEN *acciones, bonos* hold

posesión *f* DER holding, possession, INMOB possession; **~ pacífica** INMOB quiet enjoyment; **~ segura** FIN safe asset; **~ sumaria** DER summary possession; ◆ **estar en ~ de** COM GEN *carta, pago* be in receipt of

posfechado *adj* BANCA, COM GEN, FIN postdated (*P.D.*)

posfechar *vt* BANCA, FIN postdate

posgraduado, -a *m,f* COM GEN postgraduate

posguerra: **de ~** *f* ECON postwar

posibilidad *f* COM GEN possibility; **~ de deducción fiscal** FISC tax deductibility; **~ remota** COM GEN remote possibility; ♦ **no tener ninguna ~ de ganar** COM GEN be out of the running

posibilidades: **tener muchas ~ de** *fra* COM GEN stand a good chance of

posibilismo *m* POL possibilism

posible[1] *adj* COM GEN potential

posible[2]: **~ cliente(-a)** *m,f* INMOB lead (*jarg*), V&M prospective customer; **~ comprador(a)** *m,f* V&M potential buyer, prospective buyer

posibles: **~ medios de comunicación** *m pl* MEDIOS, V&M *publicidad* media options

posición *f* COM GEN position, positioning; **~ abierta** BOLSA open position; **~ acreedora** CONT creditor position; **~ del activo líquido expuesta** COM GEN exposed net asset position; **~ al contado** BOLSA spot position; **~ alcista** BOLSA bull position; **~ alfa** ECON, FISC, IMP/EXP, IND alpha position; **~ de apertura** BOLSA opening position; **~ de autoridad** RRHH position of authority; **~ bajista** BOLSA bear position; **~ cerrada** BANCA, BOLSA, FIN closed position; **~ de compensación** BANCA clearing position; **~ competitiva** COM GEN, ECON competitive position; **~ compradora larga** BOLSA long call position; **~ compradora neutral cubierta** BOLSA neutral covered call position; **~ corta** BOLSA, FIN short option position; **~ corta al descubierto sobre una opción** BOLSA naked short option position; **~ corta de apertura** BOLSA open short position; **~ corta asegurada** BOLSA covered short position; **~ corta asignada** BOLSA assigned short position; **~ corta sobre futuros** BOLSA, FIN short futures position; **~ corta sobre una opción** BOLSA, FIN short option position; **~ corta sobre opción de venta** BOLSA, FIN short call position; **~ cubierta** BOLSA *opciones* covered position; **~ en descubierto** BOLSA short account position, naked position; **~ diferencial de compraventa** BOLSA spread position; **~ dominante** ECON dominant position; **~ dura** COM GEN tough stance; **~ equilibrada** BANCA evened-out position; **~ especial** V&M special position; **~ de final abierto** BOLSA open-ended position; **~ financiera** CONT, FIN financial position; **~ fiscal** FISC fiscal position; **~ futura neta** BANCA net forward position; **~ de futuros** BOLSA futures position; **~ de futuros a largo plazo** BOLSA *opciones* long futures position; **~ de inversión neta** BANCA net investment position; **~ jurídica** DER juridical position; **~ larga** BOLSA, FIN long position; **~ larga de apertura** BOLSA, FIN open long position; **~ libre segregada** BOLSA segregated free position; **~ en el mercado** BOLSA *de moneda* market position; **~ mixta corta** BOLSA short straddle position; **~ mixta larga** BOLSA long straddle position; **~ negociadora** COM GEN negotiating position, bargaining position; **~ neta** BOLSA *compras, ventas*, FIN net position; **~ del pasivo neto arriesgado** BANCA exposed net liability position; **~ de pivote** TRANSP *vehículo de carretera* kingpin position; **~ a plazo** BOLSA forward position; **~ de precio** BOLSA *en descubierto* value position; **~ preferida** V&M preferred position; **~ presupuestaria** COM GEN budgetary position; **~ de primera línea** V&M *en el mercado* prime position; **~ de protección** TRANSP *petrolero* protective location (*PL*); **~ de riesgo** BOLSA risk position;

~ social PROT SOC social standing; **~ socioeconómica** ECON, PROT SOC socioeconomic status; **~ de tabulación** INFO tab setting; **~ de valor larga** BOLSA long value position; **~ valorada** BANCA valued position; **~ de vendedor** BOLSA short account; **~ vendedora larga** BOLSA long put position; **~ vendedora neutral cubierta** BOLSA neutral covered short; **~ de venta en descubierto** BOLSA short put position; ♦ **en una ~ peligrosa** COM GEN an exposed position; **en última ~** COM GEN in last position

posicional *adj* COM GEN positional

posicionamiento *m* COM GEN positioning; **~ de marca** V&M brand positioning; **~ del producto** V&M product positioning; **~ selectivo** V&M selective positioning

posicionamientos *m pl* INFO settings

posicionar *vt* BOLSA, COM GEN position

posiciones: **~ acaparadoras** *f pl* BOLSA longs; **~ cortas** *f pl* BOLSA shorts; **~ de las opciones renovables** *f pl* BOLSA *opciones sobre futuros en eurodólares* rolling options positions

poskeynesiano *m* ECON post-Keynesians

posponer *vt* COM GEN postpone, leave over

poste: **~ esquinero** *m* TRANSP corner post; **~ indicador de señales** *m* TRANSP signpost; **~ de telégrafos** *m* COMS telegraph pole

posterior *adj* COM GEN later; ♦ **~ a la elección** COM GEN, POL post-election; **~ a la liquidación** FISC post-assessing; **~ a la quiebra** FISC post-bankruptcy

postor *m* COM GEN, FIN *subasta* bidder; **~ más bajo** BOLSA lowest bidder

postura *f* COM GEN *sobre una cuestión* stance; **~ alcista** BOLSA bullish stance; **~ antiinflacionaria** ECON, POL anti-inflationary stance; **~ fiscal** FISC fiscal stance

posventa *adj* V&M after-sales

potencia: **~ al freno** *f* TRANSP brake horsepower (*bhp*); **~ de ciar** *f* TRANSP astern power; **~ efectiva en caballos** *f* IND, TRANSP effective horsepower (*ehp*); **~ efectiva media** *f* COM GEN mean effective pressure (*mep*); **~ en el eje** *f* TRANSP *turbina* shaft horsepower (*shp*); **~ indicada en caballos de vapor** *f* COM GEN indicated horsepower (*ihp*); **~ de masa** *f* TRANSP power-to-weight ratio; **~ de onda** *f* IND, MED AMB wave power; **~ solar** *f* IND, MED AMB solar power; **tercera ~** *f* POL third force (*jarg*)

potencial[1] *adj* COM GEN potential

potencial[2] *m* COM GEN potential; **~ administrativo** GES management potential; **~ ascendente** FIN upside potential; **~ de beneficio** BOLSA profit potential; **~ de beneficios crecientes** BOLSA *opciones* upside profit potential; **~ de crecimiento** COM GEN, ECON growth potential; **~ de desarrollo** COM GEN, ECON development potential; **~ de dirección** GES management potential; **~ de endeudamiento** COM GEN borrowing potential; **~ del mercado** V&M market potential; **~ productivo** ECON productive potential; **~ de tráfico** TRANSP traffic potential; **~ de ventas** V&M sales potential

potencialmente *adv* COM GEN potentially

potentado, -a *m,f* COM GEN fat cat *infrml*; **~ comercial** FIN business magnate

potestad: **~ administrativa** *f* COM GEN administrative authority

pozo: **~ comercial** *m* MED AMB commercial well

ppm *abr* (*palabras por minuto*) ADMIN, RRHH wpm (*words per minute*)

ppp *abr* (*puntos por pie*) INFO dpi (*dots per inch*)

práctica[1]: ~ **abusiva** *f* V&M *del vendedor* abusive practice; ~ **administrativa** *f* GES management practice; ~ **anticompetitiva** *f* ECON anticompetitive practice; ~ **comercial** *f* COM GEN trade practice, business practice; ~ **comercial honesta** *f* COM GEN fair business practice; ~ **comercial leal** *f* COM GEN fair business practice; ~ **comercial restrictiva** *f* DER, IND, RRHH restrictive practice; ~ **contable** *f* CONT accounting practice; ~ **ilegal** *f* DER illegal practice; ~ **de inversión normal** *f* FIN normal investment practice; ~ **laboral** *f* COM GEN working practice; ~ **laboral injusta** *f* RRHH unfair labor practice (*AmE*), unfair labour practice (*BrE*); ~ **de negocio sucio** *f* COM GEN unfair trading practice; ~ **política** *f* POL political practice; ~ **de representación del personal por los sindicatos** *f* RRHH union-only practice (*BrE*); ~ **restrictiva** *f* DER, ECON, RRHH, SEG restrictive practice; ~ **de simple reconocimiento** *f* RRHH recognition-only practice

práctica[2]: **en la** ~ *fra* COM GEN in practice; **es la** ~ **habitual** *fra* COM GEN it is standard practice to do so

practicar *vt* FIN practise (*BrE*), practice (*AmE*)

practicable *adj* COM GEN feasible; ♦ ~ **cohecho** DER graft (*infrml*)

prácticas: ~ **en una empresa** *f pl* RRHH placement

práctico *adj* RRHH hands-on, V&M hard-headed

pragmáticamente *adv* COM GEN pragmatically

pragmático *adj* COM GEN pragmatic

preacuerdo *m* RRHH presettlement

preámbulo *m* COM GEN, PATENT *a un acuerdo, contrato* preamble

preanunciar *vt* COM GEN give notice

prearrendar *vt* INMOB prelease

preaviso *m* DER advance notice; ♦ **con un** ~ **de 2 días** COM GEN at 2 days notice

prebenda *f* RRHH sinecure

precalcular *vt* BANCA, FIN *interés en préstamo a plazos* precompute

precario *adj* COM GEN precarious

precarización *f* RRHH precarization

precedente[1] *adj* COM GEN preceding, precedent

precedente[2]: **que sentó un** ~ **histórico** *fra* DER *proceso* landmark

precedentes: **sin** ~ *adj* COM GEN record-high, unprecedented, ECON *beneficios, desempleo* record-high

preceder *vt* COM GEN precede; ♦ ~ **en prioridad a** COM GEN take priority over

preceptivo *adj* DER mandatory; **no** ~ DER *directrices* nonmandatory

precepto *m* DER, GES rule; ~ **legal** DER rule of law

precinto: ~ **aduanero** *m* IMP/EXP, TRANSP customs seal

precio[1]: **de** ~ **excesivo** *adj* V&M overpriced

precio[2] *m* COM GEN price (*pr.*);

▪ **a** ~ **de abastecimiento** ECON supply price; ~ **abierto** BOLSA open price; ~ **del acarreo** TRANSP *navegación* carriage charge; ~ **aceptable** COM GEN acceptable price; ~ **de aceptación** BANCA acceptance price; ~ **actual** CONT, ECON, V&M actual price, current price; ~ **actual de mercado** BOLSA current market price; ~ **administrado** V&M *teoría* administered price; ~ **de adquisición** CONT historical cost, FIN acquisition price;

~ **ajustado al ejercicio económico** BOLSA adjusted exercise price; ~ **al alza** BOLSA rising bottom (*jarg*); ~ **al consumidor** V&M consumer price; ~ **al por mayor** BOLSA trade price, V&M wholesale price; ~ **al por menor sugerido** V&M suggested retail price; ~ **al mercado** BOLSA at market price; ~ **al productor** MED AMB, V&M producer price; ~ **del alquiler** FISC *de propiedad*, INMOB, PROT SOC rent cost; ~ **de apertura** BOLSA opening price; ~ **en aplicación** COM GEN price on application; ~ **aprobado** COM GEN approved price; ~ **aproximado** BOLSA approximate price; ~ **de los artículos al por mayor** BOLSA, V&M commodity price; ~ **asequible** V&M affordable price;

▪ **b** ~ **bajo** BOLSA *futuros monetarios*, V&M low price; ~ **base** BOLSA *operaciones con lotes sueltos* basis price, COM GEN, FISC base price; ~ **de los bonos** BOLSA bond price;

▪ **c** ~ **de calle principal** V&M high street price (*BrE*), main street price (*AmE*); ~ **de catálogo** COM GEN catalogue price (*BrE*), catalog price (*AmE*), V&M *minorista* list price; ~ **de cesión** COM GEN transfer price; ~ **de cierre diario** BOLSA daily settlement price; ~ **competitivo** COM GEN, V&M competitive pricing; ~ **de compra** COM GEN buying price, *de activos* purchase cost, acquisition cost, purchase price; ~ **comprador** BOLSA bid price, FIN buying rate; ~ **de compraventa** BOLSA bid-and-offered price; ~ **de compuerta** ECON sluice-gate price (*jarg*); ~ **compuesto** COM GEN composite price; ~ **en condiciones de igualdad** CONT arm's-length price; ~ **constante** COM GEN, ECON, V&M constant price, uniform price; ~ **contable** BANCA accounting price; ~ **contractual** FISC *venta a plazos* contract price; ~ **convenido** COM GEN agreed price; ~ **de conversión** BOLSA, FIN conversion price; ~ **corrido** IMP/EXP through charge; ~ **corriente** COM GEN, ECON, V&M current price, ruling price, standard price; ~ **corrupto** ECON perverse price; ~ **de coste** *Esp* (*cf precio de costo AmL*) COM GEN cost price, CONT original cost; ~ **de coste estricto** *Esp* (*cf precio de costo estricto AmL*) CONT strict cost price; ~ **de coste obligatorio** *Esp* (*cf precio de costo obligatorio AmL*) CONT strict cost price; ~ **de costo** *AmL* (*cf precio de coste Esp*) COM GEN cost price, CONT original cost; ~ **de costo estricto** *AmL* (*cf precio de coste estricto Esp*) CONT strict cost price; ~ **de costo obligatorio** *AmL* (*cf precio de coste obligatorio Esp*) CONT strict cost price; ~ **de cotización** BOLSA quoted price, ECON *del petróleo* posted price (*jarg*);

▪ **d** ~ **descendente** ECON falling price; ~ **con descuento** FIN discount price; ~ **sin descuento** RRHH full rate; ~ **diferencial** ECON, V&M differential price; ~ **diferido** V&M delayed price; ~ **en dólares del ECU** BOLSA dollar price of the ECU;

▪ **e** ~ **económico** V&M economic price; ~ **de ejecución de la compraventa** BOLSA *opciones* fill price; ~ **de ejecución de una opción** BOLSA call strike price; ~ **de ejercicio** BOLSA strike price, exercise price; ~ **de ejercicio al alza** BOLSA long exercise price; ~ **de ejercicio de la opción** BOLSA option strike price; ~ **de ejercicio de opción de venta** BOLSA call option exercise price; ~ **elevado** BOLSA *futuros* high price; ~ **de emisión** BOLSA issue price, MED AMB emission charges; ~ **de emisión de bonos** BOLSA bond issuing price; ~ **de entrada** BOLSA *futuros* entry price; ~ **de entrada actual** CONT current entry price; ~ **entregado** V&M delivered price; ~ **de equilibrio** BOLSA break-even price, ECON equilibrium price; ~ **estabilizado** ECON stabilized price; ~ **estable** COM GEN, ECON pegged price; ~ **estándar** COM GEN, ECON, V&M standard price; ~ **estimulante** ECON price incentive; ~ **excedido** ECON overshooting price; ~ **de exportación** ECON, IMP/EXP export price; ~ **expuesto** ECON, V&M displayed price;

~ f ~ **en fábrica** COM GEN price ex-works; ~ **del fabricante** V&M *ventas* manufacturer's price; ~ **de factura** BOLSA invoice price; ~ **fijo** BOLSA *opciones de venta,* COM GEN, CONT fixed price, ECON fixed price, pegged price *(jarg)*; ~ **final** BOLSA terminal price; ~ **final de cierre del contrato** BOLSA *futuros* final contract settlement price; ~ **final de liquidación** BOLSA final settlement price; ~ **firme** COM GEN wellhead price; ~ **flexible** ECON flexprice; ~ **flotante** BOLSA afloat price; ~ **franco fábrica** V&M ex-works price; ~ **fuera de embarcadero** IMP/EXP *carga,* TRANSP ex-wharf price; ~ **fuera de horas** BOLSA price after hours; ~ **de futuros** BOLSA futures price; ~ **de futuros de los tipos de interés** BOLSA interest rate futures price;

~ g ~ **de garantía** ECON *agrícola* support price; ~ **garantizado** FIN guaranteed price; ~ **global** COM GEN lump-sum price, all-round price; ~ **global del ejercicio** BOLSA aggregate exercise price; ~ **guía** COM GEN guide price;

~ h ~ **hedónico** ECON hedonic price; ~ **de homologación** BOLSA probate price;

~ i ~ **de importación** ECON, IMP/EXP import price; ~ **de incentivo** V&M premium price; ~ **indicativo** COM GEN target price; ~ **índice** BOLSA index price; ~ **inferior** BOLSA lower price; ~ **ínfimo** BOLSA lowest price; ~ **inicial** BOLSA starting price; ~ **íntegro** RRHH full rate; ~ **de intervención** COM GEN trigger price, ECON, FIN intervention price, IMP/EXP trigger price; ~ **de introducción** V&M introductory price;

~ j ~ **justificado** BOLSA justified price; ~ **justo** ECON just price;

~ l ~ **límite** ECON price ceiling, limit price, TRANSP *navegación* trading limit; ~ **de Lindahl** ECON Lindahl price; ~ **de liquidación** BOLSA settlement price, COM GEN shutdown price; ~ **de liquidación de entrega de divisas** BOLSA exchange delivery settlement price; ~ **listado** COM GEN scheduled price;

~ m ~ **marcado** V&M marked price; ~ **más bajo posible** COM GEN, V&M rock-bottom price; ~ **máximo** BOLSA maximum price, COM GEN, ECON, V&M *mercadotecnia* maximum price, top price; ~ **medio** BOLSA, ECON, V&M average price; ~ **medio de ejercicio** BOLSA *opciones* middle-strike price; ~ **medio de mercado** COM GEN average market price; ~ **de mercado** COM GEN arm's-length price, market price; ~ **de mercado negociado** ECON, V&M negotiated market price; ~ **mínimo** BOLSA bottom price, COM GEN *venta en subasta* upset price *(AmE),* knockdown price, ECON price floor, floor price, V&M *ventas en subasta* reservation price; ~ **mínimo de la oferta laboral** ECON minimum supply price of labor *(AmE),* minimum supply price of labour *(BrE)*; ~ **mínimo en subasta** BOLSA stop-out price; ~ **de monopolio** ECON monopoly price; ~ **en el muelle** TRANSP *distribución* ex-wharf price; ~ **mundial** ECON world price;

~ n ~ **natural** ECON natural price; ~ **negociado** ECON, V&M negotiated price; ~ **neto** V&M net price; ~ **nominal** CONT, FIN nominal price; ~ **normal** COM GEN, ECON, V&M normal price;

~ o ~ **de la oferta y la demanda** BOLSA bid-and-asked price; ~ **ofrecido** BOLSA price offered; ~ **de opción** BOLSA option price; ~ **de la opción de compra** BOLSA call option price; ~ **para operaciones a término** BOLSA forward rate; ~ **de oportunidad** COM GEN bargain price; ~ **orientado a la baja** BOLSA bear strike price; ~ **del oro** BOLSA gold price; ~ **del oro fijado en Londres** BANCA London gold fixing;

~ p ~ **de paridad** COM GEN, ECON parity price; ~ **del petróleo** ECON, FIN, IND oil price; ~ **por pieza** COM GEN piece rate, unit price, RRHH piece rate, V&M unit price; ~ **popular** V&M popular price; ~ **predeterminado** BOLSA, V&M predetermined price; ~ **prescrito** COM GEN prescribed price; ~ **del préstamo a la vista para el corredor** BOLSA broker call-loan rate; ~ **de prestigio** V&M prestige pricing; ~ **de productos básicos** BOLSA primary commodity price; ~ **propio** ECON eigenprice; ~ **psicológico** V&M psychological price; ~ **publicado** COM GEN published price; ~ **publicitario** FIN, V&M advertising price; ~ **público** ECON public pricing; ~ **del punto** BOLSA *opciones* point price; ~ **de punto muerto** ECON break-even pricing;

~ q ~ **que rige** COM GEN, ECON, V&M ruling price;

~ r ~ **de Ramsey** ECON Ramsey price; ~ **razonable** COM GEN reasonable price; ~ **real** CONT, ECON, V&M actual price; ~ **rebajado** V&M reduced price; ~ **recomendado por el fabricante** V&M manufacturer's recommended price *(MRP)*; ~ **del recorrido** TRANSP track-price; ~ **de redención de ejercicio** BOLSA call exercise price; ~ **reducido** OCIO concessionary rate, V&M cut price, *precio especialmente reducido* budget price; ~ **relativo** ECON relative price; ~ **de rescate** BOLSA redemption price, call price; ~ **de reventa** ECON, FIN, V&M resale price; ~ **rígido** ECON sticky price;

~ s ~ **de salida** BOLSA hammer price *(jarg),* exit price; ~ **según la categoría** COM GEN station price; ~ **según el trabajo** RRHH rate for the job; ~ **sensible a la información** ECON, V&M price-sensitive information; ~ **sobre vagón** TRANSP price on rail; ~ **de subasta** BOLSA hammer price *(jarg);* ~ **de suscripción** BOLSA, COM GEN subscription price; ~ **de sustitución** V&M replacement price;

~ t ~ **con tendencia al alza** BOLSA long strike price; ~ **con tendencia alcista** BOLSA bull strike price; ~ **a tipo fijo** COM GEN flat-rate price; ~ **todo incluido** COM GEN all-inclusive price; ~ **del trabajo** ECON workfare; ~ **tras el cierre** BOLSA after-hours price;

~ u ~ **umbral** COM GEN threshold price; ~ **uniforme** COM GEN, ECON, V&M uniform price; ~ **unitario** COM GEN, RRHH, V&M piece rate, unit price;

~ v ~ **de valoración** BOLSA valuation price; ~ **del vendedor** BOLSA, CONT, FIN asking price; ~ **de venta** BOLSA offering price, COM GEN bargain price, sales price, selling price, CONT asking price ECON, RRHH supply price, V&M sales price; ~ **de venta ajustado** CONT adjusted selling price; ~ **por venta a granel** COM GEN bulk price; ~ **de venta al público** *(P.V.R.)* COM GEN recommended retail price *(RRP);* ~ **de venta regulado** CONT adjusted selling price; ~ **en vigor en el mercado** BOLSA prevailing market price; ~ **de la vivienda** INMOB house price

precio[3]: **al** ~ *fra* BOLSA, FIN at-the-money *(ATM);* **a un** ~ **de** *fra* COM GEN at a price of; ~ **de la calle** *fra* BOLSA, COM GEN price in the street; **al** ~ **de contado** *fra* BOLSA, FIN at-the-money *(ATM);* **a** ~ **de mercado** *fra* BOLSA,

FIN at the market price; **a un ~ muy bajo** *fra* V&M on bargain-basement terms; **el ~ se ha debilitado más** *fra* COM GEN the price has weakened

precios[1]: **~ contables** *m pl* ECON, FIN shadow prices; **~ controlados** *m pl* ECON administered pricing; **~ escalonados** *m pl* ECON staggered prices; **~ especiales para espacio publicitario** *m pl* V&M off-card rate; **~ fantasmas** *m pl* ECON, FIN shadow prices; **~ de oferta** *m pl* COM GEN sale price

precios[2]: **los ~ han sido ajustados a la baja** *fra* BOLSA prices have been marked down; **los ~ pueden tanto bajar como subir** *fra* COM GEN prices can go down as well as up

precio/venta: **~ para la cuenta** *m* BANCA price/sale for the account

precipitación: **~ ácida** *f* MED AMB *nieve, granizo, niebla* acid rain

precisión *f* COM GEN *informes, documentos, objetivos* accuracy; **~ simple** INFO single precision

preciso *adj* COM GEN accurate

preclusión: **~ jurídica** *f* DER estoppel

precodificado *adj* V&M precoded

precursor *adj* COM GEN trailblazing

predador, a *m,f* COM GEN, V&M predator

predecesor, a: **~ legal** *m,f* DER, PATENT legal predecessor

predecible *adj* COM GEN predictable

predecir *vt* COM GEN predict

predefinido *adj* ECON built-in, INFO preset

predeterminado *adj* COM GEN predetermined

predeterminar *vt* COM GEN predetermine

predicción *f* COM GEN forecast; **~ normativa** COM GEN normative forecasting; **~ de programa** COM GEN program forecast (*AmE*), programme forecast (*BrE*); **~ tecnológica** COM GEN, IND technological forecasting

predicho *adj* COM GEN predicted

predio: **~ comercial** *m* COM GEN, INMOB commercial property; **~ dominante** *m* INMOB dominant tenement

predominante *adj* COM GEN, V&M prevailing

predominar *vi* COM GEN, V&M prevail

preeminente *adj* COM GEN, V&M pre-eminent, prevailing

preencuesta *f* V&M pretest

preestablecido *adj* COM GEN pre-arranged

preestreno *m* MEDIOS sneak preview

prefabricado *adj* INMOB prefabricated

prefacio *m* MEDIOS standfirst (*jarg*)

preferencia *f* COM GEN preference (*pref.*); **~ del consumidor** COM GEN, V&M consumer preference; **~ de liquidez** ECON liquidity preference; **~ manifiesta** ECON revealed preference; **~ de marca** V&M brand preference

preferencial *adj* COM GEN preferential, INFO foreground

preferencias: **~ colectivas** *f pl* PROT SOC social wants

pregunta *f* COM GEN query; **~ abierta** COM GEN, V&M open-ended question; **~ cerrada** COM GEN, V&M *investigación de mercado* closed question; **~ de control** COM GEN, V&M control question; **~ de elección múltiple** COM GEN, V&M multiple-choice question; **~ hipotética** COM GEN hypothetical question; **~ inductiva** COM GEN, V&M leading question

preguntar *vt* COM GEN ask

prejubilado, -a *m,f* FIN preretiree

prejuicio *m* COM GEN *idea preconcebida* preconception, *percualidad* prejudice; ♦ **sin ~** SEG without prejudice (*wp*)

prejuzgar: **sin ~** *fra* SEG without prejudice (*wp*)

prematuro *adj* COM GEN premature

premio *m* FISC prize; **~ contenido en el envase** V&M in-pack premium; **~ orgánico** ECON organic premium; **~ en títulos** BOLSA bonus stock

premisa *f* COM GEN premise

prenda *f* COM GEN pledge, security; **~ de vestir** IND clothing

prensa *f* COM GEN, MEDIOS press; **~ amarilla** MEDIOS gutter press, tabloid press; **~ para comerciantes** MEDIOS trade press; **~ especializada** MEDIOS, V&M technical press; **~ de imprimir** MEDIOS printing press; **~ local** MEDIOS, V&M local press; **~ nacional** MEDIOS, V&M national press; **~ profesional** MEDIOS, V&M business press; **~ de provincia** MEDIOS, V&M provincial press, regional press; **~ regional** MEDIOS, V&M regional press; **~ sensacionalista** MEDIOS gutter press, tabloid press

prepago *m* CONT prepayment

preparación[1]: **sin ~** *adj* PROT SOC untrained

preparación[2] *f* COM GEN preparation, INFO setup; **~ de datos** ADMIN, INFO data preparation; **~ del presupuesto** CONT budget preparation; **~ del terreno** MED AMB *vaciamiento* site development

preparar *vt* COM GEN prepare, GES *conferencia* stage, POL draw up, V&M make ready; ♦ **~ una declaración** FISC prepare a return; **~ el terreno para** COM GEN pave the way for

prequiebra *f* FISC pre-bankruptcy

prerrequisito *m* COM GEN prerequisite

prerrogativa *f* COM GEN prerogative; **~ de la dirección** GES, RRHH management prerogative, managerial prerogative; **~ de los directivos** GES, RRHH management prerogative, managerial prerogative

prescribir *vt* DER prescribe, GES enjoin

prescripción *f* DER time bar, GES, INMOB prescription; **~ adquisitiva** DER adverse possession

prescrito *adj* COM GEN prescribed, DER time-barred, prescribed

presencia *f* V&M presence; **~ en el mercado** V&M market presence

presentación *f* BANCA *de letra de cambio* presentation, CONT layout, reporting, FISC filing of a return, GES presentation, INFO *documento procesado* layout, V&M presentation, PATENT filing; **~ anticipada** FISC *de declaración* early filing; **~ del balance** BOLSA filing statement; **~ para cancelaciones de deudas** BANCA submission for deletions of debts; **~ del caso** DER case file; **~ comercial** V&M sales presentation; **~ en computador** *AmL ver presentación en computadora AmL*; **~ en computadora** *AmL* (*cf presentación en ordenador Esp*) INFO computer presentation; **~ correcta** CONT fair presentation; **~ de documentos** ADMIN, IMP/EXP presentation of documents; **~ engañosa de un producto** V&M slack fill (*jarg*); **~ equitativa** CONT fair presentation; **~ estándar** V&M canned presentation; **~ fuera de plazo** FISC *de declaraciones* late filing, late rendering; **~ gráfica** V&M pictorial presentation; **~ ilustrada** V&M pictorial presentation; **~ justa** CONT fair presentation (*AmE*); **~ leal** CONT fair presentation (*AmE*); **~ de ofertas** COM GEN submission of bids; **~ en ordenador** *Esp* (*cf presentación en computadora AmL*) INFO computer presentation; **~ del plan operativo**

plurianual de primavera FIN, POL spring multi-year operational plan submission; **~ presupuestaria** CONT budgetary submission; **~ del presupuesto** ECON, POL Budget speech (*BrE*); **~ de referencias** V&M credentials presentation; **~ de ventas estandarizada** V&M standardized sales presentation

presentador, a *m,f* MEDIOS frontman, *radiodifusión, diarios hablados* presenter; **~ de noticias** MEDIOS anchorman, newscaster; **~ de televisión** MEDIOS television announcer

presentar *vt* ADMIN, COM GEN *solicitud, documento* file, present, shelve *oferta, protesta* make, *queja* lodge, *propuesta* lay before, DER *demanda* set up, GES *conferencia* stage, submit, PATENT enter, submit, POL *moción, proposición* table; ◆ **~ un alegato** DER put in a plea, enter a plea; **~ una apelación** DER enter an appeal; **~ un balance de** CONT show a balance of; **~ un cheque al cobro** BANCA present a check for payment (*AmE*), present a cheque for payment (*BrE*); **~ un contrainforme** DER, INMOB *compensación de tierras* serve counternotice; **~ la declaración de la renta** FISC file one's tax return; **~ una declaración de siniestro** SEG file a damage report, file a loss report; **~ un escrito** DER enter a writ; **~ una factura para el descuento** BANCA present a bill for discount; **~ una factura para recepción** BANCA present a bill for reception; **~ una letra para su aceptación** BANCA present a draft for acceptance; **~ una petición en las instancias adecuadas** COM GEN make a request to the appropriate authority; **~ propuestas** COM GEN, GES put forward proposals; **~ una declaración de quiebra** CONT file for bankruptcy; **~ una reclamación** DER put in a claim; **~ una solicitud de empleo** RRHH put in an application for a job; **~ razonablemente** CONT present fairly; **~ una solicitud** *Esp* (*cf meter una solicitud AmL*) put in an application; **~ su dimisión** *Esp* (*cf presentar su renuncia AmL*) RRHH hand in one's resignation; **~ su renuncia** *AmL* (*cf presentar su dimisión Esp*) RRHH hand in one's resignation

presentarse: **~ segunda vez a** *fra* PROT SOC retake; **~ para la elección** *fra* COM GEN, POL stand for election

presente: **estar ~** *fra* RRHH *en alerta* be on, stand by; **tener ~** *fra* COM GEN bear in mind; **por la ~ testifico que** *fra* DER I hereby testify that

presentes: **entre los ~** *fra* COM GEN among those present, inter praesentes

presidenta *f* COM GEN, GES, RRHH chairwoman

presidente, -a *m,f* COM GEN chair, chairman, convenor, director (*dir.*), *de comisión* president (*pres.*), POL, RRHH president (*pres.*); **~ del consejo** *m* GES, RRHH chairman of the board; **~ del consejo de administración** *m* GES, RRHH chairman of the administrative board, chairman of the board of directors, chairman of the executive board, chairman of the executive committee, President of the Group Executive Board (*AmE*), chairman of the board of management; **~ del consejo y director general** *m* GES, RRHH chairman and chief executive (*AmE*), chairman and managing director (*BrE*); **~ del consejo del tesoro** FIN President of the Treasury Board (*AmE*); **~ y director ejecutivo** *m* GES, RRHH chairman and chief executive (*AmE*), chairman and general manager, chairman and managing director (*BrE*); **~ y director general** *m* GES, RRHH chairman and general manager; **~ y director gerente** *m* GES, RRHH chairman and chief executive (*AmE*), chairman

and general manager, chairman and managing director (*BrE*); **~ ejecutivo** *m* GES, RRHH chief executive officer (*AmE*) (*CEO*); **~ electo** *m* GES, RRHH chairman elect; **~ honorario** *m* RRHH honorary chairman, honorary president; **~ honorario de la junta de directores** *m* GES, RRHH honorary chairman of the board of directors; **~ de la junta directiva** *m* GES, RRHH chairman of the board of directors, chairman of the executive board, chairman of the executive committee, chairman of the board of management, chairman of the management board, president of the group executive board (*AmE*); **~ de la junta supervisora** *m* GES, RRHH chairman of the supervisory board

Presidente, -a: **~ del Gobierno** *m,f* POL ≈ President of the Government (*AmE*), ≈ Prime Minister (*BrE*)

presidir *vt* COM GEN, GES preside over, *junta* chair, *reuniones* be in the chair

presión *f* COM GEN pressure, POL lobbying; **~ ascendente** ECON *sobre presupuesto* upward pressure; **~ de austeridad** ECON contractionary pressure; **~ a la baja** ECON *divisa, tipos de interés* downward pressure; **~ del consumidor** COM GEN consumer pressure; **~ deflacionaria** ECON deflationary pressure; **~ fiscal** ECON, FISC tax pressure; **~ inflacionista** ECON, FIN inflationary pressure; **~ media efectiva al freno** TRANSP brake mean effective pressure (*bmep*); **~ de los precios** ECON price pressure; **~ del tanque** TRANSP tank pressure; **~ de trabajo** TRANSP working pressure

presionar: **~ a alguien** *vt* COM GEN put pressure on sb; **~ y congelar** *vt* ECON squeeze and freeze (*jarg*)

prestable *adj* BANCA lendable, loanable

prestación *f* BANCA loan, COM GEN, GES *a los empleados*, RRHH benefit; **~ agrícola** *f pl* BANCA, ECON agricultural loan; **~ en especie** FISC *del empleo* benefit in kind; **~ ex gratia** COM GEN, SEG ex gratia payment; **~ de servicios** COM GEN provision of services, service delivery; **~ social** PROT SOC, RRHH welfare payment, income support (*BrE*), RRHH welfare payment

prestaciones: **~ imponibles de la seguridad social** *f pl* FISC, PROT SOC taxable social security benefits; **~ de jubilación anticipada** *f pl* FIN, PROT SOC, RRHH early retirement benefits; **~ y pagos diferidos** *f pl* SEG deferred benefits and payments; **~ sanitarias** *f pl* PROT SOC health benefits; **~ por servicios pretéritos** *f* FIN *plan de pensiones privado* past service benefit (*AmE*); **~ en vida del seguro de vida** *f pl* SEG living benefits of life insurance

prestamista *mf* BANCA, FIN lender, money lender; **~ hipotecario(-a)** *m,f* BANCA mortgage lender; **~ institucional** BANCA, FIN institutional lender; **~ privado(-a)** *m,f* BANCA, FIN private lender; **~ residual** BANCA, FIN residual lender; **~ del sector privado** *m,f* BANCA, FIN private sector borrower; **~ sobre prenda** FIN pawnbroker; **~ de última instancia** BANCA, FIN lender of last resort

préstamo *m* COM GEN loan;

~ a **~ acreditado** BANCA, ECON seasoned loan; **~ a la agricultura** BANCA, ECON farm loan; **~ de ajuste estructural** BANCA, ECON *internacional* structural adjustment loan; **~ de ajuste de la política industrial y comercial** BANCA, ECON industrial and trade policy adjustment loan (*ITPAL*); **~ de ajuste de programa** BANCA, ECON program adjustment loan (*AmE*) (*PAL*), programme adjustment loan (*BrE*) (*PAL*); **~ de ajuste del sector** BANCA, FIN sector adjustment loan

(*SECAL*); ~ **al cliente** BANCA call money; ~ **al consumidor** BANCA, FIN consumer lending; ~ **al desarrollo** BANCA development loan; ~ **amortizable** BANCA amortization loan; ~ **con amortización al vencimiento** BANCA, FIN interest-only loan; ~ **ampliado** BANCA step-up loan; ~**-arriendo** INMOB lease-lend; ~ **de asistencia técnica** BANCA, FIN technical assistance loan (*TAL*); ~ **atado** BANCA, FIN tied loan; ~ **para automóvil** BANCA car loan; ~ **con aval** BANCA, FIN recourse loan; ~ **de ayuda** BANCA *al desarrollo* aid loan; ~ **de ayuda al desarrollo** BANCA aid development loan;

▪ b ~ **a bajo interés** BANCA, FIN low-interest loan; ~ **bajo mano** ECON backdoor lending; ~ **bajo palabra** BANCA loan on trust; ~ **bancario** BANCA, COM GEN, CONT bank loan; ~ **barato** BANCA low-cost loan; ~ **bilateral** BANCA bilateral loan;

▪ c ~ **de calidad** BANCA quality loan; ~ **de capitales** BANCA, FIN hire of money; ~ **con caución** BANCA collateral loan (*BrE*), Lombard loan (*AmE*), secured loan; ~ **comercial** BANCA commercial lending, commercial loan; ~ **a una compañía del grupo** CONT *cuentas anuales* loan to related company; ~ **para compra de vivienda** BANCA, INMOB home purchase loan; ~ **concatenado** BANCA, FIN piggyback loan; ~ **de consolidación** BANCA, FIN consolidation loan; ~ **para la construcción** BANCA, INMOB construction loan; ~ **para la construcción de vivienda** BANCA, INMOB house-building loan; ~ **a la construcción de viviendas** BANCA housing loan; ~ **contingente** BANCA, FIN standby loan; ~ **de contrapartida** BANCA, FIN back-to-back loan; ~ **controlado** BANCA managed loan; ~ **a una corporación** BANCA, BOLSA, FIN corporate loan; ~ **corporativo** BANCA, FIN *autoridades locales* corporation loan; ~ **de corredor** BOLSA broker's loan; ~ **a corto plazo** BANCA short-term loan; ~ **en cuenta corriente** BANCA current account loan;

▪ d ~ **para el desarrollo profesional** BANCA, PROT SOC, RRHH Career Development Loan (*CDL*); ~ **descontado** BANCA discounted loan; ~ **diario** BANCA daily loan; ~ **diario de dinero** BANCA day loan; ~ **directo** BANCA straight loan; ~ **en divisas** BANCA currency borrowing;

▪ e ~ **de embarque** BANCA shipping loan; ~ **a una empresa** BANCA, BOLSA, FIN corporate loan; ~ **de equipos** ECON equipment leasing; ~ **específico para inversión** BANCA, FIN specific investment loan (*SIL*); ~ **específico respaldado** BANCA, BOLSA purpose loan; ~ **de estudiante** BANCA, FIN student loan; ~ **en eurodivisas** BANCA eurocurrency loan; ~ **a la exportación** BANCA, IMP/EXP export loan;

▪ f ~ **fiduciario** BANCA uncovered loan; ~ **fijo** BANCA fixed loan; ~ **sin finalidad declarada** BANCA, FIN nonpurpose loan; ~ **financiero** FIN financial lease; ~ **para fines comerciales** BANCA, COM GEN, IND business loan; ~ **para fines industriales** BANCA, COM GEN, IND business loan; ~ **en firme** BANCA hard loan; ~ **con fondo de amortización** CONT sinking fund loan;

▪ g ~ **con garantía** BANCA collateral loan (*BrE*), Lombard loan (*AmE*), secured loan; ~ **sin garantía** BANCA uncovered loan, unsecured loan; ~ **con garantía pignoraticia** COM GEN advance against security; ~ **garantizado** BANCA secured loan; ~ **general y acuerdo de garantía** BOLSA general loan and collateral agreement; ~ **de gran cuantía** BANCA jumbo loan;

~ **grande** BANCA jumbo loan; ~ **gratuito** BANCA, FIN gratuitous loan, nonrecourse loan;

▪ h ~ **hipotecario** BANCA, FIN, INMOB mortgage loan, bond loan; ~ **hipotecario ajustable** BANCA, FIN, INMOB adjustable mortgage loan (*AML*); ~ **hipotecario amortizado** BANCA, FIN, INMOB amortized mortgage loan; ~ **hipotecario pendiente** BANCA, FIN, INMOB outstanding mortgage loan; ~ **hipotecario residencial** BANCA, FIN, INMOB home mortgage loan;

▪ i ~ **improductivo** BANCA nonproductive loan; ~ **incobrable** BANCA, CONT bad loan; ~ **indexado** BANCA indexed loan; ~ **indirecto** ECON, FIN backdoor lending; ~ **industrial** BANCA production loan, BOLSA industrial loan, IND production loan; ~ **inicial** BANCA, FIN front-end loan; ~ **inmobiliario** BANCA, INMOB construction loan; ~ **interbancario** BANCA bank-to-bank lending; ~ **a interés fijo** BANCA, FIN fixed-interest loan; ~ **de interés fijo** BANCA, FIN fixed-rate loan; ~ **a interés preferencial** BANCA, FIN prime-rate loan; ~ **sin intereses** BANCA, FIN interest-free loan; ~ **intermediario financiero** BANCA, FIN financial intermediary loan (*FIL*); ~ **de inversión específico** BANCA, FIN specific investment loan (*SIL*);

▪ l ~ **a largo plazo** BANCA long-term loan;

▪ m ~ **mancomunado** BANCA joint loan; ~ **marítimo** FIN maritime loan; ~ **a medio plazo** BANCA, FIN medium-term loan (*MTL*), intermediate loan; ~ **para mejoras en la vivienda** BANCA home improvement loan; ~ **del mercado de descuento** BANCA, BOLSA, FIN discount market loan; ~ **mínimo** BANCA, FIN floor loan; ~ **monetario** ECON monetary accommodation; ~ **en mora** BANCA, FIN loan default; ~ **multidivisa** BANCA multicurrency loan; ~ **de mutuo respaldo** BANCA back-to-back loan;

▪ n ~ **neto** BANCA, ECON net lending; ~ **no acumulable** BANCA nonaccruing loan; ~ **no denunciable** BANCA, FIN uncallable loan; ~ **no ejecutable** BANCA nonperforming loan; ~ **no totalmente ejecutado** BANCA quasi-performing loan; ~ **nocturno** BANCA overnight loan;

▪ o ~ **oficial** BANCA, FIN government loan;

▪ p ~ **de pago invariable** BANCA constant-payment loan; ~ **de pago total al vencimiento** BANCA balloon loan; ~ **paralelo** BANCA, ECON, FIN parallel loan; ~ **de participación** BANCA participation loan; ~ **pendiente** BANCA outstanding loan; ~ **perdonable** BANCA, FIN forgivable loan; ~ **periódico** BANCA seasoned loan; ~ **personal** BANCA, FIN personal loan; ~ **personal garantizado** BANCA secured personal loan; ~ **a plazo** BANCA term loan; ~ **a plazo fijo** BANCA fixed-term loan; ~ **a plazo fijo no garantizado** BANCA unsecured fixed-term loan; ~ **a plazos** BANCA instalment loan (*BrE*), installment loan (*AmE*); ~ **a plazos al consumo** BANCA consumer installment loan (*AmE*), consumer instalment loan (*BrE*); ~ **a plazos para el consumidor** BANCA consumer installment loan (*AmE*), consumer instalment loan (*BrE*); ~ **polivalente** BANCA fuzzy loan; ~ **a prima** FIN *de intermediario* lending at a premium; ~ **con primas** BANCA premium loan; ~ **de primera hipoteca** BANCA, FIN, INMOB first mortgage loan; ~ **principal** BANCA senior loan; ~ **prioritario** BANCA senior loan; ~ **provisional** BANCA interim loan; ~ **puente** BANCA bridge loan, swing loan;

▪ q ~ **que no devenga interés** BANCA, FIN interest-free loan;

~ r **~ de racionalización de la empresa pública** BANCA, FIN public enterprise rationalization loan (*PERL*); **~ de rápido desembolso** BANCA quick-disbursing loan; **~ reajustable** BANCA, FIN index-tied loan; **~ recíproco al descubierto** BANCA bridge loan, swing loan; **~ de reconstrucción de emergencia** FIN emergency reconstruction loan (*ERL*); **~ reestructurado** BANCA restructured loan; **~ de reforma de la empresa pública** BANCA, FIN public enterprise reform loan (*PERL*); **~ de regulación de la exportación** ECON, IMP/EXP export adjustment loan (*EAL*); **~ de regulación del sector agrícola** ECON, FIN agricultural sector adjustment loan (*BrE*) (*ASAL*); **~ de rehabilitación de la importación** FIN, IMP/EXP rehabilitation import loan (*RIL*); **~ reincidente** BANCA, FIN repeater loan; **~ de la Reserva Federal a instituciones financieras** BANCA discount window lending (*AmE*); **~ residencial hipotecario** BANCA, INMOB residential mortgage loan; **~ de riesgo supremo** BANCA sovereign risk loan;

~ s **~ sectorial de inversión y mantenimiento** BANCA, FIN sector investment and maintenance loan (*SIM*); **~ con segunda hipoteca** *f* BANCA, FIN, INMOB second mortgage lending, home equity loan; **~ sobre excedentes agrícolas** BANCA, FIN nonrecourse loan; **~ sobre una póliza** SEG policy loan; **~ sobregirado** BANCA overdraft lending; **~ a una sociedad** BANCA, BOLSA, FIN corporate loan; **~ subordinado** BANCA, FIN subordinated loan; **~ subordinado convertible** BANCA, FIN convertible subordinated loan; **~ de una subsidiaria a la empresa matriz** BANCA, FIN upstream loan (*jarg*); **~ supremo** BANCA, FIN sovereign loan;

~ t **~ de tasa flotante** BANCA floating-rate loan; **~ de tasa variable** BANCA floating-rate loan; **~ temporal** BANCA seasoned loan; **~ a término fijo garantizado** BANCA secured fixed-term loan; **~ con tipo variable** BANCA roll-over loan; **~ de títulos** BOLSA share borrowing, stock borrowing; **~ con tope máximo del tipo de interés** BOLSA *futuros* cap-rate loan (*AmE*); **~ totalmente utilizado** BANCA fully-performing loan; **~ de transferencia** BANCA, FIN pass-through loan; **~ de transición** BANCA bridging advance;

~ v **~ en valores** BANCA, BOLSA, FIN securities lending, securities borrowing; **~ de valores entre operadores** BANCA, BOLSA, FIN securities loan; **~ vencido** BANCA noncurrent loan; **~ vinculado** BOLSA self-dealing; **~ a la vista** BANCA, BOLSA call loan; **~ de vivienda** BANCA home loan

préstamos: **~, inversiones y anticipos** *m pl* CONT, FIN loans, investments and advances; **~ netos** *m pl* ECON, FIN, POL net borrowing; **~ netos del sector público** *m pl* BANCA, ECON, POL net lending by the public sector

prestar *vt* BANCA, BOLSA lend, COM GEN *servicio* deliver, FIN lend; **~ una fianza a alguien** BANCA stand surety for sb; **~ con garantía** BOLSA lend on security; **~ juramento** DER swear; ◆ **~ dinero** FIN lend money **~ sobre un valor** BOLSA lend against security; **~ testimonio en nombre de** DER give witness on behalf of

prestatario, -a *m,f* BANCA borrower; **~ con calificación triple A** BOLSA triple-A-rated borrower; **~ de primera clase** BANCA prime borrower (*AmE*), premier borrower (*BrE*); **~ supremo(-a)** BANCA, FIN sovereign borrower

prestigio *m* COM GEN, V&M good name, kudos, prestige

prestigioso *adj* COM GEN, V&M prestigious

presunción *f* COM GEN, DER assumption, presumption

presunto *adj* DER alleged

presupuestación: **~ del capital** *f* CONT capital budgeting; **~ de ejecución** *f* CONT, FIN, RRHH performance budgeting; **~ de obligaciones** *f* CONT responsibility budgeting; **~ de producción** *f* CONT *nacional*, FIN, POL output budgeting; **~ de programas** *f* CONT, FIN program budgeting (*AmE*), programme budgeting (*BrE*); **~ de responsabilidad** *f* CONT responsibility budgeting

presupuestar *vt* COM GEN budget

presupuestario[1] *adj* COM GEN budgetary; **no ~** COM GEN nonbudgetary

presupuestario[2] *m* COM GEN budget item

presupuesto *m* COM GEN budget; **~ de activo fijo** CONT, ECON, FIN capital budget; **~ actual** CONT, ECON, FIN, POL actual budget; **~ actualizado** CONT, ECON, FIN, POL actual budget; **~ ajustado** CONT, ECON, FIN tight budget; **~ anual** ECON budget year; **~ asignado a la publicidad** V&M advertising allocation budget; **~ base** CONT, ECON, FIN base budget; **~ de caja** CONT, ECON, FIN cash budget, cash forecast; **~ de capital** CONT, ECON, FIN capital budget; **~ comunitario** ECON *UE* Community budget; **~ contingente** CONT, ECON, FIN contingent budget; **~ continuo** CONT, ECON, FIN continuous budget; **~ APPEND** CONT, ECON, FIN, POL actual budget; **~ de ejecución** CONT, FIN, RRHH performance budget; **~ equilibrado** ECON, FIN balanced budget; **el ~ del Estado** ECON, POL the Budget (*BrE*); **~ eventual** CONT, ECON, FIN contingent budget; **~ de explotación** CONT, ECON, FIN operating budget; **~ familiar** ECON, V&M family budget; **~ flexible** ECON flexible budget, variable budget; **~ de gasto de capital** FIN, CONT, ECON capital budget; **~ de gastos** COM GEN expenditure budget, CONT expense budget; **~ de gastos de capital** COM GEN capital expenditure budget; **~ global** CONT, ECON, FIN comprehensive budget; **~ de ingresos** CONT income budget, revenue budget; **~ de inversiones** CONT, ECON, FIN investment budget; **~ para la investigación** COM GEN research budget; **~ a largo plazo** CONT, ECON, FIN long-term budget; **~ maestro** CONT, ECON, FIN master budget; **~ de marketing** V&M marketing budget; **~ de medios de comunicación** MEDIOS media budget; **~ modesto** COM GEN low-cost; **~ neutro** POL neutral budget; **~ oculto** POL budget purdah; **~ de operaciones** CONT, ECON, FIN operational budget; **~ original** CONT, ECON, FIN master budget; **~ participativo** GES participative budgeting; **~ de pleno empleo** CONT, ECON, POL full-employment budget; **~ principal** CONT, ECON, FIN master budget; **~ por programas** COM GEN planning-programming-budgeting system (*PPBS*); **~ promocional** V&M promotional budget; **~ proporcionado** CONT, ECON, FIN sizeable budget; **~ de publicidad** V&M advertising appropriation; **~ publicitario** V&M advertising budget; **~ suplementario** CONT, ECON, FIN supplementary budget; **~ de ventas** V&M sales budget; **~ del viaje** TRANSP voyage estimate; ◆ **de bajo ~** COM GEN, MEDIOS low-budget

Presupuesto: **~ de la Unión Europea** *m* ECON, POL European Union Budget

presupuestos: **~ de misiones** *m pl* V&M mission budgets

pretensión *f* COM GEN *reclamación* claim; **~ competitiva** V&M competitive claim

pretributación *f* FISC pre-assessing

prevención: **~ de accidentes** *f* RRHH, SEG accident

prevention; **~ del despilfarro** *f* MED AMB waste prevention; **~ del fraude marítimo** *f* SEG, TRANSP maritime fraud prevention; **~ de incendios** *f* PROT SOC, RRHH, SEG fire prevention; **~ de reclamaciones** *f* SEG claims prevention

prevenido: **estar ~ contra** *fra* COM GEN *riesgo* guard against

prevenir *vt* COM GEN foresee, prevent, warn sb against doing sth

preventa *f* INMOB presale

prever *vt* COM GEN forecast, foresee, *problema, retraso* anticipate

previo[1]: **~ pago al contado** *m* CONT cash received basis

previo[2]: **~ a** *prep* COM GEN prior to

previsión *f* COM GEN anticipation, forecast, forecasting; **~ de beneficios** COM GEN, FIN earnings forecast; **~ comercial** COM GEN, ECON business forecasting; **~ de costes** *Esp* (*cf previsión de costos AmL*) CONT cost forecast; **~ de costos** *AmL* (*cf previsión de costes Esp*) CONT cost forecast; **~ de la demanda** V&M demand forecasting; **~ económica** ECON economic forecasting; **~ de flujos de caja** CONT cash flow forecast; **~ de fondos** CONT cash flow forecast; **~ de la fuerza de trabajo** RRHH manpower forecast, staff forecasting; **~ a largo plazo** COM GEN long-range forecast; **~ de personal** RRHH manpower forecast, staff forecasting; **~ del programa** COM GEN program forecast (*AmE*), programme forecast (*BrE*); **~ de tesorería** CONT cash flow forecast, cash forecast; **~ de ventas** ECON, V&M sales forecast; ◆ **con ~ de futuro** COM GEN forward-thinking; **en ~ de** COM GEN as a precaution against

previsiones: **~ financieras** *f pl* FIN financial forecasts; **~ de gasto público** *f pl* ECON public spending plans; **~ presupuestarias suplementarias** *f pl* POL supplementary estimates

previsor, a *m,f* COM GEN forecaster

previsto *adj* COM GEN anticipated, foreseen; ◆ **estar ~** COM GEN be on schedule, be on the cards (*infrml*); **estar ~ para** COM GEN be scheduled for; **según línea ~** COM GEN according to schedule, as anticipated, TRANSP, V&M as anticipated

previsualizar *vt* INFO *documento* preview

PRH *abr* (*planificación de los recursos humanos*) RRHH HRP (*human resource planning*)

prima[1]: **con ~** *adj* COM GEN above par

prima[2] *f* COM GEN premium; **~ de aceleración** RRHH acceleration premium (*AmE*); **~ al comisionista** COM GEN del credere; **~ de amortización** CONT redemption premium; **~ por antigüedad** RRHH seniority bonus, seniority premium; **~ anual** SEG annual premium; **~ por asistencia** RRHH attendance bonus; **~ automovilística** SEG motor premium; **~ basada en riesgos** SEG risk-based premium; **~ base** SEG basic premium; **~ de cancelación** CONT redemption premium; **~ de carga** FISC *navegación* primage, TRANSP hat money (*infrml*), *navegación* primage; **~ de celeridad pagadera en origen y destino** TRANSP *navegación* dispatch money payable both ends (*dbe*); **~ de cláusula de aceleración** BANCA, FIN acceleration clause premium; **~ por cláusula de vencimiento anticipado** DER acceleration clause premium; **~ combinada** SEG combined premium; **~ complementaria** SEG additional premium (*AP*); **~ para el comprador** BOLSA, COM GEN buyer's option; **~ de contratación** RRHH golden hello (*infrml*);

~ de conversión BOLSA conversion premium; **~ debida por el periodo corrido del seguro** BOLSA time premium; **~ decreciente** SEG *marítimo* premiums reducing; **~ de depósito** SEG deposit premium; **~ y descuento de cambio** FIN premium and discount on exchange; **~ por despacho rápido** TRANSP *navegación* dispatch money; **~ devengada** SEG earned premium; **~ del dólar** BOLSA *opciones* dollar premium; **~ de ejecución** FIN performance bonus; **~ de emisión** BOLSA, CONT *balances*, ECON, FIN capital surplus (*AmE*), share premium (*BrE*); **~ de emisión de acciones** BOLSA stock issue bonus; **~ de explotación** TRANSP operating subsidy; **~ fija** SEG fixed premium; **~ por grupos** RRHH group bonus; **~ por horas extraordinarias** RRHH overtime premium; **~ de incentivo** RRHH incentive bonus; **~ por lealtad** BOLSA loyalty bonus; **~ media** SEG average premium; **~ neta** BOLSA *opciones*, SEG net premium; **~ neta modificada** SEG modified net premium; **~ nivelada** SEG level premium; **~ no cobrada** FIN, FISC unearned premium; **~ no ganada** FIN, FISC unearned premium; **~ de opción** BOLSA option premium; **~ de opción de rescate** BOLSA call option premium; **~ de opción a vender** BOLSA seller's option (*s.o.*); **~ pagada por adelantado** SEG advance premium; **~ de permanencia** COM GEN golden handcuffs (*infrml*); **~ de producción** SEG production bonus; **~ pronta descarga** TRANSP *navegación* dispatch money; **~ por reconversión** RRHH redeployment premium; **~ de rendimiento** SEG acceleration premium; **~ de rescate** BOLSA call premium, CONT redemption premium; **~ de rescate de un bono** BOLSA, CONT bond redemption premium; **~ por retraso** BOLSA backwardation; **~ del riesgo** SEG risk premium; **~ por riesgo de mercado** BOLSA market risk premium; **~ salarial** RRHH wage bonus; **~ de seguro de enfermedad** RRHH sickness insurance premium; **~ de seguros** SEG insurance premium; **~ sobre bonos** BOLSA bond premium; **~ sobre el valor del bono** BOLSA premium over bond value; **~ sobre el valor de conversión** BOLSA premium over conversion value; **~ de tipo fijo** RRHH flat-rate bonus; **~ única** COM GEN single premium; **~ de venta** BOLSA put premium; **~ vinculada al riesgo** SEG risk-related premium; ◆ **estar a ~** BOLSA be at a premium; **sobre una ~** FIN at a premium

Prima-1 *f* BANCA Prime-1

primario *adj* COM GEN primary

primer: **~ año** *m* COM GEN initial year; **~ aviso de convocatoria** *m* BOLSA first call date; **~ borrador** *m* DER rough draft; **~ día de operaciones** *m* BOLSA first dealing day; **~ dueño de los derechos de autor** *m* DER, PATENT first owner of copyright; **~ mes de cotización** *m* BOLSA spot month; **~ mundo** *m* POL *mundo desarrollado* first world; **~ navío disponible** *m* TRANSP first available vessel (*firavv*); **~ préstamo hipotecario para la vivienda** *m* BANCA, FIN, INMOB whole loan; **~ propietario de los derechos** *m* DER, PATENT *propiedad intelectual* first owner of copyright; **~ transportista** *m* TRANSP first carrier; **~ trimestre** *m* COM GEN first quarter

primera[1]: **de ~ calidad** *adj* COM GEN high-quality; **de ~ categoría** *adj* COM GEN top-flight, top-ranking, TRANSP *Registro de Buques de Lloyd's* A1; **de ~ clase** *adj* COM GEN, OCIO high-class; **de ~ línea** *adj* COMS, V&M first-rate

primera[2] *f* OCIO, TRANSP first class; ~ **clase** OCIO, TRANSP first class; ~ **copia de una película** MEDIOS film rush; ~ **dueña de los derechos de autor** PATENT first owner of copyright; ~ **emisión** BOLSA primary distribution; ~ **generación** IND, INFO, MEDIOS first generation; ~ **hipoteca** BANCA, INMOB first mortgage, first lien; ~ **línea** POL frontline (*jarg*) (*BrE*); ~ **parte** COM GEN first half; ~ **prueba** V&M *publicidad* pull (*jarg*); ~ **vivienda** INMOB starter home

primera[3]: **en ~ instancia** *fra* COM GEN in the first instance

primeramente *adv* COM GEN primarily

primerísima: **de ~ clase** *adj* BOLSA gilt-edged

primero[1]: **el ~** *m* COM GEN the former

primero[2]: **ser ~ de cartel** *fra* OCIO get top billing; ~ **en entrar, primero en salir** (*PEPS*) *fra* COM GEN, CONT *método de inventario* first in, first out (*FIFO*); ~ **en entrar, último en salir** (*PEUS*) *fra* CONT first in, last out (*FILO*)

primicia: ~ **informativa** *f* MEDIOS *edición* scoop

principal *m* BANCA, FIN *finanzas, seguros* prime (*AmE*), prime rate (*BrE*), principal sum; ~ **de la acumulación** CONT principal of accrual; ~ **del bono** BOLSA bond principal; ~ **socio-a comercial** *m,f* ECON main trading partner

principio *m* COM GEN principle, INFO *archivo* start, MAT principle; ~ **de aceleración** ECON *inversión* acceleration principle; ~ **del acelerador** ECON *inversión* accelerator principle; ~ **de acumulación** CONT accrual principle; ~ **de ajuste del precio** BOLSA stock adjustment principle; ~ **de antigüedad** RRHH seniority principle; ~ **de auditoría** CONT auditing principle; ~ **del beneficio** FISC benefit principle; ~ **de buena fe** COM GEN, DER, SEG utmost good faith; ~ **de compensación** FISC principle of equalization; ~ **de compensación social** ECON compensation principle; ~ **de conservadurismo** CONT conservatism principle; ~ **de consistencia** CONT consistency principle; ~ **de contabilidad** CONT accounting principle; ~ **de continuidad** CONT consistency principle; ~ **de coste histórico** *Esp* (*cf principio de costo histórico AmL*) CONT historical cost principle; ~ **de costo histórico** *AmL* (*cf principio de coste histórico Esp*) CONT historical cost principle; ~ **de cumplimiento voluntario** FISC principle of voluntary compliance; ~ **de descomposición jerárquica** GES hierarchical decomposition principle; ~ **del devengo** CONT accrual principle; ~ **de la diferencia rawlsiana** ECON Rawlsian difference principle; ~ **director** COM GEN governing principle, guiding principle; ~ **de empresa en funcionamiento** CONT going-concern principle; ~ **de empresa en marcha** CONT going-concern principle; ~ **de equilibrio** CONT *entre costes e ingresos* matching principle; ~ **de exclusión** ECON exclusion principle; ~ **de la garantía de recuperación de la inversión** FIN guaranteed recovery of investment principle (*GRIP*); ~ **de gestión continuada** CONT going-concern concept, going-concern principle; ~ **de la igualdad de oportunidades** COM GEN arm's-length principle; ~ **invariable de Ricardo** ECON Ricardo invariance principle; ~ **marginal de la situación** ECON marginal principle of allocation (*MPA*); ~ **del minimax** GES minimax principle; ~ **del multiplicador** ECON multiplier principle; ~ **de Peter** RRHH Peter principle; ~ **de precaución** MED AMB precautionary principle; ~ **de responsabilidad del país contaminante** MED

AMB *internacional* polluter pays principle; ~ **de uniformidad** CONT consistency principle; ~ **de Valdez** MED AMB Valdez principle; ~ **de valoración** CONT valuation principle; ◆ **de ~** COM GEN on principle

Principio: ~ **de Compensación de Kaldor-Hicks** *m* ECON Kaldor-Hicks Compensation Principle; ~ **de Equidad en Remuneración** *m* DER, RRHH Equal Pay Act (*EqPA*)

Principios: ~ **de Contabilidad Generalmente Aceptados** *m pl* (*PCGA*) ADMIN Generally Accepted Accounting Principles (*GAAP*)

priori: **a ~** *fra* COM GEN a priori

prioridad *f* COM GEN, PATENT priority; ~ **principal** COM GEN number one priority

prioritario *adj* COM GEN priority

priorización *f* FISC grandfathering

priorizar *vt* COM GEN, GES prioritize

prisión: ~ **preventiva** *f* DER preventive detention; ~ **provisional** *f* DER preventive detention

privado *adj* COM GEN private, DER deprived

privatización *f* COM GEN, ECON, POL privatization; ~ **de los resultados** ECON privatization proceeds; ◆ **de reciente ~** COM GEN newly privatized

privatizar *vt* COM GEN, ECON, POL privatize; ◆ ~ **parcialmente** ECON *empresa* hive off (*infrml*)

privatizarse *v refl* COM GEN go private (*infrml*)

privilegiado *adj* COM GEN concessional, DER, FIN privileged

privilegio[1]: ~ **en el cambio de divisas** *m* BOLSA exchange privilege; ~ **del constructor** *m* INMOB mechanic's lien; ~ **fiscal** *m* FISC tax privilege; ~ **general** *m* INMOB general lien; ~ **hipotecario** *m* BANCA, DER, INMOB mortgage lien; ~ **marítimo** *m* DER maritime lien; ~ **de omisión de pago** *m* BANCA, FIN skip-payment privilege; ~ **de pago anticipado** *m* BANCA, FIN prepayment privilege; ~ **de reinversión** *m* BOLSA reinvestment privilege; ~ **de suscripción** *m* BOLSA subscription privilege

privilegio[2]: ~ **del puesto** *fra* RRHH perk of the job (*infrml*); **sin ~** *fra* COM GEN without privileges (*x-pri*)

pro[1]: ~**-americano** *adj* POL pro-American; ~ **forma** *adj* ADMIN pro forma

pro[2] *m* COM GEN plus

pro[3]: **en ~ de** *fra* COM GEN in favor of (*AmE*), in favour of (*BrE*)

proa: **a ~** *adv* TRANSP forward

proactivo *adj* COM GEN, GES proactive

probabilidad *f* MAT probability; ~ **ponderada** FIN, MAT corrected probability

probable *adj* COM GEN, MAT probable, V&M *cliente* prospective

probador *m* COM GEN fitting room

probar *vt* COM GEN prove, test, INFO test; ◆ ~ **a alguien** COM GEN give sb a trial; ~ **una reclamación** DER substantiate a claim

probatorio *adj* DER evidenciary

problema *m* COM GEN problem; ~ **de la agregación de datos** CONT, ECON *macroeconomía* aggregation problem; ~ **añadido** CONT, ECON aggregation problem; ~ **básico** POL, PROT SOC bread-and-butter issue (*BrE*) (*infrml*), pocketbook issue (*AmE*); ~ **de la deuda mundial** ECON, POL world debt problem; ~ **de ensayo** COM GEN test problem; ~ **de identificación** ECON identification problem; **~ de liquidez** BANCA liquidity problem, CONT liquidity problem, cash flow problem, ECON cash flow problem, FIN liquidity problem, cash flow problem; **~ medioambiental** MED AMB environmental problem; **~ de optimización** MAT optimization problem; **~ de préstamo** BANCA, FIN problem loan; **~ de procedimiento** COM GEN procedural issue; **~ de relaciones humanas** COM GEN, RRHH personnel problem; **~ técnico** INFO *sistemas abiertos* glitch; **~ de tesorería** CONT, ECON, FIN cash flow problem; **~ de transformación** ECON transformation problem; **~ de traspaso** ECON transfer problem; ◆ **sin ~** COM GEN trouble-free

procedimiento *m* COM GEN modus operandi, procedure, modus operandi, DER proceeding; **~ aduanero** IMP/EXP customs formality; **~ de agravio** DER, RRHH grievance procedure; **~ de agravio colectivo** DER, RRHH collective grievance procedure; **~ de agravio individual** DER, RRHH individual grievance procedure; **~ de apelación** DER, RRHH appeals procedure; **~ de arbitraje** SEG arbitration proceedings; **~ de auditoría** CONT auditing procedure; **~ de certificación de aduanas simplificado** IMP/EXP simplified clearance procedure (*SCP*); **~ de cobro de oficio** FISC jeopardy collection procedure; **~ conciliatorio** RRHH conciliation procedure (*BrE*); **~ de contabilidad** CONT accounting procedure; **~ de control** INFO control procedure; **~ de control administrativo** ADMIN administrative control procedure; **~ de corte** CONT cut-off procedures; **~ de desahucio** DER dispossess proceedings; **~ de despido** RRHH dismissal procedure, redundancy procedure; **~ disciplinario** RRHH discipline procedure; **~ documental de exportación** ADMIN, IMP/EXP export documentation procedure; **~ ejecutivo hipotecario** DER, INMOB foreclosure; **~ ejecutorio** COM GEN enforcement procedure; **~ de ejercicio** BOLSA *opciones* exercise procedure; **~ empírico** COM GEN rule of thumb; **~ de escucha de la parte contraria** COM GEN audita altera parte procedure; **~ para evitar disputas** RRHH procedure for the avoidance of disputes; **~ externo** TRANSP external procedure; **~ interno** TRANSP internal procedure; **~ judicial** DER court procedure, judicial proceedings, legal proceedings; **~ legal** DER court procedure, proceeding; **~ para mensajes de información sobre cargas** TRANSP Cargo Information Message Procedure; **~ de negociación** COM GEN, RRHH negotiating procedure; **~ oral** PATENT oral proceeding; **~ parlamentario** GES, POL parliamentary procedure; **~ de prueba** SEG testing procedure; **~ de quiebra** DER bankruptcy proceedings; **~ de reclamación** COM GEN, DER complaints procedure, SEG claims procedure; **~ de reclamación de la carga** TRANSP cargo claim procedure; **~ de resolución de litigios** RRHH dispute procedure; **~ simplificado de transporte de mercancías por ferrocarril** TRANSP simplified procedure for goods carried by rail (*SPGER*); **~ vigente** COM GEN standing procedure

procedimientos: **~ de la conferencia** *m pl* GES conference proceedings; **~ y normas generales** *m pl* COM GEN envelope procedures and rules

procesable *adj* COM GEN *observación, delito, alegación*, DER, RRHH actionable; **no ~** INFO unprocessable

procesado: **~ de texto** *m AmL* (*cf procesador de textos Esp*) (*WP*) ADMIN, INFO word processor (*WP*)

procesador *m* INFO processor; **~ frontal** INFO front-end computer; **~ de sonido** INFO speech processing; **~ de textos** *Esp* (*cf procesado de texto AmL*) (*WP*) ADMIN, INFO word processor (*WP*); **~ vectorial** INFO array processor (*AP*)

procesal *adj* COM GEN, DER, GES procedural

procesamiento *f* BANCA *de cheques* processing; **~ de alimentos** *m* IND food processing; **~ de antecedentes** *m* RRHH *hoja de servicios* background processing (*AmE*); **~ electrónico de datos** *m* (*PED*) INFO electronic data processing (*EDP*); **~ remoto** *m* INFO remote processing; **~ en serie** *m* INFO serial processing; **~ simultáneo** *m* INFO *de tareas* parallel processing

procesar[1]: **sin ~** *adj* INFO unprocessed

procesar[2] *vt* DER prosecute, IND, INFO *datos* process; ◆ **~ a alguien por falsificación** DER sb prosecute for forgery

proceso *m* COM GEN process, DER action, IND *producción*, INFO *datos* process; **~ de adopción** V&M *de producto* adoption process; **~ analítico** GES, RRHH analytic process; **~ de armonización** COM GEN harmonization process; **~ automático de datos** (*PAD*) INFO automatic data processing (*ADP*); **~ civil** DER civil action; **~ competitivo** ECON competitive process; **~ de compra** COM GEN buying process; **~ de computador** *AmL*, **~ de computadora** *AmL* (*cf proceso de ordenador Esp*) INFO computer processing; **~ concurrente** INFO concurrent processing; **~ continuo** ECON, IND, V&M continuous process; **~ contra alguien** DER action against sb; **~ de datos** ADMIN, INFO data processing; **~ de datos comerciales** INFO business data processing; **~ de datos gráficos** INFO graphic data processing; **~ de decisión** GES decision-making process; **~ estocástico** COM GEN stochastic process; **~ de fabricación** IND manufacturing process; **~ legal** DER legal suit; **~ logístico** IND, MAT logistic process; **~ por lotes** INFO batch processing; **~ por lotes a distancia** INFO remote batch processing; **~ no prioritario** INFO background processing; **~ de ordenador** *Esp* (*cf proceso de computador AmL, proceso de computadora AmL*) INFO computer processing; **~ de producción** IND production process; **~ de recepción** IMP/EXP inward processing; **~ de selección** RRHH screening process; **~ simultáneo** INFO concurrent processing; **~ de supervivencia** COM GEN, ECON survival process; **~ técnico** COM GEN engineering process; **~ de transacción** INFO transaction processing; **~ a viva voz** BOLSA open outcry action; ◆ **estar en ~** COM GEN be in process

procomunista *adj* POL pro-communist

procuración *f* COM GEN procurement

procurador, a *m,f* BANCA, COM GEN, DER *trámites burocráticos* ≈ solicitor (*BrE*)

pródigo *adj* COM GEN spendthrift

producción *f* COM GEN production, INFO throughput; **~ por acre** ECON *agricultura* yield per acre; **~ agrícola** ECON agricultural production; **~ azucarera** COM GEN, IND sugar production; **~ de bienes de capital** ECON indirect production; **~ casera** IND home production; **~ conjunta** ECON joint production; **~ continua** IND continuous production; **~ deficitaria** IND underproduction; **~ directa** ECON, IND direct production; **~ de estados** FIN reporting; **~ experimental** COM GEN, GES, IND pilot production; **~ global** ECON aggregate production; **~ en gran escala** IND mass production; **~ por hora** IND output per hour; **~ industrial** ECON, IND industrial production; ~ **de ingresos** COM GEN revenue production; ~ **integrada por computador** *AmL ver* *producción integrada por computadora AmL*; ~ **integrada por computadora** *AmL* (*cf producción integrada por ordenador Esp*) IND, INFO computer-integrated manufacturing (*CIM*); ~ **integrada por ordenador** *Esp* (*cf producción integrada por computadora AmL*) IND, INFO computer-integrated manufacturing (*CIM*); ~ **intensiva** ECON, IND intensive production; ~ **interior** ECON, IND domestic output; ~ **intermitente** IND intermittent production; ~ **justo a tiempo** *AmL* (*cf producción según demanda Esp*) IND just-in-time production (*JIT production*); ~ **local** IND home production; ~ **en lotes** IND batch production; ~ **en masa** IND mass production; ~ **máxima** ECON, IND maximum output; ~ **modular** IND, MAT modular production; ~ **nacional** ECON home production; ~ **neta** ECON, POL net output; ~ **normal** CONT performance standard; ~ **piloto** COM GEN, GES, IND pilot production; ~ **potencial** ECON, IND potential output; ~ **de proceso continuo** ECON, IND, V&M continuous process production; ~ **según demanda** *Esp* (*cf producción justo a tiempo AmL*) IND just-in-time production (*JIT production*); ~ **en serie** ECON, IND chain production, large-scale production, line production; ~ **total** COM GEN outlay; ~ **con utilización intensiva de acero** IND steel-intensive production

producir *vt* CONT bear, ECON produce, *confianza* breed; ♦ ~ **un beneficio** BOLSA yield a profit, CONT make a profit; ~ **un incremento de capital** COM GEN make a capital gain; ~ **una pérdida** BOLSA yield a loss

productividad *f* COM GEN productivity, CONT throughput; ~ **marginal** ECON, IND marginal productivity

productivo *adj* CONT, FIN profitable, GES, RRHH productive; **no** ~ CONT, FIN nonprofitable, GES, RRHH nonproductive

producto *m* BOLSA physical commodity, COM GEN product, CONT output, ECON produce, output; ~ **acabado** COM GEN finished product, ECON, IND final good; ~ **agrícola** ECON agricultural product, farm produce; ~ **al contado** BOLSA spot commodity; ~ **alimenticio** COM GEN foodstuff; ~ **alimenticio elaborado** COM GEN, IND processed food; ~ **alimenticio orgánico** MED AMB organic foodstuff; ~ **alimenticio de primera necesidad** COM GEN essential foodstuff; ~ **de alta calidad** V&M up-market product, high-quality product; ~ **de alto valor añadido** ECON, FISC high added-value product; ~ **auténtico** COM GEN genuine article; ~ **básico** BOLSA, COM GEN, IND commodity (*cmdty*), V&M core product; ~ **básico controlado** BOLSA regulated commodity; ~ **de calidad** COM GEN quality good; ~ **con código de barras** INFO, V&M bar-coded product; ~ **compensador** IMP/EXP compensating product; ~ **complementario** V&M complementary product; ~ **consolidado** V&M established product; ~ **de consumo** COM GEN consumer product; ~ **de consumo popular** BOLSA, COM GEN, IND commodity (*cmdty*); ~ **de conveniencia** COM GEN convenience product; ~ **derivado** V&M derivative product; ~ **diferenciado** V&M differentiated product; ~ **directo** BANCA, BOLSA direct yield; ~ **duradero** ECON, IND hard commodity; ~ **ecológico** MED AMB environmentally-friendly product; ~ **equivalente corporativo** FISC corporate equivalent yield; ~ **estatal bruto** ECON gross state product; ~ **estrella** V&M star product; ~ **final** COM GEN final product, end product; ~ **físico marginal** ECON marginal physical product; ~ **de gama baja** V&M down market product; ~ **de gancho** COM GEN appeal product; ~ **de gran aceptación** MEDIOS, V&M hot property (*jarg*), *publicidad* property (*jarg*); ~ **de gran valor agregado** FISC, IND high added-value product; ~ **homogéneo** IND homogeneous good; ~ **de un impuesto** FISC yield of a tax; ~ **interior bruto** (*PIB*) ECON gross domestic product (*GDP*); ~ **interno bruto** (*PIB*) ECON gross domestic product (*GDP*); ~ **interior bruto al coste de los factores** *Esp* (*cf producto interior bruto al costo de los factores AmL*) CONT, ECON gross domestic product at factor cost; ~ **interior bruto al costo de los factores** *AmL* (*cf producto interior bruto al coste de los factores Esp*) CONT, ECON gross domestic product at factor cost; ~ **interior bruto a precios de mercado** CONT, ECON gross domestic product at market prices; ~ **interior neto** (*PIN*) ECON net domestic product (*NDP*); ~ **limpio** MED AMB clean product; ~ **marginal** ECON, IND marginal product; ~ **marginal del trabajo** ECON, IND marginal product of labour (*BrE*), marginal product of labor (*AmE*); ~ **nacional bruto** (*PNB*) ECON gross national product (*GNP*); ~ **neto** INMOB *venta* net proceeds (*np*); ~ **obsoleto** V&M obsolescent product; ~ **orientado al consumidor** V&M consumer-oriented product; ~ **per cápita** IND output per head; ~ **pionero** V&M pioneer product; ~ **de primera categoría** COM GEN, V&M top-rank product; ~ **principal** COM GEN, V&M staple product; ~ **que no daña el medio ambiente** MED AMB environmentally-friendly product; ~ **que se vende con sobreprecio** COM GEN premium grade; ~ **de la renta fija** BOLSA bond proceeds; ~ **de la reventa** COM GEN proceeds from resale; ~ **secundario** ECON, IND secondary product, spin-off product; ~ **de segunda generación** V&M second-generation product; ~ **semielaborado** COM GEN, IND, V&M semifinished product; ~ **semimanufacturado** COM GEN, IND, V&M semifinished product; ~ **social** ECON social product; ~ **social bruto** ECON gross social product; ~ **terciario** ECON *industria de servicios* tertiary product; ~ **de las ventas** COM GEN proceeds of sales; ~ **voluminoso** COM GEN bulky good; ♦ **este** ~ **tiene un precio demasiado alto** COM GEN this product is overpriced

productor, a *m,f* COM GEN business canvasser; ~ **cinematográfico(-a)** MEDIOS *emisión* film-maker; ~ **complementario(-a)** IND swing producer; ~ **importante** IND major producer; ~ **marginal** ECON, IND marginal producer; ~ **de oro** IND gold producer; ~ **de pérdidas** V&M lossmaker; ~ **principal** ECON *de un artículo* major producer

productos: ~ **comunitarios** *m pl* IMP/EXP Community goods; ~ **controlados** *m pl* BOLSA controlled commodities; ~ **cuya compra debe ser muy meditada** *m pl* V&M high involvement products; ~ **derivados del petróleo** *m pl* FISC mineral oil products; ~ **de diseño** *m pl* V&M designer products; ~ **duraderos para el hogar** *m pl* V&M household durables; ~ **de economato** *m pl* IMP/EXP commissary goods; ~ **elaborados** *m pl* IND manufactured goods; ~ **específicos** *m pl* BANCA specifics; ~ **exclusivos** *m pl* COM GEN proprietary goods; ~ **exentos de IVA** *m pl* V&M exempt rating; ~ **farmacéuticos** *m pl* COM GEN, IND, V&M pharmaceuticals; ~ **genéricos** *m pl* V&M generic products; ~ **para el hogar** *m pl* COM GEN home products;

~ **indiferenciados** *m pl* V&M undifferentiated products; ~ **industriales** *m pl* ECON, IND industrial goods, industrial products; ~ **inferiores** *m pl* IND inferior goods; ~ **de la línea amarilla** *m pl* COM GEN yellow goods (*jarg*); ~ **nacionales** *m pl* COM GEN home products; ~ **no lujosos** *m pl* V&M nonluxury goods; ~ **de la PAC** *m pl* ECON CAP goods; ~ **peligrosos** *m pl* COM GEN, TRANSP dangerous goods; ~ **perecederos** *m pl* V&M nondurables; ~ **pirateados** *m pl* MEDIOS, V&M pirated products; ~ **pirotécnicos** *m pl* TRANSP *carga como peligrosa* pyrotechnic substance; ~ **de primera necesidad** *m pl* V&M essential commodities; ~ **en proceso** *m pl* COM GEN goods in process, IND partly-finished goods, V&M goods in process; ~ **químicos** *m pl* IND chemicals; ~ **semiacabados** *m pl* COM GEN partly-finished goods; ~ **semielaborados** *m pl* COM GEN semiprocessed products, partly-finished goods; ~ **semimanufacturados** *m pl* COM GEN semifinished goods; ~ **semiterminados** *m pl* COM GEN semifinished goods; ~ **y servicios nocivos** *m pl* ECON illth; ~ **terminados** *m pl* COM GEN finished goods; ~ **a la venta** *m pl* V&M sales goods

profano, a *m,f* RRHH *en materia* outsider (*BrE*)

profecía: ~ **de cumplimiento inevitable** *f* COM GEN self-fulfilling prophecy

profesión: ~ **contable** *f* CONT accountancy profession; ~ **estrechamente conectada** *f* RRHH closely connected profession

profesional[1] *adj* COM GEN, RRHH occupational, professional

profesional[2] *mf* COM GEN, OCIO *deporte* professional; ~ **de la publicidad** RRHH adman (*infrml*) (*advertising man*)

profesionalismo *m* COM GEN professionalism

profesionalización *f* COM GEN professionalization

profesor, a *m,f* PROT SOC, RRHH *universidad* lecturer, *escuela* teacher; ~ **asociado(-a)** PROT SOC, RRHH associate lecturer; ~ **a tiempo completo** PROT SOC, RRHH full-time lecturer; ~ **a tiempo parcial** PROT SOC, RRHH part-time lecturer

profundamente: ~ **arraigado** *adj* COM GEN *problemas* deep-seated

profundidad[1]: **en** ~ *adv* COM GEN in-depth

profundidad[2]: ~ **del puesto** *f* RRHH job depth

programa *m* COM GEN program (*AmE*), programme (*BrE*), INFO program; ~ **de acción** COM GEN UE action program (*AmE*), action programme (*BrE*); ~ **de acción medioambiental** ECON, MED AMB environmental action program (*AmE*), environmental action programme (*BrE*); ~ **accionado por parámetros** INFO parameter-driven software; ~ **de actuación** COM GEN development program (*AmE*), development programme (*BrE*); ~ **de ahorro de jubilación** COM GEN retirement savings program (*AmE*), retirement savings programme (*BrE*); ~ **de ahorro para pensión** COM GEN retirement savings program (*AmE*), retirement savings programme (*BrE*); ~ **de alimentación mundial** ECON, POL World Food Programme (*WFP*); ~ **de alta prioridad** INFO foreground program; ~ **ampliado** COM GEN extended program (*AmE*), extended programme (*BrE*); ~ **antivirus** INFO antivirus software; ~ **de aprendizaje asistido por computador** AmL ver *programa de aprendizaje asistido por computadora AmL*; ~ **de aprendizaje asistido por computadora** AmL (*cf programa*

de aprendizaje asistido por ordenador Esp) INFO computer-assisted learning program; ~ **de aprendizaje asistido por ordenador** *Esp* (*cf programa de aprendizaje asistido por computadora AmL*) INFO computer-assisted learning program; ~ **de auditoría** CONT audit program (*AmE*), audit programme (*BrE*), audit schedule; ~ **de ayuda** BANCA *desarrollo*, ECON aid program (*AmE*), aid programme (*BrE*); ~ **por cable** COMS, MEDIOS cable program (*AmE*), cable programme (*BrE*); ~ **de capacitación** AmL (*cf programa de formación Esp*) RRHH training program (*AmE*), training programme (*BrE*) ~ **de capital** CONT, ECON, FIN capital program (*AmE*), capital programme (*BrE*); ~ **comercial** COM GEN trading program (*AmE*), trading programme (*BrE*), ECON program deal (*AmE*), programme deal (*BrE*), FIN trading program (*AmE*), trading programme (*BrE*); ~ **comunitario** PROT SOC UE Community Program (*AmE*) (*CP*), Community Programme (*BrE*) (*CP*); ~ **de conclusión** MED AMB completion program (*AmE*), completion programme (*BrE*); ~ **de consulta** INFO inquiry program; ~ **de control** INFO control program; ~ **de copias de seguridad** INFO backup utility program; ~ **de costes compartidos** *Esp* (*cf programa de costos compartidos AmL*) POL cost-shared program (*AmE*), cost-shared programme (*BrE*); ~ **de costos compartidos** AmL (*cf programa de costes compartidos Esp*) POL cost-shared program (*AmE*), cost-shared programme (*BrE*); ~ **de demanda macroeconómico** ECON macroeconomic demand schedule; ~ **departamental** GES departmental program (*AmE*), departmental programme (*BrE*); ~ **de desarrollo** COM GEN development program (*AmE*), development programme (*BrE*); ~ **de dibujo** INFO drawing software; ~ **en directo** COMS, MEDIOS live program (*AmE*), live programme (*BrE*); ~ **enlatado** INFO canned program; ~ **de ensamblaje** COM GEN assembly program (*AmE*), assembly programme (*BrE*); ~ **de entradas del periodo** IMP/EXP *Reino Unido* period entry scheme (*BrE*); ~ **especial de proyectos de recuperación de capital** COM GEN Special Recovery Capital Projects Program (*AmE*) (*SRCPP*); ~ **de estadística** INFO, MAT *ordenador* statistical software; ~ **estatutario** POL statutory program (*AmE*), statutory programme (*BrE*); ~ **de explotación** TRANSP operating schedule; ~ **de exportación privada** IMP/EXP personal export scheme; ~ **de financiación centralizada** CONT, ECON, FIN centrally financed program (*AmE*), centrally financed programme (*BrE*); ~ **financiado centralmente** CONT, ECON, FIN centrally financed program (*AmE*), centrally financed programme (*BrE*); ~ **financiero federal** CONT, ECON federal financial program (*AmE*), federal financial programme (*BrE*); ~ **de fiscalización** CONT audit program (*AmE*), audit programme (*BrE*); ~ **de formación** *Esp* (*cf programa de capacitación AmL*) RRHH training program (*AmE*), training programme (*BrE*); ~ **de formación experimental** ECON developmental drilling program (*AmE*), developmental drilling programme (*BrE*); ~ **de formación orientado al desarrollo** ECON developmental drilling program (*AmE*), developmental drilling programme (*BrE*); ~ **fuente** INFO source program; ~ **de garantías del arrendador** IND homeowner warranty program (*AmE*); ~ **de gastos directos** CONT *gobierno*, POL direct spending program (*AmE*), direct spending programme (*BrE*); ~ **de gestión de redes** INFO networking software; ~ **de gestión de** transacciones INFO transaction management software; ~ **inaugural** TRANSP inaugural schedule; ~ **informático** INFO computer program; ~ **de inserción obligatoria** MEDIOS mandated program (*AmE*), mandated programme (*BrE*); ~ **de instrucción** INFO instruction program; ~ **de inversión** BANCA, CONT, FIN investment program (*AmE*), investment programme (*BrE*); ~ **de investigación** IND research program (*AmE*), research programme (*BrE*); ~ **legal** POL statutory program (*AmE*), statutory programme (*BrE*); ~ **lineal** MAT linear program (*AmE*), linear programme (*BrE*); ~ **de llamada** INFO calling program; ~ **de llamadas** COMS, MEDIOS phone-in program (*AmE*), phone-in programme (*BrE*); ~ **de medios de comunicación** MEDIOS media schedule; ~ **no apalancado** FIN unleveraged program (*AmE*), unleveraged programme (*BrE*); ~ **de obras públicas** COM GEN public works program (*AmE*), public works programme (*BrE*); ~ **de optimización de equipajes** TRANSP baggage improvement program (*AmE*) (*BIP*), baggage improvement programme (*BrE*) (*BIP*); ~ **de participación directa** FIN direct participation program (*AmE*), direct participation programme (*BrE*); ~ **de perforaciones** MED AMB drilling program (*AmE*), drilling programme (*BrE*); ~ **de planificación financiera personal** FIN, INFO personal financial planning software; ~ **de privatización** ECON, POL privatization program (*AmE*), privatization programme (*BrE*); ~ **de procesamiento de textos** INFO word-processing software; ~ **de proceso de mensajes** INFO message processing program (*MPP*); ~ **de producción** GES, IND production schedule; ~ **de racionalización** ECON, FIN, IND rationalization program (*AmE*), rationalization programme (*BrE*); ~ **de radio** MEDIOS radio program (*AmE*), radio programme (*BrE*); ~ **de rearranque** INFO restart program; ~ **de reconocimiento de la voz** INFO speech recognition software; ~ **de recuperación** COM GEN recovery scheme; ~ **de reforma** ECON reform program (*AmE*), reform programme (*BrE*); ~ **reforzado** COM GEN enriched program (*AmE*), enriched programme (*BrE*); ~ **de renovación** FIN *administración de flota* rolling program (*AmE*), rolling programme (*BrE*); ~ **de la reunión** COM GEN assembly program (*AmE*), assembly programme (*BrE*); ~ **de rotación** FIN *gestión de flota* rolling program (*AmE*), rolling programme (*BrE*); ~ **de simulación financiera** FIN, INFO financial simulation software; ~ **de sugerencias** GES suggestion scheme; ~ **de tarifas** COM GEN tariff schedule; ~ **de trabajo** GES work schedule; ~ **de trabajo de auditoría** CONT audit work schedule; ~ **de traductor** INFO translation program; ~ **para el tratamiento de datos fiscales** FISC, INFO tax software; ~ **de usuario** INFO user friendliness; ~ **de utilidades** INFO utility program; ~ **de vencimiento** CONT lapsing schedule; ~ **en vivo** MEDIOS *radiodifusión* live program (*AmE*), live programme (*BrE*)

Programa: ~ **de Acceso Directo** *m* INFO Direct Access Software; ~ **Mundial de Alimentación** *f* ECON, POL, PROT SOC World Food Programme (*WFP*); ~ **de las Naciones Unidas para el Desarrollo** *m* (*PNUD*) ECON, POL United Nations Development Programme (*UNDP*); ~ **y Tecnología para la Protección Medioambiental** *f* MED AMB Science and Technology for Environmental Protection Programme (*STEP*); ~ **de Recuperación Europea** *m* ECON European Recovery Plan (*ERP*), European Recovery Programme (*ERP*)

programación *f* COM GEN, INFO programming; ~ **científica** INFO, MAT scientific programming; ~ **dinámica** COM GEN, INFO, MAT dynamic programming; ~ **económica** ECON economic programming; ~ **estructurada** INFO structured programming; ~ **del horario** TRANSP timetable planning; ~ **informática** INFO, MAT computer programming; ~ **lineal** ECON *econometría*, INFO, MAT linear programming; ~ **matemática** MAT, INFO mathematical programming; ~ **de metas** GES goal programming; ~ **no lineal** INFO, MAT nonlinear programming; ~ **de objetivos** GES goal programming; ~ **del ordenador** *Esp* (*cf software de la computadora AmL*) INFO computer software; ~ **de ordenadores** INFO, MAT computer programming; ~ **paramétrica** INFO, MAT parametric programming; ~ **de la producción** GES, IND production scheduling; ~ **de sistemas** INFO systems programming; ~ **de tareas** COM GEN task scheduling

programado *adj* COM GEN scheduled, INFO programmed; ◆ **no** ~ COM GEN unscheduled, nonscheduled, INFO unprogrammed; **según línea** ~ COM GEN as scheduled

programador, a: ~ **de aplicaciones** *m,f* INFO applications programmer; ~ **aprendiz(a)** *m,f* INFO trainee programmer; ~ **de computadores** *m,f* AmL *ver programador de computadoras AmL*; ~ **de computadoras** *m,f* AmL (*cf programador de ordenadores Esp*) INFO computer programmer; ~ **de ordenadores** *m,f* Esp (*cf programador de computadoras AmL*) INFO computer programmer; ~ **en prácticas** *m,f* INFO trainee programmer; ~ **de sistemas** *m,f* INFO systems programmer; ~ **de vuelos** *m,f* TRANSP flight scheduler

programar *vt* COM GEN schedule, INFO program

programas *m pl* INFO software; ~ **de base** INFO system software; ~ **de contabilidad** CONT, INFO accounting software; ~ **de diseño gráfico** INFO graphic-design software; ~ **de dominio público** INFO public domain software; ~ **de emulación** INFO emulation software; ~ **de liderazgo industrial** GES *relaciones públicas* industry leadership programs (*AmE*), industry leadership programmes (*BrE*); ~ **puente** INFO bridging software; ~ **de traspaso** INFO bridgeware

progresión: ~ **aritmética** *f* MAT arithmetic progression; ~ **geométrica** *f* MAT geometric progression

progresivamente *adv* COM GEN progressively

progreso *m* COM GEN advance, progress; ~ **técnico** ECON technical progress; ~ **técnico inducido** ECON induced technical progress; ~ **técnico neutral** ECON neutral technical progress; ~ **técnico que aumenta el rendimiento del trabajo** ECON labor-augmenting technical progress (*AmE*), labour-augmenting technical progress (*BrE*); ~ **tecnológico rápido** ECON, IND rapid technological progress

prohibe: **se** ~ **fumar** *fra* COM GEN no smoking

prohibición *f* COM GEN, DER prohibition, ban; ~ **de pago de intereses** BANCA ban on interest payments; ~ **de tiempo extra** RRHH overtime ban

prohibida: ~ **la entrada** *fra* COM GEN no admittance

prohibido: ~ **el paso** *fra* DER no trespassing, trespassers will be prosecuted

prohibir *vt* COM GEN bar, DER, INFO prohibit

proletariado *m* ECON, POL proletariat

proletarización *f* ECON, POL proletarianization

prolongación *f* COM GEN extension

prolongado *adj* COM GEN lengthened, prolonged

prolongar *vt* COM GEN lengthen, prolong

promediado: **~ hacia atrás** *m* FISC backward averaging

promediador, a *m,f* BOLSA averager

promediar *vt* BOLSA, FIN *coste, beneficio* average out; ◆ **~ al alza** BOLSA average up; **~ a la baja** BOLSA average down

promedio *m* COM GEN average (*av.*), average rate, averaging; **~ anual de horas trabajadas** RRHH annualized woring hours; **~ común** SEG common average; **~ con efecto retroactivo** FISC backward averaging; **~ del fondo monetario Donoghue** BOLSA Donoghue's money fund average; **~ general** COM GEN general average (*G/A*), FISC *de ingresos* general averaging; **~ general exterior** COM GEN general foreign average (*FGA*); **~ general total** SEG *mercancías aseguradas* general average in full; **~ de grupo** FISC block averaging; **~ de ingresos** FIN, FISC income averaging; **~ de lectores de una edición** MEDIOS, V&M average issue readership; **~ Nikkei** BOLSA Nikkei Average, Nikkei index; **~ PIBOR** BANCA *tipo interbancario ofrecido en Paris* average PIBOR; **~ ponderado** COM GEN, ECON, MAT weighted average; **~ de todo el sector** ECON *crecimiento* all-sector average; **~ de utilidad** BOLSA utility average; **~ variable** BOLSA averaging; ◆ **hacer un ~** COM GEN take an average

promesa *f* COM GEN promise; **~ de pago** COM GEN promise to pay; **~ vinculante** COM GEN binding promise; ◆ **~ de vender** V&M promise to sell

prometedor: **poco ~** *adj* ECON *panorama* bleak

prometer *vt* COM GEN promise

prominente *adj* COM GEN, V&M prominent, high-profile

promoción *f* COM GEN *a un puesto de trabajo superior* promotion, V&M *de producto, servicio* promotion (*promo*); **~ de altos cargos** GES executive advancement; **~ combinada** MEDIOS, V&M tie-in promotion; **~ conjunta** MEDIOS, V&M tie-in display; **~ continua** MEDIOS, V&M continuous promotion; **~ de ejecutivos** GES, RRHH executive promotion; **~ de una empresa** BOLSA company promotion; **~ de lanzamiento** MEDIOS, V&M hype; **~ de marca** V&M brand promotion; **~ con producto añadido** V&M piggyback promotion; **~ en el punto de venta** V&M point-of-sale promotion; **~ rápida** RRHH fast tracking; **~ con regalo** V&M *publicidad* gift promotion; **~ en tienda** V&M in-store promotion; **~ de ventas** V&M sales promotion; **~ vertical** RRHH vertical promotion; **~ de la vivienda** INMOB housing development; ◆ **lo mejor de la ~** RRHH cream of the crop (*infrml*)

promocional *adj* COM GEN, V&M promotional

promocionar *vt* COM GEN, V&M promote, push

promotor, a *m,f* COM GEN *de planes*, FISC promoter, INMOB developer; **~ comercial** COM GEN commercial developer, FIN backer; **~ de demanda** ECON sponsor demand; **~ financiero(-a)** FIN financial backer; **~ e impulsor(a)** GES mover and shaker (*infrml*); **~ inmobiliario(-a)** COM GEN, INMOB land developer, property developer; **~ de multipropiedades** INMOB timeshare developer; **~ de refugios fiscales** FISC tax shelter promoter; **~ teatral** COM GEN angel (*infrml*)

promover *vt* BANCA *desarrollo, compañía* aid, COM GEN pioneer, promote, develop, RRHH *a un empleado* promote; ◆ **~ la eficiencia** COM GEN promote efficiency

promulgado: **~ por** *fra* DER, FISC enacted by

pronóstico *m* COM GEN forecasting; **~ ambiental** MED AMB environmental forecasting; **~ empresarial** COM GEN, ECON business forecasting; **~ del mercado** V&M market forecast; **~ de recursos humanos** RRHH manpower forecasting; **~ tecnológico** COM GEN, IND technological forecast

pronto[1] *adj* COM GEN prompt; ◆ **tan ~ como sea posible** COM GEN, COMS as soon as possible (*a.s.a.p.*)

pronto[2]: **~ pago de las facturas** *m* FIN prompt payment of invoices

pronunciar *vt* MAT *curva* steepen; ◆ **~ un discurso** GES make a speech; **~ un fallo favorable a alguien** COM GEN give a ruling in favor of sb (*AmE*), give a ruling in favour of sb (*BrE*); **~ una sentencia** DER pass judgment; **~ una sentencia condenatoria** DER *contra alguien* pass sentence; **~ un veredicto** DER return a verdict

propaganda *f AmL* (*cf anuncio publicitario Esp*) COM GEN advertising, *TV, radio* commercial, MEDIOS, V&M commercial; **~ de buzón** COMS, V&M junk mail; **~ por correo** *Esp* (*cf buzoneo AmL*) INFO *publicidad, promoción*, V&M mailing; **~ excesiva** V&M overselling; **~ publicitaria** V&M *publicidad* blurb

propensión *f* COM GEN propensity; **~ a ahorrar** ECON propensity to save; **~ al trabajo** ECON propensity to work; **~ a consumir** ECON propensity to consume; **~ a invertir** ECON, FIN propensity to invest; **~ marginal** ECON marginal propensity; **~ marginal al ahorro** ECON marginal propensity to save; **~ marginal al consumo** ECON marginal propensity to consume; **~ marginal a la importación** ECON, IMP/EXP marginal propensity to import (*MPI*); **~ marginal a la inversión** ECON, FIN marginal propensity to invest; **~ media al ahorro** CONT, ECON *contabilidad económica* average propensity to save (*APS*); **~ media al consumo** ECON, V&M average propensity to consume (*APC*)

propenso: **estar ~ a** *fra* COM GEN be subject to

propiedad *f* FISC estate, INMOB immovable property, property, homestead (*AmE*), farmstead (*BrE*); **~ absoluta** INMOB freehold property; **~ absoluta de un inmueble** INMOB fee simple, fee simple absolute; **~ adquirida** DER acquest, INMOB property acquired; **~ de adquisición posterior** DER *insolvencia*, INMOB after-acquired property; **~ alquilada** INMOB let property; **~ amortizable** CONT depreciable property; **~ arrendada** INMOB leasehold; **~ en arriendo** INMOB leasehold property; **~ por bancarrota** FIN, INMOB bankruptcy property; **~ del capital** FISC, INMOB capital property; **~ de casas** INMOB home ownership; **~ comercial** COM GEN, INMOB commercial property; **~ compartida** DER partial taking; **~ comunal** INMOB communal ownership; **~ consolidada** INMOB funded property; **~ cruzada** COM GEN, INMOB cross-ownership; **~ declarada** FISC, INMOB certified property; **~ depreciable** INMOB depreciable real estate; **~ designada** FISC, INMOB designated property; **~ desnuda** INMOB, SEG bare ownership; **~ embargada** INMOB distressed property; **~ especificada** FISC specified property; **~ del Estado** POL state ownership; **~ estatal** ECON state ownership; **~ excluida** FISC excluded property; **~ de explotación** INMOB income property; **~ extranjera** FISC, INMOB foreign-owned property, foreign property; **~ sin gravamen** INMOB unencumbered estate property; **~ heredada** DER,

INMOB inherited property; ~ **individual** INMOB estate in severalty; ~ **industrial** COM GEN, IND, INMOB, PATENT industrial property; ~ **intangible** DER, INMOB incorporeal property; ~ **intelectual** DER, PATENT intellectual property; ~ **de inversión** INMOB investment property; ~ **libre de cargas** CONT *cuentas anuales* freehold property; ~ **mancomunada** DER, INMOB joint estate, property held in joint names; ~ **marginal** INMOB marginal property; ~ **de la mayoría** BOLSA majority ownership; ~ **mixta** MEDIOS cross-ownership; ~ **no repartida** INMOB undivided property; ~ **de la pequeña empresa** FISC small business property; ~ **privada** DER private property; ~ **pública** FIN public ownership; ~ **por quiebra** DER, INMOB bankruptcy property; ~ **de reemplazo** FISC, INMOB replacement property; ~ **residual** INMOB residuary estate; ~ **del seguro** SEG insurance property; ~ **similar** FISC, INMOB like-kind property; ~ **suplente** FISC, INMOB substituted property; ~ **de la tierra** ECON land ownership; ~ **de tierras** INMOB tenure in land; ~ **total** FIN, INMOB absolute ownership; ~ **en usufructo** FISC beneficial ownership; ~ **de venta al detalle** INMOB retail property

propietario, -a *m,f* COM GEN, INMOB proprietor, owner, homeowner, property owner; ~ **absentista** DER, INMOB absentee owner; ~ **absoluto(-a)** INMOB freehold owner, freeholder; ~ **ausente** DER, INMOB absentee owner; ~ **beneficiario(-a)** BOLSA, DER beneficial owner; ~ **desnudo(-a)** FIN remainderman, INMOB bare owner; ~**-gerente** RRHH *navegación* managing owner; ~ **de hotel** INMOB hotel proprietor; ~ **legítimo(-a)** DER, INMOB true owner, rightful owner; ~ **no ocupante** INMOB nonoccupying owner; ~ **nominal** BOLSA *de bono* registered owner; ~**-ocupante** DER, INMOB owner-occupier; ~ **original** FISC original owner; ~ **de una patente** PATENT patent proprietor; ~ **principal** RRHH main owner, master owner; ~ **registrado(-a)** DER, INMOB registered proprietor; ~ **de restaurante** RRHH restaurant proprietor; ~ **único(-a)** GES sole proprietor

propietarios: los ~ *m pl* INMOB propertied class; ~ **de los medios de comunicación** *m pl* V&M media owners

propina *f* COM GEN, OCIO tip

propio: ~ **del mercado secundario** *adj* BOLSA aftermarket

proponente *mf* COM GEN proposer

proponer *vt* COM GEN propose; ♦ ~ **una convocatoria** BOLSA *ejercer* tender notice

proporción *f* COM GEN proportion, ratio, ECON *de población* size; ~ **de acciones preferentes** BOLSA preferred stock ratio; ~ **de activo disponible a pasivo corriente** CONT quick ratio; ~ **del ahorro** ECON, FIN savings ratio; ~ **de apalancamiento** FIN gearing ratio (*BrE*), leverage ratio (*AmE*); ~ **de beneficio en libros** CONT book rate of return; ~ **de beneficios a capital invertido** FIN rate of return; ~ **beneficio-volumen** FIN profit-volume ratio (*P/V*); ~ **de capital a activos inmovilizados** CONT capital to asset ratio; ~ **de capital base a apalancamiento** BANCA base capital leverage ratio; ~ **de capital total compensado** BANCA, FIN adjusted total capital ratio; ~ **capital-producto** ECON, FIN, IND capital-output ratio; ~ **capital-trabajo** ECON, FIN, IND capital-labor ratio (*AmE*), capital-labour ratio (*BrE*); ~ **del circulante** CONT, FIN current ratio; ~ **clave** ECON key rate; ~ **de cobertura** BOLSA hedge ratio, FIN cover ratio; ~ **de cobertura de deuda** CONT debt coverage ratio; ~ **de cobertura del dividendo** BOLSA

dividend coverage ratio; ~ **de colocaciones** FIN placement ratio; ~ **de concentración de N-empresas** ECON N-firm concentration ratio; ~ **contable** CONT accounting ratio; ~ **de conversión** BOLSA conversion ratio; ~ **de correlación** BOLSA *futuros* correlation ratio; ~ **corriente** CONT, FIN current ratio; ~ **de coste** *Esp* (*cf proporción de costo AmL*) CONT cost ratio; ~ **de costo** *AmL* (*cf proporción de coste Esp*) CONT cost ratio; ~ **de crecimiento económico sostenible** ECON, FIN, POL sustainable economic growth rate; ~ **de cuentas a cobrar** CONT collection ratio; ~ **de desembolso de dividendos** BOLSA, CONT dividend payout ratio; ~ **de la deuda exterior** ECON external debt ratio; ~ **de deuda externa por exportaciones** ECON, IMP/EXP ratio of external debt to exports; ~ **deudora** FIN debit ratio; ~ **de dimensión** COM GEN aspect ratio; ~ **de dirección** FIN management ratio; ~ **directiva** GES management ratio; ~ **dividendo-precio de la acción** BOLSA, FIN dividend-price ratio; ~ **efectiva de asistencia** ECON effective rate of assistance; ~ **efectiva de protección** ECON, IND effective rate of protection; ~ **de eficiencia** ECON efficiency ratio; ~ **de empleados** RRHH employee ratio; ~ **de endeudamiento** CONT, FIN borrowing ratio, debt ratio; ~ **endeudamiento-capital propio** BOLSA, CONT, FIN gearing; ~ **de existencias** CONT stock ratio; ~ **de explotación** ECON rate of exploitation; ~ **de financiación** FIN financial ratio; ~ **de fondo de maniobra** FIN working capital ratio; ~ **de fuerzas** COM GEN balance of power; ~ **de gasto** BOLSA, ECON expense ratio (*AmE*); ~ **del gasto público** ECON public spending ratio; ~ **de impuestos directos e indirectos** ECON, FISC direct-indirect taxes ratio; ~ **incremental capital-producto** ECON, FIN incremental capital-output ratio (*ICOR*); ~ **de inflación básica** ECON core inflation rate; ~ **de inflación subyacente** ECON underlying inflation rate; ~ **de ingresos netos a patrimonio neto** CONT net income to net worth ratio; ~ **de intercambio dual** ECON dual exchange rate; ~ **de intercambio-ingreso** ECON *intercambio* income terms of trade; ~ **de interés puro** COM GEN, ECON pure interest rate; ~ **del liderazgo empresarial** ECON leading firms ratio; ~ **de liquidez** ECON cash-deposits ratio; ~ **de liquidez inmediata** CONT quick ratio; ~ **de penetración de las importaciones** IMP/EXP import penetration ratio; ~ **piso-superficie** INMOB, MAT floor-area ratio; ~ **principal** ECON primary ratio, *de inflación* headline rate; ~ **de rentabilidad** CONT, FIN profitability ratio; ~ **renta/volumen de facturación** CONT rental/turnover ratio; ~ **de rotación** COM GEN turnover ratio; ~ **salario-renta** ECON wage rental ratio; ~ **de solvencia** CONT, FIN solvency ratio; ~ **subyacente** ECON underlying rate; ~ **de suscripción** BOLSA subscription ratio; ~ **de sustitución marginal decreciente** ECON diminishing marginal rate of substitution; ~ **de utilidad bruta** CONT gross profit ratio; ~ **de valor en la base** BOLSA *futuros* basis point value ratio; ~ **de valoración** INMOB assessment ratio; ~ **de venta en descubierto de un especialista** BOLSA specialist's short-sale ratio; ~ **de venta en descubierto de pequeños lotes** BOLSA odd-lot short-sale ratio; ~ **de ventas** V&M sales ratio; ~ **de ventas a crédito** CONT accounts receivable turnover; ~ **volumen de trabajo** ECON volume ratio; ♦ **en** ~ **a** COM GEN, MAT in proportion to; **como** ~ **de** COM GEN as a proportion of

proporcionado *adj* COM GEN commensurate, proportionate, ECON *presupuesto* sizeable

proporcionalidad *f* COM GEN proportionality; ~ **de la culpa** DER comparative negligence;

proporcionalmente *adv* COM GEN proportionately

proporcionar *vt* COM GEN provide; ◆ ~ **un mercado para** BOLSA *acciones circulantes* provide a market for

proporciones *f pl* COM GEN proportions; ~ **relativas** RRHH relativities; ◆ **en diferentes** ~ COM GEN in varying degrees; **en iguales** ~ COM GEN in equal proportions

proposición *f* COM GEN proposition; ~ **alternativa** GES alternative proposal; ~ **firme de arbitraje** DER final offer arbitration; ~ **única de venta** V&M unique selling proposition (*USP*); ◆ **nuestra** ~ **sigue en pie** COM GEN our proposal still stands

propósito *m* COM GEN purpose, aim, goal; ~ **especificado** FISC specified purpose; ~ **inmediato** COM GEN immediate aim

propiedad: ~ **estatal** *f* ECON, POL state ownership

propuesta *f* COM GEN proposal, submission; ~ **de alta dirección** GES, RRHH top management approach; ~**-borrador** TRANSP slip sheet; ~**-borrador abierta** TRANSP *navegación* open slip sheet; ~ **comercial de venta** V&M sales approach; ~ **de compra al cien por cien** BOLSA buyout proposal; ~ **de contrato** COM GEN tender to contract (*TTC*); ~ **de negocio** COM GEN business proposition; ~ **de valor** FIN value proposal; ~ **de venta** V&M selling proposition

propuestas: ~ **fiscales** *f pl* ECON, FISC tax proposals

propuesto *adj* COM GEN *nombre de una empresa* proposed

propulsión: ~ **del buque asistida por el viento** *f* TRANSP wind assisted ship propulsion (*WASP*); ~ **a carbón** *f* TRANSP coal propulsion; ~ **a hélice** *f* TRANSP screw propulsion

prorrata[1]**: a** ~ *adv* COM GEN, RRHH pro rata

prorrata[2] *f* COM GEN, RRHH prorate

prorratear *vt* BOLSA, CONT *costes* apportion, *dinero, obligaciones* allocate, INMOB *tierra, propiedades* apportion; ◆ ~ **la avería** SEG *marina* apportion the average

prorrateo *m* FIN averaging, TRANSP proration; ~ **del coste** *Esp* (*cf prorrateo del costo AmL*) CONT cost apportionment; ~ **del costo** *AmL* (*cf prorrateo del coste Esp*) CONT cost apportionment

prórroga *f* BANCA, DER, PATENT extension

prorrogar *vt* BANCA, DER, PATENT *normas* extend

pros: ~ **y contras** *fra* COM GEN pros and cons

proscribir *vt* DER outlaw

proseguir *vt* PATENT *solicitud* prosecute

prospección *f* COM GEN prospecting; ~ **petrolífera** MED AMB oil prospection

prospectiva *f* COM GEN prospecting

prospecto *m* COM GEN leaflet, prospectus; ~ **definitivo** BOLSA final prospectus; ~ **de emisión preliminar** BOLSA preliminary prospectus; ~ **preliminar** BOLSA red-herring prospectus; ~ **rectificado** BOLSA amended prospectus

prosperar *vi* COM GEN flourish

prosperidad *f* COM GEN prosperity

próspero *adj* COM GEN thriving, ECON prosperous

protección *f* COM GEN protection; ~ **arancelaria** ECON, FISC, IMP/EXP tariff protection; ~ **de archivos** INFO file protection; ~ **del cambio de divisas** CONT, FIN foreign exchange hedge; ~ **catódica** TRANSP *navegación* cathodic protection; ~ **condicionada** PATENT conditional protection; ~ **del consumidor** DER, V&M consumer

protection; ~ **contra rescate anticipado** BOLSA call protection; ~ **contra sobregiro** BANCA overdraft protection; ~ **de datos** INFO data protection; ~ **de ficheros** INFO file protection; ~ **e indemnización** TRANSP protection and indemnity (*P&I*); ~ **industrial** IND industrial security; ~ **del inversor** BOLSA investor protection; ~ **a la maternidad** RRHH, SEG maternity protection; ~ **del medio ambiente** COM GEN, MED AMB environmental protection; ~ **de patentes** DER, PATENT patent protection; ~ **del precio** BOLSA price protection; ~ **de la propiedad industrial** IND, INMOB industrial property protection; ~ **provisional** PATENT provisional protection; ~ **segura** BOLSA safe hedge; ~ **total** PATENT full protection; ~ **unidireccional** BOLSA one-way protection; ◆ **bajo la** ~ **de** COM GEN under the umbrella of

proteccionismo *m* ECON protectionism, RRHH featherbedding (*infrml*); ~ **comercial** ECON trade protectionism; ~ **costero** TRANSP offshore protectionism

proteccionista *mf* ECON protectionist

protector: ~ **de cheques** *m* BANCA, FIN check protector (*AmE*), cheque protector (*BrE*)

proteger *vt* BOLSA hedge, *moneda* shadow, COM GEN shield, ECON protect, MED AMB conserve; ◆ ~ **de escritura** INFO write-protect; ~ **los intereses de** COM GEN *país, productores, consumidores* protect the interests of

protegerse *v refl* COM GEN protect oneself

protegido *adj* COM GEN *financieramente* secure; **no** ~ COM GEN unscreened; ◆ ~ **contra copia** INFO copy-protected

protesta: ~ **de mar** *f* DER ship's protest; ~ **encarnizada** *f* COM GEN sharp protest

protestado: **no** ~ *adj* FIN unprotested

protoindustrialización *f* RRHH protoindustrialization

protoproletariado *m* ECON protoproletariat

protocolo *m* COM GEN *diplomacia, etiquette*, INFO protocol

protocolos *m pl* CONT records

prototipo *m* COM GEN, V&M prototype

provecho *m* COM GEN benefit

provechoso *adj* COM GEN beneficial, profitable, lucrative

proveedor, a *m,f* COM GEN supplier, ECON provider; ~ **de efectos navales** TRANSP *compra* ship's chandler

proveer *vt* COM GEN, FIN *fondos* provide; ~ **contra** COM GEN provide against

provenir: ~ **de** *vi* COM GEN stem from

providencia *f* DER court order

provincia *f* POL territory governed as a unit with certain degree of autonomy, ≈ county (*BrE*), region

provincial *adj* COM GEN, FISC provincial

provisión *f* COM GEN, DER, FISC allowance, provision, funding, TRANSP catering; ~ **de capital inicial** FIN initial funding; ~ **para créditos no pagados** BANCA, FIN loan loss provision; ~ **por depreciación** CONT depreciation allowance; ~ **para deudas de cobro dudoso** BANCA, CONT, FIN doubtful debt provision; ~ **para deudas dudosas** BANCA, CONT, FIN doubtful debt provision, bad-debt provision; ~ **para deudas irrecuperables** BANCA, CONT, FIN bad-debt provision; ~ **especial para pérdidas fuera del país** BANCA, CONT, FIN special provision for losses on transborder claims; ~ **específica** BANCA, CONT, FIN specific provision; ~ **excesiva de fondos** POL overfunding; ~ **en exceso**

ECON overprovision; ~ **fiscal** CONT, FISC tax provision; ~ **para fluctuaciones en el cambio** CONT allowance for exchange fluctuations; ~ **de fondos** COM GEN funding; ~ **de fondos de capital** FIN, POL capital funding; ~ **para gastos de mantenimiento** FISC allowance for living expenses; ~ **general** COM GEN *para deudas* general provision; ~ **para impuestos** BANCA, CONT, FISC tax provision; ~ **para impuestos del periodo** CONT, FISC intraperiod tax provision; ~ **para incobrables** BANCA, CONT, FIN bad-debt provision; ~ **para insolvencias** BANCA, CONT, FIN doubtful debt provision; ~ **de intermediación** BOLSA brokerage allowance; ~ **de una letra** BANCA bill cover; ~ **de pago** FIN payback provision; ~ **para pérdidas** COM GEN loss provision, provision for bad debts; ~ **para pérdidas de préstamos** BANCA provision for loan loss; ~ **para préstamo dudoso** BANCA bad-loan provision; ~ **de rescate** BOLSA call provision; ~ **para riesgos y gastos** BANCA, CONT, FISC provision for contingency

provisional *adj* COM GEN interim, provisional, DER ad interim, POL drafted

provisionalmente *adv* COM GEN provisionally, DER *juicio* ad interim

provisionar *vt* BANCA, FIN *préstamo* fund

provocación: ~ **de incendios** *f* SEG incendiarism

provocar *vt* COM GEN touch off, *coste* trigger, POL trigger

próxima: ~ **liquidación** *f* BOLSA new time

próximo *adj* (*pmo.*) COM GEN proximo (*prox.*); ◆ **el ~ día hábil a partir de mañana** BOLSA from tomorrow to the next business day (*tom/next*)

próximos: **los ~ movimientos** *m pl* COM GEN the next move

proyección *f* COM GEN, MAT projection; ~ **de beneficios** COM GEN profit projection; ~ **fiscal** FISC fiscal projection; ~ **de imagen** V&M image projection; ~ **monetaria** ECON monetary overhang; ~ **del peor caso posible** ECON worst-case projection; ~ **de la respuesta** V&M *publicidad* response projection; ~ **de ventas** V&M sales projection

proyectil *m* TRANSP *carga clasificada como peligrosa* projectile

proyecto *m* COM GEN project; ~ **aprobado** FISC approved project; ~ **de carrera** RRHH career planning; ~ **de contrato** COM GEN draft agreement, draft contract; ~ **de desarrollo** ECON, POL development project; ~ **de explotación de la propiedad** INMOB property development project; ~ **de financiación de una empresa** FIN corporate financing project; ~ **financiado con ayuda** BANCA *desarrollo* aid-financed project; ~ **innecesario** RRHH futile project, boondoggle (*infrml*) (*AmE*); ~ **de inversión** ECON, FIN capital project, investment project; ~ **de ley** DER bill; ~ **de ley de asignación presupuestaria** CONT, DER, ECON appropriation bill; ~ **de ley de consignaciones** CONT, DER, ECON appropriation bill; ~ **de ley financiero** ECON, FIN finance bill *BrE*; ~ **de ley de provisión de fondos** CONT, DER, ECON appropriation bill; ~ **de ley sobre asignación de crédito** CONT, DER, ECON appropriation bill; ~ **de ley sobre concesión** CONT, DER, ECON appropriation bill; ~ **piloto** GES pilot project; ~ **preliminar** COM GEN draft project; ~ **de presupuesto** CONT budget proposal; ~ **registrado** DER registered design; ~ **de resolución** DER draft resolution; ~ **de riesgo** CONT exposure draft; ~ **de sugerencias** GES suggestion scheme

proyector: ~ **de acetatos** *m* GES *reuniones*, MEDIOS overhead projector; ~ **de diapositivas** *m* MEDIOS slide projector; ~ **de luz concentrada** *m* COM GEN spotlight

prudente *adj* COM GEN prudent

prudentemente *adv* COM GEN prudently

prueba *f* COM GEN evidence, test run, DER proof, INFO test, MEDIOS *de imprenta, fotográfica* proof, V&M dry run, test, test run; ~ **de aceptación** IND, TRANSP, V&M acceptance trial, trial; ~ **de acogida** V&M acceptance test; ~ **activa de recursos empresariales** FISC active business asset test; ~ **de admisión** IND, TRANSP, V&M acceptance trial; ~ **alfa** INFO alpha-test; ~ **anónima de un producto** V&M anonymous product testing; ~ **de aptitud** COM GEN tryout, aptitude test; ~ **beta** INFO beta-test; ~ **de bloques** CONT block testing; ~ **de capacidad** BANCA eligibility test; ~ **de carretera** TRANSP test drive; ~ **a ciegas** V&M blind test; ~ **a ciegas de un producto** V&M blind product test; ~ **cinematográfica** MEDIOS film test; ~ **circunstancial** DER circumstancial evidence; ~ **de comparación** COM GEN comparison test; ~ **conceptual** V&M concept test; ~ **del consumidor** V&M consumer test; ~ **de desempeño** IND *empaquetamiento* performance testing; ~ **de discriminación** V&M discrimination test; ~ **de doble cola** MAT two-tailed test; ~ **documental** COM GEN documentary evidence; ~ **de efectividad de las ventas** V&M sales effectiveness test; ~ **de emisión** IND issue voucher; ~ **de encuesta** V&M inquiry test; ~ **de endeudamiento** FISC evidence of debt; ~ **de entrega** TRANSP proof of delivery (*POD*); ~ **escrita** DER written evidence; ~ **de las fases** COM GEN phasing out; ~ **de fiabilidad** COM GEN reliability test; ~ **final** MEDIOS final proof; ~ **de fuego** *jarg* COM GEN, CONT, FIN acid test; ~ **de los hechos** DER factual evidence; ~ **de imagen en pantalla** MEDIOS screen test; ~ **de imprenta** V&M *publicidad* art pull; ~ **de ingresos** CONT, FISC revenue test; ~ **de ingresos brutos** CONT, FISC gross revenue test; ~ **integrada** INFO built-in test; ~ **judicial** DER judgment proof; ~ **de memorización asistida** V&M *investigación de mercado* aided recall test; ~ **de un mensaje publicitario** V&M copy test; ~ **de mercado** V&M market test, market testing; ~ **municipal** V&M town hall test; ~ **no destructiva** IND nondestructive testing; ~ **de observación** CONT *auditoría* observation test; ~ **de panel** V&M *investigación de mercado* panel testing; ~ **de paquetes** CONT block testing; ~ **de pertenencia** BOLSA *de acciones nominativas* proof of ownership; ~ **preliminar** V&M pretesting; ~ **presunta** DER prima facie evidence; ~ **del producto** V&M product testing; ~ **del programa** INFO program testing; ~ **de propiedad** DER proof of title; ~ **de propiedad recíproca** FISC cross-ownership test; ~ **de proyección** V&M projective test; ~ **psicológica** RRHH, V&M psychological test; ~ **psicométrica** MAT, RRHH, V&M psychometric test; ~ **publicitaria** V&M advertising test; ~ **de recepción** TRANSP acceptance trial; ~ **de reconocimiento** V&M recognition test; ~ **de rendimiento** IND *empaquetamiento* performance testing; ~ **en sala** V&M *investigación de mercado* hall test; ~ **de selección** RRHH employment test; ~ **de significación** *Esp* (*cf prueba de significancia AmL*) MAT significance test; ~ **de significancia** *AmL* (*cf prueba de significación Esp*) MAT significance test; ~ **del siniestro** SEG proof of loss; ~ **sobre el terreno** V&M field testing; ~ **de sonido** COMS sound check; ~ **en**

sucio V&M dirty proof; **~ testimonial** CONT vouch mark; **~ en tránsito** TRANSP test transit; **~ unilateral** MAT one-tailed test; **~ de uso** PATENT evidence of use; **~ de uso ampliado** V&M extended use test; **~ de valor** FISC value test; **~ de ventas** V&M sales test; ◆ **a ~ de desgarro** COM GEN tear-proof; **a ~ de destrozos** COM GEN tamper-proof; **a ~ de humedad** COM GEN damp-proof; **a ~ de incendios** COM GEN fire-resistant (*BrE*), fire-resistive (*AmE*); **a ~ de piratas** INFO *sistema* hacker-proof (*infrml*); **a ~ de robo** COM GEN theft proof

pruebas *f pl* DER evidence, IND *de productos* testing; **~ concluyentes** PATENT conclusive evidence; **~ de imprenta para reproducción** V&M repro pulls; **~ de página** MEDIOS, V&M page proofs; **~ que fundamentan una presunción** DER prima facie evidence; **~ de selección** RRHH *selección* employment test

psicográficos *m pl* V&M *publicidad* psychographics

psicología *f* COM GEN psychology; **~ industrial** GES, IND industrial psychology, RRHH personnel psychology; **~ de mercado** V&M market psychology; **~ organizacional** GES organizational psychology; **~ de la venta** V&M psychology of selling

psicometría *f* COM GEN, RRHH psychometrics

psicosis: **~ de guerra** *f* COM GEN war fever

PTU *abr* (*participación de los trabajadores en los beneficios*) GES, RRHH profit sharing

publicación[1]: **de ~ mensual** *adj* MEDIOS published monthly

publicación[2]: **~ agraria** *f* MEDIOS agricultural publication; **~ de aniversario** *f* MEDIOS anniversary publication; **~ anticipada** *f* PATENT early publication; **~ comercial** *f* MEDIOS *imprenta* trade paperback (*jarg*), trade publication; **~ de dividendo** *f* BOLSA declaration of dividend; **~ electrónica** *f* INFO, MEDIOS electronic publishing; **~ vertical** *f* MEDIOS *imprenta* vertical publication

publicar *vt* COM GEN publish, INFO *versión de programas, productos* release; ◆ **~ unas declaraciones** MEDIOS put out a statement

publicidad *f* COM GEN advertisement (*ad*), advertising, publicity, MEDIOS, V&M advertisement (*ad*); **contra ~** V&M counter-advertising; **~ de acción directa** V&M direct action advertising; **~ aérea** V&M aerial advertising; **~ en los aeropuertos** V&M airport advertising; **~ agresiva** V&M hard selling; **~ de ambiente** V&M mood advertising; **~ anticíclica** V&M anticyclical advertising; **~ anticipada** MEDIOS, V&M advance publicity; **~ de apoyo** V&M advocacy advertising; **~ basada en la imagen** V&M image advertising; **~ boca a boca** V&M word-of-mouth advertising; **~ ciega** V&M blind advertisement; **~ en los cines** V&M screen advertising; **~ codificada** V&M keyed advertisement; **~ comercial** V&M trade advertising; **~ comparativa** V&M comparative advertising; **~ para el consumidor** V&M consumer advertising; **~ cooperativa** V&M *acuerdo en la venta minorista* cooperative advertising (*co-op advertising*); **~ corporativa** V&M corporate advertising; **~ por correo** V&M mailing; **~ didáctica** V&M educational advertising; **~ directa por correo** V&M direct-mail advertising; **~ a doble página** MEDIOS, V&M double-spread advertising; **~ editorial** MEDIOS, V&M editorial publicity; **~ de una empresa a otra** V&M business-to-business advertising; **~ engañosa** COM GEN, MEDIOS misleading advertising; **~ especializada** V&M speciality advertising (*BrE*), specialty advertising (*AmE*); **~ ética** V&M ethical advertising; **~ de exposición** V&M display advertising; **~ de exposición clasificada** V&M classified display advertising; **~ exterior** V&M outdoor advertising; **~ falsa** V&M false advertising; **~ financiera** V&M financial advertising; **~ con globos** V&M balloon advertising; **~ a gran escala** V&M large display advertisement; **~ incidental** MEDIOS, V&M plug (*infrml*); **~ industrial** V&M industrial advertising; **~ informativa** V&M educational advertising, informative advertising; **~ institucional** V&M institutional advertising; **~ intensiva** V&M burst advertising; **~ de intriga** V&M teaser ad; **~ en laterales de autobuses** V&M bus side; **~ de una línea aérea** V&M airline advertising; **~ de marca** V&M brand advertising; **~ de masas** V&M mass advertising; **~ masiva** V&M heavy advertising; **~ en medios de transporte** V&M transport advertising; **~ de una película** OCIO, V&M motion picture advertising (*AmE*), film advertising (*BrE*); **~ de perímetro** V&M perimeter advertising; **~ en periódicos** MEDIOS, V&M newspaper advertising; **~ poscompra** V&M post-purchase advertising; **~ en la prensa** MEDIOS, V&M press advertising; **~ de prestigio** V&M prestige advertising; **~ del producto** V&M product advertising; **~ del productor** V&M producer advertising; **~ en los puntos de venta** V&M point-of-sale advertising (POS advertising); **~ en la radio** MEDIOS, V&M radio advertising; **~ de reclutamiento** V&M recruitment advertising; **~ recordatoria** V&M reminder advertising; **~ de la redacción** V&M editorial advertising; **~ de respuesta directa** V&M direct response advertising; **~ secundaria** V&M accessory advertising; **~ semiintensiva** V&M semi-display advertising; **~ de un servicio público** V&M public service advertising; **~ subliminal** V&M subliminal advertising; **~ televisiva** MEDIOS, V&M television advertising; **~ temática** V&M theme advertising

publicista *mf* RRHH publicity man

publicitario *adj* COM GEN, MEDIOS commercial, V&M advertising, commercial

público[1] *adj* COM GEN public

público[2] *m* COM GEN public, MEDIOS, V&M audience; **el ~ en general** COM GEN the public at large; **~ objetivo** V&M target audience

publireportaje *m* V&M advertorial

puente *m* COM GEN bridge, RRHH *con días festivos* long weekend; **~ aéreo** TRANSP *vuelo* shuttle; **~ alto** TRANSP flying bridge; **~-báscula** TRANSP *cargas* weighbridge; **~ de fijación** TRANSP *carga* dog bone bridge; **~ inferior** TRANSP *aeronaves, barcos* lower deck; **~ de peaje** TRANSP tollbridge; **~ de tierra transiberiano** TRANSP Trans-Siberian landbridge; ◆ **hacer ~** COM GEN, RRHH have a long weekend

puericultura *f* PROT SOC child care

puerta *f* COMS *redes de área extendida* gateway, INFO port, TRANSP *aviación* gateway, gate; **~ de embarque** TRANSP boarding gate; **~ de impresora** INFO printer port; **~ a puerta** V&M cold canvass; **~ en serie** INFO serial port; **~ de servicio** COM GEN service entrance (*AmE*), tradesman's entrance (*BrE*); ◆ **de ~ a almacén** TRANSP door/depot; **a ~ cerrada** DER, POL *reunión* in camera; **de ~ a puerta** COM GEN door to door, TRANSP house to house, V&M door to door

puertas: **~ abiertas** *f pl* COM GEN open day (*BrE*), open house (*AmE*)

puerto *m* TRANSP *navegación* harbour (*BrE*), harbor (*AmE*); **~ de aerodeslizadores** TRANSP hoverport;

~ **de aguas profundas** TRANSP deepwater harbor (*AmE*), deepwater harbour (*BrE*); ~ **autónomo** TRANSP self-governing port; ~ **de carga** TRANSP load port; ~ **cerrado** TRANSP enclosed port; ~ **comercial** TRANSP trading port, commercial port; ~ **convenido** TRANSP treaty port (*obs*); ~ **de descarga** TRANSP discharge port, port of discharge; ~ **de destino** TRANSP port of destination; ~ **directo** TRANSP direct port (*dp*); ~ **de embarque** COM GEN, IMP/EXP, TRANSP port of loading, port of shipment; ~ **de entrada** IMP/EXP, TRANSP port of entry; ~ **franco** IMP/EXP, TRANSP free port, open port; ~ **de inscripción** IMP/EXP, TRANSP port of entry; ~ **interior** TRANSP inner harbor (*AmE*), inner harbour (*BrE*); ~ **de llegada** IMP/EXP, TRANSP port of arrival; ~ **de mar** TRANSP seaport; ~ **marítimo** TRANSP seaport; ~ **de matrícula** IMP/EXP, TRANSP port of registry; ~ **de necesidad** TRANSP port of necessity; ~ **pesquero** IND fishing port; ~ **petrolero** TRANSP bunker port; ~ **seguro** TRANSP safe port; ~ **para un único usuario** TRANSP single user port; ◆ **de ~ a puerto** IMP/EXP, TRANSP port to port (*p to p*)

puertos: en los ~ *adv* FISC ex docks

puesta: ~ en escena *f* RRHH staging; ~ **en marcha** *f* BOLSA, COM GEN *de capital riesgo* start-up, ECON *de un negocio* business start-up; ~ **en práctica de estrategias** *f* COM GEN, GES strategy implementation; ~ **a punto** *f* ECON fine tuning

puesto[1]: ~ **sobre vagón** *adj* IMP/EXP *ferrocarril*, TRANSP free on rail (*f.o.r.*)

puesto[2] *m* RRHH position, post, situation (*sit.*); ~ **de aduanas fronterizo** IMP/EXP frontier customs post; ~ **de atraque para graneles líquidos** TRANSP *navegación* bulk liquid-cargo berth; ~ **de atraque para graneles secos** TRANSP *navegación* bulk dry-cargo berth; ~ **directivo** GES, RRHH managerial position; ~ **inactivo** BOLSA inactive post; ~ **menor** RRHH junior position; ~ **de oficinista** RRHH office job; ~ **de operaciones** BOLSA trading post (*jarg*); ~ **operativo** RRHH *cadena de producción* line position; ~ **permanente** RRHH tenured post; ~ **del servicio diplomático** RRHH diplomatic service post; ~ **de trabajo** COM GEN, RRHH job; ~ **de trabajo de nivel inicial** RRHH entry-level job; ~ **de trabajo de oficina** RRHH white-collar job; ◆ **en un ~ difícil** RRHH in the hot seat

puestos: ~ vacantes *m pl* RRHH situations vacant (*BrE*) (*sits. vac.*)

puja *f* COM GEN bid

pujar *vt* COM GEN bid, *en subasta* bid for

pulgada *f* COM GEN inch (*in*); ~ **de columna** MEDIOS *imprenta* column inch; ~ **de columna de a uno** MEDIOS single column inch (*SCI*); ~ **cúbica** COM GEN cubic inch

pulman *m* TRANSP *ferrocarril* Pullman

pulsación *f* INFO keystroke

pulsar *vt* COM GEN *mercado* tap, INFO press

punta[1]: **de ~** *adj AmL* (*cf puntera Esp*) IND state-of-the-art

punta[2]: ~ **fija superior** *f* TRANSP top dead center (*AmE*) (*TDC*), top dead centre (*BrE*) (*TDC*);~ **del iceberg** *f* COM GEN tip of the iceberg; ~ **nocturna** *f* COM GEN evening peak

puntal: ~ para cargas pesadas *m* TRANSP *manejo de cargas* jumbo derrick

puntear: ~ la caja *vt* COM GEN tick the box

punteo *m* COM GEN, CONT tick mark (*BrE*)

puntera *adj Esp* (*cf de punta AmL*) IND *tecnología* state-of-the-art

puntero *m* COM GEN, INFO pointer

punto[1]: ~ **menos que perfecto** *adj* COM GEN less-than-perfect

punto[2]: **después del ~ máximo** *adv* V&M post-peak

punto[3] *m* COM GEN *de discusión* point, CONT item, INFO, MAT dot; ~ **de ajuste automático** *salarios* automatic adjustment point; ~ **básico** BOLSA tick, basis point, FIN, MAT basis point; ~ **beta de la cartera** BOLSA *volatilidad* portfolio beta score; ~ **de Bliss** PROT SOC *bienestar social* bliss point; ~ **de cabecera** TRANSP *aviación* headline point; ~ **central** COM GEN focus; ~ **y coma** COM GEN semicolon; ~ **de conexión** ECON takeoff point; ~ **de control** INFO, TRANSP check point; ~ **crítico** COM GEN, CONT break-even point; ~ **de entrada** IMP/EXP *en país* point of entry; ~ **de entrada del oro** FIN, IMP/EXP gold import point; ~ **de equilibrio** COM GEN break-even level of income, FIN, IND break-even point; ~ **de equilibrio al alza** BOLSA upside break-even point; ~ **de equilibrio descendiente** BOLSA *opciones* downside break-even point; ~ **de exportación** IMP/EXP point of export; ~ **de exportación de oro** FIN, IMP/EXP gold export point; ~ **de flexión** COM GEN, ECON turning point; ~ **focal** COM GEN focal point; ~ **grueso** INFO bullet point; ~ **hipotético** OCIO *aerolínea* hypothetical point; ~ **de importación de oro** FIN, IMP/EXP gold import point; ~ **de índice** BOLSA index point; ~ **de inflexión** ECON saddle point; ~ **de interrupción** INFO, TRANSP breakpoint; ~ **límite** ECON *presupuestación del capital* cutoff point; ~ **máximo** ECON peak; ~ **de la memoria** CONT memo item, memorandum item; ~ **muerto** COM GEN break-even level of income, break-even point, deadlock, RRHH standoff, V&M deadlock; ~ **neurálgico** GES nerve center (*AmE*), nerve centre (*BrE*); ~ **de origen** TRANSP point of origin; ~ **oro** IMP/EXP gold point; ~ **de partida** COM GEN starting point, IMP/EXP, TRANSP point of departure; ~ **peligroso** COM GEN danger point; ~ **porcentual** FIN percentage point; ~ **prominente** INMOB landmark; ~ **de provocación** COM GEN trigger point; ~ **de prueba** V&M sampling point; ~ **de reaprovisionamiento** COM GEN, CONT reorder point; ~ **de recepción** OCIO reception point; ~ **de referencia** COM GEN, CONT, ECON bench mark; ~ **de referencia de grupo** COM GEN group reference point (*GRP*); ~ **de rentabilidad** ADMIN, CONT break-even point; ~ **de retención** COM GEN sticking point; ~ **de reunión** BOLSA rallying point, COM GEN rallying point, *conferencia* venue; ~ **de riesgo** ECON, IMP/EXP peril point (*jarg*); ~ **de salida del oro** FIN, IMP/EXP gold export point; ~ **de saturación** COM GEN saturation point; ~ **sin resolver** COM GEN open question; ~ **de umbral** BOLSA threshold point; ~ **de venta** COM GEN, V&M point of sale (*POS*); ~ **de venta electrónico** COM GEN, V&M electronic point of sale (*EPOS*); ~ **de vía secundaria** TRANSP *tarifa de carga* sideline point; ~ **de vista** COM GEN point of view; ~ **de vista de la administración** GES administrative point of view (*APV*); ~ **de vista administrativo** GES administrative point of view (*APV*); ~ **vital** COM GEN key point

puntos: ~ de descuento *m pl* BANCA discount points; ~ **numéricos** *m pl* COM GEN specie point; ~ **por pie** *m pl* (*ppp*) INFO dots per inch (*dpi*); **~ suspensivos** *m pl* MEDIOS ellipsis

puntuación: **~ del personal** *f* RRHH scale of points value; **~ umbral** *f* COM GEN target

puntual *adj* COM GEN *tren* on schedule

puntualidad *f* TRANSP punctuality

pura: **~ economía de mercado** *f* POL pure market economy

P.V.P. *abr* (*precio de venta al público*) COM GEN recommended retail price

PYME *abr* (*pequeña y mediana empresa*) ECON SME (*small and medium-size enterprise*)

Q

qt *abr* (*cuarto*) COM GEN qt (*quart*)

quebrado *adj* BANCA, COM GEN bankrupt

quebrantamiento: ~ **del secreto del sumario** *m* DER contempt of court

quebrar *vi* COM GEN *persona, compañía* go bankrupt, fail, go out of business, TRANSP crash

quebrarse *v refl* INFO crash (*jarg*)

quedar *vi* COM GEN remain; ◆ ~ **afectado** COM GEN, DER, ECON be affected; ~ **anticuado** COM GEN become obsolete; ~ **bajo propiedad pública** ECON, IND, POL come under public ownership; ~ **a bordo** TRANSP *carga* remain on board (*ROB*); ~ **pendiente** COM GEN stand over, remain in suspense

quedarse: ~ **sin** *v refl* COM GEN run out of; ~ **atrás** *v refl* COM GEN, ECON, FIN lag behind

queja *f* COM GEN complaint, RRHH grievance; ~ **financiera** CONT, FIN financial claim; ◆ **tener** ~ **de alguien** COM GEN have a grievance against sb

quejarse *v refl* COM GEN complain

querella *f* DER lawsuit, libel suit

quiebra *f* BANCA bankruptcy, BOLSA crash, COM GEN, CONT bankruptcy, INFO crash (*jarg*), TRANSP crash; ~ **bancaria** BANCA bank failure; ~ **comercial** COM GEN business failure; ~ **fraudulenta** COM GEN fraudulent bankruptcy; ~ **involuntaria** COM GEN involuntary bankruptcy; ◆ **estar en** ~ COM GEN be bankrupt; **ir a la** ~ COM GEN go bust (*infrml*)

quilate *m Esp* (*cf carate AmL*) COM GEN carat

química *f* COM GEN, IND chemistry

quincalla *f* COM GEN hardware

quincenal *adj* COM GEN fortnightly, half-monthly

quincenalmente *adv* COM GEN fortnightly, half-monthly

quinielas *f pl Esp* OCIO ≈ football pools (*BrE*), ≈ pools (*BrE*)

quintal *m* COM GEN hundredweight (*cwt*); ~ **métrico** COM GEN quintal

quitar: ~ **del mercado** *fra* COM GEN take off the market; ~ **hierro a** *fra* POL soft-pedal (*jarg*)

quorum *m* COM GEN, DER, GES quorum

R

R *abr* TRANSP (*refrigeración*) R (*refrigeration*)

rabino *m* POL rabbi (*jarg*) (*AmE*)

RAC *abr* (*Real Automóvil Club*) TRANSP Spanish organization for motorists, ≈ AA (*BrE*) (*Automobile Association*), ≈ AAA (*AmE*) (*American Automobile Association*), ≈ RAC (*BrE*) (*Royal Automobile Club*)

racha: ~ **de suerte** *f* COM GEN lucky break (*infrml*); ~ **de triunfos** *f* COM GEN winning streak (*infrml*)

racional *adj* COM GEN rational

racionalización *f* COM GEN rationalization, GES streamlining; ~ **de la flota** TRANSP fleet rationalization; ~ **de la marca** V&M brand rationalization; ~ **salarial** RRHH broad banding (*BrE*)

racionalizar *vt* COM GEN rationalize, GES streamline

racionamiento *m* BANCA, ECON rationing; ~ **del capital** BANCA, ECON capital rationing; ~ **del crédito** BANCA, ECON credit rationing

radar *m* TRANSP radar

radiación *f* MED AMB *nuclear* fallout, radiation

radicación *f* COM GEN location

radical *adj* COM GEN radical, *cambio* sweeping

radio: ~ **celular** *f* COMS, MEDIOS cellular radio; ~ **comercial** *f* COMS, MEDIOS commercial radio; ~ **local independiente** *f* COMS, MEDIOS independent local radio; ~ **pirata** *f* MEDIOS pirate radio

Radio: ~ **Televisión Española** *f* (*RTVE*) MEDIOS Spanish national broadcasting company, ≈ British Broadcasting Corporation (*BBC*)

radiodifusión *f* MEDIOS broadcasting

radiotelefonía *f* COMS, MEDIOS, TRANSP radiotelephony (*RT*); ~ **de alta frecuencia** COMS, MEDIOS, TRANSP high frequency radiotelephony (*RTh*); ~ **de frecuencia media** COMS, MEDIOS, TRANSP medium frequency radiotelephony (*RTm*)

radioteléfono *m* COMS, MEDIOS, TRANSP radiotelephone; ~ **portátil** COMS, TRANSP walkie-talkie

radiotelegrafía *f* COMS radiotelegraphy

radiotelegrafista *mf* RRHH, TRANSP radio officer

radiotelegrama *m* COMS radiotelegram

radioyente *mf* COMS, MEDIOS listener

raíz *f* INFO root

RAL *abr* (*red de área local*) INFO LAN (*local area network*)

ralentizar *vt* COM GEN slow

ralentizarse *v refl* COM GEN, ECON decelerate, slow down

RAM: ~ **dinámica** *f* INFO dynamic random access memory (*DRAM*)

rama: ~ **principal** *f* BANCA main branch

ramal *m* TRANSP *ferrocarril* branch line, feeder line

ramas: por ~ **familiares** *fra* DER *reparto una heredad* per stirpes

ramillete *m* COM GEN cluster

ramo *m* BANCA, COM GEN branch

rampa *f* TRANSP ramp; ~ **de transbordador** TRANSP ferry ramp

rango: ~ **de depreciación de activos** *m* CONT, FIN, INMOB asset depreciation range; ~ **percentil** *m* MAT percentile ranking; ~ **semiintercuartílico** *m* ECON *econometría* quartile deviation

ranura *f* COM GEN, INFO, TRANSP *navegación* slot

rápido[1]: ~ **aumento** *m* BOLSA expectativas de una moneda fast rise

rápido[2]: **tan** ~ **como pueda** *fra* TRANSP *carga, descarga* fast as can (*fac*)

rappel *m* COM GEN rappel

rasgo: ~ **clave** *m* COM GEN key feature; ~ **saliente** *m* COM GEN highlight

rastrear *vt* COM GEN, TRANSP trace, track down

rastreo: ~ **de auditoría** *m* CONT audit trail

ratificación *f* COM GEN ratification

ratificar *vt* COM GEN *tratado* ratify

ratio *m* COM GEN ratio; ~ **de activo disponible a pasivo corriente** CONT quick ratio; ~ **de beneficio según libros** CONT book rate of return; ~ **de capital a activos inmovilizados** CONT capital-to-asset ratio; ~ **del circulante** CONT, FIN current ratio; ~ **corriente** CONT, FIN current ratio; ~ **de cuentas a cobrar** CONT collection ratio; ~ **endeudamiento-capital propio** BOLSA, CONT, FIN gearing; ~ **de gestión** GES management ratio; ~ **de ingresos netos a patrimonio neto** CONT net income-to-net worth ratio; ~ **de liquidez inmediata** CONT quick ratio, acid test ratio; ~ **precio-beneficio** COM GEN price-earnings ratio (*PER*); ~ **de ventas a crédito** CONT accounts receivable turnover

ratón *m* INFO mouse

rayo: ~ **láser** *m* IND laser beam

razón[1]: **sin** ~ *adv* COM GEN wrongly

razón[2] *f* COM GEN reason; ~ **de apalancamiento financiero** FIN financial leverage ratio; ~ **de capacidad** IND capacity ratio; ~ **capital-mano de obra** ECON, FIN, IND capital-labor ratio (*AmE*), capital-labour ratio (*BrE*); ~ **de comportamiento de los precios** *m* COM GEN price-performance ratio; ~ **de la decisión** COM GEN ratio decidendi; ~ **de estado** POL national interest; ~ **recíproca** MAT reciprocal ratio; ~ **social** COM GEN business name, trade name, corporate name, DER legal name, ECON stylized fact; ♦ **con más** ~ COM GEN a fortiori; **por ninguna** ~ COM GEN for no reason; **tener** ~ COM GEN be in the right; **en** ~ **de la conveniencia** COM GEN on grounds of expediency

razonable *adj* COM GEN, DER equitable, reasonable

razonablemente *adv* COM GEN reasonably

razonamiento: ~ **deductivo** *m* COM GEN, GES deductive reasoning; ~ **horizontal** *m* COM GEN, GES lateral thinking; ~ **inductivo** *m* COM GEN, GES clear thinking, inductive reasoning; ~ **lúcido** *m* COM GEN clear thinking

razones: ~ **médicas** *f pl* RRHH medical grounds; ~ **de productividad** *f pl* IND factor productivity

RD *abr* BANCA (*dirigirse al librador*) RD (*refer to drawer*), COM GEN (*dirigirse al librador, devuélvase al firmante*) RD (*refer to drawer*)

RDP *abr* (*recibo de depósito del portador*) BANCA BDR (*bearer depository receipt*)

reabrir *vt* CONT bring down (*b*/*d*)

reacción *f* COM GEN reaction; **~ del consumidor** V&M consumer reaction; **~ negativa** ECON, INFO negative feedback; **~ positiva** ECON, INFO positive feedback;

reaccionar *vi* BOLSA, COM GEN react; ◆ **~ bien estando bajo tensión** COM GEN, RRHH react well under stress

reaccionario *m* POL reactionary

reachique *m* TRANSP stripping

reacio *adj* COM GEN reluctant

reacondicionado *adj* COM GEN, INMOB, TRANSP reconditioned (*R*), refurbished

reacondicionamiento *m* COM GEN, INMOB, TRANSP refurbishment

reactivación *f* COM GEN *recuperación* recovery, *economía, mercado* growth, INFO *de programas* reactivation; **~ de la economía** COM GEN, ECON pump priming (*jarg*); **~ estimulada** COM GEN, ECON pump priming (*jarg*)

reactivar *vt* COM GEN *la economía* reflate, pump prime (*jarg*), INFO *programas* reactivate

reactivarse *v refl* BOLSA, COM GEN rally

reactivo *m* COM GEN reactive

reactor: **~ de gran tonelaje** *m* TRANSP heavy jet; **~ nuclear** *m* MED AMB nuclear reactor (*NR*)

reafirmar *vt* COM GEN reaffirm

reaganomía *f* ECON, POL Reaganomics

reaganomics *m* ECON, POL Reaganomics

reagrupar *vt* COM GEN regroup

reajustado: **~ según la estación** *adj* COM GEN, ECON, RRHH seasonally-adjusted

reajustar *vt* COM GEN adjust, INFO tweak; ◆ **~ con referencia a** BOLSA write against

reajuste *m* COM GEN, ECON readjustment, RRHH dehiring (*AmE*), laying off (*BrE*); **~ del calendario de la deuda** BANCA, FIN rescheduling of debt; **~ de financiación** BANCA, FIN financing adjustment; **~ impositivo** COM GEN, FISC tax adjustment; **~ de personal** RRHH decruitment, lay-off; **~ del valor de los activos** CONT valuation adjustment

real[1] *adj* COM GEN *del rey* royal, *verdadero* actual, real

real[2]: **~ decreto** *m* COM GEN royal decree

Real: **~ Automóvil Club** *m* (*RAC*) TRANSP Spanish organization for motorists, ≈ American Automobile Association (*AmE*) (*AAA*), ≈ Automobile Association (*BrE*) (*AA*), ≈ Royal Automobile Club (*BrE*) (*RAC*)

realce *m* INFO highlighting

realismo *m* COM GEN, DER, POL realism

realista *adj* COM GEN, DER, POL realistic, V&M hard-headed

realizable *adj* COM GEN, COMS, FIN *sentido financiero* realizable; **no ~** CONT illiquid

realización *f* BOLSA *de beneficios*, COM GEN *objetivos* achievement, CONT *de la empresa* performance, realization, OCIO *cine* production, V&M *liquidación* sale, clearance; **~ de activos** CONT realization of assets; **~ de beneficios** CONT earnings performance, ECON profit taking; **~ personal** RRHH self-actualization

realizar *vt* BOLSA *beneficios* realize, COM GEN *compromisos, obligaciones* fulfil (*BrE*), fulfill (*AmE*), *hacer real* achieve, CONT *beneficio* realize, perform, OCIO produce, V&M sell, clear; ◆ **~ una conferencia** GES hold a conference; **~ indagaciones** COM GEN make enquiries; **~ órdenes** BOLSA execute orders; **~ un pedido de**

compra COM GEN *de productos extranjeros* indent (*BrE*); **~ una transacción** COM GEN make a transaction

realmacenaje *m* TRANSP restowage

reanudación *f* INFO restart

reanudar *vt* INFO *reiniciar* restart, resume

rearrancar *vt* INFO restart

rearranque *m* INFO restart

rearriendo: **~ al vendedor** *m* COM GEN, INMOB lease-back

reaseguro *m* BOLSA, SEG reinsurance, underwriting; **~ activo** SEG active reinsurance; **~ de cartera de valores** SEG portfolio reinsurance; **~ por exceso de línea** SEG excess of line reinsurance; **~ de exceso de pérdida** SEG excess of loss reinsurance; **~ limitador de pérdidas** SEG stop-loss reinsurance; **~ de línea fija** SEG flat line reinsurance

reasentamiento *m* COM GEN resettlement

reasignación *f* FIN reallocation, INFO reassignment

reasignar *vt* FIN reallocate, INFO reassign

rebaja *f* COM GEN abatement, *a precios reducidos* (*cf barata AmL*) sale, rebate, abatement, discount; **~ arancelaria** ECON, FISC, IMP/EXP tariff cut; **~ de interés** BANCA interest rebate; **~ de precios** V&M pricing down; **~ de la tasa de interés** BANCA interest rate rebate

rebajar *vt* COM GEN *impuestos, precios* lower, abate, discount, knock down, mark down; ◆ **~ un cargo** BANCA charge off; **~ el exceso de oferta agregada** ECON take up the slack (*infrml*)

rebasamiento *m* ECON *de presupuesto* overrun

rebasar *vt* COM GEN overshoot

rebatiña: **~ del oro** *f* COM GEN gold rush

rebeldía: **en ~** *fra* DER in contempt of court

rebobinar *vt* INFO *cinta*, MEDIOS *cassette, cinta* rewind

recadero *m* RRHH office boy

recalcular *vt* MAT recalculate

recalentador: **~ intermedio** *m* TRANSP *máquinas* reheater

recalentamiento: **~ de la coyuntura** *m* ECON overheating

recapitalización *f* BOLSA, FIN recapitalization

recapitulación: **~ de la situación** *f* COM GEN summary of the situation, CONT, FIN consolidated statement of condition (*AmE*)

recargar *vt* INFO *programa* reload

recargo *m* BANCA, COM GEN overcharge (*o/c*), CONT extra charge, RRHH loading (*jarg*), TRANSP surcharge value; **~ por exceso de equipaje** OCIO, TRANSP excess baggage charge; **~ por incumplimiento de pago** FISC default penalty (*AmE*), default surcharge (*BrE*); **~ por matrimonio** FISC marriage penalty; **~ por pago fuera de plazo** FISC penalty for late tax payment; **~ de primer incidente** FISC first occurrence penalty; **~ por segunda o siguientes presentaciones** FISC second or further occurrence penalty

recaudación: **~ de derechos de aduanas** *f* FISC, IMP/EXP collection of customs duties; **~ de dinero público** *f* FISC collection of public money; **~ de fondos** *f* FIN, PROT SOC fundraising; **~ de fondos para beneficencia** *f* FIN, PROT SOC charity fundraising; **~ impositiva** *f* FISC tax receipt; **~ de impuestos** *f* FISC levying of taxes, tax collection; **~ de la PAC** *f* ECON CAP levy; **~ de la Política Agrícola Común** *f* ECON Common Agricultural Policy levy; **~ provisional de impuestos** *f* FISC provisional collection of taxes; **~ tributaria** *f* FISC tax receipts, tax revenue, tax yield

recaudador, a *m,f* COM GEN receiver, FISC taxman; **~ de aduanas** IMP/EXP customs collector; **~ de contribuciones** ADMIN, FISC, RRHH collector of taxes; **~ de impuestos** FISC, RRHH tax collector

recaudar: ~ fondos *fra* COM GEN raise funds; **~ fondos externos** *fra* COM GEN raise external funds; **~ un impuesto** *fra* FISC levy a tax; **~ pagos** *fra* COM GEN collect payments; **~ las sumas vencidas** *fra* FIN collect sums due

recepción *f* COM GEN front office, reception desk; **~ en almacén** V&M *carga* warehouse receipt; **~ definitiva** COM GEN *artículos* final acceptance; **~ de mercancías** TRANSP *carga* receipt of goods (*ROG*); ♦ **a la ~ de** COM GEN on receipt of

recepcionista *mf* RRHH receptionist

receptáculo: ~ semirrígido *m* COM GEN semirigid receptacle

receptividad: ~ del mercado *f* BOLSA *de valores*, V&M market receptiveness

receptivo *adj* INFO case-sensitive

receptor[1]: **~ telefónico** *m* COMS telephone receiver; **~ transmisor síncrono** *m* COM GEN synchronous transmitter receiver

receptor[2],**a**: **~ y administrador(a)** *m,f* DER *bancarrota* receiver and manager; **~ de ingresos** *m,f* ECON revenue earner; **~ de una oferta** *m,f* COM GEN offeree; **~ del préstamo** *m,f* BANCA, FIN loan recipient

recesión *f* BOLSA downturn, COM GEN recession; **~ económica** ECON recession

recesionario *adj* COM GEN recessionary

receso: ~ estival *f* COM GEN *Parlamento*, POL summer recess

receta: ~ médica *f* PROT SOC prescription

rechazado *adj* BANCA *cheque* dishonored (*AmE*), dishonoured (*BrE*)

rechazar *vt* BANCA *cheque* bounce (*infrml*), dishonour, COM GEN reject, TRANSP *pasajero* refuse; ♦ **~ la aceptación de una letra** BANCA refuse acceptance of a draft

rechazo *m* BANCA *de letra o pagaré* nonacceptance, COM GEN rejection; **~ a la exportación** IMP/EXP export reject; **~ de un pasajero** TRANSP *aviones* pushback

recibido *adj* COM GEN received (*rcvd*)

recibimiento *m* ADMIN reception

recibir *vt* COM GEN receive; ♦ **no ~** BOLSA fail to receive; **~ un abono en cuenta** BANCA, CONT, FIN be credited to; **~ contra pago** BANCA, FIN receive against payment; **~ una impresión desfavorable** COM GEN be unfavorably impressed (*AmE*), be unfavourably impressed (*BrE*); **~ prestaciones de la Seguridad Social** PROT SOC go on benefits (*BrE*), go on the dole (*infrml*) (*BrE*), go on welfare (*AmE*); **~ una proporción de** RRHH be paid a rate of; **~ sobornos** COM GEN take bribes

recibo *m* BANCA, COM GEN receipt (*rept*); **~ del agente expedidor** IMP/EXP, TRANSP forwarding agent's receipt; **~ de almacén** BOLSA stock receipt, TRANSP, V&M warehouse receipt (*WR*); **~ del alquiler** INMOB rent receipt; **~ bancario** *Esp* (*cf boleta del banco AmL*) BANCA banker's ticket; **~ en blanco** COM GEN blank receipt; **~ de caja** *f* COM GEN, V&M sales slip, till receipt; **~ de cajero automático** BANCA automated teller machine statement; **~ contable** CONT accountable receipt; **~ de débito** COM GEN charge ticket; **~ de depósito** BANCA deposit receipt (*DR*), deposit slip;

~ de depósito del portador (*RDP*) BANCA bearer depository receipt (*BDR*); **~ de derechos de tonelaje** TRANSP *navegación* tonnage dues slip; **~ de los documentos** PATENT receipt for documents; **~ de efectivo** BANCA, FIN cash acknowledgement; **~ de embarque** TRANSP shipment received (*SR*), TRANSP *navegación* mate's receipt (*MR*); **~ de entrega** TRANSP delivery receipt; **~ de finiquito** DER quitclaim deed; **~ implícito** FISC constructive receipt; **~ implícito de la renta** FISC constructive receipt of income; **~ de muelle** TRANSP dock receipt; **~ oficial** FISC official receipt; **~ de reintegro** COM GEN refund slip; **~ secundario** COM GEN supporting receipt; **~ de ventas** V&M sales receipt; ♦ **sin acuse de ~** COM GEN *facturas* unreceipted

reciclable *adj* MED AMB recyclable; **no ~** MED AMB nonrecyclable

reciclado: ~ de residuos *m* MED AMB waste recycling

reciclaje *m* MED AMB recycling; **~ profesional** RRHH retraining

reciclar *vt* MED AMB recycle, RRHH retrain

recipiente *m* V&M jar

recíproca *f* MAT reciprocal

reciprocidad *f* ECON reciprocity; **~ del contrato** DER mutuality of contract

recíproco *adj* COM GEN reciprocal

reclamación *f* COM GEN claim; **~ de carga** TRANSP cargo claim; **~ de compensación** DER claim for compensation; **~ condicionada** CONT contingent claim; **~ contingente** CONT contingent claim; **~ de devolución** FISC repayment claim; **~ de devolución del impuesto sobre la renta** FISC income tax repayment claim; **~ de dividendos** BOLSA, CONT dividend requirement; **~ financiera** CONT financial claim; **~ fiscal** FISC tax claim; **~ de gastos de viaje** COM GEN travel expense claim; **~ global combinada** FISC combined total claim; **~ de indemnización** SEG claim for indemnification; **~ legal** DER legal claim; **~ máxima** FISC maximum claim; **~ retrospectiva** SEG retrospective claim; **~ salarial** RRHH wage claim; **~ secundaria** CONT secondary claim; **~ del seguro** SEG insurer's claim; **~ solventada** ECON adjusted claim; **~ de tercero sobre bienes embargados** DER adverse claim; **~ a terceros** DER third-party claim; **~ vencida** CONT past due claim; ♦ **desistir de una ~** DER abandon a claim

reclamante *mf* COM GEN, DER claimant

reclamar *vt* COM GEN claim, demand, MED AMB *tierras* reclaim; ♦ **~ a** DER claim against; **~ como carga familiar** FISC claim as a dependant; **~ daños y perjuicios** DER claim damages; **~ una exención personal** FISC claim personal exemption

reclame *m AmL* (*cf anuncio Esp*) COM GEN *aviso* announcement, *medios de comunicación* advert, advertisement (*ad*), commercial

reclamo *m* DER claim; **~ publicitario** V&M advertising appeal

reclasificación *f* COM GEN reclassification

reclasificar *vt* COM GEN reclassify

reclutamiento *m* RRHH *de personal* recruitment

reclutar *vt* RRHH recruit

recobrar *vt* CONT recapture, recover

recobro: ~ del agotamiento *m* CONT depletion recapture; **~ de una deuda incobrable** *m* CONT bad-debt recovery

recogedor: ~ **de papel** *m* INFO paper stacker

recoger *vt* COM GEN collect, rake in (*infrml*), TRANSP *carga* pick up

recogida: ~ **de basuras** *f* COM GEN refuse collection; ~ **de datos** *f* INFO, V&M data collection, data gathering; ~ **a domicilio** *f* TRANSP collection on wheels (*COW*); ~ **de servicio** *f* TRANSP service pick up

recogido: ~ **y entregado** *adj* COM GEN collected and delivered (*C&D*)

recolección *f* COM GEN gathering

recolocación *f* GES, RRHH secondment

recoltar: ~ **proporcionalmente** *vt* V&M scale down

recomendación *f* COM GEN recommendation; ~ **general** BOLSA, COM GEN blanket recommendation

recomendaciones: **tener excelentes** ~ *fra* RRHH have excellent testimonials

recomendar *vt* COM GEN advocate, recommend; ◆ ~ **a alguien para un puesto** RRHH put sb in for a job

recompensa *f* COM GEN, V&M reward; ◆ **como** ~ **por** COM GEN as a reward for

recompra *f* BOLSA *de opción*, COM GEN recall; ~ **inversa** BANCA, FIN reverse repurchase

recomprar *vt* BOLSA buy back, *opción* recall, COM GEN *deuda* buy back, repurchase, DER buy back, V&M rebuy

reconciliación: ~ **bancaria** *f* BANCA, CONT bank reconciliation; ~ **de cuentas** *f* BANCA, CONT reconciliation of accounts

reconciliar *vt* BANCA, COM GEN, CONT reconcile

reconfiguración *f* COM GEN reconfiguration

reconocer *vt* COM GEN recognize, *error* acknowledge, RRHH *sindicato* recognize

reconocido *adj* COM GEN acknowledged, recognized; **no** ~ COM GEN unacknowledged, unrecognized

reconocimiento *m* COM GEN acknowledgement, recognition; ~ **aéreo** TRANSP aerial survey; ~ **de deuda** BANCA, COM GEN, FIN acknowledgement of debt, acknowledgement of indebtness; ~ **legal** DER legal recognition; ~ **de marca** V&M brand recognition; ~ **de mercado** V&M market recognition; ~ **mutuo** DER, POL *de leyes nacionales dentro de la UE* mutual recognition; ~ **óptico de caracteres** INFO optical character recognition (*OCR*); ~ **de pérdidas** CONT recognition of loss; ~ **de un sindicato** RRHH trade union recognition (*BrE*); ~ **de la voz** INFO voice recognition, speech recognition

reconsiderar *vt* COM GEN rethink, reconsider; ◆ ~ **una liquidación** FISC reconsider an assessment

reconstrucción *f* COM GEN retracement, reconstruction, ECON, IND reconstruction; ~ **de la empresa** COM GEN company reconstruction

reconstruido *adj* COM GEN, INFO rebuilt (*RBT*)

reconstruir *vt* COM GEN, INFO rebuild

reconversión *f* COM GEN reconversion, *de divisas* retranslation, restructiring, INFO reconversion

reconvertir *vt* COM GEN restructure, *fuerza laboral* slim down, INFO reconvert

recopilación *f* INFO recompilation; ~ **de datos** INFO data gathering

recopilar *vt* INFO recompile

récord: ~ **histórico** *m* COM GEN all-time record

recordatorio *m* COM GEN follow-up, aide-mémoire, DER refresher; ~ **de anuncio** V&M spot recall

recordman *m* RRHH record breaker

recorrido[1]: ~ **electoral** *m* POL campaign trail; ~ **de las instalaciones** *m* POL facility trip (*jarg*); ~ **prorrateado** *m* TRANSP proration mileage; ~ **semi-intercuartílico** *m* MAT semi-interquartile range; ~ **turístico** *m* OCIO tour

recorrido[2]: **de corto** ~ *fra* TRANSP short-haul; **de largo** ~ *fra* TRANSP long-haul

recortar *vt* COM GEN reduce, ECON cut; ◆ ~ **el programa de inversión** FIN trim the investment program (*AmE*), trim the investment programme (*BrE*)

recorte *m* BANCA reduction, clipping, BOLSA killing (*infrml*), ECON *crédito* containment, FIN *en tipos de interés* reduction, MEDIOS *de periódico* clipping (*AmE*), cutting (*BrE*); ~ **de gastos** CONT breakdown of expenses; ~ **de precios** ECON price cutting, price cut, RRHH rate cutting (*BrE*), V&M price cutting, price cut; ~ **de prensa** MEDIOS press clipping (*AmE*), press cutting (*BrE*); ~ **presupuestario** CONT budget cut, budgetary cut; ~ **del presupuesto** CONT budget cut, budgetary cut

rectificación *f* COM GEN correction, rectification

rectificar *vt* COM GEN correct, rectify

recto *m* MEDIOS recto

rector, a *m,f* RRHH vice chancellor

recuadro *m* COM GEN, INFO check box (*AmE*), box (*BrE*)

recubierto *adj* COM GEN wrapped

recuento: ~ **de circulación** *m* V&M traffic count; ~ **de existencias** *m* COM GEN stocktaking; ~ **general** *m* POL depth polling; ~ **de palabras** *m* INFO word count; ~ **de población** *m* COM GEN population count

recuerdo: ~ **asistido** *m* V&M *investigación de mercado* aided recall; ~ **espontáneo** *m* V&M spontaneous recall

recuperación *f*, COM GEN *economía* recovery, *de precios* rally, *de inversión* payback, INFO *fichero perdido, datos* recovery, TRANSP *de carga, equipaje* reclamation; ~ **del agotamiento** CONT depletion recapture; ~ **de la base** FISC base recovery; ~ **cíclica moderada** ECON modest cyclical recovery; ~ **de datos** INFO data retrieval; ~ **de la depreciación** CONT, FISC depreciation recapture; ~ **de deudas incobrables** BANCA, CONT, FIN bad-debt recovery; ~ **económica inducida por la exportación** ECON, IMP/EXP export-led economic recovery; ~ **de energía** MED AMB energy recovery; ~ **de errores** INFO error recovery; ~ **fuera de horas** BOLSA after-hours rally; ~ **de gastos** CONT, FIN recovery of expenses; ~ **de gastos generales** CONT, FIN overheads recovery; ~ **de gastos indirectos** CONT, FIN overheads recovery; ~ **de la información** INFO information retrieval; ~ **de la inversión** CONT, FIN payback; ~ **del mercado** BOLSA, COM GEN rally, market recovery; ~ **del mercado de renta fija** BOLSA bond market rally; ~ **del negocio** COM GEN business recovery; ~ **de parte de los costes fijos** *Esp* (*cf recuperación de parte de los costos fijos AmL*) CONT, FIN partial recovery of overhead costs; ~ **de parte de los costos fijos** *AmL* (*cf recuperación de parte de los costes fijos Esp*) CONT, FIN partial recovery of overhead costs; ~ **de parte de los gastos generales** CONT, FIN partial recovery of overhead costs; ~ **de préstamo** BANCA, FIN loan recovery; ~ **primaria** FISC primary recovery; ~ **técnica** BOLSA technical rally

recuperar *vt* ECON pick up, INFO *datos, archivos* retrieve; ◆ ~ **el tiempo perdido** COM GEN make up for lost time

recuperarse *v refl* COM GEN *de una enfermedad* recover, *el mercado* rally, bounce back

recurrir *vt* DER appeal; ◆ ~ **a** COM GEN resort to, fall back on; ~ **una sentencia** DER appeal against a judgment

recurso *m* COM GEN resource, resort, DER appeal, recourse, FISC resource; ~ **de capital** FIN capital resource; ~ **de emergencia** COM GEN fallback; ~ **explotado** MED AMB exploited resource; ~ **fiscal** FISC tax appeal; ~ **a fuentes externas** GES outsourcing; ~ **no renovable** ECON nonrenewable resource; ~ **primario** MED AMB primary resource; ◆ **donde hay un ~ hay un derecho** COM GEN ubi remedium ibi jus

recursos *m pl* COM GEN resources, CONT *en sentido financiero* capital, ECON means, RRHH resources; ~ **de acceso común** ECON common access resources; ~ **agotables** ECON depletable resources; ~ **de caja** ECON, FIN cash resources; ~ **a corto plazo** BANCA bridging facility; ~ **disponibles** COM GEN available funds; ~ **económicos** ECON economic resources; ~ **energéticos** *m* MED AMB energy resources; ~ **financieros** CONT capital; ~ **fuera del balance general** FIN off-balance-sheet financing; ~ **generados por acción** BOLSA cash flow per share; ~ **generados antes de impuestos** CONT before-tax cash flow; ~ **humanos** (*RRHH*) RRHH human resources (*IIRM*); ~ **legales** DER lawful means; ~ **minerales** FISC, MED AMB mineral resources; ~ **naturales** COM GEN natural resources; ~ **naturales no renovables** COM GEN, MED AMB nonrenewable natural resources; ~ **de las operaciones** CONT funds from operations; ~ **propios** BOLSA common equities, ECON, POL own resources; ~ **propios basados en el PNB** ECON GNP-based own resources; ~ **públicos** COM GEN public resources; ~ **renovables** COM GEN, ECON renewable resources

recusación *f* COM GEN challenge

red *f* COM GEN, INFO network; ~ **de alimentación** IND, INFO mains (*BrE*), supply network (*AmE*); ~ **de área extendida** GES, INFO wide area network (*WAN*); ~ **de área local** (*RAL*) INFO local area network (*LAN*); ~ **bancaria** BANCA banking network; ~ **de bandejas de carga** TRANSP pallet net; ~ **de carreteras** TRANSP road network; ~ **de computadoras** *AmL* (*cf red de ordenadores Esp*) INFO computer network; ~ **de computadores** *AmL ver red de computadoras AmL*; ~ **de comunicación** COMS, INFO communications network; ~ **de comunicaciones** COMS, INFO communications network; ~ **comunitaria** COMS community network; ~ **de concesionarios de venta** V&M network of sales outlets; ~ **corporativa** INFO corporate network; ~ **de corredores de bolsa** BOLSA dealer network; ~ **de créditos recíprocos** *m* BOLSA swop network; ~ **de datos** INFO data network; ~ **de datos abierta** INFO open network; ~ **digital de servicios integrados** COMS integrated services digital network (*ISDN*); ~ **de distribución** COM GEN, INFO distribution network; ~ **para elevar cargas** *m* TRANSP cargo net; ~ **en estrella** INFO star network; ~ **de expertos** COM GEN expert network; ~ **de ferrocarriles** TRANSP railroad network (*AmE*), railroad system (*AmE*), railway network (*BrE*), railway system (*BrE*); ~ **ferroviaria** TRANSP rail network; ~ **de gran amplitud** INFO wide area network (*WAN*); ~ **de información** INFO information network; ~ **de minoristas** V&M retail network; ~ **de ordenadores** *Esp* (*cf red de computadoras AmL*) INFO computer network; ~ **de plataformas de carga** TRANSP pallet net; ~ **de sucursales** BANCA branch network; ~ **de swops** BOLSA swop network; ~ **de**

telecomunicaciones COMS telecommunication network; ~ **transeuropea** COM GEN, COMS, TRANSP transeuropean network; ~ **de valor añadido** INFO value-added network (*VAN*); ~ **de ventas** V&M sales network

Red: la ~ *f* COMS, INFO Internet, the Net, the Web; ~ **Nacional de Ferrocarriles Españoles** *f* (*RENFE*) COM GEN, TRANSP Spanish national rail network, ≈ British Rail (*obs*) (*BR*)

redacción *f* COM GEN editorial staff, editorship, *de un contrato* wording, DER wording, MEDIOS newsroom

redactado *adj* COM GEN, DER drafted

redactar *vt* COM GEN *escribir* write, *periódico* edit, draft, DER *escritura de propiedad* draw up, draft; ◆ ~ **un borrador** DER draw up a draft, draft; ~ **un estado de cuenta** BANCA draw up a statement of account; ~ **una lista de candidatos seleccionados** RRHH draw up a shortlist

redactor(a): ~ jefe(-a) *m,f* MEDIOS, RRHH news editor, *imprenta* editor in chief; ~ **jefe(-a) de un periódico** *m,f* MEDIOS, RRHH newspaper publisher; ~ **de textos publicitarios** *m,f* COM GEN, V&M copy writer

redención *f* FIN redemption; ~ **de la deuda** FIN, FISC retirement of debt, POL debt relief; ~ **parcial** DER, INMOB partial release

redepositar *vt* BANCA redeposit

redescontable *adj* BANCA, CONT, FIN rediscountable

redescontador *m* BANCA, CONT, FIN rediscounter

redescuento *m* BANCA, CONT, FIN discount rate (*BrE*), discount window (*AmE*), rediscounting

redimensionamiento *m* GES resizing

redimible *adj* BOLSA callable; **no** ~ BOLSA noncallable

rediseñar *vt* COM GEN redesign

redistribución *f* COM GEN redistribution, redeployment; ~ **de la renta** ECON income redistribution

redistribuir *vt* COM GEN redeploy, redistribute, CONT reallocate

rédito *m* BANCA, BOLSA, COM GEN *dinero* interest (*i, int.*); ~ **anual** FIN *de acciones* annual return; ~ **corriente** BOLSA current yield; ~ **de inversiones** BOLSA *aseguradores*, SEG investment revenue; ~ **normal** BANCA current yield

redondear *vt* CONT, FIN *números* round off; ◆ ~ **por exceso** MAT round up

reducción *f* COM GEN abatement, reduction, ECON rebate, FIN abatement, *de pago al contado* rebate, FISC abatement, GES, RRHH downsizing, V&M *de ventas, precio* mark-down; ~ **de la actividad comercial** ECON business slowdown; ~ **de capital** BOLSA reduction of capital; ~ **de categoría laboral** RRHH downgrading; ~ **de costes** *Esp* (*cf reducción de costos AmL*) ECON, FIN cost reduction; ~ **de costos** *AmL* (*cf reducción de costes Esp*) ECON, FIN cost reduction; ~ **directa de la hipoteca** BANCA direct reduction mortgage; ~ **de eje** TRANSP *vehículos* hub reduction; ~ **de los empleos secundarios** RRHH reduction in force (*RIF*); ~ **enorme** V&M *ventas* mammoth reduction; ~ **fiscal no utilizada** FISC unused tax credit; ~ **fiscal para los pequeños productores** FISC small producers' tax credit; ~ **del flujo de caja** COM GEN, CONT cash-flow squeeze; ~ **de las ganancias** ECON profit squeeze; ~ **impositiva** FISC mitigation of taxes, tax reduction; ~ **impositiva no ordinaria** FISC nonstandard tax relief; ~ **del impuesto sobre la renta de las personas físicas** FISC personal income tax credit, personal tax credit; **~ de impuestos** ECON, FISC, POL tax cut; **~ de impuestos federales** FISC federal tax reduction; **~ incontrolable de plantilla** RRHH *por jubilación, enfermedad, muerte y relocalización* attrition; **~ de ingresos** COM GEN, FISC revenue dilution; **~ de intereses** BANCA, ECON, FIN interest rebate; **~ del margen** CONT margin shrinkage; **~ de márgenes en los beneficios** ECON profit squeeze; **~ marginal del impuesto** FISC marginal abatement of tax; **~ de personal** GES, RRHH downsizing, staff cutback; **~ del precio de una acción** BOLSA discounted share price; **~ de precios** COM GEN, V&M price-cutting; **~ de la presión fiscal** FISC lowering of taxation; **~ presupuestaria** CONT budget reduction; **~ del riesgo** SEG decrease of risk; **~ de la señal** COM GEN bounce-back; **~ de tarifas** TRANSP rate dilution; **~ para la tercera edad** FISC reduction for senior citizens; **~ del tipo impositivo** FISC tax abatement, abatement; **~ del tipo impositivo federal** FISC federal tax abatement; **~ de tipos** COM GEN, ECON variety reduction; **~ de los tipos de interés** COM GEN interest rate rebate, interest rate reduction; **~ de la zona** INMOB downzoning; **triple ~** COM GEN triple reduction (*TR*)

reducido *adj* COM GEN reduced

reducir *vt* BOLSA scale down, COM GEN abate, decrease, lessen, reduce, lower, GES, RRHH downsize, V&M *el mercado* segment; ◆ **~ la mano de obra** RRHH trim the workforce; **~ poco a poco** COM GEN *costes, comisiones* whittle down; **~ el precio de** V&M *artículos* mark down; **~ el valor contable de** CONT write down

reducirse *v refl* ECON decline; ◆ **~ el valor** BOLSA go down in value

reducto: ~ europeo *m* POL fortress Europe (*jarg*)

redundancia *f* COM GEN, INFO redundancy

redundante *adj* COM GEN *innecesario*, INFO redundant

reeditar *vt* MEDIOS *imprenta* republish

reeducación: ~ profesional *f* COM GEN, RRHH retraining

reeducar *vt* COM GEN, RRHH re-educate

reelección *f* COM GEN, POL re-election

reembarcarse *v refl* COM GEN re-embark

reembolsable *adj* COM GEN redeemable (*red.*), refundable, repayable; **no ~** COM GEN nonrefundable

reembolsar *vt* COM GEN reimburse

reembolso *m* COM GEN refund; **~ anticipado** BOLSA *títulos del Estado* advance refunding, COM GEN advance repayment, FIN redemption before due date; **~ automático** BOLSA automatic withdrawal; **~ por cancelación** SEG *marina* canceling return (*AmE*), cancelling return (*BrE*); **~ de un certificado de depósito** BANCA certificate of deposit rollover; **~ de derechos** COM GEN drawback (*Dbk*); **~ diferido** TRANSP deferred rebate; **~ inmediato** BANCA bullet repayment; **~ menor** FIN junior refunding; **~ parcial** BOLSA partial withdrawal

reempaquetar *vt* IMP/EXP repack

reemplazar *vt* COM GEN replace

reempleo *m* RRHH re-employment

reencaminamiento *m AmL* (*cf desvío Esp*) TRANSP rerouting, **~ de la ruta** *AmL* (*cf desvío de la ruta Esp*) TRANSP route diversion

reendoso *m* BANCA re-endorsement

reensacado *m* TRANSP rebagging

reenvío: ~ automático *m* COMS automatic call forwarding

reescribir *vt* INFO *programas*, MEDIOS *prensa* rewrite

reestructuración *f* COM GEN restructuring, *de compañía* reconstruction, *de préstamo* rescheduling; **~ industrial** IND restructuring of industry

reestructurado *adj* BANCA *préstamo* rescheduled, COM GEN rescheduled, restructured

reestructurar *vt* BANCA *préstamo* reschedule, COM GEN reschedule, restructure

reevaluación: ~ de activos *f* FIN re-evaluation of assets; **~ fiscal** *f* FISC reassessment; **~ de impuestos** *f* FISC reassessment of tax; **~ de intereses** *f* FISC reassessment of interests; **~ de recargos** *f* FISC reassessment of penalties

reevaluar *vt* FISC reassess

reexamen *m* COM GEN re-examination, *de directrices* revision

reexaminar *vt* COM GEN re-examine

reexpedición *f* TRANSP reforwarding

reexportación *f* IMP/EXP re-exportation

reexportador, a *m,f* IMP/EXP re-exporter

referencia *f* COM GEN, RRHH reference (*ref.*); **~ del banco** BANCA banker's reference; ◆ **su ~** COMS your reference (*your ref.*); **con ~ a** COMS regarding (*re.*), with reference to; **más allá de la ~ de** COM GEN outside the reference of

referéndum *m* COM GEN, POL referendum

referido: ~ a *fra* COM GEN by referral to, referring to

referir: ~ al aceptante *vt* BANCA refer to acceptor (*R/A*)

referirse *v refl* PATENT *a demanda previa* refer

refinación *f* IND refining

refinado *adj* IND refined

refinanciación *f* BANCA, COM GEN, FIN refinancing, FISC rollover

refinanciar *vt* BANCA, COM GEN, FIN refinance, FISC roll over

refinería *f* IND refinery; **~ de petróleo** IND oil refinery

reflejar *vt* COM GEN reflect

reflejarse: ~ en *v refl* COM GEN be reflected in

reflexibilidad: ~ media *f* INFO brightness

reflotamiento *m* BOLSA, FIN refloating

reflujo *m* TRANSP tidal fall

reforestación *f* MED AMB reafforestation

reforma *f* COM GEN, DER reform; **~ agraria** ECON land reform; **~ económica** ECON, POL economic reform; **~ fiscal** ECON, FISC tax reform; **~ general fiscal** ECON, FISC comprehensive tax reform; **~ de ley Douglas** BANCA Douglas Amendment (*AmE*); **~ monetaria** ECON, FIN currency reform

reformación *f* COM GEN reform, DER amendment

reformado *adj* COM GEN reformed, DER amended

reformar *vt* COM GEN reform, DER amend

reformatear *vt* INFO *disco* reformat

reformismo *m* POL reformism

reforzado *adj* COM GEN, ECON reinforced, strengthened

reforzamiento *m* COM GEN, ECON *de moneda* strengthening, reinforcement; **~ de marca** V&M brand reinforcement

reforzar *vt* COM GEN boost, strengthen, *efecto, impacto* reinforce; ◆ **~ la confianza de alguien** COM GEN bolster sb's confidence

refrenado *adj* COM GEN *aumento del precio* bottled-up

refrescar *vt* INFO *la memoria* refresh

refrigeración *f* (*R*) TRANSP refrigeration (*R*)

refrigerado *adj* TRANSP refrigerated

refrigerador: **~ intermedio** *m* TRANSP intercooler; **~ portátil** *m* TRANSP clip-on unit (*COU*)

refuerzo *m* COM GEN reinforcement, boost; **~ continuo** RRHH continuous reinforcement

refugiado, -a *m,f* COM GEN refugee

refugio *m* FISC tax shelter

refundir: **~ una deuda** *fra* FIN recast a debt

regalar *vt* V&M give away

regalías *f pl* COM GEN royalties

regalo *m* V&M giveaway; **~ comercial** V&M business gift; **~ gratuito** V&M free gift

regatear *vi* COM GEN haggle; ♦ **~ por dinero** BOLSA bargain for cash; **~ sobre** COM GEN haggle over

régimen *m* COM GEN regime; **~ clearing** BANCA, BOLSA clearing system; **~ comercial** ECON, POL trade regime; **~ dictatorial** POL authoritarian society; **~ político** COM GEN, POL political system; **~ temporal** DER temporary status; **~ de los tipos de cambio** ECON exchange rate regime; ♦ **en ~ de descuentos** BOLSA on a discount basis

región *f* COM GEN, POL territory governed as a unit with certain degree of autonomy, ≈ county (*BrE*), ≈ province, region; **~ central** ECON core region; **~ crítica** MAT critical region; **~ deprimida** ECON, PROT SOC depressed region; **~ desarrollada** ECON, POL, PROT SOC development region; **~ en desarrollo** ECON, POL, PROT SOC development region; **~ designada** FISC designated region; **~ con problemas** COM GEN problem area; **~ viticultora** COM GEN vine-growing district

regional *adj* COM GEN regional

regionalmente *adv* COM GEN regionally

regir *vt* DER govern

registrable: **no ~** *adj* CONT unpostable

registrado *adj* COMS registered (*regd.*), IMP/EXP entered in; **~ desempleado** PROT SOC, RRHH registered unemployed; **no ~** BOLSA over-the-counter (*OTC*), unregistered, COM GEN *propiedad intelectual* unregistered

registrador[1] BOLSA *títulos* register; **~ ambiental** *m* MED AMB environment scan; **~ de la propiedad** *Esp* (*cf registro público de la propiedad y del comercio AmL*) DER register of deeds; **~ de video** *AmL ver registrador de vídeo Esp*; **~ de vídeo** *Esp* INFO videotape recorder

registrador[2]**,a** BOLSA *títulos* registrant; **~ de transferencias** *m* FIN registrar of transfers

registrar *vt* BOLSA *un precio superior o inferior* record, COM GEN *nombre de empresa* register; ♦ **~ un alza** BOLSA register a high; **~ una escritura** CONT start an entry; **~ mercancías para almacenarlas** COM GEN enter goods for warehousing; **~ una reunión** COM GEN record a meeting

registrarse *v refl* COM GEN *asistencia social*, PROT SOC, RRHH sign on (*BrE*)

registro *m* COM GEN *libro* register, *acto* registration, *lista* record, INMOB valuation, OCIO *deporte* book, PATENT *investigación* search; **~ abierto** TRANSP *navegación* open registry (*OR*); **~ de acciones** BOLSA share register, stock register; **~ de accionistas** DER Register of Members; **~ agrario** INMOB plot book (*AmE*); **~ de**

asiento de apertura CONT book of prime entry; **~ automático** BOLSA shelf registration; **~ de automóviles** TRANSP car registration; **~ bursátil** BOLSA stock record; **~ de castigos** ECON *marina* black books; **~ de cheques** BANCA, CONT check register (*AmE*), cheque register (*BrE*); **~ civil** DER civil status; **~ de clientes** V&M customer records; **~ de comercio** COM GEN trade register; **~ concatenado** BOLSA piggyback registration; **~ contable** CONT book entry; **~ contable auxiliar** CONT subsidiary accounting record; **~ del control de caja** CONT cash control record; **~ cronológico** CONT *teneduría de libros* original entry; **~ de cuentas** COM GEN tally register; **~ en detalle** BANCA spread; **~ domiciliario** DER house search; **~ duplicado** INFO duplicated record; **~ electoral** COM GEN, POL electoral register, electoral roll; **~ de empleo** RRHH employment record; **~ de escrituras** DER, INMOB registry of deeds; **~ final** OCIO final check-in; **~ fiscal** FISC tax record; **~ de la hora de entrada** IND, RRHH clocking-in (*BrE*); **~ de hotel** OCIO hotel register; **~ de identificación del buque** TRANSP carving note; **~ internacional** PATENT international registration; **~ de inventario de cajas jaula** TRANSP cage inventory record (*CIR*); **~ de letras** BOLSA bill diary; **~ de letras aceptadas** BANCA acceptance register; **~ Lloyd's de embarques marítimos** SEG Lloyd's Register of Shipping; **~ mercantil** IND register of companies; **~ de miembros** COM GEN Register of Members; **~ náutico** TRANSP nautical regristration; **~ de navegación** TRANSP registry of shipping; **~ neto** FIN net register; **~ de obligaciones** DER commitment record; **~ de patentes** COM GEN trading; **~ posterior** IMP/EXP, TRANSP post-entry; **~ previo** IMP/EXP pre-entry; **~ de la propiedad** DER, INMOB Land Register, register of mortgages, registry of deeds; **~ de la propiedad inmobiliaria** DER, INMOB land registry; **~ público de la propiedad y del comercio** *AmL* (*cf registrador de la propiedad Esp*) DER register of deeds; **~ de socios** COM GEN Register of Members; **~ telefónico** COMS, MEDIOS phone-in poll; **~ de transferencias** BOLSA transfer register; **~ de trayectoria** COM GEN track record; **~ de valores gestionados** BOLSA *futuros* street book (*jarg*); **~ del vehículo del agente** TRANSP agent's vehicle record (*AVR*); **~ de ventas** V&M sales record

Registro: **~ Central** *m* BOLSA Central Register (*BrE*); **~ de Equipo para Lenguaje Universal de Máquina** *m* TRANSP Universal Machine Language Equipment Register (*UMLER*); **~ Español de Buques** *m* COM GEN, TRANSP Spanish Register of Shipping; **~ Europeo de Comercio** *m* COM GEN European Registry of Commerce (*ERC*); **~ de Información Fiscal** *m* (*RIF*) FISC Tax Information Registry; **~ Lloyds** *m* SEG *marina* Lloyd's Register (*LR*); **~ Marítimo Internacional** *m* TRANSP International Maritime Bureau (*IMB*); **~ Mercantil Central** *m* BOLSA Central Register (*BrE*); **~ de patentes y marcas** *m* PATENT Patent Office (*PO*); **~ de la Propiedad** *m* INMOB, RRHH Registrar General (*BrE*); **~ de la propiedad industrial** *m* PATENT Patent Office (*PO*); **~ de Proyectos** *m* DER *propiedad intelectual*, PATENT Designs Registry

registros *m pl* CONT records; **~ de contabilidad** CONT accounting records; **~ de costes** *Esp* (*cf registros de costos AmL*) BOLSA, CONT cost records (*BrE*); **~ de costos** *AmL* (*cf registros de costes Esp*) BOLSA, CONT cost records (*BrE*)

regla *f* COM GEN rule; ~ **de aptitud** FIN suitability rule; ~ **de cálculo** COM GEN, MAT slide rule; ~ **del cinco por ciento** BOLSA five percent rule; ~ **de los cinco mil dólares** BOLSA five hundred dollar rule (*AmE*); ~ **cuantitativa** BOLSA quantitative rule; ~ **de la elasticidad inversa** ECON inverse elasticity rule; ~ **general** COM GEN rule of thumb; ~ **del hombre prudente** BOLSA, COM GEN prudent-man rule; ~ **de la mayoría** POL majority rule; ~ **de la mediana** COM GEN median rule; ~ **de los nueve bonos** BOLSA *Bolsa de Nueva York* nine-bond rule; ~ **de oro** ECON golden rule; ~ **de prioridad absoluta** FIN absolute priority rule; ~ **de prorrateo** FISC *desgravación fiscal de ingresos* apportionment rule; ~ **de la venta al descubierto** BOLSA short-sale rule

reglamentación: ~ **de desguace y construcción** *f* TRANSP scrap and build regulation; ~ **de exportación** *f* IMP/EXP export regulations; ~ **de precios** *f* COM GEN price fixing

Reglamentación: ~ **de la Reforma Legal del Transporte Marítimo de Materias Peligrosas** *f* DER, TRANSP Merchant Shipping Dangerous Goods Amendment Rules; ~ **del Transporte Marítimo** *f* TRANSP Merchant Shipping Regulations

reglamentario *adj* COM GEN, DER, POL regulatory

reglamento *m* COM GEN regulation, DER by-law; ~ **de higiene** DER, RRHH health regulation; ~ **laboral** RRHH works regulation; ~ **de mando y control** ADMIN command and control regulation; ~ **menor** FIN petty regulation; ~ **publicitario** V&M advertising regulation; ~ **de tarifas internacionales** IMP/EXP, TRANSP overseas tariff regulations; ~ **del trabajo** RRHH job regulation; ~ **unilateral** RRHH unilateral regulation

Reglamento: ~ **de Artículos Restringidos** *m* TRANSP Restricted Articles Regulations (*RAR*); ~ **del Impuesto sobre la Renta** *m* FISC Income Tax Regulations

reglas: ~ **permanentes del servicio** *f pl* COM GEN standard operating procedure (*s.o.p.*); ~ **sobre discreción** *f pl* ECON rules versus discretion; ~ **uniformes de cobro** *f pl* BANCA uniform rules for collections

Reglas: ~ **de Bridlington** *f pl* RRHH Bridlington Rules (*BrE*); ~ **de Hamburgo** *f pl* TRANSP *navegación* Hamburg Rules; ~ **de La Haya** *f pl* TRANSP *navegación* The Hague Rules; ~ **de Visby** *f pl* TRANSP Visby Rules; ~ **de York Amberes** *f pl* SEG York Antwerp Rules (*YA, YAR*)

regresión *f* MAT regression; ~ **lineal** MAT linear regression; ~ **lineal simple** CONT, MAT simple linear regression; ~ **múltiple** MAT multiple regression

regreso: ~ **en lastre** *m* TRANSP deadheading (*AmE*)

regulable *adj* COM GEN adjustable

regulación: ~ **bancaria** *f* BANCA banking regulation; ~ **del dominio y el control** *f* DER command and control regulation; ~ **de pedidos** *f* TRANSP order regulation; ~ **de precios** *f* ECON price regulation; ~ **salarial** *f* ECON, RRHH wage control; ~ **sanitaria** *f* DER, RRHH health regulation; ~ **del uso de la tierra** *f* INMOB land-use regulation; ~ **Z** *f* ECON, FIN Regulation Z

regulado: ~ **por el Estado** *fra* POL government-regulated

regulador *m* DER, FISC regulator; ~ **de voltaje** MED AMB voltage regulator

regular *vt* COM GEN adjust, regulate

regularización *f* CONT year-end adjustment

rehabilitación *f* COM GEN re-establishment, rehabilitation, MED AMB rehabilitation; ~ **del quebrado** DER, FIN discharge of bankruptcy

rehabilitar *vt* COM GEN *una reputación, empresa* rehabilitate

rehusar *vt* COM GEN refuse; ♦ ~ **la aceptación de una letra** BANCA refuse acceptance of a draft

reinado *m* COM GEN reign

reincidencia *m* DER second offence (*BrE*), second offense (*AmE*)

reiniciación *f* INFO rebooting

reinicializar *vt* INFO reboot

reiniciar *vt* COM GEN reinitiate

reintegrable: **no** ~ *adj* BOLSA nonrefundable

reintegrar *vt* BANCA pay back, FIN *deuda, dinero* pay back, repay

reintegro: ~ **de bonos** *m* BOLSA bond refunding

reintroducción *f* FIN reinfusion

reintroducir: ~ **por teclado** *vt* INFO re-enter, retype

reinversión *f* BOLSA, COM GEN reinvestment, CONT, FIN ploughback; ~ **automática** BOLSA automatic reinvestment; ~ **de dividendos** BOLSA, CONT dividend reinvestment

reinvertir *vt* BANCA rollover, BOLSA, COM GEN reinvest

reinyección: ~ **de capital** *f* ECON capital reswitching

reiterar *vt* COM GEN reiterate

reivindicación *f* DER replevin; ~ **independiente** PATENT independent claim

relación *f* BOLSA link, COM GEN ratio, relation, relationship; ~ **de activos líquidos** BANCA, BOLSA, CONT, FIN liquid assets ratio; ~ **de activos de rápida realización** BANCA, FIN quick assets ratio; ~ **de activos de reserva** BANCA, FIN reserve-assets ratio; ~ **de acuerdo con el common law** DER common-law relationship; ~ **administración-producción** ADMIN, FIN, IND administration-production ratio; ~ **de apalancamiento** FIN gearing ratio (*BrE*), leverage ratio (*AmE*); ~ **base capital** BANCA base capital ratio; ~ **de bienes recibidos** TRANSP goods received note; ~ **calidad-precio** COM GEN, V&M quality-price ratio; ~ **de capital** BANCA, FIN capital ratio; ~ **de capital ajustado** BANCA adjusted capital ratio; ~ **de capital total compensado** BANCA, FIN adjusted total capital ratio; ~ **capital-producto** ECON, FIN, IND capital-output ratio; ~ **capital-trabajo** ECON, FIN, IND capital-labor ratio (*AmE*), capital-labour ratio (*BrE*); ~ **de cobertura** FIN cover ratio; ~ **de colocaciones** FIN placement ratio; ~ **comercial** COM GEN, GES business relation; ~ **contractual** COM GEN contractual relationship, DER, RRHH privity; ~ **coste-eficacia** *Esp* (*cf relación costo-eficacia AmL*) COM GEN, ECON cost effectiveness; ~ **costo-eficacia** *AmL* (*cf relación coste-eficacia Esp*) COM GEN, ECON cost effectiveness; ~ **cronológica** CONT ageing schedule; ~ **cualificada** FISC qualified relation; ~ **curvilínea** MAT curvilinear relationship; ~ **de débito** FIN debit ratio; ~ **de deuda** CONT, FIN debt ratio; ~ **de deuda externa a exportaciones** ECON, IMP/EXP ratio of external debt to exports; ~ **diaria de visitas** V&M daily report of calls; ~ **de dirección** FIN management ratio; ~ **dividendo-precio** BOLSA, FIN dividend-price ratio; ~ **de empleo** RRHH employment relationship; ~ **endeudamiento-capital propio** BOLSA, CONT, FIN gearing; ~ **entre distintos rangos** GES line relationship; ~ **externa** COM GEN, GES external relation; ~ **de financiación** FIN financial ratio; ~ **funcional** COM

GEN, GES functional relation; ~ **gubernamental** POL government relation; ~ **humana** GES, RRHH human relation; ~ **de los ingresos que se ahorran** FIN savings-to-income ratio; ~ **intergrupal** RRHH intergroup relation; ~ **intragrupal** RRHH intragroup relation; ~ **laboral** ECON, RRHH labor relations (*AmE*), labour relations (*BrE*); ~ **laboral positiva** ECON, RRHH positive labor relations (*AmE*), positive labour relations (*BrE*); ~ **de línea** COM GEN line relation; ~ **lineal** RRHH linear relationship; ~ **de liquidez internacional** BANCA international liquidity ratio; ~ **con los medios de comunicación** MEDIOS, V&M media relation; ~ **de mercancías** IND bill of goods; ~ **de negocios** COM GEN, GES business relation; ~ **neta de trueque** IMP/EXP net barter terms of trade; ~ **normal** BOLSA normal relationship; ~ **de paridad** BOLSA parity ratio; ~ **con el personal** RRHH employee relation; ~ **del personal** RRHH personnel roster, staff list; ~ **plural** POL *desarrollo por separado* plural relation (*obs*); ~ **precio-beneficio** COM GEN price-earnings ratio (*PER*); ~ **con la prensa** MEDIOS press relation; ~ **préstamo-valor** FIN loan-to-value ratio (*LTV*); ~ **real de intercambio** ECON factorial terms of trade, *internacional* double factorial terms of trade; ~ **de rentabilidad** CONT, FIN profitability ratio; ~ **de tarjetas invalidadas** BANCA hot card list; ~ **de transferencia de materiales** *AmL* (*cf hoja de transferencia de materiales Esp*) COM GEN materials transfer note; ~ **del valor añadido** CONT value added statement; ~ **valor bajo por peso grande** TRANSP low value to high weight ratio; ~ **valor elevado por peso bajo** TRANSP high value to low weight ratio; ~ **valores-productos** BOLSA stock-output ratio; ~ **valor-peso** TRANSP value to weight ratio; ~ **de ventas** V&M sales ratio; ~ **del volumen de beneficios** FIN profit-volume ratio; ◆ **en ~ con** COM GEN in relation to

relacionado: ~ **con** *adj* COM GEN associated with, FISC connected with; ~ **con el comercio** *adj* COM GEN, ECON, V&M trade-related

relacionar *vt* BOLSA *tipos de cambios* link

relaciones: ~ **con los clientes** *f pl* RRHH customer relations; ~ **comerciales y exportaciones** *f pl* IMP/EXP Commercial Relations and Exports (*BrE*) (*CRE*); ~ **laborales** *f pl* RRHH industrial relations (*IR*); ~ **públicas** *f pl* MEDIOS, RRHH, V&M public relations (*PR*)

relajación *f* COM GEN relaxation

relajar *vt* COM GEN relax

relanzamiento *m* COM GEN, V&M relaunch

relanzar *vt* COM GEN, V&M relaunch

relativamente *adv* COM GEN relatively

relativo *adj* COM GEN relative; ~ **a** COM GEN relative to

rellenar *vt* COM GEN *una orden* fill in, TRANSP rellenar; ◆ ~ **un cheque** BANCA make out a check (*AmE*), make out a cheque (*BrE*)

relleno *m* COM GEN padding, MEDIOS *prensa* filler, TRANSP padding, stuffing, V&M *prensa* filler; ~ **de formularios** COM GEN form-filling; ~ **de impresos** COM GEN form-filling

relocalizable *adj* INFO *área de memoria* relocatable

relocalización *f* COM GEN, INFO, RRHH relocation

reloj *m* INFO timer; ~ **de control de asistencia** SEG time clock

remachado *adj* COM GEN, TRANSP riveted (*R*); ◆ ~ **y soldado** TRANSP riveted and welded (*RW*)

remanente: ~ **de impuestos mínimo** *m* FISC minimum tax carryover; ~ **de mercaderías** *f pl* COM GEN carryover stocks

remanentes *m pl* COM GEN remnants

remapeo *m* INFO remapping

rematar *vt* *AmL* COM GEN auction off

remesa *f* COM GEN remittance, *de facturas* batch, MEDIOS *cartas* batch, TRANSP consignment (*cnmt*); ~ **bancaria** BANCA bank remittance; ~ **de cobro** BANCA remittance for collection; ~ **documentaria** BANCA documentary remittance; ~ **del impuesto** FISC remittance of tax; ~ **mixta** TRANSP mixed consignment; ~ **neta** FISC net remittance

remisión *f* DER remand, cross-reference; ~ **de un impuesto** FISC remission of tax; ~ **incondicional** FIN *de una deuda* unconditional remission

remitente *mf* (*rte.*) COMS *en un sobre* sender

remitir *vt* COMS *documento* forward (*fwd*), *paquete, sobre* address, IMP/EXP forward (*fwd*), PATENT *a demanda previa* refer; ◆ ~ **a** DER refer to; ~ **al aceptante** ECON refer to acceptor (*R/A*)

remoción *f* COM GEN removal; ~ **de escombro** MED AMB debris removal, SEG clearance of debris, debris removal

remodelación: ~ **urbana** *f* COM GEN urban renewal

remolcador *m* TRANSP *buque* towboat, tug boat, tug; ~ **de puerto** TRANSP pilotage tug

remolque *m* IMP/EXP, OCIO, TRANSP trailer; ~ **de buques mercantes** IMP/EXP, TRANSP merchant haulage (*MH*); ~ **de camión** TRANSP drawbar trailer; ~ **compuesto** TRANSP composite trailer

remontarse: ~ **a** *v refl* COM GEN trace back

rémora: ~ **fiscal** *f* ECON, FISC taxflation

remoto *adj* INFO remote

remuneración *f* BOLSA consideration, COM GEN, RRHH remuneration, SEG consideration; ~ **por acción** BOLSA, FIN return on equity (*ROE*); ~ **bruta** RRHH gross pay; ~ **complementaria** RRHH make-up pay; ~ **dependiente del rendimiento** RRHH incentive pay, performance-related pay (*PRP*); ~ **por despido** RRHH severance wage; ~ **por desplazamiento** RRHH portal-to-portal pay; ~ **de los ejecutivos** RRHH executive remuneration; ~ **excluida** FISC excluded consideration; ~ **financiera** BOLSA financial reward; ~ **igual** RRHH equal pay; ~ **intangible** RRHH intangible reward; ~ **justa de un día de trabajo** RRHH fair day's pay; ~ **media** RRHH average pay; ~ **por unidad de tiempo** RRHH time rate; ~ **valiosa** COM GEN valuable consideration; ~ **vinculada a los beneficios** RRHH profit-related pay (*PRP*)

remunerador: **poco ~** *adj* COM GEN unremunerative

rendidor: ~ **de interés** *adj* BANCA interest-bearing

rendimiento *m* COM GEN, GES performance; ~ **del activo** FIN *índice de análisis* asset turnover; ~ **de los activos** COM GEN return on assets (*ROA*); ~ **actual** BOLSA *título, inversión* actual yield; ~ **acumulable** FISC concurrent return; ~ **acumulado de la propiedad** FISC accrual property income; ~ **aditivo** BOLSA add-on yield; ~ **al vencimiento** BANCA, BOLSA, FIN yield to maturity (*YTM*); ~ **alto** CONT *de inversión* good return; ~ **anual** CONT annual yield, FIN *de acciones* annual return; ~ **de la aportación** CONT contribution profit; ~ **a la baja** COM GEN yield to worst; ~ **bajo** CONT *de inversión* low return; ~ **del banco** BANCA bank return; ~ **básico** BOLSA *de futuros* floor return; ~ **de los bienes inmuebles** INMOB return on real estate; ~ **del bono**

BOLSA bond yield; **~ de los bonos después de impuestos** FISC after-tax bond yield; **~ bruto** BOLSA, COM GEN, ECON gross dividend yield; **~ bruto de una inversión** FISC gross investment revenue; **~ bursátil** BOLSA stock yield; **~ del capital** COM GEN return on capital (*ROC*); **~ del capital invertido** BANCA, CONT, ECON, FIN capital gains, return on capital employed (*ROCE*); **~ del combustible** MED AMB fuel efficiency; **~ comercial** COM GEN trade return; **~ corriente** BOLSA current return; **~ creciente de escala** ECON increasing return to scale; **~ del cupón** BOLSA coupon yield, current yield; **~ decreciente** ECON diminishing returns; **~ directo** BANCA, BOLSA direct yield; **~ en dividendos** BOLSA dividend yield; **~ económico** MED AMB commercial efficiency; **~ del ejercicio** BOLSA *de futuros* strike yield; **~ del empresario** FISC employer's return; **~ equivalente de bonos a tres meses** BOLSA three-month bond equivalent yield; **~ de escala** ECON returns to scale; **~ de explotación** CONT operating income; **~ financiero** BOLSA, CONT, FIN yield; **~ financiero necesario** BOLSA, CONT, FIN indicated yield; **~ fiscal** FISC tax yield, tax proceeds; **~ de ganancias** FIN earnings yield; **~ hedónico** ECON hedonic output; **~ histórico** BOLSA historical yield; **~ inicial** BOLSA historical yield; **~ de interés neto** BANCA, FIN net interest yield; **~ de la inversión** CONT, BANCA, ECON, FIN investment yield, return on investment (*ROI*); **~ de las inversiones a plazo** BOLSA *futuros* forward investment return; **~ justo** CONT, ECON, FIN fair return; **~ marginal del capital** FIN marginal return on capital; **~ medio** BOLSA, FIN average yield; **~ mensual** BANCA, CONT, FIN monthly return; **~ del mercado de capitales** BOLSA, CONT, ECON, FIN capital market yield; **~ del mercado monetario** BOLSA money market return; **~ mínimo obtenido** BOLSA *futuros* realized minimum return; **~ mixto** BANCA composite yield; **~ de los negocios** FISC income from business; **~ neto** CONT *de acción* net yield; **~ neto por cada acción ordinaria** CONT net income per share of common stock; **~ neto del capital** FISC net capital gain; **~ no pecuniario** RRHH nonpecuniary returns; **~ nominal** BOLSA nominal yield; **~ normal** BOLSA current yield, RRHH standard performance; **~ positivo a tres meses** BOLSA three-month add-on yield; **~ del precio de una acción** BOLSA share price performance; **~ principal** FIN, FISC relevant earnings; **~ productivo** BOLSA *futuros* interest-bearing yield; **~ del producto** V&M product performance; **~ promedio** FIN average yield; **~ de la propiedad inmobiliaria** FISC real estate gain; **~ real** BOLSA effective yield; **~ semanal** BANCA, FIN weekly return; **~ simple** BOLSA simple yield; **~ sobre acción** BOLSA return on equity (*ROE*); **~ sobre el capital** COM GEN return on capital (*ROC*); **~ sobre capital invertido** COM GEN return on invested capital (*ROIC*); **~ sobre el patrimonio** FIN return on equity (*ROE*); **~ sobre pedido** COM GEN yield to call; **~ total** ECON aggregate output, FIN, IND throughput; **~ del tráfico** TRANSP traffic yield; **~ de ventas** CONT, FIN, V&M sales performance, return on sales; **~ en votos** FIN vote netting; ♦ **tener bajo ~** COM GEN underperform; **con ~ de intereses** BANCA interest-bearing; **sin ~ de intereses** BANCA noninterest-bearing

Rendimiento: **~ Equivalente del Bono** *m* BOLSA Bond Equivalent Yield

rendimientos: **~ y descuentos de las compras** *m pl* V&M purchase returns and allowances

rendir *vt* COM GEN net, *producir ganancias* render, yield; ♦ **~ cuenta de** COM GEN account for; **~ menos de lo normal** ECON underperform

rendirse *v refl* COM GEN, IND give up

rendu *m* SEG rendu

renegociación *f* COM GEN renegociation

renegociar *vt* COM GEN renegotiate

RENFE *abr* (*Red Nacional de Ferrocarriles Españoles*) COM GEN, TRANSP Spanish national rail network, ≈ BR (*obs*) (*British Rail*)

renombrado *adj* COM GEN renowned

renombrar *vt* INFO rename

renombre *m* COM GEN renown

renovación *f* COM GEN renewal, FISC rollover, INFO *memoria* wraparound, INMOB refurbishment, MEDIOS *de suscripción* renewal; **~ del activo exigible** FIN receivables turnover; **~ a la baja** BOLSA roll down; **~ del capital social** BOLSA equity turnover; **~ del crédito** FIN credit revolving; **~ de cuenta de jubilación individual** FISC individual retirement account rollover (*AmE*) (*IRA rollover*); **~ de hipoteca** BANCA, INMOB renewal of mortgage; **~ tácita** COM GEN tacit renewal

renovado *adj* COM GEN renovated, renewed

renovar *vt* COM GEN revive, renew, INMOB refurbish, MEDIOS renew, V&M *imagen del producto* revamp; ♦ **~ el tipo de interés** BANCA rollover; **~ existencias** V&M restock

renta *f* CONT income, INMOB, PROT SOC rent; **~ acumulada** CONT retained income; **~ acumulativa** FISC cumulative income; **~ anual** FISC annuity income; **~ por arrendamiento** FISC rental income; **~ baja** FISC low rent; **~ bruta** *Esp* (*cf utilidad bruta AmL*) CONT, FIN gross earnings, gross income, trading income, FISC gross rent; **~ consolidada** FIN consolidated annuities (*BrE*); **~ contable** CONT *ganancias* accounting income; **~ después de impuestos** *m* CONT, FISC after-tax profit; **~ diferencial** ECON economic rent; **~ directa** BANCA, BOLSA direct yield; **~ discrecional** ECON discretionary income; **~ disponible para gastos fijos** CONT income available for fixed charges; **~ económica pura** ECON pure economic rent; **~ elástica** ECON elastic income (*jarg*); **~ empresarial** FISC business income; **~ del Estado** FIN government annuity; **~ de explotación** CONT operating income; **~ fija** BOLSA fixed income; **~ gravable** *Esp* (*cf utilidad gravable AmL*) COM GEN, ECON, FISC taxable income, taxable profit; **~ imponible** FISC assessable income; **~ imprevista** ECON transitory income; **~ imputada** CONT imputed income; **~ de mercado** ECON market rent; **~ monetaria** FISC money income; **~ nacional** ECON, POL national income; **~ nacional bruta** (*RNB*) ECON gross national income; **~ neta** CONT, FISC clear income, net income; **~ neta por comisiones** CONT net commission income; **~ neta de los recursos** CONT net resource income; **~ no distribuida** ECON undistributed income; **~ por noventa y nueve años** BANCA, INMOB ninety-nine-year lease; **~ pasiva** FISC passive income; **~ patrimonial** FISC estate income; **~ del patrimonio** DER estate revenue; **~ per cápita** ECON per capita income, income per head; **~ percibida** FISC income received; **~ percibida en el extranjero** FISC income earned overseas; **~ personal** ECON, FISC personal income; **~ de la propiedad** FISC,

INMOB property income; ~ **de una propiedad** FIN estate revenue; ~ **psíquica** ECON psychic income (*jarg*); ~ **de publicidad** FIN, V&M advertising revenue; ~ **real** CONT, ECON, RRHH real income; ~ **de terreno** FIN land rent; ~ **de transferencia** ECON transfer income; ~ **de valores** CONT income from securities; ~ **vitalicia** DER life interest, SEG survivorship annuity

rentas *f pl* FIN private means

Renta: ~ **Nacional del Ahorro** *f* BANCA National Savings Income (*BrE*)

rentabilidad *f* COM GEN, ECON cost effectiveness, profitability; ~ **de los activos** BANCA, CONT, ECON, FIN return on assets (*ROA*); ~ **del capital** CONT return on equity (*ROE*); ~ **corporativa** COM GEN corporate earning power; ~ **económica** COM GEN earning power; ~ **exigida al capital** ECON required rental on capital; ~ **hasta el rescate** BOLSA yield to redemption; ~ **del préstamo** BANCA, FIN loan yield; ~ **del producto** CONT, FIN, V&M product profitability; ~ **a vida media** BOLSA yield to average life; ♦ **de baja** ~ BOLSA low-yielding

rentable *adj* COM GEN cost-effective, profitable

rentar *vt* INMOB rent

rentista *mf* FISC annuitant, rentier, life annuitant

renuncia *f* DER disclaimer, *sentencia, deuda* remittal, PATENT waiving; ~ **al reconocimiento** DER release of recognizance

renunciar *vt* COM GEN waive; ♦ ~ **a** COM GEN renounce, *poder, libertad* relinquish; ~ **al derecho de cobro** BANCA, CONT forgo collection of a debt; ~ **a una herencia** DER forgo an inheritance

reoferta *f* BOLSA retendering

reordenación *f* COM GEN, ECON reorganization

reorganización *f* COM GEN, ECON reorganization, GES shake-up, INMOB redevelopment, RRHH redeployment, shake-up; ~ **del capital** BOLSA, FIN capital reorganization; ~ **de la dirección** GES management reshuffle; ~ **gubernamental** POL cabinet reshuffle

reorganizar *vt* COM GEN, GES shake up, INMOB redevelop, RRHH redeploy, shake up

reorientación: ~ **profesional** *f* RRHH retraining

repagar *vt* COM GEN repay

reparación *f* DER redress; ~ **de edificios** INMOB building repair; ~ **del inquilino** DER, INMOB, PROT SOC tenant's repair; ~ **legal** DER legal redress; ~ **positiva** DER affirmative relief

repartición *f* ADMIN *oficina*, INMOB partition, SEG adjustment, apportionment; ~ **inmobiliaria** INMOB estate distribution

repartir *vt* BOLSA allot, COM GEN *tareas, recursos* allocate, allot, appropriate, earmark; ♦ **no** ~ BOLSA *títulos* fail to deliver; ~ **acciones** BOLSA allot shares; ~ **el coste** *Esp* (*cf repartir el costo AmL*) CONT spread the cost; ~ **el costo** *AmL* (*cf repartir el coste Esp*) CONT spread the cost; ~ **un proyecto** COM GEN chunk a project; ~ **el riesgo** SEG spread the risk

repartirse *v refl* BOLSA *comisión* give up

reparto *m* BOLSA allotment, COM GEN *dinero, obligaciones* allocation, allotment, DER, INMOB partition; ~ **de acciones** COM GEN split-off, BOLSA allotment of shares, share allotment, FIN spin-off; ~ **de bonos** IND allotment of bonus; ~ **equitativo** COM GEN fair share; ~ **de ganancias** CONT, RRHH profit sharing; ~ **de trabajo** GES, RRHH allocation of work

repasar *vt* COM GEN review

repatriación *f* ECON, FIN repatriation; ~ **de beneficios** ECON, FIN repatriation of profits; ~ **de capital** ECON, FIN repatriation of capital; ~ **de fondos** ECON, FIN repatriation of funds; ~ **de fondos extranjeros** ECON, FIN repatriation of overseas funds

repatriar *vt* ECON, FIN repatriate

repercusión *f* COM GEN bounce-back, repercussion, knock-on effect, V&M *efecto* spin off; ~ **de la carga tributaria** FISC shifting of the tax burden; ~ **contra ejercicios anteriores** FISC carry-back; ~ **excesiva del impuesto** FISC tax pyramiding; ~ **de los impuestos** FISC shifting of taxes

repercusiones *f pl* COM GEN fallout

repertorio *m* INFO *de instrucciones* repertoire

repetición *f* V&M *TV* playback

repetir *vt* COM GEN repeat, INFO replay

réplica *f* DER answer, reply, MEDIOS copy, replica; ~ **de los lectores** V&M readership replication

repo[1] *abr* (*pacto de recompra*) BOLSA repo (*repurchase agreement*), RP (*repurchase agreement*)

repo[2]: ~ **a un día** *m* BOLSA overnight repo

repoblación: ~ **forestal** *f* MED AMB reafforestation

reponer *vt* COM GEN *ahorros* top up (*BrE*); ~ **las existencias** COM GEN replenish one's stocks

reportaje: ~ **editorial** *m* V&M editorial write-up

reporte *m* *AmL* (*cf informe Esp*) COM GEN briefing, report, brief, CONT statement, reporting, brief, briefing, report; ~ **de la actividad diaria** *Esp* (*cf reporte de la actividad diaria AmL*) COM GEN daily activity report; ~ **de aduanas** *Esp* (*cf reporte de aduanas AmL*) IMP/EXP customs house report; ~ **anual** *Esp* (*cf reporte anual AmL*) CONT annual report; ~ **de los auditores** *Esp* (*cf reporte de los auditores AmL*) CONT auditor's report; ~ **de auditoría** *Esp* (*cf reporte de auditoría AmL*) CONT auditor's certificate, audit report; ~ **de averías** *Esp* (*cf reporte de averías AmL*) SEG survey report, *marítimo* damage report; ~ **Brundtland** *Esp* (*cf reporte de Brundtland AmL*) ECON, POL *desarrollo sostenido* Brundtland Report; ~ **Bullock** *Esp* (*cf reporte Bullock AmL*) RRHH *democracia industrial* Bullock report (*BrE*); ~ **comercial** ECON trade brief; ~ **de la condición** GES status report; ~ **de la conferencia** *Esp* (*cf reporte de la conferencia AmL*) COM GEN conference report; ~ **confidencial** *Esp* (*cf reporte confidencial AmL*) BOLSA insider report, COM GEN tip-off, *consejo* tip, FISC tip; ~ **contable** *Esp* (*cf reporte contable AmL*) CONT accounting report; ~ **de contactos** *Esp* (*cf reporte de contactos AmL*) V&M contact report; ~ **sin correcciones** *Esp* (*cf reporte sin correcciones AmL*) DER clean record; ~ **crediticio** *Esp* (*cf reporte crediticio AmL*) COM GEN credit report; ~ **del director** *Esp* (*cf reporte del director AmL*) COM GEN director's report; ~ **del ejercicio** *Esp* (*cf reporte del ejercicio AmL*) COM GEN, GES debriefing; ~ **de entrada de buque** *Esp* (*cf reporte de entrada de buque AmL*) IMP/EXP, TRANSP ship's inward report; ~ **escolar** *Esp* (*cf reporte escolar AmL*) COM GEN school report; ~ **del estado** GES status report; ~ **de evaluación** *Esp* (*cf reporte de evaluaciónAmL*) COM GEN appraisal report; ~ **externo** *Esp* (*cf reporte externoAmL*) COM GEN external report; ~ **financiero estimado** *Esp* (*cf reporte financiero estimado AmL*) FIN estimated financial report; ~ **de gastos** *Esp* (*cf reporte de gastos AmL*) CONT expense report; **~ de gastos del viaje** *Esp* (*cf reporte de gastos de viajes AmL*) TRANSP voyage account report; **~ de la gestión financiera** *Esp* (*cf reporte de la gestión financiera AmL*) FIN financial management report; **~ global financiero anual** *Esp* (*cf reporte global financiero anual AmL*) COM GEN, ECON, FIN, GES comprehensive annual financial report (*CAFR*); **~ del gobierno** *Esp* (*cf reporte del gobierno AmL*) COM GEN, POL government report; **~ del impacto ambiental** *Esp* (*cf reporte del impacto ambiental AmL*) MED AMB environmental impact statement; **~ intermedio** *Esp* (*cf reporte intermedio AmL*) CONT interim report; **~ de intervención** *Esp* (*cf reporte de intervención AmL*) INFO call report (*BrE*); **~ de los interventores de cuentas** *Esp* (*cf reporte de los inventores de cuentas AmL*) CONT auditor's report; **~ de irregularidad** *Esp* (*cf reporte de irregularidad AmL*) TRANSP irregularity report; **~ legal** *Esp* (*cf reporte legal AmL*) COM GEN statutory report; **~ limpio de los datos** *Esp* (*cf reporte limpio de datos AmL*) TRANSP clean report of findings; **~ de liquidación** *Esp* (*cf reporte de liquidación AmL*) BANCA clearing report; **~ en lugar del folleto de emisión** *Esp* (*cf reporte en lugar de folleto de emisión AmL*) BOLSA statement in lieu of prospectus; **~ meteorológico** *Esp* (*cf reporte meteorológico AmL*) COM GEN weather report; **~ Pearson** *Esp* (*cf reporte Pearson AmL*) ECON *inversion por países en vías de desarrollo* Pearson Report; **~ de la posición neta** *Esp* (*cf reporte de la posición neta AmL*) BOLSA net position report; **~ del presidente** *Esp* (*cf reporte del presidente AmL*) GES chairman's brief; **~ provisional** *Esp* (*cf reporte provisional AmL*) COM GEN interim statement, CONT interim report, FIN interim statement; **~ provisional de riesgo** *Esp* (*cf reporte provisional de riesgo AmL*) CONT exposure draft; **~ a punto de caducar** *Esp* (*cf reporte a punto de caaducar AmL*) POL sunset report; **~ Radcliffe** *Esp* (*cf reporte Radcliffe AmL*) ECON *sistema monetario en R.U.* Radcliffe Report (*BrE*); **~ resumido** *Esp* (*cf reporte resumido AmL*) COM GEN summary report, condensed report; **~ de saldos para transacciones** *Esp* (*cf reporte de saldos para transacciones AmL*) CONT transaction balance report; **~ con salvedades** *Esp* (*cf reporte con salvedades AmL*) CONT qualified report; **~ sectorial** CONT segmental reporting; **~ segmentado** *Esp* (*cf reporte segmentado AmL*) CONT segmental reporting; **~ de la situación** *Esp* (*cf reporte de la situación AmL*) COM GEN situation report, GES status report; **~ sobre el estado de la técnica** *Esp* (*cf reporte sobre el estado de la técnica AmL*) PATENT search report; **~ sobre la labor realizada** *Esp* (*cf reporte sobre la labor realizada AmL*) COM GEN progress report, status report; **~ sobre el mercado** *Esp* (*cf reporte sobre el mercado AmL*) V&M market report; **~ tabular** *Esp* (*cf reporte tabular AmL*) COM GEN tabular report; **~ del tesorero** *Esp* (*cf reporte del tesorero AmL*) FIN treasurer's report; **~ Thomson** *Esp* (*cf reporte Thomson AmL*) ECON *política regional in UE* Thomson Report; **~ de viabilidad** *Esp* (*cf reporte de viabilidad AmL*) COM GEN feasibility report; **~ del viaje** *Esp* (*cf reporte del viaje AmL*) TRANSP voyage report; **~ de visita** *Esp* (*cf reporte de visita AmL*) V&M call report, contact report; **~ de Werner** *Esp* (*cf reporte de Werner AmL*) ECON *unión economíca y monetaria* Werner Report

reposición *f* COM GEN reinstatement, CONT *de asientos* reversal, OCIO *teatro* revival; **~ de información** COM GEN rewrite

reposicionamiento *m* V&M repositioning

reposo: en ~ *fra* INFO on standby

repostado: ~ de combustible *m* TRANSP refueling (*AmE*), refuelling (*BrE*), *náutica* bunkering

repostaje *m* TRANSP refueling (*AmE*), refuelling (*BrE*)

represalia: como ~ *fra* COM GEN in retaliation

represalias *f pl* RRHH victimization; ♦ **que toma ~** COM GEN retaliatory

representación *f* COM GEN, DER representation; **~ análoga** COM GEN analog representation; **~ analógica** COM GEN analog representation; **~ aparente** DER apparent authority; **~ colectiva** COM GEN, GES, RRHH joint representation; **~ comercial** COM GEN commercial representation; **~ en común** COM GEN, GES, RRHH joint representation; **~ conjunta** COM GEN, GES, RRHH joint representation; **~ exclusiva** COM GEN sole agency; **~ internacional** COM GEN international representation; **~ con modelo estadístico** MAT statistical modeling (*AmE*), statistical modelling (*BrE*); **~ de un papel** GES role-playing; **~ proporcional** POL proportional representation; **~ por ratificación** DER agency by ratification; **~ regional** V&M regional representation; **~ de los trabajadores** RRHH worker representation; **~ visual** COMS, INFO display

representante *mf* COM GEN agent (*agt*), representative (*rep.*), sales representative (*rep.*); **~ de agencia** INMOB agency representative; **~ comercial** RRHH, V&M sales representative (*rep*); **~ autorizado(-a)** *m,f* BOLSA, COM GEN, RRHH authorized representative, registered representative; **~ de comercio** COM GEN commercial agent, RRHH trade representative; **~ exclusivo(-a)** *m,f* COM GEN, ECON, V&M sole agent **~ en el extranjero** COM GEN foreign agent; **~ de un fabricante** V&M manufacturer's agent; **~ legal** DER legal representative; **~ de Lloyd's** TRANSP *navegación* Lloyd's Agent (*L/A*); **~ obrero(-a)** *m,f* IND, RRHH shop steward; **~ permanente del Reino Unido en la Unión Europea** *f* POL United Kingdom Permanent Representative to the European Union (*UKREP*); **~ del personal** RRHH staff representative; **~ del personal obrero** IND, RRHH shop steward; **~ del público** COM GEN member of the public; **~ de seguridad** RRHH safety representative; **~ del servicio al cliente** RRHH customer service representative; **~ sindical** GES convenor, IND, RRHH shop steward, *en el lugar de trabajo* convenor, union representative; **~ único(-a)** *m,f* COM GEN, ECON, V&M sole agent; **~ de ventas** RRHH, V&M sales representative (*rep*)

representar *vt* COM GEN represent; ♦ **~ al comité** COM GEN stand for the committee; **~ algo** COM GEN *iniciales* stand for sthg; **~ insuficientemente** COM GEN underrepresent

representativo, -a *m,f* COM GEN representative (*rep.*)

represivo *adj* COM GEN *política* restrictive

représtamo *m* FIN on-lending

reprivatización *f* ECON, POL reprivatization

reprivatizar *vt* ECON, POL reprivatize

reprocesar *vt* COM GEN, INFO rerun

reproducción *f* COM GEN reproduction

reprografía *f* COM GEN, MEDIOS reprography

reprogramación: ~ de la deuda *f* BANCA, COM GEN debt rescheduling

reprogramar *vt* INFO reprogram

reproyección *f* INFO remapping

repudiar *vt* RRHH *acción laboral* repudiate

repuestos *m pl* IND spares

reputación *f* COM GEN, V&M reputation

requerimiento[1]: **a ~** *adv* CONT, DER on demand

requerimiento[2] *m* DER subpoena; **~ de caja** CONT cash requirement; **~ de capital de operación** COM GEN operating capital requirement; **~ de cheque** BANCA, CONT check requisition (*AmE*), cheque requisition (*BrE*); **~ de equipo** INFO hardware requirement; **~ de pago** CONT payment requisition; **~ de sistema** INFO system requirement

requerir *vt* COM GEN demand, require; ◆ **~ el pago** FISC demand payment

requiere: que ~ mucho tiempo *fra* COM GEN time-consuming

requisa *f* INMOB condemnation

requisito *m* COM GEN requirement, RRHH *para trabajo* qualification; **~ administrativo** ADMIN office requisite; **~ bancario** BANCA bank requirement; **~ del consumidor** V&M consumer requirement; **~ de crédito** V&M credit requirement; **~ de la declaración** FISC reporting requirement; **~ financiero** FIN financial requirement; **~ de ingresos brutos** FISC gross revenue requirement; **~ legal** DER, POL legal requirement, statutory requirement; **~ de licencia** IMP/EXP licensing requirement; **~ de mantenimiento de la empresa** BOLSA house maintenance requirement; **~ para ofertar** COM GEN bidding requirement; **~ de preinspección** BANCA pre-inspection requirement; **~ de préstamo** BANCA, FIN borrowing requirement; **~ de préstamo del servicio público** BANCA, FIN public service borrowing requirement (*PSBR*); **~ previo** COM GEN prerequisite; **~ previo para la publicación en las listas** BOLSA listing requirement; **~ para publicación** COM GEN *de cuentas sociales* disclosure requirement; **~ del puesto** RRHH job requirement; **~ de reserva** BANCA reserve requirement; **~ de retención** FISC retention requirement; **~ de revelación** BOLSA disclosure requirement; **~ de seguridad** COM GEN, IND, V&M *para los productos* safety requirement; **~ para ser convocado** COM GEN eligibility requirement

requisitos *m pl* COM GEN requirements; **~ de financiación del gobierno central** ECON, FIN, POL central government borrowing requirements; **~ de financiación del sistema central** ECON, FIN, POL central government borrowing requirements; **~ para la presentación de ofertas** COM GEN *concursos, subastas* competing requirements; ◆ **con los ~ establecidos** COM GEN, DER with the usual proviso

resaltado *adj* INFO *calidad, rasgos*, V&M enhanced

resarcirse: ~ de *v refl* COM GEN *compensar* compensate, *pagar* repay

rescatado *adj* BOLSA *acción*, CONT redeemed

rescatar *vt* BOLSA, CONT redeem, FIN buy back

rescate *m* BOLSA, CONT redemption, FIN buyback; **~ de una acción** BOLSA share redemption; **~ anticipado** BOLSA, FIN early redemption; ◆ **para ~** BOLSA *títulos* for surrender

rescindible *adj* COM GEN terminable

rescindir *vt* COM GEN annul, *una oferta* withdraw, DER annul, rescind; ◆ **~ el contrato a alguien** RRHH terminate sb's employment

rescisión *f* COM GEN annulment, withdrawal, DER rescission, termination

rescripción *f* BOLSA *letras y papel del mercado monetario* rescription

reseña *f* MEDIOS *impresa en su funda* blurb (*jarg*)

reserva *f* COM GEN *natural* reserve, OCIO *de entradas* booking, reservation, V&M *de espacio publicitario* booking; **~ agregada obligatoria** BANCA prescribed aggregate reserve (*PAR*); **~ de amortización** FIN amortization reserve; **~ anticipada** OCIO advance booking (*BrE*), advance reservation (*AmE*); **~ del balance general** FIN balance sheet reserve; **~ en banco central** BANCA vault reserve (*AmE*); **~ de los bienes de capital** FISC capital gains reserve; **~ en bloque** V&M block booking; **~ para bonificación** COM GEN bonus reserve; **~ para bonus** COM GEN bonus reserve; **~ de capital** CONT *sin distribuir* capital reserve; **~ de carbón** MED AMB coal reserve; **~ de carga** TRANSP reservation of cargo; **~ complementaria** BANCA supplementary reserve; **~ para contingencias** FIN, GES contingency reserve; **~ para conversión de divisas** CONT *cuentas anuales* foreign currency translation reserve; **~ de crédito** FIN credit reserve; **~ para cuentas dudosas** BANCA, CONT, FIN allowance for bad debts; **~ directa** OCIO direct booking; **~ en disminución** ECON draining reserve; **~ de divisa** ECON commodity reserve currency; **~ de divisas** ECON foreign exchange reserves, currency holding, FIN currency holding; **~ de efectivo** BANCA, CONT cash reserve; **~ energética** IND, MED AMB energy reserve; **~ para errores de caja** BANCA, COM GEN cashier's error allowance; **~ especial** CONT special reserve; **~ del excedente** FIN surplus reserve; **~ en exceso** BANCA excess reserve; **~ extraíble** MED AMB *recursos energéticos* extractable reserve; **~ extraordinaria** BANCA excess reserve; **~ de fondos** ECON earmarking, ringfencing; **~ de garantía** SEG reserve liability; **~ del impuesto aplazado sobre la renta** FISC deferred income tax reserve, reserve for deferred income tax; **~ para impuestos** CONT, FISC tax provision; **~ para inflación** CONT allowance for inflation; **~ internacional** ECON international reserve; **~ legal** CONT, DER legal reserve; **~ mínima obligatoria** ECON *internacional* minimum reserve requirements (*MRR*); **~ monetaria** BANCA, ECON monetary reserve; **~ monetaria de respaldo** BOLSA backing; **~ natural nacional** MED AMB national nature reserve; **~ negativa** CONT negative reserve; **~ no distribuible** CONT undistributable reserve (*BrE*), restricted surplus (*AmE*), *reservas sin distribuir* capital reserve; **~ de nuevos pedidos** COM GEN booking of new orders; **~ obligatoria** BANCA required reserve, CONT legal reserve; **~ oculta** BANCA, CONT hidden reserve, secret reserve; **~ en oro** ECON gold reserve; **~ de oro** COM GEN stock of bullion; **~ parcial** BANCA fractional reserve; **~ de pasivo de plan de pensiones** FIN pension plan liability reserve; **~ para pérdidas de créditos de riesgo** BANCA reserve for credit risk losses; **~ de póliza** SEG policy reserve; **~ postal** CONT postal remittance; **~ prestada** BANCA borrowed reserve; **~ primaria** BANCA primary reserve; **~ de primas** FIN premium reserve; **~ publicada** CONT disclosed reserve; **~ para reclamaciones sin pagar** SEG reserve for unpaid claims; **~ para reclamaciones pendientes** SEG unpaid claim reserve; **~ recuperable** MED AMB *de minerales* recoverable reserve; **~ referenciada** BANCA benchmark reserve (*AmE*); **~ de revalorización** CONT allowance for inflation, revaluation reserve; **~ de riesgo con**

transferencia variable FIN allocated transfer risk reserve (*ATRR*); ~ **para riesgos catastróficos** SEG catastrophe reserve; ~ **para siniestros** SEG claims reserve; ~ **con tarjeta de crédito** OCIO credit-card booking (*BrE*), credit-card reservation (*AmE*); ~ **por teléfono** OCIO telephone booking (*BrE*), telephone reservation (*AmE*); ~ **de valor** ECON store of value; ~ **visible** ECON general reserve; ~ **de vuelo abierta** OCIO, TRANSP open-ended flight reservation; ◆ **a ~ de** COM GEN except for; **de ~** RRHH *responsabilidad sustitutiva* stand-by (*BrE*)

Reserva: ~ **Federal** *f* ECON Federal Reserve (*the Fed*) (*AmE*)

reservable *adj* BANCA reservable

reservado *adj* COM GEN booked; ~ **con exceso** TRANSP *vuelos* overbooked

reservar *vt* CONT, ECON, FIN earmark, OCIO, TRANSP *boletos* book, reserve; ◆ ~ **con antelación** COM GEN book early; ~ **con anticipación** *vi* COM GEN book early; ~ **contra un riesgo** SEG provide against a risk; ~ **fondos** ECON ringfence; ~ **para** COM GEN allow for; ~ **la totalidad de** COM GEN *hoteles* book up

reservarse: ~ **el derecho de** *fra* BANCA reserve the right to; ~ **el fallo** *fra* DER reserve judgment; ~ **la opinión** *fra* DER reserve judgment

resguardo *m* BOLSA *de una acción* ticket (*jarg*), COM GEN receipt (*rept*); ~ **del agente expedidor** IMP/EXP, TRANSP forwarding agent's receipt; ~ **de control** TRANSP control ticket; ~ **de ingreso** BANCA stub; ~ **de muelle** IMP/EXP, TRANSP dock warrant (*D/W*); ~ **de un pago** COM GEN receipt for payment; ~ **de transporte por tren** TRANSP railway bill of lading (*BrE*), railroad bill of lading (*AmE*); ~ **de ventas** V&M sales receipt

residencia *f* BANCA *de depositante* residency, COM GEN residence, DER, FISC, INMOB place of abode, place of residence; ~ **de ancianos** PROT SOC nursing home; ~ **permanente** DER, FISC, INMOB permanent residence; ~ **principal** DER, FISC, INMOB principal residence, main residence; ~ **por separado** FISC, INMOB separate residence; ~ **temporal** DER *permiso*, FISC, INMOB temporary residence; ~ **urbana** INMOB town house

residencial *adj* INMOB *construcción* residential

residente[1] *adj* INFO resident; **no ~** BANCA nonresident; ~ **en memoria** INFO memory-resident

residente[2] *mf* COM GEN, FISC resident; **no ~** COM GEN, FISC nonresident; ~ **ordinario(-a)** *m,f* DER, FISC ordinary resident; ~ **permanente** DER, FISC, INMOB permanent resident; ~ **temporal** DER, FISC, INMOB temporary resident

residualización *f* PROT SOC residualization

residuo: ~ **de Solow** *m* ECON Solow residual

residuos *m pl* MED AMB *de producción industrial* residue; ~ **industriales** ECON, IND, MED AMB industrial waste; ~ **peligrosos** IND, MED AMB dangerous waste; ~ **tóxicos** IND, MED AMB toxic waste

resistencia *f* COM GEN resistance, FIN staying power; ~ **del consumo** V&M consumer resistance; ~ **de materiales** IND strength of materials; ~ **del mercado** V&M market resistance; ~ **a la venta** V&M sales resistance; ◆ **de gran ~** COM GEN high-strength (*HS*)

resistente *adj* COM GEN resistant; ~ **al fuego** COM GEN fire-resistant (*BrE*), fire-resistive (*AmE*); ~ **a la corrosión** IND corrosion-resistant

resolución *f* COM GEN decision, resolution, DER determi-

nation, resolution, INFO resolution; ~ **de disputa** RRHH dispute resolution; ~ **fiscal** FISC revenue ruling; ~ **de fusión corporativa** ECON Resolution Trust Corporation (*AmE*) (*RTC*); ~ **privada** FISC private ruling; ~ **del problema** GES, MAT problem solving; ~ **de problemas** GES, MAT problem solving

resolver *vt* COM GEN *problemas* solve; ◆ **por ~** COM GEN outstanding, pending; ~ **una disputa mediante arbitraje** IND settle a dispute by arbitration; ~ **un problema hablando** COM GEN have it out with sb

respaldado: **no ~** *adj* BANCA unbacked; ~ **por** *adj* FIN backed by, supported by; ~ **por el Gobierno** *adj* FIN government-backed

respaldar *vt* COM GEN back, back up

respaldo *m* COM GEN *apoyo* backup, IND backstop, INFO backup; ~ **financiero** FIN financial backing

respectivamente *adv* COM GEN respectively

respecto *m* COM GEN respect; ◆ **a este ~** COM GEN in this respect; **con ~ a** COM GEN by reference to

respetar *vt* DER respect; ◆ ~ **los márgenes** COM GEN, ECON, FIN hold margins

respiro: **sin ~** *fra* COMS *trabajar* without respite

responder: ~ **por** *fra* COM GEN *seguridad de producto* answer for; ~ **a las necesidades de** *fra* COM GEN meet the needs of

responsabilidad *f* COM GEN accountability, liability, responsibility; ~ **actuarial** DER, SEG actuarial liability; ~ **acumulativa** SEG cumulative liability; ~ **en la administración** GES accountability in management; ~ **del armador** TRANSP shipowner's liability (*SOL*); ~ **civil** DER *ante la jurisprudencia*, SEG liability; ~ **civil del armador** DER, TRANSP shipowner's liability (*SOL*); ~ **civil del arquitecto** INMOB, SEG architect's liability; ~ **civil de la autoridad portuaria** DER wharf owner's liability (*WOL*); ~ **civil de la empresa** COM GEN business liability; ~ **civil por exposición de la empresa** COM GEN business exposures liability; ~ **civil subsidiaria** DER vicarious liability; ~ **civil de terceros** DER third-party liability; ~ **comercial** DER, SEG business liability; ~ **conjunta** BANCA, DER, FISC joint liability; ~ **contractual** DER contractual liability; ~ **corporativa** COM GEN corporate accountability; ~ **de corto plazo** SEG *riesgo* short tail; ~ **cruzada** SEG cross liability; ~ **directa** DER direct liability; ~ **excedente** SEG *naval* excess liability; ~ **fiscal** FISC liability for tax; ~ **funcional** COM GEN, GES functional responsibility; ~ **de funciones** COM GEN, GES functional responsibility; ~ **general** COM GEN comprehensive responsibility; ~ **en la gestión** GES accountability in management; ~ **ilimitada** COM GEN unlimited liability, SEG unlimited liability; ~ **jurídica** DER legal liability; ~ **de largo plazo** SEG long tail; ~ **legal** DER, SEG liability; ~ **legal del producto** COM GEN product liability; ~ **por lesión jurídica** DER tort liability; ~ **limitada** COM GEN limited liability; ~ **de línea** COM GEN line responsibility; ~ **lineal** GES, MAT linear responsibility; ~ **mancomunada** BANCA, DER, FISC joint liability; ~ **mínima de pensiones** FIN minimum pension liability; ~ **objetiva** DER absolute liability; ~ **penal** SEG criminal liability; ~ **de pensión mínima** FIN minimum pension liability; ~ **personal** COM GEN personal liability; ~ **profesional** DER professional liability; ~ **respecto al impuesto sobre la renta** FISC income-tax liability; ~ **por riesgos comerciales** DER business exposures liability; ~ **sindical** RRHH trade union liability (*BrE*); ~ **solidaria** BANCA joint liability, DER joint liability, joint and several liability, FISC joint liability; ~ **subsidiaria** DER *comercial* master-servant rule; ~ **subsidiaria del principal** COM GEN, DER respondeat superior; ~ **subsidiaria del superior** COM GEN, DER respondeat superior; ~ **del trabajador** FISC employee's liability; ~ **del transportista** SEG, TRANSP carrier's liability; ◆ **bajo la ~ del armador** COM GEN, SEG, TRANSP at owner's risk; **sin ~ por nuestra parte** COM GEN without any liability on our part

responsable[1] *adj* COM GEN responsible, answerable, DER liable; ◆ **ser ~ de** COM GEN be in charge of; ~ **ante la ley** DER responsible in law; ~ **mancomunadamente** COM GEN, DER jointly liable; ~ **solidariamente** BOLSA, DER severally liable

responsable[2]: ~ **del almacén** *mf* RRHH stock controller; ~ **de compras** *mf* V&M head buyer; ~ **de información** *mf* RRHH information officer; ~ **de investigación** *mf* RRHH investigation officer

respuesta *f* COM GEN answer, response; ~ **anticipada** COM GEN anticipatory response; ~ **del comprador** V&M buyer response; ~ **del consumidor** V&M consumer response; ~ **desfasada** ECON lag response; ~ **directa** COM GEN direct response; ~ **espontánea** V&M unprompted response; ~ **pagada** COMS reply paid; ~ **positiva** COM GEN positive response; ~ **previsora** ECON anticipatory response; ~ **publicitaria** V&M advertising response; ~ **con retraso** COM GEN lag response; ◆ **no hay ~** COM GEN there's no reply; **en ~ a su carta** COMS further to your letter, in reply to your letter; **en ~ a su llamada telefónica** COMS further to your telephone call

resquicio: ~ **de oportunidad** *m* COM GEN window of opportunity

restablecer: ~ **un gravamen** *fra* FISC restore an assessment; ~ **el equilibrio del balance** *fra* CONT redress the balance; ~ **el orden público** *fra* DER restore law and order

restablecimiento: ~ **automático** *m* INFO automatic reset; ~ **de la demanda de cobertura complementaria** *m* BOLSA *operaciones con divisas* margin call-replenish to initial level

restar *vt* CONT, MAT subtract; ◆ ~ **importancia a** POL soft-pedal (*jarg*)

restauración *f* COM GEN restoration, INFO reset

restaurante *m* COM GEN, OCIO restaurant; ~ **para los empleados** RRHH staff canteen

restaurar *vt* INFO *fichero, directorio* restore

restitución *f* INMOB reconveyance

restituir *vt* BANCA, FIN pay back, INFO undelete

resto *m* FIN residue, MAT remainder; ~ **del mundo** ECON Rest Of the World (*ROW*); ~ **de un naufragio** TRANSP wrecked ship

restricción *f* COM GEN, DER restriction, ECON *precios* squeeze, POL corset, TRANSP restriction; ~ **al comercio** POL trade restriction; ~ **comercial** COM GEN trade restriction, trade restraint; ~ **crediticia** FIN restriction of credit; ~ **del crédito** BANCA, FIN credit squeeze; ~ **cuantitativa** ECON quantitative restriction (*QR*); ~ **de divisas** ECON, FIN currency restriction; ~ **de la enajenación de bienes** DER restraint of alienation; ~ **fiscal** FISC tax restriction; ~ **a la información** MEDIOS reporting restriction; ~ **a la inversión** ECON investment restriction; ~ **monetaria** ECON monetary restriction,

money restraint; ~ **en los planes de jubilación** FIN curtailment in pension plan; ~ **de planificación** DER, INMOB planning restriction; ~ **presupuestaria** CONT budget constraint, budgetary constraint; ~ **de recorrido** TRANSP travel restriction; ~ **de tiempo** RRHH time constraint; ~ **en transacciones** COM GEN dealing restriction; ~ **de la transferencia de dominio** DER restraint of alienation; ~ **de valoración** ECON *de divisa* valuation restriction; ~ **de venta** ECON dealing restriction; ◆ **sin ~** COM GEN *competición, derechos* uncurtailed

restringido *adj* COM GEN restricted

restringir *vt* COM GEN restrict, ECON squeeze; ◆ ~ **a los bajistas** BOLSA squeeze the bears (*infrml*)

resuelto *adj* COM GEN resolved; ◆ ~ **a** COM GEN determined to; **estar ~ a hacer algo** COM GEN be set on doing sth

resultado *m* COM GEN result, CONT *de la empresa*, FIN performance; ~ **de beneficios** CONT, FIN profit performance; ~ **bruto** *Esp* (*cf utilidad bruta AmL*) CONT, FIN gross earnings, trading income; ~ **de la compañía** COM GEN company performance; ~ **del ejercicio** COM GEN bottom line (*infrml*); ~ **electoral** COM GEN, GES, POL election result; ~ **de los exámenes** COM GEN exam result; ~ **de explotación** CONT operating income; ~ **de las exportaciones** IMP/EXP export performance; ~ **final** COM GEN end result, payoff; ~ **mixto** COM GEN mixed result; ~ **óptimo** COM GEN *en negociaciones* successful outcome; ~ **sin precedentes** COM GEN record result; ~ **prometedor** COM GEN *de negociaciones* likely outcome; ~ **real** COM GEN actual outcome; ~ **rentable** COM GEN earning performance; ~ **superior** BOLSA, ECON outperformance; ~ **de la transcripción** INFO dump; ◆ **como ~** COM GEN as a result; **con el ~ de que** COM GEN with the result that

resultados *m pl* COM GEN bottom line, CONT *cifras comerciales* results

resultar: ~ **aceptable** *fra* BOLSA *venta* stand good; ~ **acertado** *fra* COM GEN prove right; ~ **equivocado** *fra* COM GEN prove wrong

resumen *m* COM GEN, ECON, FIN *sumario* abstract, GES briefing, wrap-up (*AmE*), V&M briefing; ~ **anual de estadística** ECON, MAT annual abstract of statistics; ~ **anual estadístico** ECON, MAT annual abstract of statistics; ~ **de los autos** DER abstract of record; ~ **y conformidad bancaria** BANCA bank summary and agreement; ~ **de los factores de producción** ECON *formulario PEMS* summary of input factors; ~ **financiero** FIN financial summary; ~ **de impuestos y deducciones** FISC summary of tax and credits; ~ **informativo** MEDIOS news round-up; ~ **de un texto** V&M copy brief

resumir *vt* COM GEN summarize, CONT sum up

resurgimiento *m* COM GEN *precios* resurgence; ~ **sostenible** ECON *del crecimiento* sustained resurgence

retales *m pl* COM GEN, V&M oddments

retardar *vt* ECON *recuperación* slacken

retardo *m* COM GEN lag; ~ **administrativo** ADMIN, ECON administration lag

retención *f* COM GEN retention, INMOB holdback, retainage; ~ **de factura** COM GEN bill sticking; ~ **fiscal** FISC tax withholding; ~ **fiscal sobre dividendos** FISC dividend tax withholding; ~ **fraudulenta** BOLSA *de valores, impuestos* withholding; ~ **de garantía** COM

GEN retention money; ~ **de mercancías** COMS, IMP/EXP, TRANSP stoppage in transit; ~ **neta** SEG net line; ~ **obligada** SEG *marítimo* oblige line; ~ **retroactiva** FISC backup withholding; ~ **salarial** RRHH wage withholding; ~ **sobre el sueldo** RRHH retention on wages; ~ **de tipo fijo** FISC flat-rate withholding

retener *vt* BOLSA *acciones* retain, FISC *impuestos* withhold; ◆ ~ **la línea** COMS *en conversación telefónica* hold the line

retirada *f* COM GEN withdrawal; ~ **de la cantidad media acumulada** FISC accumulated averaging amount withdrawal; ~ **del contrato** DER gazumping (*BrE*) (*jarg*); ~ **de dividendos** FIN profit taking; ~ **de existencias** COM GEN withdrawal from stocks; ~ **de fondos por pánico** BANCA bank runner; ~ **de una objeción** FISC withdrawal of an objection; ~ **de reclamación** FISC withdrawal of appeal

retirar *vt* BANCA *fondos* withdraw, BOLSA retire, withdraw, COM GEN pull, withdraw; ◆ ~ **el apoyo** BOLSA pull the plug (*jarg*); ~ **un cheque** BANCA draw a cheque (*BrE*), draw a check (*AmE*)

retirarse *v refl* COM GEN back off, back out, retire, ECON *de la actividad comercial* withdraw, POL stand down; ◆ ~ **de** COM GEN *contrato* back out of; ~ **del negocio** COM GEN retire from business

retiro *m* BANCA drawing, BOLSA *acciones* withdrawal, COM GEN, IND, RRHH retirement; ~ **de capital** BANCA withdrawal of capital; ~ **de una deuda** CONT debt retirement; ~ **de fondos** BANCA cash withdrawal, withdrawal

reto *m* COM GEN challenge; ~ **del trabajo** GES job challenge

retocar *vt* INFO tweak, V&M retouch

retórica *f* ECON rhetoric

retornable *adj* COM GEN, MED AMB, V&M *botellas* returnable

retorno *m* TRANSP redelivery; ~ **de carro** COM GEN, INFO carriage return (*CR*); ~ **de cursor** INFO wraparound; ~ **manual** INFO hard return

retornos: ~ **a escalas constantes** *m pl* ECON constant returns to scale

retractable *adj* BOLSA, FIN retractable

retractación *f* BOLSA, FIN retraction

retractar *vt* COM GEN take back

retraerse *v refl* COM GEN hold off

retransmisión: ~ **en diferido** *f* MEDIOS prerecorded broadcast

retrasado *adj* COM GEN delayed

retrasarse *v refl* COM GEN fall behind schedule

retraso *m* COM GEN *demora* delay, lag, RRHH *tardanza* lateness; ~ **interior** ECON inside lag; ~ **en el plazo de entrega** COM GEN lead-time delay; ◆ **pagar con un mes de** ~ COM GEN pay one month in arrears

retribución *f* RRHH payoff; ~ **en especie** COM GEN allowance in kind; ~ **por hora** RRHH hourly compensation; ~ **no financiera** COM GEN nonfinancial reward; ~ **con prima** BOLSA, RRHH premium bonus; ~ **prudencial** BANCA prudential consideration

retribuciones: ~ **y beneficios gravables** *f pl* FISC taxable allowances and benefits

retroactividad *f* FISC reachback

retroactivo *adj* COM GEN retroactive

retroalimentación *f* INFO feedback

retroceder *vi* BOLSA run back, COM GEN *en la competencia* lose ground, *retirarse* step back, *abandonar, renunciar* give up, ECON retrogress, INFO backspace, back up; **no** ~ COM GEN stand firm

retrocesión *f* CONT *de asientos* reversal

retroceso *m* COM GEN recession, INFO backspace

retrogresión *f* ECON retrogression

retrospección *f* FISC hindsight

retroventa *f* V&M *investigación de mercado* backselling

reubicación *f* INFO reallocation

reunión *f* BOLSA rallying, COM GEN meeting, rallying, GES meeting, INMOB *de tierras* assemblage; ~ **de aseguradores** BOLSA, ECON, SEG pool; ~ **del comité** COM GEN committee meeting; ~ **del directorio** GES board meeting; ~ **de empresa** COM GEN company meeting; ~ **extraordinaria** COM GEN, GES special meeting; ~ **del G-7** COM GEN, ECON, POL G-7 meeting; ~ **informal** ADMIN, COM GEN informal meeting; ~ **informal sobre intercambios** ECON, POL trade talk; ~ **secundaria** POL fringe meeting; ~ **de trabajo** POL, RRHH working party; ~ **de trabajo colectiva** POL, RRHH joint working party (*JWP*); ~ **de ventas** V&M sales meeting; ◆ **la** ~ **está grabada** COM GEN the meeting is on tape; **la** ~ **se disolvió** COM GEN the meeting broke up

reunir *vt* BOLSA raise, COM GEN *información* gather, *dinero, información* collect, *personas* bring together; ◆ ~ **el dinero que falta** COM GEN, FIN make up the odd money

reunirse: ~ **en sesión parlamentaria** *v refl Esp* (*cf sesionar AmL*) POL sit

reutilizable: **no** ~ *adj* MED AMB nonreusable

reutilización: ~ **de las ganancias de capital** *f* FISC capital gains rollover

reutilizar *vt* MED AMB reuse

revaloración *f* BOLSA, FISC appreciation

revalorar *vt* COM GEN revalue

revalorización *f* COM GEN appreciation, revaluation, revalorization; ~ **de activos** CONT, FIN revaluation of assets; ~ **del capital** ECON, FIN capital appreciation; ~ **excesiva** COM GEN, CONT, ECON overvaluation; ~ **legal** CONT, DER legal revaluation; ~ **de la moneda** ECON appreciation of currency; ~ **monetaria** ECON currency revaluation, *internacional* currency appreciation

revalorizar *vt* CONT write up, *bienes* revalue, ECON, FIN revalue

revaluación *f* COM GEN write-up, revaluation; ~ **legal** CONT, DER legal revaluation; ~ **de la tasa de cambio** BANCA, ECON, FIN revaluation of exchange rate

revaluarse *v refl* CONT *propiedades* appreciate

revelación: ~ **de información** *f* RRHH disclosure of information

revelar *vt* COM GEN disclose, OCIO *fotografía* develop; ~ **de nuevo** ECON redevelop

revendedor(a) *m,f* OCIO *de billetes* ticket tout; ~ **de valor añadido** *m* INFO value-added reseller (*VAR*)

revender *vt* BOLSA, COM GEN sell back

reventa *f* COM GEN resale; ~ **fraccionada** BOLSA *de acciones* secondary distribution

reversible *adj* TRANSP *póliza de flete* reversible

reversión *f* INMOB estate in reversion; ~ **de bienes raíces** DER, INMOB estate in reversion; ~ **de expropiación** DER, INMOB inverse condemnation (*AmE*); ~ **de**

propiedad DER, INMOB escheat; **~ de tendencia** COM GEN trend reversal

revertir: **~ un pase** *fra* BOLSA reverse a swop

revestimiento: **~ de la máquina** *m* TRANSP engine casing; **~ de panel** *m* COM GEN panel envelope; **~ reforzado con vidrio** *m* TRANSP glass-reinforced cladding

revisable *adj* CONT *auditoría* auditable

revisado *adj* (*ex*) COM GEN examined (*ex, exd.*)

revisar *vt* COM GEN examine, review, look over, CONT audit, DER revise, GES review

revisión *f* COM GEN check, CONT, FIN audit, FISC *buques* survey, audit, GES *examen* review, TRANSP *en aduanas* examination; **~ al alza** COM GEN *de precios* upward revision; **~ analítica** CONT analytical review; **~ del año de gracia** TRANSP year of grace survey (*YGS*); **~ anual de ventas** FIN, V&M annual sales review; **~ base A** CONT A-base review; **~ de cuentas** CONT *de un balance* accounts certification; **~ de cumplimiento** CONT performance review; **~ extraordinaria** TRANSP special survey (*SS*); **~ extraordinaria de un buque** TRANSP ship's special survey (*SS*); **~ extraordinaria intermedia** TRANSP special intermediate survey (*SIS*); **~ de las inversiones** FIN investment review; **~ de licencia** COM GEN *comercial* licensing examination; **~ del mercado** FIN market review; **~ de precios** V&M pricing review; **~ presupuestaria** CONT budget review; **~ del presupuesto de publicidad** CONT, FIN, V&M advertising budget review; **~ de rendimientos** CONT, COM GEN performance review; **~ salarial** RRHH pay review, salary review; **~ salarial anual** RRHH annual salary review; **~ del salario** RRHH pay review, salary review; **~ de tarifas** TRANSP rates review; ♦ **bajo ~** COM GEN under review

revisionismo *m* POL revisionism

revisor, a *m,f* COM GEN ticket collector

revista *f* COM GEN mag, magazine; **~ de abordo** MEDIOS, TRANSP in-flight magazine; **~ de admiradores** MEDIOS, OCIO fanzine; **~ de clase** V&M class magazine; **~ comercial** COM GEN trade magazine; **~ del consumidor** COM GEN, V&M consumer magazine; **~ de distribución gratuita** MEDIOS free circulation magazine; **~ económica** ECON, MEDIOS economic journal; **~ de empresa** MEDIOS house magazine; **~ ilustrada** MEDIOS illustrated magazine; **~ impresa en papel satinado** MEDIOS glossy magazine (*glossy*); **~ de lujo** MEDIOS glossy magazine (*glossy*); **~ de modas** MEDIOS fashion magazine; **~ de producción ajena** MEDIOS, V&M external house magazine; **~ de producción interna** MEDIOS, V&M internal house magazine

revitalización *f* COM GEN revitalization

revocable *adj* COM GEN revocable

revocación *f* FIN *de plan de pensiones*, PATENT revocation

revocado: **no ~** *adj* COM GEN, DER unrepealed

revocar *vt* COM GEN countermand, FIN, PATENT *mandamiento judicial* revoke

revolución: **~ en la administración y dirección de la empresa** *f* GES managerial revolution; **~ administrativa** *f* GES managerial revolution; **~ blanca** *f* ECON *India* white revolution; **~ cultural** *f* POL cultural revolution; **~ demográfica** *f* ECON vital revolution; **~ ecológica** *f* ECON, MED AMB green revolution; **~ gerencial** *f* GES managerial revolution; **~ industrial** *f* IND industrial revolution; **~ verde** *f* ECON, MED AMB *agrícola* green revolution

revolver *vt* BANCA churn

revuelta: **~ popular** *f* POL civil riots

rezagado *m* BOLSA laggard (*jarg*)

rezagarse *v refl* COM GEN fall behind

rezago: **~ salarial** *m* AmL (*cf desfase salarial Esp*) RRHH wage lag

rico *adj* COM GEN rich; **~ en petróleo** ECON *países*, MED AMB oil-rich

riel *m* TRANSP rail

riendas: **~ flojas** *f pl* GES loose rein; **~ sueltas** *f pl* GES loose rein

riesgo *m* COM GEN hazard, risk, FIN *en compañía* stake, SEG *marítimo* peril, venture; **~ de accidente** SEG accident risk; **~ de activos** BANCA asset exposure; **~ acumulativo** SEG accumulation risk; **~ afín** SEG allied peril; **~ agravado** SEG aggravated risk; **~ agregado** COM GEN aggregate risk; **~ ascendente** BOLSA *opciones* upside risk; **~ asegurable** SEG insurable risk; **~ asegurado** SEG insured peril; **~ de auditoría** CONT audit risk; **~ de aviación** SEG, TRANSP aviation risk; **~ por baja en los tipos de cambio** BOLSA downside risk; **~ de base** BOLSA, COM GEN basis risk; **~ básico** COM GEN basic risk; **~ calculado** BOLSA calculated risk; **~ cambiario** ECON, FIN foreign exchange risk; **~ de cambio** ECON, FIN foreign exchange risk; **~ del capital** FIN capital risk; **~ de catástrofe** SEG catastrophe hazard; **~ catastrófico** SEG catastrophe risk; **~ colectivo** SEG mass risk; **~ comercial** COM GEN business risk, commercial risk, GES commercial venture, SEG business risk; **~ compartido** BOLSA joint venture (*JV*), SEG risk pooling, risk sharing; **~ constante** SEG constant risk; **~ del crédito** BANCA, FIN credit risk; **~ de crédito bueno** BANCA, FIN good credit risk; **~ cruzado entre divisas** ECON *comercio internacional* cross currency exposure; **~ cubierto** SEG covered peril; **~ en curso** ECON current risk; **~ de descarga** COM GEN unloading risk; **~ de una divisa** ECON *macroeconomía* currency risk; **~ doméstico** SEG household risk; **~ empresarial** COM GEN, ECON entrepreneurial risk, GES business venture; **~ esperado** SEG expected peril; **~ estático** MAT static risk; **~ excluido** SEG exclusion clause; **~ de final abierto** BOLSA *opciones* open-ended risk; **~ financiero** BOLSA, COM GEN, FIN financial risk, basis risk; **~ de guerra** SEG *marítimo* war risk; **~ del hombre de negocios** BOLSA businessman's risk; **~ de incendio en la carga** SEG, TRANSP fire risk on freight (*frof*); **~ inherente** BOLSA inherent risk; **~ de interés** FIN interest risk; **~ laboral** IND, RRHH occupational hazard; **~ limitado** BOLSA limited risk; **~ de liquidez** BOLSA cash risk; **~ de litigio** CONT litigation risk; **~ de mar** TRANSP sea risk; **~ marítimo** SEG maritime risk, maritime peril; **~ máximo** BANCA maximum risk, ultimate risk, BOLSA *opciones*, FIN maximum risk; **~ de mercado** BOLSA market risk; **~ de las mercancías** DER, TRANSP risk in the goods; **~ meta** SEG target risk; **~ mixto** SEG mixed peril; **~ moral** SEG moral hazard; **~ de muerte** SEG death risk; **~ de negocios** COM GEN, GES business venture; **~ de no pago** BANCA risk of nonrepayment; **~ no sistemático** COM GEN unsystematic risk; **~ no vinculado** BOLSA *de futuros* unbounded risk; **~ ocupacional** RRHH occupational hazard; **~ de país** FIN *provisiones* country risk; **~ de perfil** FIN profile risk; **~ poco seguro** COM GEN unsound risk; **~ político** COM GEN, POL political risk; **~ preferente** SEG preferred risk; **~ de préstamos**

BANCA, FIN loan exposure; ~ **previsible** BOLSA foreseeable risk; ~ **relacionado con un desfase** BANCA lag risk; ~ **relacionado con el margen** BOLSA spread risk; ~ **relacionado con la refinanciación** BANCA, FIN refinancing risk; ~ **de robo** SEG theft risk; ~ **de ruptura de cristales** SEG breakage of glass risk; ~ **para la salud** IND, PROT SOC health risk, health hazard; ~ **de seguridad** COM GEN *altos cargos* security risk; ~ **sistemático** BOLSA systematic risk; ~ **soberano** FIN sovereign risk; ~ **sobre tipo de interés a corto plazo** BOLSA *instrumentos financieros a plazo* short-term interest rate risk; ~ **sustancial** BOLSA substantial risk; ~ **de tasa** BANCA, CONT, FIN rate risk; ~ **de la tasa de interés** BANCA, CONT, FIN interest rate risk; ~ **temporal** SEG time risk; ~ **de terceros** SEG third-party risk; ~ **de los tipos de interés** *f* BOLSA *de futuros* interest-rate exposure; ~ **de la transacción** BOLSA transaction risk; ~ **del transportista** TRANSP carrier's risk; ~ **ventajoso** SEG good risk; ◆ **a ~** BOLSA at risk; **todo ~** SEG all peril, all risks (*A*/*R*); **a todo ~** SEG against all risks (*AAR*), comprehensive; **contra todo ~** SEG against all risks (*AAR*); **a ~ del comprador** BOLSA at buyer's risk; **sin ~ después de la descarga** SEG no risk after discharge (*nrad*); **sólo ~ de guerra** SEG war risk only (*wro*); **sin ~ hasta la confirmación** SEG no risk until confirmed (*nr*); **de ~ mínimo** BOLSA risk-minimizing; **a ~ del suscriptor** DER caveat subscriptor

riesgos: **los ~ son altos** *fra* COM GEN the stakes are high

RIF *abr* (*Registro de Información Fiscal*) FISC Tax Information Registry

rigidez: ~ **del mercado laboral** *f* ECON labor market rigidity (*AmE*), labour market rigidity (*BrE*); ~ **de precios** *f* ECON price rigidity; ~ **salarial** *f* ECON wage rigidity

riqueza *f* COM GEN wealth; ~ **intangible** ECON intangible wealth; ~ **nacional** ECON national wealth; ~ **de las naciones** ECON Wealth of Nations; ~ **tangible** ECON tangible wealth

ritmo *m* COM GEN *del cambio* pace

robar: ~ **la caja** *vt* COM GEN rob the till

robo *m* RRHH *de personal* poaching; ~ **con escalo** DER burglary

robot *m* IND robot, RRHH steel-collar worker

robótica *f* IND robotics

robotizar *vt* IND robotize

rodaje *m* MEDIOS, OCIO, V&M *publicidad, películas* shooting

rodamiento *m* TRANSP *vehículo* roll-out

rodar *vt* MEDIOS, OCIO *películas* shoot, TRANSP roll, V&M *películas, publicidad* shoot

rodeado: ~ **de tierra** *fra* INMOB landlocked

rodillo *m* POL machtpolitik (*jarg*)

rogar *vt* COM GEN appeal to, plead

rol *m* COM GEN role

rollo: ~ **de papel de máquina de calcular** *m* COM GEN tally-roll; ~ **publicitario** *m* V&M sales pitch

romper *vt* COM GEN *negociaciones, conversaciones* break off, DER *contrato* break; ◆ ~ **el estancamiento** COM GEN break the stalemate; ~ **filas** RRHH break ranks; ~ **una huelga** POL, RRHH break a strike; ~ **una manifestación** POL, RRHH cross a picket line; ~ **las negociaciones** COM GEN break off negotiations; ~ **relaciones con** ECON, POL sever links with; ~ **el**

sindicato BOLSA break the syndicate; ~ **el techo** FIN break the ceiling

romperse *v refl* RRHH *las negociaciones, relaciones* break down

ronda *f* ECON round, TRANSP ring road; ~ **negociadora** IMP/EXP round

Ronda: ~ **Dillon** *f* ECON Dillon Round; ~ **Kennedy** *f* ECON Kennedy Round; ~ **de Tokio** *f* ECON Tokyo Round; ~ **Uruguay** *f* ECON Uruguay Round

ro/ro *abr* (*embarque y desembarque autopropulsado*) TRANSP ro/ro (*roll-on/roll-off*)

rotación *f* COM GEN turnover; ~ **de activos** CONT, FIN asset turnover; ~ **de anuncios** V&M copy rotation; ~ **de la cuenta** CONT account turnover; ~ **de cultivos** ECON, MED AMB crop rotation; ~ **de existencias** COM GEN stock rotation, stock turnover; ~ **de inventarios** COM GEN stock turnover; ~ **de mano de obra** RRHH labor turnover (*AmE*), labour turnover (*BrE*), staff turnover; ~ **de personal** RRHH labor turnover (*AmE*), labour turnover (*BrE*), staff turnover; ~ **de publicidad** CONT, FIN, MEDIOS, V&M advertising turnover; ~ **de puestos** ECON, RRHH efficient job mobility; ~ **de títulos** BOLSA stock turnover; ~ **de trabajos** RRHH job rotation; ~ **en tres ciclos** ECON *agricultura* three-course rotation

rotafolios *m* ADMIN flip chart

rotonda *f* INMOB roundhouse, TRANSP roundabout (*BrE*), traffic circle (*AmE*)

rotulación *f* MEDIOS *imprenta* lettering

rótulo *m* COM GEN show card; ~ **comercial** COM GEN trade sign; ~ **de neón** COM GEN neon sign

rotura: ~ **de cabeza** *f jarg* INFO head crash (*jarg*)

royalty *m* COM GEN royalties

rozamiento *m* COM GEN friction

RRHH *abr* (*recursos humanos*) RRHH HRM (*human resource management*)

rte. *abr* (*remitente*) COMS *en un sobre* sender

RTVE *abr* (*Radio Televisión Española*) MEDIOS Spanish national broadcasting company, ≈ BBC (*British Broadcasting Corporation*)

rueda: ~ **de cheques** *f* BANCA *sobre fondos ficticios* check-kiting (*AmE*), cheque-kiting (*BrE*); ~ **lateral** *f* TRANSP side wheel (*SDW*); ~ **de prensa** *f* MEDIOS, V&M press conference; ~ **de respeto deslizable** *f* TRANSP sliding fifth wheel

ruegos: ~ **y preguntas** *fra* COM GEN any other business (*AOB*), any other competent business (*AOCB*)

ruido *m* COM GEN noise; ~ **blanco** MAT white noise

rumor *m* COM GEN rumor (*AmE*), rumour (*BrE*), buzz (*infrml*)

ruptura *f* BOLSA breakout, COM GEN *de relaciones* breaking-off, *interrupción* disruption, RRHH *negociaciones* breakdown; ~ **desafortunada** COM GEN bad break (*infrml*); ~ **en dos direcciones** COM GEN two-way split; ~ **del matrimonio** DER marriage breakdown

ruta *f* COM GEN route; ~ **aérea** TRANSP air lane; ~ **comercial** ECON, TRANSP trade route; ~ **comercial internacional** TRANSP world trade route; ~ **directa** TRANSP direct route; ~ **indirecta** TRANSP indirect route; ~ **marítima** TRANSP sea route; ~ **multiusuario** TRANSP multiuser route; ~ **de navegación** TRANSP shipping lane; ~ **de navegación en alta mar** TRANSP deep-sea shipping lane; ◆ **en ~** TRANSP en route

rutas *f pl* TRANSP *navegación* roads

rutina *f* COM GEN routine, GES norm, rule, INFO routine; ~ **administrativa** COM GEN, GES, POL red tape; ~ **de diagnóstico** COM GEN diagnostic routine; ~ **de oficina** COM GEN office routine; ◆ **por** ~ COM GEN as a matter of routine

rutinario *adj* COM GEN routine

S

S.A. *abr* (*sociedad anónima*) COM GEN ≈ Inc. (*AmE*) (*incorporated business company*), ≈ Ltd (*BrE*) (*limited company*), ≈ plc (*BrE*) (*public limited company*)

S.A.A. *abr* (*sociedad anónima por acciones*) COM GEN ≈ Inc. (*AmE*) (*incorporated business company*), ≈ Ltd (*BrE*) (*limited company*), ≈ plc (*BrE*) (*public limited company*)

sacar *vt* COM GEN issue, *retirar* pull out, *conclusión* draw, MEDIOS *prospecto* issue; ◆ **~ de** COM GEN *recursos, mercado* tap into; **~ beneficio de** COM GEN capitalize on; **~ una conclusión** COM GEN draw a conclusion; **~ dinero a** COM GEN bleed (*infrml*); **~ por impresora** ADMIN, INFO print out; **~ a licitación** COM GEN put out for tender, put up for tender; **~ a la luz** COM GEN bring to light; **~ la matrícula** *AmL* (*cf sacar la patente Esp*) COM GEN license a motor vehicle; **~ la patente** *Esp* (*cf sacar la matrícula AmL*) COM GEN license a motor vehicle

sacarle: ~ información a alguien *fra* COM GEN drag information out of sb (*infrml*)

sacrificar *vt* COM GEN sacrifice

sacudida *f* BOLSA, COM GEN, SEG shake-out

sagaz *adj* COM GEN far-sighted

sala *f* COM GEN room, DER chamber; **~ de cálculo** INFO computing room; **~ de computadoras** *AmL* (*cf sala de ordenadores Esp*) INFO computer room; **~ de computadores** *AmL ver sala de computadoras AmL*; **~ del consejo** ADMIN, GES boardroom; **~ de consejo directivo** GES, ADMIN boardroom; **~ de cotizaciones** BOLSA boardroom; **~ de exposiciones** COM GEN exhibition room; **~ de noticias** MEDIOS newsroom; **~ de juntas** ADMIN, GES boardroom; **~ de ordenadores** *Esp* (*cf sala de computadoras AmL*) INFO computer room; **~ de pasajeros** OCIO, TRANSP passenger lounge; **~ de subastas** COM GEN auction room; **~ de tránsito** OCIO transit lounge; **~ de visionado** MEDIOS viewing room

salario *m* COM GEN, RRHH pay, salary, wage, wages; **~ anual** COM GEN, RRHH annual wage; **~ anual garantizado** RRHH guaranteed annual wage (*GAW*); **~ bajo** RRHH low pay; **~ base** FIN, RRHH earnings base, basic salary; **~ bruto** RRHH gross wage; **~ por contrato** COM GEN, RRHH contract hire; **~ a destajo** RRHH piece wage; **~ por eficiencia** ECON, RRHH efficiency wage; **~ eficiente** ECON, RRHH efficiency wage; **~ escalonado** RRHH graduated wage; **~ fijo** RRHH fixed salary; **~ garantizado** RRHH guaranteed wage; **~ hedónico** ECON hedonic wage; **~ por horas** RRHH hourly rate; **~ inicial** RRHH starting salary, starting wage; **~ justo** ECON, RRHH just wage; **~ medio** ECON, RRHH average wage; **~ mínimo** ECON, RRHH minimum wage; **~ mínimo garantizado** ECON, RRHH guaranteed minimum wage; **~ mínimo interprofesional** ECON, RRHH minimum wage; **~ mínimo legal** DER, ECON, RRHH statutory minimum wage; **~ mínimo vital** ECON, RRHH minimum living wage; **~ neto** RRHH net pay; **~ nominal** RRHH nominal wages; **~ de paro** COM GEN, PROT SOC, RRHH fallback pay; **~ real** ECON, RRHH real wages; **~ real por eficiencia** ECON, RRHH efficiency real wage; **~ real eficiente** ECON, RRHH efficiency real wage; **~ semanal** RRHH weekly wage; **~ social** RRHH social wage; **~ de subsistencia** PROT SOC living wage; **~ tope** FIN, RRHH earnings ceiling

salarios: ~, sueldos y beneficios complementarios *m pl* RRHH salaries, wages and fringe benefits

saldar *vt* BANCA *cuenta* balance, COM GEN *factura* pay, CONT balance, RRHH pay off, V&M *existencias* sell off; ◆ **~ costes** *Esp* (*cf saldar costos AmL*) meet costs; **~ costos** *AmL* (*cf saldar costes Esp*) FIN meet costs; **~ las cuentas** CONT balance the books (*infrml*); **~ las propias cuentas** CONT make up one's accounts

saldo *m* COM GEN payment (*PYT*), *balances* balance (*bal.*), CONT *de cuenta* balance (*bal.*), V&M *liquidación* clearance sale; **~ acumulado** FISC accumulated balance; **~ anterior** CONT carry-over; **~ de apertura** BANCA opening balance; **~ de artículos** COM GEN job lot; **~ en el banco** BANCA balance in bank; **~ de caja** CONT cash balance; **~ de caja no utilizado** CONT *contabilidad gubernamental* unspent cash balance; **~ sin cargas** CONT *gobierno* unencumbered balance; **~ de cierre** BANCA, CONT, FIN closing balance, INMOB closing statement; **~ de cierre diario** BANCA, CONT, FIN daily closing balance; **~ comercial** ECON balance of trade, trade balance; **~ compensatorio** BANCA compensating balance; **~ corriente** FIN current expenditure; **~ de crédito mínimo** BANCA minimum credit balance; **~ de cuenta** COM GEN balance of account, account statement; **~ en cuenta corriente** ECON balance on current account; **~ a cuenta nueva** CONT balance carried forward, carry-forward; **~ del depósito** BANCA, FIN deposit balance; **~ desfavorable** BANCA minus tick; **~ deudor** BOLSA, BANCA, FIN debit balance, FISC balance due; **~ deudor neto del cliente** BOLSA customers' net debit balance; **~ disponible** BANCA, CONT, FIN available balance; **~ en dólares** BANCA, ECON, FIN dollar balance; **~ externo** ECON external balance; **~ en el extranjero** BANCA balance abroad; **~ favorable** BANCA favorable balance (*AmE*), favourable balance (*BrE*); **~ favorable al acreedor** BANCA balance due to creditor; **~ favorable al deudor** BANCA balance due to debitor; **~ final** BANCA, CONT bottom line, final balance; **~ de incertidumbre** BANCA suspense balance; **~ insuficiente** BANCA, FIN insufficient funds; **~ en libras esterlinas** BANCA, ECON, FIN sterling balance; **~ del mayor** BANCA, CONT, FIN ledger balance; **~ mínimo** BANCA minimum balance; **~ negativo** BANCA minus tick; **~ no distribuido** CONT undistributed balance; **~ no gastado** FIN *de asignación* unexpended balance; **~ no reclamado** BANCA unclaimed balance; **~ ocioso** FIN idle balance; **~ operativo** BANCA operational balance; **~ pendiente** BANCA, CONT outstanding balance; **~ principal pendiente de pago** BANCA, CONT outstanding principal balance; **~ promedio** BANCA *cargo de intereses* average balance; **~ transitorio** BANCA suspense balance; ◆ **~ a su favor** BANCA balance in your favor (*AmE*), balance in your favour (*BrE*)

salida *f* CONT *de fondos* outflow, INFO output, TRANSP, V&M *de producto* outlet; **~ de campo** PROT SOC field trip; **~ de capital** CONT, ECON capital outflow; **~ de computador** *AmL ver salida de computadora AmL*; **~ de computadora** *AmL* (*cf salida de ordenador Esp*) INFO computer output; **~ de datos** INFO data output; **~ diaria** PROT SOC day release; **~ de divisas extranjeras** ECON foreign currency outflow; **~ en efectivo** CONT, FIN cash outflow; **~ de emergencia** RRHH emergency exit; **~ de fábrica** TRANSP ex mill; **~ impresa** INFO print out; **~ de incendios** RRHH fire exit; **~ de ordenador** *Esp* (*cf salida de computadora AmL*) INFO computer output; **~ de recursos líquidos** CONT, FIN cash outflow; ♦ **sin ~ para poder comprar o vender** BOLSA locked-in

salir *vi* INFO exit; ♦ **~ de apuros** COM GEN get out of trouble; **~ fiador de alguien** FIN bail sb out (*infrml*); **~ del país** ECON *dinero* flow out of the country; **~ en titulares** MEDIOS hit the headlines

salón: **~ de clase ejecutivo** *m* COM GEN, TRANSP executive lounge; **~ de fumar** *m* OCIO, RRHH smoking room

salpicadura *f* MEDIOS *prensa* splash

saltar *vt* INFO skip; ♦ **~ por encima** RRHH leapfrog (*jarg*)

saltarse: **~ los detalles** *fra* COM GEN skip the details; **~ las normas** *fra* RRHH step over the mark

salto *m* BOLSA, COM GEN jump, INFO skip; **~ de impreso** INFO form feed (*FF*); **~ de línea** INFO word wrap, line feed (*lf*); **~ de página forzado** INFO *documento procesado* hard page break; **~ de papel** INFO paper throw

salud *f* COM GEN, PROT SOC health; **~ ocupacional** COM GEN, PROT SOC, occupational health; **~ pública** COM GEN, PROT SOC public health

saluda: **le ~ atentamente** *fra* COMS Yours sincerely, Yours faithfully

saludos *m pl* COMS greetings

salvaguardar *vt* COM GEN *los activos* safeguard

salvaguardarse *v refl* COM GEN safeguard; ♦ **~ contra la inflación** ECON safeguard against inflation

salvamento *m* COM GEN *recuperar*, TRANSP *navegación* salvage

salvar *vt* COM GEN salvage, save, *brecha, vacante* bridge, INFO *datos almacenar* save, TRANSP salvage

salvedades: **sin ~** *fra* CONT clean

salvo[1] *adj* COM GEN safe; ♦ **estar a ~** COM GEN be out of the woods

salvo[2] *prep* COM GEN except; ♦ **~ convenio contrario** COM GEN unless otherwise agreed; **~ disposición contraria** FISC except as otherwise provided; **~ domingos y días festivos** COM GEN, OCIO, TRANSP Sundays and holidays excepted; **~ error u omisión** (*s.e.u.o.*) COM GEN errors and omissions excepted (*e.&o.e.*); **~ indicación de lo contrario** COM GEN except otherwise herein provided (*eohp*); **~ que se acuerde lo contrario** COM GEN unless otherwise agreed; **~ si se utilizó** TRANSP *navegación, fletamento* unless used; **~ viernes y días festivos** COM GEN, OCIO, TRANSP Fridays and holidays excepted (*FHEx*)

sanción *f* COM GEN sanction; **~ comercial** ECON, POL trade sanction; **~ por declaración incorrecta** FISC serious misdeclaration penalty (*BrE*); **~ económica** ECON, POL economic sanction; **~ fiscal** FISC tax penalty; **~ por retirada anticipada** BOLSA, FIN early-withdrawal penalty

sancionable *adj* FISC liable to a penalty

sangrar *vt infrml* COM GEN bleed (*infrml*)

sangría *f* INFO indentation

sano *adj* COM GEN healthy

S.A.R. *abr Esp* (*Su Alteza Real*) COM GEN ≈ HRH (*BrE*) (*Her Royal Highness, His Royal Highness*)

sastre *mf* COM GEN tailor

satélite *m* COMS, MEDIOS satellite; **~ de comunicaciones** COMS, MEDIOS communications satellite

satisfacción: **~ del consumidor** *f* COM GEN, V&M consumer satisfaction; **~ del trabajo** *f* GES, RRHH job satisfaction

satisfacer *vt* COM GEN satisfy, CONT *costos*, FIN, GES *exigencias* meet

satisfactorio *adj* COM GEN satisfactory

satisfecho *adj* COM GEN satisfied

saturación *f* COM GEN, ECON, INFO, V&M *del mercado* saturation; **~ del mercado** COM GEN, V&M market saturation; **~ del petróleo** MED AMB oil glut; **~ publicitaria** V&M advertising wearout; **~ en el transporte** TRANSP shipping overcapacity

saturado *adj* BOLSA oversold

saturar *vt* COM GEN, ECON *economía, mercado*, INFO, V&M saturate

screening *m* MAT screening

sección *f* COM GEN section; **~ de cartera** BOLSA, FIN portfolio section; **~ económica** ECON, MEDIOS *de periódico* economic section; **~ extranjera** BOLSA foreign section; **~ de rebajas** V&M bargain basement, bargain counter; **~ de ruta** TRANSP routes section; **~ de servicios diplomáticos** COM GEN, POL diplomatic service department; **~ transversal** COM GEN cross section; **~ de última página** COM GEN, MEDIOS *de revistas* back section

secretaría *f* ADMIN, RRHH *plantilla* secretariat

Secretaría: **~ Internacional de la Lana** *f* IND International Wool Secretariat (*IWS*)

secretariado *m* POL *gobierno* secretariat

Secretariado: **~ del Consejo del Tesoro** *m* POL Treasury Board Secretariat

secretario, -a *m,f* COM GEN, RRHH secretary (*sec*): **~ de asuntos sociales** RRHH social secretary; **~ de confianza** RRHH confidential secretary; **~ ejecutivo(-a)** RRHH executive secretary; **~ de la empresa** ADMIN *organización comercial*, RRHH company secretary; **~ de estado para el transporte** POL, TRANSP Secretary of State for Transport (*BrE*); **~ general** RRHH general secretary, company secretary; **~ interino(-a)** ADMIN, RRHH temporary secretary; **~ particular** ADMIN, RRHH private secretary; **~ personal** COM GEN, RRHH personal secretary (*P.S.*), personal assistant (*PA*), private secretary; **~ de redacción** MEDIOS, RRHH sub-editor (*sub*); **~ temporal** ADMIN, RRHH temporary secretary

Secretario, -a: **~ de Estado** *m,f* POL Secretary of State; **~ General** *m,f* RRHH *de un sindicato* General Secretary; **~ Jefe(-a) del Tesoro** *m,f* ECON Chief Secretary to the Treasury (*BrE*)

secreto[1] *adj* COM GEN secret

secreto[2] *m* COM GEN secrecy, secret, POL cover-up; **~ de fabricación** COM GEN trade secret; **~ profesional de los funcionarios** COM GEN professional secret

sector *m* COM GEN sector; **~ de actividad** FISC field of endeavor (*AmE*), field of endeavour (*BrE*); **~ agrícola** ECON agricultural sector; **~ de agricultura** ECON agricultural sector; **~ de apoyo a la electricidad** IND electricity support industry; **~ de la atención médica** IND health care industry; **~ bancario** BANCA, FIN banking sector; **~ de carreteras** ECON, TRANSP road sector; **~ de la construcción** IND, INMOB construction industry; **~ deteriorado** INFO bad sector; **~ de electricidad** IND electricity sector; **~ empresarial** COM GEN business sector, ECON company sector; **~ excluido** IND excluded sector; **~ de exportación** IMP/EXP, TRANSP export sector; **~ expuesto** COM GEN exposed sector; **~ financiero** FIN financial sector; **~ frigorífico** ECON, TRANSP reefer trade; **~ industrial** IND industrial sector; **~ manufacturero** IND manufacturing sector; **~ de mercado** V&M market sector; **~ del metal** IND metal industry; **~ nacionalizado** ECON, IND, POL nationalized sector; **~ no bancario** BANCA, FIN nonbanking sector; **~ no comercializado** ECON nonmarket sector; **~ no manufacturero** IND nonmanufacturing sector; **~ del ocio** OCIO entertainment industry; **~ personal** ECON personal sector; **~ de pesca** ECON, IND fishing sector; **~ pesquero** ECON, IND fishing industry; **~ del petróleo** IND petroleum sector, petroleum industry; **~ petrolero** IND oil sector; **~ poco atractivo** ECON, FIN, IND out-of-favor industry (*AmE*), out-of-favour industry (*BrE*); **~ primario** ECON, IND primary sector; **~ privado** IND private sector; **~ de procesamiento de alimentos** ECON, IND food-processing industry; **~ de los productos básicos** COM GEN basic goods sector; **~ público** ECON public sector; **~ rural** IND rural sector; **~ sanitario** PROT SOC health sector; **~ secundario** ECON, IND secondary sector, secondary production industry; **~ de seguros** SEG insurance business, insurance industry; **~ de servicios** ECON, IND, RRHH service sector; **~ de servicios públicos** IND utilities sector; **~ terciario** ECON, IND tertiary sector; **~ de tributación** FISC field of taxation; **~ tributario** FISC tax field; **~ de la vivienda** IND, INMOB housing industry

sectorial *adj* CONT, ECON, GES sectoral

sectorización: **~ lógica** *f* INFO soft sectoring

sectorizar *vt* INFO *disco* sector

secuencia *f* COM GEN sequence; **~ de abandono** INFO escape sequence; **~ por clave** INFO key sequence; **~ de intercalación** INFO collating sequence

secuencial *adj* COM GEN sequential

secuestro *m* DER, FIN sequestration

secundar *vt* COM GEN *moción* second

sede: **~ central** *f* BANCA main branch, COM GEN *de empresa* headquarters (*HQ, h.q.*); **~ de una conferencia** *f* GES conference site location; **~ principal** *f* COM GEN head office (*H.O.*), headquarters (*HQ, h.q.*); **~ social** *f* COM GEN, DER registered office

seductor *m* BOLSA wolf (*jarg*)

segmentación *f* COM GEN segmentation, INFO partition; **~ por estilos de vida** V&M lifestyle segmentation; **~ de mercado** V&M market segmentation

segmentar *vt* COM GEN segment, FISC *desgravación fiscal* taper, GES *política* segment

segmento *m* COM GEN segment; **~ de base** INFO root segment; **~ objetivo** V&M target segment

segregación: **~ laboral** *f* ECON occupational segregation; **~ racial** *f* COM GEN segregation

segregado *adj* COM GEN segregated

seguido *adj* COM GEN continued (*cont'd*)

seguidor, a *m,f* COM GEN follower

seguimiento[1]: **de ~ rápido** *adj* COM GEN fast-tracked

seguimiento[2] *m* COM GEN tracking, V&M follow-up

seguir *vt* COM GEN continue to, *gasto* track, *política* pursue, GES *un curso* follow, MAT *curva de demanda* follow, V&M follow up; ♦ **~ el ejemplo** COM GEN follow suit; **~ un modelo similar** COM GEN *demanda* follow a similar pattern; **~ el ritmo de** COM GEN *pagos* keep up with; **~ el trámite de** COM GEN *proyecto, esquema* follow through

segunda[1]: **~ generación** *f jarg* COM GEN second generation (*jarg*); **~ hipoteca** *f* BANCA, FIN, INMOB junior mortgage (*AmE*), second mortgage (*BrE*); **~ obligación** *f* BANCA, FIN second debenture; **~ residencia** *f* FISC second home, INMOB second residence

segunda[2]: **de ~ mano** *fra* COM GEN *bienes* second-hand

segundo[1] *adj* COM GEN second; ♦ **de ~ grado** COM GEN second-grade; **de ~ orden** ECON off-prime; **en ~ lugar** COM GEN secondly

segundo[2]: **el ~** *m* COM GEN the latter; **~ transportista** *m,f* TRANSP second carrier

seguridad *f* COM GEN safety, security; **~ de auditoría** CONT audit assurance; **~ en la carretera** TRANSP road safety; **~ sin cupón** BOLSA stripped security; **~ de los datos** INFO data security; **~ del equipo** INFO hardware security; **~ e higiene** PROT SOC, RRHH health and safety; **~ industrial** IND, RRHH industrial safety; **~ de las máquinas** IND machine safety; **~ de posesión** INMOB security of tenure; **~ del puesto de trabajo** RRHH job security; ♦ **tenga la ~ de que** COMS rest assured that

Seguridad: **~ Social** *f* FISC, PROT SOC ≈ National Insurance (*BrE*) (*NI*)

seguro[1] *adj* COM GEN riskless, safe, secure; ♦ **estar más ~** COM GEN be on the safe side

seguro[2] *m* COM GEN, SEG insurance;

~ a **~ abierto** SEG blanket insurance; **~ de abonado** COM GEN, SEG subscriber's insurance policy; **~ de abordaje** SEG collision insurance; **~ de abstemio** SEG abstainer's insurance; **~ de accidentes y de enfermedad** SEG accident and health insurance; **~ de actividades concluidas** INMOB, SEG completed operations insurance; **~ agrícola** SEG agricultural insurance; **~ de arrendamiento** SEG leasehold insurance; **~ del automóvil sin culpa** SEG *compromiso* no-fault automobile insurance (*AmE*), no-fault car insurance (*BrE*); **~ de automóviles** SEG automobile insurance (*AmE*), car insurance (*BrE*), motor vehicle insurance; **~ de aviación** SEG aviation insurance;

~ c **~ de cambio** CONT, FIN foreign exchange hedge; **~ de capital diferido** SEG endowment insurance; **~ de capitalización** SEG life assurance (*BrE*), life insurance; **~ de cartera** BOLSA, SEG portfolio insurance; **~ de cascos** SEG *marítimo* hull insurance; **~ de cascos de aviación** SEG aircraft hull insurance; **~ por cierre de negocio** SEG business closure insurance; **~ con cobertura contra responsabilidad civil** SEG third-party insurance cover; **~ de cobertura general** SEG umbrella liability insurance; **~ colectivo** SEG collective insurance; **~ colectivo de accidentes** SEG collective accident insurance; **~ colectivo y conjunto** SEG joint insurance; **~ colectivo de enfermedad** SEG group health insurance; **~ colectivo de gastos médicos** SEG blanket medical expense insurance; **~ colectivo de incapacidad** SEG group disability insurance; **~ colectivo de vida y enfermedad** SEG blanket life and health insurance; ~ **combinado de comercios** SEG combined shop insurance; ~ **de compensaciones laborales** RRHH, SEG worker compensation insurance; ~ **complementario de excedente** COM GEN, SEG excess insurance; ~ **de compra por invalidez de un socio** SEG disability buy-out insurance; ~ **compuesto** SEG composite insurance; ~ **condicionado a cese de negocio** SEG contingent business interruption insurance; ~ **contra accidentes** SEG accident insurance, casualty insurance; ~ **contra accidentes de un ascensor** SEG elevator liability insurance (*AmE*), lift liability insurance (*BrE*); ~ **contra cambio en las condiciones** SEG difference in conditions insurance; ~ **contra cesación de negocios** SEG business interruption insurance; ~ **contra daños de empleados desleales** SEG blanket fidelity bond; ~ **contra daños en la propiedad comercial** SEG business crime insurance; ~ **contra delito informático** INFO, SEG computer crime insurance; ~ **contra diferencia en los límites** SEG difference in limits insurance; ~ **contra diferencia en el valor** SEG difference in value insurance; ~ **contra estafas de empleados** SEG fidelity bond; ~ **contra extorsión** SEG extortion insurance; ~ **contra falsificaciones** SEG depositor's forgery insurance; ~ **contra gastos adicionales** SEG additional expense insurance; ~ **contra gastos de incineración** SEG cremation expenses insurance; ~ **contra hechos dolosos y vandálicos** SEG vandalism and malicious mischief insurance; ~ **contra hurto y robo de oficinas** SEG office burglary and robbery insurance; ~ **contra responsabilidad civil de directivos** GES, SEG directors' and officers' liability insurance; ~ **contra responsabilidad civil de propietarios y contratistas** SEG owners' and contractors' protective liability insurance; ~ **contra responsabilidad civil de propietarios, arrendadores e inquilinos** SEG owners', landlords', and tenants' liability policy; ~ **contra riesgo de inundación** SEG flood insurance; ~ **contra riesgos múltiples** SEG all risk insurance; ~ **contra robo de caja fuerte** SEG *empresa* mercantile safe burglary insurance; ~ **contra robo a mensajeros** SEG messenger robbery insurance; ~ **contra robo de mercancías expuestas en almacenes** SEG mercantile open-stock burglary insurance; ~ **contra robos mercantiles** SEG mercantile robbery insurance; ~ **contra rotura de lunas** SEG glass insurance; ~ **contra secuestro** SEG kidnap insurance; ~ **contra seísmos** SEG earthquake insurance; ~ **contra todo riesgo** SEG comprehensive insurance, hazard insurance; ~ **de crédito** SEG credit insurance; ~ **de crédito colectivo** SEG group credit insurance; ~ **de crédito comercial** SEG commercial credit insurance; ~ **de crédito a la exportación** SEG export credit insurance;

~ d ~ **de decesos** *AmL* (*cf seguro de vida Esp*) SEG life insurance; ~ **dental** SEG dental insurance; ~ **de depósito bancario** BANCA, SEG bank deposit insurance; ~ **de desempleo** ECON, POL, PROT SOC, RRHH unemployment benefit (*BrE*), unemployment compensation (*AmE*), unemployment insurance, SEG unemployment insurance; ~ **directo** SEG direct insurance; ~ **dotal** SEG child's deferred assurance; ~ **dotal vencido** SEG matured endowment;

~ e ~ **de enfermedad** SEG sickness insurance, health insurance; ~ **de enfermedad privado** SEG commercial health insurance; ~ **especial multirriesgo** SEG special multiperil insurance (*SMP*); ~ **de expoliación** SEG cash messenger insurance; ~ **de exposiciones** SEG exhibition risks insurance;

~ f ~ **de fidelidad** SEG fidelity insurance; ~ **de flete** SEG, TRANSP freight insurance;

~ g ~ **para gastos de estudios** SEG educational endowment; ~ **de gastos jurídicos** DER, SEG legal expense insurance; ~ **general de responsabilidad personal** SEG comprehensive personal liability insurance; ~ **global** SEG blanket insurance;

~ h ~ **de hipotecas** SEG mortgage insurance;

~ i ~ **de incapacidad laboral** SEG *subsidio* income replacement insurance; ~ **de instalación** SEG installation insurance; ~ **de invalidez** SEG disability insurance;

~ m ~ **de máquinas distribuidoras** SEG coin-machine insurance; ~ **marino de protección e indemnización** SEG ocean marine protection and indemnity insurance; ~ **marítimo** SEG marine insurance, sea insurance; ~ **médico** SEG medical insurance; ~ **de medidas preventivas** DER, SEG sue and labor insurance (*AmE*), sue and labour insurance (*BrE*); ~ **de mercancías** SEG, TRANSP cargo insurance; ~ **mixto** SEG endowment assurance; ~ **multirriesgo** SEG multiple-risk insurance; ~ **multirriesgo contra rotura de cristales** SEG comprehensive glass insurance; ~ **mutuo** SEG mutual insurance;

~ n ~ **de navegación interior** SEG, TRANSP inland marine insurance; ~ **no de vida** SEG nonlife insurance;

~ o ~ **obligatorio** SEG compulsory insurance; ~ **obligatorio de responsabilidad civil** SEG compulsory third party insurance;

~ p ~ **de paquetes postales** COMS, SEG parcel post insurance; ~ **de paro** PROT SOC, SEG unemployment insurance; ~ **de pasajeros de aviones** OCIO, SEG aircraft passenger insurance; ~ **patrimonial** SEG proprietary insurance; ~ **de pedrisco** SEG crop hail insurance; ~ **de pensión que cubre al asegurado y a su cónyuge** SEG joint and survivor annuity (*AmE*); ~ **de pérdidas de ingresos** SEG loss of income insurance; ~ **a plazo renovable por anualidades** SEG renewable annual term insurance; ~ **de préstamo** FIN, SEG loan insurance; ~ **privado sobre hipoteca** SEG private mortgage insurance; ~ **de la producción para los fabricantes** SEG *empresa* manufacturers' output insurance; ~ **de protección del crédito** SEG credit protection insurance; ~ **de protección de título** SEG title protection insurance;

~ r ~ **de renta vitalicia** SEG annuity insurance, annuity assurance; ~ **de responsabilidad** SEG liability insurance; ~ **de responsabilidad del almacenista** SEG storekeeper's liability insurance; ~ **de responsabilidad civil** SEG general liability insurance; ~ **de responsabilidad civil de automóviles** SEG automobile liability insurance (*AmE*), car liability insurance (*BrE*); ~ **de responsabilidad comercial** DER, SEG business liability insurance; ~ **de responsabilidad contra terceros, incendios y robos** SEG third-party fire and theft insurance; ~ **de responsabilidad de fabricantes y contratistas** SEG *empresa* manufacturers' and contractors liability insurance; ~ **de responsabilidad general** SEG comprehensive general liability insurance; ~ **de responsabilidad legal en caso de incendio** SEG fire legal liability insurance; ~ **de responsabilidad profesional del contable** CONT, SEG accountant's professional liability insurance; ~ **de responsabilidad a todo riesgo** SEG comprehensive liability insurance;

~ **de robo de cobradores** SEG cash messenger insurance;

■ **s** ~ **de salud y actividad comercial** SEG business life and health insurance; ~ **sanitario a todo riesgo** SEG comprehensive health insurance; ~ **sobre bonos municipales** SEG municipal bond insurance; ~ **sobre la carga de camiones** SEG motor lorry cargo insurance (*BrE*), motor truck cargo insurance (*AmE*); ~ **sobre depreciación de una propiedad** SEG property depreciation insurance; ~ **sobre documentos de valor** SEG valuable papers insurance; ~ **sobre medios para el proceso de datos** INFO, SEG data processing insurance; ~ **sobre mejoras en la propiedad** SEG improvements and betterments insurance; ~ **sobre mercancías en consignación** SEG, TRANSP consignment insurance; ~ **sobre productos y operaciones terminadas** SEG products and completed operations insurance; ~ **sobre riesgos domésticos** SEG homeowner's policy; ~ **social** FISC, PROT SOC, RRHH social insurance; ~ **de subsidio por incapacidad laboral** SEG disability income insurance (*AmE*); ~ **de supervivencia** SEG survivorship insurance; ~ **de suscriptor** COM GEN, SEG subscriber's insurance policy; ~ **suscrito con una mutua** SEG participating insurance;

■ **t** ~ **técnico** SEG engineering assurance; ~ **temporal** SEG term insurance; ~ **temporal de vida** SEG term life insurance; ~ **de título** SEG title insurance; ~ **a todo riesgo** SEG multiple-peril insurance; ~ **a todo riesgo del contratista** SEG contractor's all risks insurance; ~ **a todo riesgo para distribuidores de equipos** SEG equipment dealers' insurance; ~ **a todo riesgo sobre mercancías dadas como garantía** SEG floor plan insurance; ~ **de transporte aéreo** SEG, TRANSP air transport insurance; ~ **de transportes** SEG, TRANSP transport insurance; ~ **de transportes fluviales** SEG, TRANSP inland marine insurance;

■ **u** ~ **de utilidades** SEG profits insurance;

■ **v** ~ **por vacaciones y ocio** OCIO, SEG holiday and leisure insurance (*BrE*), vacation and leisure insurance (*AmE*); ~ **de valor convenido** SEG agreed value insurance; ~ **de vida** *Esp* (*cf seguro de decesos AmL*) SEG life insurance, life assurance; ~ **de vida actualizado** SEG indexed life insurance; ~ **de vida colectivo** SEG group life insurance; ~ **de vida entera** SEG whole life insurance; ~ **de vida con hipoteca** SEG mortgage life insurance; ~ **de vida individual** SEG individual life insurance; ~ **de vida modificable** SEG adjustable life insurance; ~ **de vida modificado** SEG modified life insurance; ~ **de vida de pago compartido por empleador y empleado** SEG split dollar life insurance; ~ **de vida de pagos limitados** SEG limited payment life insurance; ~ **de vida con prima indeterminada** SEG indeterminate premium life insurance; ~ **de vida de prima única** SEG single-premium life insurance; ~ **de vida y de salud por riesgos empresariales** SEG business exposures life and health insurance; ~ **de vida y de salud de un trabajador clave** SEG key person life and health insurance; ~ **de vida temporal con derecho a total** SEG convertible term life insurance; ~ **de vida total con base actual** SEG current assumption whole life insurance; ~ **de vida universal** SEG universal life insurance; ~ **de vida para usos comerciales** SEG business uses life insurance; ~ **de vida con valor en efectivo** SEG cash value life insurance; ~ **de vida variable** SEG variable life insurance; ~ **de vida para**

viajes en avión SEG aviation-trip life insurance; ~ **en vigor** SEG current insurance, insurance in force; ~ **voluntario** SEG voluntary insurance

seguro³: **cubierto por** ~ *fra* SEG covered by insurance; **con** ~ **insuficiente** *fra* SEG *negocios* insurance-poor (*jarg*); ~ **y transporte gratuitos** *fra* IMP/EXP, SEG free insurance cover (*FIC*)

selección *f* COM GEN *de candidatos* screening, *datos, información* selection, RRHH *de candidatos* screening; ~ **adversa** SEG adverse selection; ~ **al azar** MAT random selection; ~ **automática a distancia del abonado** COMS subscriber trunk dialing (*AmE*) (*STD*), subscriber trunk dialling (*BrE*) (*STD*); ~ **automática internacional** COMS international direct dialing (*AmE*), international direct dialling (*BrE*); ~ **de canal** MEDIOS, OCIO, V&M channel selection; ~ **de cartera** BOLSA, FIN portfolio selection; ~ **del emplazamiento** MED AMB *para el vertido* site selection; ~ **limitada** V&M narrowcasting; ~ **de medios de comunicación** MEDIOS, V&M media selection; ~ **de mercados extranjeros** ECON market selection overseas; ~ **de objetivos de mercado** V&M market target selection

seleccionado *adj* COM GEN selected

seleccionar *vt* COM GEN select, single out, INFO *valor predefinido* set, *para un trabajo* screen; ◆ ~ **y ordenar** COM GEN sort out; ~ **en salida** ADMIN select out

Selectividad *f* PROT SOC Spanish university entrance examination, ≈ Advanced Level General Certificate of Education (*A level*), ≈ Advanced Supplementary Level General Certificate of Education (*AS level*)

sellado: ~ **fiscal** *m* FISC stamp duty (*BrE*)

sellar *vt* COM GEN *pacto* seal, put one's seal to, COMS affix a seal

sello *m* ADMIN seal, COMS *Esp* (*cf estampilla AmL*) stamp, MEDIOS *compañía discográfica* label; ~ **de calidad** COM GEN, V&M seal of quality; ~ **de correos** *Esp* (*cf estampilla AmL*) COMS postage stamp; ~ **de la empresa** BANCA corporate seal, COM GEN, DER company seal; ~ **de endoso** BANCA, COM GEN endorsement stamp; ~ **de entrada** IMP/EXP *al llegar a un nuevo país* entry stamp; ~ **de goma** COM GEN rubber stamp; ~ **oficial** DER common seal; ~ **de plenos** SEG line stamp; ~ **de premio** *AmL* (*cf cupón con prima Esp*) COM GEN trading stamp; ~ **de recibo** COMS receipt stamp; ~ **de remesa** BANCA remittance seal

selva: ~ **tropical** *f* MED AMB rainforest

semana¹: ~ **de alta productividad** *f* IND, RRHH bull week; ~ **garantizada** *f* RRHH guaranteed week; ~ **laborable** *f* RRHH working week (*BrE*), workweek (*AmE*); ~ **laborable media** *f* RRHH average working week (*BrE*), average workweek (*AmE*); ~ **muy productiva** *f* IND, RRHH bull week

semana²: **una** ~ **por adelantado** *fra* COM GEN a week in advance; **de aquí a una** ~ *fra* COM GEN a week from now

semejante: **en** ~ **ocasión** *fra* COM GEN on a similar occasion

semestral *adj* COM GEN half-yearly, biannual

semestralmente *adv* COM GEN half-yearly

semestre *m* COM GEN half year

semianual *adj* COM GEN semiannual

semiconductor *m* IND, INFO semiconductor

semicualificado *adj* ECON, RRHH semiskilled

semidesarmado *adj* TRANSP semi-knocked down (*SKD*)

semiduplex *adj* INFO half-duplex

semiestructurado *adj* COM GEN semistructured

semifabricante *m* *Esp* (*cf maquiladora AmL*) IND *cadenas minoristas* quasi-manufacturer

semiindustrializado *adj* ECON, IND, POL semi-industrialized

seminario *m* COM GEN, GES seminar

seminuevo *adj* COM GEN *automóviles* pre-owned, second-hand

semirremolque *m* TRANSP semitrailer

semisumadora *f* INFO *equipo* half adder

Senado: El ~ *m* POL upper house of Spanish parliament, ≈ The Senate (*AmE*)

sencillo *adj* COM GEN straightforward

senda: ~ de crecimiento *f* COM GEN growth path

sensibilidad: ~ al interés *f* ECON interest sensitivity; **~ al precio** *f* ECON, V&M price sensitivity; **~ del mercado** *f* COM GEN, V&M market sensitivity; **~ a los tipos de interés** *f* ECON interest rate sensitivity

sensibilizar *vt* COM GEN sensitize

sensible *adj* COM GEN *mercado* sensitive; ◆ **~ al contexto** INFO context-sensitive; **~ al coste** *Esp* (*cf sensible al costo AmL*) COM GEN, ECON cost-sensitive; **~ al costo** *AmL* (*cf sensible al coste Esp*) COM GEN, ECON cost-sensitive; **~ al mercado** V&M market-sensitive; **~ al precio** V&M price sensitive

sentada *f* RRHH *acción laboral* sit-in

sentar: ~ las bases *fra* COM GEN lay the basis; **~ una partida en el libro mayor** *fra* COM GEN enter an item in the ledger

sentencia *f* DER decree; **~ de bancarrota** COM GEN, DER decree of bankruptcy; **~ condenatoria** DER conviction; **~ de divorcio firme** DER decree absolute; **~ de embargo** DER garnishment

sentido: ~ comercial *m* COM GEN business sense; **~ común** *m* COM GEN common sense; **~ del mercado** *m* COM GEN feel of the market; **~ de responsabilidad** *m* COM GEN sense of responsibility; ◆ **tener ~** COM GEN make sense; **en ~ contrario al mercado** BOLSA away from the market

señal *f* COM GEN *indicación* signal; **~ de alerta** COM GEN alarm signal; **~ de compra** V&M buying signal; **~ mixta** COM GEN mixed signal; **~ de parada** INFO, TRANSP, stop signal; **~ de peligro** COM GEN warning sign; **~ de reloj** INFO clock signal; **~ sonora** INFO *de aviso* beep; **~ telegráfica de cambio de amplitud** TRANSP *navegación* amplitude change telegraphic signal, (*ACTS*); **~ de tráfico** TRANSP traffic sign

señalar *vt* COM GEN *fecha, lugar* appoint, *indicar* point to; ◆ **~ a un precio más bajo** COM GEN, V&M underprice

señalización *f* COM GEN signalling (*BrE*), signaling (*AmE*)

Señor: ~ don *m* (*Sr.D.*) COM GEN *título de encabezamiento de carta* esquire (*Esq.*)

señoras: ~ y señores *fra* COM GEN ladies and gentlemen

separación *f* COM GEN, ECON demerger, INMOB *de tierras* severance; **~ de colores** INFO, MEDIOS, V&M color separation (*AmE*), colour separation (*BrE*); **~ de deberes** GES segregation of duties; **~ de funciones** GES segregation of duties; **~ judicial** DER judicial separation; **~ legal** DER legal separation

separadamente *adv* COM GEN seriatim, separadamente

separador *m* INFO separator, *para papel* burster

septentrional *adj* COM GEN northern

Séptima: ~ Directiva sobre el derecho de Sociedades *f* DER, POL *UE* Seventh Company Law Directive; **~ Directiva sobre Sociedades** *f* DER, POL Seventh Company Law Directive; **~ Directiva de la UE** *f* CONT *regulaciones sobre contabilidad*, DER, POL Seventh EU Directive

sequía *f* MED AMB drought

SER *abr* (*Sociedad Española de Radiodifusión*) COMS, MEDIOS Spanish broadcasting association

serial: ~-paralelo *adj* INFO serial-parallel

serie¹**: en ~** *adj* INFO serial

serie² *f* COM GEN series, run, V&M array; **~ cronológica** COM GEN, ECON, MAT *estadística* time series; **~ de negociaciones salariales** RRHH pay round, wage round (*BrE*); **~ de opciones** BOLSA series of options, option series; **~ temporal** COM GEN, ECON, MAT *estadística* time series

series: en ~ de *fra* COM GEN in sets of

serigrafía *m* V&M silk screening

serio, -a: ~ competidor(a) *m,f* COM GEN tough competitor

serpiente *f* ECON snake

servicio¹**: sin ~ de comidas** *adj* OCIO *apartamento, vacaciones* self-catering

servicio² *m* COM GEN service; **~ adicional** V&M accessorial service; **~ de administración** ADMIN, FIN, GES management service; **~ administrativo** ADMIN, FIN, GES management service; **~ al cliente** ADMIN, COM GEN, V&M customer service; **~ de alquiler de coches** TRANSP car-hire service; **~ de alta calidad** V&M up-market service; **~ de apoyo** COM GEN, POL support service, TRANSP *envíos* backup service; **~ de asesoramiento** COM GEN, FIN, GES advisory service; **~ de asesoramiento al consumidor** COM GEN, V&M consumer advisory service; **~ de asesoría de cambio de divisas** BANCA foreign exchange advisory service; **~ de atención al público** ADMIN, COM GEN, V&M customer service; **~ automático de radiotélex marítimo** TRANSP automatic maritime radio telex service; **~ automático de transferencia** BANCA automatic transfer service (*BrE*) (*ATS*); **~ auxiliar** COM GEN ancillary service; **~ de banca electrónica** BANCA electronic banking service; **~ bancario** BANCA, CONT bank facility, banking service; **~ bancario personal** BANCA personal banking service; **~ de biblioteca** PROT SOC library service; **~ de bienestar social** PROT SOC, RRHH welfare service; **~ a bordo** OCIO, TRANSP shipboard facility; **~ de carga consolidada** TRANSP consolidate-cargo service (*CCS*); **~ de carga y paquetes postales** *Esp* COMS, TRANSP freight and parcel service; **~ comercial agrícola** ECON Agricultural Marketing Service; **~ de comercialización** V&M merchandising service; **~ de comida durante el vuelo** OCIO, TRANSP in-flight catering; **~ a comisión** BANCA fee-based service; **~ de compra de emisiones** BOLSA, FIN purchase issue facility (*PIF*); **~ de compra de suscripciones** BOLSA, FIN purchase underwriting facility (*PUF*); **~ común para los usuarios** COM GEN common user facility; **~ conjunto** TRANSP joint service; **~ de consulta** COM GEN advisory service, service consultancy; **~ de consultoría** COM GEN consulting service; **~ de consumo** COM GEN consumer service; **~ contable** CONT accountancy service; **~ de contenedores** TRANSP container service; ~ **de contenedores para carga consolidada** TRANSP consolidate-cargo container service; ~ **de contenedores colectivos** TRANSP joint container service (*JCS*); ~ **de correos** COM GEN, COMS postal service; ~ **de datos directo** INFO on-line data service; ~ **deficiente** COM GEN, V&M defective service, poor service; ~ **de depósitos financieros** BANCA deposit facility; ~ **de la deuda** BANCA, CONT debt service; ~ **de deuda anual** BANCA, CONT annual debt service; ~ **de la deuda en cuotas iguales** FISC *título municipal* level debt service (*AmE*); ~ **de la deuda pública** FIN public debt service; ~ **de distribución** TRANSP distribution service; ~ **de documentación** V&M clipping service; ~ **durante el vuelo** OCIO, TRANSP in-flight facilities; ~ **de emergencia** PROT SOC emergency service; ~ **a empresas** COM GEN business service; ~ **de envío urgente** COM GEN, COMS express delivery service; ~ **extendido a todo el mundo** TRANSP round the world service (*Rws*); ~ **de extensión** FIN, GES extension service; ~ **exterior** FIN, GES extension service; ~ **de ferrocarril** TRANSP railroad service (*AmE*), railway service (*BrE*); ~ **fijo del fondo consolidado** ECON consolidated fund standing service (*BrE*); ~ **de financiación de opción múltiple** BOLSA multioption financing facility (*MOFF*); ~ **financiero** FIN financial service; ~ **financiero de aceptación** BANCA acceptance facility; ~ **financiero de suscripción parcial** BOLSA tranche underwritten facility (*TUF*); ~ **de fondos ampliados** FIN extended fund facility; ~ **de gama baja** V&M down market service; ~ **general** FISC utility; ~ **general del Estado** ECON *balanza comercial* general government service; ~ **de gestión de la cartera de valores** BANCA, BOLSA portfolio management service; ~ **de habitaciones** OCIO room service; ~ **hipotecario** BANCA, FIN mortgage servicing; ~ **importado** FISC imported service; ~ **industrial** IND industrial service; ~ **de informática** INFO computer department; ~ **a intervalos** TRANSP interval service; ~ **de inversión** FIN investment service; ~ **de localización precisa** TRANSP precise positioning service (*PPS*); ~ **marítimo** TRANSP maritime service; ~ **de marketing** V&M marketing service; ~ **mecanográfico** ADMIN typing service; ~ **de mensajería** COM GEN, COMS courier service; ~ **mercante** TRANSP merchant service; ~ **mínimo** TRANSP skeleton service; ~ **nodriza** TRANSP parent service; ~ **de opción múltiple** BOLSA multioption facility (*MOF*); ~ **de paquetes postales** COMS parcel post; ~ **personalizado** V&M customized service; ~ **de perspectivas de mercado** V&M market prospects service; ~ **de posventa** V&M after-sales service, backup service, post-sales service; ~ **de preparación de proyectos** (*SPP*) FIN project preparation facility (*PPF*); ~ **de préstamo respaldado** BANCA, FIN backstop loan facility; ~ **de preventa** V&M presales service; ~ **profesional** COM GEN professional service; ~ **programado** OCIO, TRANSP scheduled service; ~ **público** COM GEN public utility, public service; ~ **de recogida y reparto a domicilio** TRANSP pick-up service; ~ **regular** OCIO, TRANSP regular service, scheduled service; ~ **de reparto** TRANSP delivery service; ~ **de respuesta** COM GEN answering service; ~ **de respuesta comercial** V&M business reply service; ~ **de respuesta telefónica** COM GEN, COMS, V&M telephone answering service; ~ **de ría** TRANSP estuarial service; ~ **rural de entrega gratuita** COMS rural free delivery service (*RFDS*); ~ **de seguridad** PROT SOC security service;

~ **del tanque de carga** TRANSP cargo tank common (*CTX*); ~ **técnico** ECON technical assistance; ~ **de tráfico de buques** TRANSP vessel traffic service; ~ **de transbordadores** TRANSP shuttle service; ~ **de transporte en camión** TRANSP lorry service (*BrE*), truck service (*AmE*); ~ **de transporte esporádico** TRANSP sporadic service; ~ **de transporte multimodal** TRANSP multimodal transport service; ~ **de transporte urgente** COM GEN, COMS, TRANSP express delivery service; ~ **triangular** TRANSP triangle service; ~ **universitario mundial** PROT SOC World University Service (*WUS*); ~ **urgente de correos** COM GEN, COMS express mail service; ~ **de 24 horas** COM GEN around-the-clock service (*AmE*), round-the-clock service (*BrE*), twenty-four hour service; ~ **de ventas** V&M sales service; ~ **de viajeros** OCIO, TRANSP passenger service; ~ **de viajes** ECON, OCIO travel service; ◆ **estar fuera de** ~ COM GEN, COMS, IND *teléfono, máquina* be out of action, be out of service; ~ **no incluido** COM GEN, OCIO service not included; **al** ~ **de Su Majestad** COM GEN On Her Majesty's Service (*OHMS*)

Servicio: ~ **de Aduanas** *m* IMP/EXP Spanish excise department, ≈ Customs & Excise Department (*BrE*) (*C&E*), ≈ Her Majesty's Customs and Excise (*BrE*) (*HMC&E*); ~ **de Asesoramiento de Inversiones** *m* BOLSA Investment Advisory Service; ~ **Conjunto de Contenedores de Líneas Marítimas Europeas y Británicas** *m* COM GEN, TRANSP British & European Shipping Lines Joint Container Service (*BEACON*); **el** ~ **Diplomático** *m* ADMIN, POL ≈ the Diplomatic Service (*BrE*); ~ **de Intercambio de Información Jurídica** *m* DER Legal Exchange Information Service (*LEXIS*); ~ **Internacional de Información Marítima** *m* TRANSP International Shipping Information Service (*ISIS*); ~ **Internacional para Investigación Agrícola Nacional** *m* ECON *agricultura* International Service for National Agricultural Research (*ISNAR*); ~ **de Investigación de la Recaudación** *m* FISC Collection Investigation Unit; ~ **de Protección al Consumidor y al Medio Ambiente** *m* MED AMB, PROT SOC Environment and Consumer Protection Service (*ECPS*); ~ **de Rescate** *m* PROT SOC Search and Rescue (*SAR*); ~ **Rescate Internacional** *m* PROT SOC International Search and Rescue (*International SAR*); ~ **Social Internacional** *m* PROT SOC International Social Service (*ISS*)

servicios: **sólo** ~ **administrativos** *fra* ADMIN, FIN administrative services only; **por** ~ **prestados** *fra* COM GEN for services rendered

Servicios: ~ **Integrados para el Empleo** *m* (*SIPE*) RRHH ≈ Jobcentre (*BrE*)

servidor *m* INFO host computer, mainframe, server; ~ **de ficheros** INFO file server

servidumbre *f* DER, INMOB easement; ~ **de paso** DER right-of-way; ~ **tácita** DER implied easement; ~ **turística** INMOB scenic easement

servir 1. *vt* BOLSA *pedidos* execute, COM GEN, V&M *al mercado* serve; **2.** *vi* COM GEN serve; ◆ ~ **para el caso** COM GEN serve the purpose; ~ **como garante de alguien** FIN stand as guarantor for sb

sesgo *m* TRANSP bias

sesión *f* COM GEN, INFO session; ~ **de calentamiento** GES warm-up session; ~ **de cierre** BOLSA closing session; ~ **de contratación** BOLSA trading session; ~ **informativa** COM GEN briefing session; ~ **de noche**

OCIO evening performance, late show; **~ plenaria** COM GEN plenum; **~ práctica** POL hands-on session; **~ de trabajo** CONT working session; **última ~ bursátil** BOLSA last trading day

sesionar *vi AmL* (*cf reunirse en sesión parlamentaria Esp*) POL *parlamento* sit

SEU *abr* (*Sindicato de Estudiantes Universitarios*) PROT SOC ≈ NUS (*National Union of Students*)

seudónimo *m* INFO alias

seudoprueba: ~ de producto *f* V&M pseudo product testing

s.e.u.o. *abr* (*salvo error u omisión*) COM GEN e.&o.e. (*errors and omissions excepted*)

SGBD *abr* (*sistema de gestión de base de datos*) INFO DBMS (*database management system*)

si: ~, como y cuando *adv* COM GEN if, as and when; **~ no intervienen otros factores** *fra* COM GEN all else being equal

SICAV *abr* (*sociedad de inversión de capital variable*) BOLSA, FIN unit trust

siempre: ~ y cuando *fra* COM GEN provided that

sierra: ~ sinfín *f* IND band saw

Siete: ~ intermedio *m* CONT Middle Seven

SIG *abr* (*sistema de información para la gestión*) GES MIS (*management information system*)

sigla *f* COM GEN acronym

signatario *m* COM GEN maker

significación: ~ marginal *f* ECON marginal significance

significado: ~ secundario *m* V&M secondary meaning

significante *adj* COM GEN significant

significar *vt* COM GEN *indicar* signify

significativo *adj* COM GEN significant

signo *m* COM GEN sign; **~ del indicador electrónico** BOLSA ticker symbol; **~ de inserción** MEDIOS, V&M caret; **~ monetario** ECON counter signatory (*CS*); **~ de referencia** PATENT reference sign; **~ de resta** MAT minus sign; **~ de suma** MAT plus sign; **~ técnico** BOLSA technical sign

silvicultura *f* COM GEN forestry

símbolo *m* COM GEN symbol; **~ corporativo** COM GEN organizational symbol; **~ para el marcaje de la carga** TRANSP cargo marking symbol; **~ monetario** COM GEN currency symbol; **~ de prestigio** COM GEN status symbol

simpatizante *mf* COM GEN sympathiser

simplificación: ~ de puestos *f* GES, RRHH job simplification; **~ del trabajo** *f* GES, RRHH work simplification

simplificar *vt* COM GEN simplify; **~ cuestiones** COM GEN simplify matters

simposio *m* COM GEN symposium

simulación *f* COM GEN, INFO simulation; **~ por computador** *AmL ver simulación por computadora AmL*; **~ por computadora** *AmL* (*cf simulación por ordenador Esp*) INFO computer simulation; **~ estocástica** GES stochastic simulation; **~ por ordenador** *Esp* (*cf simulación por computadora AmL*) INFO computer simulation; **~ del viaje de un buque de línea regular** TRANSP liner voyage simulation

simular *vt* COM GEN, INFO simulate

simultaneidad: ~ de periféricos *f* INFO spooling

simultáneo *adj* COM GEN simultaneous

sin[1]: con y ~ *adj* BOLSA cum and ex

sin[2] *prep* COM GEN without (*w/o*); **~ número** (*s/n*) COM GEN, COMS no number

sinceridad *f* COM GEN sincerity

sincero *adj* COM GEN above-board, RRHH straightforward

sincronización *f* COM GEN synchronization (*sync*); **~ del mercado** BOLSA market timing

sincronizado *adj* COM GEN synchronized; ♦ **no ~** COM GEN out of sync

sincronizar *vt* BOLSA lock in

síncrono *adj* INFO synchronous

sindicado *adj* RRHH unionized, V&M syndicated; **no ~** RRHH non-union

sindicalismo *m* POL, RRHH syndicalism, trade unionism (*BrE*)

sindicalista *mf* POL, RRHH union member

sindicalización *f* POL, RRHH unionization

sindicar *vt* BANCA *préstamo* syndicate

sindicato *m* COM GEN union, trade union (*BrE*) (*TU*), syndicate (*AmE*); **~ abierto** RRHH open union; **~ afiliado** RRHH affiliated trade union; **~ bancario** BANCA banking syndicate, syndicate; **~ blanco** *AmL* (*cf sindicato de empresa Esp*) RRIII company union, enterprise union; **~ de compra** V&M buying syndicate; **~ cualificado** RRHH skilled union; **~ distribuidor** BOLSA distributing syndicate; **~ de empleados** RRHH white-collar union; **~ de empresa** *Esp* (*cf sindicato blanco AmL*) RRHH company union, enterprise union; **~ esquirol** *infrml* RRHH scab union (*infrml*); **~ fragmentado** RRHH splinter union; **~ general** RRHH general union; **~ genuino** RRHH bona fide trade union; **~ independiente** COM GEN, RRHH independent union, independent trade union; **~ de industria** RRHH industrial union; **~ internacional** BANCA, ECON international syndication, international union; **~ de inversores** BOLSA syndicate of investors; **~ laboral** RRHH occupational union; **~ local de impresores** RRHH chapel (*BrE*); **~ nacional** RRHH national union; **~ no afiliado** RRHH unaffiliated union; **~ obrero** COM GEN, RRHH direct labor organization (*AmE*), direct labour organization (*BrE*), labor union (*AmE*), labour union (*BrE*); **~ de periódicos** MEDIOS *prensa* newspaper syndicate; **~ periodístico** MEDIOS *prensa* newspaper syndicate; **~ profesional** RRHH horizontal union; **~ reconocido** POL, RRHH recognized trade union (*BrE*), recognized labor union (*AmE*); **~ separatista** RRHH breakaway union; **~ de trabajadores** RRHH labor union (*AmE*), Trade Union (*BrE*) (*TU*); **~ de trabajadores manuales** RRHH manual union; **~ de trabajadores no manuales** RRHH nonmanual union; **~ vertical** RRHH vertical union

Sindicato: ~ de Electricistas *m* RRHH Electrical Trades Union (*ETU*); **~ de Estudiantes Universitarios** *m* (*SEU*) PROT SOC ≈ National Union of Students (*NUS*); **~ General de Agricultores y Ganaderos** *m Esp* ECON, RRHH ≈ National Farmers Union (*BrE*) (*NFU*); **~ de Gremios Eléctricos** *m* RRHH Electrical Trades Union (*ETU*); **~ Internacional de Ferrocarriles** *m* TRANSP International Union of Railways (*IUR*); **~ Internacional de Organizaciones de Viajes Oficiales** *m* TRANSP International Union of Official Travel Organizations (*IUOTO*); **~ Internacional de Transporte por Carretera** *m* TRANSP International Road Transport Union (*IRU*); **~ de Trabajadores de**

la **Industria Automotriz** *m* RRHH ≈ United Automobile Workers (*AmE*) (*UAW*)

síndico[1]**,-a** *m,f* BOLSA government broker, trustee, COM GEN receiver, trustee; **~ y administrador(a)** COM GEN *bancarrota* receiver and manager; **~ de la bolsa** BOLSA government broker; **~ oficial** COM GEN official receiver; **~ en quiebra** BANCA trustee in bankruptcy

síndico[2]: **~ bancario** *m* BANCA, BOLSA syndicate

síndrome: **~ del edificio enfermo** *m* PROT SOC sick building syndrome

sinecura *f* RRHH sinecure

sinergía *f* COM GEN, ECON synergy

sinergismo *m* COM GEN, ECON synergism

siniestro: **~ al contado** *m* COM GEN cash loss; **~ catastrófico** *m* COM GEN catastrophic loss; **~ conocido** *m* SEG known loss; **~ pagado** *m* SEG claim paid; **~ total** *m* FIN write-off

sinopsis *f* COM GEN synopsis

sintaxis *f* INFO syntax

síntesis *f* COM GEN synthesis

sintético *adj* COM GEN synthetic, IND man-made

sintonización: **~ fina automática** *f* INFO automatic fine tuning (*AFT*); **~ precisa** *f* INFO fine tuning

SIPE *abr* (*Servicios Integrados para el Empleo*) RRHH ≈ Jobcentre (*BrE*)

sistema *m* COM GEN system;

~ a **~ de activos de riesgo** BANCA risk asset system; **~ de acuñación** ECON coinage system; **~ de administración** GES management system; **~ de administración financiera** FIN financial administration system; **~ administrativo** GES management system; **~ administrativo sobre la marcha** GES operations administration system; **~ de admisión temporal** IMP/EXP carnet system; **~ de ajuste mensual de la paridad del cambio** ECON crawling peg system; **~ alodial** DER allodial system; **~ altavoces** COM GEN, COMS public address system (*PA system*); **~ de amortización** ECON medium of redemption; **~ por antigüedad** RRHH seniority system; **~ antivegetativo** TRANSP *navegación* anti-fouling system; **~ anualizado de horas** RRHH annualized hours system; **~ arancelario** ECON, FISC, IMP/EXP, POL tariff system; **~ de archivo** ADMIN filing system; **~ autex** BOLSA autex system; **~ de autoliquidación** FISC self-assessing system; **~ autónomo** INFO stand-alone system;

~ b **~ bancario** BANCA banking system; **~ bancario Goldsmith** BANCA Goldsmith banking system (*BrE*); **~ bancario interno** BANCA domestic banking system; **~ bancario con sucursales** BANCA branch banking system; **~ bidireccional** TRANSP two-way scheme; **~ de bienestar social** PROT SOC social system; **~ de bonificación fiscal** FISC tax-credit system; **~ de botadura** TRANSP floating production system (*FPS*);

~ c **~ de caja chica** *AmL* (*cf sistema de fondo fijo Esp*) CONT imprest system; **~ de carga sobre residuos** TRANSP *petrolero* load-on-top system; **~ central de reservas** OCIO central reservation system; **~ centro periferia** ECON center peryphery system (*AmE*), centre periphery system (*BrE*); **~ de codificación** CONT coding system; **~ de colas** ECON queueing system; **~ de comisiones** RRHH commission system; **~ de compensación** BANCA, BOLSA clearing system; **~ de compensación de cheques** BANCA cheque-clearing system (*BrE*), check-clearing system (*AmE*); **~ de**

compensación mutua BOLSA Mutual Offset System; **~ de compra de un pagaré garantizado** BOLSA securitized note commitment facility (*SNCF*); **~ común** FISC *UE* common system; **~ concesiones mutuas** MEDIOS logrolling (*infrml*) (*AmE*); **~ de conexión entre intermediarios** BOLSA interdealer-broker system (*IDBS*); **~ de conferencias** COM GEN, GES conference system; **~ de contabilidad automatizado** CONT, INFO computerized accounting system, electronic accounting system; **~ de contabilidad auxiliar** CONT subsidiary accounting system; **~ de contabilidad computadorizada** *AmL* CONT, INFO computer accounting, electronic accounting system; **~ de contabilidad computadorizado** *AmL* CONT, INFO computer accounting, electronic accounting system; **~ de contabilidad informatizada** *Esp* CONT computer accounting, electronic accounting system, INFO computer accounting; **~ de contabilidad informatizado** *Esp* CONT, INFO computerized accounting system; **~ de contabilidad principal** CONT principal accounting system; **~ de contabilidad suplementario** CONT supplementary accounting system; **~ contable** CONT accounting system; **~ de control de caja** CONT cash control system; **~ de control del tráfico aéreo** TRANSP air-traffic control system; **~ de coste estándar** *Esp* (*cf sistema de costo estándar AmL*) COM GEN standard-cost system; **~ de costes estimados** *Esp* (*cf sistema de costos estimados AmL*) CONT estimated costs system; **~ de costes por órdenes de trabajo** *Esp* (*cf sistema de costos por órdenes de trabajo AmL*) CONT job cost system; **~ de costo estándar** *AmL* (*cf sistema de coste estándar Esp*) COM GEN standard-cost system; **~ de costos estimados** *AmL* (*cf sistema de costes estimados Esp*) CONT estimated costs system; **~ de costos por órdenes de trabajo** *AmL* (*cf sistema de costes por órdenes de trabajo Esp*) CONT job cost system; **~ de cotización consolidada** BOLSA consolidated quotation system; **~ de crédito por giro bancario** BANCA bank giro credit system *BrE*; **~ de cuenta doble** CONT double account system; **~ de cuentas** CONT system of accounts; **~ de cumplimiento de las obligaciones tributarias** FISC compliance system; **~ de cuotas** COM GEN quota system; **~ de cupos** IMP/EXP quota system;

~ d **~ desmontable** TRANSP demountable system; **~ de dirección** GES management system, TRANSP steering system; **~ de distribución de costes de servicios comunes** *Esp* (*cf sistema de distribución de costos de servicios comunes AmL*) CONT common service cost distribution system; **~ de distribución de costos de servicios comunes** *AmL* (*cf sistema de distribución de costes de servicios comunes Esp*) CONT common service cost distribution system; **~ distribuido** INFO distributed system; **~ de doble tarifa** FISC two-rate system; **~ de dos niveles** COM GEN two-tier system;

~ e **~ de economía mixta** ECON, POL mixed economic system; **~ económico** ECON, POL business system, economic system; **~ económico avanzado** ECON advanced organic economy; **~ electrónico de transferencia de fondos** BANCA electronic funds transfer system (*EFTS*); **~ de emisión aprobado** BOLSA approved delivery facility; **~ de emisión de un pagaré a corto plazo** BOLSA short-term note issuance facility (*SNIF*); **~ empresarial** COM GEN business system; **~ energético** IND energy system; **~ de entrega** BOLSA *de futuros* delivery system; **~ escalonado de**

participación *f* POL ladder of participation (*jarg*); ~ **de estimación presunta** FISC forfeit system; ~ **experto** COM GEN, INFO expert system (*ES*), knowledge-based system (*KBS*);

~ f ~ **de fabricación** IND manufacturing system; ~ **financiero** FIN financial system; ~ **fiscal** ECON, FISC, POL fiscal system, tax system, taxation system; ~ **de flotación controlada** ECON managed floating system; ~ **de fondo fijo** *Esp* (*cf sistema de caja chica AmL*) CONT imprest system;

~ g ~ **de gas inerte** COM GEN inert gas system (*IGS*); ~ **general de preferencias** ECON, IMP/EXP generalized system of preferences (*GSP*); ~ **generalizado de tarifas y preferencias** ECON, IMP/EXP generalized system of tariffs and preferences (*GSTP*); ~ **de gestión ambiental** MED AMB Environmental Management System; ~ **de gestión y auditoría ecológica** MED AMB eco audit and management system; ~ **de gestión de base de datos** (*SGBD*) INFO database management system (*DBMS*); ~ **de gestión de caja** BANCA cash management system; ~ **de gestión financiera** FIN financial management system; ~ **de gestión de gastos y política** FIN policy and expenditure management system; ~ **de gestión integrado** GES integrated management system; ~ **de gestión del tráfico de buques** TRANSP vessel traffic management system (*VTMS*); ~ **global de atención sanitaria** PROT SOC comprehensive health-care system;

~ h ~ **del hombre y la máquina** IND man-machine system;

~ i ~ **impositivo** ECON, FISC, POL fiscal system, tax system, taxation system, system of taxation; ~ **indefectible** INFO fault-tolerant system; ~ **industrial** IND industrial system; ~ **de información** INFO information system; ~ **de información administrativo** GES management information system (*MIS*); ~ **de información automatizada de apertura** BOLSA opening automated report system (*OARS*); ~ **de información departamental** ADMIN departmental reporting system; ~ **de información para la gestión** (*SIG*) GES management information system (*MIS*); ~ **de información de marketing** V&M *estudio* marketing information system (*MIS*); ~ **de información y presupuestación financiera** FIN financial information and budgeting system (*FIBS*); ~ **informático** INFO computer system; ~ **informatizado de sincronización del mercado** BOLSA, INFO computerized market timing system; ~ **de informes** FIN reporting system; ~ **interactivo** INFO interactive system;

~ l ~ **legal** DER legal system; ~ **de libre empresa** ECON, free enterprise system; ~ **de libre mercado** ECON free market system; ~ **de límite de crédito** BANCA, FIN credit rating system; ~ **en línea** INFO on-line system; ~ **de liquidación bancaria** BANCA bank settlement system; ~ **Lloyd's de compatibilidad instantánea** SEG Lloyd's Instantaneous Accounting System (*LIARS*); ~ **LOT** TRANSP *tanque de gasolina* LOT system;

~ m ~ **manual** COM GEN manual system (*MS*); ~ **mayoritario** POL majority rule; ~ **de mercado** COM GEN market system; ~ **métrico** COM GEN metric system; ~ **monetario internacional** ECON international monetary system; ~ **monetario mundial** ECON, FIN world monetary system; ~ **monetario de mercancía patrón** ECON commodity standard;

~ n ~ **nacional** ECON domestic system; ~ **nacional de**

mercado BOLSA National Market System (*NMS*); ~ **de negociación asistido por computador** *AmL ver sistema de negociación asistido por computadora AmL*; ~ **de negociación asistido por computadora** *AmL* (*cf sistema de negociación asistido por ordenador Esp*) BOLSA, INFO computer-assisted trading system (*CATS*); ~ **de negociación asistido por ordenador** *Esp* (*cf sistema de negociación asistido por computadora AmL*) BOLSA, INFO computer-assisted trading system (*CATS*); ~ **de negocios** COM GEN business system; ~ **normalizado de clasificación industrial** IND standard industrial classification system;

~ o ~ **de objetivos** FISC goal system; ~ **operativo** (*SO*) INFO operation system (*OS*); ~ **operativo de administración** GES management operating system; ~ **operativo de discos** (*DOS*) INFO disk operating system (*DOS*); ~ **operativo entre mercados** BOLSA Intermarket Trading System (*AmE*);

~ p ~ **de pago por cheque** BANCA check payment system (*AmE*), cheque payment system (*BrE*); ~ **de pago a destajo** *AmL* (*cf sistema de pago por pieza Esp*) RRHH piecework system; ~ **de pago no al contado** BANCA cashless payment system, noncash payment system; ~ **de pago por pieza** *Esp* (*cf sistema de pago a destajo AmL*) RRHH piecework system; ~ **de pagos** ECON payment system; ~ **de pagos automáticos de compensación** BANCA Clearing House Automatic Payments System (*CHAPS*); ~ **de periferia axial** ECON center periphery system (*AmE*), centre periphery system (*BrE*); ~ **de planificación, programación y presupuesto** CONT, FIN planning-programming-budgeting system; ~ **de precios** ECON price system; ~ **predeterminado de movimiento-tiempo** COM GEN, ECON, FIN, GES predetermined motion-time system (*PMTS*); ~ **presupuestario** CONT budget system; ~ **del presupuesto** CONT budget system; ~ **de primas medias** SEG average premium system; ~ **privado de empresa** ECON private enterprise system; ~ **de procesamiento de datos** INFO data processing system (*DPS*); ~ **de procesamiento de texto** INFO word-processing system; ~ **de producción a bordo** TRANSP floating production system (*FPS*); ~ **progresivo de impuesto sobre la renta** FISC progressive income tax system; ~ **progresivo de tributación** FISC progressive tax system; ~ **propio** INFO in-house system; ~**-proveedor** FIN system-provider; ~ **de punto de pedido** TRANSP order point system;

~ r ~ **de recompensas** POL *corrupción* spoils system (*AmE*); ~ **de recuperación acelerada de costes** *Esp* (*cf sistema de recuperación acelerada de costos AmL*) CONT, FIN accelerated cost recovery system (*ACRS*); ~ **de recuperación acelerada de costos** *AmL* (*cf sistema de recuperación acelerada de costes Esp*) CONT, FIN accelerated cost recovery system (*ACRS*); ~ **de recuperación de documentos** INFO document retrieval system; ~ **de recuperación de información** INFO information retrieval system; ~ **recursivo** ECON recursive system; ~ **de refinanciación de dividendos** BOLSA dividend rollover plan; ~ **regulador** DER regulatory system; ~ **de remuneración por incentivos** RRHH incentive payment system; ~ **de repercusión contra ejercicios anteriores** FISC carry-back system; ~ **de repercusión contra ejercicios posteriores** FISC carry-forward system; ~ **de reserva** COM GEN, OCIO, V&M reservation system, booking system; ~ **de reserva de**

inversión FIN investment reserve system; **~ de reserva de plazas** OCIO seat reservation system; **~ de respaldo** BOLSA *para opciones* backup system; **~ rojo y verde** IMP/EXP *declaración en aduanas* red and green system;

~ s **~ salarial** RRHH wage system; **~ de seguimiento** COM GEN tracking system; **~ de seguridad de la armadura sólida** TRANSP solid frame securing system; **~ de separación del tráfico** TRANSP traffic separation scheme; **~ sincrónico** TRANSP synchronous system; **~ sincronizado** TRANSP synchronous system; **~ sociotécnico** COM GEN sociotechnical system; **~ STABEX** ECON *agricultura* stabex system; **~ de sugerencias** COM GEN suggestion scheme;

~ t **~ de tablón de anuncios** COMS bulletin board system (*BBS*); **~ de transferencia bancaria** BANCA banking transfer system; **~ de tránsito rápido** TRANSP rapid transit system; **~ de transporte** TRANSP transport system; **~ de transporte colectivo** TRANSP mass transit system; **~ de transporte intermodal** TRANSP intermodal transport system; **~ de transporte público** TRANSP public transport system, mass transit system; **~ de transporte total** TRANSP through transport system; **~ tributario** ECON, FISC, POL fiscal system, tax system, taxation system; **~ tributario del impuesto sobre la renta** ECON, FISC, POL income tax system;

~ u **~ de usuarios múltiples** INFO multiuser system;

~ v **~ de vales** V&M voucher system; **~ de venta pública** BOLSA open outcry system

Sistema: **el ~** *m* COM GEN, POL the Establishment (*BrE*); **~ Bancario de Compensación Automática** *m* BANCA Banks Automated Clearing System (*BACS*); **~ para el Control y Seguimiento del Medio Ambiente** *m* MED AMB Global Environment Monitoring System; **~ de Crédito Agrícola** *m* ECON Farm Credit System; **~ de Cuentas Nacionales** *m* CONT System of National Accounts (*SNA*); **~ Departamental de Procesamiento de las Entradas** *m* IMP/EXP Departmental Entry processing System (*DEPS*); **~ Económico Latinoamericano** *m* ECON Latin American economic system; **~ Europeo de Bancos Centrales** *m* BANCA, ECON European System of Central Banks; **~ Global para Casos de Peligro y Seguridad Marítimos** *m* TRANSP Global Maritime Distress and Safety System (*GMDSS*); **~ de Liquidación de Compensación Automatizado** *m* BANCA Automated Clearing Settlement System (*ACSS*); **~ de Liquidación de la Cuentas de Carga** *m* TRANSP Cargo Accounts Settlement System (*CASS*); **~ de Mercados de Capital del Banco Mundial** *m* BANCA, BOLSA World Bank Capital Markets System (*CMS*); **~ Monetario Europeo** *m* (*SME*) ECON, POL European Monetary System (*EMS*); **~ Terminal de Artículos Restringidos** *m* TRANSP Restricted Articles Terminal System (*RATS*)

sistemas[1]: **~ y procedimientos** *m pl* COM GEN, INFO systems and procedures

sistemas[2]: **un país, dos ~** *fra* ECON one country, two systems

sistemático *adj* COM GEN systematic

sistematización: **~ de datos** *f* INFO information processing

sistematizar *vt* COM GEN systematize

SITF *abr* (*Sociedad Internacional de Telecomunicaciones Financieras*) BANCA, COMS SWIFT (*Society for Worldwide Interbank Financial Telecommunications*)

sitio *m* COM GEN, IND site

situación *f* COM GEN position; **~ aislada** ECON isolated state; **~ de la bolsa al cierre** BOLSA closing stock; **~ comercial** COM GEN business situation; **~ económica** COM GEN, ECON, POL economic situation; **~ de efectivo** CONT cash position; **~ de la empresa** RRHH corporate status; **~ especial** COM GEN special situation; **~ financiera** CONT, FIN financial situation; **~ fiscal** FISC tax position; **~ hipotética** COM GEN hypothetical situation; **~ de los instrumentos emitidos** BANCA statement of instruments issued; **~ jurídica** DER legal status; **~ laboral** COM GEN, RRHH employment situation; **~ de liquidez y deudas** BANCA cash and debt position; **~ del mercado** COM GEN market situation; **~ migratoria** DER migrant status; **~ del personal** RRHH staff status; **~ política** COM GEN, POL political situation; **~ precaria** FISC extreme hardship; **~ presupuestaria** FIN, POL budgetary statement; **~ de residencia** FISC residence status; **~ del riesgo** SEG description of risk; **~ de la teoría de la propiedad** DER title theory state; **~ de tesorería** CONT cash position; **~ de transacción** COM GEN, IND, V&M transaction status; ◆ **cualquier ~** SEG *marino* any one location (*AOLOC*); **en la ~ actual** COM GEN in the present state of affairs; **tener la ~ bajo control** COM GEN have the situation well in hand; **en ~ de estancamiento** COM GEN in the doldrums; **en ~ de excedente financiero** ECON, FIN in financial surplus; **en ~ de superávit financiero** ECON, FIN in financial surplus

situarse: **~ por delante de** *fra* BOLSA *mercado bursátil*, FIN advance

S.L. *abr* (*sociedad limitada*) COM GEN ≈ private limited company

slogan *m* MEDIOS, V&M *anuncios* advertising slogan, slogan

SME *abr* (*Sistema Monetario Europeo*) ECON, POL EMS (*European Monetary System*)

SMMD *abr* (*sociedad mediadora en el mercado de dinero*) BOLSA discount store (*BrE*), discount house (*AmE*)

s/n *abr* (*sin número*) COM GEN, COMS no number

SO *abr* (*sistema operativo*) INFO OS (*operation system*)

soberano *m* COM GEN *moneda*, POL *el Rey* sovereign

sobornar *vt* COM GEN bribe, buy (*infrml*)

soborno *m Esp* (*cf coima AmL*) COM GEN, DER, FIN, POL, RRHH bribe, graft (*infrml*) (*BrE*), kickback (*infrml*) (*AmE*), V&M *publicidad* payola (*infrml*) (*AmE*), bribe (*BrE*)

sobrante *m* SEG excess; ◆ **con ~ de liquidez** COM GEN awash with cash (*infrml*)

sobre: **~ acolchado** *m* COM GEN Jiffy bag®; **~ de bolsillo** *m* V&M pocket envelope; **~ impreso con franqueo pagado** *m* V&M business reply envelope (*BRE*); **~ de la paga** *m* COM GEN, RRHH pay packet, pay slip; **~ de respuesta comercial** *m* COMS business reply envelope (*BRE*); **~ con ventanilla** *m* ADMIN, COMS window envelope; ◆ **en ~ cerrado** ADMIN, COMS in a sealed envelope

sobreacumulación *f* ECON overaccumulation

sobreasegurado *adj* SEG over insured

sobrecapitalizado *adj* COM GEN overcapitalized

sobrecarga *f* COMS *líneas telefónicas* congestion, TRANSP overstuffing; **~ por congestión** TRANSP congestion surcharge; **~ de gasóleo** TRANSP fuel surcharge; **~ de**

petróleo TRANSP bunkering surcharge; ~ **sensorial** GES sensory overload

sobrecolocación *f* BANCA overplacing

sobrecomisión *f* OCIO *mercado turístico*, SEG *aseguramiento* overriding commission

sobrecomprado *adj* BOLSA overbought

sobrecontratación *f* TRANSP overbooking

sobrecontratado *adj* TRANSP *vuelos* overbooked

sobrecoste *m Esp* (*cf* sobrecosto *AmL*) ECON cost overrun

sobrecosto *m AmL* (*cf* sobrecoste *Esp*) ECON cost overrun

sobrecubierta *f* MEDIOS jacket

sobredependencia *f* COM GEN overdependence

sobredimensionado *adj* COM GEN top-heavy

sobreembalaje *m* TRANSP overpack

sobreempleo *m* COM GEN, RRHH excess employment

sobreendeudamiento *m* BANCA overindebtedness

sobreestadía *f* TRANSP demurrage

sobreestimar *vt* COM GEN overestimate

sobreestimular *vt* COM GEN overstimulate

sobreexplotación *f* COM GEN overexploitation

sobreextendido *adj* COM GEN overextended

sobreflete *m* COM GEN extra freight

sobregasto *m* INMOB carrying charge

sobregirado *adj* BANCA overdrawn (*O/D*)

sobregirar *vt* BANCA overdraw

sobregiro *m* BANCA, FIN overdraft; ~ **bancario** BANCA bank overdraft; ~ **no garantizado** BANCA unsecured overdraft

sobreimpresión *f* V&M overprint

sobreinversión *f* BOLSA overtrading

sobreoferta: ~ **de trabajo** *f* RRHH high employment surplus

sobrepasar *vt* ADMIN, COM GEN exceed; ◆ ~ **el límite máximo** BOLSA break the ceiling

sobrepastoreo *m* MED AMB overgrazing

sobreprima *f jarg* RRHH loading (*jarg*)

sobreproducir *vt* ECON, IND overproduce

sobrepujar *vt* V&M outbid

sobrerrepresentación *f* V&M *en el mercado* overrepresentation

sobrerrepresentar *vt* V&M overrepresent

sobres: **en** ~ **separados** *fra* COMS *correo* under separate cover

sobresaliente *adj* COM GEN top-flight

sobrestante *mf* RRHH foreman

sobresuscrito *adj* BOLSA oversubscribed

sobretasa *f* COM GEN surcharge, FISC surtax; ~ **por acumulación** FISC congestion surcharge; ~ **aérea** TRANSP air fee; ~ **portuaria** TRANSP port surcharge; ~ **postal** COMS additional postage

sobreurbanización *f* ECON, MED AMB overurbanization

sobrevaloración *f* BOLSA *internacional* overvaluation

sobrevalorado *adj* BOLSA, COM GEN, ECON overvalued

sobrevaluar *vt* BOLSA, COM GEN, ECON overvalue

sobreventa *f* TRANSP overbooking

sobrevivir *vi* COM GEN, ECON survive

socavar *vt* ECON *a un competidor* undercut

social *adj* COM GEN social

socialdemocracia *f* ECON, POL social democracy

socialismo *m* POL socialism; ~ **gremial** RRHH guild socialism (*BrE*)

socialista *mf* POL socialist

socialización *f* PROT SOC, RRHH socialization

sociedad *f* COM GEN association, society; ~ **sin acciones** BOLSA nonstock company (*BrE*), nonstock corporation (*AmE*); ~ **de acciones cotizadas en bolsa** BANCA, BOLSA clearing corporation; ~ **anónima** (*S.A.*) COM GEN ≈ incorporated business company (*AmE*) (*Inc.*), ≈ limited company (*BrE*) (*Ltd*), ≈ public limited company (*BrE*) (*plc*); ~ **anónima por acciones** (*S.A.A.*) COM GEN ≈ incorporated business company (*AmE*) (*Inc.*), ≈ limited company (*BrE*) (*Ltd*), ≈ public limited company (*BrE*) (*plc*); ~ **anónima extranjera** DER alien corporation; ~ **anónima de seguros** BOLSA stock insurance company; ~ **de arrendamiento** INMOB leasing company; ~ **autoritaria** ECON authoritarian society; ~ **bancaria por acciones** BANCA incorporated bank (*AmE*); ~ **de beneficencia** FIN benefit society (*AmE*), friendly society (*BrE*); ~ **de cartera** BANCA, BOLSA, FIN holding company, holding corporation; ~ **de cartera de actividad mixta** BOLSA mixed activity holding company; ~ **de cartera financiera** FIN financial holding company; ~ **de clasificación de buques** COM GEN, TRANSP classification society; ~ **de colocación de valores** BOLSA issuing house; ~ **en comandita por acciones** BOLSA, COM GEN joint stock company; ~ **comanditaria** BOLSA, DER *comercial* limited partnership; ~ **comercial** COM GEN trading company, FISC corporate entity, IMP/EXP trading company; ~ **compasiva** ECON, POL, PROT SOC caring society; ~ **de consumidores** ECON, POL, V&M consumer society; ~ **de consumo** ECON, POL, V&M consumer society; ~ **de contrapartida** BOLSA market maker; ~ **de control** BANCA, BOLSA holding company, holding corporation, COM GEN controlling company, FIN holding company, holding corporation; ~ **de control del banco** BANCA bank holding company; ~ **cooperativa** COM GEN cooperative society; ~ **defraudadora de impuestos** FISC collapsible corporation (*AmE*), collapsible company (*BrE*); **la** ~ **del despilfarro** COM GEN the waste society; ~ **sin dinero** COM GEN cashless society; ~ **disuelta** ECON defunct company; ~ **envejecida** ECON grey society (*BrE*); ~ **de especulación dirigida con plenos poderes** FIN blind pool; ~ **exenta de contribución** FISC, SEG tax-exempt corporation; ~ **exenta de tributación** FISC, SEG tax-exempt corporation; ~ **extranjera** COM GEN, DER foreign company (*BrE*), foreign corporation (*AmE*); ~ **extraterritorial** DER out-of-state corporation; ~ **de facto** ECON de facto corporation; ~ **fantasma** COM GEN bogus company; ~ **fiduciaria de ultramar** DER offshore trust; ~ **filial** COM GEN, CONT, ECON, RRHH affiliated company; ~ **financiera cautiva** ECON, FIN captive finance company; ~ **financiera para la exportación** FIN export finance house; ~ **de gestión abierta** FIN, GES open-end management company; ~ **de gestión administrativa** FIN, GES administrative management society; ~ **gestora de capital limitado** FIN, GES closed-end management company; ~ **grande** ECON Great Society (*AmE*); ~ **hermana** COM GEN sister company; ~ **hipotecaria** BANCA, INMOB mortgage company; ~ **ilimitada** COM GEN unlimited company; ~ **industrial** ECON, IND industrial society; ~ **inmobiliaria** COM GEN, INMOB property company, real estate company; ~ **inquieta** ECON, POL, PROT SOC caring society; ~ **de intermediación bursátil** BOLSA stock brokerage firm; ~ **de intermediación miembro** BOLSA member corporation, member firm; ~ **interpuesta** BOLSA nominee, nominee company; ~ **de inversión abierta** BOLSA, FIN open-end investment company (*OEIC*); ~ **de inversión de capital variable** (*SICAV*) BOLSA, FIN unit trust; ~ **de inversión con cartera variable** BOLSA open-end investment company (*AmE*); ~ **de inversión cerrada** FIN closed-end investment company (*CEIC*); ~ **de inversión mobiliaria de capital fijo** BOLSA closed-end mutual fund (*AmE*); ~ **de inversiones energéticas** IND energy mutual fund; ~ **de inversiones de renta** FIN income investment company; ~ **inversora de capital limitado** BOLSA, FIN closed-end investment trust; ~ **inversora por obligaciones** BOLSA, FIN unit trust; ~ **legalmente constituida** COM GEN registered company; ~ **limitada** (*S.L.*) COM GEN ≈ private limited company; ~ **limitada de capital de riesgo** FIN venture capital limited partnership; ~ **limitada con cotización en bolsa** BOLSA public limited partnership; ~ **limitada sin cotización en bolsa** BOLSA private limited partnership; ~ **limitada de investigación y desarrollo** COM GEN research and development limited partnership; ~ **limitada principal** COM GEN master limited partnership; ~ **limitada de resindicación** INMOB resyndication limited partnership; ~ **mayorista en cooperativa** COM GEN Cooperative Wholesale Society (*CWS*); ~ **mediadora en el mercado de dinero** (*SMMD*) BOLSA discount house (*AmE*), discount store (*BrE*); ~ **mediadora en el mercado de dinero** (*SMMD*) BOLSA discount house (*AmE*), discount store (*BrE*); ~ **de minas** IND mining company; ~ **mutua** FIN, SEG mutual company, mutual corporation; ~ **opulenta** COM GEN affluent society; ~ **personal** COM GEN partnership; ~ **posindustrial** ECON, POL post-industrial society; ~ **principal** BANCA pure holding company; ~ **pública** COM GEN public corporation; ~ **que no cotiza en bolsa** BOLSA unlisted company; ~ **que realiza ciertas prácticas bancarias** BANCA, BOLSA nonbank bank; ~ **de reorganización industrial** IND industrial reorganization company (*IRC*); ~ **representante** CONT agent corporation; ~ **de responsabilidad ilimitada** COM GEN partnership; ~ **de responsabilidad limitada** (*S.R.L.*) COM GEN ≈ limited company (*Ltd*) (*BrE*), ≈ incorporated business company (*Inc.*) (*AmE*); ~ **de seguros sobre bonos municipales** SEG municipal bond insurance association; ~ **de servicios públicos** COM GEN public utility company; ~ **tenedora** FIN propietary company; ~ **de valores y bolsa** BOLSA full-service broker

Sociedad: ~ **Española de Radiodifusión** *f* (*SER*) COMS, MEDIOS Spanish broadcasting association; ~ **para las Telecomunicaciones Financieras Interbancarias Internacionales** *f* BANCA, COMS Society for Worldwide Interbank Financial Telecommunications (*SWIFT*)

socio, -a *m,f* COM GEN, RRHH partner; ~ **activo(-a)** BOLSA *de bolsa* trading member, GES active partner; ~ **administrador(a)** RRHH managing partner; ~ **colectivo(-a)** BOLSA, RRHH general partner; ~ **comanditario(-a)** DER limited owner, limited liability partner, commercial limited partner; ~ **comanditario(-a) inactivo(-a)** COM GEN sleeping partner; ~ **comercial** ECON, POL trading partner; ~ **corporativo(-a)** ECON corporate affiliate; ~ **director(a)** RRHH managing part-

ner; ~ **en funciones** GES acting partner; ~ **inactivo(-a)** DER sleeping partner (*BrE*); ~ **limitado(-a)** COM GEN limited partner; ~ **mejor posicionado(-a)** GES best positioned partner; ~ **menor** COM GEN junior partner; ~ **con participación mayoritaria** BOLSA majority interest partner; ~ **de servicios generales** CONT *empresa contable* general service partner

sociocultural *adj* PROT SOC, V&M sociocultural

socioeconómico *adj* ECON, PROT SOC, V&M socioeconomic

sociometría *f* MAT, V&M sociometry

sociométrico *adj* MAT, V&M sociometric

sofisticación *f* V&M *en el mercado* sophistication

software *m* INFO software; ~ **de auditoría** CONT, INFO audit software; ~ **del computador** *AmL ver software de la computadora AmL*; ~ **de la computadora** *AmL* (*cf programación del ordenador Esp*) INFO computer software; ~ **de contabilidad** CONT, INFO accounting software; ~ **de estadística** INFO, MAT statistical software; ~ **de gestión de transacciones** INFO transaction management software; ~ **de gestión de redes** INFO networking software; ~ **interno** INFO in-house software; ~ **de planificación financiera personal** FIN, INFO personal financial planning software; ~ **de procesamiento de textos** INFO word-processing software; ~ **de proceso de mensajes** INFO message processing program (*MPP*); ~ **de reconocimiento de la voz** INFO speech recognition software; ~ **de simulación financiera** FIN, INFO financial simulation software; ~ **para el tratamiento de datos fiscales** FISC, INFO tax software

solar *m* INMOB building lot, *de tierra* plot; ~ **desocupado** INMOB vacant lot

solicitación *f* V&M solicitation

solicitado *adj* COM GEN sought-after; **no** ~ COM GEN, DER, RRHH, V&M unsolicited

solicitante *mf* COM GEN applicant; ~ **de cotización** BOLSA applicant for registration

solicitar *vt* COM GEN *aprobación* seek, *un empleo, un puesto* apply for, MEDIOS, V&M advertise for; ◆ ~ **afiliación** COM GEN apply for membership; ~ **asesoramiento jurídico** DER seek legal advice; ~ **consejo jurídico** DER seek legal advice; ~ **una deducción** FISC claim a deduction; ~ **ofertas** BOLSA invite tenders; ~ **ofertas públicamente** V&M advertise for bids; ~ **personalmente** COM GEN, RRHH apply in person; ~ **un préstamo** BANCA, FIN apply for a loan; ~ **un préstamo sin intereses** BANCA borrow interest-free

solicitud *f* COM GEN application, appeal; ~ **admisible** PATENT admissible claim; ~ **de admisión** BOLSA application for admission; ~ **de capital** COM GEN appeal for funds; ~ **de cheque** BANCA, CONT check requisition (*AmE*), cheque requisition (*BrE*); ~ **de cheque de ventanilla** BANCA, FIN counter check form (*AmE*), counter cheque form (*BrE*); ~ **de cheques** BANCA, FIN check form (*AmE*), cheque form (*BrE*); ~ **de cotización** BOLSA application for listing; ~ **de desembolsos pendientes** BOLSA, CONT dividend requirement; ~ **de devolución** FISC claim for refund; ~ **de empleo** RRHH job application; ~ **de exención** FISC bill of sufferance; ~ **de fondos** FIN appeal for funds; ~ **no pedida** RRHH unsolicited application; ~ **de un nuevo pedido** COM GEN reorder form; ~ **de oferta** BOLSA offer wanted; ~ **de ofertas** COM GEN appeal for tenders, FIN request for proposals; ~ **de préstamo** BANCA loan demand, loan application, FIN loan demand; ~ **de préstamos por parte de los bancos** BANCA borrowing by banks; ~ **de subsidios** COM GEN application for subsidies; ~ **de trabajo especulativa** RRHH speculative application

solidariamente: ~ **pero no mancomunadamente** *fra* BOLSA, DER severally but not jointly

solidaridad *f* ECON, POL solidarity

solidario *adj* COM GEN *obligación* mutually binding

solidarismo *m* ECON, POL solidarism

solidez *f* COM GEN *mercado, acciones* firmness

solidificado *adj* V&M set solid

sólido[1] *adj* COM GEN strong, *argumento* solid

sólido[2]: ~ **suspendido** *m* IND suspended solid

solo *adj* COM GEN sole

soltar: ~ **amarras** *vt* TRANSP unmoor

soltero, a *m,f* COM GEN, DER single person

solución *f* COM GEN solution, *legal, financiero* remedy; ~ **alternativa** COM GEN alternative solution; ~ **de compromiso** COM GEN compromise solution; ~ **de esquina** ECON *programación lineal* corner solution; ~ **improvisada** COM GEN makeshift solution

solucionar *vt* COM GEN *abusos* remedy

solvencia *f* BANCA, CONT, FIN solvency, V&M credit standing; ~ **crediticia** BANCA, FIN credit scoring

solventar *vt* SEG *reclamación* adjust

solvente *adj* BANCA, COM GEN, CONT, FIN creditworthy, solvent

sombra *f* COM GEN shadow; ◆ **no hay ~ de corrupción** DER there is no suggestion of corruption

sombreado *m* INFO, MEDIOS *ilustración* shading

someter *vt* COM GEN submit; ◆ ~ **algo a votación** POL, RRHH take a ballot on sth; ~ **a aprobación una enmienda** DER table an amendment (*BrE*); ~ **a arbitraje** COM GEN submit to arbitration; ~ **a una presión excesiva** FISC *a contribuyente* impose undue hardship

someterse: ~ **al reglamento** *v refl* BOLSA go under the rule (*jarg*) (*AmE*)

sometido: ~ **a contingente** *fra* COM GEN subject to quota; **ser ~ a escrutinio** *fra* COM GEN come under scrutiny; ~ **a la prueba de los ingresos** *fra* FISC income-tested

sonda: ~ **de profundidad** *f* MED AMB depth sounder (*DS*)

sondear *vt* COM GEN sound out, POL, V&M canvass

sondeo *m* COM GEN, V&M survey, poll; ~ **de Gallup** V&M *investigación de mercado* Gallup poll; ~ **de opinión** V&M *investigación de mercado* opinion polling

sonido *m* INFO sound

sonoemisión *f* MED AMB noise emission

sopesar *vt* COM GEN balance; ◆ ~ **algo con algo** COM GEN balance sth against sth; ~ **los pros y los contras** COM GEN weigh up the pros and cons

soportar *vt* COM GEN *carga, responsabilidad* bear, DER *pérdida, daño* sustain; ◆ ~ **un cargo** CONT *cuenta* be debited to

soporte *m* INFO carrier; ~ **de datos** INFO data carrier; ~ **lógico** INFO software; ~ **publicitario** MEDIOS, V&M advertising medium; ~ **televisivo** MEDIOS, V&M *publicidad* television support; ~ **transitorio** V&M transient medium

sostén *m* FISC *de familiar dependiente* support

sostener *vt* BOLSA *el mercado* hold, COM GEN *gastos, objetivos* meet, CONT *pérdidas* sustain

sostenimiento: ~ **de los ingresos** *m* PROT SOC, RRHH income support (*BrE*); ~ **de los precios agrícolas** *m* ECON agricultural price support

spot *m* COM GEN, MEDIOS, V&M advertisement (*ad*)

SPP *abr* (*servicio de preparación de proyectos*) FIN PPF (*project preparation facility*)

S.R.L. *abr* (*sociedad de responsabilidad limitada*) COM GEN ≈ Ltd (*limited company*) (*BrE*), ≈ Inc. (*incorporated business company*) (*AmE*)

stagflación *f* ECON stagflation

stand *m* V&M *en exposición* stand (*jarg*)

stock: ~ **de seguridad** *m* BOLSA, ECON safety stock

straddle *f* BOLSA straddle

strangle: ~ **corta** *f* BOLSA *opciones* short strangle; ~ **delta-neutral** *f* BOLSA *opciones* delta-neutral strangle; ~ **larga** *f* BOLSA *opciones* long strangle

strip *m* BOLSA strip bond

suavemente *adv* COM GEN smoothly

suavizar *vt* COM GEN smooth out, ECON *política económica* ease, FISC relieve, GES *política* relax

subactividad *f* COM GEN, ECON subactivity

subagente *mf* COM GEN subagent

subalterno[1] *adj* RRHH subordinate

subalterno[2],**-a** *m,f infrml* COM GEN subaltern (*BrE*) (*sub*)

subarchivo *m* INFO subfile

subarrendatario, -a *m,f* INMOB subtenant, underlessee

subarriendo *m* COM GEN, INMOB sublease

subasignación *f* POL suballotment

subasta *f* COM GEN auction; ~ **a la baja** V&M Dutch auction; ~ **de conexión entre intermediarios** BOLSA interdealer-broker system (*IDBS*); ~ **híbrida** BOLSA hybrid auction

subastar *vt* COM GEN auction off

subcapacidad *f* COM GEN, IND undercapacity

subcapitalizado *adj* COM GEN, FIN, IND undercapitalized

subcapítulo *m* FISC subchapter

subclase *f* ECON underclass

Subcomité: ~ **Aeroportuario de Equipos de Manipulación** *m* TRANSP Airport Handling Equipment Sub-Committee (*AHESC*); ~ **Aeroportuario Sobre Manipulación de Carga** *m* TRANSP Airport Handling Agreements Sub-Committee (*AHASC*); ~ **de Asesoría Técnica** *m* TRANSP Technical Advisory Sub-Committee (*TASC*); ~ **de Procedimientos de Manipulación Aeroportuaria** *m* TRANSP Airport Handling Procedures Sub-Committee (*AHPSC*)

subcompacto *adj* COM GEN subcompact

subconcesión *f* COM GEN, PATENT sublicence (*BrE*), sublicense (*AmE*)

subconjunto *m* COM GEN subset

subconsumo *m* ECON underconsumption

subcontratación *f* COM GEN contracting out (*BrE*), subcontracting; ~ **exclusivamente de mano de obra** RRHH labor-only subcontracting (*AmE*), labour-only subcontracting (*BrE*)

subcontratar *vt* COM GEN subcontract, contract out, farm out (*infrml*), TRANSP subcharter

subcontratista *mf* COM GEN subcontractor

subcontrato *m* COM GEN subcontract

subcuenta *f* BANCA, CONT subsidiary account

subcustodia *f* FIN subcustody

subdirección *f* GES junior management

subdirector, a *m,f* COM GEN assistant director, assistant manager, deputy manager; **~ general** GES, RRHH assistant general manager; **~ gerente** GES, RRHH deputy managing director

subdirectorio *m* INFO subdirectory

subdividido *adj* COM GEN subdivided

subdivisión *f* COM GEN subdivision

subempleado *adj* RRHH underemployed

subempleo *m* ECON subemployment (*jarg*), RRHH underemployment

subentrada *f* INFO sub-entry

subestimación *f* BOLSA *de acciones* undervalue; **~ de la renta** FISC understatement of income

subestimar *vt* COM GEN underestimate

subgerente *mf* BANCA, GES, RRHH assistant manager

subgrupo *m* COM GEN subgroup

subholding *m* COM GEN subholding company

subida *f* COM GEN roll up, rise, CONT rise, V&M *de precios* increase, mark-up; **~ sin efecto** COM GEN *ventas* dead rise (*DR*); **~ gradual de los precios** ECON, V&M price escalation; **~ de precios** COM GEN, ECON, V&M price increase

subinciso *m* ADMIN subparagraph

subíndice *m* INFO subscript

subinversión *f* BANCA underinvestment

subir 1. *vt* COM GEN *oferta* up; ♦ **~ los tipos de interés** FIN give an upward thrust to interest rates **2.** *vi* COM GEN rise, *el precio* bounce up; ♦ **el mercado sube como la espuma** BOLSA the market is rallying strongly; **~ en el escalafón** RRHH climb the promotion ladder; **~ poco a poco** ECON *precios* edge up; **~ rápidamente** COM GEN skyrocket (*infrml*), *precios* escalate

sublicencia *f* COM GEN, PATENT sublicence (*BrE*), sublicense (*AmE*)

submarginal *m* ECON submarginal

suboficina *f* ADMIN, COM GEN suboffice

suboptimización *f* COM GEN, ECON, FIN suboptimization

subordinado, -a *m,f* RRHH underling

subordinar *vt* COM GEN subordinate

subproducción *f* IND underproduction

subproducto *m* COM GEN by-product

subprograma *m* INFO subprogram

subrayar *vt* COM GEN, INFO *texto* underscore; ♦ **~ un argumento** COM GEN hammer home an argument

subrutina *f* COM GEN subroutine, INFO subprogram

subsecretario, -a *mf* POL, RRHH undersecretary

subsector *m* COM GEN subsector

subsidiado *adj* COM GEN subsidized

subsidiaria: **~ bancaria** *f* BANCA bank subsidiary; **~ nacional** *f* ECON domestic subsidiary; **~ en propiedad absoluta** *f* BOLSA wholly-owned subsidiary

subsidiaridad *f* COM GEN, ECON, POL subsidiarity

subsidiario *adj* BOLSA underlying, COM GEN, DER accessory

subsidio *m* ECON, FIN grant, FISC allowance, POL grant-in-aid, RRHH *pago* benefit; **~ agrario** ECON, POL farm subsidy; **~ agrícola** ECON, POL agricultural subsidy; **~ de ajuste** ECON, FISC, POL corrective subsidy; **~ de alojamiento** COM GEN, RRHH accommodation allow-

ance; **~ de astillero** TRANSP *gubernamental* shipyard subsidy; **~ por aumento del coste de vida** *Esp* (*cf subsidio por aumento del costo de vida AmL*) RRHH cost-of-living allowance; **~ por aumento del costo de vida** *AmL* (*cf subsidio por aumento del coste de vida Esp*) RRHH cost-of-living allowance; **~ básico** POL sustaining grant; **~ de bienestar social** PROT SOC, RRHH welfare benefit; **~ para comida** RRHH meal allowance; **~ de la compañía** RRHH company benefits; **~ de construcción** TRANSP construction subsidy; **~ correctivo** ECON, FISC, POL corrective subsidy; **~ cruzado** FIN cross-subsidy; **~ de desempleo** ECON, POL, PROT SOC, RRHH unemployment benefit (*BrE*), unemployment compensation (*AmE*); **~ disponible para las personas** ECON current grant to persons; **~ para los empleados** CONT, ECON, FIN, RRHH *cuando es un pago* fringe benefit; **~ de enfermedad** PROT SOC, RRHH sick allowance, sickness benefit; **~ de enfermedad obligatorio** PROT SOC, RRHH, SEG statutory sick pay (*SSP*); **~ estatal** ECON, POL, PROT SOC state subsidy; **~ a la exportación** IMP/EXP export subsidy; **~ a la exportación agrícola** ECON, IMP/EXP agricultural export subsidy; **~ familiar** FISC, PROT SOC, RRHH family allowance; **~ para familias con hijos** ECON, PROT SOC Aid to Families with Dependant Children (*AFDC*), child allowance (*AmE*), child benefit (*BrE*); **~ de huelga** RRHH strike benefits; **~ imponible** FISC taxable allowance; **~ para jubilaciones anticipadas** RRHH early retirement benefit; **~ libre de impuestos** FISC, IMP/EXP duty-free discount; **~ marginal del empleo** ECON marginal employment subsidy; **~ por maternidad** PROT SOC, RRHH maternity benefit; **~ mínimo** POL sustaining grant; **~ municipal** COM GEN, POL *ayudas estatales* City Grant (*BrE*); **~ para el pago de alquiler** INMOB, PROT SOC rent allowance; **~ de paro** PROT SOC, RRHH dole (*infrml*) (*BrE*), unemployment pay; **~ personal** FISC personal benefit; **~ del riesgo** FIN risk weighting; **~ salarial** ECON wage subsidy; **~ de la seguridad social** PROT SOC, RRHH social security benefit; **~ sindical de paro** COM GEN redundancy payment; **~ transitorio** FISC transitional relief; **~ para vivienda** PROT SOC, RRHH housing allowance, housing subsidy

subsidios: **~ y prestaciones gravables** *m pl* FISC taxable allowances and benefits

subsistencia *f* PROT SOC subsistence

substituir *vt* COM GEN supersede

substracción: **~ de ganancias** *f* COM GEN skimming

subtítulo *m* MEDIOS, V&M sidehead, sub-head

subtotal *m* CONT, MAT subtotal

subvaloración *f* BOLSA, COM GEN, ECON, FIN undervaluation

subvalorar *vt* BOLSA, COM GEN, ECON, FIN undervalue

subvención *f* COM GEN, FIN subsidy, subsidization, grant; **~ del buque** TRANSP ship subsidy; **~ para la capacitación industrial** *AmL* (*cf subvención para la formación industrial Esp*) FIN industrial training grant; **~ para compensar el déficit** ECON *agricultura* deficiency payment compensation; **~ cruzada** COM GEN, FIN cross-subsidization; **~ a donaciones** FISC Gift Aid; **~ de empresa** FIN enterprise allowance (*BrE*); **~ equivalente a la producción** ECON producer subsidy equivalent; **~ de explotación** CONT operating grant; **~ fija** PROT SOC flat grant; **~ para la formación industrial** *Esp* (*cf subvención para la capacitación industrial AmL*) FIN industrial training grant; **~ global**

ADMIN block grant (*BrE*); ~ **del gobierno** ECON government grant; ~ **gubernamental para investigación** FIN government research grant; ~ **para inversiones** CONT investment grant; ~ **paralela** FIN matching grant; ~ **de Pigou** ECON Pigouvian subsidy; ~ **proporcionada** ECON proportionate grant; ~ **por tipo de interés** FIN interest rate subsidy; ~ **de la tripulación** TRANSP crew subsidization

subvencionado *adj* COM GEN subsidized; **no** ~ COM GEN unsubsidized; ~ **por el Estado** POL, PROT SOC state-aided

subyacente *adj* BOLSA underlying

sucedáneo *m* COM GEN ersatz; ~ **perfecto** ECON perfect substitute

sucesión *f* COM GEN, DER, INMOB, FISC succession, *herencia* inheritance; ~ **rápida** FISC quick succession; ~ **en el uso de la tierra** INMOB land-use succession; ~ **vacante** DER, FISC estate in abeyance

sucesivo[1] *adj* COM GEN successive

sucesivo[2]: **en lo** ~ *fra* COM GEN in future

suceso *m* COM GEN event; ~ **manipulador del mercado** BOLSA market rigger; ~ **subsecuente** COM GEN subsequent event; ◆ **de** ~ **arriesgado** ECON touch and go

sucesor: ~ **en el título de propiedad** *m* PATENT successor in title

sucursal *f* COM GEN branch office (*B.O.*); ~ **de banco** BANCA bank branch; ~ **comercial** RRHH multiple shop; ~ **en el extranjero** BANCA foreign branch, IMP/EXP *comercialización por exportación directa* overseas branch; ~ **de mayor actividad** BANCA hub branch; ~ **principal** BANCA main branch

sueldo *m* COM GEN, RRHH salary, wage; ~ **base** RRHH base pay (*AmE*), base wage (*AmE*), basic pay (*BrE*), basic wage (*BrE*); ~ **y condiciones** RRHH pay and conditions; ~ **inicial** RRHH starting salary; ~ **negociable** RRHH salary to be negotiated; ~ **neto** RRHH take-home pay

sueldos: ~ **y jornales** *m pl* RRHH salaries and wages; ~ **y salarios totales** *m pl* CONT, RRHH total wages and salaries; ~ **del sector público** *m pl* ECON public sector pay

suelo *m* ECON floor; ~ **industrial** IND factory floor; ~ **de operaciones** BOLSA dealing floor

suelos: ~ **y techos** *m pl* ECON grounds and floors

suelto *m* COM GEN *moneda* small change

suficiencia: ~ **de capital** *f* BANCA, ECON, FIN capital adequacy; ~ **de la liquidez** *f* CONT liquidity adequacy

sufragar 1. *vt* CONT, FIN *costes* meet; ◆ ~ **los gastos de** COM GEN stand the cost of; **2.** *vi AmL* (*cf votar Esp*) CONT *costos* vote

sufragio *m* POL franchise; ~ **universal** POL universal suffrage

sufrir *vt* COM GEN undergo, *consecuencias, daños* suffer; ◆ ~ **un batacazo** BOLSA take a bath (*jarg*); ~ **una gran pérdida** BOLSA slump; ~ **una pérdida** COM GEN, DER suffer a loss; ~ **un revés** COM GEN suffer a setback

sugerencia *f* COM GEN suggestion

sujeción *f* INMOB binder (*AmE*)

sujeto *adj* COM GEN *a multa*, FISC *a impuesto* liable; ◆ **estar** ~ **a** COM GEN be subject to; ~ **al cambio** COM GEN subject to change; ~ **a aprobación** COM GEN, V&M subject to approval; ~ **a la aprobación de CFTC** BOLSA subject to CFTC approval; ~ **a aprobación sin riesgo**

SEG subject approval no risk (*SANR*); ~ **a avería simple** SEG subject to particular average (*SPA*); ~ **a controles de precios** ECON subject to price controls; ~ **a gravamen** COM GEN encumbered; ~ **a hipoteca** INMOB subject to mortgage; ~ **a impuesto** FISC liable for tax, taxable, subject to taxation; ~ **a indemnización por rotura** SEG subject to breakage; ~ **a interés** BANCA interest-linked

suma *f* CONT addition, FISC gross-up, INFO, MAT addition; ~ **agregada a la póliza de seguro** SEG dividend addition; ~ **anterior** BANCA, CONT amount carried forward, carried down (*c/d*); ~ **de aportación** FISC amount contributed; ~ **asegurada** BANCA sum assured; ~ **de capital** FIN capital sum; ~ **cierta** COM GEN amount due; ~ **convenida** COM GEN agreed sum; ~ **enorme** FIN vast sum; ~ **global** COM GEN lump sum (*ls*); ~ **invertida** *m* COM GEN amount invested; ~ **no rehabilitada** FIN undisclosed sum; ~ **de verificación** INFO *transferencia de datos* checksum; ◆ ~ **y sigue** BANCA, CONT brought forward (*b/f*), carried down (*c/d*), carried forward (*c/f*), carried over

sumador *m* CONT adder; ~ **completo** INFO *equipo* full adder

sumadora *f* MAT adding machine; ~ **con impresora** COM GEN add listing machine

sumamente *adv* COM GEN *gravado* heavily

sumar *vt* COM GEN add up; ◆ ~ **simultáneamente** COM GEN *cifras, totales* add together

sumario: ~ **del proceso** *m* COM GEN summary of the proceedings

sumas: ~ **horizontales** *f pl* MAT *hoja de análisis* cross-footing

suministrable *adj* ECON, V&M affordable

suministrado: ~ **sin impuestos** *adj* FISC, IMP/EXP delivered duty unpaid (*DDU*)

suministrar *vt* COM GEN afford, *información* supply, ECON afford, TRANSP supply; ◆ ~ **bienes a crédito** COM GEN supply goods on trust

suministro *m* COM GEN supply; ~ **de agua** MED AMB water supply; ~ **elástico** ECON, V&M elastic supply; ~ **de energía** COM GEN, IND energy supply; ~ **de servicios** ECON supply of services

suministros: ~ **exentos** *m pl* FISC exempt supplies

super: ~ **oferta** *f* V&M premium offer

superabundancia *f* COM GEN, ECON glut

superación: ~ **de objeciones** *f* V&M overcoming objections

superadaptador: ~ **videográfico** *m* (*SVGA*) INFO super video graphics adaptor (*SVGA*)

superado *adj* V&M overcoming

superahorrador *m* COM GEN super saver

superar *vt* BOLSA outperform, COM GEN overcome, surpass, ECON *demanda, oferta* exceed, *una economía a otra* outperform; ◆ ~ **en valor a** COM GEN outweigh

superávit *m* CONT cash surplus, surplus of assets over liabilities, surplus; ~ **acumulado** CONT accumulated surplus; ~ **aportado en acciones** BOLSA donated surplus; ~ **de la balanza comercial** ECON trade surplus; ~ **de la balanza de pagos** BANCA, ECON balance of payments surplus, external surplus; ~ **de capital** BOLSA, CONT, ECON, FIN capital surplus (*AmE*), share premium (*BrE*); ~ **del comercio exterior** ECON foreign trade surplus; ~ **del consumidor** ECON, V&M consumer surplus; ~ **de cuenta corriente** BANCA, ECON current account surplus; ~ **disponible** COM GEN, FIN unappropriated surplus; ~ **exento** FISC exempt surplus; ~ **fiscal** FISC fiscal surplus; ~ **neto** FIN net surplus; ~ **obtenido** FIN acquired surplus; ~ **presupuestario** ECON, FIN, POL budget surplus, budgetary surplus; ~ **de presupuesto** ECON, FIN, POL budget surplus; ~ **del productor** ECON producer's surplus; ~ **restringido** CONT undistributable reserve (*BrE*); ~ **por revalorización** CONT appreciated surplus; ~ **de tesorería** CONT *liquidez, efectivo, caja* cash-rich

supercapacidad *f* COM GEN overcapacity

supercomputador *AmL ver supercomputadora AmL*

supercomputadora *AmL* (*cf superordenador Esp*) *f* INFO supercomputer

superdirecta *f* TRANSP overdrive

superdotado *adj* PROT SOC over-gifted

superestructura *f* COM GEN superstructure (*super*)

superficie *f* COM GEN acreage, ECON, INMOB, MAT, PATENT surface; ~ **de apoyo** TRANSP bearing surface; ~ **arrendable global** INMOB gross leasable area; ~ **calefactora** COM GEN heating surface (*HS*); ~ **cultivada** FISC, MED AMB cultivated acreage; ~ **de descarga** TRANSP apron; ~ **de estacionamiento de aeronaves** TRANSP apron; ~ **de exploración** INFO scan area; ~ **habitable** INMOB floor space; ~ **minorista** COM GEN, V&M retail floorspace; ~ **en pies cuadrados** INMOB *construcción* square footage; ~ **de presentación** V&M facing

superintendente: ~ **de marina** *mf* RRHH marine superintendant; ~ **naval** *mf* RRHH naval superintendent; ~ **de seguros** *mf* RRHH, SEG Superintendent of Insurance; ~ **de tráfico** *mf* RRHH, TRANSP district traffic superintendent (*DTS*), traffic superintendent

superior[1] *adj* COM GEN *posición* senior (*Snr*), *producto* upmarket, RRHH *posición* senior (*Snr*)

superior[2] *mf* RRHH senior

supermercado *m* V&M supermarket; ~ **financiero** FIN financial supermarket

superneutralidad *f* ECON superneutrality

supernumerario *m* RRHH supernumerary

superordenador *m Esp* (*cf supercomputadora AmL*) INFO supercomputer

superpetrolero *m* MED AMB supertanker, TRANSP ultra large crude carrier (*ULCC*)

superposición *f* V&M overlap

superpotencia *f* COM GEN, POL superpower

superproducción *f* ECON, IND overproduction

superutilización *f* ECON overuse

supervalorar *vt* ECON overvalue

supervisar *vt* COM GEN, GES supervise, oversee, TRANSP *tarifas* monitor; ♦ ~ **una actuación** COM GEN, GES, RRHH monitor performance

supervisión[1]: **de** ~ *adj* INFO supervisory

supervisión[2] *f* COM GEN supervision; ~ **de la actuación** COM GEN performance monitoring; ~ **del desempeño** COM GEN performance monitoring; ~ **del gasto público** COM GEN public expenditure survey; ~ **de las instituciones de crédito** FIN supervision of credit institutions; ~ **del riesgo** *m* GES risk monitoring

supervisor, a *m,f* GES first line manager, INFO, RRHH supervisor, TRANSP *aviación* dispatcher (*AmE*); ~ **adjunto(-a) de tráfico** RRHH assistant traffic supervisor (*ATS*); ~ **de almacén** COM GEN warehouse supervisor; ~ **de carga** RRHH, TRANSP cargo surveyor; ~ **de cobro** BANCA, FIN, RRHH credit controller; ~ **de documentación de importación** RRHH import documentation supervisor; ~ **en jefe** COM GEN, RRHH chief supervisor, *construcción* head foreman; ~ **de línea** RRHH line supervisor; ~ **de primera línea** GES first line manager, first line supervisor; ~ **de quiebras** COM GEN, DER *comercial* Superintendent of Bankruptcy; ~ **de reservas** COM GEN book reviewer; ~ **de tráfico** RRHH traffic supervisor

supervivencia *f* DER, INMOB, SEG survivorship

suplantar *vt* COM GEN supersede

suplementario *adj* COM GEN supplementary, extra

suplementarios *m pl* POL supplementaries

suplemento *m* CONT additional charge, DER addendum, MEDIOS *revistas, periódicos* supplement, OCIO excess fare, V&M supplement; ~ **en color** MEDIOS, V&M colour supplement (*BrE*), color supplement (*AmE*); ~ **garantizado de ingresos** FISC guaranteed income supplement; ~ **por habitación individual** OCIO single-room supplement; ~ **nivelador de altura** TRANSP *contenedores* leveling pedestal (*AmE*), levelling pedestal (*BrE*); ~ **publicitario** MEDIOS, V&M advertising supplement

suplente *mf* POL *en lista electoral* surrogate (*jarg*) (*AmE*), RRHH stand-in, acting member, deputy member of the board of management

súplica *f* COM GEN petition

suplicar 1. *vt* COM GEN, DER petition, appeal to; **2.** *vi* COM GEN plead

suplir *vt* COM GEN *compensar* make up for

SUPR *abr* (*carácter de borrado*) INFO DEL (*delete character*)

supra *adv* COM GEN supra

supranacional *adj* COM GEN supranational

supraorganización *f* COM GEN supraorganization

supremacía: ~ **del consumidor** *f* ECON, V&M consumer sovereignty

supresión *f* COM GEN *de controles de comercio* abolition, DER *de provisiones en estatutos* deletion, ECON *de barreras* dismantling, INFO abort

suprimir *vt* COM GEN supersede, weed out, edit out, *omitir* leave out, INFO delete, *eliminar* suppress

surfear *vt* COMS, INFO *internet* surf

surtido: ~ **de mercancías** *m* COM GEN assortment of goods

surtidor: ~ **de gasolina** *m* MED AMB gas station (*AmE*), petrol station (*BrE*)

susceptible: ~ **de aplicación industrial** *adj* PATENT susceptible of industrial application; ~ **de diversas interpretaciones** *adj* COM GEN open to several interpretations

suscitar *vt* COM GEN *asunto nuevo* bring up

suscribir 1. *vt* COM GEN apply for; ♦ ~ **el contrato** DER exchange contracts; ~ **una opción de compra de acciones** BOLSA write a stock option; ~ **una póliza de seguros** SEG take out an insurance policy; ~ **un préstamo** BANCA apply for a loan; **2.** *vi* COM GEN subscribe

suscribirse *v refl* COM GEN take out a subscription

suscripción *f* BOLSA overwriting, COM GEN subscription; ~ **de acciones** BOLSA application for shares, subscription for shares; ~ **anual** COM GEN annual subscription;

~ **a una asociación** COM GEN association subscription; ~ **de bonos** BOLSA bond underwriting; ~ **de bonos del Tesoro** FIN takeup of Treasury bills; ~ **de capital** CONT, FIN capital commitment; ~ **de compromiso en firme** BOLSA firm commitment underwriting; ~ **sin garantía** BOLSA writing naked; ~ **gratuita** COM GEN complimentary subscription; ~ **inflada** BOLSA staggism; ~ **de una opción de compra** BOLSA call writing; ~ **de opciones de venta con depósito en dinero** BOLSA writing cash-secured puts; ~ **de pantalla plana** FIN flat-rate subscription; ~ **de prueba a una publicación** MEDIOS trial subscription (*TS*); ~ **a tanto alzado** FIN flat-rate subscription

suscripciones: ~ **para el Fondo Monetario Internacional** *f pl* POL subscriptions to the International Monetary Fund

suscriptor, a *m,f* COM GEN subscriber; ~ **cubierto(-a)** BOLSA covered writer; ~ **supletorio(-a)** FIN *valores, préstamos* standby underwriter

suscriptores *m pl* BOLSA takers-in

suscrito *adj* BANCA, BOLSA, FIN, SEG underwritten; ◆ ~ **de forma insuficiente** FIN undersubscribed

susodicho *adj* COMS above-mentioned

suspender *vt* BOLSA suspend, COM GEN cease, *comercio, autorización* suspend, DER *caso, juicio,* GES *reunión* adjourn, RRHH dehire (*AmE*), lay off (*BrE*); ◆ ~ **un capital en acciones** BOLSA stop a stock (*jarg*); ~ **el pago de un cheque** BANCA stop payment of a check (*AmE*), stop payment of a cheque (*BrE*)

suspensión *f* DER, GES *decisión* adjournment, RRHH suspension; ~ **antibalance** TRANSP anti-roll suspension; ~ **de la apelación** DER stay of appeal; ~ **de arancel** IMP/EXP duty suspension; ~ **de cotización** BOLSA delisting; ~ **del funcionamiento de una planta** COM GEN, IND plant interruption; ~ **del negocio** COM GEN stoppage of trade; ~ **de operaciones** BOLSA suspension of trading; ~ **del plan** FISC discontinuance of plan; ~ **simbólica** RRHH token stoppage

suspenso: **en ~** *fra* DER, INMOB in abeyance

sustancia *f* COM GEN substance; ~ **contaminante** MED AMB pollutant; ~ **explosiva** TRANSP substance explosive; ~ **higroscópica** MED AMB hygroscopic substance; ~ **peligrosa** MED AMB dangerous substance; ~ **peligrosa contaminante** MED AMB, TRANSP hazardous polluting substance (*HPS*); ~ **química peligrosa** MED AMB, TRANSP hazardous chemical (*hazchem*); ~ **con riesgo de polución** MED AMB, TRANSP hazardous polluting substance (*HPS*); ~ **sobre forma** CONT substance over form; ~ **tóxica** MED AMB hazardous substance

sustitución *f* COM GEN replacement, CONT *de asientos* reversal, ECON substitution; ~ **de importaciones** IMP/EXP import substitution

sustituir: ~ **a alguien** *fra* COM GEN take over from sb, RRHH stand in for sb

sustitutivo *adj* RRHH *responsabilidad* stand-by (*BrE*), substitute

sustituto, -a *m,f* IND substitute, POL *en lista electoral* surrogate (*jarg*) (*AmE*), RRHH stand-in

sustraerse *v refl* FISC shelter

sustraído: ~ **de cuenta** *adj* BANCA, CONT *balance* carried down (*c/d*)

SVGA *abr* (*conjunto de gráficos de supervídeo Esp, conjunto de gráficos de supervideo AmL*) INFO SVGA (*super video graphics array*)

swop *m* BANCA, BOLSA *instrumento de tipo de interés*, FIN swop; ~ **futuro** BANCA, BOLSA, FIN forward swop

T

T. *abr* (*tara*) COM GEN t. (*tare*)

tabaco *m* COM GEN tobacco

tabla *f* COM GEN table; ~ **agregada** SEG aggregate table; ~ **de consulta** INFO lookup table; ~ **de contingencia** ECON contingency table; ~ **de decisión** COM GEN decision table; ~ **de deducciones** CONT *fiscal, impuestos* derivation schedule; ~ **de encajes** CONT encashment schedule; ~ **de entradas y salidas** COM GEN input-output table; ~ **de frecuencias** MAT frequency table; ~ **de mortalidad** SEG mortality table; ~ **de valores nominales** BOLSA table of par values

tablas: ~ **y barrotes de pino** *f pl* IND *madera de construcción* deals and battens; **~, barrotes, tableros** *f pl* IND *madera de construcción* deals, battens, boards; ~ **de cambio de divisas** *f pl* BANCA, ECON, FIN foreign exchange tables; ~ **de estiba** *f pl* TRANSP dunnage

tablero *m* INFO *equipo* board; ~ **automático de cotizaciones** BOLSA ticker; ~ **de avisos** COMS, RRHH bulletin board (*AmE*), notice board (*BrE*); ~ **de control** COM GEN, IND, INFO control panel; ~ **de cotización** BOLSA quotation board; ~ **cuadriculado** COM GEN plotting table; ~ **de dibujo** GES drawing board, INFO plotting board; ~ **de diseño** V&M *publicidad* art board; ~ **de distribución** INFO switchboard; ~ **electrónico de la bolsa** BOLSA exchange screen; ~ **indicador** BOLSA annunciator board (*AmE*)

tabloide *m* MEDIOS *prensa* tabloid

tablón: ~ **de anuncios** *m Esp* (*cf cartelera AmL*) COMS, RRHH bulletin board (*BB*), notice board (*BrE*)

tablones: ~ **contra corrimiento de estiba** *m pl* TRANSP shifting board

tabulación *f* ADMIN, INFO tabulation (*tab*); ~ **horizontal** MAT cross tabulation

tabular *vt* ADMIN, INFO tab

TAC *abr* (*tasa anual compuesta*) BANCA, FIN CAR (*compound annual rate*)

tachadura *m* INFO scratch

tachar *vt* COM GEN fault

tacógrafo *m* TRANSP tachograph

táctica: ~ **competitiva** *f* ECON, GES, V&M competitive tactic; ~ **dilatoria** *f* COM GEN delaying tactic; ~ **de fijación de precios** *f* V&M pricing tactic; ~ **publicitaria** *f* V&M advertising tactic

táctil *adj* INFO touch-sensitive

TAE *abr* (*tasa anual equivalente*) BANCA, FIN effective annual rate of interest

talento *m* RRHH accomplishment

talla: de ~ estándar *adj* INFO standard-size

taller *m* COM GEN workshop, IND workshop, toolroom, V&M *agencia publicitaria* shop (*BrE*); ~ **agremiado** RRHH union shop; ~ **artesanal** IND workshop; ~ **de carrocería** COM GEN body shop; ~ **de fundición** IND smelting works; ~ **de maquinaria** COM GEN, IND engineering works; ~ **oportunista** IND runaway shop (*AmE*); ~ **de reparación** COM GEN repair shop

talón *m* BANCA *de letra de cambio* allonge, *de cheque* stub, BOLSA counterfoil, talon, ~ **bancario contra el cheque** BANCA, FIN counter check (*AmE*), counter cheque (*BrE*); ~ **de cheque** BANCA check stub (*AmE*), cheque stub (*BrE*); ~ **de embarque** IMP/EXP, TRANSP shipping note (*S/N*); ~ **de embarque normalizado** IMP/EXP, TRANSP standard shipping note

talonario *m* BANCA *de cheques* checkbook (*AmE*), chequebook (*BrE*), COM GEN, OCIO *de billetes* book; ~ **de recibos** COM GEN receipt book

tamaño *m* COM GEN size; ~ **aleatorio** COM GEN random size; ~ **base** COM GEN basic size; ~ **de carteles** V&M poster size; ~ **económico** COM GEN, V&M economy size; ~ **económico de lote** IND economic batch size; ~ **especial** IND *producción* odd size; ~ **de lote** IND batch size; ~ **de papel ISO** MEDIOS, V&M ISO paper size

tambaleante *adj* COM GEN *recuperación* wobbly

tambo *f AmL* (*cf granja lechera Esp*) ECON dairy farm

tambor *m* COM GEN barrel, INFO, TRANSP drum

tampón: ~ **para sellos** *m* COM GEN stamp pad

tándem *m* TRANSP tandem

tangible *adj* COM GEN tangible

tanque *m* TRANSP tank (*TK*); ~ **bajo cubierta** TRANSP under deck tank (*Un Dk*); ~ **de carga** TRANSP cargo tank (*CT*); ~ **contenedor** TRANSP tanktainer; ~ **inferior** TRANSP deep tank (*DT*); ~ **inferior central** TRANSP midship deep tank (*DTm*); ~ **inferior central delantero** TRANSP midship deep tank forward (*DTmf*); ~ **inferior central trasero** TRANSP midship deep tank aft (*DTma*); ~ **inferior de popa** TRANSP deep tank aft (*DTa*); ~ **inferior de proa** TRANSP deep tank forward (*DTf*); ~ **de lastre** TRANSP ballast tank

tantear: ~ **el mercado en busca de** *fra* BOLSA tap the market for

tanteo *m* COM GEN guesstimate (*infrml*)

tanto: al ~ *adv* COM GEN au fait

tantos: en ~ porciento *fra* COM GEN in percentage terms

tap *f* BOLSA tap (*jarg*)

tapa[1]**: con ~ dura** *adj* MEDIOS *libro* hardback; **de ~ dura** *adj* MEDIOS casebound

tapa[2]**:** ~ **de acero** *f* TRANSP steel cover; ~ **de la escotilla** *f* TRANSP hatch covering; ~ **de tanque** *f* TRANSP tank top (*TT*)

tapar *vt* COM GEN, POL cover up

taquigrafía *f* ADMIN, COM GEN shorthand, stenography

taquigrafiar *vt* ADMIN, COM GEN take down in shorthand

taquígrafo, -a *m,f* ADMIN, RRHH stenographer

taquilla *f* OCIO *espectáculos* box office; ~ **para equipajes en consigna** COM GEN baggage locker (*AmE*), left-luggage locker (*BrE*); ~ **de venta anticipada** OCIO advance booking office

taquimecanógrafo, -a *m,f* ADMIN, COM GEN, RRHH shorthand typist

tara *f* (*T.*) COM GEN, TRANSP *embalaje* tare (*t.*); ~ **acostumbrada** FISC customary tare; ~ **extra** COM GEN extra tare

taraje *m* COM GEN, TRANSP tare weight; ~ **bruto** COM GEN, TRANSP gross tare weight

tarea *f* COM GEN task, undertaking, INFO task, job, RRHH labor (*AmE*), labour (*BrE*), task; ~ **por lotes** INFO batch job; ~ **secundaria** INFO *de baja prioridad* background task

tarifa *f* COM GEN tariff, ECON *de precios* rate; ~ **aceptada** BOLSA, COM GEN *acciones* takeup rate; ~ **acordada** TRANSP *de cargamento* agreed rate; ~ **actual** COM GEN current rate; ~ **ad valórem** CONT ad valorem rate; ~ **adicional por servicio** TRANSP supplementary service tariff (*SST*); ~ **aduanera** ECON, IMP/EXP, POL tariff; ~ **de adulto** COM GEN, TRANSP adult fare; ~ **aérea** OCIO air fare; ~ **alta** COM GEN, COMS peak rate; ~ **anunciada** TRANSP published fare; ~ **de arrendamiento** INMOB, PROT SOC rental rate; ~ **bajo costes** *Esp* (*cf tarifa bajo costos AmL*) TRANSP rate below cost; ~ **bajo costos** *AmL* (*cf tarifa bajo costes Esp*) TRANSP rate below cost; ~ **de biblioteca** PROT SOC library rate; ~ **bruta** TRANSP gross rate; ~ **de buque de línea regular** TRANSP liner rate; ~ **cablegráfica** ECON cable rate; ~ **de carga autopropulsada** IMP/EXP, TRANSP *tarifas marítimas* ro/ro rate; ~ **de carga requerida** IMP/EXP, TRANSP required freight rate (*RFR*); ~ **clave** ECON key rate; ~ **combinada de transportes** TRANSP combination rate; ~ **de compensación** COMS *Correos* compensation fee; ~ **competitiva** V&M *precio* competitive rate; ~ **conjunta** TRANSP joint fare; ~ **por debajo del flete** TRANSP under cost freight rate; ~ **de dos elementos** ECON *uno variable y otro fijo* two-part tariff; ~ **económica** OCIO economy fare; ~ **por espacio publicitario** V&M *publicidad* space rates; ~ **especial** RRHH golden rate, TRANSP commodity rate, V&M bargain rate; ~ **especificada** TRANSP specified rate; ~ **para excursiones** OCIO excursion fare; ~ **exterior común** ECON common external tariff (*CET*), IMP/EXP UE common customs tariff (*CCT*); ~ **familiar** OCIO, TRANSP family fare; ~ **ferroviaria** OCIO, TRANSP train fare; ~ **fija** PATENT flat-rate fee; ~ **de flete estable** TRANSP stable rate; ~ **de fletes** TRANSP freight tariff; ~ **de fletes para fines de semana** TRANSP weekend freight tariff; ~ **fuera de las horas picos** *AmL* (*cf tarifa fuera de las horas puntas Esp*) TRANSP off-peak fare; ~ **fuera de las horas puntas** *Esp* (*cf tarifa fuera de las horas picos AmL*) TRANSP off-peak fare; ~ **general** CONT, TRANSP blanket rate; ~ **general de carga** TRANSP general cargo rate; ~ **general de productos** BOLSA general commodity rate (*GCR*); ~ **por hora** ECON time rate; ~ **IATA** TRANSP IATA rate; ~ **de ida** OCIO, TRANSP one-way fare; ~ **de ida y vuelta** OCIO, TRANSP return fare (*BrE*), round-trip fare (*AmE*); ~ **de ida y vuelta para fin de semana** OCIO, TRANSP weekend return fare (*BrE*), weekend round-trip fare (*AmE*); ~ **del impuesto** FISC tax rate schedule, tax rate structure; ~ **de impuesto especial** TRANSP *flete aéreo* specific commodity rate; ~ **incentivada** TRANSP incentive rate; ~ **interna** OCIO internal fare; ~ **por kilómetro** TRANSP per-kilometer rate (*AmE*), per-kilometre rate (*BrE*); ~ **en línea** TRANSP *tarifa de flete aéreo* on-line rate; ~ **mínima** COM GEN minimum charge, RRHH threshold rate, TRANSP minimum charge; ~ **nacional** TRANSP domestic rate; ~ **no comunicada** TRANSP rate not reported (*RNR*); ~ **normal** TRANSP normal rate; ~ **óptima** ECON, IMP/EXP optimal tariff; ~ **por página** MEDIOS, V&M page rate; ~ **de pasajeros** OCIO, TRANSP passenger tariff; ~ **portuaria** TRANSP port tariff; ~ **postal** COMS postage rate; ~ **de precios** COM GEN price list, fare pricing; ~ **proporcional** TRANSP proportional rate; ~ **provocadora** FIN teaser rate; ~ **publicitaria** V&M

adrate, rate card; ~ **reducida** OCIO, TRANSP reduced fare; ~ **regional** TRANSP sectional rate; ~ **según contador** COM GEN meter rate; ~ **de servicio de contenedores** TRANSP container service tariff (*CST*); ~ **sobre las aguas residuales** ECON effluent fee; ~ **de una sola emisión** V&M *publicidad* one-time rate; ~ **de temporada** V&M seasonal rate; ~ **de temporada alta** OCIO high-season fare; ~ **de temporada baja** OCIO low-season fare; ~ **total** TRANSP through fare; ~ **de transporte terrestre** TRANSP *entre dos transportes marítimos* land bridge rate; ~ **turista** OCIO tourist fare; ~ **unificada** TRANSP consolidated rate; ~ **por vagón completo** TRANSP wagonload rate (*AmE*), carload rate (*BrE*); ~ **de viaje de ida y vuelta** TRANSP round trip rate (*AmE*), return rate (*BrE*); ~ **de viajeros** OCIO, TRANSP passenger fare

tarifación *f* BOLSA, FIN, FISC rating; ~ **prospectiva** SEG prospective rating

tarifas *f pl* COM GEN fees, honorarium (*frml*), TRANSP rates; ~ **del Atlántico Norte** TRANSP North Atlantic rates; ~ **del Atlántico Sur** TRANSP South Atlantic rates; ~ **contables** CONT accounting fees; ~ **de clasificación de mercancías** TRANSP commodity classification rates (*CCR*); ~ **y clasificaciones** COMS rates and classifications; ~ **del Pacífico sur** TRANSP South Pacific rates; ~ **de publicidad** FIN, V&M advertising rates; ~ **y regulaciones internacionales** IMP/EXP, TRANSP overseas tariff and regulations (*OTAR*)

tarjeta *f* INFO *equipo* card; ~ **aceleradora** INFO accelerator card; ~ **bancaria** BANCA bank card; ~ **de banco automático** BANCA autobank card; ~ **para cajero automático** BANCA automated teller card, bank teller card, cash card; ~ **de caracteres** INFO character card; ~ **de cargo** BANCA charge card; ~ **de cheque** BANCA check card (*AmE*), cheque card (*BrE*); ~ **con chip** INFO chip card; ~ **con circuito de memoria** INFO chip-based card; ~ **de cliente** COM GEN client card, customer card; ~ **comercial** COM GEN business card; ~ **de control del cursor** INFO cursor control pad; ~ **de crédito** BANCA, FIN credit card; ~ **de crédito corporativa** BANCA, FIN corporate credit card; ~ **de crédito de empresa** BANCA, FIN, FISC company credit card; ~ **de crédito de una tienda específica** BANCA, FIN store card; ~ **de desembarque** TRANSP landing card; ~ **de embarque** COM GEN embarkation card, TRANSP boarding card; ~ **de emulación** INFO emulation card, emulation board; ~ **de entrada** COM GEN entrance card; ~ **de expansión** INFO expansion card, expansion board; ~ **de expansión de memoria** INFO memory expansion card; ~ **externa** INFO add-on board, add-on card; ~ **de fichar** RRHH time card; ~ **de firma** BANCA signature card; ~ **de garantía** BANCA warranty card; ~ **de gráficos** INFO graphics board; ~ **de identificación** DER, POL identity card (*ID card*); ~ **de identificación extranjera** POL, PROT SOC alien registration card (*AmE*); ~ **informativa** SEG *marítimo* advice card; ~ **inteligente** COM GEN smart card; ~ **maestra** INFO master card; ~ **magnética** INFO magnetic card; ~ **de memoria** INFO memory card; ~ **de muestra de firma** BANCA specimen signature card; ~ **de muestra de firma normalizada** BANCA standard specimen signature card; ~ **multifilar** INFO cage card; ~ **del negocio** COM GEN business card; ~ **oro** BANCA gold card; ~ **de pedido** V&M order card; ~ **perforada** COM GEN, INFO punch card, punched card; ~ **prepagada** V&M prepaid card; ~ **de presentación** COM GEN business card; ~ **reloj** RRHH time card; ~ **de respuesta comercial** COMS business reply card (*BRC*); ~ **de servicio** INFO service card; ~ **de servicio al lector** V&M reader service card; ~ **de tránsito** OCIO transit card; ~ **de transporte de emergencia** TRANSP transport emergency card; ~ **VGA** INFO VGA card; ~ **de video** *AmL*, ~ **de vídeo** *Esp* INFO video card; ~ **de visita** COM GEN visiting card, business card

Tarjeta: ~ **Europea** *f* BANCA Eurocard®

tasa[1] *f* ECON rate;

~ a ~ **de abandono del empleo** ECON quit rate; ~ **de actividad** COM GEN activity ratio; ~ **aduanera** FISC, IMP/EXP duty; ~ **aeroportuaria** FISC airport tax; ~ **de agrupamiento** TRANSP groupage rate; ~ **de ahorro de bonos** BANCA bonus savings rate; ~ **de amortización** BOLSA redemption fee; ~ **anual** COM GEN, FIN annual rate; ~ **anual compuesta** (*TAC*) BANCA, FIN compound annual rate (*CAR*); ~ **anual equivalente** (*TAE*) BANCA, FIN effective annual rate of interest; ~ **anunciada** TRANSP published rate; ~ **aproximada de beneficios** CONT approximate rate of return;

~ b ~ **bancaria** BANCA, FIN bank rate; ~ **base** BANCA, FIN base rate; ~ **base bancaria** BANCA, FIN bank base rate; ~ **base de una casa financiera** FIN finance house base rate (*FHBR*); ~ **de beneficio después de impuestos** CONT, FISC after-tax rate of return; ~ **de bonos de interés** BANCA bonus rate of interest; ~ **bruta de la población** ECON crude population rate;

~ c ~ **de cambio al contado** BOLSA spot rate; ~ **de cambio estabilizada** ECON, FIN pegged exchange rate; ~ **de cambio a fecha futura** BOLSA, ECON forward exchange rate; ~ **de cambio real** COM GEN real exchange rate; ~ **de capitalización** CONT, ECON capitalization rate (*cap rate*); ~ **combinada** BANCA *de interés* blended rate; ~ **de comisión** BANCA commission rate; ~ **compensadora** IMP/EXP compensatory levy; ~ **de compra** BOLSA buyer's rate; ~ **contractual de los préstamos** BOLSA *futuros sobre eurodólares* contractual loan rate; ~ **del control de los tipos de cambio** ECON Exchange Control Rate (*ECR*); ~ **controlada** BANCA, BOLSA, ECON, FIN controlled rate; ~ **de conversión** BANCA, ECON translation rate, conversion rate; ~ **corriente** COM GEN going rate; ~ **de costo combinado a largo plazo** *AmL* (*cf tipo de coste combinado a largo plazo Esp*) FIN long-term blended cost rate (*LTB*); ~ **de crecimiento compuesto** ECON, FIN compound growth rate; ~ **de crecimiento económico sostenible** ECON, FIN, POL sustainable economic growth rate; ~ **de crecimiento garantizada** ECON warranted rate of growth; ~ **crítica de rendimiento** ECON, FIN hurdle rate of return; ~ **crítica de rentabilidad** ECON *gastos de capital*, FIN hurdle rate; ~ **cruzada** ECON, FIN cross rate; ~ **de cuarentena** COM GEN, IMP/EXP quarantine due;

~ d ~ **decreciente** FIN decreasing rate; ~ **de dependencia** PROT SOC dependency ratio; ~ **de depósito** BANCA deposit rate; ~ **de depósito bancario** BANCA bank deposit rate, banker's deposit rate; ~ **de depreciación** CONT rate of depreciation; ~ **de descuento** BANCA, CONT, FIN discount rate (*BrE*), discount window (*AmE*); ~ **de descuento ajustado a riesgo** BANCA, FIN risk-adjusted discount rate; ~ **de descuento bancario** BANCA, FIN bank discount rate; ~ **de desempleo** COM GEN unemployment rate; ~ **de desgaste** COM GEN attrition rate; ~ **de deuda externa** POL external debt ratio; ~ **de devolución** BANCA rate of

return, MEDIOS *imprenta* remit rate; ~ **de dimisión del empleo** ECON quit rate; ~ **de dinero a la vista** BANCA call money rate, daily money rate; ~ **dual** TRANSP dual rate;

~ e ~ **efectiva** CONT effective rate; ~ **de efluentes** MED AMB effluent fee; ~ **de emisión** MED AMB emission fee; ~ **de empresa preferencial** BANCA prime business rate; ~ **de error** INFO error rate; ~ **de eurodólares** ECON *divisas* Eurodollar rate;

~ f ~ **de fecundidad total** ECON total fertility rate (*TRF*); ~ **de financiación** BOLSA financing rate; ~ **de financiación a corto plazo** BOLSA *de futuros* short date financing rate; ~ **flotante** BANCA floating rate;

~ g ~ **de gastos estándar** FIN Standard Spending Assessment (*SSA*); ~ **global de beneficio** CONT overall rate of return;

~ h ~ **de hipoteca reestructurada** BANCA renegotiated mortgage rate; ~ **hipotecaria** BANCA, FIN mortgage rate;

~ i ~ **de incorporación** FISC *para ganancias y pérdidas de capital* inclusion rate; ~ **de incremento** ECON rate of increase; ~ **de inflación** ECON, POL inflation rate; ~ **interbancaria** BANCA interbank rate; ~ **de interés** COM GEN rate of interest; ~ **de interés absoluta** ECON, COM GEN pure interest rate; ~ **de interés acumulado** COM GEN accumulated rate of interest (*ARI*), CONT accrued interst rate; ~ **de interés de la bonificación** COM GEN backwardation rate; ~ **de interés del consumo** COM GEN consumption rate of interest (*CRI*); ~ **de interés de cuenta** COM GEN, CONT, FIN accounting rate of interest (*ARI*); ~ **de interés de la demanda** BANCA, BOLSA, ECON, FIN *acciones, participaciones* call rate; ~ **de interés devengado** CONT accrual interest rate; ~ **de interés diferencial** BANCA interest rate differential; ~ **de interés de disminución** COM GEN declining interest rate; ~ **de interés efectivo** BANCA effective interest rate; ~ **de interés facial** BANCA face interest rate; ~ **de interés flotante** BANCA floating interest rate; ~ **de interés del mercado** BOLSA market rate; ~ **de interés preferencial** BANCA preferential interest rate, prime rate; ~ **de interés de los préstamos** BANCA lending rate; ~ **de interés promedio** BANCA average interest rate; ~ **de interés propia** ECON own interest rate; ~ **de interés real** COM GEN real interest rate; ~ **de interés sobre préstamos a corto plazo** BANCA, BOLSA, ECON, FIN call rate; ~ **de interés tope** BANCA interest rate ceiling; ~ **de interés variable** COM GEN variable interest rate; ~ **de intereses** COM GEN interest rate; ~ **interna de descuento** CONT internal rate of discount;

~ l ~ **de letras de cambio** FIN bill rate; ~ **de licitaciones interbancarias de Londres** BANCA, BOLSA London Interbank Bid Rate (*LIBID*); ~ **de liquidación de futuros** BOLSA futures liquidation rate; ~ **Lombard** BANCA Lombard rate;

~ m ~ **marginal** FISC marginal rate; ~ **marginal de sustitución** ECON marginal rate of substitution (*MRS*); ~ **marginal de transformación** ECON marginal rate of transformation; ~ **máxima** BOLSA ceiling rate, COM GEN maximum rate; ~ **media** CONT average rate; ~ **media del mercado monetario mensual** BOLSA average monthly money market rate; ~ **media ponderada** BOLSA average weighted rate; ~ **del mercado de obligaciones** BOLSA bond market rate; ~ **mínima** BANCA, BOLSA *de futuros* ECON, FIN floor rate, rate floor;

~ n ~ **natural de crecimiento** ECON natural rate of growth; ~ **natural de empleo** ECON, PROT SOC natural rate of employment; ~ **natural de interés** ECON natural rate of interest; ~ **neta** BANCA *del interés sobre préstamo* net rate, V&M flat rate; ~ **neta de todos los cargos** FIN all charges net rate; ~ **no ajustable** BANCA nonadjustable rate; ~ **nominal de interés** BANCA, BOLSA, FIN nominal interest rate;

~ o ~ **ofrecida interbancaria** BANCA interbank offered rate (*IBOR*);

~ p ~ **de participación de la mano de obra** ECON labor force participation rate (*AmE*) (*LFPR*), labour force participation rate (*BrE*) (*LFPR*); ~ **de penalización** DER penalty rate; ~ **de Pigou** ECON Pigouvian tax; ~ **de porcentaje anual** BANCA, COM GEN, FIN annualized percentage rate (*APR*); ~ **porcentual por año** BANCA, COM GEN, FIN annualized percentage rate (*APR*); ~ **de precios** ECON price rate; ~ **preferencial** BANCA *de interés sobre un préstamo* preferential rate; ~ **preferencial de interés** BANCA prime rate of interest; ~ **preferente** BANCA *de interés sobre un préstamo* preferential rate; ~ **de préstamo de amortización** BOLSA call loan rate; ~ **de préstamo mínimo** BANCA minimum lending rate (*MLR*); ~ **de préstamo nominal** BANCA, FIN nominal loan rate; ~ **de préstamo preferencial** BANCA, FIN prime lending rate; ~ **de préstamo variable** BANCA, FIN variable lending rate (*VLR*); ~ **de préstamos** BANCA, FIN borrowing rate; ~ **de préstamos comerciales preferenciales** BANCA, FIN prime business loan rate; ~ **de prima** BOLSA premium rate; ~ **privada de descuento** BANCA private rate of discount; ~ **prorrateada** TRANSP proration rate; ~ **provocadora** FIN teaser rate;

~ r ~ **real de devolución** COM GEN, FIN real rate of return (*RRR*); ~ **real de rendimiento** COM GEN, FIN real rate of return (*RRR*); ~ **real de rentabilidad después de impuestos** FISC after-tax real rate of return; ~ **de recargo** BANCA flat; ~ **de reclamación** FIN, PROT SOC *subsidio* take-up rate; ~ **de recompra** BANCA repurchase rate; ~ **de recursos propios** INMOB equity rate (*AmE*); ~ **de reducción de clase** TRANSP *de fletes aéreos* reduce class rate; ~ **de reinversión** BOLSA *de futuros*, COM GEN reinvestment rate; ~ **de relevo** RRHH standby rate (*BrE*); ~ **de rendimiento** BANCA rate of return, BOLSA earnings yield; ~ **de rendimiento del capital invertido** BANCA, CONT, ECON, FIN rate of return on capital employed (*RORCE*); ~ **de rendimiento contable** CONT accounting rate of return (*ARR*); ~ **de rendimiento interna** (*TRI*) FIN internal rate of return (*IRR*); ~ **de rendimiento justo** BOLSA, CONT, FIN fair rate of return; ~ **de rendimiento requerida** FIN required rate of return; ~ **de renovación** BOLSA rate of rolling, PATENT renewal fee; ~ **de rentabilidad** CONT rate of return, FISC pretax rate of return; ~ **de rentabilidad de la gestión financiera** FIN financial management rate of return (*FMRR*); ~ **de rentabilidad interna** FIN internal rate of return (*IRR*); ~ **de reposición** PROT SOC replacement ratio; ~ **de reproducción** COM GEN reproduction rate; ~ **de reserva** BANCA reserve rate; ~ **de rotación de personal** RRHH quit rate;

~ s ~ **de servicio** COM GEN service fee; ~ **social de descuento** FIN social rate of discount;

~ t ~ **de Tobin** ECON, FISC Tobin tax; ~ **tope** BANCA, FIN rate ceiling; ~ **trimestral** FIN three-months' rate;

~ u ~ **unitaria** ECON tax unit; ~ **por uso de bienes y servicios públicos** TRANSP *navegación* fixture rate;

~ v ~ **de valor superávit** BANCA rate of surplus value; ~ **variable** BANCA, FIN variable rate; ~ **de venta bancaria** BANCA bank selling rate; ~ **a la vista** BANCA, BOLSA, ECON, FIN call rate

tasa^2: ~ **a acordar** *fra* TRANSP rate to be agreed (*RTBA*); **a una ~ anual** *fra* COM GEN at an annual rate

tasación *f Esp* (*cf avalúo AmL*) BOLSA *acciones* valuation, COM GEN valuation report, assessment, COM GEN, CONT *propiedades* appreciation, FIN appraisal, appraisement; ~ **excesiva** COM GEN, CONT, ECON overvaluation; ~ **de Hulbert** FIN Hulbert rating; ~ **inmobiliaria** FISC real estate appraisal

tasado: ~ **íntegramente** *adj* BOLSA fully valued

tasador, a *m,f Esp* (*cf valuador AmL*) FIN, INMOB appraiser, SEG adjuster; ~ **de aduanas** IMP/EXP examiner; ~ **de Hacienda** FISC tax assessor; ~ **oficial** DER official valuer; ~ **de pérdidas** RRHH, SEG *seguros* loss adjuster

tasar *vt* COM GEN *bienes* valorize

tasas: ~ **de eurodivisas** *f* ECON Eurocurrency Rates

TAV *abr* (*Tren de Alta Velocidad*) TRANSP ≈ HST (*high-speed train*)

taxi *m* TRANSP taxi

taylorismo *m* ECON, RRHH Taylorism

TC *abr* (*tonelaje cúbico*) TRANSP CT (*cubic tonnage*)

techo *m* BOLSA, COM GEN, ECON, FIN *tipo de interés* cap; ~ **de crédito** BANCA, FIN credit ceiling; ~ **de los ingresos por jubilación** FISC pension earnings cap; ~ **máximo** BOLSA peak level; ~ **presupuestario** CONT budget ceiling; ~ **del tipo de interés** COM GEN interest rate ceiling; ♦ **de alto ~** INMOB *edificio* high-rise

tecla: ~ **activación** *f* INFO hot key; ~ **alt** *f* (*tecla alternativa*) INFO Alt key (*Alternate key*); ~ **alternativa** *f* (*tecla alt*) INFO Alternate key (*Alt key*); ~ **de ayuda** *f* INFO help key; ~ **de barra inversa** *f* INFO backslash key; ~ **de comando** *f* INFO command key; ~ **de contacto** *f* INFO touch key; ~ **CTRL** *f* (*tecla de mando*) INFO CTRL key (*control key*); ~ **desactivada** *f* ADMIN, INFO dead key; ~ **de función** *f* INFO function key (*F key*); ~ **maestra** *f* INFO master key; ~ **de mando** *f* (*tecla CTRL*) INFO control key (*CTRL key*); ~ **de mayúsculas** *f* INFO shift key

teclado *m* INFO keyboard; ~ **de entrada** INFO input keyboard; ~ **en función programable** INFO soft keyboard; ~ **numérico** INFO keypad, numeric keypad; ~ **personalizado** INFO customized keyboard; ~ **QWERTY** INFO QWERTY keyboard; ~ **táctil** INFO tactile keyboard

teclear *vt* INFO key in, *tecla, botón del ratón* click

técnica *f* COM GEN technique; ~ **de administración** GES management technique; ~ **administrativa** GES management technique; ~ **administrativa de dinero** GES cash management technique; ~ **del aerógrafo** MEDIOS, V&M *publicidad* air brush technique; ~ **anterior** PATENT prior art; ~ **de auditoría** CONT auditing technique, audit technique; ~ **de comunicación** RRHH communication skill; ~ **Delphi** GES Delphi technique; ~ **electrónica** COM GEN electronic engineer; ~ **de evaluación y revisión del programa** GES program evaluation and review technique (*AmE*) (*PERT*), programme evaluation and review technique (*BrE*) (*PERT*); ~ **de fabricación** IND process engineering; ~ **interpersonal**

RRHH interpersonal skill; **~ de laboratorio** V&M laboratory technique (*jarg*); **~ de licitación** COM GEN, V&M bidding technique; **~ de producción** IND production technique; **~ publicitaria** V&M advertising technique; **~ de las relaciones humanas** RRHH human engineering; **~ de secretariado** ADMIN, RRHH secretarial skill; **~ de subasta** ECON bidding technique; **~ de la venta segura** COM GEN, V&M bread-and-butter technique (*infrml*); **~ de ventas** V&M sales technique

tecnicidad *f* COM GEN, DER technicality

técnico[1] *adj* COM GEN technical; **poco ~** COM GEN, IND low-tech

técnico[2] *m* COM GEN repair man

técnico[3]**,-a** *m,f* RRHH engineer; **~ asesor(a)** COM GEN consulting engineer; **~ electrónico(-a)** COM GEN electronic engineer; **~ financiero(-a) principal** CONT senior financial officer

tecnocracia *f* COM GEN, ECON technocracy

tecnócrata *mf* COM GEN, ECON technocrat

tecnocrático *adj* COM GEN, ECON technocratic

tecnoestructura *f* ECON technostructure

tecnología *f* COM GEN technology, know-how (*infrml*); **~ alternativa** IND alternative technology; **~ apropiada** ECON appropriate technology; **~ de avance** COM GEN, INFO advanced technology; **~ avanzada** COM GEN, INFO advanced technology; **~ complementaria** COM GEN complementary technology; **~ de los computadores** *m AmL ver* tecnología de las computadoras *AmL*; **~ de las computadoras** *AmL* (*cf* tecnología de los ordenadores *Esp*) INFO computer environment; **~ de la comunicación** COMS communication technology; **~ flexible** MED AMB soft technology; **~ incremental** COM GEN incremental technology; **~ informática** COM GEN INFO computer technology; **~ intermedia** IND *producción* intermediate technology; **~ limpia** MED AMB clean technology; **~ nueva** COM GEN new technology; **~ de oficina** ADMIN, INFO office technology; **~ de los ordenadores** *Esp* (*cf* tecnología de las computadoras *AmL*) INFO computer environment; **~ PAL/SECAM** COM GEN, MEDIOS *transmisión por vía satélite* PAL/SECAM technology; **~ de las plataformas petrolíferas** IND offshore technology; **~ sustituta** COM GEN replacement technology

tecnológicamente: ~ avanzado *adj* COM GEN technologically advanced

tejeduría *f* IND weaving mill

tejido: ~ a mano *adj* IND hand-woven

telar *m* IND weaving loom

Telaraña: la ~ *f* INFO Internet, the Net, the Web; **~ mundial** *f* INFO World Wide Web (*WWW*)

telebanca *f* BANCA telebanking

telecomunicaciones *f pl* COMS telecommunications; **~ por satélite** COMS satellite communications

teleconferencia *f* COMS, INFO, V&M teleconference; **~ por computador** *AmL* (*cf* teleconferencia por computadora *Aml*), **~ por computadora** *AmL* (*cf* teleconferencia por ordenador *Esp*) INFO computer conferencing; **~ por ordenador** *Esp* (*cf* teleconferencia por computadora *AmL*) INFO computer conferencing

telecopiadora *f* ADMIN, COMS telewriter

teléf. *abr* (*teléfono*) ADMIN, COMS tel. (*telephone*)

telefonía *f* ADMIN, COMS telephony

telefónico *adj* COMS telephonic

telefonista *mf* COMS, RRHH telephone operator, switchboard operator

teléfono *m* (*teléf.*) COMS telephone (*tel.*); **~ de botonera** *AmL* (*cf* teléfono de teclado *Esp*) COMS push-button telephone; **~ celular** COM GEN, COMS cellphone; **~ gratuito** COMS, V&M Freefone® (*BrE*); **~ móvil** COM GEN mobil telephone; **~ de pago** COMS pay phone (*BrE*), pay station (*AmE*); **~ portátil** COMS mobile phone, mobile telephone, portable phone; **~ público** COMS pay phone (*BrE*), pay station (*AmE*); **~ con teclado** COMS touch-tone phone; **~ de teclado** *Esp* (*cf* teléfono de botonera *AmL*) COMS push-button telephone; **~ visual** COMS visual telephone

telegrafiar *vt* COMS cable

telegrama *m* BOLSA, COMS cable; **~ internacional** COMS international telegram; **~ de madrugada** COMS night letter (*AmE*)

teleimpresión *f* INFO, MEDIOS remote printing

teleimpresora *f* INFO, MEDIOS teleprinter

teleinformática *f* INFO computer communication

telemando *m* COMS remote control

telemarket *m* FIN, GES, V&M telemarket

telemarketing *m* FIN, GES, V&M telemarketing

telemática *f* COM GEN, COMS, INFO telematics

telemercado *m* FIN, V&M telemarketing

telepedido *m* COMS, INFO, V&M teleordering

teleproceso *m* COM GEN, INFO teleprocessing (*TP*)

teleregistro *m* COMS telerecording

telespectadores *m pl* MEDIOS, V&M television audience, viewers

teletexto *m* COMS, INFO, MEDIOS teletext

teletrabajador, a *m,f* COMS, ECON, RRHH teleworker

teletrabajo *m* COM GEN, COMS, RRHH telework, teleworking

teletranscripción *f* ADMIN, COMS telewriting

teletranscriptor *m* ADMIN, COMS telex machine

televentas *f pl* FIN, V&M telesales

televisión *f* (*TV*) MEDIOS television (*TV*); **~ de alta densidad parcialmente digital** (*TVAD parcialmente digital*) MEDIOS partially digital HDTV (*partially digital high-density television*); **~ por cable** MEDIOS, V&M cable television; **~ comercial** MEDIOS, V&M commercial television; **~ patrocinada** MEDIOS, V&M sponsored television; **~ por satélite** MEDIOS *radio y televisión* satellite television; **~ privada de pago**

telón: ~ de bambú *m* POL bamboo curtain; **~ de fondo** *m* COM GEN *de la situación* backdrop

tema: ~ musical *m* MEDIOS *radio y televisión* theme tune; **~ publicitario** *m* V&M advertising theme

temas: ~ medioambientales *m pl* MED AMB environmental issues

temperatura: ~ ambiente *f* COM GEN ambient temperature, room temperature; **~ de autoinflamación** *f* COM GEN spontaneous ignition temperature; **~ de ebullición inicial** *f* COM GEN initial boiling point; **~ mínima** *f* COM GEN minimum temperature (*MT*)

temporada[1]**: ~ alta** *f* COM GEN, ECON peak season; **~ baja** *f* COM GEN off season, MEDIOS *prensa, radiodifusión* closed season; **~ importadora alta** *f* IMP/EXP peak importing season; **~ inactiva** *f* COM GEN off season

temporada[2]**: fuera de ~** *fra* COM GEN off season, out of season; **de ~ baja** *fra* COM GEN off-peak

temporero[1] *adj* COM GEN temporary

temporero^2**,-a** *m,f* RRHH casual worker, seasonal worker, temporary (*temp.*)

tenaz *adj* ECON steep

tenazas: ~ **de elevación** *f pl* TRANSP *equipo de cargas* tongs

tendencia *f* COM GEN *ascendente, rendimiento* run, ECON trend; ~ **al alza** BOLSA rising trend, bullish tendency, upward trend, ECON uptrend; ~ **alcista** BOLSA bullish tendency, rising trend, upward trend; ~ **básica** COM GEN basic trend; ~ **central** MAT central tendency; ~ **comercial** COM GEN business trend; ~ **de las compras** V&M purchasing pattern; ~ **de consumo** V&M consumer trend; ~ **declinante** COM GEN, ECON downtrend; ~ **dominante** COM GEN, ECON major trend; ~ **económica** ECON, POL economic trend; ~ **económica actual** ECON, POL current economic trend; ~ **exponencial** COM GEN exponential trend; ~ **del flujo de pedidos** V&M order flow pattern; ~ **futura** COM GEN future trend; ~ **inflacionaria** ECON inflationary trend; ~ **a largo plazo** COM GEN long-term trend; ~ **del mercado** COM GEN, ECON, V&M market trend; ~ **nacional** COM GEN national trend; ~ **oculta** COM GEN underlying tendency; ~ **del precio** COM GEN, FIN price trend; ~ **a privilegiar el corto plazo** BOLSA short termism; ~ **regional** ECON, V&M regional trend; ~ **secular** ECON secular trend; ~ **subyacente** COM GEN underlying trend; ~ **de tarifa** TRANSP rate trend; ~ **del tráfico** TRANSP traffic trend

tender *vt* COM GEN *en dirección* tend; ♦ ~ **a** COM GEN *cifra, nivel* tend toward; ~ **hacia** COM GEN lean toward

tenderetes *m pl* BOLSA stands (*jarg*)

tendero, -a *m,f* V&M shopkeeper (*BrE*), storekeeper (*AmE*)

tenedor, a *m,f* BANCA bearer; BOLSA holder; ~ **de buena fe** BANCA *de letra de cambio*, DER holder in due course; ~ **de contrato** FIN contracting holder; ~ **de cuenta** BANCA account payee; ~**indiviso(-a)** BOLSA joint holder; ~ **legítimo(-a)** BANCA, DER holder in due course; ~ **de libros** RRHH bookkeeper; ~ **de una obligación** DER obligee; ~ **de una opción** BOLSA option holder; ~ **registrado(-a)** BOLSA holder of record; ~ **de reversión** RRHH reversioner; ~ **a título oneroso** BANCA, DER holder for value; ~ **de títulos** BOLSA security holder; ~ **unitario(-a)** BOLSA unit holder

teneduría: ~ **de libros** *f* ADMIN, CONT book-keeping

tenemos: ~ **las manos atadas** *fra* COM GEN our hands are tied

tenencia *f* DER, INMOB holding, occupation; ~ **de bonos** BOLSA, FIN bond holding; ~ **cruzada entre empresas** BOLSA cross holding between companies; ~ **de una letra** BANCA bill holding; ~ **por el propietario** INMOB owner occupation; ~ **de valores** BOLSA security holding, holding of securities

tener: ~ **una cuenta con** *fra* BANCA bank with; ~ **éxito** *fra* COM GEN come off, succeed; ~ **lugar** *fra* COM GEN take place; ~ **manía a** *fra* COM GEN be down on (*infrml*); ~ **necesidad urgente de** *fra* COM GEN be in urgent need of; ~ **una participación en un negocio** *fra* COM GEN have a share in a business; ~ **posibilidades de** *fra* COM GEN *para el ascenso* be in the running for

tensión *f* IND power, RRHH stress; ♦ **con ~ eléctrica** INFO power on

tenso *adj* COM GEN strained

tensor *m* TRANSP twistlock, screw; ~ **de cadena** TRANSP chain tensioner; ~ **descentrado** TRANSP *látigo* over-center tensioner (*AmE*), overcentre tensioner (*BrE*); ~ **neumático** TRANSP pneumatic tensioner; ~ **de palanca** TRANSP lever tensioner

teonomía *f* ECON theonomy

teorema: ~ **de la autopista** *m* ECON turnpike theorem; ~ **de la bañera** *m* ECON bathtub theorem; ~ **de Bayes** *m* ECON *probabilidad* Bayes theorem; ~ **comercial de Heckscher-Ohlin** *m* ECON *comercio internacional* Heckscher-Ohlin trade theorem; ~ **de Coase** *m* ECON *renta nacional* Coase theorem; ~ **de equivalencia ricardiana** *m* ECON *teoría laboral del valor* Ricardian equivalence theorem; ~ **de Euler** *m* ECON *rendimiento de escala* Euler's theorem; ~ **del exceso de capacidad** *m* ECON excess capacity theorem; ~ **de Fisher** *m* ECON *inflación* Fisher theorem; ~ **Heckscher-Ohlin** *m* ECON Heckscher-Ohlin theorem; ~ **de la igualdad del precio de los factores** *m* ECON factor price equalization theorem; ~ **de la imposibilidad** *m* ECON impossibility theorem; ~ **de Rybczynski** *m* ECON *condiciones del intercambio* Rybczynski theorem; ~ **de Stolper-Samuelson** *m* ECON *libre comercio, efecto de aumento* Stolper Samuelson theorem; ~ **de la Telaraña** *m* ECON Cobweb Theorem

teoría^1: ~ **de la administración** *f* ADMIN, GES administrative theory; ~ **administrativa** *f* ADMIN, GES administrative theory, management theory; ~ **de la agencia** *f* ECON agency theory; ~ **bayesiana de la decisión** *f* V&M Bayesian decision theory; ~ **del camino aleatorio** *f* BOLSA, ECON random walk theory; ~ **del camino crítico** *f* GES critical path theory; ~ **de campo de la motivación** *f* RRHH field theory of motivation; ~ **del caos** *f* ECON chaos theory; ~ **del capital** *f* ECON capital theory; ~ **característica de la demanda del consumidor** *f* ECON characteristics theory; ~ **de la cartera de valores** *f* BOLSA portfolio theory; ~ **de catástrofes** *f* MAT catastrophe theory; ~ **central de la localización** *f* ECON central place theory; ~ **del ciclo de elecciones presidenciales** *f* BOLSA presidential election cycle theory; ~ **clásica del ahorro** *f* ECON classical savings theory; ~ **de las colas** *f* ECON, MAT queueing theory (*BrE*), waiting line theory (*AmE*); ~ **de las comunicaciones** *f* GES communications theory; ~ **de contingencia** *f* GES contingency theory; ~ **del contrato implícito** *f* ECON implicit contract theory; ~ **de convenios salariales** *f* RRHH bargaining theory of wages; ~ **de costes comparativos** *f Esp* (*cf teoría de costos comparativos AmL*) ECON theory of comparative costs; ~ **de costos comparativos** *f AmL* (*cf teoría de costes comparativos Esp*) ECON theory of comparative costs; ~ **de crecimiento de la empresa** *f* ECON growth theory of the firm; ~ **cuantitativa del dinero** *f* BANCA, CONT, ECON, FIN quantity theory of money; ~ **de la decisión** *f* GES decision theory; ~ **de la dependencia** *f* ECON, POL, PROT SOC, RRHH dependency theory; ~ **diferencial de la renta** *f* ECON differential theory of rent; ~ **de Dow** *f* BOLSA Dow theory; ~ **económica** *f* COM GEN, ECON economic theory; ~ **de elección pública** *f* ECON public choice theory; ~ **de la elección social** *f* ECON social choice theory; ~ **de equipo** *f* ECON, RRHH team theory; ~ **de establecimiento de precios por arbitraje** *f* BOLSA arbitrage pricing theory (*APT*); ~ **de estado** *f* ECON state theory; ~ **de etapas** *f* ECON stages theory; ~ **de la evolución de la empresa** *f* ECON evolutionary theory of the firm; ~ **de la expectativa-valencia** *f* RRHH *motivación* expectancy theory of motivation; **~ de la filtración** *f* ECON trickle down theory; **~ del fondo de salarios** *f* ECON wages fund theory; **~ de fondos de préstamo** *f* FIN loanable funds theory; **~ de Ford** *f* ECON *literatura* Fordism; **~ general de Keynes** *f* ECON Keynes' General Theory; **~ de la gestión de cartera de valores** *f* BOLSA portfolio management theory; **~ de grupos** *f* ECON theory of clubs; **~ del habitat preferente** *f* FIN preferred habitat theory; **~ de la información** *f* COM GEN *estadística* information theory; **~ del interés basada en la especulación** *f* BOLSA agio theory of interest; **~ del interés reducido** *f* BANCA, BOLSA short-interest theory; **~ internacional del comercio** *f* ECON international trade theory; **~ de juegos** *f* ECON, GES, RRHH game theory; **~ laboral del valor** *f* ECON labor theory of value (*AmE*), labour theory of value (*BrE*); **~ de la localización** *f* ECON location theory; **~ de las manchas solares** *f* ECON sunspot theory; **~ marginal de la productividad** *f* ECON marginal productivity theory; **~ de los medios y las metas** *f* GES path-goal theory; **~ del mercado laboral segmentado** *f* ECON segmented labor market theory (*AmE*), segmented labour market theory (*BrE*); **~ moderna de la cartera** *f* BOLSA modern portfolio theory (*MPT*); **~ de la motivación por expectativas** *f* RRHH expectancy theory of motivation, VIE theory; **~ neoricardiana** *f* ECON neo-Ricardian theory; **~ de la onda** *f* COM GEN wave theory; **~ de la organización** *f* ECON, GES organization theory; **~ organizativa** *f* COM GEN organizational theory; **~ de los pequeños lotes** *f* BOLSA odd-lot theory; **~ posicional** *f* V&M positioning theory; **~ de la probabilidad** *f* GES, MAT probability theory; **~ del proceso laboral** *f* RRHH labor process theory (*AmE*), labour process theory (*BrE*); **~ de reglamentación** *f* COM GEN capture theory; **~ reguladora** *f* COM GEN regulatory theory; **~ ricardiana del valor** *f* ECON Ricardian theory of value; **~ del sacrificio** *f* ECON *venta sin beneficio* sacrifice theory; **~ salarial** *f* ECON, RRHH wage theory; **~ del salario de subsistencia** *f* ECON subsistence theory of wages; **~ de sistemas** *f* GES systems theory; **~ de los tipos de ahorro** *f* ECON class savings theory; **~ de la valoración de opciones** *f* BOLSA option pricing theory; **~ X** *f* RRHH theory X (*jarg*)

teoría²: en ~ *fra* COM GEN in theory

teórico¹ *adj* COM GEN theoretical

teórico²,a: ~ de las opciones *m,f* BOLSA option theorist

tercer¹ *adj* COM GEN third

tercer²: ~ mundo *m* COM GEN Third World; **~ transportista** *mf* TRANSP third carrier; **~ trimestre** *m* COM GEN third quarter

tercera: ~ era *f* ECON third age; **~ persona** *f* COM GEN third person

terceras *f pl* DER, PATENT, SEG third party

terceros *m pl* COM GEN third party

terminación *f* COM GEN completion, GES *reunión* adjournment

terminado *adj* COM GEN, DER completed

terminal¹ *f* TRANSP terminal; **~ aérea** TRANSP air terminal; **~ de carga** TRANSP freight terminal; **~ de carga general y contenedor** TRANSP general cargo and container berth; **~ para contenedores** TRANSP container terminal; **~ ferroviaria** TRANSP rail terminal; **~ granelera** TRANSP grain terminal; **~ marítima**

TRANSP maritime terminal; **~ de pasajeros** OCIO, TRANSP passenger terminal; **~ de petroleros** TRANSP oil terminal; **~ portuaria de contenedores** TRANSP container port; **~ refrigerada** TRANSP cold store terminal; **~ de tierra** MED AMB onshore terminal

terminal² *m* INFO terminal; **~ de aplicaciones** INFO applications terminal; **~ básico** INFO dumb terminal; **~ de computador** *ver terminal de computadora AmL*; **~ de computadora** *AmL* (*cf terminal de ordenador Esp*) INFO computer terminal; **~ de entrada de datos** INFO data entry terminal; **~ de información** INFO report terminal; **~ inteligente** INFO intelligent terminal, smart terminal; **~ mudo** INFO dumb terminal; **~ no inteligente** INFO dumb terminal; **~ de ordenador** *Esp* (*cf terminal de computadora AmL*) INFO computer terminal; **~ de pago electrónico** COM GEN electronic payment terminal (*EPT*); **~ con pantalla de visualización** INFO visual display terminal (*VDT*); **~ en punto de venta** BANCA, V&M point-of-sale terminal; **~ de representación gráfica** INFO graphic display terminal; **~ teleescritor** INFO teletypewriter (*AmE*); **~ de video** *AmL*, **~ de vídeo** *Esp* INFO video terminal

terminar *vt* COM GEN finish, terminate, GES *reunión* adjourn; ♦ **~ con beneficio potencial** BOLSA finish in the money; **~ la comunicación** INFO log out; **~ gradualmente** COM GEN, FIN wind down; **~ su alegato** DER rest one's case

término¹: ~ de carga de línea regular *m* TRANSP liner term; **~ estocástico** *m* MAT stochastic term; **~ explícito** *m* COM GEN, DER *de contrato* express term; **~ expreso** *m* COM GEN, DER *de contrato* express term; **~ implícito** *m* COM GEN, DER *de un contrato* implied term; **~ particular** *m* COM GEN private term (*pt*); **~ de perturbación** *m* MAT *estadística* disturbance term; **~ secundario libre** *m* IMP/EXP, TRANSP free out term (*fo*); **~ de un voto** *m* BANCA wording of a vote

término²: por ~ medio *fra* COM GEN at an average, in the medium term

terminología *f* COM GEN terminology

términos *m pl* COM GEN terms; **~ del intercambio** COM GEN terms of trade; ♦ **en los mismos ~** COM GEN in the same terms, on equal terms; **en ~ absolutos** ECON in absolute terms; **en ~ americanos** ECON *cambio de divisas* in American terms; **según los ~ del contrato** DER under the terms of the contract; **en ~ relativos** ECON in relative terms

termómetro: ~ publicitario *m* V&M advertising thermometer

terotecnología *f* ECON terotechnology

terrateniente *m* INMOB landowner

terreno *m* INMOB plot, land; **~ de abono** MED AMB dumping ground; **~ afecto a una vivienda** DER, INMOB curtilage; **~ agrícola** MED AMB agricultural land; **~ alrededor de la casa** DER, INMOB curtilage; **~ sin calificar** INMOB *planificación territorial* white land (*jarg*); **~ de explotación agrícola** MED AMB, COM GEN farmland; **~ de explotación ganadera** MED AMB, COM GEN farmland; **~ inocupado** INMOB vacant land; **~ interior** INMOB inside lot; **~ inundable** INMOB flood plain; **~ mejorado** INMOB improved land; **~ no acondicionado** INMOB raw land; **~ rural** INMOB rural land

terrenos: ~ bancarios *m pl* BANCA, FIN land banking; **~,**

viviendas y herencias *m pl* DER, INMOB land, tenements and hereditaments

terrestre *adj* COM GEN onshore, *tecnología de transmisiones* terrestrial, MEDIOS terrestrial

territorio *m* COM GEN territory, *de vendedor* pitch, POL territory; **~ de ventas** V&M sales territory

terrorismo *m* POL terrorism

tesis: ~ de continuidad *f* ECON continuity thesis; **~ de convergencia** *f* ECON, POL convergence thesis; **~ de disponibilidad** *f* ECON availability thesis; **~ de mercado discutible** *f* ECON, V&M contestable markets thesis; **~ de Prebisch-Singer** *f* ECON Prebisch-Singer thesis

tesorería *f* CONT cash assets

tesorero, -a: ~ de la empresa *m,f* RRHH corporate treasurer

tesoro: ~ público *m* ECON, FIN public purse

Tesoro: el ~ *m* ECON, FIN, POL Treasury; **~ Público** *m* FIN National Treasury, Treasury

test: ~ del chi-cuadrado *m* MAT *método estadístico* chi-square test; **~ de conocimientos específicos** *m* COM GEN achievement test; **~ de inversión de Scitovsky** *m* ECON Scitovsky reversal test; **~ de la tasa de descuento** *m* ECON test rate of discount

testaferro *m* COM GEN, DER dummy

testamento *m* DER will, last will and testament

testificación *f* DER attestation

testificar *vi* DER testify

testigo: ~ de cargo *m* DER witness for the prosecution; **~ de la defensa** *m* DER witness for the defence (*BrE*), witness for the defense (*AmE*); **~ de descargo** *m* DER witness for the defence (*BrE*), witness for the defense (*AmE*); **~ no solicitado** *m* DER unsolicited testimonial; **~ ocular** *m* DER eye witness; **~ pericial** *m* DER expert witness; **~ que no comparece** *m* DER defaulting witness

testimonio *m* DER testimony; **~ adjunto** DER affixed testimonial; **~ contradictorio** DER conflicting evidence; **~ falso** DER false testimony; **~ irrefutable** DER *circunstancias esenciales* res gestae; **~ de oídas** DER hearsay; ◆ **en ~ de lo cual** DER in witness whereof

tetrapak *m* V&M tetrapak

textiles *m pl* COM GEN, IND textiles

texto *m* MEDIOS, V&M text; **~ completo** COM GEN text in full; **~ impreso** MEDIOS, V&M letterpress; **~ de presentación** MEDIOS blurb (*jarg*); **~ publicitario** MEDIOS, V&M advertising text; **~ suelto** V&M body matter; ◆ **contra ~** V&M *publicidad* against text

Thatcherismo *m* ECON, POL Thatcherism

tiburón *m* BOLSA, FIN corporate raider, raider; **~ corporativo** BOLSA, FIN corporate raider

tiempo *m* COM GEN *duración* time, *meteriológico* weather; **~ de acceso** *Esp* (*cf tiempo de ingreso AmL*) INFO access time; **~ de acceso múltiple** *Esp* (*cf tiempo de ingreso múltiple AmL*) INFO multiple access time (*MAT*); **~ de antena** MEDIOS airtime; **~ de antena disponible** MEDIOS *radio* availability; **~ de audiencia primaria** MEDIOS *radiodifusión* prime listening time; **~ de carga y descarga** TRANSP turnaround time (*AmE*), turnround time (*BrE*); **~ de carga y descarga de automóviles** TRANSP vehicle turnaround time (*AmE*), vehicle turnround time (*BrE*); **~ compartido** INFO, RRHH time-sharing (*TS*); **~ de compensación** RRHH compensatory time; **~ concedido** RRHH *trabajo*

allowed time; **~ de conducción** V&M drive time; **~ de conexión** INFO connection time; **~ disponible** INFO available time; **~ de ejecución** COM GEN operation time, INFO execution time; **~ de emisión** MEDIOS airtime; **~ entre entrada y salida de un puerto** TRANSP port turnaround time (*AmE*), port turnround time (*BrE*); **~ de entrega reducido** IND reduced lead time; **~ de espera** COM GEN waiting time, IND lead time; **~ estimado** GES time budget; **~ de ida y vuelta del barco** TRANSP ship turnaround time (*AmE*), ship turnround time (*BrE*); **~ de inactividad** COM GEN down time; **~ inactivo** INFO idle time; **~ de indisponibilidad** COM GEN down time; **~ de ingreso** *AmL* (*cf tiempo de acceso Esp*) INFO access time; **~ de ingreso múltiple** *AmL* (*cf tiempo de acceso múltiple Esp*) INFO multiple access time (*MAT*); **~ libre** COM GEN, OCIO, RRHH leisure time, time off; **~ libre fuera del trabajo** COM GEN, OCIO, RRHH time off work; **~ de máquina** INFO computer time; **~ máximo para realizar una tarea** ECON time span; **~ medio** (*TM*) COM GEN mean time (*MT*); **~ medio de acceso** INFO average access time; **~ medio entre averías** INFO mean time between failures (*MTBF*); **~ mínimo** RRHH core time; **~ mínimo de conexión** TRANSP minimum connecting time (*MCT*); **~ muerto** RRHH dead time; **~ de parada** INFO stop time; **~ de parado a parado** TRANSP *aviación* block time; **~ de pasada** COM GEN run time; **~ de plancha definido** TRANSP *navegación* definite laytime; **~ de prescripción** COM GEN term of limitation; **~ prestado de servicio** RRHH time served; **~ previsto** COM GEN prescribed time, TRANSP *salida, llegada* right time; **~ previsto de llegada** TRANSP estimated time of arrival (*ETA*); **~ de proceso** INFO run time; **~ para publicidad** V&M advertising time; **~ en radio** MEDIOS airtime; **~ de reacción** IND reaction time; **~ real** COM GEN real time; **~ de recorrido** COM GEN turnaround time (*AmE*), turnround time (*BrE*); **~ de recuperación** INFO retrieval time; **~ de recurso** COM GEN resource time; **~ reducido de aparcamiento de vehículos** TRANSP short-term vehicle park (*STVP*); **~ de retorno al puerto** TRANSP port turnaround time (*AmE*), port turnround time (*BrE*); **~ de retorno de un vehículo** TRANSP vehicle turnaround time (*AmE*), vehicle turnround time (*BrE*); **~ en riesgo** SEG time on risk; **~ transcurrido** INFO elapsed time; **~ de tránsito** TRANSP transit time; **~ del turno de atraque** *puerto* turn time; **~ en TV** MEDIOS *para publicidad* airtime; **~ del viaje de ida y vuelta** TRANSP return journey time (*BrE*), round trip time (*AmE*); **~ de viaje redondo** TRANSP ship turnaround time (*AmE*), ship turnround time (*BrE*); **~ de viaje redondo de un avión** TRANSP aircraft turnaround time (*AmE*), aircraft turnround time (*BrE*); **~ de vuelo** OCIO, TRANSP flight time, airborne time; ◆ **a ~** COM GEN on time; **todo ~ ahorrado** TRANSP *navegación* all time saved; **a ~ completo** RRHH full-time; **en un ~ determinado** COM GEN at a given time; **el ~ es oro** COM GEN time is money; **en un ~ futuro** COM GEN at a given time in the future; **si el ~ lo permite** COM GEN, TRANSP weather permitting (*WP*); **con ~ de sobra** COM GEN with time to spare

tienda *f* COM GEN shop (*BrE*), store (*AmE*); **~ en las afueras** V&M out-of-town shop (*BrE*), out-of-town store (*AmE*); **~ de alimentación** V&M food shop (*BrE*), food store (*AmE*); **~ de alimentación del centro** V&M town-center food store (*AmE*), town-centre food shop (*BrE*); ~ **de artículos de segunda mano** COM GEN, V&M second-hand shop (*BrE*), thrift shop (*AmE*); ~ **de autoservicio** V&M self-service shop (*BrE*), self-service store (*AmE*); ~ **de barrio** V&M neighborhood store (*AmE*), local shop (*BrE*), corner shop (*BrE*); ~ **de una cadena** COM GEN franchise, chain-store; ~ **de conveniencia** V&M convenience shop (*BrE*), convenience store (*AmE*); ~ **de descuento** BOLSA, COM GEN, FIN, V&M discount house (*AmE*), discount store (*BrE*); ~ **franquiciada** ECON, V&M tied house (*BrE*); ~ **independiente** COM GEN independent store; ~ **insignia** V&M flagship store; ~ **de licores** COM GEN liquor store (*AmE*), off-licence (*BrE*), package store (*AmE*); ~ **libre de impuestos** FISC, IMP/EXP, OCIO, V&M duty-free shop; ~ **de modas** COM GEN fashion house; ~ **múltiple** V&M multivariety store; ~ **de saldos** BOLSA, COM GEN *que vende artículos a precios rebajados*, FIN, V&M discount house (*AmE*), discount store (*BrE*); ~ **urbana** V&M in-town store; ~ **de venta al público** V&M outlet store

tierra: ~ **baldía** *f* INMOB, MED AMB waste land; ~ **de cultivo redundante** *f* MED AMB redundant farmland

tierras: ~ **en curso de adquisición** *f pl* DER, INMOB land in abeyance; ~ **en explotación ocupadas por su propietario** *f pl* INMOB owner-occupied farmland; ~ **en suspenso** *f pl* DER, INMOB land in abeyance; ~ **sin titular** *f pl* DER, INMOB land in abeyance

tildar *vt* BANCA tick up

timador, a *m,f* COM GEN confidence man, confidence trickster, DER crook (*infrml*)

timbre: ~ **de alarma** *m* COM GEN alarm bell; ~ **postal** *m* COMS postmark

timo *m* COM GEN confidence game (*AmE*), confidence trick (*BrE*)

tinglado: ~ **de importación** *m* IMP/EXP import shed

tinte: ~ **mecánico** *m* V&M mechanical tint

típicamente *adv* COM GEN typically

tipificación *f* COM GEN standardization

tipificar *vt* COM GEN typify

tipo *m* COM GEN, DER standard (*Std*), ECON *de cambio* rate, INFO standard (*Std*), *tipografía* type; ~ **actual** COM GEN current rate; ~ **ajustado a los antecedentes del asegurado** SEG experience rating; ~ **de alquiler** INMOB, PROT SOC rental rate; ~ **anual con ajuste estacional** ECON seasonally-adjusted annual rate (*s.a.a.r.*); ~ **de aportación de los asalariados** FISC *Seguridad Social* employee rate (*BrE*); ~ **de aportación del empresario** FISC employer rate; ~ **de arancel** *f* ECON, FISC, IMP/EXP, POL tariff rate; ~ **básico del impuesto de sociedades** FISC basic corporate tax rate; ~ **de beneficio después de impuestos** CONT, FISC after-tax rate of return; **todo** ~ **de bienes inmuebles** DER, INMOB land, tenements, and hereditaments; ~ **de cambio** COM GEN, ECON exchange rate, rate of exchange; ~ **de cambio al contado** ECON cash exchange rate, spot exchange rate; ~ **de cambio comercial especial** ECON special commercial exchange rate; ~ **de cambio cruzado** ECON *divisas* exchange cross rate; ~ **de cambio descentrado** ECON misaligned rate of exchange (*BrE*), misaligned rate of exchange (*AmE*); ~ **de cambio efectivo** ECON, FIN effective exchange rate; ~ **de cambio extranjero** BANCA foreign exchange rate; ~ **de cambio a fecha futura** BOLSA, ECON forward exchange rate; ~ **de cambio ficticio** ECON artificial exchange rate; ~ **de cambio**

flexible ECON flexible exchange rate; ~ **de cambio histórico** ECON historical exchange rate; ~ **de cambio interbancario** BANCA, ECON interbank exchange rate; ~ **de cambio medido según la importancia del comercio** COM GEN, ECON trade-weighted exchange rate; ~ **de cambio múltiple** ECON multiple exchange rate; ~ **de cambio a plazo** BOLSA forward rate; ~ **de cambio para turistas** ECON tourist exchange rate; ~ **de capitalización** CONT, ECON capitalization rate (*cap rate*); ~ **central** ECON central rate; ~ **combinado** COM GEN composite rate; ~ **competitivo** BANCA, V&M *intereses* competitive rate; ~ **de compra de divisas** BANCA buying rate of exchange; ~ **comprador** BANCA bid rate; ~ **concedido** COM GEN concessionary rate; ~ **concertado** FISC *Seguridad Social* contracted-in rate (*BrE*); ~ **controlado** BANCA, BOLSA, ECON, FIN controlled rate; ~ **de conversión** BANCA, ECON, FIN conversion rate; ~ **a corto plazo** FIN, V&M *intereses* short rate; ~ **de coste combinado a largo plazo** *Esp* (*cf tasa de costo combinado a largo plazo AmL*) FIN long-term blended cost rate (*LTB*); ~ **de costes** *Esp* (*cf tipo de costos AmL*) FIN type of costs; ~ **de costos** *AmL* (*cf tipo de costes Esp*) FIN type of costs; ~ **cruzado** ECON *internacional*, FIN cross rate; ~ **de datos** INFO data type; ~ **decreciente** FIN decreasing rate; ~ **de la deducción** FISC rate of relief; ~ **de depreciación** CONT rate of depreciation; ~ **de descuento** BOLSA, FIN, COM GEN rate of discount; ~ **de descuento ajustado a riesgo** FIN risk-adjusted discount rate; ~ **de descuento del mercado** BOLSA, FIN market rate of discount; ~ **diferencial** BANCA spread; ~ **para el dinero que se pide a plazo** BOLSA *futuros sobre divisas* forward borrowing rate; ~ **efectivo** CONT effective rate; ~ **de escritura** ADMIN, INFO, MEDIOS typeface; ~ **establecido** FISC *Seguridad Social* contracted-out rate; ~ **expandido** V&M expanded type; ~ **favorable** ECON favourable rate (*BrE*), favorable rate (*AmE*); ~ **fijo** FISC flat rate; ~ **fijo de cambio** ECON, FIN pegged exchange rate; ~ **flotante** ECON *de cambio* floating rate; ~ **flotante de cambio de divisas** ECON floating currency exchange rate; ~ **global de beneficio** CONT overall rate of return; ~ **impositivo** FISC rate of tax, rate of taxation, tax rate; ~ **impositivo aparente** FISC apparent tax rate; ~ **impositivo compuesto** FISC composite tax rate; ~ **impositivo efectivo** FISC effective tax rate; ~ **impositivo empresarial básico** FISC basic corporate tax rate; ~ **impositivo especial** FISC special tax rate; ~ **impositivo fijo** FISC fixed tax rate; ~ **impositivo legal** FISC statutory tax rate; ~ **impositivo marginal** FISC marginal tax rate; ~ **impositivo máximo** FISC ceiling tax rate; ~ **impositivo medio** FISC average tax rate; ~ **impositivo nominal** FISC nominal tax rate; ~ **impositivo real** FISC actual tax rate; ~ **impositivo para la vivienda** FISC residential tax rate; ~ **del impuesto** FISC rate of taxation, tax rate; ~ **del impuesto sobre la renta** FISC income tax rate; ~ **indicativo adecuado** CONT adequate target rate; ~ **interbancario** BANCA *mercado de dinero* interbank rate; ~ **de interés** BANCA lending rate, COM GEN interest rate; ~ **de interés acumulado** CONT accrual interest rate; ~ **de interés en aumento** COM GEN rising interest rate; ~ **de interés de la bonificación** FIN backwardation rate; ~ **de interés del bono** BOLSA bond rate; ~ **de interés a corto plazo** BANCA, COM GEN short-term interest rate; ~ **de interés de cuenta** *f* COM GEN, CONT, FIN accounting rate of interest (*ARI*); ~ **de interés**

deprimido ECON depression pole; ~ **de interés en descenso** COM GEN declining interest rate; ~ **de interés devengado** CONT accrual interest rate; ~ **de interés a largo plazo** COM GEN long-term interest rate; ~ **de interés del mercado** ECON, FIN market interest rate; ~ **de interés del mercado según cotización general** ECON, FIN generally quoted market interest rate; ~ **de interés nominal** BOLSA nominal interest rate; ~ **de interés para préstamos a la vista** BANCA, BOLSA, ECON, FIN call rate; ~ **de interés vigente** FISC standard rate or interest (*BrE*); ~ **interno de descuento** CONT internal rate of discount; ~ **legal** FISC statutory rate; ~ **de letra** ADMIN lettertype; ~ **de letras de cambio** FIN bill rate; ~ **marginal del impuesto sobre la renta** FISC marginal income tax rate; ~ **más alejado** COM GEN switching out rate; ~ **más cercano** COM GEN switching in rate; ~ **máximo** BOLSA *de futuros* ceiling rate, CONT, ECON *de interés* capitalization rate (*cap rate*); ~ **máximo del impuesto** FISC top rate of tax; ~ **medio** ECON middle rate; ~ **del mercado de contado** BOLSA cash market rate; ~ **mínimo** COM GEN rate floor; ~ **mínimo garantizado** ECON rate support grant (*RSG*); ~ **negrita** INFO bold type; ~ **normalizado** COM GEN standard grade; ~ **objetivo** BOLSA, CONT *futuros sobre tipos de interés* target rate; ~ **objetivo adecuado** CONT adequate target rate; ~ **oficial de cambio** ECON official exchange rate; ~ **de porcentaje actual** BANCA, COM GEN annual percentage rate (*APR*); ~ **preestablecido** FISC prescribed rate; ~ **preferencial** COM GEN preferred rate; ~ **preferencial para préstamos** BANCA, FIN prime lending rate; ~ **preferente canadiense** ECON Canadian Prime Rate; ~ **de préstamo variable** BANCA, FIN variable lending rate (*VLR*); ~ **de prima** SEG premium rate; ~ **de provisión efectiva de fondos** BOLSA *de futuro* effective funding rate; ~ **de redescuento** BANCA banking rate, CONT, FIN rediscount rate; ~ **reducido** FISC *Seguridad Social* reduced rate; ~ **de reinversión** BOLSA *de futuros*, COM GEN reinvestment rate; ~ **de rendimiento contable** CONT accounting rate of return (*ARR*); ~ **de rendimiento justo** BOLSA, CONT, FIN fair rate of return; ~ **renovable** BOLSA, FIN rolling rate; ~ **repo implícito** FIN *recompra* implied repo rate (*infrml*) (*AmE*); ~ **de salario de equilibrio** ECON equilibrium wage rate; ~ **de segunda generación** INMOB *de un almacén* second generation type; ~ **de sueldo por hora** RRHH base pay rate (*AmE*), basic pay rate (*BrE*); ~ **de transporte** TRANSP transport mode; ~ **uniforme de salarios** RRHH flat rate of pay; ~ **volátil** BOLSA gliding rate; ◆ **a un ~ actual** COM GEN at a current rate; **a un ~ anual** COM GEN at an annual rate; **ser ~ cero para el IVA** FISC be zero rated for VAT; **de ~ fijo** ECON *precios* flat-rate; **al ~ más alto** FISC at the top rate

Tipo: ~ **de Interés Interbancario de Tokio** *m* BANCA, ECON Tokyo Interbank Offered Rate (*TIBOR*)

tipógrafo, -a *m,f* COM GEN, V&M typographer

tipología *f* COM GEN typology

Tipos: ~ **del Impuesto de Sociedades** *m pl* FISC ≈ Corporation Tax rates (*BrE*)

tira *f* COM GEN strip; ~ **y afloja** COM GEN *entre varios* tug-of-war; ~ **de película** MEDIOS film strip; ~ **posterior** MEDIOS backstrip; ~ **de rasgado** COM GEN tear strip

tirada *f* MEDIOS printing, print run; ~ **controlada** V&M controlled circulation; ~ **en cuatricromía** MEDIOS four-colour set (*BrE*), four-color set (*AmE*); ~ **suscrita** V&M subscribed circulation; ~ **total** V&M gross circulation; ~ **vertical** V&M vertical circulation

tiro: ~ **natural** *m* ECON *agrícola* natural draft

tirón: ~ **de un bloque de emisión** *m* V&M block pull; ~ **de la inflación** *m* ECON cost-pull inflation; ~ **de los precios** *m* COM GEN pull of prices; ~ **de precios** *m* ECON price twist

titulación *f* RRHH qualifications

titular[1] *mf* BOLSA rights holder, PATENT *de una patente* owner, RRHH *de puesto de trabajo* occupant; ~ **anterior** BANCA advance holder; ~ **de un certificado** BOLSA *para compra de acciones* warrant holder; ~ **del cargo** POL incumbent; ~ **de una cuenta corriente** BANCA current account holder; ~ **de una cuenta** BANCA account holder; ~ **de una cuenta corriente** BANCA current account holder; ~ **de derechos** BOLSA rights holder; ~ **de los derechos** FISC royalty holder; ~ **de un documento** COM GEN document holder; ~ **de una licencia** COM GEN licence holder (*BrE*), license holder (*AmE*); ~ **de una organización** RRHH titular head of an organization; ~ **del pasaporte** COM GEN passport holder; ~ **de un préstamo** BANCA, FIN loan holder; ~ **de tarjeta** COM GEN cardholder; ~ **de tarjeta de crédito** BANCA cardholder; ~ **verdadero(-a)** *m,f* DER, INMOB true owner

titular[2] *m* MEDIOS headline (*head*); ~ **en bandera** MEDIOS *prensa* streamer; ~ **del cargo** POL incumbent; ~ **en grandes caracteres** MEDIOS screamline (*jarg*); ~ **sensacionalista** MEDIOS *prensa* screamline (*jarg*); ~ **a toda página** MEDIOS *imprenta* banner headline

titularidad: ~ **de acciones** *f* BOLSA share ownership, stock ownership

titulización *f* BANCA, BOLSA, FIN securitization

titulizar *vt* BANCA, BOLSA, FIN securitize

título *m* BANCA security, BOLSA bond, CONT *hoja de balance* heading, FIN security, MEDIOS *revistas* title, RRHH *académico* qualification, V&M title; ~ **al portador** BOLSA bearer security; ~ **al portador de gran liquidez** BOLSA active bond; ~ **de alto rendimiento** BOLSA gilt-edged security; ~ **aparente** INMOB color of title (*AmE*), colour of title (*BrE*); ~ **asegurable** SEG insurable title; ~ **atrayente** V&M *publicidad* catch line; ~ **del capítulo presupuestario** POL vote title; ~ **comprado con acuerdo de reventa** FIN *hoja de balance* note purchased under resale agreement; ~ **condicional** BANCA *internacional* conditional bond; ~ **convertible** BOLSA convertible security; ~ **a corto plazo** BOLSA short-term security; ~ **cotizado** BOLSA listed security, quoted security; ~ **de crédito** V&M credit title; ~ **de una cuenta** BANCA, CONT title of an account; ~ **entregable** BOLSA deliverable security; ~ **del Estado** BOLSA government security; ~ **en eurodólares** ECON Eurodollar bond; ~ **en garantía** BANCA pledge security; ~ **de garantía preferente** BOLSA preference qualification shares, senior security; ~ **garantizado** BOLSA underlying security; ~ **genérico del puesto de trabajo** RRHH generic job title; ~ **imperfecto** DER, INMOB bad title; ~ **inactivo** BOLSA inactive bond; ~ **indexado** BOLSA indexed security; ~ **industrial** FIN industrial security; ~ **con intereses** BOLSA interest-bearing security; ~ **con intereses acumulados en la cotización** BOLSA flat bond; ~ **intransferible** INMOB nonmarketable title (*BrE*), nonmerchantable title (*AmE*); ~ **limpio** DER clear title (*AmE*); ~ **del mercado monetario** BOLSA money market paper; ~ **ministerial**

BOLSA cabinet security; ~ **negociable** BANCA, FIN negotiable instrument, INMOB marketable title (*BrE*), merchantable title; ~ **no asegurable** SEG uninsurable title; ~ **no negociable** INMOB nonmarketable title (*BrE*), nonmerchantable title (*AmE*); ~ **no válido** DER, INMOB bad title; ~ **nominativo** MEDIOS registered title; ~ **parcial** BOLSA participating security; ~ **de participación en una sociedad** BOLSA equity security; ~ **perfeccionado** BANCA perfected security; ~ **en pie de página** INFO, MEDIOS footer; ~ **prioritario** BOLSA underlying bond; ~ **de propiedad** DER, INMOB title deed, PATENT certificate of registration; ~ **de propiedad de los bienes** COM GEN, DER title to the goods; ~ **de propiedad con defecto de forma** DER defective title; ~ **de propiedad imperfecto** DER, INMOB bad title; ~ **de propiedad incontestable** DER, INMOB good title; ~ **de propiedad limpio** DER clear title; ~ **de próximo vencimiento** BOLSA maturing security; ~ **redescontable con prima** BOLSA option eligible security; ~ **redimido** BOLSA called security; ~ **registrado** BOLSA registered security, MEDIOS registered title; ~ **con rendimiento** BOLSA income debenture; ~ **de renta fija** BOLSA fixed-income security, fixed-interest security, fixed-yield security; ~ **respaldado por una hipoteca** BOLSA, FIN mortgage-backed security (*AmE*) (*MBS*); ~ **de segunda categoría** FIN second-class paper; ~ **sobre los bienes** COM GEN, DER title to the goods; ~ **subordinado** BOLSA junior security; ~ **subrogado** BANCA, FIN pass-through security; ~ **de tipo fijo** BOLSA fixed-rate security; ~ **totalmente en regla** BOLSA fully registered security; ~ **universitario** PROT SOC degree; ~ **válido** DER, INMOB good title; ◆ **a ~ de ensayo** COM GEN *en la forma* on approval (*BrE*) (*on appro.*); **a ~ honorífico** RRHH in an honorary capacity; **a ~ de reciprocidad** COM GEN reciprocally

Título: ~ **de Bachiller** *m* COM GEN Spanish school leavers' certificate, ≈ General Certificate of Education (*obs*) (*BrE*) (*GCE*), ≈ General Certificate of Secondary Education (*BrE*) (*GCSE*)

títulos: ~ **acreditativos** *m pl* DER, INMOB muniments of title; ~ **de bolsa** *m pl* BOLSA listed securities; ~ **en cartera** *m pl* BOLSA securities in portfolio; ~ **de la cuenta de inversión** *m pl* BANCA investment account securities; ~ **documentarios** *m pl* DER documents of title; ~ **estables** *m pl* BOLSA defensive securities; ~ **del Estado** *m pl* BOLSA government stock (*BrE*); ~ **estadounidenses** *m pl* BOLSA Yankees (*jarg*); ~ **exentos** *m pl* BOLSA exempt securities; ~ **garantizados** *m pl* BOLSA guaranteed securities; ~ **negociables** *m pl* BOLSA marketable securities, negotiable securities; ~ **en préstamo** *m pl* BOLSA, FIN lending securities; ~ **de propiedad** *m pl* DER, INMOB muniments of title; ~ **respaldados por activos** *m pl* BOLSA, FIN asset-backed securities; ~ **valores** *m pl* COM GEN securities, shares (*shs*)

TLC *abr* (*Tratado de Libre Comercio*) ECON, POL NAFTA (*North American Free Trade Agreement*)

tm *abr* (*tonelada métrica*) COM GEN mton (*metric ton*)

TM *abr* (*tiempo medio*) COM GEN MT (*mean time*)

TNC *abr* (*corporación transnacional*) ECON, IND, POL TNC (*transnational corporation*)

tocar: ~ **algo de oído** *fra* COM GEN play sth by ear; ~ **fondo** *fra* BOLSA bottom, COM GEN *mercado, precios, gráficos* bottom out; ~ **resortes** *fra* COM GEN pull strings (*BrE*), pull wires (*AmE*)

todólogo, -a *m,f* COM GEN business generalist

tolerancia *f* COM GEN tolerance

tolerante: ~ **a fallos** *adj* INFO fault-tolerant

toma *f* INFO *de datos* capture; ~ **de control** BOLSA, ECON, FIN takeover; ~ **de control amistosa** BOLSA, ECON, FIN friendly takeover; ~ **de control pactada** BOLSA, ECON, FIN agreed takeover; ~ **de datos** INFO data capture; ~ **de decisiones** GES decision making; ~ **de fuerza** TRANSP power take-off (*PTO*); ~ **parcial** DER, INMOB partial taking; ~ **de posesión violenta** DER forcible entry; ~ **de posición** BOLSA buy-in; ~ **de prueba** MEDIOS *película* test shot

tomador, a *m,f* BOLSA taker; ~ **de opción de venta y compra** BOLSA taker for a put and call; ~ **de seguro** SEG policyholder

tomar *vt* BOLSA *acciones* take up, COM GEN raise; ◆ ~ **conciencia** MED AMB raise awareness; ~ **en consideración** COM GEN take into account; ~ **el control** COM GEN take control; ~ **el control administrativo de una compañía** COM GEN, GES take administrative control of a company; ~ **en cuenta** COM GEN take into consideration; ~ **una decisión** COM GEN make a decision; ~ **una decisión rápida** COM GEN make a snap decision; ~ **dinero prestado** BANCA, FIN borrow money; ~ **la iniciativa** GES, RRHH take the initiative; ~ **medidas** COM GEN take measures; ~ **una muestra** MAT, V&M take a sample; ~ **nota de** COM GEN take account of; ~ **parte en** COM GEN play a part in, take part in; ~ **una participación en** COM GEN acquire an interest in; ~ **partido por** COM GEN take sides with; ~ **posesión** INMOB take possession; ~ **posición** BOLSA take a position; ~ **prestado** COM GEN borrow; ~ **prestado a la vista** BANCA borrow at call; ~ **un préstamo en el Euromercado** COM GEN borrow in the Euromarket; ~ **un préstamo en el extranjero** COM GEN borrow abroad; ~ **un socio** COM GEN take a partner; ~ **a su cargo** COM GEN undertake

tomarse: ~ **un día libre** *fra* COM GEN, RRHH take a day off; ~ **muchas molestias** *fra* COM GEN go to a lot of trouble; ~ **unas vacaciones** *fra* RRHH take a holiday (*BrE*), take a vacation (*AmE*)

tombstone *m* BOLSA tombstone, tombstone ad

tonalizador *m* INFO *para fax, fotocopiadora* toner

tonel *m* TRANSP cask (*ck*)

tonelada *f* COM GEN ton, tonne; ~ **americana** COM GEN American short ton, American short tonne; ~ **de arqueo** COM GEN, TRANSP net register ton (*NRT*), net register tonne (*NRT*), measurement ton, measurement tonne; ~ **de arqueo bruto** COM GEN, TRANSP gross register ton (*GRT*), gross register tonne (*GRT*); ~ **bruta** COM GEN gross ton (*GT*), gross tonne (*GT*); ~ **por centímetro** COM GEN ton per centimetre (*BrE*) (*TPC*), tonne per centimetre (*BrE*) (*TPC*), ton per centimeter (*AmE*) (*TPC*), tonne per centimeter (*AmE*) (*TPC*); ~ **del conocimiento de embarque** IMP/EXP, TRANSP bill of lading ton (*B/L ton*), bill of lading tonne (*B/L ton*); ~ **por kilómetro** COM GEN ton kilometre (*BrE*), tonne kilometre (*BrE*), ton kilometer (*AmE*), tonne kilometer (*AmE*); ~ **larga** COM GEN long ton, long tonne; ~ **marítima** TRANSP shipping ton, shipping ton; ~ **métrica** (*tm*) COM GEN metric ton (*mton*), metric tonne (*mton*); ~ **por milla** COM GEN, TRANSP ton mile, tonne mile; ~ **de peso** COM GEN weight ton, weight tonne; ~ **de peso muerto** TRANSP deadweight tonnage (*dwt*)

toneladas: ~ **por milla y hora** *f pl* TRANSP tonne miles per vehicle hour, ton miles per vehicle hour; ~ **de peso muerto** *f pl* TRANSP tons deadweight (*TDW*), tonnes deadweight (*TDW*)

tonelaje: ~ **amarrado** *m* TRANSP laid-up tonnage; ~ **bajo bandera nacional** *m* TRANSP national flag tonnage; ~ **bajo cubierta** *m* TRANSP under deck tonnage; ~ **bruto** *m* COM GEN gross tonnage (*GT*); ~ **bruto registrado** *m* COM GEN, TRANSP gross register tonnage (*GRT*); ~ **de carga** *m* TRANSP cargo tonnage; ~ **construido de encargo** *m* TRANSP purpose-built tonnage; ~ **cúbico** *m* (*TC*) TRANSP cubic tonnage (*CT*); ~ **de desplazamiento** *m* TRANSP displacement tonnage; ~ **inmovilizado** *m* TRANSP idle tonnage; ~ **neto registrado** *m* COM GEN, TRANSP net registered tonnage (*NRT*); ~ **registrado** *m* COM GEN, TRANSP registered ton; ~ **de registro** *m* COM GEN *marítimo*, TRANSP register tonnage; ~ **de segunda mano** *m* TRANSP second-hand tonnage; ~ **total** *m* COM GEN, TRANSP deadweight tonnage (*dwt*)

tonelería *f* TRANSP cooperage

tongada: ~ **de cadena estibada** *f* TRANSP tier

tono: ~ **alcista** *m* BOLSA *del mercado* bullish tone; ~ **bajista** *m* BOLSA *del mercado* bearish tone; ~ **de discado** *m* COMS dial tone (*AmE*), dialling tone (*BrE*); ~ **del mercado** *m* BOLSA market tone; ~ **de ocupado** *m* COMS engaged tone (*BrE*)

tontina *f* DER, ECON *seguros* tontine

topar: ~ **con las autoridades** *fra* COM GEN run foul of the authorities

tope *m* BANCA, FIN *cap*, V&M *publicidad* stopper; ~ **de endeudamiento** COM GEN borrowing ceiling; ~ **fiscal** FISC roof tax; ~ **de hipoteca** BANCA, INMOB mortgage ceiling; ~ **máximo** FISC *deducción* upper cap; ~ **máximo de oscilación de precio** BOLSA limit up; ~ **de préstamo** COM GEN lending ceiling

topes: ~ **máximos** *m pl* BOLSA descending tops

topógrafo, -a *m,f* RRHH surveyor

topograma: ~ **de la memoria** *m* INFO storage map

torre *f* TRANSP steeple; ~ **de control de tráfico** TRANSP traffic control tower; ~ **de perforación** IND, MED AMB oil rig

tortuguismo: ~ **laboral** *m* AmL IND job action (*jarg*)

total[1] *adj* COM GEN complete, all-inclusive, MAT total, SEG *seguro* all-in

total[2] *m* COM GEN total; ~ **de la actividad** COM GEN activity total; ~ **actualizado** COM GEN running total; ~ **anual móvil** MAT moving annual total (*MAT*); ~ **de las bases de coste ajustadas** *Esp* (*cf total de las bases de costo ajustadas AmL*) FISC aggregate of the adjusted cost bases; ~ **de las bases de costo ajustadas** *AmL* (*cf total de las bases de coste ajustadas Esp*) FISC aggregate of the adjusted cost bases; ~ **a la fecha** FIN total to date; ~ **general** COM GEN grand total; ~ **hasta la fecha** COM GEN running total; ~ **no presupuestario** FIN non-budgetary total; ~ **presupuestario** FIN budgetary total; ~ **de votos emitidos** COM GEN, POL, RRHH *elección* total votes cast

total[3]: **en** ~ *fra* COM GEN in the aggregate; ~ **y exclusivamente** *fra* DER wholly and exclusively

totales: ~ **monetarios** *m pl* ECON monetary aggregates (*M*)

totalidad *f* COM GEN totality, CONT *datos* completeness, MAT gross

totalizador *m* COM GEN totalizator

totalizar *vt* COM GEN add up, totalize

totalmente[1]: ~ **gravado** *adj* FISC *rendimiento* clean assessed

totalmente[2] *adv* COM GEN in full, *completamente* in toto

tour: ~ **operador(a)** *m,f* OCIO, TRANSP tour operator

TOVALOP *abr* (*Acuerdo Voluntario de Armadores de Petroleros sobre la Responsabilidad por Contaminación de Crudos*) MED AMB, TRANSP TOVALOP (*Tanker Owners' Voluntary Agreement Concerning Liability for Oil Pollution*)

toxicidad *f* COM GEN toxicity

tóxico[1] *adj* COM GEN toxic

tóxico[2] *m* COM GEN poison

toxicológico *adj* COM GEN toxicological

traba: ~ **fiscal** *f* FISC fiscal drag

trabador: ~ **del diferencial** *m* TRANSP differential lock

trabajador, a *m,f* RRHH worker; ~ **agrícola** MED AMB, FISC, RRHH farm labourer (*BrE*), farm laborer (*AmE*); ~ **atípico(-a)** RRHH atypical worker; ~ **autónomo(-a)** FISC, RRHH self-employed person, self-employed worker, freelance worker; ~ **en cadena** IND, RRHH assembly line worker; ~ **clandestino(-a)** RRHH moonlighter; ~ **por cuenta ajena** RRHH employee; ~ **por cuenta propia** FISC, RRHH self-employed person, self-employed worker, freelance worker; ~ **desanimado(-a)** RRHH discouraged worker; ~ **directo(-a)** RRHH direct worker; ~ **diurno(-a)** RRHH dayworker; ~ **sin documentación** DER undocumented worker; ~ **domiciliario(-a)** RRHH homeworker; ~ **eventual** RRHH casual laborer (*AmE*), casual labourer (*BrE*), occasional worker, casual worker; ~ **extranjero(-a)** RRHH foreign worker; ~ **fronterizo(-a)** RRHH frontier worker; ~ **por horas** RRHH hourly worker; ~ **incapacitado(-a)** RRHH disabled worker; ~ **indirecto(-a)** RRHH indirect worker; ~ **indocumentado(-a)** RRHH undocumented worker; ~ **inmigrante** PROT SOC, RRHH immigrant worker; ~ **invitado(-a)** RRHH guest-worker; ~ **itinerante** RRHH itinerant worker, mobile worker; ~ **joven** RRHH young worker; ~ **manual** RRHH manual worker; ~ **marginal** RRHH marginal worker; ~ **migratorio(-a)** RRHH migrant worker, migratory worker; ~ **muy ambicioso(-a) y diligente** *Esp* (*cf trabajador muy empeñoso AmL*) RRHH eager beaver (*infrml*); ~ **muy empeñoso(-a)** *AmL* (*cf trabajador muy ambicioso y diligente Esp*) RRHH eager beaver (*infrml*); ~ **no cualificado(-a)** RRHH threshold worker (*jarg*) (*AmE*); ~ **no declarado(-a)** RRHH moonlighter; ~ **de oficina** RRHH clerical worker; ~ **portuario(-a)** COM GEN, RRHH, TRANSP docker (*BrE*); ~ **de primera línea** RRHH front-line employee; ~ **semiespecializado(-a)** ECON, RRHH semiskilled worker; ~ **social** RRHH social worker; ~ **temporal** RRHH short-term worker, temp; ~ **a tiempo completo** RRHH full-time worker (*BrE*), full-timer; ~ **a tiempo parcial** RRHH part-time worker, part-timer; ~ **tipo** COM GEN *compañía* pacesetter; ~ **transitorio(-a)** RRHH transient worker; ~ **por turnos** RRHH shift worker

trabajar *vi* COM GEN work, *en comité* serve, GES operate, RRHH labor (*AmE*), labour (*BrE*), work; ♦ ~ **en** COM GEN work on; ~ **codo con codo** COM GEN work alongside; ~ **como** COM GEN trade as; ~ **como parte de un equipo** RRHH work as part of a team; ~ **para la compañía** RRHH serve the company; ~ **en equipo** GES operate in tandem; ~ **en estrecha colaboración con** COM GEN,

RRHH work closely with; ~ **fines de semana alternos** COM GEN, RRHH work alternate weekends; ~ **fuera** RRHH work out; ~ **para ganarse la vida** PROT SOC work for a living; ~ **en un horario muy preciso** COM GEN work to a very tight schedule; ~ **en horarios insociables** RRHH work unsocial hours; ~ **horas extras** RRHH work overtime; ~ **incansablemente** RRHH work like a beaver (*infrml*); ~ **juntos** COM GEN work together; ~ **a medias con** COM GEN work in tandem with; ~ **en medios de comunicación** RRHH, MEDIOS work in the media; ~ **moderadamente** ECON slow-down; ~ **en sociedad con** GES work in partnership with; ~ **a tiempo completo** RRHH work full time; ~ **por turnos** RRHH work in shifts

trabajo *m* COM GEN, RRHH *tarea* work, labor (*AmE*), labour (*BrE*), task; ~ **abstracto** RRHH abstract labor (*AmE*), abstract labour (*BrE*); ~ **adicional** RRHH additional labor (*AmE*), additional labour (*BrE*); ~ **administrativo** ADMIN, RRHH administrative work; ~ **agrícola** RRHH agricultural job; ~ **agropecuario** RRHH agricultural job; ~ **de alto coste** *Esp* (*cf trabajo de alto costo AmL*) RRHH *tarea* high-cost labor (*AmE*), high-cost labour (*BrE*); ~ **de alto costo** *AmL* (*cf trabajo de alto coste Esp*) *tarea* high cost labour (*AmE*), high cost labour (*BrE*); ~ **de asesor** COM GEN, RRHH consultancy work; ~ **de asesoramiento** RRHH advisory work; ~ **sin atención al público** ADMIN back-of-the-house job; ~ **atrasado** COM GEN arrears of work; ~ **de baja categoría** RRHH menial work; ~ **de campo** V&M fieldwork; ~ **bajo contrato** RRHH contract work; ~ **clandestino** RRHH moonlighting (*infrml*); ~ **colectivo** ECON community job; ~ **compartido** RRHH job share, job sharing, work sharing; ~ **común** RRHH *tarea* common labor (*AmE*), common labour (*BrE*); ~ **concreto** RRHH concrete labor (*AmE*), concrete labour (*BrE*); ~ **continuo** RRHH continuous labor (*AmE*), continuous labour (*BrE*); ~ **contratado** RRHH *tarea* contract labor (*AmE*), contract labour (*BrE*); ~ **corriente** RRHH *tarea* common labor (*AmE*), common labour (*BrE*); ~ **de coste elevado** *Esp* (*cf trabajo costo elevado AmL*) RRHH *tarea* high-cost labor (*AmE*), high-cost labour (*BrE*); ~ **de costo elevado** *AmL* (*cf trabajo coste elevado Esp*) RRHH *tarea* high-cost labor (*AmE*), high-cost labour (*BrE*); ~ **cualificado** ECON, RRHH skilled labor (*AmE*), skilled labour (*BrE*); ~ **por cuenta propia** FISC, RRHH self-employment; ~ **en curso** COM GEN work-in-process (*AmE*), work-in-progress (*BrE*); ~ **en curso de ejecución** COM GEN work-in-process (*AmE*), work-in-progress (*BrE*); ~ **en desarrollo** COM GEN work-in-process (*AmE*) work-in-progress (*BrE*); ~ **a destajo** *AmL* COM GEN, IND jobbing, RRHH piecework; ~ **a destajo por equipos** RRHH gang piecework, group piecework; ~ **a destajo por grupos** RRHH group piecework; ~ **directo** CONT, ECON, RRHH *tarea* direct labor (*AmE*), direct labour (*BrE*); ~ **sin discriminación** RRHH fair employment; ~ **a distancia** ECON *mediante fax, teléfono*, RRHH *por red informática* telecommuting; ~ **diurno** RRHH day-work; ~ **diverso** RRHH odd job; ~ **a domicilio** RRHH homework, *por red informática* telecommuting; ~ **duro** RRHH hard graft, slog; ~ **en equipo** RRHH teamwork; ~ **escalonado** RRHH spreadover working (*jarg*); ~ **especializado** ECON, RRHH skilled labor (*AmE*), skilled labour (*BrE*); ~ **eventual** RRHH casual labor (*AmE*), casual labour (*BrE*), temporary work; ~ **explotador** PROT SOC, RRHH *tarea* sweated labor

(*AmE*), sweated labour (*BrE*); ~ **forzoso** FISC, RRHH forced labour (*BrE*), forced labor (*AmE*); ~ **de grupo** RRHH group working; ~ **de impresión** MEDIOS printing work; ~ **indirecto** RRHH *tarea* indirect labor (*AmE*), indirect labour (*BrE*); ~ **indispensable** RRHH *tarea* indispensable labor (*AmE*), indispensable labour (*BrE*); ~ **local** RRHH *tarea* local labor (*AmE*), local labour (*BrE*); ~ **manual** RRHH manual labor (*AmE*), manual labour (*BrE*), manual work; ~ **materializado** RRHH materialized labor (*AmE*), materialized labour (*BrE*); ~ **medio de un día** RRHH fair day's work; ~ **de medio tiempo** RRHH part-time work; ~ **de misionero** RRHH missionary work; ~ **muy mal pagado** PROT SOC, RRHH sweated labor (*AmE*), sweated labour (*BrE*); ~ **necesario** RRHH necessary labor (*AmE*), necessary labour (*BrE*); ~ **no especializado** RRHH *tarea* unskilled labor (*AmE*), unskilled labour (*BrE*); ~ **no productivo** RRHH unproductive labor (*AmE*), unproductive labour (*BrE*); ~ **no registrado** RRHH unregistered labor (*AmE*), unregistered labour (*BrE*); ~ **nocturno** RRHH night work; ~ **ocasional** RRHH casual labor (*AmE*), casual labour (*BrE*), temporary work; ~ **de oficina** ADMIN, RRHH clerical work, office work; ~ **organizado** RRHH organized labor (*AmE*), organized labour (*BrE*); ~ **pagado por horas** RRHH time work; ~ **para persona semiexperta** ECON, RRHH *tarea* semiskilled labor (*AmE*), semiskilled labour (*BrE*); ~ **sin perspectivas de avance** RRHH blind-alley job, dead-end job; ~ **por pieza** *Esp* RRHH piecework; ~ **en proceso** CONT work-in-process (*AmE*) work-in-progress (*BrE*); ~ **productivo** RRHH productive labor (*AmE*), productive labour (*BrE*); ~ **que compensa** RRHH rewarding job; ~ **sin restricciones** RRHH unrestricted labor (*AmE*), unrestricted labour (*BrE*); ~ **en el sector servicios** RRHH service sector job; ~ **secundario** RRHH sideline job; ~ **seguro** RRHH secure job; ~ **simple** ECON, RRHH simple labour; ~ **social** PROT SOC, RRHH community job; ~ **temporal** RRHH temporary work; ~ **temporero** RRHH casual labor (*AmE*), casual labour (*BrE*), casual work; ~ **terminal** RRHH blind-alley job; ~ **en el terreno** V&M fieldwork; ~ **de tiempo completo** RRHH full-time employment, full-time job; ~ **a tiempo parcial** RRHH part-time employment, part-time job; ~ **por turnos** RRHH shift work; ~ **urgente** COM GEN rush job; ~ **voluntario** RRHH voluntary work; ◆ **sin ~** PROT SOC, RRHH out-of-work; **tener el ~ al día** RRHH be on top of one's work

tractor: ~ **para remolque** *m* TRANSP towing dolly

tradeunionismo *m* RRHH trade unionism (*BrE*)

tradición *f* COM GEN tradition

tradicional *adj* COM GEN traditional

traducción *f* COM GEN, COMS translation; ~ **asistida por computador** *AmL*, ~ **asistida por computadora** *AmL* (*cf traducción asistida por ordenador Esp*) INFO computer-aided translation (*CAT*), computer-assisted translation (*CAT*); ~ **asistida por ordenador** *Esp* (*cf traducción asistida por computadora AmL*) INFO computer-aided translation (*CAT*), computer-assisted translation (*CAT*); ~ **automática** INFO machine-assisted translation (*MAT*); ~ **simultánea** COM GEN simultaneous translation

traducir *vt* COM GEN, ECON *monedas* translate

traductor, a *m,f* COM GEN translator

traer *vt* *AmL* (*cf extraer Esp*) COM GEN bring, INFO fetch

traficante *mf* COM GEN trafficker

traficar *vt* COM GEN, ECON trade; ~ **en** COM GEN traffic in

tráfico *m* TRANSP traffic; ~ **aéreo** TRANSP air traffic; ~ **de almacén** V&M store traffic; ~ **complementario** TRANSP filler traffic; ~ **diseminado** V&M spread traffic; ~ **de drogas** COM GEN drug trade; ~ **de la estación de carga** TRANSP terminal traffic; ~ **de ferrocarril** TRANSP rail traffic; ~ **de fletes** TRANSP freight traffic; ~ **de mercancías pesadas** TRANSP heavy goods traffic; ~ **de pasillo** V&M corridor traffic; ~ **portuario** TRANSP port traffic; ~ **reglamentario** TRANSP booked traffic; ~ **de remolques por ferrocarril** TRANSP piggyback traffic *(jarg)* *(AmE)*; ~ **sobre neumáticos** TRANSP rubber-tired traffic *(AmE)*, rubber-tyred traffic *(BrE)*; ~ **tasado de pasajeros** TRANSP passenger rated traffic; ~ **de tienda** V&M shop traffic; ~ **total en una estación de carga** TRANSP terminal throughput; ~ **en tránsito** TRANSP transit traffic

tragar *vt* COM GEN buy *(infrml)*

trailer: ~ **basculante** *m* TRANSP tilt trailer *(Tt)*

trama *f* INFO raster; ~ **gruesa** V&M coarse screen

tramitación *f* FISC processing; ~ **de un juicio** DER conduct of law suit

trámite *m* PATENT *de una aplicación* processing; ~ **de autorización** BANCA approval process; ◆ **en** ~ COM GEN *proyecto* in the pipeline *(jarg)*

trámites: ~ **burocráticos** *m pl* COM GEN, GES, POL red tape; ~ **de cierre de ejercicio** *m pl* COM GEN year-end procedures; ~ **de transportes** *m pl* SEG instrumentalities of transportation

tramo *m* BOLSA *de margen* leg, COM GEN *de precios, impositivo* bracket; ~ **de crédito** FIN credit tranche; ~ **de cuatro carriles** TRANSP four-track band; ~ **de depreciación de activos** CONT, FIN, INMOB asset depreciation range; ~ **del impuesto progresivo** FISC bracket creep, tax-bracket creep; ~ **de renta** FISC income bracket

tramos *m pl* COM GEN pieces *(pcs)*

trampa: ~ **del bienestar** *f* PROT SOC welfare trap; ~ **del desempleo** *f* PROT SOC, RRHH unemployment trap; ~ **fiscal** *f* FISC tax gimmick; ~ **de la liquidez** *f* ECON liquidity trap; ~ **de la movilidad** *f* ECON mobility trap; ~ **de la pobreza** *f* PROT SOC poverty trap

tranquilo *adj* COM GEN *mercado, negocios* quiet

transacción *f* BOLSA bargain, COM GEN dealings, transaction; ~ **de acciones** BOLSA bundled deal; ~ **del banco central** BANCA, ECON central bank transaction; ~ **condicional** BOLSA conditional transaction; ~ **al contado** BANCA, CONT cash transaction; ~ **al margen de la bolsa** BOLSA upstairs market *(AmE)*; ~ **de arbitraje** BOLSA arbitration transaction, ECON *internacional* switch dealing *(jarg)*; ~ **bancaria** BANCA bank transaction; ~ **de capital** BANCA, FIN capital transaction; ~ **de cierre** BOLSA closing transaction; ~ **combinada de compraventa** BOLSA matched trade; ~ **comercial** COM GEN business transaction; ~ **comercial sin favor** COM GEN non-arm's-length transaction; ~ **compensatoria** BOLSA offsetting transaction; ~ **complicada** BANCA complex transaction; ~ **de compra al cierre** BOLSA closing purchase transaction; ~ **contraria** COM GEN opposite transaction; ~ **a cuenta** CONT, FIN account transaction; ~ **en cuenta** CONT, FIN account transaction, dealing within the account; ~ **de depósito directo** BANCA direct deposit transaction; ~ **en divisas** BOLSA foreign exchange deal,

ECON foreign currency transaction; ~ **de divisas a plazo a plazo** ECON *comercio internacional* forward-forward currency deal; ~ **doble cerrada** BOLSA *comisión* round turn; ~ **en efectivo** COM GEN cash operation; ~ **entre empresas interrelacionadas** BANCA, COMS arm's-length transaction; ~ **exenta de riesgo** BOLSA riskless transaction; ~ **por facsímil** COM GEN, COMS facsimile transaction; ~ **ficticia** BOLSA wash sale; ~ **financiera transfronteriza** FIN cross-border financial transaction; ~ **fuera del corro** BOLSA ex-pit transaction; ~ **en igualdad de condiciones** COM GEN arm's-length transaction; ~ **con información privilegiada** BOLSA, FIN insider dealing; ~ **interbancaria** BANCA interbank transaction; ~ **interna** CONT internal transaction; ~ **leonina** DER unconscionable bargain; ~ **de liquidación** BOLSA settlement transaction; ~ **en el mercado de opciones** BOLSA option bargain; ~ **neta** BOLSA net transaction; ~ **no registrada en bolsa** BOLSA over-the-counter dealings *(OTC)*; ~ **sin papel** INFO paperless trading; ~ **en planos** FISC step transaction; ~ **en posición abierta** BOLSA open trading; ~ **de respaldo mutuo** BANCA back-to-back transaction; ~ **sobre futuros** BOLSA futures transaction; ~ **con tarjeta de crédito** BANCA credit card transaction; ~ **THS** BOLSA THS transaction; ~ **de títulos** BOLSA securities transaction; ~ **transfronteriza** FIN cross-border transaction; ~ **de venta al cierre** BOLSA closing sale transaction; ~ **vinculada** ECON interlinked transaction

transaccional *adj* COM GEN transactional

transatlántico *m* TRANSP ocean liner

transbordador *m* TRANSP *buque* ferry; ~ **espacial** TRANSP space shuttle; ~ **de pasajeros** OCIO, TRANSP passenger ferry; ~ **de trenes** TRANSP train ferry; ~ **de vehículos** TRANSP car ferry; ~ **para vehículos de pasajeros** OCIO, TRANSP passenger vehicle ferry

transbordar *vt* TRANSP break bulk, tranship

transbordo *m* TRANSP transfer *(tr., trf.)*, transhipment; ~ **de carga** TRANSP cargo transfer; ~ **directo** TRANSP direct transhipment; ~ **a otro vehículo** IMP/EXP, TRANSP vehicle transhipment

transcodificador *m* COMS transcoder

transcodificar *vt* COMS transcode

transcribir *vt* COM GEN, COMS, INFO transcribe

transcripción *f* COM GEN, COMS, INFO transcription

transcurrir *vt* ECON elapse

transductor *m* COMS transducer

transeúnte *mf* V&M passer-by

transeuropeo *adj* COM GEN transeuropean

transferencia *f* BANCA transfer *(tr., trf.)*, BOLSA, COM GEN, DER transfer *(tr., trf.)*, ECON *en divisas* move, INFO *programas* porting, TRANSP transfer *(tr., trf.)*; ~ **a la actividad comercial** COM GEN transfer to business; ~ **de activo** COM GEN, ECON spin-off *(jarg)* *(AmE)*; ~ **de activos** CONT transfer of assets; ~ **al contado** BANCA, CONT cash transfer; ~ **automática** BANCA automatic transfer; ~ **bancaria** BANCA bank transfer; ~ **del banco** BANCA banker's transfer; ~ **de beneficios** SEG *fondo de pensiones* buyout; ~ **por bloques** INFO block transfer; ~ **cablegráfica** COMS telegraphic transfer *(TT)*; ~ **de capital** BANCA, FIN capital transfer; ~ **de compromiso** RRHH transfer of undertaking *(BrE)*; ~ **de contrato** RRHH transfer of engagement *(BrE)*; ~ **por correo** COMS *comercio internacional* mail transfer *(MT)*;

~ **por correo aéreo** BANCA, COM GEN air mail transfer (*AMT*); ~ **de crédito** BANCA, FIN credit transfer; ~ **de un crédito bancario** BANCA bank credit transfer; ~ **de efectivo** BANCA, CONT cash transfer; ~ **por endoso** BANCA transfer by endorsement; ~ **entre almacenes** TRANSP interdepot transfer; ~ **entre votos** FIN inter vote transfer; ~ **de fondos** BANCA, CONT, FIN transfer of funds, funds transfer; ~ **de fondos automática** BANCA, CONT, FIN automatic funds transfer (*AFT*); ~ **de fondos directa** BANCA, CONT, FIN direct fund transfer (*DFT*); ~ **de fondos electrónica** BANCA, CONT, FIN electronic funds transfer (*EFT*); ~ **de fondos electrónica en punto de venta** BANCA, V&M electronic funds transfer at point of sale (*EFTPOS*); ~ **gratuita** FISC *derechos de sucesión* gratuitous transfer; ~ **de informaciones** INFO information transfer; ~ **legal** BOLSA *de acciones* legal transfer; ~ **mínima** COM GEN minimum transfer (*MT*); ~ **monetaria inmediata** BANCA, FIN immediate money transfer (*IMT*); ~ **monetaria telegráfica urgente** BANCA, FIN express telegraphic money transfer; ~ **de pago** BANCA payment transfer; ~ **de participación** BOLSA share transfer; ~ **de personal** RRHH staff transfer; ~ **potencialmente exenta** FISC potentially exempt transfer (*PET*); ~ **de prima** SEG premium transfer; ~ **de respaldo mutuo** BANCA back-to-back transfer; ~ **de riesgo** SEG passing of risk; ~ **de tecnología** COM GEN technology transfer (*TT*); ~ **telegráfica** COMS telegraphic transfer (*TT*)

transferible *adj* BOLSA *opciones* transferable, COM GEN assignable, INFO *programas* portable

transferidor *m* BANCA transferor

transferir *vt* BANCA, ECON *fondos, dinero* transfer, INFO download; ♦ ~ **por cable** BANCA transfer by wire; ~ **a disco** COM GEN roll out; ~ **la propiedad de** INMOB transfer ownership of

transformación *f* COM GEN conversion

transformar *vt* COM GEN transform

transfronterizo *adj* COM GEN cross-border

transición: ~ **demográfica** *f* ECON demographic transition

transistor: ~ **bipolar** *m* INFO *equipo* bipolar transistor

transitario, -a *m,f* TRANSP, V&M forwarding agent

tránsito *m* TRANSP transit; ~ **controlado** TRANSP controlled transit; ~ **rápido masivo** TRANSP mass rapid transit (*MRT*); ♦ **en** ~ BANCA, COM GEN in transit

transitorio *adj* COM GEN transitional

transmisibilidad *f* BOLSA *de acciones nominales* transferability

transmisión *f* COM GEN, COMS transmission, INFO transmission, broadcasting, INMOB, PATENT assignment; ~ **de datos** COMS, INFO data broadcasting; ~ **en diferido** MEDIOS prerecorded broadcast; ~ **facsimilar** ADMIN, COMS facsimile transmission; ~ **por fax** ADMIN, COMS fax transmission; ~ **simultánea** MEDIOS *radio y TV* simultaneous broadcast (*simulcast*); ~ **de tecnología** ECON *internacional* transfer of technology, IND technological transfer; ~ **testamentaria** FISC gift by will; ~ **por vía satélite** COM GEN, MEDIOS satellite broadcasting

transmisor *adj* COM GEN, COMS, INFO transmitting

transmitir *vt* COM GEN, COMS transmit, INMOB assign, INFO transmit; ♦ ~ **por telecomunicaciones** COMS telecommunicate

transmitirse: ~ **con la tierra** *fra* DER run with the land

transnacional *adj* COM GEN transnational

transpaleta *f* TRANSP hand pallet transporter

transparencia *f* COM GEN *proyector* acetate, overhead transparency, transparency (*jarg*); ~ **fiscal** FISC tax transparency, *de cuenta, dividendos* flow-through; ~ **informativa** POL transparency of information (*jarg*); ~ **del mercado** COM GEN market transparency

transparente *adj* COM GEN, INFO *dispositivo, red* transparent

transportabilidad *f* INFO portability

transportable *adj* COM GEN transportable

transportado: ~ **directamente** *adj* IMP/EXP, TRANSP directly transported; ~ **por mar** *adj* TRANSP seaborne; ~ **sin transbordos** *adj* IMP/EXP, TRANSP directly transported

transportador: ~ **de coches** *m* TRANSP car carrier; ~ **de contenedores** *m* TRANSP spreader

transportar: ~ **por avión** *vt* TRANSP transport by air

transporte *m* TRANSP transport; ~ **adicional** TRANSP overhaul; ~ **aéreo** TRANSP air transport; ~ **por agua** TRANSP water transportation; ~ **en autobús** TRANSP bus shuttle; ~ **de automóviles** TRANSP vehicular ferry; ~ **por carretera** TRANSP road transport, trucking (*AmE*); ~ **combinado** TRANSP combined transport (*CT*); ~ **combinado por carretera y ferrocarril** TRANSP road-rail transport; ~ **comercial** IMP/EXP, TRANSP merchant haulage (*MH*); ~ **en contenedores** TRANSP container transport; ~ **discrecional** TRANSP multiple drop; ~ **de una exposición** IMP/EXP, TRANSP exhibition forwarding; ~ **por ferrocarril** TRANSP rail shipment, rail transport; ~ **a granel** TRANSP forwarding in bulk; ~ **intermodal** TRANSP intermodal transport; ~ **internacional** IMP/EXP, TRANSP international traffic; ~ **internacional por carretera** IMP/EXP, TRANSP Transport International Routier (*TIR*); ~ **ligero** TRANSP lighter carrier; ~ **marítimo** TRANSP maritime shipping; ~ **de mercancías** TRANSP freight transport; ~ **mercante** IMP/EXP, TRANSP merchant haulage (*MH*); ~ **por el mismo mar y costa** TRANSP same sea and coast (*SS&C*); ~ **por el mismo mar y país** TRANSP same sea and country (*SS&C*); ~ **multimodal** TRANSP multimodal transport; ~ **pagado** TRANSP carriage paid (*carr pd*), carriage paid transport (*CPT*); ~ **propio del cliente** TRANSP customers' own transport (*COT*), carriage paid transport (*CPT*); ~ **público** TRANSP public transport; ~ **a temperatura controlada** TRANSP temperature-controlled transport; ~ **terrestre** TRANSP overland transport; ~ **por tierra** TRANSP ground transportation, land carriage; ~ **de tierra transiberiano** TRANSP Trans-Siberian landbridge (*TSL*); ~ **en travesías cortas** TRANSP short sea shipping; ~ **ulterior** TRANSP on-carriage; ~ **urgente** COM GEN express delivery; ~ **de volumen** TRANSP volume shipping

transportista *mf* TRANSP *buque* carrier; ~ **de crudos** TRANSP crude-oil carrier; ~ **de enlace** TRANSP connecting carrier; ~ **entre compañías** TRANSP interline carrier; ~ **expedidor** TRANSP issuing carrier; ~ **final** TRANSP carrier last; ~ **en general** TRANSP omnicarrier; ~ **LPG** TRANSP *envíos* LPG carrier; ~ **participante** TRANSP participating carrier; ~ **de petróleo** TRANSP oil carrier; ~ **principal** TRANSP principal carrier; ~ **privado** V&M private carrier; ~ **que no posee buques** TRANSP non-vessel-owning carrier; ~ **real** TRANSP actual carrier; ~ **receptor** TRANSP receiving carrier; ~ **de tercera bandera** TRANSP third flag carrier

transversal *adj* COM GEN transverse

trapichero, -a *m,f infrml* COM GEN wheeler-dealer (*infrml*)

traslación *f* ECON *de monedas* translation, TRANSP racking

trasladado: ~ **a cuenta nueva** *adj* BANCA, CONT *balance de cuentas* carried forward (*c/f*)

trasladar *vt* COM GEN pass off, pass on, FIN *saldos* carry, TRANSP *de un tren a otro* transfer; ◆ ~ **a alguien** RRHH *a otra sucursal* transfer sb

traslado *m* BANCA, CONT amount brought forward; ~ **negativo** FIN negative carry; ~ **de pérdidas a ejercicios anteriores** CONT, FISC loss carry-back; ~ **de pérdidas a ejercicios futuros** CONT, FISC *balances* loss carry-forward; ~ **temporal** RRHH secondment; ~ **transfronterizo** IMP/EXP, TRANSP *de desechos peligrosos* cross-frontier transfer

traspasar *vt* BANCA, BOLSA, CONT transfer, DER, INMOB assign, convey, PATENT assign; ◆ ~ **al periodo anterior** CONT, FISC carry back; ~ **al periodo futuro** CONT, FISC carry forward

traspaso *m* BOLSA *de acciones* delivery (*D, dely*), COM GEN transfer (*tr., trf.*), INMOB *de propiedad* transfer, assignment, OCIO transfer fee; ~ **del banco** BANCA banker's transfer; ~ **del banco central** BANCA, ECON central bank transaction; ~ **de deudas** CONT assignment of debts; ~ **de dinero** BANCA money transmission; ~ **ilegal** DER unlawful trespass

trasposición *f* DER transposal

trastienda *f* BOLSA cage (*AmE*), *establecimientos* back office

trastornar *vt* COM GEN, GES, RRHH shake up

tratado *m* COM GEN *política* treaty, agreement; ~ **comercial** COM GEN, DER, ECON commercial treaty, commodity agreement; ~ **comercial bilateral** ECON, POL bilateral trade treaty; ~ **de comercio bilateral** ECON, POL bilateral trade treaty; ~ **multilateral** COM GEN convention; ~ **particular** INMOB private treaty; ~ **de reaseguro de exceso de pérdida** SEG excess of loss reinsurance treaty; ~ **de trueque** DER, ECON *comercio internacional* barter agreement

Tratado: ~ **de Cooperación sobre Patentes** *m* DER *propiedad intelectual*, PATENT Patent Cooperation Treaty (*PCT*); ~ **de Libre Comercio** *m* (*TLC*) ECON, POL North American Free Trade Agreement (*NAFTA*); ~ **Monetario Europeo** *m* COM GEN, POL European Monetary Agreement (*EMA*); ~ **de Roma** *m* ECON, POL Treaty of Rome; ~ **de la Unión Europea** *m* COM GEN, POL European Union Treaty

tratamiento *m* COM GEN treatment; ~ **del agua** MED AMB water treatment; ~ **comunitario** IMP/EXP Community treatment; ~ **contable** CONT accounting treatment; ~ **fiscal** FISC tax treatment; ~ **en hospital privado** PROT SOC private hospital treatment; ~ **de informes** CONT reporting treatment; ~ **interactivo** INFO interactive processing; ~ **médico gratuito** PROT SOC free medical treatment; ~ **de nación más favorecida** ECON, POL *comercio internacional* most-favored nation treatment (*AmE*), most-favoured nation treatment (*BrE*); ~ **preliminar** MED AMB *de desperdicios* pretreatment; ~ **de los residuos** MED AMB waste treatment; ~ **de texto** ADMIN, INFO word processing

tratar *vt* COM GEN process, treat; ◆ ~ **de pasar desapercibido** COM GEN keep a low profile

trato *m* COM GEN deal; ~ **en firme** COM GEN firm deal; ~ **de Nash** ECON Nash bargaining; ~ **preferencial** COM GEN preferential treatment; ◆ **se acabó el** ~ COM GEN the deal is off

través: **a** ~ **del sistema** *fra* V&M across-the-network

travesaño *m* TRANSP *de contenedor* crossbar

travesía: ~ **de barco** *f* TRANSP vessel crossing

traviesa *f* TRANSP *de ferrocarril* crosstie (*AmE*), sleeper (*BrE*)

trayecto: ~ **de ida** *m* OCIO, TRANSP outward leg; ~ **de vuelta** *m* OCIO, TRANSP return leg

trayectoria: ~ **de la industria** *f* TRANSP industry track; ~ **profesional** *f* RRHH career

trazado: ~ **portuario** *m* IMP/EXP, TRANSP port layout; ~ **total** *m* MAT *en gráfico* solid line

trazador *m* COM GEN tracer, INFO plotter; ~ **de curvas X-Y** ADMIN X-Y plotter; ~ **de gráficos** INFO graph plotter; ~ **de tambor** INFO drum plotter

trazar *vt* MAT *gráfico* plot

trazo[1]: **de** ~ **fino** *adj* INFO slim-line

trazo[2]: ~ **terminal** *m* INFO, MEDIOS *tipografía* serif

tregua: ~ **laboral** *f* BOLSA, RRHH cooling-off period; ~ **tributaria** *f* FISC tax holiday

tren: ~ **de carga** *m* TRANSP freight train (*AmE*), goods train (*BrE*); ~ **de carretera** *m* TRANSP road train; ~ **de cercanías** *m* TRANSP commuter train; ~ **directo** *m* TRANSP through train; ~ **eléctrico** *m* TRANSP electric train; ~ **interurbano** *m* TRANSP InterCity (*BrE*); ~ **de mercancías** *m* TRANSP freight train (*AmE*), goods train (*BrE*); ~ **de pasajeros** *m* OCIO, TRANSP passenger train

Tren: ~ **de Alta Velocidad** *m* (*TAV*) TRANSP high-speed train (*HST*)

trepar *vt* COM GEN climb

tres: **de** ~ **hélices** *adj* TRANSP triple screw (*Tr*)

TRI *abr* (*tasa de rendimiento interna*) FIN IRR (*internal rate of return*)

triangulación *f* IMP/EXP triangulation

triangular *adj* COM GEN triangular

triángulo: ~ **dorado** *m* ECON Golden Triangle

tribuna: ~ **de redacción** *f* COM GEN copy platform

tribunal *m* DER bar, court; ~ **de apelación** DER appeal court, court of appeal; ~ **de arbitraje** DER court of arbitration; ~ **arbitral** COM GEN arbitration tribunal; ~ **competente** DER court entitled to adjudicate; ~ **de consulta** DER tribunal of enquiry; ~ **federal** DER, RRHH federal tribunal; ~ **fiscal** DER, FISC tax court; ~ **judicial ordinario** DER court of law; ~ **de menores** DER juvenile court; ~ **oficial del Estado** RRHH state government tribunal; ~ **de primera instancia** DER, POL trial court; ~ **de quiebras** DER bankruptcy court; ~ **de sucesiones** DER probate court

Tribunal: **el** ~ *m* DER the Bench; ~ **Constitucional** *m* DER, POL Constitutional Tribunal; ~ **de Cuentas** *m* Esp (*cf Oficina General de Contabilidad AmL*) CONT ≈ General Accounting Office (*AmE*) (*GAO*), Audit Office (*BrE*); ~ **Europeo** *m* DER, POL European Court; ~ **Europeo de Justicia** *m* DER, POL European Court of Justice; ~ **de la Haya** *m* DER, ECON, POL Hague Tribunal; ~ **Internacional de Justicia** *m* DER, POL International Court of Justice (*ICJ*); ~ **de Justicia** *m* DER, POL Court of Justice; ~ **Superior de Justicia** *m* DER High Court of Justice; ~ **Supremo** *m* DER, POL High Court (*BrE*), Supreme Court (*AmE*)

tributación: **~ arbitraria** *f* FISC arbitrary taxation; **~ discriminatoria de los extranjeros** *f* FISC discriminatory taxation of foreigners; **~ excesiva** *f* FISC overtax; **~ independiente** *f* FISC independent taxation

tributo: **~ municipal** *m* FISC local tax

trimensualidad *f* FIN three-months'rate

trimestral[1] *adj* BOLSA, COM GEN quarterly

trimestral[2] *m* MEDIOS *prensa* quarterly

trimestralmente *adv* COM GEN quarterly

trimestre *m* COM GEN calendar quarter, quarter (*qtr*); **~ fiscal** FISC fiscal quarter; **segundo ~** COM GEN second quarter

trinca *f* V&M dog

tripartismo *m* RRHH tripartism

triple: **~ hora bruja** *f* COM GEN triple witching hour

triplicado *adj* COM GEN triplicate; ◆ **por ~** COM GEN in triplicate

triplicar *vt* MAT triple

tripulación[1]: **~ de un avión** *f* TRANSP aircrew; **~ de un solo miembro** *f* TRANSP single manning

tripulación[2]: **con ~ incompleta** *fra* TRANSP undermanned

tripular *vt* RRHH *barco* man

triunfador, a *m,f* COM GEN achiever

triunfar *vi* COM GEN succeed

triunfo *m* COM GEN success

trocar *vt* ECON barter

troika *f* POL troika (*jarg*)

tropiezo: **sin ningún ~** *fra* COM GEN without a hitch

truco *m* COM GEN, FISC gimmick; **~ fiscal** FISC tax gimmick; **~ publicitario** V&M publicity stunt, advertising gimmick

trueque *m* COM GEN exchange; **~ de capital de la deuda** FIN debt-equity swop

truncamiento *m* BANCA, COM GEN, INFO truncation

truncar *vt* BANCA, COM GEN, INFO truncate

trust *m* ADMIN trust; **~ de cerebros** RRHH brains trust

trustificación *f* COM GEN, DER trustification

trustificar *vt* COM GEN, DER trustify

tubería *f* IND pipeline; **~ de descarga** TRANSP flow line

tubo: **~ de rayos catódicos** *m* INFO, MEDIOS *electrónica, informática* cathode ray tube (*CRT*); **~ de salida** *m* TRANSP spout

tubular *m* TRANSP *neumático* cushion tire (*AmE*), cushion tyre (*BrE*)

tumultos: **~ y agitaciones sociales** *m pl* PROT SOC riots and civil commotions (*R&CC*)

túnel *m* ECON, TRANSP tunnel

Túnel: **~ del Canal de la Mancha** *m* TRANSP Channel Tunnel

turboeléctrico *adj* TRANSP turbo-electric (*TE*)

turbulencias *f pl* BOLSA *mercado* ups and downs

Turespaña *f Esp* OCIO Spanish tourist board, ≈ English Tourist Board (*ETB*)

turismo *m* COM GEN, OCIO tourism; **~ extranjero** COM GEN, OCIO overseas tourism; **~ rural** OCIO rural tourism

turista *mf* COM GEN, OCIO tourist; **~ extranjero(-a)** *m,f* COM GEN, OCIO overseas tourist

turno *m* RRHH shift; **~ de día** RRHH day shift; **~ con horario flexible** RRHH gliding shift (*jarg*); **~ de media noche** RRHH graveyard shift (*infrml*); **~ de noche** RRHH night shift; **~ de relevo** RRHH relief shift, swing shift; **~ rotativo** RRHH rotating shift; **~ vespertino** RRHH twilight shift; ◆ **por ~** COM GEN in rotation

turnos: **~ alternos** *m pl* RRHH alternating shifts

tutelar *vt* COM GEN *intereses nacionales* protect

tutor, a *m,f* COM GEN guardian, DER custodian

TV[1] *abr* (*televisión*) MEDIOS TV (*television*)

TV[2]: **~ privada de pago** *f* V&M pay-per-view TV

TVAD: **~ parcialmente digital** *f* (*televisión alta densidad parcialmente digital*) MEDIOS *transmisión por vía satélite* partially digital HDTV (*partially digital high-density television*)

U

ubicación *f* COM GEN location; ~ **indeterminada** MEDIOS *imprenta*, V&M run-of-paper; ~ **de la planta** COM GEN plant location; ~ **de primer orden** INMOB prime location; ◆ **cualquier** ~ SEG *marino* any one location (*AOLOC*)

UE *abr* (*Unión Europea*) ECON, POL EU (*European Union*)

UEO *abr* (*Unión Europea Occidental*) ECON, POL WEU (*Western European Union*)

UEP *abr* (*Unión Europea de Pagos*) ECON, POL EPU (*European Payments Union*)

UEPS *abr* (*último en entrar, primero en salir*) COM GEN, CONT LIFO (*last in, first out*)

UER *abr* (*Unión Europea de Radiodifusión*) COMS, MEDIOS EBU (*European Broadcasting Union*)

UIT *abr* (*Unión Internacional de Telecomunicaciones*) COMS ITU (*International Telecommunications Union*)

última: ~ **advertencia** *f* RRHH final warning; ~ **franja horaria de emisión** *f* MEDIOS *radio* late fringe (*jarg*) (*AmE*); ~ **reclamación** *f* FISC final demand; ~ **venta** *f* V&M last sale

último¹ *adj* COM GEN last, latter; ◆ ~ **en entrar, primero en salir** (*UEPS*) COM GEN, CONT last in, first out (*LIFO*)

último²: ~ **día de operaciones** *m* BOLSA final trading day, last day of trading; ~ **día del seguro** *m* SEG *naval* last safe day (*lsd*); ~ **pago** *m* FIN late payment; ~ **transportista** *m,f* TRANSP last carrier

ultramar: **de** ~ *adj* BANCA offshore, COM GEN overseas

umbral *m* COM GEN threshold; ~ **divergente** ECON divergence threshold; ~ **de excedentes** SEG excess point; ~ **impositivo** ECON, FIN, FISC tax threshold; ~ **de población** ECON threshold population; ~ **de pobreza** PROT SOC poverty line; ~ **de propiedad recíproca** FISC cross-ownership threshold; ~ **publicitario** V&M advertising threshold; ~ **de rentabilidad** CONT break-even point

UME *abr* (*Unión Monetaria Europea*) ECON, POL EMU (*European Monetary Union*)

unánime *adj* COM GEN *decisión* unanimous, *voto* solid

unanimidad *f* COM GEN unanimity; ◆ **por** ~ COM GEN unanimously

UNCTAD *abr* (*Conferencia de las Naciones Unidas sobre Comercio y Desarrollo*) ECON, POL UNCTAD (*United Nations Conference on Trade and Development*)

UNED *abr Esp* (*Universidad Nacional de Educación a Distancia*) PROT SOC ≈ OU (*Open University*) (*BrE*)

UNICEF *abr* (*Agencia de las Naciones Unidas para la Ayuda a la Infancia*) POL, PROT SOC UNICEF (*United Nations Children's Fund*)

único *adj* COM GEN one-off, sole

unidad *f* COM GEN unit; ~ **de almacenamiento** COM GEN stockkeeping unit; ~ **de arrastre** TRANSP transport unit; ~ **de base** COM GEN basic unit; ~ **con capacidad de decisión** V&M decision-making unit; ~ **de carga stakrak** TRANSP stakrak cargo unit; ~ **central de procesamiento** INFO central processing unit; ~ **de cinta** COM GEN tape unit, INFO tape drive; ~ **de**

contratación BOLSA round lot (*jarg*) (*AmE*), **de opciones en eurodólares** trading unit; ~ **de decisión** COM GEN decision unit; ~ **de disco duro** INFO hard disk drive, hard disk unit; ~ **de disco flexible** INFO floppy disk drive; ~ **de discos** INFO disk unit; ~ **de una empresa de inversión colectiva** FIN unit of a collective investment undertaking; ~ **equivalente a una tonelada** TRANSP *envíos* ton equivalent unit, tonne equivalent unit; ~ **de escritorio** INFO desktop unit; ~ **estratégica de negocio** COM GEN, ECON, GES strategic business unit; ~ **europea de cuenta** ECON European Unit of Account (*EUA*); ~ **familiar** COM GEN, ECON household; ~ **fiduciaria** BOLSA trust unit; ~ **impositiva** FISC tax unit; ~ **de impresión** COM GEN printing unit, INFO print driver; ~ **de invento** PATENT unity of invention; ~ **monetaria** BANCA, CONT, ECON, FIN currency unit, monetary unit; ~ **monetaria combinada** ECON composite currency unit; ~ **monetaria extranjera** BANCA, CONT, ECON, FIN foreign currency unit; ~ **de negociación** BOLSA unit of trading; ~ **de negocio estratégico** COM GEN strategic business unit; ~ **de negocios** COM GEN business unit; ~ **normal de negociación** BOLSA normal trading unit; ~ **de organización** ADMIN organizational unit; ~ **organizacional** ADMIN organizational unit; ~ **de pantalla** INFO screen driver; ~ **de patentes europeas** PATENT unity of European patent; ~ **de perforación costera móvil** IND mobile offshore drilling unit (*MODU*); ~ **de planificación económica** ECON economic planning unit; ~ **principal** INMOB prime unit; ~ **de ratón** INFO mouse driver; ~ **de representación visual** INFO visual display unit (*VDU*), display device; ~ **salarial** RRHH wage unit; ~ **de tracción** TRANSP tractive unit; ~ **de tratamiento de entradas** IMP/EXP entry processing unit (*EPU*); ~ **de venta** V&M shop unit; ~ **de visualización** INFO display unit; ~ **de visualización de video** AmL ver unidad de visualización de vídeo Esp; ~ **de visualización de vídeo** Esp INFO video display unit; ◆ **por** ~ COM GEN apiece

Unidad: ~ **Compuesta Europea** *f* FIN European Composite Unit (*EURCO*); ~ **de Cooperación de Productos** *f* IMP/EXP Product Co-operation Unit (*PCU*); ~ **de Inteligencia Económica** *f* ECON Economist Intelligence Unit (*EIU*); ~ **Internacional de Reclutamiento** *f* RRHH International Recruitment Unit (*IRU*); ~ **de Investigación de la Recaudación** *f* FISC Collection Investigation Unit; ~ **Monetaria Europea** *f* (*ECU*) ECON, POL European Currency Unit (*ECU*)

unidades: ~ **periféricas** *f pl* COM GEN, INFO peripherals

unidimensional *adj* COM GEN unidimensional

unidireccional *adj* INFO *transmisión* simplex

unido¹: ~ **al suelo** *adj* FISC affixed to land

unido²: ~ **al párrafo anterior** *fra* V&M *texto* run-on

unificación *f* POL unification; ~ **de graneles** TRANSP *navegación* bulk unitization

unificar *vt* POL unify

uniformación: ~ **exponencial** *f* COM GEN exponential smoothing

uniformar *vt* COM GEN, DER standardize
uniforme *adj* BOLSA flat, COM GEN uniform
uniformemente: ~ **distribuido** *adj* COM GEN evenly spread
uniformidad *f* COM GEN consistency, uniformity
unilateral *adj* COM GEN, ECON, RRHH unilateral
unilateralmente *adv* COM GEN, ECON, RRHH unilaterally
unión: ~ **aduanera** *f* DER, ECON, IMP/EXP customs union; ~ **de aseguradoras** *f* FIN, SEG pool; ~ **de crédito** *f* BANCA, FIN credit union (*BrE*); ~ **económica** *f* ECON *internacional*, POL economic union; ~ **política** *f* ECON, POL *Comunidad Europea* political union; ~ **de trabajadores** *f* RRHH labor union (*AmE*), trade union (*BrE*) (*TU*); ~ **de vendedores** *f* V&M bonding of salespeople
Unión: ~ **Económica y Monetaria** *f* ECON, POL Economic and Monetary Union; ~ **Europea** *f* ECON, POL (*UE*) European Union (*EU*); ~ **Europea Occidental** *f* (*UEO*) ECON, POL Western European Union (*WEU*); ~ **Europea de Pagos** *f* (*UEP*) ECON, POL European Payments Union (*EPU*); ~ **Europea de Radiodifusión** *f* (*UER*) COMS, MEDIOS European Broadcasting Union (*EBU*); ~ **Internacional de Compensación** *f* BANCA, ECON International Clearing Union (*ICU*); ~ **Internacional de Telecomunicaciones** *f* (*UIT*) COMS International Telecommunications Union (*ITU*); ~ **Monetaria Europea** *f* (*UME*) ECON, POL European Monetary Union (*EMU*); ~ **Postal Universal** *f* (*UPU*) COMS Universal Postal Union (*UPU*)
unir *vt* DER bind
UNITAR *abr* (*Instituto de las Naciones Unidas para la Formación Profesional y la Investigación*) POL, PROT SOC, RRHH UNITAR (*United Nations Institute for Training and Research*)
universal *adj* COM GEN general purpose (*GP*), worldwide
universalismo *m* COM GEN, PROT SOC universalism
universalmente *adv* COM GEN worldwide
universidad *f* COM GEN university
Universidad: ~ **Nacional de Educación a Distancia** *m Esp* (*UNED*) PROT SOC ≈ Open University *BrE* (*OU*)
universo *m* V&M universe
uno: ~ **por uno** *fra* BOLSA *relación de precio* one-for-one
untar: ~ **a alguien** *vt* COM GEN oil sb's palm (*infrml*)
uñero *m* COM GEN thumb index
UPU *abr* (*Unión Postal Universal*) COMS UPU (*Universal Postal Union*)
urbanismo *m* COM GEN town planning, urban planning
urbanista *mf* COM GEN town planner, urban planner
urbanización *f* COM GEN urbanization
urbanizar *vt* COM GEN urbanize
urbanizarse *v refl* INMOB build up
urgente *adj* COM GEN, COMS, TRANSP urgent, *servicio* express
urna: ~ **electoral** *f* POL, RRHH ballot box
usar: ~ **algo** *fra* COM GEN have the use of sth
uso *m* COM GEN, PATENT use; ~ **alternativo** INMOB alternative use; ~ **anterior** PATENT prior use; ~ **compartido de datos** INFO data sharing; ~ **del contenedor** TRANSP container use; ~ **económico de los recursos** ECON economical use of resources; ~ **de los fondos** BANCA, CONT, FIN use of funds; ~ **horario** COM GEN time zone; ~ **indebido de autoridad** COM GEN exercise of undue authority; ~ **indebido de patente** DER, PATENT patent infringement; ~ **no agrícola** INMOB, MED AMB nonagricultural use; ~ **no conforme** DER, INMOB nonconforming use; ~ **preexistente** INMOB pre-existing use; ~ **público** PATENT public use; ◆ **hacer** ~ **de** COM GEN make use of; ~ **y desgaste** COM GEN wear and tear; ~ **y desgaste normales** COM GEN normal wear and tear; **de** ~ **fácil** COM GEN, INFO user-friendly; **hacer** ~ **de la fuerza** COM GEN use strong-arm tactics; **sólo para** ~ **interno** ADMIN for office use only; **hacer** ~ **pleno de** COM GEN make full use of
usos: ~ **de compra** *m pl* COM GEN buying habits; ~ **y costumbres** *m pl* IND, RRHH custom and practice; ~ **y prácticas normalizados de créditos documentarios** *m pl* COM GEN uniform customs and practice for documentary credits (*UC&P*)
usuario, -a *m,f* COM GEN, INFO user; ~ **continuo(-a)** INFO heavy user; ~ **final** V&M end consumer, end user; ~ **potencial** V&M potential user; ~ **registrado(-a)** DER, PATENT registered user; ~ **de un servicio sin pagar** ECON easy rider; ~ **de terminal** INFO terminal user
usucapir *vt* DER prescribe
usufructo *m* DER usufruct, INMOB life estate; ◆ **con derecho a** ~ FISC beneficially interested
usufructuador, a *m,f* DER usufructuary
usufructuario, -a *m,f* DER usufructuary, INMOB limited owner
usura *f* BANCA, FIN usury
usurario *adj* BANCA, FIN usurious
usurero, -a *m,f* BANCA, FIN loan shark (*infrml*), usurer
usurpar *vt* DER encroach on
utilidad *f* COM GEN utility, CONT profit; ~ **absoluta** CONT pure profit; ~ **acumulada** CONT accumulated profit; ~ **anticipada** FIN anticipated profit; ~ **bruta** CONT gross earnings, trading income, FISC (*cf renta bruta*) gross rent; ~ **cambiaria** BANCA banker's turn; ~ **de capital** BANCA, CONT, FIN capital profit; ~ **cardinal** ECON cardinal utility; ~ **por distribuir** CONT, FIN undistributed profit; ~ **entre compañías** CONT, FIN intercompany profit; ~ **de explotación** CONT operating profit; ~ **gravable** CONT, ECON, FISC taxable profit; ~ **del lugar** ECON place utility; ~ **marginal** ECON marginal utility; ~ **neta de operación** CONT net operating profit; ~ **no realizada** BOLSA, CONT, FIN paper profit; ~ **ordinal** ECON ordinal utility; ~ **superior a lo normal** CONT, FIN supernormal profit
utilitarismo *m* ECON utilitarianism, *método Bentham* felicific calculus
utilización *f* COM GEN use, utility, PATENT use; ~ **de la capacidad industrial** IND industrial capacity utilization; ~ **en común de ficheros** INFO file sharing; ~ **del contenedor** TRANSP container utilization; ~ **de la flota** TRANSP fleet utilization; ~ **racional** INFO enhancement; ~ **de la tierra** MED AMB land use; ◆ **con** ~ **intensiva de mano de obra** RRHH labor-intensive (*AmE*), labour-intensive (*BrE*)
utilizado: **no** ~ *adj* COM GEN, FISC unused
utilizar *vt* COM GEN use, utilize
utillaje *m* COM GEN tool

V

v *abr* (*voltio*) COM GEN V (*volt*)

vacaciones *f pl* OCIO, RRHH holidays (*BrE*), vacations (*AmE*); **~ anuales** RRHH annual leave; **~ escalonadas** OCIO, RRHH staggered holidays (*BrE*), staggered vacations (*AmE*); **~ establecidas** COM GEN, RRHH statutory holidays (*BrE*), statutory vacations (*AmE*); **~ remuneradas** OCIO, RRHH paid holidays (*BrE*), paid vacations (*AmE*); **~ con todo organizado** OCIO, TRANSP package holiday (*BrE*); ♦ **de ~** RRHH on furlough; **ir de ~** OCIO go on holiday (*BrE*), take a vacation (*AmE*)

vacante *f* BANCA, IND, RRHH vacancy; **~ no cubierta** RRHH unfilled vacancy; **~ de puesto de trabajo** RRHH job vacancy

vaciado: **~ del contenedor** *m* TRANSP devanning, container unstuffing; **~ de memoria** *m* INFO memory dump; **~ de pantalla** *m* INFO screen dump

vaciar *vt* COM GEN *contenido* empty out, INFO dump

vacilación *f* BOLSA *transacción bursátil* halt

vacilar *vi* ECON falter

vacío: **~ de comunicación** *m* COM GEN communication gap; **~ legal** *m* DER loophole; **~ tecnológico** *m* IND technological gap

vacunación *f* IMP/EXP, PROT SOC vaccination

vagón *m* TRANSP carriage; **~ basculante** TRANSP tipper; **~ de cemento** TRANSP cement wagon; **~ cerrado** TRANSP *tren* box wagon (*BrE*), boxcar (*AmE*); **~ de ferrocarril** TRANSP railcar (*AmE*), railway carriage (*BrE*); **~ frigorífico** TRANSP insulated van; **~ plataforma** TRANSP *tren* flat car (*AmE*), flat wagon (*BrE*); **~ plataforma plana** TRANSP trailer on flat car (*TOFC*); **~ portacontenedores** TRANSP *tren* container car (*AmE*), container wagon (*BrE*); **~ raso** TRANSP *vagón ferroviario* flat car (*AmE*), flat wagon (*BrE*); **~ para transporte de contenedores** TRANSP *ferrocarril* container wagon (*BrE*), container car (*AmE*); **~ de tren** TRANSP railcar (*AmE*), railway coach (*BrE*)

vaivenes *m pl* COM GEN *del mercado* swing

vale *m* COM GEN *cupón* voucher; **~ canjeable** (*cf boleta AmL*) BOLSA scrip (*jarg*), voucher; **~ de comida** FISC, RRHH luncheon voucher (*BrE*) (*LV*), meal ticket (*AmE*); **~ para compra de libros** OCIO, V&M book token; **~ para comprar un regalo** OCIO, V&M gift token; **~ por pronto pago de bono** BOLSA bond anticipation note (*BAN*)

valer *vt* COM GEN be worth; ♦ **no ~ un duro** *Esp infrml* COM GEN not worth a bean (*infrml*), not worth a penny; **~ la pena** COM GEN worthwhile; **~ un potosí** COM GEN worth a mint

valía *f* RRHH worth; ♦ **de gran ~** RRHH *personal* high-caliber (*AmE*), high-calibre (*BrE*)

validación *f* COM GEN vetting, validation, INFO validation

validar *vt* COM GEN *documento, reclamación*, INFO validate

validez *f* COM GEN, FISC, PATENT validity; **~ legal** DER legal force

válido *adj* COM GEN, INFO *argumento, excusa* valid

valija: **~ diplomática** *f* COMS diplomatic pouch (*AmE*), diplomatic bag (*BrE*)

valla: **~ publicitaria** *f* V&M billboard, poster site; **~ publicitaria en carretera** *f* V&M roadside site

valor[1]: **sin ~** *adj* COM GEN worthless, valueless; **con ~ agregado** *adj* IND added-value; **sin ~ comercial** *adj* COM GEN no business value (*NBV*); **sin ~ nominal** *adj* BOLSA no-par value (*n.p.v.*); **sin ~ a la par** *adj* BOLSA no-par value (*n.p.v.*)

valor[2] *m* COM GEN, ECON stock (*stck, stk*), value, worth;

■ a **~ absoluto del excedente** ECON absolute surplus value; **~ de las acciones en el balance** BOLSA, CONT balance sheet value of shares; **~ de activo** CONT, ECON, FIN asset value; **~ del activo intangible** CONT, ECON, FIN intangible asset worth; **~ de activo neto** (*VAN*) CONT, FIN net asset value (*NAV*); **~ actual** COM GEN, CONT, ECON, FIN current value; **~ actual descontado** FIN discounted present value; **~ actual neto** (*VAN*) CONT, FIN net present value (*NPV*); **~ actual de venta** COM GEN actual cash value (*ACV*); **~ acumulable** BOLSA cumulative security; **~ de adquisición** COM GEN acquisition value; **~ aduanero por kilogramo bruto** IMP/EXP customs value per gross kilogram (*AmE*) (*CVGK*), customs value per gross kilogramme (*BrE*) (*CVGK*); **~ aduanero por libra bruta** IMP/EXP customs value per gross pound (*CVGP*); **~ de afección** SEG affection value; **~ agregado** *AmL* (*cf valor añadido Esp*) COM GEN, CONT, ECON, FISC, V&M added value, value-added; **~ al cobro** CONT value for collection; **~ al coste** *Esp* (*cf valor al costo AmL*) CONT value at cost; **~ al costo** *AmL* (*cf valor al coste Esp*) CONT value at cost; **~ al vencimiento** BOLSA maturity value; **~ de altura** BOLSA high-flying stock; **~ amortizado** CONT amortized value, written-down value; **~ añadido** *Esp* (*cf valor agregado AmL*) COM GEN added value, value-added; **~ añadido de la cadena de servicios** ECON value added network service; **~ añadido relativo** ECON relative surplus value; **~ anticipado** BOLSA advance security; **~ de arrendamiento** FIN leasehold value, FISC, INMOB rental value; **~ del arrendamiento** INMOB leasehold value; **~ de arrendamiento razonable** INMOB fair rental value; **~ asegurado** SEG aggregate indemnity; **~ de atención** V&M *publicidad* attention value; **~ atípico** MAT outlier;

■ b **~ de bolsa que promete rápidos beneficios** FIN go-go fund (*jarg*);

■ c **~ caducado** SEG forfeited security; **~ de cambio** BOLSA, ECON exchange value; **~ capital** ECON, FIN capital value; **~ del capital** ECON, FIN capital value; **~ capitalizado** ECON, FIN capitalized value; **~ cercano a su vencimiento** BOLSA maturing value; **~ por cobrar** CONT receivable; **~ por cobrar por suscripción** BOLSA subscription receivable; **~ comerciable** V&M marketable value; **~ comercial** CONT market value; **~ comercial actual** CONT, V&M current market value; **~ como póliza marina** SEG value as marine policy (*VMP*); **~ comparable** RRHH comparable worth (*CW*); **~ de compra** BOLSA bid value; **~ constante** COM GEN, CONT, ECON, FIN current value; **~ contable agregado** CONT aggregate book value; **~ contable de la inversión** CONT book value of investment; **~ del contrato** BOLSA *futuros* contract value; ~ **contribuyente** SEG contributory value; ~ **convenido** SEG agreed value; ~ **cotizable** BOLSA listed security; ~ **de cotización** BOLSA quote value; ~ **sin cotización** BOLSA, FIN unlisted security; ~ **crítico** MAT critical value;

■ **d** ~ **declarado** CONT stated value; ~ **declarado en aduanas** IMP/EXP, TRANSP declared value for customs; ~ **declarado por porte** IMP/EXP, TRANSP declared value for carriage; ~ **descontado** FIN present value; ~ **a un día** BOLSA overnight security; ~ **del dinero** ECON value of money; ~ **de disolución** CONT break-up value; ~ **disponible** CONT cash assets; ~ **en dólares** BOLSA dollar value;

■ **e** ~ **económico** ECON economic value; ~ **en efectivo** BANCA, CONT, FIN cash value; ~ **equitativo de venta** BOLSA, COM GEN, CONT *activos* fair market value, fair value; ~ **de escasez** ECON scarcity value; ~ **de escisión** CONT break-up value; ~ **esperado** MAT expected value; ~ **estimado** INMOB appraised value, SEG estimated value; ~ **estrella** BOLSA leading share; ~ **del excedente** CONT, ECON surplus value; ~ **exento** BOLSA, FISC tax-exempt security; ~ **externo ponderado según el comercio exterior** ECON *de divisa* trade-weighted external value; ~ **extrínseco** BOLSA *opciones*, ECON *opciones* extrinsic value;

■ **f** ~ **facial** BOLSA face value; ~ **de factura** COM GEN invoice value;

■ **g** ~ **de garantía** BOLSA margin security; ~ **de gran aceptación** BOLSA glamour stock (*BrE*);

■ **i** ~ **ilusorio del dinero** ECON money illusion; ~ **imponible** FISC *de propiedad*, INMOB assessed valuation (*AmE*), rateable value (*BrE*), taxable value (*BrE*); ~ **imputado** CONT imputed value; ~ **intangible** CONT intangible value; ~ **interno actual** ECON, IMP/EXP current domestic value (*CDV*); ~ **intrínseco** BOLSA, ECON intrinsic value; ~ **de inventario** CONT stocktaking value; ~ **de inversión por acción** BOLSA asset value per share; ~ **de inversión de un título convertible** BOLSA investment value of a convertible security;

■ **j** ~ **justo** CONT *activos* fair value;

■ **l** ~ **en libros** CONT, FIN book value; ~ **de liquidación** CONT *de compañía* liquidating value;

■ **m** ~ **medio** MAT mean value; ~ **de mercado** COM GEN market value; ~ **mínimo de variación** BOLSA tick; ~ **del mismo día** BANCA same-day value; ~ **mixto** BOLSA blended value; ~ **mobiliario** BOLSA, FIN transferable security; ~ **monetario** ECON currency value;

■ **n** ~ **negativo** ECON value subtractor; ~ **del negocio establecido** CONT going-concern value; ~ **del negocio en funcionamiento** CONT going-concern value; ~ **neto** BOLSA stockholders' equity, CONT net value; ~ **neto contable** CONT carrying value; ~ **neto del déficit** ECON deficit net worth; ~ **neto en libros** CONT, FIN net book value; ~ **neto negativo** ECON negative net worth; ~ **no cotizado en la bolsa** BOLSA, FIN unlisted security; ~ **nominal** BOLSA face value, par value, nominal value, denomination (*denom.*), CONT nominal value, par value, ECON *obligaciones* denomination (*denom.*), SEG face amount; ~ **nominal del bono** BOLSA bond denomination; ~ **nominal del PIB** ECON nominal GDP; ~ **de novedad** V&M novelty value;

■ **o** ~ **objetivo** ECON objective value; ~ **oculto** V&M hidden value;

■ **p** ~ **pagadero a la liquidación** CONT amount payable

on settlement; ~ **a la par** BOLSA, CONT par value (*p.v.*); ~ **a la par de una moneda** BOLSA, CONT par value of currency; ~ **a plazo** BOLSA forward security; ~ **de la plusvalía** CONT, ECON surplus value; ~ **de la póliza** SEG face of policy; ~ **de la póliza marina** SEG value as in original policy (*VOP*); ~ **en posición cubierta bloqueada** BOLSA *de acciones adjudicadas a empleados* locked-in value; ~ **presente** CONT, ECON, FIN present value; ~ **presente neto** (*VAN*) CONT, FIN net present value (*NPV*); ~ **para préstamo** BANCA, SEG loan value; ~ **de préstamo de los títulos** BOLSA borrowing power of securities; ~ **de primer orden** FIN gilt-edged security; ~ **de primera clase** BOLSA, FIN blue chip; ~ **principal** BOLSA principal value, COM GEN chief value (*cv*); ~ **de privación** ECON deprival value; ~ **de propiedades arrendadas** FIN, INMOB leasehold value; ~ **propuesto** CONT value proposal; ~ **publicitario** V&M advertising value; ~ **de un punto** BOLSA value of one point;

■ **r** ~ **razonable de venta** CONT *activos* fair value; ~ **real en efectivo** COM GEN actual cash value (*ACV*); ~ **real de venta** COM GEN actual cash value (*ACV*); ~ **realizable estimado** BANCA, CONT, FIN, V&M estimated realizable value; ~ **realizable neto** BANCA, CONT, FIN, V&M net realizable value (*NRV*); ~ **de realización inmediata** CONT, FIN break-up value; ~ **de reposición** CONT replacement value; ~ **de rescate** BOLSA redemption value, CONT surrender value; ~ **de rescate al contado** SEG cash surrender value; ~ **residual** ECON salvage value, FISC residual value; ~ **respaldado por una hipoteca** BOLSA, FIN mortgage-backed security (*MBS*); ~ **de reventa** COM GEN resale value; ~ **reversible** INMOB reversionary value;

■ **s** ~ **semejante** BOLSA equal value; ~ **de Shapley** ECON Shapley value; ~ **del superávit** CONT, ECON surplus value;

■ **t** ~ **techo** BOLSA topping out; ~ **teórico de las acciones según balance** CONT balance sheet value of shares; ~ **tiempo** BOLSA *opciones* time value; ~ **total** CONT, FISC *del patrimonio* aggregate value; ~ **total contable** CONT aggregate book value; ~ **del trabajo** COM GEN work content; ~ **transferible de suscripción renovable** BOLSA transferable revolving underwriting security (*TRUF*);

■ **u** ~ **de umbral** INFO threshold value; ~ **de la unidad de construcción** TRANSP construction unit value (*CUV*); ~ **unitario** COM GEN, ECON unit value; ~ **de uso** ECON value in use; ~ **en uso** ECON use value;

■ **v** ~ **por valor** BOLSA mark to mark (*jarg*); ~ **valuado** FIN appraised value; ~ **de venta** V&M sale value

valor[3]: **sobre el ~** *fra* COM GEN *impuestos* ad valorem (*ad val*); **sin ~ en aduana** *fra* IMP/EXP no customs value (*NCV*); **sin ~ comercial** *fra* COM GEN *de distribución gratuita* no commercial value (*n.c.v.*), no business value (*NBV*); **por encima del ~ nominal** *fra* BOLSA *precio*, COM GEN *precio de las obligaciones*, CONT above par

valoración *f* COM GEN appraisal, appreciation, CONT *propiedades* appreciation, DER *de compensación* assessment, RRHH appraisal; ~ **de la actuación** FIN *inversión* performance rating; ~ **en aduana** IMP/EXP customs valuation; ~ **arbitraria** FISC arbitrary assessment; ~ **de bonos** BOLSA bond valuation; ~ **de la calidad** GES, SEG quality assessment; ~ **a coste total** (*cf valoración a costo total AmL*) BANCA, CONT full costing, ECON, V&M full-cost pricing; ~ **a costo total** *AmL* (*cf valoración a coste total Esp*) BANCA, CONT full costing; ~ **diferencial**

ECON differential pricing; **~ de la economía industrial** ECON, GES, IND economic manufacturing quantity; **~ eventual** ECON contingent valuation; **~ excesiva** COM GEN, CONT, ECON overvaluation; **~ de existencias** COM GEN, CONT stock valuation; **~ de inventario** COM GEN, CONT inventory valuation; **~ de mercado** BOLSA market valuation; **~ de méritos** COM GEN, RRHH merit rating; **~ del orden económico** ECON, MAT economic order quantity (*EOQ*); **~ de un problema** COM GEN, GES problem assessment; **~ de proyecto** *Esp* (*cf avalúo del proyecto AmL*) COM GEN project assessment; **~ de recursos** COM GEN resource appraisal; **~ de rendimientos** RRHH performance appraisal; **~ de resultados** RRHH performance appraisal; **~ tributaria** FISC income tax assessment; ◆ **en la más alta ~** COM GEN at the highest estimate; **en la más baja ~** COM GEN at the lowest estimate

valorado: **estar ~ en** *fra* BOLSA be valued at

valorador, a *m,f* INMOB appraiser

valorar *vt* COM GEN, INMOB assess

valores *m pl* BANCA shares (*shs*), BOLSA equities, COM GEN securities, valuables, CONT shares (*shs*), FIN shares (*shs*), paper (*infrml*); **~ activos** BOLSA active securities; **~ anotados** BOLSA book-entry securities; **~ de anticipo sobre recursos propios a largo plazo** BOLSA long-term equity anticipation securities (*LEAPS*); **~ de arbitraje** BOLSA arbitrage stocks; **~ bancarios** BANCA bankable paper, bank paper; **~ basados en el activo neto** CONT net asset based values; **~ en cartera** BOLSA holdings; **~ en cartera actuales** BOLSA current holdings; **~ continuos** BOLSA tap bills; **~ de control** BOLSA control stock; **~ cotizados** BOLSA listed securities, quoted securities, quoted shares; **~ con derecho de voto** BOLSA voting security; **~ de distribución** BOLSA distribution stock; **~ entregables** BOLSA deliverable bills; **~ especulativos** BOLSA cats and dogs, speculative securities; **~ del Estado** BOLSA, ECON gilt-edged stocks (*BrE*), government securities (*AmE*); **~ extranjeros** BOLSA foreign securities; **~ ferroviarios** BOLSA railroad securities (*AmE*), railway securities (*BrE*); **~ financieros** FIN financial paper; **~ financieros de la compañía** FIN finance company paper; **~ en flotación** BOLSA floating securities; **~ industriales de primera clase** BOLSA blue-chip industrials; **~ sin límite** BOLSA unlimited securities; **~ a mayor plazo de oferta continua** BOLSA Continuously Offered Longer-Term Securities (*COLTS*); **~ mineros** BOLSA mining shares; **~ mobiliarios** COM GEN securities, ECON chattel paper; **~ negociables** BANCA eligible paper; **~ no cotizables en bolsa** BOLSA unlisted securities, unquoted shares; **~ no cotizados** BOLSA unquoted securities; **~ no inscritos en la bolsa** BOLSA unlisted securities; **~ no negociados** BANCA ineligible paper; **~ a nombre del propio operador** BOLSA street name; **~ ordinarios** BOLSA current stock; **~ petrolíferos** BOLSA oil shares; **~ de primera clase** BOLSA blue-chip securities; **~ seguros** BOLSA blue chips, steel securities; **~ en un trust** BOLSA securities held in trust; **~ vendidos con acuerdo de recompra** BOLSA securities sold under repurchase agreement; **~ vendidos antes de la emisión** BOLSA bonds sold prior to issue; ◆ **se necesitan ~** BOLSA securities wanted

valorización *f* BANCA, BOLSA securitization, COM GEN, ECON valorization, FIN securitization

valuación *f* BOLSA, FISC appreciation, RRHH appraisal

(*BrE*); **~ de gastos de capital** *Esp* (*cf avalúo de gastos de capital AmL*) ECON, FIN capital expenditure appraisal

valuador, a *m,f AmL* (*cf tasador Esp*) FIN appraiser

válvula: **~ de presión** *f* TRANSP pressure valve; **~ de seguridad del recalentador** *f* TRANSP superheater safety valve (*SHSV*); **~ de seguridad de vacío** *f* TRANSP vacuum relief valve (*PV*)

VAN *abr* CONT, FIN (*valor de activo neto*) NAV (*net asset value*), (*valor actual neto, valor presente neto*) NPV (*net present value*)

vanguardia *f* COM GEN spearhead, V&M leading edge; ◆ **a la ~** COM GEN in the vanguard; **de ~** COM GEN state-of-the-art, *de investigación y desarrollo* at the cutting edge, at the forefront

vanguardista *adj* COM GEN state-of-the-art

vapor *m* TRANSP steam (*STM*); **~ de agua** TRANSP steam (*STM*); **cualquier ~** SEG *marino*, TRANSP any one steamer (*AOS*)

varado *adj* TRANSP aground

varar *vi* TRANSP *barco* run aground

variabilidad *f* MAT variability

variable[1]: **no ~** *adj* BANCA, COM GEN nonvariable; **~ hacia arriba** *adj* COM GEN upwardly mobile

variable[2] *f* COM GEN, FIN, INFO variable; **~ aleatoria** INFO, MAT random variable; **~ booleana** INFO boolean variable; **~ compleja** COM GEN complex variable; **~ común** INFO global variable; **~ continua** MAT continuous variable; **~ desfasada** MAT lagged variable; **~ discreta** MAT discrete variable; **~ endógena** ECON endogenous variable; **~ ex ante** ECON ex ante variable; **~ exógena** ECON exogenous variable; **~ ex post** ECON ex post variable; **~ ficticia** ECON dummy variable; **~ independiente** MAT independent variable; **~ local** INFO local variable; **~ objetivo** ECON target variable, POL goal variable

variación *f* BOLSA, COM GEN, FIN *renta, gasto* variation, MAT variance; **~ al cierre** BOLSA closing range; **~ aleatoria** ECON random variation; **~ oíclica** COM GEN, ECON cyclical variation, cyclic variation; **~ del coste** *Esp* (*cf variación del costo AmL*) CONT, FIN cost variance; **~ del coste de marketing** *Esp* (*cf variación del costo de marketing AmL*) V&M marketing cost variance; **~ del costo** *AmL* (*cf variación del coste Esp*) CONT, FIN cost variance; **~ del costo de marketing** *AmL* (*cf variación del coste de marketing Esp*) V&M marketing cost variance; **~ en eficiencia** FIN efficiency variance; **~ estacional** ECON seasonal variation; **~ favorable** CONT favorable variance (*AmE*), favourable variance (*BrE*); **~ gradual** RRHH tapering; **~ de mercado** BOLSA trading variation; **~ mercantil** BOLSA trading variation; **~ mínima del precio** BOLSA *mercado de divisas* price tick; **~ de muestreo** MAT *estadística* sampling variance; **~ neta** BOLSA *títulos* net change; **~ porcentual** FIN percentage change; **~ del precio** COM GEN price variance; **~ presupuestaria** FIN budget variance; **~ de rendimiento** COM GEN yield variance; **~ de los resultados** MAT output variance

variante *f* COM GEN alternative

variar *vt* COM GEN vary; ◆ **~ según** COM GEN vary with

variedad: **~ de demandas** *f* PATENT claims of different categories; **~ de monedas** *f* FIN currency cocktail

variedades: **~ vegetales** *f pl* PATENT plant varieties

vario *adj* COM GEN miscellaneous (*misc.*)

variómetro *m* SEG variometer

varios *m pl* CONT sundries, *hoja de balance* miscellaneous

vasto *adj* COM GEN far-flung

véase: ~ **a la vuelta** *fra* MEDIOS *prensa* see overleaf

vecindario *m* COM GEN neighbourhood (*BrE*), neighborhood (*AmE*)

vector *m* COM GEN vector

vega *m* BOLSA *coeficiente* vega

vehículo *m* TRANSP vehicle; ~ **con amortiguación por aire** TRANSP air cushion vehicle (*ACV*); ~ **articulado** TRANSP articulated vehicle; ~ **automotor interno** TRANSP internal motor vehicle (*IMV*); ~ **de carga con plataforma baja** TRANSP low loader (*lo*); ~ **para cargas pesadas** TRANSP heavy goods vehicle (*HGV*); ~ **de carretera con motor diesel** TRANSP diesel-engined road vehicle (*DERV*); ~ **comercial** TRANSP trade car, commercial vehicle; ~ **construido de encargo** TRANSP purpose-built vehicle; ~ **de dos ejes** TRANSP two-axle vehicle; ~ **para equipajes** OCIO, TRANSP baggage vehicle; ~ **con horquilla elevadora tipo pescante de grúa** TRANSP crane-jib-type fork-lift truck; ~ **industrial** TRANSP industrial vehicle; ~ **de licitación** COM GEN bid vehicle; ~ **de motor** TRANSP motor vehicle; ~ **de pasajeros** OCIO, TRANSP passenger vehicle; ~ **plataforma** TRANSP platform vehicle; ~ **publicitario** MEDIOS, V&M advertising vehicle; ~ **recuperador** TRANSP recovery vehicle; ~ **remolque autocargador** TRANSP self-loading trailer; ~ **rígido** TRANSP rigid vehicle; ~ **de servicio público** TRANSP public service vehicle (*PSV*); ~ **con sus accesorios ya instalados** TRANSP built-up vehicle; ~ **de transporte** TRANSP transportation car; ~ **de transporte por carretera** TRANSP road haulage vehicle (*RHV*); ~ **de transporte para minerales/graneles/petróleo/productos** TRANSP product/oil/bulk/ore carrier (*PROBO*); ~ **con tres ejes** TRANSP three axle vehicle

velocidad *f* COM GEN *de tendencia* pace, velocity, ECON, FIN velocity, INFO rate, speed, TRANSP velocity; ~ **de arrastre** INFO feed rate; ~ **de cálculo** INFO computing speed; ~ **de circulación** FIN velocity of circulation; ~ **de circulación monetaria** FIN velocity of circulation of money; ~ **del dinero** ECON, FIN velocity of money; ~ **de impresión** INFO printing speed; ~ **mecanográfica** ADMIN, COM GEN, INFO typing speed; ~ **de reloj** INFO clock rate; ~ **de transferencia** INFO transfer rate; ~ **de transferencia de bitios** INFO bit rate; ~ **de tratamiento de documentos** INFO document rate

vencer *vi* BOLSA, ECON, FIN mature

vencido *adj* COM GEN matured, overdue, mature; ~ **e impagado** FISC due and unpaid

vencimiento *m* BANCA *de préstamo* term, maturity, BOLSA, COM GEN *fecha* expiration, redemption date, maturity, COMS term, CONT recoverable date, ECON maturity; ~ **del acuerdo** RRHH expiry of agreement; ~ **desfasado** BANCA mismatched maturity; ~ **desigual** BANCA maturity mismatch; ~ **a fecha fija** BANCA fixed maturity; ~ **medio** BANCA, BOLSA, FIN average maturity; ~ **original** BANCA, BOLSA, FIN original maturity; ~ **de una póliza** SEG termination of a policy; ~ **de la prima** ECON term premium; ♦ **al** ~ BANCA, BOLSA, COM GEN, FIN at due date; **antes del** ~ BANCA, BOLSA, FIN before maturity; **con** ~ **a medio plazo** BOLSA medium-dated

vencimientos: ~ **comerciales cómodos** *m pl* ECON commodity terms of trade; ~ **escalonados** *m pl* BOLSA staggering maturities

vende: **se** ~ **oficina** *fra* INMOB office for sale

vendedor, a *m,f* COM GEN, RRHH, V&M trader, seller, vendor, salesman, saleswoman, salesperson, *puerta a puerta* knocker (*infrml*) ~ **al descubierto** BOLSA short seller; ~ **ambulante** V&M huckster (*infrml*) (*AmE*), pedlar (*BrE*); ~ **callejero(-a)** COM GEN, V&M street trader (*BrE*), street vendor (*AmE*); ~ **de carrera** RRHH, V&M career salesperson; ~ **a comisión** RRHH commission salesman; ~ **de contratos de compra y venta** BOLSA straddle writer; ~ **a domicilio** RRHH, V&M door-to-door salesman; ~ **especializado(-a)** RRHH, V&M speciality salesperson (*BrE*), specialty salesperson (*AmE*); ~ **en firme** BOLSA firm seller; ~ **con opción de compra y venta** BOLSA straddle seller; ~ **de promoción** RRHH, V&M missionary salesperson; ~ **robotizado(-a)** RRHH, V&M robot salesperson; ~ **silencioso(-a)** RRHH, V&M silent salesperson; ~ **técnico(-a)** V&M technical salesperson; ~ **de televentas** FIN, V&M telesales person; ~ **de zona** COM GEN area sales executive

vender 1. *vt* BOLSA *futuros* sell out, COM GEN sell; ♦ ~ **al cierre** BOLSA *futuros* sell on close (*jarg*); ~ **al descubierto** BOLSA sell short; ~ **algo como chatarra** COM GEN sell sth for scrap; ~ **algo mediante acuerdo privado** COM GEN sell sth by private treaty; ~ **algo en subasta** COM GEN sell sth by auction; ~ **las mercancías** COM GEN sell one's wares; ~ **títulos en el mercado** BOLSA unload stocks on the market; ~ **una opción sobre** BOLSA write an option against; ~ **a plazo en firme** BOLSA sell a bear; ~ **a precio de mercado** BOLSA sell at market price; ~ **en régimen de franquicia** V&M exercise a franchise; ~ **a término** BOLSA sell for the settlement; ~ **todas las existencias** COM GEN, FIN, V&M sell out; **2.** *vi* COM GEN, V&M *producto* sell; ♦ ~ **al contado** BOLSA sell spot; ~ **a comisión** V&M sell on commission; ~ **a crédito** V&M sell on credit, sell on trust; ~ **a cuenta** BOLSA sell for the account; ~ **directamente al público** COM GEN, V&M sell directly to the public; ~ **a futuro** BOLSA, COM GEN sell forward; ~ **a granel** V&M sell in bulk; ~ **con pérdida** COM GEN sell at a loss; ~ **a un precio más elevado que el de mercado** V&M price oneself out of the market; ~ **totalmente** COM GEN, V&M sell up

vendible *adj* COM GEN marketable, vendible

vendido: **no** ~ *adj* COM GEN *existencias* undisposed of; ~ **a un precio demasiado bajo** *adj* V&M underpriced

venidero *adj* COM GEN coming

venir *vi* COM GEN come along; ♦ ~ **a parar en** COM GEN result in

venirse: ~ **abajo** *fra* COM GEN *economía* go to rack and ruin (*infrml*)

venta *f* COM GEN sale, selling, FISC disposal; ~ **de acciones incestuosa** BOLSA incestuous share dealing; ~ **acoplada** COM GEN, V&M tie-in sale; ~ **de activos** BOLSA, COM GEN, CONT asset sale; ~ **con acuerdo de alquiler** COM GEN, CONT sale and leaseback; ~ **agresiva** V&M high-pressure selling, hard selling; ~ **al alza** BOLSA long put; ~ **de comando** V&M commando selling; ~ **al contado** COM GEN cash and carry; ~ **al descubierto** BOLSA short sale, bear sale, sell short; ~ **al por mayor** V&M wholesaling; ~ **al por menor** COM GEN, IND, V&M retail sale, retailing; ~ **al precio de mercado** BOLSA at-the-money put; ~ **ambulante** COM GEN back peddling, V&M field selling; ~ **anticipada** BOLSA *valor* advance selling, OCIO *teatro, restaurante* advance booking, advance reservation; ~ **aparente** BOLSA wash sale

(*AmE*); ~ **y arriendo al vendedor** COM GEN sale and leaseback; ~ **de artículos sin repuestos** V&M closed stock; ~ **automática** COM GEN automatic selling; ~ **bajo mano** V&M under-the-counter sale; ~ **bajo presión** V&M pressure selling; ~ **de bienes** V&M sale of goods; ~ **condicionada a una llegada** V&M sale subject to safe arrival; ~ **condicional** V&M conditional sale; ~ **por consignación** V&M consignment selling; ~ **por contacto directo** V&M face-to-face selling; ~ **contra la caja fuerte** BOLSA against the box; ~ **por convencimiento** V&M soft sell; ~ **por correspondencia** COMS, V&M mail order selling; *empresa* mail order business; ~ **a corto** BOLSA short selling; ~ **a crédito** V&M credit sale; ~ **a crédito partido** V&M split credit sale; ~ **en depósito** TRANSP, V&M consignment sale; ~ **en descubierto** BOLSA selling short; ~ **en descubierto protegida** BOLSA hedged short sale; ~ **dinámica** V&M high-pressure selling; ~ **directa** V&M direct sale, direct selling, *mercadeo* drop-shipping (*AmE*); ~ **directa por correo** COMS, V&M direct mailing; ~ **domiciliaria** V&M door-to-door selling; ~ **a domicilio** V&M house-to-house selling; ~ **de embargo** INMOB scavenger sale (*infrml*); ~ **con entrega aplazada** BOLSA sale for delivery; ~ **de equilibrio** FIN breakpoint sale; ~ **especializada** V&M speciality selling (*BrE*), specialty selling (*AmE*); ~ **excelente** V&M record sale; ~ **de exploración** V&M pioneer selling; ~ **de exportación** V&M foreign sale; ~ **extensiva** V&M extensive selling; ~ **fácil** COM GEN, V&M quick sale; ~ **de fin de temporada** COM GEN, V&M end-of-season sale; ~ **forzosa de existencias** COM GEN, DER, V&M forced sale of stock; ~ **forzosa de mercancías** COM GEN, DER, V&M forced sale of goods; ~ **fuera de horas** BOLSA, FIN after-hours dealing; ~ **futura** COM GEN, V&M future sale; ~ **en grandes almacenes** V&M department store sale; ~ **impulsiva** V&M impulse sale; ~ **industrial** IND, V&M industrial selling; ~ **por inercia** V&M inertia selling; ~ **ínfima** V&M one-cent sale (*AmE*); ~ **inicial** V&M initial sale, sell-in; ~ **inmediata** COM GEN, V&M spot business; ~ **intensiva** V&M intensive selling; ~ **intercontable** CONT, FIN inter-account dealing; ~ **irrevocable** V&M absolute sale; ~ **judicial** DER judicial foreclosure, judicial sale; ~ **por juicio hipotecario** V&M foreclosure sale; ~ **de liquidación** COM GEN winding-up sale; ~ **de líquidos envasados** COM GEN wet sell (*jarg*); ~ **mediante licitación pública** V&M sale by tender; ~ **mensual** V&M monthly sale; ~ **de mercancías** V&M sale of goods; ~ **minorista** V&M over-the-counter retailing; ~ **minorista de alimentos** V&M food retailing; ~ **minorista directa** V&M nonstore retailing; ~ **nacional** V&M domestic sale, home sale; ~ **objetiva** V&M objective selling; ~ **de objetos usados** V&M jumble sale (*BrE*), rummage sale (*AmE*); ~ **para obtener plusvalía** ECON vent for surplus; ~ **de opción de compra cubierta** BOLSA covered call write; ~ **parcial** V&M party selling; ~ **personal** V&M personal selling; ~ **por persuasión** V&M soft sell; ~ **pionera** V&M pioneer selling; ~ **piramidal** V&M pyramid selling; ~ **planificada** V&M planned selling; ~ **a plazos** COM GEN tally trade, INMOB, V&M installment sale (*AmE*), instalment sale (*BrE*); ~ **poco apremiante** V&M low-pressure selling; ~ **posbalance** COM GEN stocktaking sale; ~ **a un precio más bajo** V&M underselling; ~ **a precios superiores** V&M trading up; ~ **precipitada** BOLSA sell-off; ~ **de prendas usadas** V&M jumble sale (*BrE*), rummage sale (*AmE*); ~ **prevista** V&M anticipated sale; ~ **de promo-**

ción simultánea de dos productos V&M piggyback selling; ~ **a prueba** V&M sale on approval; ~ **de puestos de trabajo** V&M job selling; ~ **rápida** FIN, TRANSP quick returns, V&M blowout (*AmE*); ~ **de rendimiento nulo** FIN breakpoint sale; ~ **de saldos** COM GEN, V&M end-of-season sale; ~ **secreta** V&M backdoor selling; ~ **selectiva** V&M selective selling; ~ **simulada** *m* FISC bypass trust; ~ **sintética a largo** BOLSA *opciones* synthetic long put; ~ **por sugerencia** V&M suggestion selling; ~ **sujeta a impuesto** FISC, V&M taxable sale; ~ **telefónica** V&M telephone selling; ~ **por teléfono** V&M telephone sale; ~ **de terceros** V&M third-party sale; ~ **a término cubierta** BOLSA covered short; ~ **de títulos** BOLSA disposal of securities, security disposal; ~ **de títulos sin reinversión inmediata** BOLSA switching (*AmE*); ~ **de un valor para comprar otro con mejor perspectiva** BOLSA switch selling; ~ **de valores no oficial** BOLSA street dealing; ~ **de valores de renta fija** BOLSA bond sale; ◆ **estar a la ~** COM GEN be on sale

ventaja *f* COM GEN plus, advantage; ~ **absoluta** ECON absolute advantage; ~ **adicional de los ejecutivos** GES, RRHH executive perk (*infrml*), executive perquisite (*frml*); ~ **comercial** COM GEN commercial advantage; ~ **comparativa** ECON comparative advantage; ~ **competitiva** ECON competitive advantage, V&M competitive edge; ~ **para el consumidor** COM GEN, V&M consumer benefit; ~ **diferencial** ECON differential advantage; ~ **para los empleados** CONT, ECON, FIN, RRHH employee benefit, fringe benefit; ~ **fiscal** FISC tax advantage; ~ **en materia de vivienda** ECON housing start; ~ **de operación** CONT operating gearing (*BrE*), operating leverage (*AmE*); ~ **de precio** BOLSA *mercado del eurodólar* price advantage; ~ **en relación con la clientela del negocio** CONT goodwill; ~ **remunerativa** BOLSA yield advantage; ◆ **tener ~** COM GEN have the upper hand, have a head start; **última ~** BOLSA last sale

ventajoso *adj* COM GEN advantageous

ventana *f* INFO window; ~ **guía** TRANSP window-guidance; ~ **de intervención** INFO audit window; ~ **de oportunidad** COM GEN window of opportunity; ◆ **por la ~** BOLSA out the window

ventanilla *f* BANCA counter, COM GEN, COMS *sobre* window; ~ **de dinero** BANCA money desk

ventas *f pl* COM GEN sales; ~ **brutas** CONT gross sales; ~ **netas** CONT net sales; ~ **repetidas** V&M repeat sales; ~ **totales** COM GEN, V&M total sales

ventilador: ~ **termostático** *m* IND thermostatic fan

veracidad *f* CONT truthfulness; ~ **en contratos de préstamo** BANCA, DER, FIN truth in lending (*jarg*) (*AmE*)

veraneante *mf* OCIO holiday-maker (*BrE*), vacationer (*AmE*)

verbigracia *adv* (*v.gr.*) COM GEN namely (*viz*)

verdadero *adj* CONT *aplicado a los números* actual; ~ **y equitativo** CONT *auditoría, contabilidad* true and fair

verde *adj* MED AMB green

verdes: **los ~** *m pl* POL the Greens

veredicto: ~ **dictado por el juez** *m* DER directed verdict; ~ **mayoritario** *m* DER majority verdict

verificable *adj* COM GEN verifiable, CONT *auditoría* auditable, verifiable

verificación *f* COM GEN verification, CONT verification, *de declaraciones sobre la renta* audit, FIN audit, FISC monitoring, audit; ~ **de aduana** IMP/EXP, TRANSP customs check; ~ **de los conocimientos de embarque** TRANSP sighting bills of lading; ~ **cruzada** COM GEN, IMP/EXP cross check; ~ **de cuentas** CONT verification of accounts, *de un balance* accounts certification; ~ **de una hipótesis** MAT hypothesis testing; ~ **por redundancia** INFO redundancy check; ~ **retrospectiva** INFO audit trail

verificado: **no** ~ *adj* COM GEN unverified

verificador[1]**,a** *m,f* RRHH, V&M checker

verificador[2]: ~ **ortográfico** *m* INFO spellcheck

verificar *vt* COM GEN ascertain, verify, CONT audit, verify, INFO audit; ◆ ~ **la identidad de alguien** DER prove sb's identity

versal *f* INFO, MEDIOS capital letter (*caps*)

versatilidad *f* INFO versatility

versión *f* COM GEN, INFO version; ~ **avanzada** INFO advanced version; ~ **beta** INFO beta version; ~ **de un programa** INFO software release; ~ **revisada** MEDIOS *imprenta* revised version

versus *prep* COM GEN versus

vert *abr* (*vertical*) COM GEN vert (*vertical*)

vertedero *m* MED AMB landfill site

verter *vt* MED AMB *residuos en el mar* dump

vertical *adj* (*vert*) COM GEN vertical (*vert*)

vertido *m* MED AMB spillage, *de residuos* dumping; ~ **de desperdicios** MED AMB waste dumping; ~ **de petróleo** MED AMB oil spill, oil spillage

vertiente: ~ **tecnológica** *f* COM GEN technological edge

vertiginosamente *adv* COM GEN steeply

vetar *vt* COM GEN veto, put a veto on

veterano *adj* COM GEN, RRHH senior (*Snr*)

veto *m* COM GEN veto; ~ **de una cámara** POL one-house veto (*AmE*)

vez: **en** ~ **de** *prep* COM GEN in lieu of

VGA *abr* (*adaptador de gráficos de vídeo Esp, adaptador de gráficos de video AmL, adaptador videográfico*) INFO VGA (*video graphics adaptor*)

v.gr. *abr* (*verbigracia*) COM GEN viz (*namely*)

VHF *abr* (*frecuencia muy alta*) COMS VHF (*very high frequency*)

vía[1]: ~ **aérea** *f* TRANSP *ruta* airway (*AWY*), AWY (*airway*); ~ **interior de navegación** *f* TRANSP inland waterway; ~ **muerta** *f* TRANSP side track (*AmE*), siding (*BrE*); ~ **principal** *f* TRANSP *ferrocarriles* main line; ~ **rápida** *f* COM GEN fast track, TRANSP fast lane; ~ **secundaria** *f* TRANSP side track (*AmE*), siding (*BrE*);

vía[2]: **por la** ~ **amistosa** *fra* DER *cancelar, ceder* amicably; **en la** ~ *fra* TRANSP *ferrocarril* on track (*ot*)

viabilidad *f* COM GEN viability; ~ **económica** ECON, FIN economic viability

viabilización: ~ **de tierras** *f* INMOB land development

viable *adj* COM GEN viable

viajante *mf* COM GEN, RRHH, V&M salesman; ~ **de comercio** COM GEN commercial traveler (*AmE*), commercial traveller (*BrE*), PROT SOC bagman (*jarg*) (*AmE*), RRHH, V&M sales representative (*rep*), traveling salesman (*AmE*), travelling salesman (*BrE*)

viajar *vi* TRANSP travel

viaje *m* COM GEN trip, TRANSP junket (*infrml*) (*AmE*), voyage, trip; ~ **aéreo** OCIO, TRANSP air travel; ~ **comercial** COM GEN business trip; ~ **con descuento** OCIO discount travel; ~ **de estudios** PROT SOC study trip; ~ **en grupo** OCIO group travel; ~ **hasta la zona de trabajo** COM GEN travel to work area; ~ **de ida** COM GEN, TRANSP outward voyage; ~ **de ida y vuelta** COM GEN, TRANSP return trip (*BrE*), round trip (*AmE*); ~ **inaugural** TRANSP maiden voyage; ~ **internacional** COM GEN, TRANSP international travel; ~ **internacional corto** COM GEN, TRANSP short international voyage; ~ **en lastre** TRANSP ballast trip; ~ **de negocios** COM GEN business trip; ~ **nocturno** OCIO overnight travel; ~ **organizado** OCIO package holiday (*BrE*); ~ **de retorno** TRANSP back haul; ~ **subvencionado** OCIO, TRANSP subsidized travel; ~ **de vuelta** COM GEN, TRANSP homeward voyage, return trip

viajero, -a *m,f* OCIO traveler (*AmE*), traveller (*BrE*); ~ **abonado(-a)** COM GEN, TRANSP commuter; ~ **de ferrocarril** OCIO, TRANSP rail traveler (*AmE*), rail traveller (*BrE*); ~ **de una línea aérea** OCIO, TRANSP air traveler (*AmE*), air traveller (*BrE*)

viáticos *m pl AmL* (*cf dietas de viaje Esp*) COM GEN traveling expenses (*AmE*), travelling expenses (*BrE*), traveling allowance (*AmE*), travelling allowance (*BrE*); ~ **para regreso a casa en fines de semana** *AmL* COM GEN weekend travel home allowance

vicepresidente, -a *m,f* (*VP*) GES, RRHH deputy chairman (*BrE*), vice chairman (*AmE*), vice president (*AmE*) (*VP*), POL vice president (*VP*); ~ **adjunto(-a)** GES senior vice president (*AmE*); ~ **del consejo** GES, RRHH deputy chairman of the supervisory board, deputy chairman of the board of management; ~ **ejecutivo(-a)** GES, RRHH executive vice president; ~ **primero(-a)** RRHH first vice president; ~ **principal** RRHH senior vice president (*AmE*)

vicesecretario, -a *m,f* POL, RRHH undersecretary, vice secretary

viceversa *adv* COM GEN vice versa

vicio: ~ **de consentimiento** *m* COM GEN bilateral mistake; ~ **oculto** *m* DER, INMOB latent defect; ~ **propio** *m* COM GEN, TRANSP inherent vice

víctima *f* COM GEN victim

víctimas: ~ **de accidentes en carretera** *f pl* TRANSP road fatalities

victoria: ~ **fácil** *f* COM GEN walkover (*infrml*)

vida *f* BOLSA *de opción*, COM GEN life; ~ **del activo** CONT asset life; ~ **amortizable** ECON depreciable life; ~ **económica** CONT, ECON, V&M economic life; ~ **económica útil** CONT, ECON useful economic life; ~ **efectiva** BOLSA lifetime; ~ **en estantería** V&M *de producto* shelf life; ~ **estimable** CONT *de fondos comerciales* predictable life; ~ **media** BOLSA half-life (*infrml*), COM GEN average life; ~ **previsible** CONT *de fondos comerciales* predictable life; ~ **de un producto** V&M product life; ~ **de una transacción** BOLSA *futuros* trading life; ~ **útil** CONT *de activo* useful life, FIN economic life, FISC depreciable life, IND *de una máquina* useful life

video *AmL ver* **vídeo** *Esp*

vídeo *m Esp* MEDIOS video

videocámara *f* MEDIOS video camera

videoconferencia *f* COMS, MEDIOS video conference, video conferencing

videodisco *m* INFO video disk

videograbadora: ~ **de casete** *f* INFO video cassette recorder

videopantalla *f* INFO view screen

videopiratería *f* COM GEN video piracy

videoteléfono *m* COMS videophone

viento *m* COM GEN wind

vientos: ~ **de cambio** *m pl* COM GEN winds of change

viernes[1]: ~ **negro** *m* BOLSA Black Friday

viernes[2]: ~ **y vacaciones incluidos** *fra* COM GEN, OCIO, TRANSP Fridays and holidays included

vigencia *f* BOLSA *de opción* life; ~ **de una patente** DER, PATENT patent life

vigente *adj* COM GEN, DER valid, unexpired, INFO valid

vigilancia *f* DER surveillance; ~ **activa** BOLSA radar alert; ~ **de la contaminación** IND, MED AMB pollution monitoring

vigilante *mf* RRHH watchman; ~ **de almacén** COM GEN warehouse keeper; ~ **de carga y descarga de buques** TRANSP *puerto* ship's clerk

vigilar *vt* BOLSA *el valor*, COM GEN watch; ◆ ~ **a alguien** COM GEN put a guard on sb; ~ **atentamente** COM GEN keep a close watch on

vigor: **en** ~ *fra* DER in force

vigueta: ~ **de izado de grandes pesos** *f* TRANSP heavy lifting beam

vinatero, -a *m,f* COM GEN, RRHH vintner, wine merchant

vinculación: ~ **hacia atrás** *f* ECON, IND backward linkage; ~ **a un índice** *f* ECON, IND index linkage

vinculado *adj* BOLSA linked; ◆ **estar** ~ COM GEN be tied to

vinculante *adj* DER *decisión* binding

vincular *vt* BOLSA peg, COM GEN link, DER bind, ECON, FIN *moneda, precios* peg

vínculo *m* COM GEN link, DER entail; ~ **móvil** ECON *internacional* crawling peg

viña *f* COM GEN vineyard

viñeta *f* V&M *publicidad* vignette

violación *f* COM GEN violation; ~ **del honor profesional** COM GEN breach of professional etiquette; ~ **de patente** DER, PATENT patent infringement; ~ **de secreto** COM GEN breach of secrecy; ~ **de la seguridad** DER safety violation; ◆ **en** ~ **de** DER in violation of

violar *vt* COM GEN, DER break, violate; ◆ ~ **la sindicación** BOLSA break the syndicate

violencia: ~ **familiar** *f* PROT SOC family violence

virtual *adj* INFO virtual

virtud: **en** ~ **de** *fra* COM GEN by virtue of; **en** ~ **de su puesto** *fra* COM GEN virtute officii

virus *m* INFO virus; ◆ **sin** ~ INFO virus-free

visado[1] *adj* SEG *marítimo* approved

visado[2] *m* COM GEN *aprovación, firma* scratching, OCIO visa; ~ **de doble entrada** OCIO, POL double-entry visa; ~ **de entrada** OCIO, POL entrance visa, entry visa; ~ **de entradas múltiples** OCIO, POL multiple-entry visa; ~ **de residencia** DER, POL, RRHH green card (*AmE*), residence visa (*BrE*); ~ **de residencia temporal** DER, POL, RRHH temporary residence visa; ~ **para una sola entrada** OCIO, POL single-entry visa; ~ **turístico** OCIO tourist visa

visar *vt* SEG approve

viscosidad *f* ECON viscosity

visibilidad: ~ **financiera** *f* FIN financial visibility

visibles *m pl* ECON visibles

visión *f* COM GEN, GES vision; ◆ **con** ~ **de futuro** COM GEN *persona, proyecto* forward-looking

visionar *vt* INFO view

visita *f* V&M visit, call; ~ **de instalación** V&M facility visit; ~ **de negocios** COM GEN business call; ~ **sin preparación previa** V&M cold call; ~ **relámpago** COM GEN flying visit; ~ **de venta** V&M sales call; ◆ **hacer una** ~ **a** COM GEN pay a call on

visitante[1] *adj* COM GEN visiting

visitante[2] *mf* COM GEN visitor; ~ **con autorización de estudios** FISC visitor with student authorization; ~ **extranjero(-a)** *m,f* COM GEN overseas visitor

vista *f* DER hearing; ~ **de conjunto** FIN conspectus; ~ **despiezada** V&M exploded view; ~ **privada** COM GEN private hearing; ~ **general** FIN conspectus; ◆ **a la** ~ COM GEN at sight (*a/s*)

visual *adj* COM GEN visual

visualización: ~ **de archivos** *f* INFO display file; ~ **en color** *f* INFO color display (*AmE*), colour display (*BrE*)

visualizador, a *m,f* INFO, V&M visualizer

visualizar *vt* INFO display

vitrina *f* COM GEN *exposición* showcase

viudedad *f* DER dower, FIN widow's pension

viudo, -a *m,f* COM GEN widower, widow

vivienda *f* COM GEN housing, living accommodation, INMOB tenement; ~ **de estilo ejecutivo** INMOB executive-style housing; ~ **modular** INMOB modular housing; ~ **multifamiliar** INMOB, PROT SOC multifamily housing; ~ **privada** COM GEN private household; ~ **de protección oficial** (*VPO*) INMOB, PROT SOC council house (*BrE*), housing project (*AmE*); ~ **unifamiliar** FISC, INMOB, PROT SOC single-family dwelling, single-family home (*AmE*), single-family house (*BrE*); ~ **unipersonal** FISC, V&M single-person household

vivir: ~ **por encima de las posibilidades** *fra* COM GEN live beyond one's means; ~ **en la miseria** *fra* COM GEN be on the breadline; ~ **de subsidios sociales** *fra* PROT SOC, RRHH be on benefits (*BrE*), be on welfare (*AmE*)

vivos: **entre** ~ *adv* DER inter vivos

vocación *f* PROT SOC, RRHH vocation

volante *m* ADMIN *nota* note, COMS handbill, TRANSP *vehículo* steering wheel, V&M *publicidad* leaflet (*jarg*)

volátil *adj* COM GEN volatile

volatilidad *f* COM GEN volatility; ~ **histórica** BOLSA historical volatility; ~ **implícita** BOLSA implied volatility; ~ **del precio de una acción** BOLSA price volatility of a share

volcado *m* INFO dumping; ~ **de la memoria** INFO storage dump; ~ **de modificaciones** INFO change dump

volcoa *abr* (*contrato por volumen del flete*) TRANSP volcoa (*volume contract of affreightment*)

voltio *m* (*v*) COM GEN volt (*V*)

volumen *m* COM GEN volume (*vol.*); ~ **borrado** BOLSA volume deleted; ~ **comercial** ECON trade volume; ~ **compensatorio** ECON *internacional* compensatory amount; ~ **de contratación** COM GEN trading volume; ~ **de contrato** BOLSA contract size; ~ **de demanda** ECON, V&M backlog of demand; ~ **diario** BOLSA daily volume; ~ **de exportaciones** ECON, IMP/EXP, TRANSP volume of exports; ~ **de facturación** COM GEN, FIN invoicing amount; ~ **de las ganancias** FISC earnings amount; ~ **de ingresos** FISC income amounts; ~ **de inversión de la pequeña empresa** FISC small business investment amount; ~ **de negocio** COM GEN amount of business; ~ **de negocios** COM GEN turnover, business volume; ~ **de negocios anual** COM GEN, CONT annual turnover; ~ **de obligaciones** BOLSA bond pool; ~ **de pedidos** COM GEN volume of orders; ~ **de producción** COM GEN output volume, IND production volume; ~ **real** IND *de producción* actual volume; ~ **del riesgo** FISC at-risk amount; ~ **de siniestros** COM GEN burden of losses; ~ **total negociado** BOLSA weekly volume; ~ **de trabajo pendiente** COM GEN, IND work backlog; ~ **de tráfico** TRANSP traffic flow; ~ **de venta** COM GEN turnover, ~ **de ventas** COM GEN, CONT, V&M sales volume; ~ **de ventas al por mayor** ECON, V&M volume of wholesale; ~ **de ventas al por menor** COM GEN, ECON, V&M volume of retail sales

voluminoso *adj* COM GEN bulky

voluntario[1] *adj* COM GEN noncompulsory

voluntario[2]**,-a** *m,f* RRHH volunteer

voluntarismo *m* RRHH voluntarism (*jarg*)

volver *vi* COM GEN return; ◆ ~ **al punto de partida** COM GEN to come full circle; ~ **atrás una operación** BOLSA unwind a tape; ~ **dentro de una hora** COM GEN be back within an hour; ~ **a emitir un préstamo** BANCA refloat a loan; ~ **a escena** COM GEN make a comeback; ~ **a imponer** COM GEN reimpose; ~ **a insistir en** COM GEN re-emphasize; ~ **a inventar la rueda** COM GEN reinvent the wheel; ~ **a llamar** V&M call back; ~ **a presentarse para un trabajo** RRHH reapply for a job; ~ **a puerto para recibir órdenes** TRANSP return to port for orders (*R/p*); ~ **sigilosamente** COM GEN slip back; ~ **a sumar** MAT *suma* add back; ~ **a tomar aliento** COM GEN get one's second wind

volverse: ~ **atrás** *vi* COM GEN back-pedal, GES *en discusión* back down

votación *f* COM GEN, GES *en las juntas*, POL *apropiación* vote, voting, ballot, RRHH *sindicatos* ballot; ~ **acumulativa** BOLSA *de accionistas* cumulative voting; ~ **en bloque** RRHH block voting; ~ **por correo** POL postal vote, RRHH postal ballot (*BrE*); ~ **de gastos imprevistos** FIN contingencies vote; ~ **de huelga** RRHH strike ballot, strike vote; ~ **por el método de la mayoría** BOLSA majority rule voting; ~ **neta** FIN net voting; ~ **secreta** RRHH secret ballot; ~ **de tanteo** POL *investigación de mercado* straw vote, straw poll

votante: ~ **indeciso(-a)** *m,f* POL floating voter (*BrE*), swing voter (*jarg*)

votar 1. *vt* COM GEN, INFO *proyecto, reglamento* approve, POL *candidato, partido* vote for, ballot, RRHH ballot; ◆

~ **un fondo provisional** POL vote interim supply; ~ **un fondo total** POL vote full supply; **2.** *vi Esp* (*cf sufragar AmL*) CONT vote; ◆ ~ **a mano alzada** RRHH vote by show of hands (*BrE*)

voto *m* COM GEN, POL vote; ~ **al voto** POL franchise; ~ **aproximado** POL proxy vote; ~ **en blanco** POL blank ballot; ~ **en bloque** RRHH block vote; ~ **colectivo** RRHH block vote; ~ **en contra** POL vote against; ~ **por correo** POL postal vote, RRHH postal ballot; ~ **a favor** POL vote in favor (*AmE*), vote in favour (*BrE*); ~ **mayoritario** COM GEN majority vote; ~ **mayoritario cualificado** COM GEN qualified majority vote; ~ **obligatorio** DER statutory voting; ~ **parlamentario** CONT, POL parliamentary vote; ~ **de protesta** POL protest vote

votos: ~ **contrapuestos** *m pl* POL opposing votes

voz *f* COMS, INFO, RRHH voice; ~ **en off** MEDIOS, V&M voice-over; ◆ **tener ~ y voto** COM GEN have a say in sth

VP *abr* (*vicepresidente*) GES, POL, RRHH VP (*vice president*)

VPO *abr* (*vivienda de protección oficial*) INMOB, PROT SOC council house (*BrE*), housing project (*AmE*)

VTR *abr* (*grabación en video AmL, grabación en vídeo Esp*) COMS VTR (*video tape recording*)

vuelco *m* COM GEN *en tendencia* turnaround (*AmE*), turnround (*BrE*), TRANSP tipping

vuelo: ~ **chárter** *m* OCIO, TRANSP charter flight; ~ **de conexión** *m* OCIO, TRANSP connecting flight; ~ **económico** *m* OCIO, TRANSP economy flight; ~ **sin escalas** *m* TRANSP nonstop flight; ~ **inaugural** *m* TRANSP inaugural flight; ~ **de intercambio** *m* TRANSP interchange flight; ~ **nacional** *m* OCIO, TRANSP internal flight, domestic flight; ~ **perdido** *m* TRANSP missing flight; ~ **programado** *m* OCIO, TRANSP scheduled flight; ~ **de reexpedición** *m* TRANSP onward flight; ~ **de vuelta** *m* OCIO, TRANSP return flight

vuelta[1]: **de ~** *adj* TRANSP inboard

vuelta[2]: ~ **rápida a la baja** *f* BOLSA bear squeeze; ~ **rápida a corto** *f* BOLSA short squeeze; **segunda ~** *f* POL runoff (*AmE*), *elección* run-off election (*jarg*) (*AmE*)

vuelta[3]: **a ~ de correo** *fra* COMS by return of post

vuelto: ~ **al servicio** *adj* COM GEN recommissioned (*recmd*)

vulgarizar *vt* COM GEN vulgarize

vulnerable *adj* COM GEN vulnerable

vulnerar *vt* DER, PATENT infringe

W X Y

warrant *m* BOLSA warrant
Web: **la ~** *f* INFO Internet, the Net, the Web
WP *abr* (*procesado de texto AmL, procesador de textos Esp*) ADMIN, INFO WP (*word processor*)

xerografiar *vt* ADMIN Xerox®
xerográfico *adj* ADMIN xerographic

yacimiento: **~ petrolífero controlado** *m* MED AMB controlled wildcat drilling
yanquis *m pl* BOLSA *bonos* yankees (*jarg*)
yarda *f* COM GEN, ECON yard (*yd*)
yermo *m* MED AMB, INMOB waste land

Z

zarpar: ~ **desde** *fra* TRANSP sail from

zócalo *m* V&M plinth

zona *f* COM GEN *región* area; ~ **de acumulación** BOLSA accumulation area; ~ **del agente** V&M agent's territory; ~ **ambientalmente sensible** MED AMB environmentally-sensitive area; ~ **arrendable** INMOB rentable area; ~ **arrendable neta** INMOB net leasable area; ~ **de ayuda** ECON, POL, PROT SOC assisted area; ~ **de los barrios exteriores** COM GEN, INMOB commuter belt; ~ **de captación** PROT SOC, V&M catchment area; ~ **del centro de la ciudad** COM GEN, INMOB inner-city area; ~ **comercial** COM GEN, V&M trading area; ~ **comercial peatonal** COM GEN shopping mall (*AmE*), shopping precinct (*BrE*); ~ **de comercio** V&M *tiendas* trading area; ~ **común** INMOB common area; ~ **de comunicaciones del disco** INFO disk communication area; ~ **de conflagración** SEG conflagration area; ~ **densamente poblada** ECON densely-populated area; ~ **de desarrollo industrial** ECON, IND, RRHH enterprise zone (*EZ*); ~ **de desarrollo rural** ECON Rural Development Area (*BrE*) (*RDA*); ~ **de descarga** TRANSP wharf apron; ~ **desertizada** INMOB *de ciudad*, MED AMB, PROT SOC blighted area; ~ **de distribución** BOLSA distribution area; ~ **económica especial** ECON, POL special economic zone; ~ **de estabilidad** PROT SOC stability zone; ~ **estadística metropolitana normalizada** MAT Standard Metropolitan Statistical Area (*SMSA*); ~ **forestal** COM GEN woodland; ~ **franca** ECON, IMP/EXP, POL free zone, free-trade zone; ~ **franca portuaria** TRANSP free port zone (*FPZ*); ~ **de franquicia** ECON franchise gap; ~ **industrial** IND, INMOB industrial estate (*BrE*), industrial park (*AmE*); ~ **intermedia** INFO buffer area; ~ **de la libra esterlina** FIN Sterling Area; ~ **de libre comercio** ECON, IMP/EXP free-trade zone (*FTZ*); ~ **de libre mercado** ECON, IMP/EXP, POL free market zone; ~ **de línea de carga** TRANSP load line zone; ~ **meta** ECON *tipos de cambio* target zone; ~ **meta de los tipos de cambio** ECON exchange rate target zone; ~ **monetaria óptima** ECON *internacional* optimum currency area; ~ **no intervenida** ECON, IMP/EXP, POL free zone; ~ **de no libre comercio** COM GEN Non Free-Trade Zone (*NFTZ*); ~ **de parcelación mínima** INMOB minimum lot area; ~ **de pruebas** COM GEN testbed, V&M *mercadotecnia* test area; ~ **publicitaria** V&M advertising zone; ~ **de puerto franco** TRANSP free port zone (*FPZ*); ~ **de recogida de equipaje** OCIO, TRANSP baggage reclaim area; ~ **reservada para carga peligrosa** TRANSP dangerous cargo compound; ~ **restringida** TRANSP restricted area; ~ **salarial** RRHH wage zone; ~ **sensible** MED AMB sensitive zone; ~ **tapón** INMOB buffer zone; ~ **tipo** V&M type area; ~ **de trabajo** INFO working area, scratch area, RRHH *en una oficina* working area; ~ **urbanizada** COM GEN, INMOB built-up area; ~ **de ventas** V&M *en almacenes* sales area; ◆ **de ~ verde** MED AMB greenfield

Apéndice español–inglés/
Spanish–English appendix

Índice de contenidos/Contents

Correspondencia y documentos del mundo de los negocios/ Business correspondence and documents

Carta de solicitud de empleo/Job application

Ref: Traductor (825/97)

Estimada señora González Blanco:

Me dirijo a usted con motivo del anuncio publicado en el diario *El Norte* el día 8 de abril de 1997, en el que necesitan a una persona para ocupar el puesto de Traductor.

Como se puede observar en el *curriculum vitae* adjunto, poseo amplia experiencia en el campo de la traducción. Fui intérprete de conferencia para la Comisión Europea y he hecho algunos trabajos como traductor freelance para varias empresas. Esto me convierte en un candidato idóneo para cubrir la plaza que ustedes ofertan.

Asimismo, soy miembro de la asociación APETI y durante el año pasado trabajé como traductor freelance para empresas tales como la British Rail en Londres e IBM en Barcelona. Estoy muy interesado en poder trabajar en Madrid y pienso que puedo aportar gran experiencia a su empresa.

Le agradecería mucho que me concediera la oportunidad de tener una entrevista para poder presentarle mi historial académico y profesional con mayor detalle.

Quedo a su disposición para cualquier consulta que requiera.

En espera de sus noticias, le saluda muy atentamente,

Luis Gutiérrez Moreno

Curriculum vitae

Nombre:	**GUTIÉRREZ MORENO, Luis**
Dirección:	C/ Jorge Juan nº 10, 7º B, 08009 Toledo
Teléfono:	(91) 98 30 89
Fecha de nacimiento:	21 de marzo de 1966
Lugar de nacimiento:	Salamanca
D.N.I.- N.I.F.:	8.329.657-T
Estado civil:	soltero

ESTUDIOS

1996 – Ingreso como miembro en la Asociación Española de Traductores APETI.

1984–1988 – Licenciado en Filología inglesa y francesa por la Universidad de Salamanca.

1978–1984 – Bachillerato en el I.E.S. San Francisco Javier, Salamanca.

EXPERIENCIA PROFESIONAL

1996–1997 – Traductor freelance (inglés-español/español-inglés). Campos especializados: derecho, gestión de empresa, comercio exterior, tecnología informática y transportes.
1993–1996 – Traductor contratado por la organización británica de ferrocarriles, British Rail, para la traducción de textos especializados en transporte, derecho y gestión.

1992–1993 – Intérprete de conferencia (en cabina) para la Comisión Europea, Bruselas.
1991–1992 – Traductor a tiempo completo en la empresa IBM, Barcelona.

1989–1991 – Auxiliar Administrativo para la Editorial Libros, en Salamanca. Las responsabilidades diarias consistían en el procesamiento de datos, la elaboración de correspondencia comercial y el archivo de documentos de la empresa.

1988 – Hotel San Sebastián, camarero en la barra del bar durante el verano.

CONOCIMIENTOS ESPECIALES

Manejo de Word for Windows 6.0, Lotus 123 y de la base de datos Babel.

Dominio del francés e inglés; conocimientos del portugués para negocios; manejo del italiano a nivel elemental.

OTROS INTERESES

Me gusta la lectura, ir al cine y al teatro, y soy capitán del equipo de fútbol de la Universidad de Salamanca.

Contrato de trabajo/Offer of employment

ARRENDAMIENTO DE SERVICIOS

En Madrid, a 25 de julio de 1997.

REUNIDOS

De una parte, **Don Fernando García Jiménez**, mayor de edad, soltero, de profesión Abogado, domiciliado en Madrid, en Avda. Santa Marina nº 28 y con D.N.I.-N.I.F. nº 8.937.485-L.

Y de otra parte, **Don Luis Gutiérrez Moreno**, mayor de edad, casado, en régimen de gananciales, de profesión Traductor e Intérprete, y vecino de Toledo en la calle Jorge Juan nº 10, 7º B y con D.N.I.-N.I.F. nº 8.329.657-T.

INTERVIENEN

Ambos en nombre propio, acreditando su identidad por los documentos indicados. Se reconocen mutuamente capacidad y legitimación para celebrar el presente contrato de arrendamiento de servicios que se regirá por los siguientes

PACTOS

PRIMERO.-CONSENTIMIENTO. Don Fernando García Jiménez contrata los servicios profesionales de Don Luis Gutiérrez Moreno que se enumeran en el pacto 2º y ésta acepta.

SEGUNDO.-OBLIGACIONES DEL ARRENDATARIO. Don Luis Gutiérrez Moreno se obliga a prestar los servicios profesionales que se enumeran a continuación:

1º.- Traducir documentos técnicos.
2º.- Redactar informes en distintas lenguas.
3º.- Acudir a conferencias como intérprete simultáneo.
4º.- Trabajar como guía turístico para turistas extranjeros.
5º.- Todo lo concerniente a estos cuatro apartados será en lengua inglesa, francesa y portuguesa.

TERCERO.-OBLIGACIONES DEL ARRENDADOR. Don Fernando García Jiménez se obliga a pagar por los citados servicios la cantidad de 5.000 pesetas por hora, incrementada con el IVA del 16%, no pudiendo exceder en más de 300 horas al año. Dicha cantidad será abonable cada trimestre, la cual se ingresará en la Caja Postal de Toledo en el nº de cuenta 0-456-678-90-C.

CUARTO.-DURACIÓN. La duración del contrato será de un año a partir del día 1/12/97. No obstante, el contrato podrá ser resuelto en cualquier momento por cualquiera de las partes, previa denuncia comunicada verbalmente o por escrito con un mes de anticipación.

Igualmente, antes del mes de la finalización del contrato, y si ambas partes están de acuerdo, se podrá considerar su renovación por período de otro año. Y en prueba de conformidad los contratantes firman por duplicado el presente documento en el lugar y fecha arriba indicados.

Fdo. .... Fdo. ....

Hoja de balance/Balance sheet

CUENTAS ANUALES
BALANCE
Ejercicio........

No de Cuentas	Activo	Ejercicio N	Ejercicio N-1
110, 111, 112	A) Accionistas (socios) por desembolsos no exigidos		
	B) Inmovilizado		
30	I. Gastos de establecimiento		
	II. Inmovilizaciones inmateriales		
31, 32, 33, 34	1. Fondo de comercio		
(113)	2. Provisiones		
114, 115	3. Gastos de investigación y desarrollo		
	III. Inmovilizaciones materiales		
116, 117, 118	1. Instalaciones técnicas y maquinaria		
37	2. Provisiones		
	IV. Inmovilizaciones financieras		
200, 201	1. Créditos a empresas del grupo		
202, 203, 204, 205	2. Otros créditos		
38	V. Acciones propias		
39	C) Gastos a distribuir en varios ejercicios		
	D) Activo circulante		
206, 207	I. Accionistas por desembolsos exigidos		
(119)	II. Existencias		
120, 121	1. Comerciales		
122, 123, 124	2. Provisiones		
40	3. Materias primas y otros aprovisionamientos		
	III. Deudores		
41, (42)	1. Empresas del grupo, deudores		
43, 44, 45	2. Personal		
46, 47	3. Administraciones públicas		
	IV. Inversiones financieras temporales		
125, 126, 127	1. Participaciones en empresas del grupo		
(128)	2. Créditos a empresas del grupo		
	3. Depósitos y fianzas constituidos a corto plazo		
	V. Acciones propias a corto plazo		
48	VI. Tesorería		
49, 50	VII. Ajustes por periodificación		
	TOTAL GENERAL (A + B + C + D)		

Hoja de balance/Balance sheet

CUENTAS ANUALES
BALANCE
Ejercicio........

No de Cuentas	Pasivo	Ejercicio N	Ejercicio N-1
	A) Fondos propios		
5	I. Capital suscrito		
6, 7	II. Prima de emisiœn		
105	III. Reserva de revalorización		
	IV. Reservas		
106	1. Reserva legal		
107	2. Reservas por acciones propias		
120	3. Reservas estatutarias		
	V. Resultados de ejercicios anteriores		
121, 122	1. Remanente		
	2. Resultados negativos de ejercicios anteriores		
123	VI. Pérdidas y ganancias (Beneficio o pérdida)		
(124)	VII. Dividendo a cuenta entregado en el ejercicio		
	B) Ingresos a distribuir en varios ejercicios		
108, 109	1. Subvenciones de capital		
110	2. Diferencias positivas de cambio		
111	3. Otros ingresos a distribuir en varios ejercicios		
	C) Provisiones para riesgos y gastos		
112	1. Provisiones para pensiones y obligaciones similares		
113, 114	2. Provisiones para impuestos		
	D) Acreedores a largo plazo		
	I. Emisiones de obligaciones y otros valores negociables		
115	1. Obligaciones no convertibles		
125	II. Deudas con entidades de crédito		
126, 127	III. Deudas con empresas del grupo y asociadas		
	IV. Otros acreedores		
128	1. Fianzas y depósitos recibidos a largo plazo		
	V. Desembolsos pendientes sobre acciones no exigidas		
116, 117	1. De empresas del grupo		
130, 131	2. De empresas asociadas		
	3. De otras empresas		

No de Cuentas	Pasivo	Ejercicio N	Ejercicio N-1
132	E) Acreedores a corto plazo I. Emisiones de obligaciones y otros valores negociables		
133, 134	II. Deudas con entidades de crédito 1. Préstamos y otras deudas		
401, 402, 403, 404	III. Deudas con empresas del grupo		
405 406, (407), 408	IV. Acreedores comerciales 1. Anticipios recibidos por pedidos 2. Deudas por compras o prestaciones de servicio		
135 136	V. Otras deudas no comerciales 1. Administraciones Públicas 2. Remuneración pendientes de pago		
137	VI. Provisiones para operaciones de tráfico		
138, 139	VII. Ajustes por periodificación		
	TOTAL GENERAL (A + B + C + D + E)		

Profesiones dentro del mundo de los negocios/ Job titles used in business

en España y América Latina *in Spain and Latin America*	en el R.U. y los EE.UU. *in the UK and US*
accionista *mf*	shareholder *BrE*, stockholder *AmE*
administrador,a *m,f*	administrator, *propiedades* bailiff
administrador,a de activos *m,f*	asset manager
administrador,a de bienes *m,f*	estate manager
administrador,a fiducidario(-a) *m,f*	trustee
administrador,a de fincas *m,f*	estate manager, land agent, realtor *AmE*
administrador,a de herencias *m,f*	estate manager
administrador,a de marketing *m,f Esp*	marketing officer
administrador,a de mercadotecnia *m,f LAm*	marketing officer
administrador,a de propiedades *m,f*	estate manager
administrativo,-a *m,f*	administrator, white-collar worker, administrative assistant
administrativo,-a superior *m,f*	senior clerk
agente de aduanas *mf*	customs broker, customs officer
agente de agrupamiento de importaciones *mf*	import groupage operator
agente de almacén *mf*	stockist agent, stock agent
agente asalariado(-a) *m,f*	salaried agent
agente de carga *mf*	loading agent
agente de compraventa *mf*	sales and purchase broker
agente consignatario(-a) *m,f*	receiver agent
agente de despacho de aduanas *mf*	clearance agent, customs clearance agent
agente de existencias *mf*	stockist agent, stock agent
agente de exportación *mf*	export agent
agente inmobiliario(-a) *m,f*	estate agent *BrE*, realtor *AmE*
agente de proyecto *mf*	project agent
agente de transportes marítimos *mf*	shipping and fowarding agent
agente de transporte multimodal *mf*	multimodal transport operator
agente de ventas *mf*	sales agent
agente de viajes *mf*	travel agent
agregado,-a cultural *m,f*	cultural attaché
agregado,-a de defensa *m,f*	defence attaché *BrE*, defense attaché *AmE*
agregado,-a militar *m,f*	defence attaché *BrE*, defense attaché *AmE*
agregado,-a de prensa *m,f*	press officer
agrimensor,a *m,f*	*terrenos* surveyor
almacenista *mf*	storeman *BrE*, stockman *AmE*, warehouseman *AmE*, warehouse keeper *AmE*
alto(-a) ejecutivo,-a *m,f*	senior executive, top executive
analista de mercados *mf*	market analyst
analista de ventas *mf*	sales analyst
apoderado,-a *m,f*	manager, supervisor, *banca* official, *derecho* attorney-in-fact *AmE*, private attorney, proxy holder

en España y América Latina	en el R.U. y los EE.UU.
in Spain and Latin America	*in the UK and US*

asesor,a de selección *m,f*	recruitment consultant
asistente de línea *mf*	line assistant
asistente técnico(-a) *m,f*	technical assistant
auditor,a *m,f*	auditor
auxiliar administrativo(-a) *m,f*	administrative assistant
ayudante,-a de línea *m,f*	line assistant
ayudante,-a técnico(-a) *m,f*	technical assistant
broker *mf*	broker, *bolsa* stockbroker
capacitador,a *m,f AmL*	training officer
capataz,a *m,f*	foreman, charge hand, overseer
catedrático,-a adjunto(-a) *m,f*	associate professor *BrE*, adjunct professor *AmE*
coauditor,a *m,f*	joint auditor
cobrador,a *m,f*	collector
codirector,a *m,f*	co-director, co-manager, joint director
codueño,-a *m,f*	co-owner, joint owner
cogerente *mf*	joint manager
comanditario,-a *m,f*	limited partner, limited liability partner, limited owner
comerciante *mf*	merchant, trader, businessman, merchandiser, dealer
comisionario,-a *m,f*	commissionaire
comisionista *mf*	commission agent, commission merchant, *bolsa* broker, commission broker
comisionista de exportación *mf*	export agent
condómino,-a *m,f*	co-owner, joint owner
conferenciante *mf*	lecturer
conferencista *mf*	lecturer
consejero,-a *m,f*	director, advisor, consultant
consejero,-a de administración *m,f*	managing director, director
consejero,-a de defensa *m,f*	defence advisor *BrE*, defense advisor *AmE*
consejero,-a presidente *m,f*	director
consejero,-a vocacional *m,f*	careers officer, careers advisor
consignatario,-a de línea marítima *m,f*	liner broker
contable colegiado(-a) *m,f Esp*	certified accountant, chartered accountant
contable financiero(-a) *m,f Esp*	financial accountant
contable principal *mf Esp*	chief clerk, chief accountant
contador,a colegiado(-a) *m,f AmL*	certified accountant, chartered accountant
contador,a financiero(-a) *m,f AmL*	financial accountant
contador,a principal *m,f AmL*	chief clerk, chief accountant
contralor,a *m,f AmL*	comptroller, controller
contratista *mf*	contracts officer, contractor
controlador,a de almacén *m,f*	stock controller
controlador,a de existencias *m,f*	stock controller
controlador,a de transporte *m,f*	transport controller
coordinador,a de exportación *m,f*	export coordinator
copropietario,-a *m,f*	co-owner, joint owner
corredor,a de bolsa *m,f*	broker, stockjobber *AmE*, trader
corredor,a de fincas *m,f*	land agent, realtor *AmE*
delegado,-a gremial *m,f*	shop steward
directivo,-a comercial *m,f*	business manager, commercial manager, traffic executive, commercial director
directivo,-a medio(-a) *m,f*	middle manager
director,a *m,f*	director, manager

en España y América Latina   en el R.U. y los EE.UU.

in Spain and Latin America   *in the UK and US*

---

director,a adjunto(-a) *m,f*   assistant director, assistant manager, deputy director,
                                                    deputy manager, associate manager, associate
                                                    director, deputy chief executive

director,a administrativo(-a) *m,f*   *recursos humanos* managing director, *general*
                                                    comptroller, controller

director,a artístico(-a) *m,f*   artistic director

director,a de atención al cliente *m,f*   customer relations manager, consumer relations
                                                    manager

director,a comercial *m,f*   commercial manager, commercial director,
                                                    merchandising director, business manager

director,a comercial y de desarrollo *m,f*   commercial and development manager

director,a de compras *m,f*   head buyer, purchasing manager

director,a de contratos *m,f*   contracts manager

director,a de cuentas *m,f*   *finanzas* account executive, *marketing* account
                                                    manager

director,a de cuentas nacionales *m,f*   national accounts manager

director,a de departamento *m,f*   *compañías* department head, *universidad* head of
                                                    department

director,a de desarrollo *m,f*   development director, development manager

director,a de división *m,f*   division head, division manager, head of section

director,a ejecutivo(-a) *m,f*   executive director, executive manager, chief executive
                                                    manager, senior manager

director,a ejecutivo(-a) adjunto(-a) *m,f*   deputy chief executive, deputy managing director

director,a de exportación *m,f*   export director

director,a externo(-a) *m,f*   outside director, external director

director,a de fábrica *m,f*   plant manager, works manager

director,a de finanzas *m,f*   chief financial officer

director,a sin funciones ejecutivas *m,f*   nonexecutive director

director,a general *m,f*   chief executive officer *AmE*, chief operating officer,
                                                    director-general, general manager, senior manager

director,a general adjunto(-a) *m,f*   assistant director general, assistant general manager

director,a general de correos *m,f*   postmaster general *BrE*

director,a general ejecutivo(-a) *m,f*   general executive manager

director,a general de operaciones *m,f*   chief operating officer

director,a gerente *m,f*   managing director

director,a de importación *m,f*   import manager

director,a de información *m,f*   senior information officer, chief information officer

director,a de investigación *m,f*   research director

director,a jurídico(-a) *m,f*   head of legal department *BrE*, general counsel *AmE*

director,a de línea de transbordadores *m,f*   ferry line manager

director,a de marketing *m,f Esp*   marketing director, marketing manager

director,a de marketing para la exportación *m,f*   export marketing manager

director,a de mercadotecnia *m,f AmL*   marketing director, marketing manager

director,a de oficina *m,f*   office manager

director,a de operaciones *m,f*   operational manager, operations manager,operations
                                                    director

director,a de personal *m,f*   head of personnel, personnel director, personnel
                                                    manager

director,a de planta *m,f*   *fábricas* works manager, *compañías* departmental
                                                    head, head of section

director,a de posventa *m,f*   after-sales manager

director,a de prácticas *m,f*   training manager

director,a de producción *m,f*   production director, production manager

en España y América Latina	en el R.U. y los EE.UU.
in Spain and Latin America	*in the UK and US*

director,a provincial *m,f*	district manager, regional manager, sectorial manager
director,a de proyecto *m,f*	project leader, project manager
director,a de publicidad *m,f*	advertising director, publicity manager
director,a de puerto *m,f*	port director, port manager
director,a de reclamaciones *m,f*	claims manager
director,a de recursos humanos *m,f*	human resources director
director,a regional *m,f*	regional manager, sectorial manager
director,a de relaciones industriales *m,f*	industrial relations director
director,a de relaciones laborales *m,f*	director of labour relations *BrE,* director of labor relations *AmE*
director,a de relaciones públicas *m,f*	director of public relations
director,a técnico(-a) *m,f*	engineering manager, technical director, technical manager
director,a sectorial *m,f*	regional manager
director,a de ventas *m,f*	sales director, sales manager
director,a de ventas de campo *m,f*	field sales manager
dueño,-a de restaurante *m,f*	restaurant proprietor, restaurateur
ejecutivo,-a de una corporación *m,f*	corporate executive
ejecutivo,-a de cuentas *m,f*	*finanzas* account executive, *marketing* account manager
ejecutivo,-a de empresa *m,f*	corporate executive
ejecutivo,-a de línea *m,f*	line executive
ejecutivo, -a de marketing *m.f*	marketing executive
ejecutivo,-a de reclutamiento *m,f*	recruiting officer, recruitment officer
ejecutivo,-a de ventas *m,f*	sales executive
ejecutivo,-a de ventas de importación *m,f*	import sales executive
empleado,-a de exportación *m,f*	export clerk
empleado,-a postal *m,f*	postal clerk *BrE,* mail clerk *AmE*
empresario,-a *m,f*	businessman, entrepreneur, employer
encargado,-a *m,f*	*gestión* first line manager, *obras* foreman
encargado,-a de posoperaciones *m,f*	post operations officer
enlace sindical *mf*	shop steward
expedidor,a *m,f*	forwarding clerk, forwarder, consignor, dispatcher, shipper, shipping clerk, shipping officer
experto,-a en marketing *m,f Esp*	marketeer
experto,-a en mercadotecnia *m,f AmL*	marketeer
exportador,a *m,f*	export merchant, exporter
formador,a *m,f Esp*	training officer
funcionario,-a *m,f*	*Administración* civil servant, officer, official
funcionario,-a de la Administración *m,f*	civil servant
funcionario,-a de capacitación *m,f AmL*	training officer
funcionario,-a de formación *m,f Esp*	training officer
funcionario,-a de importación *m,f*	import clerk
funcionario,-a de inmigración *m,f*	immigration officer
funcionario,-a principal de exportación *m,f*	senior export clerk
funcionario,-a principal de importación *m,f*	senior import clerk
funcionario,-a público(-a) *m,f*	civil servant
funcionario,-a de rango superior *m,f*	senior officer
funcionario,-a de relaciones públicas *m,f*	public relations officer
funcionario,-a superior *m,f*	senior officer
funcionario,-a de tarifas *m,f*	rates clerk, rates officer
gerente *mf*	manager

en España y América Latina

in Spain and Latin America

en el R.U. y los EE.UU.

in the UK and US

gerente adjunto(-a) *m,f*	deputy manager
gerente de área *mf*	area manager, section manager
gerente de contratación *mf*	recruitment manager
gerente de cuentas *mf*	account manager
gerente de departamento *mf*	department manager, departmental manager
gerente de división *mf*	division head, division manager, head of section
gerente ejecutivo(-a) *m,f*	executive manager
gerente de fábrica *mf*	plant manager, works manager
gerente financiero(-a) *m,f*	financial manager
gerente general *mf*	chief executive officer *AmE*, chief executive
gerente general ejecutivo(-a) *m,f*	general executive manager
gerente intermediario(-a) *mf*	middle manager
gerente de línea *mf*	line manager
gerente medio(-a) *m,f*	middle manager
gerente de operaciones *mf*	operational manager, operations manager, operations director
gerente de personal *mf*	staff manager, personnel manager, personnel officer
gerente de primera línea *mf*	first line manager
gerente de producción *mf*	production manager
gerente propietario,-a *m,f*	owner manager
gerente de publicidad *mf AmL*	advertising manager
gerente regional *mf*	district manager, sectorial manager
gerente de relaciones industriales *mf*	industrial relations manager, industrial relations director
gerente técnico(-a) *m,f*	technical manager
gerente de territorio *mf*	district manager
gerente de tráfico *mf*	traffic manager
gerente de ventas *mf*	sales manager
gerente de zona *mf*	area manager
gestor,a *m,f*	administrator
gestor,a administrativo(-a) *m,f*	administrative agent
gestor,a de cuentas *m,f*	account manager
guarda de almacén *mf*	storeman *BrE*, stockman *AmE*, warehouseman *AmE*, warehouse keeper *AmE*
hombre de negocios *m*	businessman
ingeniero,-a de funcionamiento *m,f*	service engineer
ingeniero,-a de reparaciones *m,f*	service engineer
ingeniero,-a de servicio *m,f*	service engineer
ingeniero,-a de ventas *m,f*	sales engineer, sales executive
inspector,a *m,f*	comptroller, controller, inspector, *propiedad* surveyor
inspector,a de carga *m,f*	cargo superintendent, cargo inspector
inspector,a general de banca *m,f*	inspector general of banks
inspector,a de Hacienda *m,f*	inspector of taxes
inspector,a jefe(-a) *m,f*	chief inspector
inspector,a de sanidad *m,f*	health officer
interventor,a *m,f Esp*	comptroller, controller, compliance accountant, financial accountant
interventor,a adjunto(-a) *m,f Esp*	assistant controller
interventor,a de cuentas *m,f Esp*	auditor
interventor,a general adjunto(-a) *m,f Esp*	deputy receiver general
jefe,-a *m,f*	manager, leader, chief, head
jefe,-a administrativo(-a) *m,f*	administration officer, senior clerk

en España y América Latina	en el R.U. y los EE.UU.
in Spain and Latin America	*in the UK and US*

jefe,-a de almacén *m,f*	stock controller, stockman *AmE*, storeman *BrE*
jefe,-a auxiliar de sección *m,f*	assistant head of section
jefe,-a de caja *m,f*	cash manager
jefe,-a de capacitación *m,f AmL*	training officer
jefe,-a comercial *m,f*	commercial manager, commercial director
jefe,-a de compras *m,f*	chief buyer, head buyer, procurement manager
jefe,-a de contabilidad *m,f*	accountant general, chief accountant
jefe,-a de contratación *m,f*	recruitment manager
jefe,-a de contratos *m,f*	contracts manager
jefe,-a de cuentas *m,f*	*finanzas* accountant general, chief accountant, *marketing* account manager
jefe,-a de departamento *m,f*	department head, head of department
jefe,-a de distrito *m,f*	district manager
jefe,-a de división *m,f*	division head, division manager, head of section
jefe,-a ejecutivo(-a) *m,f*	chief executive officer *AmE*
jefe,-a de equipo *m,f*	team leader
jefe,-a de Estado Mayor *m,f*	*ejército* Chief of Staff
jefe,-a de exportación *m,f*	export manager
jefe,-a de formación *m,f Esp*	training officer
jefe,-a de grupo *m,f*	group leader
jefe,-a de importación *m,f*	import manager
jefe,-a de información *m,f*	chief information officer
jefe,-a de inmigración *m,f*	chief immigration officer
jefe,-a de movimiento *m,f*	traffic manager
jefe,-a de negociado *m,f*	human resources manager, personnel manager, head of personnel
jefe,-a de oficina *m,f*	head clerk, office manager
jefe,-a de oficina de ventas *m,f*	sales office manager
jefe,-a de personal *m,f*	personnel officer, personnel manager, staff manager, human resources manager
jefe,-a de planta *m,f*	floor manager *BrE*, floorwalker *AmE*
jefe,-a de producto *m,f*	product manager
jefe,-a de proyecto *m,f*	project manager, project leader, project director
jefe,-a de publicidad *m,f*	advertising manager
jefe,-a de reclamaciones *m,f*	claims manager
jefe,-a de reclutamiento *m,f*	recruiting officer
jefe,-a de relaciones industriales *m,f*	industrial relations manager
jefe,-a de sección *m,f*	division head, division manager, head of section, head of department, *de grandes superficies* floor manager *BrE*, floorwalker *AmE*
jefe,-a de unidad *m,f*	head of unit
jefe,-a de taller *m,f*	head foreman
líder del equipo *mf*	team leader
líder del grupo *mf*	group leader
listero,-a *m,f*	*obras* contracts manager
manager *mf*	manager
maquinista *mf*	machine operator
mensajero,-a *m,f*	runner, messenger, *transporte* courier
miembro del consejo de administración *mf*	member of the board of management
miembro del consejo de supervisión *mf*	member of the supervisory board
mujer de negocios *f*	businesswoman
obrero,-a manual *m,f*	production worker

en España y América Latina

in Spain and Latin America

en el R.U. y los EE.UU.

in the UK and US

oficial,a de aduanas *m,f*	customs officer, customs broker
oficial,a de capacitación *m,f AmL*	training officer
oficial,a de control de divisas *m,f*	exchange control officer
oficial,a de descarga *m,f*	landing officer *BrE*
oficial,a de desembarque *m,f*	landing officer *BrE*
oficial,a de distrito *m,f*	district officer
oficial,a ejecutivo(-a) *m,f*	executive officer
oficial,a de exportación *m,f*	export clerk
oficial,a de formación *m,f Esp*	training officer
oficial,a de formación de distrito *m,f*	district training officer
oficial,a de guardia *m,f*	duty officer
oficial,a de prensa *m,f*	press officer
oficial,a de transporte motorizado *m,f*	motor transport officer
operador,a de teléfonos *m,f*	switchboard operator
organizador,a de una reunión *m,f*	convenor, organizer
orientador,a vocacional *m,f*	careers advisor
pagador,a *m,f*	paymaster, disburser, payer *BrE*, payor *AmE*
patrón,-ona *m,f*	employer
presidente,-a *m,f*	chairman, convenor, director, president
presidente,-a del consejo *m,f*	chairman of the board
presidente,-a del consejo de administración *m,f*	chairman of the administrative board, chairman of the board of directors, chairman of the executive board, chairman of the executive committee, chairman of the board of management, president of the group executive board *AmE*
presidente,-a del consejo del tesoro *m,f*	President of the Treasury *AmE*
presidente,-a y director,a ejecutivo(-a) *m,f*	chairman and chief executive *AmE*, chairman and managing director *BrE*, chairman and general manager
presidente,-a y director,a general *m,f*	chairman and chief executive *AmE*, chairman and managing director *BrE*, chairman and general manager
presidente,-a y director,a gerente *m,f*	chairman and chief executive *AmE*, chairman and managing director *BrE*, chairman and general manager
presidente,-a ejecutivo(-a) *m,f*	chief executive officer *AmE*
presidente,-a del gobierno *m,f*	President of the Government *AmE*
presidente,-a honorario(-a) *m,f*	honorary chairman, honorary president
presidente,-a honorario(-a) de la junta de directores *m,f*	honorary chairman of the board of directors
presidente,-a de la junta directiva *m,f*	chairman of the administrative board, chairman of the board of directors, chairman of the executive board, chairman of the executive committee, chairman of the board of management, president of the group executive board *AmE*
presidente,-a de la junta supervisora *m,f*	chairman of the supervisory board
profesor,a *m,f*	*universidad* lecturer, *educación obligatoria* teacher
profesor,a asociado(-a) *m,f*	associate lecturer
profesor,a a tiempo completo *m,f*	full-time lecturer
profesor,a a tiempo parcial *m,f*	part-time lecturer
propietario,-a *m,f*	proprietor, *inmobiliaria* property owner
propietario,-a principal *m,f*	master owner, main owner
propietario,-a de restaurante *m,f*	restaurant proprietor, restaurateur
rector,a *m,f*	vice chancellor *BrE*

en España y América Latina

in Spain and Latin America

en el R.U. y los EE.UU.

in the UK and US

representante de agencia *mf*	agency representative
representante autorizado(-a) *m,f*	authorized representative, registered representative
representante de comercio *mf*	trade representative, commercial agent
representante obrero *mf*	shop steward
representante del personal *mf*	shop steward
representante sindical *mf*	convenor
representante de ventas *mf*	sales representative
responsable de compras *mf*	head buyer
responsable de información *mf*	information officer
revisor,a *m,f*	*control de calidad* checker
secretario,-a de confianza *m,f*	confidential secretary
secretario,-a de la empresa *m,f*	company secretary
secretario,-a general *m,f*	company secretary, general secretary
secretario,-a interino(-a) *m,f*	temporary secretary
secretario,-a particular *m,f*	private secretary, personal assistant
secretario,-a personal *m,f*	personal secretary, personal assistant
secretario,-a temporal *m,f*	temporary secretary
sobrestante *mf*	foreman
socio,-a *m,f*	partner, member
socio,-a administrador(a) *m,f*	managing partner
socio,-a colectivo(-a) *m,f*	general partner
socio,-a comanditario(-a) *m,f*	limited partner, limited owner, limited liability partner
socio,-a director,a *m,f*	managing partner
socio,-a limitado(-a) *m,f*	limited partner
subdirector,a *m,f*	assistant director, assistant manager, deputy director, deputy manager
subdirector,a general *m,f*	assistant general director, assistant general manager
subdirector,a gerente *m,f*	deputy managing director
subgerente *mf*	assistant manager, deputy director, deputy manager
subsecretario,-a *m,f*	undersecretary
superintendente de tráfico *mf*	district traffic superintendent, traffic superintendent
supervisor,a *m,f*	supervisor, first-line manager
supervisor,a de carga *m,f*	cargo surveyor
supervisor,a de cobro *m,f*	credit controller
supervisor,a de crédito *m,f*	credit controller
supervisor,a de documentación de importación *m,f*	import documentation supervisor
supervisor,a en jefe *m,f*	head foreman, chief supervisor
supervisor,a de línea *m,f*	line supervisor
supervisor,a de primera línea *m,f*	first-line supervisor, first-line manager
supervisor,a de tráfico *m,f*	traffic supervisor
suplente *mf*	deputy, acting member
suplente de la junta directiva *mf*	deputy member of the board of management
tasador,a de pérdidas *m,f*	*seguros* loss adjuster
topógrafo,-a *m,f*	surveyor
transportista *mf*	shipping and forwarding agent
urbanista *mf*	town planner, urban planner
vendedor,a *m,f*	salesman
vendedor,a a comisión *m,f*	commission salesman
vendedor,a a domicilio *m,f*	door-to-door salesman
verificador,a *m,f*	*control de calidad* checker
viajante *mf*	salesman

en España y América Latina	en el R.U. y los EE.UU.
in Spain and Latin America	*in the UK and US*

viajante de comercio *mf*	sales representative, travelling salesman *BrE*, traveling salesman *AmE*, commercial traveller *BrE*, commercial traveler *AmE*
vicepresidente,-a *m,f*	deputy chairman *BrE*, vice chairman *AmE*, vice president
vicepresidente,-a adjunto(-a) *m,f*	senior vice president
vicepresidente,-a del consejo *m,f*	deputy chairman of the board of management, deputy chairman of the supervisory board
vicepresidente,-a ejecutivo(-a) *m,f*	executive vice president
vicepresidente,-a primero(-a) *m,f*	first vice president
vicepresidente,-a principal *m,f*	senior vice president
vicesecretario,-a *m,f*	undersecretary, vice secretary
vigilante *mf*	watchman

Bolsas/Stock exchanges

Nombre español *Spanish name*	País, ciudad *Country, city*	Nombre inglés *English name*
	R.U. *UK*	
Asociación Internacional de Entidades del Mercado Primario de Bonos *f*	Londres	International Primary Market Association
Bolsa de Contratación de Materias Primas de Londres *f*	Londres	London Commodity Exchange
Bolsa de Contratos Futuros sobre Metales *f*	Londres	London Metal Exchange
Bolsa Internacional *f*	Londres	London Stock Exchange
Bolsa Internacional Báltica de Futuros de Fletes *f*	Londres	Baltic International Freight Futures Exchange
Bolsa de Valores de Belfast *f*	Belfast	Belfast Stock Exchange
Bolsa de Valores de Birmingham *f*	Birmingham	Birmingham Stock Exchange
Bolsa de Valores de Glasgow *f*	Glasgow	Glasgow Stock Exchange
Bolsa de Valores de Liverpool *f*	Liverpool	Liverpool Stock Exchange
Bolsa de Valores de Londres *f*	Londres	London Stock Exchange
cotización automatizada del Mercado de Valores *f*	Londres	Stock Exchange Automated Quotation
Federación de Bolsas del Reino Unido *f*	Londres	United Kingdom Stock Exchanges
Junta Directiva de la Bolsa de Valores de Londres *f*	Londres	London Stock Exchange Board
Mercado de Futuros Báltico *m*	Londres	Baltic Futures Exchange
Mercado de Futuros Financieros de Londres *m*	Londres	London International Financial Futures Exchange
Mercado Internacional del Petróleo *m*	Londres	International Petroleum Exchange
Mercado Londinense de Valores Extranjeros *m*	Londres	London Foreign Exchange Market
Mercado de Londres de Opciones Negociadas *m*	Londres	London Traded Options Market
Mercado de Mercaderías de Liverpool *m*	Liverpool	Liverpool Commodity Exchange
Mercado Internacional del Petróleo *m*	Londres	International Petroleum Exchange
Mercado de Mercaderías de Manchester *m*	Manchester	Manchester Commodity Exchange
Mercado de Opciones y Futuros de Londres *m*	Londres	London Futures and Options Exchange
Mercado de Valores no Cotizados *m*	Londres	Unlisted Securities Market
Sistema Operativo de Cotizaciones *m*	Londres	Stock Exchange Alternative Trading Service

Nombre español	País, ciudad	Nombre inglés
Spanish name	*Country, city*	*English name*

	EE.UU.	
	US	
Bolsa Americana de Valores *f*	Nueva York	American Stock Exchange
Bolsa de Arroz y Algodón de Chicago *f*	Chicago	Chicago Rice and Cotton Exchange
Bolsa de Café, Azúcar y Cacao de Nueva York *f*	Nueva York	New York Coffee, Sugar and Cocoa Exchange
Bolsa de Contratación Amex *f*	Nueva York	Amex Commodity Exchange
Bolsa Mercantil de Chicago *f*	Chicago	Chicago Mercantile Exchange
Bolsa Mercantil de Nueva York *f*	Nueva York	New York Mercantile Exchange
Bolsa de Nueva York *f*	Nueva York	New York Stock Exchange
Bolsa de Productos Amex *f*	Nueva York	Amex Commodity Exchange
Bolsa de Productos Básicos de Medio América *f*	Chicago	Mid-America Commodity Exchange
Bolsa Secundaria de Nueva York *f*	Nueva York	New York Curb Exchange
Bolsa de Valores de Boston *f*	Boston	Boston Stock Exchange
Bolsa de Valores de Chicago *f*	Chicago	Chicago Stock Exchange
Bolsa de Valores del Medio Oeste *f*	Chicago	Midwest Stock Exchange
Bosla de Valores de Cincinnatti *f*	Cincinnatti	Cincinnatti Stock Exchange
Bolsa de Valores de Filadelfia *f*	Filadelfia	Philadelphia Stock Exchange
Bolsa de Valores del Pacífico *f*	Los Angeles y San Francisco	Pacific Stock Exchange (Los Angeles Stock Exchange *and* San Francisco Stock Exchange)
Bolsa de Valores de Salt Lake *f*	Salt Lake City	Salt Lake City Stock Exchange
Bolsa de Valores de Spokane *f*	Spokane	Spokane Stock Exchange
Mercado de Algodón de Nueva York *m*	Nueva York	New York Cotton Exchange
Mercado de Algodón, Petróleo y Asociados de Cítricos *m*	Nueva York	New York Cotton Exchange and Petroleum and Citrus Associates
Mercado del Cereal de Minneapolis *m*	Minneapolis	Minneapolis Grain Exchange
Mercado de Contratación de Derivados de Nueva York *m*	Nueva York	Commodity Exchange Inc. of New York
Mercado de Futuros de Chicago *m*	Chicago	Chicago Board of Trade
Mercado de Futuros de Nueva York *m*	Nueva York	New York Futures Exchange
Mercado de Mercaderías de Nueva Orleans *m*	Nueva Orleans	New Orleans Commodity Exchange
Mercado de Opciones de Chicago *m*	Chicago	Chicago Board Options Exchange
Mercado Monetario Internacional *m*	Chicago	International Monetary Market

Nombre español	País, ciudad	Nombre inglés
Spanish name	*Country, city*	*English name*

	América Latina	
	Latin America	
Bolsa de Argentina *f*	Buenos Aires	Merval Stock Exchange
Bolsa de Méjico *f*	Ciudad de Méjico	Mexico City Stock Exchange
Bolsa de Montevideo f	Montevideo	Montevideo Stock Exchange
Bolsa de Santiago *f*	Santiago	Santiago Stock Exchange
Bolsa de Lima *f*	Lima	Lima Stock Exchange
	Bélgica	
	Belgium	
Cámara de Compensación de Eurobonos *f*	Bruselas	Euroclear
	España	
	Spain	
Bolsa de Barcelona *f*	Barcelona	Barcelona Stock Exchange
Bolsa de Bilbao *f*	Bilbao	Bilbao Stock Exchange
Bolsa de Madrid *f*	Madrid	Madrid Stock Exchange
Bolsa de Valencia *f*	Valencia	Valencia Stock Exchange
Cámara de Compensación y Liquidación *f*	Madrid	association for payment clearing services
Comisión de Estudios del Mercado Monetario *f*	Madrid	Spanish commission of main institutions that regulate the monetary market
Comisión Nacional del Mercado de Valores *f*	Madrid	Spanish national securities and investment board
Mercado Español de Futuros Financieros *m*	Madrid	Spanish financial futures market
	Países Bajos	
	Netherlands	
Mercado Europeo de Opciones *m*	Amsterdam	European Options Exchange

Índices financieros y económicos/
Financial and economic indexes

Nombre español	Nombre inglés
Spanish name	*English name*

Cobertura general
General coverage

cotización de bonos *f*	bond index
índice de acciones de las minas *m*	golds index
índice adelantado compuesto *m*	composite leading index
índice de mercaderías *m*	commodities index
índice bursátil *m*	stock market index
índice de calidad física de vida *m*	physical quality of life index
índice de capitalización bursátil *m*	market capitalization index
índice del coste de la construcción *m*	construction cost index
índice del coste de la vida *m*	cost-of-living index
índice de cotización de acciones en bolsa *m*	share index
índice de cotización bursátil *m*	stock price index
índice de crecimiento *m*	growth index
índice de difusión *m*	diffusion index
índice de escasez *m*	scarcity index
índice Herfindahl-Hirschman *m*	Herfindahl-Hirschman Index
índice de indicadores adelantados *m*	index of leading indicators
índice de indicadores muy adelantados *m*	index of longer leading indicators
índice de indicadores poco adelantados *m*	index of shorter leading indicators
índice de indicadores anticipados *m*	index of leading indicators
índice de indicadores coincidentes *m*	index of coincident indicators
índice de indicadores retardados *m*	index of lagging indicators
índice de Laspeyres *m*	Laspeyre's Index
índice de Lerner *m*	Lerner Index
índice de malestar *m*	discomfort index
índice del mercado *m*	market index
índice del mercado de valores *m*	stock market index
índice mixto *m*	composite index
índice de Paasche *m*	Paasche Index
índice ponderado *m*	weighted index
índice de precios *m*	price index
índice de precios de la bolsa de valores *m*	stock exchange price index
índice de precios bursátiles *m*	stock exchange price index, stock market price index
índice de precios al consumo *m*	consumer price index
índice de precios implícitos *m*	implied price index
índice de precios del mercado de valores *m*	stock market price index
índice de precios ponderados *m*	price-weighted index
índice de precios al por mayor *m*	wholesale price index
índice de precios al por menor *m*	retail price index
índice de precios a la producción *m*	producer price index

Nombre español	Nombre inglés
Spanish name	*English name*

índice de valores estimados del mercado *m*	market value-weighted index
índice de valor unitario *m*	unit value index

Australia
Australia

índice All Ordinaries *m*	All Ordinaries Index

Bélgica
Belgium

índice del eurodólar *m*	Eurodollar Index

EE.UU.
US

índice bursátil de fecha valor *m*	value line stock index
índice compuesto de la Bolsa de Nueva York *m*	New York Stock Exchange Composite Index
índice compuesto de fecha valor *m*	value line composite index
índice de confianza de Barron *m*	Barron's Confidence Index
índice Dow Jones *m*	Dow Jones index

España
Spain

índice IBEX 35 *m*	IBEX 35 Index

Hong Kong
Hong Kong

índice Hang Seng *m*	Hang Seng Index

Internacional
International

índice de certificados de depósito del mercado monetario internacional *m*	international monetary market certificate of deposit index
índice de compra a plazo a tres meses del mercado monetario internacional *m*	international monetary market three-month add-on index
índice de descuento a tres meses del mercado monetario internacional *m*	international monetary market three-month discount index
índice de divisa *m*	Forex Index
índice de letras del tesoro del mercado monetario *m*	international monetary market treasury-bill index
Índice Mundial del Capital Internacional *m*	Capital International World Index
promedio del fondo monetario Donoghue *m*	Donoghue's Money Fund Average

Japón
Japan

índice Nikkei *m*	Nikkei average, Nikkei index
promedio Nikkei *m*	Nikkei average, Nikkei index

Países Bajos
Netherlands

índice de valores CBS *m*	CBS Tendency Index

Nombre español	Nombre inglés
Spanish name	*English name*

R.U.
UK

índice bursátil de valores industriales del Financial Times *m*	Financial Times Industrial Ordinary Share Index
índice de cotización de Treinta Valores *m*	Thirty-Share Index
índice del Financial Times *m*, índice del FT *m*	Financial Times Index, FT Index
índice Footsie *m*	Financial Times Stock Exchange 100 Share Index, FT-SE 100, Footsie
índice Footsie Eurotrack 100 *m*	Financial Times Stock Exchange Eurotrack 100 Index, FT-SE Eurotrack 100 Index
índice Footsie Eurotrack 200 *m*	Financial Times Stock Exchange Eurotrack 200 Index, FT-SE Eurotrack 200 Index
índice de precios de valores de los actuarios del Financial Times *m*	Financial Times Actuaries All Share Index, All Share Index
índice de producción industrial *m*	index of industrial production

Suiza
Switzerland

| índice del Crédito Suizo *m* | Credit Suisse Index |

Países y dependencias principales/
Countries and principal dependencies

Países y dependencias principales	Capital	Habitante	Lengua(s) oficial(es)	Moneda
Countries and principal dependencies *	*Capital*	*Inhabitant* **	*Official language(s)* ***	Currency
Afganistán	Kabul	afgano,-a *m,f*	pashtu, dari	afganí *m*
Afghanistan	*Kabul*	*Afghan*	*Pashto/Pushtu, Dari*	*afghani*
Albania	Tirana	albano,-a *m,f*/ albanés,-esa *m,f*	albanés	lek *m*
Albania	*Tirana*	*Albanian*	*Albanian*	*lek*
Alemania	Berlín	alemán,-ana *m,f*	alemán	marco alemán *m*
Germany	*Berlin*	*German*	*German*	*German Mark*
Andorra	Andorra la Vella	andorrano,-a *m,f*	catalán, francés, español	franco francés *m*, peseta *f*
Andorra	*Andorra la Vella*	*Andorran*	*Catalan, French, Spanish*	*French franc, peseta*
Angola	Luanda	angoleño,-a *m,f*	portugués	kwanza *f*
Angola	*Luanda*	*Angolan*	*Portuguese*	*kwanza*
Antigua y Barbuda	St. Johns	de Antigua y Barbuda	inglés	dólar del Caribe Oriental *m*
Antigua and Barbuda	*St. John's*	*Antiguan/Barbudan*	*English*	*East Caribbean dollar*
Angulia/Anguila (R.U.)	The Valley	de Anguila	inglés, criollo	dólar del Caribe Oriental *m*
Anguilla (UK)	*The Valley*	*Anguillan*	*English, Creole*	*East Caribbean dollar*
Antillas Holandesas (Holanda)	Willemstad	de las Antillas Holandesas	holandés	florín *m*
Netherlands Antilles (Netherlands)	*Willemstad*	*from Netherlands Antilles*	*Dutch*	*guilder*
Arabia Saudí	Riyadh	saudí *mf*/árabe saudita *mf*	árabe	rial saudí *m*
Saudi Arabia	*Riyadh*	*Saudi/Saudi Arabian*	*Arabic*	*Saudi riyal*
Argelia	Argel	argelino,-a *m,f*	árabe	dinar argelino *m*
Algeria	*Algiers*	*Algerian*	*Arabic*	*dinar*
Argentina	Buenos Aires	argentino,-a *m,f*	español	peso *m*
Argentina	*Buenos Aires*	*Argentinian/ Argentine*	*Spanish*	*peso*
Armenia	Yereván	armenio,-a *m,f*	armenio	dram *m*
Armenia	*Yerevan*	*Armenian*	*Armenian*	*dram*
Aruba (Países Bajos)	Oranjestad	arubeño,-a *m,f*	holandés	florín *m*
Aruba (Netherlands)	*Oranjestad*	*Aruban*	*Dutch*	*guilder*
Australia	Canberra	australiano,-a *m,f*	inglés	dólar australiano *m*
Australia	*Canberra*	*Australian*	*English*	*Australian dollar*
Austria	Viena	austriaco,-a *m,f*	alemán	chelín *m*
Austria	*Vienna*	*Austrian*	*German*	*schilling*

Países y dependencias principales	Capital	Habitante	Lengua(s) oficial(es)	Moneda
*Countries and principal dependencies *****	*Capital*	*Inhabitant ******	*Official language(s) ******	Currency
Azerbaiyán	Bakú	azerbaiyano -a *m,f*	azerí, ruso	manat *m*
Azerbaijan	*Baku*	*Azeri/Azerbaijani*	*Azeri, Russian*	*manat*
Bahamas	Nassau	bahamense *mfl* bahamés,-esa *m,fl* bahameño,-a *m,f*	inglés	dólar de Bahamas *m*
Bahamas	*Nassau*	*Bahamian*	*English*	*Bahamian dollar*
Bahrein	Manama	bahreiní *mf*	árabe	dinar de Bahrein *m*
Bahrain/Bahrein	*Manama*	*Bahraini*	*Arabic*	*Bahrain dinar*
Bangladesh	Dacca/Dhaka	bangladesí *mf*	bengalí, inglés	taka *m*
Bangladesh	*Dhaka*	*Bangladeshi*	*Bengali, English*	*taka*
Barbados	Bridgetown	barbadense *mf*	inglés	dólar de Barbados *m*
Barbados	*Bridgetown*	*Barbadian*	*English*	*Barbados dollar*
Bélgica	Bruselas	belga *mf*	francés, flamenco, alemán	franco belga *m*
Belgium	*Brussels*	*Belgian*	*French, Flemish, German*	*Belgian franc*
Belice	Belmopán	beliceño,-a *m,f*	inglés, español	dólar de Belice *m*
Belize	*Belmopan*	*Belizean*	*English, Spanish*	*Belize dollar*
Benín	Porto Novo	beninés,-esa *m,fl* aboense *mf*	francés	franco CFA *m*
Benin	*Porto Novo*	*Beninese*	*French*	*CFA franc*
Bermudas (R.U.)	Hamilton	de Bermudas	inglés	dólar de Bermudas *m*
Bermuda (UK)	*Hamilton*	*Bermudan/ Bermudian*	*English*	*Bermudian dollar*
Bielorrusia	Minsk	bielorruso,-a *m,f*	bielorruso	rublo bielorruso *m*
Belarus	*Minsk*	*Belarussian*	*Belarussian*	*Belarussian rouble*
Bolivia	La Paz *(sede del gobierno)*, Sucre *(sede legal y judicial)*	boliviano,-a *m,f*	español, quechua, aimará	boliviano *m*
Bolivia	*La Paz (seat of government), Sucre (legal and judicial seat)*	*Bolivian*	*Spanish, Quechua, Aymara*	*boliviano*
Bosnia-Herzegovina	Sarajevo	bosnio,-a *mf*	bosnio	dinar bosnio *m*
Bosnia-Herzegovina	*Sarajevo*	*Bosnian*	*Bosnian*	*Bosnian dinar*
Botswana	Gaborone	botsuano,-a *m,fl* botsuanés,-esa *m,f*	inglés, setswana	pula *m*
Botswana	*Gaborone*	*Botswanan*	*English, Setswana*	*pula*
Brasil	Brasilia	brasileño,-a *m,f*	portugués	cruzeiro *m*
Brazil	*Brasilia*	*Brazilian*	*Portuguese*	*cruzeiro*
Brunei	Bandar Seri Begawan	de Brunei	malayo, inglés	dólar de Brunei *m*
Brunei	*Bandar Seri Begawan*	*Bruneian*	*Malay, English*	*Brunei dollar*
Bulgaria	Sofía	búlgaro,-a *m,f*	búlgaro	lev *m*
Bulgaria	*Sofia*	*Bulgarian*	*Bulgarian*	*lev*

Países y dependencias principales	Capital	Habitante	Lengua(s) oficial(es)	Moneda
Countries and principal dependencies *	*Capital*	*Inhabitant ***	*Official language(s) ****	Currency
Burkina Faso	Uagadugú	voltense *mf*	francés, mossi	franco CFA *m*
Burkina Faso	*Ouagadougou*	*Burkinabe*	*French, Mossi*	*CFA franc*
Burundi	Bujumbura	burundés,-esa *m,f*	kirundi, francés	franco Burundés *m*
Burundi	*Bujumbura*	*Burundian*	*Kirundi, French*	*Burundi franc*
Bután	Thimbu	butanés,-esa *m,f*	dzong-kha	ngultrum *m*, rupia india *f*
Bhutan	*Thimphu*	*Bhutanese*	*Dzongka*	*ngultrum, Indian rupee*
Cabo Verde	Praia	caboverdiano,-a *m,f*	portugués	escudo Caboverdianos *m*
Cape Verde Islands	*Praia*	*Cape Verdean*	*Portuguese*	*Cape Verdean escudo*
Camboya	Phnom Penh	camboyano,-a *m,f*	khmer	riel *m*
Cambodia	*Phnom Penh*	*Cambodian*	*Khmer*	*riel*
Camerún	Yaoundé	camerunés,-esa *m,f*	francés, inglés	franco CFA *m*
Cameroon	*Yaoundé*	*Cameroonian*	*French, English*	*CFA franc*
Canadá	Ottawa	canadiense *mf*	inglés, francés	dólar canadiense *m*
Canada	*Ottawa*	*Canadian*	*English, French*	*Canadian dollar*
Chad	N'Djamena	chadí *mf*/ chadiano,-a *m,f*	árabe, francés	franco CFA *m*
Chad	*N'Djamena*	*Chadian*	*Arabic, French*	*CFA franc*
Chile	Santiago	chileno,-a *m,f*	español	peso *m*
Chile	*Santiago*	*Chilean*	*Spanish*	*peso*
China	Pekín	chino,-a *m,f*	mandarín, chino	yuan *m*
China	*Beijing*	*Chinese*	*Mandarin, Chinese*	*yuan*
Chipre	Nicosia	chipriota *mf*	griego, turco	libra chipriota *f*
Cyprus	*Nicosia*	*Cypriot*	*Greek, Turkish*	*Cyprus pound*
Christmas (Australia)	dependen políticamente de Canberra	de Christmas	inglés	dólar australiano *m*
Christmas Island (Australia)	*politically dependent on Canberra*	*Christmas Islander*	*English*	*Australian dollar*
Colombia	Bogotá	colombiano,-a *m,f*	español	peso colombiano *m*
Colombia	*Bogotá*	*Colombian*	*Spanish*	*Colombian peso*
Comoros	Moroni	comorano,-a *m,f*	francés, árabe	franco CFA *m*
Comoras	*Moroni*	*Comorian*	*French, Arabic*	*CFA franc*
Congo	Brazzaville	congoleño,-a *m,f*/ congolés,-esa *m,f*	francés	franco CFA *m*
Congo	*Brazzaville*	*Congolese*	*French*	*CFA franc*
Corea del Norte/ República Democrática Popular de Corea	Piongyang	norcoreano,-a *m,f*	coreano	won *m*
North Korea/ Democratic People's Republic of Korea	*Pyongyang*	*North Korean*	*Korean*	*won*

Países y dependencias principales	Capital	Habitante	Lengua(s) oficial(es)	Moneda
Countries and principal dependencies *	*Capital*	*Inhabitant* **	*Official language(s)* ***	Currency
Corea del Sur/ República de Corea/Corea	Seúl	surcoreano,-a *m,f*	coreano	won *m*
South Korea/ Republic of Korea/ Korea	*Seoul*	*South Korean*	*Korean*	*won*
Costa de Marfil	Yamaussoukro	marfileño,-a *m,f*	francés	franco CFA *m*
Ivory Coast	*Yamoussoukro*	*Ivoirian*	*French*	*CFA franc*
Costa Rica	San José	costarricense *mf*	español	colón *m*
Costa Rica	*San José*	*Costa Rican*	*Spanish*	*colón*
Croacia, República de	Zagreb	croata *mf*	croata	kuna *f*
Croatia, Republic of	*Zagreb*	*Croat/Croatian*	*Croatian*	*kuna*
Cuba	La Habana	cubano,-a *m,f*	español	peso cubano *m*
Cuba	*Havana*	*Cuban*	*Spanish*	*Cuban peso*
Dinamarca	Copenhague	danés,-esa *m,f*	danés	corona danesa *f*
Denmark	*Copenhagen*	*Dane*	*Danish*	*Danish krone*
Dominica	Roseau	dominicano,-a *m,f*	inglés	dólar del Caribe Oriental *m*
Dominica	*Roseau*	*Dominican*	*English*	*East Caribbean dollar*
Ecuador	Quito	ecuatoriano,-a *m,f*	español	sucre *m*
Ecuador	*Quito*	*Ecuadorian/ Ecuadoran*	*Spanish*	*sucre*
Egipto	El Cairo	egipcio,-a *m,f*	árabe	libra egipcia *f*
Egypt	*Cairo*	*Egyptian*	*Arabic*	Egyptian pound
El Salvador	San Salvador	salvadoreño,-a *m,f*	español	colón *m*
El Salvador	*San Salvador*	*Salvadoran*	*Spanish*	*colón*
Emiratos Arabes Unidos/Unión de Emiratos Arabes *f*	Abu Dhabi	de los Emiratos Arabes Unidos	árabe	dirham *m*
United Arab Emirates	*Abu Dhabi*	*Emirian*	*Arabic*	*dirham*
Eritrea	Asmara	de Eritrea	árabe, inglés	birr *m*
Eritrea	*Asmara*	*Eritrean*	*Arabic, English*	*birr*
Escocia	Edimburgo	escocés,-esa *m,f*	inglés	libra esterlina *f*
Scotland	*Edinburgh*	*Scot/Scotsman, Scotswoman*	*English*	*Sterling pound*
Eslovaquia	Bratislava	eslovaco,-a *m,f*	eslovaco	corona eslovaca *f*
Slovakia	*Bratislava*	*Slovak*	*Slovak*	*Slovak koruna*
Eslovenia	Ljubljana	esloveno,-a *m,f*	esloveno	tólar *m*
Slovenia	*Lubliana*	*Slovenian/Slovene*	*Slovenian*	*tolar*
España	Madrid	español,a *m,f*	español	peseta *f*
Spain	*Madrid*	*Spaniard*	*Spanish*	*peseta*
Estados Unidos de América	Washington, D.C.	estadounidense *mf*	inglés	dólar americano *m*
United States of America	*Washington, D.C.*	*from the United States*	*English*	*US dollar*

Países y dependencias principales	Capital	Habitante	Lengua(s) oficial(es)	Moneda
Countries and principal dependencies *	*Capital*	*Inhabitant* **	*Official language(s)* ***	Currency

Estonia	Tallin	estoniano,-a *m,f*	estonio	corona *f*
Estonia	*Tallinn*	*Estonian*	*Estonian*	*kroon*
Etiopía	Addis Abeba	etíope *mf*/etiope *mf*/ abisinio,-a *m,f*	amárico/amhárico	birr *m*
Ethiopia	*Addis Ababa*	*Ethiopian*	*Amharic*	*birr*
Fiji	Suva	fijiano,- a *m,f*	inglés	dólar de Fiji *m*
Fiji	*Suva*	*Fijian*	*English*	*Fiji dollar*
Filipinas	Manila	filipino,-a *m,f*	filipino, inglés	peso filipino *m*
Philippines	*Manila*	*Filipino*	*Filipino, English*	*Philippine peso*
Finlandia	Helsinki	finlandés,-esa *m,f*/ finés,-esa *m,f*	finlandés, sueco	marco *m*
Finland	*Helsinki*	*Finn*	*Finnish, Swedish*	*markka*
Francia	París	francés,-esa *m,f*	francés	franco francés *m*
France	*Paris*	*Frenchman, Frenchwoman*	*French*	*French franc*
Gabón	Libreville	gabonés,-esa *m,f*	francés	franco CFA *m*
Gabon	*Libreville*	*Gabonese*	*French*	*CFA franc*
Gambia	Banjul	gambiano,-a *m,f*	inglés	dalasi *m*
Gambia	*Banjul*	*Gambian*	*English*	*dalasi*
Georgia	Tiflis	georgiano,-a *m,f*	georgiano	lari *m*
Georgia	*Tbilisi*	*Georgian*	*Georgian*	*lari*
Ghana	Acra	ghanés,-esa *m,f*	inglés	cedi *m*
Ghana	*Accra*	*Ghanaian*	*English*	*cedi*
Gibraltar (R.U.)	Gibraltar	gibraltareño,-a *m,f*	inglés	libra esterlina *f*
Gibraltar (UK)	*Gibraltar*	*Gibraltarian*	*English*	*Sterling pound*
Grecia	Atenas	griego,-a *m,f*/ heleno,-a *m,f*	griego	dracma *m*
Greece	*Athens*	*Greek*	*Greek*	*drachma*
Granada	St. Georges	granadino,-a *m,f*	inglés	dólar del Caribe Oriental *m*
Grenada	*St. George's*	*Grenadian*	*English*	*East Caribbean dollar*
Groenlandia (Dinamarca)	Nuuk	groenlandés,-esa *m,f*	danés, esquimal	corona danesa *f*
Greenland (Denmark)	*Nuuk*	*Greenlander*	*Danish, Eskimo*	*Danish krone*
Guadalupe (Francia)	Basse-Terre	guadalupeño,-a *m,f*	francés	franco francés *m*
Guadeloupe (France)	*Basse-Terre*	*from Guadeloupe*	*French*	*French franc*
Guam (EE.UU.)	Agaña	de Guam	inglés, chamorro	dólar americano *m*
Guam (US)	*Agaña*	*Guamanian*	*English, Chamorro*	*US dollar*
Guatemala	Ciudad de Guatemala	guatemalteco,-a *m,f*	español	quetzal *m*
Guatemala	*Guatemala City*	*Guatemalan*	*Spanish*	*quetzal*

Países y dependencias principales	Capital	Habitante	Lengua(s) oficial(es)	Moneda
Countries and principal dependencies *	*Capital*	*Inhabitant* **	*Official language(s)* ***	Currency
Guayana Francesa (Francia)	Cayena	de la Guayana Francesa	francés	franco francés *m*
French Guiana (France)	*Cayenne*	*French Guianese/ Guianan*	*French*	*French franc*
Guinea	Konakry	guineo,-a *m,f/* guineano,-a *m,f*	francés	franco guineano *m*
Guinea	*Conakry*	*Guinean*	*French*	*Guinean franc*
Guinea-Bissau	Bissau	de Guinea-Bissau	portugués	peso de Guinea-Bissau *m*
Guinea-Bissau	*Bissau*	*from Guinea-Bissau*	*Portuguese*	*Guinea-Bissau peso*
Guinea Ecuatorial	Malabo	ecuatoguineano,-a *m,f*	español	franco CFA *m*
Equatorial Guinea	*Malabo*	*Equatorial Guinean*	*Spanish*	*CFA franc*
Guyana	Georgetown	guyanés,-esa *m,f*	inglés	dólar guyanés *m*
Guyana	*Georgetown*	*Guyanese*	*English*	*Guyana dollar*
Haití	Port-au-Prince	haitiano,-a *m,f*	francés	gourde *m*
Haiti	*Port-au-Prince*	*Haitian*	*French*	*gourde*
Holanda/Países Bajos	Amsterdam, La Haya *(sede del gobierno)*	holandés,-esa *m,f/* neerlandés,-esa *m,f*	holandés	florín *m*
Holland/ Netherlands, the	*Amsterdam, The Hague (seat of government)*	*Dutchman, Dutchwoman/ Netherlander*	*Dutch*	*guilder*
Honduras	Tegucigalpa	hondureño,-a *m,f*	español	lempira *f*
Honduras	*Tegucigalpa*	*Honduran*	*Spanish*	*lempira*
Hong Kong (China)	Victoria	de Hong Kong	inglés, chino	dólar de Hong Kong *m*
Hong Kong (China)	*Victoria*	*from Hong Kong*	*English, Chinese*	*Hong Kong dollar*
Hungría	Budapest	húngaro,-a *m,f*	magyar, húngaro	florín *m*
Hungary	*Budapest*	*Hungarian*	*Magyar, Hungarian*	*forint*
India	Nueva Delhi	indio,-a *m,f*	hindi, inglés	rupia india *f*
India	*New Delhi*	*Indian*	*Hindi, English*	*Indian rupee*
Indonesia	Yakarta	indonesio,-a *m,f*	bahasa indonesio	rupia indonesia *f*
Indonesia	*Jakarta*	*Indonesian*	*Bahasa Indonesia*	*Indonesian rupiah*
Inglaterra	Londres	inglés,-esa *m,f*	inglés	libra esterlina *f*
England	*London*	*Englishman, Englishwoman*	*English*	*Sterling pound*
Irán	Teherán	iraní *mf*	farsi	rial *m*
Iran	*Tehran/Teheran*	*Iranian*	*Farsi*	*rial*
Iraq/Irak	Bagdad	iraquí *mf*	árabe	dinar iraquí m
Iraq/Irak	*Baghdad*	*Iraqi/Iraki*	*Arabic*	*Iraqi dinar/Iraki dinar*
Irlanda del Norte	Belfast	de Irlanda del Norte	inglés	libra esterlina *f*
Northern Ireland	*Belfast*	*from Northern Ireland*	*English*	*Sterling pound*
Islandia	Reykiavik	islandés,-esa *m,f*	islandés	corona *f*
Iceland	*Reykjavik*	*Icelander*	*Icelandic*	*Icelandic krona*

Países y dependencias principales	Capital	Habitante	Lengua(s) oficial(es)	Moneda
*Countries and principal dependencies**	*Capital*	*Inhabitant ***	*Official language(s) ****	Currency
Islas Caimán (R.U.)	George Town	de Caimán	inglés	dólar americano *m*
Cayman Islands (UK)	*George Town*	*Caymanian*	*English*	*US dollar*
Islas Cocos/Islas Keeling (Australia)	dependen políticamente de Canberra	de Cocos	inglés	dólar australiano *m*
Cocos Islands/ Keeling Islands (Australia)	*politically dependent on Canberra*	*Cocos Malay/Cocos Islander*	*English*	*Australian dollar*
Islas Cook (Nueva Zelanda)	Avarua	de Cook	inglés, rarotongano	dólar neozelandés *m*
Cook Islands (New Zealand)	*Avarua*	*Cook islander*	*English, Rarotongan*	*New Zealand dollar*
Islas Feroe (Dinamarca)	Thorshavn	de Islas Feroe	feroés, danés	corona danesa *f*
Faeroe Islands/ Faeroes (Denmark)	*Tórshavn*	*Faeroese*	*Faeroese, Danish*	*Danish krone*
Islas Malvinas (R.U.)	Stanley	malvinense *mf*	inglés	libra esterlina *f*
Falkland Islands (UK)	*Stanley*	*Falklander*	*English*	*Sterling pound*
Islas Marianas (EE.UU.)	Garapan	de las Islas Marianas	inglés, chamorro	dólar americano *m*
Northern Marianas (US)	*Chalan Kanoa*	*from Northern Marianas*	*English, Chamorro*	*US dollar*
Islas Marshall *f*	Dalap-Uliga-Darrit	de las Islas Marshall	marshalés	dólar americano *m*
Marshall Islands	*Dalap-Uliga-Darrit*	*Marshallese*	*Marshallese*	*US dollar*
Islas Salomón	Honiara	de Islas Salomón	inglés	dólar de Salomón *m*
Solomon Islands	*Honiara*	*Solomon islander*	*English*	*Solomon Islands dollar*
Islas Vírgenes (EE.UU.)	Charlotte Amalie	de las Islas Vírgenes	inglés	dólar americano *m*
Virgin Islands (US)	*Charlotte Amalie*	*from the Virgin Islands*	*English*	*US dollar*
Islas Vírgenes (R.U.)	Road Town	de las Islas Vírgenes	inglés	dólar americano *m*
Virgin Islands, British (UK)	*Road Town*	*from the Virgin Islands*	*English*	*US dollar*
Israel	Jerusalén	israelí/israelita *mf*	hebreo, árabe	shekel *m*, siclo *m*
Israel	*Jerusalem*	*Israeli/Israelite*	*Hebrew, Arabic*	*New shekel*
Italia	Roma	italiano,-a *m,f*	italiano	lira *f*
Italy	*Rome*	*Italian*	*Italian*	*lira*
Jamaica	Kingston	jamaicano,-a *m,f*/ jamaiquino,-a *m,f*	inglés	dólar jamaicano *m*
Jamaica	*Kingston*	*Jamaican*	*English*	*Jamaican dollar*
Japón	Tokio	japonés,-esa *m,f*	japonés	yen *m*
Japan	*Tokyo*	*Japanese*	*Japanese*	*yen*
Jordania	Ammán	jordano,-a *m,f*	árabe	dinar jordano *m*
Jordan	*Amman*	*Jordanian*	*Arabic*	*Jordanian dinar*

Países y dependencias principales	Capital	Habitante	Lengua(s) oficial(es)	Moneda
Countries and principal dependencies *	*Capital*	*Inhabitant* **	*Official language(s)* ***	Currency
Kazajstán	Alma-Ata	kazajo,-a *m,f*	kazajo, ruso	tenge *m*
Kazakhstan	*Alma-Ata*	*Kazakh/Kazak*	*Kazakh, Russian*	*tenge*
Kenia/Kenya	Nairobi	keniata *mf*/ kenyano,-a *m,f*	suahili, inglés	chelín de Kenya *m*
Kenya	*Nairobi*	*Kenyan*	*Swahili, English*	*Kenyan shilling*
Kirgüizistán	Pishpek	kirguiz *mf*	kirguiz	som *m*
Kyrgyzstan	*Bishkek*	*Kyrgyzstani*	*Kyrgyz*	*som*
Kiribati	Bairiki	kiribatiano,-a *m,f*	inglés, gilbertés	dólar autraliano *m*
Kiribati	*Bairiki*	*Kiribatian*	*English, Gilbertese*	*Australian dollar*
Kuwait/Koweit	Al-Kuwait	kuwaití *mf*	árabe	dinar kuwaití *m*
Kuwait	*Kuwait City*	*Kuwaiti*	*Arabic*	*Kuwaiti dinar*
Laos	Vientiane	lao,-a *m,fl* laosiano,-a *m,f*	laosiano	kip *m*
Laos	*Vientiane*	*Laotian*	*Lao*	*kip*
Lesoto	Maseru	basoto,-a *m,f*	sesotho, inglés	loti *m*
Lesotho	*Maseru*	*Basotho*	*Sesotho, English*	*loti*
Letonia	Riga	letón,a *m,f*	letón	lat *m*
Latvia	*Riga*	*Latvian*	*Latvian/Lettish*	*lat*
Líbano	Beirut	libanés,-esa *m,f*	árabe	libra libanesa *f*
Lebanon	*Beirut*	*Lebanese*	*Arabic*	*Lebanese pound*
Liberia	Monrovia	liberiano,-a *m,f*	inglés	dólar liberiano *m*
Liberia	*Monrovia*	*Liberian*	*English*	*Liberian dollar*
Libia	Trípoli	libio,-a *m,f*	árabe	dinar libio *m*
Libya	*Tripoli*	*Libyan*	*Arabic*	*Libyan dinar*
Liechtenstein	Vaduz	liechtenstiense *mf*	alemán	franco suizo *m*
Liechtenstein	*Vaduz*	*Liechtensteiner*	*German*	*Swiss franc*
Lithuania	Vilna	lituano,-a *m,f*	lituano	lita lituana *f*
Lituania	*Vilnius*	*Lithuanian*	*Lithuanian*	*Lithuanian lita*
Luxemburgo	Luxemburgo	luxemburgués,-esa *m,f*	francés, alemán	franco belga *m*
Luxembourg	*Luxembourg*	*Luxemburger*	*French, German*	*Belgian franc*
Macao (Portugal)	Ciudad de Macao	de Macao	portugués, cantonés	pataca *f*
Macao (Portugal)	*Macao City*	*Macanese*	*Portugese, Cantonese*	*pataca*
Macedonia, República de	Skopje	macedonio,-a *m,f*	macedonio	dinar *m*
Macedonia, Republic of	*Skopje*	*Macedonian*	*Macedonian*	*dinar*
Madagascar	Antananarivo	malgache *mf*	malgache, francés	franco malgache *m*
Madagascar	*Antananarivo*	*Malagasy*	*Malagasy, French*	*Malagasy franc*
Malasia	Kuala Lumpur	malasio,-a *m,fl* malayo,-a *m,f*	malayo	ringgit de Malasia *m*
Malaysia	*Kuala Lumpur*	*Malaysian/Malay*	*Malay*	*Malaysian ringgit*
Malawi	Lilongwe	malawiano,-a *m,fl* malawí *mf*	inglés, chichewa	kwacha *m*
Malawi	*Lilongwe*	*Malawian*	*English, Chichewa*	*kwacha*

Países y dependencias principales	Capital	Habitante	Lengua(s) oficial(es)	Moneda
Countries and principal dependencies *	*Capital*	*Inhabitant* **	*Official language(s)* ***	Currency
Maldivas	Male	maldivo,-a *m,f*	maldivo	rupia maldiva *f*
Maldives	*Malé*	*Maldivian*	*Divehi*	*Maldivian rupee*
Malí	Bamako	maliense *mf*	francés	franco CFA *m*
Mali	*Bamako*	*Malian*	*French*	*CFA franc*
Malta	La Valetta	maltense *mf*/ maltés,-esa *m,f*	maltés, inglés	libra maltesa *f*
Malta	*Valletta*	*Maltese*	*Maltese, English*	*Maltese pound*
Marruecos	Rabat	marroquí *mf*	árabe	dirham marroquí *m*
Morocco	*Rabat*	*Moroccan*	*Arabic*	*dirham*
Martinica (Francia)	Fort-de-France	de Martinica/ martiniqueño,-a *m,f*	francés	franco francés *m*
Martinique (France)	*Fort-de-France*	*Martinican*	*French*	*French franc*
Mauricio	Port Louis	mauriciano,-a *m,f*	inglés	rupia de Mauricio *f*
Mauritius	*Port Louis*	*Mauritian*	*English*	*Mauritian rupee*
Mauritania	Nouakchott	mauritano,-a *m,f*	árabe	ouguiya *m*
Mauritania	*Nouakchott*	*Mauritanian*	*Arabic*	*ouguiya*
Mayotte (Francia)	Mamoutzu	de Mayotte	francés, mahoriano	franco francés *m*
Mayotte (France)	*Mamoutzu*	*from Mayotte*	*French, Mahorian*	*French franc*
Méjico/México	Ciudad de México	mejicano,-a *m,f*/ mexicano,-a *m,f*	español	peso *m*
Mexico	*Mexico City*	*Mexican*	*Spanish*	*Mexican peso*
Mianmar	Yangón	burmano,-a *m,f*	burmés	kyat *m*
Myanmar	*Yangon*	*Burmese*	*Burmese*	*kyat*
Micronesia, Estados Federados de	Palikir	de los Estados Federados de Micronesia	inglés	dólar americano *m*
Micronesia, Federated States of	*Palikir*	*from the Federated States of Micronesia*	*English*	*US dollar*
Moldavia/Moldova	Chisinau	moldavo,-a *m,f*	moldavo	leu moldavo *m*
Moldova/Moldavia	*Kishinev*	*Moldovan*	*Moldovan*	*Moldovan leu*
Mónaco	Mónaco	monegasco,-a *m,f*	francés	franco francés *m*
Monaco	*Monaco*	*Monegasque*	*French*	*French franc*
Mongolia	Ulan Bator	mongol,a *m,f*	mongol khalkha	tugrik *m*
Mongolia	*Ulaanbaatar/Ulan Bator*	*Mongolian*	*Khalkha Mongol*	*tugrik*
Montserrat (R.U.)	Plymouth	de Montserrat	inglés	dólar del Caribe Oriental *m*
Montserrat (UK)	*Plymouth*	*Montserratian*	*English*	*East Caribbean dollar*
Mozambique	Maputo	mozambiqueño,-a *m,f*/ mozambiqués,-esa *m,f*	portugués	metical *m*
Mozambique	*Maputo*	*Mozambican*	*Portuguese*	*metical*
Namibia	Windhoek	namibio,-a *m,f*	inglés, africaans	dólar namibio *m*
Namibia	*Windhoek*	*Namibian*	*English, Afrikaans*	*Namibian dollar*

Países y dependencias principales	Capital	Habitante	Lengua(s) oficial(es)	Moneda
Countries and principal dependencies *	*Capital*	*Inhabitant* **	*Official language(s)* ***	Currency
Nauru	Yaren	nauruano,-a *m,f*	inglés, nauruano	dólar australiano *m*
Nauru	*Yaren District*	*Nauruan*	*English, Naurian*	*Australian dollar*
Nepal	Katmandú	nepalés,-esa *m,fl* nepalí *mf*	nepalí	rupia nepalí *f*
Nepal	*Kathmandu*	*Nepalese/Nepali*	*Nepali*	*Nepali rupee*
Nicaragua	Managua	nicaragüense *mf*	español	córdoba *m*
Nicaragua	*Managua*	*Nicaraguan*	*Spanish*	*córdoba*
Niger	Niamey	nigerino,-a *m,f*	francés	franco CFA *m*
Níger	*Niamey*	*Nigerien*	*French*	*CFA franc*
Nigeria	Abuja	nigerino,-a *m,f*	inglés	naira nigeriana *f*
Nigeria	*Abuja*	*Nigerian*	*English*	*naira*
Niue (Nueva Zelanda)	Alofi	de Niue	inglés	dólar neozelandés *m*
Niue (New Zealand)	*Alofi*	*from Niue*	*English*	*New Zealand dollar*
Norfolk (Australia)	Kingston	de Norfolk	inglés	dólar australiano *m*
Norfolk Island (Australia)	*Kingston*	*Norfolk Islander*	*English*	*Australian dollar*
Noruega	Oslo	noruego,-a *m,f*	noruego	corona noruega *f*
Norway	*Oslo*	*Norse/Norwegian*	*Norwegian*	*Norwegian krone*
Nueva Caledonia (Francia)	Nouméa	de Nueva Caledonia	francés	franco del Pacífico *m*
New Caledonia (France)	*Nouméa*	*from New Caledonia*	*French*	*Pacific franc*
Nueva Zelanda	Wellington	neozelandés,-esa *m,f*	inglés, maorí	dólar neozelandés *m*
New Zealand	*Wellington*	*New Zealander*	*English, Maori*	*New Zealand dollar*
Omán	Mascate	omaní *m,f*	árabe	rial omaní *m*
Oman	*Muscat*	*Omani*	*Arabic*	*Omani rial*
País de Gales	Cardiff	galés,-esa *m,f*	inglés, galés	libra esterlina f
Wales	*Cardiff*	*Welshman, Welshwoman*	*English, Welsh*	*Sterling pound*
Países Bajos/ Holanda	Amsterdam, La Haya *(sede del gobierno)*	holandés,-esa *m,fl* neerlandés,-esa *m,f*	holandés	florín *m*
Netherlands, the/ Holland	*Amsterdam, The Hague (seat of government)*	*Dutchman, Dutchwoman/ Netherlander*	*Dutch*	*guilder*
Palaos (EE.UU.)	Koror	de Palaos	inglés, sonsorolese-tobiano	dólar americano *m*
Palau (US)	*Koror*	*Palavan*	*English, Sonsorolese-Tobian*	*US dollar*
Panamá	Panamá	panameño,-a *m,f*	español	balboa *m*
Panama	*Panama City*	*Panamanian*	*Spanish*	*balboa*
Papua Nueva Guinea	Port Moresby	papuano,-a *m,fl* papú *mf*	inglés	kina *f*
Papua New Guinea	*Port Moresby*	*Papua New Guinean, Papuan*	*English*	*kina*

Países y dependencias principales	Capital	Habitante	Lengua(s) oficial(es)	Moneda
Countries and principal dependencies *	*Capital*	*Inhabitant* **	*Official language(s)* ***	Currency

Paquistán/Pakistán	Islamabad	paquistaní *mf*	urdu, inglés	rupia paquistaní *f*
Pakistan	*Islamabad*	*Pakistani*	*Urdu, English*	*Pakistan rupee*
Paraguay	Asunción	paraguayo,-a *m,f*	español	guaraní paraguayo *m*
Paraguay	*Asunción*	*Paraguayan*	*Spanish*	*guaraní*
Perú	Lima	peruano,-a *m,f*	español, quechua	sol *m*
Peru	*Lima*	*Peruvian*	*Spanish, Quechua*	*nuevo sol*
Pitcairn (R.U.)	Adamstown	de Pitcairn	inglés	dólar neozelandés *m*
Pitcairn Islands (UK)	*Adamstown*	*from Pitcairn*	*English*	*New Zealand dollar*
Polinesia Francesa (Francia)	Papeete	de la Polinesia Francesa	francés	franco del Pacífico *m*
French Polynesia (France)	*Papeete*	*French Polynesian*	*French*	*Pacific franc*
Polonia	Varsovia	polonés,-esa *m,f/* polaco,-a *m,f*	polaco	zloty *m*
Poland	*Warsaw*	*Pole*	*Polish*	*zloty*
Portugal	Lisboa	portugués,-esa *m,f*	portugués	escudo *m*
Portugal	*Lisbon*	*Portuguese*	*portuguese*	*escudo*
Puerto Rico (EE.UU.)	San Juan	puertorriqueño,-a *m,f*	español, inglés	dólar americano *m*
Puerto Rico (US)	*San Juan*	*Puerto Rican*	*Spanish, English*	*US dollar*
Qatar/Katar	Doha	qatarí *mf/* katarí *mf*	árabe	rial de Qatar *m*
Qatar	*Doha*	*Qatari*	*Arabic*	*Qatar riyal*
Reino Unido	Londres	británico,-a *m,f*	inglés	libra esterlina *f*
United Kingdom	*London*	*Briton*	*English*	*Sterling pound*
República Centroafricana	Bangui	centroafricano,-a *m,f/*de la República Centroafricana	francés, sango	franco CFA *m*
Central African Republic	*Bangui*	*from the Central African Republic*	*French, Sango*	*CFA franc*
República Checa	Praga	checo,-a *m,f*	checo	corona checa *f*
Czech Republic	*Prague*	*Czech*	*Czech*	*czech koruna*
República Dominicana	Santo Domingo	dominicano,-a *m,f*	español	peso dominicano *m*
Dominican Republic	*Santo Domingo*	*Dominican*	*Spanish*	*Dominican peso*
República de Irlanda	Dublín	irlandés,-esa *m,f*	gaélico irlandés, inglés	libra irlandesa *f*
Republic of Ireland	*Dublin*	*Irishman, Irishwoman*	*Irish Gaelic, English*	*Irish pound/punt*
Reunión (Francia)	Saint-Denis	de Reunión	francés, criollo	franco francés *m*
Réunion (France)	*Saint Denis*	*from Réunion*	*French, Creole*	*French franc*
Ruanda	Kigali	ruandés,-esa *m,f*	francés, kinyaruanda	franco ruandés *m*
Rwanda	*Kigali*	*Rwandese/Rwandan*	*French, Kinyarwanda*	*Rwanda franc*

Países y dependencias principales	Capital	Habitante	Lengua(s) oficial(es)	Moneda
Countries and principal dependencies *	*Capital*	*Inhabitant* **	*Official language(s)* ***	Currency
Rumanía	Bucarest	rumano,-a *m,f*	rumano	leu *m*
Romania/Rumania	*Bucharest*	*Romanian/ Rumanian*	*Romanian*	*Romanian leu*
Rusia	Moscú	ruso,-a *m,f*	ruso	rublo *m*
Russia	*Moscow*	*Russian*	*Russian*	*rouble*
Sáhara Occidental (Marruecos)	El Aaiún	Saharaui *mf*	árabe	dirham *m*
Western Sahara (Morocco)	*Al-Aioun*	*Saharaui*	*Arabic*	*dirham*
Saint Kitts y Nevis	Basseterre	de Saint Kitts y Nevis	inglés	dólar del Caribe Oriental *m*
Saint Kitts and Nevis	*Basseterre*	*Kittsian and Nevisian*	*English*	*East Caribbean dollar*
Samoa Estadounidense (EE.UU.)	Fagatogo	samoano,-a *m,f*	inglés, samoano	dólar americano *m*
American Samoa (US)	*Fagatogo*	*Samoan*	*English, Samoan*	*US dollar*
Samoa Occidental	Apia	samoano,-a *m,f*	inglés, samoano	tala *m*
Western Samoa	*Apia*	*Western Samoan*	*English, Samoan*	*tala*
San Vicente y Granadinas	Kingstown	de San Vicente	inglés	dólar del Caribe Oriental *m*
Saint Vincent and the Grenadines	*Kingstown*	*St. Vincentian*	*English*	*East Caribbean dollar*
San Marino	San Marino	sanmarinense *mf,* sanmarinés,-esa *m,f*	italiano	lira italiana *f,* lira de San Marino *f*
San Marino	*San Marino*	*San Marinese*	*Italian*	*Italian lira, San Marino lira*
Santa Helena y dependencias (R.U.)	Jamestown	de Santa Helena	inglés	libra esterlina *f*
St. Helena and dependencies (UK)	*Jamestown*	*from St. Helena*	*English*	*Sterling pound*
Santa Lucía	Castries	santalucense *mf*	inglés	dólar del Caribe Oriental *m*
Saint Lucia	*Castries*	*Saint Lucian*	*English*	*East Caribbean dollar*
St. Pierre y Miquelon (Francia)	St. Pierre	de St. Pierre	francés	franco francés *m*
St. Pierre and Miquelon (France)	*St. Pierre*	*from St. Pierre*	*French*	*French franc*
Santo Tomé y Principe	Santo Tomé	santomense *mf*	portugués	dobra *f*
São Tomé and Principe	*São Tomé*	*São Toméan*	*Portuguese*	*dobra*
Senegal	Dakar	senegalés,-esa *m,f*	francés	franco CFA *m*
Senegal	*Dakar*	*Senegalese*	*French*	*CFA franc*

Países y dependencias principales	Capital	Habitante	Lengua(s) oficial(es)	Moneda
Countries and principal dependencies *	*Capital*	*Inhabitant* **	*Official language(s)* ***	Currency
Seychelles	Victoria	de Seychelles	inglés, francés, criollo	rupia de Seychelles *f*
Seychelles	*Victoria*	*Seychellois*	*English, French, Creole*	*Seychelles rupee*
Sierra Leona	Freetown	sierraleonense *mf* sierraleonés,-esa *m,f*	inglés	leone *m*
Sierra Leone	*Freetown*	*Sierra Leonean*	*English*	*leone*
Singapore/Singapur	Singapur	singapurense *mf*	chino, malayo, inglés, tamil	dólar de Singapur *m*
Singapore	*Singapore*	*Singaporean*	*Chinese, Malay, English, Tamil*	*Singapore dollar*
Siria	Damasco	sirio,-a *mf*	árabe	libra siria *f*
Syria	*Damascus*	*Syrian*	*Arabic*	*Syrian pound*
Somalia	Mogadiscio	somalí *mf*	somalí	chelín somalí *m*
Somalia	*Mogadishu*	*Somali*	*Somali*	*Somali shilling*
Sri Lanka	Colombo	srilanqués,-esa, *m,f* cingalés,-esa *m,f*	cingalés, tamil	rupia de Sri Lanka *f*
Sri Lanka	*Colombo*	*Sri Lankan*	*Singhala, Tamil*	*Sri Lanka rupee*
Sudáfrica/ República Sudafricana	Pretoria (administrativa), Ciudad del Cabo (legislativa)	sudafricano,-a *m,f*	afrikaans, inglés	rand sudafricano *m*
South Africa	*Pretoria (administrative), Cape Town (legislative)*	*South African*	*Afrikaans, English*	*South African rand*
Sudán	Jartum	sudanés,-esa *m,f*	árabe	libra sudanesa *f*
Sudan	*Khartoum*	*Sudanese*	*Arabic*	*Sudanese pound*
Suecia	Estocolmo	sueco,-a *m,f*	sueco	corona sueca *f*
Sweden	*Stockholm*	*Swede*	*Swedish*	*Swedish krona*
Suiza	Berna	suizo,-a *m,f*	francés, alemán, italiano, romanche	franco suizo *m*
Switzerland	*Bern*	*Swiss*	*French, German, Italian, Romansch*	*Swiss franc*
Surinam	Paramaribo	surinamés,-esa *m,f* surinamita *mf*	holandés	florín de Surinam *m*
Suriname	*Paramaribo*	*Surinamese*	*Dutch*	*Suriname guilder*
Svalbard (Noruega)	Longyearbyen	de Svalbard	noruego, ruso	corona noruega *f*
Svalbard (Norway)	*Longyearbyen*	*from Svalbard*	*Norwegian, Russian*	*Norwegian krone*
Swazilandia	Mbabane	suazi *mf* swazilandés,-esa *m,f*	siswati, inglés	lilangeni *m*
Swaziland	*Mbabane*	*Swazi*	*Siswati, English*	*lilangeni*
Tailandia	Bangkok	tailandés,-esa *m,f*	tai	baht *m*
Thailand	*Bangkok*	*Thai*	*Thai*	*baht*
Taiwán	Taipei/Taipeh	taiwanés,-esa *m,f*	chino mandarín	nuevo dolár de Taiwán *m*
Taiwan	*Taipei*	*Taiwanese*	*Mandarin Chinese*	*New Taiwan dollar*

Países y dependencias principales	Capital	Habitante	Lengua(s) oficial(es)	Moneda
Countries and principal dependencies *	*Capital*	*Inhabitant* **	*Official language(s)* ***	Currency
Tanzania	Dodoma	tanzanés,-esa *m,f*/ tanzano,-a *m,f*	suahili, inglés	chelín de Tanzania *m*
Tanzania	*Dodoma*	*Tanzanian*	*Swahili, English*	*Tanzanian shilling*
Tayikistán	Dushanbe	tayiko,-a *m,f*	tayiko	rublo *m*
Tajikistan	*Dushanbe*	*Tajikistani*	*Tajik*	*rouble*
Togo	Lomé	togolés,-esa *m,f*	francés	franco CFA *m*
Togo	*Lomé*	*Togolese*	*French*	*CFA franc*
Tonga	Nuku'alofa	tongano,-a *m,f*	inglés, tongano	pa'anga *m*
Tonga	*Nuku'alofa*	*Tongan*	*English, Tongan*	*pa'anga*
Trinidad y Tobago	Puerto España	trinidense *m,f*/de Trinidad y Tobago/ trinitario,-a *m,f*	inglés	dólar de Trinidad y Tobago *m*
Trinidad and Tobago	*Port of Spain*	*Trinidadian/ Tobagoan/ Tobagodian*	*English*	*Trinidad and Tobago dollar*
Tunicia	Túnez	tunecino,-a *m,f*	árabe	dinar tunecino *m*
Tunisia	*Tunis*	*Tunisian*	*Arabic*	*Tunisian dinar*
Turcas y Caicos (R.U.)	Cockburn Town	de las Islas Turcas	inglés	dólar americano *m*
Turks and Caicos Islands (UK)	*Cockburn Town*	*from the Turks and Caicos Islands*	*English*	*US dollar*
Turkmenistán	Asjabad	turkmeno,-a *m,f*	turkmeno, ruso	manat *m*
Turkmenistan	*Ashkhabad*	*Turkmenistani*	*Turkmen, Russian*	*manat*
Turquía	Ankara	turco,-a *m,f*	turco	lira turca *f*
Turkey	*Ankara*	*Turk*	*Turkish*	*Turkish lira*
Tuvalu	Vaiaku	de Tuvalu	inglés, tuvalu	dólar australiano *m*
Tuvalu	*Funafuti*	*Tuvaluan*	*English, Tuvaluan*	*Australian dollar*
Ucrania	Kiev	ucranio,-a *m,f*/ ucraniano,-a *m,f*	ucraniano, ruso	hryvnia *m*
Ukraine	*Kiev*	*Ukrainian*	*Ukrainian, Russian*	*hryvnia*
Uganda	Kampala	ugandés,-esa *m,f*	inglés	nuevo chelín ugandés *m*
Uganda	*Kampala*	*Ugandan*	*English*	*New Uganda shilling*
Uruguay	Montevideo	uruguayo,-a *m,f*	español	nuevo peso uruguayo *m*
Uruguay	*Montevideo*	*Uruguayan*	*Spanish*	*Uruguayan peso*
Uzbekistán	Tashkent	uzbeko,-a *m,f*	uzbeko	som *m*
Uzbekistan	*Tashkent*	*Uzbekistani*	*Uzbek*	*som*
Vanuatu	Port Vila	de Vanuatu	inglés, francés, bislama	vatu *m*
Vanuatu	*Port Vila*	*Vanuatuan*	*English, French, Bislama*	*vatu*
Venezuela	Caracas	venezolano,-a *m,f*	español	bolívar *m*
Venezuela	*Caracas*	*Venezuelan*	*Spanish*	*bolivar*
Vietnam	Hanoi	vietnamita *m,f*	vietnamita	dong *m*
Vietnam	*Hanoi*	*Vietnamese*	*Vietnamese*	*dong*

Países y dependencias principales	Capital	Habitante	Lengua(s) oficial(es)	Moneda
Countries and principal dependencies *	*Capital*	*Inhabitant* **	*Official language(s)* ***	Currency
Wallis y Futuna (Francia)	Mata-Utu	de Wallis y Futuna	francés, uveano	franco francés *m*
Wallis and Futuna Islands (France)	*Mata-Utu*	*from Wallis and Fortuna*	*French, Uvean*	*French franc*
Yemen, República del	Sana'a (*administrativa*), Adén (*comercial*)	yemení *mf*	árabe	rial del Yemen *m*, dinar yemení *m*
Yemen	*Sana'a (administrative), Aden (commercial)*	*Yemeni*	*Arabic*	*Yemeni riyal, dinar*
Yibuti	Yibuti	de Yibuti	árabe, francés	franco de Yibuti *m*
Djibouti	*Djibouti*	*Djibuti/Djibutian*	*Arabic, French*	*Djibouti franc*
Yugoslavia, República Federal de	Belgrado	yugoslavo,-a *m,f*	Serbian	dinar *m*
Yugoslavia, Federal Republic of	*Belgrade*	*Yugoslavian*	*serbio*	*dinar*
Zaire	Kinshasa	zairense *mf/* zaireño,-a *m,f*	francés	zaïre *m*
Zaïre	*Kinshasa*	*Zaïrese/Zairean*	*French*	*zaïre*
Zambia	Lusaka	zambiano,-a *m,f*	inglés	kwacha de Zambia *m*
Zambia	*Lusaka*	*Zambian*	*English*	*kwacha*
Zimbabwe/ Zimbabue	Harare	zimbabuense *mf/* zimababuo,-a *m,f*	inglés	dólar de Zimbabwe *m*
Zimbabwe	*Harare*	*Zimbabwean*	*English*	*Zimbabwe dollar*

*Las dependencias y colonias llevan en paréntesis el país del que dependen/Controlling countries of dependencies and colonies are shown in brackets

**Cuando no existe un gentilicio, se utiliza la forma '(ser) de + nombre del país o dependencia'/Where no name exists for the inhabitant of a country, the form '(to be) from + country/dependency' is used in place of the noun

***Todas las lenguas oficiales de este listado aparecen en masculino/All official languages listed in this table are given in the masculine form

Husos horarios/Time zones

Nombre español *Spanish name*	Nombre inglés *English name*
diferencias horarias internacionales *f pl*	international time differences
hora británica *f*	British Standard Time
hora centroeuropea *f*	Central European Time
hora central establecida *f*	Central Standard Time
hora de la Costa Oeste *f*	Pacific Standard Time
hora local *f*	local time
hora media de Greenwich *f*	Greenwich Mean Time
hora del meridiano de Greenwich *f*	Greenwich Mean Time
hora del meridiano 75 al oeste de Greenwich *f*	Eastern Standard Time
hora de las Montañas Rocosas *f*	Mountain Standard Time
hora universal coordinada *f*	coordinated universal time
horario de Europa Oriental *m*	Eastern European Time
horario de verano británico *m*	British Summer Time
huso horario internacional *m*	international time zone

ENGLISH–SPANISH DICTIONARY

DICCIONARIO INGLÉS–ESPAÑOL

A

A¹ *abbr* (*A-road*) TRANSP N (*carretera nacional*)

A²: **~ level** *n* (*Advanced Level General Certificate of Education*) WEL examen británico a nivel de bachillerato superior, ≈ Selectividad *f*, ≈ C.O.U. (*Curso de Orientación Universitaria*); **~ shares** *n pl* BrE FIN, STOCK acciones clase A *f pl*

AA *abbr* INS (*average adjuster*) ajustador(a) de averías *m,f*, árbitro(-a) de seguros marítimos *m,f*; TRANSP BrE (*Automobile Association*) organización británica para el automovilista, ≈ ADA (*Esp*) (*Ayuda del Automovilista*), ≈ RAC (*Real Automóvil Club*)

AAA¹ *abbr* INS (*Association of Average Adjusters*) asociación de tasadores de daños, TRANSP (*American Automobile Association*) organización estadounidense para el automovilista, ≈ ADA (*Esp*) (*Ayuda del Automovilista*), ≈ RAC (*Real Automóvil Club*)

AAA²: **~ bond** *n* FIN, STOCK *Standard & Poor's* bono clase AAA *m*

AAAA *abbr* (*American Association of Advertising Agencies*) S&M asociación estadounidense de agencias de publicidad

AACC *abbr* (*Airport Associations Coordinating Council*) TRANSP consejo coordinador de asociaciones aeroportuarias, ≈ AENA (*Aeropuertos Españoles y Navegación Aérea*)

AACCA *abbr* (*Associate of the Association of Certified and Corporate Accountants*) ACC miembro de la asociación de contables de empresas autorizados

AAD *abbr* (*at a discount*) FIN *forward markets* por debajo del cambio, S&M con descuento

AAIA *abbr* (*Associate of the Association of International Accountants*) ACC miembro de la asociación de contables internacionales

AAR *abbr* (*against all risks*) INS a todo riesgo, contra todo riesgo

AAS *abbr* (*annual automated controls survey*) TRANSP *shipping* inspección anual de controles automatizados *f*

AASO *abbr* (*Association of American Shipowners*) TRANSP asociación estadounidense de armadores

AAT *abbr* (*Association of Accounting Technicians*) ACC organización de técnicos contables

ABAA *abbr* (*Associate of the British Association of Accountants & Auditors*) ACC miembro asociado de la asociación británica de contables y auditores

abandon *vt* GEN COMM ceder, abandonar, IMP/EXP *goods in customs*, PATENTS, STOCK *option* abandonar; ◆ **~ a claim** LAW desistir de una reclamación; **~ ship** TRANSP abandonar el buque

abandoned *adj* GEN COMM abandonado

abandonment *n* IND *complaint*, INS *marine*, LAW, S&M *complaint*, STOCK *option* abandono *m*; **~ clause** INS *marine* cláusula de abandono *f*

A-base *n* ACC base A *f*; **~ review** ACC revisión base A *f*

abate *vt* FIN *levy* reducir, GEN COMM *taxes, prices* rebajar, reducir, disminuir, LAW extinguir, TAX reducir

abatement *n* FIN *levy* reducción *f*, GEN COMM *taxes, prices* reducción *f*, rebaja *f*, disminución *f*, LAW *of contract* extinción *f*, TAX reducción del tipo impositivo *f*

abbreviate *vt* GEN COMM abreviar

abbreviation *n* GEN COMM abreviatura *f*

ABC¹ *abbr* ACC (*activity-based costing*) cálculo de costes basado en la actividad *m* (*Esp*), cálculo de costos basado en la actividad *m* (*AmL*), MEDIA (*Australian Broadcasting Corporation*) organismo de radiodifusión australiana, S&M (*Audit Bureau of Circulation*) OJD (*Oficina de Justificación de la Difusión*), TRANSP (*Advance Booking Charter*) flete reservado por adelantado *m*

ABC²: **~ method** *n* ACC, MGMNT *inventory management* método ABC *m*

ABCC *abbr* ECON, IND (*Association of British Chambers of Commerce*) asociación de cámaras de comercio británicas

abeyance: **in ~** *phr* GEN COMM en desuso, LAW, PROP en suspenso

abide by *vt* GEN COMM *rule, decision* atenerse a

abilities *n* GEN COMM aptitudes *f pl*

ability *n* ECON, GEN COMM capacidad *f*; **~ grouping** WEL agrupación por aptitud *f*; **~ level** WEL nivel de aptitud *m*, nivel de capacidad *m*; **~ to earn** GEN COMM facultad para ganar *f*; **~ to pay** HRM, LAW, TAX capacidad de pago *f*; **~ to repay** BANK capacidad de pago *f*

able: **~ to work** *adj* HRM apto para el trabajo

abnormal¹ *adj* GEN COMM anormal

abnormal²: **~ indivisible load** *n* TRANSP carga irregular indivisible *f*; **~ profit** *n* ACC, HRM beneficio extraordinario *m*

aboard *adv* GEN COMM a bordo

abolish *vt* GEN COMM, POL *frontier controls* abolir, derogar

abolition *n* GEN COMM *of trade controls* supresión *f*, abolición *f*, derogación *f*, LAW, POL abolición *f*

abort¹ *n* COMP cancelación *f*, supresión *f*

abort² *vt* COMP *program, operation* interrumpir, *program* cancelar, abandonar, GEN COMM *mission, trial, launch* interrumpir

abortive: **~ benefits** *n pl* TAX beneficios frustrados *m pl*

above¹: **~-average** *adj* GEN COMM por encima de la media; **~-board** *adj* GEN COMM *action, deal* legítimo, *person* sincero; **~-deck** *adj* (*AD*) TRANSP sobre cubierta; **~-mentioned** *adj* COMMS susodicho, antes citado; **~-named** *adj* COMMS arriba mencionado; **~ par** *adj* ACC por encima del valor nominal, sobre la par, GEN COMM con prima, sobre la par, STOCK *price of bonds* por encima del valor nominal, sobre la par

above²: **~-market price** *n* STOCK *options on currency futures* por encima del precio de mercado

above³: **the ~ address** *phr* COMMS, GEN COMM la dirección arriba indicada

ABP *abbr* (*Associated British Ports*) TRANSP asociación británica de puertos

abreaction: **~ channels** *n pl* HRM, MGMNT canales de abreacción *m pl*, canales de expresión *m pl*

abreast: be ~ of *phr* GEN COMM *developments* mantenerse informado de

abroad *adv* GEN COMM fuera

abrogate *vt* LAW, TAX abrogar

abrogation *n* LAW, TAX abrogación *f*

ABS *abbr* (*American Bureau of Shipping*) TRANSP sociedad clasificadora de buques

abscond *vi* LAW fugarse

absence *n* GEN COMM ausencia *f*, LAW ausencia *f*, incomparecencia *f*, S&M ausencia *f*; **~ of consideration** FIN, GEN COMM falta de consideración *f*; **~ without leave** HRM ausencia sin permiso *f*; ◆ **in the ~ of** GEN COMM *information* ante la ausencia de, *news* a falta de, *person* en ausencia de; **in the ~ of evidence to the contrary** LAW a falta de pruebas en contra

absent *adj* GEN COMM, LAW ausente

absentee *n* GEN COMM, LAW ausentado(-a) *m,f*, absentista *mf*; **~ owner** LAW, PROP propietario(-a) absentista *m,f*, propietario(-a) ausente *m,f*; **~ rate** GEN COMM, HRM nivel de absentismo *m*

absenteeism *n* HRM absentismo *m*

absolute[1] *adj* LAW *contracts* firme, *court order, decree* definitivo; ◆ **in ~ terms** ECON en términos absolutos

absolute[2]: **~ address** *n* COMMS, COMP dirección absoluta *f*; **~ addressing** *n* COMP direccionamiento absoluto *m*; **~ advantage** *n* ECON ventaja absoluta *f*; **~ concentration** *n* ECON concentración absoluta *f*; **~ endorsement** *n* BANK, GEN COMM endoso absoluto *m*; **~ error** *n* MATH error absoluto *m*; **~ frequency** *n* MATH frecuencia absoluta *f*; **~ income hypothesis** *n* ECON hipótesis de la renta absoluta *f*; **~ liability** *n* LAW responsabilidad objetiva *f*; **~ majority** *n* POL mayoría absoluta *f*; **~ monopoly** *n* ECON, FIN, S&M monopolio absoluto *m*; **~ ownership** *n* FIN, PROP propiedad total *f*; **~ poor** *n pl* ECON, HRM, WEL personas en situación de pobreza absoluta *f pl*; **~ poverty** *n* ECON, WEL miseria absoluta *f*, pobreza absoluta *f*; **~ priority rule** *n* FIN regla de prioridad absoluta *f*; **~ sale** *n* S&M venta irrevocable *f*; **~ scarcity** *n* ECON escasez absoluta *f*; **~ surplus value** *n* ECON valor absoluto del excedente *m*; **~ tax incidence** *n* TAX incidencia fiscal total *f*; **~ title** *n* PROP derecho absoluto *m*

absolutely: ~ or contingently *phr* TAX absoluta o contingentemente

absorb *vt* ACC, GEN COMM, STOCK *costs, profits*, POL *vote* absorber; ◆ **~ overheads** ACC absorber gastos generales; **~ a surplus** GEN COMM absorber un excedente

absorbed[1] *adj* ACC *cost*, ECON, GEN COMM, STOCK *securities* absorbido

absorbed[2]: **~ cost** *n* ACC coste absorbido *m* (*Esp*), costo absorbido *m* (*AmL*)

absorbing: ~ capacity *n* STOCK *security market* capacidad de absorción *f*; **~ company** *n* ECON empresa absorbente *f*

absorption *n* GEN COMM *costs, profits, business*, POL absorción *f*; **~ approach** ECON enfoque de la absorción *m*; **~ costing** ACC cálculo de costes de absorción *m* (*Esp*), cálculo de costos de absorción *m* (*AmL*), costeo por absorción *m* (*AmL*); **~ rate** S&M índice de absorción *m*

absorptive: ~ capacity *n* ECON capacidad de absorción *f*

abstain *vi* POL *in election* abstenerse

abstainer: ~'s insurance *n* INS seguro de abstemio *m*

abstention *n* POL abstención *f*

abstinence *n* ECON abstención *f*

abstract *n* ECON, FIN, GEN COMM *summary* resumen *m*, extracto *m*, LAW compendio *m*, extracto *m*; **~ of accounts** BANK, FIN extracto de cuentas *m*; **~ labor** *AmE*, **~ labour** *BrE* HRM trabajo abstracto *m*; **~ of record** LAW resumen de los autos *m*; **~ of title** LAW documento que señala los antecedentes de propiedad de un inmueble desde su primer asiento registral

ABT *abbr* (*American Board of Trade*) ECON, IND Cámara de Comercio Americana *f*

ABTA *abbr* (*Association of British Travel Agents*) LEIS asociación británica de agentes de viaje

ABTC *abbr* (*Australian British Trade Association*) ECON, IND asociación comercial australiano-británica

abundance *n* GEN COMM abundancia *f*

abundant *adj* GEN COMM abundante

abuse[1] *n* GEN COMM, LAW, PATENTS abuso *m*; **~ administrative authority** LAW abuso de autoridad administrativa *m*; **~ of authority** LAW abuso de autoridad *f*; **~ of confidence** LAW abuso de confianza *m*; **~ of power** LAW abuso de poder *m*; **~ of rights** LAW abuso de derecho *m*; **~ of trust** LAW abuso de confianza *m*

abuse[2] *vt* GEN COMM, LAW, PATENTS abusar

abusive: ~ practice *n* S&M *of the seller* práctica abusiva *f*

ac *abbr* (*airfreight container*) TRANSP contenedor de flete aéreo *m*

a/c *abbr* (*account*) ACC, BANK, FIN c/, cta. (*cuenta*)

AC *abbr* ECON (*advanced country*) país desarrollado *m*, GEN COMM (*authorization under consideration*) autorización en trámite *f*, HRM, TRANSP (*assistant controller*) interventor(a) adjunto(-a) *m,f*

ACA *abbr* (*Accredited Chartered Accountant*) ACC ≈ Contable Colegiado(-a) *m,f* (*Esp*), ≈ Contador(a) Autorizado(-a) Colegiado(-a) *m,f* (*AmL*)

academic[1] *adj* WEL académico

academic[2]: **~ research** *n* WEL investigación académica *f*

ACAS *abbr* (*Advisory, Conciliation and Arbitration Service*) HRM, MGMNT *industrial relations* organismo independiente británico que media entre dos partes confrontadas, ≈ IMAC (*Instituto de Mediación, Arbitraje y Conciliación*)

ACB *abbr* (*adjusted cost basis*) ACC, TAX base de coste ajustada *f* (*Esp*), base de coste corregida *f* (*Esp*), base de costo ajustada *f* (*AmL*), base de costo corregida *f* (*AmL*)

Acc *abbr* (*accountancy*) ACC contabilidad *f*

ACC *abbr* IND (*American Chamber of Commerce*) Cámara de Comercio Americana *f*, TRANSP (*automatic control certified*) control automático autorizado *m*

ACCA *abbr* ACC (*Associate of the Chartered Association of Certified Accountants*) miembro asociado del colegio de contables, TAX (*accelerated capital cost allowance*) amortiguaciones fiscales rápidas *f pl*

accelerable: ~ guarantee *n* FIN garantía acelerable *f*

accelerate 1. *vt* GEN COMM acelerar, adelantar; **2.** *vi* GEN COMM acelerar

accelerated[1] *adj* GEN COMM *training courses* acelerado

accelerated[2]: **~ amortization** *n* ACC, GEN COMM amortización acelerada *f*; **~ capital cost allowance** *n* (*ACCA*) TAX amortiguaciones fiscales rápidas *f pl*, deducción por amortizaciones fiscales rápidas *f*; **~ conversion** *n*

BANK *debentures* conversión acelerada *f*; ~ **cost recovery system** *n* (*ACRS*) ACC, FIN *economic accounting* sistema de recuperación acelerada de costes *m* (*Esp*), sistema de recuperación acelerada de costos *m* (*AmL*); ~ **depreciation** *n* ACC, FIN, GEN COMM *economic accounting* amortización acelerada *f*, depreciación acelerada *f*; ~ **motion** *n* S&M cámara rápida *f*; ~ **redemption** *n* GEN COMM amortización acelerada *f*; ~ **surface post** *n* COMMS *by land or sea* correspondencia rápida *f*; ~ **training course** *n* GEN COMM curso acelerado *m*

acceleration *n* GEN COMM *real estate* aceleración *f*; ~ **clause** BANK *mortgages* cláusula de aceleración *f*, PROP *mortgages* cláusula de reintegro del salto pendiente *f*; ~ **clause premium** BANK, FIN prima de cláusula de aceleración *f*, LAW prima por cláusula de vencimiento anticipado *f*; ~ **of maturity** BANK anticipación del vencimiento *f*; ~ **premium** HRM prima de aceleración *f*, IND prima de rendimiento *f*; ~ **principle** ECON *investment* principio de aceleración *m*

accelerator *n* ECON *investment* acelerador *m*; ~ **card** COMP tarjeta aceleradora *f*; ~ **principle** ECON *investment* principio del acelerador *m*

accentuate *vt* GEN COMM poner el acento en

accept *vt* BANK *credit card*, COMMS *call*, GEN COMM *request, suggestion, wish* aceptar; ◆ ~ **apologies** COMMS aceptar disculpas; ~ **a bid** GEN COMM, STOCK aceptar una oferta; ~ **a bill** GEN COMM comprometerse a pagar una factura; ~ **cash payments only** GEN COMM, HRM cobrar al contado; ~ **a collect call** *AmE* (*cf accept a reverse-charge call BrE*) COMMS aceptar una llamada a cobro revertido; ~ **delivery** GEN COMM aceptar la entrega; ~ **liability** GEN COMM aceptar la obligación; ~ **no liability** GEN COMM no aceptar ninguna responsabilidad; ~ **on presentation** GEN COMM aceptar a su presentación; ~ **payment** BANK, FIN aceptar en pago; ~ **a reverse-charge call** *BrE* (*cf accept a collect call AmE*) COMMS aceptar una llamada a cobro revertido; ~ **a tender** GEN COMM, STOCK aceptar una oferta

acceptability *n* GEN COMM aceptabilidad *f*, admisibilidad *f*, LAW *of evidence* admisibilidad *f*

acceptable[1] *adj* GEN COMM aceptable; ◆ **of ~ quality** GEN COMM de calidad aceptable

acceptable[2]: ~ **container condition** *n* (*ACC*) TRANSP *shipping* estado aceptable del contenedor *m*; ~ **investment** *n* TAX inversión aceptable *f*; ~ **price** *n* GEN COMM precio aceptable *m*

acceptance *n* GEN COMM *of brand* aceptación *f*; ~ **account** BANK cuenta de aceptación *f*; ~ **against documents** BANK aceptación contra documentos *f*; ~ **bill** BANK, GEN COMM letra aceptada *f*; ~ **by intervention** GEN COMM aceptación por intervención *f*; ~ **certificate** TRANSP certificado de aceptación *m*; ~ **commission** BANK comisión de aceptación *f*; ~ **credit** BANK crédito de aceptación *m*; ~ **of delivery** GEN COMM, STOCK aceptación de entrega *f*; ~ **duty** BANK derechos de aceptación *m pl*, impuesto de aceptación *m*; ~ **facility** BANK servicio financiero de aceptación *m*; ~ **fee** BANK comisión de aceptación *f*, cuota de aceptación *f*; ~ **for honour** GEN COMM aceptación por el honor de la firma *f*; ~ **house** BANK banco de aceptación *m*; ~ **ledger** ACC libro de letras aceptadas *m*; ~ **line** BANK línea de aceptación *f*; ~ **of lump-sum settlement** GEN COMM aceptación de pago a tanto alzado *f*; ~ **market** BANK mercado de efectos

aceptados *m*; ~ **price** BANK precio de aceptación *m*; ~ **register** BANK registro de letras aceptadas *m*; ~ **sampling** S&M *quality control* muestreo para aceptación *m*; ~ **slip** INS borderó de aceptación *m*; ~ **supra protest** BANK, FIN aceptación después del protesto *f*, GEN COMM aceptación bajo protesta *f*; ~ **test** S&M prueba de acogida *f*; ~ **trial** IND, S&M, TRANSP prueba de recepción *f*, prueba de aceptación *f*, prueba de admisión *f*

accepted[1] *adj* GEN COMM aceptado (*acept.*)

accepted[2]: ~ **draft** *n* BANK giro aceptado *m*; ~ **liability** *n* ACC, BANK pasivo aceptado *m*; ~ **pairing** *n* S&M *market research* paridad aceptada *f*

accepting: ~ **bank** *n* BANK banco de aceptación *m*; ~ **banker** *n* BANK bancario(-a) de aceptación *m,f*; ~ **house** *n* BANK, FIN casa de aceptaciones *f*

acceptor *n* BANK *bill* aceptante *m,f*

access[1] *n* COMP, GEN COMM acceso *m* (*Esp*), ingreso *m* (*AmL*); ~ **code** COMP código de acceso *m* (*Esp*), código de ingreso *m* (*AmL*); ~ **control** COMP *auditing* control de acceso *m* (*Esp*), control de ingreso *m* (*AmL*); ~ **cycle** BANK, FIN, GEN COMM, MGMNT ciclo de acceso *m* (*Esp*), ciclo de ingreso *m* (*AmL*); ~ **differential** ECON diferencial de acceso *m* (*Esp*), diferencial de ingreso *m* (*AmL*); ~ **right** COMP, LAW, PROP derecho de acceso *m* (*Esp*), derecho de ingreso (*AmL*); ~ **time** COMP tiempo de acceso *m* (*Esp*), tiempo de ingreso *m* (*AmL*)

access[2] *vt* COMP *database* acceder

accessibility *n* GEN COMM *of information, to public places* accesibilidad *f*

accessible[1] *adj* GEN COMM accesible

accessible[2]: **always ~** *phr* TRANSP siempre accesible

accession *n* POL *to the EU* adhesión *f*, PROP acceso *m*

accessorial: ~ **service** *n* S&M servicio adicional *m*

accessory[1] *adj* GEN COMM, LAW accesorio, subsidiario

accessory[2]: ~ **advertising** *n* S&M publicidad secundaria *f*

accident *n* GEN COMM accidente *m*; ~ **and health insurance** INS seguro de accidentes y de enfermedad *m*; ~ **insurance** INS seguro contra accidentes *m*; ~ **prevention** HRM, INS prevención de accidentes *f*; ~ **risk** INS riesgo de accidente *m*; ~ **to conveyance** INS accidente durante el transporte *m*

accidents: ~ **at sea** *n pl* INS accidentes en el mar *m pl*

accommodate *vt* BANK *sb with loan* favorecer, GEN COMM *in office* alojar, acomodar, WEL *lodging* admitir

accommodating: ~ **credit** *n* ACC crédito ajustado *m*, crédito de favor *m*

accommodation *n* BANK, FIN crédito *m*, GEN COMM *compromise* arreglo *m*, LEIS, PROP, TAX, WEL *lodging* alojamiento *m*; ~ **acceptance** GEN COMM aceptación de complacencia *f*; ~ **address** COMMS dirección temporal *f*; ~ **agency** WEL agencia de alojamiento *f*; ~ **allowance** GEN COMM, HRM subsidio de alojamiento *m*, asignación para vivienda *f*, WEL asignación para vivienda *f*; ~ **berth** TRANSP fondeadero *m*; ~ **bill** BANK, FIN, GEN COMM pagaré de favor *m*; ~ **bureau** WEL oficina de alojamiento *f*; ~ **draft** BANK giro avalado *m*, FIN, GEN COMM giro de favor *m*; ~ **endorsement** BANK, FIN, GEN COMM endoso de favor *m*, endoso de crédito *m*, endoso de garantía *m*, endoso por aval *m*; ~ **endorser** FIN endosante por aval *m*; ~ **maker** FIN librador(a) de un pagaré de favor *m,f*; ~ **note** BANK pagaré avalado *m*; ~ **paper** BANK, GEN COMM documento de garantía *m*, papel avalado *m*; ~ **party** FIN firmante de favor *mf*;

~ **payment** FIN pago por aval *m*, GEN COMM pago de deferencia *m*; ~ **road** TRANSP camino de servicio *m*

accommodatory: ~ **credit** *n* IMP/EXP crédito con garantía personal *m*

accompanied[1]: ~ **baggage** *n* TRANSP equipaje acompañado *m*

accompanied[2]: ~ **by** *phr* GEN COMM acompañado por

accompany *vt* GEN COMM *escort* acompañar

accompanying: ~ **document** *n* ADMIN, COMMS documento adjunto *m*; ~ **letter** *n* ADMIN, COMMS carta de compañía *f*

accomplish *vt* GEN COMM *task* cumplir, efectuar, lograr, HRM conseguir

accomplishment *n* GEN COMM *of task* cumplimiento *m*, HRM *of aim* consecución *f*, logro *m*, *skill* talento *m*, mérito *m*

accord *n* GEN COMM acuerdo *m*; ~ **and satisfaction** FIN *bond, debenture* acuerdo y satisfacción *m*

accordance: **in** ~ **with** *phr* ACC *accounting principles*, GEN COMM de conformidad con; **in** ~ **with your instructions** *phr* GEN COMM de acuerdo con sus instrucciones

according: ~ **to** *phr* GEN COMM en función de, *in agreement with* conforme a, de acuerdo con, *document, person* según; ~ **to the norm** *phr* LAW conforme a la norma; ~ **to plan** *phr* GEN COMM conforme al plan; ~ **to schedule** *phr* GEN COMM según lo previsto, de acuerdo al horario, de acuerdo al programa

accordingly *adv* GEN COMM de conformidad

account *n* (*a/c, c/, acct.*) ACC, BANK, COMP, FIN, GEN COMM, TAX cuenta *f* (*cta.*); ~ **activity** BANK movimiento de la cuenta *m*; ~ **activity charge** BANK cargo por el movimiento de la cuenta *m*; ~ **analysis** BANK análisis de cuentas *m*; ~ **book** ACC libro de cuentas *m*; ~ **card** ACC ficha de cuenta *f*; ~ **conflict** S&M conflicto contable *m*; ~ **day** FIN día de cuenta *m*; ~ **executive** HRM ejecutivo(-a) de cuentas *m,f*, jefe(-a) de cuentas *m,f*, MEDIA *advertising* ejecutivo(-a) de cuentas *m,f*, STOCK *brokerage firm* director(a) de cuentas *m,f*, ejecutivo(-a) de cuentas *m,f*; ~ **form** ACC estado de cuentas *m*, *balance sheet* balance de cuentas *m*; ~ **format** ACC formato de cuenta *m*; ~ **group** S&M grupo de cuentas *m*; ~ **holder** BANK titular de una cuenta *mf*; ~ **maintenance charge** BANK cargo por mantenimiento de la cuenta *m*; ~ **maintenance fee** BANK comisión de mantenimiento de cuenta *f*, cuota de mantenimiento de cuenta *f*; ~ **management** BANK administración de una cuenta *f*, gestión de una cuenta *f*; ~ **manager** BANK gestor(a) de cuentas *m,f*, HRM ejecutivo(-a) de cuentas *m,f*, MEDIA *advertising* gerente de cuentas *mf*, S&M *advertising* director(a) de cuentas *m,f*; ~ **market** STOCK mercado contable *m*; ~ **movements** *n pl* ACC movimientos de la cuenta *m pl*; ~ **name** ACC, BANK nombre de cuenta *m*; ~ **number** ACC código contable *m*, número de cuenta *m*, BANK, TAX número de cuenta *m*; ~**-only check** *AmE*, ~**-only cheque** *BrE* BANK, FIN cheque sólo para depositar *m*; ~ **operation** BANK manejo de una cuenta *m*; ~ **operation charge** BANK cargo por las operaciones en cuenta *m*; ~ **payee** BANK *on cheque* tenedor(a) de cuenta *m,f*; ~ **period** STOCK periodo de contratación bursátil a crédito *m*, periodo de contratación bursátil a cuenta *m*; ~ **planning** MEDIA *advertising*, S&M planificación contable *f*; ~ **reconcilement** ACC conciliación de cuentas *f*; ~ **reconciliation** ACC conciliación de cuentas *f*;

~ **rendered** BANK cuenta pendiente de aprobación *f*; ~ **settled** ACC, BANK, FIN cuenta saldada *f*; ~ **statement** GEN COMM estado de cuentas *m*, *figure itself* estado de cuenta *m*, saldo de cuenta *m*; ~ **title** ACC, BANK denominación de una cuenta *f*; ~ **transaction** ACC, FIN transacción a cuenta *f*, transacción en cuenta *f*; ~ **turnover** ACC movimiento de la cuenta *m*, rotación de la cuenta *f*; ♦ **my** ~ (*m/a*) BANK mi cuenta; ~ **of** GEN COMM cuenta de; **on** ~ GEN COMM, S&M en cuenta; **on** ~ **of** GEN COMM a cuenta de, debido a, por causa de, a favor de, en favor de; **on no** ~ GEN COMM en ningún caso

account for *vt* GEN COMM rendir cuenta de

accountability *n* GEN COMM responsabilidad *f*; ~ **in management** MGMNT responsabilidad en la administración *f*, responsabilidad en la gestión *f*

accountable: ~ **advance** *n* ACC anticipo contable *m*; ~ **officer** *n* ACC funcionario(-a) responsable *m,f*; ~ **receipt** *n* ACC recibo contable *m*

accountancy *n* (*Acc*) ACC, GEN COMM contabilidad *f*, contaduría *f*; ~ **fees** ACC minutas contables *f pl*; ~ **profession** ACC profesión contable *f*; ~ **service** ACC servicio contable *m*

accountant *n* ACC contable *mf* (*Esp*), contador(a) *m,f* (*AmL*); ~ **general** (*A.G.*) ACC jefe(-a) de contabilidad *m,f*; ~**'s professional liability insurance** ACC, INS seguro de responsabilidad profesional del contable *m*

accounting *n* ACC contabilidad *f*, contabilización *f*; ~ **adjustment** ACC ajuste contable *m*; ~ **analysis** ACC análisis contable *m*; ~ **balance of payments** ACC, ECON contabilidad de la balanza de pagos *f*, balanza de pagos *f*; ~ **change** ACC cambio contable *m*, modificación contable *f*; ~ **clerk** ACC empleado(-a) de contabilidad *m*; ~ **control** ACC *auditing* control contable *m*; ~ **convention** ACC práctica contable *f*; ~ **costs** *n pl* ACC costes contables *m pl* (*Esp*), costos contables *m pl* (*AmL*); ~ **cycle** ACC ciclo contable *m*; ~ **data** *n pl* ACC datos contables *m pl*; ~ **department** ACC departamento de contabilidad *m* (*Esp*), contaduría *f* (*AmL*); ~ **doctrines** *n pl* ACC doctrinas contables *f pl*; ~ **effect** ACC *rules application* efecto contable *m*; ~ **entity** ACC entidad contable *f*; ~ **entry** ACC asiento contable *m*; ~ **equation** ACC ecuación contable *f*; ~ **error** ACC error contable *m*; ~ **evaluation** ACC evaluación contable *f*; ~ **fees** *n pl* ACC tarifas contables *f pl*; ~ **file** ACC fichero contable *m*; ~ **firm** ACC firma contable *f*; ~ **harmonization** ACC armonización contable *f*; ~ **identity** ACC identidad contable *f*; ~ **income** ACC *revenue*, TAX ingreso contable *m*, renta contable *f*; ~ **law** LAW ley contable *f*, ley de contabilidad *f*; ~ **method** ACC método contable *m*; ~ **model** ACC, FIN modelo contable *m*; ~ **office** ACC *of government department* contaduría *f* (*AmL*), departamento de contabilidad *m* (*Esp*), oficina de contabilidad *f* (*Esp*); ~ **officer** ACC, HRM jefe(-a) de contabilidad *m,f*; ~ **package** ACC, COMP conjunto de programas de contabilidad *m*, paquete de contabilidad, *m*, paquete contable *m*, FIN conjunto de programas de contabilidad *m,f*; ~ **papers** *n pl* ACC papeles contables *m pl*; ~ **period** ACC, FIN periodo contable *m*; ~ **plan** ACC plan de contabilidad *m*; ~ **policy** ACC política contable *f*; ~ **practice** ACC práctica contable *f*; ~ **price** BANK precio contable *m*; ~ **principle** ACC principio de contabilidad *m*; ~ **procedure** ACC procedimiento de contabilidad *m*; ~ **profit** ACC beneficio contable *m*, beneficio del ejercicio *m*; ~ **rate of interest** (*ARI*) ACC, FIN, GEN COMM tasa de interés de cuenta *f*, tipo de interés de cuenta *f*, tasa de interés acumulado *f*; ~ **rate of return** (*ARR*) ACC tasa de rendimiento contable *f*, tipo de rendimiento contable *m*; ~ **ratio** ACC proporción contable *f*, FIN coeficiente contable *m*; ~ **records** *n pl* ACC registros de contabilidad *m pl*; ~ **report** ACC estado contable *m*, informe contable *m*, (*Esp*), reporte contable *m* (*AmL*); ~ **return** ACC beneficio contable *m*; ~ **software** ACC, COMP aplicación informática para contabilidad *f*, programas de contabilidad *m pl*, software de contabilidad *m*; ~ **standard** ACC norma contable *f*, norma de contabilidad *f*; ~ **standard setting** ACC establecimiento de normas de contabilidad *m*; ~ **system** ACC sistema contable *m*; ~ **treatment** ACC tratamiento contable *m*; ~ **year** ACC, ECON, FIN año contable *m*; ~ **year then ended** ACC año contable finalizado *m*; ◆ **for ~ purposes** ACC a efectos contables

Accounting: ~ **Principles Board** *n AmE* (*APB, cf Accounting Standards Board BrE*) ACC junta reguladora estadounidense de los estándars de contabilidad; ~ **Standards Board** *n BrE* (*cf Accounting Principles Board AmE*) ACC junta reguladora británica de los estándars de contabilidad

accounts *n pl* FIN *of the company* GEN COMM cuentas *f pl*; ~ **appraisal** *n* ACC *auditing* estimación contable *f*; ~ **certification** *n* ACC *auditing* certificación de cuentas *f*, revisión de cuentas *f*, verificación de cuentas *f*; ~ **close-off** *n* BANK bloqueo de cuentas *m*; ~ **department** *n* ACC departamento de contabilidad *m* (*Esp*), contaduría *f* (*AmL*); ~ **payable** ACC cuentas a pagar *f pl*; ~ **payable clerk** *n* ACC auxiliar de cuentas a pagar *mf*, empleado(-a) de cuentas a pagar *m,f*; ~ **payable ledger** *n* ACC libro mayor de compras *m*, libro mayor de cuentas a pagar *m*, libro mayor de proveedores *m*; ~ **receivable** ACC cuentas a cobrar *f pl*; ~ **receivable financing** *n* ACC financiación mediante cuentas a cobrar *f*; ~ **receivable ledger** *n* ACC libro mayor de clientes *m*, libro mayor de cuentas a cobrar *m*, libro mayor de ventas *m*; ~ **receivable statement** *n* ACC estado de cuentas a cobrar *m*; ~ **receivable turnover** *n* ACC proporción de ventas a crédito *f*, ratio de ventas a crédito *m*

accrd. int. *abbr* (*accrued interest*) BANK interés acumulado *m*, interés devengado *m*

accredit *vt* GEN COMM *representative, official* dar credenciales a, *guarantee* acreditar, WEL *guarantee* acreditar

accreditation *n* GEN COMM, WEL *institution, qualification* acreditación *f*

accredited[1] *adj* GEN COMM, WEL acreditado

accredited[2]: ~ **investor** *n* STOCK inversor(a) acreditado(-a) *m*

Accredited: ~ **Chartered Accountant** *n* (*ACA*) ACC ≈ Contable Colegiado(-a) *m,f* (*Esp*), ≈ Contador(a) Autorizado(-a) Colegiado(-a) *m,f* (*AmL*)

accretion *n* ACC, GEN COMM acrecimiento *m*, STOCK aumento *m*

accrual *n* ACC, BANK, FIN acumulación *f*, devengo *m*; ~ **accounting** ACC contabilidad a base de ingresos y gastos *f*, contabilidad acumulativa *f*, contabilidad diferida *f*, contabilidad en valores devengables *f*; ~ **basis** ACC base de acumulación *f*; ~ **basis of accounting** ACC base acumulable de contabilidad *f*; ~ **concept** ACC concepto de acumulación *m*; ~ **date**

ACC fecha de acumulación *f*, fecha de devengo *f*; ~ **of exchange** ECON afluencia de divisas *f*; ~ **of interest** BANK acumulación de intereses *f*; ~ **interest rate** ACC tasa de interés acumulado *f*, tasa de interés devengado *f*, tipo de interés devengado *m*; ~ **method** ACC método de acumulación *m*; ~ **principle** ACC principio de acumulación *m*, principio del devengo *m*; ~ **property income** TAX rendimiento acumulado de la propiedad *m*

accruals *n pl* ACC, BANK, FIN acumulaciones *f pl*

accrue 1. *vt* ACC, BANK, FIN acumular, devengar; ◆ ~ **interest** BANK acumular interés; 2. *vi* ACC, BANK *expense*, FIN acumular, devengar

accrued[1] *adj* GEN COMM *interest* acumulado, devengado

accrued[2]: ~ **asset** *n* ACC activo acumulado *m*, activo devengado *m*; ~ **charge** *n* ACC, BANK, FIN cargo devengado *m*; ~ **charges** *n pl* BANK cargos acumulados *m pl*; ~ **compound interest** *n* BANK interés compuesto acumulado *m*; ~ **dividend** *n* ACC, STOCK dividendo acumulado *m*, dividendo devengado *m*; ~ **expense** *n* ACC gasto acumulado *m*, gasto devengado *m*; ~ **expenses** *n pl* GEN COMM gastos devengados *m pl*; ~ **income** *n* ACC ingresos acumulados *m pl*; ~ **interest** *n* (*accrd. int., AI*) BANK interés acumulado *m*, interés devengado *m*; ~ **interest payable** *n* ACC, BANK intereses acumulados por pagar *m pl*; ~ **interest receivable** *n* ACC, BANK intereses acumulados por cobrar *m pl*; ~ **liability** *n* ACC, BANK pasivo acumulado *m*, pasivo devengado *m*; ~ **receivable and pre-paid expenses** *n pl* ACC efectos a cobrar acumulados y gastos anticipados *m pl*; ~ **revenue** *n* ACC ingresos acumulados *m pl*; ~ **taxes** *n* TAX impuestos acumulados *m pl*

accruing *adj* ACC, FIN *interests* devengado

acct. *abbr* (*account*) ACC, BANK, FIN cuenta *f* (*cta.*)

accumulate 1. *vt* ACC, BANK, FIN acumular, GEN COMM *products* acopiar; 2. *vi* GEN COMM acumularse

accumulated[1] *adj* ACC *expenses, revenue*, BANK *interest*, FIN *expenses, revenue* acumulado, GEN COMM acopiado

accumulated[2]: ~ **averaging amount** *n* TAX cantidad media acumulada *f*; ~ **averaging amount withdrawal** *n* TAX retirada de la cantidad media acumulada *f*; ~ **balance** *n* TAX saldo acumulado *m*; ~ **deficit** *n* ACC, FIN, TAX déficit acumulado *m*; ~ **depletion** *n* ACC, FIN, STOCK amortización acumulada *f*, depreciación acumulada *f*; ~ **depreciation** *n* ACC depreciación acumulada *f*; ~ **dividend** *n* ACC, STOCK dividendo acumulado *m*; ~ **earnings tax** *n* TAX impuesto sobre las ganancias acumuladas *m*; ~ **interest** *n* (*AI*) GEN COMM interés acumulado *m*; ~ **profit** *n* ACC beneficio acumulado *m* (*Esp*), utilidad acumulada *f* (*AmL*); ~ **profits tax** *n* TAX impuesto sobre los beneficios acumulados *m*; ~ **surplus** *n* ACC excedente acumulado *m*, plusvalía acumulada *f*, superávit acumulado *m*

accumulating: ~ **fund** *n* TAX fondo acumulativo *m*; ~ **income** *n* TAX ingreso acumulativo *m*; ~ **income of the trust** *n* TAX ingreso acumulativo del fideicomiso *m*

accumulation *n* ACC, BANK, FIN acumulación *f*, GEN COMM *of capital, wealth, interest* acopio *m*; ~ **area** STOCK zona de acumulación *f*; ~ **factor** ECON factor de acumulación *m*; ~ **of risk** INS acumulación de riesgos *f*; ~ **risk** INS riesgo acumulativo *m*

accumulative *adj* GEN COMM *dividends* acumulativo

accuracy *n* ACC *figures, statement* exactitud *f*, GEN COMM *judgment* justeza *f*, *figures, data* exactitud *f*, *report, document, aim* precisión *f*, MATH exactitud *f*

accurate *adj* GEN COMM *description* ajustado, *figures, judgment* preciso, *report, aim* justo

accurately *adv* GEN COMM cabalmente

accusation *n* LAW acusación *f*; ◆ **bring an ~ against sb** LAW acusar a alguien

accuse *vt* LAW acusar

ACD *abbr* (*automated cash dispenser*) BANK cajero automático *m*, cajero bancario *m*

ACE *abbr* (*Amex Commodities Exchange*) STOCK Bolsa de Contratación Amex *f*, Bolsa de Productos Amex *f*

acetate *n* GEN COMM *projector* transparencia *f*

ACGI *abbr* BrE (*Associate of the City and Guilds of London Institute*) GEN COMM miembro asociado del Instituto City and Guilds de Londres

ACH *abbr* (*Automated Clearing House*) BANK Cámara de Compensación Automatizada *f*

achievable *adj* GEN COMM factible

achieve *vt* GEN COMM *growth, level, objective* lograr, obtener, *make real* realizar

achievement *n* GEN COMM *success* logro *m*, *of goal* realización *f*; ~ **motive** HRM motivo para el éxito *m*; ~ **quotient** GEN COMM coeficiente de rendimiento *m*; ~ **test** GEN COMM test de conocimientos específicos *m*

achiever *n* GEN COMM triunfador(a) *m,f*

acid: ~ **deposit** *n* ENVIR depósito de ácido *m*; ~ **rain** *n* ENVIR lluvia ácida *f*; ~ **rain pollution** *n* ENVIR contaminación por lluvia ácida *f*; ~ **test** *n* ACC, FIN, GEN COMM prueba de fuego *f* (*jarg*); ~ **test ratio** *n* ACC coeficiente de liquidez *m*, ratio de liquidez inmediata *m*

ACIS *abbr* (*Associate of the Chartered Institute of Secretaries*) HRM miembro asociado del colegio de secretarios

acknowledge *vt* GEN COMM admitir, *arrival* confirmar, *mistake* reconocer; ◆ ~ **receipt of** COMMS *letter, cheque,* FIN, GEN COMM *mail, goods* acusar recibo de; ~ **receipt by letter** COMMS, GEN COMM acusar recibo por carta

acknowledgement *n* (*Ackt.*) COMMS *on document* aceptación *f*, GEN COMM acuse de recibo *m*, *of payment* reconocimiento *m*, documento de aceptación *m*, LAW *of contract* documento de aceptación *m*; ~ **of debt** BANK, FIN, GEN COMM acuse de recepción de deuda *m*, reconocimiento de deuda *m*; ~ **of indebtness** BANK, FIN, GEN COMM reconocimiento de deuda *m*; ~ **of order** COMMS, GEN COMM confirmación de pedido *f*; ~ **of receipt** (*Ackt.*) COMMS, GEN COMM *payment* acuse de recibo *m*

Ackt. *abbr* COMMS (*acknowledgement of receipt*), GEN COMM (*acknowledgement*) acuse de recibo *m*

ACMA *abbr* (*Associate of the Chartered Institute of Management Accountants*) ACC miembro asociado del Colegio de Contables de gestión

ACOP *abbr* (*approved code of practice*) GEN COMM código de procedimiento aprobado *m*

acquaint: ~ **sb with the situation** *phr* GEN COMM advertir a uno de la situación, poner a uno al corriente de la situación

acquaintance *n* GEN COMM *person* conocido(-a) *m,f*

acquainted: **be ~ with** *phr* GEN COMM *fact, situation* conocer

acquest *n* LAW propiedad adquirida *f*

acquire *vt* GEN COMM adquirir; ◆ ~ **an interest** GEN COMM adquirir una participación, tomar una participación en; ~ **an option** STOCK adquirir una opción

acquired[1] *adj* GEN COMM adquirido

acquired[2]: ~ **company** *n* ECON empresa adquirida *f*; ~ **share** *n* AmE (*cf acquired stock BrE*) FIN, STOCK acción adquirida *f*; ~ **stock** *n* BrE (*cf acquired share AmE*) FIN, STOCK acción adquirida *f*; ~ **surplus** *n* FIN superávit obtenido *m*

acquiring: ~ **authority** *n* PROP *compulsory purchase* autoridad de adquisición *f*, centro de adquisición *m*; ~ **company** *n* GEN COMM *corporate takeover* compañía adquirente *f*

acquisition *n* ACC *subsidiary acquired by takeover,* FIN, GEN COMM *of company* compra *f*, adquisición *f*; ~ **accounting** ACC contabilidad de adquisiciones *f*, contabilidad de compras *f*; ~ **agent** GEN COMM agente comprador(a) *m,f*; ~ **of assets** ACC adquisición de activos *f*; ~ **commission** INS, STOCK comisión de adquisición *f*; ~ **contract** TAX contrato de adquisición *m*; ~ **cost** ACC, TAX coste de adquisición *m* (*Esp*), costo de adquisición *m* (*AmL*), precio de compra *m*; ~ **costs** *n pl* ACC, GEN COMM gastos de adquisición *m pl*; ~ **fee** ACC, GEN COMM gastos de adquisición *m pl*, INS, STOCK comisión de adquisición *f*; ~ **financing** FIN financiación de compra *f*; ~ **of goods** TAX adquisición de mercancías *f*; ~ **policy** STOCK política de adquisición *f*; ~ **price** FIN precio de adquisición *m*; ~ **profile** BANK *merchant* perfil de adquisición *m*; ~ **of shareholdings** STOCK adquisición de participación en acciones *f*; ~ **of stock** STOCK adquisición de acciones *f*; ~ **value** GEN COMM valor de adquisición *m*

acquisitive[1] *adj* FIN *company* codicioso

acquisitive[2]: ~ **instinct** *n* GEN COMM instinto adquisitivo *m*

acquit *vt* GEN COMM, LAW absolver, *debt, duty* descargar, pagar

acquittal *n* GEN COMM, LAW *of debt* descargo *m*, *of duty* desempeño *m*, *of the accused* absolución *f*

acquittance *n* LAW *confirmation* carta de pago *f*, *of debt* descargo *m*

acreage *n* GEN COMM superficie *f*

acronym *n* GEN COMM sigla *f*

across[1]: ~-**the-board** *adj* GEN COMM, HRM *reduction, increase* igual para todas las categorías, MGMNT *changes* que cubre todo, que cubre todo en general; ~-**the-counter** *adj* GEN COMM *purchases* bursátil, *sales* al contado (*Esp*), de contado AmL; ~-**the-network** *adj* S&M a través del sistema

across[2]: ~-**the-board** *adv* GEN COMM para todas las categorías

ACRS *abbr* (*accelerated cost recovery system*) ACC, FIN sistema de recuperación acelerada de costes *m* (*Esp*), sistema de recuperación acelerada de costos *m* (*AmL*)

ACS *abbr* (*Australian Container Service*) TRANSP *shipping* servicio australiano de contenedores

ACSS *abbr* (*Automated Clearing Settlement System*) BANK Sistema de Liquidación de Compensación Automatizado *m*

act[1] *n* GEN COMM acto *m*, LAW, POL ley *f*, ley parlamentaria *f*, acto *m*; ~ **of acknowledgement** LAW acto de reconocimiento *m*; ~ **of appraising damages** GEN COMM acto de daños tasados *m*; ~ **of bankruptcy** ACC, BANK acto de quiebra *m*; ~ **of cession** GEN COMM acto de cesión *m*; ~ **of honor** AmE, ~ **of honour** BrE LAW aceptación haciendo honor a la firma

act[2] *vi* GEN COMM actuar; ◆ ~ **bona fide** LAW actuar de buena fe; ~ **in the capacity of** GEN COMM actuar en calidad de; ~ **in good faith** LAW actuar de buena fe; ~ **on behalf of** LAW actuar en nombre de

act on *vt* GEN COMM *advice, suggestion* decidir

act upon *vt* GEN COMM *letter* actuar sobre

Act: ~ **of Congress** *n* *AmE* LAW, POL ≈ Ley de las Cortes *f*, ≈ Ley del Congreso *f*; ~ **of the House of Commons** *n* *BrE* LAW, POL ≈ Ley de las Cortes *f*, ≈ Ley del Congreso *f*; ~ **of Parliament** *n* *BrE* LAW Ley del Parlamento *f*

ACT *abbr* (*advance corporation tax*) TAX impuesto anticipado de sociedades *m*

acting: ~ **allowance** *n* GEN COMM asignación interina *f*; ~ **director** *n* HRM, MGMNT director(a) interino(-a) *m,f*; ~ **member** *n* HRM suplente *mf*; ~ **partner** *n* MGMNT socio(-a) en funciones *m,f*

actio in personam *phr* LAW acción contra persona *f*

actio in rem *phr* LAW acción contra la cosa *f*, acción contra la cosa misma *f*, acción in rem *f*

action[1]: ~-**oriented** *adj* GEN COMM de acción

action[2] *n* LAW proceso *m*; ~ **against sb** LAW proceso contra alguien *m*; ~ **code** COMP código de intervención *m*; ~ **for cancelation** *AmE*, ~ **for cancellation** *BrE* LAW condición resolutoria *f*; ~ **for damages** INS, LAW acción por daños y perjuicios *f*; ~ **for libel** LAW demanda por difamación *f*; ~ **message** COMP mensaje de intervención *m*; ~ **plan** GEN COMM plan de contingencia *m*, plan de acción *m*; ~ **program** *AmE*, ~ **programme** *BrE* GEN COMM programa de acción *m*; ~ **recourse** INS acción de recurso *f*; ~ **research** MGMNT búsqueda de acción *f*, investigación de acción *f*; ~ **statement** BANK, INS, LAW cláusula de decisión *f*; ◆ **bring an** ~ LAW iniciar un juicio, interponer una acción; **be out of** ~ COMMS, GEN COMM, IND *telephone, machine* estar fuera de servicio

actionable *adj* GEN COMM, HRM, LAW *claim* justiciable, *remark, offence, allegation* procesable

activate *vt* COMP *window, field*, GEN COMM activar

activated *adj* COMP, IND, MGMNT activado

active[1] *adj* GEN COMM en actividad, activo; ◆ **in** ~ **employment** HRM en empleo activo

active[2]: ~ **account** *n* ACC, BANK cuenta activa *f*; ~ **bond** *n* STOCK título al portador de gran liquidez *m*; ~ **bond crowd** *n* STOCK cantidad importante de obligaciones *f*, cantidad importante de títulos a interés fijo *f*; ~ **business** *n* GEN COMM comercio activo *m*; ~ **business asset test** *n* TAX prueba activa de recursos empresariales *f*; ~ **capital** *n* FIN capital activo *m*; ~ **computer** *n* COMP computador activo (*AmL*), computadora activa *f* (*AmL*), ordenador activo *m* (*Esp*); ~ **corps of executives** *n* HRM cuerpo ejecutivo activo *m*; ~ **dealing** *n* STOCK negociación activa *f*; ~ **demand** *n* ECON demanda activa *f*; ~ **file** *n* COMP fichero activo *m*; ~ **financing** *n* FIN financiación activa *f*; ~ **fiscal policy** *n* TAX política fiscal activa *f*; ~ **income** *n* TAX ingreso activo *m*; ~ **investment** *n* STOCK inversión activa *f*; ~ **investor** *n* STOCK inversor(a) activo(-a) *m,f*; ~ **management** *n* GEN COMM, MGMNT administración activa *f*, gestión activa *f*; ~ **market** *n* STOCK mercado activo *m*; ~ **money** *n* FIN dinero productivo *m*; ~ **partner** *n* MGMNT socio(-a) activo(-a) *m,f*; ~ **reinsurance** *n* INS reaseguro activo *m*; ~ **securities** *n pl* STOCK valores activos *m pl*; ~ **shares** *n pl* STOCK acciones activas *f pl*; ~ **trader** *n* S&M comerciante activo(-a) *m,f*; ~ **trading** *n* STOCK negociación activa *f*

actively: ~ **trade** *phr* *BrE* STOCK *shares* realizar un fuerte volumen de transacciones

activist *n* ECON militante *mf*, POL activista *mf*

activity *n* BANK *account*, GEN COMM actividad *f*; ~ **analysis** GEN COMM análisis de actividades *m*; ~-**based costing** (*ABC*) ACC cálculo de costes basado en la actividad *m* (*Esp*), cálculo de costos basado en la actividad *m* (*AmL*); ~ **charges** *n pl* BANK cargos por actividad *m pl*, gastos bancarios *m pl*; ~ **chart** MGMNT diagrama de actividad *m*; ~ **classification** ACC clasificación de actividad *f*; ~ **coding** ACC código de actividad *m*; ~ **element** ACC elemento de actividad *m*; ~ **factor** ECON factor de actividad *m*; ~ **rate** GEN COMM nivel de actividad *f*; ~ **ratio** GEN COMM tasa de actividad *f*; ~ **sampling** MATH *statistics* muestreo de una actividad *m*, MGMNT ejemplo de actividad *m*, S&M *market research* muestreo de una actividad *m*; ~ **total** GEN COMM total de la actividad *m*

ACTU *abbr* (*Australian Council of Trade Unions*) HRM confederación de sindicatos australianos

actual[1] *adj* ACC *figure* efectivo, verdadero, GEN COMM *physical commodity* efectivo, real

actual[2]: ~ **address** *n* COMP dirección real *f*; ~ **amount** *n* ACC *outlay, expenditure* cantidad real *f*, importe efectivo *m*; ~ **budget** *n* ACC, ECON, FIN, POL presupuesto actual *m*, presupuesto actualizado *m*, presupuesto corriente *m*; ~ **carrier** *n* TRANSP transportista real *mf*; ~ **cash disbursement** *n* ACC efectivo realmente desembolsado *m*; ~ **cash value** *n* (*ACV*) GEN COMM valor actual de venta *m*, valor real de venta *m*, valor real en efectivo *m*; ~ **cost** *n* ACC, TAX coste real *m* (*Esp*), costo real *m* (*AmL*); ~ **deficit** *n* ECON déficit actualizado *m*; ~ **earnings** *n pl* ACC, TAX ganancias corrientes *f pl*, ingresos corrientes *m pl*; ~ **eviction** *n* LAW desahucio efectivo *m*, PROP expulsión efectiva *f*; ~ **expenditures** *n pl* ACC gastos reales *m pl*; ~ **expense** *n* ACC gasto actual *m*; ~ **figures** *n pl* ECON cifras reales *f pl*; ~ **gross weight** *n* GEN COMM, TRANSP peso bruto real *m*; ~ **instruction** *n* COMP instrucción real *f*; ~ **inventory** *n* GEN COMM inventario actual *m*; ~ **investment** *n* BANK inversión real *f*; ~ **level of unemployment** *n* ECON, POL nivel actual de desempleo *m*, nivel real de desempleo *m*; ~ **loan loss** *n* BANK pérdidas totales por préstamos *f pl*; ~ **loan loss experience** *n* BANK antecedentes de pérdidas actuales por préstamos *m pl*; ~ **loss** *n* ACC pérdida real *f*; ~ **outcome** *n* GEN COMM resultado real *m*; ~ **payload** *n* TRANSP *net weight* carga útil real *f*; ~ **price** *n* ACC, ECON, S&M precio actual *m*, precio real *m*; ~ **quotation** *n* STOCK cotización real *f*; ~ **stock** *n* GEN COMM existencias reales *f pl*; ~ **tax rate** *n* TAX tipo impositivo real *m*; ~ **total loss** *n* INS *abandonment clauses* pérdida efectiva total *f*; ~ **volume** *n* IND *of production* volumen real *m*; ~ **yield** *n* STOCK *bond, investment* rendimiento actual *m*

actualize *vt* GEN COMM *represent realistically* actualizar

actuals *n pl* ACC, FIN, STOCK *physical commodity* disponibilidades *f pl*, efectivos *m pl*

actuarial[1] *adj* INS actuarial

actuarial[2]: ~ **basis** *n* ACC, BANK base actuarial *f*; ~ **certificate** *n* INS certificado actuarial *m*; ~ **deficit** *n* INS déficit actuarial *m*; ~ **department** *n* LAW departamento actuarial *m*; ~ **liability** *n* INS, LAW responsabilidad actuarial *f*; ~ **life expectation** *n* INS esperanza matemática de vida *f*; ~ **loss** *n* INS pérdida actuarial *f*; ~ **science** *n* INS ciencia actuarial *f*; ~ **statistics** *n* MATH estadística actuarial *f*

actuary *n* INS actuario(-a) *m,f*; ~**'s valuation** INS cálculo actuarial *m*

actuate *vt* GEN COMM, LEIS *person* actuar

actus reus *phr* LAW acción u omisión que constituyen delito

acute: ~ **awareness** *n* GEN COMM conocimiento profundo *m*

ACV *abbr* GEN COMM (*actual cash value*) valor actual de venta *m*, valor real de venta *m*, valor real en efectivo *m*, TRANSP (*air cushion vehicle*) vehículo con amortiguación por aire *m*

ad *n* (*advertisement*) GEN COMM, MEDIA, S&M anuncio *m* (*Esp*), cuña publicitaria *f* (*AmL*)

A/D *abbr* (*after date*) GEN COMM después de fecha, postdatado

Adam: ~ **Smith Institute** *n* BrE ECON, POL gabinete británico de estrategia económico y político

adapt *vt* COMP, GEN COMM, S&M adaptar

adaptability *n* COMP, GEN COMM adaptabilidad *f*, *of technology, procedure, project* adecuación *f*

adaptable *adj* COMP adaptable, GEN COMM adaptable, acomodadizo

adaptation *n* COMP, GEN COMM adaptación *f*

adapted *adj* COMP, GEN COMM, S&M adaptado

adaptive: ~ **control** *n* MGMNT control por adaptación *m*; ~ **expectations** *n pl* ECON expectativas adaptivas *f pl*

adaptor *n* COMP, GEN COMM adaptador *m*

AD-AS *abbr* (*aggregate demand-aggregate supply*) ECON, FIN demanda agregada-oferta agregada *f*

ADC *abbr* COMP (*analog-to-digital converter*) *hardware* conversor de analógico a digital *m*, GEN COMM (*advice of duration and/or change*) aviso de duración y/o cambio *m*

add[1]: ~ **listing machine** *n* GEN COMM sumadora con impresora *f*

add[2] *vt* ACC *figures*, STOCK añadir

add back *vt* MATH *sum* volver a sumar

add in *vt* GEN COMM *details, figures, statement* añadir

add together *vt* GEN COMM *figures, sums* sumar simultáneamente

add up *vt* GEN COMM totalizar, *figures, results* añadir, sumar

Add. *abbr* (*address*) COMMS, COMP Dir., dirección *f*

added[1]: ~**value** *adj* IND con valor agregado

added[2]: ~ **value** *n* GEN COMM valor añadido *m* (*Esp*), valor agregado *m* (*AmL*)

addendum *n* LAW anexo *m*, apéndice *m*, suplemento *m*, MEDIA *text amendment* adición *f*

adder *n* ACC sumador *m*

adding *n* MATH adición *f*; ~ **circuit** COMP circuito adicionador *m*; ~ **machine** COMP, GEN COMM máquina de sumar *f*, MATH sumadora *f*; ~**-up controversy** ECON controversia de la productividad marginal *f*

addition *n* ACC *to fixed assets, new asset*, COMP suma *f*, GEN COMM incremento *m*, MATH suma *f*, MEDIA *text amendment* adición *f*; ~ **to stock** ADMIN, S&M incremento de las existencias *m*; ♦ **no ~, no correction** GEN COMM sin adición, sin corrección; **in ~ to** GEN COMM además de

additional[1] *adj* GEN COMM, LAW accesorio

additional[2]: ~ **assessment** *n* TAX impuesto adicional *m*;

~ **charge** *n* ACC carga adicional *f*, coste adicional *m* (*Esp*), costo adicional *m* (*AmL*), gasto adicional *m*, suplemento *m*; ~ **clause** *n* LAW cláusula adicional *f*; ~ **conditions** *n pl* INS condiciones complementarias *f pl*; ~ **expense insurance** *n* INS seguro contra gastos adicionales *m*; ~ **facilities** *n pl* ECON *balance of payments* facilidades complementarias de crédito *f*; ~ **feature** *n* PATENTS, S&M característica adicional *f*; ~ **first-year depreciation** *n* AmE TAX amortización adicional del primer año *f*; ~ **interest** *n* ACC interés adicional *m*; ~ **labor** AmE, ~ **labour** BrE *n* HRM *task* trabajo adicional *m*, mano de obra adicional *f*, mano de obra suplementaria *f*; ~ **margin** *n* STOCK margen adicional *m*; ~ **mark-on** *n* S&M *retail merchandise price* margen adicional *m*; ~ **matter** *n* PATENTS cuestión adicional *f*; ~ **paid-in capital** AmE *n* (*cf additional paid-up capital BrE*) ACC capital adicional desembolsado (*Esp*), capital adicional integrado (*AmL*); ~ **paid-up capital** BrE *n* (*cf additional paid-in capital AmE*) ACC capital adicional desembolsado *m* (*Esp*), capital adicional integrado (*AmL*); ~ **pay** *n* HRM paga adicional *f*; ~ **personal allowance** *n* TAX desgravación personal adicional *f*; ~ **postage** *n* COMMS sobretasa postal *f*; ~ **premium** *n* (*AP*) INS prima complementaria *f*; ~ **security** *n* INS garantía suplementaria *f*; ~ **tax** *n* TAX impuesto complementario *m*; ~ **voluntary contributions** *n pl* BrE (*AVCs*) TAX cuotas voluntarias adicionales *f pl*; ~ **worker hypothesis** *n* ECON, HRM hipótesis del trabajador adicional *f*

additive: ~**-free** *adj* GEN COMM sin aditivos

add-on[1] *adj* BANK añadido, COMP incorporable, GEN COMM añadido

add-on[2] *n* BANK, GEN COMM añadido *m*; ~ **basis** GEN COMM base de tipo aditivo *f*; ~ **board** COMP tarjeta externa *f*; ~ **card** COMP tarjeta externa *f*; ~ **CDs** *n pl* BrE STOCK certificados de depósito aditivos *m pl*; ~ **certificates of deposit** *n pl* BrE (*add-on CDs*) STOCK certificados de depósito aditivos *m pl*; ~ **costs** *n pl* ACC costes incorporados *m pl* (*Esp*), costos incorporados *m pl* (*AmL*), MGMNT costes agregados *m pl* (*Esp*), costos agregados *m pl* (*AmL*); ~ **domestic certificates of deposit** *n pl* BrE (*add-on CDs*) STOCK certificados de depósito aditivos *m pl*, certificados nacionales de depósito aditivos *m pl*; ~ **equipment** COMP material complementario incorporable *m*, MGMNT equipo complementario *m*; ~ **interest** BANK interés aditivo *m*; ~ **memory** COMP memoria adicional *f*, memoria externa *f*; ~ **minimum tax** TAX impuesto mínimo añadido *m*; ~ **sales** *n pl* BrE S&M *market research* ventas subsecuentes a un cliente satisfecho; ~ **yield** STOCK rendimiento aditivo *m*; ~ **yield equivalent** STOCK *Treasury bills* equivalente de un rendimiento de tipo adicional

address[1] *n* (*Add.*) COMMS, COMP dirección *f*; ~ **book** COMMS libro de direcciones *m*; ~ **bus** COMP bus común de dirección *m*; ~ **commission** IMP/EXP, TRANSP comisión por solicitud *f*; ~ **field** COMP campo de dirección *m*; ~ **file** COMP fichero de direcciones *m*; ~ **label** COMMS etiqueta postal *f*; ~ **line** S&M línea para la dirección *f*

address[2] *vt* COMMS *parcel, envelope* remitir, *speech, talk* dirigir, *meeting* dirigirse a, GEN COMM *issue, problem* orientar, LAW dirigir; ♦ ~ **oneself to** GEN COMM *issue, problem* dedicarse a; ~ **complaints to** GEN COMM dirigir sus reclamaciones a

addressable *adj* COMMS direccionable

addressee *n* COMMS destinatario(-a) *m,f*

addressing *n* COMMS, COMP direccionamiento *m*; **~ machine** COMMS máquina de imprimir direcciones

Addressograph® *n* GEN COMM máquina de imprimir direcciones

adduce *vt* LAW *proof, reason* aducir

adequacy: **~ of coverage** *n* INS cobertura apropiada *f*

adequate[1] *adj* GEN COMM *funds, supply, explanation* adecuado

adequate[2]: **~ target rate** *n* ACC tipo indicativo adecuado *m*, tipo objetivo adecuado *m*

adequately: **~ funded** *adj* ACC adecuadamente fundado, GEN COMM con fondos adecuados

ADG *abbr* (*assistant director general*) HRM, MGMNT director(-a) *m,f*

adhere to *vt* GEN COMM *contracts* adherir a, *principle* atenerse a

adhesion: **~ contract** *n* LAW contrato de adhesión *m*; **~ insurance contract** *n* LAW contrato de seguros de adhesión *m*

ad hoc *adj* GEN COMM ad hoc; **~ committee** *n* GEN COMM comisión ad hoc *f*

ad idem *adv* GEN COMM al mismo efecto

ad infinitum *adv* GEN COMM al infinito

ad interim *adj* LAW *judgment* provisional

adjective: **~ law** *n* LAW derecho adjetivo *m*, derecho procesal *m*

adjoining *adj* GEN COMM contiguo

adjourn *vt* GEN COMM aplazar, LAW *case, trial* aplazar, levantar, suspender, MGMNT *meeting* aplazar, clausurar, suspender, terminar, PROP levantar; ♦ **~ sentence** LAW diferir sentencia

adjournment *n* GEN COMM aplazamiento *m*, LAW aplazamiento *m*, suspensión *f*, MGMNT *decision* aplazamiento *m*, suspensión *f*, *meeting* terminación *f*, clausura *f*; **~ debate** *BrE* POL *Parliament* debate de aplazamiento *m*

adjudge *vt* LAW *decree* decretar; ♦ **~ heavy damages** LAW declarar judicialmente fuertes daños

adjudicate *vt* GEN COMM, LAW *auctions, contracts* decidir, *contest* adjudicar, *claim* determinar judicialmente, S&M *auctions, contracts* adjudicar; ♦ **~ bankruptcy** ACC adjudicar una quiebra; **~ sb bankrupt** ACC declarar a alguien en bancarrota, declarar a alguien en quiebra

adjudication *n* ACC, GEN COMM adjudicación *f*, LAW adjudicación *f*, fallo *m*; **~ of bankruptcy order** ACC, FIN, GEN COMM, LAW declaración judicial de quiebra *f*, adjudicación de quiebra *f*

adjudicator *n* GEN COMM adjudicador(a) *m,f*

adjunct *n* GEN COMM ayudante(-a) *m,f*; **~ professor** *AmE* (*cf associate professor BrE*) HRM catedrático(-a) adjunto(-a) *m,f*

adjust *vt* ECON *price, amount, timetable* ajustar, GEN COMM regular, *mechanism, component, level* reajustar, ajustar, IND, INS ajustar, *claim* solventar; MATH *figures, error* corregir, ajustar, STOCK *price, amount, timetable* ajustar; ♦ **~ downwards** ECON, MATH ajustar a la baja; **~ oneself to** GEN COMM *situation* adaptarse a; **~ to** GEN COMM ajustar a; **~ upwards** ECON, MATH ajustar al alza

adjustable[1] *adj* FIN *mortgage rate, insurance policy* ajustable, GEN COMM regulable, *hours, rate* ajustable

adjustable[2]: **~ life insurance** *n* INS seguro de vida modificable *m*; **~ mortgage loan** *n* (*AML*) BANK, FIN,

PROP préstamo hipotecario ajustable *m*; **~ peg** *n* ECON *Bretton Woods agreement* ajuste del tipo de cambio *m*; **~ rate mortgage** *n* (*ARM*) BANK, FIN, PROP hipoteca de tasa ajustable *f*; **~ rate preferred stock** *n* (*ARP*) STOCK acción preferente de tipo ajustable *f*

adjusted[1] *adj* GEN COMM ajustado, MATH corregido, TAX ajustado

adjusted[2]: **~ basis** *n* TAX base ajustada *f*; **~ capital ratio** *n* BANK relación de capital ajustado *f*; **~ claim** *n* ECON reclamación solventada *f*; **~ cost base** *n* (*ACB*) ACC, TAX base de coste ajustada *f* (*Esp*), base de coste corregida *f* (*Esp*), base de costo ajustada *f* (*AmL*), base de costo corregida *f* (*AmL*); **~ cost basis** *n* (*ACB*) ACC, TAX base de coste ajustada *f* (*Esp*), base de coste corregida *f* (*Esp*), base de costo ajustada *f* (*AmL*), base de costo corregida *f* (*AmL*); **~ exercise price** *n* STOCK precio ajustado al ejercicio económico *m*; **~ gross income** *n* ACC, TAX ingreso bruto ajustado *m*; **~ income** *n* TAX ingreso ajustado *m*; **~ principal amount** *n* TAX cantidad principal ajustada *f*; **~ selling price** *n* ACC precio de venta ajustado *m*, precio de venta regulado *m*; **~ tax base** *n* TAX base imponible ajustada *f*; **~ tax payable** *n* TAX deuda tributaria ajustada *f*; **~ taxable income** *n* TAX ingreso imponible ajustado *m*; **~ total capital ratio** *n* BANK, FIN proporción de capital total compensado *f*, relación de capital total compensado *f*; **~ trial balance** *n* ACC balance de comprobación ajustado *m*, balance de comprobación de saldos con cuentas regularizadas *m*

adjuster *n* INS tasador(a) *m,f*

adjusting: **~ entry** *n* ACC asiento de actualización *m*, asiento de ajuste *m*, contrapartida *f*

adjustment *n* ACC *of statistics, error, accrual accounting*, ECON *of prices, rates, charges, wages* ajuste *m*, GEN COMM adaptación *f*, *of position, speed* ajuste *m*, *to situation* adecuación *f*, INS repartición *f*, MATH *of value* corrección *f*; **~ account** ACC cuenta de ajuste *f*, cuenta de regulación *f*; **~ of accounts receivable** ACC ajuste de las cuentas a cobrar *m*; **~ bond** FIN, STOCK bono secundario *m*; **~ center** *AmE*, **~ centre** *BrE* WEL centro de ajuste *m*; **~ clause** INS cláusula de finiquito *f*; **~ costs** *n pl* INS gastos de liquidación *m pl*; **~ gap** ECON ajuste del déficit *m*; **~ limit** TAX límite de ajuste *m*; **~ premium at maturity** INS ajuste de prima al vencimiento *m*; **~ speed** ECON ajuste de la velocidad en la tasa de producción *m*; **~ to cost base** TAX ajuste al coste base *m* (*Esp*), ajuste al costo base *m* (*AmL*); **~ trigger** GEN COMM activador de ajuste *m*

adman *n infrml* (*advertising man*) HRM *professional working in advertising* hombre anuncio *m*, profesional de la publicidad *mf*

admass *adj* GEN COMM *culture, society* cautivo de la publicidad

admin. *abbr* (*administration*) ADMIN, GEN COMM, HRM, MGMNT admón. (*administración*)

administer *vt* GEN COMM administrar, controlar

administered[1] *adj* GEN COMM controlado, administrado

administered[2]: **~ inflation** *n* ECON inflación controlada *f*; **~ price** *n* S&M *theory* precio administrado *m*; **~ pricing** *n* ECON precios controlados *m pl*

administration *n* (*admin.*) ADMIN, GEN COMM, HRM, MGMNT administración *f* (*admón.*), gestión *f*, POL *ministry* administración pública *f*, PROP *of estate, inheritance* administración *f*; **~ costs** *n pl* ACC, ADMIN gastos de administración *m pl*; ~ **expenses** *n pl* ACC, ADMIN gastos de administración *m pl*; ~ **lag** ADMIN, ECON retardo administrativo *m*; ~ **letter** ACC, ADMIN, BANK carta administrativa *f*; ~ **officer** (*AO*) HRM jefe(-a) administrativo(-a) *m,f*; ~ **order** ADMIN, LAW orden administrativa *f*; ~-**production ratio** ADMIN, FIN, IND relación administración-producción *f*

administrative[1] *adj* GEN COMM administrativo; ◆ **take ~ control of a company** GEN COMM, MGMNT tomar el control administrativo de una compañía

administrative[2]: ~ **activity element** *n* ACC elemento de la actividad administrativa *m*; ~ **agent** *n* ADMIN, HRM gestor(a) administrativo(-a) *m,f*; ~ **assistant** *n* ADMIN, HRM auxiliar administrativo(-a) *m,f*; ~ **audit** *n* ACC, HRM auditoría administrativa *f*; ~ **authority** *n* GEN COMM potestad administrativa *f*; ~ **board** *n* HRM consejo administrativo *m*; ~ **burden** *n* ACC, ADMIN gastos administrativos *m pl*; ~ **center** *AmE*, ~ **centre** *BrE n* ADMIN centro administrativo *m*; ~ **charge** *n* INS gasto administrativo *m*; ~ **control procedure** *n* ADMIN procedimiento de control administrativo *m*; ~ **cost** *n* TAX coste administrativo *m* (*Esp*), costo administrativo *m* (*AmL*); ~ **costs** *n* ADMIN, GEN COMM costes administrativos *m pl* (*Esp*), costos administrativos *m pl* (*AmL*); ~ **expenses** *n pl* ACC, ADMIN gastos administrativos *m pl*; ~ **file** *n* ADMIN expediente administrativo *m*; ~ **law** *n* LAW derecho administrativo *m*; ~ **machinery** *n* GEN COMM aparato administrativo *m*; ~ **management society** *n* FIN, MGMNT sociedad de gestión administrativa *f*; ~ **and organizational controls** *n pl* ACC *auditing* controles administrativos y organizacionales *m pl*; ~ **overheads** *n pl* FIN, GEN COMM gastos generales de administración *m pl*; ~ **point of view** *n* (*APV*) ADMIN, MGMNT punto de vista administrativo *m*, punto de vista de la administración *m*; ~ **services only** *n* ADMIN, FIN sólo servicios administrativos; ~ **staff** *n pl* HRM personal administrativo *m*; ~ **theory** *n* ADMIN, MGMNT teoría de la administración *f*, teoría administrativa *f*; ~ **work** *n* ADMIN, HRM trabajo administrativo *m*

administrator *n* ADMIN administrador(a) *m,f*, COMP *software* gestor(a) *m,f*, GEN COMM, HRM, LAW, PROP *of estate, inheritance* administrador(a) *m,f*; ~'**s deed** LAW escritura del administrador *f*

admissibility *n* ECON *of money*, GEN COMM, LAW admisibilidad *f*

admissible[1] *adj* ECON, GEN COMM, LAW admisible

admissible[2]: ~ **claim** *n* PATENTS solicitud admisible *f*

admission *n* GEN COMM, HRM, IMP/EXP *customs* admisión *f*, LAW *of crime* confesión *f*; ~ **fee** GEN COMM derechos de admisión *m pl*; ~ **free** LEIS admisión gratuita *f*; ~ **of securities** FIN admisión de acciones, bonos y valores *f*; ~ **to listing** STOCK admisión a la cotización *f*; ~ **to quotation** STOCK admisión a la cotización *f*; ◆ **by his own ~** GEN COMM por su propia admisión

admit *vt* GEN COMM admitir, *request, suggestion, wish* aceptar, HRM *new partners to business*, INS *claim* admitir; ◆ ~ **to the Bar** LAW admitir en el Colegio de abogados

admittance: no ~ *phr* GEN COMM prohibida la entrada

admitted: ~ **company** *n* FIN, GEN COMM, HRM compañía autorizada *f*

adopt *vt* ECON, GEN COMM *procedures, resolutions*, MGMNT adoptar; ◆ ~ **a joint stance** GEN COMM adoptar una postura conjunta

adoption *n* ECON *of single currency*, MGMNT adopción *f*; ~ **process** S&M *of product* proceso de adopción *m*

ADP *abbr* (*automatic data processing*) COMP PAD (*proceso automático de datos*)

ADR *abbr* ACC (*asset depreciation range*) escala de amortización de activos *f*, FIN (*American Depositary Receipt*) recibo estadounidense de depósito de acciones

adrail *n* S&M *railway station* panel publicitario *m*

adrate *n* S&M tarifa publicitaria *f*

adrift *adj* TRANSP a la deriva

adshel *n* S&M *bus stop* panel publicitario *m*

adult[1] *adj* LAW mayor de edad

adult[2]: ~ **fare** *n* GEN COMM, TRANSP tarifa de adulto *f*; ~ **population** *n* GEN COMM población adulta *f*

adulteration: ~ **of proceedings** *n* LAW falsificación de actas *f*

ADV *abbr* (*advice enclosed*) COMMS contiene carta de aviso, contiene aviso

ad val *abbr* (*ad valorem*) GEN COMM ad valórem, sobre el valor

ad valorem[1] *adj* (*ad val*) GEN COMM, TAX ad valórem, sobre el valor

ad valorem[2]: ~ **bill of lading** *n* IMP/EXP, TRANSP conocimiento de embarque sobre el valor *m*; ~ **duty** *n* ACC, IMP/EXP, TRANSP arancel sobre el valor *m*, derecho de aduana ad valórem *m*; ~ **freight** *n* TRANSP flete sobre el valor *m*; ~ **rate** *n* ACC tarifa ad valórem *f*; ~ **tax** *n* ACC, IMP/EXP impuesto ad valórem *m*

advance[1]: **in** ~ *adv* GEN COMM por adelantado, por anticipado

advance[2] *n* BANK anticipo *m*, GEN COMM *in technology* adelanto *m*, *loan* anticipo *m*, *of civilization, in science* progreso *m*, STOCK anticipo *m*, *of prices* alza *m*; ~ **account** ACC cuenta de anticipos *f*; ~ **against goods** GEN COMM anticipo contra entrega de productos *m*; ~ **against security** GEN COMM préstamo con garantía pignoraticia *m*; ~ **arrangement** TRANSP *shipping* acuerdo anticipado *m*, acuerdo de anticipo *m*; ~ **bill** FIN efecto anticipado *m*; ~ **billing** ACC facturación anticipada *f*; ~ **booking** *BrE* (*cf advance reservation AmE*) LEIS *hotel* reserva anticipada *f*, *theatre, restaurant* venta anticipada *f*; ~ **booking office** LEIS taquilla de venta anticipada *f*; ~ **freight** (*AF*) IMP/EXP, TRANSP anticipo sobre el flete *m*, flete pagado por adelantado; ~-**funded pension plan** FIN *personal* plan de pensiones dotado por adelantado *m*; ~ **guarantee** STOCK garantía anticipada *f*; ~ **guaranty** *see advance guarantee*; ~ **holder** BANK titular anterior *mf*; ~ **income tax ruling** TAX decisión sobre el impuesto de la renta que sirve como precedente; ~ **corporation tax** (*ACT*) TAX impuesto anticipado de sociedades *m*; ~ **notice** LAW preaviso *m*; ~ **on goods** GEN COMM adelanto sobre mercancías *m*; ~ **on salary** HRM anticipo salarial *m*; ~ **on securities** *BrE* STOCK anticipo sobre valores *m*; ~ **payment** GEN COMM pago anticipado *m*; ~ **payment bond** FIN, STOCK bono de pago anticipado *m*; ~ **payment guarantee** IMP/EXP garantía con pago anticipado *f*; ~ **premium** INS prima pagada por adelantado *f*; ~ **publicity** MEDIA, S&M *product launch* publicidad anticipada *f*; ~ **refunding** STOCK *government securities* reembolso anticipado *m*; ~ **repayment** GEN COMM reembolso anticipado *m*; ~ **reservation** *AmE* (*cf advance booking BrE*) LEIS *hotel* reserva anticipada *f*, *theatre, restaurant* venta anticipada; ~ **royalty payment**

TAX pago anticipado de derechos *m*; ~ **security** STOCK valor anticipado *m*; ~ **selling** STOCK *security* venta anticipada *f*; ~ **of special survey** TRANSP avance de reconocimiento extraordinario *m*

advance[3] **1.** *vt* ADMIN adelantar, COMP *tape* avanzar, GEN COMM avanzar, adelantar; ♦ ~ **a loan** BANK anticipar un préstamo; **2.** *vi* FIN *market* situarse por delante de, GEN COMM *person, society, civilization* ascender, STOCK *market* situarse por delante de

Advance: ~ **Booking Charter** *n* (*ABC*) TRANSP flete reservado por adelantado *m*

advanced[1] *adj* COMP *software, system*, GEN COMM avanzado

advanced[2]: ~ **charge** *n* TRANSP cobro por adelantado *m*; ~ **collection** *n* TAX cobro anticipado *m*; ~ **country** *n* (*AC*) ECON, POL país desarrollado *m*; ~ **disbursement** *n* TRANSP desembolso por adelantado *m*; ~ **economy** *n* GEN COMM economía avanzada *f*; ~ **education** *n* WEL educación superior *f*; ~ **engineering** *n* IND ingeniería avanzada *f*; ~ **factory** *n* ENVIR, IND fábrica avanzada *f*; ~ **language** *n* COMP lenguaje avanzado *m*; ~ **organic economy** *n* ECON *agricultural* sistema económico avanzado *m*; ~ **technology** *n* COMP, GEN COMM tecnología avanzada *f*, tecnología de avance *f*; ~ **training** *n* HRM capacitación superior *f* (*AmL*), formación superior *f* (*Esp*); ~ **version** *n* COMP versión avanzada *f*

Advanced: ~ **Level General Certificate of Education** *n* (*A level*) WEL examen británico a nivel de bachillerato superior, ≈ Curso de Orientación Universitaria *m* (*Esp*) (*C.O.U.*), ≈ Selectividad *f* (*Esp*); ~ **Supplementary Level General Certificate of Education** *n* (*AS level*) WEL examen británico a nivel de bachillerato superior, ≈ Curso de Orientación Universitaria *m* (*Esp*) (*C.O.U.*), ≈ Selectividad *f* (*Esp*)

advancement *n* ADMIN, GEN COMM adelantamiento *m*, avance *m*

advances *n pl* BANK anticipos *m pl*; ~ **received** ACC anticipos recibidos *m pl*

advantage *n* GEN COMM ventaja *f*

advantageous *adj* GEN COMM ventajoso

adventure *n* ECON, FIN, GEN COMM, STOCK especulación aislada *f*, especulación eventual *f*

adversary *n* LAW adversario(-a) *m,f*

adverse[1] *adj* GEN COMM *balance* desfavorable, *consequences, influence* negativo, adverso

adverse[2]: ~ **balance of trade** *n* ECON balanza comercial negativa *f*; ~ **claim** *n* LAW reclamación de tercero sobre bienes embargados *f*; ~ **movement** *n* STOCK *price of bonds* movimiento adverso *m*; ~ **opinion** *n* ACC opinión adversa *f*, opinión desfavorable *f*, opinión negativa *f*; ~ **possession** *n* LAW prescripción adquisitiva *f*; ~ **price movement** *n* ECON evolución adversa de los precios *f*; ~ **selection** *n* INS selección adversa *f*; ~ **supply shock** *n* ECON choque adverso de la oferta *m*; ~ **trading conditions** *n pl* ECON condiciones comerciales adversas *f pl*; ~ **weather** *n* GEN COMM, TRANSP condiciones adversas *f pl*

adversely: ~ **affected** *adj* GEN COMM afectado adversamente

advert *n* GEN COMM, MEDIA, S&M *mass media* anuncio publicitario *m* (*Esp*), reclame *m* (*AmL*)

advertise *vt* S&M anunciar; ♦ ~ **a job** HRM, MEDIA anunciar un empleo, poner un anuncio de empleo, anunciar un trabajo

advertise for *vt* GEN COMM, MEDIA, S&M anunciar, anunciarse para, buscar por medios publicitarios, hacer publicidad de, poner un anuncio; ♦ ~ **bids** S&M solicitar ofertas públicamente

advertised[1] *adj* GEN COMM anunciado; ♦ **as ~ on TV** S&M según anunciado en televisión

advertised[2]: ~ **bidding** *n* S&M oferta publicitada *f*

advertisement *n* (*ad*) GEN COMM, MEDIA, S&M cuña publicitaria *f*, publicidad *f*, spot *m*, *mass media* anuncio *m* (*Esp*), reclame *m* (*AmL*)

advertiser *n* S&M anunciante *mf*

advertising[1] *adj* S&M publicitario

advertising[2] *n* GEN COMM propaganda *f* (*AmL*), publicidad *f*; ~ **agency** MEDIA, S&M agencia de publicidad *f*; ~ **agent** S&M agente de publicidad *mf*; ~ **allocation budget** S&M presupuesto asignado a la publicidad *m*; ~ **appeal** S&M reclamo publicitario *m*; ~ **appropriation** FIN asignación para publicidad *f*, S&M presupuesto de publicidad *m*; ~ **budget** S&M presupuesto publicitario *m*; ~ **budget review** ACC, FIN, S&M revisión del presupuesto de publicidad *f*; ~ **campaign** MEDIA, S&M campaña publicitaria *f*; ~ **channel** MEDIA, S&M canal publicitario *m*; ~ **code** S&M código publicitario *m*; ~ **commission** S&M comisión por publicidad *f*; ~ **concept** S&M concepto publicitario *m*; ~ **conversion rate** S&M índice de conversión publicitaria *m*; ~ **copy** MEDIA original del anuncio *m*, S&M mensaje publicitario *m*; ~ **cost per product sale** ACC, S&M coste publicitario por venta de producto *m* (*Esp*), costo publicitario por venta de producto *m* (*AmL*); ~ **coverage** S&M cobertura publicitaria *f*; ~ **criteria** *n pl* S&M criterios publicitarios *m pl*; ~ **department** MEDIA, S&M *of magazine* departamento de publicidad *m*; ~ **director** HRM, S&M director(a) de publicidad *m,f*; ~ **effectiveness** S&M efectividad del anuncio *f*, eficacia publicitaria *f*; ~ **expenditure** FIN, S&M gastos de publicidad *m pl*; ~ **expenses** *n pl* ACC, FIN, S&M gastos de publicidad *m pl*, gastos publicitarios *m pl*; ~ **gimmick** S&M truco publicitario *m*; ~ **industry** ECON, S&M industria de la publicidad *f*; ~ **jingle** MEDIA, S&M jingle publicitario *m*, melodía publicitaria *f*; ~ **man** (*adman*) HRM hombre anuncio *m*, profesional de la publicidad *m*; ~ **manager** HRM, S&M gerente de publicidad *mf*, jefe(-a) de publicidad *m,f*; ~ **media** *n pl* MEDIA, S&M medios publicitarios *m pl*; ~ **medium** MEDIA, S&M medio publicitario *m*, soporte publicitario *m*; ~ **message** S&M mensaje publicitario *m*; ~ **overkill** S&M exceso de medios publicitarios *m*; ~ **policy** S&M política publicitaria *f*; ~ **price** FIN, S&M precio publicitario *m*; ~ **program objective** AmE, ~ **programme objective** BrE S&M objetivo de un programa publicitario *m*; ~ **rates** *n pl* FIN, S&M tarifas de publicidad *f pl*; ~ **reach** S&M alcance publicitario *m*; ~ **regulation** S&M reglamento publicitario *m*; ~ **research** S&M investigación publicitaria *f*; ~ **response** S&M respuesta publicitaria *f*; ~ **revenue** FIN, MEDIA, S&M ingresos publicitarios *m pl*, renta de publicidad *f*; ~ **revenue by media** FIN, MEDIA, S&M ingresos publicitarios de los medios de comunicación *m pl*; ~ **schedule** MEDIA, S&M plan publicitario *m*; ~ **slogan** MEDIA, S&M eslogan publicitario *m*, slogan *m*; ~ **space** MEDIA, S&M espacio publicitario *m*; ~ **space buyer** MEDIA, S&M comprador(a) de espacio publicitario *m,f*; ~ **statistics** *n pl* S&M estadísticas de publicidad *f pl*; ~ **strategy** S&M estrategia publicitaria *f*; ~ **supplement** S&M suplemento publicitario *m*; ~ **tactic** S&M táctica publicitaria *f*; ~ **talk** S&M jerga de publicidad *f*; ~ **technique** S&M técnica publicitaria *f*; ~ **test** S&M prueba publicitaria *f*; ~ **text** MEDIA, S&M texto publicitario *m*; ~ **theme** S&M tema publicitario *m*; ~ **thermometer** S&M termómetro publicitario *m*; ~ **threshold** S&M umbral publicitario *m*; ~ **time** S&M tiempo para publicidad *m*; ~ **tour** S&M gira publicitaria *f*; ~ **tower** S&M columna publicitaria *f*; ~ **turnover** ACC, FIN, MEDIA, S&M facturación de publicidad *f*, rotación de publicidad *f*; ~ **value** S&M valor publicitario *m*; ~ **vehicle** MEDIA, S&M medio publicitario *m*, vehículo publicitario *m*; ~ **weapon** S&M arma publicitaria *f*; ~ **wearout** S&M saturación publicitaria *f*; ~ **zone** S&M zona publicitaria *f*

Advertising: ~ **Association** *n* S&M asociación británica de agencias de publicidad; ~ **Standards Authority** *n* (*ASA*) MEDIA, S&M organización británica para la regulación de la publicidad

advertorial *n* S&M publireportaje *m*

advice *n* GEN COMM *notification* aviso *m*, *counsel* consejo *m*; ~ **of arrival** COMMS aviso de llegada *m*; ~ **card** INS *marine* tarjeta informativa *f*; ~ **of collection** BANK aviso de cobro *m*; ~ **of deal** STOCK asesoramiento de una operación *m*; ~ **of delivery** COMMS aviso de entrega *m*; ~ **of duration and/or change** (*ADC*) GEN COMM aviso de duración y/o cambio *m*; ~ **note** COMMS carta de aviso *f*; ◆ **no** ~ (*N/A*) GEN COMM sin aviso; ~ **enclosed** (*ADV*) COMMS contiene carta de aviso; **until further** ~ GEN COMM hasta nuevo aviso

advisable *adj* GEN COMM, LAW, MGMNT aconsejable, conveniente

advise *vt* COMMS *inform* avisar, informar, GEN COMM asesorar, avisar, aconsejar, advertir, HRM advertir, MGMNT informar, advertir, avisar; ◆ ~ **a draft** BANK notificar un giro

advised[1]: ~ **bill** *n* BANK nota de aviso *f*

advised[2]: **be well** ~ *phr* GEN COMM estar bien aconsejado

advising: ~ **bank** *n* BANK banco girador *m*, banco ordenante *m*

advisor *n* GEN COMM, HRM, MGMNT asesor(a) *m,f*, consejero(-a) *m,f*, TAX asesor(a) *m,f*

advisory[1] *adj* GEN COMM *role* consultivo; ◆ **in an** ~ **capacity** GEN COMM en calidad de asesor

advisory[2]: ~ **account** *n* FIN cuenta no discrecional *f*; ~ **board** *n* ECON, FIN, GEN COMM, HRM junta consultiva *f*; ~ **body** *n* GEN COMM *committees and boards* órgano consultivo *m*; ~ **capacity** *n* HRM capacidad asesora *f*; ~ **committee** *n* BrE (*cf prudential committee AmE*) BANK, FIN *for rescheduling of debt*, GEN COMM, HRM, POL comisión asesora *f*, comité asesor *m*; ~ **function** *n* HRM función asesora *f*; ~ **funds** *n pl* STOCK fondos de colocación no discrecional *m pl*; ~ **group** *n* GEN COMM grupo asesor *m*; ~ **service** *n* FIN servicio de asesoramiento *m*, GEN COMM, MGMNT servicio de asesoramiento *m*, servicio de consulta *m*; ~ **voice** *n* GEN COMM asesoramiento *m*; ~ **work** *n* HRM trabajo de asesoramiento *m*

Advisory: ~, **Conciliation and Arbitration Service** *n* BrE (*ACAS*) HRM, MGMNT organismo independiente británico que media entre dos partes confrontadas, ≈ Instituto de Mediación, Arbitraje y Conciliación *m* (*IMAC*)

advocacy: ~ **advertising** *n* S&M publicidad de apoyo *f*

advocate[1] *n* LAW *in Scottish legal system* ≈ abogado(-a) *m,f*

advocate[2] *vt* GEN COMM recomendar

AERE *abbr* (*Atomic Energy Research Establishment*) ENVIR ≈ CONEA (*AmL*) (*Comisión Nacional de Energía Atómica*)

aerial: ~ **advertising** *n* S&M publicidad aérea *f*; ~ **survey** *n* TRANSP aerofotogrametría *f*, aerofotometría *f*, reconocimiento aéreo *m*

aerodrome *n* BrE TRANSP aeródromo *m*, aeropuerto *m*

aerogram *n* COMMS aerograma *m*

aeroplane *n* BrE TRANSP aeronave *f*, aeroplano *m*, avión *m*; ~ **banner** BrE S&M *advertising* avioneta con anuncio publicitario *f*, estandarte aéreo *m*

aerospace *adj* IND aeroespacial

AF *abbr* (*advance freight*) IMP/EXP, TRANSP anticipo sobre el flete *m*

AFBD *abbr* (*Association of Futures Brokers and Dealers*) STOCK Asociación de Agentes y Corredores de Futuros *f*

AFDC *abbr AmE* (*Aid to Families with Dependent Children*) ECON, WEL subsidio para familias con hijos

affair *n* GEN COMM *incident, event* asunto *m*

affairs *n pl* GEN COMM asuntos *m pl*

affect *vt* GEN COMM, ECON, LAW *supply of money, findings* afectar

affected: **be** ~ *phr* ECON, GEN COMM, LAW quedar afectado

affection: ~ **value** *n* INS valor de afección *m*

affective: ~ **behavior** *AmE*, ~ **behaviour** *BrE n* GEN COMM comportamiento afectivo *m*, conducta afectiva *f*

affidavit *n* LAW acta notarial *f*, declaración jurada por escrito *f*

affiliate[1] *n* ACC filial *f*, GEN COMM *company* filial *f*, afiliado(-a) *m,f*, HRM filial *f*; ~ **member** GEN COMM miembro afiliado *m*

affiliate[2] **1.** *vt* GEN COMM afiliar; **2.** ~ **to** *vi* GEN COMM afiliarse a, asociarse a

affiliated[1]: ~ **to** *adj* GEN COMM asociado a

affiliated[2]: ~ **bank** *n* BANK banco filial *m*; ~ **chain** *n* S&M cadena afiliada *f*; ~ **company** *n* GEN COMM compañía asociada *f*, compañía filial *f*, sociedad filial *f*, empresa afiliada *f*, filial *f*; ~ **firm** *n* GEN COMM casa filial *f*; ~ **group** *n* GEN COMM grupo asociado *m*; ~ **person** *n* GEN COMM *in society* persona afiliada *f*; ~ **retailer** *n* S&M minorista afiliado(-a) *m,f*; ~ **trade union** *n* HRM sindicato afiliado *m*; ~ **wholesaler** *n* S&M mayorista afiliado(-a) *m,f*

affiliation *n* GEN COMM afiliación *f*; ~ **fee** HRM cuota de afiliación *f*

affirmative: ~ **relief** *n* LAW reparación positiva *f*

affix *vt* GEN COMM *label* adherir, *stamp* pegar, *seal* estampar, *notice, poster, bill* fijar; ◆ ~ **a seal** COMMS sellar

affixed[1]: ~ **to land** *adj* TAX unido al suelo

affixed[2]: ~ **document** *n* ADMIN, GEN COMM *mail* anexo *m*, documento adjunto *m*; ~ **testimonial** *n* LAW testimonio adjunto *m*

affluence *n* GEN COMM abundancia *f*, opulencia *f*

affluent[1] *adj* GEN COMM abundante

affluent[2]: ~ **society** *n* GEN COMM sociedad opulenta *f*

AFFM *abbr* (*Australian Financial Futures Market*) STOCK mercado de futuros financieros australiano

afford *vt* ECON, GEN COMM *provide* aprovisionar, suministrar

affordable[1] *adj* ECON, S&M suministrable

affordable[2]: ~ **price** *n* S&M precio asequible *m*

affreightment *n* LAW fletamento *m*, TRANSP fletamento *m*, fletamiento *m*

AFL-CIO *abbr* (*American Federation of Labor-Congress of Industrial Organizations*) HRM, IND federación estadounidense de trabajadores-congreso de organizaciones industriales

afloat[1] *adj* GEN COMM *business*, STOCK boyante

afloat[2]: ~ **price** *n* STOCK precio flotante *m*

afloat[3]: **not always ~ but safe aground** *phr* TRANSP no siempre a flote pero seguro encallado

aforementioned *adj* COMMS antes mencionado

a fortiori *phr* GEN COMM con más razón

AFT *abbr* ACC, BANK (*automatic funds transfer*) transferencia de fondos automática *f*, COMP (*automatic fine tuning*) sintonización fina automática *f*

after[1]: ~**-hours** *adj* STOCK después de horas de oficina; ~**-market** *adj* STOCK propio del mercado secundario; ~**-sales** *adj* S&M postventa, posventa

after[2]: ~ **acceptance** *n* BANK, FIN aceptación a posteriori *f*; ~**-acquired clause** *n* BANK *in mortgage agreement* cláusula de adquisición posterior *f*; ~**-acquired property** *n* LAW *bankruptcy* propiedad de adquisición posterior *f*, *commercial* bienes gananciales *m pl*, PROP propiedad de adquisición posterior *f*; ~**-effect** *n* GEN COMM efecto tardío *m*; ~**-hours dealing** *n* FIN, STOCK negociación tras el cierre *f*, venta fuera de horas *f*; ~**-hours market** *n* STOCK mercado tras el cierre *m*, mercado fuera de horas *m*; ~**-hours price** *n* STOCK precio tras el cierre *m*, precio fuera de horas *m*; ~**-hours rally** *n* STOCK recuperación fuera de horas *f*, recuperación tras el cierre *f*; ~**-hours trading** *n* STOCK negociación fuera de horas *f*, negociación tras el cierre *f*; ~**-profits tax** *n* ACC, TAX impuesto después de beneficios *m*; ~**-sales manager** *n* HRM director(a) de posventa *m,f*; ~**-sales service** *n* S&M servicio de posventa *m*; ~**-tax basis** *n* TAX base después de impuestos *f*; ~**-tax bond yield** *n* TAX rendimiento de los bonos después de impuestos *m*; ~**-tax capital gain** *n* ACC beneficio del capital después de impuestos *m*; ~**-tax cash flow** *n* TAX flujo de dinero después de impuestos *m*; ~**-tax dividend** *n* TAX dividendo después de impuestos *m*; ~**-tax financing** *n* TAX financiación después de impuestos *f*; ~**-tax income** *n* TAX beneficio después de impuestos *m*; ~**-tax profit** *n* ACC, TAX renta después de impuestos *m*; ~**-tax rate of return** *n* ACC, TAX tasa de beneficio después de impuestos *f*, tipo de beneficio después de impuestos *m*; ~**-tax real rate of return** *n* TAX porcentaje real de devolución después de impuestos *m*, tasa real de rentabilidad después de impuestos *f*; ~**-tax yield** *n* TAX beneficio después de impuestos *m*

afteracceptance *n* BANK, FIN aceptación a posteriori *f*

afterimage *n* S&M *advertising* imagen secundaria *f*

aftermath: in the ~ of *phr* GEN COMM en el periodo subsiguiente a

A.G. *abbr* (*accountant general*) ACC jefe(-a) de contabilidad *m,f*

against: ~ **all risks** *phr* (*AAR*) INS a todo riesgo, contra todo riesgo; ~ **documents** *phr* GEN COMM contra entrega de documentos; ~ **one's judgment** *phr* GEN COMM contra su propio parecer; ~ **payment** *phr* GEN COMM contra pago; ~ **text** *phr* S&M *advertising* contra texto; ~ **policy** *phr* GEN COMM en contra de costumbre

agcy *abbr* (*agency*) ADMIN, BANK, FIN *trust institutions* agencia *f*, *government departments* gestoría *f*, GEN COMM, HRM agencia *f*

age[1] *n* GEN COMM *epoch* edad *f*, era *f*; ~ **allowance** BrE TAX desgravación a la tercera edad; ~ **at entry** INS edad de ingreso *f*; ~ **at expiry** INS edad al vencimiento *f*; ~ **bracket** S&M *market research* grupo etario *m*; ~ **discrimination** HRM, LAW, WEL discriminación por edad *f*; ~ **distribution** ECON distribución según edad *f*; ~**-earnings profile** HRM perfil de ingresos por edad *m*; ~ **exemption** TAX exención por edad *f*; ~ **group** GEN COMM, S&M *market research, statistics* grupo etario *m*; ~ **inventories** ACC envejecimiento de las existencias *m*; ~ **limit** GEN COMM límite de edad *m*; ~ **pyramid** ECON pirámide de población *f*

age[2] **1.** *vt* ACC clasificar por fecha, ordenar por antigüedad, ordenar por fecha; ◆ ~ **stocks** ACC dar antigüedad a las mercaderías, fechar las mercaderías; **2.** *vi* GEN COMM deteriorarse

aged: ~ **account** *n* ACC cuenta vencida *f*; ~ **trial balance** *n* ACC balance de comprobación vencido *m*

ageing: ~ **of accounts receivable** *n* ACC ordenación cronológica de las cuentas a cobrar *f*; ~ **population** *n* ECON población que envejece *m*; ~ **of receivables** *n* ACC análisis de la antigüedad de las cuentas a cobrar *m*, análisis de las cuentas a cobrar según su antigüedad *m pl*, antigüedad de las cuentas a cobrar *f*; ~ **schedule** *n* ACC lista cronológica *f*, relación cronológica *f*

ageism *n* ECON, HRM, LAW discriminación por motivo de edad *f*

agency *n* (*agcy, agy.*) GEN COMM agencia *f*, *bureaucratic administration* gestoría *f*, mediación *f*, HRM agencia *f*; ~ **account** ACC cuenta de agencia *f*; ~ **agreement** LAW contrato de representación *m*; ~ **audit** S&M auditoría de agencia *f*; ~ **auditing** S&M auditoría de agencia *f*; ~ **bank** BANK banco representante *m*; ~ **billing** MEDIA facturación de agencia *f*; ~ **broker** STOCK broker de bolsa *mf*, intermediario(-a) de bolsa *m,f*; ~ **by necessity** LAW mediación por necesidad *f*; ~ **by ratification** LAW representación por ratificación *f*; ~ **cost** STOCK costes de corretaje *m pl* (*Esp*), costos de corretaje *m pl* (*AmL*); ~ **experience** S&M *advertising* experiencia en agencia *f*; ~ **fee** BANK, GEN COMM comisión de gestión *f*, cuota de gestión *f*, TRANSP *paid by shipowner to agents* gasto de agencia *m*, gasto de representación *m*; ~ **with full service** MEDIA, S&M *advertising* agencia con servicios plenos *f*; ~ **fund** GEN COMM fondo de agencia *m*, LAW fondo de acción *m*, MEDIA fondo de agencia *m*; ~ **law** LAW ley de representación *f*; ~ **relationship** ACC relación de agencia *f*; ~ **representative** PROP representante de agencia *mf*; ~ **shop** HRM empresa con plantilla sindicada *f*; ~ **theory** ECON teoría de la agencia *f*

Agency: ~ **for International Development** *n AmE* ECON agencia para el desarrollo internacional

agenda *n* ADMIN, GEN COMM, MGMNT agenda; ◆ **be on the ~** ADMIN, GEN COMM, MGMNT estar en el orden del día, estar en la agenda

agent *n* (*agt*) GEN COMM, S&M agente *mf*, representante *mf*; ~ **bank** BANK banco agente *m*; ~**'s commission** S&M comisión del agente *f*; ~ **corporation** ACC compañía representante *f*, sociedad representante *f*; ~-**general** HRM *representative post* apoderado(-a) general *m,f*; ~**'s territory** S&M *advertising* zona del agente *f*; ~**'s vehicle record** (*AVR*) TRANSP registro del vehículo del agente *m*

agglomeration *n* ECON aglomeración *f*; ~ **diseconomy** ECON deseconomía de aglomeración *f*; ~ **economy** ECON economía de concentración *f*

aggravated: ~ **risk** *n* INS riesgo agravado *m*

aggregate[1] *adj* ECON *amount, demand,* GEN COMM, MATH agregado, global

aggregate[2] *n* ECON, MATH monto global *m*; ~ **of the adjusted cost bases** TAX total de las bases de coste ajustadas *m* (*Esp*), total de las bases de costo ajustadas *m* (*AmL*); ~ **balance** ACC balance consolidado *m*; ~ **book value** ACC valor contable agregado *m*, valor total contable *m*; ~ **concentration** ECON concentración agregada *f*; ~ **data** ACC datos agregados *m pl*; ~ **demand** ECON, FIN demanda agregada *f*, demanda global *f*; ~ **demand-aggregate supply** (*AD-AS*) ECON, FIN demanda agregada-oferta agregada *f*; ~ **exercise price** STOCK precio global del ejercicio *m*; ~ **income** ACC, ECON, TAX ingresos totales *m pl*; ~ **indemnity** INS *aggregate limit* capital total asegurado por siniestro *m*, valor asegurado *m*; ~ **liability index** INS ficha de acumulación de riesgos *f*; ~ **output** ECON rendimiento total *m*; ~ **production** ECON producción global *f*; ~ **risk** GEN COMM riesgo agregado *m*; ~ **statement** ACC estado de cuentas global *m*; ~ **supply** ECON oferta agregada *f*; ~ **table** INS tabla agregada *f*; ~ **value** ACC, TAX *of estate* valor total *m*; ~ **sales listings** *n pl BrE* (*ASL*) TAX inventario total de ventas *m*; ◆ **in the** ~ GEN COMM en total

aggregate[3] *vt* ECON, GEN COMM, MATH agregar, globalizar

aggregation: ~ **problem** *n* ACC, ECON problema añadido *m*, problema de la agregación de datos *m*

aggressive[1] *adj* GEN COMM, S&M *strategy* agresivo

aggressive[2]: ~ **executive** *n* GEN COMM ejecutivo(-a) agresivo(-a) *m,f*; ~ **investment** *n* STOCK inversión agresiva *f*; ~ **marketing** *n* S&M marketing agresivo *m*; ~ **pricing** *n* S&M fijación de precios agresiva *f*

agio *n* ECON, STOCK *foreign bills of exchange* agio *m*; ~ **account** ECON, STOCK cuenta de agio *f*; ~ **theory of interest** ECON, STOCK teoría del interés basada en la especulación *f*

agiotage *n* GEN COMM *foreign bills of exchange* especulación *f*

AGM *abbr* (*annual general meeting*) GEN COMM, MGMNT asamblea anual *f*, junta anual *f*

AGNP *abbr* (*augmented gross national product*) ECON aumento del producto interior bruto *m*

agree 1. *vt* GEN COMM acordar, *accounts, books* cuadrar; ◆ ~ **the accounts** ACC, FIN aceptar las cuentas; ~ **the books** GEN COMM aceptar los libros; ~ **by consensus** GEN COMM consensuar; **2.** *vi* GEN COMM acceder, entenderse, pactar, *opinion, idea* asentir, *reach mutual understanding* ponerse de acuerdo

agree on *vt* GEN COMM *price, terms of sale* estar de acuerdo en

agree to *vt* GEN COMM estar de acuerdo con, *project, plan* otorgar, *consent* consentir a

agree upon *vt* GEN COMM *price, terms of sale* convenir

agree with *vt* GEN COMM estar de acuerdo con

agreed[1] *adj* GEN COMM *time, place, total* convenido; ◆ **as** ~ GEN COMM según lo convenido; **be** ~ GEN COMM *plan, report* estar acordado

agreed[2]: ~ **portion** *n* TAX parte convenida *f*; ~ **price** *n* GEN COMM precio convenido *m*; ~ **rate** *n* TRANSP *of freight* tarifa acordada *f*; ~ **sum** *n* GEN COMM suma convenida *f*; ~ **takeover** *n* ECON, FIN, STOCK toma de control pactada *f*; ~ **valuation clause** *n* INS cláusula de valor convenido *f*; ~ **value** *n* INS valor convenido *m*; ~ **value insurance** *n* INS seguro de valor convenido *m*

agreement[1]: **in** ~ *adj* GEN COMM, LAW conforme

agreement[2] *n* GEN COMM, LAW acuerdo *m*, pacto *m*, tratado *m*, *formal agreement, treaty* convenio *m*, *contract* contrato *m*; ~ **among underwriters** BANK acuerdo entre garantes *m*, acuerdo entre suscriptores *m*; ~ **of clearing** BANK acuerdo de compensación *m*; ~ **for exclusiveness** LAW contrato de exclusividad *m*; ~ **with no strings attached** GEN COMM acuerdo sin condiciones *m*; ~ **on double taxation** TAX convenio de doble imposición *m*

Agreement: ~ **on International Goods Traffic by Rail** *n* TRANSP acuerdo sobre el transporte internacional de mercancías por ferrocarril

agribusiness *n* ECON, ENVIR, IND industria agropecuaria *f*, agroindustria *f*

agricultural[1] *adj* ECON, ENVIR agrícola, agrario

agricultural[2]: ~ **bank** *n* BANK, ECON banco agrícola *m*; ~ **buildings** *n pl* ECON, PROP construcciones agrícolas *f pl*; ~ **cooperative** *n* HRM cooperativa agrícola *f*; ~ **credit** *n* GEN COMM crédito agrícola *m*; ~ **credit bank** *n* BANK ≈ caja rural *f*; ~ **engineering** *n* ENVIR, IND ingeniería agrícola *f*; ~ **export subsidy** *n* ECON, IMP/EXP subsidio a la exportación agrícola *m*; ~ **futures contract** *n* STOCK contrato sobre futuros agrícolas *m*; ~ **household** *n* ECON, WEL comunidad agrícola *f*; ~ **insurance** *n* INS seguro agrícola *m*; ~ **job** *n* HRM trabajo agrícola *m*, trabajo agropecuario *m*; ~ **land** *n* ENVIR terreno agrícola *m*; ~ **levy** *n* ECON impuesto agrario *m*; ~ **loan** *n* BANK, ECON prestación agrícola *f*; ~ **paper** *n* ECON documento agrícola *m*; ~ **policy** *n* ECON, POL política agraria *f*; ~ **price support** *n* ECON sostenimiento de los precios agrícolas *m*; ~ **product** *n* ECON producto agrícola *m*; ~ **production** *n* ECON producción agrícola *f*; ~ **publication** *n* MEDIA publicación agraria *f*; ~ **sector** *n* ECON sector agrícola *m*, sector de agricultura *m*; ~ **sector adjustment loan** *n* BrE (*ASAL*) ECON, FIN préstamo de regulación del sector agrícola *m*; ~ **show** *n* ECON, S&M feria agrícola *f*; ~ **subsidy** *n* ECON, POL subsidio agrícola *m*; ~ **tenant** *n* GEN COMM arrendatario(-a) agrícola *m,f*; ~ **unit** *n* ECON explotación agrícola *f*; ~ **wages board** *n* HRM junta de salarios agrarios *f*; ~ **warrant** *n* ECON garantía agrícola *f*

Agricultural: ~ **Holdings Act** *n BrE* LAW Ley de Propiedades Agrícolas *f*; ~ **Marketing Service** *n* ECON servicio comercial agrícola *m*

agriculturalist *n* GEN COMM agrónomo(-a) *m,f*, agricultor(a) *m,f*

agriculture *n* GEN COMM agricultura *f*, agronomía *f*

Agriculture: ~ **Act** *n BrE* ENVIR, LAW Ley Agrícola *f*

agriculturist *n* GEN COMM agrónomo(-a) *m,f*, agricultor(a) *m,f*

agrifood: ~ **industry** *n* ECON, IND industria agrícola-alimentaria *f*

agrifoodstuffs *n pl* ECON materias primas agrícolas *f pl*

agrochemical *adj* ECON, ENVIR, IND agroquímico

agroforestry *n* ECON, ENVIR agrosilvicultura *f*

agroindustry *n* ECON, ENVIR, IND agroindustria *f*

agronomist *n* ECON, ENVIR agrónomo(-a) *m,f*

agronomy *n* ECON, ENVIR agronomía *f*

aground *adj* TRANSP varado, encallado

agt *abbr* (*agent*) GEN COMM, S&M agente *mf*, representante *mf*

agy. *abbr* (*agency*) ADMIN, BANK, FIN *trust institutions* agencia *f*, *government departments* gestoría *f*, GEN COMM, HRM agencia *f*

AHASC *abbr* (*Airport Handling Agreements Sub-Committee*) TRANSP Subcomité Aeroportuario Sobre Manipulación de Carga *m*

AHC[1] *abbr* (*Airport Handling Committee*) TRANSP Comité Aeroportuario de Carga y Descarga *m*

AHC[2]: **~ Banks** *n pl* BANK bancos AHC *m pl*

AHESC *abbr* (*Airport Handling Equipment Sub-Committee*) TRANSP Subcomité Aeroportuario de Equipos de Manipulación *m*

AHM *abbr* (*Airport Handling Manual*) TRANSP Manual de Carga y Descarga en Aeropuertos *m*

AHPSC *abbr* (*Airport Handling Procedures Sub-Committee*) TRANSP Subcomité de Procedimientos de Manipulación Aeroportuaria *m*

AHS *abbr* (*assistant head of section*) HRM, MGMNT jefe(-a) auxiliar de sección *m,f*

AI *abbr* BANK (*accrued interest*) interés acumulado *m*, (*accumulated interest*) interés devengado *m*, COMP (*artificial intelligence*) IA (*inteligencia artificial*), FIN, GEN COMM, STOCK (*accrued interest*) interés acumulado *m*, (*accumulated interest*) interés devengado *m*

AIA *abbr* (*Associate of the Institute of Actuaries*) INS miembro del instituto de actuarios

AIB *abbr* AmE (*American Institute of Bankers, cf CIB BrE*) BANK instituto estadounidense de banqueros

AIBD *abbr* (*Association of International Bond Dealers*) STOCK Asociación de Intermediarios Internacionales de Bonos *f*

AICPA *abbr* (*American Institute of Certified Public Accountants*) ACC asociación profesional estadounidense de expertos contables

AICS *abbr* (*Associate Institute of Chartered Shipbrokers*) HRM, TRANSP instituto afiliado de corredores marítimos colegiados *m*

aid[1] *n* BANK *help*, COMP, ECON asistencia *f*, GEN COMM amparo *m*, POL asistencia *f*; **~ development loan** BANK préstamo de ayuda al desarrollo *m*; **~ donor** BANK donante de ayuda *m*; **~-financed project** BANK proyecto financiado con ayuda *m*; **~ in kind** BANK *cooperation and development* ayuda en especie *f*; **~ loan** BANK préstamo de ayuda *m*; **~ money** BANK dinero de ayuda *m*, ayuda monetaria *f*; **~ program** AmE, **~ programme** BrE BANK, ECON programa de ayuda *m*; **~ scheme** BANK plan de ayuda *m*

aid[2] *vt* BANK *understanding* favorecer, *development* ayudar, *company* promover, *person* asistir, apoyar, GEN COMM *financially* ayudar, POL promover; **~ and abet** LAW coadyuvar, cooperar en

Aid: **~ to Families with Dependent Children** *n AmE* (*AFDC*) ECON, WEL subsidio para familias con hijos *m*

AIDA *abbr* (*attention, interest, desire, action*) GEN COMM atención, interés, deseo, acción

aide *n* GEN COMM asesor(a) privado(-a) *m,f*; **~-mémoire** GEN COMM recordatorio *m*

aided: **~ recall** *n* S&M *market research* recuerdo asistido *m*; **~ recall test** *n* S&M *market research* prueba de memorización asistida *f*

AIFTA *abbr* ECON (*Anglo-Irish Free Trade Area Agreement*) acuerdo anglo-irlandés de área de libre comercio, HRM (*Associate Institute Freight Trades Association*) instituto afiliado de la asociación de tráfico de mercancías

ailing[1] *adj* GEN COMM averiado

ailing[2]: **~ bank** *n* BANK banco en dificultades *m*; **~ economy** *n* ECON, POL economía débil *f*, economía enferma *f*; **~ industry** *n* ECON, IND industria decadente *f*

aim[1] *n* GEN COMM propósito *m*

aim[2] *vt* GEN COMM *criticism, product, programme* dirigir

AIMS *abbr AmE* (*American Institute of Merchant Shipping*) TRANSP instituto estadounidense de la marina mercante

ACIM *abbr* (*Associate of the Chartered Institute of Marketing*) HRM miembro asociado del instituto de marketing

air[1]: **~-conditioned** *adj* WEL climatizado

air[2]: **~ bill** *n* IMP/EXP, TRANSP conocimiento de embarque aéreo *m*; **~ bill of lading** *n* IMP/EXP, TRANSP carta de porte aéreo *f*, conocimiento de embarque aéreo *m*, guía de flete aéreo *f*; **~ brush technique** *n* MEDIA, S&M *advertising* técnica del aerógrafo *f*; **~ cargo** *n* TRANSP flete aéreo *m*; **~ carrier** *n* TRANSP empresa de transporte aéreo *f*; **~ check** *n* MEDIA control de un programa *m*, copia de archivo *f*; **~ conditioning** *n* WEL climatización *f*; **~ consignment note** *n* IMP/EXP, TRANSP carta de porte aéreo *f*; **~ cruise** *n* LEIS crucero aéreo *m*; **~ cushion vehicle** *n* (*ACV*) TRANSP vehículo con amortiguación por aire *m*; **~ date** *n* S&M fecha de emisión *f*; **~ fare** *n* LEIS tarifa aérea *f*; **~ fee** *n* TRANSP sobretasa aérea *f*; **~ freight** *n* TRANSP flete aéreo *m*; **~ freight consolidation** *n* TRANSP consolidación de flete aéreo *f*; **~ freighter** *n* TRANSP avión de carga *m*, avión cargero *m*; **~ hostess** *n* LEIS, TRANSP azafata *f* (*Esp*), aeromoza *f* (*AmL*); **~ lane** *n* TRANSP ruta aérea *f*; **~ mail transfer** *n* (*AMT*) BANK, GEN COMM transferencia por correo aéreo *f*; **~ mode container** *n* TRANSP contenedor de modalidad aérea *m*; **~ pocket stock** *n infrml* STOCK acciones o valores que caen en picado al entrar en un bache; **~ pollution** *n* ENVIR contaminación del aire *f*; **~ rights** *n* LAW derechos de vuelo *m pl*, MEDIA derechos de antena *m pl*, derechos de emisión *m pl*, TRANSP derechos de vuelo *m pl*; **~ show** *n* TRANSP exhibición aérea *f*; **~ terminal** *n* TRANSP terminal aérea *f*; **~-time buyer** *n* MEDIA, S&M *radio, TV* comprador(a) de espacio en medios audiovisuales *m,f*; **~ traffic** *n* TRANSP tráfico aéreo *m*; **~-traffic control** *n* (*ATC*) TRANSP control de tráfico aéreo *m*; **~-traffic control system** *n* TRANSP sistema de control de tráfico aéreo *m*; **~-traffic controller** *n* TRANSP controlador(a) de tráfico aéreo *m,f*; **~ transport** *n* TRANSP transporte aéreo *m*; **~ transport insurance** *n* INS, TRANSP seguro de transporte aéreo *m*; **~ transportation tax** *n* (*ATT*) TAX impuesto sobre el transporte aéreo *m*; **~ travel** *n* LEIS, TRANSP viaje aéreo *m*; **~ traveler** *AmE*, **~ traveller** *BrE n* LEIS, TRANSP pasajero(-a) de vía aérea *m,f*, viajero(-a) de una línea aérea *m,f;* ~ **waybill** *n* (*AWB*) IMP/EXP, TRANSP conocimiento de embarque aéreo *m*

air³ *vt* GEN COMM *idea, proposal* dar a conocer, *opinion, view* airear, divulgar; ◆ ~ **one's opinions** GEN COMM divulgar las propias opiniones; ~ **one's views** GEN COMM divulgar los propios puntos de vista

air⁴: **by** ~ *phr* TRANSP por avión; **on the** ~ *phr* COMMS, MEDIA, S&M en el aire

Air: ~ **Transport Association** *n AmE* (*ATA*) TRANSP asociación estadounidense de transporte aéreo

airborne: ~ **time** *n* LEIS, TRANSP tiempo de vuelo *m*

airbus *n* TRANSP aerobús *m*, airbus *m*

aircraft *n* TRANSP aeronave *f*, aeroplano *m*, avión *m*; ~ **charter agreement** TRANSP contrato de flete aéreo *m*; ~ **hull insurance** INS seguro de cascos de aviación *m*; ~ **industry** ECON, IND industria aeronáutica *f*; ~ **manifest** TRANSP declaración de una aeronave *f*; ~ **movement message** (*MVT*) TRANSP mensaje de movimiento de aeronave *m*; ~ **operator** HRM, TRANSP operador(a) aéreo(-a) *m,f;* ~ **passenger insurance** INS, LEIS seguro de pasajeros de aviones *m*; ~ **turnaround time** *AmE*, ~ **turnround time** *BrE* TRANSP tiempo de viaje redondo de un avión *m*

aircrew *n* TRANSP tripulación de un avión *f*

airdrome *AmE see* aerodrome *BrE*

airflex: ~ **clutch** *n* (*AFC*) TRANSP embrague airflex *m*

airfreight: ~ **container** *n* (*ac*) TRANSP contenedor de flete aéreo *m*

airline *n* TRANSP línea aérea *f;* ~ **advertising** S&M publicidad de una línea aérea *f;* ~ **guide** LEIS guía de línea aérea *f*

Airline: ~ **Schedules and Interline Availability Study** *n* (*ASIAS*) TRANSP estudio de planes de vuelo y disponibilidad *m*

airliner *n* TRANSP avión comercial *m*, avión de línea *m*, avión de pasajeros *m*

airmail¹: **by** ~ *adv* COMMS por correo aéreo

airmail² *n* COMMS correo aéreo *m;* ~ **letter** COMMS carta por correo aéreo *f*, carta por vía aérea *f;* ~ **paper** COMMS papel para correo aéreo *m*

airmail³ *vt* COMMS enviar por correo aéreo

airplane *AmE see* aeroplane *BrE*

airport *n* TRANSP aeródromo *m*, aeropuerto *m;* ~ **advertising** S&M publicidad en los aeropuertos *f;* ~ **tax** TAX tasa aeroportuaria *f*

Airport: ~ **Associations Coordinating Council** *n* (*AACC*) TRANSP consejo coordinador de asociaciones aeroportuarias, ≈ Aeropuertos Españoles y Navegación Aérea *m pl* (*AENA*); ~ **Handling Agreements Sub-Committee** *n* (*AHASC*) TRANSP Subcomité Aeroportuario Sobre Manipulación de Carga *m;* ~ **Handling Committee** *n* (*AHC*) TRANSP Comité Aeroportuario de Carga y Descarga *m;* ~ **Handling Equipment Sub-Committee** *n* (*AHESC*) TRANSP Subcomité Aeroportuario de Equipos de Manipulación *m;* ~ **Handling Manual** *n* (*AHM*) TRANSP Manual de Carga y Descarga en Aeropuertos *m;* ~ **Handling Procedures Sub-Committee** *n* (*AHPSC*) TRANSP Subcomité de Procedimientos de Manipulación Aeroportuaria *m*

airtight *adj* GEN COMM *container, seal* hermético

airtime *n* MEDIA *for advertising* tiempo de emisión *m*, tiempo de antena *m*, *radio* tiempo en radio *m*, *television* tiempo en TV *m*, espacio publicitario *m*

airway *n* (*AWY*) TRANSP vía aérea *f*

airworthiness: ~ **certification** *n* TRANSP certificado de aeronavegabilidad *m*

airworthy *adj* TRANSP en condiciones de vuelo

aisle *n* GEN COMM *in cinema, shop, train* pasillo *m*

a.k.a. *abbr* (*also known as*) GEN COMM alias, también conocido como

AKA *abbr* (*also known as*) GEN COMM alias, también conocido como

alarm *n* GEN COMM alarma *f;* ~ **bell** GEN COMM timbre de alarma *m;* ~ **call** GEN COMM llamada de alarma *f;* ~ **signal** GEN COMM señal de alerta *f*

alcoholic: ~ **drink** *n* TAX bebida alcohólica *f*

aleatory: ~ **contract** *n* INS contrato aleatorio *m*

alert *n* GEN COMM alerta *f;* ◆ **be on the** ~ GEN COMM estar sobre aviso

algorithm *n* COMP, MATH algoritmo *m*

algorithmic *adj* COMP, MATH algorítmico

alias¹ *adv* GEN COMM alias, también conocido como

alias² *n* COMP seudónimo *m*, GEN COMM alias *m*

alien¹: ~ **from** *adj* GEN COMM ajeno a; ~ **to** *adj* GEN COMM ajeno a

alien² *n* LAW extranjero(-a) *m,f;* ~ **corporation** GEN COMM, LAW compañía extranjera *f*, empresa extranjera *f*, LAW sociedad anónima extranjera *f;* ~ **registration card** *AmE* (*cf foreign identity card BrE*) POL, WEL tarjeta de identificación extranjera *f*

alienable *adj* GEN COMM, HRM, LAW alienable, enajenable

alienate *vt* GEN COMM, HRM, LAW alienar, enajenar

alienation *n* GEN COMM, HRM, LAW alienación *f*, enajenación *f;* ~ **effect** S&M *advertising* efecto de alienación *m*

alienee *n* LAW persona que adquiere el bien o derecho enajenado

align *vt* COMP, GEN COMM, LAW alinear

aligned: ~ **forms** *n pl* ADMIN formularios alineados *m pl*

alignment *n* COMP, GEN COMM, LAW alineación *f*

alimony *n* LAW manutención *f*, pensión alimenticia *f;* ~ **income** TAX ingresos por pensión alimenticia *m pl;* ~ **paid** TAX pensión alimenticia *f*

all: ~ **things being equal** *phr* GEN COMM permaneciendo invariable todo lo demás

All: ~ **Ordinaries Index** *n* STOCK índice All Ordinaries *m;* ~ **Share Index** *n BrE* STOCK índice del Financial Times

all-day: ~ **trading** *n* STOCK mercado continuo *m*

allegation *n* LAW alegación *f*

alleged *adj* LAW presunto

all-employee: ~ **option scheme** *n* HRM, STOCK plan de opción para todo el personal *m*

alleviate *vt* GEN COMM *problems* mitigar

alleviation *n* GEN COMM *of problem* mitigación *f*

alliance *n* GEN COMM, POL acuerdo *m*, alianza *f*

allied: ~ **industries** *n pl* IND industrias afines *f pl;* ~ **member** *n* STOCK miembro aliado *m;* ~ **peril** *n* INS riesgo afín *m;* ~ **trades** *n pl* GEN COMM, IND negocios afines *m pl*

alligator: ~ **spread** *n* STOCK *investment banking, securities, options* margen de cocodrilo *m*

all-in *adj* GEN COMM *price* todo comprendido, todo incluido, INS *insurance* total

all-inclusive¹ *adj* GEN COMM *rate, price* todo incluido, total

all-inclusive[2]: ~ **price** n GEN COMM precio todo incluido m

all-loss: ~, **all-risk** adj INS a toda pérdida, a todo riesgo

allocate vt ACC, ECON money, securities adjudicar, consignar, funds, resources destinar, prorratear, FIN contract adjudicar, afectar, destinar, imputar, GEN COMM work asignar, repartir, LAW money, securities, contracts adjudicar; ◆ ~ **costs to the appropriate accounts** ACC aplicar los costes en las cuentas apropiadas (Esp), aplicar los costos en las cuentas apropiadas (AmL), asignar los costes a las cuentas apropiadas (Esp), asignar los costos a las cuentas apropiadas (AmL)

allocated: ~ **benefit** n ACC personal beneficio distribuido m; ~ **exemption limit** n TAX límite asignado de exención m; ~ **material** n TRANSP material asignado m; ~ **transfer risk reserve** n (ATRR) FIN reserva de riesgo con transferencia variable f

allocation n ACC, ECON of funds aplicación f, adjudicación f, traspaso m, FIN money, duties imputación f, adjudicación f, afectación f, GEN COMM contract asignación f, distribución f, money, duties reparto m, LAW of contracts, STOCK adjudicación f, TRANSP localización f; ~ **of costs** ACC asignación de costes f (Esp), asignación de costos f (AmL); ~ **of earnings** ACC, HRM distribución de las ganancias f, distribución de los beneficios f; ~ **of exemption limit** TAX asignación del límite de exención f; ~ **of funds** FIN, TAX consignación presupuestaria f; ~ **to the lowest tenderer** S&M adjudicación al postor que presenta la oferta más baja f; ~ **in proportion to patronage** TAX asignación proporcional al patrocinio f; ~ **to reserves** ACC asignación a reservas f, atribución a reservas f, dotación a reservas f; ~ **of responsibilities** FIN, HRM, MGMNT asignación de responsabilidades f, distribución de responsabilidades f; ~ **of special drawing rights** BANK asignación de derechos especiales de giro f; ~ **by tender** STOCK adjudicación por licitación f; ~ **of work** HRM, MGMNT distribución de trabajo f, reparto de trabajo m

allocative: ~ **efficiency** n ECON, FIN eficiencia de localización f

allocatur n BANK, ECON, FIN, GEN COMM certificado de autorización de gastos m

allodial[1] adj LAW alodial

allodial[2]: ~ **system** n LAW sistema alodial m

allonge n BANK on bill of exchange talón m

all-or-nothing: ~ **clause** n BrE (AON clause) STOCK cláusula de todo o nada f

allot vt ACC consignar, GEN COMM asignar, distribuir, repartir, STOCK entregar, repartir, TRANSP entregar; ◆ ~ **shares** STOCK to employees repartir acciones

allotment n ACC public accountancy consignación f, GEN COMM asignación f, reparto m, distribución f, STOCK shares entrega f, reparto m, TRANSP shipping entrega f; ~ **of bonus** INS reparto de bonos m; ~ **letter** FIN, STOCK carta de asignación f, notificación de reparto f; ~ **price** FIN asignación de precio f; ~ **of securities** STOCK adjudicación de valores f; ~ **of shares** STOCK reparto de acciones m

allotted: ~ **share** n FIN, STOCK acción asignada f

allottee n STOCK beneficiario(-a) m,f

all-out: ~ **effort** n GEN COMM esfuerzo a toda potencia m; ~ **strike** n HRM, IND huelga general f

allow vt GEN COMM admitir, grant money, resources ceder, person, organization, action, change autorizar, INS claim admitir

allow for vt GEN COMM reservar para, hacer provisión para; ◆ ~ **a margin of error** GEN COMM permitir un margen de error, aceptar un margen de errores

allowable[1] adj GEN COMM lícito

allowable[2]: ~ **business investment loss** n BrE (cf deductible business investment loss AmE) TAX pérdida deducible en inversiones empresariales f; ~ **capital loss** n STOCK pérdida de capital reembolsable f; ~ **claim** n INS demanda admisible f; ~ **credit** n TAX crédito justo m, crédito reembolsable m; ~ **deduction** n ACC deducción autorizada f, TAX deducción admisible f; ~ **exemption** n TAX exención admisible f; ~ **expenses** n pl ACC, TAX gastos autorizables m pl, gastos deducibles m pl; ~ **liquid assets** n TAX of corporation, partnership activos líquidos desgravables m pl; ~ **refund** n TAX devolución deducible f; ~ **refundable tax on hand** n TAX impuesto sobre el disponible reembolsable y desgravable m; ~ **tax credit** n TAX deducción de la cuota permitida f

allowance n GEN COMM provisión f, deducción f, S&M for damaged or lost goods indemnización f, TAX provisión f, desgravación f, subsidio m, deducción f; ~ **for bad debts** ACC, BANK, FIN reserva para cuentas dudosas f; ~ **for depreciation** ACC deducción por amortización f; ~ **for exchange fluctuations** ACC provisión para fluctuaciones en el cambio f; ~ **for inflation** ACC reserva de revalorización f, reserva para inflación f; ~ **for living expenses** TAX deducción por gastos corrientes f, provisión para gastos de mantenimiento f; ~ **for personal expenses** TAX desgravación de gastos personales f; ~ **for traveling expenses** AmE, ~ **for travelling expenses** BrE TAX deducción por gastos de viaje f; ~ **in kind** GEN COMM indemnización en especie f, retribución en especie f

allowed[1] adj GEN COMM deduction permitido

allowed[2]: ~ **discount** n ACC, GEN COMM bonificación de descuento f; ~ **time** n HRM work tiempo concedido m

alloy: ~ **container** n TRANSP contenedor de mezcla m

all-round: ~ **price** n GEN COMM precio global m

all-savers: ~ **certificate** n BANK certificado de ahorros universal m

all-sector: ~ **average** n ECON growth promedio de todo el sector m

all-time: ~ **high** n GEN COMM, STOCK máximo histórico m; ~ **low** n GEN COMM, STOCK mínimo histórico m; ~ **record** n GEN COMM, STOCK récord histórico m

ALM abbr (asset-liability management) BANK, FIN, MGMNT GAP (gestión de activos y pasivos)

alongside[1] adv (a/s) TRANSP al costado

alongside[2]: ~ **bill of lading** n IMP/EXP, TRANSP conocimiento de embarque al costado del buque m

alongside[3] prep GEN COMM al lado de

aloof adj TRANSP ship apartado

alpha[1] adj STOCK alfa

alpha[2]: ~ **position** n ECON, IMP/EXP, IND, TAX posición alfa f; ~ **share** n STOCK acción alfa f; ~ **stage** n FIN etapa alfa f; ~ **stock** n STOCK acciones alfa f pl; ~-**test** n COMP prueba alfa f

alphabetical: **in** ~ **order** phr GEN COMM en orden alfabético

alphanumeric[1] *adj* (*A/N*) COMP, GEN COMM alfanumérico (*A/N*)

alphanumeric[2]: **~ character** *n* COMP carácter alfanumérico *m*

Alpine: **~ countries** *n pl* GEN COMM países alpinos *m pl*

alt. *abbr* (*altered*) GEN COMM mod. (*modificado*)

Alt: **~ key** *n* (*Alternate key*) COMP tecla alt (*tecla alternativa*)

alter *vt* GEN COMM alterar

alteration *n* GEN COMM alteración *f*; **~ of capital** GEN COMM alteración de capital *f*

alterations: **~ and improvements** *n pl* ACC *annual accounts* modificaciones y mejoras *f pl*

altered *adj* (*alt.*) GEN COMM modificado (*mod.*)

alternate[1] *adj* GEN COMM *by turns, successive* alterno; ◆ **on ~ days** GEN COMM en días alternos

alternate[2] *n AmE* (*cf substitute BrE*) GEN COMM *stand-in* alternativo(-a) *m,f*; **~ demand** ECON, S&M demanda de bienes sustitutivos *f*

alternate[3] *vt* GEN COMM alternar

Alternate: **~ key** *n* (*Alt key*) COMP tecla alternativa *f* (*tecla alt*)

alternating: **~ shifts** *n pl* HRM turnos alternos *m pl*

alternative *n* GEN COMM alternativa *f*, variante *f*; **~ cost** FIN coste alternativo *m* (*Esp*), costo alternativo *m* (*AmL*); **~ economic strategy** ECON, POL estrategia económica alternativa *f*; **~ energy** ENVIR energía alternativa *f*; **~ funding** FIN asignación de fondos alternativa *f*; **~ hypothesis** MATH *statistical testing* hipótesis alternativa *f*; **~ minimum tax** TAX impuesto mínimo alternativo *m*; **~ mortgage instrument** BANK instrumento hipotecario alternativo *m*; **~ order** GEN COMM orden alternativa *f*; **~ participation instrument** (*API*) STOCK instrumento de participación alternativa *m*; **~ payee** GEN COMM beneficiario(-a) alternativo(-a) *m,f*; **~ proposal** MGMNT proposición alternativa *f*; **~ solution** GEN COMM solución alternativa *f*; **~ technology** IND tecnología alternativa *f*; **~ use** PROP uso alternativo *m*; ◆ **there is no ~** (*TINA*) GEN COMM no hay alternativa

altruism *n* ECON, GEN COMM altruismo *m*

aluminium *n BrE* ENVIR aluminio *m*; **~ covers** *n pl BrE* TRANSP *shipping* cubiertas de aluminio *f pl*

aluminum *AmE see aluminium BrE*

a.m. *abbr* (*ante meridiem*) GEN COMM a.m. (*ante meridiem*)

AMA *abbr* (*Asset Management Account*) ACC, FIN cuenta de gestión de activos *f*

amalgamate *vt* GEN COMM *companies, activities, shares* amalgamar, fusionar

amalgamated: **~ bank** *n* BANK banco fusionado *m*; **~ body corporate** *n* GEN COMM, TAX compañía fusionada *f*; **~ corporation** *n* BANK, GEN COMM, TAX corporación fusionada *f*, compañía fusionada *f*

amalgamating: **~ body corporate** *n* GEN COMM compañía en vías de fusión *f*

amalgamation *n* GEN COMM fusión *f*, amalgamación *f*; **~ agreement** STOCK contrato de fusión *m*

amass *vt* GEN COMM amasar

ambassador *n* GEN COMM, POL embajador(a) *m,f*

ambient: **~ standard** *n* ENVIR *pollution* norma ambiental *f*; **~ temperature** *n* GEN COMM temperatura ambiente *f*

ambition *n* GEN COMM ambición *f*

ambitious *adj* GEN COMM ambicioso

amend *vt* LAW enmendar, reformar, PATENTS, POL modificar, enmendar, STOCK, TAX corregir

amended[1] *adj* LAW enmendado, reformado, PATENTS, POL, enmendado, modificado, STOCK, TAX corregido

amended[2]: **~ act** *n* LAW ley reformada *f*; **~ prospectus** *n* STOCK prospecto rectificado *m*; **~ tax return** *n* TAX porcentaje de devolución corregido *m*

amendment *n* LAW enmienda *f*, reformación *f*, PATENTS, POL modificación *f*, enmienda *f*, STOCK, TAX cambio *m*

amenities *n pl* PROP *appraisal* comodidades *f pl*

American[1]: **~ Association of Advertising Agencies** *n* (*AAAA*) S&M asociación estadounidense de agencias de publicidad; **~ Automobile Association** *n* (*AAA, cf Royal Automobile Club, Automobile Association BrE*) TRANSP organización estadounidense para el automovilista, ≈ Ayuda del Automovilista *f* (*Esp*) (*ADA*), ≈ Real Automóvil Club *m* (*RAC*), ≈ Real Automóvil Club *m* (*RAC*); **~ Board of Trade** *n* (*ABT*) GEN COMM, IND Cámara de Comercio de los Estados Unidos de America *f*; **~ Bureau of Shipping** *n* (*ABS*) TRANSP sociedad clasificadora de buques; **~ Chamber of Commerce** *n* (*ACC*) GEN COMM, IND Cámara de Comercio de los Estados Unidos de America *f*; **~ clause** *n* INS cláusula estadounidense en seguros marítimos; **~ Depositary Receipt** *n* (*ADR*) FIN recibo estadounidense de depósito de acciones; **~ dry quart** *n* GEN COMM cuarto estadounidense para áridos *m*; **~ Federation of Labor-Congress of Industrial Organizations** *n* (*AFL-CIO*) HRM federación estadounidense de trabajadores-congreso de organizaciones industriales; **~ Institute of Accountants** *n* ACC instituto estadounidense de contables; **~ Institute of Bankers** *n* (*AIB, cf Chartered Institute of Bankers BrE*) BANK instituto estadounidense de banqueros; **~ Institute of Certified Public Accountants** *n* (*AICPA*) ACC asociación profesional estadounidense de expertos contables; **~ Institute of Merchant Shipping** *n* (*AIMS*) TRANSP instituto estadounidense de la marina mercante; **~ liquid quart** *n* GEN COMM cuarto estadounidense para líquidos *m*; **~ Merchant Marine Institute** *n* (*AMMI*) TRANSP instituto estadounidense de la marina mercante; **~ National Standards Institution** *n* (*ANSI*) GEN COMM, IND, LAW instituto nacional estadounidense de normalización, ≈ Asociación Española de Normalización y Certificación *f* (*AENOR*); **~ option** *n* STOCK opción a la americana *f*; **~ short ton** *n* GEN COMM tonelada americana *f*; **~ Society for Testing and Materials** *n* (*ASTM*) GEN COMM sociedad estadounidense de evaluación y materiales; **~ Standard Code for Information Interchange** *n* (*ASCII*) COMP código estadounidense normalizado de intercambio de información; **~ Standards Association** *n* (*ASA, cf British Standards Institution*) GEN COMM, PATENTS asociación estadounidense de normalización, ≈ Asociación Española de Normalización y Certificación (*AENOR*); **~ Stock Exchange** *n* (*ASE, AMEX*) FIN, STOCK bolsa estadounidense de valores

American[2]: **in ~ terms** *phr* ECON *currency exchange* en términos americanos

Americanized-European: **~ option** *n* STOCK opción europea americanizada *f*

AMEX *abbr* (*American Stock Exchange*) STOCK bolsa americana de valores

Amex: **~ Commodities Exchange** *n* (*ACE*) FIN, STOCK

Bolsa de Contratación Amex *f*, Bolsa de Productos Amex *f*

AMI Ex *abbr* (*Associate Member of the Institute of Export*) IMP/EXP, HRM miembro asociado del instituto de exportación

amicable[1] *adj* GEN COMM amigable

amicable[2]: **~ settlement** *n* GEN COMM composición amigable *f*

amicably *adv* LAW *settle, part* por la vía amistosa

AMIME *abbr* (*Associate Member of the Institute of Marine Engineers*) HRM, TRANSP miembro asociado del instituto de ingenieros marítimos

AML *abbr* (*adjustable mortgage loan*) BANK, FIN, PROP préstamo hipotecario ajustable *m*

AMMI *abbr* (*American Merchant Marine Institute*) TRANSP instituto estadounidense de la marina mercante

amortizable[1] *adj* ACC, FIN, GEN COMM amortizable

amortizable[2]: **~ debt** *n* ACC, FIN, GEN COMM deuda amortizable *f*

amortization *n* GEN COMM, TAX amortización *f*; **~ adjustment** INS ajuste de la amortización *m*; **~ expense** ACC coste de amortización *m* (*Esp*), costo de amortización *m* (*AmL*); **~ fund** FIN, STOCK fondo de amortización *m*; **~ loan** BANK préstamo amortizable *m*; **~ method** ACC método de amortización *m*; **~ on a straight-line basis** ACC amortización constante *f*, amortización sobre la base de cuota fija *f*, amortización uniforme *f*, método de amortización lineal *m*; **~ payment** FIN pago de amortización *m*; **~ reserve** FIN reserva de amortización *f*; **~ schedule** ACC, BANK, FIN cuadro de amortización *m*, plan de amortización *m*

amortize *vt* ACC *asset*, BANK, FIN amortizar

amortized: **~ capital** *n* ACC, ECON, FIN, GEN COMM capital amortizado *m*; **~ cost** *n* ACC, TAX coste amortizado *m* (*Esp*), coste depreciado *m* (*Esp*), costo amortizado *m* (*AmL*), costo depreciado *m* (*AmL*); **~ mortgage loan** *n* BANK, FIN, PROP préstamo hipotecario amortizado *m*; **~ value** *n* ACC valor amortizado *m*

amortizement *n* GEN COMM, STOCK depreciación *f*

amount *n* (*amt*) ACC, ADMIN, GEN COMM cuantía *f*, montante *m*, cantidad *f* (*ctdad*), *of bill* importe *m*, monto *m*, MATH cuantía *f*; **~ brought forward** ACC traslado *m*; **~ of business** GEN COMM volumen de negocio *m*; **~ carried forward** ACC cantidad llevada a cuenta nueva *f*, suma anterior *f*; **~ charged** GEN COMM cantidad cargada *f*; **~ contributed** TAX suma de aportación *f*; **~ credited to an account** BANK cantidad ingresada en una cuenta *f*; **~ of damage** INS importe del daño *m*; **~ due** GEN COMM cantidad a pagar *f*, cantidad adeudada *f*, suma cierta *f*; **~ exported** GEN COMM cantidad exportada *f*; **~ invested** GEN COMM suma invertida *m*; **~ of loss** INS monto de la pérdida *m*; **~ outstanding** ACC, BANK, FIN cantidad pendiente *f*, deuda pendiente *f*, montón insoluto *m*, pago pendiente *m*; **~ overdue** ACC, BANK, FIN cantidad no pagada al vencimiento *f*, cuantía no pagada al vencimiento *f*, importe no pagado al vencimiento *m*; **~ overpaid** ACC, BANK, FIN cantidad pagada de más *f*; **~ paid** ACC, BANK, FIN cantidad pagada *f*; **~ paid by installments** *AmE*, **~ paid by instalments** *BrE* TAX cantidad pagada a plazos *f*; **~ paid out** ACC cantidad desembolsada *f*; **~ payable** ACC cuenta pagadera *f*, efectos a pagar *m pl*, obligación pagadera *f*, TAX cantidad pagadera *f*; **~ payable on settlement** ACC valor pagadero a la liquidación *m*; **~ repayable** ACC cantidad reembolsable *f*; **~ secured** TAX cantidad asegurada *f*; **~ secured by a charge upon property** FIN cantidad asegurada mediante una carga sobre la propiedad *f*; **~ to be invested** BANK cantidad por invertir *f*; **~ to be made good** INS cantidad a demostrar *f*; **~ underpaid** ACC, BANK, FIN cantidad pagada de menos *f*

amount to *vt* GEN COMM *bill* ascender a

amplitude: **~ change telegraphic signal** *n* (*ACTS*) TRANSP señal telegráfica de cambio de amplitud *f*; **~ of cycle** *n* GEN COMM amplitud del ciclo *f*

amt *abbr* (*amount*) GEN COMM monto *m*

AMT *abbr* (*air mail transfer*) BANK, COMMS, TRANSP transferencia por correo aéreo *f*

A/N *abbr* (*alphanumeric*) COMP, GEN COMM A/N (*alfanumérico*)

analog[1] *adj* COMP análogo; **~-to-digital** COMP analógico a digital

analog[2]: **~ channel** *n* COMP canal analógico *m*; **~ computer** *n* COMP computador analógico *m* (*AmL*), computadora analógica *f* (*AmL*), ordenador analógico *m* (*Esp*); **~ monitor** *n* COMP *hardware* monitor analógico *m*; **~ representation** *n* GEN COMM representación análoga *f*, representación analógica *f*; **~-to-digital converter** *n* (*ADC*) COMP *hardware* conversor de analógico a digital *m*

analogical *adj* COMP analógico

analyse *vt* *BrE* GEN COMM analizar

analyser *n* *BrE* COMP analizador *m*

analysis *n* GEN COMM *account, report*, HRM, MGMNT análisis *m*; **~ book** ACC libro de análisis *m*; **~ of cost variances** ACC análisis de las desviaciones del coste *m* (*Esp*), análisis de las desviaciones del costo *m* (*AmL*); **~ of costs by nature** ACC *annual accounts* análisis de costes por naturaleza *m* (*Esp*), análisis de costos por naturaleza *m* (*AmL*); **~ of variance** (*ANOVA*) MATH análisis de varianza *m*

analyst *n* BANK, HRM, MGMNT analista *mf*

analytic[1] *adj* GEN COMM analítico

analytic[2]: **~ process** *n* HRM, MGMNT proceso analítico *m*

analytical[1] *adj* GEN COMM analítico

analytical[2]: **~ accounting** *n* ACC contabilidad analítica *f*; **~ audit** *n* ACC auditoría analítica *f*; **~ auditing** *n* ACC auditoría analítica *f*; **~ review** *n* ACC revisión analítica *f*; **~ training** *n* HRM, MGMNT capacitación analítica *f* (*AmL*), formación analítica *f* (*Esp*)

analyze *AmE see* **analyse** *BrE*

analyzer *AmE see* **analyser** *BrE*

anarcho: **~-communism** *n* POL anarco-comunismo *m*; **~-syndicalism** *n* POL anarco-sindicalismo *m*

anarchy: **~ of production** *n* POL anarquía de la producción *f*

anchor: **~ bracket** *n* TRANSP *rail* anclaje de esquina *m*; **~-handling tug supply vessel** *n* TRANSP navío de suministros, remolque y enmienda de anclas *m*; **~ tenant** *n* PROP inquilino(-a) inamovible *m,f*

anchorage *n* GEN COMM, TRANSP anclaje *m*; **~ charges** *n pl* GEN COMM, TRANSP derechos de anclaje *m pl*

anchorman *n* MEDIA presentador(a) de noticias *m,f*

anchorwoman *n* MEDIA presentadora de telediario *f*

ancillary[1] *adj* GEN COMM *costs* auxiliar

ancillary[2]: **~ and incidental activities** *n pl* TAX actividades secundarias e incidentales *f pl*; **~ operation** *n* GEN

COMM, MGMNT operación subsidiaria *f*, operación auxiliar *f*; ~ **service** *n* GEN COMM servicio auxiliar *m*

ANF *abbr* (*arrival notification form*) TRANSP formulario de notificación de arribada *m*

angel *n infrml* GEN COMM promotor(a) teatral *m,f*

angle *n* MATH, TRANSP ángulo *m*; ~ **of repose** TRANSP ángulo de reposo *m*

Anglo-Irish: ~ **Free Trade Area Agreement** *n* (*AIFTA*) ECON acuerdo anglo-irlandés de área de libre comercio

animatic *n* S&M *advertising* esbozo de anuncio para TV *m*

animation *n* MEDIA *advertising* animación *f*

ankled *adj jarg* HRM *from job* despedido

annex[1] *n AmE see* **annexe** *BrE*

annex[2] *vt* GEN COMM, POL anexionar

annexe *n BrE* GEN COMM, LAW anexo *m*

anniversary *n* GEN COMM aniversario *m*; ~ **offer** S&M oferta aniversario *f*; ~ **publication** MEDIA publicación de aniversario *f*

announce *vt* GEN COMM *cut, details* anunciar

announcement *n* GEN COMM *advertisement* reclame *m* (*AmL*), anuncio *m* (*Esp*), *statement* declaración *f*; ~ **of a tax burden** TAX declaración de la carga fiscal *f*; ~ **effect** POL efecto anuncio *m*; ~ **of sale** MEDIA, S&M anuncio de venta *m*

annual[1] *adj* GEN COMM anual; ◆ **on an ~ basis** GEN COMM sobre una base anual

annual[2] *n* S&M anuario *m*; ~ **abstract of statistics** ECON, MATH resumen anual estadístico *m*, resumen anual de estadística *m*; ~ **accounts** *n pl* ACC cuentas anuales *f pl*; ~ **adjustment** TAX ajuste anual *m*; ~ **amortization** INS amortización anual *f*; ~ **annuity amount** TAX importe del pago anual *m*; ~ **appropriation** ACC asignación anual *f*; ~ **audit plan** ACC plan anual de auditoría *m*, plan de revisión anual *m*; ~ **automated controls survey** (*AAS*) TRANSP *shipping* inspección anual de controles automatizados *f*; ~ **basis** MATH *statistics* base anual *f*; ~ **cash flow** ACC flujo anual de tesorería *m*; ~ **certificate** ACC *audit* certificado anual *m*; ~ **closing** ACC, BANK, FIN, GEN COMM cierre anual *m*; ~ **debt service** ACC, BANK servicio de deuda anual *m*; ~ **depreciation** ACC depreciación anual *f*; ~ **depreciation charge** ACC cargo por depreciación anual *m*, gasto por depreciación anual *m*; ~ **dividend** GEN COMM dividendo anual *m*; ~ **earnings** *n pl* ACC ganancias anuales *f pl*; ~ **evaluation plan** FIN plan anual de evaluación *m*; ~ **exemption** TAX exención anual *f*; ~ **fee** ACC, FIN, GEN COMM, INS cuota anual *f*; ~ **gains limit** TAX límite de las ganancias anuales *m*; ~ **general meeting** (*AGM*) GEN COMM, MGMNT asamblea general anual *f*, junta general anual *f*; ~ **hours contract** HRM contrato anual por horas *m*; ~ **inert gas system survey** (*AIGSS*) ENVIR estudio anual del sistema de gas inerte *m*; ~ **installment** *AmE*, ~ **instalment** *BrE* ACC, FIN, GEN COMM cuota anual *f*, entrega anual *f*, plazo anual *m*, INS cuota anual *f*; ~ **leave** HRM vacaciones anuales *f pl*; ~ **meeting** GEN COMM, MGMNT asamblea anual *f*, junta anual *f*; ~ **meeting of shareholders** STOCK junta anual de accionistas *f*; ~ **mortgage constant** BANK, FIN, MATH, PROP hipoteca anual constante *f*; ~ **net cash inflow** ACC entrada anual neta de efectivo *f*; ~ **net profit** ACC beneficio neto anual *m*; ~ **order** GEN COMM, S&M pedido anual *m*; ~ **payment** GEN COMM pago anual *m*; ~ **percentage rate** (*APR*) BANK, FIN, GEN COMM tasa de porcentaje anual *f*, tasa porcentual por año *f*;

~ **premium** INS prima anual *f*; ~ **rate** FIN, GEN COMM *interest, growth* tasa anual *f*; ~ **rate bond** FIN, STOCK bono de tipo de interés anual *m*; ~ **rental charges** *n pl* TAX gastos anuales de alquiler *m pl*; ~ **repayment** GEN COMM devolución anual *f*; ~ **report** ACC informe anual *m* (*Esp*), reporte anual *m* (*AmL*), FIN memoria anual *f*; ~ **return** FIN *shares* rendimiento anual *m*, rédito anual *m*; ~ **salary review** HRM revisión salarial anual *f*; ~ **sales conference** MGMNT, S&M conferencia anual de ventas *f*; ~ **sales review** FIN, S&M revisión anual de ventas *f*; ~ **statement** ACC estado anual *m*; ~ **subscription** GEN COMM suscripción anual *f*; ~ **turnover** ACC, GEN COMM cifra de negocios anual *f*, cifra de ventas anual *f*, facturación anual *f*, volumen de negocios anual *m*; ~ **wage** HRM salario anual *m*; ~ **yield** ACC interés anual *m*, rendimiento anual *m*

annualize *vt* GEN COMM anualizar

annualized[1] *adj* GEN COMM anualizado

annualized[2]: ~ **working hours** *n pl* HRM promedio anual de horas trabajadas *m*; ~ **hours system** *n* HRM sistema anualizado de horas *m*; ~ **percentage rate** *n* (*APR*) BANK, FIN, GEN COMM tasa porcentual por año *f*, tasa de porcentaje anual *f*

annually *adv* GEN COMM anualmente

annuitant *n* GEN COMM beneficiario(-a) de una anualidad *m,f*, beneficiario(-a) de una renta *m,f*, TAX rentista *mf*

annuity *n* GEN COMM anualidad *f*; ~ **assurance** INS seguro de renta vitalicia *m*; ~ **bond** FIN, STOCK bono de renta vitalicia *m*; ~ **contract** TAX contrato de anualidad *m*; ~ **due** INS anualidad vencida *f*; ~ **factor** INS factor de pensión *m*; ~ **fund** INS fondo de anualidad *m*; ~ **income** TAX renta anual *f*; ~ **installment** *AmE*, ~ **instalment** *BrE* INS plazo de anualidad *m*; ~ **insurance** INS seguro de renta vitalicia *m*; ~ **payable in advance** INS anualidad pagadera por anticipado *f*; ~ **payable in arrears** INS anualidad pagadera a plazo vencido *f*; ~ **payment** TAX pago anual *m*, pago de anualidad *m*; ~ **plan** INS plan de anualidades *m*; ~ **policy** INS póliza de anualidades *f*

annul *vt* ECON, FIN cancelar, GEN COMM *decision*, LAW anular, cancelar, rescindir

annulling[1] *adj* GEN COMM, LAW *decision, action* anulado

annulling[2]: ~ **clause** *n* LAW cláusula abrogatoria *f*

annulment *n* GEN COMM *of contract* cancelación *f*, *of decision* anulación *f*, rescisión *f*

annunciator: ~ **board** *n AmE* STOCK tablero indicador *m*

anomaly *n* GEN COMM anomalía *f*; ~ **switch** STOCK cambio irregular *m*

anonymity *n* GEN COMM anonimato *m*

anonymous[1] *adj* GEN COMM anónimo

anonymous[2]: ~ **product testing** *n* S&M prueba anónima de un producto *f*

ANOVA *abbr* (*analysis of variance*) MATH análisis de varianza *m*

Ansaphone® *n* COMMS, GEN COMM Ansaphone® *m*

ANSI *abbr* (*American National Standards Institution*) GEN COMM, IND, LAW instituto nacional estadounidense de normalización, ≈ AENOR (*Asociación Española de Normalización y Certificación*)

answer[1] *n* GEN COMM, LAW contestación a la demanda *f*, defensa *f*, réplica *f*, respuesta *f*, contestación *f*; ~ **mode** COMP modalidad de respuesta *f*, modo respuesta *m*; ~ **print** S&M copia cero *f*

answer[2] **1.** *vt* GEN COMM contestar; ◆ **~ the telephone** COMMS contestar al teléfono; **2.** *vi* GEN COMM contestar

answer for *vt* GEN COMM *safety of product* responder por

answer to *vt* GEN COMM contestar a

answerable *adj* GEN COMM responsable

answerback: ~ code *n* ADMIN código de respuesta *m*

answering: ~ machine *n* COMMS, COMP, GEN COMM contestador *m*, contestador automático *m*; **~ service** *n* GEN COMM servicio de respuesta *m*

answerphone *n* COMMS, COMP, GEN COMM contestador telefónico *m*, *device* contestador automático *m*

antagonistic: ~ conditions of distribution *n pl* POL condiciones de distribución antagónicas *f pl*; **~ growth** *n* ECON crecimiento contrario *m*

ante[1]: **~-natal tax** *n* TAX impuesto prenatal *m*

ante[2] *prep* GEN COMM ante

antedate *vt* GEN COMM *document, cheque, event* antedatar

ante meridiem *phr* (*a.m.*) GEN COMM ante meridiem (*a.m.*)

anti-avoidance: ~ legislation *n* FIN, LAW, STOCK, TAX legislación antievasión *f*; **~ rule** *n* TAX norma contra la evasión fiscal *f*

anticipate *vt* GEN COMM *bill, debt* anticipar, *problem, delay* prever

anticipated[1] *adj* GEN COMM anticipado, previsto; ◆ **as ~** GEN COMM, S&M, TRANSP según lo previsto

anticipated[2]: **~ cost** *n* ACC coste previsto *m* (*Esp*), costo previsto *m* (*AmL*); **~ demand** *n* ECON, S&M demanda prevista *f*; **~ holding period** *n* STOCK periodo de espera previsto *m*; **~ profit** *n* FIN utilidad anticipada *f*; **~ repayment** *n* GEN COMM *of debt* amortización anticipada *f*; **~ sale** *n* S&M venta prevista *f*

anticipation *n* GEN COMM *of profits, income* previsión *f*, anticipación *f*; **~ equivalence** IMP/EXP equivalencia por anticipo *f*

anticipatory: ~ breach *n* LAW desistimiento de contrato *m*; **~ hedge** *n* STOCK cobertura anticipada *f*; **~ pricing** *n* ECON fijación de precios anticipada *f*; **~ purchase** *n* FIN, GEN COMM, S&M, STOCK compra de previsión *f*; **~ response** *n* ECON respuesta previsora *f*, GEN COMM respuesta anticipada *f*

anticompetitive[1] *adj* GEN COMM no competitivo

anticompetitive[2]: **~ practice** *n* ECON práctica anticompetitiva *f*

anticyclical[1] *adj* ECON *policy*, S&M anticíclico

anticyclical[2]: **~ advertising** *n* S&M publicidad anticíclica *f*

antidumping[1] *adj* ENVIR antidumping

antidumping[2]: **~ agreement** *n* ENVIR, IND, POL acuerdo antidumping *m*, convenio antidumping *m*

anti-fouling: ~ system *n* TRANSP sistema antivegetativo *m*

anti-inflation: ~ fight *n* ECON, POL lucha antiinflacionista *f*

anti-inflationary[1] *adj* ECON, POL antiinflacionista

anti-inflationary[2]: **~ stance** *n* ECON, POL postura antiinflacionaria *f*

anti-inflationist *adj* ECON, POL antiinflacionista

antimarket *adj* GEN COMM antimercadista

antimonopoly: ~ laws *n pl* GEN COMM, LAW, S&M leyes antimonopolio *f pl*

antiquated *adj* GEN COMM anticuado

antirecession *adj* GEN COMM antirecesión

anti-roll: ~ suspension *n* TRANSP suspensión antibalance *f*

antitheft: ~ device *n* TRANSP *on motor vehicles* dispositivo antirrobo *m*

antitrust[1] *adj* ADMIN antitrust, LAW antimonopolista, antimonopolio

antitrust[2]: **~ act** *n* LAW ley antimonopolio *f*; **~ law** *n* LAW legislación antimonopolio *f*

antivirus: ~ software *n* COMP programa antivirus *m*

ANZTAC *abbr* (*Australia and New Zealand Trade Advisory Committee*) ECON comité asesor de comercio de Australia y Nueva Zelanda

AO *abbr* (*administration officer*) HRM jefe(-a) administrativo(-a) *m,f*

AOB *abbr* GEN COMM (*any other business*) ruegos y preguntas, INS (*any one bottom*) *marine* cualquier fondo *m*

AOCB *abbr* (*any other competent business*) GEN COMM ruegos y preguntas

AOCTs *abbr* (*associated overseas countries and territories*) ECON, POL países y territorios asociados de ultramar *m pl*

AOLOC *abbr* (*any one location*) INS *marine* cualquier ubicación *f*

AON: ~ clause *n* (*all-or-nothing clause*) STOCK cláusula de todo o nada *f*

A1 *adj* TRANSP *Lloyd's Register of Shipping* de primera categoría, A1

AOS *abbr* (*any one steamer*) INS *marine*, TRANSP cualquier vapor *m*

AOV *abbr* (*any one vessel*) INS *marine* cualquier navío *m*

AP *abbr* COMP (*array processor*) computador vectorial *m* (*AmL*), computadora vectorial *f* (*AmL*), ordenador vectorial *m* (*Esp*), procesador vectorial *m*, INS (*additional premium*) prima complementaria *f*, MEDIA (*Associated Press*) agencia de noticias estadounidense, STOCK (*associated person*) persona asociada *f*

apartment *n* AmE (*cf flat BrE*) PROP apartamento *m* (*AmL*) (*Apt., Apto.*), departamento *m* (*AmL*) (*dpto.*), piso *m* (*Esp*); **~ building** PROP edificio de apartamentos *m*

APB *abbr* AmE (*Accounting Principles Board*) ACC comisión de principios contables *f*

APC *abbr* (*average propensity to consume*) ECON, S&M propensión media al consumo *f*

APEC *abbr* (*Asia Pacific Economic Cooperation*) ECON, POL CEAP (*Cooperación Económica de Asia y los Países del Pacífico*)

aphorism *n* GEN COMM aforismo *m*

API *abbr* (*alternative participation instrument*) STOCK instrumento de participación negativa *m*

apiece *adv* GEN COMM por unidad

apologies *n pl* GEN COMM disculpas *f pl*

apologize *vi* GEN COMM disculparse; ◆ **~ to sb for sth** GEN COMM disculparse ante alguien por algo

apologize for *vt* GEN COMM disculparse por

apology *n* GEN COMM apología *f* (*AmL*), disculpa *f* (*Esp*)

apparatus *n* GEN COMM dispositivo *m*, IND aparato *m*

apparel *n* GEN COMM equipo *m*; **~ industry** IND industria de la ropa *f*, industria indumentaria *f*; **~ wool** IND lana para confección *f*

apparent: ~ **authority** *n* LAW representación aparente *f*, poder aparente *m*; ~ **good order of the goods** *n* TRANSP buen orden aparente de las mercancías *m*; ~ **tax rate** *n* TAX tipo impositivo aparente *m*; ~ **time at ship** *n* (*ATS*) TRANSP hora aparente en el barco *f*

appeal[1] *n* GEN COMM solicitud *f*, *to public* alzada *f*, *of plan, idea* atractivo *m*, LAW *against judicial decision* recurso *m*, apelación *f*, S&M *of product* atractivo *m*; ~ **bond** LAW fianza de apelación *f*; ~ **court** LAW tribunal de apelación *m*; ~ **for funds** FIN solicitud de fondos *f*, solicitud de capital *f*; ~ **for tenders** GEN COMM solicitud de ofertas *f*; ~ **proceedings** *n pl* LAW autos de apelación *m pl*; ~ **product** GEN COMM producto de gancho *m*

appeal[2] *vi* GEN COMM, LAW apelar

appeal against *vt* LAW recurrir; ♦ ~ **a judgment** LAW recurrir una sentencia

appeal to *vt* GEN COMM *call* rogar, suplicar, S&M *attract* atraer

appeals: ~ **procedure** *n* HRM, LAW procedimiento de apelación *m*

appear *vi* GEN COMM *item in catalogue* figurar *seem* parecer, LAW *in court* comparecer

append *vt* COMP añadir, GEN COMM *document* añadir, *signature* estampar

appendix *n* GEN COMM apéndice *m*, MEDIA anexo *m*, apéndice *m*

appliance *n* GEN COMM dispositivo *m*

appliances *n pl* GEN COMM *domestic* electrodomésticos *m pl*

applicable: **not** ~ *adj* (*N/A*) GEN COMM no aplicable, no pertinente; ~ **to** *adj* GEN COMM aplicable a

applicant *n* GEN COMM solicitante *mf*; ~ **entrepreneur** GEN COMM empresario(-a) solicitante *m,f*; ~ **for registration** STOCK solicitante de cotización *mf*

application *n* COMP *software* aplicación *f*, GEN COMM *for job* solicitud *f*, *of technique, law* aplicación *f*; ~ **of accounting rules in good faith** ACC aplicación de buena fe de las normas contables; ~ **control** ACC *auditing* control de aplicación *m*, control de cumplimiento *m*; ~ **fee** BANK *share issue* cuota de suscripción *f*, derecho de suscripción *m*; ~ **for admission** STOCK solicitud de admisión *f*; ~ **for listing** STOCK solicitud de cotización *f*; ~ **for shares** STOCK suscripción de acciones *f*; ~ **for subsidies** GEN COMM solicitud de subsidios *f*; ~ **form** GEN COMM, HRM forma de solicitud *f*, formulario de solicitud *m*; ~ **of funds** ACC aplicación de fondos *f*; ~ **of funds statement** ACC declaración de aplicación de fondos *f*, estado de aplicación de fondos *m*; ~ **money** STOCK petición de fondos en la suscripción de acciones *f*; ~ **right** STOCK derecho de suscripción *m*

applications: ~ **package** *n* COMP paquete de aplicaciones *m*; ~ **program** *n* COMP *software* aplicación informática *f*; ~ **programmer** *n* COMP *software* programador(a) de aplicaciones *m,f*; ~ **software** *n* COMP aplicaciones informáticas *f pl*; ~ **terminal** *n* COMP terminal de aplicaciones *m*

applied[1] *adj* GEN COMM *research* aplicado

applied[2]: ~ **cost** *n* ACC, ECON, FIN coste aplicado *m* (*Esp*), costo aplicado *m* (*AmL*); ~ **economics** *n* ECON economía aplicada *f*; ~ **overheads** *n pl* GEN COMM gastos generales aplicados *m pl*, gastos generales reales *m pl*; ~ **research** *n* GEN COMM investigación aplicada *f*; ~ **research cost** *n* GEN COMM coste de investigación

aplicada *m* (*Esp*), costo de investigación aplicada *m* (*AmL*)

apply 1. *vt* COMP *to affect, to touch*, GEN COMM *accounting principle*, LAW aplicar; **2.** *vi* GEN COMM *rule* aplicarse; ♦ ~ **at the office** GEN COMM destinar a la oficina; ~ **in person** GEN COMM, HRM solicitar personalmente

apply against *vt* ACC imputar a

apply for *vt* GEN COMM suscribir, *post, job* solicitar; ♦ ~ **membership** GEN COMM solicitar afiliación; ~ **a loan** BANK suscribir un préstamo; ~ **shares** STOCK suscribir acciones

applying: **in** ~ *phr* TAX en aplicación

appoint *vt* GEN COMM *date, place* concertar, designar, señalar, *person* nombrar

appointed[1] *adj* GEN COMM *agent, chairman*, HRM nombrado

appointed[2]: ~ **day** *n* GEN COMM día designado *m*; ~ **executor** *n* FIN administrador(a) de herencia *m,f*; ~ **guardian** *n* FIN *of trust* administrador(a) de herencia *m,f*; ~ **space** *n* MEDIA, S&M *advertising* espacio adjudicado *m*, espacio designado *m*; ~ **stockist** *n* S&M distribuidor(a) designado(-a) *m,f*; ~ **time** *n* GEN COMM momento concertado *m*

appointee *n* GEN COMM *executive or junior*, LAW persona designada *f*, designado(-a) *m,f*

appointment *n* GEN COMM *of date* designación *f*, *of employee* nombramiento *m*, *arrangement to meet* cita *f*, HRM nombramiento *m*, PATENTS designación *f*; ♦ **by** ~ **only** GEN COMM sólo con cita previa; **arrange an** ~ GEN COMM, MGMNT concertar una cita, hacer una cita

appointments: ~ **vacant** *n pl* HRM empleos vacantes *m pl*

apportion *vt* ACC *costs*, PROP *land, property*, STOCK *shares* prorratear; ♦ ~ **the average** INS *marine* prorratear la avería; ~ **budget funds** FIN consignar fondos presupuestarios

apportioned: ~ **contract** *n* LAW contrato adjudicado *m*

apportionment *n* ACC, ECON, FIN consignación *f*, consignación en cuanta *f*, imputación *f*, INS repartición *f*, PATENTS derrama *f*; ~ **of funds** FIN *government agency, project* imputación de fondos *f*; ~ **rule** TAX *input tax credit* regla de prorrateo *f*

appraisal *n* FIN avalúo *m* (*AmL*), tasación *f* (*Esp*), GEN COMM, HRM *evaluation* justiprecio *m*, valoración *f*, *by expert, of project* evaluación *f*; ~ **clause** ECON *agricultural* cláusula de tasación *f*; ~ **of damage** INS evaluación del daño *f*; ~ **increment** ACC incrementos por revalorización *m pl*, GEN COMM incremento por apreciación *m*; ~ **report** GEN COMM informe de evaluación *m* (*Esp*), reporte de evaluación *m* (*AmL*); ~ **rights** *n pl AmE* STOCK derechos de tasación *m pl*

appraise *vt* GEN COMM evaluar, PROP estimar

appraised: ~ **value** *n* FIN valor valuado *m*, PROP valor estimado *m*

appraisement *n* FIN avalúo *m* (*AmL*), tasación *f* (*Esp*)

appraiser *n* FIN, PROP tasador(a) *m,f* (*Esp*), valuador(a) *m,f* (*AmL*), valorador(a) *m,f*

appreciable *adj* GEN COMM apreciable

appreciate 1. *vt* GEN COMM *understand the significance of sth* apreciar, *welcome* estimar; **2.** *vi* ACC revaluarse, PROP *asset, property*, STOCK ganar valor

appreciated: ~ **surplus** *n* GEN COMM plusvalía *f*, superávit por revalorización *m*

appreciation *n* ACC, GEN COMM estimación *f*, revalorización *f*, tasación *f*, valoración *f*, PROP, STOCK *currency, share,* TAX revaloración *f*, valuación *f*; **~ of currency** ECON revalorización de la moneda *f*

apprentice *n* HRM aprendiz(a) *m,f*

apprenticeship *n* HRM aprendizaje *m*

approach[1] *n* GEN COMM *bringing together* acercamiento *m*, aproximación *f*, MGMNT *plan of action* enfoque *m*, planteamiento *m*, acercamiento *m*, aproximación *f*

approach[2] *vt* GEN COMM *problem* abordar; ◆ **~ sb about sth** GEN COMM abordar a alguien sobre algo

appropriate[1]: **~ for** *adj* GEN COMM adecuado para

appropriate[2]: **~ funds** *n pl* ACC fondos asignados *m pl*; **~ percentage** *n* TAX porcentaje apropiado *m*; **~ technology** *n* ECON, ENVIR tecnología apropiada *f*

appropriate[3] *vt* ACC, ECON, FIN *funds* adjudicarse, apropiarse, consignar, destinar, incautarse de, GEN COMM asignar, repartir, afectar, LAW afectar, apoderarse de

appropriateness *n* GEN COMM aptitud *f*

appropriation *n* ACC *of funds* consignación *f*, dotación *f*, ECON *of funds to reserve* afectación *f*, FIN *of funds* adjudicación *f*, GEN COMM distribución *f*, asignación *f*, LAW, TAX dotación *f*; **~ account** ACC cuenta de aplicación *f*, cuenta de consignación *f*, cuenta de dotación *f*; **~ bill** ACC, ECON, LAW proyecto de ley de asignación presupuestaria *m*, proyecto de ley de consignaciones *m*, proyecto de ley de provisión de fondos *m*, proyecto de ley sobre asignación de crédito *m*, proyecto de ley sobre concesión *m*; **~ of income** ACC, ECON, TAX distribución de ingresos *f*; **~ to a reserve** ACC asignación a una reserva *f*

Appropriation: **~ Act** *n* BrE (*cf Appropriation Bill AmE*) FIN Decreto de Presupuestos *m*; **~ Bill** *n* AmE (*cf Appropriation Act BrE*) FIN Decreto de Presupuestos *m*

appropriations: **~ for contingencies** *n* TAX dotación para contingencias *f*

approval *n* GEN COMM *acceptance* aprobación *f*, conformidad *f*, autorización *f*; **~ of the accounts** ACC aprobación de cuentas *f*; **~ mark** TRANSP *vehicles* marca de aprobación *f*; **~ process** BANK trámite de autorización *m*; ◆ **on ~** (*on appro.*) GEN COMM *goods* a título de ensayo; **have the ~ of** GEN COMM contar con la aprobación de

approve *vt* COMP, GEN COMM votar, *action, accounts, decision* aprobar, INS visar, TAX aprobar

approved[1] *adj* COMP *device, software,* GEN COMM *decision, document* aprobado, INS *marine* visado, TAX aprobado

approved[2]: **~ code of practice** *n* (*ACOP*) GEN COMM código de procedimiento aprobado *m*; **~ delivery facility** *n* STOCK sistema de emisión aprobado *m*; **~ depository** *n* BANK depositario(-a) autorizado(-a) *m,f*; **~ list** *n* STOCK *of investments* lista aprobada *f*; **~ place** *n* ADMIN plaza confirmada *f*; **~ premises** *n pl* IMP/EXP, PROP local autorizado *m*; **~ price** *n* GEN COMM precio aprobado *m*; **~ profit-sharing scheme** *n* HRM plan aprobado de participación en los beneficios *m*; **~ project** *n* TAX proyecto aprobado *m*; **~ research institute** *n* TAX instituto de investigación aprobado *m*; **~ share** *n* STOCK acción admitida *f*; **~ status** *n* BrE TAX *by the Inland Revenue* categoría aprobada *f*

approx. *abbr* (*approximately*) GEN COMM aproximadamente

approximate[1]: **~ price** *n* STOCK precio aproximado *m*;

~ range *n* MATH cifra aproximada *f*; **~ rate of return** *n* ACC tasa aproximada de beneficios *f*

approximate[2] *vt* MATH aproximar

approximately *adv* (*approx.*) GEN COMM aproximadamente

approximation *n* GEN COMM, MGMNT acercamiento *m*, POL *of international policies* acercamiento *m*, aproximación *f*

appurtenant[1] *adj* LAW aparejado

appurtenant[2]: **~ structures** *n pl* INS estructuras accesorias *f pl*

APR *abbr* (*annual percentage rate*) BANK, FIN, GEN COMM tasa anual equivalente *f*, tasa porcentual por año *f*

aprioristic: **~ conjecture** *n* ACC, FIN, HRM cálculo apriorístico *m*

apron *n* TRANSP superficie de estacionamiento de aeronaves *f*, superficie de descarga *f*; **~ wharf** TRANSP *shipping* muelle de protección *m*

APS *abbr* (*average propensity to save*) ACC, ECON *economic accounting* propensión media al ahorro *f*

APT *abbr* (*arbitrage pricing theory*) STOCK teoría de establecimiento de precios por arbitraje *f*

aptitude *n* GEN COMM, HRM *of individual* aptitud *f*; **~ test** GEN COMM prueba de aptitud *f*, HRM, S&M examen de aptitud profesional *m*

APV *abbr* (*administrative point of view*) ADMIN, MGMNT punto de vista administrativo *m*, punto de vista de la administración *m*

AR *abbr* (*Average Revenue*) ACC, FIN, LEIS beneficios medios *m pl*, ingresos medios *m pl*

A/R *abbr* (*all risks*) INS todo riesgo

Arab: **~ Common Market** *n* ECON, POL Mercado Común Árabe *m*

Arabian-American: **~ Oil Company** *n* (*ARAMCO*) ECON compañía arábico-americana del petróleo

ARAMCO *abbr* (*Arabian-American Oil Company*) ECON compañía arábico-americana del petróleo

arb *abbr* (*arbiter*) LAW, STOCK árbitro(-a) *m,f*

arbiter *n* (*arb*) LAW, STOCK árbitro(-a) *m,f*

arbitrage *n* BANK arbitraje de cambio *m*, GEN COMM arbitraje *m*, STOCK arbitraje de cambio *m*; **~ bonds** *n pl* AmE STOCK bonos de arbitraje *m pl*; **~ dealer** GEN COMM arbitrajista *mf*, STOCK operador(a) de arbitraje *m,f*, arbitrajista *mf*; **~ dealing** STOCK operación de arbitraje *f*; **~ house** BANK, FIN, STOCK casa de arbitraje *f*; **~ in securities** BrE STOCK arbitraje de valores *m*; **~ margin** BrE STOCK margen de arbitraje *m*; **~ pricing theory** (*APT*) STOCK teoría de establecimiento de precios por arbitraje *f*; **~ stocks** *n pl* STOCK valores de arbitraje *m pl*; **~ trader** STOCK intermediario(-a) de arbitraje *m,f*; **~ trading** STOCK operación de arbitraje *f*

arbitrageur *n* GEN COMM cambista *mf*, árbitro(-a) *m,f*, cambista de divisas *mf*, arbitrajista *mf*

arbitral[1] *adj* GEN COMM arbitral

arbitral[2]: **~ award** *n* GEN COMM laudo arbitral *m*

arbitrary[1] *adj* GEN COMM arbitrario

arbitrary[2]: **~ assessment** *n* TAX valoración arbitraria *f*; **~ income** *n* TAX ingreso arbitrario *m*; **~ taxation** *n* TAX tributación arbitraria *f*

arbitrate *vi* GEN COMM arbitrar

arbitrate in *vt* GEN COMM arbitrar

arbitration *n* GEN COMM arbitraje *m*; **~ agreement** GEN COMM acuerdo de arbitraje *m*; **~ board** GEN COMM,

HRM junta arbitral *f*; **~ clause** GEN COMM, LAW cláusula de arbitraje *f*; **~ committee** GEN COMM comité de arbitraje *m*; **~ of exchange** FIN arbitraje de tipo de cambio *m*, pago con letra de cambio extranjera *m*; **~ proceedings** *n pl* IND procedimiento de arbitraje *m*; **~ transaction** STOCK transacción de arbitraje *f*; **~ tribunal** GEN COMM tribunal arbitral *m*

arbitrator *n* LAW, STOCK árbitro(-a) *m,f*

arc: **~ elasticity** *n* ECON elasticidad arco *f*

arcade *n* GEN COMM *shopping* galería *f*

architect *n* PROP arquitecto(-a) *m,f*; **~'s liability** INS, PROP responsabilidad civil del arquitecto *f*

archival: **~ storage** *n* COMP almacenamiento de archivos *m*

archive[1] *n* ADMIN, COMP, GEN COMM, LAW archivo *m*; **~ file** ADMIN, COMP, GEN COMM, LAW fichero *m*; **~ storage** ADMIN, COMP, GEN COMM, LAW almacenamiento de archivos *m*

archive[2] *vt* ADMIN, COMP, GEN COMM, LAW archivar

archiving *n* ADMIN, COMP, GEN COMM, LAW archivo *m*

archivist *n* ADMIN, HRM archivador(a) *m,f* (*Esp*), archivero(-a) *m,f* (*AmL*), archivista *mf*

arcsin *n* MATH *function* arc sen *m*

arctan *n* MATH *function* arc tg *m*

area *n* COMP campo *m*, ECON *surface size* área *f*, GEN COMM *space, extent, surface size* área *f*, barrio *m*, *of knowledge* campo *m*, IND *region* zona *f*, *of knowledge* campo *m*; **~ code** COMMS *telephone* código de área *m*; **~ of expertise** GEN COMM *of professional* área de conocimientos especializados *f*; **~ manager** HRM gerente de área *mf*; **~ office** BANK oficina de zona *f*; **~ of responsibility** HRM, MGMNT área de responsabilidad *f*; **~ sales executive** GEN COMM vendedor(a) de zona *m,f*; **~ sample** S&M muestreo por áreas *m*

arguments *n* PATENTS *for opposition, revocation* alegaciones *f*

ARI *abbr* (*accounting rate of interest*) ACC, BANK, FIN tasa de interés de cuenta *f*, tipo de interés de cuenta *f*

Ariel *abbr* (*Automated Real-Time Investments Exchange*) STOCK Bolsa de Valores Automatizada Tiempo Real *f*

arise from *vt* GEN COMM obedecer a

arithmetic: **~ mean** *n* MATH media aritmética *f*; **~ progression** *n* MATH progresión aritmética *f*

arm[1]: **at ~'s-length** *phr* ACC en condiciones de igualdad, en pie de igualdad, GEN COMM a distancia, TAX en pie de igualdad

arm[2] *n* ECON brazo *m*; **~'s-length competition** GEN COMM competencia en pie de igualdad *f*; **~'s-length price** ACC precio de mercado *m*, precio en condiciones de igualdad *m*, GEN COMM precio de mercado *m*; **~'s-length principle** GEN COMM principio de la igualdad de oportunidades *m*; **~'s-length transaction** BANK, COMMS transacción entre empresas interrelacionadas *f*, GEN COMM competencia en pie de igualdad *f*, transacción en igualdad de condiciones *f*

ARM *abbr* (*adjustable rate mortgage*) BANK, FIN, PROP hipoteca de tasa ajustable *f*

armchair: **~ critic** *n infrml* GEN COMM crítico de salón *m*

A-road *n BrE* (*A*) (*cf highway AmE*) TRANSP carretera nacional *f* (*N*)

around[1]: **~-the-clock** *adj AmE* (*cf round-the-clock BrE*) GEN COMM continuo

around[2]: **~-the-clock** *adv AmE* (*cf round-the-clock BrE*) GEN COMM continuamente

around[3]: **~-the-clock service** *n AmE* (*cf round-the-clock service BrE*) GEN COMM servicio de 24 horas *m*

ARP *abbr* (*adjustable rate preferred stock*) STOCK acción preferente de tipo ajustable *f*

ARR *abbr* (*accounting rate of return*) ACC tasa de rendimiento contable *f*, tipo de rendimiento contable *m*

arrange *vt* BANK disponer, GEN COMM concertar; **~ an appointment** GEN COMM, MGMNT concertar una cita

arranged: **~ total loss** *n* FIN, GEN COMM, INS *marine* pérdida total concertada *f*

arrangement *n* COMP clasificación *f*, FIN, GEN COMM, LAW convenio *m*; **~ fee** BANK gastos de gestión *m pl*; ♦ **by ~** GEN COMM por acuerdo

arranger *n* FIN facilitador(a) *m,f*

array *n* COMP *of figures, data* matriz *f*, S&M *products* serie *f*; **~ processor** (*AP*) COMP ordenador vectorial *m* (*Esp*), computador vectorial *m* (*AmL*), computadora vectorial *f* (*AmL*), procesador vectorial *m*

arrearage *n* FIN atrasos *m pl*, STOCK demora en el pago *f*

arrears *n pl* ACC importe atrasado *m*, BANK deuda atrasada *f*, FIN morosidad *f*, STOCK deuda atrasada *f*, *dividend or interest still owed* atrasos *m pl*; **~ of work** GEN COMM trabajo atrasado *m*; ♦ **in ~** BANK, FIN en mora; **be in ~** GEN COMM tener atrasos; **pay one month in ~** GEN COMM pagar con un mes de retraso

arrest *n* INS *marine*, LAW detención *f*

arrival *n* GEN COMM, TRANSP llegada *f*; **~ date** TRANSP fecha de llegada *f*; **~ notification form** (*ANF*) TRANSP *marine* formulario de notificación de arribada *m*; ♦ **reachable on ~** TRANSP *shipping* accesible a la llegada

arrived: **~ notification form** *n* TRANSP formulario de notificación de buque arribado *m*; **~ ship** *n* TRANSP buque arribado *m*

arson *n* INS, LAW incendio provocado *m*

art: **~ board** *n* S&M *advertising* tablero de diseño *m*; **~ buyer** *n* GEN COMM comprador(a) de obras de arte *m,f*; **~ department** *n* S&M *advertising* departamento gráfico *m*; **~ designer** *n* GEN COMM, HRM, S&M *advertising* creativo(-a) *m,f*, dibujante *mf*; **~ matt paper** *n* S&M *advertising* papel cuché mate *m*; **the ~ of the possible** *n* POL el arte de lo posible *m*; **~ print** *n* S&M *advertising* impresión artística *f*; **~ pull** *n* S&M *advertising* prueba de imprenta *f*

article[1]: **under ~** *adj* LAW, PROP escriturado

article[2] *n* GEN COMM *small object* artículo *m*, MEDIA *in newspaper* crónica *f*; **~ of consumption** GEN COMM artículo de consumo *m*

Article *n* LAW artículo *m*

articled: **~ clerk** *n* GEN COMM, LAW ≈ pasante *mf*

articles: **~ of agreement** *n pl* TRANSP *between shipowner and crew* convenio *m*, estipulaciones del convenio *f pl*; **~ of association** *n pl* LAW estatutos *m pl*; **~ of incorporation** *n pl* LAW escritura de constitución *f*; **~ for personal use** *n pl* GEN COMM *customs* artículos de uso personal *m pl*

articulated: **~ vehicle** *n* TRANSP vehículo articulado *m*

artifice *n* GEN COMM ardid *m*

artificial[1] *adj* GEN COMM ficticio

artificial[2]: **~ barrier to entry** *n* ECON *trade between different markets*, IMP/EXP, S&M barreras artificiales de entrada *f pl*; **~ currency** *n* ECON moneda artificial *f*;

~ **exchange rate** *n* ECON tipo de cambio ficticio *m*;
~ **intelligence** *n* (*AI*) COMP inteligencia artificial *f* (*IA*);
~ **obsolescence** *n* S&M caída en desuso artificial *f*,
caducidad artificial *f*

artisan: ~ **fair** *n* GEN COMM feria de artesanía *f*

artistic: ~ **director** *n* S&M *advertising* director(a) artístico(-a) *m,f*

arts: ~ **sponsor** *n* LEIS, S&M patrocinador(a) de arte *m,f*;
~ **sponsorship** *n* LEIS, S&M patrocinio de arte *m*

artwork *n* GEN COMM *of text* ilustraciones *f pl*

a/s *abbr* ACC, BANK (*account sales*) cuenta de ventas *f*,
GEN COMM (*at sight*) a la vista, a vista, (*account sales*)
cuenta de ventas *f*, S&M (*account sales*) cuenta de ventas
f, TRANSP (*alongside*) al costado

AS: ~ **level** *n* (*Advanced Supplementary Level General
Certificate of Education*) WEL examen británico a nivel de
bachillerato superior, ≈ Curso de Orientación Universitaria *m* (*Esp*) (*C.O.U.*), ≈ Selectividad *f* (*Esp*)

ASA *abbr* GEN COMM, IND (*American Standards
Association*) ≈ Asociación Española de Normalización
y Certificación (*AENOR*), MEDIA (*Advertising Standards Authority*) organización británica para la regulación
de la publicidad, PATENTS (*American Standards
Association*) ≈ Asociación Española de Normalización
y Certificación (*AENOR*), S&M (*Advertising Standards
Authority*) organización británica para la regulación de la
publicidad

ASAL *abbr BrE* (*agricultural sector adjustment loan*)
ECON, FIN préstamo de regulación del sector agrícola *m*

a.s.a.p. *abbr* (*as soon as possible*) COMMS, GEN COMM tan
pronto como sea posible, con la mayor brevedad
posible

ascending[1] *adj* GEN COMM ascendente; ◆ **in** ~ **order** GEN
COMM en orden ascendente

ascending[2]: ~ **top** *n* STOCK límite ascendente *m*

ascertain *vt* ACC *cost* establecer, GEN COMM verificar, *fact*
averiguar, *price* determinar

ascertainable *adj* TAX *group or person* investigable

ascertained: ~ **fact** *n* GEN COMM hecho verificado *m*;
~ **goods** *n pl* GEN COMM mercancías comprobadas *f pl*

ascertainment *n* GEN COMM averiguación *f*; ~ **error**
COMP error de observación *m*

ASCII[1] *abbr* (*American Standard Code for Information
Interchange*) COMP código americano normalizado de
intercambio de información

ASCII[2]: ~ **file** *n* COMP archivo ASCII *m*

ascribe: ~ **sth to sb** *phr* GEN COMM atribuir algo a
alguien

ASE *abbr* (*American Stock Exchange*) STOCK bolsa
americana de valores

Asia: ~ **Pacific Economic Cooperation** *n* (*APEC*) ECON,
POL Cooperación Económica de Asia y los Países del
Pacífico *f* (*CEAP*)

ASIAS *abbr* (*Airline Schedules and Interline Availability
Study*) TRANSP estudio de planes de vuelo y disponibilidad *m*

Asiatic: ~ **mode of production** *n* ECON, IND modelo de
producción asiático *m*

ask 1. *vt* GEN COMM preguntar; **2.** *vi* GEN COMM preguntar

ask for *vt* GEN COMM pedir

asked: ~ **and bid** *adj* STOCK *buying, selling price*
demandado y ofertado

asking: ~ **price** *n* ACC, FIN, STOCK precio del vendedor *m*,
precio de venta *m*

ASL *abbr* (*aggregate sales listings*) TAX inventario total de
ventas *m*

aspect *n* GEN COMM aspecto *m*; ~ **ratio** GEN COMM
proporción de dimensión *f*

aspiration: ~ **level** *n* S&M nivel de aspiración *f*

assay: ~ **mark** *n AmE* (*cf hallmark BrE*) BANK marca de
aleación *f*

assemblage *n* PROP *of land* reunión *f*

assembler *n* COMP *assembly language*, GEN COMM
ensamblador *m*

assembling *n* COMP, GEN COMM ensamblaje *m*

assembly *n* GEN COMM *parliament* asamblea *f*; ~ **cargo**
TRANSP carga concentrada *f*; ~ **line** HRM, IND *production* cadena de producción *f*, línea de montaje *f*, cadena
de ensamblaje *f*, cadena de montaje *f*; ~ **line worker**
HRM, IND obrero(-a) de línea *m,f*, trabajador(a) en
cadena *m,f*; ~ **plant** HRM, IND planta de montaje *f*,
planta armadora *f* (*Esp*), planta de ensamblado *f* (*Esp*);
~ **program** *AmE*, ~ **programme** *BrE* GEN COMM
programa de ensamblaje *m*, programa de la reunión *m*

assent *n* POL *of parliament* aquiescencia *f*

assertion *n* GEN COMM afirmación *f*

assertiveness: ~ **training** *n* HRM, WEL capacitación
asertiva *f* (*AmL*), formación asertiva *f* (*Esp*)

assess *vt* GEN COMM, PROP valorar, TAX *penalty* imponer,
taxpayer gravar

assessable: ~ **income** *n* TAX renta imponible *f*

assessed: ~ **tax** *n* TAX impuesto liquidable *m*; ~ **tax
arrears** *n pl* TAX atrasos del impuesto liquidable *m pl*;
~ **valuation** *n AmE* (*cf rateable value BrE*) PROP, TAX
property valor imponible *m*

assessing: ~ **action** *n* TAX acción impositiva *f*; ~ **tax** *n*
TAX cuota liquidable *f*

assessment *n* GEN COMM evaluación *f*, tasación *f*, LAW *of
compensation* valoración *f*, PROP *of compensation*
estimación *f*, TAX evaluación fiscal *f*, liquidación *f*, *of
penalty* imposición *f*; ~ **center** *AmE*, ~ **centre** *BrE*
HRM centro de evaluación *m*; ~ **of deficiency** TAX
estimación de la irregularidad *f*; ~ **of duty** IMP/EXP,
TAX fijación de derechos de aduana *f*; ~ **notice** TAX
aviso de imposición *m*; ~ **ratio** PROP proporción de
valoración *f*; ~ **roll** PROP, TAX lista de contribuyentes *f*

assessor *n* INS *marine* evaluador(a) *m,f*, TAX asesor(a)
m,f

asset *n* GEN COMM activo *m*, bien *m*, STOCK activo *m*,
elemento del activo *m*; ~ **account** ACC, BANK cuenta
activa *f*; ~ **allocation** STOCK asignación de activos *f*;
~-**backed finance** FIN finanzas respaldadas por activos
f pl; ~-**backed investment** FIN inversión respaldada
por activos *f*; ~-**backed securities** *n pl* FIN, STOCK
títulos respaldados por activos *m pl*; ~-**based financing**
FIN financiación basada en activos *f*; ~-**based
investment** STOCK inversión basada en activos *f*;
~ **coverage** ACC garantía con activos *f*, STOCK cobertura de activos *f*; ~ **depreciation range** (*ADR*) ACC,
FIN, PROP escala de amortización de activos *f*, rango de
depreciación de activos *m*, tramo de depreciación de
activos *m*; ~ **diversification** FIN diversificación de
activos *f*; ~ **exposure** BANK riesgo de activos *m*; ~ **held
abroad** GEN COMM activo exterior *m*; ~ **item** ACC
partida de activo *f*; ~-**liability management** (*ALM*)
BANK, FIN, MGMNT gestión de activos y pasivos *f*

(*GAP*); ~ **life** ACC vida del activo *f*; ~ **management** ACC, FIN administración de activos *f*, gestión de activos *f*; ~ **management company** FIN compañía de gestión de activos *f*; ~ **manager** STOCK administrador(a) de activos *m,f*; ~ **mix** ACC combinación de activos *f*, diversidad de activos *f*; ~ **motive** ECON *monetary economics* motivación del activo *f*; ~ **portfolio** FIN, STOCK cartera de activos *f*; ~ **price inflation** ACC, ECON inflación del precio de un activo *f*; ~ **quality** FIN *financial analysis* calidad del activo *f*; ~ **sale** ACC, GEN COMM, STOCK venta de activos *f*; ~ **specificity** ECON especificidad de activos *f*; ~ **stripping** ACC, ECON, FIN desglose de activos *m*, liquidación de activos *f*; ~ **swop** BANK canje de activos *m*; ~ **sweating** *AmE* BANK explotación del activo *f*; ~ **turnover** ACC, FIN movimiento de activos *m*, rotación de activos *f*; ~ **value** ACC, ECON, FIN valor de activo *m*; ~ **value per share** STOCK valor de inversión por acción *m*; ~ **write-down** ACC amortización de un activo *f*

Asset: ~ **Management Account** *n* (*AMA*) FIN cuenta de gestión de activos *f*

assets *n pl* ACC bienes *m pl*, capital *m*, ECON, FIN capital *m*, GEN COMM activos *m pl*, capital *m*; ~ **and drawbacks** GEN COMM *market economy* activos y devoluciones *m pl*; ~ **eligible for the money market** BANK activos elegibles para el mercado de dinero *m pl*; ~ **and liabilities management** *n* ACC, FIN, MGMNT administración de activos y pasivos *f*; ~ **and liabilities statement** *n* ACC, FIN balance de activo y pasivo *m*, balance de situación *m*; ~ **under construction** ACC *annual accounts* activos en construcción *m pl*, activos en curso *m pl*

assign *vt* ACC *costs* aplicar, imputar, INS *transfer* ceder, LAW, PATENTS ceder, traspasar, PROP traspasar, transmitir, STOCK ceder

assignable[1] *adj* GEN COMM transferible

assignable[2]: ~ **credit** *n* ACC, BANK crédito transferible *m*

assigned: ~ **account** *n* BANK cuenta cedida en calidad de empeño *f*, cuenta en garantía *f*; ~ **short position** *n* FIN, STOCK posición corta asignada *f*

assignee *n* GEN COMM cesionario(-a) *m,f*; ~ **in bankruptcy** BANK apoderado(-a) en bancarrota *m,f*

assignment *n* ACC *receivables* cesión *f*, traspaso *m*, INS cesión *f*, LAW, PATENTS cesión *f*, transmisión *f*, PROP traspaso *m*, escritura de cesión de bienes *f*, transmisión *f*, STOCK cesión *f*; ~ **of advertising expenditure** FIN, S&M asignación de gastos publicitarios *f*; ~ **day** STOCK día de notificación *m*, *options* día de cesión *m*; ~ **of debts** ACC cesión de deudas *f*, traspaso de deudas *m*; ~ **of income** TAX cesión de ingresos *f*; ~ **of lease** LAW cesión de arriendo *f*; ~ **man** MEDIA hombre con misión encomendada *m*; ~ **notice** STOCK aviso de asignación *m*; ~ **of patent** LAW, PROP cesión de una patente *f*; ~ **of rights** INS cesión de derechos *f*

assignor *n* INS, LAW, PATENTS cedente *mf*

assimilation *n* LAW *of laws*, STOCK asimilación *f*

assistance *n* ECON asistencia *f*, GEN COMM, LAW, POL, TAX ayuda *f*

assistant *n* (*asst*) GEN COMM auxiliar administrativo(-a) *m,f*, ayudante(-a) *m,f*, HRM asistente(-a) *m,f*, auxiliar administrativo(-a) *m,f*, ayudante(-a) *m,f*, *in shop* dependiente *mf*; ~ **administrator** GEN COMM, HRM auxiliar administrativo(-a) *m,f*; ~ **cashier** *BrE* (*cf assistant teller AmE*) BANK cajero(-a) adjunto(-a) *m,f*; ~ **controller**

(*AC*) HRM, TRANSP *shipping* interventor(a) adjunto(-a) *m,f* (*Esp*), contralor(a) adjunto(-a) *m,f* (*AmL*); ~ **director** BANK director(a) adjunto(-a) *m,f*, GEN COMM subdirector(a) *m,f*, HRM, MGMNT director(a) adjunto(-a) *m,f*; ~ **director general** (*ADG*) HRM, MGMNT director(a) general adjunto(-a) *m,f*; ~ **general director** BANK, HRM, MGMNT director(a) adjunto(-a) *m,f*; ~ **general manager** HRM, MGMNT director(a) general adjunto(-a) *m,f*, subdirector(a) general *m,f*; ~ **head of section** (*AHS*) HRM, MGMNT jefe(-a) auxiliar de sección *m,f*; ~ **manager** BANK director(a) adjunto(-a) *m,f*, subgerente *mf*, GEN COMM subdirector(a) *m,f*, HRM, MGMNT director(a) adjunto(-a) *m,f*, subgerente *mf*; ~ **teller** *AmE* (*cf assistant cashier BrE*) BANK cajero(-a) adjunto(-a) *m,f*; ~ **to manager** HRM, MGMNT asistente(-a) ejecutivo(-a) *m,f*; ~ **traffic supervisor** (*ATS*) HRM supervisor(a) adjunto(-a) de tráfico *m,f*

assisted: ~ **area** *n* ECON, POL, WEL zona de ayuda *f*

associate: ~ **company** *n* GEN COMM compañía asociada *f*, empresa asociada *f*, empresa filial *f*; ~ **director** *n* MGMNT director(a) adjunto(-a) *m,f*; ~ **editor** *n* MEDIA jefe(-a) de redacción adjunto(-a) *m,f*; ~ **lecturer** *n* HRM, WEL profesor(a) asociado(-a) *m,f*; ~ **manager** *n* MGMNT director(a) adjunto(-a) *m,f*; ~ **professor** *n* *BrE* (*cf adjunct professor AmE*) catedrático(-a) adjunto(-a) *m,f*

associate with *vt* GEN COMM asociarse con

Associate: ~ **of the Association of Certified and Corporate Accountants** *n* (*AACCA*) ACC miembro de la asociación de contables de empresas autorizados; ~ **of the Association of International Accountants** *n* (*AAIA*) ACC miembro de la asociación de contables internacionales; ~ **of the British Association of Accounts & Auditors** (*ABAA*) ACC miembro asociado de la asociación británica de contables y auditores; ~ **of the Chartered Association of Certified Accountants** *n* (*ACCA*) ACC miembro asociado del colegio de contables; ~ **of the Chartered Institute of Management Accountants** *n* *BrE* (*ACMA*) ACC miembro asociado del colegio de contables de gestión; ~ **of the Chartered Institute of Marketing** *n* (*ACIM*) HRM miembro asociado del instituto de marketing; ~ **of the Chartered Institute of Secretaries** *n* (*ACIS*) HRM miembro asociado del colegio de secretarias; ~ **of the City and Guilds of London Institute** *n* *BrE* (*ACGI*) GEN COMM miembro asociado del Instituto City and Guilds de Londres; ~ **of the Institute of Actuaries** *n* *BrE* (*AIA*) INS miembro del instituto de actuarios; ~ **Institute of Chartered Shipbrokers** *n* (*AICS*) HRM, TRANSP instituto afiliado de corredores marítimos colegiados; ~ **Institute Freight Trades Association** *n* (*AIFTA*) HRM instituto afiliado de la asociación de tráfico de mercancía; ~ **Member of the Institute of Export** *n* (*AMI Ex*) HRM miembro asociado del instituto de exportación; ~ **Member of the Institute of Marine Engineers** *n* (*AMIME*) HRM miembro asociado del instituto de ingenieros marítimos

associated[1] *adj* GEN COMM asociado; ~ **with** GEN COMM relacionado con

associated[2]: ~ **account** *n* BANK cuenta asociada *f*; ~ **company** *n* GEN COMM compañía asociada *f*; ~ **company abroad** *n* GEN COMM compañía asociada del extranjero *f*; ~ **employer** *n* HRM empresario(-a) asociado(-a) *m,f*, patrón(a) asociado(-a) *m,f*; ~ **mark** *n* GEN COMM marca derivada *f*; ~ **overseas countries and territories** *n pl* (*AOCTs*) ECON, POL *international trade* países y territorios asociados de ultramar *m pl*; ~ **person** *n* (*AP*) STOCK persona asociada *f*

Associated: ~ **British Ports** *n* (*ABP*) TRANSP asociación británica de puertos; ~ **Press** *n* (*AP*) MEDIA agencia de noticias estadounidense

association *n* ADMIN, ECON entidad sin fines de lucro *f*, GEN COMM asociación *f*, sociedad *f*; ~ **bargaining** HRM negociación de asociación *f*; ~ **subscription** GEN COMM suscripción a una asociación *f*; ♦ **in ~ with** GEN COMM asociado con

Association: ~ **of Accounting Technicians** *n* (*AAT*) ACC organización de técnicos contables; ~ **of American Shipowners** *n* (*AASO*) TRANSP asociación estadounidense de armadores; ~ **of Average Adjusters** *n* (*AAA*) INS asociación de tasadores de daños; ~ **of British Chambers of Commerce** *n* (*ABCC*) IND asociación de cámaras de comercio británicas; ~ **of British Travel Agents** *n* (*ABTA*) LEIS asociación británica de agentes de viaje; ~ **of European Steel Producers** *n* (*Euro Fer*) IND Asociación Europea de Productores de Acero *f*; ~ **of Futures Brokers and Dealers** *n* (*AFBD*) STOCK Asociación de Agentes y Corredores de Futuros *f*; ~ **of International Bond Dealers** *n* (*AIBD*) STOCK organismo autorregulador del mercado de eurobonos; ~ **of Scientific, Technical and Managerial Staff** *n* (*ASTMS*) HRM asociación de personal científico, técnico y de dirección; ~ **of Shipbrokers and Agents** *n AmE* TRANSP asociación de consignatarios y agentes de los Estados Unidos; ~ **of South-East Asian Nations** *n* (*ASEAN*) ECON Asociación de Naciones del Sureste Asiático

assortment: ~ **of goods** *n* GEN COMM surtido de mercancías *m*

asst *abbr* (*assistant*) HRM asistente(-a) *m,f*, auxiliar administrativo(-a) *m,f*, ayudante(-a) *m,f*, *in shop* dependiente (-a) *m,f*

assume *vt* GEN COMM *risk, power* asumir; ♦ ~ **responsibility for** GEN COMM asumir la responsabilidad de

assumption *n* GEN COMM, LAW presunción *f*; ~ **of mortgage** BANK aceptación de hipoteca *f*

assured[1] *adj* INS asegurado

assured[2]: ~ **capital** *n* ECON, INS capital asegurado *m*, cantidad asegurada *f*

astern: ~ **power** *n* TRANSP potencia de ciar *f*

ASTM *abbr* (*American Society for Testing and Materials*) GEN COMM sociedad estadounidense de evaluación y materiales

ASTMS *abbr* (*Association of Scientific, Technical and Managerial Staff*) HRM asociación de personal científico, técnico y de dirección

asylum *n* GEN COMM, POL, WEL asilo *m*

asymmetric: ~ **information** *n* GEN COMM información asimétrica *f*

asymmetry *n* GEN COMM asimetría *f*

asynchronous *adj* COMP asincrónico

at[1]: ~ **call** *adv* FIN, STOCK sobre demanda

at[2]: **as ~** *phr* BANK, GEN COMM a fecha

ATA *abbr AmE* (*Air Transport Association*) TRANSP asociación estadounidense de transporte aéreo, ≈ AENA *abbr* (*Aeropuertos Españoles y Navegación Aérea*) (*Esp*)

ATC *abbr* (*air-traffic control*) TRANSP control de tráfico aéreo *m*

ATC/IATA: ~ **Reservations Interline Message Proce-** dures **Manual** *n* TRANSP Manual de Procedimientos para Mensajes de Reservas *m*

ATM *abbr AmE* BANK (*automated teller machine*) cajero bancario *m*, cajero automático *m*, FIN, STOCK (*at-the-money*) al precio de contado, al precio

atmosphere *n* ENVIR, GEN COMM atmósfera *f*, ambiente *m*

atomic: ~ **energy** *n* ENVIR, IND energía atómica *f*

Atomic: ~ **Energy Research Establishment** *n* (*AERE*) ENVIR ≈ Comisión Nacional de Energía Atómica *f* (*AmL*) (*CONEA*)

atomistic: ~ **competition** *n* ECON competencia atomizada *f*

at-risk: ~ **amount** *n* TAX volumen del riesgo *m*; ~ **rule** *n* TAX norma de riesgo *f*

ATRR *abbr* (*allocated transfer risk reserve*) FIN reserva de riesgo con transferencia variable *f*

ATS *abbr* BANK (*automatic transfer service*) cuentas enlazadas automáticamente *f pl*, servicio automático de transferencia *m*, HRM (*assistant traffic supervisor*) supervisor(a) adjunto(-a) de tráfico *m,f*, TRANSP (*apparent time at ship*) hora aparente en el barco *f*

ATT *abbr* (*air transportation tax*) TAX, TRANSP impuesto sobre el transporte aéreo *m*

attach *vt* COMP interconectarse, COMMS *document, copy*, GEN COMM adjuntar

attached: ~ **account** *n* BANK cuenta adjunta *f*; ~ **copy of letter** *n* COMMS copia adjunta de la carta *f*, copia de la carta adjunta *f*

attachment *n* COMP interconexión *f*, INS anexo *m*; ~ **bond** FIN, LAW fianza de embargo *f*; ~ **date** INS *marine* fecha de efectiva *f*

attack[1] *n* GEN COMM ataque *m*

attack[2] *vt* GEN COMM *problems* acometer

attained: ~ **age** *n* INS edad cumplida *f*

attempt[1] *n* GEN COMM intento *m*

attempt[2] *vt* GEN COMM intentar, ensayar

attend *vt* HRM, MGMNT *meeting* asistir

attend to *vt* GEN COMM cumplir algo; ♦ ~ **a customer** GEN COMM atender a un cliente

attendance: ~ **bonus** *n* HRM prima por asistencia *f*; ~ **fees** *n pl* HRM cuotas de asistencia *f pl*; ~ **money** *n* HRM cuotas de asistencia *f pl*, dietas por asistencia *f pl*

attention[1] *n* GEN COMM, S&M atención *f*; ~ **factor** S&M *advertising* factor de atención *m*; ~~**getter** S&M *advertising* anuncio publicitario que capta la atención del público; ~ **value** S&M *advertising* valor de atención *m*; ♦ **for the ~ of** (*FAO*) GEN COMM *in fax* a la atención de

attention[2]: ~, **interest, desire, action** *phr* (*AIDA*) GEN COMM atención, interés, deseo, acción

attest *vt* LAW atestar, dar fe de

attest to: ~ **sth** *phr* GEN COMM dar fe de algo

attestation *n* LAW testificación *f*; ~ **clause** INS *marine* cláusula de ratificación de compromiso *f*

at-the-money[1] *adv* (*ATM*) FIN, STOCK al precio *m* al precio de contado *m*, sin beneficio ni pérdida

at-the-money[2]: ~ **call** *n* STOCK compra a precio corriente *f*; ~ **call option** *n* STOCK opción de compra a precio corriente *f*; ~ **option** *n* STOCK opción indiferente *f*; ~ **put** *n* STOCK venta al precio de mercado *f*; ~ **put option** *n* STOCK opción de venta a precio de mercado *f*

attitude *n* GEN COMM, MGMNT, S&M actitud *f*; ~ **scale**

S&M *market research* escala de actitudes *f*; ~ **survey** S&M *market research* estudio de actitudes *m*

attornment *n* LAW reconocimiento de los derechos un nuevo terrateniente

attorney *n* GEN COMM, LAW ≈ abogado(-a) *m,f*; **~-at-law** GEN COMM, LAW ≈ abogado(-a) *m,f*; **~-in-fact** *AmE* LAW ≈ apoderado(-a) *m,f*

attract *vt* GEN COMM atraer; ♦ **~ new business** GEN COMM atraer nuevos negocios; **~ sb's attention** GEN COMM llamar la atención de alguien, atraer la atención de alguien

attractive[1] *adj* GEN COMM *for investors* atractivo, STOCK *in vogue* de moda

attractive[2]: **~ nuisance** *n AmE* LAW *property*, PROP fuente de peligro para los niños involucrando la responsabilidad del propietario; **~ offer** *n* GEN COMM oferta atractiva *f*; **~ terms** *n pl* GEN COMM condiciones atractivas *f pl*

attributable: **~ to** *adj* GEN COMM atribuible a

attribute[1] *n* COMP *language*, GEN COMM atributo *m*; **~ sampling** ACC *auditing*, MATH *statistics* muestreo de atributos *m*, MEDIA *market research* muestreo característico *m*, S&M muestreo de atributos *m*

attribute[2]: **~ sth to sb** *phr* GEN COMM atribuir algo a alguien; **~ sth to sth** *phr* GEN COMM atribuir algo a algo

attributed: **~ to** *adj* GEN COMM atribuido a

attribution[1]: **~ rule** *n* TAX norma de atribución *f*

attribution[2]: **not for ~** *phr jarg* MEDIA *print* no atribuible

attrition *n* HRM *due to retirement, sickness, death and relocation* reducción incontrolable de plantilla *f*; **~ rate** GEN COMM tasa de desgaste *f*

atypical: **~ worker** *n* HRM trabajador(a) atípico(-a) *m,f*

au fait *adj* GEN COMM al tanto

auction *n* GEN COMM subasta *f*; **~ market** STOCK mercado de subasta *m*; **~ room** GEN COMM sala de subastas *f*

auction off *vt* GEN COMM subastar, rematar (*AmL*)

audi: **~ alteram partem** *phr* GEN COMM escuchar a la parte contraria

audience *n* GEN COMM audiencia *f*, MEDIA, S&M *advertising* audiencia *f*, público *m*

audio: **~ conference** *n* COMMS, COMP audioconferencia *f*; **~ conferencing** *n* COMMS, COMP audioconferencia *f*

audiotyping *n* GEN COMM audiomecanografía *f*

audiovisual[1] *adj* (*av*) COMMS, MEDIA, S&M audiovisual

audiovisual[2]: **~ aids** *n pl* COMMS, MEDIA ayudas audiovisuales *f pl*, medios audiovisuales *m pl*; **~ display** *n* S&M exhibición audiovisual *f*; **~ equipment** *n* S&M equipo audiovisual *m*

audit[1] *n* ACC, FIN, TAX censura de cuentas *f*, *of tax returns* revisión *f*, verificación *f*, auditoría *f*; **~ activity** ACC actividad de auditoría *f*, desarrollo de una auditoría *m*; **~ assurance** ACC nivel de confianza *m*, seguridad de auditoría *f*; **~ certificate** ACC certificado de auditoría *m*; **~ client** ACC cliente de auditoría *mf*; **~ committee** ACC comité de auditoría *m*; **~ costs** *n pl* ACC costes de auditoría *m pl* (*Esp*), costos de auditoría *m pl* (*AmL*); **~ coverage** ACC alcance de la auditoría *m*; **~ engagement** ACC compromiso de auditoría *m*, contratación de auditoría *f*, encargo de auditoría *m*; **~ evidence** ACC evidencia de auditoría *f*; **~ examination** ACC examen de auditoría *m*; **~ file** ACC archivo de auditoría *m*, archivo de revisión contable *m*, archivo de verificación contable *m*; **~ function** ACC, TAX función fiscalizadora *f*; **~ group** ACC grupo de auditoría

m; **~ guide** ACC guía de auditoría *f*; **~ head** ACC jefe(-a) de auditoría *m,f*; **~ independence** ACC independencia en auditoría *f*; **~ officer** ACC funcionario(-a) auditor(a) *m,f*; **~ plan** ACC plan de auditoría *m*; **~ program** *AmE*, **~ programme** *BrE* ACC programa de auditoría *m*, programa de fiscalización *m*; **~ report** ACC informe de auditoría *m* (*Esp*), reporte de auditoría *m* (*AmL*); **~ risk** ACC riesgo de auditoría *m*; **~ schedule** ACC programa de auditoría *m*; **~ scope** ACC ámbito de revisión contable *m*; **~ software** ACC, COMP aplicación informática para auditoría *f*, software de auditoría *m*; **~ staff** ACC personal de auditoría *m*; **~ standard** ACC norma de auditoría *f*; **~ team** ACC equipo de auditores *m*; **~ technique** ACC técnica de auditoría *f*; **~ trail** ACC rastreo de auditoría *m*, COMP verificación retrospectiva *f*; **~ window** COMP ventana de intervención *f*; **~ work schedule** ACC programa de trabajo de auditoría *m*; **~ working papers** *n pl* ACC papeles de trabajo de auditoría *m pl*

audit[2] *vt* ACC auditar, revisar, verificar, *accounts* censurar, COMP verificar, FIN censurar, auditar, TAX auditar

Audit: **~ Bureau of Circulation** *n* (*ABC*) S&M Oficina de Justificación de la Difusión *f* (*OJD*); **~ Office** *n BrE* ACC, POL Tribunal de Cuentas *m* (*Esp*)

audita altera parte: **~ procedure** *n* GEN COMM procedimiento de escucha de la parte contraria *m*

auditability *n* ACC auditabilidad *f*

auditable *adj* ACC auditable, revisable, verificable

audited: **~ circulation** *n* S&M difusión auditada *f*; **~ statement** *n* ACC estado auditado *m*, estado revisado *m*, estado verificado *m*

auditee *n* ACC auditado(-a) *m,f*

auditing *n* ACC, FIN auditoría *f*, censura de cuentas *f*, TAX auditoría *f*; **~ department** ACC *of company* departamento de auditoría *m*; **~ manual** ACC manual de auditoría *m*; **~ principle** ACC principio de auditoría *m*; **~ procedure** ACC procedimiento de auditoría *m*; **~ standard** ACC norma de auditoría *f*; **~ technique** ACC técnica de auditoría *f*

auditor *n* ACC auditor(a) *m,f*, interventor(a) de cuentas *m,f* (*Esp*), contralor(a) de cuentas *m,f* (*AmL*), FIN, TAX auditor(a) *m,f*; **~'s certificate** ACC dictamen de auditoría *m*, informe de auditoría *m* (*Esp*), reporte de auditoría *m* (*AmL*); **~'s opinion** ACC opinión del auditor *f*; **~'s report** ACC informe del auditor *m* (*Esp*), informe del interventor de cuentas *m* (*Esp*), reporte de los auditores *m* (*AmL*), reporte de los interventores de cuentas *m* (*AmL*)

Auditor: **~'s Operational Standard** *n* ACC norma de operación del auditor *f*

augmented: **~ gross national product** *n* (*AGNP*) ECON *economic accounting* aumento del PIB *m*, aumento del producto interior bruto *m*

Australia: **~ and New Zealand Trade Advisory Committee** *n* (*ANZTAC*) ECON comité asesor de comercio de Australia y Nueva Zelanda

Australian: **~ British Trade Association** *n* (*ABTC*) IND sociedad comercial australiano-británica; **~ Broadcasting Corporation** *n* (*ABC*) MEDIA organismo de radiodifusión australiana; **~ Conciliation and Arbitration Commission** *n* HRM cómite australiano de arbitraje y de conciliación; **~ Container Service** *n* (*ACS*) TRANSP servicio australiano de contenedores; **~ Council of Trade Unions** *n* (*ACTU*) HRM confederación de sindicatos australianos; ~ **Financial Futures Market** n (*AFFM*) STOCK mercado de futuros financieros australiano; ~ **Stock Exchange** n STOCK bolsa de valores australiana

Austrian: ~ **Economics** n ECON economía austríaca f; ~ **School of Economics** n pl ECON escuela austríaca de economía f

autarchy n ECON, POL autarquía f

autex: ~ **system** n STOCK sistema autex m

authenticated: ~ **signature** n BANK, LAW firma autentificada f, firma certificada f

authentification n LAW, STOCK autentificación f

author: ~'s **note** n GEN COMM nota del autor f (*N.A.*); ~ **royalties** n GEN COMM, MEDIA, S&M derechos de autor m pl

authoritarian: ~ **management** n HRM, MGMNT administración autoritaria f, gestión autoritaria f; ~ **society** n ECON sociedad autoritaria f, POL régimen dictatorial m; ~ **state** n ECON estado autoritario m

authoritative adj GEN COMM *version* autoritativo

authorities n pl BANK, GEN COMM autoridades f pl; ~ **to purchase** TRANSP autorizaciones de compra f pl

authority n GEN COMM competencia f, autoridad f, HRM autoridad f, LAW *national* competencia f, poder m, PATENTS jurisdicción f, POL poder m; ~ **bond** AmE STOCK obligación de organismo público f; ~ **structure** GEN COMM estructura de autoridad f; ~ **to buy** GEN COMM *of third party* autoridad para comprar f; ◆ **have signing** ~ BANK tener autoridad para firmar

authorization n GEN COMM permiso m, LAW autorización f, legalización f; ~ **center** AmE, ~ **centre** BrE BANK centro de autorización m; ~ **code** BANK código de autorización m; ~ **for expenditure** ACC autorización del gasto f; ~ **number** BANK número de autorización m; ~ **under consideration** (*AC*) GEN COMM autorización en trámite f

authorize vt GEN COMM autorizar, LAW legalizar

authorized¹: ~ **agent** n GEN COMM agente autorizado(-a) m,f, LAW agente oficial mf; ~ **bank** n BANK banco autorizado m; ~ **bond** n FIN, STOCK bono autorizado m; ~ **capital** n ACC, ECON, FIN capital autorizado m; ~ **capital stock** n STOCK capital social autorizado m; ~ **clerk** n STOCK empleado(-a) de bolsa m,f; ~ **credit** n BANK crédito autorizado m; ~ **dealer** n BANK agente autorizado(-a) m,f, STOCK intermediario(-a) autorizado(-a) m,f; ~ **person** n TAX persona autorizada f; ~ **representative** n GEN COMM, HRM, STOCK representante autorizado(-a) m,f; ~ **share** n FIN, STOCK acción autorizada f; ~ **share capital** n ACC, ECON, FIN capital accionario autorizado m, capital autorizado m, capital accionario autorizado m; ~ **signature** n BANK firma autorizada f; ~ **stock** n STOCK emisión autorizada f

authorized²: **be** ~ **to sign** phr BANK tener firma autorizada

auto: ~ **rental** n AmE (*cf car hire* BrE) TRANSP alquiler de coches m

autobank: ~ **card** n BANK tarjeta de banco automático f

autoboot n COMP autoarranque m

autocorrelation n ECON *econometrics* autocorrelación f

autodidact n WEL autodidacta mf

autoduplication n COMP duplicación automática f

auto-economy n ECON economía de autosuficiencia f

autofeeder n COMP alimentador automático m

autofinancing n ACC, FIN autofinanciación f

autogeny n GEN COMM generación espontánea f

autoloader n COMP autocargador m

autologin n COMP carga automática f

autologon n COMP entrada automática al sistema f

automate vt COMP, GEN COMM, IND automatizar

automated¹ adj GEN COMM, IND automatizado

automated²: ~ **cash dispenser** n BrE (*cf automated teller machine* AmE) BANK cajero automático m, cajero bancario m, dispensador de dinero en efectivo m; ~ **quotation** n STOCK cotización mecanizada f; ~ **teller card** n BANK tarjeta para cajero automático f; ~ **teller machine** n AmE (*cf automated cash dispenser* BrE) BANK cajero automático m, cajero bancario m, dispensador de dinero en efectivo m; ~ **teller machine statement** n BANK recibo de cajero automático m

Automated: ~ **Clearing House** n (*ACH*) BANK, FIN Cámara de Compensación Automatizada f; ~ **Clearing Settlement System** n (*ACSS*) BANK Sistema de Liquidación de Compensación Automatizado m; ~ **Pit Trading** n STOCK *CBOT, LIFFE* operación de corro automatizada f; ~ **Real-Time Investments Exchange** n (*Ariel*) STOCK Bolsa de Valores Automatizada a Tiempo Real f

automatic¹ adj GEN COMM automático

automatic²: ~ **adjustment point** n HRM *salaries* punto de ajuste automático m; ~ **call forwarding** COMMS reenvío automático m; ~ **cash dispenser** n BrE (*ACD*) (*cf automatic telling machine* AmE) BANK cajero automático m, cajero bancario m, dispensador de dinero en efectivo m; ~ **check** n COMP comprobación automática f; ~ **check-off** n ECON *labour economics* comprobación automática f; ~ **control** n COMP mando automático m; ~ **control certified** n (*ACC*) TRANSP control automático autorizado m; ~ **control certified for unattended engine room** n TRANSP control automático aprobado de maquinaria no operativa m; ~ **coupling** n TRANSP *road transport* acoplamiento automático m; ~ **data processing** n (*ADP*) COMP proceso automático de datos m (*PAD*); ~ **fare collection** n TRANSP cobro automático de tarifas m; ~ **feeder** n ADMIN *office equipment* alimentador automático m; ~ **fine tuning** n (*AFT*) COMP sintonización fina automática f; ~ **funds transfer** n (*AFT*) ACC, BANK, FIN transferencia de fondos automática f; ~ **maritime radio telex service** n TRANSP servicio automático de radiotélex marítimo m; ~ **merchandising** n S&M comercialización automática f; ~ **payment through a bank** n BANK, FIN domiciliación bancaria f; ~ **redialing** AmE, ~ **redialling** BrE n COMMS *button* botón de rellamada m; ~ **reinvestment** n STOCK reinversión automática f; ~ **reset** n COMP restablecimiento automático m; ~ **selling** n GEN COMM venta automática f; ~ **stabilizer** n ECON *government spending*, POL estabilizador automático m; ~ **teller** n AmE (*cf automatic cash dispenser* BrE) BANK cajero automático m; ~ **telling machine** n AmE (*cf automatic cash dispenser* BrE) BANK cajero automático m, cajero bancario m, dispensador de dinero en efectivo m; ~ **transfer** n BANK transferencia automática f; ~ **transfer service** n BrE (*ATS*) BANK cuentas enlazadas automáticamente f pl, servicio automático de transferencia m; ~ **typewriter** n ADMIN máquina de escribir automática f; ~ **updating** n COMP *data* actualización automática f; ~ **watch keeper** n TRANSP *shipping* maquinista de guardia automático mf; ~ **withdrawal** n STOCK reembolso automático m

automation *n* GEN COMM automatización *f*

automobile: ~ **benefit** *n* AmE TAX beneficio por automóvil *m*; ~ **insurance** *n* AmE (*cf car insurance* BrE) INS seguro de automóviles *m*; ~ **liability insurance** *n* AmE (*cf car liability insurance* BrE) INS seguro de responsabilidad civil de automóviles *m*; ~ **policies insuring agreement** *n* INS convenio asegurador del sector del automóvil *m*

Automobile: ~ **Association** *n* BrE (*AA*, *cf American Automobile Association*) TRANSP organización británica para el automovilista, ≈ Ayuda del Automovilista *f* (*Esp*) (*ADA*), ≈ Real Automóvil Club *m* (*RAC*)

automotive: ~ **industry** *n* AmE (*cf car industry* BrE) ECON, IND industria de la automoción *f*, industria automotriz *f*

autonomous: ~ **consumption** *n* ECON consumo autónomo *m*; ~ **expenditure** *n* ECON gasto autónomo *m*; ~ **investment** *n* STOCK inversión autónoma *f*; ~ **work group** *n* HRM grupo autónomo de trabajo *m*

autonomy *n* GEN COMM autonomía *f*

autopark *n* COMP *of heads of hard disk drive* estacionamiento automático *m*

autopilot *n* TRANSP piloto automático *m*

auto-regressive: ~ **moving-average model** *n* MATH modelo de promedio móvil autorregresivo *m*

autorestart *n* COMP autoarranque *m*

autosave *n* COMP autoalmacenamiento *m*

autostart *n* COMP autoarranque *m*

aux. *abbr* (*auxiliary*) TRANSP auxiliar *mf*

auxiliary[1] *adj* GEN COMM auxiliar

auxiliary[2] *n* (*aux.*) TRANSP auxiliar *mf*; ~ **banking services undertaking** FIN garantía de servicios bancarios auxiliares *f*; ~ **boiler** TRANSP caldera auxiliar *f*; ~ **equipment** COMP, HRM equipo auxiliar *m*; ~ **memory** COMP memoria auxiliar *f*; ~ **storage** COMP *hardware* memoria auxiliar *f*

av[1] *abbr* (*audiovisual*) COMMS, MEDIA, S&M audiovisual

av[2]: ~-**commercial** *n* MEDIA, S&M anuncio audiovisual *m*

av. *abbr* (*average*) GEN COMM media *f*, promedio *m*

availability *n* COMP, GEN COMM disponibilidad *f*, MEDIA *radio* tiempo de antena disponible *m*, S&M *radio, TV* disponibilidad *f*; ~ **clause** BANK, INS, LAW cláusula de disponibilidad *f*; ~ **thesis** ECON *international* tesis de disponibilidad *f*

available[1] *adj* COMP, GEN COMM, MEDIA, S&M disponible; ♦ **not** ~ (*N/A*) GEN COMM no disponible; ~ **at short notice** GEN COMM disponible a corto plazo; ~ **on a current basis** GEN COMM disponible actualmente

available[2]: ~ **asset** *n* STOCK activo disponible *m*; ~ **balance** *n* ACC, BANK, FIN saldo disponible *m*; ~ **cash** *n* ACC efectivo disponible *m*, efectivo en caja *m*; ~ **cash flow** *n* ACC efectivo disponible *m*, efectivo en caja *m*; ~ **funds** *n pl* GEN COMM fondos disponibles *m pl*, recursos disponibles *m pl*; ~ **sites list** *n* S&M *advertising* lista de emplazamientos disponibles *f*; ~ **space** *n* COMP *on hard disk* espacio aprovechable *m*; ~ **time** *n* COMP tiempo disponible *m*

aval *n* BANK, GEN COMM endoso especial de garantía *m*

AVCs *n pl* BrE (*additional voluntary contributions*) TAX cuotas voluntarias adicionales *f pl*

avdp. *abbr* (*avoirdupois*) GEN COMM sistema de pesas y medidas basado en el antiguo sistema británico

average[1] *adj* GEN COMM medio, mediano, regular

average[2] *n* (*av.*) ACC avería *f*, GEN COMM media *f*, promedio *m*; ~ **access time** COMP tiempo medio de acceso *m*; ~ **adjuster** (*AA*) INS *marine* ajustador(a) de averías *m,f*, árbitro(-a) de seguros marítimos *m,f*; ~ **amount** GEN COMM cantidad media *f*; ~ **balance** BANK *interest charges* saldo promedio *m*; ~ **bond** INS fianza de avería *f*; ~ **claim** INS coste medio por siniestro *m* (*Esp*), costo medio por siniestro *m* (*AmL*); ~ **clause** INS cláusula de proporcionalidad *f*; ~ **collection period** ACC periodo medio de cobro *m*; ~ **compensation** ACC compensación media *f*; ~ **cost** ACC coste medio *m* (*Esp*), costo medio *m* (*AmL*), coste promedio *m* (*Esp*), costo promedio *m* (*AmL*); ~ **cost of claims** INS coste medio por siniestro *m* (*Esp*), costo medio por siniestro *m* (*AmL*); ~ **deposit** FIN depósito de averías *m*; ~ **deviation** MATH desviación media *f*; ~ **duration of life** INS, WEL duración media de vida *f*; ~ **earnings** *n pl* HRM ingresos medios *m pl*; ~ **equity** STOCK acciones de rendimiento medio *f pl*; ~ **fixed cost** ACC coste fijo medio *m* (*Esp*), costo fijo medio *m* (*AmL*); ~ **hourly earnings** *n pl* GEN COMM, HRM ingresos medios por hora *m pl*; ~ **income** HRM ingresos medios *m pl*; ~ **incremental cost** ECON media incremental del coste *f* (*Esp*), media incremental del costo *f* (*AmL*); ~ **interest rate** BANK tasa de interés promedio *f*; ~ **issue readership** MEDIA, S&M número medio de lectores de una edición *m*, promedio de lectores de una edición *m*; ~ **laytime** TRANSP *shipping* plancha por avería *f*; ~ **LIBOR** (*London interbank offered rate*) BrE BANK LIBOR promedio *m*; ~ **life** GEN COMM vida media *f*; ~ **market price** GEN COMM precio medio de mercado *m*; ~ **maturity** BANK, FIN, STOCK *security* vencimiento medio *m*; ~ **monthly money market rate** STOCK tasa media del mercado monetario mensual *f*; ~ **net income** ACC, TAX ingresos netos medios *m pl*; ~ **pay** HRM remuneración media *f*; ~ **PIBOR** (*Paris interbank offered rate*) BANK promedio PIBOR *m*; ~ **premium** INS prima media *f*; ~ **premium system** INS sistema de primas medias *m*; ~ **price** ECON, S&M, STOCK precio medio *m*; ~ **propensity to consume** (*APC*) ECON, S&M propensión media al consumo *f*; ~ **propensity to save** (*APS*) ACC, ECON *economic accounting* propensión media al ahorro *f*; ~ **rate** ACC índice medio *m*, GEN COMM promedio *m*, tasa media *f*; ~ **revenue** (*AR*) ACC, FIN ingreso promedio *m*, LEIS beneficios medios *m pl*, ingresos medios *m pl*; ~ **settlement** INS liquidación de averías *f*; ~ **sold circulation** GEN COMM circulación media colocada *f*; ~ **tax** TAX impuesto medio *m*; ~ **tax rate** TAX tipo impositivo medio *m*; ~ **total cost** ACC coste medio total *m* (*Esp*), costo medio total *m* (*AmL*); ~ **unit cost** ACC coste unitario medio *m* (*Esp*), costo unitario medio *m* (*AmL*); ~ **wage** ECON, HRM salario medio *m*; ~ **weighted rate** STOCK tasa media ponderada *f*; ~ **working week** BrE, ~ **workweek** AmE HRM semana laborable media *f*; ~ **yield** FIN, STOCK rendimiento promedio *m*, rendimiento medio *m*; ♦ **at an** ~ GEN COMM por término medio; **with** ~ (*W.A.*) INS con avería; **with particular** ~ (*W.P.A*) INS con avería particular; **take an** ~ GEN COMM hacer un promedio

average down *vt* STOCK bajar el promedio, promediar a la baja

average out *vt* FIN *cost, profit*, STOCK promediar

average up *vt* STOCK promediar al alza, *price of securities* compensar

averager *n* STOCK promediador(a) *m,f*

averaging *n* FIN prorrateo *m*, GEN COMM promedio *m*, STOCK promedio variable *m*; ~ **amount** TAX cantidad promediada *f*; ~ **down** FIN, GEN COMM, S&M, STOCK compra de títulos a bajo precio *f*; ~ **formula** BANK fórmula del promedio *f*, fórmula del término medio *f*; ~ **period** TAX periodo de pago del impuesto *m*

aviation: ~ **fuel** *n* TRANSP gasolina para aviación *f*; ~ **insurance** *n* INS seguro de aviación *m*; ~ **risk** *n* INS, TRANSP riesgo de aviación *m*; ~**-trip life insurance** *n* INS seguro de vida para viajes en avión *m*; ~ **turbine fuel** *n* TRANSP combustible para turbinas de avión *m*

avoid *vt* GEN COMM evitar, TAX eludir, evadir

avoidable: ~ **costs** *n pl* GEN COMM costes evitables *m pl* (*Esp*), costos evitables *m pl* (*AmL*)

avoidance *n* GEN COMM *contract* anulación *f*; ~ **of tax** ECON, TAX evasión fiscal *f*

avoirdupois *n* (*avpd.*) GEN COMM sistema de pesas y medidas basado en el antiguo sistema británico

AVR *abbr* (*agent's vehicle record*) TRANSP registro del vehículo del agente *m*

avulsion *n* PROP avulsión *f*

award[1] *n* GEN COMM *of contract* adjudicación *f*, HRM fallo *m*, laudo *m*; ~ **incomes** TAX ingresos por concesión *m pl*; ~ **letter** TAX carta de adjudicación *f*

award[2] *vt* GEN COMM *contract* conceder, LAW *contract* adjudicar; ◆ ~ **a salary increase** HRM conceder un aumento salarial

awarder *n* GEN COMM juez(a) árbitro(-a) *m,f*

awarding: ~ **of costs** *n* LAW condena a pagar los gastos *f*, PATENTS obligación de pagar los gastos *f*

aware *adj* GEN COMM consciente

away: ~**-from-home expenses** *n pl* ACC, TAX gastos por residir fuera del domicilio familiar *m pl*

AWB *abbr* (*air waybill*) IMP/EXP, TRANSP conocimiento de embarque aéreo *m*

AWD *abbr* (*awning deck*) TRANSP cubierta de abrigo *f*, cubierta de toldilla *f*

awning *n* GEN COMM *advertising* marquesina *f*; ~ **deck** (*AWD*) TRANSP cubierta de abrigo *f*, cubierta de toldilla *f*

AWY *abbr* (*airway*) TRANSP vía aérea *f*

axial: ~ **composition** *n* GEN COMM *advertising* composición axial *f*

axioms: ~ **of preference** *n pl* ECON axiomas de preferencia *m pl*

axis *n* MATH, TRANSP eje *m*

axle: ~ **weight** *n* GEN COMM peso del eje *m*

B

b *abbr* (*barrels*) TRANSP barriles *m pl*

B *abbr* (*bale capacity*) TRANSP espacio para carga general *m*

BA *abbr* (*Bachelor of Arts*) HRM, WEL ≈ licenciado (-a) en Humanidades *m,f*

BAA *abbr* (*British Airports Association*) TRANSP asociación aeroportuaria británica

Bachelor: ~ **of Arts** *n* (*BA*) HRM, WEL ≈ licenciado(-a) en Humanidades *m,f*; ~ **of Business Administration** *n* HRM, WEL licenciado(-a) en Administración de Empresas *m,f*; ~ **of Commerce** *n* (*BCom*) HRM, WEL licenciado(-a) en Comercio *m,f*; ~ **of Economics** *n* (*BEcon*) HRM, WEL licenciado(-a) en Economía *m,f*; ~ **of Industrial Design** *n* (*BID*) HRM, WEL licenciado(-a) en Dibujo Técnico *m,f*, licenciado(-a) en Diseño Industrial *f*; ~ **of Laws** *n* (*LLB*) HRM, LAW ≈ licenciado(-a) en Derecho *m,f*; ~ **of Science** *n* (*BSc*) HRM, WEL ≈ licenciado(-a) en Ciencias *m,f*; ~ **of Science in Business Administration** *n* (*BSBA*) HRM, WEL licenciado(-a) en Administración de Empresas *m,f*, licenciado(-a) en Ciencias Empresariales *m,f*; ~ **of Science in Industrial Relations** *n* (*BSIR*) HRM, WEL licenciado(-a) en Relaciones Laborales *m,f*

back[1]: ~ **arrow** *n* COMP flecha de retroceso *f*; ~ **cover** *n* MEDIA contracubierta del libro *f*; ~**-end load** *n* STOCK comisión por cancelación anticipada *f*; ~ **freight** *n* TRANSP flete de vuelta *m*; ~ **haul** *n* TRANSP *return journey* acarreo *m*, viaje de retorno *m*; ~ **interest** *n* ACC, BANK intereses atrasados *m pl*; ~ **issue** *n* MEDIA *of newspaper, magazine* edición atrasada *f*, número atrasado *m*; ~ **load** *n* TRANSP carga posterior *f*, carga de retorno *f*; ~ **margin** *n* MEDIA *print* blanco de salida *m*, margen posterior *m*; ~ **number** *n* MEDIA *newspaper, magazine* número atrasado *m*; ~ **office** *n* ADMIN oficina de apoyo *f*, STOCK *settlements* trastienda *f*; ~**-of-the-house job** *n* ADMIN, HRM trabajo sin atención al público *m*; ~ **order** *n* GEN COMM, S&M pedido en espera *m*, pedido retrasado *m*; ~ **pay** *n* HRM pago de atrasos *m*; ~ **payment** *n* FIN pago pendiente de ejecución *m*, GEN COMM atrasos *m pl*, HRM, S&M devolución *f*; ~ **peddling** *n* GEN COMM venta ambulante *f*; ~ **rent** *n* PROP alquiler atrasado *m*; ~ **section** *n* GEN COMM, MEDIA *magazine* sección de última página *f*; ~ **taxes** *n pl* ACC, TAX *balance sheet* impuestos atrasados *m pl*, impuestos vencidos *m pl*; ~**-to-back credit** *n* BANK crédito subsidiario *m*; ~**-to-back loan** *n* BANK préstamo de contrapartida *m*, préstamo de mutuo respaldo *m*, empréstito de contrapartida *m*, FIN préstamo de contrapartida *m*; ~**-to-back placement** *n* STOCK colocación directa *f*; ~**-to-back transaction** *n* BANK transacción de respaldo mutuo *f*; ~**-to-back transfer** *n* BANK transferencia de respaldo mutuo *f*

back[2] *vt* GEN COMM *project* respaldar

back down *vi* MGMNT *in argument* retractarse, volverse atrás

back off *vi* GEN COMM retirarse

back out *vi* GEN COMM retirarse; ♦ ~ **of** GEN COMM *contract, deal* retirarse de

back up 1. *vt* COMP *make a copy of file, data* hacer una copia de seguridad, GEN COMM apoyar, respaldar; **2.** *vi* COMP retroceder

backbench: ~ **MP** *n BrE* POL *parliament* diputado(-a) de fila *m,f*

backbencher *n BrE* POL *parliament* diputado(-a) de fila *m,f*

backbenches *n pl BrE* POL *parliament* escaños de los diputados que no son ministros

backbiting *n* GEN COMM maledicencia *f*

backbone: ~ **of the economy** *n* ECON columna vertebral de la economía *f*

backchannels *n pl AmE* POL canales de comunicación sólo conocidos por algunos miembros del gobierno

backdate *vt* GEN COMM *cheque, contract* antedatar

backdated[1] *adj* GEN COMM con efecto retroactivo

backdated[2]: ~ **pay increase** *n* HRM aumento salarial retroactivo *m*

backdating *n* GEN COMM entrada en vigor con efecto retroactivo *f*

backdoor: ~ **financing** *n* ECON financiación clandestina *f*, FIN financiación secreta *f*; ~ **lending** *n* ECON préstamo bajo mano *m*, préstamo indirecto *m*, FIN préstamo indirecto *m*; ~ **operation** *n* ECON operación bajo cuerda *f*, FIN operación furtiva *f*; ~ **selling** *n* S&M venta secreta *f*

backdrop *n* GEN COMM *to situation* telón de fondo *m*

backed[1]: ~ **by** *adj* FIN respaldado por

backed[2]: ~ **bill of exchange** *n* BANK, STOCK letra de cambio avalada *f*

backer *n* FIN promotor(a) comercial *m,f*

background *n* GEN COMM, HRM *personal information* antecedentes *m pl*; ~ **color** *AmE*, ~ **colour** *BrE* COMP color de fondo *m*; ~ **information** GEN COMM información básica *f*; ~ **investigation** HRM *of applicant* investigación de antecedentes *f*; ~ **paper** FIN, MEDIA documento de antecedentes *m*; ~ **pollution** ENVIR polución base *f*; ~ **printing** COMP impresión sin prioridad *f*; ~ **processing** COMP proceso no prioritario *m*, HRM *job history* procesamiento de antecedentes *m*; ~ **story** MEDIA *print, newspaper* historia documental *f*; ~ **task** COMP *of low priority* tarea secundaria *f*

backhander *n infrml* S&M astilla *f* (*infrml*)

backing *n* GEN COMM *bank-note issue* garantía *f*, *support* apoyo financiero *m*, STOCK *bank-note issue* garantía *f*, reserva monetaria de respaldo *f*; ~ **storage** COMP almacenamiento de archivos *m*; ~ **up** MEDIA *print* impresión de la segunda cara *f*

backlog *n* GEN COMM acumulación *f*; ~ **demand** GEN COMM demanda acumulada *f*; ~ **of demand** ECON, S&M volumen de demanda *m*; ~ **of final orders** GEN COMM acumulación de pedidos finales *f*; ~ **order books** *n pl* GEN COMM libros de pedidos acumulados *m pl*; ~ **of orders** ACC, BANK, FIN cartera de pedidos atrasados *f*, GEN COMM exceso de pedidos *m*; ~ **of payments** ACC cartera de pagos *f*; ~ **of work** GEN COMM acumulación de trabajo *f*

backlogged: ~ **order** n GEN COMM pedido acumulado m

back-pedal vi GEN COMM volverse atrás

backselling n S&M *market research* retroventa f

backslash n COMP barra inversa f; ~ **key** COMP tecla de barra inversa f

backspace[1] n COMP retroceso m; ~ **character** COMP carácter de retroceso m

backspace[2] vi COMP retroceder

backspread n STOCK *options* liquidación de un arbitraje f

backstop n IND respaldo m; ~ **loan facility** BANK, FIN servicio de préstamo respaldado m

backstrip n MEDIA *of book* tira posterior f

backtrack vi GEN COMM *from plan, promise* echarse atrás

backup[1] adj COMP duplicado

backup[2] n COMP respaldo m, copia de reserva f, GEN COMM *support* respaldo m; ~ **battery** COMP batería de seguridad f; ~ **copy** COMP copia de seguridad f; ~ **credit line** BANK línea de crédito de respaldo f; ~ **facility** COMP instalación de apoyo f; ~ **file** COMP archivo de protección m; ~ **line** BANK línea de respaldo f, FIN línea de apoyo f; ~ **material** GEN COMM material de apoyo m; ~ **memory** COMP memoria de apoyo f; ~ **service** S&M servicio de post-venta m, TRANSP servicio de apoyo m; ~ **support** STOCK apoyo de reserva m; ~ **system** STOCK *for options* sistema de respaldo m; ~ **utility program** COMP programa de copias de seguridad m; ~ **withholding** TAX retención retroactiva f

backward: ~ **averaging** n TAX promediado hacia atrás m, promedio con efecto retroactivo m; ~~**bending labor supply curve** AmE, ~~**bending labour supply curve** BrE n ECON curva de oferta de trabajo retroflexionada f, curva flexionada de la oferta de trabajo f; ~~**bending supply curve** n ECON curva de oferta retroflexionada f; ~ **integration** n GEN COMM integración regresiva f; ~ **linkage** n ECON, IND vinculación hacia atrás f; ~ **scheduling** n MGMNT horario regresivo m; ~ **vertical integration** n GEN COMM integración vertical decreciente f

backwardation n STOCK margen de cobertura m, prima por retraso f; ~ **business** STOCK contrato de deport m; ~ **rate** FIN tasa de interés de la bonificación f, tipo de interés de la bonificación m

backwash: ~ **effect** n ECON efecto backwash m

backyard: **not in my** ~ phr jarg (*NIMBY*) ENVIR *protest slogan* en mi patio no

BACS abbr (*Banks Automated Clearing System*) BANK Sistema Bancario de Compensación Automática m

bad: ~ **bargain** n GEN COMM mal negocio m; ~ **break** n infrml GEN COMM ruptura desafortunada f; ~ **buy** n GEN COMM mala compra f; ~ **check** AmE, ~ **cheque** BrE n BANK, FIN cheque sin fondos m, cheque incobrable m; ~ **debt** n ACC, BANK, GEN COMM deuda fallida f, deuda incobrable f, insolvencia f; ~~**debt losses** n pl ACC, BANK, ECON, FIN pérdidas por débitos fallidos f pl, pérdidas por insolvencias f pl, pérdidas de cuentas incobrables f pl; ~~**debt provision** n ACC, BANK, FIN provisión para deudas irrecuperables f, provisión para incobrables f, provisión para insolvencias f, provisión para deudas dudosas f; ~~**debt recovery** n ACC recobro de una deuda incobrable m; ~~**debt recovery** n ACC, BANK, FIN recuperación de deudas incobrables f; ~ **debtor** n BANK deudor moroso m; ~ **delivery** n STOCK mala entrega f; ~ **and doubtful debt** n (*B&D*) ACC, BANK, GEN COMM deuda mala y dudosa f, deuda

incobrable f; ~ **investment** n BANK inversión malograda f; ~ **loan** n ACC, BANK préstamo incobrable m; ~~**loan provision** n BANK provisión para préstamo dudoso f; ~ **management** n MGMNT mala administración f, mala gestión f; ~ **name** n GEN COMM *poor reputation* mal nombre m; ~ **news** n GEN COMM malas noticias f pl; ~ **paper** n infrml BANK documento incobrable m; ~ **sector** n COMP sector deteriorado m; ~ **title** n LAW, PROP título de propiedad imperfecto m, título imperfecto m, título no válido m; ~ **will** n ACC *consolidated accounts* fondo de comercio negativo m, GEN COMM mala voluntad f; ~ **work** n GEN COMM obra defectuosa f

BAEC abbr (*British Agricultural Export Council*) IMP/EXP consejo británico de exportaciones agrícolas

BAF abbr TRANSP (*bunker adjustment factor*) ajuste por combustible m, factor de ajuste del suministro de combustible m

baggage n LEIS, TRANSP equipaje m; ~ **allowance** TRANSP equipaje permitido m; ~ **cart** AmE (*cf luggage trolley* BrE) LEIS, TRANSP carro de equipajes m; ~ **checked** TRANSP equipaje controlado m; ~ **handling** TRANSP carga y descarga del equipaje f; ~ **improvement program** AmE, ~ **improvement programme** BrE (*BIP*) TRANSP programa de optimización de equipajes m; ~ **locker** AmE (*cf left-luggage locker* BrE) GEN COMM taquilla para equipajes en consigna f; ~ **reclaim area** LEIS, TRANSP zona de recogida de equipaje f; ~ **tag** LEIS etiqueta de equipaje f; ~ **trolley** LEIS, TRANSP carro para equipaje m; ~ **vehicle** LEIS, TRANSP vehículo para equipajes m

bagging: ~ **of cargo** n TRANSP ensacado de la carga m

bagman n AmE jarg POL persona contratada por la mafia para cobrar dinero, S&M viajante de comercio mf

bail[1]: ~ **bond** n FIN bono depositario m, GEN COMM compromiso de fianza m, escritura de fianza f, LAW compromiso de fianza m, fianza f, escritura de afianzamiento f, escritura de caución f, STOCK bono depositario m; ~~**out** n GEN COMM ayuda financiera f; ~~**out period** n BANK, FIN periodo de respaldo financiero m

bail[2]: ~ **sb out** vt infrml FIN avalar a alguien, salir fiador de alguien, LAW pagar una fianza a alguien

bailee n LAW depositario(-a) m,f

bailer n BANK depositante mf

bailiff n LAW *officer* agente judicial mf, PROP *on estate* administrador(a) m,f

bailment n GEN COMM caución f, LAW depósito m

bailor n BANK *in safekeeping*, GEN COMM fiador(a) m,f

bait: ~ **advertising** n AmE S&M anuncio gancho m; ~ **and switch advertising** n AmE S&M artículo gancho f

Baker: ~ **Plan** n ECON *international, financial aid* plan Baker m

bal. abbr (*balance*) ACC, BANK, FIN balance m

balance[1] n (*bal.*) ACC balance m, saldo m, FIN balance m, GEN COMM saldo m; ~ **abroad** BANK saldo en el extranjero m; ~ **of account** GEN COMM estado de cuenta m, saldo de cuenta m; ~ **book** FIN libro de balances m; ~ **brought down** (*b/d.*) ACC balance a cuenta nueva m; ~ **brought forward** ACC balance llevado a cuenta nueva m; ~ **carried forward** ACC saldo a cuenta nueva m; ~ **due** TAX saldo deudor m; ~ **due to creditor** BANK saldo favorable al acreedor m; ~ **due to debitor** BANK saldo favorable al deudor m; ~ **for official financing**

(*BOF*) ACC balance para financiación oficial *m*, ECON balanza de financiación oficial *f*; ~ **in bank** BANK saldo en el banco *m*; ~ **of invisible items** ECON balanza de servicios *f*; ~ **of invoice** ACC balanza de facturación *f*; ~ **item** ACC detalle del balance *m*; ~ **on current account** BANK balance de una cuenta corriente *m*, ECON saldo en cuenta corriente *m*; ~ **order settlement** STOCK cancelación de orden de saldo *f*; ~ **of payments** (*BOP*) ECON, POL balanza de pagos *f*; ~ **of payments deficit** (*BP deficit*) ECON déficit de la balanza de pagos *m*; ~ **of payments equilibrium** ECON equilibrio de la balanza de pagos *m*; ~ **of payments surplus** BANK, ECON superávit de la balanza de pagos *m*; ~ **of power** GEN COMM proporción de fuerzas *f*; ~ **sheet** (*B/S*) ACC, FIN balance *m*, balance de ejercicio *m*, balance de situación *m*, balance general *m*; ~ **sheet account** ACC cuenta de balance *f*; ~ **sheet equation** ACC ecuación del balance *f*; ~ **sheet item** ACC partida del balance *f*; ~ **sheet reserve** INS reserva del balance general *f*; ~ **sheet value of shares** ACC valor de las acciones en el balance *m*, *shareholder's equity* estado contable del valor de las acciones *m*, valor teórico de las acciones según balance *m*, STOCK valor de las acciones en el balance *m*; ~ **of trade** ECON balanza comercial *f*, saldo comercial *m*; ◆ ~ **in your favor** *AmE*, ~ **in your favour** *BrE* BANK saldo a su favor; **off the ~ sheet** ACC fuera del balance general *m*

balance[2] *vt* ACC, BANK *account* saldar, GEN COMM cuadrar, sopesar; ~ **the books** *infrml* ACC saldar las cuentas; ~ **sth against sth** GEN COMM sopesar algo con algo

balance out *vt* ACC compensar, neutralizar, FIN compensar

balance with *vt* GEN COMM equilibrar con

Balance: ~ for Official Financing *n* (*BOF*) ECON *balance of payments* balanza de financiación oficial *f*

balanced[1] *adj* ACC compensado, equilibrado, GEN COMM equilibrado

balanced[2]: ~ **article** *n* LAW artículo equilibrado *m*; ~ **budget** *n* ECON, FIN presupuesto equilibrado *m*; ~ **budget multiplier** *n* ECON multiplicador de presupuesto equilibrado *m*; ~ **growth** *n* ECON, FIN crecimiento equilibrado *m*; ~ **mutual fund** *n* FIN, STOCK fondo de inversión equilibrado *m*; ~ **portfolio** *n* FIN, STOCK cartera equilibrada *f*

Balanced: ~ Budget and Emergency Deficit Control Act *n* *AmE* ECON ley del presupuesto equilibrado y control de emergencia del déficit

balancing: ~ item *n* ECON contrapartida *f*; ~ **of portfolio** *n* GEN COMM compensación de riesgos *f*

balderdash *n* GEN COMM disparate *m*

bale[1] *n* GEN COMM, IMP/EXP, TRANSP bala *f*; ~ **capacity** (*B*) TRANSP espacio para carga general *m*; ~ **cubic meters** *AmE*, ~ **cubic metres** *BrE* *n pl* GEN COMM metros cúbicos embalados *m pl*, metros cúbicos para balas *m pl*; ~ **space** TRANSP espacio para balas *m*

bale[2] *vt* GEN COMM, IMP/EXP, TRANSP embalar

baling *n* GEN COMM, IMP/EXP, TRANSP embalaje *m*

ballast *n* TRANSP *shipping* lastre *m*; ~ **sailing** TRANSP navegación en lastre *f*; ~ **space** TRANSP *in vessel* espacio de lastre *m*; ~ **tank** TRANSP tanque de lastre *m*; ~ **trip** TRANSP *by empty vessel* viaje en lastre *m*

balloon: ~ advertising *n* S&M publicidad con globos *f*; ~ **interest** *n* STOCK interés creciente *m*; ~ **loan** *n* BANK

préstamo de pago total al vencimiento *m*; ~ **note** *n* BANK pagaré especial *m*; ~ **payment** *n* BANK pago especial *m*, pago extraordinario *m*, STOCK *bonds* pago final superior al promedio *m*; ~ **repayment** *n* BANK devolución en un solo pago *f*

ballot[1] *n* HRM votación *f*, POL votación *f*; ~ **box** HRM, POL urna electoral *f*; ~ **paper** HRM *union election*, POL papeleta *f*, papeleta de votación *f*, papeleta de voto *f*; ◆ **take a ~ on sth** HRM, POL someter algo a votación

ballot[2] **1.** *vt* HRM *members* invitar a votar; **2.** *vi* HRM, POL votar, acudir a las urnas

Baltic: ~ Exchange *n BrE* STOCK mercado báltico; ~ **Freight Index** *n* (*BFI*) TRANSP *shipping* índice de Fletes del Báltico *m*; ~ **Futures Exchange** *n BrE* (*BFE*) STOCK mercado de futuros báltico; ~ **International Freight Futures Exchange** *n BrE* (*BIFFEX*) STOCK, TRANSP bolsa internacional báltica de futuros de fletes

BAM *abbr* (*bulk air mail*) COMMS correo aéreo de grandes dimensiones *m*

bamboo: ~ curtain *n* POL telón de bambú *m*

ban *n* GEN COMM, LAW prohibición *f*; ~ **on interest payments** BANK prohibición de pago de intereses *f*

BAN *abbr* (*bond anticipation note*) STOCK vale por pronto pago de bono *m*

band *n* TAX *VAT* banda *f*; ~ **advertising** S&M *two products* banda publicitaria *f*; ~ **of fluctuation** ECON *currency rate* banda de fluctuación *f*; ~ **saw** IND sierra sinfín *f*

B&B *abbr* (*bed and breakfast*) LEIS alojamiento y desayuno en casa particular, pensión con desayuno incluido *f*

B&D *abbr* (*bad and doubtful debt*) ACC, BANK, GEN COMM deuda mala y dudosa *f*, deuda incobrable *f*

banded: ~ offer *n* S&M *two products* oferta asociada *f*; ~ **pack** *n* S&M *for the same product* envase conjunto *m*; ~ **packs** *n pl* GEN COMM *of notes* fajos de billetes *m pl*

banding *n* HRM calificación *f*

bandwidth *n* COMP, HRM, MEDIA amplitud de banda *f*, anchura de banda *f*

bank[1] *adj* (*bk*) BANK bancario; ~**-endorsed** BANK endosado por un banco; ~**-financed** BANK financiado por un banco

bank[2] *n* (*bk*) BANK banco *m*; ~ **acceptance** BANK aceptación bancaria *f*; ~ **accommodation** BANK crédito bancario *m*; ~ **account** BANK, FIN cuenta bancaria *f*; ~ **address** BANK domicilio bancario *m*; ~ **advance** BANK anticipo bancario *m*; ~ **advice** BANK asesoramiento bancario *m*; ~ **agreement** BANK convenio de préstamo *m*; ~ **annuities** *n pl* BANK anualidades bancarias *f pl*; ~ **assets** BANK activos bancarios *m pl*; ~ **balance** ACC, BANK, FIN estado de cuentas *m*; ~ **base rate** BANK, FIN tasa base bancaria *f*; ~ **bill** BANK *AmE* (*cf banknote BrE*) billete de banco *m*, pagaré bancario *m*; ~ **board** BANK consejo bancario *m*; ~ **bond** BANK bono bancario *m*; ~ **bookkeeping** BANK contabilidad bancaria *f*; ~ **branch** BANK sucursal de banco *f*; ~ **capital** BANK capital bancario *m*; ~ **card** BANK tarjeta bancaria *f*; ~ **cash ratio** BANK coeficiente bancario de caja *m*; ~**'s cash reserve** BANK reserva en efectivo de un banco *f*; ~ **certificate** BANK certificado bancario *m*; ~ **charge** BANK cargo del banco *m*; ~ **charges** *n pl* BANK, FIN cargos bancarios *m pl*; ~ **charter** BANK documento legal que autoriza la constitución de un banco *m*; ~ **check** *AmE*, ~ **cheque** *BrE* BANK, FIN cheque bancario *m*; ~ **clearing** BANK compensación bancaria *f*; ~ **clerk** BANK empleado(-a) bancario(-a) *m,f*; ~ **code** BANK *routing* código bancario *m*; ~ **commission** BANK comisión bancaria *f*; ~ **credit** BANK crédito bancario *m*; ~ **credit transfer** BANK transferencia de un crédito bancario *f*; ~ **debenture** ACC, BANK, STOCK obligación bancaria *f*; ~ **debts** *n pl* BANK deudas bancarias *f pl*; ~ **demand deposits** *n pl* BANK depósitos bancarios a la vista *m pl*; ~ **deposit** BANK depósito bancario *m*; ~ **deposit insurance** BANK, INS seguro de depósito bancario *m*; ~ **deposit money** BANK dinero depositado en un banco *m*; ~ **deposit rate** BANK tasa de depósito bancario *f*; ~ **discount** BANK descuento bancario *m*; ~ **discount rate** BANK, FIN tasa de descuento bancario *f*; ~ **draft** (*B/D*) BANK giro bancario *m*; ~ **efficiency** BANK eficiencia bancaria *f*; ~ **employee** BANK, HRM banquero(-a) *m,f*, empleado(-a) de banco *m*; ~ **endorsement** BANK, GEN COMM endoso bancario *m*; ~ **examination** BANK inspección oficial de un banco *f*; ~ **examiner** *BrE* (*cf commissioner of banking AmE*) BANK inspector(a) oficial de bancos *m,f*; ~ **facility** ACC, BANK servicio bancario *m*; ~ **failure** BANK quiebra bancaria *f*; ~ **financing** BANK, FIN financiación bancaria *f*; ~ **float** BANK flotación bancaria *f*, emisión bancaria *f*; ~ **giro** *BrE* BANK giro bancario *m*; ~ **giro credit** *BrE* BANK abono de un giro bancario *m*; ~ **giro credit system** *BrE* BANK sistema de crédito por giro bancario *m*; ~ **group** *AmE* (*cf banking group BrE*) BANK cadena de bancos *f*, grupo bancario *m*; ~ **guarantee** BANK garantía bancaria *f*; ~ **holding company** BANK sociedad de control del banco *f*, GEN COMM empresa de holding bancario *f*; ~ **holiday** *BrE* (*cf legal holiday AmE*) GEN COMM cierre bancario *m*, día no laborable *m*, HRM día de asueto *m* (*frml*), día de descanso obligatorio *m*, fiesta oficial *f*, día inhábil *m*, LAW día inhábil *m*, fiesta oficial *f*, LEIS día de asueto *m* (*frml*), día de descanso obligatorio *m*, fiesta oficial *f*, día inhábil *m*; ~ **interest** ACC, BANK interés bancario *m*, intereses bancarios *m pl*; ~ **of issue** BANK banco de emisión *m*; ~ **lending policy** BANK política de préstamos de un banco *f*; ~ **lending rate** BANK interés sobre préstamos bancarios *m*; ~ **lien** BANK gravamen bancario en prevención *m*; ~ **line** BANK *of credit* línea bancaria *f*; ~ **liquidity** BANK liquidez de un banco *f*; ~ **loan** ACC, BANK, GEN COMM préstamo bancario *m*; ~ **loan rate** BANK interés sobre préstamos de un banco *m*; ~ **manager** BANK, MGMNT director(a) de banco *m,f*; ~ **messenger** BANK mensajero(-a) bancario(-a) *m,f*; ~ **money** BANK dinero bancario *m*; ~ **-note trading** BANK compraventa de billetes bancarios *f*; ~ **officer** BANK empleado(-a) bancario(-a) *m,f*; ~ **overdraft** BANK descubierto bancario *m*, sobregiro bancario *m*; ~ **paper** BANK valores bancarios *m pl*; ~ **place** BANK plaza bancaria *f*; ~ **postbill** BANK cuenta de cargo bancaria *f*; ~ **rate** BANK, FIN tasa bancaria *f*; ~ **reconciliation** ACC, BANK comprobación del estado de la cuenta *f*, conciliación bancaria *f*, reconciliación bancaria *f*; ~ **reconciliation statement** BANK estado de conciliación de bancos *m*; ~ **remittance** BANK remesa bancaria *f*; ~ **requirement** BANK requisito bancario *m*; ~ **reserve** BANK fondo de reserva *m*; ~ **return** BANK rendimiento del banco *m*; ~ **run** BANK corrida sobre un banco *f*; ~ **runner** BANK retirada de fondos por pánico *f*; ~ **security** BANK garantía bancaria *f*; ~ **selling rate** BANK tasa de venta bancaria *f*; ~ **service charge** BANK cargo por servicio bancario *m*, comisión por servicio bancario *f*; ~ **settlement system** BANK sistema de

liquidación bancaria *m*; ~ **settlement voucher** BANK comprobante de pago de la liquidación bancaria *m*; ~ **shares** *n pl* BANK acciones bancarias *f pl*; ~ **statement** BANK estado bancario *m*, estado de cuentas bancario *m*; ~ **subsidiary** BANK subsidiaria bancaria *f*; ~ **summary and agreement** BANK resumen y conformidad bancaria *m*; ~ **switching** COMP conmutación de bancos *f*; ~ **teller** BANK *person* cajero(-a) bancario(-a) *m*, *machine* cajero automático *m*; ~ **teller card** BANK tarjeta para cajero automático *f*; ~**-to-bank lending** BANK préstamo interbancario *m*; ~ **transaction** BANK transacción bancaria *f*; ~ **transfer** BANK transferencia bancaria *f*; ~ **trust department** BANK departamento fiduciario del banco *m*; ~ **vault** BANK cámara acorazada *f*, caja de seguridad bancaria *f*, caja fuerte *f*

bank[3] *vt* BANK *money* depositar, ingresar

bank on *vt* GEN COMM *rely on* contar con

bank with *vt* BANK *have account with* tener una cuenta en

Bank: ~ **Charter Act** *n BrE* BANK *historical financial legislation* ley del capítulo bancario *f*; ~ **of England** *n* (*BE*) BANK banco central del Reino Unido, ≈ Banco de España *m* (*Esp*); ~ **for International Settlements** *n* (*BIS*) BANK, ECON Banco de Pagos Internacionales *m* (*BPI*); ~ **Giro** *n BrE* FIN servicio nacional británico de cheques postales

bankable[1] *adj* BANK financiable, GEN COMM descontable

bankable[2]: ~ **assets** *n pl* BANK activos descontables *m pl*; ~ **bill** *n* BANK letra descontable *f*; ~ **paper** *n* BANK valores bancarios *m pl*

bankbook *n* BANK, FIN *for customers* libreta de banco *f*

banker *n* BANK, HRM banquero(-a) *m,f*; ~**'s acceptance** BANK aceptación bancaria *f*; ~**'s bill** BANK letra bancaria *f*; ~**'s check** *AmE*, ~**'s cheque** *BrE* BANK, FIN cheque bancario *m*; ~**'s deposit rate** BANK tasa de depósito bancario *f*; ~**'s discount** BANK descuento bancario *m*; ~**'s draft** BANK, FIN cheque de banco *m*; ~**'s order** BANK, FIN domiciliación bancaria de pagos *f*; ~**'s ramp** *jarg* BANK estafa bancaria *f*; ~**'s reference** BANK referencia del banco *f*; ~**'s ticket** BANK boleta del banco *f* (*AmL*), recibo bancario *m* (*Esp*); ~**'s transfer** BANK transferencia del banco *f*, traspaso del banco *m*; ~**'s trust company** BANK banco fiduciario *m*; ~**'s turn** BANK utilidad cambiaria *f*

banking[1] *adj* (*bkg*) BANK bancario

banking[2] *n* (*bkg*) BANK banca *f*; ~ **account** BANK, FIN cuenta bancaria *f*; ~ **activity** BANK actividad bancaria *f*; ~ **arrangements** *n pl* BANK acuerdos bancarios *m pl*; ~ **business** BANK negocios bancarios *m pl*; ~ **center** *AmE*, ~ **centre** *BrE* BANK centro bancario *m*; ~ **charges** *n pl* BANK, FIN cargos bancarios *m pl*; ~ **circles** *n pl* BANK círculos bancarios *m pl*; ~ **commission** BANK comisión bancaria *f*; ~ **community** BANK comunidad bancaria *f*; ~ **day** ACC, BANK día de bancos *m*, día hábil bancario *m*; ~ **establishment** BANK establecimiento bancario *m*; ~ **group** *BrE* (*cf bank group AmE*) BANK cadena de bancos *f*, grupo bancario *m*, grupo de bancos *m*; ~ **hours** *n pl* BANK horario bancario *m*; ~ **house** BANK casa de banca *f*; ~ **industry** BANK industria bancaria *f*; ~ **institution** BANK institución bancaria *f*; ~ **law** BANK, LAW ley bancaria *f*; ~ **network** BANK red bancaria *f*; ~ **operation** BANK operación bancaria *f*; ~ **rate** BANK tipo de redescuento *m*; ~ **ratio** BANK, ECON, FIN, STOCK coeficiente bancario *m*; ~ **regulation** BANK regulación bancaria *f*; ~ **sector** BANK, FIN sector bancario *m*;

~ **service** BANK servicio bancario *m*; ~ **subsidiary** BANK filial bancaria *f*; ~ **syndicate** BANK sindicato bancario *m*; ~ **system** BANK sistema bancario *m*; ~ **transfer system** BANK sistema de transferencia bancaria *m*

Banking: ~ **Ombudsman** *n* BANK Defensor(a) del Cliente *m,f*; ~ **School** *n* BrE BANK escuela bancaria *f*; ~ **Supervision Division** *n* BrE BANK división de supervisión bancaria del Banco de Inglaterra

banknote *n* BrE (*cf bank bill AmE*) BANK billete de banco *m*

bankroll[1] *n* AmE BANK *financial resources* fortuna *f*

bankroll[2] *vt* infrml BANK financiar

bankrupt[1] *adj* ACC, BANK, FIN, HRM arruinado, insolvente, quebrado, en quiebra; ◆ **go** ~ ACC, BANK, FIN, HRM ir a la bancarrota

bankrupt[2]: ~ **firm** *n* GEN COMM firma en bancarrota *f*

bankrupt[3] *vt* ACC, BANK, FIN, HRM ir a la bancarrota, arruinarse, quebrar

bankruptcy *n* GEN COMM bancarrota *f*, insolvencia *f*, quiebra *f*; ~ **court** FIN juzgado para la bancarrota *m*, LAW tribunal de quiebras *m*; ~ **estate** FIN, LAW conjunto de bienes de una quiebra *m*; ~ **notice** BANK, HRM, IND aviso de quiebra *m*, LAW notificación de quiebra *f*; ~ **proceedings** *n pl* LAW procedimiento de quiebra *m*; ~ **property** FIN propiedad por bancarrota *f*, LAW, PROP bienes puestos en quiebra *m pl*, propiedad por quiebra *f*

Bankruptcy: ~ **Act** *n* FIN, LAW Ley de Quiebras *f*; ~ **Law** *n* FIN, LAW Ley de Quiebras *f*

Banks: ~ **Automated Clearing System** *n* (*BACS*) BANK Sistema Bancario de Compensación Automática *m*

banner: ~ **headline** *n* MEDIA titular a toda página *m*; ~ **year** *n* GEN COMM año insignia *m*

bar[1] *n* COMP barra *f*, LAW jurado *m*, tribunal *m*, MEDIA barra *f*; ~ **chart** GEN COMM gráfico de barras *m*; ~ **code** BrE (*cf bar graphics AmE*) COMP código de barras *m*; ~ **code marking** COMP, S&M marcaje con código de barras *m*; ~ **code scanner** COMP lector óptico de código de barras *m*, lector de código de barras *m*, S&M lector de código de barras *m*; ~**-coded identification number** COMP, S&M número de identificación mediante código de barras *m*; ~**-coded product** COMP, S&M producto con código de barras *m*; ~ **graph** GEN COMM gráfico de barras *m*; ~ **graphics** *n pl* AmE (*cf bar code BrE*) COMP código de barras *m*

bar[2] *vt* GEN COMM excluir, prohibir; ◆ ~ **sb** GEN COMM excluir a alguien

Bar: ~ **Association** *n* AmE (*cf Law Society BrE*) BANK, GEN COMM, LAW ≈ Colegio de Abogados *m*

BARB *abbr* (*Broadcasters Audience Research Board*) MEDIA, S&M junta de investigación de audiencia de la radiodifusión

Barber: ~ **boom** *n* BrE ECON boom de Barber *m*

Barcelona: ~ **Stock Exchange** *n* STOCK Bolsa de Barcelona *f*

Barclays: ~ **Index** *n* STOCK Índice de Barclays *m*

bare[1] *adj* INS desnudo

bare[2]: ~**-boat charter** *n* TRANSP contrato con entrega *m*, fletamento sin tripulación *m*; ~**-boat charter party** *n* TRANSP contrato de fletamento a casco desnudo *m*; ~**-boat consignee** *n* TRANSP destinatario del casco desnudo *m*; ~ **contract** *n* GEN COMM contrato sin causa

m; ~ **owner** *n* PROP proprietario desnudo *m*; ~ **ownership** *n* INS, PROP propiedad desnuda *f*

bargain[1] *n* FIN *agreement* convenio *m*, GEN COMM ganga *f*, *agreement* convenio *m*, LAW *agreement* convenio *m*, STOCK *deal* transacción *f*; ~ **basement** S&M *in shop* sección de rebajas *f*; ~ **book** STOCK libro de transacciones *m*; ~ **counter** S&M sección de rebajas *f*; ~ **hunter** STOCK cazador(a) de gangas *m,f*; ~ **price** GEN COMM precio de oferta *m*, precio de oportunidad *m*; ~ **rate** S&M tarifa especial *f*; ~ **and sale** PROP compraventa *f*

bargain[2] *vt* HRM negociar

bargain away *vt* GEN COMM malvender

bargain down *vt* GEN COMM *seller* negociar a la baja

bargain for *vt* GEN COMM *anticipate* esperar, contar con, *negotiate* negociar; ◆ ~ **an account** STOCK negociar a través de una cuenta; ~ **cash** STOCK regatear por dinero

bargainer *n* GEN COMM negociador(a) *m,f*

bargaining *n* GEN COMM, HRM, STOCK negociación *f*; ~ **agent** HRM *unions* agente negociador(a) *m,f*; ~ **chip** infrml POL concesión o compromiso que se puede ofrecer en una negociación; ~ **form** HRM forma de negociación *f*; ~ **level** HRM nivel de negociación *m*; ~ **party** GEN COMM contratante comprador(a) *m,f*; ~ **position** GEN COMM posición negociadora *f*; ~ **power** GEN COMM poder negociador *m*; ~ **scope** HRM alcance de la negociación *m*; ~ **structure** HRM estructura de negociación *f*; ~ **table** GEN COMM mesa de negociaciones *f*; ~ **theory of wages** HRM teoría de convenios salariales *f*; ~ **unit** HRM grupo negociador en convenios colectivos *m*

barge *n* TRANSP barcaza *f*, gabarra *f*; ~ **carrier** TRANSP buque portabarcazas *m*; ~**-carrying vessel** (*BCV*) TRANSP navío portabarcazas *m*; ~ **forwarding** TRANSP *off-loading of containers* envío de barcazas *m*

barometer *n* ECON *measuring of trends* barómetro *m*; ~ **stock** STOCK barómetro bursátil *m*

barometric: ~ **firm leadership** *n* ECON medida de liderazgo de una empresa *f*

barratry *n* LAW *fraud* baratería *f*

barrel *n* (*bbl.*) ENVIR, TRANSP tambor *m*, barril *m*; ~ **handler** TRANSP *fork-lift truck* manipulador de barriles *m*; ~ **hook** TRANSP *cargo* grapón de barril *m*

barrels: ~ **per day** *n pl* (*b/d*) ECON, IND *petroleum production* barriles por día *m pl*

barren: ~ **money** *n* ACC deuda sin interés *f*

barrier *n* GEN COMM barrera *f*; ~ **to entry** ECON, IMP/EXP barrera de entrada *f*; ~ **to exit** ECON, IMP/EXP barrera de salida *f*; ~ **to trade** ECON, IMP/EXP, POL barrera al comercio *f*

barrister *n* GEN COMM, LAW ≈ abogado(-a) *m,f*

barristers': ~ **chambers** *n* BrE LAW cámara de abogados *f*, despacho de abogados *m*

Barron: ~**'s Confidence Index** *n* AmE STOCK Índice de Confianza de Barron *m*; ~**'s Group Stock Average** *n* AmE STOCK media bursátil del grupo Barron *f*

barter[1]: ~ **agreement** *n* ECON, LAW acuerdo de trueque *m*, tratado de trueque *m*; ~ **economy** *n* ECON economía de permuta *f*; ~ **trade** *n* ECON comercio de trueque *m*; ~ **transaction** *n* ECON operación de trueque *f*

barter[2] **1.** *vt* ECON bartear, permutar, trocar, GEN COMM bartear; **2.** *vi* ECON hacer trueques

BASATA *abbr* (*British and South Asian Trade Association*) ECON, POL asociación comercial de Gran Bretaña y el sur de Asia

base[1] *adj* COMP *hardware* básico

base[2] *n* GEN COMM base *f*; **~ address** COMP dirección de base *f*; **~ amount** TAX cantidad base *f*; **~ broadening** TAX ampliación de la base *f*; **~ budget** ACC, ECON, FIN presupuesto base *m*; **~ of calculation** FIN, GEN COMM base de cálculo *f*; **~ capital** ECON, FIN capital base *m*; **~ capital leverage ratio** BANK proporción de capital base a apalancamiento *f*; **~ capital ratio** BANK relación base capital *f*; **~ configuration** COMP configuración básica *f*; **~ date** STOCK *prices* fecha base *f*; **~ lending rate** BANK interés básico sobre préstamos *m*; **~ level deduction** TAX *of corporation* deducción de nivel básica *f*; **~-load power station** IND central eléctrica de carga fundamental *f*; **~ pay** *AmE* (*cf basic pay BrE*) HRM salario base *m*, sueldo base *m*; **~ pay rate** *AmE* (*cf basic pay rate BrE*) HRM tipo de sueldo por hora *m*; **~ period** TAX periodo base *m*; **~ point pricing** ECON fijación de precios al punto base *f*; **~ price** GEN COMM, TAX precio base *m*; **~ rate** BANK, FIN tasa base *f*; **~ rent** PROP alquiler básico *m*; **~ sheet** MEDIA *print* hoja base *f*, hoja de montaje *f*; **~ recovery** TAX recuperación de la base *f*; **~ stock** STOCK acciones de base *f pl*; **~ wage** *AmE* (*cf basic wage BrE*) HRM sueldo base *m*; **~ year** ECON, FIN año base *m*; **~ year analysis** ECON análisis año-base *m*

base[3] *vt* GEN COMM basar; **~ on** GEN COMM *decision* basar en

baseband *n* COMP banda de base *f*

based: ~ on *adj* GEN COMM basado en

baseline *n* COMP *of diagram* línea de referencia *f*, MATH *of diagram* línea base *f*, línea de referencia *f*

basic: ~ agreement *n* LAW acuerdo marco *m*; **~ amount** *n* GEN COMM cantidad básica *f*; **~ books** *n pl* FIN libros básicos *m pl*; **~ commodity** *n* ECON, S&M bien de primera necesidad *m*; **~ concept** *n* GEN COMM concepto básico *m*; **~ corporate tax rate** *n* TAX tipo básico del impuesto de sociedades *m*, tipo impositivo empresarial básico *m*; **~ credit allowance** *n* TAX deducción de crédito básica *f*; **~ currency** *n* ECON, FIN medio de cambio básico *f*; **~ definition** *n* GEN COMM definición básica *f*; **~ earnings per share** *n pl* FIN ganancia básica por acción *f*; **~ exemption** *n* TAX exención básica *f*; **~ foodstuffs** *n pl* GEN COMM, IND alimentos básicos *m pl*; **~ goods sector** *n* GEN COMM sector de los productos básicos *m*; **~ grade** *n* HRM, IND calidad normal *f*; **~ income** *n* ACC, FIN ingreso básico *m*; **~ income level** *n* (*BIL*) TAX nivel de ingresos básicos *m*; **~ industry** *n* ECON, IND industria básica *f*; **~ liability limit** *n* INS límite básico de responsabilidad *m*; **~ material** *n* ECON material básico *m*; **~ media** *n pl* MEDIA medios básicos *m pl*; **~ medium** *n* MEDIA medio básico *m*; **~ message** *n* S&M *advertising* mensaje básico *m*; **~ need** *n* ECON necesidad básica *f*; **~ pay** *n BrE* (*cf base pay AmE*) HRM salario base *m*, sueldo base *m*; **~ pay rate** *n BrE* (*cf base pay rate AmE*) HRM tipo de sueldo por hora *m*; **~ personal exemption** *n* TAX exención personal básica *f*; **~ premium** *n* INS prima base *f*; **~ rate** *n* BANK, ECON, FIN interés base *m*; **~-rate tax** *n* TAX impuesto de tipo básico *m*; **~ rating** *n* BANK aplicación de tarifa básica *f*; **~ relief** *n* TAX desgravación básica *f*; **~ rent** *n* PROP alquiler básico *m*; **~ research** *n* GEN COMM investigación básica *f*; **~ research cost** *n* GEN COMM, S&M coste de investigación básica *m* (*Esp*), costo de investigación básica *m* (*AmL*); **~ risk** *n* GEN COMM riesgo básico *m*; **~ salary** *n* HRM salario base *m*, sueldo base *m*; **~ size** *n* GEN COMM dimensión nominal *f*, tamaño base *m*; **~ tax**

n TAX impuesto básico *m*; **~ time limit** *n* GEN COMM límite temporal básico *m*; **~ trend** *n* GEN COMM tendencia básica *f*; **~ unit** *n* GEN COMM unidad de base *f*; **~ wage** *n BrE* (*cf base wage AmE*) HRM sueldo base *m*; **~ weight scales** *n pl* GEN COMM escalas de pesos básica *f pl*

BASIC *abbr* (*Beginner's All-Purpose Symbolic Instruction Code*) COMP BASIC (*código de instrucciones simbólicas de carácter general para principiantes*)

Basic: ~ Research in Industrial Technologies for Europe *n* (*BRITE*) IND Investigación Básica de Tecnologías Industriales para Europa *f*

basics *n pl* GEN COMM fundamentos *m pl*

basin *n* TRANSP *harbour* dársena *f*, dique *m*

basis *n* GEN COMM base *f*; **~ of an agreement** GEN COMM base de un acuerdo *f*; **~ for discussion** GEN COMM base para la discusión *f*; **~ point** FIN, MATH, STOCK punto básico *m*; **~ point value ratio** STOCK *futures* proporción de valor en la base *f*; **~ of premium calculation** INS base para el cálculo de las primas *f*; **~ price** STOCK *odd-lot trading* precio base *m*; **~ risk** FIN, GEN COMM, STOCK riesgo financiero, riesgo de base *m*; ◆ **on the ~ of** GEN COMM a base de; **on a daily ~** GEN COMM a base diaria

basket *n* GEN COMM cesta *f*; **~ of currencies** ECON cesta de monedas *f*, FIN canasta de monedas *f*; **~ of goods** ECON cesta de productos *f*; **~ hitch** TRANSP *cargo handling* embrague en cesta *m*; **~ of products** ECON cesta de productos *f*; **~ purchase** FIN compra de conjunto *f*, compra global *f*, GEN COMM, S&M, STOCK compra global *f*; **~ of rates** FIN canasta de dinero *f*, IND cesta de tipos *f*; **~ trading** STOCK negociación sobre un conjunto de valores *f*

Basle: ~ Concordat on Banking Supervision *n* BANK Concordato Basle sobre la Supervisión Bancaria *m*

bastard: ~ face *n* MEDIA *printing* bastardilla *f*; **~ Keynesianism** *n* ECON keynesianismo falso *m*

batch *n* ACC *invoices* remesa *f*, lote *m*, COMP, IND lote *m*, MEDIA *letters* remesa *f*; **~ computer** COMP computador por lotes *m* (*AmL*), computadora por lotes *f* (*AmL*), ordenador por lotes *m* (*Esp*); **~ control** IND control de lotes *m*; **~ file** COMP fichero secuencial *m*; **~ job** COMP tarea por lotes *f*; **~ processing** COMP proceso por lotes *m*; **~ production** IND producción en lotes *f*; **~ size** IND tamaño de lote *m*

bath *n jarg* STOCK batacazo *m* (*jarg*); ◆ **take a ~** *jarg* STOCK sufrir un batacazo

bathtub: ~ theorem *n* ECON teorema de la bañera *m*

battered: ~ letter *n* S&M carta defectuosa *f*

battery[1]: **~-backed** *adj* COMP con batería de seguridad

battery[2] *n* COMP batería *f*, IND *automobile* batería *f*, *for torch, radio* pila *f*

baud *n* COMP baudio *m*

bay *n* TRANSP *rail* compartimento *m*

Bayes: ~ theorem *n* ECON *probability* teorema de Bayes *m*

Bayesian: ~ approach to decision-making *n* MGMNT enfoque bayesiano para la toma de decisiones *m*; **~ decision theory** *n* S&M teoría bayesiana de la decisión *f*; **~ method** *n* MATH método bayesiano *m*

BB *abbr* COMMS, COMP (*bulletin board*) cartelera *m* (*AmL*), tablón de anuncios *m* (*Esp*), ECON, POL (*Bureau of the Budget*) Oficina del Presupuesto *f*

BBA *abbr* (*British Bankers Association*) BANK asociación de banqueros británicos

BBAISR *abbr* (*British Bankers Association Interest Settlement Rate*) BANK, STOCK tipo de interés básico acordado por la asociación bancaria británica

BBC *abbr* (*British Broadcasting Corporation*) MEDIA la BBC, ≈ RTVE (*Radio Televisión Española*)

bbl. *abbr* (*barrel*) ENVIR, TRANSP barril *m*, tambor *m*

BBS *abbr* (*bulletin board system*) COMMS, COMP sistema de tablón de anuncios *m*

BC *abbr* (*budgetary control*) ACC, FIN control presupuestario *m*

BCom *abbr* (*Bachelor of Commerce*) HRM, WEL licenciado(-a) en Comercio *m,f*

BCV *abbr* (*barge-carrying vessel*) TRANSP navío portabarcazas *m*

b/d *abbr* ACC (*bring down*) llevar a cuenta nueva, reabrir, IND (*barrels per day*) barriles por día *m pl*

b/d. *abbr* ACC (*balance brought down*) balance a cuenta nueva *m*

B/D *abbr* (*bank draft*) BANK giro bancario

bdi *abbr* (*both dates inclusive*) GEN COMM ambas fechas inclusive

bdl *abbr* (*bundle*) TRANSP fardo *m*

BDO *abbr* (*bottom dropped out*) STOCK desplome del fondo *m*

BDR *abbr* (*bearer depository receipt*) BANK RDP (*recibo de depósito del portador*)

B/E *abbr* BANK, (*bill of exchange*) letra de cambio *f*, IMP/ EXP, TRANSP (*bill of entry*) *customs duty* conocimiento de entrada *m*, declaración de aduana *f*

BEA *abbr* (*Bureau of Economic Analysis*) ECON departamento de análisis económico *m*

beacon *n* TRANSP fanal *m*

BEACON *abbr* (*British & European Shipping Lines Joint Container Service*) IMP/EXP, TRANSP Servicio Conjunto de Contenedores de Líneas Marítimas Europeas y Británicas *m*

beancounter *n infrml* ACC cabeza contable *f*

bear[1] *n* ACC, BANK, STOCK bajista *m*; ~ **account** STOCK cuenta de especulaciones a la baja *f*; ~ **call spread** STOCK margen de compra a la baja *m*; ~ **campaign** STOCK campaña bajista *f*; ~ **closing** STOCK cierre a la baja *m*; ~ **covering** STOCK compra para cubrir ventas al descubierto *f*; ~ **hug** *jarg* FIN, STOCK *corporate takeover* compra de una sociedad por otra más grande; ~ **market** STOCK mercado bajista *m*, mercado con tendencia a la baja *m*; ~ **operation** STOCK operación a la baja *f*; ~ **position** STOCK posición bajista *f*; ~ **put spread** STOCK margen de venta a la baja *m*; ~ **raid** STOCK compra agresiva a la baja *f*, manipulación a la baja *f*; ~ **raiding** STOCK manipulación a la baja *f*; ~ **sale** STOCK venta al descubierto *f*; ~ **speculation** STOCK especulación a la baja *f*; ~ **spread** STOCK diferencia a la baja *f*; ~ **squeeze** STOCK vuelta rápida a la baja *f*; ~ **strike price** STOCK precio orientado a la baja *m*; ~ **transaction** STOCK operación a la baja *f*

bear[2] *vt* ACC *interest* devengar, producir, GEN COMM *burden, responsibility* soportar, STOCK correr con; ◆ ~ **the cost of** ACC correr con el coste de (*Esp*), correr con el costo de (*AmL*); ~ **the costs** GEN COMM asumir los costes (*Esp*), asumir los costos (*AmL*); ~ **a date** GEN

COMM asumir una fecha; ~ **in mind** GEN COMM tener presente, tener en cuenta

bearer *n* BANK portador(a) *m,f*, tenedor(a) *m,f*; ~ **bill** STOCK efectos al portador *m pl*; ~ **bond** FIN, STOCK bono al portador *m*; ~ **certificate** STOCK certificado al portador *m*; ~ **check** *AmE*, ~ **cheque** *BrE* BANK, FIN cheque al portador *m*; ~ **clause** STOCK cláusula al portador *f*; ~ **coupon** TAX cupón al portador *m*; ~ **depository receipt** (*BDR*) BANK recibo de depósito del portador *m* (*RDP*); ~ **form** STOCK documento al portador *m*, impreso al portador *m*; ~ **marketable bond** FIN, STOCK bono negociable al portador *m*; ~ **proxy** STOCK poder al portador *m*; ~ **security** STOCK título al portador *m*; ~ **share** ACC, FIN, STOCK acción al portador *f*; ~ **stock** ACC, FIN, STOCK acción al portador *f*; ~ **warrant** STOCK opción de compra al portador *f*

bearing: ~ **surface** *n* TRANSP *shipping* superficie de apoyo *f*

bearish[1] *adj* STOCK bajista; ◆ **be** ~ STOCK estar a la baja

bearish[2]: ~ **market** *n* STOCK mercado a la baja *m*; ~ **movement** *n* STOCK movimiento a la baja *m*; ~ **signal information** *n* STOCK *analysis* información de signo pesimista *f*; ~ **spread** *n* STOCK diferencial a la baja *m*; ~ **tone** *n* STOCK tono bajista *m*

beat down *vt* GEN COMM conseguir que baje el precio de algo

Beaufort: ~ **scale** *n* GEN COMM escala Beaufort *f*

BEcon *abbr* (*Bachelor of Economics*) HRM, WEL licenciado(-a) en Economía *m,f*

bed: ~ **and breakfast** *n* (*B&B*) LEIS alojamiento y desayuno en casa particular, pensión con desayuno incluido *f*; ~ **and breakfast deal** *n jarg* STOCK venta con recompra al día siguiente para evadir impuestos

bedroom: ~ **community** *n AmE* (*cf dormitory town BrE*) GEN COMM ciudad dormitorio *f*

Beeb: **the** ~ *n BrE jarg* MEDIA la BBC

beep[1] *n* COMP *warning* señal sonora *f*

beep[2] *vi* COMP emitir un señal sonora

before[1]: ~ **hours** *adv* STOCK antes de horas de oficina; ~ **maturity** *adv* BANK, FIN, GEN COMM, STOCK antes del vencimiento

before[2]: ~**hours dealing** *n* STOCK negociación previa a la apertura *f*; ~**tax cash flow** *n* ACC cash-flow antes de impuestos *m*, recursos generados antes de impuestos *m pl*

beforehand *adv* GEN COMM por anticipado

beggar: ~**my-neighbor policy** *AmE*, ~**my-neighbour policy** *BrE n* GEN COMM política económica para empobrecer al vecino

begin *vi* GEN COMM empezar

Beginner: ~**'s All-Purpose Symbolic Instruction Code** *n* (*BASIC*) COMP código de instrucciones simbólicas de carácter general para principiantes *m* (*BASIC*)

beginning *n* GEN COMM comienzo *m*; ~ **inventory** ACC inventario de apertura *m*, inventario de entrada *m*, inventario inicial *m*; ~ **of the year** ACC comienzo del año *m*

BEHA *abbr* (*British Export Houses Association*) IMP/EXP asociación de compañías importadoras británicas

behalf: **on** ~ **of** *prep* GEN COMM de parte de, en nombre de

behavior *AmE see* behaviour *BrE*

behavioral *AmE see* behavioural *BrE*

behaviour *n* *BrE* GEN COMM, HRM comportamiento *m*; ~ **line** *BrE* ECON *microeconomics* línea de comportamiento *f*, línea de conducta *f*; ~ **modification** *BrE* HRM modificación de la conducta *f*

behavioural: ~ **research** *n* *BrE* S&M investigación conductista *f*; ~ **science** *n* *BrE* MGMNT, S&M ciencia del comportamiento *f*

belated: ~ **claim** *n* INS daño diferido *m*

Belfast: ~ **Stock Exchange** *n* STOCK Bolsa de Valores de Belfast *f*

belief *n* GEN COMM fe *f*, S&M *advertising* opinión *f*

believe *vt* GEN COMM creer

bell: ~-**shaped curve** *n* MATH curva en forma de campana *f*

bellwether *n* STOCK indicador de tendencia *m*

belly *n* TRANSP panza *f*; ~ **container** TRANSP contenedor en la panza *m*

below[1]: ~ **average** *adj* GEN COMM por debajo de la media; ~-**market price** *adj* S&M, STOCK inferior al precio de mercado; ~ **par** *adj* ACC, GEN COMM, STOCK bajo la par; ~-**the-line** *adj* *jarg* MEDIA, S&M *commissionable advertising media* gastos en publicidad indirecta *m pl*

below[2] *adv* GEN COMM *letter, document* abajo

below[3]: ~-**the-line credit** *n* *jarg* FIN financiación mediante préstamo *f*; ~-**the-line item** *n* ECON partida extraordinaria *f*; ~-**the-line revenue** *n* ACC ingresos bajo la línea *m pl*

belship *n* TRANSP buque transatlántico de mercancías *m*

bench: ~ **mark** *n* ACC punto de referencia *m*, COMP *test of software* banco de pruebas *m*, ECON punto de referencia *m*, FIN parámetros *m pl*, criterio de referencia *m*, GEN COMM punto de referencia *m*; ~ **method** *n* FIN método de comparación *m*, método de comprobación *m*; ~ **reserve** *n* *AmE* BANK reserva referenciada *f*; ~ **statistics** *n pl* MATH estadísticas de referencia *f pl*; ~ **test** *n* COMP ensayo en banco de pruebas *m*

Bench: **the** ~ *n* LAW el Tribunal *m*

beneficial[1] *adj* GEN COMM provechoso

beneficial[2]: ~ **interest** *n* LAW, TAX intereses patrimoniales *m pl*; ~ **owner** *n* LAW, STOCK propietario(-a) beneficiario(-a) *m,f*; ~ **ownership** *n* TAX propiedad en usufructo *f*

beneficially: ~ **interested** *adj* TAX con derecho a usufructo

beneficiary *n* GEN COMM beneficiario(-a) *m,f*; ~ **clause** INS cláusula de beneficiario *f*; ~ **under a trust** TAX beneficiario(-a) bajo un fideicomiso *m,f*

beneficium cedendarum actionum *n* ACC, ECON, FIN beneficio de cesión de acciones *m*

benefit[1] *n* GEN COMM beneficio *m*, ganancia *f*, *welfare* prestación *m*, provecho *m*, HRM subsidio *m*, prestación *f*, INS *from plans*, MGMNT *to employees* prestación *f*, TAX ganancia *f*; ~ **approach to taxation** TAX enfoque de la tributación desde los beneficios *m*; ~-**based pension plan** INS plan de jubilación basado en prestaciones *m*; ~ **club** FIN club de beneficios mutuos *m*; ~-**cost analysis** ACC análisis de beneficios y costes *m pl* (*Esp*), análisis de beneficios y costos *m pl* (*AmL*); ~ **in kind** TAX *from employment* prestación en especie *f*; ~ **of insurance clause** INS *marine* cláusula de beneficio del seguro *f*; ~ **principle** TAX principio del beneficio *m*; ~ **society** *AmE* (*cf friendly society BrE*) FIN mutualidad *f*, sociedad de beneficiencia *f*; ~ **tax** ACC, TAX impuesto sobre beneficios *m*; ♦ **in** ~ HRM incluido en las prestaciones

benefit[2] **1.** *vt* GEN COMM beneficiar; **2.** *vi* GEN COMM beneficiarse

benefits: **be on** ~ *phr* *BrE* (*cf be on welfare AmE*) HRM, WEL vivir de subsidios sociales

benevolent[1] *adj* HRM *organization* benévolo, IND, POL, WEL *organization* benevolente; ~-**authoritative** MGMNT *Likert's leadership* benevolente-autoritario

benevolent[2]: ~ **capitalism** *n* ECON, IND, POL capitalismo benevolente *m*

bequeath *vt* LAW legar

bequest *n* LAW legado *m*

Bergson: ~ **social welfare function** *n* ECON, HRM, WEL función de bienestar social bergsonia *f*

Bermuda: ~ **Agreement** *n* ECON, POL Acuerdo de las Bermudas *m*

Berne: ~ **Union** *n* INS sindicato internacional de aseguradoras de créditos e inversiones

Bernoulli: ~ **box** *n* COMP caja de Bernoulli *f*; ~ **distribution** *n* MATH distribución de Bernoulli *f*; ~'s **hypothesis** *n* MATH hipótesis de Bernouilli *f*

berth *n* TRANSP *shipping, train* fondeadero *m*; ~ **accommodation** LEIS, TRANSP alojamiento de pasajeros *m*; ~ **charter** TRANSP póliza de atraque *f*

berthing: ~ **of ships** *n* TRANSP atraque al muelle *m*

Bertrand: ~ **duopoly model** *n* ECON modelo duopolista de Bertrand *m*

best[1]: ~ **alternative** *n* GEN COMM mejor alternativa *f*; ~ **bid** *n* GEN COMM mejor oferta *f*; ~ **bidder** *n* GEN COMM, STOCK mejor postor(a) *m,f*; ~-**case scenario** *n* GEN COMM argumento de supuesto óptimo *m*, escenario para el mejor de los casos *m*; ~ **estimate** *n* GEN COMM estimación óptima *f*; ~ **linear unbiased estimator** *n* (*BLUE*) ECON estimador lineal insesgado óptimo *m* (*ELIO*); ~ **positioned partner** *n* MGMNT socio(-a) mejor posicionado(-a) *m,f*; ~ **practical means** *n pl* (*bpm*) GEN COMM medios prácticos más adecuados *m pl*; ~ **price** *n* GEN COMM mejor precio *m*; ~ **profferer** *n* GEN COMM mejor comunicante *mf*

best[2]: **at** ~ *phr* STOCK *price, order* al mejor; ~ **efforts** *phr* STOCK *of underwriter* acuerdo de colocación de una emisión; ~ **time available** *phr* S&M disponible en el mejor tiempo

Best: ~'s **Rating** *n* *AmE* INS Clasificación del Best *f*

bestseller *n* MEDIA, S&M *book* best seller *m*, más vendido

beta: ~ **coefficient** *n* STOCK coeficiente beta de regresión *m*; ~ **factor** *n* STOCK factor beta *m*; ~ **share** *n* FIN, STOCK acción beta *f*; ~ **stock** *n* STOCK acciones beta *f pl*; ~-**test** *n* COMP prueba beta *f*; ~ **version** *n* COMP versión beta *f*

BETA *abbr* *BrE* (*Business Equipment Trade Association*) IND sociedad de comerciantes de equipamiento para oficinas

better: ~ **than average** *adj* GEN COMM por encima de la media

betterment *n* PROP mejora *f*, plusvalía *f*; ~ **tax** TAX impuesto sobre la plusvalía *m*

betting *n* LEIS *sport* apuesta *f*

BEX: ~ **35 Index** *n* STOCK Índice BEX 35 *m* (*Esp*)

beyond: ~ **repair** *adj* GEN COMM que no tiene arreglo

b/f *abbr* (*brought forward*) ACC *balance sheet* llevado a cuenta nueva, suma y sigue

BFE *abbr* (*Baltic Futures Exchange*) STOCK mercado báltico de futuros

BFI *abbr* (*Baltic Freight Index*) TRANSP *shipping* Índice de Fletes del Báltico *m*

BFO *abbr* (*bunker fuel oil*) TRANSP combustible para calderas *m*

b/g *abbr* (*bonded goods*) ECON, IMP/EXP, TAX mercancías en almacén de aduanas *f pl*, mercancías en depósisto *f pl*

BH *abbr* (*Bill of Health*) WEL certificado médico *m*

BHC *abbr* (*British High Commission*) POL alto comisionado británico

bhp *abbr* (*brake horsepower*) TRANSP potencia al freno *f*

BHRA *abbr* (*British Hotels and Restaurants Association*) LEIS asociación de hoteles y restaurantes británicos

biannual *adj* GEN COMM semestral

bias[1]: **~-belted** *adj* TRANSP *pneumatic tyre* encintado al sesgo

bias[2] *n* GEN COMM *prejudice* prejuicio *m*, TRANSP *pneumatic tyre* sesgo *m*

biased *adj* GEN COMM parcial

BIC *abbr* (*British Importers Confederation*) IMP/EXP confederación de importadores británicos

bid[1] *adj* GEN COMM, STOCK ofertado

bid[2] *n* GEN COMM oferta *f*, puja *f*; **~-and-asked price** STOCK precio de la oferta y la demanda *m*; **~-and-offered price** STOCK precio de compraventa *m*; **~-ask spread** STOCK margen entre oferta y demanda *m*; **~ bond** FIN fianza de la oferta *f*, GEN COMM, STOCK fianza de licitación *f*; **~ closing** STOCK cierre de licitación *m*; **~-closing date** STOCK fecha de cierre de licitación *f*; **~-offer spread** STOCK diferencial de demanda y oferta *m*; **~ opening** GEN COMM apertura de plicas *f*; **~ price** STOCK precio comprador *m*; **~ rate** BANK tipo comprador *m*; **~ rent** PROP alquiler puesto en subasta *m*; **~ value** STOCK valor de compra *m*; **~ vehicle** GEN COMM instrumento de licitación *m*, vehículo de licitación *m*; ♦ **make a ~** GEN COMM hacer una oferta

bid[3] **1.** *vt* GEN COMM *order* mandar, ordenar, ofertar, STOCK ofertar; **2.** *vi* GEN COMM *at auction* pujar, licitar, MGMNT *projects, contracts* licitar, STOCK hacer una oferta

bid for *vt* GEN COMM *at auction* pujar

bid on *vi AmE* GEN COMM *contract* ofrecer más

BID *abbr* (*Bachelor of Industrial Design*) HRM, WEL licenciado(-a) en Dibujo Técnico *m,f*, licenciado(-a) en Diseño Industrial *m,f*

bidder *n* FIN *tender, offer*, GEN COMM postor *m*

bidding *n* GEN COMM *submission of bids* licitación *f*; **~ requirement** GEN COMM requisito para ofertar *m*; **~ technique** ECON técnica de subasta *f*, GEN COMM, S&M método de licitación *m*, técnica de licitación *f*; **~ up** STOCK oferta al alza *f*

bidirectional: **~ printer** *n* COMP impresora bidireccional *f*

BIDS *abbr* (*British Institute of Dealers in Securities*) STOCK instituto británico de operadores de valores

biennial *adj* GEN COMM bienal

BIF *abbr* (*British Industries Fair*) IND feria industrial británica

BIFFEX *abbr* (*Baltic International Freight Futures Exchange*) STOCK, TRANSP bolsa báltica internacional de futuros de fletes

big: **~ banks** *n pl* BANK bancos importantes *m pl*, grandes bancos *m pl*; **~ business** *n* GEN COMM empresas de gran magnitud *f pl*; **~ customer** *n* GEN COMM cliente importante *mf*; **~ figure** *n* STOCK *dealer's term* gran cifra *f*; **~ income earner** *n* GEN COMM gran perceptor(a) de renta *m,f*; **~ industrial user** *n* GEN COMM gran usuario(-a) industrial *m,f*; **~ investor** *n* FIN gran inversor(a) *m,f*; **~ issue** *n* GEN COMM emisión importante *f*; **~ name** *n* GEN COMM personaje *mf*; **~ tent** *n AmE jarg* POL gran bazar *m*

Big: **~ Bang** *n BrE* STOCK Big Bang *m*; **~ Blue** *n infrml* COMP *IBM society* Gigante Azul *m*; **the ~ Five** *n* POL las cinco Grandes *f pl*; **the ~ Four** *n BrE* BANK *Barclays, Lloyds, Midland, National Westminster* las cuatro mayores corporaciones bancarias del Reino Unido; **~ Six** *n BrE* ACC las seis firmas de auditoría más importantes a nivel internacional

BIL *abbr* TAX (*basic income level*) nivel de ingresos básicos *m*, (*business investment loss*) pérdidas de inversión empresarial *f pl*

bilateral[1] *adj* GEN COMM bilateral

bilateral[2]: **~ agreement** *n* ECON convenio bilateral *m*; **~ aid** *n* ECON, POL *tied aid* ayuda bilateral *f*; **~ contract** *n* LAW contrato bilateral *m*, contrato sinalagmático *m*; **~ disbursement** *n* ECON *development assistance* desembolso bilateral *m*, POL pago bilateral *m*; **~ donor** *n* ECON *of development assistance*, POL donante bilateral *m*; **~ loan** *n* BANK *development* préstamo bilateral *m*; **~ mistake** *n* GEN COMM vicio de consentimiento *m*; **~ monopoly** *n* ECON monopolio bilateral *m*; **~ reference** *n* HRM consulta bilateral *f*; **~ road agreement** *n* TRANSP acuerdo bilateral de carreteras *m*; **~ trade** *n* ECON comercio bilateral *m*; **~ trade agreement** *n* ECON, POL acuerdo comercial bilateral *m*; **~ trade treaty** *n* ECON, POL tratado de comercio bilateral *m*, tratado comercial bilateral *m*

bilateralism *n* ECON, POL bilateralismo *m*

bilaterals *n pl* ECON bilaterales *m pl*

Bilbao: **~ Stock Exchange** *n* STOCK Bolsa de Bilbao *f*

bill *n* BANK pagaré *m*, *AmE* (*cf note BrE*) *banknote* billete de banco *m*, FIN *invoice* factura *f*, pagaré *m*, *payable, receivable* efecto *m*, GEN COMM *BrE* (*cf check AmE*) *invoice* cuenta *f*, LAW *legislation* proyecto de ley *m*, ley *f*, MEDIA *advertising* cartel publicitario *m*, POL ley *f*, S&M *invoice* factura *f*; **~ at double usance** GEN COMM letra de cambio al doble uso *f*; **~ book** ACC libro de facturas *m*, libro de letras *m*; **~ broker** STOCK casa de descuento *f*; **~ of costs** FIN cuenta de gastos *f*; **~ cover** BANK provisión de una letra *f*; **~ diary** STOCK registro de letras *m*; **~ discounted** BANK documento descontado *m*, letra descontada *f*; **~ of entry** (*B/E*) IMP/EXP, TRANSP conocimiento de entrada *m*, declaración de aduana *f*, *customs* declaración detallada *f*, declaración de aduana *f*; **~ of exchange** (*B/E*) BANK, IMP/EXP letra de cambio *f*; **~ for collection** BANK letra al cobro *f*; **~ of freight** IMP/EXP, TRANSP carta de porte *f*; **~ of goods** IND relación de mercancías *f*; **~ holding** BANK tenencia de una letra *f*; **~ of lading** (*B/L*) IMP/EXP, INS, TRANSP conocimiento de carga *m*, conocimiento a bordo *m*, conocimiento embarcado *m*, conocimiento de embarque *m*, conocimiento de carga *m*; **~ of lading clause** BANK, INS, LAW cláusula del conocimiento de embarque *f*; **~ of lading form** IMP/EXP, TRANSP formulario de conocimiento de embarque *m*; ~ **of lading fraud** IMP/ EXP, TRANSP fraude en el conocimiento de embarque *m*; ~ **of lading issued to a named party** IMP/EXP, TRANSP conocimiento de embarque nominativo *m*, conocimiento de embarque emitido a una parte determinada *m*; ~ **of lading ton** (*B/L ton*) IMP/EXP, TRANSP tonelada del conocimiento de embarque *f*; ~ **market** STOCK mercado de letras *m*; ~ **of materials** IND *production* lista de materiales *f*; ~ **merchant** BANK, FIN, STOCK corredor(a) de cambios *m,f*; ~ **payable** ACC efecto a pagar *m*; ~ **payable at sight** ACC, BANK letra pagadera a la vista *f*; ~ **portfolio** BANK cartera de efectos *f*; ~ **rate** FIN tasa de letras de cambio *f*, tipo de letras de cambio *m*; ~ **of sight** IMP/EXP declaración provisional *f*; ~ **sticking** GEN COMM retención de factura *f*; ~ **of store** IMP/EXP permiso de reimportación libre *m*; ~ **of sufferance** ACC, ADMIN, BANK carta de exención *f*, TAX solicitud de exención *f*; ~ **to order** BANK instrumento al portador *m*

Bill: ~ **of Health** *n* (*BH*) WEL certificado médico *m*

billback *n* STOCK aporte posterior de dinero *m*, efecto como aval *m*

billboard *n* S&M valla publicitaria *f*

biller *n* GEN COMM *machine* facturador *m*

billing *n* GEN COMM facturación *f*, S&M *advertising* importe total de negocios *m*; ~ **cycle** GEN COMM ciclo de facturación *m*; ~ **date** *AmE* (*cf invoice date BrE*) GEN COMM fecha de facturación *f*; ~ **day** ACC día de facturación *m*; ~ **department** *AmE* (*cf invoicing department BrE*) GEN COMM departamento de facturación *m*; ~ **for the time spent** GEN COMM facturación por tiempo *f*

billion *n* (*bn*) BANK, GEN COMM mil millones *m pl*

bills *n pl* BANK letras *f pl*; ~ **discounted** ACC efectos descontados *m pl*; ~ **in a set** FIN letra con varios ejemplares *f*; ~ **purchased under resale agreement** ACC, FIN *balance sheet* efectos comprados bajo acuerdo de reventa *m pl*, efectos comprados con pacto de recompra *m pl*; ~ **receivable** ACC cuentas a cobrar *f pl*, efectos a cobrar *m pl*, facturas a cobrar *f pl*, letras a cobrar *f pl*

BIM *abbr* (*British Institute of Management*) MGMNT instituto británico de gestión empresarial

bimetallic[1] *adj* ECON, ENVIR, IND bimetálico

bimetallic[2]: ~ **standard** *n* ENVIR modelo bimetálico *m*

bimetallism *n* ECON bimetalismo *m*

bimodal: ~ **distribution** *n* MATH distribución bimodal *f*; ~ **frequency curve** *n* MATH curva de frecuencias bimodal *f*

bimonthly *adj* GEN COMM, MEDIA bimensual

bin: ~ **container** *n* TRANSP contenedor tolva *m*

binary[1] *adj* COMP binario

binary[2]: ~ **code** *n* COMP código binario *m*; ~**-coded decimal** *n* COMP decimal en código binario *m*; ~ **coding** *n* COMP codificación binaria *f*; ~ **digit** *n* COMP dígito binario *m*; ~ **number** *n* COMP, MATH número binario *m*; ~ **operator** *n* COMP operador binario *m*; ~ **search** *n* COMP búsqueda binaria *f*; ~**-to-decimal conversion** *n* COMP conversión binario a decimal *f*

bind 1. *vt* LAW unir, vincular, escriturar, PROP escriturar; ~ **oneself to** GEN COMM *agree to* comprometerse a; **2.** *vi* IND agarrotarse (*Esp*), engarrotarse (*AmL*), pegarse (*Esp*)

binder *n* *AmE* INS póliza de seguro provisional *f*, PROP sujeción *f*

binding[1] *adj* LAW vinculante

binding[2]: ~ **agreement** *n* LAW acuerdo vinculante *m*; ~ **arbitration** *n* LAW arbitraje vinculante *m*; ~ **offer** *n* GEN COMM oferta vinculante *f*; ~ **promise** *n* GEN COMM promesa vinculante *f*; ~ **tender** *n* GEN COMM oferta vinculante *f*

binomial[1] *adj* ECON, MATH binomial

binomial[2]: ~ **charge** *n* ECON cargo binomial *m*

biochip *n* COMP chip biológico *m*

biocontrol *n* ENVIR biocontrol *m*

biodegradability *n* ENVIR biodegradabilidad *f*

bioeconomics *n* ECON bioeconomía *f*

bioengineering *n* IND ingeniería biológica *f*

biographical: ~ **data** *n* HRM datos biográficos *m pl*

biotope *n* ENVIR biotopo *m*

BIP *abbr* (*baggage improvement programme*) TRANSP programa de optimización de equipajes *m*

bipolar[1] *adj* COMP bipolar

bipolar[2]: ~ **transistor** *n* COMP *hardware* transistor bipolar *m*

birdwatchers *n pl* GEN COMM asistentes a una subasta *m pl*

Birmingham: ~ **Sotck Exchange** *n* STOCK Bolsa de Valores de Birmingham *f*

birth: ~ **certificate** *n* GEN COMM, LAW certificado de nacimiento, partida de nacimiento *f*

BIS *abbr* (*Bank for International Settlements*) BANK, ECON BPI (*Banco de Pagos Internacionales*)

bisque: ~ **clause** *n* BANK, INS, LAW cláusula de modificación parcial *f*

BISRA *abbr* (*British Iron & Steel Research Association*) IND asociación británica para la investigación del hierro y el acero

bit *n* COMP bit *m*, bitio *m*, MATH bit *m*; ~ **configuration** COMP configuración binaria *f*; ~ **density** COMP densidad en dígitos binarios *f*; ~ **location** COMP celda binaria *f*; ~ **rate** COMP velocidad de transferencia de bitios *f*; ~ **string** COMP cadena de bitios *f*

bits: ~ **per inch** *n pl* (*bpi*) COMP bitios por pulgada *phr* (*bpp*); ~ **per second** *n pl* (*bps*) COMP bitios por segundo *phr* (*bps*)

biweekly *adj* GEN COMM, MEDIA bisemanal

bk *abbr* (*bank*) BANK banco *m*

bkg *abbr* (*banking*) BANK banca *f*

BL *abbr* (*British Library*) GEN COMM ≈ BN *Esp* (*Biblioteca Nacional*)

B/L *abbr* (*bill of lading*) IMP/EXP, INS, TRANSP conocimiento de embarque *m*, conocimiento de carga *m*, conocimiento a bordo *m*, conocimiento embarcado *m*

black: ~ **books** *n pl* ECON *takeover bids* registro de castigos *m*; ~ **box** *n* COMP, TRANSP caja negra *f*; ~ **capitalism** *n* GEN COMM capitalismo salvaje *m*, capitalismo tardío *m*; ~ **economy** *n* ECON, FIN economía clandestina *f*, economía sumergida *f*; ~ **gold** *n* ENVIR oro negro *m*; ~ **market** *n* ECON mercado negro *m*; ~ **money** *n* TAX, TRANSP dinero negro *m*; ~ **powder** *n* ENVIR pólvora negra *f*; ~ **trading** *n* GEN COMM comercio clandestino *m*

Black: ~ **Friday** *n* STOCK viernes negro *m*; ~ **Monday** *n* STOCK lunes negro *m*; ~ **Thursday** *n* STOCK jueves negro *m*; ~ **Wednesday** *n* STOCK miércoles negro *m*

blackboard: ~ **trading** *n* STOCK operación a precio puesto *f*, operación con pizarra *f*

blacking *n* HRM boicoteo contra la contratación de personal no sindicalizado

blackleg *n* BrE *infrml* HRM esquirol *mf* (*infrml*)

blacklist[1] *n* GEN COMM, HRM, IND lista negra *f*

blacklist[2] *vt* GEN COMM, HRM, IND poner en la lista negra

blacklisted *adj* GEN COMM, HRM, IND incluido en la lista negra

blackmail[1] *n* GEN COMM chantaje *m*

blackmail[2] *vt* GEN COMM chantajear

blackout *n* COMP *of electrical supply* apagón *m*

Black-Scholes: ~ **option pricing model** *n* STOCK modelo de tarificación de opciones Black Scholes *m*

blank[1] *adj* GEN COMM blanco

blank[2] *n* COMP blanco *m*; ~ **acceptance** BANK, FIN aceptación en blanco *f*; ~ **ballot** POL voto en blanco *m*; ~ **character** COMP carácter en blanco *m*; ~ **check** AmE, ~ **cheque** BrE BANK, FIN cheque en blanco *m*; ~ **credit** BANK, FIN crédito al descubierto *m*, crédito en blanco *m*; ~ **endorsement** GEN COMM, STOCK endoso en blanco *m*; ~ **form** GEN COMM formulario en blanco *m*; ~ **order** GEN COMM, S&M pedido en blanco *m*; ~ **receipt** GEN COMM recibo en blanco *m*; ~ **signature** BANK firma en blanco *f*

blank[3] *vt* COMP ocultar, borrar

blanket[1] *adj* GEN COMM general, global, LAW *licences* de cobertura total

blanket[2]: ~ **agreement** *n* GEN COMM, HRM acuerdo general *m*; ~ **amount** *n* GEN COMM cantidad general *f*; ~ **ban** *n* GEN COMM exclusión general *f*; ~ **bond** *n* INS fianza colectiva *f*, fianza general *f*; ~ **coverage** *n* S&M cobertura general *f*; ~ **fidelity bond** *n* INS seguro contra daños de empleados desleales *m*; ~ **insurance** *n* INS seguro abierto *m*, seguro global *m*; ~ **life and health insurance** *n* INS seguro colectivo de vida y enfermedad *m*; ~ **medical expense insurance** *n* INS seguro colectivo de gastos médicos *m*; ~ **mortgage** *n* BANK, PROP hipoteca colectiva *f*; ~ **order** *n* GEN COMM orden de compra abierta *f*; ~ **policy** *n* INS póliza abierta *f*; ~ **rate** *n* ACC, TRANSP tarifa general *f*; ~ **recommendation** *n* GEN COMM, STOCK recomendación general *f*; ~ **statement** *n* GEN COMM declaración general *f*; ~ **statute** *n* GEN COMM estatuto colectivo *m*

blanking *n* COMP ocultación *f*

bleak *adj* ECON *outlook* poco prometedor

bleed *vt infrml* GEN COMM sacar dinero a, sangrar (*infrml*)

blended: ~ **rate** *n* BANK *of interest* tasa combinada *f*; ~ **value** *n* STOCK valor mixto *m*

blending *n* ENVIR, IND mezcla *f*; ~ **plant** ENVIR planta mezcladora *f*

blight: ~ **notice** *n* PROP notificación de plaga *f*

blighted: ~ **area** *n* ENVIR, PROP *of city*, WEL zona desertizada *f*

blind: ~ **advertisement** *n* S&M publicidad ciega *f*; ~~**alley job** *n* HRM trabajo sin perspectivas de avance *m*, trabajo terminal *m*; ~ **date** *n* GEN COMM fecha a ciegas *f*; ~ **faith** *n* GEN COMM fe ciega *f*; ~ **figure** *n* GEN COMM cifra confusa *f*; ~ **pool** *n* FIN sociedad de especulación dirigida con plenos poderes *f*; ~ **product test** *n* S&M prueba a ciegas de un producto *f*; ~ **test** *n* S&M prueba a ciegas *f*; ~ **trust** *n* LAW fideicomiso ciego *m*

blink[1] *n* COMP, S&M parpadeo *m*

blink[2] *vi* COMP parpadear

blink-meter *n* S&M medidor de parpadeos *m*

bliss: ~ **point** *n* WEL *social welfare* punto de Bliss *m*

blister: ~ **packaging** *n* S&M embalaje con papel de burbujas *m*

block[1] *n* GEN COMM bloque *m*, FIN *of shares* paquete *m*, PROP *between intersecting streets* manzana *f*, STOCK paquete *m*, TRANSP picadero *m*; ~ **averaging** TAX promedio de grupo *m*; ~ **booking** S&M reserva en bloque *f*; ~ **code** COMP código de bloques *m*; ~ **diagram** COMP esquema funcional *m*; ~ **funding** ACC *public sector* asignación de fondos en bloque *f*, FIN *public sector* inversión en paquetes *f*, POL asignación de fondos en bloque *f*, TAX *public sector* fondo en bloque *m*; ~ **grant** ADMIN subvención global *f*; ~ **move** COMP *data, word processing* desplazamiento de bloque *m*; ~ **policy** INS póliza conjunta *f*; ~ **positioner** STOCK colocador(a) de paquetes *m,f*; ~ **pull** S&M tirón de un bloque de emisión *m*; ~ **purchase** STOCK compra de un lote *f*; ~ **sampling** ACC muestreo en bloque *m*; ~ **of shares** STOCK paquete de acciones *m*; ~ **stock trader** STOCK intermediario(-a) por lotes *m,f*; ~ **testing** ACC *auditing* comprobación de bloques *f*, prueba de bloques *f*, prueba de paquetes *f*; ~ **time** TRANSP *aviation* tiempo de parado a parado *m*; ~ **trade** STOCK contratación por bloque *f*; ~ **trades** *n pl* STOCK comercio con paquetes de acciones *m*; ~ **transfer** COMP transferencia por bloques *f*; ~ **vote** HRM voto colectivo *m*, voto en bloque *m*; ~ **voting** HRM votación en bloque *f*; ◆ **in** ~ **mode** COMP en modo de bloque

block[2] *vt* GEN COMM *competition* bloquear, detener

blockade *n* GEN COMM bloqueo *m*

blockbuster *n infrml* MEDIA, S&M éxito de taquilla *m*, bomba *f*

blockbusting *n* AmE *jarg* ENVIR explosivo *m*

blocked[1] *adj* GEN COMM bloqueado

blocked[2]: ~ **account** *n* BANK cuenta bloqueada *f*; ~ **funds** *n pl* ACC, BANK, FIN fondos bloqueados *m pl*, fondos congelados *m pl*; ~ **grant** *n* POL ayuda bloqueada *f*

blocking *n* COMP agrupación en bloque *f*; ~ **off** TRANSP *of cargo* acuñamiento de la carga *m*

blood: ~ **money** *n jarg* GEN COMM *paid to victim's family* dinero manchado de sangre *m*, *ill-gotten gains* dinero sucio *m*

blow *vt infrml* GEN COMM *money* fundir

blowout *n* AmE S&M venta rápida *f*

blue: ~ **book** *n* AmE ACC, POL informe sobre la situación financiera; ~ **button** *n* BrE *jarg* STOCK empleado(-a) de bolsa *m,f*; ~ **chip** *n* FIN, STOCK valor de primera clase *m*; ~~**chip company** *n* STOCK compañía de acciones de primera clase *f*; ~~**chip customer** *n* GEN COMM cliente de primer orden *mf*; ~~**chip industrials** *n pl* STOCK valores industriales de primera clase *m pl*; ~~**chip securities** *n pl* STOCK valores de primera clase *m pl*; ~~**chip stock** *n* STOCK acciones de primer orden *f pl*; ~ **chips** *n pl* FIN acciones selectas *f pl*, STOCK valores seguros *m pl*; ~~**collar worker** *n* HRM obrero(-a) *m,f*; ~ **economy** *n* BrE ECON economía oficial *f*; ~ **laws** *n pl* AmE LAW, S&M *Sunday trading* leyes de prohibición comercial en los domingos, ley de regulación del horario comercial *f*; ~~**sky** *n* AmE GEN COMM *phoney, of no value* inversión monetaria insegura *f*; ~~**sky bargaining** *n* AmE HRM negociación sin valor *f*; ~~**sky law** *n* AmE

LAW, STOCK legislación en los Estados Unidos sobre emisión y venta de valores *f*; **~-sky research** *n* HRM investigación pura *f*

Blue: **~ Cross** *n AmE* INS *hospital plan* Cruz Azul *f*

BLUE *abbr* (*best linear unbiased estimator*) ECON ELIO (*estimador lineal insesgado óptimo*)

blueprint *n* ADMIN *printing* copia heliográfica *f*, GEN COMM anteproyecto *m*, copia *f*, heliográfica *f*, LAW, POL anteproyecto *m*

blurb *n* MEDIA reseña *f*, texto de presentación *m*, S&M *publicity* propaganda publicitaria *f*

BMEG *abbr* (*Building Materials Export Group*) IMP/EXP grupo de exportación de materiales para la construcción

bmep *abbr* (*brake mean effective pressure*) TRANSP presión media efectiva al freno *f*

BMLA *abbr* (*British Maritime Law Association*) LAW asociación británica de derecho marítimo

B-movie *n* LEIS película de la serie B *f*

BMRB *abbr* (*British Market Research Bureau*) S&M departamento de estudios de mercado del Reino Unido

bn *abbr* (*billion*) GEN COMM mil millones *m pl*

B.O. *abbr* (*branch office*) GEN COMM filial *f*, sucursal *f*

BOAG *abbr* (*British Overseas Aid Group*) WEL grupo británico de ayuda a países de ultramar

board *n* COMP *hardware* tablero *m*, GEN COMM, HRM, MGMNT consejo *m*, consejo de administración *m*, comité *m*, POL comité *m*; **~ of accounting** ACC comisión contable *f*; **~ of arbitration** GEN COMM junta de arbitraje *f*, HRM comisión de arbitraje *f*, junta de arbitraje *f*, STOCK comisión de arbitraje *f*; **~ broker** STOCK corredor(a) de bolsa con mesa *m,f*; **~ of conciliation** GEN COMM, HRM junta de conciliación *f*, junta de conciliación y arbitraje *f*; **~ control** MGMNT control del consejo *m*; **~ of directors** ACC, GEN COMM consejo de administración *m*, consejo de control *m*, consejo administrativo *m*, consejo de administración *m*, consejo directivo *m*, cuadro directivo *m*, mesa directiva *f* (*Esp*); **~ of equalization** TAX junta de revisión de avalúos *f*; **~ of management** GEN COMM consejo de dirección *m*; **~ meeting** GEN COMM junta de consejo *f* (*AmL*), junta de consejo de administración *f*, junta de consejo directivo *f*, MGMNT reunión de los directivos *f*, reunión del directorio *f*, junta de consejo *f* (*AmL*) de la mesa directiva *f* (*Esp*); **~ of realtors** *AmE* PROP comisión de agentes inmobiliarios *f*; **~ of trade** ECON *international* junta de comercio *f*; **~ of trustees** ECON, FIN, HRM consejo de fideicomisarios *m*

Board: **~ of Investment** *n* (*BOI*) GEN COMM Consejo de Inversiones *m*; **~ of Trade** *n BrE* (*BOT*) ECON, POL ≈ Junta de Comercio *f* (*Esp*)

boarding: **~ card** *n* TRANSP tarjeta de embarque *f*; **~ gate** *n* TRANSP puerta de embarque *f*

boardroom *n* ADMIN, MGMNT sala del consejo *f*, sala de consejo directivo *f*, sala de juntas *f*, STOCK sala de cotizaciones *f*

boatload *n* TRANSP barcada *f*

bodily: **~ injury** *n* INS daño corporal *m*

body *n* GEN COMM cuerpo *m*; **~ of creditors** ACC masa de acreedores *f*; **~ language** HRM, MGMNT lenguaje corporal *m*, lenguaje no verbal *m*; **~ matter** S&M texto suelto *m*; **~ shop** GEN COMM taller de carrocería *m*; **~-shopping** HRM atractivo personal *m*

BOF *abbr* (*balance for official financing*) ACC, ECON

balance para financiación oficial *m*, balanza de financiación oficial *f*

bogie *n* TRANSP *railways* carretilla *f*; **~ lift** TRANSP elevador de carretones *m*

bogus: **~ bank** *n* BANK banco fraudulento *m*; **~ company** *n* GEN COMM sociedad fantasma *f*

BOI *abbr* (*Board of Investment*) GEN COMM Consejo de Inversiones *m*

boiler: **~ room** *n AmE* STOCK cabina desde donde telefonean los especuladores ilegales de valores

boilerplate *n* ADMIN, MEDIA cliché *m*, GEN COMM *standardized language* modelo de contrato *m*

bold: **~ face** *n* MEDIA negrita *f*; **~-face character** *n* COMP, MEDIA carácter en negrita *m*; **~ printing** *n* COMP escritura en negrilla *f*; **~ type** *n* COMP tipo negrita *m*, MEDIA negrita *f*

bollard *n* TRANSP *for mooring purposes* bita *f*

bolster *vt* GEN COMM *morale* alentar, reforzar; ♦ **~ sb's confidence** GEN COMM reforzar la confianza de alguien

bomb: **~ scare** *n* GEN COMM amenaza de bomba *f*

bona fide[1] *adj* GEN COMM de buena fe

bona fide[2]: **~ clause** *n* GEN COMM cláusula de buena fe *f*; **~ holder** *n* STOCK contable honrado(-a) *m,f Esp* (*cf contador honrado AmL*); **~ offer** *n* GEN COMM oferta de buena fe *f*; **~ purchaser** *n* GEN COMM comprador(a) de buena fe *m,f*; **~ trade union** *n* HRM sindicato genuino *m*

bona vacantia *n* LAW, PROP bienes vacantes *m pl*

bonanza *n* IND *mining* bonanza *f*

bond *n* ACC obligación *f*, ECON bono *m*, FIN obligación *f*, bono *m*, STOCK obligación *f*, título *m*; **~ anticipation note** (*BAN*) STOCK vale por pronto pago de bono *m*; **~ with bond-buying warrant** FIN, STOCK bono con garantía de compra *f*; **~ broker** BANK, FIN, STOCK corredor(a) de cambios *m,f*, corredor(a) de comercio *m,f*; **~ call option** STOCK opción de compra de bonos *f*; **~ capital** STOCK capital de renta fija *m*; **~ certificate** BANK, ECON, GEN COMM certificado nominativo *m*, STOCK certificado de bono *m*; **~ conversion** STOCK conversión de renta fija *f*; **~ coupon** STOCK cupón de un bono *m*; **~ creditor** STOCK acreedor(a) con caución *m,f*, acreedor(-a) garantizado(-a) por fianza *m,f*; **~ crowd** STOCK lote de bonos *m*; **~ cum warrant** STOCK bono con garantía *m*; **~ dealer** STOCK colocador(a) de bonos *m,f*; **~ dealing** STOCK operación con renta fija *f*; **~ debt** STOCK deuda representada por bonos *f*; **~ denomination** STOCK valor nominal del bono *m*; **~ discount** STOCK descuento sobre bonos *m*; **~ ex warrants** *n pl* FIN, STOCK bono sin certificado *m*; **~ features** *n pl* STOCK características del bono *f pl*; **~ financing** STOCK financiación mediante emisión de obligaciones *f*; **~ fund** FIN, STOCK fondo de bonos *m*; **~ futures contract** STOCK contrato de futuros sobre renta fija *m*; **~ guarantee** FIN fianza de bonos *f*; **~ holding** FIN, STOCK bonos en cartera *m pl*, tenencia de bonos *f*; **~ indenture** STOCK contrato de emisión de bonos *m*; **~ index** STOCK cotización de bonos *f*; **~ interest** STOCK interés del bono *m*, pago de intereses sobre bonos *m*; **~ with interest paid in advance** FIN, STOCK bono con pago de intereses anticipado *m*; **~ interest tax allowance** TAX desgravación fiscal de intereses de bonos *f*; **~ issue** STOCK emisión de bonos *f*; **~ issue expenses** *n pl* ACC, STOCK gastos de emisión de bonos *m pl*; **~ issue operation** STOCK operación de emisión de bonos *f*; **~ issuing price** STOCK precio de emisión de bonos *m*; ~ **liability** FIN, STOCK pasivo de obligaciones *m*; ~ **loan** BANK, FIN, PROP préstamo hipotecario *m*; ~ **market** STOCK mercado de bonos *m*, mercado de obligaciones de renta fija *m*; ~ **market rally** STOCK recuperación del mercado de renta fija *f*; ~ **market rate** STOCK tasa del mercado de obligaciones *f*; ~ **with monthly-paid interest** FIN, STOCK bono con pago mensual de intereses *m*; ~ **number** BANK, STOCK número de bono *m*; ~ **option** STOCK opción de bonos *f*; ~ **options market** STOCK mercado de opciones sobre bonos *m*; ~ **payable** FIN, STOCK bono pagadero *m*; ~ **pool** STOCK volumen de obligaciones *m*; ~ **portfolio** STOCK cartera de valores de renta fija *f*; ~ **power** STOCK poder para asegurar la transferencia de bonos; ~ **premium** STOCK prima sobre bonos *f*; ~ **price** STOCK precio de los bonos *m*; ~ **principal** STOCK principal del bono *m*; ~ **proceeds** *n pl* STOCK producto de la renta fija *m*; ~ **put option** STOCK opción de venta de bonos *f*; ~ **rate** STOCK tipo de interés del bono *m*; ~ **rating** STOCK clasificación de títulos *f*; ~ **rating agency** STOCK agencia de rating *f*; ~ **redemption premium** ACC, STOCK fondo para redención de premios *m*, prima de rescate de un bono *f*; ~ **refunding** STOCK reintegro de bonos *m*; ~ **sale** STOCK venta de valores de renta fija *f*; ~ **sinking fund** STOCK fondo para amortización de obligaciones *m*; ~ **specialist** STOCK especialista en bonos *mf*; ~ **switch** STOCK canje de bonos *m*; ~ **switching** STOCK conmutación de bonos *f*; ~ **terms** *n pl* FIN, STOCK bono con condiciones *m*; ~ **trader** STOCK intermediario(-a) de renta fija *m,f*; ~ **trading** STOCK operación con bonos *f*; ~ **trading department** FIN, STOCK departamento de operaciones con bonos *m*; ~ **turnover** STOCK movimiento de los valores de renta fija *m*; ~ **underwriting** STOCK suscripción de bonos *f*; ~ **valuation** STOCK valoración de bonos *f*; ~ **warrant** STOCK certificado de depósito *m* (*c.d.*, *CD*); ~ **with warrants** FIN, STOCK bono con certificado *m*; ~ **with warrants attached** FIN, STOCK bono con certificado adjunto *m*; ~ **washing** FIN compra y venta en bolsa de títulos para obtener desgravación fiscal, invocando la baja del valor; ~-**year basis** TAX base bono-año *f*; ~ **yield** STOCK rendimiento del bono *m*; ◆ **in ~** (*IB*) IMP/EXP en aduana, en depósito, LAW, en aduana, TRANSP bajo precinto aduanero, en aduana

Bond: ~ **Equivalent Yield** *n* STOCK Rendimiento Equivalente del Bono *m*; ~ **Traders Association** *n BrE* STOCK asociación de operadores de obligaciones

bonded: ~ **cargo** *n* GEN COMM, TRANSP carga almacenada en depósito *f*; ~ **debt** *n* STOCK deuda garantizada con bonos *f*; ~ **elevator** *n* GEN COMM elevador garantizado *m*; ~ **goods** *n pl* (*b/g*) ECON, IMP/EXP, TAX mercancías en almacén de aduanas *f pl*, mercancías en depósito *f pl*; ~ **store** *n* GEN COMM almacén de depósito *m*; ~ **warehouse** *n* ECON, IMP/EXP, TAX almacén de depósito *m*, depósito de aduana *m*

bondholder *n* BANK, STOCK obligacionista *mf*

bonding: ~ **cost** *n* STOCK coste de emisión *m* (*Esp*), costo de emisión *m* (*AmL*); ~ **of salespeople** *n* S&M unión de vendedores *f*

bonds *n pl* BANK obligaciones *f pl*; ~ **sold prior to issue** STOCK valores vendidos antes de la emisión *m pl*

bone: ~ **of contention** *n* GEN COMM manzana de la discordia *f*

bonus *n* GEN COMM *wages* sobrepaga, bonificación, HRM *m*, INS prima *f*, STOCK *to shareholders* dividendo extraordinario *m*; ~ **certificate** BANK, ECON, FIN, GEN COMM certificado de prima *m*; ~ **interest payment** TAX pago de interés del bono *m*; ~ **issue** *BrE* (cf *capitalization issue BrE, scrip issue BrE, stock dividend AmE, stock split AmE*) ACC, STOCK dividendo en acciones *m*, emisión de acciones liberadas *f*; ~ **pack** S&M envase con premio *m*; ~ **payment** STOCK pago de prima *m*; ~ **rate of interest** BANK tasa de bonos de interés *f*; ~ **reserve** GEN COMM reserva para bonificación *f*, reserva para bonus *f*; ~ **savings account** BANK cuenta de ahorro de primas *f*; ~ **savings rate** BANK tasa de ahorro de bonos *f*; ~ **scheme** HRM plan de bonificaciones *m*; ~ **share** FIN, STOCK acción gratuita *f*; ~ **stock** STOCK premio en títulos *m*

BONUS *abbr* (*borrower's option for notes and unwritten standby*) FIN opción del tomador a títulos y créditos no emitidos *f*

book[1] *n* ACC libro de contabilidad *m*, GEN COMM, LEIS *of notes* talonario *m*, LEIS registro *m*, STOCK libro de contabilidad *m*, *foreign exchange market* libro *m*, *underwriting of securities* libro de anotaciones *m*; ~ **cost** ACC coste en libros *m* (*Esp*), costo en libros *m* (*AmL*); ~ **debt** ACC deuda contabilizada *f*; ~ **depreciation** ACC amortización en libros *f*, depreciación en libros *f*; ~ **entry** ACC apunte contable *m*, asiento contable *m*, asiento en libros *m*, registro contable *m*; ~-**entry securities** *n pl* STOCK valores anotados *m pl*; ~ **of final entry** ACC libro de últimas entradas *m*; ~ **of first entry** ACC anotación del asiento de apertura *f*, asiento de apertura *m*; ~ **inventory** STOCK inventario en libros *m*; ~-**keeping** ACC contabilidad *f*, teneduría de libros *f*, ADMIN teneduría de libros *f*; ~ **loss** ACC pérdida contable *f*, pérdida según libros *f*; ~ **on final entry** ACC anotación del asiento de cierre *f*, asiento de cierre *m*; ~ **of original entry** ACC libro de asiento original *m*; ~ **of prime entry** ACC registro de asiento de apertura *m*; ~ **profit** ACC beneficio aparente *m*, beneficio contable *m*, beneficio según libros *m*; ~ **rate of return** ACC proporción de beneficio en libros *f*, ratio de beneficio según libros *m*; ~ **reviewer** GEN COMM supervisor(a) de reservas *m,f*; ~ **squaring** STOCK balance de los libros *m*, cuadrado de los libros *m*; ~ **token** LEIS, S&M vale para compra de libros *m*; ~ **value** ACC, FIN valor en libros *m*; ~ **value of investment** ACC valor contable de la inversión *m*; ◆ **by the ~** GEN COMM con apego exacto, STOCK según las normas, según las reglas

book[2] *vt* ACC *book-keeping* contabilizar, LEIS, TRANSP *reserve* reservar; ◆ ~ **early** GEN COMM reservar con anticipación, reservar con antelación

book in *vi* GEN COMM *at hotel* firmar el registro, MGMNT firmar a la entrada

book out *vi* GEN COMM *at hotel* despedirse, MGMNT firmar a la salida

book up *vt* GEN COMM *hotels* reservar la totalidad de

booked[1] *adj* GEN COMM reservado

booked[2]: ~ **traffic** *n* TRANSP tráfico reglamentario *m*

booking *n* GEN COMM, LEIS, S&M reserva *f*; ~ **fee** GEN COMM cuota de reserva *f*; ~ **of new orders** GEN COMM reserva de nuevos pedidos *f*; ~ **note** TRANSP nota de reserva *f*; ~ **office** LEIS, TRANSP despacho de billetes *m*; ~ **order** GEN COMM orden de reserva *f*; ~ **system** GEN COMM, LEIS, S&M sistema de reserva *m*; ~ **of unpaid checks** *AmE*, ~ **of unpaid cheques** *BrE* BANK contabilización de cheques no pagados *f*, libro de cheques no pagados *m*

bookkeeper *n* ACC, ADMIN tenedor(a) de libros *m,f*

bookmaker *n* LEIS *sport* corredor(a) de apuestas *m,f*

books *n pl* ACC libros contables *m pl*, libros de contabilidad *m pl*; ◆ **cook the ~** ACC falsificar las cuentas

Boolean[1] *adj* COMP booleano

Boolean[2]: **~ algebra** *n* COMP, MATH álgebra de Boole *f*; **~ search** *n* COMP búsqueda de Boole *f*; **~ variable** *n* COMP variable booleana *f*

boom[1] *n* ECON, GEN COMM alza extraordinaria *f*, alza rápida *f*, auge *m*, aumento repentino *m*, boom *m*

boom[2] *vi* ECON, GEN COMM estar en auge

boomlet *n* ECON, GEN COMM mini boom *m*, periodo breve de prosperidad *m*

boondoggle *n AmE infrml* HRM proyecto innecesario *m*

boost[1] *n* GEN COMM refuerzo *m*, estímulo *m*, impulso *m*, aumento *m*

boost[2] *vt* GEN COMM reforzar, alentar, aumentar sustancialmente, animar, *growth, interest rate* estimular, S&M *sales* aumentar

booster *n* TRANSP *cargo* acelerador de refuerzo *m*, bomba elevadora de presión *f*; **~ training** HRM capacitación complementaria *f* (*AmL*), formación complementaria *f* (*Esp*)

boot: **~ disk** *n* COMP disco de arranque *m*; **~-up** *n* COMP arranque *m*

boot out *vt infrml* GEN COMM echar, poner de patitas en la calle (*infrml*)

boot up *vt* COMP *computer* arrancar, inicializar

booth *n* S&M barraca *f*

bootstrap *vt* COMP cargar instrucciones

boot-up *n* COMP arranque *m*

BOP *abbr* (*balance of payments*) ECON, POL balanza de pagos *f*

border: **~ control** *n* ECON, IMP/EXP control fronterizo *m*; **~ trade** *n* IMP/EXP comercio fronterizo *m*

borderline: **~ case** *n* GEN COMM caso dudoso *m*, caso cuestionable *m*

born: **~ leader** *n* HRM líder nato(-a) *m,f*

borough *n* GEN COMM barrio *m*, POL municipio *m*, *local authority* Ayuntamiento *m*

borrow[1]: **~ funds** *n pl* BANK fondos de préstamo *m pl*

borrow[2] *vt* GEN COMM pedir prestado, tomar prestado, *idea* adoptar, apropiar; ◆ **~ abroad** GEN COMM tomar un préstamo en el extranjero; **~ external funds** GEN COMM pedir prestados fondos exteriores; **~ funds** BANK pedir fondos prestados; **~ in the Euromarket** GEN COMM tomar un préstamo en el Euromercado; **~ interest-free** BANK solicitar un préstamo sin intereses; **~ money from sb** GEN COMM pedir dinero prestado a alguien; **~ money** BANK, FIN tomar dinero prestado; **~ stock** STOCK pedir acciones en préstamo; **~ at call** BANK tomar prestado a la vista; **~ at interest** BANK pedir prestado con intereses; **~ long** STOCK pedir prestado a largo plazo; **~ on securities** STOCK pedir un préstamo sobre valores; **~ short** STOCK pedir prestado a corto plazo

borrow from *vt* BANK pedir prestado de

borrowed: **~ capital** *n* BANK capital ajeno a la sociedad *m*; **~ funds** *n pl* BANK, FIN fondos prestados *m pl*; **~ money** *n* BANK, TAX dinero prestado *m*; **~ reserve** *n*

BANK reserva prestada *f*; **~ stock** *n* STOCK acciones a préstamo *f pl*

borrower *n* BANK prestatario(-a) *m,f*; **~ country** ECON país prestatario *m*; **~'s option for notes and unwritten standby** (*BONUS*) FIN opción del tomador a títulos y créditos no emitidos *f*

borrowing *n* BANK, STOCK empréstito *m*; **~ abroad** FIN endeudamiento externo *m*, obtención de créditos en el exterior *f*; **~ allocation** GEN COMM adjudicación de préstamos *f*; **~ authority** GEN COMM autoridad de préstamo *f*; **~ bank** BANK banco prestatario *m*; **~ by banks** BANK solicitud de préstamos por parte de los bancos *f*; **~ ceiling** GEN COMM tope de endeudamiento *m*; **~ cost** BANK, GEN COMM coste de un préstamo *m* (*Esp*), costo de un préstamo *m* (*AmL*); **~ customer** BANK, GEN COMM cliente(-a) que solicita un préstamo *m,f*; **~ facilities** *n pl* BANK facilidades de crédito *f pl*; **~ facility** BANK instalación de crédito *f*; **~ fee** GEN COMM cargo por el empréstito *m*; **~ in the money market** FIN endeudamiento en el mercado monetario *m*, STOCK endeudamiento en el mercado del dinero *m*; **~ limit** GEN COMM límite de endeudamiento *m*; **~ potential** GEN COMM potencial de endeudamiento *m*; **~ power** GEN COMM capacidad de endeudamiento *f*; **~ power of securities** STOCK valor de préstamo de los títulos *m*; **~ powers** *n pl* BANK, GEN COMM poderes para solicitar préstamos *m pl*; **~ rate** BANK, FIN tasa de préstamos *f*; **~ ratio** ACC coeficiente de empréstitos *m*, proporción de endeudamiento *f*, FIN proporción de endeudamiento *f*; **~ requirement** BANK necesidad de crédito *f*, requisito de préstamo *m*, FIN requisito de préstamo *m*

borrowings *n pl* BANK, STOCK empréstitos *m pl*

boss *n infrml* HRM jefe(-a) *m,f*

Boston: **~ box** *n* S&M *branch* matriz de Boston *f*; **~ Stock Exchange** *n* STOCK bolsa de valores de Boston

BOT *abbr* (*Board of Trade*) ECON, POL ≈ Junta de Comercio *f* (*Esp*)

both: **~-to-blame collision clause** *n* INS *maritime insurance* cláusula ambos culpables de colisión *f*; **~ dates inclusive** *phr* (*bdi*) GEN COMM ambas fechas inclusive

bottled: **~-up** *adj* GEN COMM *price increase* refrenado

bottleneck *n* GEN COMM, IND cuello de botella *m*, estrangulamiento *m*, TRANSP *traffic jam* embotellamiento *m*; **~ inflation** ECON inflación de demanda *f*

bottom[1] *n* GEN COMM fondo *m*, HRM *of organization* nivel inferior *m*, TRANSP *of ship* carena *f*; **~ dropped out** (*BDO*) STOCK desplome del fondo *m*; **~ end of the range** S&M extremo más bajo de la gama *m*, parte más baja de la gama *f*; **~ fisher** STOCK inversor(a) de oportunidades *m,f*; **~ line** ACC balance final *f*, saldo final *m*, GEN COMM resultados *m pl*, resultado del ejercicio *m*; **~ profit margin** ACC, FIN margen de beneficio final *m*, margen de beneficios del resultado final *m*; **~ price** STOCK precio mínimo *m*; **~ rung** HRM *of organization* nivel básico *m*, nivel inferior *m*; **~-up approach to investing** FIN enfoque invertido de la inversión *m*; **~-up management** MGMNT dirección ascendente *f*; ◆ **the ~ has fallen out of the market** GEN COMM se ha hundido el mercado, se ha derrumbado el mercado; **the ~ line is** GEN COMM al fin y al cabo; **any one ~** (*AOB*) INS *marine* cualquier fondo *m*

bottom[2] *vi* STOCK tocar fondo

bottom out *vi* GEN COMM *market, prices, graph* tocar fondo

bottomry: **~ bond** *n* INS *marine insurance* hipoteca a la gruesa *f*, LAW, TRANSP contrato a la gruesa *m*

bought: **~ book** *n* ACC libro de compras *m*; **~ contract** *n* STOCK escritura de compraventa *f*; **~ day book** *n* ACC libro diario de compras *m*; **~ deal** *n* STOCK emisión precolocada *f*; **~ journal** *n* ACC libro diario de compras *m*; **~ ledger** *n* ACC mayor de compras *m*; **~ note** *n* STOCK *of broker* documento de contrato de compras de valores *m*

Boulewarism *n* HRM negociación de contrato colectivo

bounce 1. *vt infrml* BANK *cheque* rechazar; **2.** *vi infrml* BANK *cheque* impagar

bounce back *vi* GEN COMM recuperarse

bounce-back *n* GEN COMM repercusión *f*

bounced: **~ check** *infrml AmE*, **~ cheque** *BrE n* BANK, FIN cheque devuelto *m*, cheque impagado por falta de fondos *m*, cheque incobrable por falta de fondos *m*

bound: **~ for** *phr* TRANSP con destino a

boundary *n* PROP límite *m*, límite de propiedad *m*, linde *f*; **~ constraint** MATH condición de contorno *f*

bourgeoisie *n* ECON, POL burguesía *f*

boutique *n* GEN COMM, S&M boutique *f*

box *n* S&M estuche *m*; **~ container** TRANSP contenedor para cargas apiladas *m*; **~ number** MEDIA *of printed advert* número de referencia *m*; **~ office** LEIS *cinema, theatre* taquilla *f*; **~-office draw** LEIS película taquillera *f* (*jarg*); **~-office success** *n pl* LEIS película taquillera *f* (*jarg*); **~ pallet** TRANSP bandeja de carga cerrada *f*; **~ spread** STOCK margen de depósito *m*; **~ trailer** TRANSP *for maximum security shipping* camión remolcador *m*; **~ wagon** *BrE* (*cf boxcar AmE*) TRANSP vagón cerrado *m*

boxcar *n AmE* (*cf box wagon BrE*) TRANSP vagón cerrado *m*

boycott[1] *n* GEN COMM, HRM boicot *m*, boicoteo *m*

boycott[2] *vt* GEN COMM, HRM boicotear

BP: **~ deficit** *n* (*balance of payments deficit*) ECON déficit de la balanza de pagos *m*

BPA *abbr* (*British Ports Association*) TRANSP asociación británica de puertos

BPF *abbr* (*British Plastics Federation*) IND federación británica de plásticos

bpi *abbr* (*bits per inch*) COMP bpp (*bitios por pulgada*)

bpm *abbr* (*best practical means*) GEN COMM medios prácticos más adecuados *m pl*

bps *abbr* (*bits per second*) COMP bps (*bitios por segundo*)

BR *abbr obs* (*British Rail*) GEN COMM, TRANSP red nacional británica de ferrocarriles, ≈ RENFE (*Red Nacional de Ferrocarriles Españoles*)

bracket *n* GEN COMM *price, tax* tramo *m*; **~ creep** ECON, TAX tramo del impuesto progresivo *m*, paso al siguiente tramo impositivo *m*

Brady: **~ Commission** *n AmE* STOCK Comisión Brady *f*

brain: **~ drain** *n infrml* HRM éxodo de profesionales *m*, fuga de cerebros *f* (*infrml*)

brainchild *n infrml* GEN COMM *design* creación *f*

brains: **~ trust** *n* HRM grupo de expertos *m*, trust de cerebros *m*

brainstorm[1] *n* MGMNT idea genial *f*, frenesí *m*

brainstorm[2] *vi* MGMNT brainstorm

brainstorming *n* MGMNT brainstorming *m*

brake: **~ horsepower** *n* (*bhp*) TRANSP potencia al freno *f*; **~ mean effective pressure** *n* (*bmep*) TRANSP presión media efectiva al freno *f*

branch *n* BANK *of credit institution, bank* sucursal *f*, ramo *m*, COMP bifurcación *f*, GEN COMM sucursal *f*, ramo *m*; **~ address** COMP dirección de bifurcación *f*; **~ banking** BANK banca con sucursales *f*; **~ banking system** BANK sistema bancario con sucursales *m*; **~ economy** ECON economía dependiente *f*; **~ line** TRANSP *rail* ramal *m*; **~ manager** BANK, MGMNT director(a) de sucursal *m,f*; **~ network** BANK red de sucursales *f*; **~ number** BANK número de sucursal *m*; **~ office** (*BO*) GEN COMM sucursal *f*, filial *f*; **~ office manager** HRM gerente de sucursal *mf*; **~ operation** GEN COMM funcionamiento de una sucursal *m*

brand[1]: **~-new** *adj* GEN COMM flamante

brand[2] *n* S&M *of product, service* marca *f*; **~ acceptance** S&M aceptación de marca *f*; **~ advertising** S&M publicidad de marca *f*; **~ association** S&M asociación de marca *f*; **~ awareness** GEN COMM conocimiento de marca *m*; **~ development** S&M desarrollo de marca *m*; **~ differentiation** S&M diferenciación de marca *f*; **~ extension** S&M extensión de la marca *f*; **~ identification** S&M identificación de marca *f*; **~ image** S&M imagen de marca *f*; **~ leader** GEN COMM, S&M marca líder *f*; **~ loyalty** S&M fidelidad a una marca *f*, lealtad a una marca *f*; **~ management** S&M gestión de la marca *f*; **~ manager** HRM, S&M gerente de marcas *mf*; **~ marketing** S&M marketing de marca *m*; **~ name** S&M nombre comercial *m*; **~ personality** S&M personalidad de marca *f*; **~ portfolio** FIN cartera de marcas comerciales *f*, S&M, STOCK cartera de marcas *f*; **~ positioning** S&M posicionamiento de marca *m*; **~ preference** S&M preferencia de marca *f*; **~ promotion** S&M promoción de marca *f*; **~ rationalization** S&M racionalización de la marca *f*; **~ recognition** S&M reconocimiento de marca *m*; **~ reinforcement** S&M reforzamiento de marca *m*; **~ share** S&M cuota de marca *f*; **~ strategy** FIN, S&M estrategia de marca *f*

branded: **~ good** *n* GEN COMM artículo de marca *m*

BRAS *abbr* (*Building Research Advisory Service*) IND servicio de asesoría de investigadores de la construcción

brass *n infrml* GEN COMM, HRM, MGMNT alto ejecutivo *m*

BRC *abbr* (*business reply card*) COMMS tarjeta de respuesta comercial *f*

BRE *abbr* (*business reply envelope*) COMMS sobre de respuesta comercial *m*, S&M sobre impreso con franqueo pagado *m*

breach[1] *n* LAW incumplimiento *m*; **~ of contract** HRM, LAW incumplimiento de contrato *m*; **~ of duty** LAW incumplimiento del deber *m*; **~ of professional etiquette** GEN COMM violación del honor profesional *f*; **~ of secrecy** GEN COMM violación de secreto *f*; **~ of trust** GEN COMM abuso de confianza *m*; **~ of warranty** LAW incumplimiento de garantía *m*

breach[2] *vt* GEN COMM *market* abrir brecha en, LAW incumplir

bread *n infrml* GEN COMM *money* guita *f* (*infrml*), pasta *f* (*Esp*) (*infrml*), lana *f* (*AmL*) (*infrml*); **~-and-butter issue** *BrE infrml* (*cf pocketbook issue AmE*) POL, WEL cuestión relacionada con los ingresos básicos *f*, problema básico *m*; **~-and-butter letter** *infrml* GEN

COMM breve misiva de agradecimiento *f*; **~-and-butter technique** *infrml* GEN COMM, S&M técnica de la venta segura *f*

breadline *n infrml* GEN COMM nivel de subsistencia *m*; ◆ **be on the ~** GEN COMM vivir en la miseria

breadwinner *n* WEL mantenedor(a) de la familia *m,f*

break[1] *n* GEN COMM *good luck* golpe de suerte *m* (*infrml*), HRM pausa *f*, STOCK bajada de precios *f*, *fall* desplome *m*; **~ bulk agent** TRANSP agente de carga fraccionada *mf*; **~ bulk cargo** TRANSP *goods shipped loose* carga desarrumada *f*, carga fraccionada *f*; **~ bulk center** *AmE*, **~ bulk centre** *BrE* TRANSP centro de descarga *m*, centro de inicio de la descarga *m*; **~-even analysis** ECON, FIN análisis del punto muerto *m*, análisis del punto crítico *m*; **~-even level of income** ACC cifra de ingresos del punto muerto *f*, ECON nivel de ingresos de punto muerto *m*; **~-even point** ACC punto crítico *m*, punto de rentabilidad *m*, umbral de rentabilidad *m*, FIN punto de equilibrio *m*, GEN COMM punto crítico *m*, punto de equilibrio *m* punto muerto *m*, IND punto de equilibrio *m*; **~-even price** STOCK precio de equilibrio *m*; **~-even pricing** ECON precio de punto muerto *m*, S&M fijación de precios para cubrir los gastos *f*; **~-even quantity** ECON cantidad de punto muerto *f*, IND cantidad para cubrir gastos *f*, MGMNT cantidad de paridad *f*; **~ in the market** GEN COMM baja en el mercado *f*; **~ a strike** HRM, POL *strike* romper una huelga; **~-up** GEN COMM disolución *f*; **~-up value** ACC valor de disolución *m*, valor de escisión *m*, valor de realización inmediata *m*, FIN valor de realización inmediata *m*; **~ weight** TRANSP carga de rotura *f*

break[2] *vt* COMMS *interrupt* interrumpir, *news* comunicar, GEN COMM violar, LAW *contract, law* violar, infringir, romper; ◆ **~ bulk** TRANSP desarrumar, descargar, fraccionar la carga, transbordar; **~ the ceiling** FIN romper el techo, STOCK sobrepasar el límite máximo; **~ even** ACC, ECON, FIN, S&M equilibrar; **~ new ground** GEN COMM abrir brecha; **~ ranks** HRM romper filas; **~ the stalemate** GEN COMM romper el estancamiento; **~ the syndicate** STOCK romper el sindicato

break down 1. *vt* ACC *allocate expenses* asignar, *costs* desagregar, desglosar, BANK, GEN COMM desglosar; **2.** *vi* COMP averiarse, GEN COMM averiarse, malfuncionar, HRM *negotiations, relations* descomponer, romperse, POL descomponer

break into *vt* GEN COMM *market* irrumpir

break off *vt* GEN COMM romper; ◆ **~ negotiations** GEN COMM romper las negociaciones

break up *vi* GEN COMM *meeting* disolver

breakage: **~ clause** *n* INS cláusula de rotura *f*; **~ of glass risk** *n* INS riesgo de ruptura de cristales *m*

breakaway: **~ union** *n* HRM sindicato separatista *m*

breakdown *n* COMP *malfunction* avería *f*, GEN COMM *failure* fracaso *m*, avería *f*, colapso *m*, HRM *of negotiations* interrupción *f*, ruptura *f*, fracaso *m*, *personal* crisis nerviosa *f*, IND desglose *m*, STOCK colapso *m*, TRANSP *rail* interrupción del servicio *f*; **~ of expenses** ACC recorte de gastos *m*; **~ of tasks** HRM descomposición del trabajo en fases *f*; **~ van** *BrE* (*cf tow truck AmE*) TRANSP furgoneta de socorro *f*

breaking: **~ load** *n* TRANSP inicio de la descarga *m*; **~-off** *n* GEN COMM *of relationships* ruptura *f*

breakout *n* STOCK ruptura *f*

breakpoint *n* COMP, TRANSP punto de interrupción *m*;

~ instruction COMP instrucción de reenvío *f*; **~ sale** FIN venta de equilibrio *f*, venta de rendimiento nulo *f*

breakthrough *n* ECON descubrimiento importante *m*, GEN COMM avance extraordinario *m*

breech: **~ base** *n* TRANSP base de cerrojo para trincaje de contenedores *f*

breed *vt* ECON *confidence* producir

Bretton: **~ Woods Agreement** *n* ECON, POL acuerdo de Bretton Woods *m*

bribe[1] *n* GEN COMM cohecho *m* (*Esp*), coima *f* (*AmL*), comisión ilícita *f*, soborno *m* (*Esp*)

bribe[2] *vt* GEN COMM cohacer, sobornar

briber *n* GEN COMM cohacedor(a) *m,f*

bribes: **take ~** *phr* GEN COMM recibir sobornos

bridge[1] *n* GEN COMM puente *m*; **~ financing** FIN financiación puente *f*, financiación transitoria *f*; **~ loan** BANK préstamo puente *m*, préstamo recíproco al descubierto *m*

bridge[2] *vt* GEN COMM *gap* llenar, salvar

bridgeware *n* COMP programas de traspaso *m pl*

bridging: **~ advance** *n* BANK préstamo de transición *m*; **~ credit** *n* BANK, FIN crédito de empalme *m*; **~ facility** *n* BANK recursos a corto plazo *m pl*; **~ pension scheme** *n* FIN, HRM plan de pensiones transitorio *m*; **~ software** *n* COMP programas puente *m pl*

Bridlington: **~ agreement** *n BrE* HRM *on trade union recruitment* acuerdo Bridlington *m*; **~ Rules** *n pl BrE* HRM reglas de Bridlington *f pl*

brief[1] *n* GEN COMM informe *m* (*Esp*), reporte *m* (*AmL*), LAW *puesto* abogado(-a) *m,f*, *escrito* instrucciones *fpl*; **~ audit** ACC auditoría limitada *f*; **~ summary** GEN COMM resumen corto *m*

brief[2] *vt* GEN COMM informar, *lawyer* instruir

briefing *n* GEN COMM *training* briefing *m*, *document* informe *m* (*Esp*), reporte *m* (*AmL*), MGMNT, S&M resumen *m*, session GEN COMM sesión informativa *f*

brightness *n* COMP reflexibilidad media *f*

bring *vt* GEN COMM *person* llevar, conducir, *news, object* traer (*AmL*), extraer (*Esp*); ◆ **~ to bear against** GEN COMM apuntar contra, LAW aplicar contra alguien; **~ into fashion** GEN COMM poner de moda; **~ pressure to bear on** GEN COMM ejercer presión sobre; **~ sb up to date on sth** GEN COMM poner a alguien al tanto de algo; **~ to an end** GEN COMM alcanzar una conclusión; **~ to light** GEN COMM sacar a la luz; **~ under control** ECON *inflation, unemployment* poner bajo control; **~ up to date** GEN COMM poner al día

bring back *vt* STOCK *futures* devolver

bring down *vt* ACC (*b/d*) llevar a cuenta nueva, reabrir, GEN COMM *prices, inflation rate* hacer bajar

bring forward *vt* ACC arrastrar saldos, llevar a cuenta nueva

bring in *vt* GEN COMM *revenue* aportar

bring out *vt* MEDIA, STOCK *new issue* lanzar

bring together *vt* GEN COMM reunir

bring up *vt* GEN COMM *new subject* suscitar

brisk[1] *adj* GEN COMM *pace* rápido, *trade* animado, activo; ◆ **business is ~** GEN COMM el negocio va bien

brisk[2]: **~ commerce** *n* ECON comercio floreciente *m*; **~ demand** *n* GEN COMM demanda animada *f*; **~ market** *n* STOCK mercado animado *m*; **~ trading** *n* STOCK negociación ágil *f*

BRITE *abbr* (*Basic Research in Industrial Technologies for*

Europe) IND Investigación Básica de Tecnologías Industriales para Europa *f*

British: ~ **Agricultural Export Council** *n* (*BAEC*) IMP/EXP consejo británico de exportaciones agrícolas; ~ **Airports Association** *n* (*BAA*) TRANSP asociación aeroportuaria británica; ~ **American Chamber of Commerce** *n* ECON Cámara de Comercio Británico-Estadounidense *f*; ~ **Bankers Association** *n* (*BBA*) BANK asociación de banqueros británicos; ~ **Bankers Association Interest Settlement Rate** *n* (*BBAISR*) STOCK tipo de interés básico acordado por la asociación bancaria británica; ~ **Broadcasting Corporation** *n* (*BBC*) MEDIA la BBC, ≈ Radio Televisión Española *f* (*RTVE*); ~ **Chamber of Commerce** *n* GEN COMM ≈ Cámara de Comercio Española *f* (*Esp*); ~ **Code of Advertising Practice** *n* S&M normas que regulan la publicidad británica; ~ **Code of Promotion Practice** *n* S&M normas que regulan la promoción británica; ~ **Export Houses Association** *n* (*BEHA*) IMP/EXP asociación de compañías importadoras británicas; ~ **High Commission** *n* (*BHC*) POL alto comisionado británico; ~ **Hotels and Restaurants Association** *n* (*BHRA*) LEIS asociación de hoteles y restaurantes británicos; ~ **Importers Confederation** *n* (*BIC*) IMP/EXP confederación de importadores británicos; ~ **Industries Fair** *n* (*BIF*) IND feria industrial británica; ~ **Institute of Dealers in Securities** *n* (*BIDS*) STOCK instituto británico de operadores de valores; ~ **Institute of Management** *n* (*BIM*) MGMNT instituto británico de gestión empresarial; ~ **Iron & Steel Research Association** *n* (*BISRA*) IND asociación británica para la investigación del hierro y el acero; ~ **Library** *n* (*BL*) GEN COMM ≈ Biblioteca Nacional *f* (*Esp*) (*BN*); ~ **Maritime Law Association** *n* (*BMLA*) LAW asociación británica de derecho marítimo; ~ **Market Research Bureau** *n* (*BMRB*) S&M departamento de estudios de mercado del Reino Unido; ~ **Overseas Aid Group** *n* (*BOAG*) WEL grupo británico de ayuda a países de ultramar; ~ **Plastics Federation** *n* (*BPF*) IND federación británica de plásticos; ~ **Ports Association** *n* (*BPA*) TRANSP asociación británica de puertos; ~ **problem** *n* *EU* situación de tira y afloja en las contribuciones del gobierno británico a las partidas presupuestarias de la Unión Europea; ~ **quart** *n* GEN COMM cuarto de galón británico *m*; ~ **Rail** *n* *obs* (*BR*) GEN COMM, TRANSP red nacional británica de ferrocarriles, ≈ Red Nacional de Ferrocarriles Españoles *f* (*RENFE*); ~ **Savings Bonds** *n* *BrE* STOCK títulos de ahorro británicos; ~ **Shippers Council** *n* (*BSC*) TRANSP consejo británico de cargadores de buques; ~ **Shipping Federation** *n* (*BSF*) TRANSP federación de empresas navieras británicas; ~ **and South Asian Trade Association** *n* (*BASATA*) ECON asociación comercial de Gran Bretaña y el sur de Asia; ~ **Standard Code of Practice** *n* (*BSCP*) LAW código británico de procedimiento normalizado; ~ **Standards Institution** *n* (*BSI, cf American Standards Association*) GEN COMM, PATENTS ≈ Asociación Española de Normalización y Certificación *f* (*AENOR*); ~ **Standards Specification** *n* (*BSS*) IND, LAW especificación de normas británicas; ~ **Summer Time** *n* (*BST*) GEN COMM hora británica *f*, horario de verano británico *m*; ~ **Technology Group** *n* (*BTG*) IND grupo británico de tecnología; ~ **Telecom** *n* (*BT*) COMMS red nacional británica de telecomunicaciones, ≈ Compañía Telefónica Nacional de España *f* (*CTNE*); ~ **Travel Association** *n* (*BTA*) LEIS, TRANSP asociación británica de empresas del transporte; ~ **United Provident Association** *n* (*BUPA*) INS asociación privada de seguros

médicos del REino Unido; ~ **Venture Capital Association** *n* FIN asociación británica de capital de riesgo; ~ **Waterways Board** *n* (*BWB*) TRANSP consejo británico para vías navegables; ~ **& European Shipping Lines Joint Container Service** *n* (*BEACON*) GEN COMM, TRANSP Servicio Conjunto de Contenedores de Líneas Marítimas Europeas y Británicas *m*

BRM *abbr AmE* (*business reply mail*) COMMS correo de respuesta comercial *m*

broad[1]: ~**-based** *adj* TAX de amplia base; ~**-brush** *adj* POL sin perfilar

broad[2]: ~ **banding** *n* *BrE* HRM racionalización salarial *f*; ~ **market** *n* STOCK mercado amplio *m*; ~ **masses** *n pl* POL grandes masas *f pl*; ~ **money** *n* BANK dinero en sentido amplio *m*; ~ **tape** *n* *jarg* STOCK agencia de prensa financiera, *insurance, real estate, securities* franja de información banda amplia *f*

broadband *n* COMP, MEDIA banda ancha *f*

broadcast[1] *n* MEDIA emisión *f*

broadcast[2] *vt* MEDIA emitir

Broadcasters: ~ **Audience Research Board** *n* (*BARB*) S&M junta de investigación de audiencia de la radiodifusión

broadcasting *n* COMP, GEN COMM transmisión *f*, MEDIA radiodifusión *f*

broaden: ~ **the tax base** *phr* ECON, TAX ampliar la base del impuesto

broadsheet *n* GEN COMM, MEDIA *newspaper* periódico de calidad *m*, periódico de gran formato *m print* página asabanada *f*

brochure *n* GEN COMM, LEIS folleto *m*

broke[1] *adj infrml* HRM bruja (*infrml*) (*AmL*), sin un duro (*infrml*) (*Esp*), sin blanca (*infrml*); ◆ be ~ *infrml* GEN COMM quedarse sin blanca; **go** ~ *infrml* GEN COMM *fail*, HRM arruinarse, quebrar

broke[2] *vi* STOCK *trade* operar

broken: ~ **amount** *n* STOCK cantidad inactiva *f*; ~ **lot** *n* S&M, STOCK lote suelto *m*

broker *n* FIN broker *mf*, comisionista *mf*, GEN COMM corredor(a) de bolsa *m,f*, INS agente *mf*, STOCK comisionista *mf*, corredor(a) de bolsa *m,f*, intermediario(-a) *m,f*; ~ **call-loan rate** STOCK precio del préstamo a la vista para el corredor *m*; ~**'s commission** STOCK comisión del corredor de bolsa *f*; ~**-dealer** STOCK corredor(a)-intermediario(-a) de cambio y bolsa *m,f*; ~ **fund** GEN COMM fondo del corredor de comercio *m*; ~**'s loan** STOCK préstamo de corredor *m*; ~**'s note** GEN COMM, LAW, STOCK contrato de corretaje *m*; ~**'s order** GEN COMM, S&M pedido del corredor de comercio *m*, STOCK orden del agente de bolsa *f*; ~**'s statement** GEN COMM declaración del corredor de comercio *f*

brokerage *n* STOCK corretaje *m*; ~ **account** STOCK cuenta de corretaje *f*; ~ **allowance** STOCK provisión de intermediación *f*; ~ **commission** STOCK comisión de corretaje *f*; ~ **fee** STOCK comisión de corretaje *f*; ~ **firm** STOCK empresa de intermediación *f*; ~ **house** STOCK firma de corretaje en bolsa *f*, firma de inversión *f*; ~ **statement** STOCK declaración de gastos de corretaje *f*

brokered: ~ **deposit** *n* STOCK depósito de corretaje hecho *m*

broking *n* STOCK corretaje *m*; ~ **house** STOCK correduría de bolsa *f*

Brookings: ~ **Institution** *n* *AmE* ECON institución Brookings *f*

brought: ~ **forward** *phr* (*blf*) ACC *balance sheet* llevado a cuenta nueva, suma y sigue

brown: ~ **book** *n* *BrE jarg* GEN COMM, POL libro marrón *m*; ~ **goods** *n pl* GEN COMM línea marrón *f*, S&M *small appliances* electrodomésticos *m pl*

brownout *n* COMP *of electric power* caída *f*

browse *vt* COMP *document* hojear

browsing *n* COMP lectura *f*

Brundtland: ~ **Report** *n* ECON, POL *on sustainable development* informe Brundtland *m* (*Esp*), reporte de auditoría *m* (*AmL*)

brush up *vt infrml* GEN COMM *experience, skill* poner al día; ◆ ~ **on** GEN COMM dar un repaso a (*infrml*), ponerse al corriente de

B/S *abbr* (*balance sheet*) ACC, FIN balance de ejercicio *m*, balance de situación *m*, hoja de balance *f*

BSBA *abbr* (*Bachelor of Science in Business Administration*) HRM, WEL licenciado(-a) en Administración de Empresas *m,f*, licenciado(-a) en Ciencias Empresariales *m,f*

BSc *abbr* (*Bachelor of Science*) HRM, WEL licenciado(-a) en Ciencias *m,f*

BSC *abbr* (*British Shippers Council*) TRANSP consejo británico de cargadores de buques

BSCP *abbr* (*British Standard Code of Practice*) LAW código británico de procedimiento normalizado

BSF *abbr* (*British Shipping Federation*) TRANSP federación de empresas navieras británicas

BSI *abbr* (*British Standards Institution*) GEN COMM, IND, PATENTS ≈ AENOR (*Asociación Española de Normalización y Certificación*)

BSIR *abbr* (*Bachelor of Science in Industrial Relations*) HRM, WEL licenciado(-a) en Relaciones Laborales *m,f*

BSS *abbr* (*British Standards Specification*) GEN COMM, IND especificación de normas británicas

BST *abbr* (*British Summer Time*) GEN COMM hora británica *f*, horario de verano británico *m*

BT *abbr* (*British Telecom*) COMMS red nacional británica de telecomunicaciones, ≈ CTNE (*Compañía Telefónica Nacional de España, Telefónica*)

BTA *abbr* (*British Travel Association*) LEIS, TRANSP asociación británica de empresas del transporte

BTG *abbr* (*British Technology Group*) IND grupo británico de tecnología

bubble *n* GEN COMM estafa *f*, STOCK burbuja *f*, estafa *f*; ~ **memory** COMP memoria de burbujas *f*; ~ **pack** S&M envase de burbujas *m*; ~ **sort** COMP clasificación por cribadura *f*

buck: ~ **the trend** *phr infrml* GEN COMM ir en contra de la tendencia

bucket: ~ **elevator** *n* TRANSP elevador de cangilones *m*, montacargas de cubetas *m*; ~ **shop** *n* LEIS agencia de viajes con precios reducidos *f*

Buddhist: ~ **economics** *n* ECON economía budista *f*

budget[1] *adj* S&M *inexpensive* económico

budget[2] *n* GEN COMM presupuesto *m*; ~ **account** ACC, FIN cuenta presupuestaria *f*; ~ **analysis** ACC análisis presupuestario *m*; ~ **appropriation** BANK crédito presupuestario *m*, ECON asignación presupuestaria *f*, FIN crédito presupuestario *m*, *governmental accounting* asignación presupuestaria *f*, POL asignación presupuestaria *f*; ~ **ceiling** ACC techo presupuestario *m*; ~ **constraint** ACC restricción presupuestaria *f*;

~ **control** ACC, FIN, TAX control presupuestario *m*; ~ **cut** ACC recorte del presupuesto *m*, recorte presupuestario *m*; ~ **cycle** BANK, FIN, GEN COMM, MGMNT ciclo presupuestario *m*; ~ **deficit** GEN COMM déficit presupuestario *m*; ~ **document** ACC, FIN cuenta del presupuesto *f*; ~ **equilibrium** ACC, ECON equilibrio presupuestario *m*; ~ **estimate** ACC, POL estimación presupuestaria *f*; ~ **expenditure** ECON, FIN gasto presupuestario *m*, POL gasto presupuestado *m*; ~ **incidence** ECON alcance del presupuesto *m*; ~ **item** GEN COMM capítulo *m*, partida presupuestaria *f*, presupuestario *m*; ~ **level** ACC nivel presupuestario *m*; ~ **management** ACC, MGMNT, POL gestión presupuestaria *f*; ~ **mortgage** BANK, PROP hipoteca presupuestaria *f*; ~ **payment** ECON *development aid*, POL pago presupuestado *m*, pago presupuestario *m*; ~ **period** ECON, FIN, POL periodo del presupuesto *m*; ~ **preparation** ACC elaboración del presupuesto *f*, preparación del presupuesto *f*; ~ **price** S&M *reduced price* precio reducido *m*; ~ **proposal** ACC proyecto de presupuesto *m*; ~ **reduction** *n pl* ACC reducción presupuestaria *f*; ~ **resolution** ECON, FIN, POL decisión presupuestaria *f*; ~ **review** ACC revisión presupuestaria *f*; ~ **standard** ACC estándar presupuestario *m*, FIN norma presupuestaria *f*; ~ **surplus** ECON, FIN, POL superávit de presupuesto *m*, superávit presupuestario *m*; ~ **system** ACC sistema del presupuesto *m*, sistema presupuestario *m*; ~ **variance** FIN variación presupuestaria *f*; ~ **year** ECON presupuesto anual *m*, POL ejercicio presupuestario *m*; ~ **year operational plan** ACC plan operativo del año presupuestario *m*

budget[3] *vt* ACC, ECON, GEN COMM presupuestar

budget for *vt* ACC incluir en el presupuesto

Budget: **the ~** *n* *BrE* ECON, POL el presupuesto del Estado *m*; ~ **Box** *n* *BrE* ECON, POL apartado presupuestario *m*; ~ **Bureau Certificate** *n* IMP/EXP Certificado de la Oficina del Presupuesto *m*; ~ **Papers** *n* ECON, POL *governmental* documentos presupuestarios *m pl*; ~ **purdah** *n* ECON, POL cuarentena presupuestaria *f*, presupuesto oculto *m*; ~ **speech** *n* *BrE* ECON, POL presentación del presupuesto *f*

budgetary[1] *adj* GEN COMM presupuestario

budgetary[2]: ~ **account** *n* ACC, FIN cuenta presupuestaria *f*; ~ **adjustment** *n* ACC ajuste presupuestario *m*; ~ **appropriation** *n* ECON, FIN, POL *governmental* asignación presupuestaria *f*; ~ **constraint** *n* ACC restricción presupuestaria *f*; ~ **control** *n* (*BC*) ACC, FIN, TAX control presupuestario *m*; ~ **costs** *n pl* ECON, POL costes presupuestarios *m pl* (*Esp*), costos presupuestarios *m pl* (*AmL*); ~ **cut** *n* ACC recorte del presupuesto *m*, recorte presupuestario *m*; ~ **deficit** *n* GEN COMM déficit presupuestario *m*; ~ **expenditure** *n* POL *governmental* desembolso presupuestario *m*; ~ **period** *n* ECON, FIN, POL periodo presupuestario *m*; ~ **planning** *n* ECON, FIN, POL *governmental* planificación presupuestaria *f*; ~ **policy** *n* ECON, POL política presupuestaria *f*; ~ **position** *n* GEN COMM posición presupuestaria *f*; ~ **powers** *n pl* ECON, POL atribuciones presupuestarias *f pl*; ~ **revenue** *n* ECON, POL ingresos presupuestarios *m pl*; ~ **statement** *n* ECON memoria presupuestaria *f*, FIN estado presupuestario *m*, situación presupuestaria *f*, POL declaración presupuestaria *f*, situación presupuestaria *f*; ~ **submission** *n* ACC presentación presupuestaria *f*; ~ **surplus** *n* FIN excedente presupuestario *m*, POL superávit presupuestario *m*; ~ **total** *n* FIN total presupuestario *m*

budgeted: ~ **cost** *n* ACC coste presupuestado *m* (*Esp*), costo presupuestado *m* (*AmL*); ~ **income** *n* ACC, TAX ingresos presupuestados *m pl*; ~ **profit** *n* ACC beneficios esperados *m pl*, beneficios presupuestados *m pl*, beneficios prospectivos *m pl*

budgeting *n* ACC confección del presupuesto *f*, elaboración del presupuesto *f*; ~ **control** ACC control de la elaboración del presupuesto *m*

buffer *n* COMP *circuit* memoria tampón *f*, *temporary storage area for data* memoria intermedia *f*; ~ **area** COMP zona intermedia *f*; ~ **state** POL estado protector *m*; ~ **stock** ECON, STOCK fondo de regulación *m*, TRANSP existencia reguladora *f*; ~ **storage** COMP almacenamiento intermedio *m*; ~ **store** COMP memoria de tránsito *f*, memoria interfaz *f*; ~ **zone** PROP zona tapón *f*

bug *n* COMP *program* error *m*

build *vt* GEN COMM construir, PROP construir, edificar; ◆ ~ **links with** GEN COMM establecer vínculos con

build into *vt* LAW *contract, clause* incorporar

build up 1. *vt* GEN COMM *firm* fomentar, fundar, *reputation* crear, conseguir; **2.** *vi* PROP urbanizarse

building *n* GEN COMM, PROP edificio *m*; ~ **code** PROP código de edificación *m*; ~ **cycle** BANK, FIN, GEN COMM ciclo de construcción *m*; ~ **line** PROP límite de construcción *m*; ~ **loan agreement** BANK acuerdo de préstamo para la construcción *m*; ~ **and loan association** *AmE* BANK asociación de préstamos y construcción *f*, banco de crédito hipotecario *m*, banco hipotecario *m*; ~ **lot** PROP solar *m*; ~ **materials** *n pl* IND, INS materiales de construcción *m pl*; ~ **permit** *AmE* (*cf planning permission BrE*) PROP permiso para construir *m*; ~ **regulations** *n pl* IND, LAW legislación sobre construcciones *f*; ~ **repair** PROP reparación de edificios *f*; ~ **site** IND obra *f*; ~ **society** *BrE* (*cf savings and loan association AmE*) BANK banco de crédito hipotecario *m*, banco hipotecario *m*

Building: ~ **Materials Export Group** *n BrE* (*BMEG*) IMP/EXP grupo de exportación de materiales para la construcción; ~ **Research Advisory Service** *n* (*BRAS*) IND servicio de asesoría de investigadores de la construcción; ~ **Societies Act** *n BrE* BANK ley de sociedades hipotecarias; ~ **Societies Association** *n BrE* BANK asociación de sociedades hipotecarias; ~ **Societies Commission** *n* FIN Comisión de Empresas Hipotecarias *f*

built[1]: ~**-in** *adj* COMP incorporado, integrado, ECON predefinido

built[2]: ~**-in check** *n* COMP comprobación automática *f*; ~**-in obsolescence** *n* ECON *product*, IND obsolescencia planeada *f*, S&M caducidad programada *f*; ~**-in stabilizers** *n* ECON estabilizadores incorporados *m pl*; ~**-in test** *n* COMP prueba integrada *f*; ~**-up area** *n* GEN COMM, PROP área edificada *f*, zona urbanizada *f*; ~**-up vehicle** *n* TRANSP vehículo con sus accesorios ya instalados *m*

bulge *n* STOCK comba *f*

bulk *n* GEN COMM *of holdings* grueso *m*, *volume* granel *m*, TRANSP *items to be carried* granel *m*; ~ **air mail** (*BAM*) COMMS correo aéreo de grandes dimensiones *m*; ~ **billing** *jarg* WEL acto por el cual un médico factura a la administración pública por sus servicios, y no a su paciente;

~ **business** GEN COMM negocio granel *m*; ~ **buyer** GEN COMM comprador(a) de graneles *m,f*; ~ **buying** GEN COMM compras a granel *f pl*; ~ **capacity** TRANSP capacidad para graneles *f*; ~ **cargo** TRANSP carga a granel *f*; ~ **carrier** TRANSP carguero de graneles *m*; ~ **commodity** GEN COMM mercancías a granel *f pl*; ~ **container** TRANSP contenedor a granel *m*; ~ **container ship** TRANSP buque para graneles *m*; ~ **discount** GEN COMM descuento por compra a granel *m*; ~ **dry-cargo berth** TRANSP *shipping* puesto de atraque para graneles secos *m*; ~ **freight container** TRANSP contenedor para graneles *m*; ~ **goods** *n pl* GEN COMM, S&M artículos de mucho consumo *m pl*; ~ **input/output** COMP entrada/salida masivas *f*; ~ **licence** *BrE*, ~ **license** *AmE* IMP/EXP licencia para graneles *f*; ~ **liquid-cargo berth** TRANSP *shipping* puesto de atraque para graneles líquidos *m*; ~ **liquid container** TRANSP contenedor de graneles líquidos *m*; ~ **mail** GEN COMM envío postal de gran volumen *m*; ~ **material** GEN COMM material a granel *m*; ~ **order** GEN COMM, S&M pedido a granel *m*; ~ **package** GEN COMM envase de gran tamaño *m*; ~ **price** GEN COMM precio por venta a granel *m*; ~ **purchaser** GEN COMM comprador(a) de graneles *m,f*; ~ **shipment** TRANSP cargamento a granel *m*; ~ **storage** COMP *data*, GEN COMM almacenamiento de gran capacidad *m*; ~ **transhipment center** *AmE*, ~ **transhipment centre** *BrE* TRANSP centro de trasbordo de graneles *m*; ~ **unitization** TRANSP *shipping* unificación de graneles *f*; ◆ **in** ~ GEN COMM a granel

bulktainer *n* TRANSP contenedor para graneles *m*

bulky[1] *adj* GEN COMM voluminoso

bulky[2]: ~ **cargo** *n* GEN COMM carga voluminosa *f*; ~ **good** *n* GEN COMM producto voluminoso *m*; ~ **goods** *n pl* S&M *specialist retailer* mercancías voluminosas *f pl*

bull *n* FIN, STOCK alza *f*; ~ **account** STOCK cuenta alcista *f*; ~ **and bear** STOCK alzas y bajas *f pl*; ~**-and-bear bond** *BrE* FIN, STOCK bono alcista y bajista *m*; ~ **buying** STOCK compra de alcista *f*; ~ **call spread** STOCK margen de compra a la alza *m*; ~ **campaign** STOCK campaña alcista *f*; ~ **commitment** STOCK compra al alza *f*; ~ **market** STOCK mercado al alza *m*, mercado alcista *m*, mercado sostenido *m*; ~ **operation** STOCK operación al alza *f*; ~ **operator** STOCK operador(a) alcista *m,f*; ~ **position** STOCK posición alcista *f*; ~ **purchase** FIN, GEN COMM, S&M compra al descubierto *f*, STOCK compra de alcista *f*, compra al descubierto *f*; ~ **put spread** STOCK margen de venta al alza *m*; ~ **speculation** STOCK especulación alcista *f*; ~ **speculator** STOCK especulador(a) alcista *m,f*; ~ **spread** STOCK margen alcista *m*; ~ **strike price** STOCK precio con tendencia alcista *m*; ~ **transaction** STOCK operación alcista *f*; ~ **week** HRM, IND semana muy productiva *f*, semana de alta productividad *f*; ◆ **go a** ~ STOCK especular al alza

bulldog: ~ **bond** *n BrE* FIN obligación en libras esterlinas emitida por una sociedad extranjera en el Reino Unido; ~ **edition** *n AmE* MEDIA *print* edición matinal *f*; ~ **issue** *n BrE* STOCK emisión en libras esterlinas de una sociedad extranjera en el Reino Unido; ~ **loan** *n BrE* BANK crédito en libras esterlinas emitido por una sociedad extranjera en el Reino Unido

bullet *n jarg* BANK amortización única *f*; ~ **point** COMP punto grueso *m*; ~ **repayment** BANK reembolso inmediato *m*; ~ **vote** POL el hecho de votar a un candidato sin contrastar con otros candidatos y sin una reflexión previa

bulletin n COMMS, S&M boletín m; ~ **board** (*BB*) COMMS, HRM tablón de anuncios m, tablero de avisos m; ~ **board system** (*BBS*) COMMS sistema de tablón de anuncios m

bullion n BANK oro y plata en lingotes m; ~ **market** STOCK mercado del oro y la plata m

Bullionist: ~ **controversy** n *BrE* BANK controversia de oro f, controversia dorada f

bullish[1] adj STOCK alcista

bullish[2]: ~ **market** n STOCK mercado alcista m; ~ **movement** n STOCK movimiento alcista m; ~ **spread** n STOCK diferencial al alza m; ~ **stance** n STOCK postura alcista f; ~ **stock** n STOCK acciones en alza f pl; ~ **tendency** n STOCK tendencia al alza f, tendencia alcista f; ~ **tone** n STOCK tono alcista m; ~ **vertical call spread** n STOCK margen vertical alcista de opción de compra m; ~ **vertical put spread** n STOCK margen vertical alcista de opción de venta m

bullishness n STOCK alcismo m

Bullock: ~ **report** n *BrE* HRM *industrial democracy* informe Bullock m (*Esp*), reporte Bullock m (*AmL*)

bumboat n TRANSP *supplies* buceta f

bump n *infrml* TRANSP cancelación de un billete de avión por un error de sobrecontrata

bumper: ~ **year** n GEN COMM año floreciente m

bunch: ~ **map** n MATH diagrama radial m

bunching n TAX acumulación f

Bundesbank n BANK *banco central alemán* Bundesbank m

bundle n (*bdl*) TRANSP fardo m; ~**-of-rights theory** PROP teoría exponiendo las prerogativas dadas por el derecho de la propiedad

bundled: ~ **deal** n STOCK transacción de acciones f

bundling n S&M agrupamiento m; ~ **yard** TRANSP parque de empaquetado m

bunker: ~ **adjustment factor** n (*BAF*) TRANSP ajuste por combustible m; ~ **fuel oil** n (*BFO*) TRANSP combustible para calderas m; ~ **port** n TRANSP puerto petrolero m

bunkering n TRANSP repostado de combustible m; ~ **adjustment factor** (*BAF*) TRANSP factor de ajuste del suministro de combustible m; ~ **barge** TRANSP lanchón para suministro de combustible en puerto; ~ **surcharge** TRANSP sobrecarga de petróleo f

bunkers n TRANSP carboneras f pl

bunny: ~ **bond** n *jarg* FIN, STOCK bono reinvertible m

buoyancy n STOCK dinamismo m

buoyant[1] adj ECON boyante, STOCK *supply, demand* intensivo

buoyant[2]: ~ **market** n STOCK mercado al alza m, mercado sostenido m

BUPA abbr (*British United Provident Association*) INS, WEL asociación privada de seguros médicos del Reino Unido

burden[1] n ECON gravamen m, TAX carga f; ~ **center** *AmE*, ~ **centre** *BrE* ACC, BANK centro de carga m, centro de costos m (*AmL*), centro de costes m (*Esp*), centro de gastos generales m; ~ **of losses** GEN COMM volumen de siniestros m; ~ **of payment** TAX obligación de pago f; ~ **of proof** HRM, LAW peso de la prueba m, carga de la prueba f; ~ **of taxation** TAX carga impositiva f; ◆ **the ~ of proof lies with the prosecution** LAW el peso de la prueba recae en la acusación, la carga de la prueba recae en la acusación

burden[2] vt GEN COMM *with debt* cargar

bureau n ADMIN, GEN COMM oficina f; ~ **of standards** COMP dirección de normalización f

Bureau: ~ **of the Budget** n (*BB*) ECON, POL Oficina del Presupuesto f; ~ **of Economic Analysis** n (*BEA*) ECON departamento de análisis económico m; ~ **of Labour Statistics** n HRM, MATH oficina de estadística laboral f

bureaucracy n HRM, POL burocracia f

bureaucrat n HRM, POL burócrata mf

bureaucratic adj HRM, POL burocrático

bureaucratization n HRM, POL burocratización m

burglary n LAW allanamiento de morada m, robo con escalo m

burning: ~ **cost** n INS coste de pérdida neta m (*Esp*), costo de pérdida neta m (*AmL*)

burnout n HRM agotamiento m, TAX extinción f

burst: ~ **advertising** n S&M publicidad intensiva f; ~ **campaign** n S&M *advertising* campaña de saturación f; ~ **mode** n COMP modalidad en ráfagas f, modo en ráfagas m

burster n COMP *for paper* separador m, TRANSP *dangerous cargo* carga explosiva f

bus n COMP *hardware* bus m; ~ **mailing** COMP envío en bus m, ECON, FIN canal de correspondencia m; ~ **shuttle** TRANSP transporte en autobús m; ~ **side** S&M publicidad en laterales de autobuses f

bushing n TRANSP *container securing* anclaje circular m

business[1]: ~**-oriented** adj GEN COMM, HRM empresarial, orientado hacia los negocios, de orientación comercial

business[2] n GEN COMM *affairs* negocios m pl, *company* firma f, negocio m, empresa f;

[a] ~ **account** BANK cuenta de negocios f; ~ **activity** GEN COMM, TAX actividad comercial f; ~ **acumen** MGMNT perspicacia empresarial f, perspicacia en los negocios f; ~ **address** COMMS dirección profesional f, GEN COMM dirección profesional f, dirección comercial f; ~ **administration** GEN COMM administración de empresas f, dirección de empresas f, gestión de empresas f; ~ **agent** GEN COMM delegado(-a) del gremio m,f; ~ **assets** n pl ACC capital de negocio m; ~ **automobile policy** *AmE* (cf *company car policy BrE*) INS póliza de automóviles comerciales f;

[b] ~ **bank** BANK banco comercial m; ~ **barometer** GEN COMM *index* barómetro económico m;

[c] ~ **call** GEN COMM llamada de negocios f, visita de negocios f; ~ **canvasser** GEN COMM productor(a) m,f; ~ **card** GEN COMM tarjeta comercial f, tarjeta de visita f, tarjeta de presentación f, tarjeta del negocio f; ~ **center** *AmE*, ~ **centre** *BrE* GEN COMM centro financiero m, centro de negocios m; ~ **charges** ACC, GEN COMM cargas comerciales f pl, gastos comerciales m pl, S&M gastos comerciales m pl; ~ **circles** n pl GEN COMM círculos económicos m pl; ~ **class** LEIS, TRANSP clase preferente f; ~ **closure insurance** INS seguro por cierre de negocio m; ~ **college** HRM academia de negocios f; ~ **combination** ACC combinación mercantil f; ~ **community** GEN COMM esferas empresariales f pl; ~ **computer** COMP computador comercial m (*AmL*), computadora comercial f (*AmL*), ordenador comercial m (*Esp*); ~ **computing** COMP computación de gestión f, informática de gestión f; ~ **concern** GEN COMM empresa especulativa f, entidad comercial f; ~ **conditions** n pl ECON condiciones comerciales f pl; ~ **connection** GEN COMM conexión comercial f; ~ **consultant** GEN COMM

empresólogo(-a) *m,f*; ~ **convention** GEN COMM convención de negocios *f*; ~ **corporation** ECON corporación mercantil *f*, GEN COMM empresa mercantil *f*; ~ **creation** ECON, GEN COMM creación comercial *f*; ~ **crime insurance** INS seguro contra daños en la propiedad comercial *m*; ~ **cycle** ECON ciclo económico *m*, GEN COMM ciclo de negocios *m*;

~ d ~ **data processing** COMP proceso de datos comerciales *m*; ~ **day** GEN COMM día laborable *m*; ~ **decision** GEN COMM decisión comercial *f*; ~ **development** GEN COMM, MGMNT desarrollo empresarial *m*; ~ **diversification** GEN COMM, MGMNT diversificación de los negocios *f*;

~ e ~ **economics** GEN COMM economía de empresa *f*; ~ **economist** GEN COMM economista mercantil *mf*; ~ **enterprise** GEN COMM empresa comercial *f*; ~ **environment** GEN COMM medio comercial *m*; ~ **ethics** *n pl* GEN COMM ética comercial *f*; ~ **etiquette** GEN COMM etiqueta comercial *f*; ~ **expansion** GEN COMM, MGMNT expansión del negocio *f*; ~ **expenses** *n pl* GEN COMM gastos del negocio *m pl*; ~ **experience** GEN COMM experiencia comercial *f*; ~ **exposures liability** GEN COMM responsabilidad civil por exposición de la empresa *f*, LAW *commercial* responsabilidad por riesgos comerciales *f*; ~ **exposures life and health insurance** INS seguro de vida y de salud por riesgos empresariales *m*;

~ f ~ **failure** GEN COMM quiebra comercial *f*; ~ **finance** FIN financiación comercial *f*; ~ **forecasting** ECON, GEN COMM previsión comercial *f*, pronóstico empresarial *m*; ~ **form** GEN COMM impreso mecanográfico *m*;

~ g ~ **game** ECON, HRM juego de empresas *m*, juego de negocios *m*; ~ **generalist** GEN COMM todólogo(-a) *m,f*; ~ **gift** S&M regalo comercial *m*; ~ **goods** *n pl* ACC bienes comerciales *m pl*; ~ **graphics** *n pl* GEN COMM gráficos comerciales *m pl*, COMP gráficas de gestión *f pl*, GEN COMM gráficos de gestión *m pl*;

~ h ~ **hours** *n pl* GEN COMM horas de comercio *f pl*; ~ **house** GEN COMM establecimiento comercial *m*;

~ i ~ **income** TAX renta empresarial *f*; ~ **income tax** TAX impuesto de sociedades *m*, impuesto sobre los beneficios empresariales *m*; ~ **indicator** ECON, GEN COMM indicador comercial *m*; ~ **interest** GEN COMM interés comercial *m*; ~ **interruption** GEN COMM interrupción de actividades *f*; ~ **interruption insurance** INS seguro contra cesación de negocios *m*; ~ **interruption policy** INS póliza de interrupción comercial *f*; ~ **investment loss** (*BIL*) TAX nivel de ingresos básico *m*, pérdidas de inversión empresarial *f pl*; ~ **investment tax** TAX impuesto sobre las inversiones empresariales *m* (*Esp*), impuesto sobre los insumos empresariales *m* (*AmL*); ~ **investment tax allowance** TAX desgravación de la inversión empresarial *f*; ~ **investment tax credit** TAX deducción por activos de crédito *f*;

~ l ~ **law** LAW derecho mercantil *m*; ~ **letter** COMMS, GEN COMM carta comercial *f*; ~ **liability** GEN COMM responsabilidad civil de la empresa *f*, INS, LAW responsabilidad comercial *f*; ~ **liability insurance** INS, LAW seguro de responsabilidad comercial *m*; ~ **library** GEN COMM *public services* biblioteca empresarial *f*; ~ **life and health insurance** INS seguro de salud y actividad comercial *m*; ~ **loan** BANK, GEN COMM, IND préstamo para fines comerciales *m*, préstamo para fines industriales *m*; ~ **losses** *n pl* ACC pérdidas de explotación *f*

pl; ~ **lunch** GEN COMM almuerzo de negocios *m*, comida de negocios *f*;

~ m ~ **machine** GEN COMM máquina de oficina *f*; ~ **magnate** FIN potentado(-a) comercial *m,f*; ~ **management** GEN COMM administración de empresas *f*, dirección de empresas *f*, gestión de empresas *f*; ~ **manager** HRM director(a) de empresa *m,f*; ~ **meeting** GEN COMM encuentro de negocios *m*;

~ n ~ **name** GEN COMM razón social *f*;

~ o ~ **objective** S&M objetivo de negocios *m*; ~ **office** ADMIN oficina comercial *f*; ~ **opportunity** GEN COMM, MGMNT oportunidad comercial *f*, oportunidad de negocios *f*; ~ **organization** GEN COMM organización de la empresa *f*, organización de negocios *f*; ~ **outlook** GEN COMM perspectiva empresarial *f*, perspectivas de negocio *f pl*;

~ p ~ **package** ACC paquete comercial *m*, COMP paquete de gestión *m*, FIN paquete comercial *m*; ~ **pages** *n pl* GEN COMM *of newspaper* páginas de negocios *f pl*; ~ **park** GEN COMM parque industrial *m*; ~ **plan** BANK, GEN COMM, MGMNT plan comercial *m*, plan de negocios *m*; ~ **plan consulting** GEN COMM consultoría de planificación de empresa *f* (*Esp*); ~ **planning** GEN COMM, MGMNT planificación de la empresa *f* (*Esp*), planificación de negocios *f* (*Esp*); ~ **policy** ECON, GEN COMM, MGMNT política empresarial *f*; ~ **portfolio** ECON cartera empresarial *f*, FIN, STOCK cartera de negocios *f*; ~ **practice** GEN COMM práctica comercial *f*; ~ **premises** *n pl* GEN COMM, PROP local comercial *m*; ~ **press** MEDIA, S&M prensa profesional *f*; ~ **property and liability insurance package** INS póliza paquete de seguro de daños materiales y responsabilidad civil para empresas *f*; ~ **proposition** GEN COMM propuesta de negocio *f*;

~ r ~ **recovery** GEN COMM recuperación del negocio *f*; ~ **regulations** *n pl* GEN COMM normativa comercial *f*; ~ **relation** GEN COMM, MGMNT relación comercial *f* relación de negocios *f*; ~ **reply card** (*BRC*) COMMS tarjeta de respuesta comercial *f*; ~ **reply envelope** (*BRE*) COMMS sobre de respuesta comercial *m*, S&M sobre impreso con franqueo pagado *m*; ~ **reply mail** (*BRM*) COMMS correo de respuesta comercial *m*; ~ **reply service** S&M servicio de respuesta comercial *m*; ~ **risk** GEN COMM, INS riesgo comercial *m*; ~ **risk exclusion** GEN COMM, INS exclusión de riesgos comerciales *f*, exclusión de riesgos empresariales *f*;

~ s ~ **school** GEN COMM escuela de negocios *f*; ~ **sector** GEN COMM sector empresarial *m*; ~ **segment reporting** ACC información sobre el sector *f*, información sobre un segmento del negocio *f*; ~ **sense** GEN COMM sentido comercial *m*; ~ **service** GEN COMM servicio a empresas *m*; ~ **situation** GEN COMM situación comercial *f*; ~ **slowdown** ECON reducción de la actividad comercial *f*, GEN COMM baja en las ventas *f*; ~ **start-up** ECON puesta en marcha *f*; ~ **strategy** ECON, GEN COMM, MGMNT estrategia comercial *f*, estrategia empresarial *f*; ~ **stream** ECON corriente empresarial *f*, GEN COMM flujo de negocio *m*; ~ **structure** ECON estructura económica *f*; ~ **studies** *n pl* ECON estudios económicos *m pl*, GEN COMM *education* estudios empresariales *m pl*, WEL estudios de mercado *m pl*; ~ **system** ECON sistema económico *m*, GEN COMM sistema de negocios *m*, sistema empresarial *m*, POL sistema ecónomico *m*;

~ t ~ **tax** TAX impuesto comercial *m*; ~**-to-business advertising** S&M publicidad de una empresa a otra *f*;

~-to-business marketing S&M marketing negocio a negocio *m*; ~ **tout** GEN COMM corredor(a) comercial *m,f*; ~ **transaction** GEN COMM transacción comercial *f*; ~ **travel market** LEIS mercado de los viajes de negocios *m*; ~ **trend** GEN COMM tendencia comercial *f*; ~ **trip** GEN COMM viaje comercial *m*, viaje de negocios *m*;

██ **u** ~ **unit** GEN COMM unidad de negocios *f*; ~ **uses life insurance** INS seguro de vida para usos comerciales *m*;

██ **v** ~ **venture** GEN COMM, MGMNT riesgo de negocios *m*, riesgo empresarial *m*; ~ **volume** GEN COMM volumen de negocios *m*;

██ **w** ~ **world** GEN COMM mundo comercial *m*, mundo de los negocios *m*;

██ **y** ~ **year** GEN COMM ejercicio anual *m*

business³: **any other** ~ *phr* (*AOB*) GEN COMM ruegos y preguntas; **any other competent** ~ *phr* (*AOCB*) GEN COMM *in meeting* ruegos y preguntas; **go out of** ~ *phr* GEN COMM ir a la quiebra, quebrar; **to be on** ~ *phr* GEN COMM estar de negocios; **do** ~ *phr* GEN COMM hacer negocios; **do** ~ **over the phone** *phr* GEN COMM hacer negocios por teléfono; ~ **to be transacted** *phr* GEN COMM negocio por tramitar; ~ **transferred to** *phr* GEN COMM negocio trasladado a; **no** ~ **value** *phr* (*NBV*) FIN sin valor comercial

Business: ~ **Equipment Trade Association** *n* BrE (*BETA*) IND sociedad de comerciantes de equipamiento para oficinas; ~ **School** *n* ECON, GEN COMM Escuela de Comercio *f*

businessman *n* BANK comerciante *m*, GEN COMM comerciante *m*, empresario *m*, hombre de negocios *m*, HRM, S&M comerciante *m*; **~'s risk** STOCK riesgo del hombre de negocios *m*

businessowners': ~ **policy** *n* AmE INS póliza de directores de empresa *f*

businesswoman *n* BANK, GEN COMM comerciante *f*, empresaria *f*, mujer de negocios *f*, HRM, S&M comerciante *f*

bust¹: **~-up acquisition** *n* STOCK *of corporation* adquisición fracasada *f*

bust²: **go** ~ *vi infrml* GEN COMM ir a la quiebra

busy *adj* COMMS *line*, COMP *tone or signal* comunicando, GEN COMM *person* ocupado, atareado, *schedule* apretado

butane *n* ENVIR butano *m*

Butskellism *n* BrE ECON *policy*, POL economía mixta *f*

butterfly: ~ **effect** *n* STOCK efecto dominó *m*; ~ **spread** *n* STOCK margen de mariposa *m*

button *n* COMP *on device* botón *m*

buttress *n* TRANSP *containers* arbotante *m*

buy¹: **~-and-hold strategy** *n* STOCK estrategia de compra y retención *f*; **~-and-sell agreement** *n* ECON, STOCK acuerdo de compraventa *m*; **~-and-write strategy** *n* STOCK estrategia de compra y suscripción *f*; **~-back agreement** *n* ECON *international trade* acuerdo de recompra *m*, LAW *contract* pacto de retrocompra *m*; **~-back clause** *n* LAW cláusula de retrocompra *f*; **~-back option** *n* STOCK opción de recompra *f*; ~ **classes** *n pl* S&M clases de compra *f pl*; **~-in** *n* STOCK toma de posición *f*, *securities* compra por intermediación *f*; ~ **minus** *n* STOCK compra reducida *f*; ~ **order** *n* STOCK orden de compra *f*; **~-out** *n* STOCK compra total *f*; ~ **transaction** *n* STOCK operación de compra *f*

buy² *vt* ECON *prices* comprar, GEN COMM comprar, *infrml accept as true* tragar, creer, *bribe* sobornar, POL comprar, *bribe* sobornar, S&M comprar; ◆ ~ **airtime** MEDIA *TV, radio* comprar espacio publicitario; ~ **a bull** STOCK comprar al alza; ~ **at market** STOCK comprar a precio de mercado; ~ **at a reduced price** GEN COMM comprar a precio reducido; ~ **at the top of the market** STOCK comprar a precio alto; ~ **for the account** STOCK comprar a término; ~ **for future delivery** GEN COMM comprar a entrega futura; ~ **for a rise** STOCK comprar al alza; ~ **in installments** AmE, ~ **in instalments** BrE GEN COMM comprar a plazos; ~ **low and sell high** STOCK comprar a la baja y vender al alza; ~ **on the bad news** STOCK comprar con malas noticias; ~ **on bid** STOCK comprar a precio de oferta; ~ **on the black market** ECON comprar en el mercado negro; ~ **on close** STOCK comprar al cierre; ~ **on a fall** STOCK comprar a la baja; ~ **on a falling market** STOCK comprar en un mercado a la baja; ~ **on hire purchase** GEN COMM comprar a plazos; ~ **on margin** FIN, STOCK comprar al margen; ~ **on a rise** STOCK comprar al alza; ~ **shares on the open market** STOCK comprar acciones en el mercado abierto; ~ **sth on approval** GEN COMM comprar algo a condición; ~ **sth on credit** GEN COMM comprar algo a crédito; ~ **sth on tick** BrE *infrml* GEN COMM comprar algo a crédito

buy back *vt* FIN rescatar, GEN COMM, LAW, STOCK recomprar

buy down *vt* BANK anticipar, PROP comprar a la baja

buy in *vt* GEN COMM *goods* aprovisionarse de, STOCK comprar

buy into *vt* GEN COMM *idea* apoyar, STOCK *company* comprar acciones de

buy out *vt* GEN COMM *partner* comprar la parte de

buy up *vt* FIN, GEN COMM, S&M, STOCK acaparar

buyback *n* FIN rescate *m*

buyer *n* ECON, GEN COMM, S&M, STOCK comprador(a) *m,f*; ~ **behavior** AmE, ~ **behaviour** BrE S&M comportamiento del comprador *m*; ~ **concentration** S&M concentración de compradores *f*; ~ **credit** BANK, FIN crédito al consumidor *m*; **~'s option** GEN COMM, STOCK prima para el comprador *f*; **~'s rate** STOCK tasa de compra *f*; ~ **response** S&M respuesta del comprador *f*; ◆ **at ~'s risk** STOCK a riesgo del comprador

buyers: ~ **over** *phr* STOCK mercado agotado

buyers': ~ **market** *n* GEN COMM mercado de compradores *m*

buying: ~ **behavior** AmE, ~ **behaviour** BrE *n* S&M comportamiento de compra *m*, comportamiento de las compras *m*; ~ **commission** *n* S&M comisión de compra *f*; ~ **end** *n* ACC, BANK, FIN, GEN COMM cierre de la operación *m*, cierre de la operación *m*; ~ **habits** *n pl* GEN COMM usos de compra *m pl*; ~ **hedge** *n* STOCK cobertura de compra *f*; ~ **house** *n* S&M casa compradora *f*; **~-in price** *n* ECON *EC* cambio de rescate *m*; ~ **motive** *n* S&M motivo de compra *m*; ~ **order** *n* STOCK orden de compra *f*; ~ **pattern** *n* S&M modelo de compra *m*; ~ **power** *n* GEN COMM poder adquisitivo *m*; ~ **price** *n* GEN COMM precio de compra *m*; ~ **process** *n* GEN COMM proceso de compra *m*; ~ **rate** *n* FIN precio comprador *m*; ~ **rate of exchange** *n* BANK tipo de compra de divisas *m*; ~ **signal** *n* S&M señal de compra *f*; ~ **surge** *n* GEN COMM oleada de compras *f*; ~ **syndicate** *n* S&M sindicato de compra *m*

buyout *n* FIN compra de la parte de un socio *f*, oferta de compras *f*, INS transferencia de beneficios *f*, STOCK compra de control *f*; ~ **proposal** STOCK propuesta de compra al cien por cien *f*

buzz *n infrml* COMMS *telephone call* llamada *f*, GEN COMM *rumour* rumor *m*; ◆ **give sb a ~** *infrml* COMMS *telephone* llamar a alguien

buzzword *n infrml* GEN COMM palabra de moda *f*

BWB *abbr* (*British Waterways Board*) TRANSP consejo británico para vías navegables

by-election *n* POL elección parcial *f*

by-law *n* BANK *of bank* estatuto *m*, LAW *subsidiary law* estatuto *m*, estatutos sociales *m pl*, reglamento *m*

by-line *n* MEDIA pie de autor *m*

bypass: ~ **trust** *n* TAX venta simulada *m*

by-product *n* GEN COMM subproducto *m*

byte *n* COMP byte *m*, octeto *m*; ~ **mode** COMP modalidad byte a byte *f*

C

c *abbr* (*cage container*) TRANSP contenedor para cajas jaula *m*

c. *abbr* (*coupon*) GEN COMM cupón *m*

C *abbr* ECON, GEN COMM (*consumption*) consumo *m*, (*centigrade*) C (*centígrado*)

C/- *abbr* (*case packaging*) TRANSP empaquetado de cajas *m*

c/a *abbr* (*current account BrE, checking account AmE*) ACC, BANK c/c (*cuenta corriente*)

CA *abbr* ACC (*certified accountant*) contable autorizado(-a) *m,f* (*Esp*), contable certificado(-a) *m,f* (*Esp*), contable colegiado(-a) *m,f* (*Esp*), contable diplomado(-a) *m,f* (*Esp*), contable público(-a) *m,f* (*Esp*), contable registrado(-a) *m,f* (*Esp*), contador(a) autorizado(-a) *m,f* (*AmL*), contador(a) certificado(-a) *m,f* (*AmL*), contador(a) colegiado(-a) *m,f* (*AmL*), contador(a) diplomado(-a) *m,f* (*AmL*), contador(a) público(-a) *m,f* (*AmL*), contador(a) registrado(-a) *m,f* (*AmL*), ENVIR (*controlled atmosphere*) atmósfera controlada *f*, GEN COMM *BrE* (*Consumers' Association, cf CAC AmE*) oficina de asesoramiento al consumidor, ≈ OCU (*Organización de Consumidores y Usuarios*), MATH (*confluence analysis*) análisis confluente *m*, WEL *BrE* (*Consumers' Association, cf CAC AmE*) oficina de asesoramiento al consumidor, ≈ OCU (*Organización de Consumidores y Usuarios*)

C/A *abbr* ACC, BANK, FIN (*capital account*) cuenta de capital *f*, (*credit account*) cuenta de crédito *f*

CAA *abbr* (*Civil Aviation Authority*) TRANSP jurisdicción de aviación civil

CAB *abbr* TRANSP (*Civil Aeronautics Board*) consejo aeronáutico civil, WEL (*Citizens Advice Bureau*) organización voluntaria británica que asesora legal o financieramente

cabin *n* TRANSP cabina *f*; **~ staff** TRANSP personal de cabina *m*

cabinet *n* POL gabinete *m*; **~ crowd** *jarg* STOCK pandilla de los archivadores *m pl* (*jarg*); **~ reshuffle** POL reorganización gubernamental *f*; **~ security** STOCK título ministerial *m*; **~ minister** POL ministro(-a) del gobierno *m,f*

Cabinet *n* POL ≈ Consejo de Ministros *m*; **~ Committee on Social Development** POL, WEL comisión del gobierno británico sobre desarrollo social

cable[1] *n* COMMS, STOCK telegrama *m*; **~ address** COMMS dirección cablegráfica *f*; **~ program** *AmE*, **~ programme** *BrE* COMMS, MEDIA programa por cable *m*; **~ rate** ECON *international trade* tarifa cablegráfica *f*; **~ television** MEDIA, S&M televisión por cable *f*; **~ transfer** COMMS giro cablegráfico *m*

cable[2] *vt* COMMS telegrafiar

cablegram *n* COMMS cablegrama *m*

cabotage *n* TRANSP cabotaje *m*

CAC *abbr* HRM (*Central Arbitration Committee*) Junta Federal de Conciliación y Arbitraje *f*, Comité Central de Arbitraje *m*, IMP/EXP (*Customs Additional Code*) Código Adicional de Aduanas *m*, STOCK (*Central Arbitration Committee*) Comité Central de Arbitraje *m*, WEL *AmE* (*Consumers' Advisory Council, cf CA BrE*)

oficina de asesoramiento al consumidor, ≈ OCU (*Organización de Consumidores y Usuarios*)

cache: **~ buffer** *n* COMP antememoria *f*; **~ memory** *n* COMP memoria temporal *f*

CACM *abbr* (*Central American Common Market*) ECON Mercado Común de América Central *m*

c.a.d. *abbr* (*cash against documents*) IMP/EXP pago contra documentación *m*

CAD *abbr* COMP, IND (*Control-Alternate-Delete*) Control-Alternar-Suprimir *m*, (*computer-aided design*) CAD (*diseño asistido por computador AmL, diseño asistido por computadora AmL, diseño asistido por ordenador Esp*)

cadastral *adj* LAW, PROP, TAX catastral; **~ survey** *n* TAX, PROP inspección catastral *f*

cadastre *n* LAW, PROP, TAX catastro *m*

CADD *abbr* (*computer-aided design and drafting*) COMP, IND CADD (*diseño y dibujo asistido por computador AmL, diseño y dibujo asistido por computadora AmL, diseño y dibujo asistido por ordenador Esp*)

cadre *n* HRM ejecutivo *m,f*, POL cuadro *m*

CAE *abbr* (*computer-assisted engineering*) COMP ingeniería asistida por computador *f* (*AmL*), ingeniería asistida por computadora *f* (*AmL*), ingeniería asistida por ordenador *f* (*Esp*)

CAF *abbr* IMP/EXP (*currency adjustment factor*) aumento por cambio de divisas, TRANSP (*cost and freight*) C&F (*coste y flete Esp, costo y flete AmL*)

CAFR *abbr* (*comprehensive annual financial report*) ECON, FIN, MGMNT informe global financiero anual *m* (*Esp*), reporte global financiero anual *m* (*AmL*)

cage *n* STOCK *AmE* trastienda *f*; **~ card** COMP tarjeta multifilar *f*; **~ container** (*c*) TRANSP contenedor para cajas jaula *m*; **~ inventory record** (*CIR*) TRANSP registro de inventario de cajas jaula *m*; **~-tainer** TRANSP jaula *f*

CAI *abbr* COMP CAI (*instrucción asistida por computador AmL, instrucción asistida por computadora AmL, instrucción asistida por ordenador Esp*)

Cairn: **~'s Group** *n* ECON *agricultural* grupo de Cairn *m*

CAL *abbr* (*computer-aided learning*) COMP aprendizaje asistido por computador *m* (*AmL*), aprendizaje asistido por computadora *m* (*AmL*), aprendizaje asistido por ordenador *m* (*Esp*)

calculable *adj* COMP, GEN COMM, MATH calculable

calculate *vt* COMP, GEN COMM, MATH calcular

calculated: **~ risk** *n* STOCK riesgo calculado *m*

calculating: **~ machine** *n* COMP, GEN COMM máquina calculadora *f*

calculation *n* GEN COMM cálculo *m*; **~ of prices** ACC, FIN, HRM cálculo de precios *m*

calculator *n* COMP, GEN COMM, MATH calculadora *f*

calculus: **~ of probabilities** *n* MATH cálculo de probabilidades *m*

calendar *n* GEN COMM, MGMNT, TRANSP calendario *m*; **~ day** GEN COMM día de calendario *m*, LAW *contract* día natural *f*; **~ management** MGMNT gestión del calendario *f*; ~ **month** GEN COMM mes calendario *m*; ~ **quarter** GEN COMM trimestre *m*; ~ **spread** STOCK diferencial en el tiempo *m*; ~ **year** GEN COMM año natural *m*

caliber *AmE see* calibre *BrE*

calibre *n BrE* HRM *of staff* calibre *m*, capacidad *f*

call[1] *n* ACC obligación *f*, BANK petición de devolución *f*, COMMS *by telephone*, COMP llamada *f*, GEN COMM comunicación *f*, visita *f*, FIN *capital*, S&M demanda *f*, *visit* visita, STOCK cupón cero *m*, obligación *f*; ~ **account** BANK cuenta a la vista *f*, cuenta de suscripciones pagaderas *f*; ~ **analysis** S&M análisis de la visita *m*; ~ **to the Bar** *BrE* LAW ceremonia de ingreso en el Colegio de Abogados; ~ **box** *AmE* (*cf telephone box BrE*) COMMS cabina de teléfono *f* (*Esp*), locutorio *m* (*AmL*); ~ **buyer** STOCK comprador(a) de una opción de compra *m,f*; ~ **charge** COMMS cargo de llamadas *m*; ~ **date** BANK fecha de vencimiento *f*; ~ **exercise price** STOCK precio de redención de ejercicio *m*; ~ **for bids** GEN COMM *for contract* llamada a licitación *f*; ~ **for tenders** GEN COMM *for contract* llamada a licitación *f*; ~ **forwarding** COMMS *telephony* desvío de llamada *m*; ~ **frequency** S&M frecuencia de las visitas *f*; ~ **loan** BANK, STOCK préstamo a la vista *m*; ~ **loan rate** STOCK tasa de préstamo de amortización *f*; ~ **money** BANK préstamo al cliente *m*; ~ **money rate** BANK tasa de dinero a la vista *f*; ~ **notice** STOCK aviso de opción de compra *m*; ~ **option** STOCK opción de compra *f*; ~ **option exercise price** STOCK precio de ejercicio de opción de venta *m*; ~ **option premium** STOCK prima de opción de rescate *f*; ~ **option price** STOCK precio de la opción de compra *m*; ~ **option writer** STOCK emisor(a) de opciones de compra *m,f*; ~ **premium** STOCK prima de rescate *f*; ~ **price** STOCK precio de rescate *m*; ~ **protection** STOCK protección contra rescate anticipado *f*; ~ **provision** STOCK provisión de rescate *f*; ~ **purchase** STOCK adquisición de una opción de compra *f*; ~ **and put option** STOCK opción de compra y venta *f*; ~ **rate** BANK, ECON, FIN, STOCK tasa a la vista *f*, tasa de interés sobre préstamos a corto plazo *f*, *interest rates* tipo de interés para préstamos a la vista *m*, *of stock, shares* tasa de interés de la demanda *f*; ~ **ratio backspread** STOCK margen a ratio comprador inverso *m*; ~ **report** COMP informe de intervención *m* (*Esp*), reporte de intervención *m* (*AmL*), S&M informe de visita *m* (*Esp*), reporte de visita *m* (*AmL*); ~ **selling hedge** STOCK cobertura de venta de opciones de compra *f*; ~ **sign** TRANSP *shipping* indicativo de llamada *m*; ~ **spread** STOCK margen de rescate *m*; ~ **strike** STOCK ejercicio de una opción de compra *m*; ~ **strike price** STOCK precio de ejecución de una opción *m*; ~ **waiting** COMMS *telephony* llamada en espera *f*; ~ **warrant** STOCK garantía de una opción de compra *f*; ~ **writer** STOCK emisor(a) de opciones de compra *m,f*; ~ **writing** STOCK suscripción de una opción de compra *f*

call[2] *vt* BANK cobrar, exigir el pago, COMMS llamar, GEN COMM cobrar, LEIS *theatre* llamar; ◆ ~ **away options** GEN COMM, LAW, S&M, STOCK cancelar opciones; ~ **as a witness** LAW llamar a alguien como testigo; ~ **bonds** BANK amortizar bonos por anticipado; ~ **sb** COMMS llamar a alguien; ~ **on a Freefone**® **number** *BrE* (*cf call toll-free AmE*) llamar sin pagar tasas; ~ **sb over the intercom** COMMS llamar a alguien por el intercomunicador; ~ **sb to account** GEN COMM pedir cuentas a alguien; ~ **toll-free** *AmE* (*cf call on a Freefone number BrE*) COMMS llamar sin pagar tasas; ~ **securities for**

redemption ACC demandar títulos para rescate; ~ **a strike** HRM declarar una huelga

call back *vi* S&M volver a llamar

call collect *vi AmE* (*cf make a reverse charge call BrE*) COMMS llamar a cobro revertido

call for *vt* GEN COMM convocar

call up *vt* COMMS llamar por teléfono

CALL *abbr* (*computer-assisted language learning*) COMP aprendizaje de idiomas asistido por computador *m* (*AmL*), aprendizaje de idiomas asistido por computadora *m* (*AmL*), aprendizaje de idiomas asistido por ordenador *m* (*Esp*)

callable[1] *adj* STOCK amortizable, redimible

callable[2]: ~ **bond** *n* FIN, STOCK bono amortizable anticipadamente *m*, bono redimible antes del vencimiento *m*; ~ **capital** *n* BANK capital a la vista *m*; ~ **preferred stock** *n* STOCK acciones preferentes amortizables *f pl*

called[1]: ~ **away** *adj* STOCK *bonds* amortizado; **so-~** *adj* GEN COMM así llamado

called[2]: ~ **security** *n* STOCK título redimido *m*; **~-up share capital** *n* ACC capital social exigido *m*, desembolsos exigidos sobre acciones *m pl*

calligraphy *n* MEDIA, S&M caligrafía *f*

calling *n* GEN COMM convocatoria *f*; ~ **cycle** S&M ciclo de visitas *m*; ~ **forward notice** TRANSP notificación anticipada de escala *f*; ~ **program** COMP programa de llamada *m*

calls: ~ **and puts** *n pl* STOCK compras y ventas *f pl*

calumniate *vi* GEN COMM, LAW calumniar

calumniation *n* GEN COMM, LAW calumnia *f*

calumny *n* GEN COMM, LAW calumnia *f*

CAM *abbr* (*computer-aided manufacturing*) COMP, IND CAM (*fabricación asistida por computador AmL, fabricación asistida por computadora AmL, fabricación asistida por ordenador Esp*)

cambist *n* STOCK cambista de divisas *mf*

cambistry *n* STOCK cambios de divisas *m pl*

Cambridge: ~ **controversies** *n* ECON controversias de Cambridge *f pl*; ~ **Economic Policy Group** *n* ECON Grupo de Política Económica de Cambridge *m*; ~ **school** *n* ECON escuela de Cambridge *f*

CAMEL *abbr* (*capital, assets, management, earnings, liquidity*) FIN capital, activos, administración, ganancias, liquidez

camera[1]: **~-ready** *adj* MEDIA listo para fotografiar

camera[2]: **in ~** *adv* LAW, POL *meeting* a puerta cerrada

camera[3]: **~-ready copy** *n* (*CRC*) MEDIA boceto publicitario listo para fotografiar *m*

camp: **~-on** *adj* COMMS *of calls* en espera

campaign *n* GEN COMM, POL, S&M campaña *f*; ~ **plan** GEN COMM, S&M plan de campaña *m*; ~ **trail** POL recorrido electoral *m*; ◆ **conduct a ~** POL emprender una campaña

can: ~ **crowd** *n infrml* STOCK grupo cerrado de inversores *m*

Canada: ~ **Deposit Insurance Corporation** *n* (*CDIC*) INS Corporación Canadiense de Seguro de Depósitos *f*; **~-United Kingdom Chamber of Commerce** *n* (*CUKCC*) ECON Cámara de Comercio Anglo-Canadiense *f*

Canadian: ~ **Chamber of Commerce** *n* (*CCC*) ECON Cámara de Comercio Canadiense *f*; ~ **Institute of Chartered Accountants** *n* (*CICA*) ACC instituto canadiense de contables registrados; ~ **Prime Rate** *n* ECON tipo preferente canadiense *m*

canal *n* TRANSP canal *m*; ~ **dues** *n pl* TRANSP derechos de canal *m pl*

cancel[1]: ~ **order** *n* STOCK orden de cancelación *f*

cancel[2] *vt* GEN COMM cancelar; ◆ ~ **options** GEN COMM cancelar opciones

cancel out *vt* GEN COMM *factor* anular

canceled *AmE see* cancelled *BrE*

canceling *AmE see* cancelling *BrE*

cancellation *n* GEN COMM anulación *f*, cancelación *f*; ~ **clause** LAW *in contract* cláusula abrogatoria *f*, cláusula de rescisión *f*, cláusula resolutoria *f*; ~ **fee** GEN COMM gastos de cancelación *m pl*; ~ **notice** STOCK aviso de cancelación *m*; ~ **of premium** INS anulación de prima *f*; ~ **provision clause** INS cláusula de provisión para cancelaciones *f*; ~ **of registration** TAX *VAT* cancelación de la inscripción *f*

cancelled: ~ **check** *AmE*, ~ **cheque** *BrE n* BANK, FIN cheque anulado *m*, cheque cancelado *m*; ~ **debt** *n BrE* ACC, BANK, FIN, GEN COMM deuda anulada *f*; ~ **share** *n BrE* FIN, STOCK acción cancelada *f*

cancelling: ~ **clause** *n BrE* LAW cláusula abrogatoria *f*, cláusula de rescisión *f*, cláusula resolutoria *f*; ~ **date** *n BrE* TRANSP fecha de anulación *f*; ~ **entry** *n BrE* ACC asiento cancelado *m*; ~ **return** *n BrE* INS *marine* reembolso por cancelación *m*

C&D *abbr* (*collected and delivered*) GEN COMM recogido y entregado, *cheques, drafts* cobrado y entregado

C&E *abbr BrE* (*Customs & Excise Department*) IMP/EXP departamento británico aduanero, ≈ Departamento de Aduanas y Tributos *m*, ≈ Servicio de Aduanas *m*

c&f *abbr* (*cost and freight*) IMP/EXP, TRANSP c&f (*coste y flete Esp, costo y flete AmL*)

C&I *abbr* (*cost and insurance*) IMP/EXP, INS, TRANSP coste y seguro *m* (*Esp*), costo y seguro *m* (*AmL*)

candidacy *n* HRM, LAW, POL candidatura *f*

candidate *n* HRM, LAW, POL candidato(-a) *m,f*

candidature *n* HRM, LAW, POL *in election* candidatura *f*

C&U: ~ **regulation** *n* (*construction and use regulation*) TRANSP normativa de construcción y explotación *f*

canned: ~ **presentation** *n* S&M presentación estándar *f*; ~ **program** *n* COMP programa enlatado *m*

canton *n* POL cantón *m*

canvass *vt* POL, S&M hacer una encuesta, sondear

canvasser *n* GEN COMM corredor(a) *m,f*

cap[1] *n* BANK tope *m*, ECON techo *m*, FIN *interest rate* techo *m*, tope *m*, GEN COMM, STOCK techo *m*; ~ **issue** (*capitalization issue*) STOCK dividendo en acciones *m*, emisión de acciones liberadas *f*; ~ **rate** (*capitalization rate*) ACC, ECON tasa de capitalización *f*, tipo de capitalización *m*, tipo máximo *m*; ~~**rate loan** *AmE* STOCK *futures* préstamo con tope máximo del tipo de interés *m*; ~~**type primer** TRANSP *carrying of dangerous classified cargo* bomba principal tipo casquete *f*

cap[2] *vt* GEN COMM coronar; ◆ ~ **interest rates** BANK, ECON, FIN poner tope a las tasas de interés, poner un límite a los tipos de interés

CAP[1] *abbr* (*Common Agricultural Policy*) ECON, POL PAC (*Política Agrícola Común*)

CAP[2]: ~ **charges** *n pl* ECON *international* cargos de la PAC *m pl*; ~ **goods** *n pl* ECON productos de la PAC *m pl*; ~ **levy** *n* ECON recaudación de la PAC *f*

capability *n* ECON, GEN COMM capacidad *f*

capacity *n* ECON *production*, GEN COMM, HRM, IND capacidad *f*; ~ **charge** ECON cargo adicional *m*; ~ **effect** ECON efecto de la capacidad productiva *m*; ~ **factor** ECON factor de capacidad *m*; ~ **of penetration** S&M capacidad de penetración *f*; ~ **ratio** ECON, HRM índice de capacidad *m*, IND razón de capacidad *f*; ~ **to work** GEN COMM, HRM aptitud física para el trabajo *f*; ~ **utilization** BANK, ECON, FIN, IND capacidad utilizada *f*; ~ **utilization rate** ECON, IND grado de utilización de la capacidad productiva *m*; ◆ **at full ~** GEN COMM a plena capacidad

capex *abbr* (*capital expenditure*) GEN COMM gasto de capital *m*, inversión en capital fijo *f*

capital[1]: ~~**intensive** *adj* IND intensivo en capital

capital[2] *n* ACC activos de capital *m pl*, financiaciones *f pl*, fondos financieros *m pl*, recursos *m pl*, recursos financieros *m pl*, capital *m*, ECON, FIN, GEN COMM capital *m*;

■ **a** ~ **account** (*C/A*) ACC, BANK, ECON, FIN cuenta de capital *f*; ~ **accumulation** ECON, FIN acumulación de capital *f*, inversión en capital productivo *f*; ~ **adequacy** BANK, ECON, FIN *of investment firms and credit institutions* suficiencia de capital *f*; ~ **aid** ECON, POL *developing countries* ayuda financiera *f*, capital de ayuda *m*; ~ **allotment** FIN *governmental*, POL asignación de capital *f*; ~ **allowance** ACC, TAX desgravación sobre bienes de capital *f*; ~ **appreciation** ECON, FIN revalorización del capital *f*, alza de capital *m*; ~ **appropriations** *n pl* PROP adquisición de una empresa *f*; ~ **asset** ECON activo fijo *m*; ~ **asset account** BANK cuenta de activo de capital *f*; ~ **asset pricing model** (*CAPM*) ECON, FIN, STOCK modelo de fijación de precios de los activos de capital *m* (*MOFIPAC*); ~ **assets** *n pl* FIN *investment* activos de capital *m pl*, TAX bienes de capital *m pl*; ~, **assets, management, earnings, liquidity** (*CAMEL*) FIN capital, activos, administración, ganancias, liquidez; ~~**augmenting technical progress** ECON aumento de producción debido al progreso técnico *m*;

■ **b** ~ **base** BANK, STOCK base de capital *f*; ~ **bonus** FIN, STOCK bono de capital *m*, gratificación de capital *f*; ~ **budget** ACC, ECON, FIN presupuesto de activo fijo *m*, presupuesto de capital *m*, presupuesto de gasto de capital *m*; ~ **budgeting** ACC presupuestación del capital *f*, ECON análisis de inversiones *f*;

■ **c** ~ **commitment** ACC, FIN asunción de capital *f*, suscripción de capital *f*; ~ **component** ECON, FIN componente de capital *m*; ~ **consolidation** ECON, FIN consolidación del capital *f*; ~ **consumption** ECON, FIN consumo de capital *m*; ~ **consumption allowance** ECON, FIN amortización del consumo de capital *f*; ~ **contributed in excess of par value** ACC, STOCK capital aportado que excede el valor nominal *m*; ~ **contribution** FIN aporte de capital *m*; ~ **cost** TAX coste de inversión *m* (*Esp*), costo de inversión *m* (*AmL*); ~ **cost allowance** (*CCA*) TAX desgravación de los costes de inversión *f* (*Esp*), desgravación de los costos de inversión *f* (*AmL*); ~ **cost allowance class** TAX grupo de desgravación de los gastos de capital *m*; ~ **cost allowance schedule** TAX baremo de desgravación de los gastos de capital *m*; ~ **costs** *n pl* ECON, FIN coste de capital *m* (*Esp*), costo de capital *m* (*AmL*); ~ **cover** BANK capital cubierto *m*;

■ **d** ~ **deduction** TAX deducción de capital *f*; ~ **deepening** ECON intensificación del capital *f*;

~ **dividend** STOCK dividendo de capital *m*; ~ **dividend account** (*CDA*) BANK, STOCK, TAX cuenta de dividendo de capital *f* (*CDA*);

e ~ **endorsement** ACC, FIN, STOCK dotación de capital *f*; ~ **equipment** MGMNT equipo capital *m*; ~ **expenditure** (*capex*) GEN COMM gasto de capital *m*, inversión en capital fijo *f*; ~ **expenditure appraisal** ECON, FIN avalúo de gastos de capital *m* (*AmL*), estimación de gastos de capital *f* (*Esp*), valuación de gastos de capital *f* (*Esp*); ~ **expenditure budget** GEN COMM presupuesto de gastos de capital *m*; ~ **expenditure vote** POL *governmental* capítulo presupuestario de gastos de capital *f*; ~ **export** IMP/EXP exportación de capital *f*;

f ~ **financing** FIN financiación del capital *f*; ~ **flight** ECON evasión de divisas *f*; ~ **flow** STOCK corriente de capital *f*; ~ **flows** *n pl* FIN flujos de capital *m pl*; ~ **formation** ACC, ECON formación de capital *f*; ~ **fund** ACC, FIN *investments* fondo de capital *m*; ~ **funding** FIN, POL provisión de fondos de capital *f*; ~ **funding planning** FIN plan de financiación del capital *f*;

g ~ **gains** *n pl* ACC, BANK, ECON, FIN ganancias de capital *f pl*, rendimiento del capital invertido *m*; ~ **gains distribution** STOCK distribución de plusvalías *f*; ~ **gains dividend** TAX dividendo de los rendimientos del capital *m*; ~ **gains exemption** TAX exención de las ganancias del capital *f*; ~ **gains redemption** TAX amortización de los rendimientos del capital *f*; ~ **gains refund** TAX devolución de las ganancias de capital *f*; ~ **gains reserve** TAX reserva de los bienes de capital *f*; ~ **gains rollover** TAX reutilización de las ganancias de capital *f*; ~ **gains tax** (*CGT*) TAX impuesto sobre la plusvalía *m*; ~ **gearing** BrE (*cf capital leverage AmE*) STOCK apalancamiento de capital *m*; ~ **goods** *n pl* ECON, GEN COMM bienes de capital *m pl*; ~ **growth** ECON, STOCK crecimiento del capital *m*;

i ~ **import** IMP/EXP, STOCK importación de capital *f*; ~ **improvement** ECON aumento de capital *m*; ~ **income tax** TAX impuesto sobre la renta del capital *m*; ~ **increase** GEN COMM capitalización *f*; ~ **inflow** ECON, STOCK afluencia de capital *f*, entrada de capital *f*; ~ **injection** ECON, FIN inyección de capital *f*; ~ **instrument** FIN instrumento de capital *m*; ~ **-intensive industry** ECON, IND industria con alto coeficiente de capital *f*, industria con empleo intensivo de capital *f*, industria intensiva en capital *f*; ~ **interest** TAX *in trust* intereses del capital *m pl*; ~ **investment** STOCK inversión de capital *f*; ~ **investment appraisal** FIN evaluación de la inversión de capital *f*; ~ **investment strategy** FIN estrategia de inversión *f*;

l ~ **-labor ratio** *AmE*, ~ **-labour ratio** *BrE* ECON, FIN, IND proporción capital-trabajo *f*, razón capital-mano de obra *f*, relación capital-trabajo *f*; ~ **lease** ACC arrendamiento de capital *m*, GEN COMM arriendo financiero de capital *m*; ~ **lease agreement** GEN COMM arrendamiento de capital *m*; ~ **letter** COMP, MEDIA letra mayúscula *f*; ~ **letters** *n pl* (*caps*) COMP, MEDIA mayúsculas *f pl*, versal *f*; ~ **leverage** *AmE* (*cf capital gearing BrE*) STOCK apalancamiento de capital *m*; ~ **liabilities** ACC, ECON, FIN, GEN COMM capital pasivo *m*; ~ **loss** ACC, ECON, FIN, GEN COMM minusvalías *f pl*, pérdida de capital *f*;

m ~ **market** ACC, ECON, FIN, STOCK mercado de capitales *m*; ~ **market influence** ACC, FIN, STOCK *theory, practice* influencia del mercado de capitales *f*; ~ **market**

yield ACC, ECON, FIN, STOCK rendimiento del mercado de capitales *m*;

n ~ **needs** *n pl* ECON, FIN, GEN COMM necesidades del capital *f pl*; ~ **net worth** ACC, ECON, FIN, GEN COMM capital neto *m*;

o ~ **outflow** ACC, ECON salida de capital *f*; ~ **outlay** ECON, FIN desembolso de capital *m*, gastos de operación *m pl*; ~ **-outlay ratio** FIN coeficiente de capital desembolsado *m*; ~ **-output ratio** ECON, FIN, IND proporción capital-producto *f*, relación capital-producto *f*;

p ~ **paid in excess of par value** ACC capital pagado que excede el valor nominal *m*; ~ **profit** ACC, BANK, FIN utilidad de capital *f* (*AmL*), beneficio de capital *f* (*AmL*); ~ **program** *AmE*, ~ **programme** *BrE* ACC, ECON, FIN programa de capital *m*; ~ **project** ECON, FIN proyecto de inversión *m*; ~ **project evaluation** ECON, FIN evaluación de proyectos de capital *f*, evaluación del proyecto de capital *f*; ~ **property** PROP, TAX propiedad del capital *f*;

r ~ **raising** BANK, FIN captación de capital *f*, STOCK obtención de capital *f*; ~ **-raising operation** BANK, FIN operación de captación de capital *f*; ~ **ratio** BANK, FIN relación de capital *f*; ~ **rationing** BANK, ECON racionamiento del capital *m*, FIN control del capital *m*; ~ **reorganization** FIN, STOCK reorganización del capital *f*; ~ **requirement** ECON, STOCK exigencia de capital *f*; ~ **requirements** *n pl* ACC necesidades de financiación *f pl*, ECON, FIN necesidades del capital *f pl*, GEN COMM necesidades de financiación *f pl*, necesidades del capital *f pl*; ~ **reserve** ACC *undistributed reserves* reserva de capital *f*, reserva no distribuible *f*; ~ **and reserves** ACC capital y reservas *m*; ~ **resource** FIN recurso de capital *m*; ~ **resources** *n pl* ECON bienes de equipo *m pl*; ~ **reswitching** ECON reinyección de capital *f*; ~ **risk** FIN riesgo del capital *m*;

s ~ **shares** *n pl* STOCK acciones de capital *f pl*; ~ **shortage** ACC, FIN, STOCK escasez de capital *f*; ~ **spending** ECON gasto de capital *m*, FIN consumo de capital *m*; ~ **stock** *BrE* (*cf equity capital AmE*) ACC, STOCK capital social en acciones *m*, existencias de capital *f pl*; ~ **strategy** FIN estrategia de inversión *f*; ~ **structure** ACC *arrangement of long-term funds*, ECON, FIN estructura de capital *f*; ~ **sum** FIN suma de capital *f*; ~ **surplus** *AmE* (*cf share premium BrE*) ACC, ECON, FIN, STOCK prima de emisión *f*, excedente de capital *m*, plusvalía de capital *f*, superávit de capital *m*; ~ **surplus on hand** TAX excedente de capital disponible *m*;

t ~ **tax** TAX impuesto sobre el capital *m*; ~ **theory** ECON teoría del capital *f*; ~ **-to-asset ratio** ACC proporción de capital a activos inmovilizados *f*, ratio de capital a activos inmovilizados *m*; ~ **transaction** BANK, FIN transacción de capital *f*; ~ **transfer** BANK, FIN transferencia de capital *f*; ~ **transfer tax** (*CTT*) TAX impuesto sobre las transferencias de capital *m*;

u ~ **utilization rate** ECON grado de utilización del capital *m*;

v ~ **value** ECON, FIN valor capital *m*, valor del capital *m*;

w ~ **widening** ECON ampliación del capital *f*

capital³: **make a ~ gain** *phr* GEN COMM producir un incremento de capital

Capital: ~ **International World Index** *n* STOCK Índice Mundial del Capital Internacional *m*

capitalism *n* ECON, IND, POL capitalismo *m*

capitalist[1] *adj* ECON, IND, POL capitalista

capitalist[2]: ~ **class** *n* ECON, POL clase capitalista *f*; ~ **imperialism** *n* ECON, POL imperialismo capitalista *m*

capitalistic *adj* ECON, IND, POL capitalista

capitalization *n* GEN COMM capitalización *f*; ~ **effect of a tax** ECON, TAX efecto capitalizador de un impuesto *m*; ~ **of income** GEN COMM capitalización de la renta *f*; ~ **of interest** FIN capitalización del interés *f*; ~ **issue** (*cap issue, cf bonus issue BrE, scrip issue BrE, stock dividend AmE, stock split AmE*) ACC, STOCK dividendo en acciones *m*, emisión de acciones liberadas *f*; ~ **of leases** ACC capitalización de los arrendamientos *f*; ~ **rate** (*cap rate*) ACC, ECON tasa de capitalización *f*, tipo de capitalización *m*, tipo máximo *m*; ~ **ratio** FIN coeficiente de capitalización *m*; ~ **of reserves** STOCK incorporación de reservas *f*; ~ **shares** *n pl* STOCK acciones de capitalización *f pl*

capitalize *vt* GEN COMM capitalizar

capitalize on *vt* GEN COMM sacar beneficio de, capitalizar

capitalized[1] *adj* GEN COMM capitalizado

capitalized[2]: ~ **cost** *n* ACC coste capitalizado *m* (*Esp*), costo capitalizado *m* (*AmL*); ~ **interest** *n* STOCK interés capitalizado *m*; ~ **value** *n* ECON, FIN valor capitalizado *m*

capitation *n* ECON, TAX capitación *f*; ~ **tax** ECON, TAX impuesto de capitación *m*, impuesto por persona *m*

CAPM *abbr* (*capital asset pricing model*) ECON, FIN, STOCK MOFIPAC (*modelo de fijación de precios de los activos de capital*)

caps *abbr* (*capital letters*) COMP, MEDIA mayúsculas *f pl*, versal *f*

capstan *n* TRANSP cabrestante *m*

captain *n* HRM, TRANSP capitán *m*; ~ **of industry** HRM, IND capitán de empresa *m*; ~**'s imperfect entry** (*CIE*) TRANSP declaración defectuosa del capitán *f*

caption *n* COMMS encabezamiento *m*, MEDIA *under illustration* pie *m*

captive: ~ **audience** *n* S&M audiencia cautiva *f*; ~ **candidate** *n* POL candidato(-a) cautivo(-a) *m,f*; ~ **finance company** *n* ECON, FIN sociedad financiera cautiva *f*; ~ **insurance company** *n* INS empresa de seguros cautiva *f*; ~ **market** *n* S&M mercado cautivo *m*

capture[1] *n* COMP *of data* toma *f*; ~ **theory** GEN COMM teoría de reglamentación *f*

capture[2] *vt* GEN COMM *market* ganar

car: ~ **allowance** *n* GEN COMM dietas de transporte *f pl*; ~ **carrier** *n* TRANSP transportador de coches *m*; ~ **exhaust emissions** *n pl* ENVIR emisión de gases de automóviles *f*; ~ **ferry** *n* TRANSP transbordador de vehículos *m*; ~ **hire** *n* (*cf auto rental AmE*) TRANSP alquiler de coches *m*; ~**-hire operator** *n* LEIS, TRANSP agente de coches de alquiler *mf*; ~**-hire service** *n* TRANSP servicio de alquiler de coches *m*; ~ **industry** *n* BrE (*cf automotive industry AmE*) ECON, IND industria de la automoción *f*, industria automotriz *f*; ~ **insurance** *n* BrE (*cf automobile insurance AmE*) INS seguro de automóviles *m*; ~ **liability insurance** *n* BrE (*cf automobile liability insurance AmE*) INS seguro de responsabilidad civil de automóviles *m*; ~ **loan** *n* BANK, FIN préstamo para automóvil *m*; ~ **manufacturer** *n* HRM, IND, TRANSP fabricante de coches *mf*; ~ **park** *n* BrE (*cf parking lot AmE*) GEN COMM, LEIS, TRANSP aparcamiento *m*, estacionamiento *m*; ~ **parking** *n* GEN COMM, LEIS aparcamiento *m*; ~ **pool** *n* TRANSP consor-

cio de coches *m*; ~ **registration** *n* TRANSP registro de automóviles *m*; ~ **tax** *n* TAX impuesto sobre el automóvil *m*

CAR *abbr* (*compound annual rate*) BANK, FIN TAC (*tasa anual compuesta*)

carat *n* GEN COMM *of gold* carate *m* (*AmL*), quilate *m* (*Esp*)

caravan *n* LEIS, PROP caravana *f*

carbon *n* IND carbón *m*; ~ **copy** (*cc*) ADMIN, COMMS copia mecanográfica *f*; ~ **dioxide emission** ENVIR, IND emisión de dióxido de carbono *m*; ~ **emission** ENVIR, IND emisión de carbono *f*; ~ **monoxide** ENVIR, IND monóxido de carbono *m*; ~ **paper** ADMIN, COMMS papel carbón *m*

carboy *n* TRANSP bombona para ácidos *f*

card *n* COMP *hardware* tarjeta *f*; ~ **bin** COMP casillero para fichas *m*; ~ **catalog** ADMIN, COMP caja de fichas *f*; ~ **file** ADMIN, COMP fichero de tarjetas *m*, fichero *m*; ~**-holder** GEN COMM titular de tarjeta *mf*; **identity** ~ (*ID card*) LAW, POL documento nacional de identidad *m* (*DNI*), tarjeta de identificación *f*; ~ **index** GEN COMM fichero *m*; ~ **issuer** GEN COMM emisor(a) de la tarjeta *m,f*; ~ **punch** GEN COMM perforadora de tarjetas *f*; ~ **reader** COMP lectora de tarjetas *f*; ~ **sorter** COMP clasificadora de tarjetas *f*

CARD *abbr* (*certificate of amortized revolving debt*) BANK, FIN certificado de deuda renovable amortizada *m*

cardboard *n* GEN COMM, IND, S&M, TRANSP cartón *m*

cardholder *n* BANK titular de tarjeta de crédito *mf*; ~ **fee** BANK gastos del titular de la tarjeta *m pl*

cardinal: ~ **utility** *n* ECON utilidad cardinal *f* (*AmL*), beneficio cardinal *f* (*Esp*)

cards: **be on the** ~ *phr infrml* GEN COMM *anticipated event* estar previsto; ~ **per minute** *phr* GEN COMM fichas por minuto

care[1] *n* GEN COMM cuidado *m*; ~ **and control** WEL atención y control *f*

care[2]: ~ **of** *phr* (*c/o*) COMMS, GEN COMM casa de (*c/d*)

career[1]: ~**-oriented** *adj* GEN COMM, HRM de orientación profesional

career[2] *n* HRM trayectoria profesional *f*; ~ **advancement** HRM desarrollo profesional *m*; ~ **development** HRM desarrollo profesional *m*; ~ **expectations** *n pl* HRM expectativas profesionales *f pl*; ~ **goals** *n pl* HRM metas profesionales *f pl*; ~ **guidance** HRM guía de carrera *f*; ~ **ladder** HRM, S&M jerarquía profesional *f*; ~ **management** HRM, MGMNT administración del desarrollo profesional *f*, gestión de la carrera *f*, gestión del desarrollo profesional *f*; ~ **planning** HRM proyecto de carrera *m*; ~ **prospects** *n pl* HRM perspectivas de desarrollo profesional *f pl*; ~ **record** HRM expediente académico *m*; ~ **salesperson** HRM, S&M vendedor(a) de carrera *m,f*; ~ **vitae** HRM currículum profesional *m*

Career: ~ **Development Loan** *n* (*CDL*) BANK, HRM, WEL préstamo para el desarrollo profesional *m*

careers: ~ **advisor** *n* HRM consejero(-a) de salidas profesionales *m,f*, orientador(a) vocacional *m,f*; ~ **officer** *n* HRM consejero(-a) de salidas profesionales *m,f*, orientador(a) vocacional *m,f*

caret *n* MEDIA, S&M signo de inserción *m*

cargo *n* TRANSP carga *f*; ~ **accounting device** TRANSP dispositivo contabilizador de carga *m*; ~ **aircraft** TRANSP avión de carga *m*, avión cargero *m*; ~ **assembly** TRANSP concentración de la carga *f*;

~ boat TRANSP barco de carga *m*, barco de transporte *m*; **~ capacity** (*CC*) TRANSP capacidad de carga *f*; **~ center** *AmE*, **~ centre** *BrE* TRANSP centro de carga *m*; **~ claim** TRANSP reclamación de carga *f*; **~ claim procedure** TRANSP procedimiento de reclamación de la carga *m*; **~ clearance** IMP/EXP, TRANSP expedición de carga *f*; **~ configuration** TRANSP configuración de la carga *f*; **~ declaration** IMP/EXP, TRANSP manifiesto de carga *m*; **~ delivery terms** *n pl* TRANSP condiciones de entrega de la carga *f pl*; **~ derrick** TRANSP *shipping* pescante de carga *m*; **~ disassembly** TRANSP desconcentración de la carga *f*, disgregación de la carga *f*; **~ dues** *n pl* TRANSP *shipping* derechos de la carga *m pl*; **~ handling charges** *n pl* (*CHC*) TRANSP gastos de carga y descarga *m pl*, gastos de manipulación de la carga *m pl*; **~ handling equipment** TRANSP equipo de carga y descarga *m*; **~ in isolation** TRANSP carga aislada *f*; **~ inspector** HRM, TRANSP inspector(a) de carga *m,f*; **~ insurance** INS, TRANSP seguro de mercancías *m*; **~ liner** TRANSP buque de carga de línea regular *m*; **~ manifest** TRANSP manifiesto de carga *m*; **~ marking symbol** TRANSP símbolo para el marcaje de la carga *m*; **~ mix** TRANSP composición de la carga *f*; **~ net** TRANSP red para elevar cargas *m*; **~ plan** TRANSP plan de estiba *m*; **~ plane** *infrml* TRANSP avión carguero *m*, avión de carga *m*; **~ ship** *BrE* (*cf freighter AmE*) TRANSP buque de carga *m* (*Esp*), fletero *m* (*AmL*); **~ ship safety equipment certificate** TRANSP certificado del equipo de seguridad de buques de carga *m*; **~ shut out** TRANSP mercancías no embarcadas por falta de espacio *f pl*; **~ stowage** TRANSP estibaje de la carga *m*; **~ superintendent** HRM, TRANSP inspector(a) de carga *m,f*; **~ surveyor** HRM, TRANSP supervisor(a) de carga *m,f*; **~ tag** TRANSP etiquetado de origen *m*; **~ tank** (*CT*) TRANSP tanque de carga *m*; **~ tank center** *AmE*, **~ tank centre** *BrE* TRANSP centro del tanque de carga *m*; **~ tank common** (*CTX*) TRANSP servicio del tanque de carga *m*; **~ tonnage** TRANSP tonelaje de carga *m*; **~ transfer** TRANSP transbordo de carga *m*; **~ transit** TRANSP mercancías en tránsito *f pl*; **~ tray** TRANSP *handling equipment* bandeja para carga *f*; **~ vessel** *BrE* (*cf freighter AmE*) TRANSP buque de carga *m* (*Esp*), fletero *m* (*AmL*)

Cargo: **~ Accounts Settlement System** *n* (*CASS*) TRANSP Sistema de Liquidación de la Cuentas de Carga *m*; **~ Information Message Procedure** *n* TRANSP procedimiento para mensajes de información sobre cargas *m*; **~ Systems and Procedures Committee** *n* (*CSPC*) TRANSP Comité de Sistemas y Procedimientos de Carga *m*; **~ Traffic Procedures Committee** *n* (*CTPC*) TRANSP Comité de Procedimientos para el Tráfico de Carga *m*

Caribbean: **~ Development Bank** *n* (*CDB*) BANK, ECON, POL banco para el desarrollo del Caribe

caring: **~ capitalism** *n* ECON, IND, POL capitalismo benevolente *m*; **~ society** *n* ECON, POL, WEL sociedad compasiva *f*, sociedad inquieta *f*

carload: **~ rate** *n BrE* (*cf wagonload rate AmE*) TRANSP *rail* tarifa de vagón completo *f*, tarifa por vagón completo *f*

carnet *n* IMP/EXP *customs* guía *m*; **~ system** IMP/EXP sistema de admisión temporal *m*

carr fwd *abbr* (*carriage forward*) IMP/EXP, TRANSP porte debido *m*

carr pd *abbr* (*carriage paid*) IMP/EXP, TRANSP flete pagado *m*, transporte pagado *m*

carriage *n* TRANSP porte *m*, *rail* acarreo *m*, vagón *m*; **~ charge** TRANSP precio del acarreo *m*; **~ expenses** *n pl* TRANSP gastos de transporte *m pl*; **~ return** (*CR*) COMP, GEN COMM retorno de carro *m*; ◆ **~ forward** (*carr fwd, CF*) IMP/EXP, TRANSP porte debido; **~ and insurance paid** (*CIP*) IMP/EXP, TRANSP flete y seguro pagados, porte y seguro pagados; **~ paid** (*carr pd*) IMP/EXP, TRANSP flete pagado, transporte pagado; **~ paid home** IMP/EXP, TRANSP franco a domicilio; **~ paid transport** (*CPT*) TRANSP transporte pagado

Carriage: **~ of Goods by Road Act** *n* LAW, TRANSP 1965 Ley de Transporte de Mercancía por Carretera *f*; **~ of Goods by Sea Act** *n* (*COGSA*) LAW, TRANSP 1924, 1971 Ley de Transporte Marítimo *f*

carriageway *n* TRANSP calzada *f*

carried[1]: **~ back** *adj* ACC *balance sheet*, BANK arrastrado a cuentas anteriores; **~ down** *adj* (*c/d*) ACC *balance sheet*, BANK suma anterior *f*, suma y sigue, sustraído de cuenta; **~ forward** *adj* (*c/f*) ACC *balance sheet*, BANK llevado a cuenta nueva, suma y sigue, trasladado a cuenta nueva; **~ over** *adj* ACC *balance sheet*, BANK llevado a cuenta nueva, suma y sigue

carried[2]: **~ interest** *n* BANK interés resultante *m*

carrier *n* COMP soporte *m*, TRANSP *firm* transportista *mf*; **~'s haulage** TRANSP gastos de acarreo del transportista *m pl*; **~ last** TRANSP transportista final *mf*; **~'s liability** INS, TRANSP responsabilidad del transportista *f*; **~'s lien** TRANSP gravamen de transportista *m*; **~'s risk** TRANSP riesgo del transportista *m*

carrot: **~ and stick** *n infrml* MGMNT *negotiations* meta y cumplimiento

carry[1]: **~ back** *n* ACC existencias en efectivo *f pl*; **~-back** *n* TAX compensación con ejercicios anteriores *f*, repercusión contra ejercicios anteriores *f*; **~-back loss** *n* ACC, TAX pérdida traspasada al periodo anterior *f* pérdidas con efecto retroactivo *f*, traslado de pérdidas a ejercicios anteriores *m*; **~-back system** *n* TAX sistema de repercusión contra ejercicios anteriores *m*; **~-forward** *n* ACC distribución en ejercicios posteriores *f*, saldo a cuenta nueva *m*; **~-forward system** *n* TAX sistema de repercusión contra ejercicios posteriores *m*; **~-over** *n* ACC saldo anterior *m*; **~-over business** *n* STOCK negocio de remanente *m*; **~-over effect** *n* MEDIA *print* efecto remanencia del mensaje publicitario *m*; **~-over loss** *n* ACC pérdida traspasada al año siguiente *f*; **~-over rate** *n* STOCK índice de remanente *m*; **~-over stocks** *n pl* GEN COMM remanente de mercaderías *f pl*

carry[2] *vt* FIN *balances* trasladar, STOCK *risk* asumir, TRANSP acarrear; ◆ **~ information on** GEN COMM llevar información sobre; **~ a loss** FIN arrastrar una pérdida; **~ a report** GEN COMM, MEDIA *newspaper* contener un informe

carry back *vt* ACC, TAX traspasar al periodo anterior

carry forward *vt* ACC distribuir en ejercicios posteriores, traspasar al periodo futuro, TAX traspasar al periodo futuro

carry out *vt* GEN COMM *order* cumplir, *plan, policy* llevar a cabo; ◆ **~ a survey** GEN COMM hacer una encuesta

carrying: **~ cable** *n* COMP cable de suspensión *m*; **~ capacity** *n* ECON *population* capacidad de carga *f*, TRANSP *of container vessel* capacidad de transporte *f*, carga útil *f*; **~ cash** *n* FIN efectivo útil *m*; **~ charge** *n*

PROP sobregasto *m*, TRANSP gasto de transporte *m*; ~ **charges** *n pl* STOCK gastos de corretaje en operaciones a crédito *m pl*, gastos incidentales *m pl*; ~ **cost** *n* STOCK coste incidental *m* (*Esp*), costo incidental *m* (*AmL*); ~ **value** *n* ACC valor neto contable *m*

cars: ~ **available for private use** *n pl* TAX *benefits* automóviles disponibles para uso privado *m pl*

cartage *n* TRANSP acarreo *m*, camionaje *m*

carte: ~-**blanche** *n* ACC, BANK, GEN COMM carta blanca *f*

cartel *n* ECON cartel *m*, HRM cartel *m*, asociación de fabricantes *f*, INS asociación de fabricantes *f*

cartelization *n* ADMIN cartelización *f*

carton *n* GEN COMM, IND, S&M, TRANSP cartón *m*

cartouche *n* TRANSP cartela *f*, cartucho *m*

cartridge *n* TRANSP cargador *m*

carve: ~-**out rule** *n* TAX norma establecida *f*

carving: ~ **note** *n* TRANSP *shipping* registro de identificación del buque *m*

cascade: **in** ~ *adj* TAX en cascada

case¹: ~-**sensitive** *adj* COMP receptivo

case² *n* LAW caso *m*, LEIS caja *f*; ~ **file** LAW presentación del caso *f*; ~ **history** GEN COMM carpeta de antecedentes *f*, expediente de antecedentes *m*, S&M *advertising* ejemplo típico *m*; ~ **law** LAW derecho jurisprudencial *m*, jurisprudencia *f*; ~ **notes** *n pl* GEN COMM expediente *m*; ~ **packaging** (*Cl*-) TRANSP empaquetado de cajas *m*; ~ **papers** *n pl* GEN COMM documentos del caso *m pl*; ~ **shift** COMP inversión *f*; ~ **study** MGMNT, S&M estudio de casos *m*, estudio de casos prácticos *m*; ~-**study method** MGMNT, S&M *formulation of policy* método de estudio de casos *m*; ◆ **argue one's own** ~ LAW defender el propio caso

CASE *abbr* (*computer-assisted software engineering*) COMP ingeniería de programas asistida por computador *f* (*AmL*), ingeniería de programas asistida por computadora *f* (*AmL*), ingeniería de programas asistida por ordenador *f* (*Esp*)

casebound *adj* MEDIA *book* de tapa dura, en cartoné

cases *n pl* (*c/s*) TRANSP cajones *m pl*

cash¹: ~ **poor** *adj* FIN con efectivo insuficiente; ~ **rich** *adj* FIN con efectivo abundante; ~ **settled** *adj* GEN COMM pagado al contado; ~ **strapped** *adj* ACC, FIN con falta de liquidez

cash² *n* GEN COMM metálico *m*, dinero en efectivo *m*, contado *m*, *amount available immediately* liquidez *f*, *available capital* líquido *m*, dinero en metálico *m*, *funds* efectivo *m*, *legal tender* dinero *m*; ~ **account** ACC cuenta de caja *f*, BANK cuenta de débito directo *f*, GEN COMM *clients* cuenta de caja *f*; ~ **accounting** ACC contabilidad de caja *f*; ~ **acknowledgement** BANK recibo de efectivo *m*, FIN acuse de recibo de efectivo *m*, recibo de efectivo *m*; ~ **advance** GEN COMM anticipo en efectivo *m*; ~ **against documents** (*c.a.d.*) IMP/EXP pago contra documentación *m*; ~ **asset** ACC, FIN, PROP activo líquido *m*; ~ **assets** *n pl* ACC activos disponibles *m pl*, activos líquidos *m pl*, tesorería *f*, valor disponible *m*, BANK, FIN, STOCK activos disponibles *m pl*, activos líquidos *m pl*; ~ **available** FIN activo disponible *m*; ~ **balance** ACC saldo de caja *m*; ~ **bargain** STOCK contrato en firme *m*; ~ **basis** ACC, BANK base de caja *f*, base de efectivo *f*, método de caja *m*, método de efectivo *m*; ~ **basis of accounting** ACC, BANK contabilidad de caja *f*; ~ **before delivery** (*CBD*) ECON, FIN, GEN COMM pago antes de la entrega *m*, cobro antes de la

entrega *m*; ~ **benefit** GEN COMM, TAX beneficio líquido *m*; ~ **bonus** GEN COMM bonificación en efectivo *f*, STOCK *on bonds* dividendo extraordinario en efectivo *m*, TAX bonificación en efectivo *f*; ~ **book** ACC caja *f*, diario de caja *m*, libro de caja *m*; ~ **box** ACC, BANK, GEN COMM caja *f*; ~ **budget** ACC, ECON, FIN presupuesto de caja *m*; ~ **budgeting** ACC, ECON elaboración del presupuesto de caja *f*, elaboración del presupuesto de tesorería *f*; ~ **buyer** S&M comprador(a) al contado *m,f*; ~ **card** BANK tarjeta para cajero automático *f*; ~ **and carry** GEN COMM pago al contado *m*, venta al contado *f*; ~ **and carry arbitrage** STOCK arbitraje de pago al contado *m*; ~ **and carry wholesaler** S&M mayorista de venta al contado *mf*; ~ **certificate** FIN certificado de caja *m*; ~ **collection** FIN acopio de efectivo *m*; ~ **commodity** FIN mercancía al contado *f*; ~ **contribution** ACC aportación dineraria *f*; ~ **control** ACC control de caja *m*; ~ **control record** ACC registro del control de caja *m*; ~ **control system** ACC sistema de control de caja *m*; ~ **conversion cycle** FIN ciclo de conversión en efectivo *m*; ~ **cow** *jarg* ECON fuente de ingresos *f*; ~ **credit** GEN COMM crédito de caja *m*; ~ **crop** ECON, ENVIR cultivo comercial *m*; ~ **and debt position** BANK situación de liquidez y deudas *f*; ~ **deficit** ACC déficit de caja *m*; ~-**delivery option** STOCK opción al contado *f*, opción librada al contado *f*; ~ **department** ADMIN, FIN, GEN COMM departamento de caja *m*; ~ **deposit acknowledgement** FIN *of receipt of order* acuse de depósito de efectivo *m*; ~-**deposits ratio** ECON proporción de liquidez *f*; ~ **desk** ACC, BANK caja *f*; ~ **disbursement** ACC desembolsos de caja *m pl*, gastos netos *m pl*; ~ **discount** S&M descuento por pago al contado *m*; ~ **dispenser** BANK cajero automático *m*, dispensador de dinero en efectivo *m*; ~-**dispensing machine** BANK cajero automático *m*, dispensador de dinero en efectivo *m*, máquina dispensadora de dinero *f*; ~ **dividend** ACC, FIN, STOCK dividendo en efectivo *m*; ~ **drawdown** ACC *government* disposición de la liquidez *f*, disposición de tesorería *f*; ~ **earnings** *n pl* ACC, FIN ingresos en efectivo *m pl*; ~ **economy** ECON economía monetaria *f*; ~ **equivalence** S&M equivalencia en efectivo *f*; ~ **equivalents** *n pl* FIN equivalentes de caja *m pl*; ~ **exchange rate** ECON tipo de cambio al contado *m*; ~ **flow** ACC, ECON, FIN beneficio neto más amortizaciones *m*, cash-flow *m*, flujo de caja *m*, flujo de dinero *m*, margen bruto de autofinanciación *m*; ~ **flow accounting** ACC, BANK, FIN contabilidad del flujo de caja *f*, contabilidad del flujo de efectivo *f*, contabilidad del flujo de tesorería *f*; ~ **flow forecast** ACC previsión de flujos de caja *f*, previsión de fondos *f*, previsión de tesorería *f*; ~ **flow per share** STOCK recursos generados por acción *m pl*; ~ **flow problem** ACC, ECON, FIN problema de liquidez *m*, problema de tesorería *m*; ~-**flow squeeze** ACC, GEN COMM reducción del flujo de caja *f*; ~ **flow statement** *n pl* ACC estado de cash-flow *m*, estado de flujos de caja *m*, estado de variación de tesorería *m*; ~ **forecast** ACC previsión de tesorería *f*, FIN estimación de caja *f*, presupuesto de caja *m*; ~ **holdings** ACC, GEN COMM efectivo en caja *m*, disponibilidad en efectivo *f*; ~ **in advance** ACC pago adelantado *m*; ~ **in bank** BANK efectivo en bancos; ~ **in hand** ACC disponibilidad en efectivo *f*, efectivo de caja *m*, efectivo disponible *m*, BANK cuenta de débito directo *f*, GEN COMM efectivo disponible *m*, existencias en caja *f pl*; ~ **in transit** ACC efectivo en tránsito *m*; ~ **inflow** FIN entrada en efectivo *f*; ~ **journal** ACC diario de caja *m*, libro de caja *m*; **~ limit** BANK, ECON, HRM límite de efectivo *m*, límite de liquidez *m*, límite de tesorería *m*; **~ loss** GEN COMM siniestro al contado *m*; **~ management** ACC, MGMNT dirección de la tesorería *f*, gestión de caja *f*, gestión de liquidez *f*, gestión de tesorería *f*; **~ management account** (*CMA*) BANK, FIN cuenta de administración de fondos *f*; **~ management system** BANK sistema de gestión de caja *m*; **~ management technique** MGMNT técnica administrativa de dinero *f*; **~ manager** HRM jefe(-a) de caja *m,f*; **~ market** STOCK mercado al contado *m*; **~ market rate** STOCK tipo del mercado de contado *m*; **~ messenger insurance** INS seguro de expoliación *m*, seguro de robo de cobradores *m*; **~ needs** *n pl* ACC necesidades de caja *f pl*, necesidades de efectivo *f pl*, necesidades de liquidez *f pl*; **~ office** ADMIN, FIN, GEN COMM departamento de caja *m*; **~ on delivery** (*COD*) GEN COMM entrega contra reembolso; **~ on hand** ACC efectivo en caja *m*, existencia en caja *f*; **~ on shipment** (*COS*) TRANSP pago contra embarque *m*; **~ operation** GEN COMM operación al contado *f*, transacción en efectivo *f*; **~ order** (*co*) GEN COMM pedido al contado *m*; **~ with order** (*c.w.o.*) GEN COMM pago al hacer el pedido *m*; **~ outflow** ACC, FIN pago *m*, salida de recursos líquidos *f*, salida en efectivo *f*; **~ payment** GEN COMM pago al contado *m*; **~ payments journal** ACC diario de pagos al contado *m*; **~ position** ACC dinero efectivo en caja *m*, situación de efectivo *f*, situación de tesorería *f*; **~ purchase** GEN COMM compra al contado *f*; **~ ratio** BANK, FIN coeficiente de caja *m*; **~ receipts** *n pl* ACC cobros *m pl*, entradas de caja *f pl*, entradas de efectivo *f pl*, entradas en metálico *f pl*; **~ receipts journal** ACC diario de cobros al contado *m*, diario de entradas en caja *m*; **~ received basis** ACC previo pago al contado *m*; **~ refunding date** STOCK *futures* límite de reembolso del efectivo *m*; **~ register** S&M caja registradora *f*; **~ requirement** ACC requerimiento de caja *m*; **~ reserve** ACC, BANK encaje excedente *m*, existencias en efectivo *f pl*, reserva de efectivo *f*; **~ resources** ECON, FIN recursos de caja *m pl*; **~ risk** STOCK riesgo de liquidez *m*; **~-settled option** STOCK opción pagada al contado *f*; **~ short** ACC déficit de caja *m*; **~ statement** ACC estado de efectivo *m*, estado de tesorería *m*, estado del efectivo de caja *m*; **~ surplus** ACC excedente de efectivo *m*, superávit *m*; **~ surrender value** INS valor de rescate al contado *m*; **~ transaction** ACC, BANK transacción al contado *f*; **~ transfer** ACC, BANK transferencia al contado *f*, transferencia de efectivo *f*; **~ value** ACC, BANK, FIN valor en efectivo *m*; **~ value life insurance** INS seguro de vida con valor en efectivo *m*; **~ voucher** ACC comprobante de caja *m*; **~ withdrawal** BANK retiro de fondos *m*; ◆ **awash with ~** *infrml* GEN COMM con sobrante de liquidez; **for ~** (*f.c.*) GEN COMM al contado (*Esp*), de contado (*AmL*); **have ~ in hand** FIN tener dinero en mano

cash³ *vt* BANK, FIN cobrar; ◆ **~ a check** *AmE*, **~ a cheque** *BrE* BANK cobrar un cheque

cash in *vt* STOCK *bonds* hacer efectivo; ◆ **~ on** FIN, S&M *demand* aprovechar

cash up *vi* ACC, BANK cobrar, hacer arqueo, hacer caja

cashable *adj* BANK, FIN canjeable

cashier *n* HRM cajero(-a) *m,f*; **~'s check** *AmE*, **~'s cheque** *BrE* BANK, FIN cheque de caja *m*; **~'s department** ADMIN, FIN, GEN COMM departamento de caja *m*; **~'s error allowance** BANK, GEN COMM reserva para errores de caja *f*

cashiering: **~ department** *n* ADMIN, FIN, GEN COMM departamento de caja *m*

cashless: **~ payment system** *n* BANK sistema de pago no al contado *m*; **~ society** *n* GEN COMM sociedad sin dinero *f*

cask *n* (*ck*) TRANSP tonel *m*

CASS *abbr* (*Cargo Accounts Settlement System*) TRANSP Sistema de Liquidación de la Cuentas de Carga *m*

cassette *n* COMP, MEDIA casete *f*; **~ tape recorder** COMP, MEDIA grabadora de casetes *f*

cast off *vt* MEDIA, S&M *advertising* calcular el espacio tipográfico, calcular espacio

casual: **~ labor** *AmE see casual labour BrE*; **~ laborer** *AmE see casual labourer BrE*; **~ labour** *BrE n* HRM trabajo eventual *m*, trabajo ocasional *m*, *seasonal* trabajo temporero *m*; **~ labourer** *n BrE* HRM trabajador(a) eventual *m,f*; **~ work** *n* HRM *seasonal* trabajo temporero *m*; **~ worker** *n* HRM jornalero(-a) *m,f*, temporero(-a) *m,f*, trabajador(a) eventual *m,f*

casualty: **~ insurance** *n* INS seguro contra accidentes *m*

CAT *abbr* COMP (*computer-assisted testing*) comprobación asistida por computador *f* (*AmL*), comprobación asistida por computadora *f* (*AmL*), comprobación asistida por ordenador *f* (*Esp*), (*computer-assisted translation*) traducción asistida por computador *f* (*AmL*), traducción asistida por computadora *f* (*AmL*), traducción asistida por ordenador *f* (*Esp*)

catalog *AmE see catalogue BrE*

catalogue¹ *n BrE* COMP, GEN COMM catálogo *m*; **~ buying** *BrE* S&M compra por catálogo *f*; **~ of errors** *BrE* GEN COMM lista de errores *f*; **~ price** *BrE* GEN COMM precio de catálogo *m*

catalogue² *vt BrE* GEN COMM catalogar

catalyst *n* GEN COMM catalizador *m*

catalytic: **~ converter** *n* ENVIR, TRANSP *in vehicle* conversor catalítico *m*, convertidor catalítico *m*; **~ policy mix** *n* ECON combinación de políticas principales y subsidiarias *m*

catastrophe: **~ cover** *n* INS cobertura contra catástrofe *f*; **~ hazard** *n* INS riesgo de catástrofe *m*; **~ policy** *n* INS póliza de catástrofe *f*; **~ reserve** *n* INS reserva para riesgos catastróficos *f*; **~ risk** *n* INS riesgo catastrófico *m*; **~ theory** *n* MATH teoría de catástrofes *f*

catastrophic: **~ loss** *n* GEN COMM siniestro catastrófico *m*

catch: **~-all account** *n* BANK cuenta general *f*; **~ line** *n* S&M *advertising* título atrayente *m*; **~-up demand** *n* ECON demanda adquirida *f*; **~-up effect** *n* HRM efecto de alcance *m*; **~-up increase** *n* HRM aumento de actualización *m*

catch up *vi* GEN COMM ponerse al día

catching: **~-up hypothesis** *n* ECON hipótesis de actualización tecnológica *f*

catchment: **~ area** *n* S&M, WEL *for schools* zona de captación *f*

categorical: **~ grant** *n* POL ayuda incondicionada *f*

categorically: **~ needy** *adj* WEL indigente absoluto

categories: **~ of construction types** *n pl* INS categorías de tipos de construcción *f pl*

categorization *n* ECON, GEN COMM, LAW, PATENTS categorización *f*

categorize *vt* ECON, GEN COMM, LAW, PATENTS clasificar

category *n* ECON, GEN COMM, LAW, PATENTS categoría *f*, clase *f*; **~ A share** FIN, STOCK acción de clase A *f*

cater for *vt* GEN COMM atender a

catering *n* LEIS catering *m*, hostelería *f*, TRANSP abastecimiento *m*, aprovisionamiento *m*, provisión *f*; **~ trade** LEIS negocio de aprovisionamiento *m*

cathode: ~ ray tube *n* (*CRT*) COMP, MEDIA tubo de rayos catódicos *m*

cathodic: ~ protection *n* TRANSP *shipping* protección catódica *f*

cats: ~ and dogs *n pl* STOCK valores especulativos *m pl*

CATS *abbr* COMP (*computer-assisted trading system*) sistema de negociación asistido por computador *m* (*AmL*), sistema de negociación asistido por computadora *m* (*AmL*), sistema de negociación asistido asistido por ordenador *m* (*Esp*), STOCK (*Certificate of Accrual on Treasury Securities*) Certificado de Réditos sobre Letras del Tesoro *m*

cattle: ~ container *n* TRANSP contenedor para ganado *m*; **~ float** *n* TRANSP barcaza para ganado *f*; **~ lorry** *n* BrE (*cf cattle truck AmE*) TRANSP camión para ganado *m*; **~ truck** *n* AmE (*cf cattle lorry BrE*) TRANSP camión para ganado *m*

cause[1] *n* GEN COMM causa *f*, ocasión *f*; **~ of action** LAW *claim* causa de acción *m*; **~ of cancellation of policy** INS causa de anulación de póliza *f*; **~ of loss** GEN COMM causa de la pérdida *f*

cause[2] *vt* GEN COMM causar; ♦ **~ undue hardship** TAX ejercer una presión excesiva

causes: ~ of unemployment *n* HRM causas del desempleo *f pl*

caution: ~ money *n* GEN COMM, LAW cantidad depositada en garantía *f*

cautionary *adj* LAW cautelar

cautious *adj* GEN COMM cauteloso; **~ optimism** GEN COMM optimismo cauto *m*

caveat: ~ emptor *phr* LAW por cuenta y riesgo del comprador; **~ subscriptor** *phr* LAW a riesgo del suscriptor; **~ venditor** *phr* LAW por cuenta y riesgo del vendedor

CB *abbr* (*current blend*) STOCK combinación circulante *f*

CBD *abbr* GEN COMM (*central business district*) distrito financiero *m*, (*cash before delivery*) pago antes de la entrega *m*, cobro antes de la entrega *m*

CBI *abbr* (*Confederation of British Industry*) IND ≈ CEOE (*Confederación Española de Organizaciones Empresariales*)

cbm *abbr* (*cubic meter AmE, cubic metre BrE*) GEN COMM metro cúbico *m*

CBO *abbr* AmE (*Congressional Budget Office*) FIN, POL comisión de presupuestos del congreso

CBOE *abbr* (*Chicago Board Options Exchange*) STOCK mercado de opciones de Chicago

CBOT *abbr* (*Chicago Board of Trade*) STOCK mercado de Chicago

CBS: ~ Tendency Index *n* ECON, FIN índice de valores CBS *m*

cc *abbr* ADMIN, COMMS (*carbon copy*) copia mecanográfica *f*, GEN COMM (*cubic centimeter AmE, cubic centimetre BrE*) cc (*centímetro cúbico*), (*cubic capacity*) capacidad cúbica *f*

CC *abbr* INS (*civil commotion*) conmoción civil *f*,

(*continuation clause*) cláusula sobre prórroga *f*, TRANSP (*cargo capacity*) capacidad de carga *f*, (*container control*) control de contenedores *m*

CCA *abbr* ACC, ECON, TAX (*current cost accounting*) contabilidad de costes corrientes *f* (*Esp*), contabilidad de costos corrientes *f* (*AmL*), estados financieros a costes actuales *m pl* (*Esp*), estados financieros a costos actuales *m pl* (*AmL*), contabilidad de gastos corrientes *f*, (*capital cost allowance*) desgravación de los costes de inversión *f* (*Esp*), desgravación de los costos de inversión *f* (*AmL*)

CCC *abbr* ECON (*Commodity Credit Corporation*) Compañía de Crédito al Consumo *f*, (*Canadian Chamber of Commerce*) Cámara de Comercio Canadiense *f*, IMP/EXP (*Customs Cooperation Council*) consejo de cooperación aduanera

CCCN *abbr* (*Customs Cooperation Council nomenclature*) IMP/EXP nomenclatura del consejo de cooperación aduanera

CCI *abbr* (*Chamber of Commerce and Industry*) ECON, IND CCI (*Cámara de Comercio e Industria*)

CCL *abbr* (*customs clearance*) IMP/EXP despacho aduanero *m*, despacho de aduanas *m*

CCLN *abbr* (*consignment note control label number*) TRANSP número de etiqueta de control de la hoja de embarque *m*

CC/O *abbr* (*certificate of consignment/origin*) IMP/EXP, TRANSP certificado de consignación/origen *m*

CCR *abbr* (*commodity classification rates*) TRANSP tarifas de clasificación de mercancías *f pl*

CCS *abbr* IMP/EXP (*Customs Clearance Status*) Categoría del Despacho Aduanero *f*, TRANSP (*consolidate-cargo service*) servicio de carga consolidada *m*

CCT *abbr* ECON (*compensating common tariff*) arancel común de compensación *m*, IMP/EXP (*common customs tariff*) tarifa exterior común *f*

cd *abbr* (*cum dividend*) STOCK con dividendo

c.d. *abbr* (*certificate of deposit*) FIN, STOCK c.d. (*certificado de depósito*)

c/d *abbr* (*carried down*) ACC *balance sheet*, BANK suma anterior *f*, suma y sigue, sustraído de cuenta

CD *abbr* BANK, FIN (*certificate of deposit*) CD (*certificado de depósito*), IMP/EXP (*customs declaration*) declaración de aduana *f*, declaración arancelaria *f*, STOCK (*certificate of deposit*) CD (*certificado de depósito*), TRANSP (*commercial dock*) depósito comercial *m*, (*customs declaration*) declaración arancelaria *f*

CDA *abbr* (*capital dividend account*) BANK, STOCK, TAX CDA (*cuenta de dividendo de capital*)

CDB *abbr* (*Caribbean Development Bank*) BANK, ECON, POL banco para el desarrollo del Caribe

CDC *abbr* (*Commonwealth Development Corporation*) ECON, POL CDC (*Corporación para el Desarrollo de la Commonwealth*)

CD-I *abbr* (*compact disk interactive*) COMP CD-I (*disco compacto interactivo*)

CDIC *abbr* (*Canada Deposit Insurance Corporation*) INS Corporación Canadiense de Seguro de Depósitos *f*

CDL *abbr* (*Career Development Loan*) BANK, HRM, WEL préstamo para el desarrollo profesional *m*

CD-ROM *abbr* (*compact disk read-only memory*) COMP CD-ROM (*disco compacto con memoria sólo de lectura*)

CDV *abbr* (*current domestic value*) ECON, IMP/EXP valor interno actual *m*

CE *abbr* (*Council of Europe*) ECON, POL CE (*Consejo de Europa*)

CEA *abbr* ECON (*Council of Economic Advisers*) Consejo de Asesores Económicos *m*, Junta de Asesores Económicos *f*, STOCK (*Commodity Exchange Authority*) organismo oficial encargado de los mercados de materias primas

cease[1]: **~-trading order** *n* STOCK orden de compra de futuros con entrega de lo disponible *f*

cease[2] **1.** *vt* GEN COMM suspender; **2.** *vi* GEN COMM cesar, dejar; ♦ **~ to be extant** TAX dejar de existir; **~ to have effect** LAW *contract* dejar de tener efecto

CEC *abbr* ECON (*Commission of the European Communities*) Comisión de las Comunidades Europeas *f*, IMP/EXP (*Clothing Export Council*) consejo de exportaciones de ropa

cedant *n* INS, LAW, PATENTS cedente *mf*

cede *vt* INS, LAW, PATENTS ceder

ceding: **~ company** *n* INS, LAW, PATENTS compañía cedente *f*

CEEC *abbr* (*Council for European Economic Co-operation*) ECON, POL Consejo para la Cooperación Económica Europea *m*

Ceefax® *n* BrE COMMS sistema de teletexto de la BBC

CEIC *abbr* (*closed-end investment company*) FIN sociedad de inversión cerrada *f*

CEIF *abbr* (*Council of European Industrial Federations*) ECON, IND, POL Consejo de Federaciones Industriales Europeas *m*

ceiling *n* GEN COMM *upper limit* límite máximo *m*; **~ rate** STOCK *of futures* tasa máxima *f*, tipo máximo *m*; **~ tax rate** TAX tipo impositivo máximo *m*

cell *n* COMP, TRANSP *containers* celda *f*; **~ guide** TRANSP *container* guía celular *f*; **~ organization** IND *production* organización celular *f*

cellphone *n* COMMS, GEN COMM teléfono celular *m*

cellular: **~ container ship** *n* TRANSP buque celular de contenedores *m*; **~ radio** *n* COMMS, MEDIA radio celular *f*

Celsius *adj* GEN COMM celsius

cement: **~ wagon** *n* TRANSP vagón de cemento *m*

CEN *abbr* (*European Committee for Standardization*) ECON, IND CEN (*Comité Europeo para la Normalización*)

CENE *abbr* (*Commission on Energy and the Environment*) ENVIR Comisión de la Energía y el Medio Ambiente *f*

CENIS *abbr* (*Centre for International Studies*) HRM, WEL Centro de Estudios Internacionales *m*

censure *vt* GEN COMM censurar

census *n* GEN COMM censo *m*; **~ of business** AmE ECON censo de empresas *m*; **~ of manufacturers** AmE IND censo de fabricantes industriales *m*; **~ of retail trade** ECON, S&M censo del comercio al por menor *m*

cent *n* BANK centavo *m*

center AmE *see* centre BrE

centigrade (*C*) *adj* GEN COMM centígrado (*C*)

centiliter AmE *see* centilitre BrE

centilitre *n* BrE GEN COMM centilitro *m* (*cl*)

centimeter AmE *see* centimetre BrE

centimetre *n* BrE GEN COMM centímetro *m* (*cm*)

central[1] *adj* GEN COMM central, S&M céntrico

central[2]: **~ bank** *n* BANK, ECON, FIN banco central *m*, banco emisor *m*; **~ bank transaction** *n* BANK, ECON transacción del banco central *f*, traspaso del banco central *m*; **~ business district** *n* (*CBD*) GEN COMM distrito financiero *m*; **~ buying** *n* S&M compra centralizada *f*; **~ freight booking office** *n* TRANSP *aviation* oficina central de contratación de fletes *f*; **~ freight bureau** *n* (*CFB*) TRANSP oficina central de fletes *f*; **~ government** *n* GEN COMM, POL gobierno central *m*; **~ government borrowing requirements** *n pl* ECON, FIN, POL necesidades de financiación del gobierno central *f pl*, necesidades de financiación del sistema central *f pl*, requisitos de financiación del sistema central *m pl*, requisitos de financiación del gobierno central *m pl*; **~ occupation** *n* HRM ocupación central *f*; **~ place theory** *n* ECON *population* teoría central de la localización *f*; **~ planning** *n* GEN COMM, MGMNT planificación central *f*; **~ processing unit** *n* COMP *hardware* unidad central de procesamiento *f*; **~ rate** *n* ECON tipo central *m*; **~ reservation office** *n* LEIS oficina central de reservas *f*; **~ reservation system** *n* LEIS sistema central de reservas *m*; **~ supplies depot** *n* GEN COMM depósito central de abastecimiento *m*; **~ tendency** *n* MATH tendencia central *f*

Central: **~ African Customs and Economics Union** *n* (*UDEAC*) ECON, IMP/EXP unión aduanera y económica de Africa Central; **~ American Common Market** *n* (*CACM*) ECON Mercado Común de América Central *m*; **~ Arbitration Committee** *n* (*CAC*) STOCK Comité Central de Arbitraje *m*; **~ Bank Facility** *n* BrE BANK, ECON, FIN Facilidad de Banco Central *f*; **~ Bureau of Statistics** *n* ECON, MATH Oficina Central de Estadística *f*; **~ European Time** *n* (*CET*) GEN COMM hora centroeuropea *f*; **~ Office of Information** *n* BrE (*COI*) POL oficina central británica de información; **~ Register** *n* BrE STOCK Registro Central *m*, Registro Mercantil Central *m*; **~ Standard Time** *n* (*CST*) GEN COMM hora central establecida *f*; **~ Statistical Office** *n* BrE (*CSO*) ECON ≈ Instituto Nacional de Estadística *m* (*INE*)

centralize *vt* GEN COMM centralizar

centralized[1] *adj* GEN COMM centralizado

centralized[2]: **~ institution** *n* GEN COMM institución centralizada *f*; **~ money** *n* BANK dinero centralizado *m*

centrally: **~ financed program** AmE, **~ financed programme** *n* BrE ACC, ECON, FIN programa de financiación centralizada *m*, programa financiado centralmente *m*; **~ planned economy** *n* (*CPE*) ECON, POL economía de planificación centralizada *f*

centre *n* BrE GEN COMM, IND centro *m*; **~ of gravity** BrE TRANSP centro de gravedad *m*; **~ periphery system** BrE ECON sistema centro periferia *m*; **~ spread** BrE MEDIA *print*, S&M *advertising* anuncio en doble página central *m*

Centre: **~ for Economic and Social Information** *n* (*CESI*) ECON, WEL centro de información económica y social, ≈ Centro de Investigaciones Sociológicas *m* (*Esp*) (*CIS*); **~ for International Studies** *n* BrE (*CENIS*) ECON, HRM, WEL Centro de Estudios Internacionales *m*; **~ for Policy Studies** *n* (*CPS*) ECON centro independiente de investigación socio-económica; **~ for Political Studies** *n* POL centro de estudios políticos

Centronics: **~ interface**® *n* COMP interfaz Centronics ® *m*

CEO *abbr* AmE (*chief executive officer*) HRM, MGMNT DG (*director general*), gerente general *mf*, jefe(-a) ejecutivo(-a) *m,f*, presidente(-a) ejecutivo(-a) *m,f*

CERF *abbr* (*Council of Europe Resettlement Fund*) ECON, POL fondo de restablecimiento del Consejo Europeo *m*

cert. *abbr* (*certificate*) GEN COMM certificado *m*

certain: ~ **conditions** *n pl* GEN COMM determinadas condiciones *f pl*

certainty *n* GEN COMM certidumbre *f*

certificate *n* (*cert.*) GEN COMM certificado *m*; ~ **of accrual** *AmE* ECON *treaty securities* certificado de acumulación *m*; ~ **of amortized revolving debt** (*CARD*) BANK, FIN certificado de deuda renovable amortizada *m*; ~ **of analysis** TRANSP certificado de análisis *m*; ~ **of clearing inwards** BANK, ECON, GEN COMM certificado de llegada *m*; ~ **of clearing outwards** BANK, ECON, GEN COMM certificado de salida *m*; ~ **of competency** TRANSP certificado de competencia *m*; ~ **of conditioning** TRANSP certificado de climatización *m*; ~ **of consignment/origin** (*CC/O*) IMP/EXP, TRANSP certificado de consignación/origen *m*; ~ **of deposit** BANK, FIN, STOCK (*c.d.*, *CD*) certificado de depósito *m* (*c.d.*, *CD*); ~ **of deposit rollover** BANK reembolso de un certificado de depósito *m*; ~ **of existence** INS certificado de vida *m*; ~ **of health** WEL certificado de salud *m*, certificado médico *m*; ~ **of incorporation** BANK, GEN COMM, LAW certificado de organización de una sociedad *m*; ~ **of indebtedness** BANK certificado de depósito *m*, TAX certificado de deuda *f*; ~ **of independence** HRM certificado de independencia *m*; ~ **of inspection** TRANSP certificado de inspección *m*; ~ **of insurance** (*c/i*) INS certificado de seguro *m*; ~ **of manufacture** IND certificado de fabricación *m*; ~ **of occupancy** PROP certificado de ocupación *m*; ~ **of origin** (*c/o*) FIN, IMP/EXP certificado de origen *m*; ~ **of origin and consignment** (*C/OC*) IMP/EXP certificado de origen y consignación *m*; ~ **of ownership** GEN COMM, LAW, PROP certificado de propiedad *m*; ~ **of posting** COMMS certificado de franqueo *m*; ~ **of pratique** IMP/EXP, TRANSP certificado de sanidad *m*; ~ **of protest** BANK, ECON, FIN, GEN COMM certificado de protesta *m*; ~ **of quality** GEN COMM, IMP/EXP, TRANSP certificado de calidad *m*; ~ **of registration** LAW certificado de registro *m*, PATENTS título de propiedad *m*, TAX certificado de inscripción *m*; ~ **of registry** TRANSP *shipping* certificado de registro *m*; ~ **of shipment** TRANSP certificado de expedición *m*; ~ **of survey** TRANSP certificado de inspección *m*; ~ **of tax deposit** *BrE* (*CTD*) TAX certificado de pago de impuestos *m*, comprobante de depósito del impuesto *m*; ~ **of title** LAW, PROP certificado de título *m*; ~ **of use** PROP certificado de uso *m*; ~ **of value** (*C/V*) IMP/EXP certificado de valor *m*; ~ **of value and origin** (*CVO*) IMP/EXP certificado de valor y origen *m*; ~ **of weight** TRANSP certificado de peso *m*

Certificate: ~ **of Accrual on Treasury Securities** *n AmE* (*CATS*) STOCK Certificado de Réditos sobre Letras del Tesoro *m*

certificateless: ~ **municipals** *n pl* STOCK bonos municipales sin certificado *m pl*

certification *n* GEN COMM certificación *f*; ~ **by spouse** TAX certificación del cónyuge *f*; ~ **mark** BANK *on gold and silver* marca de verificación *f*, HRM *labour relations* homologación *f*, marca de certificación *f*, IMP/EXP homologación *f*, IND, LAW, PATENTS marca de certificación, marca de identificación *f*, marca comercial *f*

Certification: ~ **Officer** *n* (*CO*) HRM Director(a) de Certificaciones *m,f*

certified[1]: ~ **accountant** *n BrE* (*CA*) ACC contable autorizado(-a) *m,f* (*Esp*), contable certificado(-a) *m,f* (*Esp*), contable colegiado(-a) *m,f* (*Esp*), contable diplomado(-a) *m,f* (*Esp*), contable público(-a) *m,f* (*Esp*), contable registrado(-a) *m,f* (*Esp*), contador(a) autorizado(-a) *m,f* (*AmL*), contador(a) certificado(-a) *m,f* (*AmL*), contador(a) colegiado(-a) *m,f* (*AmL*), contador(a) diplomado(-a) *m,f* (*AmL*), contador público(a) *m,f* (*AmL*), contador(a) registrado(-a) *m,f* (*AmL*); ~ **accounts** *n pl* ACC cuentas autorizadas *f pl*, cuentas certificadas *f pl*, cuentas fiscalizadas *f pl*, cuentas intervenidas *f pl*; ~ **administration manager** *n* HRM gerente administrativo(-a) diplomado(-a) *m,f*; ~ **check** *AmE*, ~ **cheque** *BrE n* BANK, FIN cheque certificado *m*; ~ **copy** *n* LAW copia certificada *f*; ~ **declaration of origin** *n* IMP/EXP declaración de origen certificada *f*, ~ **employee benefit specialist** *n AmE* HRM especialista diplomado(-a) en subsidios laborales *m,f*; ~ **financial planner** *n* FIN, STOCK planificador(a) financiero(-a) diplomado(-a) *m,f*; ~ **financial statement** *n* ACC estado financiero certificado *m*; ~ **general accountant** *n* ACC contable general autorizado(-a) *m,f(Esp)*, contable general certificado(-a) *m,f* (*Esp*), contable general registrado(-a) *m,f* (*Esp*), contador(a) general autorizado(-a) *m,f(AmL)*, contador(a) general certificado(-a) *m,f* (*AmL*), contador(a) general registrado(-a) *m,f* (*AmL*); ~ **institution** *n* TAX institución reconocida *f*; ~ **invoice** *n* ACC factura certificada *f*; ~ **mail** *n AmE* (*cf registered post BrE*) COMMS correo certificado *m*; ~ **property** *n* PROP, TAX propiedad declarada *f*; ~ **true copy** *n* LAW copia fiel y auténtica *f*

certified[2]: ~ **as a true copy** *phr* LAW autentificado como copia fiel

Certified: ~ **Public Accountant** *n AmE* (*C.P.A.*) ACC contable público(-a) certificado(-a) *m,f* (*Esp*), contable público(-a) titulado(-a) *m,f* (*Esp*), contador(a) público(-a) certificado(-a) *m,f* (*AmL*), contador(a) público(-a) titulado(-a) *m,f* (*AmL*)

certifying: ~ **officer** *n* HRM empleado(-a) diplomado(-a) *m,f*

CES *abbr* (*Committee of European Shipowners*) TRANSP Comité de Armadores de Europa *m*

CESI *abbr* (*Centre for Economic and Social Information*) ECON, WEL centro de información económica y social, ≈ CIS *Esp* (*Centro de Investigaciones Sociológicas*)

cessation: ~ **of interest** *n* BANK cesación de interés *f*; ~ **of payment of premiums** *n* INS cesación de pago de las primas *f*

cesser: ~ **clause** *n* LAW, TRANSP *shipping* cláusula de fin de la responsabilidad *f*

cession *n* GEN COMM cesión de reaseguro *f*; ~ **of portfolio** GEN COMM cesión de cartera *f*

CET *abbr* ECON (*common external tariff*) tarifa exterior común *f*, GEN COMM (*Central European Time*) hora centroeuropea *f*

CETA *abbr AmE* (*Comprehensive Employment and Training Act*) HRM ley de trabajo y formación

ceteris paribus *phr* GEN COMM ceteris paribus

c/f *abbr* (*carried forward*) ACC *balance sheet*, BANK llevado a cuenta nueva, suma y sigue, trasladado a cuenta nueva

CF *abbr* IMP/EXP, TRANSP (*cost and freight*) C&F (*coste y*

flete Esp, costo y flete AmL), (*carriage forward*) porte debido *m*

CFB *abbr* (*central freight bureau*) TRANSP oficina central de fletes *f*

CFBH *abbr* (*Corporation of Foreign Bondholders*) STOCK corporación de la sociedad de cartera de títulos extranjeros

CFC *abbr* (*chlorofluorocarbon*) ENVIR CFC (*clorofluorocarbono*)

CFE *abbr* (*college of further education*) WEL ≈ Centro de Formación Profesional *m* (*Esp*), ≈ Instituto de Educación Secundaria *m* (*Esp*)

CFF *abbr* (*compensatory financial facility*) FIN mecanismo financiero compensatorio *m*

CFO *abbr* (*chief financial officer*) HRM director(a) de finanzas *m,f*

CFS *abbr* (*container freight station*) TRANSP centro de contenedores para fletes *m*

CFTC *abbr* ECON, POL (*Commonwealth Fund for Technical Cooperation*) *overseas development* Fondo de la Comunidad para la Cooperación Técnica *m*, STOCK (*Commodity Futures Trading Commission*) agencia para la regulacion del mercado de futuros

CG *abbr* HRM (*coastguard*) guardacostas *mf*, TRANSP (*clearance group*) grupo de despacho *m*

CGA *abbr* (*color/graphics adaptor AmE, colour/graphics adaptor BrE*) COMP CGA (*adaptador color/gráficos*)

CGI *abbr* (*City and Guilds Institute*) WEL cuerpo de evaluadores de exámenes de carácter técnico o manual

CGT *abbr* (*capital gains tax*) TAX impuesto sobre la plusvalía *m*

chain *n* GEN COMM *of businesses*, TRANSP *cargo handling* cadena *f*; ~ **of command** MGMNT cadena de órdenes *f*; ~ **of distribution** IND cadena de distribución *f*; ~ **feeding** COMP alimentación de cadena *f*; ~**-index method** ACC, ECON método del índice en cadena *m*; ~ **lashing** TRANSP amarre con cadena *m*; ~ **mall** *AmE* (*cf chain superstore BrE*) S&M centro comercial de una cadena *m*; ~ **production** ECON, IND producción en serie *f*; ~ **sling** TRANSP *cargo handling* eslinga de cadena *f*; ~**-store** GEN COMM, S&M centro comercial de una cadena *m*; ~ **superstore** *BrE* (*cf chain mall AmE*) S&M hipermercado perteneciente a una cadena *m*; ~ **tensioner** TRANSP tensor de cadena *m*

chair[1] *n* GEN COMM, HRM *meeting, conference, company*, MGMNT presidente(-a) *m,f*; ♦ **be in the** ~ GEN COMM presidir

chair[2] *vt* GEN COMM, HRM, MGMNT *meeting* presidir

chairman *n* GEN COMM, HRM, MGMNT presidente *m*; ~ **of the administrative board** HRM, MGMNT presidente del consejo de administración *m*; ~ **of the board** HRM, MGMNT presidente del consejo *m*; ~ **of the board of directors** HRM, MGMNT presidente de la junta directiva *m*, presidente del consejo de administración *m*; ~ **of the board of management** HRM, MGMNT presidente de la junta directiva *m*, presidente del consejo de administración *m*; ~**'s brief** MGMNT informe del presidente *m* (*Esp*), reporte del presidente *m* (*AmL*); ~ **and chief executive** *AmE* (*cf chairman and managing director BrE*) HRM, MGMNT, HRM presidente del consejo y director general *m*, presidente y director ejecutivo *m*, presidente y director gerente *m*; ~ **elect** HRM, MGMNT presidente electo *m*; ~ **of the executive board** HRM, MGMNT presidente de la junta directiva *m*, presidente del consejo de administración *m*; ~ **of the executive**

committee HRM, MGMNT presidente de la junta directiva *m*, presidente del consejo de administración *m*; ~ **and general manager** MGMNT presidente y director ejecutivo *m*, presidente y director general *m*, presidente y director gerente *m*; ~ **of the management board** HRM, MGMNT presidente de la junta directiva *m*; ~ **and managing director** *BrE* (*cf chairman and chief executive AmE*) HRM, MGMNT presidente del consejo y director general *m*, presidente y director ejecutivo *m*, presidente y director gerente *m*; ~ **of the supervisory board** HRM, MGMNT presidente de la junta supervisora *m*

chairwoman *n* GEN COMM, HRM, MGMNT presidenta *f*

challenge[1] *n* GEN COMM recusación *f*, reto *m*

challenge[2] *vt* GEN COMM, HRM desafiar

chamber *n* LAW, POL *meetings, trials* cámara *f*, sala *f*

Chamber: ~ **of Commerce** *n* ECON, GEN COMM, IMP/EXP Cámara de Comercio *f*; ~ **of Commerce and Industry** *n* (*CCI*) ECON, IND Cámara de Comercio e Industria *f* (*CCI*)

chance *n* GEN COMM ocasión *f*

Chancellor: ~ **of the Exchequer** *n BrE* ECON, POL, TAX ≈ Ministro(-a) de Economía y Hacienda *m,f* (*Esp*)

chancery *n* LAW cancillería *f*

change[1] *n* COMP, ECON, GEN COMM *in price* cambio *m*; ~ **of address** COMMS cambio de dirección *m*; ~ **of beneficiary provision** INS disposición de cambio de beneficiario *f*; ~ **dispenser** BANK dispensador de cambio *m*; ~ **dump** COMP volcado de modificaciones *m*; ~ **files** COMP ficheros de movimiento *m pl*; ~ **in the risk** GEN COMM cambio en el riesgo *m*; ~ **in the tendency** GEN COMM cambio de tendencia *m*; ~ **management** MGMNT dirección del cambio *f*, gestión del cambio *f*

change[2] **1.** *vt* GEN COMM cambiar; **2.** *vi* GEN COMM cambiar de, cambiarse; ♦ ~ **hands** GEN COMM, S&M *goods, business* cambiar de dueño

channel *n* COMP, GEN COMM, MEDIA *broadcast* canal *m*; ~ **capacity** BANK, ECON, GEN COMM, IND capacidad de canal *f*; ~ **of communication** COMMS, GEN COMM, S&M canal de comunicación *m*; ~ **of distribution** IMP/EXP, S&M, TRANSP canal de distribución *m*; ~ **for orders** S&M canal de pedidos *m*; ~ **management** MGMNT dirección de canales *f*, gerencia de canales *f*; ~ **of sales** S&M canal de ventas *m*; ~ **selection** LEIS *TV, Radio*, MEDIA, S&M selección de canal *f*

channel into *vt* FIN, GEN COMM *funds* canalizar hacia

channel through *vt* GEN COMM canalizar a través de

Channel: ~ **Tunnel** *n* TRANSP Túnel del Canal de la Mancha *m*

channels: ~ **of communication** *n pl* COMMS canales de comunicación *m pl*

chaos: ~ **theory** *n* ECON teoría del caos *f*

chapel *n BrE* HRM *printing industry* sindicato local de impresores *m*

CHAPS *abbr* (*Clearing House Automatic Payments System*) BANK sistema de pagos automáticos de compensación *m*

chapter *n* GEN COMM, LAW, MEDIA *book* capítulo *m*

character *n* COMP, GEN COMM, S&M *of area, shop, product* carácter *m*; ~ **array** COMP conjunto de caracteres *m*; ~ **card** COMP tarjeta de caracteres *f*; ~ **density** COMP densidad en caracteres *f*; ~ **file** COMP archivo de caracteres *m*; **~ merchandising** S&M *advertising* comercialización de un personaje *f*; **~ pitch** ADMIN paso de carácter *m*; **~ set** COMP conjunto de caracteres *m*, juego de caracteres *m*; **~ string** COMP cadena de caracteres *f*

characteristics: **~ theory** *n* ECON *of consumer demand* teoría característica de la demanda del consumidor *f*

characterizing: **~ portion** *n* PATENTS parte característica *f*

charcoal *n* ENVIR, IND carbón vegetal *m*

charge[1]: **in ~** *adj* HRM encargado

charge[2] *n* ACC, BANK cargo *m*, ECON, FIN, GEN COMM, IND carga *f*, cargo *m*, gasto *m*, LAW acusación *f*, cargo *m*, extracto de los debates *m*, STOCK cargo *m*, TAX gasto *m*; **~ account** BANK cuenta corriente a la vista *f*, GEN COMM cuenta de cargo *f*; **~-back** *AmE* BANK cargo al usuario *m*; **~ buyer** *BrE* (*cf credit buyer AmE*) S&M comprador(a) a crédito *m,f*; **~ card** BANK tarjeta de cargo *f*; **~ hand** HRM, PROP capataz(a) *m,f*; **~-off** ACC disminución de un cargo *f*, extorno del activo *m*, rebaja de un cargo *f*; **~ on land** TAX impuesto sobre la tierra *m*; **~ published** TRANSP gasto publicado *m*; **~ of stocks** ECON, IMP/EXP, TAX arbitraje de cartera *m*; **~ ticket** GEN COMM recibo de débito *m*; **~ upon a property** TAX impuesto sobre la propiedad *m*; ◆ **be in ~ of** GEN COMM ser responsable de, estar encargado de

charge[3] *vt* GEN COMM cobrar, *fee* cargar, S&M cobrar; ◆ **~ an expense to an account** BANK, FIN cargar un gasto a una cuenta; **~ interest** BANK cargar interés; **~ on top** TAX gravar adicionalmente

charge against *vt* GEN COMM adeudar

charge off *vt* ACC cancelar, BANK rebajar un cargo

charge to *vt* GEN COMM *expenses* cargar a

chargeable[1] *adj* GEN COMM, TAX imputable; **~ to tax** TAX imputable a impuestos

chargeable[2]: **~ assets** *n pl* TAX *capital gains* activos imponibles *m pl*; **~ capital gains** *n pl* TAX ganancias de capital imponibles *f pl*; **~ staff** *n pl* HRM personal a cargo *m*

charges *n pl* ACC cargas *f pl*, cargos *m pl*, BANK *on banking transactions* comisiones *f pl*; **~ prepaid** IMP/EXP gastos prepagados *m pl*, TRANSP gastos anticipados *m pl*; ◆ **no ~ for packing** S&M embalaje gratuito *m*; **all ~ net rate** FIN tasa neta de todos los cargos *f*

charging: **~ wharf** *n* TRANSP muelle de carga *m*

charitable: **~ activity** *n* TAX, WEL actividad benéfica *f*; **~ donation** *n* TAX, WEL donativo benéfico *m*; **~ foundation** *n* TAX, WEL fundación benéfica *f*; **~ gift** *n* TAX, WEL donación a un centro benéfico *f*; **~ organization** *n* TAX, WEL organización benéfica *f*; **~ organizations** *n pl* HRM, WEL asociaciones caritativas *f pl*; **~ purposes** *n pl* TAX, WEL fines benéficos *m pl*; **~ trust** *n* TAX fideicomiso benéfico *m*

charity *n* HRM, INS asociación caritiva *f*, TAX institución benéfica *f*; **~ fundraising** FIN, WEL recaudación de fondos para beneficencia *f*; **~ funds** TAX, WEL fondos de beneficencia *m pl*; **~ number** TAX número de la institución benéfica *m*; **~ sponsorship** WEL patrocinio de la beneficencia *m*

chart[1] *n* GEN COMM *diagram, graph* gráfica *f*, gráfico *m*, grafo *m*; **~ of accounts** ACC cuadro de cuentas *m*, plan contable *m*

chart[2] *vt* GEN COMM *progress* diagramar, graficar

charter[1] *n* LAW, TRANSP fletamento *m*, fletamiento *m*, *flights* chárter *m*; **~ broker** TRANSP agente de fletamen-

to *mf*; **~ contract** TRANSP contrato de fletamento *m*; **~ flight** LEIS, TRANSP vuelo chárter *m*; **~ party** (*C/P*) TRANSP *shipowner's contractual agreement* póliza de fletamento *f*; **~ party bill of lading** (*C/P b/lading*) IMP/EXP, TRANSP *shipping* conocimiento de embarque bajo condiciones de la póliza de fletamento *m*; **~ party fraud** IMP/EXP, TRANSP fraude en el contrato de fletamento *m*; **~ party freight** TRANSP portes del contrato de fletamento *m pl*; **~ plane** LEIS, TRANSP avión chárter *m*

charter[2] *vt* GEN COMM, TRANSP *vehicle* fletar

chartered: **~ accountant** *n* ACC contable autorizado(-a) *m,f* (*Esp*), contable colegiado(-a) *m,f* (*Esp*), contable público(-a) *m,f*, contador(a) autorizado(-a) *m,f* (*AmL*), contador(a) colegiado(-a) *m,f* (*AmL*); **~ bank** *n AmE* BANK banco registrado *m*; **~ financial consultant** *n AmE* FIN consultor(a) financiero(-a) autorizado(-a) *m,f*; **~ life underwriter** *n* INS asegurador(a) de vida colegiado(-a) *m,f*; **~ life underwriting company** *n* INS compañía aseguradora de vida colegiada *f*; **~ plane** *n* LEIS, TRANSP avión chárter *m*; **~ property and casualty underwriter** *n* INS asegurador(a) registrado(-a) de bienes y accidentes *m,f*; **~ property and casualty underwriting company** *n* INS compañía aseguradora registrada de bienes y accidentes *f*

Chartered: **~ Institute of Bankers** *n BrE* (*CIB, cf American Institute of Bankers*) instituto británico de banqueros; **~ Institute of Secretaries** *n* (*CIS*) HRM colegio de secretarios; **~ Institute of Transport** *n BrE* TRANSP instituto colegiado de transporte

charterer *n* IMP/EXP, TRANSP fletador(a) *m,f*; **~'s account** TRANSP cuenta del fletador *f*; **~'s pay dues** (*cpd*) TRANSP derechos pagados por el fletador *m pl*

chartering *n* LAW, TRANSP fletamento *m*, fletamiento *m*; **~ agent** TRANSP *shipping* agente de fletes *mf*; **~ broker** TRANSP *shipping* corredor(-a) fletador(-a) *m,f*

chartism *n* ECON, STOCK chartismo *m*

chartist *n* ECON, STOCK analista de bolsa *mf*, analista de inversiones bursátiles *mf*, grafista de bolsa *mf*

chase: **~ eighths** *n jarg* STOCK especulador bursátil satisfecho con obtener el octavo de los beneficios

chat *n* GEN COMM charla *f*

chattel: **~ mortgage** *n* BANK, PROP hipoteca sobre bienes muebles *f*; **~ paper** *n* ECON valores mobiliarios *m pl*

chattels *n pl* LAW, PROP bienes muebles *m pl*

CHC *abbr* (*cargo handling charges*) TRANSP gastos de carga y descarga *m pl*, gastos de manipulación de la carga *m pl*

cheap[1] *adj* GEN COMM barato

cheap[2]: **~ execution** *n BrE* STOCK ejecución a bajo interés *f*; **~ money** *n* BANK dinero barato *m*; **~ money policy** *n* BANK política de dinero barato *f*

cheapest: **~ to deliver** *phr* (*CTD*) STOCK más bajo por entregar

check[1] *n* BANK *AmE see cheque BrE*, COMP *verification* comprobación *f*, FIN *AmE see cheque BrE*, GEN COMM *AmE see cheque BrE*, (*cf bill BrE*) *invoice* cuenta *f*, *examination, test* control *m*, revisión *f*, comprobación *f*, *of machinery, equipment* inspección *f*; **~ bit** COMP bitio de control *m*; **~ box** *AmE* (*cf box BrE*) COMP, GEN COMM casilla *f*, recuadro *m*; **~ character** COMP carácter de control *m*; **~ digit** COMP, GEN COMM dígito de comprobación *m*; **~-kiting** *AmE* BANK circulación de cheques en descubierto *f*, circulación de cheques sin fondos *f*; ~~-off HRM cuota sindical *f*; ~ **point** COMP *IBM*, TRANSP punto de control *m*

check² *vt* GEN COMM cotejar, *fact* averiguar

check in 1. *vt* GEN COMM *luggage* facturar, HRM, IND *for work* checar (*AmL*); **2.** *vi* HRM, IND checar (*AmL*), fichar (*Esp*), LEIS *hotels* firmar el registro, *airport* facturar

checkbook *AmE see* chequebook *BrE*

checker *n* HRM, S&M verificador(a) *m,f*

checking: ~ **account** *n* *AmE* (*cf* current account *BrE*) ACC, BANK cuenta corriente *f* (*clc*), cuenta de cheques *f*, cuenta de depósitos a la vista *f*, FIN cuenta corriente (*clc*)

checklist *n* GEN COMM lista de control *f*

checkout *n* S&M caja *f*; ~ **clerk** HRM cajero(-a) *m,f*; ~ **lane** S&M fila de caja *f*

checkroom *n* *AmE* (*cf* left-luggage office *BrE*) TRANSP *stations* consigna *f*, oficina de consigna *f*

checksum *n* COMP *data transfer* suma de verificación *f*

chemical: ~ **industry** *n* ECON, IND industria química *f*; ~ **input** *n* ENVIR *agriculture* insumos químicos *m pl*; ~ **works** *n* IND fábrica de productos químicos *f*

Chemical: ~ **Industries Association** *n* IND asociación de industrias químicas

chemicals *n pl* IND productos químicos *m pl*

chemistry *n* GEN COMM, IND química *f*

cheque *n* *BrE* BANK, FIN, GEN COMM cheque *m*; ~ **book** *BrE* BANK, FIN, GEN COMM chequera *f*; ~ **card** *BrE* BANK, FIN tarjeta de cheque *f*; ~ **clearing** *BrE* BANK compensación de cheques *f*; ~~-clearing system *BrE* BANK sistema de compensación de cheques *m*; ~ **counterfoil** *BrE* BANK matriz de cheque *f*; ~ **credit** *BrE* BANK crédito por cheque *m*; ~ **form** *BrE* BANK solicitud de cheques *f*; ~ **in favour of** *BrE* BANK, FIN cheque a favor de *m*; ~ **issue** *BrE* ACC, BANK, FIN, GEN COMM emisión de cheques *f*; ~~-kiting BANK rueda de cheques *f*; ~ **made to cash** *BrE* BANK, FIN cheque para cobrar en efectivo *m*; ~ **payment** *BrE* BANK pago de un cheque *m*; ~ **payment system** *BrE* BANK sistema de pago por cheque *m*; ~ **protector** *BrE* BANK, FIN protector de cheques *m*; ~ **register** *BrE* ACC, BANK registro de cheques *m*; ~ **requisition** *BrE* ACC, BANK requerimiento de cheque *m*, solicitud de cheque *f*; ~ **signer** *BrE* ADMIN, BANK, FIN firmante del cheque *mf*, girador(a) *m,f*; ~ **stub** *BrE* BANK talón de cheque *m*; ~ **to the amount of** *BrE* BANK, FIN cheque por la cantidad de *m*, cheque por valor de *m*; ♦ **make a** ~ **payable to sb** *BrE* BANK emitir un cheque a favor de alguien, emitir un cheque pagadero a alguien

chequebook *n* *BrE* BANK talonario *m*; ~ **journalism** *n* *BrE* *infrml* MEDIA periodismo sensacionalista *m*

chi: ~ **square** *n* MATH chi-cuadrado *m*; ~~-square test *n* MATH test del chi-cuadrado *m*; ~~-squared distribution *n* MATH distribución chi cuadrado *f*

Chicago: ~ **Board Options Exchange** *n* (*CBOE*) STOCK mercado de opciones de Chicago; ~ **Board of Trade** *n* STOCK Mercado de Futuros de Chicago *m*; ~ **Mercantile Exchange** *n* (*CME*) STOCK bolsa mercantil de Chicago; ~ **Rice and Cotton Exchange** *n* STOCK bolsa de arroz y algodón de Chicago; ~ **School** *n* ECON escuela de Chicago *f*; ~ **Stock Exchange** *n* ECON Bolsa de Valores de Chicago *f*

chief *n* HRM jefe(-a) *m,f*; ~ **accountant** ACC contable jefe(-a) *m,f* (*Esp*), contador(a) jefe(-a) *m,f* (*AmL*),

jefe(-a) de contabilidad *m,f*, jefe(-a) de cuentas *m,f*; ~ **accounting officer** ACC director(a) de contabilidad *m,f*; ~ **assets** *n pl* STOCK activos principales *m pl*; ~ **buyer** S&M jefe(-a) de compras *m,f*; ~ **clerk** HRM contable principal *mf* (*Esp*), contador(a) principal *m,f* (*AmL*); ~ **economist** ECON, GEN COMM economista jefe(-a) *m,f*; ~ **editor** MEDIA jefe(-a) de redacción *m,f*; ~ **executive** HRM, MGMNT director(a) ejecutivo(-a) *m,f*; ~ **executive officer** *AmE* (*CEO*) HRM, MGMNT director(a) general *m,f* (*DG*), gerente general *mf*, jefe(-a) ejecutivo(-a) *m,f*, presidente(-a) ejecutivo(-a) *m,f*; ~ **financial officer** (*CFO*) HRM director(a) de finanzas *m,f*; ~ **immigration officer** (*CIO*) HRM jefe(-a) de inmigración *m,f*; ~ **information officer** (*CIO*) HRM director(a) general de información *m,f*, jefe(-a) de información *m,f*; ~ **inspector** (*CI*) HRM inspector(a) jefe(-a) *m,f*; ~ **operating officer** (*COO*) HRM director(a) general *m,f* (*DG*), director(a) general de operaciones *m,f*; ~ **place of business** GEN COMM negocio de primer orden *m*; ~ **of staff** HRM jefe(-a) de personal *m,f*; ~ **sub** *BrE* *jarg* (*chief sub-editor*) MEDIA *print* editor(a) en jefe(-a) adjunto(-a) *m,f*; ~ **sub-editor** *BrE* (*chief sub*) MEDIA *print* editor(a) en jefe(-a) adjunto(-a) *m,f*; ~ **supervisor** GEN COMM, HRM supervisor(a) en jefe *m,f*; ~ **traffic controller** HRM, TRANSP jefe(-a) de control de tráfico *m,f*; ~ **value** (*cv*) GEN COMM valor principal *m*

Chief: ~ **Commissioner** *n* *BrE* HRM *police* ≈ Director General de la Policía *m*; ~ **Secretary to the Treasury** *n* *BrE* ECON Secretario(-a) Jefe(-a) del Tesoro *m,f*; ~ **of Staff** *n* POL *military* Jefe(-a) del Estado Mayor *m,f*

child¹: ~~-centered *AmE*, ~~-centred *BrE* *adj* WEL concebido en función del niño

child² *n* GEN COMM hijo *m*; ~ **allowance** *AmE* (*cf* child benefit *BrE*) ECON, WEL subsidio para familias con hijos *m*, asignación familiar *f*; ~ **benefit** *BrE* (*cf* child allowance *AmE*) ECON, WEL subsidio para familias con hijos *m*, asignación familiar *f*; ~ **care** WEL puericultura *f*; ~'s **deferred assurance** INS seguro dotal *m*; ~ **and dependent care credit** TAX deducción por niños y cargas familiares *f*; ~ **maintenance payment** LAW, TAX pago de la pensión alimenticia de los hijos *m*; ~ **tax credit** TAX deducción familiar por los hijos *f*

childcare: ~ **expense deduction** *n* TAX deducción por cargas familiares *f*; ~ **expenses** *n* TAX gastos por cuidado de menores *m pl*; ~ **facilities** *n pl* TAX, WEL instalaciones de atención infantil *f pl*

children: ~'s **court** *n* LAW Juzgado de Letras de Menores *m*

Chinese: ~ **money** *n* *BrE* *jarg* STOCK pago efectuado en valores; ~ **wall** *n* BANK *insider trading* pared china *f*; ~ **walls** *n pl* FIN *insider trading* intramuros *m pl*

chip *n* COMP chip *m*, microplaqueta *f*; ~~-based card COMP tarjeta con circuito de memoria *f*; ~ **card** COMP tarjeta con chip *f*

chipboard *n* GEN COMM cartón ordinario *m*

chlorofluorocarbon *n* (*CFC*) ENVIR clorofluorocarbono *m* (*CFC*)

choice *n* GEN COMM elección *f*; ~ **variable** ACC, ECON elección variable *f*

chose *n* LAW objeto en propiedad; ~ **in action** LAW derecho de acción *m*

Christmas: ~ **bonus** *n* HRM paga extraordinaria de Navidad *f*

chronic: ~ **unemployment** *n* ECON, HRM, WEL desempleo crónico *m*

chunk: ~ **a project** *phr* FIN despedazar un proyecto, GEN COMM repartir un proyecto, MGMNT dividir un proyecto

churn *vt* BANK *broker* agitar, revolver, FIN, STOCK inflar el mercado, inflar la bolsa

c/i *abbr* (*certificate of insurance*) INS certificado de seguro *m*

CI *abbr* (*chief inspector*) HRM inspector(a) jefe(-a) *m,f*

CIB *abbr* (*Chartered Institute of Bankers, cf AIB AmE*) BANK instituto británico de banqueros

CIC *abbr* (*Committee for Industrial Cooperation*) IND comité de cooperación industrial *m*

CICA *abbr* (*Canadian Institute of Chartered Accountants*) ACC instituto canadiense de contables registrados

CIE *abbr* IMP/EXP (*Committee on Invisible Exports*), comité de exportaciones invisibles, TRANSP (*captain's imperfect entry*) declaración defectuosa del capitán *f*

CI&F¹ *abbr* (*cost, insurance and freight*) IMP/EXP, INS, TRANSP CI&F (*coste, seguro y flete Esp, costo, seguro y flete AmL*)

CI&F²: ~ **contract** *n* IMP/EXP contrato con coste, seguro y flete *m*; ~ **landed** *n* IMP/EXP CIF desembarcado *m*

CIF&C *abbr* (*cost, insurance, freight and commission*) IMP/EXP, INS, TRANSP coste, seguro, flete y comisión *m* (*Esp*), costo, seguro, flete y comisión *m* (*AmL*)

CIF&I *abbr* (*cost, insurance, freight and interest*) IMP/EXP, INS, TRANSP coste, seguro, flete e interés *m* (*Esp*), costo, seguro, flete e interés *m* (*AmL*)

CIFAS *abbr BrE* (*Credit Industry Fraud Avoidance System*) FIN sistema de prevención de fraudes en el sector de créditos *m*

CIFC&E *abbr* (*cost, insurance, freight, commission and exchange*) IMP/EXP, INS coste, seguro, flete, comisión y cambio *m* (*Esp*), costo, seguro, flete, comisión y cambio *m* (*AmL*)

CIFC&I *abbr* (*cost, insurance, freight, commission and interest*) IMP/EXP coste, seguro, flete, comisión e intereses *m* (*Esp*), costo, seguro, flete, comisión e intereses *m* (*AmL*)

CIFI&E *abbr* (*cost, insurance, freight, interest and exchange*) IMP/EXP, INS, TRANSP coste, seguro, flete, interés y cambio *m* (*Esp*), costo, seguro, flete, interés y cambio *m* (*AmL*)

CIM *abbr* COMP, IND (*computer-integrated manufacture*) fabricación integrada por computador *f* (*AmL*), fabricación integrada por computadora *f* (*AmL*), fabricación integrada por ordenador *f* (*Esp*), (*computer-integrated manufacturing*) producción integrada por computador *f* (*AmL*), producción integrada por computadora *f* (*AmL*), producción integrada por ordenador *f* (*Esp*)

Cincinnatti: ~ **Stock Exchange** *n* STOCK Bolsa de Valores de Cincinnatti *f*

CIO *abbr* GEN COMM *AmE* (*Congress of Industrial Organizations*) congreso de organizaciones profesionales, HRM (*chief immigration officer*) jefe(-a) de inmigración *m,f*, (*chief information officer*) director(a) general de información *m,f*, jefe(-a) de información *m,f*

CIP *abbr* (*carriage and insurance paid*) IMP/EXP, TRANSP flete y seguro pagados, porte y seguro pagados

cipher *n* COMMS *coded message* cifra *f*; ~ **code** COMP código cifrado *m*

CIR *abbr* (*cage inventory record*) TRANSP registro de inventario de cajas jaula *m*

circle *n* GEN COMM *business, political* círculo *m*; ◆ **to come full** ~ GEN COMM volver al punto de partida

circuit *n* COMP circuito *m*, LAW *for judges* distrito judicial *m*; ~ **breaker mechanism** COMP mecanismo de sistema automatizado *m*; ~ **terminating equipment** COMP equipo de conmutación de circuitos *m*; ~ **working** TRANSP funcionamiento del circuito *m*

circular *n* ADMIN, COMMS circular *f*; ~ **calculations** TAX cálculos circulares *m pl*; ~ **flow** ECON flujo circular *m*; ~ **letter** ADMIN, COMMS circular *f*; ~ **migration** ECON *population* migración circular *f*

circulate *vt* COMMS *information, news* divulgar

circulating: ~ **capital** *n* BANK, ECON, FIN, GEN COMM capital circulante *m*; ~ **medium** *n* FIN instrumento de cambio *m*

circulation *n* ECON, GEN COMM, MEDIA *of newspapers* circulación *f*; ~ **breakdown** GEN COMM colapso de circulación *m*; ~ **department** MEDIA *print* departamento de circulación *m*; ~ **manager** MEDIA *print* jefe(-a) de circulación *m,f*

circumflex *n* COMP, MEDIA circunflejo *m*

circumstances *n pl* GEN COMM circunstancias *f pl*; ◆ **under the** ~ GEN COMM en estas circunstancias

circumstancial: ~ **evidence** *n* LAW conjetura *f*, prueba circunstancial *f*

CIS *abbr* (*Chartered Institute of Secretaries*) HRM colegio de secretarios

citation *n* LAW, PATENTS plazamiento judicial *m*, citación *f*, citación judicial *f*

cite *vt* LAW, PATENTS citar, emplazar judicialmente

citizen *n* POL ciudadano(-a) *m,f*; ~ **bonds** *n pl* STOCK bono emitido por las colectividades locales

Citizen: ~**'s Charter** *n* POL Carta de Derechos del Ciudadano *f*

Citizens: ~ **Advice Bureau** *n BrE* (*CAB*) WEL organización voluntaria británica que asesora legal o financieramente

citizenship *n* POL ciudadanía *f*

city: ~ **center** *AmE*, ~ **centre** *BrE n* GEN COMM centro de la ciudad *m*; ~ **hall** *n AmE* (*cf town hall BrE*) GEN COMM, POL Ayuntamiento *m*

City: the ~ *n BrE* ACC, BANK, FIN, STOCK *London* la City *f*; ~ **Grant** *n BrE* GEN COMM, POL *government aid* subsidio municipal *m*; ~ **and Guilds Institute** *n* (*CGI*) WEL cuerpo de evaluadores de exámenes de carácter técnico o manual

civil: ~ **action** *n* LAW demanda legal *f*, proceso civil *m*; ~ **assessment** *n* TAX gravamen municipal *m*; ~ **aviation** *n* ECON, TRANSP aviación civil *f*; ~ **code** *n* GEN COMM, LAW código civil *m*; ~ **commotion** *n* (*CC*) INS conmoción civil *f*; ~ **engineer** *n* IND ingeniero(-a) industrial *m,f*; ~ **law** *n* LAW derecho civil *m*; ~ **lawyer** *n* BANK, GEN COMM, LAW ≈ abogado(-a) civilista *m,f*; ~ **penalty** *n* LAW multa civil *f*; ~ **rights** *n pl* LAW, POL, WEL derechos civiles *m pl*; ~ **riots** *n* POL alborotos populares *m pl*, revuelta popular *f*; ~ **servant** *n* HRM funcionario(-a) *m,f*, funcionario(-a) público(-a) *m,f*; ~ **status** *n* LAW registro civil *m*; ~ **wrong** *n* LAW ilícito civil *m*

Civil: ~ **Aeronautics Board** *n AmE* (*CAB*) (*cf Civil Aviation Authority BrE*) TRANSP consejo aeronáutico civil; ~ **Aviation Authority** *n BrE* (*CAA*) (*cf Civil*

Aeronautics Board AmE) TRANSP consejo de aviación civil; **~ Rights Act** *n AmE* ECON, LAW *of 1964* Ley de los Derechos Civiles *f*; **~ Service** *n BrE* (*CS*) POL administración pública *f*; **~ Service Commission** *n BrE* (*CSC*) POL comisión británica de funcionarios

civilian: **~ employment** *n* HRM empleo civil *m*

ck *abbr* (*cask*) TRANSP tonel *m*

CKD *abbr* (*completely knocked down*) TRANSP completamente desmontado

cl *abbr* (*centiliter AmE, centilitre BrE*) GEN COMM cl (*centilitro*)

c/l *abbr* (*craft loss*) TRANSP pérdida de la embarcación *f*

CL *abbr* INS (*Corporation of Lloyd's*) asociación de aseguradoras y agencias de seguros, TRANSP (*continuous liner*) buque de pasaje en servicio continuo

claim¹ *n* GEN COMM demanda *f*, reclamación *f*, HRM *trade union request made to employer* pretensión *f*, LAW reclamo *m*, TAX *for relief* petición *f*; **~ for compensation** LAW reclamación de compensación *f*; **~ for damages** LAW demanda por daños *f*; **~ for indemnification** INS reclamación de indemnización *f*; **~ for refund** TAX solicitud de devolución *f*; **~ form** INS formulario de reclamación *m*; **~ letter** ACC, ADMIN, BANK carta de reclamación *f*; **~ notice** BANK, HRM, IND aviso de reclamación *m*; **~ paid** INS siniestro pagado *m*; **~ payment** INS pago de la reclamación *m*; **~ settlement** INS liquidación de daños *f*, liquidación de siniestro *f*

claim² *vt* GEN COMM, INS, LAW, TAX demandar, reclamar; ♦ **~ an amount** TAX exigir una cantidad; **~ as a dependant** TAX reclamar como carga familiar; **~ damages** INS exigir indemnización por daños, LAW reclamar daños y perjuicios; **~ a deduction** TAX solicitar una deducción; **~ personal exemption** TAX reclamar una exención personal; **~ immunity from tax** TAX alegar exención fiscal

claim against *vt* LAW reclamar a

claimant *n* GEN COMM, LAW demandante *mf*, reclamante *mf*

claims: **~ adjuster** *n* INS ajustador(a) de reclamaciones *m,f*; **~ adjustment** *n* INS ajuste de daños *m*; **~ department** *n* INS departamento de reclamaciones *m*; **~ of different categories** *n pl* PATENTS variedad de demandas *f*; **~ expenses** *n pl* INS gastos de liquidación *m pl*; **~ inspector** *n* HRM inspector(a) de quejas *m,f*; **~ and liabilities** *n pl* ACC demandas y obligaciones *f pl*; **~ manager** *n* HRM director(a) de reclamaciones *m,f*, jefe(-a) de reclamaciones *m,f*; **~ payment** *n* INS pago de reclamaciones *m*; **~ prevention** *n* INS prevención de reclamaciones *f*; **~ procedure** *n* INS procedimiento de reclamación *m*; **~ reserve** *n* INS reserva para siniestros *f*; **~ of the same category** *n pl* PATENTS demandas del mismo tipo *f pl*; **~ settlement fund** *n* INS fondo de liquidación de siniestros *m*

clamp: **~-on** *adj* COMMS en espera

clarification *n* GEN COMM, MGMNT aclaración *f*

clarify *vt* GEN COMM, MGMNT *policy* aclarar

class *n* GEN COMM clase *f*, *type* tipo *m*, *category* categoría *f*; **~ action** LAW acción de grupo en la que se hacen valer individualmente intereses compartidos por varios sujetos; **~ A share** FIN, STOCK acción de clase A *f*; **~ of business** TAX clase de negocio *f*; **~ of construction** INS clase de construcción *f*; **~ of employment** TAX clase de empleo *f*; **~ of insurance** INS clase de seguro *f*; **~ magazine** S&M revista de clase *f*; **~ object** GEN COMM

objeto de clase *m*; **~ of options** STOCK clase de opciones *f*; **~ of payments** TAX clase de pagos *f*; **~ of property** PROP, TAX clase de propiedad *f*; **~ of risk** INS categoría del riesgo *f*; **~ savings theory** ECON *econometrics* teoría de los tipos de ahorro *f*; **~ war** ECON, POL lucha de clases *f*

classic: **~ example** *n* GEN COMM ejemplo clásico *m*; **~ school** *n* ECON, GEN COMM escuela clásica *f*

classical: **~ dichotomy** *n* ECON dicotomía clásica *f*; **~ economics** *n* ECON *1752–82* economía clásica *f*; **~ model** *n* ECON modelo clásico *m*; **~ savings theory** *n* ECON *econometrics* teoría clásica del ahorro *f*; **~ school of economics** *n* ECON escuela clásica de economía *f*

classification *n* ACC, ADMIN, ECON, GEN COMM clasificación *f*; **~ of accounts** ACC clasificación de cuentas *f*; **~ by object** GEN COMM clasificación por objetivos *f*; **~ certificate** TRANSP certificado de clasificación *m*; **~ of risks** INS clasificación de los riesgos *f*; **~ society** GEN COMM, TRANSP sociedad de clasificación de buques *f*

classified: **~ ad** *n* MEDIA, S&M anuncio por palabras *m*; **~ advertisement** *n* MEDIA, S&M anuncio por palabras *m*; **~ directory** *n* S&M guía clasificada *f*; **~ display advertising** *n* S&M publicidad de exposición clasificada *f*; **~ return** *n* TAX declaración clasificada *f*; **~ stock** *n* STOCK acciones clasificadas *f pl*

classify *vt* ACC, ADMIN, ECON, GEN COMM clasificar

clause *n* GEN COMM, HRM, INS, LAW cláusula *f*

claused: **~ bill of health** *n* TRANSP *shipping* patente de sanidad sucia *f*; **~ bill of lading** *n* ECON, IMP/EXP, TRANSP *shipping* conocimiento de embarque sucio *m*, conocimiento de embarque con cláusula *m*

clawback *n* FIN, TAX *of capital gains tax relief* desgravación por devolución de impuestos *f*

clay: **~ ore** *n* ENVIR, IND mineral de arcilla *m*

Clayton: **~ Act** *n AmE* ECON, LAW *1914* Ley de Clayton *f*

Cld *abbr* (*cleared*) BANK compensado

clean¹ *adj* ACC sin observaciones, sin salvedades, ECON *international trade*, ENVIR limpio, GEN COMM, STOCK sin garantía escrita; **~ assessed** TAX *return* totalmente gravado; **not ~ assessed** TAX *return* no gravado por completo

clean²: **~ acceptance** *n* BANK aceptación absoluta *f*, aceptación directa *f*; **~ bill** *n* ECON, FIN letra limpia *f*; **~ bill of health** *n* GEN COMM, WEL certificado médico positivo de no padecer enfermedad *f*, patente de sanidad limpia *f*; **~ bill of lading** *n* ECON, IMP/EXP, TRANSP conocimiento de embarque limpio *m*, conocimiento de embarque neto *m*, conocimiento de embarque sin restricciones *m*; **~ float** *n* ECON *international* flotación limpia *f*; **~ hands** *n pl* GEN COMM, LAW manos limpias *f pl*, conducta intachable *f*; **~ letter of credit** *n* BANK, FIN carta de crédito abierta *f*, carta de crédito simple *f*; **~ opinion** *n infrml* ACC opinión clara *f*, opinión favorable *f*, opinión limpia *f*; **~ payment** *n* BANK, FIN pago simple *m*; **~ product** *n* ENVIR producto limpio *m*; **~ record** *n* LAW informe sin correcciones *m* (*Esp*), reporte sin correciones *m* (*AmL*); **~ report of findings** *n* TRANSP informe limpio de los datos *m* (*Esp*), reporte limpio de los datos *m* (*AmL*); **~ signature** *n* GEN COMM firma clara y sin alteraciones *f*; **~ technology** *n* ENVIR tecnología limpia *f*

clean up *vt* ENVIR limpiar

cleaning: **~-up operation** *n* ENVIR operación de limpieza *f*

cleanup: ~ **campaign** n ENVIR campaña de limpieza f; ~ **fund** n INS fondo de restablecimiento m

clear[1]: ~ **of debts** adj ACC, BANK, FIN, GEN COMM libre de deudas

clear[2]: ~ **days** n pl GEN COMM, TRANSP días completos m pl; ~ **income** n ECON, TAX ingreso neto m, renta neta f; ~ **loss** n FIN pérdida líquida f; ~ **profit** n FIN ganancia neta f; ~ **thinking** n GEN COMM razonamiento lúcido m, MGMNT razonamiento inductivo m; ~ **title** n LAW título de propiedad limpio m, título limpio m

clear[3] vt BANK cheque compensar, cobrar, funds liquidar, COMP wipe out, erase borrar, S&M clear, STOCK securities liquidar, TRANSP transhipment permit extender; ♦ ~ **the market** STOCK equilibrar el mercado

clearance n BANK, ECON, GEN COMM certificado de despacho m, autorización f, S&M liquidación f, realización f; ~ **agent** HRM customs, IMP/EXP agente de despacho de aduanas mf; ~ **of cargo goods** IMP/EXP, TRANSP despacho de carga de mercancías m; ~ **of debris** INS remoción de escombro f; ~ **group** (CG) TRANSP grupo de despacho m; ~ **inwards** IMP/EXP, TRANSP despacho de entrada m; ~ **outward of a vessel** IMP/EXP, TRANSP despacho de un buque hacia el exterior m; ~ **outwards** IMP/EXP, TRANSP despacho de salida m; ~ **papers** IMP/EXP, TRANSP certificado de autorización de salida de buque m; ~ **sale** S&M liquidación f, saldo m; ~ **of ship** IMP/EXP, TRANSP despacho de barco m

cleared[1] adj (Cld) BANK compensado; ~ **without examination** (CWE) IMP/EXP desaduanado sin inspección

cleared[2]: ~ **check** AmE, ~ **cheque** BrE n BANK, FIN cheque compensado m; ~ **reject** n TAX denegación despachada f

clearer n infrml BANK banco adscrito a la Cámara de Compensación bancaria de Londres

clearing[1] n BANK compensación f, ECON international trade liquidación de balances f, FIN of debt compensación bancaria f; ~ **account** ECON international trade cuenta de compensación f; ~ **agent** BANK agente de compensación mf; ~ **agreement** ECON international trade convenio de compensación m, GEN COMM convenio de liquidación m; ~ **balance statement** BANK estado de cuentas de compensación m; ~ **bank** BANK, FIN banco adscrito a la Cámara de Compensación bancaria de Londres; ~ **center** AmE, ~ **centre** BrE BANK centro de compensación m; ~ **corporation** BANK, STOCK sociedad de acciones cotizadas en bolsa f; ~ **day** BANK día de compensación m; ~ **entry** BANK entrada en compensación f; ~ **house** BANK, ECON, FIN, STOCK cámara de compensación f, casa de liquidación f; ~ **house funds** n pl BANK fondos de una cámara de compensación m pl; ~ **market** ECON mercado de liquidación m; ~ **member** FIN, STOCK currency options miembro de la cámara compensatoria m, miembro de la cámara de compensación m; ~ **position** BANK posición de compensación f; ~ **process** BANK operación de compensación f; ~ **report** BANK informe de liquidación m (Esp), reporte de liquidación m (AmL); ~ **statement** BANK estado de la cámara de compensación m; ~ **system** BANK, STOCK régimen clearing m, sistema de compensación m

Clearing: ~ **House Automatic Payments System** n (CHAPS) BANK sistema de pagos automáticos de compensación m; ~ **House Interbank Payment System** (CHIPS) n STOCK sistema de compensación y liquidación en el que intervienen más de 130 bancos, trabajando con divisas y Eurodólares

CLECAT abbr (European Communities Freight Forwarders Association) TRANSP Asociación de Transportistas de las Comunidades Europeas f

clerical: ~ **error** n ACC, ADMIN error de oficina m, error del personal de oficina m; ~ **personnel** n ADMIN, HRM personal de oficina m; ~ **staff** n ADMIN, HRM personal de oficina m; ~ **work** n ADMIN, HRM trabajo de oficina m; ~ **work measurement** n (CWM) ADMIN, HRM medición del trabajo de oficina f (MTO); ~ **worker** n HRM trabajador(a) de oficina m,f

clerk n HRM oficinista mf, empleado(-a) m,f

click vt COMP key, mouse button teclear

client n BANK, GEN COMM, MEDIA, S&M of advertising agency cliente mf; ~ **account** ACC cuenta del cliente f, cuenta de la cliente f; ~ **base** S&M base de clientes f; ~ **card** GEN COMM tarjeta de cliente f; ~ **firm** S&M firma del cliente f, firma de la cliente f; ~**-led marketing policy** S&M política de marketing dirigida por el consumidor f; ~**'s previous record** ACC, BANK, FIN antecedentes crediticios m pl; ~ **ledger** ACC mayor de clientes m

Client: ~ **Agreement Letter** n FIN Carta de Acuerdo del Cliente f

clientele n GEN COMM clientela f

client/server n COMP cliente/servidor m

climb 1. vt GEN COMM trepar; ♦ ~ **the promotion ladder** HRM subir en el escalafón; **2.** vi ECON increase aumentar

clip: ~**-on unit** n (COU) TRANSP refrigerador portátil m

clipping n BANK, MEDIA from newspaper recorte m; ~ **service** S&M servicio de documentación m

cloakroom n BrE (cf restroom AmE) LEIS, TRANSP guardarropa m

clock: ~ **card** n HRM, IND ficha de control de asistencia f; ~ **rate** n COMP velocidad de reloj f; ~ **signal** n COMP señal de reloj f

clock in vi HRM, IND checar la tarjeta (AmL), fichar la entrada (Esp)

clock off vi BrE (cf punch out AmE) HRM, IND checar la tarjeta (AmL), fichar la salida (Esp)

clock on vi BrE (cf punch in AmE) HRM, IND checar la tarjeta (AmL), fichar la entrada (Esp)

clock out vi HRM, IND checar la tarjeta (AmL), fichar la salida (Esp)

clocking: ~**-in** n HRM, IND registro de la hora de entrada m

clone[1] n COMP, GEN COMM clon m

clone[2] vt COMP, GEN COMM clonar

close[1] adj GEN COMM cooperation, relationship estrecho; ♦ **in** ~ **contact** GEN COMM en estrecho contacto

close[2] n GEN COMM cierre m, STOCK cierre m, final de la sesión m; ~ **of business** ACC, BANK, FIN, GEN COMM cierre de operaciones m, cierre del negocio m; ~ **company** BrE GEN COMM sociedad controlada por un máximo de cinco personas; ~ **corporation plan** BrE STOCK deceased stockholder plan de sociedad cerrada m; ~ **correlation** MATH correlación exacta f; ~**-down** MEDIA broadcast cierre de la emisión m; ~ **examination** GEN COMM examen atento m; ~ **of the market** ACC, BANK, FIN, GEN COMM, STOCK cierre del mercado m; ~**-out price** GEN COMM cambio de liquidación m

close³ *vt* GEN COMM cerrar; ◆ ~ **a deal** STOCK cerrar un acuerdo; ~ **the gap** FIN acabar con el déficit; ~ **a position** FIN, STOCK cerrar una posición; ~ **a sale** S&M cerrar una venta

close down 1. *vt* GEN COMM *companies, branches* cerrar; **2.** *vi* GEN COMM *companies, branches* cerrar

close out *vt* GEN COMM liquidar

closed: ~ **account** *n* ACC, BANK, FIN cuenta cancelada *f*, cuenta cerrada *f*, cuenta saldada *f*; ~ **circuit** *n* COMP circuito cerrado *m*; ~ **corporation** *n* AmE ECON compañía cerrada *f*; ~ **economy** *n* ECON economía cerrada *f*; ~~**end fund** *n* FIN *investment* fondo con número de acciones fijo *f*; ~~**end investment company** *n* (CEIC) FIN sociedad de inversión cerrada *f*; ~~**end investment fund** *n* FIN, STOCK fondo de inversión cerrado *f*; ~~**end investment trust** *n* FIN, STOCK sociedad inversora de capital limitado *f*; ~~**end management company** *n* FIN, MGMNT sociedad gestora de capital limitado *f*; ~~**end mortgage** *n* BANK, PROP hipoteca limitada *f*, hipoteca cerrada *f*; ~~**end mutual fund** *n* AmE STOCK sociedad de inversión mobiliaria de capital fijo *f*; ~ **height** *n* TRANSP *of fork-lift* altura cerrada *f*; ~ **population** *n* ECON población cerrada *f*; ~ **position** *n* FIN, STOCK posición cerrada *f*; ~ **question** *n* GEN COMM, S&M *market research* pregunta cerrada *f*; ~ **season** *n* MEDIA *broadcast* temporada baja *f*; ~ **shop** *n* HRM monopolio sindical *m*; ~ **stock** *n* S&M venta de artículos sin repuestos *f*; ~ **union** *n* HRM sindicato de afiliación restringida o cerrada

closely: ~~**connected profession** *n* HRM profesión estrechamente conectada *f*; ~~**held corporation** *n* ECON, STOCK compañía estrechamente controlada *f*

closing *n* GEN COMM cierre *m*; ~ **agreement** AmE TAX convenio final *m*; ~ **balance** ACC, BANK, FIN balance de cierre *m*, saldo de cierre *m*; ~ **bid** GEN COMM oferta definitiva *f*; ~ **the books** ACC, BANK, FIN, GEN COMM cierre de libros *m*; ~ **cost** PROP *real estate* gastos de cierre *m pl*, gastos de formalización *m pl*; ~ **costs** *n pl* BANK, FIN costes de cierre *m pl* (Esp), costos de cierre *m pl* (AmL); ~ **date** GEN COMM, PROP fecha de cierre *f*; ~~**down costs** GEN COMM costes de clausura *m pl* (Esp), costes de liquidación *m pl* (Esp), costos de clausura *m pl* (AmL), costos de liquidación *m pl* (AmL); ~ **entry** ACC asiento de cierre *m*; ~ **inventory** ACC inventario de cierre *m*, inventario final *m*; ~ **price** FIN, STOCK cotización de cierre *f*; ~ **purchase** STOCK compra al cierre *f*; ~ **purchase transaction** STOCK transacción de compra al cierre *f*; ~ **quotation** FIN, STOCK cotización de cierre *f*; ~ **range** STOCK variación al cierre *f*; ~ **rate method** BrE (cf current rate method AmE) ACC *currency translation* método del cambio de cierre *m*, método del salario real *m*; ~ **sale transaction** STOCK transacción de venta al cierre *f*; ~ **session** STOCK sesión de cierre *f*; ~ **statement** PROP saldo de cierre *m*; ~ **stock** STOCK situación de la bolsa al cierre *f*; ~ **of the Stock Exchange** ACC, FIN, GEN COMM, STOCK cierre de la Bolsa *m*; ~ **time** GEN COMM horario de cierre *m*; ~ **trade** STOCK negociación tras el cierre *f*, operación al cierre *f*; ~ **transaction** STOCK transacción de cierre *f*; ◆ **at** ~ STOCK al cierre

closure *n* GEN COMM cierre *m*

clothing *n* IND prenda de vestir *f*

Clothing: ~ **Export Council** *n* BrE (CEC) IMP/EXP consejo de exportaciones de ropa

cloud: ~ **on title** *n* AmE PROP imperfección del título *f*

CLSB *abbr* (Committee of London and Scottish Bankers) BANK comité de banqueros londinenses y escoceses *m*

club: ~ **class** *n* LEIS, TRANSP clase club *f*; ~ **good** *n* ECON conjunto de bienes públicos y privados *m*

Club: ~ **of Rome** *n* ECON 1968 onwards Club de Roma *m*

cluster *n* GEN COMM ramillete *m*; ~ **analysis** S&M *market research* análisis de grupos *m pl*; ~ **controller** COMP controlador(a) de grupo *m,f*; ~ **of countries** S&M agrupación de países *f*; ~ **housing** PROP conjunto residencial *m*; ~ **sample** S&M *market research* muestra por segmentos *f*, muestra por universos *f*; ~ **sampling** S&M *market research* muestreo por segmentos *m*, muestreo por universos *m*

clustering *n* S&M agrupación *f*

cm *abbr* (centimeter AmE, centimetre BrE) GEN COMM cm (centímetro)

CM *abbr* ECON, POL (Common Market) mercado común *m*, TRANSP (condition monitoring) control del estado de las mercancías *m*

CMA *abbr* (cash management account) BANK, FIN cuenta de administración de fondos *f*

cmdty *abbr* (commodity) GEN COMM bien *m*, bien de consumo *m*, mercancía *f*, producto básico *m*, producto de consumo popular *m*

CME¹ *abbr* (Chicago Mercantile Exchange) STOCK bolsa mercantil de Chicago

CME²: ~ **Clearing House** *n* STOCK cámara de compensación de la bolsa de comercio de Chicago

CMEA *abbr obs* (Council for Mutual Economic Aid) ECON Consejo de Asistencia Mutua Económica *m*

CMO *abbr* (collateralized mortgage obligation) BANK, FIN obligación hipotecaria con garantía prendaria *f*, obligación hipotecaria garantizada *f*

CMS *abbr* (World Bank Capital Markets System) STOCK Sistema de Mercados de Capital del Banco Mundial *m*

CMSA *abbr* AmE (Consolidated Metropolitan Statistical Area) POL área estadística metropolitana consolidada

CN *abbr* (credit note) ACC, BANK, FIN, GEN COMM nota de abono *f*, nota de crédito *f*

C/N *abbr* INS (cover note) aviso de cobertura *m*, TRANSP (consignment note) hoja de embarque *f*

cnee *abbr* (consignee) TRANSP consignatario *m,f*

cnmt *abbr* (consignment) TRANSP remesa *f*

CNS *abbr* BrE (continuous net settlement) STOCK liquidación neta continua *f*

co *abbr* (cash order) GEN COMM pedido al contado *m*

c/o *abbr* COMMS, GEN COMM (care of) c/d (casa de), IMP/EXP (certificate of origin) certificado de origen *m*

Co.¹ *abbr* (company) GEN COMM Cía (compañía)

Co.²: **and** ~ *phr* GEN COMM y compañía

CO *abbr* (Certification Officer) HRM Director(a) de Certificaciones *m,f*

coal *n* ECON, ENVIR, IND, TRANSP carbón *m*; ~ **carrier** TRANSP buque carbonero *m*; ~ **deposit** ENVIR depósito de carbón *m*; ~~**fired power station** IND planta generadora alimentada por carbón *f*; ~ **industry** ECON, IND industria del carbón *f*; ~ **mine** IND mina de carbón *f*; ~ **mining** ENVIR, IND extracción de carbón *f*, minería del carbón *f*; ~ **propulsion** TRANSP propulsión a carbón *f*; ~ **reserve** ENVIR reserva de carbón *f*

coalition *n* POL *government* coalición *f*; ~ **alliance** POL acuerdo de coalición *m*; ~ **government** POL gobierno de coalición *m*

coarse: ~ **screen** n S&M trama gruesa f

Coase: ~ **theorem** n ECON *national income* teorema de Coase m

coastal: ~ **pollution** n ENVIR contaminación de las costas f; ~ **trading** n TRANSP comercio costero m

coaster n TRANSP barco de cabotaje m, buque costero m

coastguard n (*CG*) HRM guardacostas mf

coasting n TRANSP cabotaje m; ~ **broker** TRANSP agente de cabotaje mf; ~ **trade** TRANSP comercio de cabotaje m

coaxial: ~ **cable** n COMP *hardware* cable coaxial m (*Esp*), cable coaxil m (*AmL*)

Cobb: ~ **Douglas production function** n ECON función de producción de Cobb-Douglas f

COBOL abbr (*Common Business Oriented Language*) COMP COBOL (*lenguaje común orientado a la gestión y los negocios*)

Cobweb: ~ **Theorem** n ECON teorema de la Telaraña m

C/OC abbr (*certificate of origin and consignment*) IMP/EXP certificado de origen y consignación m

Cocom abbr (*Coordinating Committee for Multilateral Export Controls*) IMP/EXP Comité de Coordinación del Control Multilateral de las Exportaciones m

COD abbr (*cash on delivery*) GEN COMM entrega contra reembolso

code n GEN COMM código m, norma f; ~ **of accounts** ACC código de cuentas m; ~ **address** COMP dirección codificada f; ~ **of arbitration** STOCK código de arbitraje m; ~ **box** IMP/EXP casilla del código f; ~ **check** COMP comprobador de código m; ~ **of conduct** GEN COMM código deontológico m; ~ **of conduct on ships** TRANSP código de conducta a bordo m; ~ **element** COMP clave f; ~ **of ethics** GEN COMM código de ética m; ~ **line** COMP línea de código f; ~ **name** COMP nombre codificado m; ~ **of practice** GEN COMM código de práctica m, LAW código de conducta m; ~ **of procedure** STOCK código de procedimiento m; ~ **set** COMP conjunto de código m; ~ **sheet** COMP hoja de programación f

codec n COMP codificador-descodificador m

coded: ~ **data entry** n COMP introducción de datos codificados f

codetermination n HRM codeterminación f, cogestión f; ~ **rights** n pl STOCK derechos de cogestión m pl

code-UN n IMP/EXP código de la ONU m

codicil n LAW *in will* codicilo m

coding n COMP *programming language* codificación f; ~ **of accounts** ACC *identification* codificación de cuentas f; ~ **error** COMP error de codificación m; ~ **manual** ACC manual de codificación m; ~ **system** ACC sistema de codificación m

co-director n BANK, HRM, MGMNT codirector(a) m,f

co-ed abbr (*coeducational*) WEL mixto

coeducational[1] adj (*co-ed*) WEL mixto

coeducational[2]: ~ **high school** n WEL instituto mixto de enseñanza secundaria m

coefficient n MATH coeficiente m; ~ **of association** HRM coeficiente de asociación m; ~ **of contingency** BANK, ECON, STOCK coeficiente de contingencia m; ~ **of correlation** MATH coeficiente de correlación m; ~ **of determination** MATH coeficiente de determinación m; ~ **of multiple correlation** MATH coeficiente de correlación múltiple m; ~ **of multiple determination** MATH coeficiente de determinación múltiple m; ~ **of variation** MATH coeficiente de variación m

coemption n FIN, GEN COMM acaparamiento de toda la oferta m

Coffee: ~, **Sugar and Cocoa Exchange Inc. of New York** n STOCK mercado de productos de Nueva York que opera con contratos de futuros y con opciones

cofferdam n TRANSP *shipping* dique de presa m

co-finance vt BANK, ECON, FIN cofinanciar

co-financing n BANK, ECON, FIN cofinanciación f

cognate: ~ **disciplines** n pl WEL disciplinas análogas f pl

cognition n GEN COMM, MGMNT cognición f, conocimiento m, entendimiento m, percepción f

cognitive: ~ **behavior** AmE, ~ **behaviour** BrE n S&M comportamiento cognitivo m; ~ **consonance** n ECON consonancia cognitiva f; ~ **dissonance** n ECON disonancia cognitiva f; ~ **ergonomics** n pl GEN COMM, HRM ergonomía cognitiva f

COGSA abbr (*Carriage of Goods by Sea Act*) LAW, TRANSP Ley de Transporte Marítimo f

cohesion n GEN COMM cohesión f; ~ **fund** ECON fondo de cohesión m

COI abbr BrE (*Central Office of Information*) POL oficina central británica de información

coin n GEN COMM moneda f; ~-**machine insurance** INS seguro de máquinas distribuidoras m; ~ **wrapper** BANK cartucho de monedas m

coinage n BANK, ECON acuñación f; ~ **system** ECON sistema de acuñación m

coincide vi GEN COMM, HRM coincidir

coincident: ~ **indicator** n ECON *econometrics* indicador coincidente m

coinsurance n INS coaseguro m, coseguro m

coinsured adj INS coasegurado

coinsurer n INS coasegurador(a) m,f

col abbr (*collision*) TRANSP colisión f

col. abbr (*column*) ACC *figures*, GEN COMM, MEDIA *printed matter* columna f

COLA abbr (*cost-of-living adjustment*) ECON ajuste del coste de vida m (*Esp*), ajuste del costo de vida m (*AmL*)

Colbertism n POL Colbertismo m

cold: ~ **boot** n COMP arranque en frío m; ~ **call** n S&M visita sin preparación previa f; ~ **calling** n S&M visitas o llamadas de venta sin cita; ~ **canvass** n GEN COMM campaña de mercadotecnia para captar nuevos clientes, S&M puerta a puerta f; ~ **mailing** n S&M *advertising* envío de folletas por correo sin preparación previa; ~ **start** n COMP, GEN COMM arranque en frío m; ~ **storage** n GEN COMM, IND, TRANSP almacenamiento refrigerado m; ~ **storage plant** n GEN COMM, IND planta frigorífica f; ~ **store** n GEN COMM, TRANSP almacén frigorífico m; ~ **store terminal** n TRANSP terminal refrigerada f; ~ **type** n ADMIN, MEDIA *printing* composición no tipográfica f

coll abbr (*collision*) TRANSP colisión f

collaborate vi GEN COMM, MGMNT colaborar

collaboration n GEN COMM, MGMNT colaboración f

collaborative adj GEN COMM, MGMNT *action* colaborador

collaborator n GEN COMM, MGMNT colaborador(a) m,f

collage n S&M collage m

collapse[1] n GEN COMM *prices* colapso m, desastre m, caída f, STOCK *market* caída en picado f, colapso m; ~ **of a currency** ECON, STOCK caída de una moneda f; ~ **of prices** ECON, STOCK caída fuerte de los precios f

collapse[2] *vi* GEN COMM *system* derrumbarse

collapsed *adj* GEN COMM *companies* hundido

collapsible: ~ **container** *n* (*coltainer*) TRANSP contenedor abatible *m*; ~ **company** *n* BrE (*cf collapsible corporation AmE*) TAX sociedad defraudadora de impuestos *f*; ~ **corporation** *n* AmE (*cf collapsible company BrE*) TAX sociedad defraudadora de impuestos *f*

collar *n* ECON banda *f*, STOCK contrato de cobertura *m*

collate *vt* GEN COMM, S&M cotejar

collated *adj* COMP intercalado

collateral[1] *adj* BANK, FIN, GEN COMM, MATH colateral

collateral[2] *n* BANK, ECON aval *m*, FIN colateral *m*, garantía subsidiaria *f*, GEN COMM *loans* garantía *f*, colateral *m*; ~ **acceptance** BANK, FIN aceptación colateral *f*; ~ **assignment** INS cesión de garantía *f*; ~ **bill** STOCK cuenta colateral *f*, cuenta con garantía prendaria *f*; ~ **loan** BrE (*cf Lombard loan AmE*) BANK empréstito con garantía *m*, préstamo con caución *m*, préstamo con garantía *m*; ~ **security** ECON, FIN garantía adicional *f*; ~ **trust bond** FIN, INS, STOCK bono con garantía prendaria *m*, bono de garantía colateral *m*; ~ **trust certificate** BANK, ECON, FIN, GEN COMM certificado con garantía de prenda *m*, certificado con garantía prendaria *m*

collateralize *vt* GEN COMM garantizar

collateralized: ~ **mortgage obligation** *n* (*CMO*) BANK, FIN obligación hipotecaria con garantía prendaria *f*, obligación hipotecaria garantizada *f*; ~ **preferred share** *n* STOCK, TAX acción preferente con garantía prendaria *f*

collating: ~ **sequence** *n* COMP secuencia de intercalación *f*

collation *n* COMP intercalación *f*

collator *n* COMP compaginadora de documentos *f*, interclasificadora *f*; ~ **code** COMP código de cotejo *m*; ~ **number** COMP número de cotejo *m*

colleague *n* HRM compañero(-a) *m,f*

collect[1]: ~ **call** *n* AmE (*cf reverse-charge call BrE*) COMMS *telephone* comunicación de cobro revertido *f*, conferencia a cobro revertido *f*, llamada a cobro revertido *f* (*Esp*), llamada pagadera en destino *f* (*AmL*)

collect[2] *vt* GEN COMM *statistics, information* reunir, recoger, STOCK *premium* cobrar; ♦ ~ **commission** INS cobrar comisión; ~ **a debt** FIN cobrar una deuda; ~ **payments** GEN COMM recaudar pagos; ~ **sums due** FIN recaudar las sumas vencidas; ~ **taxes** TAX recaudar impuestos

collected: ~ **and delivered** *adj* (*C&D*) GEN COMM recogido y entregado, *cheques, drafts* cobrado y entregado

collectible *adj* GEN COMM cobrable

collecting: ~ **agency** *n* BANK banco de cobro *m*; ~ **bank** *n* BANK banco de cobranzas *m*; ~ **charge** *n* GEN COMM cargo recaudador *m*

collection[1]: **for** ~ *adj* STOCK *security* al cobro

collection[2] *n* GEN COMM cobranza *f*, cobro *m*; ~ **of accounts** ACC cobro de cuentas *m*; ~ **against documents** BANK, ECON, FIN, GEN COMM cobro contra documentación *m*; ~ **agent** TAX inspector(a) recaudador(a) *m,f*; ~ **agreement** TAX acuerdo de cobro *m*; ~ **banker** BANK banquero(-a) de cobro de cobro *m,f*; ~ **of a bill** ACC, BANK cobro de un efecto *m*, cobro de una letra de cambio *m*; ~ **charge** GEN COMM cargo por

cobranza *m*, TRANSP gastos de cobro *m pl*; ~ **of checks** AmE, ~ **of cheques** BrE BANK, ECON, FIN, GEN COMM cobro de cheques *m*; ~ **costs** *n pl* GEN COMM costes de recaudación *m pl* (*Esp*), costos de recaudación *m pl* (*AmL*); ~ **of customs duties** IMP/EXP, TAX recaudación de derechos de aduanas *f*; ~ **letter** ACC, ADMIN, BANK, FIN carta de cobro *f*; ~ **on wheels** (*COW*) TRANSP recogida a domicilio *f*; **~-only check** AmE, **~-only cheque** BrE BANK, FIN cheque pagadero sólo por ventanilla *m*; ~ **payable** BANK, ECON, FIN, GEN COMM cobro a reembolsar *m*; ~ **of premiums** INS cobranza de primas *f*, cobro de primas *m*; ~ **of public money** TAX recaudación de dinero público *f*; ~ **ratio** ACC proporción de cuentas a cobrar *f*, ratio de cuentas a cobrar *m*; ~ **tariff** IMP/EXP arancel de recaudación *m*

Collection: ~ **Investigation Unit** *n* TAX Servicio de Investigación de la Recaudación *m*, Unidad de Investigación de la Recaudación *f*

collective[1] *adj* GEN COMM colectivo

collective[2]: ~ **accident insurance** *n* INS seguro colectivo de accidentes *m*; ~ **agreement** *n* HRM contrato colectivo *m*, convenio colectivo *m*; ~ **bargaining** *n* HRM convenio colectivo *m*, negociación colectiva *f*; ~ **bargaining agreement** *n* HRM, IND, LAW contrato colectivo *m*; ~ **conciliation** *n* BrE HRM conciliación colectiva *f*; ~ **dismissal** *n* BrE HRM despido colectivo *m*; ~ **good** *n* ECON, GEN COMM bien colectivo *m*; ~ **grievance procedure** *n* HRM, LAW procedimiento de agravio colectivo *m*; ~ **insurance** *n* INS seguro colectivo *m*; ~ **investment undertaking** *n* FIN portafolio colectivo de inversión *m*; ~ **investment undertaking other than of the closed-end type** *n* FIN portafolio colectivo de inversión abierto *m*; ~ **mark** *n* PATENTS marca colectiva *f*; ~ **pay agreement** *n* HRM acuerdo de pago colectivo *m*; ~ **severance pay** *n* HRM, WEL indemnización por despido colectivo *f*

collectively *adv* GEN COMM colectivamente

collectivization: ~ **of agriculture** *n* ECON colectivización de la agricultura *f*

collector *n* GEN COMM cobrador(a) *m,f*, colector(a) *m,f*, HRM *customs* cobrador(a) *m,f*; ~ **of customs** HRM, IMP/EXP administrador(a) de aduanas *m,f*; **~'s office** IMP/EXP, TAX oficina de recaudación *f*, oficina recaudadora *f*; ~ **of taxes** ADMIN, HRM, TAX recaudador(a) de contribuciones *m,f*

college: ~ **of further education** *n* (*CFE*) WEL ≈ Centro de Formación Profesional *m* (*Esp*), ≈ Instituto de Educación Secundaria *m* (*Esp*)

College: ~ **of Arts** *n* ECON, GEN COMM Escuela de Artes Aplicadas y Oficios Artísticos *f*

collier *n* TRANSP buque carbonero *m*

colliery *n* IND mina de carbón *f*

collision *n* (*col, coll*) TRANSP colisión *f*; ~ **clause** INS *marine* cláusula de colisión *f*; ~ **coverage** INS cobertura de colisión *f*; ~ **insurance** INS seguro de abordaje *m*

colloquium *n* GEN COMM coloquio *m*

collusion *n* GEN COMM, ECON, LAW colusión *f*

collusive: ~ **oligopoly** *n* ECON oligopolio colusorio *m*

colony *n* POL colonia *f*

color AmE see *colour* BrE

color/graphics: ~ **adaptor** AmE see *colour/graphics adaptor* BrE

colour *n* BrE COMP color *m*; ~ **display** BrE COMP pantalla a color *f*, visualización en color *f*;

~ **separation** *BrE* COMP, MEDIA, S&M separación de colores *f*; ~ **supplement** *BrE* MEDIA, S&M suplemento en color *m*; ~ **of title** *BrE* PROP título aparente *m*

colour/graphics: ~ **adaptor** *n BrE* COMP adaptador color/gráficos *m* (*CGA*)

coltainer *abbr* (*collapsible container*) TRANSP contenedor abatible *m*

COLTS *abbr* (*Continuously Offered Longer-Term Securities*) STOCK valores a mayor plazo de oferta continua *m pl*

column *n* (*col.*) ACC *figures*, GEN COMM, MEDIA columna *f*; ~ **centimeters** *AmE*, ~ **centimetres** *BrE n pl* MEDIA centímetros de columna *m pl*; ~ **heading** ACC encabezamiento de columnas *m*; ~ **inch** *n pl* MEDIA pulgada de columna *f*

columnar: ~ **journal** *n* ACC diario en columnas *m*

co-manager *n* BANK, HRM, MGMNT *international banking* codirector(a) *m,f*, director(a) adjunto(-a) *m,f*

COMB *abbr* (*combination*) GEN COMM combinación *f*

combat *vt* GEN COMM *unemployment, drug trafficking* combatir

combi: ~ **carrier** *n* TRANSP transportista combinado(-a) *m,f*; ~ **ship** *n* TRANSP buque combinado *m*

combination *n* (*COMB*) GEN COMM combinación *f*; ~ **charge** TRANSP gasto por concentración *m*; ~ **of charges** TRANSP combinación de gastos *f*; ~ **rate** TRANSP tarifa combinada de transportes *f*; ~ **of rates** TRANSP combinación de tarifas *f*

Combination: ~ **Acts** *n BrE* HRM *British legislation of 1799 and 1800* leyes de combinación

combinations *n pl* MATH combinaciones *f pl*

combine *vt* GEN COMM combinar

combine with *vt* GEN COMM combinar con

combined: ~ **amount** *n* TAX cantidad combinada *f*; ~ **balance sheet** *n* FIN balance de situación combinado *m*; ~ **committee** *n* HRM comité mixto *m*; ~ **financial statement** *n* FIN estado financiero combinado *m*; ~ **issue** *n* MEDIA *print* edición combinada *f*; ~ **mark** *n* PATENTS marca mixta *f*; ~ **premium** *n* INS prima combinada *f*; ~ **shop insurance** *n* INS seguro combinado de comercios *m*; ~ **statement of income** *n* ACC cuenta de pérdidas y ganancias combinada *f*; ~ **ticket** *n* LEIS billete combinado *m*; ~ **total claim** *n* TAX reclamación global combinada *f*; ~ **trade** *n* GEN COMM comercio combinado *m*; ~ **transport** *n* (*CT*) IMP/EXP, TRANSP transporte combinado *m*; ~ **transport bill of lading** *n* (*CTBL*) TRANSP conocimiento de transporte combinado *m*; ~ **transport document** *n* (*CTD*) TRANSP documento de transporte combinado *m*; ~ **transport operation** *n* TRANSP operación combinada de transporte *f*; ~ **transport operator** *n* (*CTO*) TRANSP operador(a) de transporte combinado *m,f*

combustion: ~ **plant** *n* ENVIR, IND planta de combustión *f*

come *vi* GEN COMM acudir; ◆ ~ **before a court** LAW comparecer ante un tribunal; ~ **into effect** LAW entrar en vigor; ~ **into force** GEN COMM aplicarse, LAW entrar en vigor; ~ **into office** HRM, INS, MGMNT asumir un cargo; ~ **into operation** LAW entrar en funcionamiento; ~ **into play** GEN COMM *factors* entrar en juego; ~ **on stream** IND *oil* llegar a una operación normal; ~ **onto the market** S&M entrar en el mercado; ~ **out on strike** HRM declarar la huelga; ~ **under public ownership** ECON, IND, POL quedar bajo propiedad pública

come across *vt* GEN COMM encontrarse con

come along *vi* GEN COMM venir

come down *vi* HRM, WEL *from university* licenciarse

come off *vi* GEN COMM tener éxito

come to *vt* GEN COMM *amount to* equivaler a, *bill* ascender a; ◆ ~ **an agreement** GEN COMM alcanzar un acuerdo; ~ **the fore** GEN COMM empezar a destacar; ~ **fruition** GEN COMM llegar a concretarse; ~ **hand** GEN COMM llegar a su destino; ~ **maturity** GEN COMM llegar al vencimiento; ~ **an understanding** GEN COMM llegar a un entendimiento

comeback: **make a** ~ *phr* GEN COMM volver a escena

COMECON *abbr obs* (*Council for Mutual Economic Aid*) ECON Consejo de Asistencia Mutua Económica *m*

COMET *abbr* ECON (*Committee of Middle East Trade*) Comité Internacional de Oriente Medio *m*, (*Common Market Medium Term Model*) *econometrics* Modelo del Mercado Común a Medio Plazo *m*

COMEX *abbr* (*Commodity Exchange of New York*) STOCK mercado de contratación de derivados de metales preciosos de Nueva York

comfort: ~ **letter** *n* BANK, FIN carta de apoyo *f*, carta de recomendación *f*

coming *adj* GEN COMM venidero

Comit: ~ **Index** *n* STOCK índice de las principales acciones de la bolsa de Milán

comm. *abbr* (*commission*) STOCK comisión *f*

command[1] *n* COMP comando *m*, GEN COMM, HRM mandato *m*; ~ **and control regulation** ADMIN reglamento de mando y control *m*, LAW regulación del dominio y el control *f*; ~ **economy** ECON, POL economía dirigida *f*, economía planificada *f*; ~ **file** COMP archivo de comandos *m*; ~ **key** COMP tecla de comando *f*; ~ **line** COMP línea de comandos *f*

command[2] *vt* ECON *certain price* imponer, GEN COMM mandar

commando: ~ **selling** *n* S&M venta de comando *f*

commencement *n* GEN COMM inicio *m*; ~ **of coverage** INS inicio de la cobertura *m*; ~ **of a policy** INS inicio de vigencia de una póliza *m*

commensurate[1] *adj* GEN COMM proporcionado

commensurate[2]: ~ **charge** *n* GEN COMM *EU* cargo proporcionado *m*; ~ **taxation** *n* TAX equivalencia de las cargas fiscales *f*

comment *n* GEN COMM comentario *m*

comment on *vt* GEN COMM comentar

commentary *n* GEN COMM comentario *m*

commerce *n* ECON, GEN COMM, S&M comercio *m*; ~ **clause** BANK, INS, LAW cláusula comercial *f*

commercial[1] *n* GEN COMM, MEDIA, S&M *mass media* anuncio *m* (*Esp*), anuncio publicitario *m* (*Esp*), comercial *m* (*AmL*), reclame *m* (*AmL*); ~ **accounts** *n pl* ACC cuentas de comercio *f pl*; ~ **activity** GEN COMM, TAX actividad comercial *f*; ~ **acumen** GEN COMM, MGMNT perspicacia comercial *f*; ~ **advantage** GEN COMM ventaja comercial *f*; ~ **agent** GEN COMM representante de comercio *m,f*; ~ **analysis** FIN análisis comercial *m*; ~ **artist** HRM, S&M *advertising* dibujante publicitario(-a) *m,f*; ~ **banking** BANK banca comercial *f*; ~ **bill** *AmE* BANK *retail* letra de cambio comercial *f*; ~ **break** MEDIA *television*, S&M cuña publicitaria *f*; ~ **broker** *AmE* PROP corredor(a) de comercio *m,f*; ~ **cargo** TRANSP carga comercial *f*; ~ **center** *AmE*,

~ **centre** *BrE* S&M centro comercial *m*; ~ **code** GEN COMM, LAW código de comercio *m*; ~ **computer** COMP computador comercial *m* (*AmL*), computadora comercial *f* (*AmL*), ordenador comercial *m* (*Esp*); ~ **concern** GEN COMM negocio comercial *m*; ~ **contract** GEN COMM, LAW contrato comercial *m*; ~ **counsellor** ECON, FIN, GEN COMM consejero(-a) comercial *m,f*; ~ **credit insurance** INS seguro de crédito comercial *m*; ~ **designer** MEDIA, S&M *advertising* diseñador(a) comercial *m,f*; ~ **development** GEN COMM, PROP desarrollo comercial *m*; ~ **and development manager** HRM, MGMNT director(a) comercial y de desarrollo *m,f*; ~ **director** HRM, MGMNT director(a) comercial *m,f*, jefe(-a) comercial *m,f*; ~ **distribution** S&M distribución comercial *f*; ~ **dock** (*CD*) TRANSP depósito comercial *m*; ~ **efficiency** ENVIR rendimiento económico *m*; ~ **establishment** GEN COMM fondo de comercio *m*; ~ **forgery policy** INS póliza de cobertura de falsificaciones *f*; ~ **form** INS *covering risks* póliza comercial *f*; ~ **health insurance** INS seguro de enfermedad privado *m*; ~ **hedgers** *n pl* STOCK cubridores comerciales *m pl*; ~ **interest** GEN COMM interés comercial *m*; ~ **invoice** ACC factura comercial *f*; ~ **law** LAW derecho mercantil *m*; ~ **lawyer** BANK, GEN COMM, LAW ≈ abogado(-a) mercantilista *m,f*; ~ **lease** GEN COMM arrendamiento comercial *m*; ~ **lending** BANK préstamo comercial *m*; ~ **lending power** BANK capacidad de crédito comercial *f*; ~ **letting** PROP alquiler comercial *m*; ~ **limited partner** LAW socio(-a) comanditario(-a) *m,f*; ~ **loan** BANK préstamo comercial *m*; ~ **manager** HRM, MGMNT director(a) comercial *m,f*, jefe(-a) comercial *m,f*; ~ **market** GEN COMM mercado comercial *m*; ~ **occupancy** PROP ocupación comercial *f*; ~ **paper** (*CP*) GEN COMM papel comercial *m*, instrumentos negociables *m pl*; ~ **policy** GEN COMM política comercial *f*; ~ **port** TRANSP puerto comercial *m*; ~ **property** GEN COMM, PROP predio comercial *m*, propiedad comercial *f*; ~ **property policy** INS póliza de daños materiales para empresas *f*; ~ **radio** COMMS, MEDIA radio comercial *f*; ~ **radio station** MEDIA emisora de radio comercial *f*; ~ **representation** GEN COMM representación comercial *f*; ~ **research** GEN COMM investigación comercial *f*; ~ **risk** GEN COMM riesgo comercial *m*; ~ **risk analysis** FIN, INS análisis del riesgo comercial *m*; ~ **sickness insurance policy** INS, WEL póliza comercial de seguro de enfermedad *f*; ~ **stocks** *n pl* GEN COMM existencias comerciales *f pl*; ~ **storage** TRANSP almacenaje comercial *m*; ~ **strategy** ECON, GEN COMM estrategia comercial *f*; ~ **target** GEN COMM, S&M objetivo de ventas *m*; ~ **television** MEDIA, S&M televisión comercial *f*; ~ **television channel** MEDIA canal comercial de televisión *m*; ~ **trade** ECON operación comercial *f*; ~ **traveler** *AmE*, ~ **traveller** *BrE* GEN COMM viajante de comercio *mf*; ~ **treaty** GEN COMM tratado comercial *m*; ~ **trust** TAX fideicomiso comercial *m*; ~ **value movement order** (*CVMO*) GEN COMM orden de cambio de valor comercial *f*; ~ **vehicle** TRANSP vehículo comercial *m*; ~ **venture** MGMNT riesgo comercial *m*; ~ **weight** TRANSP peso comercial *m*; ~ **well** ENVIR pozo comercial *m*; ~ **world** GEN COMM mundo del comercio *m*

commercial[2]: **no ~ value** *phr* (*n.c.v.*) GEN COMM sin valor comercial

Commercial: ~ **Relations and Exports** *n pl BrE* (*CRE*) IMP/EXP relaciones comerciales y exportaciones *f pl*

commercialism *n* GEN COMM comercialidad *f*

commercialization *n* ECON, GEN COMM, S&M, STOCK comercialización *f*

commercialize *vt* GEN COMM comercializar

commercially *adv* GEN COMM comercialmente; ~ **viable** GEN COMM comercialmente viable

commingling *n* BANK, STOCK *securities, trust banking* mezcla *f*

commissary *n AmE* ADMIN, S&M comisario *m*; ~ **goods** *n pl* IMP/EXP productos de economato *m pl*

commission[1] *n* BANK, GEN COMM, STOCK (*comm.*) comisión *f*; ~ **account** BANK cuenta de comisión *f*; ~ **agent** HRM comisionista *mf*; ~ **broker** STOCK comisionista *mf*, comisionista en bolsa de comercio *mf*; ~ **for acceptance** BANK comisión de aceptación *f*; ~ **house** STOCK casa de comisiones *f*; ~ **of inquiry** HRM comisión de indagación *f*; ~ **merchant** HRM comisionista *mf*; ~ **rate** BANK tasa de comisión *f*; ~ **salesman** HRM, S&M vendedor(a) a comisión *m,f*; ~ **system** HRM sistema de comisiones *m*

commission[2] *vt* ADMIN *request, empower*, GEN COMM, HRM, MEDIA *book* comisionar

Commission: ~ **of the European Communities** *n* (*CEC*) ECON Comisión de las Comunidades Europeas *f*; ~ **on Energy and the Environment** *n* (*CENE*) ENVIR Comisión de la Energía y el Medio Ambiente *f*; ~ **White Paper** *n* LAW, POL *European Union* Libro Blanco de la Comisión *m*

commissioner *n* ADMIN liquidador(a) de averías *m,f*; ~ **of banking** *AmE* (*cf bank examiner BrE*) BANK inspector(a) oficial de bancos *m,f*; ~ **of deeds** HRM, LAW funcionario(-a) notarial *m,f*

Commissioner: ~ **of the Inland Revenue** *n BrE* TAX inspector(a)-recaudador(a) de la Administración Fiscal *m,f*; ~ **for the Rights of Trade Union Members** *n* (*CROTUM*) HRM comisionado para los derechos de miembros de los sindicatos m

Commissioners: ~ **of Customs and Excise** *n* TAX Comisarios de Aduanas y Contribuciones Indirectas *m pl*

commissioning *n* TRANSP armamento *m*

commissionaire *n* HRM comisionario(-a) *m,f*

commit: ~ **oneself to** *phr* GEN COMM comprometerse a

commitment *n* GEN COMM *promise, pledge* compromiso *m*, LAW auto de prisión *m*, auto de procesamiento *m*, compromiso *m*, POL compromiso *m*; ~ **accounting** ACC *governmental* contabilidad de compromisos *f*, contabilidad de créditos comprometidos *f*; ~ **acknowledgement clause** INS cláusula de ratificación de compromiso *f*; ~ **authority** FIN facultad para contraer compromisos *f*; ~ **control** LAW control de obligaciones *m*; ~ **document** LAW documento de compromiso *m*; ~ **fee** BANK comisión de apertura *f*, comisión de compromiso *f*, comisión de disponibilidad *f*; ~ **record** LAW registro de obligaciones m

committed[1] *adj* GEN COMM comprometido

committed[2]: ~ **costs** *n pl* ACC costes obligados *m pl* (*Esp*), costos obligados *m pl* (*AmL*)

committee *n* GEN COMM, MGMNT, POL *group of people* comisión *f*, comité *m*; ~ **of inquiry** POL comisión investigadora *f*; ~ **of inspection** LAW comité de inspección *m*; ~ **meeting** GEN COMM reunión del comité *f*; ~ **member** GEN COMM miembro del comité *m*

Committee: ~ **of European Shipowners** *n* (*CES*)

TRANSP Comité de Armadores de Europa *m*; **~ for Industrial Cooperation** *n* (*CIC*) IND comité de cooperación industrial *m*; **~ for the Simplification of International Trade Procedures** *n* (*SIPROCOM*) ECON, POL Comisión para la Simplificación del Comercio Internacional *f*; **~ of London and Scottish Bankers** *n* (*CLSB*) BANK comité de banqueros londinenses y escoceses *m*; **~ of Middle East Trade** *n* (*COMET*) ECON Comité Internacional de Oriente Medio *m*; **~ on Invisible Exports** *n BrE* (*CIE*) IMP/EXP comité de exportaciones invisibles; **~ on Scientific and Technical Research** *n* (*CREST*) IND comité de investigación científica y técnica; **~ of Permanent Representatives of the EU** *n* (*COREPER*) ECON, POL Comité de los Representantes Permanentes de la UE *m*; **~ of Shipowners Associations of the European Community** *n* TRANSP Comisión de Asociaciones de Navieros de la Comunidad Europea *f*; **~ of Twenty** *n* (*C-20*) GEN COMM Comité de los Veinte *m* (*C-20*); **~ of Ways and Means** *n AmE* POL Comisión de Medios y Arbitrios *f*

commodities: **~ futures** *n pl* STOCK futuros sobre productos básicos *m pl*; **~ index** *n* STOCK índice de mercaderías *m*; **~ trading** *n* STOCK comercialización de mercancías *f*

Commodities: **~ Exchange** *n AmE* STOCK mercado de materias primas de Nueva York

commodity *n* (*cmdty*) GEN COMM *food product, raw material* bien *m*, *consumer good* bien de consumo *m*, mercancía *f*, producto de consumo popular *m*, producto básico *m*; **~ agreement** ECON, GEN COMM, LAW tratado comercial *m*, acuerdo sobre mercancías *m*, acuerdo sobre un producto básico *m*; **~ analysis** STOCK análisis de productos básicos *m*; **~ approach** S&M enfoque de productos *m*; **~ broker** FIN, STOCK corredor(a) de mercancías *m,f*, corredor(a) de productos *m,f*; **~ cartel** ECON cartel de productos *m*; **~ classification rates** *n pl* (*CCR*) TRANSP tarifas de clasificación de mercancías *f pl*; **~ contract** STOCK contrato de productos *m*; **~ credit** BANK crédito de mercancía *m*; **~ currency** STOCK dinero de mercancía *m*; **~ exchange** FIN, STOCK Bolsa de Comercio *f*, bolsa de contratación *f*; **~ fetishism** ECON, S&M fetichismo de la mercancía *m*, fetichismo de los bienes *m*; **~ flow** GEN COMM flujo de bienes *m*; **~ futures market** STOCK mercado de productos a futuro *m*; **~ futures trading** STOCK mercado de futuros sobre productos básicos *m*; **~ market** FIN, STOCK bolsa de contratación *f*; **~ mix** TRANSP composición de la carga *f*; **~ paper** STOCK efectos garantizados con mercancías *m pl*; **~ price** S&M, STOCK precio de los artículos al por mayor *m*; **~ pricing** S&M, STOCK fijación de precios de los productos básicos *f*; **~ rate** TRANSP tarifa especial *f*; **~ reserve currency** ECON reserva de divisa *f*; **~ stabilization schemes** ECON *international* esquemas de estabilización del comercio de mercancías *m pl*; **~ standard** ECON sistema monetario de mercancía patrón *m*; **~ tax** TAX impuesto sobre mercancías *m*; **~ terms of trade** ECON *international* vencimientos comerciales cómodos *m pl*; **~ trade structure** ECON *international* estructura comercial de las existencias *f*; **~ trades** ECON *international trade* mercancías comercializables *f pl*; **~ trading** STOCK comercio de productos *m*

Commodity: **~ Credit Corporation** *n AmE* (*CCC*) ECON Compañía de Crédito al Consumo *f*; **~ Exchange**

Authority *n* (*CEA*) STOCK autoridad del mercado de materias primas; **~ Exchange of New York** *n* (*COMEX*) STOCK mercado de contratación de derivados de Nueva York; **~ Futures Trading Commission** *n AmE* (*CFTC*) STOCK agencia para la regulación de mercados futuros

common[1] *adj* GEN COMM común; ◆ **by ~ consent** GEN COMM, LAW de común acuerdo

common[2]: **~ access resources** *n* ECON recursos de acceso común *m pl*; **~ area** *n* PROP zona común *f*; **~ average** *n* INS promedio común *m*; **~ carrier** *n* IND *European networks* empresa de servicios públicos *f*, TRANSP distribuidor(a) común *m,f*; **~ code of practice** *n* GEN COMM código de procedimiento común *m*; **~ cost** *n* ECON coste común *m* (*Esp*), costo común *m* (*AmL*); **~ currency** *n* ECON *international*, POL moneda común *f*; **~ customs tariff** *n* (*CCT*) IMP/EXP tarifa exterior común *f*; **~ denominator** *n* GEN COMM *decision making, discussions* denominador común *m*; **~ directive** *n* LAW, POL *from European union* directiva común *f*, directriz común *f*; **~ distinguishing factor** *n* HRM factor común de distinción *m*; **~ dividend** *n* STOCK dividendo ordinario *m*; **~ elements** *n* PROP *in condominium* elementos comunes *m pl*; **~ equities** *n pl* STOCK recursos propios *m pl*; **~ external tariff** *n* (*CET*) ECON tarifa exterior común *f*; **~ labor** *AmE*, **~ labour** *BrE n* HRM mano de obra común *f*, *task* trabajo común *m*, trabajo corriente *m*; **~ law** *n* LAW derecho angloamericano *m*; **~-law relationship** *n* LAW relación de acuerdo con el common law *f*; **~-law spouse** *n* LAW cónyuge de hecho *mf*; **~-law wife** *n* LAW esposa de hecho *f*; **~ learnings** *n pl* WEL aprendizaje común *m*; **~ ownership** *n* GEN COMM condominio *m*; **~ policy** *n* GEN COMM, POL política común *f*; **~ pricing** *n* GEN COMM, S&M fijación común de precios *m*; **~ revenue** *n* ACC ingreso habitual *m*; **~ seal** *n* LAW sello oficial *m*; **~ sense** *n* GEN COMM sentido común *m*; **~ service agency** *n* ADMIN agencia de servicios generales *f*; **~ service cost distribution system** *n* ACC sistema de distribución de costes de servicios comunes *m* (*Esp*), sistema de distribución de costos de servicios comunes *m* (*AmL*); **~ share certificate** *n BrE* (*cf common stock certificate AmE*) STOCK certificado de acción ordinaria *m*; **~ share dividend** *n BrE* (*cf common stock dividend AmE*) STOCK dividendo de acción ordinaria *m*; **~ share investment** *n BrE* (*cf common stock investment AmE*) STOCK inversión en acciones ordinarias *f*; **~ shareholder** *n BrE* (*cf common stockholder AmE*) STOCK accionista ordinario(-a) *m,f*; **~ shareholders' equities** *n pl BrE* (*cf common stockholders' equities AmE*) ACC, ECON, STOCK acciones ordinarias *f pl*; **~ shares** *n pl BrE* (*cf common stock AmE*) ACC, ECON, STOCK acciones comunes *f pl*, acciones ordinarias *f pl*; **~ shares equivalent** *n BrE* (*cf common stock equivalent AmE*) STOCK equivalente de acciones ordinarias *m*; **~ shares fund** *n BrE* (*cf common stock fund AmE*) STOCK fondo de acciones ordinarias *m*; **~ stock** *n* (*cf common shares BrE*) ACC, ECON, STOCK acciones ordinarias *f pl*, acciones comunes *f pl*; **~ stock certificate** *n AmE* (*cf common share certificate BrE*) STOCK certificado de acción ordinaria *m*; **~ stock dividend** *n AmE* (*cf common share dividend BrE*) STOCK dividendo de acción ordinaria *m*; **~ stock equivalent** *n AmE* (*cf common shares equivalent BrE*) STOCK equivalente de acciones ordinarias *m*; **~ stock fund** *n AmE* (*cf common shares fund BrE*) STOCK fondo de acciones ordinarias *m*; **~ stock investment** *n AmE* (*cf common* *share investment BrE*) STOCK inversión en acciones ordinarias *f*; **~ stockholder** *n AmE* (*cf common shareholder BrE*) STOCK accionista ordinario(-a) *m,f*; **~ stockholders' equities** *n pl* (*cf common shareholders' equities BrE*) ACC, ECON, STOCK acciones ordinarias *f pl*; **~ system** *n* TAX *EU* sistema común *m*; **~ user facility** *n* GEN COMM servicio común para los usuarios *m*

Common: **~ Agricultural Policy** *n* (*CAP*) ECON, POL Política Agrícola Común *f* (*PAC*); **~ Agricultural Policy levy** *n* ECON recaudación de la Política Agrícola Común *f*; **~ Business Oriented Language** *n* (*COBOL*) COMP lenguaje común orientado a la gestión y los negocios *m* (*COBOL*); **~ Market** *n* (*CM*) ECON, POL mercado común *m*; **~ Market Medium Term Model** *n* (*COMET*) ECON *econometrics* Modelo del Mercado Común a Medio Plazo *m*

Commons *n pl BrE* POL Cámara de los Comunes *f*

Commonwealth: **~ Development Corporation** *n* (*CDC*) ECON, POL Corporación para el Desarrollo de la Commonwealth *f* (*CDC*); **~ Fund for Technical Cooperation** *n* (*CFTC*) POL *overseas development* Fondo de la Comunidad para la Cooperación Técnica *m*; **~ Grants Commission** *n* ECON comisión de subsidios de la Commonwealth; **~ of Independent States** *n* ECON estados independientes de la Commonwealth *m pl*; **~ Preference** *n BrE* IMP/EXP preferencias arancelarias para países de la Commonwealth

communal[1] *adj* ECON, GEN COMM, POL, PROP comunal

communal[2]: **~ economy** *n* ECON economía comunal *f*; **~ ownership** *n* PROP propiedad comunal *f*

commune *n* ECON, GEN COMM, POL comuna *f*

communicate *vt* GEN COMM comunicar

communication *n* GEN COMM comunicación *f*; **~ barrier** GEN COMM barrera de comunicación *f*; **~ gap** GEN COMM vacío de comunicación *m*; **~ link** GEN COMM enlace de comunicación *m*; **~ management** MEDIA, MGMNT dirección de las comunicaciones *f*, gerencia de las comunicaciones *f*; **~ media** MEDIA medios de comunicación *m pl*; **~ mix** S&M combinación de estrategias de comunicación *f*; **~ objective** S&M objetivo de comunicación *m*; **~ skill** HRM técnica de comunicación *f*; **~ strategy** COMMS estrategia de comunicación *f*; **~ technology** COMMS tecnología de la comunicación *f*

communications *n pl* GEN COMM comunicaciones *f pl*; **~ network** *n* COMMS, COMP red de comunicaciones *f*; **~ satellite** *n* COMMS, MEDIA satélite de comunicaciones *m*; **~ theory** *n* MGMNT teoría de las comunicaciones *f*

communicator *n* COMMS comunicante *m*

communiqué *n* COMMS comunicado *m*

communism *n* ECON, POL comunismo *m*

community *n* GEN COMM comunidad *f*; **~ association** PROP asociación de vecinos *f*; **~ debt** ACC, FIN, GEN COMM deuda conjunta *f*; **~ of goods** GEN COMM comunidad de bienes *f*; **~ of interests** GEN COMM comunidad de intereses *f*; **~ job** ECON, HRM, WEL trabajo colectivo *m*, trabajo social *m*; **~ network** COMMS red comunitaria *f*; **~ property** LAW bienes gananciales *m pl*; **~ quota** IMP/EXP, POL contingente comunitario *m*; **~ spirit** GEN COMM espíritu comunitario *m*; **~ tariff quota** IMP/EXP, POL contingente arancelario comunitario *m*

Community: **~ Action** *n* GEN COMM *EU* Acción Comunitaria *f*; **~ Aid** *n* ECON *EU* Ayuda Comunitaria *f*; **~ budget** *n* ECON *EU* presupuesto comunitario *m*;

~ Charter of Fundamental Social Rights of Workers *n* HRM, WEL *EU* Carta Comunitaria de Derechos Sociales Fundamentales de los Trabajadores *f*; **~ goods** *n pl* IMP/EXP productos comunitarios *m pl*; **~ imports** *n pl* IMP/EXP importaciones de la Comunidad *f pl*; **~ Program** *AmE*, **~ Programme** *BrE n* (*CP*) WEL *EU* programa comunitario *m*; **~ Trade Mark Office** *n* LAW *EU* Oficina de Marcas Registradas de la Comunidad *f*; **~ treatment** *n* IMP/EXP tratamiento comunitario *m*

communization *n* PROP *of land* colectivización *f*, comunización *f*

communize *vt* PROP *land* comunizar

commutability *n* GEN COMM conmutabilidad *f*

commutable *adj* GEN COMM conmutable

commutation *n* GEN COMM conmutación *f*; **~ right** INS derecho de conmutación *m*; **~ ticket** *AmE* (*cf season ticket BrE*) GEN COMM abono *m*, TRANSP abono *m*, abono ferroviario *m*

commute *vt* LAW conmutar

commuter *n* GEN COMM, TRANSP viajero(-a) abonado(-a) *m,f*, *aircraft* conmutador *m*; **~ airline** TRANSP línea aérea de cabotaje *f*; **~ belt** GEN COMM, PROP cercanías *f pl*, zona de los barrios exteriores *f*; **~ suburb** GEN COMM ciudad dormitorio *f*; **~ tax** *AmE* TAX impuesto sobre los viajeros de abono *m*; **~ train** TRANSP tren de cercanías *m*

compact: **~ disk** *n* COMP disco compacto *m*; **~ disk interactive** *n* (*CD-I*) COMP disco compacto interactivo *m* (*CD-I*); **~ disk read-only memory** *n* (*CD-ROM*) COMP disco compacto con memoria sólo de lectura *m* (*CD-ROM*)

companies: **~ included within consolidation** *n pl* ACC compañías incluidas en la consolidación *f pl*

Companies: **~ Act** *n pl BrE* (*cf Companies Bill AmE*) GEN COMM, IND, LAW Decreto de Sociedades Mercantiles *m*, Ley de Sociedades Mercantiles *f*; **~ Bill** *n pl AmE* (*cf Companies Act BrE*) GEN COMM, IND, LAW Decreto de Sociedades Mercantiles *m*, Ley de Sociedades Mercantiles *f*; **~ Code** *n* LAW Código de Empresa *m*

company *n* (*Co.*) GEN COMM compañía *f* (*Cía.*); **~ accounts** *n pl* ACC cuentas de la empresa *f pl*, cuentas empresariales *f pl*; **~'s affairs** *n pl* GEN COMM asuntos de la compañía *m pl*; **~ agreement** HRM acuerdo de empresa *m*, contrato de empresa *m*; **~ bargaining** HRM negociación de empresa *f*; **~ benefits** *n pl* HRM subsidio de la compañía *m*; **~ car** GEN COMM, TRANSP *fringe benefit* coche de la empresa *m*, automóvil de la empresa *m*; **~ car policy** *BrE* (*cf business automobile policy AmE*) INS póliza de automóviles comerciales *f*; **~ credit card** BANK, FIN, TAX tarjeta de crédito de empresa *f*; **~ director** MEDIA director(a) de empresa *m,f*; **~ executive** HRM ejecutivo(-a) de la compañía *m,f*; **~ formation** GEN COMM formación de una empresa *f*; **~ goal** GEN COMM meta de la empresa *f*; **~ law** GEN COMM, LAW derecho de sociedades *m*; **~ lawyer** BANK, GEN COMM, LAW ≈ abogado(-a) mercantilista *m,f*; **~ level agreement** *BrE* HRM acuerdo del ámbito de una empresa *m*; **~ liquidity** FIN liquidez de empresa *f*; **~ logo** GEN COMM, S&M logo de la compañía *m*, logotipo de la empresa *m*; **~ manager** HRM, MGMNT director(a) de la compañía *m,f*; **~ meeting** GEN COMM reunión de empresa *f*; **~ model** GEN COMM modelo de empresa *m*; **~ objective** GEN COMM objetivo de la empresa *m*; **~'s own field organization** IMP/EXP, IND organización en el propio campo de la empresa *f*;

~ **performance** GEN COMM resultado de la compañía *m*; ~ **philosophy** GEN COMM filosofía de la empresa *f*; ~ **planning** GEN COMM, MGMNT planificación de la empresa *f*; ~ **policy** GEN COMM política de la empresa *f*; ~ **profile** GEN COMM perfil de la empresa *m*; ~ **promotion** STOCK promoción de una empresa *f*; ~ **quotation** ECON cotización empresarial *f*; ~ **reconstruction** GEN COMM reconstrucción de la empresa *f*; ~ **seal** GEN COMM, LAW sello de la empresa *m*; ~ **secretary** ADMIN, HRM *commercial organization* secretarío(-a) de la empresa *m,f*, secretario(-a) general *m,f*; ~ **sector** ECON sector empresarial *m*; ~ **service contract** TRANSP contrato de servicio de la compañía *m*; ~'**s sickness insurance scheme** HRM, INS fondo de pensiones para enfermedad *m*; ~ **strategy** GEN COMM estrategia de la empresa *f*; ~ **structure** GEN COMM estructura de la empresa *f*; ~ **tax** TAX impuesto de sociedades *m*; ~ **town** ECON ciudad cuya economía depende de una sola empresa; ~ **union** HRM sindicato blanco *m* (*AmL*), sindicato de empresa *m* (*Esp*); ♦ **this ~ is rated triple-A** STOCK esta empresa está clasificada como triple A

Company: ~ **Law** *n* LAW Ley de Sociedades Mercantiles *f*

comparability *n* HRM comparabilidad *f*

comparable: ~ **basis** *n* ACC *of reporting* base comparable *f*; ~ **worth** *n* (*CW*) HRM valor comparable *m*

comparables *n pl* PROP comparables *m pl*

comparative[1] *adj* GEN COMM *value* comparativo

comparative[2]: ~ **advantage** *n* ECON *international* ventaja comparativa *f*; ~ **advertising** *n* S&M publicidad comparativa *f*; ~ **balance sheet** *n* ACC, FIN balance de situación comparativo *m*; ~ **financial statement** *n* ACC estado financiero comparativo *m*; ~ **negligence** *n* LAW proporcionalidad de la culpa *f*; ~ **statement** *n* ACC, FIN balance de situación comparativo *m*, estado de situación comparativo *m*; ~ **statics** *n* ECON *dynamic economics* estática comparativa *f*

comparatively *adv* GEN COMM comparativamente

compare *vt* GEN COMM comparar; ♦ ~ **sth to sth** GEN COMM comparar algo con algo

comparison *n* GEN COMM comparación *f*; ~ **shopping** S&M compra comparativa *f*; ~ **test** GEN COMM prueba de comparación *f*

compartmentalization *n* GEN COMM, MGMNT compartimentación *f*, división en compartimentos *f*

compartmentalize *vt* GEN COMM, MGMNT compartimentalizar, dividir en compartimentos

compatibility *n* COMP *of software*, ECON, GEN COMM, IND *of products* compatibilidad *f*

compatible *adj* COMP, ECON, GEN COMM, IND compatible

compensate *vt* GEN COMM *sb for sth* compensar, resarcirse de, INS, LAW *pay* compensar, indemnizar; ♦ ~ **for damage** LAW indemnizar por daños y perjuicios

compensated: ~ **demand curve** *n* ECON curva de demanda compensada *f*

compensating[1] *adj* GEN COMM compensatorio

compensating[2]: ~ **balance** *n* BANK saldo compensatorio *m*; ~ **common tariff** *n* (*CCT*) ECON arancel común de compensación *m*; ~ **depreciation** *n* ACC, GEN COMM depreciación compensatoria *f*; ~ **error** *n* ACC error de compensación *m*; ~ **income** *n* BrE STOCK ingreso compensatorio *m*; ~ **loss** *n* STOCK pérdida compensatoria *f*; ~ **product** *n* IMP/EXP producto compensador *m*;

~ **wage differential** *n* HRM diferencial para compensar diferencias salariales *m*

compensation *n* GEN COMM compensación *f*, pago compensatorio *m*; ~ **agreement** ECON *international trade* acuerdo de compensación *m*; ~ **fee** COMMS tarifa de compensación *f*; ~ **for industrial injury** LAW, WEL *loss of earning-power* indemnización por accidente laboral *f*; ~ **for loss or damage** INS compensación por pérdida o daño *f*; ~ **fund** STOCK fondo de compensación *m*; ~ **money** GEN COMM, HRM dinero de compensación *m*; ~ **principle** ECON principio de compensación social *m*; ~ **settlement** LAW acuerdo de compensación *m*, acuerdo de indemnización *m*; ~ **stocks** *n pl BrE* STOCK acciones de compensación *f pl*; ~ **tax** TAX impuesto de compensación *m*

compensatory[1] *adj* GEN COMM compensatorio

compensatory[2]: ~ **amount** *n* ECON *international* volumen compensatorio *m*; ~ **damages** *n pl* LAW, WEL indemnización compensatoria *f*; ~ **finance** *n* FIN, POL financiación compensatoria *f*; ~ **financial facility** *n* (*CFF*) FIN mecanismo financiero compensatorio *m*; ~ **fiscal policy** *n* ECON, POL, TAX política fiscal compensatoria *f*; ~ **levy** *n* IMP/EXP tasa compensadora *f*; ~ **stock option** *n* STOCK opción sobre acciones compensatorias *f*; ~ **time** *n* HRM tiempo de compensación *m*

compete *vi* GEN COMM competir

compete against *vt* GEN COMM competir contra

competence *n* GEN COMM competencia *f*

competency: ~ **of court** *n* LAW jurisdicción del tribunal *f*

competent: ~ **party** *n* LAW *contract* parte cualificada *f*

competing: ~ **bid** *n* GEN COMM *tender offers* invitación para la presentación de ofertas *f*; ~ **requirements** *n pl* GEN COMM *tender offers* requisitos para la presentación de ofertas *m pl*

competition *n* GEN COMM competencia *f*; ~ **act** LAW, POL ley de competencia *f*; **no ~ competition pact** LAW, S&M pacto de no competencia *m*; ~ **policy** POL política sobre libre competencia *f*, S&M política de competencia *f*

Competition: ~ **and Credit Control** *n* ECON control de competencia y crédito *m*

competitive[1] *adj* GEN COMM competitivo

competitive[2]: ~ **advantage** *n* ECON ventaja competitiva *f*; ~ **bidding** *n* GEN COMM licitación pública *f*; ~ **business** *n* GEN COMM negocio competitivo *m*; ~ **claim** *n* S&M pretensión competitiva *f*; ~ **demand** *n* S&M demanda competitiva *f*; ~ **edge** *n* ECON margen favorable competitivo *m*, S&M ventaja competitiva *f*; ~ **fringe** *n* ECON franja competitiva *f*; ~ **parity** *n* S&M paridad competitiva *f*; ~**-parity method** *n* S&M método de paridad competitiva *m*; ~ **position** *n* ECON, GEN COMM posición competitiva *f*; ~ **power** *n* BANK, GEN COMM, S&M capacidad competitiva *f*; ~ **pricing** *n* GEN COMM, S&M precio competitivo *m*; ~ **process** *n* ECON proceso competitivo *m*; ~ **rate** *n* BANK tipo competitivo *m*, S&M tarifa competitiva *f*, tipo competitivo *m*; ~ **stimulus** *n* ECON, S&M estímulo competitivo *m*; ~ **strategy** *n* ECON, GEN COMM, S&M estrategia competitiva *f*; ~ **tactic** *n* ECON, MGMNT, S&M táctica competitiva *f*; ~ **tendering** *n* ECON, GEN COMM licitación competitiva *f*, oferta competitiva *f*; ~ **thrust** *n* ECON impulso competitivo *m*; ~ **trading** *n* ECON, IND, S&M comercio competitivo *m*

competitiveness *n* GEN COMM capacidad competitiva *f*, competitividad *f*

competitor *n* GEN COMM competidor(a) *m,f*; **~ analysis** S&M análisis de competidores *m*

compile *vt* COMP, GEN COMM compilar

compiler *n* COMP, GEN COMM compilador(a) *m,f*

complain *vi* GEN COMM quejarse

complaint *n* GEN COMM demanda *f*, queja *f*, LAW *civil action* denuncia *f*

complaints: **~ procedure** *n* GEN COMM, LAW demanda *f*, procedimiento de reclamación *m*

complement *n* COMP, ECON, GEN COMM, S&M complemento *m*

complementary[1] *adj* GEN COMM complementario

complementary[2]: **~ demand** *n* S&M demanda complementaria *f*; **~ product** *n* S&M producto complementario *m*; **~ technology** *n* GEN COMM tecnología complementaria *f*

complete[1] *adj* GEN COMM completo, total, cumplido, ejecutado

complete[2]: **~ audit** *n* ACC auditoría completa *f*, auditoría total *f*; **~ refund offer** *n* S&M oferta de reembolso total *f*

complete[3] *vt* GEN COMM consumar, completar, cumplir; ◆ **~ a sale** PROP cerrar una venta

completed[1] *adj* GEN COMM, LAW consumado, terminado

completed[2]: **~ contract method** *n* ACC método de contrato completo *m*, método de contrato cumplido *m*, método de contrato ejecutado *m*, método de contrato terminado *m*; **~ operations insurance** *n* INS, PROP seguro de actividades concluidas *m*

completely[1] *adv* GEN COMM completamente

completely[2]: **~ knocked down** *phr* (*CKD*) TRANSP completamente desmontado

completeness *n* ACC *data* integridad *f*, totalidad *f*

completion *n* GEN COMM conclusión *f*, terminación *f*; **~ basis** ACC base de cumplimiento *f*; **~ bond** LAW, PROP garantía de cumplimiento *f* (*Esp*), garantía de realización *f* (*AmL*); **~ date** GEN COMM fecha de terminación *f*; **~ of end use** *BrE* IMP/EXP utilización de acuerdo con la indicación de uso final; **~ program** *AmE*, **~ programme** *BrE* ENVIR programa de conclusión *m*

complex[1] *adj* GEN COMM, POL *issue, decision* complicado, complejo

complex[2]: **~ capital structure** *n* ECON estructura compleja del capital *f*; **~ economy** *n* ECON economía compleja *f*; **~ transaction** *n* BANK transacción complicada *f*; **~ trust** *n* LAW fideicomiso complejo *m*; **~ variable** *n* GEN COMM variable compleja *f*

complexity *n* GEN COMM complejidad *f*

compliance *n* GEN COMM adhesión *f*, LAW conformidad *f*, cumplimiento *m*; **~ accountant** GEN COMM interventor(a) *m,f* (*Esp*), contralor(a) *m,f* (*AmL*); **~ audit** ACC, GEN COMM, MGMNT auditoría de cumplimiento *f*; **~ cost** ACC, ADMIN, TAX coste de cumplimiento *m* (*Esp*), costo de cumplimiento *m* (*AmL*); **~ department** STOCK departamento administrativo *m*, departamento de cumplimiento *m*; **~ system** TAX sistema de cumplimiento de las obligaciones tributarias *m*; ◆ **in ~ with** LAW *regulations* conforme a

complication *n* GEN COMM complicación *f*

compliment: **~ slip** *n* COMMS, GEN COMM, S&M papeleta de saludos *f*

complimentary: **~ close** *n* COMMS fórmula de cortesía *f*;

~ copy *n* GEN COMM, MEDIA ejemplar de regalo *m*; **~ subscription** *n* GEN COMM suscripción gratuita *f*

compliments: **~ slip** *n* ADMIN, COMMS hoja de cumplido *f*

comply *vi* LAW, POL adherir

comply with *vt* LAW atenderse a, cumplir con; ◆ **~ a clause** LAW cumplir con una cláusula

component[1] *adj* GEN COMM, IND componente

component[2] *n* GEN COMM componente *m*, pieza *f*; **~ factory** ENVIR, IND fábrica de componentes *f*

compose *vt* GEN COMM componer

composite[1] *adj* GEN COMM compuesto

composite[2]: **~ commodity** *n* ECON bien compuesto *m*; **~ currency** *n* ECON monedas combinadas *f pl*; **~ currency unit** *n* ECON unidad monetaria combinada *f*; **~ depreciation** *n* FIN depreciación combinada *f*; **~ index** *n* ECON índice compuesto *m*, FIN índice mixto *m*; **~ insurance** *n* INS seguro compuesto *m*; **~ insurance company** *n* INS compañía mixta de seguros *f*; **~ leading index** *n* STOCK índice compuesto adelantado *m*; **~ leading indicator** *n* STOCK indicador adelantado compuesto *m*; **~ mark** *n* PATENTS marca mixta *f*; **~ package** *n* S&M paquete compuesto *m*; **~ packaging** *n* TRANSP empaquetado compuesto *m*; **~ price** *n* GEN COMM precio compuesto *m*; **~ rate** *n* GEN COMM tipo combinado *m*; **~ spread** *n* BANK *of risk* diversificación mixta *f*; **~ tax rate** *n* TAX tipo impositivo compuesto *m*; **~ trailer** *n* TRANSP *road transport* remolque compuesto *m*; **~ yield** *n* BANK rendimiento mixto *m*

composition *n* COMP, GEN COMM composición *f*, LAW *with creditor* arreglo *m*, MEDIA composición *f*; **~ of creditors** FIN convenio de acreedores *m*

compound[1]: **~ annual growth** *n* ECON, FIN crecimiento anual compuesto *m*; **~ annual rate** *n* (*CAR*) BANK, FIN *of interest* tasa anual compuesta *f* (*TAC*); **~ bonus** *n* ACC, GEN COMM bonificación compuesta *f*; **~ deferment** *n* IMP/EXP aplazamiento compuesto *m*; **~ duty** *n* IMP/EXP *customs* derecho compuesto *m*; **~ entry** *n* ACC apunte compuesto *m*, asiento compuesto *m*; **~ growth rate** *n* ECON, FIN índice de crecimiento compuesto *m*, tasa de crecimiento compuesto *f*; **~ interest** *n* BANK interés combinado *m*, interés compuesto *m*; **~ interest bond** *n* BANK, ECON, FIN, STOCK obligación de interés compuesto *f*; **~ journal entry** *n* ACC asiento compuesto en el diario *m*; **~ yield** *n* FIN ingreso compuesto *m*

compound[2] *vt* BANK, FIN capitalizar, GEN COMM *exacerbate* agravar, exacerbar, LAW capitalizar; ◆ **~ a debt** BANK, FIN, LAW componer una deuda, concertar una deuda

comprehensive[1] *adj* GEN COMM *report, review* completo, *answer* global, INS a todo riesgo, completo

comprehensive[2]: **~ agreement** *n* HRM acuerdo global *m*; **~ annual financial report** *n* (*CAFR*) ECON, FIN, GEN COMM, MGMNT informe global financiero anual *m* (*Esp*), reporte global financiero anual *m* (*AmL*); **~ bank guarantee** *n* BANK garantía bancaria por la totalidad *f*; **~ budget** *n* ACC, ECON, FIN presupuesto global *m*; **~ crime endorsement** *n* INS endoso de cobertura amplia contra actos criminales *m*; **~ extended term banker's guarantee** *n* (*CXBG*) BANK ampliación del plazo de una garantía bancaria total *f*; **~ general liability insurance** *n* INS seguro de responsabilidad general *m*; **~ glass insurance** *n* INS seguro multirriesgo contra rotura de cristales *m*; ~ **health insurance** *n* INS seguro sanitario a todo riesgo *m*; ~ **health-care system** *n* WEL sistema global de atención sanitaria *m*; ~ **insurance** *n* INS seguro contra todo riesgo *m*; ~ **insurance policy** *n* GEN COMM, INS póliza de seguros global *f*, INS *automobile* póliza de seguro a todo riesgo *f*; ~ **liability insurance** *n* INS seguro de responsabilidad a todo riesgo *m*; ~ **personal liability insurance** *n* INS seguro general de responsabilidad personal *m*; ~ **policy** *n* INS póliza combinada *f*; ~ **responsibility** *n* GEN COMM responsabilidad general *f*; ~ **tax reform** *n* ECON, TAX reforma general fiscal *f*

Comprehensive: ~ **Employment and Training Act** *n AmE* (*CETA*) HRM ley de trabajo y formación

compress *vt* COMP *file, data* comprimir

compression *n* COMP compresión *f*

comprise *vt* GEN COMM abarcar, constar de

comprised: ~ **total loss** *n* FIN, GEN COMM, INS *marine* pérdida total incluida *f*

compromise[1] *n* GEN COMM, LAW, POL compromiso *m*; ~ **agreement** GEN COMM acuerdo conciliatorio *m*; ~ **decision** GEN COMM decisión de compromiso *f*; ~ **solution** GEN COMM solución de compromiso *f*

compromise[2] **1.** *vt* GEN COMM *project* exponer; **2.** *vi* GEN COMM comprometer

comptroller *see controller*

Comptroller: ~ **Of The Currency** *n AmE* BANK organismo estadounidense para el control y seguimiento de las actividades bancarias; ~ **General** *n AmE* ACC inspector(a) general *m,f*

compulsive: ~ **buying** *n* S&M compra compulsiva *f*

compulsory[1] *adj* GEN COMM obligatorio, *power* coercitivo, *regulation* coactivo, obligatorio

compulsory[2]: ~ **arbitration** *n BrE* HRM *labour disputes* arbitraje necesario *m*, arbitraje obligatorio *m*; ~ **competitive tendering** *n BrE* GEN COMM licitación competitiva obligatoria *f*, POL obligación de vender con carácter competitivo; ~ **deduction** *n* GEN COMM deducción forzosa *f*; ~ **expenditure** *n* ECON gasto obligatorio *m*; ~ **insurance** *n* INS seguro obligatorio *m*; ~ **licence** *BrE*, ~ **license** *AmE n* LAW, PATENTS licencia obligatoria *f*; ~ **liquidation** *n* ACC, FIN, GEN COMM liquidación forzosa *f*, liquidación obligatoria *f*; ~ **margin** *n BrE* STOCK margen obligatorio *m*; ~ **purchase** *n* GEN COMM, LAW, PROP compra obligatoria *f*; ~ **purchase order** *n* LAW, PROP orden de compra obligatoria *f*; ~ **redundancy** *n* HRM despido obligatorio *m*; ~ **retirement** *n BrE* (*cf mandatory retirement AmE*) HRM jubilación forzosa *f*, jubilación obligatoria *f*; ~ **saving** *n BrE* BANK, ECON, FIN ahorro forzoso *m*; ~ **surrender** *n* LAW cesión obligatoria *f*; ~ **third party insurance** *n* INS seguro obligatorio de responsabilidad civil *m*

Compulsory: ~ **Purchase Act** *n BrE* LAW Ley de Compra Forzosa *f*

computation *n* GEN COMM cálculo *m*; ~ **of errors** GEN COMM cálculo de errores *m*

computational: ~ **error** *n* COMP error de cálculo *m*

compute *vt* GEN COMM computar

computer[1]: ~~**aided** *adj* COMP, IND asistido por computador (*AmL*), asistido por computadora (*AmL*), asistido por ordenador (*Esp*); ~~**assisted** *adj* COMP asistido por computador (*AmL*), asistido por computadora (*AmL*), asistido por ordenador (*Esp*); ~~**based**

adj COMP basado en computador (*AmL*), basado en computadora (*AmL*), basado en ordenador (*Esp*), computadorizado (*AmL*), informatizado (*Esp*); ~~**controlled** *adj* COMP controlado por computador (*AmL*), controlado por computadora (*AmL*), controlado por ordenador (*Esp*); ~~**driven** *adj* COMP dirigido por computador (*AmL*), dirigido por computadora (*AmL*), dirigido por ordenador (*Esp*); ~~**operated** *adj* COMP manejado por computador (*AmL*), manejado por computadora (*AmL*), manejado por ordenador (*Esp*); ~~**oriented** *adj* COMP ejecutado por computador (*AmL*), ejecutado por computadora (*AmL*), ejecutado por ordenador (*Esp*)

computer[2] *n* COMP computador *m* (*AmL*), computadora *f* (*AmL*), ordenador *m* (*Esp*); ~ **accounting** ACC, COMP contabilidad informatizada *f* (*Esp*), contabilidad computadorizada (*AmL*), contabilidad por computador *f* (*AmL*), contabilidad por ordenador *f* (*Esp*), sistema de contabilidad informatizada *f* (*Esp*); ~ **age** COMP era de las computadoras *f* (*AmL*), era de los computadores *f* (*AmL*), era de los ordenadores *f* (*Esp*); ~~**aided design** (*CAD*) COMP, IND diseño asistido por computador *m* (*AmL*) (*CAD*), diseño asistido por computadora *m* (*AmL*) (*CAD*), diseño asistido por ordenador *m* (*Esp*) (*CAD*); ~~**aided design and drafting** (*CADD*) COMP, IND diseño y dibujo asistido por computador *m* (*AmL*) (*CADD*), diseño y dibujo asistido por computadora *m* (*AmL*) (*CADD*), diseño y dibujo asistido por ordenador *m* (*Esp*) (*CADD*); ~~**aided engineering** (*CAE*) COMP ingeniería asistida por computador *f* (*AmL*), ingeniería asistida por computadora *f* (*AmL*), ingeniería asistida por ordenador *f* (*Esp*); ~~**aided instruction** (*CAI*) COMP instrucción asistida por computador *f* (*AmL*), instrucción asistida por computadora *f* (*AmL*), instrucción asistida por ordenador *f* (*Esp*) (*CAI*); ~~**aided language learning** (*CALL*) COMP aprendizaje de idiomas asistido por computador *m* (*AmL*), aprendizaje de idiomas asistido por computadora *m* (*AmL*), aprendizaje de idiomas asistido por ordenador *m* (*Esp*); ~~**aided learning** (*CAL*) COMP aprendizaje asistido por computador *m* (*AmL*), aprendizaje asistido por computadora *m* (*AmL*), aprendizaje asistido por ordenador *m* (*Esp*); ~~**aided manufacturing** (*CAM*) COMP, IND fabricación asistida por computador *f* (*AmL*) (*CAM*), fabricación asistida por computadora *f* (*AmL*) (*CAM*), fabricación asistida por ordenador *f* (*Esp*) (*CAM*); ~~**assisted engineering** (*CAE*) COMP ingeniería asistida por computador *f* (*AmL*), ingeniería asistida por computadora *f* (*AmL*), ingeniería asistida por ordenador *f* (*Esp*); ~~**assisted language learning** (*CALL*) COMP aprendizaje de idiomas asistido por computador *m* (*AmL*), aprendizaje de idiomas asistido por computadora *m* (*AmL*), aprendizaje de idiomas asistido por ordenador *m* (*Esp*); ~~**assisted learning program** COMP programa de aprendizaje asistido por computador *m* (*AmL*), programa de aprendizaje asistido por computadora *m* (*AmL*), programa de aprendizaje asistido por ordenador *m* (*Esp*); ~~**assisted software engineering** (*CASE*) COMP ingeniería de programas asistida por computador *f* (*AmL*), ingeniería de programas asistida por computadora *f* (*AmL*), ingeniería de programas asistida por ordenador *f* (*Esp*); ~~**assisted testing** (*CAT*) COMP comprobación asistida por computador *f* (*AmL*), comprobación asistida por computadora *f* (*AmL*), comprobación asistida por

ordenador *f* (*Esp*); **~-assisted trading system** (*CATS*)
COMP, STOCK sistema de negociación asistido por
computador *m* (*AmL*), sistema de negociación asistido
por computadora *m* (*AmL*), sistema de negociación
asistido por ordenador *m* (*Esp*); **~-assisted translation**
COMP traducción asistida por computador *f* (*AmL*),
traducción asistida por computadora *f* (*AmL*), traducción asistida por ordenador *f* (*Esp*); **~ bank** BANK
banco computerizado *m*; **~-based training** HRM
formación por ordenador (*Esp*), capacitación por
computador (*AmL*), capacitación por computadora
(*AmL*); **~ center** *AmE*, **~ centre** *BrE* COMP centro de
procesamiento de datos *m*; **~ circles** COMP *IT industry
professionals* círculos informáticos *m pl*; **~ code** COMP
código de calculadora *m*; **~ communication** COMP
teleinformática *f*; **~ company** COMP empresa de computadoras *f* (*AmL*), empresa de computadores *f* (*AmL*),
empresa de ordenadores *f* (*Esp*); **~ conferencing** COMP
teleconferencia por computador *f* (*AmL*), teleconferencia por computadora *f* (*AmL*), teleconferencia por
ordenador *f* (*Esp*); **~ consultant** COMP asesor(a) de
informática *m,f*; **~ control** COMP *stocks* control por
computador *m* (*AmL*), control por computadora *m*
(*AmL*), control por ordenador *m* (*Esp*); **~ crime
insurance** INS, COMP seguro contra delito informático
m; **~ department** COMP servicio de informática *m*;
~ engineer COMP, HRM ingeniero(-a) informático(-a)
m,f; **~ environment** COMP tecnología de las computadoras *f* (*AmL*), tecnologia de los computadores *m*
(*AmL*), tecnología de los ordenadores *f* (*Esp*); **~ file**
COMP fichero de computador *m* (*AmL*), fichero de
computadora *m* (*AmL*), fichero de ordenador *m* (*Esp*);
~ fraud COMP, LAW fraude informático *m*; **~ graphics** *n
pl* COMP infografía *f*, computación gráfica *f* informática
gráfica *f*; **~ instruction** COMP instrucción de máquina *f*;
~-integrated manufacture (*CIM*) COMP, IND fabricación integrada por computador *f* (*AmL*), fabricación
integrada por computadora *f* (*AmL*), fabricación
integrada por ordenador *f* (*Esp*); **~-integrated manufacturing** (*CIM*) COMP, IND producción integrada por
computador *f* (*AmL*), producción integrada por
computadora *f* (*AmL*), producción integrada por
ordenador *f* (*Esp*); **~ language** COMP lenguaje de
máquina *m*; **~ law** COMP, LAW derecho aplicable a la
informática *m*; **~ leasing business** COMP empresa de
alquiler de computadoras *f* (*AmL*), empresa de alquiler
de computadores *f* (*AmL*), empresa de alquiler de
ordenadores *f* (*Esp*); **~ leasing firm** COMP firma de
alquiler de computadoras *f* (*AmL*), firma de alquiler de
computadores *f* (*AmL*), firma de alquiler de ordenadores *f* (*Esp*); **~ line** COMP línea de computador *f*
(*AmL*), línea de computadora *f* (*AmL*), línea de
ordenador *f* (*Esp*); **~ literacy** COMP capacidad de operar
con un ordenador *f*, familiarización con la informática
f; **~ log** COMP diario de máquina *m*; **~ mail** ADMIN,
COMP correo electrónico *m*; **~ map** COMP esquema de la
computadora *m* (*AmL*), esquema del computador *m*
(*AmL*), esquema del ordenador *m* (*Esp*); **~ memory**
COMP memoria del computador *f* (*AmL*), memoria de la
computadora *f* (*AmL*), memoria del ordenador *f* (*Esp*);
~ network COMP red de computadoras *f* (*AmL*), red de
computadores *f* (*AmL*), red de ordenadores *f* (*Esp*);
~ operation COMP manejo de la computadora *m*
(*AmL*), manejo del computador *m* (*AmL*), manejo del
ordenador *m* (*Esp*); **~ operator** COMP, HRM operador(a)
informático(-a) *m,f*; **~ output** COMP salida de compu-

tador *f* (*AmL*), salida de computadora *f* (*AmL*), salida
de ordenador *f* (*Esp*); **~ package** COMP paquete
informático *m*; **~ phobia** COMP fobia informática *f*;
~ presentation COMP presentación en computador *f*
(*AmL*), presentación en computadora *f* (*AmL*), presentación en ordenador *f* (*Esp*); **~ print-out** COMP
impresión por computador *f* (*AmL*), impresión por
computadora *f* (*AmL*), impresión por ordenador *f*
(*Esp*); **~ processing** COMP proceso de computador *m*
(*AmL*), proceso de computadora *m* (*AmL*), proceso de
ordenador *m* (*Esp*); **~ program** COMP programa informático *m*; **~ programmer** COMP programador(a) de
computadoras *m,f* (*AmL*), programador(a) de ordenadores *m,f* (*Esp*), programador(a) de computadores *m,f*
(*AmL*); **~ programming** COMP, MATH programación de
ordenadores *f*, programación informática *f*; **~ return**
COMP, TAX declaración por computador *f* (*AmL*),
declaración por computadora *f* (*AmL*), declaración
por ordenador *f* (*Esp*); **~ room** COMP sala de computadoras *f* (*AmL*), sala de computadores *f* (*AmL*), sala de
ordenadores *f* (*Esp*); **~ run** COMP ejecución en computador *f* (*AmL*), ejecución en computadora *f* (*AmL*),
ejecución en ordenador *f* (*Esp*), pasada de ordenador *f*
(*Esp*), pasada en computadora *f* (*AmL*), pasada en
computadora *f* (*AmL*); **~ science** COMP computación *f*,
informática *f*; **~ scientist** COMP especialista en informática *mf*; **~ screen** COMP pantalla de computador *f*
(*AmL*), pantalla de computadora *f* (*AmL*), pantalla de
ordenador *f* (*Esp*); **~ simulation** COMP simulación por
computador *f* (*AmL*), simulación por computadora *f*
(*AmL*), simulación por ordenador *f* (*Esp*); **~ software**
COMP programación del ordenador *f* (*Esp*), software de
la computador *m* (*AmL*), software de la computadora
m (*AmL*); **~ software licence** *BrE*, **~ software license**
AmE COMP licencia de programas de computador *f*
(*AmL*), licencia de programas de computadora *f*
(*AmL*), licencia de programas de ordenador *f* (*Esp*);
~ strategy COMP estrategia informática *f*; **~ system**
COMP sistema informático *m*; **~ technology** COMP
ingeniería informática *f*, tecnología informática *f*;
~ terminal COMP terminal de computador *m* (*AmL*),
terminal de computadora *m* (*AmL*), terminal de
ordenador *m* (*Esp*); **~ time** COMP tiempo de máquina
m; **~ trading** COMP, ECON comercio informático *m*;
~ vendor COMP vendedor(a) de ordenadores *m,f*;
~ whizz kid *jarg* COMP joven prodigio(-a) en materia
de computación *m,f* (*jarg*); **~ wizard** COMP experto(-a)
en informática *m,f*

computerization *n* COMP informatización *f*

computerize *vt* COMP automatiizar, computadorizar
(*AmL*), computerizar, informatizar (*Esp*)

computerized[1] *adj* COMP computadorizado (*AmL*),
computerizado, informatizado (*Esp*), automatizado

computerized[2]: **~ accounting system** *n* ACC, COMP
sistema de contabilidad automatizado *m*, sistema de
contabilidad informatizado *m*; **~ banking** *n* BANK,
COMP banca automática *f*, banca computerizada *f*;
~ file *n* COMP fichero informatizado *m*; **~ market
timing system** *n* COMP, STOCK sistema informatizado
de sincronización del mercado *m*

computing *n* COMP informatización *f*, computación *f*,
informática *f*; **~ center** *AmE*, **~ centre** *BrE* COMP
centro de cálculo *m*; **~ company** COMP compañía de
computadoras *f* (*AmL*), compañía de computadores *f*
(*AmL*), compañía de ordenadores *f* (*Esp*); **~ power**

COMP capacidad de cálculo *f*; ~ **room** COMP sala de cálculo *f*; ~ **speed** COMP velocidad de cálculo *f*

con: ~ **artist** *n infrml* GEN COMM estafador(a) *m,f*; ~ **man** *n infrml* GEN COMM estafador *m*

concatenation *n* COMP *programming language* concatenación *f*

conceal *vt* LAW ocultar

concealed: ~ **asset** *n* ACC, FIN activo oculto *m*; ~ **employment** *n* ECON, HRM empleo encubierto *m*; ~ **unemployment** *n* ECON, HRM, WEL desempleo encubierto *m*, paro encubierto *m*

concealment *n* LAW *of information* ocultación *f*; ~ **of losses** ACC, STOCK ocultación de pérdidas *f*

concentrate: ~ **attention on** *phr* GEN COMM centrar la atención en

concentrate on *vt* GEN COMM concentrar en

concentration *n* ECON, FIN, GEN COMM concentración *f*; ~ **banking** BANK banca de concentración *f*; ~ **curve** MATH curva de concentración *f*; ~ **economy** ECON economía de concentración *f*; ~ **of industry** IND concentración industrial *f*; ~ **ratio** ECON grado de concentración *m*

concept *n* GEN COMM, S&M *publicity campaign* concepto *m*; ~ **test** S&M prueba conceptual *f*

conceptual: ~ **framework** *n* ACC *of standards* estructura conceptual *f*, marco conceptual *m*

concern *n* GEN COMM *business organization* empresa *f*

concerted: ~ **effort** *n* GEN COMM esfuerzo concertado *m*

concession *n* GEN COMM cesión *f*, *distribution right* concesión *f*

concessionaire *n* GEN COMM concesionario(-a) *m,f*

concessional[1] *adj* GEN COMM privilegiado

concessional[2]: ~ **aid** *n* ECON *development assistance* ayuda financiera *f*; ~ **fee** *n* WEL *courses* matrícula reducida *f*; ~ **exports** *n pl* IMP/EXP exportaciones de favor *f pl*, POL exportación productos básicos por los que los receptores no deben pagar; ~ **terms** *n pl* GEN COMM condiciones muy favorables *f pl*

concessionary[1] *adj* GEN COMM concesionario

concessionary[2]: ~ **rate** *n* GEN COMM tipo concedido *m*, LEIS precio reducido *m*

conciliate *vt* GEN COMM, HRM, LAW conciliar

conciliation *n* GEN COMM, HRM *labour disputes*, LAW conciliación *f*; ~ **board** GEN COMM, HRM junta de conciliación *f*, junta de conciliación y arbitraje *f*; ~ **officer** *BrE* HRM funcionario(-a) de conciliación *m,f*; ~ **procedure** *BrE* HRM procedimiento conciliatorio *m*

conciliator *n* HRM *labour disputes* conciliador(a) *m,f*

conclude *vt* GEN COMM concluir

conclude from *vt* GEN COMM llegar a la conclusión a partir de

conclusion *n* ACC, GEN COMM *of agreement* cierre *m*, *of contract* conclusión *f*

conclusive[1] *adj* GEN COMM conclusivo

conclusive[2]: ~ **evidence** *n* LAW indicios indudables *m pl*, PATENTS pruebas concluyentes *f pl*

CONCORP *abbr* (*construction corporation*) GEN COMM empresa constructora *f*

concrete: ~ **evidence** *n* LAW indicios concretos *m pl*; ~ **labor** *AmE*, ~ **labour** *BrE* *n* HRM trabajo concreto *m*

concur *vi* GEN COMM concurrir, LAW convenir

concurrency *n* HRM, S&M competencia *f*

concurrent: ~ **processing** *n* COMP proceso concurrente *m*, proceso simultáneo *m*; ~ **return** *n* TAX rendimiento acumulable *m*

concurrents *n pl* TAX concurrentes *m pl*

condemn *vt* GEN COMM condenar

condemnation *n* PROP requisa *f*

condensed[1] *adj* ACC, S&M condensado

condensed[2]: ~ **report** *n* GEN COMM informe resumido *m* (*Esp*), reporte resumido *m* (*AmL*); ~ **statement** *n* ACC estado condensado *m*

condition *n* GEN COMM, LAW condición *f*; ~ **of collection** ECON, GEN COMM condición de cobro *f*; ~ **monitoring** (*CM*) TRANSP control del estado de las mercancías *m*; ~ **precedent** *AmE* LAW condición suspensiva *f*; ~ **subsequent** *AmE* LAW condición resolutoria *f*; ◆ **on** ~ **that** GEN COMM a condición de que; **on the** ~ **that** GEN COMM con la condición de que

conditional: ~ **acceptance** *n* BANK, FIN aceptación condicional *f*; ~ **bond** *n* BANK *international* título condicional *m*; ~ **branch** *n* COMP *programming language* bifurcación condicional *f*; ~ **clause** *n* LAW cláusula onerosa *f*; ~ **contract** *n* LAW contrato condicional *m*; ~ **endorsement** *n* FIN endoso condicional *m*; ~ **market order** *n BrE* STOCK *futures* orden de mercado condicional *f*; ~ **protection** *n* PATENTS protección condicionada *f*; ~ **sale** *n* S&M venta condicional *f*; ~ **sales agreement** *n* S&M acuerdo condicional de ventas *m*; ~ **transactions** *n pl* STOCK transacciones condicionales *f pl*

conditionality *n* BANK carácter condicional *m*, limitación *f*

conditioned *adj* GEN COMM condicionado

conditions *n pl* GEN COMM condiciones *f pl*; ~ **of carriage** TRANSP condiciones del transporte *f pl*; ~ **of contract** GEN COMM, LAW, TRANSP condiciones del contrato *f pl*; ~ **of employment** HRM condiciones de empleo *f pl*; ~ **of sale** ECON, GEN COMM, IMP/EXP, S&M condiciones de venta *f pl*; ~ **of tender** GEN COMM condiciones de la oferta *f pl*; ~ **of use** GEN COMM condiciones de uso *f pl*

condominium *n* GEN COMM condominio *m*, cooperativa *f*, edificio en copropiedad *m*

Condorcet: ~ **paradox** *n* POL paradoja de Condorcet *f*

conducive: ~ **to** *adj* GEN COMM *growth* conducente a

conduct[1] *n* HRM conducta *f*; ~ **of law suit** LAW tramitación de un juicio *f*; ~ **money** GEN COMM dinero de gestión *m*

conduct[2] *vt* GEN COMM *share sale, meeting, trade, survey* conducir

confectioner: ~, **tobacconist and newsagent** *n* (*CTN*) S&M confitero, estanquero y vendedor de periódicos *m*

confederation *n* GEN COMM, POL confederación *f*

Confederation: ~ **of British Industry** *n* (*CBI*) IND ≈ Confederación Española de Organizaciones Empresariales *f* (*CEOE*)

confer *vt* GEN COMM, LAW *rights* conferir; ◆ ~ **the right** GEN COMM otorgar el derecho

conference *n* GEN COMM, MGMNT, POL conferencia *f*; ~ **board** HRM junta de conferencias *f*; ~ **call** COMMS *audio* llamada tridireccional *f*; ~ **delegate** HRM, MGMNT delegado(-a) a una conferencia *m,f*; ~ **line** TRANSP *shipping* línea de conferencia *f*; ~ **member** MGMNT miembro de conferencia *m*; ~ **proceedings** *n pl*

MGMNT procedimientos de la conferencia *m pl*; ~ **report** GEN COMM informe de la conferencia *m* (*Esp*), reporte de conferencia *m* (*AmL*); ~ **site location** MGMNT sede de una conferencia *f*; ~ **system** GEN COMM, MGMNT sistema de conferencias *m*; ~ **table** MGMNT mesa de conferencias *f*; ~ **venue** GEN COMM, MGMNT lugar de la conferencia *m*

confessed: ~ **judgment note** *n AmE* GEN COMM documento de enjuiciamiento reconocido *m*

confession *n* GEN COMM, LAW *of crime* confesión *f*

confidence *n* GEN COMM confianza *f*; ~ **coefficient** MATH coeficiente de confianza *m*; ~ **game** *AmE* (*cf confidence trick BrE*) GEN COMM timo *m*; ~ **interval** MATH intervalo de confianza *m*; ~ **level** MATH nivel de confianza *m*; ~ **man** GEN COMM timador *m*; ~ **trick** *BrE* (*cf confidence game AmE*) GEN COMM timo *m*; ~ **trickster** GEN COMM embaucador(a) *m,f*, timador(a) *m,f*

confidential[1] *adj* BANK, GEN COMM *correspondence*, LAW, POL, TAX confidencial

confidential[2]: ~ **clerk** *n* GEN COMM empleado(-a) de confianza *m,f*; ~ **information** *n* LAW información confidencial *f*; ~ **secretary** *n* HRM secretario(-a) de confianza *m,f*

confidentiality *n* GEN COMM, LAW, TAX confidencialidad *f*; ~ **agreement** LAW, PATENTS acuerdo de confidencialidad *m*

configuration *n* COMP configuración *f*; ~ **control** COMP control de la configuración *m*

configure *vt* COMMS, COMP configurar

configured *adj* COMMS, COMP configurado

confirm *vt* GEN COMM, TAX *assessment* confirmar

confirmation *n* GEN COMM confirmación *f*; ~ **notice** COMMS, GEN COMM aviso de confirmación *m*; ~ **of order** COMMS, GEN COMM confirmación de pedido *f*; ~ **of renewal** INS confirmación de renovación *f*

confirmed: ~ **credit** *n* BANK crédito confirmado *m*; ~ **irrevocable credit** *n* BANK crédito irrevocable confirmado *m*; ~ **letter of credit** *n* BANK, FIN carta de crédito confirmada *f*

confirming: ~ **bank** *n* BANK banco que confirma un crédito; ~ **house** *n* BANK, ECON *international trade* casa de confirmación *f*; ~ **letter** *n* ACC, ADMIN, BANK carta de confirmación *f*

confiscate *vt* GEN COMM confiscar, incautar

confiscation *n* GEN COMM confiscación *f*, incautación *f*

conflagration: ~ **area** *n* INS zona de conflagración *f*

conflict *n* GEN COMM lucha *f* conflicto *m*; ~ **of interest** GEN COMM, POL conflicto de intereses *m*; ~ **of laws** LAW derecho internacional privado *m*, conflicto de leyes *m*

conflicting: ~ **evidence** *n* LAW testimonio contradictorio *m*; ~ **interests** *n* GEN COMM intereses opuestos *m pl*

confluence *n* GEN COMM *interest* confluencia *f*; ~ **analysis** (*CA*) MATH análisis confluente *m*

conform to *vt* GEN COMM *standards* ajustarse a

conformed: ~ **copy** *n* LAW *of legal document* copia conformada *f*

conformity *n* GEN COMM conformidad *f*; ~ **to accounting rules** ACC conformidad con las normas contables *f*; ◆ **in ~ with** ACC *accounting principles*, GEN COMM de conformidad con

confront *vt* GEN COMM hacer frente a

confrontation *n* GEN COMM, LAW careo *m*, confrontación *f*

congestion *n* COMMS *telephone lines* sobrecarga *f*, *market* aglomeración *f*, GEN COMM *market*, S&M congestión *f*; ~ **surcharge** TAX sobretasa por acumulación *f*, TRANSP *shipping* sobrecarga por congestión *f*

conglomerate *n* ECON, FIN conglomeración *f*, conglomerado *m*, conglomerado de empresas *m*; ~ **diversification** ECON, FIN diversificación conglomerada *f*, diversificación de conglomerado *f*; ~ **merger** ECON, FIN fusión de conglomerados *f*

congress *n* GEN COMM congreso *m*

Congress *n AmE* (*cf Parliament BrE*) POL ≈ Las Cortes *f pl* (*Esp*); ~ **of Industrial Organizations** *AmE* (*CIO*) GEN COMM congreso de organizaciones profesionales

Congressional[1] *adj AmE* POL del congreso

Congressional[2]: ~ **Budget and Impoundment Control Act** *n AmE* POL ley del Congreso de Estados Unidos para controlar el presupuesto y los gastos fiscales; ~ **Budget Office** *n AmE* (*CBO*) FIN, POL comisión de presupuestos del congreso

Congressman *n AmE* (*cf Member of Parliament BrE*) POL ≈ diputado *m*, ≈ Miembro del Congreso *m*

Congresswoman *n AmE* (*cf Member of Parliament BrE*) POL ≈ diputada *f*, ≈ Miembro del Congreso *f*

congruence *n* GEN COMM congruencia *f*

congruent *adj* GEN COMM conforme

conjunction[1]: ~ **of circumstances** *n* GEN COMM cúmulo de circunstancias *m*

conjunction[2]: **in ~ with** *phr* GEN COMM en conjunción con *f*

conjuncture *n* GEN COMM coyuntura *f*

connect *vt* COMP, GEN COMM conectar

connected: ~ **with** *adj* TAX relacionado con; ~ **by blood relationship** *adj* TAX emparentado por lazos de sangre

connecting: ~ **carrier** *n* TRANSP transportista de enlace *mf*; ~ **flight** *n* LEIS, TRANSP vuelo de conexión *m*

connection *n* COMP, GEN COMM, TRANSP *airlines* conexión *f*; ~ **time** COMP tiempo de conexión *m*

cons. *abbr* (*consolidated*) GEN COMM consolidado

consecutive[1] *adj* GEN COMM consecutivo

consecutive[2]: ~ **days** *n pl* GEN COMM días consecutivos *m pl*

consensus *n* GEN COMM consenso *m*; ~ **agreement** GEN COMM acuerdo unánime *m*

consent[1] *n* GEN COMM consentimiento *m*; ~ **decree** LAW avenencia sujeta a aprobación de un tribunal *f*; ~ **executed** TAX consentimiento ejecutado *m*

consent[2] *vi* GEN COMM acceder

consequence *n* GEN COMM consecuencia *f*

consequential: ~ **damage** *n* INS, TRANSP daño consecuencial *m*, daño indirecto *m*; ~ **effect** *n* LAW *of court action* efecto resultante *m*; ~ **loss** *n* INS pérdida consecuencial *f*; ~**-loss policy** *n* INS póliza con repercusión en pérdidas *f*

conservation *n* ENVIR conservación *f*; ~ **camp** ENVIR, POL grupo conservacionista *m*; ~ **of portfolio** GEN COMM conservación de cartera *f*

conservationist *n* ENVIR conservacionista *mf*

conservatism *n* GEN COMM conservadurismo *m*; ~ **principle** ACC principio de conservadurismo *m*

conservative[1] *adj* GEN COMM *spending, estimate*, POL conservador

conservative[2]: ~ **accounting** *n* ACC contabilidad basada en el principio de prudencia *f*, contabilidad previsora *f*; **~ estimate** *n* GEN COMM evaluación prudente *m*

Conservative: **~ Party** *n BrE* POL Partido Conservador *m*

conserve *vt* GEN COMM, ENVIR conservar

consgt *abbr* (*consignation*) TRANSP consignación *f*, expedición *f*

consideration *n* INS *payment* remuneración *f*, LAW causa contractual *f*, contrapartida de un contrato *f*, contraprestación *f*, STOCK remuneración *f*; **~ for sale** GEN COMM consideración para la venta *f*; ◆ **take into ~** GEN COMM tomar en cuenta; **upon further ~** GEN COMM considerándolo más detenidamente

consign *vt* TRANSP *goods* consignar

consignation *n* (*consgt*) TRANSP consignación *f*, expedición *f*

consignee *n* (*cnee*) TRANSP consignatario(-a) *m,f*

consigner *n* TRANSP consignador(a) *m,f*, expedidor(a) *m,f*

consignment *n* (*cnmt*) TRANSP remesa *f*; **~ insurance** INS, TRANSP seguro sobre mercancías en consignación *m*; **~ note** (*C/N*) TRANSP hoja de embarque *f*; **~ note control label number** (*CCLN*) TRANSP número de etiqueta de control de la hoja de embarque *m*; **~ sale** S&M, TRANSP venta en depósito *f*; **~ selling** S&M venta por consignación *f*; ◆ **on ~** TRANSP en comisión, en consignación

consignor *n* TRANSP expedidor(a) *m,f*

consistency *n* GEN COMM coherencia *f*, consistencia *f*, continuidad *f*, uniformidad *f*, MGMNT, S&M continuidad *f*; **~ check** GEN COMM control de conformidad *m*; **~ principle** ACC principio de consistencia *m*, principio de continuidad *m*, principio de uniformidad *m*

consistent *adj* GEN COMM coherente, consecuente, consistente

consistently *adv* GEN COMM conformemente

consol. *abbr* (*consolidated*) GEN COMM consolidado

CONSOL *abbr BrE* (*consolidated annuity*) STOCK bono a largo plazo del gobierno británico

consolidate[1]: **~-cargo container service** *n* TRANSP servicio de contenedores para carga consolidada *m*; **~-cargo service** *n* (*CCS*) TRANSP servicio de carga consolidada *m*

consolidate[2] *vt* GEN COMM *position, agreement* consolidar

consolidated[1] *adj* (*cons., consol.*) GEN COMM consolidado; ◆ **on a ~ basis** FIN sobre bases consolidadas

consolidated[2]: **~ accounting** *n* ACC contabilidad consolidada *f*; **~ accounts** *n pl* ACC cuentas consolidadas *f pl*; **~ annuities** *n pl BrE* FIN anualidades consolidadas *f pl*, renta consolidada *f*; **~ annuity** *n BrE* (*CONSOL*) STOCK bono a largo plazo del gobierno británico; **~ audited accounts** *n pl* ACC cuentas consolidadas auditadas *f pl*; **~ balance sheet** *n* ACC balance consolidado *m*, balance de situación consolidado *m*; **~ base capital** *n* GEN COMM capital de base consolidado *m*; **~ bond** *n* FIN, STOCK bono consolidado *m*; **~ branch** *n* GEN COMM, IND filial consolidada *f*; **~ cash flow statement** *n* ACC estado consolidado del activo líquido, estado de cash flow consolidado *m*, estado de flujos de caja consolidado *m*, estado de tesorería consolidado *m*; **~ data plate** *n* TRANSP placa de características unificadas *f*; **~ debenture stock** *n BrE* FIN, STOCK acción irredimible consolidada *f*; **~ debt** *n* ACC, FIN, GEN COMM deuda consolidada *f*; **~ delivery** *n* TRANSP entrega consolidada

f; **~ figures** *n pl* ACC cifras consolidadas *f pl*; **~ financial statement** *n* ACC estado financiero consolidado *m*; **~ fund** *n* ECON, FIN, TAX fondo consolidado *m*; **~ fund standing service** *n BrE* ECON servicio fijo del fondo consolidado *m*; **~ loan** *n* BANK empréstito consolidado *m*; **~ net profit** *n* ACC beneficio neto consolidado *m*; **~ quotation system** *n* STOCK sistema de cotización consolidada *m*; **~ rate** *n* TRANSP cuota combinada *f*, tarifa unificada *f*; **~ statement** *n* ACC, FIN estado consolidado *m*; **~ statement of condition** *n AmE* ACC, FIN estado de contabilidad consolidado *m*, recapitulación de la situación *f*; **~ stock** *n BrE* FIN existencias consolidadas *f pl*; **~ tape** *n* STOCK cinta consolidada *f*; **~ tax return** *n* TAX *affiliated companies* declaración de la renta consolidada *f*

Consolidated: **~ Metropolitan Statistical Area** *n AmE* (*CMSA*) POL área estadística metropolitana consolidada; **~ Revenue Fund** *n* FIN Fondo Consolidado de Ingresos *m*

consolidation *n* GEN COMM consolidación *f*; **~ of balances** ACC consolidación de balances *f*; **~ depot** TRANSP almacén de consolidación *m*; **~ of funds** BANK, FIN consolidación de fondos *f*; **~ of interests** BANK, FIN consolidación de intereses *f*; **~ loan** BANK, FIN préstamo de consolidación *m*; **~ method** ACC método de consolidación *m*; **~ of shares** STOCK consolidación de acciones *f*

consolidator *n* TRANSP agrupador(a) *m,f*

consortium *n* GEN COMM consorcio *m*, grupo de empresas *m*, HRM consorcio *m*; **~ bank** BANK, FIN banco de consorcio *m*; **~ of banks** *n pl* BANK, FIN consorcio de bancos *m*

conspectus *n* FIN vista de conjunto *f*, vista general *f*, GEN COMM estudio de conjunto *m*

conspicuous: **~ consumption** *n* ECON, S&M consumo conspicuo *m*, consumo ostentoso *m*

constant *n* COMP, MATH constante *f*; **~ capital** ECON capital constante *m*; **~ dollars** ECON dólares de poder adquisitivo constante *m pl*; **~ elasticity of substitution** (*CES*) ECON elasticidad de sustitución constante *f*; **~-payment loan** BANK préstamo de pago invariable *m*; **~ price** ECON, GEN COMM, S&M precio constante *m*; **~ returns to scale** *n pl* ECON retornos a escalas constantes *m pl*; **~ risk** INS riesgo constante *m*

constituent: **~ company** *n* STOCK compañía constituyente *f*

constituted *adj* GEN COMM, LAW *trust* constituido

constitution *n* LAW, POL constitución *f*

constitutional: **~ foundation** *n* ADMIN fundamento constitucional *m*; **~ law** *n* LAW derecho constitucional *m*; **~ strike** *n* HRM, IND, LAW huelga legal *f*

Constitutional: **~ Tribunal** *n* LAW, POL Tribunal Constitucional *m*

constr *abbr* (*construction*) GEN COMM, PROP construcción *f*

constrained: **~ cycle** *n* BANK, FIN, GEN COMM, MGMNT ciclo restringido *m*; **~ market pricing** *n AmE* (*cf stand alone cost BrE*) ECON fijación restrictiva de precios de mercado *f*

constraining: **~ factor** *n* ECON *restricting production, sale*, S&M factor constrictor *m*

constraint *n* ECON, POL *on monetary policy* contención *f*

construct *vt* GEN COMM, PROP construir

construction *n* (*constr*) GEN COMM, PROP construcción *f*;

~ **activities** *n pl* GEN COMM, PROP actividades de la construcción *f pl*; ~ **corporation** (*CONCORP*) GEN COMM empresa constructora *f*; ~ **cost index** STOCK índice del coste de la construcción *m* (*Esp*), índice del costo de la construcción *m* (*AmL*); ~ **industry** IND, PROP sector de la construcción *m*; ~ **loan** BANK, PROP préstamo inmobiliario *m*, préstamo para la construcción *m*; ~ **rate** TRANSP índice de construcción *m*; ~ **subsidy** TRANSP subsidio de construcción *m*; ~ **unit value** (*CUV*) TRANSP valor de la unidad de construcción *m*; ~ **and use** *BrE* LAW construcción y uso; ~ **and use regulation** (*C&U regulation*) TRANSP normativa de construcción y explotación *f*; ~ **worker** HRM, IND obrero(-a) de la construcción *m,f*; ◆ **under** ~ IND, PROP en construcción

constructive: ~ **delivery** *n* GEN COMM entrega implícita *f*; ~ **dismissal** *n* HRM despido constructivo *m*; ~ **eviction** *n* LAW desalojo constructivo *m*, PROP desalojo constructivo *m*, expulsión constructiva *f*; ~ **notice** *n AmE* LAW notificación sobreentendida *f*; ~ **receipt** *n* TAX recibo implícito *m*; ~ **receipt of income** *n* TAX recibo implícito de la renta *m*; ~ **total loss** *n* (*CTL*) GEN COMM, INS pérdida total implícita *f*, TRANSP *maritime insurance* pérdida total constructiva *f*; ~ **total loss only** *n* (*CTLO*) GEN COMM, INS sólo pérdida total implícita *f*

consul *n* GEN COMM, POL cónsul *mf*; ~ **general** POL cónsul general *mf*

consulage *n* IMP/EXP derechos consulares *m pl*

consular: ~ **fees** *n pl* ADMIN, IMP/EXP derechos consulares *m pl*

consulate *n* GEN COMM, POL consulado *m*

consult *vt* COMP, GEN COMM, HRM, MGMNT consultar

consultancy *n* GEN COMM, HRM, MGMNT, S&M consultoría *f*; ~ **work** GEN COMM, HRM trabajo de asesor *m*

consultant *n* GEN COMM, HRM, MGMNT asesor(a) *m,f*, consejero(-a) *m,f*, consultor(a) *m,f*; ~ **engineer** GEN COMM, HRM asesor(a) técnico(-a) *m,f*, ingeniero(-a) consultor(a) *m,f*

consultation *n* COMP, GEN COMM, HRM, MGMNT, S&M consulta *f*; ◆ **in** ~ **with** GEN COMM en consulta con

consultative[1] *adj* GEN COMM consultivo; ~-**democratic** MGMNT consultivo-democrático

consultative[2]: ~ **body** *n* GEN COMM, MGMNT *committees and boards* organismo consultivo *m*; ~ **committee** *n* ADMIN comité consultivo *m*; ~ **group** *n* POL grupo consultivo *m*; ~ **shipping group** *n* (*CSG*) TRANSP grupo naviero consultivo *m*

consulting: ~ **division** *n* HRM división de consultoría *f*; ~ **engineer** *n* GEN COMM técnico(-a) asesor(a) *m,f*; ~ **firm** *n* GEN COMM, HRM, MGMNT consulting *m*, consultoría *f*, firma consultora *f*; ~ **office** *n* HRM despacho de consultoría *m*; ~ **service** *n* GEN COMM servicio de consultoría *m*

consume *vt* GEN COMM consumir

consumer[1]: ~-**oriented** *adj* GEN COMM orientado al consumidor

consumer[2] *n* GEN COMM consumidor(a) *m,f*; ~ **acceptance** S&M aceptación del consumidor *f*; ~ **advertising** S&M publicidad para el consumidor *f*; ~ **advisory service** GEN COMM, S&M servicio de asesoramiento al consumidor *m*; ~ **age group** S&M grupo de edades de consumidores *m*; ~ **banking** BANK banca orientada al consumo *f*; ~ **behavior** *AmE*, ~ **behaviour** *BrE* S&M comportamiento del consumidor

m; ~ **benefit** GEN COMM, S&M ventaja para el consumidor *f*; ~ **brand** S&M marca de consumo *f*; ~ **buying power** S&M poder adquisitivo del consumidor *m*; ~ **choice** S&M elección del consumidor *f*, opción del consumidor *f*; ~ **company** GEN COMM empresa de consumo *f*; ~ **cooperative** HRM cooperativa de consumidores *f*; ~ **credit** BANK, FIN crédito al consumo *m*; ~ **credit market** BANK, FIN mercado de crédito al consumo *m*; ~ **demand** S&M demanda de los consumidores *f*; ~ **durables** *n pl* ECON, S&M bienes de consumo duraderos *m pl*, bienes duraderos *m pl*; ~ **equilibrium** ECON, S&M equilibrio del consumidor *m*; ~ **expectations** *n pl* GEN COMM expectativas del consumidor *f pl*; ~ **expenditure** ECON, S&M gasto de consumo *m*; ~ **expenditure survey** ECON, FIN estudio del gasto del consumidor *m*, Índice de Precios al Detalle *m* (*IPC*); ~ **finance company** FIN compañía financiera de consumo *f*; ~ **goods** ECON, S&M bienes de consumo *m pl*; ~ **habits** *n pl* S&M hábitos del consumidor *m pl*, hábitos de consumo *m pl*; ~ **hardgoods** *n pl* GEN COMM, S&M bienes de consumo duraderos *m pl*; ~ **index price** ECON índice de precios al consumo *m*; ~ **installment loan** *AmE*, ~ **instalment loan** *BrE* BANK préstamo a plazos al consumo *m*, préstamo a plazos para el consumidor *m*; ~ **issue** S&M cuestión de consumo *f*; ~ **leasing** BANK arrendamiento financiero al consumidor *m*; ~ **lending** BANK, FIN préstamo al consumidor *m*; ~ **loan** BANK, FIN crédito al consumidor *m*; ~ **loan institute** BANK, FIN establecimiento de créditos personales *m*, instituto de préstamos al consumidor *m*; ~ **loyalty** S&M lealtad del consumidor *f*; ~ **magazine** GEN COMM, S&M revista del consumidor *f*; ~ **market** S&M mercado de consumo *m*; ~ **marketing** S&M marketing de consumo *m*; ~ **nondurables** *n pl* S&M bienes no duraderos *m pl*; ~ **organization** S&M organización del consumidor *f*; ~ **orientation** S&M orientación del consumo *f*; ~-**oriented product** S&M producto orientado al consumidor *m*; ~ **panel** S&M *market research* panel de consumidores *m*; ~ **pattern** S&M modelo de consumo *m*; ~ **policy** GEN COMM *EU*, S&M política de consumo *f*; ~ **preference** GEN COMM, S&M preferencia del consumidor *f*; ~ **pressure** GEN COMM presión del consumidor *f*; ~ **price** S&M precio al consumidor *m*; ~ **product** GEN COMM producto de consumo *m*; ~ **profile** S&M perfil del consumidor *m*; ~ **protection** LAW, S&M protección del consumidor *f*; ~-**protection legislation** LAW, S&M legislación de protección al consumidor *f*; ~ **reaction** S&M reacción del consumidor *f*; ~ **relations manager** HRM, S&M director(a) de atención al cliente *m,f*; ~ **requirement** S&M requisito del consumidor *m*; ~ **research** S&M investigación del consumidor *f*; ~ **resistance** S&M resistencia del consumo *f*; ~ **response** S&M respuesta del consumidor *f*; ~ **satisfaction** GEN COMM, S&M satisfacción del consumidor *f*; ~ **service** TAX servicio de consumo *m*; ~ **society** ECON, POL, S&M sociedad de consumidores *f*, sociedad de consumo *f*; ~ **sovereignty** ECON, S&M dominio del consumo *m*, supremacía del consumidor *f*; ~ **spending** ECON, GEN COMM consumo privado *m*; ~ **surplus** ECON, S&M superávit del consumidor *m*; ~ **survey** S&M encuesta de consumidores *f*; ~ **test** S&M prueba del consumidor *f*; ~ **trend** S&M tendencia de consumo *f*; ~ **want** S&M deseo del consumidor *m*

Consumer: ~ **Credit Act** *n* LAW, POL, S&M Ley de Crédito al Consumo *f*; ~ **Credit Protection Act** *n AmE* ADMIN,

LAW, S&M acta de protección del consumidor en materia de crédito al consumo; **~ Protection Advisory Committee** *n* ECON *European Union* Comité Asesor de Protección al Consumo *m*; **~ Price Index** *n* *BrE* (*CPI*) ECON, FIN Índice de Precios al Consumo *m* (*IPC*);

consumerism *n* ECON, GEN COMM, S&M consumismo *m*

consumerist *n* ECON, GEN COMM, S&M consumista *mf*

Consumers': **~ Advisory Council** *n* *AmE* (*CAC, cf Consumers' Association BrE*) WEL oficina de asesoramiento al consumidor, ≈ Organización de Consumidores y Usuarios *f* (*OCU*); **~ Association** *n* *BrE* (*CA, cf Consumers' Advisory Council AmE*) WEL oficina de asesoramiento al consumidor, ≈ Organización de Consumidores y Usuarios *f* (*OCU*)

consummate *vt* GEN COMM, LAW consumar

consummated *adj* GEN COMM, LAW consumado

consumption *n* (*C*) ECON, GEN COMM, S&M consumo *m*; **~ function** ECON función de consumo *f*; **~ goods** *n pl* ECON, S&M bienes de consumo *m pl*; **~ pattern** ECON, S&M estructura del consumo *f*; **~ per capita** ECON consumo por persona *m*; **~ rate of interest** (*CRI*) GEN COMM tasa de interés del consumo *f*; **~ tax** TAX impuesto sobre el consumo *m*

contact *n* GEN COMM *person* contacto *m*; **~ damage** TRANSP daño por contacto *m*; **~ report** S&M informe de contactos *m*, informe de visita *m* (*Esp*), reporte de contactos *m* (*AmL*), reporte de visita *m* (*AmL*); ♦ **make ~ with** GEN COMM ponerse en contacto con

contain *vt* ECON, GEN COMM *demand, inflation* contener

container *n* TRANSP *ISO unit* contáiner *m*, contenedor *m*; **~ berth** TRANSP *shipping* muelle para carga y descarga de contenedores *m*; **~ bill of lading** IMP/EXP *shipping*, TRANSP conocimiento de embarque de contenedores *m*; **~ block** TRANSP bloque de contenedores *m*; **~ car** *AmE* (*cf container wagon BrE*) TRANSP *rail* vagón para transporte de contenedores *m*, vagón portacontenedores *m*; **~ control** (*CC*) TRANSP control de contenedores *m*; **~ depot** TRANSP depósito de contenedores *m*; **~ dock** TRANSP depósito de contenedores *m*; **~ dues** *n pl* TRANSP *shipping* derechos por contenedor *m pl*; **~ frame** TRANSP armazón del contenedor *m*; **~ freight station** (*CFS*) TRANSP centro de contenedores para fletes *m*; **~ head** TRANSP cabeza del contenedor *f*; **~ import cargo manifest** IMP/EXP, TRANSP declaración de la carga de importación del contenedor *f*; **~ leasing** TRANSP arrendamiento de contenedores *m*; **~ line** TRANSP línea de contenedores *f*; **~ load** TRANSP carga completa *f*; **~ market** TRANSP mercado de contenedores *m*; **~ on flat car** *AmE* (*cf container on flat wagon BrE*) TRANSP contenedor sobre vagón plataforma *m*, contenedor sobre vagón raso *m*; **~ on flat wagon** *BrE* (*cf container on flat car AmE*) TRANSP contenedor sobre vagón plataforma *m*, contenedor sobre vagón raso *m*; **~ operator** TRANSP operador(a) de contenedores *m,f*; **~ packing certificate** TRANSP certificado de embalaje del contenedor *m*; **~ park** TRANSP depósito de contenedores *m*; **~ partload** TRANSP carga incompleta del contenedor *f*; **~ pool** TRANSP consorcio de contenedores *m*; **~ port** TRANSP terminal portuaria de contenedores *f*; **~ safety convention** (*CSC*) TRANSP convención sobre seguridad de los contenedores *f*; **~ service** TRANSP servicio de contenedores *m*; **~ service tariff** (*CST*) TRANSP tarifa de servicio de contenedores *f*; **~ ship** TRANSP buque portacontenedores *m*; **~ space allocation** TRANSP adjudicación de espacio para contenedores *f*; **~ stack** TRANSP pila de contenedores *f*; **~ stuffing** TRANSP llenado del contenedor *m*; **~ terminal** TRANSP terminal para contenedores *f*; **~ transport** TRANSP transporte en contenedores *m*; **~ unstuffing** TRANSP vaciado del contenedor *m*; **~ use** TRANSP uso del contenedor *m*; **~ user analysis** TRANSP análisis del uso del contenedor *m*; **~ utilization** TRANSP utilización del contenedor *f*; **~ wagon** *BrE* (*cf container car AmE*) TRANSP *rail* vagón para transporte de contenedores *m*, vagón portacontenedores *m*; **~ yard** (*CY*) TRANSP muelle de contenedores *m*

containerization *n* TRANSP contenedorización *f*

containerize *vt* TRANSP contenedorizar

containerized[1] *adj* TRANSP contenedorizado

containerized[2]: **~ shipping** *n* TRANSP despacho contenedorizado *m*, despacho en contenedores *m*, envío en contenedores *m*

containment *n* ECON *credit* recorte *m*, *demand* contención *f*, POL *on monetary policy* contención *f*

contaminate *vt* ENVIR contaminar

contaminated *adj* ENVIR contaminado; **~ site** *n* ENVIR lugar contaminado *m*

contamination *n* ENVIR, IND *of product* contaminación *f*

contango *n* BANK comisión de aplazamiento *f*, FIN interés de aplazamiento *m*, STOCK reporte *m* (*AmL*); **~ business** *BrE* STOCK operación con interés de aplazamiento *f*, operación de reporte *f*; **~ day** *BrE* STOCK día del reporte *m*; **~ market** STOCK mercado de contangos *m*

cont'd *abbr* (*continued*) GEN COMM *written documents* continúa, seguido

contemporaneous: **~ externality** *n* ECON externalidad contemporánea *f*

contempt[1]: **~ of court** *n* LAW desacato *m*, desobediencia *f*, quebrantamiento del secreto del sumario *m*

contempt[2]: **in ~ of court** *phr* LAW *witness* en rebeldía

content *n* GEN COMM contenido *m*

contents *n* GEN COMM contenido *m*

contest[1] *n* GEN COMM concurso *m*

contest[2] *vt* LAW *will* impugnar

contestable: **~ clause** *n* INS, LAW cláusula disputable *f*; **~ markets thesis** *n* ECON, S&M tesis de mercado discutible *f*

contested *adj* S&M competido *m*

context[1]: **~-sensitive** *adj* COMP sensible al contexto

context[2] *n* COMP, GEN COMM contexto *m*

contiguous *adj* COMP contiguo

Continent: the ~ *n* GEN COMM, POL *mainland Europe* el continente *m*

continental[1] *adj* GEN COMM continental

continental[2]: **~ trade** *n* ECON, S&M comercio continental *m*

contingencies: **~ vote** *n pl* FIN votación de gastos imprevistos *f*

contingency *n* GEN COMM contingencia *f*; **~ arrangements** *n pl* GEN COMM acuerdos para imprevistos *m pl*; **~ clause** BANK, INS, LAW cláusula condicional *f*; **~ fund** FIN *personal budgets* fondo de imprevistos *m*; **~ management** MGMNT administración por contingencia *f*, dirección por contingencia *f*, gestión por contingencia *f*; **~ order** STOCK orden de contingencia *f*; **~ payment** ACC, BANK pago condicionado *m*, pago contingente *m*, pago eventual *m*; **~ plan** GEN

COMM plan de contingencia *m*, plan de emergencia *m*; ~ **planning** GEN COMM plan de contingencia *m*, planificación de contingencia *f*, planificación de emergencia *f*; ~ **reserve** FIN, MGMNT reserva para contingencias *f*; ~ **table** ECON tabla de contingencia *f*; ~ **theory** MGMNT teoría de contingencia *f*

contingent[1] *adj* GEN COMM *liability* contingente

contingent[2]: ~ **asset** *n* ACC, FIN, PROP activo condicionado *m*, activo contingente *m*, activo realizable *m*; ~ **budget** *n* ACC presupuesto contingente *m*, ECON presupuesto eventual *m*, presupuesto contingente *m*, FIN presupuesto eventual *m*; ~ **business interruption insurance** *n* INS seguro condicionado a cese de negocio *m*; ~ **charge** *n* ACC, BANK, FIN cargo contingente *m*; ~ **claim** *n* ACC reclamación condicionada *f*, reclamación contingente *f*; ~ **consideration** *n* GEN COMM consideración condicional *f*; ~ **cost** *n* ACC coste contingente *m* (*Esp*), costo contingente *m* (*AmL*); ~ **expenses** *n pl* ACC gastos contingentes *m pl*; ~ **fee** *n* GEN COMM comisión por cobranza *f*; ~ **liability** *n* ACC, FIN, LAW pasivo eventual *m*, pasivo contingente *m*; ~ **market** *n* INS mercado contingente *m*; ~ **obligation** *n* TAX obligación contingente *f*; ~ **order** *n* STOCK pedido imprevisto *m*; ~ **valuation** *n* ECON valoración eventual *f*

contingently *adv* GEN COMM eventualmente

continual: ~ **professional education** *n* HRM capacitación profesional permanente *f* (*AmL*), educación profesional permanente *f*, formación profesional permanente *f* (*Esp*)

continuation *n* STOCK continuación *f*; ~ **clause** (*CC*) INS cláusula sobre prórroga *f*; ~ **day** STOCK día de reportes *m*

continue *vi* GEN COMM continuar

continue to *vi* GEN COMM seguir

continued[1] *adj* (*cont'd*) GEN COMM *written documents* continua, seguido

continued[2]: ~ **bond** *n* FIN, STOCK bono de vencimiento aplazado *m*; ~ **success** *n* GEN COMM *of person, company, product* éxito permanente *m*

continuing[1] *adj* GEN COMM *interest, support* continuo

continuing[2]: ~ **appropriation authority** *n pl* FIN organismo de asignación presupuestaria *m*; ~ **commitment** *n* GEN COMM compromiso permanente *m*; ~ **cost** *n* ACC coste continuo *m* (*Esp*), costo continuo *m* (*AmL*); ~ **guarantee** *n* BANK, GEN COMM, LAW garantía permanente *f*

continuity *n* ACC, GEN COMM, MGMNT, S&M continuidad *f*; ~ **of employment** *BrE* HRM continuidad en el empleo *f*; ~ **thesis** ECON tesis de continuidad *f*

continuous: ~ **assessment** *n* HRM, WEL evaluación continua *f*; ~ **audit** *n* ACC auditoría continua *f*, fiscalización continua *f*, intervención continua *f*; ~ **budget** *n* ACC, ECON, FIN presupuesto continuo *m*; ~ **form** *n pl* GEN COMM formulario continuo *m*; ~ **inventory** *n* ACC, GEN COMM, ECON inventario continuo *m*; ~ **labor** *AmE*, ~ **labour** *BrE* HRM trabajo continuo *m*; ~ **liner** *n* (*CL*) TRANSP buque de pasaje en servicio continuo; ~ **market** *n* STOCK mercado continuo *m*; ~ **net settlement** *n BrE* (*CNS*) STOCK liquidación neta continua *f*; ~ **process** *n* ECON, IND, S&M proceso continuo *m*; ~ **process production** *n* ECON, IND, S&M producción de proceso continuo *f*; ~ **production** *n* IND producción continua *f*; ~ **promotion** *n* MEDIA, S&M *advertising* promoción continua *f*; ~ **reinforcement** *n*

HRM refuerzo continuo *m*; ~ **research** *n* MGMNT, S&M investigación permanente *f*; ~ **stationery** *n* COMP papel continuo *m*; ~ **stocktaking** *n* ACC, GEN COMM, ECON inventario continuo *m*; ~ **survey** *n* S&M *market research* encuesta permanente *f*; ~ **survey cycle** *n* (*CSC*) GEN COMM ciclo de peritaje continuo *m*; ~ **variable** *n* MATH variable continua *f*

Continuously: ~ **Offered Longer-Term Securities** *n pl* (*COLTS*) STOCK valores a mayor plazo de oferta continua *m pl*

contr. *abbr* (*contractor*) GEN COMM contratista *mf*

contra *n* ACC, BANK contrapartida *f*; ~ **account** ACC contrapartida *f*; ~-**deal** S&M contraoferta *f*; ~ **entry** ACC, BANK contraasiento *m*

contraband *n* GEN COMM contrabando *m*

contrabandist *n* GEN COMM contrabandista *mf*

contract[1] *n* GEN COMM contrato *m*; ~ **agreement** LAW acuerdo de contrato *m*; ~ **bargaining** HRM negociación de contrato *f*; ~ **bond** GEN COMM fianza de contratista *f*; ~ **carrier** TRANSP empresa de transportes por contrato *f*; ~ **clause** BANK, INS, LAW cláusula de un contrato *f*; ~ **compliance** HRM, LAW cumplimiento de contrato *m*; ~ **curve** ECON curva de contrato *f*; ~ **delivery date** STOCK *currency futures* fecha de entrega *f*; ~ **delivery month** STOCK *currency futures* mes de entrega *m*; ~ **of employment** HRM contrato de trabajo *m*; ~ **for the sale of goods** LAW, S&M contrato para la venta de mercancías *m*; ~ **for services** COMP, GEN COMM, HRM, LAW contrato de servicios *m*; ~ **grade** STOCK *Eurodollar futures* calidad aceptada *f*; ~ **hire** GEN COMM, HRM contratación *f*, salario por contrato *m*; ~ **holdback** GEN COMM obstáculo contractual *m*; ~ **holder** FIN portador(a) de contrato *m,f*, tenedor de contrato *m,f*; ~ **of indemnity** INS, PROP *liability* contrato de indemnización *m*; ~ **joint venture** GEN COMM asociación temporal de empresas contractual *f*; ~ **labor** *AmE*, ~ **labour** *BrE* HRM mano de obra contratada *f*, *task* trabajo contratado *m*; ~ **licence** *BrE*, ~ **license** *AmE* IMP/EXP licencia por contrato *f*; ~ **maintenance** GEN COMM mantenimiento del contrato *m*; ~ **month** GEN COMM, STOCK *futures* mes del contrato *m*; ~ **note** STOCK nota de contrato *f*; ~ **payment** ACC pago contractual *m*; ~ **price** TAX *instalment sale* precio contractual *m*; ~ **print** S&M impresión del contrato *f*; ~ **rent** PROP alquiler contractual *m*; ~ **size** STOCK *currency futures* volumen de contrato *m*; ~ **specifications** *n pl* LAW especificaciones contractuales *f pl*; ~ **value** STOCK *futures* valor del contrato *m*; ~ **work** HRM trabajo bajo contrato *m*; ♦ **this ~ is ultravires** LAW este contrato se celebró en exceso de las facultades de las partes contratantes

contract[2] **1.** *vt* FIN *loan* contraer; ♦ ~ **sb** GEN COMM contratar a alguien; **2.** *vi* ECON, GEN COMM contratar, *growth* contraerse

contract out *vt* GEN COMM subcontratar

contract to *vi* GEN COMM contratar para

contracted: ~-**in rate** *n BrE* TAX *National Insurance* tipo concertado *m*; ~-**out rate** *n* TAX *National Insurance* tipo establecido *m*

contracting: ~ **in** *n BrE* GEN COMM, HRM contratante *m*; ~ **out** *BrE n* GEN COMM subcontratación *f*; ~ **out clause** *n BrE* LAW cláusula de formalización de un plan de pensiones que se sale del plan nacional *f*; ~ **party** *n* LAW parte contratante *f*; ~ **state** *n* PATENTS licencia contractual *f*

contraction *n* ECON contracción *f*; ~ **of demand** S&M *for product* contracción de la demanda *m*, disminución de la demanda *f*

contractionary: ~ **national income gap** *n* ECON *econometrics* brecha restrictiva del ingreso nacional *f*; ~ **pressure** *n* ECON presión de austeridad *f*

contractor *n* (*contr*) GEN COMM contratista *mf*; ~'s **all risks insurance** INS seguro a todo riesgo del contratista *m*; ~'s **yard** PROP obra de material de construcción *f*

contracts: ~ **manager** *n* HRM, MGMNT director(a) de contratos *m,f*; ~ **officer** *n* HRM, GEN COMM, IND, LAW, PROP contratista *mf*

contractual: ~ **liability** *n* LAW responsabilidad contractual *f*; ~ **loan rate** *n* STOCK *Eurodollar futures* tasa contractual de los préstamos *f*; ~ **obligation** *n* LAW obligación contractual *f*; ~ **payment** *n* ACC pago contractual *m*; ~ **provision** *n* LAW disposición contractual *f*; ~ **relationship** *n* GEN COMM relación contractual *f*; ~ **savings** *n* BANK, ECON, FIN ahorros contractuales *m pl*

contracyclical: ~ **policy** *n* ECON política anticíclica *f*

contrarian *n* STOCK inversor(a) contracorriente *m,f*

contrast *n* COMP, GEN COMM contraste *m*

contribute *vt* GEN COMM contribuir

contributed: ~ **capital** *n* STOCK capital aportado *m*

contribution *n* GEN COMM *personal, financial* contribución *f*; ~ **analysis** FIN, GEN COMM análisis de contribución *m*; ~ **of capital** FIN aportación de capital *f*; ~ **margin** ACC margen de contribución *m*; ~ **payable on self-employed earnings** TAX aportación sobre las ganancias de un trabajador por cuenta propia *f*; ~ **profit** ACC beneficio de la contribución *m*, rendimiento de la aportación *m*; ~ **standard** ECON contribución tipo *f*; ◆ **make a** ~ GEN COMM aportar una contribución

contributions: ~ **through employment** *n pl* TAX *pensions* aportaciones a través del empleo *f pl*

contributor *n* ECON, GEN COMM colaborador(a) *m,f*, TAX contribuyente *mf*; ~ **of capital** GEN COMM capitalista *mf*

contributory[1] *adj* LAW contribuyente, parcial

contributory[2]: ~ **earnings from employment** *n* ACC, TAX *pensions* ingresos salariales sujetos a aportación *m pl*; ~ **negligence** *n* LAW negligencia concurrente *f*; ~ **pension fund** *n* FIN, HRM, TAX, WEL fondo de pensión contributivo *m*; ~ **pension plan** *n* FIN, HRM, TAX plan de pensión contributiva *m*; ~ **pension scheme** *n* FIN, HRM, TAX esquema de pensión contributoria *m*, plan de pensión contributiva *m*; ~ **self-employed earnings** *n* TAX *pensions* ganancias del trabajador por cuenta propia sujetas a aportación *f pl*; ~ **sickness fund** *n* GEN COMM, HRM fondo contributivo para enfermedad *m*, fondo contributivo para invalidez *m*; ~ **value** *n* INS valor contribuyente *m*

control[1] *n* GEN COMM control *m*; ~ **account** ACC, MGMNT cuenta de control *f*; ~ **ball** COMP bola rodante *f*; ~ **block** STOCK bloque de control *m*; ~ **change** GEN COMM cambio de control *m*; ~ **character** COMP carácter de verificación *f*; ~ **command** COMP comando de control *m*; ~ **cycle** BANK, FIN, GEN COMM, MGMNT ciclo de control *m*; ~ **data** COMP datos de control *m pl*; ~ **group** S&M grupo de control *m*; ~ **information** GEN COMM información de control *f*; ~ **key** (*CTRL key*) COMP tecla

de mando *f* (*tecla CTRL*); ~ **law** LAW ley de control *f*; ~ **of line limits** GEN COMM control de los límites de una línea *m*; ~ **panel** COMP, GEN COMM, IND tablero de control *m*; ~ **procedure** COMP procedimiento de control *m*; ~ **program** COMP programa de control *m*; ~ **question** GEN COMM, S&M pregunta de control *f*; ~ **stock** STOCK valores de control *m pl*; ~ **structure** ADMIN, S&M estructura de control *f*; ~ **ticket** TRANSP resguardo de control *m*; ◆ **take** ~ GEN COMM tomar el control

control[2] *vt* ECON *inflation* contener, GEN COMM *demand* controlar; ◆ ~ **a market** FIN controlar un mercado; ~ **the purse strings** FIN controlar los gastos

Control: ~ **of Substances Hazardous To Health Regulations** *n BrE* (*COSHH*) WEL normativa de control de sustancias peligrosas para la salud

Control-Alternate-Delete *n* (*CAD*) COMP Control-Alternar-Suprimir *m*

controllable: ~ **cost** *n* ACC costo controlable *m* (*AmL*), coste controlable *m* (*Esp*)

controlled[1] *adj* GEN COMM controlado

controlled[2]: ~ **atmosphere** *n* (*CA*) ENVIR atmósfera controlada *f*; ~ **circulation** *n* S&M tirada controlada *f*; ~ **commodities** *n pl BrE* STOCK productos controlados *m pl*; ~ **company** *n* GEN COMM compañía filial *f*; ~ **corporation** *n* STOCK empresa controlada *f*; ~ **economy** *n* ECON economía dirigida *f*; ~ **market** *n* ECON mercado intervenido *m*; ~ **rate** *n* BANK, ECON, FIN, STOCK tipo controlado *m*, tasa controlada *f*; ~ **transit** *n* TRANSP tránsito controlado *m*; ~ **wildcat drilling** *n* ENVIR yacimiento petrolífero controlado *m*

controller *n* FIN director(a) financiero(-a) *m,f*, GEN COMM controlador(a) *m,f*, director(a) administrativo(-a) *m,f*, director(a) financiero(-a) *m,f*, inspector(a) *m,f*, interventor(a) *m,f* (*Esp*); HRM, MGMNT director(a) financiero(-a) *m,f*

controlling: ~ **account** *n* ACC cuenta de mayor *f*; ~ **company** *n* GEN COMM sociedad de control *f*; ~ **corporation** *n* GEN COMM compañía matriz *f*; ~ **interest** *n* HRM, STOCK inversión dominante *f*, participación controladora *f*; ~ **shareholder** *n* STOCK accionista mayoritario(-a) *m,f*

controversial *adj* GEN COMM, MEDIA, POL controvertido

controversy *n* GEN COMM, MEDIA, POL controversia *f*

convene *vt* GEN COMM, HRM, MGMNT *meeting* convocar

convenience: ~ **bill** *n* GEN COMM factura de prueba *f*; ~ **food** *n* S&M platos precocinados *m pl*; ~ **goods** *n pl* S&M artículos de consumo corriente *m pl*; ~ **product** *n* GEN COMM producto de conveniencia *m*; ~ **sampling** *n* S&M muestreo aleatorio *m*; ~ **shop** *n BrE* (*cf convenience store AmE*) S&M tienda de conveniencia *f*; ~ **store** *n AmE* (*cf convenience shop BrE*) S&M tienda de conveniencia *f*

convenor *n* GEN COMM presidente(-a) *m,f*, HRM, MGMNT *of committee* organizador(a) de una reunión *m,f*, presidente(-a) *m,f*, *in the workplace* representante sindical *mf*

convention *n* ACC convención *f*, GEN COMM tratado multilateral *m*, *accepted behaviour, rule* norma aceptada *f*, convención *f*, MGMNT convención *f*

Convention: ~ **on the Contract for the International Carriage of Goods by Road** *n* GEN COMM, TRANSP Convención sobre el Contrato para el Transporte Internacional de Mercancías por Carretera *f*

conventional: ~ **cargo** n TRANSP carga convencional f; ~ **lien** n TAX gravamen convenido m; ~ **mortgage** n BANK, PROP hipoteca convencional f

converge vi GEN COMM *ideas, activities* converger

convergence n GEN COMM convergencia f; ~ **hypothesis** ECON, POL hipótesis de convergencia f; ~ **thesis** ECON, POL tesis de convergencia f

conversational: ~ **entry** n COMP entrada conversacional f; ~ **mode** n COMP modalidad dialogada f, modo conversación m

conversationally adv COMP en modo de conversación

conversely adv GEN COMM a la inversa

conversion n GEN COMM conversión f, transformación f, STOCK conversión de títulos m; ~ **cost** ACC coste de transformación m (*Esp*), coste directo más gastos generales m (*Esp*), costo de transformación m (*AmL*), costo directo más gastos generales m (*AmL*); ~ **date** STOCK fecha de conversión f; ~ **factor** MATH, STOCK factor de conversión m; ~ **factor for employee contributions** INS *pension plan* factor de conversión para las aportaciones del empleado m; ~ **issue** FIN emisión convertible f, STOCK emisión de conversión f; ~ **loan** FIN empréstito de conversión m; ~ **parity** STOCK paridad de conversión f; ~ **premium** STOCK prima de conversión f; ~ **price** FIN, STOCK precio de conversión m; ~ **privilege** BANK, INS, LAW cláusula de conversión f; ~ **rate** BANK, ECON, FIN tasa de conversión f, tipo de conversión m; ~ **ratio** STOCK proporción de conversión f; ~ **rights** STOCK derechos de conversión m pl; ~ **to the metric system** GEN COMM adopción del sistema métrico decimal f

convert vt GEN COMM convertir; ◆ ~ **into capital** GEN COMM convertir en capital; ~ **into cash** GEN COMM convertir en dinero

converted adj GEN COMM convertido

convertibility n BANK, FIN canjeabilidad f

convertible[1] adj GEN COMM convertible

convertible[2]: ~ **bond** n FIN, STOCK bono convertible m, obligación convertible f; ~ **currency** n BANK, ECON *econometrics*, FIN moneda convertible f; ~ **debenture** n FIN, STOCK obligación convertible f; ~ **issue** n FIN emisión convertible m; ~ **loan** n BANK empréstito convertible m; ~ **preferred share** n STOCK acción preferente convertible f; ~ **preferred stock** n STOCK acciones preferentes convertibles f pl; ~ **security** n FIN garantía convertible f, STOCK título convertible m; ~ **share** n FIN, STOCK acción convertible f; ~ **stock** n FIN, STOCK acciones convertibles f; ~ **subordinated loan** n BANK, FIN préstamo subordinado convertible m; ~ **term life insurance** n INS seguro de vida temporal con derecho a total m

convey vt LAW, PROP traspasar

conveyor: ~ **belt** n TRANSP cinta transportadora f (*Esp*), máquina transportadora f (*AmL*), correa transportadora f (*Esp*)

conviction n LAW sentencia condenatoria f

convolute: ~ **winding** n TRANSP *fibre drum* enrollamiento en espiral m

COO abbr HRM (*chief operating officer*) DG (*director general*), director(a) general de operaciones m,f, IMP/EXP (*country of origin*) país de origen m

cool down vt ECON enfriar

cooling: ~~**off period** n GEN COMM periodo de reflexión m, HRM, STOCK tregua laboral f

co-op[1] abbr (*cooperative*) GEN COMM condominio m, cooperativa f, edificio en copropiedad m

co-op[2]: ~ **advertising** n (*cooperative advertising*) S&M publicidad cooperativa f

cooperage n TRANSP tonelería f

cooperate vi GEN COMM cooperar

cooperation n GEN COMM cooperación f; ~ **agreement** GEN COMM, POL *between nations* acuerdo de cooperación m

cooperative n (*co-op*) GEN COMM condominio m, cooperativa f, edificio en copropiedad m; ~ **advertising** (*co-op advertising*) S&M publicidad cooperativa f; ~ **apartment** PROP apartamento en copropiedad m; ~ **association** HRM, INS asociación cooperativa f; ~ **bank** BANK ≈ Banco de Crédito Agrícola m; ~ **credit association** GEN COMM asociación de crédito cooperativo f; ~ **credit institution** BANK, FIN institución de crédito cooperativo f; ~ **education** WEL educación coordinada f; ~ **farm** ECON, POL granja cooperativa f; ~ **federalism** POL federalismo cooperativo m; ~ **marketing** S&M marketing cooperativo m; ~ **retail society** HRM cooperativa de consumo f; ~ **society** GEN COMM sociedad cooperativa f

Cooperative: ~ **Wholesale Society** n (*CWS*) GEN COMM sociedad mayorista en cooperativa f

cooperatives n pl GEN COMM, MGMNT colaboradores m pl

coordinate vt GEN COMM, HRM, MGMNT, TRANSP coordinar

coordinated[1] adj GEN COMM coordinado

coordinated[2]: ~ **universal time** n (*UTC*) GEN COMM hora universal coordinada f (*HUC*)

Coordinating: ~ **Committee for Multilateral Export Controls** n (*Cocom*) IMP/EXP Comité de Coordinación del Control Multilateral de las Exportaciones m

coordination n GEN COMM coordinación f

coordinator n GEN COMM coordinador(a) m,f

co-owner n GEN COMM codueño(-a) m,f, condómino(-a) m,f, copropietario(-a) m,f

co-ownership n GEN COMM copropiedad f

copier n ADMIN copiadora f

copper: ~ **ore** n ENVIR, IND mineral de cobre m

coppers n pl FIN, STOCK calderilla f

coprocessor n COMP *hardware* coprocesador m

copy[1]: ~~**protected** adj COMP protegido contra copia

copy[2] n COMP copia f, GEN COMM duplicado m (*dupdo.*), *advertising* ejemplar m, *material, text* copia f, MEDIA réplica f; ~~**adaptor** GEN COMM adaptador de copia m; ~ **appeal** S&M *advertising* atractivo del anuncio publicitario f; ~ **body** S&M *of advert* cuerpo del texto m; ~ **brief** S&M resumen de un texto m; ~ **chief** MEDIA *print* jefe(-a) de redacción m,f; ~ **claim** S&M afirmación del mensaje publicitario f; ~ **clearance** S&M aprobación de una cuña radiofónica f; ~ **date** GEN COMM fecha de redacción f; ~ **deadline** GEN COMM hora límite de redacción f, MEDIA cierre de edición m; ~ **editor** MEDIA editor(a) m,f, corrector(a) m,f; ~ **platform** GEN COMM tribuna de redacción f; ~~**protected disk** COMP disco protegido contra copias m; ~ **reader** MEDIA *print* corrector(a) de estilo m,f; ~ **rotation** S&M *advertising* rotación de anuncios f; ~ **strategy** S&M *advertising* estrategia de mensaje publicitario f; ~ **test** S&M *advertising* prueba de un mensaje publicitario f;

~ **writer** GEN COMM, S&M redactor(a) de textos publicitarios *m,f*

copy³ *vt* COMP *software*, GEN COMM *photocopy* copiar; ◆ ~ **from the original** GEN COMM copiar del original

copyright *n* LAW copyright *m*; ◆ ~ **reserved** LAW, PATENTS todos los derechos reservados

Copyright: ~ **Act** *n* GEN COMM, LAW, PATENTS Ley de Derechos de Autor *f*

copywriting *n* GEN COMM, S&M escritura de material publicitario *f*

co-rates *n pl* TRANSP *air freight* cotarifas *f pl*

cordless¹ *adj* COMMS *mechanism* inalámbrico

cordless²: ~ **digital telecommunications** *n pl* COMMS comunicaciones digitales inalámbricas *f pl*, comunicaciones digitales móviles *f pl*

core *n* GEN COMM *essential element* núcleo *m*; ~ **business** ECON, GEN COMM negocio básico *m*; ~ **consumer price inflation** ECON inflación básica de los precios al consumo *f*; ~ **definition** GEN COMM definición esencial *f*; ~ **economy** ECON *international* núcleo de la economía *m*; ~ **firm** GEN COMM compañía central *f*, compañía matriz *f*; ~ **funding** FIN financiación básica *f*; ~ **hours** *n pl* IND horas centrales *f pl*; ~ **inflation** ECON inflación básica *f*; ~ **inflation rate** ECON proporción de inflación básica *f*; ~ **memory** COMP memoria de núcleos *f*; ~**periphery** ECON periferia del núcleo *f*; ~ **product** S&M producto básico *m*; ~ **region** ECON región central *f*; ~ **size** COMP capacidad de la memoria de núcleos *f*; ~ **storage** COMP memoria de núcleos *f*; ~ **time** HRM tiempo mínimo *m*; ~ **workforce** HRM mano de obra imprescindible *f*

COREPER *abbr* (*Committee of Permanent Representatives of the EU*) ECON, POL Comité de los Representantes Permanentes de la UE *m*

corn: ~ **model** *n* ECON leyes de granos *f pl*

corner¹ *n* GEN COMM esquina *f*; ~ **casting** TRANSP enganche de grúa en el contenedor *m*; ~ **post** TRANSP esquinal *m*, montante de esquina *m*, poste esquinero *m*; ~ **shop** *BrE* (*cf neighborhood store AmE*) GEN COMM, S&M tienda de barrio *f*; ~ **solution** ECON solución de esquina *f*

corner² *vt* GEN COMM *the market* acaparar

cornered *adj* GEN COMM acaparado

cornerer *n* GEN COMM acaparador(a) *m,f*

cornering *n* GEN COMM acaparamiento *m*; ~ **of goods** GEN COMM acaparamiento de bienes *m*, acaparamiento de mercancías *m*; ~ **the market** GEN COMM monopolización del mercado *f*

cornerstone *n* GEN COMM piedra de toque *f*

corp. *abbr* (*corporation*) GEN COMM corp. (*corporación*)

corporate¹ *adj* GEN COMM corporativo

corporate²: ~ **account deposit** *n* BANK depósito en la cuenta corporativa *m*; ~ **accountability** *n* GEN COMM responsabilidad corporativa *f*; ~ **advertising** *n* S&M publicidad corporativa *f*; ~ **affairs** *n pl* S&M asuntos corporativos *m pl*; ~ **affiliate** *n* ECON *employee* socio(-a) corporativo(-a) *m,f*, GEN COMM *company* corporación afiliada *f*; ~ **assets** *n pl* ACC activos sociales *m pl*, bienes sociales *m pl*; ~ **association** *n* HRM, INS asociación corporativa *f*; ~ **banking** *n* BANK banca corporativa *f*; ~ **beneficiary** *n* TAX beneficiario(-a) corporativo(-a) *m,f*; ~ **bond** *n* *AmE* STOCK obligación societaria *f*; ~ **campaign** *n* S&M campaña corporativa *f*; ~ **client** *n* BANK cliente corporativo(-a) *m,f*; ~ **credit** *n* BANK

crédito corporativo *m*; ~ **credit card** *n* BANK, FIN tarjeta de crédito corporativa *f*; ~ **credit manager** *n* BANK gerente de créditos corporativos *mf*; ~ **culture** *n* GEN COMM cultura corporativa *f*; ~ **customer** *n* BANK cliente corporativo(-a) *m,f*, ~ **data center** *AmE*, ~ **data centre** *BrE* *n* COMP centro de datos corporativo *m*, centro informático de empresa *m*; ~ **database** *n* COMP base de datos corporativa *f*; ~ **debenture** *n* BANK, STOCK obligación de empresa *f*; ~ **debt securities** *n* BANK deuda de acciones, bonos y valores de empresa *f*; ~ **earning power** *n* GEN COMM rentabilidad corporativa *f*; ~ **earnings** *n pl* ACC ganancias corporativas *f pl*; ~ **entity** *n* TAX sociedad comercial *f*; ~ **equivalent yield** *n* TAX producto equivalente corporativo *m*; ~ **executive** *n* MGMNT ejecutivo(-a) de empresa *m,f*; ~ **finance** *n* FIN finanza corporativa *f*; ~ **financing** *n* FIN financiación corporativa *f*; ~ **financing committee** *n* FIN comité financiero de una empresa *m*; ~ **financing project** *n* FIN proyecto de financiación de una empresa *m*; ~ **goal** *n* GEN COMM meta corporativa *f*; ~ **governance** *n* ADMIN, MGMNT autoridad corporativa *f*; ~ **group** *n* GEN COMM grupo de empresas *m*; ~ **growth** *n* GEN COMM crecimiento corporativo *m*; ~ **identity** *n* S&M identidad corporativa *f*; ~ **image** *n* GEN COMM imagen corporativa *f*; ~ **income tax** *n* TAX impuesto sobre la renta de sociedades *m*; ~ **insider** *n* GEN COMM empleado que maneja información reservada; ~ **investment** *n* FIN inversión en sociedades *f*; ~ **investor** *n* STOCK inversor(a) corporativo(-a) *m,f*; ~ **issue** *n* FIN, STOCK emisión de acciones de una compañía *f*; ~ **lending** *n* BANK empréstito corporativo *m*; ~ **lending market** *n* BANK, FIN mercado de préstamos corporativos *m*; ~ **loan** *n* BANK, FIN, STOCK préstamo a una corporación *m*, préstamo a una empresa *m*, préstamo a una sociedad *m*; ~ **management** *n* MGMNT dirección corporativa *f*, gerencia corporativa *f*; ~ **member** *n* STOCK miembro corporativo(-a) *m,f*; ~ **mission** *n* GEN COMM, MGMNT misión corporativa *f*; ~ **model** *n* ACC, FIN, GEN COMM modelo corporativo *m*; ~ **morality** *n* GEN COMM moralidad corporativa *f*; ~ **name** *n* GEN COMM razón social *f*; ~ **network** *n* COMP red corporativa *f*; ~ **objective** *n* GEN COMM objetivo corporativo *m*; ~ **plagiarism** *n* GEN COMM plagio empresarial *m*; ~ **planning** *n* GEN COMM planificación empresarial *f*; ~ **purchaser** *n* S&M, TAX comprador(a) de una sociedad *m,f*; ~ **purchasing** *n* S&M, TAX compra corporativa *f*; ~ **raider** *n* FIN, STOCK especulador(a) corporativo(-a) *m,f*, tiburón *m*, tiburón corporativo *m*; ~ **raiding** *n* FIN, STOCK especulación agresiva sobre una empresa; ~ **savings** *n pl* BANK, ECON, FIN ahorros colectivos *m pl*; ~ **seal** *n* BANK sello de la empresa *m*; ~ **spending** *n* TAX gasto de sociedad *m*; ~ **sponsorship** *n* S&M *promotion* patrocinio corporativo *m*; ~ **state** *n* POL estado corporativo *m*; ~ **status** *n* HRM situación de la empresa *f*; ~ **strategic planning** *n* GEN COMM, MGMNT planificación estratégica corporativa *f*; ~ **strategy** *n* GEN COMM, MGMNT estrategia corporativa *f*; ~ **structure** *n* GEN COMM estructura corporativa *f*; ~ **surtax** *n* TAX impuesto adicional de sociedades *m*; ~ **tax** *n* TAX impuesto de sociedades *m*, impuesto sobre la renta de sociedades *m* (*ISRS*); ~ **tax credit** *n* TAX desgravación empresarial *f*; ~ **taxation** *n* TAX impuesto de sociedades *m*; ~ **treasurer** *n* HRM tesorero(-a) de la empresa *m,f*; ~ **turnaround** *n* GEN COMM cambio completo corporativo *m*; ~ **veil** *n jarg* GEN COMM encubrimiento corporativo *m*

Corporate: ~ **Law** *n* GEN COMM, IND, LAW Ley de Sociedades Mercantiles *f*

corporation *n* (*corp.*) GEN COMM corporación *f* (*corp.*); ~ **income tax** TAX impuesto sobre los beneficios empresariales *m*, impuesto sobre la renta de sociedades *m*; ~ **investment allowance** TAX desgravación de la inversión empresarial *f*; ~ **law** GEN COMM, LAW derecho de sociedades *m*; ~ **loan** BANK, FIN *local government* préstamo corporativo *m*; ~ **surtax** TAX impuesto adicional de sociedades *m*; ~ **tax** TAX impuesto de sociedades *m*; ~ **tax liability** TAX deuda fiscal de una sociedad *f*

Corporation: ~ **of Foreign Bondholders** *n* (*CFBH*) STOCK corporación de la sociedad de cartera de títulos extranjeros; ~ **Law** *n* GEN COMM, IND, LAW Ley de Sociedades Mercantiles *f*; ~ **of Lloyd's** *n* (*CL*) INS asociación de aseguradoras y agencias de seguros; ~ **tax rates** *n pl* BrE TAX tipos del impuesto de sociedades *m pl*

corporatism *n* POL corporativismo *m*

corporeal[1] *adj* GEN COMM corpóreo *m*

corporeal[2]: ~ **hereditaments** *n pl* LAW bienes materiales por heredar *m pl*

corpus *n* ACC, ECON, FIN, patrimonio de un fideicomiso *m*, bienes fideicometidos *m pl*, LAW cuerpo *m*

corr. *abbr* (*correspondence*) COMMS, GEN COMM correspondencia *f*

correct[1] *adj* GEN COMM correcto, exacto

correct[2] *vt* GEN COMM *errors* corregir, rectificar, *proofs* leer

corrected[1] *adj* GEN COMM corregido

corrected[2]: ~ **invoice** *n* ACC, FIN factura rectificada *f*; ~ **probability** *n* FIN, MATH probabilidad ponderada *f*

correcting: ~ **entry** *n* ACC contraasiento *m*

correction *n* GEN COMM corrección *f*, rectificación *f*, PATENTS, POL rectificación *f*; ~ **maintenance** GEN COMM mantenimiento de corrección *m*

corrective: ~ **action** *n* GEN COMM operación de corrección *f*; ~ **subsidy** *n* ECON, POL, TAX subsidio correctivo *m*, subsidio de ajuste *m*; ~ **tax** *n* TAX impuesto corrector *m*

correlate *vt* MATH correlacionar

correlation *n* MATH correlación *f*; ~ **coefficient** MATH coeficiente de correlación *m*; ~ **ratio** STOCK *futures* proporción de correlación *f*

correspond *vi* COMMS *by letter* tener correspondencia con, MATH corresponder

correspond to *vt* GEN COMM corresponder a

correspond with *vi* COMMS, GEN COMM *communicate by letter* corresponder con

correspondence *n* (*corr.*) COMMS *letters* correspondencia *f*; ~ **school** HRM, WEL centro de educación a distancia *m*

correspondent *n* BANK corresponsal *m*; ~ **bank** BANK banca corresponsal *f*

corresponding *adj* GEN COMM *equivalent* correspondiente

corridor: ~ **traffic** *n* S&M tráfico de pasillo *m*

corrosion[1]: ~-**resistant** *adj* IND anticorrosivo, resistente a la corrosión

corrosion[2] *n* IND, INS corrosión *f*; ~ **damage** INS daños por corrosión *m pl*; ~-**resistant material** IND, TRANSP material anticorrosión *m*

corrugated: ~ **board** *n* S&M cartón ondulado *m*;

~ **container** *n* TRANSP contenedor de chapa ondulada *m*

corruption *n* LAW corrupción *f*

corset *n* ECON corsé *m*, POL limitación *f*, restricción *f*

cos *abbr* (*cosine*) MATH cos (*coseno*)

COS *abbr* (*cash on shipment*) TRANSP pago contra embarque *m*

COSHH *abbr* BrE (*Control of Substances Hazardous To Health Regulations*) WEL normativa de control de sustancias peligrosas para la salud

cosign *vt* LAW firmar conjuntamente

cosine *n* (*cos*) MATH coseno *m* (*cos*)

cost[1]: ~-**effective** *adj* ACC, GEN COMM eficaz en relación con el coste (*Esp*), eficaz en relación con el costo (*AmL*), rentable; ~-**efficient** *adj* ACC coste-eficiente (*Esp*), costo-eficiente (*AmL*); ~-**sensitive** *adj* ECON, GEN COMM sensible al coste (*Esp*), sensible al costo (*AmL*)

cost[2] *n* GEN COMM coste *m* (*Esp*), costo *m* (*AmL*); ~ **accountant** ACC contable de costes *mf* (*Esp*), contador(a) de costos *m,f* (*AmL*); ~ **accounting** ACC contabilidad de costes *f* (*Esp*), contabilidad de costos *f* (*AmL*); ~ **allocation** ACC asignación de costes *f* (*Esp*), asignación de costos *f* (*AmL*), imputación de costes *f* (*Esp*), imputación de costos *f* (*AmL*); ~ **amount** TAX importe del coste *m* (*Esp*), importe del costo *m* (*AmL*); ~ **analysis** ACC, FIN análisis de los costes *m* (*Esp*), análisis de los costos *m* (*AmL*); ~ **application** ECON aplicación de costes *f* (*Esp*), aplicación de costos *f* (*AmL*); ~ **apportionment** ACC prorrateo del coste *m* (*Esp*), prorrateo del costo *m* (*AmL*); ~ **approach** ACC método de coste *m* (*Esp*), método de costo *m* (*AmL*), FIN aproximación de coste *f* (*Esp*), aproximación de costo *f* (*AmL*), PROP método de coste *m* (*Esp*), método de costo *m* (*AmL*); ~ **awareness** GEN COMM conscienciación del coste *f* (*Esp*), conscienciación del costo *f* (*AmL*); ~ **base** ACC, TAX base del coste *f* (*Esp*), base del costo *f* (*AmL*); ~-**benefit analysis** ACC, ECON *project appraisal* análisis de coste-beneficio *m* (*Esp*), análisis de costo-beneficio *m* (*AmL*); ~ **of borrowing** BANK, GEN COMM coste de un empréstito *m* (*Esp*), coste de un préstamo *m* (*Esp*), costo de un empréstito *m* (*AmL*), costo de un préstamo *m* (*AmL*); ~ **of capital** STOCK coste de capital *m* (*Esp*), costo de capital *m* (*AmL*); ~ **of carriage** TRANSP coste de transporte *m* (*Esp*), costo de transporte *m* (*AmL*); ~ **center** AmE, ~ **centre** BrE ACC, BANK centro de costes *m* (*Esp*), centro de costos *m* (*AmL*); ~ **of compliance** ENVIR coste de acatamiento *m* (*Esp*), costo de acatamiento *m* (*AmL*); ~ **consciousness** GEN COMM, S&M conciencia del coste *f* (*Esp*), conciencia del costo *f* (*AmL*); ~ **containment** ECON contención de los costes *f* (*Esp*), contención de los costos *f* (*AmL*); ~ **control** ACC control de costes *m* (*Esp*), control de costos *m* (*AmL*); ~ **curve** ACC curva de costes *f* (*Esp*), curva de costos *f* (*AmL*); ~ **distribution** ACC distribución de costes *f* (*Esp*), distribución de costos *f* (*AmL*); ~ **effectiveness** ECON, GEN COMM relación coste-eficacia *f* (*Esp*), relación costo-eficacia *f* (*AmL*), rentabilidad *f*; ~-**effectiveness analysis** ECON, S&M análisis de la rentabilidad *m*; ~ **escalation cover** BrE INS cobertura de aumento de coste *f* (*Esp*), cobertura de aumento de costo *f* (*AmL*); ~ **estimate** GEN COMM estimación de costes *f* (*Esp*), estimación de costos *f* (*AmL*); ~ **factor** ACC, ECON componente del precio de coste *m* (*Esp*), componente del precio de costo *m* (*AmL*), elemento del coste *m* (*Esp*), elemento del costo *m* (*AmL*), factor del coste *m* (*Esp*), factor del costo *m* (*AmL*); ~ **flow** ACC, ECON fluctuación de costes *f* (*Esp*), fluctuación de costos *f* (*AmL*); ~ **forecast** ACC previsión de costes *f* (*Esp*), previsión de costos *f* (*AmL*); ~ **and freight** (*c&f*) IMP/EXP, TRANSP coste y flete *m* (*Esp*) (*c&f*), costo y flete *m* (*AmL*) (*c&f*); ~ **of freight** TRANSP coste del flete *m* (*Esp*), costo del flete *m* (*AmL*); **under ~ freight rate** TRANSP *distribution* tarifa por debajo del flete *f*; ~ **function** ACC función de costes *f* (*Esp*), función de costos *f* (*AmL*); ~ **of funds** FIN coste de los fondos *m* (*Esp*), costo de los fondos *m* (*AmL*); ~ **of funds plus** BANK coste del plus de fondos *m* (*Esp*), costo del plus de fondos *m* (*AmL*); ~ **of goods manufactured** ACC, ECON, IND coste de las mercancías fabricadas *m* (*Esp*), costo de las mercancías fabricadas *m* (*AmL*); ~ **of goods sold** ACC, ECON coste de las mercancías vendidas *m* (*Esp*), costo de las mercancías vendidas *m* (*AmL*); ~ **and insurance** (*C&I*) IMP/EXP, INS, TRANSP coste y seguro *m* (*Esp*), costo y seguro *m* (*AmL*); ~, **insurance and freight** (*CI&F*) IMP/EXP, INS, TRANSP coste, seguro y flete *m* (*Esp*) (*CI&F*), costo, seguro y flete *m* (*AmL*) (*CI&F*); ~, **insurance, freight and commission** (*CIFC&C*) IMP/EXP, INS, TRANSP coste, seguro, flete y comisión *m* (*Esp*), costo, seguro, flete y comisión *m* (*AmL*); ~, **insurance, freight, commission and exchange** (*CIFC&E*) IMP/EXP, INS coste, seguro, flete, comisión y cambio *m* (*Esp*), costo, seguro, flete, comisión y cambio *m* (*AmL*); ~, **insurance, freight, commission and interest** (*CIFC&I*) IMP/EXP, INS, TRANSP coste, seguro, flete, comisión e intereses *m* (*Esp*), costo, seguro, flete, comisión e intereses *m* (*AmL*); ~, **insurance and freight contract** IMP/EXP, INS, TRANSP contrato con coste, seguro y flete *m* (*Esp*), contrato con costo, seguro y flete *m* (*AmL*); ~, **insurance, freight and interest** (*CIF&I*) IMP/EXP, INS, TRANSP coste, seguro, flete e interés *m* (*Esp*), costo, seguro, flete e interés *m* (*AmL*); ~, **insurance, freight, interest and exchange** (*CIFI&E*) IMP/EXP, INS, TRANSP coste, seguro, flete, interés y cambio *m* (*Esp*), costo, seguro, flete, interés y cambio *m* (*AmL*); ~ **of labor** *AmE*, ~ **of labour** *BrE* HRM coste de la mano de obra *m* (*Esp*), costo de la mano de obra *m* (*AmL*); ~ **leader** ECON guía de coste *f* (*Esp*), guía de costo *f* (*AmL*); ~ **of living** ECON, GEN COMM coste de la vida *m* (*Esp*), costo de la vida *m* (*AmL*); ~**-of-living index** ECON, FIN índice del coste de la vida *m* (*Esp*), índice del costo de la vida *m* (*AmL*); ~ **of a loan** BANK, GEN COMM coste de un empréstito *m* (*Esp*), costo de un préstamo *m* (*Esp*), costo de un empréstito *m* (*AmL*), costo de un préstamo *m* (*AmL*); ~ **of manufacturing and processing capital** IND, TAX costes del capital de manufacturación y procesamiento *m pl* (*Esp*), costos del capital de manufacturación y procesamiento *m pl* (*AmL*); ~ **of meals and lodging** TAX coste de la alimentación y del alojamiento *m* (*Esp*), costo de la alimentación y del alojamiento *m* (*AmL*); ~ **of medical treatment** INS gastos de tratamiento médico *m pl*; ~ **method** ACC, FIN *inventory* método de coste *m* (*Esp*), método de costo *m* (*AmL*); ~ **objective** ECON objetivo de costes *m* (*Esp*), objetivo de costos *m* (*AmL*); ~**-of-living adjustment** (*COLA*) ECON ajuste del costo de vida *m* (*AmL*), ajuste del costo de vida *m* (*AmL*); ~**-of-living allowance** HRM, WEL subsidio por aumento del coste de vida *m* (*Esp*), subsidio por aumento del costo de vida *m* (*AmL*); ~**-of-**

living index ECON, WEL índice de la vida *m* (*Esp*), índice del costo de la vida *m* (*AmL*); ~**-of-living tax credit** TAX desgravación fiscal de coste de vida *f* (*Esp*), desgravación fiscal de costo de vida *f* (*AmL*); ~ **overrun** ECON sobrecoste *m* (*Esp*), sobrecosto *m* (*AmL*); ~ **per inquiry** S&M coste por información requerida *m* (*Esp*), costo por información requerida *m* (*AmL*); ~ **per thousand** S&M coste por mil *m* (*Esp*), costo por mil *m* (*AmL*); ~ **per vehicle** TRANSP coste por vehículo *m* (*Esp*), costo por vehículo *m* (*AmL*); ~**-plus contract** GEN COMM contrato al coste más honorarios *m* (*Esp*), contrato al costo más honorarios *m* (*AmL*); ~ **price** GEN COMM, S&M precio de coste *m* (*Esp*), precio de costo *m* (*AmL*); ~ **pricing** ACC fijación del coste *f* (*Esp*), fijación del costo *f* (*AmL*); ~ **of proceedings** GEN COMM, LAW coste del proceso *m* (*Esp*), costo del proceso *m* (*AmL*); ~ **of production** ACC, ECON, INS coste de producción *m* (*Esp*), costo de producción *m* (*AmL*); ~**-pull inflation** ECON tirón de la inflación *m*; ~**-push inflation** ECON inflación de costes *f* (*Esp*), inflación de costos *f* (*AmL*); ~ **ratio** ACC proporción de coste *f* (*Esp*), proporción de costo *f* (*AmL*); ~ **records** *n pl* ACC, STOCK registros de costes *m pl* (*Esp*), registros de costos *m pl* (*AmL*); ~ **reduction** ECON, FIN reducción de costes *f* (*Esp*), reducción de costos *f* (*AmL*); ~ **of sales** ACC, ECON, S&M coste de ventas *m* (*Esp*), costo de ventas *m* (*AmL*); ~**-shared program** *AmE*, ~**-shared programme** *BrE* POL programa de costes compartidos *m* (*Esp*), programa de costos compartidos *m* (*AmL*); ~ **standard** ACC, FIN estándar de costes *m* (*Esp*), estándar de costos *m* (*AmL*), modelo de costes *m* (*Esp*), modelo de costos *m* (*AmL*), norma de costes *f* (*Esp*), norma de costos *f* (*AmL*); ~ **structure** ACC, FIN composición del coste *f* (*Esp*), composición del costo *f* (*AmL*), estructura del coste *f* (*Esp*), estructura del costo *f* (*AmL*); ~ **trimming** GEN COMM desglose de gastos *m*, distribución de gastos *f*; ~ **variance** ACC, FIN variación del coste *f* (*Esp*), variación del costo *f* (*AmL*); ~**-volume-profit analysis** ACC, FIN análisis de coste-volumen-beneficio *m* (*Esp*), análisis de costo-volumen-beneficio *m* (*AmL*); ♦ **at ~** GEN COMM al coste (*Esp*), al costo (*AmL*)

cost[3] *vt* ACC *calculate expenditure* establecer el precio de coste

COST *abbr* (*European Cooperation in Science and Technology*) IND, POL COST (*Cooperación Europea en Ciencia y Tecnología*)

costing *n* ACC cálculo de costes *m* (*Esp*), cálculo de costos *m* (*AmL*)

costly *adj* GEN COMM caro, costoso

costs *n pl* GEN COMM costes *m pl* (*Esp*), costos *m pl* (*AmL*), cuenta de costes *f* (*Esp*), cuenta de costos *f* (*AmL*); ~ **account** *n* ACC cuenta de costes *f* (*Esp*), cuenta de costos *f* (*AmL*); ~ **taxable to sb** TAX costes gravables a alguien *m pl* (*Esp*), costos gravables a alguien *m pl* (*AmL*)

COT *abbr* (*customer's own transport*) TRANSP transporte propio del cliente

cotenancy *n* PROP arrendamiento conjunto *m*

co-tenant: ~ **finance** *n* PROP financiación coarrendataria *f*

cottage: ~ **industry** *n* ECON, IND industria familiar *f*

CO$_2$: ~ **tax** *n* ENVIR, TAX impuesto por contaminación del aire

COU *abbr* (*clip-on unit*) TRANSP refrigerador portátil *m*

couchette *n* LEIS, TRANSP *on train* litera *f*

council *n* GEN COMM *of meeting* consejo *m*; ~ **of economic advisers** (*CEA*) ECON junta de asesores económicos *f*; ~ **house** *BrE* (*cf housing project AmE*) PROP, WEL vivienda de protección oficial *f* (*VPO*); ~ **tax** *BrE* GEN COMM contribución urbana *f*, TAX impuesto municipal *m*

Council: ~ **of Economic Advisers** *n* (*CEA*) ECON Consejo de Asesores Económicos *m*, Junta de Asesores Económicos *f*; ~ **of Europe** *n* (*CE*) ECON, POL Consejo de Europa *m* (*CE*); ~ **of Europe Resettlement Fund** *n* (*CERF*) ECON, POL fondo de restablecimiento del Consejo Europeo *m*; ~ **of European Industrial Federations** *n* (*CEIF*) ECON, IND, POL Consejo de Federaciones Industriales Europeas *m*; ~ **for European Economic Co-operation** (*CEEC*) ECON, POL Consejo para la Cooperación Económica Europea *m*; ~ **for Mutual Economic Aid** *n obs* (*CMEA, COMECON*) ECON Consejo de Asistencia Mutua Económica *m*; ~ **of Ministers** *n* ECON *in European Union* Consejo de Ministros *m*; ~ **of the Stock Exchange** *n BrE* STOCK sociedad rectora de la bolsa

counsel[1] *n* LAW asesoramiento *m*, *lawyer* asesor(a) legal *m,f*

counsel[2] *vt* LAW *advise* asesorar, *criminal* instigar

count *vt* MATH, POL *votes* contar; ~ **on** GEN COMM contar con

countable: ~ **set** *n* MATH conjunto contable *m*

counter[1] *n* BANK ventanilla *f*, GEN COMM *in supermarket* mostrador de caja *m*; ~**-advertising** S&M contra publicidad *f*; ~ **check** *AmE see counter cheque BrE*; ~ **check form** *AmE see counter cheque form BrE*; ~ **cheque** *BrE* BANK, FIN cheque contra la cuenta propia *m*, cheque de mostrador *m*, cheque de ventanilla *m*, talón bancario contra el cheque *m*; ~ **cheque form** *BrE* BANK, FIN solicitud de cheque de ventanilla *f*; ~ **deal** BANK operación recíproca *f*; ~ **purchase** *international trade* compras de contrapartida *f pl*; ~ **signatory** (*CS*) ECON signo monetario *m*; ~ **trade** ECON contracomercio *m*

counter[2] *vt* GEN COMM oponerse a

counteract *vt* GEN COMM contrarrestar

counterbalance[1] *n* ECON cuenta de compensación *f*

counterbalance[2] *vt* ECON contrarrestar

counterclaim *n* LAW contrademanda *f*

countercyclical: ~ **policy** *n* ECON política contracíclica *f*

counterfeit *n* BANK, GEN COMM billete falso *m*, falsificación *f*, moneda falsa *f*; ~ **copies** *n pl* IND copias falsificadas *f pl*; ~ **goods** *n pl* IND *fashion sector* imitaciones ilegales *f pl*

counterfoil *n* STOCK talón *m*

countermand *vt* GEN COMM revocar

countermeasure *n* GEN COMM contramedida *f*

counteroffer *n* S&M contraoferta *f*

counterpack *n* S&M contrapaquete *m*

counterpart *n* ECON contrapartida *f*

counterparty *n BrE* STOCK contraparte *f*; ~ **capital** FIN capital de la contraparte *m*

countervailing *n* IMP/EXP compensación *f*; ~ **duties** *n pl* IMP/EXP derechos compensatorios *m pl*; ~ **power** ECON poder compensador *m*

country[1]: ~**-specific** *adj* ECON *development aid* específico del país

country[2]: ~ **club at the top** *n jarg* MGMNT altos cargos con conexiones en la esfera política, social y económica; ~ **code** *n* BANK código de país *m*; ~ **of destination** *n* IMP/EXP país de destino *m*; ~ **exposure** *n* ECON exposición crediticia por país *f*; ~ **fund** *n BrE* STOCK *en bolsa* fondos de inversión nacionales; ~ **of origin** *n* (*COO*) IMP/EXP país de origen *m*; ~ **planning** *n* GEN COMM ordenación rural *f*; ~ **report** *n* ECON informe sobre las perspectivas políticas y económicas de un país; ~ **of residence** *n* POL, TAX país de residencia *m*; ~ **risk** *n* FIN *provisions* riesgo de país *m*; ~ **of ultimate risk** *n* GEN COMM país de riesgo límite *m*

Country: ~ **Bank** *n* BANK Caja Rural *f*

Countryside: ~ **Commission** *n BrE* ENVIR comisión del distrito rural; ~ **Council for Wales** *n BrE* ENVIR consejo del distrito rural de Gales

county *n* GEN COMM, POL unidad administrativa equivalente a una provincia, ≈ Comunidad Autónoma *f* (*Esp*) (*CA*); ~ **court** LAW tribunal de condado

coupled: ~ **with** *adj* COMP acoplado con, GEN COMM emparejado con

coupon *n* (*c., cp.*) GEN COMM cupón *m*; ~ **bond** FIN, STOCK bono al portador con cupones *m*; ~ **rate** BANK, FIN, STOCK interés nominal *m*; ~ **registered bond** FIN, STOCK bono nominativo con cupón *m*; ~ **yield** STOCK rendimiento del cupón *m*

courier *n* COMMS estafeta *f*, mensajero(-a) *m,f*; ~ **agency** COMMS, GEN COMM agencia de transporte urgente *f*; ~ **firm** COMMS, GEN COMM empresa de mensajería *f*; ~ **service** COMMS, GEN COMM servicio de mensajería *m*

Cournot: ~**'s duopoly model** *n* ECON modelo duopolista de Cournot *m*

course *n* GEN COMM curso *m*; ~ **of action** MGMNT curso de acción *m*; ♦ **in the** ~ **of** GEN COMM *negotiations* en el curso de, durante; **in due** ~ GEN COMM a su debido tiempo

court *n* LAW juzgado *m*, tribunal *m*; ~ **of appeal** LAW tribunal de apelación *m*; ~**-appointed attorney** LAW ≈ abogado de oficio; ~ **of arbitration** LAW tribunal de arbitraje *m*; ~ **entitled to adjudicate** LAW tribunal competente *m*; ~ **of inquiry** *BrE* HRM, POL comisión parlamentaria de investigación *f*; ~ **of law** LAW tribunal judicial ordinario *m*; ~ **lawyer** GEN COMM, LAW ≈ abogado(-a) *m,f*; ~ **order** LAW auto *m*, orden del tribunal *f*, providencia *f*; ~ **procedure** LAW norma procesal *f*, procedimiento judicial *m*, procedimiento legal *m*; ~ **of record** *AmE* LAW tribunal que guarda constancia de los autos o del sumario; ♦ **the** ~ **is now in session** LAW la audiencia está abierta

Court: ~ **of Justice** *n* LAW, POL Tribunal de Justicia *m*

covariance *n* MATH covarianza *f*

covenant *n* LAW, TAX concierto *m*, contrato *m*

covenantor *n* LAW parte contratante *f*

covenants *n pl* LAW *affirmative or negative* obligaciones *f pl*

cover[1] *n* (*C'vr*) GEN COMM cubierta *f*, cobertura *f*, INS cobertura *f*; ~ **against stranding** INS cobertura contra encalladura *f*; ~ **note** (*C/N*) INS aviso de cobertura *m*; ~ **page** MEDIA, S&M portada *f*; ~ **ratio** FIN proporción de cobertura *f*, relación de cobertura *f*; ~**-up** POL secreto *m*; ♦ **under separate** ~ COMMS *envelope* en sobres separados

cover[2] *vt* GEN COMM cubrir; ◆ ~ **public expenditure** ECON, POL atender al gasto público

cover up *vt* GEN COMM, POL *conceal fact* ocultar, tapar

coverage *n* GEN COMM cobertura *f*; ~ **fees** *n pl* LEIS *sport* cuota de cobertura *f*

covered[1] *adj* GEN COMM, STOCK *put and call* cubierto; ◆ ~ **by insurance** INS *damage, loss* cubierto por seguro

covered[2]: ~ **call option** *n* STOCK opción de compra cubierta *f*; ~ **call write** *n* STOCK venta de opción de compra cubierta *f*; ~ **dry container** *n* TRANSP contenedor cerrado sin aislamiento térmico *m*; ~ **long** *n* STOCK *options* largo cubierto *m*; ~ **option** *n* STOCK opción con garantía *f*; ~ **option writing** *n* STOCK emisión de opciones cubiertas *f*; ~ **peril** *n* INS riesgo cubierto *m*; ~ **position** *n* STOCK *options* posición cubierta *f*; ~ **put** *n* STOCK opción de venta cubierta *f*; ~ **short** *n* STOCK *options* venta a término cubierta *f*; ~ **short position** *n* STOCK posición corta asegurada *f*; ~ **warrant** *n* FIN garantía cubierta *f*; ~ **writer** *n* STOCK suscriptor(a) cubierto(-a) *m,f*

covering: ~ **deed** *n* ACC, BANK acto de garantía *m*, GEN COMM acta de garantía *f*; ~ **letter** *n* ADMIN, COMMS, GEN COMM carátula *f* (*AmL*), carta de presentación *f* (*Esp*); ~ **warrant** *n* BANK, ECON, FIN, GEN COMM certificado de cobertura *m*

COW *abbr* TRANSP (*crude oil washing*) lavado de crudos *m*, (*collection on wheels*) recogida a domicilio *f*

cowboy *n infrml* IND chapucero(-a) *m,f*; ~ **economy** *AmE infrml* ECON economía del despilfarro y la irresponsabilidad

cp. *abbr* (*coupon*) GEN COMM cupón *m*

CP *abbr* GEN COMM (*commercial paper*) papel comercial *m*, instrumentos negociables *m pl*, WEL EU (*Community Program AmE, Community Programme BrE*) programa comunitario *m*

C/P[1] *abbr* (*charter party*) TRANSP *shipowner's contractual agreement* póliza de fletamento *f*

C/P[2]: ~ **b/lading** *n* (*charter party bill of lading*) IMP/EXP, TRANSP conocimiento de embarque bajo condiciones de la póliza de fletamento *m*

CPA *abbr* (*critical path analysis*) MGMNT análisis del camino crítico *m*

C.P.A. *abbr* (*Certified Public Accountant*) ACC contable público(-a) certificado(-a) *m,f* (*Esp*), contable público(-a) titulado(-a) *m,f* (*Esp*), contador(a) público(-a) certificado(-a) *m,f* (*AmL*), contador(a) público(-a) titulado(-a) *m,f* (*AmL*)

cpd *abbr* (*charterer's pay dues*) TRANSP derechos pagados por el fletador *m pl*

CPE *abbr* (*centrally-planned economy*) ECON, POL economía de planificación centralizada *f*

CPI *abbr BrE* (*consumer price index*) ECON, FIN IPC (*Índice de Precios al Consumo*)

CPM *abbr* (*critical path method*) MGMNT método del camino crítico *m*

CPP *abbr* (*current purchasing power*) ECON poder adquisitivo actual *m*

CPS *abbr* ECON (*current population survey*) estudio de la población circulante *m*, (*Centre for Policy Studies*) centro independiente de investigación socio-económica

CPT *abbr* (*carriage paid transport*) TRANSP transporte pagado *m*

cr *abbr* GEN COMM (*credit*) crédito *m*, (*creditor*) acreedor(a) *m,f*

Cr *abbr* (*crane*) TRANSP grúa *f*

CR *abbr* COMP, GEN COMM (*carriage return*) retorno de carro *m*

crack *n* STOCK crac *m*

craft: ~ **loss** *n* (*c/l*) TRANSP pérdida de la embarcación *f*; ~ **organizations** *n pl* HRM asociaciones artesanales *f pl*; ~ **union** *n* HRM gremio *m*

craftsman *n* HRM artesano *m*

crane *n* (*Cr*) TRANSP grúa *f*; ~-**jib-type fork-lift truck** TRANSP *cargo* vehículo con horquilla elevadora tipo pescante de grúa *m*

crash[1] *n* COMP *system* quiebra *f*, STOCK crac *m*, quiebra *f*, desplome *m*, TRANSP quiebra *f*

crash[2] *vi* COMP quebrarse, STOCK *prices* hundirse, TRANSP quebrar

crate *n* TRANSP jaula de embalaje *f*

crawling: ~ **peg** *n* ECON *international* vínculo móvil *m*; ~ **peg system** *n* ECON sistema de ajuste mensual de la paridad del cambio *m*

CRC *abbr* (*camera-ready copy*) MEDIA boceto publicitario listo para fotografiar *m*

CRE *abbr BrE* (*Commercial Relations and Exports*) IMP/EXP relaciones comerciales y exportaciones *f pl*

cream[1]: ~ **of the crop** *n infrml* HRM lo mejor de la promoción

cream[2]: ~ **off the best** *phr infrml* GEN COMM *money, demand* hacerse con lo mejor

create *vt* ECON *demand*, GEN COMM *opportunities, agency*, S&M *market* crear

creation *n* GEN COMM creación *f*

creative[1] *adj* GEN COMM, S&M creativo

creative[2]: ~ **accounting** *n* ACC contabilidad creativa *f*; ~ **department** *n* S&M departamento creativo *m*; ~ **destruction** *n* ECON destrucción creativa *f*; ~ **federalism** *n* POL federalismo creativo *m*; ~ **financing** *n* FIN financiación innovadora *f*; ~ **group** *n* S&M grupo creativo *m*; ~ **hot shops** *n pl* S&M agencias publicitarias creativas *f pl*; ~ **marketing** *n* S&M marketing creativo *m*; ~ **strategy** *n* S&M *advertising* estrategia creativa *f*; ~ **thinking** *n* GEN COMM, MGMNT, S&M *strategy* pensamiento creativo *m*

creativity *n* GEN COMM, S&M creatividad *f*

credentials *n pl* HRM carta credencial *f*; ~ **presentation** *n* S&M presentación de referencias *f*

credibility *n* GEN COMM, S&M credibilidad *f*; ~ **gap** S&M pérdida de credibilidad *f*

credit[1]: ~-**enhanced** *adj* STOCK *securities* de crédito mejorado

credit[2] *n* (*cr*) GEN COMM crédito *m*; ~ **account** (*C/A*) ACC, BANK, ECON, FIN cuenta de crédito *f*; ~ **account voucher** BANK comprobante de cuenta de crédito *m*; ~ **advisor** FIN asesor(a) de crédito *m,f*, consejero(-a) de crédito *m,f*; ~ **agency** FIN agencia de crédito *f*; ~ **agreement** FIN convenio de crédito *m*; ~ **analysis** BANK, FIN análisis del crédito *m*; ~ **analyst** BANK, FIN analista de créditos *mf*; ~ **association** BANK, FIN entidad de crédito *f*; ~ **balance** BANK haber *m*; ~ **bank** BANK inmobiliaria *f*; ~ **bureau** BANK, FIN, oficina de crédito *f*; ~ **buyer** *AmE* (*cf charge buyer BrE*) S&M comprador(a) a crédito *m,f*; ~ **card** BANK, FIN tarjeta de crédito *f*; ~-**card booking** *BrE* (*cf credit-*

card reservation AmE) LEIS reserva con tarjeta de crédito *f*; ~ **card imprinter** BANK, FIN impresora de tarjetas de crédito *f*; ~ **card issuer** BANK, FIN emisor de tarjetas de crédito *m*; ~ **card payment** GEN COMM pago con tarjeta de crédito *m*; ~ **card portfolio** BANK cartera de tarjetas de crédito *m*; **~card reservation** *AmE* (*cf credit-card booking BrE*) LEIS reserva con tarjeta de crédito *f*; ~ **card transaction** BANK transacción con tarjeta de crédito *f*; ~ **ceiling** BANK, FIN límite del crédito *m*, techo de crédito *m*; ~ **column** BANK, FIN columna del haber *f*; ~ **conditions** *n pl* BANK, FIN condiciones de crédito *f pl*; ~ **control** BANK, ECON, FIN control de crédito *m*; ~ **controller** BANK, FIN, HRM supervisor(a) de cobro *m,f*, supervisor(a) de crédito *m,f*; ~ **counsellor** FIN asesor(a) de crédito *m,f*; ~ **crunch** BANK dificultades crediticias *f pl*; ~ **demand** BANK, FIN petición de crédito *f*; ~ **department** BANK, FIN departamento de crédito *m*; ~ **enhancement** BANK, FIN acrecentamiento del crédito *m*, aumento del crédito *m*; ~ **entry** ACC abono *m*, asiento de abono *m*, BANK, FIN asiento de abono *m*; ~ **expansion** BANK expansión del crédito *f*; ~ **facilities** *n pl* BANK condiciones de pago aplazado *f pl*; ~ **facilities at a bank** *n pl* BANK facilidades crediticias de un banco *f pl*; ~ **for mental or physical impairment** TAX deducción por disminución mental o física *f*, desgravación fiscal por disminución mental o física *f*; ~ **freeze** BANK congelación de créditos *f*; ~ **granting** BANK concesión de crédito *f*; ~ **guarantee** BANK garantía de crédito *f*; ~ **guarantor** BANK garante de un crédito *mf*; ~ **history** BANK, FIN historial del crédito *m*; ~ **information** ACC, BANK, FIN antecedentes crediticios *m pl*, información sobre créditos *f*; ~ **institution** BANK, FIN institución crediticia *f*; ~ **instrument** STOCK *interest rate futures* instrumento de crédito *m*; ~ **insurance** INS seguro de crédito *m*; ~ **limit** BANK, FIN límite del crédito *m*; ~ **line** BANK, FIN línea de crédito *f*; ~ **loss** BANK, FIN pérdida de crédito *f*; ~ **management** ACC, FIN gestión de crédito *f*; ~ **market** GEN COMM mercado crediticio *m*; ~ **memorandum** BANK, FIN memorándum de crédito *m*; ~ **multiplier** FIN multiplicador del crédito *m*; ~ **note** (*CN*) ACC, BANK, FIN, GEN COMM nota de abono *f*, nota de crédito *f*; ~ **officer** FIN jefe(-a) de créditos *m,f*; ~ **order** GEN COMM, S&M pedido a crédito *m*; ~ **package** BANK crédito combinado *m*; ~ **policy** GEN COMM política crediticia *f*; ~ **protection insurance** INS seguro de protección del crédito *m*; ~ **quality** BANK calidad del crédito *f*; ~ **rating** BANK, FIN grado de solvencia estimado *m*, límite del crédito *m*; ~ **rating system** BANK, FIN sistema de límite de crédito *m*; ~ **rationing** BANK, ECON racionamiento del crédito *m*; ~ **reference agency** FIN agencia de referencias de crédito *f*; ~ **report** GEN COMM informe crediticio *m* (*Esp*), reporte crediticio *m* (*AmL*); ~ **requirement** S&M requisito de crédito *m*; ~ **reserve** FIN reserva de crédito *f*; ~ **revolving** FIN renovación del crédito *f*; ~ **risk** BANK, FIN riesgo del crédito *m*; ~ **sale** S&M venta a crédito *f*; ~ **score** BANK, FIN *calculated by finance house* calificación de solvencia *f*; ~ **scoring** BANK, FIN solvencia crediticia *f*; ~ **side** FIN haber *m*; ~ **slip** BANK, FIN, GEN COMM nota de crédito *f*, ficha de pago *f*; ~ **squeeze** BANK, FIN estrechamiento del crédito *m*, restricción del crédito *m*; ~ **standing** S&M solvencia *f*; ~ **swing** BANK movimiento crediticio *m*; ~ **terms** *n pl* BANK, FIN condiciones crediticias *f pl*, condiciones de crédito *f pl*; ~ **title** S&M título de crédito *m*; ~ **tranche**

FIN parte del crédito *f*, tramo de crédito *m*; ~ **tranche facility** BANK, FIN ayuda crediticia *f*; ~ **transfer** BANK, FIN transferencia de crédito *f*; ~ **union** *BrE* BANK, FIN cooperativa de crédito *f*, unión de crédito *f*; ~ **voucher** BANK, GEN COMM comprobante de crédito *m*

credit[3] *vt* GEN COMM *cuenta* abonar

Credit: ~ **Clearing** *n BrE* BANK compensación de créditos *f*; ~ **Industry Fraud Avoidance System** *n BrE* (*CIFAS*) FIN sistema de prevención de fraudes en el sector de créditos *m*; ~ **Suisse index** *n* STOCK índice del Crédito Suizo *m*

creditable[1] *adj* TAX fidedigno

creditable[2]: ~ **input tax** *n* TAX impuesto reembolsable sobre insumos *m* (*AmL*), impuesto reembolsable sobre inversiones *m* (*Esp*)

credited[1]: ~ **to** *adj* ACC, BANK, FIN *account* acreditado para

credited[2]: **be ~ to** *phr* ACC, BANK, FIN recibir un abono en cuenta

creditor *n* (*cr*) GEN COMM acreedor(a) *m,f*; ~ **account** ACC cuenta acreedora *f*; ~ **beneficiary** INS *life insurance* acreedor(a) beneficiario(-a) *m,f*; ~ **department** ADMIN departamento acreedor *m*; ~ **position** ACC posición acreedora *f*; ~ **rights life assurance** INS derechos del beneficiario en los seguros de vida *m pl*; ~ **rights life insurance** INS derechos del beneficiario en los seguros de vida *m pl*

creditors': ~ **committee** *n* FIN comisión de acreedores *f*; ~ **ledger** *n* ACC mayor de acreedores *m*; ~ **meeting** *n* ACC, FIN, GEN COMM, MGMNT asamblea de acreedores *f*

credits *n pl* GEN COMM *options on futures* créditos *m pl*; ~ **outstanding** *n* ACC, BANK créditos pendientes *m pl*, créditos vigentes *m pl*, cuentas pendientes *f pl*

creditworthiness *n* BANK, FIN capacidad crediticia *f*

creditworthy *adj* BANK, FIN solvente

creeping: ~ **inflation** *n* ECON inflación reptante *f*; ~ **tender** *n* FIN, STOCK *takeovers* oferta progresiva *f*

cremation: ~ **expenses insurance** *n* INS seguro contra gastos de incineración *m*

CREST *abbr* (*Committee on Scientific and Technical Research*) IND comité de investigación científica y técnica

crew: ~ **agreement** *n BrE* TRANSP acuerdo de tripulación *m*; ~ **manifest** *n* TRANSP manifiesto de tripulación *m*; ~ **subsidization** *n* TRANSP subvención de la tripulación *f*

CRI *abbr* (*consumption rate of interest*) GEN COMM tasa de interés del consumo *f*

crime *n* LAW delito *m*

criminal: ~ **lawyer** *n* BANK, GEN COMM, LAW ≈ abogado(-a) penalista *m,f*; ~ **liability** *n* INS responsabilidad penal *f*; ~ **negligence** *n* LAW negligencia susceptible de configurar un delito *f*; ~ **offence** *n* LAW delito *m*

crisis *n* ECON, GEN COMM, POL crisis *f*; ~ **management** MGMNT gestión de crisis *f*

criteria *n pl* GEN COMM criterios *m pl*

criterion *n* GEN COMM criterio *m*, constante de comparación *f*

critical[1] *adj* COMP, GEN COMM crítico

critical[2]: ~ **level** *n* GEN COMM nivel crítico *m*; ~ **mass** *n* ECON, GEN COMM, S&M masa crítica *f*; ~ **path** *n* MGMNT *planning* camino crítico *m*; ~ **path analysis** *n* (*CPA*) MGMNT análisis del camino crítico *m*; ~ **path method** *n* (*CPM*) MGMNT método del camino crítico *m*; ~ **path**

theory *n* MGMNT teoría del camino crítico *f*; **~ region** *n* MATH *statistical testing* región crítica *f*; **~ success** *n* LEIS *theatre* éxito crítico *m*; **~ value** *n* MATH *statistics* valor crítico *m*

criticize *vt* GEN COMM criticar

CRN *abbr* (*customs registered number*) IMP/EXP número registrado en aduanas *m*

crook *n infrml* LAW timador(a) *m,f*

crop *n* ENVIR, GEN COMM cosecha *f*; **~ failure** ECON *agricultural*, ENVIR mala cosecha *f*; **~ hail insurance** INS seguro de pedrisco *m*; **~ rotation** ECON, ENVIR rotación de cultivos *f*

cross¹: **~-border** *adj* GEN COMM transfronterizo

cross² *n* STOCK cruce *m*; **~ assembler** COMP ensamblador cruzado *m*, ensamblador de referencias cruzadas *m*; **~ book** ECON, GEN COMM, STOCK especulación mixta *f*; **~-border demergers** *n pl* ECON, POL disolución de fusiones internacionales *f*; **~-border financial transaction** FIN transacción financiera transfronteriza *f*; **~-border joint venture** FIN alianza estratégica transfronteriza *f*, coinversión transfronteriza *f*, empresa conjunta transfronteriza *f*; **~-border merger** FIN, IMP/EXP consorcio transfronterizo *m*, fusión transfronteriza *f*; **~-border trade** ECON comercio transfronterizo *m*; **~ border trading** ECON comercio transfronterizo *m*; **~-border transaction** FIN transacción transfronteriza *f*; **~ check** GEN COMM, IMP/EXP verificación cruzada *f*; **~ currency exposure** ECON *international trade* riesgo cruzado entre divisas *m*; **~-current** GEN COMM contracorriente *f*; **~ default** BANK, FIN falta de pago cruzado *f*; **~ demand** TAX contrademanda *f*; **~-elasticity of demand** S&M elasticidad cruzada de la demanda *f*; **~-footing** MATH *spreadsheet* sumas horizontales *f pl*; **~-frontier transfer** IMP/EXP, TRANSP *of hazardous waste* traslado transfronterizo *m*; **~ guarantee** BANK garantía cruzada *f*; **~ hedge** STOCK cobertura cruzada *f*; **~ hedging** STOCK cobertura cruzada *f*; **~ holding between companies** STOCK participación recíproca *f*, tenencia cruzada entre empresas *f*; **~ liability** INS responsabilidad cruzada *f*; **~-licensing** COMP *of technology transfer*, GEN COMM, LAW explotación mutua de derechos de patente *f*; **~ merchandising** S&M comercialización cruzada *f*; **~-ownership** GEN COMM propiedad cruzada *f*, MEDIA propiedad mixta *f*, PROP propiedad cruzada *f*; **~-ownership test** TAX prueba de propiedad recíproca *f*; **~-ownership threshold** TAX nivel de propiedad recíproca *m*, umbral de propiedad recíproca *m*; **~ rate** ECON *international*, FIN tasa cruzada *f*, tipo cruzado *m*; **~-reference** COMP remisión *f*; **~-reference listing** COMP lista de remisiones *f*; **~ section** GEN COMM sección transversal *f*; **~-section analysis** GEN COMM análisis de corte transversal *m*, análisis de datos transversales *m*; **~-section data** ECON *econometrics* datos de corte transversal *f*; **~-subsidization** FIN, GEN COMM subvención cruzada *m*; **~-subsidy** FIN subsidio cruzado *m*; **~ tabulation** MATH *statistical technique* tabulación horizontal *f*; **~ trade** TRANSP comercio entre países extranjeros *m*

cross³ *vt* GEN COMM, IMP/EXP cruzar; ◆ **~ international frontiers** IMP/EXP atravesar las fronteras internacionales; **~ a picket line** HRM, POL *demonstration* romper una manifestación; **~ specially** BANK *cheque* cruzar especialmente

crossbar *n* TRANSP *of container* travesaño *m*

crossed: **~ check** *AmE*; **~ cheque** *n BrE* BANK cheque cruzado *m*; **~ loan** *n* BANK, FIN crédito cruzado *m*; **~ trade** *n* STOCK negocio cruzado *m*

cross-fade *vi* MEDIA, S&M *radio, television* fundir sonoro

crossover: **~ vote** *n AmE* POL cambio de voto entre las elecciones primarias y las elecciones generales

crosstie *n AmE* (*cf sleeper BrE*) TRANSP *rail* traviesa *f*

CROTUM *abbr BrE* (*Commissioner for the Rights of Trade Union Members*) HRM comisionado para los derechos de miembros de los sindicatos

crowd *n* STOCK corro *m*

crowd out *vt* ECON *borrowers, investors*, FIN, GEN COMM excluir

crowding: **~ hypothesis** *n* ECON hipótesis de la aglomeración *f*; **~ out** *n* ECON, FIN, GEN COMM exclusión *f*, *of borrowing, investment* efecto de exclusión *m*; **~-out effect** *n* ECON efecto crowding-out *m*

crown: **~ jewels** *n infrml* ECON joyas de la corona *f pl*

Crown: **~ charges** *n pl BrE* TAX gastos de la Corona *m pl*; **~ corporation** *n* LAW empresa pública *f*; **~ loan** *n* TAX crédito de la Corona *m*; **~ royalty** *n* TAX derecho de la corona *m*; **~ share** *n* TAX participación de Estado *f*

CRT *abbr* (*cathode ray tube*) COMP, MEDIA tubo de rayos catódicos *m*

crude: **~ goods** *n pl* GEN COMM mercancías en bruto *f pl*; **~ oil** *n* ENVIR, IND, TRANSP crudo *m*, petróleo crudo *m*; **~-oil carrier** *n* TRANSP transportista de crudos *mf*; **~-oil washing** *n* (*COW*) TRANSP lavado de crudos *m*; **~ petroleum** *n* ENVIR, IND, TRANSP petróleo bruto *m*; **~ population rate** *n* ECON tasa bruta de la población *f*

c/s *abbr* (*cases*) TRANSP cajones *m pl*

CS *abbr* ECON (*counter signatory*) signo monetario *m*, POL (*Civil Service*) administración pública *f*

CSC *abbr* GEN COMM (*continuous survey cycle*) ciclo de peritaje continuo *m*, POL (*Civil Service Commission*) comisión británica de funcionarios, TRANSP (*container safety convention*) convención sobre seguridad de los contenedores *f*

CSG *abbr* (*consultative shipping group*) TRANSP grupo naviero consultivo *m*

CSO *abbr BrE* (*Central Statistical Office*) ECON ≈ INE (*Instituto Nacional de Estadística*)

CSPC *abbr* (*Cargo Systems and Procedures Committee*) TRANSP Comité de Sistemas y Procedimientos de Carga *m*

CST *abbr* GEN COMM (*Central Standard Time*) hora central establecida *f*, TRANSP (*container service tariff*) tarifa de servicio de contenedores *f*

CT *abbr* IMP/EXP (*Community transit*) tránsito comunitario *m*, (*customs transaction code*) código de transacciones aduaneras *m*, TRANSP (*cubic tonnage*) TC (*tonelaje cúbico*), (*combined transport*) transporte combinado *m*, (*cargo tank*) tanque de carga *m*, (*customs transaction code*) código de transacciones aduaneras *m*

CTBL *abbr* (*combined transport bill of lading*) TRANSP conocimiento de transporte combinado *m*

CTC *abbr* (*cargo tank center AmE, cargo tank centre BrE*) TRANSP centro del tanque de carga *m*

CTD *abbr* STOCK (*cheapest to deliver*) más bajo por entregar, TAX (*certificate of tax deposit BrE*) certificado de pago de impuestos *m*, comprobante de depósito del impuesto *m*, IMP/EXP, TRANSP (*combined transport document*) documento de transporte combinado *m*

CTL *abbr* (*constructive total loss*) GEN COMM, INS pérdida total implícita *f*, TRANSP *maritime insurance* pérdida total constructiva *f*

CTLO *abbr* (*constructive total loss only*) GEN COMM, INS sólo pérdida total implícita *f*

CTN *abbr* (*confectioner, tobacconist and newsagent*) S&M confitero, estanquero y vendedor de periódicos *m*

CTO *abbr* (*combined transport operator*) TRANSP operador(a) de transporte combinado *m,f*

CTPC *abbr* (*Cargo Traffic Procedures Committee*) TRANSP Comité de Procedimientos para el Tráfico de Carga *m*

ctr *abbr* (*cutter*) TRANSP guardacostas *m*

CTRL: ~ **key** *n* (*control key*) COMP tecla CTRL *f* (*tecla de mando*)

CTT *abbr* (*capital transfer tax*) TAX impuesto sobre las transferencias de capital *m*

CTX *abbr* (*cargo tank common*) TRANSP servicio del tanque de carga *m*

cu *abbr* (*cubic*) GEN COMM cúbico

cube *n* TRANSP cubo *m*

cube out *vi* TRANSP cubicar

cubic[1] *adj* (*cu*) GEN COMM cúbico

cubic[2]: ~ **capacity** *n* (*cc*) GEN COMM capacidad cúbica *f*; ~ **centimeter** *AmE*, ~ **centimetre** *BrE n* (*cc*) GEN COMM centímetro cúbico *m* (*cc*); ~ **inch** *n* GEN COMM pulgada cúbica *f*; ~ **meter** *AmE*, ~ **metre** *BrE n* (*cbm*) GEN COMM metro cúbico *m*; ~ **tonnage** *n* (*CT*) TRANSP tonelaje cúbico *m* (*TC*)

CUKCC *abbr* (*Canada-United Kingdom Chamber of Commerce*) ECON Cámara de Comercio Anglo-Canadiense *f*

cul-de-sac *n* PROP callejón sin salida *m*

culminate in *vi* GEN COMM, POL *discussions* culminar en

culpability *n* LAW culpabilidad *f*

culpable *adj* LAW *action* culposo, *person* culpable

cultivated: ~ **acreage** *n* ENVIR, TAX superficie cultivada *f*

cultivation *n* ECON *agricultural economics* cultivo *m*

cultural[1] *adj* GEN COMM cultural

cultural[2]: ~ **attaché** *n* HRM agregado(-a) cultural *m,f*, ~ **center** *AmE*, ~ **centre** *BrE n* GEN COMM centro cultural *m*; ~ **revolution** *n* POL revolución cultural *f*

culture *n* GEN COMM cultura *f*; ~ **shock** GEN COMM choque cultural *m*

cum. *abbr* (*cumulative*) GEN COMM acumulativo

cum[1]: ~ **and ex** *adj* STOCK con y sin

cum[2] *adv* STOCK con; ~ **coupon** STOCK con cupón; ~ **dividend** (*cd*) STOCK con dividendo; ~ **warrant** GEN COMM con garantía

cum[3]: ~**rights period** *n* STOCK periodo con derechos *m*

cum[4]: ~ **rights** *phr* STOCK con derechos

cumulative[1] *adj* (*cum.*) GEN COMM acumulativo

cumulative[2]: ~ **audience** *n* S&M audiencia acumulativa *f*; ~ **deduction account** *n* TAX cuenta de deducción acumulativa *f*; ~ **dividend** *n* STOCK dividendo acumulativo *m*; ~ **eligible capital** *n* TAX capital redescontable acumulativo *m*; ~ **frequency** *n* MATH frecuencia acumulativa *f*; ~ **gains limit** *n* TAX límite acumulativo de ganancias *m*; ~ **imputed amount** *n* TAX cantidad acumulativa imputada *f*; ~ **income** *n* TAX renta acumulativa *f*; ~ **liability** *n* INS responsabilidad acumulativa *f*; ~ **net capital loss** *n* FIN pérdida acumulativa de capital neto *f*; ~ **net investment loss** *n* TAX pérdida

acumulativa de inversión neta *f*; ~ **net taxable capital gain** *n* TAX ganancia acumulativa del capital neto imponible *f*; ~ **offset account** *n* TAX cuenta de compensación acumulativa *f*; ~ **penetration** *n* S&M penetración acumulativa *f*; ~ **preference share** *n* *BrE* (*cf cumulative preferred stock AmE*) FIN, STOCK acción preferente de dividendo acumulable *f*, acción privilegiada de dividendo acumulable *f*; ~ **preferred stock** *n* *AmE* (*cf cumulative preference share BrE*) STOCK acciones privilegiadas de dividendo acumulativo *f pl*; ~ **reach** *n* S&M alcance acumulativo *m*; ~ **security** *n* STOCK valor acumulativo *m*; ~ **small business gains account** *n* TAX cuenta acumulativa de ganancias de la pequeña empresa *f*; ~ **tax** *n* TAX impuesto acumulativo *m*; ~ **voting** *n* STOCK votación acumulativa *f*

curable: ~ **depreciation** *n* ECON depreciación recuperable *f*

curator *n* LAW *bankruptcy* administrador(a) *m,f*

cure: **no** ~ **no pay** *phr* INS *marine* pago al buen fin *m*

currency *n* (*cy.*) GEN COMM divisa *f*, FIN moneda circulante *f*; ~ **account** FIN cuenta en divisas *f*; ~ **adjustment factor** (*CAF*) IMP/EXP, TRANSP aumento por cambio de divisas *m*; ~ **appreciation** ECON *international* revalorización monetaria *f*, FIN alza de la moneda circulante *f*; ~ **arbitrage** STOCK arbitraje de divisas *m*; ~ **at a discount** BANK, ECON *international* divisa bajo la par *f*; ~ **at a premium** BANK, ECON divisa por encima de la par *f*; ~ **of a bill** ACC periodo de validez de una letra de cambio *m*; ~ **borrowing** BANK préstamo en divisas *m*; ~ **call option** STOCK opción de compra de divisas *f*; ~ **clause** BANK, INS, LAW cláusula monetaria *f*; ~ **cocktail** FIN variedad de monedas *f*; ~ **code** BANK código de divisa *m*; ~ **contract** STOCK *money market* contrato sobre divisas *m*; ~ **deposits** *n pl* BANK, FIN depósitos en divisas *m pl*; ~ **depreciation** ECON *international*, FIN depreciación de la moneda circulante *f*, depreciación monetaria *f*; ~ **devaluation** ECON *international*, FIN devaluación monetaria *f*; ~ **draft** BANK giro en divisas *m*; ~ **futures** *n pl* STOCK futuros sobre divisa *m pl*; ~ **futures contract** STOCK contrato sobre futuros de divisas *m*; ~ **futures market** FIN, STOCK mercado de futuros en divisas *m*; ~ **holding** ECON, FIN reserva de divisas *f*; ~ **in circulation** ECON moneda de curso legal *f*; ~ **issue** BANK emisión de papel moneda *f*; ~**-linked** FIN indexado de la moneda *m*; ~ **market** ECON, FIN, STOCK *international* mercado de divisas *m*; ~ **mix** BANK combinación de divisas *f*; ~ **option** STOCK opción sobre divisas *f*; ~ **options contract** STOCK contrato de opciones de divisas *m*; ~ **options seller** STOCK vendedor(a) de opciones de divisas *m,f*; ~ **options writer** STOCK emisor(a) de opciones de divisas *m,f*; ~ **put option** STOCK opción de venta de divisas *f*; ~ **reform** ECON, FIN reforma monetaria *f*; ~ **restriction** ECON, FIN restricción de divisas *f*; ~ **revaluation** ECON *international* revalorización monetaria *f*; ~ **risk** ECON *macroeconomics* riesgo de una divisa *m*; ~ **stabilization scheme** ECON *international* esquema de estabilización monetaria *m*; ~ **standard** STOCK patrón monetario *m*; ~ **swop** FIN intercambio de monedas *m*; ~ **symbol** GEN COMM símbolo monetario *m*; ~ **unit** ACC, BANK, ECON, FIN unidad monetaria *f*; ~ **value** ECON valor monetario *m*

current[1] *adj* BANK, GEN COMM *exchange rate* actual

current[2]: ~ **account** *n* *BrE* (*cf checking account AmE*) ACC, BANK (*c/a*) *balance of payments* cuenta corriente *f* (*clc*), cuenta de cheques *f*; ~ **account balance** *n* BANK, GEN COMM balanza por cuenta corriente *f*; ~ **account customer** *n* BANK cliente de cuenta corriente *mf*; ~ **account deficit** *n* ACC, BANK déficit en cuenta corriente *m*; ~ **account holder** *n* BANK titular de una cuenta corriente *mf*; ~ **account loan** *n* BANK préstamo en cuenta corriente *m*; ~ **account surplus** *n* BANK, ECON superávit de cuenta corriente *m*; ~ **adaptor** *n* AmE (*cf mains adaptor BrE*) COMP, IND adaptador a la red *m*, adaptador de corriente *m*; ~ **affairs** *n pl* MEDIA, POL noticias de actualidad *f*; ~ **annuity** *n* INS anualidad en curso *f*; ~ **asset** *n* ACC, FIN, PROP activo circulante *m*, activo realizable *m*; ~ **asset cycle** *n* BANK, FIN, GEN COMM, MGMNT ciclo del activo circulante *m*; ~ **assumption whole life insurance** *n* INS seguro de vida total con base actual *m*; ~ **blend** *n* (*CB*) STOCK combinación circulante *f*; ~ **business year** *n* ACC año mercantil en curso *m*, ejercicio económico actual *m*, ejercicio económico en curso *m*, ejercicio económico vigente *m*; ~ **cost** *n* ACC, FIN, GEN COMM coste corriente *m* (*Esp*), coste de reposición *m* (*Esp*), costo corriente *m* (*AmL*), costo de reposición *m* (*AmL*); ~ **cost accounting** *n* (*CCA*) ACC, ECON, TAX contabilidad de costes corrientes *f* (*Esp*), contabilidad de costos corrientes *f* (*AmL*), estados financieros a costes actuales *m pl* (*Esp*), estados financieros a costos actuales *m pl* (*AmL*), contabilidad de gastos corrientes *f*; ~ **cost basis** *n* ACC, TAX base del coste corriente *f* (*Esp*), base del costo corriente *f* (*AmL*); ~ **demand** *n* S&M demanda actual *f*; ~ **dollars** *n* ACC, ECON dólares corrientes *m pl*, dólares actuales *m pl*; ~ **domestic value** *n* (*CDV*) ECON, IMP/EXP valor interno actual *m*; ~ **economic trend** *n* ECON, POL tendencia económica actual *f*; ~ **entry price** *n* ACC precio de entrada actual *m*; ~ **expenditure** *n* FIN saldo corriente *m*; ~ **fiscal plan** *n* TAX plan fiscal actual *m*; ~ **fiscal year** *n* TAX año fiscal en curso *m*; ~ **grant to persons** *n* ECON subsidio disponible para las personas *m*; ~ **holdings** *n pl* STOCK valores en cartera actuales *m pl*; ~ **insurance** *n* INS seguro en vigor *m*; ~ **level of unemployment** *n* ECON, POL nivel real de desempleo *m*; ~ **liability** *n* ACC, BANK pasivo corriente *m*; ~ **loop** *n* COMP *older teletypewriters* bucle de corriente *m*; ~ **market price** *n* STOCK precio actual de mercado *m*; ~ **market value** *n* ACC, S&M valor comercial actual *m*; ~ **operating profit** *n* ACC beneficio corriente de explotación *m*, beneficio de las actividades ordinarias *m*, beneficio de operaciones corrientes *m*; ~ **population survey** *n* (*CPS*) ECON estudio de la población circulante *m*; ~ **price** *n* ECON, GEN COMM, S&M precio actual *m*, precio corriente *m*; ~ **purchasing power** *n* (*CPP*) ECON poder adquisitivo actual *m*; ~ **rate** *n* GEN COMM tarifa actual *f*, tipo actual *m*; ~ **rate method** *n* AmE (*cf closing rate method BrE*) ACC *currency translation* método del cambio de cierre *m*, método del salario real *m*; ~ **ratio** *n* ACC, FIN proporción corriente *f*, proporción del circulante *f*, ratio corriente *m*, ratio del circulante *m*; ~ **return** *n* STOCK rendimiento corriente *m*; ~ **revenues** *n pl* ACC ingresos corrientes *m pl*; ~ **risk** *n* ECON riesgo en curso *m*; ~ **savings account** *n* BANK cuenta de ahorro a la vista *f*; ~ **spending** *n* ECON gasto corriente *m*; ~ **stock** *n* STOCK valores ordinarios *m pl*; ~ **value** *n* ACC, ECON, FIN, GEN COMM valor constante *m*, *in the case of investment other than land and buildings* valor actual *m*; ~ **value accounting** *n* ACC contabilización del valor actual *f*; ~ **year** *n* GEN COMM año en curso *m*; ~ **year disposition** *n* TAX disposición del año

en curso *f*; ~ **yield** *n* BANK rédito normal *m*, STOCK rédito corriente *m*, rendimiento del cupón *m*, rendimiento normal *m*

curriculum *n* GEN COMM *education* curriculum *m*, WEL plan de estudios *m*; ~ **vitae** (*CV*) BrE (*cf résumé AmE*) HRM curriculum vitae *m*, datos biográficos *m pl*

cursor *n* COMP *comp keyboard* cursor *m*; ~ **control pad** COMP tarjeta de control del cursor *f*

curtailment: ~ **in pension plan** *n* FIN restricción en los planes de jubilación *f*

curtilage *n* LAW, PROP terreno afecto a una vivienda *m*, terreno alrededor de la casa *m*

curve *n* GEN COMM curva *f*

curvilinear: ~ **relationship** *n* MATH relación curvilínea *f*

cushion: ~ **tire** AmE, ~ **tyre** BrE *n* TRANSP tubular *m*

custodial: ~ **account** *n* BANK cuenta de custodia *f*

custodian *n* LAW tutor(a) *m,f*, STOCK custodio(-a) *m,f*; ~ **account fee** BANK comisión de cuenta de custodia *f*, cuota de cuenta de custodia *f*; ~ **fee** BANK comisión de custodia *f*, cuota de custodia *f*; ~ **of property** LAW administrador(a) de la propiedad *m,f*

custodianship: ~ **account** *n* BANK cuenta de custodia *f*

custody *n* GEN COMM, LAW custodia *f*; ~ **account** BANK cuenta de custodia *f*; ~ **account charge** BANK cargo por cuenta de custodia *m*; ~ **charge** BANK cargo por custodia *m*; ~ **and control** LAW *of child* custodia y control *f*; ~ **of shares** STOCK custodia de acciones *f*

custom[1]: ~**-made** *adj* GEN COMM, IND hecho de encargo

custom[2] *n* GEN COMM *trade* clientela *f*, *habit* costumbre *f*; ~ **builder** PROP constructor(a) por encargo *m,f*; ~ **and practice** HRM, IND costumbres y prácticas *f pl*, usos y costumbres *m pl*

customary: ~ **despatch** *n* TRANSP expedición habitual *f*; ~ **tare** *n* TAX tara acostumbrada *f*

customer[1]: ~**-driven** *adj* COMP personalizado; ~**-oriented** *adj* GEN COMM orientado al cliente

customer[2] *n* GEN COMM cliente *mf*; ~ **account** ACC cuenta de cliente *f*; ~ **awareness** S&M conciencia del cliente *f*; ~ **base** S&M base de clientes *f*; ~ **billing** ACC facturación al cliente *f*; ~ **card** GEN COMM tarjeta de cliente *f*; ~ **care** S&M atención al cliente *f*; ~ **confidence** S&M confianza del cliente *f*; ~ **deposit** BANK depósito del cliente *m*; ~ **flow** ECON, GEN COMM fluctuación de clientela *f*; ~ **liaison** GEN COMM enlace con el cliente *m*; ~ **ledger** ACC mayor de clientes *m*; ~**s' net debit balance** STOCK saldo deudor neto del cliente *m*; ~ **orientation** S&M orientación del cliente *f*; ~**'s own transport** (*COT*) TRANSP transporte propio del cliente *m*; ~ **profile** S&M perfil del cliente *m*; ~ **records** *n pl* S&M registro de clientes *m*; ~ **relations** *n pl* HRM relaciones con los clientes *f pl*; ~ **relations manager** HRM, S&M director(a) de atención al cliente *m,f*; ~ **research** S&M investigación de clientes *f*; ~ **service** ADMIN, GEN COMM, S&M servicio al cliente *m*, servicio de atención al público *m*; ~ **service department** ADMIN, GEN COMM, S&M departamento de atención al cliente *m*, departamento de servicio al cliente *m*; ~ **service representative** HRM representante del servicio al cliente *mf*

customize *vt* GEN COMM hacer a medida, personalizar, IND *production* modificar sobre pedido, personalizar, S&M hacer a medida, personalizar

customized[1] *adj* GEN COMM, S&M hecho a medida,

personalizado, IND modificado sobre pedido, a la medida del cliente, hecho a medida, personalizado

customized²: ~ **keyboard** n COMP teclado personalizado m; ~ **service** n S&M servicio personalizado m

customs n GEN COMM aduana f; ~ **agency** ECON, IMP/EXP, TAX agencia de aduanas f; ~ **arrangement** IMP/EXP, POL, TAX, TRANSP acuerdo aduanero m; ~ **authorities** IMP/EXP arancel aduanero m; ~ **barriers** IMP/EXP barrera aduanera f; ~ **broker** IMP/EXP agente de aduanas mf; ~ **cargo clearance** IMP/EXP, TRANSP despacho de carga por aduanas m; ~ **check** IMP/EXP, TRANSP verificación de aduana f; ~ **clearance** (*CCL*) IMP/EXP despacho aduanero m, despacho de aduanas m; ~ **clearance agent** IMP/EXP agente de despacho de aduanas mf; ~ **collector** IMP/EXP recaudador(a) de aduanas m,f; ~ **consignee** IMP/EXP consignatario(-a) de aduanas m,f; ~ **control** IMP/EXP control aduanero m; ~ **court** IMP/EXP, LAW tribunal aduanero m; ~ **declaration** IMP/EXP, TRANSP (*CD*) declaración de aduana f, declaración arancelaria f; ~ **duties** n pl IMP/EXP, TAX derechos aduaneros m pl, derechos arancelarios m pl, impuestos aduaneros m pl; ~ **entry** IMP/EXP, TRANSP declaración de entrada en aduana f; ~ **formality** IMP/EXP formalidad aduanera f, procedimiento aduanero m; ~ **house report** IMP/EXP informe de aduanas m (*Esp*), reporte aduanas m (*AmL*); ~ **inspection** IMP/EXP, LAW inspección aduanera f; ~ **invoice** IMP/EXP factura de aduanas f; ~ **inwards** n pl TRANSP derechos de entrada m pl; ~ **jurisdiction** LAW jurisdicción aduanera f; ~ **manifest** GEN COMM, IMP/EXP guía de aduanas f; ~ **officer** HRM, IMP/EXP, TAX aduanero(-a) m,f, oficial(a) de aduanas m,f; ~ **pre-entry exports** n pl IMP/EXP exportaciones aún no declaradas f pl; ~ **pre-entry imports** n pl IMP/EXP importaciones aún no declaradas f pl; ~ **procedure** IMP/EXP formalidades aduaneras f pl; ~ **registered number** (*CRN*) IMP/EXP número registrado en aduanas m; ~ **regulations** n pl IMP/EXP disposiciones aduaneras m pl; ~ **seal** IMP/EXP, TRANSP precinto aduanero m; ~ **tariff** IMP/EXP arancel aduanero m; ~ **transaction code** (*CT*) IMP/EXP código de transacciones aduaneras m; ~ **union** ECON international, IMP/EXP, LAW unión aduanera f; ~ **valuation** IMP/EXP valoración en aduana f; ~ **value per gross kilogram** AmE, ~ **value per gross kilogramme** BrE (*CVGK*) IMP/EXP valor aduanero por kilogramo bruto m; ~ **value per gross pound** (*CVGP*) IMP/EXP valor aduanero por libra bruta m; ~ **warehouse** IMP/EXP, TRANSP depósito aduanero m; ♦ **no ~ value** (*NCV*) IMP/EXP sin valor en aduana

Customs: ~ **Additional Code** n (*CAC*) IMP/EXP Código Adicional de Aduanas m; ~ **Clearance Status** n (*CCS*) IMP/EXP Categoría del Despacho Aduanero f; ~ **Cooperation Council** n BrE (*CCC*) IMP/EXP consejo de cooperación aduanera; ~ **Cooperation Council nomenclature** n BrE (*CCCN*) IMP/EXP nomenclatura del consejo de cooperación aduanera; ~ **& Excise Department** n BrE (*C&E*) IMP/EXP departamento británico aduanero, ≈ Departamento de Aduanas y Tributos m, ≈ Servicio de Aduanas m

cut¹: ~**-off** n ACC cierre de libros m, cierre de libros para inventario m, GEN COMM cierre m; ~**-off bank reconciliation** n BANK conciliación bancaria de cierre f; ~**-off date** n BANK, FIN, STOCK fecha límite f; ~ **point** n ECON capital budgeting punto límite m; ~**-off procedures** n pl ACC corte de operaciones m, procedimiento de corte m; ~**-off time** n MGMNT fecha límite f;

~ **paper** n COMP papel cortado m; ~ **price** n S&M precio reducido m; ~**-throat competition** n GEN COMM competencia intensa f

cut² vt COMP edit software cortar, ECON prices recortar, GEN COMM cortar; ♦ ~ **one's losses** GEN COMM cortar por lo sano

cutback n FIN cese repentino m

cutter n (*ctr*) TRANSP guardacostas m

cutting n BrE MEDIA from newspaper recorte m

CUV abbr (*construction unit value*) TRANSP valor de la unidad de construcción m

cv abbr GEN COMM (*chief value*) valor principal m

CV abbr BrE (*curriculum vitae, cf résumé AmE*) HRM curriculum vitae m, datos biográficos m pl

C'vr abbr (*cover*) GEN COMM cobertura f, cubierta f, INS cobertura f

C/V abbr (*certificate of value*) IMP/EXP certificado de valor m

CVGK abbr (*customs value per gross kilogram AmE, customs value per gross kilogramme BrE*) IMP/EXP valor aduanero por kilogramo bruto m

CVGP abbr (*customs value per gross pound*) IMP/EXP valor aduanero por libra bruta m

CVMO abbr (*commercial value movement order*) GEN COMM orden de cambio de valor comercial f

CVO abbr (*certificate of value and origin*) IMP/EXP certificado de valor y origen m

CW abbr ECON (*commercial weight*) peso comercial m, HRM (*comparable worth*) valor comparable m

CWE abbr (*cleared without examination*) IMP/EXP desaduanado sin inspección

CWM abbr (*clerical work measurement*) ADMIN, HRM MTO (*medición del trabajo de oficina*)

c.w.o. abbr (*cash with order*) GEN COMM pago al hacer el pedido m

CWS abbr (*Cooperative Wholesale Society*) GEN COMM sociedad mayorista en cooperativa f

cwt abbr (*hundredweight*) GEN COMM quintal m

CXBG abbr (*comprehensive extended term banker's guarantee*) BANK ampliación del plazo de una garantía bancaria total f

cy. abbr (*currency*) FIN divisa f, GEN COMM divisa f

Cy abbr (*cylinder*) COMP, TRANSP cilindro m

CY abbr TRANSP (*container yard*) muelle de contenedores m

cybernetics n COMP cibernética f

cyberspace n COMP ciberespacio m

cycle n ECON, GEN COMM ciclo m; ~ **stock** STOCK acciones cíclicas f pl

cyclic: ~ **code** n COMP código cíclico m; ~ **variation** n ECON, GEN COMM variación cíclica f

cyclical¹ adj GEN COMM, STOCK stock performance cíclico

cyclical²: ~ **company** n STOCK empresa sensible a los ciclos económicos; ~ **demand** n ECON demanda cíclica f; ~ **demand industry** n ECON, IND industria cíclica f, industria de demanda cíclica f; ~ **factor** n ECON factor cíclico m; ~ **fluctuation** n ECON, GEN COMM, STOCK commodity prices fluctuación cíclica f; ~ **shares** n pl ECON, STOCK acciones cíclicas f pl; ~ **stock** n ECON, STOCK acciones cíclicas f pl; ~ **trade** n ECON comercio cíclico m; ~ **unemployment** n ECON, HRM, WEL desempleo cíclico *m*; ~ **variation** *n* ECON, GEN COMM variación cíclica *f*

cylinder *n* (*Cy*) COMP, TRANSP cilindro *m*

cymogene *n* IND *associated with movement of dangerous classified cargo* cimógeno *m*

cymometer *n* IND cimómetro *m*

D

d *abbr* (*dry bulk container*) TRANSP *shipping* contenedor de graneles secos *m*

D *abbr* COMMS, GEN COMM, STOCK (*delivered*) entregado, (*delivery*) entrega *f*, TRANSP (*diagonal engine*) máquina diagonal *f*

DA *abbr* COMP (*design automation, drawing automation*) AD (*automatización del dibujo*), HRM (*defence attaché BrE, defense attaché AmE*) agregado(-a) de defensa *m,f*, agregado(-a) militar *m,f*, LAW (*District Attorney*) fiscal *mf*

D/A *abbr* BANK (*deposit account*) cuenta de ahorros *f*, cuenta a plazo *f*, cuenta de depósito *f*, COMP (*digital/analog*) D/A (*digital/analógico*), GEN COMM (*documents against acceptance*) documentos contra aceptación *m pl*, (*days after acceptance*) días transcurridos desde la aceptación *m pl*, TRANSP (*discharge afloat*) *shipping* descarga a flote *f*

dabbler *n* STOCK especulador(a) en bolsa *m,f*

DAC *abbr* (*Development Assistance Committee*) POL CAD (*Comité de Ayuda al Desarrollo*)

DAF *abbr* (*delivered at frontier*) IMP/EXP entregado en frontera

daily[1] *adj* GEN COMM por día

daily[2] *adv* GEN COMM diariamente

daily[3]: **~ activity report** *n* GEN COMM informe de la actividad diaria *m* (*Esp*), reporte de la actividad diaria *m* (*AmL*); **~ allowance** *n* GEN COMM, HRM dieta *f*, INS indemnización diaria *f*; **~ balance interest calculation** *n* BANK cálculo de intereses sobre saldos diarios *m*; **~ closing balance** *n* ACC, BANK, FIN saldo de cierre diario *m*; **~ compensation** *n* INS indemnización diaria *f*; **~ deposit** *n* BANK depósito diario *m*; **~ interest** *n* BANK interés diario *m*; **~ interest account** *n* BANK cuenta de abono diario de intereses *f*; **~ interest deposit** *n* BANK depósito con intereses diarios *m*; **~ interest savings account** *n* BANK cuenta de ahorro con interés diario *f*; **~ limit** *n* BANK, STOCK límite diario *m*; **~ loan** *n* BANK préstamo diario *m*; **~ money rate** *n* BANK tasa de dinero a la vista *f*; **~ newspaper** *n* GEN COMM, MEDIA periódico *m*; **~ position statement** *n* ACC balance de la posición diaria *m*, estado de posición diaria *m*; **~ report of calls** *n* S&M relación diaria de visitas *f*; **~ settlement** *n* STOCK liquidación diaria *f*; **~ settlement price** *n* STOCK precio de cierre diario *m*; **~ trading limit** *n* STOCK límite de negocio diario *m*; **~ volume** *n* STOCK volumen diario *m*

Daily: ~ Range Factor *n* (*DRF*) FIN, STOCK factor de alcance diario *m*, factor de la banda diaria *m*

dairy: ~ farm *n* ECON granja lechera *f* (*Esp*), tambo *m* (*AmL*)

daisy: ~ chain *n* STOCK cadena de compra y venta para manipular el mercado *f*

daisywheel: ~ printer *n* COMP impresora a rueda de mariposa *f* (*AmL*), impresora de margarita *f* (*Esp*)

damage *n* GEN COMM *company, reputation* daño *m*, LAW agravio *m*, pérdida *f*; **~ caused by pharmaceutical products** INS daño causado por productos farmacéuticos *m*; **~ caused by radiation** INS daño causado por radiaciones *m*; **~ caused in extinguishing fire** INS daño causado por extinción de incendio *m*; **~ control** IND, TRANSP control de daños *m*; **~ limitation** GEN COMM limitación de las averías *f*, limitación de los daños *f*; **~ report** INS *marine* informe de averías *m* (*Esp*), reporte de auditoría *m* (*AmL*); **~ to goods in custody** IMP/EXP, INS, TRANSP daño a mercancías en custodia *m*; **~ to health** INS daño para la salud *m*; **~ to rented property** INS, PROP daño contra propiedad alquilada *m*; **~ to rural land** INS daño a terrenos rústicos *m*; **~ whilst loading and unloading** INS daño durante carga y descarga *m*

damaged: ~ in transit *adj* TRANSP dañado en tránsito, deteriorado en tránsito

damages *n pl* HRM daños y perjuicios *m pl*, LAW daños y perjuicios *m pl*, *compensation* indemnización *f*

damnum sine injuria *phr* GEN COMM damnum sine injuria

damp: ~-proof *adj* GEN COMM a prueba de humedad

dampen *vt* ECON *growth* amortiguar, GEN COMM *enthusiasm* moderar

danger *n* HRM, WEL peligro *m*; **~ point** GEN COMM punto peligroso *m*; ◆ **in ~ of** GEN COMM en peligro de

dangerous: ~ cargo *n* TRANSP carga peligrosa *f*; **~ cargo compound** *n* TRANSP zona reservada para carga peligrosa *f*; **~ goods** *n pl* GEN COMM, TRANSP mercancías peligrosas *f pl*, productos peligrosos *m pl*; **~ goods authority form** *n* GEN COMM, TRANSP formulario para la autorización de carga peligrosa *m*; **~ goods note** *n* (*DGN*) GEN COMM, TRANSP nota de mercancías peligrosas *f*; **~ goods rate** *n* GEN COMM, TRANSP índice de mercancías peligrosas *m*; **~ goods regulations** *n pl* IMP/EXP, TRANSP normativa sobre mercancías peligrosas *f*; **~ substance** *n* ENVIR sustancia peligrosa *f*; **~ waste** *n* ENVIR, IND residuos peligrosos *m pl*

Dangerous: ~ Goods Board *n* (*DGB*) GEN COMM, TRANSP directiva de mercancías peligrosas *f*

DAP *abbr* (*documents against payment*) GEN COMM documentos contra pago *m pl*

dash *n* MEDIA *typography* guión *m*

dashed: ~ line *n* COMP, GEN COMM línea de rayas *f*

data *n* GEN COMM datos *m pl*; **~ acquisition** COMP, ECON captación de datos *f*; **~ bank** COMP banco de datos *m*; **~ bit** COMP bitio de datos *m*; **~ broadcasting** COMMS, COMP transmisión de datos *f*; **~ bus** COMP bus de datos *m*, enlace común de datos *m*; **~ capture** COMP captura de datos *f*, toma de datos *f*; **~ card** COMP ficha de datos *f*; **~ carrier** COMP soporte de datos *m*; **~ collection** COMP, S&M recogida de datos *f*; **~ communication** COMP *data transferred between computers* comunicación de datos *f*; **~ communications equipment** (*DCE*) COMP equipo de comunicación de datos *m*; **~ compression** COMP *software* compresión de datos *f*; **~ conversion** COMP conversión de datos *f*; **~ entry** COMP entrada de datos *f*; **~ entry operator** COMP grabador(a) de datos *m,f*; **~ entry terminal** COMP terminal de entrada de datos *m*; **~ field** COMP campo de datos *m*; **~ file** COMP fichero de datos *m*; **~ flow**

COMP, GEN COMM flujo de datos *m*; **~ flow chart** COMP diagrama de flujo de datos *m*; **~ freight receipt** (*DFR*) TRANSP fecha de recepción del flete *f*; **~ gathering** COMP recogida de datos *f*, recopilación de datos *f*, S&M recogida de datos *f*; **~ input** COMP introducción de datos *f*; **~ integrity** COMP integridad de los datos *f*; **~ link** COMP enlace de datos *m*; **~ management** COMP gestión de datos *f*; **~-mining** ECON *econometrics* intentos continuados de encontrar una relación entre variables; **~ network** COMP red de datos *f*; **~ output** COMP salida de datos *f*; **~ plate** TRANSP *on container* chapa de datos *f*; **~ post** *BrE* COMMS correo de datos *m*; **~ preparation** ADMIN, COMP preparación de datos *f*; **~ processing** ADMIN, COMP proceso de datos *m*; **~ processing insurance** COMP, INS seguro sobre medios para el proceso de datos *m*; **~ processing system** (*DPS*) COMP sistema de procesamiento de datos *m*; **~ protection** COMP protección de datos *f*; **~ retrieval** COMP recuperación de datos *f*; **~ security** COMP seguridad de los datos *f*; **~ set** COMP conjunto de datos *m*; **~ sharing** COMP uso compartido de datos *m*; **~ sheet** S&M hoja de datos *f*; **~ storage** COMP almacenamiento de datos *m*; **~ stream** COMP, GEN COMM flujo de datos *m*; **~ structure** COMP estructura de datos *f*, matriz *f*; **~ terminal equipment** (*DTE*) COMP *hardware* equipo terminal de datos *m*; **~ transfer rate** COMP caudal de transferencia de datos *m*; **~ type** COMP tipo de datos *m*; ◆ **~ post on demand** (*DCD*) COMMS correo de datos por pedido

Data: ~ Protection Act *n BrE* LAW Ley de Protección de Datos *f*

database *n* COMP base de datos *f*; **~ management system** (*DBMS*) COMP sistema de gestión de base de datos *m* (*SGBD*)

dataphone *n* COMMS datáfono *m*

date *n* GEN COMM fecha *f*; **~ of acquisition** GEN COMM fecha de adquisición *f*; **~ of exercise** GEN COMM *of right*, STOCK *of option* fecha de ejercicio *f*; **~ of filing** PATENTS fecha de presentación *f*; **~ of grant** PATENTS fecha de concesión de una patente *f*, STOCK *of shares for employees* fecha de concesión *f*; **~ of invoice** GEN COMM fecha de la factura *f*; **~ of issue** INS, STOCK fecha de emisión *f*; **~-marking** GEN COMM, S&M *prepackaged goods* fechado *m*; **~ of maturity** GEN COMM, STOCK fecha de vencimiento *f*; **~ of payment** GEN COMM, STOCK día de pago *m*; **~ of record** LAW fecha de registro *f*; **~ of registration** PATENTS fecha de registro *f*; ◆ **after ~** (*A/D*) GEN COMM después de fecha, postdatado; **at due ~** BANK, FIN, GEN COMM, STOCK al vencimiento; **at a later ~** GEN COMM en fecha posterior; **at some future ~** GEN COMM en una fecha por determinar; **at a subsequent ~** GEN COMM en fecha posterior; **to ~** GEN COMM hasta la fecha

dated: ~ bond *n* FIN, STOCK bono de vencimiento fijo *m*; **~ date** *n* FIN fecha atrasada *f*

dating *n* GEN COMM datación *f*

davit *n* TRANSP *shipping* pescante para botes *m*

dawn: ~ raid *n* FIN, STOCK *shares sale* incursión al amanecer *f*

DAX: ~ index *n* STOCK índice de acciones de la bolsa de Francfort

day[1]: **~-to-day** *adj* GEN COMM diario

day[2] *n* GEN COMM día *m*; **~ loan** BANK préstamo diario de dinero *m*; **~ off** HRM día libre *m*; **~ order** STOCK orden de compra para un solo día *f*; **~ release** WEL salida diaria *f*; **~ shift** HRM turno de día *m*; **~ of shipment** TRANSP día de embarque *m*; **~-to-day funding activity** FIN actividad diaria de consolidación *f*; **~-to-day money** BANK dinero a la vista *m*; **~ trader** STOCK operador(a) de posiciones diarias *m,f*; **all ~ trading** *BrE* GEN COMM, STOCK mercado continuo *m*, negociación ininterrumpida *f*; **~ trading** STOCK negociación del día *f*; ◆ **~ by day** GEN COMM día a día; **take a ~ off** GEN COMM, HRM tomarse un día libre

daybook *n* (*db*) ACC libro de entradas y salidas *m*, libro diario *m*, GEN COMM diario *m*

daylight: ~ saving *n* GEN COMM horario de verano *f*

days: ~ after acceptance *n pl* (*D/A*) GEN COMM días transcurridos desde la aceptación *m pl*; **~ after date** *n pl* (*dd*) GEN COMM días transcurridos desde el vencimiento *m pl*, días transcurridos desde la fecha *m pl*; **~ after sight** *n pl* (*DS*) TRANSP días vista; **~ to delivery** *n pl* STOCK *currency futures* días hasta la entrega *m pl*; **~ to maturity** *n pl* STOCK días hasta el vencimiento *m pl*

daywork *n* HRM trabajo diurno *m*

dayworker *n* HRM trabajador(a) diurno(-a) *m,f*

db *abbr* ACC (*daybook*) libro de entradas y salidas *m*, libro diario *m*, (*debenture*) empréstito *m*, obligación *f*, ACC, BANK, FIN, STOCK (*debenture*) empréstito *m*, obligación *f*, GEN COMM (*daybook*) diario *m*

dB *abbr* (*decibel*) GEN COMM decibelio *m*

DB *abbr* TRANSP (*double bottom*) doble fondo *m*, (*double-ended*) anfídromo, de dos frentes

DBA *abbr* (*doing business as*) GEN COMM nombre que se adopta para transacciones de negocios

dbe *abbr* (*dispatch money payable both ends*) TRANSP prima de celeridad pagadera en origen y destino *f*

Dbk *abbr* (*drawback*) GEN COMM reembolso de derechos *m*

DBMS *abbr* (*database management system*) COMP SGBD (*sistema de gestión de base de datos*)

DC *abbr* (*developed country*) ECON, POL país desarrollado *m*

D/C *abbr* (*deviation clause*) INS *marine* cláusula de desvío *f*

DCA *abbr* (*debt collection agency*) FIN agencia de cobro de deudas *f*

DCD *abbr* (*data post on demand*) COMMS correo de datos por pedido *m*

DCE *abbr* COMP (*data communications equipment*) *hardware* equipo de comunicación de datos *m*, ECON (*domestic credit expansion*) expansión del crédito interior *f*

DCF *abbr* (*discounted cash flow*) ACC, BANK, FIN flujo de efectivo descontado *m*

DCO *abbr* (*debt collection order*) FIN orden de cobro de deudas *f*

DCom *abbr* (*Doctor of Commerce*) GEN COMM Doctor(a) en Comercio *m,f*

DComL *abbr* (*Doctor of Commercial Law*) GEN COMM, LAW Doctor(a) en Derecho Comercial *m,f*

DCP *abbr* (*droppages, cancellations, and prepayments*) GEN COMM bajas, cancelaciones y pagos anticipados

dd *abbr* GEN COMM (*delivered*) entregado, (*days after date*) días transcurridos desde la fecha *m pl*, días transcurridos desde el vencimiento *m pl*, STOCK (*due date*) fecha de vencimiento *f*

DD *abbr* BANK (*direct debit*) CD (*cargo directo*), (*demand draft*) giro a la vista *m*, TRANSP (*dry docking*) dique seco *m*

DDA *abbr* (*Duty Deposit Account*) IMP/EXP, TAX cuenta de depósito de derechos *f*

DDB *abbr* (*distributed database*) COMP DDB (*base de datos distribuida*)

DDD *abbr* (*direct distance dialing AmE, direct distance dialling BrE*) COMMS discado directo a distancia *m*

DDE *abbr* (*direct data entry*) COMP entrada directa de datos *f*

DDO *abbr* (*dispatch discharging only*) TRANSP despacho adelantado de la descarga únicamente *f*

DDP *abbr* (*delivered duty paid*) IMP/EXP, TAX entregado derechos pagados

DDU *abbr* (*delivered duty unpaid*) IMP/EXP, TAX suministrado sin impuestos

D-E *abbr* (*diesel-electric*) TRANSP diesel-eléctrico

dead: **~ account** *n* BANK, S&M cuenta inactiva *f*, cuenta muerta *f*; **~-end job** *n* HRM trabajo sin perspectivas de avance *m*; **~ key** *n* ADMIN *on keyboard*, COMP tecla desactivada *f*; **~ letter** *n* COMMS carta rehusada *f*; **~ load** *n* GEN COMM carga permanente *f*; **~ matter** *n* S&M conjunto de ideas irrelevantes *m*; **~ rise** *n* (*DR*) GEN COMM *sales* subida sin efecto *f*; **~ stock** *n* ACC existencias inmovilizadas *f pl*, S&M capital improductivo *m*; **~ time** *n* HRM tiempo muerto *m*

deadbeat *n* S&M mal(a) pagador(a) *m,f*

deadfreight *n* (*df*) TRANSP falso flete *m*

deadhead *vi AmE* TRANSP *drive empty vehicle* conducir sin carga

deadheading *n AmE* TRANSP regreso en lastre *m*

deadline *n* GEN COMM, STOCK fecha de vencimiento *f*

deadlock¹ *n* COMP bloqueo *m*, GEN COMM, S&M *in negotiations, stalemate* punto muerto *m*

deadlock² *vt* POL estancar

deadlocked *adj* POL estancado

deadrise *n* TRANSP *deck* astilla muerta *f*

deadweight *n* (*dw*) GEN COMM, TRANSP peso muerto *m*; **~ all told** (*dwat*) TRANSP peso muerto total *m*; **~ capacity** (*dwc*) TRANSP capacidad de carga *f*; **~ cargo** GEN COMM, TRANSP *shipping* cargamento de peso muerto *m*, cargamento pesado *m*; **~ cargo capacity** (*dwcc*) TRANSP capacidad máxima de carga *f*; **~ loss** ECON pérdida del excedente *f*; **~ tonnage** (*dwt*) TRANSP tonelada de peso muerto *f*, tonelaje total *m*

deal¹ *n* GEN COMM negociación *f*, *contract* trato *m*; ♦ **make a ~** GEN COMM cerrar un trato, conseguir un trato; **the ~ is off** GEN COMM se acabó el trato

deal² *vt* GEN COMM negociar, STOCK operar

deal with *vt* COMMS *the mail*, GEN COMM *arrangement, crisis* ocuparse de

dealer *n* BANK, GEN COMM, HRM, comerciante *mf*, S&M comerciante *mf*, concesionario(-a) *m,f*, dealer *m*, STOCK corredor(a) de bolsa *m,f*, intermediario(-a) *m,f*; **~ audit** ACC, S&M auditoría de comerciante *f*, auditoría de concesionario *f*, auditoría de distribuidor *f*; **~ brand** S&M marca del distribuidor *f*; **~ in securities** STOCK intermediario(-a) en valores *f*; **~ incentive** S&M incentivo para el comerciante *m*; **~ network** STOCK red de corredores de bolsa *f*

dealing *n* GEN COMM, STOCK comercio *m*, distribución *f*; **~ floor** STOCK suelo de operaciones *m*; **~ for the**

account FIN operación en cuenta *f*; **~ restriction** ECON restricción de venta *f*, GEN COMM restricción en transacciones *f*; **~ slip** STOCK boleta *f* (*AmL*), papeleta de votación *f* (*Esp*); **~ within the account** ACC, FIN transacción en cuenta *f*

dealings *n pl* GEN COMM transacciones *f pl*, STOCK transacciones no registradas *f pl*

deals: **~ and battens** *n pl* IND *timber* tablas y barrotes de pino *f pl*; **~, battens, boards** *n pl* IND *timber* tablas, barrotes, tableros *f pl*

death: **~ benefit** *n* INS compensación por defunción *f*, TAX indemnización por fallecimiento *f*; **~ certificate** *n* GEN COMM, LAW certificado de defunción *m*, partida de defunción *f*; **~ duty** *n BrE* LAW, TAX derecho de sucesión *m*; **~ risk** *n* INS riesgo de muerte *m*; **~ tax** *n* TAX derechos de sucesión *m pl*, impuesto sobre sucesiones *m*

debase *vt* ECON *currency* devaluar

debasement *n* ECON *currency* devaluación *f*

debate *vt* GEN COMM debatir

debenture *n* (*db*) ACC, BANK, FIN, STOCK empréstito *m*, obligación *f*; **~ bond** ACC, BANK, FIN, STOCK obligación hipotecaria *f*; **~ capital** ACC, BANK, FIN, STOCK capital en obligaciones *m*; **~ holder** ACC, BANK, FIN, STOCK obligacionista *mf*; **~ loan** ACC, BANK, FIN, STOCK empréstito *m*

debit¹ *n* GEN COMM débito *m*, debe *m*; **~ account** ACC cuenta deudora *f*; **~ balance** BANK, FIN, STOCK saldo deudor *m*; **~ column** ACC, BANK, FIN columna del debe *f*; **~ entry** ACC, BANK, FIN asiento de cargo *m*, débito *m*; **~ float** BANK flotación de deuda *f*; **~ interest** ACC, BANK, FIN interés deudor *m*; **~ memorandum** BANK, FIN memorándum de débito *m*; **~ note** (*D/N*) GEN COMM nota de cargo *f*; **~ ratio** FIN proporción deudora *f*, relación de débito *f*; **~ return** TAX declaración negativa *f*; **~ side** ACC, GEN COMM, PROP debe *m*

debit² *vt* GEN COMM adeudar, cargar

debited: **be ~ to** *vi* ACC *account* soportar un cargo

de bonis non administratis *phr* PROP bienes no administrados *m pl*

debrief *vt* GEN COMM, MGMNT pedir y recibir informe (*Esp*), pedir y recibir reporte (*AmL*)

debriefing *n* GEN COMM, MGMNT informe del ejercicio *m* (*Esp*), reporte del ejercicio *m* (*AmL*)

debris: **~ removal** *n* ENVIR, INS remoción de escombro *f*

debt *n* ACC, BANK, FIN obligación *f*, GEN COMM deuda *f*, deuda pasiva *f*, STOCK obligación *f*; **~ burden** ECON peso de la deuda *m*, carga de la deuda *f*; **~ capital** GEN COMM capital de empréstito *m*; **~ certificate** GEN COMM certificado de adeudo *m*; **~ charges** *n pl* GEN COMM cargos de la deuda *m pl*, gastos de la deuda *m pl*; **~ collection** FIN cobro de una deuda *m*; **~ collection agency** (*DCA*) FIN agencia de cobro de deudas *f*; **~ collection order** (*DCO*) FIN orden de cobro de deudas *f*; **~ collector** FIN cobrador(a) de deudas *m,f*; **~ consolidation** BANK, FIN, STOCK consolidación de la deuda *f*; **~ conversion** FIN conversión de la deuda *f*; **~ coverage ratio** ACC índice de cobertura de deuda *m*, coeficiente de cobertura de deuda *m*, proporción de cobertura de deuda *f*; **~ due to solvent debt** ACC deuda vencida *f*; **~-equity ratio** FIN coeficiente de endeudamiento *m*; **~-equity swop** FIN trueque de capital de la deuda *m*, canje de deuda/títulos *m*; **~ factoring** FIN descuento de deudas *m*; **~ financing** FIN financiación de la deuda *f*; **~-for-equity swop** FIN canje de deuda por títulos *m*; ~ **forgiveness** FIN cancelación de la deuda *f*; ~ **instrument** GEN COMM instrumento de la deuda *m*; ~ **manager** HRM administrador(a) de la deuda *m,f*; ~ **obligation** ACC, TAX obligación de la deuda *f*; ~ **ratio** ACC, FIN proporción de endeudamiento *f*, relación de deuda *f*; ~ **recovery period** ACC, ECON, TAX periodo de recuperación de la deuda *m*; ~ **relief** ACC, ECON, TAX alivio de la deuda *m*, POL redención de la deuda *f*; ~ **rescheduling** BANK, GEN COMM reprogramación de la deuda *f*; ~ **retirement** ACC amortización de deuda *f*, retiro de una deuda *m*; ~ **security** GEN COMM garantía de deuda *f*; ~ **service** ACC, BANK servicio de la deuda *m*; ~ **service indicator** ECON indicador de servicio de la deuda *m*; ~ **swop** FIN intercambio de la deuda *m*; ♦ ~ **owed to** ACC deuda debida a

debtor *n* (*Dr*) GEN COMM deudor(a) *m,f* (*Dr*); ~ **department** ADMIN departamento deudor *m*

debug *vt* COMP depurar

debugging *n* COMP depuración *f*

decade *n* GEN COMM década *f*

deceased[1] *adj* LAW difunto

deceased[2]: ~ **person** *n* LAW persona fallecida *f*

decedent: ~'s **estate** *n* LAW patrimonio sucesorio *m*

deceive *vt* GEN COMM embaucar, engañar, LAW, S&M engañar

decelerate *vi* ECON *growth*, GEN COMM ralentizarse, desacelerar

deceleration *n* ECON, GEN COMM *of the economy* desaceleración *f*

decentralization *n* GEN COMM descentralización *f*

decentralize *vt* GEN COMM descentralizar

decentralized: ~ **government** *n* POL *regional assemblies* gobierno descentralizado *m*; ~ **management** *n* MGMNT, POL administración descentralizada *f*, gestión descentralizada *f*; ~ **market economy** *n* (*DME*) ECON economía de mercado descentralizada *f*

deception *n* GEN COMM engaño *m*

deceptive[1] *adj* GEN COMM, LAW, S&M engañoso

deceptive[2]: ~ **entry** *n* TAX entrada fraudulenta *f*; ~ **packaging** *n* S&M envase engañoso *m*

decibel *n* (*dB*) GEN COMM decibelio *m*

decimal: ~ **digit** *n* COMP dígito decimal *m*; ~ **notation** *n* COMP notación decimal *f*; ~ **number** *n* COMP número decimal *m*; ~ **point** *n* COMP, MATH coma decimal *f*; ~ **sorting** *n* COMP, GEN COMM clasificación decimal *f*; ~**-to-binary conversion** *n* COMP conversión de decimal a binario *f*

decision *n* GEN COMM decisión *f*, resolución *f*; ~ **aids** GEN COMM ayudas para la toma de decisión *f pl*; ~ **analysis** MGMNT análisis de decisión *m*; ~ **maker** MGMNT persona responsable de tomar decisiones; ~ **making** MGMNT toma de decisiones *f*; ~**-making process** MGMNT proceso de decisión *m*; ~**-making unit** S&M unidad con capacidad de decisión *f*; ~ **model** MGMNT modelo de decisión *m*; ~ **package** FIN, MGMNT paquete de decisiones *m*; ~ **table** GEN COMM tabla de decisión *f*; ~ **theory** MGMNT teoría de la decisión *f*; ~ **tree** HRM árbol de decisión *m*; ~ **unit** GEN COMM unidad de decisión *f*; ♦ **make a** ~ GEN COMM tomar una decisión

decisive *adj* GEN COMM *measures* decisivo

deck *n* COMP *for magnetic tapes* platina *f*; **on-~ bill of lading** IMP/EXP, TRANSP conocimiento de embarque

sobre cubierta *m*; ~ **cargo** TRANSP carga de cubierta *f*; ~ **cargo certificate** TRANSP certificado de carga en cubierta *m*; ~ **girder** TRANSP *ship* eslora de cubierta *f*; ~ **load** TRANSP carga de cubierta *f*; ~ **socket** TRANSP *of container* fijación de cubierta *f*; **under** ~ **tank** (*Un Dk*) TRANSP tanque bajo cubierta *m*; **under** ~ **tonnage** TRANSP *shipping* tonelaje bajo cubierta *m*

declaration *n* LAW alegato *m*, declaración *f*, TRANSP declaración *f*; ~ **of bankruptcy** ACC, BANK declaración de quiebra *f*, declaración de bancarrota *f*, declaración de cese de pago *f*; ~ **of dividend** STOCK publicación de dividendo *f*; ~ **of entry** IMP/EXP, TRANSP declaración de entrada *f*; ~ **of estimated tax** TAX declaración estimativa del impuesto *f*; ~ **of membership** LAW declaración de adhesión *f*; ~ **of options** STOCK declaración de primas *f*; ~ **of origin** IMP/EXP declaración de origen *f*; ~ **of trust** LAW declaración de fideicomiso *f*

declare *vt* GEN COMM declarar; ♦ ~ **on oath** LAW declarar bajo juramento; ~ **oneself bankrupt** ACC declararse en bancarrota, declararse en quiebra; ~ **an option** STOCK ejecutar una opción

declared: ~ **dividend** *n* STOCK dividendo declarado *m*; ~ **value for carriage** *n* IMP/EXP, TRANSP valor declarado por porte *m*; ~ **value for customs** *n* IMP/EXP, TRANSP valor declarado en aduanas *m*

declination *n* GEN COMM declive *m*

decline[1] *n* FIN *in interest rates* disminución *f*; ~ **in investments** ACC, FIN disminución de las inversiones *f*

decline[2] **1.** *vt* ECON, GEN COMM declinar; **2.** *vi* ECON reducirse, GEN COMM *price* bajar

declining: ~ **balance depreciation** *n* ACC, FIN amortización de balance decreciente *f*, depreciación de balance decreciente *f*, depreciación de saldo decreciente *f*; ~ **balance method** *n* ACC método de depreciación de saldos decrecientes *m*; ~ **industrial area** *n* ECON, IND área industrial decreciente *f*, área industrial en declive *f*; ~ **industry** *n* ECON, IND industria en desaparición *f*; ~ **interest rate** *n* GEN COMM tasa de interés de disminución *f*, tipo de interés en descenso *m*; ~ **market** *n* STOCK mercado bajista *m*; ~ **share** *n* ECON, FIN, STOCK acción de índice decreciente *f*, acción declinante *f*

decode *vt* COMP decodificar

decoder *n* COMP decodificador *m*

decoding *n* COMP decodificación *f*

decommission *vt* ENVIR, POL decomisar

decommissioning *n* ENVIR *of nuclear plant*, POL decomisación *f*

decommitment *n* ACC cancelación de compromiso *f*

decompartmentalization *n* STOCK descompartimentalización *f*

DEcon *abbr* (*Doctor of Economics*) ECON, GEN COMM Doctor(a) en Economía *m,f*

decrease[1]: ~ **in value** *n* GEN COMM disminución del valor *f*; ~ **of risk** *n* INS reducción del riesgo *f*

decrease[2] *vi* GEN COMM mermar, reducir, disminuir

decreasing: ~ **liquidity order** *n* ACC orden de liquidez decreciente *f*; ~ **order** *n* COMP orden decreciente *m*; ~ **rate** *n* FIN tasa decreciente *f*, tipo decreciente *m*; ~ **tax** *n* TAX impuesto decreciente *m*

decree *n* GEN COMM decreto *m*, LAW auto *m*, fallo *m*, sentencia *f*; ~ **absolute** LAW sentencia de divorcio firme *f*; ~ **of bankruptcy** GEN COMM, LAW sentencia de bancarrota *f*; ~ **nisi** LAW fallo de divorcio condicional *m*

decruitment *n* HRM descontratación *f*, reajuste de personal *m*

decrypt *vt* COMMS, COMP, GEN COMM descifrar

decryption *n* COMMS, COMP, GEN COMM *software* descifrado *m*, desciframiento *m*

dedicated *adj* COMP *hardware*, GEN COMM *for specific purpose* dedicado

dedomiciling *n* GEN COMM, TAX desdomiciliación *f*

deduce *vt* GEN COMM deducir

deduct *vt* GEN COMM descontar, INS, MATH, TAX deducir

deductibility *n* HRM, INS, TAX deducibilidad *f*; **~ of employer contributions** TAX deducibilidad de aportación patronal *f*

deductible[1] *adj* INS, TAX deducible

deductible[2]: **~ business investment loss** *n* *AmE* (*cf allowable business investment loss BrE*) TAX pérdida deducible en inversiones empresariales *f*; **~ farm loss** *n* TAX pérdidas deducibles de la explotación agraria *f pl*

deduction *n* ACC importe deducible *m*, INS, TAX deducción *f*; **~ at source** FIN deducción en origen *f*; **~ for business meals** TAX deducción por comidas de negocios *f*; **~ for gifts** TAX deducción por regalos *f*; **~ for lending assets** TAX deducción por activos de crédito *f*; **~ for loan losses** TAX deducción por préstamos incobrables *f*; **~ for uncollectable loans** TAX deducción por préstamos incobrables *f*; **~ transferred eligible for cost of living tax credit** TAX *credit* deducción transferida desgravable por la carestía de la vida *f*; ◆ **make a ~** TAX hacer una deducción

deductive: **~ reasoning** *n* GEN COMM, MGMNT razonamiento deductivo *m*

de-duped *adj* COMP deduplicado

deed *n* LAW, PROP escritura *f*, escritura pública *f*; **~ of assignation** GEN COMM, LAW escritura de cesión *f*; **~ of conveyance** LAW escritura de traslación de dominio *f*; **~ of covenant** *BrE* TAX escritura de garantía *f*; **~ of foundation** LAW, PROP escritura fundacional *f*; **~ in lieu of foreclosure** LAW, PROP escritura en sustitución de embargo de bienes hipotecados *f*, escritura de extinción de derecho de redimir *f*; **~ of partnership** LAW escritura de constitución de una sociedad colectiva *f*; **~ restriction** LAW, PROP limitación de una escritura *f*; **~ of trust** LAW escritura de fideicomiso *f*

deem: **~ necessary** *vt* GEN COMM estimar necesario

deemed[1] *adj* GEN COMM, MATH, TAX estimado

deemed[2]: **~ disposition** *n* TAX norma aplicable *f*

deep[1]: **~-seated** *adj* GEN COMM *problems* profundamente arraigado

deep[2]: **~ discount bond** *n* FIN, STOCK bono con alto descuento *m*, bono de descuento intensivo *m*; **~ discounts** *n pl* TAX descuentos considerables *m pl*; **~-out-of-the-money option** *n* STOCK opción por encima del precio de mercado *f*; **~-sea shipping lane** *n* TRANSP ruta de navegación en alta mar *f*; **~ tank** *n* (*DT*) TRANSP tanque inferior *m*; **~ tank aft** *n* (*DTa*) TRANSP tanque inferior de popa *m*; **~ tank forward** *n* (*DTf*) TRANSP tanque inferior de proa *m*

deepwater[1] *adj* TRANSP de alta mar

deepwater[2]: **~ berth** *n* TRANSP *shipping* fondeadero en aguas profundas *m*; **~ harbor** *AmE*, **~ harbour** *BrE* *n* TRANSP puerto de aguas profundas *m*

def. *abbr* (*deferred*) GEN COMM diferido, aplazado

de facto *n* LAW de hecho, **~ corporation** ECON sociedad de facto *f*, GEN COMM empresa de hecho *f*; **~ manager** HRM gerente en funciones *mf*; **~ population** ECON población de facto *f*

defamation *n* LAW difamación *f*

default[1] *adj* COMP por omisión; **by ~** COMP por defecto

default[2] *n* COMP *operational systems* asignación implícita *f*, GEN COMM mora *f*; **~ bonds** *n pl* STOCK bonos defectuosos *m pl*, bonos en bancarrota *m pl*; **~ device** COMP dispositivo implícito *m*; **~ interest** BANK interés por falta de pago *m*; **~ judgment** LAW fallo por incomparecencia de la parte *m*; **~ option** COMP opción por defecto *f*; **~ of payment** BANK falta de pago *f*; **~ penalty** *AmE* (*cf default surcharge BrE*) TAX recargo por incumplimiento de pago *m*; **~ surcharge** *BrE* (*cf default penalty AmE*) TAX recargo por incumplimiento de pago *m*; ◆ **be in ~ in filing** TAX no haber presentado la declaración

defaulted: **~ bond** *n* FIN, STOCK bono de interés en mora *m*, bono en mora *m*

defaulting: **~ witness** *n* LAW testigo que no comparece *m*

defeasance *n* STOCK *corporate finance, general* abrogación *f*, anulación *f*

defeat *vt* GEN COMM desbaratar

defect *vi* POL cambiar de partido

defective[1] *adj* GEN COMM defectuoso

defective[2]: **~ packaging** *n* S&M embalaje defectuoso *m*; **~ service** *n* COMMS, GEN COMM *consumer protection* servicio deficiente *m*; **~ title** *n* LAW título de propiedad con defecto de forma *m*

defence: **~ advisor** *n* *BrE* (*DA*) HRM consejero(-a) de la defensa *m,f*; **~ attaché** *n* *BrE* HRM agregado(-a) de defensa *m,f*, agregado(-a) militar *m,f*; **~ envelope** *n* *BrE* FIN apartado de defensa *m*; **~ production revolving fund** *n* *BrE* FIN fondo renovable para la producción orientada a la defensa *m*; **~ of suit against insured** *n* *BrE* INS defensa del juicio contra el asegurado *f*, defensa del pleito contra el asegurado *f*

defend: **~ oneself** *phr* LAW defender el propio caso

defendant *n* LAW demandado(-a) *m,f*

defense *AmE* see **defence** *BrE*

defensive: **~ budgeting** *n* *BrE* S&M elaboración de un presupuesto para ponerse al nivel de la competencia; **~ cushion** *n* GEN COMM colchón defensivo *m*; **~ securities** *n* STOCK títulos estables *m pl*; **~ spending** *n* S&M gasto justificado *m*; **~ strategy** *n* GEN COMM estrategia defensiva *f*

defer *vt* GEN COMM aplazar, diferir; ◆ **~ a debt** ACC diferir una deuda; **~ payment** ACC diferir el pago; **~ tax payment** TAX aplazar el pago de impuestos

deferment *n* ACC, GEN COMM, TAX aplazamiento *m*

deferral *n* GEN COMM, TAX aplazamiento *m*

deferred[1] *adj* (*def.*) GEN COMM diferido, aplazado

deferred[2]: **~ account** *n* *AmE* TAX cuenta diferida *f*; **~ amount** *n* TAX cantidad aplazada *f*; **~ annuity** *n* INS anualidad diferida *f*; **~ asset** *n* ACC activo diferido *m*; **~ benefits and payments** *n pl* INS prestaciones y pagos diferidos *f pl*; **~ billing** *n* S&M facturación diferida *f*; **~ charge** *n* ACC, BANK, FIN cargo diferido *m*; **~ charges** *n pl* ACC gastos diferidos *m pl*; **~ compensation** *n* HRM *salary* compensación diferida *f*; **~ compensation plan** *n* HRM plan de compensaciones diferidas *m*; **~ contribution plan** *n* HRM plan de contribución diferida *m*; **~ credit** *n* ACC crédito diferido *m*; ~ **demand** *n* ECON, LAW demanda aplazada *f*; ~ **dividend** *n* FIN dividendo diferido *m*; ~ **futures** *n pl* FIN, STOCK futuros diferidos *m pl*; ~ **group annuity** *n* HRM anualidad colectiva diferida *f*; ~ **income** *n* ACC ingresos diferidos *m pl*; ~ **income tax** *n* TAX impuesto sobre la renta diferido *m*; ~ **income tax reserve** *n* TAX reserva del impuesto aplazado sobre la renta *f*; ~ **interest bond** *n* STOCK bono de interés diferido *m*; ~ **maintenance** *n* PROP *appraisal* mantenimiento diferido *m*; ~ **payment** *n* GEN COMM pago diferido *m*; ~**-payment annuity** *n* INS anualidad diferida *f*; ~ **profit-sharing plan** *n* HRM, TAX plan diferido de participación en los beneficios *m*; ~ **profit-sharing** *n* HRM participación diferida en beneficios *f*; ~ **rebate** *n* TRANSP reembolso diferido *m*; ~ **retirement** *n* HRM jubilación diferida *f*; ~ **retirement credit** *n* HRM crédito de jubilación diferido *m*; ~ **revenue** *n* ACC beneficios diferidos *m pl*; ~ **share** *n* FIN, STOCK acción diferida *f*, acción de dividendo diferido *f*; ~ **stock** *n* STOCK capital en acciones diferidas *m*; ~ **tax** *n* TAX impuesto aplazado *m*, impuesto diferido *m*; ~ **tax accounting** *n* TAX contabilidad del impuesto aplazado *f*; ~ **tax assets** *n pl* ACC, TAX haberes de impuestos diferidos *m pl*; ~ **tax liabilities** *n pl* ACC, TAX obligaciones de impuestos diferidos *f pl*; ~ **taxation** *n* ACC, TAX impuestos diferidos *m pl*; ~ **wage increase** *n* HRM aumento salarial diferido *m*

deficiency *n* GEN COMM déficit *m*, deficiencia *f*, TAX descubierto *m*; ~ **judgment** LAW fallo de deficiencia *m*; ~ **letter** ACC, ADMIN, BANK carta de deficiencias *f*, STOCK carta de la comisión de operaciones de la bolsa pidiendo una revisión del prospecto; ~ **payment** ECON *agriculture* pago compensatorio *m*, subvención para compensar el déficit *f*

deficient[1] *adj* GEN COMM deficiente

deficient[2]: ~ **tax installment** *AmE*, ~ **tax instalment** *BrE* *n* TAX pago fraccionario incorrecto del impuesto *m*

deficit[1] *adj* GEN COMM deficitario

deficit[2] *n* GEN COMM déficit *m*; ~ **balance of payments** ECON balanza de pagos deficitaria *f*; ~ **financing** ECON, FIN financiación mediante déficit *f*; ~ **net worth** ECON valor neto del déficit *m*; ~ **spending** ECON gastos deficitarios *m pl*; ~ **spending policy** ACC, ECON, POL política de gastos deficitarios *f*

define *vt* GEN COMM, HRM *framework, limit* delimitar

defined: ~**-benefit pension plan** *n* GEN COMM plan de jubilación con prestaciones definidas *m*, plan de pensiones de beneficios definidos *m*; ~ **contribution pension plan** *n* GEN COMM plan de jubilación con aportación definida *m*

definite: ~ **laytime** *n* TRANSP *shipping* tiempo de plancha definido *m*

definition *n* GEN COMM definición *f*, delimitación *f*, HRM delimitación *f*; ~ **of items** INS definición de artículos *f*; ~ **of limits** INS definición de límites *f*

deflagrating: ~ **explosive** *n* TRANSP *dangerous goods* explosivo deflagrante *m*

deflate *vt* ECON *the economy* deflacionar

deflation *n* ECON deflación *f*, desinflación *f*

deflationary[1] *adj* ECON deflacionario

deflationary[2]: ~ **gap** *n* ECON *econometrics* brecha deflacionaria *f*, déficit deflacionario *m*, diferencia deflacionaria *f*; ~ **pressure** *n* ECON presión deflacionaria *f*

deflator *n* MATH coeficiente de deflación *m*

deforestation *n* ENVIR desforestación *f*

deform *vt* GEN COMM deformar

deformation *n* GEN COMM deformación *f*

defraud *vt* GEN COMM defraudar

defraudation *n* GEN COMM fraude *m*

defrauded: ~ **tax** *n* TAX defraudación fiscal *f*

defunct: ~ **company** *n* ECON sociedad disuelta *f*, GEN COMM compañía desaparecida *f*, compañía disuelta *f*

degear *vt* FIN desarmonizar

degradation *n* ENVIR *of cities* degradación *f*

degrade *vt* ENVIR degradar

degree *n* GEN COMM *measure*, HRM grado *m*, WEL *education* título universitario *m*; ~ **of accuracy** GEN COMM grado de exactitud *m*; ~ **of correlation** MATH grado de correlación *m*; ~ **of damage** INS grado del daño *m*; ~ **of disablement** INS grado de invalidez *m*; ~ **of fluctuation** STOCK *futures price* grado de fluctuación *m*; ~ **measure** MATH medida en grados *f*; ~ **of monopoly** ECON grado de monopolio *m*; ~ **of risk** GEN COMM, STOCK grado de riesgo *m*

degression *n* MATH degresión *f*

degressive: ~ **tax** *n* TAX impuesto degresivo *m*

dehire *vt* *AmE* (*cf lay off BrE*) GEN COMM, HRM *workers* despedir, suspender

dehiring *n* *AmE* (*cf laying off BrE*) HRM desocupación *f*, reajuste *m*

deindustrialization *n* ECON, IND desindustrialización *f*

deintensified: ~ **farming** *n* ECON, ENVIR cultivo no intensivo *m*

de jure *n* LAW de derecho; ~ **population** ECON población de derecho *f*

del. *abbr* (*delegation*) GEN COMM delegación *f*

DEL *abbr* (*delete character*) COMP SUPR (*carácter de borrado*)

del credere *n* GEN COMM prima al comisionista *f*; ~ **agent** GEN COMM, S&M agente de garantía *mf*

delay[1] *n* COMP demora *f*, GEN COMM retraso *m*, LAW mora *f*

delay[2] *vt* GEN COMM *obstruct* impedir, *postpone* demorar

delayed[1] *adj* GEN COMM retrasado

delayed[2]: ~ **delivery** *n* STOCK entrega aplazada *f*; ~ **price** *n* S&M precio diferido *m*

delaying: ~ **tactic** *n* GEN COMM táctica dilatoria *f*

delegate[1] *n* GEN COMM delegado(-a) *m,f*, HRM compromisario(-a) *m,f*

delegate[2] *vt* GEN COMM, HRM, LAW, MGMNT delegar; ♦ ~ **authority to** GEN COMM delegar la autoridad en

delegation *n* (*del.*) GEN COMM delegación *f*; ~ **of authorization** GEN COMM delegación de autorización *f*; ~ **of signing authority** GEN COMM delegación de firma *f*

delete[1]: ~ **character** *n* (*DEL*) COMP carácter de borrado *m* (*SUPR*)

delete[2] *vt* ACC *debt* anular, COMP suprimir

deletion *n* LAW *of provisions in by-laws* supresión *m*; ~ **of a debt** ACC, GEN COMM cancelación de una deuda *f*, eliminación de una deuda *f*

delict *n* LAW *Scots law* agravio *m*

delimit *vt* GEN COMM, HRM delimitar

delinquency *n* ACC, LAW, TAX morosidad *f*

delinquent: ~ **account** *n* ACC cuenta morosa *f*; ~ **return** *n*

LAW declaración morosa *f*; ~ **taxpayer** *n* TAX contribuyente moroso(-a) *m,f*

delisting *n* STOCK suspensión de cotización *f*

deliver *vt* GEN COMM *speech* entregar, *service* prestar, POL exponer, STOCK *shares* emitir; ◆ ~ **a lecture** WEL *at university* dar una clase

deliverable[1] *adj* STOCK *T-bills* entregable

deliverable[2]: ~ **bills** *n pl* STOCK valores entregables *m pl*; ~ **security** *n* STOCK título entregable *m*

delivered[1] *adj* (*D, dd*) COMMS, GEN COMM, STOCK entregado; ◆ ~ **at docks** (*DD*) TRANSP entregado en dársenas; ~ **at frontier** (*DAF*) IMP/EXP entregado en frontera; ~ **duty paid** (*DDP*) IMP/EXP, TAX entregado derechos pagados; ~ **duty unpaid** (*DDU*) IMP/EXP, TAX suministrado sin impuestos; ~ **ex quay** (*DEQ*) IMP/EXP *duty paid* entregado en muelle; ~ **ex ship** (*DES*) IMP/EXP *port* entregado en buque

delivered[2]: ~ **dock** *n* TRANSP dique de entrega *m*; ~ **domicile** *n* TRANSP domicilio de entrega *m*; ~ **frontier** *n* IMP/EXP frontera de entrega *f*; ~ **price** *n* S&M precio entregado *m*

delivering: ~ **carrier** *n* TRANSP transportista entregador *m*

delivery *n* (*D, dely*) COMMS *of post* entrega *f*, envío *m*, GEN COMM entrega *f*, STOCK *of shares* entrega *f*, *transfer* traspaso *m*; ~ **broker** STOCK intermediario(-a) de bolsa de entrega *m,f*; ~ **charge** TRANSP gastos de entrega *m pl*; ~ **date** STOCK fecha de entrega *f*; ~ **day** STOCK día de entrega *m*; ~ **month** STOCK *futures* mes de entrega *m*; ~ **note** ACC, IMP/EXP, TRANSP nota de entrega *f*; ~ **on wheels** (*DOW*) TRANSP *by road* entrega a domicilio *f*; ~ **order** (*D/O*) TRANSP orden de entrega *f*; ~ **performance** TRANSP nivel de servicio *m*; ~ **period** GEN COMM plazo de entrega *m*; ~ **receipt** TRANSP recibo de entrega *m*; ~ **service** TRANSP servicio de reparto *m*; ~ **system** STOCK *futures* sistema de entrega *m*; ~ **terms** *n pl* TRANSP condiciones de entrega *f pl*; ~ **terms of sale** *n pl* IMP/EXP condiciones de entrega de la venta *f pl*; ~ **time** GEN COMM plazo de entrega *m*; ~ **turnround** GEN COMM cambio completo en la distribución *m*; ~ **versus payment** STOCK entrega contra reembolso; ◆ **take** ~ STOCK aceptar la entrega; ~ **and re-delivery** (*dely&re-dely*) TRANSP entrega y devolución

Delors: ~ **Plan** *n* ECON plan Delors *m*

Delphi: ~ **technique** *n* MGMNT técnica Delphi *f*

delta[1]: ~**-neutral** *adj* STOCK *options on Eurodollar futures* delta-neutral

delta[2] *n* FIN, STOCK delta *m*; ~ **call** STOCK delta de una opción de compra *m*; ~ **factor** *BrE* STOCK factor delta *m*; ~ **hedging** FIN compensación triangular *f*; ~ **net** STOCK delta neto de la posición *m*; ~ **net position** STOCK *options* delta neto de la posición *m*; ~**-neutral straddle** STOCK opción doble delta-neutral *f*; ~**-neutral strangle** STOCK *options* strangle delta-neutral *f*; ~ **put** STOCK delta de una opción de venta *m*; ~ **share** FIN, STOCK acción delta *f*; ~ **stock** *BrE* STOCK acciones delta *f pl*

de luxe *adj* MEDIA de lujo

dely *abbr* (*delivery*) COMMS, GEN COMM, STOCK entrega *f*

dely&re-dely *abbr* (*delivery and re-delivery*) TRANSP entrega y devolución

DEM *abbr* (*Domestic Equities Market*) STOCK Mercado Nacional de Títulos *m*

demand[1]: **on** ~ *adv* ACC, LAW a requerimiento

demand[2] *n* GEN COMM *request*, TAX demanda *f*; ~ **account** BANK cuenta a la vista *f*; ~ **assessment** ECON evaluación de la demanda *f*; **on** ~ **bond** BANK *merchant* bono a la demanda *m*; ~ **curve** ECON curva de demanda *f*; ~ **deposit** BANK depósito a la vista *m*, depósito exigible a la vista *m*; ~ **draft** (*DD*) BANK giro a la vista *m*; ~ **for goods** ECON demanda de mercancías *f*; ~ **for money** ECON *speculative* demanda de dinero *f*; ~ **forecasting** S&M previsión de la demanda *f*; ~ **function** ECON función de demanda *f*; ~**-led growth** GEN COMM crecimiento arrastrado por la demanda *m*; ~ **money** BANK dinero a la vista *m*; ~ **note** GEN COMM *instrument* pagaré a la vista *m*; ~ **pattern** ECON pauta de la demanda *f*; ~**-pull inflation** ECON, GEN COMM inflación de demanda *f*; ~ **rate** GEN COMM cambio a la vista *m*; ~ **schedule** ECON calendario de demanda *m*; ◆ **by popular** ~ GEN COMM por demanda popular; **in** ~ GEN COMM, HRM en demanda

demand[3] *vt* GEN COMM reclamar, exigir; ◆ ~ **payment** TAX requerir el pago

demarcation *n* GEN COMM, HRM delimitación *f*; ~ **dispute** *BrE* HRM conflicto intergremial *m*

demarketing *n* S&M desmarketing *m*

dematerialization *n* ECON, STOCK desmaterialización *f*

dematerialized *adj* ECON, STOCK *certificates of deposit* desmaterializado

demerger *n* ECON *of companies*, GEN COMM separación *f*

demerit: ~ **goods** *n pl* ECON bienes no deseables *m pl*

demijohn *n* TRANSP bombona para ácidos *f*, damajuana *f*

de minimis *phr* LAW insignificante

demise: ~ **charter party** *n* TRANSP póliza de fletamento de traspaso *f*

demised: ~ **premises** *n pl* GEN COMM, PROP local alquilado *m*

democracy *n* GEN COMM, POL democracia *f*

democratic[1] *adj* GEN COMM, POL democrático

democratic[2]: ~ **centralism** *n* POL centralismo democrático *m*; ~ **management** *n* HRM, POL administración democrática *f*, gestión democrática *f*

democratically *adv* GEN COMM, POL democráticamente

demogrant *n* HRM demogrant *m*

demographic[1] *adj* ECON, S&M, WEL demográfico

demographic[2]: ~ **accounting** *n* ACC, ECON contabilidad demográfica *f*; ~ **transition** *n* ECON transición demográfica *f*

demography *n* ECON, S&M, WEL demografía *f*

demolition *n* PROP demolición *m*; ~ **costs** *n pl* GEN COMM, PROP costes de demolición *m pl* (*Esp*), costos de demolición *m pl* (*AmL*)

demonetization *n* ECON desmonetización *f*

demonstrate *vt* GEN COMM *by table, graph*, S&M demostrar

demonstration *n* GEN COMM, S&M demostración *f*

demoralize *vt* HRM desmoralizar

demote *vt* HRM degradar, depreciar

demotion *n* HRM depreción *f*

demotivate *vt* HRM desanimar, desmoralizar, desmotivar

demotivation *n* HRM desánimo *m*, desmotivación *f*

demountable: ~ **system** *n* TRANSP sistema desmontable *m*

demurrage *n* TRANSP sobreestadía *f*

demurrer *n* LAW excepción de falta de acción *f*

denationalization n POL desnacionalización f

denationalized: ~ **money** n BANK, ECON dinero desnacionalizado m

denial n LAW negación f; ~ **of opinion** GEN COMM denegación de opinión f

Dennison: ~'s **Law** n ECON Ley de Dennison f

denom. abbr (denomination) BANK, ECON notes valor nominal m

denominate vt ECON expresar

denominated: ~ **quantity** n GEN COMM cantidad predeterminada f

denomination n (denom.) BANK, ECON notes valor nominal m

denominator n GEN COMM denominador m

densely[1]: ~**populated** adj ECON, GEN COMM densamente poblado

densely[2]: ~**populated area** n ECON zona densamente poblada f

density n ECON, PROP densidad f; ~ **zoning** AmE LAW, PROP plan de urbanización regulando estrictamente el uso del terreno

dental: ~ **insurance** n INS seguro dental m

de novo phr LAW de nuevo

deny vt LAW entitlement to something negar

department n (dept.) GEN COMM departamento m (dpto.); ~ **head** HRM, MGMNT company director(a) de departamento m,f; ~ **manager** S&M department store, shop jefe(-a) de departamento m,f; ~ **store** S&M gran almacén m; ~ **store chain** S&M cadena de grandes almacenes f; ~ **store sale** S&M venta en grandes almacenes f

departmental: ~ **account** n ADMIN cuenta departamental f, BANK cuenta bancaria departamental f; ~ **assets** n pl ACC activos departamentales m pl, bienes departamentales m pl; ~ **bank account** n ACC, BANK cuenta bancaria departamental f; ~ **corporation** n ADMIN empresa departamental f; ~ **head** n GEN COMM jefe(-a) de departamento m,f; ~ **line object** n ADMIN objetivo de la línea departamental f; ~ **management** n GEN COMM, MGMNT dirección por departamentos f, gerencia departamental f, gerencia por departamentos f; ~ **manager** n HRM gerente del departamento mf, gerente departamental mf, jefe(-a) de servicio m,f; ~ **objective** n MGMNT objetivo departamental m; ~ **plan** n GEN COMM, MGMNT plan departamental m; ~ **program** AmE, ~ **programme** BrE n MGMNT programa departamental m; ~ **reporting system** n ADMIN sistema de información departamental m

Departmental: ~ **Entry Processing System** n (DEPS) IMP/EXP Sistema Departamental de Procesamiento de las Entradas m

departmentalization n GEN COMM división departamental f

departure: ~ **lounge** n TRANSP antesala de salida f; ~ **tax** n TAX impuesto de salida del país; ~ **time** n TRANSP hora de salida f

depend on vt GEN COMM person, PATENTS claim depender de

dependant n TAX carga familiar f, persona a cargo f; ~ **tax credit** TAX deducción por carga familiar f

dependency: ~ **culture** n jarg WEL cultura de la dependencia f; ~ **ratio** n WEL tasa de dependencia f; ~ **theory** n ECON international, HRM, POL, WEL teoría de la dependencia f

dependent: ~ **child** n TAX hijo dependiente m; ~ **claim** n PATENTS demanda dependiente f; ~ **coverage** n INS cobertura de dependientes f; ~ **economy** n ECON international economía dependiente f; ~ **patent** n LAW, PATENTS patente dependiente f

de-planing n AmE TRANSP desembarque m

depletable: ~ **externality** n ECON externalidad agotable f; ~ **resources** n pl ECON recursos agotables m pl

depletion n ACC, ECON of resources, GEN COMM, TAX depreciación por agotamiento f; ~ **allowance** ECON factor de agotamiento m, TAX deducción sobre el activo agotable f; ~ **base** TAX base de reducción f; ~ **recapture** ACC recobro del agotamiento m, recuperación del agotamiento f

deploy 1. vt GEN COMM desplegar, distribuir; **2.** vi HRM disponer

deployment n GEN COMM, HRM despliegue m

deponent n LAW declarante mf

depopulation n GEN COMM despoblación f

deposit[1] n GEN COMM, LAW depósito m, S&M ingreso m; ~ **account** (D/A) BANK, cuenta de ahorros f, cuenta de depósito f, cuenta a plazo f; ~ **administration plan** FIN pensions plan de administración de depósitos m; ~ **agreement** LAW acuerdo de depósito m; ~ **balance** BANK, FIN saldo del depósito m; ~ **bank** BANK banco comercial m, banco de depósitos m; ~ **base** ECON base monetaria f; ~ **bonds** n pl BrE BANK bonos de depósito m pl; ~ **book** BANK libreta bancaria f; ~ **certificate** GEN COMM certificado de depósito m (c.d., CD); ~ **facility** BANK servicio de depósitos financieros m; ~ **freeze** BANK congelamiento de depósitos m; ~ **in transit** BANK depósito en línea m; ~ **institution** BANK, FIN institución de depósito f; ~ **instrument** BANK instrumento de depósito m; ~ **interest** BANK interés sobre depósitos m; ~ **liability** ACC, BANK pasivo por depósitos m; ~ **money** BANK dinero en depósito m; ~ **multiplier** ECON econometrics multiplicador de depósitos m; ~ **note** BANK formulario de depósito m; ~ **passbook** BANK libreta de depósitos f; ~ **premium** INS prima de depósito f; ~ **rate** BANK tasa de depósito f; ~ **receipt** (DR) BANK recibo de depósito m; ~ **slip** BANK recibo de depósito m; ~ **surety** INS garantía del depósito f; ~ **and trust account** BANK depósito y cuenta fiduciaria; ◆ **take a ~** STOCK aceptar un depósito

deposit[2] vt BANK depositar

Deposit: ~ **Protection Fund** n BANK UK Banking Act fondo de protección de depósitos

deposition n LAW deposición f, declaración f

depositor n BANK depositante mf; ~'s **forgery insurance** INS seguro contra falsificaciones m

depository n BANK, TAX depositario(-a) m,f

depot n GEN COMM building depósito m; ~ **charges** n pl IMP/EXP gastos de almacén m pl

depreciable: ~ **amount** n ACC cantidad amortizable f; ~ **asset** n ACC activo amortizable m; ~ **basis** n ACC base amortizable m; ~ **cost** n ACC, TAX coste amortizable m (Esp), coste de depreciación m (Esp), costo amortizable m (AmL), costo de depreciación m (AmL); ~ **life** n ECON vida amortizable f, TAX vida útil f; ~ **property** n ACC, PROP propiedad amortizable f; ~ **real estate** n PROP bienes raíces depreciables m pl, propiedad depreciable f

depreciate 1. *vt* ACC *investment, assets* amortizar, GEN COMM *currency* depreciar; **2.** *vi* GEN COMM depreciarse

depreciated: **~ cost** *n* ACC, TAX coste amortizado *m* (*Esp*), coste depreciado *m* (*Esp*), costo amortizado *m* (*AmL*), costo depreciado *m* (*AmL*)

depreciation *n* ACC, BANK, ECON, FIN amortización *f*, GEN COMM amortización *f*, depreciación *f*; **~ adjustment** ACC ajuste de amortización *m*; **~ allowance** ACC provisión por depreciación *f*; **~ expenses** *n pl* ACC gastos de depreciación *m pl*; **~ of fixed assets** BANK depreciación de activos fijos *f*; **~ rate** BANK, ECON, FIN, STOCK coeficiente de amortización *m*; **~ recapture** ACC, TAX recuperación de la depreciación *f*; **~ reserve** ACC, FIN, STOCK amortización acumulada *f*, fondo de amortización *m*; **~ schedule** ACC cuadro de amortización *m*, cuadro de depreciación *m*, planilla de depreciación *f* (*AmL*)

depressed[1] *adj* ECON *industry*, STOCK *prices* deprimido

depressed[2]: **~ region** *n* ECON, WEL región deprimida *f*

depression *n* ECON depresión *f*; **~ pole** ECON tipo de interés deprimido *m*

deprival: **~ value** *n* ECON valor de privación *m*

deprived *adj* LAW *of assets through sequestration* privado

DEPS *abbr* (*Departmental Entry Processing System*) IMP/EXP Sistema Departamental de Procesamiento de las Entradas *m*

dept. *abbr* (*department*) GEN COMM dpto. (*departamento*)

depth: **~ alongside** *n* TRANSP altura del agua *f*; **~ analysis** *n* GEN COMM, MGMNT análisis a fondo *m*; **~ interview** *n* S&M *research technique* entrevista en profundidad *f*; **~ polling** *n* POL escrutinio en profundidad *m*, recuento general *m*; **~ sounder** *n* (*DS*) ENVIR sonda de profundidad *f*

depurate *vt* ENVIR depurar

deputy: **~ chairman** *n* HRM, MGMNT vicepresidente(-a) *m,f* (*VP*); **~ chairman of the board of management** *n* HRM, MGMNT vicepresidente(-a) del consejo *m,f*; **~ chairman of the supervisory board** *n* HRM, MGMNT vicepresidente(-a) del consejo *m,f*; **~ chief executive** *n* HRM, MGMNT director(a) ejecutivo(-a) adjunto(-a) *m,f*; **~ director** *n* BANK, HRM, MGMNT director(a) adjunto(-a) *m,f*; **~ manager** *n* BANK director(a) adjunto(-a) *m,f*, GEN COMM subdirector(a) *m,f*, HRM, MGMNT director(a) adjunto(-a) *m,f*, gerente adjunto(-a) *m,f*; **~ managing director** *n* HRM, MGMNT director(a) ejecutivo(-a) adjunto(-a) *m,f*, subdirector(a) gerente *m,f*; **~ member of the board of management** *n* HRM suplente *mf*; **~ receiver general** *n* ADMIN, HRM interventor(a) general adjunto(-a) *m,f*, (*Esp*), contralor(a) general adjunto(-a) *m,f* (*AmL*)

DEQ *abbr* (*delivered ex quay*) IMP/EXP entregado en muelle

derecognition *n* HRM desreconocimiento *m*

deregistration *n* FIN *of pension plan* baja *f*

deregulate *vt* ECON, GEN COMM, POL desregular

deregulation *n* ECON *of international trade*, GEN COMM, POL desregulación *f*

dereliction: **~ of duty** *n* LAW abandono del servicio *m*

derival: **~ statistics** *n pl* MATH estadística derival *f*

derivation: **~ schedule** *n* ACC tabla de deducciones *f*

derivative *n* STOCK derivada *f*; **~ instrument** FIN instrumento derivado *m*; **~ product** S&M producto derivado *m*

derived: **~ demand** *n* ECON demanda derivada *f*

derogation *n* LAW derogación *f*

derogate *vt* GEN COMM, LAW derogar

derogatory: **~ stipulation** *n* LAW estipulación derogatoria *f*

DERV[1] *abbr* (*diesel-engined road vehicle*) TRANSP vehículo de carretera con motor diesel *m*

DERV[2]: **~ fuel** *n* TRANSP combustible para vehículos diesel *m*

DES *abbr* (*delivered ex ship*) IMP/EXP entregado en buque

descending: **~ tops** *n pl* STOCK máximos descendentes *m pl*, topes máximos *m pl*

descent *n* LAW, PROP sucesión *f*

describe *vt* GEN COMM describir

description *n* GEN COMM descripción *f*; **~ of operational risk** INS descripción de riesgo operativo *f*; **~ of risk** INS situación del riesgo *f*

descriptive[1] *adj* GEN COMM descriptivo

descriptive[2]: **~ statistics** *n pl* MATH estadística descriptiva *f*

deselect *vt* HRM despedir a una persona en formación antes de que haya acabado el programa

desertification *n* ENVIR desertificación *f*

design *n* GEN COMM *appearance* diseño *m*; **~ aids** *n pl* GEN COMM ayudas de diseño *f pl*; **~ automation** (*DA*) COMP automatización del dibujo *f* (*AD*); **~ draft** TRANSP boceto de diseño *m*; **~ editor** HRM editor(a) de diseño *m,f*; **~ engineer** GEN COMM, HRM ingeniero(-a) de diseño *m,f*; **~ engineering** COMP, GEN COMM estudio de diseño *m*; **~ and layout** S&M *of store* diseño y composición; **~ office** GEN COMM oficina de estudios *f*, oficina de proyectos *f*; **~ right** LAW derecho del proyecto *m*; **~ weight** IND peso de diseño *m*

designate *vt* GEN COMM designar

designated[1] *adj* GEN COMM, HRM nombrado

designated[2]: **~ amount** *n* TAX cantidad designada *f*; **~ beneficiary** *n* TAX beneficiario(-a) designado(-a) *m,f*; **~ benefit** *n* TAX beneficio designado *m*; **~ corporation** *n* TAX compañía designada *f*; **~ educational institution** *n* WEL institución educativa designada *f*; **~ income** *n* ACC, TAX ingresos previstos *m pl*; **~ investment exchange** *n* BrE STOCK bolsa de inversión designada *f*; **~ office** *n* PATENTS oficina designada *f*; **~ person** *n* TAX persona designada *f*; **~ property** *n* PROP, TAX propiedad designada *f*; **~ region** *n* TAX región designada *f*; **~ shareholder** *n* STOCK accionista designado(-a) *m,f*; **~ stockholder** *n* STOCK accionista designado(-a) *m,f*; **~ surplus** *n* TAX excedente previsto *m*

designation *n* GEN COMM, PATENTS designación *f*

designer: **~ products** *n pl* S&M productos de diseño *m pl*

Designs: **~ Registry** *n* LAW, PATENTS *intellectual property* Registro de Proyectos *m*

desire: **~ to purchase** *n* GEN COMM, S&M deseo de comprar *m*

desk *n* ADMIN, COMP escritorio *m*; **~ clerk** ADMIN, HRM empleado(-a) administrativo(-a) *m,f*; **~ planner** ADMIN organizador(a) de escritorio *m,f*; **~ research** GEN COMM investigación de datos ya existentes *f*; **~ trader** STOCK corredor(a) de despacho *m,f*

deskilling *n* HRM descalificación *f*, descualificación *f*

desktop[1] *adj* COMP de escritorio, de mesa

desktop[2]: **~ publishing** *n* (*DTP*) COMP, MEDIA auto-edición *f*; **~ unit** *n* COMP unidad de escritorio *f*

despite *adv* GEN COMM independientemente de

destabilize *vt* GEN COMM desestabilizar

destination *n* COMP, TRANSP destino *m*; **~ airport** TRANSP aeropuerto de destino *m*; **~ marketing** S&M marketing de destino *m*, marketing de persuasión *m*; **~ port** TRANSP puerto de destino *m*

destruction *n* ENVIR *rainforests* destrucción *f*

destructive: **~ competition** *n* ECON competencia ruinosa *f*

detachable: **~ front end** *n* TRANSP *trailer* cara anterior desmontable *f*, frontal desmontable *m*; **~ warrant** *n* STOCK certificado separable *m*

detailed: **~ account** *n* GEN COMM inventario contable *m*; **~ tax calculation** *n* TAX cálculo fiscal detallado *m*

details[1]: **~ of dependant** *n pl* TAX datos de la carga familiar *m pl*

details[2]: **for further ~** *phr* COMMS, GEN COMM para más información

detention *n* GEN COMM, TRANSP *of ship, cargo* detención *f*

deter *vt* GEN COMM disuadir

deteriorate *vi* GEN COMM deteriorarse

deterioration *n* GEN COMM deterioro *m*

determination *n* LAW *in tribunal* resolución *f*, TAX determinación *f*

determine *vt* GEN COMM determinar

determined: **~ to** *adj* GEN COMM resuelto a

deterrent *n* GEN COMM factor disuasorio *m*

detonating: **~ explosive** *n* TRANSP *dangerous goods* explosivo detonante *m*

detonator *n* TRANSP detonador *m*

detour *n* GEN COMM desvío *m* (*Esp*), reencaminamiento *m* (*AmL*)

detriment: **to the ~ of** *phr* GEN COMM en detrimento de

de-unionization *n BrE* HRM desindicalización *f*

devalorization *n* ECON desvalorización *f*

devaluation *n* ECON *international* devaluación *f*

devalue 1. *vt* ECON devaluar; **2.** *vi* ECON devaluarse

devanning *n* TRANSP vaciado del contenedor *m*

develop *vt* COMP *system, software* desarrollar, GEN COMM promover, IND *prototype, new model* crear, desarrollar, LEIS *photograph* revelar, TRANSP *prototype, new model* desarrollar

developed: **~ country** *n* (*DC*) ECON, POL país desarrollado *m*; **~ market** *n* S&M mercado desarrollado *m*

developer *n* PROP promotor(a) *m,f*

developing[1] *adj* GEN COMM en desarrollo

developing[2]: **~ country** *n* GEN COMM país en desarrollo *m*, país en vías de desarrollo *m*

development *n* GEN COMM desarrollo *m*; **~ aid** ECON, POL ayuda al desarrollo *f*; **~ area** *BrE* ECON *assisted areas in UK* área de desarrollo *f*; **~ assistance** ECON, POL ayuda al desarrollo *f*; **~ bank** BANK banco de desarrollo *m*; **~ charges** *n pl* ACC gastos de ampliación *m pl*; **~ credit agreement** BANK, FIN convenio de crédito de fomento *m*; **~ director** HRM, MGMNT director(a) de desarrollo *m,f*; **~ economics** ECON *international*, POL desarrollo económico *m*, economía del desarrollo *f*; **~ expenditures** *n pl* ACC gastos de desarrollo *m pl*; **~ loan** BANK préstamo al desarrollo *m*; **~ management** GEN COMM, MGMNT gerencia de desarrollo *f*;

~ manager HRM, MGMNT director(a) de desarrollo *m,f*; **~ planning** ECON *international*, POL planificación del desarrollo *f*; **~ policy** ECON, POL política de desarrollo *f*; **~ potential** GEN COMM potencial de desarrollo *m*; **~ program** *AmE*, **~ programme** *BrE* GEN COMM programa de actuación *m*, programa de desarrollo *m*; **~ project** ECON, POL proyecto de desarrollo *m*; **~ region** ECON, POL, WEL región desarrollada *f*, región en desarrollo *f*; **~ stage enterprise** ECON, POL empresa en fase de ampliación *f*, empresa en vías de consolidación *f*; **~ strategy** MGMNT estrategia de desarrollo *f*

Development: **~ Assistance Committee** *n* (*DAC*) ECON OECD, POL Comité de Ayuda al Desarrollo *m* (*CAD*)

developmental[1] *adj* GEN COMM en desarrollo, evolutivo

developmental[2]: **~ drilling program** *AmE*, **~ drilling programme** *BrE n* ECON programa de formación experimental *m*, programa de formación orientado al desarrollo *m*; **~ economics** *n* ECON, POL economía de países en vías de desarrollo

deviation *n* LAW desviación *f*; **~ clause** (*D/C*) INS *marine* cláusula de desvío *f*; **~ fraud** TRANSP *shipping* fraude por cambio de derrota *m*; **~ policy** MGMNT política de desviación *f*

device[1]: **~-independent** *adj* COMP independiente del tipo de dispositivo; **~-specific** *adj* COMP específico de un dispositivo

device[2] *n* GEN COMM aparato *m*, dispositivo *m*; **~ mark** PATENTS marca del invento *f*

devise[1] *n* LAW, PROP *clause in will* disposición testamentaria *f*, herencia *f*, legado *m*, TAX herencia *f*

devise[2] *vt* GEN COMM, IND *systems, technology*, POL idear, inventar

devisee *n* LAW, PROP legatario(a) *m,f*

df *abbr* (*deadfreight*) TRANSP falso flete *m*

DFR *abbr* (*data freight receipt*) TRANSP fecha de recepción del flete *f*

dft *abbr* (*draft*) BANK, FIN, GEN COMM cheque *m*

DFT *abbr* (*direct fund transfer*) ACC, BANK, FIN transferencia de fondos directa *f*

DGB *abbr* (*Dangerous Goods Board*) GEN COMM, TRANSP directiva de mercancías peligrosas *f*

DGN *abbr* (*dangerous goods note*) GEN COMM, TRANSP nota de mercancías peligrosas *f*

diagnosis *n* GEN COMM diagnosis *f*

diagnostic *n* COMP diagnóstico *m*, detección de averías *f*; **~ message** COMP *programming language* mensaje de diagnóstico *m*; **~ routine** GEN COMM rutina de diagnóstico *f*

diagonal: **~ engine** *n* (*D*) TRANSP máquina diagonal *f*; **~ expansion** *n* ECON expansión comercial de nuevos productos con la misma maquinaria *f*; **~ spread** *n* STOCK diferencial diagonal *m*

dial: **~ tone** *n AmE* (*cf dialling tone BrE*) COMMS tono de discado *m*

dialing: **~ code** *AmE see dialling code BrE*

dialling: **~ code** *n BrE* COMMS, GEN COMM *telephone* código de discado *m*; **~ tone** *n BrE* (*cf dial tone AmE*) COMMS tono de discado *m*

dialog *n* COMP diálogo *m*; **~ box** COMP caja de diálogo *f*

diamond: **~ investment trust** *n* STOCK compañía de inversiones en diamantes *f*

diary *n* GEN COMM agenda *f*

dictate *vt* ADMIN *shorthand*, GEN COMM dictar

DIDMCA *abbr* (*Depository Institutions Deregulation and Monetary Control Act*) ECON, LAW, POL ley de 1980 de desregulación y control monetario de las instituciones de déposito

die: ~ **intestate** *phr* LAW morir intestado

diesel[1]: **~-electric** *adj* (*D-E*) TRANSP *machinery* diesel-eléctrico

diesel[2]: **~-electric engine** *n* TRANSP máquina diesel-eléctrica *f*, motor diesel-eléctrico *m*; **~-engined road vehicle** *n* (*DERV*) TRANSP vehículo de carretera con motor diesel *m*; ~ **oil** *n* (*DO*) ENVIR, TRANSP gasóleo para motores diesel *m*, gasoil para motores diesel *m*

dieselization *n* ECON dieselización *f*

differ *vt* ACC, GEN COMM diferir

difference *n* GEN COMM diferencia *f*; ~ **equation** ECON *econometrics* ecuación en diferencias *f*; ~ **in conditions insurance** INS seguro contra cambio en las condiciones *m*; ~ **in limits insurance** INS seguro contra diferencia en los límites *m*; ~ **in value insurance** INS seguro contra diferencia en el valor *m*

differential *n* GEN COMM *yield*, HRM, TRANSP *road transport* diferencial *m*; ~ **advantage** ECON ventaja diferencial *f*; ~ **analysis** MGMNT análisis diferencial *m*; ~ **calculus** ACC, FIN, HRM, MATH cálculo diferencial *m*; ~ **cost** ACC coste diferencial *m* (*Esp*), costo diferencial *m* (*AmL*); ~ **lock** TRANSP trabador del diferencial *m*; ~ **margin** ECON margen diferencial *m*; ~ **price** ECON, S&M precio diferencial *m*; ~ **pricing** ECON valoración diferencial *f*, S&M fijación diferencial de precios *f*; ~ **profit** ACC, ECON, FIN beneficio diferencial *m*; ~ **sampling** MATH, S&M muestreo diferencial *m*; ~ **tax incidence** TAX incidencia del impuesto diferencial *f*; ~ **theory of rent** ECON teoría diferencial de la renta *f*

differentiate *vt* GEN COMM diferenciar

differentiate between *vt* GEN COMM distinguir entre

differentiated: ~ **marketing** *n* S&M marketing diferenciado *m*; ~ **product** *n* S&M producto diferenciado *m*

differentiation *n* S&M diferenciación *f*; ~ **strategy** S&M estrategia de diferenciación *f*

diffusion: ~ **index** *n* ECON *econometrics* índice de difusión *m*; ~ **of innovation** *n* S&M difusión de innovación *f*; ~ **rate** *n* IND *production* índice de difusión *m*

digit *n* COMP dígito *m*

digital[1] *adj* COMMS, COMP, GEN COMM digital

digital[2]: ~ **data** *n* COMP datos digitales *m pl*; ~ **selective calling** *n* (*DSC*) COMMS llamada selectiva digital *f*; ~ **sort** *n* COMP clasificación numérica *f*; **~-to-analog converter** *n* (*DAC*) COMP convertidor de digital a analógico *m*

digital/analog *adj* (*D*/*A*) COMP digital/analógico

digitize *vt* COMMS, COMP, GEN COMM digitalizar

digits: ~ **deleted** *n pl* STOCK dígitos borrados *m pl*

dilapidation *n* PROP dilapidación *f*

Dillon: ~ **Round** *n* ECON Ronda Dillon *f*

diluted: ~ **capital** *n* ACC, ECON, FIN, GEN COMM capital desvalorizado *m*

dilution *n* HRM, STOCK dilución *f*; ~ **of equity** STOCK desvalorización del capital propio *f*; ~ **of labor** *AmE*, ~ **of labour** *BrE* HRM dilución del trabajo *f*, dilución de la mano de obra *f*

DIM *abbr* (*Diploma in Industrial Management*) GEN COMM, WEL ≈ Diploma en Dirección de Empresa *m*

dime *n* *AmE infrml* FIN moneda de diez centavos

diminish **1.** *vt* GEN COMM disminuir, hacer mella; **2.** *vi* GEN COMM disminuir, mermar

diminishing: **~-balance method** *n* ACC método de saldo decreciente *m*; ~ **marginal rate of substitution** *n* ECON proporción de sustitución marginal decreciente *f*; ~ **returns** *n pl* ECON rendimiento decreciente *m*

Dinks *abbr infrml* (*Double Income no Kids*) ECON pareja de profesionales independientes con altos ingresos y sin hijos

diode *n* COMP *hardware* diodo *m*

dip *vi* GEN COMM *profits* bajar

DipCOM *abbr* (*Diploma of Commerce*) GEN COMM, WEL ≈ Diploma en Comercio *m*

DipEcon *abbr* (*Diploma of Economics*) GEN COMM, WEL ≈ Diploma en Economía *m*

diploma *n* WEL diploma *m*

Diploma: ~ **of Commerce** *n* (*DipCOM*) GEN COMM, WEL ≈ Diploma en Comercio *m*; ~ **of Economics** *n* (*DipEcon*) GEN COMM, WEL ≈ Diploma en Economía *m*; ~ **in Industrial Management** *n* (*DIM*) GEN COMM, WEL ≈ Diploma en Dirección de Empresa *m*; ~ **in Public Administration** *n* (*DipPA*) GEN COMM, WEL ≈ Diploma en Administración Pública *m*; ~ **in Technology** *n* (*DipTech*) GEN COMM, WEL ≈ Diploma en Tecnología *m*

diplomacy *n* MGMNT diplomacia *f*

diplomatic: ~ **bag** *n* *BrE* (*cf diplomatic pouch AmE*) COMMS valija diplomática *f*; ~ **mission** *n* POL misión diplomática *m*; ~ **pouch** *n* *AmE* (*cf diplomatic bag BrE*) COMMS valija diplomática *f*; ~ **service department** *n* GEN COMM, POL sección de servicios diplomáticos *m*; ~ **service post** *n* HRM puesto del servicio diplomático *m*

Diplomatic: **the ~ Service** *n* *BrE* ADMIN, POL el Servicio Diplomático *m*

DipPA *abbr* (*Diploma in Public Administration*) GEN COMM, WEL ≈ Diploma en Administración Pública *m*

DipTech *abbr* (*Diploma in Technology*) GEN COMM, WEL ≈ Diploma en Tecnología *m*

dir. *abbr* (*director*) GEN COMM, HRM director(a) *m,f*, gte. (*gerente*), presidente(-a) *m,f*, consejero(-a) de administración *m,f*

DIR *abbr* (*direct*) TRANSP directo

direct[1] *adj* (*DIR*) TRANSP *route* directo; ◆ ~ **or held covered** INS *marine* directo o con cobertura mantenida

direct[2]: ~ **access** *n* COMP acceso directo *m*; ~ **action advertising** *n* S&M publicidad de acción directa *f*; ~ **bill of lading** *n* IMP/EXP, TRANSP *shipping* conocimiento de embarque directo *m*, conocimiento sin trasbordos *m*; ~ **booking** *n* *BrE* (*cf direct reservation AmE*) LEIS reserva directa *f*; ~ **call** *n* COMMS llamada directa *f*; ~ **charge-off method** *n* ACC *bad debt* método de descuento directo *m*; ~ **clearer** *n* BANK compensador directo *m*; ~ **clearing member** *n* BANK miembro compensador(a) directo(-a) *m,f*; ~ **cost** *n* ECON, S&M coste directo *m* (*Esp*), costo directo *m* (*AmL*); ~ **cost of sales** *n* GEN COMM coste directo de las ventas *m* (*Esp*), costo directo de las ventas *m* (*AmL*); ~ **costing** *n* ACC cálculo de costes directos *m* (*Esp*), cálculo de costos directos *m* (*AmL*); ~ **costs** *n pl* ACC, FIN costes directos *m pl* (*Esp*), costos directos *m pl* (*AmL*); ~ **current** *n* GEN COMM corriente continua *f*; ~ **data entry** *n* (*DDE*) COMP entrada directa de datos *f*; ~ **debit** *n* (*DD*) BANK cargo directo *m* (*CD*), débito directo *m*, domiciliación bancaria *f*; ~ **delivery** *n* TRANSP entrega directa *f*, entrega sin trasbordos *f*; ~ **deposit** *n* BANK depósito directo *m*; ~ **deposit transaction** *n* BANK transacción de depósito directo *f*; ~ **dialing** *AmE*, ~ **dialling** *BrE n* COMMS discado directo *m*; ~ **discrimination** *n* HRM discriminación directa *f*; ~ **distance dialing** *AmE*, ~ **distance dialling** *BrE n* (*DDD*) COMMS discado directo a distancia *m*; ~ **equity** *n* TAX patrimonio directo *m*; ~ **expenses** *n pl* ACC, FIN costes directos *m pl* (*Esp*), costos directos *m pl* (*AmL*); ~ **export trading** *n* IMP/EXP comercio mayorista de exportación *m*; ~ **exporting** *n* IMP/EXP exportación directa *f*; ~ **financial leasing** *n* ECON arrendamiento financiero directo *m*; ~ **foreign investment** *n* FIN *international* inversión extranjera directa *f*; ~ **fund transfer** *n* (*DFT*) ACC, BANK, FIN transferencia de fondos directa *f*; ~ **and indirect tax evasion** *n* ECON, TAX evasión fiscal directa e indirecta *f*; ~ **and indirect taxation** *n* ECON, TAX fiscalización directa e indirecta *f*; ~ **and indirect taxes ratio** *n* ECON *tax structure*, TAX proporción de impuestos directos e indirectos *f*; ~ **insurance** *n* INS seguro directo *m*; ~ **insurer** *n* INS asegurador(a) directo(-a) *m,f*; ~ **insuring company** *n* INS aseguradora directa *f*; ~ **investment** *n* STOCK inversión directa *f*; ~ **labor** *AmE see direct labour BrE*; ~ **labor costs** *AmE see direct labour costs BrE*; ~ **labor organization** *AmE see direct labour organization BrE*; ~ **labour** *BrE n* ACC, ECON *task* trabajo directo *m*, HRM mano de obra directa *f*, *task* trabajo directo *m*; ~ **labour costs** *BrE n pl* ACC costes de personal directos *m pl* (*Esp*), costos de personal directos *m pl* (*AmL*), costes laborales directos *m pl* (*Esp*), costos laborales directos *m pl* (*AmL*); ~ **labour organization** *BrE n* GEN COMM, HRM sindicato obrero *m*; ~ **liability** *n* LAW responsabilidad directa *f*; ~ **mail** *n* ADMIN, S&M correo directo *m*; ~-**mail advertising** *n* S&M publicidad directa por correo *f*; ~ **mail shot** *n* S&M envío de folletos publicitarios por correo a posibles clientes; ~ **mailing** *n* COMMS, S&M venta directa por correo *f*; ~ **marketing** *n* S&M marketing directo *m*; ~ **material** *n* ECON material directo *m*; ~ **obligation** *n* BANK obligación directa *f*; ~ **overheads** *n pl* GEN COMM, FIN gastos generales directos *m pl*; ~ **participation program** *AmE*, ~ **participation programme** *BrE n* FIN programa de participación directa *m*; ~ **payment** *n* ECON *grants* pago directo *m*; ~ **placement** *n* BANK colocación directa a los inversores de una emisión de títulos *f*; ~ **port** *n* (*dp*) TRANSP puerto directo *m*; ~ **production** *n* ECON, IND producción directa *f*; ~ **reduction mortgage** *n* BANK reducción directa de la hipoteca *f*; ~ **reservation** *n AmE* (*cf direct booking BrE*) LEIS reserva directa *f*; ~ **response** *n* GEN COMM respuesta directa *f*; ~ **response advertising** *n* S&M publicidad de respuesta directa *f*; ~ **response marketing** *n* S&M marketing de respuesta directa *m*; ~ **route** *n* TRANSP ruta directa *f*; ~ **sale** *n* S&M venta directa *f*; ~ **selling** *n* S&M venta directa *f*; ~ **spending envelope** *n* FIN apartado de gasto directo *m*; ~ **spending program** *AmE*, ~ **spending programme** *BrE n* ACC *government*, POL programa de gastos directos *m*; ~ **tax** *n* TAX impuesto directo *m*; ~ **taxation** *n* TAX imposición directa *f*; ~ **trader input** *n* (*DTI*) IMP/EXP compra de un mayorista *f*; ~ **transhipment** *n* TRANSP transbordo directo *m*; ~ **worker** *n* HRM trabajador(a) directo(-a) *m,f*; ~ **yield** *n* BANK, STOCK ingreso directo *m*, producto directo *m*, rendimiento directo *m*, renta directa *f*

direct[3] *vt* GEN COMM dirigir

Direct: ~ **Access Software** *n* COMP, GEN COMM Programa de Acceso Directo *m*; ~ **Marketing Association** *n* (*DMA*) S&M asociación de marketing directo; ~ **Trading Corporation** *n* (*DTC*) GEN COMM Corporación de Comercialización Directa *f*

directed: ~ **interview** *n* S&M *market research* entrevista dirigida *f*; ~ **verdict** *n* LAW veredicto dictado por el juez *m*

direction *n* ECON *of interest rates*, GEN COMM dirección *f*, HRM, MGMNT administración *f*, dirección *f*

directions: ~ **for use** *n pl* GEN COMM modo de empleo *m*

directly[1]: ~ **related to** *adj* GEN COMM directamente relacionado con; ~ **responsible for** *adj* GEN COMM directamente responsable de; ~ **transported** *adj* IMP/EXP, TRANSP *EU* transportado directamente, transportado sin transbordos

directly[2] *adv* GEN COMM directamente

directly[3]: ~ **unproductive profit-seeking activities** *n pl* (*DUP*) ECON actividades directamente improductivas con fines lucrativos *f pl*

director *n* (*dir.*) GEN COMM, HRM director(a) *m,f*, gte. (*gerente*), presidente(-a) *m,f*, consejero(-a) de administración *m,f*; ~'s **circular** GEN COMM circular del director *f*; ~-**general** HRM, MGMNT director(a) general *m,f* (*DG*); ~ **of labor relations** *AmE*, ~ **of labour relations** *BrE* HRM director(a) de relaciones laborales *m,f*; ~ **of public relations** (*DPR*) HRM director(a) de relaciones públicas *m,f*; ~'s **report** GEN COMM informe del director *m*, (*Esp*), reporte del director *m* (*AmL*)

Director: ~ **of Public Prosecutions** *n BrE* (*DPP*) LAW ≈ Fiscal Jefe(-a) del Servicio de Acusación Pública *m,f* (*AmL*), ≈ Fiscal General del Estado *mf* (*Esp*); ~ **of Studies** *n* (*DOS*) WEL *education* jefe(-a) de estudios *m,f*

directorate *n* GEN COMM, HRM, MGMNT consejo de administración *m*

directors': ~ **fees** *n pl* HRM honorarios de los directores *m pl*; ~ **and officers' liability insurance** *n pl* INS, MGMNT seguro contra responsabilidad civil de directivos *m*; ~ **shares** *n pl* STOCK acciones del Consejo de Administración *f pl*

directorship *n* HRM dirección *f*

directory *n* COMP, GEN COMM directorio *m*

dirty: ~ **bill** *n* IMP/EXP, TRANSP conocimiento con reservas *m*, *shipping* conocimiento sucio *m*; ~ **bill of lading** *n* IMP/EXP, TRANSP *shipping* conocimiento de embarque con reservas *m*; ~ **float** *n* ECON *international* flotación dirigida *f*, flotación sucia *f*; ~ **money** *n* TAX, TRANSP *shipping* dinero negro *m*; ~ **proof** *n* S&M prueba en sucio *f*

dis *abbr* (*discount*) GEN COMM dto. (*descuento*)

disability *n* HRM *of employee* incapacidad *f*; ~ **allowance** TAX deducción por invalidez *f*; ~ **annuity** INS anualidad de invalidez *f*; ~ **benefit** HRM, WEL indemnización de invalidez *f*; ~ **buy-out insurance** INS seguro de compra por invalidez de un socio *m*; ~ **income insurance** *AmE* INS seguro de subsidio por incapacidad laboral *m*; ~ **insurance** INS seguro de invalidez *m*; ~ **pension** FIN, INS pensión de invalidez *f*; ~ **percentage table** INS baremo de invalidez *m*; ~ **tax credit** TAX deducción por incapacidad *f*

disabled[1] *adj* COMP desactivado

disabled[2]: ~ **quota** *n* HRM cuota de incapacitados *f*; ~ **worker** *n* HRM trabajador(a) incapacitado(-a) *m,f*

disadvantage *n* ECON, GEN COMM, POL desventaja *f*

disadvantaged *adj* ECON, GEN COMM, POL desventajado

disadvantageous *adj* ECON, GEN COMM, POL desventajoso

disaffirm *vt* GEN COMM negar

disaffirmation *n* GEN COMM negación *f*

disagree *vi* GEN COMM disentir

disagreement *n* GEN COMM *dispute* desacuerdo *m*; ♦ **be in** ~ GEN COMM estar en desacuerdo

disallow *vt* GEN COMM, TAX denegar

disallowable: ~ **items** *n pl* BrE TAX artículos no desgravables *m pl*

disallowance *n* GEN COMM, TAX denegación *f*

disappointing *adj* GEN COMM decepcionante

disaster: ~ **clause** *n* BANK, INS, LAW cláusula de salvaguardia *f*

disbursable *adj* ACC, ECON, FIN desembolsable

disburse *vt* ACC, ECON, FIN desembolsar

disbursement *n* ACC, ECON, FIN desembolso *m*; ~ **commission** GEN COMM comisión de gastos *f*; ~ **excess** TAX *charities* exceso de desembolso *m*; ~ **quota** TAX *charities* cuota de desembolso *f*

disburser *n* FIN pagador(a) *m,f*

disbursing: ~ **account** *n* ACC cuenta de pagos *f*

disc. *abbr* (*discount*) GEN COMM dto. (*descuento*)

DISC *abbr* AmE (*Domestic International Sales Corporation*) GEN COMM corporación nacional de ventas internacionales

discharge[1] *n* LAW *of contract* extinción *f*; ~ **afloat** (*D/A*) TRANSP *shipping* descarga a flote *m*; ~ **of bankruptcy** FIN, LAW rehabilitación del quebrado *f*; ~ **for cause** BrE HRM despido justificado *m*, despido motivado *m*; ~ **of lien** LAW levantamiento de embargo *m*; ~ **of mortgage** BANK cancelación de una hipoteca *f*; ~ **port** TRANSP puerto de descarga *m*; ~ **of the trustee** LAW despido del fideicomisario *m*

discharge[2] *vt* HRM *staff* despedir, LAW eximir, extinguir; ♦ ~ **sb** HRM poner a alguien de patitas en la calle (*infrml*)

discharging: ~ **berth** *n* TRANSP *shipping* atraque de descarga *m*; ~ **wharf** *n* TRANSP muelle de descarga *m*

disciplinary: ~ **layoff** *n* HRM despido disciplinario *m*; ~ **measure** *n* GEN COMM medida disciplinaria *f*; ~ **rule** *n* HRM norma disciplinaria *f*

discipline[1] *n* GEN COMM disciplina *f*; ~ **procedure** HRM procedimiento disciplinario *m*

discipline[2] *vt* GEN COMM, HRM, LAW disciplinar

disciplined: ~ **movement** *n* TRANSP movimiento disciplinado *m*

disclaimer *n* GEN COMM denegación *f*, INS declinación de responsabilidad *f*, LAW *property, right* abandono *m*, renuncia *f*, TAX denegación *f*; ~ **of opinion** ACC abstención de opinión *f*

disclose *vt* GEN COMM revelar

disclosed: ~ **reserve** *n* ACC reserva publicada *f*

disclosure *n* STOCK descripción del riesgo *f*; ~ **of information** HRM revelación de información *f*; ~ **requirement** GEN COMM *of social account* requisito para publicación *m*, STOCK requisito de revelación *m*

discomfort: ~ **index** *n* ECON índice de malestar *m*

discontent: ~ **in the workplace** *n* HRM descontento en el lugar de trabajo *m*

discontinuance: ~ **of plan** *n* TAX suspensión del plan *f*

discontinue: ~ **an appeal** *vt* TAX desistir de una apelación

discontinued: ~ **operation** *n* ACC operación discontinua *f*, operación no continuada *f*

discount[1] *n* (*disc.*) GEN COMM descuento *m* (*dto.*), rebaja *m*; ~ **bill** ACC, BANK letra de descuento *f*; ~ **bond** FIN, STOCK bono descontado *m*; ~ **broker** STOCK corredor(a) de préstamos *m,f*; ~ **brokerage** STOCK corretaje de descuento *m*; ~ **center** AmE, ~ **centre** BrE FIN centro de descuento *m*; ~ **charges** *n pl* ACC gastos de descuento *m pl*; ~ **credit** FIN crédito de descuento *m*; ~ **dividend reinvestment plan** FIN, STOCK plan de reinversión del dividendo de descuento *m*; ~ **forex** ECON *international* cambio para descuento *m*; ~ **house** AmE (*cf discount store BrE*) STOCK tienda de descuento *f*, tienda de saldos *f*, sociedad mediadora en el mercado de dinero *f* (*SMMD*); ~ **instrument** STOCK instrumento de descuento *m*; ~ **market** FIN, STOCK mercado de descuento *m*; ~ **market loan** BANK, FIN, STOCK préstamo del mercado de descuento *m*; ~ **mechanism** FIN mecanismo de descuento *m*; ~ **points** *n pl* BANK puntos de descuento *m pl*; ~ **price** FIN precio con descuento *m*; ~ **rate** BrE (*cf discount window AmE*) ACC, BANK, FIN redescuento *m*, tasa de descuento *f*; ~ **stock broker** STOCK intermediario(-a) de cambio de descuento *m,f*; ~ **store** BrE (*cf discount house AmE*) STOCK tienda de descuento *f*, tienda de saldos *f*, sociedad mediadora en el mercado de dinero *f* (*SMMD*); ~ **travel** LEIS viaje con descuento *m*; ~ **window** AmE (*cf discount rate BrE*) ACC, BANK, FIN redescuento *m*, tasa de descuento *f*; ~ **window lending** AmE BANK préstamo de la Reserva Federal a instituciones financieras *m*; ♦ **at a** ~ (*AAD*) FIN *forward markets* por debajo del cambio, S&M con descuento; **no** ~ (*ND*) S&M sin descuento; **on a** ~ **basis** STOCK en régimen de descuentos

discount[2] *vt* FIN bonificar, GEN COMM descontar, hacer descuento, rebajar

discountable *adj* GEN COMM descontable

discounted[1] *adj* GEN COMM descontado

discounted[2]: ~ **bill** *n* BANK letra descontada *f*; ~ **bond** *n* FIN, STOCK bono emitido a descuento *m*; ~ **cash flow** *n* (*DCF*) ACC, BANK, FIN flujo de efectivo descontado *m*; ~ **loan** *n* BANK préstamo descontado *m*; ~ **present value** *n* FIN valor actual descontado *m*; ~ **share price** *n* STOCK reducción del precio de una acción *f*

discounting *n* GEN COMM descuento *m* (*dto.*); ~ **bank** BANK banco de descuento *m*; ~ **of bills** BrE (*cf discounting of notes AmE*) ACC descuento de efectos *m*; ~ **of notes** AmE (*cf discounting of bills BrE*) ACC descuento de efectos *m*

discourage *vt* GEN COMM desalentar

discouraged: ~ **worker** *n* HRM trabajador(a) desanimado(-a) *m,f*

discovery *n* LAW conjunto de actos procesales destinados a que las partes de un litigio obtengan información y pruebas sobre los hechos relativos a tal litigio, mediante interrogatorios, exhibición de documentos y otros medios; ~ **sampling** MATH muestreo descubridor *m*

discrepancy *n* GEN COMM discrepancia *f*, desviación *f*

discrete: ~ **variable** *n* MATH *statistics* variable discreta *f*

discretion: **at the** ~ **of** *phr* GEN COMM según se estime oportuno

discretionary[1] *adj* GEN COMM *fiscal policy* discrecional

discretionary[2]: **~ account** *n* BANK, FIN cuenta discrecional *f*; **~ authority** *n* BANK autoridad discrecional *f*; **~ buying power** *n* S&M poder adquisitivo discrecional *m*; **~ cost** *n* ECON coste discrecional *m* (*Esp*), costo discrecional *m* (*AmL*); **~ deduction** *n* TAX deducción discrecional *f*; **~ fiscal policy** *n* ECON, POL, TAX política fiscal discrecional *f*; **~ income** *n* ECON renta discrecional *f*; **~ limit** *n* BANK límite discrecional *m*; **~ period** *n* GEN COMM periodo de discreción *m*; **~ policy** *n* ECON, POL política discrecional *f*; **~ share** *n* STOCK participación discrecional *f*; **~ spending power** *n* ECON *of government*, POL capacidad de gasto discrecional *f*; **~ trust** *n* LAW, STOCK fideicomiso discrecional *m*

discriminate *vi* GEN COMM discriminar

discriminate against *vt* GEN COMM discriminar a

discriminating: **~ monopoly** *n* ECON monopolio discriminante *m*

discrimination *n* GEN COMM discriminación *f*; **~ test** S&M prueba de discriminación *f*; ◆ **no ~ factor** GEN COMM factor de no discriminación *m*

discriminatory: **~ taxation of foreigners** *n* TAX tributación discriminatoria de los extranjeros *f*

discuss *vt* GEN COMM hablar de, comentar, exponer

discussion *n* GEN COMM discusión *f*; **~ group** S&M grupo de discusión *m*

diseconomy *n* ECON deseconomía *f*; **~ of scale** ECON deseconomía de escala *f*

disembarkation *n* TRANSP desembarque *m*

disequilibrium *n* ECON desequilibrio *m*

disguised: **~ unemployment** *n* ECON, HRM, WEL desempleo disfrazado *m*

dishonest *adj* GEN COMM ímprobo

dishonor *AmE see* dishonour *BrE*

dishonored *AmE see* dishonoured *BrE*

dishonour[1] *n BrE* BANK falta de pago *f*; **~ at maturity** *BrE* ACC, FIN falta de pago al vencimiento *f*

dishonour[2] *vt* BANK rechazar; ◆ **~ a cheque** *BrE* BANK *said of the drawee* desatender el pago de un cheque, no pagar un cheque

dishonoured[1] *adj BrE* BANK *cheque* rechazado

dishonoured[2]: **~ bill** *n BrE* BANK, STOCK letra impagada *f*; **~ bill of exchange** *n BrE* IMP/EXP letra de cambio no atendida *f*; **~ cheque** *n BrE* BANK, FIN cheque impagado *m*, cheque no pagado *m*, cheque rehusado *m*

disincentive *n* ECON desincentivo *m*; **~ effect** ECON efecto desincentivador *m*

disinflation *n* ECON deflación *f*

disinformation *n* POL desinformación *f*

disintegration *n* ECON, GEN COMM, POL desintegración *f*

disintermediation *n* BANK, ECON, FIN desintermediación *f*

disinvest *vt* FIN desinvertir

disinvestment *n* FIN desinversión *f*

disinvestor *n* FIN desinversor(a) *m,f*

disjoint: **~ events** *n pl* GEN COMM hechos no consecutivos *m pl*

disk *n* COMP disco *m*; **~ communication area** COMP zona de comunicaciones del disco *f*; **~ drive** COMP *hardware* mecanismo impulsor de disco *m*; **~ operating system** (*DOS*) COMP sistema operativo de discos *m* (*DOS*); **~ pack** COMP pila de discos *f*; **~ space** COMP espacio del disco *m*; **~ unit** COMP unidad de discos *f*

diskette *n* COMP disquete *m*; **~ drive** COMP disquetera *f*

dismantling *n* ECON *of barriers* supresión *f*

dismiss *vt* HRM *staff* cesar, despedir, echar; ◆ **~ sb** HRM cesar a alguien, poner a alguien de patitas en la calle (*infrml*)

dismissal *n* HRM desocupación *f*, despido *m*; **~ procedure** HRM procedimiento de despido *m*; **~ wage** HRM indemnización por despido *f*

disorderly: **~ market** *n* ECON, STOCK mercado indeciso *m*, mercado inestable *m*

disparaging: **~ copy** *n* S&M mensaje publicitario despectivo *m*; **~ statements** *n pl* PATENTS informes promovidos por el registro de la propiedad industrial cuando el invento no es patentable

disparity *n* GEN COMM disparidad *f*

dispatch[1] *n* TRANSP *shipping* despacho *m*, envío *m*, expedición *f*; **~ bay** TRANSP compuerta de expedición *f*, nave de expedición *f*; **~ department** TRANSP departamento de expedición *m*; **~ money** TRANSP *shipping* prima por despacho rápido *f*, prima pronta descarga *f*; **~ money payable both ends** (*dbe*) TRANSP *shipping* prima de celeridad pagadera en origen y destino *f*; **~ note** COMMS nota de envío *f*, TRANSP carta de expedición *f*, nota de envío *f*; ◆ **~ discharging only** (*DDO*) TRANSP despacho adelantado de la descarga únicamente *f*; **~ half demurrage** (*d1/2D*) TRANSP *shipping* media penalización por demora en el despacho *f*; **~ loading only** (*DLO*) TRANSP despacho adelantado de carga únicamente *m*

dispatch[2] *vt* COMP encaminar, TRANSP *traffic* despachar, diligenciar

dispatcher *n* TRANSP expedidor(a) *m,f*, *aviation* supervisor(a) *m,f*

dispatching *n* TRANSP expedición *f*, *aviation* despacho *m*; **~ charge** GEN COMM gasto de expedición *m*

dispensation *n* LAW dispensa *f*

dispense with *vt* GEN COMM hacer caso omiso de

displacement: **~ load** *n* TRANSP *shipping* carga por desplazamiento *f*; **~ tonnage** *n* TRANSP *shipping* tonelaje de desplazamiento *m*

display[1]: **~ classified** *adj* S&M clasificado para exposición

display[2] *n* COMMS, COMP representación visual *f*, S&M *sales conference, promotion* exposición *f*; **~ advertising** S&M publicidad de exposición *f*; **~ device** COMP unidad de representación visual *f*; **~ file** COMP visualización de archivos *f*; **~ monitor** COMP monitor visualizador *m*; **~ outer** S&M exposición exterior *f*; **~ pack** S&M paquete de exposición *m*; **~ unit** COMP unidad de visualización *f*

display[3] *vt* COMP visualizar

displayed: **~ price** *n* ECON, S&M precio expuesto *m*

disponent: **~ owner** *n* TRANSP *shipping* fletador(a) *m,f*

disposable: **~ income** *n* ECON, TAX ingreso disponible *m*; **~ real income** *n* (*DRY*) ECON, TAX ingreso real disponible *m*

disposal *n* TAX cesión *f*, disposición *f*, venta *f*; **~ facility** ENVIR *waste* medio de eliminación *m*; **~ of securities** STOCK venta de títulos *f*

dispose of *vi* STOCK, TAX disponer de; ◆ **~ stock** S&M deshacerse de las existencias, disponer de las existencias

disposition *n* TAX disposición *f*

dispossess[1]: **~ proceedings** *n pl* LAW procedimiento de desahucio *m*, PATENTS procedimientos para la declaración de la nulidad y caducidad de la patente

dispossess² *vt* LAW, PROP desahuciar

dispute¹ *n* GEN COMM *boardroom, labour* conflicto *m*; ~ **procedure** HRM procedimiento de resolución de litigios *m*; ~ **resolution** HRM resolución de disputa *f*; ◆ **in ~** GEN COMM en litigio, HRM *with employer* en discusión

dispute² *vt* LAW *claim* impugnar; ◆ ~ **a will** LAW disputar un testamento

disputed: ~ **tax** *n* TAX impuesto impugnado *m*

Disputes: ~ **Committee** *n BrE* HRM Comité de Litigios *m*

disruption *n* GEN COMM ruptura *f*

dissaving *n* ECON desahorro *m*

disseminate *vt* TRANSP *containers* diseminar

dissemination *n* GEN COMM *of information* difusión *f*

dissolution *n* GEN COMM *of company*, POL *of parliament* disolución *f*

dissolve *vt* GEN COMM *partnership, parliament* disolver

distance: ~ **education center** *AmE*, ~ **education centre** *BrE n* HRM, WEL centro de educación a distancia *m*; ~ **freight** *n* TRANSP *shipping* flete por distancia *m*; ~ **learning** *n* WEL educación a distancia *f*

distancing *n* GEN COMM, HRM distanciamiento *m*

distilling *n* GEN COMM destilación *f*

distinction *n* GEN COMM distinción *f*, WEL *in examination* mención especial *f*; ◆ **make a ~** GEN COMM hacer una distinción

distinctive *adj* COMP, PATENTS distintivo

distinctiveness *n* COMP, PATENTS característica *f*

distinguished *adj* HRM *career* eminente

distort *vt* GEN COMM *figures* deformar, distorsionar

distorting *adj* GEN COMM deformante

distortion *n* ECON distorsión *f*, GEN COMM deformación *f*

distortionary: ~ **tax** *n* TAX distorsión fiscal *f*

distraint *n* LAW, PROP embargo *m*; ~ **of property** LAW, PROP embargo de propiedad *m*

distressed: ~ **property** *n* PROP propiedad embargada *f*

distributable: ~ **profit** *n* ACC beneficios distribuibles *m pl*, beneficios repartibles *m pl*

distribute *vt* GEN COMM *information* distribuir

distributed¹ *adj* GEN COMM distribuido

distributed²: ~ **computing** *n* COMP cálculo repartido *m*; ~ **database** *n* (*DDB*) COMP base de datos distribuida *f* (*DDB*); ~ **profit** *n* ACC beneficio distribuido *m*; ~ **system** *n* COMP sistema distribuido *m*

distributing: ~ **syndicate** *n* STOCK sindicato distribuidor *m*

distribution *n* GEN COMM, HRM, TRANSP distribución *f*; ~ **allowance** S&M concesión de distribución *f*, descuento de distribución *m*; ~ **area** STOCK zona de distribución *f*; ~ **of capital** TAX distribución del capital *f*; ~ **center** *AmE*, ~ **centre** *BrE* TRANSP centro de distribución *m*, centro distribuidor *m*; ~ **channel** GEN COMM, S&M canal de comercialización *m*; ~ **check** S&M control de distribución *m*; ~ **cost analysis** S&M análisis de costes de distribución *m* (*Esp*), análisis de costos de distribución *m* (*AmL*); ~ **costs** *n pl* ACC, TRANSP costes de distribución *m pl* (*Esp*), costos de distribución *m pl* (*AmL*); ~ **depot** TRANSP depósito para distribución *m*; ~ **of dividends** ACC distribución de dividendos *f*;

~ **manager** HRM, MGMNT, TRANSP director(a) de distribución *m,f*, gerente de distribución *mf*, jefe(-a) de distribución *m,f*; ~ **of net profit** ACC distribución del beneficio neto *f*; ~ **network** COMP, GEN COMM *sales* red de distribución *f*; ~ **office** (*DO*) TRANSP oficina de distribución *f*; ~ **planning** GEN COMM planificación de la distribución *f*, TRANSP plan de distribución *m*; ~ **policy** GEN COMM, TRANSP política de distribución *f*; ~ **of risks** INS distribución de riesgos *f*; ~ **service** TRANSP servicio de distribución *m*; ~ **stock** STOCK valores de distribución *m pl*; ~ **of wealth** ECON distribución de la riqueza *f*

distributive: ~ **ability** *n* TRANSP capacidad distributiva *f*

distributor *n* IMP/EXP, TRANSP distribuidor(a) *m,f*

distributors': ~ **brand** *n* S&M marca de los distribuidores *f*

district *n* POL distrito *m*; ~ **agreement** HRM acuerdo por distritos *m*, contrato por distritos *m*; ~ **court** *AmE* LAW juzgado de distrito *m*; ~ **manager** HRM, MGMNT director(a) provincial *m,f*, gerente de distrito *mf*, gerente regional *mf*, gerente de territorio *mf*, jefe(-a) de distrito *m,f*; ~ **officer** (*DO*) HRM oficial(a) de distrito *m,f*; ~ **traffic superintendent** (*DTS*) HRM, TRANSP *railway* superintendente de tráfico *mf*; ~ **training officer** (*DTO*) HRM oficial(a) de formación de distrito *m,f*

District: ~ **Attorney** *n AmE* (*DA*) LAW fiscal *mf*; ~ **Council** *n BrE* GEN COMM, POL ≈ Ayuntamiento *m* (*Esp*)

disturbance: ~ **term** *n* MATH *statistics* término de perturbación *m*

disutility *n* ECON desutilidad *f*

ditto *adv* (*do.*) GEN COMM ídem (*íd.*)

div. *abbr* (*dividend*) STOCK dividendo *m*

diverge *vi* ECON, GEN COMM divergir

divergence *n* ECON, GEN COMM divergencia *f*; ~ **indicator** ECON *international* indicador divergente *m*; ~ **threshold** ECON *international* umbral divergente *m*

divergent: ~ **marketing** *n* S&M marketing divergente *m*; ~ **thinking** *n* MGMNT pensamiento divergente *m*

diverse *adj* GEN COMM diverso

diversification *n* GEN COMM diversificación *f*; ~ **strategy** S&M estrategia de diversificación *f*

diversified: ~ **company** *n* ECON, GEN COMM, MGMNT empresa diversificada *f*

diversify *vt* ECON, GEN COMM, MGMNT diversificar; ◆ ~ **risks** STOCK diversificar riesgos

diversion *n* TRANSP *traffic* desvío *m* (*Esp*), reencaminamiento *m* (*AmL*)

diversity: ~ **of opinions** *n* GEN COMM pluralidad de opiniones *f*

divest: ~ **oneself of sth** *phr* TAX deshacerse de algo

divestiture *n* LAW desposeimiento *m*

divide *vt* COMP, MATH dividir

divided¹: ~ **by** *adj* MATH dividido por

divided²: ~ **coverage** *n* STOCK cobertura repartida entre varias aseguradoras *f*

dividend *n* (*div.*) STOCK dividendo activo *m*; ~ **addition** INS suma agregada a la póliza de seguro *f*; ~ **allowance** TAX deducción de dividendo *f*; ~ **announcement** STOCK anuncio de dividendo *m*; ~ **bond** FIN, STOCK bono de dividendo *m*; ~ **control** ACC, STOCK control de dividendos *m*; ~ **coupon** STOCK cupón de dividendo *f*; ~ **cover**

ACC, STOCK beneficio por acción *m*, cobertura de dividendos *f*; **~ coverage ratio** STOCK proporción de cobertura del dividendo *f*; **~ declaration** STOCK declaración de dividendo *f*; **~ exclusion** *AmE* TAX exclusión del dividendo *f*; **~ fund** ACC, STOCK fondo de dividendo *m*; **~ gross-up** ACC, STOCK bloque de dividendos *m*; **~ in arrears** ACC, FIN, STOCK dividendo atrasado *m*; **~ in kind** ACC, STOCK dividendo en especie *m*; **~ income** ACC, STOCK ingreso por dividendos *m*; **~ net** ACC, STOCK dividendo neto *m*; **~ payable** ACC, STOCK dividendo a pagar *m*, dividendo pagadero *m*; **~ payout ratio** ACC, STOCK índice de desembolso de dividendos *m*, coeficiente de desembolso de dividendos *m*, proporción de desembolso de dividendos *f*; **~ per share** ACC, STOCK dividendo por acción *m*; **~ policy** FIN, STOCK política de dividendos *f*; **~-price ratio** FIN, STOCK proporción dividendo-precio de la acción *f*, relación dividendo-precio *f*; **~ reinvestment** ACC, STOCK reinversión de dividendos *f*; **~ reinvestment plan** ACC, STOCK plan de reinversión de dividendos *m*; **~ requirement** ACC, STOCK exigencia de dividendos *f*, reclamación de dividendos *f*, solicitud de desembolsos pendientes *f*; **~ rollover plan** STOCK sistema de refinanciación de dividendos *m*; **~ stripping** *jarg* FIN, TAX desdoblamiento de dividendos *m*; **~ tax** TAX impuesto sobre dividendos *m*; **~ tax credit** TAX desgravación de dividendo *f*; **~ tax withholding** TAX impuesto sobre retención de dividendos *m*, retención fiscal sobre dividendos *f*; **~ trading** STOCK lavado de dividendos *m*; **~ voucher** STOCK comprobante de dividendos *m*; **~ warrant** BANK, FIN cheque en pago de dividendos *m*; **~ yield** STOCK rendimiento en dividendos *m*

dividends: **~ check** *AmE*, **~ cheque** *BrE n* BANK, FIN cheque de dividendos *m*; **~ eligible for interest** *n pl* STOCK dividendos elegibles por interés *m pl*; **~ income deduction** *n* STOCK, TAX deducción del ingreso por dividendos *f*

Divisia: **~ money index** *n* ECON índice de Divisia *m*

divisibility *n* GEN COMM divisibilidad *f*

divisible *adj* GEN COMM divisible

division *n* GEN COMM *of the market* división *f*; **~ head** HRM, MGMNT director(a) de división *m,f*, director(a) divisional *m,f*, gerente de división *mf*, jefe(-a) de división *m,f*, jefe(-a) de sección *m,f*; **~ of labor** *AmE*, **~ of labour** *BrE* ECON, HRM división del trabajo *f*; **~ manager** HRM, MGMNT director(a) de división *m,f*, director(a) divisional *m,f*, gerente de división *mf*, jefe(-a) de división *m,f*, jefe(-a) de sección *m,f*; **~ of powers** GEN COMM división de poderes *f*

divisional: **~ management** *n* GEN COMM, MGMNT gestión por departamentos *f*

divisionalization *n* GEN COMM divisionalización *f*

divorced: **~ spouse** *n* LAW cónyuge divorciado(-a) *m,f*

DJ *abbr* (*Dow Jones*) STOCK institución bursátil estadounidense

DLO *abbr* (*dispatch loading only*) TRANSP despacho adelantado de carga únicamente *m*

DMA *abbr* S&M (*Direct Marketing Association*) asociación de marketing directo

DME *abbr* (*decentralized market economy*) ECON economía de mercado descentralizada *f*

D/N *abbr* (*debit note*) GEN COMM nota de cargo *f*

do. *abbr* (*ditto*) GEN COMM íd. (*ídem*)

DO *abbr* ENVIR (*diesel oil*) gasóleo para motores diesel *m*,

gasoil para motores diesel *m*, HRM (*district officer*) oficial(a) de distrito *m,f*, (*duty officer*) oficial(a) de guardia *m,f*, TRANSP (*distribution office*) oficina de distribución *f*, (*dock operation*) operación portuaria *f*, (*duty officer*) oficial(a) de guardia *m,f*, (*diesel oil*) gasóleo para motores diesel *m*, gasoil para motores diesel *m*

D/O *abbr* (*delivery order*) TRANSP orden de entrega *f*

DOC[1] *abbr* (*Drive Other Car insurance*) INS seguro que cubre al titular cuando conduce un coche ajeno

DOC[2]: **~ credits** *n pl* IMP/EXP créditos DOC *m pl*

dock[1] *n* TRANSP *shipping* dique *m*, dock *m*; **~ charges** *n pl* TRANSP derechos de atraque *m pl*; **~ charter** TRANSP contrato con mención de dique *m*; **~ container park** TRANSP parque portuario de contenedores *m*; **~ dues** *n pl* TRANSP derechos de muelle *m pl*; **~ operation** (*DO*) TRANSP operación portuaria *f*; **~ receipt** TRANSP recibo de muelle *m*; **~ warrant** (*D/W*) IMP/EXP, TRANSP conocimiento de depósito *m*, *issued by Dock Authorities for warehouse goods* conocimiento de muelle *m*, resguardo de muelle *m*

dock[2] *vi* TRANSP *shipping* atracar al muelle, entrar en dique

docker *n* *BrE* GEN COMM, HRM, TRANSP alijador(a) *m,f* (*AmL*), estibador(a) *m,f* (*Esp*), trabajador(a) portuario(-a) *m,f*

dockers *n pl* GEN COMM, HRM, TRANSP estibadores *m pl* (*Esp*), alijadores *m pl* (*AmL*)

docking *n* HRM paga con un descuento en concepto de sanción; **~ survey** TRANSP inspección portuaria *f*

doctor *n* WEL doctor(a) *m,f*

Doctor *n* (*Dr*) GEN COMM *title* Doctor(a) *m,f* (*Dr*); **~ of Business Management** GEN COMM, MGMNT Doctor(a) en Administración Empresarial *m,f*; **~ of Commerce** (*DCom*) GEN COMM Doctor(a) en Comercio *m,f*; **~ of Commercial Law** (*DComL*) GEN COMM, LAW Doctor(a) en Derecho Comercial *m,f*; **~ of Economics** (*DEcon*) ECON, GEN COMM Doctor(a) en Economía *m,f*; **~ of Laws** (*LLD*) HRM, LAW Doctor(a) en Derecho *m,f*

doctrine: **~ of comparative costs** *n* ACC doctrina de los costes comparativos *f* (*Esp*), doctrina de los costos comparativos *f* (*AmL*); **~ of strict compliance** *n* BANK doctrina de estricta conformidad *f*; **~ of substantial performance** *n* LAW doctrina de cumplimiento sustancial *f*

document *n* GEN COMM documento *m*, LAW *article of incorporation, deed, bylaw* escritura pública *f*; **~ code** COMP código del documento *m*; **~ feeder** COMP dispositivo de alimentación de documentos *m*; **~ holder** GEN COMM titular de un documento *mf*; **~ name** COMP nombre del documento *m*; **~ rate** COMP velocidad de tratamiento de documentos *f*; **~ reader** COMP lectora de documentos *f*; **~ retrieval system** COMP sistema de recuperación de documentos *m*

documentary *n* MEDIA, S&M documental *m*; **~ credit** BANK, FIN, IMP/EXP crédito documentario *m*; **~ draft** BANK, IMP/EXP, TRANSP giro documentario *m*, letra documentaria *f*; **~ evidence** GEN COMM prueba documental *f*; **~ fraud** GEN COMM fraude documental *m*; **~ letter of credit** BANK, FIN, IMP/EXP carta de crédito documentaria *f*; **~ remittance** BANK remesa documentaria *f*

documentation *n* COMP, GEN COMM documentación *f*

documents: **~ against acceptance** *n pl* (*D/A*) GEN

COMM documentos contra aceptación *m pl*; ~ **against payment** *n pl* (*DP*) GEN COMM documentos contra pago *m pl*; ~ **of title** *n pl* LAW documentos de propiedad *m pl*, títulos documentarios *m pl*

dodge *vt infrml* GEN COMM defraudar

dog *n* S&M trinca *f*; ~ **bone bridge** TRANSP *cargo handling* puente de fijación *m*; ~ **hooks** *n pl* TRANSP *cargo handling* patas de eslinga *f pl*

doing: ~ **business as** *phr* (*DBA*) GEN COMM nombre que se adopta para transacciones de negocios

doldrums: in the ~ *phr* GEN COMM en situación de estancamiento

dole *n BrE infrml* HRM, WEL subsidio de paro *m*; ◆ **be on the** ~ *infrml BrE* (*cf be on welfare AmE*) GEN COMM, HRM estar en el paro, WEL vivir de subsidios sociales

dollar: ~ **area** *n* ECON área de influencia del dólar *f*; ~ **balance** *n* BANK, ECON, FIN saldo en dólares *m*; ~ **bid** *n* STOCK *options* oferta de compra de dólares *f*; ~ **cost averaging** *n* STOCK política para asegurar riesgos sobre el cambio del dólar; ~ **drain** *n* ECON déficit en dólares del comercio exterior de Estados Unidos; ~**-for-dollar offset** *n* STOCK liquidación mediante compensación dólar por dólar *f*; ~ **gap** *n* ECON brecha de dólares *f*; ~ **premium** *n* STOCK *options* prima del dólar *f*; ~ **price** *n* STOCK cotización del dólar *f*; ~ **price of the ECU** *n* STOCK precio en dólares del ECU *m*; ~ **shortage** *n* STOCK escasez de dólares *f*; ~ **spot and forward** *n* FIN dólar al contado y a plazo *m*; ~ **standard** *n* ECON, FIN patrón dólar *m*; ~ **value** *n* STOCK valor en dólares *m*

dollarization *n* ECON, GEN COMM *international* dolarización *f*

dolly *n* TRANSP carretilla *f*

domain *n* GEN COMM, MATH ámbito *m*, dominio *m*

domestic[1] *adj* ECON, TRANSP *network* nacional

domestic[2]: ~ **absorption** *n* ECON *international* absorción nacional *f*; ~ **affairs** *n pl* POL asuntos internos *m pl*; ~ **agreement** *n BrE* HRM acuerdo interno *m*; ~ **airline** *n* LEIS, TRANSP línea aérea interna *f*; ~ **asset** *n* BANK activo interno *m*; ~ **bank** *n* BANK, ECON banco interno *m*, banco nacional *m*; ~ **banking system** *n* BANK sistema bancario interno *m*; ~ **business** *n* GEN COMM negocio familiar *m*; ~ **consumption** *n* ECON, ENVIR consumo doméstico *m*, consumo interior *m*; ~ **corporation** *n* ECON, GEN COMM corporación nacional *f*, empresa nacional *f*; ~ **credit expansion** *n* (*DCE*) ECON *international* expansión del crédito interior *f*; ~ **demand** *n* ECON demanda interna *f*; ~ **exchange** *n* GEN COMM cambio interior *m*; ~ **export financing** *n* FIN, IMP/EXP financiación de la exportación nacional *f*; ~ **financing** *n* ACC, FIN, GEN COMM financiación interna *f*; ~ **flight** *n* LEIS, TRANSP vuelo nacional *m*; ~ **industry** *n* ECON, IND industria nacional *f*; ~ **investment** *n* ECON inversión interna *f*; ~ **issue** *n* STOCK emisión interior *f*, emisión nacional *f*; ~ **liabilities** *n pl* ACC, BANK pasivos internos *m pl*; ~ **market** *n* ECON, S&M mercado doméstico *m*, mercado interno *m*, mercado nacional *m*; ~ **money market** *n* ECON, FIN mercado de dinero doméstico *m*, mercado de dinero interno *m*, mercado de dinero local *m*; ~ **output** *n* ECON, IND producción interior *f*; ~ **rate** *n* TRANSP tarifa nacional *f*; ~ **resource cost** *n* (*DRC*) ECON costo en recursos internos *m* (*AmL*), coste en recursos internos *m* (*Esp*); ~ **sale** *n* S&M venta nacional *f*; ~ **securities market** *n* STOCK mercado interior de títulos *m*; ~ **subsidiary** *n* ECON

subsidiaria nacional *f*; ~ **system** *n* ECON sistema nacional *m*; ~ **trade** *n* GEN COMM comercio interno *m*, comercio interior *m*; ~ **waste** *n* ENVIR desperdicios domésticos *m pl*

Domestic: ~ **Equities Market** *n* (*DEM*) STOCK Mercado Nacional de Títulos *m*; ~ **International Sales Corporation** *n AmE* (*DISC*) GEN COMM corporación nacional de ventas internacionales

domicile *n* LAW, PROP domicilio *m*; ~ **taxation** TAX fiscalidad de la vivienda *f*

domiciled *adj* LAW, PROP domiciliado

dominant[1] *adj* ECON, GEN COMM, S&M dominante

dominant[2]: ~ **firm** *n* ECON empresa dominante *f*; ~ **position** *n* ECON posición dominante *f*; ~ **tenement** *n* PROP predio dominante *m*

dominate *vt* ECON *the market*, GEN COMM, S&M dominar

domination *n* ECON, GEN COMM, S&M dominación *f*

donate *vt* TAX donar

donated[1] *adj* TAX donado

donated[2]: ~ **stock** *n* STOCK acciones restituidas por los fundadores; ~ **surplus** *n* STOCK superávit aportado en acciones *m*

donation *n* TAX donación *f*; ~ **in kind** TAX donación en especie *f*; ~ **pledged** TAX donación pignorada *f*

donee *n* TAX donatario(-a) *m,f*; ~ **beneficiary** ACC, FIN, GEN COMM, INS, LAW beneficiario(-a) por donación *m,f*

d1/2D *abbr* (*dispatch half demurrage*) TRANSP *shipping* media penalización por demora en el despacho *f*

dongle *n* COMP dongle *m*

Donoghue: ~**'s Money Fund Average** *n AmE* STOCK Promedio del Fondo Monetario Donoghue *m*

donor: ~ **agency** *n* WEL agencia donante *f*; ~ **aid** *n* ECON *development assistance*, POL ayuda sin contraprestación *f*, dotación de ayuda *f*; ~ **country** *n* ECON *of overseas aid*, POL país donante *m*

Donovan: ~ **Commission** *n BrE* HRM Comisión Donovan *f*

door[1]: ~**-to-door clause** *n* INS cláusula puerta a puerta *f*; ~**-to-door salesman** *n* HRM, S&M vendedor(a) a domicilio *m,f*; ~**-to-door selling** *n* S&M venta domiciliaria *f*

door[2]: ~ **to door** *phr* GEN COMM, S&M de puerta a puerta

door/depot *phr* TRANSP de puerta a almacén

dormant: ~ **account** *n* BANK, S&M cuenta inactiva *f*, cuenta sin movimiento *f*

dormitory: ~ **town** *n BrE* (*cf bedroom community AmE*) GEN COMM ciudad dormitorio *f*

DOS[1] *abbr* COMP (*disk operating system*) DOS (*sistema operativo de discos*), WEL (*Director of Studies*) jefe(-a) de estudios *m,f*

DOS[2]: ~ **prompt** *n* COMP guía del DOS *f*

dossier *n* ADMIN legajo *m*

dot *n* COMP, MATH punto *m*; ~ **chart** COMP, MATH gráfico de puntos *m*; ~ **command** COMP comando puntual *m*; ~**-matrix printer** COMP *hardware* impresora de matriz de puntos *f*, impresora por puntos *f*; ~ **printer** COMP impresora matricial *f*

dots: ~ **per inch** *n pl* (*dpi*) COMP *typeface* puntos por pie *m pl* (*ppp*)

dotted: ~ **line** *n* COMP, GEN COMM, MATH *on graph* línea punteada *f*

double[1] *adj* MATH doble; ~ **acting** IND *machinery* de doble acción; **~-barreled** *AmE*, **~-barrelled** *BrE* STOCK de doble garantía; **~ decker** TRANSP de dos niveles; **~-ended** (*DB*) TRANSP *boiler* anfidromo, de dos frentes; **~-income** ECON *family, household* de doble ingreso; **~ precision** COMP de doble precisión; **~-sided** COMP de doble cara

double²: **~ account system** *n* ACC sistema de cuenta doble *m*; **~-barreled bond** *AmE*, **~-barrelled bond** *BrE* *n* FIN, STOCK bono con doble garantía *m*; **~ bottom** *n* (*DB*) TRANSP *of ship* doble fondo *m*; **~ column** *n* S&M doble columna *f*; **~ counting** *n* FIN doble contabilización *f*; **~ crown** *n* S&M doble corona *f*; **~ damages** *n pl* LAW *award* indemnización doble *f*; **~-decked pallet** *n* TRANSP bandeja de carga de dos pisos *f* (*Esp*), palét de carga de dos pisos *f* (*AmL*), paleta de carga de dos pisos *f* (*AmL*), bandeja de carga reversible *f* (*Esp*), palét de carga reversible *f* (*AmL*), paleta de carga reversible *f* (*AmL*); **~-decker bus** *n* LEIS, TRANSP autobús de dos pisos *m*; **~-declining balance** *n* ACC amortización doble de saldo decreciente *f*; **~ density** *n* COMP doble densidad *f*; **~-digit inflation** *n* ECON, FIN inflación de dos dígitos *f*; **~ dip** *n jarg* ECON *general* doble depresión *f*; **~-dipper** *n jarg* HRM persona con dos empleos *f*; **~-dipping** *n* HRM infidelidad reincidente *f*; **~ distribution** *n* GEN COMM doble distribución *f*; **~ eagle** *n AmE* FIN moneda de oro de veinte dólares; **~-edged sword** *n BrE* (*cf whipsaw AmE*) HRM arma de doble filo *m*; **~ entry** *n* ACC, ECON doble entrada *f*; **~-entry accounting** *n* ACC, ECON contabilidad por partida doble *f*; **~-entry book-keeping** *n* ACC, ECON contabilidad por partida doble *f*; **~-entry method** *n* ACC, ECON *book-keeping* método de contabilidad por partida doble *m*, método de partida doble *m*; **~-entry visa** *n* LEIS, POL visado de doble entrada *m*; **~ factorial terms of trade** *n* ECON *international* relación real de intercambio *f*; **~-figure inflation** *n* ECON inflación de dos cifras *f*; **~ front** *n* S&M doble frontal *f*; **~ insurance** *n* INS doble seguro *m*; **~ manning** *n* HRM, IND doble dotación de personal *f*; **~ option** *n* STOCK doble opción *f*; **~ reduction** *n* GEN COMM doble reducción *f*; **~ room** *n* LEIS habitación doble *f*; **~-sided disk** *n* COMP *software* disco de dos caras *m*; **~ space** *n* COMP doble espacio *m*; **~ spacing** *n* COMP espacio doble *m*; **~-spread advertising** *n* MEDIA, S&M anuncio a doble página *m*, publicidad a doble página *f*; **~ stack** *n* TRANSP doble pila *f*; **~ stacker** *n* TRANSP *containers* bicono fijador *m*; **~ stacking** *n* TRANSP apilamiento doble *m*; **~ strike** *n* COMP doble tecleo *m*; **~ switching** *n* ECON doble arbitraje *m*; **~ tax agreement** *n* TAX acuerdo de doble fiscalidad *m*; **~ taxation** *n* TAX doble imposición *f*; **~ taxation agreement** *n* TAX acuerdo de doble imposición *m*; **~ taxation relief** *n* (*DTR*) TAX deducción por doble imposición *f*; **~ taxation of savings** *n* TAX doble imposición de los ahorros *f*; **~ time** *n* HRM hora contada doble *f*; **~ width gangway** *n* TRANSP *shipping* escalerilla de doble ancho *f*, portalón de doble ancho *m*

double³: **~ stack** *vt* TRANSP *containers* apilar en dos niveles

Double: **~ Income no Kids** *phr infrml* (*Dinks*) ECON pareja de profesionales independientes con altos ingresos y sin hijos

doubtful: **~ debt** *n* ACC, BANK, FIN deuda de cobro dudoso *f*; **~ debt provision** *n* ACC, BANK, FIN provisión para deudas de cobro dudoso *f*, provisión para deudas

dudosas *f*, provisión para insolvencias *f*; **~ debtor** *n* ACC, BANK, FIN deudor(a) dudoso(-a) *m,f*

Douglas: **~ Amendment** *n AmE* BANK reforma de ley Douglas *f*

Dow: **~ Jones** *n* (*DJ*) STOCK institución bursátil estadounidense; **~ Jones index** *n* STOCK índice Dow Jones *m*; **~ Jones Industrial Average** *n* STOCK media Industrial Dow Jones *f*; **~ theory** *n* STOCK teoría de Dow *f*

DOW *abbr* (*delivery on wheels*) TRANSP entrega a domicilio *f*

dower *n* LAW cuota vidual *f*, viudedad *f*

down¹ *adj* COMP *direction, position* descendente, *system* fuera de funcionamiento; **~-market** GEN COMM, S&M *product* de baja gama, inferior

down²: **~ arrow** *n* COMP *keyboard* flecha hacia abajo *f*; **~ market product** *n* S&M producto de gama baja *m*; **~ market service** *n* S&M servicio de gama baja *m*; **~ payment** *n* BANK, GEN COMM, S&M depósito inicial *m*, adelanto a cuenta *m*, pago inicial *m*; **~ period** *n* ACC, BANK, FIN, GEN COMM cierre por reforma *m*; **~-the-line personnel** *n* HRM personal subalterno *m*; **~ tick** *n* STOCK *AmE* venta de un título a un precio inferior al de la cotización precedente; **~ time** *n* GEN COMM tiempo de indisponibilidad *m*, tiempo de inactividad *m*

down³: **be ~ on** *vt infrml* GEN COMM tener manía a; ◆ **~ tools** HRM *strike* dejar de trabajar

downgrade *vt* HRM *job* depreciar

downgrading *n* HRM reducción de categoría laboral *f*

download *vt* COMP transferir

downloadable: **~ font** *n* COMP fuente cargable por teleproceso *f*

downside: **~ break-even** *n* STOCK *options* punto de equilibrio descendente *m*; **~ break-even point** *n* STOCK *options* punto de equilibrio descendente *m*; **~ risk** *n* STOCK riesgo por baja en los tipos de cambio *m*

downsize *vt* HRM *workforce*, MGMNT reducir

downsizing *n* HRM *of the workforce*, MGMNT reducción de personal *f*, reducción *f*

downstream¹ *adv* GEN COMM hacia abajo

downstream²: **~ float** *n* GEN COMM flotación descendente *f*

downswing *n* ECON, GEN COMM baja *f*, descenso *m*, fase descendente *f*

downtown *n AmE* (*cf town centre BrE*) GEN COMM centro de la ciudad *m*

downtrend *n* ECON, GEN COMM tendencia declinante *f*

downturn *n* ECON, GEN COMM baja *f*, descenso *m*, fase descendente *f*, STOCK recesión *f*

downward¹ *adj* COMP *computer screen*, GEN COMM *trend* descendente

downward² *adv AmE* (*cf downwards BrE*) GEN COMM hacia abajo

downward³: **~ communication** *n* MGMNT comunicación descendente *f*; **~ compatibility** *n* COMP compatibilidad descendente *f*; **~ correction** *n* STOCK corrección a la baja *f*; **~ movement** *n* ECON, GEN COMM movimiento descendente *m*; **~ pressure** *n* ECON *currency, interest rates* presión a la baja *f*; **~ spiral** *n* GEN COMM *in wages, prices* espiral descendente *f*

downwards *adv BrE* (*cf downward AmE*) GEN COMM hacia abajo

downzoning *n* PROP reducción de la zona *f*

dowry n PROP dote f

dp abbr (direct port) TRANSP shipping puerto directo m

DP abbr GEN COMM (dynamic positioning) localización dinámica f, (documents against payment) documentos contra pago m pl

dpi abbr (dots per inch) COMP ppp (puntos por pie)

DPP abbr BrE (Director of Public Prosecutions) LAW ≈ Fiscal General del Estado mf (Esp), ≈ Fiscal Jefe(-a) del Servicio de Acusación Pública m,f (AmL)

DPR abbr (director of public relations) HRM director(a) de relaciones públicas m,f

DPS abbr (data processing system) COMP sistema de procesamiento de datos m

DR abbr (dead rise) GEN COMM subida sin efecto f

Dr abbr GEN COMM (Doctor) title Dr (Doctor), (debtor) Dr (deudor)

draft[1] n (dft) BANK cheque m, libranza f, COMP borrador m, FIN, GEN COMM borderó m, cheque m, INS borderó m, POL borrador m, TRANSP AmE see draught BrE; **~ agreement** GEN COMM proyecto de contrato m; **~ amendments** n pl POL enmiendas al borrador f pl; **~ budget** ACC borrador de presupuesto m; **~ clause** LAW bill borrador de artículo m, borrador de cláusula m; **~ contract** GEN COMM proyecto de contrato m, LAW borrador de un contrato m; **~ directive** LAW EU borrador de directiva m; **~ for collection** BANK letra al cobro f; **~ mode** COMP modo borrador m; **~ order** LAW compulsory purchase borrador de decreto m; **~ printing** COMP anteproyecto m; **~ project** GEN COMM proyecto preliminar m; **~ prospectus** STOCK borrador de prospecto m; **~ resolution** LAW proyecto de resolución m; **~ stage** LAW fase de redacción f, POL fase de borrador f; ◆ **in ~ form** GEN COMM en borrador, en forma de borrador

draft[2] vt GEN COMM, LAW girar, redactar

drafted adj GEN COMM, LAW redactado, POL provisional

drag: **~ information out of sb** phr infrml GEN COMM sacarle información a alguien

drain n COMP hardware consumo m, ECON of resources drenaje m, INS desagüe m

draining: **~ reserve** n ECON reserva en disminución f

Dram: **~ Shop Act** n AmE LAW Ley de Tabernas f

DRAM abbr (dynamic random access memory) COMP hardware RAM dinámica f

drastic: **~ measure** n GEN COMM medida drástica f

draught n BrE TRANSP shipping calado m

draw[1]: **~-down** n BANK aprovechamiento de fondos prestados m

draw[2] vt BANK librar, GEN COMM sacar, stock agotar, MATH, S&M dibujar (Esp), graficar (AmL); ◆ **~ a check** AmE, **~ a cheque** BrE BANK hacer un cheque, librar un cheque, retirar un cheque; **~ a conclusion** GEN COMM sacar una conclusión; **~ a distinction between** GEN COMM establecer una diferencia entre; **~ from** HRM cobrar de; **~ on savings** FIN girar contra los ahorros; **~ sickness insurance** HRM cobrar el seguro de enfermedad

draw up vt GEN COMM plan, will formular, LAW deed redactar, white paper elaborar, levantar, POL white paper preparar; ◆ **~ an agenda** MGMNT establecer un orden del día; **~ a balance sheet** ACC hacer balance; **~ a draft** LAW redactar un documento; **~ a shortlist** HRM redactar una lista de candidatos seleccionados; **~ a**

statement of account BANK redactar un estado de cuenta

drawback n (Dbk) GEN COMM reembolso de derechos m, devolución de derechos f, IMP/EXP drawback m; **~ debenture** BANK, ECON, GEN COMM certificado para reintegro m

drawbar: **~ combination** n TRANSP combinación de barra tractora f; **~ trailer** n TRANSP remolque de camión m

drawee n ADMIN, BANK, FIN girado(-a) m,f, librado(-a) m,f

drawer n ADMIN, BANK, FIN girador(a) m,f, librador(a) m,f

drawing n BANK on loan retiro m, PATENTS libranza f; **~ account** ACC, BANK, FIN cuenta corriente f (c/c), cuenta de depósitos a la vista f; **~ automation** (DA) COMP automatización del dibujo f (AD); **~ of bill** BANK extensión de una letra f, giro de una letra m; **~ board** MGMNT tablero de dibujo m; **~ down of stocks** ACC, GEN COMM disminución de las existencias f; **~ file** COMP archivo de diseño m; **~ officer** BANK jefe(-a) de cobros m,f; **~ software** COMP programa de dibujo m; **~ up** PATENTS of report elaboración f

drawn: **~ bill** n ECON letra de cambio emitida f; **~ bond** n STOCK bono sorteado m

DRC abbr (domestic resource cost) ECON international coste en recursos internos m (Esp), costo en recursos internos m (AmL)

dredging: **~ anchor** n TRANSP shipping ancla de dragado f

dressed: **~ return** n TAX declaración falsificada f

dressing n GEN COMM, S&M, TRANSP embalaje m

DRF abbr (Daily Range Factor) STOCK factor de la banda diaria m

drilling: **~ installation** n S&M estación de sondeos f; **~ platform** n ENVIR plataforma de perforación f; **~ program** AmE, **~ programme** BrE n ENVIR programa de perforaciones m

drinking: **~ water** n ENVIR agua potable f

drip n S&M goteo m

drive[1] n COMP accionamiento m, GEN COMM concerted effort impulso m; **~ time** S&M tiempo de conducción m

drive[2]: **~ a hard bargain** phr GEN COMM hacer un trato provechoso

drive down vt ECON price arrastrar hacia abajo

Drive: **~ Other Car insurance** n (DOC) INS seguro que cubre al titular cuando conduce un coche ajeno

driven adj GEN COMM impulsado; **~ by** GEN COMM impulsado por

driver n COMP software módulo de gestión m, hardware circuito de arranque m, HRM conductor(a) m,f, operador(a) m,f; **~'s cab** TRANSP cabina del conductor f

Driver: **~ and Vehicle Licensing Centre** n BrE (DVLC) TRANSP centro emisor de permisos de conducir y de circulación

driving: **~ force** n GEN COMM fuerza motriz f; **~'s licence** BrE, **~'s license** AmE n ADMIN, TRANSP carnet de conducir m (Esp), permiso de conducir m (Esp), licencia de conducir f (AmL)

drop[1] n ECON in spending, orders, GEN COMM caída f; **~ in investments** ECON, STOCK caída en las inversiones f; **~ in production** IND caída de la producción f; **~ leg** TRANSP cargo handling pata abatible f; **~-lock stock**

STOCK chicharros *m pl*; **~-out** COMP pérdida de información *f*; **~-shipping** *AmE* S&M *merchandising* venta directa *f*

drop[2] *vi* ECON, GEN COMM caer

droppages: ~, cancellations, and prepayments *phr* (*DCP*) GEN COMM bajas, cancelaciones y pagos anticipados

drought *n* ENVIR sequía *f*

drug *n* GEN COMM *medication* medicamento *m*, *narcotic* droga *f*; **~ economy** ECON economía basada en los beneficios obtenidos por la venta de drogas legales; **~ trade** GEN COMM tráfico de drogas *m*, narcotráfico *m*

drum *n* COMP, TRANSP tambor *m*; **~ plotter** COMP trazador de tambor *m*; **~ printer** COMP impresora de tambor *f*

drummer *n* *AmE infrml* HRM corredor(a) de comercio *m,f*

dry: ~ barrel *n* TRANSP barril de áridos *m*; **~ battery** *n* TRANSP *shipping* pila seca *f*; **~ bulk cargo** *n* TRANSP carga a granel seca *f*; **~ bulk container** *n* (*d*) TRANSP contenedor de graneles secos *m*; **~ cargo** *n* TRANSP carga seca *f*; **~ dock** *n* TRANSP dique seco *m*; **~ docking** *n* (*DD*) TRANSP dique seco *m*; **~ freight** *n* TRANSP carga seca *f*; **~ goods** *n pl* S&M artículos de corte y confección *m pl*, artículos de mercería *m pl*; **~ measure** *n* GEN COMM medida para áridos *f*; **~ run** *n* S&M prueba *f*; **~ trust** *n* LAW fideicomiso pasivo *m*; **~ weight** *n* TRANSP peso en seco *m*

DRY *abbr* (*disposable real income*) ECON ingreso real disponible *m*

DS *abbr* ENVIR (*depth sounder*) sonda de profundidad *f*, TRANSP (*days after sight*) días vista *m pl*

DSC *abbr* (*digital selective calling*) COMMS llamada selectiva digital *f*

DT *abbr* (*deep tank*) TRANSP tanque inferior *m*

DTa *abbr* (*deep tank aft*) TRANSP tanque inferior de popa *m*

DTC *abbr* (*Direct Trading Corporation*) GEN COMM Corporación de Comercialización Directa *f*

DTE *abbr* (*data terminal equipment*) COMP *hardware* equipo terminal de datos *m*

DTf *abbr* (*deep tank forward*) TRANSP tanque inferior de proa *m*

DTm *abbr* (*midship deep tank*) TRANSP tanque inferior central *m*

DTma *abbr* (*midship deep tank aft*) TRANSP tanque inferior central trasero *m*

DTmf *abbr* (*midship deep tank forward*) TRANSP tanque inferior central delantero *m*

DTO *abbr* (*district training officer*) HRM oficial(a) de formación de distrito *m,f*

DTP *abbr* (*desktop publishing*) COMP, MEDIA *print* autoedición *f*

DTR *abbr* (*double taxation relief*) TAX deducción por doble imposición *f*

DTS *abbr* (*district traffic superintendent*) HRM, TRANSP superintendente de tráfico *mf*

Du Pont: ~ formula *n* FIN fórmula Du Pont *f*

dual: ~ banking *n* BANK banca dual *f*; **~ capacity** *n* STOCK doble capacidad *f*; **~ contract** *n* LAW contrato doble *m*; **~ decision hypothesis** *n* ECON hipótesis de la decisión dual *f*; **~ economy** *n* ECON economía dual *f*, POL economía de trueque *f*; **~ exchange rate** *n* ECON *international* proporción de intercambio dual *f*;

~ federalism *n* POL doble federalismo *m*; **~ job holding** *n* HRM pluriempleo *m*; **~ listing** *n* STOCK cotización dual *f*; **~ pitch** *n* ADMIN espaciado doble *m*; **~ purpose fund** *n* STOCK fondo de doble finalidad *m*; **~ rate** *n* TRANSP *shipping* tasa dual *f*; **~ residence** *n* TAX doble residencia *f*; **~ responsibility** *n* HRM *EU* doble responsabilidad *f*; **~ skilling** *n* HRM cualificación doble *f*, multihabilidades *f pl*; **~ sourcing** *n* GEN COMM doble fuente *m*; **~ valuation clause** *n* INS *marine* cláusula sobre doble valoración *f*

dubbing *n* MEDIA, S&M doblaje *m*

dubious: ~ account *n* ACC, BANK cuenta de valor dudoso *f*

dud: ~ check *AmE*, **~ cheque** *BrE n infrml* BANK, FIN cheque sin fondos *m*

due[1] *adj* GEN COMM *outstanding amount* debido; ♦ **~ to** GEN COMM *as a result of* por causa de, debido a; **~ and unpaid** TAX vencido e impagado

due[2]**: ~ bill** *n* TRANSP pagaré *m*; **~ capital** *n* FIN capital exigible *m*; **~ date of filing** *n* TAX *of return* fecha límite de presentación *m*; **~ date of premium** *n* INS fecha de vencimiento de la prima *f*; **~ date of renewal** *n* INS fecha tope de la renovación *f*; **~ diligence** *n* FIN, INS debida diligencia *f*; **~ diligence expenses** *n pl* FIN, INS gastos de debida diligencia *m pl*; **~-on-sale clause** *n* *AmE* BANK, FIN cláusula pagadera a la venta *f*

dues *n pl* HRM cuotas *f pl*

dull: ~ market *n* STOCK mercado con escasez de operaciones *m*, mercado flojo *m*

dumb: ~ craft *n* TRANSP *shipping* embarcación no propulsada *f*; **~ terminal** *n* COMP terminal básico *m*, terminal mudo *m*, terminal no inteligente *m*

dummy *n* GEN COMM, LAW testaferro *m*; **~ activity** *n* GEN COMM actividad ficticia *f*; **~ employee** *n* HRM empleado(-a) fantasma *m,f*, empleado(-a) inútil *m,f*; **~ variable** *n* ECON *econometrics* variable ficticia *f*

dump[1] *n* COMP *data transfer* resultado de la transcripción *m*; **~ bin** GEN COMM papelera *f*, S&M estantes de presentación independiente, con frecuencia para libros

dump[2] *vt* COMP vaciar, ENVIR *waste at sea* verter

dumping *n* COMP volcado *m*, ENVIR *of waste* vertido *m*, GEN COMM competencia desleal *f*; **~ ground** ENVIR terreno de abono *m*; **~ standard** GEN COMM norma de la competencia desleal *f*

dunnage *n* TRANSP tablas de estiba *f pl*

dunning: ~ letter *n* ACC, ADMIN, BANK carta de cobranza *f*

Dun: ~'s market identifier *n* *AmE* FIN identificador de mercado de Dun *m*; **~ Number** *n* FIN número de Dun *m*

duopoly *n* ECON duopolio *m*

DUP *abbr* (*directly unproductive profit-seeking activities*) ECON actividades directamente improductivas con fines lucrativos *f pl*

dupe *n jarg* S&M *advertising* copia *f*, duplicado *m* (*dupdo.*)

duplex[1] *adj* COMP *printing* bidireccional

duplex[2] *n* *AmE* (*cf semidetached house BrE*) PROP casa semiseparada *f*, casa adosada *f*; **~ computer** COMP computador en tándem *m* (*AmL*), computadora en tándem *f* (*AmL*), ordenador en tándem *m* (*Esp*)

duplicate[1] *n* COMP, GEN COMM duplicado *m* (*dupdo.*); **~ sailing** TRANSP navegación doble *f*; **~ taxation** TAX doble imposición *f*

duplicate[2] *vt* COMP, GEN COMM duplicar

duplicated: ~ **record** n COMP registro duplicado m

duplication n COMP, GEN COMM duplicación f; ~ **of benefits** INS duplicación de prestaciones f

duplicatory adj COMP, GEN COMM duplicatorio

durable: ~ **goods** n pl S&M bienes duraderos m pl; ~ **household goods** n pl ECON bienes de uso doméstico duraderos m pl, IND aparatos domésticos m pl

durables n pl S&M bienes duraderos m pl

duration n GEN COMM duración f; ~ **of benefits** INS duración de las prestaciones f; ~ **of guarantee** GEN COMM duración de la garantía f; ~ **of guaranty** see duration of guarantee

duress n LAW coacción f

dust: ~ **cover** n COMP guardapolvo m

dustbin: ~ **check** n S&M control de consumo por medio de envases vacíos

Dutch: ~ **auction** n S&M subasta a la baja f; ~ **disease** n ECON enfermedad holandesa f

dutiable: ~ **cargo** n IMP/EXP, TRANSP carga sujeta a derechos de aduana f; ~ **cargo list** n IMP/EXP, TRANSP lista de carga sujeta a derechos de aduana f; ~ **goods** n pl TAX mercancías imponibles f pl, mercancías sujetas a aranceles f pl

duties: ~ **under the employment contract** n pl HRM deberes establecidos en el contrato de empleo m pl

duty[1]: ~-**free** adj IMP/EXP, TAX libre de impuestos, exento de derechos

duty[2] n IMP/EXP derecho aduanero m, tasa aduanera f, LAW obligación f, TAX derecho aduanero m, derechos arancelarios m pl; ~ **of assured clause** INS derecho de claúsula de seguro m; ~-**free allowance** BrE IMP/EXP cantidades autorizadas de productos libres de impuestos; ~-**free discount** IMP/EXP, TAX subsidio libre de impuestos m; ~-**free goods** IMP/EXP, TAX bienes libres de impuestos m pl; ~-**free shop** IMP/EXP, LEIS, S&M, TAX tienda libre de impuestos f; ~ **officer** (DO) HRM, TRANSP oficial(a) de guardia m,f; ~ **suspension** IMP/EXP suspensión de arancel f

Duty: ~ **Deposit Account** n (DDA) IMP/EXP, TAX cuenta de depósito de derechos f

DVLC abbr BrE (Driver and Vehicle Licensing Centre) TRANSP centro emisor de permisos de conducir y de circulación

dw abbr (deadweight) TRANSP peso muerto m

D/W abbr (dock warrant) TRANSP conocimiento de muelle m, resguardo de muelle m

dwat abbr (deadweight all told) TRANSP peso muerto total m

dwc abbr (deadweight capacity) TRANSP capacidad de carga f

dwcc abbr (deadweight cargo capacity) TRANSP capacidad máxima de carga f

dwindle vi ECON growth, GEN COMM demand decaer

dwt abbr (deadweight tonnage) TRANSP tonelada de peso muerto f, tonelaje total m

dynamic[1] adj GEN COMM growth, personality dinámico

dynamic[2]: ~ **economics** n ECON economía dinámica f; ~ **evaluation** n GEN COMM evaluación dinámica f; ~ **hedging** n FIN compensación dinámica f; ~ **management model** n MGMNT modelo de administración dinámico m; ~ **obsolescence** n S&M caída en desuso dinámica f; ~ **positioning** n (DP) GEN COMM localización dinámica f; ~ **programming** n COMP, GEN COMM, MATH programación dinámica f; ~ **random access memory** n (DRAM) COMP hardware RAM dinámica f

dynamically: ~ **inconsistent policy** n POL política dinámicamente inconsistente f

dynamism n GEN COMM dinamismo m

E

EA *abbr BrE* (*Employment Act*) HRM, LAW ley de empleo, ≈ Ley de Contrato de Trabajo *f* (*Esp*)

EAAA *abbr* (*European Association of Advertising Agencies*) S&M AEAP (*Asociación Europea de Agencias de Publicidad*)

EABC *abbr* (*European/ASEAN Business Council*) ECON, POL Consejo Comercial Europeo-ASEAN *m*

EAC *abbr* (*European Agency for Cooperation*) LAW, POL AEC (*Agencia Europea para la Cooperación*)

EAEC *abbr* (*European Atomic Energy Community*) ECON, POL CEEA (*Comunidad Europea de Energía Atómica*)

eager: ~ **beaver** *n infrml* HRM *person* trabajador(a) muy ambicioso(-a) y diligente *m,f* (*Esp*), trabajador(a) muy empeñoso(-a) *m,f* (*AmL*)

EAGGF *abbr* (*European Agricultural Guidance and Guarantee Fund*) ECON, POL FEOGA (*Fondo Europeo de Orientación y Garantía Agrícola*)

eagle *n AmE* FIN ten dollars águila *f*

EAL *abbr* (*export adjustment loan*) ECON, IMP/EXP préstamo de regulación de la exportación *m*

e.&o.e. *abbr* (*errors and omissions excepted*) GEN COMM s.e.u.o. (*salvo error u omisión*)

earlier: ~ **application** *n* PATENTS aplicación anterior *f*

early: ~ **adopter** *n jarg* S&M consumidor que compra un producto nuevo muy pronto; ~ **closing day** *n* GEN COMM día de cierre anticipado *m*; ~ **exercise** *n* STOCK *options* ejercicio anticipado de una opción *m*; ~ **filing** *n* TAX *of return* presentación anticipada *f*; ~ **fringe** *n* MEDIA *television* franja horaria de primera hora de la tarde *f*; ~ **majority** *n* S&M mayoría precoz *f*; ~ **penalty** *n* BANK penalización por reembolso anticipado *f*; ~ **publication** *n* PATENTS publicación anticipada *f*; ~ **redemption** *n* FIN, STOCK rescate anticipado *m*, amortización anticipada *f*; ~ **retirement** *n* HRM jubilación anticipada *f*, jubilación temprana *f*; ~ **retirement annuities** *n pl* FIN *EU* anualidades de jubilación anticipada *f pl*; ~ **retirement benefit** *n* FIN, HRM, WEL prestaciones de jubilación anticipada *f pl*, subsidio para jubilación anticipada *m*; ~ **settlement rebate** *n* FIN *consumer credit* bonificación por pago anticipado *f*; ~ **withdrawal penalty** *n* BANK, FIN, STOCK penalización por amortización anticipada *f*, penalización por retirada anticipada *f*, sanción por retirada anticipada *f*

earmark *vt* ACC, ECON, FIN destinar, reservar, GEN COMM *sb for promotion* repartir; ◆ ~ **funds** FIN asignar fondos

earmarked: ~ **account** *n* ACC cuenta reservada *f*; ~ **check** *AmE*, ~ **cheque** *BrE n* BANK, FIN cheque destinado a un determinado pago *m*, cheque reservado *m*; ~ **gold** *n* ECON oro depositado como garantía *m*, oro en custodia *m*; ~ **tax** *n* TAX impuesto afectado *m*

earmarking *n* ECON *of public funds* reserva de fondos *f*

earn *vt* GEN COMM *reputation* ganar, HRM cobrar; ◆ ~ **a fast buck** *infrml* GEN COMM ganar un dinero rápido; ~ **interest** ACC, BANK, FIN devengar intereses; ~ **a living** ECON ganarse la vida

earned: ~ **depletion** *n* TAX deducción devengada sobre activos agotables *f*; ~ **income** *n* TAX ingreso percibido *m*; ~ **income allowance** *n* TAX abono de ingresos salariales *m*, estimación para ingresos devengados *f*; ~ **interest** *n* BANK interés devengado *m*; ~ **premium** *n* INS prima devengada *f*; ~ **surplus** *n* ACC beneficio acumulado *m* (*Esp*), IND excedente de explotación *m*

earnest: ~ **money** *n* PROP depósito de garantía *m*

earning: ~ **capacity** *n* ACC, BANK, WEL grado de rendimiento *m*; ~ **per share** *n* (*EPS*) ACC, FIN, STOCK beneficio por acción *m* (*BPA*), dividendo por acción *m*, ganancia por acción *f*; ~ **performance** *n* GEN COMM resultado rentable *m*; ~ **power** *n* GEN COMM capacidad de beneficio *f*, capacidad de obtención de ingresos *f*, rentabilidad económica *f*; ~ **streams** *n pl* FIN flujos de ganancias *m pl*

earnings *n* FIN, HRM beneficios distribuibles *m pl*; ~ **amount** TAX volumen de las ganancias *m*; ~ **base** FIN, HRM salario base *m*; ~ **ceiling** FIN, HRM salario tope *m*; ~ **differential** HRM diferencial de sueldo *m*; ~ **drift** HRM inestabilidad de los salarios *f*; ~ **forecasts** *n pl* FIN estimaciones de ganancias *f pl*, estimaciones de sueldos *f pl*, estimaciones de utilidades *f pl*; ~ **on assets** ACC ganancias en activos *f pl*; ~ **performance** ACC realización de beneficios *f*, FIN *of stock* evaluación de ganancias *f*, HRM comportamiento de los beneficios *m*; ~ **period** TAX periodo de beneficios *m*; ~ **ratio** STOCK media de ganancias *f*; ~ **report** FIN balance de resultados *m*; ~ **test** TAX comprobación de beneficios *f*; ~ **yield** FIN rendimiento de ganancias *m*, STOCK tasa de rendimiento *f*

earphone *n* GEN COMM auricular *m*

earpiece *n* S&M mancheta *f*

earthquake: ~ **insurance** *n* INS seguro contra seísmos *m*

ease[1]**:** ~ **of handling** *n* TRANSP facilidad de manejo *f*

ease[2] *vt* ECON *credit controls* facilitar, *economic policy* suavizar, GEN COMM facilitar

ease off *vi* GEN COMM *demand* bajar gradualmente

easement *n* LAW, PROP servidumbre *f*

EASI *abbr* (*European Association for Shipping Information*) TRANSP Asociación Europea para Información de Transporte Marítimo *f*

easing *n* ECON *of policy*, POL moderación *f*; ~ **of capital market** STOCK expansión de mercado de capitales *f*

East: ~ **Caribbean Common Market** *n* (*ECCM*) ECON, POL Mercado Común del Caribe Oriental (*MCCO*); ~ **European Trade Council** *n* IMP/EXP Consejo de Comercio del Este de Europa *m*

Eastern: ~ **Bloc** *n* POL bloque del Este *m*; ~ **Europe** *n* POL Europa del Este *f*; ~ **European Time** *n* (*EET*) GEN COMM horario de Europa Oriental *m*; ~ **Standard Time** *n* (*EST*) GEN COMM hora estándar del este *f*

easy: ~ **money** *n* ECON dinero abundante *m*; ~ **money policy** *n* ECON política monetaria expansiva *f*; ~ **option** *n* MGMNT opción fácil *f*; ~ **payments** *n pl* BANK facilidades de pago *f pl*; ~ **rider** *n* ECON usuario(-a) de un servicio sin pagar *m*; ~ **terms** *n pl* BANK facilidades de pago *f pl*

eat into *vt* GEN COMM *savings, reserves* correr

EAT *abbr BrE* (*Employment Appeal Tribunal*) HRM tribunal de apelación para asuntos laborales, ≈ Tribunal Constitucional *m* (*Esp*)

ebb: ~ **tide** *n* TRANSP marea menguante *f*

EBRD *abbr* (*European Bank for Reconstruction and Development*) BANK, ECON BERD (*Banco Europeo para Reconstrucción y Desarrollo*)

EBU *abbr* (*European Broadcasting Union*) COMMS, MEDIA UER (*Unión Europea de Radiodifusión*)

EC *abbr obs* (*European Community*) ECON, POL CE (*obs*) (*Comunidad Europea*)

ECB *abbr* (*European Central Bank*) BANK, ECON, POL BCE (*Banco Central Europeo*)

ECCM *abbr* (*East Caribbean Common Market*) ECON, POL MCCO (*Mercado Común del Caribe Oriental*)

ECDC *abbr* (*Economic Cooperation among Developing Countries*) ECON, POL Cooperación Económica entre Países en Desarrollo *f*

ECE *abbr* (*Economic Commission for Europe*) ECON, POL CEPE (*Comisión Económica para Europa*)

ECG *abbr* (*European Cooperation Grouping*) ECON, POL ACE (*Agrupación de Cooperación Europea*)

ECGD *abbr* (*Export Credit Guarantee Department*) IMP/EXP departamento de garantía de créditos a la exportación

echelon *n* HRM escalón *m*

ECI *abbr* (*export consignment identification*) IMP/EXP identificación de remesa de exportación *f*

ECLA *abbr* (*Economic Commission for Latin America*) ECON, POL Comisión Económica para América Latina *f*

ECM *abbr* (*European Mercantile Exchange*) STOCK Bolsa Mercantil Europea *f*

ECMT: ~ **permit** *n* TRANSP *road haulage* permiso ECMT *m*

eco: ~ **audit and management system** *n* ENVIR sistema de gestión y auditoría ecológica *m*

ECOCOM *abbr* (*Economic Commission for Europe for Trade and Technology Division*) ECON, POL División de la Comisión Económica Europea de Comercio Internacional y Tecnología *f*

ECOFIN *abbr* (*European Community Finance Ministers*) ECON, POL ECOFIN (*Consejo Europeo de los Ministros de Finanzas*)

ecolabeling *AmE see* **ecolabelling** *BrE*

ecolabelling *n BrE* ENVIR etiquetado ecológico *m*, etiquetado ecologista *m*

ecological[1] *adj* ENVIR ecológico

ecological[2]: ~ **character** *n* ENVIR, GEN COMM carácter ecológico *m*; ~ **indicator** *n* ENVIR, GEN COMM indicador ecológico *m*

ecology *n* ENVIR, GEN COMM ecología *f*

econometric *adj* ECON, GEN COMM econométrico

econometrician *n* ECON, GEN COMM econometrista *mf*

econometrics *n* ECON, GEN COMM econometría *f*

economic[1] *adj* ECON económico

economic[2]: ~ **activity** *n* ECON actividad económica *f*; ~ **advancement** *n* GEN COMM avance económico *m*; ~ **adviser** *n* ECON, POL asesor(a) económico(-a) *m,f*; ~ **affairs** *n pl* ECON asuntos económicos *m*; ~ **agent** *n* ECON agente económico(-a) *m,f*; ~ **aid** *n* BANK, ECON, MGMNT ayuda económica *f*; ~ **analysis** *n* ECON, FIN análisis económico *m*; ~ **appraisal** *n* ECON evaluación económica *f*; ~ **austerity** *n* ECON austeridad económica *f*; ~ **base** *n* ECON base económica *f*; ~ **batch quantity** *n* ECON cantidad económica por lotes *f*; ~ **batch size** *n*

IND tamaño económico de lote *m*; ~ **benefit** *n* ECON beneficio económico *m*; ~ **boom** *n* ECON, POL auge económico *m*, boom económico *m*; ~ **capacity** *n* ACC, BANK, ECON, GEN COMM capacidad económica *f*; ~ **climate** *n* ECON, GEN COMM, POL clima económico *m*; ~ **conditions** *n pl* ECON condiciones económicas *f pl*; ~ **conjuncture** *n* ECON, GEN COMM, POL coyuntura económica *f*; ~ **conservation** *n* ENVIR conservación económica *f*; ~ **cost** *n* ECON, FIN coste económico *m* (*Esp*), costo económico *m* (*AmL*); ~ **crime** *n* ECON, LAW delito económico *m*; ~ **criteria** *n pl* ECON criterios económicos *m pl*; ~ **cycle** *n* ECON ciclo económico *m*; ~ **data** *n* ECON datos económicos *m pl*; ~ **depreciation** *n* ECON *real estate*, PROP depreciación económica *f*; ~ **development** *n* ECON, POL desarrollo económico *m*; ~ **devolution** *n* ECON devolución económica *f*; ~ **disaster** *n* ECON desastre económico; ~ **disequilibrium** *n* ECON desequilibrio económico *m*; ~ **efficiency** *n* ECON, ENVIR eficiencia económica *f*; ~ **expansion** *n* ECON, POL expansión económica *f*; ~ **federalism** *n* ECON, HRM, POL federalismo económico *m*; ~ **fluctuation** *n* ECON, GEN COMM fluctuación económica *f*; ~ **forecasting** *n* ECON previsión económica *f*; ~ **framework** *n* ECON entorno económico *m*; ~ **freedom** *n* ECON, POL libertad económica *f*; ~ **geography** *n* ECON geografía económica *f*; ~ **good** *n* ECON bien económico *m*; ~ **grants** *n pl* ECON concesiones económicas *f pl*; ~ **growth** *n* ECON crecimiento económico *m*; ~ **growth rate** *n* ECON índice de crecimiento económico *m*; ~ **incentive** *n* ECON incentivo económico *m*; ~ **incidence** *n* TAX incidencia económica *f*; ~ **indicator** *n* ECON, POL *econometrics* indicador económico *m*; ~ **institution** *n* ECON institución económica *f*; ~ **integration** *n* GEN COMM integración económica *f*; ~ **intelligence** *n* ECON inteligencia económica *f*; ~ **journal** *n* ECON, MEDIA periódico económico *m*, revista económica *f*; ~ **law** *n* ECON, LAW legislación económica *f*, ley económica *f*; ~ **life** *n* ACC, ECON vida económica *f*, FIN vida útil *f*, S&M vida económica *f*; ~ **loss** *n* ECON pérdida económica *f*; ~ **manufacturing quality** *n* IND calidad de fabricación económica *f*; ~ **manufacturing quantity** *n* ECON, IND, MGMNT cantidad de fabricación económica *f*, valoración de la economía industrial *f*; ~ **method** *n* ECON método económico *m*; ~ **methodology** *n* ECON metodología económica *f*; ~ **mission** *n* ECON, MGMNT misión económica *f*; ~ **model** *n* ECON modelo económico *m*; ~ **news** *n* ECON, MEDIA noticias económicas *f pl*; ~ **obsolescence** *n* ECON obsolescencia económica *f*; ~ **order quantity** *n* (*EOQ*) ECON, MATH cantidad de orden económico *f*, valoración del orden económico *f*; ~ **paradigm** *n* ECON paradigma económico *m*; ~ **pattern** *n* ECON esquema económico *m*; ~ **planning** *n* ECON, ENVIR, POL planificación económica *f*; ~ **planning unit** *n* ECON unidad de planificación económica *f*; ~ **position** *n* ECON posición económica *f*; ~ **price** *n* S&M precio económico *m*; ~ **profit** *n* ECON beneficio económico *m*; ~ **programming** *n* ECON programación económica *f*; ~ **prospects** *n pl* ECON perspectivas de la coyuntura económica *f pl*, POL expectativas económicas *f pl*; ~ **reform** *n* ECON, POL reforma económica *f*; ~ **rent** *n* ECON renta diferencial *f*; ~ **reports** *n pl* ECON informes económicos *m pl*; ~ **research** *n* ECON investigación económica *f*; ~ **resources** *n pl* ECON recursos económicos *m pl*; ~ **sanction** *n* ECON, POL sanción económica *f*; ~ **section** *n* MEDIA *of newspaper* sección económica *f*; **~ situation** *n* ECON, GEN COMM, POL coyuntura económica *f*, situación económica *f*; **~ slowdown** *n* ECON estancamiento económico *m*, GEN COMM contracción de la economía *f*, IND estancamiento del mercado *m*; **~ stability** *n* ECON estabilización económica *f*; **~ strategy** *n* ECON, POL estrategia económica *f*; **~ structure** *n* ECON, POL estructura económica *f*; **~ summit** *n* ECON, POL cumbre económica *f*; **~ system** *n* ECON, POL sistema económico *m*; **~ theory** *n* ECON, GEN COMM teoría económica *f*; **~ transaction cost** *n* ECON coste de transacción económica *m* (*Esp*), costo de transacción económica *m* (*AmL*); **~ trend** *n* ECON, GEN COMM, POL coyuntura económica *f*, tendencia económica *f*; **~ union** *n* ECON, POL unión económica *f*; **~ value** *n* ECON valor económico *m*; **~ viability** *n* ECON, FIN viabilidad económica *f*; **~ weather** *n* ECON, GEN COMM, POL clima económico *m*; **~ welfare** *n* WEL bienestar económico *m*; **~ well-being** *n* ECON, POL bienestar económico *m*

Economic: **~ Commission for Europe** *n* (*ECE*) ECON, POL Comisión Económica para Europa *f* (*CEPE*); **~ Commission for Europe for Trade and Technology Division** *n* (*ECOCOM*) ECON, POL División de la Comisión Económica Europea de Comercio Internacional y Tecnología *f*; **~ Commission for Latin America** *n* (*ECLA*) ECON, POL Comisión Económica para América Latina *f*; **~ Commission for Western Asia** *n* (*ECWA*) ECON, POL Comisión Económica para Asia Occidental *f* (*CEPAO*); **~ Community of West African States** *n* (*ECOWAS*) ECON, POL Comunidad Económica de Estados Africanos Occidentales *f* (*CEDEAO*); **~ Cooperation among Developing Countries** *n* (*ECDC*) ECON, POL Cooperación Económica entre Países en Desarrollo *f*; **~ Cooperation for Africa** *n* ECON Cooperación Económica para África *f*; **~ and Monetary Union** *n* ECON, POL Unión Económica y Monetaria *f*; **~ and Social Committee** *n* (*ESC*) ECON, WEL Comité Económico y Social *m*; **~ and Social Council** *n* (*ECOSOC*) ECON Consejo Económico y Social *m* (*ECOSOC*); **~ Trends Annual Survey** *n* BrE (*ETAS*) ECON *econometrics* estudio anual de la evolución económica *m*

economical[1] *adj* GEN COMM económico

economical[2]: **~ use of resources** *n* ECON uso económico de los recursos *m*

economically[1] *adv* ECON, FIN, S&M económicamente

economically[2]: **~ backward area** *n* ECON, POL área económicamente subdesarrollada *f*, área retrasada económicamente *f*

economics *n* BANK, POL, WEL economía *f*; **~ as rhetoric** ECON la economía como retórica *f*; **~ and psychology** ECON, WEL economía y psicología *f*

economies: **~ of scale** *n pl* ECON economías de escala *f pl*

economism *n* ECON, POL economismo *m*

economist *n* ECON, POL economista *mf*

Economist: **~ Intelligence Unit** *n* (*EIU*) ECON Unidad de Inteligencia Económica *f*

economize **1.** *vt* GEN COMM economizar; **2.** *vi* GEN COMM economizar

economy *n* BANK, POL, WEL economía *f*; **~ of abundance** ECON economía de la abundancia *f*; **~ class** LEIS, TRANSP clase económica *f*; **~ fare** LEIS tarifa económica *f*; **~ flight** LEIS, TRANSP vuelo económico *m*; **~ pack**

GEN COMM paquete económico *m*; **~ of size** ECON, IND economía de escala *f*, economía de tamaño *f*; **~ size** GEN COMM, S&M tamaño económico *m*; **~ thrust** ECON impulso económico *m*; **~ ticket** LEIS billete económico *m*

ECOSOC *abbr* (*Economic and Social Council*) ECON ECOSOC (*Consejo Económico y Social*)

ecosystem *n* ENVIR ecosistema *m*

ecotoxicological *adj* ENVIR ecotoxicológico

ECOWAS *abbr* (*Economic Community of West African States*) ECON, POL CEDEAO (*Comunidad Económica de Estados Africanos Occidentales*)

ECP *abbr* (*Eurocommercial paper*) STOCK efectos comerciales en eurodivisas *m pl*

ECPD *abbr* (*export cargo packing declaration*) IMP/EXP, TRANSP declaración de embalaje de carga para exportación *f*

ECPS *abbr* (*Environment and Consumer Protection Service*) ENVIR, WEL Servicio de Protección al Consumidor y al Medio Ambiente *m*

ECR *abbr* (*Exchange Control Rate*) ECON tasa del control de los tipos de cambio *f*

ECSC *abbr* (*European Coal and Steel Community*) ECON, INS CECA (*Comunidad Europea del Carbón y el Acero*)

ECSI *abbr* (*export cargo shipping instruction*) IMP/EXP, TRANSP instrucción de expedición de carga para exportación *f*

ECU *abbr* (*European Currency Unit*) ECON, POL ECU (*Unidad Monetaria Europea*)

ECWA *abbr* (*Economic Commission for Western Asia*) ECON, POL CEPAO (*Comisión Económica para Asia Occidental*)

ed. *abbr* (*edition*) COMP, GEN COMM edición *f*

Ed. *abbr* (*editor's note*) GEN COMM N.R. (*nota de la redacción*)

ED *abbr* ECON (*Eurodollar*) ED (*eurodólar*), IND (*engine designer*) diseñador(a) de motores *m,f*, STOCK (*Eurodollar*) ED (*eurodólar*)

EDF *abbr* (*European Development Fund*) ECON, POL Fondo Europeo de Desarrollo *m*

edge up *vi* ECON *prices* aumentar lentamente, subir poco a poco

edge: **at the cutting ~** *phr* GEN COMM de vanguardia; **have the ~ over sb** *phr* GEN COMM llevar ventaja a alguien

Edgeworth: **~ Box** *n* ECON *theory* caja de Edgeworth *f*

EDI *abbr* COMMS (*electronic document interchange*) intercambio electrónico de documentos *m*, COMP (*electronic data interchange*) intercambio electrónico de datos *m*

edict *n* GEN COMM auto *m*

edit[1]: **~ mode** *n* COMP modalidad de edición *f*, modo edición *m*

edit[2] *vt* COMP *data, document, text* editar, GEN COMM redactar

edit out *vt* GEN COMM suprimir, *párrafo* eliminar

edited[1] *adj* COMP *data, documents, text* editado

edited[2]: **~ return** *n* TAX declaración impresa *f*

editing: **~-out** *n* GEN COMM eliminación *f*

edition *n* (*ed.*) COMP, GEN COMM edición *f*

editor *n* COMP *software* editor(a) *m,f*; **~ in chief** HRM,

MEDIA *print* redactor(a) jefe(-a) *m,f;* ~**'s note** *(Ed.)* GEN COMM nota de la redacción *f (N.R.)*

editorial *n* GEN COMM, MEDIA artículo de fondo *m*, editorial *m;* ~ **advertisement** MEDIA, S&M anuncio de publicidad editorial *m;* ~ **advertising** S&M publicidad de la redacción *f;* ~ **board** MEDIA consejo de redacción *m;* ~ **column** MEDIA, S&M columna editorial *f;* ~ **matter** S&M material editorial *m;* ~ **mention** S&M mención editorial *f;* ~ **publicity** MEDIA, S&M publicidad editorial *f;* ~ **staff** GEN COMM redacción *f;* ~ **write-up** S&M reportaje editorial *m*

editorialist *n* GEN COMM editorialista *mf*

editorship *n* GEN COMM redacción *f*

EDP *abbr (electronic data processing)* COMP PED *(procesamiento electrónico de datos)*

educated *adj* HRM culto

education *n* WEL educación *f;* ~ **credit** TAX deducción por gastos de educación *f*

educational: ~ **advertising** *n* S&M publicidad didáctica *f*, publicidad informativa *f;* ~ **background** *n* WEL antecedentes educativos *m pl;* ~ **development** *n* GEN COMM, WEL desarrollo educativo *m;* ~ **endowment** *n* INS seguro para gastos de estudios *m;* ~ **establishment** *n* WEL establecimiento docente *m;* ~ **institution** *n* WEL institución educativa *f;* ~ **organization** *n* TAX, WEL organización educativa *f*

EEA *abbr* BANK *(Exchange Equalization Account)* cuenta de compensación de cambios *f*, cuenta de igualación de tipo de cambio *f,* IND *(Electronic Engineering Association)* sociedad de ingenieros en electrónica

EEB *abbr (European Environment Bureau)* ENVIR, POL Oficina Europea para el Medio Ambiente *f*

EEC *abbr obs (European Economic Community)* ECON, POL CEE *(obs) (Comunidad Económica Europea)*

EEIG *abbr (European Economic Interest Grouping)* ECON, POL Agrupación Europea de Intereses Económicos *f*

EEOC *abbr (Equal Employment Opportunity Commission)* HRM comisión que promueve la igualdad de oportunidades sin distinción de raza, credo ni orientación sexual

EET *abbr (Eastern European Time)* GEN COMM horario de Europa Oriental *m*

EF *abbr (European Foundation)* POL Fundación Europea *f*

effect[1] *n* ECON, GEN COMM efecto *m;* ◆ **with ~ from** *(w.e.f.)* GEN COMM efectivo desde el día

effect[2] *vt* GEN COMM *settlement* efectuar

effective[1] *adj* COMP efectivo, GEN COMM eficaz

effective[2]: ~ **annual rate of interest** *n* BANK, FIN tasa anual equivalente *f (TAE);* ~ **control** *n* FIN, GEN COMM control efectivo *m;* ~ **cover** *n* S&M *of advertisement* cobertura eficaz *f;* ~ **date** *n* GEN COMM fecha de entrada en vigor *f;* ~ **debt** *n* BANK deuda vigente *f;* ~ **demand** *n* ECON, S&M demanda efectiva *f;* ~ **exchange rate** *n* ECON, FIN *international* tipo de cambio efectivo *m;* ~ **funding rate** *n* STOCK *of futures* tipo de provisión efectiva de fondos *m;* ~ **horsepower** *n (ehp)* IND potencia efectiva en caballos *f;* ~ **interest date** *n* TAX fecha del interés efectivo *f;* ~ **interest rate** *n* BANK tasa de interés efectivo *f;* ~ **management** *n* HRM, MGMNT administración efectiva *f*, gestión efectiva *f;* ~ **net worth** *n* ACC activo neto real *m;* ~ **rate** *n* ACC tasa efectiva *f*, tipo efectivo *m;* ~ **rate of assistance** *n* ECON proporción efectiva de asistencia *f;* ~ **rate of protection** *n* ECON, IND índice efectivo de protección *m*, proporción efectiva de protección *f;* ~ **tax rate** *n* TAX tipo

impositivo efectivo *m;* ~ **yield** *n* STOCK rendimiento real *m*

effectively[1]: ~ **closed** *adj* TRANSP *packing* cerrado eficazmente

effectively[2] *adv* GEN COMM efectivamente

effects: no ~ *phr (NE)* GEN COMM sin efectos

effectual: ~ **demand** *n* ECON, S&M demanda efectiva *f*

efficiency *n* GEN COMM eficacia *f*, eficiencia *f;* ~ **agreement** HRM acuerdo de eficiencia *m*, contrato de eficiencia *m;* ~ **audit** ACC auditoría de eficiencia *f;* ~ **engineer** MGMNT ingeniero(-a) en eficiencia *m,f;* ~ **ratio** ECON, ENVIR proporción de eficiencia *f;* ~ **real wage** ECON, HRM salario real eficiente *m*, salario real por eficiencia *m;* ~ **variance** FIN variación en eficiencia *f;* ~ **wage** ECON, HRM salario eficiente *m*, salario por eficiencia *m*

efficient[1] *adj* COMP, GEN COMM eficiente

efficient[2]: ~ **allocation** *n* ECON asignación eficiente *f;* ~ **estimator** *n* ECON estimador eficiente *m;* ~ **job mobility** *n* ECON, HRM movilidad laboral eficiente *f*, rotación de puestos *f;* ~ **market** *n* ECON *theory* mercado eficiente *m;* ~ **portfolio** *n* STOCK cartera eficiente *f*

effluence *n* ENVIR desagüe *m*

effluent *n* ENVIR emisario *m;* ~ **fee** ECON tarifa sobre las aguas residuales *f,* ENVIR tasa de efluentes *f*

EFL *abbr (external financing limit)* FIN límite de financiación externa *m*

EFT *abbr (electronic funds transfer)* ACC, BANK, FIN transferencia de fondos electrónica *f*

EFTA *abbr (European Free Trade Association)* ECON, POL AELC *(Asociación Europea de Libre Comercio)*

EFTPOS *abbr (electronic funds transfer at point of sale)* BANK, S&M transferencia de fondos electrónica en punto de venta *f*

EFTS *abbr (electronic funds transfer system)* BANK sistema electrónico de transferencia de fondos *m*

e.g. *abbr (for example, exempli gratia)* GEN COMM p. ej. *(por ejemplo)*

egalitarianism *n* POL igualitarismo *m*

EGM *abbr (extraordinary general meeting)* GEN COMM, MGMNT junta general extraordinaria *f*

ehp *abbr (effective horsepower)* IND potencia efectiva en caballos *f*

EI *abbr (employee involvement)* HRM implicación de los empleados *f*, implicación de los trabajadores *f*

EIB *abbr (European Investment Bank)* BANK, ECON BEI *(Banco Europeo de Inversiones)*

EIC *abbr (Energy Industries Council)* IND consejo de industrias de generación de energía

eigenprice *n* ECON precio propio *m*

EIM *abbr (European Interprofessional Market)* STOCK mercado interprofesional europeo *m*

EITZ *abbr (English Inshore Traffic Zone)* TRANSP *shipping* zona de tráfico del interior de Inglaterra

EIU *abbr (Economist Intelligence Unit)* ECON Unidad de Inteligencia Económica *f*

eject *vt* COMP *card, disk* expulsar

ejectment *n* AmE LAW *property* diligencias de lanzamiento *f pl,* PROP desahucio *m*

ejusdem generis *phr* GEN COMM del mismo género

elapse *vi* ECON transcurrir

elapsed: ~ **time** *n* COMP tiempo transcurrido *m*

elastic: ~ **demand** *n* ECON, S&M demanda elástica *f*; ~ **income** *n jarg* ECON renta elástica *f*; ~ **supply** *n* ECON, S&M oferta elástica *f*, suministro elástico *m*

elasticity *n* ECON elasticidad *f*; ~ **of anticipation** ECON elasticidad de la previsión *f*; ~ **of demand** ECON, S&M elasticidad de la demanda *f*; ~ **of demand and supply** ECON, S&M elasticidad de la demanda y del suministro *f*, elasticidad de la oferta y la demanda *f*; ~ **of expectations** ECON elasticidad de expectativas *f*; ~ **of substitution** ECON elasticidad de sustitución *f*; ~ **of supply** ECON, S&M elasticidad de la oferta *f*, elasticidad del suministro *f*

ELB *abbr* (*export licensing branch*) IMP/EXP oficina de licencias de exportación *f*

ELEC *abbr* (*European League for Economic Cooperation*) ECON Liga Europea para la Cooperación Económica *f*

elect *vt* POL elegir; ◆ ~ **sb to the board** GEN COMM elegir a alguien para la junta

elected office *n* POL cargo elegido *m*

election *n* GEN COMM, MGMNT, POL, TAX elección *f*; ~ **campaign** POL campaña electoral *f*; ~ **meeting** ACC, FIN, GEN COMM, MGMNT asamblea electoral *f*; ~ **result** GEN COMM, MGMNT, POL resultado electoral *m*

elective[1] *adj* GEN COMM, MGMNT, POL electivo

elective[2]: ~ **income** *n* ACC, TAX ingresos facultativos *m pl*, ingresos opcionales *m pl*

electoral: ~ **college** *n* AmE POL colegio electoral *m*; ~ **register** *n* GEN COMM, POL censo electoral *m*, registro electoral *m*; ~ **roll** *n* GEN COMM, POL censo electoral *m*, registro electoral *m*

electorate *n* GEN COMM *politics* electorado *m*

electric: ~ **power** *n* IND energía eléctrica *f*; ~ **train** *n* TRANSP tren eléctrico *m*

electrical: ~ **appliance** *n* GEN COMM aparato eléctrico *m*; ~ **engineering** *n* IND ingeniería eléctrica *f*; ~ **damage clause** *n* INS *property insurance* cláusula que excluye los daños por electricidad *f*; ~ **propulsion builder** *n* TRANSP *marine engine* constructor de propulsión eléctrica *m*

Electrical: ~ **Trades Union** *n* (*ETU*) HRM Sindicato de Electricistas *m*, Sindicato de Gremios Eléctricos *m*

electricity: ~ **consumption** *n* ENVIR, IND consumo de electricidad *m*; ~ **generation** *n* BrE (*cf power generation AmE*) IND generación de electricidad *f*; ~ **industry** *n* ECON, IND industria de la electricidad *f*; ~ **sector** *n* IND sector de electricidad *m*; ~ **support industry** *n* IND sector de apoyo a la electricidad *m*

electrification *n* TRANSP *of railways* electrificación *f*

electronic: ~ **accounting system** *n* ACC, COMP contabilidad computadorizada *f AmL*, contabilidad informatizada *Esp f*, COMP sistema de contabilidad computadorizado *f* (*AmL*), sistema de contabilidad informatizado *m* (*Esp*); ~ **bank** *n* BANK banco electrónico *m*; ~ **banking** *n* BANK banca electrónica *f*; ~ **banking service** *n* BANK servicio de banca electrónica *m*; ~ **calculator** *n* COMP calculadora electrónica *f*; ~ **component** *n* COMP *hardware* componente electrónico *m*; ~ **data interchange** *n* (*EDI*) COMMS, COMP intercambio electrónico de datos *m*; ~ **data processing** *n* (*EDP*) COMP procesamiento electrónico de datos *m* (*PED*); ~ **document interchange** *n* (*EDI*) COMMS intercambio de documentos electrónicos *m*; ~ **engineer** *n* GEN COMM técnico(-a) electrónico(-a) *m,f*; ~ **funds transfer** *n* (*EFT*) ACC, BANK, FIN transferencia de fondos electrónica *f*; ~ **funds transfer at point of sale** *n* (*EFTPOS*) BANK, S&M transferencia de fondos electrónica en punto de venta *f*; ~ **funds transfer system** *n* (*EFTS*) BANK sistema electrónico de transferencia de fondos *m*; ~ **home banking** *n* BANK banca domiciliaria electrónica *f*; ~ **mail** *n* (*e-mail*) COMMS, COMP *network* correo electrónico *m*; ~ **media** *n* S&M medios electrónicos *m pl*; ~ **news gathering** *n* GEN COMM periodismo electrónico *m*; ~ **office** *n* ADMIN, COMP, GEN COMM oficina electrónica *f*; ~ **payment** *n* BANK, FIN pago electrónico *m*; ~ **payment terminal** *n* (*EPT*) GEN COMM terminal de pago electrónico *m*; ~ **point of sale** *n* (*EPOS*) GEN COMM punto de venta electrónico *m*; ~ **posting board** *n* STOCK pantalla de precios electrónica *f*; ~ **publishing** *n* COMP, MEDIA publicación electrónica *f*; ~ **shopping** *n* COMP, GEN COMM compra electrónica *f*; ~ **typewriter** *n* ADMIN máquina de escribir electrónica *f*

Electronic: ~ **Engineering Association** *n* BrE (*EEA*) IND sociedad de ingenieros en electrónica

electronically: ~ **programmable read only memory** *n* (*EPROM*) COMP memoria sólo de lectura programable electrónicamente *f*

electronics *n* IND electrónica *f*

electrostatic[1] *adj* COMP electrostático

electrostatic[2]: ~ **printer** *n* COMP *hardware* impresora electrostática *f*

electrotype *n* S&M electrotipo *m*

element *n* GEN COMM *factor* elemento *m*; ~ **of risk** GEN COMM elemento de riesgo *m*

elementary: ~ **loss** *n* INS pérdida elemental *f*

elephant: ~**'s foot** *n* TRANSP *fixed lashing* pie de elefante *m*

elevator: ~ **liability insurance** *n* AmE (*cf lift liability insurance BrE*) INS seguro contra accidentes de un ascensor *m*

eligibility *n* GEN COMM idoneidad *f*, POL elegibilidad *f*, TAX elegibilidad *f*, habilitación *f*; ~ **requirement** GEN COMM requisito para ser convocado *m*; ~ **rule** TAX norma de la elegibilidad *f*; ~ **test** BANK prueba de capacidad *f*

eligible[1] *adj* BANK aceptable, capacitado, elegible, idóneo, GEN COMM aceptable; ◆ ~ **to adjudicate** LAW con derecho a ajudicar *phr*; **be ~ for** GEN COMM *grants, subsidies* poder optar a, tener derecho a; ~ **for retirement** HRM habilitado para el retiro; ~ **for tax relief** TAX desgravable

eligible[2]: ~ **asset** *n* FIN activo elegible *m*; ~ **bills** *n pl BrE* BANK letras aceptables para el redescuento *f pl*; ~ **expense** *n* TAX gasto computable *m*; ~ **individual** *n* TAX individuo computable *m*; ~ **paper** *n* BANK valores negociables *m pl*

eliminate *vt* GEN COMM eliminar

ellipsis *n* MEDIA puntos suspensivos *m pl*

em: ~ **dash** *n* MEDIA *typography* cuadratín *m*; ~ **space** *n* MEDIA *typography* espacio de la eme *f*

EMA *abbr* (*European Monetary Agreement*) GEN COMM, POL Tratado Monetario Europeo *m*

e-mail[1] *abbr* (*electronic mail*) COMMS, COMP correo electrónico *m*

e-mail[2]: ~ **address** *n* COMMS, COMP casilla electrónica *f*, dirección electrónica *f*

emancipation *n* LAW, POL emancipación *f*

embargo *n* TRANSP embargo *m*

embark on *vi* GEN COMM *course of action* embarcarse en

embarkation *n* TRANSP *of passengers* embarque *m*; ~ **card** GEN COMM tarjeta de embarque *f*

embassy *n* GEN COMM, POL embajada *f*

embed *vt* COMP intercalar

embedded[1] *adj* COMP intercalado

embedded[2]: ~ **command** *n* COMP comando integrado *m*; ~ **option** *n* STOCK opción intercalada *f*

embezzle *vt* FIN, GEN COMM, LAW desfalcar

embezzlement *n* FIN, GEN COMM, LAW desfalco *m*

embezzler *n* FIN, GEN COMM, LAW desfalcador(a) *m,f*

embodied: ~ **technical progress** *n* IND avance técnico incorporado *m*

embossing *n* S&M estampación *f*

EMCF *abbr* (*European Monetary Cooperation Fund*) ECON, POL FECOM (*Fondo Europeo para la Cooperación Monetaria*)

emergency *n* (*emy*) GEN COMM emergencia *f*; ~ **aid** ECON, POL ayuda de emergencia *f*; ~ **exit** HRM salida de emergencia *f*; ~ **powers** *n pl* HRM atribuciones de emergencia *f pl*; ~ **reconstruction loan** (*ERL*) BANK, ECON, FIN préstamo de reconstrucción de emergencia *m*; ~ **service** WEL servicio de emergencia *m*

Emerging: ~ **Markets Growth Fund** *n* (*EMGF*) ECON Fondo de Desarrollo para Mercados Emergentes *m*; ~ **Markets Investment Fund** *n* (*EMIF*) FIN, POL Fondo de Inversión para Mercados Emergentes *m*

EMGF *abbr* (*Emerging Markets Growth Fund*) FIN Fondo de Desarrollo para Mercados Emergentes *m*

EMI *abbr* (*European Monetary Institute*) ECON, POL IME (*Instituto Monetario Europeo*)

EMIF *abbr* (*Emerging Markets Investment Fund*) ECON, POL Fondo de Inversión para Mercados Emergentes *m*

eminent: ~ **domain** *n* PROP derecho de expropiación *m*

emission *n* ENVIR *of gases* emisión *f*; ~ **charges** *n pl* ENVIR precio de emisión *m*; ~ **fee** ENVIR tasa de emisión *f*; ~ **limit** ENVIR límite de emisión *m*; ~ **reductions banking** ENVIR banca de reducción de emisión *f*; ~ **standard** ENVIR estándar de emisión *m*

emotional: ~ **appeal** *n* S&M *of product, advertisement* atractivo emocional *m*

emphasis *n* GEN COMM acento *m*

emphasize *vt* GEN COMM enfatizar, poner énfasis sobre

emphatic *adj* GEN COMM categórico

empirical[1] *adj* ECON empírico

empirical[2]: ~ **study** *n* ECON estudio empírico *m*

empirics *n* ECON empírico *m*

employ *vt* GEN COMM, HRM *method* emplear

employable *adj* HRM capacitado para trabajar

employed *adj* GEN COMM empleado; ~**capital** *n* ACC, FIN capital en uso *m*

employee *n* HRM empleado(-a) *m,f*, trabajador(a) por cuenta ajena *m,f*; ~ **association** HRM asociación de empleados *f*; ~ **benefit** ACC, ECON, FIN, HRM beneficio adicional para los empleados *m*, ventaja para los empleados *f*; ~ **benefit plan** HRM plan de beneficios para los empleados *m*; ~ **'s buyout** GEN COMM, FIN compra de la empresa por los empleados *f*; ~ **communications** *n pl* HRM comunicaciones con los empleados *f pl*; ~ **contributions** *n pl* HRM aportaciones de los empleados *f pl*; ~ **counseling** *AmE*,

~ **counselling** *BrE* HRM asesoramiento a los empleados *m*; ~ **involvement** (*EI*) HRM *in organization's activities* implicación de los empleados *f*, implicación de los trabajadores *f*; ~ **involvement and participation** HRM *in organization, activities* participación e implicación de los empleados *f*, participación del trabajador *f*; ~**'s job history** HRM antecedentes laborales del empleado *m pl*; ~**'s liability** TAX responsabilidad del trabajador *f*; ~**-owned firm** MGMNT empresa que pertenece a los empleados *f*, empresa administrada por los obreros *f*; ~ **participation** HRM participación de los empleados *f*; ~ **pension plan** HRM, INS plan de pensión para los empleados *m*; ~ **profile** HRM perfil del empleado *m*; ~ **profit sharing** HRM participación de los empleados en los beneficios *f*; ~**s' profit sharing plan** HRM, STOCK plan de reparto de beneficios entre los empleados *m*; ~ **rate** *BrE* TAX *National Insurance* tipo de aportación de los asalariados *m*; ~ **ratio** HRM proporción de empleados *f*; ~ **relation** HRM relación con el personal *f*; ~ **retirement income security act** *AmE* HRM ley de garantía de pensiones a los trabajadores *f*; ~ **shareholding scheme** HRM, STOCK plan de participación accionaria de los empleados *m*; ~ **share ownership trust** (*ESOT*) STOCK trust de personal propietario de acciones; ~ **stock option** HRM, STOCK opción de compra de acciones para los empleados *f*; ~ **stock option plan** HRM, STOCK plan de opción de acciones para el personal *m*; ~ **stock ownership plan** (*ESOP*) HRM, STOCK plan de propiedad de acciones de los empleados *m*, plan de venta de acciones a empleados *m*; ~ **trust** TAX fideicomiso de empleados *m*

employees': ~ **commitment** *n* HRM *with the organization* compromiso de los empleados *m*; ~ **committee** *n* ACC, HRM comité de empleados *m*; ~ **provident fund** *n* ACC, HRM, WEL fondo de ayuda a los trabajadores *m*; ~ **stock purchase plan** *n* STOCK plan de compra de acciones por el personal de la compañía *m*

employer *n* HRM empresario(-a) *m,f*, patrón(a) *m,f*; ~**'s contribution** ACC, TAX cuota patronal *f*; ~ **express term** HRM condición expresa del empresario *f*; ~ **interference** HRM interferencia del empresario *f*; ~**'s occupational pension scheme** ACC, HRM, TAX plan de pensión laboral del empresario *m*; ~ **rate** TAX *National Insurance* porcentaje de contribución del empresario *m*, tipo de aportación del empresario *m*; ~**'s return** TAX declaración del empresario *f*, rendimiento del empresario *m*; ~ **taxation number** TAX número de identificación fiscal de la empresa *m*

employers': ~ **association** *n* HRM asociación patronal *f*; ~ **federation** *n* GEN COMM, HRM federación patronal *f*; ~ **legal obligation to fund** *n* HRM, LAW *pension* obligación legal de aportación de los empresarios *f*; ~ **liability coverage** *n* INS, LAW cobertura contra responsabilidad del empleador *f* (*AmL*), cobertura contra responsabilidad del empresario *f* (*Esp*)

employment *n* ECON, HRM, POL empleo *m*; ~ **agency** GEN COMM, HRM agencia de empleo *f*, agencia de trabajo *f*, oficina de colocaciones *f*, oficina de empleo *f*; ~ **bureau** GEN COMM, HRM agencia de empleo *f*, agencia de trabajo *f*, oficina de colocaciones *f*, oficina de empleo *f*; ~ **expenses** *n pl* GEN COMM gastos de empleados *m pl*; ~ **figure** ECON, POL indicador de empleo *m*; ~ **figures** *n pl* HRM, POL, WEL cifras de empleo *f pl*; ~ **function** ECON función de empleo *f*; ~ **income** ACC, TAX ingresos por empleo *m pl*; ~ **law** HRM, LAW, POL legislación laboral *f*, ley de empleo *f*, ley del trabajo *f*; ~ **multiplier** ECON multiplicador de empleo *m*; ~ **offer** HRM oferta de empleo *f*, oferta de trabajo *f*; ~ **office** *BrE* GEN COMM, HRM oficina de empleo *f*; ~ **record** HRM registro de empleo *m*; ~ **relationship** HRM *EU* relación de empleo *f*; ~ **situation** GEN COMM, HRM situación laboral *f*; ~ **tax** TAX impuesto sobre el empleo *m*; ~ **tax credit** TAX desgravación fiscal del empleo *f*; ~ **tax deduction** TAX deducción fiscal del empleo *f*; ~ **test** HRM *selection* prueba de selección *f*; ~ **training** (*ET*) HRM, WEL capacitación ocupacional *f* (*AmL*), formación ocupacional *f* (*Esp*); ◆ **on the ~ front** HRM en el ámbito del empleo

Employment: ~ **Act** *n BrE* (*EA*) HRM, LAW ley de empleo, ≈ Ley de Contrato de Trabajo *f* (*Esp*); ~ **Appeal Tribunal** *n BrE* (*EAT*) HRM, LAW tribunal de apelación para asuntos laborales, tribunalde apelación para la conciliación y el arbitraje ≈ Tribunal Constitucional *m* (*Esp*); ~ **Protection Act** *n* (*EPA*) LAW, WEL ley de protección del empleo; ~ **Protection Consolidation Act** *n* (*EPCA*) HRM, LAW ley de consolidación de protección del empleo; ~ **Retirement Income Security Act** *n* (*ERISA*) LAW, WEL ley de garantía de las pensiones por jubilación, ≈ Ley de Jubilación *f* (*Esp*); ~ **Service** *n BrE* HRM, WEL oficina gubernamental para el empleo, ≈ Instituto Nacional de Empleo *m* (*INEM*)

emporium *n* GEN COMM centro comercial *m*

empty *n* S&M envase vacío *m*; ~ **nester** *infrml* ECON persona sin cargas familiares *f*

empty out *vt* GEN COMM vaciar

EMS *abbr* (*European Monetary System*) ECON, POL SME (*Sistema Monetario Europeo*)

EMU *abbr* (*European Monetary Union*) ECON, POL UME (*Unión Monetaria Europea*)

emulate *vt* COMP *software, protocol*, GEN COMM emular

emulation *n* COMP emulación *f*; ~ **board** COMP tarjeta de emulación *f*; ~ **card** COMP tarjeta de emulación *f*; ~ **software** COMP programas de emulación *m pl*

emulator *n* COMP emulador *m*

emy *abbr* (*emergency*) GEN COMM emergencia *f*

enable *vt* COMP *hardware* encender, *software* activar

enabling: ~ **clause** *n* LAW cláusula de autorización *f*

enact *vt* LAW decretar, POL aprobar

enacted: ~ **by** *phr* LAW, TAX promulgado por

enactment *n* LAW estatuto *m*, POL aprobación *f*

encashable *adj* ACC, BANK convertible en efectivo

encashing: ~ **agent** *n* TAX inspector(a) recaudador(a) *m,f*

encashment *n* ACC, BANK cobro en efectivo *m*, cobro en metálico *m*; ~ **schedule** ACC tabla de encajes *f*

encl. *abbr* (*enclosed*) COMMS, GEN COMM adj. (*adjunto*)

enclave: ~ **economy** *n* ECON economía aislada *f*

enclose *vt* COMMS, GEN COMM adjuntar

enclosed[1] *adj* (*encl.*) COMMS, GEN COMM adjunto (*adj.*); ◆ ~ **copy of letter** COMMS, GEN COMM adjunta copia de la carta

enclosed[2]: ~ **dock** *n* TRANSP *shipping* dique cerrado *m*; ~ **document** *n* ADMIN, COMMS, GEN COMM anexo *m*, documento adjunto *m*; ~ **port** *n* TRANSP *shipping* puerto cerrado *m*

encode *vt* BANK, COMP poner en clave

encoding *n* BANK, COMMS, COMP cifrado *m*, codificado *m*

encompass *vt* GEN COMM abarcar

encourage *vt* ECON, GEN COMM, HRM fomentar, S&M incentivar

encouragement *n* ECON, GEN COMM, HRM fomento *m*, S&M incentivación *f*

encouraging *adj* GEN COMM alentador

encroach on *vt* LAW usurpar

encroachment *n* LAW intrusión *f*

encryption *n* BANK, COMMS cifrado *m*, COMP cifrado *m*, *programming language* codificación *f*

encumbered *adj* GEN COMM gravado, sujeto a gravamen

encumbrance *n* GEN COMM carga *f*, LAW *property* carga real *f*, gravamen *m*

end *n* GEN COMM, S&M fin *m*, final *m*; ~ **consumer** S&M consumidor(a) final *m,f*, usuario(-a) final *m,f*; ~ **of file** (*EOF*) COMP fin de archivo *m* (*FDA*); ~ **of financial year** ACC final de año contable *m*, final del ejercicio contable *m*; ~ **of message** (*EOM*) COMP fin de mensaje *m* (*FDM*); ~ **of month** ACC fin de mes *m*; ~**-of-line goods** *n pl* GEN COMM, S&M artículos de fin de serie *m pl*; ~**-of-file mark** COMP marca de fin de archivo *f*; ~**-of-month account** ACC, BANK cuenta de periodo mensual *f*; ~**-of-season sale** GEN COMM, S&M venta de fin de temporada *f*, venta de saldos *f*; ~ **product** GEN COMM producto final *m*; ~ **of programe** *AmE*, ~ **of programme** *BrE* HRM fin de programa *m*; ~ **result** GEN COMM resultado final *m*; ~ **of the taxation year** ACC, TAX cierre del año fiscal *m*; ~**-use goods** *n pl* IMP/EXP bienes de uso final *m pl*, bienes finales *m pl*; ~**-use trader** IMP/EXP comerciante(-a) de bienes finales *m,f*; ~ **user** GEN COMM consumidor(a) final *m,f*, usuario(-a) final *m,f*; ~**-user computing** COMP computación de usuario final *f*, informática de usuario final *f*; ◆ **at the top ~** GEN COMM *of scale* en el extremo superior

endanger *vt* GEN COMM arriesgar

endeavor *AmE see* endeavour *BrE*

endeavour *n BrE* GEN COMM esfuerzo *m*, intento *m*

endemic *adj* GEN COMM endémico

ending: ~ **balance** *n* ACC, BANK, FIN balance de cierre *m*, balance final *m*; ~ **inventory** *n* ACC inventario final *m*

endless: ~ **SWR sling** *n* TRANSP *cargo handling equipment* eslinga SWR sinfín *f*

endogenizing: ~ **the exogenous** *phr* ECON *econometrics* endogenizar lo exógeno

endogenous: ~ **factor** *n* ECON factor endógeno *m*; ~ **variable** *n* ECON *econometrics* variable endógena *f*

endorse *vt* BANK endosar, GEN COMM *employee* ayudar con un aval, *warrant* endosar; ◆ ~ **sb** GEN COMM ayudar a alguien con un aval

endorse back *vt* BANK contraendosar

endorsee *n* BANK, GEN COMM endosatario(-a) *m,f*

endorsement *n* GEN COMM endoso *m*, S&M *product* aprobación *f*; ~ **of a note** BANK, GEN COMM endoso de un pagaré *m*; ~ **stamp** BANK, GEN COMM sello de endoso *m*

endorser *n* BANK, GEN COMM endosante(-a) *m,f*

endowment *n* ACC dotación *f*, LAW *gift* donación *f*, TAX dotación *f*; ~ **assurance** INS seguro mixto *m*; ~ **effect** BANK efecto dotal *m*; ~ **fund** ACC, FIN, INS fondo de beneficiencia *m*; ~ **insurance** INS seguro de capital diferido *m*

ENEA *abbr* (*European Nuclear Energy Authority*) IND, POL Autoridad Europea de Energía Nuclear *f*

energy *n* IND energía *f*; ~ **conservation** ENVIR, IND conservación de la energía *f*; ~ **crisis** ENVIR, IND crisis energética *f*; ~ **efficiency** ENVIR, IND eficiencia de la energía *f*; ~ **management** ENVIR, IND, MGMNT dirección de energía *f*, gerencia de energía *f*; ~ **mutual fund** ENVIR, IND sociedad de inversiones energéticas *f*; ~ **recovery** ENVIR *recycling* recuperación de energía *f*; ~ **reserve** ENVIR, IND reserva energética *f*; ~ **resources** *n pl* ENVIR recursos energéticos *m pl*; ~ **source** ENVIR, GEN COMM, IND fuente energética *f*; ~ **supply** ENVIR, GEN COMM, IND suministro de energía *m*; ~ **system** IND sistema energético *m*; ~ **tax credit** IND, TAX deducción fiscal para la energía *f*

Energy: ~ **Industries Council** *n* (*EIC*) IND consejo de industrias de generación de energía

ENF *abbr* (*enforcement*) LAW aplicación de la ley *f*, cumplimiento de la ley *m*

enforce *vt* GEN COMM *one's rights* ejercer, LAW hacer cumplir

enforceable *adj* LAW ejecutable, ejecutorio

enforced[1] *adj* GEN COMM coercitivo

enforced[2]: ~ **collection** *n* GEN COMM cobro coercitivo *m*

enforcement *n* (*ENF*) LAW aplicación de la ley *f*, cumplimiento de la ley *m*; ~ **action** TAX acción coercitiva *f*; ~ **order** GEN COMM orden ejecutoria *f*; ~ **procedure** GEN COMM procedimiento ejecutorio *m*

enfranchise *vt* GEN COMM franquear

ENG *abbr* (*engine*) TRANSP motor *m*

engage *vt* HRM *staff* contratar; ◆ ~ **in a campaign** POL emprender una campaña

engaged[1] *adj* COMMS *telephone line*, COMP *tone or signal*, GEN COMM ocupado; ◆ **be** ~ **in** MGMNT *activity* estar comprometido en

engaged[2]: ~ **signal** *n BrE* COMMS *telephone* señal de ocupación *f*, señal de ocupado *f*; ~ **tone** *n BrE* COMMS *telephone* tono de ocupado *m*

engagement *n* GEN COMM, HRM contratación *f*

Engel: ~ **coefficient** *n* ECON coeficiente de Engel *m*; ~**'s Law** *n* ECON Ley de Engel *f*

engine *n* (*ENG*) TRANSP motor *m*; ~ **casing** TRANSP *shipping* cárter del motor *m*, revestimiento de la máquina *m*; ~ **designer** (*ED*) IND *ships machinery* diseñador(a) de motores *m,f*; ~ **of growth** ECON motor del crecimiento *m*; ~ **transplant** TRANSP cambio de motor *m*

engineer *n* HRM técnico(-a) *m,f*

engineering *n* IND ingeniería *f*; ~ **assurance** INS seguro técnico *m*; ~ **department** GEN COMM departamento de ingeniería *m*; ~ **design** GEN COMM diseño técnico *m*; ~ **and design department** GEN COMM departamento de ingeniería y diseño *m*; ~ **firm** GEN COMM firma de ingeniería *f*; ~ **manager** COMP, HRM, MGMNT director(a) técnico(-a) *m,f*, gerente de ingeniería *mf*; ~ **process** GEN COMM proceso técnico *m*; ~ **works** *n pl* GEN COMM, IND taller de maquinaria *m*

English: ~ **Heritage** *n* ENVIR organización encargada del mantenimiento del patrimonio histórico de Inglaterra; ~ **Inshore Traffic Zone** *n* (*EITZ*) TRANSP *shipping* zona de tráfico del interior de Inglaterra; ~~**speaking world** *n* GEN COMM mundo de habla inglesa *m*; ~ **Tourist Board** *n* (*ETB*) LEIS oficina de turismo de Inglaterra, ≈ Oficina de Turismo de España *f*, ≈ Turespaña *f*

engraved: ~ **form** *n* GEN COMM formulario impreso *m*

enhance *vt* ECON *purchasing power* aumentar

enhanced[1] *adj* COMP *quality, features*, S&M resaltado

enhanced[2]: ~ **graphics array** *n* COMP matriz de gráficos realzada *f*

Enhanced: ~ **Structural Adjustment Facility** *n* (*ESAF*) FIN mecanismo de ajuste estructural mejorado *f*

enhancement *n* COMP *computer system* utilización racional *f*

enjoin *vt* MGMNT imponer, ordenar, prescribir

enlarged: ~ **copy** *n* GEN COMM copia ampliada *f*; ~ **edition** *n* GEN COMM edición ampliada *f*

enlargement *n* GEN COMM ampliación *f*

enough: **be** ~ *phr* GEN COMM llegar

enquiry *n* GEN COMM consulta *f*; ~ **desk** GEN COMM oficina de investigaciones *f*

enriched: ~ **program** *AmE*, ~ **programme** *BrE n* GEN COMM programa reforzado *m*; ~ **tax expenditure** *n* TAX gasto fiscal aumentado *m*

enrichment *n* GEN COMM *job* enriquecimiento *m*

enrollment *AmE see* enrolment *BrE*

enrolment *n BrE* GEN COMM *act* adscripción *f*, *number* inscripción *f*

entail *n* LAW vínculo *m*

enter 1. *vt* GEN COMM *market* introducirse en, presentar, LAW *plea, appeal, writ* presentar; ◆ ~ **an appeal** LAW presentar una apelación; ~ **business** GEN COMM entrar en negocios; ~ **goods** IMP/EXP declarar mercancías; ~ **goods for warehousing** GEN COMM registrar mercancías para almacenarlas; ~ **in the accounts** ACC contabilizar; ~ **information onto a register** GEN COMM introducir información en un registro; ~ **an item in the ledger** GEN COMM sentar una partida en el libro mayor; ~ **the labor market** *AmE*, ~ **the labour market** *BrE* GEN COMM ingresar al mercado del trabajo; ~ **the market** GEN COMM introducirse en el mercado; ~ **a plea** LAW presentar un alegato; ~ **politics** GEN COMM, POL entrar en política; ~ **recession** ECON entrar en recesión; ~ **a writ** LAW presentar un escrito; **2.** *vi* GEN COMM entrar

enter into *vt* GEN COMM entrar en; ◆ ~ **an agreement** GEN COMM celebrar un convenio; ~ **a contract with** GEN COMM establecer un contrato con

entered: ~ **in** *adj* IMP/EXP registrado

enterprise *n BrE* GEN COMM empresa *f*; ~ **allowance** *BrE* FIN subvención de empresa *f*; ~ **union** HRM sindicato blanco *m* (*AmL*), sindicato de empresa *m* (*Esp*); ~ **zone** (*EZ*) ECON, HRM, IND zona de desarrollo industrial *f*

enterprising *adj* GEN COMM emprendedor

entertain *vt* GEN COMM *client* atender

entertainment *n* GEN COMM, LEIS espectáculos *m pl*; ~ **complex** LEIS complejo para espectáculos *m*; ~ **industry** LEIS sector del ocio *m*; ~ **on board** LEIS, TRANSP entretenimiento a bordo *m*

enticing *adj* GEN COMM *offer* atractivo

entitle *vt* GEN COMM autorizar, LAW dar derecho

entitlement *n* GEN COMM derecho *m*

entity *n* LAW entidad *f*; ~ **convention** ACC asamblea de la entidad *f*, asamblea general *f*

entrance: ~ **card** *n* GEN COMM tarjeta de entrada *f*; ~ **examination** *n* GEN COMM examen de ingreso *m*; ~ **fee** *n* GEN COMM derechos de entrada *m pl*; ~ **ticket** *n* GEN COMM billete de entrada *m*; ~ **visa** *n* LEIS, POL visado de entrada *m*

entrepreneur *n* ECON, GEN COMM, MGMNT empresario(-a) *m,f*

entrepreneurial[1] *adj* ECON, GEN COMM, MGMNT empresarial

entrepreneurial[2]: **~ risk** *n* ECON, GEN COMM riesgo empresarial *m*; **~ spirit** *n* GEN COMM, MGMNT espíritu empresarial *m*

entrepreneurship *n* GEN COMM, MGMNT capacidad empresarial *f*

entry *n* ACC asiento *m*, GEN COMM entrada *f*, IMP/EXP partida *f*; **~ acceptance data** *n pl* COMP datos de aceptación de entrada *m pl*; **~ barrier** ECON, IMP/EXP barrera de entrada *f*; **~ into force** PATENTS entrada en vigor *f*; **~-level job** HRM puesto de trabajo de nivel inicial *m*; **~ outwards** IMP/EXP, TRANSP declaración de salida *f*; **~ permit** GEN COMM, POL permiso de entrada *m*; **~ price** STOCK *futures* precio de entrada *m*; **~ processing unit** *(EPU)* IMP/EXP unidad de tratamiento de entradas *f*; **~ stamp** IMP/EXP *on arrival in new country* sello de entrada *m*; **~ visa** LEIS, POL visado de entrada *m*

enumerate *vt* GEN COMM enumerar

enumeration *n* GEN COMM enumeración *f*

envelope: **~ curve** *n* ECON curva envolvente *f*; **~ procedures and rules** *n pl* GEN COMM procedimientos y normas generales *m pl*

Envireg *n* ENVIR Envireg *f*

environment *n* COMP entorno *m*, ENVIR medio ambiente *m*, ambiente *m*, GEN COMM ambiente *m*; **~ policy** ENVIR, POL política medioambiental *f*; **~ scan** ENVIR registrador ambiental *m*

Environment: **~ and Consumer Protection Service** *n* *(ECPS)* ENVIR, WEL Servicio de Protección al Consumidor y al Medio Ambiente *m*

environmental: **~ accounting** *n* ENVIR contabilidad medioambiental *f*, contabilidad verde *f*; **~ action program** *AmE*, **~ action programme** *BrE n* ECON, ENVIR programa de acción medioambiental *m*; **~ analysis** *n* ENVIR, MGMNT análisis del medio ambiente *m*; **~ assessment** *n* ENVIR, MGMNT diagnóstico ambiental *m*; **~ conditions** *n pl* ENVIR condiciones ambientales *f pl*; **~ control** *n* ENVIR control ambiental *m*; **~ damage** *n* ENVIR daño ambiental *m*; **~ determinism** *n* ENVIR determinismo ambiental *m*; **~ development** *n* ENVIR fomento del medio ambiente *m*; **~ forecasting** *n* ENVIR pronóstico ambiental *m*; **~ goods** *n pl* ENVIR, GEN COMM mercancías ambientales *f pl*; **~ hygiene** *n* ENVIR higiene medioambiental *f*; **~ impact** *n* ENVIR impacto ambiental *m*; **~ impact assessment** *n* ENVIR evaluación de impacto medioambiental *f*; **~ impact statement** *n* ENVIR balance del impacto ambiental *m*, informe del impacto ambiental *m* *(Esp)*, declaración de impacto medioambiental *f*, reporte del impacto ambiental *m* *(AmL)*; **~ issues** *n pl* ENVIR temas medioambientales *m pl*; **~ lobby** *n* ENVIR, POL grupo de presión ecologista *m*; **~ management** *n* ENVIR, MGMNT dirección del medio ambiente *f*, gerencia del medio ambiente *f*; **~ policy** *n* ENVIR, POL política ambiental *f*; **~ problem** *n* ENVIR problema medioambiental *m*; **~ protection** *n* ENVIR, MGMNT protección del medio ambiente *f*; **~ quality standard** *n* ENVIR norma de calidad ambiental *f*; **~ scanner** *n* ENVIR explorador medioambiental *m*; **~ scanning** *n* ENVIR exploración medioambiental *f*;

~ standard *n* ENVIR norma medioambiental *f*; **~ tax** *n* ENVIR *pollution* impuesto ambiental *m*

Environmental: **~ Health Officer** *n BrE* GEN COMM Director(a) de Sanidad Ambiental *m,f*; **~ Management System** *n* ENVIR sistema de gestión ambiental *m*; **~ Protection Act** *n BrE* ENVIR, LAW Ley de Protección Ambiental de 1990 *f*; **~ Protection Agency** *n AmE* *(EPA)* ENVIR *pollution* Organismo de Protección del Medio Ambiente *m*

environmentalism *n* ENVIR ambientalismo *m*

environmentalist *n* ENVIR ecologista *mf*

environmentally[1]: **~ friendly** *adj* ENVIR *goods* ecológico, que no daña el medio ambiente

environmentally[2]: **~-friendly product** *n* ENVIR producto ecológico *m*, producto que no daña el medio ambiente *m*; **~-sensitive area** *n* ENVIR zona ambientalmente sensible *f*; **~-sensitive zone** *n* ENVIR zona ambientalmente sensible *f*

e.o. *abbr* *(ex officio)* HRM de oficio

EO *abbr* *(executive officer)* HRM, MGMNT director(a) ejecutivo(-a) *m,f*

EOC *abbr BrE* *(Equal Opportunities Commission)* HRM comisión de igualdad en oportunidades en el empleo

EOE *abbr* *(European Options Exchange)* ECON, STOCK mercado de opciones europeo *m*

EOF *abbr* *(end of file)* COMP FDA *(fin de archivo)*

eohp *abbr* *(except otherwise herein provided)* GEN COMM salvo indicación de lo contrario

EOM *abbr* *(end of message)* COMP FDM *(fin de mensaje)*

EOP *abbr* *(Equal Opportunities Policy)* HRM política de igualdad de oportunidades *f*

EOQ *abbr* *(economic order quantity)* ECON, MATH valoración del orden económico *f*, cantidad de orden económico *f*

EPA *abbr* ENVIR *(Environmental Protection Agency)* Agencia de Protección del Medio Ambiente *f*, ECON, POL *(European Productivity Agency)* AEP *(Agencia Europea para la Productividad)*, LAW *(Employment Protection Act)* ley de protección del empleo

EPCA *abbr* *(Employment Protection Consolidation Act)* HRM, LAW ley de consolidación de protección del empleo

ephemeralization *n jarg* ECON efemeralización *f*

EPOS *abbr* *(electronic point of sale)* GEN COMM, S&M punto de venta electrónico *m*

EPROM *abbr* COMP *(electronically programmable read only memory)* memoria sólo de lectura programable electrónicamente *f*, *(erasable programmable read only memory)* memoria sólo de lectura programable y que puede borrarse *f*

EPS *abbr* *(earning per share)* ACC, FIN, STOCK BPA *(beneficio por acción)*, dividendo por acción *m*, ganancia por acción *f*

EPT *abbr* *(electronic payment terminal)* GEN COMM terminal de pago electrónico *m*

EPU *abbr* ECON, POL *(European Payments Union)* UEP *(Unión Europea de Pagos)*, IMP/EXP *(entry processing unit)* unidad de tratamiento de entradas *f*

EPZA *abbr* *(export processing zone authority)* IMP/EXP autoridad zonal de tratamiento de la exportación *f*

EqPA *abbr* *(Equal Pay Act)* HRM, LAW, WEL Principio de Equidad en Remuneración *f*

equal[1] *adj* GEN COMM igual; ♦ **all else being ~** GEN COMM si no intervienen otros factores, sin que lo demás se modifique; **on an ~ footing** *n* GEN COMM en pie de igualdad, en iguales condiciones; **~ and opposite** GEN COMM igual y opuesto; **~ pay for work of equal value** *BrE* HRM a trabajo de igual valor igual remuneración; **in ~ proportions** GEN COMM en iguales proporciones; **on ~ terms** GEN COMM en los mismos términos

equal² *n* MATH igual *m*; **~ employment opportunity** HRM igualdad de oportunidad de empleo *f*; **~ opportunity** *BrE* (*cf affirmative action AmE*) HRM plan del gobierno para promover el empleo entre los minorías, igualdad de oportunidades *f*; **~ opportunity employer** HRM empresario(-a) que aplica la igualdad de oportunidades *m,f*; **~ pay** HRM pago igual *m*, remuneración igual *f*; **~ pay directive** HRM *1975* directriz de paga igual *f*; **~ product curve** ECON curva de igual producción *f*; **~ value** STOCK *currency futures prices* valor semejante *m*; **~ value amendment** *BrE* HRM enmienda de igual valor *f*; **~ voting rights** *n pl* POL igualdad de derechos de voto *f*, iguales derechos a voto *m pl*

Equal: ~ Credit Opportunity Act *n AmE* LAW *anti-discrimination* ley de igualdad de oportunidades crediticias; **~ Opportunities Commission** *n BrE* HRM *in recruiting* comisión que promueve la igualdad de oportunidades sin distinción de raza, credo ni orientación sexual; **~ Opportunities Policy** *n* (*EOP*) HRM política de igualdad de oportunidades *f*; **~ Pay Act** *n* (*EqPA*) HRM, LAW Principio de Equidad en Remuneración *m*; **~ Protection of the Laws** *n AmE* LAW *constitution* igual protección de la ley; **~ Worth Equal Pay Act** *n* HRM ley de igual valor igual pago

equality *n* GEN COMM igualdad *f*; **~ standard** POL estándar de igualdad *m*

equalization *n* ECON, GEN COMM igualación *f*, compensación *f*, TAX compensación *f*; **~ fund** INS fondo de compensación *m*; **~ payment** TAX pago de compensación *m*; **~ of revenue and expenditure** FIN compensación de ingresos y gastos *f*; **~ of taxes** TAX compensación tributaria *f*; **~ of wage differentials** ECON igualación de diferencias salariales *f*

equalize *vt* GEN COMM compensar

equalized *adj* GEN COMM igualado

equalizing: ~ dividend *n* ACC, FIN, STOCK dividendo de regulación *m*

equation *n* MATH ecuación *f*

equilibrium *n* GEN COMM equilibrio *m*; **~ basis** STOCK *currency futures* base de equilibrio *f*; **~ GNP** ECON equilibrio del PNB *m*; **~ price** ECON precio de equilibrio *m*; **~ quantity** ECON cantidad de equilibrio *f*; **~ wage rate** ECON tipo de salario de equilibrio *m*

equip *vt* GEN COMM equipar

equipment *n* GEN COMM equipamiento *m*; **~ dealers' insurance** INS seguro a todo riesgo para distribuidores de equipos *m*; **~ failure** GEN COMM avería de máquina *f*; **~ goods** *n pl* ECON bienes de equipo *m pl*; **~ handover agreement** IND acuerdo de entrega de equipos *m*; **~ hire** GEN COMM alquiler *m*; **~ leasing** ECON préstamo de equipos *m*, IND, PROP alquiler con opción a compra de material *m*, arrendamiento de equipo *m*, leasing de material *m*; **~ trust bond** FIN certificado de fideicomiso de equipo *m*; **~ trust certification** FIN certificado de fideicomiso de equipo *m*

equitable¹ *adj* GEN COMM *fair* razonable, LAW equitativo, razonable

equitable²: ~ distribution *n* GEN COMM distribución equitativa *f*; **~ lien** *n* TAX gravamen equitativo *m*

equities *n pl* FIN valores *m pl*

equity *n* ACC acción *f*, activo neto *m*, BANK acción *f*, fondos propios *m pl*, ECON *fairness* equidad *f*, FIN acción *f*, activo neto *m*, GEN COMM acción *f*, PROP equidad *f*, STOCK acción *f*, fondos propios *m pl*, neto patrimonial *m*; **~ accounting** ACC contabilidad del activo neto *f*, contabilidad del capital social *f*, contabilidad del patrimonio neto *f*; **~ base** ACC base de recursos propios *f*; **~ capital** *BrE* (*cf capital stock AmE*) ACC, STOCK capital social en acciones *m*, existencias de capital *f pl*, capital propio *m*; **~ capital base** BANK, STOCK base de capital accionario *f*; **~ dilution** ACC, FIN, STOCK dilución del capital *f*; **~ financing** FIN financiación por venta de participación *f*; **~ funds** *n pl* ACC, STOCK fondos en títulos *m pl*; **~ holder** STOCK accionista ordinario(-a) *m,f*; **~ holdings** *n pl* FIN, GEN COMM, STOCK cartera de valores *f*; **~ investment** GEN COMM, STOCK inversión en acciones *f*; **~ investment funds** *n pl* FIN, STOCK fondos de inversión en acciones *m pl*; **~ investor** STOCK inversor(-a) en acciones *m,f*; **~ issue** STOCK emisión de títulos *f*; **~ joint venture** GEN COMM coinversión por acciones *f*; **~ kicker** STOCK hipoteca vinculada al capital *f*; **~-linked policy** STOCK política ligada al mercado de acciones *f*; **~ market** STOCK mercado de valores *m*, mercado de valores de renta variable *m*; **~ method** ACC método de participación *m*; **~ method of accounting** ACC método de contabilidad patrimonial *m*; **~ option** STOCK opción sobre el neto *f*; **~ ownership** STOCK participación en el capital social *f*; **~ rate** *AmE* PROP tasa de recursos propios *f*; **~ of redemption** BANK derecho de rescate *m*; **~-related bonds** *n pl* STOCK acciones garantizadas *f pl*; **~-related futures** *n pl* STOCK futuros relacionados con el neto patrimonial *m pl*; **~ security** *n pl* STOCK título de participación en una sociedad *m*; **~ share** ACC, FIN, STOCK, TAX acción ordinaria *f*; **~ taxation** TAX equidad fiscal *f*; **~ trading** STOCK operación de bolsa *f*; **~ turnover** STOCK renovación del capital social *f*; **~ value** BANK capital contable de la participación *m*; **~ warrant** STOCK derecho de adquisición de capital social *m*, derecho especial de suscripción de capital *m*; ♦ **take an ~ stake** STOCK adquirir una participación

equivalence *n* GEN COMM equivalencia *f*

equivalent *n* GEN COMM equivalente *m*; **~ taxable yield** *AmE* ACC, TAX beneficio imponible equivalente *m*

era *n* GEN COMM era *f*

eradicate *vt* GEN COMM erradicar

erasable: ~ programmable read only memory *n* (*EPROM*) COMP memoria sólo de lectura programable y que puede borrarse *f*

erase¹: ~ head *n* COMP cabeza de borrado *f*

erase² *vt* COMP borrar

ERC *abbr* (*European Registry of Commerce*) GEN COMM Registro Europeo de Comercio *m*

ERDF *abbr* (*European Regional Development Fund*) ECON, POL FEDER (*Fondo Europeo para el Desarrollo Regional*)

erect *vt* GEN COMM *customs barriers* levantar

ergonometric *adj* GEN COMM, HRM ergonométrico

ergonometrics *n* GEN COMM, HRM ergonometría *f*

ergonomic *adj* GEN COMM, HRM ergonómico

ergonomically[1]: **~-designed** *adj* COMP *work station* de diseño ergonómico

ergonomically[2] *adv* GEN COMM, HRM ergonómicamente

ergonomics *n* GEN COMM, HRM ergonomía *f*

ergonomist *n* GEN COMM, HRM ergonomista *mf*

ergophobia *n* GEN COMM, HRM ergofobia *f*

ERISA *abbr* (*Employment Retirement Income Security Act*) LAW, WEL ley de garantía de las pensiones por jubilación, ≈ Ley de Jubilación *f*

ERL *abbr* BANK, ECON (*economic recovery loan*) préstamo de recuperación económica *m*, FIN (*emergency reconstruction loan*) préstamo de reconstrucción de emergencia *m*

ERM *abbr* (*Exchange Rate Mechanism*) ECON MAC (*mecanismo de ajuste de cambios*), mecanismo de los tipos de cambio *m*

erode *vt* ENVIR, GEN COMM *power* erosionar

erosion *n* ENVIR *of land*, GEN COMM erosión *f*

ERP *abbr* (*European Recovery Programme*) ECON, POL Programa de Recuperación Europea *m*

err *vi* GEN COMM *in judgment* errar

erratum *n* COMP, GEN COMM, MEDIA errata *f*

erroneous *adj* GEN COMM erróneo

error[1]: **~-free** *adj* COMP sin errores

error[2] *n* GEN COMM error *m*; **~ control** COMP control de errores *m*; **~ of law** LAW error de derecho *m*; **~ message** COMP mensaje de error *m*; **~ rate** COMP tasa de error *f*; **~ recovery** COMP recuperación de errores *f*; **~ report** COMP lista de errores *f*

errors[1]: **~ and omissions** *n pl* GEN COMM errores y omisiones *m pl*; **~ and omissions clause** *n* INS cláusula de errores y omisiones *f*

errors[2]: **~ and omissions excepted** *phr* (*e.&o.e.*) GEN COMM salvo error u omisión (*s.e.u.o.*)

ersatz *n* GEN COMM sucedáneo *m*

ES *abbr* (*expert system*) COMP sistema experto *m*

ESA *abbr* (*European Space Agency*) IND, POL Agencia Espacial Europea *f*

ESAF *abbr* (*Enhanced Structural Adjustment Facility*) FIN mecanismo de ajuste estructural mejorado *f*

Esc *abbr* (*escape key*) COMP *keyboard* escape *m*

ESC *abbr* (*Economic and Social Committee*) ECON, WEL Comité Económico y Social *m*

escalate *vi* GEN COMM *prices* subir rápidamente

escalation: **~ clause** *n* INS cláusula de reajuste *f*

escalator *n* GEN COMM *moving staircase* escalera mecánica *f*; **~ cards** *n pl* S&M anuncios a los lados de las escaleras mecánicas *m pl*; **~ clause** BANK, HRM, INS, LAW cláusula de revisión salarial automática *f*

escape: **~ character** *n* COMP carácter de cambio de código *m*; **~ clause** *n* BANK, INS, LAW cláusula de elusión *f*, cláusula de evasión *f*, cláusula de salvaguardia *f*; **~ key** *n* (*Esc*) COMP *keyboard* escape *m*; **~ sequence** *n* COMP secuencia de abandono *f*

escheat *n* LAW, PROP reversión de bienes abintestados al Estado, reversión de propiedad *f*

escort[1] *n* GEN COMM acompañante *mf*

escort[2] *vt* GEN COMM *visitor* acompañar

escrow *n* FIN documento depositado en garantía *m*; **~ account** BANK cuenta de depósito en garantía *f*; **~ agent** FIN depositario legal de documentos *m*; **~ agreement** LAW acuerdo en plica *m*; **~ clause**

TRANSP *in charter party* cláusula de depósito *f*; ◆ **in ~** GEN COMM en depósito

ESD *abbr* (*echo sounding device*) TRANSP *shipping* sonda acústica *f*

ESF *abbr* (*European Social Fund*) ECON, POL FSE (*Fondo Social Europeo*)

ESOP *abbr* (*employee stock ownership plan*) HRM, STOCK plan de venta de acciones a empleados *m*

ESOT *abbr* (*employee share ownership trust*) STOCK trust de personal de propietario de acciones

esp. *abbr* (*especially*) GEN COMM esp. (*especialmente*)

especially *adv* (*esp.*) GEN COMM especialmente (*esp.*)

espionage *n* GEN COMM espionaje *m*

esprit: **~ de corps** *n* GEN COMM, HRM espíritu de equipo *m*

Esq. *abbr* (*esquire*) GEN COMM *form of address in letter writing* Sr.D. (*Señor don*)

esquire *n* (*Esq.*) GEN COMM *form of address in letter writing* Señor don *m* (*Sr.D.*)

ESRO *abbr* (*European Space Research Organization*) IND, POL Organización Europea de Investigaciones Espaciales *f*

essential: **~ commodities** *n pl* S&M productos de primera necesidad *m pl*; **~ condition** *n* GEN COMM, LAW condición indispensable *f*; **~ feature** *n* GEN COMM, PATENTS, S&M característica principal *f*; **~ foodstuff** *n* GEN COMM producto alimenticio de primera necesidad *m*; **~ industry** *n* ECON, IND industria esencial *f*, industria vital *f*

est. *abbr* (*established*) GEN COMM establecido

EST *abbr* (*Eastern Standard Time*) GEN COMM hora estándar del este *f*

establish *vt* ECON, GEN COMM, LAW establecer, fundar; ◆ **~ a direct link with** COMMS establecer comunicación directa con

established[1] *adj* (*est.*) GEN COMM establecido

established[2]: **~ brand** *n* S&M marca establecida *f*; **~ image** *n* S&M imagen consolidada *f*; **~ market** *n* S&M mercado consolidado *m*; **~ product** *n* S&M producto consolidado *m*; **~ programs financing** *n* FIN financiación de programas establecidos *f*

establishment *n* GEN COMM, HRM establecimiento *m*; **~-level bargaining** HRM negociación a nivel del establecimiento *f*

Establishment: **the ~** *n* BrE GEN COMM, POL el Establishment *m*, los poderes fácticos *m pl*, el Sistema *m*

estate *n* GEN COMM parque *m*, PROP, TAX propiedad *f*; **~ agency** BrE (*cf real estate agency AmE*) PROP agencia inmobiliaria *f*; **~ agent** BrE (*cf realtor AmE*) GEN COMM, PROP administrador(a) de fincas *m,f*, agente inmobiliario(-a) *m,f*; **~ of bankrupt** TAX masa de la quiebra *f*; **~ distribution** PROP distribución inmobiliaria *f*, repartición inmobiliaria *f*; **~ duty** TAX derechos de sucesión *m pl*, impuesto sobre herencias *m*, impuesto sobre sucesiones *m*; **~ economy** ECON economía de haciendas *f*; **~ executor** LAW albacea testamentario(-a) *m,f*; **~ freezing** TAX congelación de la propiedad *f*; **~ in abeyance** LAW, TAX cosa nullius *f*, sucesión vacante *f*; **~ in reversion** LAW *property* reversión de bienes raíces *f*, PROP bienes con reversión *m pl*, reversión *f*; **~ in severalty** PROP propiedad individual *f*; **~ income** TAX renta patrimonial *f*; **~ manager** FIN administrador(a) de bienes *m,f*, administrador(-a) de herencia *m,f*, administrador(-a) de propiedades *m,f*; ~ **planning** FIN, LAW *wills* disposiciones sucesorias *f pl*; ~ **revenue** FIN renta de una propiedad *f*, LAW renta del patrimonio *f*; ~ **tax** TAX impuesto sobre transmisiones patrimoniales *m (ITP)*

estimate[1] *n* GEN COMM estimación *f*; ~ **of expenditure** ACC estimación de gastos *f*; ◆ **at the highest** ~ GEN COMM en la más alta valoración; **at the lowest** ~ GEN COMM en la más baja valoración

estimate[2] *vt* GEN COMM estimar

estimated[1] *adj* GEN COMM, MATH, TAX estimado

estimated[2]: ~ **amount** *n* GEN COMM cantidad estimada *f*; ~ **charges** *n pl* ACC, BANK, FIN cargos estimados *m pl*, gastos estimados *m pl*; ~ **cost** *n* ACC coste estimado *m* (*Esp*), costo estimado *m* (*AmL*); ~ **costs system** *n* ACC sistema de costes estimados *m* (*Esp*), sistema de costos estimados *m* (*AmL*); ~ **deduction** *n* TAX deducción estimada *f*; ~ **financial report** *n* FIN informe financiero estimado *m* (*Esp*), reporte financiero estimado *m* (*AmL*); ~ **lapse** *n* ACC periodo estimado *m*; ~ **realizable value** *n* ACC, BANK, FIN, S&M valor realizable estimado *m*; ~ **revenue** *n* ACC entradas brutas estimadas *f pl*, ingresos estimados *m pl*; ~ **systems costs** *n pl* FIN costes estimados de los sistemas *m pl* (*Esp*), costos estimados de los sistemas *m pl* (*AmL*); ~ **tax** *n* TAX impuesto estimado *m*; ~ **time of arrival** *n* (*ETA*) GEN COMM, TRANSP hora prevista de llegada *f*; ~ **time of departure** *n* (*ETD*) GEN COMM, TRANSP hora prevista de salida *f*; ~ **time of sailing** *n* (*ETS*) GEN COMM, TRANSP hora prevista de salida de un barco *f*; ~ **trading account** *n* FIN cuenta comercial estimada *f*; ~ **value** *n* INS valor estimado *m*

estimates *n pl* FIN cálculos *m pl*

estimation: ~ **sampling** *n* MATH *statistics* muestreo de estimación *m*

estimator *n* S&M estimador *m*

estoppel *n* LAW impedimento legal *m*, preclusión jurídica *f*; ~ **certificate** BANK certificado de impedimento legal *m*

estovers *n pl* LAW, PROP derecho del arrendentario de cortar madera de la propiedad para el mantenimiento de la misma

estranged: ~ **spouse** *n* LAW cónyuge separado(-a) *m,f*

estuarial: ~ **service** *n* TRANSP *shipping* servicio de ría *m*

estuary *n* TRANSP *shipping* estuario *m*

ET *abbr* (*employment training*) HRM, WEL capacitación ocupacional *f* (*AmL*), formación ocupacional *f* (*Esp*)

ETA *abbr* (*estimated time of arrival*) GEN COMM, TRANSP hora prevista de llegada *f*

ETAS *abbr BrE* (*Economic Trends Annual Survey*) ECON *econometrics* estudio anual de la evolución económica *m*

ETB *abbr* (*English Tourist Board*) LEIS oficina de turismo de Inglaterra, ≈ Oficina de Turismo de España *f*, ≈ Turespaña *f*

ETD *abbr* (*estimated time of departure*) GEN COMM, TRANSP hora prevista de salida *f*

Ethernet® *n* COMP *network* Ethernet® *m*

ethical[1] *adj* GEN COMM ético

ethical[2]: ~ **advertising** *n* S&M publicidad ética *f*; ~ **investment** *n* POL, STOCK inversión ética *f*

ethics *n pl* GEN COMM *business conduct* ética *f*, éticas *f pl*

ethnic: ~ **monitoring** *n* HRM política en contra de la discriminación racial en el proceso de selección y promoción de los empleados

ETO *abbr* (*European Transport Organization*) TRANSP OET (*Organización Europea de Transportes*)

ETPO *abbr* (*European Trade Promotion Organization*) ECON, POL Organización Europea de Fomento Comercial *f*

ETS *abbr* (*estimated time of sailing*) GEN COMM, TRANSP hora prevista de salida de un barco *f*

ETSI *abbr* (*European Telecommunications Standards Institute*) COMMS Instituto Europeo de Normas de Telecomunicaciones *m*

ETU *abbr* (*Electrical Trades Union*) GEN COMM Sindicato de Electricistas *m*, Sindicato de Gremios Eléctricos *m*

ETUC *abbr* (*European Trade Union Confederation*) HRM Confederación de Sindicatos Europeos *f*

et ux *phr* LAW *old legal documents* y su esposa

EU[1] *abbr* (*European Union*) ECON, POL UE (*Unión Europea*)

EU[2]: ~ **directive** *n* LAW, POL directiva de la UE *f*; ~~**mark** *n* IND *on toys* marca de la UE *f*; ~ **transit form** *n* TRANSP formulario de tránsito por la UE *m*

EUA *abbr* (*European Unit of Account*) ECON unidad europea de cuenta *f*

Euler: ~'s **theorem** *n* ECON *returns to scale* teorema de Euler *m*

EURATOM *abbr* (*European Atomic Energy Community*) ECON, POL CEEA (*Comunidad Europea de Energía Atómica*)

EURCO *abbr* (*European Composite Unit*) FIN Unidad Compuesta Europea *f*

euro: ~ **commercial paper** *n* BANK, FIN papel comercial europeo *m*

Euro[1]: ~ **Co-op** *n* (*European Community of Consumers' Cooperatives*) ECON Comunidad Europea de Cooperativas de Consumidores *f*; ~ **MP** *n* (*European Member of Parliament*) POL Eurodiputado(-a) *m,f*, parlamentario(-a) europeo(-a) *m,f*; ~~**rates** *n pl* BANK eurotasas *f pl*; ~~**security** *n* FIN garantía europea *f*

Eurobank *n* BANK Eurobanco *m*

Eurobond *n* BANK, STOCK eurobono *m*; ~ **issue** STOCK emisión de eurobonos *f*; ~ **market** ECON, STOCK mercado de eurobonos *m*

Euro-Canadian: ~ **dollar issue** *n* STOCK emisión del dólar eurocanadiense *f*

Eurocapital: ~ **market issue** *n* ECON, STOCK emisión en el mercado de eurocapitales *f*

Eurocard *n* BANK Tarjeta Europea *f*

eurocentric *adj* GEN COMM eurocéntrico

eurocheque *n* ECON *for international use* eurocheque *m*

Euroclear *n* STOCK Cámara de Compensación de Eurobonos *f*

Eurocommercial: ~ **paper** *n* (*ECP*) STOCK *money market* efectos comerciales en eurodivisas *m pl*

eurocurrency *n* BANK, ECON eurodivisa *f*; ~ **issue** ECON euroemisión *f*; ~ **loan** BANK préstamo en eurodivisas *m*; ~ **market** ECON, STOCK mercado de eurodivisas *m*

Eurocurrency: ~ **Rates** *n* ECON tasas de eurodivisas *f pl*

Eurodollar *n* (*ED*) ECON eurodólar *m* (*ED*); ~ **bond** ECON título en eurodólares *m*, STOCK bono en eurodólares *m*; ~ **certificate of deposit** BANK certificado de depósito en eurodólares *m*; ~ **deposit** BANK depósito de eurodólares *m*; ~ **future** FIN, STOCK opción de futuro en eurodólares *f*; ~ **index** STOCK índice del eurodólar *m*; ~ **market** ECON, FIN, STOCK mercado del eurodólar *m*; ~ **rate** ECON *currency* tasa de eurodólares *f*; ~ **time deposit** BANK, STOCK depósito a plazo en eurodólares *m*; ~ **time deposit funds** *n pl* STOCK fondos de depósito a plazo en eurodólares *m pl*; ~ **time deposit futures contract** STOCK contrato de futuros sobre depósitos a plazo en eurodólares *m*

Euroequity *n* ECON euroequidad *f*

Euro Fer *n* (*Association of European Steel Producers*) IND Asociación Europea de Productores de Acero *f*

Eurofranc *n* ECON eurofranco *m*

Euromarket *n* ECON euromercado *m*

Euromoney *n* BANK eurodinero *m*, euromoneda *f*; ~ **deposit** BANK, ECON depósito euromonetario *m*

Euronet *n* COMMS Euronet *f*

Europallet *n* GEN COMM europaleta *f*

European[1] *adj* GEN COMM europeo

European[2]: ~ **affairs** *n pl* GEN COMM asuntos europeos *m pl*; ~ **Agency for Cooperation** *n* (*EAC*) LAW, POL Agencia Europea para la Cooperación *f* (*AEC*); ~ **Agricultural Fund** *n* ECON, POL Fondo Europeo Agrícola *m*; ~ **Agricultural Guidance and Guarantee Fund** *n* (*EAGGF*) ECON, POL Fondo Europeo de Orientación y Garantía Agrícola *m* (*FEOGA*); ~ **Association of Advertising Agencies** *n* (*EAAA*) S&M Asociación Europea de Agencias de Publicidad *f* (*AEAP*); ~ **Association for Shipping Information** *n* (*EASI*) TRANSP Asociación Europea para Información de Transporte Marítimo *f*; ~ **Atomic Energy Community** *n* ECON, POL (*EAEC, EURATOM*) Comunidad Europea de Energía Atómica *f* (*CEEA*); ~ **Bank for Reconstruction and Development** *n* (*EBRD*) BANK, ECON Banco Europeo para Reconstrucción y Desarrollo *m* (*BERD*); ~ **Broadcasting Union** *n* (*EBU*) COMMS, MEDIA Unión Europea de Radiodifusión *f* (*UER*); ~ **Central Bank** *n* (*ECB*) BANK, ECON, POL Banco Central Europeo *m* (*BCE*); ~ **Coal and Steel Community** *n* (*ECSC*) ECON, IND Comunidad Europea del Carbón y el Acero *f* (*CECA*); ~ **Commission** *n* ECON Comisión Europea *f*; ~ **Committee for Standardization** *n* (*CEN*) ECON, IND Comité Europeo para la Normalización *m* (*CEN*); ~ **Committee of Legal Cooperation** *n* LAW Comité Europeo de Cooperación Jurídica *m*; ~ **Communities Freight Forwarders Association** *n* (*CLECAT*) TRANSP Asociación de Transportistas de las Comunidades Europeas *f*; ~ **Community** *n obs* (*EC*) ECON, POL Comunidad Europea *f* (*obs*) (*CE*); ~ **Community of Consumers' Cooperatives** *n* (*Euro Co-op*) ECON Comunidad Europea de Cooperativas de Consumidores *f*; ~ **Community Finance Ministers** *n pl* (*ECOFIN*) ECON, POL Consejo Europeo de los Ministros de Finanzas *m* (*ECOFIN*); ~ **Composite Unit** *n* (*EURCO*) FIN Unidad Compuesta Europea *f*; ~ **Convention on Human Rights** *n* WEL Convención Europea de Derechos Humanos *f*; ~ **Cooperation Grouping** *n* (*ECG*) ECON, POL Agrupación de Cooperación Europea *f* (*ACE*); ~ **Cooperation in Science and Technology** *n* (*COST*) IND, POL Cooperación Europea en Ciencia y Tecnología *f* (*COST*); ~ **Court** *n* LAW, POL Corte Europea *f*, Tribunal Europeo *m*; ~ **Court of Justice** *n* LAW, POL Tribunal Europeo de Justicia *m*; ~ **Currency Unit** *n* (*ECU*) ECON, POL Unidad Monetaria Europea *f* (*ECU*); ~ **Development Fund** *n* (*EDF*) ECON, POL Fondo Europeo de

Desarrollo *m*; ~ **Economic Area** *n obs* ECON Área Económica Europea *f* (*obs*); ~ **Economic Community** *n obs* (*EEC*) ECON, POL Comunidad Económica Europea *f* (*obs*) (*CEE*); ~ **Economic Interest Grouping** *n* (*EEIG*) ECON, POL Agrupación Europea de Intereses Económicos *f*; ~ **Economic Space** *n* ECON Espacio Económico Europeo *m*; ~ **Environment Bureau** *n* (*EEB*) ENVIR, POL Oficina Europea para el Medio Ambiente *f*; ~ **Foundation** *n* (*EF*) POL Fundación Europea *f*; ~ **Free Trade Association** *n* (*EFTA*) ECON, POL Asociación Europea de Libre Comercio *f* (*AELC*); ~ **Insurance Committee** *n* INS Comité Europeo de Seguros *m*; ~ **Interprofessional Market** *n* (*EIM*) STOCK mercado interprofesional europeo *m*; ~ **Investment Bank** *n* (*EIB*) BANK, ECON *merchant* Banco Europeo de Inversiones *m* (*BEI*); ~ **League for Economic Cooperation** *n* (*ELEC*) ECON Liga Europea para la Cooperación Económica *f*; ~ **Member of Parliament** *n* (*Euro MP*) POL Eurodiputado(-a) *m,f*, parlamentario(-a) europeo(-a) *m,f*; ~ **Mercantile Exchange** *n* (*ECM*) STOCK Bolsa Mercantil Europea *f*; ~ **Monetary Agreement** *n* (*EMA*) GEN COMM, POL Tratado Monetario Europeo *m*; ~ **monetary cooperation** *n* ECON, POL cooperación monetaria europea *f*; ~ **Monetary Cooperation Fund** *n* (*EMCF*) ECON, POL Fondo Europeo para la Cooperación Monetaria *m* (*FECOM*); ~ **Monetary Fund** *n* BANK, ECON, POL Fondo Monetario Europeo *m*; ~ **Monetary Institute** *n* (*EMI*) ECON, POL Instituto Monetario Europeo *m* (*IME*); ~ **Monetary System** *n* (*EMS*) ECON, POL Sistema Monetario Europeo *m* (*SME*); ~ **Monetary Union** *n* (*EMU*) ECON, POL Unión Monetaria Europea *f* (*UME*); ~ **Nuclear Energy Authority** *n* (*ENEA*) IND, POL Autoridad Europea de Energía Nuclear *f*; ~ **option** *n* STOCK opción a la europea *f*; ~ **Options Exchange** *n* (*EOE*) ECON, STOCK Mercado Europeo de Opciones *m*; ~ **Organization for Quality Control** *n* (*EOQC*) GEN COMM, POL Organización Europea de Control de Calidad *f*; ~ **Organization for Testing and Certification** *n* GEN COMM Organización Europea de Pruebas y Certificaciones *f*; ~ **pallet pool** *n* TRANSP consorcio europeo de plataformas de transporte *m*; ~ **patent application** *n* PATENTS aplicación de patente europea *f*; ~ **Patent Convention** *n* LAW, PATENTS *intellectual property* Convención Europea de Patentes *f*; ~ **Patent Organization** *n* (*EPO*) LAW, PATENTS Organización Europea de Patentes *f*; ~ **Payments Union** *n* (*EPU*) ECON, POL Unión Europea de Pagos *f* (*UEP*); ~ **Productivity Agency** *n* (*EPA*) ECON, POL Agencia Europea para la Productividad *f* (*AEP*); ~ **Recovery Plan** *n* (*ERP*) ECON Programa de Recuperación Europea *m*; ~ **Recovery Programme** *n* (*ERP*) ECON, POL Programa de Recuperación Europea *m*; ~ **Regional Development Fund** *n* (*ERDF*) ECON, POL Fondo Europeo para el Desarrollo Regional *m* (*FEDER*); ~ **Registry of Commerce** *n* (*ERC*) GEN COMM Registro Europeo de Comercio *m*; ~ **Shippers' Council** *n* TRANSP Consejo Europeo de Cargadores de Buques *m*; ~ **Single Market** *n* ECON, GEN COMM, POL Mercado Único Europeo *m*; ~ **Social Charter** *n* ECON, POL Carta Social Europea *f*; ~ **Social Fund** *n* (*ESF*) ECON, POL Fondo Social Europeo *m* (*FSE*); ~ **Space Agency** *n* (*ESA*) IND, POL Agencia Espacial Europea *f*; ~ **Space Research Organization** *n* (*ESRO*) IND, POL Organización Europea de Investigaciones Espaciales *f*; ~ **style option** *n* STOCK opción de tipo europeo *f*;

~ System of Central Banks *n* BANK, ECON Sistema Europeo de Bancos Centrales *m*; **~ Telecommunications Standards Institute** *n* (*ETSI*) COMMS Instituto Europeo de Normas de Telecomunicaciones *m*; **~ terms** *n pl* ECON *currency trading* modalidad europea *f*; **~ Trade Promotion Organization** *n* (*ETPO*) ECON, POL Organización Europea de Fomento Comercial *f*; **~ Trade Union Confederation** *n* (*ETUC*) HRM Confederación de Sindicatos Europeos *f*; **~ Transport Organization** *n* (*ETO*) TRANSP Organización Europea de Transportes *f* (*OET*); **~ Union** *n* (*EU*) ECON, POL Unión Europea *f* (*UE*); **~ Union Budget** *n* ECON, POL Presupuesto de la Unión Europea *m*; **~ Union Market** *n* ECON Mercado de la Unión Europea *m*; **~ Union Treaty** *n* GEN COMM, POL Tratado de la Unión Europea *m*; **~ Unit of Account** *n* (*EUA*) ECON unidad europea de cuenta *f*; **~ Year of the Environment** *n* ENVIR Año Europeo del Medio Ambiente *m*; **~ zone charge** *n* (*EZC*) TRANSP *haulage* costes de zona europea *m pl* (*Esp*), costos de zona europea *m pl* (*AmL*)

European/ASEAN: ~ Business Council *n* (*EABC*) ECON, POL Consejo Comercial Europeo-ASEAN *m*

Europeseta *n* BANK europeseta *f*

europhile *adj* GEN COMM eurófilo

europhobic *adj* GEN COMM eurófobo

Europortfolio *n* BANK eurocartera *f*

Eurorebel *n* GEN COMM eurorrebelde *mf*

Eurosceptic *n* GEN COMM euroescéptico(-a) *m,f*

eurosceptical *adj* GEN COMM euroescéptico

Eurovision *n* MEDIA Eurovisión *f*

Eurowindow *n* POL euroventana *f*

evade *vt* TAX evadir

evaluate *vt* GEN COMM evaluar

evaluation *n* GEN COMM evaluación *f*; **~ questionnaire** GEN COMM cuestionario de evaluación *m*

evasion *n* TAX evasión *f*

evasive *adj* GEN COMM *reply* evasivo

even[1] *adj* COMP par; **~-numbered** GEN COMM de numeración par

even[2]: **~ parity** *n* COMP paridad par *f*

even out *vi* GEN COMM *prices* igualar

even up *vt* GEN COMM compensar

evened: ~-out position *n* BANK posición equilibrada *f*

evening: ~ class *n* GEN COMM clase nocturna *f*; **~ peak** *n* GEN COMM punta nocturna *f*; **~ performance** *n* LEIS sesión de noche *f*; **~ trade** *n* STOCK operación próxima al cierre del mercado *f*

evenly: ~ spread *adj* GEN COMM uniformemente distribuido

event *n* COMP evento *m*, GEN COMM suceso *n*; **~ of default** BANK, FIN caso de incumplimiento *m*

events: ~ subsequent to the closing date *phr* ACC hechos posteriores a la fecha de cierre *m*

eventuality *n* GEN COMM eventualidad *f*

eventually *adv* GEN COMM finalmente

eventuate *vi* GEN COMM acontecer

evergreen[1] *adj* FIN de actualidad

evergreen[2]: **~ credit** *n* BANK crédito permanente *m*

evict *vt* GEN COMM despojar, LAW desalojar, expulsar, PROP desalojar

eviction *n* LAW desahucio *m*, desalojo *m*, expulsión *f*, PROP desahucio *m*, desalojo *m*; **~ order** GEN COMM, LAW, PROP orden de desahucio *f*

evidence *n* GEN COMM evidencia *f*, prueba *f*, LAW pruebas *f pl*; **~ of debt** TAX prueba de endeudamiento *f*; **~ of title** LAW, PROP escritura de propiedad *f*; **~ of use** PATENTS prueba de uso *f*; **~ accounts** *n pl* ECON *international trade* cuentas testimoniales *f pl*; ◆ **be in ~** GEN COMM ponerse en evidencia

evidenciary *adj* LAW probatorio

evident *adj* GEN COMM evidente

evolution *n* GEN COMM *price* evolución *f*

evolutionary: ~ theory of the firm *n* ECON teoría de la evolución de la empresa *f*

ex[1] *abbr* GEN COMM (*executed*) ejecutado, (*examined*) ex (*revisado*), (*excluding*) excepto

ex[2]: **~ ante** *adj* ECON ex ante; **~ coupon** *adj* (*ex cp.*) STOCK sin cupón; **~ gratia** *adj* GEN COMM por gracia; **~ parte** *adj* GEN COMM de una parte; **~ post** *adj* STOCK ex post, sin derecho de subscripción; **~-rights** *adj* STOCK ex derecho, sin derecho de subscripción; **~-warrant** *adj* GEN COMM sin derecho de compra

ex[3] *adv* STOCK sin; **~ allotment** FIN sin asignación; **~ dividend** (*ex div.*) FIN, STOCK ex-dividendo, sin dividendo, sin derecho a dividendo; **~ docks** TAX en los puertos; **~ hypothesi** GEN COMM ex hipótesis; **~ officio** (*e.o.*) HRM de oficio; **~ plantation** IMP/EXP *cargo* fuera de plantación, TRANSP *delivery term* en plantación; **~-quay** (*x-quay, ExQ*) IMP/EXP, TRANSP en el muelle, franco muelle; **~ warehouse** GEN COMM fuera de almacén; **~-wharf** (*x-wharf*) GEN COMM, IMP/EXP, TRANSP en el embarcadero, sobre embarcadero; **~-works** (*ExW*) GEN COMM, IMP/EXP, TRANSP ex fábrica, franco fábrica

ex[4]: **~ ante variable** *n* ECON variable ex ante *f*; **~ claim** *n* LAW por derecho; **~-dividend date** *n* STOCK fecha sin dividendos *f*; **~-employee** *n* HRM ex empleado(-a) *m,f*; **~ gratia payment** *n* FIN, GEN COMM pago ex gratia *m*, INS prestación ex gratia *f*; **~-officio member** *n* HRM miembro ex oficio *mf*; **~ parte application** *n* TAX aplicación unilateral *f*; **~-pit transaction** *n* STOCK transacción fuera del corro *f*; **~ post variable** *n* ECON variable ex post *f*; **~-rights date** *n* STOCK fecha sin derechos *f*; **~-rights period** *n* STOCK periodo sin derechos *f*; **~-wharf price** *n* IMP/EXP, TRANSP *cargo* precio fuera de embarcadero *m*, TRANSP *delivery* precio en el muelle *m*; **~ works export packing** *n* IMP/EXP *cargo* embalaje para exportación franco de fábrica *m*, TRANSP *cargo* embalaje de exportación en la fábrica *m*; **~-works price** *n* S&M precio franco fábrica *m*

ex. *abbr* GEN COMM (*extra*) extra, (*example*) ej. (*ejemplo*)

exacerbate *vt* GEN COMM exacerbar

exact[1] *adj* GEN COMM correcto, exacto

exact[2]: **~ interest** *n* BANK interés a 365 días *m*, interés anual *m*

exaggerated *adj* GEN COMM extremado

exam: ~ result *n* GEN COMM resultado de los exámenes *m*

examination *n* GEN COMM, HRM examen *m*, IMP/EXP *by customs* revisión *f*, PATENTS interrogatorio *m*; **~ of proposal** INS examen de proposición *m*

examine *vt* GEN COMM *application* examinar, revisar; ◆ **~ in depth** GEN COMM examinar en profundidad

examined *adj* (*exd.*) GEN COMM revisado (*ex*)

examiner *n* GEN COMM, HRM *of candidate* examinador(a) *m,f*, IMP/EXP *customs* tasador(a) de aduanas *m,f*, inspector(a) de aduanas *m,f*, PATENTS examinador(a) *m,f*

example[2] *n* (*ex.*) GEN COMM ejemplo *m* (*ej.*); ◆ **for ~** (*e.g.*) GEN COMM por ejemplo (*p.ej.*)

exceed *vt* ACC exceder, ADMIN sobrepasar, ECON *supply, demand* superar, GEN COMM sobrepasar

exceeding: **not ~** *phr* GEN COMM sin que exceda

except *prep* GEN COMM salvo; ◆ **~ as otherwise provided** TAX salvo disposición contraria; **~ for** GEN COMM a reserva de; **~ otherwise herein provided** (*eohp*) GEN COMM salvo indicación de lo contrario

excepted *adj* TRANSP exceptuado

exception *n* GEN COMM *case* excepción *f*; ◆ **with the ~ of** GEN COMM con la excepción de

exceptional[1] *adj* GEN COMM *case, circumstances* excepcional

exceptional[2]: **~ expenses** *n pl* ACC *balance sheet* gastos extraordinarios *m pl*; **~ item** *n* TRANSP elemento excepcional *m*

exceptions: **~ clause** *n* LAW *shipping* cláusula de excepción *f*

excess *n* GEN COMM exceso *m*, INS franquicia *f*, sobrante *m*; **~ amount** GEN COMM, TAX cantidad en exceso *f*; **~ baggage** GEN COMM, LEIS, TRANSP exceso de equipaje *m*; **~ baggage charge** LEIS, TRANSP cargo por exceso de equipaje *m*, recargo por exceso de equipaje *m*, pago por exceso de equipaje *m*; **~ bank reserves** *n pl* BANK exceso de depósito *m*; **~ burden of a tax** TAX exceso de gravamen fiscal *m*; **~ capacity** ECON, IND capacidad excedente *f*, excedente de capacidad *m*; **~ capacity theorem** ECON teorema del exceso de capacidad *m*; **~ cash** ACC exceso de efectivo *m*, exceso de liquidez *m*; **~ contribution** TAX contribución excesiva *f*; **~ demand** ECON, S&M demanda excedente *f*, exceso de demanda *m*; **~ employment** GEN COMM, HRM sobreempleo *m*; **~ fare** LEIS suplemento *m*; **~ insurance** GEN COMM, INS seguro complementario de excedente *m*; **~ liability** INS *marine* responsabilidad excedente *f*; **~ of line reinsurance** INS reaseguro por exceso de línea *m*; **~ of loss** INS exceso de pérdidas *m*; **~ of loss reinsurance** INS reaseguro de exceso de pérdida *m*; **~ of loss reinsurance treaty** INS tratado de reaseguro de exceso de pérdida *m*; **~ mortality** INS exceso de mortalidad *m*; **~ point** INS umbral de excedentes *m*; **~ profits tax** TAX impuesto sobre beneficios extraordinarios *m*; **~ purchasing power** ECON exceso de poder adquisitivo *m*; **~ reserve** BANK reserva extraordinaria *f*, reserva en exceso *f*; **~ revenue allotment** FIN distribución del ingreso excedente *f*; **~ shares** *n pl* STOCK excedente de acciones *m*; **~ supply** ECON, S&M exceso de oferta *m*, exceso de suministro *m*

excessive[1] *adj* GEN COMM excesivo

excessive[2]: **~ taxation** *n* TAX imposición excesiva *f*

excessively *adv* GEN COMM excesivamente

Exch *abbr* (*Exchange*) STOCK bolsa *f*

exchange[1] *n* COMMS *telephone* centralita *f*, ECON lonja *f*, GEN COMM cambio *m*, intercambio *m*, trueque *m*; **~ arbitrage** BANK, STOCK arbitraje de cambio *m*; **~ certificate** BANK, ECON, FIN, GEN COMM certificado de cambio monetario *m*; **~ charge** BANK cargo por diferencia de cambios *m*; **~ contract** LAW contrato de cambios *m*; **~ of contracts** GEN COMM intercambio de contratos *m*; **~ control** BANK, ECON, POL control de divisas *m*, control de cambios *m*; **~ control officer** HRM

oficial(a) de control de divisas *m,f*; **~ cross rate** ECON *currency* tipo de cambio cruzado *m*; **~ delivery settlement price** STOCK precio de liquidación de entrega de divisas *m*; **~ department** STOCK departamento de cambios *m*; **~ difference** ECON diferencia de cambio *f*; **~ discount** STOCK descuento de cambio *m*; **~ efficiency** ECON eficiencia de la bolsa *f*; **~ equalization account** BANK cuenta de igualación de cambios *f*; **~ fund** STOCK fondo de cambio *m*; **~ of information** GEN COMM intercambio de información *m*; **~ offer** STOCK oferta de divisas *f*; **~ office** BANK casa de cambio *m*; **~ privilege** STOCK privilegio en el cambio de divisas *m*; **~ rate** GEN COMM, ECON tipo de cambio *m*; **~ rate agreement** ECON acuerdo sobre los tipos de cambio *m*; **~ rate fluctuation** ECON, FIN fluctuación del tipo de cambio *f*; **~ rate movements** *n pl* ECON, GEN COMM oscilaciones de los tipos de cambio *m pl*; **~ rate regime** ECON régimen de los tipos de cambio *m*; **~ rate target zone** ECON zona meta de los tipos de cambio *f*; **~ risk guarantee scheme** BANK plan de garantía de riesgo de cambio *m*; **~ screen** STOCK tablero electrónico de la bolsa *m*; **~ of securities** STOCK operaciones con títulos *f pl*; **~ value** ECON, STOCK valor de cambio *m*; ◆ **in ~** ACC a cambio

exchange[2] *vt* COMMS *information, views* intercambiar, GEN COMM cambiar; ◆ **~ contracts** LAW suscribir el contrato

Exchange *n* (*Exch*) STOCK bolsa *f*; **~ Control Rate** (*ECR*) ECON tasa del control de los tipos de cambio *f*; **~ Equalization Account** (*EEA*) BANK cuenta de compensación de cambios *f*, cuenta de igualación de tipo de cambio *f*; **~ Rate Mechanism** (*ERM*) ECON mecanismo de ajuste de cambios *m* (*MAC*)

exchanged: **~ share** *n* FIN, STOCK acción intercambiada *f*

Exchequer *n BrE* FIN ≈ fisco *m*

excisable: **~ good** *n* TAX artículo imponible *m*

excise: **~ duty** *n* IMP/EXP contribución indirecta *f*, derecho arancelario *m*, derechos de aduana *m pl*, TAX impuesto sobre consumos específicos, derecho arancelario *m*, derechos de aduana *m pl*; **~ tax** *n* TAX impuesto sobre consumos específicos

excite: **~ interest** *phr* FIN, GEN COMM ser motivo de interés

excl. *abbr* GEN COMM (*excluding*) excepto, (*exclusive*) exclusivo

exclude *vt* GEN COMM excluir

excluded: **~ consideration** *n* TAX remuneración excluida *f*; **~ corporation** *n* TAX compañía excluida *f*; **~ dividend** *n* TAX dividendo excluido *m*; **~ obligation** *n* TAX obligación excluida *f*; **~ period** *n* TAX periodo excluido *m*; **~ property** *n* TAX propiedad excluida *f*; **~ sector** *n* IND sector excluido *m*

excluding *prep* (*excl.*) GEN COMM excepto

exclusion *n* TAX exención *f*; **~ clause** INS riesgo excluido *m*; **~ principle** ECON principio de exclusión *m*; ◆ **to the ~ of** GEN COMM con la exclusión de

exclusive[1] *adj* (*excl.*) GEN COMM exclusivo; ◆ **~ of tax** ECON, FIN, TAX exento de impuestos; **~ of loading and unloading** (*xl&ul*) IMP/EXP, TRANSP exceptuando la carga y descarga, exclusivo de carga y descarga; **~ of post and packing** GEN COMM exclusivo de envío y embalaje

exclusive[2]: **~ agency agreement** *n* LAW acuerdo de agencia exclusivo *m*; **~ agency listing** *n* PROP *brokers* listado de agencia exclusivo *m*; ~ **distribution** *n jarg* (*exdis*) POL material que sólo circula entre algunos ministros del gobierno norteamericano; ~ **licence** *BrE*, ~ **license** *AmE n* PATENTS licencia exclusiva *f*; ~ **monopoly** *n* ECON monopolio exclusivo *m*; ~ **right** *n* LAW, PATENTS derecho exclusivo *m*; ~ **right to sell listing** *n* PROP contrato de venta exclusivo *m*; ~ **taxation** *n* TAX imposición exclusiva *f*

exclusivity *n* S&M *of product* exclusividad *f*

ex cp. *abbr* (*ex coupon*) STOCK sin cupón

exculpatory *adj* BANK, LAW eximente

excursion: ~ **fare** *n* LEIS tarifa para excursiones *f*

exd. *abbr* (*examined*) GEN COMM revisado (*ex*)

exdis *abbr jarg* (*exclusive distribution*) POL material que sólo circula entre algunos ministros del gobierno estadounidense

ex div. *abbr* (*ex dividend*) FIN, STOCK ex-dividendo, sin dividendo, sin derecho a dividendo

exec. *abbr* GEN COMM, HRM (*executive*) ejecutivo(-a) *m,f*, LAW (*executor*) albacea testamentario(-a) *m,f*

execute *vt* GEN COMM ejecutar, STOCK servir pedidos; ◆ ~ **orders** STOCK ejecutar órdenes, realizar órdenes

executed: ~ **contract** *n* LAW contrato perfeccionado *m*

execution *n* GEN COMM ejecución *f*; ~ **time** COMP tiempo de ejecución *m*

executive[1] *adj* MGMNT, POL ejecutivo

executive[2] *n* (*exec.*) GEN COMM ejecutivo(-a) *m,f*; **the** ~ POL el ejecutivo *m*, el poder ejecutivo *m*; ~ **advancement** MGMNT promoción de altos cargos *f*; ~ **assistant** GEN COMM auxiliar ejecutivo(-a) *m,f*; ~ **board** GEN COMM, HRM, MGMNT consejo de administración *m*, consejo ejecutivo *m*; ~ **class** LEIS, TRANSP clase ejecutiva *f*; ~ **committee** HRM *of union* comisión ejecutiva *f*, comité ejecutivo *m*, MGMNT *decision-making* comité ejecutivo *m*; ~ **compensation** MGMNT *travelling expenses* compensación a ejecutivos *f*; ~ **competence** MGMNT competencia ejecutiva *f*; ~ **development** GEN COMM, MGMNT desarrollo de ejecutivos *m*; ~ **director** HRM, MGMNT director(a) ejecutivo(-a) *m,f*; ~ **grade** HRM categoría ejecutiva *f*; ~ **leasing** MGMNT *of vehicles for company business* alquiler ejecutivo *m* (*Esp*), arrendamiento ejecutivo *m* (*AmL*); ~ **lounge** GEN COMM, TRANSP *air, ship* salón de clase ejecutivo *m*; ~ **manager** HRM, MGMNT director(a) ejecutivo(-a) *m,f*, gerente ejecutivo(-a) *m,f*; ~ **manpower strategy** HRM, MGMNT estrategia de la fuerza de trabajo ejecutiva *f*, estrategia laboral para altos cargos *f*; ~ **officer** (*EO*) HRM, MGMNT director(a) ejecutivo(-a) *m,f*; ~ **option scheme** HRM, MGMNT, STOCK plan de opción para los ejecutivos *m*; ~ **perk** *infrml* HRM, MGMNT ventaja adicional de los ejecutivos *f*; ~ **perquisite** HRM, MGMNT ventaja adicional de los ejecutivos *f*; ~ **power** POL poder ejecutivo *m*; ~ **promotion** HRM, MGMNT promoción de ejecutivos *f*; ~ **remuneration** HRM remuneración de los ejecutivos *f*; ~ **search** HRM, MGMNT búsqueda ejecutiva *f*; ~ **search firm** HRM *headhunter* compañía de búsqueda de ejecutivos *f*, empresa para captación de ejecutivos *f*; ~ **secretary** HRM secretario(-a) ejecutivo(-a) *m,f*; ~ **share option scheme** HRM, STOCK plan de opción sobre acciones para ejecutivos *m*; ~ **stress** HRM estrés del ejecutivo *m*; ~-**style housing** PROP vivienda de estilo ejecutivo *f*; ~ **training** HRM, MGMNT capacitación de ejecutivos *f* (*AmL*), capacitación ejecutiva *f* (*AmL*), formación de ejecutivos *f* (*Esp*), formación ejecutiva *f* (*Esp*); ~ **vice president** HRM, MGMNT vicepresidente(-a) ejecutivo(-a) *m,f*

executor *n* (*exor, exec.*) LAW *of will* albacea testamentario(-a) *m,f*

executory *adj* LAW ejecutorio

executrix *n* LAW albacea testamentaria *f*

exempli gratia *adv* (*e.g.*) GEN COMM por ejemplo (*p.ej.*)

exempt[1] *adj* GEN COMM, TAX exento

exempt[2]: ~ **assets** *n pl* TAX activos exentos *m pl*; ~ **corporation** *n* TAX compañía exenta *f*; ~ **deficit** *n* TAX déficit exento *m*; ~ **dividend** *n* STOCK dividendo exento *m*; ~ **earnings** *n pl* TAX ganancias exentas *f pl*; ~ **employees** *n pl AmE* HRM empleados exentos *m pl*; ~ **income** *n* ACC, TAX ingresos exentos de impuestos *m pl*; ~ **interest** *n* TAX interés exento *m*; ~ **organization** *n* LAW, TAX entidad exenta *f*; ~ **percentage** *n* TAX porcentaje exento *m*; ~ **period** *n* ACC, ECON, FIN periodo exento *m*; ~ **rating** *n* S&M productos exentos de IVA *m pl*; ~ **securities** *n pl* STOCK títulos exentos *m pl*; ~ **supplies** *n pl* TAX suministros exentos *m pl*; ~ **surplus** *n* TAX superávit exento *m*

exempt[3] *vt* GEN COMM, HRM eximir, TAX *dividend* pagar en origen

exempted: ~ **sum** *n* TAX cantidad exenta *f*, cantidad eximida *f*

exemption *n* GEN COMM exención *f*, TAX exención *f*, inmunidad fiscal *f*; ~ **certificate** TAX certificado de exención *m*; ~ **clause** GEN COMM *contract clause* cláusula de exención *f*; ~ **for dependent children** TAX exención por tener hijos al cargo *f*; ~ **for dependents** TAX exención por personas a cargo *f*; ~ **from payment of premium** INS exención de prima *f*

exemptions *n pl* HRM exenciones *f pl*

exercisable *adj* GEN COMM ejecutable

exercise[1] *n* GEN COMM, STOCK *option* ejercicio *m*; ~ **date** GEN COMM *right* fecha de comunicación *f*, STOCK *option* fecha de ejecución *f*; ~ **deadline** STOCK fecha límite del ejercicio *f*, límite del ejercicio *m*; ~ **limit** STOCK límite del ejercicio *m*; ~ **notice** STOCK notificación de ejercicio *f*; ~ **of an option** STOCK ejercicio de una opción *m*; ~ **price** STOCK precio de ejercicio *m*; ~ **procedure** STOCK *options* procedimiento de ejercicio *m*; ~ **of rights** STOCK ejercicio de los derechos *m*; ~ **of undue authority** GEN COMM uso indebido de autoridad *m*

exercise[2] *vt* LAW *right*, STOCK *option, right* ejercer; ◆ ~ **a franchise** S&M vender en régimen de franquicia

exert *vt* GEN COMM *effect* ejercer

exhaust[1]: ~ **emission** *n* ENVIR emisión de gases *f*; ~ **gas** *n* ENVIR *from vehicles* gas de escape *m*

exhaust[2] *vt* GEN COMM *resources* agotar

exhaustive *adj* GEN COMM exhaustivo

exhibit[1] *n* INS anexo *m*, LAW *proof in court* documento *m*, objeto *m*

exhibit[2] *vt* GEN COMM *goods* mostrar

exhibition *n* LAW, LEIS exhibición *f*, S&M exposición *f*; ~ **center** *AmE*, ~ **centre** *BrE* GEN COMM centro de exposición *m*; ~ **forwarding** IMP/EXP, TRANSP transporte de una exposición *m*; ~ **risks insurance** INS seguro de exposiciones *m*; ~ **room** GEN COMM sala de exposiciones *f*

EXIM *abbr* (*export-import bank*) IMP/EXP banco de exportaciones e importaciones *m*

exit[1]: **~ barrier** *n* ECON, IMP/EXP barrera de salida *f*; **~ interview** *n* HRM entrevista de salida *f*; **~ price** *n* STOCK precio de salida *m*; **~ voice** *n* ECON, HRM forma de revelar las preferencias *f*

exit[2] *vi* COMP salir

ex nudo pacto non oritur actio *phr* GEN COMM ex nudo pacto non oritur actio

exogenous: **~ expectations** *n pl* ECON expectativas exógenas *f pl*; **~ factor** *n* ECON factor exógeno *m*; **~ variable** *n* ECON variable exógena *f*

exor *abbr* (*executor*) LAW albacea testamentario(-a) *m,f*

exotic: **~ currency** *n* BANK, ECON *international* divisa exótica *f*

exotics *n pl* STOCK exóticas *f pl*

exp. *abbr* (*export*) IMP/EXP exportación *f*

expand *vt* GEN COMM *activities* ampliar, alargar

expandable *adj* COMP *hardware, software* ampliable

expanded[1] *adj* GEN COMM alargado

expanded[2]: **~ type** *n* S&M tipo expandido *m*

expanding *adj* GEN COMM expansionario, expansivo

expansion *n* GEN COMM, IND ampliación *f*, *of company* expansión *f*; **~ board** COMP tarjeta de expansión *f*; **~ business cycle** ECON fase expansiva del ciclo económico *f*; **~ card** COMP tarjeta de expansión *f*; **~ of demand** S&M expansión de la demanda *f*; **~ strategy** GEN COMM estrategia de expansión *f*

expansionary *adj* GEN COMM *fiscal policy* expansionista

expansive *adj* GEN COMM expansivo

expatriate *n* GEN COMM expatriado(-a) *m,f*; **~ executive** GEN COMM ejecutivo(-a) desplazado(-a) al extranjero *m,f*

expect *vt* GEN COMM anticipar

expectancy: **~ theory of motivation** *n* HRM teoría de la expectativa-valencia *f*, teoría de la motivación por expectativas *f*

expectation *n* GEN COMM, MATH *expected value* expectativa *f*; ◆ **in ~ of** GEN COMM en espera de

expected[1] *adj* GEN COMM *result, outcome* esperado

expected[2]: **~ actual capacity** *n* ECON capacidad real estimada *f*; **~ date** *n* GEN COMM fecha esperada *f*, fecha prevista *f*; **~ mortality** *n* INS mortalidad prevista *f*; **~ peril** *n* INS riesgo esperado *m*; **~ value** *n* MATH valor esperado *m*

expediency *n* GEN COMM aptitud *f*

expedite *vt* GEN COMM apresurar

Expedited: **~ Funds Availability** *n* (*EFA*) BANK, FIN disponibilidad de fondos expeditados *f*

expendable[1] *adj* GEN COMM consumible

expendable[2]: **~ goods** *n pl* GEN COMM bienes consumibles *m pl*; **~ pallet** *n* TRANSP plataforma de carga no recuperable *f*

expendables *n pl* COMP *paper, peripherals* consumibles *m pl*

expenditure *n* GEN COMM egreso *m*, desembolso *m*, gasto *m*; **~ base** TAX base del gasto *f*; **~ budget** GEN COMM presupuesto de gastos *m*; **~ function** ECON función de gastos *f*; **~ limit** TAX límite del gasto *m*; **~ tax** ECON, TAX impuesto sobre los gastos *m*

expense *n* GEN COMM gasto *m*; **~ account** ACC, GEN COMM cuenta de gastos *f*; **~ allowance** TAX deducción de gastos *f*; **~ budget** ACC presupuesto de gastos *m*; **~ center** *AmE*, **~ centre** *BrE* ACC centro de gastos *m*;

~ ratio ECON, STOCK proporción de gasto *f*; **~ report** ACC informe de gastos *m* (*Esp*), reporte de gastos *m* (*AmL*)

expenses *n pl* ACC, GEN COMM costes *m pl* (*Esp*), costos *m pl* (*AmL*), gastos *m pl*; **~ control** *n* ACC control de gastos *m*; **~ incurred** ACC, FIN gastos incurridos *m pl*; ◆ **all ~ paid** GEN COMM todos los gastos pagados

expensive[1] *adj* GEN COMM caro

expensive[2]: **~ easy money** *n* FIN dinero fácil costoso *m*

experience[1] *n* GEN COMM, HRM experiencia *f*; **~ curve** ECON curva de experiencia *f*; **~ deficiency** INS deficiencia de experiencia *f*; **~ good** ECON bien que el consumidor compra para encontrarle cada vez más utilidades; **~ rating** INS tipo ajustado a los antecedentes del asegurado *m*; **~ refund** INS devolución por experiencia *f*

experience[2] *vt* GEN COMM, HRM *growth* experimentar

experienced[1] *adj* GEN COMM, HRM experimentado

experienced[2]: **~ investor** *n* STOCK inversor(a) con experiencia *m,f*; **~ workforce** *n* HRM mano de obra con experiencia *f*

experiment *n* GEN COMM experimento *m*

expert[1] *adj* GEN COMM, HRM experto; ◆ **take ~ advice** GEN COMM pedir una opinion cualificada

expert[2]: **~ accountant** *n* ACC perito(-a) contable *m,f*, experto(-a) contable *m,f*; **~ network** *n* GEN COMM red de expertos *f*; **~ system** *n* (*ES*) COMP, GEN COMM sistema experto *m*; **~ witness** *n* LAW testigo pericial *m*

expertise *n* GEN COMM conocimiento experto *m*, experiencia *f*

expiration *n* GEN COMM expiración *f*, *date* vencimiento *m*, STOCK vencimiento *m*; **~ cycle** STOCK ciclo de caducidad *m*, ciclo de vencimiento *m*; **~ date** STOCK fecha de caducidad *f*; **~ month** STOCK *currency futures* mes de vencimiento *m*; **~ notice** INS *policy* notificación de expiración *f*

expire *vi* ACC caducar, GEN COMM *lapse* expirar, INS, STOCK caducar; ◆ **~ in-the-money** STOCK llegar al vencimiento con beneficio potencial; **~ worthless** STOCK llegar al vencimiento sin valor alguno

expired *adj* ACC, INS, STOCK caducado

expiring: **~ of a policy** *n* INS expiración de una póliza *f*

expiry *n* ACC caducidad *f*, GEN COMM expiración *f*, INS, STOCK caducidad *f*; **~ of agreement** HRM vencimiento del acuerdo *m*; **~ date** GEN COMM, STOCK fecha de vencimiento *f*; **~ month** STOCK mes de vencimiento *m*

explain *vt* GEN COMM explicar, aclarar, MGMNT aclarar

explanation *n* ACC *notes* explicación *f*, GEN COMM aclaración *f*, nota *f*, MGMNT aclaración *f*

explicit[1] *adj* GEN COMM explícito

explicit[2]: **~ contract** *n* LAW contrato explícito *m*; **~ cost** *n* ECON coste explícito *m* (*Esp*), costo explícito *m* (*AmL*)

explode *vi* COMP estallar

exploded: **~ view** *n* S&M vista despiezada *f*

exploit *vt* GEN COMM explotar

exploitation *n* GEN COMM explotación *f*; **~ in industry** IND, PATENTS explotación industrial *f*; **~ of a patent** PATENTS explotación de una patente *f*

exploitative: **~-authoritative** *adj* MGMNT *Likert's leadership* autoridad de explotación *f*, autoridad de explotador *f*

exploited: **~ resource** *n* ENVIR recurso explotado *m*

exploration: **~ and development expense tax credit** *n*

TAX desgravación de gastos de exploración y explotación *f*

explosive: ~ **article** *n* TRANSP artículo explosivo *m*

exponent *n* MATH exponente *m*

exponential: ~ **function** *n* COMP, MATH *computer programmer* función exponencial *f*; ~ **notation** *n* MATH notación exponencial *f*; ~ **smoothing** *n* GEN COMM nivelación exponencial *f*, uniformación exponencial *f*, MATH *forecasting technique* aproximación exponencial *f*; ~ **trend** *n* GEN COMM tendencia exponencial *f*

export *n* (*exp.*) IMP/EXP exportación *f*; ~ **adjustment loan** (*EAL*) ECON, IMP/EXP préstamo de regulación de la exportación *m*; ~ **agent** HRM agente de exportación *mf*, comisionista de exportación *mf*; ~ **berth** TRANSP *shipping* muelle de exportación *m*; ~ **capacity** BANK, GEN COMM, ECON, IMP/EXP capacidad exportadora *f*; ~ **cargo packing declaration** (*ECPD*) IMP/EXP, TRANSP declaración de embalaje de carga para exportación *f*; ~ **cargo shipping instruction** (*ECSI*) IMP/EXP, TRANSP instrucción de expedición de carga para exportación *f*; ~ **clerk** HRM, IMP/EXP, TRANSP empleado(-a) de exportación *m,f*, oficial(a) de exportación *m,f*; ~ **club** IMP/EXP club de exportadores *m*; ~ **consignment identification** (*ECI*) IMP/EXP identificación de remesa de exportación *m*; ~ **control** IMP/EXP control a la exportación *m*; ~ **coordinator** HRM coordinador(a) de exportación *m,f*; ~ **credit** IMP/EXP crédito a la exportación *m*; ~ **credit insurance** INS seguro de crédito a la exportación *m*; ~ **data folder** IMP/EXP expediente de exportación *m*; ~ **depot charges** *n pl* IMP/EXP gastos de almacén de la exportación *m pl*; ~ **director** HRM, IMP/EXP, MGMNT director(a) de exportación *m,f*, jefe(-a) de exportación *m,f*; ~ **documentation** IMP/EXP documentación de exportación *f*; ~ **documentation procedure** ADMIN, IMP/EXP procedimiento documental de exportación *m*; ~ **earnings** *n pl* ECON ingresos por exportación *m pl*, IMP/EXP ganancias de la exportación *f pl*, ingresos por exportación *m pl*; ~ **facilitation organization** IMP/EXP organización de ayuda a la exportación *f*; ~ **factoring** IMP/EXP factoraje de exportación *m*; ~ **figures** *n pl* ECON, IMP/EXP cifras de exportación *f pl*; ~ **finance** FIN, IMP/EXP financiación de la exportación *f*; ~ **finance house** FIN sociedad financiera para la exportación *f*; ~ **financing** FIN, IMP/EXP financiación de la exportación *f*; ~ **goods fair** IMP/EXP feria de la exportación *f*; ~ **of goods order** IMP/EXP, TRANSP pedido de exportación de bienes *m*; ~ **house** IMP/EXP casa exportadora *f*; ~ **invoice** IMP/EXP, TRANSP factura para exportación *f*; ~**-led economic recovery** ECON, IMP/EXP recuperación económica inducida por la exportación *f*; ~**-led growth** IMP/EXP crecimiento inducido por las exportaciones *m*; ~ **licence** *BrE* IMP/EXP permiso de exportación *m*; ~ **licence expiry date** *BrE* IMP/EXP fecha de expiración de licencia de exportación *f*, fecha de vencimiento de licencia de exportación *f*; ~ **licence number** *BrE* IMP/EXP, TRANSP número de licencia de exportación *m*; ~ **license** *AmE see export licence BrE*; ~ **license expiry date** *AmE see export licence expiry date BrE*; ~ **license number** *AmE see export licence number BrE*; ~ **licensing branch** (*ELB*) IMP/EXP oficina de licencias de exportación *f*; ~ **loan** BANK, IMP/EXP préstamo a la exportación *m*; ~ **manager** HRM, IMP/EXP, MGMNT director(a) de exportación *m,f*, jefe(-a) de exportación *m,f*; ~ **man-**

agement company IMP/EXP compañía de gestión de la exportación *f*; ~ **of manufactures** IMP/EXP exportación de productos industriales *f*; ~ **market** IMP/EXP mercado de exportación *m*; ~ **market research** IMP/EXP, S&M investigación de mercados exteriores *f*; ~ **marketing** IMP/EXP, S&M marketing de exportación *m*; ~ **marketing manager** HRM, MGMNT, S&M director(a) de marketing para la exportación *m,f*; ~ **merchant** ECON, GEN COMM, HRM, S&M exportador(a) *m,f*; ~ **office** IMP/EXP, TRANSP oficina de exportación *f*; ~ **order check list** IMP/EXP lista de comprobación del pedido de exportación *f*; ~ **packer** IMP/EXP embalador(-a) de exportación *m,f*; ~ **performance** IMP/EXP resultado de las exportaciones *m*; ~ **permit** IMP/EXP licencia de exportación *f*; ~ **price** ECON, IMP/EXP precio de exportación *m*; ~ **processing zone authority** (*EPZA*) IMP/EXP autoridad zonal de tratamiento de la exportación *f*; ~ **promotion** IMP/EXP fomento de la exportación *m*; ~ **regulations** *n pl* IMP/EXP reglamentación de exportación *f*; ~ **reject** IMP/EXP rechazo a la exportación *m*; ~ **sales** *n pl* GEN COMM exportaciones *f pl*; ~ **sales manager** S&M jefe(-a) de ventas de exportación *m,f*; ~ **sector** IMP/EXP, TRANSP sector de exportación *m*; ~ **services voucher** IMP/EXP comprobante de servicios de exportación *m*; ~ **shed** IMP/EXP almacén de exportación *m*; ~ **subsidy** IMP/EXP subsidio a la exportación *m*; ~ **surplus** IMP/EXP excedente de exportación *m*; ~ **tax** TAX impuesto sobre la exportación *m*; ~ **turnover** IMP/EXP facturación de exportación *f*

Export: ~ **Credit Guarantee Department** *n* (*ECGD*) IMP/EXP departamento de garantía de créditos a la exportación; ~ **Representative Service** *n BrE* IMP/EXP servicio de representación a la exportación

exportation *n* GEN COMM, IMP/EXP exportación *f*

exported *adj* ECON, IMP/EXP exportado

exporter *n* ECON, GEN COMM, HRM, S&M exportador(a) *m,f*; ~**'s acceptance credit** BANK crédito de aceptación del exportador *m*; ~ **credit** BANK, IMP/EXP crédito de exportador *m*; ~ **status** ACC, BANK, IMP/EXP carta de exportador *f*

export-import: ~ **bank** *n AmE* (*EXIM*) IMP/EXP banco de exportaciones e importaciones *m*

exporting *adj* GEN COMM, IMP/EXP exportador

EXPORTIT *abbr* (*Information Technology Export Organization*) IMP/EXP organización de exportación de tecnología de la información

exports *n pl* GEN COMM exportaciones *f pl*; ~ **good fair** *n* GEN COMM feria de la exportación *f*

expose *vt* GEN COMM, STOCK exponer; ♦ ~ **to** GEN COMM *pressures* exponer a

exposed[1]: ~ **net asset position** *n* GEN COMM posición del activo líquido expuesta *f*; ~ **net liability position** *n* BANK posición del pasivo neto arriesgado *f*; ~ **sector** *n* GEN COMM sector expuesto *m*

exposed[2]: **in an** ~ **position** *phr* GEN COMM en una posición peligrosa *f*

exposition *n* GEN COMM, STOCK exposición *f*

ex post facto *phr* LAW de hechos posteriores

expostulatory: ~ **letter** *n* ACC, ADMIN, BANK carta de amonestación *f*

exposure *n* FIN compromisos netos *m pl*, S&M *advertising* exposición *f*, STOCK extensión del riesgo *f*; ~ **draft** ACC borrador de riesgo *m*, informe provisional de riesgo *m* (*Esp*), proyecto de riesgo *m*, reporte crediticio *m* (*AmL*)

express[1] *adj* COMMS, GEN COMM, TRANSP *intent* expreso, *service* urgente

express[2]: **~ agency** *n* GEN COMM agencia de mensajería *f*; **~ authority** *n* GEN COMM autorización expresa *f*; **~ condition** *n* GEN COMM, HRM condición expresa *f*; **~ contract** *n* LAW contrato expreso *m*; **~ delivery** *n* GEN COMM envío urgente *m*, transporte urgente *m*; **~ delivery service** *n* COMMS, GEN COMM servicio de envío urgente *m*, servicio de transporte urgente *m*, TRANSP servicio de transporte urgente *m*; **~ mail service** *n* COMMS, GEN COMM servicio urgente de correos *m*; **~ telegraphic money transfer** *n* BANK, FIN transferencia monetaria telegráfica urgente *f*; **~ term** *n* GEN COMM *of contract* término explícito *m*, término expreso *m*, condición expresa *f*, HRM condición expresa *f*, LAW *of contract* término explícito *m*, término expreso *m*; **~ warranty** *n* GEN COMM garantía expresa *f*

expressage *n* GEN COMM porte por tren expreso *m*

expression *n* COMP *programming language* expresión *f*

expressway *n* TRANSP autopista *f*

expropriate *vt* LAW, PROP expropriar

expropriation: **~ asset** *n* TAX activo de la expropiación *m*

expunge *vt* TRANSP cancelar

ExQ *abbr* (*ex-quay*) GEN COMM en el muelle, IMP/EXP *shipping*, TRANSP franco muelle

extend *vt* BANK *payment* prorrogar, GEN COMM *power* extender, *research, study, knowledge* ampliar, LAW *rules, contract* prorrogar, PATENTS prorrogar; ◆ **~ a loan** BANK conceder un crédito; **~ the time limit** GEN COMM ampliar el límite de tiempo

extended: **~ coverage** *n* INS cobertura ampliada *f*; **~ coverage endorsement** *n* INS endoso de extensión de cobertura *m*; **~ credit** *n* S&M crédito ampliado *m*; **~ deferment** *n* ACC *of credits, debits* aplazamiento ampliado *m*, novación *f*; **~ fund facility** *n* FIN servicio de fondos ampliados *m*; **~ guarantee** *n* S&M garantía prolongada *f*; **~ payment** *n* ACC, FIN pago prorrogado *m*; **~ program** *AmE*, **~ programme** *BrE* *n* GEN COMM programa ampliado *m*; **~ term** *n* BANK plazo alargado *m*; **~ use test** *n* S&M prueba de uso ampliado *f*

extendible: **~ bond** *n* FIN, STOCK bono de vencimiento ajustable *m*

extensibility *n* GEN COMM capacidad de ampliación *f*

extension *n* BANK prórroga *f*, COMP *file name* extensión *f*, GEN COMM prolongación *f*, LAW, PATENTS *time limits* prórroga *f*; **~ costs** *n pl* INS costes de ampliación *m pl* (*Esp*), costos de ampliación *m pl* (*AmL*); **~ fee** BANK comisión de renegociación *f*, cuota de renegociación *f*; **~ for returns** TAX ampliación para los beneficios *f*; **~ fork** TRANSP desviación secundaria *f*; **~ service** FIN, MGMNT servicio de extensión *m*, servicio exterior *m*; **~ of time** TAX *to file return* prolongación del plazo *m*; **~ to a building** TAX ampliación a una construcción *f*

extensive: **~ farming** *n* ECON, ENVIR *agricultural* cultivo extensivo *m*; **~ selling** *n* S&M venta extensiva *f*

extent *n* PATENTS *of protection* grado *m*; **~ of damage** INS extensión del daño *f*; **~ of cover** GEN COMM amplitud de cobertura *f*; ◆ **to a certain ~** GEN COMM en cierta medida; **to a large ~** GEN COMM en mayor medida, en gran parte; **to a lesser ~** GEN COMM en menor medida

extenuating: **~ circumstances** *n pl* LAW circunstancias atenuantes *f pl*

external: **~ account** *n* ECON cuenta de transacciones exteriores *f*, POL cuenta externa *f*; **~ audit** *n* ACC auditoría externa *f*; **~ balance** *n* ECON saldo externo *m*, POL balanza externa *f*; **~ border** *n* GEN COMM frontera exterior *f*; **~ borrowings** *n pl* FIN endeudamiento externo *m*; **~ consumption** *n* ECON consumo externo *m*; **~ cost** *n* ACC coste externo *m* (*Esp*), costo externo *m* (*AmL*); **~ debt** *n* ECON, POL deuda exterior *f*; **~ debt ratio** *n* ECON proporción de la deuda exterior *f*, POL tasa de deuda externa *f*; **~ debtor** *n* ACC deudor(a) exterior *m,f*, deudor(a) externo(-a) *m,f*; **~ device** *n* COMP dispositivo externo *f*; **~ director** *n* HRM, MGMNT director(a) externo(-a) *m,f*; **~ document** *n* GEN COMM documento externo *m*; **~ economy** *n* GEN COMM economía exterior *f*; **~ economy of scale** *n* ECON economía externa de escala *f*; **~ financing** *n* ACC, FIN financiación externa *f*; **~ financing limit** *n* (*EFL*) FIN límite de financiación externa *m*; **~ funds** *n pl* FIN fondos externos *m pl*; **~ government policy** *n* ECON, POL política exterior del gobierno *f*; **~ house magazine** *n* MEDIA, S&M revista de producción ajena *f*; **~ labor market** *AmE*, **~ labour market** *BrE* *n* ECON mercado laboral externo *m*; **~ procedure** *n* TRANSP procedimiento externo *m*; **~ relation** *n* GEN COMM, MGMNT relación externa *f*; **~ report** *n* GEN COMM informe externo *m* (*Esp*), reporte externo *m* (*AmL*); **~ shock** *n* ECON *of offer* choque externo *m*; **~ surplus** *n* BANK, ECON superávit de la balanza de pagos *m*; **~ trade guarantee** *n* INS garantía de comercio exterior *f*; **~ trade indicator** *n* ECON, IMP/EXP indicador de comercio exterior *m*

externality *n* ECON *third-party effect* externalidad *f*

externalize *vt* ECON externalizar

externally: **~ funded pension** *n* *BrE* FIN pensión no contributiva *f*

extinction *n* ENVIR extinción *f*, LAW *of action* anulación *f*

extinguish *vt* ENVIR extinguir

extort *vt* FIN, GEN COMM extorsionar

extortion: **~ insurance** *n* INS seguro contra extorsión *m*

extra[1] *adj* GEN COMM extra, suplementario; **~-territorial** GEN COMM extraterritorial

extra[2] *n* (*ex.*) GEN COMM extra *m*; **~-billing** ACC facturación extra *f*; **~ charge** ACC recargo *m*; **~ dividend** STOCK dividendo extraordinario *m*; **~ freight** GEN COMM sobreflete *m*; **~ interest** GEN COMM interés extraordinario *m*; **~ pay** HRM paga extra *f*; **~ postage** GEN COMM porte suplementario *m*; **~-special quality steel cable** TRANSP *ship's equipment* cable de acero de calidad especial extra *m*; **~ tare** GEN COMM tara extra *f*

extract[1] *n* GEN COMM *from document* extracto *m*; **~ from the register** PATENTS extracto del registro *m*

extract[2] *vt* FIN, GEN COMM, LAW extraer

extractable: **~ reserve** *n* ENVIR *energy resources* reserva extraíble *f*

extraction *n* GEN COMM extracción *f*

extractive: **~ industry** *n* IND *mining* industria de extracción *f*

extrajudicially *adv* LAW extrajudicialmente

extramarginal *adj* ECON extramarginal

extraofficial *adj* GEN COMM extraoficial

extraofficially *adv* GEN COMM extraoficialmente

extraordinary: ~ **charges** *n* ACC *balance sheets* cargas extraordinarias *f pl*, cargo extraordinario *m*, gastos extraordinarios *m pl*; ~ **dividend** *n* STOCK dividendo extraordinario *m*; ~ **expenditure** *n* ACC gastos extraordinarios *m pl*; ~ **expenses** *n pl* ACC gastos extraordinarios *m pl*; ~ **gain** *n* ACC ganancia extraordinaria *f*; ~ **general meeting** *n* (*EGM*) GEN COMM, MGMNT junta general extraordinaria *f*; ~ **item** *n* GEN COMM partida extraordinaria *f*; ~ **loss** *n* ACC pérdida extraordinaria *f*; ~ **meeting** *n* GEN COMM asamblea extraordinaria *f*

extrapolation *n* MATH extrapolación *f*

extrapolative: ~ **expectations** *n pl* ECON expectativas extrapoladas *f pl*

extraterritorial: ~ **enforcement** *n* LAW ejecución extraterritorial *f*

extravagance *n* TAX despilfarro *m*

extreme: ~ **hardship** *n* TAX situación precaria *f*

extremum *n* ECON extremo *m*

extrinsic: ~ **motivation** *n* HRM motivación extrínseca *f*; ~ **value** *n* ECON, STOCK *options* valor extrínseco *m*

ExW *abbr* (*ex-works*) GEN COMM, IMP/EXP, TRANSP ex fábrica, franco fábrica

eye[1]: ~-**catching** *adj* S&M llamativo

eye[2]: ~ **bolt** *n* TRANSP *container-securing* armella *f*; ~ **contact** *n* S&M contacto visual *m*; ~-**movement camera** *n* S&M cámara de movimiento ocular *f*; ~-**observation camera** *n* S&M cámara de observación ocular *f*; ~ **wash** *n* *infrml* S&M *of product* alabanzas desmesuradas; ~ **witness** *n* LAW testigo ocular *m*

eyes: **in the** ~ **of the law** *phr* LAW a los ojos de la ley

EZ *abbr* (*enterprise zone*) ECON, HRM, IND zona de desarrollo industrial *f*

EZC *abbr* (*European zone charge*) TRANSP costes de zona europea *m pl* (*Esp*), costos de zona europea *m pl* (*AmL*)

F

F[1] *abbr* (*fahrenheit*) GEN COMM F (*grados fahrenheit*)

F[2]: **~ key** *n* (*function key*) COMP tecla de función *f*

f.a.a. *abbr* (*free of all average*) GEN COMM libre de toda avería

FAA *abbr* (*Federal Aviation Administration*) TRANSP administración federal de aviación

fabricate *vt* GEN COMM, IND fabricar

fabricator *n* GEN COMM fabricante *mf*

fac *abbr* TRANSP (*fast as can*) *loading, discharging* tan rápido como pueda, (*forwarding agent's commission*) comisión de agente expedidor *f*

facade *n* PROP *of building* fachada *f*

face[1]: **~ amount** *n* INS valor nominal *m*; **~ interest rate** *n* BANK tasa de interés facial *f*; **~ of policy** *n* INS valor de la póliza *m*; **~-to-face selling** *n* S&M venta por contacto directo *f*; **~ value** *n* STOCK valor facial *m*, valor nominal *m*

face[2] *vt* GEN COMM *criticism, attacks, future* afrontar, hacer frente a; ◆ **~ the facts** GEN COMM afrontar los hechos; **~ risks** STOCK afrontar riesgos

face up: **~ to sth** *phr* GEN COMM *problems, responsibilities* hacer frente a algo; **~ to sb** *phr* GEN COMM encarar a alguien

facilitate *vt* ECON *credit controls*, GEN COMM facilitar

facilitation *n* ECON *of credit controls*, GEN COMM facilitación *f*, facilitamiento *m*

facilities *n pl* GEN COMM instalaciones *f pl*

facility *n* COMP instalación *f*, GEN COMM línea de crédito *f*; **~ letter** IMP/EXP carta de servicios *f*; **~ trip** *jarg* POL recorrido de las instalaciones *m*; **~ visit** S&M visita de instalación *f*

facing *n* S&M superficie de presentación *f*; **~ matter** S&M anuncio colocado en la página opuesta al editorial

facsimile *n* (*fax*) GEN COMM facsímil *m* (*fax*); **~ signature** GEN COMM firma facsimilar *f*; **~ transaction** COMMS, GEN COMM transacción por facsímil *f*; **~ transmission** ADMIN, COMMS transmisión facsimilar *f*

fact: **~-finding** *n* LAW determinación de los hechos *f*; **~-finding mission** *n* GEN COMM misión de investigación *f*

faction *n* HRM facción *f*

factoblig *abbr* (*facultative/obligatory*) INS *re-insurance* opcional/obligatorio

factor *n* ECON coeficiente *m*, GEN COMM factor *m*; **~ analysis** MATH análisis factorial *m*, análisis de factores *m*; **~ cost** ACC, ECON, IND coste de los factores *m* (*Esp*), costo de los factores *m* (*AmL*); **~ endowment** ECON dotación de factores *f*; **~ income** ECON ingreso de los factores *m*; **~ market** ECON mercado de factores de producción *m*; **~ price equalization theorem** ECON teorema de la igualdad del precio de los factores *m*; **~ of production** ECON, IND factor de producción *m*; **~ of productivity** ECON factor de productividad *m*, IND razones de productividad *f pl*; **~ tax** ECON, TAX factor impositivo *m*; ◆ **be a ~ in** GEN COMM ser un factor de

factorage *n* FIN *percentage* comisión *f*

factorial *n* MATH factorial *m*; **~ terms of trade** ECON relación real de intercambio *f*

factoring *n* ACC *of debts*, FIN factorización *f*, factoraje *m*, GEN COMM cobro de deudas de otra persona *m*, MATH factoraje *m*, MGMNT factoring *m*

factors: **~ of production** *n pl* ECON, IND factores de producción *m pl*

factory *n* GEN COMM, HRM, IND fábrica *f*, factoría *f*; **~ costs** *n pl* IND costes de fabricación *m pl* (*Esp*), costos de fabricación *m pl* (*AmL*); **~ farming** ECON, ENVIR cultivo industrializado *m*; **~ floor** IND suelo industrial *m*; **~ hand** HRM, IND operario(-a) de fábrica *m,f*, operario(-a) de factoría *m,f*; **~ incentive scheme** HRM plan de incentivo en fábrica *m*, plan de incentivo en factoría *m*, plan de incentivo en planta *m*; **~ inspector** HRM, IND inspector(a) de fábrica *m,f*, inspector(a) de factoría *m,f*; **~ overheads** *n pl* ACC gastos indirectos de fábrica *m pl*, gastos indirectos de factoría *m pl*, gastos generales de fábrica *m pl*, gastos generales de factoría *m pl*; **~ supplies** *n pl* ACC materiales auxiliares *m pl*, materiales de fábrica *m pl*, materiales de factoría *m pl*

Factory: **~ Inspectorate** *n BrE* WEL cuerpo de inspectores sociales

facts: **~ and figures** *n pl* GEN COMM hechos y números *m pl*

factual[1] *adj* GEN COMM fáctico

factual[2]: **~ error** *n* GEN COMM error de hecho *m*; **~ evidence** *n* LAW prueba de los hechos *f*

facultative[1] *adj* GEN COMM facultativo

facultative[2]: **~ placing** *n* INS *marine* colocación facultativa *f*

facultative/obligatory *adj* (*factoblig*) INS *re-insurance* opcional/obligatorio

faculty: **~ of actuaries** *n* LAW facultad de actuarios *f*

fad *n* ECON novedad *f*

fahrenheit *n* (*F*) GEN COMM grados fahrenheit *m pl* (*F*)

fail *vi* BANK faltar a la obligación, COMP *break down* averiarse, GEN COMM fracasar, fallar, *business* quebrar; ◆ **~ to deliver** STOCK *securities* no repartir; **~ to observe the law** LAW incumplir la ley; **~ to reach agreement** GEN COMM no llegar a un acuerdo; **~ to receive** STOCK no recibir

failed: **~ delivery** *n* STOCK entrega fallida *f*

failing: **~ institution** *n* GEN COMM institución en quiebra *f*

failure *n* COMP, GEN COMM *of firm* fallo *m*; **~ analysis** MGMNT análisis de fallos *m*; **~ in payment** GEN COMM falta de pago *f*; **~ rate** GEN COMM frecuencia de fallos *f*; **~ to accept** GEN COMM falta de aceptación *f*; **~ to agree** (*FTA*) HRM incapacidad de llegar a un acuerdo *f*; **~ to appear** LAW incomparecencia *f*; **~ to comply** LAW, TAX falta de cumplimiento *f*; **~ to deliver** GEN COMM falta de entrega *f*; **~ to deliver a security on value date** STOCK incumplimiento en la entrega de un título el día de pago *m*

fair[1] *adj* GEN COMM, LAW justo

fair[2]: **~ average quality** *n* (*f.a.q.*) GEN COMM calidad regular *f*; **~ business practice** *n* GEN COMM práctica comercial honesta *f*; ~ **competition** *n* ECON, GEN COMM competencia equitativa *f*, competencia justa *f*, competencia leal *f*, LAW *commercial*, S&M competencia leal *f*; ~ **day's pay** *n* HRM remuneración justa de un día de trabajo *f*; ~ **day's work** *n* HRM trabajo medio de un día *m*; ~ **dismissal** *n* HRM despido justificado *m*; ~ **employment** *n* HRM trabajo sin discriminación *m*; ~ **market rent** *n* PROP alquiler a precio de mercado *m*; ~ **market value** *n* ACC, GEN COMM, STOCK valor equitativo de venta *m*; ~ **play** *n* GEN COMM juego limpio *m*; ~ **presentation** *n* AmE ACC presentación correcta *f*, presentación equitativa *f*, presentación justa *f*, presentación leal *f*; ~ **rate of return** *n* ACC, FIN, STOCK tasa de rendimiento justo *f*, tipo de rendimiento justo *m*; ~ **rent** *n* PROP alquiler razonable *m*; ~ **rental value** *n* PROP valor de arrendamiento razonable *m*; ~ **representation** *n* AmE (*cf true and fair view BrE*) ACC imagen fiel *f*; ~ **return** *n* ACC, ECON, FIN beneficio justo *m*, rendimiento justo *m*; ~ **sample** *n* GEN COMM muestra regular *f*; ~ **share** *n* GEN COMM reparto equitativo *m*; ~ **trade** *n* S&M *pricing* comercio equitativo *m*; ~ **trading** *n* ECON, LAW *international* comercio legal *m*, mercado equitativo *m*; ~ **value** *n* ACC *assets* valor equitativo de venta *m*, valor justo *m*, valor razonable de venta *m*, GEN COMM, STOCK valor equitativo de venta *m*; ~ **value adjustments** *n pl* ACC *of subsidiary* compensaciones por valor justo *f pl*; ~ **wear and tear** *n* GEN COMM desgaste natural *m*

Fair: ~ **Access To Insurance Requirements Plan** *n* AmE (*FAIR plan*) INS plan gubernamental para facilitar la suscripción de seguros; ~ **Credit Reporting Act** *n* AmE LAW ley de garantía de equidad crediticia; ~ **Employment Commission** *n* (*FEC*) HRM, WEL *Northern Ireland* comisión que promueve la igualdad de oportunidades sin distinción de raza, credo ni orientación sexual; ~ **Labor Standards Act** *n* AmE (*FLSA*) LAW estatuto de normas laborales equitativas; ~ **Trade Acts** *n* AmE S&M ley de comercio equitativo; ~ **Wages Resolution** *n* BrE ECON resolución salarial justa

FAIR: ~ **plan** *n* AmE (*Fair Access To Insurance Requirements Plan*) INS plan gubernamental para facilitar la suscripción de seguros

fairway *n* TRANSP *shipping* canal de acceso *m*

fait: ~ **accompli** *n* GEN COMM hecho consumado *m*

faith *n* GEN COMM fe *f*; ◆ **in bad** ~ LAW de mala fe; **in good** ~ LAW de buena fe

faithful *adj* GEN COMM fiel

fake: ~ **the marks** *phr infrml* STOCK imitar las marcas, operar con acciones a precios ficticios

fall[1]: ~ **of currency** *n* ECON caída de la divisa *f*; ~ **guy** *n* AmE infrml (*cf scapegoat BrE*) STOCK cabeza de turco *f* (*infrml*); ~ **in the bank rate** *n* ECON caída en los tipos bancarios *f*; ~ **in foreign exchange reserves** *n* STOCK descenso en la reserva de divisas *m*; ~ **in population** *n* ECON descenso de la población *m*; ~ **in price** *n* GEN COMM abaratamiento *m*; ~ **in production** *n* IND caída de la producción *f*; ~ **in supplies** *n* ECON descenso de suministros *m*; ~ **in value** *n* STOCK depreciación *f*

fall[2] *vi* GEN COMM *prices* caer, descender, disminuir *government* caer; ◆ ~ **foul of** GEN COMM indisponerse con; ~ **foul of the law** LAW chocar con la ley; ~ **in value** GEN COMM depreciarse; ~ **into abeyance** LAW caer en desuso; ~ **short of** GEN COMM *expectations, target* no alcanzar; ~ **within the scope of** PATENTS estar dentro del alcance de

fall apart *vi* GEN COMM *plan, negociations* fracasar

fall away *vi* GEN COMM *numbers* bajar, *trade* decaer

fall back *vi* GEN COMM *price* bajar; ~ **on sth** GEN COMM *resources* recurrir a algo

fall behind *vi* GEN COMM rezagarse; ◆ ~ **schedule** GEN COMM retrasarse; ~ **with payments** BANK, FIN atrasarse en los pagos

fall down *vi* GEN COMM *plans, buildings* derrumbarse, *fail* fracasar

fall in: ~ **with** *vt* GEN COMM *proposal* encontrarse con

fallacy *n* LAW falacia *f*

fallback *n* GEN COMM recurso de emergencia *m*; ~ **option** MGMNT opción de base *f*, opción de reserva *f*; ~ **pay** GEN COMM, HRM, WEL salario de paro *m*; ~ **position** POL exposición de unas medidas por parte del político en el que se acepta desde el primer momento su disposición a retirarlas

fallen: ~ **angel** *n* STOCK angel caído *m*; ~ **building clause** *n* INS, PROP cláusula de edificios en ruinas *f*

fallibility *n* GEN COMM falibilidad *f*

fallible *adj* GEN COMM falible

falling: ~ **price** *n* ECON precio descendente *m*

fallout *n* ENVIR *nuclear* radiación *f*, GEN COMM *disagreement* desacuerdo *m* (*infrml*), pelea *f* (*infrml*), *consequences* repercusiones *f pl*, consecuencias *f pl*

fallow *adj* ECON *agricultural* barbecho *m*

false: ~ **advertising** *n* S&M publicidad falsa *f*; ~ **advertising claim** *n* S&M falsa afirmación publicitaria *f*; ~ **alarm** *n* GEN COMM falsa alarma *f*; ~ **declaration** *n* TAX declaración falsa *f*; ~ **economy** *n* ECON, GEN COMM economía falsa *f*; ~ **entry** *n* TAX entrada falsa *f*; ~ **information** *n* LAW información falsa *f*; ~ **return** *n* TAX declaración falsa *f*; ~ **statement** *n* TAX balance falso *m*, declaración falsa *f*; ~ **testimony** *n* LAW testimonio falso *m*

falsification *n* GEN COMM *accounts* falsificación *f*

falsify *vt* ACC, LAW falsificar

falter *vi* ECON vacilar

familiarity *n* GEN COMM, S&M familiaridad *f*

family *n* GEN COMM *of products* familia *f*; ~ **allowance** HRM, TAX, WEL subsidio familiar *m*; ~ **allowance payment** TAX pago por subsidio familiar *m*; ~ **brand** S&M marca familiar *f*; ~ **budget** ECON, S&M presupuesto familiar *m*; ~ **business** S&M negocio familiar *m*; ~ **circumstances** *n pl* HRM circunstancias familiares *f pl*; ~ **fare** LEIS, TRANSP tarifa familiar *f*; ~ **farm corporation** TAX compañía agraria familiar *f*; ~ **of funds** STOCK familia de fondos de inversión *f*; ~ **house** MEDIA *broadcast* casa familiar *f*; ~ **income** ACC, TAX ingresos familiares *m pl*; ~ **income policy** INS póliza de renta familiar *f*; ~ **income threshold** TAX nivel de los ingresos familiares *m*; ~ **life cycle** S&M ciclo de la vida familiar *m*; ~ **lifestyle** S&M estilo de vida familiar *m*; ~**-size pack** GEN COMM paquete familiar *m*; ~**-size package** GEN COMM envase de tamaño familiar *m*; ~ **tree** GEN COMM, MGMNT árbol genealógico *m*; ~ **violence** WEL violencia familiar *f*

Family: ~ **Expenditure Survey** *n* (*FES*) ECON *econometrics* informe sobre el gasto familiar

fan *n* IND abanico *m*

fancy: ~ **accounting** *n* BANK contabilidad ficticia *f*

F&D *abbr* (*freight and demurrage*) IMP/EXP, TRANSP flete y sobrestadías

Fannie: ~ **Mae** *n infrml* (*Federal National Mortgage Association*) BANK, FIN asociación nacional federal de hipotecas

fanzine *n* MEDIA, LEIS revista de admiradores *f*

FAO *abbr* ECON (*Food and Agriculture Organization*) FAO (*Organización de las Naciones Unidas para la Agricultura y Alimentación*), GEN COMM (*for the attention of*) a la atención de, POL (*Food and Agriculture Organization*) FAO (*Organización de las Naciones Unidas para la Agricultura y Alimentación*)

FAP *abbr* (*fixed annual percentage*) BANK, FIN PAF (*porcentaje anual fijo*)

f.a.q. *abbr* (*fair average quality*) GEN COMM calidad regular *f*

FAQ *abbr* (*free alongside quay*) IMP/EXP, TRANSP franco al lado del muelle

far: ~-**flung** *adj* GEN COMM *business empire* vasto; ~-**reaching** *adj* GEN COMM de gran alcance; ~-**sighted** *adj* GEN COMM perspicaz, sagaz

fare: ~ **database** *n* TRANSP base de datos de tarifas *f*; ~ **pricing** *n* GEN COMM tarifa de precios *f*; ~ **war** *n* TRANSP guerra de precios *f*

farm: ~ **equipment** *n* ECON *agricultural* equipo agrícola *m*; ~ **implements** *n pl* ECON *agricultural* aperos de labranza *m pl*; ~ **income** *n* ECON *agricultural* ingresos agrícolas *m pl*; ~ **labourer** *AmE*, ~ **labourer** *BrE n* ENVIR, HRM, TAX trabajador(a) agrícola *m,f*; ~ **loan** *n* BANK, ECON préstamo a la agricultura *m*; ~ **lobby** *n* POL grupo de presión de los agricultores *m*; ~ **losses** *n* TAX pérdidas agrarias *f pl*; ~ **policy** *n* ECON, POL *agricultural* política agrícola *f*; ~ **produce** *n* ECON, GEN COMM, IMP/EXP producto agrícola *m*; ~ **shop** *n BrE* S&M tienda de productos agrícolas en una granja; ~ **subsidy** *n* ECON, POL subsidio agrario *m*; ~ **surplus** *n* ECON excedente agrícola *m*; ~ **tenancy** *n* PROP arrendamiento agrícola *m*

farm out *vt infrml* GEN COMM *piece of work* subcontratar

Farm: ~ **Credit System** *n* ECON Sistema de Crédito Agrícola *m*; ~ **Loan Bank** *n* BANK ≈ Banco de Crédito Agrícola *m*

farmer *n* GEN COMM, HRM agricultor(a) *m,f*, campesino(-a) *m,f*

farmers': ~ **association** *n* HRM asociación agrícola *f*

farmhand *n* GEN COMM, HRM campesino(-a) *m,f*, labrador(a) *m,f*

farming *n* GEN COMM *of animals* crianza de animales *f*, *of land* cultivo *m*, labranza *f*; ~ **business** ECON empresa agrícola *f*, empresa ganadera *f*; ~ **income** ECON ingresos agrícolas *m pl*, ingresos por explotación ganadera *m pl*; ~ **method** GEN COMM método de cultivo *m*, método de explotación ganadera *m*

farmland *n* ENVIR, GEN COMM terreno de explotación agrícola *m*, terreno de explotación ganadera *m*

farmstead *n BrE* (*cf homestead AmE*) PROP propiedad *f*

farther: ~ **in** *adv* STOCK *options* más cerca; ~ **out** *adv* STOCK *options* más lejos

f.a.s. *abbr* (*free alongside vessel*) IMP/EXP, TRANSP franco al costado, franco al costado del buque

FASB *abbr* (*Financial Accounting Standards Board*) ACC junta de normas de contabilidad financiera

fascism *n* POL fascismo *m*

fashion *n* S&M moda *f*; ~ **designer** GEN COMM diseñador(a) de modas *m,f*; ~ **editor** GEN COMM director(a) de modas *m,f*; ~ **goods** *n pl* S&M artículos de moda *m pl*;

~ **house** GEN COMM tienda de modas *f*; ~ **magazine** MEDIA revista de modas *f*; ~ **model** GEN COMM modelo de moda *mf*; ~ **parade** GEN COMM desfile de modas *m*; ~ **show** GEN COMM pase de modelos *m*; ♦ **in** ~ GEN COMM de moda; **out of** ~ GEN COMM pasado de moda

fast[1]: ~-**growing** *adj* ECON de crecimiento rápido; ~-**tracked** *adj* GEN COMM de seguimiento rápido

fast[2]: ~ **decline** *n* FIN, STOCK *currency expectations* caída rápida *f*; ~ **food** *n* S&M comida rápida *f*; ~ **lane** *n* TRANSP vía rápida *f*; ~ **market** *n* STOCK mercado rápido *m*; ~-**moving article** *n* S&M artículo de venta fácil *m*; ~-**moving consumer goods** *n pl* (*FMG*) S&M mercancías de venta fácil *f pl*; ~ **rise** *n* STOCK *currency expectations* rápido aumento *m*; ~ **track** *n* GEN COMM vía rápida *f*; ~ **tracking** *n* HRM ascensión rápida *f*, promoción rápida *f*

fast[3]: ~ **as can** *phr* (*fac*) TRANSP *loading/discharging* tan rápido como pueda

fasten *vt* GEN COMM amarrar

fastening *n* GEN COMM fijación *f*

FAT *abbr* (*file allocation table*) COMP listado de archivos *m*

fat: ~ **cat** *n* GEN COMM potentado *m*, pez gordo *mf* (*infrml*)

fatal: ~ **error** *n* COMP error grave *m*

fatality *n* WEL fatalidad *f*

father: ~ **of the chapel** *n BrE* HRM, MEDIA *publishing, printing trade unions* cabecilla sindical *mf*; ~ **file** *n* COMP fichero padre *m*

fault[1]: ~-**tolerant** *adj* COMP insensible a los fallos, tolerante a fallos

fault[2] *n* COMP fallo *m*, avería *f*, GEN COMM *in system* avería *f*, fallo *m*, falta *f*; ~-**tolerant system** COMP sistema indefectible *m*; ~ **tree analysis** GEN COMM análisis de árbol de fallas *m*, análisis en árbol de los fallos *m*; ♦ **no** ~ **of** INS *damage* sin culpa de

fault[3] *vt* GEN COMM encontrar defectos en, tachar

faultless *adj* GEN COMM sin defecto

faults: ~ **diagnosis clinic** *n* MGMNT centro de diagnosis de fallas *m*

faulty[1] *adj* GEN COMM defectuoso

faulty[2]: ~ **good** *n* S&M artículo defectuoso *m*; ~ **installation** *n* INS instalación defectuosa *f*

favor *AmE see favour BrE*

favorability *AmE see favourability BrE*

favorable *AmE see favourable BrE*

favour[1] *vt BrE* GEN COMM *course of action* favorecer

favour[2]: **in** ~ **of** *phr BrE* GEN COMM a favor de, en pro de

favourability *n BrE* GEN COMM favorabilidad *f*

favourable[1] *adj BrE* GEN COMM *price, conditions* favorable

favourable[2]: ~ **balance** *n BrE* BANK balance favorable *m*; ~ **difference** *n BrE* ACC diferencia a favor *f*; ~ **economic climate** *n BrE* ECON clima económico favorable *m*; ~ **economic conditions** *n pl BrE* ECON condiciones económicas favorables *f pl*; ~ **exchange** *n BrE* STOCK cambio favorable *m*; ~ **rate** *n BrE* ECON tipo favorable *m*; ~ **trade balance** *n BrE* ECON balanza comercial favorable *f*; ~ **variance** *n BrE* ACC desviación favorable *f*, variación favorable *f*

FAWB *abbr* (*forwarder air waybill*) IMP/EXP, TRANSP hoja de ruta aérea *f*, conocimiento de embarque aéreo del expedidor *m*

fax[1] *n* (*facsimile*) COMMS, GEN COMM fax *m* (*facsímil*);

~ **machine** ADMIN, COMMS, COMP *hardware* aparato de fax *m*; ~ **transmission** ADMIN, COMMS transmisión por fax *f*

fax[2] *vt* ADMIN, COMMS, COMP, GEN COMM enviar por fax

FBD *abbr* (*freeboard*) TRANSP *shipping* francobordo *m*

FBIM *abbr* (*Fellow of the British Institute of Management*) HRM, MGMNT miembro del instituto británico de gestión administrativa

f.c. *abbr* (*for cash*) GEN COMM al contado (*Esp*), de contado (*AmL*)

f.c.a. *abbr* (*free carrier*) IMP/EXP, TRANSP franco porteador *m*

fc&s *abbr* (*free of capture and seizure*) INS libre de actos de la autoridad

FCAR *abbr* (*free of claim for reported accident*) INS *marine* libre de reclamaciones por el accidente informado

FCC *abbr* (*fully cellular container ship*) TRANSP buque contenedor compartimentado *m*, portacontenedor celular *m*

FCCA *abbr* (*Fellow of the Chartered Association of Certified Accountants*) ACC, HRM miembro de la asociación colegiada de contables diplomados

FCGI *abbr* (*Fellow of the City and Guilds of London Institute*) HRM miembro del instituto City and Guilds de Londres

FCL *abbr* (*full container load*) TRANSP contenedor completo *m*

FCMA *abbr* (*Fellow of the Institute of Chatered Management Accountants*) ACC, HRM miembro del instituto colegiado de contables de gestión

fco. *abbr* (*franco*) IMP/EXP, TRANSP franco

FCO *abbr* (*Foreign and Commonwealth Office*) POL oficina para asuntos exteriores de la Mancomunidad Británica

FCR *abbr* (*forwarder's certificate of receipt*) IMP/EXP, TRANSP certificado de recibo de expedición *m*, certificado de recibo del expedidor *m*

fcsrcc *abbr* (*free of capture, seizure and riots, and civil commotions*) INS libre de actos de la autoridad, motines y conmoción civil

FCT *abbr* (*freight forwarder's combined transport bill of lading*) IMP/EXP, TRANSP conocimiento de embarque de transporte combinado del expedidor del flete *m*, conocimiento de embarque del expedidor para transporte combinado *m*

fd *abbr* IMP/EXP, TRANSP (*free delivery*) entrega exenta *f*, (*free dock*) dique franco *m*, muelle franco *m*, muelle libre *m*

f.d. *abbr* (*free dispatch*) IMP/EXP, TRANSP franco de consignación *m*

FDA *abbr* AmE (*Food and Drug Administration*) WEL oficina de control de alimentos y fármacos

FD&D[1] *abbr* (*freight, demurrage and defence BrE, freight, demurrage and defense AmE*) INS, TRANSP flete, sobrestadía y defensa

FD&D[2]: ~ **cover** *n* INS, TRANSP cobertura por flete, sobreestadía y defensa *f*

FDIC *abbr* AmE (*Federal Deposit Insurance Corporation*) INS *company* corporación aseguradora de depósitos federales

FDX *abbr* (*full-duplex*) COMP dúplex integral *m*, dúplex completo *m*

feasibility: ~ **report** *n* GEN COMM informe de viabilidad *m* (*Esp*), reporte de viabilidad *m* (*AmL*); ~ **study** *n* GEN COMM estudio de factibilidad *m* estudio de viabilidad *m*; ~ **survey** *n* GEN COMM estudio de factibilidad *m* estudio de viabilidad *m*

feasible *adj* GEN COMM practicable

featherbedding *n* HRM exceso de trabajadores *m*, proteccionismo *m*

feature *n* GEN COMM característica *f*, MEDIA *in newspaper* crónica *f*; ~ **article** MEDIA *print* artículo periodístico firmado *m*; ~ **film** LEIS largometraje *m*

FEC *abbr* (*Fair Employment Commission*) HRM, WEL *Northern Ireland* comisión de igualdad en el empleo

fed: ~ **funds** *n pl* BANK *money mark* fondos federales *m pl*

fed. *abbr* (*federal*) POL federal

Fed: **the** ~ *n* AmE (*Federal Reserve*) BANK, FIN Reserva Federal *f*

federal[1] *adj* (*fed.*) GEN COMM, POL federal

federal[2]: ~ **agency issue** *n* AmE FIN emisión de la agencia federal; ~ **agency security** *n* AmE FIN valor de la agencia federal; ~ **aid** *n* BANK, ECON, MGMNT ayuda federal *f*; ~ **deficit** *n* ECON déficit federal *m*; ~ **dividend tax credit** *n* TAX desgravación federal de dividendos *f*; ~ **election** *n* POL elección federal *f*; ~ **finance** *n* FIN finanzas federales *f pl*; ~ **financial program** *AmE*, ~ **financial programme** *n BrE* ACC, ECON programa financiero federal *m*; ~ **foreign tax credit** *n* TAX desgravación federal de impuestos pagados en el exterior *f*; ~ **funds** *n AmE* BANK *money market* fondos federales *m pl*; ~ **funds market** *n AmE* BANK mercado de fondos federales *m*; ~ **funds rate** *n AmE* BANK interés de fondos federales *m*; ~ **government** *n* POL gobierno federal *m*; ~ **government bond** *n AmE* FIN, STOCK bono del gobierno federal *m*; ~ **investment tax credit** *n* TAX desgravación federal de inversiones *f*; ~ **non-business foreign tax credit** *n* TAX desgravación federal de un impuesto extranjero no mercantil *f*; ~ **political contribution tax** *n AmE* TAX impuesto federal sobre contribuciones políticas; ~ **retail sales tax** *n AmE* TAX impuesto federal de ventas al por menor; ~ **sales tax** *n* TAX impuesto federal sobre ventas *m*; ~ **sales tax credit** *n* TAX desgravación federal de las ventas *f*; ~ **tax abatement** *n* TAX reducción del tipo impositivo federal *f*; ~ **tax lien** *n* TAX embargo fiscal federal *m*; ~ **tax reduction** *n* TAX reducción de impuestos federales *f*; ~ **tribunal** *n* HRM, LAW tribunal federal *m*

Federal: ~ **Aviation Administration** *n* (*FAA*) TRANSP administración federal de aviación; ~ **Deposit Insurance Corporation** *n AmE* (*FDIC*) INS *company* organismo general de garantía de depósitos bancarios; ~ **Farm Credit System** *n AmE* ECON sistema federal de crédito agrícola; ~ **Flood Insurance** *n AmE* INS seguro federal contra inundaciones; ~ **Home Loan Bank Board** *n AmE* BANK comité del banco federal para préstamos a la vivienda; ~ **Home Loan Bank System** *n pl AmE* FIN sistema del banco federal que facilita créditos a sociedades de ahorro y crédito inmobiliario; ~ **Home Loan Mortgage Corporation** *n* (*FHLMC, Freddie Mac*) BANK, FIN corporación federal de créditos hipotecarios a la vivienda; ~ **Housing Administration** *n AmE* (*FHA*) PROP administración federal para la vivienda; ~ **Insurance Contributions Act** *n* (*FICA*) INS ley federal de contribuciones de seguros; ~ **Intermediate Credit Bank** *n AmE* FIN banco federal de crédito a medio plazo; ~ **Land Bank** *n AmE* BANK banco federal de crédito agrícola; ~ **Maritime Board** *n* (*FMB*) IND dirección marítima de los Estados Unidos; ~ **Maritime Commission** *n* (*FMC*)

TRANSP comisión marítima federal; ~ **National Mortgage Association** n (*Fannie Mae, FNMA*) BANK, FIN asociación nacional federal de hipotecas; ~ **Open Market Committee** n AmE (*FOMC*) STOCK comité federal de mercado abierto; ~ **Parliament** n POL Parlamento Federal m; ~ **Power Commission** n (*FPC*) IND comisión federal de energía; ~ **Reserve** n AmE (*the Fed*) ECON Reserva Federal f; ~ **Reserve Bank** n AmE BANK, ECON banco de la Reserva Federal m; ~ **Reserve Board** n (*FRB*) BANK, ECON Comisión de la Reserva Federal; ~ **Reserve Open Market Committee** n AmE FIN comité del mercado abierto de la Reserva Federal; ~ **Reserve System** n AmE (*the Fed*) BANK, FIN sistema de la Reserva Federal que facilita crédito a los bancos comerciales; ~ **Savings and Loan Insurance Corporation** n (*FSLIC*) BANK sociedad federal de seguro de crédito; ~ **Trade Commission Act** n AmE LAW, POL ley sobre la comisión federal de comercio

federalism n GEN COMM, POL federalismo m

federally[1]: ~ **regulated** adj TAX federalmente regulado

federally[2]: ~ **regulated exchange** n AmE STOCK bolsa regida por las leyes federales f

federated: ~ **company** n HRM empresa federada f

federation n HRM, POL federación f; ~ **of mutual societies** HRM federación de mutualidades f; ~ **of trade union** HRM federación de sindicatos f

Federation: ~ **of National Associations of Shipbrokers and Agents** n (*FONASBA*) TRANSP federación de asociaciones nacionales de agentes y consignatarios

fee n ACC honorarios m pl, GEN COMM cargo m, comisión f, cuota f, WEL *courses* matrícula; ~**-based service** BANK servicio a comisión m; ~ **income** ACC honorarios m pl, ingreso por comisión m, PATENTS honorarios m pl; ~ **simple** PROP dominio absoluto m, propiedad absoluta de un inmueble f; ~ **simple absolute** PROP dominio absoluto m, propiedad absoluta de un inmueble f; ~ **split** ACC *in accountancy firm* división de la comisión f, fraccionamiento de los honorarios m

feed[1] n COMP alimentación f; ~ **circuit** COMP circuito de alimentación m; ~ **rate** COMP velocidad de arrastre f

feed[2] vt COMP alimentar

feedback n COMP feedback m, retroalimentación f, GEN COMM intercambio de información m

feeder n TRANSP *shipping* buque distribuidor de contenedores m; ~ **line** TRANSP línea secundaria de transporte f, ramal m; ~ **organization** GEN COMM empresa proveedora f; ~ **ship** TRANSP buque alimentador m; ~ **vessel** TRANSP buque alimentador m

feedstuffs n pl ECON *agricultural* forrajes m pl

feel[1]: ~ **of the market** n GEN COMM sentido del mercado m

feel[2]: ~ **the pinch** phr infrml ECON pasar apuros

fees n pl GEN COMM tarifas f pl

felicific calculus n ECON *Bentham method* utilitarismo m

fellow: ~**-worker** n HRM compañero(-a) de trabajo m,f

Fellow: ~ **of the British Association of Accountants and Auditors** n ACC miembro de la asociación británica de contables y auditores; ~ **of the British Institute of Management** n (*FBIM*) HRM, MGMNT miembro del instituto británico de gestión empresarial; ~ **of the Chartered Association of Certified Accountants** n (*FCCA*) ACC, HRM miembro de la asociación colegiada de contables diplomados; ~ **of the City and Guilds of London Institute** n (*FCGI*) HRM miembro del Instituto City and Guilds de Londres; ~ **of the Institute of Actuaries** n (*FIA*) FIN, HRM ≈ Miembro del Instituto de Actuarios mf; ~ **of the Incorporated Society of Valuers and Auctioneers** n (*FSVA*) GEN COMM, HRM ≈ Miembro de la Sociedad de Tasadores y Subastadores mf; ~ **of the Institute of Bankers** n (*FIB*) BANK, HRM ≈ Miembro del Instituto de Banqueros mf; ~ **of the Institute of Chartered Management Accountants** n (*FCMA*) ACC, HRM miembro del instituto colegiado de contables de gestión; ~ **of the Institute of Chartered Shipbrokers** n (*FICS*) HRM ≈ Miembro del Instituto de Consignatarios Colegiados mf; ~ **of the Institute of Commerce** n (*FIC*) GEN COMM ≈ Miembro del Instituto de Comercio mf; ~ **of the Institute of Company Accountants** n BrE (*FICA*) ACC, HRM ≈ Miembro del Instituto de Contables de Empresa mf; ~ **of the Institute of Export** n (*FIEx*) HRM, IMP/EXP ≈ Miembro del Instituto de Exportación mf; ~ **of the Institute of Insurance Agents** n INS ≈ Miembro del Instituto de Agentes de Seguros mf; ~ **of the Institute of Marine Engineers** n (*FIME*) HRM ≈ Miembro del Instituto de Ingenieros Navales mf; ~ **of the Institute of Personnel Management** n (*FIPM*) HRM, MGMNT ≈ Miembro del Instituto de Dirección de Personal mf; ~ **of the Royal Institute of Chartered Surveyors** n (*FRICS*) HRM, PROP colegiado del real instituto de expertos inmobiliarios

felonious adj LAW criminal

ferrous adj ENVIR, IND ferroso

ferry n TRANSP transbordador m; ~ **berth** TRANSP muelle de transbordador m; ~ **line manager** HRM, TRANSP director(a) de línea de transbordadores m,f; ~ **ramp** TRANSP rampa de transbordador f

fertilize vt ENVIR *agriculture* fertilizar

fertilizer n ENVIR *agriculture* fertilizante m

FES abbr (*Family Expenditure Survey*) ECON *econometrics* informe sobre el gasto familiar

fetch vt COMP extraer (*Esp*), traer (*AmL*), GEN COMM *price* deducir

feudalism n POL feudalismo m

FF[1] abbr (*form feed*) COMP avance de formato m, salto de impreso m

FF[2]: ~ **curve** n ECON curva FF f

FFA abbr (*free foreign agency*) TRANSP agencia extranjera libre f

FFCR abbr (*freight forwarder's certificate of receipt*) IMP/EXP, TRANSP certificado de recibo de expedición de flete m, certificado de recibo del expedidor del flete m

FFI abbr (*for further instructions*) GEN COMM para instrucciones adicionales

FGA abbr (*foreign general average*) GEN COMM promedio general exterior m

FHA abbr BANK, FIN (*Finance Houses Association*) asociación de compañías financieras, PROP (*Federal Housing Administration AmE*) administración federal para la vivienda

FHBR abbr (*Finance House Base Rate*) FIN tasa base de una casa financiera f

FHEx abbr (*Fridays and holidays excepted*) GEN COMM, LEIS, TRANSP salvo viernes y días festivos

FHLMC abbr (*Federal Home Loan Mortgage Corporation*) BANK, FIN corporación federal de créditos hipotecarios a la vivienda

f.i. abbr (*free in*) IMP/EXP, TRANSP franco de carga

fia *abbr* (*full interest admitted*) GEN COMM, TRANSP interés total admitido

FIA *abbr* (*Fellow of the Institute of Actuaries*) FIN, HRM ≈ Miembro del Instituto de Actuarios *mf*

fias *abbr* (*free in and stowed*) TRANSP libre para el buque la carga y estiba

FIAS *abbr* (*Foreign Investment Advisory Service*) STOCK servicio de asesoramiento para inversiones en el extranjero

fiat: ~ **money** *n AmE* (*cf token money BrE*) BANK, FIN moneda despreciada *f*, moneda fiduciaria *f*, moneda nominal *f*; ~ **standard** *n* LAW moneda fiduciaria *f*

f.i.b. *abbr* IMP/EXP, TRANSP (*free into bunkers*) franco en pañoles, (*free into barges*) franco en barcaza

FIB *abbr* (*Fellow of the Institute of Bankers*) BANK, HRM ≈ Miembro del Instituto de Banqueros *mf*

FIBC *abbr* (*flexible intermediate and bulk container*) TRANSP contenedor polivalente intermedio y masivo *m*

fiber *AmE see* fibre *BrE*

fiberboard *AmE see* fibreboard *BrE*

fiberglass *AmE see* fibreglass *BrE*

fibre: ~-**optic cable** *n BrE* COMMS, COMP, IND cable de fibra óptica *m*; ~ **optics** *n BrE* COMMS, COMP, IND óptica de fibra *f*, fibroóptica, fibra óptica *f*

fibreboard *n BrE* IND aglomerado *m*, cartón de pasta de madera *m*, cartón duro *m*; ~ **can** *BrE* TRANSP envase de fibra *m*; ~ **case** *BrE* S&M caja de madera conglomerada *f*

fibreglass *n BrE* IND fibra de vidrio *f*

FIBS *abbr* (*financial information and budgeting system*) FIN sistema de información y presupuestación financiera *m*

f.i.c. *abbr* (*free insurance and carriage*) IMP/EXP, TRANSP franco de seguro y porte

FIC *abbr* GEN COMM (*Fellow of the Institute of Commerce*) ≈ Miembro del Instituto de Comercio *mf*, IMP/EXP, TRANSP (*free insurance and carriage*) franco de seguro y porte

FICA *abbr* ACC, HRM (*Fellow of the Institute of Company Accountants BrE*) ≈ Miembro del Instituto de Contables de Empresa *mf*, INS (*Federal Insurance Contributions Act*) ley federal de contribuciones de seguros

FICS *abbr* (*Fellow of the Institute of Chartered Shipbrokers*) HRM ≈ Miembro del Instituto de Consignatarios Colegiados *mf*

fictitious[1] *adj* GEN COMM falso

fictitious[2]: ~ **capital** *n* FIN, STOCK capital ficticio *m*

fiddle *vt infrml* GEN COMM desfalcar, mal usar, malgastar

fidelity *n* GEN COMM fidelidad *f*; ~ **bond** INS seguro contra estafas de empleados *m*, fianza *f*; ~ **guarantee** INS fianza *f*; ~ **insurance** INS seguro de fidelidad *m*

fiduciarily *adv* LAW fiduciariamente

fiduciary[1] *adj* LAW fiduciario

fiduciary[2]: ~ **account** *n* BANK cuenta fiduciaria *f*; ~ **accounting** *n* BANK contabilidad fiduciaria *f*; ~ **activities** *n pl* LAW actividades fiduciarias *f pl*; ~ **banking** *n* BANK banca fiduciaria *f*; ~ **bond** *n* INS fianza *f*; ~ **currency** *n* BANK, FIN moneda fiduciaria *f*, dinero fiduciario *m*; ~ **investment** *n* BANK inversión fiduciaria *f*; ~ **issue** *n* BANK emisión fiduciaria *f*; ~ **operation** *n* BANK *investment banking* operación fiduciaria *f*

field *n* COMP *word or data processing*, GEN COMM, IND *of research* campo *m*; ~ **audit** TAX auditoría externa *f*, intervención externa *f*; ~ **of endeavor** *AmE*, ~ **of endeavour** *BrE* TAX sector de actividad *m*; ~ **force** S&M equipo de campo *m*, personal de campo *m*; ~ **investigator** S&M *market research* investigador(a) de campo *m,f*; ~ **operator** GEN COMM operador(a) de campo *m,f*; ~ **organization** GEN COMM organización exterior *f*; ~ **research** S&M *of market* investigación de campo *f*; ~ **sales manager** HRM, MGMNT, S&M director(a) de ventas de campo *m,f*; ~ **selling** S&M venta ambulante *f*; ~ **staff** HRM personal de campo *m*; ~ **support** GEN COMM apoyo de campo *m*; ~ **survey** S&M *market research* encuesta de campo *f*; ~ **of taxation** TAX sector de tributación *m*; ~ **testing** S&M prueba sobre el terreno *f*; ~ **theory of motivation** HRM teoría de campo de la motivación *f*; ~ **trip** WEL salida de campo *f*; ~ **work** GEN COMM trabajo de campo *m*, trabajo en el terreno *m*; ~ **worker** GEN COMM investigador que trabaja en el terreno

fierce *adj* GEN COMM *competition* fiero

FIEx *abbr* (*Fellow of the Institute of Export*) HRM, IMP/EXP ≈ Miembro del Instituto de Exportación *mf*

FIFO *abbr* (*first in, first out*) ACC, GEN COMM PEPS (*primero en entrar, primero en salir*)

fifth: ~-**generation computer** *n* COMP computador de quinta generación *m* (*AmL*), computadora de quinta generación *f* (*AmL*), ordenador de quinta generación *m* (*Esp*)

fight *vt* GEN COMM luchar; ♦ ~ **a losing battle against** GEN COMM librar una batalla perdida contra

fight back *vi* GEN COMM contraatacar

figurative: ~ **device** *n* PATENTS aparato figurativo *m*

figure *n* ECON, FIN, GEN COMM, MATH, PATENTS *of drawing* cifra *f*; ~ **number** GEN COMM número de cifras *m*

figures *n pl* GEN COMM cifras; ~ **adjusted for seasonal variations** FIN, GEN COMM cifras ajustadas a los cambios estacionales *f pl*; ♦ **in round** ~ GEN COMM en cifras redondas; **your** ~ **are in agreement with ours** ACC sus cifras concuerdan con las nuestras

f.i.h. *abbr* (*free in harbor AmE, free in harbour BrE*) IMP/EXP, TRANSP franco en puerto

FIL *abbr* (*financial intermediary loan*) BANK, FIN préstamo intermediario financiero *m*

file[1] *n* GEN COMM fichero *m*, archivo *m*, LAW archivo *m*; ~ **allocation table** (*FAT*) COMP listado de archivos *m*; ~ **clerk** ADMIN, HRM archivador(a) *m,f* (*Esp*), archivero(-a) *m,f* (*AmL*), archivista *mf*; ~ **compression** COMP compresión de fichero *f*; ~ **conversion** COMP conversión de fichero *f*; ~ **copy** ADMIN copia para archivo *f*; ~ **directory** COMP directorio de ficheros *m*; ~ **management** COMP gestión de ficheros *f*; ~ **menu** COMP menú de archivos *m*, menú de ficheros *m*; ~ **protection** COMP protección de archivos *f*, protección de ficheros *f*; ~ **server** COMP servidor de ficheros *m*; ~ **sharing** COMP utilización en común de ficheros *f*; ♦ ~ **not found** COMP fichero no encontrado

file[2] **1.** *vt* GEN COMM *application, document* archivar, presentar, formular, instar, LAW *claim* elevar, archivar; ♦ ~ **a claim for damages** LAW entablar una demanda por daños y perjuicios; ~ **a damage report** INS presentar una declaración de siniestro; ~ **a loss report** INS presentar una declaración de siniestro; ~ **one's tax return** TAX presentar la declaración de la renta; ~ **a return** TAX archivar una declaración; **2.** *vi* GEN COMM archivar; ◆ **~ for bankruptcy** ACC presentar una declaración de quiebra

file away *vt* GEN COMM archivar

filed *adj* GEN COMM archivado

filer *n* TAX declarante *mf*

filing *n* GEN COMM, archivo *m*, PATENTS *of application* presentación *f*; **~ basket** ADMIN cestilla de archivo *f*; **~ cabinet** ADMIN archivador *m* (*Esp*), archivero *m* (*AmL*); **~ drawer** ADMIN cajón clasificador *m*; **~ of a return** TAX presentación *f*; **~ statement** STOCK presentación del balance *f*; **~ system** ADMIN sistema de archivo *m*

fill[1]: **~-in** *n* HRM, S&M cumplimentación *f*; **~ price** *n* STOCK *options* precio de ejecución de la compraventa *m*

fill[2] *vt* GEN COMM *gap, vacancy* llenar; ◆ **~-or-kill** *AmE* (*FOK*) STOCK cancelar inmediatamente, cumplimentar inmediatamente; **~ a position** HRM cubrir un puesto; **~ a vacancy** HRM cubrir una vacante

fill in *vt* GEN COMM *form* rellenar, HRM cumplimentar

filler *n* MEDIA, S&M relleno *m*; **~ traffic** TRANSP tráfico complementario *m*

fillers *n pl* MEDIA *print* artículos de relleno *m pl*

film *n* *BrE* (*cf motion picture AmE, cf movie AmE*) LEIS, MEDIA película *f*; **~ advertising** *BrE* LEIS, S&M publicidad de una película *f*; **~ festival** MEDIA festival cinematográfico *m*; **~ industry** *BrE* (*cf motion-picture industry AmE*) ECON, LEIS, MEDIA industria cinematográfica *f*, industria del cine *f*; **~-maker** MEDIA *broadcast* productor(a) cinematográfico(-a) *m,f*; **~ production costs** *n pl* TAX costes de producción de películas *m pl* (*Esp*), costos de producción de películas *m pl* (*AmL*); **~ rights** *n pl* LAW, MEDIA derechos cinematográficos *m pl*; **~ rush** MEDIA primera copia de una película *f*; **~ script** MEDIA guión cinematográfico *m*; **~ strip** MEDIA tira de película *f*; **~ test** MEDIA prueba cinematográfica *f*

filmsetter *n* MEDIA *print* máquina de componer fotográficamente *f*

filmsetting *n* MEDIA *print* composición fotográfica *f*, fotocomposición *f*

FILO *abbr* (*first in, last out*) ACC, GEN COMM PEUS (*primero en entrar, último en salir*)

filter *n* COMP, ECON, FIN filtro *m*

filtering *n* COMP, ECON, FIN filtración *f*; **~ down** PROP divulgación *f*

FIMBRA *abbr* (*Financial Intermediaries, Managers and Brokers Regulatory Association*) FIN asociación profesional de intermediarios, gestores y agentes financieros

FIME *abbr* (*Fellow of the Institute of Marine Engineers*) HRM ≈ Miembro del Instituto de Ingenieros Navales *mf*

FIML *abbr* (*full-information maximum likelihood*) ECON *econometrics* método de estimación de modelos econométricos con ecuaciones simultáneas

final[1]: **~ and conclusive** *adj* TAX *determination* final y concluyente

final[2] *n* GEN COMM, S&M final *m*; **~ acceptance** GEN COMM *of goods* recepción definitiva *f*; **~ accounts** *n pl* ACC cuentas finales *f pl*; **~ assembly** GEN COMM, IND montaje final *m*; **~ balance** ACC, BANK saldo final *m*; **~ check-in** LEIS registro final *m*; **~ consumption** COMP, ENVIR consumo final *m*; **~ contract settlement price** STOCK *futures* precio final de cierre del contrato *m*;

~ demand ECON, S&M demanda final *f*, TAX última reclamación *f*; **~ dividend** STOCK dividendo final *m*; **~ good** ECON, IND producto acabado *m*; **~ income** FIN ingreso neto *m*; **~ installment** *AmE*, **~ instalment** *BrE* BANK, FIN plazo final *m*; **~ mortgage payment** FIN liquidación de una hipoteca *f*; **~ offer arbitration** ECON arbitraje de la oferta final *m*, LAW proposición firme de arbitraje *f*; **~ product** GEN COMM producto final *m*; **~ proof** MEDIA *printing, photography* prueba final *f*; **~ prospectus** STOCK prospecto definitivo *m*; **~ settlement price** STOCK precio final de liquidación *m*; **~ trading day** STOCK último día de operaciones *m*; **~ warning** HRM última advertencia *f*

finalize *vt* GEN COMM finalizar

finalized *adj* GEN COMM finalizado

finance[1] *n* GEN COMM finanzas *f pl*; **~ charge** BANK carga financiera *f*; **~ charges** *n pl* ACC gastos financieros *m pl*; **~ company** FIN financiera *f*; **~ company paper** FIN valores financieros de la compañía *m pl*; **~ department** FIN departamento financiero *m*; **~ house** *BrE* FIN empresa financiera *f*; **~ lease** ACC arrendamiento financiero *m*; **~ paper** FIN papel financiero *m*

finance[2] *vt* GEN COMM financiar; ◆ **~ the difference** ECON financiar la diferencia; **~ directly** GEN COMM financiar directamente

Finance: ~ Act *n* *BrE* LAW Ley de Finanzas *f*; **~ Bill** *n* *BrE* ECON, FIN proyecto de ley financiero *m*; **~ Houses Association** *n* (*FHA*) BANK, FIN asociación de compañías financieras; **~ house base rate** *n* (*FHBR*) FIN tasa base de una casa financiera *f*

financial[1] *adj* GEN COMM económico, financiero

financial[2]: **~ account** *n* ACC, FIN cuenta financiera *f*; **~ accountant** *n* GEN COMM contable financiero(-a) *m,f* (*Esp*), contador(a) financiero(-a) *m,f* (*AmL*), interventor(a) *m,f* (*Esp*), contralor(a) *m,f* (*AmL*); **~ accounting** *n* ACC, FIN contabilidad financiera *f*; **~ adjustment policy** *n* ECON, POL política de ajuste monetario *f*; **~ administration** *n* FIN administración financiera *f*, gestión financiera *f*; **~ administration system** *n* FIN sistema de administración financiera *m*; **~ advertising** *n* S&M publicidad financiera *f*; **~ agent** *n* FIN agente financiero(-a) *m,f*; **~ aid** *n* ECON, POL *development* ayuda financiera *f*; **~ analysis** *n* FIN, GEN COMM análisis financiero *m*; **~ appraisal** *n* FIN evaluación financiera *f*; **~ asset** *n* FIN activo financiero *m*; **~ assistance** *n* ECON, POL ayuda financiera *f*, asistencia financiera *f*;

■ b **~ backer** *n* FIN promotor(a) financiero(-a) *m,f*; **~ backing** *n* FIN respaldo financiero *m*; **~ balance** *n* ECON balanza financiera *f*; **~ burden** *n* FIN carga financiera *f*;

■ c **~ capacity** *n* FIN capacidad financiera *f*; **~ capital** *n* FIN capital financiero *m*; **~ center** *AmE*, **~ centre** *BrE* *n* ECON, FIN centro de finanzas *m*, centro financiero *m*; **~ circles** *n pl* FIN círculos financieros *m pl*; **~ claim** *n* ACC, FIN demanda financiera *f*, petición financiera *f*, queja financiera *f*, reclamación financiera *f*; **~ climate** *n* ECON clima financiero *m*; **~ company** *n* FIN compañía financiera *f*; **~ conglomerate** *n* FIN conglomeración financiera *f*; **~ control** *n* FIN control financiero *m*; **~ controller** *n* FIN, GEN COMM *of organization*, HRM, MGMNT director(a) financiero(-a) *m,f*; **~ costs** *n pl* ACC, FIN costes de financiación *m pl* (*Esp*), costos de financiación *m pl* (*AmL*); **~ credit** *n* BANK, FIN crédito de financiación *m*; **~ crisis** *n* FIN crisis financiera *f*;

~ d ~ **director** n FIN, GEN COMM, HRM, MGMNT director(a) financiero(-a) m,f; ~ **disclosure** n FIN divulgación de información financiera f; ~ **disequilibrium** n ECON desequilibrio monetario m, desequilibrio de precios m;

~ e ~ **economy** n FIN economía financiera f; ~ **encumbrance** n FIN gravamen financiero m; ~ **engineering** n IND ingeniería financiera f; ~ **enterprise** n FIN empresa financiera f;

~ f ~ **field** n FIN ámbito financiero m; ~ **firm** n FIN firma financiera f; ~ **flow** n ACC, ECON, FIN corriente financiera f, fluctuación financiera f; ~ **forecasts** n pl FIN estimaciones financieras f pl, previsiones financieras f pl; ~ **future** n STOCK futuro financiero m; ~ **futures** n pl FIN, STOCK futuros financieros m pl; ~ **futures contract** n FIN, STOCK contrato de futuros financieros m; ~ **futures market** n FIN, STOCK mercado de futuros financieros m;

~ g ~ **gearing** n BrE STOCK apalancamiento financiero m;

~ h ~ **highlights** n pl ACC hitos financieros m pl; ~ **history** n FIN historia financiera f; ~ **holding company** n FIN casa matriz financiera f, sociedad de cartera financiera f; ~ **holding group** n FIN grupo empresarial financiero m;

~ i ~ **incentive** n FIN incentivo financiero m; ~ **industry** n ECON, FIN industria financiera f, FIN industria f; ~ **information and budgeting system** n (FIBS) FIN sistema de información y presupuestación financiera m; ~ **institution** n FIN institución financiera f; ~ **instrument** n FIN instrumento financiero m; ~ **intermediary** n FIN intermediario(-a) financiero(-a) m,f; ~ **intermediary loan** n (FIL) BANK, FIN préstamo intermediario financiero m; ~ **intermediation** n FIN intermediación financiera f; ~ **investment** n FIN inversión financiera f; ~ **involvement** n FIN implicación financiera f;

~ j ~ **journalism** n FIN periodismo financiero m;

~ l ~ **lease** n FIN arrendamiento financiero m, préstamo financiero m; ~ **leasing** n FIN arrendamiento financiero m; ~ **leverage** n AmE STOCK apalancamiento financiero m; ~ **leverage ratio** n FIN razón de apalancamiento financiero f; ~ **losses** n pl ACC, FIN pérdidas financieras f pl;

~ m ~ **magnate** n FIN magnate financiero(-a) m,f; ~ **management** n FIN administración financiera f, dirección financiera f, gestión financiera f, gerencia financiera f; ~ **management rate of return** n (FMRR) FIN tasa de rentabilidad de la gestión financiera f; ~ **management report** n FIN informe de la gestión financiera m (Esp), reporte de la gestión financiera m (AmL); ~ **management system** n FIN sistema de gestión financiera m; ~ **manager** n HRM gerente financiero(-a) m,f; ~ **market** n FIN, STOCK mercado financiero m; ~ **marketplace** n FIN, STOCK plaza financiera f; ~ **means** n pl FIN medios financieros m pl; ~ **muscle** n FIN fuerza financiera f;

~ n ~ **news** n pl FIN crónica financiera f;

~ o ~ **officer** n FIN, GEN COMM, HRM, MGMNT director(a) financiero(-a) m,f;

~ p ~ **package** n BANK, FIN plan de financiación m; ~ **panic** n FIN pánico financiero m; ~ **paper** n FIN valores financieros m pl; ~ **participation scheme** n BrE HRM plan de participación financiera m; ~ **period**

n ACC, ECON, FIN ejercicio contable m, ejercicio económico m, GEN COMM periodo financiero m; ~ **perspective** n FIN perspectiva financiera f; ~ **planner** n FIN, MGMNT planificador(a) financiero(-a) m,f; ~ **planning** n ACC, FIN, MGMNT planificación financiera f; ~ **policy** n FIN política financiera f; ~ **position** n ACC, FIN posición financiera f; ~ **profit** n ACC annual accounts beneficios financieros m pl; ~ **pyramid** n FIN pirámide financiera f;

~ r ~ **ratio** n FIN proporción de financiación f, relación de financiación f; ~ **reporting** n FIN información financiera f; ~ **reporting standard** n (FRS) ACC modelo de estado financiero m, norma de informes financieros f; ~ **requirement** n FIN necesidades financieras f pl, requisito financiero m; ~ **responsibility clause** n INS automobiles cláusula de responsabilidad financiera f; ~ **review** n FIN, GEN COMM análisis financiero m; ~ **reward** n STOCK remuneración financiera f; ~ **risk** n FIN, GEN COMM, STOCK riesgo financiero m; ~ **roundness** n ECON equilibrio cíclico m;

~ s ~ **sector** n FIN sector financiero m; ~ **service** n FIN servicio financiero m; ~ **services industry** n ECON, FIN industria de servicios financieros f; ~ **settlement** n BANK, FIN, LAW arreglo financiero m, convenio financiero m; ~ **signing authority** n FIN organismo financiero ejecutivo m; ~ **simulation software** n COMP, FIN programa de simulación financiera m, software de simulación financiera m; ~ **situation** n ACC, FIN situación financiera f; ~ **sophistication** n FIN complejidad financiera f; ~ **stability** n FIN estabilidad financiera f; ~ **standard** n FIN, GEN COMM norma financiera f; ~ **standing** n FIN of firm capacidad financiera f; ~ **statement** n ACC balance m, estado contable m, estado financiero m, BANK estado de la situación financiera m, FIN balance m; ~ **statement analysis** n ACC análisis de balances m, análisis de estados contables m, análisis de estados financieros m, análisis del estado de cuentas m; ~ **strategy** n FIN, GEN COMM estrategia financiera f; ~ **strength** n BANK of bank capacidad financiera f; ~ **structure** n ACC balance sheet estructura financiera f; ~ **summary** n FIN resumen financiero m; ~ **supermarket** n FIN supermercado financiero m; ~ **support** n ECON apoyo financiero m, ayuda financiera f, POL ayuda financiera f; ~ **support staff** n FIN equipo de apoyo financiero m; ~ **system** n FIN sistema financiero m;

~ v ~ **visibility** n FIN visibilidad financiera f;

~ w ~ **wizard** n infrml GEN COMM mago(-a) de las finanzas m,f;

~ y ~ **year** n (FY) FIN año financiero m, ejercicio económico m, ejercicio financiero m

Financial: ~ **Accounting Standards Board** n (FASB) ACC junta de normas de contabilidad financiera; ~ **Administration Act** n LAW Ley de Administración Fiscal f; ~ **Intermediaries, Managers and Brokers Regulatory Association** n (FIMBRA) FIN asociación profesional de intermediarios, gestores y agentes financieros; ~ **Reporting Council** n BrE ACC consejo de informes financieros; ~ **Services Act** n (FSA) FIN 1986 ley de servicios financieros; ~ **Statement and Budget Report** n (FSBR) FIN informe del estado financiero y presupuestario; ~ **Times Actuaries All Shares Index** n BrE STOCK índice de precios de valores de los actuarios del Financial Times; ~ **Times Index** n (FT Index) STOCK Índice del Financial Times m (índice del FT); ~ **Times**

Industrial Ordinary Share Index n (*FT-30*) STOCK índice bursátil de valores industriales del Financial Times m; ~ **Times Stock-Exchange Eurotrack 100 Index** n (*FTSE Eurotrack 100 Index*) STOCK índice Footsie Eurotrack 100 m; ~ **Times Stock-Exchange Eurotrack 200 Index** n (*FTSE Eurotrack 200 Index*) STOCK índice Footsie Eurotrack 200 m; ~ **Times Stock-Exchange 100 Share Index** n (*Footsie, FTSE 100*) STOCK índice bursátil del Financial Times de los valores de las 100 mayores entidades de la Bolsa de Londres, índice Footsie m; ~ **Times Stock-Exchange Index** n STOCK índice bursátil del Financial Times m

financially: ~ **sound** adj GEN COMM económicamente sólido, financieramente sólido

financier n FIN financista mf

financing n GEN COMM financiación f, financiamiento m; ~ **adjustment** BANK, FIN reajuste de financiación m; ~ **of capital projects** FIN financiación de inversiones f; ~ **charges** n pl ACC, FIN costes de financiación m pl (*Esp*), costos de financiación m pl (*AmL*); ~ **expenses** n pl ACC, FIN gastos de financiación m pl; ~ **package** FIN paquete financiero m; ~ **plan** BANK, FIN plan de financiación m; ~ **rate** STOCK *futures pricing* tasa de financiación f

find vt COMP, GEN COMM encontrar; ♦ ~ **the balance** STOCK conseguir un equilibrio; ~ **fault with** GEN COMM criticar; ~ **sth wanting** GEN COMM encontrar algo deficiente

finder: ~**'s fee** n GEN COMM, S&M honorarios del intermediario m pl

finding n LAW laudo m

findings n pl LAW *of investigation, tribunal* conclusiones f pl

fine[1] n GEN COMM, LAW multa f; ~ **screen** S&M cribado fino m; ~ **tuning** COMP sintonización precisa f, ECON puesta a punto f

fine[2]: ~**-tune** vt COMP *program*, ECON poner a punto

finish vt GEN COMM terminar; ♦ ~ **in the money** STOCK terminar con beneficio potencial; ~ **work** GEN COMM acabar el trabajo

finished: ~ **goods** n pl GEN COMM productos terminados m pl, artículos terminados m pl; ~ **product** n GEN COMM producto acabado m

finishing n GEN COMM acabado m

finite[1] adj ENVIR, MATH finito

finite[2]: ~ **life real estate investment trust** n FIN compañía de inversiones inmobiliarias de vida finita f; ~ **set** n MATH conjunto finito m

f.i.&o. abbr (*free in and out*) IMP/EXP, TRANSP franco de carga y descarga, franco dentro y fuera

f.i.o.&s. abbr (*free in, out and stowed*) IMP/EXP, TRANSP franco de carga, descarga y estibado

f.i.o.s.&t. abbr (*free in, out, stowed and trimmed*) IMP/EXP, TRANSP franco de carga, descarga, estibado y asentado

f.i.o.&t. abbr (*free in, out and trimmed*) IMP/EXP, TRANSP franco de carga, descarga y asentado

FIPM abbr (*Fellow of the Institute of Personnel Management*) HRM, MGMNT ≈ Miembro del Instituto de Dirección de Personal mf

firavv abbr (*first available vessel*) TRANSP primer navío disponible m

fire[1]: ~**-resistant** adj BrE (cf *fire-resistive AmE*) GEN COMM ignífugo, resistente al fuego, a prueba de incendios; ~**-resistive** adj AmE (cf *fire-resistant BrE*) GEN COMM ignífugo, resistente al fuego, a prueba de incendios

fire[2]: ~ **drill** n HRM ejercicio de contraincendio m; ~ **escape** n HRM, INS, PROP escalera de incendios f; ~ **exit** n HRM salida de incendios f; ~ **hazard** n HRM, WEL peligro de incendio m; ~ **insuring agreement** n AmE INS convenio asegurador contra incendios m; ~ **legal liability insurance** n INS seguro de responsabilidad legal en caso de incendio m; ~ **prevention** n HRM, INS, WEL prevención de incendios f; ~ **regulations** n pl LAW normas en caso de incendio f pl; ~**-resistant construction** n BrE (cf *fire-resistive construction AmE*) INS construcción a prueba de incendios; ~**-resistive construction** n AmE (cf *fire-resistant construction BrE*) INS construcción a prueba de incendios f; ~ **risk on freight** n (*frof*) INS, TRANSP riesgo de incendio en la carga m

fire[3] vt infrml HRM *staff* cesar, despedir, echar; ♦ ~ **sb** HRM poner a alguien de patitas en la calle (*infrml*)

fired adj infrml HRM despedido

fireproof adj GEN COMM incombustible

firing n infrml HRM *of staff* despido m, cese m

firm[1] adj GEN COMM *order* en firme; ♦ **make a ~ bid** STOCK hacer una oferta en firme

firm[2] n GEN COMM *organization* firma f; ~ **belief** GEN COMM opinión en firme f; ~ **bid** GEN COMM, STOCK oferta en firme f; ~ **buyer** STOCK comprador(a) en firme m,f; ~ **commitment** STOCK *securities underwriting* compromiso en firme m; ~ **commitment underwriting** STOCK suscripción de compromiso en firme f; ~ **consumption** ECON consumo empresarial m; ~ **deal** GEN COMM trato en firme m; ~ **offer** GEN COMM, STOCK oferta en firme f; ~ **order** S&M pedido en firme m; ~ **quote** STOCK cotización en firme f; ~ **seller** STOCK vendedor(a) en firme m,f

firm up vi GEN COMM *currency* afirmarse

firmness n GEN COMM *market, shares* solidez f

firmware n COMP microprogramación f

first[1]: ~**-rate** adj GEN COMM excelente, S&M de primera línea

first[2]: ~**-aid kit** n GEN COMM botiquín de primeros auxilios m; ~ **available vessel** n (*firavv*) TRANSP primer navío disponible m; ~**-best economy** n ECON modelo de economía real con optimización de parámetros; ~ **call date** n STOCK primer aviso de convocatoria m; ~ **carrier** n TRANSP primer(a) transportista m,f; ~ **class** n LEIS, TRANSP primera f, primera clase f; ~**-class mail** AmE, ~**-class post** BrE n COMMS correo preferencial m; ~ **dealing day** n STOCK primer día de operaciones m; ~ **degree murder** n AmE LAW asesinato con premeditación m; ~ **degree price discrimination** n GEN COMM, S&M discriminación de precios de primer grado f; ~ **generation** n COMP, IND, MEDIA primera generación f; ~**-generation computer** n COMP computador de primera generación m (*AmL*), computadora de primera generación f (*AmL*), ordenador de primera generación m (*Esp*); ~ **half** n GEN COMM *of the month, of the year* primera parte f; ~ **lien** n BANK, PROP primera hipoteca f; ~**-line management** n MGMNT gestión directa f, dirección de contacto directo f, dirección de primera línea f, gerencia de primera línea f; ~ **line manager** n HRM, MGMNT encargado(-a) m,f (*Esp*), supervisor(a) m,f, gerente de primera línea mf, supervisor(a) de primera línea *m,f*; ~ **line supervisor** *n* MGMNT supervisor(a) de primera línea *m,f*; ~ **mortgage** *n* BANK, PROP primera hipoteca *f*; ~ **mortgage loan** *n* BANK, FIN, PROP préstamo de primera hipoteca *m*; ~ **occurrence penalty** *n* TAX penalización por primera incidencia *f*, recargo de primer incidente *m*; ~ **order goods** *n pl* GEN COMM, S&M artículos de consumo de primera necesidad *m pl*; ~ **owner of copyright** *n* LAW, PATENTS primer(a) dueño(-a) de los derechos de autor *m,f*; ~ **preferred stock** *n* STOCK acciones de preferencia *f pl*; ~ **quarter** *n* GEN COMM primer trimestre *m*; ~ **vice president** *n* HRM vicepresidente(-a) primero(-a) *m,f*; ~ **World countries** *n* GEN COMM países industrializados *m pl*, países desarrollados *m pl*

first³: ~ **in, first out** *phr* (*FIFO*) ACC, GEN COMM primero en entrar, primero en salir (*PEPS*); ~ **in, last out** *phr* (*FILO*) ACC, GEN COMM primero en entrar, último en salir (*PEUS*); **in the** ~ **instance** *phr* GEN COMM en primera instancia

FIS *abbr* (*freight, insurance and shipping charges*) IMP/EXP, TRANSP cargos por flete, seguro y embarque *m pl*

fiscal¹ *adj* ECON, FIN, POL, TAX fiscal

fiscal²: ~ **agent** *n* STOCK intermediario fiscal(-a) *m,f*; ~ **approximation** *n* TAX aproximación fiscal *f*; ~ **austerity** *n* ECON austeridad fiscal *f*; ~ **authorities** *n pl* TAX autoridades fiscales *f pl*; ~ **barrier** *n* ECON barrera fiscal *f*; ~ **burden** *n* ACC, ECON, TAX carga fiscal *f*; ~ **crisis** *n* TAX crisis fiscal *f*; ~ **deficit** *n* GEN COMM déficit fiscal *m*; ~ **dividend** *n* TAX dividendo fiscal *m*; ~ **domicile** *n* LAW, TAX domiciliación fiscal *f*; ~ **drag** *n* TAX traba fiscal *f*; ~ **equalization** *n* TAX compensación fiscal *f*; ~ **federalism** *n* ECON, POL federalismo fiscal *m*; ~ **frontiers** *n pl* ECON, POL *trade* fronteras fiscales *f pl*; ~ **illusion** *n* TAX ilusión fiscal *f*; ~ **incidence** *n* TAX incidencia fiscal *f*; ~ **indicator** *n* TAX indicador fiscal *m*; ~ **inducement** *n* TAX incentivo fiscal *m*; ~ **law** *n* LAW, TAX derecho fiscal *m*; ~ **matter** *n* LAW, TAX asunto fiscal *m*; ~ **mobility** *n* ECON movilidad fiscal *f*; ~ **month** *n* TAX mes fiscal *m*; ~ **multiplier** *n* ECON multiplicador fiscal *m*; ~ **neutrality** *n* TAX neutralidad fiscal *f*; ~ **offset** *n* TAX compensación fiscal *f*; ~ **opacity** *n* TAX opacidad fiscal *f*; ~ **period** *n* GEN COMM ejercicio financiero *m*, ejercicio fiscal *m*, periodo fiscal *m*; ~ **planning** *n* TAX gestión fiscal *f*; ~ **policy** *n* POL política fiscal *f*; ~ **position** *n* TAX posición fiscal *f*; ~ **projection** *n* TAX proyección fiscal *f*; ~ **projections** *n pl* TAX ampliaciones fiscales *f pl*; ~ **quarter** *n* TAX trimestre fiscal *m*; ~ **rectitude** *n* TAX integridad fiscal *f*; ~ **stance** *n* TAX postura fiscal *f*; ~ **surplus** *n* TAX superávit fiscal *m*; ~ **system** *n* ECON, POL, TAX sistema fiscal *m*, sistema impositivo *m*, sistema tributario *m*; ~ **year** *n* (*FY*) TAX año fiscal *m*, ejercicio fiscal *m*; ~ **year ended** *n* GEN COMM año fiscal finalizado *m*; ~ **year then ended** *n* GEN COMM año fiscal finalizado *m*

fiscalist *n* TAX fiscalista *mf*

fiscally: ~ **opaque** *adj* TAX fiscalmente opaco

fish: ~ **farm** *n* ECON *agricultural* piscifactoría *f*; ~ **farming** *n* ECON *agricultural* piscicultura *f*

Fisher: ~ **effect** *n* ECON efecto Fisher *m*; ~ **equation** *n* MATH ecuación de Fisher *f*; ~ **theorem** *n* ECON *inflation* teorema de Fisher *m*

fishery *n* ECON, IND *agricultural* industria pesquera *f*

fishing: ~ **grounds** *n pl* ECON *agricultural* caladeros *m pl*; ~ **industry** *n* ECON, IND sector pesquero *m*; ~ **port** *n* IND

puerto pesquero *m*; ~ **sector** *n* ECON, IND sector de pesca *m*

fit¹: ~ **and proper** *adj* LAW apto

fit² *n* STOCK ajuste *m*; ~ **investment** STOCK inversión oportuna *f*

fit³ *vt* GEN COMM equipar

f.i.t. *abbr* (*free of income tax*) TAX exento de impuestos sobre la renta

fitness *n* WEL aptitud *f*

fitting: ~ **room** *n* GEN COMM cuarto de prueba *m*, probador *m*

five: ~ **hundred dollar rule** *n* *AmE* STOCK regla de los cinco mil dólares *f*; ~ **percent rule** *n* STOCK método del cinco por ciento *m*, regla del cinco por ciento *f*; ~ **spot** *n* *AmE infrml* FIN billete de cinco dólares; ~**-year block averaging** *n* TAX bloque quinquenal promediado *m*; ~**-year plan** *n* ACC, BANK plan a cinco años *m*; plan quinquenal *m*; ~**-year straight-line amortization** *n* TAX amortización constante durante cinco años *f*, amortización quinquenal de variación lineal *f*

fix¹ *n* FIN fijo *m*

fix² *vt* ECON *secure* fijar, GEN COMM *arrange* arreglar, STOCK fijar; ♦ ~ **an appointment** GEN COMM concertar una cita; ~ **the claim** TAX fijar la indemnización; ~ **quotas** IMP/EXP *for import* fijar contingentes

fixed: ~ **advance** *n* ACC, BANK anticipo fijo *m*; ~ **annual percentage** *n* (*FAP*) BANK, FIN porcentaje anual fijo *m* (*PAF*); ~ **annuity** *n* INS anualidad fija *f*; ~ **asset** *n* ACC activo inmovilizado *m*, GEN COMM *land, properties, buildings* activo fijo *m*; ~ **asset assessment** *n* ACC determinación del activo fijo *f*, evaluación del activo fijo *f*; ~ **asset policies** *n pl* ACC políticas de los activos fijos *f pl*; ~ **assets** *n pl* ACC, FIN activos fijos *m pl*, capital fijo *m*; ~ **benefits** *n pl* GEN COMM beneficios fijos *m pl*; ~ **capital** *n* ACC, FIN capital fijo *m*, capital inmovilizado *m*; ~ **charge** *n* ACC cargo fijo *m*, gasto fijo *m*; ~ **charge coverage** *n* ACC cobertura de cargo fijo *f*, cobertura de gastos fijos *f*; ~ **charges** *n pl* ACC, BANK, FIN cargas fijas *f pl*; ~ **cost** *n* ECON, GEN COMM coste fijo *m* (*Esp*), costo fijo *m* (*AmL*); ~ **crane** *n* TRANSP grúa fija *f*; ~ **deposit** *n* BANK depósito a plazo fijo *m*; ~ **disk** *n* COMP *hardware* disco fijo *m*; ~ **duty** *n* TAX impuesto fijo *m*; ~ **exchange rate** *n* ECON cambio fijo *m*; ~ **expenses** *n pl* ACC gastos fijos *m pl*; ~ **expiration date** *n* STOCK *options* fecha fija de vencimiento *f*; ~ **factor** *n* ECON factor fijo *m*; ~ **fee** *n* GEN COMM honorario fijo *m*; ~ **hedge** *n* STOCK cobertura fija *f*; ~ **income** *n* STOCK renta fija *f*; ~**-income fund** *n* STOCK fondo de inversión de renta fija *m*; ~**-income investment** *n* STOCK inversión en renta fija *f*; ~**-income securities market** *n* STOCK mercado de valores de renta fija *m*; ~**-income security** *n* STOCK título de renta fija *m*; ~ **installment** *AmE*, ~ **instalment** *BrE* *n* BANK, FIN plazo fijo *m*; ~**-interest bond** *n* STOCK bono de interés fijo *m*, obligación de renta fija *f*; ~**-interest loan** *n* BANK, FIN préstamo a interés fijo *m*; ~**-interest security** *n* STOCK título de renta fija *m*; ~ **liability** *n* ACC, BANK pasivo fijo consolidado *m*; ~ **loan** *n* BANK préstamo fijo *m*; ~ **maturity** *n* BANK vencimiento a fecha fija *m*; ~ **overheads** *n pl* ACC gastos generales fijos *m pl*; ~ **penalties** *n pl* TAX *return* fianza de incumplimiento *f*; ~**-period deposit** *n* BANK depósito en periodo fijo *m*; ~ **place of business** *n* GEN COMM, TAX domicilio social fijo *m*; ~ **plant** *n* IND planta fija *f*, planta de producto fijo *f*; ~**-point number** *n* MATH número de coma fija *m*; ~ **premium** *n* INS prima fija *f*; ~ **price** *n* ACC, ECON, STOCK *put options* precio fijo *m*; ~**-price contract** *n* S&M contrato de precio fijado *m*; ~**-price offering** *n* STOCK oferta a precio fijo *f*; ~**-rate bond** *n* FIN, STOCK bono de tipo de interés fijo *m*; ~**-rate loan** *n* BANK, FIN préstamo de interés fijo *m*; ~**-rate mortgage** *n* BANK crédito hipotecario a interés fijo *m*; ~**-rate security** *n* STOCK título de tipo fijo *m*; ~ **route** *n* TRANSP itinerario fijo *m*; ~ **salary** *n* HRM salario fijo *m*; ~ **spot** *n* S&M espacio fijo *m*; ~ **supply** *n* ECON abastecimiento fijo *m*, aprovisionamiento fijo *m*; ~ **tax rate** *n* TAX tipo impositivo fijo *m*; ~**-term agreement** *n* HRM acuerdo por tiempo establecido *m*, contrato por tiempo establecido *m*; ~**-term annuity** *n* FIN anualidad con vencimiento fijo *f*; ~**-term contract** *n* HRM contrato de plazo fijo *m*; ~**-term deal** *n* HRM acuerdo por tiempo establecido *m*, contrato por tiempo establecido *m*; ~**-term deposit** *n* BrE (*cf time deposit AmE*) BANK depósito a plazo fijo *m*; ~**-term loan** *n* BANK préstamo a plazo fijo *m*; ~**-yield security** *n* STOCK título de renta fija *m*

fixing *n* ECON fijación *f*, GEN COMM cambio base *m*, STOCK *prices* fijación *f*; ~ **of costs** STOCK determinación de los costes *f* (*Esp*), determinación de los costos *f* (*AmL*); ~ **rate** BANK fixing *m*; ~**-up expense** *infrml* PROP *of residence* gastos de acondicionamiento *m pl*, gastos de arreglo *m pl*

fixture *n* PROP instalación *f*; ~ **rate** TRANSP *chartered vessel hire* tasa por uso de bienes y servicios públicos *f*

fixtures: ~ **and fittings** *n pl* ACC bienes inmuebles y enseres *m pl*, GEN COMM, PROP accesorios e instalaciones *m pl*

flag[1] *n* COMP indicador *m*, TRANSP *shipping* pabellón *m*; ~ **of convenience** TRANSP *shipping* bandera de conveniencia *f*

flag[2] *vt* COMP indicar

flagging *n* TRANSP *ship* abanderizamiento *m*

flagship: ~ **store** *n* S&M tienda insignia *f*

flash: ~ **of inspiration** *n* GEN COMM golpe de inspiración *m*; ~ **pack** *n* S&M envase con reducción de precio en lugar destacado *m*

flat[1] *adj* FIN fijo, GEN COMM *dull* invariable, *surface* plano, *unchanged* fijo, STOCK fijo, uniforme, plano; ~ **broke** *infrml* HRM bruja (*infrml*) (*AmL*), sin un duro (*infrml*) (*Esp*); ~**-rate** ECON *prices* de tipo fijo

flat[2] *n* BANK tasa de recargo *f*, PROP BrE (*cf apartment AmE*) apartamento *m* (*AmL*) (*Apt., Apto.*), departamento *m* (*AmL*) (*dpto.*), piso *m* (*Esp*); ~ **bed** TRANSP plataforma *f*; ~ **bond** STOCK título con intereses acumulados en la cotización *m*; ~ **car** AmE (*cf flat wagon BrE*) TRANSP *rail* coche plataforma *m*, vagón plataforma *m*, vagón raso *m*; ~ **container** TRANSP contenedor de cubierta plana *m*; ~ **fee** BANK, FIN comisión fija *f*; ~ **grant** WEL subvención fija *f*; ~ **line reinsurance** INS reaseguro de línea fija *m*; ~ **market** STOCK mercado sinátono *m*; ~ **organization** MGMNT organización horizontal *f*; ~ **quotation** STOCK cotización sin interés *f*; ~ **rack** TRANSP contenedor abierto abatible *m*; ~ **rate** S&M tasa neta *f*, TAX tipo fijo *m*; ~**-rate bonus** HRM prima de tipo fijo *f*; ~**-rate fee** PATENTS tarifa fija *f*; ~ **rate of pay** HRM tipo uniforme de salarios *m*; ~**-rate price** GEN COMM precio a tipo fijo *m*; ~**-rate subscription** FIN suscripción a tanto alzado *f*, suscripción de pantalla plana *f*; ~**-rate tax** TAX impuesto de tipo fijo *m*; ~**-rate withholding** TAX

retención de tipo fijo *f*; ~**-rate withholding tax** TAX impuesto de retención de tasa fija *m*; ~ **scale** HRM escala uniforme *f*; ~ **tax** TAX impuesto de tipo fijo *m*; ~ **wagon** BrE (*cf flat car AmE*) TRANSP *rail* coche plataforma *m*, vagón plataforma *m*, vagón raso *m*

flatten *vi* MATH *curve* achatar

flaunt *vt* GEN COMM ostentar

flaw *n* GEN COMM defecto *m*

flawed *adj* GEN COMM defectuoso

fledgling: ~ **commercial field** *n* GEN COMM campo comercial nuevo *m*

fleet *n* TRANSP *of company cars* parque *m*, *shipping* flota *f*; ~ **manager** HRM, TRANSP director(a) de flota *m,f*, *cars* gerente de flotilla *mf*, jefe(-a) de parque de coches *m,f*, *engines* jefe(-a) de flota *m,f*, *planes, ships* jefe(-a) de flotilla *m,f*; ~ **planning** TRANSP *shipping* planificación de la flota *f*; ~ **policy** INS póliza de flotilla *f*, póliza para un grupo de coches *f*; ~ **rationalization** TRANSP racionalización de la flota *f*; ~ **utilization** TRANSP utilización de la flota *f*

Fleet: ~ **Street** *n* BrE, MEDIA calle londinense famosa por ser el centro de la industria periodística nacional

flexibility *n* GEN COMM flexibilidad *f*; ~ **of time** HRM flexibilidad de horario *f*

flexible[1] *adj* GEN COMM flexible

flexible[2]: ~ **accelerator** *n* ECON acelerador flexible *m*; ~ **budget** *n* ECON presupuesto flexible *m*; ~ **exchange rate** *n* ECON tipo de cambio flexible *m*; ~ **firm** *n* GEN COMM empresa flexible *f*; ~ **intermediate and bulk container** *n* (*FIBC*) TRANSP contenedor polivalente intermedio y masivo *m*; ~ **mark-up pricing** *n* ECON fijación flexible de precios *f*; ~**-payment mortgage** *n* (*FPM*) BANK, FIN hipoteca de pagos variables *f*, hipoteca de pagos flexibles *f*; ~ **plant** *n* IND equipo flexible *m*, planta de producto flexible *f*; ~ **pricing** *n* ECON fijación flexible de precios *f*; ~**-rate term deposit** *n* BANK depósito a plazo con interés variable *m*; ~ **schedule** *n* HRM horario flexible *m*; ~ **time** *n* HRM horario flexible *m*; ~ **working hours** *n pl* HRM horario de trabajo flexible *m*, horario flexible *m*, horario móvil *m*

flexitime *n* HRM horario de trabajo flexible *m*, horario flexible *m*, horario móvil *m*

flexography *n* MEDIA flexografía *f*

flexprice *n* ECON precio flexible *m*

flextime *n* HRM horario de trabajo flexible *m*, horario móvil *m*, horario flexible *m*

flicker[1] *n* COMP *screen* parpadeo *m*

flicker[2] *vi* COMP *screen* parpadear

flier *n* AmE STOCK especulación peligrosa *f*; ◆ **take a** ~ AmE STOCK especular

flight: ~ **attendant** *n* LEIS, TRANSP auxiliar de vuelo *mf*; ~ **of capital** *n* ECON huida de capitales *f*; ~ **coupon** *n* LEIS, TRANSP cupón de vuelo *m*; ~ **from the dollar** *n* ECON conversión del dólar con otras divisas *f*; ~ **from money** *n* ECON conversión de la moneda *f*; ~ **information** *n* LEIS, TRANSP información de vuelo *f*; ~ **number** *n* LEIS, TRANSP número de vuelo *m*; ~ **scheduler** *n* TRANSP programador(a) de vuelo *m,f*; ~ **stage** *n* TRANSP etapa de vuelo *f*; ~ **strategy** *n* TRANSP estrategia de vuelo *f*; ~ **time** *n* LEIS, TRANSP tiempo de vuelo *m*; ~ **time information** *n* LEIS, TRANSP información del tiempo de vuelo *f*; ~ **to quality** *n* STOCK huida hacia la calidad *f*

flip: **~ chart** *n* ADMIN rotafolios *m*; **~-flop** *n* COMP *hardware* circuito biestable *m*

float[1] *n* BANK *uncollected cheques* cheques no canjeados *m pl*, GEN COMM dinero en caja *m*, efectivo disponible *m*, efectivo en caja *m*; **~ time** BANK fecha de negociación *f*, IMP/EXP periodo de emisión *m*

float[2] *vt* BANK, FIN, STOCK flotar, *new issue* lanzar; ◆ **~ a loan** STOCK emitir un empréstito; **~ securities** STOCK emitir obligaciones

floater *n* AmE (*cf floating-rate note BrE*) STOCK obligación de interés variable *f*

floating[1] *adj* BANK, FIN, STOCK *interest rate, exchange rate* flotante

floating[2] *n* BANK, FIN *of currency*, STOCK flotación *f*, *of new issue* lanzamiento *m*; **~ asset** ACC activo flotante *m*; **~ berth** TRANSP amarradero flotante *m*; **~ capital** ACC, ECON, FIN, GEN COMM capital flotante *m*; **~ cargo policy** INS póliza de cargamento marítimo *f*, TRANSP póliza flotante de carga *f*; **~ cash reserve** ACC encaje circulante *m*, encaje flotante *m*; **~ currency** ECON, FIN moneda flotante *f*; **~ currency exchange rate** ECON tipo flotante de cambio de divisas *m*; **~ debt** ACC, BANK deuda flotante *f*, pasivo flotante *m*; **~ dock** TRANSP *shipping* dique flotante *m*; **~ exchange** GEN COMM cambio flotante *m*; **~ exchange rate** ECON cambios flotantes *m pl*; **~ interest rate** BANK tasa de interés flotante *f*; **~ lien** TAX gravamen continuado *m*; **~ marine policy** (*FP*) INS, TRANSP póliza marina flotante *f*, póliza marítima flotante *f*; **~-point number** MATH número de coma flotante *m*; **~ policy** WEL póliza flotante *f*, póliza variable *f*; **~ production system** (*FPS*) TRANSP sistema de botadura *m*, sistema de producción a bordo *m*; **~ production vessel** TRANSP *shipping* navío de producción a bordo *m*; **~ rate** BANK tasa flotante *f*, ECON *of exchange* tipo flotante *m*; **~-rate debenture** STOCK obligación de tipo flotante *f*; **~-rate deposit** STOCK *futures* depósito de interés variable *m*; **~-rate investment** STOCK *of futures* inversión a interés variable *f*; **~-rate loan** BANK préstamo de tasa flotante *m*, préstamo de tasa variable *m*; **~-rate note** (*FRN*) (*cf floater AmE*), STOCK obligación de interés variable *f*; **~-rate preferred share** STOCK acción preferente de tipo flotante *f*; **~ securities** *n pl* STOCK valores en flotación *m pl*; **~ stock** STOCK acciones flotantes *f pl*; **~ supply** STOCK oferta fluctuante *f*; **~ treasury stock** STOCK autocartera flotante *f*; **~ voter** BrE POL votante indeciso(-a) *m,f*

flood: **~ insurance** *n* INS seguro contra riesgo de inundación *m*; **~ plain** *n* PROP terreno inundable *m*

flooded: **~ market** *n* GEN COMM mercado saturado *m*

floor *n* ECON *fluctuation of interests* suelo *m*, PROP planta *f*, STOCK parqué *m*; **~-area ratio** MATH, PROP proporción piso-superficie *f*; **~ broker** STOCK agente auxiliar de bolsa *mf*, comisionista bursátil *mf*; **~ loading** TRANSP *ship* carga sobre el suelo *f*; **~ loan** BANK, FIN préstamo mínimo *m*; **~ manager** BrE (*cf floorwalker AmE*) S&M *of department store* jefe(-a) de sección *m,f*; **~ official** STOCK empleado(-a) del parqué *m,f*; **~ plan insurance** INS seguro a todo riesgo sobre mercancías dadas como garantía *m*; **~ price** ECON precio mínimo *m*; **~ rate** BANK, ECON, FIN, STOCK *of futures* tasa mínima *f*; **~ return** STOCK *of futures* rendimiento básico *m*; **~ space** PROP superficie habitable *f*; **~ trader** STOCK *exchange trading* corredor(a) de bolsa independiente *m,f*

floorwalker *n* AmE (*cf floor manager BrE*) S&M *of department store* jefe(-a) de sección *m,f*

flop *n* infrml GEN COMM fracaso *m* (*infrml*)

floppy *n* COMP disco flexible *m*, disquete flexible *m*; **~ disk** COMP disco flexible *m*, disquete flexible *m*; **~ disk drive** COMP unidad de disco flexible *f*

flotation *n* BANK *interest rate, exchange rate*, FIN *of currency* flotación *f*, STOCK emisión de bonos *f*, flotación *f*; **~ cost** STOCK coste de flotación *m* (*Esp*), costo de flotación *m* (*AmL*); **~ costs** *n pl* STOCK gastos de emisión *m pl*

flourish *vi* GEN COMM *business, competition* florecer, prosperar

flow *n* ACC *of funds*, COMP *of data* flujo *m*, GEN COMM *of operations* desarrollo *m*, TRANSP *of goods, passenger traffic* flujo *m*; **~ concepts** *n pl* STOCK conceptos de flujo *m pl*; **~ control** COMP control de flujo *m*; **~ diagram** MATH diagrama del proceso de fabricación *m*; **~ of funds** ACC, ECON, FIN, STOCK flujo de fondos *m*; **~ of funds account** ACC, ECON, FIN estado de cuentas del flujo de fondos *m*; **~ of investments** ACC, ECON fluctuación de inversiones *f*; **~ of money** ECON, GEN COMM flujo monetario *m*; **~-of-funds table** FIN *national accounts* cuadro de corrientes financieras *m*; **~ line** GEN COMM cadena de producción *f*; **~ of orders** GEN COMM incremento de pedidos *m*; **~ process chart** MATH diagrama de proceso *m*, MGMNT diagrama de flujo de proceso *m*; **~ production** IND fabricación en cadena *f*; **~-through** TAX *of account, dividends* transparencia fiscal *f*; **~-through basis** TAX base de transparencia fiscal *f*; **~-through share** STOCK acción de transparencia fiscal *f*; ◆ **go with the ~** infrml HRM ir con la corriente; **~ out of the country** ECON *money* salir del país

flowchart *n* ACC gráfico de circulación *m*, GEN COMM diagrama de flujo *m*, flujograma *m*, organigrama *m*, organigrama funcional *m*

flower: **~ bond** *n* AmE STOCK bonos del tesoro aceptados a la par después de la muerte del titular, =bono flor *m*

fl.oz. *abbr* (*fluid ounce*) GEN COMM onza fluida *f*

FLSA *abbr* AmE (*Fair Labor Standards Act*) LAW estatuto de normas laborales equitativas

FLT *abbr* (*fork-lift truck*) TRANSP carretilla de horquilla elevadora *f*

fluctuate *vi* ECON, FIN *share price, rate of exchange* fluctuar, GEN COMM *prices* oscilar, STOCK *share price, rate of exchange* fluctuar

fluctuating: **~ currency** *n* BANK, ECON, FIN divisa fluctuante *f*

fluctuation *n* ECON, FIN, STOCK *prices, interest rates* fluctuación *f*; **~ band** ECON *currency rate* banda de fluctuación *f*; **~ limit** STOCK límite de fluctuación *m*

fluid: **~ ounce** *n* (*fl.oz.*) GEN COMM onza fluida *f*

flurry: **~ of activity** *n* STOCK agitación de la actividad *f*

flush[1]: **~ left** *adj* COMMS, COMP, MEDIA *document layout* justificado a la izquierda; **~ right** *adj* COMMS, COMP, MEDIA *document layout* justificado a la derecha

flush[2] *vt* COMP, MEDIA *document layout* justificar

flux *n* GEN COMM flujo *m*

fly: **~-posting** *n* S&M anuncio ilegal *m*

flyer *n* MEDIA, S&M *advertisement* octavilla *f*

flying: **~ bridge** *n* TRANSP *shipping* puente alto *m*; **~ doctor** *n* WEL médico que se desplaza en avión;

~ picket *n* HRM piquete de huelga *m*, piquete móvil *m*; **~ visit** *n* GEN COMM visita relámpago *f*

FMB *abbr* (*Federal Maritime Board*) IND dirección marítima de los Estados Unidos

FMC *abbr* (*Federal Maritime Commission*) TRANSP comisión marítima de los Estados Unidos

FMF *abbr* (*Food Manufacturers' Federation*) IND federación de fabricantes de alimentos

FMG *abbr* (*fast-moving consumer goods*) S&M mercancías de venta fácil *f pl*

FMRR *abbr* (*financial management rate of return*) FIN tasa de rentabilidad de la gestión financiera *f*

FNMA *abbr* (*Federal National Mortgage Association*) BANK, FIN asociación nacional federal de hipotecas

fo *abbr* GEN COMM (*for orders*) a órdenes, IMP/EXP, TRANSP (*free out term*) término secundario libre *m*

f.o.a. *abbr* (*free on aircraft*) IMP/EXP, TRANSP franco avión

FOA *abbr* AmE (*Foreign Operations Administration*) GEN COMM dirección de operaciones con el exterior

f.o.b. *abbr* (*free on board*) IMP/EXP, TRANSP franco a bordo

f.o.b.&t *abbr* (*free on board and trimmed*) IMP/EXP, TRANSP franco a bordo y asentado, franco a bordo y carga equilibrada

FOC *abbr* (*free of charge*) GEN COMM libre de gastos

focal: ~ point *n* GEN COMM *of discussion* punto focal *m*

focus[1] *n* GEN COMM punto central *m*; **~ group** S&M *market research* grupo analizado *m*, grupo estudiado *m*; **~ group survey** S&M encuesta de un grupo enfocado *f*

focus[2] *vt* GEN COMM fijar

focus on *vt* GEN COMM fijar, centrar en

fod *abbr* (*free of damage*) GEN COMM libre de daños

FOIA *abbr* AmE (*Freedom of Information Act*) LAW ley de libertad de información

foil: ~ stamping *n* MEDIA estampación sobre metal *f*

FOK *abbr* AmE (*fill-or-kill*) STOCK cancelar inmediatamente, cumplimentar inmediatamente

folder *n* ADMIN legajo *m*, carpeta *f*

folio *n* MEDIA folio *m*

follow[1]: **~-up** *n* GEN COMM recordatorio *m*, S&M seguimiento *m*; **~-up of invoices** *n* ACC control de cobros *m*; **~-up letter** *n* ADMIN, COMMS, GEN COMM carta de insistencia *f*, carta recordatoria *f*, S&M carta de seguimiento *f*; **~-up of orders** *n* S&M control de pedidos *m*

follow[2] *vt* MATH *curve of demand*, MGMNT seguir; ♦ **~ a similar pattern** GEN COMM *demand* seguir un modelo similar; **~ suit** GEN COMM seguir el ejemplo

follow through *vi* GEN COMM *project, scheme* seguir el trámite de

follow up *vt* GEN COMM controlar, S&M seguir

follower *n* GEN COMM, POL partidario(-a) *m,f*, seguidor(a) *m,f*

FOMC *abbr* AmE (*Federal Open Market Committee*) STOCK comité federal de mercado abierto

FONASBA *abbr* (*Federation of National Associations of Shipbrokers and Agents*) TRANSP federación de asociaciones nacionales de agentes y consignatarios

font *n* COMP, MEDIA *typography* juego de caracteres *m*; **~ family** COMP, MEDIA *typography* familia de tipos *f*

Fontainebleau: ~ abatement *n* ECON Cancelación de Fontainebleau *f*

food: ~ aid *n* ECON, POL ayuda alimentaria *f*, ayuda alimenticia *f*; **~ chain** *n* ECON, ENVIR cadena alimenticia *f*; **~ law** *n* LAW ley de productos alimentarios *f*; **~ processing** *n* IND procesamiento de alimentos *m*; **~-processing industry** *n* ECON, IND industria alimenticia *f*, sector de procesamiento de alimentos *m*; **~ retailing** *n* S&M venta minorista de alimentos *f*; **~ store** *n* S&M tienda de alimentación *f*; **~ surplus** *n* ECON excedentes alimentarios *m pl*

Food: ~ and Agriculture Organization *n* (*FAO*) ECON, POL Organización de las Naciones Unidas para la Agricultura y Alimentación *f* (*FAO*); **~ and Drug Administration** *n* AmE (*FDA*) WEL oficina de control de alimentos y fármacos; **~ Manufacturers' Federation** *n* (*FMF*) IND federación de fabricantes de alimentos

foodstuff *n* GEN COMM producto alimenticio *m*

foot *n* (*ft*) GEN COMM pie *m*

footage *n* MEDIA metraje *m*

football: ~ pools *n pl* BrE LEIS ≈ quinielas *f pl* (*Esp*)

footer *n* COMP, MEDIA título en pie de página *m*

footing: be on an equal ~ *phr* GEN COMM, HRM estar en iguales condiciones

footnote *n* COMP *document* nota a pie de página *f*, nota al pie *f*, anotación a pie de página *f*; **~ disclosure** ACC exposición en nota al pie *f*

Footsie *n* (*Financial Times-Stock Exchange 100 Share Index*) STOCK índice Footsie *m*, índice bursátil del Financial Times de los valores de las 100 mayores entidades de la Bolsa de Londres

f.o.q. *abbr* (*free on quay*) IMP/EXP, TRANSP franco muelle

f.o.q.-f.o.q. *abbr* (*free on quay to free on quay*) IMP/EXP, TRANSP franco de muelle a muelle

f.o.r. *abbr* (*free on rail*) IMP/EXP, TRANSP franco sobre vagón, puesto sobre vagón

force[1]: **~ majeure** *n* LAW fuerza mayor *f*

force[2] *vt* GEN COMM obligar; ♦ **~ into early retirement** HRM obligar a una jubilación anticipada; **~ an issue** GEN COMM forzar una salida

force[3]: **in ~** *phr* LAW en vigor

force down *vt* ECON *interest rates* forzar el descenso de

forced: ~ currency *n* ECON, FIN moneda forzada *f*, STOCK moneda forzosa *f*; **~ labor** AmE, **~ labour** BrE *n* TAX trabajo forzoso *m*; **~ landing** *n* LEIS, TRANSP aterrizaje forzoso *m*; **~ sale of stock** *n* GEN COMM, LAW, S&M venta forzosa de existencias *f*, venta forzosa de mercancías *f*; **~ saving** *n* BANK, ECON, FIN ahorro forzoso *m*

forceful *adj* ECON, GEN COMM *argument* fuerte

forcible: ~ entry *n* LAW *by police* toma de posesión violenta *f*

Fordism *n* ECON teoría de Ford *f*

fore: ~ and aft *phr* TRANSP *shipping* de popa a proa

forecast[1] *n* GEN COMM previsión *f*, predicción *f*

forecast[2] *vt* GEN COMM prever

forecaster *n* GEN COMM previsor(a) *m,f*

forecasting *n* GEN COMM previsión *f*, pronóstico *m*

foreclose *vt* FIN *mortgage* ejecutar

foreclosure *n* LAW, PROP procedimiento ejecutivo hipotecario *m*; **~ sale** S&M venta por juicio hipotecario *f*

foredate *vt* GEN COMM antefechar

forefront: at the ~ *phr* GEN COMM *of research and development* de vanguardia

foreground[1] *adj* COMP preferencial

foreground[2]: ~ **program** *n* COMP programa de alta prioridad *m*

foreign: ~ **account** *n* BANK cuenta con el exterior *f*, cuenta extranjera *f*; ~ **accrual tax** *n* TAX impuesto acumulativo pagado en el extranjero *m*; ~ **affairs** *n pl* POL asuntos exteriores *m pl*, asuntos internacionales *m pl*; ~ **affiliate** *n* STOCK asociado(-a) extranjero(-a) *m,f*; ~ **agent** *n* GEN COMM representante en el extranjero *mf*; ~ **aid** *n* ECON, POL ayuda exterior *f*, ayuda externa *f*; ~ **assets** *n pl* STOCK activos en divisas *m pl*; ~ **balance** *n* ECON balanza exterior *f*; ~ **bank** *n* BANK banco extranjero *m*; ~ **banking** *n* BANK banca extranjera *f*; ~ **bill** *n* BANK letra extranjera *f*, letra sobre el exterior *f*; ~ **bond** *n* FIN, STOCK bono extranjero *m*; ~ **borrowing** *n* BANK empréstito extranjero *m*; ~ **branch** *n* BANK sucursal en el extranjero *f*; ~ **buying house** *n* IMP/EXP casa compradora extranjera *f*; ~ **capital** *n* ACC, ECON, FIN, GEN COMM capital externo *m*; ~ **check issue** *AmE*, ~ **cheque issue** *BrE n* BANK emisión de cheques extranjeros *f*; ~ **company** *n* GEN COMM, LAW sociedad extranjera *f*, compañía extranjera *f*; ~ **competitor** *n* GEN COMM competidor(a) extranjero(-a) *m,f*; ~**controlled bank** *n* BANK banco bajo control extranjero *m*; ~**controlled enterprise** *n* GEN COMM empresa controlada desde el exterior *f*; ~ **corporation** *n* GEN COMM, LAW compañía extranjera *f*, sociedad extranjera *f*; ~ **correspondent** *n* MEDIA corresponsal en el extranjero *mf*; ~ **currency** *n* GEN COMM divisa extranjera *f*; ~ **currency allowance** *n* FIN asignación en divisas *f*; ~ **currency conversion** *n* ECON conversión a una moneda extranjera *f*; ~ **currency issue** *n* STOCK emisión en divisas *f*; ~ **currency loan** *n* ECON, FIN crédito en divisas *m*; ~ **currency market** *n* FIN, STOCK bolsa de divisas *f*; ~ **currency outflow** *n* ECON salida de divisas extranjeras *f*; ~ **currency transaction** *n* BANK, ECON transacción en divisas *f*; ~ **currency translation reserve** *n* ACC *annual accounts* reserva para conversión de divisas *f*; ~ **currency unit** *n* ACC, BANK, ECON, FIN unidad monetaria extranjera *f*; ~ **debt** *n* ECON, POL deuda externa *f*; ~ **demand** *n* ECON, S&M demanda exterior *f*; ~ **dividends** *n pl* STOCK dividendos extranjeros *m pl*; ~ **exchange** *n* (*forex*) GEN COMM divisa extranjera *f*, cambio extranjero *m*; ~ **exchange account** *n* BANK cuenta en divisas *f*; ~ **exchange advisory service** *n* BANK servicio de asesoría de cambio de divisas *m*; ~ **exchange broker** *n* BANK, FIN, STOCK corredor(a) de cambios *m,f*; ~ **exchange deal** *n* STOCK transacción en divisas *f*; ~ **exchange dealer** *n* BANK, FIN, STOCK cambista *mf*; ~ **exchange department** *n* BANK mesa de cambios *f*; ~ **exchange earner** *n* GEN COMM ganador(a) de divisas *m,f*, persona remunerada en divisas extranjeras *f*; ~ **exchange hedge** *n* ACC, FIN cobertura del cambio de divisas *f*, protección del cambio de divisas *f*, seguro de cambio *m*; ~ **exchange holding** *n* BANK participación en cambio de divisas *f*; ~ **exchange market** *n* ECON, FIN, STOCK *international* mercado de divisas *m*; ~ **exchange office** *n* BANK, LEIS oficina de cambio *f*; ~ **exchange rate** *n* BANK tipo de cambio extranjero *m*; ~ **exchange reserves** *n pl* ECON reserva de divisas *f*; ~ **exchange risk** *n* ECON, FIN riesgo cambiario *m*, riesgo de cambio *m*; ~ **exchange tables** *n pl* BANK, ECON, FIN tablas de cambio de divisas *f pl*; ~ **exchange trader** *n* STOCK corredor(a) de divisas *m,f*; ~ **flag** *n* TRANSP *shipping* bandera extranjera *f*; ~**going**

passenger ship *n* TRANSP buque de altura de transporte de pasajeros *m*; ~ **identity card** *n* BrE (*cf alien registration card AmE*) POL, WEL tarjeta de identificación extranjera *f*; ~ **income** *n* ACC, TAX ingresos procedentes del exterior *m pl*; ~ **investment** *n* FIN inversión extranjera *f*; ~ **investment income** *n* ACC, TAX ingresos por inversiones extranjeras *m pl*; ~ **investment limit** *n* TAX límite de la inversión extranjera *m*; ~ **investor** *n* STOCK inversor(a) extranjero(-a) *m,f*; ~ **merger** *n* STOCK fusión extranjera *f*; ~ **money order** *n* BANK orden de moneda extranjera *f*; ~ **national** *n* HRM persona de nacionalidad extranjera *f*; ~**owned bank** *n* BANK banco de propiedad extranjera *m*; ~**owned container** *n* TRANSP contenedor de propiedad extranjera *m*; ~**owned property** *n* PROP, TAX propiedad extranjera *f*; ~ **property** *n* PROP, TAX propiedad extranjera *f*; ~ **sale** *n* S&M venta de exportación *f*; ~ **section** *n* STOCK sección extranjera *f*; ~ **securities** *n pl* STOCK valores extranjeros *m pl*; ~ **share** *n* FIN, STOCK acción extranjera *f*; ~ **stock** *n* STOCK acciones extranjeras *f pl*; ~ **student** *n* WEL estudiante extranjero(-a) *m,f*; ~ **tax** *n* ACC, TAX impuestos pagados en el extranjero *m pl*; ~ **tax carryover** *n* TAX impuesto pagado en el extranjero llevado al año siguiente *m*; ~ **tax credit** *n* TAX desgravación de impuestos pagados en el extranjero *f*; ~ **trade** *n* ECON, IMP/EXP comercio exterior *m*; ~ **trade bank** *n* BANK banco de comercio exterior *m*; ~ **trade multiplier** *n* ECON multiplicador del comercio exterior *m*; ~ **trade surplus** *n* ECON superávit del comercio exterior *m*; ~ **venture** *n* GEN COMM operación arriesgada en el extranjero *f*; ~ **worker** *n* HRM trabajador(a) extranjero(-a) *m,f*

Foreign: ~ **and Commonwealth Office** *n* (*FCO*) POL oficina para asuntos exteriores de la Commonwealth; ~ **Exchange Administration Technical Office** *n* ECON, POL Oficina Técnica de Administración Cambiaria *f* (*OTAC*); ~ **Investment Advisory Service** *n* (*FIAS*) STOCK servicio de asesoramiento para inversiones en el extranjero; ~ **Operations Administration** *n* AmE (*FOA*) GEN COMM dirección de operaciones con el exterior; ~ **Minister** *n* POL Ministro(-a) de Asuntos Exteriores *m,f*

foreigner *n* GEN COMM extranjero(-a) *m,f*

foreman *n* HRM, PROP capataz(a) *m,f*, sobrestante *mf*

forename *n* HRM nombre *m*

foresee *vt* GEN COMM prevenir, prever

foreseeable: ~ **future** *n* GEN COMM futuro previsible *m*; ~ **risk** *n* STOCK riesgo previsible *m*

foreseen *adj* GEN COMM previsto

foreshore *n* LAW anteplaya *f*

forestry *n* GEN COMM silvicultura *f*; ~ **industry** ECON, IND industria forestal *f*

Forestry: ~ **Commission** *n* BrE ENVIR, IND Comisión Forestal *f*

forex[1] *abbr* (*foreign exchange*) GEN COMM cambio extranjero *m*, divisa extranjera *f*

forex[2]: ~ **option** *n* STOCK opción sobre divisas *f*; ~ **trading** *n* BANK *merchant* operación de compra-venta extranjera *f*

Forex: ~ **index** *n* ECON, FIN índice de divisas *m*

forfaiting *n* ECON *international trade* compra de efectos a cobrar *f*

forfeit: ~ **system** *n* TAX sistema de estimación presunta *m*

forfeited: ~ **security** *n* INS valor caducado *m*

forfeiting n GEN COMM forfeiting m

forfeiture n LAW confiscación f, pérdida legal del derecho de un bien f; **~ of a debt** FIN extinción de una obligación o deuda f

forge vt GEN COMM, LAW falsificar

forged: **~ bill** n AmE (cf forged note BrE) BANK, GEN COMM billete falso m; **~ check** AmE, **~ cheque** BrE n BANK, FIN cheque falsificado m, cheque falso m; **~ note** n BrE (cf forged bill AmE) BANK, GEN COMM billete falso m

forgery n GEN COMM falsificación f

forgivable: **~ loan** n BANK, FIN préstamo perdonable m

forgive vt GEN COMM perdonar

forgiveness: **~ of tax** n TAX exención del impuesto f

forgo: **~ collection of** phr ACC a debt abstenerse de cobrar, perdonar, renunciar al derecho de cobro; **~ an inheritance** phr LAW renunciar a una herencia

fork: **~-lift truck** n (FLT) TRANSP carretilla de horquilla elevadora f

form[1] n GEN COMM of the abstract forma f, printed formulario m; **~ feed** (FF) COMP avance de formato m, salto de impreso m; **~-filling** GEN COMM relleno de formularios m, relleno de impresos m; ♦ **In the ~ of** GEN COMM en forma de

form[2] vt GEN COMM committee, alliance constituir, subsidiary crear; ♦ **~ a partnership** GEN COMM constituir una sociedad; **~ a quorum** MGMNT constituir quorum

formal[1] adj GEN COMM formal

formal[2]: **~ agreement** n GEN COMM acuerdo formal m; **~ communication** n COMMS comunicación formal f; **~ economy** n ECON economía formal f; **~ indexation** n TAX indexación formal f; **~ management development** n MGMNT desarrollo formal de la administración m; **~ notice** n GEN COMM admonición por mora f; **~ receipt** n GEN COMM factura formal f; **~ submission date** n FIN fecha formal de presentación f

formality n GEN COMM formalidad f

formalization n GEN COMM, HRM formalización f

formalize vt GEN COMM, HRM formalizar, agreement concuir

format[1] n ADMIN, COMP descripción de formato f, of document formato m

format[2] vt COMP disk formatear

formation: **~ of a corporation** n STOCK constitución de una compañía f, formación de una sociedad f; **~ expense** n ACC gastos de establecimiento m pl

formatting n COMP formateado m

former[1] adj GEN COMM antiguo

former[2]: **the ~** n GEN COMM el primero m; **~ buyer** n S&M comprador(a) anterior m,f; **~ spouse** n LAW antiguo(-a) cónyuge m,f

forms: **~ design sheet** n ADMIN hoja de diseño de formularios f

formula n GEN COMM fórmula f; **~ funding** FIN financiación ponderada f; **~ investing** STOCK inversión por fórmula f

formulate vt GEN COMM, MGMNT policy formular

formulation n GEN COMM, MGMNT of policy formulación f

fortnightly[1] adj GEN COMM bimensual, quincenal

fortnightly[2] adv GEN COMM bimensualmente, quincenalmente

fortress: **~ Europe** n jarg POL fortaleza europea f, reducto europeo m

fortuitous: **~ event** n GEN COMM, LAW hecho fortuito m

forum n POL foro m

forward[1]: **~-forward** adj STOCK a plazo con tipo de interés convenido; **~-looking** adj GEN COMM person, project con visión de futuro; **~-thinking** adj GEN COMM con previsión de futuro

forward[2] adv TRANSP a proa

forward[3]: **~ accounting** n BANK contabilidad especulativa f; **~ averaging** n TAX pago adelantado del impuesto m; **~ averaging tax** n TAX pago adelantado del impuesto m; **~ borrowing rate** n STOCK currency futures tipo para el dinero que se pide a plazo m; **~ buying** n ECON, GEN COMM compra anticipada f, STOCK compras para el futuro f pl; **~ contract** n STOCK contrato a plazo m; **~ cover** n STOCK cobertura a futuro f; **~ dealing** n STOCK operación a futuros f, operación a término f; **~ delivery** n STOCK entrega futura f; **~ discount** n GEN COMM descuento a término m; **~ exchange** n ECON divisas a plazo f pl; **~ exchange contract** n BANK currency exchange contract contrato de divisas a plazo m; **~ exchange market** n STOCK mercado de futuros m; **~ exchange rate** n ECON, STOCK tipo de cambio a fecha futura m, tasa de cambio a fecha futura f; **~-forward currency deal** n ECON transacción de divisas a plazo f; **~ integration** n GEN COMM integración progresiva f; **~ investment return** n STOCK futures rendimiento de las inversiones a plazo m; **~ linkage** n ECON efecto de propulsión m; **~ margin** n ECON margen futuro m; **~ market** n STOCK mercado de futuros m; **~ operation** n STOCK operación a plazo f; **~ planning** n GEN COMM, FIN, MGMNT planeación a largo plazo f (AmL), planeación anticipada f (AmL), planeación de largo alcance f (AmL), planificación a largo plazo f (Esp), planificación anticipada f (Esp), planificación de largo alcance f (Esp); **~ position** n STOCK posición a plazo f; **~ price** n GEN COMM cambio a plazo m; **~ pricing** n STOCK cotización de precio a término f; **~ purchase contract** n GEN COMM contrato de compra a futuro m; **~ rate** n ECON, FIN, GEN COMM cambio a plazo m, STOCK cotización a plazo f, tipo de cambio a plazo m, currency futures precio para operaciones a término m; **~ rate agreement** n (FRA) STOCK acuerdo de interés a término m; **~ rate spread** n STOCK margen de tipo a futuros m; **~ sales contract** n GEN COMM contrato de venta para entrega en el futuro m; **~ security** n STOCK valor a plazo m; **~ spread agreement** n (FSA) STOCK acuerdo del diferencial futuro m; **~ stock** n AmE S&M género trasladado m; **~ swop** n BANK, FIN, STOCK crédito recíproco futuro m, swop futuro m; **~ transaction** n STOCK operación a vencimiento f; **~ vertical integration** n GEN COMM integración vertical progresista f

forward[4] vt (fwd) COMMS package, document remitir, enviar

forward average vi TAX adelantar el impuesto efectivo, adelantar el pago del impuesto

forwarder n (fwdr) COMMS, IMP/EXP embarcador(a) m,f, expedidor(a) m,f; **~ air waybill** (FAWB) IMP/EXP, TRANSP conocimiento de embarque aéreo del expedidor m, hoja de ruta aérea f; **~'s bill of lading** IMP/EXP, TRANSP carta de embarque del remitente f, conocimiento de embarque del expedidor m; **~'s certificate of**

receipt (*FCR*) IMP/EXP, TRANSP certificado de recibo de expedición *m*, certificado de recibo del expedidor *m*

forwarding *n* STOCK expedición *f*; ~ **address** COMMS dirección de reenvío *f*; ~ **agency** TRANSP casa de expedición *f*; ~ **agent** S&M, TRANSP transitario(-a) *m,f*; ~ **agent's bill of lading** IMP/EXP, TRANSP conocimiento de embarque del agente expedidor *m*; ~ **agent's commission** (*fac*) TRANSP comisión de agente expedidor *f*; ~ **agent's receipt** IMP/EXP, TRANSP recibo del agente expedidor *m*, resguardo del agente expedidor *m*; ~ **clerk** HRM expedidor(a) *m,f*; ~ **company** IMP/EXP, TRANSP empresa expedidora *f*; ~ **department** TRANSP departamento de envíos *m*; ~ **in bulk** TRANSP transporte a granel *m*; ~ **instruction** COMMS instrucción de envío *f*; ~ **station** TRANSP *rail* estación de envío *f*

f.o.s. *abbr* (*free on ship*) IMP/EXP, TRANSP franco en buque

fossil: ~ **fuel** *n* ENVIR combustible fósil *m*

foster *vt* GEN COMM *environment, relationship* mantener

f.o.t. *abbr* (*free on truck*) IMP/EXP, TRANSP *rail* franco camión

foul: ~ **bill of lading** *n* IMP/EXP, TRANSP conocimiento de embarque con reservas *m*, conocimiento de embarque sucio *m*

foundation *n* ECON, GEN COMM, POL entidad privada sin fines de lucro *f*, fundación *f*; ~ **fund** ACC, FIN, STOCK fondo fundacional *m*

foundations *n pl* PROP cimiento frontal *m*

founder: ~ **member** *n* GEN COMM miembro fundador(-a) *m,f*

founders': ~ **shares** *n pl* STOCK acciones de los promotores *f pl*

founding: ~ **company** *n* GEN COMM compañía fundadora *f*

fountain: ~ **pen** *n* GEN COMM pluma estilográfica *f*, pluma fuente *f*

four: ~-**cabin** *n* TRANSP camarote para cuatro *m*; ~-**color set** *AmE*, ~-**colour set** *BrE* *n* MEDIA tirada en cuatricromía *f*; ~ **freedoms** *n pl* ECON cuatro libertades *f pl*; ~ **sheet** *n* S&M anuncio de 1 x 1,5 metros; ~-**star gasoline** *n* *AmE* (*cf four-star petrol BrE*) ENVIR gasolina súper *f* (*Esp*), nafta súper (*AmL*), ~-**star petrol** *n* *BrE* (*cf four-star gasoline AmE*) ENVIR gasolina súper *f* (*Esp*), nafta súper *f* (*AmL*); ~-**track band** *n* TRANSP tramo de cuatro carriles *m*; ~-**way entry pallet** *n* TRANSP plataforma de carga de cuatro entradas *f*; ~-**way pallet** *n* TRANSP plataforma de carga de cuatro entradas *f*

fourth: ~ **cover** *n* S&M *advertising* contraportada *f*; ~-**generation computer** *n* COMP computador de cuarta generación *m* (*AmL*), computadora de cuarta generación *f* (*AmL*), ordenador de cuarta generación *m* (*Esp*); ~ **market** *n* STOCK cuarto mercado *m*; ~ **quarter** *n* GEN COMM cuarto trimestre *m*

Fourth: ~ **Company Law Directive** LAW Cuarta Directiva de la Ley de Sociedades Anónimas *f*; ~ **Directive of the European Union** *n* ACC Cuarta Directiva de la Unión Europea *f*; ~ **European Directive** *n* ACC Cuarta Directiva Europea *f*; ~ **World** *n* ECON, POL cuarto mundo *m*

f.p. *abbr* (*fully paid*) GEN COMM totalmente pagado

FP *abbr* (*floating marine policy*) INS, TRANSP póliza marina flotante *f*, póliza marítima flotante *f*

f.p.a. *abbr* (*free of particular average*) INS libre de avería simple, libre de avería particular

FPC *abbr* (*Federal Power Commission*) IND comisión federal de energía

FPM *abbr* (*flexible-payment mortgage*) BANK, FIN hipoteca de pagos variables *f*, hipoteca de pagos flexibles *f*

FPS *abbr* (*floating production system*) TRANSP sistema de botadura *m*, sistema de producción a bordo *m*

FPZ *abbr* (*free port zone*) TRANSP zona de puerto franco *f*, zona franca portuaria *f*

F/R *abbr* (*freight release*) IMP/EXP, TRANSP autorización de descarga *f*, liberación por pago de flete *f*

FRA *abbr* (*forward rate agreement*) STOCK acuerdo de interés a término *m*

fraction *n* MATH fracción *f*

fractional: ~ **cash reserve** *n* BANK coeficiente obligatorio de caja *m*; ~ **discretion order** *n* STOCK orden discrecional fraccionaria *f*; ~ **lot** *n* GEN COMM lote fraccionario *m*; ~ **reserve** *n* BANK reserva parcial *f*; ~ **reserve banking** *n* BANK banco de reserva múltiple *m*; ~ **share** *n* FIN, STOCK acción fraccionaria *f*

fractionalize *vt* MATH fraccionar

fragile *adj* TRANSP frágil

fragmentation *n* COMP *disk*, ECON *of the market* fragmentación *f*

fragmented: ~ **bargaining** *n* HRM negociación fragmentada *f*; ~ **market** *n* ECON mercado fragmentado *m*

frame *n* COMP encuadre *m*; ~ **of mind** GEN COMM estado de ánimo *m*

framework *n* GEN COMM armazón *m*, marco *m*; ~ **agreement** LAW acuerdo marco *m*; ◆ **in the** ~ **of** GEN COMM en el marco de

franchise *n* LAW franquicia *f*, POL sufragio *m*, derecho al voto *m*, S&M franquicia *f*, tienda de una cadena *f*; ~ **agreement** LAW acuerdo de franquicia *m*; ~ **clause** BANK, INS, LAW cláusula de franquicia *f*; ~ **financing** FIN financiación de franquicia *f*; ~ **gap** ECON zona de franquicia *f*; ~ **tax** *AmE* TAX impuesto de franquicia *m*

franchised: ~ **dealer** *n* *BrE* LAW agente autorizado(-a) *m,f*, distribuidor(a) oficial *m,f*

franchisee *n* LAW, S&M franquiciado(-a) *m,f*

franchising *n* LAW, S&M franquicia *f*

franchisor *n* LAW, S&M franquiciador(a) *m,f*

franco *adj* (*fco.*) IMP/EXP, TRANSP franco; ◆ ~ **quay** IMP/EXP, TRANSP franco muelle

fr&cc *abbr* (*free of riots and civil commotions*) INS libre de disturbios y altercados civiles, libre de tumultos y desórdenes

frank[1]: ~ **discussions** *n pl* POL discusiones francas *f pl*

frank[2] *vt* ADMIN, COMMS *letter, parcel* franquear

franked: ~ **letter** *n* ADMIN, COMMS carta franqueada *f*

franking: ~ **machine** *n* ADMIN, COMMS máquina franqueadora *f*

fraud *n* GEN COMM fraude *m*; ~ **pocket** TAX bolsa de fraude *f*

fraudulence *n* LAW fraudulencia *f*

fraudulent: ~ **bankruptcy** *n* GEN COMM quiebra fraudulenta *f*; ~ **entry** *n* LAW apunte fraudulento *m*; ~ **misrepresentation** *n* INS declaración fraudulenta *f*; ~ **statement** *n* TAX balance fraudulento *m*

fraudulently *adv* LAW fraudulentamente

FRB *abbr* (*Federal Reserve Board*) BANK, ECON Comisión de la Reserva Federal

Freddie: ~ **Mac** *n* *infrml* (*Federal Home Loan Mortgage*

Corporation) BANK, FIN corporación federal de créditos hipotecarios a la vivienda

free[1] *adj* COMP exento, GEN COMM *at no cost* gratuito, *unoccupied* libre, IMP/EXP, TRANSP franco; **~-standing** COMP autónomo; ♦ **~ of address** TRANSP libre de comisión por solicitud; **~ of all additives** GEN COMM sin aditivos; **~ of all average** (*f.a.a.*) GEN COMM libre de toda avería; **~ of all taxation** TAX exento de todo impuesto; **~ alongside** IMP/EXP, TRANSP franco al costado; **~ alongside quay** (*FAQ*) IMP/EXP franco al lado del muelle; **~ alongside vessel** (*f.a.s.*) IMP/EXP, TRANSP franco al costado del buque; **~ of capture and seizure** (*fc&s*) INS libre de actos de la autoridad; **~ of capture, seizure and riots, and civil commotions** (*fcsrcc*) INS libre de actos de la autoridad, motines y conmoción civil; **~ carrier** (*f.c.a.*) TRANSP franco porteador; **~ of charge** (*FOC*) GEN COMM libre de gastos; **~ of claim for reported accident** (*FCAR*) INS *marine* libre de reclamaciones por el accidente informado; **~ and clear** *AmE* LAW, PROP *title to property* no gravado; **~ of damage** (*fod*) GEN COMM libre de daños; **~ discharge** (*fd*) IMP/EXP, TRANSP sin gastos de descarga; **~ dispatch** (*f.d.*) IMP/EXP, TRANSP franco de consignación; **~ format** COMP de formato libre; **~ in** (*fi*) IMP/EXP, TRANSP franco de carga; **~ of income tax** (*f.i.t.*) TAX exento de impuestos sobre la renta; **~ in harbor** *AmE*, **~ in harbour** *BrE* IMP/EXP, TRANSP franco en puerto; **~ in and out** (*f.i.&o.*) IMP/EXP, TRANSP franco de carga y descarga, franco dentro y fuera; **~ in, out and stowed** (*f.i.o.&s.*) IMP/EXP, TRANSP franco de carga, descarga y estibado; **~ in, out, stowed and trimmed** (*f.i.o.s.&t.*) IMP/EXP, TRANSP franco de carga, descarga, estibado y asentado; **~ in, out and trimmed** IMP/EXP *shipping* franco de carga, descarga y asentado; **~ in and stowed** (*fias*) TRANSP libre para el buque la carga y estiba; **~ insurance and carriage** (*f.i.c.*, *FIC*) IMP/EXP, TRANSP franco de seguro y porte; **~ into barge** (*f.i.b.*) IMP/EXP, TRANSP franco en barcaza; **~ into bunkers** (*f.i.b.*) IMP/EXP, TRANSP *shipping* franco en pañoles; **~ on aircraft** (*f.o.a.*) IMP/EXP, TRANSP franco avión; **~ on board** (*f.o.b.*) IMP/EXP, TRANSP franco a bordo; **~ on board airport** IMP/EXP, TRANSP franco a bordo en aeropuerto; **~ on board and trimmed** (*f.o.b.&t.*) IMP/EXP, TRANSP franco a bordo y asentado, franco a bordo y carga equilibrada; **~ on quay** (*f.o.q.*) IMP/EXP, TRANSP franco muelle; **~ on quay to free on quay** (*f.o.q.-f.o.q.*) IMP/EXP, TRANSP franco de muelle a muelle; **~ on rail** (*f.o.r.*) IMP/EXP, TRANSP franco sobre vagón, puesto sobre vagón; **~ on ship** (*f.o.s.*) IMP/EXP, TRANSP franco en buque; **~ overboard** IMP/EXP, TRANSP franco por la borda; **~ of particular average** (*f.p.a.*) INS libre de avería particular, libre de avería simple; **~ of riots and civil commotions** (*fr&cc*) INS libre de disturbios y altercados civiles, libre de tumultos y desórdenes; **~ of term** TRANSP *shipping, chartering term* libre de plazo

free[2]: **~ access and choice** *n* GEN COMM libre acceso y elección *m*; **~ admission** *n* LEIS entrada gratuita *f*, entrada libre *f*; **~ baggage allowance** *n* IMP/EXP, TRANSP franquicia de equipaje *f*, equipaje admisible sin cargo *m*; **~ banking** *n* BANK banca libre *f*; **~ carrier** *n* (*f.c.a.*) IMP/EXP, TRANSP franco porteador *m*; **~ circulation** *n* ECON, POL libre circulación *f*; **~ circulation of goods and services** *n* LAW *EU* libre circulación de bienes y servicios *f*; **~ circulation magazine** *n* MEDIA revista de distribución gratuita *f*; **~ competition** *n*

ECON, S&M libre competencia *f*; **~ delivery** *n* (*fd*) IMP/EXP, TRANSP entrega exenta *f*; **~ depreciation** *n* FIN depreciación libre *f*; **~ dock** *n* (*fd*) IMP/EXP, TRANSP *tax exempt* dique franco *m*, muelle franco *m*, muelle libre *m*; **~ domicile** *n* IMP/EXP *cargo* domicilio franco *m*; **~ economy** *n* ECON libre economía *f*; **~ enterprise** *n* ECON libre empresa *f*; **~ enterprise economy** *n* ECON economía competitiva *f*, economía de mercado *f*, economía sin intervención *f*; **~ enterprise market** *n* ECON, S&M mercado de libre empresa *m*, mercado no intervenido *m*; **~ enterprise system** *n* ECON sistema de libre empresa *m*; **~ foreign agency** *n* (*FFA*) TRANSP agencia extranjera libre *f*; **~ gift** *n* S&M regalo gratuito *m*; **~ good** *n* ECON bien gratuito *m*; **~ house** *n* IMP/EXP, TRANSP *cargo* casa franca *f*; **~ in clause** *n* IMP/EXP, TRANSP *shipping* cláusula de franco dentro *f*; **~ insurance cover** *n* (*FIC*) IMP/EXP seguro y transporte gratuitos; **~ issue** *n* TRANSP entrega gratuita *f*; **~ lodging** *n* TAX alojamiento exento *m*; **~ market** *n* ECON, POL, S&M mercado libre *m*, mercado sin intervención *m*; **~ market system** *n* ECON sistema de libre mercado *m*; **~ market zone** *n* ECON, IMP/EXP, IND zona de libre comercio *f*; **~ medical treatment** *n* WEL tratamiento médico gratuito *m*; **~ movement of goods** *n* LAW *EU* libre circulación de mercancías *f*; **~ movement of labor** *AmE*, **~ movement of labour** *BrE n* LAW *EU* libre circulación de mano de obra *f*; **~ newspaper** *n* GEN COMM, MEDIA periódico independiente *m*; **~ and open market** *n* ECON, S&M mercado libre y abierto *m*; **~ out term** *n* (*fo*) IMP/EXP, TRANSP término secundario libre *m*; **~ play** *n* ACC, BANK, GEN COMM carta blanca *f*; **~ port** *n* IMP/EXP, TRANSP puerto franco *m*; **~ port zone** *n* (*FPZ*) TRANSP zona de puerto franco *f*, zona franca portuaria *f*; **~-rein leadership** *n* HRM liderazgo incontestable *m*; **~ ride** *n infrml* STOCK canon sin gastos *m*; **~ rider** *n infrml* ECON, HRM, WEL beneficiario(-a) gratuito(-a) *m,f*, parásito *mf* (*infrml*); **~ riding** *n* STOCK movimiento libre *m*; **~ right of exchange** *n* STOCK libre derecho de cambio *m*; **~ sale agreement** *n* TRANSP acuerdo de venta libre *m*; **~ sample** *n* GEN COMM, S&M muestra gratuita *f*; **~ sea carrier** *n* IMP/EXP, TRANSP *cargo delivery* buque amarrado disponible *m*; **~ trade** *n* ECON, IMP/EXP, POL libre cambio *m*, libre comercio *m*; **~-trade area** *n* ECON, IMP/EXP, POL área de libre comercio *f*; **~-trade zone** *n* (*FTZ*) ECON, IMP/EXP zona franca, zona de libre comercio *f*; **~ zone** *n* ECON, IMP/EXP, POL zona de libre mercado *f*, zona franca *f*, zona no intervenida *f*

free[3] *vi* ECON liberar; ♦ **~ load** HRM beneficiarse gratuitamente

Free: **~ Banking School** *n BrE* BANK escuela bancaria sin costo; **~ Trade Agreement** *n* (*FTA*) POL *international trade* Acuerdo de Libre Comercio *m*

freeboard *n* (*FBD*) TRANSP *shipping* francobordo *m*

freed[1]: **~ up** *adj* STOCK *securities* liberado

freed[2]: **~ up capital** *n* GEN COMM capital mobiliario *m*

freedom *n* LAW libertad *f*; **~ of action** LAW libertad de acción *f*; **~ of association** GEN COMM, LAW libertad de asociación *f*; **~ of choice** GEN COMM, POL libertad de elección *f*; **~ of competition** ECON, GEN COMM libertad de competencia *f*; **~ of establishment** POL *in EU* libertad de establecimiento *f*; **~ of movement** ECON, POL *of goods, services*, libre circulación *f*; **~ ship** TRANSP barco con libertad de acción *m*

Freedom: ~ **of Information Act** n AmE (FOIA) LAW ley de libertad de información

freehold: ~ **owner** n PROP propietario(-a) absoluto(-a) m,f; ~ **property** n ACC annual accounts propiedad libre de cargas f, PROP propiedad absoluta f

freeholder n PROP propietario(-a) absoluto(-a) m,f

freelance n HRM freelance mf, independiente mf; ~ **contract** HRM contrato de trabajador autónomo m; ~ **correspondent** MEDIA corresponsal independiente mf; ~ **worker** HRM, TAX trabajador(a) por cuenta propia m,f, trabajador(a) autónomo(-a) m,f; ~ **writer** MEDIA journalism escritor(a) independiente m,f, escritor(a) freelance m,f

freely: ~ **negotiable credit** n ECON, FIN international trade crédito negociable sin condiciones m

freeness: ~ **of the market** n S&M extensión del mercado f

Freefone® n BrE COMMS, S&M teléfono gratuito m; ~ **number** BrE COMMS número exento de pago m

Freepost® n COMMS, S&M correo gratuito m

freesheet n GEN COMM periódico independiente m

freeway n AmE (cf motorway BrE) TRANSP autopista f

freeze[1] n ECON wages, prices, FIN credit, TAX congelación f

freeze[2] vt ECON, wages, prices FIN credit, TAX congelar; ◆ ~ **an account** BANK congelar una cuenta

freezing n ECON, wages, prices, FIN credit, TAX congelación f

freight n (frt) GEN COMM, TRANSP carga f, flete m; ~ **aircraft** TRANSP avión de transporte de mercancías m; ~ **all kinds** TRANSP flete a peso m; ~ **collection** COMMS, TRANSP cobro de portes m; ~ **container** TRANSP contenedor de mercancías m; ~ **and demurrage** (F&D) IMP/EXP, TRANSP flete y sobrestadías m; ~, **demurrage and defence** BrE, ~, **demurrage and defense** AmE (FD&D) INS, TRANSP flete, sobrestadía y defensa m; ~, **demurrage and defence cover** BrE, ~, **demurrage and defense cover** AmE (FD&D cover) INS, TRANSP cobertura por flete, sobreestadía y defensa f; ~ **forwarder** IMP/EXP, TRANSP agente de transportes mf; ~ **forwarder's certificate of receipt** (FFCR) IMP/EXP, TRANSP certificado de recibo de expedición de flete m, certificado de recibo del expedidor del flete m; ~ **forwarder's combined transport bill of lading** (FCT) IMP/EXP, TRANSP conocimiento de embarque de transporte combinado del expedidor del flete m, conocimiento de embarque del expedidor para transporte combinado m; ~ **futures contract** FIN contrato de flete a futuro m; ~ **futures market** STOCK mercado de fletes a plazo m; ~ **insurance** INS, TRANSP seguro de flete m; ~, **insurance and shipping charges** n pl (FIS) IMP/EXP, TRANSP cargos por flete, seguro y embarque m pl; ~ **manifest** TRANSP manifiesto de flete m; ~ **market** STOCK mercado de fletes m; ~ **and parcel service** COMMS, TRANSP servicio de carga y paquetes postales m (Esp); ~ **plane** AmE TRANSP avión carguero m, avión de carga m; ~ **policy** INS póliza de flete f; ~ **prepaid** (frt ppd) IMP/EXP, TRANSP carga prepagada f, flete pagado por anticipado m, portes pagados m pl; ~ **release** (F/R) IMP/EXP, TRANSP liberación por pago de flete f, autorización de descarga f; ~ **strategy** TRANSP estrategia de fletes f; ~ **tariff** TRANSP tarifa de fletes f; ~ **terminal** TRANSP terminal de carga f; ~ **ton**, ~ **tonne** (F/T, frt ton) TRANSP flete-tonelada m; ~ **traffic** TRANSP tráfico de fletes m; ~ **train** AmE (cf goods train BrE)

TRANSP tren de carga m, tren de mercancías m; ~ **transport** TRANSP transporte de mercancías m; ◆ ~ **forward** (frt fwd) IMP/EXP, TRANSP portes debidos; ~ **and insurance paid** IMP/EXP, TRANSP flete y seguro pagados, porte y seguro pagados; ~ **paid** IMP/EXP, TRANSP to named place flete pagado

Freight: ~ **Transport Association** n (FTA) TRANSP sociedad de transportistas de carga

freighter n TRANSP aviation carguero m, AmE (cf cargo ship BrE, cargo vessel BrE) shipping buque de carga m (Esp), fletero m (AmL)

frequency n MATH, MEDIA frecuencia f; ~ **curve** MATH curva de frecuencias f; ~ **distribution** MATH statistics distribución de frecuencias f; ~ **modulation** COMMS modulación de frecuencias f; ~ **polygon** MATH polígono de frecuencias m; ~ **table** MATH tabla de frecuencias f

fresh: ~ **food** n GEN COMM alimentos frescos m pl, alimentos sin procesar m pl; ~ **money** n GEN COMM dinero fresco m; ~ **water** n (FW) ENVIR, TRANSP agua dulce f

FRICS abbr (Fellow of the Royal Institute of Chartered Surveyors) HRM, PROP miembro del real instituto de expertos inmobiliarios

friction n GEN COMM between parties rozamiento m; ~ **feed** COMP alimentación por fricción f

frictional: ~ **unemployment** n ECON, HRM, WEL desempleo conjuntural m, desempleo friccional m, paro conyuntural m

Fridays: ~ **and holidays excepted** phr (FHEx) GEN COMM, LEIS, TRANSP salvo viernes y días festivos; ~ **and holidays included** phr GEN COMM, LEIS, TRANSP viernes y vacaciones incluidos

friendly: ~ **agreement** n GEN COMM, LAW acuerdo amistoso m; ~ **society** n BrE (cf benefit society AmE) FIN mutualidad f, sociedad de beneficencia f; ~ **suit** n LAW acción amigable f; ~ **takeover** n ECON, FIN, STOCK toma de control amistosa f

Friends: ~ **of the Earth** n pl ENVIR ≈ Amigos de la Tierra m pl

fringe n GEN COMM franja f; ~ **bank** BANK banco periférico m; ~ **banking crisis** BANK crisis bancaria secundaria f; ~ **benefit** ACC, ECON, FIN, HRM beneficio adicional para los empleados m, beneficio complementario m, beneficio extraordinario m, subsidio para los empleados m; ~ **benefits tax** TAX impuesto sobre beneficios complementarios m; ~ **market** S&M, STOCK mercado marginal m, mercado periférico m; ~ **meeting** POL reunión secundaria f

fringes n pl GEN COMM márgenes m pl

FRN abbr (floating-rate note) STOCK obligación de interés variable f

frof abbr (fire risk on freight) INS, TRANSP riesgo de incendio en la carga m

front[1]: ~-**end** adj COMP central

front[2] n jarg MEDIA frente m; ~ **cover** MEDIA, S&M portada f; ~ **desk** ADMIN mostrador de recepción m; ~-**end computer** COMP computador frontal m (AmL), ordenador frontal m (Esp), computadora frontal f (AmL), procesador frontal m; ~-**end costs** n pl ACC, ECON, FIN costes de puesta en marcha m pl (Esp), costos de puesta en marcha m pl (AmL); ~-**end fee** GEN COMM comisión inicial f; ~-**end finance** FIN financiación de la puesta en marcha f; ~-**end financing** FIN financiación sin garantía f; ~-**end load** STOCK cobro inicial m; ~-**end**

loading FIN concentración del gasto al principio de un periodo *f*; **~-end loan** BANK, FIN préstamo inicial *m*; **~-end money** FIN dinero inicial *m*; **~-end payment** HRM pago inicial *m*; **~ foot** *AmE* PROP cimiento frontal *m*; **~-line employee** HRM empleado(-a) de primera línea *m,f*, trabajador(a) de primera línea *m,f*; **~ money** FIN, GEN COMM capital inicial para lanzar un proyecto empresarial *f*; **~ office** ADMIN alta dirección *f*, alta gerencia *f*, GEN COMM recepción *f*, STOCK piso de remates *m*; **~ office clerk** ADMIN empleado(-a) de la oficina de dirección *m,f*; **~ office personnel** ADMIN personal de alta dirección *m*; **~-page news** MEDIA noticias de primera plana *f pl*; **~-runner** POL cabeza de lista *mf*; **~ running** STOCK inversión anticipada en valores por parte de un corredor o agente para su uso propio

frontage *n* PROP extensión de tierras *f*

frontier *n* GEN COMM, POL frontera *f*; **~ control** ECON, IMP/EXP control fronterizo *m*; **~ customs post** IMP/EXP puesto de aduanas fronterizo *m*; **~ station** TRANSP estación fronteriza *f*; **~ worker** HRM trabajador(a) fronterizo *m,f*

fronting *n* INS *marine* confrontación *f*

frontline *n BrE jarg* POL primera línea *f*

frontman *n* MEDIA *broadcast* presentador(a) *m,f*

frozen[1] *adj* ECON, FIN, TAX *assets, credits* congelado

frozen[2]: **~ account** *n* BANK cuenta bloqueada *f*; **~ asset** *n* FIN activo congelado *m*; **~ capital** *n* ACC, ECON, FIN, GEN COMM capital bloqueado *m*; **~ credit** *n* BANK, FIN crédito congelado *f*; **~ receivables** *n pl* FIN *balance sheet* efectos por cobrar congelados *m pl*

FRS *abbr* (*financial reporting standard*) ACC modelo de estado financiero *f*, norma de informes financieros *f*

frt *abbr* (*freight*) GEN COMM, TRANSP carga *f*, flete *m*

frt fwd *abbr* (*freight forward*) IMP/EXP, TRANSP portes debidos *m pl*

frt ppd *abbr* (*freight prepaid*) IMP/EXP, TRANSP carga prepagada *f*, flete pagado por anticipado *m*, portes pagados *m pl*

frt ton *abbr* (*freight ton, freight tonne*) TRANSP flete-tonelada *m*

fruitless *adj* GEN COMM infructuoso

frustration *n* LAW frustración *f*; **~ of contract** LAW frustración de contrato *f*

FSA *abbr* FIN (*Financial Services Act*) *1986* ley de servicios financieros, STOCK (*forward spread agreement*) acuerdo del diferencial futuro *m*

FSBR *abbr BrE* (*Financial Statement and Budget Report*) FIN informe del estado financiero y presupuestario

FSLIC *abbr* (*Federal Savings and Loan Insurance Corporation*) BANK sociedad federal de seguro de crédito

FSVA *abbr* (*Fellow of the Incorporated Society of Valuers and Auctioneers*) GEN COMM, HRM ≈ Miembro de la Sociedad de Tasadores y Subastadores *mf*

ft *abbr* (*fuel terms*) TRANSP condiciones sobre el combustible *f pl*

FT: **~ Index** *n* (*Financial Times Index*) STOCK Índice del FT *m* (*Índice del Financial Times*); **~-30** *n* (*Financial Times Industrial Ordinary Share Index*) STOCK índice bursátil de valores industriales del Financial Times

F/T *abbr* (*freight ton, freight tonne*) TRANSP flete-tonelada *m*

FTA *abbr* HRM (*failure to agree*) incapacidad de llegar a un acuerdo *f*, POL (*Free Trade Agreement*) *international trade* Acuerdo de Libre Comercio *m*, TRANSP (*Freight Transport Association*) sociedad de transportistas de carga

FTO *abbr* (*full-time official*) HRM funcionario(-a) a tiempo completo *m,f*

FTSE[1] *abbr* (*Financial Times Stock Exchange Index*) STOCK índice bursátil del Financial Times

FTSE[2]: **~ Eurotrack 100 Index** *n* (*Financial Times-Stock Exchange Eurotrack 100 Index*) STOCK índice Footsie Eurotrack 100; **~ Eurotrack 200 Index** *n* (*Financial Times-Stock Exchange Eurotrack 200 Index*) STOCK índice Footsie Eurotrack 200; **~ 100** *n* (*Financial Times-Stock Exchange 100 Share Index*) STOCK índice Footsie *m*, índice bursátil del Financial Times de los valores de las 100 mayores entidades de la Bolsa de Londres

FTZ *abbr* (*free-trade zone*) ECON, IMP/EXP zona de libre comercio *f*, zona franca *f*

fuel[1]: **~ benefits** *n pl* TAX desgravación de los combustibles *f*; **~ duty rebate** *n BrE* TAX *rural transport* bonificación en la tasa de combustible *f*; **~ efficiency** *n* ENVIR eficiencia del combustible *f*, rendimiento del combustible *m*; **~ surcharge** *n* TRANSP *shipping* sobrecarga de gasóleo *f*; **~ tax** *n* TAX impuesto sobre el combustible *m*; **~ terms** *n pl* (*ft*) TRANSP condiciones sobre el combustible *f pl*

fuel[2] *vt* GEN COMM *inflation* alimentar; ◆ **~ an advance** ECON *market* estimular un avance, impulsar una subida; **~ inflation** ECON estimular la inflación

fulcrum *n* GEN COMM fulcro *m*

fulfil *vt BrE* GEN COMM *commitments, obligations* cumplir, realizar; ◆ **~ the requirements** GEN COMM llenar los requisitos

fulfill *AmE see* fulfil *BrE*

fulfillment *AmE see* fulfilment *BrE*

fulfilment *n BrE* HRM, S&M *subscriptions* cumplimentación *f*, cumplimiento *m*

full[1]: **~ screen** *adj* COMP a toda pantalla; **~-time** *adj* HRM *job* a tiempo completo, de plena dedicación, *worker* de jornada completa

full[2]: **in ~** *adv* GEN COMM totalmente

full[3]: **~ adder** *n* COMP *hardware* sumador completo *m*; **~ amount** *n* ACC importe total *m*; **~ basis** *n* ACC *on road vehicle* base total *f*; **~ board** *n* LEIS pensión completa *f*; **~-capacity load** *n* IND carga a toda capacidad *f*; **~ container load** *n* (*FCL*) TRANSP contenedor completo *m*; **~-cost method** *n* ACC, FIN método de coste total *m* (*Esp*), método de costo total *m* (*AmL*), método de full-cost *m*; **~-cost pricing** *n* ACC fijación de precios según los costes *f* (*Esp*), fijación de presios según los costos (*AmL*) ECON, S&M valoración a coste total *f* (*Esp*), valoración a costo total *f* (*AmL*); **~ costing** *n* ACC, BANK valoración a coste total *f* (*Esp*), valoración a costo total *f* (*AmL*); **~ coupon bond** *n* FIN, STOCK bono por el que se paga el interés completo; **~ coverage** *n* GEN COMM *news*, INS, MEDIA *event* cobertura total *f*; **~ disclosure** *n* LAW divulgación completa *f*; **~-duplex** *n* (*FDX*) COMP dúplex integral *m*, dúplex completo *m*; **~ employment** *n* ECON, HRM, POL, WEL pleno empleo *m*; **~-employment budget** *n* ACC, ECON, POL presupuesto de pleno empleo *m*; **~ exemption** *n* TAX exención total *f*; **~ faith and credit** *AmE* STOCK garantía solidaria *f*; **~ fare** *n* GEN COMM billete completo *m*; **~ implications** *n pl* GEN COMM implicaciones plenas *f pl*; **~-information maximum likelihood** *n* (*FIML*) ECON *econometrics* método de estimación de modelos econométricos con ecuaciones simultáneas; **~ lot** *n jarg* ACC lote completo *m*; **~ member** *n* GEN COMM miembro de pleno derecho *mf*; **~ name** *n* GEN COMM, HRM nombre y apellidos *m*; **~-page advertisement** *n* MEDIA, S&M anuncio a toda página *m*, anuncio de página entera *m*, anuncio desplegado de una plana *m*; **~ protection** *n* PATENTS protección total *f*; **~ quotation** *n* STOCK cotización plena *f*; **~ rate** *n* HRM precio íntegro *m*, precio sin descuento *m*; **~-scale investigation** *n* TAX investigación sin restricciones *f*; **~-service agency** *n* MEDIA, S&M *advertising* agencia de publicidad global *f*; **~-service broker** *n* STOCK sociedad de valores y bolsa *f*; **~ share** *n* STOCK acción con valor a la par *f*; **~ taxation year** *n* TAX año de tributación máxima *m*; **~-time attendance** *n* TAX asistencia de jornada completa *f*; **~-time attendant** *n* TAX asistente(-a) de dedicación completa *m,f*; **~-time employment** *n* HRM trabajo de tiempo completo *m*; **~-time job** *n* HRM trabajo de tiempo completo *m*; **~-time lecturer** *n* HRM, WEL profesor(a) a tiempo completo *m,f*; **~-time official** *n* (*FTO*) HRM funcionario(-a) a tiempo completo *m,f*; **~-timer** *n* HRM trabajador(a) a tiempo completo *m,f*; **~-time worker** *n* HRM trabajador(a) a tiempo completo; **~ weight** *n* GEN COMM peso completo *m*

fully[1]: **~ comp** *abbr infrml* (*fully comprehensive cover*) INS cobertura total *f*

fully[2]: **~ distributed** *adj* STOCK distribuido íntegramente; **~ paid** *adj* (*f.p.*) GEN COMM totalmente pagado; **~ valued** *adj* STOCK tasado íntegramente

fully[3]: **~ cellular container ship** *n* (*FCC*) TRANSP buque contenedor compartimentado *m*, portacontenedor celular *m*; **~ comprehensive cover** *n* (*fully comp*) INS cobertura total *f*; **~ comprehensive insurance policy** *n* INS póliza de seguros de cobertura total *f*; **~ diluted earnings per share** *n pl* STOCK ganancias por acción totalmente diluidas *f pl*; **~-paid policy** *n* INS *of life* póliza cubierta *f*; **~-paid share** *n* FIN, STOCK acción cubierta *f*; **~ paid-up capital** *n* ACC, ECON, FIN, GEN COMM capital totalmente desembolsado *m*; **~-performing loan** *n* BANK préstamo totalmente utilizado *m*; **~ quoted company** *n* STOCK empresa de cotización plena *f*; **~ registered bond** *n* FIN, STOCK bono debidamente registrado *m*; **~ registered security** *n* STOCK título totalmente en regla *m*

fumes *n pl* ENVIR, IND humos *m pl*

function *n* COMP, GEN COMM función *f*; **~ key** (*F key*) COMP tecla de función *f*; ◆ **as a ~ of** GEN COMM como una función de

functional[1] *adj* GEN COMM funcional

functional[2]: **~ analysis** *n* GEN COMM análisis funcional *m*; **~ analysis of costs** *n* ACC *annual accounts* análisis funcional de costes *m* (*Esp*), análisis funcional de costos *m* (*AmL*); **~ approach** *n* GEN COMM enfoque funcional *m*; **~ authority** *n* HRM autoridad funcional *f*; **~ costing** *n* ACC cálculo de costes funcionales *m* (*Esp*), cálculo de costos funcionales *m* (*AmL*); **~ currency** *n* ECON moneda funcional *f*; **~ financing** *n* FIN financiación funcional *f*; **~ flexibility** *n* HRM flexibilidad funcional *f*; **~ income distribution** *n* ECON distribución funcional del ingreso *f*; **~ layout** *n* GEN COMM disposición según la función *f*; **~ management** *n* MGMNT dirección de funciones *f*, gerencia de funciones *f*, gestión funcional *f*; **~ obsolescence** *n* S&M caída en desuso funcional *f*;

~ organization *n* GEN COMM, MGMNT organización funcional *f*; **~ relation** *n* GEN COMM, MGMNT relación funcional *f*; **~ responsibility** *n* GEN COMM, MGMNT responsabilidad de funciones *f*, responsabilidad funcional *f*

functioning *n* GEN COMM funcionamiento *m*

fund[1] *n* STOCK fondo *m*; **~ accounting** ACC contabilidad de fondos *f*; **~ appropriation** ACC *governmental*, POL asignación de fondos *f*; **~ management** BANK *investment banking* administración de fondos *f*, gestión de fondos *f*; **~ manager** BANK *investment banking* gestor(a) de fondos *m,f*

fund[2] *vt* BANK, FIN *loan* provisionar

fundamental[1] *adj* GEN COMM fundamental

fundamental[2]: **~ analysis** *n* FIN *financial statements, investments*, STOCK análisis fundamental *m*; **~ disequilibrium** *n* ECON desequilibrio estructural *m*, desequilibrio fundamental *m*; **~ equilibrium** *n* ECON equilibrio general *m*

funded: **~ debt** *n* ACC, BANK deuda consolidada *f*, pasivo consolidado *m*; **~ pension plan** *n* BrE (*cf funded retirement plan AmE*) HRM fondos de pensiones *m pl*; **~ property** *n* PROP propiedad consolidada *f*; **~ retirement plan** *n* (*cf funded pension plan BrE*) AmE HRM fondos de pensiones *m pl*

funding *n* GEN COMM financiación *f*, financiamiento *m*, consolidación de la deuda *f*, provisión de fondos *f*; **~ agency** FIN organismo de financiación *m*; **~ bond** FIN, STOCK bono de consolidación *m*; **~ gap** ACC, FIN déficit de fondos *m*; **~ group** FIN grupo de fondos *m*; **~ source** ACC, FIN fuente de financiación *f*

fundraising *n* FIN, WEL recaudación de fondos *f*

funds *n pl* GEN COMM fondos *m pl*; **~ abroad** BANK fondos en el extranjero *m pl*; **~ flow** *n* ACC, ECON, FIN, STOCK flujo de fondos *m*, corriente de fondos *f*; **~ from operations** ACC fondos resultantes de las operaciones *m pl*, recursos de las operaciones *m pl*; **~ statement** *n* ACC estado de flujos *m*, estado de fondos *m*; **~ transfer** *n* ACC, BANK, FIN transferencia de fondos *f*; ◆ **no ~** (*N/F*) GEN COMM sin fondos; **lack the necessary ~** FIN faltar los fondos necesarios

funeral: **~ expenses** *n pl* INS gastos de inhumación *m pl*

fungibility *n* LAW fungibilidad *f*

fungible[1] *adj* LAW fungible

fungible[2]: **~ asset** *n* FIN activo fungible *m*

fungibles *n pl* LAW bienes fungibles *m pl*

funnel *vt* GEN COMM canalizar

furlough *n* HRM *Armed Forces* licencia *f*, permiso *m*; ◆ **on ~** HRM con permiso, de vacaciones

furniture: **~ depot** *n* GEN COMM depósito de muebles *m*; **~ and fittings** *n pl* TAX enseres *m pl*, mobiliario e instalación *m*; **~ warehouse** *n* GEN COMM guardamuebles *m*

further[1]: **~ education** *n* BrE WEL educación post-escolar que no comprende la universidad

further[2]: **for ~ instructions** *phr* (*FFI*) GEN COMM para instrucciones adicionales *f pl*; **~ to your letter** *phr* COMMS en respuesta a su carta; **~ to your telephone call** *phr* COMMS en respuesta a su llamada telefónica

fuse *vt* ECON, FIN, STOCK fusionar

fusion *n* GEN COMM fusión *f*

futile: **~ project** *n* HRM proyecto innecesario *m*

future[1] *adj* GEN COMM *contract* futuro; ◆ **in ~** GEN COMM en lo sucesivo, en el futuro

future[2] *n* STOCK futuro *m*; **~ gains** *n pl* TAX ganancias futuras *f pl*; **~ goods** *n pl* GEN COMM mercaderías futuras *f pl*; **~ interest** GEN COMM *in property, trust* interés futuro *m*; **~ order** GEN COMM, S&M pedido futuro *m*; **~ rate agreement** FIN, STOCK contrato sobre tipos futuros *m*; **~ sale** GEN COMM, S&M venta futura *f*; **~ tax credits** *n pl* ACC, TAX créditos fiscales futuros *m pl*; **~ trading** STOCK mercado de futuros *m*; **~ trading market** STOCK mercado a plazo *m*; **~ trend** GEN COMM tendencia futura *f*

futures *n pl* STOCK futuros *m pl*, operación a término *f*; **~ contract** *n* STOCK contrato de futuros *m*; **~ exchange council** *n* STOCK consejo de la bolsa de futuros *m*; **~ expiry date** *n* STOCK fecha de vencimiento de futuros *f*; **~ liquidation rate** *n* STOCK tasa de liquidación de futuros *f*; **~ market** *n* STOCK mercado de futuros *m*; **~ option contract** *n* STOCK contrato de opción sobre futuros *m*; **~ position** *n* STOCK posición de futuros *f*; **~ price** *n* STOCK precio de futuros *m*; **~ price change** *n* STOCK modificación en el precio de futuros *f*; **~-registered broker** *n* STOCK corredor(a) autorizado(-a) de futuros *m,f*; **~ trading** *n* STOCK compraventa de futuros *f*; **~ transaction** *n* STOCK transacción sobre futuros *f*; ◆ **long in ~** STOCK largo en futuros; **short in ~** STOCK corto en futuros

fuzzy: **~ loan** *n* BANK préstamo polivalente *m*

FW *abbr* (*fresh water*) ENVIR, TRANSP agua dulce *f*

fwd *abbr* (*forward*) COMMS, IMP/EXP *package document* remitir, enviar

fwdr *abbr* (*forwarder*) COMMS, IMP/EXP embarcador(a) *m,f*, expedidor(a) *m,f*

FY *abbr* FIN (*financial year*) ejercicio económico *m*, año financiero *m*, ejercicio financiero *m*, TAX (*fiscal year*) año fiscal *m*, ejercicio fiscal *m*

FYI *abbr* (*for your information*) GEN COMM para su información

G

g *abbr* (*gram, gramme*) GEN COMM gr. (*gramo*)

G *abbr* (*gross mass*) GEN COMM masa bruta *f*

GA *abbr* GEN COMM (*general assembly*) asamblea general *f*, TRANSP (*general arrangement plan*) plan general de estiba *m*

G/A *abbr* (*general average*) INS avería común *f*, avería gruesa *f*, MATH promedio general *m*

G/A con *abbr* (*general average contribution*) INS contribución a la avería gruesa *f*

G/A dep *abbr* (*general average deposit*) GEN COMM depósito de avería gruesa *m*

GAAP *abbr* (*Generally Accepted Accounting Principles*) ACC PCGA (*Principios de Contabilidad Generalmente Aceptados*)

GAAS *abbr* (*Generally Accepted Auditing Standards*) ACC normativas de auditoría generalmente aceptadas

GAB *abbr* (*general agreement to borrow*) ECON, FIN acuerdo general de préstamos *m*, acuerdo general sobre créditos *m*

gadget *n* GEN COMM artilugio *m*

GAFTA[1] *abbr* (*Grain and Free Trade Association*) IMP/EXP asociación que controla las transacciones comerciales de grano y patatas en el Mercado de Contratación del Báltico

GAFTA[2]: **~ Clearing House** *n* (*GCH*) FIN cámara de compensación de GAFTA

gag: **~ order** *n AmE jarg* (*cf gagging order BrE*) LAW orden judicial de control de la información periodística; **~ rule** *n AmE* POL disposiciones aprobadas por el parlamento para limitar sus debates

gage *AmE see* gauge *BrE*

gagging: **~ order** *n BrE jarg* (*cf gag order AmE*) LAW orden judicial de control de la información periodística

gain[1] *n* GEN COMM beneficio *m*, ganancia *f*, MGMNT beneficio *m*, STOCK *on position values*, TAX ganancia *f*; **~ contingency** ACC, FIN contingencia de beneficio *f*, contingencia de ganancia *f*

gain[2] **1.** *vt* STOCK *increase value* aumentar; ◆ **~ entry to** FIN conseguir acceso a; **~ formal approval from** GEN COMM obtener la aprobación formal de; **~ ground** GEN COMM ganar terreno; **~ momentum** ECON empezar a avanzar, GEN COMM *trend* cobrar impulso, empezar a avanzar; **~ value** STOCK aumentar de valor; **2.** *vi* STOCK ganar

gains: **~ from trade** *n pl* ECON ganancias comerciales *f pl*; **~ on disposal** *n pl BrE* TAX ganancias por traspaso *f pl*

gal *abbr* (*gallon*) GEN COMM galón *m*

galley *n* MEDIA *print* galera *f*

gallon *n* (*gal*) GEN COMM galón *m*

galloping: **~ inflation** *n* ECON inflación galopante *f*

Gallup: **~ poll** *n* S&M *research* sondeo de Gallup *m*

gamble: **~ on the stock exchange** *phr* STOCK jugar en bolsa

gambling: **~ debts** *n pl* GEN COMM deudas de juego *f pl*

game *n* GEN COMM juego *m*; **~ plan** GEN COMM plan del juego *m*; **~ theory** ECON, HRM, MGMNT teoría de juegos *f*

gamesmanship *n* GEN COMM astucia *f*

gaming *n* GEN COMM juego *m*

gamma *n* STOCK gamma *f*; **~ share** FIN, STOCK acción gamma *f*; **~ stock** *BrE* STOCK acciones gamma *f pl*

gang: **~ piecework** *n* HRM trabajo a destajo por equipos *m*

gangway: **below the ~** *phr BrE* POL en el pasillo

gantry *n* TRANSP *cargo handling* grúa de pórtico *f*; **~ crane** TRANSP *cargo handling* grúa de pórtico *f*

Gantt: **~ chart** *n* COMP diagrama de Gantt *m*

GAO *abbr AmE* (*General Accounting Office*) ACC ≈ Oficina General de Contabilidad *f* (*AmL*), ≈ Tribunal de Cuentas *m* (*Esp*)

gap *n* ECON bache *m*, gap *m*, GEN COMM déficit *m*, diferencia *f*, S&M *in the market* gap, STOCK diferencial *m*, gap *m*; **~ analysis** BANK análisis del desfase *m*; **~ filler** TAX ajustador(a) de déficit *m,f*; **~ financing** ECON, FIN financiación del déficit *f*; **~ in coverage** MEDIA déficit de cobertura *m*; **~ loan** FIN crédito intermedio *m*; **~ sheet** *jarg* HRM ficha personal de trabajo *f*; **~ study** GEN COMM, S&M estudio del déficit *m*

garage *n* STOCK nombre dado al piso añadido al norte del "parquet" de la Bolsa de Nueva York

garbage *n* COMP basura *f*; **~-in/garbage-out** (*GIGO*) COMP entrada descontrolada/salida descontrolada *f* (*GIGO*)

garden: **~ apartment** *n AmE* (*cf garden flat BrE*) PROP piso con jardín en planta baja *m*; **~ flat** *n BrE* (*cf garden apartment AmE*) PROP piso con jardín en planta baja *m*

Garn: **~ St Germain Depository Institutions Act** *n AmE* BANK ley de instituciones de depósito Garn St Germain

garnish *vt* LAW embargar

garnishee *n* LAW depositario(-a) de bienes embargados *m,f*, depositario(-a) de bienes sujetos a embargo *m,f*

garnishment *n* LAW embargo *m*, interdicto *m*, sentencia de embargo *f*

gas *n* GEN COMM gas *m*; **~ company** ENVIR compañía del gas *f*; **~ exploitation** IND explotación de gas *f*; **~ exploration licence** *BrE*, **~ exploration license** *AmE* ENVIR, IND licencia de exploración de gas *f*, licencia de prospección de gas *f*; **~ industry** ECON, IND industria del gas *f*; **~ oil** ENVIR gasóleo *m*; **~ station** *AmE* (*cf petrol station BrE*) GEN COMM, TRANSP estación de servicic *f*, gasolinera *f*, surtidor de gasolina *m*; **~ turbine ship** (*GT*) TRANSP buque de turbina de gas *m*; **~ turbo electric ship** (*GT-E*) TRANSP buque de propulsión eléctrica por turbina de gas *m*; **~ works** *n pl* ENVIR, IND fábrica de gas *f* (*Esp*), factoría de gas industrial *f* (*AmL*)

GASB *abbr AmE* (*Governmental Accounting Standards Board*) ACC ≈ Consejo Oficial de Normas Contables *m*, ≈ Junta Gubernamental de Normas Contables *f*

gasoline *n AmE* (*cf petrol BrE*) TRANSP gasolina *f* (*Esp*), nafta *f* (*AmL*); **~ expenses** *n pl AmE* TAX gastos de combustible *m pl*

gate *n* LEIS *takings* entrada *f*, puerta *f*, TRANSP *aviation* puerta *f*; **~ number** TRANSP *aviation* número de puerta *m*

gatefold *n* MEDIA desplegable *m*

gateway *n* COMMS *wide-area networks*, TRANSP *aviation* puerta *f*

gather *vt* GEN COMM *information* reunir, STOCK acumular; ◆ ~ **in the stops** STOCK acumular en las pausas

gathered *adj* STOCK acumulado

gathering *n* GEN COMM recolección *f*

GATT *abbr* (*General Agreement on Tariffs and Trade*) ECON, POL Acuerdo GATT *m* (*Acuerdo General sobre Aranceles y Comercio*)

gauge[1] *n BrE* GEN COMM *of trends* indicador *m*; ◆ **out of ~** *BrE* (*OOG*) TRANSP fuera de gálibo

gauge[2] *vt BrE* GEN COMM estimar

Gaussian: ~ **curve** *n* MATH curva de Gauss *f*

gavel *n* GEN COMM *auctioneer* martillo *m*

GAW *abbr* (*guaranteed annual wage*) HRM salario anual garantizado *m*

gazump *vt BrE jarg* LAW, PROP anular un compromiso de venta para vender a un mejor postor

gazumping *n BrE jarg* LAW, PROP retirada del contrato *f*, ruptura de las negociaciones contractuales

Gb *abbr* (*gigabyte*) COMP gigaocteto *m*

GBL *abbr* (*government bill of lading*) IMP/EXP, TRANSP conocimiento de embarque gubernamental *m*

GC *abbr* TRANSP (*general cargo*) mercancía general *f*, (*gyrocompass*) girocompás *m*, (*grain cubic*) cubicación de grano *f*

GCA *abbr* (*gold clause agreement*) TRANSP acuerdo con cláusula de pago en oro *m*

GCBS *abbr BrE* (*General Council of British Shipping*) TRANSP consejo general de empresas navieras británicas

GCE *abbr obs* (*General Certificate of Education*) GEN COMM ≈ Certificado de Educación Secundaria *m*, ≈ Graduado Escolar *m* (*obs*), ≈ Título de Bachiller *m*

GCH *abbr* (*GAFTA Clearing House*) FIN cámara de compensación de GAFTA

GCM *abbr* (*general clearing member*) STOCK cámara de compensación *f*, miembro compensador general *m*

GCR *abbr* (*general commodity rate*) STOCK tarifa general de productos *f*

GCSE *abbr* (*General Certificate of Secondary Education*) GEN COMM ≈ Certificado de Educación Secundaria *m*, ≈ Graduado Escolar *m* (*obs*), ≈ Título de Bachiller *m*

GCW *abbr* (*gross combination weight*) TRANSP peso bruto de combinado *m*

GDP[1] *abbr* (*gross domestic product*) ECON PIB (*producto interior bruto, producto interno bruto*)

GDP[2]: ~ **per capita** *n* ECON PIB per capita *m*; ~ **per head** *n* ECON PIB per capita *m*

gds *abbr* (*goods*) GEN COMM bienes *m pl*, mercancías *f pl*

GE *abbr* (*general equilibrium*) ECON equilibrio general *m*

gear[1]: ~ **manufacturer** *n* TRANSP constructor de equipos *m*

gear[2]: ~ **towards** *phr* MGMNT orientar hacia

gearing *n BrE* (*cf leverage AmE*) ACC, FIN, STOCK apalancamiento *m*, ratio endeudamiento-capital propio *m*, relación endeudamiento-capital propio *f*, proporción endeudamiento-capital propio *f*; ~ **adjustment** *BrE* (*cf leverage adjustment AmE*) FIN ajuste de apalancamiento *m*; ~ **lease** *BrE* (*cf leverage lease AmE*) FIN arrendamiento ventajoso *m*; ~ **ratio** *BrE* (*cf leverage ratio AmE*)

FIN proporción de apalancamiento *f*, relación de apalancamiento *f*

gears *n pl* (*GRS*) TRANSP engranaje *m*

GEM *abbr* (*growing-equity mortgage*) BANK, FIN hipoteca de amortización rápida *f*

GEMM *abbr* (*gilt-edged market makers*) STOCK creadores de mercado de valores de primerísima clase *m pl*

gender: ~ **discrimination** *n* HRM, LAW, WEL discriminación sexual *f*

general[1]: ~ **purpose** *adj* (*GP*) GEN COMM universal, de aplicación general

general[2]: ~ **acceptance** *n* BANK, GEN COMM *document* aceptación general *f*; ~ **accounting officer** *n* (*GAO*) ACC funcionario(-a) general contable *m,f*; ~ **administrative expenses** *n pl* HRM gastos generales de administración *m pl*; ~ **agent** *n* LAW agente general *mf*; ~ **agreement to borrow** *n* (*GAB*) ECON, FIN acuerdo general sobre créditos *m*, acuerdo general de préstamos *m*; ~ **anti-avoidance provision** *n* TAX disposición general contra la evasión legal *f*, norma general contra la evasión fiscal *f*; ~ **anti-avoidance rule** *n* TAX disposición general contra la evasión legal *f*; ~ **arrangement plan** *n* (*GA*) TRANSP plan general de estiba *m*; ~ **assembly** *n* (*GA*) GEN COMM asamblea general *f*; ~ **authorization** *n* GEN COMM autorización general *f*; ~ **average** *n* INS (*G/A*) avería común *f*, avería gruesa *f*, MATH (*G/A*) promedio general *m*; ~ **average act** *n* INS *marine* acto de avería gruesa *m*; ~ **average certificate** *n* (*GAC*) INS certificado de avería gruesa *m*; ~ **average contribution** *n* (*G/A con*) INS contribución a la avería gruesa *f*; ~ **average deposit** *n* (*G/A dep*) INS depósito de avería gruesa *m*; ~ **average guarantee** *n* INS *marine* garantía de avería gruesa *f*; ~ **average in full** *n* INS *assurance merchandises* promedio general total *m*; ~ **averaging** *n* TAX *of income* promedio general *m*; ~ **cargo** *n* (*GC*) TRANSP mercancía general *f*; ~ **cargo berth** *n* TRANSP amarradero de carga general *m*; ~ **cargo and container berth** *n* TRANSP *shipping* terminal de carga general y contenedor *f*; ~ **cargo rate** *n* TRANSP tarifa general de carga *f*; ~ **cargo ship** *n* TRANSP buque de carga general *m*, buque de mercancía general *m*; ~ **clearing member** *n* (*GCM*) STOCK cámara de compensación *f*, miembro compensador general *m*; ~ **commodity rate** *n* (*GCR*) STOCK tarifa general de productos *f*; ~ **contractor** *n* GEN COMM contratista principal *mf*; ~ **counsel** *n AmE* (*cf head of legal department BrE*) HRM, LAW director(a) jurídico(-a) *m,f*; ~ **creditor** *n* ACC acreedor(a) ordinario(-a) *m,f*; ~ **equilibrium** *n* (*GE*) ECON equilibrio general *m*, equilibrio walrasiano *m*; ~ **equilibrium analysis** *n* ECON *theoretical model* análisis de equilibrio general *m*; ~ **exclusions clause** *n* INS *marine* cláusula de exclusiones generales *f*; ~ **executive manager** *n* HRM, MGMNT director(a) general ejecutivo(-a) *m,f*, gerente general ejecutivo(-a) *m,f*; ~ **expenses** *n pl* ACC, GEN COMM gastos generales *m pl*; ~ **foreign average** *n* GEN COMM promedio general exterior *m*; ~ **fund** *n* FIN fondo de libre disposición *m*; ~ **government expenditure** *n* (*GGE*) ECON, POL gasto general del Estado *m*; ~ **government service** *n* ECON *balance of trade* servicio general del Estado *m*; ~ **holdover relief** *n* TAX deducción general por horas extraordinarias *f*; ~ **holiday** *n* HRM asueto general *m*, festivo general *m*; ~ **income tax** *n* TAX impuesto general sobre la renta *m*; ~ **journal** *n* ACC diario general *m*; ~ **ledger** *n* ACC libro mayor general *m*, libro mayor principal *m*; **~ liability insurance** *n* INS seguro de responsabilidad civil *m*; **~ lien** *n* PROP derecho general de retención *m*, privilegio general *m*; **~ loan and collateral agreement** *n* STOCK préstamo general y acuerdo de garantía *m*; **~ management** *n* HRM, MGMNT administración general *f*, gestión general *f*, alta gerencia *f*, dirección general *f*, gerencia general *f*; **~ manager** *n* (*GM*) HRM, MGMNT director(a) general *m,f* (*DG*); **~ meeting of members** *n* ACC, FIN, GEN COMM, MGMNT asamblea de socios *f*; **~ meeting of shareholders** *n* STOCK junta general de accionistas *f*; **~ merchandise** *n* TRANSP carga general *f*; **~ mortgage** *n* BANK, PROP hipoteca general *f*; **~ mortgage bond** *n* FIN, STOCK bono hipotecario *m*, obligación con garantía hipotecaria *f*; **~ obligation bond** *n* AmE (*G-O bond*) STOCK bono de responsabilidad general *m*; **~ partner** *n* HRM, STOCK socio(-a) colectivo(-a) *m,f*; **~ price level** *n* GEN COMM nivel general de precios *m*; **~ price level accounting** *n* (*GPLA*) ACC contabilidad del nivel general de precios *f*; **~ property tax** *n* TAX impuesto sobre el patrimonio *m*; **~ provision** *n* GEN COMM *for debts* provisión general *f*; **~ purpose berth** *n* TRANSP amarradero de propósito general *m*; **~ purpose freight container** *n* TRANSP contenedor de uso general *m*; **~ reserve** *n* ECON reserva visible *f*; **~ revenue** *n* TAX impuesto general sobre la renta *m*; **~ revenue sharing** *n* TAX participación en los ingresos tributarios federales *f*; **~ sales tax** *n* TAX impuesto general sobre las ventas *m*; **~ secretary** *n* HRM secretario(-a) general *m,f*; **~ service contract** *n* BrE TRANSP *shipping* contrato de servicio general *m*; **~ service partner** *n* ACC *accountancy firm* socio(-a) de servicios generales *m,f*; **~ statement** *n* GEN COMM *accounts* estado general *m*; **~ strike** *n* HRM, IND huelga general *f*; **~ trader** *n* TRANSP *shipping* comerciante de mercancía general *mf*; **~ training** *n* HRM capacitación general *f* (*AmL*), formación general *f* (*Esp*); **~ transire** *n* IMP/EXP permiso aduanero general *m*; **~ union** *n* HRM sindicato general *m*; **~ warranty deed** *n* AmE PROP escritura de garantía total *f*

General: **~ Accounting Office** *n* AmE (*GAO*) ACC ≈ Oficina General de Contabilidad *f* (*AmL*), ≈ Tribunal de Cuentas *m* (*Esp*); **~ Agreement on Tariffs and Trade** *n* (*GATT*) ECON, POL Acuerdo General sobre Aranceles y Comercio *m* (*Acuerdo GATT*); **~ Certificate of Education** *n* BrE obs (*GCE*) GEN COMM ≈ Certificado de Educación Secundaria *m*, ≈ Graduado Escolar *m* (*obs*), ≈ Título de Bachiller *m*; **~ Certificate of Secondary Education** *n* BrE (*GCSE*) GEN COMM ≈ Certificado de Educación Secundaria *m*, ≈ Graduado Escolar *m* (*obs*), ≈ Título de Bachiller *m*; **~ Commissioners** *n pl* BrE TAX interventores generales *m pl*; **~ Conference on Weights and Measures** *n* GEN COMM Conferencia General de Pesos y Medidas *f* (*CGPM*); **~ Council of British Shipping** *n* (*GCBS*) TRANSP consejo general de empresas navieras británicas; **~ Council of the Judicial Power** *n* POL ≈ Consejo General del Poder Judicial *m*; **~ Household Survey** *n* (*GHS*) ECON *econometrics* encuesta general del núcleo familiar; **~ Secretary** *n* HRM *of a union* Secretario(-a) General *m,f*

generalist *n* HRM generalista *mf*

generalized: **~ least squares** *n pl* ECON *econometrics* mínimos cuadrados generalizados *m pl*; **~ medium** *n* ECON medio generalizado *m*; **~ system of preferences** *n* (*GSP*) ECON, IMP/EXP sistema general de preferencias *m*; **~ system of tariffs and preferences** *n* (*GSTP*) IMP/EXP sistema generalizado de tarifas y preferencias *m*

generally: **~ quoted market interest rate** *n* ECON, FIN tipo de interés del mercado según cotización general *m*

Generally: **~ Accepted Accounting Principles** *n pl* (*GAAP*) ACC Principios de Contabilidad Generalmente Aceptados *m pl* (*PCGA*); **~ Accepted Auditing Standards** *n pl* (*GAAS*) ACC normativas de auditoría generalmente aceptadas

generate *vt* GEN COMM *ideas, income, profits* generar

generating: **~ station** *n* ENVIR estación generadora *f*

generation *n* GEN COMM *profits* generación *f*; **~ gap** WEL desfase entre generaciones *m*

generative: **~ city** *n* ECON ciudad generatriz *f*

generator *n* GEN COMM generador *m*

generic[1] *adj* GEN COMM, S&M genérico

generic[2]: **~ appeal** *n* S&M interés genérico *m*; **~ brand** *n* S&M marca genérica *f*; **~ business plan** *n* GEN COMM plan genérico de negocios *m*; **~ job grades** *n pl* BrE HRM categorías genéricas de puestos de trabajo *f pl*; **~ job title** *n* HRM título genérico del puesto de trabajo *m*; **~ market** *n* S&M mercado genérico *m*; **~ products** *n pl* S&M productos genéricos *m pl*

generous *adj* TAX generoso

genetic: **~ engineering** *n* POL ingeniería genética *f*

gentleman: **~'s agreement** *n* GEN COMM, LAW pacto de caballeros *m*

genuine: **~ article** *n* GEN COMM producto auténtico *m*; **~ occupational qualification** *n* (*GOQ*) HRM, WEL cualificación ocupacional genuina *f*

geodemography *n* S&M *research* geodemografía *f*

geographic *adj* GEN COMM geográfico

geographical[1] *adj* GEN COMM geográfico

geographical[2]: **~ area** *n* GEN COMM, IMP/EXP área geográfica *f*; **~ trade structure** *n* ECON estructura geográfica comercial *f*

geometric: **~ mean** *n* (*GM*) MATH media geométrica *f*; **~ progression** *n* MATH progresión geométrica *f*

geopolitical *adj* POL geopolítico

German: **~ Historical School** *n* ECON Escuela Histórica alemana *f*

gerrymander *vt* POL dividir arbitrariamente

gerrymandering *n* POL falsificación de elecciones *f*

Gerschenkron: **~ effect** *n* ECON efecto Gerschenkron *m*

gestation: **~ period** *n* ECON periodo de gestación *m*

get 1. *vt* GEN COMM *after effort* conseguir, *obtain* obtener; ◆ **~ a first** GEN COMM, MEDIA conseguir una primicia informativa; **~ good value for money** ECON conseguir un buen valor por el dinero; **~ justice** LAW obtener justicia; **~ one's second wind** GEN COMM volver a tomar aliento; **~ a pay rise** HRM conseguir un aumento de sueldo; **~ results** HRM conseguir resultados; **~ rid of** GEN COMM librarse de; **~ the sack** *infrml* HRM ser despedido; **~ sth straight** *infrml* GEN COMM entender bien algo; **~ a toehold in the market** GEN COMM asentarse en el mercado, conseguir un punto de apoyo en el mercado; **~ top billing** LEIS ser primero de cartel; **2.** *vi* GEN COMM *reach* llegar; ◆ **~ bogged down** *infrml* GEN COMM empantanarse; **~ down to** GEN COMM *business* llegar a; **~ down to specifics** GEN COMM ir al grano; **~ down to work** GEN COMM ponerse a trabajar; **~ into debt** *infrml* BANK, ECON, FIN meterse en deudas, obtener deudas (*infrml*), endeudarse; **~ off the ground** *infrml* GEN COMM *business, project* iniciar el despegue; **~ off to a flying start** *infrml* GEN COMM *business, project* entrar con buen pie; **~ out of trouble** GEN COMM salir de apuros; **~ rich** *infrml* GEN COMM hacerse rico; **~ sidetracked** GEN COMM ser apartado; **~ through to sb** COMMS conseguir comunicarse con alguien

GGE *abbr* (*general government expenditure*) ECON, POL GGE (*Esp*) (*gasto general del Estado*)

ghost *n* *AmE* *infrml* HRM beneficiario(-a) gratuito(-a) *m,f*, parásito *mf* (*infrml*)

ghostwriter *n* *jarg* S&M negro(-a) *m,f* (*jarg*)

GHS *abbr* (*General Household Survey*) ECON *econometrics* encuesta general del núcleo familiar

GIC *abbr* FIN (*guaranteed investment contract*) condiciones generales del seguro *f pl*, contrato de inversión garantizado *m*, INS (*guaranteed income contract*) póliza de ingresos garantizados *f*

Giffen: **~ effect** *n* S&M efecto Giffen *m*; **~ paradox** *n* ECON paradoja de Giffen *f*

gift *n* TAX donación *f*; **~ by will** TAX transmisión testamentaria *f*; **~ causa mortis** LAW donación mortis causa *f*; **~ certificate** *AmE* GEN COMM bono de regalo *m*; **~ deed** LAW escritura de donación *f*; **~ inter vivos** LAW donación entre vivos *f*; **~ promotion** S&M *advertising* promoción con regalo *f*; **~ of property** TAX donación de propiedades *f*; **~ tax** TAX impuesto sobre donaciones *m*; **~ tax return** TAX declaración de impuestos sobre donativos *f*; **~ token** LEIS, S&M vale para comprar un regalo *m*; **~ voucher** GEN COMM bono de regalo *m*; **~ with reservation** TAX donación con retención *f*

Gift: **~ Aid** *n* TAX deducción por donaciones *f*, subvención a donaciones *f*

gifted *adj* WEL *child* dotado

gigabyte *n* (*Gb*) COMP gigaocteto *m*

gigantomania *n* *jarg* HRM gigantomanía *f*

gigantomaniac *adj* *jarg* HRM gigantomaníaco

GIGO *abbr* *jarg* (*garbage-in/garbage-out*) COMP GIGO (*entrada descontrolada/salida descontrolada*)

gilt[1]: **~-edged** *adj* STOCK de primerísima clase

gilt[2] *n* *BrE* STOCK papel del Estado *m*; **~-edged bill of exchange** STOCK letra de cambio de primera clase *f*, letra del Tesoro del Reino Unido *f*; **~-edged market** STOCK *government securities* mercado de valores de primera *m*; **~-edged market makers** *n pl* (*GEMM*) STOCK creadores de mercado de valores de primerísima clase *m pl*; **~-edged security** FIN valor de primer orden *m*, STOCK título de alto rendimiento *m*; **~-edged stock** STOCK acciones de alto rendimiento *f pl*; **~-edged stocks** *n pl* *BrE* (*cf government securities AmE*) ECON, STOCK fondos públicos *m pl*, valores del Estado *m pl*

gimmick *n* GEN COMM, TAX truco *m*

gin out *vt* *infrml* GEN COMM despejar

Gini: **~ coefficient** *n* ECON *econometrics* coeficiente de Gini *m*

Ginnie Mae *abbr* *AmE* *infrml* (*Government National Mortgage Association*) BANK, FIN asociación gubernamental hipotecaria

giro *n* GEN COMM giro postal *m*

Girobank *n* BANK, FIN banco especializado en giros bancarios

give *vt* GEN COMM dar; ◆ **~ advice** GEN COMM asesorar;

~ the alert GEN COMM poner sobreaviso; **~ bond** GEN COMM dar fianza; **~ bribes** GEN COMM dar sobornos; **~ consent** GEN COMM dar el consentimiento; **~ the employees a day off** HRM dar un día libre a los empleados; **~ evidence** LAW declarar, prestar declaración; **~ evidence on oath** LAW declarar bajo juramento; **~ evidence under oath** LAW declarar bajo juramento; **~ free rein to** GEN COMM dar rienda suelta a; **~ a loose interpretation of sth** GEN COMM interpretar algo con flexibilidad; **~ media coverage** MEDIA dar cobertura en los medios de comunicación; **~ notice** GEN COMM preanunciar; **~ notice to quit** PROP *to landlord, tenant* dar aviso de desalojo, dar aviso de expulsión; **~ priority to** GEN COMM, MGMNT dar prioridad a; **~ record of** GEN COMM *expenses, deficit* dejar constancia de; **~ a ruling in favor of sb** *AmE*, **~ a ruling in favour of sb** *BrE* GEN COMM fallar en favor de alguien, pronunciar un fallo favorable a alguien; **~ sb access to** GEN COMM permitir a alguien el acceso a; **~ sb the opportunity to** GEN COMM dar a alguien la oportunidad de; **~ sb the right to** GEN COMM otorgar a alguien el derecho a; **~ sb their cards** *BrE* *infrml* HRM *staff* cesar a alguien, despedir, echar, poner a alguien de patitas en la calle (*infrml*); **~ sb the sack** *BrE* *infrml* HRM *staff* cesar a alguien, despedir, echar, poner a alguien de patitas en la calle (*infrml*); **~ sb a trial** GEN COMM probar a alguien; **~ sb an ultimatum** GEN COMM dar a alguien un ultimátum; **~ an upward thrust to interest rates** FIN subir los tipos de interés; **~ witness on behalf of** LAW prestar testimonio en nombre de

give away *vt* S&M regalar

give back *vi* *jarg* HRM *industrial relations* devolver

give in to *vt* GEN COMM condescender con

give up 1. *vt* *jarg* STOCK abandonar; **2.** *vi* GEN COMM rendirse, retroceder, IND claudicar, rendirse, STOCK repartirse

giveaway *n* S&M regalo *m*

given: **~ the circumstances** *phr* GEN COMM dadas las circunstancias

giver *n* STOCK dador(a) *m,f*; **~ for a call** STOCK dador(a) de una opción de compra *m,f*; **~ for a call of more** STOCK comprador(a) para una opción a adquirir el doble *m,f*, dador(a) de la facultad de comprar el doble *m,f*; **~ for a put** STOCK dador(a) de una opción de venta *m,f*; **~ for a put and call** STOCK dador(a) de una opción de venta y de compra *m,f*; **~ on stock** STOCK dador(a) de capital social *m,f*; **~ of option money** STOCK dador(a) de suma de opción *m,f*

GLAM *abbr* *infrml* (*Gray, Leisured, Affluent, Married AmE, Grey, Leisured, Affluent, Married BrE*) ECON *econometrics* viejo, ocioso, rico, casado

glamor *AmE* *see* **glamour** *BrE*

glamour: **~ issue** *n* *BrE* *jarg* STOCK emisión atractiva *f*, emisión de moda *f*; **~ stock** *n* *BrE* STOCK acción de moda *f*, valor de gran aceptación *m*

glare: **~-free** *adj* COMP *screen* sin brillo

Glasgow: **~ Stock Exchange** *n* STOCK Bolsa de Valores de Glasgow *f*

glass: **~ insurance** *n* INS seguro contra rotura de lunas *m*; **~-reinforced cladding** *n* TRANSP revestimiento reforzado con vidrio *m*; **~-reinforced plastic** *n* IND, TRANSP *lifeboats* plástico reforzado con vidrio *m*; **~ wool** *n* TRANSP lana de vidrio *f*

Glass: ~ **Steagall Act** n BANK on credit ley Glass Steagall f

gliding: ~ **rate** n STOCK tipo volátil m; ~ **shift** n jarg HRM turno con horario flexible m; ~ **time** n jarg HRM horario de trabajo flexible m, horario móvil m

glitch n COMP interferencia f, problema técnico m, POL fallo técnico que estropea la intervención de un candidato

global[1] adj GEN COMM global, mundial

global[2]: ~ **balance** n ENVIR balance global m; ~ **communications** n pl COMMS comunicaciones globales f pl; ~ **custody** n FIN custodia global f; ~ **deregulation** n ECON desregulación global f; ~ **financial center** AmE, ~ **financial centre** BrE n ECON centro financiero global m, centro financiero mundial m; ~ **financial market** n ECON, FIN mercado financiero global m; ~ **harmonization** n ACC armonización mundial f; ~ **image** n S&M imagen global f; ~ **marketing** n S&M marketing global m; ~ **memory** n COMP memoria global f; ~ **monetarism** n ECON, POL monetarismo global m; ~ **search** n COMP document, data búsqueda automática f; ~ **strategy** n GEN COMM estrategia global f; ~ **variable** n COMP variable común f

Global: ~ **Environment Monitoring System** n ENVIR Sistema para el Control y Seguimiento del Medio Ambiente m; ~ **Maritime Distress and Safety System** n (GMDSS) TRANSP shipping Sistema Global para Casos de Peligro y Seguridad Marítimos m; ~ **Positioning System** n (GPS) TRANSP shipping sistema de localización global

globalization n GEN COMM of markets mundialización f, globalización f

globalize vt GEN COMM globalizar

gloom n ECON, GEN COMM pesimismo m

glossary n GEN COMM glosario m

glossy[1] adj infrml MEDIA de lujo

glossy[2] n infrml (glossy magazine) MEDIA revista de lujo f, revista impresa en papel satinado f; ~ **magazine** (glossy) MEDIA revista de lujo f, revista impresa en papel satinado f; ~ **paper** COMMS, GEN COMM, MEDIA papel glaseado m, papel satinado m

glut n ECON, GEN COMM exceso m, superabundancia f

GM abbr ECON (gross margin) margen bruto m, FIN (gross margin) margen bruto m, GEN COMM (group mark) marca de grupo f, HRM (general manager) DG (director general), MATH (geometric mean) media geométrica f, MGMNT (general manager) DG (director general)

GMB abbr (good marketable brand) GEN COMM marca comercializable f

GMT abbr (Greenwich Mean Time) GEN COMM hora media de Greenwich f

GNI abbr (gross national Income) ECON INB (ingreso nacional bruto)

GNMA abbr AmE (Government National Mortgage Association) BANK, FIN asociación gubernamental hipotecaria

GNP[1] abbr (gross national product) ECON PNB (producto nacional bruto)

GNP[2]: ~~**based own resources** n pl ECON recursos propios basados en el PNB m pl

go[1] vi GEN COMM pasar, LEIS, TRANSP ir, viajar; ♦ ~ **on benefits** BrE (cf go on welfare AmE) WEL recibir prestaciones de la Seguridad Social; ~ **on the dole** infrml BrE (cf go on welfare AmE) WEL recibir prestaciones de la Seguridad Social; ~ **about one's daily business** GEN COMM ocuparse de las cosas diarias; ~ **along with** GEN COMM estar de acuerdo con; ~ **down in value** STOCK reducirse el valor; ~ **downhill** GEN COMM business ir cuesta abajo; ~ **into voluntary liquidation** GEN COMM hacer la liquidación voluntaria; ~ **long** STOCK estar largo; ~ **on one's note** AmE GEN COMM ayudar a alguien con un aval; ~ **on welfare** AmE (cf go on the dole BrE, go on benefits BrE) WEL recibir prestaciones de la Seguridad Social; ~ **out in sympathy with** HRM strikers ir a la huelga en solidaridad con; ~ **out on strike** BrE HRM ir a la huelga; ~ **private** infrml GEN COMM privatizarse, WEL medicine acudir a un hospital o médico privado; ~ **public** STOCK cotizar en bolsa, poner en bolsa; ~ **through the proper channels** GEN COMM company canalizar debidamente, pasar por los canales debidos; ~ **to the expense of** GEN COMM correr por cuenta de; ~ **to great expense** GEN COMM meterse en mayores gastos; ~ **to a lot of trouble** GEN COMM tomarse muchas molestias; ~ **to press** MEDIA print entrar en máquina; ~ **to rack and ruin** infrml GEN COMM venirse abajo; ~ **to the wall** infrml GEN COMM ir a la bancarrota, irse a pique (infrml), company llegar al límite; ~ **under the rule** AmE jarg STOCK someterse al reglamento; ~ **upstream** GEN COMM ir a contracorriente

go[2]: **make a** ~ **of sth** phr infrml tener éxito en algo

go against vt STOCK ir en contra de; ♦ ~ **the current** GEN COMM ir a contracorriente; ~ **the tide** GEN COMM ir a contracorriente

go down vi jarg WEL from university salir de la universidad

go under vi GEN COMM company, TRANSP boat naufragar

go up vi jarg WEL to university entrar en la universidad

G-O: ~ **bond** n AmE (general obligation bond) STOCK bono de responsabilidad general m

goal n GEN COMM propósito m, meta f, IND meta f, MGMNT objective fin m, finalidad f, meta f, propósito m, S&M meta f; ~ **congruence** MGMNT congruencia de objetivos f; ~ **equilibrium** ECON equilibrio meta m; ~ **programming** MGMNT programación de metas f, programación de objetivos f; ~ **seeking** GEN COMM, MGMNT búsqueda de metas f; ~ **setting** GEN COMM, MGMNT establecimiento de metas m, fijación de objetivos f; ~ **system** TAX sistema de objetivos m; ~ **variable** POL variable objetivo f

gods n pl LEIS theatre gallinero m, paraíso m

go-go: ~ **fund** n jarg FIN valor de bolsa que promete rápidos beneficios m

GOH abbr (goods on hand) TRANSP mercancías en almacén f pl

going: ~ **concern** n ACC, GEN COMM empresa en funcionamiento f, empresa en marcha f; ~~**concern concept** n ACC concepto de empresa en funcionamiento m, concepto de empresa establecida m, principio de gestión continuada m; ~~**concern principle** n ACC principio de empresa en funcionamiento m, principio de empresa en marcha m, principio de gestión continuada m; ~~**concern value** n ACC valor del negocio en funcionamiento m, valor del negocio establecido m; ~ **rate** n GEN COMM tasa corriente f

gold: ~ **bullion standard** n ECON, FIN patrón lingote oro m; ~ **card** n BANK tarjeta oro f; ~ **clause agreement** n (GCA) TRANSP shipping acuerdo con cláusula de pago en oro *m*; ~ **coin** *n* BANK moneda de oro *f*; ~ **cover** *n* ECON cobertura oro *f*; ~ **credit** *n* STOCK crédito valor oro *m*; ~ **currency** *n* BANK, ECON divisa oro *f*; ~ **demonetization** *n* ECON desmonetización del oro *f*; ~ **disc** *BrE*, ~ **disk** *AmE n* MEDIA *album sales* disco de oro *m*; ~ **exchange standard** *n* ECON, FIN patrón de cambio del oro *m*; ~ **export point** *n* FIN, IMP/EXP punto de exportación de oro *m*, punto de salida del oro *m*; ~ **fixing** *n* BANK cotización diaria del oro *f*; ~ **franc** *n* ECON franco oro *m*; ~ **import point** *n* FIN, IMP/EXP punto de entrada del oro *m*, punto de importación de oro *m*; ~ **market** *n* ECON, STOCK mercado del oro *m*; ~ **mining** *n* IND explotación aurífera *f*; ~**mining company** *n* ENVIR empresa de explotación aurífera *f*; ~ **mutual fund** *n* STOCK fondo de pensiones del oro *m*; ~ **ore** *n* ENVIR mineral de oro *m*; ~ **parity** *n* FIN paridad oro *f*; ~ **point** *n* IMP/EXP punto oro *m*; ~ **price** *n* STOCK precio del oro *m*; ~ **producer** *n* IND productor(a) de oro *m,f*; ~ **reserve** *n* ECON reserva en oro *f*; ~ **rush** *n* GEN COMM rebatiña del oro *f*; ~ **shortage** *n* ECON escasez de oro *f*; ~ **standard** *n* ECON, FIN patrón oro *m*

golden: ~ **age** *n* ECON edad de oro *f*; ~ **formula** *n BrE* HRM fórmula de oro *f*; ~ **handcuffs** *n pl infrml* GEN COMM prima de permanencia *f*; ~ **handshake** *n infrml* HRM despido con una compensación en metálico; ~ **hello** *n infrml* HRM prima de contratación *f*; ~ **parachute** *n infrml* FIN contrato blindado *f*; ~ **rate** *n* HRM tarifa especial *f*; ~ **rule** *n* ECON, GEN COMM regla de oro *f*, norma de oro *f*; ~ **share** *n* STOCK acción de primera clase *f*

Golden: ~ **Triangle** *n* ECON triángulo dorado *m*

golds: ~ **index** *n* STOCK índice de acciones de las minas

Goldsmith: ~ **banking system** *n BrE* BANK sistema bancario Goldsmith *m*

gondola *n* S&M *shop fitting*, TRANSP *rail* góndola *f*; ~ **flat** TRANSP *container* piso góndola *m*

good[1]: **not in** ~ **delivery** *adj* STOCK *unmatched trade* no conforme al reglamento; ~ **sound merchantable** *adj BrE* (*gsm*) GEN COMM *quality* totalmente aprovechable

good[2]: ~ **bargain** *n* GEN COMM buen negocio *m*; ~ **box office** *n* LEIS *theatre, cinema* buena recaudación de taquilla *f*; ~ **business background** *n* GEN COMM buenos antecedentes mercantiles *m pl*; ~ **credit risk** *n* BANK, FIN riesgo de crédito bueno *m*; ~ **delivery** *n* STOCK buena entrega *f*; ~ **fair average** *n* (*gfa*) GEN COMM buen promedio *m*; ~ **faith** *n* GEN COMM, INS buena fe *f*; ~~**faith bargaining** *n* HRM negociación de buena fe *f*; ~~**faith deposit** *n* STOCK depósito de buena fe *m*, depósito hecho de buena fe *m*; ~ **housekeeping** *n* MGMNT buena administración interna *f*; ~ **marketable brand** *n* (*GMB*) GEN COMM marca comercializable *f*; ~ **money** *n* BANK dinero de disposición inmediata *m*, ECON *Gresham's Law* buena moneda *f*; ~ **name** *n* GEN COMM, S&M prestigio *m*, reputación *f*; ~ **news** *n* GEN COMM buenas noticias *f pl*; ~ **return** *n* ACC *on investment* rendimiento alto *m*; ~ **risk** *n* INS riesgo ventajoso *m*; ~~**till-canceled order** *AmE*, ~~**till-cancelled order** *BrE n* (*GTC order*) STOCK orden vigente hasta su cancelación *f* (*orden GTC*), orden de compraventa vigente hasta su cancelación *f* (*orden GTC*); ~~**till-date order** *n* (*GTD order*) STOCK orden vigente hasta su fecha *f* (*orden GTD*); ~ **title** *n* LAW, PROP título de propiedad incontestable *m*, título válido *m*

Goodhart: ~**'s Law** *n* ECON, LAW Ley de Goodhart *f*

goods *n pl* (*gds*) GEN COMM bienes *m pl*, mercancías *f pl*;

~ **account** *n* ACC cuenta de mercaderías *f*; ~ **called forward** TRANSP bienes con opción de futuro *m pl*; ~ **and chattels** PROP, TAX bienes muebles *m pl*; ~ **covered by warrant** GEN COMM bienes garantizados *m pl*; ~ **department** *n* GEN COMM departamento de mercancías *m*; ~ **depot** *n* GEN COMM depósito de mercancías *m*; ~ **for re-export** IMP/EXP bienes para la reexportación *m pl*; ~ **held for re-sale** ACC bienes sujetos a reventa *m pl*; ~ **in process** GEN COMM, S&M productos en proceso *m pl*, artículos en proceso *m pl*; ~ **on approval** GEN COMM, S&M géneros a condición; ~ **on consignment** S&M bienes en consignación *m pl*; ~ **on hand** (*GOH*) TRANSP mercancías en almacén *f pl*; ~ **received note** *n* TRANSP aviso de recibo de mercancías *m*, nota de recepción *f*, nota de recepción de mercancías *f*; ~ **and services** GEN COMM bienes y servicios *m pl*; ~ **and services tax** *n* (*GST*) TAX impuesto sobre bienes y servicios *m*; ~ **and services tax credit** *n* TAX desgravación de bienes y servicios *f*; ~ **train** *n BrE* (*cf freight train AmE*) TRANSP tren de carga *m*, tren de mercancías *m*; ◆ **the** ~ **remain undelivered** GEN COMM las mercancías todavía no se han entregado

goodwill *n* ACC fondo de comercio positivo *m*, ventaja en relación con la clientela del negocio *f*, crédito mercantil *m*; ~ **amortization** ACC *credits* amortización del fondo de comercio *f*, amortización del saldo de cuentas de clientes *f*; ~ **on consolidation** ACC crédito comercial en consolidación *m*, fondo de comercio de la consolidación *m*

GOP *abbr AmE infrml* (*Grand Old Party*) POL el partido republicano

GOQ *abbr* (*genuine occupational qualification*) HRM, WEL cualificación ocupacional genuina *f*

gorilla *n BrE infrml* GEN COMM persona en posición de poder e influencia; ~ **scale** *jarg* HRM jerarquía de cuadros directivos *f*

go-slow *n BrE* ECON, HRM huelga de brazos caídos *f*

govern *vt* LAW *by regulations* regir

governing: ~ **principle** *n* GEN COMM principio director *m*

government[1]: ~~**backed** *adj* FIN respaldado por el Gobierno; ~~**financed** *adj* FIN financiado por el Estado; ~~**owned** *adj* GEN COMM *company* estatal; ~~**regulated** *adj* POL regulado por el Estado; ~~**sponsored** *adj* FIN *project* patrocinado por el Estado; ~~**supported** *adj* FIN *project* apoyado por el Estado; ~~**to-government** *adj* GEN COMM de gobierno a gobierno

government[2] *n* (*govt*) ECON, POL administración pública *f*, gobierno *m*; ~ **accounting** ACC, POL cuentas del estado *f pl*, cuentas públicas *f pl*; ~ **agency** HRM, POL dependencia del gobierno *f*; ~ **annuity** FIN anualidades de gobierno *f pl*, renta del Estado *f*; ~ **assistance** TAX ayuda del Estado *f*; ~ **bill of lading** (*GBL*) IMP/EXP, TRANSP conocimiento de embarque gubernamental *m*; ~ **bond** *AmE* (*cf yearling BrE*) ECON, STOCK bono del Estado *m*; ~ **broker** STOCK síndico(-a) *m,f*, síndico(-a) de la bolsa *m,f*; ~ **contract** LAW contrato de la administración *m*; ~~**controlled corporation** POL empresa controlada por el gobierno *f*, empresa paraestatal *f*; ~ **defence appropriations** *BrE*, ~ **defense appropriations** *AmE n pl* POL asignaciones nacionales de defensa *f pl*, dotación presupuestaria para defensa *f*; ~ **enterprise** ECON empresa estatal *f*; ~ **expenditure** ECON gasto del Estado *m*, gasto público *m*; ~ **finance** FIN hacienda pública *f*; ~ **form** (*GF*) TRANSP *charter* *party* formulario oficial *m*; **~ grant** ECON, POL, TAX subvención del gobierno *f*, donación gubernamental *f*; **~ intervention** ECON, POL intervención estatal *f*; **~ investment** BANK, FIN colocación del estado *f*; **~ loan** BANK, FIN préstamo oficial *m*; **~ obligation** ECON obligación del Estado *f*; **~ relation** POL relación gubernamental *f*; **~ report** GEN COMM, POL informe del gobierno *m* (*Esp*), reporte del gobierno *m* (*AmL*); **~ research grant** FIN subvención gubernamental para investigación *f*; **~ securities** *AmE n pl* (*cf gilt-edged stocks BrE*) ECON valores del Estado *m pl*, POL efectos públicos *m pl*, STOCK valores del Estado *m pl*; **~ security** STOCK título del Estado *m*; **~sponsored enterprise** FIN empresa patrocinada por el gobierno *f*; **~ stock** *BrE* STOCK títulos del Estado *m pl*

Government: the ~ *n* POL el Gobierno *m*; **~ lawyer** *n* LAW ≈ abogado(-a) del Estado *m,f*; **~ National Mortgage Association** *n AmE* BANK, FIN (*GNMA, Ginnie Mae*) asociación gubernamental hipotecaria; **~ State Secretariat** *n* POL Secretaría de Estado del Gobierno *f*

governmental[1] *adj* GEN COMM, POL gubernamental

governmental[2]: **~ accounting** *n* ACC, BANK contabilidad gubernamental *f*, contabilidad pública *f*

Governmental: ~ Accounting Standards Board *n AmE* (*GASB*) ACC ≈ Consejo Oficial de Normas Contables *m*, ≈ Junta Gubernamental de Normas Contables *f*

Governor: ~ of the Bank of England *n* ECON ≈ Gobernador(a) del Banco de España *m,f*; **~ General** *n* POL Gobernador(a) *m,f*

govt *abbr* (*government*) ECON, POL gobierno *m*, administración pública *f*

GP *abbr* (*general purpose*) GEN COMM universal, de aplicación general

GPS *abbr* (*Global Positioning System*) TRANSP *shipping* sistema de localización global

grab[1] *n* TRANSP *cargo* cuchara *f*

grab[2] *vt* GEN COMM *attention* atraer

grace: ~ days *n pl* ACC días de gracia *m pl*; **~ period** *n* ACC periodo de gracia *m*

grade *n* HRM clase *f*; **~ creep** *jarg* HRM escalamiento de categorías *m*; **~ drift** HRM cambio de categoría *m*; **~ standard** ACC, BANK base estándar *f*

graded: ~ by size *phr* GEN COMM *produce* clasificado por tamaño

gradual *adj* GEN COMM gradual

gradualism *n* POL gradualismo *m*

gradualist: ~ monetarism *n* ECON monetarismo gradual *m*

gradually *adv* GEN COMM gradualmente

graduate[1] *n* HRM graduado *m*; **~ school of business** WEL escuela superior de negocios *f*

graduate[2] *vt* FIN escalonar

graduated[1]: **in ~ stages** *adv* GEN COMM en pasos escalonados

graduated[2]: **~ income tax** *n* TAX impuesto sobre la renta escalonado *m*; **~ interest** BANK interés escalonado *m*; **~ lease** *n* PROP alquiler progresivo *m*, arrendamiento progresivo *m*; **~ payment mortgage** *n* BANK, PROP hipoteca de pagos proporcionales *f*; **~ pension scheme** *n* HRM, INS plan de pensión graduado *m*; **~ tax** *n* TAX impuesto escalonado *m*; **~ wage** *n* HRM salario escalonado *m*

graft[1] *n BrE infrml* GEN COMM soborno *m* (*Esp*), LAW chanchullo *m*, corrupción *f*

graft[2] *vi infrml* LAW practicar cohecho

Graham: ~ and Dodd investing method *n* STOCK método Graham y Dodd de inversión *m*

grain: ~ certificate *n* TRANSP *shipping* certificado de grano *m*; **~ charter party** *n* TRANSP contrato de fletamento de grano *m*; **~ crop** *n* ECON *agriculture* cosecha de cereales *f*; **~ cubic** *n* (*GC*) TRANSP *shipping* cubicación de grano *f*; **~ elevator** *n* TRANSP *cargo handling* elevador de grano *m*; **~ exchange** *n* STOCK bolsa de cereales *f*; **~ terminal** *n* TRANSP *shipping* terminal granelera *f*

Grain: ~ and Free Trade Association *n* (*GAFTA*) IMP/EXP asociación que controla las transacciones comerciales de grano y patatas en el Mercado de Contratación del Báltico

gram *n* (*g*) GEN COMM gramo *m* (*gr.*)

Gramm: ~ Rudman Hollings Act *AmE n* LAW, POL *US* Ley Gramm Rudman Hollings *f*

gramme *see* gram

Grammy *n AmE jarg* LEIS, MEDIA *broadcast award* premio para programas y gente de la televisión americana

granary *n* TRANSP granero *m*

grand: ~ jury *n AmE* LAW jurado de acusación *m*; **~ larceny** *n AmE* (*cf serious crime BrE*) LAW hurto mayor *m*; **~ total** *n* GEN COMM total general *m*

Grand: ~ Old Party *n AmE infrml* (*GOP*) POL el partido republicano

grandfather: ~ clause *n infrml* BANK, INS, LAW cláusula limitativa de participación en holdings *f*, cláusula de exención *f*, disposición excepcional *f*

grandfathering *n* TAX priorización *f*

granny: ~ bond *n BrE infrml* STOCK bono a largo plazo *m*

grant[1] *n* ECON, FIN, GEN COMM subsidio *m*, subvención *f*, PROP cesión *f*, WEL beca *f*; **~-in-aid** POL subsidio *m*; ◆ **in ~ form** FIN a modo de subvención

grant[2] *vt* BANK otorgar, GEN COMM dar, *concessions* garantizar, conceder, PATENTS *licence* conceder, otorgar, PROP *tenancy* conceder; ◆ **~ extended credit** FIN garantizar la ampliación de un crédito; **~ an extension** GEN COMM conceder una prórroga; **~ interim supply** ACC garantizar un abastecimiento provisional; **~ an option** STOCK garantizar una opción

grantee *n* GEN COMM, LAW beneficiario(-a) *m,f*, PROP, STOCK, TAX cesionario(-a) *m,f*

granting: ~ of credit *n* BANK concesión de crédito *f*; **~ of patents** *n* PATENTS concesión de la patente *f*

grantor *n* ACC cesionista *mf*, LAW, PROP otorgante *mf*, STOCK cesionista *mf*; **~ trust** LAW, PROP fideicomiso con responsabilidad fiscal del otorgante *m*

grants: ~ expenditures *n pl* FIN gastos de subvenciones *m pl*

grapevine *n* COMMS, GEN COMM *information source* medio de comunicación clandestina *m*, comunicación oficiosa *f*

graph[1] *n* GEN COMM grafo *m*; **~ plotter** COMP trazador de gráficos *m*

graph[2] *vt* MATH, S&M dibujar (*Esp*), graficar (*AmL*)

graphic[1] *adj* GEN COMM gráfico *m*

graphic[2]: **~ character** *n* COMP carácter gráfico *m*; **~ data processing** *n* COMP proceso de datos gráficos *m*; **~ database** *n* COMP base de datos gráfica *f*; **~ design**

n MEDIA, S&M diseño gráfico *m*; **~-design software** *n* COMP programas de diseño gráfico *m pl*; **~ designer** *n* MEDIA, S&M diseñador(a) gráfico(-a) *m,f*; **~ display terminal** *n* COMP terminal de representación gráfica *m*

graphical: **~ editing** *n* COMP, MEDIA *print* edición gráfica *f*

graphically: **~ illustrated** *adj* GEN COMM con grabados

graphics *n pl* GEN COMM gráficos *m pl*; **~ board** *n* COMP tarjeta de gráficos *f*; **~ file** *n* COMP archivo gráfico *m*; **~ mode** *n* COMP modo gráfico *m*; **~ printer** *n* COMP impresora de gráficos *f*

grass: **~-roots movement** *n* POL movimiento de base popular *m*; **~-roots support** *n* POL apoyo popular *m*

gratis *adv* GEN COMM gratis

gratuitous[1] *adj* GEN COMM gratuito

gratuitous[2]: **~ loan** *n* BANK, FIN préstamo gratuito *m*; **~ transfer** *n* TAX *inheritance* transferencia gratuita *f*

gratuity *n* TAX gratificación *f*

graveyard: **~ market** *n* STOCK mercado muerto *m*; **~ shift** *n* infrml HRM turno de media noche *m*

graving: **~ dock** *n* TRANSP *shipping* dique de carenas *m*, dique seco *m*

gravity: **~ model** *n* ECON modelo de gravedad *m*

gray *AmE see* **grey** *BrE*

grazing *n AmE jarg* GEN COMM digerir alimentos robados en el interior de un establecimiento mientras se está comprando

Great: **~ Depression** *n* ECON *during 1930s* Gran Depresión *f*; **~ Leap Forward** *n* ECON *agricultural* gran salto hacia adelante *m*; **~ Society** *n AmE* ECON sociedad grande *f*

green[1] *adj* ENVIR verde; **~-conscious** ENVIR *consumers* con conciencia ecológica

green[2]: **~ accounting** *n* ENVIR contabilidad medioambiental *f*, contabilidad verde *f*; **~ ban** *n* HRM negativa sindical a trabajar en proyectos que dañen el medio ambiente; **~ belt** *n* ENVIR *around towns* cinturón ecológico *m*, cinturón verde *m*; **~ card** *n AmE* (*cf residence visa BrE*) HRM, INS, LAW, POL visado de residencia *m*, carta verde *f*; **~ conditionality** *n* ENVIR condicionalidad ecológica *f*; **~ currency** *n* ECON moneda agropecuaria *f*; **~ energy** *n* ENVIR energía ecológica *f*; **~ issue** *n* ENVIR edición ecológica *f*; **~ labeling scheme** *AmE*, **~ labelling scheme** *BrE n* ENVIR, S&M plan de etiquetado ecológico *m*; **~ light** *n* GEN COMM *authorization* luz verde *f*; **~ lobby** *n* ENVIR, POL grupo de presión verde *m*; **~ revolution** *n* ECON, ENVIR *agricultural* revolución verde *f*, revolución ecológica *f*

Green: **~ Discussion Paper** *n* LAW, POL Libro Verde *m*; **~ Paper** *n BrE* LAW anteproyecto de ley *m*; **~ Party** *n* ENVIR, POL Partido Verde *m*

greenback *n AmE* BANK, ECON, FIN billete de un dólar

greenfield[1] *adj* ENVIR de zona verde

greenfield[2]: **~ site** *n* GEN COMM negocio en el que los beneficios son una perspectiva, pero no una realidad actual; **~ site company** *n* HRM empresa situada en un área no desarrollada *f*, empresa situada en zona verde *f*

greenhouse: **~ effect** *n* ENVIR efecto de invernadero *m*

greening *n jarg* ENVIR *of public opinion* enverdecimiento *m*

greenlining *n AmE jarg* ENVIR línea ecológica *f*, WEL permiso para realizar una actividad *m*

greenmail *n AmE* STOCK pago de acciones para evitar una absorción, pago de rescate *m*

greenmailer *n* STOCK inversor(a) hostil *m,f*, chantajista *mf*

Greens: **the ~** *n pl* POL los verdes *m pl*

Greenwich: **~ Mean Time** *n* (*GMT*) GEN COMM hora media de Greenwich *f*

greetings *n pl* COMMS saludos *m pl*

Gresham: **~'s Law** *n* ECON, LAW Ley de Gresham *f*

grey: **~ belt** *n BrE infrml* ECON, LEIS área de población mayoritariamente jubilada *f*; **~ market** *n BrE* STOCK mercado gris *m*; **~ Monday** *n BrE* STOCK lunes gris *m*; **~ society** *n BrE* ECON sociedad envejecida *f*

Grey: **~, Leisured, Affluent, Married** *phr BrE infrml* (*GLAM*) ECON *econometrics* viejo, ocioso, rico, casado

grid *n* COMP parrilla *f*, GEN COMM, IND cuadrícula *f*, matriz *f*; **~ structure** *n* FIN estructura en rejilla *f*, GEN COMM estructura de matriz *f*

grievance *n* HRM queja *f*, LAW agravio *m*; **~ arbitration** *n* HRM arbitraje de agravios *m*; **~ procedure** *n* HRM, LAW procedimiento de agravio *m*

GRIP *abbr* (*guaranteed recovery of investment principle*) FIN principio de la garantía de recuperación de la inversión *m*

GRM *abbr* (*gross rent multiplier*) PROP multiplicador del arrendamiento bruto *m*

gross[1] *adj* ACC, FIN, GEN COMM bruto

gross[2] *n* MATH totalidad *f*; **~ amount** *n* ACC importe bruto *m*; **~ billing** *n AmE* S&M facturación bruta *f*; **~ cash flow** *n* GEN COMM, FIN flujo bruto en efectivo *m*; **~ circulation** *n* S&M tirada total *f*; **~ combination weight** *n* (*GCW*) TRANSP *articulated vehicle* peso bruto de combinado *m*; **~ cost** *n* TAX coste bruto *m* (*Esp*), costo bruto *m* (*AmL*); **~ cover** *n* S&M cobertura bruta *f*; **~ debt** *n* BANK, FIN deuda bruta *f*; **~ dividend** *n* ACC dividendo bruto *m*; **~ dividend yield** *n* ECON, GEN COMM, STOCK rendimiento bruto *m*; **~ domestic product** *n* (*GDP*) ECON producto interior bruto, producto interno bruto *m* (*PIB*); **~ domestic product at factor cost** *n* ACC, ECON producto interior bruto al coste de los factores *m* (*Esp*), producto interior bruto al costo de los factores *m* (*AmL*); **~ domestic product at market prices** *n* ACC, ECON producto interior bruto a precios de mercado *m*; **~ earnings** *n pl* ACC, FIN beneficio bruto *m* (*Esp*), ganancia bruta *f*, renta bruta *f* (*Esp*), resultado bruto *m* (*Esp*), utilidad bruta *f* (*AmL*), HRM ganancias brutas *f pl*; **~ estate** *n* TAX patrimonio bruto *m*; **~ excess reinsurance policy** *n* INS póliza de reaseguro de excedente bruto *f*; **~ Federal debt** *n AmE* ECON deuda bruta federal *f*; **~ fixed capital formation** *n* GEN COMM formación bruta de capital fijo *f*; **~ form of charter** *n* TRANSP *maritime* condiciones brutas *f pl*; **~ income** *n* ACC, TAX ingreso bruto *m*, renta bruta *f* (*Esp*); **~ investment** *n* STOCK inversión bruta *f*; **~ investment revenue** *n* TAX rendimiento bruto de una inversión *m*; **~ leasable area** *n* PROP superficie arrendable global *f*; **~ lease** *n* PROP arriendo bruto *m*; **~ margin** *n* (*GM*) ACC, ECON, FIN margen bruto *m*; **~ mass** *n* (*G*) GEN COMM masa bruta *f*; **~ miscarriage of justice** *n* LAW error judicial de envergadura *m*; **~ misconduct** *n* HRM falta grave *f*; **~ national expenditure** *n* ECON Gasto Nacional Bruto *m*; **~ national income** *n* (*GNI*) ACC, ECON, FIN ingreso nacional bruto *m* (*INB*), renta nacional bruta *f* (*RNB*); **~ national product** *n* (*GNP*) ECON producto nacional

bruto *m* (*PNB*); ~ **negligence** LAW imprudencia temeraria *f*, negligencia grave *f*, culpa grave *f*; ~ **operating**
income ACC beneficio bruto de explotación *m*; ~ **oper-**
ating spread STOCK margen bruto de la emisión *m*;
~ **pay** HRM remuneración bruta *f*; ~ **profit** ACC, FIN
beneficio bruto *m*, ganancia bruta *f*; ~ **profit margin**
ACC, FIN margen de beneficio bruto *m*; ~ **profit method**
ACC, FIN método de la utilidad bruta *m*; ~ **profit ratio**
ACC, FIN índice de utilidad bruta *m*, coeficiente de
utilidad bruta *m*, proporción de utilidad bruta *f*; ~ **rate**
TRANSP tarifa bruta *f*; ~ **reach** S&M alcance bruto *m*;
~ **receipts pool** TRANSP *shipping* consorcio de ingresos
brutos *m*; ~ **register ton** (*GRT*) GEN COMM, TRANSP
tonelada de arqueo bruto *f*; ~ **registered tonnage**
(*GRT*) GEN COMM, TRANSP *shipping* tonelaje bruto
registrado *m*; ~ **rent** TAX renta bruta *f* (*Esp*), utilidad
bruta *f* (*AmL*); ~ **rent multiplier** (*GRM*) PROP multiplicador del arrendamiento bruto *m*; ~ **revenue** ACC,
TAX entrada bruta *f*, ingreso bruto *m*; ~ **revenue**
requirement TAX requisito de ingresos brutos *m*;
~ **revenue test** ACC, TAX prueba de ingresos brutos *f*;
~ **sales** *n pl* ACC ventas brutas *f pl*; ~ **savings** *n pl*
BANK, ECON, FIN ahorro bruto *m*; ~ **social product**
ECON producto social bruto *m*; ~ **state product** ECON
producto estatal bruto *m*; ~ **taking** GEN COMM entrega
bruta *f*; ~ **tare weight** GEN COMM, TRANSP peso de tara
bruto *m*, taraje bruto *m*; ~ **terms** *n pl* TRANSP
condiciones brutas *f pl*; ~ **ton** (*GT*) GEN COMM *maritime*
tonelada bruta *f*; ~ **train weight** (*GTW*) TRANSP peso
bruto del tren *m*; ~**-up** TAX suma *f*; ~ **vehicle weight**
(*GVW*) TRANSP peso bruto del vehículo *m*; ~ **wage**
HRM salario bruto *m*; ~ **weight** (*gr.wt.*) GEN COMM peso
bruto *m*

gross up *vt* ACC hallar el bruto

Gross: ~ **National Debt** *n* ECON deuda pública bruta *f*

grossed: ~**-up dividend** *n* FIN dividendo con adición del
impuesto *m*, STOCK dividendo pagado en bloque *m*

ground[1]: ~ **level** *adj* PROP a planta baja

ground[2]: ~ **control** *n* COMMS identificación desde tierra *f*;
~ **crew** *n* COMMS personal de tierra *m*; ~ **handling** *n*
TRANSP *aviation* manipulación de la carga en tierra *f*;
~ **handling agent** *n* TRANSP *aviation* agente de carga y
descarga en tierra *mf*; ~ **lease** *n* PROP arriendo para
tierras; ~ **plan** *n* GEN COMM plano fundamental *m*;
~ **rent** *n* PROP alquiler de la tierra *m*; ~ **rule** *n* GEN COMM
business pratice norma básica *f*; ~ **transportation** *n*
TRANSP transporte por tierra *m*; ~ **zero** *n* GEN COMM
base cero *f*

groundage *n* TRANSP derecho de andaje o de puerto *m*

grounding: ~ **cord** *n* COMP cable de conexión a tierra *m*

groundless *adj* GEN COMM infundado

grounds *n pl* PATENTS *for opposition, revocation* alegaciones *f*; ~ **and floors** ECON suelos y techos *m pl*; ~ **for**
dismissal HRM motivo de despido *m*; ♦ **on ~ of**
expediency GEN COMM en razón de la conveniencia;
on ~ of ill health HRM *retirement, leave* por motivos de
mala salud

groundwork *n* GEN COMM fundamento *m*

group *n* GEN COMM grupo *m*; ~ **accounts** *n pl* ACC
cuentas del grupo *f pl*; ~ **of affiliated companies** GEN
COMM grupo de empresas asociadas *m*; ~ **of assets** ACC
grupo de activos *m*; ~ **banking** BANK consorcio
bancario *m*; ~ **of banks** BANK grupo bancario *m*, grupo
de bancos *m*; ~ **bonus** HRM prima por grupos *f*; ~ **chief**

accountant ACC jefe(-a) contable de grupo *m,f*; ~ **of**
companies GEN COMM grupo de compañías *m*; ~ **of**
connected clients GEN COMM grupo de clientes
conectados *m*; ~ **contract** GEN COMM contrato de
grupo *m*; ~ **credit insurance** INS seguro de crédito
colectivo *m*; ~ **disability insurance** INS seguro colectivo
de incapacidad *m*; ~ **discussion** S&M discusión de
grupo *f*; ~ **dynamics** *n pl* HRM dinámica de grupo *f*;
~ **health insurance** INS seguro colectivo de enfermedad
m; ~ **incentive** HRM incentivo de grupo *m*; ~ **incentive**
scheme HRM plan de incentivo de grupo *m*;
~ **interview** GEN COMM entrevista grupal *f*; ~ **leader**
HRM jefe(-a) de grupo *m,f*, líder del grupo *mf*; ~ **life**
insurance INS seguro de vida colectivo *m*; ~ **mark**
(*GM*) GEN COMM marca de grupo *f*; ~ **piecework** HRM
trabajo a destajo por equipos *m*, trabajo a destajo por
grupos *m*; ~ **profit** ACC beneficio del grupo *m*; ~ **refer-**
ence point (*GRP*) GEN COMM punto de referencia de
grupo *m*; ~ **structure** GEN COMM estructura de grupo *f*;
~ **of taxpayers** TAX conjunto de contribuyentes *m*;
~ **training** HRM capacitación grupal *f* (*AmL*), entrenamiento grupal *m*, formación grupal *f* (*Esp*); ~ **travel**
LEIS viaje en grupo *m*; ~ **working** HRM trabajo de grupo
m

Group: ~ **Executive Board** *n* HRM Consejo Ejecutivo del
Grupo *m*; ~ **of Seven** *n* (*G-7*) ECON, GEN COMM, POL
Grupo de los Siete *m* (*G-7*)

groupage *n* TRANSP grupaje *m*; ~ **agent** TRANSP agente
de grupage *mf*; ~ **bill of lading** IMP/EXP, TRANSP
conocimiento de embarque agrupado *m*, conocimiento
de embarque de agrupamiento *m*; ~ **depot** TRANSP
depósito de grupaje *m*; ~ **operator** HRM, IMP/EXP,
TRANSP operador(a) de grupo *m,f*, operador(a) de
agrupamiento *m,f*; ~ **rate** TRANSP tasa de agrupamiento
f

grouping *n* GEN COMM agrupación *f*, MATH agrupamiento
m, clasificación *f*

growing: ~ **budget deficit** *n* GEN COMM déficit presupuestario creciente *m*; ~ **demand** *n* ECON demanda
creciente *f*; ~**-equity mortgage** *n* (*GEM*) BANK, FIN
hipoteca de amortización rápida *f*

growth *n* GEN COMM acrecentamiento *m*, crecimiento *m*,
reactivación *f*; ~ **accounting** ECON contabilidad del
crecimiento *f*; ~ **curve** ECON curva de crecimiento *f*;
~ **figures** *n pl* ECON, GEN COMM índices de crecimiento
m pl, cifras de crecimiento *f pl*; ~ **fund** STOCK fondo de
crecimiento *m*; ~ **in value** STOCK *shares legislation*
aumento de valor *m*; ~ **index** ECON índice de crecimiento *m*; ~ **industry** ECON, IND industria en
crecimiento *f*, industria en desarrollo *f*; ~ **path** GEN
COMM senda de crecimiento *f*; ~ **pole** ECON política
regional de crecimiento *f*, IND polo de desarrollo *m*;
~ **potential** ECON, GEN COMM potencial de crecimiento
m; ~ **rate** ECON, STOCK índice de crecimiento *m*;
~ **savings certificate** BANK certificado de ahorro con
crecimiento *m*; ~ **stock** STOCK acciones de compañía de
gran futuro *f pl*; ~ **strategy** ECON, GEN COMM estrategia
de crecimiento *f*; ~ **theory of the firm** ECON teoría de
crecimiento de la empresa *f*

GRP *abbr* (*group reference point*) S&M punto de referencia
de grupo *m*

GRS *abbr* (*gears*) TRANSP engranaje *m*

GRT *abbr* GEN COMM, TRANSP (*gross register ton*) tonelada
de arqueo bruto *f*, (*gross registered tonnage*) tonelaje
bruto registrado *m*

gr.wt. *abbr* (*gross weight*) GEN COMM peso bruto *m*

G-7[1] *abbr* (*Group of Seven*) ECON G-7 (*Grupo de los Siete*)

G-7[2]: **~ meeting** *n* GEN COMM reunión del G-7 *f*

gsm *abbr BrE* (*good sound merchantable*) GEN COMM *quality* totalmente aprovechable

GSP *abbr* (*generalized system of preferences*) ECON, IMP/EXP sistema general de preferencias *m*

G-spool *n* S&M *advertising* copia vídeo de un anuncio que se manda a varias cadenas de televisión para su uso, carrete G *m*

GST[1] *abbr* (*goods and services tax*) TAX impuesto sobre bienes y servicios *m*

GST[2]: **~ credit** *n* TAX desgravación de bienes y servicios *f*

GSTP *abbr* (*generalized system of tariffs and preferences*) ECON, IMP/EXP sistema generalizado de tarifas y preferencias *m*

GT *abbr* GEN COMM (*gross ton*) tonelada bruta *f*, TRANSP (*gas turbine ship*) buque de turbina de gas *m*

GTC: **~ order** *n* (*good-till-canceled order AmE, good-till-cancelled order BrE*) STOCK orden GTC *f* (*orden vigente hasta su cancelación, orden de compraventa vigente hasta su cancelación*)

GTD: **~ order** *n* (*good-till-date order*) STOCK orden GTD *f* (*orden vigente hasta su fecha*)

GT-E *abbr* (*gas turbo electric ship*) TRANSP buque de propulsión eléctrica por turbina de gas *m*

GTW *abbr* (*gross train weight*) TRANSP peso bruto del tren *m*

guar. *abbr* (*guaranteed*) GEN COMM garantizado

guarantee[1] *n* GEN COMM garantía *f*, aval *m*; **~ agreement** BANK acuerdo de garantía *m*, STOCK contrato de garantía *m*; **~ bond** GEN COMM fianza comercial *f*, STOCK fianza de garantía *f*; **~ capital** ACC, ECON, FIN, GEN COMM capital de garantía *m*; **~ deed** BANK escritura de garantía *f*; **~ from vice** INS garantía contra todo defecto *f*; **~ fund** BANK fondo de garantía *m*; **~ letter** STOCK carta de garantía *f*; **~ pay** HRM paga de garantía *f*; **~ payment** HRM pago de garantía *m*; **~ savings bank** BANK banco de ahorros en garantía *m*; **~ of signature** BANK aval de la firma *m*; ◆ **under ~** GEN COMM bajo garantía

guarantee[2] *vt* BANK afianzar, endosar, FIN afianzar, avalar, GEN COMM *loan* endosar, dar fianza, garantizar, *document* avalar

guaranteed[1] *adj* (*guar.*) GEN COMM garantizado

guaranteed[2]: **~ annual wage** *n* (*GAW*) HRM salario anual garantizado *m*; **~ bill** *n* STOCK letra avalada *f*; **~ bond** *n* FIN, STOCK bono garantizado *m*; **~ delivery** *n* STOCK entrega garantizada *f*; **~ facility** *n* FIN línea de crédito garantizada *f*; **~ income** *n* FIN ingreso garantizado *m*; **~ income contract** *n* (*GIC*) INS póliza de ingresos garantizados *f*; **~ income supplement** *n* TAX suplemento garantizado de ingresos *m*; **~ insurability** *n* INS asegurabilidad garantizada *f*; **~ investment** *n* FIN inversión garantizada *f*; **~ investment certificate** *n* FIN certificado de inversión garantizado *m*; **~ investment contract** *n* (*GIC*) FIN condiciones generales del seguro *f pl*, contrato de inversión garantizado *m*; **~ issue** *n*

STOCK emisión garantizada *f*; **~ letter of credit** *n* BANK, FIN carta de crédito garantizada *f*; **~ liability** *n* ACC, BANK pasivo de garantía *m*; **~ minimum wage** *n* ECON, HRM salario mínimo garantizado *m*; **~ mortgage** *n* BANK, PROP hipoteca garantizada *f*; **~ mortgage certificate** *n* BANK certificado con garantía de hipoteca *m*, certificado con garantía hipotecaria *m*; **~ price** *n* FIN precio garantizado *m*; **~ recovery of investment principle** *n* (*GRIP*) FIN principio de la garantía de recuperación de la inversión *m*; **~ securities** *n pl* STOCK títulos garantizados *m pl*; **~ share** *n* STOCK acción garantizada *f*; **~ stock** *n* STOCK acciones con intereses garantizados *f pl*; **~ term** *n* BANK plazo garantizado *m*; **~ wage** *n* HRM salario garantizado *m*; **~ week** *n* HRM semana garantizada *f*

guarantor *n* BANK, GEN COMM avalista *mf*, garante *mf*; **~ underwritten note** (*GUN*) STOCK nota de compromiso de avalista *f*

guaranty *see* guarantee

guard: **~ books** *n pl jarg* S&M *advertising* libros de resguardo *m pl*

guard against *vt* GEN COMM *risk* estar prevenido contra

guardian *n* GEN COMM tutor(a) *m,f*; **~ deed** PROP escritura de tutoría *f*

guesstimate[1] *n infrml* GEN COMM tanteo *m*

guesstimate[2] *vt infrml* GEN COMM estimar por aproximación

guestworker *n* HRM trabajador(a) invitado(a) *m,f*

guide *n* GEN COMM *manual* guía *m*; **~ price** GEN COMM precio guía *m*

guidelines *n pl* GEN COMM *working practices* directrices *f pl*

guiding: **~ principle** *n* GEN COMM principio director *m*

guild *n* HRM gremio *m*; **~ socialism** *BrE* HRM socialismo gremial *m*

guilty[1] *adj* LAW culpable

guilty[2]: **~ person** *n* LAW culpable *mf*

Gulf: **~ Plus** *n* ECON acuerdo secreto del precio del petróleo; **~ War** *n* POL Guerra del Golfo *f*

gun[1]: **~ jumping** *n* STOCK operación basada en la información confidencial e ilegal

gun[2] *vt jarg* STOCK provocar la cesión forzada de cierta cantidad de acciones por un rival

GUN *abbr* (*guarantor underwritten note*) STOCK nota de compromiso de avalista *f*

gut: **~ feeling** *n infrml* S&M instinto *m*

gutter *n* MEDIA *print* medianil *m*; **~ politics** POL política sensacionalista *f*; **~ press** MEDIA prensa amarilla *f*, prensa sensacionalista *f*

guttersnipe *n jarg* S&M *advertising* pequeño poster puesto en la calle

guy *n* TRANSP *rope* obenque *m*

GVW *abbr* (*gross vehicle weight*) TRANSP peso bruto del vehículo *m*

gypsy *n* TRANSP *loading* capirón *m*

gyrocompass *n* (*GC*) TRANSP *navigation* girocompás *m*

H

ha *abbr* (*hectare*) GEN COMM ha (*hectárea*)

habeas corpus *n* LAW *criminal* habeas corpus *m*

habendum *n* LAW cláusula de una escritura donde se determina la identidad y extensión de los derechos transferidos

habitat *n* ENVIR *of wildlife* hábitat *m*

hack *vt infrml* COMP *break into systems* piratear

hacker[1]: **~-proof** *adj infrml* COMP *system* a prueba de piratas

hacker[2] *n infrml* COMP pirata informático(-a) *m,f*

hacking *n infrml* COMP pirateo informático *m*

haggle *vi* GEN COMM regatear; ◆ **~ over** GEN COMM regatear sobre

Hague: The ~ Rules *n pl* TRANSP *shipping* Reglas de La Haya *f pl*; **~ Tribunal** *n* ECON, LAW Tribunal de la Haya *m*; **~ Visby Rule** *n* TRANSP *shipping* Norma Visby de la Haya *f*

Haigh: ~ Simons definition of income *n* ECON definición del ingreso según Haigh Simons *f*

half[1]: **~-duplex** *adj* COMP semiduplex; **~-monthly** *adj* GEN COMM *fortnightly* quincenal; **~-yearly** *adj* GEN COMM semestral

half[2]: **~-monthly** *adv* GEN COMM quincenalmente; **~-yearly** *adv* GEN COMM semestralmente

half[3]: **~ adder** *n* COMP *hardware* semisumadora *f*; **~ board** *n* LEIS media pensión *f*; **~ fare** *n* GEN COMM media tarifa *f*; **~ height** *n* (*H/H*) TRANSP *container* media altura *f*; **~-life** *n infrml* STOCK vida media *f*; **~ a strike price interval** *n* STOCK *Eurodollar options* intervalo a mitad de precio de ejercicio *m*; **~-tilt container** *n* (*ht*) TRANSP contenedor con media cubierta de lona *m*; **~ year** *n* GEN COMM semestre *m*; **~-year rule** *n* TAX norma del medio año *f*; **~-yearly dividend** *n* STOCK dividendo semestral *m*; ◆ **on ~-time** GEN COMM a media jornada

halftone *n* MEDIA medios tonos *m pl*

hall: ~ test *n* S&M *research* prueba en sala *f*

hallmark *n BrE* (*cf assay mark AmE*) BANK marca de aleación *f*

halo *n jarg* S&M *advertising* halo *m*

Halsey: ~ Premium Plan *n* HRM plan Halsey de primas *m*

halt *n* STOCK *trading* vacilación *f*

halve *vt* GEN COMM dividir en dos partes

Hamburg: ~ Rules *n pl* TRANSP *shipping* Reglas de Hamburgo *f pl*

hammer[1]: **~ price** *n jarg* STOCK precio de salida *m*, precio de subasta *m*

hammer[2]: **~ home an argument** *phr* GEN COMM *point of view* subrayar un argumento; **~ the market** *phr* STOCK machacar el mercado

hammered *adj jarg* STOCK insolvente

hamper *vt* GEN COMM *growth* obstaculizar

hand[1]: **by ~** *adj* GEN COMM a mano; **~-held** *adj* COMP manipulado, S&M en mano; **~-woven** *adj* IND tejido a mano

hand[2]: **~ barrow** *n* TRANSP carretón de mano *m*; **~ calculator** *n* COMP calculadora mecánica *f*; **~-eye**

span *n* ADMIN lapso ojo-mano *m*; **~ pallet transporter** *n* TRANSP *cargo handling equipment* transpaleta *f*

hand[3]: **have the upper ~** *phr* GEN COMM tener ventaja; **~ in one's resignation** *phr* HRM presentar su dimisión (*Esp*), presentar su renuncia (*AmL*); **on the other ~** *phr* GEN COMM por otro lado

handbill *n* COMMS volante *m*

handbook *n* GEN COMM folleto *m*

handle[1] *n* COMP manejo *m*

handle[2] *vt* COMP, FIN, GEN COMM, TRANSP manejar; ◆ **~ with care** GEN COMM, TRANSP *notice on parcels* manejar con cuidado; **~ large sums of money** FIN manejar grandes sumas de dinero

handling *n* COMP manejo *m*, TRANSP *of goods* manipulación *f*; **~ allowance** STOCK descuento de transferencia *m*; **~ charge** S&M coste de manipulación *m* (*Esp*), costo de manipulación *m* (*AmL*); **~ charges** *n pl* ACC, BANK, FIN, GEN COMM cargos por tramitación *m pl*, gastos de transferencia *m pl*

handmade *adj* GEN COMM, IND, S&M hecho a mano

handout *n* S&M folleto *m*

hands[1]: **~-on** *adj* HRM *experience* práctico

hands[2]: **~-off policy** *n* ECON, POL política de no intervención *f*; **~-on experience** *n* HRM *practical learning* experiencia práctica *f*; **~-on session** *n* POL sesión práctica *f*; **~-on training** *n* HRM entrenamiento práctico *m*

hands[3]: **in the ~ of** *phr* GEN COMM en las manos de; **be in the ~ of a receiver** *phr* GEN COMM estar en manos de un liquidador, estar en manos de un síndico, estar en manos de un recaudador; **in the ~ of a third party** *phr* GEN COMM en manos de terceros; **our ~ are tied** *phr* GEN COMM tenemos las manos atadas

handshaking *n* COMP, COMMS establecimiento de comunicación *m*

handwritten *adj* COMMS manuscrito

handyman *n* HRM ayudante(-a) general *m,f*, hombre para todo *m*

Hang: ~ Seng Index *n* STOCK índice Hang Seng *m*

hangout *n AmE infrml* PROP balance restante de un préstamo cuando el plazo del préstamo es más amplio que el plazo del arriendo

hansom: ~ cab economy *n* ECON tipo de economía que propugna el mantenimiento de la industria tradicional

harbor *AmE see* **harbour** *BrE*

harbour *n BrE* TRANSP puerto *m*; **~ authority** *BrE* TRANSP autoridad portuaria *f*; **~ dues** *n pl BrE* IMP/ EXP, TAX, TRANSP *shipping* derechos de puerto *m pl*; **~ facilities** *n pl BrE* TRANSP instalaciones portuarias *f pl*; **~ master** *BrE* HRM capitán de puerto *m*; **~ station** *BrE* TRANSP estación marítima *f*

hard[1] *adj* GEN COMM *data, facts* malo, *rigid* firme; **~-boiled** HRM *attitude*, S&M duro; **~ and fast** GEN COMM *rules* estricto; **~-headed** S&M práctico, realista; **~ hit** GEN COMM *by loss* muy afectado

hard[2]: **~ bargaining** *n* GEN COMM negociación dura *f*; **~ cash** *n* GEN COMM *funds* dinero en efectivo *m*, efectivo *m*; **~ commodity** *n* ECON, IND bien duradero *m*, producto duradero *m*; **~ copy** *n* COMP *printout of file* copia directa en papel *f*; **~ core** *n* ACC, ECON *of shareholders*, STOCK núcleo duro *m*; **~ cost** *n* FIN *construction, real estate* coste gravoso *m* (*Esp*), costo gravoso *m* (*AmL*); **~ currency** *n* ECON moneda fuerte *f*; **~ discount** *n* FIN descuento en efectivo *m*; **~ discounter** *n* FIN el que descuenta en fijo; **~ disk** *n* COMP disco duro *m*; **~ disk drive** *n* COMP unidad de disco duro *f*; **~ disk unit** *n* COMP unidad de disco duro *f*; **~ dollars** *n pl* ECON dólares fuertes *m pl*; **~ error** *n* COMP error de máquina *m*; **~ goods** *n pl* GEN COMM, S&M bienes de consumo duraderos *m pl*; **~ graft** *n* HRM trabajo duro *m*; **~ hat** *n* HRM, IND casco protector *m*; **~ loan** *n* BANK préstamo en firme *m*; **~ money** *n* GEN COMM dinero en efectivo *m*, dinero en metálico *m*, WEL dinero destinado por el gobierno a educación; **~ page break** *n* COMP *word processing* salto de página forzado *m*; **~ return** *n* COMP retorno manual *m*; **~ selling** *n* S&M publicidad agresiva *f*, venta agresiva *f*

hardback *adj* MEDIA *book* con tapa dura

hardening: **~ market** *n* GEN COMM mercado con tendencia firme *m*

hardliner *n* POL persona inflexible que no acepta cambios

hardship *n* WEL dificultades excepcionales gravosas *f pl*; **~ categories** *n pl* WEL categorías de dificultad *f pl*

hardware *n* COMP equipo físico *m*, hardware *m*, GEN COMM quincalla *f*; **~ compatibility** COMP compatibilidad de equipos *f*; **~ configuration** COMP configuración del equipo *f*; **~ device** COMP dispositivo automático *m*; **~ failure** COMP fallo del equipo *m*; **~ firm** COMP firma de componentes electrónicos *f*; **~ requirement** COMP requerimiento de equipo *m*; **~ security** COMP seguridad del equipo *f*; **~ specialist** COMP especialista en equipo físico *mf*

harmonic: **~ mean** *n* MATH media armónica *f*

harmonization *n* GEN COMM armonización *f*; **~ conference** TRANSP conferencia de armonización *f*; **~ of excise duties** IMP/EXP armonización de impuestos sobre el consumo *f*; **~ process** GEN COMM proceso de armonización *m*

harmonize *vt* GEN COMM armonizar

Harrod: **~ Domar model** *n* ECON modelo de Harrod Domar *m*

harsh: **~ competition** *n* ECON competencia sin cuartel *f*

hat: **~ money** *n infrml* TRANSP prima de carga *f*

hatch: **~ covering** *n* TRANSP tapa de la escotilla *f*

hatchman *n* HRM, TRANSP *navegación* escotillero *m*

hatchway *n* HRM escotilla *f*, TRANSP compuerta de esclusa *f*

haulage: **~ company** *n* TRANSP compañía de transportes *f*; **~ contractor** *n* TRANSP contratista de transportes *mf*

Havana: **~ Charter** *n* ECON *international* estatuto de La Habana *m*

have: **~ access to information** *phr* GEN COMM tener acceso a la información; **~ a competitive advantage over sb** *phr* ECON competir ventajosamente con alguien; **~ an equity interest** *phr* STOCK tener un interés propio; **~ a grievance against sb** *phr* HRM tener queja de alguien; **~ a head start** *phr* GEN COMM tener ventaja; **~ holdings in a company** *phr* GEN COMM tener participaciones en una empresa; **~ it out with sb** *phr* GEN COMM resolver un problema hablando; **~ a share in a business** *phr* GEN COMM tener una participación en

un negocio; **they ~ the exclusive agency for our firm** *phr* GEN COMM tienen la representación exclusiva de nuestra firma

HAWB *abbr* (*house air waybill*) IMP/EXP, TRANSP *aviation* conocimiento de embarque aéreo local *m*

hazard *n* GEN COMM riesgo *m*; **~ bonus** ACC, FIN, GEN COMM, TAX bonificación por riesgo *f*; **~ insurance** INS seguro contra todo riesgo *m*

hazardous: **~ cargo** *n* TRANSP cargamento peligroso *m*; **~ chemical** *n* (*hazchem*) ENVIR, TRANSP sustancia química peligrosa *f*; **~ polluting substance** *n* (*HPS*) ENVIR, TRANSP sustancia con riesgo de polución *f*, sustancia peligrosa contaminante *f*; **~ substance** *n* ENVIR sustancia tóxica *f*

hazchem[1] *abbr* (*hazardous chemical*) ENVIR, TRANSP sustancia química peligrosa *f*

hazchem[2]: **~ code** *n* TRANSP código hazchem *m*

h.b. *abbr* (*hours of business*) GEN COMM horas de oficina *f pl*

HC *abbr* POL *BrE* (*House of Commons*) Cámara de los Comunes *f*, ≈ Cámara Baja *f* (*Esp*), ≈ Congreso *m* (*Esp*), ≈ Congreso de los Diputados *m* (*Esp*), TRANSP (*hydraulic coupling*) acoplamiento hidráulico *m*

head[1] *abbr jarg* (*headline*) MEDIA titular *m*

head[2] *n* ACC *of negociating team*, COMP, GEN COMM cabeza *f*, HRM jefe(-a) *m,f*, MEDIA *of page* cabecera *f*; **~ accountant** ACC jefe(-a) contable *m,f*; **~ of the audit group** ACC director(a) del equipo auditor *m,f*; **~ buyer** HRM, MGMNT, S&M director(a) de compras *m,f*, jefe(-a) de compras *m,f*, responsable de compras *mf*; **~ clerk** HRM, LAW, MGMNT jefe(-a) de oficina *m,f*; **~ crash** *jarg* COMP fractura de cabeza *f* (*jarg*), rotura de cabeza *f* (*jarg*); **~ of department** (*HoD*) HRM jefe(-a) de departamento *m,f*, jefe(-a) de sección *m,f*; **~ foreman** GEN COMM, HRM jefe(-a) de taller *m,f*, supervisor(a) en jefe *m,f*; **~ of household** TAX cabeza de familia *f*; **~ lease** LAW contrato de arrendamiento principal *m*; **~ of legal department** *BrE* (*cf general counsel AmE*) HRM, LAW director(a) jurídico *m,f*; **~ office** (*H.O.*) GEN COMM casa matriz *f*, oficina central *f*, oficina matriz *f*, oficina principal *f*, sede principal *f*; **~ of personnel** HRM, MGMNT director(a) de personal *m,f*; **~ of section** HRM jefe(-a) de sección *m,f*; **~ and shoulders** ECON cabeza y hombros; **~ of state** POL jefe(-a) de estado *f*; **~ tax** ECON, TAX impuesto de capitación *m*; **~ of unit** HRM jefe(-a) de unidad *m,f*

Head: **~ of State** *n* POL Jefe(-a) del Estado *m,f*

header *n* ADMIN cabecera *f*, COMP *typography* encabezamiento *m*, GEN COMM, MEDIA *broadcast* cabecera *f*; **~ bar** TRANSP *container* barra desmontable *f*

headhunt[1] *n* HRM caza de talentos *f*

headhunt[2] *vi* HRM buscar

headhunter *n* HRM cazatalentos *mf*

heading[1] *n* ACC *balance sheet* encabezamiento *m* (*Esp*), epígrafe *m* (*Esp*), título *m*, COMMS, GEN COMM membrete *m*

heading[2]: **be ~ for** *phr* GEN COMM estar encabezado por

headline *n* (*head*) MEDIA *newspaper* titular *m*; **~ point** TRANSP *aviation* punto de cabecera *m*; **~ rate** ECON *of inflation* proporción principal *f*

headquarter *vt AmE* ADMIN establecer la sede

headquarters *n* (*h.q.*, *HQ*) GEN COMM oficina principal *f*, sede principal *f*, *of company* sede central *f*, HRM, IND dirección central *f*

health *n* GEN COMM, WEL salud *f*; ~ **care** GEN COMM atención de la salud *f*; ~ **benefits** *n pl* WEL prestaciones sanitarias *f pl*; ~ **care industry** IND sector de la atención médica *m*; ~ **center** *AmE*, ~ **centre** *BrE* WEL ambulatorio *m*, centro de salud *m*; ~ **club** LEIS club de salud *m*; ~ **economics** ECON, HRM economía de la salud *f*; ~ **education** GEN COMM educación sanitaria *f*; ~ **farm** WEL centro de salud *m*; ~ **foods** *n pl* GEN COMM, S&M alimentos naturales *m pl*; ~ **hazard** IND, WEL riesgo para la salud *m*; ~ **insurance** INS seguro de enfermedad *m*; ~ **insurance scheme** HRM, INS plan de seguros de enfermedad *m*; ~ **maintenance organization** *AmE* (*HMO*) INS organización estadounidense para la preservación de la salud; ~ **officer** HRM, WEL inspector(a) de sanidad *m,f*; ~ **record** WEL historial médico *m*; ~ **regulation** HRM, LAW reglamento de higiene *m*, regulación sanitaria *f*, norma sanitaria *f*; ~ **risk** WEL riesgo para la salud *m*; ~ **and safety** HRM, WEL seguridad e higiene *f*; ~ **sector** WEL sector sanitario *m*; ~ **services plan** INS, WEL plan de servicios de salud *m*; ~ **standard** LAW norma sanitaria *f*

Health: ~ **Authority** *n BrE* GEN COMM autoridad sanitaria *f*; ~ **and Safety at Work Act** *n* (*HSWA*) HRM, LAW, WEL ley británica de higiene y seguridad en el trabajo; ~ **and Safety Executive** *n BrE* (*HSE*) WEL oficina británica para la defensa de la seguridad y salud en el lugar de trabajo; ~ **and Safety Inspectorate** *n BrE* WEL cuerpo de inspectores sociales

healthy *adj* GEN COMM *competition, market* sano

hear: ~ **a case in chambers** *phr* LAW ver una causa a puerta cerrada; ~ **sth through the grapevine** *phr infrml* COMMS enterarse por fuente no identificada

hearing *n* LAW audiencia *f*, vista *f*

hearsay *n* LAW testimonio de oídas *m*

heated: ~ **container** *n* TRANSP contenedor calorífico *m*

heater *n* (*htr*) GEN COMM calentador *m*

heating: ~ **boiler plant** *n* IND planta de calefacción *f*; ~ **industry** *n* ECON, IND industria de calefacción *f*; ~ **power station** *n* IND central de calefacción *f*; ~ **surface** *n* (*HS*) GEN COMM superficie calefactora *f*

heavily[1]: ~ **traded** *adj* STOCK muy negociado

heavily[2] *adv* GEN COMM sumamente, *concentrate* altamente, TAX excesivamente

heavy[1] *adj* ECON, GEN COMM fuerte, STOCK *market* derrimido

heavy[2]: ~ **advertising** *n* S&M publicidad masiva *f*; ~ **demand** *n* S&M fuerte demanda *f*; ~ **duties** *n pl* TAX derechos elevados *m pl*; ~ **engineering** *n* IND ingeniería pesada *f*; ~ **fall of prices** *n* ECON, STOCK caída fuerte de los precios *f*; ~ **fuel** *n* ENVIR combustible pesado *m*; ~ **goods traffic** *n* TRANSP tráfico de mercancías pesadas *m*; ~ **goods vehicle** *n* (*HGV*) TRANSP vehículo para cargas pesadas *m*; ~ **industrial plant** *n* IND planta de industria pesada *f*; ~ **industry** *n* ECON, IND industria pesada *f*; ~ **jet** *n* TRANSP *wide-body aircraft* reactor de gran tonelaje *m*; ~ **lift** *n* (*h/lift*) TRANSP *handling* carga pesada *f*; ~ **lift mast crane** *n* TRANSP *shipping* grúa de mástil para cargas pesadas *f*; ~ **lift ship** *n* TRANSP buque para cargas pesadas *m*; ~ **lifting beam** *n* TRANSP *shipping* vigueta de izado de grandes pesos *f*; ~ **metal concentration** *n* ENVIR concentración de metales pesados *f*; ~ **share** *n* FIN, STOCK acción cotizada a menos de un dolar *f*; ~ **user** *n* COMP usuario(-a)

continuo(-a) *m,f*; ~ **viewer** *n* S&M persona que ve mucha TV

Heckscher-Ohlin: ~ **theorem** *n* ECON teorema Heckscher-Ohlin *m*; ~ **trade theorem** *n* ECON teorema comercial de Heckscher-Ohlin *m*

hectare *n* (*ha*) GEN COMM hectárea *f* (*ha*)

hedge[1] *n* STOCK cerca *f*; ~ **clause** STOCK cláusula de protección *f*; ~ **cost** STOCK coste cubierto *m* (*Esp*), costo cubierto *m* (*AmL*); ~ **fund** *jarg* STOCK fondo especulativo *m*; ~ **management** STOCK manipulación de la cobertura *f*; ~ **manager** STOCK administrador(a) de la cobertura *m,f*; ~ **period** STOCK periodo de protección *m*; ~ **ratio** STOCK proporción de cobertura *f*; ~ **trading** STOCK operación de cobertura *f*

hedge[2] *vt* STOCK proteger; ♦ ~ **one's bets** GEN COMM invertir con cobertura; ~ **the risk** STOCK cubrir el riesgo

hedged: ~ **asset** *n* ACC activo protegido *m*; ~ **liability** *n* ACC, FIN pasivo protegido *m*; ~ **short sale** *n* STOCK venta en descubierto protegida *f*; ~ **tender** *n* STOCK oferta afianzada *f*, oferta garantizada *f*

hedging *n* BANK hedging *m*, ECON arbitraje de cartera *m*, GEN COMM cobertura *f*, IMP/EXP, LAW arbitraje de cartera *m*, STOCK cobertura contra cambio de precios *f*, TAX arbitraje de cartera *m*; ~ **goal** STOCK objetivo de cobertura *m*; ~ **operation** FIN, STOCK operación de protección cambiaria *f*, operación de cobertura *f*; ~ **strategy** STOCK estrategia de cobertura contra cambios de precio

hedonic: ~ **output** *n* ECON rendimiento hedónico *m*; ~ **price** *n* ECON precio hedónico *m*; ~ **wage** *n* ECON salario hedónico *m*

hefty *adj* ECON, GEN COMM *price, debt* fuerte

hegemony *n* POL hegemonía *f*

heighten *vt* GEN COMM elevar

heir *n* LAW, PROP, TAX heredero(-a) *m,f*

heirs: ~ **and assigns** *n pl* LAW *deeds and wills* herederos y sucesores *m pl*

held: **not** ~ *adj* STOCK no detentado

helicopter: ~ **money** *n jarg* ECON incremento en las existencias de dinero que hace incrementar la demanda y el precio de los bienes

heliport *n* TRANSP helipuerto *m*

helistop *n* TRANSP heliestación *f*

help *n* GEN COMM ayuda *f*; ~ **key** COMP tecla de ayuda *f*; ~ **mode** COMP modo de ayuda *m*

hereby: **I** ~ **testify that** *phr* LAW por la presente testifico que

herein *adv* COMMS aquí dentro

hereof *adv* COMMS de aquí

hereto *adv* COMMS a esto

hereunder *adv* COMMS más abajo

Herfindahl-Hirschman: ~ **index** *n* ECON index de Herfindahl-Hirschman *m*

Hermes: ~ **model** *n* ECON modelo de Hermes *m*

hesiflation *n jarg* ECON *macroeconomics* inflación subyacente *f*

heterogeneous[1] *adj* GEN COMM heterogéneo

heterogeneous[2]: ~ **cargo** *n* TRANSP carga heterogénea *f*

heteroscedasticity *n* MATH heteroscedasticidad *f*

heuristic *adj* COMP, GEN COMM, MGMNT *problem solving* heurístico

heuristics *n pl* COMP, GEN COMM, MGMNT heurística *f*

H-form *n* ECON *business organization division* forma H *f*

H/H *abbr* (*half height*) TRANSP *container* media altura *f*

hiccup *n* GEN COMM *setback* bache *m*

Hicks: ~ **Charts** *n pl* ECON gráficas de Hicks *f pl*

Hicksian: ~ **income measure** *n* ECON medida del ingreso de Hicks *f*

hidden: ~ **agenda** *n* GEN COMM, MGMNT agenda oculta *f*; ~ **asset** *n* ACC, FIN activo oculto *m*; ~ **damage** *n* INS *maritime* avería oculta *f*; ~ **decision** *n* GEN COMM decisión secreta *f*; ~ **file** *n* COMP fichero oculto *m*; ~ **inflation** *n* ECON inflación larvada *f*; ~ **price increase** *n* S&M aumento de precio oculto *m*; ~ **reserve** *n* ACC, BANK reserva oculta *f*; ~ **tax** *n* TAX impuesto encubierto *m*; ~ **unemployment** *n* ECON, HRM desempleo encubierto *m*; ~ **value** *n* S&M valor oculto *m*

hide *vt* GEN COMM ocultar

hiding: ~ **hand** *n* ECON mano oculta *f*

hierarchical: ~ **decomposition principle** *n* MGMNT principio de descomposición jerárquica *m*; ~ **task analysis** *n* (*HTA*) MGMNT análisis de tareas jerárquicos *m*

hierarchy *n* HRM jerarquía *f*; ~ **of effects** S&M jerarquía de efectos *f*; ~ **of needs** HRM jerarquía de necesidades *f*; ~ **of objectives** GEN COMM jerarquía de objetivos *f*

high[1] *adj* STOCK alto; ~**-caliber** *AmE*, ~**-calibre** *BrE* HRM *staff* de alto potencial, de gran valía; ~**-class** GEN COMM, LEIS *hotel* de primera clase; ~**-profile** GEN COMM, S&M prominente, de primera línea; ~**-quality** GEN COMM de alta calidad; ~**-return** STOCK de alto rendimiento; ~**-rise** PROP *building* de alto techo; ~**-risk** FIN, STOCK de alto riesgo; ~**-strength** (*HS*) GEN COMM de gran resistencia; ~**-volume** STOCK de gran volumen; ~**-yielding** STOCK de alto rendimiento

high[2]: ~ **achiever** *n* GEN COMM, HRM persona de elevado desempeño *f*, persona de elevado rendimiento *f*, persona de buen rendimiento *f*; ~ **added-value product** *n* ECON, IND, TAX producto de gran valor añadido *m*, producto de alto valor añadido *m*; ~**-cost labor** *AmE*, ~**-cost labour** *BrE n* HRM mano de obra de coste elevado *f* (*Esp*), mano de obra de costo elevado *f* (*AmL*), trabajo de alto coste *m* (*Esp*), trabajo de alto costo *m* (*AmL*), trabajo de coste elevado *m* (*Esp*), trabajo de costo elevado *m* (*AmL*); ~ **cost of living** *n* ECON alto coste de la vida *m* (*Esp*), alto costo de vida *m* (*AmL*); ~ **costs** *n pl* FIN costes elevados *m pl* (*Esp*), costos elevados *m pl* (*AmL*); ~ **credit** *n* BANK, FIN crédito elevado *m*; ~ **cube** *n* (*HC*) TRANSP cubo elevado *m*, *container* depósito superior *m*; ~ **density** *n* COMP alta densidad *f*; ~**-density cargo** *n* TRANSP carga de alta densidad *f*; ~**-density disk** *n* COMP disco de alta densidad *m*; ~**-density freight** *n* TRANSP flete de alta densidad *m*; ~ **employment surplus** *n* ECON plusvalía elevada de empleo *f*, HRM sobreoferta de trabajo *f*; ~**-end computer** *n* COMP computador de nivel superior *f* (*AmL*), computadora de nivel superior *f* (*AmL*), ordenador del nivel superior *m* (*Esp*); ~**-end computing** *n* COMP computación de alto nivel *f*, informática de alto nivel *f*; ~ **end of the range** *n* STOCK extremo alto de la banda *m*; ~ **executive** *n* GEN COMM, HRM, MGMNT alto(-a) ejecutivo(-a) *m,f*; ~ **finance** *n* FIN las altas finanzas *f pl*; ~**-flier** *n* GEN COMM, HRM persona de buen rendimiento *f*, MGMNT *person* persona con éxito personal *f*, STOCK valor cuyo precio crece muy rápidamente; ~**-flying stock** *n* STOCK valor de altura *m*;

very ~ **frequency** *n* (*VHF*) COMMS *of radio* frecuencia muy alta *f* (*VHF*); ~ **frequency radiotelephony** *n* (*RTh*) COMMS, MEDIA, TRANSP *shipping* radiotelefonía de alta frecuencia *f*; ~ **gearing** *n BrE* (*cf high leverage AmE*) ACC apalancamiento alto *m*, nivel elevado de endeudamiento *m*; ~**-grade bond** *n* FIN, STOCK bono de primera clase *m*; ~ **image** *n jarg* GEN COMM imagen sobresaliente *f*; ~ **impact case** *n* TAX caso de gran repercusión *m*; ~**-income taxpayer** *n* TAX contribuyente de ingresos elevados *mf*; ~ **involvement products** *n pl* S&M productos cuya compra debe ser muy meditada *m pl*; ~ **-level decision** *n* GEN COMM decisión de alto nivel *f*; ~**-level design** *n* MGMNT diseño de alto nivel *m*; ~**-level language** *n* (*HLL*) COMP lenguaje de alto nivel *m* (*LAN*); ~ **leverage** *n AmE* (*cf high gearing BrE*) ACC apalancamiento alto *m*, nivel elevado de endeudamiento *m*; ~**-leveraged takeover** *n AmE* (*HLT*) GEN COMM compra de alto apalancamiento *f*; ~ **loader** *n* TRANSP *vehicle* cargador elevado *m*; ~ **office** *n* HRM alto cargo *m*; ~**-order language** *n* COMP lenguaje de orden superior *m*; ~**-powered money** *n* ECON dinero de alta potencia *m*; ~**-premium convertible debenture** *n* FIN, STOCK obligación convertible de prima alta *f*; ~**-pressure selling** *n* S&M venta agresiva *f*, venta dinámica *f*; ~ **price** *n* STOCK *futures* precio elevado *m*; ~ **rate of investment** *n* ECON, FIN índice elevado de inversión *m*; ~ **resolution** *n* COMP, MEDIA alta definición *f*; ~**-risk venture** *n* GEN COMM empresa de alto riesgo *f*; ~**-season fare** *n* LEIS tarifa de temporada alta *f*; ~**-speed memory** *n* COMP memoria de alta velocidad *f*; ~**-speed printer** *n* COMP impresora de alta velocidad *f*; ~**-speed train** *n* (*HST*) TRANSP Tren de Alta Velocidad *m* (*TAV*); ~ **standard of living** *n* WEL alto nivel de vida *m*; ~ **standards** *n pl* GEN COMM altos niveles *m pl*; ~ **stowage factor** *n* TRANSP factor de estiba alto *m*; ~**-stream industry** *n* ECON, IND industria de alta tecnología *f*; ~ **street** *n BrE* (*cf main street AmE*) S&M *of town* calle céntrica y comercial *f*, calle mayor *f*, calle principal *f*; ~ **street price** *n BrE* (*cf main street price AmE*) GEN COMM, S&M precio de calle principal *m*; ~ **street share shop** *n BrE* STOCK centro de inversiones situado en lugar céntrico *m*; ~ **street spending** *n BrE* (*cf main street spending AmE*) ECON gastos de calle mayor *m pl*; ~**-tech stock** *n* STOCK acciones de empresas de alta tecnología *f pl*; ~ **technology** *n* GEN COMM, IND alta tecnología *f*; ~**-value clearings** *n BrE* BANK compensaciones de valor elevado *f pl*; ~ **value to low weight ratio** *n* TRANSP relación valor elevado por peso bajo *f*; ~ **volume paper clearings** *n pl BrE* BANK compensaciones en papel de gran volumen *f*; ~**-water mark** *n* (*HWM*) TRANSP *maritime* nivel de la pleamar *m*; ~**-yield financing** *n* FIN financiación de alto rendimiento *f*

High: ~ **Court** *n BrE* (*cf Supreme Court AmE*) LAW, POL Tribunal Supremo *m*, ≈ Audiencia Nacional *f* (*Esp*); ~ **Court of Justice** *n* LAW Tribunal Superior de Justicia *m*

higher: ~ **education** *n* GEN COMM, WEL educación superior *f*; ~ **income bracket** *n* ECON grupo de ingresos más altos *m*

Higher: ~ **National Certificate** *n BrE* (*HNC*) WEL certificado de estudios superiores; ~ **National Diploma** *n BrE* (*HND*) WEL diploma de estudios superiores

highest: ~ **and best use** *n* PROP *appraisal* mejor uso posible *m*; ~ **bid** *n* STOCK oferta más elevada *f*; ~ **bidder**

n GEN COMM, STOCK mejor postor(a) *m,f*; **~ price** *n* STOCK mayor precio *m*; **~ tender** *n* GEN COMM oferta más alta *f*

highlight[1] *n* GEN COMM rasgo saliente *m*

highlight[2] *vt* COMP *word processed document*, GEN COMM *differences* destacar

highlighting *n* COMP realce *m*

highly: **~ competitive** *adj* GEN COMM sumamente competitivo, altamente competitivo; **~-geared** *adj* BANK, FIN, STOCK con índice de endeudamiento elevado; **~-skilled** *adj* HRM altamente cualificado

highs *n pl* STOCK cotizaciones máximas *f pl*

highway *n AmE* (*cf trunk road BrE, A-road BrE*) TRANSP carretera nacional *f*, carretera principal *f*; **~ order** LAW, PROP *compulsory purchase* orden de expropiación por causa de utilidad pública

hike[1] *n* ACC, ECON, FIN *in price*, GEN COMM aumento *m*

hike[2] *vt* ACC, ECON, FIN *price*, GEN COMM aumentar

Himalaya: **~ clause** *n* TRANSP *shipping* cláusula Himalaya *f*

hinder *vt* GEN COMM obstaculizar

hindrance *n* GEN COMM estorbo *m*

hindsight *n* TAX retrospección *f*

hinge on *vt* GEN COMM depender de

hint *n* GEN COMM pista *f*

hire[1]: **~ of money** *n* BANK, FIN préstamo de capitales *m*; **~ purchase** *n* (*HP, cf installment purchase AmE*) GEN COMM, S&M compra a plazos *f*; **~ purchase agreement** *n* FIN contrato de compra a plazos *m*; **~ and reward operator** *n* TRANSP *road haulage* operador(a) con salario y bonificación *m,f*

hire[2] *vt* GEN COMM alquilar, HRM *staff* contratar, PROP *accommodation* alquilar; ◆ **~ and fire** HRM contratar y despedir

hire[2]: **for ~** *phr* PROP en alquiler; **on ~ purchase** *phr BrE* FIN en alquiler con derecho a compra

histogram *n* MATH diagrama de frecuencia *m*, histograma *m*

historic[1] *adj* GEN COMM histórico

historic[2]: **~ structure** *n* PROP estructura histórica *f*

historical: **~ cost** *n* ACC coste histórico *m* (*Esp*), costo histórico *m* (*AmL*), precio de adquisición *m*; **~ cost principle** *n* ACC criterios del precio de adquisición *m pl*, principio de coste histórico *m* (*Esp*), principio de costo histórico *m* (*AmL*); **~ exchange rate** *n* ECON tipo de cambio histórico *m*; **~ loss** *n* ACC pérdida inicial *f*; **~ trade** *n* TRANSP comercio histórico *m*; **~ volatility** *n* STOCK volatilidad histórica *f*; **~ yield** *n* STOCK rendimiento histórico *m*, rendimiento inicial *m*

Historical: **~ School** *n* ECON Escuela Histórica *f*

historically *adv* GEN COMM históricamente

hit[1]: **~-or-miss** *adj infrml* GEN COMM *method* al azar

hit[2]: **~-and-run strike** *n* HRM, IND huelga relámpago *f*; **~ list** *n infrml* POL lista de objetivos a cubrir, S&M lista de éxitos *f*; **~ order** *n* STOCK orden de venta a un precio dado *f*; **~ rate** *n* S&M índice de éxito *m*

hit[3] *vt* ECON corresponder; ◆ **~ the bid** STOCK mejorar la oferta; **~ the bricks** *AmE infrml* HRM ir a la huelga; **~ the headlines** MEDIA salir en titulares; **~ the jackpot** GEN COMM dar en el blanco; **~ rock bottom** ECON alcanzar el punto más bajo

hive off *vt infrml* ECON *company* privatizar parcialmente

hive-off *n BrE jarg* GEN COMM empresa derivada *f*

HL *abbr BrE* (*House of Lords*) POL cámara de los Lores, ≈ Cámara Alta *f* (*Esp*)

H/L *abbr* (*heavy lift*) TRANSP carga pesada *f*

h/lift *abbr* (*heavy lift*) TRANSP carga pesada *f*

HLL *abbr* (*high-level language*) COMP LAN (*lenguaje de alto nivel*)

HLT *abbr* (*high-leveraged takeover*) GEN COMM compra de alto apalancamiento *f*

HMC&E *abbr BrE* (*Her Majesty's Customs and Excise*) IMP/EXP departamento de impuestos de aduanas sobre el consumo, ≈ Servicio de Aduanas *m*

HMG *abbr BrE* (*Her Majesty's Government*) POL el gobierno británico

HMO *abbr AmE* (*health maintenance organization*) INS organización para la preservación de la salud

HMS *abbr* (*Her Majesty's Ship*) TRANSP embarcación de la monarquía británica

HMSO *abbr BrE* (*Her Majesty's Stationery Office*) GEN COMM suministros de papelería de la monarquía británica

HNC *abbr BrE* (*Higher National Certificate*) WEL certificado de estudios superiores

HND *abbr BrE* (*Higher National Diploma*) WEL diploma nacional de estudios superiores

H.O. *abbr* (*head office*) GEN COMM oficina matriz *f*, oficina principal *f*, sede principal *f*,

hoard *vt* FIN, GEN COMM, S&M, STOCK atesorar, acaparar

hoarded *adj* GEN COMM acaparado

hoarding *n* GEN COMM acaparamiento *m*; **~ of goods** FIN, GEN COMM, S&M, STOCK acaparamiento de bienes *m*, acaparamiento de mercancías *m*; **~ site** S&M lugar con vallas publicitarias *m*

hobby: **~ loss** *n* TAX pérdida de aficionado *f*

HoD *abbr* (*head of department*) HRM jefe(-a) de departamento *m,f*, jefe(-a) de sección *m,f*

hog: **~ cycle** *n* ECON ciclo del cerdo *m*

hogshead *n* (*hhd*) TRANSP bocoy *m*

hoist *n* TRANSP *cargo handling* polipasto *m*

hold[1] *n* TRANSP *for cargo* bodega *f*; **~-harmless agreements** *n pl* LAW acuerdos que eximen de responsabilidad *m pl*; **~-harmless clause** LAW *contract* cláusula eximente de responsabilidad *f*; **~-harmless provision** *BrE jarg* POL medida de exención de responsabilidad

hold[2] *vt* BANK *funds*, mantener, GEN COMM *enquiry* hacer, *referendum* celebrar, STOCK *the market* sostener, poseer, *a position* mantener; ◆ **~ as a security** BANK, FIN, INS mantener como garantía; **~ center stage** *AmE*, **~ centre stage** *BrE* GEN COMM dominar la situación; **~ a conference** MGMNT celebrar una conferencia, llevar a cabo una conferencia, realizar una conferencia; **~ funds for a check** *AmE*, **~ funds for a cheque** *BrE* BANK inmovilizar fondos para un cheque; **~ in check** ECON *prices* controlar estrictamente, mantener a raya; **~ the line** COMMS *on phone* retener la línea; **~ margins** ECON, FIN, GEN COMM respetar los márgenes, mantener los márgenes; **~ the market** STOCK vender o comprar para mantener estable el precio; **~ one's ground** GEN COMM mantenerse firme; **~ power** POL detentar el poder; **~ the purse strings** GEN COMM manejar los cuartos; **~ sb liable for sth** GEN COMM hacer responsable a alguien de algo; **~ sb responsible for sth** GEN COMM hacer responsable a alguien de algo; **~ a share** FIN participar; **~ a summit** POL celebrar una cumbre; **~ a**

survey GEN COMM hacer una encuesta; **~ water** GEN COMM estar bien fundado

hold off *vi* GEN COMM retraerse

holdback *n* PROP retención *f*; **~ pay** HRM descuentos en nómina *m pl*

holder *n* GEN COMM, PROP arrendatario(-a) *m,f*, STOCK tenedor(a) *m,f*; **~ for value** BANK *bill of exchange*, LAW tenedor(a) a título oneroso *m,f*; **~ in due course** BANK, LAW tenedor(a) de buena fe *m,f*, tenedor(a) legítimo(-a) *m,f*; **~ of record** STOCK tenedor(a) registrado(-a) *m,f*

holding *n* GEN COMM consorcio *m*, participación *f*, LAW, PROP posesión *m*, tenencia *f*; **~ company** BANK, FIN, STOCK compañía tenedora *f*, sociedad de control *f*, holding *m*, sociedad de cartera *f*; **~ of bonds** ACC, BANK, FIN cartera de bonos *f*; **~ corporation** BANK, FIN, STOCK compañía tenedora *f*, sociedad de control *f*, holding *m*, sociedad de cartera *f*; **~ gain** ACC, FIN beneficios retenidos *m pl*; **~ gains** *n pl* ACC beneficios de la sociedad tenedora *m pl*; **~ in a bank** BANK participación en un banco *f*; **~ pattern** *jarg* FIN, GEN COMM, STOCK compás de espera *m* (*jarg*), estancamiento *m* (*jarg*); **~ period** STOCK periodo de tenencia *m*; **~ of securities** STOCK tenencia de valores *f*

holdings *n pl* STOCK valores en cartera *m pl*

holdover: **~ effect** *n* GEN COMM efecto de aplazamiento *m*; **~ relief** *n BrE* TAX deducción por horas extraordinarias; **~ tenant** *n AmE* PROP inquilino(-a) en posesión *m,f*

holiday *n BrE* (*cf vacation AmE*) GEN COMM *public holiday* fiesta *f*, día festivo *m*, *leave* vacaciones *f pl*; **~ accommodation** *BrE* (*cf vacation accommodation AmE*) LEIS, PROP alojamiento de vacaciones *m*; **~ entitlement** *BrE* (*cf vacation entitlement AmE*) HRM derecho a vacaciones *m*; **~ leave** *BrE* (*cf vacation leave AmE*) HRM permiso de vacaciones *m*; **~ and leisure insurance** *BrE* (*cf vacation and leisure insurance AmE*) INS, LEIS seguro por vacaciones y ocio *m*; **~-maker** *BrE* (*cf vacationer AmE*) LEIS veraneante *mf*; **~ pay** *BrE* (*cf vacation pay AmE*) HRM paga de vacaciones *m*; **~ period** *BrE* (*cf vacation period AmE*) HRM, LEIS periodo de vacaciones *m*; ◆ **go on ~** *BrE* (*cf go on vacation AmE*) LEIS ir de vacaciones; **take a ~** *BrE* (*cf take a vacation AmE*) HRM tomarse unas vacaciones

holidays *n pl BrE* (*cf vacations AmE*) HRM, LEIS vacaciones *f pl*

home[1]: **~-grown** *adj* GEN COMM de origen nacional

home[2]: **~ affairs** *n pl* POL asuntos internos *m pl*; **~ audit** *n* S&M auditoría doméstica *f*; **~ banking** *n* BANK *by telephone* banca telefónica *f*; **~ computer** *n* COMP computador doméstico *m* (*AmL*), computadora doméstica *f* (*AmL*), ordenador doméstico *m* (*Esp*); **~ consumption** *n* ECON autoconsumo *m*; **~ country** *n* GEN COMM, IMP/EXP país sede *m*; **~-country control** *n* FIN control del país de origen *m*; **~ equity loan** *n* BANK, FIN, PROP préstamo con segunda hipoteca *m*; **~ improvement** *n* PROP mejora de la casa *f*; **~ improvement loan** *n* BANK préstamo para mejoras en la vivienda *m*; **~ loan** *n* BANK préstamo de vivienda *m*; **~ mortgage** *n* BANK, PROP hipoteca de la residencia *f*, hipoteca de la vivienda *f*; **~ mortgage loan** *n* BANK, FIN, PROP préstamo hipotecario residencial *m*; **~ office expense deduction** *n* TAX deducción por gastos de la casa matriz *f*; **~ ownership** *n* PROP propiedad de casas *f*; **~ page** *n* COMP *Internet* página frontal *f*, página principal *f*; **~ production** *n* ECON producción nacional

f, IND producción casera *f*, producción local *f*; **~ products** *n pl* GEN COMM *domestic* productos nacionales *m pl*, *household* productos para el hogar *m pl*; **~ purchase loan** *n* BANK, PROP préstamo para compra de vivienda *m*; **~ sale** *n* S&M venta nacional *f*; **~ trade passenger ship** *n* TRANSP buque de transporte nacional de pasajeros *m*; **~ trade ship** *n* TRANSP buque de comercio nacional *m*; **~ use entry** *n* ADMIN, IMP/EXP declaración de entrada en un país *f*

Home: **~ Office expenses** *n pl BrE* TAX gastos del departamento del interior *m pl*

homeowner *n* TAX propietario(-a) *m,f*; **~ warranty program** *AmE*, **~ warranty programme** *BrE* INS garantía del arrendador *f*, programa de garantías del arrendador *m*; **~'s equity account** BANK cuenta patrimonial del propietario de una vivienda *f*; **~'s policy** INS seguro sobre riesgos domésticos *m*

homeowners': **~ association** *n* PROP asociación de propietarios *f*

homestead *n AmE* PROP hacienda *f*, (*cf farmstead BrE*) propiedad *f*; **~ tax exemption** *AmE* TAX ≈ exención fiscal para explotaciones rurales *f*

homeward: **~ cargo** *n* TRANSP cargamento de vuelta *m*; **~ voyage** *n* GEN COMM, TRANSP viaje de vuelta *m*

homework *n* HRM trabajo a domicilio *m*

homeworker *n* HRM trabajador(a) domiciliario(-a) *m,f*

homogeneous[1] *adj* GEN COMM homogéneo

homogeneous[2]: **~ cargo** *n* TRANSP carga homogénea *f*; **~ good** *n* ECON bien homogéneo *m*, IND producto homogéneo *m*; **~ market** *n* S&M mercado homogéneo *m*; **~ oligopoly** *n* ECON oligopolio homogéneo *m*

homologation *n* HRM, IMP/EXP homologación *f*

honest: **~ broker** *n* POL corredor(a) honesto(-a) *m,f*

honeycomb: **~ slip** *n* FIN borderó de casillas *m*, INS, STOCK *underwriting* borderó de cajetines *m*

honor *AmE see* **honour** *BrE*

honorarium *n frml* GEN COMM honorarios *m pl*, tarifas *f pl*

honorary[1]: **~ chairman** *n* HRM presidente honorario *m*; **~ chairman of the board of directors** *n* HRM, MGMNT presidente honorario de la junta de directores *m*; **~ chairwoman** *n* HRM presidenta honoraria *f*; **~ chairwoman of the board of directors** *n* HRM, MGMNT presidenta honoraria de la junta de directores *f*; **~ contract** *n* GEN COMM, LAW contrato honorario *m*; **~ membership** *n* HRM ingreso honorario *m* (*Esp*), membresía honoraria *f* (*AmL*); **~ president** *n* HRM presidente(-a) honorario(-a) *m,f*

honorary[2]: **in an ~ capacity** *phr* HRM a título honorífico

honors *AmE see* **honours** *BrE*

honour[1] *n BrE* GEN COMM honor *m*; **~ policy** LAW póliza no aceptable como evidencia en un tribunal

honour[2] *vt BrE* BANK *debt* atender, GEN COMM honrar

honours: **~ graduate** *n BrE* GEN COMM graduado cum laude *m*

hood *n* COMP cubierta *f*

hook[1]: **~ cycle** *n* TRANSP periodo de izada *m*; **~ damage** *n* TRANSP *cargo handling* desgarro causado por ganchos *m*

hook[2] *vt* COMP, TRANSP enganchar

hooking *n* COMP, TRANSP enganche *m*

hopper: **~ container** *n* TRANSP contenedor tolva *m*

hoppertainer *n* TRANSP vagón tolva *m*

hor *abbr* (*horizontal*) COMP, GEN COMM horizontal

horizon[1]: ~ **analysis** *n* FIN análisis horizontal *m*

horizon[2]: **on the** ~ *phr* GEN COMM en perspectiva

horizontal[1] *adj* (*hor*) COMP, GEN COMM horizontal

horizontal[2]: ~ **amalgamation** *n* ECON, GEN COMM fusión horizontal *f*; ~ **analysis** *n* ACC análisis horizontal *m*; ~ **balance sheet** *n* ACC balance en forma de cuenta *m*, balance horizontal *m*, hoja de balance horizontal *f*; ~ **channel integration** *n* MGMNT integración horizontal de los canales *f*; ~ **combination** *n* ECON consolidación horizontal de empresas *f*; ~ **communication** *n* GEN COMM comunicación horizontal *f*; ~ **discrimination** *n* ECON discriminación horizontal *f*; ~ **divestiture** *n jarg* IND desposeimiento horizontal *m*; ~ **equity** *n* ECON participación horizontal *f*, TAX patrimonio horizontal *m*; ~ **expansion** *n* GEN COMM integración horizontal *f*; ~ **integration** *n* GEN COMM integración horizontal *f*; ~ **merger** *n* ECON, GEN COMM fusión horizontal *f*; ~ **publication** *n* MEDIA *print* publicación empresarial dedicada a todo tipo de empresas *f*; ~ **specialization** *n* MGMNT especialización horizontal *f*; ~ **spread** *n* STOCK diferencial en el tiempo *m*; ~ **union** *n* HRM sindicato profesional *m*; ~**vertical amalgamation** *n* ECON, GEN COMM fusión horizontal/vertical *f*

horse: ~**trading** *n infrml* POL intercambio de favores *m*

horsepower *n* (*h.p.*) TRANSP caballaje *m* (*AmL*) (*CV*), caballo de vapor *m* (*Esp*) (*CV*)

hospital: ~ **care insurance plan** *n* INS, WEL plan de seguro de hospitalización *m*; ~ **expenses** *n pl* TAX gastos de hospitalización *m pl*; ~ **revenue bond** *n* FIN título a corto plazo por anticipación de ingresos de un hospital

hospitalization: ~ **plan** *n* INS, WEL plan de hospitalización *m*

host[1]: ~**driven** *adj* COMP centralizado

host[2] *n* COMP huésped *m*; ~ **city** GEN COMM ciudad anfitriona *f*; ~ **computer** COMP servidor *m*; ~ **country** GEN COMM, LEIS país anfitrión *m*

hostile: ~ **fire** *n* INS incendio *m*; ~ **takeover bid** *n* GEN COMM, STOCK oferta pública de adquisición hostil *f* (*OPAH*)

hot[1] *adj jarg* HRM *industrial relations* conflictivo; ♦ **in the ~ seat** HRM en un puesto difícil

hot[2]: ~ **bill** *n infrml* ACC, BANK, FIN efecto a la vista *m* billete nuevo *m*, efecto de vencimiento a corto plazo *m*; ~ **card list** *n* BANK relación de tarjetas invalidadas *f*; ~ **cargo clause** *n* HRM, TRANSP cláusula de carga peligrosa *f*; ~ **issue** *n AmE jarg* STOCK cuestión candente *f*; ~ **key** *n* COMP tecla activación *f*, clave directa *f*; ~ **line** *n* COMMS *phone* línea de prioridad *f*, *politics* línea de comunicación directa *f*; ~ **list** *n* BANK lista de invalidaciones *f*; ~ **money** *n* ECON capital especulativo *m*, STOCK capitales febriles *m pl*, dinero caliente *m*; ~ **property** *n jarg* MEDIA *advertising*, S&M *popular product* producto de gran aceptación *m*, *person* personaje de gran éxito *mf*, personaje taquillero *mf* (*jarg*); ~ **shop** *n jarg* S&M *advertising* agencia creativa *f*, agencia de creación *f*; ~ **stock** *n jarg* FIN, STOCK acción especulativa *f*

hotel: ~ **accommodation** *n* LEIS alojamiento hotelero *m*; ~ **manager** *n* LEIS, MGMNT director(a) de hotel *m,f*; ~ **proprietor** *n* PROP propietario(-a) de hotel *m,f*; ~ **register** *n* LEIS registro de hotel *m*

hotelier *n* LEIS hotelero(-a) *m,f*

hourly[1]: ~ **paid** *adj* HRM pagado por hora

hourly[2]: ~ **compensation** *n* HRM retribución por hora *f*; ~ **rate** *n* HRM salario por horas *m*; ~ **worker** *n* HRM trabajador(a) por horas *m,f*; ~ **workers** *n pl* HRM personal obrero *m*

hours: ~ **of business** *n pl* (*h.b.*) GEN COMM horas de oficina *f pl*; ~ **purpose** *n* TRANSP *shipping* objetivo horario *m*

house *n* PROP casa *f*, STOCK sociedad de valores o inversión bancaria, ≈ Cámara *f*; ~ **account** STOCK cuenta de empresa *f*; ~ **air waybill** (*HAWB*) IMP/EXP, TRANSP conocimiento de embarque aéreo local *m*; ~ **bill of lading** IMP/EXP, TRANSP conocimiento de embarque de compañía *m*; ~**building loan** BANK, PROP préstamo para la construcción de vivienda *m*; ~ **journal** MEDIA boletín de empresa *m*; ~ **magazine** MEDIA revista de empresa *f*; ~ **mailing** S&M correo interno *m*; ~ **maintenance requirement** STOCK requisito de mantenimiento de la empresa *m*; ~ **mortgage** BANK, PROP hipoteca sobre vivienda *f*; ~ **price** PROP precio de la vivienda *m*; ~ **purchase** PROP compra de vivienda *f*; ~ **search** LAW registro domiciliario *m*; ~ **style** GEN COMM, MEDIA *editorial* estilo de la casa *m*; ~**to-house sampling** S&M muestreo domiciliario *m*; ~**to-house selling** S&M venta a domicilio *f*; ♦ ~ **to house** TRANSP de puerta a puerta

House: ~ **of Commons** *n BrE* (*HC*) POL Cámara de los Comunes *f*, ≈ Cámara Baja *f* (*Esp*), ≈ El Congreso *m* (*Esp*); ~ **of Lords** *n BrE* (*HL*) POL Cámara de los Lores *f*, ≈ Cámara Alta *f* (*Esp*); ~ **of Representatives** *n AmE* POL ≈ Cámara Baja *f* (*Esp*), ≈ El Congreso *m* (*Esp*)

house/depot *phr* IMP/EXP, TRANSP casa/depósito *f*, firma/ depósito *f*

household *n* ECON, GEN COMM unidad familiar *f*; ~ **appliances** *n pl* GEN COMM electrodomésticos *m pl*, aparatos domésticos *m pl*; ~ **behavior** *AmE*, ~ **behaviour** *BrE* ECON comportamiento de la unidad familiar *m*; ~ **commodities** *n pl* GEN COMM bienes domésticos *m pl*; ~ **decision making** ECON grupo de toma de decisiones *m*; ~ **durables** *n pl* S&M productos duraderos para el hogar *m pl*; ~ **effects** *n pl* GEN COMM enseres domésticos *m pl*; ~ **goods** *n pl* GEN COMM mobiliario y efectos domésticos *m pl*; ~ **name** S&M nombre familiar *m*; ~ **risk** INS riesgo doméstico *m*

Houses: **the ~ of Parliament** *n pl BrE* POL parlamento británico, ≈ Las Cortes *f pl* (*Esp*)

housing *n* GEN COMM vivienda *f*, LEIS, PROP, TAX, WEL alojamiento *m*; ~ **allowance** HRM, WEL asignación para vivienda *f*, subsidio para vivienda *m*; ~ **bond** PROP bono vivienda *m*; ~ **code** LAW ordenanza de seguridad e higiene en viviendas *f*, PROP código de construcción *m*, código de edificación *m*; ~ **complex** PROP complejo residencial *m*; ~ **corporation** TAX compañía constructora de viviendas *f*; ~ **development** PROP promoción de la vivienda *f*; ~ **estate** *BrE* (*cf housing project AmE*) PROP, WEL complejo de viviendas subvencionadas *m*; ~ **industry** IND, PROP sector de la vivienda *m*; ~ **loan** BANK, PROP préstamo a la construcción de viviendas *m*; ~ **market** PROP mercado de la vivienda *m*; ~ **project** *AmE* PROP, WEL (*cf council house BrE*) vivienda de protección oficial *f* (*VPO*), (*cf housing estate BrE*) complejo de viviendas subvencionadas *m*; ~ **scheme** WEL plan de vivienda *m*; ~ **shortage** PROP escasez de viviendas *f*; **~ start** ECON ventaja en materia de vivienda *f*; **~ subsidy** HRM, WEL subsidio para vivienda *m*

Housing: ~ and Urban Development Department *n* AmE (*HUD Department*) PROP departamento de desarrollo de la vivienda y urbanismo

hovercraft *n* TRANSP aerodeslizador *m*

hoverport *n* TRANSP puerto de aerodeslizadores *m*

h.p. *abbr* (*horsepower*) TRANSP CV (*caballaje AmL, caballo de vapor Esp*)

HP *abbr BrE* (*hire purchase*) S&M compra a plazos *f*

HPS *abbr* (*hazardous polluting substance*) ENVIR, TRANSP sustancia con riesgo de polución *f*, sustancia peligrosa contaminante *f*

h.q. *abbr* (*headquarters*) GEN COMM oficina principal *f*, sede principal *f*, *of company* sede central *f*, HRM, IND dirección central *f*

HQ *abbr* (*headquarters*) GEN COMM oficina principal *f*, sede principal *f*, *of company* sede central *f*, HRM, IND dirección central *f*

HRD *abbr* (*human resource development*) HRM DRH (*desarrollo de recursos humanos*)

HRH *abbr BrE* (*His Royal Highness, Her Royal Highness*) GEN COMM ≈ S.A.R. (*Esp*) (*Su Alteza Real*)

HRM *abbr* (*human resource management*) HRM RRHH (*recursos humanos*)

HRP *abbr* (*human resource planning*) HRM, MGMNT PRH (*planificación de los recursos humanos*)

HS *abbr* (*high-strength*) GEN COMM superficie calefactora *f*

HSE *abbr* (*Health and Safety Executive*) WEL oficina para la defensa de la seguridad y salud en el lugar de trabajo

HST *abbr* (*high-speed train*) TRANSP ≈ TAV (*Tren de Alta Velocidad*)

HSWA *abbr BrE* (*Health and Safety at Work Act*) HRM, LAW, WEL ley de higiene y seguridad en el trabajo

HTA *abbr* (*hierarchical task analysis*) MGMNT análisis de tareas jerárquicos *m*

hub: ~ of activity *n* GEN COMM centro de actividad *m*; **~ branch** *n* BANK sucursal de mayor actividad *f*; **~ reduction** *n* TRANSP *vehicles* reducción de eje *f*

huckster *n AmE infrml* (*cf pedlar BrE*) S&M vendedor(a) ambulante *m,f*, *advertising* buhonero *m*

HUD: ~ Department *n AmE* (*Housing and Urban Development Department*) PROP departamento de desarrollo de la vivienda y urbanismo

huge *adj* GEN COMM *debt, order* colosal

Hulbert: ~ rating *n* FIN tasación de Hulbert *f*

hull *n* TRANSP *of ship* casco *m*; **~ insurance** INS *marine* seguro de cascos *m*; **~ underwriter** INS *marine* asegurador(a) de cascos de buques *m,f*; **~ underwriting company** INS compañía aseguradora de cascos de buques *f*

human: ~ asset accounting *n* HRM contabilidad de activos humanos *f*; **~ capital** *n* HRM capital humano *m*; **~ consumption** *n* ENVIR *of water* consumo humano *m*; **~ engineering** *n* HRM técnica de las relaciones humanas *f*; **~ factors** *n pl* HRM *industrial psychology* factores humanos *m pl*; **~ relation** *n* HRM, MGMNT relación humana *f*; **~ resource accounting** *n* HRM contabilidad de recursos humanos *f*; **~ resource administration** *n* HRM, MGMNT administración de recursos humanos *f*, dirección de recursos humanos *f*, gestión de recursos humanos *f*; **~ resource development** *n* (*HRD*) HRM

desarrollo de recursos humanos *m* (*DRH*); **~ resource management** *n* (*HRM*) HRM recursos humanos (*RRHH*); **~ resource planning** *n* (*HRP*) HRM planificación de los recursos humanos *f* (*PRH*); **~ resources** *n pl* HRM mano de obra *f*, *persons, workers* fuerza de trabajo *f*, fuerza laboral *f*, recursos humanos *m pl* (*RRHH*); **~ resources director** *n* HRM, MGMNT director(a) de recursos humanos *m,f*; **~ resources manager** *n* HRM jefe(-a) de negociado *m,f*; **~ rights** *n pl* LAW derechos del hombre *m pl*; **~ scale economics** *n* ECON escala económica humana *f*

Humphrey-Hawkins: ~ Act *n AmE* LAW, POL Ley de Humphrey-Hawkins *f*

hundredweight *n* (*cwt*) GEN COMM quintal *m*

hurdle *n* GEN COMM obstáculo *m*; **~ rate** ECON, FIN *budgeting capital expenditures* tasa crítica de rentabilidad *f*; **~ rate of return** ECON, FIN tasa crítica de rendimiento *f*

hustle: ~ and bustle *n* GEN COMM ajetreo *m*

hybrid[1] *adj* COMP híbrido

hybrid[2]**: ~ annuity** *n* INS anualidad mixta *f*; **~ auction** *n* STOCK subasta híbrida *f*; **~ computer** *n* COMP computador híbrido *m* (*AmL*), computadora híbrida *f* (*AmL*), ordenador híbrido *m* (*Esp*); **~ income tax** *n* TAX impuesto mixto sobre la renta *m*

HYC *abbr* (*hydraulic coupling*) TRANSP acoplamiento hidráulico *m*

hydraulic: ~ coupling *n* (*HC, HYC*) TRANSP acoplamiento hidráulico *m*; **~ power** *n* ENVIR, IND energía hidráulica *f*

hydro *abbr* (*hydroelectric*) ENVIR, IND *power* hidroeléctrico

hydrocarbon *n* ENVIR hidrocarburo *m*

hydroelectric[1] *adj* (*hydro*) ENVIR, IND *power* hidroeléctrico

hydroelectric[2]**: ~ power** *n* ENVIR, IND energía hidroeléctrica *f*; **~ power station** *n* IND central hidroeléctrica *f*

hydrofoil *n* TRANSP hidroala *f*

hydrometer *n* ENVIR densímetro *m*

hygiene: ~ standard *n* WEL norma de higiene *f*

hygroscopic: ~ substance *n* ENVIR sustancia higroscópica *f*

hype *n* MEDIA, S&M gran despliegue publicitario *m*, promoción de lanzamiento *f*

hyperinflation *n* ECON hiperinflación *f*

hyperinflationist *n* ECON hiperinflacionista *mf*

hypermarket *n* S&M hipermercado *m*

hyphenation *n* COMP guionado *m*

hypothecate *vt* LAW hipotecar

hypothecation *n* ECON *expenditure* hipoteca *f*, pignoración *f*

hypothesis *n* GEN COMM hipótesis *f*; **~ testing** MATH verificación de una hipótesis *f*

hypothetical[1] *adj* GEN COMM hipotético

hypothetical[2]**: ~ circumstances** *n pl* GEN COMM circunstancias hipotéticas *f pl*; **~ conditions** *n pl* GEN COMM condiciones hipotéticas *f pl*; **~ point** *n* GEN COMM punto hipotético *m*; **~ question** *n* GEN COMM pregunta hipotética *f*; **~ situation** *n* GEN COMM situación hipotética *f*

hysteresis *n* ECON histéresis *f*

I

i *abbr* (*interest*) GEN COMM interés *m*, rédito *m*

I: **~ owe you** *n* (*IOU*) GEN COMM pagaré *m*

IACS *abbr* (*International Association of Classification Societies*) GEN COMM asociación internacional de sociedades de clasificación

IADB *abbr* (*Inter-American Development Bank*) BANK BID (*Banco Interamericano de Desarrollo*)

IAEC *abbr* (*International Association of Environmental Co-ordinators*) ENVIR Asociación Internacional de Coordinadoras del Medio Ambiente *f*

IAM *abbr* (*Institute of Administrative Management*) MGMNT instituto británico de gestión administrativa

IAPC *abbr* (*International Auditing Practices Committee*) ACC, BANK Comité Internacional de Prácticas de Auditoría *m*

IAPH *abbr* (*International Association of Ports and Harbours*) IMP/EXP, TRANSP Organización Internacional de Puertos *f*

IAPIP *abbr* (*International Association for the Protection of Industrial Property*) LAW, PROP Asociación Internacional para la Protección de Propiedad Industrial *f*

IARA *abbr* (*International Agricultural Research Institute*) IND Instituto Internacional de Investigación Agrícola *m*

IAS *abbr* (*International Auditing Standard*) ACC Norma Internacional de Auditoría *f*

IASC *abbr* (*International Accounting Standards Committee*) ACC Comité Internacional de Normas Contables *m*

IATA[1] *abbr* (*International Air Transport Association*) TRANSP IATA (*Asociación Internacional de Transporte Aéreo*)

IATA[2]: **~ air waybill** *n* TRANSP conocimiento de embarque aéreo de IATA *m*; **~ Airport Handling Manual** *n* TRANSP Manual de la IATA para Carga y Descarga Aeroportuaria *m*; **~ cargo agent** *n* TRANSP agente de fletes de IATA *mf*; **~ clearing house** *n* TRANSP cámara de compensación de IATA *f*; **~ container** *n* TRANSP contenedor IATA *m*; **~ rate** *n* TRANSP tarifa IATA *f*

IBC *abbr* (*intermediate bulk container*) TRANSP contenedor intermedio para graneles *m*

IBEC *abbr* BANK, ECON (*International Bank for Economic Cooperation*) Banco Internacional para la Cooperación Económica *m* (*IBEC*)

IBF *abbr* (*international banking facility*) BANK facilidad bancaria internacional *f*

ibid. *abbr* (*ibidem*) GEN COMM ibid. (*ibidem*)

ibidem *phr* (*ibid.*) GEN COMM ibidem (*ibid.*)

IBM[1]: **~-compatible** *adj* COMP compatible con IBM

IBM[2]: **~ personal computer** *n* COMP computador personal IBM *m* (*AmL*), computadora personal IBM *f* (*AmL*), ordenador personal IBM *m* (*Esp*)

IBOR *abbr* (*interbank offered rate*) BANK tasa ofrecida interbancaria *f*

IBRC *abbr* BrE (*Insurance Brokers' Registration Council*) INS consejo de registro de agencias de seguros

IBRD *abbr* (*International Bank for Reconstruction and Development*) BANK, ECON BIRD (*Banco Internacional para la Reconstrucción y el Desarrollo*)

IC *abbr* COMP (*integrated circuit*) CI (*circuito integrado*), FIN (*Investment Committee*) comité de inversiones de la asociación de aseguradores británicos

ICA *abbr* ACC (*Institute of Chartered Accountants*) instituto de contables colegiados, POL (*International Cooperation Administration*) administración de cooperación internacional

ICAC *abbr* (*International Cotton Advisory Committee*) IND Comité Internacional de Consultoría del Algodón *m*

ICAEW *abbr* (*Institute of Chartered Accountants in England and Wales*) ACC instituto de contables colegiados de Inglaterra y Gales

ICAI *abbr* (*Institute of Chartered Accountants in Ireland*) ACC instituto de contables colegiados de Irlanda

ICAO *abbr* (*International Civil Aviation Organization*) TRANSP Organización de Aviación Civil Internacional *f*

ICAS *abbr* (*Institute of Chartered Accountants of Scotland*) ACC instituto de contables colegiados de Escocia

ICC *abbr* ECON (*income-consumption curve*) curva de renta-consumo *f*, (*Interstate Commerce Commission*) comisión de comercio interestatal, (*International Chamber of Commerce*) Cámara de Comercio Internacional *f*, GEN COMM (*International Control Centre*) Centro Internacional de Control *m*, (*industrial and commercial company*) empresa manufacturera y comercializadora *f*, TRANSP (*Institute Cargo Clause*) Cláusula de Fletes del Instituto *f*

ICCH *abbr* (*International Commodities Clearing House*) STOCK Cámara de Compensación de Productos Internacionales *f*

ICCICA *abbr* (*Interim Co-ordinating Committee for International Commodity Arrangements*) STOCK Comité Provisional de Coordinación para Convenios Comerciales Internacionales *m*

ICCO *abbr* (*International Council of Containership Operators*) TRANSP Consejo Internacional de Operadores de Contenedores de Carga *m*

ICD *abbr* (*inland clearance depot*) IMP/EXP, TRANSP depósito aduanero interior *m*

iceberg: **~ company** *n jarg* GEN COMM empresa mayor de lo aparente *f*

ICEM *abbr* (*Intergovernmental Committee for European Migration*) POL, WEL Comité Intergubernamental sobre Migraciones en Europa *m*

ICETT *abbr* (*Industrial Council for Educational & Training Technology*) IND, WEL comité industrial de educación y aprendizaje de nuevas tecnologías

ICFC *abbr* (*Industrial and Commercial Finance Corporation.*) IND, FIN Corporación de Finanzas Industrial y Comercial *f*

ICFTU *abbr* (*International Confederation of Free Trade Unions*) HRM Confederación Internacional de Sindicatos Independientes *f*

ICHCA *abbr* (*International Cargo Handling Coordination*

Association) TRANSP Asociación Internacional Coordinadora de Transporte de Cargamento *f*

ICIE *abbr* (*International Centre for Industry and the Environment*) ENVIR, IND Centro Internacional para la Industria y el Medio Ambiente *m*

ICITO *abbr* (*Interim Commission of the International Trade Organization*) ECON, IMP/EXP, POL comisión intermediaria de comercio internacional

ICJ *abbr* (*International Court of Justice*) LAW, POL Tribunal Internacional de Justicia *m*

ICMA *abbr* (*Institute of Cost and Management Accountants*) ACC instituto de contables de costes y gestión

icon *n* COMP, GEN COMM icono *m*

ICOR *abbr* (*incremental capital-output ratio*) ECON, FIN proporción incremental capital-producto *f*

ICS *abbr* (*International Chamber of Shipping*) TRANSP Cámara Internacional de Comercio Marítimo *f*

ICTB *abbr* (*International Customs Tariffs Bureau*) IMP/EXP, TRANSP Oficina Internacional de Tarifas Aduaneras *f*

ICU *abbr* (*International Clearing Union*) BANK, ECON Unión Internacional de Compensación *f*

id. *abbr* (*idem*) GEN COMM id. (*ídem*)

ID[1] *abbr* COMP (*identifier*) identificador *m*, IMP/EXP, TAX (*import duty*) derechos fiscales sobre la importación *m pl*

ID[2]: **~ card** *n* (*identity card*) LAW, POL documento nacional de identidad *m* (*DNI*), tarjeta de identificación *f*; **~ number** *n* COMP número ID *m*

IDA *abbr* ECON (*International Development Association*) AIF (*Asociación Internacional de Fomento*), IMP/EXP (*Import Duty Act*) Ley Arancelaria *f*, IND (*Industrial Development Authority*) autoridad para el desarrollo industrial, TAX (*Import Duty Act*) Ley Arancelaria *f*

IDB *abbr* BANK, ECON (*Inter-American Development Bank*) BID (*Banco Interamericano de Desarrollo*), STOCK (*interdealer broker*) CI (*corredor intermediario*)

IDBS *abbr* (*interdealer-broker system*) STOCK subasta de conexión entre intermediarios *f*

ideal: **~ capacity** *n* ECON capacidad ideal *f*; **~ limit** *n* ECON límite ideal *m*

idem *adj* (*id.*) GEN COMM ídem (*id.*)

identification *n* COMP, TAX *of returns* identificación *f*; **~ problem** ECON problema de identificación *m*

identifier *n* (*ID*) COMP identificador *m*

id est *phr* (*i.e.*) GEN COMM id est

idle[1] *adj* GEN COMM inactivo, HRM improductivo, ocioso, *machine* muerto; ♦ **lying ~** *infrml* BANK *money* inactivo

idle[2]: **~ balance** *n* FIN saldo ocioso *m*; **~ capacity** *n* ECON, IND capacidad ociosa *f*; **~ capital** *n* ACC, ECON, FIN, GEN COMM capital inactivo *m*; **~ cash** *n* ECON, FIN, STOCK dinero inactivo *m*; **~ cycle** *n* BANK, FIN, MGMNT ciclo en vacío *m*; **~ money** *n* ECON, FIN, STOCK dinero inactivo *m*; **~ shipping** *n* TRANSP navegación de vacío *f*; **~ time** *n* COMP tiempo inactivo *m*; **~ tonnage** *n* TRANSP *shipping* tonelaje inmovilizado *m*

IDRC *abbr* (*International Development Research Centre*) WEL centro internacional de investigación y desarrollo

i.e. *abbr* (*id est*) GEN COMM id est

IEA *abbr* ECON (*Institute of Economic Affairs*) Instituto de Asuntos Económicos *m*, ENVIR (*International Energy Agency*) AIE (*Agencia Internacional de la Energía*)

IEE *abbr* (*Institute of Electrical Engineers*) HRM, IND instituto de ingenieros eléctricos

IEM *abbr* (*International Equities Market*) STOCK Mercado Internacional de Acciones *m*

IET *abbr* (*Interest Equalization Tax*) TAX impuesto de igualación de los tipos de interés

if: **~, as and when** *adv* GEN COMM si, como y cuando

IFAP *abbr* (*International Federation of Agricultural Producers*) ECON, POL Federación Internacional de Productores Agrícolas *f*

IFC *abbr* (*International Finance Corporation*) FIN CFI (*Corporación de Finanzas Internacionales*)

IFD *abbr* (*International Federation for Documentation*) GEN COMM Federación Internacional de Documentación *f*

IFS *abbr* (*Institute of Fiscal Studies*) TAX, WEL Instituto de Estudios Fiscales *m*

IFSE *abbr* (*International Federation of Stock Exchanges*) STOCK Federación Internacional de Bolsas de Valores *f*

IFTU *abbr* (*International Federation of Trade Unions*) HRM federación internacional de sindicatos

igloo *n* TRANSP *aviation* iglú *m*

igniter *n* GEN COMM, TRANSP encendedor *m*

IIB *abbr* (*International Investment Bank*) BANK Banco de Inversión Internacional *m*

IIF *abbr* (*Institute for International Finance*) FIN Instituto para Finanzas Internacionales *m*

I/L *abbr* (*import licence BrE, import license AmE*) IMP/EXP licencia de importación *f*

ILA *abbr* (*International Longshoremen's Association*) TRANSP asociación international de estibadores

ill: **~-health** *n* GEN COMM mala salud; **~ will** *n* GEN COMM mala voluntad *f*

illegal[1] *adj* LAW ilegal

illegal[2]: **~ alien** *n* LAW extranjero(-a) ilegal *m,f*; **~ character** *n* COMP carácter ilegal *m*; **~ dividend** *n* LAW dividendo ilegal *m*; **~ immigrant** *n* POL, WEL inmigrante ilegal *mf*; **~ immigration** *n* POL inmigración ilegal *f*; **~ operation** *n* COMP operación no válida *f*; **~ practice** *n* LAW práctica ilegal *f*; **~ seizure** *n* LAW apropiación indebida *f*; **~ strike** *n* HRM, IND, LAW huelga ilegal *f*

illegally *adv* LAW ilegalmente

illiquid[1] *adj* ACC no realizable, BANK ilíquido

illiquid[2]: **~ assets** *n pl* ACC activos difícilmente liquidables *m pl*, activos difícilmente realizables *m pl*, activos no líquidos *m pl*

illth *n* ECON productos y servicios nocivos *m pl*

illusory: **~ profit** *n* FIN beneficio ilusorio *m*

illustrate *vt* GEN COMM, MEDIA ilustrar

illustrated: **~ magazine** *n* MEDIA revista ilustrada *f*

illustration *n* GEN COMM aclaración *f*, MEDIA *example, picture* ilustración *f*, MGMNT aclaración *f*

ILO[1] *abbr* (*International Labor Organization AmE, International Labour Organization BrE*) HRM, POL, WEL OIT (*Organización Internacional de Trabajo*)

ILO[2]: **~ Conventions** *n pl* HRM Convenciones de la OIT *f pl*

image *n* COMP, S&M imagen *f*; **~ advertising** S&M publicidad basada en la imagen *f*; **~ audit** S&M auditoría de imagen *f*; **~ file** COMP fichero de imagen *m*; **~ projection** S&M proyección de imagen *f*

imaging *n* COMP, S&M formación de imágenes *f*

IMB *abbr* (*International Maritime Bureau*) TRANSP Registro Marítimo Internacional *m*

imbalance *n* ECON desequilibrio *m*; ~ **of orders** STOCK desequilibrio de órdenes *m*; ~ **of trade** ECON desequilibrio de intercambios *m*

imbalanced: ~ **working** *n* TRANSP funcionamiento desequilibrado *m*

IMC *abbr* (*International Maritime Committee*) TRANSP Comité Marítimo Internacional *m*

IMDGC *abbr* (*International Maritime Dangerous Goods Code*) TRANSP Código Marítimo Internacional de Productos Peligrosos *m*

IME *abbr* (*Institute of Maritime Engineers*) TRANSP instituto de ingenieros náuticos

I Mech E *abbr* (*Institute of Mechanical Engineers*) IND instituto de ingenieros mecánicos

IMF *abbr* (*International Monetary Fund*) ECON, POL FMI (*Fondo Monetario Internacional*)

IMM[1] *abbr* (*International Monetary Market*) ECON, POL, STOCK Mercado Monetario Internacional *m*

IMM[2]: ~ **CD index** *n* (*International Monetary Market certificate of deposit index*) STOCK índice de certificados de depósito del IMM *m* (*índice de certificados de depósito del Mercado Monetario Internacional*); ~ **T-bill index** *n* (*International Monetary Market Treasury bill index*) STOCK Índice de Letras del Tesoro del IMM *m*; ~ **Three-Month Discount Index** *n* STOCK índice de Descuento IMM a Tres Meses *m*

immediate: ~ **access** *n* COMP acceso directo *m*; ~ **aim** *n* GEN COMM propósito inmediato *m*; ~ **capital gain** *n* TAX ganancia inmediata del capital *f*; ~ **family** *n* STOCK familia inmediata *f*; ~ **money transfer** *n* (*IMT*) BANK, FIN transferencia monetaria inmediata *f*; ~ **occupancy** *n* PROP entrega inmediata *f*; ~**-or-cancel order** *n* (*IOC*) FIN orden de ejecución inmediata o cancelación *f*; ~ **possession** *n* PROP llave en mano *f*, WEL entrada inmediata *f*; ~ **rebate** *n* TRANSP descuento inmediato *m*; ◆ **for** ~ **attention** *phr* GEN COMM para atención inmediata *f*; **for** ~ **delivery** *phr* GEN COMM para entrega inmediata

immigrant *n* POL, WEL inmigrante *mf*; ~ **worker** HRM, WEL trabajador(a) inmigrante *m,f*

immigration *n* ECON, LAW inmigración *f*; ~ **control** POL, WEL control de inmigración *m*; ~ **law** LAW, POL ley de inmigración *f*; ~ **officer** (*IO*) HRM, IMP/EXP funcionario(-a) de inmigración *m,f*; ~ **policy** LAW, POL política de inmigración *f*

imminent: ~ **peril** *n* INS peligro inminente *m*

immiseration *n* ECON pobreza creciente de las clases trabajadoras

immiserizing: ~ **growth** *n* ECON crecimiento de la pérdida de bienestar económico *m*, crecimiento empobrecedor *m*

immovable: ~ **capital** *n* GEN COMM capital inmobiliario *m*; ~ **estate** *n* LAW, PROP bienes inmuebles *m pl*; ~ **property** *n* PROP propiedad *f*

immunities *n pl* BrE HRM exenciones *f pl*

immunity *n* LAW, TAX inmunidad *f*; ~ **from taxation** TAX inmunidad tributaria *f*

immunization *n* FIN, WEL inmunización *f*

immunize *vt* FIN, WEL inmunizar

IMO *abbr* IND (*International Miners' Organization*) Organización Internacional de Mineros *f*, TRANSP (*International Maritime Organization*) Organización Marítima Internacional *f*

imp. *abbr* (*import, importation*) IMP/EXP importación *f*

impact *n* ECON, GEN COMM efecto *m*; ~ **effect** ECON efecto inmediato *m*; ~ **of a loss** TAX impacto de una pérdida *m*; ~ **multiplier** ECON impacto multiplicador *m*; ~ **printer** COMP impresora de percusión *f*; ~ **study** S&M estudio de impacto *m*; ◆ **have an** ~ **on** GEN COMM ejercer influencia sobre

impacted: ~ **area** *n* TAX área afectada *f*

impair *vt* ECON, FIN *currency* deteriorar

impaired: ~ **capital** *n* FIN capital no respaldado por activo equivalente *m*

impairment *n* BANK *of value* disminución *f*, TAX deterioro *m*, menoscabo *m*

impartial *adj* GEN COMM imparcial

impasse *n* GEN COMM callejón sin salida *m*

impede *vt* GEN COMM *growth* poner un impedimento a

imperfect: ~ **competition** *n* ECON, S&M competencia imperfecta *f*; ~ **market** *n* ECON, S&M mercado imperfecto *m*; ~ **obligation** *n* LAW obligación imperfecta *f*

imperial: ~ **gallon** *n* GEN COMM galón normalizado *m*

imperialism *n* POL imperialismo *m*

impetus *n* GEN COMM impulso *m*

impinge: ~ **on sb's rights** *phr* LAW chocar con los derechos de alguien

implement *vt* COMP *system* instrumentar, GEN COMM *contract* hacer efectivo, *policy* poner en práctica

implementation: ~ **of an article** *n* FIN implementación de un artículo *f*; ~ **lag** *n* ECON implementación desfasada *f*; ~ **of a treaty** *n* FIN implementación de un tratado *f*

implications *n pl* GEN COMM consecuencias *f pl*

implicit: ~ **contract theory** *n* ECON teoría del contrato implícito *f*; ~ **cost** *n* ECON coste implícito *m* (*Esp*), costo implícito *m* (*AmL*); ~ **marginal income** *n* ECON, FIN ingreso marginal implícito *m*; ~ **price deflator** *n* ECON deflactor implícito de precios *m*

implied[1] *adj* GEN COMM *conditions* implícito

implied[2]: ~ **acceptance** *n* BANK, FIN aceptación implícita *f*; ~ **agency** *n* GEN COMM agencia implícita *f*; ~ **condition** *n* GEN COMM condición implícita *f*; ~ **contract** *n* GEN COMM, LAW contrato sobreentendido *m*, contrato tácito *m*; ~ **easement** *n* LAW servidumbre tácita *f*; ~ **in fact contract** *n* LAW contrato implícito de hecho *m*; ~ **obligation** *n* GEN COMM obligación implícita *f*; ~ **price index** *n* ECON, S&M índice de precios implícitos *m*; ~ **repo rate** *n* AmE infrml FIN repurchase tipo repo implícito *m*; ~ **term** *n* GEN COMM, LAW *of contract* término implícito *m*; ~ **terms** *n pl* HRM condiciones implícitas *f pl*; ~ **volatility** *n* STOCK volatilidad implícita *f*; ~ **warranty** *n* GEN COMM garantía tácita *f*, LAW garantía implícita *f*

imply *vt* GEN COMM implicar

import[1] *n* (*imp.*) IMP/EXP importación *f*; ~ **allowance** ECON concesión de importación *m*, IMP/EXP autorización de importación *f*; ~ **berth** TRANSP *shipping* muelle de importaciones *m*; ~ **capacity** BANK, ECON, GEN COMM, IMP/EXP capacidad importadora *f*; ~ **clerk** HRM, IMP/EXP funcionario(-a) de importación *m,f*; ~ **control** IMP/EXP control a la importación *m*; ~ **credit** IMP/EXP crédito a la importación *m*;

~ **demand** ECON, IMP/EXP demanda de importaciones *f*; ~ **depot charge** IMP/EXP gasto de almacén de la importación *m*; ~ **documentation supervisor** HRM supervisor(a) de documentación de importación *m,f*; ~ **duty** (*ID*) IMP/EXP, TAX derechos fiscales sobre la importación *m pl*; ~**-export** COMP importación-exportación *f*; ~ **gold** IMP/EXP importación de oro *f*; ~ **groupage operator** HRM agente de agrupamiento de importaciones *mf*; ~ **letter of credit** BANK, FIN, IMP/EXP carta de crédito para importación *f*; ~ **licence** *BrE*, ~ **license** *AmE* (*I/L*) IMP/EXP licencia de importación *f*; ~ **licensing** IMP/EXP concesión de licencia de importación *f*; ~ **manager** HRM, MGMNT director(a) de importación *m,f*; ~ **penetration ratio** IMP/EXP proporción de penetración de las importaciones *f*; ~ **permit** IMP/EXP autorización de importación *f*; ~ **price** ECON, IMP/EXP precio de importación *m*; ~ **quota** IMP/EXP contingente arancelario *m*, cuota de importaciones *f*; ~ **release note** (*IRN*) IMP/EXP aviso de despacho de importación *m*; ~ **sales executive** HRM ejecutivo(-a) de ventas de importación *m,f*; ~ **shed** IMP/EXP tinglado de importación *m*; ~ **substitution** IMP/EXP sustitución de importaciones *f*; ~ **surplus** IMP/EXP excedente de importación *m*; ~ **tariff** IMP/EXP arancel de importación *m*; ~ **trade** IMP/EXP comercio de importación *m*

import[2] *vt* COMP *data*, GEN COMM, IMP/EXP importar

Import: ~ **Duty Act** *n* (*IDA*) TAX Ley Arancelaria *f*

importance: **attach** ~ **to** *phr* GEN COMM adjudicar importancia a

important: **very** ~ **cargo** *n* (*VIC*) TRANSP carga muy importante *f*; ~ **office** *n* HRM cargo importante *m*; **very** ~ **person** *n* (*VIP*) GEN COMM persona muy destacada *f*

importation *n* (*imp.*) IMP/EXP importación *f*

imported[1] *adj* IMP/EXP importado, de importación

imported[2]: ~ **goods** *n pl* IMP/EXP mercancías importadas *f pl*; ~ **inflation** *n* ECON inflación importada *f*; ~ **service** *n* TAX servicio importado *m*

importer *n* IMP/EXP importador(a) *m,f*

impose *vt* GEN COMM, TAX imponer; ~ **a tax on sth** TAX gravar un impuesto sobre algo; ~ **undue hardship** TAX **on taxpayer** someter a una presión excesiva

imposition *n* GEN COMM *burden, request* imposición *f*

impossibility: ~ **theorem** *n* ECON teorema de la imposibilidad *m*

impound *vt* LAW incautar

impounding *n* LAW incautación *f*, TRANSP *ships* almacenamiento *m*

impoverished *adj* FIN empobrecido

impression *n* GEN COMM *opinion* impresión *f*

impressive *adj* GEN COMM *increase* impresionante

imprest: ~ **account** *n* ACC cuenta de anticipos *f*; ~ **fund** *n* ACC fondo fijo *m*; ~ **system** *n* ACC sistema de caja chica *m* (*AmL*), sistema de fondo fijo *m* (*Esp*)

imprint *n* MEDIA, S&M pie de imprenta *m*

imprinter *n* GEN COMM impresora *f*

imprison *vt* LAW encarcelar

imprisonment *n* LAW encarcelamiento *m*

improved: ~ **land** *n* PROP terreno mejorado *m*

improvement *n* GEN COMM mejora *f*, *system* mejoramiento *m*; ~**notice** *BrE* HRM *health and safety* apercibimiento de mejoras *m*; ~ **patent** PATENTS adición *f*

improvements: ~ **and betterments insurance** *n* INS seguro sobre mejoras en la propiedad *m*

impulse: ~ **buy** *n* S&M compra de impulso *f*, compra impulsiva *f*; ~ **buyer** *n* S&M comprador(a) por impulso *m,f*; ~ **buying** *n* S&M compra impulsiva *f*; ~ **goods** *n pl* S&M artículos de compra impulsiva *m pl*; ~ **purchase** *n* S&M compra de impulso *f*; ~ **sale** *n* S&M venta impulsiva *f*

impure: ~ **public good** *n* ECON bien semipúblico *m*

imputation *n* ACC, ECON, FIN imputación *f*

imputed: ~ **cost** *n* ECON, FIN coste imputado *m* (*Esp*), costo imputado *m* (*AmL*); ~ **income** *n* ACC ingreso imputado *m*, renta imputada *f*, ECON ingreso imputado *m*; ~ **interest** *n* TAX interés atribuido *m*; ~ **value** *n* ACC valor imputado *m*

IMRO *abbr* (*Investment Managers' Regulatory Organization*) STOCK organización reguladora de gestores de inversiones

IMRS *abbr* (*Industrial Market Research Services*) S&M servicios de investigación de mercado industrial

IMS *abbr* (*Institute of Manpower Studies*) HRM, WEL instituto de estudios laborales

IMV *abbr* (*internal motor vehicle*) TRANSP vehículo automotor interno *m*

in *abbr* (*inch*) GEN COMM pulgada *f*

inability: ~ **to work** *n* HRM incapacidad para trabajar *f*

inaccuracy *n* GEN COMM inexactitud *f*

inactive[1] *adj* GEN COMM inactivo

inactive[2]: ~ **account** *n* BANK, S&M cuenta inactiva *f*; ~ **asset** *n* STOCK activo sin movimiento *m*; ~ **bond** *n* STOCK título inactivo *m*; ~ **post** *n* STOCK puesto inactivo *m*; ~ **stock** *n* STOCK acciones inmovilizadas *f pl*

inadvertently *adv* GEN COMM inadvertidamente

inaugural: ~ **cruise** *n* TRANSP *shipping* crucero inaugural *m*; ~ **flight** *n* TRANSP vuelo inaugural *m*; ~ **sailing** *n* TRANSP navegación inaugural *f*; ~ **schedule** *n* TRANSP programa inaugural *m*; ~ **voyage** *n* TRANSP programa inaugural *m*

inboard *adj* TRANSP *motor* de vuelta

in-bond: ~ **manufacturing** *n* IMP/EXP manufacturas en depósito *f pl*

inbound: ~ **investor** *n* STOCK inversor(a) extranjero(-a) *m,f*

Inc. *abbr* *AmE* (*incorporated business company*) GEN COMM ≈ S.A. (*sociedad anónima*), ≈ S.A.A. (*sociedad anónima por acciones*), ≈ S.L.R. (*sociedad de responsabilidad limitada*)

incapacity *n* GEN COMM incapacidad *f*

ince *abbr* (*insurance*) GEN COMM, INS seguro *m*

incendiarism *n* INS provocación de incendios *f*

incentive *n* GEN COMM incentivo *m*; ~ **bonus** HRM prima de incentivo *f*; ~ **commission** S&M comisión de incentivo *f*; ~ **compatible** ECON incentivo compatible *m*; ~ **contract** GEN COMM contrato incentivo *m*; ~ **contracting** GEN COMM contratación por incentivos *f*; ~ **effect** ECON efecto incentivador *m*, efectos de incentivo *m pl*; ~ **fee** S&M honorarios de incentivo *m pl*; ~ **packs** *n pl* S&M envases con incentivo *m pl*; ~ **pay** HRM remuneración dependiente del rendimiento *f*; ~ **pay scheme** HRM paga por incentivos *f*; ~ **payment system** HRM sistema de remuneración por incentivos *m*; ~ **plan** HRM plan de incentivo *m*; ~ **rate** TRANSP *freight* tarifa incentivada *f*; ~ **stock option** *AmE* (*ISO*)

TAX incentivo fiscal sobre opciones *m* (*ISO*); **~ wage plan** HRM plan de incentivos salariales *m*

incestuous: **~ share dealing** *n* STOCK venta de acciones incestuosa *f*

inch *n* (*in*) GEN COMM pulgada *f*

Inchmaree: **~ Clause** *n* INS *in hull policy* Cláusula Inchmaree *f*

inchoate *adj* LAW incompleto

incidence *n* TAX incidencia *f*

incidental[1] *adj* GEN COMM contingente

incidental[2]: **~ charges** *n pl* ACC, GEN COMM gastos imprevistos *m pl*; **~ damages** *n pl* LAW, HRM daños y perjuicios incidentales *m pl*; **~ expenses** *n pl* ACC, GEN COMM gastos imprevistos *m pl*

incidentals: **~ allowance** *n* ACC asignación para gastos imprevistos *f*

incineration *n* ENVIR *of waste* incineración *f*; **~ plant** ENVIR, IND planta de incineración *f*

incitative: **~ planning** *n jarg* POL *socialist countries* planificación de estímulo *f*

incl. *abbr* GEN COMM (*inclusive*) comprendido, inclusivo, (*included*) comprendido, incluido

include *vt* GEN COMM incluir

included[1] *adj* (*incl.*) GEN COMM comprendido, incluido

included[2]: **~ angle** *n* TRANSP *cargo handling* ángulo de eslinga *m*

including *prep* GEN COMM incluido, comprendido

inclusion *n* GEN COMM inclusión *f*; **~ rate** TAX *for capital gains and losses* tasa de incorporación *f*

inclusive[1] *adv* (*incl.*) GEN COMM inclusivo, comprendido

inclusive[2]: **~ tour** *n* (*IT*) LEIS, TRANSP excursión con gastos incluidos *m*

income[1]: **~-tested** *adj* TAX sometido a la prueba de los ingresos

income[2] *n* ACC ingreso *m*, renta *f*, ECON ingreso *m*, TAX ingreso *m*, ingresos *m pl*; **~ accounts** *n pl* ACC cuentas de ganancias *f pl*, cuentas de ingresos *f pl*; **~ amounts** *n pl* TAX volumen de ingresos *m*; **~ approach** PROP método de rendimiento *m*; **~ available for fixed charges** ACC renta disponible para gastos fijos *f*; **~ averaging** FIN, TAX promedio de ingresos *m*; **~ band** TAX banda de ingresos *f*; **~ blank** ACC, TAX formulario del impuesto sobre la renta *m*; **~ bond** FIN, STOCK bono amortizable con los ingresos *m*; **~ bracket** TAX tramo de renta *m*; **~ budget** ACC presupuesto de ingresos *m*; **~-consumption curve** (*ICC*) ECON curva de renta-consumo *f*; **~ debenture** STOCK título con rendimiento *m*; **~ differential** ECON ingreso diferencial *m*; **~ distribution** ACC, ECON, TAX distribución de ingresos *f*; **~ earned overseas** TAX renta percibida en el extranjero *f*; **~ effect** ECON efecto de ingreso *m*; **~ elasticity of demand** ECON elasticidad-renta de la demanda *f*, S&M elasticidad-ingreso de la demanda *f*; **~ and expenditure account** ACC cuenta de ingresos y gastos *f*; **~ for the year** TAX ingresos anuales *m pl*; **~ from business** TAX rendimiento de los negocios *m*; **~ from discounting** BANK beneficios por descuento *m pl*; **~ from employment** ACC, TAX ingresos salariales *m pl*; **~ from interest** ACC, TAX ingresos por intereses *m pl*; **~ from participations** ACC, FIN ingresos de participaciones *m pl*; **~ from securities** ACC, TAX ingresos por valores *m pl*, renta de valores *f*; **~ from services** ACC, TAX ingresos de servicios *m pl*; **~ from trades and**

professions ACC, TAX ingresos procedentes de oficios y profesiones *m pl*; **~ gain** ACC aumento de beneficios *m*; **~ gains** *n pl* ACC ganancias de renta *f pl*; **~ group** S&M *market research* grupo de ingresos *m*; **~ in respect of a decedent** ACC, TAX ingresos procedentes de un fallecido *m pl*; **~ investment company** FIN sociedad de inversiones de renta *f*; **~ per head** ECON renta per cápita *f*; **~ property** *AmE* PROP propiedad de explotación *f*; **~ range** TAX banda de ingresos *f*, nivel de renta *m*; **~ received** TAX renta percibida *f*; **~ received under deduction of tax** TAX ingresos recibidos por deducción fiscal *m pl*; **~ receiver** GEN COMM beneficiario de rentas *m*; **~ redistribution** ECON redistribución de la renta *f*; **~ replacement insurance** INS *disability* seguro de incapacidad laboral *m*; **~ smoothing** ACC ajuste de ingresos *m*; **~ splitting** TAX participación de la renta *f*; **~ splitting system** TAX participación de renta a efectos tributarios *f*; **~ spread** FIN banda de ingresos *f*; **~ statement** ACC balance de resultados *m*, cuenta de pérdidas y ganancias *f*, cuenta de resultados *f*; **~ stream** ECON flujo de ingresos *m*; **~ subject to tax** TAX ingresos sujetos a imposición *m pl*; **~ and substitution effects** *n pl* ECON efectos de renta y sustitución *m pl*; **~ support** *BrE* HRM, WEL *social security payment* sostenimiento de los ingresos *m*, prestación social *f*; **~ tax assessment** TAX cálculo del impuesto sobre la renta *m*, valoración tributaria *f*; **~ tax deferral** TAX aplazamiento del impuesto sobre la renta *m*; **~-tax liability** TAX responsabilidad respecto al impuesto sobre la renta *f*; **~-tax package** TAX conjunto de medidas sobre el impuesto sobre la renta *m*, paquete del impuesto sobre la renta *m*; **~ tax rate** TAX tipo del impuesto sobre la renta *m*; **~ tax rate band** TAX banda de tipos del impuesto sobre la renta *f*; **~ tax refund** TAX devolución del impuesto sobre la renta *f*; **~ tax repayment claim** TAX reclamación de devolución del impuesto sobre la renta *f*; **~ tax return** ACC declaración del impuesto sobre la renta *f*, declaración sobre la renta *f*, TAX declaración a hacienda *f*, declaración del impuesto sobre la renta *f*, declaración sobre la renta *f*; **~ tax scale** TAX escala del impuesto sobre la renta *f*; **~ tax system** ECON, POL, TAX sistema tributario del impuesto sobre la renta *m*; **~ taxed at a lower rate** ACC, TAX ingresos gravados con un tipo más bajo *m pl*; **~ terms of trade** ECON proporción de intercambio-ingreso *f*; **~ test** TAX comprobación de los ingresos *f*; **~-tested supplement** WEL complemento salarial según ingresos *m*; **~ threshold** TAX nivel de ingresos *m*; ♦ **for ~ tax purposes** TAX para el impuesto sobre la renta; **take into ~** ACC incluir en los ingresos

Income: **~ and Corporation Taxes Act** *n AmE* LAW, TAX Ley de Impuestos sobre la Renta y Sociedades *f*; **~ Tax** *n* (*IT*) TAX ≈ Impuesto sobre la Renta *m* (*IRPF*); **~ Tax Act** *n* LAW, TAX Ley del Impuesto Sobre la Renta *f*; **~ Tax Regulations** *n pl* TAX Reglamento del Impuesto sobre la Renta *m*

incomes: **~ policies** *n pl jarg* HRM políticas de rentas *f pl*; **~ policy** *n* GEN COMM política de rentas *f*, FIN política de ingresos *f*

incoming: **~ call** *n* COMMS *phone* llamada de entrada *f*; **~ data** *n* COMP datos de entrada *m pl*; **~ goods** *n pl* COMMS artículos recibidos *m pl*, GEN COMM artículos nuevos *m pl*; **~ mail** *n AmE* COMMS correo entrante *m*; **~ order** *n* S&M nuevo pedido *m*; **~ post** *n BrE* COMMS correo entrante *m*

in-company: ~ **training** *n* HRM, IND capacitación interna *f* (*AmL*), formación interna *f* (*Esp*)

incompatible *adj* GEN COMM incompatible

incompetent *adj* HRM incompetente, LAW incapaz

incomplete *adj* GEN COMM incompleto

incontestable: ~ **clause** *n* INS cláusula irrecusable *f*

inconvertible: ~ **money** *n* ECON dinero no convertible *m*

incorporate *vt* GEN COMM incorporar, LAW, STOCK constituir

incorporated[1] *adj* GEN COMM constituido, incorporado

incorporated[2]: ~ **bank** *n* AmE BANK banco por acciones *m*, sociedad bancaria por acciones *f*; ~ **business company** *n* AmE (*Inc., cf limited company BrE*) ≈ sociedad anónima *f* (*S.A.*), ≈ sociedad anónima por acciones *f* (*S.A.A.*), ≈ sociedad de responsabilidad limitada *f* (*S.L.R.*)

incorporation *n* GEN COMM, LAW *of company* constitución *f*, STOCK constitución en sociedad anónima *f*, *of company* asociación *f*

incorporeal[1] *adj* GEN COMM incorpóreo

incorporeal[2]: ~ **hereditaments** *n pl* LAW bienes inmateriales por heredar *m pl*; ~ **property** *n* LAW propiedad intangible *f*, PROP bien incorporal *m*, propiedad intangible *f*

INCOTERM *abbr* (*International Commercial Term*) ECON, IMP/EXP INCOTERM (*cláusulas comerciales internacionales*)

increase[1] *n* ACC aumento *m*, incremento *m*, subida *f*, FIN aumento *m*, GEN COMM incremento *m*, acrecentamiento *m*, aumento *m*, crecimiento *m*; ~ **in capital** ECON ampliación del capital *f*; ~ **in cost of capital** FIN aumento en el coste de capital *m* (*Esp*), aumento en el costo de capital *m* (*AmL*)

increase[2] *vt* ACC aumentar, GEN COMM incrementar, aumentar; ♦ ~ **production** IND incrementar la producción; ~ **the supply** ECON aumentar la oferta; ~ **tenfold** GEN COMM aumentar diez veces; ~ **twofold** GEN COMM aumentar el doble; 2. *vi* GEN COMM incrementarse

increasing: ~ **budget deficit** *n* GEN COMM déficit presupuestario creciente *m*; ~ **liquidity order** *n* ACC método de aumento de liquidez *m*; ~ **opportunity costs law** *n* ECON ley de costes de oportunidad crecientes *f* (*Esp*), ley de costos de oportunidad crecientes *f* (*AmL*); ~ **return to scale** *n* ECON rendimiento creciente de escala *m*

increment *n* GEN COMM incremento *m*

incremental[1] *adj* COMP, GEN COMM *cost* incremental

incremental[2]: ~ **analysis** *n* ACC, GEN COMM análisis incremental *m*, MGMNT análisis de crecimiento *m*, TAX análisis incremental *m*; ~ **capital-output ratio** *n* (*ICOR*) ECON, FIN proporción incremental capital-producto *f*; ~ **cash flow** *n* ACC, FIN flujo de caja incremental *m*, FIN flujo de efectivo en aumento *m*; ~ **cost** *n* ACC, ECON, FIN coste marginal *m* (*Esp*), costo marginal *m* (*AmL*); ~ **oil revenue tax** *n* (*IORT*) TAX impuesto progresivo sobre los ingresos del petróleo *m*; ~ **payment** *n* ACC, FIN pago progresivo *m*; ~ **scale** *n* HRM escala progresiva *f*; ~ **spending** *n* S&M gasto incremental *m*; ~ **tax** *n* TAX impuesto adicional *m*; ~ **technology** *n* GEN COMM tecnología incremental *f*

incumbent *adj* POL *minister* titular del cargo *mf*

incur *vt* ACC *debts* contraer, GEN COMM *expenses* incurrir

incurable: ~ **depreciation** *n* PROP *appraisal* depreciación irremediable *f*

incurred: ~ **costs** *n pl* ACC, FIN costes incurridos *m pl* (*Esp*), costes realizados *m pl* (*Esp*), costos incurridos *m pl* (*AmL*), costos realizados *m pl* (*AmL*); ~ **expenses** *n pl* ACC, FIN gastos incurridos *m pl*, gastos realizados *m pl*

indebted *adj* ECON, FIN endeudado; ♦ ~ **to** GEN COMM endeudado con

indebtedness *n* ECON, FIN endeudamiento *m*

indefinite[1] *adj* GEN COMM indefinido

indefinite[2]: ~ **laytime** *n* TRANSP *shipping* estadía indefinida *f*

indemnify *vt* INS, LAW indemnizar

indemnity *n* INS, LAW indemnización *f*; ~ **bond** INS fianza de indemnización *f*; ~ **fund** HRM fondo de indemnizaciones *m*

indent[1] *n* BrE GEN COMM orden de compra *f*; ~ **house** GEN COMM agencia de importación *f*

indent[2] *vt* BrE GEN COMM *foreign goods* realizar un pedido de compra

indentation *n* COMP sangría *f*

indenture *n* LAW contrato *m*, STOCK contrato con el comisariado *m*; ~ **of apprenticeship** GEN COMM, LAW contrato de aprendizaje *m*

independence *n* ACC, ECON, GEN COMM, POL independencia *f*

independent[1] *adj* GEN COMM *arbitrator*, POL independiente; ♦ ~ **of** GEN COMM con independencia de, independiente de

independent[2]: ~ **accountant** *n* ACC contable independiente *mf* (*Esp*), contador(a) independiente *m,f* (*AmL*); ~ **adjuster** *n* INS ajustador(a) independiente *m,f*; ~ **auditors** *n pl* ACC, FIN, TAX auditores independientes *m pl*; ~ **broker** *n* STOCK corredor(a) independiente *m,f*; ~ **claim** *n* PATENTS reivindicación independiente *f*; ~ **contractor** *n* TAX contratista independiente *mf*; ~ **expert** *n* HRM experto(-a) independiente *m,f*; ~ **inquiry** *n* LAW investigación independiente *f*; ~ **local radio** *n* COMMS, MEDIA radio local independiente *f*; ~ **retailer** *n* S&M minorista independiente *mf*; ~ **store** *n* GEN COMM tienda independiente *f*; ~ **tank** *n* (*IT*) TRANSP *liquefied natural gas* cuba independiente *f*; ~ **tank center** *AmE*, ~ **tank centre** *BrE n* (*ITC*) TRANSP centro de tanque independiente *m*; ~ **taxation** *n* TAX tributación independiente *f*; ~ **television commission** *n* MEDIA, S&M comisión de la televisión independiente *f*; ~ **trade union** *n* GEN COMM, HRM sindicato independiente *m*; ~ **union** *n* GEN COMM, HRM sindicato independiente *m*; ~ **variable** *n* MATH variable independiente *f*

Independent: ~ **Review Committee** *n* BrE HRM Comité Independiente de Revisión *m*; ~ **Television Publications** *n* (*ITP*) MEDIA publicaciones de la televisión independiente de Gran Bretaña

independently: ~ **of** *adv* GEN COMM independientemente de

in-depth[1] *adv* GEN COMM en profundidad

in-depth[2]: ~ **analysis** *n* GEN COMM, MGMNT análisis a fondo *m*, análisis en profundidad *m*; ~ **business plan** *n* GEN COMM plan exhaustivo de negocios *m*; ~ **discussion** *n* GEN COMM discusión en profundidad *m*; ~ **interview** *n* S&M entrevista en profundidad *f*; ~ **study** *n* GEN COMM estudio pormenorizado *m*

indeterminate: ~ **premium life insurance** *n* INS seguro de vida con prima indeterminada *m*

index[1]: ~**-linked** *adj* HRM ajustable

index[2] *n* GEN COMM índice *m*; ~ **basis** MATH *comparative calculation* base de ajuste del índice *f*; ~**-card file** GEN COMM fichero *m*; ~ **of coincident indicators** FIN índice de indicadores coincidentes *m*; ~ **file** COMP, GEN COMM archivo índice *m*; ~ **fund** STOCK fondo indexado *m*; ~ **futures** *n pl* STOCK futuros sobre índices *m pl*; ~ **of industrial production** ECON índice de producción industrial *m*; ~ **of lagging indicators** ECON índice de indicadores retardados *m*; ~ **of leading indicators** STOCK índice de indicadores adelantados *m*, índice de indicadores anticipados *m*; ~ **lease** PROP alquiler de referencia *m*, arrendamiento indexado *m*; ~ **linkage** ECON, IND vinculación a un índice *f*; ~**-linked gilt** STOCK obligación del Estado indiciada *f*; ~**-linked investments** *n pl* ACC, ECON, STOCK ajustes referenciados a un índice *m pl*; ~**-linked stock** BrE FIN acciones indexadas *m*; ~ **linking** ECON articulación de índices *f*; ~**-linking** FIN, HRM indización *f*; ~ **of longer leading indicators** ECON, FIN índice de indicadores muy adelantados *m*; ~ **number** ECON, MATH número índice *m*; ~ **option** STOCK opción índice *f*; ~ **point** STOCK punto de índice *m*; ~ **price** STOCK precio índice *m*; ~ **of shorter leading indicators** ECON, FIN índice de indicadores poco adelantados *m*; ~**-tied loan** BANK, FIN préstamo reajustable *m*; ~**-tracking fund** FIN fondo que siguen la bolsa de valores *m*

Index: ~ **and Option Market division** *n AmE (IOM division)* STOCK *of the Chicago Mercantile Exchange* departamento de cotización y mercado de opciones

indexation *n* ECON corrección monetaria *f*, HRM indexación *f*; ~ **allowance** TAX desgravación por indexación *f*; ~ **relief** TAX *gains* deducción por indexación *f*

indexed[1] *adj* MATH indexado

indexed[2]: ~ **bond** *n* STOCK bono indizado *m*; ~ **currency option note** *n (ICON)* STOCK apunte de opción sobre divisas indexadas *m*; ~ **file** *n* COMP, GEN COMM fichero indexado *m*; ~ **life insurance** *n* INS seguro de vida actualizado *m*; ~ **loan** *n* BANK préstamo indexado *m*; ~ **security** *n* STOCK título indexado *m*; ~ **security investment plan** *n* STOCK plan indexado de inversión en valores *m*

indexing *n* ECON, STOCK indexación *f*

indicated: ~ **horsepower** *n (ihp)* GEN COMM potencia indicada en caballos de vapor *f*, potencia nominal *f*; ~ **yield** *n* ACC, FIN, STOCK rendimiento financiero necesario *m*

indication: ~ **of interest** *n* STOCK indicación de interés *f*

indicative[1]: ~ **of** *adj* GEN COMM indicativo de

indicative[2]: ~ **planning** *n* ECON planificación indicativa *f*, MGMNT planificación de dirección *f*, planificación indicativa *f*

indicator *n* ECON indicador *m*; ~ **variable** ECON indicador variable *m*

indictment: **by** ~ *phr* LAW conforme al auto de procesamiento

indifference: ~ **analysis** *n* MATH análisis de indiferencia *m*; ~ **curve** *n* ECON curva de indiferencia *f*

indirect: ~ **authorization** *n* BANK autorización indirecta *f*; ~ **cost** *n* ECON, FIN coste indirecto *m (Esp)*, costo indirecto *m (AmL)*; ~ **costs** *n pl* ACC, FIN, IND costes indirectos *m pl (Esp)*, costos indirectos *m pl (AmL)*;

~ **discrimination** *n* HRM discriminación indirecta *f*; ~ **expenses** *n pl* ACC, FIN gastos indirectos *m pl*; ~ **export trading** *n* IMP/EXP comercio de exportación indirecto *m*; ~ **exporting** *n* IMP/EXP exportación indirecta *f*; ~ **labor** *AmE see indirect labour BrE*; ~ **labor costs** *AmE see indirect labour costs BrE*; ~ **labour** BrE *n* ACC, ECON *task* trabajo indirecto *m*, HRM mano de obra indirecta *f*, *task* trabajo indirecto *m*; ~ **labour costs** *n pl* BrE ACC costes de personal indirectos *m pl (Esp)*, costos de personal indirectos *m pl (AmL)*; ~ **production** *n* ECON producción de bienes de capital *f*; ~ **route** *n* TRANSP ruta indirecta *f*; ~ **tax** *n* TAX impuesto indirecto *m*; ~ **taxation** *n* TAX imposición indirecta *f*; ~ **worker** *n* HRM trabajador(a) indirecto(-a) *m,f*

indirectly *adv* GEN COMM indirectamente

indiscountable *adj* GEN COMM no descontable

indispensable: ~ **labor** *AmE*, ~ **labour** *BrE n* HRM *task* trabajo indispensable *m*, *person* mano de obra indispensable *f*

individual[1] *adj* GEN COMM individuo

individual[2] *n* GEN COMM *person* individuo *m*; ~ **annuity policy** INS póliza individual de rentas anuales *f*; ~ **bargaining** HRM contrato individual *m*; ~ **clearing member** STOCK miembro compensador individual *m*; ~ **company accounts** *n pl* ACC cuentas de empresa individual *f pl*; ~ **company audited accounts** *n pl* ACC cuentas auditadas de empresa individual *f pl*; ~ **conciliation** HRM conciliación individual *f*; ~ **consumer** GEN COMM consumidor(a) individual *m,f*; ~ **firm** GEN COMM empresa individual *f*; ~ **grievance procedure** HRM, LAW procedimiento de agravio individual *m*; ~ **import licence** BrE, ~ **import license** AmE IMP/EXP licencia individual de importación *f*, licencia personal de importación *f*; ~ **income tax return** ACC, TAX declaración individual del impuesto sobre la renta *f*; ~ **investor** STOCK inversor(a) individual *m,f*; ~ **licence** BrE, ~ **license** AmE IMP/EXP licencia individual *f*, licencia personal *f*; ~ **life insurance** INS seguro de vida individual *m*; ~ **retirement account** AmE TAX cuenta de jubilación individual *f*; ~ **retirement account rollover** AmE *(IRA rollover)* TAX renovación de cuenta de jubilación individual *f*; ~ **rights** *n pl* HRM derechos individuales *m pl*

individualism *n* HRM *of employee or manager* individualismo *m*

individualization *n* WEL individualización *f*

individually *adv* GEN COMM individualmente

indivisibility *n* ECON indivisibilidad *f*

indivisible: ~ **exports** *n pl* IMP/EXP exportaciones indivisibles *f pl*; ~ **load** *n* TRANSP carga indivisible *f*

indorse *see endorse*

indorser *see endorser*

indorsor *see endorser*

induce *vt* LAW incitar

induced: ~ **draft** *n* FIN efecto inducido *m*; ~ **technical progress** *n* ECON progreso técnico inducido *m*

inducement *n* LAW *to break the law* incitación *f*; ~ **good** ECON bien inducido *m*; ~ **mechanism** ECON mecanismo de inducción *m*; ~ **payment** TAX pago de incentivo *m*

induction *n* GEN COMM, HRM, IMP/EXP admisión *f*; ~ **course** HRM, WEL curso de introducción *m*

inductive: ~ **reasoning** *n* GEN COMM, MGMNT razonamiento inductivo *m*; ~ **statistics** *n pl* MATH estadística inductiva *f*

indulgency: ~ **pattern** *n jarg* HRM, MGMNT *industrial relations* patrón indulgente *m*

industrial[1] *adj* ECON, IND industrial; ♦ **take ~ action** HRM emprender acciones laborales

industrial[2]: ~ **accident** *n* HRM, IND accidente industrial *m*; ~ **action** *n* GEN COMM acción reivindicativa *f*, huelga *f*, medida de presión *f*; ~ **activity** *n* IND actividad industrial *f*; ~ **advertising** *n* S&M publicidad industrial *f*; ~ **application** *n* IND *of machine*, PATENTS aplicación industrial *f*; ~ **arbitration** *n* HRM arbitraje industrial *m*; ~ **bank** *n* BANK banco industrial *m*; ~ **base** *n* IND base industrial *f*; ~ **capacity utilization** *n* IND utilización de la capacidad industrial *f*; ~ **capitalism** *n* ECON, IND, POL capitalismo industrial *m*; ~ **carrier** *n* TRANSP *shipping* buque de transporte industrial *m*; ~ **center** *AmE*, ~ **centre** *BrE n* IND centro industrial *m*; ~ **and commercial company** *n* (*ICC*) GEN COMM empresa manufacturera y comercializadora *f*; ~ **concentration** *n* IND concentración industrial *f*; ~ **conflict** *n* HRM conflicto industrial *m*; ~ **cooperation** *n* IND cooperación industrial *f*; ~ **court** *n BrE* (*cf labor court AmE*) HRM, IND Juzgado de lo Social *m*; ~ **demand** *n* IND demanda industrial *f*; ~ **democracy** *n* GEN COMM, HRM, POL democracia industrial *f*; ~ **development bond** *n* STOCK bono de desarrollo industrial *m*; ~ **discharge** *n* ENVIR desagüe industrial *m*; ~ **disease** *n* HRM enfermedad laboral *f*; ~ **dispute** *n* ECON, HRM, POL conflicto colectivo *m*, conflicto laboral *m*; ~ **dynamics** *n pl* IND dinámica industrial *f*; ~ **economics** *n pl* ECON economía industrial *f*; ~ **engineer** *n* GEN COMM, HRM, IND ingeniero(-a) industrial *m,f*; ~ **engineering** *n* GEN COMM, HRM ingeniería industrial *f*; ~ **equipment** *n* ACC equipo industrial *m*; ~ **espionage** *n* GEN COMM, IND espionaje comercial *m*, espionaje industrial *m*; ~ **estate** *n BrE* (*cf industrial park AmE*) IND, PROP complejo industrial *m*, parque industrial *m*, zona industrial *f*; ~ **expansion** *n* INS expansión industrial *f*; ~ **fatigue** *n* HRM fatiga industrial *f*; ~ **finance** *n* FIN, IND financiación industrial *f*; ~ **gas works** *n* IND fábrica de gas industrial *f*; ~ **goods** *n pl* ECON, GEN COMM, IND bienes industriales *m pl*, productos industriales *m pl*; ~ **health** *n* HRM higiene industrial *f*; ~ **hygiene** *n* HRM higiene en el trabajo *f*, higiene industrial *f*; ~ **incident** *n* HRM incidente laboral *m*; ~ **inertia** *n* IND inercia industrial *f*; ~ **injury** *n* HRM, IND accidente laboral *m*; ~ **loan** *n* STOCK préstamo industrial *m*; ~ **marketing** *n* S&M marketing industrial *m*; ~ **nation** *n* ECON, POL nación industrializada *f*; ~ **organization** *n* (*IO*) IND organización industrial *f*; ~ **overspill area** *n* IND polígono de descongestión *m*; ~ **park** *n AmE* (*cf industrial estate BrE*) IND, PROP complejo industrial *m*, parque industrial *m*, zona industrial *f*; ~ **plant** *n* IND planta industrial *f*; ~ **policy** *n* IND política industrial *f*; ~ **production** *n* ECON, IND producción industrial *f*; ~ **products** *n pl* ECON, IND productos industriales *m pl*; ~ **property** *n* GEN COMM, IND, PATENTS, PROP propiedad industrial *f*; ~ **property protection** *n* IND, PROP protección de la propiedad industrial *f*; ~ **psychology** *n* IND, MGMNT psicología industrial *f*; ~ **refuse** *n* ENVIR, IND desechos industriales *m pl*; ~ **relation** *n* (*IR*) ECON, HRM relación laboral *f*; ~ **relations director** *n* HRM, IND director(a) de relaciones industriales *m,f*; ~ **relations manager** *n* HRM gerente de relaciones industriales *mf*;

~ **rent** *n* IND, PROP arrendamiento industrial *m*, alquiler industrial *m*; ~ **reorganization company** *n* (*IRC*) IND sociedad de reorganización industrial *f*; ~ **research** *n* IND, S&M *of market* investigación industrial *f*; ~ **revolution** *n* IND revolución industrial *f*; ~ **safety** *n* HRM, IND seguridad industrial *f*; ~ **sector** *n* IND sector industrial *m*; ~ **security** *n* FIN garantía industrial *f*, título industrial *m*, IND protección industrial *f*; ~ **selling** *n* IND, S&M venta industrial *f*; ~ **service** *n* IND servicio industrial *m*; ~ **share** *n* FIN, STOCK acción industrial *f*; ~ **site** *n* IND enclave industrial *m*; ~ **society** *n* ECON, IND sociedad industrial *f*; ~ **source** *n* ENVIR *of pollution* foco industrial *m*; ~ **spirits** *n pl* IND alcoholes industriales *m pl*; ~ **strife** *n* HRM disputas profesionales *f pl*; ~ **system** *n* IND sistema industrial *m*; ~ **and trade policy adjustment loan** *n* (*ITPAL*) BANK, ECON préstamo de ajuste de la política industrial y comercial *m*; ~ **training** *n* HRM, IND capacitación industrial *f* (*AmL*), formación industrial *f* (*Esp*); ~ **training grant** *n* FIN subvención para la capacitación industrial *f* (*AmL*), subvención para la formación industrial *f* (*Esp*); ~ **tribunal** *n BrE* (*IT*) HRM, IND, LAW Juzgado de lo Social *m* (*Esp*), Magistratura de Trabajo *f* (*Esp*); ~ **union** *n* HRM sindicato de industria *m*; ~ **vehicle** *n* TRANSP vehículo industrial *m*; ~ **waste** *n* ECON, ENVIR, IND residuos industriales *m pl*; ~ **zone** *n* IND polígono industrial *m*

Industrial: ~ **and Commercial Finance Corporation** *n* (*ICFC*) IND, FIN Corporación de Finanzas Industrial y Comercial *f*; ~ **Council for Educational & Training Technology** *n* (*ICETT*) IND, WEL comité industrial de educación y aprendizaje de nuevas tecnologías; ~ **Development Authority** *n* (*IDA*) IND autoridad para el desarrollo industrial; ~ **Development Certificate** *n* IND Certificado de Promoción Industrial *m*; ~ **Market Research Services** *n* (*IMRS*) S&M servicios de investigación de mercado industrial; ~ **Planning Department** *n* IND ≈ Departamento de Planeación Industrial *m* (*AmL*), ≈ Departamento de Planificación Industrial *m* (*Esp*); ~ **Relations Policy Committee** *n* (*IRPC*) HRM comité de política de relaciones industriales

industrialism *n* ECON, IND industrialismo *m*

industrialist *n* ECON, IND empresario(a) industrial *m,f*, industrialista *mf*

industrialization *n* ECON, IND industrialización *f*

industrialize *vt* ECON, IND industrializar

industrialized[1] *adj* ECON, IND industrializado

industrialized[2]: ~ **countries** *n pl* GEN COMM países industrializados *m pl*

industry *n* GEN COMM industria *f*; ~ **leadership programs** *AmE*, ~ **leadership programmes** *BrE n pl* MGMNT *public relations* programas de liderazgo industrial *m pl*; ~ **standard** ECON, IND norma industrial *f*; ~ **track** TRANSP trayectoria de la industria *f*; ~**-wide agreement** HRM *EU* acuerdo sectorial *m*

inefficiency *n* GEN COMM ineficacia *f*, ineficiencia *f*

inefficient *adj* GEN COMM ineficiente

inelastic: ~ **demand** *n* ECON demanda inelástica *f*; ~ **supply** *n* ECON, S&M oferta inelástica *f*

inelasticity *n* ECON inelasticidad *f*; ~ **of demand** ECON inelasticidad de la demanda *f*; ~ **of supply** ECON inelasticidad de la oferta *f*

ineligible: ~ **paper** *n* BANK valores no negociados *m pl*

inequality *n* ECON, HRM, POL desigualdad *f*

inert: ~ **gas system** *n* (*IGS*) GEN COMM sistema de gas inerte *m*

inertia: ~ **salesman** *n* S&M vendedor por inercia *m*; ~ **selling** *n* S&M venta por inercia *f*

inertial: ~ **effect** *n* POL efecto inercia *m*; ~ **inflation** *n* ECON inflación inerte *f*

inevitably *adv* GEN COMM inevitablemente

INF *abbr* (*information*) GEN COMM información *f*

infant: ~ **industry** *n* ECON, IND industria incipiente *f*; ~ **industry argument** *n* IND argumento de la industria naciente *m*; ~ **mortality** *n* WEL mortalidad infantil *f*

infected: ~ **ship** *n* TRANSP barco contaminado *m*

inferential: ~ **statistics** *n pl* MATH estadística deductiva *f*

inferior: ~ **goods** *n pl* GEN COMM, IND bienes inferiores *m pl*, productos inferiores *m pl*

inferred: ~ **authority** *n* HRM autoridad estimada *f*

infession *n jarg* ECON inflación debida a un fallo en el sistema monetario

infinite *adj* GEN COMM infinito

infinitesimal: ~ **calculus** *n* ACC, FIN, MATH cálculo infinitesimal *m*

infirm *adj* TAX enfermo

inflame *vt* GEN COMM encender

inflatable: ~ **life raft** *n* TRANSP balsa salvavidas inflable *f*

inflate *vt* ECON, GEN COMM *economy* inflar

inflation *n* ECON, FIN, POL inflación *f*; ~ **accounting** ACC, ECON contabilidad de reposición *f*; ~**-adjusted deficit** TAX déficit inflacionario ajustado *m*; ~**-adjusted income** ACC ingreso ajustado a la inflación *m*; ~ **endorsement** INS, PROP endorso de ajuste por inflación *m*; ~ **illusion** ECON ilusión inflacionaria *f*; ~ **rate** ECON, POL tasa de inflación *f*; ~ **shock** ECON choque de la inflación *m*; ~ **tax** TAX impuesto sobre la inflación *m*

inflationary[1] *adj* ECON, FIN, POL inflacionario

inflationary[2]: ~ **expectations** *n pl* ECON expectativas inflacionarias *f pl*; ~ **gap** *n* ECON bache inflacionista *m*, brecha inflacionaria *f*, déficit inflacionario *m*; ~ **pressure** *n* ECON, FIN presión inflacionista *f*; ~ **spiral** *n* ECON espiral inflacionista *f*; ~ **trend** *n* ECON *decrease* tendencia inflacionaria *f*

inflationist *adj* ECON, FIN, POL inflacionista

in-flight: ~ **catering** *n* LEIS, TRANSP servicio de comida durante el vuelo *m*; ~ **entertainment** *n* LEIS, TRANSP espectáculos durante el vuelo *m pl*; ~ **facilities** *n pl* LEIS, TRANSP servicio durante el vuelo *m*; ~ **film** *n* BrE (*cf in-flight movie AmE*) LEIS, TRANSP película durante el vuelo *f*; ~ **information** *n* LEIS, TRANSP información durante el vuelo *f*; ~ **magazine** *n* MEDIA, TRANSP revista de abordo *f*; ~ **meal** *n* LEIS, TRANSP comida durante el vuelo *f*; ~ **movie** *n* AmE (*cf in-flight film BrE*) LEIS, TRANSP película durante el vuelo *f*

inflow *n* GEN COMM entrada *f*; ~ **of currency** ECON entrada de divisas *m*

influence *vt* GEN COMM *costs* influir, *decision* influenciar

influential *adj* GEN COMM influyente

info. *abbr* (*information*) GEN COMM información *f*

inform *vt* GEN COMM *advise* aconsejar, *by letter* informar, notificar, avisar, comunicar

informal[1] *adj* GEN COMM informal

informal[2]: ~ **arrangement** *n* GEN COMM acuerdo informal *m*; ~ **economy** *n* ECON economía informal *f*; ~ **interview** *n* HRM entrevista informal *f*; ~ **leader** *n* HRM líder informal *mf*; ~ **meeting** *n* ADMIN, GEN COMM reunión informal *f*; ~ **organization** *n* GEN COMM *society, management*, MGMNT organización informal *f*

informality *n* HRM informalidad *f*

informant *n* TAX declarante *mf*; ~ **letter** ACC, ADMIN, BANK carta de denuncia *f*

informatics *n* COMP computación *f*, informática *f*

information *n* (*info., INF*) GEN COMM información *f*; ~ **agreement** GEN COMM contrato de información *m*; ~ **bit** COMP bitio de información *m*; ~ **channel** COMP canal de información *m*; ~ **desk** ADMIN, GEN COMM, LEIS oficina de información *f*; ~ **flow** COMP, GEN COMM *company* circulación de la información *f*; ~ **handling** COMP, GEN COMM manejo de la información *m*; ~ **highway** COMP autopista de la información *f*, infopista *f*, infovía *f*; ~ **network** COMP red de información *f*; ~ **officer** HRM responsable de información *mf*; ~ **processing** COMP sistematización de datos *f*; ~ **retrieval** COMP recuperación de la información *f*; ~ **retrieval system** COMP sistema de recuperación de información *m*; ~ **return** TAX formulario con información salarial *m*; ~ **storage** COMP, GEN COMM compilación de datos *f*; ~ **system** COMP sistema de información *m*; ~ **technology** (*IT*) COMP informática *f*; ~ **technology company** COMP, IND empresa de tecnología de la información *f*; ~ **theory** GEN COMM teoría de la información *f*; ~ **transfer** COMP transferencia de informaciones *f*; ♦ **for further** ~ GEN COMM para más información; **for your** ~ (*FYI*) GEN COMM para su información

Information: ~ **Technology Export Organization** *n* (*EXPORTIT*) IMP/EXP organización de exportación de tecnología de la información

informative: ~ **advertising** *n* S&M publicidad informativa *f*; ~ **labeling** *AmE*, ~ **labelling** *BrE n* S&M etiquetado informativo *m*

informed *adj* GEN COMM *decision, argument, public* informado

infra- *pref* GEN COMM infra-

infrastructure *n* ECON, GEN COMM infraestructura *f*

infringe *vt* LAW, PATENTS infringir, vulnerar

infringement *n* LAW, PATENTS infracción *f*

infringer *n* LAW, PATENTS infractor(a) *m,f*

ingenuity *n* GEN COMM ingeniosidad *f*

ingot *n* GEN COMM lingote *m*

ingress: ~ **and egress** *n* GEN COMM ingresos y egresos *m pl*

inhabitant *n* GEN COMM habitante *mf*

inherent: ~ **defect** *n* GEN COMM defecto inherente *m*; ~ **error** *n* GEN COMM error inherente *m*; ~ **explosion clause** *n* INS *properties* cláusula por riesgo intrínseco de explosión *f*; ~ **risk** *n* STOCK riesgo inherente *m*; ~ **vice** *n* GEN COMM, TRANSP vicio propio *m*

inherit *vt* LAW, PROP, TAX heredar

inheritance *n* LAW, PROP, TAX herencia *f*, sucesión *f*; ~ **tax** TAX derecho de sucesiones *m*, impuesto de sucesiones *m*, impuesto sobre herencias *m*

inherited: ~ **audience** *n jarg* MEDIA *broadcast* audiencia heredada *f*; ~ **property** *n* LAW, PROP propiedad heredada *f*

inhibit *vt* GEN COMM bloquear

in-home: ~ **banking** *n* BANK banco interno *m*

inhospitable *adj* GEN COMM inhóspito

in-house[1] *adj* COMP *service, worker*, GEN COMM *translator*, HRM interno

in-house[2]: **~ lawyer** *n* BANK, GEN COMM, LAW ≈ abogado(-a) de empresa *m,f*, asesor(a) jurídico(-a) *m,f*; **~ operation** *n* STOCK operación interna *f*; **~ software** *n* COMP software interno *m*; **~ system** *n* COMP sistema propio *m*; **~ training** *n* HRM, IND capacitación dentro de la empresa *f* (*AmL*), capacitación interna *f* (*AmL*), formación dentro de la empresa *f* (*Esp*), formación interna *f* (*Esp*); **~ valuation** *n* PROP evaluación interna *f*

initial[1] *adj* GEN COMM inicial

initial[2]: **~ assessment** *n* TAX gravamen inicial *m*; **~ boiling point** *n* GEN COMM temperatura de ebullición inicial *f*; **~ capital** *n* FIN, STOCK capital inicial *m*; **~ expenditure** *n* FIN gastos de instalación *m pl*; **~ funding** *n* FIN provisión de capital inicial *f*; **~ inventory** *n* ACC inventario inicial *m*; **~ margin** *n* STOCK margen inicial *m*; **~ margin level** *n* STOCK nivel del margen inicial *m*; **~ margin requirement** *n* STOCK necesidad de garantía inicial *f*; **~ outlay** *n* ACC *of purchase* anticipo *m*, desembolso inicial *m*, entrega inicial *f*, pago inicial *m*, FIN desembolso inicial *m*; **~ public offering** *f* (*IPO*) GEN COMM oferta pública inicial *f* (*OPI*); **~ quantity** *n* GEN COMM cantidad inicial *f*; **~ sale** *n* S&M venta inicial *f*; **~ year** *n* GEN COMM primer año *m*

initialize *vt* COMP *operating system* inicializar

initiate *vt* COMP *software* iniciar

initiating: **~ explosive** *n* TRANSP *dangerous goods* explosivo iniciador *m*

initiation: **~ dues** *n pl* TAX cuotas de ingreso *f pl*; **~ fees** *n pl* TAX cuotas de ingreso *f pl*

initiative *n* HRM, MGMNT iniciativa *f*; ◆ **take the ~** HRM, MGMNT tomar la iniciativa

initiator *n* POL iniciador(a) *m,f*

inject *vt* GEN COMM *funds* inyectar

injection *n* ECON, FIN inyección *f*

injunction *n* LAW interdicto *m*; **~ bond** LAW fianza de entredicho *f*

injured: **~ party** *n* LAW parte agraviada *f*, parte ofendida *f*, parte perjudicada *f*

injurious: **~ affection** *n* LAW constitución lesiva de hipoteca *f*

injury *n* HRM, WEL *of employee* lesión corporal *f*; **~ independent of all other means** INS daño al margen de toda otra causa *m*

ink: **~-jet printer** *n* COMP impresora a chorro de tinta *f*

in-kind: **~ transfer** *n* WEL ayuda en especie *f*

inland: **~ carrier** *n* IMP/EXP, TRANSP empresa de transporte interior *f*; **~ clearance depot** *n* (*ICD*) IMP/EXP, TRANSP depósito aduanero interior *m*; **~ container** *n* (*IC*) TRANSP contenedor terrestre *m*; **~ haulage** *n* IMP/EXP, TRANSP *shipping* desplazamiento interior *m*; **~ marine insurance** *n* INS, TRANSP seguro de navegación interior *m*, seguro de transportes fluviales *m*; **~ navigation** *n* INS, TRANSP navegación fluvial *f*; **~ rail depot** *n* (*IRD*) TRANSP almacén ferroviario interior *m*; **~ waterway** *n* TRANSP vía interior de navegación *f*; **~ waterway vessel** *n* TRANSP embarcación fluvial *f*

Inland: **~ Revenue** *n* BrE (*IR*) TAX departamento gubernamental británico para regular los impuestos, ≈ Dirección General de Tributos *f* (*Esp*); **~ Revenue Office** *n* BrE (*IRO*) TAX departamento gubernamental

británico para regular los impuestos, ≈ Dirección General de Tributos *f* (*Esp*)

INMARSAT *abbr* (*International Maritime Satellite Organization*) COMMS, TRANSP INMARSAT (*Organización Internacional Marítima de Satélites*)

inner: **~ city** *n* ENVIR centro de la ciudad *m*; **~-city area** *n* ENVIR, GEN COMM, PROP zona del centro de la ciudad *f*; **~ code** *n* TAX código interior *m*; **~ harbor** *AmE*, **~ harbour** *BrE n* TRANSP dársena *f*, puerto interior *m*; **~ pack** *n* S&M envase interior *m*

innocent *adj* LAW inocente

innovate *vi* GEN COMM, IND, S&M innovar

innovation *n* GEN COMM, IND innovación *f*; **~ center** *AmE*, **~ centre** *BrE* IND centro de innovación *m*; **~ possibility frontier** ECON frontera de posibilidades de innovación *f*

innovative *adj* GEN COMM, IND, S&M innovador

innovator *n* GEN COMM, IND, S&M innovador(a) *m,f*, novador(a) *m,f*

inoperative: **~ clause** *n* LAW cláusula inoperante *f*

in-pack: **~ premium** *n* S&M premio contenido en el envase *m*

in pari delicto *phr* LAW a igual delito

in personam *phr* LAW in personam

in-plant: **~ training** *n* HRM, IND capacitación en la propia fábrica *f* (*AmL*), formación en la propia fábrica *f* (*Esp*)

input *n* ECON input *m*, GEN COMM entrada *f*; **~ cost** ACC coste de insumos *m* (*Esp*), costo de insumos *m* (*AmL*); **~ data** COMP datos de entrada *m pl*; **~ device** COMP dispositivo de entrada *m*; **~ factor** FIN factor de insumo *m*; **~ keyboard** COMP teclado de entrada *m*; **~ message** COMP mensaje de entrada *m*; **~-output** ECON input-output *f pl*; **~-output analysis** COMP análisis de entrada/salida *m*, ECON análisis input-output *m*, FIN, IND análisis de insumo/producto *m*, análisis de insumos y producción *m pl*, MATH análisis de entrada y salida *m*, análisis factor-producto *m*; **~-output table** COMP, ECON, FIN, GEN COMM tabla de entradas y salidas *f*; **~ tax** TAX impuesto sobre los factores de producción *m*; **~ tax credit** TAX desgravación de insumos *f*

input/output *n* (*I/O*) COMP entrada/salida *f* (*E/S*)

inputs *n pl* COMP entradas *f pl*, ECON factores de producción *m pl*, IND insumos *m pl*, INS factores de producción *m pl*, LAW insumos *m pl*

inquiry *n* COMP interrogación *f*, GEN COMM, S&M encuesta *f*, TAX encuesta *f*, petición *f*; **~ form** GEN COMM formulario de encuesta *m*; **~ program** COMP programa de consulta *m*; **~ test** S&M prueba de encuesta *f*

INSA *abbr* (*International Shipowners' Association*) TRANSP Asociación Internacional de Armadores *f*

insert *vt* COMP, S&M *advertising* insertar

in-service: **~ training** *n* HRM capacitación en el trabajo *f* (*AmL*), formación en el trabajo *f* (*Esp*)

inside: **~ back cover** *n* MEDIA *print* interior de la contraportada *m*; **~ front** *n* S&M *advertising* cobertura interna *f*; **~ front cover** *n* MEDIA *print* interior de la portada *m*; **~ information** *n* FIN, STOCK información privilegiada *f*; **~ lag** *n* ECON retraso interior *m*; **~ lot** *n* PROP terreno interior *m*; **~ money** *n* ECON dinero interior *m*

insider *n* STOCK empleado(-a) con información confidencial *m,f*; **~ dealing** FIN, STOCK transacciones con información privilegiada *f pl*; ~ **report** STOCK informe confidencial *m* (*Esp*), reporte confidencial *m* (*AmL*)

insolvable *adj* GEN COMM insoluble

insolvency *n* GEN COMM insolvencia *f*; ~ **clause** INS cláusula de insolvencia *f*; ~ **legislation** GEN COMM, IND, LAW legislación sobre insolvencia *f*

insolvent *adj* ACC insolvente

inspection *n* GEN COMM *product* inspección *f*; ~ **of files** PATENTS *of application* inspección de expedientes *f*

inspector *n* HRM inspector(a) *m,f*; ~ **of taxes** *BrE* TAX inspector(a) de Hacienda *m,f*

Inspector: ~ **General of Banks** *n* BANK inspector(a) general de banca *m,f*

inspectorate *n* WEL *office* cuerpo de inspectores *m*

inst. *abbr* (*instant*) GEN COMM cte. (*corriente*)

install *vt* COMP *software, peripherals* instalar, *system, network* implantar, GEN COMM colocar

installation *n* COMP *of system* instalación *f*; ~ **diskette** COMP disquete de instalación *m*; ~ **insurance** INS seguro de instalación *m*

installed *adj* (*inst.*) COMP, GEN COMM instalado

installment *AmE see* instalment *BrE*; ~ **purchase** *n AmE* (*cf hire purchase BrE*) GEN COMM, S&M compra a plazos *f*

installments: **in** ~ *AmE see* in instalments *BrE*

instalment *n BrE* BANK, GEN COMM plazo *m*, mensualidad *f*; ~ **base** *BrE* ACC modalidad aplazada *f*; ~ **contract** *BrE* LAW contrato de venta a plazos *m*, contrato de venta en cuotas *m*; ~ **credit** *BrE* BANK, FIN crédito a plazos *m*; ~ **loan** *BrE* BANK préstamo a plazos *m*; ~ **payment** *BrE* BANK, FIN pago a plazos *m*, pago aplazado *m*; ~ **repayment schedule** *BrE* BANK plan de pago a plazos *m*; ~ **sale** *BrE* PROP, S&M venta a plazos *f*

instalments: **in** ~ *adv BrE* GEN COMM en cuotas

instance: **in this** ~ *phr* GEN COMM en esta instancia

instant *n* (*inst.*) GEN COMM corriente *m* (*cte.*); ~ **monetarism** ECON monetarismo instantáneo *m*

instinct *n* S&M instinto *m*

institute *n* (*inst.*) GEN COMM instituto *m*; ~ **clause** INS *marine* cláusula de instituto *f*; ~ **warranty** INS garantía de instituto *f*

Institute: ~ **of Administrative Management** *n* (*IAM*) MGMNT instituto británico de gestión administrativa; ~ **of Bankers** *n* (*IOB*) BANK Instituto de Banqueros *m*; ~ **Cargo Clause** *n* (*ICC*) TRANSP Cláusula de Fletes del Instituto *f*; ~ **of Chartered Accountants** *n* (*ICA*) ACC instituto de contables colegiados; ~ **of Chartered Accountants in England and Wales** *n* (*ICAEW*) ACC instituto de contables colegiados de Inglaterra y Gales; ~ **of Chartered Accountants in Ireland** *n* (*ICAI*) ACC instituto de contables colegiados de Irlanda; ~ **of Chartered Accountants of Scotland** *n* (*ICAS*) ACC instituto de contables colegiados de Escocia; ~ **of Cost and Management Accountants** *n* (*ICMA*) ACC instituto de contables de costes y gestión; ~ **of Economic Affairs** *n BrE* (*IEA*) ECON Instituto de Asuntos Económicos *m*; ~ **of Electrical Engineers** *n* (*IEE*) HRM, IND instituto de ingenieros eléctricos; ~ **of Fiscal Studies** *n* (*IFS*) TAX, WEL Instituto de Estudios Fiscales *m*; ~ **for International Economics** *n* ECON Instituto de Economía Internacional *m*; ~ **for International Finance** *n* (*IIF*) FIN Instituto para Finanzas Internacionales *m*; ~ **of London Underwriters** *n* INS instituto de aseguradores de

Londres; ~ **of Manpower Studies** *n* (*IMS*) HRM, WEL instituto de estudios laborales; ~ **of Maritime Engineers** *n* (*IME*) TRANSP instituto de ingenieros náuticos; ~ **of Mechanical Engineers** *n* (*I Mech E*) IND instituto de ingenieros mecánicos; ~ **of Office Management** *n* (*IOM*) MGMNT instituto de administración de oficinas; ~ **of Personnel Management** *n BrE* (*IPM*) MGMNT instituto de administración de personal; ~ **of Practitioners in Advertising** *n* (*IPA*) S&M instituto de profesionales de publicidad; ~ **of Public Relations** *n BrE* (*IPR*) S&M instituto de relaciones públicas; ~ **of Shipping and Forwarding Agents** *n* (*ISFA*) TRANSP instituto de agentes consignatarios y transitarios; ~ **of Transport Administration** *n BrE* TRANSP instituto de gestión de transporte; ~ **of Travel Agents** *n BrE* LEIS instituto de agentes de viaje

institution *n* ECON, GEN COMM institución *f*; ~ **of an appeal** TAX interposición de una apelación *f*

institutional: ~ **advertising** *n* S&M publicidad institucional *f*; ~ **economics** *n* ECON economía institucional *f*; ~ **investor** *n* STOCK inversor(a) institucional *m,f*; ~ **lender** *n* BANK, FIN prestamista institucional *mf*

in-store: ~ **merchandising** *n* S&M comercialización en tiendas *f*; ~ **promotion** *n* S&M promoción en tienda *f*

instruction *n* COMP *program* instrucción *f*; ~ **book** GEN COMM manual de instrucciones *m*; ~ **leaflet** GEN COMM folleto de instrucciones *m*; ~ **manual** GEN COMM manual de instrucciones *m*; ~ **program** COMP programa de instrucción *m*

instrument *n* GEN COMM instrumento *m*, LAW documento *m*, instrumento *m*; ~ **variable** ECON instrumento variable *m*

instrumental *adj* GEN COMM *capital* instrumental

instrumentalities: ~ **of transportation** *n pl* INS trámites de transportes *m pl*

instrumentality *n* FIN, GEN COMM instrumentalidad *f*

insufficient: ~ **funds** *n pl* BANK saldo insuficiente *m*, ECON falta de fondos *f*, FIN saldo insuficiente *m*

insulate *vt* ECON, GEN COMM, STOCK aislar

insulated: ~ **capacity** *n* TRANSP *of container* capacidad termoaislada *f*; ~ **container** *n* TRANSP contenedor frigorífico *m*; ~ **tank container** *n* TRANSP contenedor de cuba refrigerada *m*; ~ **van** *n* TRANSP furgón frigorífico *m*, vagón frigorífico *m*

insurability *n* INS asegurabilidad *f*

insurable: ~ **interest** *n* INS interés asegurable *m*; ~ **risk** *n* INS riesgo asegurable *m*; ~ **title** *n* INS título asegurable *m*

insurance[1]: **~~poor** *adj jarg* INS *business* con seguro insuficiente

insurance[2] *n* (*ince*) GEN COMM, INS seguro *m*; ~ **annuity payment** INS pago de anualidad del seguro *m*; ~ **broker** INS agente de seguros *mf*, corredor(a) de seguros *m,f*; ~ **brokerage** INS correduría de seguros *f*; ~ **broking** INS correduría de seguros *f*; ~ **business** INS actividad aseguradora *f*, sector de seguros *m*; ~ **certificate** INS póliza de seguro *f*; ~ **charge** INS cargo del seguro *m*; ~ **company** INS aseguradora *f* (*AmL*), compañía de seguros *f* (*Esp*); ~ **consultant** ACC, FIN, INS, LAW asesor(a) de seguros *m,f*; ~ **contract** INS contrato de seguros *m*; ~ **corporation** INS aseguradora *f* (*AmL*), compañía de seguros *f* (*Esp*); ~ **cost** INS coste de seguro *m* (*Esp*), costo de seguro *m* (*AmL*); ~ **cover** *BrE* (*cf insurance coverage AmE*) INS cobertura del seguro *f*; ~ **coverage** *AmE* (*cf insurance cover BrE*) INS cobertura del seguro *f*; ~ **factoring** INS factoraje de seguros *m*; ~ **in force** INS seguro en vigor *m*; ~ **industry** INS sector de seguros *m*; ~ **market** INS mercado de seguros *m*; ~ **policy** INS póliza de seguro *f*; ~ **premium** INS prima de seguros *f*; ~ **proceeds** *n pl* INS ingresos de seguros *m pl*; ~ **property** INS propiedad del seguro *f*; ~ **report** INS declaración de siniestro *f*; ~ **settlement** INS liquidación del seguro *f*; ◆ **take out an ~ policy** INS suscribir una póliza de seguros

Insurance: ~ **Brokers' Registration Council** *n BrE* (*IBRC*) INS consejo de registro de agencias de seguros; ~ **Contributions Act Date** *n AmE* (*FICA*) LAW Ley Federal de Contribuciones de Seguros *f*; ~ **Ombuds-man Bureau** *n BrE* (*IOB*) INS oficina mediadora de seguros

insure *vt* INS asegurar; ◆ **not to ~ clause** INS cláusula de no asegurar; ~ **against fire** INS asegurar contra incendios

insured[1] *adj* INS asegurado; **over ~** INS sobreasegurado; ◆ **be ~** INS estar asegurado

insured[2]: ~ **account** *n* FIN, INS cuenta asegurada *f*; ~ **liability** *n* ACC, BANK pasivo asegurado *m*; ~ **mail** *n AmE* (*cf insured post BrE*) INS correo asegurado *m*; ~ **peril** *n* INS riesgo asegurado *m*; ~ **post** *n BrE* (*cf insured mail AmE*) INS correo asegurado *m*

insurer *n* INS asegurador(a) *m,f*; ~ **claim** INS reclamación del seguro *f*

insurgent *n* GEN COMM insurrecto(-a) *m,f*

int. *abbr* (*interest*) GEN COMM interés *m*, rédito *m*

intake *n* GEN COMM *of new orders* entrada *f*, *of students* admisión *f*, HRM, IMP/EXP *entry* admisión *f*

intangible: ~ **asset** *n* ACC, ECON activo intangible *m*, activo inmaterial *m*, bien inmaterial *m*, bien intangible *m*; ~ **asset worth** *n* ACC, ECON, FIN valor del activo intangible *m*; ~ **assets** *n pl* ACC, FIN bienes intangibles *m pl*, inmovilizado inmaterial *m*; ~ **contribution** *n* GEN COMM aportación intangible *f*; ~ **drilling and develop-ment cost** *n* ACC coste intangible de perforación y explotación *m* (*Esp*), costo intangible de perforación y explotación *m* (*AmL*); ~ **fixed assets** *n pl* ACC activos fijos inmateriales *m pl*, activos fijos intangibles *m pl*; ~ **good** *n* ACC, ECON bien inmaterial *m*, bien intangible *m*; ~ **property** *n* ACC bienes intangibles *m pl*; ~ **reward** *n* HRM gratificación intangible *f*, remuneración intangi-ble *f*; ~ **value** *n* ACC valor intangible *m*; ~ **wealth** *n* ECON riqueza intangible *f*

integral[1] *adj* TRANSP integral

integral[2] *n* TRANSP *type of container* integral *m*; ~ **calculus** *n* ACC, FIN, MATH cálculo integral *m*; ~ **part** *n* GEN COMM parte integrante *f*

integrate *vt* GEN COMM integrar

integrated[1] *adj* ECON integrado

integrated[2]: ~ **circuit** *n* (*IC*) COMP circuito integrado *m* (*CI*); ~ **company** *n* GEN COMM compañía integrada *f*; ~ **management system** *n* MGMNT sistema de gestión integrado *m*; ~ **project management** *n* (*IPM*) FIN gestión integrada de proyectos *f*; ~ **services digital network** *n* (*ISDN*) COMMS red digital de servicios integrados *f*

integration *n* GEN COMM integración *f*

integrative: ~ **bargaining** *n* HRM negociación integrativa *f*

integrator *n* IMP/EXP, TRANSP integrador(a) *m,f*

integrity *n* GEN COMM integridad *f*

intellectual: ~ **property** *n* LAW, PATENTS propiedad intelectual *f*; ~ **property rights** *n pl* LAW, PATENTS derechos sobre la propiedad intelectual *m pl*

intelligent: ~ **terminal** *n* COMP terminal inteligente *m*

intensification *n* ECON *of farming techniques* intensifica-ción *f*

intensify 1. *vt* GEN COMM *effort* intensificar; **2.** *vi* GEN COMM *slowdown, competition* intensificarse

intensive[1] *adj* GEN COMM intensivo

intensive[2]: ~ **farming** *n* ECON, GEN COMM *agriculture* cultivo intensivo *m*; ~ **livestock farming** *n* ECON *agriculture* ganadería intensiva *f*; ~ **production** *n* ECON *farming*, IND producción intensiva *f*; ~ **selling** *n* S&M venta intensiva *f*

intention *n* GEN COMM intención *f*

inter: ~ **availability** *n* LEIS posibilidad de cambiar de itinerario usando eventualmente los servicios de otra compañía; ~ **vote transfer** *n* FIN transferencia entre votos *f*

inter-account: ~ **dealing** *n* ACC, FIN venta intercontable *f*

interaction: ~ **matrix** *n* MGMNT matriz interactiva *f*

interactive[1] *adj* COMP, GEN COMM interactivo

interactive[2]: ~ **computing** *n* COMP computación interac-tiva *f*, informática interactiva *f*; ~ **mode** *n* COMP modalidad interactiva *f*, modo interactivo *m*; ~ **processing** *n* COMP tratamiento interactivo *m*; ~ **stock** *n* ACC existencias inmovilizadas *f pl*; ~ **system** *n* COMP sistema interactivo *m*

Inter-American: ~ **Development Bank** *n AmE* (*IDB*) BANK, ECON Banco Interamericano de Desarrollo *m* (*BID*)

interbank: ~ **business** *n* BANK negocios interbancarios *m pl*; ~ **deposit** *n* BANK depósito interbancario *m*; ~ **exchange rate** *n* BANK, ECON tipo de cambio interbancario *m*; ~ **market** *n* BANK, ECON mercado interbancario *m*; ~ **offered rate** *n* (*IBOR*) BANK tasa ofrecida interbancaria *f*; ~ **rate** *n* BANK tipo interban-cario *m*, tasa interbancaria *f*; ~ **transactions** *n pl* BANK operaciones interbancarias *f pl*, transacciones interban-carias *f pl*

interchange: ~ **container** *n* TRANSP contenedor de intercambio *m*; ~ **flight** *n* TRANSP vuelo de intercambio *m*; ~ **of letters** *n* COMMS intercambio de cartas *m*

InterCity *n BrE* TRANSP *train* interurbano *m*

intercoastal[1] *adj* TRANSP de cabotaje, intercostero

intercoastal[2]: ~ **tanker** *n* TRANSP buque cisterna de cabotaje *m*

intercommodity: ~ **spread** *n* STOCK margen entre los productos *m*

intercommunity: ~ **trade** *n* ECON, S&M comercio interco-munitario *m*

intercompany: ~ **market** *n* STOCK mercado interempre-sarial *m*; ~ **profit** *n* ACC, FIN utilidad entre compañías *f* (*AmL*), beneficio entre compañías *f* (*Esp*)

interconnection *n* GEN COMM interconexión *f*

intercontinental *adj* TRANSP intercontinental

intercooler *n* TRANSP refrigerador intermedio *m*

interdealer: ~ **broker** *n BrE* (*IDB*) STOCK corredor intermediario *mf* (*CI*); ~**broker system** *n* (*IDBS*) STOCK sistema de conexión entre intermediarios *m*

interdelivery: ~ **spread** *n* STOCK *currency futures* margen entre entregas *m*

interdepartmental[1] *adj* ADMIN, GEN COMM, POL interdepartamental

interdepartmental[2]: ~ **flexibility** *n* (*IDF*) HRM flexibilidad interdepartamental *f*; ~ **settlement** *n* LAW acuerdo entre departamentos *m*; ~ **settlement advice** *n* FIN notificación interdepartamental de liquidación *f*

interdependence *n* ECON, POL interdependencia *f*

interdependent[1] *adj* GEN COMM interdependiente

interdependent[2]: ~ **economy** *n* ECON, POL economía interdependiente *f*

interdepot: ~ **transfer** *n* TRANSP transferencia entre almacenes *f*

interest[1]: ~-**bearing** *adj* BANK con interés, rendidor de interés, con rendimiento de intereses; ~-**free** *adj* BANK sin intereses; ~-**linked** *adj* BANK sujeto a interés

interest[2] *n* GEN COMM (*i, int.*) interés *m*, rédito *m*; ~ **accrued** GEN COMM interés acumulado *m*, interés devengado *m*; ~ **arrearage** ACC, BANK intereses atrasados *m pl*; ~-**bearing deposits** *n pl* BANK depósitos que devengan interés *m pl*; ~-**bearing eligible liabilities** *n pl* BANK obligaciones aceptables con interés *f pl*; ~-**bearing instrument** STOCK instrumento que devenga interés *m*; ~-**bearing liabilities** *n pl* ACC obligaciones que devengan intereses *f pl*; ~-**bearing security** STOCK título con intereses *m*; ~-**bearing trading portfolio** STOCK cartera de operaciones que devenga interés *f*; ~-**bearing yield** STOCK *futures* rendimiento productivo *m*; ~ **charge** FIN cargo en concepto de intereses *m*; ~ **charges** *n pl* ACC *on loan* gastos de intereses *m*; ~ **check** *AmE*, ~ **cheque** *BrE* BANK, FIN cheque con intereses *m*; ~ **coupon** FIN cupón de intereses *m*; ~ **and dividend income deduction** TAX, STOCK deducción de los ingresos por dividendos e intereses *f*; ~ **earned** ACC intereses recibidos *m pl*; ~ **elasticity of savings** ECON elasticidad del interés de los ahorros *f*; ~ **formula** BANK cuadro de interés *m*, formula de interés *f*; ~-**free deposit** BANK depósito sin intereses *m*; ~-**free loan** BANK, FIN préstamo que no devenga interés *m*, préstamo sin intereses *m*; ~ **group** GEN COMM grupo de interés *m*; ~ **in a bank** BANK *shares held* interés en un banco *m*; ~ **in a company** GEN COMM participación en una compañía *f*; ~ **in a life insurance policy** INS participación en una póliza de seguro de vida *f*; ~ **in a partnership** STOCK participación en una sociedad *f*; ~ **in real property** STOCK participación en bienes raíces *f*; ~ **income** BANK ingresos por interés *m pl*, interés devengado *m*; ~ **margin** BANK margen de interés neto *m*; ~ **on arrears** BANK interés de moratorio *m*; ~ **on bonds** STOCK interés sobre bonos *m*; ~-**only loan** BANK, FIN préstamo con amortización al vencimiento *m*; ~ **operation** ACC operación con intereses *f*; ~ **and other investment income tax** TAX impuesto sobre la renta de intereses y otras inversiones *m*; ~ **paid** ACC, BANK intereses pagados *m pl*; ~ **payment** BANK pago de intereses *m*; ~ **penalty** BANK penalización en los intereses *f*; ~, **profit and dividends** *n pl* (*IPD*) ECON interés, beneficio y dividendos *m*; ~ **rate** GEN COMM tipo de interés *m*, tasa de intereses *f*; ~ **rate adjustment** BANK ajuste de la tasa de interés *m*, ECON ajuste del tipo de interés *m*; ~ **rate cartel** *BrE* BANK cartel de la tasa de interés *m*; ~ **rate ceiling** BANK tasa de interés tope *f*, GEN COMM techo del tipo de interés *m*; ~ **rate contract** STOCK contrato sobre tipo de interés *m*; ~ **rate differential** BANK tasa de interés diferencial *f*, ECON

diferencial de tipos de interés *m*; ~-**rate exposure** STOCK *of futures* riesgo de los tipos de interés *f*; ~ **rate future** FIN, STOCK futuros de tipos de interés *m pl*; ~ **rate futures contract** STOCK contrato de futuros de tipos de interés *m*; ~ **rate futures price** STOCK precio de futuros de los tipos de interés *m*; ~ **rate instrument** STOCK instrumento de tipo de interés *m*; ~ **rate movement** BANK movimiento de la tasa de interés *m*, ECON cambio del tipo de interés *m*; ~-**rate option** STOCK opción de tipo de interés *f*; ~ **rate quotation** BANK cotización de la tasa de interés *f*, ECON cotización del tipo de interés *f*; ~ **rate rebate** BANK rebaja de la tasa de interés *f*, GEN COMM reducción de los tipos de interés *f*; ~ **rate reduction** GEN COMM reducción de los tipos de interés *f*; ~ **rate risk** ACC, BANK, FIN riesgo de la tasa de interés *m*; ~ **rate sensitivity** ECON sensibilidad a los tipos de interés *f*; ~ **rate subsidy** FIN subvención por tipo de interés *f*; ~ **rate swop** FIN, STOCK permuta financiera de tipos de interés *f*; ~ **rebate** BANK rebaja de interés *f*, reducción de intereses *f*, ECON reducción de intereses *f*, FIN bonificación de interés *f*, descuento de interés *m*, reducción de intereses *f*; ~ **received** BANK interés recibido *m*; ~ **relief** ECON desgravación de los intereses *f*; ~ **risk** FIN riesgo de interés *m*; ~ **rollover date** BANK fecha de cambio de interés *f*; ~-**sensitive expenditure** FIN gasto volátil de intereses *m*; ~-**sensitive policy** INS póliza en la que el asegurado tiene un interés real; ~ **sensitivity** ECON sensibilidad al interés *f*; ~ **spread** BANK márgenes de variación de intereses *m pl*; ◆ **full ~ admitted** (*fia*) TRANSP interés total admitido; **have a vested ~ in sth** GEN COMM tener intereses en algo

Interest: ~ **Equalization Tax** *n* (*IET*) TAX impuesto de igualación de los tipos de interés

interested: ~ **party** *n* GEN COMM, LAW interesado(-a) *m,f*

interface[1] *n* COMP interfaz *m*; ~ **limit line** TRANSP *shipping* línea límite de apoyo *f*

interface[2] **1.** *vt* COMP, GEN COMM conectar; **2.** *vi* COMP interconectar

interfere with *vt* LAW *contract* intervenir en

interference *n* COMP, GEN COMM, LAW interferencia *f*; ~ **with contract** HRM interferencia con el contrato *f*

inter-firm: ~ **comparison** *n* GEN COMM comparación entre empresas *f*, comparación inter-empresas *f*

interfund *n* ECON interfondo *m*

intergenerational: ~ **distribution of income** *n* ECON distribución intergeneracional del ingreso *f*; ~ **equity** *n* ECON equidad intergeneracional *f*

intergovernmental *adj* POL intergubernamental

Intergovernmental: ~ **Committee for European Migration** *n* (*ICEM*) POL, WEL Comité Intergubernamental sobre Migraciones en Europa *m*

intergroup[1] *adj* HRM intergrupal

intergroup[2]: ~ **relation** *n* HRM relación intergrupal *f*

interim[1] *adj* GEN COMM *report, job* provisional

interim[2] *n* GEN COMM intermedio *n*; ~ **accounts** *n pl* ACC contabilidad provisional *f*, cuentas interinas *f pl*, cuentas intermedias *f pl*; ~ **agreement** GEN COMM acuerdo provisional *m*; ~ **audit** ACC auditoría interina *f*; ~ **certificate** STOCK certificado provisional *m*; ~ **closing** ACC, BANK, FIN, GEN COMM cierre intermedio *m*; ~ **dividend** ACC, FIN, STOCK dividendo a cuenta *m*, dividendo anticipado *m*, dividendo provisional *m*; ~ **financing** FIN financiación temporal *f*; ~ **injunction**

LAW interdicto *m*, PATENTS tipo de medida cautelar que acompaña a la demanda, o posterior a ella; ~ **loan** BANK préstamo provisional *m*; ~ **pension** FIN pensión interina *f*; ~ **relief** HRM, LAW medida cautelar de suspensión de una ley o reglamento; ~ **report** ACC informe intermedio *m*, informe provisional *m* (*Esp*), reporte provisional *m* (*AmL*); ~ **statement** FIN, GEN COMM informe provisional *m* (*Esp*), reporte provisional *m* (*AmL*); ~ **statements** ACC estados intermedios *m pl*, estados provisionales *m pl*; ◆ **in the ~** GEN COMM entretanto

Interim: ~ **Commission of the International Trade Organization** *n* (*ICITO*) ECON, IMP/EXP, POL comisión intermediaria de comercio internacional; ~ **Co-ordinating Committee for International Commodity Arrangements** *n* (*ICCICA*) STOCK Comité Provisional de Coordinación para Convenios Comerciales Internacionales *m*

interindustry: ~ **competition** *n* ECON, IND competencia entre empresas del mismo ramo *f*, competencia entre industrias *f*; ~ **trade** *n* IND comercio entre industrias *m*, comercio interindustrial *m*

interior: ~ **robbery policy** *n* INS póliza contra robo interno *f*

interline: ~ **agreement** *n* TRANSP *aviation* acuerdo entre compañías aéreas *m*; ~ **carrier** *n* TRANSP *aviation* transportista entre compañías *mf*

interliner *n jarg* LEIS persona que pasa de una línea aérea a otra en un aeropuerto

INTERLINK *n* ECON modelo de previsión económica

interlinked: ~ **transaction** *n* ECON *package deal* transacción vinculada *f*

interlocking: ~ **directorate** *n* LAW consejos de administración coincidentes *m pl*, MGMNT junta directiva vinculada *f*; ~ **directorship** *n* GEN COMM, MGMNT dirección mancomunada *f*

interlocutory[1] *adj* PATENTS interlocutorio

interlocutory[2]: ~ **decree** *n* LAW auto interlocutorio *m*

Intermarket: ~ **Trading System** *n AmE* STOCK sistema operativo entre mercados *m*

intermedia: ~ **comparisons** *n pl* S&M comparaciones entre medios de comunicación *f pl*

intermediary[1] *adj* GEN COMM intermediario

intermediary[2] *n* FIN, GEN COMM intermediario(-a) *m,f*; ~ **corporation** GEN COMM corporación intermediaria *f*; ~ **goods** *n pl* GEN COMM bienes intermediarios *m pl*

intermediate[1] *adj* GEN COMM intermedio

intermediate[2]: ~ **bulk container** *n* (*IBC*) TRANSP *goods* contenedor intermedio para graneles *m*; ~ **consumption** *n* COMP, ENVIR consumo intermedio *m*; ~ **container** *n* TRANSP contenedor intermedio *m*; ~ **credit** *n* BANK, FIN crédito a medio plazo *m*; ~ **financing** *n* BANK, FIN financiación a medio plazo *f*; ~ **goods** *n pl* IND bienes intermedios *m pl*; ~ **loan** *n* BANK préstamo a medio plazo *m*; ~ **stage** *n* FIN fase intermedia *f*; ~ **survey** *n* (*INT*) INS inspección intermedia *f*; ~ **target** *n* POL objetivo intermedio *m*; ~ **technology** *n* IND *production* tecnología intermedia *f*; ~ **term** *n* GEN COMM periodo intermedio *m*; ~**-term credit** *n* BANK, FIN crédito a medio plazo *m*

intermediation *n* FIN intermediación *f*

intermittent[1] *adj* GEN COMM intermitente

intermittent[2]: ~ **production** *n* IND producción intermitente *f*

intermodal[1] *adj* TRANSP intermodal

intermodal[2]: ~ **container** *n* TRANSP contenedor intermodal *m*; ~ **packaging** *n* TRANSP embalaje intermodal *m*; ~ **transport** *n* TRANSP transporte intermodal *m*; ~ **transport law** *n* LAW, TRANSP ley de transporte intermodal *f*; ~ **transport system** *n* TRANSP sistema de transporte intermodal *m*

internal[1] *adj* GEN COMM, HRM interno

internal[2]: ~ **audit** *n* ACC intervención interior de cuentas *f*; ~ **balance** *n* ECON equilibrio interno *m*; ~ **check** *n* GEN COMM comprobación interna *f*; ~ **communications** *n pl* COMMS comunicaciones internas *f pl*; ~ **consumption** *n* ECON, ENVIR consumo interno *m*; ~ **control** *n* ACC control interno *m*; ~ **debt** *n* ECON deuda interna *f*; ~ **debt ratio** *n* ECON, POL porcentaje de deuda interna *m*; ~ **economy** *n* GEN COMM economía interna *f*; ~ **economy of scale** *n* ECON, IND economía de escala interna *f*; ~ **expansion** *n* ECON expansión interna *f*; ~ **fare** *n* LEIS tarifa interna *f*; ~ **financing** *n* ACC, FIN, GEN COMM financiación interna *f*; ~ **flight** *n* LEIS, TRANSP vuelo nacional *m*; ~ **frontier** *n* GEN COMM frontera interna *f*; ~ **funding** *n* ACC, FIN asignación interna de fondos *f*, autofinanciación *f*, financiación interna *f*; ~ **government policy** *n* POL política interior del gobierno *f*; ~ **house magazine** *n* MEDIA, S&M revista de producción interna *f*; ~ **labor market** *AmE see internal labour market BrE*; ~ **labor market contracting** *AmE see internal labour market contracting BrE*; ~ **labour market** *n BrE* ECON *of company* mercado laboral interno *m*, POL mercado de trabajo doméstico *m*; ~ **labour market contracting** *n BrE* ECON contratación del mercado laboral interno *f*; ~ **market** *n* ECON mercado interno *m*; ~ **motor vehicle** *n* (*IMV*) TRANSP vehículo automotor interno *m*; ~ **orientation** *n* HRM, MGMNT orientación interna *f*; ~ **policy** *n* ECON, POL política interior *f*; ~ **procedure** *n* TRANSP procedimiento interno *m*; ~ **rate of discount** *n* ACC tasa interna de descuento *f*, tipo interno de descuento *m*; ~ **rate of return** *n* (*IRR*) FIN tasa de rendimiento interna *f* (*TRI*); ~ **revenue code** *n* TAX código de impuestos interiores *m*; ~ **sales manager** *n* HRM, S&M director(a) de ventas internas *m,f*; ~ **school assessment** *n* WEL evaluación en el propio centro educativo *f*; ~ **search** *n* HRM *for staff* contratación interna *f*; ~ **storage** *n* COMP memoria interna *f*; ~ **transactions** *n pl* ACC transacciones internas *f pl*

Internal: ~ **Revenue Service** *n AmE* (*IRS*) TAX departamento gubernamental estadounidense para regular los impuestos, ≈ Dirección General de Tributos *f* (*Esp*)

internalization *n* GEN COMM internalización *f*

internalize *vt* GEN COMM internalizar; ◆ ~ **an externality** ECON interiorizar una externalidad

internally: ~**-funded pension** *n* HRM pensión de financiación interna *f*; ~**-generated funds** *n pl* ACC fondos generados internamente *m pl*

inter-nation: ~ **equity** *n* ECON equidad inter-nación *f*

international[1] *adj* (*intl*) BANK, GEN COMM internacional

international[2]: ~ **affairs** *n pl* POL asuntos internacionales *m pl*; ~ **agency** *n* GEN COMM organismo internacional *m*; ~ **agreement** *n* LAW, POL acuerdo internacional *m*; ~ **airline** *n* TRANSP línea aérea internacional *f*; ~ **airport** *n* TRANSP aeropuerto internacional *m*; ~ **application** *n* PATENTS aplicación internacional *f*; ~ **banking** *n* BANK banca internacional *f*; ~ **banking facility** *n* (*IBF*) BANK facilidad bancaria internacional *f*; ~ **bond** *n* STOCK obligación internacional *f*; ~ **business** *n* ECON, MGMNT comercio internacional *m*; ~ **call** *n* COMMS llamada internacional *f*; ~ **capital market** *n* STOCK mercado internacional de capitales *m*; ~ **cartel** *n* ECON cartel internacional *m*; ~ **clearing house** *n* BANK cámara de compensación internacional *f*; ~ **comparisons** *n pl* ECON comparaciones internacionales *f pl*; ~ **comparisons of the cost of living** *n pl* ECON comparaciones internacionales del coste de vida *f pl* (*Esp*), comparaciones internacionales del costo de vida *f pl* (*AmL*); ~ **competitiveness** *n* ECON competencia internacional *f*; ~ **conference** *n* MGMNT conferencia internacional *f*; ~ **credit** *n* BANK crédito internacional *m*; ~ **direct dialing** *AmE*, ~ **direct dialling** *BrE* *n* COMMS discado internacional directo *m*, selección automática internacional *f*; ~ **driver's licence** *BrE*, ~ **driver's license** *AmE* *n* ADMIN licencia de conducir internacional *f* (*AmL*), carnet de conducir internacional *m* (*Esp*), permiso de conducir internacional *m* (*Esp*); ~ **driving permit** *n* ADMIN licencia de conducir internacional *f* (*AmL*), carnet de conducir internacional *m* (*Esp*), permiso de conducir internacional *m* (*Esp*); ~ **economic cooperation** *n* ECON cooperación económica internacional *f*; ~ **financial management** *n* FIN gestión financiera internacional *f*; ~ **freight forwarder** *n* TRANSP agente expedidor(a) internacional *m,f*; ~ **gateway** *n* TRANSP *aviation* entrada internacional *f*; ~ **goods regulations** *n pl* IMP/EXP, TRANSP normativa internacional sobre mercancías *f*; ~ **law** *n* LAW, POL derecho internacional *m*, ley internacional *f*; ~ **liquidity** *n* ECON liquidez internacional *f*; ~ **liquidity ratio** *n* BANK relación de liquidez internacional *f*; ~ **management** *n* MGMNT gerencia internacional *f*; ~ **marketing** *n* S&M marketing internacional *m*; ~ **monetary market certificate of deposit index** *n* STOCK índice de certificados del depósito del mercado monetario internacional *m*; ~ **monetary market three-month add-on index** *n* FIN índice de compra a plazo a tres meses del mercado monetario internacional *m*; ~ **monetary system** *n* ECON sistema monetario internacional *m*; ~ **money draft** *n* BANK giro monetario internacional *m*; ~ **money flow** *n* ECON, GEN COMM flujo monetario internacional *m*; ~ **money order** *n* (*IMO*) BANK giro postal internacional *m*; ~ **payment** *n* ECON pago internacional *m*; ~ **payment order** *n* (*IPO*) ACC, BANK orden de pago internacional *f*; ~ **preliminary examining authority** *n* PATENTS autoridad internacional encargada del examen preliminar *f*; ~ **registration** *n* PATENTS registro internacional *m*; ~ **representation** *n* GEN COMM representación internacional *f*; ~ **reserve** *n* ECON reserva internacional *f*; ~ **road haulage permit** *n* IMP/EXP, TRANSP permiso internacional de transporte por carretera *m*; ~ **standard** *n* GEN COMM norma internacional *f*; ~ **syndication** *n* BANK, ECON, MGMNT sindicato internacional *m*; ~ **telegram** *n* COMMS telegrama internacional *m*; ~ **trade** *n* ECON comercio internacional *m*; ~ **trade theory** *n* ECON teoría internacional del comercio *f*; ~ **trading certificate** *n* ECON certificado de comercio internacional *m*; ~ **traffic** *n* IMP/EXP, TRANSP transporte internacional *m*; ~ **travel** *n* GEN COMM, TRANSP viaje internacional *m*; ~ **union** *n* BANK, ECON sindicato internacional *m*; ~ **union federation** *n* HRM federación internacional de sindicatos *f*; ~ **wage levels** *n pl* ECON niveles salariales internacionales *m pl*

International: ~ **Accounting Standards Committee** *n* (*IASC*) ACC Comité Internacional de Normas Con-

tables *m*; ~ **Agricultural Research Institute** *n* (*IARA*) IND Instituto Internacional de Investigación Agrícola *m*; ~ **Aid and Loan Bulletin** *n* BANK Boletín Internacional de Ayuda y Préstamo *m*; ~ **Air Transport Association** *n* (*IATA*) TRANSP Asociación Internacional de Transporte Aéreo *f* (*IATA*); ~ **Association of Classification Societies** *n* (*IACS*) GEN COMM asociación internacional de sociedades de clasificación; ~ **Association of Environmental Co-ordinators** *n* (*IAEC*) ENVIR Asociación Internacional de Coordinadoras del Medio Ambiente *f*; ~ **Association for the Distribution of Food Products** *n* S&M Asociación Internacional para la Distribución de Productos Alimenticios *f*; ~ **Association for the Protection of Industrial Property** *n* (*IAPIP*) LAW, PROP Asociación Internacional para la Protección de Propiedad Industrial *f*; ~ **Association of Ports and Harbours** *n* (*IAPH*) IMP/EXP, TRANSP Organización Internacional de Puertos *f*; ~ **Auditing Practices Committee** *n* (*IAPC*) ACC, BANK Comité Internacional de Prácticas de Auditoría *m*; ~ **Auditing Standard** *n* (*IAS*) ACC Norma Internacional de Auditoría *f*; ~ **Bank for Economic Cooperation** *n* (*IBEC*) BANK Banco Internacional para la Cooperación Económica *m* (*IBEC*); ~ **Bank for Reconstruction and Development** *n* (*IBRD*) BANK, ECON Banco Internacional para la Reconstrucción y el Desarrollo *m* (*BIRD*); ~ **Banking Act** *n* BANK, LAW *1978* ley bancaria internacional *f*; ~ **Cargo Handling Coordination Association** *n* (*ICHCA*) TRANSP Asociación Internacional Coordinadora de Transporte de Cargamento *f*; ~ **Centre for Industry and the Environment** *n* (*ICIE*) ENVIR, IND Centro Internacional para la Industria y el Medio Ambiente *m*; ~ **Centre of Tropical Agriculture** *n* ECON Centro Internacional de Agricultura Tropical *m*; ~ **Chamber of Commerce** *n* (*ICC*) ECON Cámara de Comercio Internacional *f*; ~ **Chamber of Shipping** *n* (*ICS*) TRANSP Cámara Internacional de Comercio Marítimo *f*; ~ **Civil Aviation Organization** *n* (*ICAO*) TRANSP Organización de Aviación Civil Internacional *f*; ~ **Clearing Union** *n* (*ICU*) BANK, ECON Unión Internacional de Compensación *f*; ~ **Commercial Term** *n* (*INCOTERM*) ECON, IMP/EXP cláusulas comerciales internacionales *f pl* (*INCOTERM*); ~ **Commodities Clearing House** *n* (*ICCH*) STOCK Cámara de Compensación de Productos Internacionales *f*; ~ **Commodity Agreements** *n pl* (*ICA's*) STOCK Acuerdos Internacionales sobre Comercio *m pl*; ~ **Confederation of Free Trade Unions** *n* (*ICFTU*) HRM Confederación Internacional de Sindicatos Independientes *f*; ~ **Control Centre** *n* (*ICC*) GEN COMM Centro Internacional de Control *m*; ~ **Convention on Carriage of Goods by Rail** *n* GEN COMM, TRANSP Convención Internacional de Transporte de Mercancías por Ferrocarril *f*; ~ **Cooperation Administration** *n* (*ICA*) POL administración de cooperación internacional; ~ **Cotton Advisory Committee** *n* (*ICAC*) IND Comité Internacional de Consultoría del Algodón *m*; ~ **Council of Containership Operators** *n* (*ICCO*) TRANSP Consejo Internacional de Operadores de Contenedores de Carga *m*; ~ **Court of Justice** *n* (*ICJ*) LAW, POL Tribunal Internacional de Justicia *m*; ~ **Customs Tariffs Bureau** *n* *BrE* (*ICTB*) IMP/EXP, TRANSP Oficina Internacional de Tarifas Aduaneras *f*; ~ **Development Agency** *n* ECON Agencia de Desarrollo Internacional *f*; ~ **Development Association** *n* (*IDA*) ECON Asociación Internacional de Fomento *f* (*AIF*);

~ **Development Research Centre** n (*IDRC*) WEL centro internacional de investigación y desarrollo; ~ **Energy Agency** n (*IEA*) ENVIR Agencia Internacional de la Energía f (*AIE*); ~ **Equities Market** n (*IEM*) STOCK Mercado Internacional de Acciones m; ~ **Federation of Agricultural Producers** n (*IFAP*) ECON, POL Federación Internacional de Productores Agrícolas f; ~ **Federation for Documentation** n (*IFD*) GEN COMM Federación Internacional de Documentación f; ~ **Federation of Forwarding Agents' Associations** n TRANSP Federación Internacional de Asociaciones de Agentes de Transitorios f; ~ **Federation of Freight Forwarders' Associations** n TRANSP Federación Internacional de Asociaciones de Agentes de Transporte f; ~ **Federation of Stock Exchanges** n (*IFSE*) STOCK Federación Internacional de Bolsas de Valores f; ~ **Federation of Trade Unions** n (*IFTU*) HRM federación internacional de sindicatos; ~ **Finance Corporation** n (*IFC*) FIN Corporación de Finanzas Internacionales f (*CFI*); ~ **Hotel Association** n LEIS Asociación Internacional de Hoteles f; ~ **Institute for Unification of Private Law** n LAW Instituto Internacional para la Unificación del Derecho Privado m; ~ **Investment Bank** n (*IIB*) BANK Banco de Inversión Internacional m; ~ **Labor Organization** AmE, ~ **Labour Organization** BrE n (*ILO*) HRM, POL, WEL Organización Internacional de Trabajo f (*OIT*); ~ **Load Line Certificate** n TRANSP *shipping* Certificado de Franco a Bordo Internacional m; ~ **Longshoremen's Association** n (*ILA*) TRANSP asociación international de estibadores; ~ **Maritime Bureau** n (*IMB*) TRANSP Registro Marítimo Internacional m; ~ **Maritime Committee** n (*IMC*) TRANSP Comité Marítimo Internacional m; ~ **Maritime Dangerous Goods Code** n (*IMDGC*) TRANSP Código Marítimo Internacional de Productos Peligrosos m; ~ **Maritime Organization** n (*IMO*) TRANSP Organización Marítima Internacional f; ~ **Maritime Satellite Organization** n (*INMARSAT*) COMMS, TRANSP Organización Internacional Marítima de Satélites f (*INMARSAT*); ~ **Miners' Organization** n (*IMO*) IND Organización Internacional de Mineros f; ~ **Monetary Fund** n (*IMF*) ECON, POL Fondo Monetario Internacional m (*FMI*); ~ **Monetary Market** n (*IMM*) ECON, POL, STOCK Mercado Monetario Internacional m; ~ **Monetary Market certificate of deposit index** n (*IMM CD index*) STOCK índice de certificados de depósito del Mercado Monetario Internacional m; ~ **Monetary Market three-month discount index** n FIN índice de descuento a tres meses del Mercado Monetario Internacional m; ~ **Monetary Market Treasury bill index** n (*IMM T-bill index*) STOCK Índice de Letras del Tesoro del Mercado Monetario Internacional m; ~ **Oil Pollution Compensation Fund** n (*IOPC Fund*) BANK, ENVIR Fondo de Compensación Internacional para la Contaminación Producida por Petróleo m; ~ **Oil Tanker and Terminal Safety Group** n (*IOTTSG*) TRANSP Grupo Internacional para la Seguridad de los Petroleros y las Terminales m; ~ **Options Market** n (*IOM*) STOCK Mercado Internacional de Opciones m; ~ **Organization of Employers** n (*IOE*) HRM Organización Internacional Patronal f; ~ **Organization for Legal Metrology** n (*OIML*) GEN COMM Organización Internacional de Metrología Legal f (*OIML*); ~ **Organization of Securities Commissions** n (*IOSCO*) STOCK Organización Internacional de Comisiones de Valores f; ~ **Petroleum Exchange** n (*IPE*)

STOCK Mercado Internacional del Petróleo m; ~ **Press Institute** n (*IPI*) MEDIA Instituto Internacional de Prensa m; ~ **Primary Market Association** n (*IPMA*) STOCK Asociación Internacional de Entidades del Mercado Primario de Bonos f; ~ **Radio-Maritime Committee** n COMMS Comité Radiomarítimo Internacional m; ~ **Recruitment Unit** n (*IRU*) HRM Unidad Internacional de Reclutamiento f; ~ **Road Transport Union** n (*IRU*) TRANSP Sindicato Internacional de Transporte por Carretera m; ~ **SAR** n (*International Search and Rescue*) WEL Servicio de Rescate Internacional m; ~ **Search and Rescue** n (*International SAR*) WEL Servicio de Rescate Internacional m; ~ **Securities Market Association** n (*ISMA*) STOCK Asociación Internacional de Mercados de Valores f; ~ **Securities Regulatory Organization** n (*ISRO*) STOCK Organización Internacional Reguladora de Valores f; ~ **Service for National Agricultural Research** n (*ISNAR*) ECON Servicio Internacional para Investigación Agrícola Nacional m; ~ **Shipowners' Association** n (*INSA*) TRANSP Asociación Internacional de Armadores f; ~ **Shipping Federation** n (*ISF*) TRANSP Federación Internacional de Compañías Navieras f; ~ **Shipping Information Service** n (*ISIS*) TRANSP Servicio Internacional de Información Marítima m; ~ **Social Service** n (*ISS*) WEL Servicio Social Internacional m; ~ **Standard Book Number** n (*ISBN*) MEDIA Numeración Internacional Normalizada de Libros f (*ISBN*); ~ **Standard Classification of Occupations** n (*ISCO*) ECON Clasificación Internacional del Empleo f; ~ **Standard Serial Number** n (*ISSN*) MEDIA *print* número de serie de la Norma Internacional m; ~ **Standards Industrial Classification** n (*ISIC*) IND Clasificación Industrial según Normas Internacionales f; ~ **Standards Organization** n (*ISO*) GEN COMM Organización Internacional de Normalización f (*OIN*); ~ **Statistical Institute** n (*ISI*) GEN COMM, MATH Instituto Internacional de Estadística m; ~ **Stock Exchange** n BrE (*ISE*) STOCK Bolsa Internacional f, Bolsa Internacional de Valores f; ~ **Sugar Council** n (*ISC*) IND Consejo Internacional del Azúcar m; ~ **Swap Dealers' Association** n (*ISDA*) STOCK Asociación Internacional de Operadores de Swap f; ~ **Telecommunications Union** n (*ITU*) COMMS Unión Internacional de Telecomunicaciones f (*UIT*); ~ **Tin Council** n (*ITC*) IND Consejo Internacional del Estaño m; ~ **Trade Center** AmE, ~ **Trade Centre** BrE n GEN COMM Centro de Comercio Internacional m; ~ **Trade Law** n ECON, LAW, POL, S&M Derecho Comercial Internacional m; ~ **Trade Organization** n (*ITO*) GEN COMM Organización Internacional de Comercio f (*OIC*); ~ **Transport Workers' Federation** n (*ITF*) TRANSP federación internacional de trabajadores del transporte; ~ **Union of Official Travel Organizations** n (*IUOTO*) LEIS, TRANSP Sindicato Internacional de Organizaciones de Viajes Oficiales m; ~ **Union of Railways** n (*IUR*) TRANSP Sindicato Internacional de Ferrocarriles m; ~ **Wheat Council** n BrE (*IWC*) IND Consejo Internacional del Trigo m; ~ **Wool Secretariat** n (*IWS*) IND Secretaría Internacional de la Lana f

internationalism n POL internacionalismo m

internationalization n GEN COMM internacionalización f

internationalize vt GEN COMM internacionalizar

Internet n COMMS, COMP, GEN COMM Internet m, la Web f, la Red f, la Telaraña f interoperability *n* COMP, FIN, IND interoperabilidad *f*

Inter-Parliamentary: ~ Union *n* POL unión inter-parlamentaria

interperiod: ~ income tax allocation *n* TAX distribución periódica del impuesto sobre la renta *f*

interpersonal: ~ skill *n* HRM técnica interpersonal *f*; ~ utility comparisons *n pl* ECON comparaciones de la utilidad interpersonales *f pl*

interplay *n* GEN COMM efecto recíproco *m*

interpleader *n* LAW admisión de tercero en juicio *f*

interpolation *n* MATH interpolación *f*

inter praesentes *adv* GEN COMM entre los presentes

interpret *vt* GEN COMM interpretar

interpretation *n* GEN COMM interpretación *f*

interpreter *n* COMMS *languages* intérprete *mf*, COMP *programming* interpretador *m*

interpreting *n* COMMS *languages* interpretación *f*

interrelation *n* MATH interrelación *f*

interrogatories *n pl* LAW interrogatorios *m pl*

interruption *n* GEN COMM interrupción *f*

interstate[1] *adj AmE* GEN COMM interestatal

interstate[2]: ~ commerce *n AmE* GEN COMM comercio entre estados *m*

Interstate: ~ Commerce Commission *n AmE* (*ICC*) ECON comisión de comercio interestatal; ~ Land Sales Act *n AmE* PROP ley interestatal de ventas de tierras

interunion: ~ disputes *n pl BrE* HRM disputas entre sindicatos *f pl*

interval: ~ estimate *n* MATH estimación de intervalo *f*; ~ scale *n* GEN COMM escala de intervalo *f*; ~ service *n* TRANSP servicio a intervalos *m*

intervene *vi* ECON, GEN COMM, POL intervenir; ♦ ~ in GEN COMM intervenir en

intervention *n* GEN COMM intervención *f*; ~ currency ECON intervención monetaria *f*, FIN moneda de intervención *f*; ~ price ECON, FIN precio de intervención *m*

interventionist *adj* POL intervencionista

interview *n* HRM, MEDIA, S&M entrevista *f*; ~ guide HRM guía del entrevistador *f*; ♦ arrange an ~ HRM concertar una entrevista

interviewee *n* HRM, MEDIA, S&M entrevistado(-a) *m,f*

interviewer *n* HRM, MEDIA, S&M entrevistador(a) *m,f*; ~ bias MEDIA, S&M parcialidad del entrevistador *f*

inter vivos[1] *adv* LAW entre vivos

inter vivos[2]: ~ trust *n* LAW fideicomiso entre vivos *m*

intestate *adj* LAW intestado

in-the-money[1] *adj* STOCK dentro del precio

in-the-money[2]: ~ call *n* STOCK opción de compra indiferente *f*; ~ call option *n* STOCK opción de compra dentro del precio *f*; ~ option *n* STOCK opción con beneficio potencial *f*; ~ put *n* STOCK opción de venta indiferente *f*; ~ put option *n* STOCK opción de venta dentro del precio *f*

intimidation *n* HRM intimidación *f*

in-town: ~ store *n* S&M tienda urbana *f*

intra: ~ number *n* ADMIN número interno *m*

intracommodity: ~ spread *n* STOCK margen dentro del mismo producto *m*

intra-Community: ~ trade *n* ECON comercio intracomunitario *m*

intradepartmental *adj* ADMIN intradepartamental

intra-EU: ~ trade *n* ECON, POL comercio interior de la UE *m*

intragroup: ~ relation *n* HRM relación intragrupal *f*

intramedia: ~ comparisons *n pl* S&M comparaciones dentro de los medios de comunicación *f pl*

intraperiod: ~ tax provision *n* ACC, TAX provisión para impuestos del periodo *f*

intrastate *adj AmE* GEN COMM intraestatal

intra vires *adj* LAW dentro de su competencia

in-tray *n* GEN COMM bandeja *f*; ~ exercise *jarg* ADMIN ejercicio en curso *m*

intrinsic: ~ motivation *n* HRM motivación intrínseca *f*; ~ value *n* ECON, STOCK valor intrínseco *m*

introduce *vt* GEN COMM, LAW introducir

introduction *n* GEN COMM *to book, speech* introducción *f*, STOCK nueva emisión de valores no directamente en bolsa

introductory: ~ course *n* WEL curso introductorio *m*, curso preliminar *m*; ~ offer *n* MEDIA, S&M *advertising* oferta de lanzamiento *f*; ~ price *n* S&M precio de introducción *m*; ~ stage *n* S&M fase de lanzamiento *f*

intrusive *adj* COMMS, S&M *radio* intruso

intuitive: ~ management *n* HRM, MGMNT administración intuitiva *f*, gestión intuitiva *f*

inure 1. *vt* PROP habituar; 2. *vi frml* GEN COMM tener efecto

inv. *abbr* (*invoice*) ACC, FIN, GEN COMM, S&M factura *f*

invalidate *vt* GEN COMM invalidar

invalidated: ~ bond *n* FIN, STOCK bono cancelado *m*

invalidation *n* GEN COMM anulación *f*, invalidación *f*

invaluable *adj* GEN COMM inapreciable

invent *vt* IND inventar

invention *n* ECON, IND, PATENTS invención *f*

inventive: ~ step *n* PATENTS fase del invento *f*

inventor *n* GEN COMM inventor(a) *m,f*

inventory *n* ACC, COMP, ECON, FIN inventario *m*, GEN COMM inventario *m*, existencias *f pl*, STOCK inventario *m*; ~ allowance TAX desgravación por inventario *f*; ~ analysis ACC análisis de inventarios *m*; ~ book ACC libro de almacén *m*, libro de inventario *m*; ~ certificate ACC certificado de inventarios *m*; ~ computation GEN COMM cómputo de inventario *m*; ~ control ACC control de inventarios *m*, fiscalización de las existencias *f*, control de existencias *f*, ECON, FIN fiscalización de las existencias *f*; ~ controller GEN COMM controlador(a) de inventario *m,f*; ~ costing ACC cálculo de costes de inventario *m* (*Esp*), cálculo de costos de inventario *m* (*AmL*); ~ count ACC, S&M existencias en inventario *f pl*; ~ cycle GEN COMM ciclo de inventario *m*; ~ evaluation ACC valoración de inventario *f*; ~ file GEN COMM fichero de existencias *m*; ~ financing ACC financiación del inventario *f*; ~ investment cycle BANK, FIN, GEN COMM, MGMNT ciclo de inversión en existencias *m*; ~ item GEN COMM inventario de artículos *m*; ~ management ACC gestión de inventarios *f*, FIN, IND administración de existencias *f*, gestión de existencias *f*, MGMNT dirección de inventario *f*, gerencia de inventario *f*; ~ planning ECON planificación del inventario *f*; ~ pricing ACC fijación de precios del inventario *f*; ~ sheet ACC estado de existencias *m*, formulario del inventario *m*; ~ shortage ECON merma en el inventario *f*; ~ shrinkage ECON merma en el inventario *f*; ~ turnover GEN COMM facturación *f*, rotación de existencias *f*; ~ valuation ACC, GEN COMM valoración de inventario *f*; ~ **valuation adjustment** ACC, MATH ajuste en la valoración de existencias *m*

inverse[1] *adj* MATH inverso

inverse[2]: ~ **condemnation** *n AmE* LAW, PROP expropiación recíproca *f*, reversión de expropiación *f*; ~ **elasticity rule** *n* ECON regla de la elasticidad inversa *f*

inversely *adv* MATH inversamente

invert *vt* COMP invertir

inverted: ~ **commas** *n pl* GEN COMM comillas *f pl*; ~ **market** *n jarg* STOCK mercado invertido *m*; ~ **scale** *n* STOCK escala invertida *f*; ~ **yield curve** *n* ECON curva de rendimiento invertida *f*

invest *vt* ECON, GEN COMM, STOCK invertir; ♦ ~ **in an annuity** FIN invertir en una renta anual; ~ **in bonds** STOCK invertir en obligaciones; ~ **in property** PROP invertir en propiedades; ~ **in shares** STOCK invertir en acciones; ~ **money in** STOCK invertir dinero en

invested[1] *adj* GEN COMM invertido

invested[2]: ~ **capital** *n* GEN COMM capital invertido *m*

investee *n* FIN participado *m*

investible *adj* FIN invertible

investigate *vt* GEN COMM *question*, LAW *crime* investigar

investigating: ~ **committee** *n* LAW comisión investigadora *f*

investigation: ~ **officer** *n* HRM responsable de investigación *mf*

investigative: ~ **approach** *n* TAX *to field audits* método indagatorio *m*

investigatory: ~ **powers** *n pl* LAW *of court* poderes indagatorios *m pl*

investment *n* GEN COMM, IND inversión *f*; ~ **abroad** GEN COMM inversión exterior *f*; ~ **account** BANK cuenta de inversiones *f*; ~ **account securities** *n pl* BANK títulos de la cuenta de inversión *m pl*; ~ **activity** ECON actividad inversionista *f*; ~ **advice** STOCK notificación de inversión *f*; ~ **adviser** ACC, FIN, INS, LAW asesor(a) de inversiones *m,f*, asesor(a) financiero(-a) *m,f*, STOCK consultor(a) de inversiones *m,f*; ~ **allowance** TAX desgravación por inversión *f*; ~ **analysis** FIN estudio de rentabilidad *m*; ~ **appraisal** FIN evaluación de inversiones *f*; ~ **bank** *AmE* (*cf merchant bank BrE*) BANK, FIN banco de emisión de valores *m*, banco de inversiones *m*, banco de negocios *m*, banco financiero *m*, banco mercantil *m*; ~ **banker** *AmE* (*cf merchant banker BrE*) BANK, FIN banquero(-a) comercial *m,f*; ~ **banking** *AmE* (*cf merchant banking BrE*) BANK banca financiera *f*, banca mercantil *f*, banca de negocios *f*; ~ **base** BANK base de inversión *f*; ~ **budget** ACC, ECON, FIN presupuesto de inversiones *m*; ~ **business** STOCK compañía inversora *f*; ~ **capital** ACC, ECON, FIN, GEN COMM capital de inversión *m*; ~ **center** *AmE*, ~ **centre** *BrE* FIN centro de inversiones *m*, centro inversor *m*; ~ **certificate** BANK, FIN, STOCK certificado de inversión *m*; ~ **climate** ECON clima inversor *m*; ~ **club** STOCK club de inversión *m*; ~ **company** FIN, STOCK compañía inversionista *f*; ~ **contract** STOCK contrato de inversión *m*; ~ **corporation** FIN, STOCK compañía inversionista *f*; ~ **counsel** ECON, FIN, GEN COMM consejero(-a) de inversiones *m,f*, STOCK consejo de inversiones *m*; ~ **counseling** *AmE*, ~ **counselling** *BrE* FIN asesoramiento de inversiones *m*, asesoramiento financiero *m*; ~ **credit** BANK, FIN crédito a la inversión *m*; ~ **criteria** *n pl* FIN criterios de inversión *m pl*; ~ **currency** FIN moneda de inversión *f*; ~ **dealer** FIN comisionista en

colocaciones *mf*; ~ **demand** FIN demanda de inversión *f*; ~ **dollar pool system** ECON método de control de los tipos de cambio *m*; ~ **expansion** FIN, STOCK expansión de las inversiones *f*; ~ **expense** GEN COMM, TAX gastos de inversión *m pl*; ~ **expert** FIN, STOCK experto(-a) en inversiones *m,f*; ~ **firm** FIN compañía de inversión *f*; ~ **function** FIN función de inversión *f*; ~ **fund** BANK, FIN, STOCK fondo de inversión *m*; ~ **fund for shares** FIN, STOCK fondo de inversión para acciones *m*; ~ **gap** FIN déficit de inversión *m*; ~ **gold coin** FIN moneda de oro para inversión *f*; ~ **goods** *n pl* FIN, S&M bienes de inversión *m pl*; ~ **grade** STOCK categoría de la inversión *f*; ~ **grant** ACC subvención para inversiones *f*; ~ **hedger** STOCK coberturista de inversiones *mf*; ~ **history** BANK, FIN historial de inversión *m*; ~ **horizon** FIN horizonte de inversión *m*; ~ **incentive** BANK incentivo a la inversión *m*; ~ **income** STOCK ingresos derivados de inversiones *m pl*; ~ **income deduction** TAX deducción de los ingresos por inversión *f*; ~ **income tax** TAX impuesto sobre inversiones *m* (*Esp*), impuesto sobre insumos *m* (*AmL*); ~ **interest expense** TAX gastos por intereses de una inversión *m pl*; ~ **life cycle** STOCK ciclo vital de la inversión *m*; ~ **loss** STOCK pérdidas de inversión *f pl*; ~ **management** FIN, MGMNT administración de inversiones *f*, gestión de inversiones *f*, dirección de inversiones *f*, gerencia de inversiones *f*; ~ **mix** FIN inversión mixta *f*; ~ **multiplier** ECON *econometrics* multiplicador de inversión *m*; ~ **objective** ACC, BANK, FIN objetivo de inversiones *m*; ~ **opportunity** ACC, BANK, FIN, STOCK oportunidad de inversión *f*; ~ **policy** FIN, POL política de inversión *f*; ~ **portfolio** BANK, FIN cartera de inversiones *f*; ~ **program** *AmE*, ~ **programme** *BrE* ACC, BANK, FIN programa de inversión *m*; ~ **project** ECON, FIN proyecto de inversión *m*; ~ **property** PROP propiedad de inversión *f*; ~ **reserve system** FIN sistema de reserva de inversión *m*; ~ **restriction** ECON restricción a la inversión *f*; ~ **revenue** INS, STOCK rédito de inversiones *m*; ~ **review** FIN revisión de las inversiones *f*; ~ **savings account** BANK cuenta de ahorro para inversión *f*; ~ **service** FIN servicio de inversión *m*; ~ **software** COMP, FIN aplicaciones informáticas para inversión *f pl*; ~ **spending** GEN COMM, TAX gastos de inversión *m pl*; ~ **strategy** STOCK estrategia de inversión *f*; ~ **strategy committee** FIN comité estratégico para inversiones *m*; ~ **surplus** FIN excedente de inversiones *m*; ~ **tax credit** TAX bonificación tributaria a la inversión *f*; ~ **trust** FIN compañía inversionista *f*, HRM cooperativa de inversiones *f*, STOCK compañía inversionista *f*; ~ **value of a convertible security** STOCK valor de inversión de un título convertible *m*; ~ **yield** BANK rendimiento de la inversión *m*

Investment: ~ **Advisers Act** *n* FIN, LAW Ley de Asesores de Inversión *f*; ~ **Advisory Service** *n* STOCK Servicio de Asesoramiento de Inversiones *m*; ~ **Committee** *n* (*IC*) FIN comité de inversiones *m*; ~ **Management Regulatory Organization** *n AmE* STOCK organización reguladora de gestores de inversiones; ~ **Managers' Regulatory Organization** *n BrE* (*IMRO*) STOCK organización reguladora de gestores de inversiones; ~ **Company Act** *n* FIN, LAW Ley de Sociedades de Inversión de 1940 *f*

investments *n pl* STOCK inversiones *f pl*

investor *n* ECON, FIN, STOCK inversor(a) *m,f*, inversionista *mf*; ~ **group** FIN grupo de inversión *m*; ~ **protection** STOCK protección del inversor *f*; ~ **relations**

department STOCK departamento de relaciones con el inversor *m*

investors': ~ **indemnity account** *n* BANK cuenta de indemnización de inversionistas *f*; ~ **service bureau** *n* FIN oficina de atención a los inversores *f*

Investors': ~ **Compensation Scheme** *n* BrE STOCK plan de compensación de los inversores

invisible: ~ **balance** *n* FIN balanza de invisibles *f*; ~ **earnings** *n pl* FIN ganancias invisibles *f pl*; ~ **export** *n* IMP/EXP exportación invisible *f*; ~ **exports** *n pl jarg* ECON *balance of trade* exportaciones invisibles *f pl*; ~ **hand** *n jarg* ECON mano invisible *f*; ~ **import** *n* IMP/EXP importación invisible *f*; ~ **supply** *n* GEN COMM oferta invisible *f*; ~ **trade** *n* ECON comercio invisible *m*; ~ **trade balance** *n* ECON balanza comercial invisible *f*

invisibles *n pl* ECON, GEN COMM partidas invisibles *f pl*

invitation *n* GEN COMM invitación *f*; ~ **to treat** LAW invitación a negociar *f*

invite: ~ **subscriptions for sth** *phr* GEN COMM pedir adhesiones para algo; ~ **tenders** *phr* STOCK solicitar ofertas

invoice *n* (*inv.*) ACC, FIN, GEN COMM, S&M factura *f*; ~ **amount** FIN importe de la factura *m*; ~ **book** (*IB*) GEN COMM libro de facturas *m*; ~ **clerk** GEN COMM encargado(-a) de facturación *m,f*; ~ **cost and charges** *n pl* ACC costes y gastos según factura *m pl* (*Esp*), costos y gastos según factura *m pl* (*AmL*); ~ **date** BrE (*cf billing date AmE*) GEN COMM fecha de facturación *f*; ~ **discount** S&M descuento en factura *m*; ~ **in the currency of the overseas buyer** ACC factura en la divisa del comprador extranjero *f*; ~ **in the currency of the overseas seller** ACC factura en la divisa del vendedor extranjero *f*; ~ **payable** ACC, FIN factura a pagar *f*; ~ **price** STOCK precio de factura *m*; ~ **receivable** ACC, FIN factura a cobrar *f*; ~ **value** GEN COMM valor de factura *m*

invoices: ~ **inwards** *n pl* ACC, FIN, GEN COMM facturas recibidas *f pl*

invoicing *n* GEN COMM facturación *f*; ~ **amount** FIN, GEN COMM volumen de facturación *m*; ~ **department** BrE (*cf billing department AmE*) GEN COMM departamento de facturación *m*

invoke *vt* GEN COMM *law, penalty* invocar

involuntary: ~ **bankruptcy** *n* GEN COMM quiebra involuntaria *f*; ~ **conversion** *n* INS conversión forzosa *f*, PROP conversión involuntaria *f*; ~ **employment** *n* ECON empleo involuntario *m*; ~ **investment** *n* FIN inversión forzosa *f*; ~ **lien** *n* LAW garantía real involuntaria *f*; ~ **liquidation** *n* ACC, FIN, GEN COMM liquidación involuntaria *f*; ~ **trust** *n* LAW fideicomiso implícito *m*; ~ **unemployment** *n* ECON, HRM, WEL desempleo involuntario *m*

involve *vt* GEN COMM *expenses* ocasionar, PATENTS *inventive step* implicar

involved *adj* PATENTS implícito

involvement: ~ **of employees** *n* HRM implicación de los trabajadores *f*

inward: ~ **bill of lading** *n* IMP/EXP, TRANSP conocimiento de embarque en la entrada *m*; ~ **cargo** *n* IMP/EXP carga de entrada *f*; ~ **charges** *n pl* TRANSP derechos de entrada *m pl*; ~ **clearing bill** *n* IMP/EXP cédula de liquidación de entrada *f*; ~ **freight department** *n* IMP/EXP, TRANSP departamento de fletes de entrada *m*;

~ **investment** *n* FIN inversión interna *f*; ~ **investor** *n* STOCK inversor(a) extranjero(-a) *m,f*; ~ **payment** *n* FIN pago interno *m*; ~ **processing** *n* IMP/EXP proceso de recepción *m*; ~ **processing relief** *n* (*IPR*) TAX deducción interior por transformación *f*, desgravación interior por transformación *f*

inwards: ~ **mission** *n* S&M misión interna *f*

Inwood: ~ **Annuity Factor** *n* INS Factor Inwood de Periodicidad Anual *m*

IO *abbr* HRM, IMP/EXP (*immigration officer*) funcionario(-a) de inmigración *m,f*, IND (*industrial organization*) organización industrial *f*

I/O *abbr* (*input/output*) COMP E/S (*entrada/salida*)

IOB *abbr* BANK (*Institute of Bankers*) Instituto de Banqueros *m*, INS (*Insurance Ombudsman Bureau*) oficina mediadora de seguros

IOC *abbr* (*immediate-or-cancel order*) FIN orden de ejecución inmediata o cancelación *f*

IOE *abbr* (*International Organization of Employers*) HRM Organización Internacional Patronal *f*

IOM[1] *abbr* MGMNT (*Institute of Office Management*) instituto de gestión de oficinas, STOCK (*International Options Market*) Mercado Internacional de Opciones *m*

IOM[2]: ~ **division** *n* AmE (*Index and Option Market division*) STOCK *of the Chicago Mercantile Exchange* departamento de cotización y mercado de opciones

IOPC: ~ **Fund** *n* (*International Oil Pollution Compensation Fund*) BANK, ENVIR Fondo de Compensación Internacional para la Contaminación Producida por Petróleo *m*

IORT *abbr* (*incremental oil revenue tax*) TAX impuesto progresivo sobre los ingresos del petróleo *m*

IOSCO *abbr* (*International Organization of Securities Commissions*) STOCK Organización Internacional de Comisiones de Valores *f*

IOTTSG *abbr* (*International Oil Tanker and Terminal Safety Group*) TRANSP Grupo Internacional para la Seguridad de los Petroleros y las Terminales *m*

IOU *abbr* (*I owe you*) GEN COMM pagaré *m*

IPA *abbr* (*Institute of Practitioners in Advertising*) S&M instituto de profesionales de publicidad

IPE *abbr* (*International Petroleum Exchange*) STOCK Mercado Internacional del Petróleo *m*

IPI *abbr* (*International Press Institute*) MEDIA Instituto Internacional de Prensa *m*

IPM *abbr* FIN (*integrated project management*) gestión integrada de proyectos *f*, MGMNT (*Institute of Personnel Management*) instituto de administración de personal

IPMA *abbr* (*International Primary Market Association*) STOCK Asociación Internacional de Mercados de Emisión *f*

IPO *abbr* (*initial public offering*) GEN COMM OPI (*oferta pública inicial*)

IPR *abbr* S&M (*Institute of Public Relations*) instituto de relaciones públicas, TAX (*inward processing relief*) deducción interior por transformación *f*, desgravación interior por transformación *f*

IR *abbr* HRM (*industrial relation*) relaciones industriales *f*, TAX BrE (*Inland Revenue*) departamento gubernamental británico para regular los impuestos, ≈ Dirección General de Tributos *f*

IRA: ~ **rollover** *n* AmE (*individual retirement account*

rollover) TAX renovación de cuenta de jubilación individual *f*

IRC *abbr* (*industrial reorganization company*) IND sociedad de reorganización industrial *f*

IRD *abbr* (*inland rail depot*) TRANSP almacén ferroviario interior *m*

IRN *abbr* (*import release note*) IMP/EXP aviso de despacho de importación *m*

IRO *abbr BrE* (*Inland Revenue Office*) TAX departamento gubernamental británico para regular los impuestos, ≈ Dirección General de Tributos *f*

iron: ~ **law of wages** *n* ECON, LAW ley de hierro de los salarios *f*; ~ **ore** *n* ENVIR mineral de fierro *m* (*AmL*), mineral de hierro *m* (*Esp*); ~ **ore carrier** *n* TRANSP *shipping* carguero de mineral de fierro *m* (*AmL*), carguero de mineral de hierro *m* (*Esp*); ~ **and steel industry** *n* ECON, IND industria siderúrgica *f*; ~ **and steel plant** *n* IND acería *f*

IRPC *abbr* (*Industrial Relations Policy Committee*) HRM comité de política de relaciones industriales

IRR *abbr* (*internal rate return*) FIN TRI (*tasa de rendimiento interna*)

irrebuttable *adj* LAW irrefutable

irredeemable *adj* STOCK irrescatable, no ejecutable

irreducible *adj* GEN COMM irreductible

irregular: ~ **market** *n* STOCK mercado irregular *m*

irregularity *n* GEN COMM, LAW irregularidad *f*; ~ **report** TRANSP informe de irregularidad *m* (*Esp*), reporte de irregularidad *m* (*AmL*)

irrelevant *adj* GEN COMM, LAW irrelevante

irreparable[1] *adj* GEN COMM, LAW irreparable

irreparable[2]: ~ **damage** *n* LAW daño irreparable *m*; ~ **harm** *n* LAW daño irreparable *m*

irreplaceable *adj* GEN COMM irreemplazable

irrespective: ~ **of** *adv* GEN COMM con independencia de

irreversible *adj* GEN COMM *decision* irrevocable, *strategy* irreversible

irrevocable[1] *adj* LAW irrevocable

irrevocable[2]: ~ **credit** *n* BANK crédito irrevocable *m*; ~ **credit line** *n* BANK línea de crédito irrevocable *f*; ~ **letter of credit** *n* (*ILOC*) BANK, FIN carta de crédito irrevocable *f*, crédito documentario irrevocable *m*; ~ **settlement** *n* LAW acuerdo irrevocable *m*; ~ **trust** *n* LAW fideicomiso irrevocable *m*; ~ **trust fund** *n* GEN COMM fondo fiduciario irrevocable *m*

IRS *abbr AmE* (*Internal Revenue Service*) TAX departamento gubernamental estadounidense para regular los impuestos, ≈ Dirección General de Tributos *f*

IRU *abbr* HRM (*International Recruitment Unit*) Unidad Internacional de Reclutamiento *f*, TRANSP (*International Road Transport Union*) Sindicato Internacional de Transporte por Carretera *m*

IS: ~ **curve** *n* ECON curva IS *f*

ISBN *abbr* (*International Standard Book Number*) MEDIA ISBN (*Numeración Internacional Normalizada de Libros*)

ISC *abbr* (*International Sugar Council*) IND Consejo Internacional del Azúcar *m*

ISCO *abbr* (*International Standard Classification of Occupations*) ECON Clasificación Internacional del Empleo *f*

ISDA *abbr* (*International Swap Dealers' Association*) STOCK Asociación Internacional de Operadores de Swap *f*

ISE *abbr* (*International Stock Exchange*) STOCK bolsa internacional *f*, Bolsa Internacional de Valores *f*

ISF *abbr* (*International Shipping Federation*) TRANSP Federación Internacional de Compañías Navieras *f*

ISFA *abbr* (*Institute of Shipping and Forwarding Agents*) TRANSP instituto de agentes consignatarios y transitarios

ISI *abbr* (*International Statistical Institute*) GEN COMM, MATH Instituto Internacional de Estadística *m*

ISIS *abbr* (*International Shipping Information Service*) TRANSP Servicio Internacional de Información Marítima *m*

island *n* ECON isla de venta *f*; ~ **display** S&M mercancía expuesta fuera de los estantes en una tienda; ~ **site** *jarg* S&M *advertising* anuncio fuera de espacio publicitario *m*

IS-LM: ~ **curves** *n pl* ECON curvas IS-LM *f pl*

ISMA *abbr* (*International Securities Market Association*) STOCK Asociación Internacional de Mercados de Valores *f*

iso: ~~**outlay curve** *n* ECON curva isocoste *f*

ISO[1] *abbr* GEN COMM (*International Standards Organization*) OIN (*Organización Internacional de Normalización*), IND (*International Sugar Organization*) Organización Internacional del Azúcar *f*, STOCK (*incentive stock option*) ISO (*incentivo fiscal sobre opciones*)

ISO[2]: ~ **base** *n* TRANSP *of containers* cono ISO *m*; ~ **paper size** *n* MEDIA, S&M tamaño de papel ISO *m*

isocost *n* ECON isocosto *m*; ~ **curve** ECON curva isocoste *f*

isolate *vt* ECON, GEN COMM, STOCK aislar

isolated[1] *adj* ECON, GEN COMM, STOCK aislado

isolated[2]: ~ **market equilibrium** *n* ECON equilibrio de mercado aislado *m*; ~ **state** *n* ECON situación aislada *f*

isolationist *adj* POL aislacionista

isoproduct: ~ **curve** *n* ECON *map* curva isocuanta *f*, línea isocuanta *f*

isoquant *n* ECON isocuanta *f*

ISRO *abbr* (*International Securities Regulatory Organization*) STOCK Organización Internacional Reguladora de Valores *f*

ISS *abbr* (*International Social Service*) WEL Servicio Social Internacional *m*

issuance *n* TAX coste de emisión *m* (*Esp*), costo de emisión *m* (*AmL*); ~ **facility** FIN mecanismo de emisión *m*

issue[1] *n* GEN COMM asunto *m*, controversia *f*, cuestión *f*, LAW descendientes *m pl*, cuestión *f*, MEDIA controversia *f*, *print* edición *f*, ejemplar *m*, número *m* (*n.º*), MGMNT asunto *m*, POL controversia *f*, STOCK *shares* emisión *f*; ~ **by tender** FIN distribución por licitación *f*; ~ **card** IND ficha de salida *f*; ~ **of checks** *AmE*, ~ **of cheques** *BrE* BANK libramiento de cheques *m*; ~ **date** S&M fecha de emisión *f*; ~ **of debentures** STOCK emisión de obligaciones *f*; ~ **management** *jarg* S&M *public relations* control de un asunto *m*, gestión de un asunto *f*; ~ **market** ECON, STOCK *futures* mercado de emisiones *m*, mercado primario *m*; ~ **price** STOCK precio de emisión *m*; ~ **readership** MEDIA, S&M número total de lectores de una edición *m*; ~ **voucher** IND prueba de emisión *f*; ◆ **at** ~ GEN COMM en litigio; **the** ~ **was undersubscribed** STOCK la emisión no fue suscrita en su totalidad; **take over an** ~ STOCK hacerse cargo de una emisión

issue[2] *vt* COMP *message,* FIN *cheques, shares, bonds, bank notes* emitir, GEN COMM editar, MEDIA *magazine, newspaper* editar, *prospectus* sacar, STOCK emitir; ♦ ~ **bad checks** *AmE,* ~ **bad cheques** *BrE* BANK extender cheques sin fondos; ~ **bank notes** BANK, STOCK emitir billetes; ~ **a letter of credit** BANK, IMP/EXP abrir una carta de crédito; ~ **a loan** BANK, STOCK emitir un empréstito; ~ **a policy** INS extender una póliza; ~ **shares at a discount** STOCK emitir acciones al descuento; ~ **shares at par** STOCK emitir acciones a la par; ~ **a writ against sb** LAW dictar un auto contra alguien

issued[1] *adj* GEN COMM editado, STOCK emitido; ~ **and in circulation** STOCK emitido y en circulación

issued[2]: ~ **capital** *n* STOCK capital emitido *m*; ~ **share capital** *n* ACC capital social emitido *m*, FIN capital de acciones emitidas *m*

issuer *n* FIN, GEN COMM, STOCK emisor(a) *m,f*

issues *n pl* GEN COMM asuntos *m pl*; ~ **with currency options** STOCK emisiones con opción en efectivo *f pl*; ~ **of necessity** STOCK emisión de valores *f*

issuing: ~ **authority** *n* POL *passport* autoridad expedidora *f*; ~ **bank** *n* BANK banco de emisión *m*; ~ **carrier** *n* TRANSP transportista expedidor *m*; ~ **company** *n* STOCK compañía emisora *f*; ~ **house** *n* BANK banco de emisión de valores *m*, casa emisora *f*, STOCK sociedad de colocación de valores *f*

IT[1] *abbr* COMP (*information technology*) informática *f*, HRM, LAW (*industrial tribunal*) Juzgado de lo Social *m* (*Esp*), Magistratura de Trabajo *f* (*Esp*), LEIS (*inclusive tour*) excursión con gastos incluidos *m*, TAX (*Income Tax*) ≈ IRPF (*Impuesto sobre la Renta*), TRANSP (*independent tank*) contenedor de cuba refrigerada *m*

IT[2]: ~ **company** *n* (*information technology company*) COMP, IND empresa de tecnología de la información *f*

italic *n* COMP, MEDIA *typography* cursiva *f*

italics *n* COMP, MEDIA *typography* bastardilla *f*

ITC *abbr* IND (*International Tin Council*) Consejo Internacional del Estaño *m*, TRANSP (*independent tank center AmE, independent tank centre BrE*) centro de tanque independiente *m*

item *n* ACC ítem *m*, detalle *m*, partida *f*, punto *m*, GEN COMM artículo *m*, detalle *m*; ~ **analysis** MATH análisis por casos *m*; ~ **of expenditure** ACC partida de gastos *f*

itemization *n* ACC, GEN COMM *invoice* detalle *m*

itemize *vt* ACC itemizar

itemized: ~ **deduction** *n* TAX deducción en el sobre de paga *f*; ~ **invoice** *n* ACC, FIN factura detallada *f*; ~ **pay statement** *n* HRM declaración de pago por partidas *f*; ~ **statement** *n* GEN COMM estado de cuenta pormenorizado *m*

items: ~ **on the agenda** *n pl* GEN COMM asuntos de la agenda *m pl*

iteration *n* COMP iteración *f*

iterative: ~ **warnings** *n pl* COMP advertencias iterativas *f pl*

ITF *abbr* (*International Transport Workers' Federation*) TRANSP federación internacional de trabajadores del transporte

itinerant: ~ **worker** *n* HRM trabajador(a) itinerante *m,f*

itinerary *n* GEN COMM itinerario *m*

ITM *abbr* (*in-the-money*) STOCK dentro del precio

ITO *abbr* (*International Trade Organization*) GEN COMM OIC (*Organización Internacional de Comercio*)

ITP *abbr* (*Independent Television Publications*) MEDIA publicaciones de televisión independientes de Gran Bretaña

ITPAL *abbr* (*industrial and trade policy adjustment loan*) BANK, ECON, FIN préstamo de ajuste de la política industrial y comercial *m*

ITU *abbr* (*International Telecommunications Union*) COMMS UIT (*Unión Internacional de Telecomunicaciones*)

ITW *abbr* (*independent task wing*) TRANSP ala de tanque independiente *f*

IUOTO *abbr* (*International Union of Official Travel Organizations*) TRANSP Sindicato Internacional de Organizaciones de Viajes Oficiales *m*

IUR *abbr* (*International Union of Railways*) TRANSP Sindicato Internacional de Ferrocarriles *m*

ius gentium *n* LAW derecho de gentes *m*

IWC *abbr* (*International Wheat Council*) IND Consejo Internacional del Trigo *m*

IWS *abbr* (*International Wool Secretariat*) IND Secretaría Internacional de la Lana *f*

J

J: **~ curve** *n* ECON curva en J *f*

J/A *abbr* (*joint account*) BANK cuenta conjunta *f*

jacket *n* COMP *disk* cubierta exterior *f*, MEDIA *on book* camisa *f*, sobrecubierta *f*

jam *n* COMP *printer* atasco *m*

Jamaica: **~ Agreement** *n* ECON acuerdo de Jamaica *m*

Jane: **~ Doe** *n* AmE *infrml* LAW Fulana de Tal *f*

Janson: **~ Clause** *n* INS *marine* cláusula Janson *f*

japanization *n* ECON, FIN *international trade* japonización *f*

jar *n* S&M recipiente *m*

jargon *n* GEN COMM jerga *f*

jawbone *vi* AmE *jarg* POL obtener reducidos aumentos salariales en las negociaciones patronal-sindicatos

jawboning *n* AmE *jarg* POL arenga *f*, discurso *m*

JCCC *abbr* (*Joint Customs Consultative Committee*) IMP/EXP comité de consultas aduaneras

JCS *abbr* (*joint container service*) TRANSP servicio de contenedores colectivos *m*

JDI *abbr* (*joint declaration of interest*) BANK declaración conjunta de interés *f*

JEC *abbr* AmE (*Joint Economic Committee of Congress*) ECON comité mixto económico del congreso americano

jeopardize *vt* GEN COMM *situation* arriesgar

jeopardy: **~ assessment** *n* TAX liquidación de oficio *f*; **~ collection procedure** *n* TAX procedimiento de cobro de oficio *m*

jerque: **~ note** *n* IMP/EXP certificado de declaración de entrada *m*, nota de inspección *f*

jet[1]: **~ foil** *n* TRANSP deslizador propulsado a reacción *m*

jet[2]: **~ lagged** *phr* TRANSP desfasado por el viaje

JICCAR *abbr* (*Joint Industry Committee for Cable Audience Research*) MEDIA, S&M comité conjunto del sector para la investigación de la audiencia por cable

JICNARS *abbr* (*Joint Industry Committee for National Readership Surveys*) MEDIA, S&M comité mixto del sector para encuestas nacionales de lectores

JICRAR *abbr* (*Joint Industry Committee for Radio Audience Research*) MEDIA, S&M comité mixto del sector para la investigación de la audiencia radiofónica

JICTAR *abbr* (*Joint Industrial Committee for Television Advertising Research*) MEDIA, S&M comité mixto del sector para la investigación de la publicidad en TV

Jiffy: **~ bag**® *n* COMMS, GEN COMM sobre acolchado *m*

JIT[1] *abbr* (*just-in-time*) IND JIT (*justo a tiempo*) (*AmL*)

JIT[2]: **~ production** *n* IND producción justo a tiempo *f* (*AmL*), producción según demanda *f* (*Esp*)

JMC *abbr* (*Joint Maritime Commission*) TRANSP comisión marítima conjunta

jnr. *abbr* (*junior*) GEN COMM hijo *m*

job *n* COMP *task* tarea *f*, GEN COMM, HRM *post* plaza *f*, puesto de trabajo *m*; **~ acceptance schedule** ECON listas de aceptación de trabajo *f pl*; **~ advertisement** HRM anuncio de empleo *m*; **~ analysis** HRM análisis de puestos *m*, análisis del puesto de trabajo *m*; **~ application** HRM solicitud de empleo *f*; **~ appraisal** HRM estimación de empleo *f*, evaluación del puesto *f*; **~ assignment** GEN COMM asignación de empleo *f*, HRM asignación de puestos *f*; **~ bank** HRM banco de trabajo *m*; **~ breakdown** HRM *responsibilities of given post* desglose del trabajo *m*, *distribution of tasks* distribución de trabajo *f*; **~ card** HRM bono de trabajo *m*; **~ challenge** HRM desafío en el puesto *m*, desafío en el trabajo *m*, reto del trabajo *m*; **~ characteristics** *n pl* HRM características del puesto *f pl*; **~ classification** HRM clasificación del puesto de trabajo *f*; **~ club** BrE HRM grupo de asesoramiento para desempleados; **~ cluster** ECON agrupación laboral *f*; **~ competence** HRM capacidad para el puesto *f*; **~ content** HRM contenido del puesto *m*; **~ control** HRM control de trabajos *m*; **~ control unionism** HRM sindicalismo controlador de empleos; **~ cost sheet** ECON hoja de costes por órdenes de trabajo *f* (*Esp*), hoja de costos por órdenes de trabajo *f* (*AmL*); **~ cost system** ACC sistema de costes por órdenes de trabajo *m* (*Esp*), sistema de costos por órdenes de trabajo *m* (*AmL*); **~ costing** HRM coste del trabajo *m* (*Esp*), costo del trabajo *m* (*AmL*); **~ creation** HRM creación de empleos *f*; **~ depth** HRM profundidad del puesto *f*; **~ description** HRM descripción del puesto *f*; **~ design** HRM *duties* diseño de un puesto de trabajo *m*; **~ enlargement** HRM, MGMNT enriquecimiento del trabajo *m*, expansión del trabajo *f*; **~ entry** COMP entrada de trabajo *f*; **~ evaluation** HRM evaloración de puestos de trabajo *f*; **~ evaluation scale** HRM escala de evaluación de los puestos de trabajo *f*; **~ evaluation scheme** HRM plan de evaloración de los puestos de trabajo *m*, plan de evaluación del trabajo *m*; **~ expectations** *n pl* HRM expectativas de empleo *f pl*; **~ and finish** *jarg* HRM *industrial relations* acuerdo por el cual un trabajador acepta realizar una tarea en un día, independientemente de su horario regular de trabajo; **~ flexibility** HRM flexibilidad del puesto de trabajo *f*; **~ freeze** HRM congelación de empleo *f*; **~ hopper** HRM persona que cambia frecuentemente de trabajo; **~ hopping** HRM cambio frecuente de trabajo; **~ hunter** HRM persona que busca empleo *f*; **~ hunting** HRM búsqueda de empleo *f*; **~ improvement** HRM mejora del puesto *f*; **~ interest** HRM interés en el puesto *m*; **~ jumper** HRM persona que cambia frecuentemente de trabajo; **~ legislation** HRM, LAW, POL ley de empleo *f*, ley del trabajo *f*; **~ lot** GEN COMM saldo de artículos *m*; **~ market** ECON, HRM mercado de trabajo *m*, mercado laboral *m*; **~ mobility** ECON, HRM movilidad de trabajo *f*, movilidad laboral *f*; **~ offer** HRM oferta de empleo *f*, oferta de trabajo *f*; **~ opportunity** HRM oportunidad de empleo *f*; **~ order** HRM, IND orden de trabajo *f*; **~ order costing** IND coste por orden de trabajo *m* (*Esp*), costo por orden de trabajo *m* (*AmL*); **~ performance** HRM desempeño del puesto *f*, ejecución del trabajo *f*; **~ placement** HRM prácticas de trabajo *f pl*; **~ profile** HRM perfil del puesto *m*; **~ prospects** *n pl* HRM, WEL perspectivas de empleo *f pl*, perspectivas laborales *f pl*; **~ queue** COMP *at printer* cola de espera de trabajos *f*; **~ regulation** HRM reglamento del trabajo *m*; **~-related accommodation** HRM, PROP hospedaje relacionado con el trabajo *m*, alojamiento vinculado al puesto de

trabajo *m*; ~-**related injury** HRM, INS *worker's compensation* lesión laboral *f*; ~ **requirement** HRM requisito del puesto *m*; ~ **retraining course** HRM curso de reactualización profesional *m*; ~ **rotation** HRM rotación de trabajos *f*; ~ **satisfaction** HRM, MGMNT satisfacción del trabajo *f*; ~ **search** HRM búsqueda de puesto de trabajo *f*; ~ **security** HRM seguridad del puesto de trabajo *f*; ~ **security agreement** HRM acuerdo de seguridad de empleo *m*; ~ **selling** S&M venta de puestos de trabajo *f*; ~ **share** HRM trabajo compartido *m*; ~ **share scheme** HRM plan de empleo compartido *m*; ~ **sharing** HRM trabajo compartido *m*; ~ **simplification** HRM, MGMNT simplificación de puestos *f*; ~ **skills** *n pl* HRM capacidad profesional *f*; ~ **spec** *infrml* HRM detalles del puesto *m pl*, perfil del puesto *m*; ~ **specialization** HRM especialización laboral *f*; ~ **specification** HRM detalles del puesto *m pl*, perfil del puesto *m*; ~ **splitting** HRM división del puesto de trabajo *f*; ~ **study** HRM estudio laboral *m*; ~ **ticket** HRM bono de trabajo *m*; ~ **title** HRM denominación del puesto *f*; ~ **training** HRM capacitación en el puesto de trabajo *f* (*AmL*), formación en el puesto de trabajo *f* (*Esp*); ~ **vacancy** HRM vacante de puesto de trabajo *f*; ◆ **take a ~** HRM aceptar un trabajo
job backwards *vi jarg* STOCK especular en contratos de futuros
job share *vi* HRM compartir el trabajo
Job: ~ **Corps** *n AmE* HRM cuerpo de trabajo *m*
jobber *n jarg* STOCK operador(a) de la bolsa *m,f*, corredor(a) intermediario(-a) *m,f*; ~'**s spread** STOCK margen del agente *m*, margen del corredor de bolsa *m*; ~'**s turn** STOCK ganancia del intermediario *f*
jobbery *n* ECON *foreign bills of exchange*, STOCK *bills of exchange* agiotaje *m*
jobbing *n* GEN COMM especulación *f*, trabajo a destajo *m* (*AmL*), HRM *non-permanent work* maquila *f* (*AmL*), trabajo temporal *m* (*Esp*), IND trabajo a destajo *m*; ◆ ~ **in contangos** STOCK negocio mayorista en primas por gastos *m*
Jobcentre *n BrE* HRM oficina estatal de empleo, ≈ Servicios Integrados para el Empleo *m* (*SIPE*)
jobless[1] *adj* ECON, GEN COMM, HRM desempleado, parado
jobless[2]: **the** ~ *n pl* ECON, GEN COMM, HRM los desempleados *m pl*
jobsworth *n infrml* GEN COMM *officious employee* una persona oficial con poca autoridad que utiliza su poder para implantar su ley
jockey *n jarg* FIN maniobrero *m*
jogging *n jarg* BANK *storing information* batido de las fichas para alineamiento *m*
John: ~ **Doe** *n AmE infrml* LAW Fulano de Tal *m*
join *vt* GEN COMM afiliar; ◆ ~ **the dole queue** *BrE infrml* HRM unirse a la fila de gente que cobra subsidio de desempleo; ~ **a union** HRM afiliarse a un sindicato
join together *vi* GEN COMM *companies* juntarse
joinder *n* HRM incorporación *f*; ~ **of appeals** TAX acumulación de apelaciones *f*
joint[1] *adj* GEN COMM *communiqué* conjunto
joint[2]: ~ **account** *n* (*J/A*) BANK cuenta conjunta *f*; ~ **account agreement** *n* BANK acuerdo de cuenta conjunta *m*; ~ **action** *n* LAW acción conjunta *f*; ~ **assignment** *n* GEN COMM cesión conjunta *f*; ~ **auditor** *n* ACC coauditor(a) *m,f*; ~ **authorization** *n* BANK autorización mancomunada *f*; ~ **bank account** *n* BANK cuenta bancaria conjunta *f*; ~ **bond** *n* FIN, STOCK

bono de deuda solidaria *m*; ~ **charge** *n* TRANSP gasto combinado *m*; ~ **committee** *n* HRM comisión mixta *f*, comité paritario *m*; ~ **consultation** *n* HRM coconsulta *f*, MGMNT consulta conjunta *f*, consulta en común *f*, consulta colectiva *f*; ~ **container service** *n* (*JCS*) TRANSP servicio de contenedores colectivos *m*; ~ **cost** *n pl* ECON coste conjunto *m* (*Esp*), costo conjunto *m* (*AmL*); ~ **custody** *n* BANK custodia conjunta *f*; ~ **debtor** *n* ACC, BANK deudor(a) solidario(-a) *m,f*; ~ **declaration of interest** *n* (*JDI*) BANK declaración conjunta de interés *f*; ~ **demand** *n* ECON demanda conjunta *f*; ~ **designation** *n* PATENTS designación conjunta *f*; ~ **director** *n* BANK, HRM, MGMNT codirector(a) *m,f*; ~ **equity venture company** *n* ACC, GEN COMM empresa conjunta *f*; ~ **estate** *n* LAW, PROP copropiedad *f*, propiedad mancomunada *f*; ~ **fare** *n* TRANSP tarifa conjunta *f*; ~ **financing** *n* FIN financiación conjunta *f*; ~ **guarantee** *n* FIN garantía solidaria *f*; ~ **holder** *n* STOCK tenedor(a) indiviso(-a) *m,f*; ~ **insurance** *n* INS seguro colectivo y conjunto *m*; ~ **liability** *n* BANK, LAW, TAX responsabilidad mancomunada *f*, responsabilidad conjunta *f*, responsabilidad solidaria *f*; ~ **loan** *n* BANK préstamo mancomunado *m*; ~ **management** *n* HRM, MGMNT codirección *f*; ~ **manager** *n* HRM cogerente *m,f*; ~ **negotiation** *n* GEN COMM, HRM, MGMNT *industrial relations* negociación colectiva *f*, negociación conjunta *f*, negociación en común *f*, STOCK negociación conjunta *f*; ~ **obligation** *n* TAX obligación solidaria *f*; ~ **occupancy** *n* PROP, TAX ocupación conjunta *f*; ~ **operator** *n* IND cooperador, a *m,f*, operador(a) conjunto(-a) *m,f*; ~ **owner** *n* GEN COMM codueño(-a) *m,f*, copropietario(-a) *m,f*, condómino(-a) *m,f*; ~ **ownership** *n* GEN COMM condominio *m*, copropiedad *f*; ~ **partnership** *n* GEN COMM coasociación *f*; ~ **product cost** *n* ACC coste conjunto *m* (*Esp*), coste de producción conjunta *m* (*Esp*), costes mancomunados del producto *m pl* (*Esp*), costo conjunto *m* (*AmL*), costo de producción conjunta *m* (*AmL*), costos mancomunados del producto *m pl* (*AmL*); ~ **production committee** *n* HRM comité conjunto de producción *m*; ~ **production** *n* ECON producción conjunta *f*; ~ **promissory note** *n* FIN pagaré solidario *m*; ~ **regulation** *n* HRM normativa conjunta *f*; ~ **representation** *n* GEN COMM, HRM, MGMNT representación colectiva *f*, representación en común *f*, representación conjunta; ~ **return** *n* TAX *tax return* declaración conjunta sobre la renta *f*; ~ **service** *n* TRANSP servicio conjunto *m*; ~ **and several liability** *n* LAW responsabilidad solidaria *f*; ~ **signature** *n* BANK firma conjunta *f*; ~ **statement** *n* GEN COMM, LAW, POL declaración conjunta *f*; ~-**stock bank** *n* BANK banco de acción mancomunada *m*, banco de accionistas *m*; ~ **stock company** *n* GEN COMM, STOCK sociedad en comandita por acciones *f*; ~ **and survivor annuity** *n AmE* INS seguro de pensión que cubre al asegurado y a su cónyuge *m*; ~ **tenancy** *n* PROP coarriendo *m*; ~ **tenant with right of survivorship** *n* STOCK coarrendatario(-a) con derecho de supervivencia *m,f*; ~ **venture** *n* (*JV*) GEN COMM alianza estratégica *f*, coinversión *f*, empresa conjunta *f*, empresas mixtas *f pl*, STOCK agrupación de empresas *f*, riesgo compartido *m*; ~-**venture bank** *n* BANK banco de coinversión *m*; ~-**venture company** *n* ECON, GEN COMM, MGMNT compañía de coinversión *f*, compañía de inversión conjunta *f*, STOCK agrupación de empresas *f*; ~-**venture investment bank** *n AmE* BANK banco de inversión participado por otras entidades financieras *m*, banco mercantil participado por otras instituciones financieras *m*; **~ venture merchant bank** *BrE n* (*cf joint-venture investment bank AmE*) BANK banco de inversión participado por otras entidades financieras *m*, banco mercantil participado por otras instituciones financieras *m*; **~ ventures** *n pl* HRM, INS asociación de empresas en participación *f*; **~ working party** *n* (*JWP*) HRM, POL reunión de trabajo colectiva *f*

Joint: **~ Cargo Committee** *n* TRANSP comité conjunto de carga; **~ Consultative Committee** *n* HRM Comisión Consultiva Mixta *f*, Comisión Mixta Obrero-patronal *f*; **~ Customs Consultative Committee** *n* (*JCCC*) IMP/EXP comité de consultas aduaneras; **~ Economic Committee of Congress** *n AmE* (*JEC*) ECON comité mixto económico del congreso estadounidense; **~ Industrial Committee for Television Advertising Research** *n* (*JICTAR*) MEDIA, S&M comité mixto del sector para la investigación de la publicidad en TV; **~ Industrial Council** *n BrE* IND consejo industrial mancomunado; **~ Industry Committee for Cable Audience Research** *n* (*JICCAR*) MEDIA, S&M comité conjunto del sector para la investigación de la audiencia por cable; **~ Industry Committee for National Readership Surveys** *n* (*JICNARS*) MEDIA, S&M comité mixto del sector para encuestas nacionales de lectores; **~ Industry Committee for Radio Audience Research** *n* (*JICRAR*) MEDIA, S&M comité mixto del sector para la investigación de la audiencia radiofónica; **~ Maritime Commission** *n* (*JMC*) TRANSP comisión marítima conjunta; **~ Research Centre** *n* IND centro mancomunado de investigación; **~ Traffic Conference** *n* TRANSP conferencia conjunta de tráfico

jointly[1]: **~ liable** *adj* GEN COMM, LAW responsable mancomunadamente

jointly[2] *adv* TAX mancomunadamente; **~ and severally** LAW *liability* mancomunada y solidariamente

joker *n AmE* LAW disposición engañosa *f*

jot down *vt* GEN COMM anotar

journal *n* GEN COMM diario *m*; **~ entry** ACC anotación en el libro diario *f*, apunte en el libro diario *m*, asiento en el libro diario *m*; **~ voucher** ACC comprobante de diario *m*

journalize *vt* ACC contabilizar

journey: **~ cycle** *n* S&M ciclo de viaje *m*; **~ planner** *n* TRANSP planificador de viaje *m*; **~ planning** *n* TRANSP plan de viaje *m*

joystick *n* COMP *computer games* palanca de mando *f*

JP *abbr* (*Justice of the Peace*) HRM juez(a) de paz *m,f*

jr. *abbr* (*junior*) GEN COMM hijo *m*

J-shaped: **~ frequency curve** *n* MATH *statistics* curva de frecuencias en forma de J *f*

judge *n* LAW juez(a) *m,f*; **~'s rules** *n pl BrE jarg* LAW directrices del juez *f pl*

judgment *n* GEN COMM juicio *m*, LAW decisión judicial *f*, PROP indemnización *f*; **~ creditor** FIN acreedor(a) judicial *m,f*, acreedor(a) por sentencia firme *m,f*, LAW acreedor(a) en virtud de una sentencia *m,f*; **~ debtor** FIN, LAW deudor(a) judicial *m,f*, deudor(a) por sentencia firme *m,f*, deudor(a) en virtud de una sentencia; **~ lien** *AmE* LAW gravamen por fallo *m*, gravamen por juicio *m*; **~ proof** LAW prueba judicial *f*; **~ sample** LAW muestra de comparación *f*

judicature *n* POL *body* judicatura *f*

judicial[1] *adj* LAW judicial

judicial[2]: **~ affairs** *n pl* LAW asuntos judiciales *m pl*; **~ arbitrator** *n* LAW árbitro(-a) judicial *m,f*; **~ bond** *n* LAW fianza judicial *f*; **~ foreclosure** *n* LAW aprobación de remate *f*, venta judicial *f*; **~ notice** *n* LAW citación judicial *f*; **~ proceedings** *n pl* LAW procedimiento judicial *m*; **~ sale** *n* LAW aprobación de remate *f*, venta judicial *f*; **~ separation** *n* LAW separación judicial *f*

judiciary *n* LAW, POL *body* judicatura *f*; **the ~** LAW, POL poder judicial *m*

juggernaut *n* TRANSP camión gigante *m*

Juglar: **~ cycle** *n* ECON ciclo Juglar *m*

jumble: **~ sale** *n BrE* (*cf rummage sale AmE*) S&M venta de objetos usados *f*, venta de prendas usadas *f*

jumbo *n infrml* (*jumbo jet*) TRANSP jumbo *m*; **~ certificate of deposit** STOCK certificado de depósito de mayor cuantía *m*; **~ derrick** TRANSP *cargo handling* puntal para cargas pesadas *m*; **~ jet** (*jumbo*) TRANSP avión jumbo *m*; **~ loan** BANK préstamo de gran cuantía *m*, préstamo grande *m*; **~ pack** S&M envase gigante *m*

jumboization *n jarg* TRANSP alargamiento en un petrolero de la parte central, conservando la popa y proa primitivas

jumboize *vt jarg* TRANSP ampliar la capacidad de una embarcación mediante la utilización de la cubierta

jump *n* GEN COMM, STOCK *in prices* salto *m*

jumpy *adj* ECON, STOCK *market* indeciso, inestable

June: **~ call** *n* STOCK *options* opción de compra en junio *f*; **~ put** *n* STOCK *options* opción de venta en junio *f*

junior *n* GEN COMM *employee* auxiliar *mf*, (*jnr., jr.*) hijo *m*; **~ creditor** BANK acreedor(a) en segunda instancia *m,f*; **~ debt** FIN, STOCK deuda subordinada *f*; **~ issue** *AmE* STOCK emisión de deuda subordinada *f*; **~ lien** LAW gravamen inferior *m*; **~ management** MGMNT subdirección *f*; **~ manager** BANK director(a) adjunto(-a) *m,f*, HRM, MGMNT director(a) adjunto(-a) *m,f*, gerente adjunto(-a) *m,f*, gerente medio(-a) *m,f*; **~ mortgage** *AmE* (*cf second mortgage BrE*) BANK, PROP hipoteca en segundo grado *f*, segunda hipoteca *f*; **~ partner** GEN COMM socio(-a) menor *m,f*; **~ position** HRM cargo auxiliar *m*, puesto menor *m*; **~ refunding** FIN reembolso menor *m*; **~ security** STOCK título subordinado *m*; **~ share** STOCK acción subordinada *f*

junk *n* ACC existencias inmovilizadas *f pl*; **~ bond** FIN, STOCK *blue chip* bono basura *m*; **~ mail** COMMS, S&M propaganda de buzón *f*

junket[1] *n AmE infrml* TRANSP *on public expenses for private purposes* excursión *f*, viaje *m*

junket[2] *vi AmE infrml* TRANSP *on public expenses for private purposes* ir de excursión

juridical: **~ position** *n* LAW posición jurídica *f*

juridification *n* HRM, LAW judicialización *f*

jurisdiction *n* LAW *geographic, political*, PATENTS jurisdicción *f*, POL competencia *f*, jurisdicción *f*; **~ dispute** HRM disputa jurisdiccional *f*

jurisdictional: **~ strike** *n* HRM huelga de competencias *f*

jurisprudence *n* LAW filosofía del derecho *f*, ciencia del derecho *f*

jurist *n* BANK, GEN COMM, LAW jurista *mf*

jury *n* LAW jurado *m*; **~ of executive opinion** MATH jurado de opinión ejecutiva *m*; **~ trial** LAW juicio con jurado *m*

jus disponendi *n* GEN COMM derecho a disponer *m*

just[1]: **~-in-time** *adj* (*JIT*) IND justo a tiempo (*JIT*) (*AmL*)

just[2]: **~ cause dismissal** *n* HRM despido por causa justa *m*; **~ compensation** *n* LAW *property* indemnización justa por daños y perjuicios *f*, PROP compensación equitable *f*, compensación razonable *f*; **~-in-time model** *n* IND modelo de justo a tiempo *m*; **~-in-time production** *n* (*JIT production*) IND producción justo a tiempo *f* (*AmL*), producción según demanda *f* (*Esp*); **~ price** *n* ECON precio justo *m*; **~ wage** *n* ECON, HRM salario justo *m*

Justice: **~ of the Peace** *n* *BrE* (*JP*) HRM juez(a) de paz *m,f*

justification *n* COMP *of text*, GEN COMM *reason* justifica-ción *f*; **~ character** COMP carácter de encuadramiento *m*

justified[1] *adj* COMP *to the right, left*, GEN COMM *reason* justificado

justified[2]: **~ price** *n* STOCK precio justificado *m*

justify *vt* COMP *text*, LAW *action* justificar

juvenile: **~ court** *n* LAW tribunal de menores *m*

JV *abbr* (*joint venture*) GEN COMM alianza estratégica *f*, coinversión *f*, empresa conjunta *f*, empresas mixtas *f pl*, STOCK agrupación de empresas *f*, riesgo compartido *m*

K

Kaldor: ~'s laws *n pl* ECON leyes de Kaldor *f pl*

Kaldor-Hicks: ~ **Compensation Principle** *n* ECON Principio de Compensación de Kaldor-Hicks *m*

kanban *n* INS ficha de reposición *f*

kangaroo: ~ **crane** *n* TRANSP *cargo* grúa canguro *f*; ~ **ticket** *n AmE infrml* POL candidatura en la que el vicepresidente tiene más "gancho" que el presidente

Katona: ~ **effect** *n* ECON efecto Katona *m*

KBS *abbr* (*knowledge-based system*) COMP sistema experto *m*

keep *vt* GEN COMM *retain* guardar, mantener; ♦ ~ **abreast of** GEN COMM *conditions, legislation* mantenerse al corriente de, mantenerse informado de; ~ **afloat** GEN COMM *business* mantenerse a flote; ~ **an appointment** GEN COMM asistir a una cita; ~ **a close watch on** GEN COMM vigilar atentamente; ~ **the filing up to date** ADMIN mantener el archivo al día; ~ **in reserve** GEN COMM guardar en reserva; ~ **in step with one's competitors** GEN COMM ir al mismo ritmo que los competidores; ~ **in touch with** GEN COMM *acquaintances, contacts* mantenerse en contacto con, *new developments* mantenerse al corriente de; ~ **inflation down** ECON mantener baja la inflación; ~ **a low profile** GEN COMM tratar de pasar desapercibido; ~ **a note** GEN COMM llevar nota; ~ **pace with** GEN COMM *developments, progress* mantenerse al tanto de; ~ **sb informed** COMMS, GEN COMM mantener informado a alguien; ~ **sth under wraps** *infrml* GEN COMM mantener algo en secreto; ~ **tally of** GEN COMM llevar la cuenta de; ~ **track of** GEN COMM llevar un control de; ~ **up with** GEN COMM *developments* continuar con, *payments* seguir el ritmo de, *standards* atenderse a; ~ **up payment on one's mortgage** BANK, FIN estar al día en el pago de la hipoteca; ~ **within the law** LAW mantenerse dentro de la ley

keg *n* TRANSP cuñete *m*

Kennedy: ~ **Round** *n* ECON Ronda Kennedy *f*

Keogh: ~ **Plan** *n* FIN *pension* plan Keogh *m*

kerb: ~ **market** *n* STOCK *unlisted market* bolsín *m*; ~ **weight** *n* TRANSP *motor trade* peso en orden de marcha *m*

kerbside: ~ **conference** *n* S&M discusión de técnicas de venta entre alumno e instructor; ~ **weight** *n* TRANSP peso en orden de marcha *m*

key *n* COMP clave *f*; ~~**area evaluation** MGMNT evaluación de área clave *f*; ~ **currency** ECON divisa de referencia *f*; ~ **data** *n pl* GEN COMM datos básicos *m pl*; ~ **feature** GEN COMM rasgo clave *m*; ~ **industry** ECON, IND industria clave *f*; ~ **issue** GEN COMM cuestión clave *f*; ~ **money** GEN COMM *flat* dinero dado como señal *m*; ~ **pallet** TRANSP plataforma maestra de carga *f*; ~ **person life and health insurance** INS seguro de vida y de salud de un trabajador clave *m*; ~ **point** GEN COMM punto vital *m*; ~ **prospects** *n pl* S&M perspectivas claves *f pl*; ~ **rate** ECON *interest* proporción clave *f*, *wage* tarifa clave *f*; ~ **sequence** COMP secuencia por clave *f*; ~ **stage** GEN COMM *in process* fase clave *f*

key in *vt* COMP teclear, introducir por teclado

keyboard[1]: ~~**operated** *adj* COMP manejado mediante teclado

keyboard[2] *n* COMP teclado *m*; ~ **operator** COMP, HRM operador(a) de teclado *m,f*

keyed: ~ **advertisement** *n* S&M publicidad codificada *f*

keyhole: ~ **socket** *n* TRANSP *containers* encastre en U *m*

keylock *n* COMP cerradura de seguridad *f*

Keynes: ~ **effect** *n* ECON efecto Keynes *m*; ~ **expectations** *n pl* ECON expectativas de Keynes *f pl*; ~ **Plan** *n* ECON Plan Keynes *m*

Keynes': ~ **General Theory** *n* ECON teoría general de Keynes *f*

Keynesian: ~ **cross diagram** *n* ECON diagrama cruzado de Keynes *m*; ~ **economics** *n* ECON economía keynesiana *f*; ~ **equilibrium** *n* ECON equilibrio keynesiano *m*; ~ **multiplier** *n* ECON *investment* multiplicador de Keynes *m*; ~ **policy** *n* ECON política keynesiana *f*

keypad *n* COMP teclado numérico *m*

keypunch *n* COMP perforadora de teclado *f*

keypuncher *n* COMP perforista *mf*

keystroke *n* COMP pulsación *f*; ~ **rate** ADMIN coeficiente de pulsaciones *m*

keyword *n* COMP palabra clave *f*; ~ **search** COMP búsqueda de palabra clave *f*

kickback *n AmE infrml* FIN, HRM, LAW, POL cohecho *m* (*Esp*), coima *f* (*AmL*), comisión ilícita *f*, soborno *m* (*Esp*)

kiddie: ~ **tax** *n AmE infrml* TAX impuesto según la Ley de Reforma Fiscal de 1986 por el que los niños menores de 14 años deben pagar un impuesto por intereses y dividendos superiores a $1000 según la tasa de impuesto marginal más alta de sus padres

kidnap: ~ **insurance** *n* INS seguro contra secuestro *m*

kill: ~ **demand** *phr* S&M matar la demanda

killer: ~ **bond** *n* STOCK bono matador *m*

killing *n infrml* STOCK *profit* recorte *m*

kind: in ~ *adj* GEN COMM *payment, benefits*, LAW en especie

king: ~ **post** *n* TRANSP *shipping* pendolón *m*

kingpin: ~ **position** *n* TRANSP *road vehicle* posición de pivote *f*

King: ~'s **warehouse** *n BrE* IMP/EXP almacén público nacional *m*

kinked: ~ **demand curve** *n* ECON curva de demanda quebrada *f*

Kitchin: ~ **cycle** *n* ECON ciclo de Kitchin *m*

kite *n jarg* FIN, STOCK letra de colisión *f*, letra de pelota *f*

kiting *n AmE* BANK, circulación de cheques en descubierto *f*, circulación de cheques sin fondos *f*

kneeling *adj* TRANSP *road vehicle* articulado

knock[1] *n* GEN COMM golpe *m*; ~~**for-knock** *jarg* INS golpe por golpe; ~~**on effect** GEN COMM repercusión *f*; ~~**out axle** TRANSP *road trailer* eje roto *m*

knock[2] *vt jarg* TRANSP *car trade* chocar

knock down *vt* GEN COMM, S&M *auctions, contracts* adjudicar, *prices* rebajar, hundirse

knock off *vi infrml* GEN COMM *finish work* cesar el trabajo

knockdown: ~ **price** *n* GEN COMM precio mínimo *m*

knocker *n infrml* S&M vendedor(a) *m,f*

knocking: ~ **competition** *n* S&M competencia que denigra los productos de los demás; ~ **copy** *n* S&M anuncio destinado a denigrar el producto de la competencia

knockoffs *n pl infrml* IND *fashion sector* imitaciones *f pl*

knockout *n infrml* GEN COMM acuerdo entre los concursantes *m*; ~ **agreement** *infrml* GEN COMM acuerdo de competencia *m*; ~ **competition** GEN COMM concurso eliminatorio *m*

knot *n* GEN COMM nudo *m*

know: ~-**how** *n* GEN COMM *technical* know-how *m* (*infrml*), tecnología *f*, LAW pericia *f*; ~-**how agreement** *n* LAW, PATENTS acuerdo de asistencia técnica *f*

knowledge[1]: ~-**intensive** *adj* GEN COMM con aplicación intensiva de conocimientos, intensivo en conocimientos

knowledge[2] *n* GEN COMM, MGMNT conocimiento *m*; ~ **base** ACC, WEL *social work* base de conocimiento *f*; ~-**based industry** ECON, IND industria basada en el conocimiento *f*; ~-**based system** (*KBS*) COMP, GEN COMM sistema experto *m*; ♦ **have a working** ~ **of** HRM tener un conocimiento práctico de

knowledgeable *adj* GEN COMM inteligente

known[1] *adj* GEN COMM conocido; ♦ **also** ~ **as** (*a.k.a.*, *AKA*) GEN COMM alias, también conocido como; ~ **by name** GEN COMM conocido por su nombre

known[2]: ~ **loss** *n* INS siniestro conocido *m*

Kondratieff: ~ **cycle** *n* ECON ciclo de Kondratieff *m*; ~ **wave** *n* ECON onda de Kondratieff *f*

kudos *n* GEN COMM, S&M prestigio *m*

kurtosis *n* MATH curtosis *f*

Kuznets: ~ **curve** *n* ECON curva de Kuznets *f*; ~ **cycle** *n* ECON ciclo Kuznets *m*

L

L/A *abbr* GEN COMM (*letter of authority*) carta de autorización *f*, TRANSP (*Lloyd's Agent*) *shipping* representante de Lloyds *mf*, (*landing account*) cuenta de desembarque *f*

lab *n infrml* (*laboratory*) IND laboratorio *m*

LAB *abbr* (*live animals on board*) TRANSP animales vivos a bordo

label¹ *n* COMP etiqueta *f*, MEDIA *record company* sello *m*, S&M, TRANSP *identification of cargo* etiqueta *f*; **~ clause** (*LC*) GEN COMM cláusula sobre etiquetas *f*; **~ of quality** GEN COMM marchamo de calidad *m*

label² *vt* COMP, S&M, TRANSP etiquetar

labeled *AmE see* **labelled** *BrE*

labeling *AmE see* **labelling** *BrE*

labelled: ~ file *n BrE* COMP fichero con etiqueta *m*

labelling *n BrE* COMP, S&M etiquetado *m*

labor *AmE see* **labour** *BrE*

Labor: ~ Management Relations Act *n AmE* HRM *1947* ley de relaciones obrero-patronales; **~ Management Reporting and Disclosure Act** *n AmE* HRM *1959* ley de relaciones laborales que obliga a la información

laboratory *n* (*lab*) IND laboratorio *m*; **~ experience** WEL experimento de laboratorio *m*; **~ technique** S&M técnica de laboratorio *f*

laborer *AmE see* **labourer** *BrE*

labour¹: **~-intensive** *adj BrE* HRM, IND *production* de alto coeficiente de mano de obra, intensivo en cuanto a mano de obra; **~-saving** *adj BrE* HRM, IND que ahorra trabajo

labour² *n BrE* GEN COMM, HRM *workforce* mano de obra *f*, *persons* obreros *m pl*, *task* tarea *f*, *work* trabajo *m*; **~ administration** *BrE* HRM administración laboral *f*, gestión laboral *f*; **~ agreement** *BrE* HRM acuerdo laboral *m*, IND, LAW convenio colectivo de trabajo *m*; **~-augmenting technical progress** *BrE* ECON progreso técnico que aumenta el rendimiento del trabajo *m*; **~ clause** *BrE* HRM cláusula laboral *f*; **~ code** *BrE* HRM, LAW código del trabajo *m*, ley federal del trabajo *f*; **~ contract** *BrE* GEN COMM, HRM contrato de trabajo *m*; **~ cost** *BrE* ECON, HRM coste laboral *m* (*Esp*), costo laboral *m* (*AmL*); **~ costs** *n pl BrE* ECON costes de mano de obra *m pl* (*Esp*), costes de personal *m pl* (*Esp*), costos de mano de obra *m pl* (*AmL*), costos de personal *m pl* (*AmL*); **~ demand** *BrE* ECON demanda de mano de obra *f*, demanda laboral *f*; **~ dispute** *BrE* ECON, HRM, POL conflicto colectivo *m*, conflicto laboral *m*; **~ efficiency** *BrE* HRM eficiencia laboral *f*; **~ force** *BrE* ECON *workforce* población activa *f*, plantilla de personal *f*, GEN COMM, HRM *persons* obreros *m pl*, *workforce* mano de obra *f*, plantilla de personal *f*, IND población activa *f*; **~ force participation** *BrE* HRM participación de la mano de obra *f*; **~ force participation rate** *BrE* (*LFPR*) ECON tasa de participación de la mano de obra *f*; **~ inspector** *BrE* HRM, WEL inspector(a) de trabajo *m,f*; **~-intensive industry** *BrE* ECON, HRM, IND industria con uso intensivo de mano de obra *f*; **~ law** *BrE* HRM ley laboral *f*, LAW derecho del trabajo *m*, derecho laboral *m*, ley laboral *f*; **~ law lawyer** *BrE* BANK, GEN COMM, LAW ≈ abogado(-a) laborista *m,f*; **~-managed firm** *BrE* MGMNT empresa administrada por los obreros *f*, empresa que pertenece a los empleados *f*; **~ market** *BrE* ECON, HRM mercado de trabajo *m*, mercado laboral *m*; **~-market policy** *BrE* POL política de mercado laboral *f*; **~ market rigidity** *BrE* ECON rigidez del mercado laboral *f*; **~ mobility** *BrE* ECON, HRM movilidad de la mano de obra *f*, movilidad laboral *f*; **~ movement** *BrE* HRM, POL laborismo *m*, movimiento obrero *m*; **~-only subcontracting** *BrE* HRM subcontratación exclusiva de mano de obra *f*; **~ piracy** *BrE* HRM intrusismo laboral *m*; **~ pool** *BrE* HRM bolsa de trabajo *f*; **~ power** *BrE* HRM poder de la mano de obra *m*, poder obrero *m*; **~ process theory** *BrE* HRM teoría del proceso laboral *f*; **~ relations** *BrE* ECON, HRM relación laboral *f*; **~ relations manager** *BrE* HRM gerente de relaciones laborales *m*; **~ shed** *BrE* ECON aportación de mano de obra *f*, HRM nave industrial *f*; **~ shedding** *BrE* HRM cambio de empleo *m*; **~ shortage** *BrE* HRM escasez de mano de obra *f*; **~ standard** *BrE* ECON norma laboral *f*; **~ supply** *BrE* ECON oferta laboral *f*, oferta de trabajo *f*; **~ theory of value** *BrE* ECON teoría laboral del valor *f*; **~ troubles** *n pl BrE* HRM dificultades laborales *f pl*; **~ turnover** *BrE* HRM rotación de mano de obra *f*, rotación de personal *f*; **~ union** *BrE* GEN COMM, HRM sindicato obrero *m*; **~ unrest** *BrE* HRM descontento del personal *m*, inquietud laboral *f*

labour³ *vi BrE* HRM trabajar

Labour: ~ Party *n BrE* POL Partido Laborista *m*; **~ Representation Committee** *n* (*LRC*) HRM comité de representación laboral

labourer *n BrE* GEN COMM operario(-a) *m,f*

LAC *abbr* (*Lights Advisory Committee*) TRANSP comité de consulta de faros y boyas

laches *n pl* LAW incuria *f*, negligencia en el ejercicio de un derecho *f*

lack¹ *n* ECON falta *f*, GEN COMM *scarcity* escasez *f*, ausencia *f*, carencia *f*, LAW ausencia *f*; **~ of competence** ECON falta de competencia *f*; **~ of inventory** ECON falta de existencias *f*; **~ of raw material** ENVIR falta de materia prima *f*; **◆ for ~ of** GEN COMM por falta de

lack² *vi* GEN COMM, S&M *confidence, support* carecer, faltar

ladder: ~ of participation *n jarg* POL sistema escalonado de participación *f*

ladies: ~ and gentlemen *phr* GEN COMM *as introduction* señoras y señores

Laffer: ~ curve *n* ECON curva de Laffer *f*

LAFTA *abbr obs before 1981* (*Latin American Free Trade Association*) ECON, POL ALALC (*Asociación Latinoamericana de Libre Comercio*)

lag *n* ECON desfase *m*, demora *f*, GEN COMM retardo *m*, retraso *m*; **~ response** ECON respuesta desfasada *f*, GEN COMM respuesta con retraso *f*; **~ risk** BANK riesgo relacionado con un desfase *m*

lag behind *vi* ECON, FIN, GEN COMM quedarse atrás

laggard *n jarg* S&M consumidor(a) conservador(a) *m,f*, STOCK rezagado *m*

lagged: ~ **variable** *n* MATH variable desfasada *f*

lagging: ~ **indicator** *n* ECON *econometrics* indicador de retardo *m*

LAIA *abbr* (*Latin American Integration Association*) ECON, POL ≈ ALALC (*Asociación Latinoamericana de Libre Comercio*)

laid[1]: ~-**up** *adj* GEN COMM *ship, car* fuera de circulación, TRANSP *shipping* desarmado

laid[2]: ~-**up tonnage** *n* TRANSP *shipping* tonelaje amarrado *m*

laissez: ~-**faire** *n* ECON laissez faire *m*, POL laissez faire *m*, librecambismo *m*; ~-**faire economy** *n* ECON economía liberal *f*

lame: ~ **duck** *n jarg* GEN COMM *company* deudor(a) insolvente *m,f*, STOCK especulador(a) insolvente *m,f*

LAN *abbr* (*local area network*) COMP RAL (*red de área local*)

land *n* PROP finca *f*, terreno *m*; ~ **agent** GEN COMM, PROP corredor(a) de fincas *m,f*; ~ **bank** BANK banco rural *m*; ~ **banking** BANK, FIN, PROP operación bancaria de tierras *f*; ~ **bridge** TRANSP conexión a tierra *f*; ~ **bridge rate** TRANSP tarifa de transporte terrestre *f*; ~ **carriage** TRANSP transporte por tierra *m*; ~ **certificate** LAW, PROP certificado de tierras *m*, certificado expedido por el registro de la propiedad inmobiliaria *m*; ~ **compensation** LAW compensación de tierras *f*; ~ **compensation code** PROP código de compensación de tierras *m*; ~ **contract** PROP contrato de compraventa de un bien inmueble *m*; ~ **developer** GEN COMM, PROP promotor(a) inmobiliario(-a) *m,f*; ~ **development** ENVIR explotación de la tierra *f*, PROP viabilización de tierras *f*; ~ **economy** ECON economía de la tierra *f*; ~ **end for orders** (*LEFO*) TRANSP final de los pedidos *m*; ~ **grant** PROP concesión de terrenos *f*; ~ **improvement** ENVIR mejoramiento de la tierra *m*, PROP bonificación de tierras *f*; ~ **in abeyance** LAW, PROP tierras sin titular *f pl*, tierras en curso de adquisición *f pl*, tierras en suspenso *f pl*; ~ **lease** PROP arrendamiento de tierras *m*; ~ **office** ADMIN oficina del catastro *f*; ~ **ownership** ECON propiedad de la tierra *f*; ~ **reform** ECON *agricultural*, ENVIR reforma agraria *f*; ~ **register** LAW, PROP, TAX catastro *m*; ~ **registration** LAW, PROP, TAX catastro *m*; ~ **registry** LAW, PROP, TAX catastro *m*, registro de la propiedad inmobiliaria *m*; ~ **rent** FIN renta de terreno *f*, PROP alquiler de la tierra *m*; ~ **tax** TAX contribución territorial *f*; ~ **trust** LAW *property* fideicomiso de bienes *m*, fideicomiso de bienes raíces *m*, PROP fideicomiso de bienes *m*; ~ **trust certificate** LAW certificado de fideicomiso de tierras *m*; ~ **use** ENVIR utilización de la tierra *f*; ~-**use intensity** ENVIR intensidad del uso de la tierra *f*; ~-**use planning** ECON planificación de tierras *f*; ~-**use regulation** LAW normativa sobre el uso del suelo *f*, PROP regulación del uso de la tierra *f*; ~-**use succession** PROP sucesión en el uso de la tierra *f*; ~ **value tax** TAX impuesto sobre el valor de la tierra *m*; ◆ ~, **tenements and hereditaments** LAW, PROP terrenos, viviendas y herencias, todo tipo de bienes inmuebles

Land: ~ **Bank** *n* BANK Caja Rural *f*; ~ **Compensation Act** *n BrE* LAW ley de compensación de tierras; ~ **Register** *n* LAW, PROP registro de la propiedad *m*

landed: ~ **cost** *n* IMP/EXP, TRANSP coste descargado *m* (*Esp*), costo descargado *m* (*AmL*); ~ **freight insurance cost** *n* TRANSP *of goods* coste de seguro de flete descargado *m* (*Esp*), costo de seguro de flete descargado

m (*AmL*); ~ **property** *n* LAW, PROP bienes raíces *m pl*; ~ **terms** *n pl* IMP/EXP, TRANSP condiciones de descarga *f pl*

landfill: ~ **site** *n* ENVIR vertedero *m*

landing[1]: ~ **account** *n* (*L/A*) TRANSP *shipping* cuenta de desembarque *f*; ~ **card** *n* TRANSP *shipping* tarjeta de desembarque *f*; ~ **certificate** *n* TRANSP certificado de descarga *m*; ~ **charge** *n* TRANSP *shipping* gasto de desembarque *f*; ~ **gear** *n* TRANSP *on trailer* mecanismo de descarga *m*; ~ **officer** *n* HRM, TRANSP oficial(a) de desembarque *m,f*, *shipping* oficial(a) de descarga *m,f*; ~ **order** *n* TRANSP *shipping* orden de desembarque *f*; ~ **permit** *n* TRANSP permiso de descarga *m*; ~ **stage** *n* TRANSP desembarcadero *m*; ~ **storage delivery** *n* (*LSD*) IMP/EXP entrega de productos almacenados al desembarque *f*, TRANSP entrega de la carga a tierra *f*

landing[2]: ~ **and delivering cargo** *phr* TRANSP *shipping* flete desembarcado y entregado

landlady *n* PROP arrendadora *f*

landlocked[1] *adj* ENVIR sin acceso al mar, PROP rodeado de tierra

landlocked[2]: ~ **country** *n* ENVIR país sin acceso al mar *m*, país sin litoral *m*, país sin salida al mar *m*

landlord *n* PROP arrendador *m*

landmark[1] *adj* LAW *case* que hizo época, que sentó un precedente histórico

landmark[2] *n* PROP punto prominente *m*

landowner *n* PROP terrateniente *mf*, hacendado(-a) *m,f*

Landrum-Griffin: ~ **Act** *n AmE* HRM, LAW Ley Landrum-Griffin *f*

landscape[1] *adj jarg* COMP *document layout*, GEN COMM horizontal

landscape[2] *n jarg* ADMIN, COMP, MEDIA, S&M formato horizontal *m*, formato apaisado *m*

landscape[3] *vt jarg* ADMIN crear una oficina de planificación abierta

language *n* COMP, S&M *advertising* lenguaje *m*; ~ **arts** *n pl* WEL artes del lenguaje *f pl*; ◆ **in plain** ~ GEN COMM *document, leaflet* en lenguaje claro

Lanham: ~ **Act** *n AmE* LAW Ley Lanham *f*

Lapanov: ~ **equilibrium** *n* ECON equilibrio de Lapanov *m*

lapping *n* ACC falseamiento de la cuenta de clientes *m*

lapse[1] *n* ACC *time* caducidad *f*, GEN COMM *error* equivocación *f*, *time* lapso *m*, INS, STOCK caducidad *f*; ~ **clause** INS cláusula de caducidad *f*; ~ **of a patent** PATENTS expiración de una patente *f*; ~ **of time** GEN COMM lapso de tiempo *m*

lapse[2] *vi* ACC, INS, STOCK caducar

lapsed[1] *adj* ACC, INS, STOCK caducado

lapsed[2]: ~ **discount** *n* GEN COMM descuento caducado *m*; ~ **funds** *n pl* ACC fondos caducados *m pl*; ~ **option** *n* STOCK opción caducada *f*

lapsing *n* ACC, INS, STOCK caducidad *f*; ~ **appropriation** ACC aplicación caducada *f*; ~ **resources** ACC *governmental* carestía de recursos *f*, descenso de recursos *m*, falta de recursos *f*; ~ **schedule** ACC cédula de caducidad *f*, cuadro de amortización *m*, cuadro de periodificación *m*, programa de vencimiento *m*

laptop *n* COMP computador portátil *m* (*AmL*), computadora portátil *f* (*AmL*), ordenador portátil *m* (*Esp*), laptop *m*

large[1]: ~-**scale** *adj* ECON, GEN COMM *project* a gran escala; **in ~ quantities** GEN COMM en grandes cantidades

large[2]: **~ display advertisement** *n* MEDIA, S&M anuncio resaltado *m*, S&M publicidad a gran escala *f*; **~ exposure** *n* FIN gastos a gran escala *m pl*; **~ market** *n* STOCK mercado amplio *m*; **~ order** *n* GEN COMM, S&M pedido importante *m*; **~ risks** *n pl* INS grandes riesgos *m pl*; **~-scale exporter** *n* ECON exportador(a) a gran escala *m,f*; **~-scale farming** *n* ECON agricultura a gran escala *f*; **~-scale industry** *n* IND industria a gran escala *f*; **~-scale integration** *n* (*LSI*) COMP gran escala de integración *f* (*LSI*); **~-scale model** *n* ECON *econometrics* modelo de gran escala *m*; **~-scale production** *n* ECON, IND producción en serie *f*

largely *adv* GEN COMM en gran parte, ampliamente

largest: **~ investor** *n* STOCK gran inversor(a) *m,f*, mayor inversor(a) *m,f*

laser: **~ banking** *n* BANK banco de conveniencia *m*; **~ beam** *n* IND rayo láser *m*; **~ personalization** *n* S&M personalización por láser *f*; **~ printer** *n* COMP impresora de rayo láser *f*, impresora láser *f*; **~ scanner** *n* MEDIA print lector óptico *m*

lash: **~ end fitting** *n* TRANSP *containers* fijación de trinca *f*

lash out *vt jarg* ACC, ECON, FIN *spend* desembolsar

LASH *abbr* (*lighter aboard ship*) TRANSP buque portagabarras *m*

lashing *n* TRANSP amarre *m*; **~ cage** TRANSP cesta de amarre *f*; **~ eye** TRANSP atadura del extremo de trinca *f*

Laspeyre: **~'s index** *n* ECON *econometrics* índice de Laspeyres *m*

last[1] *adj* GEN COMM último; ◆ **~ in, first out** (*LIFO*) ACC, GEN COMM último en entrar, primero en salir (*UEPS*)

last[2]: **~ carrier** *n* TRANSP último transportista *m*; **~ day hours** *n pl* STOCK últimas horas del día *f pl*; **~ day of trading** *n* STOCK último día de operaciones *m*; **~-minute decision** *n* GEN COMM decisión de última hora *f*; **~ notice day** *n* FIN día de la última comunicación *m*; **~-offer arbitration** *n* IIRM arbitraje de última oferta *m*; **~ safe day** *n* (*lsd*) INS *marine* último día del seguro *m*; **~ sale** *n* S&M, STOCK última venta *f*; **~ trading day** *n* STOCK última sesión bursátil *f*; **~ will and testament** *n* LAW testamento *m*

last[3] *vi* GEN COMM durar, permanecer

last out *vi* GEN COMM *money, resources* durar

lat. *abbr* (*latitude*) GEN COMM latitud *f*

LATAG *abbr* (*Latin American Trade Advisory Group*) ECON, POL Grupo Consultor de Comercio Latinoamericano *m*

late: **~ capitalism** *n* ECON, IND, POL capitalismo tardío *m*; **~ filer** *n* TAX declarante fuera de plazo *m*; **~ filing** *n* TAX *of returns* presentación fuera de plazo *f*; **~ fringe** *n* AmE *jarg* MEDIA *broadcast* última franja horaria de emisión *f*; **~ majority** *n* S&M mayoría tardía *f*; **~-night bus** *n* TRANSP autobús a última hora de la noche *m*; **~-night news** *n* MEDIA *broadcast* edición de noticias de última hora de la noche *f*; **~-night show** *n* LEIS sesión de noche *f*; **~ payment** *n* ACC, FIN último pago *m*, pago tardío *m*; **~ rendering** *n* TAX *VAT return* presentación fuera de plazo *f*; **~ tape** *n* STOCK grabación reciente *f*

lateness *n* HRM retraso *m*

latent: **~ defect** *n* LAW vicio oculto *m*, PROP defecto latente *m*, vicio oculto *m*; **~ demand** *n* S&M demanda latente *f*; **~ tax** *n* TAX impuesto latente *m*

lateral: **~ integration** *n* GEN COMM integración lateral *f*;

~ thinking *n* COMMS, GEN COMM, MGMNT pensamiento lateral *m*, razonamiento horizontal *m*

latest[1]: **~ addition** *n* GEN COMM *product range* novedad más reciente *f*; **~ date** *n* GEN COMM fecha más reciente *f*; **~ estimate** *n* (*L/E*) GEN COMM última estimación *f*, estimación más reciente *f*; **~ fashion** *n* GEN COMM última moda *f*

latest[2]: **at the ~** *phr* GEN COMM a más tardar; **the ~ statistics show that** *phr* MATH *statistics* las últimas estadísticas muestran que

Latin: **~ American Free Trade Association** *n obs before 1981* (*LAFTA*) ECON, POL ≈ Asociación Latinoamericana de Libre Comercio *f* (*ALALC*); **~ American Integration Association** *n* (*LAIA*) ECON, POL ≈ Asociación Latinoamericana de Libre Comercio *f* (*ALALC*); **~ American Trade Advisory Group** *n* (*LATAG*) ECON, POL Grupo Consultor de Comercio Latinoamericano *m*

latitude *n* (*lat.*) GEN COMM latitud *f*, MGMNT *of thinking* anchura *f*, latitud *f*

latter *adj* GEN COMM *later* posterior, último, *of two* segundo

lattice: **~-sided container** *n* TRANSP contenedor con enrejado lateral *m*

launch[1] *n* COMP lanzamiento *m*, LEIS *of film* estreno *m*, S&M lanzamiento *m*, *of product* estreno *m*, TRANSP *vessel* lancha *f*; **~ offer** MEDIA, S&M oferta de lanzamiento *f*; **~ party** MEDIA *book* fiesta de lanzamiento *f*

launch[2] *vt* COMP lanzar, GEN COMM *company* crear, fundar, LEIS *new film* estrenar, S&M *into marketplace* iniciar, *product* lanzar, STOCK lanzar, TRANSP *new vessel* botar; ◆ **~ a bond issue** STOCK lanzar una emisión de bonos

launching *n* COMP lanzamiento *m*, MEDIA *of book*, S&M lanzamiento *m*, TRANSP *of new vessel* botadura *f*, inauguración *f*

launder *vt* BANK, FIN, GEN COMM *money* lavar

laundry: **~ list** *n* AmE *jarg* POL lista de cuestiones por resolver *f*

Lausanne: **~ School** *n* ECON, GEN COMM Escuela de Lausana *f*

Lautro *abbr* (*Life Assurance and Unit Trust Regulatory Organization*) FIN organización regulatoria de seguros de vida y de fondos de inversiones

law *n* HRM *course of study* derecho *m*, LAW, POL *system, statute* ley *f*; **~ of comparative advantage** ECON, LAW *international trade* ley de ventaja comparativa *f*; **~ of diminishing marginal utility** ECON, LAW ley de utilidad marginal decreciente *f*; **~ of diminishing returns** ECON ley de rendimientos decrecientes *f*; **~ enforcement official** LAW funcionario(-a) encargado(-a) de la ejecución de la ley *m,f*; **~ firm** LAW bufete de abogados *m*; **~ of the flag** GEN COMM, LAW ley de banderas *f*, ley del pabellón *f*; **~ of increasing costs** ECON ley de los costes *f* (*Esp*), ley de los costos *f* (*AmL*); **~-making power** ECON, LAW, POL competencia legislativa *f*; **~ and order** LAW orden público *m*; **~ practice** LAW ejercicio del derecho *m*, abogacía *f*; **~ of reciprocal demand** ECON *international* ley de la demanda recíproca *f*; **~ of reflux** BANK, LAW ley de reflejo *f*; **~ report** LAW acta de proceso *f*; **~ of satiable wants** ECON ley de la saciedad de las necesidades *f*; **~ school** LAW, WEL facultad de derecho *f*; **~ of supply and demand** GEN COMM ley de la oferta y la demanda *f*; **~ of taxation** LAW, TAX ley fiscal *f*; **~ of**

value ECON, LAW ley del valor *f*; **~ of variable proportions** ECON, LAW ley de las proporciones variables *f*; ◆ **as the ~ stands at present** LAW según la legislación vigente; **as required by ~** LAW conforme exige la ley

Law: **~ Lords** *n pl* LAW, POL jueces que son miembros de la Cámara de los Lores; **~ Society** *n BrE* (*cf Bar Association AmE*) BANK, GEN COMM, LAW ≈ Colegio de Abogados *m*

lawful[1] *adj* LAW lícito

lawful[2]: **~ means** *n pl* LAW recursos legales *m pl*; **~ money** *n AmE* (*cf legal tender BrE*) FIN curso legal *m*

lawsuit *n* LAW pleito *m*, causa *f*, querella *f*; ◆ **bring a ~ against sb** LAW entablar un pleito contra alguien

lawyer *n* BANK, GEN COMM, LAW abogado(-a) *m,f*, letrado(-a) *m,f*; **~ specializing in European Community law** BANK, GEN COMM, LAW abogado(-a) especialista en derecho comunitario *m,f*; **~ specializing in international law** BANK, GEN COMM, LAW ≈ abogado(-a) especialista en derecho internacional *m,f*

lay[1]: **~ day** *n* TRANSP *shipping* estadía *f*, plancha *f*; **~ members** *n pl* HRM asesores no juristas *m pl*; **~-off** *n* HRM despido de personal *m*, reajuste de personal *m*; **~ official** *n* HRM *industrial relations* funcionario(-a) no profesional *m,f*; **~-up berth** *n* TRANSP *shipping* muelle de desarmamento *m*; **~-up return** *n* INS *marine* extorno por amarre *m*

lay[2] *vt* GEN COMM imponer, *blame* echar, *plans* formar, *complaint* formular; ◆ **~ the basis** GEN COMM sentar las bases; **~ claim to** LAW demandar; **~ the emphasis on** GEN COMM poner el acento en; **~ the ground for** GEN COMM allanar el camino para

lay before *vt* GEN COMM *proposal* presentar

lay down *vt* GEN COMM *rules* establecer, LAW dictar

lay off *vt BrE* (*cf dehire AmE*) GEN COMM, HRM *workers* despedir, suspender

lay on *vt* GEN COMM *provide* instalar, TAX imponer

lay out *vt* GEN COMM *money* gastar, *investment* invertir

lay up *vt* TRANSP amarrar, desarmar

layer *n* COMP *network* capa *f*

laying: **~ off** *n BrE* (*cf dehiring AmE*) HRM reajuste *m*

layoff *n* BANK depósito temporal *m*; **~ pay** HRM *redundancy payment* indemnización por despido *f*

layout *n* ACC disposición *f*, implantación *f*, presentación *f*, ADMIN disposición *f*, distribución *f*, COMP *word-processed document* presentación *f*; **~ character** COMP carácter de encuadramiento *m*; **~ chart** MGMNT esquema de disposición *m*

laytime *n* TRANSP *shipping* plancha *f*; **~ saved** TRANSP *shipping* días de plancha ahorrados *m pl*

lazaret *n* IMP/EXP lazareto *m*

lazaretto *n* IMP/EXP lazareto *m*

lb *abbr* (*pound*) GEN COMM *weight* libra *f*

LBO *abbr* (*leveraged buyout*) GEN COMM, STOCK compra apalancada *f*

l/c *abbr* (*letter of credit*) BANK, FIN carta de crédito *f*

LC *abbr* GEN COMM (*label clause*) cláusula sobre etiquetas *f*, (*Library of Congress*) biblioteca del congreso de los Estados Unidos, ≈ Biblioteca Nacional *f Esp* (*BN*)

L/C *abbr* (*letter of credit*) BANK, FIN carta de crédito *f*

LCE *abbr obs* (*London Commodity Exchange*) STOCK antiguo nombre de la bolsa de materias primas de Londres conocido desde 1987 como London Futures and Options Exchange

LCH *abbr* ECON (*life-cycle hypothesis*) hipótesis cíclica de la vida *f*, STOCK (*London Clearing House*) cámara de compensación de Londres

LCL: **~ depot** *n* TRANSP depósito LCL *m*

LDC *abbr* (*less-developed country*) ECON, POL país en desarrollo *m*

ldg *abbr* (*loading*) TRANSP carga *f*

ldg&dly *abbr* (*loading and delivery*) TRANSP carga y distribución *f*

LDMA *abbr* (*London Discount Market Association*) BANK, FIN asociación del mercado de descuento de Londres

L/E *abbr* (*latest estimate*) GEN COMM última estimación *f*, estimación más reciente *f*

LEA *abbr BrE* (*Local Education Authority*) POL, WEL unidad administrativa equivalente a una provincia

lead[1] *n* MEDIA *main news story* artículo principal *m*, editorial *m*, entradilla *f*, PROP posible cliente(-a) *m,f*; **~ article** MEDIA párrafo inicial *m*; **~ bank** BANK banco director *m*; **~-free fuel** ENVIR carburante sin plomo *m*; **~-free gasoline** *AmE* (*cf lead-free petrol BrE*) TRANSP gasolina sin plomo *f* (*Esp*), nafta sin plomo *f* (*AmL*); **~-free petrol** *BrE* (*cf lead-free gasoline AmE*) TRANSP gasolina sin plomo *f* (*Esp*), nafta sin plomo *f* (*AmL*); **~ management** S&M gestión avanzada *f*; **~ manager** S&M director(a) de la emisión *m,f*; **~ ore** ENVIR, IND filón *m*; **~ slip** TRANSP amarradero principal *m*, atracadero principal *m*; **~ time** GEN COMM, IND tiempo de espera *m*, plazo de espera *m*, plazo de entrega *m*, S&M *of new product* plazo de entrega *m*, *stock* margen de tiempo *m*, TRANSP plazo de espera *m*; **~-time delay** GEN COMM retraso en el plazo de entrega *m*

lead[2]: **~ for the defence** *BrE*, **~ for the defense** *AmE* *phr* LAW llevar la defensa

leader *n* GEN COMM *person* jefe(-a) *m,f*, dirigente *mf*, HRM líder *mf*, MEDIA párrafo *m*, MGMNT, S&M líder *mf*, guía *mf*; **~ merchandising** S&M venta forzada de artículos más caros que los que están en promoción; **~ pricing** S&M *sales* fijación de precios orientativos *f*; **~ writer** MEDIA *newspapers* editorialista *mf*

leaders: **~ and laggards** *n pl* STOCK adelantados y rezagados *m pl*

leadership *n* HRM, MGMNT liderazgo *m*

leading[1] *adj* S&M líder

leading[2]: **~ article** *n* MEDIA *in newspaper* editorial *m*; **~ edge** *n* S&M vanguardia *f*; **~ firms ratio** *n* ECON proporción del liderazgo empresarial *f*; **~ indicator** *n* ECON *econometrics* indicador anticipado *m*, indicador básico *m*, MATH indicador anticipado *m*; **~ industries** *n pl* IND industrias avanzadas *f pl*; **~ line** *n* S&M línea principal *f*; **~ question** *n* S&M pregunta inductiva *f*; **~ share** *n* STOCK valor estrella *m*; **~ underwriters' agreement** *n* INS acuerdo de asegurador principal *m*; **~ underwriters' agreement for marine cargo business** *n* (*LUAMC*) INS acuerdo de primeros aseguradores para fletes marítimos *m*; **~ underwriters' agreement for marine hull business** *n* (*LUAMH*) INS convenio de aseguradores principales para seguro del casco del buque *m*

leaf *n* BANK *of cheque book* hoja *f*

leaflet *n* GEN COMM octavilla *f*, prospecto *m*, S&M folleto *m*, *advertising* volante *m*

league *n* GEN COMM liga *f*

League: ~ International for Creditors n (*LIC*) BANK liga internacional de acreedores

leak[1] n COMP, ECON filtraciones *f pl*, GEN COMM *pipe* pérdida de agua *f*, MEDIA *in the press* filtraciones *f pl*

leak[2] vt *infrml* GEN COMM *information* gotear, filtrar

leakage n ECON merma *f*; ◆ **~ and breakage** (*lkg & bkg*) TRANSP mermas de mercancía durante el transporte

lean: ~ year n ECON año de carestía *m*, año pobre *m*

lean towards vt GEN COMM tender hacia

leap: ~ year n GEN COMM año bisiesto *m*

leapfrog vi *jarg* HRM saltar por encima

leapfrogging n HRM demanda alternativa de aumento de remuneraciones *f*

learning: ~ curve n ECON, HRM, WEL curva de aprendizaje *f*; **~ effect** n ECON, HRM efecto de aprendizaje *m*

lease[1] n BANK, PROP leasing *m*, GEN COMM *agreement* arrendamiento *m*, LAW inquilinato *m*, arriendo *m*, PROP arriendo *m*, alquiler *m*; **~ acquisition cost** FIN coste de adquisición de un alquiler *m* (*Esp*), costo de adquisición de un alquiler *m* (*AmL*); **~ agreement** GEN COMM acuerdo de arrendamiento *m*; **~-lend** PROP préstamo-arriendo *m*; **~ option** PROP opción de arrendamiento *f*; **~ with option to purchase** PROP arrendamiento con opción a compra *m*

lease[2] vt GEN COMM, PROP arrendar

leaseback n FIN arrendamiento-compra *m*, cesión-arrendamiento *f*, GEN COMM, PROP rearriendo al vendedor *m*

leased[1] adj GEN COMM, PROP arrendado

leased[2]: **~ line** n COMP línea especializada *f*

leasee n GEN COMM, PROP arrendador(a) *m,f*

leasehold n LAW inquilinato *m*, PROP *contract* arriendo *m*, arrendamiento *m*, propiedad arrendada *f*; **~ estate** GEN COMM bienes forales *m pl*; **~ improvement** PROP mejora de inmueble arrendado *f*; **~ insurance** INS seguro de arrendamiento *m*; **~ interest** PROP interés de arrendamiento *m*; **~ mortgage** BANK, PROP hipoteca sobre inmueble arrendado *f*; **~ property** PROP propiedad en arriendo *f*; **~ value** FIN, PROP valor de propiedades arrendadas *m*, valor del arrendamiento *m*

leaseholder n GEN COMM, PROP arrendatario(-a) *m,f*

leasing n FIN *option to buy* alquiler con opción a compra *m*, arrendamiento *m*, alquiler *m*, PROP leasing *m*; **~ agreement** GEN COMM acuerdo de arrendamiento *m*; **~ company** PROP sociedad de arrendamiento *f*; **~ corporation** FIN compañía de arrendamiento financiero *f*

least: ~ squares method n MATH *statistics* método de los mínimos cuadrados *m*

leave[1]: **~ of absence** n GEN COMM falta con permiso *f*, HRM ausencia con permiso *f*

leave[2] vt GEN COMM dejar, LAW *bequeath* legar, dejar; ◆ **~ open** GEN COMM *matter* dejar abierto; **~ port** TRANSP abandonar el puerto; **~ a space** COMP dejar un espacio

leave[3]: **on ~** phr HRM *civilian* de permiso

leave aside vt GEN COMM dejar de lado, omitir

leave behind vt GEN COMM *outdistance* dejar atrás

leave out vt GEN COMM *omit* omitir, suprimir

leave over vt GEN COMM *postpone* posponer

LEC abbr (*Local Export Control*) IMP/EXP, TAX consejo local de control de la exportación

lecturer n HRM, WEL *university* profesor(a) *m,f*, *visitor* conferenciante *mf*, conferencista *mf*

LED abbr (*light-emitting diode*) COMP diodo electro-luminiscente *m*, diodo emisor de luz *m*

ledger n ACC *bookkeeping* libro mayor *m*; **~ account** ACC cuenta del mayor *f*; **~ balance** ACC, BANK, FIN balance del mayor *m*, saldo del mayor *m*; **~ card** ACC ficha contable *f*; **~ entry** ACC asiento del mayor *m*; **~ posting** ACC, ADMIN pase de asientos al libro mayor *m*

left[1] adj POL izquierdista, de izquierdas; **~-justified** COMMS, MEDIA *word-processed document* justificado a la izquierda; **~-wing** POL izquierdista, de izquierdas

left[2]: **~ column** n ACC, GEN COMM columna izquierda *f*; **~-hand column** n ACC, GEN COMM columna izquierda *f*; **~-luggage locker** n BrE (*cf baggage locker AmE*) GEN COMM taquilla para equipajes en consigna *f*, **~-luggage office** n BrE (*cf checkroom AmE*) TRANSP oficina de consigna *f*, consigna *f*; **~ shift** n COMP desplazamiento a la izquierda *m*

left[3]: **~ justify** vt COMMS, MEDIA *document* justificar a la izquierda

leftism n POL izquierdismo *m*

leg n MEDIA *print* informante *mf*, STOCK *of spread* tramo *m*

legacy n LAW legado *m*; **~ duty** BrE (*cf legacy tax AmE*) TAX impuesto sobre la renta de sucesiones; **~ tax** AmE (*cf legacy duty BrE*) TAX impuesto sobre la renta de sucesiones

legal[1] adj LAW legal, lícito; ◆ **take ~ action** HRM emprender acción legal; **take ~ advice** LAW aceptar asesoramiento jurídico; **be under ~ obligation to** LAW estar obligado legalmente a

legal[2]: **~ action** n HRM acción legal *f*, LAW acción legal, actuación judicial *f*; **~ advice** n LAW asesoramiento jurídico *f*; **~ adviser** n LAW asesor(a) legal *m,f*; **~ aid** n WEL asesoramiento legal *m*; **~ capital** n ACC, ECON, FIN, GEN COMM capital legal *m*; **~ charges** n pl LAW gastos judiciales *m pl*; **~ claim** n LAW reclamación legal *f*; **~ consultancy** n GEN COMM, LAW asesoría jurídica *f*; **~ costs** n pl LAW, TAX *awarded by the court* costas judiciales *f pl*; **~ department** n LAW departamento jurídico *m*; **~ description** n LAW descripción legal *f*; **~ document** n LAW documento legal *m*; **~ effect** n TAX efecto legal *m*; **~ enactment** n LAW disposición legal *f*; **~ enforceability of collective agreement** n HRM, LAW fuerza legal de un acuerdo colectivo *f*, obligatoriedad legal del contrato colectivo *f*; **~ entity** n LAW ente de existencia jurídica *f*, persona jurídica *f*, persona moral *f*; **~ expense insurance** n LAW *personal* seguro de gastos jurídicos *m*; **~ expenses** n pl LAW, PATENTS, TAX costas judiciales *f pl*; **~ fees** n pl LAW honorarios del letrado *m pl*; **~ force** n LAW validez legal *f*; **~ formalities** n pl LAW formalidades legales *f pl*; **~ framework** n LAW marco jurídico *m*; **~ harmonization** n LAW armonización legal *f*, POL armonización de legislaciones *f*; **~ holiday** n AmE (*cf bank holiday BrE*) GEN COMM cierre bancario *m*, día no laborable *m*, HRM día de asueto *m* (*frml*), día de descanso obligatorio *m*, fiesta oficial *f*, día inhábil *m*, LAW día inhábil *m*, fiesta oficial *f*, LEIS día de asueto *m* (*frml*), día de descanso obligatorio *m*, fiesta oficial *f*, día inhábil *m*; **~ immunity** n HRM, LAW inmunidad legal *f*; **~ investment** n STOCK inversión legal *f*; **~ liability** n LAW responsabilidad jurídica *f*; **~ list** n AmE STOCK lista de valores de alta calidad *f*; **~ monopoly** n ECON monopolio legal *m*; **~ name** n LAW nombre legal *m*, razón social *f*, *administrative* denominación legal *f*;

~ **notice** *n* LAW notificación legal *f*; ~ **obligation** *n* LAW obligación legal *f*; ~ **officer** *n* LAW funcionario(-a) judicial *m,f*; ~ **opinion** *n* GEN COMM *commercial* opinión legal *f*, LAW dictamen jurídico *m*; ~ **person** *n* LAW persona jurídica *f*; ~ **predecessor** *n* LAW, PATENTS antecesor(a) legal *m,f*, predecesor(a) legal *m,f*; ~ **proceedings** *n pl* LAW procedimiento judicial *m*; ~ **profession** *n* BANK, COMMS, LAW ≈ abogacía *f*; ~ **recognition** *n* LAW reconocimiento legal *m*; ~ **redress** *n* LAW reparación legal *f*; ~ **representative** *n* LAW representante legal *mf*; ~ **requirement** *n* LAW, POL requisito legal *m*; ~ **reserve** *n* ACC encaje legal *m*, reserva legal *f*, reserva obligatoria *f*, LAW reserva legal *f*; ~ **reserve life insurance company** *n* INS empresa de seguros de vida con reserva legal *f*; ~ **residence** *n* LAW domicilio legal *m*; ~ **revaluation** *n* ACC, LAW revalorización legal *f*, revaluación legal *f*; ~ **right** *n* LAW derecho legal *m*; ~ **section** *n* LAW artículo de una ley *m*; ~ **separation** *n* LAW separación legal *f*; ~ **services** *n pl* LAW asistencia jurídica *f*; ~ **settlement** *n* LAW acuerdo legal *m*; ~ **status** *n* LAW situación jurídica *f*; ~ **suit** *n* LAW proceso legal *m*; ~ **system** *n* LAW sistema legal *m*; ~ **tender** *n* BrE (*cf lawful money AmE*) FIN curso legal *m*; ~ **transfer** *n* STOCK *of shares* transferencia legal *f*; ~ **wrong** *n* LAW acto ilícito *m*

Legal: ~ **Exchange Information Service** *n* (*LEXIS*) LAW Servicio de Intercambio de Información Jurídica *m*

legalistic *adj* LAW legalista

legalization *n* LAW legalización *f*

legalize *vt* LAW legalizar

legally: ~**-binding** *adj* LAW de obligado cumplimiento, legalmente vinculante; ~ **bound** *adj* LAW legalmente obligado; ~ **married** *adj* LAW casado legalmente

legatee *n* LAW, PROP legatario(-a) *m,f*

legislate *vi* LAW legislar

legislation *n* LAW legislación *f*, normativa *f*; ◆ **bring in** ~ LAW introducir en la legislación

legislative[1] *adj* LAW legislativo

legislative[2]: ~ **power** *n* LAW poder legislativo *m*, POL cuerpo legislativo *m*, poder legislativo *m*

legislature *n* LAW legislatura *f*

legless *adj jarg* LEIS *film* sin gancho

Lehman: ~ **Investment Opportunity Notes** *n pl* (*LIONs*) STOCK apuntes de Lehman sobre oportunidades de inversión *m pl*

leisure *n* LEIS ocio *m*; ~ **center** *AmE*, ~ **centre** *BrE* LEIS centro de ocio *m*; ~ **development** *jarg* LEIS fomento del tiempo libre *m*; ~ **facility** LEIS instalaciones para el ocio *f pl*; ~ **industry** LEIS industria de recreación *f*, industria del ocio *f*; ~ **time** HRM, LEIS tiempo libre *m*; ◆ **at** ~ LEIS ocioso

lemonade: ~ **stand capitalism** *n* ECON, IND, POL capitalismo de competencia perfecta *m*

lemons: ~ **market** *n* ECON mercado de coches usados *m*

lend *vt* BANK, FIN, STOCK prestar; ◆ ~ **against security** STOCK prestar sobre un valor; ~ **money** FIN prestar dinero; ~ **on security** STOCK prestar con garantía; ~ **weight to** GEN COMM *argument, assumption* otorgar importancia a

lendable[1] *adj* BANK prestable

lendable[2]: ~ **funds** *n pl* BANK fondos para préstamos *m pl*

lender *n* BANK, FIN prestamista *mf*; ~ **of last resort** BANK prestamista de última instancia *mf*; ~'s **holder-in-due-**

course insurance INS *personal* seguro de tenedor legal del prestamista *m*

lending *n* BANK concesión de préstamos *f*; ~ **at a premium** FIN *of intermediary* préstamo a prima *m*; ~ **bank** BANK banco de crédito *m*; ~ **business** BANK operación de préstamo *f*; ~ **ceiling** GEN COMM tope de préstamo *m*; ~ **institution** BANK, FIN institución de crédito *f*; ~ **officer** BANK empleado de créditos *m*; ~ **policy** BANK política de préstamos *f*; ~ **power** BANK capacidad de crédito *f*; ~ **rate** BANK tipo de interés *m*, tasa de interés de los préstamos *f*; ~ **securities** *n pl* FIN, STOCK títulos en préstamo *m pl*

length: ~ **of service** *n* HRM duración del servicio *f*

lengthen *vt* GEN COMM alargar, prolongar

lengthened *adj* GEN COMM alargado, prolongado

Leontief: ~ **matrix** *n* ECON matriz de Leontief *f*; ~ **paradox** *n* ECON *international* paradoja de Leontief *f*

Lerner: ~ **effect** *n* ECON efecto Lerner *m*; ~ **index** *n* ECON índice de Lerner *m*

less[1]: ~**-than-perfect** *adj* GEN COMM poco menos que perfecto, punto menos que perfecto

less[2]: ~**-developed country** *n* (*LDC*) ECON, POL país en desarrollo *m*; ~**-favored area** *AmE*, ~**-favoured area** *BrE* ECON *agriculture* área menos favorecida *f*

less[3] *prep* ACC *profit and loss account* menos

lessee *n* GEN COMM arrendatario(-a) *m,f*, LAW inquilino(-a) *m,f*, PROP arrendatario(-a) *m,f*

lessen *vt* GEN COMM mermar, disminuir, reducir

lessor *n* GEN COMM, PROP arrendador(a) *m,f*

let[1] *n* PROP alquiler *m*; ~ **property** PROP propiedad alquilada *f*

let[2] *vt* PROP alquilar; ◆ **to** ~ *BrE* (*cf for rent AmE*) PROP se alquila

letter *n* COMMS carta *f*; ~ **of advice** COMMS carta de aviso *f*; ~ **of allotment** COMMS, STOCK carta de adjudicación *f*; ~ **of apology** COMMS carta de disculpas *f*; ~ **of application** COMMS *candidate* carta de solicitud *f*; ~ **of appointment** HRM carta de nombramiento *f*; ~ **of assignment** GEN COMM *of business* carta de cesión *f*, *to job* carta de asignación *f*; ~ **of attorney** LAW carta de poder *f*; ~ **of authority** (*L/A*) GEN COMM carta de autorización *f*; ~ **box** *BrE* (*cf mailbox AmE*) COMMS buzón *m*; ~ **of comfort** GEN COMM carta de seguridades *f*; ~ **of commitment** GEN COMM carta de garantía *f*; ~ **of complaint** GEN COMM carta de reclamación *f*; ~ **of consent** GEN COMM carta de aceptación *f*; ~ **of content** COMMS carta de contenido *f*; ~ **of cooperation** COMMS, GEN COMM carta de cooperación *f*; ~ **of credit** (*L/C*) BANK, FIN carta de crédito *f*; ~ **of delegation** ACC, BANK, GEN COMM carta de delegación *f*; ~ **of deposit** ACC, BANK, FIN carta de depósito *f*; ~ **of direction** GEN COMM carta de dirección *f*; ~ **of hypothecation** ACC, BANK, LAW carta de pignoración *f*, carta de hipoteca *f*; ~ **of indemnity** (*L/I*) BANK, GEN COMM carta de indemnización *f*, INS garantía de indemnización *f*; ~ **of indication** ACC, BANK, GEN COMM carta de identificación *f*; ~ **of inquiry** COMMS carta de solicitud de informes *f*; ~ **of intent** GEN COMM, MGMNT carta de intención *f*, STOCK carta de intenciones *f*; ~ **of introduction** COMMS, GEN COMM carta de introducción *f*; ~ **quality** (*LQ*) COMP, MEDIA calidad de letra *f*; ~**-quality printer** COMP impresora de alta calidad *f*; ~ **of recommendation** HRM carta de recomendación *f*; ~ **of renunciation** STOCK *rights issue* carta de renuncia *f*;

~ of resignation COMMS, HRM carta de dimisión *f*; **~ of respite** ACC carta de moratoria *f*, BANK, LAW carta de gracia *f*, carta de moratoria *f*; **~ spacing** S&M espaciado de letras *m*; **~ stock** STOCK acciones no cotizadas en bolsa *f pl*; **~ of subordination** COMMS carta de subrogación *f*; **~ of subrogation** COMMS carta de subrogación *f*; **~ of transmittal** LAW carta de remisión *f*; **~ of undertaking** ACC, BANK, LAW carta de compromiso *f*

letterfoot *n* COMMS despedida *f*

letterhead *n* COMMS, GEN COMM membrete *m*

lettering *n* MEDIA *printing* rotulación *f*

letterpress *n* MEDIA texto impreso *m*

letters: **~ to the editor** *n pl* MEDIA cartas al director *f pl*

lettertype *n* ADMIN tipo de letra *m*

letting *n* PROP arriendo *m*

level[1] *n* COMP nivel *m*, GEN COMM *of interest rates* nivel *m*, *position* plano *m*; **~ of consumption** ECON grado de consumo *m*; **~ debt service** *AmE* TAX *municipal charter* servicio de la deuda en cuotas iguales *m*; **~ of expenditure** ECON nivel de gasto *m*; **~ of investment** GEN COMM nivel de inversiones *m*; **~ money** GEN COMM, HRM dinero de compensación *m*; **~ of orders** S&M nivel de pedidos *m*; **~ payment** BANK devolución en cuotas iguales *f*; **~-payment mortgage** *AmE* BANK, FIN plan para pagos nivelados de la hipoteca *m*; **~ premium** INS prima nivelada *f*; **~ repayment** BANK devolución en cuotas iguales *f*; **~ of return** TAX nivel de beneficios *m*; **~ of significance** MATH nivel de significación *m*; ◆ **at international ~** GEN COMM a nivel internacional

level[2]: **~ criticism at sb** *phr* GEN COMM dirigir críticas a alguien

level off *vi* ECON nivelar

level out *vi* ECON *production* nivelar

leveling *AmE see* levelling *BrE*

levelling: **~-out** *n BrE* FIN nivelación *f*; **~ pedestal** *n BrE* TRANSP *container* suplemento nivelador de altura *m*

lever: **~ scale** *n* TRANSP báscula *f*; **~ tensioner** *n* TRANSP tensor de palanca *m*

leverage *n AmE* (*cf gearing BrE*) ACC, FIN apalancamiento *m*, palanca financiera *f*, POL influencia *f*, STOCK palanca financiera *f*; **~ adjustment** *AmE* (*cf gearing adjustment BrE*) FIN ajuste de apalancamiento *m*; **~ lease** *AmE* (*cf gearing lease BrE*) FIN arrendamiento ventajoso *m*; **~ ratio** *AmE* (*cf gearing ratio BrE*) FIN proporción de apalancamiento *f*, relación de apalancamiento *f*

leverage up *vi* ACC, FIN, STOCK apalancar

leveraged: **~ bid** *n* STOCK oferta apalancada *f*; **~ buyout** *n* (*LBO*) FIN adquisiciones apalancadas *f pl*, compra apalancada de empresas *f*, GEN COMM, STOCK compra apalancada *f*; **~ company** *n* ACC compañía apalancada *f*; **~ lease** *n* PROP arrendamiento de deuda *m*; **~ management buy-in** *n* (*LMBI*) FIN, MGMNT compra con influencia administrativa *f*; **~ management buy-out** *n* (*LMBO*) MGMNT compra con apalancamiento por la dirección *f*, compra apalancada por ejecutivos *f* (*CAPE*); **~ stock** *n* FIN acciones apalancadas *f pl*

levy[1] *n* GEN COMM impuesto *m*, IMP/EXP contribución *f*, gravamen *m*, TAX gravamen tributario *m*

levy[2] *vt* GEN COMM *raise, collect*, LAW *seize* embargar, gravar, TAX gravar; ◆ **~ a tax** TAX exigir un impuesto, recaudar un impuesto

levying: **~ of taxes** *n* TAX exigencia de impuestos *f*, recaudación de impuestos *f*

Lewis-Fei-Ranis: **~ model** *n* ECON *international* modelo de Lewis-Rei-Ranis *m*

lex mercatoria *n* GEN COMM lex mercatoria *f*

lex scripta *n* GEN COMM derecho escrito *m*

lex non cogit ad impossibilia *phr* GEN COMM la ley no obliga a nadie a hacer cosas imposibles

LEXIS *abbr* (*Legal Exchange Information Service*) LAW Servicio de Intercambio de Información Jurídica *m*

lf *abbr* (*line feed*) COMP avance de línea *m*, salto de línea *m*

LFPR *abbr* (*labour force participation rate*) ECON tasa de participación de la mano de obra *f*

LGS *abbr* (*liquid assets and government securities*) ECON, FIN, POL activos líquidos y garantías gubernamentales *m pl*

L/I *abbr* (*letter of indemnity*) GEN COMM carta de indemnización *f*

liabilities *n pl* ACC deudas *f pl*, BANK obligaciones *f pl*

liability *n* GEN COMM deuda *f*, responsabilidad *f*, INS, LAW *under the act* responsabilidad civil *f*, responsabilidad legal *f*; **~ certificate** BANK, ECON, FIN, GEN COMM certificado pasivo *m*; **~ cost** STOCK coste del pasivo *m* (*Esp*), costo del pasivo *m* (*AmL*); **~ dividend** ACC dividendo pasivo *m*; **~ for tax** TAX responsabilidad fiscal *f*; **~ insurance** INS seguro de responsabilidad *m*; **~ insuring agreement** INS convenio asegurador de responsabilidad civil *m*; **~ issuer** STOCK emisor de pasivos *m*; **~ item** ACC partida del pasivo *f*; **~ ledger** ACC libro mayor del pasivo *m*; **~ management** BANK gestión del pasivo *f*; **~ manager** STOCK administrador(a) de pasivos *m,f*; **~ method** ACC *of deferred tax* método de la cuota *m*, método de la deuda *m*, método de pasivo *m*, TAX método de la cuota *m*; **~ rate** STOCK *futures* coeficiente del pasivo *f*

liable *adj* LAW responsable, TAX sujeto; ◆ **~ for tax** TAX sujeto a impuesto; **~ to a penalty** TAX sancionable

liaise with *vt* GEN COMM enlazar con

liaison *n* COMMS, COMP, GEN COMM enlace *m*

LIARS *abbr* (*Lloyd's Instantaneous Accounting Record System*) INS sistema Lloyd's de compatibilidad instantánea *m*

libel *n* LAW libelo *m*; **~ laws** *n pl* LAW leyes antilibelo *f pl*; **~ proceedings** *n pl* LAW juicio por difamación *m*; **~ suit** LAW pleito *m*, querella *f*

libeling *AmE see* libelling *BrE*

libelling *n* LAW alegación por deuda *f*

libellous *adj BrE* LAW difamante, difamatorio

libelous *AmE see* libellous *BrE*

liberal[1] *adj* GEN COMM liberal

liberal[2]: **~ economics** *n* ECON economía liberal *f*

liberalization *n* ECON liberalización *f*; **~ code** POL código de liberación *m*; **~ of trade** ECON liberalización del comercio *f*

liberalize *vt* ECON liberalizar

liberalizing *adj* ECON liberalizador

libertarian: **~ economics** *n* ECON economía libertaria *f*

liberty[1]: **~ ship** *n* TRANSP buque franco *m*

liberty[2]: **at ~** *phr jarg* LAW libre

LIBID *abbr* (*London Interbank Bid Rate*) BANK, STOCK tasa de licitaciones interbancarias de Londres *f*

LIBOR[1] *abbr* (*London Interbank Offered Rate*) BANK,

STOCK tasa de interés ofrecida en el mercado interbancario de Londres

LIBOR[2]: **~ futures contract** n STOCK contrato de futuros LIBOR m

library n COMP, WEL biblioteca f; **~ rate** WEL tarifa de biblioteca f; **~ service** WEL servicio de biblioteca m

Library: **~ of Congress** n AmE (*LC, cf British Library*) GEN COMM biblioteca del congreso de los Estados Unidos, ≈ Biblioteca Nacional f Esp (*BN*)

LIC abbr (*League International for Creditors*) BANK liga internacional de acreedores

licence[1]: **under ~** adj BrE LAW, PATENTS con licencia

licence[2] n BrE BANK *of bank* autorización f, licencia f, GEN COMM permiso m, LAW *for activity* autorización f, cédula f, PATENTS *for activity* licencia f, PROP autorización f; **~ bond** BrE LAW *commercial* escritura de autorización f; **~ contract** BrE GEN COMM, LAW contrato de licencia m; **~ holder** BrE GEN COMM titular de una licencia mf; **~ law** n pl BrE LAW *commercial* ley para la concesión de licencias f

licensable adj IMP/EXP permisible

license[1] n AmE *see* licence BrE; **~ plate** AmE (*cf number plate BrE*) TRANSP chapa de matrícula f, placa de matrícula f

license[2] vt GEN COMM dar permiso a, licenciar

licensed adj LAW, PATENTS autorizado, licenciado

licensee n GEN COMM concesionario(-a) m,f, LAW licenciatario(-a) m,f, PATENTS persona autorizada f

licensing n ECON *international trade* concesión de licencia f; **~ agreement** LAW acuerdo de licencia m; **~ examination** GEN COMM examen para licencia m, LAW *commercial* examen para la concesión de licencias m, revisión de licencia f; **~ requirement** IMP/EXP requisito de licencia m; **~ standard** ENVIR criterio de concesión de autorizaciones m

licensor n PATENTS concedente mf

LICOM abbr (*London Interbank Currency Options Market*) STOCK mercado interbancario de opciones sobre divisas de Londres

lidding: **~ document** n BANK, LAW, STOCK documento de liquidación m

lien n LAW derecho prendario m, embargo preventivo m, gravamen m; **~-theory states** n pl LAW estados que adoptan la teoría del derecho de retención

liens: **~ for taxes** n pl TAX embargos fiscales m pl; **~ tax** n TAX embargos fiscales m pl

lieu[1]: **~ day** n HRM trabajo en horas extras para compensar un tiempo laboral tomado de vacaciones

lieu[2]: **in ~ of** phr GEN COMM en lugar de, en vez de

life n GEN COMM vida f, STOCK *of option* vida f, vigencia f; **~ annuitant** TAX rentista mf; **~ assurance** INS *personal* seguro de capitalización m, seguro de vida m; **~ assurance policy** INS póliza de seguro de vida f; **~ cycle** S&M *of product* ciclo de vida m; **~-cycle analysis** S&M análisis de ciclo de vida m; **~-cycle hypothesis** (*LCH*) ECON hipótesis cíclica de la vida f; **~ estate** PROP dominio vitalicio m, usufructo m; **~ expectancy** HRM *person* esperanza de vida f; **~ imprisonment** LAW cadena perpetua f; **~ insurance** INS *personal* seguro de decesos m (*AmL*), seguro de vida m (*Esp*), seguro de capitalización m; **~ insurance company** INS compañía de seguros de vida f **~ insurance policy** INS póliza de seguro de vida f; **~ insurer** INS asegurador(a) de vida

m,f; **~ insuring company** INS aseguradora de vida f; **~ interest** LAW renta vitalicia f; **~ savings** n pl BANK, ECON, FIN ahorro de patrimonio m, ahorro de seguridad m; **~ tenancy** PROP derecho de arrendamiento vitalicio m, ocupación vitalicia f; **~ tenant** PROP inquilino(-a) vitalicio(-a) m,f

Life: **~ Assurance and Unit Trust Regulatory Organization** n (*LAUTRO*) FIN organización regulatoria de seguros de vida y de fondos de inversiones; **~ Cycle Assessment** n (*LCA*) ENVIR evaluación del ciclo vital f

lifeboat n TRANSP bote salvavidas m; **~ ethics** n pl infrml POL decisiones políticas basadas más en un interés político que social; **~ operation** infrml BANK operación salvavidas f

lifeless adj STOCK inanimado, muerto

lifestyle n GEN COMM, S&M estilo de vida m; **~ concept** S&M concepto de estilo de vida m; **~ merchandising** S&M comercialización de un estilo de vida f; **~ segmentation** S&M segmentación por estilos de vida f

lifetime n STOCK vida efectiva f; **~ averaging** ECON *taxation of income*, TAX media de vida f; **~ employment** HRM empleo vitalicio m

LIFFE abbr (*London International Financial Futures Exchange*) STOCK bolsa de opciones y futuros de Londres

LIFO abbr (*last in, first out*) ACC, GEN COMM UEPS (*último en entrar, primero en salir*)

lift[1] n STOCK alza f; **~ liability insurance** BrE (*cf elevator liability insurance AmE*) INS seguro contra accidentes de un ascensor m; **~ unit frame** (*LUF*) TRANSP armazón de unidad montacargas m

lift[2] vt GEN COMM *sanctions* elevar, levantar, LAW *restrictions*, PROP *mortgage* levantar; ◆ **~ a leg** STOCK cerrar un lado; **~ a short** STOCK cerrar una posición corta

LIFT abbr (*London International Freight Terminal*) TRANSP terminal internacional de carga de Londres

lifting n GEN COMM *restrictions, laws*, TRANSP *car* levantamiento m

light[1] adj GEN COMM *interest, trading* bajo, MEDIA light

light[2]: **~ cable** n COMP cable de sustentación m; **~ cargo** n TRANSP cargamento ligero m; **~ displacement** n TRANSP desplazamiento en lastre m; **~ dues** n pl TRANSP *shipping* derechos de faro m pl; **~-emitting diode** n (*LED*) COMP diodo electroluminiscente m, diodo emisor de luz m; **~ engineering** n IND ingeniería ligera f; **~ industry** n ECON, IND industria ligera f; **~ pen** n COMP lápiz óptico m; **~ vessel** n (*LTV*) TRANSP buque en lastre m

lighter n TRANSP gabarra f, lancha f; **~ aboard ship** (*LASH*) TRANSP buque portagabarras m; **~ carrier** TRANSP *shipping* transporte ligero m

lighterage n TRANSP gabarraje m; **~ berth** TRANSP *shipping* muelle para barcazas m

lightning: **~ strike** n HRM, IND huelga relámpago f, huelga sin previo aviso f

Lights: **~ Advisory Committee** n (*LAC*) TRANSP comité de consulta de faros y bollas

like: **~-kind property** n PROP, TAX propiedad similar f

likely: **~ outcome** n GEN COMM *of negotiations* resultado prometedor m

Lima: **~ Stock Exchange** n STOCK Bolsa de Lima f

limit[1] n GEN COMM *prices*, STOCK límite m; **~ price** ECON precio límite *m*; ♦ **~ up** STOCK tope máximo de oscilación de precio

limit[2] *vt* GEN COMM *risk* limitar

limited: ~ annual statements *n pl* ACC estados contables anuales limitados *m pl*; **~ audit** *n* ACC *auditing* auditoría limitada *f*; **~ authorization** *n* IMP/EXP autorización limitada *f*; **~ check** *AmE*, **~ cheque** *BrE n* BANK, FIN, LAW cheque limitado *m*; **~ company** *n BrE* (*Ltd, cf incorporated business company AmE*) GEN COMM ≈ sociedad anónima *f* (*S.A.*), ≈ sociedad anónima por acciones *f* (*S.A.A.*), ≈ sociedad de responsabilidad limitada (*S.L.R.*); **~ discretion** *n* STOCK discreción limitada *f*; **~ distribution** *n* TRANSP *distribution* circulación limitada *f*; **~ liability** *n* GEN COMM responsabilidad limitada *f*; **~ liability partner** *n* LAW socio(-a) comanditario(-a) *m,f*; **~ market** *n* ECON mercado con escaso movimiento *m*; **~ occupancy agreement** *n* LAW, PROP acuerdo de ocupación limitada *m*; **~ order** *n* GEN COMM, S&M pedido limitado *m*; **~ owner** *n* LAW socio(-a) comandatario(-a) *m,f*, PROP usufructuario(-a) *m,f*; **~ partner** *n* GEN COMM socio(-a) limitado(-a) *m,f*, comanditario(-a) *m,f*, HRM comanditario(-a) *m,f*, LAW *commercial* socio(-a) comanditario(-a) *m,f*; **~ partnership** *n* LAW *commercial*, STOCK sociedad comanditaria *f*; **~ payment life insurance** *n* INS *personal* seguro de vida de pagos limitados *m*; **~ policy** *n* INS póliza limitada *f*; **~ postponed accounting** *n* IMP/EXP contabilización diferida y limitada *f*; **~-recourse debt** *n* BANK deuda de recurso limitado *f*; **~-recourse finance** *n* BANK financiación con limitación de reclamaciones *f*; **~-recourse financing** *n* BANK, FIN financiación con limitación de reclamaciones *f*; **~ risk** *n* STOCK riesgo limitado *m*; **~ tax bond** *n* TAX bono con gravamen limitado *m*; **~ terms** *n pl* INS condiciones limitadas *f pl*; **~ trading authorization** *n* STOCK autorización de negociación limitada *f*

limousine: ~ liberalism *n jarg* POL liberalismo de lujo *m*

Lindahl: ~ equilibrium *n* ECON equilibrio de Lindahl *m*; **~ price** *n* ECON precio de Lindahl *m*

line *n* GEN COMM línea *f*, S&M *advertising* línea *f* (*jarg*), orientación *f*; **~ assistant** HRM asistente(-a) de línea *m,f*, ayudante(-a) de línea *m,f*; **~ of attack** GEN COMM línea de ataque *f*; **~ authority** HRM, MGMNT autoridad de línea *f*, autoridad lineal *f*; **~ block** S&M clisé de trazo *m*; **~ of business** GEN COMM giro del negocio *m*; **~ of command** MGMNT línea jerárquica *f*; **~ control** MGMNT control de línea *m*; **~ of credit** BANK, FIN línea de crédito *f*; **~ drawing** S&M dibujo lineal *m*; **~ executive** HRM ejecutivo(-a) de línea *m,f*; **~ extension** S&M ampliación de la gama *f*; **~ feed** (*lf*) COMP avance de línea *m*, salto de línea *m*; **~ function** GEN COMM función directiva y ejecutiva *f*; **~ of least resistance** GEN COMM línea de menor resistencia *f*; **~ management** HRM, MGMNT gerencia de línea *f*; **~ manager** HRM gerente de línea *mf*; **~ object** ADMIN objeto de la línea *m*; **~ organization** GEN COMM organización lineal *f*, HRM organización de cuadros directivos *f*, MGMNT organización lineal *f*; **~ position** HRM *assembling* puesto operativo *m*; **~ printer** COMP impresora de líneas *f*; **~ production** ECON producción en serie *f*, IND cadena continua de montaje *f*, *production* producción en serie *f*; **~ relation** GEN COMM relación de línea *f*; **~ relationship** MGMNT relación entre distintos rangos *f*; **~ responsibility** GEN COMM responsabilidad de línea *f*;

~ slip INS borderó de línea *m*; **~ space** MEDIA *printing* interlínea *f*; **~ spacing** COMMS espacio entre líneas *m*; **~ and staff** HRM línea y staff *f*, organigrama de jerarquización intermedia *f* (*Esp*); **~ and staff management** HRM gerencia de línea y staff *f* (*AmL*), gestión lineal y funcional *f*; **~ and staff organization** HRM, MGMNT organización de cuadros y personal subalterno *f*, organización de línea y personal *f*; **~ stamp** INS sello de plenos *m*; **~-stretching** IND extensión de la línea de productos *f*; **~ supervisor** HRM supervisor(a) de línea *m,f*; ♦ **in ~ with** GEN COMM *expectations* acorde con, *inflation, expectations* en línea con

lineage *n* MEDIA lineaje *m*, número de líneas de un espacio publicitario *m*, S&M linaje *m*

linear: ~ correlation *n* MATH correlación lineal *f*; **~ measure** *n* GEN COMM medida de longitud *f*; **~ program** *AmE*, **~ programme** *BrE n* MATH programa lineal *m*; **~ programming** *n* COMP, ECON, MATH programación lineal *f*; **~ regression** *n* MATH *statistics* regresión lineal *f*; **~ relationship** *n* HRM relación lineal *f*; **~ responsibility** *n* MATH, MGMNT responsabilidad lineal *f*

liner *n* TRANSP buque de pasajeros *m*; **~ broker** HRM consignatario(-a) de línea marítima *m,f*; **~ conference** TRANSP conferencia de líneas regulares *f*; **~ conference code** TRANSP código de conferencia de buque de línea *m*; **~ consortium** TRANSP consorcio de líneas marítimas *m*; **~ rate** TRANSP tarifa de buque de línea regular *f*; **~ term** TRANSP término de carga de línea regular *m*; **~ voyage simulation** TRANSP simulación del viaje de un buque de línea regular *f*

lingua: ~ franca *n* GEN COMM lengua franca *f*

link[1] *n* COMMS, COMP enlace *m*, GEN COMM enlace *m*, vínculo *m*, STOCK relación *f*

link[2] *vt* COMMS, COMP enlazar, GEN COMM enlazar, vincular, STOCK relacionar

linkage *n* GEN COMM eslabonamiento *m*; **~ model** ECON modelo de previsión *m*

linked *adj* STOCK vinculado

lion: ~'s share *n* GEN COMM *the largest portion* parte del león *f*

liquid[1] *adj* BANK *funds* líquido

liquid[2]: **~ assets** *n* ACC, BANK, FIN, STOCK activos líquidos *m pl*, disponibilidades *f pl*, activos disponibles *m pl*; **~ assets and government securities** *n pl* (*LGS*) ECON, FIN, ECON activos líquidos y garantías gubernamentales *m pl*; **~ assets ratio** *n* ACC, BANK, FIN, STOCK relación de activos líquidos *f*; **~ bulk cargo ship** *n* TRANSP buque para cargamentos líquidos *m*; **~ capital** *n* STOCK capital líquido *m*; **~ debt** *n* FIN deuda vencida *f*; **~ funds** *n pl* ACC, BANK, FIN fondos en efectivo *m pl*, fondos líquidos *m pl*; **~ market** *n* STOCK mercado fluido *m*; **~ measure** *n* GEN COMM medición de líquidos *f*; **~ petroleum gas** *n* (*LPG*) IND, TRANSP gas licuado de petróleo *m* (*LPG*); **~ petroleum gas carrier** *n* TRANSP carguero de gas licuado de petróleo *m*; **~ ratio** *n* ACC coeficiente de liquidez *m*; **~ savings** *n pl* BANK, ECON, FIN ahorros líquidos *m pl*; **~ yield option note** *n* (*LYON*) STOCK apunte de opción sobre rendimientos líquidos *m*

liquidate *vt* ACC, GEN COMM, LAW, STOCK *position, options* liquidar

liquidated[1] *adj* ACC, GEN COMM, LAW, STOCK *position, options* liquidado

liquidated[2]: ~ **damages** *n pl* LAW estimación de daños y perjuicios *f*; ~ **debt** *n* ACC deuda saldada *f*

liquidating: ~ **dividend** *n* FIN dividendo de capital *m*; ~ **value** *n* ACC *of company* valor de liquidación *m*

liquidation *n* ACC, BANK, FIN, STOCK liquidación *f*; ~ **dividend** ACC dividendo de liquidación *m*

liquidator *n* ACC, BANK, FIN, STOCK liquidador(a) *m,f*

liquidity *n* ACC, BANK, FIN, STOCK liquidez *f*; ~ **adequacy** ACC suficiencia de la liquidez *f*; ~ **control** ACC, GEN COMM control de liquidez *m*; ~ **crisis** BANK, GEN COMM crisis de liquidez *f*; ~ **diversification** STOCK diversificación de la liquidez *f*; ~ **famine** ACC, BANK, FIN carestía de liquidez *f*; ~ **portfolio** ACC, BANK, FIN cartera líquida *f*; ~ **preference** ECON preferencia de liquidez *f*; ~ **problem** ACC, BANK, FIN problema de liquidez *m*; ~ **ratio** ACC, BANK, FIN coeficiente de liquidez *m*; ~ **squeeze** FIN iliquidez *f*; ~ **trap** ECON trampa de la liquidez *f*

liquidization *n jarg* STOCK licuidificación *f*

liquor: ~ **store** *n AmE* (*cf off-licence BrE, package store AmE*) GEN COMM *shop* tienda de licores *f*

lis pendens *n* LAW litispendencia *f*

list[1] *n* GEN COMM lista *f*, PROP nómina *f*; ~ **broker** GEN COMM agente de direcciones *mf*; ~ **of candidates** *BrE* POL lista de candidatos *f*; ~ **of deliverable bonds** STOCK lista de obligaciones entregables *f*; ~ **head** POL cabeza de lista *mf*; ~ **manager** S&M jefe(-a) de lista *m,f*; ~ **price** S&M *retail* precio de catálogo *m*; ◆ **be top of the ~** GEN COMM estar a la cabeza de la lista

list[2] *vt* GEN COMM listar, cotizar

List: ~ **of Addresses** *n BrE* HRM Lista de Domicilios *f*

listed[1] *adj* COMP, GEN COMM listado, STOCK cotizado; ~ **on the stock exchange** STOCK cotizado en la bolsa

listed[2]: ~ **bank** *n* BANK banco listado *m*; ~ **company** *n* STOCK empresa que cotiza en bolsa *f*; ~ **option** *n* STOCK opción admitida a cotización *f*, opción cotizada *f*; ~ **securities** *n pl* STOCK títulos de bolsa *m pl*, valores cotizados *m pl*; ~ **security** *n* STOCK título cotizado *m*, valor cotizable *m*; ~ **share** *n* STOCK acciones cotizables *f pl*

listener *n* COMMS, MEDIA radioyente *mf*

listening: ~ **time** *n* MEDIA *broadcast* hora de audiencia *f*

listing *n* COMP, ECON, FIN, GEN COMM inventario *m*, PROP listado *m*, STOCK inventario *m*, admisión de un valor en bolsa *f*; ~ **agent** *AmE* PROP agente de registros *mf*; ~ **broker** *BrE* (*cf listing agent AmE*) PROP agente de registros *mf*; ~ **particulars** *n pl* STOCK peculiaridades del listado *f pl*; ~ **requirement** STOCK requisito previo para la publicación en las listas *m*

listless *adj* STOCK *market, trading* indiferente

literal *n* COMP, GEN COMM, MEDIA *printing* errata *f*

litigant *n* LAW litigante *mf*

litigation *n* LAW litigio *m*; ~ **risk** ACC *provisions* riesgo de litigio *m*

litigator *n* LAW abogado que se dedica a los litigios

little: ~ **dragons** *n pl infrml* ECON *Asian countries* pequeños dragones *m pl*

live[1] *adj* LEIS *sport* en directo

live[2]: ~ **customers** *n pl* S&M clientes existentes *m pl*; ~ **labor** *AmE*, ~ **labour** *BrE n jarg* HRM *persons, workers* mano de obra activa *f*; ~ **program** *AmE*, ~ **programme**

BrE n COMMS programa en directo *m*, MEDIA *broadcast* programa en directo *m*, programa en vivo *m*

live[3]: ~ **animals on board** *phr* (*LAB*) TRANSP animales vivos a bordo

Liverpool: ~ **Commodity Exchange** *n* STOCK Mercado de Mercaderías de Liverpool *m*; ~ **Stock Exchange** *n* STOCK Bolsa de Valores de Liverpool *m*

livery: ~ **company** *n* GEN COMM, S&M gremio de Londres

livestock *n* GEN COMM crianza de animales *f*

living: ~ **accommodation** *n* GEN COMM vivienda *f*; ~ **benefits of life insurance** *n* INS prestaciones en vida del seguro de vida *f pl*; ~ **conditions** *n pl* WEL condiciones de vida *f pl*; ~ **dead** *n jarg* STOCK muerto viviente *m*; ~ **expenses** *n pl* WEL gastos de mantenimiento *m pl*; ~ **space** *n* WEL espacio vital *m*; ~ **trust** *n AmE* LAW fideicomiso activo *m*; ~ **wage** *n* WEL salario de subsistencia *m*

lkg & bkg *abbr* (*leakage and breakage*) TRANSP mermas de mercancía durante el transporte

LLB *abbr* (*Bachelor of Laws*) HRM, LAW ≈ licenciado(-a) en Derecho *m,f*

LLD *abbr* (*Doctor of Laws*) HRM, LAW Doctor(a) en Derecho *m,f*

Lloyd's: ~ **Agent** *n* (*L/A*) TRANSP *shipping* representante de Lloyd's *mf*; ~ **Corporation** *n BrE* INS *marine* Compañía Lloyd's *f*; ~ **Instantaneous Accounting Record System** *n* (*LIARS*) INS sistema Lloyd's de compatibilidad instantánea *m*; ~ **List** *n* TRANSP *shipping* lista de Lloyd's *f*; ~ **of London** *n* INS compañía de seguros Lloyd's; ~ **Loading List** *n* TRANSP *shipping* lista de carga de Lloyd's *f*; ~ **Register** *n* (*LR*) INS *marine* Registro Lloyd's *m*; ~ **Register of Shipping** *n* INS registro Lloyd's de embarques marítimos *m*

LM: ~ **curve** *n* ECON curva LM *f*

LMBO *abbr* (*leveraged management buy-out*) MGMNT CAPE (*compra apalancada por ejecutivos*)

LME *abbr* (*London Metal Exchange*) STOCK mercado de metales de Londres

load[1] *n* STOCK carga *f*; ~ **bulge** TRANSP exceso de carga *m*; ~ **factor** ECON *manufacturing* factor de consumo *m*, GEN COMM coeficiente de carga *m*, factor de carga *m*, factor de ocupación *m*, factor de consumo *m*, MATH grado de saturación *m*, TRANSP *airline* factor de ocupación *m*, coeficiente de carga *m*, densidad de ocupación *f*; ~ **fund** STOCK *mutual fund* fondo de inversión que cobra una comisión *m*; ~ **line** (*LL*) TRANSP línea de carga *f*; ~ **line certificate** TRANSP certificado de línea de carga *m*; ~ **line convention** TRANSP *rules governing freeboard* convención de línea de carga *f*; ~ **line zone** TRANSP *shipping* zona de línea de carga *f*; ~**-on-top system** TRANSP *oil tanker* sistema de carga sobre residuos *m*; ~ **plan** TRANSP plan de carga *m*; ~ **port** TRANSP *shipping* puerto de carga *m*; ~ **sheet** TRANSP declaración de la carga *f*; ◆ **under ~** TRANSP con carga

load[2] *vt* COMP *software*, TRANSP *cargo* cargar

loading *n* (*ldg*) HRM recargo *m*, sobreprima *f* (*jarg*), TRANSP carga *f*; ~ **agent** IMP/EXP, TRANSP *shipping* agente de carga *mf*; ~ **allocation** TRANSP distribución de carga *f*, localización de la carga *f*; ~ **broker** HRM corredor(a) de fletes *m,f*; ~ **date** TRANSP *shipping* fecha de carga *f*; ~ **dock** TRANSP muelle de carga *m*; ~ **overside** TRANSP exceso de carga *m*; ~ **space** GEN

COMM espacio de carga *m*; ◆ ~ **and delivery** (*ldg&dly*) TRANSP carga y distribución *f*

loadmate *n* TRANSP oficial(a) de carga *m,f*

loan *n* BANK prestación *f*, GEN COMM crédito *m*, préstamo *m*, empréstito *m*, STOCK empréstito *m*; ~ **account** BANK cuenta del préstamo *f*, cuenta de empréstitos *f*, STOCK cuenta de empréstitos *f*; ~ **agreement** BANK, GEN COMM, LAW contrato de préstamo *m*; ~ **application** BANK solicitud de préstamo *f*; ~ **authorization** BANK autorización de préstamo *f*; ~ **capital** ACC, BANK, ECON, FIN fondos ajenos *m pl*, capital de empréstito *m*; ~ **certificate** FIN certificado de préstamos *m*; ~ **commitment** BANK compromiso de préstamo *m*; ~ **company** FIN compañía prestamista *f*; ~ **crowd** STOCK grupo prestamista *m*; ~ **default** BANK, FIN préstamo en mora *m*; ~ **demand** BANK, FIN solicitud de préstamo *f*; ~ **department** BANK, FIN departamento de crédito *m*; ~ **exposure** BANK, FIN riesgo de préstamos *m*; ~ **fee** BANK gastos de préstamo *m pl*; ~ **guarantee** BANK, FIN garantía de préstamo *f*; ~ **guarantee scheme** *BrE* FIN *rural development* plan de garantía de préstamos; ~ **holder** BANK, FIN titular de un préstamo *mf*; ~ **insurance** FIN, INS seguro de préstamo *m*; ~ **investment** BANK, FIN inversión en forma de préstamo *f*; ~ **loss** BANK, FIN pérdidas de préstamos *f pl*; ~ **loss provision** BANK, FIN provisión para créditos no pagados *f*; ~ **market** BANK, FIN mercado de préstamos *m*; ~ **officer** BANK director(a) de préstamos *m,f*; ~ **on trust** BANK préstamo bajo palabra *m*; ~ **origination fee** BANK gastos de emisión de un préstamo *m pl*; ~ **portfolio** BANK cartera de préstamos *f*; ~ **-pricing date** STOCK fecha de valoración de un préstamo *f*; ~ **recipient** BANK, FIN receptor(a) del préstamo *m,f*; ~ **recovery** BANK, FIN recuperación de préstamo *f*; ~ **repayment** BANK, FIN devolución de préstamo *f*; ~ **repayment schedule** BANK, FIN plan de amortizaciones del préstamo *m*; ~ **shark** *infrml* BANK, FIN, extorsionador(a) *m,f*, usurero(-a) *m,f*; ~ **stock** BANK, STOCK fondos de préstamo *m pl*; ~ **to related company** ACC préstamo a una compañía del grupo *m*; ~ **-to-value ratio** (*LTV*) FIN relación préstamo-valor *f*; ~ **value** BANK, INS valor para préstamo *m*; ~ **write-off** BANK cancelación de préstamo *f*; ~ **yield** BANK, FIN rentabilidad del préstamo *f*; ◆ **apply for a** ~ BANK, FIN solicitar un préstamo; **approval of a** ~ BANK, FIN aprobación de un préstamo; **arrange a** ~ BANK, FIN disponer un préstamo; **take a** ~ **out** BANK, FIN disponer de un préstamo

loanable[1] *adj* BANK prestable

loanable[2]: ~ **funds theory** *n* FIN teoría de fondos de préstamo *f*

loaned: ~ **flat** *n* STOCK depósitos sin interés en operaciones con acciones

loans: ~, **investments and advances** *n pl* ACC, FIN préstamos, inversiones y anticipos *m pl*

lobby[1]: ~ **group** *n* POL grupo de presión *m*

lobby[2]: **on** ~ **terms** *phr BrE* POL según las condiciones de un grupo de presión

lobbying *n* POL presión *f*

lobbyist *n* POL miembro de un grupo de presión

local[1] *adj* COMP, GEN COMM local

local[2] *n jarg* STOCK local *m*; ~ **agreement** HRM acuerdo local *m*; ~ **area network** (*LAN*) COMP red de área local *f* (*RAL*); ~ **authority** POL autoridad local *f*; ~ **authority**

bill (*LAB*) STOCK certificado de la autoridad local *m*; ~ **authority bond** (*LAB*) STOCK obligación de la administración local *f*; ~ **charge** TAX impuesto local *m*, TRANSP gravamen local *m*, impuesto local *m*; ~ **custody** FIN custodia local *f*; ~ **election** GEN COMM elecciones locales *f pl*; ~ **export control** IMP/EXP control local de exportaciones *m*; ~ **government** POL administración local *f*; ~ **firm** GEN COMM firma local *f*; ~ **government finance** FIN, POL financiación de la administración local *f*; ~ **handicraft** HRM artesanía local *f*; ~ **import control** (*LIC*) IMP/EXP control local de las importaciones *m*; ~ **industry** ECON, IND industria local *f*; ~ **labor** *AmE see local labour BrE*; ~ **labor market** *AmE see local labour market BrE*, ~ **labour** *BrE* ECON *task* trabajo local *m*, HRM mano de obra local *f*, *task* trabajo local *m*; ~ **labour market** *BrE* ECON, HRM mercado laboral local *m*; ~ **monopoly** ECON monopolio local *m*; ~ **newspaper** GEN COMM, MEDIA periódico local *m*; ~ **press** MEDIA, S&M prensa local *f*; ~ **public good** ECON bien público local *m*; ~ **shop** S&M tienda de barrio *f*; ~ **skills** *n pl* HRM conocimientos prácticos locales *m pl*; ~ **tax** TAX impuesto municipal *m*, tributo municipal *m*; ~ **time** GEN COMM, MEDIA *broadcast* hora local *f*; ~ **union** HRM delegación local de un sindicato *f*; ~ **variable** COMP variable local *f*

Local: ~ **Education Authority** *n* (*LEA*) POL, WEL territorio administrativo para fines educativos; ~ **Enterprise Agency** *n* WEL oficina de asistencia a empresas locales; ~ **Export Control** *n BrE* (*LEC*) IMP/EXP, TAX consejo local de control de la exportación; ~ **VAT Office Inquiry Team** *n* (*LVOIT*) TAX equipo de información de la oficina local del IVA

localization *n* COMP *software* localización *f*

location *n* GEN COMM radicación *f*, ubicación *f*, IND emplazamiento *m*; ~ **clause** TRANSP cláusula sobre el emplazamiento *f*; ~ **theory** ECON teoría de la localización *f*; ◆ **any one** ~ (*AOLOC*) INS *marine* cualquier ubicación

locator *n* TRANSP localizador(a) *m,f*

LOCH *abbr* (*London Options Clearing House*) STOCK cámara de compensación de opciones de Londres

lock[1]: ~ **-chamber** *n* TRANSP *waterway* cámara de esclusas *f*; ~ **-out** *n* ADMIN cierre patronal *m*; ~ **-up option** *n* FIN opción de cierre *f*, STOCK *corporate takeover* opción inmovilizada *f*; ~ **-up premises** *n pl* GEN COMM, PROP local sin trastienda *m*

lock[2] *vt* COMP desactivar, bloquear, TRANSP *containers* fijar, enclavar

lock away *vt jarg* STOCK guardar bajo llave

lock in *vt* STOCK sincronizar, encerrar; ◆ ~ **a rate** STOCK *futures* cerrar en un tipo

locked[1]: ~ **-in** *adj* STOCK sin salida para poder comprar o vender

locked[2]: ~ **canal** *n* TRANSP canal con esclusas *m*; ~ **-in capital** *n* ACC, ECON, FIN, GEN COMM capital retraído *m*; ~ **-in effect** *n* STOCK efecto inmovilizado *m*; ~ **-in industry** *n* ECON, IND industria cerrada *f*; ~ **-in knowledge** *n* ECON conocimiento alcanzado *m*; ~ **-in value** *n* STOCK *of shares allocated to employees* valor en posición cubierta bloqueada *m*; ~ **market** *n* STOCK mercado inmovilizado *m*

locking *n* TRANSP *of containers* enclavamiento *m*, fijación *f*

lockmatic: ~ **stacker** n TRANSP *containers* apiladora de cierre automático f

lockout n GEN COMM, HRM *industrial dispute* cierre empresarial m

lodge vi GEN COMM presentar, *reside* alojarse, hospedarse; ◆ ~ **a complaint** GEN COMM hacer una reclamación

log n COMP diario de operaciones m, TRANSP cuaderno de bitácora m; ~ **file** COMP archivo de registro m

log in vi COMP ejecutar el procedimiento de entrada

log off vi COMP finalizar la comunicación

log on vi COMP iniciar la conexión

log out vi COMP terminar la comunicación

logbook n TRANSP cuaderno de bitácora m, libro de vuelos m

logging n GEN COMM descarga f

logic: ~ **circuit** n COMP circuito lógico m; ~ **device** n COMP dispositivo lógico f

logistic: ~ **cycle** n ECON ciclo logístico m; ~ **process** n IND, MATH proceso logístico m

logistical adj COMP, GEN COMM, MATH logístico

logistically adv COMP, GEN COMM, MATH logísticamente

logistics n pl COMP, GEN COMM, MATH logística f; ~ **industry** n ECON, IND industria de la logística f

logo n (*logotype*) GEN COMM, S&M logotipo m

logoptics n GEN COMM logóptica f

logotype n (*logo*) GEN COMM, S&M logotipo m

logrolling n AmE infrml POL sistema de concesiones mutuas m, intercambio de favores m

Lombard: ~ **loan** n AmE (*cf collateral loan BrE*) BANK empréstito con garantía m, préstamo con caución m, préstamo con garantía m; ~ **rate** n BANK tasa Lombard f

Lomé: ~ **Convention** n ECON *trade* Convención de Lomé f

London: ~ **clause** n (*LC*) GEN COMM cláusula de desembarco f; ~ **Clearing House** n (*LCH*) STOCK cámara de compensación de materias primas de Londres; ~ **Commodity Exchange** n obs (*LCE*) STOCK bolsa de contratación de materias primas de Londres; ~ **Discount Market Association** n (*LDMA*) BANK, FIN asociación del mercado de descuento de Londres; ~ **Foreign Exchange Market** n STOCK mercado de valores extranjeros de Londres; ~ **Futures and Options Exchange** n (*FOX*) STOCK mercado de opciones y futuros de Londres; ~ **gold fixing** n BANK precio del oro fijado en Londres m; ~ **Interbank Bid Rate** n (*LIBID*) BANK, STOCK tasa de licitaciones interbancarias de Londres f; ~ **Interbank Currency Options Market** n (*LICOM*) STOCK mercado interbancario de opciones sobre divisas de Londres; ~ **Interbank Offered Rate** n (*LIBOR*) BANK, STOCK tipo de interés ofrecido en el mercado interbancario de Londres; ~ **International Financial Futures Exchange** n (*LIFFE*) STOCK mercado de futuros financieros de Londres; ~ **International Freight Terminal** n (*LIFT*) TRANSP terminal internacional de carga de Londres; ~ **Landed Terms** n pl IMP/EXP condiciones en muelle de descarga de Londres; ~ **Metal Exchange** n (*LME*) STOCK bolsa de contratos futuros sobre metales; ~ **Options Clearing House** n (*LOCH*) STOCK cámara de compensación de opciones de Londres; ~ **Regional Transport** n (*LRT*) TRANSP servicio londinense de transporte público; ~ **School of Economics** n (*LSE*) WEL Universidad londinense de estudios económicos y

sociales; ~ **Stock Exchange** n (*LSE*) STOCK Bolsa de Valores de Londres; ~ **Stock Exchange Board** n STOCK junta directiva de la Bolsa de Valores de Londres; ~ **Traded Options Market** n (*LTOM*) STOCK mercado de Londres de opciones negociadas; ~ **weighting** n WEL subido por residir en Londres

long[1]: ~**-distance** adj COMMS *telephone call* a larga distancia; ~**-established** adj GEN COMM muy arraigado; ~**-haul** adj TRANSP de largo recorrido; ~**-range** adj GEN COMM *planning, forecast* de largo alcance; ~**-standing** adj GEN COMM antiguo; ~**-term** adj GEN COMM a largo plazo

long[2]: ~**-distance** adv COMMS *call* a larga distancia; **in the** ~**-term** adv GEN COMM a largo plazo

long[3]: ~ **bond** n STOCK bono a largo plazo m; ~ **butterfly** n STOCK *options* mariposa comprada f; ~ **call** n STOCK compra al alza f, opción de compra a largo plazo f; ~ **call position** n STOCK posición compradora larga f; ~ **coupon** n STOCK cupón a largo plazo m; ~ **cycle** n GEN COMM ciclo de larga duración m; ~**-distance call** n COMMS conferencia interurbana f, llamada de larga distancia f, comunicación interurbana f; ~ **exercise price** n STOCK precio de ejercicio al alza m; ~ **form** n IMP/EXP *bill of lading* formulario extenso m, TRANSP *bill of lading* formulario ordinario m; ~ **fraud** n GEN COMM fraude al proveedor m; ~ **futures position** n STOCK *options* posición de futuros a largo plazo f; ~ **hedge** n STOCK cobertura de una posición larga f; ~ **in a currency** n ECON *international trade* largo en una divisa m; ~ **lease** n FIN enfiteusis f; ~ **leg** n STOCK parte alcista f; ~ **period** n ECON periodo largo m; ~ **position** n FIN, STOCK posición larga f; ~ **put** n STOCK venta al alza f; ~ **put position** n STOCK posición vendedora larga f; ~**-range forecast** n GEN COMM previsión a largo plazo f; ~**-range planning** n GEN COMM, FIN, MGMNT planificación a largo plazo f, planificación de largo alcance f; ~ **room** n BrE IMP/EXP espacio amplio m; ~**-run equilibrium** n ECON equilibrio a largo plazo m; ~ **straddle** n STOCK *options* estructura de deribados al alza f; ~ **straddle position** n STOCK posición mixta larga f; ~ **strangle** n STOCK *options* strangle larga f; ~ **strike price** n STOCK precio con tendencia al alza m; ~ **tail** n INS responsabilidad de largo plazo f; **in the** ~ **term** n GEN COMM a largo plazo m; ~**-term blended cost rate** n (*LTB*) FIN tasa de costo combinado a largo plazo f (*AmL*), tipo de coste combinado a largo plazo m (*Esp*); ~**-term bond** n STOCK bono a largo plazo m; ~**-term bond option** n STOCK opción de bonos a largo plazo f; ~**-term budget** n ACC, ECON, FIN presupuesto a largo plazo m; ~**-term capital** n ACC, ECON, FIN, GEN COMM capital a largo plazo m; ~**-term credit** n BANK, FIN crédito a largo plazo m; ~**-term credit bank** n BANK banco de crédito a largo plazo m; ~**-term debt** n ACC, BANK, FIN deuda a largo plazo f; ~**-term deposit** n BANK depósito a largo plazo m; ~**-term equity anticipation securities** n pl (*LEAPS*) STOCK valores de anticipo sobre recursos propios a largo plazo m pl; ~**-term financial investment** n ACC, BANK, FIN *annual accounts* inversión financiera a largo plazo f; ~**-term financing** n BANK, FIN financiación a largo plazo f; ~**-term gain** n TAX ganancia a largo plazo f; ~**-term government bond** n STOCK bono del Estado a largo plazo m; ~**-term income averaging** n TAX pago a largo plazo del impuesto sobre la renta m; ~**-term interest rate** n GEN COMM tipo de interés a largo plazo m;

~-term liability n ACC, BANK deudas a largo plazo f pl, FIN deudas a largo plazo f pl, pasivo a largo plazo m; **~-term loan** n BANK, FIN préstamo a largo plazo m; **~-term loss** n TAX pérdida a largo plazo f pl; **~-term objective** n GEN COMM objetivo a largo plazo m; **~-term planning** n FIN, GEN COMM, MGMNT planificación a largo plazo f, planificación de largo alcance f; **~-term prime rate** n (*LTPR*) FIN interés preferencial a largo plazo m; **~-term security** n STOCK obligación a largo plazo f; **~-term team** n WEL *social work* equipo a largo plazo m; **~-term trend** n GEN COMM tendencia a largo plazo f; **~-term unemployed** n pl (*LTU*) ECON, HRM, WEL persona que ha estado desempleada por largo tiempo; **~-term unemployment** n ECON, HRM desempleo de larga duración m, paro de larga duración m, WEL desempleo de larga duración m; **~ ton** n GEN COMM tonelada larga f; **~ value position** n STOCK posición de valor larga f; **~ wave** n MEDIA *radio* onda larga f (*OL*); **~ wave cycle** n GEN COMM ciclo de larga duración m, ciclo amplio m; **~ weekend** n HRM puente m

Long: ~ Boom n ECON gran boom económico m

longer: ~-term asset n STOCK activo a largo plazo m; **~-term option** n STOCK opción a más largo plazo f

longevity: ~ pay n HRM paga de antigüedad f

longitudinal[1] adj GEN COMM longitudinal

longitudinal[2]**: ~ framing** n TRANSP *shipping* disposición estructural longitudinal f, estructura longitudinal f

longs n pl STOCK posiciones acaparadoras f pl

look: ~ promising phr GEN COMM tener buenas perspectivas

look at vt GEN COMM *consider* considerar, examinar

look into vt GEN COMM *investigate* investigar

look out: ~ for vt GEN COMM estar en la búsqueda de

look over vt GEN COMM examinar, revisar

look to vt GEN COMM *attend to* ocuparse de; ♦ **~ the future** GEN COMM poner la mira en el futuro; **~ sb for sth** GEN COMM contar con alguien para algo

look up vi GEN COMM *improve* mejorar

lookup: ~ table n COMP tabla de consulta f

loop n AmE obs POL *Reagan administration* bucle m

loophole n LAW vacío legal m

loose[1]**: ~-leaf** adj GEN COMM de hoja suelta

loose[2]**: ~ cargo** n TRANSP cargamento suelto m; **~ inserts** n pl MEDIA encartes m pl; **~ order reports** n pl S&M informes de pedidos perdidos m pl; **~ rein** n MGMNT riendas flojas f pl, riendas sueltas f pl

Lorenz: ~ curve n ECON curva de Lorenz f

lorry n BrE (*cf truck AmE*) TRANSP camión m; **~ driver** BrE (*cf teamster AmE*) TRANSP camionero(-a) m,f, conductor(a) de camión m,f; **~-mounted crane** BrE (*cf truck-mounted crane AmE*) TRANSP grúa sobre camión f; **~ reception area** BrE (*cf truck reception area AmE*) TRANSP área de recepción de camiones f; **~ service** BrE (*cf truck service AmE*) TRANSP servicio de transporte en camión m

lose vt GEN COMM, LAW *protection* perder; ♦ **~ ground** GEN COMM *in competition* perder terreno, retroceder; **~ one's job** HRM perder el empleo

loss n BANK *capital*, GEN COMM pérdida f; **~ adjuster** HRM, INS tasador(a) de pérdidas m,f; **~ adjustment expense** INS gasto de ajuste por pérdidas m; **~ carryback** ACC, TAX pérdidas con efecto retroactivo f, traslado de pérdidas a ejercicios anteriores m; **~ car-**

ry-forward ACC *balance sheets*, TAX traslado de pérdidas a ejercicios futuros m; **~ of claim** LAW pérdida del derecho f; **~ coefficient** BANK, ECON, FIN, STOCK coeficiente de pérdida m; **~ contingency** ACC, FIN *balance sheets* contingencia de pérdidas f; **~ of custom** GEN COMM, S&M pérdida de la clientela f; **~ of earnings** HRM pérdida de sueldo f; **~ function** MATH *statistics* función de pérdida f; **~ in transit** TRANSP pérdida en tránsito f; **~ in value of assets** ACC, BANK, ECON, FIN pérdida de valor de los activos f; **~ of income insurance** INS *personal* seguro de pérdidas de ingresos m; **~ leader** S&M artículo de reclamo m; **~ leader pricing** S&M determinación de precios de venta con pérdida f; **~ limitation** FIN limitación de la pérdida f; **~ of market** GEN COMM pérdida de mercado f; **~ on depreciable property** ACC pérdida en la propiedad amortizable f; **~ of pay** HRM pérdida de remuneración f; **~-pricing** jarg S&M fijación de precios con pérdida para promover la venta; **~ of priority** PATENTS pérdida de prioridad f; **~ provision** GEN COMM provisión para pérdidas f; **~ ratio** BANK, INS índice de siniestralidad m; ♦ **sell at a ~** GEN COMM vender con pérdida; **take a ~** STOCK asumir una pérdida

losses: ~ carried forward n pl ACC pérdidas llevadas a cuenta nueva f pl; **~ suffered** n pl LAW pérdidas sufridas f pl

lossmaker n S&M productor(a) de pérdidas m,f

lot: ~ line n PROP línea de parcelación f

LOT: ~ system n TRANSP *oil tanker* sistema LOT m

Lotharingian: ~ axis n ECON eje de Lothar m

lottery n GEN COMM lotería f; **~ ticket** GEN COMM boleto de lotería m

Louvre: ~ Accord n ECON *international agreement on stabilization of exchange rates* acuerdo de El Louvre m

low[1] adj GEN COMM, STOCK *futures, price* bajo; **~-budget** GEN COMM, MEDIA *film* de bajo presupuesto; **~-cost** GEN COMM barato, de presupuesto modesto; **~-geared** STOCK bajo apalancamiento; **~-grade** S&M *quality* de baja calidad; **~-key** GEN COMM moderado; **~-paid** HRM de bajo ingreso, mal pagado, mal remunerado; **the ~-paid** HRM los mal pagados m pl; **~-polluting** ENVIR poco contaminante; **~-priced** GEN COMM barato; **~-profile** S&M discreto, de perfil discreto; **~-quality goods** n GEN COMM, S&M bienes de baja calidad m pl; **~-stream** jarg IND de bajo índice de operación; **~-tech** GEN COMM, IND poco técnico; **~-yielding** STOCK de baja rentabilidad

low[2]**: ~ abstraction** n jarg HRM bajo índice de concentración m; **~ achiever** n GEN COMM, HRM persona de bajo desempeño f, persona de bajo rendimiento f, deficiente en desempeño mf; **~-cost loan** n BANK préstamo barato m; **~ density cargo** n TRANSP carga de baja densidad f; **~ end of the market** n S&M gama baja del mercado m; **~ end of the range** n STOCK extremo bajo de la banda m; **~-flier** n GEN COMM, HRM persona de baja desempeño f, persona de bajo rendimiento f, MGMNT persona de baja estima f; **~-geared capital** n FIN capital con bajo apalancamiento m; **~-income household** n S&M market research familia con ingresos reducidos f; **~-income taxpayer** n TAX contribuyente de bajos ingresos mf; **~-interest loan** n BANK, FIN préstamo a bajo interés m; **~ loader** n (*lo*) TRANSP vehículo de carga con plataforma baja m; **~-margin high-space goods** n pl S&M mercancías que ocupan mucho espacio y dejan poco margen m; **~ memory** n

COMP memoria baja *f*; ~ **pay** *n* HRM ingreso bajo *m*, salario bajo *m*; ~ **pressure** *n* (*LP*) GEN COMM baja presión *f*; **~-pressure selling** *n* S&M venta poco apremiante *f*; ~ **price** *n* S&M, STOCK *currency futures* precio bajo *m*; ~ **profile** *n* S&M perfil discreto *m*; ~ **profile coaster** *n* TRANSP buque de cabotaje de puntal bajo *m*; ~ **rent** *n* PROP alquiler bajo *m*, renta baja *f*; ~ **return** *n* ACC *on investment* rendimiento bajo *m*; **~-season fare** *n* LEIS tarifa de temporada baja *f*; ~ **stowage factor** *n* TRANSP factor de estibaje bajo *m*; ~ **value to high weight ratio** *n* TRANSP relación valor bajo por peso grande *f*; ~ **water** *n* (*lw*) TRANSP bajamar *f*; ~ **water ordinary spring tide** *n* (*LWOST*) TRANSP *shipping* bajamar de marea de sigicia ordinaria *f*; **~-yield bond** *n* FIN, STOCK bono de bajo rendimiento *m*

lowballer *n jarg* STOCK *company* empresa con objetivos modestos de gestión *f*, *individual* inversor(a) de teoría contraria *m,f*

lower[1] *adj* GEN COMM inferior, más bajo

lower[2]: ~ **case letter** *n* COMP letra minúscula *f*; ~ **classes** *n pl* GEN COMM, POL clase baja *f*; ~ **deck** *n* TRANSP *aircraft, ship* puente inferior *m*; ~ **deck container** *n* TRANSP contenedor de cubierta inferior *m*; ~ **income bracket** *n* ECON grupo de ingresos más bajos *m*; ~ **of market** *n* ACC mínimo de mercado *m*; ~ **price** *n* STOCK precio inferior *m*; ~ **quartile** *n* MATH *statistics* cuartil inferior *m*

lower[3] *vt* GEN COMM *reduce* reducir, disminuir, *price* rebajar, TRANSP *boat* lanzar

lowering: ~ **of taxation** *n* TAX reducción de la presión fiscal *f*

lowest: ~ **bidder** *n* STOCK postor más bajo *m*; ~ **common denominator** *n* GEN COMM mínimo común denominador *m*; ~ **price** *n* STOCK precio ínfimo *m*; ~ **tender** *n* GEN COMM oferta más baja *f*

loyalty *n* GEN COMM *customer, employee* lealtad *f*, fidelidad *f*; ~ **bonus** STOCK prima por lealtad *f*; ~ **factor** S&M *of product* factor de lealtad *m*

LPG[1] *abbr* (*liquid petroleum gas*) IND, TRANSP LPG (*gas licuado de petróleo*)

LPG[2]: ~ **carrier** *n* TRANSP *vessel* transportista LPG *m*

LQ *abbr* (*letter quality*) COMP, MEDIA calidad de letra *f*

LRC *abbr* (*Labour Representation Committee*) HRM comité de representación laboral

LRT *abbr* (*London Regional Transport*) TRANSP servicio londinense de transporte público

ls *abbr* (*lump sum*) GEN COMM suma global *f*

lsd *abbr* (*last safe day*) INS *marine* último día del seguro *m*

LSD *abbr* (*landing storage delivery*) IMP/EXP entrega de productos almacenados al desembarque *f*, TRANSP entrega de la carga a tierra *f*

LSE *abbr* ECON (*London School of Economics*) universidad londinense de estudios económicos y sociales, STOCK (*London Stock Exchange*) bolsa de valores de Londres

LSI *abbr* (*large-scale integration*) COMP LSI (*gran escala de integración*)

LTB *abbr* (*long-term blended cost rate*) FIN tasa de costo combinado a largo plazo *f* (*AmL*), tipo de coste combinado a largo plazo *m* (*Esp*)

Ltd *abbr* BrE (*limited company*) GEN COMM ≈ S.A. (*sociedad anónima*), ≈ S.A.A. (*sociedad anónima por acciones*), ≈ S.L.R. (*sociedad de responsabilidad limitada*)

LTOM *abbr* (*London Trader Options Market*) STOCK mercado de opciones de Londres

LTPR *abbr* (*long-term prime rate*) FIN interés preferencial a largo plazo *m*

LTU *abbr* (*long-term unemployed*) ECON, HRM, WEL persona que ha estado desempleada por largo tiempo

LTV *abbr* (*light vessel*) TRANSP buque en lastre *m*

LUAMC *abbr* (*leading underwriters' agreement for marine cargo business*) INS acuerdo de primeros aseguradores para fletes marítimos *m*

LUAMH *abbr* (*leading underwriters' agreement for marine hull business*) INS convenio de aseguradores principales para seguro del casco del buque *m*

Lucas: ~ **supply function** *n* ECON función de oferta de Lucas *f*

lucky: ~ **break** *n infrml* GEN COMM *chance* racha de suerte *f*

lucrative *adj* GEN COMM lucrativo, provechoso

Luddism *n* HRM Luddismo *m*

Luddite *n* HRM Luddita *m*

luffing: ~ **crane** *n* TRANSP *cargo* grúa de inclinación variable *f*

luggage *n* LEIS, TRANSP equipaje *m*; ~ **trolley** BrE (*cf baggage cart AmE*) LEIS, TRANSP carro de equipajes *m*

lugger *n* TRANSP *vessel* lugre *m*

lull *n* GEN COMM *diminished activity* calma *f*

lumber *n AmE* (*cf timber BrE*) IND *prepared* madera *f*; ~ **industry** *AmE* (*cf timber industry BrE*) ECON, IND industria maderera *f*

lump *n* HRM *contract work* destajo *m*; **the ~** BrE HRM, TAX *building trade* el lumpen *m*; ~ **sum** (*ls*) GEN COMM suma global *f*; **~-sum contract** HRM contrato a precio alzado *m*, contrato por precio global *m*; **~-sum distribution** STOCK distribución global *f*; **~-sum freight** TRANSP flete pagadero por entero *m*; **~-sum price** GEN COMM precio global *m*; **~-sum purchase** FIN compra a tanto alzado *f*; **~-sum tax** TAX contribución a tasa fija *f*, impuesto global *m*

lunch: **~-hour** *n* GEN COMM hora de comer *f*

luncheon: ~ **voucher** *n* (*LV*) BrE (*cf meal ticket AmE*) HRM, TAX vale de comida *m*

Lundberg: ~ **lag** *n* ECON ajuste de Lundberg *m*

Luxemburg: ~ **effect** *n* ECON efecto luxemburgo *m*

luxury[1] *adj* S&M de lujo

luxury[2]: ~ **goods** *n pl* ECON, S&M bienes de lujo *m pl*; ~ **tax** *n* TAX impuesto de lujo *m*

LV *abbr* (*luncheon voucher*) HRM, TAX vale de comida *m*

LVOIT *abbr* (*Local VAT Office Inquiry Team*) TAX equipo de información de la oficina local del IVA

lw *abbr* (*low water*) TRANSP bajamar *f*

LW *abbr* (*long wave*) MEDIA *radio* onda larga *f* (*OL*)

LWOST *abbr* (*low water ordinary spring tide*) TRANSP bajamar de marea de sigicia ordinaria *f*

M

m *abbr* (*midship*) TRANSP medio del buque *m*

M[1] *abbr* ECON (*monetary aggregates*) totales monetarios *m pl*, GEN COMM (*money*) dinero *m*, *supply* oferta monetaria *f*, TRANSP *BrE* (*motorway*) (autopista *f*

M[2]: **~ factors** *n pl* ECON factores M *m pl*

m/a *abbr* (*my account*) BANK mi cuenta

Maastricht: ~ summit *n* GEN COMM *UE* cumbre de Maastricht *f*

MABP *abbr* (*monetary approach to the balance of payments*) ECON enfoque monetario de la balanza de pagos *m*

machine[1]: **~-based** *adj* COMP, GEN COMM automático, IND automático, mecanizado; **~-made** *adj* GEN COMM, IND hecho a máquina; **~-readable** *adj* COMP, S&M *bar codes* legible mecánicamente

machine[2] *n* IND máquina *f*; **~ accounting** ACC, COMP contabilidad computadorizada *f* (*AmL*), contabilidad informatizada *f* (*Esp*) , contabilidad mecanizada *f*; **~ address** COMP dirección de máquina *f*; **~-assisted translation** (*MAT*) COMP traducción automática *f*; **~ code** IND código de máquina *m*; **~ dynamics** *n pl* IND dinámica de las máquinas *f*; **~ load** IND carga de una máquina *f*; **~ operator** HRM maquinista *mf*; **~ proof** S&M impresión de control *f*; **~ readable code** S&M código legible por máquina *m*; **~ run** COMP, TRANSP pasada de máquina *f*; **~ safety** IND seguridad de las máquinas *f*

machinery *n* (*mchy*) GEN COMM maquinaria *f*, LAW aparato *m*; **~ damage co-ins clause** INS *hull clause* cláusula coaseguro de daños maquinaria *f*; **~ survey** (*MS*) TRANSP *shipping* inspección de la maquinaria *f*

macho: ~ management *n* HRM, MGMNT administración impositiva *f*, gestión impositiva *f*

machtpolitik *n jarg* POL política de fuerza *f*, rodillo *m*

Macmillan: ~ Gap *n* FIN Brecha Macmillan *f*

macro *n* COMP, GEN COMM macroinstrucción *f*

macrocompany *n* MGMNT macroempresa *f*

macrocomputing *n* COMP macroinformática *f*

macrodistribution *n* ECON macrodistribución *f*

macroeconomic[1] *adj* ECON macroeconómico

macroeconomic[2]: **~ demand schedule** *n* ECON programa de demanda macroeconómico *m*; **~ policy** *n* ECON, POL política macroeconómica *f*

macroeconomics *n* ECON macroeconomía *f*

macroenvironment *n* GEN COMM macroambiente *m*

macromarketing *n* S&M macromarketing *m*

macroproject *n* MGMNT macroproyecto *m*

made[1]: **~ to last** *adj* GEN COMM, IND hecho para durar

made[2]: **~ bill** *n jarg* ECON letra endosada *f*

measure[1]: **made to ~** *adj* GEN COMM, IND, S&M *individual purchaser* hecho a medida

measure[2] *n* GEN COMM medida *f*

Madison: ~ Avenue *n* *AmE* S&M *advertising* avenida neoyorkina famosa por sus agencias de publicidad

Madrid: ~ Stock Exchange *n* STOCK Bolsa de Madrid *f*

mag *n infrml* (*magazine*) GEN COMM revista *f*

magazine *n* (*mag*) GEN COMM revista *f*

magic: ~ square *n* ECON cuadrilátero mágico *m*

magistrate *n* LAW juez(a) de primera instancia e instrucción *m,f*, magistrado(-a) *m,f*; **~ entitled to adjudicate** LAW magistrado(-a) autorizado(-a) para adjudicar *m,f*

magistrates': ~ court *n* LAW juzgado de paz *m*

magnate *n* GEN COMM magnate *mf*

magnetic: ~ card *n* COMP tarjeta magnética *f*, GEN COMM, IND ficha magnética *f*; **~ core** *n* COMP núcleo magnético *m*; **~ disk** *n* COMP disco magnético *m*; **~ film** *n* S&M filme magnético *m*; **~ head** *n* COMP cabeza magnética *f*; **~ soundtrack** *n* MEDIA, S&M banda sonora magnética *f*; **~ storage** *n* COMP memoria magnética *f*; **~ tape** *n* COMP cinta magnética *f*; **~ tape recorder** *n* COMP grabadora de cinta *f*, magnetofón *m*

magnitude *n* MATH magnitud *f*; **~ of a right** LAW amplitud de un derecho *f*

Mahalanobis: ~ model *n* POL modelo Mahalanobis *m*

maiden: ~ voyage *n* TRANSP viaje inaugural *m*

mail[1] *n* *AmE* (*cf post BrE*) GEN COMM correo *m*; **~ clerk** *AmE* (*cf postal clerk BrE*) HRM empleado(-a) postal *m,f*; **~ fraud** S&M *advertising* fraude en una promoción por correo; **~ order** (*MO*) S&M pedido por correo *m*, pedido por correspondencia *m*; **~ order business** S&M negocio por correspondencia *m*, venta por correspondencia *f*; **~ order catalog** *AmE*, **~ order catalogue** *BrE* S&M catálogo de venta por correo *m*; **~ order selling** S&M venta por correspondencia *f*; **~ shot** COMMS, S&M carta cicular *f*, mailing *m*, envío de folletos por correo a posibles clientes; **~ transfer** (*MT*) ECON, GEN COMM transferencia por correo *f*, giro postal *m*; **~ van** *BrE* (*cf mailcar AmE*) COMMS, TRANSP furgón postal *m*; ♦ **by ~** *AmE* (*cf by post BrE*) COMMS por correo; **through the ~** *AmE* (*cf through the post BrE*) COMMS por correo

mail[2] *vt* *AmE* (*cf post BrE*) ADMIN, COMMS enviar por correo, franquear, GEN COMM *notices*

mailbox *n* *AmE* (*cf postbox BrE*) COMMS buzón *m*

mailcar *n* *AmE* (*cf post van BrE, mail van BrE*) COMMS, TRANSP furgón postal *m*

mailing *n* ADMIN, COMMS correo *m*, mailing *m*, envío por correo *m*, S&M buzoneo de propaganda *m* (*AmL*), envío publicitario *m*, propaganda por correo *f*, publicidad por correo *f*; **~ address** COMMS domicilio postal *m*; **~ list** COMMS, S&M buzoneo *m* (*AmL*), lista de clientes *f*, lista de direcciones *f*, mailing *m* (*Esp*); **~ piece** S&M envío de publicidad a domicilio *m*; **~shot** COMMS carta circular *f*, envío de publicidad a domicilio *m*

mailman *n* *AmE* (*cf postman BrE*) COMMS cartero *m*

mailmerge *n* ADMIN, COMP fusión de correo *f*, fusión de ficheros de direcciones *f*

mailshot *n* COMMS, S&M *advertising* mailing *m*; ♦ **do a ~** COMMS hacer un mailing

main: ~ branch *n* BANK rama principal *f*, sede central *f*, sucursal principal *f*; **~ file** *n* COMP fichero principal *m*; **~ line** *n* TRANSP *rail* línea principal *f*, vía principal *f*; **~ menu** *n* COMP menú principal *m*; **~ owner** *n* HRM propietario(-a) principal *m,f*; **~ residence** *n* LAW, PROP,

TAX residencia principal *f*; ~ **street** *n AmE* (*cf high street BrE*) S&M calle céntrica y comercial *f*, calle mayor *f* (*Esp*); ~ **street price** *n AmE* (*cf high street price BrE*) S&M precio de calle principal *m*; ~ **street spending** *n AmE* (*cf high street spending BrE*) ECON gastos de calle mayor *m pl*; ~ **trading partner** *n* ECON principal socio(-a) comercial *m,f*

mainframe *n* COMP servidor *m*

mains *n pl BrE* (*cf supply network AmE*) COMP, IND línea principal *f*, red de alimentación *f*; ~ **adaptor** *n BrE* (*cf current adaptor AmE*) COMP, IND adaptador a la red *m*, adaptador de corriente *m*

mainstream: ~ **corporation tax** *n* (*MCT*) TAX impuesto corporativo total *m*; ~ **economics** *n pl* ECON línea central del pensamiento económico *f*

mainstreaming *n* WEL línea central *f*

mainstreeting *n* POL campaña en la calle principal *f*

maintain *vt* GEN COMM mantener

maintenance *n* ACC ingresos por pensión alimenticia *m pl*, COMP, GEN COMM, IND mantenimiento *m*, LAW *of spouse, child* pensión *f*; ~ **allowance** LAW pensión alimenticia *f*; ~ **bond** GEN COMM, LAW fianza de cumplimiento *f*, *commercial* fianza de conservación *f*; ~ **charges** *n pl* GEN COMM, TAX gastos de conservación *m pl*; ~ **crew** HRM, IND cuadrilla de mantenimiento *f*; ~ **engineer** HRM, IND ingeniero(-a) de mantenimiento *m,f*; ~ **equipment** GEN COMM, HRM, IND equipo de mantenimiento *m*; ~ **expenses** *n pl* WEL gastos de mantenimiento *m pl*; ~ **fee** BANK *for keeping account* cargo de mantenimiento *m*, PROP honorarios por mantenimiento *m pl*; ~ **margin** STOCK margen de mantenimiento *m*; ~ **of membership** HRM continuidad en la afiliación sindical *f*; ~ **payment** LAW, TAX pago de pensión alimenticia *m*; ~ **personnel** HRM equipo de mantenimiento *m*; ~ **schedule** GEN COMM calendario de mantenimiento *m*; ~ **staff** HRM equipo de mantenimiento *m*; ◆ ~, **repair and overhaul** (*MRO*) TRANSP mantenimiento, reparación y revisión

Majesty[1]: **Her ~'s Customs and Excise** *n BrE* (*HMC&E*) IMP/EXP ≈ Servicio de Aduanas *m*, departamento de impuestos de aduanas sobre el consumo; **Her ~'s Government** *n BrE* (*HMG*) POL el gobierno británico; **Her ~'s Ship** *n* (*HMS*) TRANSP embarcación de la monarquía británica; **Her ~'s Stationery Office** *n* GEN COMM suministros de papelería de la monarquía británica

Majesty[2]: **On Her ~'s Service** *phr BrE* (*OHMS*) GEN COMM al servicio de Su Majestad

major[1] *adj* GEN COMM mayor

major[2]: ~ **account** *n* GEN COMM cuenta principal *f*; ~ **currency** *n* BANK, ECON divisa principal *f*; ~ **cycle** *n* BANK, FIN, MGMNT ciclo principal *m*; ~ **foreign exchange market** *n* FIN mercado principal de divisas *m*; ~ **producer** *n* ECON, IND *of commodity* productor principal *m*, productor importante *m*; ~ **road** *n* TRANSP carretera de abundante tránsito *f*, carretera nacional *f*, carretera principal *f*; ~ **trend** *n* ECON, GEN COMM tendencia dominante *f*

Major: ~ **Market Index** *n* (*MMI*) STOCK índice del mercado de valores *m*

majority *n* LAW *of age*, POL *in vote* mayoría *f*; ~ **decision** GEN COMM decisión mayoritaria *f*; ~ **holding** STOCK participación mayoritaria *f*; ~ **interest** GEN COMM interés mayoritario *m*, interés de la mayoría *m*; ~ **interest partner** STOCK socio(-a) con participación

mayoritaria *m,f*; ~ **ownership** STOCK propiedad de la mayoría *f*; ~ **rule** POL sistema mayoritario *m*, regla de la mayoría *f*; ~ **rule voting** STOCK votación por el método de la mayoría *f*; ~ **shareholder** STOCK accionista mayoritario(-a) *m,f*; ~ **shareholding** STOCK accionariado(-a) mayoritario(-a) *m,f*; ~ **stake** GEN COMM interés de la mayoría *m*, interés mayoritario *m*, STOCK paquete mayoritario *m*; ~ **stockholder** STOCK accionista mayoritario(-a) *m,f*; ~ **verdict** LAW veredicto mayoritario *m*; ~ **vote** GEN COMM voto mayoritario *m*

make[1] *n* S&M *of vehicle* marca *f*; ~**-or-buy decision** GEN COMM decisión de fabricar o comprar *m*; ~**-up** ACC falseación *f* (*infrml*), manipulación contable *f*, maquillaje de balance *m* (*jarg*), maquillaje *m*; ~**-up pay** HRM remuneración complementaria *f*

make[2] *vt* GEN COMM manufacturar, presentar, IND manufacturar, PATENTS *invention* fraguar, S&M crear; ◆ ~ **an advance** BANK *of money* anticipar; ~ **an advance payment** BANK anticipar un pago; ~ **an allowance** GEN COMM hacer una concesión; ~ **allowances** GEN COMM *exceptional occurrences* hacer provisiones; ~ **an appointment** GEN COMM, MGMNT concertar una cita; ~ **an appraisal of future needs** GEN COMM evaluar las necesidades futuras; ~ **available** GEN COMM *money* poner a disposición; ~ **a benefit** GEN COMM obtener beneficio; ~ **clear** GEN COMM dejar claro; ~ **delivery** STOCK *of currency* hacer entrega; ~ **enquiries** GEN COMM realizar indagaciones, hacer averiguaciones; ~ **an entry against sb** ACC hacer un asiento contra alguien; ~ **an error** GEN COMM cometer un error; ~ **an exception** GEN COMM hacer una excepción; ~ **the first move** GEN COMM hacer la primera jugada; ~ **full use of** GEN COMM hacer uso pleno de; ~ **gains on sth** STOCK obtener beneficios sobre algo; ~ **good** GEN COMM *damage* compensar; ~ **a good deal by** GEN COMM *goods, products* llegar a un buen acuerdo; ~ **headway** GEN COMM hacer progresos; ~ **inroads** GEN COMM hacer incursiones; ~ **it** *infrml* GEN COMM *succeed* llegar; ~ **a killing** *infrml* FIN hacer una cancelación; ~ **a list** GEN COMM hacer una lista; ~ **a living** ECON ganarse la vida; ~ **a loan** BANK hacer un préstamo; ~ **money** GEN COMM hacer dinero; ~ **an objection** GEN COMM hacer una objeción *f*; ~ **an offer** GEN COMM presentar una oferta; ~ **payable to** BANK hacer pagadero a; ~ **a payment** BANK, GEN COMM hacer un pago; ~ **a pig's ear of sth** *infrml* GEN COMM hacer algo muy mal (*infrml*); ~ **a point of** GEN COMM insistir en; ~ **port** TRANSP *shipping* llegar a puerto; ~ **a profit** ACC producir un beneficio; ~ **a promissory note** FIN extender un pagaré; ~ **a protest** GEN COMM presentar una protesta; ~ **provision for** GEN COMM apartar fondos para; ~ **a purchase** GEN COMM hacer una compra; ~ **quick progress** GEN COMM hacer rápidos progresos; ~ **ready** S&M preparar; ~ **redundant** HRM *staff* cesar, despedir, echar, poner a alguien de patitas en la calle (*infrml*); ~ **regulations** LAW establecer las normas; ~ **a request** GEN COMM hacer una petición; ~ **a request to the appropriate authority** GEN COMM presentar una petición en las instancias adecuadas; ~ **a sale** STOCK hacer una venta; ~ **sb's acquaintance** GEN COMM conocer a alguien; ~ **a scoop** *infrml* MEDIA conseguir una primicia informativa; ~ **sense** GEN COMM tener sentido; ~ **a snap decision** GEN COMM tomar una decisión rápida; ~ **a speech** MGMNT pronunciar un discurso; ~ **a statement** LAW hacer una declaración; ~ **a suggestion** GEN COMM hacer una sugerencia; ~ **things rough for sb** GEN COMM ponerle las cosas difíciles a alguien; ~ **a transaction** GEN COMM realizar una transacción; ~ **use of** GEN COMM hacer uso de; ~ **a valuation of sth** GEN COMM hacer una evaluación de algo; ~ **void** GEN COMM invalidar

make out *vt* BANK librar, GEN COMM *invoice* extender; ◆ ~ **a check** *AmE*, ~ **a cheque** *BrE* BANK emitir un cheque, rellenar un cheque; ~ **a cheque to** *BrE* BANK extender un cheque; ~ **an invoice** GEN COMM extender una factura; ~ **in** BANK *dollars* expresar en

make up *vt* BANK, ECON, FIN ajustar, GEN COMM componer, STOCK ajustar; ◆ ~ **the difference** GEN COMM compensar la diferencia; ~ **for** GEN COMM *compensate* suplir; ~ **for lost time** GEN COMM recuperar el tiempo perdido; ~ **one's accounts** ACC saldar las propias cuentas; ~ **the odd money** FIN, GEN COMM reunir el dinero que falta

maker *n* GEN COMM signatario(-a) *m,f*, LAW *of note* firmante *mf*

makeshift: ~ **solution** *n* GEN COMM solución improvisada *f*

making *n* ACC *of profit* obtención *f*, HRM *of position* fijación *f*, IND *of paper* fabricación *f*, *of clothes* confección *f*; ~-**up** ACC *for losses*, BANK *of accounts*, FIN *of balance sheet* compensación *f*, STOCK compensación *f*, constitución de nuevos títulos valores *f*

mala fide *adj* LAW de mala fe

malfunction *n* GEN COMM fallo de funcionamiento *m*

malicious: ~ **acts clause** *n* INS *hull policy* cláusula sobre actos dolosos *f*; ~ **damage clause** *n* INS *marine, cargo policy* cláusula de daños de mala fe *f*; ~ **mischief** *n* LAW agravio malicioso *m*; ~ **prosecution** *n* LAW demanda de mala fe *f*

maliciously *adv* LAW con alevosía, de mala fe

malingerer *n* HRM falso(-a) enfermo(-a) *m,f*

malingering *n* HRM enfermedad ficticia *f*

mall *n* *AmE* (*cf commercial centre* *BrE*) S&M *shopping* centro comercial *m*

malleable: ~ **capital** *n* ACC, ECON, GEN COMM, FIN capital maleable *m*

Maloney: ~ **Act** *n* LAW, STOCK Ley Maloney *f*

malpractice *n* LAW negligencia profesional *f*

Malthusian: ~ **law of population** *n* ECON ley maltusiana de la población *f*

Malthusianism *n* ECON maltusianismo *m*

mammoth: ~ **reduction** *n* S&M reducción enorme *f*

man¹: ~-**made** *adj* IND artificial, sintético

man²: ~-**hour** *n* HRM, MGMNT hora-hombre *f*; **the** ~ **in the street** *n* S&M el ciudadano de a pie *m*, el ciudadano medio *m*; ~-**machine system** *n* IND sistema del hombre y la máquina *m*; ~-**made fiber** *AmE*, ~-**made fibre** *BrE* *n* ENVIR, IND fibra sintética *f*

man³ *vt* HRM *machine* manejar, *ship* tripular; ◆ ~ **a night-shift** HRM dirigir un turno de noche

manage *vt* ADMIN, GEN COMM, MGMNT administrar, dirigir, manejar; ◆ ~ **sb's affairs** GEN COMM, MGMNT administrar los negocios de alguien

manageable *adj* GEN COMM manejable

managed: ~ **account** *n* ACC cuenta administrada *f*, cuenta controlada *f*; ~ **bond** *n* ECON bono administrativo *m*; ~ **cost** *n* ACC, FIN coste controlado *m* (*Esp*), costo controlado *m* (*AmL*); ~ **costs** *n pl* ACC, FIN costes

administrados *m pl* (*Esp*), costes gestionados *m pl* (*Esp*), costos administrados *m pl* (*AmL*), costos gestionados *m pl* (*AmL*); ~ **currency** *n* BANK, ECON divisa controlada *f*; ~ **currency funds** *n pl* FIN fondos de moneda circulante administrados *m pl*; ~ **economy** *n* ECON economía dirigida *f*, economía intervenida *f*; ~ **floating system** *n* ECON sistema de flotación controlada *m*; ~ **loan** *n* BANK préstamo controlado *m*; ~ **news** *n pl jarg* MEDIA, POL noticias manipuladas *f pl*; ~ **trade** *n* ECON comercio controlado *m*

management *n* ECON *of interest rates* dirección *f*, GEN COMM, MGMNT *concept* administración *f* (*admón.*), gestión *f*, dirección *f*, gerencia *f*; ~ **accountancy** ACC contabilidad de gestión *f*, contabilidad directiva *f*, FIN, HRM contabilidad directiva *f*; ~ **accountant** ACC contable de gestión *mf* (*Esp*), contador(a) de gestión *m,f* (*AmL*); ~ **accounting** ACC, FIN, HRM contabilidad de gestión *f*, contabilidad directiva *f*; ~ **accounts** *n pl* ACC cuentas de gestión *f pl*; ~ **agreement** MGMNT acuerdo de gestión *m*; ~ **aid** MGMNT ayuda administrativa *f*; ~ **audit** ACC, HRM auditoría administrativa *f*, auditoría de gestión *f*; ~ **board** HRM, MGMNT consejo de administración *m*, consejo directivo *m* (*Esp*), junta directiva *f*, mesa directiva *f* (*AmL*); ~ **buy-in** GEN COMM, FIN, MGMNT compra financiada de acciones de una empresa por personas ajenas a ella; ~ **buyout** (*MBO*) MGMNT compra por ejecutivos (*CPE*); ~ **by crisis** MGMNT administración por crisis *f*, dirección por crisis *f*; ~ **by exception** MGMNT dirección por excepción *f*, gerencia por excepción *f*; ~ **by objectives** (*MBO*) MGMNT administración por objetivos *f*, dirección por objetivos *f*, gestión por objetivos *f*; ~ **by walking around** (*MBWA*) MGMNT dirección por contacto directo *f*; ~ **of change** MGMNT administración del cambio *f*; ~ **chart** ADMIN, MGMNT diagrama de gestión *m*, organigrama administrativo *m*; ~ **committee** MGMNT comité administrativo *m*, comité de gerencia *m*, POL comisión de gestión *f*, comisión gestora *f*; ~ **competence** MGMNT aptitud administrativa *f*; ~ **computing** COMP computación de gestión *f*, informática de gestión *f*; ~ **consultancy** MGMNT asesoría de empresas *f*, consultoría de gestión *f*, consultoría administrativa *f*; ~ **consultant** MGMNT asesor(a) administrativo(-a) *m,f*, consultor(a) en administración de empresas *m,f*, consultor(a) administrativo(-a) *m,f*, consultor(a) en administración *m,f*; ~ **contract** MGMNT contrato administrativo *m*, contrato de gestión *m*; ~ **control** ACC *auditing* control de gestión *m*; ~ **cycle** MGMNT ciclo administrativo *m*; ~ **development** MGMNT desarrollo administrativo *m*; ~ **education** MGMNT educación administrativa *f*; ~ **expenses** *n pl* ACC gastos de gerencia *m pl*; ~ **fee** BANK comisión de administración *f*, cuota administrativa *f*, PROP *for managing real estate* honorarios de administración *m pl*, STOCK *for managing portfolio* comisión de administración *f*; ~ **game** MGMNT juego de la administración *m*; ~ **group** MGMNT grupo de dirección *m*; ~ **guide** MGMNT guía administrativa *f*; ~ **information** MGMNT información de la gestión *f*, información para la administración *f*, información para la dirección *f*; ~ **information system** (*MIS*) MGMNT sistema de información para la gestión *m* (*SIG*), sistema de información administrativo *m*; ~ **method** MGMNT método administrativo *m*; ~ **office staff** ADMIN personal de la oficina de dirección *m*; ~ **operating system** MGMNT sistema operativo de administración *m*;

~ **operation** MGMNT operación administrativa *f*; ~ **organization** HRM organización de la gestión *f*; ~ **potential** MGMNT potencial de dirección *m*, potencial administrativo *m*; ~ **practice** MGMNT práctica administrativa *f*, experiencia en la dirección *f*; ~ **prerogative** HRM, MGMNT prerrogativa de la dirección *f*, prerrogativa de los directivos *f*; ~ **ratio** FIN proporción de dirección *f*, relación de dirección *f*, MGMNT coeficiente de gestión *m*, proporción directiva *f*, ratio de gestión *m*; ~ **reshuffle** MGMNT reorganización de la dirección *f*; ~ **science** GEN COMM ciencias empresariales *f pl*, MGMNT ciencia administrativa *f*; ~ **service** ADMIN, FIN, MGMNT servicio de administración *m*, servicio administrativo *m*; ~ **skill** HRM, MGMNT habilidad administrativa *f*; ~ **staff** HRM, MGMNT personal administrativo *m*, personal directivo *m*; ~ **structure** HRM, MGMNT estructura administrativa *f*, estructura directiva *f*, estructura de la gestión *f*; ~ **style** MGMNT estilo administrativo *m*, estilo de gerencia *m*; ~ **succession planning** MGMNT plan de sucesión en los cargos administrativos *m* (*Esp*), planificación de la sucesión administrativa *f* (*AmL*); ~ **support** HRM apoyo gerencial *m*; ~ **survey** MGMNT estudio de gerencia *m*; ~ **system** MGMNT sistema administrativo *m*, sistema de administración *m*, sistema de dirección *m*; ~ **team** HRM, MGMNT equipo administrativo *m*, equipo de gestión *m*; ~ **technique** MGMNT técnica administrativa *f*, técnica de administración *f*; ~ **theory** MGMNT teoría administrativa *f*; ~ **training** HRM, MGMNT capacitación de mandos *f* (*AmL*), capacitación gerencial *f* (*AmL*), formación de mandos *f* (*Esp*); ◆ **under new** ~ MGMNT bajo nueva dirección; **the** ~ **regrets any inconvenience caused** GEN COMM la dirección se disculpa por las molestias causadas

Management: ~ **Consultants Association** *n* (*MCA*) MGMNT asociación de consultorías de administración

manager *n* (*MGR*) HRM, MGMNT director(a) *m,f*, gerente *mf* (*gte.*), gestor(a) *m,f*, jefe(-a) *m,f*, mánager *mf*; ~**'s office** HRM, MGMNT oficina del gerente *f*

manageress *n* (*MGR*) HRM, MGMNT directora *f*, gerente *f* (*gte.*), gestora *f*, jefa *f*, mánager *f*

managerial[1] *adj* MGMNT gerencial

managerial[2]: ~ **accounting** *n* ACC contabilidad administrativa *f*, contabilidad de gestión *f*, contabilidad directiva *f*; ~ **control** *n* MGMNT control administrativo *m*, control directivo *m*; ~ **effectiveness** *n* MGMNT eficacia administrativa *f*; ~ **function** *n* MGMNT función directiva *f*; ~ **grid** *n* MGMNT *leadership behaviour* cuadrícula administrativa *f*, parrilla de gestión *f*; ~ **model of the firm** *n* MGMNT modelo administrativo de la empresa *m*; ~ **position** *n* HRM, MGMNT cargo ejecutivo *m*, cargo directivo *m*, puesto directivo *m*; ~ **prerogative** *n* HRM, MGMNT prerrogativa de la dirección *f*, prerrogativa de los directivos *f*; ~ **revolution** *n* MGMNT revolución administrativa *f*, revolución gerencial *f*, revolución en la administración y dirección de la empresa *f*; ~ **staff** *n* HRM, MGMNT personal directivo *m*; ~ **structure** *n* MGMNT estructura administrativa *f*, estructura de la gestión *f*; ~ **style** *n* GEN COMM, MGMNT estilo administrativo *m*

managers: ~ **and workers** *n pl* HRM, MGMNT gerentes y empleados *m pl*, directores y empleados *m pl*

managing[1] *adj* MGMNT directivo

managing[2]: ~ **agent** *n* MGMNT agente administrador(a) *m,f*; ~ **director** *n* (*MD*) HRM, MGMNT director(a)

gerente *m,f*, consejero(-a) delegado(-a) *m,f*, director(a) administrativo(-a) *m,f*; ~ **owner** *n* HRM *responsible for ship operation* propietario(-a)-gerente *m,f*; ~ **partner** *n* HRM socio(-a) administrador(a) *m,f*, socio(-a) director(a) *m,f*; ~ **underwriter** *n* BANK garante administrador(a) *m,f*

Manchester: ~ **Commodity Exchange** *n* STOCK Mercado de Mercaderías de Manchester *m*

M&A *abbr* (*mergers and acquisitions*) ECON fusiones y adquisiciones *f pl*

mandarin *n* POL *government* mandarín *m*

mandate *n* LAW mandato *m*

mandated: ~ **program** *AmE*, ~ **programme** *BrE n* MEDIA programa de inserción obligatoria *m*

mandatory[1] *adj* LAW mandatario, preceptivo

mandatory[2]: ~ **accounting plans** *n pl* ACC planes contables coercitivos *m pl*, planes contables imperativos *m pl*, planes contables obligatorios *m pl*, planes contables preceptivos *m pl*; ~ **copy** *n* S&M *advertising* material publicitario obligatorio *m*; ~ **injunction** *n* LAW interdicto mandatario *m*; ~ **provision** *n* INS cláusula obligatoria *f*; ~ **quote period** *n* STOCK periodo obligatorio de cotización *m*; ~ **retirement** *n* *AmE* (*cf compulsory retirement BrE*) HRM jubilación forzosa *f*, jubilación obligatoria *f*

manifest *n* IMP/EXP, TRANSP manifiesto *m*; ~ **of cargo** IMP/EXP, TRANSP manifiesto del cargamento *m*; ~ **clerk** HRM funcionario(-a) de manifiesto *m,f*; ~ **crisis** POL crisis manifiesta *f*

manifold *n* GEN COMM papel de copia *m*

manipulate *vt* GEN COMM *market* manipular; ◆ ~ **accounts** ACC manipular una contabilidad

manipulation *n* GEN COMM *of market* manipulación *f*

manipulator *n* GEN COMM *of market* manipulador(a) *m,f*

manned *adj* HRM *service* dotado de personal

manning: ~ **level** *n* HRM nivel de personal *m*

manpower *n* HRM mano de obra *f*; ~ **aid** HRM ayuda en mano de obra *f*; ~ **audit** ACC, HRM auditoría de la mano de obra *f*, auditoría de recursos humanos *f*; ~ **cost** HRM coste de la mano de obra *m* (*Esp*), costo de la mano de obra *m* (*AmL*); ~ **forecast** HRM previsión de la fuerza de trabajo *f*, previsión de personal *f*; ~ **forecasting** HRM pronóstico de recursos humanos *m*; ~ **management** HRM, MGMNT dirección de recursos humanos *f*; ~ **planning** HRM, MGMNT planificación de la mano de obra *f*, planificación del potencial humano disponible *f*

Manpower: ~ **Services Commission** *n* *BrE obs* (*MSC*) HRM comisión de servicios laborales

manual[1] *adj* GEN COMM manual

manual[2] *n* GEN COMM *for reference* manual *m*; ~ **labor** *AmE*, ~ **labour** *BrE* HRM trabajo manual *m*; ~ **mode** MATH *of calculation* modo manual *m*; ~ **skill** HRM destreza *f*, habilidad manual *f*; ~ **system** (*MS*) GEN COMM sistema manual *m*; ~ **union** HRM sindicato de trabajadores manuales *m*; ~ **work** HRM trabajo manual *m*; ~ **worker** HRM trabajador(a) manual *m,f*

manually *adv* GEN COMM manualmente

manufacture[1] *n* GEN COMM, IND confección *f*, construcción *f*, manufactura *f*, *of articles* fabricación *f*

manufacture[2] *vt* GEN COMM, IND fabricar, manufacturar, elaborar; ◆ ~ **under licence** *BrE*, ~ **under license** *AmE* IND *production* fabricar bajo licencia

manufactured[1] *adj* (*mfd*) GEN COMM, IND fabricado, manufacturado

manufactured[2]: **~ goods** *n pl* IND productos elaborados *m pl*, bienes manufacturados *m pl*; **~ home** *n* PROP casa prefabricada *f*

manufacturer *n* (*mfr*) GEN COMM fabricante *mf*; **~'s agent** S&M agente de un fabricante *mf*, representante de un fabricante *mf*; **~'s brand** S&M marca de fábrica *f*; **~'s export agent** IMP/EXP agente de exportaciones del fabricante *mf*; **~'s price** S&M *sales* precio del fabricante *m*; **~'s recommended price** (*MRP*) S&M precio recomendado por el fabricante *m*

manufacturers': **~ and contractors liability insurance** *n* INS *company* seguro de responsabilidad de fabricantes y contratistas *m*; **~ output insurance** *n* INS *company* seguro de la producción para los fabricantes *m*; **~ sales tax** *n* TAX impuesto sobre las ventas de los fabricantes *m*

manufactures *n pl* ECON bienes manufacturados *m pl*, IND manufacturas *f pl*

manufacturing[1] *adj* GEN COMM, IND fabril

manufacturing[2] *n* GEN COMM, IND fabricación *f*; **~ activity** IND actividad fabril *f*; **~ base** IND base industrial *f*; **~-based economy** ECON economía de carácter manufacturero *f*; **~ capacity** IND capacidad de fabricación *f*; **~ control** IND control de producción *m*; **~ cost** ACC, ECON, GEN COMM coste de fabricación *m* (*Esp*), costo de fabricación *m* (*AmL*); **~ department** IND departamento de producción *m*; **~ expenses** *n pl* ACC gastos de fabricación *m pl*, gastos de transformación *m pl*; **~ industries** *n pl* ECON, IND industrias de transformación *f pl*; **~ industry** ECON, IND industria manufacturera *f*; **~ inventory** IND inventario de producción *m*; **~ order** GEN COMM, IND, S&M pedido de fabricación *m*; **~ overheads** *n pl* ACC gastos de fabricación *m pl*, gastos de transformación *m pl*, IND costes indirectos de manufactura *m pl* (*Esp*), costes indirectos de producción *m pl* (*Esp*), costos indirectos de manufactura *m pl* (*AmL*), costos indirectos de producción *m pl* (*AmL*); **~ process** IND proceso de fabricación *m*; **~ and processing profits** ACC, TAX beneficios de fabricación y procesamiento *m pl*; **~ profits** *n pl* ACC, TAX beneficios industriales *m pl*; **~ rights** *n pl* IND, LAW, PATENTS derechos de fabricación *m pl*; **~ sector** IND sector manufacturero *m*; **~ system** IND sistema de fabricación *m*; **~ under licence** BrE, **~ under license** AmE INS, IND fabricación con licencia *f*; **~ workforce** HRM mano de obra de fábrica *f*, personal de fábrica *m*

manuscript *n* (*MS*) MEDIA manuscrito *m*

map *n* COMP mapa *m*, GEN COMM *of city* plano *m*

MAP *abbr* (*market anti-inflation plan*) ECON plan anti-inflacionario del mercado *m*

MAR: **~ policy** *n* INS *of cargo* póliza MAR *f*

margin *n* COMP cobertura *f*, GEN COMM cobertura *f*, margen *m*, STOCK cobertura *f*; **~ account** STOCK cuenta de adelantos *f*; **~ buying** FIN, GEN COMM, S&M, STOCK compra al descubierto *f*; **~ call** STOCK demanda de cobertura suplementaria *f*; **~ call-replenish to initial level** STOCK *currency trading* restablecimiento de la demanda de cobertura complementaria *m*; **~ department** STOCK departamento de margen *m*; **~ deposit** STOCK *currency futures* depósito de garantía *m*; **~ of error** ACC margen de error *m*; **~ gearing** BrE (*cf

margin leverage AmE) STOCK *futures* apalancamiento de margen *m*; **~ leverage** AmE (*cf margin gearing BrE*) STOCK *futures* apalancamiento de margen *m*; **~ maintenance** STOCK conservación del margen *f*; **~ purchase** STOCK compra parcialmente a crédito *f*; **~ requirement** BANK parte de la adquisición de valores pagadera al contado *f*, STOCK margen obligatorio *m*; **~ of safety** GEN COMM margen de seguridad *m*; **~ security** STOCK valor de garantía *m*; **~ shrinkage** ACC reducción del margen *f*; **~ trading** STOCK margen comercial *m*

marginal[1] *adj* GEN COMM marginal

marginal[2]: **~ abatement of tax** *n* TAX reducción marginal del impuesto *f*; **~ account** *n* BANK cuenta marginal *f*; **~ analysis** *n* ACC, ECON, FIN análisis marginal *m*; **~ constituency** *n* POL distrito electoral marginal *m*; **~ cost** *n* ACC, ECON, FIN coste marginal *m* (*Esp*), costo marginal *m* (*AmL*); **~ cost of abatement** *n* ECON coste marginal de supresión *m* (*Esp*), costo marginal de supresión *m* (*AmL*); **~ cost of acquisition** *n* ACC coste marginal de adquisición *m* (*Esp*), costo marginal de adquisición *m* (*AmL*); **~ cost curve** *n* ECON curva de coste marginal *f* (*Esp*), curva de costo marginal *f* (*AmL*); **~ cost pricing** *n* ACC, ECON fijación del precio conforme al coste marginal *f* (*Esp*), fijación del precio conforme al costo marginal *f* (*AmL*); **~ costing** *n* ACC, ECON, FIN cálculo de costes diferenciales *m* (*Esp*), cálculo de costes marginales *m* (*Esp*), cálculo de costos diferenciales *m* (*AmL*), cálculo de costos marginales *m* (*AmL*); **~ costs** *n pl* ACC, ECON, FIN costes marginales *m pl* (*Esp*), costos marginales *m pl* (*AmL*); **~ efficiency of capital** *n* ECON eficiencia marginal del capital *f*; **~ efficiency of investment** *n* ECON eficiencia marginal de la inversión *f*; **~ employment subsidy** *n* ECON subsidio marginal del empleo *m*; **~ firm** *n* ECON empresa marginal *f*; **~ income tax rate** *n* TAX tipo marginal del impuesto sobre la renta *m*; **~ note** *n* ADMIN nota marginal *f*; **~ physical product** *n* ECON producto físico marginal *m*; **~ pricing** *n* ACC, ECON, FIN, S&M fijación marginal de precios *f*; **~ principle of allocation** *n* (*MPA*) ECON principio marginal de la situación *m*; **~ private cost** *n* ECON coste privado marginal *m* (*Esp*), costo privado marginal *m* (*AmL*); **~ private damage** *n* (*MPD*) ECON perjuicios privados no relevantes *m pl*; **~ producer** *n* ECON, IND productor(a) marginal *m,f*; **~ product** *n* ECON, IND producto marginal *m*; **~ product of labor** AmE, **~ product of labour** BrE *n* ECON, IND producto marginal del trabajo *m*; **~ productivity** *n* ECON, IND productividad marginal *f*; **~ productivity theory** *n* ECON teoría marginal de la productividad *f*; **~ profit** *n* ECON beneficio marginal *m*; **~ propensity** *n* ECON propensión marginal *f*; **~ propensity to consume** *n* ECON propensión marginal al consumo *f*; **~ propensity to import** *n* (*MPI*) ECON, IMP/EXP propensión marginal a la importación *f*; **~ propensity to invest** *n* ECON, FIN propensión marginal a la inversión *f*; **~ propensity to save** *n* ECON propensión marginal al ahorro *f*; **~ property** *n* PROP propiedad marginal *f*; **~ rate** *n* TAX tasa marginal *f*; **~ rate of substitution** *n* (*MRS*) ECON tasa marginal de sustitución *f*; **~ rate of transformation** *n* ECON tasa marginal de transformación *f*; **~ return on capital** *n* FIN rendimiento marginal del capital *m*; **~ revenue** *n* ECON, FIN ingreso marginal *m*; **~ revenue product** *n* (*MRP*) ECON ingreso del producto marginal *m*; **~ significance** *n* ECON significación marginal *f*; ~ **social cost** *n* ECON coste social marginal *m* (*Esp*), costo social marginal *m* (*AmL*); ~ **social damage** *n* (*MSD*) ECON perjuicios sociales no relevantes *m pl*; ~ **tax rate** *n* TAX tipo impositivo marginal *m*; ~ **utility** *n* ECON utilidad marginal *f*; ~ **worker** *n* HRM trabajador(a) marginal *m,f*

Marginal: ~ **Utility School of Economics** *n* ECON Escuela Económica de la Utilidad Marginal *f*

marginalism *n* ECON marginalismo *m*

Marginalists *n pl* ECON marginalistas *m pl*

marginalize *vt* GEN COMM marginalizar

marginally *adv* GEN COMM al margen

marine[1] *adj* TRANSP marino

marine[2]: ~ **diesel oil** *n* TRANSP gasóleo marino *m*; ~ **engineer** *n* HRM, TRANSP ingeniero(-a) naval *m,f*; ~ **insurance** *n* INS seguro marítimo *m*; ~ **insurance fraud** *n* INS defraudación de seguro marítimo *f*; ~ **insurance policy** *n* (*MIP*) INS póliza de seguro marítimo *f*; ~ **insurance policy certificate** *n* INS certificado de póliza de seguros marítimos *m*; ~ **piracy** *n* TRANSP piratería marítima *f*; ~ **pollution** *n* ENVIR polución marítima *f*; ~ **risk analyst** *n* HRM, INS analista de riesgo marítimo *mf*; ~ **superintendant** *n* HRM superintendente de marina *mf*

marital: ~ **deduction** *n* TAX deducción fiscal al fallecer un cónyuge *f*; ~ **status** *n* LAW, TAX estado civil *m*

maritime[1] *adj* TRANSP marítimo

maritime[2]: ~ **canal** *n* TRANSP canal marítimo *m*; ~ **fraud** *n* TRANSP fraude marítimo *m*; ~ **fraud prevention** *n* INS, TRANSP prevención del fraude marítimo *f*; ~ **law** *n* LAW derecho marítimo *m*; ~ **lien** *n* LAW gravamen marítimo *m*, privilegio marítimo *m*; ~ **loan** *n* FIN préstamo marítimo *m*; ~ **peril** *n* INS riesgo marítimo *m*; ~ **risk** *n* INS riesgo marítimo *m*; ~ **service** *n* TRANSP servicio marítimo *m*; ~ **shipping** *n* TRANSP transporte marítimo *m*; ~ **terminal** *n* TRANSP terminal marítima *f*; ~ **trade** *n* GEN COMM negocio marítimo *m*, comercio marítimo *m*

Maritime: ~ **Industrial Development Area** *n* (*MIDA*) IND Área de Desarrollo Industrial Marítimo *f*; ~ **Pollution** *n* (*MARPOL*) ENVIR *1978 convention* programa internacional de Naciones Unidas para tratar la contaminación del petróleo en el medio ambiente marino; ~ **Transport Committee** *n* (*MTC*) TRANSP *OECD* comité de transporte marítimo

mark[1] *n* PATENTS, STOCK marca *f*; ~**down** GEN COMM descuento en precios *m*, S&M *sales, in price* reducción *f*; ~ **to market** STOCK acomodación continua al mercado *f*; ~**to-the-market** STOCK liquidación diaria de pérdidas y ganancias *f*; ~**up** GEN COMM margen de utilidad *m*, MEDIA *print* margen de utilidad *m*, S&M *of prices* subida *f*; ~**up inflation** ECON margen de beneficio de la inflación *m*; ~**up pricing** ECON fijación del precio al coste medio recargado *f* (*Esp*), fijación del precio al costo medio recargado *f* (*AmL*); ◆ **no** ~ (*n/m*) TRANSP *shipping* sin marca; ~ **to mark** *jarg* STOCK valor por valor *m*

mark[2]: ~ **stock** *phr* ACC cotizar valores en bolsa; ~ **to the market** *phr* STOCK ajustar al valor del mercado, liquidar diariamente pérdidas y ganancias

mark down *vt* S&M *sales, goods* rebajar, reducir el precio de

mark off *vt* ACC cancelar

mark up *vt* S&M *prices* aumentar

marked[1] *adj* GEN COMM *decline, difference* marcado; ~**to-market** STOCK *futures* ajustado al valor de mercado

marked[2]: ~ **check** *AmE*, ~ **cheque** *BrE* *n* BANK, FIN cheque confirmado *m*; ~ **price** *n* S&M precio marcado *m*

market[1]: ~**driven** *adj* S&M impulsado por el mercado; ~**oriented** *adj* S&M orientado al mercado; ~**sensitive** *adj* S&M sensible al mercado

market[2] *n* GEN COMM mercado *m*;

~ a ~ **acceptance** S&M aceptación del mercado *f*; ~ **adjustment** ECON ajuste del mercado *m*; ~ **aggregation** ECON concentración del mercado *f*; ~ **aim** S&M meta comercial *f*; ~ **analysis** S&M, STOCK análisis de mercado *m*; ~ **analyst** HRM analista de mercados *mf*; ~ **anti-inflation plan** (*MAP*) ECON plan antiinflacionario del mercado *m*; ~ **appraisal** GEN COMM, S&M *market research* estimación del mercado *f*; ~ **attrition** S&M desgaste del mercado *m*; ~ **awareness** S&M conocimiento del mercado *m*;

~ b ~ **balance of payments** ECON balanza de pagos del mercado *f*; ~ **base** S&M base del mercado *f*; ~ **basket** ECON, GEN COMM cesta de la compra *f*; ~ **behavior** *AmE*, ~ **behaviour** *BrE* S&M comportamiento del mercado *m*;

~ c ~ **capitalization** GEN COMM capitalización de mercado *f*, STOCK capitalización bursátil *f*; ~ **capitalization index** ECON, STOCK índice de capitalización bursátil *m* (*ICB*); ~ **clearing** ECON desatascamiento del mercado *m*; ~ **clearing price** ECON precios que devuelven el equilibrio al mercado; ~ **close** ACC, BANK, FIN, GEN COMM, STOCK cierre del mercado *m*; ~ **comparison approach** GEN COMM, PROP método de comparación de mercados *m*; ~ **concentration** ECON concentración de mercados *f*; ~ **conditions** *n pl* GEN COMM condiciones del mercado *f pl*; ~ **confidence** S&M confianza del mercado *f*; ~ **connection** S&M conexión en el mercado *f*; ~ **correction** STOCK corrección del mercado *f*; ~ **coverage** S&M cobertura de mercado *f*; ~ **creation** S&M creación de mercado *f*; ~ **cycle** GEN COMM ciclo del mercado *m*;

~ d ~ **day** STOCK día del mercado *m*; ~ **dealing** FIN operación de mercado *f*; ~ **demand** ECON demanda de mercado *f*; ~ **development** S&M desarrollo de mercado *m*; ~ **disclosure** STOCK información sobre el mercado *f*; ~ **discrimination coefficient** ECON coeficiente de discriminación del mercado *m*; ~ **distortion** ECON distorsión del mercado *f*; ~ **downturn** STOCK fase de depresión del mercado *f*;

~ e ~ **economy** ECON, POL economía de mercado *f*; ~ **entry** S&M entrada en el mercado *f*; ~ **entry guarantee scheme** S&M esquema garante de la entrada en el mercado *m*; ~ **entry option** IMP/EXP opción de entrada en el mercado *f*; ~ **environment** S&M entorno del mercado *m*; ~ **equilibrium** ECON equilibrio del mercado *m*; ~ **evaluation** S&M evaluación del mercado *f*; ~ **expansion** S&M expansión del mercado *f*; ~ **exploration** S&M exploración del mercado *f*;

~ f ~ **failure** ECON fallo del mercado *m*; ~ **fluctuation** ECON, GEN COMM fluctuación de mercado *f*; ~ **forces** *n pl* ECON, S&M fuerzas del mercado *f pl*; ~ **forecast** S&M perspectivas de mercado *f pl*, pronóstico del mercado *m*; ~ **form** ECON, S&M estructura del mercado *f*; ~ **fragmentation** ECON fragmentación del mercado *f*, hueco en el mercado *m*;

~ g ~ **gap** S&M brecha en el mercado *f*; ~ **gardener** *BrE* (*cf* truck farmer *AmE*) ECON *agricultural* hortelano(-a) *m,f*; **~ gardening** *BrE* (*cf truck farming AmE*) ECON *agricultural* horticultura comercial *f*;

~ h **~ holding** STOCK *pricing strategy technique* dominio del mercado *m*; **~ hours** *n pl* STOCK horario del mercado *m*;

~ i **~–if-touched order** (*MIT order*) STOCK orden de compra o venta si se alcanza un precio *f* (*orden MIT*); **~ index** STOCK índice del mercado *m*; **~ indicator** GEN COMM indicador del mercado *m*; **~ intelligence** S&M información sobre el mercado *f*; **~ interest rate** ECON, FIN tipo de interés del mercado *m*;

~ l **~ leader** GEN COMM, S&M artículo líder *m*, líder del mercado *mf*, STOCK valor bursátil importante *m*; **~ leadership** S&M liderazgo del mercado *m*; **~ letter** STOCK carta circular de información sobre valores *f*; **~ level** STOCK nivel del mercado de valores *m*;

~ m **~ maker** STOCK creador(a) de mercados *m,f*, sociedad de contrapartida *f*; **~ management** S&M dirección del mercado *f*, gerencia del mercado *f*, gestión del mercado *f*; **~ mechanism** ECON mecanismo del mercado *m*;

~ n **~ niche** S&M nicho de mercado *m*, hueco abierto para el mercado de un producto;

~ o **~ objective** S&M objetivo de mercado *m*; **~ opening** S&M apertura del mercado *f*; **~ opportunity** S&M oportunidad de mercado *f*; **~ order** STOCK orden al mercado *f*; **~ order on the close** (*MOC*) STOCK orden de mercado al cierre *f*; **~ out clause** BANK, INS, LAW cláusula de abandono de mercado *f*;

~ p **~ penetration** S&M penetración en el mercado *f*; **~ place** GEN COMM, S&M área comercial *f*; **~ plan** S&M plan de mercado *m*; **~ planning** S&M planificación de mercado *f*; **~ position** STOCK posición en el mercado *f*; **~ potential** S&M potencial del mercado *m*; **~ power** ECON poder de mercado *m*; **~ presence** S&M presencia en el mercado *f*; **~ price** GEN COMM precio de mercado *m*; **~ pricing** GEN COMM determinación de precios del mercado *f*, fijación de precios del mercado *f*; **~ profile** GEN COMM, S&M perfil de mercado *m*; **~ prospects** *n pl* S&M perspectivas de mercado *f pl*; **~ prospects service** S&M servicio de perspectivas de mercado *m*; **~ psychology** S&M psicología de mercado *f*;

~ r **~ rate** STOCK tipo de interés del mercado *m*; **~ rate of discount** FIN, STOCK tipo de descuento del mercado *m*; **~ rating** S&M índice del mercado *m*; **~ reach** S&M alcance de mercado *m*; **~ receptiveness** S&M, STOCK receptividad del mercado *f*; **~ recognition** S&M reconocimiento de mercado *m*; **~ recovery** GEN COMM, STOCK recuperación del mercado *f*; **~ rent** ECON renta de mercado *f*, PROP alquiler de mercado *m*, arriendo de mercado *m*; **~ report** S&M informe sobre el mercado *m* (*Esp*), reporte sobre el mercado *m* (*AmL*); **~ research** S&M estudio de mercado *m*; **~ resistance** S&M resistencia del mercado *f*; **~ review** FIN análisis del mercado *m*, revisión del mercado *f*; **~ rigger** STOCK suceso manipulador del mercado *m*; **~ rigging** STOCK manipulación del mercado *f*; **~ risk** STOCK riesgo de mercado *m*; **~ risk premium** STOCK prima por riesgo de mercado *f*;

~ s **~ saturation** GEN COMM, S&M saturación del mercado *f*; **~ sealing** GEN COMM cierre del mercado *m*; **~ sector** S&M sector de mercado *m*; **~ segmentation** S&M segmentación de mercado *f*; **~ selection overseas** ECON selección de mercados extranjeros *f*; **~ sensitivity** GEN COMM, S&M sensibilidad del mercado *f*; **~ share** ECON, S&M cuota de mercado *f*, participación en el

mercado *f*; **~ situation** GEN COMM situación del mercado *f*; **~ size** STOCK amplitud del mercado *f*; **~ skimming** S&M *pricing* esquilmado del mercado *m*; **~ slump** ECON, STOCK caída en picado del mercado *f*, hundimiento del mercado *m*; **~ structure** ECON, S&M estructura del mercado *f*; **~ study** GEN COMM, S&M estudio de mercado *m*; **~ support** S&M apoyo del mercado *m*; **~ survey** S&M estudio de mercado *m*; **~ system** GEN COMM sistema de mercado *m*;

~ t **~ target selection** S&M selección de objetivos de mercado *f*; **~ test** S&M prueba de mercado *f*; **~ testing** S&M prueba de mercado *f*; **~ timing** STOCK sincronización del mercado *f*; **~ tone** STOCK tono del mercado *m*; **~ transparency** GEN COMM transparencia del mercado *f*; **~ trend** ECON, GEN COMM, S&M tendencia del mercado *f*;

~ v **~ valuation** STOCK valoración de mercado *f*; **~ value** GEN COMM valor comercial *m*, valor de mercado *m*; **~ value clause** INS, PROP cláusula de valor en mercado *f*; **~ value-weighted index** STOCK índice de valores estimados del mercado *m*; **~ view** STOCK panorama del mercado *m*;

~ w **~ watcher** GEN COMM observador(a) del mercado *m,f*; **~ weight** S&M peso del mercado *m*

market[3] *vt* GEN COMM comercializar

market[4]: **away from the ~** *phr* STOCK en sentido contrario al mercado; **no ~** *phr* STOCK *broker's term* sin mercado; **on the ~** *phr* PROP en el mercado; **at the ~ call** *phr BrE* STOCK según la demanda; **at the ~ price** *phr* FIN, STOCK a precio de mercado *m*

Market: ~ Eye *n* STOCK organismo de vigilancia de la Bolsa de Valores de Londres; **~ and Opinion Research International** *n* (*MORI*) POL, S&M compañía británica de sondeo de la opinión pública, ≈ Demoscopia *m* (*Esp*); **~ Research Corporation of America** *n* (*MRCA*) S&M sociedad estadounidense de estudios de mercado; **~ and Trading Information System** *n BrE* (*MANTIS*) STOCK sistema de información de la Bolsa de Valores de Londres para la ejecución automática de transacciones

marketability *n* STOCK bursatilidad *f*

marketable[1] *adj* GEN COMM comerciable, comercializable, vendible

marketable[2]: **~ bond** *n* STOCK obligación ordinaria *f*; **~ discharge permit** *n* ENVIR, GEN COMM concesión transferible *f*; **~ securities** *n pl* STOCK títulos negociables *m pl*; **~ title** *n BrE* PROP título negociable *m*; **~ value** *n* S&M valor comercial *m*

marketeer *n* HRM experto(-a) en marketing *m,f* (*Esp*), experto(-a) en mercadotecnia *m,f* (*AmL*), POL partidario(-a) del Mercado Común *m,f*

marketing *n* S&M marketing *m*; **~ agreement** S&M acuerdo comercial *m*; **~ appropriation** S&M apropiación marketing *f*; **~ audit** S&M auditoría de marketing *f*; **~ authorization** S&M *for pharmaceuticals* autorización de comercialización *f*; **~ budget** S&M presupuesto de marketing *m*; **~ chain** S&M cadena de marketing *f*; **~ channel** GEN COMM, S&M canal de comercialización *m*; **~ communications** *n pl* S&M comunicaciones de marketing *f pl*; **~ communications channel** S&M canal de comunicaciones de marketing *m*; **~ communications manager** MGMNT, S&M director(a) de comunicaciones de marketing *m,f*; **~ communications mix** S&M combinación de estrategias de comunicaciones de marketing *f*; **~ concept** S&M concepto de marketing *m*; ~ **conference** S&M conferencia de marketing *f*; ~ **cost** S&M coste de marketing *m* (*Esp*), costo de marketing *m* (*AmL*); ~ **cost variance** S&M variación del coste de marketing *f* (*Esp*), variación del costo de marketing *f* (*AmL*); ~ **department** S&M departamento de marketing *m*; ~ **director** HRM, MGMNT, S&M director(a) de marketing *m,f* (*Esp*), director(a) de mercadotecnia *m,f* (*AmL*); ~ **executive** HRM ejecutivo(-a)) de marketing *m,f* (*Esp*), ejecutivo(-a) de mercadotecnia *m,f* (*AmL*); ~ **information system** (*MIS*) S&M *research* sistema de información de marketing *m*; ~ **intelligence** S&M información de marketing *f*; ~ **manager** S&M director(a) de marketing *m,f* (*Esp*), director(a) de mercadotecnia *m,f* (*AmL*); ~ **mix** S&M mezcla de estrategias marketing *f*; ~ **model** S&M modelo de marketing *m*; ~ **objective** S&M objetivo de marketing *m*; ~ **officer** HRM administrador(a) de marketing *m,f* (*Esp*), administrador(a) de mercadotecnia *m,f* (*AmL*); ~ **orientation** S&M orientación de marketing *f*; ~ **plan** S&M plan de marketing *m*; ~ **policy** S&M política comercial *f*; ~ **profile** S&M perfil de marketing *m*; ~ **research** S&M investigación de mercado *f*; ~ **and sales plan** S&M plan de marketing y ventas *m*; ~ **service** S&M servicio de marketing *m*; ~ **services manager** HRM, MGMNT, S&M director(a) de servicios de marketing *m,f*; ~ **strategy** S&M estrategia de marketing *f*; ~ **tool** S&M herramienta de marketing *f*; ~ **transport operator** GEN COMM agente de transporte multimodal *m,f*

marketplace *n* GEN COMM mercado *m*, plaza comercial *f*

marking *n* FIN marcación *f*

Markov: ~ **chain model** *n* MATH modelo de cadena de Markov *m*

MARPOL *abbr* (*Maritime Pollution*) ENVIR *1978 convention* programa internacional de Naciones Unidas para tratar la contaminación del petróleo en el medio ambiente marino

marriage: ~ **allowance** *n* TAX deducción por matrimonio *f*; ~ **breakdown** *n* LAW ruptura del matrimonio *f*; ~ **deduction** *n* TAX deducción por matrimonio *f*; ~ **penalty** *n* TAX recargo por matrimonio *m*

married[1] *adj* LAW casado

married[2]: ~ **couples' allowance** *n* BrE TAX desgravación al matrimonio *f*; ~ **exemption** *n* TAX exención por matrimonio *f*; ~ **man** *n* ADMIN, LAW *administrative*, TAX hombre casado *m*; ~ **print** *n* S&M copia cero cinematográfica *f*

marry *vt* LAW, STOCK casar

marry up *vt* S&M *sales, auction* conjugar

Marshall: ~ **Plan** *n* ECON plan Marshall *m*

Marshall-Lerner: ~ **condition** *n* ECON condición de Marshall-Lerner *f*

mart *n* AmE infrml S&M centro comercial *m*

martingale *n* MATH martingala *f*

Marxian: ~ **economics** *n* ECON economía marxista *f*; ~ **school** *n* ECON escuela Marxista *f*

Marxism *n* ECON, POL marxismo *m*

mask *vt* S&M *advertising* ocultar

Maslow: ~'**s hierarchy of needs** *n* MGMNT *motivation theory* jerarquía de necesidades de Maslow *f*

mass[1]: ~ **advertising** *n* S&M publicidad de masas *f*; ~ **appeal** *n* S&M atracción masiva *f*; ~ **communication** *n* MEDIA comunicación de masas *f*; ~ **dismissal** *n* HRM despido colectivo *m*; ~ **mailing** *n* COMP carteo masivo

m; ~ **market** *n* S&M mercado de masas *m*; ~ **marketing** *n* S&M marketing de masa *m*; ~ **media** *n pl* MEDIA medios de comunicación *m pl*, medios de comunicación al público *m pl*; ~ **memory** *n* COMP memoria de masa *f*; ~ **production** *n* IND fabricación en serie *f*, producción en masa *f*, producción en gran escala *f*; ~ **rapid transit** *n* (*MRT*) TRANSP tránsito rápido masivo *m*; ~ **redundancy** *n* HRM despido masivo *m*; ~ **risk** *n* INS riesgo colectivo *m*; ~ **storage** *n* COMP almacenamiento de gran capacidad *m*, almacenamiento masivo *m*; ~ **storage device** *n* COMP dispositivo de memoria masiva *m*; ~ **transit railroad** *n* AmE (*MTR, cf mass transit railway BrE*) TRANSP ferrocarril de tránsito masivo *m*; ~ **transit railway** *n* BrE (*MTR cf mass transit railroad AmE*) TRANSP ferrocarril de tránsito masivo *m*; ~ **transit system** *n* TRANSP sistema de transporte colectivo *m*, sistema de transporte público *m*; ~ **unemployment** *n* ECON, HRM, POL, WEL desempleo masivo *m*

mass[2]: ~-**produce** *vt* IND fabricar en serie

massage: ~ **the figures** *phr* ACC, FIN maquillar los números

massive *adj* GEN COMM masivo

master *n* MEDIA *copy* original *m*, TRANSP *ship* capitán *m*; ~ **air waybill** (*MAWB*) IMP/EXP, TRANSP conocimiento de embarque aéreo del capitán *m*; ~ **budget** ACC, ECON, FIN presupuesto maestro *m*, presupuesto original *m*, presupuesto principal *m*; ~ **card** COMP tarjeta maestra *f*; ~'**s certificate** TRANSP certificado de patrón *m*; ~ **change** (*MC*) TRANSP *aviation* cambio de comandante *m*; ~ **copy** COMP, GEN COMM copia maestra *f*; ~ **document** COMP documento maestro *m*; ~ **file** COMP, GEN COMM fichero maestro *m*; ~ **key** COMP tecla maestra *f*; ~ **lease** PROP arrendamiento principal *m*; ~ **limited partnership** GEN COMM sociedad limitada principal *f*; ~ **owner** HRM propietario(-a) principal *m,f*; ~ **pallet** TRANSP bandeja de carga estibadora *f*; ~ **plan** ECON plan básico *m*, MGMNT plan maestro *m*, plan principal *m*; ~ **policy** AmE INS *company* póliza colectiva *f*; ~-**servant rule** LAW *commercial* responsabilidad subsidiaria *f*

Master: ~ **of Business Administration** *n* (*MBA*) HRM, WEL Master en Dirección y Administración de Empresas *m* (*MBA*); ~ **of Commerce** *n* (*MCom*) WEL Master de Comercio *m*; ~ **of Economics** *n* (*MEcon*) WEL Master de Economía *m*; ~ **of Science** *n* (*MSc*) WEL Master de Ciencias *m*

masthead *n* MEDIA *in newspaper* mancheta *f*

MAT *abbr* (*multiple access time*) COMP tiempo de acceso múltiple *m*

match *vt* GEN COMM *results* igualar, S&M *quality*, STOCK comparar

match up to *vt* GEN COMM igualar

matched[1] *adj* GEN COMM igualado

matched[2]: ~ **book** *n* STOCK libro equilibrado *m*; ~ **orders** *n pl* STOCK órdenes casadas *f pl*, órdenes emparejadas *f pl*; ~ **sale-purchase transaction** *n* STOCK compra y venta coincidente *f*; ~ **samples** *n pl* S&M muestras emparejadas *f pl*; ~ **trade** *n* STOCK transacción combinada de compraventa *f*

matching: ~ **grant** *n* FIN subvención paralela *f*; ~ **principle** *n* ACC *costs with revenues* principio de equilibrio *m*; ~ **of a product line** *n* MEDIA armonización de una gama de productos *f*

material[1] *adj* GEN COMM material

material[2] *n* ENVIR materia *f*, GEN COMM *information* material *m*; ~ **balance** ECON equilibrio volumétrico *m*; ~ **barrier** POL *EU* barrera física *f*, barrera material *f*; ~ **circumstance** INS *marine* circunstancia material *f*; ~ **fact** GEN COMM hecho material *m*; ~ **good** ECON, IND bien material *m*; ~ **interest** STOCK *in company* interés material *m*; ~ **purchase** FIN, GEN COMM, S&M, STOCK compra de materias primas *f*; ~ **representation** INS *marine* declaración y presentación material de hechos *f*

materialism *n* POL materialismo *m*

materiality *n* ACC *accounting reports* importancia relativa *f*, materialidad *f*; ~ **level** ACC nivel de importancia relativa *m*, nivel de materialidad *m*

materialize *vi* GEN COMM materializarse

materialized: ~ **labor** *AmE jarg*, ~ **labour** *BrE jarg n* HRM mano de obra concreta *f*

materials: ~ **accounting** *n* ACC contabilidad de materiales *f*; ~ **handling** *n* GEN COMM movimiento de materiales *m*; ~ **management** *n* TRANSP administración de materiales *f*, gestión de materiales *f*; ~ **transfer note** *n* GEN COMM hoja de transferencia de materiales *f* (*Esp*), relación de transferencia de materiales *f* (*AmL*)

maternity: ~ **allowance** *n* HRM, WEL bonificación por maternidad *f*; ~ **benefit** *n* HRM, WEL subsidio por maternidad *m*; ~ **leave** *n* HRM licencia de maternidad *m*, baja de maternidad *f* (*infrml*); ~ **pay** *n* HRM, WEL paga por maternidad *f*; ~ **protection** *n* HRM, INS protección a la maternidad *f*

mate: ~**'s receipt** *n* (*MR*) TRANSP *for loaded cargo* billete de embarque *m*, recibo de embarque *m*

mathematical: ~ **programming** *n* COMP, MATH programación matemática *f*

matrix: ~ **analysis** *n* ECON análisis matricial *m*; ~ **management** *n* MATH gestión por matrices *f*, MGMNT dirección de la matriz *f*, gerencia de la matriz *f*; ~ **organization** *n* MGMNT organización matriz *f*, organización matricial *f*; ~ **printer** *n* COMP impresora matricial *f*; ~ **trading** *n* STOCK intercambio de valores *m*

matter *n* GEN COMM, MGMNT *affair* asunto *m*; ~ **of urgency** GEN COMM asunto urgente *m*; ◆ **the ~ in hand** GEN COMM el asunto de que se trata; **the ~ is closed** GEN COMM el asunto está concluido

mature[1] *adj* FIN, STOCK pagadero, vencido

mature[2]: ~ **economy** *n* ECON economía completa *f*, economía madura *f*; ~ **market** *n* S&M, STOCK mercado maduro *m*

mature[3] *vi* ECON, FIN, STOCK vencer

matured[1] *adj* ECON, FIN, STOCK vencido

matured[2]: ~ **bond** *n* STOCK obligación vencida *f*; ~ **capital** *n* ACC, ECON, FIN capital vencido *m*; ~ **coupon** *n* STOCK cupón vencido *m*; ~ **debt** *n* FIN deuda vencida *f*; ~ **endowment** *n* INS *personal* seguro dotal vencido *m*

maturing: ~ **security** *n* STOCK título de próximo vencimiento *m*; ~ **value** *n* STOCK valor cercano a su vencimiento *m*

maturity *n* BANK, GEN COMM, ECON, STOCK vencimiento *m*; ~ **bands** *n pl* ECON bandas de vencimiento *f pl*; ~ **date** BANK, ECON, STOCK fecha de vencimiento *f*; ~ **mismatch** BANK vencimiento desigual *m*; ~ **structure of debt** BANK, ECON estructura de los vencimientos de la deuda *f*; ~ **value** STOCK valor al vencimiento *m*; ~ **yield** STOCK beneficio al vencimiento *m*

MAWB *abbr* (*master air waybill*) IMP/EXP, TRANSP conocimiento de embarque aéreo del capitán *m*

max. *abbr* (*maximum*) GEN COMM máximo

maximal[1] *adj* MATH máximo

maximal[2]: ~ **awareness** *n* S&M conciencia máxima *f*

maximin *n* ECON maximin *m*

maximization *n* GEN COMM maximización *f*

maximize *vt* GEN COMM maximizar

maximum[1] *adj* (*max.*) GEN COMM máximo

maximum[2] *n* GEN COMM máximo *m*; ~ **allowable deduction** TAX deducción máxima permitida *f*; ~ **brand exposure** S&M exposición máxima de la marca *f*; ~ **capacity** IND capacidad máxima *f*; ~ **capital gains mutual fund** STOCK fondo de pensiones de ganancias máximas de capital *m*; ~ **claim** TAX reclamación máxima *f*; ~ **coverage** STOCK cobertura máxima *f*; ~ **efficiency** ECON máxima eficiencia *f*; ~ **likelihood estimator** (*MLE*) MATH estimador de verosimilitud máxima *m*; ~ **load** TRANSP límite de carga *m*; ~ **output** ECON, IND producción máxima *f*; ~ **permissible concentration** (*MPC*) ECON concentración máxima admisible *f*; ~ **practical capacity** ECON capacidad máxima práctica *f*; ~ **price** ECON, GEN COMM, S&M, STOCK precio máximo *m*; ~ **price fluctuation** STOCK fluctuación máxima del precio *f*; ~ **rate** GEN COMM tasa máxima *f*; ~ **return** BANK, FIN, STOCK beneficio máximo *m*; ~ **risk** BANK, FIN, STOCK *options* riesgo máximo *m*; ~ **stock** ACC, S&M existencias máximas *f pl*; ◆ **up to a ~ of** GEN COMM hasta un máximo de

Mayday *n* STOCK *New York Stock Exchange* mayday *m*

Mb *abbr* (*megabyte*) COMP Mb (*megabyte*)

MBA *abbr* (*Master of Business Administration*) HRM, WEL MBA (*Master en Dirección y Administración de Empresas*)

MBIM *abbr* (*Member of the British Institute of Management*) MGMNT miembro del instituto británico de dirección

MBO *abbr* GEN COMM, MGMNT (*management buyout*) CEP (*compra por ejecutivos*), (*management by objectives*) administración por objetivos *f*, dirección por objetivos *f*, gestión por objetivos *f*

MBS *abbr* (*mortgage-backed security*) FIN, STOCK título respaldado por una hipoteca *m*, valor respaldado por una hipoteca *m*

MBWA *abbr* (*management by walking around*) MGMNT dirección por contacto directo *f*

MCA *abbr* FIN (*monetary compensation amount*) cantidad monetaria compensatoria *f*, monto de la compensación monetaria *m*, MGMNT (*Management Consultants Association*) asociación de consultorías de administración

M-CATS *abbr* (*municipal certificate of accrual on treasury securities*) STOCK certificado municipal de acumulación de bonos del tesoro *m*

McFadden: ~ **Act** *n* *AmE* BANK, LAW Ley McFadden *f*

mcht *abbr* (*merchant*) BANK, GEN COMM, comerciante *mf*

mchy *abbr* (*machinery*) GEN COMM maquinaria *f*

MCM *abbr* (*multi-country economic model*) ECON modelo económico multipaís *m*

MCO *abbr* (*miscellaneous charges order*) TRANSP orden por gastos varios *f*

MCom *abbr* (*Master of Commerce*) WEL Master de Comercio *m*

MCSI: ~ **Index** *n* (*Morgan Stanley Capital International*

Index) STOCK parámetros internacionales para la comparación de índices de futuros financieros

MCT *abbr* TAX (*mainstream corporation tax*) impuesto corporativo total *m*, TRANSP (*minimum connecting time*) tiempo mínimo de conexión *m*

MD *abbr* (*managing director*) HRM, MGMNT director(a) gerente *m,f*, consejero(-a) delegado(-a) *m,f*, director(a) administrativo(-a) *m,f*

MDW *abbr* (*measured daywork*) HRM jornada controlada *f*

meal: ~ **allowance** *n* HRM subsidio para comida *m*; ~ **ticket** *n AmE* (*cf luncheon voucher, LV BrE*) HRM vale de comida *m*

meals: ~ **on wheels** *n pl* WEL comidas a domicilio *f pl*

mean *n* MATH media *f*; ~ **amount on deposit** INS cantidad media en depósito *f*; ~ **audit date** ACC, S&M fecha media de auditoría *f*; ~ **cost** ACC coste medio *m* (*Esp*), costo medio *m* (*AmL*); ~ **deviation** MATH desviación media *f*; ~ **effective pressure** (*mep*) GEN COMM potencia efectiva media *f*; ~ **low water** (*MLW*) TRANSP bajamar media *f*; ~ **sea level** TRANSP nivel medio del mar *m*; ~ **time** (*MT*) GEN COMM tiempo medio *m* (*TM*); ~ **time between failures** (*MTBF*) COMP tiempo medio entre averías *m*; ~ **value** MATH valor medio *m*

means *n pl* ECON recursos *m pl*, medios *m pl*; ~ **of payment** *n* ECON medios de pago *m pl*; ~ **test** *n* TAX, WEL comprobación de medios de vida *f*; ◆ **as a ~ of** GEN COMM como medio de; **have the ~ to** GEN COMM contar con los medios para; **live beyond one's ~** GEN COMM vivir por encima de las posibilidades

measure¹ *n* GEN COMM, S&M, TRANSP *nautical, cargo* medida *f*; ~ **of control** ECON *prices* medida de control *f*; ~ **of economic welfare** (*MEW*) ECON, HRM *econometrics* medida de la riqueza económica *f*; ~ **of indemnity** INS cuantificación de la indemnización *f*; ◆ **as a precautionary ~** GEN COMM como medida precautoria

measure² *vt* ECON medir; ◆ ~ **sb's performance** HRM medir el desempeño de alguien

measured: ~ **daywork** *n* (*MDW*) HRM *job evaluation* jornada controlada *f*

measurement *n* (*met*) GEN COMM, MATH, TRANSP medición *f*; ~ **bill** BANK, ECON, FIN, GEN COMM certificado de arqueo *m*; ~ **freight** TRANSP flete por volumen *m*; ~ **goods** *n pl* TRANSP artículos tarifados por volumen *m pl*; ~ **ton** TRANSP *shipping* tonelada de arqueo *f*

measures: **take ~** *phr* GEN COMM tomar medidas

measuring: ~ **tape** *n* GEN COMM cinta para medir *f*

mechanical: ~ **binding** *n* S&M encuadernación mecánica *f*; ~ **data** *n* S&M datos mecánicos *m pl*; ~ **handling equipment** *n* (*MHE*) TRANSP *cargo* equipo de manipulación mecánica *m*; ~ **tint** *n* S&M tinte mecánico *m*

mechanically: ~ **ventilated container** *n* TRANSP contenedor de ventilación mecánica *m*

mechanic: ~**'s lien** *n* IND dominio de la mecánica *m*, PROP privilegio del constructor *m*

mechanism *n* GEN COMM, IND mecanismo *m*

mechanization *n* IND mecanización *f*; ~ **of cargo handling** TRANSP mecanización de la manipulación de la carga *f*

mechanize *vt* GEN COMM, IND mecanizar

mechanized *adj* GEN COMM, IND mecanizado

MEcon *abbr* (*Master of Economics*) WEL Master de Economía *m*

media¹ *adj* MEDIA medios de comunicación *m pl*; ~ **independent** MEDIA, S&M independiente de los medios de comunicación

media² *n pl* MEDIA medios de comunicación *m pl*; ~ **analysis** *n* MEDIA, S&M análisis de los medios de comunicación *m*; ~ **analyst** *n* MEDIA, S&M analista de medios de comunicación *mf*; ~ **broker** *n* MEDIA, S&M agente de publicidad *mf*; ~ **budget** *n* MEDIA presupuesto de medios de comunicación *m*; ~ **buyer** *n* HRM, MEDIA, S&M *advertising* comprador(a) de medios de comunicación *m,f*; ~ **buying** *n* MEDIA, S&M *advertising* compra de espacios en medios de comunicación *f*; ~ **commission** *n* MEDIA, S&M comisión de los medios de comunicación *f*; ~ **coverage** *n* MEDIA, S&M cobertura en los medios de comunicación *f*; ~ **evaluation** *n* MEDIA, S&M evaluación de medios de comunicación *f*; ~ **event** *n* MEDIA acontecimiento mediático *m*; ~ **fragmentation** *n* MEDIA, S&M *advertising* fragmentación de los medios de comunicación *f*; ~ **mix** *n* MEDIA, S&M combinación de estrategias de medios de comunicación *f*; ~ **options** MEDIA, S&M *advertising* posibles medios de comunicación *m pl*; ~ **owners** S&M propietarios de los medios de comunicación *m pl*; ~ **plan** *n* MEDIA, S&M *advertising* plan de medios de comunicación *m*; ~ **planner** *n* MEDIA, S&M *advertising* planificador(a) de medios de comunicación *m,f*; ~ **planning** *n* MEDIA *advertising*, S&M planificación de medios *f*; ~ **relation** *n* MEDIA, S&M relación con los medios de comunicación *f*; ~ **research** *n* MEDIA, S&M estudio de medios de comunicación *m*; ~ **schedule** *n* MEDIA programa de medios de comunicación *m*; ~ **selection** *n* MEDIA, S&M selección de medios de comunicación *f*; ~ **strategy** *n* S&M estrategia de los medios de comunicación *f*; ~ **studio** *n* COMMS locutorio radiofónico *m*; ~ **weight** *n* MEDIA, S&M *advertising* ponderación de los medios de comunicación *f*

median *n* MATH mediana *f*; ~ **amount** TAX cantidad media *f*; ~ **rule** GEN COMM regla de la mediana *f*

mediate *vi* GEN COMM, HRM *between parties* mediar

mediation *n* GEN COMM, HRM mediación *f*

mediator *n* GEN COMM, HRM mediador(a) *m,f*

medical¹ *adj* GEN COMM médico

medical²: ~ **assistance** *n* WEL asistencia médica *f*; ~ **care insurance plan** *n* INS, WEL plan de seguro de gastos médicos *m*; ~ **costs** *n pl* INS, WEL costes médicos *m pl* (*Esp*), costos médicos *m pl* (*AmL*); ~ **engineering** *n* IND ingeniería médica *f*; ~ **examination** *n* WEL examen médico *m*; ~ **expense credit** *n* INS, WEL desgravación de gastos de atención médica *f*; ~ **expenses** *n pl* TAX gastos médicos *m pl*; ~ **grounds** *n pl* HRM razones médicas *f pl*; ~ **insurance** *n* INS seguro médico *m*; ~ **officer of health** *n* (*MOH*) HRM oficial(a) médico(-a) *m,f*

Mediterranean: ~ **basin** *n* GEN COMM cuenca del Mediterráneo *f*; ~ **bloc** *n* GEN COMM bloque mediterráneo *m*

medium¹: ~**-dated** *adj* STOCK con vencimiento a medio plazo

medium² *n* COMMS, GEN COMM *of communication* medio *m*; ~ **of account** ACC instrumento de cuenta *m*; ~ **of exchange** ECON medio de cambio *m*; ~ **frequency radiotelephony** (*RTm*) COMMS, MEDIA, TRANSP *shipping* radiotelefonía de frecuencia media *f*; **~ of redemption** ECON sistema de amortización *m*; **in the ~ term** BANK, FIN, GEN COMM a medio plazo; **~-term credit** BANK, FIN crédito a medio plazo *m*; **~-term deposit** BANK, FIN depósito a medio plazo *m*; **~-term Euronote** STOCK *money market* Eurobillete a medio plazo *m*; **~-term financial strategy** (*MTFS*) ECON estrategia financiera a medio plazo *f*; **~-term instrument** STOCK instrumento a medio plazo *m*; **~-term loan** (*MTL*) BANK, FIN préstamo a medio plazo *m*; **~-term note** (*MTN*) BANK bono a medio plazo *m*, documento a medio plazo *m*, nota a medio plazo *f*

mediums *n pl* STOCK medios *m pl*

meet *vt* ACC, FIN *costs* sufragar, satisfacer, cubrir, GEN COMM *requirements* atender, *targets* sostener, INS cubrir, MGMNT satisfacer, STOCK cubrir; ◆ **~ a claim** GEN COMM atender una reclamación; **~ costs** GEN COMM saldar costes (*Esp*), saldar costos (*AmL*); **~ a draft** FIN, LAW atender una letra; **~ a goal** MGMNT cumplir un objetivo; **~ the needs of** GEN COMM responder a las necesidades de; **~ one's obligations** GEN COMM atender a sus obligaciones

meeting *n* GEN COMM reunión *f*, *face to face* careo *m*, MGMNT junta *f*, reunión *f*; **~ of minds** GEN COMM mutuo acuerdo *m*, LAW *commercial* acuerdo de voluntades *m*, concierto de voluntades *m*; **~ of sub-committee** GEN COMM, MGMNT asamblea de delegados *f*; ◆ **the ~ broke up** GEN COMM la reunión se disolvió; **the ~ is on tape** GEN COMM la reunión está grabada

megabucks *n pl infrml* GEN COMM pasta gansa *f* (*infrml*)

megabyte *n* (*Mb*) COMP megabyte *m* (*Mb*)

megacorp *n jarg* GEN COMM megaempresa *f*

mega-corporation *n* GEN COMM megaempresa *f*

member *n* GEN COMM *of company*, HRM *of union* miembro *mf*; **~ of the board** HRM miembro de la junta directiva *mf*, miembro del consejo *mf*; **~ of the board of management** HRM miembro del consejo de administración *mf*; **~ corporation** STOCK sociedad miembro *f*; **~ firm** STOCK empresa miembro de una bolsa *f*; **~ of the public** GEN COMM representante del público *mf*; **~ short sale ratio** STOCK *New York Stock Exchange* ratio de venta en descubierto de un miembro; **~ state** (*MS*) POL estado miembro *m*; **~ of the supervisory board** HRM miembro del consejo de supervisión *mf*; **~ of a syndicate** HRM miembro de un sindicato *mf*; **~ of a trade union** HRM miembro de un sindicato *mf*

Member: **~ of the British Institute of Management** *n* (*MBIM*) MGMNT miembro del instituto británico de dirección; **~ of Congress** *n AmE* (*cf Member of Parliament BrE*) POL ≈ diputado(-a) *m,f*, ≈ Miembro del Congreso *mf*; **~ of the European Parliament** *n* (*MEP*) POL Miembro del Parlamento Europeo *mf*, eurodiputado(-a) *m,f* (*Euro MP*); **~ of the Institute of Chartered Accountants** *n* (*MICA*) GEN COMM miembro del instituto de contables públicos titulados; **~ of Parliament** *n BrE* (*MP, cf Member of Congress AmE, Congressman AmE, Congresswoman AmE*) POL ≈ diputado(-a) *m,f*, ≈ Miembro del Congreso *mf*

membership *n* ECON, GEN COMM, HRM condición de afiliación *f*; **~ dues** *n pl* TAX cuota de participación *f*

memo *n* (*memorandum*) GEN COMM memorándum *m*

memorandum *n* (*frml*) (*memo*) GEN COMM memorándum *m* (*memo*); **~ account** ACC cuenta en orden *f*; **~ allocation** GEN COMM asignación por memoria *f*;

~ and articles *n pl* LAW escritura y estatutos *f*; **~ and articles of association** *n pl* LAW escritura de constitución y estatutos *f*, estatutos de una sociedad mercantil *m pl*; **~ of association** LAW *of trading corporation* escritura de constitución *f*; **~ check** *AmE*, **~ cheque** *BrE* BANK, FIN cheque en garantía *m*; **~ clause** BANK, INS, LAW cláusula de límite de responsabilidad *f*; **~ of deposit** BANK, LAW documento de depósito *m*; **~ of intent** GEN COMM memorándum de intención *m*; **~ item** ACC partida del memorandum *f*, punto de la memoria *m*

memory[1]: **~-resident** *adj* COMP residente en memoria

memory[2] *n* COMP memoria *f*; **~ bank** COMP banco de memoria *m*; **~ capacity** COMP capacidad de memoria *f*; **~ card** COMP tarjeta de memoria *f*; **~ chip** COMP chip de memoria *m*; **~ decay** S&M decaimiento de la memoria *m*; **~ dump** COMP vaciado de memoria *m*; **~ expansion card** COMP tarjeta de expansión de memoria *m*; **~ extension** COMP ampliación de la memoria *f*; **~ lapse** S&M error de memoria *m*; **~ operation** COMP operación de la memoria *f*; **~ print-out** COMP impresión de la memoria *f*; **~ typewriter** ADMIN máquina de escribir con memoria *f*

menial[1] *adj* HRM de baja categoría

menial[2]: **~ work** *n* HRM trabajo de baja categoría *m*

mental: **~ handicap** *n* WEL minusvalía mental *f*; **~ impairment** *n* WEL minusvalía mental *f*; **~ or physical impairment tax credit** *n* TAX desgravación fiscal por disminución mental o física *f*

mention *vt* GEN COMM avisar, mencionar

mentioned: **as ~ above** *phr* COMMS según arriba se menciona

menu[1]: **~-driven** *adj* COMP dirigido por menú

menu[2] *n* COMP menú *m*; **~ costs of inflation** ECON minuta de los costes de inflación *f* (*Esp*), minuta de los costos de inflación *f* (*AmL*)

MEP *abbr* (*Member of the European Parliament*) POL Miembro del Parlamento Europeo *m*

mercantile[1] *adj* ECON mercantil

mercantile[2]: **~ affairs** *n pl* GEN COMM asuntos mercantiles *m pl*; **~ agency** *n* S&M agencia mercantil *f*; **~ bank** *n* BANK banco de comercio *m*, banco mercantil *m*; **~ character** *n* ECON, GEN COMM condición de comerciante *f*; **~ doctrine** *n* ECON doctrina mercantilista *f*; **~ exchange** *n* STOCK intercambio mercantil *m*; **~ law** *n* LAW *commercial* derecho mercantil *m*; **~ open-stock burglary insurance** *n* INS *company* seguro contra robo de mercancías expuestas en almacenes *m*; **~ robbery insurance** *n* INS *company* seguro contra robos mercantiles *m*; **~ safe burglary insurance** *n* INS *company* seguro contra robo de caja fuerte *m*

Mercantile: **~ School of Economics** *n* ECON Escuela Mercantilista de Economía *f*

mercantilism *n* ECON mercantilismo *m*, doctrina mercantilista *f*

merchandise *n* S&M mercancías *f pl*; **~ allowance** S&M descuento de mercancías *m*; **~ balance of trade** ECON mercancías de la balanza comercial *f pl*; **~ broker** S&M corredor(a) de mercancías *m,f*; **~ control** S&M control de mercancía *m*; **~ inventory** GEN COMM *balance sheets* inventario de mercancías *m*

merchandiser *n* BANK, GEN COMM, HRM, S&M comerciante *mf*

merchandising *n* ECON, GEN COMM comercialización *f*, S&M comercialización *f*, merchandising *m*, STOCK comercialización *f*; ~ **director** HRM, MGMNT director(a) comercial *m,f*; ~ **service** S&M servicio de comercialización *m*

merchant[1] *adj* HRM mercante

merchant[2] *n* (*mcht*) BANK, GEN COMM, comerciante *mf*; ~ **bank** *BrE* (*cf investment bank AmE*) BANK, FIN banco de emisión de valores *m*, banco de inversiones *m*, banco de negocios *m*, banco financiero *m*, banco mercantil *m*; ~ **banker** *BrE* (*cf investment banker AmE*) BANK, FIN banquero(-a) comercial *m,f*; ~ **banking** *BrE* (*cf investment banking AmE*) BANK banca financiera *f*, banca de negocios *f*, banca mercantil *f*; ~ **capitalism** ECON, IND, POL capitalismo mercantil *m*; ~ **haulage** (*MH*) IMP/EXP, TRANSP transporte comercial *m*, transporte mercante *m*, remolque de buques mercantes *m*; ~ **marine** TRANSP marina mercante *f*; ~ **navy** TRANSP marina mercante *f*; ~ **service** TRANSP servicio mercante *m*; ~ **ship** TRANSP buque mercante *m*; ~ **shipping** TRANSP marina mercante *f*; ~ **trading** ECON comercio mayorista *m*; ~ **vessel** TRANSP buque mercante *m*

Merchant: ~ **Shipping Act** *n BrE* (*MSA*) TRANSP ley británica sobre marina mercante; ~ **Shipping Dangerous Goods Amendment Rules** *n pl* LAW, TRANSP Reglamentación de la Reforma Legal del Transporte Marítimo de Materias Peligrosas *f*; ~ **Shipping Regulations** *n pl* TRANSP Reglamentación del Transporte Marítimo *f*

merchantable[1] *adj* ECON, GEN COMM, S&M, STOCK comercializable

merchantable[2]: ~ **quality** *n* LAW, S&M calidad comercial *f*; ~ **title** *n* PROP título negociable *m*

merchant: ~**'s haulage** *n* (*MH*) IMP/EXP, TRANSP *shipping* remolque de buques mercantes *m*

Mercosur *n* ECON *international trade* Mercosur *m*

merge 1. *vt* COMP, ECON, FIN fusionar; ◆ ~ **and purge** *jarg* S&M *advertising* mezclar dos listas de envío quitando nombres y direcciones repetidas. **2.** *vi* STOCK fusionarse

merge into *vt* GEN COMM fusionarse a

merge with *vt* GEN COMM *company* fusionarse con

merged: ~ **company** *n* GEN COMM compañía fusionada *f*

merger *n* GEN COMM fusión *f*, consolidación de empresas *f*; ~ **accounting** *BrE* (*cf pooling of interests AmE*) ACC contabilidad de fusiones *f*, *balance sheets* fusión de intereses *f*; ~ **arbitrage** STOCK arbitraje de fusión *m*; ~ **company** FIN compañía de fusión *f*; ~ **expenses** *n pl* GEN COMM gastos de fusión *m pl*

mergers: ~ **and acquisitions** *n pl* (*M&A*) ECON, STOCK fusiones y adquisiciones *f pl*

meridian *n* GEN COMM meridiano *m*

merit: ~ **good** *n* ECON bien deseable *m*; ~ **increase** *n BrE* (*cf merit raise AmE*) HRM aumento salarial por méritos *m*; ~ **pay** *n* HRM paga por mérito *f*; ~ **raise** *n AmE* (*cf merit increase BrE*) HRM aumento salarial por méritos *m*; ~ **rating** *n* GEN COMM, HRM apreciación de méritos *f*, calificación de méritos *f*, valoración de méritos *f*; ~ **wants** *n pl* ECON necesidades preferentes *f pl*

merits: on its ~ *phr* LAW en el fondo de la cuestión

meritocracy *n* HRM meritocracia *f*

MERM *abbr* (*Multilateral Exchange Rate Model*) ECON MMTC (*modelo multilateral de tipos de cambio*)

Merval: ~ **Stock Exchange** *n* STOCK Bolsa de Argentina *f*

MES *abbr* (*minimum efficient scale*) ECON escala de mínima eficiencia *f*

mesoeconomy *n* ECON mesoeconomía *f*

message *n* GEN COMM mensaje *m*; ~ **feedback** COMMS comprobación en bucle *f*; ~ **handling** COMMS, COMP manejo de mensajes *m*; ~ **processing program** (*MPP*) COMP programa de proceso de mensajes *m*, software de proceso de mensajes *m*; ~ **source** S&M fuente de mensajes *f*; ~ **switching** COMMS conmutación de mensajes *f pl*

messenger *n* COMMS mensajero(-a) *m,f*; ~ **robbery insurance** INS *company* seguro contra robo a mensajeros *m*

metacentric: ~ **height** *n* GEN COMM altura metacéntrica *f*

metal: ~ **industry** *n* IND sector del metal *m*; ~ **market** *n* STOCK mercado de metales *m*; ~ **packaging** *n* ENVIR embalaje metálico *m*

metalliferous: ~ **ore** *n* ENVIR mineral metalífero *m*

metallist *n* ECON metalista *mf*

metallurgic *adj* HRM, IND metalúrgico

metallurgist *n* HRM, IND metalúrgico(-a) *m,f*

metamarketing *n* S&M metamarketing *m*

metayer: ~ **contract** *n* GEN COMM, LAW contrato de aparcería *m*

meter: ~ **rate** *n* GEN COMM tarifa según contador *f*, *BrE* (*cf meterage AmE*) GEN COMM medición *f*

meterage *n* AmE (*cf meter rate BrE*) GEN COMM medición *f*

metered: ~ **mail** *n* COMMS correspondencia con franqueo impreso *f*

metes: ~ **and bounds** *n pl* PROP medidas y límites

methetics *n* MATH metética *f*

method *n* GEN COMM método *m*, modo *m*; ~ **of payment** GEN COMM modo de pago *m*, metodo de pago *m*; ~ **of preparation** ACC método de preparación *m*; ~ **of taxation** TAX método de tributación *m*

methodology *n* MGMNT metodología *f*

methods: ~ **engineering** *n* GEN COMM ingeniería de métodos *f*; ~ **study** *n* GEN COMM estudio de métodos *m*; ~**-time measurement** *n* (*MTM*) MGMNT medición de métodos para tiempos *f*

methyl: ~ **bromide** *n* TRANSP *extinguishant* bromuro de metilo *m*

metric[1]: ~ **system** *n* GEN COMM sistema métrico *m*; ~ **ton** *n* (*mton*) GEN COMM tonelada métrica *f* (*tm*)

metric[2]: **go** ~ *phr* GEN COMM cambiar al sistema métrico

metricate *vi* GEN COMM cambiar al sistema métrico

metrication *n* GEN COMM adopción del sistema métrico decimal *f*

metropolitan[1] *adj* GEN COMM metropolitano

metropolitan[2]: ~ **area** *n* ECON área metropolitana *f*; ~ **town** *n* GEN COMM ciudad metropolitana *f*

MEW *abbr* (*measure of economic welfare*) ECON, HRM medida de la riqueza económica *f*

Mexico: ~ **City Stock Exchange** *n* STOCK Bolsa de Méjico *f*

mezzanine: ~ **bracket** *n* STOCK clasificación intermedia *f*; ~ **debt** *n* STOCK deuda intermedia *f*; ~ **finance** *n* FIN finanzas intermedias *f pl*; ~ **funding** *n* FIN financiamiento intermedio *m*; ~ **level** *n* FIN *venture capital* nivel de una empresa previo a la cotización en bolsa *m*

MFA *abbr* (*Multi-Fiber Arrangement AmE, Multi-Fibre Arrangement BrE*) ECON *international trade since 1973* Acuerdo Multifibra *m*

mfd *abbr* (*manufactured*) GEN COMM, IND manufacturado, fabricado

MFN *abbr* (*most-favored nation AmE*, *most-favoured nation BrE*) ECON, POL nación más favorecida *f*

M-form *n* ECON *job organization division* forma M *f*

mfr *abbr* (*manufacturer*) GEN COMM fabricante *mf*

mg *abbr* (*milligram, milligramme*) GEN COMM mg (*miligramo*)

MGR *abbr* (*manager*) GEN COMM, HRM director(a) *m,f*, gestor(a) *m,f*, jefe(-a) *m,f*, mánager *mf*

MH *abbr* (*merchant haulage*) IMP/EXP, TRANSP transporte comercial *m*, transporte mercante *m*, remolque de buques mercantes *m*

MHE *abbr* (*mechanical handling equipment*) TRANSP *cargo* equipo de manipulación mecánica *m*

MICA *abbr* (*Member of the Institute of Chartered Accountants*) GEN COMM miembro del instituto de contables públicos titulados

micro *n* COMP micro *m*

microchip *n* COMP microchip *m*

microcomputer *n* COMP microcomputador *m* (*AmL*), microcomputadora *f* (*AmL*), microordenador *m* (*Esp*)

microcomputing *n* COMP microinformática *f*

microdecision *n* ECON microdecisión *f*

microdisk *n* COMP microdisco *m*

microeconomic *adj* ECON microeconómico

microeconomics *n* ECON microeconomía *f*

microelectronic *adj* IND microelectrónico

microelectronics *n pl* IND microelectrónica *f*

microfiche *n* ADMIN microficha *f*; ~ **reader** ADMIN lector de microfichas *m*

microfilm *n* ADMIN microfilme *m*

micromarketing *n* S&M micromarketing *m*

microphone *n* COMMS micrófono *m*

microprocessor *n* COMP microprocesador *m*

micro-production: ~ **function** *n* ECON función de producción *f*

microprogram *n* COMP microprograma *m*

Microsoft®: ~ **disk-operating system** *n* (*MS-DOS*®) COMP Microsoft® disk-operating system (*MS-DOS*®)

Mid-America: ~ **Commodity Exchange** *n* STOCK bolsa de productos básicos de la zona central de los Estados Unidos, bolsa de productos básicos de medio América (*jarg*)

midcareer: ~ **plateau** *n* HRM fase de promoción bloqueada de los mandos intermedios *f*

middle: ~**-income bracket** *n* ECON grupo de ingresos medios *m*; ~**-income taxpayer** *n* TAX contribuyente de ingresos medios *mf*; ~ **management** *n* HRM, MGMNT dirección intermedia *f*, gerencia intermedia *f*, mandos intermedios *m pl*; ~ **manager** *n* HRM, MGMNT directivo(-a) medio(-a) *m,f*, mando intermedio *m*, gerente intermediario(-a) *m,f*; ~ **market business** *n* ECON operación comercial del mercado intermedio *f*; ~ **range of the market** *n* S&M gama media del mercado *f*; ~ **rate** *n* ECON tipo medio *m*; ~**-strike option** *n* STOCK opción a precio medio de ejercicio *f*; ~**-strike price** *n* STOCK *options* precio medio de ejercicio *m*

Middle: ~ **Seven** *n* ACC Siete intermedio *m*

middleman *n* MGMNT intermediario *m*

midlock *n* TRANSP *containers* cierre central *m*

midship *n* (*m*) TRANSP maestra *f*; ~ **deep tank** (*DTm*) TRANSP tanque inferior central *m*; ~ **deep tank aft**

(*DTma*) TRANSP tanque inferior central trasero *m*; ~ **deep tank forward** (*DTmf*) TRANSP tanque inferior central delantero *m*

Midwest: ~ **Stock Exchange** *n AmE* STOCK bolsa del medio oeste

MIGA *abbr* (*multinational investment guarantee agency*) FIN agencia de garantía de inversión multinacional *f*

migrant: ~ **labor** *AmE*, ~ **labour** *BrE n* HRM mano de obra migratoria *f*; ~ **status** *n* LAW situación migratoria *f*; ~ **worker** *n* HRM trabajador(a) migratorio(-a) *m,f*

migration *n* COMP *data*, ECON emigración *f*; ~**-fed unemployment** ECON desempleo alimentado por migración *m*

migratory: ~ **worker** *n* HRM trabajador(a) migratorio(-a) *m,f*

mike *n infrml* COMMS micrófono *m*

miles: ~ **per gallon** *n pl* (*mpg*) TRANSP millas por galón *f pl*; ~ **per hour** *n pl* (*mph*) TRANSP millas por hora *f pl*

military: ~ **attaché** *n* HRM agregado(-a) militar *m,f*; ~ **industrial complex** *n* POL complejo militar industrial *m*; ~ **lawyer** *n* LAW abogado(-a) jurídico(-a) militar *m,f*

milk¹: ~ **round** *n BrE* WEL reclutamiento anual de estudiantes universitarios

milk² *vt infrml* GEN COMM *opportunity* aprovechar

milking: ~ **strategy** *n* S&M estrategia de marketing a corto plazo para coger el máximo provecho de un artículo en el tiempo mínimo sin preocuparse de las posibilidades de ventas a largo plazo

mill *n AmE* TAX *tax rates* milésima *f*

milligram *n* (*mg*) GEN COMM miligramo *m* (*mg*)

milligramme *see* milligram

milliliter *AmE see* millilitre *BrE*

millilitre *n BrE* (*ml*) GEN COMM mililitro *m* (*ml*)

millimeter *AmE see* millimetre *BrE*

millimetre *n BrE* (*mm*) GEN COMM milímetro *m* (*mm*)

million *n* GEN COMM millón *m*

millionaire *n* GEN COMM millonario(-a) *m,f*; ~ **on paper** GEN COMM millonario(-a) en el papel *m,f*

millionairess *n* GEN COMM millonaria *f*; ~ **on paper** GEN COMM millonaria en el papel *f*

min. *abbr* (*minimum*) GEN COMM mínimo

min B/L *abbr* (*minimum bill of lading*) IMP/EXP, TRANSP conocimiento de embarque mínimo *m*

mine *n* IND mina *f*

mineral: ~**-based economy** *n* ECON economía basada en los recursos minerales *f*; ~ **industry** *n* ECON, ENVIR, IND industria minera *f*; ~ **oil products** *n pl* TAX productos derivados del petróleo *m pl*; ~ **resources** *n pl* ENVIR, TAX recursos minerales *m pl*; ~ **rights** *n pl* IND, LAW derechos mineros *m pl*, PROP derecho al subsuelo *m*

Mines: ~ **and Quarries Inspectorate** *n BrE* WEL cuerpo de inspección de minas y yacimientos

mini: ~**-page** *n* S&M *advertising* minipágina *f*; ~**-series** *n* MEDIA *broadcast* miniserie *f*; ~**-warehouse** *n* GEN COMM minialmacen *m*

minicomputer *n* COMP minicomputador *m* (*AmL*), minicomputadora *f* (*AmL*), miniordenador *m* (*Esp*)

minimal¹ *adj* MATH mínimo

minimal²: ~ **state intervention** *n* POL intervención mínima del Estado *f*

minimax *n* ECON minimax *m*; ~ **principle** MGMNT

principio del minimax *m*; ~ **strategy** ECON estrategia de aproximación al minimax *f*

minimization *n* ECON minimización *f*

minimize *vt* ECON, GEN COMM minimizar

minimum[1] *adj* (*min.*) GEN COMM mínimo

minimum[2]: ~ **amount** *n* TAX cantidad mínima *f*; ~ **balance** *n* BANK saldo mínimo *m*; ~ **bill of lading** *n* (*min B/L*) IMP/EXP, TRANSP conocimiento de embarque mínimo *m*; ~ **charge** *n* GEN COMM, TRANSP tarifa mínima *f*; ~ **connecting time** *n* (*MCT*) TRANSP tiempo mínimo de conexión *m*; ~ **cost** *n* ACC mínimo de coste *m* (*Esp*, mínimo de costo *m* (*AmL*); ~ **credit balance** *n* BANK saldo de crédito mínimo *m*; ~ **efficient scale** *n* (*MES*) ECON escala de mínima eficiencia *f*; ~ **grade** *n* HRM *required in exam* calificación mínima *f*; ~ **income tax** *n* TAX impuesto mínimo sobre la renta *m*; ~ **lease payment** *n* PROP *capital lease* pago de renta mínima *m*; ~ **lending rate** *n* (*MLR*) BANK *central banking* tasa de préstamo mínimo *f*; ~ **list heading** *n* BrE (*MLH*) IND estadística industrial inglesa; ~ **living wage** *n* ECON, HRM salario mínimo vital *m*; ~ **lot area** *n* PROP zona de parcelación mínima *f*; ~ **maintenance** *n* STOCK mantenimiento mínimo *m*; ~ **margin** *n* STOCK margen mínimo *m*; ~ **margin requirement** *n* STOCK cobertura obligatoria mínima *f*; ~ **pension liability** *n* FIN responsabilidad de pensión mínima *f*, responsabilidad mínima de pensiones *f*; ~ **personal income tax** *n* TAX impuesto mínimo sobre la renta de las personas físicas *m*; ~ **price change** *n* STOCK cambio mínimo en el precio *m*; ~ **price fluctuation** *n* STOCK fluctuación mínima del precio *f*; ~ **quality standard** *n* S&M norma mínima de calidad *f*; ~ **quote size** *n* (*MQS*) STOCK cotización mínima *f*; ~ **reserve requirements** *n pl* (*MRR*) ECON reserva mínima obligatoria *f*; ~ **stock** *n* ACC, S&M existencias mínimas *f pl*; ~ **supply price of labor** *AmE*, ~ **supply price of labour** *BrE n* ECON precio mínimo de la oferta laboral *m*; ~ **tax** *n* TAX impuesto mínimo *m*; ~ **tax allowance** *n* TAX deducción fiscal mínima *f*; ~ **tax carryover** *n* TAX remanente de impuestos mínimo *m*; ~ **tax credit** *n* TAX desgravación fiscal mínima *f*; ~ **temperature** *n* (*MT*) GEN COMM temperatura mínima *f*; ~ **transfer** *n* (*MT*) GEN COMM transferencia mínima *f*; ~ **wage** *n* ECON, HRM salario mínimo *m*, salario mínimo interprofesional *m*

mining *n* IND minería *f*; ~ **company** IND sociedad de minas *f*; ~ **industry** ECON, ENVIR, IND industria minera *f*; ~ **shares** *n pl* STOCK valores mineros *m pl*; ~ **tax** TAX impuesto minero *m*

Ministerial: ~ **order** *n* BrE LAW orden ministerial *f*

Ministry: ~ **of Transport Test** *n* BrE (*MOT*) TRANSP examen anual a vehículos británicos, ≈ Inspección Técnica de Vehículos *m* (*ITV*)

minivan *n* TRANSP minifurgoneta *f*

Minneapolis: ~ **Grain Exchange** *n* AmE STOCK mercado del cereal de Minneapolis

minor[1] *adj* GEN COMM menor, *under age* menor de edad

minor[2] *n* LAW *under age* menor de edad *mf*; ~ **balance status** ACC estado de cuentas auxiliar *m*; ~ **cycle** BANK, FIN, GEN COMM, MGMNT ciclo menor *m*

minority: ~ **holding** *n* GEN COMM, STOCK participación minoritaria *f*; ~ **interest** *n* GEN COMM interés minoritario *m*; ~ **interests in profit** *n* ACC participación de la minoría en beneficios *f*, participación minoritaria en los beneficios *f*; ~ **investment** *n* STOCK inversión minori-

taria *f*; ~ **participation** *n* ACC participación minoritaria *f*; ~ **shareholder** *n* STOCK accionista minoritario(-a) *m,f*; ~ **shareholding** *n* STOCK accionariado(-a) minoritario *m,f*; ~ **stake** *n* GEN COMM interés minoritario *m*, STOCK interés minoritario *m*, paquete minoritario *m*; ~ **stake in a business** *n* STOCK participación minoritaria en una empresa *f*; ~ **stockholder** *n* STOCK accionista minoritario(-a) *m,f*

mint[1] *n* BANK, ECON fábrica de la moneda *f*; ~ **par** BANK, ECON paridad intrínseca *f*; ~ **par of exchange** BANK, ECON cambio de moneda a la par *f*

mint[2] *vt* BANK, ECON acuñar, GEN COMM *phrase* inventar

Mint *n* BANK, ECON Casa de la Moneda *f*

mintage *n* BANK, ECON acuñación *f*

minus[1] *n* MATH *symbol* menos *m*; ~ **advantage** *jarg* ECON, GEN COMM, POL desventaja *f*; ~ **balance** ACC saldo negativo *m*, saldo desfavorable *m*; ~ **sign** MATH signo de resta *m*; ~ **tick** AmE STOCK venta de un título a precio inferior que el de su cotización inmediatamente anterior

minus[2] *prep* MATH menos

minute: ~ **book** *n* GEN COMM, LAW libro de actas *m*; ~ **number** *n* FIN *Treasury board* número de acta *m*

minutes *n pl* GEN COMM *of meeting* minutas *f pl*

minutiae *n pl* GEN COMM minucias *f pl*

MIS *abbr* MGMNT (*management information system*) SIG (*sistema de información para la gestión*), sistema de información administrativo *m*, S&M (*marketing information system*) sistema de información de marketing *m*

misaligned: ~ **rate of exchange** *n* BrE ECON tipo de cambio descentrado *m*

misalignment *n* GEN COMM defecto de alineación *m*, desalineación *f*, desacuerdo *m*

misalined *AmE see misaligned BrE*

misallocation *n* GEN COMM asignación inadecuada *f*

misapply *vt* LAW aplicar a destino indebido

misappropriate *vt* ACC, FIN, LAW *funds* malversar

misappropriation *n* ACC, FIN, LAW apropiación indebida *f*; ~ **of funds** ACC, FIN, LAW malversación de caudales *f*, malversación de dinero *f*, malversación de fondos *f*

misc. *abbr* (*miscellaneous*) GEN COMM misceláneo, vario

miscalculate *vt* GEN COMM calcular mal

miscalculation *n* GEN COMM error de cálculo *m*

miscarriage: ~ **of justice** *n* LAW injusticia *f*

miscellaneous[1] *adj* (*misc.*) ACC *balance sheet* diverso, vario, GEN COMM misceláneo, vario

miscellaneous[2]: ~ **charges order** *n* (*MCO*) TRANSP orden por gastos varios *f*; ~ **expenses** *n pl* ACC gastos varios *m pl*, gastos diversos *m pl*

miscoding *n* COMP error de programación *m*

misconduct *n* HRM, LAW conducta desordenada *f*

misdeclaration *n* TAX declaración incorrecta *f*

misdemeanor *AmE see misdemeanour BrE*

misdemeanour *n* BrE GEN COMM delito menor *m*

misfeasance *n* LAW infidelidad *f*, *act* infidencia *f*

misfile *vt* GEN COMM clasificar incorrectamente

mishandling *n* GEN COMM falsa maniobra *f*

mislead *vt* GEN COMM, LAW, S&M engañar

misleading[1] *adj* GEN COMM, LAW, S&M engañoso

misleading[2]: ~ **advertising** *n* GEN COMM, MEDIA publicidad engañosa *f*; ~ **information** *n* GEN COMM información equívoca *f*

mismanage *vt* MGMNT administrar mal

mismanagement *n* HRM, MGMNT mala administración *f*, dirección deficiente *f*, gestión deficiente *f*

mismatch *n* ACC desalineación *f*, descuadre *m*, desigualdad *f*; **~ case** TAX caso desequilibrado *m*

mismatched: **~ maturity** *n* BANK vencimiento desfasado *m*

mispricing *n* FIN error de precios *m*

misprint *n* COMP, GEN COMM, MEDIA errata *f*

misrepresent *vt* GEN COMM falsear, falsificar

misrepresentation *n* TAX desfiguración *f*; **~ of competition** ECON falseamiento de la competencia *m*

miss: **~ an appointment** *phr* GEN COMM faltar a una cita

missing: **~ bill of lading** *n* (*msbl*) IMP/EXP, TRANSP *shipping* conocimiento de embarque extraviado *m*; **~ cargo** *n* (*msca*) TRANSP carga extraviada *f*; **~ flight** *n* TRANSP vuelo perdido *m*; **~ market** *n* ECON mercado no existente *m*; **~ vessel** *n* TRANSP buque perdido *m*

mission *n* GEN COMM, S&M misión *f*; **~ budgets** *n pl* S&M presupuestos de misiones *m pl*; **~ costing** S&M cálculo de costes de una misión *m* (*Esp*), cálculo de costos de una misión *m* (*AmL*); **~ statement** MGMNT formulación de la misión *f*, S&M formulación de la emisión *f*

missionary: **~ salesperson** *n* HRM, S&M vendedor(a) de promoción *m,f*; **~ work** *n* HRM trabajo de misionero *m*

mistake *n* GEN COMM descuido *m*, error *m*; **~ of law** LAW error de derecho *m*

mistaken *adj* GEN COMM erróneo

mistype *vt* ADMIN hacer un error tipográfico

misunderstanding *n* GEN COMM malentendido *m*

misuse *n* FIN, LAW *of funds* malversación *f*

MIT: **~ order** *n* (*market-if-touched order*) STOCK orden MIT *f* (*orden de compra o venta si se alcanza un precio*)

mitigating: **~ circumstances** *n pl* LAW circunstancias atenuantes *f pl*

mitigation *n* LAW atenuación *f*; **~ of damages** LAW minoración de la indemnización por daños y perjuicios *f*; **~ of taxes** TAX reducción impositiva *f*

mix *n* GEN COMM, MEDIA mezcla *f*, S&M combinación de estrategias *f*

mixed: **~ account** *n* STOCK cuenta mixta *f*; **~ activity holding company** *n* STOCK sociedad de cartera de actividad mixta *f*; **~ consignment** *n* TRANSP remesa mixta *f*; **~ cost** *n* ACC coste mixto *m* (*Esp*), coste semifijo *m* (*Esp*), coste semivariable *m* (*Esp*), costo mixto *m* (*AmL*), costo semifijo *m* (*AmL*), costo semivariable *m* (*AmL*), S&M coste semifijo *m* (*Esp*), costo semifijo *m* (*AmL*); **~ credit** *n* FIN crédito mixto *m*; **~ economic system** *n* ECON, POL sistema de economía mixta *m*; **~ economy** *n* ECON, POL economía mixta *f*; **~ farming** *n* ECON policultivo *m*; **~ funds** *n pl* STOCK fondos mixtos *m pl*; **~ good** *n* ECON bien mixto *m*; **~ media** *n* S&M medios mezclados *m pl*; **~ peril** *n* INS riesgo mixto *m*; **~ policy** *n* MGMNT política mixta *f*; **~ result** *n* GEN COMM resultado mixto *m*; **~ signal** *n* GEN COMM señal mixta *f*

ml *abbr* (*millilitre*) GEN COMM ml (*mililitro*)

MLE *abbr* (*maximum likelihood estimator*) MATH *statistics* estimador de verosimilitud máxima *m*

MLH *abbr* (*minimum list heading*) IND estadística industrial inglesa

MLM *abbr* (*multilevel marketing*) S&M marketing de varios niveles *m*

MLR *abbr* (*minimum lending rate*) BANK tasa de préstamo mínimo *f*

MLS *abbr* (*multiple listing service*) PROP servicio de listado múltiple

MLW *abbr* (*mean low water*) TRANSP bajamar media *f*

mm *abbr* (*millimetre*) GEN COMM mm (*milímetro*)

MMC *abbr* ECON, FIN (*money market certificate*) certificado del mercado monetario *m*, GEN COMM (*Monopolies and Mergers Commission*) comisión de monopolios y fusiones

MMDA *abbr* (*money market deposit account*) BANK, FIN cuenta de depósito del mercado monetario *f*

MMF *abbr* (*money market fund*) BANK, FIN FIAMM (*fondo de inversión en activos del mercado monetario*)

MMI *abbr* (*Major Market Index*) STOCK índice del mercado de valores *m*

MMMF *abbr* (*money market mutual fund*) BANK, FIN FIAMM (*fondo de inversión en activos del mercado monetario*)

MNC *abbr* (*multinational corporation*) GEN COMM empresa multinacional *f*

MNEs *abbr* (*multinational enterprises*) GEN COMM empresas multinacionales *f pl*

m/o *abbr* (*my order*) GEN COMM mi orden, mi pedido

MO *abbr* GEN COMM (*money order*) orden de pago *f*, papel de pago *m*, S&M (*mail order*) pedido por correo *m*, pedido por correspondencia *m*

mobile[1] *adj* S&M móvil

mobile[2]: **~ crane** *n* (*MC*) TRANSP grúa móvil *f*; **~ home** *n* LEIS, PROP caravana *f*, casa móvil *f*; **~ home certificate** *n* AmE STOCK certificado de vivienda móvil *m*; **~-home park** *n* BrE (*cf trailer park* AmE) PROP parque de vivienda móvil *m*; **~ lift frame** *n* TRANSP *containers* estructura elevadora móvil *f*; **~ offshore drilling unit** *n* (*MODU*) IND unidad de perforación costera móvil *f*; **~ phone** *n* COMMS, GEN COMM teléfono portátil *m*, teléfono móvil *m*; **~ telephone** *n* COMMS, GEN COMM teléfono portátil *m*, teléfono móvil *m*; **~ worker** *n* HRM trabajador(a) itinerante *m,f*

mobility *n* ECON movilidad *f*; **~ clause** HRM cláusula de movilidad *f*; **~ of labor** AmE, **~ of labour** BrE ECON, HRM movilidad de trabajo *f*, movilidad laboral *f*; **~ trap** ECON trampa de la movilidad *f*

MoD *abbr* BrE (*Ministry of Defence*) POL ≈ Ministerio de Defensa *f* (*Esp*), ≈ Secretaría de la Defensa Nacional *f* (*AmL*)

mode *n* COMP modalidad *f*, modo *m*, MATH *statistics* moda *f*; **~ of transport** TRANSP modo de transporte *m*

model *n* ECON, GEN COMM, MATH modelo *m*; **~ profile** GEN COMM perfil del modelo *m*

modeling AmE *see* **modelling** BrE

modelling *n* BrE MATH modelación *f*

modem *n* (*modulator/demodulator*) COMP, MATH módem (*modulador-desmodulador*); **~ link** COMP conexión de módem *f*

moderate[1]: **~ income** *n* ACC, FIN ingreso moderado *m*

moderate[2] *vt* GEN COMM moderar

modern[1] *adj* GEN COMM moderno

modern[2]: **~ economy** *n* ECON economía moderna *f*; **~ portfolio theory** *n* (*MPT*) STOCK teoría moderna de la cartera *f*

modernization *n* GEN COMM modernización *f*

modernize *vt* GEN COMM modernizar

modest[1] *adj* GEN COMM *increase* modesto

modest[2]: ~ **cyclical recovery** *n* ECON recuperación cíclica moderada *f*

modestly *adv* GEN COMM modestamente

modification *n* GEN COMM *of data*, PROP *of buildings* modificación *f*

modifications *n pl* GEN COMM, PROP modificaciones *f pl*; ◆ **with such ~ as the circumstances require** GEN COMM con las modificaciones que las circunstancias requieran

modified: ~ **accrual** *n* ACC acumulación modificada *f*, devengo modificado *m*, BANK, FIN devengo modificado *m*; ~ **life insurance** *n* INS *personal* seguro de vida modificado *m*; ~ **net premium** *n* INS prima neta modificada *f*; ~ **re-buy** *n jarg* S&M hábitos de compra modificados; ~ **union shop** *n AmE* HRM empresa que exige sindicarse a los nuevos trabajadores

modify *vt* GEN COMM modificar

MODU *abbr* (*mobile offshore drilling unit*) IND unidad de perforación costera móvil *f*

modular: ~ **automated container handling** *n* (*MACH*) TRANSP manipulación automática modular de contenedores *f*; ~ **housing** *n* PROP vivienda modular *f*; ~ **production** *n* IND, MATH producción modular *f*

modularity *n* GEN COMM, MATH modularidad *f*

modulation *n* COMMS modulación *f*

modulator/demodulator *n* (*modem*) COMP, MATH modulador-desmodulador *m* (*módem*)

modus operandi *n* GEN COMM procedimiento *m*

MOH *abbr* (*medical officer of health*) HRM oficial(a) médico(-a) *m,f*

mold *AmE see* **mould** *BrE*

mole *n* TRANSP *harbour* malecón *m*

moments *n pl* MATH *statistics* momentos *m pl*

momentum *n* ECON impulso *m*

monadic *adj* S&M monádico

monetarism *n* ECON *quantity theory of money* monetarismo *m*

monetarist *n* ECON *econometrics* monetarista *mf*

monetary[1] *adj* GEN COMM monetario

monetary[2]: ~ **accommodation** *n* ECON préstamo monetario *m*; ~ **aggregates** *n pl* (*M*) ECON totales monetarios *m pl*; ~ **agreement** *n* LAW acuerdo monetario *m*; ~ **approach to the balance of payments** *n* (*MABP*) ECON enfoque monetario de la balanza de pagos *m*; ~ **asset** *n* ACC, FIN, PROP activo líquido *m*; ~ **assets** *n pl* ACC activos monetarios *m pl*; ~ **authorities** *n pl* BANK autoridades monetarias *f pl*; ~ **base** *n* ECON base monetaria *f*, disponibilidades líquidas *f pl*; ~ **bloc** *n* ECON, POL bloque monetario *m*; ~ **compensation amount** *n* (*MCA*) FIN cantidad monetaria compensatoria *f*, monto de la compensación monetaria *m*; ~ **compensatory amount** *n* FIN *agriculture* importe de compensación monetaria *m*; ~ **control act** *n* ECON, LAW ley de control monetario *f*; ~ **course** *n* ECON curso monetario *m*; ~ **ease** *n* ECON, FIN facilidad monetaria *f*; ~ **economics** *n pl* ECON economía monetaria *f*; ~ **expansion** *n* ECON expansión monetaria *f*; ~ **inducement** *n* FIN incentivo monetario *m*; ~ **inflation** *n* ECON inflación monetaria *f*; ~ **item** *n* ACC *balance sheets* partida monetaria *f*; ~ **overhang** *n* ECON *sleeping overhang* proyección monetaria *f*; ~ **policy** *n* ECON política monetaria *f*; ~ **reserve** *n*

BANK, ECON reserva monetaria *f*; ~ **restriction** *n* ECON restricción monetaria *f*; ~ **standard** *n* ECON patrón monetario *m*; ~ **unit** *n* ACC, BANK, ECON, FIN unidad monetaria *f*; ~ **veil** *n* ECON ilusión monetaria *f*

monetization *n* ECON monetización *f*

money *n* (*M*) GEN COMM dinero *m*, *supply* oferta monetaria *f*; ~ **at call** ECON dinero a la vista *m*; ~ **broker** *BANK*, FIN, STOCK corredor(a) de cambios *m,f*; ~ **center bank** *AmE*, ~ **centre bank** *BrE* BANK banco de los centros monetarios *m*; ~ **demand** ECON demanda monetaria *f*; ~ **desk** BANK ventanilla de dinero *f*; ~ **fund** BANK fondo de dinero *m*; ~ **illusion** ECON valor ilusorio del dinero *m*; ~ **in circulation** BANK, ECON dinero en circulación *m*; ~ **income** ECON ingresos monetarios *m pl*, TAX renta monetaria *f*; ~ **laundering** BANK, FIN, GEN COMM blanqueo de dinero *m*, lavado de dinero *m*; ~ **lender** BANK, FIN prestamista *mf*; ~ **management** FIN gestión del dinero *f*; ~ **market** BANK, STOCK mercado de dinero *m*; ~ **market certificate** (*MMC*) ECON, FIN certificado del mercado monetario *m*; ~ **market department** STOCK departamento del mercado monetario *m*; ~ **market deposit account** (*MMDA*) BANK, FIN cuenta de depósito del mercado monetario *f*; ~ **market fund** (*MMF*) BANK, FIN fondo de inversión en activos del mercado monetario *m* (*FIAMM*); ~ **market funds** *n pl* FIN, STOCK fondos de inversión en activos del mercado monetario *m pl*; ~ **market institution** FIN institución del mercado bursátil *f*; ~ **market instrument** STOCK instrumento del mercado monetario *m*; ~ **market mutual fund** (*MMMF*) BANK, FIN fondo de inversión en activos del mercado monetario *m* (*FIAMM*); ~ **market paper** STOCK título del mercado monetario *m*; ~ **market rate** STOCK índice del mercado monetario *m*; ~ **market return** STOCK rendimiento del mercado monetario *m*; ~ **market trader** FIN intermediario(-a) del mercado monetario *m,f*; ~ **matters** *n pl* GEN COMM asuntos monetarios *m pl*; ~ **measurement** FIN medición monetaria *f*; ~ **multiplier** ECON multiplicador monetario *m*; ~-**off pack** S&M envase con cupón de descuento *m*; ~ **order** (*MO*) GEN COMM orden de pago *f*, papel de pago *m*; ~ **placements** *n pl* STOCK colocaciones de dinero *f pl*; ~ **restraint** ECON restricción monetaria *f*; ~ **scarcity** ECON escasez de dinero *f*; ~ **and securities** INS *company* dinero y valores *f*; ~-**spinner** *infrml* GEN COMM, FIN fuente de dinero *f*; ~ **spread** STOCK margen neto *m*; ~ **supply** BANK oferta monetaria *f*, ECON, FIN oferta de dinero *f*, oferta monetaria *f*; ~ **transfer order** BANK, FIN orden de transferencia de dinero *f*; ~ **transmission** BANK traspaso de dinero *m*; ~ **up front** ACC, FIN, GEN COMM pago adelantado *m*, adelanto de dinero *m*; ~ **wealth capitalization** ACC, ECON, FIN, GEN COMM, STOCK capitalización monetaria *f*; ◆ **have ~ to burn** GEN COMM estar cargado de dinero

moneyed: ~ **capital** *n* ACC, ECON, FIN, GEN COMM capital reinvertido *m*

moneymaker *n* GEN COMM, FIN fuente de dinero *f*

monies: ~ **paid in** *n pl* FIN cobros *m pl*; ~ **paid out** *n pl* FIN pagos *m pl*; ~ **received** *n pl* FIN dinero recibido *m*

monitor[1] *n* COMP *screen* pantalla *f*, GEN COMM *security* monitor *m*

monitor[2] *vt* GEN COMM controlar, TRANSP *rates* supervisar; ◆ ~ **a market** S&M controlar un mercado; ~ **performance** GEN COMM, HRM, MGMNT supervisar una actuación

monitoring *n* TAX observación *f*, verificación *f*

Monnet: ~'s Law *n* ECON Ley de Monnet *f*

monochrome *adj* COMP *computer screen, peripherals* monocromo

monoeconomics *n* ECON monoeconomía *f*

monogram *n* GEN COMM monograma *m*

Monopolies: ~ and Mergers Commission *BrE n* (*MMC*) GEN COMM comisión británica de monopolios y fusiones

monopolistic: ~ competition *n* ECON competencia monopolística *f*

monopolization *n* GEN COMM acaparamiento *m*; **~ of goods** GEN COMM acaparamiento de bienes *m*, acaparamiento de mercancías *m*

monopolize *vt* FIN, GEN COMM, S&M, STOCK acaparar

monopolized *adj* GEN COMM *market* acaparado

monopolizer *n* GEN COMM acaparador(a) *m,f*

monopoly *n* ECON, FIN, S&M, STOCK monopolio *m*; **~ capital** ECON, FIN, STOCK capital monopolista *m*; **~ capitalism** ECON capitalismo monopolista *m*; **~ power** ECON poder monopolístico *m*; **~ price** ECON precio de monopolio *m*; **~ profit** ECON beneficio del monopolio *m*; **~ rent** PROP alquiler de monopolio *m*

monopsonic *adj* ECON monopsónico

monopsony *n* ECON monopsonio *m*

monorail *n* TRANSP monorrail *m*

Mont: ~ Pelerin Society *n* ECON agrupación de Mont Pelerin *f*

montage *n* S&M montaje *m*

Montevideo: ~ Stock Exchange *n* STOCK Bolsa de Montevideo *f*

month: this ~'s actuals *n pl* ACC disponibilidades del mes en curso *f pl*; **~ order** *n* STOCK orden para un mes *f*; **~-to-month tenancy** *n* LAW, PROP arrendamiento mensual *m*, arrendamiento al mes *m*, arrendamiento mes a mes *m*

monthly[1] *adj* GEN COMM mensual; ◆ **in ~ installments** *AmE*, **in ~ instalments** *BrE* ACC, BANK en cuotas mensuales, en plazos mensuales

monthly[2] *adv* GEN COMM mensualmente

monthly[3]**: ~ compounding of interest** *n* BANK ajuste mensual del interés *m*; **~ expenses** *n pl* GEN COMM gastos mensuales *m pl*; **~ installment** *AmE*, **~ instalment** *BrE n* FIN cuota mensual *f*, plazo mensual *m*; **~ investment plan** *n* FIN, STOCK plan mensual de inversión *m*; **~ rent** *n* PROP alquiler mensual *m*; **~ return** *n* ACC, BANK, FIN rendimiento mensual *m*; **~ sale** *n* S&M venta mensual *f*; **~ savings** *n pl* BANK, HRM *of employee* ahorro mensual *m*; **~ statement** *n* BANK, FIN *of account, credit card* estado mensual *m*

months: ~ after sight *n pl* (*m/s*) BANK meses vencidos *m pl*

mood: ~ advertising *n* S&M publicidad de ambiente *f*; **~ conditioning** *n* S&M condicionante del estado de ánimo *m*

Moody: ~'s investment grade *n AmE* FIN calificación de inversión de Moody *f*; **~'s investor service** *n AmE* FIN servicio de inversión de Moody *m*

moonlight: ~ economy *n* ECON economía del pluriempleo *f*

moonlighter *n infrml* HRM pluriempleado(-a) *m,f*, trabajador(a) clandestino(-a) *m,f*, trabajador(a) no declarado(-a) *m,f*

moonlighting *n infrml* HRM pluriempleo *m*, trabajo clandestino *m*

moor *vt* TRANSP amarrar

moral: ~ hazard *n* INS riesgo moral *m*; **~ law** *n* LAW ética *f*, ley moral *f*; **~ obligation bond** *n* FIN, STOCK bono con respaldo oficial *m*; **~ persuasion** *n* BANK persuasión moral *f*

morale *n* HRM moral *f*

moratorium *n* BANK, FIN, GEN COMM moratoria *f*

Morgan: ~ Stanley Capital International World Index *n* (*MCSI Index*) STOCK parámetros internacionales para la comparación de futuros financieros

MORI *abbr* (*Market and Opinion Research International*) POL, S&M compañía británica de sondeo de la opinión pública, ≈ Demoscopia *m* (*Esp*)

morphological: ~ analysis *n* FIN, MATH análisis morfológico *m*

mortality: ~ gain *n* TAX adquisición por fallecimiento *f*; **~ loss** *n* TAX pérdida por mortalidad *f*; **~ table** *n* INS tabla de mortalidad *f*

mortg. *abbr* (*mortgage*) BANK, FIN hipoteca *f*

mortgage[1] *n* (*mortg.*) BANK, FIN hipoteca *f*; **~ account** BANK cuenta hipotecaria *f*; **~ assumption** BANK aceptación de hipoteca *f*, adquisición de hipoteca *f*; **~-backed certificate** FIN certificado respaldado por una hipoteca *m*; **~-backed security** (*MBS*) FIN, STOCK título respaldado por una hipoteca *m*, valor respaldado por una hipoteca *m*; **~ bank** BANK inmobiliaria inglesa, ≈ banco de crédito hipotecario *m*, ≈ banco hipotecario *m*; **~ bond** BANK, FIN, STOCK bono con garantía *m*, bono hipotecario *m*; **~ broker** FIN corredor(a) de hipotecas *m,f*; **~ ceiling** BANK, PROP límite máximo de hipoteca *m*, tope de hipoteca *m*; **~ certificate** BANK, FIN certificado de hipoteca *m*; **~ clause** BANK, INS, LAW cláusula de hipoteca *f*; **~ commitment** BANK, FIN obligación hipotecaria *f*; **~ company** BANK, PROP sociedad hipotecaria *f*; **~ constant** BANK constante hipotecaria *f*; **~ correspondent** FIN corresponsal hipotecario(-a) *m,f*; **~ credit association** FIN asociación de crédito hipotecario *f*; **~ debt** BANK deuda hipotecaria *f*, deuda hipotecaria global *f*; **~ deed** LAW, PROP escritura de hipoteca *f*; **~ department** BANK, FIN, PROP departamento de hipotecas *m*; **~ discount** BANK, FIN, PROP descuento hipotecario *m*; **~ insurance** INS *personal* seguro de hipotecas *m*; **~ insurance policy** INS *personal* póliza de seguros por hipoteca *f*; **~ interest relief at source** BANK, FIN, TAX desgravación de intereses hipotecarios en origen *f*; **~ lender** BANK prestamista hipotecario(-a) *m,f*; **~ lien** BANK, LAW, PROP privilegio hipotecario *m*; **~ life insurance** INS *personal* seguro de vida con hipoteca *m*; **~ loan** BANK, FIN, PROP préstamo hipotecario *m*; **~ loan bank** BANK ≈ banco de crédito hipotecario *m*, ≈ banco hipotecario *m*; **~ loan company** BANK, FIN empresa de préstamos hipotecarios *f*; **~ loan corporation** BANK, FIN corporación de préstamo hipotecario *f*; **~ market** BANK, FIN mercado hipotecario *m*; **~ payable** BANK, FIN, PROP hipoteca a pagar *f*; **~ payment** BANK, FIN, PROP pago de hipoteca *m*; pago hipotecario *m*; **~ portfolio** BANK cartera hipotecaria *f*; **~ rate** BANK, FIN tasa hipotecaria *f*; **~ REIT** FIN fondo de inversión en propiedad hipotecaria *m*; **~ relief** BANK, FIN, TAX desgravación hipotecaria *f*; **~ rescue scheme** BANK, PROP plan de rescate de hipoteca *m*; **~ servicing** BANK, FIN servicio hipotecario *m*; **~ statement** BANK, FIN balance hipotecario *m*;

~ **strip** FIN anulación de la hipoteca *f*; ~ **table** BANK cuadro de amortización hipotecaria *m*

mortgage[2] *vt* BANK, FIN hipotecar

mortgage out *vt* BANK, FIN amortizar la hipoteca

mortgagee *n* BANK, FIN acreedor(a) hipotecario(-a) *m,f*

mortgager *n* BANK, FIN deudor(a) hipotecario(-a) *m,f*

most: **~-active list** *n* STOCK *stocks with the most shares traded on given day* lista de los más activos *f*; **~-favored nation** *n* AmE *see most-favoured nation BrE*; **~-favored nation clause** AmE *see most-favoured nation clause BrE*; **~-favored nation treatment** AmE *see most-favoured nation treatment BrE*, **~-favoured nation** *BrE n* ECON, POL nación más favorecida *f*; **~-favoured nation clause** *n BrE* ECON, LAW, POL cláusula de nación más favorecida *f*; **~-favoured nation treatment** *n BrE* ECON, POL tratamiento de nación más favorecida *m*

MOT *abbr* TRANSP (*Ministry of Transport Test*) examen anual a vehículos británicos, ≈ ITV (*Inspección Técnica de Vehículos*)

mother: **~ of the chapel** *n BrE* HRM, MEDIA *publishing, printing trade union* cabecilla sindical *f*; **~ ship** *n* TRANSP buque nodriza *m*

motherboard *n* COMP placa base *f*

mothercard *n* COMP placa base *f*

motif *n* GEN COMM motivo *m*

motion *n* POL moción *f*; **~ of censure** POL moción de censura *f*; **~ picture** AmE (*cf film BrE*) LEIS película *f*; **~ picture advertising** AmE LEIS, S&M publicidad de una película *f*; **~-picture industry** AmE (*cf film industry BrE*) MEDIA industria cinematográfica *f*, industria del cine *f*; **~ study** ECON, MATH, MGMNT estudio de movimientos *m*

motivate *vt* GEN COMM motivar

motivation *n* GEN COMM motivación *f*

motivational[1] *adj* GEN COMM motivacional

motivational[2]: **~ analysis** *n* HRM análisis motivacional *m*; **~ research** *n* MGMNT, S&M *of market* investigación motivacional *f*

motivator *n* GEN COMM motivador *m*

motor: **~ freight** *n* TRANSP carga motorizada *f*; **~ industry** *n* ECON, IND, INS industria de la automoción *f*, industria automotriz *f*; **~ lorry cargo insurance** *n BrE* (*cf motor truck cargo insurance AmE*) INS seguro sobre la carga de camiones *m*; **~ merchant vessel** *n* (*M/V*) TRANSP navío mercante motorizado *m*; **~ mileage allowance** *n BrE* TAX desgravación por kilometraje *f*; **~ premium** *n* INS prima automovilística *f*; **~ spirit** *n* TRANSP *fuel* gasolina para motores *f*; **~ tanker** *n* TRANSP *shipping* motopetrolero *m*; **~ transport officer** *n* (*MTO*) HRM, TRANSP oficial(a) de transporte motorizado *m,f*; **~ truck cargo insurance** *n* AmE (*cf motor lorry cargo insurance BrE*) INS seguro sobre la carga de camiones *m*; **~ vehicle** *n* TRANSP vehículo de motor *m*; **~ vehicle insurance** *n* INS seguro de automóviles *m*; **~ vessel** *n* TRANSP motonave *f*

motorist: **~ inclusive tour** *n* LEIS excursión que incluye conductor

motorway *n BrE* (*M*) (*cf freeway AmE*) TRANSP autopista *f*

mould *vt BrE* MEDIA, S&M *public opinion* moldear

mounting *adj* GEN COMM *increasing* en alza

mouse *n* COMP ratón *m*; **~ driver** COMP unidad de ratón *f*; **~ mat** COMP alfombrilla para ratón *f*

movable: **~ property** *n* LAW, PROP bienes muebles *m pl*

move[1] *n* ECON *in currency* transferencia *f*, STOCK jugada *f*

move[2]: **~ house** *phr* PROP mudarse de casa; **~ in tandem** ECON *currencies* evolucionar simultáneamente, *phr* STOCK moverse en serie; **~ into the money** *phr* STOCK pasarse a opciones dentro del precio; **~ to larger premises** *phr* ADMIN mudarse a un local más grande

moveables *n pl* ACC bienes muebles *m pl*

movement *n* GEN COMM *of price* evolución *f*, movimiento *m*; **~ certificate** IMP/EXP certificado de movimiento *m*; **~ of freight** TRANSP movimiento de fletes *m*; **~ of labor** AmE, **~ of labour** *BrE* ECON movimiento de la mano de obra *m*; **~ on shareholders' equity** ACC *annual accounts* movimiento del capital de los accionistas *m*, movimiento del capital aportado *m*

mover: **~ and shaker** *n infrml* MGMNT promotor(a) e impulsor(a) *m,f*

movie *n AmE* (*cf film BrE*) LEIS, MEDIA película *f*

moving: **~ annual total** *n* (*MAT*) MATH total anual móvil *m*; **~ average** *n* MATH media móvil *f*

MP *abbr BrE* (*Member of Parliament*) POL ≈ diputado(-a) *m,f*, ≈ Miembro del Congreso *mf*

MPC *abbr* (*maximum permissible concentration*) ECON concentración máxima admisible *f*

MPD *abbr* (*marginal private damage*) ECON perjuicios privados no relevantes *m pl*

mpg *abbr* (*miles per gallon*) TRANSP millas por galón *f pl*

mph *abbr* (*miles per hour*) TRANSP millas por hora *f pl*

MPI *abbr* (*marginal propensity to import*) ECON, IMP/EXP propensión marginal a la importación *f*

MPP *abbr* (*message processing program*) COMP programa de proceso de mensajes *m*, software de proceso de mensajes *m*

MQS *abbr* (*minimum quote size*) STOCK cotización mínima *f*

MPT *abbr* (*modern portfolio theory*) STOCK teoría moderna de la cartera *f*

MR *abbr* (*mate's receipt*) TRANSP *for loaded cargo* billete de embarque *m*, recibo de embarque *m*

MRA *abbr* (*multiple regression analysis*) ECON, FIN, MATH análisis de regresión múltiple *m*

MRCA *abbr* (*Market Research Corporation of America*) S&M sociedad estadounidense de estudios de mercado

MRO *abbr* (*maintenance, repair and overhaul*) TRANSP mantenimiento, reparación y revisión

MRP *abbr* ECON (*marginal revenue product*) ingreso del producto marginal *m*, S&M (*manufacturer's recommended price*) precio recomendado por el fabricante *m*

MRR *abbr* (*minimum reserve requirements*) ECON reserva mínima obligatoria *f*

MRS *abbr* (*marginal rate of substitution*) ECON tasa marginal de sustitución *f*

MRT *abbr* (*mass rapid transit*) TRANSP tránsito rápido masivo *m*

m/s *abbr* (*months after sight*) BANK meses vencidos *m pl*

MS *abbr* (*manuscript*) MEDIA manuscrito *m*

msbl *abbr* (*missing bill of lading*) IMP/EXP, TRANSP conocimiento de embarque extraviado *m*

MSc *abbr* (*Master of Science*) WEL Master de Ciencias *m*

MSC *abbr BrE obs* (*Manpower Services Commission*) HRM comisión de servicios laborales

MSD *abbr* (*marginal social damage*) ECON perjuicios sociales no relevantes *m pl*

MS-DOS® *abbr* (*Microsoft disk-operating system*) COMP MS-DOS®

MT *abbr* COMMS (*mail transfer*) transferencia por correo *f*, GEN COMM (*minimum transfer*) transferencia mínima *f*, (*mean time*) TM (tiempo medio)

MTBF *abbr* (*mean time between failures*) COMP tiempo medio entre averías *m*

MTC *abbr* (*Maritime Transport Committee*) TRANSP comité de transporte marítimo

MTFS *abbr* BrE (*medium-term financial strategy*) ECON estrategia financiera a medio plazo *f*

MTL *abbr* (*medium-term loan*) BANK, FIN préstamo a medio plazo *m*

MTN *abbr* BANK (*medium-term note*) bono a medio plazo *m*, nota a medio plazo *f*, documento a medio plazo *m*, ECON, POL (*multilateral trade negotiation*) negociación comercial multilateral *f*

MTO *abbr* (*motor transport officer*) HRM, TRANSP oficial(a) de transporte motorizado *m,f*

mton *abbr* (*metric ton*) GEN COMM tm (*tonelada métrica*)

MTR *abbr* (*mass transit railroad AmE*, *mass transit railway BrE*) TRANSP ferrocarril de tránsito masivo

muckraker *n* GEN COMM husmeador(a) *m,f*

Multi: -Fiber Arrangement *AmE*, **~-Fibre Arrangement** *BrE n* (*MFA*) ECON *international trade since 1973* Acuerdo Multifibra *m*

multiaccess *n* GEN COMM multiacceso *m*

multiannual *adj* GEN COMM multianual

multibrand: **~ stategy** *n* S&M estrategia multimarca *f*

multiclient: **~ survey** *n* S&M encuesta multicliente *f*

multicollinearity *n* ECON multicolinealidad *f*, MATH *statistics* colineación múltiple *f*

multi-country: **~ economic model** *n* (*MCM*) ECON modelo económico multipaís *m*

multicurrency[1] *adj* BANK, ECON multidivisa

multicurrency[2]: **~ loan** *n* BANK préstamo multidivisa *m*; **~ option** *n* BANK, INS, LAW cláusula multidivisa *f*

multidelivery *n* TRANSP destinos múltiples *m pl*

multidimensional: **~ scaling** *n* S&M evaluación multidimensional por escalas *f*

multiemployer: **~ bargaining** *n* HRM acuerdo multisectorial *m*, negociación con múltiples empresarios *f*

multifamily: **~ housing** *n* PROP, WEL vivienda multifamiliar *f*

multifunctional *adj* GEN COMM multifuncional

multijobbing *n* COMP multitarea *f*

multijurisdictional *adj* LAW multijurisdiccional

multilateral[1] *adj* ECON, POL multilateral

multilateral[2]: **~ agency** *n* ECON, POL agencia multilateral *f*; **~ agreement** *n* ECON, LAW, POL acuerdo multilateral *m*, contrato multilateral *m*; **~ aid** *n* ECON, POL ayuda multilateral *f*; **~ development bank** *n* BANK, FIN banco de desarrollo multilateral *m*; **~ disbursement** *n* ECON *of development aid* desembolso multilateral *m*; **~ donor** *n* ECON, POL *of development assistance* donante multilateral *mf*; **~ investment guarantee agency** *n* (*MIGA*) FIN agencia de garantía de inversión multilateral *f*; **~ netting** *n* BANK, FIN compensación de créditos y débitos *f*; **~ permit** *n* TRANSP *EC* permiso multilateral *m*; **~ trade agreement** *n* ECON, LAW, POL acuerdo de

comercio multilateral *m*; **~ trade negotiation** *n* (*MTN*) ECON, POL negociación comercial multilateral *f*; **~ trade organization** *n* ECON, POL organización comercial multilateral *f*

Multilateral: **~ Exchange Rate Model** *n* (*MERM*) ECON modelo multilateral de tipos de cambio *m* (*MMTC*)

multilateralism *n* ECON, POL multilateralismo *m*

multilevel: **~ marketing** *n* (*MLM*) S&M marketing de varios niveles *m*

multilingual *adj* GEN COMM multilingüe

multimedia[1] *adj* MEDIA, S&M *advertising* multimedia

multimedia[2]: **~ training** *n* HRM, MEDIA capacitación en multimedia *f* (*AmL*), formación en multimedia *f* (*Esp*)

multimillion: **~ pound deal** *n* FIN convenio multimillonario de libras *m*

multimodal[1] *adj* TRANSP multimodal

multimodal[2]: **~ distribution** *n* MATH *statistics* distribución multimodal *f*, distribución plurimodal *f*; **~ frequency curve** *n* MATH *statistics* curva de frecuencias multimodal *f*; **~ transport** *n* TRANSP transporte multimodal *m*; **~ transport law** *n* LAW, TRANSP ley del transporte multimodal *f*; **~ transport service** *n* TRANSP servicio de transporte multimodal *m*

multinational[1] *adj* GEN COMM multinacional

multinational[2]: **~ bank** *n* BANK banco multinacional *m*; **~ company** *n* GEN COMM empresa multinacional *f*; **~ corporation** *n* (*MNC*) GEN COMM empresa multinacional *f*; **~ enterprises** *n pl* (*MNEs*) GEN COMM empresas multinacionales *f pl*; **~ export credit** *n* IMP/EXP crédito a la exportación multinacional *m*; **~ trading** *n* IMP/EXP comercio multinacional *m*

multinationally *adv* GEN COMM multinacionalmente

multioption: **~ facility** *n* (*MOF*) STOCK servicio de opción múltiple *m*; **~ financing facility** *n* (*MOFF*) STOCK servicio de financiación de opción múltiple *m*

multiplant: **~ bargaining** *n* HRM acuerdo multiplanta *m*, negociación multisectorial *f*

multiple *n* MATH múltiple *m*; **~ access time** (*MAT*) tiempo de acceso múltiple *m*; **~-activity chart** COMP gráfico de actividades múltiples *m*; **~ buyer** S&M comprador(a) múltiple *m,f*; **~-choice question** GEN COMM, S&M pregunta de elección múltiple *f*; **~ correlation** MATH *statistics* correlación múltiple *f*; **~ drop** TRANSP transporte discrecional *m*; **~-entry visa** LEIS, POL visado de entradas múltiples *m*; **~ exchange rate** ECON tipo de cambio múltiple *m*; **~ general purpose line of credit** FIN *multiple contract finance* línea de crédito de general *f*; **~ listing** PROP listado múltiple *m*; **~ listing service** *AmE* (*MLS*) PROP servicio de listado múltiple; **~ locations forms** *n pl* INS formularios para ubicaciones múltiples *m pl*; **~ management** MGMNT dirección múltiple *f*, gerencia múltiple *f*; **~-management plan** MGMNT plan de gestión múltiple *m*; **~-peril insurance** INS seguro a todo riesgo *m*; **~ projected line of credit** FIN *multiple contract finance* línea de crédito de proyección *f*; **~ readership** S&M lectores múltiples *m pl*; **~ regression** MATH *statistics* regresión múltiple *f*; **~ regression analysis** (*MRA*) ECON, FIN, MATH análisis de regresión múltiple *m*; **~ regression coefficient** BANK, ECON, STOCK coeficiente de regresión múltiple *m*; **~ retirement ages** *n pl* HRM edades diferentes de jubilación *f pl*; **~-risk insurance** INS seguro multirriesgo *m*; **~ shop** HRM sucursal comercial *f*; **~ taxation** TAX imposición múltiple *f*;

~ **track plan** *jarg* WEL plan para agrupar a los estudiantes según sus aptitudes; ~ **unit pricing** S&M fijación múltiple de precios unitarios *f*; ~ **unit residential building** WEL edificio multifamiliar *m* (*AmL*), edificio residencial *m* (*Esp*)

multiplier *n* ECON multiplicador *m*; ~**-accelerator model** ECON modelo de multiplicador-acelerador *m*; ~ **effect** ECON *econometrics* efecto multiplicador *m*; ~ **principle** ECON principio del multiplicador *m*

multiply *vt* MATH multiplicar

multiport: ~ **itinerary** *n* TRANSP itinerario de distribución *m*; ~ **operation** *n* TRANSP operación multipuerto *f*

multiprocessing *n* COMP multiproceso *m*

multiprocessor *n* COMP multiprocesador *m*

multiproduct: ~ **berth** *n* TRANSP muelle multiproducto *m*

multiprogramming *n* COMP multiprogramación *f*

multipurpose[1] *adj* COMP *peripheral, software* polivalente, GEN COMM multiuso

multipurpose[2]: ~ **vessel** *n* TRANSP *shipping* buque para uso general *m*

multiquota *n* TRANSP cuota múltiple *f*

multiregional *adj* GEN COMM multiregional

multiroute *adj* TRANSP multiruta

multisector *adj* GEN COMM multisectorial

multisegmented: ~ **operation** *n* S&M operación multi-segmentada *f*

multiskilling *n* HRM cualificación múltiple *f*, polivalencia *f*

multistage: ~ **sampling** *n* MATH *statistics* muestreo multinivel *m*, muestreo por etapas *m*; ~ **tax** *n* TAX impuesto en etapas múltiples *m*

multistory *AmE see* **multistorey** *BrE*

multistorey *adj* *BrE* PROP *building, car park* de varios pisos

multitasking *n* COMP multitarea *f*

multiunion: ~ **bargaining** *n* *BrE* HRM acuerdo multisindical *m*, negociación multisindical *f*; ~ **plant** *n* HRM, IND fábrica multisindical *f*

multiunionism *n* HRM multisindicalismo *m*

multiuser: ~ **berth** *n* TRANSP amarradero multiusuario *m*; ~ **route** *n* TRANSP ruta multiusuario *f*; ~ **system** *n* COMP sistema de usuarios múltiples *m*

multivariate: ~ **analysis** *n* MATH análisis multivariable *m*

multivariety: ~ **store** *n* S&M tienda múltiple *f*

multiyear[1] *adj* GEN COMM multianual

multiyear[2]: ~ **operational plan** *n* (*MYOP*) FIN plan operacional plurianual *m*, plan plurianual de actuaciones *m*; ~ **rescheduling agreement** *n* (*MYRA*) FIN acuerdo reajustable plurianual *m*, acuerdo reestructurable plurianual *m*; ~ **resource envelope** *n* FIN partida plurianual de recursos *f*; ~ **restructuring agreement** *n* (*MYRA*) FIN acuerdo reajustable plurianual *m*, acuerdo reestructurable plurianual *m*; ~ **spending envelope** *n* FIN partida plurianual de gastos *f*

Mundell-Fleming: ~ **model** *n* ECON modelo de Mundell-Fleming *m*

municipal[1] *adj* GEN COMM municipal

municipal[2]: ~ **body** *n* TAX corporación municipal *f*; ~ **bond** *n* BANK, STOCK obligación municipal *f*; ~ **bond insurance** *n* INS seguro sobre bonos municipales *m*; ~ **bond insurance association** *n* INS sociedad de seguros sobre bonos municipales *f*; ~ **bond offering** *n*

BANK, STOCK ofrecimiento de bono municipal *m*; ~ **bonds** *n pl* BANK, STOCK empréstitos municipales *m pl*; ~ **borough** *n* POL distrito municipal *m*, municipio *m*; ~ **certificate of accrual on treasury securities** *n* (*M-CATS*) STOCK certificado municipal de acumulación de bonos del tesoro; ~ **government** *n* POL gobierno municipal *m*; ~ **notes** *n pl* BANK notas municipales *f pl*; ~ **revenue bond** *n* FIN, STOCK bono municipal que se paga por ingresos

muniment *n* LAW, PROP, STOCK documento de título *m*

muniments: ~ **of title** *n pl* LAW, PROP títulos acreditativos *m pl*, títulos de propiedad *m pl*

murder: ~ **one** *n* *AmE infrml* LAW asesinato con premeditación *m*

Murphy: **'s ~ Law** *n* GEN COMM Ley de Murphy *f*

must: ~ **fit** *n* LAW *intellectual property* ajuste obligatorio *m*; ~ **match** *n* LAW *intellectual property* ajuste obligatorio *m*

mutatis mutandis *phr* LAW por analogía

Muth-Mills: ~ **model** *n* ECON modelo de Muth-Mills *m*

mutilated: ~ **check** *AmE*, ~ **cheque** *BrE n* BANK, FIN cheque mutilado *m*; ~ **note** *n* BANK pagaré deteriorado *m*; ~ **security** *n* STOCK valor cuya impresión no es clara

mutual[1] *adj* GEN COMM mutuo; ◆ **by ~ agreement** GEN COMM, LAW de común acuerdo, de convenio mutuo; **by ~ consent** GEN COMM, LAW *general agreement* de común acuerdo, por acuerdo mutuo, por consentimiento mutuo

mutual[2]: ~ **agreement** *n* GEN COMM mutuo acuerdo *m*; ~ **aid pact** *n* ECON, POL *international trade* pacto de ayuda mutua *m*; ~ **association** *n* FIN asociación mutua *f*; ~ **benefit** *n* GEN COMM beneficio mutuo *m*; ~ **border** *n* IMP/EXP frontera común *f*; ~ **company** *n* FIN, INS compañía mutua *f*, sociedad mutua *f*; ~ **corporation** *n* FIN, INS compañía mutua *f*, sociedad mutua *f*; ~ **fund** *n* FIN fondo mutuo *m*, STOCK fondo de pensiones *m*; ~ **fund custodian** *n* BANK custodio de un fondo de inversiones *m*; ~ **improvement certificate** *n* FIN certificado de inversión en mejoras *m*; ~ **insurance** *n* INS seguro mutuo *m*; ~ **insurance company** *n* INS compañía mutua de seguros *f*; ~ **insurer** *n* INS asegurador(a) mutualista *m,f*; ~ **insuring company** *n* INS aseguradora mutualista *f*; ~ **recognition** *n* LAW *EU*, POL *of national laws in the EU* reconocimiento mutuo *m*; ~ **savings bank** *n* BANK banco mutualista de ahorros *m*

Mutual: ~ **Offset System** *n* STOCK *Eurodollar futures* sistema de compensación mutua *m*

mutuality: ~ **of contract** *n* LAW reciprocidad del contrato *f*

mutually: ~ **binding** *adj* GEN COMM solidario; ~ **exclusive** *adj* GEN COMM mutuamente excluyente

M/V *abbr* (*motor merchant vessel*) TRANSP navío mercante motorizado *m*

MYOP *abbr* (*multiyear operational plan*) FIN plan operacional plurianual *m*, plan plurianual de actuaciones *m*

MYRA *abbr* (*multiyear restructuring agreement*) FIN acuerdo reajustable plurianual *m*, acuerdo reestructurable plurianual *m*

mystery: ~ **shopper** *n jarg* S&M representante de una compañía que va a varias tiendas pidiendo un artículo específico para comprobar su calidad

N

n/a *abbr* (*no-account*) BANK sin cuenta

N/A *abbr* GEN COMM (*not applicable*) no pertinente, (*not available*) no disponible, (*no advice*) sin aviso

NAEGA *abbr* (*North American Export Grain Association*) IMP/EXP sociedad norteamericana de exportación de granos

NAFA *abbr* (*net acquisition of financial assets*) FIN adquisición neta de activos financieros *f*

NAFTA *abbr* (*North American Free Trade Agreement*) ECON, POL TLC (*Tratado de Libre Comercio*)

NAHB *abbr AmE* (*National Association of Home Builders*) PROP asociación estadounidense de constructores de viviendas

NAIC *abbr AmE* (*National Association of Insurance Commissioners*) INS sociedad estadounidense de comisionados de seguros

naked: **~ call** *n* STOCK *options* compra sin garantía *f*; **~ call option** *n* STOCK opción de compra de acciones sin garantía *f*; **~ option** *n* STOCK opción sin garantía *f*; **~ position** *n* STOCK posición en descubierto *f*; **~ put** *n* STOCK *options* opción doble sin garantía *f*; **~ short call** *n* STOCK *options* opción de compra a corto sin garantía *f*; **~ short option position** *n* STOCK posición corta al descubierto sobre una opción *f*; **~ short put** *n* STOCK opción de venta a corto sin garantía *f*; **~ writer** *n* STOCK emisor(a) de opciones abiertas *m,f*

NALGO *abbr BrE* (*National and Local Government Officers Association*) HRM, WEL sindicato británico de funcionarios de gobierno local y nacional

NAM *abbr AmE* (*National Assocation of Manufacturers*) IND asociación estadounidense de fabricantes

NAMAS *abbr* (*National Measurement Accreditation Service*) GEN COMM servicio nacional de acreditación de medidas

name *n* GEN COMM *of person, company* nombre *m*; **~ badge** GEN COMM gafete de identificación *m*; **~ brand** S&M nombre de marca *m*; **~ day** STOCK *London Stock Exchange* día anterior al de liquidación *m*; **~ position bond** INS *company* fianza de puesto laboral *f*; **~ schedule bond** INS fianza de lealtad nominal *f*; ◆ **in my ~ and on my behalf** LAW en mi nombre y representación; **in my ~, place and stead** LAW en mi nombre y representación

named: **~ client** *n* LAW cliente nominativo(-a) *m,f*; **~ peril policy** *n* INS póliza contra riesgo especificado *f*; **~ person** *n* LAW persona designada *f*

namely *adv* (*viz*) GEN COMM verbigracia (*v.gr.*)

nanny: **~ state** *n infrml* ECON *welfare state* estado del bienestar *m*

NAR *abbr AmE* (*National Association of Realtors*) PROP asociación estadounidense de agentes inmobiliarios

narcodollars *n pl infrml* ECON narcodólares *m pl* (*infrml*)

narrow[1]: **~ band** *n* ECON *EU* banda estrecha *f*; **~ margin** *n* ACC margen escaso *m*, margen estrecho *m*, margen reducido *m*; **~ market** *n* STOCK mercado con escasez de operaciones *m*, mercado flojo *m*

narrow[2] **1.** *vt* GEN COMM *gap* estrechar; **2.** *vi* STOCK *spread* estrechar

narrowcasting *n* S&M selección limitada *f*

narrowing: **~ inflation gap** *n* ECON déficit inflacionario decreciente *m*

narrows *n pl* TRANSP estrechos *m pl*

NASA *abbr AmE* (*National Aeronautics and Space Administration*) TRANSP administración estadounidense de aeronáutica y del espacio

NASD *abbr AmE* (*National Association of Securities Dealers*) STOCK asociación estadounidense de operadores de bolsa

NASDAQ *abbr AmE* (*National Association of Securities Dealers Automated Quotation*) STOCK cotización automatizada de la asociación estadounidense de operadores de bolsa

Nash: **~ bargaining** *n* ECON trato de Nash *m*

nat. *abbr* (*national*) GEN COMM nacional

NATFHE *abbr BrE* (*National Association of Teachers in Further Education*) HRM asociación británica de profesores de enseñanza media

national[1] *adj* (*nat.*) GEN COMM nacional

national[2]: **~ account** *n* S&M cuenta nacional *f*; **~ accounting** *n* ACC contabilidad nacional *f*; **~ accounts manager** *n* HRM, MGMNT director(a) de cuentas nacionales *m,f*; **~ affairs** *n pl* POL asuntos internos *m pl*; **~ association of investment clubs** *n* AmE STOCK asociación estadounidense de clubs de inversión; **~ average** *n* ECON media nacional *f*; **~ bank** *n* BANK, ECON banco nacional *m*; **~ borders** *n pl* GEN COMM fronteras nacionales *f pl*; **~ boundaries** *n pl* GEN COMM fronteras nacionales *f pl*; **~ brand** *n* S&M marca de ámbito nacional *f*; **~ campaign** *n* S&M campaña nacional *f*; **~ contingency fund** *n* FIN fondo nacional de contingencia *m*; **~ currency** *n* ECON moneda nacional *f*; **~ debt** *n BrE* (*cf public debt AmE*) ECON, POL deuda nacional *f*, deuda pública *f*; **~ debt management** *n BrE* (*cf public debt management AmE*) LAW, POL administración de la deuda pública *f*, gestión de la deuda pública *f*; **~ demand** *n* ECON demanda nacional *f*; **~ flag tonnage** *n* TRANSP *shipping* tonelaje bajo bandera nacional *m*; **~ grid** *n BrE* IND red británica de suministro de electricidad; **~ income** *n* ECON, POL renta nacional *f*; **~ insurance** *n BrE* (*NI*) TAX, WEL ≈ seguridad social *f*; **~ insurance contribution** *n* (*NIC*) WEL aportación a la seguridad social *f*, cuota de la seguridad social *f*; **~ insurance number** *n* TAX ≈ número de afiliación a la seguridad social *m*; **~ interest** *n* POL interés nacional *m*, razón de estado *f*; **~ law** *n* LAW ley nacional *f*; **~ legislation** *n* LAW legislación nacional *f*; **~ market advisory board** *n* STOCK consejo asesor del mercado nacional *m*; **~ nature reserve** *n* ENVIR reserva natural nacional *f*; **~ newspaper** *n* MEDIA periódico nacional *m*; **~ noise standard** *n* ENVIR estándar nacional de ruido *m*; **~ patent** *n* LAW, PATENTS patente nacional *f*; **~ plan** *n BrE* POL *1965* plan nacional *m*; **~ press** *n* MEDIA, S&M prensa nacional *f*; **~ quota** *n* ECON cuota nacional *f*; **~ sales tax** *n AmE* TAX impuesto nacional sobre ventas *m*; **~ savings** *n pl* BANK, ECON, FIN ahorro nacional *m*;

~ **savings certificates** *n pl BrE* BANK, FIN bonos de ahorro nacional *m pl*; ~ **savings register** *n BrE* STOCK indicador del ahorro nacional; ~ **standard shipping note** *n (NSSN)* TRANSP nota de embarque nacional normalizada *f*; ~ **subsidiary structure** *n* GEN COMM *company structure* estructura de filiales nacionales *f*; ~ **tax** *n* TAX impuesto nacional *m*; ~ **trend** *n* GEN COMM tendencia nacional *f*; ~ **union** *n* HRM sindicato nacional *m*; ~ **wage award** *n* HRM arbitraje nacional sobre salarios *m*, decisión salarial nacional *f*; ~ **wealth** *n* ECON riqueza nacional *f*

National: ~ **Aeronautics and Space Administration** *n AmE (NASA)* TRANSP administración estadounidense de aeronáutica y del espacio; ~ **Association of Manufacturers** *n AmE (NAM)* IND asociación estadounidense de fabricantes; ~ **Association of Home Builders** *n AmE (NAHB)* PROP asociación estadounidense de constructores de viviendas; ~ **Association of Insurance Commissioners** *n AmE (NAIC)* INS sociedad estadounidense de comisionados de seguros; ~ **Association of Realtors** *n AmE (NAR)* PROP asociación estadounidense de agentes inmobiliarios; ~ **Association of Securities Dealers** *n AmE (NASD)* STOCK asociación estadounidense de operadores en bolsa; ~ **Association of Securities Dealers Automated Quotation** *n AmE (NASDAQ)* STOCK cotización automatizada de la asociación estadounidense de operadores de bolsa; ~ **Association of Teachers in Further Education** *n BrE (NATFHE)* HRM asociación británica de profesores de enseñanza media; ~ **Banking Act** *n AmE* BANK ley bancaria estadounidense; ~ **Board for Prices and Incomes** *n (NBPI)* ECON Junta Nacional de Precios y Rentas *f*; ~ **Broadcasting Company** *n AmE* MEDIA compañía de televisión estadounidense; ~ **Bureau of Economic Research** *n AmE (NBER)* ECON departamento estadounidense de investigación económica; ~ **Bureau of Standards** *n AmE* GEN COMM, IND oficina estadounidense de normalización; ~ **Business Publications** *n pl AmE* MEDIA publicaciones comerciales estadounidenses; ~ **Council on International Trade Documentation** *n AmE (NCITD)* GEN COMM consejo estadounidense de documentación comercial; ~ **Council of Voluntary Organizations** *n BrE (NCVO)* WEL organización para la coordinación de asociaciones voluntarias, ≈ Consejo del Voluntariado Nacional *m (AmL)*, ≈ Plataforma Nacional del Voluntariado *f (Esp)*; ~ **Curriculum** *n BrE (NC)* WEL *education* plan de estudios a nivel nacional, ≈ Diseño Curricular Base *m (Esp) (DCB)*; ~ **Data Processing Service** *n BrE (NDPS)* COMMS *subsidiary of British Telecom* servicio británico de procesamiento de datos; ~ **Dock Labour Board** *n (NDLB)* HRM consejo nacional de trabajo portuario; ~ **Economic Development Council** *n BrE (NEDC, Neddy)* ECON consejo británico de desarrollo económico; ~ **Executive Committee** *n BrE (NEC)* POL *Labour Party* comité ejecutivo británico; ~ **Farmers Union** *n BrE (NFU)* ECON, IND ≈ Sindicato General de Agricultores y Ganaderos *m (Esp)*; ~ **Federation of American Shipping** *n (NFAS)* TRANSP federación estadounidense naviera; ~ **Futures Association** *n AmE (NFA)* STOCK asociación estadounidense de operaciones de futuros; ~ **Income and Product Accounts** *n (NIPA)* ECON cuentas de la renta y producción nacionales; ~ **Industrial Recovery Act** *n BrE* IND, LAW ley británica de recuperación industrial; ~ **Institute of Economic and Social Research** *n (NIESR)* ECON, WEL instituto nacio-

nal de investigación económica y social *m*; ~ **Joint Committee** *n BrE (NJC)* HRM comisión británica mixta; ~ **Joint Industrial Council** *n BrE (NJIC)* HRM, IND consejo nacional paritario del sector industrial; ~ **Labor Relations Act** *n AmE POL 1935* ≈ Estatuto de los Trabajadores *f (Esp)*; ~ **Labor Relations Board** *n AmE (NLRB)* HRM junta estadounidense de relaciones laborales; ~ **and Local Government Officers Association** *n BrE (NALGO)* HRM, WEL sindicato de funcionarios de gobierno local y nacional; ~ **Lottery** *n* LEIS Lotería Nacional *f*; ~ **Maritime Board** *n (NMB)* TRANSP comisión marítima nacional; ~ **Market System** *n (NMS)* STOCK sistema nacional de mercado *m*; ~ **Measurement Accreditation Service** *n (NAMAS)* GEN COMM servicio nacional de acreditación de medidas; ~ **Plan** *n BrE POL 1965* plan nacional *m*; ~ **Productivity Board** *n* IND Consejo de Productividad Nacional *m*; ~ **Savings Bank** *n BrE (NSB)* BANK banco nacional de ahorros, ≈ Caja Postal de Ahorros *f (Esp)*; ~ **Savings Income Bonds** *n BrE* BANK pagarés del Tesoro sin deducción en origen *m pl*; ~ **Savings Investment Account** *n BrE* STOCK cuenta de inversión de ahorro nacional *f*; ~ **Securities Clearing Corporation** *n AmE* STOCK ≈ Corporación Nacional de Compensación de Valores *f*; ~ **Shipping Authority** *n AmE* TRANSP autoridad marítima estadounidense; ~ **Trade Union Council** *n (NTUC)* HRM Consejo del Sindicato Nacional *m*; ~ **Treasury** *n* FIN Tesoro Público *m*; ~ **Trust** *n BrE* ENVIR organización británica para la conservación de monumentos históricos y edificios de interés cultural; ~ **Union of Marine Aviation and Shipping Transport** *n BrE (NUMAST)* HRM, TRANSP sindicato británico de aviación y transporte marítimo; ~ **Union of Mineworkers** *n BrE (NUM)* HRM sindicato británico de mineros; ~ **Union of Public Employees** *n BrE (NUPE)* HRM sindicato británico de trabajadores del estado; ~ **Union of Seamen** *n BrE (NUS)* HRM sindicato británico de marineros; ~ **Union of Students** *n BrE (NUS)* WEL unión general de estudiantes, ≈ Sindicato de Estudiantes Universitarios *m (Esp) (SEU)*; ~ **Wages Council** *n BrE (NWC)* HRM consejo británico salarial

nationalism *n* ECON, POL nacionalismo *m*

nationalization *n* ECON, POL nacionalización *f*

nationalize *vt* ECON, POL nacionalizar

nationalized: ~ **enterprise** *n* ECON, IND, POL empresa nacionalizada *f*; ~ **industry** *n* ECON, IND, POL industria nacionalizada *f*; ~ **sector** *n* ECON, IND, POL sector nacionalizado *m*

nationwide *adj* GEN COMM de ámbito nacional

native[1] *adj* LAW, POL oriundo

native[2]: ~ **industry** *n* ECON, IND industria nacional *f*

NATO *abbr (North Atlantic Treaty Organization)* POL OTAN *(Organización del Tratado del Atlántico Norte)*

natural: ~ **break** *n* S&M interrupción natural *f*; ~ **business year** *n* GEN COMM año comercial natural *m*; ~ **capital** *n* GEN COMM capital constituido por tierras *m*; ~ **draft** *n* ECON *agricultural* tiro natural *m*; ~ **gas** *n* ENVIR gas natural *m*; ~ **increase** *n* ECON incremento vegetativo *m*; ~ **monopoly** *n* ECON monopolio natural *m*; ~ **number** *n* COMP entero natural *m*; ~ **person** *n* GEN COMM persona física *f*; ~ **price** *n* ECON precio natural *m*; ~ **rate of employment** *n* ECON, WEL tasa natural de empleo *f*; ~ **rate of growth** *n* ECON *productive potential* tasa natural de crecimiento *f*; ~ **rate of interest** *n* ECON tasa natural de interés *f*; ~ **resources** *n pl* GEN COMM recursos naturales *m pl*; ~ **resources management** *n* ENVIR gestión de los recursos naturales *f*; ~ **rights** *n pl* LAW derechos naturales *m pl*; ~ **wastage** *n* ECON, ENVIR, GEN COMM merma natural *f*, desgaste natural *m*; ~ **wear and tear** *n* GEN COMM desgaste natural *m*

nature *n* GEN COMM naturaleza *f*; ~ **conservation** ENVIR conservación de la naturaleza *f*; ~ **of the invention** PATENTS naturaleza de la invención *f*

nautical: ~ **mile** *n* GEN COMM, TRANSP milla marítima *f*; ~ **regristration** *n* TRANSP registro náutico *m*

NAV *abbr* (*net asset value*) ACC, FIN VAN (*valor de activo neto*)

naval: ~ **architect** *n* HRM, TRANSP arquitecto(-a) naval *m,f*, ingeniero(-a) naval *m,f*; ~ **superintendent** *n* HRM superintendente naval *mf*

navigate *vi* TRANSP navegar

navigation *n* TRANSP navegación *f*; ~ **law** LAW, TRANSP *commercial* ley de navegación *f*

NAWFA *abbr* (*North Atlantic Westbound Freight Association*) TRANSP asociación del atlántico norte de transporte de flete con destino al oeste

NB *abbr* GEN COMM (*nota bene*) nota bene, TRANSP (*northbound*) con dirección norte

NBC *abbr AmE* (*National Broadcasting Company*) MEDIA compañía de televisión estadounidense

NBCC *abbr* (*Nigerian-British Chamber of Commerce*) GEN COMM cámara de comercio nigerio-británica

NBER *abbr AmE* (*National Bureau of Economic Research*) ECON departamento estadounidense de investigación económica

NBPI *abbr* (*National Board for Prices and Incomes*) ECON Junta Nacional de Precios y Rentas *f*

NBV *abbr* (*no business value*) FIN sin valor comercial

NC *abbr* (*noncontinuous liner*) TRANSP *shipping* buque de línea ocasional *m*, WEL *education* (*National Curriculum*) ≈ DCB (*Diseño Curricular Base*) (*Esp*)

N/C *abbr* (*new crop*) ECON *agricultural* nueva cosecha *f*

NCITD *abbr AmE* (*National Council on International Trade Documentation*) GEN COMM consejo estadounidense de documentación comercial

NCR *abbr* (*net cash requirement*) ACC, FIN necesidades de contado *f pl*

NCS *abbr* (*noncallable securities*) STOCK valores no rescatables antes de su vencimiento

n.c.v. *abbr* (*no commercial value*) GEN COMM sin valor comercial

NCV *abbr* (*no customs value*) IMP/EXP sin valor en aduana

NCVO *abbr BrE* (*National Council of Voluntary Organizations*) WEL organización para la coordinación de asociaciones voluntarias, ≈ Consejo del Voluntariado Nacional *m* (*AmL*), ≈ Plataforma Nacional del Voluntariado *f* (*Esp*)

NDLB *abbr* (*National Dock Labour Board*) HRM consejo nacional de trabajo portuario

NDP *abbr* (*net domestic product*) ECON PIN (*producto interior neto*)

NDPS *abbr* (*National Data Processing Service*) COMMS servicio nacional de procesamiento de datos

neap: ~ **tide** *n* TRANSP *shipping* marea muerta *f*

near[1]: ~**-cash items** *n pl* STOCK activos líquidos *m pl*; ~ **future** *n* GEN COMM futuro inmediato *m*; ~ **letter quality** *n* (*NLQ*) COMP calidad casi de impresión alta *f* (*NLQ*); ~ **money** *n* ECON cuasi dinero *m*

near[2]: ~ **completion** *phr* GEN COMM casi acabado; **in the** ~ **future** *phr* GEN COMM en un futuro próximo

nearby: ~ **contracts** *n pl* STOCK contratos de futuros *m pl*

nearbys *n pl jarg* STOCK *futures market* contratos de futuros *m pl*

nearest: ~ **month** *n* STOCK mes inmediato *m*

nearly: ~ **contract** *n* STOCK cuasi contrato *m*

NEB *abbr obs* (*National Enterprise Board*) ECON junta nacional empresarial, ≈ INI (*Instituto Nacional de Industria*) (*Esp*)

NEC *abbr BrE* (*National Executive Committee*) POL comité ejecutivo británico

necessary: ~ **labor** *AmE*, ~ **labour** *BrE n* HRM mano de obra indispensable *f*, mano de obra necesaria *f*, *task* trabajo necesario *m*

NEDC *abbr BrE* (*National Economic Development Council*) ECON consejo británico de desarrollo económico

Neddy *abbr BrE* (*National Economic Development Council*) ECON consejo británico de desarrollo económico

need *n* GEN COMM necesidad *f*; ~ **arousal** S&M estimulación de una necesidad *f*; ~**-to-know basis** GEN COMM, MGMNT base de necesidad de conocimiento *f*; ◆ **be in urgent** ~ **of** GEN COMM tener necesidad urgente de

needs *n pl* GEN COMM necesidades *f pl*; ~ **analysis** *n* HRM, S&M análisis de necesidades *m*; ~ **test** *n* TAX comprobación de necesidades *f*; ~ **of trade** *n* BANK necesidades comerciales *f pl*, necesidades de comercio *f pl*

needy: **the** ~ *n pl* ECON, WEL los pobres *m pl*

negative[1]: ~ **amortization** *n* FIN *of loan* amortización negativa *f*; ~ **carry** *n* FIN traslado negativo *m*; ~ **cash flow** *n* ACC, FIN cash-flow negativo *m*, flujo de caja negativo *m*, liquidez negativa *f*; ~ **correlation** *n* MATH correlación negativa *f*; ~ **elasticity** *n* ECON elasticidad negativa *f*; ~ **feedback** *n* COMP, ECON reacción negativa *f*, feedback negativo *m*; ~ **file** *n* BANK archivo negativo *m*, copia negativa *f*; ~ **financing** *n* BANK, FIN financiación negativa *f*; ~ **income tax** *n* (*NIT*) ECON, TAX impuesto negativo sobre la renta *m*; ~ **interest** *n* BANK interés negativo *m*; ~ **interest rate gap** *n* STOCK *futures* diferencial negativo del tipo de interés *m*, gap negativo del tipo de interés *m*; ~ **investment** *n* FIN inversión negativa *f*; ~ **monetary compensatory amount** *n* FIN cantidad compensatoria monetaria negativa *f*; ~ **net worth** *n* ECON valor neto negativo *m*; ~ **option** *n* GEN COMM opción negativa *f*; ~ **pledge** *n* BANK pignoración negativa *f*; ~ **pledge clause** *n* BANK cláusula de garantía negativa *f*; ~ **reserve** *n* ACC reserva negativa *f*; ~ **savings** *n* BANK, ECON, FIN ahorros negativos *m pl*; ~**-sum game** *n* ECON juego de suma negativa *m*; ~ **targeting** *n* POL campaña destinada a desacreditar políticamente a la oposición; ~ **tax expenditure** *n* TAX gasto fiscal negativo *m*; ~ **working capital** *n* ACC capital circulante negativo *m*, capital de trabajo negativo *m*, fondo de operaciones negativo *m*; ~ **yield curve** *n* ECON curva de rendimiento negativo *f*

negative[2]: **go** ~ *phr AmE jarg* POL montar una campaña destinada a mostrar las debilidades del oponente

neglect: ~ **clause** *n* INS, LAW, TRANSP cláusula de negligencia *f*

neglected *adj* GEN COMM abandonado

negligence *n* GEN COMM descuido *m*, negligencia *f*; ~ **clause** INS, LAW *marine*, TRANSP cláusula de negligencia *f*

negligent *adj* GEN COMM negligente

negligently *adv* GEN COMM negligentemente

negotiability *n* GEN COMM negociabilidad *f*

negotiable[1] *adj* GEN COMM negociable

negotiable[2]: ~ **bill** *n* BANK cuenta negociable *f*; ~ **bill of exchange** *n* BANK letra de cambio negociable *f*; ~ **bill of lading** *n* IMP/EXP, TRANSP conocimiento de embarque negociable *m*; ~ **check** *AmE*, ~ **cheque** *BrE n* BANK, FIN cheque negociable *m*; ~ **instrument** *n* BANK, FIN título negociable *m*; ~ **issue** *n* HRM cuestión negociable *f*; ~ **order of withdrawal** *n* BANK, FIN, STOCK orden negociable de retirada *f*; ~ **order of withdrawal account** *n* (*NOW account*) BANK cuenta corriente especial *f*, cuenta de ahorro a la vista con interés *f*, cuenta hipotecaria especial *f*; ~ **securities** *n pl* STOCK títulos negociables *m pl*

negotiate 1. *vt* GEN COMM, HRM negociar; ◆ ~ **with sb** GEN COMM negociar con alguien; **2.** *vi* GEN COMM, HRM negociar

negotiated: ~ **coordination** *n* ECON coordinación negociada *f*; ~ **market price** *n* ECON, S&M precio de mercado negociado *m*; ~ **price** *n* ECON, S&M precio negociado *m*; ~ **underwriting** *n* STOCK colocación negociada *f*

negotiating: ~ **bank** *n* BANK banco que negocia un crédito; ~ **machinery** *n* HRM *industrial relations* mecanismo de negociación *m*; ~ **position** *n* GEN COMM posición negociadora *f*; ~ **procedure** *n* GEN COMM, HRM procedimiento de negociación *m*; ~ **table** *n* HRM, MGMNT mesa de negociaciones *f*

negotiation *n* GEN COMM negociación *f*; ~ **fee** BANK costo de negociación *m*, gastos de tramitación *m pl*; ~ **strategy** GEN COMM, HRM, STOCK estrategia de negociación *f*

negotiator *n* GEN COMM negociador(a) *m,f*

neighborhood *AmE see neighbourhood BrE*; ~ **store** *n AmE* (*cf local shop BrE, corner shop BrE*) GEN COMM, S&M tienda de barrio *f*

neighboring: ~ **country** *AmE see neighbouring country BrE*

neighbourhood *n BrE* GEN COMM vecindario *m*; ~ **effect** *BrE* ECON efecto externo *m*

neighbouring: ~ **country** *n BrE* GEN COMM país vecino *m*

nemo dat quod no habet *phr* GEN COMM no se da lo que no se tiene

neoclassical: ~ **economics** *n* ECON economía neoclásica *f*

Neoclassical: ~ **School** *n* ECON Escuela Neoclásica *f*

neocorporatism *n* ECON, POL neocorporativismo *m*

neomalthusianism *n* ECON, POL neomaltusianismo *m*

neomercantilism *n* ECON, POL neomercantilismo *m*

neon: ~ **sign** *n* GEN COMM rótulo de neón *m*

neo-Ricardian: ~ **theory** *n* ECON teoría neoricardiana *f*

NEP *abbr* (*new economic policy*) ECON nueva política económica *f*

nepotism *n* HRM nepotismo *m*

nerve: ~ **center** *AmE*, ~ **centre** *BrE n* MGMNT centro neurálgico *m*, punto neurálgico *m*

NES *abbr* (*not elsewhere specified*) GEN COMM no especificado en otro punto

nest *vt* COMP anidar

nested *adj* COMP anidado

nesting *n* COMP anidamiento *m*; ~ **berth** TRANSP muelle jerarquizado *m*

net[1]: ~ **of** *adj* GEN COMM neto de

net[2] *n* GEN COMM neto *m*; ~ **acquisition of financial assets** (*NAFA*) FIN adquisición neta de activos financieros *f*; ~ **acquisitions** *n pl* ECON, FIN adquisiciones netas *f pl*; ~ **asset** ACC, FIN activo neto *m*; ~ **asset amount** ACC importe neto del activo *m*, montante neto del activo *m*, monto neto de los activos *m*; ~ **asset based values** *n pl* ACC valores basados en el activo neto *m pl*; ~ **asset value** (*NAV*) ACC, FIN valor de activo neto *m* (*VAN*); ~ **audience** S&M audiencia neta *f*; ~ **barter terms of trade** IMP/EXP relación neta de trueque *f*; ~ **base capital** ACC capital neto de base *m*; ~ **book value** ACC, FIN valor neto en libros *m*; ~ **borrowing** ECON, FIN, POL empréstitos netos *m pl*, préstamos netos *m pl*; ~ **capital expenditure** ECON, FIN gasto neto de capital *m*; ~ **capital gain** ECON, FIN plusvalías netas *f pl*, TAX rendimiento neto del capital *m*; ~ **capital loss** ECON, FIN minusvalías netas *f pl*; ~ **capital requirement** ECON, FIN exigencia neta del capital *f*; ~ **capital spending** ECON, FIN gasto neto de capital *m*; ~ **cash flow** GEN COMM flujo neto de caja *m*; ~ **cash requirement** (*NCR*) ACC, FIN necesidades de contado *f pl*; ~ **change** STOCK *securities* variación neta *f*; ~ **commission income** ACC ingreso neto por comisiones *m*, renta neta por comisiones *f*; ~ **contribution** GEN COMM contribución neta *f*; ~ **cost** GEN COMM coste neto *m* (*Esp*), costo neto *m* (*AmL*); ~ **cover** S&M cobertura neta *f*; ~ **credit** STOCK *options* crédito neto *m*; ~ **current asset** ACC, FIN activo neto circulante *m*; ~ **daily loss** FIN, TRANSP *chartering* pérdida neta diaria *f*; ~ **daily surplus** FIN excedente neto diario *m*, TRANSP *chartering* ganancia neta diaria *f*; ~ **debit** STOCK *options* débito neto *m*; ~ **debt** GEN COMM deuda neta *f*; ~ **dividend** ACC, STOCK dividendo neto *m*; ~ **domestic investment** ACC inversión neta interior *f*; ~ **domestic product** (*NDP*) ECON producto interior neto *m* (*PIN*); ~ **earnings** *n pl* GEN COMM ganancias netas *f pl*; ~ **employment earnings** TAX ganancias netas procedentes del empleo *f pl*; ~ **equity** ACC capital propio *m*, fondos propios *m pl*, patrimonio neto *m*; ~ **estate** *AmE* TAX acervo hereditario neto *m*; ~ **expenditure** ECON *development aid* desembolso neto *m*; ~ **federal tax** TAX impuesto federal neto *m*; ~ **foreign asset** BANK activo exterior neto *m*; ~ **foreign income** TAX ingresos netos procedentes del exterior *m pl*; ~ **foreign investment** ACC inversión extranjera neta *f*; ~ **forward position** BANK posición futura neta *f*; ~ **from charter** IMP/EXP, TRANSP condiciones netas *f pl*; ~ **gain** TAX ganancia neta *f*; ~ **gainer** ECON ganador(a) claro(-a) *m,f*; ~ **income** GEN COMM ingreso neto *m*, renta neta *f*; ~ **income per share of common stock** ACC rendimiento neto por cada acción ordinaria *m*; ~ **income-to-net worth ratio** ACC proporción de ingresos netos a patrimonio neto *f*, ratio de ingresos netos a patrimonio neto *m*; ~ **interest income** BANK interés neto devengado *m*; ~ **interest margin** ACC margen de interés neto *m*; ~ **interest yield** BANK, FIN rendimiento de interés neto *m*; ~ **investment position** BANK posición de inversión neta *f*; ~ **leasable area** PROP zona arrendable neta *f*; ~ **lease** PROP arrendamiento más gastos *m*; ~ **lending** GEN COMM préstamo neto *m*; ~ **lending by the public sector** GEN COMM préstamos netos del sector público *m pl*; ~ **line** INS retención neta *f*; ~ **liquid funds** *n pl* ACC, BANK, FIN fondos líquidos netos *m pl*; ~ **listing** PROP listado neto *m*; ~ **loss** GEN COMM pérdida neta *f*; ~ **margin** ACC, ECON, FIN margen neto *m*; ~ **operating income** ACC beneficio de explotación neto *m*; ~ **oper-**

ating loss ACC pérdida de explotación neta *f*; **~ operating profit** ACC beneficio neto de operación *m* (*Esp*), utilidad neta de operación *f* (*AmL*); **~ output** ECON, POL producción neta *f*; **~ paid circulation** S&M difusión pagada neta *f*; **~ pay** HRM salario neto *m*; **~ position** FIN, STOCK *purchases, sales* posición neta *f*; **~ position report** STOCK informe de la posición neta *m* (*Esp*), reporte de la posición neta *m* (*AmL*); **~ premium** INS, STOCK *options* prima neta *f*; **~ present value** (*NPV*) ACC, FIN valor actual neto *m* (*VAN*), valor presente neto *m* (*VAN*); **~ price** S&M precio neto *m*; **~ proceeds** *n pl* (*np*) PROP *sale* producto neto *m*; **~ profit** GEN COMM beneficio neto *m*; **~ profit for the current year** ACC beneficio neto del año en curso *m*, beneficio neto del ejercicio *m*; **~ profit margin** GEN COMM margen de beneficio neto *m*; **~ profits** *n pl* GEN COMM excedente neto *m*; **~ property income from abroad** FIN, PROP ingresos netos de bienes inmobiliarios en el extranjero *m pl*; **~ purchases** *n pl* ACC compras netas *f pl*; **~ quick asset** ACC activo neto realizable *m*; **~ rate** BANK *of interest on loan* tasa neta *f*; **~ reach** S&M alcance neto *m*; **~ realizable value** (*NRV*) GEN COMM valor realizable neto *m*; **~ realized capital gains per share** *n pl* STOCK ganancias de capital neto realizado por acción *f pl*; **~ receipts** *n pl* ACC entradas netas *f pl*, ingresos netos *m pl*; **~ receipts pool** ACC grupo de entradas netas *m*; **~ recorded assets** *n pl* ACC activos contabilizados netos *m pl*; **~ register** FIN registro neto *m*; **~ register ton, ~ register tonne** (*NRT*) GEN COMM, TRANSP tonelada de arqueo *f*; **~ registered tonnage** (*NRT*) GEN COMM, TRANSP tonelaje neto registrado *m*; **~ relevant earnings** *n pl* TAX *for pensions, retirement* ingresos netos pertinentes *m pl*; **~ remittance** TAX consignación neta *f*, remesa neta *f*; **~ reserve adjustment amount** ACC importe neto del ajuste de la reserva *m*, montante neto del ajuste de la reserva *m*, monto neto del ajuste de la reserva *m*; **~ reserve inclusion amount** ACC importe neto de las reservas *m*, montante neto de las reservas *m*, monto neto de la reducción de la reserva *m*; **~ resource income** ACC *of corporation* renta neta de los recursos *f*; **~ sales** *n pl* GEN COMM ventas netas *f pl*; **~ surplus** GEN COMM superávit neto *m*; **~ tangible assets per share** *n pl* STOCK activos tangibles netos por acción *m pl*; **~ tare weight** GEN COMM peso de tara neto *m*; **~ taxable capital gain** TAX plusvalías netas imponibles *f pl*; **~ terms** *n pl* (*Nt*) TRANSP condiciones netas *f pl*; **~ tonnage** GEN COMM, TRANSP tonelaje de registro neto *m*; **~ transaction** STOCK transacción neta *f*; **~ value** GEN COMM valor neto *m*; **~ voting** FIN votación neta *f*; **~ weight** GEN COMM, TRANSP peso neto *m*; **~ working capital** ACC capital circulante neto *m*; **~ worth** ACC, FIN activo neto *m*; **~ worth assessment** ACC determinación del activo neto *f*, determinación del valor neto *f*, evaluación del valor neto *f*; **~ yield** ACC *of share* rendimiento neto *m*

net³ *vt* GEN COMM rendir

net against *vt* BANK deducir de

Net: the ~ *n* COMMS, COMP Internet *m*, la Red *f*, la Telaraña *f*, la Web *f*

network¹ *n* COMP, GEN COMM red *f*, MEDIA *broadcasting* cadena *f*; **~ analysis** COMP, MGMNT análisis de una red *m*; **~ building** GEN COMM construcción de red *f*; **~ marketing** S&M marketing de red *m*; **~ of sales outlets** S&M red de concesionarios de venta *f*

network² **1.** *vt* COMP interconectar, GEN COMM poner en red; **2.** *vi* HRM hacer contactos en el mundo de negocios

networking *n* BANK gestión de la red *f*, COMP conexión de redes *f*, gestión de redes *f*; **~ economy** ECON economía basada en el trabajo en cadena *f*; **~ software** COMP programa de gestión de redes *m*, software de gestión de redes *m*

neutral¹ *adj* GEN COMM, POL neutral; **~ to bearish** STOCK neutral a la baja

neutral²: **~ budget** *n* POL presupuesto neutro *m*; **~ covered call position** *n* STOCK *options* posición compradora neutral cubierta *f*; **~ covered short** *n* STOCK *options* posición vendedora neutral cubierta *f*; **~ technical progress** *n* ECON progreso técnico neutral *m*

neutralism *n* GEN COMM neutralismo *m*

neutrality *n* GEN COMM, POL neutralidad *f*; **~ of money** ECON neutralidad del dinero *f*

never: ~-never *n* infrml S&M compra a plazos *f*

nevertheless *adv* GEN COMM no obstante

new: ~ account report *n* STOCK nuevo informe contable *m*; **~ business** *n* GEN COMM nuevo giro *m*; **~ charter** *n* TRANSP nuevo fletamiento *m*; **~ classical economics** *n* ECON nueva economía clásica *f*; **~ crop** *n* (*N/C*) ECON *agricultural* nueva cosecha *f*; **~ deal** *n* GEN COMM nuevo trato *m*; **~ deck** *n* (*ND*) TRANSP cubierta nueva *f*; **~ democracies** *n pl* GEN COMM, POL nuevas democracias *f pl*; **~ economic mechanism** *n* ECON nuevo mecanismo económico *m*; **~ economic policy** *n* (*NEP*) ECON *Soviet Union* nueva política económica *f*; **~ economics** *n* ECON nueva economía *f*; **~ edition** *n* MEDIA *print* nueva edición *f*; **~ federalism** *n* POL nuevo federalismo *m*; **~-for-old deduction** *n* INS deducción nuevo por viejo *f*; **~ industrial state** *n* ECON nuevo estado industrial *m*; **~ international economic order** *n* ECON, POL nuevo orden económico internacional *m*; **~ issue** *n* STOCK nueva emisión *f*; **~ Keynesianism** *n* POL nuevo keynesianismo *m*; **~ law** *n* LAW jurisprudencia reciente *f*; **~ microeconomics** *n* ECON nueva microeconomía *f*; **~ money** *n* GEN COMM dinero fresco *m*; **~-product development** *n* S&M desarrollo de nuevo producto *m*; **~ protectionism** *n* ECON nuevo proteccionismo *m*; **~ realism** *n* HRM nuevo realismo *m*; **~ share** *n* FIN, STOCK acción nueva *f*; **~ technology** *n* GEN COMM tecnología nueva *f*; **~ technology agreement** *n* GEN COMM acuerdo sobre nueva tecnología *m*, contrato sobre nueva tecnología *m*; **~ time** *n* STOCK próxima liquidación *f*; **~ world order** *n* POL nuevo orden mundial *m*; **~ year** *n* GEN COMM año nuevo *m*

New: ~ Commonwealth *n* POL nueva Commonwealth *f*; **~ Earnings Survey** *n* ECON estudio sobre los ingresos *m*; **~ International Division of Labor** *AmE*, **~ International Division of Labour** *BrE* ECON, POL nueva división internacional del trabajo *f*; **~ Investment Authority** *n* (*NIA*) STOCK autoridad sobre nuevas inversiones *f*; **~ Left** *n* POL Nueva Izquierda *f*; **~ Right** *n* POL Nueva Derecha *f*; **~ Orleans Commodity Exchange** *n* STOCK mercado de mercaderías de Nueva Orleans; **~ York Coffee, Sugar and Cocoa Exchange** *n* STOCK bolsa de café, azúcar y cacao de Nueva York; **~ York Cotton Exchange** *n* STOCK mercado de algodón de Nueva York; **~ York Cotton Exchange and Petroleum and Citrus Associates** *n* STOCK mercado de algodón, petróleo y asociados de cítricos de Nueva York; **~ York Curb Exchange** *n* STOCK bolsa secundaria de

Nueva York; ~ **York Futures Exchange** *n* (*NYFE*) STOCK mercado de futuros de Nueva York; ~ **York Mercantile Exchange** *n* (*NYMEX*) STOCK bolsa mercantil de Nueva York; ~ **York prime loan rate** *n* (*NYPLR*) BANK tasa de préstamo preferente de Nueva York; ~ **York Shipping Association** *n* (*NYSA*) TRANSP asociación naviera de Nueva York; ~ **York Stock Exchange** *n* (*NYSE*) STOCK bolsa de Nueva York *f*; ~ **York Stock Exchange Composite Index** *n* STOCK índice compuesto de la bolsa de Nueva York *m*

newly¹: ~ **elected** *adj* GEN COMM elegido recientemente; ~ **privatized** *adj* GEN COMM de reciente privatización

newly²: ~ **industrialized country** *n* (*NIC*) ECON, IND país recientemente industrializado *m*, país de reciente industrialización *m*

news *n* GEN COMM *piece of news* noticia *f*, MEDIA noticias *f pl*; ~ **adviser** MEDIA asesor(a) de noticias *m,f*; ~ **agency** *BrE* (*cf wire service AmE*) COMMS, MEDIA agencia de noticias *f*; ~ **bulletin** MEDIA espacio informativo *m*; ~ **coverage** MEDIA cobertura de noticias *f*, cobertura informativa *f*; ~ **editor** MEDIA redactor(a) jefe(-a) *m,f*; ~ **flash** MEDIA avance de noticias *m*; ~ **headline** MEDIA *of newspaper* cabecera *f*; ~ **item** GEN COMM, MEDIA noticia *f*; ~ **pictures** *n pl* MEDIA fotografías de prensa *f pl*; ~ **round-up** MEDIA resumen informativo *m*

newscaster *n* MEDIA presentador(a) de noticias *m,f*

newsletter *n* GEN COMM boletín *m*

newspaper *n* GEN COMM diario *m*; ~ **advertisement** MEDIA, S&M anuncio de periódico *m*; ~ **advertising** MEDIA, S&M publicidad en periódicos *f*; ~ **publisher** HRM, MEDIA redactor(a) jefe de un periódico *m,f*; ~ **syndicate** MEDIA sindicato periodístico *m*, sindicato de periódicos *m*

Newspaper: ~ **Publishers' Association** *n* (*NPA*) MEDIA asociación de prensa

newsroom *n* MEDIA redacción *f*, sala de noticias *f*

next: **the** ~ **move** *n* GEN COMM los próximos movimientos *m pl*; ~**-to-reading matter** *n* S&M espacio publicitario al lado de texto redaccional

NFA *abbr AmE* (*National Futures Association*) STOCK asociación estadounidense de operaciones de futuros

NFAS *abbr* (*National Federation of American Shipping*) TRANSP federación estadounidense naviera

N-firm: ~ **concentration ratio** *n* ECON proporción de concentración de N-empresas *f*

NFTZ *abbr* (*Non Free-Trade Zone*) ECON zona de no libre comercio *f*

NFU *abbr BrE* (*National Farmers Union*) ECON, HRM ≈ Sindicato General de Agricultores y Ganaderos *m* (*Esp*)

NGO *abbr* (*nongovernmental organization*) POL ONG (*organización no gubernamental*)

NHP *abbr* (*nominal horsepower*) TRANSP caballo de vapor nominal *m*

NI *abbr BrE* (*National Insurance*) TAX, WEL ≈ Seguridad Social *f*

NIA *abbr* (*New Investment Authority*) STOCK autoridad sobre nuevas inversiones *f*

NIC *abbr* (*newly industrialized country*) ECON, IND país recientemente industrializado *m*, país de reciente industrialización *m*, WEL (*national insurance contribution*) aportación a la seguridad social *f*, cuota de la seguridad social *f*

niche *n* HRM buena posición *f*, colocación conveniente *f*, S&M nicho *m*; ~ **bank** BANK banco de posición conveniente *m*; ~ **market** S&M mercado altamente especializado *m*; ~ **trading** GEN COMM mercado cautivo *m*

NICs *abbr* (*National Insurance Contributions*) TAX, WEL ≈ Aportaciones a la Seguridad Social *f pl*

NIDL *abbr* (*New International Division of Labor AmE, New International Division of Labour BrE*) ECON, POL nueva división internacional del trabajo *f*

NIESR *abbr* (*National Institute of Economic and Social Research*) ECON, WEL instituto nacional de investigación económica y social

NIF *abbr* (*note issuance facility*) FIN NIF (*mecanismo de emisión de nota*)

Nigerian: ~**-British Chamber of Commerce** *n* (*NBCC*) GEN COMM cámara de comercio nigerio-británica

night: ~ **depository** *n* BANK depósito fuera de hora *m*, depósito nocturno *m*; ~ **letter** *n AmE* COMMS telegrama de madrugada *m*; ~ **safe** *n* BANK depósito fuera de hora *m*, depósito nocturno *m*; ~ **shift** *n* HRM turno de noche *m*; ~ **work** *n* HRM trabajo nocturno *m*

Nikkei: ~ **Average** *n* STOCK promedio Nikkei *m*; ~ **Index** *n* STOCK promedio Nikkei *m*, índice Nikkei *m*; ~ **225 Index** *n* STOCK Índice Nikkei 225 *m*

Nikkeiren *n* STOCK federación japonesa de asociaciones de empleadores

nil: ~ **paid** *phr* STOCK pago nulo *m*

NIMBY *abbr* (*not in my backyard*) ENVIR *protest slogan* en mi patio no

nine: ~**-bond rule** *n* STOCK *New York Stock Exchange* regla de los nueve bonos *f*

ninety: ~**-nine-year lease** *n* BANK, PROP renta por noventa y nueve años *f*

NIPA *abbr* (*National Income and Product Accounts*) ECON cuentas de la renta y producción nacionales

NIT *abbr* (*negative income tax*) ECON, TAX impuesto negativo sobre la renta *m*

nitrogen: ~ **fertilizer** *n* ENVIR fertilizante nitrogenado *m*

NJC *abbr BrE* (*National Joint Committee*) HRM comisión británica mixta

NJIC *abbr BrE* (*National Joint Industrial Council*) HRM, IND consejo británico paritario del sector industrial

NLQ *abbr* (*near letter quality*) COMP NLQ (*calidad casi de impresión alta*)

NLRB *abbr AmE* (*National Labor Relations Board*) HRM junta estadounidense de relaciones laborales

n/m *abbr* (*no mark*) TRANSP *shipping* sin marca

NMB *abbr* (*National Maritime Board*) TRANSP comisión marítima nacional

NMS *abbr* STOCK (*normal market size*) amplitud normal del mercado *f*, (*National Market System*) sistema nacional de mercado *m*

no. *abbr* (*number*) GEN COMM n.º (*número*)

no-account *adj* (*n/a*) BANK sin cuenta

no-claim: ~ **bonus** *n BrE* INS bonificación por no tener reclamaciones *f*

node *n* COMP nodo *m*

no-fault: ~ **automobile insurance** *AmE* (*cf no-fault car insurance BrE*) INS seguro del automóvil sin culpa *m*; ~ **car insurance** *BrE n* (*cf no-fault automobile insurance AmE*) INS seguro del automóvil sin culpa *m*

no-growth *adj* ECON sin crecimiento

noise *n* GEN COMM ruido *m*; ~ **emission** ENVIR sonoemisión *f*; ~ **insulation** ENVIR aislamiento del ruido *m*; ~ **level** ENVIR nivel del ruido *m*

no-lien: ~ **affidavit** *n* LAW acta notarial de no retención *f*

no-load: ~ **fund** *n* STOCK fondo sin gastos de gestión *m*

no-loan: ~ **fund** *n* STOCK fondo de inversión no proveniente de préstamo *m*

nominal[1] *adj* GEN COMM nominativo, nominal

nominal[2]: ~ **amount** *n* ACC importe nominal *m*; ~ **asset** *n* ACC activo nominal *m*; ~ **capital** *n* ACC capital nominal *m*; ~ **cost** *n* ACC coste nominal *m* (*Esp*), costo nominal *m* (*AmL*); ~ **damages** *n pl* LAW daños nominales *m pl*, daños de poca consideración *m pl*; ~ **GDP** *n* ECON valor nominal del PIB *m*; ~ **growth** *n* ECON crecimiento nominal *m*; ~ **horsepower** *n* (*NHP*) TRANSP caballo de vapor nominal *m*; ~ **income** *n* ECON, FIN, TAX ingreso nominal *m*; ~ **interest** *n* BANK, FIN, STOCK interés nominal *m*; ~ **interest rate** *n* BANK, FIN, STOCK tasa nominal de interés *f*, tipo de interés nominal *f*; ~ **ledger** *n* ACC libro mayor nominal *m*; ~ **loan rate** *n* BANK, FIN tasa de préstamo nominal *f*; ~ **paid-up capital** *n* STOCK capital nominal pagado *m*; ~ **payment** *n* GEN COMM, HRM pago nominal *m*; ~ **price** *n* ACC, FIN precio nominal *m*; ~ **quotation** *n* STOCK cotización nominal de una acción *f*; ~ **scale** *n* GEN COMM escala nominal *f*; ~ **tax rate** *n* TAX tipo impositivo nominal *m*; ~ **value** *n* ACC, STOCK valor nominal *m*; ~ **wages** *n pl* HRM salario nominal *m*; ~ **yield** *n* STOCK rendimiento nominal *m*

nominate *vt* GEN COMM designar

nomination *n* GEN COMM nominación *f*

nominee *n* GEN COMM candidato(-a) propuesto(-a) *m,f*, nominatario(-a) *m,f*, STOCK sociedad interpuesta *f*; ~ **account** STOCK cuenta nominal *f*; ~ **company** STOCK sociedad interpuesta *f*; ~ **name** BANK, STOCK nombre del nominatario *m*, nombre del titular *m*; ~ **shareholder** STOCK accionista nominatario(-a) *m,f*; ~ **stockholder** STOCK accionista nominatario(-a) *m,f*

Non: ~ **Free-Trade Zone** *n* (*NFTZ*) GEN COMM zona de no libre comercio *f*

non est factum *phr* LAW no es obligación mía

non-accelerating: ~ **inflation rate of unemployment** *n* ECON inflación no acelerada por la tasa de desempleo *f*

non-arm[1]: ~'s-**length** *adj* LAW, TAX en desigualdad de condiciones

non-arm[2]: ~'s-**length transaction** *n* GEN COMM transacción comercial sin favor *f*

nonacceptance *n* BANK *of bill or note* rechazo *m*, GEN COMM inaceptación *f*

nonaccruing[1] *adj* BANK no acumulable

nonaccruing[2]: ~ **loan** *n* BANK préstamo no acumulable *m*

nonadjustable: ~ **rate** *n* BANK tasa no ajustable *f*

nonagricultural: ~ **use** *n* ENVIR, PROP uso no agrícola *m*

no-name *adj* STOCK de menor riesgo

nonappearance *n* LAW contumacia *f*

nonapproved[1] *adj* STOCK *options* sin aprobar

nonapproved[2]: ~ **pension scheme** *n* FIN, HRM, WEL plan de pensiones no aprobado *m*

nonattributable *adj* GEN COMM no atribuible

nonaudit *adj* TAX sin auditar

nonbank: ~ **bank** *n* BANK, STOCK sociedad que realiza ciertas prácticas bancarias *f*; ~ **financial institution** *n* FIN, STOCK institución financiera no bancaria *f*

nonbanking: ~ **sector** *n* BANK, FIN sector no bancario *m*

nonbasic: ~ **commodity** *n* ECON bien no básico *m*; ~ **industry** *n* ECON, IND industria no básica *f*

nonbudgetary *adj* GEN COMM no presupuestario; ~ **total** *n* FIN total no presupuestario *m*

nonbusiness: ~ **income tax** *n* TAX impuesto sobre la renta de actividades no comerciales *m*; ~ **income foreign tax credit** *n* TAX desgravación de ingresos no empresariales gravados en el exterior *f*

noncallable[1] *adj* STOCK no redimible

noncallable[2]: ~ **bond** *n* FIN, STOCK bono no redimible *m*; ~ **securities** *n* (*NCS*) STOCK valores no rescatables antes de su vencimiento

noncash: ~ **payment system** *n* BANK sistema de pago no al contado *m*; ~ **rewards** *n pl* HRM compensaciones en especies *f pl*; ~ **self-service** *n* GEN COMM autoservicio sin dinero *m*

noncheckable *AmE see* **nonchequable** *BrE*

nonchequable: ~ **account** *n* *BrE* BANK cuenta sin emisión de cheques *f*; ~ **deposit** *n* *BrE* BANK depósito que no admite cheques *m*

nonclearing: ~ **item** *n* BANK efecto no compensable *m*; ~ **member** *n* STOCK miembro no liquidador *m*

noncommercial: ~ **cargo** *n* TRANSP carga no comercial *f*

noncompeting: ~ **group** *n* HRM grupo no competidor *m*

noncompetitive: ~ **bid** *n* STOCK oferta sin competencia *f*

noncompliance *n* LAW incumplimiento *m*

noncompulsory[1] *adj* GEN COMM voluntario, LAW no obligatorio

noncompulsory[2]: ~ **expenditure** *n* ECON gasto no obligatorio *m*

nonconcessional *adj* GEN COMM no concesionario

nonconforming: ~ **use** *n* LAW, PROP uso no conforme *m*

nonconformity *n* GEN COMM disconformidad *f*

nonconsolidated *adj* ACC no consolidado

noncontestability: ~ **clause** *n* INS cláusula de no disputa *f*, cláusula de no objeción *f*

noncontinuous: ~ **liner** *n* (*NC*) TRANSP buque de línea ocasional *m*

noncontribution: ~ **clause** *n* INS cláusula de no contribución *f*

noncontributory: ~ **pension fund** *n* HRM, TAX, WEL fondo de pensión no contributivo *m*; ~ **pension plan** *n* HRM, TAX, WEL plan de pensión no contributivo *m*; ~ **pension scheme** *n* HRM, TAX, WEL plan de pensión no contributivo *m*

noncontrollable: ~ **cost** *n* ACC coste incontrolable *m* (*Esp*), costo incontrolable *m* (*AmL*)

nonconvertible *adj* STOCK *bond* no convertible

noncreditable: ~ **tax** *n* TAX impuesto no acreditable *m*

noncumulative[1] *adj* GEN COMM no acumulable, no acumulativo

noncumulative[2]: ~ **preferred stock** *n* STOCK acciones privilegiadas de dividendo no acumulativo *f pl*; ~ **tax** *n* TAX impuesto no acumulativo *m*

noncurrent: ~ **asset** *n* ACC activo fijo *m*, activo inmovilizado *m*, activo no circulante *m*; ~ **loan** *n* BANK préstamo vencido *m*

noncyclical *adj* STOCK *performance* acíclico

nondebugged *adj* COMP sin corregir los errores

nondeductibility: ~ **of employer contributions** *n* HRM indeducibilidad de las contribuciones del empresario *f*, no deducibilidad de las contribuciones del empresario *f*

nondemise: ~ **charter party** *n* TRANSP contrato de fletamento no transferible *m*

nondestructive: ~ **testing** *n* IND prueba no destructiva *f*

nondisclosure *n* INS encubrimiento *m*

nondiscretionary: ~ **trust** *n* LAW, STOCK fideicomiso no discrecional *m*

nondiscrimination: ~ **notice** *n* HRM apercibimiento de no discriminación *m*, notificación de no discriminación *f*

nondisturbance: ~ **clause** *n* IND *mineral rights*, PROP *mortgage contract* cláusula de inalterabilidad *f*

nondurable: ~ **goods** *n pl* S&M bienes no duraderos *m pl*

nondurables *n pl* S&M productos perecederos *m pl*

nondutiable *adj* TAX exento de derechos o aranceles

nonencashable: ~ **deposit** *n frml* BANK depósito no canjeable *m*, depósito no liquidable *m*

non-EU: ~ **national** *n* ADMIN, GEN COMM persona no perteneciente a la UE *f*

nonexecution *n* LAW incumplimiento *m*

nonexecutive[1] *adj* HRM no ejecutivo

nonexecutive[2]: ~ **director** *n* HRM director(a) sin funciones ejecutivas *m,f*

nonexempt *adj* TAX no exento

nonfeasance *n* GEN COMM incumplimiento *m*, LAW *commercial* omisión *f*

nonfiler *n* TAX contribuyente que no presenta declaración

nonfiling *n* TAX *of return, form* falta de presentación *f*

nonfinancial: ~ **reward** *n* GEN COMM retribución no financiera *f*

nonfulfillment *AmE see nonfulfilment BrE*

nonfulfilment *n BrE* LAW incumplimiento *m*; ~ **of contract** *BrE* HRM, LAW incumplimiento de contrato *m*

nonfungible: ~ **goods** *n pl* ACC activos no fungibles *m pl*, bienes no fungibles *m pl*, elementos no fungibles *m pl*

nongovernmental: ~ **organization** *n* (*NGO*) POL organización no gubernamental *f* (*ONG*)

noninterest: ~ **earnings** *adj* BANK, FIN, STOCK ganancias sin intereses *f pl*

noninterest-bearing[1] *adj* BANK, FIN, STOCK sin rendimiento de intereses, sin intereses, que no devenga interés

noninterest-bearing[2]: ~ **deposit** *n* BANK depósito que no devenga interés *m*; ~ **securities** *n pl* STOCK acciones sin intereses *f pl*

nonintervention *n* BANK, ECON, FIN desintermediación *f*, POL no intervención *f*

nonlife: ~ **insurance** *n* INS seguro no de vida *m*

nonlinear: ~ **correlation** *n* MATH *statistics* correlación no lineal *f*; ~ **pricing** *n* ECON fijación de precios no lineal *f*; ~ **programming** *n* COMP, MATH programación no lineal *f*

nonluxury: ~ **goods** *n pl* S&M productos no lujosos *m pl*

nonmandatory *adj* LAW *guidelines* no preceptivo

nonmanual: ~ **union** *n* HRM sindicato de trabajadores no manuales *m*

nonmanufacturing: ~ **sector** *n* IND sector no manufacturero *m*

nonmarket: ~ **sector** *n* ECON sector no comercializado *m*

nonmarketable: ~ **instrument** *n* BANK instrumento no negociable *m*; ~ **title** *n BrE* (*cf nonmerchantable title AmE*) PROP título no negociable *m*, título intransferible *m*

nonmember: ~ **bank** *n AmE* BANK banco que no es miembro de la Reserva Federal; ~ **corporation** *n* STOCK corporación no respaldada *f*; ~ **firm** *n* STOCK firma no reconocida *f*

nonmerchantable: ~ **title** *n AmE* (*cf nonmarketable title BrE*) PROP título intransferible *m*, título no negociable *m*

nonmetropolitan *adj* GEN COMM no metropolitano

nonmonetary: ~ **investment** *n* HRM inversión no monetaria *f*; ~ **rewards** *n pl* HRM compensaciones en especies *f pl*

non-negotiable: ~ **bill of lading** *n* IMP/EXP, TRANSP *shipping* conocimiento de embarque no negociable *m*; ~ **check** *AmE*, ~ **cheque** *BrE n* BANK, FIN cheque no negociable *m*; ~ **instrument** *n* BANK documento no negociable *m*, instrumento no negociable *m*

nonobligatory *adj* LAW no obligatorio

nonobservance: ~ **of conditions** *n* GEN COMM inobservancia de las condiciones *f*

nonoccupying: ~ **owner** *n* PROP propietario(-a) no ocupante *m,f*

nonofficial: ~ **trade organization** *n* (*NOTO*) HRM organización gremial no oficial

nonoil: ~ **balance** *n* ECON balanza sin incluir el petróleo *f*; ~ **country** *n* ENVIR país carente de petróleo *m*

nonoperating: ~ **expense** *n* ACC gasto ajeno a la explotación *m*, gasto ajeno a la operación *m*; ~ **revenue** *n* ACC ingresos ajenos a la operación *m pl*

nonparametric: ~ **statistics** *n pl* MATH estadística no paramétrica *f*

nonparticipating: ~ **preferred stock** *n* FIN, STOCK acción preferencial no participativa *f*; ~ **share** *n* STOCK acción no participativa *f*

nonpayment *n* GEN COMM impago *m*, falta de pago *f*

nonpecuniary: ~ **returns** *n pl* HRM rendimiento no pecuniario *m*

nonpenalized: ~ **adjustment** *n* TAX ajuste sin recargo *m*; ~ **taxable income** *n* TAX ingreso imponible sin recargo *m*

nonperformance *n* LAW incumplimiento *m*

nonperforming: ~ **assets** *n* STOCK activos improductivos *m pl*; ~ **credit** *n* BANK crédito en falta de cumplimiento *m*, crédito en falta de ejecución *m*, crédito en mora *m*; ~ **loan** *n* BANK préstamo no ejecutable *m*

nonprice: ~ **competition** *n* S&M competencia ajena a los precios *f*

nonproductive[1] *adj* GEN COMM improductivo, HRM, MGMNT no productivo

nonproductive[2]: ~ **loan** *n* BANK préstamo improductivo *m*

nonprofessional: ~ **behavior** *AmE*, ~ **behaviour** *BrE n* HRM comportamiento no profesional *m*

nonprofit[1] *adj AmE* (*cf non-profit-making AmE*) GEN COMM no lucrativo, sin ánimo de lucro, sin beneficio

nonprofit[2]: ~ **accounting** *AmE* (*cf non-profit-making accounting BrE*) ACC contabilidad no lucrativa *f*; ~ **association** *n AmE* (*cf non-profit-making association BrE*) GEN COMM asociación sin ánimo de lucro *f*; ~ **enterprise** *n* (*NPE*) GEN COMM empresa no lucrativa *f*; ~**-making company** *n AmE* (*cf non-profit-making company BrE*) GEN COMM compañía sub fines de lucro *f*; ~**-making organization** *n AmE* (*cf non-profit-making* *organization BrE*) GEN COMM, TAX organización sin ánimo de lucro *f*

nonprofitable *adj* GEN COMM no lucrativo, sin ánimo de lucro, sin beneficio

non-profit-making[1] *adj BrE* (*cf nonprofit AmE*) GEN COMM no lucrativo, sin ánimo de lucro, sin beneficio

non-profit-making[2]: ~ **accounting** *BrE* (*cf nonprofit accounting AmE*) *n* ACC contabilidad no lucrativa *f*; ~ **association** *n BrE* (*cf nonprofit association AmE*) GEN COMM asociación sin ánimo de lucro *f*; ~ **company** *n BrE* (*cf nonprofit company AmE*) GEN COMM compañía sin fines de lucro *f*; ~ **organization** *n BrE* (*cf nonprofit organization AmE*) GEN COMM, TAX organización sin ánimo de lucro *f*

nonproject: ~ **aid** *n* ECON asistencia no dedicada a proyectos específicos *f*, POL ayuda no finalista *f*

nonpublic: ~ **information** *n* GEN COMM información privada *f*

nonpurpose: ~ **loan** *n* BANK, FIN préstamo sin finalidad declarada *m*

nonqualifying: ~ **annuity** *n* FIN anualidad no habilitante *f*; ~ **business** *n* TAX actividad no sujeta *f*, negocios no habilitantes *m pl*; ~ **share** *n* FIN, STOCK acción no habilitante *f*; ~ **stock option** *n* STOCK opción-bono no remunerativa *f*

nonrecourse: ~ **finance** *n* FIN financiación sin posibilidad de recurso *f*; ~ **financing** *n* FIN financiación sin recursos *f*; ~ **loan** *n* BANK, FIN préstamo gratuito *m*, préstamo sobre excedentes agrícolas *m*

nonrecuperable: ~ **packing** *n* S&M envase no recuperable *m*

nonrecurring: ~ **appropriation** *n* FIN asignación extraordinaria *f*; ~ **charge** *n* ACC cargo no recurrente *m*, gasto no recurrente *m*

nonrecyclable *adj* ENVIR no reciclable

nonrefundable[1] *adj* GEN COMM no reembolsable, STOCK no reintegrable

nonrefundable[2]: ~ **deposit** *n* GEN COMM depósito no reembolsable *m*; ~ **fee** *n* GEN COMM, S&M cuota no reembolsable *f*; ~ **taxes** *n pl* ACC, TAX impuestos no reembolsables *m pl*

nonregistrant *n* TAX no inscrito(-a) *m,f*

nonrenewable: ~ **natural resources** *n pl* ENVIR, GEN COMM recursos naturales no renovables *m pl*; ~ **resource** *n* ECON recurso no renovable *m*

nonresident[1] *adj* BANK no residente

nonresident[2] *n* GEN COMM, TAX no residente *mf*; ~ **bank** BANK banco no residente *m*; ~ **company** GEN COMM, LAW compañía no residente *f*, empresa no residente *f*; ~ **tax** TAX impuesto de no residente *m*, impuesto de visitante *m*; ~ **tax deduction** TAX deducción de impuestos de permanencia *f*, impuesto retenido a los no residentes *m*; ~ **withholding tax** TAX deducción de impuestos de permanencia *f*, impuesto retenido a los no residentes *m*

nonresidential: ~ **mortgage** *n* BANK, PROP hipoteca no residencial *f*

nonreusable *adj* GEN COMM no reutilizable

nonreversible: ~ **laytime** *n* TRANSP *shipping* estadía irreversible *f*

nonroutine: ~ **decision** *n* GEN COMM decisión no rutinaria *f*

nonscheduled *adj* GEN COMM no programado

nonsegregated: ~ **account** *n* STOCK cuenta no segregada *f*

nonstandard: ~ **mail** *n* COMMS correo sin normalizar *m*; ~ **tax relief** *n* TAX reducción impositiva no ordinaria *f*

nonstatutory *adj* LAW no obligatorio

nonsterling: ~ **area** *n* (*NSA*) ECON área de no influencia de la libra esterlina *f*

nonstock: ~ **company** *n BrE* (*cf nonstock corporation AmE*) STOCK sociedad sin acciones *f*; ~ **corporation** *n AmE* (*cf nonstock company BrE*) STOCK sociedad sin acciones *f*

nonstop: ~ **flight** *n* TRANSP vuelo sin escalas *m*

nonstore: ~ **retailing** *n* S&M venta minorista directa *f*

nontariff: ~ **barrier** *n* (*NTB*) ECON, IMP/EXP, TAX barrera no arancelaria *f*; ~ **trade barrier** *n* GEN COMM barrera comercial no arancelaria *f*

nontax: ~ **receipts** *n pl* ACC, TAX ingresos no tributarios *m pl*; ~ **revenue** *n* ACC, TAX ingresos libres de impuestos *m pl*, ingresos no tributarios *m pl*

nontaxable[1] *adj* TAX no imponible

nontaxable[2]: ~ **beneficiary** *n* TAX beneficiario(-a) no imponible *m,f*; ~ **obligation** *n* TAX obligación no imponible *f*; ~ **profitable firm** *n* TAX compañía mercantil no imponible *f*; ~ **repayment supplement** *n* TAX aumento de devolución no imponible *m*; ~ **year** *n* TAX año no impositivo *m*

nontradables *n pl* GEN COMM no comerciables *m pl*

nontransferable: ~ **debentures** *n pl* BANK garantías no transferibles *f pl*

non-union[1] *adj* HRM no sindicado

non-union[2]: ~ **firm** *n* HRM empresa no sindicada *f*, empresa no sindicalizada *f*; ~ **labor** *AmE*, ~ **labour** *BrE n* HRM mano de obra no sindicada *f*

nonutilized *adj* BANK, FIN, GEN COMM *line of credit* inutilizado

nonvariable *adj* BANK, GEN COMM no variable

nonverbal: ~ **communication** *n* GEN COMM, MGMNT comunicación no verbal *f*

nonvoting: ~ **share** *n* FIN, STOCK acción sin derecho de voto *f*; ~ **stock** *n* STOCK acciones sin derecho de voto *f pl*

nonworking: ~ **spouse** *n* HRM, TAX cónyuge que no trabaja *mf*

non-zero-sum: ~ **game** *n* ECON juego de suma no nula *m*

no-par[1]: ~ **value** *adj* (*n.p.v.*) STOCK sin valor a la par, sin valor nominal

no-par[2]: ~ **stock** *n* STOCK acción sin valor nominal *f*; ~~**value share** *n* STOCK acción sin valor nominal *f*

Nordic: ~ **countries** *n pl* GEN COMM países nórdicos *m pl*

norm *n* MGMNT rutina *f*; ◆ **above the** ~ GEN COMM por encima de la norma; **below the** ~ GEN COMM bajo la norma

normal: ~ **capacity** *n* ECON, IND capacidad normal *f*; ~ **course of business** *n* GEN COMM desarrollo normal de la empresa *m*; ~ **distribution** *n* MATH *statistics* distribución normal *f*; ~ **good** *n* ECON bien normal *m*; ~ **investment practice** *n* FIN modalidad normal de inversión *f*, práctica de inversión normal *f*; ~ **laytime** *n* TRANSP *shipping* estadía normal *f*; ~ **market size** *n* (*NMS*) STOCK amplitud normal del mercado *f*; ~ **price** *n* ECON, GEN COMM, S&M precio normal *m*; ~ **profit** *n* ACC beneficio normal *m*; ~ **rate** *n* TRANSP tarifa normal *f*; ~ **relationship** *n* STOCK *in prices* relación normal *f*;

~ **retirement** *n* HRM jubilación normal *f*; ~ **retirement age** *n* HRM edad normal de jubilación *f*; ~ **tax** *n* TAX impuesto normal *m*; ~ **trading unit** *n* STOCK unidad normal de negociación *f*; ~ **wear and tear** *n* GEN COMM uso y desgaste normales

normalcy *n* AmE (*cf normality BrE*) GEN COMM normalidad *f*

normality *n* BrE (*cf normalcy AmE*) GEN COMM normalidad *f*

normative: ~ **economics** *n* ECON economía normativa *f*; ~ **forecasting** *n* GEN COMM predicción normativa *f*

Norris-La Guardia: ~ **Act** *n* AmE HRM, LAW Ley Norris-La Guardia *f*

North: ~ **American Export Grain Association** *n* (*NAEGA*) IMP/EXP sociedad norteamericana de exportación de granos; ~ **American Free Trade Agreement** *n* (*NAFTA*) ECON, POL Tratado de Libre Comercio *m* (*TLC*); ~ **Atlantic rates** *n pl* TRANSP tarifas del Atlántico Norte *f pl*; ~ **Atlantic Treaty Organization** *n* (*NATO*) POL Organización del Tratado del Atlántico Norte *f* (*OTAN*); ~ **Atlantic Westbound Freight Association** *n* (*NAWFA*) TRANSP asociación del atlántico norte de transporte de flete con destino al oeste; ~ **Sea gas** *n* ENVIR gas del Mar del Norte *m*

northern *adj* GEN COMM septentrional

no-show *n* *infrml* LEIS pasajero que no se presenta a un vuelo

no-strike: ~ **agreement** *n* HRM acuerdo de no ir a la huelga *m*; ~ **clause** *n* HRM cláusula de no declaración de huelga *f*; ~ **deal** *n* HRM acuerdo de no ir a la huelga *m*

nostro: ~ **account** *n* BANK cuenta nostro *f*

nota bene *phr* (*NB*) GEN COMM nótese bien, nota bene

notarize *vt* LAW otorgar ante notario

notary: ~ **public** *n* LAW notario público *m*

note *n* ADMIN volante *m*, BANK BrE (*cf bill AmE*) billete *m*, billete de banco *m*, GEN COMM nota *f*; ~ **of cancellation at maturity** INS aviso de cancelación al vencimiento *m*; ~ **disclosure** GEN COMM divulgación de nota *f*; ~ **issuance facility** (*NIF*) FIN mecanismo de emisión de nota *m* (*NIF*); ~ **issue** BANK emisión fiduciaria *f*; ~-**issuing bank** BANK, ECON, FIN banco emisor *m*; ~ **payable** FIN documento por pagar *m*; ~ **receivable** FIN documento por cobrar *m*; ~ **under repurchase agreement** FIN *balance sheet* pagaré con pacto de recompra *m*

notebook *n* ADMIN, GEN COMM cuaderno *m*, COMP ordenador portátil *m* (*Esp*), computadora portátil *f* (*AmL*), computador portátil *m* (*AmL*)

notes: ~ **to the accounts** *n pl* ACC notas a las cuentas *f pl*; ~ **to the financial statements** *n pl* ACC anexo a los estados financieros *m*, memoria a los estados financieros *f*, notas a los estados financieros *f pl*

notice *n* GEN COMM aviso *m*, HRM *from employer or employee* aviso de despido *m*, notificación de despido *f*, INS declaración *f*; ~ **of abandonment** INS *marine* declaración de abandono *f*; ~ **account** BANK cuenta sujeta a preaviso *f*; ~ **of appeal** PATENTS notificación de apelación *f*, TAX aviso de recurso *m*; ~ **of application** TAX aviso de demanda *m*; ~ **of arrears** GEN COMM aviso de mora *m*; ~ **of assessment** TAX aviso de imposición *m*; ~ **of assignment** STOCK *currency options* notificación de ejercicio *f*; ~ **board** BrE COMMS, HRM tablón de anuncios *m* (*Esp*), cartelera *f* (*AmL*); ~ **of call** STOCK

aviso de opción de compra *m*; ~ **of cancellation** STOCK notificación de cancelación *f*, notificación de revisión *f*; ~ **of cancellation at anniversary date** (*NCAD*) INS aviso de cancelación al vencimiento *m*; ~ **of cancellation clause** INS cláusula de aviso de cancelación *m*; ~ **of cancellation on expiry date** INS aviso de cancelación al vencimiento *m*; ~ **of default** GEN COMM aviso de falta de pago *m*; ~ **deposit** BANK depósito sujeto a preaviso *m*; ~ **of dishonor** AmE, ~ **of dishonour** BrE BANK aviso de falta de aceptación *m*, aviso de rechazo *m*; ~ **of intention** LAW aviso de intención *m*, carta de intenciones *f*; ~ **of objection** TAX aviso de objeción *m*; ~ **of opposition** PATENTS requerimiento notarial al titular de la patente para que se pronuncie sobre la oponibilidad entre la patente y la explotación industrial que el requirente lleva a cabo; ~ **of original assessment** TAX aviso de imposición inicial *m*; ~ **of protest** TRANSP aviso de protesto *m*; ~ **of readiness** TRANSP aviso de disponibilidad *m*; ~ **of reassessment** TAX aviso de reevaluación *m*; ~ **of revocation** STOCK *of option* aviso de anulación *m*; ~ **of shipment** TRANSP aviso de embarque *m*, carta de embarque *f*; ~ **to quit** PROP aviso de desocupar *m*; ~ **treaty** LAW *land compensation* acuerdo de notificación *m*; ◆ **at 2 days** ~ GEN COMM con un preaviso de 2 días; **until further** ~ GEN COMM hasta nuevo aviso

notification *n* GEN COMM notificación *f*

notify[1]: ~ **address** *n* IMP/EXP, TRANSP dirección notificada *f*, dirección para avisos *f*

notify[2] *vt* GEN COMM *of decision* notificar; ◆ ~ **sb of sth** GEN COMM dar aviso a alguien de algo, notificar algo a alguien

notifying: ~ **party** *n* IMP/EXP, TRANSP parte notificante *f*

notional[1] *adj* GEN COMM nocional

notional[2]: ~ **rent** *n* PROP alquiler nocional *m*

NOTO *abbr* (*nonofficial trade organization*) HRM organización gremial no oficial

no-trade: ~ **equilibrium** *n* ECON no equilibrio comercial *m*

notwithstanding *prep* GEN COMM, LAW no obstante (*frml*); ◆ ~ **any other provision** GEN COMM independientemente de cualquier otra disposición

novation *n* GEN COMM, LAW *commercial* novación *f*

novelty *n* PATENTS novedad *f*; ~ **value** S&M valor de novedad *m*

novo: **de** ~ *adv* LAW de nuevo

novus actus interveniens *n* GEN COMM intervención de terceras personas

NOW: ~ **account** *n* (*negotiable order of withdrawal account*) BANK cuenta corriente especial *f*, cuenta de ahorro a la vista con interés *f*, cuenta hipotecaria especial *f*

noxious: ~ **gas** *n* ENVIR gas nocivo *m*

np *abbr* (*net proceeds*) PROP producto neto *m*

NPA *abbr* (*Newspaper Publishers' Association*) MEDIA asociación de prensa

NPE *abbr* (*nonprofit enterprise*) GEN COMM empresa no lucrativa *f*

n.p.v. *abbr* (*no-par value*) STOCK sin valor a la par, sin valor nominal

NPV *abbr* (*net present value*) ACC, FIN VAN (*valor actual neto, valor presente neto*)

NR *abbr* (*nuclear reactor*) ENVIR reactor nuclear *m*

NRT *abbr* GEN COMM, TRANSP (*net registered tonnage*)

tonelaje neto registrado *m*, (*net register ton*) tonelada de arqueo *f*

NRV *abbr* (*net realizable value*) GEN COMM valor realizable neto *m*

N.S.F.[1] *abbr* (*not sufficient funds*) BANK, GEN COMM fondos insuficientes *m pl*

N.S.F.[2]: **~ check** *AmE* (*not-sufficient-funds check*); **~ cheque** *BrE n* (*not-sufficient-funds cheque*) BANK, FIN cheque con fondos insuficientes *m*, cheque sin fondos suficientes *m*, cheque sin provisión suficiente de fondos *m*

NSA *abbr* (*non-sterling area*) ECON área de no influencia de la libra esterlina *f*

NSB *abbr BrE* (*National Savings Bank*) BANK banco nacional de ahorros, ≈ Caja Postal de Ahorros *f* (*Esp*) (*obs*), ≈ argenteria *f*

NSF[1] *abbr* (*not sufficient funds*) BANK, GEN COMM fondos insuficientes *m pl*

NSF[2]: **~ check** *AmE*, **~ cheque** *BrE n* BANK, FIN cheque con fondos insuficientes *m*, cheque sin fondos suficientes *m*, cheque sin provisión suficiente de fondos *m*

nspf *abbr* (*not specially provided for*) GEN COMM no específicamente dispuesto

NSSN *abbr* (*national standard shipping note*) TRANSP nota de embarque nacional normalizada *f*

Nt *abbr* (*net terms*) IMP/EXP, TRANSP condiciones netas *f pl*

NTB *abbr* (*nontariff barrier*) ECON, IMP/EXP, TAX barrera no arancelaria *f*

NTUC *abbr* (*National Trade Union Council*) HRM Consejo del Sindicato Nacional *m*

nuclear: **~ energy** *n* ENVIR, IND energía nuclear *f*; **~ industry** *n* ENVIR, IND industria nuclear *f*; **~ plant** *n* ENVIR, IND planta nuclear *f*; **~ power** ENVIR, IND energía atómica *f*; **~ power station** *n* ENVIR, IND central de energía nuclear *f*; **~ reactor** *n* (*NR*) ENVIR reactor nuclear *m*

Nuclear: **~ Installations Inspectorate** *n BrE* WEL cuerpo de inspección de instalaciones nucleares

nudum pactum *n* GEN COMM nudo pacto *m*

nugatory: **~ payment** *n* FIN pago nulo *m*

nuisance *n* GEN COMM perjuicio *m*; **~ tax** TAX impuesto burocrático *m*

null[1]: **~ hypothesis** *n* MATH *statistics* hipótesis nula *f*

null[2]: **~ and void** *phr* LAW nulo y sin efecto

NUM *abbr BrE* (*National Union of Mineworkers*) HRM sindicato británico de mineros

NUMAST *abbr BrE* (*National Union of Marine Aviation and Shipping Transport*) HRM, TRANSP sindicato británico de aviación y transporte marítimo

number[1] *n* (*no.*) GEN COMM número *m* (*n.º*); **~ crunching** *infrml* ACC cálculo complejo; **~ of employees** HRM número de empleados *m*; **~ facts** *n pl* WEL datos numéricos *m pl*; **~ one priority** GEN COMM prioridad principal *f*; **~ plate** *BrE* (*cf license plate AmE*) TRANSP chapa de matrícula *f*, placa de identificación *f*; **~ of shares issued** STOCK número de acciones emitidas *m*

number[2]: **~ consecutively** *phr* GEN COMM numerar consecutivamente

numbered: **~ account** *n* BANK cuenta numerada *f*

numbering *n* GEN COMM numeración *f*

numeraire *adj* ECON numerario

numeric[1] *adj* COMP, MATH numérico

numeric[2]: **~ character** *n* COMP, MATH carácter numérico *m*; **~ keypad** *n* COMP teclado numérico *m*

numerical: **~ control** *n* FIN, MATH control numérico *m*; **~ filing** *n* COMP, GEN COMM archivo numérico *m*; **~ flexibility** *n* HRM flexibilidad numérica *f*

NUPE *abbr BrE* (*National Union of Public Employees*) HRM sindicato británico de trabajadores del estado

nursing: **~ home** *n* WEL residencia de ancianos *f*

NUS *abbr BrE* HRM (*National Union of Seamen*) sindicato británico de marineros, WEL (*National Union of Students*) unión general de estudiantes, ≈ SEU (*Sindicato de Estudiantes Universitarios*)

NVD *abbr* (*no value declared*) IMP/EXP sin declaración de valor

NWC *abbr BrE* (*National Wages Council*) HRM consejo británico salarial

NYFE *abbr* (*New York Futures Exchange*) STOCK mercado de futuros de Nueva York

NYME *abbr* (*New York Mercantile Exchange*) STOCK bolsa mercantil de Nueva York

NYPLR *abbr* (*New York prime loan rate*) BANK tasa de préstamo preferente de Nueva York

NYSA *abbr* (*New York Shipping Association*) TRANSP asociación naviera de Nueva York

NYSE *abbr* (*New York Stock Exchange*) STOCK bolsa de Nueva York *f*

O

oa *abbr* (*overall*) GEN COMM global

OA *abbr* (*office automation*) ADMIN, COMP AO (*automatización de oficinas*)

OAG *abbr* (*official airline guide*) TRANSP *aviation* guía oficial de aerolíneas *f*

O.A.P. *abbr* (*old age pensioner*) WEL pensionista por jubilación *mf*

OARS *abbr* (*opening automated report system*) STOCK sistema de información automatizada de apertura *m*

OASDHI *abbr* (*Old Age, Survivors, Disability and Health Insurance*) INS seguro de ancianidad, supervivientes, incapacidad y gastos médicos

oath *n* LAW juramento *m*; ◆ **under ~** LAW bajo juramento

OBE *abbr* (*Officer of the Order of the British Empire*) GEN COMM miembro de la Orden del Imperio Británico

obey *vt* GEN COMM, LAW obedecer

obiter dictum *n* GEN COMM juicio no vinculante *m*

object[1] *n* GEN COMM motivo *m*, *thing* objeto *m*

object[2] *vi* GEN COMM objetar, oponerse

object to *vt* GEN COMM *proposal* oponerse a, poner reparos a; ◆ **~ an assessment** TAX poner objeciones a una imposición

objection *n* GEN COMM objeción *f*; ◆ **~ overruled** LAW objeción denegada; **~ sustained** LAW objeción justificada; **~ to an assessment** TAX objeción a una imposición

objections: no ~ *phr* GEN COMM sin objeciones

objective *n* GEN COMM objetivo *m*; **~ budgeting** S&M elaboración objetiva de presupuesto *f*; **~ evaluation** GEN COMM estimación objetiva *f*; **~ function** MATH función objetiva *f*; **~ indicator** GEN COMM indicador objetivo *m*; **~ selling** S&M venta objetiva *f*; **~-setting** GEN COMM, MGMNT determinación de objetivos *f*, fijación de objetivos *f*; **~ value** ECON valor objetivo *m*

obligate *vt* LAW obligar

obligation *n* FIN obligación *f*; **~ bond** FIN, STOCK *mortgage bond* bono con obligación *m*; ◆ **no ~ to buy** S&M sin obligación de comprar; **be under no ~** GEN COMM no estar obligado; **be under an ~ to do sth** GEN COMM estar obligado a hacer algo

obligatory *adj* GEN COMM obligatorio

oblige[1]: **~ line** *n* INS *marine* retención obligada *f*

oblige[2] *vt* GEN COMM obligar

obliged *adj* GEN COMM obligado; ◆ **be much ~** GEN COMM estar muy agradecido, estar muy obligado

obligee *n* LAW tenedor(a) de una obligación *m,f*

obligor *n* LAW obligado(-a) *m,f*

OBRA *abbr* (*Omnibus Budget Reconciliation Act*) LAW Ley de Reconciliación Presupuestaria *f*

observance *n* GEN COMM *of rule* cumplimiento *m*, LAW acatamiento *m*

observation *n* GEN COMM observación *f*; **~ test** ACC *auditing* prueba de observación *f*

observe *vt* LAW *the law* acatar

obsolescence *n* GEN COMM obsolescencia *f*, depreciación

por desuso *f*, S&M caída en desuso *f*; **~ clause** INS cláusula de caducidad *f*

obsolescent: ~ product *n* S&M producto obsoleto *m*

obsolete *adj* GEN COMM, S&M obsoleto; ◆ **become ~** GEN COMM quedar anticuado, anticuarse

obstruct *vt* GEN COMM obstruir

obtain *vt* GEN COMM obtener; ◆ **~ permission in writing** COMMS obtener permiso por escrito; **~ security** STOCK conseguir seguridad; **~ sth by fraud** LAW obtener algo fraudulentamente

OBU *abbr* (*offshore banking unit*) BANK oficina bancaria ultramarina *f*

o/c *abbr* (*overcharge*) ACC importe en demasía *m*, BANK, GEN COMM recargo *m*, cobro excesivo *m*

OCAS *abbr* (*Organization of Central American States*) POL OEAC (*Organización de Estados Centroamericanos*)

OCC *abbr* (*options clearing corporation*) STOCK corporación de liquidación de opciones *f*

occasional[1] *adj* GEN COMM irregular

occasional[2]: **~ worker** *n* HRM trabajador(a) eventual *m,f*

occupancy *n* PROP ocupación *f*; **~ cost** TAX coste de ocupación *m* (*Esp*), costo de ocupación *m* (*AmL*); **~ level** PROP nivel de ocupación *m*

occupant *n* HRM *of post* titular *mf*, LAW, PROP, TAX ocupante *mf*

occupation *n* HRM *work*, LAW ocupación *f*, PROP tenencia *f*

occupational[1] *adj* GEN COMM, HRM laboral, profesional

occupational[2]: **~ accident** *n* HRM, IND, INS accidente de trabajo *m*; **~ analysis** *n* HRM análisis de ocupaciones *m*, análisis ocupacional *m*; **~ disease** *n* HRM enfermedad profesional *f*; **~ hazard** *n* HRM, IND riesgo laboral *m*, riesgo ocupacional *m*; **~ health** *n* GEN COMM, HRM, WEL salud ocupacional *f*; **~ illness** *n* HRM enfermedad profesional *f*; **~ mobility** *n* ECON, HRM movilidad laboral *f*; **~ pension** *n* HRM jubilación profesional *f*; **~ pension plan** *n* FIN, HRM plan profesional de retiro *m*; **~ pension scheme** *n BrE* FIN, GEN COMM, HRM plan de jubilación profesional *m*; **~ segregation** *n* ECON segregación laboral *f*; **~ union** *n* HRM sindicato laboral *m*

occupier *n* PROP inquilino(-a) *m,f*

OCD *abbr* (*other checkable deposits*) BANK, FIN otros depósitos *m pl*

ocean[1]: **~-going** *adj* TRANSP de alta mar

ocean[2]: **~ bill of lading** *n* IMP/EXP, TRANSP conocimiento de embarque marítimo *m*; **~ freight** *n* IMP/EXP, TRANSP flete marítimo *m*; **~-going ship** *n* TRANSP buque de navegación de altura *m*, buque de navegación marítima *m*; **~-going vessel** *n* TRANSP buque transatlántico *m*; **~ liner** *n* TRANSP transatlántico *m*; **~ marine protection and indemnity insurance** *n* INS, TRANSP seguro marino de protección e indemnización *m*

OCIMF *abbr* (*Oil Companies International Marine Forum*) ENVIR, TRANSP foro marítimo internacional de compañías petrolíferas

OCO: ~ **order** n (*one-cancels-the-other order*) STOCK orden condicionada f

OCR abbr (*optical character recognition*) COMP lector óptico de carácteres m

O/D abbr BANK (*overdraft*) descubierto m, (*overdrawn*) en descubierto

ODA abbr BrE (*Overseas Development Agency*) ECON, POL agencia estatal para el desarrollo exterior

odd[1] adj COMP, GEN COMM impar

odd[2]: ~ **change** n GEN COMM cambio sobrante m; ~ **job** n HRM trabajo diverso m; **~-job man** n HRM factótum m, hombre que hace de todo m; **~-lot** n jarg STOCK paquete de menos de 100 acciones m, pequeño lote m; **~-lot dealer** n STOCK operador(a) de lotes sueltos m,f; **~-lot short-sale ratio** n STOCK proporción de venta en descubierto de pequeños lotes f; **~-lot theory** n STOCK teoría de los pequeños lotes f; **~-lotter** n STOCK corredor(a) de paquete pequeño m,f; ~ **man out** n HRM excepción f; ~ **one** n GEN COMM *of pair* impar mf; ~ **size** n IND *production* tamaño especial m; **~-value pricing** n S&M fijación de precios de valor poco corriente f

oddment n GEN COMM, S&M artículo suelto m, artículo de saldo m

oddments n pl S&M retales m pl

ODI abbr (*Overseas Development Institute*) ECON instituto para el desarrollo exterior

OEC abbr (*overpaid entry certificate*) IMP/EXP, TRANSP certificado de entrada pagado en exceso m

OECD abbr (*Organization for Economic Cooperation and Development*) ECON, POL OCDE (*Organización para la Cooperación y Desarrollo Económicos*)

OECF abbr (*Overseas Economic Cooperation Fund*) ECON Fondo para la Cooperación Económica Exterior m

OEEC abbr (*Organization for European Economic Cooperation*) ECON, POL Organización para la Cooperación Económica Europea f

OF abbr (*open full*) TRANSP de apertura total

off adj COMP apagado

off-balance: ~ **sheet** n ACC, FIN fuera del balance m; ~ **sheet commitment** n ACC, FIN obligación fuera del balance general f; **-sheet financing** n ACC, FIN recursos fuera del balance general m pl

off-card: ~ **rate** n S&M precios especiales para espacio publicitario m pl

offence n LAW delito m, ofensa f

offensive: **take the** ~ phr GEN COMM ponerse a la ofensiva

offer[1] n GEN COMM oferta f; ~ **and acceptance** LAW *commercial* oferta y aceptación f; ~ **for sale** STOCK oferta de venta f; ~ **wanted** STOCK solicitud de oferta f; ◆ **nearest** ~ S&M oferta más próxima f; **on** ~ S&M en oferta; **or near** ~ S&M u oferta próxima; **or nearest** ~ (*o.n.o.*) S&M u oferta más próxima; **under** ~ PROP *house* en oferta

offer[2] vt GEN COMM, HRM ofertar, *job* ofrecer, *objection* objetar; ◆ ~ **considerable scope** GEN COMM ofrecer una magnitud considerable; ~ **one's services** GEN COMM ofrecer sus servicios

offered adj GEN COMM ofertado, STOCK ofrecido

offeree n GEN COMM receptor(a) de una oferta m,f

offering: ~ **date** n STOCK *new issue* fecha de oferta f;

~ **price** n STOCK precio de oferta m; ~ **scale** n STOCK escala de la oferta f

off-exchange: ~ **instrument** n FIN instrumento fuera de la bolsa de valores m

offhand: ~ **buying** n FIN, GEN COMM, S&M, STOCK compra directa f

office n ADMIN, GEN COMM *building* despacho m, oficina f; ~ **aide** GEN COMM, HRM auxiliar administrativo(-a) m,f; ~ **automation** (*OA*) ADMIN, COMP automatización de oficinas f (*AO*); ~ **block** BrE GEN COMM, PROP edificio de oficinas m; ~ **boy** HRM botones m, ordenanza m, recadero m; ~ **building** GEN COMM, PROP edificio de oficinas m; ~ **burglary and robbery insurance** INS seguro contra hurto y robo de oficinas m; ~ **equipment** ADMIN equipo de oficina m; ~ **expenses** n pl ACC gastos de oficina m pl; ~ **hours** n pl GEN COMM horas de oficina f pl, horas hábiles f pl, horas laborables f pl; ~ **job** HRM puesto de oficinista m; ~ **management** ADMIN, GEN COMM, MGMNT dirección de oficina f, gerencia de oficina f, organización de oficina f; ~ **manager** ADMIN, HRM, MGMNT director(a) de oficina m,f, jefe(-a) de oficina m,f; ~ **planning** ADMIN, GEN COMM, MGMNT planificación de la oficina f; ~ **premises** n pl GEN COMM, PROP local para oficina m; ~ **requisite** ADMIN requisito administrativo m; ~ **routine** GEN COMM rutina de oficina f; ~ **space** GEN COMM, PROP espacio para oficina m; ~ **staff** n pl HRM personal de oficina m; ~ **stationery** ADMIN artículos de papelería de la oficina m pl; ~ **supplies** n pl ADMIN materiales de oficina m pl; ~ **technology** ADMIN, COMP tecnología de oficina f; ~ **work** HRM trabajo de oficina m; ◆ ~ **for sale** PROP se vende oficina; **for** ~ **use only** ADMIN sólo para uso interno

Office: ~ **of Fair Trading** n (*OFT*) ECON, GEN COMM ≈ Departamento de Control de Prácticas Comerciales m ≈ Oficina de Protección al Consumidor f; ~ **of International Trade** n (*OIT*) ECON, IMP/EXP Oficina de Comercio Internacional f; ~ **of Interstate Land Sales Registration** n AmE (*OILSR*) PROP oficina de registro de ventas de tierras interestatales; ~ **of Management and Budget** n AmE (*OMB*) MGMNT oficina de administración y presupuesto; ~ **of Population Censuses and Surveys** n BrE (*OPCS*) WEL ≈ Oficina del Censo f; ~ **of Telecommunications** n (*Oftel*) COMMS oficina de telecomunicaciones

officer n HRM cargo ejecutivo(-a) m,f, funcionario(-a) m,f, oficial(a) m,f; ~ **'s check** AmE, ~ **'s cheque** BrE BANK, FIN cheque de caja m

Officer: ~ **of the Order of the British Empire** n (*OBE*) GEN COMM miembro de la Orden del Imperio Británico

official[1] adj GEN COMM oficial

official[2] n HRM apoderado(-a) m,f, funcionario(-a) m,f, oficial(a) m,f; ~ **action** HRM acción oficial f; ~ **airline guide** (*OAG*) TRANSP guía oficial de aerolíneas f; ~ **check** AmE, ~ **cheque** BrE BANK, FIN cheque de banco m; ~ **deposit** MEDIA *print* depósito oficial m; ~ **development assistance** ECON, POL asistencia oficial para el desarrollo f, ayuda oficial al desarrollo f; ~ **document** GEN COMM acta oficial f, documento oficial m; ~ **exchange rate** ECON tipo oficial de cambio m; ~ **figures** n pl GEN COMM cifras oficiales f pl; ~ **financing** ECON, FIN financiación oficial f; ~ **list** STOCK cotización oficial f; ~ **market** ECON mercado oficial m; ~ **no.** (*on*) TRANSP *ship's registration number* número oficial m; ~ **notice of sale** FIN notificación oficial de venta *f*; ~ **number** (*on*) TRANSP *shipping* número oficial *m*; ~ **quotations** *n pl* GEN COMM cotizaciones oficiales *f pl*; ~ **rate** BANK, ECON cambio oficial *m*; ~ **receipt** TAX recibo oficial *m*; ~ **receiver** GEN COMM síndico(-a) oficial *m,f*, LAW *commercial* administrador(a) *m,f*, administrador(a) judicial de una quiebra *m,f*; ~ **statement** GEN COMM comunicación oficial *f*; ~ **strike** HRM, IND, LAW huelga oficial *f*, huelga legal *f*; ~ **supported export credits** *n pl* FIN apoyo oficial de créditos de exportación *m*; ~ **valuer** LAW tasador(a) oficial *m,f*

Official: ~ **Journal** *n* (*OJ*) ECON Diario Oficial *m*

officialese *n* GEN COMM argot burocrático *m*

officially *adv* GEN COMM oficialmente

off-licence *n BrE* GEN COMM (*cf liquor store AmE, package store AmE*) *shop* tienda de licores *f*, LAW *permit* permiso para vender bebidas alcohólicas que van a consumirse fuera del establicimiento

off-limits: ~ **area** *n* GEN COMM área fuera de límites *f*

off-line *adj* COMP desconectado, autónomo

offload *vt* GEN COMM *responsibility, work*, TRANSP descargar

off-loading *n* TRANSP descarga *f*

off-peak[1] *adj* GEN COMM, LEIS de temporada baja, TRANSP mínimo

off-peak[2]: ~ **day** *n* GEN COMM día de temporada baja *m*; ~ **fare** *n* TRANSP tarifa fuera de las horas puntas *f* (*Esp*), tarifa fuera de las horas picos *f* (*AmL*); ~ **ticket** *n* TRANSP billete de temporada baja *m*; ~ **time** *n* MEDIA, S&M periodo de menor audiencia *m*, MEDIA hora de baja audiencia *f*

off-period: ~ **adjustments** *n pl* ACC ajustes después del periodo de cierre *m pl*

off-prime *adj* ECON de segundo orden

off-profile: ~ **return** *n* TAX declaración atípica *f*

off-sale: ~ **date** *n* MEDIA *broadcast* fecha de retirada de la venta *f*

offset[1] *n* ACC, FIN compensación *f*, MEDIA *print* offset *m*, STOCK compensación *f*; ~ **account** ACC, FIN cuenta de compensación *f*

offset[2] *vt* ACC *losses and gains*, FIN, STOCK compensar; ◆ ~ **a loss** STOCK compensar una pérdida

offset against *vt* ACC, FIN, STOCK compensar contra

offsetting: ~ **entry** *n* ACC, FIN, STOCK partida compensatoria *f*, asiento compensatorio *m*; ~ **transaction** *n* ACC, FIN, STOCK transacción compensatoria *f*

offshore[1] *adj* BANK internacional, de ultramar, FIN antecostero, GEN COMM extranjero

offshore[2]: ~ **banking** *n* BANK banca externa *f*, banca ultramarina *f*; ~ **banking unit** *n* (*OBU*) BANK *of investment* oficina bancaria extraterritorial *f*, oficina bancaria ultramarina *f*; ~ **center** *AmE*, ~ **centre** *BrE n* BANK centro de ultramar *m*, centro financiero extranjero con ventajas fiscales *m*, centro financiero internacional *m*; ~ **competition** *n* IMP/EXP competencia offshore *f*; ~ **dollars** *n pl* BANK dólares de ultramar *m pl*; ~ **drilling** *n* ENVIR, IND perforación costera *f*; ~ **funds** *n pl* ACC, BANK, FIN, TAX fondos colocados en paraísos fiscales *m pl*; ~ **installation** *n* TRANSP instalación en mar abierto *f*, instalación marítima separada de la costa *f*; ~ **investment** *n* BANK, FIN inversión extranjera *f*; ~ **oil field** *n* ENVIR, IND plataforma petrolífera *f*; ~ **placement** *n* BANK, FIN colocación

internacional *f*; ~ **protectionism** *n* TRANSP proteccionismo costero *m*; ~ **takeover** *n* FIN absorción supranacional *f*; ~ **technology** *n* ENVIR, IND tecnología de las plataformas petrolíferas *f*; ~ **trust** *n* FIN, LAW fideicomiso extranjero *m*, sociedad fiduciaria de ultramar *f*

off-site: ~ **cost** *n* PROP *construction* coste de instalación exterior *m* (*Esp*), costo de instalación exterior *m* (*AmL*)

off-the-board *adj* STOCK fuera de cotización

off-the-job: ~ **training** *n* HRM, IND capacitación fuera del puesto de trabajo *f* (*AmL*), entrenamiento fuera del puesto *m*, formación fuera del puesto de trabajo *f* (*Esp*)

off-the-record *adj* GEN COMM, MEDIA, POL *remark* fuera de acta, sin carácter oficial

off-the-shelf: ~ **company** *n* GEN COMM empresa de conveniencia *f*

OFT *abbr* (*Office of Fair Trading*) ECON ≈ Departamento de Control de Prácticas Comerciales *m*

Oftel *abbr* (*Office of Telecommunications*) COMMS oficina de telecomunicaciones

OGIL *abbr* (*open general import licence*) IMP/EXP, TRANSP licencia de importación general abierta *f*

OGL *abbr* (*open general licence*) IMP/EXP, TRANSP licencia general abierta *f*

OHMS *abbr BrE* (*On Her Majesty's Service*) GEN COMM al servicio de Su Majestad

OID *abbr* (*original issue discount*) STOCK emisión con descuento *f*

oil[1]: ~**-bearing** *adj* ENVIR, IND petrolífero; ~**-rich** *adj* ECON, ENVIR rico en petróleo

oil[2] *n* ENVIR, IND, TRANSP petróleo *m*; ~ **analyst** IND analista petrolífero(-a) *m,f*; ~**-bearing continuous liner** TRANSP buque petrolífero de línea continua *m*; ~ **carrier** TRANSP transportista de petróleo *mf*; ~ **company** ENVIR, IND compañía petrolera *f*; ~ **crisis** ECON, IND crisis del petróleo *f*; ~ **deposit** ENVIR, IND estrato de petróleo *m*; ~ **exploration licence** *BrE*, ~ **exploration license** *AmE* ENVIR, IND licencia de exploración de petróleo *f*, licencia de prospección petrolífera *f*; ~ **exporting country** ECON, IMP/EXP país exportador de petróleo *m*; ~ **field** IND campo petrolífero *m*; ~ **gage** *AmE see oil gauge BrE*; ~ **and gas lease** IND, LAW arrendamiento de petróleo y gas *m*, contrato de gas y petróleo *m*; ~ **and gas sampling** ENVIR, IND muestreo de petróleo y gas *m*; ~ **gauge** *BrE* ENVIR, TRANSP aforamiento del petróleo *m*, manómetro de aceite *m*; ~ **glut** ENVIR, IND saturación del petróleo *f*; ~ **industry** ECON, IND industria petrolera *f*; ~ **pipeline** ENVIR, IND oleoducto *m*; ~ **platform** ENVIR, IND plataforma petrolífera *f*; ~ **pollution** ENVIR, IND contaminación por crudos *f*, contaminación por petróleo *f*; ~ **price** GEN COMM precio del petróleo *m*; ~ **price increase** GEN COMM incremento del precio del petróleo *m*; ~**-producing country** ECON, ENVIR, POL país productor de petróleo *m*; ~ **prospection** ENVIR, IND prospección petrolífera *f*; ~ **refinery** ENVIR, IND refinería de petróleo *f*; ~ **revenue tax** TAX impuesto sobre explotaciones petrolíferas *m*; ~ **rig** ENVIR, IND plataforma petrolífera *f*, torre de perforación *f*; ~ **sector** ECON, IND sector petrolero *m*; ~ **shares** *n pl* STOCK acciones petrolíferas *f pl*, valores petrolíferos *m pl*; ~ **shortage** ECON, GEN COMM escasez de petróleo *f*; ~ **spill** ENVIR vertido de petróleo *m*; ~ **spillage** ENVIR vertido de petróleo *m*;

~ tanker TRANSP petrolero *m*; **~ terminal** ENVIR, TRANSP terminal de petroleros *f*

oil[3]: **~ sb's palm** *phr infrml* GEN COMM untar a alguien

Oil: ~ Companies International Marine Forum *n* (*OCIMF*) ENVIR foro marítimo internacional de compañías petrolíferas

OILSR *abbr AmE* (*Office of Interstate Land Sales Registration*) PROP oficina de registro de ventas de tierras interestatales

oiltight *adj* TRANSP estanco al petróleo

OIML *abbr* (*International Organization for Legal Metrology*) GEN COMM OIML (*Organización Internacional de Metrología Legal*)

OIT *abbr* (*Office of International Trade*) ECON, IMP/EXP Oficina de Comercio Internacional *f*

OJ *abbr* (*Official Journal*) ECON Diario Oficial *m*

Okun's: ~ Law *n* ECON Ley de Okun *f*

old[1]: **~-established** *adj* GEN COMM antiguo; **~-fashioned** *adj* GEN COMM anticuado

old[2]: **~ age exemption** *n* TAX exención por vejez *f*; **~-age pension** *n* FIN, WEL pensión de jubilación *f*, pensión asegurada para la tercera edad *f*, pensión de vejez *f*; **~-age pension scheme** *n* GEN COMM plan de pensiones de jubilación *m*; **~ age pensioner** *n* (*O.A.P.*) WEL pensionista por jubilación *mf*; **~-age security pension** *n* FIN, WEL pensión de vejez *f*; **~ charter** *n* (*OC*) TRANSP antiguo fletamiento *m*; **~ crop** *n* (*OC*) ECON *agricultural* cosecha vieja *f*; **~ law** *n* LAW derecho antiguo *m*, jurisprudencia antigua *f*

Old: ~ Age, Survivors, Disability and Health Insurance *n AmE* (*OASDHI*) INS seguro de ancianidad, supervivientes, incapacidad y gastos médicos; **~ Lady of Threadneedle Street** *n BrE infrml* BANK edificio del Banco de Inglaterra en Londres

OLG *abbr* (*overlapping generations model*) ECON modelo de solapación de generaciones *m*

oligopolistic *adj* ECON oligopolístico

oligopoly *n* ECON oligopolio *m*

oligopsony *n* ECON oligopsonio *m*

OLS *abbr* MATH *statistics* método de los mínimos cuadrados *m*

O&M *abbr* (*organization and methods*) MGMNT organización y métodos *f*

OM *abbr* (*options market*) STOCK mercado de opciones *m*

OMA *abbr* (*orderly market agreement*) ECON acuerdo de mercado metódico *m*

OMB *abbr AmE* (*Office of Management and Budget*) MGMNT oficina de administración y presupuesto

Ombudsman *n* STOCK Defensor(a) del Accionista *m,f*

omission *n* GEN COMM omisión *f*

omit[1] *vt* GEN COMM omitir

omit[2]: **~ to do** *phr* GEN COMM omitir hacer

omitted: ~ dividend *n* ACC dividendo omitido *m*

omnibus: ~ survey *n* S&M *market research* encuesta ómnibus *f*

Omnibus: ~ Budget Reconciliation Act *n* (*OBRA*) LAW Ley de Reconciliación Presupuestaria *f*

omnicarrier *n* TRANSP transportista en general *mf*

on *adj* COMP conectado ♦ **~ time** GEN COMM a tiempo

on-balance: ~ volume *n* STOCK balance de volumen *m*

on-board *adj* COMP interno

on-carriage *n* TRANSP transporte ulterior *m*

one[1]: **~-for-one** *adj* STOCK *price relationship* uno por uno; **~-off** *adj* GEN COMM único; **~-way** *adj* COMP de una dirección

one[2]: **~-bank holding company** *n* BANK casa matriz de banco único *f*; **~-cancels-the-other order** *n* (*OCO order*) STOCK orden condicionada *f*; **~-cent sale** *n AmE* S&M venta ínfima *f*; **~ class** *n* LEIS, TRANSP clase única *f*; **~-club policy** *n* ECON política de una sociedad *f*; **~-crop economy** *n* ECON economía de monocultivo *f*, POL economía de una cosecha *f*, economía sin fundamento *f*; **~-house veto** *n AmE* POL veto de una cámara *m*; **~-hundred-percent location** *n* S&M lugar privilegiado para facturación de ventas; **~ -hundred-percent reserve banking** *n* BANK banco de reserva al cien por ciento *m*; **~-minute manager** *n* MGMNT directivo(-a) de corta vida *m,f*; **~-off cash gift** *n pl* TAX donación en metálico realizada sólo en una ocasión *f*; **~ percent spread** *n* STOCK margen del uno por ciento *m*; **~-piece box** *n* TRANSP caja de una sola pieza *f*; **~-program-to-one-vote convention** *n AmE* FIN convención un programa-un voto *f*; **~-stop shopping** *n* S&M compras en un mismo sitio *f pl*; **~-stop shopping center** *AmE*, **~-stop shopping centre** *BrE n* GEN COMM, PROP, S&M centro comercial *m*; **~-tailed test** *n* MATH *statistics* prueba unilateral *f*; **~-time buyer** *n* S&M comprador(a) de una sola vez *m,f*; **~-time rate** *n advertising* tarifa de una sola emisión *f*; **~-to-one straddle** *n* STOCK *options* opción doble uno a uno *f*; **~-trial learning** *n* WEL sistema de enseñanza en el que sólo se hace un examen; **~-trip sling** *n* TRANSP *cargo handling* eslinga monoviaje *f*; **~-way fare** *n* LEIS, TRANSP tarifa de ida *f*; **~-way lease** *n* TRANSP alquiler de ida *m*; **~-way protection** *n* STOCK protección unidireccional *f*

one[3]: **~ country, two systems** *phr* ECON *Hong Kong after 1997* un país, dos sistemas; **~ for the shelf** *phr jarg* STOCK que debe diferirse

onerous: ~ contract *n* GEN COMM, LAW contrato leonino *m*

ongoing[1] *adj* GEN COMM en curso

ongoing[2]: **~ concern** *n* GEN COMM asunto en marcha *m*

on-lending *n* FIN représtamo *m*

on-line[1] *adj* COMP en línea, GEN COMM en conexión

on-line[2]: **~ banking** *n* BANK banca telefónica *f*; **~ data service** *n* COMP servicio de datos directo *m*; **~ database** *n* COMP base de datos en línea *f*; **~ rate** *n* TRANSP *air freight* tarifa en línea *f*; **~ system** *n* COMP sistema en línea *m*

o.n.o. *abbr* (*or nearest offer*) S&M u oferta más próxima

on-pack[1] *adj* S&M en el envase

on-pack[2]: **~ price reduction** *n* S&M reducción de precio anunciada sobre el envase

on-sale: ~ date *n* MEDIA *print* fecha de puesta a la venta *f*

onset *n* GEN COMM comienzo *m*, inicio *m*

onshore[1] *adj* GEN COMM terrestre

onshore[2]: **~ banking** *n* BANK banca en territorio nacional *f*; **~ terminal** *n* ENVIR terminal de tierra *f*

on-site: ~ manager *n* IND jefe(-a) de obra *m,f*

on-the-job: ~ training *n* HRM, IND capacitación en la empresa *f* (*AmL*), entrenamiento en el puesto *m*, formación en la empresa *f* (*Esp*)

on-the-record *adj* GEN COMM, MEDIA, POL con carácter oficioso

on-the-spot: ~ reporter *n* MEDIA reportero desplazado al lugar de los hechos

onward: **~ clearing** *n* BANK compensación progresiva *f*; **~ flight** *n* TRANSP vuelo de reexpedición *m*

o/o *abbr* (*order of*) GEN COMM orden de

O/o *abbr* (*ore/oil ship*) TRANSP buque para transporte combinado de mineral y petróleo *m*

OOG *abbr* (*out of gauge*) TRANSP fuera de gálibo

o.p. *abbr* (*out of print*) MEDIA agotado

OP *abbr* (*open cargo insurance policy*) INS póliza de seguro para cualquier carga *f*

OPCS *abbr BrE* (*Office of Population Censuses and Surveys*) WEL ≈ Oficina del Censo *f*

OPEC *abbr* (*Organization of Petroleum Exporting Countries*) IMP/EXP, POL OPEP (*Organización de los Países Exportadores de Petróleo*)

open[1] *adj* COMP *file, document, system, network*, GEN COMM *balance*, STOCK *price* abierto; **~-end** GEN COMM sin límite; **~-ended** COMP ampliable, GEN COMM abierto; **~-plan** GEN COMM *office* de plan abierto; ♦ **~ full** (*OF*) TRANSP *container* de apertura total; **~ on the print** STOCK abierto en imprenta; **~ to buy** S&M disponible para la compra; **~ to debate** GEN COMM abierto a debate; **~ to several interpretations** GEN COMM susceptible de diversas interpretaciones

open[2]: **~ account** *n* GEN COMM cuenta comercial *f*; **~ account credit** *n* GEN COMM crédito con cuenta abierta *m*; **~ admissions** *n pl* WEL ingreso libre *m*; **~ bid** *n* GEN COMM licitación abierta *f*; **~account business** *n* GEN COMM negocio con cuenta abierta *m*; **~ cargo insurance policy** *n* (*OP*) INS póliza de seguro para cualquier carga *f*; **~ cargo policy** *n* INS *marine* póliza de carga abierta *f*; **~-cast method** *n* IND *of mining* método a cielo abierto; **~ cast mining** *n BrE* (*cf strip mining AmE*) ENVIR, IND explotación a cielo abierto *f*, explotación minera a cielo abierto *f*; **~ charter** *n* (*OC*) TRANSP contrato abierto *m*; **~ check** *AmE*, **~ cheque** *BrE n* BANK, FIN cheque abierto *m*, cheque libre *m*, cheque no cruzado *m*; **~ competition** *n* ECON, LAW competencia abierta *f* (*AmL*), competición abierta *m* (*Esp*); **~ container** *n* TRANSP contenedor abierto *m*; **~ contract** *n* FIN, STOCK contrato abierto *m*; **~ contracts** *n pl* FIN, STOCK *futures market* contratos pendientes *m pl*; **~ cover** *n* (*OC*) INS cobertura abierta *f*; **~ credit** *n* BANK, FIN crédito al descubierto *m*, crédito abierto *m*; **~ dating** *n AmE* S&M señal visible de la fecha límite de consumición de un producto, fecha abierta *f*; **~ day** *n BrE* GEN COMM, WEL día en que un establecimiento educativo y científico puede ser visitado por el público; **~ deck** *n* TRANSP cubierta de intemperie *f*; **~ distribution** *n* TRANSP distribución abierta *f*; **~ dock** *n* TRANSP dársena de mareas *f*; **~-door policy** *n* GEN COMM, MGMNT, POL política de puertas abiertas *f*; **~ economy** *n* ECON, POL economía abierta *f*; **~-end contract** *n* LAW contrato de suministro abierto *m*, contrato sin límites preestablecidos *m*; **~-end fund** *n AmE* FIN fondo de inversión de capital variable *m*; **~-end investment company** *n AmE* (*OEIC*) FIN, STOCK sociedad de inversión abierta *f*, sociedad de inversión con cartera variable *f*; **~-end management company** *n* FIN, MGMNT sociedad de gestión abierta *f*; **~-ended agreement** *n* HRM acuerdo de final abierto *m*, contrato con vigencia indefinida *m*; **~-ended contract** *n* LAW, contrato de suministro abierto *m*, contrato sin límites preestablecidos *m*; **~-ended flight reservation** *n* LEIS, TRANSP reserva de vuelo abierta *f*; **~-ended fund** *n* FIN fondo sin límites *m*; **~-ended investment company** *n*

FIN compañía de capital abierto *f*; **~-ended mortgage** *n* BANK, PROP hipoteca de apertura y cierre *f*, hipoteca ampliable *f*; **~-ended position** *n* STOCK posición de final abierto *f*; **~-ended question** *n* GEN COMM, S&M *market research* pregunta abierta *f*; **~-ended risk** *n* STOCK *options* riesgo de final abierto *m*; **~ general import licence** *BrE*, **~ general import license** *AmE n* IMP/EXP licencia de importación general abierta *f*; **~ general licence** *BrE*, **~ general license** *AmE n* IMP/EXP licencia general abierta *f*; **~ house** *n AmE* GEN COMM puertas abiertas *f pl*, PROP casa abierta al público *f*; **~ individual licence** *BrE*, **~ individual license** *AmE n* IMP/EXP licencia individual abierta *f*; **~ interest** *n* STOCK interés abierto *m*; **~ letter** *n* ACC, ADMIN, BANK carta abierta *f*; **~ letter of credit** *n* BANK, FIN carta de crédito sin condiciones *f*; **~ listing** *n AmE* PROP listado abierto *m*; **~ long position** *n* FIN, STOCK posición larga de apertura *f*; **~ market** *n* ECON, GEN COMM mercado abierto *m*; **~ market committee** *n* ECON comité del mercado abierto *m*; **~ market operations** *n pl AmE* ECON, POL operaciones de mercado abierto *f pl*; **~ market rate** *n* BANK, ECON cotización del mercado libre *f*; **~ market trading** *n* ECON comercio en mercado libre *m*; **~ mortgage** *n* BANK, FIN hipoteca abierta *f*; **~ network** *n* COMP red de datos abierta *f*; **~ order** *n* STOCK orden abierta *f*; **~ outcry action** *n* STOCK proceso a viva voz *m*; **~ outcry auction market** *n* STOCK corro *m*, mercado de subastas a viva voz *m*; **~ outcry system** *n* STOCK sistema de venta pública *m*; **~-plan office** *n* ADMIN oficina de plan abierto *f*, oficina de planificación abierta *f*; **~ policy** *n* INS, TRANSP póliza abierta *f*, póliza flotante *f*; **~ population** *n* ECON población abierta *f*; **~ port** *n* IMP/EXP, TRANSP puerto franco *m*; **~ position** *n* STOCK posición abierta *f*; **~ price** *n* STOCK precio abierto *m*; **~ question** *n* GEN COMM cuestión pendiente *f*, punto sin resolver *m*; **~ registry** *n* (*OR*) TRANSP *shipping* registro abierto *m*; **~-shelf filing** *n* ADMIN archivo en anaqueles *m*; **~ shelter deck** *n* (*OSD*) TRANSP *vessel* cubierta de abrigo abierta *f*; **~ shop** *n* HRM empresa con sindicación voluntaria *f*, empresa que no exige sindicación *f*; **~ short position** *n* STOCK posición corta de apertura *f*; **~-sided container** *n* TRANSP contenedor de laterales abiertos *m*; **~ slip sheet** *n* TRANSP *shipping* propuesta-borrador abierta *f*; **~ space** *n* PROP espacio abierto *m*; **~ stock** *n* S&M artículo que pertenece a un juego pero que se puede comprar por separado; **~ storage** *n* TRANSP almacenamiento al aire libre *m*; **~ systems interconnection** *n* (*OSI*) COMP interconexión de sistemas abiertos *f* (*OSI*); **~ tax** *n* TAX impuesto abierto *m*; **~ tendering** *n* GEN COMM, MGMNT licitación abierta *f*; **~ ticket** *n* LEIS billete abierto *m*; **~-top container** *n* (*OT*) TRANSP contenedor con techo removible *m*; **~-topped container** *n* (*OT*) TRANSP contenedor de abertura superior *m*, contenedor de techo removible *m* (*OT*); **~-topped reefer** *n* TRANSP contenedor de techo aislante removible *m*; **~ trading** *n* STOCK transacción en posición abierta *f*; **~ union** *n* HRM sindicato abierto *m*; **~-wall container** *n* TRANSP contenedor de abertura lateral *m*

open[3] *vt* BANK, COMP, GEN COMM abrir; ♦ **~ an account with** BANK abrir una cuenta con; **~ the door to** GEN COMM abrir las puertas a; **~ a long position** STOCK abrir una posición larga; **~ a position** STOCK abrir una posición; **~ a short position** STOCK abrir una posición corta

open up *vt* GEN COMM *opportunities* explorar; ◆ **~ the market to competition** GEN COMM abrir el mercado a la competencia

Open: ~ University *n* *BrE* (*OU*) WEL universidad a distancia británica, ≈ Universidad Nacional de Educación a Distancia *m* *Esp* (*UNED*)

opening *n* GEN COMM *of meeting*, STOCK *trade* apertura *f*; **~ automated report system** (*OARS*) STOCK sistema de información automatizada de apertura *m*; **~ balance** ACC, BANK balance de apertura *m*, saldo de apertura *m*; **~ bank** BANK banco de apertura *m*; **~ bid** S&M oferta de apertura *f*; **~ date** GEN COMM fecha de apertura *f*; **~ entry** ACC asiento de apertura *m*; **~ hours** *n pl* GEN COMM horario de apertura *m*; **~ inventory** ACC inventario inicial *m*; **~ position** STOCK posición de apertura *f*; **~ price** STOCK precio de apertura *m*; **~ quotation** STOCK cotización de apertura *f*; **~ of tenders** GEN COMM apertura de ofertas *f*; **~ up** STOCK apertura al comercio *f*; ◆ **at the ~** STOCK a la apertura

operand *n* MATH operando *m*

operate 1. *vt* GEN COMM *business* operar, MGMNT manejar; **2.** *vi* GEN COMM *machine* funcionar, MGMNT trabajar; ◆ **~ in tandem** MGMNT trabajar en equipo

operating: ~ account *n* BANK cuenta de operación *f*, IND cuenta de explotación *f*; **~ asset** *n* ACC activo de explotación *m*; **~ budget** *n* ACC, ECON, FIN presupuesto de explotación *m*; **~ capacity** *n* ECON capacidad operativa *f*; **~ capital** *n* ACC, ECON, FIN capital de explotación *m*, capital de operación *m*; **~ capital requirement** *n* GEN COMM requerimiento de capital de operación *m*; **~ charge** *n* ACC, BANK, FIN cargo por operaciones *m*; **~ cost** *n* ACC coste de explotación *m* (*Esp*), costo de explotación *m* (*AmL*); **~ costs** *n pl* GEN COMM costes de explotación *m pl* (*Esp*), costos de explotación *m pl* (*AmL*), gastos de mantenimiento *m pl*; **~ cycle** *n* ACC ciclo de operación *m*; **~ deficit** *n* ACC déficit de explotación *m*; **~ department** *n* TRANSP *shipping* departamento técnico *m*; **~ division** *n* GEN COMM división operativa *f*; **~ efficiency** *n* TRANSP eficiencia operativa *f*; **~ expenditure vote** *n* ACC, POL *government* capítulo de gastos de funcionamiento *m*; **~ expenditures** *n* GEN COMM gastos de operaciones *m pl*, gastos de funcionamiento *m pl*; **~ gearing** *n* *BrE* (*cf operating leverage AmE*) ACC apalancamiento operativo *m*, ventaja de operación *f*; **~ grant** *n* ACC concesión de explotación *f*, subvención de explotación *f*; **~ income** *n* ACC rendimiento de explotación *m*, renta de explotación *f*, resultado de explotación *m*; **~ interest** *n* GEN COMM interés operativo *m*; **~ lease** *n* ACC, PROP alquiler de explotación *m*, arrendamiento de explotación *m*; **~ leverage** *n* *AmE* (*cf operating gearing BrE*) ACC apalancamiento operativo *m*, ventaja de operación *f*; **~ loss** *n* ACC *balance sheets* pérdida de la explotación *f*; **~ management** *n* MGMNT dirección operativa *f*, gerencia operativa *f*; **~ plan** *n* GEN COMM, TRANSP plan de explotación *m*; **~ profit** *n* ACC beneficio de explotación *m* (*Esp*), utilidad de explotación *f* (*AmL*); **~ schedule** *n* TRANSP programa de explotación *m*; **~ statement** *n* ACC estado de resultados de operación *m*; **~ strategy** *n* TRANSP estrategia operativa *f*; **~ subsidy** *n* TRANSP prima de explotación *f*

operation *n* BANK operación *f*, GEN COMM, MGMNT marcha *f*, operación *f*, STOCK operación *f*; **~ code** COMP código de orden *m*; **~ field** COMP campo de operación *m*; **~ lease** FIN arrendamiento de operación

m, TRANSP alquiler de explotación *m*; **~ system** (*OS*) COMP sistema operativo *m* (*SO*); **~ time** GEN COMM tiempo de ejecución *m*; ◆ **in ~** GEN COMM en marcha

operational[1] *adj* GEN COMM operacional

operational[2]**: ~ analysis** *n* HRM, IND análisis operativo *m*, análisis operacional *m*; **~ audit** *n* ACC, MGMNT auditoría de operaciones *f*, auditoría operacional *f*, auditoría operativa *f*; **~ balance** *n* BANK saldo operativo *m*; **~ budget** *n* ACC, ECON, FIN presupuesto de operaciones *m*; **~ control** *n* GEN COMM control operacional *m*; **~ environment** *n* COMP *software* condiciones de funcionamiento *f pl*; **~ investment** *n* ACC *in buildings, equipment* inversión de explotación *f*; **~ manager** *n* HRM, MGMNT director(a) de operaciones *m,f*, gerente de operaciones *mf*; **~ margin** *n* GEN COMM margen operacional *m*; **~ plan framework** *n* FIN marco operativo de un plan *m*; **~ planning** *n* GEN COMM planificación operacional *f*; **~ research** *n* (*OR*) MGMNT, S&M investigación operacional *f*; **~ staff** *n* GEN COMM, HRM personal operativo *m* (*Esp*), staff operativo *m* (*AmL*)

operations: ~ administration system *n* MGMNT sistema administrativo sobre la marcha *m*; **~ analysis** *n* HRM análisis de las operaciones *m*; **~ audit** *n* ACC, MGMNT auditoría de operaciones *f*, auditoría operacional *f*, auditoría operativa *f*; **~ breakdown** *n* GEN COMM colapso de las operaciones *m*, IND desglose de operaciones *m*, MGMNT interrupción de las operaciones *f*; **~ department** *n* FIN, STOCK *of brokerage firm* departamento de operaciones *m*; **~ director** *n* HRM, MGMNT, director(a) de operaciones *m,f*, gerente de operaciones *mf*; **~ management** *n* GEN COMM, MGMNT dirección de operaciones *f*, gerencia de operaciones *f*; **~ manager** *n* HRM, MGMNT director(a) de operaciones *m,f*; **~ research** *n* (*OR*) MGMNT, S&M investigación de operaciones *f*

operative *n* MGMNT operativo(-a) *m,f*

operator *n* GEN COMM operador(a) *m,f*, operario(-a) *m,f*, STOCK operador(a) *m,f*, operador(a) de la bolsa *m,f*

opinion *n* GEN COMM opinión *f*, LAW dictamen *m*; **~ leader** S&M *market research* líder de opinión *m*; **~ poll** S&M *market research* encuesta de opinión *f*; **~ polling** S&M *market research* sondeo de opinión *m*; **~ polls** *n pl* S&M encuesta de opiniones *f*; **~ survey** S&M encuesta de opinión *f*; **~ of title** LAW, PROP dictamen de propiedad *m*, certificado de validez de un título *m*, opinión de título *f*; ◆ **that's a matter of ~** GEN COMM es cuestión de opinión

OPM *abbr* (*options pricing model*) STOCK modelo de fijación de precios de las opciones

opportunism *n* POL *Marxism* oportunismo *m*

opportunist *n* GEN COMM oportunista *mf*

opportunistic: ~ behavior *AmE*, **~ behaviour** *BrE* *n* ECON, STOCK comportamiento oportunista *m*

opportunity *n* GEN COMM ocasión *f*, *report, explanation, description* oportunidad *f*; **~ cost** ACC, ECON, FIN coste de oportunidad *m* (*Esp*), costo de oportunidad *m* (*AmL*); **~ curve** ECON curva de oportunidad *f*

oppose *vt* GEN COMM oponerse, oponerse a

opposing: ~ votes *n pl* POL votos contrapuestos *m pl*

opposite: ~ number *n* HRM *in another organization* homólogo(-a) *m,f*; **~ transaction** *n* GEN COMM transacción contraria *f*

opposition *n* GEN COMM, PATENTS, POL oposición *f*;

~ **party** POL partido de la oposición *m*, ~ **proceedings** *n pl* PATENTS actos de oposición *m pl*

opt: ~**-out** *n jarg* MEDIA *broadcast* conexión *f*

opt for *vt* GEN COMM optar por

opt out *vi BrE* GEN COMM salirse del control de las autoridades regionales con competencias en educación

optical: ~ **character recognition** *n* (*OCR*) COMP reconocimiento óptico de caracteres *m*; ~ **scanner** *n* IND explorador óptico *m*; ~ **wand** *n* COMP lápiz óptico *m*

optimal: ~ **control** *n* ECON control óptimo *m*; ~ **rate** *n* ECON, FIN grado óptimo *m*; ~ **rate of pollution** *n* ENVIR grado óptimo de polución *m*; ~ **tariff** *n* ECON, IMP/EXP tarifa óptima *f*; ~ **taxation** *n* TAX imposición óptima *f*; ~ **work effort** *n* ECON esfuerzo laboral óptimo *m*

optimality *n* ECON optimalidad *f*

optimization *n* ECON, FIN, GEN COMM optimización *f*; ~ **problem** MATH problema de optimización *m*

optimize *vt* ECON, FIN, GEN COMM optimizar; ◆ ~ **the objective function** GEN COMM optimizar la función objetiva

optimum[1] *adj* GEN COMM óptimo

optimum[2]: ~ **capacity** *n* ECON, IND capacidad óptima *f*; ~ **city** *n* ECON ciudad óptima *f*; ~ **currency area** *n* ECON zona monetaria óptima *f*; ~ **firm** *n* ECON empresa óptima *f*; ~ **population** *n* ECON población óptima *f*

option *n* GEN COMM opción *f*; ~ **account** FIN cuenta opcional *f*; ~ **bargain** STOCK negocio a prima *m*, transacción en el mercado de opciones *f*; ~ **buyer** STOCK comprador(a) de opciones *m,f*; ~**-buying hedge** STOCK cobertura de compra de una opción *f*; ~ **class** STOCK clase de opción *f*; ~ **contract** STOCK contrato de opciones *m*; ~ **coverage** STOCK cobertura de opción *f*; ~ **demand** ECON demanda alternativa *f*; ~ **eligible security** STOCK título redescontable con prima *m*; ~ **exchange** STOCK intercambio de opciones *m*; ~ **exercise** STOCK ejercicio de la opción *m*; ~ **fee** FIN *purchase* comisión optativa *f*; ~ **forward contract** IMP/EXP contrato con opción de futuro *m*; ~ **holder** STOCK tenedor(a) de una opción *m,f*; ~ **market** (*OM*) STOCK mercado de opciones *m*; ~ **on currency futures** STOCK opción sobre futuros de divisas *f*; ~ **period** STOCK periodo de opción *m*; ~ **premium** STOCK prima de opción *f*; ~ **price** STOCK precio de opción *m*; ~ **pricing model** (*OPM*) STOCK modelo de fijación de precios de las opciones; ~ **pricing formula** STOCK fórmula para valorar opciones *f*; ~**-pricing parameter** STOCK parámetro de valoración de una opción *m*; ~ **pricing theory** STOCK teoría de la valoración de opciones *f*; ~ **seller** *AmE* STOCK vendedor(a) de opciones *m,f*; ~**-selling hedge** STOCK cobertura de venta de una opción *f*; ~ **series** STOCK serie de opciones *f*; ~ **spread** STOCK diferencial de opciones *m*; ~ **strike price** STOCK precio de ejercicio de la opción *m*; ~ **theorist** STOCK teórico, a de las opciones *m,f*; ~ **writer** STOCK emisor(a) de una opción *m,f*, vendedor(a) de opciones de compra y venta *m,f*

Options: ~ **Clearing Corporation** *n* (*OCC*) *AmE* STOCK cámara de compensación de opciones

optional: ~ **feature** *n* STOCK opción facultativa *f*; ~ **item** *n* FIN elemento optativo *m*; ~ **mode of settlement** *n* INS opción de liquidación *f*; ~ **payment bond** *n* FIN, STOCK bono de pago opcional *m*

optional/mandatory *adj* INS opcional/obligatorio

OR *abbr* MGMNT, S&M (*operations research*) investigación de operaciones *f*, investigación operacional *f*

oracle *n* S&M oráculo *m*

oral: ~ **contract** *n* LAW contrato verbal *m*; ~ **note** *n* POL apunte verbal *m*, comentario *m*; ~ **proceeding** *n* PATENTS procedimiento oral *m*

orange: ~ **goods** *n pl* S&M productos de duración de vida media

ord. *abbr* (*order*) GEN COMM, HRM orden *f*, LAW mandamiento *m*, orden *f*

order[1]: **on** ~ *adj* GEN COMM, S&M pedido

order[2] *n* (*ord.*) GEN COMM orden *f*, *stock* pedido *m*, LAW *from the courts* mandamiento *m*; ~ **acceptance** BANK, FIN aceptación del pedido *f*; ~ **bill of lading** IMP/EXP, TRANSP conocimiento de embarque a la orden *m*; ~ **blank** GEN COMM, S&M formulario de pedido *m*; ~ **book** GEN COMM libro de pedidos *m*; ~ **book official** STOCK funcionario(-a) de la cartera de pedidos *m,f*; ~ **buying** GEN COMM compra por pedido *f*; ~ **card** S&M tarjeta de pedido *f*; ~ **clause** BANK, LAW cláusula sobre pedidos *f*; ~ **code** ACC código de orden *m*; ~ **of discharge** TAX orden de exención *f*; ~ **entry** S&M entrada de pedido *f*; ~ **flow pattern** S&M *direct mail* tendencia del flujo de pedidos *f*; ~ **form** GEN COMM, S&M hoja de pedido *f*; ~ **letter** ACC, ADMIN, BANK carta de pedido *f*; ~ **of magnitude** MATH orden de magnitud *m*; ~ **number** GEN COMM, S&M *fulfillment* número de pedido *m*; ~ **on hand** GEN COMM, S&M pedido en existencia *m*; ~ **paper** BANK instrumento negociable endosado por el portador *m*; ~ **point system** TRANSP sistema de punto de pedido *m*; ~ **quantity** GEN COMM, S&M cantidad de pedido *f*; ~ **regulation** TRANSP regulación de pedidos *f*; ~ **to pay** ACC, BANK orden de pago *f*; ~ **valid only today** STOCK orden de compra para un solo día *f*; ◆ **my** ~ (*m/o*) GEN COMM mi orden, mi pedido; **on** ~ S&M pedido; ~ **of** (*o/o*) GEN COMM orden de *f*; **out of** ~ *adj* GEN COMM improcedente, averiado, LAW improcedente; **in** ~ **of importance** GEN COMM por orden de importancia; **in** ~ **of priority** GEN COMM en orden de prioridad; **in the** ~ **specified** GEN COMM en el orden señalado

order[3] *vt* GEN COMM pedir

orderly: ~ **market** *n* STOCK mercado tranquilo *m*; ~ **market agreement** *n* (*OMA*) ECON acuerdo de mercado metódico *m*

orders: ~ **in hand** *phr* ACC, BANK, FIN cartera de pedidos *f*; **for** ~ *phr* (*fo*) GEN COMM a órdenes; **take** ~ *phr* GEN COMM aceptar pedidos

ordinal: ~ **data entry** *n* COMP entrada de datos ordinal *f*; ~ **scale** *n* MATH ?scala ordinal *f*; ~ **utility** *n* ECON utilidad ordinal *f*

ordinance *n* LAW ordenanza *f*

ordinary: ~ **account** *n* BANK cuenta ordinaria *f*; ~ **annuity** *n* INS anualidad ordinaria *f*; ~ **business** *n* TAX negocio habitual *m*; ~ **course of business** *n* GEN COMM marcha normal de los negocios *f*; ~ **gain** *n* TAX ganancia ordinaria *f*; ~ **general meeting** *n* STOCK *of shareholders* junta general ordinaria *f*; ~ **income** *n* ACC, TAX ingresos ordinarios *m pl*; ~ **interest** *n* FIN interés ordinario *m*; ~ **loss** *n* TAX pérdida ordinaria *f*; ~ **and necessary business expenses** *n pl* TAX gastos corrientes y necesarios de explotación *m pl*; ~ **payroll exclusion endorsement** *n* INS *company* endoso de exclusión de la nómina ordinaria *m*; ~ **profit before**

taxation *n* ACC, TAX beneficios ordinarios antes de impuestos *m pl*; ~ **resident** *n* LAW, TAX residente ordinario(-a) *m,f*; ~ **return** *n* LEIS, TRANSP billete de ida y vuelta *m*; ~ **share** *n* GEN COMM acción ordinaria *f*; ~ **shareholder** *n* STOCK accionista ordinario(-a) *m,f*; ~ **single ticket** *n* LEIS, TRANSP billete sencillo *m*; ~ **spring tide** *n* (*ost*) TRANSP marea equinoccial ordinaria *f*; ~ **stockholder** *n* STOCK accionista ordinario(-a) *m,f*; ~ **ticket** *n* LEIS billete ordinario *m*

ore *n* ENVIR *deposit* mena *f*, mineral metálico *m*; ~ **carrier** TRANSP buque mineralero *m*

organic: ~ **composition of capital** *n* ECON composición orgánica del capital *f*; ~ **farming** *n* ECON, ENVIR agricultura orgánica *f*, cultivo orgánico *m*; ~ **foodstuff** *n* ENVIR producto alimenticio orgánico *m*; ~ **growth** *n* ECON, GEN COMM crecimiento orgánico *m*; ~ **material** *n* ENVIR materia orgánica *f*; ~ **premium** *n* ECON *agricultural* premio orgánico *m*

organicity *n jarg* GEN COMM organicidad *f*

organigram *n* MGMNT esquema de disposición *m*

organization *n* (*org*) GEN COMM *company* organización *f*; ~ **behavior** *AmE*, ~ **behaviour** *BrE* GEN COMM, MGMNT comportamiento de la organización *m*; ~ **chart** GEN COMM, MGMNT carta de organización *f*, esquema de disposición *m*, organigrama *m*, flujograma *m*; ~ **cost** ACC coste de organización *m* (*Esp*), costo de organización *m* (*AmL*); ~ **culture** MGMNT cultura de organización *f*; ~ **development** MGMNT desarrollo de la organización *m*; ~ **man** MGMNT hombre de la organización *m*; ~ **and methods** (*O&M*) MGMNT organización y métodos *f*; ~ **planning** GEN COMM, MGMNT planificación de la organización *f*, plan de la organización *m*, plan organizacional *m*; ~ **structure** GEN COMM, MGMNT estructura de la organización *f*; ~ **theory** ECON, MGMNT teoría de la organización *f*

Organization: ~ **of Central American States** *n* (*OCAS*) ECON, POL Organización de Estados Centroamericanos *f* (*OEAC*); ~ **for Economic Cooperation and Development** *n* (*OECD*) ECON, POL Organización para la Cooperación y Desarrollo Económicos *f* (*OCDE*); ~ **for European Economic Cooperation** *n* (*OEEC*) ECON, POL Organización para la Cooperación Económica Europea *f*; ~ **for International Exhibitions** *n* S&M Organización para las Exposiciones Internacionales *f*; ~ **for Trade Cooperation** *n* (*OTC*) ECON Organización para la Cooperación Comercial *f*; ~ **of Petroleum Exporting Countries** *n* (*OPEC*) IMP/EXP, POL Organización de los Países Exportadores de Petróleo *f* (*OPEP*)

organizational: ~ **behavior** *AmE*, ~ **behaviour** *BrE* *n* GEN COMM, MGMNT comportamiento de la organización *m*, comportamiento en las organizaciones *m*, comportamiento organizacional *m*, comportamiento organizativo *m*; ~ **change** *n* MGMNT cambio organizacional *m*; ~ **convenience** *n* GEN COMM conveniencia organizativa *f*; ~ **development** *n* MGMNT desarrollo organizacional *m*; ~ **economics** *n* ECON economía organizacional *f*; ~ **effectiveness** *n* MGMNT eficacia organizacional *f*; ~ **pathology** *n* HRM patología organizativa *f*; ~ **politics** *n pl* POL política organizativa *f*; ~ **psychology** *n* MGMNT psicología organizacional *f*; ~ **shape** *n* GEN COMM formato organizacional *m*; ~ **size** *n* GEN COMM magnitud organizativa *f*; ~ **symbol** *n* GEN COMM *logo* símbolo corporativo *m*; ~ **theory** *n* GEN COMM teoría organizativa *f*; ~ **unit** *n* ADMIN unidad de organización *f*, unidad organizacional *f*

organize *vt* GEN COMM organizar

organizer *n* ADMIN agenda personal *f*, organizador personal *m*

organized: ~ **crime** *n* LAW crimen organizado *m*; ~ **labor** *AmE*, ~ **labour** *BrE* *n* HRM trabajo organizado *m*; ~ **market** *n* ECON mercado organizado *m*

orientation *n* GEN COMM, POL orientación *f*

origin: ~ **and destination study** *n* S&M *market research* estudio de origen y destino *m*

original *n* GEN COMM, MEDIA *broadcast* original *m*; ~ **address** COMMS, COMP dirección de origen *f*; ~ **assessment** TAX imposición original *f*; ~ **bid** GEN COMM oferta original *f*; ~ **bill** GEN COMM, IMP/EXP, TRANSP factura original *f*; ~ **bill of lading** IMP/EXP, TRANSP *shipping* conocimiento de embarque original *m*; ~ **capital** FIN capital original *m*; ~ **cost** ACC coste original *m* (*Esp*), costo original *m* (*AmL*), precio de coste *m* (*Esp*), precio de costo *m* (*AmL*); ~ **device** GEN COMM dispositivo original *m*; ~ **document** GEN COMM documento de origen *m*; ~ **entry** ACC *bookkeeping* registro cronológico *m*; ~ **invoice** GEN COMM, IMP/EXP, TRANSP factura original *f*; ~ **issue discount** (*OID*) STOCK emisión con descuento *f*; ~ **issue discount bond** (*OID bond*) FIN, STOCK emisión con descuento original *f*; ~ **margin** FIN, STOCK margen original *m*; ~ **maturity** BANK, FIN, STOCK vencimiento original *m*; ~ **order** GEN COMM, S&M pedido original *m*; ~ **owner** TAX propietario(-a) original *m,f*; ~ **slip** INS borderó original *m*

originating: ~ **document** *n* TAX documento originario *m*

originator *n* BANK emisor(a) *m,f*

orthodox: ~ **school** *n* ECON escuela ortodoxa *f*

OS *abbr* (*operation system*) COMP SO (*sistema operativo*)

OSA *abbr* (*overseas sterling area*) ECON área internacional de dominio de la libra esterlina *f*

OSD *abbr* (*open shelter deck*) TRANSP cubierta de abrigo abierta *f*

OSI *abbr* (*open systems interconnection*) COMP OSI (*interconexión de sistemas abiertos*)

ost *abbr* (*ordinary spring tide*) TRANSP marea equinoccial ordinaria *f*

OT *abbr* HRM, IND (*overtime*) horas extra *f pl*, horas extraordinarias *f pl*, TRANSP (*open-top container, open-topped container*) contenedor con techo removible *m*

OTAR *abbr* (*overseas tariff and regulations*) IMP/EXP, TRANSP tarifas y regulaciones internacionales *f pl*

OTC[1] *abbr* ECON (*Organization for Trade Cooperation*) Organización para la Cooperación Comercial *f*, STOCK (*over-the-counter*) no registrado, transacciones no registradas en bolsa *f pl*, WEL (*over-the-counter*) de libre adquisición

OTC[2]: ~ **option** *abbr* STOCK opción OTC

OTCM *abbr* (*over-the-counter market*) ECON, FIN, STOCK mercado de valores extrabursátil *m*

other: ~ **assets** *n pl* FIN otros activos *m pl*; ~ **beneficiary** *n* FIN *profit sharing* otro(-a) beneficiario(-a) *m,f*; ~ **checkable deposits** *n* (*OCD*) BANK, FIN otros depósitos *m pl*; ~ **income** *n* ACC, TAX otros ingresos *m pl*; ~ **insurance clause** *n* INS cláusula de otros seguros *f*; ~ **receivables** *n pl* BANK *balance sheet* otros efectos por cobrar *m pl*

OTS *abbr BrE* (*Overseas Trade Statistics*) ECON, POL estadísticas del comercio exterior

OU *abbr BrE* (*Open University*) WEL universidad a

distancia británica, ≈ UNED (*Universidad Nacional de Educación a Distancia*) (*Esp*)

ounce *n* (*oz*) GEN COMM onza *f*

outbid *vt* S&M *at auction* hacer mejor oferta que, sobrepujar

outcry *n* GEN COMM estruendo *m*; ~ **market** STOCK mercado de subasta *m*

outdated *adj* GEN COMM *idea, product* anticuado

outdoor: ~ **advertising** *n* S&M publicidad exterior *f*

outer: ~ **code** *n* COMP código exterior *m*; ~ **pack** *n* S&M envase exterior *m*

outflow *n* ACC *of funds* salida *f*

outgoing *n*: ~ **invoices** *n pl* ACC, FIN, GEN COMM facturas enviadas *f pl*; ~ **mail** *n* (*cf outgoing post BrE*) COMMS correo saliente *m*; ~**post** *n* (*cf outgoing mail AmE*) COMMS correo saliente *m*

outgoings *n* ACC, ECON, FIN desembolso *m*

outlaw *vt* LAW proscribir

outlay *n* ACC, ECON, FIN desembolso *m*, GEN COMM, IND gasto *m*, producción total *f*, inversión *f*; ~ **creep** BANK, ECON deformación de la salida *f* (*jarg*), FIN incremento gradual de los gastos *m*, deformación de la salida *f*, POL deformación de la salida *f*

outlet *n* S&M *of article* salida *f*, TRANSP *for dangerous waste* desagüe *m*, descarga *f*, salida *f*; ~ **store** S&M tienda de venta al público *f*

outlier *n* MATH *statistics* valor atípico *m*

outline[1] *n* ADMIN, ECON, GEN COMM esquema *m*

outline[2] *vt* GEN COMM esbozar

outlook *n* GEN COMM *economic* perspectiva *f*

out-of-court: ~ **settlement** *n* LAW arreglo extrajudicial *m*

out-of-favor: ~ **industry** *AmE see out-of-favour industry BrE*

out-of-favour: ~ **industry** *n BrE* ECON, FIN, IND industria caída en desgracia *f*, sector poco atractivo *m*; ~ **stock** *n BrE* FIN, STOCK acciones sin demanda *f pl*

out-of-pocket: ~ **costs** *n* ACC, FIN, GEN COMM gastos menores *m pl*, gastos en efectivo *m pl*

out-of-state: ~ **corporation** *n* LAW sociedad extraterritorial *f*

out-of-the-money: ~ **call** *n* STOCK opción de compra con pérdida potencial *f*; ~ **option** *n* STOCK opción con precio diferente al de mercado *f*; ~ **put** *n* STOCK opción de venta con pérdida potencial *f*

out-of-town: ~ **center** *AmE*, ~ **centre** *BrE n* GEN COMM, PROP, S&M *retail development* centro comercial a las afueras *m*; ~ **shop** *n BrE* (*cf out-of-town store AmE*) S&M tienda en las afueras *f*; ~ **store** *AmE n* (*cf out-of-town shop BrE*) S&M tienda en las afueras *f*

out-of-work *adj* HRM, WEL sin trabajo

outpace *vt* GEN COMM dejar atrás

outperform *vt* ECON, STOCK superar

outperformance *n* ECON, STOCK resultado superior *m*

outplacement *n* HRM, MGMNT orientación vocacional pagada por una empresa, principalmente para los ejecutivos que han sido despedidos; ~ **agency** HRM agencia que ayuda a las personas despedidas a salir de la empresa y colocarse

output[1] *n* ACC output *m*, producto *m*, COMP salida *f*, ECON output *m*, producto *m*; ~ **bonus** HRM incentivo por productividad *m*; ~ **budgeting** ACC, FIN, POL *governmental* presupuestación de producción *f*; ~ **data** COMP

datos de salida *m pl*; ~ **device** COMP dispositivo de salida *m*; ~ **file** COMP archivo de salida *m*, fichero de impresión *m*; ~ **per head** IND producto per cápita *m*; ~ **per hour** IND producción por hora *f*; ~ **variance** MATH *statistics* variación de los resultados *f*; ~ **volume** GEN COMM volumen de producción *m*

output[2] *vt* COMP *data, text* extraer, *to printer* imprimir

outright[1] *adj* GEN COMM *ownership* incondicional

outright[2]: ~ **forward purchase** *n* ECON compra futura en firme *f*; ~ **gift** *n* TAX donación propiamente dicha *f*

outset: at the ~ *phr* GEN COMM al comienzo

outshipment *n* TRANSP envío exterior *m*

outside[1]: ~ **broadcast** *n* MEDIA emisión de exteriores *f*; ~ **director** *n* HRM, MGMNT director(a) externo(a) *m,f*; ~ **finance** *n* FIN finanzas exteriores *f pl*; ~ **money** *n* ECON dinero exterior *m*;

ouside[2]: ~ **the reference of** *phr* GEN COMM más allá de la referencia de

outsider *n* GEN COMM forastero(-a) *m,f*, HRM *in field* profano(-a) *m,f*, *in group, organization* persona independiente *f*, *in organization* intruso(-a) *m,f*, MGMNT ajeno(-a) *m,f*, extranjero(-a) *m,f*, intruso(-a) *m,f*; ~ **broker** STOCK broker independiente *mf*, intermediario(-a) independiente *m,f*; ~ **wage-setting** ECON liquidación del sueldo *f*

outsourcing *n* MGMNT recurso a fuentes externas *m*

outstanding[1] *adj* FIN *debt, amount, obligation*, GEN COMM *debt, amount, obligation* insoluto, por resolver, pendiente de pago, LAW *objection, appeal* pendiente

outstanding[2] *n* ACC, FIN montón insoluto *m*, pago pendiente *m*; ~ **accounts** *n pl* ACC, BANK cuentas pendientes *f pl*; ~ **advance** ACC anticipo pendiente *m*; ~ **balance** ACC, BANK, GEN COMM saldo pendiente *m*, déficit *m*; ~ **bill** ACC, FIN factura pendiente *f*; ~ **bond** FIN, STOCK bono en circulación *m*; ~ **capital stock** STOCK acciones de capital en circulación *f pl*; ~ **check** *AmE*, ~ **cheque** *BrE* BANK, FIN cheque pendiente *m*; ~ **commitment** ACC compromiso pendiente *m*, obligación pendiente *f*; ~ **credits** ACC, BANK créditos pendientes *m pl*, cuentas pendientes *f pl*; ~ **debt** ACC, BANK, FIN deuda pendiente de pago *f*; ~ **entry** ACC entrada pendiente *f*, ingreso pendiente *m*; ~ **item** ACC partida pendiente *f*; ~ **loan** BANK préstamo pendiente *m*; ~ **matters** *n pl* GEN COMM asuntos importantes *m pl*, asuntos pendientes *m pl*; ~ **mortgage loan** BANK, FIN, PROP préstamo hipotecario pendiente *m*; ~ **order** GEN COMM, S&M pedido sin entregar *m*; ~ **payment** ACC, BANK, FIN pago atrasado *m*; ~ **principal balance** ACC, BANK saldo principal pendiente de pago *m*

out-tray *n* GEN COMM bandeja *f*

outvote *vt* GEN COMM *other board-members* emitir más votos que

outward[1]: ~-**looking** *adj* GEN COMM *approach* abierto

outward[2]: ~ **cargo** *n* IMP/EXP, TRANSP cargamento de ida *m*; ~ **freight department** *n* IMP/EXP, TRANSP departamento de fletes de salida *m*; ~ **leg** *n* LEIS, TRANSP trayecto de ida *m*; ~ **mission** *n* IMP/EXP misión exterior *f*; ~ **payment** *n* FIN pago externo *m*; ~ **voyage** *n* TRANSP viaje de ida *m*

outweigh *vt* GEN COMM superar en valor a

overaccumulation *n* ECON sobreacumulación *f*

over-achiever *n jarg* WEL persona de rendimiento superior a lo esperado

overage *n* GEN COMM exceso de edad *m*, FIN superávit *m*,

~ loan FIN, BANK préstamo para cubrir posibles excesos de costes

overall[1] *adj* (*oa*) GEN COMM global

overall[2] *adv* GEN COMM generalmente

overall[3]: **~ deficit** *n* ECON déficit global *m*; **~ demand** *n* ECON, FIN demanda global *f*; **~ expenses method** *n* ACC método global de gastos *m*; **~ length** *n* TRANSP *shipping* eslora total *f*; **~ market price coverage** *n* STOCK cobertura global del precio de mercado *f*; **~ rate of return** *n* ACC tasa global de beneficio *f*, tipo global de beneficio *m*; **~ width** *n* TRANSP anchura total *f*

overbid *vt* STOCK ofrecer por encima del valor

overbooked *adj* TRANSP *flights* reservado con exceso, sobrecontratado

overbooking *n* GEN COMM, TRANSP overbooking *m*, sobrecontratación *f*, sobreventa *f*

overbought *adj* STOCK sobrecomprado

overcapacity *n* GEN COMM supercapacidad *f*

overcapitalized *adj* GEN COMM sobrecapitalizado

overcenter: **~ tensioner** *AmE see overcentre tensioner BrE*

overcentre: **~ tensioner** *n BrE* TRANSP *lashing* tensor descentrado *m*

overcharge[1] *n* (*o/c*) ACC importe en demasía *m*, BANK, GEN COMM recargo *m*, cobro excesivo *m*

overcharge[2] *vt* GEN COMM, S&M cobrar de más, cobrar un precio excesivo

overcome *vt* GEN COMM superar

overcoming[1] *adj* S&M superado

overcoming[2]: **~ objections** *n pl* S&M superación de objeciones *f*

overcommitment *n* FIN exceso de compromisos *m*

overcompensation *n* HRM compensación excesiva *f*

overdependence *n* GEN COMM sobredependencia *f*

overdiversification *n* STOCK diversificación excesiva *f*

overdraft *n* (*O/D*) BANK, FIN descubierto *m*, balance descubierto *m*, sobregiro *m*; **~ facility** BANK facilidad de sobregiro *f*; **~ lending** BANK préstamo sobregirado *m*; **~ protection** BANK protección contra sobregiro *f*

overdraw *vt* BANK sobregirar; ◆ **~ an account** BANK dejar una cuenta en descubierto

overdrawn[1] *adj* (*O/D*) BANK en descubierto, sobregirado

overdrawn[2]: **~ account** *n* BANK cuenta en descubierto *f*; **~ amount** *n* BANK cantidad en descubierto *f*

overdrive *n* TRANSP superdirecta *f*

overdue[1] *adj* GEN COMM vencido

overdue[2]: **~ check** *AmE*, **~ cheque** *BrE n* BANK, FIN cheque vencido *m*

overemployment *n* HRM exceso de empleo *m*

overestimate *vt* GEN COMM sobreestimar

overexploitation *n* GEN COMM sobreexplotación *f*

overextended *adj* ECON, GEN COMM *financial resources* sobreextendido

overfunding *n* POL, STOCK provisión excesiva de fondos *f*, captación excesiva de fondos *f*

over-gifted *adj* WEL superdotado

overgrazing *n* ENVIR sobrepastoreo *m*

overhang *n* STOCK exceso de oferta *m*

overhaul *n* MGMNT *of system* examen *m*, TRANSP transporte adicional *m*

overhead: **~ capital** *n* ECON capital social fijo *m*; **~ charges** *n* ACC, GEN COMM gastos generales *m pl*;

~ projector *n* MEDIA, MGMNT *meeting* proyector de acetatos *m*; **~ transparency** *n* GEN COMM transparencia *f*

overheads *n pl* GEN COMM costes indirectos *m pl* (*Esp*), costos indirectos *m pl* (*AmL*), gastos generales de fabricación *m pl*, gastos generales *m pl*; **~ recovery** *n* GEN COMM recuperación de gastos generales *f*, recuperación de gastos indirectos *f*

overheated: **~ economy** *n* ECON economía recalentada *f*

overheating *n* ECON recalentamiento de la coyuntura *m*

overheight: **~ cargo** *n* TRANSP *in open-top container* carga que sobrepasa la altura *f*

overindebtedness *n* BANK sobreendeudamiento *m*

overissue *n* BANK exceso de emisión *m*

overkill *n infrml* S&M *advertising* exceso de medios *m*, desbordamiento *m*

overland: **~ transport** *n* TRANSP transporte terrestre *m*

overlap *n* S&M superposición *f*

overlapping: **~ generations model** *n* (*OLG*) ECON modelo de solapación de generaciones *m*

overlay *n* ADMIN *guide* alza *m*

overman *vt* HRM dotar de exceso de personal

overmanned *adj* HRM con exceso de personal

overnight[1] *adj* GEN COMM nocturno

overnight[2]: **~ deposit** *n* BANK depósito nocturno *m*; **~ loan** *n* BANK préstamo nocturno *m*; **~ money** *n* BANK, FIN dinero nocturno *m*, dinero a un día *m*; **~ repo** *n* STOCK repo a un día *m*; **~ security** *n* STOCK valor a un día *m*; **~ travel** *n* LEIS viaje nocturno *m*

overpack *n* TRANSP sobreembalaje *m*

overpaid: **~ entry certificate** *n* (*OEC*) IMP/EXP certificado de entrada pagado en exceso *m*

overpass *vt* ACC exceder

overpayment *n* ACC pago en exceso *m*

overplacing *n* BANK sobrecolocación *f*

overprice *vt* S&M fijar un precio excesivo para

overpriced *adj* S&M de precio excesivo

overprint *n* S&M sobreimpresión *f*

overproduce *vt* ECON, IND sobreproducir

overproduction *n* ECON, IND superproducción *f*

overprovision *n* ECON provisión en exceso *f*

overrepresent *vt* S&M *in the market* sobrerrepresentar

overrepresentation *n* S&M *in the market* sobrerrepresentación *f*

override[1] *n* HRM compensación extraordinaria a un vendedor *f*

override[2] *vt* GEN COMM cancelar, POL anular

overriding: **~ clause** *n* BANK, INS, LAW cláusula derogatoria *f*; **~ commission** *n* INS *underwriting*, LEIS *travel trade* sobrecomisión *f*; **~ interest** *n* GEN COMM interés dominante *m*

overrule *vt* POL *decision* anular

overrun *n* ECON *budget* rebasamiento *m*, IND *production* exceso *m*

oversaving *n* BANK exceso de ahorro *m*

overseas[1] *adj* GEN COMM de ultramar

overseas[2]: **~ agent** *n* GEN COMM agente exterior *mf*; **~ aid** *n* ECON, POL ayuda exterior *f*, ayuda externa *f*; **~ asset** *n* ECON, FIN activo extranjero *m*, activos en el exterior *m pl*; **~ branch** *n* IMP/EXP sucursal en el extranjero *f*; **~ customer** *n* GEN COMM, S&M cliente extranjero(-a) *m,f*; **~ department** *n* GEN COMM departamento de ultramar *m*; **~ employment tax credit** *n* TAX deducción por empleo en ultramar *f*; **~ investment cover** *n* INS cobertura de inversión internacional *f*; **~ investor** *n* STOCK inversor(a) extranjero(a) *m,f*; **~ market** *n* GEN COMM mercado exterior *m*; **~ project fund** *n* ECON fondo para la financiación de proyectos en el extranjero *m*; **~ status report status** *n* IMP/EXP categoría del informe de la valoración internacional *f*; **~ sterling area** *n* (*OSA*) ECON área internacional de dominio de la libra esterlina *f*; **~ tariff and regulations** *n* (*OTAR*) IMP/EXP, TRANSP tarifas y regulaciones internacionales *f pl*; **~ tariff regulations** *n* IMP/EXP, TRANSP reglamento de tarifas internacionales *m*; **~ tourism** *n* GEN COMM, LEIS turismo extranjero *m*; **~ tourist** *n* GEN COMM, LEIS turista extranjero *mf*; **~ trade** *n* IMP/EXP, TRANSP comercio de ultramar *m*; **~ trade fairs and seminars** *n pl* IMP/EXP ferias y seminarios de comercio internacional *f pl*; **~ visitor** *n* GEN COMM visitante extranjero(-a) *m,f*

Overseas: **~ Development Agency** *n BrE* (*ODA*) ECON, POL agencia estatal para el desarrollo exterior; **~ Development Institute** *n* (*ODI*) ECON instituto para el desarrollo exterior; **~ Economic Cooperation Fund** *n* (*OECF*) ECON Fondos para la Cooperación Económica Exterior *m pl*; **~ Project Fund** *n* ECON Fondo de Proyecto de Ultramar *m*; **~ Service Aid Scheme** *n* (*OSAS*) ECON *ODA* Plan de Ayuda de Servicio Internacional *m*; **~ Trade Board** *n BrE* ECON junta para el comercio exterior; **~ Trade Statistics** *n pl BrE* (*OTS*) ECON, POL estadísticas de comercio exterior; **~ Union Bank** *n* BANK Banco Unido Internacional *m*

oversee *vt* GEN COMM, MGMNT supervisar

overseer *n* HRM, PROP capataz(a) *m,f*

overselling *n* S&M propaganda excesiva *f*

overshoot *vt* GEN COMM rebasar

overshooting: **~ price** *n* ECON precio excedido *m*

overside[1]: **~ loading** *n* TRANSP *shipping* carga por barcazas *f*

overside[2] *vt* GEN COMM dar de lado

oversold *adj* STOCK saturado

overspent *adj* ACC agotado

overspill: **~ town** *n* GEN COMM poblado periférico *m*

overstaffed *adj* HRM con exceso de personal

overstaffing *n* HRM exceso de personal *m*

overstepping: **~ of appropriation** *n* BANK exceso de crédito *m*

overstimulate *vt* GEN COMM sobreestimular

overstretch *vt* GEN COMM exagerar

overstuffing *n* TRANSP sobrecarga *f*

oversubscribed *adj* STOCK cubierto en exceso, sobresuscrito

oversubscription *n* STOCK *shares* exceso de peticiones de suscripción *m*

oversupply *n* ECON oferta excesiva *f*

overtax *n* TAX tributación excesiva *f*

overtaxation *n* TAX imposición excesiva *f*

over-the-counter: **~ dealings** *n* (*OTC*) STOCK transacciones de valores no registradas en bolsa en un mercado secundario *f*; **~ derivative instrument** *n AmE* FIN instrumento derivativo de mostrador *m*; **~ market** *n*

(*OTCM*) ECON, FIN, STOCK mercado de valores extrabursátil *m*; **~ medicine** *n* WEL medicamento sin receta *m*, medicamento sin prescripción *m*; **~ option** *n* (*OTC option*) STOCK opción extrabursátil *f* (*opción OTC*); **~ retailing** *n* S&M venta minorista *f*; **~ trading** *n AmE* FIN comercio legal de acciones sin cotización oficial

overtime *n* (*OT*) HRM, IND horas extra *f pl*, horas extraordinarias *f pl*; **~ ban** HRM prohibición de tiempo extra *f*; **~ hours** *n pl* HRM, IND horas extra *f pl*, horas extraordinarias *f pl*; **~ pay** HRM paga por horas extra *f*, paga por horas extraordinarias *f*; **~ premium** HRM prima por horas extraordinarias *f*

overtonnaging *n* TRANSP exceso de tonelaje *m*

overtrading *n* ECON exceso de comercialización *m*, exceso de inversión *f*, STOCK sobreinversión *f*

overurbanization *n* ECON, ENVIR sobreurbanización *f*

overuse *n* ECON superutilización *f*

overvaluation *n* GEN COMM revalorización excesiva *f*, tasación excesiva *f*, valoración excesiva *f*, sobrevaloración *f*

overvalue *vt* GEN COMM sobrevaluar

overvalued[1] *adj* GEN COMM sobrevalorado

overvalued[2]: **~ currency** *n* ECON moneda sobrevalorada *f*

overview *n* GEN COMM descripción general *f*

overwriting *n* STOCK suscripción *f*

owe *vt* ACC adeudar, GEN COMM deber algo a

own: **~ account operator** *n* TRANSP operador por cuenta propia *m*; **~ brand** *n* S&M marca propia *f*; **~interest rate** *n* ECON tasa de interés propia *f*; **~ label** *n* S&M *supermarket brand* etiqueta propia *f*; **~ resources** *n pl* ECON, POL recursos propios *m pl*

owner *n* GEN COMM dueño(-a) *m,f*, patrón(a) *m,f*, PATENTS titular *mf*, PROP, TRANSP *vessel* propietario(-a) *m,f*; **~'s account** TRANSP *chartering* cuenta del armador *f*; **~'s broker** TRANSP *shipping* corredor(a) del armador *m,f*; **~'s capital** GEN COMM capital del propietario *m*; **~-manager** HRM, MGMNT gerente-propietario(-a) *m,f*; **~ occupation** PROP tenencia por el propietario *f*; **~-occupied farmland** PROP tierras en explotación ocupadas por su propietario *f pl*; **~-occupied home** TAX casa ocupada por su propietario *f*; **~-occupier** LAW, PROP propietario(-a)-ocupante *m,f*; **~-operator** GEN COMM explotador(a) *m,f*; ◆ **at ~'s risk** GEN COMM, INS, TRANSP bajo la responsabilidad del armador

owners': **~ and contractors' protective liability insurance** *n* INS *company* seguro contra responsabilidad civil de propietarios y contratistas *m*; **~, landlords', and tenants' liability policy** *n* INS seguro contra responsabilidad civil de propietarios, arrendadores e inquilinos *m*

ownership *n* GEN COMM, LAW, PROP derecho de propiedad *m*; **~ form** LAW, PROP formulario de propiedad *m*; **~ rights under life insurance** *n pl* INS derechos de propiedad en un seguro de vida *m pl*; ◆ **under new ~** ECON cambio de propietario

oz *abbr* (*ounce*) GEN COMM onza *f*

ozone: **~ depletion** *n* ENVIR agotamiento del ozono *m*; **~ layer** *n* ENVIR capa de ozono *f*

P

p. *abbr* (*page*) GEN COMM p (*página*), pág. (*página*)

p.a. *abbr* (*per annum*) GEN COMM por año

PA[1] *abbr* GEN COMM, HRM, MGMNT (*personal assistant*) asistente(-a) personal *m,f*, ayudante(-a) personal *m,f*, secretario(-a) personal *m,f*, (*postal assistant*) ayudante postal *mf*, LAW (*by power of attorney*) poder notarial *m*, MEDIA *BrE* (*Press Association*) asociación británica de prensa

PA[2]: **~ system** *n* (*public address system*) COMMS, GEN COMM sistema altavoces *m*

P.A. *abbr* (*particular average*) INS *marine* avería particular *f*

Paasche: **~ index** *n* ECON índice de Paasche *m*

PABX *abbr BrE* (*private automatic branch exchange*) COMMS centralita automática privada unida a la red pública *f*

pace *n* GEN COMM *of change* ritmo *m*, *of trend* velocidad *f*

pacesetter *n* GEN COMM *company* trabajador tipo *m*

Pacific: **~ Stock Exchange** *n* (*PSE*) STOCK Bolsa de valores del Pacífico *f*

pacify *vt* GEN COMM, STOCK *shareholders* apaciguar

pack[1] *n* GEN COMM, IMP/EXP, S&M, TRANSP embalaje *m*; **~ shot** S&M *advertising* plano macro sobre el producto

pack[2] *vt* COMP *data* comprimir, GEN COMM, IMP/EXP, TRANSP, S&M embalar

package[1] *n* (*pkg.*) COMMS, GEN COMM envoltorio *m*, paquete *m*; **~ code** S&M código del envase *m*; **~ deal** ECON, GEN COMM conjunto de normas económicas *m*, conjunto de medidas económicas *m*, FIN *interlinked transaction*, acuerdo global *m*, HRM paquete de reivindicaciones *m*, LEIS paquete *m* (*jarg*), viaje organizado *m*; **~ design** S&M diseño del envase *m*, diseño de la envoltura *m*; **~ mortgage** BANK, FIN, PROP hipoteca para financiar la compra del inmueble y su mobiliario; **~ store** *AmE* (*cf liquor store AmE, off-licence BrE*) GEN COMM *shop* tienda de licores *f*; **~ tour** LEIS, TRANSP excursión con todo organizado *f*; **~ tour operator** *BrE* LEIS agente de viajes organizados *mf*; **~ holiday** *BrE* LEIS, TRANSP viaje organizado *m*, vacaciones con todo organizado *f pl*

package[2] *vt* GEN COMM embalar, empaquetar

packaged: **~ goods** *n pl* S&M, TRANSP mercancía empaquetada *f*; **~ timber** *n* TRANSP madera embalada *f*

packaging *n* GEN COMM, S&M, TRANSP embalaje *m*; **~ certificate** TRANSP *containers* certificado de embalaje *m*; **~ cost** GEN COMM coste de embalaje *m* (*Esp*), costo de embalaje *m* (*AmL*); **~ credit** BANK crédito paquete *m*; **~ list** IMP/EXP, TRANSP lista de embalaje *f*; **~ materials** *n pl* S&M materiales de embalaje *m pl*

packer *n* GEN COMM embalador(a) *m,f*

packet *n* (*pkt.*) COMP, GEN COMM paquete *m*

packing *n* GEN COMM, IMP/EXP, S&M, TRANSP empaquetado *m*; **~ company** IND compañía empaquetadora *f*; **~ costs** *n pl* IND, S&M gastos de embalaje *m pl*; **~ density** COMP *data* densidad de almacenamiento *f*; **~ instruction** (*pkg instr*) TRANSP instrucción de emba-laje *f*; **~ list** IMP/EXP, TRANSP lista de bultos *f*, lista de embalaje *f*

Pac-Man: **~ defence** *BrE*, **~ defense** *AmE* *n* FIN, STOCK *corporate mergers and acquisitions* defensa comecocos *f*; **~ strategy** *n* FIN, STOCK estrategia Pac-Man *f*

pact *n* GEN COMM pacto *m*

pad *n* COMP *mouse* almohadilla *f*

padding *n* ACC falsificación de nóminas, cuentas de gastos y otros documentos contables *f*, GEN COMM, TRANSP relleno *m*

paddle *n* IND, TRANSP pálet *m* (*AmL*), paleta *f* (*Esp*), bandeja *f* (*Esp*)

page[1] *n* (*p., pg.*) ADMIN, COMP, GEN COMM página *f* (*p, pág.*); **~ break** COMP cambio de página *m*; **~ exposure** MEDIA, S&M índice de lectura de la página impresa *m*; **~ length** COMP longitud de página *f*; **~ number** ADMIN, GEN COMM, MEDIA número de página *m*; **~ proofs** *n pl* MEDIA, S&M pruebas de página *f pl*; **~ rate** MEDIA, S&M tarifa por página *f*; **~ setting** MEDIA *print*, S&M composición de página *f*; **~ traffic** *BrE jarg* MEDIA, S&M *advertising* estimación del número total de lectores de una publicación; **~-turner** MEDIA *print* pasapáginas *m*

page[2] *vt* COMMS, GEN COMM, MGMNT *telecom* avisar

pages *n pl* (*pp.*) GEN COMM páginas *f pl* (*págs.*)

paginate *vt* GEN COMM paginar

pagination *n* GEN COMM paginación *f*

paging: **~ device** *n* COMP dispositivo de paginación *m*

paid[1] *adj* (*pd*) GEN COMM *amounts, dividends* pagado; ◆ **~ by agent** (*PBA*) TRANSP pagado por agente; **be ~ in cash** GEN COMM, HRM cobrar al contado; **~ on delivery** (*POD*) TRANSP pago a la entrega; **~ by the piece** HRM pagado por unidad; **~ by piece rate** HRM pagado por pieza; **be ~ a rate of** HRM recibir una proporción de

paid[2]: **~ experts** *n* HRM comisión de expertos *f*; **~ holidays** *n pl BrE* (*cf paid vacations AmE*) HRM, LEIS vacaciones remuneradas *f pl*; **~-in capital** *n* FIN, STOCK capital cubierto *m*; **~ instrument** *n* FIN instrumento liberado *m*; **~ leave** *n* HRM permiso pagado *m*; **~-out capital** *n* FIN, STOCK capital desembolsado *m*; **~-up addition** *n* INS adquisición pagada *f*; **~-up capital** *n* FIN, STOCK capital desembolsado *m*; **~-up common share** *n* FIN, STOCK acción ordinaria cubierta *f*; **~-up member** *n* HRM miembro que ha pagado su cuota *m*; **~ vacations** *n AmE* (*cf paid holidays BrE*) HRM, LEIS vacaciones remuneradas *f pl*

pail *n* TRANSP cubo *m*

painstakingly *adv* GEN COMM minuciosamente

painting: **~ the tape** *phr AmE* STOCK manipulación ilegal de un valor

paired: **~ comparisons** *n pl* GEN COMM comparaciones por parejas *f pl*; **~ shares** *n pl* STOCK acciones pareadas *f pl*

PAL *abbr* (*program adjustment loan AmE, programme adjustment loan BrE*) BANK, FIN préstamo de ajuste de programa *m*

pallet *n* IND, TRANSP pálet *m* (*AmL*), paleta *f* (*Esp*), bandeja *f* (*Esp*), plataforma, plataforma de carga *f*;

~ **fork** TRANSP *cargo handling* carretilla elevadora *f*, horquilla *f*; ~ **lorry** *BrE* (*cf pallet truck AmE*) TRANSP camión de plataformas *m*; ~ **net** TRANSP red de bandejas de carga *f*, red de plataformas de carga *f*; ~ **track** TRANSP guía de plataforma de carga *f*; ~ **truck** *AmE* (*cf pallet lorry BrE*) TRANSP camión de plataformas *m*

palletizable *adj* IND, TRANSP apilable

palletization *n* IND, TRANSP paletización *f*

palletize *vt* IND, TRANSP apilar

palletized: ~ **stowage** *n* TRANSP estibaje embandejado *m*

PAL/SECAM: ~ **technology** *n* GEN COMM, MEDIA *satellite broadcasting* tecnología PAL/SECAM *f*

pamphlet *n* GEN COMM octavilla *f*, panfleto *m*

Pan: ~ **American Tracing and Reservations System** *n* (*PANTRAC*) TRANSP *aviation* sistema panamericano de localización y reservas

Panamax: ~ **vessel** *n* TRANSP buque Panamax *m*

P&I[1] *abbr* (*protection and indemnity*) TRANSP protección e indemnización *f*

P&I[2]: ~ **club** *n* TRANSP asociación para la protección e indemnización *f*

P&L[1] *abbr* (*profit and loss*) ACC, FIN pérdidas y ganancias *f pl*

P&L[2]: ~ **account** *n* ACC cuenta de pérdidas y ganancias *f*; ~ **statement** *n* ACC *annual accounts* cuenta de pérdidas y ganancias *f*, cuenta de resultados *f*

p&p *abbr* (*postage and packing*) COMMS gastos de franqueo y empaquetado

P&S[1] *abbr* (*purchase and sale*) STOCK compra y venta *f*

P&S[2]: ~ **statement** *n* STOCK declaración de compra y venta *f*

panel *n* COMP plantilla *f*, MATH muestra *f*; ~ **data** S&M datos del panel *m pl*; ~ **envelope** GEN COMM revestimiento de panel *m*; ~ **of experts** GEN COMM grupo de expertos *m*; ~ **testing** S&M *market research* prueba de panel *f*

pan-European *adj* GEN COMM paneuropeo

PANTRAC *abbr* (*Pan American Tracing and Reservations System*) TRANSP *aviation* sistema panamericano de localización y reservas

pantry: ~ **check** *n* S&M control de despensa *m*

paper *n* FIN *infrml* efectos *m pl*, valores *m pl*, GEN COMM papel *m*; ~ **feed** COMP alimentación del papel *f*; ~ **feeder** COMP alimentador de papel *m*; ~ **gold** BANK papel oro *m*; ~ **industry** ECON, ENVIR, IND industria papelera *f*; ~ **loss** STOCK pérdida potencial *f*; ~ **mill** ENVIR, IND fábrica de papel *f*; ~ **money** BANK, ECON, FIN papel moneda *m*; ~ **profit** ACC, FIN, STOCK utilidad no realizada *f*, ganancias por realizar *f pl*; ~ **qualifications** *n pl* WEL documentos de titulación *m pl*; ~ **setting** S&M composición del papel *f*; ~ **shredder** ADMIN, COMP destructora de documentos *f*; ~ **stacker** COMP recogedor de papel *m*; ~ **tape** COMP cinta de papel *f*; ~ **throw** COMP salto de papel *m*; ~ **track** COMP pista para el papel *f*

paperback *n* GEN COMM libro de pasta blanda *m* (*AmL*), libro en rústica *m* (*Esp*)

paperless[1] *adj* STOCK *certificates of deposit* por ordenador

paperless[2]: ~ **entry** *n* BANK entrada sin dinero *f*; ~ **trading** *n* COMP transacción sin papel *f*

paperwork *n* ADMIN papeleo *m*

par *n* GEN COMM par *m*; ~ **bond** FIN, STOCK bono con valor a la par *m*; ~ **collection** GEN COMM cobro a la par *m*; ~ **delivery** STOCK entrega a la par *f*; ~ **stock** STOCK acciones a la par *f pl*; ~ **trading** STOCK cambio a la par *m*; ~ **value** (*p.v.*) ACC, STOCK valor a la par *m*, valor nominal *m*; ~ **value of currency** ACC, STOCK valor a la par de una moneda *m*; ~ **value share** STOCK acción con valor a la par *f*; ~ **value stock** STOCK acciones con valor a la par *f pl*; ♦ **at** ~ ACC, GEN COMM, STOCK a la par

PAR *abbr* (*prescribed aggregate reserve*) BANK reserva agregada obligatoria *f*

paragraph *n* ADMIN, LAW apartado *m*, párrafo *m*

paralegal *adj* LAW paralegal

parallel[1]: ~ **access** *n* COMP acceso en paralelo *m*; ~ **currency** *n* ECON divisa no oficial *f*; ~ **currency strategy** *n* ECON estrategia monetaria no oficial *f*; ~ **import** IMP/EXP importación paralela *f*; ~ **interface** *n* COMP interfaz paralelo *m*; ~ **loan** *n* BANK, ECON, FIN préstamo paralelo *m*; ~ **market economy** *n* ECON economía de mercado no oficial *f*; ~ **plant** *n* IND planta paralela *f*; ~ **pricing** *n* ECON, S&M fijación de precios no oficial *f*; ~ **processing** *n* COMP *of tasks* procesamiento simultáneo *m*; ~ **readership** *n* MEDIA, S&M número paralelo de lectores *m*; ~ **standard** *n* GEN COMM nivel paralelo *m*; ~ **trading** *n* GEN COMM comercio paralelo *m*

parallel[2]: **in** ~ **with** *phr* GEN COMM en paralelo con

parameter *n* COMP, GEN COMM, MATH *statistics* parámetro *m*; ~**-driven software** COMP programa accionado por parámetros *m*

parametric: ~ **programming** *n* COMP, MATH programación paramétrica *f*; ~ **statistics** *n pl* MATH estadística paramétrica *f*

parasitic: ~ **city** *n* ECON ciudad parasitaria *f*

parcel *n* COMMS paquete *m*, PROP *of land* parcela *f*; ~ **awaiting delivery** COMMS, GEN COMM paquete preparado para su despacho *m*; ~ **post** COMMS servicio de paquetes postales *m*; ~ **post insurance** COMMS, INS seguro de paquetes postales *m*

parcel out *vt* PROP *land* parcelar

parcels: ~ **market** *n* TRANSP mercado de paquetería *m*; ~ **van** *n* TRANSP furgoneta paquetera *f*, furgoneta para paquetes *f*

parent *n* COMP padre *m*; ~ **bank** BANK banca matriz *f*; ~ **company** GEN COMM compañía central *f*, compañía matriz *f*, empresa matriz *f*; ~ **company dividend** ACC, FIN dividendo de la compañía matriz *m*; ~ **Crown corporation** GEN COMM corporación pública matriz *f*; ~ **dividends** *n pl* ACC, FIN, STOCK dividendos de la empresa matriz *m pl*; ~ **sailing** TRANSP navegación matriz *f*; ~ **service** TRANSP servicio nodriza *m*

Pareto: ~**'s alpha coefficient** *n* ECON coeficiente alfa de Pareto; ~ **analysis** *n* ECON, GEN COMM análisis de Pareto *m*; ~ **distribution** *n* ECON, MATH distribución de Pareto *f*; ~ **efficiency** *n* ECON eficiencia de Pareto *f*; ~ **improvement** *n* ECON mejora de Pareto *f*; ~**'s Law** *n* ECON *income distribution theory*, LAW Ley de Pareto *f*; ~ **optimality** *n* ECON *top-level efficiency* optimalidad de Pareto *f*; ~ **optimum** *n* ECON óptimo de Pareto *m*

pari passu *phr* GEN COMM igualmente

Paris: ~ **Club** *n* ECON Club de París *m*; ~ **financial futures market** *n* FIN, STOCK mercado de futuros financieros de París *m*; ~ **options market** *n* FIN, STOCK mercado de opciones de París *m*

parity *n* GEN COMM paridad *f*; ~ **bit** COMP bitio de paridad *m*; ~ **bond** STOCK bono de paridad *m*; ~ **check** COMMS, COMP comprobación de paridad *f*, control de paridad *m*; ~-**check block** COMP código de control de paridad *m*; ~ **clause** INS cláusula sobre paridad *f*; ~ **of exchange** BANK paridad de tipo de cambio *f*; ~ **of rates** TRANSP paridad de tipos *f*; ~ **price** ECON, GEN COMM precio de paridad *m*; ~ **pricing** ECON, GEN COMM fijación de precios de paridad *f*; ~ **ratio** STOCK relación de paridad *f*

park[1] *n* GEN COMM parque *m*

park[2]: ~ **and ride** *phr* TRANSP estacionar y montar

parking *n* STOCK estacionamiento *m*; ~ **lot** *AmE* (*cf car park BrE*) GEN COMM, LEIS, TRANSP aparcamiento *m*, estacionamiento *m*

Parkinson: ~'**s Law** *n* HRM Ley de Parkinson *f*

parliament *n* GEN COMM parlamento *m*

Parliament *n BrE* (*cf Congress AmE*) POL ≈ Las Cortes *f pl* (*Esp*)

parliamentary: ~ **appropriation** *n* ACC, FIN, POL asignación parlamentaria *f*; ~ **procedure** *n* MGMNT, POL procedimiento parlamentario *m*; ~ **vote** *n* ACC, POL voto parlamentario *m*

part[1]: ~-**analysis training** *n* GEN COMM, HRM capacitación en análisis parcial *f* (*AmL*), formación en análisis parcial *f* (*Esp*); ~ **bunker** *n* TRANSP depósito de combustible parcial *m*; ~-**cancellation** *n* GEN COMM, LAW, PATENTS *of trade mark* cancelación parcial *f*; ~ **exchange** *n* GEN COMM intercambio de piezas *m*; ~ **load** *n* TRANSP carga parcial *f*; ~ **method** *n* WEL método del deber *m*; ~ **payment** *n* GEN COMM pago parcial *m*; ~ **shipment** *n* TRANSP embarque no completo *m*; ~-**time employee** *n* HRM empleado(-a) a tiempo parcial *m,f*; ~-**time employment** *n* HRM empleo a tiempo parcial *m*, trabajo a tiempo parcial *m* (*Esp*), trabajo a medio tiempo *m* (*AmL*); ~-**time job** *n* HRM trabajo a tiempo parcial *m* (*Esp*), trabajo a medio tiempo *m* (*AmL*); ~-**time lecturer** *n* HRM, WEL profesor(a) a tiempo parcial *m,f*; ~-**time work** *n* HRM dedicación parcial *f*, empleo de media jornada *m*, empleo de medio tiempo *m*; ~-**time worker** *n* HRM trabajador(a) a tiempo parcial *m,f*; ~-**timer** *n* HRM trabajador(a) a tiempo parcial *m,f*

part[2]: **for my** ~ *phr* GEN COMM por mi parte; **in** ~ **payment** *phr* HRM a cuenta

partial: ~ **acceptance** *n* FIN aceptación parcial *f*; ~ **basis** *n* FIN base parcial *f*; ~ **consideration** *n* ACC consideración parcial *f*; ~ **delivery** *n* STOCK entrega parcial *f*; ~ **equilibrium** *n* ECON equilibrio parcial *m*; ~ **equilibrium analysis** *n* ECON análisis parcial del equilibrio *m*; ~ **eviction** *n* LAW, PROP desalojo parcial *m*, expulsión parcial *f*; ~ **loss** *n* (*P/L*) INS pérdida parcial *f*; ~ **of overhead costs** *n* ACC, FIN recuperación de parte de los costes fijos *f* (*Esp*), recuperación de parte de los costos fijos *f* (*AmL*), recuperación de parte de los gastos generales *f*; ~ **payment agreement** *n* GEN COMM convenio de pago parcial *m*; ~ **provision basis** *n* ACC, TAX *calculating deferred taxation* base de provisión parcial *f*; ~ **release** *n* LAW, PROP redención parcial *f*; ~ **taking** *n* LAW, PROP adquisición parcial *f*, propiedad compartida *f*, toma parcial *f*; ~ **total loss** *n* (*PTL*) INS pérdida total parcial *f*; ~ **unemployment** *n* ECON, HRM, WEL paro parcial *m*; ~ **withdrawal** *n* STOCK reembolso parcial *m*; ~ **write-off** *n* ACC amortización parcial *f*

partially[1]: ~ **knocked down** *adj* (*PKD*) TRANSP *consignment* desmontado parcialmente

partially[2]: ~ **digital HDTV** *n* (*partially digital high-density television*) MEDIA *satellite broadcasting* TVAD parcialmente digital *f* (*televisión de alta densidad parcialmente digital*); ~ **digital high-density television** *n* (*partially digital HDTV*) MEDIA *satellite broadcasting* television alta densidad parcialmente digital *f* (*TVAD parcialmente digital*)

participant *n* GEN COMM, MGMNT *convention*, STOCK participante *mf*

participate *vi* GEN COMM participar

participating[1] *adj* GEN COMM participativo

participating[2]: ~ **bond** *n* STOCK obligación preferente *f*; ~ **carrier** *n* TRANSP transportista participante *mf*; ~ **insurance** *n* INS seguro suscrito con una mutua *m*; ~ **interest** *n* STOCK interés preferencial *m*; ~ **policy** *n* INS póliza con participación en los beneficios *f*; ~ **preference share** *n* STOCK acción preferente con participación *f*; ~ **preferred stock** *n* ACC, STOCK acciones privilegiadas *f pl*; ~ **security** *n* STOCK título parcial *m*

participation *n* GEN COMM participación *f*; ~ **account** ACC cuenta de participación *f*; ~ **agreement** LAW acuerdo de participación *m*; ~ **certificate** GEN COMM certificado de copropiedad *m*, STOCK *dividends* certificado de transferencia de préstamos *m*; ~ **fee** BANK comisión de participación *f*, cuota de participación *f*; ~ **loan** BANK, FIN préstamo de participación *m*, crédito sindicado *m*; ~ **rate** HRM nivel de participación *f* ~ **in a transaction** STOCK participación en una transacción *f*

participative[1]: ~-**democratic** *adj* MGMNT *Likert's leadership* participativo-democrático

participative[2]: ~ **budgeting** *n* MGMNT presupuesto participativo *m*; ~ **leadership** *n* MGMNT liderazgo participativo *m*; ~ **management** *n* MGMNT dirección participativa *f*, gerencia participativa *f*

particular: ~ **average** *n* (*P.A.*) INS, TRANSP *marine* avería particular *f*

particularity *n* GEN COMM particularidad *f*

particulars *n pl* GEN COMM, HRM coordenadas *f pl*, información personal *f*; ~ **of sale** PROP descripción de la propiedad en venta *f*

partition *n* ADMIN *office* repartición *f*, COMP partición *f*, segmentación *m*, LAW reparto *m*, PROP repartición *f*, reparto *m*, partición *f*

partly[1]: ~-**paid** *adj* STOCK *shares* parcialmente pagado

partly[2]: ~-**finished goods** *n pl* GEN COMM, IND, S&M productos en procesos *m pl*, productos semiacabados *m pl*, productos semielaborados *m pl*; ~-**paid share** *n* FIN, STOCK acción pagada parcialmente *f*, acción parcialmente liberada *f*

partner *n* ECON, GEN COMM, HRM socio(-a) *m,f*; ◆ **take a** ~ GEN COMM tomar un socio

partnership *n* GEN COMM sociedad personal *f*, sociedad de responsabilidad ilimitada *f*, POL *between countries* asociación *f*; ~ **agreement** GEN COMM, LAW contrato de sociedad *m*; ~ **income** ACC, TAX ingresos de la sociedad *m pl*

parts: ~ **per million** *n pl* (*ppm*) GEN COMM partes por millón *f pl*

party *n* LAW *in contract* parte *f*; ~ **line** COMMS *telephone service* línea compartida *f*, línea telefónica común *f*, POL *policy stance* consignas partidarias *f pl*; ~ **selling** S&M

venta parcial *f*; ~ **ticket** LEIS *for group* billete de grupo *m*; ~ **to an agreement** HRM parte de un acuerdo *f*; ~ **to a contract** LAW parte del contrato *f*; ~ **to an estate** GEN COMM copropiedad *f*; ~ **wall** GEN COMM pared medianera *f*

pass[1]: **~-along** *n jarg* S&M circulación *f*; **~-along readership** *n jarg* S&M número total de lectores que no compran la revista pero leen la copia de otra persona *f*; **~-through loan** *n* BANK, FIN préstamo de transferencia *m*; **~-through security** *n* BANK, FIN título subrogado *m*

pass[2] *vt* ACC efectuar, ECON, GEN COMM *budget* aprobar, *resolution* adoptar, pasar, LAW aprobar, *resolution* adoptar; ♦ ~ **a dividend** *jarg* FIN omitir un dividendo; ~ **for press** MEDIA *print* meter en máquina, pasar a la prensa; ~ **inspection** LAW inspeccionar; ~ **judgment** LAW pronunciar una sentencia; ~ **the proofs** MEDIA *print* pasar las pruebas; ~ **sentence** LAW *on sb* pronunciar una sentencia condenatoria; ~ **sth over in silence** GEN COMM dejar algo de lado en silencio

pass off *vt* GEN COMM *goods* trasladar

pass on *vt* COMMS *information, message* comunicar, GEN COMM *cost to the customer* trasladar

passed[1] *adj* GEN COMM pasado

passed[2]: ~ **dividend** *n* ACC dividendo impagado *m*, dividendo no repartido *m*, dividendo omitido *m*

passenger *n* LEIS, TRANSP pasajero(-a) *m,f*; ~ **aircraft** TRANSP avión de pasajeros *m*; ~ **analysis** LEIS análisis de pasajeros *m*; ~ **care** LEIS atención a los pasajeros *f*; ~ **certificate** *BrE* (*PC*) TRANSP certificado de pasajeros *m*; ~ **control** LEIS control de pasajeros *m*; ~ **coupon** LEIS, TRANSP cupón de pasajero *m*; ~ **dues** LEIS derechos a pagar por los pasajeros *m pl*; ~ **elevator** *AmE* (*cf passenger lift BrE*) GEN COMM, LEIS ascensor para pasajeros *m*; ~ **fare** LEIS, TRANSP tarifa de viajeros *f*; ~ **ferry** LEIS, TRANSP transbordador de pasajeros *m*; ~ **indemnity clause** BANK, INS, LAW cláusula de indemnización de pasajeros *f*; ~ **lift** *BrE* (*cf passenger elevator AmE*) GEN COMM, LEIS ascensor para pasajeros *m*; ~ **liner** TRANSP barco de pasajeros *m*; ~ **list** LEIS, TRANSP lista de pasajeros *f*; ~ **lounge** LEIS, TRANSP sala de pasajeros *f*; ~ **market** TRANSP mercado de pasajeros *m*; ~ **mile** TRANSP pasajeros por milla *m pl*; ~ **miles per vehicle hour** *n pl* TRANSP millas-pasajero por hora de vehículo *f pl*; ~ **number certificate** TRANSP certificado de número de pasajeros *m*; ~ **rated traffic** TRANSP tráfico tasado de pasajeros *m*; ~ **return** TRANSP lista de pasajeros *f*; ~ **safety certificate** INS, TRANSP certificado de seguridad de los pasajeros *m*; ~ **service** LEIS, TRANSP servicio de viajeros *m*; ~ **ship** TRANSP buque de pasaje *m*; ~ **strategy** TRANSP estrategia de pasajeros *f*; ~ **tariff** LEIS, TRANSP tarifa de pasajeros *f*; ~ **terminal** LEIS, TRANSP terminal de pasajeros *f*; ~ **throughput** TRANSP flujo de pasajeros *m*; ~ **toll** TRANSP peaje de pasajeros *m*; ~ **tonnage** TRANSP *shipping* capacidad de pasajeros *m*; ~ **train** LEIS, TRANSP tren de pasajeros *m*; ~ **vehicle** LEIS, TRANSP vehículo de pasajeros *m*; ~ **vehicle ferry** LEIS, TRANSP transbordador para vehículos de pasajeros *m*

passer: **~-by** *n* S&M transeúnte *mf*

passing[1]: ~ **off** *adj* S&M disimulado

passing[2]: ~ **of risk** *n* INS transferencia de riesgo *f*

passive[1] *adj* S&M *advertising* pasivo

passive[2]: ~ **activities** *n pl* TAX actividades sin intereses *f pl*; ~ **bond** *n* STOCK bono sin intereses *m*; ~ **income** *n*

TAX renta pasiva *f*; ~ **investor** *n* STOCK inversor(a) pasivo(-a) *m,f*; ~ **loss** *n* TAX pérdida pasiva *f*; ~ **trust** *n* LAW fideicomiso pasivo *m*

passport *n* GEN COMM pasaporte *m*; ~ **control** GEN COMM control de pasaporte *m*; ~ **holder** GEN COMM titular del pasaporte *mf*

password *n* COMP contraseña *f*

past: ~ **due claim** *n* ACC reclamación vencida *f*; ~ **service benefit** *n* FIN *private pension plan* prestaciones por servicios pretéritos *f*; ~ **year** *n* GEN COMM año pasado *m*

paste[1]: **~-up** *n* GEN COMM modelado *m*, MEDIA, S&M *advertising* montaje de originales *m*

paste[2] *vt* COMP *word-processed document* insertar

pasteboard *n* GEN COMM, IND, S&M, TRANSP cartón *m*

pat. *abbr* (*patent*) LAW, PATENTS patente *f*; ~ **pend.** (*patent pending*) LAW, PATENTS patente en tramitación *f*

patent[1] *n* (*pat.*) LAW, PATENTS patente *f*; ~ **agent** LAW, PATENTS agente de patentes *mf*; ~ **application** PATENTS aplicación de una patente *f*; ~ **certificate** PATENTS certificado de patente *m*; ~ **infringement** LAW, PATENTS uso indebido de patente *m*, violación de patente *f*; ~ **life** LAW, PATENTS duración de una patente *f*, vigencia de una patente *f*; ~ **monopoly** IND, PATENTS *from government to inventor* monopolio legal de patente *m*; ~ **proprietor** PATENTS propietario(-a) de una patente *m,f*; ~ **protection** LAW, PATENTS protección de patentes *f*; ~ **renewal fee** GEN COMM, PATENTS cargo por renovación de patente *m*; ~ **rights** GEN COMM, PATENTS derechos de patente *m pl*; ~ **royalties** GEN COMM, PATENTS derechos de patente *m pl*; ~ **specification** LAW, PATENTS *printed* descripción de la patente *f*; ~ **specifications** *n pl* LAW especificaciones de una patente *f pl*; ~ **trading** GEN COMM, PATENTS comercio de patentes *m*; ~ **warfare** LAW, PATENTS guerra de patentes *f*; ♦ ~ **pending** (*pat. pend.*) LAW, PATENTS patente en tramitación *f*; **take out a** ~ PATENTS sacar una patente

patent[2] *vt* LAW, PATENTS patentar

Patent: ~ **Cooperation Treaty** *n* (*PCT*) LAW, PATENTS *intellectual property* Tratado de Cooperación sobre Patentes *m*; ~ **Office** *n* (*PO*) PATENTS Registro de la propiedad industrial *m*, Registro de patentes y marcas *m*

patentability *n* LAW, PATENTS patentabilidad *f*

patentable[1] *adj* LAW, PATENTS patentable

patentable[2]: ~ **invention** *n* PATENTS invento patentable *m*

Patents: ~ **Advisory Committee** *n* ACC, PATENTS comité de patentes *m*

paternalism *n* GEN COMM, MGMNT paternalismo *m*

paternity: ~ **leave** *n* HRM, WEL licencia de paternidad *m*

path *n* COMP, GEN COMM camino *m*; **~-goal theory** MGMNT teoría de los medios y las metas *f*

patrimonial[1] *adj* POL patrimonial

patrimonial[2]: ~ **industry** *n* ECON, IND industria patrimonial *f*

pattern *n* COMP patrón *m*, GEN COMM pauta *f*; ~ **agreement** HRM acuerdo modelo *m*, contrato modelo *m*; ~ **bargaining** HRM convenio laboral sobre esquemas *m*; ~ **of economic activity** ECON modelo de actividad económica *m*; ~ **of investment** FIN estructura de la inversión *f*

patterned: ~ **interview** *n* S&M entrevista con cuestionario prefijado *f*

pave: ~ **the way for** *phr* GEN COMM preparar el terreno para

pawn *n* GEN COMM caución *f*

pawn[2] *vt* GEN COMM empeñar, dejar en prenda

pawnbroker *n* FIN prestamista sobre prenda *mf*

pawned: ~ **stock** *n* STOCK capital fiado *m*

pawnshop *n* FIN casa de empeño *f*

pay[1] *n* GEN COMM, HRM salario *m*; **~-as-paid** GEN COMM impuesto sobre el pago *m*; **~-as-paid policy** INS *damage insurance* póliza de pagos coincidentes con los ingresos *f*; ~ **as you earn** *BrE* (*PAYE, cf pay-as-you-go AmE*) TAX sistema británico de retención de impuestos en la fuente de la renta de trabajo; **~-as-you-go** *AmE* (*cf pay as you earn BrE*) TAX sistema estadounidense de retención de impuestos en la fuente de la renta de trabajo; **~-back method** BANK, FIN método de pago *m*, método de restituir *m*; ~ **check** *AmE*, ~ **cheque** *BrE* BANK cheque de la paga *m*, cheque del sueldo *m*; ~ **comparability** HRM comparabilidad de pagos *f*; ~ **and conditions** *n pl* HRM sueldo y condiciones *m*; **~-day** GEN COMM día de la paga *f*; ~ **differential** HRM diferencial de pago *m*; ~ **dispute** HRM disputa salarial *f*; ~ **and file** TAX *compliances* pago y declaración *m*; ~ **freeze** HRM congelación de salarios; ~ **in lieu of notice** HRM compensación en lugar de preaviso *f*; **~-in slip** *AmE* (*cf paying-in slip BrE*) BANK impreso de ingreso *m*; **~-out** GEN COMM, BANK, ECON, FIN amortización *f*, desembolso *m*, liquidación *m*, pago *m*, MGMNT porcentaje de dividendo *m*; **~-out date** GEN COMM fecha de desembolso *f*; **~-out period** GEN COMM periodo de recuperación *m*; ~ **packet** GEN COMM, HRM sobre de la paga *m*; ~ **pause** HRM interrupción del pago *f*; ~ **phone** *BrE* (*cf pay station AmE*) COMMS teléfono público *m*, teléfono de pago *m*; ~ **policy** HRM política de pagos *f*; ~ **review** HRM revisión del salario *f*, revisión salarial *f*; ~ **rise** HRM aumento de sueldo *m*; ~ **round** HRM serie de negociaciones salariales *f*; ~ **self check** *AmE*, ~ **self cheque** *BrE* BANK, FIN cheque nominativo *m*; ~ **settlement** HRM acuerdo salarial *m*; ~ **sheet** HRM hoja de paga *f*, lista de rayas *f*; ~ **slip** HRM sobre de la paga *m*, *recibo de pago* nómina *f*, planilla *f* (*AmL*); **statement** HRM estado de los salarios *m*; ~ **station** *AmE* (*cf pay phone BrE*) COMMS teléfono público *m*, teléfono de pago *m*; ~ **talks** *n pl* HRM, MGMNT negociaciones salariales *f pl*; **~-per-view TV** MEDIA, S&M televisión privada de pago *f*

pay[2] **1.** *vt* GEN COMM *bill* abonar, pagar, saldar, *settle* finiquitar; ♦ ~ **as cargo** INS pagar como cargamento; ~ **the bill** GEN COMM pagar la cuenta; ~ **by check** *AmE*, ~ **by cheque** *BrE* BANK pagar con un talón; ~ **expenses** GEN COMM pagar los gastos; ~ **by installments** *AmE*, ~ **by instalments** *BrE* BANK, GEN COMM pagar a plazos; ~ **a call on** GEN COMM hacer una visita a; ~ **for cargo by measurement** TRANSP pagar la carga según medición; ~ **in** BANK abonar en ventanilla; ~ **in cash** GEN COMM pagar al contado (*Esp*), pagar de contado (*AmL*); ~ **in full** GEN COMM, FIN pagar por completo, pagar totalmente; ~ **in specie** GEN COMM pagar en especie; ~ **an installment** *AmE*, ~ **an instalment** *BrE* GEN COMM pagar un plazo, pagar una cuota; ~ **lip service** GEN COMM hacer un cumplido; ~ **off a mortgage** BANK levantar una hipoteca; ~ **to the order of** BANK pagar a la orden de; ~ **top dollar for sth** *AmE* (*cf pay top whack for sth BrE*) GEN COMM pagar mucho por algo; ~ **top whack for sth** *BrE infrml* (*cf pay top dollar for sth BrE*) GEN COMM pagar mucho por algo; **2.** *vi* GEN COMM pagar; ♦ ~ **cash** GEN COMM pagar al contado (*Esp*), pagar de contado (*AmL*), pagar en metálico; ~ **by giro** BANK pagar por giro; ~ **by the hour** GEN COMM, HRM pagar por hora; ~ **in kind** GEN COMM, FIN pagar en especie; ~ **quarterly** BANK pagar trimestralmente; ~ **in ready cash** GEN COMM pagar en efectivo; ~ **weekly** BANK pagar semanalmente; ~ **yearly** GEN COMM, HRM pagar anualmente

pay back *vt* BANK, FIN devolver, pagar, reintegrar, restituir

pay in *vt* BANK pagar

pay off *vt* GEN COMM *loan, mortgage* amortizar, *debt* cancelar, liquidar, HRM *employee* pagar y despedir, saldar, finiquitar; ♦ ~ **a debt** BANK amortizar una deuda; ~ **a mortgage** BANK cancelar una hipoteca

pay out *vt* ACC, ECON, FIN desembolsar

payable[1] *adj* GEN COMM pagadero; ~ **after notice** FIN pagadero después del aviso; ~ **at maturity** GEN COMM, STOCK pagadero al vencimiento; ~ **in advance** GEN COMM pagadero anticipadamente; ~ **monthly in arrears** BANK, FIN, GEN COMM pagadero mensualmente a plazo vencido; ~ **on** BANK, FIN, GEN COMM *date* pagadero en

payable[2]: ~ **damage** *n* INS avería pagadera *f*; ~ **dividend** *n* ACC, FIN, STOCK dividendo a pagar *m*

payables: ~ **at year-end** *n pl* ACC efectos a pagar al cierre del ejercicio *m pl*

payback *n* HRM devolución *f*, MGMNT recuperación *m*, recuperación de la inversión *f*; ~ **period** ACC, HRM periodo de recuperación *m*, plazo de recuperación *m*, S&M plazo de amortización *m*; ~ **provision** FIN provisión de pago *f*

payday *n* HRM día de pago de jornales *m*, día de pago *m*

PAYE[1] *abbr BrE* (*Pay As You Earn*) TAX sistema británico de retención de impuestos en la fuente de la renta de trabajo

PAYE[2]: ~ **Audit** *n BrE* TAX *specialist section of the Inland Revenue* ≈ Auditoría de Impuestos Pagados Según Ganancias *f*; ~ **remittances** *n pl BrE* TAX aplazamiento de la retención fiscal en origen

payee *n* GEN COMM beneficiario(-a) *m,f*

payer *n BrE* GEN COMM pagador(a) *m,f*

paying: ~ **agent** *n* TAX agente de pagos *mf*; ~ **bank** *n* BANK banco pagador *m*; ~ **guest** *n* (*PG*) GEN COMM huésped *mf*; **~-in slip** *n BrE* (*cf pay-in slip AmE*) BANK impreso de ingreso *m*

payload *n* TRANSP carga rentable *f*, carga útil *f*

paymaster *n* HRM pagador *m*

payment *n* (*PYT*) GEN COMM pago *m*, saldo *m*; ~ **authorization** GEN COMM autorización de pago *f*; ~ **bond** GEN COMM, LAW *commercial* fianza de pago *f*; ~ **by incentives scheme** HRM plan de pago por incentivos *m*; ~ **by results** (*PBR*) HRM pago por resultados *m*, pago según resultados *m*; ~ **commitment** BANK *loans*, FIN obligación de pago *f*; ~ **commitments** *n pl* BANK, FIN compromisos de pago *m pl*; ~ **date** GEN COMM, STOCK fecha de pago *f*, día de pago *m*; ~ **device** FIN divisa de pago *f*; ~ **guarantee** ACC garantía de pago *f*; ~ **in arrears** ACC, BANK, FIN pago atrasado *m*; ~ **in due course** STOCK pago por procedimiento legal *m*; ~ **in full on allotment** FIN, STOCK liberación de acciones en adjudicación *f*; ~ **in kind** GEN COMM pago en especie *m*; **~-in-kind bond** (*PIK bond*) FIN, STOCK bono de pago en especie *m*;

~ **method** GEN COMM, S&M método de pago *m*; ~ **on account** BANK, GEN COMM pago en cuenta *m*; ~ **on behalf of others** ACC pago en nombre de otros *m*; ~ **order** GEN COMM orden de pago *f*; ~ **request** BANK, FIN, LAW demanda de pagar *f*; ~ **requisition** ACC requerimiento de pago *m*; ~ **system** ECON sistema de pagos *m*; ~ **terms** *n pl* BANK, GEN COMM condiciones de pago *f pl*; ~ **transfer** BANK transferencia de pago *f*; ~ **type** GEN COMM, S&M forma de pago *f*; ~ **under protest** LAW pago bajo protesta *m*, pago bajo reclamación *m*; ◆ ~ **made to** GEN COMM pago en favor de

payoff *n* GEN COMM resultado final *m*, beneficio *m*, HRM retribución *f*

payola *n AmE infrml* S&M *advertising* soborno *m* (*Esp*)

payor *AmE see* **payer** *BrE*

payout *n* BANK amortización *f*; ~ **ratio** S&M índice de reparto *m*, porcentaje de beneficios pagados como dividendos *m*

payroll *n* ACC, HRM *salaries* nómina *f*, planilla *f* (*AmL*), *list of salaried employees* plantilla *f* (*Esp*); ~ **costs** *n pl* HRM costes de nómina *m pl* (*Esp*), costos de nómina *m pl* (*AmL*); ~ **deduction** HRM *from gross earnings* deducción en nómina *f*; ~ **deduction scheme** TAX plan de deducciones en nómina *m*; ~ **deductions account** ACC cuenta de deducciones salariales *f*; ~ **department** HRM departamento de nóminas *m*; ~ **distribution** ACC distribución de la nómina *f*; ~ **savings plan** HRM, FIN plan de ahorros en nómina *m*; ~ **tax** TAX impuesto sobre el salario *m*, impuesto sobre la nómina *m*, contribución sobre salarios *f*; ◆ **be on the** ~ HRM estar en nómina, estar en planilla (*AmL*), estar en plantilla (*Esp*)

PBA *abbr* (*paid by agent*) TRANSP pagado por agente

PBR *abbr* (*payment by results*) HRM pago por resultados *m*, pago según resultados *m*

PBS *abbr AmE* (*Public Broadcasting Services*) MEDIA *broadcast* cadena pública

p.c. *abbr* (*per cent*) GEN COMM p.c. (*por ciento*)

PC[1] *abbr* (*personal computer*) COMP PC (*ordenador personal Esp, computadora personal AmL, computador personal AmL*)

PC[2]: **~-based** *adj* COMP basado en PC

PC[3]: **~-compatibility** *n* COMP compatibilidad del PC *f*

P/C *abbr* (*petty cash*) ACC, FIN caja chica *f*, caja pequeña *f*

PCC *abbr* (*price consumption curve*) ECON curva de gastos *f*

p.c.m. *abbr* (*per calendar month*) GEN COMM por mes

PCT *abbr* (*Patent Cooperation Treaty*) LAW, PATENTS Tratado de Cooperación sobre Patentes *m*

PCU *abbr* (*Product Co-operation Unit*) IMP/EXP Unidad de Cooperación de Productos *f*

pd *abbr* (*paid*) GEN COMM pagado

PD *abbr* BANK, FIN, GEN COMM (*postdated*) postfechado, con fecha adelantada, IMP/EXP, TAX, TRANSP (*port dues*) *shipping* derechos de puerto *m pl*

PDM *abbr* (*physical distribution management*) MGMNT, TRANSP gerencia de la distribución física *f*, gestión de la distribución física *f*

peace: ~ **dividend** *n* POL *the end of the cold war* dividendo de la paz *m*

peaceful: ~ **picketing** *n* HRM formación de piquetes pacíficos *f*

peak[1] *n* ECON punto máximo *m*; ~ **hour** GEN COMM hora punta *f* (*Esp*), hora pico *f* (*AmL*); ~ **importing season** IMP/EXP temporada importadora alta *f*; ~ **level** STOCK nivel máximo *m*, techo máximo *m*; **~-load pricing** ECON carga máxima *f*, demanda máxima *f*; ~ **period** ENVIR periodo de pico máximo *m*, TRANSP periodo de valores máximos *m*; ~ **rate** COMMS, GEN COMM tarifa alta *f*; ~ **season** ECON, GEN COMM estación de máxima actividad *f* temporada alta *f*; ~ **time** MEDIA, S&M hora de máxima audiencia *f*; ◆ **at ~-time** GEN COMM a la hora punta

peak[2] *vi* ECON, GEN COMM alcanzar el máximo

Pearson: ~ **Report** *n* ECON *on investment in developing countries* informe Pearson *m* (*Esp*), reporte Pearson *m* (*AmL*)

pecuniary[1] *adj* GEN COMM pecuniario

pecuniary[2]: ~ **benefit** *n* ACC, ECON, FIN beneficio pecuniario *m*; ~ **economy of scale** *n* ECON economía de escala pecuniaria *f*; ~ **external economy** *n* ECON economía externa pecuniaria *f*; ~ **returns** *n pl* ECON desembolsos monetarios *m pl*

pedestal *n* TRANSP *container securing* pedestal *m*; ~ **fitting** TRANSP *container* colocación del pedestal *m*

pedestrian *n* GEN COMM peatón *m*

pedlar *n BrE* (*cf* **huckster** *AmE*) S&M vendedor(a) ambulante *m,f*

peer: ~ **group** *n* S&M grupo paritario *m*

peg *vt* ECON, FIN, STOCK *currency, prices* vincular; ~ **the exchange** ECON fijar el cambio

pegged: ~ **exchange rate** *n* ECON, FIN cambio fijo *m*, tipo fijo de cambio *m*, tasa de cambio estabilizada *f*; ~ **price** *n* ECON, GEN COMM precio fijo *m*, precio estable *m*; ~ **rate of exchange** *n* ECON, FIN cambios fijos *m pl*

pegging *n* ECON fijación del precio de un título *f*, fijación del precio de un valor *f*; ~ **device** ECON dispositivo de estabilización artificial de precios *m*, dispositivo de fijación de precios *m*; ~ **system** ECON estabilización artificial de precios *f*, fijación de precios *f*

penalize *vt* LAW castigar

penalty *n* GEN COMM, LAW penalización *f*, multa *f*; ~ **clause** BANK, INS, LAW cláusula de penalización *f*, cláusula punitiva *f*; ~ **for breach of contract** LAW penalización por incumplimiento de contrato *f*; ~ **for late tax payment** TAX recargo por pago fuera de plazo *m*; ~ **for noncompliance** LAW penalización por incumplimiento *f*; ~ **rate** LAW tasa de penalización *f*; ~ **return** TAX devolución de recargo *f*

pending[1] *adj* GEN COMM pendiente, por resolver

pending[2]: ~ **application** *n* PATENTS pendiente de concesión *f*; ~ **business** *n* GEN COMM negocios pendientes *m pl*; ~ **tray** *n* ADMIN, GEN COMM bandeja de pendientes *f* (*Esp*), charola de pendientes *f* (*AmL*)

pendulum: ~ **arbitration** *n* HRM arbitraje pendular *m*

penetrate: ~ **the market** *phr* S&M penetrar en el mercado

penetration *n* S&M *advertising* penetración *f*; ~ **pricing** GEN COMM, S&M fijación de precios de penetración *f*; ~ **rate** S&M índice de penetración *f*

peniche *n* TRANSP *canal boat* peniche *m*

pennant *n* STOCK gallardete *m*

penny: ~ **share** *n* FIN, STOCK acción cotizada a menos de un dólar *f*; ~ **stock** *n* FIN, STOCK acciones con valor inferior a un dólar *f pl*

pension *n* GEN COMM jubilación *f*, pensión *f*; ~ **adjustment** TAX ajuste de pensión *m*; ~ **benefit**

guarantee corporation HRM empresa avalista de las prestaciones por jubilación *f*; **~ benefit guaranty corporation** *see pension benefit guarantee corporation*; **~ charges** *n pl* ACC aportaciones a fondos de pensión *f pl*, aportaciones a sistemas complementarios de pensiones *f pl*; **~ contributions** *n pl* TAX cuotas a la Seguridad Social *f pl*; **~ costs** *n pl* ACC costes de pensiones *m pl* (*Esp*), costos de pensiones *m pl* (*AmL*); **~ credit** TAX crédito por jubilación *m*, desgravación de pensión *f*; **~ earnings cap** TAX techo de los ingresos por jubilación *m*; **~ fund** ACC, GEN COMM fondo de pensiones *m*, pensión de retiro *f*, plan de jubilación *m*; **~-holder** FIN beneficiario(-a) de una pensión *m,f*; **~ income** ACC, TAX ingresos por pensión *m pl*; **~ income credit** TAX crédito por jubilación *m*, desgravación de pensión *f*; **~ liabilities** *n pl* ACC obligaciones de jubilación *f pl*; **~ payment** GEN COMM pago de la pensión *m*; **~ plan** GEN COMM plan de pensiones *m*; **~ plan funding** GEN COMM financiación de plan de pensiones *f*; **~ plan liability reserve** FIN reserva de pasivo de plan de pensiones *f*; **~ scheme** GEN COMM plan de pensiones *m*; **~ tax credit** TAX desgravación de pensión *f*

pensionable[1] *adj* FIN, HRM, WEL pensionable

pensionable[2]: **~ age** *n* HRM edad de jubilación *f*; **~ earnings** *n pl* ACC, TAX ingresos sometidos a descuento *m pl*; **~ employment** *n* HRM empleo sometido a descuentos de jubilación *m*

pensioner *n* GEN COMM, HRM, WEL jubilado(-a) *m,f*

pent: **~-up demand** *n* ECON, S&M demanda reprimida *f*, demanda contenida *f*; **~-up energy** *n* GEN COMM energía acumulada *f*

penthouse *n* PROP dúplex *m*

peon *n jarg* HRM peón *m*

people[1]: **~-intensive** *adj* HRM con alta participación de gente, intensivo en cuanto a gente

people[2]: **~ mover** *n* TRANSP movilizador de personas *m*; **~'s democracy** *n* POL democracia popular *f*

PEP *abbr BrE* (*Personal Equity Plan*) STOCK Plane Personal de Compra de Acciones *m*

per[1]: **~ capita** *adj* GEN COMM por cabeza; **~ head** *adj* GEN COMM por cabeza, por persona; **~ person** *adj* GEN COMM por persona; **~ share** *adj* STOCK por acción

per[2]: **~ annum** *adv* (*p.a.*) GEN COMM por año; **~ calendar month** *adv* GEN COMM por mes; **~ cent** *adv* (*p.c.*) GEN COMM por ciento (*p.c.*); **~ day** *adv* GEN COMM por día; **~ month** *adv* (*p.m.*) GEN COMM por mes; **~ year** *adv* GEN COMM por año

per[3]: **~-capita debt** *n* ECON deuda per capita *f*; **~ capita income** *n* ECON renta per cápita *f*; **~-contract basis** *n* STOCK *brokerage commission* base según contrato *f*; **~ diem allowance** *n* GEN COMM, HRM dieta *f*; **~-kilometer rate** *AmE*, **~-kilometre rate** *BrE n* TRANSP tarifa por kilómetro *f*

per[4]: **as ~** *phr* GEN COMM según aviso, como ha sido convenido; **as ~ from** *phr* GEN COMM por indicación de; **~ hatch per day** *phr* TRANSP por escotilla y día

PER *abbr* GEN COMM (*price-earnings ratio*) relación precio-beneficio *f*, ratio precio-beneficio *m*, STOCK (*post-execution reporting*) informe posterior a la ejecución

per procurationem *phr* (*p.p.*) LAW por poder

per se *adv* GEN COMM por sí mismo

per stirpes *phr* LAW *distribution of estate* por ramas familiares

per pro *prep* (*pp*) GEN COMM en nombre de

perceived: **~ benefit** *n* S&M beneficio percibido *m*

percentage[1] *adj* GEN COMM porcentual

percentage[2] *n* GEN COMM, MATH porcentaje *m*; **~ analysis** MATH *statistics* análisis de porcentajes *m*; **~ of capital held** ACC *balance sheet* porcentaje de capital retenido *m*; **~ change** FIN variación porcentual *f*, GEN COMM cambio porcentual *m*; **~ of depreciation** TRANSP porcentaje de depreciación *m*; **~ distribution** MATH *statistics* distribución por porcentajes *f*, distribución porcentual *f*; **~ grant** WEL ayuda en porcentaje *f*; **~ interest** GEN COMM interés porcentual *m*; **~ lease** PROP alquiler a porcentaje *m*, arrendamiento a porcentaje *m*; **~-of-completion basis** ACC base por porcentaje de cumplimiento del contrato *f*; **~-of-completion method** ACC método de porcentaje de obra ejecutada *m*; **~-of-sales method** S&M *advertising budgets* método de porcentaje de ventas *m*; **~ point** FIN punto porcentual *m*; **~ of product price spent on its promotion** S&M *advertising* porcentaje del precio del producto gastado en su promoción *m*; ♦ **in ~ terms** GEN COMM en tantos porciento

percentagewise *adv* GEN COMM, MATH a modo de porcentaje

percentile *n* MATH percentil *m*; **~ ranking** MATH *statistics* rango percentil *m*

perfect: **~ competition** *n* ECON competencia perfecta *f*; **~ hedge** *n* STOCK cobertura perfecta *f*; **~ market** *n* ECON mercado perfecto *m*; **~ monopoly** *n* ECON monopolio perfecto *m*; **~ obligation** *n* LAW obligación perfecta *f*; **~ price discrimination** *n* ECON discriminación perfecta de precios *f*; **~ substitute** *n* ECON sucedáneo perfecto *m*

perfected: **~ security** *n* BANK título perfeccionado *m*

perfectly: **~ elastic demand** *n* ECON demanda perfectamente elástica *f*; **~ inelastic demand** *n* ECON demanda perfectamente inelástica *f*

perform 1. *vt* ACC realizar, GEN COMM ejecutar; **2.** *vi* GEN COMM, LEIS *entertainment* actuar

performance *n* ACC *of company* cumplimiento *m*, resultado *m*, realización *f*, ejecución *f*, GEN COMM *of work, job* cumplimiento *m*, funcionamiento *m*, rendimiento *m*, LAW *contractual duty* cumplimiento *m*, ejecución *f*, MGMNT rendimiento *m*, S&M cumplimiento *m*; **~ against objectives** HRM, MGMNT actuación por objetivos *f*, desarrollo por objetivos *m*; **~ appraisal** HRM, MGMNT valoración de rendimientos *f*, valoración de resultados *f*, MGMNT evaluación de la actuación *f*; **~ appraisal interview** (*PAI*) HRM entrevista de evaluación del comportamiento *f*, entrevista de evaluación del desempeño *f*; **~ bond** GEN COMM, STOCK fianza de incumplimiento *f*; **~ bonus** FIN prima de ejecución *f*; **~ budget** ACC, FIN, HRM presupuesto de ejecución *m*; **~ budgeting** ACC, FIN, HRM presupuestación de ejecución *f*; **~ evaluation** MGMNT evaluación del desempeño *f*; **~ fund** STOCK fondo de alto rendimiento *m*, fondo dedicado a la especulación en acciones *m*; **~ guarantee** S&M garantía de rendimiento *f*, STOCK garantía de actuación *f*; **~ indicator** GEN COMM indicador de rendimientos, *employee* indicador de desempeño *m*, *company* indicador de resultados *m*; **~ marketing** S&M marketing de rendimiento *m*; **~ measurement** HRM, MGMNT medición de ejecución *f*, medición de realización *f*, medición del rendimiento *f*; **~ monitoring** GEN COMM control de actuación *m*, supervisión de la actuación *f*, control de funcionamiento *m*, supervisión del desempeño *f*; ~ **rating** FIN *investment* valoración de la actuación *f*; ~**-related indicator** GEN COMM indicador relacionado con los resultados *m*; ~**-related pay** (*PRP*) HRM pago según desempeño *m*, remuneración dependiente del rendimiento *f*; ~ **review** ACC, GEN COMM auditoría de cumplimiento *f*, revisión de cumplimiento *f*, revisión de rendimientos *f*, auditoría de cumplimiento *f*, análisis de resultados *m*; ~ **standard** ACC norma de cumplimiento *f*, norma de rendimiento *f*, producción normal *f*, HRM norma de rendimiento *f*; ~ **stock** STOCK acciones de alto rendimiento *f pl*; ~ **target** GEN COMM, HRM, MGMNT meta de desempeño *f*, meta de ejecución *f*, meta de realización *f*, meta de rendimiento *f*; ~ **testing** IND *packaging* prueba de desempeño *f*, prueba de rendimiento *f*

performer *n* ECON ejecutante *mf*

performing: ~ **rights** *n pl* LAW derechos de ejecución *m pl*, MEDIA derechos de interpretación *m pl*

peril[1]: **all** ~ *adj* INS todo riesgo

peril[2] *n* INS *marine* riesgo *m*; ~ **point** ECON, IMP/EXP punto de riesgo *m*

perimeter: ~ **advertising** *n* S&M publicidad de perimetro *f*

period *n* GEN COMM *of time* periodo *m*; ~ **charge** ACC, BANK, FIN cargo del periodo *m*; ~ **cost** ACC coste del periodo *m* (*Esp*), costo del periodo *m* (*AmL*), GEN COMM coste fijo *m* (*Esp*), costo fijo *m* (*AmL*); ~ **of digestion** STOCK periodo de digestión *m*; ~ **entry scheme** *BrE* IMP/EXP programa de entradas del periodo *m*; ~ **of grace** GEN COMM, LAW plazo de gracia *m*; ~ **of notice** HRM *of dismissal* periodo de notificación *m*; ~ **of payment** BANK, FIN, TAX periodo de pago *m*; ♦ **for the ~ of** GEN COMM para el periodo de; **over the ~ of** GEN COMM durante el periodo de; **over a ~ of time** GEN COMM durante un periodo de tiempo

periodgram *n* COMP, MATH gráfico cronológico *m*

periodic[1] *adj* GEN COMM, S&M periódico

periodic[2]: ~ **amounts** *n pl* TAX cantidades periódicas *f pl*; ~ **charge** *n* ACC, BANK, FIN cargo periódico *m*; ~ **inventory method** *n* ACC método de inventario periódico *m*; ~ **payment plan** *n* FIN, STOCK plan con pago periódico *m*, plan de pagos periódicos *m*; ~ **purchase deferred contract** *n* FIN contrato diferido de compra periódica *m*

periodical[1] *adj* GEN COMM, S&M periódico

periodical[2]: ~ **survey** *n* TRANSP inspección periódica *f*

peripheral[1] *adj* GEN COMM periférico

peripheral[2]: ~ **capitalism** *n* ECON, IND, POL capitalismo periférico *m*; ~ **computer** *n* COMP computador periférico *m* (*AmL*), computadora periférica *f* (*AmL*), ordenador periférico *m* (*Esp*); ~ **device** *n* COMP dispositivo periférico *f*; ~ **equipment** *n* COMP, IND equipo periférico *m*; ~ **worker** *n* HRM trabajador(a) periférico(-a) *m,f*

peripherals *n pl* COMP, GEN COMM unidades periféricas *f pl*, S&M *public relations* periféricos *m pl*

periphery: ~ **firm** *n* ECON empresa periférica *f*

perishable[1] *adj* GEN COMM, S&M *fish, fruit* perecedero

perishable[2]: ~ **goods** *n pl* GEN COMM, S&M bienes perecederos *m pl*

perishables *n pl* GEN COMM, S&M perecederos *m pl*

perjury *n* LAW perjurio *m*

perk *n infrml* GEN COMM, HRM beneficios extrasalariales *m pl*, emolumentos *m pl*, complemento salarial *m*, gratificación *f*; ♦ ~ **of the job** *infrml* HRM privilegio del puesto

PERL *abbr* (*public enterprise rehabilitation loan*) BANK, FIN préstamo de racionalización de la empresa pública *m*, préstamo de reforma de la empresa pública *m*

permanent[1] *adj* GEN COMM permanente

permanent[2]: ~ **account** *n* ACC cuenta permanente *f*; ~ **appointment** *n* GEN COMM, HRM nombramiento permanente *m*; ~ **arms economy** *n* ECON economía de armamento permanente *f*; ~ **ballast** *n* TRANSP lastre permanente *m*; ~ **bunker** *n* (*PB*) TRANSP pañol permanente *m*; ~ **customer** *n* GEN COMM cliente(-a) fijo(-a) *m,f*; ~ **employment** *n* HRM empleo permanente *m*; ~ **exhibition** *n* GEN COMM exposición permanente *f*; ~ **financing** *n* FIN financiación a largo plazo *f*; ~ **income bearing share** *n* (*PIBs*) STOCK acción productora de renta permanente *f*; ~ **income hypothesis** *n* ECON hipótesis de la renta permanente *f*; ~ **participation** *n* ACC *balance sheet* participación permanente *f*; ~ **residence** *n* LAW, PROP, TAX residencia permanente *f*; ~ **resident** *n* LAW, PROP, TAX residente permanente *mf*; ~ **staff** *n* HRM empleados fijos *m pl*, personal permanente *m*

permissible[1] *adj* GEN COMM, LAW permitido, lícito

permissible[2]: ~ **error** *n* GEN COMM error permitido *m*

permission *n* COMP, GEN COMM permiso *m*

permit[1]: ~**-free** *adj* LAW exento de licencia

permit[2] *n* GEN COMM permiso *m*; ~ **bond** LAW garantía de licencia *f*

permit[3] *vt* GEN COMM, LAW permitir

permitted *adj* GEN COMM, LAW autorizado; ~**quantity** IMP/EXP cantidad permitida *f*

permutation *n* MATH permutación *f*

perpendicular: ~ **spread** *n* STOCK diferencial perpendicular *m*

perpetual[1] *adj* GEn COMM perpetuo

perpetual[2]: ~ **bond** *n* FIN, STOCK bono perpetuo *m*; ~ **lease** *n* PROP alquiler perpetuo *m*, arrendamiento perpetuo *m*; ~ **preferred share** *n* STOCK acción preferente sin vencimiento *f*

perpetuity[1]: **in** ~ *adv* GEN COMM a perpetuidad

perpetuity[2] *n* GEN COMM, STOCK anualidad perpetua *f*

perquisite *n* ACC beneficio casual *m*, beneficio eventual *m*, HRM beneficios extrasalariales *m pl*, complemento salarial *m*, gratificación *f*

perquisites *n pl* GEN COMM, HRM emolumentos *m pl*

persistent: ~ **demand** *n* S&M demanda persistente *f*

person *n* GEN COMM *administrative* persona *f*; ~**-job fit** HRM adecuación entre una persona y su trabajo; ~ **liable to tax** TAX persona sujeta a tributación *f*; ~ **skilled in the art** PATENTS experto(-a) sobre la materia *m,f*; ~**-to-person call** COMMS llamada de persona a persona *f*

personal: ~ **allowance** *n* *BrE* (*cf personal exemption AmE*) TAX deducción personal *f*; ~ **assistant** *n* (*PA*) GEN COMM, HRM, MGMNT asistente(-a) personal *m,f*, ayudante(-a) personal *m,f*, secretario(-a) personal *m,f*; ~ **baggage** *n* IMP/EXP, TRANSP equipaje personal *m*; ~ **bank** *n* BANK banco personal *m*; ~ **banking service** *n* BANK servicio bancario personal *m*; ~ **benefit** *n* TAX subsidio personal *m*; ~ **capitalism** *n* ECON, IND, POL capitalismo personal *m*; ~ **chattels** *n pl* PROP bienes muebles personales *m pl*; **~ computer** *n* (*PC*) COMP computador personal *f* (*PC*) (*AmL*), computadora personal *f* (*PC*) (*AmL*), ordenador personal *m* (*PC*) (*Esp*); **~ credit** *n* BANK crédito personal *m*, TAX crédito personal *m*, deducción personal *f*; **~ data sheet** *n* HRM hoja de entrada *f*; **~ disposable income** *n* ECON ingreso personal disponible *m*; **~ effects** *n pl* GEN COMM efectos personales *m pl*; **~ estate** *n* LAW, PROP bienes inmuebles *m pl*, bienes personales *m pl*; **~ exemption** *n* AmE (*cf personal allowance BrE*) TAX deducción personal *f*, exención personal *f*; **~ exemption from tax** *n* TAX exención personal de impuestos *f*; **~ expenses** *n pl* TAX gastos personales *m pl*; **~ export scheme** *n* IMP/EXP programa de exportación privada *m*; **~ file** *n* HRM expediente personal *m*; **~ financial planning software** *n* COMP, FIN aplicación personalizada para la planificación financiera *f*, software de planificación financiera personal *m*; **~ growth** *n* HRM crecimiento personal *m*, desarrollo personal *m*; **~ guarantee** *n* BANK *of loan*, FIN garantía personal *f*; **~ holding company** *n* AmE (*PHC*) TAX tipo de compañía que paga una cantidad elevada de impuestos; **~ identification number** *n* (*PIN*) BANK número de identificación personal *m*; **~ income** *n* ECON, TAX renta personal *f*; **~ income distribution** *n* ECON, TAX distribución personal del ingreso *f*; **~ income tax credit** *n* TAX desgravación de los ingresos personales *f*, reducción del impuesto sobre la renta de las personas físicas *f*; **~ influence** *n* GEN COMM influencia personal *f*; **~ injury** *n* LAW lesión personal *f*; **~ interview** *n* S&M entrevista personal *f*; **~ liability** *n* GEN COMM responsabilidad personal *f*; **~ loan** *n* BANK, FIN préstamo personal *m*; **~ money** *n* BANK, FIN dinero personal *f*; **~ particulars** *n pl* HRM generales *m pl* (*AmL*), información general *f* (*Esp*); **~ pension scheme** *n* GEN COMM plan personal de jubilación *m*; **~ property** *n* PROP, TAX inmuebles personales *m pl*; **~ property floater** *n* INS póliza contra pérdidas de la propiedad personal *f*; **~ saving** *n* BANK, ECON, FIN ahorro personal *m*; **~ secretary** *n* (*P.S.*) GEN COMM, HRM secretario(-a) personal *m,f*; **~ sector** *n* ECON sector personal *m*; **~ sector liquid assets** *n* FIN activos líquidos del sector personal *m pl*; **~ selling** *n* S&M venta personal *f*; **~ services business** *n* TAX empresa de servicios personales *f*; **~ share** *n* ACC, STOCK acción nominativa *f*; **~ statute** *n* HRM estatuto personal *f*; **~ tax credit** *n* TAX desgravación de los ingresos personales *f*, reducción del impuesto sobre la renta de las personas físicas *f*; **~ wealth** *n* ECON patrimonio personal *m*

Personal: **~ Equity Plan** *n* BrE (*PEP*) STOCK Plan Personal de Compra de Acciones *m*

personality *n* MGMNT personalidad *f*; **~ promotion** BrE *jarg* S&M *advertising* promoción que utiliza a personas famosas

personalization *n jarg* S&M *advertising* personalización *f*

personalized: **~ check** *AmE*; **~ cheque** *n* BrE BANK, FIN cheque personalizado *m*; **~ letter** *n* S&M carta personalizada *f*

personally: **~ liable** *adj* LAW personalmente responsable; **~ responsible** *adj* LAW *for liabilities* personalmente responsable

personnel[1]: **~-intensive** *adj* HRM, IND con exceso de personal, con alta ocupación de personal, intensivo en cuanto a personal

personnel[2] *n* GEN COMM, HRM empleados *m pl*, personal

m, planta *f*, plantilla *f*; **~ administration** HRM, MGMNT administración del personal *f*; **~ department** GEN COMM, HRM departamento de personal *m*; **~ director** HRM, MGMNT director(a) de personal *m,f*; **~ expenses** *n pl* ACC, HRM gastos de personal *m pl*; **~ growth** GEN COMM, HRM aumento de personal *m*; **~ management** HRM, MGMNT administración del personal *f*, dirección de personal *f*, gerencia del personal *f*, gestión del personal *f*; **~ manager** HRM, MGMNT director(a) de personal *m,f*, gerente de personal *mf*; **~ officer** HRM jefe(-a) de personal *m,f*; **~ overheads** *n pl* HRM gastos generales de personal *m pl*; **~ policy** HRM, MGMNT política de personal *f*; **~ psychology** HRM psicología industrial *f*; **~ problem** GEN COMM, HRM problema de relaciones humanas *m*; **~ rating** HRM calificación del personal *f*; **~ roster** HRM relación del personal *f*; **~ specification** HRM detalle de los empleados *m*

perspective *n* GEN COMM perspectiva *f*

persuade *vt* GEN COMM convencer

persuasion *n* GEN COMM *influence* persuasión *f*

persuasive[1] *adj* GEN COMM, S&M *sales pitch* persuasivo

persuasive[2]: **~ communication** *n* S&M comunicación persuasiva *f*

PERT *abbr* (*programme evaluation and review technique*) MGMNT técnica de evaluación y revisión del programa *f*

pertain to *vt* GEN COMM corresponder a, pertenecer a

pertaining: **~ to** *prep* GEN COMM correspondiente a

pertinence: **~ chart** *n* MGMNT gráfico de correspondencia *m*, organigrama de correspondencia *m*; **~ tree** *n* MGMNT árbol de correspondencia *m*

perverse: **~ price** *n* ECON precio corrupto *m*

pessimist *n* GEN COMM pesimista *mf*

pessimistic *adj* GEN COMM *outlook* pesimista

pesticide *n* ENVIR pesticida *m*

PET *abbr* (*potentially exempt transfer*) TAX transferencia potencialmente exenta *f*

Peter: **~ principle** *n* HRM *competency of senior executives* principio de Peter *m*

petition[1] *n* GEN COMM súplica *f*, LAW escrito de súplica *m*, instancia *f*, libelo *m*

petition[2] *vt* GEN COMM, LAW suplicar

petrobond *n* STOCK petrobono *m*

petrocurrency *n* ECON, GEN COMM petrodivisa *f*

petrodollar *n* ECON, GEN COMM petrodólar *m*

petrol *n* BrE (*cf gasoline AmE*) ENVIR gasolina *f* (*Esp*), nafta *f* (*AmL*); **~ station** BrE (*cf gas station AmE*) ENVIR surtidor de gasolina *m*, GEN COMM, TRANSP gasolinera *f*

petroleum: **~ compensation** *n* FIN compensación de hidrocarburos *f*; **~ industry** *n* IND sector del petróleo *m*; **~ revenue tax** *n* (*PRT*) TAX impuesto sobre explotaciones petrolíferas *m*; **~ sector** *n* IND sector del petróleo *m*

Petroleum: **~ Compensation Revolving Fund** *n* FIN Fondo Renovable de Compensación de Hidrocarburos *m*

petty: **~ cash** *n* (*P/C*) ACC, BANK, FIN caja chica *f* (*AmL*), caja pequeña *f* (*Esp*); **~ cash book** *n* ACC diario de caja chica *m* (*AmL*), libro de caja pequeña *m* (*Esp*); **~ cash fund** *n* ACC *bookkeeping* fondo de caja chica *m* (*AmL*), fondo de caja pequeña *m* (*Esp*); **~ cash voucher** *n* ACC *bookkeeping* comprobante de caja chica *m* (*AmL*), comprobante de caja pequeña *m* (*Esp*); **~ expenses** *n pl*

ACC, FIN, GEN COMM gastos en efectivo *m pl*, gastos menores *m pl*; ~ **official** *n* HRM funcionario(-a) de bajo nivel *m,f*; ~ **regulation** *n* FIN reglamento menor *m*

Petty: ~**'s Law** *n* ECON Ley de Petty *f*

PEWP *abbr* (*Public Expenditure White Paper*) *BrE* ECON libro blanco del gasto público *m*

pg. *abbr* (*page*) GEN COMM p (*página*), pág. (*página*)

PG *abbr* (*paying guest*) GEN COMM huésped *mf*

PHA *abbr* (*port health authority*) TRANSP autoridad sanitaria del puerto *f*

phantom: ~ **capital** *n* FIN, STOCK capital ficticio *m*; ~ **income** *n* ACC, TAX ingresos ficticios *m pl*; ~ **share** *n* FIN, STOCK acción ficticia *f*; ~ **share option** *n* FIN, STOCK opción ficticia sobre acciones *f*; ~ **stock plan** *n* FIN, STOCK plan de suscripción ficticia *m*; ~ **tax** *n* TAX impuesto ficticio *m*

pharmaceutical[1] *adj* ECON, GEN COMM, IND farmacéutico

pharmaceutical[2]: ~ **industry** *n* ECON, IND industria farmacéutica *f*

pharmaceuticals *n pl* GEN COMM, IND, S&M productos farmacéuticos *m pl*

phase *n* GEN COMM fase *f*; ~ **zero** *jarg* POL fase cero *f*

phase in *vt* COMP *technology, service, system*, GEN COMM introducir progresivamente, colocar progresivamente

phase out *vt* COMP *technology, service, system*, GEN COMM eliminar progresivamente, eliminar por fases

phased: ~ **distribution** *n* S&M distribución por fases *f*

phasing: ~ **out** *n* GEN COMM prueba de las fases *f*

PHC *abbr AmE* (*personal holding company*) TAX compañía que obtiene el 60 por 100 *f*

Philadelphia: ~ **Stock Exchange** *n AmE* (*PHLX*) STOCK Bolsa de Valores de Filadelfia *f*

Phillips: ~ **curve** *n* ECON curva de Philips *f*

philosophy *n* GEN COMM filosofía *f*

phlegmitiser *n* TRANSP *of dangerous cargo* flegmitizador *m*

PHLX *abbr AmE* (*Philadelphia Stock Exchange*) STOCK Bolsa de Valores de Filadelfia *f*

phone: ~ **banking** *n* BANK banca telefónica *f*; ~ **book** *n* COMMS guía telefónica *f*; ~ **desk** *n* STOCK centralita *f*; ~**-in poll** *n* COMMS, MEDIA registro telefónico *m*; ~**-in program** *AmE*, ~**-in programme** *BrE n* COMMS, MEDIA *radio, TV* programa de llamadas *m*; ~ **number** *n* (*telephone number*) COMMS número de teléfono *m*

phosphate: ~ **berth** *n* TRANSP muelle de fosfatos *m*

photo: ~ **call** *n* S&M fotollamada *f*

photocopy[1] *n* ADMIN fotocopia *f*

photocopy[2] *vt* ADMIN fotocopiar

photogravure *n* S&M fotograbado *m*

photostat *n obs* GEN COMM fotostato *m*

physical: ~ **assets** *n pl* GEN COMM activos físicos *m pl*, activos materiales *m pl*, activos tangibles *m pl*; ~ **barrier** *n* POL *for trade in European Union* barrera física *f*; ~ **collateral** *n* BANK garantías materiales *f pl*; ~ **commodity** *n* STOCK mercancía física *f*, producto *m*; ~ **delivery** *n* STOCK entrega física *f*; ~ **depreciation** *n* ACC amortización física *f*, depreciación física *f*; ~ **deterioration** *n* ACC *annual accounts* deterioro físico *m*; ~ **distribution** *n* MGMNT, S&M, TRANSP distribución física *f*; ~ **distribution management** *n* (*PDM*) MGMNT, TRANSP gerencia de la distribución física *f*, gestión de la distribución física *f*; ~ **examination** *n* GEN COMM *of object*, WEL examen físico *m*; ~ **handicap** *n* TAX

minusvalía física *f*; ~ **impairment** *n* TAX minusvalía física *f*; ~ **injury** *n* TAX daño físico *m*; ~ **inventory** *n* ACC inventario físico *m*; ~ **market** *n* STOCK mercado físico *m*; ~ **quality of life index** *n* (*PQLI*) ECON índice de calidad física de vida *m*

physically *adv* GEN COMM físicamente

physiocratic: ~ **school** *n* ECON escuela fisiocrática *f*

Physiocrats *n* ECON fisiócratas *m pl*

pick: ~**-up** *n* MEDIA captación *f*, fonocaptor *m*; ~**-up cost** *n* TRANSP coste de recogida *m* (*Esp*), costo de recogida *m* (*AmL*); ~**-up service** *n* TRANSP servicio de recogida y reparto a domicilio *m*

pick up 1. *vt* TRANSP *cargo* recoger; ♦ ~ **the tab** *infrml* GEN COMM comprometerse a pagar una factura; **2.** *vi* ECON *strengthen* recuperar, GEN COMM *ideas, efficiency* animarse (*infrml*)

picket *n* HRM *of strike* piquete *m*

picketing *n* HRM formación de piquetes *f*

picking *n* STOCK, TRANSP pérdida de valor por partes averiadas *f*

pickup: ~ **bond** *n* STOCK bono con alto interés y pronto vencimiento *m*

pictogram *n* MATH *statistics* pictograma *m*

pictorial: ~ **presentation** *n* S&M presentación gráfica *f*, presentación ilustrada *f*

picture *n* GEN COMM *outlook, prospects* panorama *m*; ~ **caption** MEDIA, S&M pie de ilustración *m*

pie: ~ **chart** *n* COMP, GEN COMM, MATH diagrama circular *m*, diagrama sectorial *m*, gráfico circular *m*, gráfico de sectores *m*

piece: ~ **of advice** *n* MGMNT *information* consejo *m*; ~ **of information** *n* GEN COMM elemento de información *m*; ~ **of legislation** *n* LAW parte de la jurisprudencia *f*, pieza legislativa *f*; ~ **rate** *n* GEN COMM, HRM precio por pieza *m*, precio unitario *m*; ~ **wage** *n* HRM salario a destajo *m*

pieces *n pl* (*pcs*) GEN COMM tramos *m pl*

piecework *n* HRM trabajo a destajo *m* (*AmL*), trabajo por pieza *m* (*Esp*); ~ **contract** TRANSP contrato de trabajo a destajo *m*; ~ **system** HRM sistema de pago a destajo *m* (*AmL*), sistema de pago por pieza *m* (*Esp*)

pier *n* TRANSP *breakwater* espigón *m*, *landing stage* embarcadero *m*; ♦ ~ **to house** IMP/EXP muelle a puerta, TRANSP embarcadero al pie de la casa *m*; ~ **to pier** IMP/EXP, TRANSP *shipping* embarcadero a embarcadero

piggyback[1]: ~ **export schemes** *n pl* S&M planes de exportación con oferta comercial especial *m pl*; ~ **legislation** *n* LAW, POL legislación concatenada *f*; ~ **loan** *n* BANK, FIN préstamo concatenado *m*; ~ **promotion** *n* S&M promoción con producto añadido *f*; ~ **registration** *n* STOCK registro concatenado *m*; ~ **selling** *n* S&M venta de promoción simultánea de dos productos *f*; ~ **traffic** *n AmE jarg* TRANSP tráfico de remolques por ferrocarril *m*

piggyback[2] *vt jarg* TRANSP transportar remolques de carretera sobre vagones plataforma

pignorative: ~ **contract** *n* GEN COMM, LAW contrato pignoraticio *m*

Pigou: ~ **effect** *n* ECON efecto de saldo real *m*

Pigouvian: ~ **subsidy** *n* ECON subvención de Pigou *f*; ~ **tax** *n* ECON tasa de Pigou *f*

PIK: ~ **bond** *abbr* (*payment-in-kind bond*) FIN, STOCK bono de pago en especie *m*

piker *n jarg* STOCK oportunista *mf*

pilot[1] *adj* GEN COMM, TRANSP piloto

pilot[2] *n jarg* MEDIA *broadcast* piloto *m*; **~ boat** TRANSP embarcación del práctico *f*; **~ launch** S&M lanzamiento piloto *m*; **~ plant** IND *production* planta piloto *f*; **~ production** GEN COMM, IND, MGMNT producción experimental *f*, producción piloto *f*; **~ project** MGMNT proyecto piloto *m*; **~ run** GEN COMM ensayo piloto *m*; **~ scheme** GEN COMM plan piloto *m*; **~ study** GEN COMM estudio piloto *m*

pilotage: **~ slip** *n* TRANSP embarcadero del práctico *m*; **~ tug** *n* TRANSP remolcador de puerto *m*

pin *n* COMP *paper feeder* diente *m*; **~ money** GEN COMM dinero para gastos personales *m*

PIN *abbr* (*personal identification number*) BANK número de identificación personal *m*

pinch: **~ bar** *n* TRANSP *cargo handling* pie de cabra *m*

pinion *n* TRANSP piñón *m*

pink: **~ paper** *n BrE jarg* POL borrador *m*; **~ sheet market** *n AmE* GEN COMM *OTC stocks* mercado bursátil informal *m*; **~ sheets** *n pl AmE* GEN COMM *OTC stocks* publicación diaria de la oficina estadounidense de cotizaciones que contiene una relación actualizada del mercado extrabursátil; **~ slip** *n AmE* HRM aviso de despido *f*, *warning* notificación de despido *f*, *dismissal* carta de despido *f* (*Esp*), boleta de despido *f* (*AmL*)

pinlock *n* TRANSP *containers* pasador de espiga *m*

pint *n* (*pt*) GEN COMM pinta *f*

pintle *n* TRANSP *diesel engine* aguja macho *f*

pioneer[1] *n* GEN COMM, IND pionero(-a) *m,f*; **~ product** S&M producto pionero *m*; **~ selling** S&M venta de exploración *f*, venta pionera *f*

pioneer[2] *vt* GEN COMM promover

PIOPIC *abbr* (*Protection & Oil Pollution Indemnity Clause*) ENVIR cláusula de indemnización por contaminación petrolera

pip *n jarg* STOCK pipo *m* (*jarg*)

pipe: **~-laying ship** *n* TRANSP buque para tendido de conductos submarinos *m*

pipeline *n* COMMS cable coaxial *m*, IND tubería *f*; **~ information** COMMS conducto *m*; ♦ **in the ~** *jarg* GEN COMM *project* en trámite

piracy *n* GEN COMM piratería *f*

pirate: **~ copies** *n pl* IND, MEDIA copias piratas *f pl*; **~ radio** *n* MEDIA *broadcast* radio pirata *f*

pirated[1] *adj* MEDIA, S&M pirateado

pirated[2]: **~ products** *n pl* MEDIA, S&M productos pirateados *m pl*

pit *n* STOCK lonja de transacciones *f*

pitch *n* COMP espaciado *m*, GEN COMM territorio *m*

pitfall *n* GEN COMM hueco *m*

Pittsburgh: **~-plus** *n AmE* ECON precio del acero en Pittsburgh

pivot[1]: **~ weight** *n* TRANSP *aviation* peso de giro *m*

pivot[2]: **over ~ area** *phr* TRANSP *aviation* sobre el área de giro; **over ~ weight** *phr* TRANSP *aviation* sobre el peso de giro

pixel *n* COMP pixel *m*

pkg. *abbr* (*package*) COMMS, GEN COMM envoltorio *m*, paquete *m*

pkt. *abbr* (*packet*) COMMS, GEN COMM paquete *m*

P/L *abbr* (*partial loss*) INS pérdida parcial *f*

PLA *abbr* (*Port of London Authority*) TRANSP autoridad portuaria de Londres

placard *n* S&M cartel *m*

place[1]: **~ of abode** *n* LAW, PROP, TAX lugar de residencia *m*, residencia *f*; **~ of acceptance** *n* (*POA*) TRANSP lugar de recepción *m*; **~ of delivery** *n* (*POD*) TRANSP lugar de la entrega *m*; **~ of destination** *n* GEN COMM lugar de destino *m*; **~ of employment** *n* HRM lugar de empleo *m*; **~ of origin** *n* TRANSP lugar de origen *m*; **~ of payment** *n* BANK lugar de pago *m*; **~ of residence** *n* LAW, PROP, TAX residencia *f*; **~ utility** *n* ECON utilidad del lugar *f*; **~ of work** *n* GEN COMM *company, organization, building* lugar de trabajo *m*

place[2] *vt* GEN COMM *question on agenda* plantear, STOCK colocar; ♦ **~ a deposit** BANK, STOCK hacer un depósito; **~ an embargo on** GEN COMM poner embargo a; **~ emphasis on** GEN COMM poner énfasis sobre; **~ a hold on an account** BANK constituir una custodia en una cuenta; **~ in custody** LAW poner bajo custodia; **~ in trust** LAW dar en fideicomiso; **~ an order** GEN COMM, S&M hacer un pedido; **~ a question on the agenda** MGMNT incluir un asunto en el orden del día; **~ under guardianship** LAW, WEL poner bajo tutela

placement *n* HRM *work experience* prácticas en una empresa *f pl*, STOCK *bonds* colocación *f*; **~ memorandum** FIN, STOCK folleto de emisión *m*; **~ ratio** FIN proporción de colocaciones *f*, relación de colocaciones *f*; **~ test** HRM contrato de empleo a prueba *m*

placing: **~ of share issue** *n* STOCK colocación de una emisión de acciones *f*

PLACO *abbr* (*Planning Committee*) GEN COMM comité de planificación *m*

plain: **~ vanilla swop** *n infrml* FIN, STOCK permuta financiera clásica *f*

plaintiff *n* LAW demandante *mf*

plan[1] *n* GEN COMM plan *m*, *arquitecture* plano *m*; **~ position indicator** GEN COMM indicador de posición en el plan *m*

plan[2] *vt* GEN COMM planear, planificar, hacer un plano, hacer una descripción de; ♦ **~ ahead** GEN COMM hacer preparativos

planchette *n* BANK dado de estampado *m*

plane *n* GEN COMM, MATH plano *m*

planetary: **~ gear** *n* TRANSP engranaje planetario *m*

plank *n* POL principio sobre el cual un partido basa su campaña

planned: **~ capacity** *n* ECON, IND capacidad planificada *f*, capacidad planeada *f*; **~ maintenance** *n* GEN COMM mantenimiento planeado *m*; **~ obsolescence** *n* ECON, S&M depreciación planeada *f*, obsolescencia planificada *f*; **~ selling** *n* S&M venta planificada *f*; **~ unit development** *n* (*PUD*) PROP desarrollo previsto de una unidad *m*

planning: **~ approval** *n AmE* (*cf planning permission BrE*) LAW, PROP licencia de urbanización *f*, licencia de obras *f*, permiso de construcción *m*; **~ authority** *n* ENVIR organismo de planificación *m*; **~ commission** *n* ECON comisión de planificación *f*; **~ and control** *n* IND planificación y control *f*; **~ department** *n* GEN COMM, MGMNT departamento de planificación *m*; **~ element memorandum** *n* FIN memorándum de planificación de factores *m*; **~ horizon** *n* ECON *socialist countries* horizonte de planificación *m*; **~ permission** *n BrE* (*cf* *planning approval AmE*) LAW, PROP licencia de urbanización *f*, licencia de obras *f*, permiso de construcción *m*; ~ **policy** *n* GEN COMM política de planificación *f*; ~-**programming-budgeting system** *n* (*PPBS*) GEN COMM presupuesto por programas *m*, sistema de planificación, programación y presupuesto *m*; ~ **restriction** *n* LAW, PROP restricción de planificación *f*, limitación a la urbanización *f*; ~ **total** *n* BrE ECON planificación total *f*

Planning: ~ **Committee** *n* (*PLACO*) GEN COMM comité de planificación *m*

plans *n pl* GEN COMM planes *m pl*; ~ **board** *n* S&M junta directiva de planificación

plant *n* ACC *fixed assets* GEN COMM, IND planta *f*, fábrica *f*, equipo *m*, instalación *f*; ~ **agreement** HRM acuerdo de planta *m*; ~ **bargaining** GEN COMM, HRM, IND negociación de planta *f*, negociación en la fábrica *f*; ~ **capacity** GEN COMM, IND, INS capacidad de planta *f*; ~ **hire** GEN COMM, IND alquiler de planta *m*; ~ **incentive scheme** HRM, IND plan de incentivo en fábrica *m*, plan de incentivo en planta *m*; ~ **interruption** GEN COMM, IND suspensión del funcionamiento de una planta *f*; ~ **layout** IND distribución de planta *f*; ~ **layout study** IND estudio de proyección de planta *m*; ~ **location** GEN COMM ubicación de la planta *f*; ~ **and machinery** ECON, IND planta y maquinaria *f*; ~ **maintenance** GEN COMM, IND mantenimiento de las instalaciones *m*; ~ **management** IND, MGMNT dirección de fábrica *f*, gerencia de fábrica *f*; ~ **manager** HRM, IND, MGMNT director(a) de fábrica *m,f*, gerente de fábrica *mf*; ~ **manufacturing** IND manufactura de planta *f*; ~ **operator** IND encargado(-a) de la planta *m,f*; ~ **varieties** *n pl* PATENTS variedades vegetales *f pl*

plantation *n* ECON *agricultural* plantación *f*

plastic: ~ **waste** *n* ENVIR, IND desechos plásticos *m pl*

plastics *n pl* IND plásticos *m pl*

plate: ~ **lifting clamp** *n* TRANSP *cargo* fijación de acarreo de planchas *f*

plated: ~ **weight** *n* TRANSP peso del revestimiento *m*

platform *n* GEN COMM plataforma *f*; ~ **crane** (*Pc*) TRANSP grúa de plataforma *f*; ~ **vehicle** TRANSP vehículo plataforma *m*

platinum: ~ **disc** BrE, ~ **disk** AmE *n* MEDIA disco de platino *m*

play[1] *n* STOCK juego *m*; ~ **book** AmE *jarg* GEN COMM *of company* manual de actuación *m*

play[2] *vt* GEN COMM *role* desempeñar: ♦ ~ **the market** STOCK especular; ~ **a role** GEN COMM desempeñar un cometido; ~ **a part in** GEN COMM desempeñar un papel en, tomar parte en; ~ **sth by ear** GEN COMM tocar algo de oído

playback *n* S&M repetición *f*

player *n* GEN COMM *in negotiations* participante *mf*

Plaza: ~ **agreement** *n* ECON acuerdo de Plaza *m*

plc *abbr* BrE (*public limited company*) GEN COMM ≈ S.A. (*sociedad anónima*), ≈ S.A.A. (*sociedad anónima por acciones*)

plea *n* POL alegato *m*; ~ **bargain** LAW convenio entre el acusado y el fiscal para que el acusado admita su culpabilidad de ciertos cargos a cambio de la recomendación del fiscal de que no se dicte la pena máxima

plead 1. *vt* GEN COMM suplicar, rogar, LAW alegar; **2.** *vi* LAW declararse ignorante; ♦ ~ **guilty** LAW declararse culpable; ~ **ignorance** LAW alegar ignorancia

pleading *n* LAW alegación *f*, alegato *m*

pleasant: ~ **working environment** *n* HRM ambiente de trabajo agradable *m*

please: ~ **forward** *phr* COMMS despachar por favor; ~ **let us know which date suits** *phr* COMMS por favor, háganos saber que fecha le conviene; ~ **reply** *phr* (*RSVP*) COMMS se ruega respuesta; ~ **submit your quotations** *phr* GEN COMM por favor, expongan sus presupuestos; ~ **telex your confirmation** *phr* COMMS por favor, envíe su confirmación por télex

pleasure: ~ **shopping** *n* S&M compra por placer *f*

pledge[1] *n* BANK empeño *m*, gravamen *m*, pignoración *f*, prenda *f*; ~ **agreement** GEN COMM, LAW contrato de prenda *m*, contrato prendario *m*; ~ **security** BANK título en garantía *m*

pledge[2] *vt* BANK, GEN COMM *collateral* aportar

pledged: ~ **security** *n* BANK garantía en prenda *f*

pledging *n* BANK pignoración *f*

plenary *adj* POL *parliamentary session* plenario

plenum *n* GEN COMM sesión plenaria *f*

plentiful: ~ **supply of** *n* GEN COMM suficiente abastecimiento de *m*

Plimsoll: ~ **line** *n* TRANSP *on vessel* línea de máxima carga *f*, marca Plimsoll *f*

plinth *n* S&M zócalo *m*

plot[1] *n* PROP *of land* solar *m*, terreno *m*, parcela *f*; ~ **and block** PROP parcela y bloque *f*; ~ **book** AmE PROP registro agrario *m*; ~ **plan** PROP plano de terreno *m*

plot[2] *vt* MATH, S&M *graph* dibujar (*Esp*), graficar (*AmL*), trazar

plotter *n* COMP trazador *m*

plotting: ~ **board** *n* COMP tablero de dibujo *m*; ~ **pen** *n* COMP lápiz trazador *m*; ~ **table** *n* GEN COMM tablero cuadriculado *m*

ploughback *n* ACC, FIN reinversión *f*

Plowden: ~ **Committee** *n* ECON comité Plowden *m*

PLR *abbr* (*public lending right*) BANK derecho a empréstito público *m*

PLTC *abbr* (*port liner terms charge*) TRANSP coste portuario por transporte regular *m* (*Esp*), costo portuario por transporte regular *m* (*AmL*)

plug[1] *n* COMP enchufe *f*, MEDIA, S&M *advertising* publicidad incidental *f*

plug[2] *vt* COMP enchufar

plum: ~ **book** *n* AmE *jarg* POL listado de cargos ministeriales vacantes designados por el presidente del gobierno

plunge[1] *n* STOCK especulación fuerte *f*

plunge[2] *vi* STOCK arriesgar grandes sumas

plunger *n* STOCK especulador(a) fuerte *m,f*

plural: ~ **relation** *n obs* POL relación plural *f*

pluralism *n* HRM *industrial relations* pluralismo *m*

plus *n* GEN COMM *advantage* pro *m*, ventaja *f*; ~ **sign** MATH signo de suma *m*; ~ **tick** AmE STOCK venta de un título a un precio mayor que una anterior

plying: ~ **limit** *n* TRANSP *maritime* límite de navegación *m*

plywood *n* IND *timber* madera contrachapada *f* (*Esp*), madera terciada *f* (*AmL*); ~ **drum** TRANSP cilindro contrachapado en madera *m* (*Esp*), cilindro terciado en madera *m* (*AmL*)

p.m. *abbr* GEN COMM (*post meridiem*) de la tarde, (*per month*) por mes

PMG *abbr BrE* (*Postmaster General*) COMMS, HRM Director(a) General de Correos *m,f*

PMTS *abbr* (*predetermined motion-time system*) ECON, FIN, GEN COMM, MGMNT sistema predeterminado de movimiento-tiempo *m*

PN *abbr* (*promissory note*) BANK, FIN pagaré *m*

P/N *abbr* (*promissory note*) BANK, FIN pagaré *m*

pneumatic: ~ **tensioner** *n* TRANSP tensor neumático *m*

p.o. *abbr* (*postal order*) GEN COMM giro postal *m*

PO *abbr* COMMS, GEN COMM (*Post Office*) servicio nacional de correo británico, ≈ Correos *m*, ≈ Dirección General de Correos y Telégrafos *f*, PATENTS (*Patent Office*) Registro de la propiedad industrial *m*, Registro de patentes y marcas *m*

P.O. *abbr* (*purchase order*) GEN COMM O/C (*orden de compra*)

poaching *n* HRM *of staff* robo *m*

POB *abbr* (*Post Office Box*) COMMS Apdo. (*Esp*) (*apartado de correos*), casilla de correos (*AmL*)

pocket *n* ECON *of consumer* bolsillo *m*; ~ **calculator** COMP calculadora de bolsillo *f*; ~ **computer** COMP computador de bolsillo *m* (*AmL*), computadora de bolsillo *f* (*AmL*), ordenador de bolsillo *m* (*Esp*); ~ **envelope** S&M sobre de bolsillo *m*; ♦ **out of** ~ GEN COMM con pérdida

pocketbook: ~ **issue** *n AmE* (*cf bread-and-butter issue BrE*) POL, WEL cuestión pendiente *f*, problema básico *m* problema básico *m*

POD *abbr* TRANSP (*place of delivery*) lugar de la entrega *m*, (*proof of delivery*) prueba de entrega *f*, (*paid on delivery*) pago a la entrega

point *n* FIN *real estate, commercial lending* ficha *m*, GEN COMM *for discussion* punto *m*, STOCK *on index of share prices* entero *m*; ~**-and-figure chart** STOCK gráfico de punto y figura *m*; ~ **of departure** IMP/EXP, TRANSP punto de partida *m*; ~ **elasticity** ECON elasticidad de punto *f*; ~ **of entry** IMP/EXP *into country* punto de entrada *m*; ~ **estimate** MATH estimación puntual *f*; ~ **of export** IMP/EXP punto de exportación *m*; ~ **of law** LAW cuestión de derecho *f*; ~**-of-sale advertising** (*POS advertising*) S&M publicidad en los puntos de venta *f*; ~**-of-sale material** S&M material de punto de venta *m*; ~**-of-sale promotion** S&M promoción en el punto de venta *f*; ~**-of-sale terminal** (*POS terminal*) BANK, S&M terminal en punto de venta *m* (*terminal PV*); ~ **of origin** TRANSP punto de origen *m*; ~**-output model** ECON modelo de indicación de salida *m*; ~ **price** STOCK *options* precio del punto *m*; ~ **of sale** (*POS*) GEN COMM, S&M punto de venta *m*; ~ **of view** GEN COMM punto de vista *m*

point to *vt* GEN COMM *indicate* señalar

pointer *n* COMP, GEN COMM *presentation aid* puntero *m*

points: ~ **rating** *n* GEN COMM calificación por puntos *f*; ~**-rating method** *n* GEN COMM método de clasificación por puntos *m*

poison *n* ENVIR, GEN COMM, TRANSP tóxico *m*; ~ **pill** *AmE jarg* GEN COMM en adquisiciones públicas, es la estrategia por parte de la empresa objetivo de desacreditar el valor de sus acciones para no hacerlas atractivas al comprador

Poisson: ~ **distribution** *n* MATH *statistics* distribución de Poisson *f*

polarization *n* COMMS, FIN polarización *f*

police: ~ **files** *n pl* LAW, POL archivos policíacos *m pl*;

~ **force** *n* LAW fuerza pública *f*, fuerza policial *f*; ~ **intelligence** *n* LAW departamento de información de la policía *m*; ~ **power** *n* LAW, POL fuerza pública *f*, poder policial *m*; ~ **record** *n* LAW antecedentes penales *m pl*

policy *n* GEN COMM, INS póliza *f*, MGMNT política *f*; ~ **of the big stick** *infrml* POL política de fuerza *f*, política del garrote *f*; ~ **decision** GEN COMM decisión política *f*; ~ **dividend** INS dividendo de una póliza *m*; ~ **execution** GEN COMM ejecución de una póliza *f*, POL ejecución de una política *f*; ~ **and expenditure management system** FIN sistema de gestión de gastos y política *m*; ~ **formulation** GEN COMM, MGMNT formulación de una política *f*; ~ **framework paper** (*PFP*) ECON marco de referencia de la política *m*, STOCK documento marco de la política *m*; ~ **loan** INS *personal* préstamo sobre una póliza *m*; ~ **mix** MGMNT combinación de políticas *f*, política mixta *f*; ~ **proof of interest** (*PPI*) INS *marine* póliza constitutiva de prueba del interés asegurado *f*; ~ **reserve** INS reserva de póliza *f*; ~ **and resource management** GEN COMM, MGMNT gestión de recursos y políticas *f*; ~ **statement** GEN COMM declaración de política *f*; ~ **to bearer** TAX póliza al portador *f*

Policy:

policyholder *n* INS tomador(a) de seguro *m,f*

policymaker *n* GEN COMM planificador(a) *m,f*, MGMNT persona que establece la política

policymaking *n* MGMNT establecimiento de la política *m*

polipoly *n* ECON polipolio *m*

Polish: ~ **notation** *n* MATH notación polaca *f*

political[1] *adj* POL político

political[2]: ~ **affairs** *n pl* POL asuntos políticos *m pl*; ~ **business cycle** *n* ECON, POL ciclo económico-político *m*; ~ **change** *n* GEN COMM cambio político *f*; ~ **climate** *n* GEN COMM, POL clima político *m*; ~ **contribution** *n* TAX contribución política *f*; ~ **co-operation** *n* POL *EU* cooperación política *f*; ~ **donation** *n* HRM, POL donación política *f*; ~ **economy** *n* ECON, POL economía política *f*; ~ **fund** *n* HRM fondo político *m*; ~ **institution** *n* POL institución política *f*; ~ **issue** *n* GEN COMM cuestión política *f*; ~ **levy** *n BrE* HRM impuesto político *m*; ~ **party** *n* GEN COMM, POL partido político *m*; ~ **practice** *n* POL práctica política *f*; ~ **risk** *n* GEN COMM, POL riesgo político *m*; ~ **situation** *n* GEN COMM, POL situación política *f*; ~ **stability** *n* GEN COMM, POL estabilidad política *f*; ~ **strike** *n* HRM, POL huelga política *f*; ~ **system** *n* GEN COMM, POL régimen político *m*; ~ **thinking** *n* POL pensamiento político *m*; ~ **union** *n* ECON, POL *European Community* unión política *f*

politician *n* POL político(-a) *m,f*

politicize *vt* POL politizar

politics *n* POL política *f*

poll *n* GEN COMM, S&M sondeo *m*; ~ **tax** *BrE obs* TAX capitación *f*, impuesto per cápita *m*

polling *n* COMMS interrogación *f*, COMP *network, modem* invitación a emitir *f*; ~ **booth** POL cabina electoral *f*; ~ **day** POL día de elecciones *m*; ~ **station** POL colegio electoral *m*

polls: **go to the** ~ *phr* POL acudir a las urnas

pollutant *n* ENVIR contaminante *f*, sustancia contaminante *f*

pollute *vt* ENVIR contaminar

polluted *adj* ENVIR, IND contaminado

polluter: ~ **pays principle** *n* ENVIR principio de responsabilidad del país contaminante *m*

pollution *n* ENVIR, IND contaminación *f*; ~ **charge** ENVIR carga de polución *f*; ~ **control** ENVIR, IND, INS control de la contaminación *m*; ~ **monitoring** ENVIR, IND control de la contaminación *m*, vigilancia de la contaminación *f*, INS control de la contaminación *m*; ~ **tax** ENVIR, TAX impuesto por contaminación *m*

polycentrism *n* POL policentrismo *m*

polymerizable: ~ **material** *n* TRANSP *dangerous cargo* material polimerizable *m*

polytechnic *adj BrE* GEN COMM politécnico

pony *n AmE jarg* MEDIA *print* plagio *m*

POO *abbr* (*Port Operations Officer*) HRM, IMP/EXP, TRANSP oficial(a) de operaciones portuarias *m,f*

pool¹ *n* GEN COMM reunión de aseguradores *f*, unión de aseguradoras *f*, equipo *m*, HRM pool *m*, TAX consorcio *m*; ~ **schemes** *n pl* INS esquemas de agrupación *m pl*; ~ **of vehicles** TRANSP consorcio de vehículos *m*

pool² *vt* ECON, GEN COMM *resources, abilities* aunar, combinar

pooling *n* ECON pooling *m*; ~ **arrangement** LAW acuerdo de consolidación de resultados *m*; ~ **arrangements** *n pl* GEN COMM acuerdos de fondo común *m pl*; ~ **of interests** *AmE* (*cf merger accounting BrE*) ACC contabilidad de fusiones *f*, *balance sheets* fusión de intereses *f*; ~ **system** TRANSP banalización *f*

pools *n BrE* LEIS *sport* ≈ quinielas *f pl* (*Esp*)

poop: ~ **and bridge** *n pl* (*PB*) TRANSP popa y puente; ~ **and forecastle** *n pl* (*PF*) TRANSP popa y castillo de proa

poor¹ *adj* ECON *demand* pobre

poor²: ~ **bill of health** *n* GEN COMM, WEL certificado médico negativo de que se padece una enfermedad *m*; ~ **service** *n* GEN COMM, S&M servicio deficiente *m*

pop: ~**-down menu** *n* COMP menú descendente *m*; ~**-up** *n jarg* S&M *advertising* folleto que cobra relieve al abrirlo; ~**-up menu** *n* COMP menú de funciones *m*

Poplarism *n BrE jarg* POL política desmesurada de bienestar social llevada a cabo por el gobierno local

popular: ~ **capitalism** *n* ECON, IND, POL capitalismo popular *m*; ~ **price** *n* S&M precio popular *m*

popularity: ~ **rating** *n* GEN COMM lugar en popularidad *m*, orden de popularidad *m*, POL índice de popularidad *m*

population *n* GEN COMM población *f*; ~ **census** POL censo de población *m*, censo demográfico *m*; ~ **count** GEN COMM recuento de población *m*; ~ **density** ECON, POL densidad de población *f*; ~ **explosion** ECON, POL explosión demográfica *f*; ~ **policy** ECON, POL política demográfica *f*; ~ **statistics** *n pl* MATH, POL estadística demográfica *f*, estadísticas sobre población *f pl*

populist *n* POL populista *mf*

pork *n AmE infrml* POL favores políticos *m pl*; ~ **barrel** *AmE infrml* POL legislación con fines electorales *f*; ~ **chop** *AmE infrml* HRM enchufismo sindical *m*

port *n* COMP puerta *f*; ~ **access** TRANSP acceso portuario *m*; ~ **agent** TRANSP consignatario(-a) de puerto *m,f*; ~ **of arrival** IMP/EXP, TRANSP puerto de llegada *m*; ~ **charges** IMP/EXP, TAX, TRANSP derechos de puerto *m pl*; ~ **control** TRANSP control portuario *m*; ~ **of destination** TRANSP puerto de destino *m*; ~ **director** HRM, IMP/EXP, TRANSP director(a) de puerto *m,f*; ~ **disbursements** *n pl* TRANSP gastos de estancia en puerto *m pl*; ~ **of discharge** TRANSP puerto de descarga

m; ~ **dues** *n pl* (*PD*) IMP/EXP, TAX, TRANSP *shipping* derechos de puerto *m pl*; ~ **of entry** IMP/EXP puerto de entrada *m*, puerto de inscripción *m*; ~ **facilities** *n pl* TRANSP instalaciones portuarias *f pl*; ~ **health authority** (*PHA*) TRANSP autoridad sanitaria del puerto *f*; ~ **interchange** TRANSP intercambio portuario *m*; ~ **layout** IMP/EXP, TRANSP diseño portuario *m*, disposición portuaria *f*, trazado portuario *m*; ~ **liner terms charge** (*PLTC*) TRANSP coste portuario por transporte regular *m* (*Esp*), costo portuario por transporte regular *m* (*AmL*); ~ **of loading** GEN COMM, IMP/EXP, TRANSP puerto de embarque *m*; ~ **management** TRANSP gestión portuaria *f*; ~ **manager** HRM, IMP/EXP, TRANSP director(a) de puerto *m,f*; ~ **of necessity** TRANSP puerto de necesidad *m*; ~ **operation** TRANSP explotación portuaria *f*; ~ **of registry** IMP/EXP, TRANSP puerto de matrícula *m*; ~ **of shipment** GEN COMM, IMP/EXP, TRANSP puerto de embarque *m*; ~ **statistics** *n pl* TRANSP estadísticas portuarias *f pl*; ~ **surcharge** TRANSP sobretasa portuaria *f*; ~ **tariff** TRANSP tarifa portuaria *f*; ~ **tax** TAX, TRANSP impuesto portuario *m*; ~ **throughput** TRANSP flujo portuario *m*; ~ **traffic** TRANSP tráfico portuario *m*; ~ **traffic control** TRANSP control de tráfico portuario *m*; ~ **turnaround time** *AmE*, ~ **turnround time** *BrE* TRANSP tiempo entre entrada y salida de un puerto *m*, tiempo de retorno al puerto *m*; ~ **users' committee** TRANSP comité de usuarios de puerto *m*; ◆ ~ **to port** (*p to p*) IMP/EXP, TRANSP de puerto a puerto

Port: ~ **of London Authority** *n* (*PLA*) TRANSP autoridad portuaria de Londres; ~ **Operations Officer** *n* (*POO*) HRM, IMP/EXP, TRANSP oficial(a) de operaciones portuarias *m,f*

portability *n* COMP transportabilidad *f*

portable¹ *adj* COMP *hardware* portátil, *software* transferible

portable²: ~ **computer** *n* COMP computador portátil *m* (*AmL*), computadora portátil *f* (*AmL*), ordenador portátil *m* (*Esp*), laptop *m*; ~ **gangway** *n* TRANSP escalerilla desplazable *f*; ~ **phone** *n* COMMS teléfono portátil *m*

portainer: ~ **crane** *n* TRANSP *cargo* grúa de portal *f*

portal: ~ **berth** *n* TRANSP muelle de pórtico *m*; ~ **crane** *n* TRANSP *cargo* grúa de pórtico *f*; ~**-to-portal pay** *n* HRM remuneración por desplazamiento *f*

portfolio *n* FIN, GEN COMM cartera de valores *f*, POL *of government activity* cartera *f*, STOCK cartera de valores *f*, portfolio *m*; ~ **analysis** S&M análisis de cartera *m*; ~ **balance** FIN balance de la cartera *m*; ~ **beta score** STOCK punto beta de la cartera *m*; ~ **dividend** STOCK dividendo de cartera de valores *m*; ~ **income** ACC, STOCK ingresos en cartera *m pl*; ~ **insurance** INS, STOCK seguro de cartera *m*; ~ **investment** STOCK inversión de cartera *f*; ~ **of investments** ACC, BANK, FIN cartera de participaciones *f*, cartera de títulos *f*; ~ **management** GEN COMM administración de carteras *f*, gerencia de carteras *f*, FIN gestión de carteras *f*; ~ **management service** BANK, STOCK servicio de gestión de la cartera de valores *m*; ~ **management theory** STOCK *investment decision approach* teoría de la gestión de cartera de valores *f*; ~ **manager** BANK, STOCK gestor(a) de la cartera de valores *m,f*; ~ **reinsurance** INS reaseguro de cartera de valores *m*; ~ **section** FIN, STOCK sección de cartera *f*; ~ **selection** FIN, STOCK selección de cartera *f*; ~ **split** FIN, STOCK división de cartera de valores *f*; ~ **switching** STOCK intercambio de cartera *m*; ~ **theory**

STOCK *investment decision approach* teoría de la cartera de valores *f*; ~ **of trade** BANK, FIN *of investments* cartera comercial *f*; ~ **transfer** INS cesión de cartera *f*

porting *n* COMP *software* transferencia *f*

portion *n* FIN *of dividend, amount* parte *f*

portrait *n* ADMIN, COMP, MEDIA *of format*, S&M *advertising, printing* formato vertical *m*

POS[1] *abbr* (*point of sale*) GEN COMM, S&M punto de venta *m*

POS[2]: ~ **advertising** *n* S&M publicidad en los puntos de venta *f*; ~ **terminal** *n* BANK, S&M terminal en punto de venta *m*

position[1] *n* GEN COMM posición *f*, situación *f*, empleo *m*, puesto *m*; ~ **account** STOCK cuenta de posición *f*; ~ **of authority** HRM posición de autoridad *f*; ~ **closed** BANK posición cerrada *f*; ~ **fixing device** TRANSP dispositivo para fijar la situación *m*; ~ **limit** STOCK límite de posición *m*; ~ **media** S&M medios de colocación *m pl*; ~ **net credit** STOCK *options* crédito neto de la posición *m*; ~ **paper** *jarg* POL documento de situación *f*; ~**-risk capital** STOCK capital expuesto al riesgo *m*; ~ **schedule bond** INS fianza de puesto laboral y de lealtad nominal *f*; ~ **trader** STOCK operador(a) de posición *m,f*; ~ **trading** STOCK negociación de posiciones *f*; ♦ **in a ~ to do** GEN COMM en condiciones de hacer; **take a ~** STOCK tomar posición

position[2] *vt* ECON, GEN COMM posicionar, STOCK determinar una posición, *client* posicionar

positional[1] *adj* ECON posicional

positional[2]: ~ **good** *n* ECON bien posicional *m*

positioning *n* GEN COMM posición *f*, posicionamiento *m*; ~ **theory** S&M teoría posicional *f*

positive[2]: ~ **action** *n* AmE *jarg* HRM, LAW acción positiva *f*; ~ **cash-flow** *n* ACC, FIN cash flow positivo *m*, flujo de caja positivo *m*, FIN, TAX cobro *m*; ~ **confirmation** *n* ACC *auditing* confirmación positiva *f*; ~ **correlation** *n* MATH *between two variables* correlación positiva *f*; ~ **discrimination** *n* GEN COMM discriminación positiva *f*; ~ **economics** *n* ECON economía positiva *f*; ~ **feedback** *n* COMP, ECON reacción positiva *f*; ~ **file** *n* BANK archivo positivo *m*, declaración positiva *f*; ~ **gearing** *n* BrE FIN apalancamiento positivo *m*; ~ **interest-rate gap** *n* ECON diferencia positiva de tipos de interés *f*; ~ **labor relations** AmE, ~ **labour relations** BrE *n pl* ECON, HRM relación laboral positiva *f*, clima laboral sano *m*; ~ **leverage** *n* AmE FIN apalancamiento positivo *m*; ~ **monetary compensatory amount** *n* FIN cantidad compensatoria monetaria positiva *f*; ~ **neutrality** *n* POL neutralidad positiva *f*; ~ **response** *n* GEN COMM respuesta positiva *f*; ~**-sum game** *n jarg* ECON juego de suma positiva *m*; ~ **yield curve** *n* ECON curva de rendimiento positivo *f*

possession *n* LAW, PROP posesión *f*

possible: **as soon as ~** *phr* (*a.s.a.p.*) COMMS, GEN COMM tan pronto como sea posible, con la mayor brevedad posible

possibilism *n* POL posibilismo *m*

possibility *n* GEN COMM posibilidad *f*

post[1]: ~**-assessing** *adj* TAX posterior a la liquidación; ~**-bankruptcy** *adj* TAX posterior a la quiebra; ~**-election** *adj* GEN COMM, POL posterior a la elección; ~**-peak** *adj* S&M después del punto máximo

post[2] *n* ADMIN, COMMS BrE (*cf mail AmE*) correo *m*, COMP correo electrónico *m*, HRM puesto *m*; ~**-audit** TAX intervención a posteriori *f*; ~ **balance sheet event** ACC acontecimiento posterior al balance general *m*, hecho posterior al balance general *m*; ~**-closing trial balance** ACC balance de situación *m*; ~**-contractual optimism** ECON optimismo poscontractual *m*; ~**-entry** ACC asiento posterior *m*, IMP/EXP, TRANSP *shipping* asiento posterior *m*, declaración adicional *f*, registro posterior *m*; ~**-entry closed shop** HRM empresa que impone la sindicación *f*; ~**-entry discrimination** ECON discriminación posentrada *f*; ~**-execution reporting** AmE (*PER*) STOCK informe posterior a la ejecución; ~**-flight information** TRANSP información posvuelo *f*; ~**-implementation audit** GEN COMM auditoría diferida de ejecución *f*; ~**-industrial society** ECON, POL sociedad posindustrial *f*; ~**-maturity interest** BANK interés a partir del vencimiento *m*; ~ **office** ADMIN, COMMS, GEN COMM oficina de correos *f*; ~ **office savings bank** BANK banco de ahorros de la oficina de correos *m*; ~ **operations officer** HRM encargado(-a) de posoperaciones *m,f*; ~ **pallet** TRANSP plataforma de carga apilable *f*; ~**-purchase advertising** S&M publicidad poscompra *f*; ~**-purchase remorse** S&M arrepentimiento poscompra *m*; ~**-sailing information** TRANSP información de navegación *f*; ~**-sales service** S&M servicio de posventa *m*; ~**-shipment inspection** TRANSP inspección posembarque *f*; ~ **stacker** TRANSP apiladora postal *f*; ~ **van** BrE (*cf mailcar AmE*) COMMS furgón postal *m*; ~**-war boom** ECON auge de posguerra *m*; ♦ **by ~** BrE (*cf by mail AmE*) COMMS por correo; **by return of ~** COMMS a vuelta de correo; **through the ~** BrE (*cf through the mail AmE*) COMMS por correo

post[3] *vt* BrE (*cf mail AmE*) ADMIN, COMMS enviar por correo, franquear; ♦ ~ **an entry** ACC anotar, anotar una entrada, apuntar; ~ **margin** STOCK *open position by selling* contabilizar el margen; ~ **up an account** BANK poner al día una cuenta

Post: ~ **Office** *n* BrE (*PO*) COMMS servicio nacional de correo británico, ≈ Correos *m*, ≈ Dirección General de Correos y Telégrafos *f*; ~ **Office Box** *n* BrE (*POB*) COMMS apartado de correos *m* (*Esp*) (*Apdo.*), casilla de correos *f* (*AmL*); ~ **Office Giro** *n* BrE GEN COMM giro postal *m*

postage *n* ADMIN, COMMS franqueo *m*; ~ **certificate** COMMS certificado de franqueo *m*; ~**-due stamp** ADMIN, COMMS franqueo en destino *m*; ~ **meter** AmE, ~ **metre** BrE COMMS franqueadora *f*; ~ **and packing** *n pl* (*p&p*) COMMS gastos de franqueo y empaquetado; ~ **rate** COMMS tarifa postal *f*; ~ **stamp** COMMS sello *m* (*Esp*), sello de correos *m* (*Esp*), estampilla *f* (*AmL*); ~**-stamp remittance** AmE GEN COMM *method of payment* envío de sellos de correos *m*; ♦ ~ **due** ADMIN, COMMS portes debidos; ~ **paid** ADMIN, COMMS franqueo pagado, porte pagado

postal: ~ **address** *n* ADMIN, COMMS dirección postal *f*; ~ **assistant** *n* (*PA*) HRM ayudante postal *mf*; ~ **ballot** *n* BrE HRM votación por correo *f*, voto por correo *m*; ~ **check** AmE, ~ **cheque** BrE *n* BANK, FIN cheque postal *m*; ~ **clerk** *n* BrE (*cf mail clerk AmE*) HRM empleado(-a) postal *m,f*; ~ **code** *n* BrE (*cf zip code AmE*) COMMS, GEN COMM código postal *m*; ~ **export** *n* IMP/EXP exportación postal *f*; ~ **money order** *n* AmE (*cf postal order BrE*) GEN COMM giro postal *m*; ~ **order** *n* BrE (*p.o.*, *cf postal money order AmE*) GEN COMM giro postal *m*; ~ **panel** *n* S&M panel postal *m*; ~ **remittance** *n* ACC envío postal *m*, giro postal *m*, reserva postal *f*;

~ service *n* COMMS, GEN COMM servicio de correos *m*; **~ vote** *n* POL votación por correo *f*, voto por correo *m*; **~ worker** *n* HRM empleado(-a) de correos *m,f*; **~ zone** *n* COMMS distrito postal *m*

postbox *n BrE* (*cf mailbox AmE*) COMMS buzón *m*

postcode *n BrE* (*cf zip code AmE*) COMMS, GEN COMM código postal *m*

post-Communist *adj* GEN COMM poscomunista

postdate[1] *n* BANK, FIN posdata *f* (*P.D.*), posfechado *m*

postdate[2] *vt* BANK, FIN posdatar, posfechar

postdated[1] *adj* (*P.D.*) BANK, GEN COMM, FIN con fecha adelantada, posfechado

postdated[2]: **~ check** *AmE*, **~ cheque** *BrE n* BANK, FIN cheque posdatado *m*, cheque posfechado *m*

posted[1] *adj* GEN COMM, HRM nombrado

posted[2]: **~ price** *n jarg* ECON precio de cotización *m*

poster *n* S&M cartel *m*; **~ advertising** S&M pancartas publicitarias *f pl*; **~ display** S&M *advertising* pancarta publicitaria *f*; **~ site** S&M *advertising* valla publicitaria *f*; **~ site classifications** *n pl* S&M clasificaciones de emplazamiento de carteles *f pl*; **~ size** S&M tamaño de carteles *m*

postgraduate *n* GEN COMM posgraduado(-a) *m,f*

posting *n* ACC, ADMIN pase de asientos *m*, HRM *appointment* destino *m*, LAW *civil procedure* aviso público *m*, *commercial* inscripción *f*; **~ error** ACC error de pase *m*, error de registro *m*, error de transcripción *m*

post-Keynesians *n* ECON poskeynesianos *m*

postman *n BrE* (*cf mailman AmE*) COMMS cartero *m*

postmark *n* COMMS timbre postal *m*

Postmaster: **~ General** *n BrE* (*PMG*) COMMS, HRM Director(a) General de Correos *m,f*

post meridiem *phr* (*p.m.*) GEN COMM después del mediodía

postpaid *adj* (*pp*) GEN COMM porte pagado *m*

postpone *vt* GEN COMM posponer; ♦ **~ tax payment** TAX aplazar el pago de impuestos

postscript *n* (*P.S.*) COMMS posdata *f* (*P.D.*); **~ printer** COMP impresora de post scriptum *f*

postwar[1] *adj* GEN COMM de posguerra

postwar[2]: **~ period** *n* GEN COMM periodo de posguerra *m*

pot: **the ~ is clean** *phr jarg* STOCK anuncio de que se han vendido las acciones

potash: **~ berth** *n* TRANSP muelle de potasas *m*

potential[1] *adj* GEN COMM posible, potencial

potential[2] *n* GEN COMM potencial *m*; **~ buyer** S&M posible comprador(a) *m,f*; **~ commitment** GEN COMM compromiso potencial *m*; **~ demand** ECON, S&M demanda potencial *f*; **~ income** ECON ingreso potencial *m*; **~ investor** STOCK inversor(a) potencial *m,f*; **~ output** ECON, IND producción potencial *f*; **~ profit** STOCK beneficio posible *m*; **~ user** S&M usuario(-a) potencial *m,f*; ♦ **have ~** GEN COMM tener potencial

potentially[1] *adv* GEN COMM potencialmente

potentially[2]: **~ exempt transfer** *n* (*PET*) TAX transferencia potencialmente exenta *f*

pound *n* GEN COMM (*lb*) *weight* libra *f*, *currency* libra esterlina *f*; **~ spot and forward** ECON libra al contado y a plazo *f*; **~ sterling** *BrE* GEN COMM libra esterlina; ♦ **valued impressions per ~** S&M ediciones valoradas por libra *f pl*

pounds: **~ per square inch** *phr* (*PSI*) TRANSP libras por pulgada cuadrada

pour autre vie *phr* LAW uso limitado temporalmente a la vida de otra persona

poverty *n* WEL pobreza *f*; **~ line** ECON, WEL umbral de pobreza *m*; **~ pocket** WEL bolsa de pobreza *f*; **~ trap** WEL trampa de la pobreza *f*

power[1] *n* COMP energía *f*, GEN COMM *capability* poder *m*, IND tensión *f*; **~ of appointment** LAW facultad para efectuar nombramientos *f*; **~ of attorney** (*PA*) LAW *administrative* Poder General *m*, poder legal *m*; **~ failure** COMP, ENVIR corte de corriente *m*, caída de tensión *f*; **~ generation** (*cf electricity generation BrE*) IND generación de energía *f*, generación de electricidad *f*; **~ industries** *n pl* IND industrias energéticas *f pl*; **~ of the media** MEDIA poder de los medios de comunicación *m*; **~ politics** POL política de fuerza *f*; **~ of recourse** LAW poder para pleitos *m*; **~ of sale** LAW, PROP facultad de vender *f*, poder de venta *m*; **~ station** IND central eléctrica *f*, planta de electricidad *f*; **~ struggle** POL lucha por el poder *f*; **~ surge** COMP fuente de alimentación *f*; **~ take-off** (*PTO*) TRANSP toma de fuerza *f*; **~-to-weight ratio** TRANSP potencia de masa *f*; ♦ **in ~** POL *government* en el poder; **~ on** COMP con tensión eléctrica; **have the ~ to** GEN COMM tener autoridad para

power[2] *vt* COMP encender, IND impulsar

powerful *adj* GEN COMM poderoso

powers *n pl* LAW competencias *f pl*

pp *abbr* GEN COMM (*per pro*) en nombre de, GEN COMM (*postpaid*) porte pagado *m*

pp. *abbr* (*pages*) GEN COMM págs. (*páginas*)

p.p. *abbr* GEN COMM (*prepaid*) pagado por adelantado, LAW (*per procurationem*) por poder

PPBS *abbr* (*planning-programming-budgeting system*) GEN COMM presupuesto por programas *m*, sistema de planificación y presupuesto *m*

Ppd *abbr* (*prepaid*) GEN COMM pagado por adelantado

PPF *abbr* ECON (*production possibility frontier*) frontera de posibilidades de producción *f*, FIN (*project preparation facility*) SPP (*servicio de preparación de proyectos*)

PPI[1] *abbr* (*producer price index*) ECON índice de precios a la producción *m*

PPI[2]: **~ policy** *n* INS póliza PPI *f*

PPP *abbr* FIN, MGMNT (*profit and performance planning*) plan de beneficios y rendimientos *m*, WEL (*private patients plan*) plan de pacientes privados *m*,

PQLI *abbr* (*physical quality of life index*) ECON índice de calidad física de vida *m*

pr. *abbr* (*price*) GEN COMM precio *m*

PR *abbr* (*public relations*) HRM, MEDIA, S&M relaciones públicas *f pl*

PRA *abbr* (*purchase and resale agreement*) STOCK compromiso de compra y reventa *m*

practical: **~ capacity** *n* ECON capacidad práctica *f*; **~ politics** *n pl* POL política práctica *f*; **~ use** *n* HRM *of skills* aplicación práctica *f*

practice[1] *n* LAW ejercicio de una profesión *m*; ♦ **in ~** GEN COMM en la práctica *f*

practice[2] *vt AmE see practise BrE*

practise *vt BrE* FIN practicar, ejercer

pragmatic *adj* GEN COMM pragmático

pragmatically *adv* GEN COMM pragmáticamente

preacquisition: ~ **profits** n pl ACC beneficios de preadquisición m pl

preamble n GEN COMM to agreement, contract, PATENTS preámbulo m

pre-approach n S&M enfoque previo m

pre-arranged adj GEN COMM preestablecido

pre-assessing n TAX pretributación f

pre-audit n TAX intervención a priori f

pre-authorized: ~ **check** AmE, ~ **cheque** BrE n BANK, FIN cheque preautorizado m; ~ **payment** n BANK pago preautorizado m

pre-bankruptcy n GEN COMM, TAX prequiebra f

pre-bill n GEN COMM factura proforma f

Prebisch-Singer: ~ **thesis** n ECON tesis de Prebisch-Singer f

pre-campaign: ~ **exposure** n S&M exposición de pre-campaña f

precarious adj GEN COMM precario

precarization n HRM precarización f

precaution: as a ~ **against** phr GEN COMM en previsión de

precautionary: ~ **demand for money** n ECON demanda de precaución del dinero f; ~ **motive** n GEN COMM motivo de salvaguarda m; ~ **principle** n ENVIR principio de precaución m; ~ **saving** n BANK, ECON, FIN ahorro preventivo m

precede vt GEN COMM preceder

precedent adj GEN COMM precedente

preceding[1] adj GEN COMM anterior, precedente

preceding[2]: ~ **taxation year** n TAX ejercicio fiscal anterior m; ~ **year** n GEN COMM año precedente m

precious: ~ **metal** n GEN COMM metal fino m; ~ **metal account** n BANK cuenta de metales preciosos f

precise: ~ **positioning service** n (PPS) TRANSP servicio de localización precisa m

precision: ~ **engineering** n IND ingeniería de precisión f

preclosing n LAW commercial cierre anticipado m

preclude vt GEN COMM excluir

precoded adj S&M precodificado

precompute vt BANK, FIN interest in instalment loans precalcular

preconception n GEN COMM prejuicio m

precondition n GEN COMM condición previa f

predator n GEN COMM, S&M depredador(a) m,f, predador(a) m,f

predatory: ~ **competition** n GEN COMM competencia desleal f; ~ **pricing** n ECON fijación de precios depredadores f

predecessor n GEN COMM compañía predecesora f; ~ **in title** PATENTS antecesor en el título de propiedad m

predelivery: ~ **inspection** n TRANSP inspección previa a la entrega f

predetermine vt GEN COMM predeterminar

predetermined[1] adj GEN COMM predeterminado

predetermined[2]: ~ **motion-time system** n (PMTS) ECON, FIN, GEN COMM, MGMNT sistema predeterminado de movimiento-tiempo m; ~ **price** n S&M, STOCK precio predeterminado m

predict vt GEN COMM predecir

predictable[1] adj GEN COMM predecible

predictable[2]: ~ **life** n ACC of business assets vida estimable f, vida previsible f

predicted adj GEN COMM predicho

pre-eminent adj GEN COMM preeminente

pre-empt: ~ **spot** n S&M anuncio reservado de antemano a tarifa reducida m

pre-emption n LAW derecho de prioridad m, derecho preferente m; ~ **right** LAW, PATENTS, STOCK derecho de prioridad m

pre-emptive: ~ **bid** n STOCK oferta preferente f; ~ **right** n GEN COMM, LAW, PATENTS, STOCK commercial derecho de tanteo m, derecho de prioridad m, derecho del tanto m

pre-emptor n AmE LAW comprador(a) por derecho de prioridad m,f

pre-entry n IMP/EXP registro previo m; ~ **closed shop** HRM empresa que exige sindicarse a los nuevos trabajadores; ~ **discrimination** ECON discriminación antes de la entrada f

pre-existing: ~ **use** n PROP uso preexistente m

pref. abbr (preference) GEN COMM preferencia f

prefabricated adj PROP prefabricado; ~ **house** n PROP casa prefabricada f

preference n (pref.) GEN COMM preferencia f; ~ **dividend** BrE (cf preferred dividend AmE) ACC dividendo preferente m, dividendo privilegiado m; ~ **qualification shares** n pl STOCK título de garantía preferente m; ~ **share** BrE (cf preferred stock AmE) STOCK, TAX acción preferente f

preferential[1] adj GEN COMM preferencial

preferential[2]: ~ **creditor** n GEN COMM acreedor(a) preferente m,f; ~ **form** n STOCK forma preferencial f; ~ **interest rate** n BANK tasa de interés preferencial f; ~ **rate** n BANK of interest on loan tasa preferencial f, tasa preferente f; ~ **rehiring** n LAW Civil Rights derecho preferente m; ~ **shop** n GEN COMM, HRM industrial relations negocio de contratación preferencial m, empresa que prefiere trabajadores sindicados f; ~ **treatment** n GEN COMM trato preferencial m

preferred: ~ **beneficiary** n TAX beneficiario(-a) preferente m,f; ~ **creditor** n GEN COMM acreedor(a) privilegiado m,f; ~ **dividend** n AmE (cf preference dividend BrE) ACC dividendo preferente m, dividendo privilegiado m; ~ **dividend coverage** n ACC cobertura de dividendo de acciones preferentes f; ~ **habitat theory** n FIN teoría del habitat preferente f; ~ **investment certificate** n STOCK certificado de inversión preferente m; ~ **lien** n TAX gravamen preferente m; ~ **position** n S&M posición preferida f; ~ **rate** n GEN COMM tipo preferencial m; ~ **risk** n INS riesgo preferente m; ~ **stock** n ACC, STOCK, TAX acciones preferentes f pl; ~ **stock ratio** n STOCK proporción de acciones preferentes f

prefinancing: ~ **credit** n BANK crédito de prefinanciación m

pre-inspection: ~ **requirement** n BANK exigencia de preinspección f, requisito de preinspección m

prejudice n GEN COMM damage perjuicio m, prejuicio m

prejudicial adj GEN COMM perjudicial

prelease vt PROP prearrendar

preliminary: ~ **day** n STOCK día previo m; ~ **entry** n GEN COMM declaración previa f; ~ **estimate** n GEN COMM cálculo anticipado m; ~ **examination** n PATENTS interrogatorio preliminar m; ~ **expenses** n pl ACC gastos preliminares m pl; ~ **investigation** n LAW instrucción f; ~ **project** n GEN COMM anteproyecto m; ~ **prospectus** n STOCK prospecto de emisión preliminar m

preloading: ~ **inspection** *n* TRANSP inspección previa a la carga *f*

premature *adj* GEN COMM prematuro

premier: ~ **borrower** *n* *BrE* BANK prestatario(-a) de primera clase *m,f*

premise *n* GEN COMM premisa *f*; ◆ **on the ~ that** GEN COMM sobre la base de que

premises *n pl* GEN COMM local *m*

premium *n* GEN COMM prima *f*; ~ **bond** FIN, STOCK bono de prima *m*; ~ **bonus** HRM incentivo de premio *m*, retribución con prima *f*, STOCK retribución con prima *f*; ~ **and discount on exchange** FIN prima y descuento de cambio *f*; ~ **grade** GEN COMM producto que se vende con sobreprecio *m*; ~ **income** INS encaje de primas *m*; ~ **loan** BANK préstamo con primas *m*; ~ **offer** S&M super oferta *f*; ~ **over bond value** STOCK prima sobre el valor del bono *f*; ~ **over conversion value** STOCK prima sobre el valor de conversión *f*; ~ **price** S&M precio de incentivo *m*; ~ **payment** STOCK pago de prima *m*; ~ **pricing** S&M fijación de precios de incentivo *f*; ~ **quotations** *n pl* STOCK *options* cotizaciones con prima *f pl*; ~ **raid** STOCK especulación en el mercado con prima *f*; ~ **rate** INS tipo de prima *m*, STOCK tasa de prima *f*; ~ **reserve** FIN reserva de primas *f*; ~ **savings account** BANK cuenta de ahorro de primas *f*; ~ **savings bond** FIN, STOCK bono de ahorro con prima *m*; ~ **statement** FIN descuento de primas *m*; ~ **transfer** INS transferencia de prima *f*; ◆ **at a ~** FIN sobre el cambio, sobre una prima, STOCK *shares* sobre el cambio

Premium: ~ **Bond** *n* STOCK obligación con prima *f*, obligación con lotes *f*

premiums: ~ **reducing** *n* INS *marine* prima decreciente *f*

prenuptial: ~ **contract** *n* LAW contrato prematrimonial *m*

pre-owned *adj* GEN COMM *motor trade* seminuevo

prepackaged *adj* S&M *goods* empaquetado

prepaid[1] *adj* (*p.p., Ppd*) GEN COMM pagado por adelantado

prepaid[2]: ~ **card** *n* S&M tarjeta prepagada *f*; ~ **charges** *n pl* ACC gastos pagados *m pl*; ~ **expenses** *n* ACC gastos anticipados *m pl*, gastos pagados por anticipado *m pl*; ~ **interest** *n* FIN descuento por adelantado *m*; ~ **letter of credit** *n* BANK, FIN carta de crédito pagada por adelantado *f*; ~ **ticket advice** *n* (*PTA*) LEIS, TRANSP aviso de billete de pago anticipado *m*

preparation *n* GEN COMM preparación *f*

prepare *vt* GEN COMM preparar; ◆ ~ **a return** TAX preparar una declaración

prepared *adj* GEN COMM listo

prepayment *n* GEN COMM pago antes del vencimiento *m*, prepago *m*; ~ **clause** FIN cláusula de pago anticipado *f*; ~ **penalty** BANK penalización por pago anticipado *f*; ~ **privilege** BANK, FIN privilegio de pago anticipado *m*

preplanning *n* TRANSP *shipping* planificación previa *f*

pre-production: ~ **expenditure** *n* TAX gasto previo a la producción *m*

prerecorded: ~ **broadcast** *n* MEDIA retransmisión en diferido *f*, transmisión en diferido *f*

prerequisite *n* GEN COMM prerrequisito *m*, requisito previo *m*

preretiree *n* FIN prejubilado(-a) *m,f*

preretirement: ~ **pension** *n* FIN pensión de prejubilación *f*

prerogative *n* GEN COMM prerrogativa *f*

pres. *abbr* (*president*) GEN COMM, HRM, POL presidente *m,f*

presale *n* PROP preventa *f*; ~ **order** STOCK orden de venta anticipada *f*

presales: ~ **service** *n* S&M servicio de preventa *m*

preschool: ~ **center** *AmE*, ~ **centre** *BrE* *n* WEL escuela preescolar *f*

prescribe *vt* LAW prescribir, usucapir

prescribed[1] *adj* GEN COMM, LAW prescrito

prescribed[2]: ~ **aggregate reserve** *n* (*PAR*) BANK reserva agregada obligatoria *f*; ~ **contract** *n* GEN COMM, LAW contrato prescrito *m*; ~ **form** *n* TAX formulario reglamentario *m*; ~ **information** *n* TAX información reglamentaria *f*; ~ **price** *n* GEN COMM precio prescrito *m*; ~ **rate** *n* TAX tipo preestablecido *m*; ~ **share** *n* STOCK acción prescrita *f*; ~ **time** *n* GEN COMM tiempo previsto *m*; ~ **venture capital corporation** *n* FIN compañía de capital de riesgo reglamentaria *f*

prescription *n* MGMNT, PROP prescripción *f*, WEL receta médica *f*

prescriptive: ~ **right** *n* LAW, PROP derecho legal por prescripción *m*

preselected: ~ **campaign** *n* S&M campaña preseleccionada *f*

presence *n* S&M presencia *f*

present[1] *adj* GEN COMM actual, presente; ◆ **among those ~** GEN COMM entre los presentes; **in the ~ state of affairs** GEN COMM en la situación actual

present[2]: ~ **value** *n* ACC, ECON, FIN valor descontado *m*, valor presente *m*; ~ **value method** *n* ACC, ECON, FIN factor del valor presente *m*, método del valor descontado *m*, método del valor presente *m*

present[3] *vt* GEN COMM *report* presentar, *argument* objetar; ◆ ~ **a bill for discount** BANK presentar una factura para el descuento; ~ **a bill for reception** BANK presentar una factura para recepción; ~ **a check for payment** *AmE*, ~ **a cheque for payment** *BrE* BANK presentar un cheque al cobro; ~ **a draft for acceptance** BANK presentar una letra para su aceptación; ~ **fairly** ACC *auditing* mostrar claramente, mostrar con claridad, presentar razonablemente

presentation *n* GEN COMM presentación *f*; ~ **copy** MEDIA *print* ejemplar gratuito *m*; ~ **of documents** IMP/EXP presentación de documentos *f*

presenter *n* MEDIA *print, broadcast, newscasting* presentador(a) *m,f*

preservation *n* ENVIR *of habitats* conservación *f*

preservatives: **no ~** *phr* GEN COMM, S&M sin conservantes; **no ~ or additives** *phr* GEN COMM, S&M sin conservantes ni aditivos

preserve *vt* ENVIR, GEN COMM conservar

preserved: ~ **foods** *n pl* GEN COMM, IND alimentos en conserva *m pl*

preset *adj* COMP predefinido

presettlement *n* HRM preacuerdo *m*

preshipment: ~ **inspection** *n* TRANSP inspección previa al embarque *f*

preside over *vt* GEN COMM *meeting* presidir

president *n* (*pres.*) GEN COMM, HRM, POL presidente(-a) *m,f*

President: ~ **of the Government** *n* *AmE* POL ≈ Presidente(-a) del Gobierno *m,f*; ~ **of the group executive board** *n* *AmE* HRM, MGMNT presidente(-a) de la junta directiva *m,f*, presidente(-a) del consejo de administración *m,f*; **~ of the Treasury Board** *n AmE* FIN presidente(-a) del consejo del tesoro *m,f*

presidential: **~ election cycle theory** *n* STOCK teoría del ciclo de elecciones presidenciales *f*

presiding: **~ judge** *n* LAW juez(a) de turno *m,f*

presidium *n* HRM junta permanente *f*

press¹ *n* GEN COMM, MEDIA prensa *f*; **~ advertisement** MEDIA, S&M anuncio en prensa *m*; **~ advertising** MEDIA, S&M publicidad en la prensa *f*; **~ agency** MEDIA agencia de prensa *f*; **~ availability** *jarg* POL rueda de prensa abierta a las preguntas de los medios de comunicación; **~ campaign** MEDIA *print* campaña de prensa *f*; **~ clipping** *AmE* (*cf press cutting BrE*) MEDIA *print* recorte de prensa *m*; **~ conference** MEDIA *print*, S&M rueda de prensa *f*; **~ copy** MEDIA *print* ejemplar para reseña publicitaria *m*; **~ coverage** MEDIA *print* cobertura periodística *f*; **~ cutting** *BrE* (*cf press clipping AmE*) MEDIA *print* recorte de prensa *m*; **~ date** MEDIA, S&M fecha de publicación *f*; **~ edition** MEDIA *print* edición de prensa *f*; **~ flesh** *jarg* POL contacto directo *m*; **~ kit** MEDIA *print* información para la prensa *f*; **~ mentions** *n pl* S&M menciones en la prensa *f pl*; **~ officer** HRM, MEDIA, S&M agregado(-a) de prensa *m,f*, oficial(a) de prensa *m,f*; **~ pack** S&M paquete informativo *m*; **~ pass** S&M acreditación de prensa *f*; **~ photographer** MEDIA *print* fotógrafo(-a) de prensa *m,f*; **~ relation** MEDIA *print* relación con la prensa *f*; **~ release** GEN COMM boletín de prensa *m*, gacetilla *f*, comunicado de prensa *m*

press² *vt* COMP pulsar

Press: **~ Association** *n BrE* (*PA*) MEDIA asociación británica de prensa

pressure *n* GEN COMM presión *f*; **~ group** POL grupo de presión *m*; **~ selling** S&M venta bajo presión *f*; **~ valve** TRANSP válvula de presión *f*

prestige *n* GEN COMM, S&M prestigio *m*; **~ advertising** S&M publicidad de prestigio *f*; **~ goods** *n pl* GEN COMM, S&M artículos suntuarios *m pl*; **~ pricing** S&M precio de prestigio *m*, fijación de precios de prestigio *f*

prestigious *adj* GEN COMM, S&M prestigioso

presumption *n* GEN COMM *impertinence*, LAW presunción *f*

presumptive: **~ tax** *n* TAX impuesto en régimen de evaluación global; **~ assessment** *n* TAX impuesto en régimen de evaluación global

pretax: **~ earnings** *n pl* ACC, TAX ganancias antes de impuestos *f pl*; **~ rate of return** *n* TAX tasa de rentabilidad *f*; **~ yield** *n* ACC beneficio antes de impuestos *m*

pretest *n* S&M preencuesta *f*

pretesting *n* S&M prueba preliminar *f*; **~ copy** S&M mensaje publicitario de pre-encuesta *m*

pretreatment *n* ENVIR *of waste* tratamiento preliminar *m*

prevail *vi* GEN COMM, S&M predominar

prevailing¹ *adj* GEN COMM, S&M *trend* predominante, preeminente

prevailing²: **~ market price** *n* STOCK precio en vigor en el mercado *m*; **~ party** *n* LAW parte predominante *f*

prevent *vt* GEN COMM evitar, impedir, prevenir

Prevention: **~ of Fraud Act** *n BrE* FIN, LAW *investment* ley de prevención del fraude

preventive: **~ detention** *n* LAW prisión preventiva *f*, prisión provisional *f*; **~ maintenance** *n* GEN COMM, IND, MGMNT mantenimiento preventivo *m*

preview *vt* COMP *document* previsualizar

previous: **~ closing** *n* GEN COMM cierre previo *m*; **~ endorsement** *n* BANK, GEN COMM endoso anterior *m*; **~ engagement** *n* GEN COMM compromiso previo *m*; **~ history** *n* HRM historial previo *m*; **~ year** *n* GEN COMM año anterior *m*

previously: **~-mentioned** *adj* COMMS antes citado

price¹: **~ sensitive** *adj* S&M sensible al precio

price² *n* (*pr.*) STOCK *security* precio *m*; **~ advantage** STOCK *Eurodollar market* ventaja de precio *f*; **~ after hours** STOCK precio fuera de horas *m*; **~ behavior** *AmE*, **~ behaviour** *BrE* STOCK *of options* comportamiento del precio *m*; **~ ceiling** ECON precio límite *m*; **~ change** STOCK *futures* cambio de precios *m*; **~ competitiveness** S&M competitividad de los precios *f*; **~ consumption curve** (*PCC*) ECON curva de gastos *f*; **~ control** ECON control de precios *m*; **~ cue** S&M indicación de precio *f*; **~ current** GEN COMM lista de precios *f*; **~ cut** ECON, S&M recorte de precios *m*; **~ cutting** ECON, S&M recorte de precios *m*; **~-cutting** GEN COMM, S&M reducción de precios *f*; **~-demand elasticity** S&M elasticidad precio-demanda *f*; **~ deregulation** GEN COMM desregulación de precios *f*; **~ deterioration** ECON, GEN COMM deteriorización de precios *f*; **~ determinant** S&M determinante de precio *m*; **~ determination** ECON, GEN COMM, S&M formación de precios *f*, determinación de precios *f*; **~ differential** ECON, GEN COMM diferencial de inflación *m*, diferencial de precios *m*, margen entre los precios *m*, S&M margen entre los precios *m*; **~ discrimination** GEN COMM, S&M discriminación de precios *f*; **~ earnings multiple** ACC múltiplo de capitalización de beneficios *m*; **~-earnings ratio** (*PER*) GEN COMM proporción precio-beneficio *f*, ratio precio-beneficio *m*; **~ effect** ECON efecto de los precios *m*; **~ elasticity of demand** ECON elasticidad-precio de la demanda *f*; **~ escalation** ECON, S&M subida gradual de los precios *f*; **~ escalation clause** GEN COMM cláusula sobre aumento de precio *f*; **~ expectations** *n pl* GEN COMM expectativas con respecto a los precios *f pl*; **~ ex-works** GEN COMM precio en fábrica *m*; **~ factor** STOCK factor precio *m*; **~ fixing** GEN COMM estabilización de precios *f*, manipulación de precios *f*, reglamentación de precios *f*; **~ flexibility** ECON flexibilidad de precios *f*; **~ floor** ECON precio mínimo *m*; **~ freeze** ECON, GEN COMM bloqueo de los precios *m*, congelación de precios *f*; **~ gap** STOCK desajuste de precios *m*; **~ haven** S&M paraíso de precios *m*; **~ incentive** ECON precio estimulante *m*; **~ increase** ECON, GEN COMM, S&M aumento del precio *m*, subida de precios *f*; **~ index** ACC, ECON, FIN índice de precios *m*; **~ index level** STOCK nivel del índice de precios *m*; **~ inelasticity** ECON inelasticidad de los precios *f*; **~ inflation** ECON inflación de precios *f*; **~ leader** ECON, S&M fijador de precios *m*; **~ level** ECON nivel de precios *m*; **~ level accounting** ACC contabilidad del nivel de precios *f*; **~ level changes** *n pl* GEN COMM cambios en niveles de precios *m pl*; **~ limit** STOCK límite de precio *m*; **~-lining** ECON, S&M diferentes precios de un mismo artículo *m pl*; **~ list** GEN COMM lista de precios *f*, tarifa de precios *f*; **~ loss** STOCK pérdida en el precio *f*; **~ maintenance** GEN COMM mantenimiento de los precios *m*; **~ maker** ECON el que establece el precio; **~ mechanism** ECON mecanismo de precios *m*; **~ move**

STOCK movimiento de precios *m*; ~ **offered** STOCK precio ofrecido *m*; ~ **on application** GEN COMM precio en aplicación *m*; ~ **on rail** TRANSP precio sobre vagón *m*; ~-**performance ratio** GEN COMM razón de comportamiento de los precios *m*; ~ **pressure** ECON presión de los precios *f*; ~ **protection** STOCK protección del precio *f*; ~ **quotation list** GEN COMM lista de precios efectivos *f*; ~ **range** ECON, S&M escala de precios *f*; ~ **rate** ECON tasa de precios *f*; ~ **regulation** ECON control de precios *m*, regulación de precios *f*, control de precios *m*; ~ **rigging** STOCK chanchullo *m*; ~ **rigidity** ECON rigidez de precios *f*; ~ **scanner** S&M lector óptico de precios *m*; ~-**sensitive information** ECON, S&M precio sensible a la información *m*; ~ **sensitivity** ECON, S&M sensibilidad al precio *f*; ~ **sewing** ECON, GEN COMM fluctuación de precios *f*; ~ **skimming** S&M fijación de precio alto para obtener prontos beneficios *f*; ~ **spread** STOCK dispersión de precios *f*; ~ **stability** ECON estabilidad de precios *f*; ~ **stabilization** ECON estabilización de precios *f*; ~ **sticker** GEN COMM, S&M etiqueta de precio *f*; ~ **structure** ECON, FIN, S&M estructura de precios *f*; ~ **supervision** ECON inspección de precios *f*; ~ **supervisor** ECON inspector(a) de precios *m,f*; ~ **support** FIN mantenimiento de los precios *m*; ~ **system** ECON sistema de precios *m*; ~ **tick** STOCK *currency market* variación mínima del precio *f*; ~ **trend** FIN tendencia del precio *f*; ~ **twist** ECON tirón de precios *m*; ~ **variance** GEN COMM variación del precio *f*; ~ **variation clause** S&M cláusula de variación de precios *f*; ~ **volatility of a share** STOCK volatilidad del precio de una acción *f*; ~ **war** GEN COMM guerra de precios *f*; ~-**weighted index** STOCK índice de precios ponderados *m*; ♦ **at a ~ of** GEN COMM a un precio de; **the ~ has weakened further** GEN COMM el precio se ha debilitado más; ~ **in the street** GEN COMM, STOCK precio de la calle

price[3] *vt* GEN COMM fijar un precio, poner precio a, fijar precios; ♦ ~ **oneself out of the market** S&M vender a un precio más elevado que el de mercado

Price: ~ **Commission** *n BrE* ECON comisión de política de precios; ~ **Reporting Terminal Operator** *n* (*PRTO*) STOCK operador terminal de comunicación de precios *m*

pricer *n* FIN el que pone los precios m

prices[1]: ~ **and incomes agreement** *n* HRM acuerdo de precios e ingresos *m*; ~ **and incomes policy** *n* ECON, POL política de precios y rentas *f*, política de rentas y control de precios *f*; ~ **policy** *n* ECON, GEN COMM, S&M política de precios *f*

prices[2]: ~ **can go down as well as up** *phr* GEN COMM los precios pueden tanto bajar como subir; ~ **have been marked down** *phr* STOCK los precios han sido ajustados a la baja

price/sale: ~ **for the account** *n* BANK precio/venta para la cuenta *m*

pricey *adj infrml* GEN COMM caro

pricing *n* GEN COMM cálculo de precios *m*, fijación de precios *f*; ~ **arrangement** GEN COMM acuerdo sobre fijación de precios *m*; ~ **down** S&M rebaja de precios *f*; ~ **mix** S&M combinación de estrategias de precios *f*; ~ **model** STOCK modelo de valoración *m*; ~ **plateau** S&M nivel medio de precio *m*, nivelado de precio *m*; ~ **policy** ECON, GEN COMM, S&M política de precios *f*; ~ **review** S&M revisión de precios *f*; ~ **strategy** S&M estrategia de precios *f*; ~ **tactic** S&M táctica de fijación de precios *f*; ~ **up** S&M fijación de precios más altos *f*

prima facie: ~ **evidence** *n* LAW prueba presunta *f*, pruebas que fundamentan una presunción *f pl*

primage *n* TAX, TRANSP *shipping* prima de carga *f*

primarily *adv* GEN COMM primeramente

primary[1] *adj* GEN COMM primario

primary[2]: ~ **action** *n* HRM acción inicial *f*; ~ **activities** *n pl* GEN COMM actividades primarias *f pl*, actividades principales *f pl*; ~ **capital** *n* ECON, FIN capital principal *m*; ~ **commodity** *n* GEN COMM bien de primera necesidad *m*, mercancía básica *f*; ~ **commodity price** *n* STOCK precio de productos básicos *m*; ~ **data** *n* GEN COMM, S&M datos primarios *m pl*; ~ **dealer** *n* ECON corredor(a) de mercado primario *m,f*; ~ **deficit** *n* ECON déficit principal *m*; ~ **distribution** *n* STOCK primera emisión *f*; ~ **earnings per share** *n* STOCK beneficios primarios por acción *m pl*; ~ **explosive** *n* TRANSP *dangerous goods* explosivo primario *m*; ~ **industry** *n* ECON, IND industria primaria *f*; ~ **instrument of indebtedness** *n* BANK instrumento primario de endeudamiento *m*; ~ **issue** *n* STOCK emisión primaria *f*; ~ **labor market** *AmE*, ~ **labour market** *BrE n* ECON mercado de trabajo primario *m*; ~ **market** *n jarg* ECON *of issues*, STOCK *futures* mercado de emisiones *m*, mercado primario *m*; ~ **market area** *n* STOCK área del mercado primario *f*; ~ **market dealer** *n* STOCK corredor(a) de acciones en el mercado de emisión *m,f*, intermediario(-a) en el mercado primario *m,f*; ~ **offering** *n* STOCK *new issue* oferta de emisión *f*, oferta primaria *f*; ~ **package** *n* GEN COMM envase primario *m*; ~ **ratio** *n* ECON proporción principal *f*; ~ **readership** *n* MEDIA, S&M número primario de lectores *m*; ~ **recovery** *n* TAX recuperación primaria *f*; ~ **reserve** *n* BANK reserva primaria *f*; ~ **resource** *n* ENVIR recurso primario *m*; ~ **sector** *n* ECON, IND sector primario *m*; ~ **standard** *n* ENVIR norma primaria *f*

prime *n AmE* (*cf prime rate BrE*) BANK principal *m*, intereses preferenciales *m pl*, tasa de interés preferencial *f*; ~ **bank** BANK banco de primera mano *m*; ~ **borrower** BANK prestatario(-a) de primera clase *m,f*; ~ **business loan rate** BANK, FIN tasa de préstamos comerciales preferenciales *f*; ~ **business rate** BANK tasa de empresa preferencial *f*; ~ **contract** LAW contrato principal *m*; ~ **contractor** GEN COMM contratista principal *mf*; ~ **cost** ACC, ECON, INS coste de producción *m* (*Esp*), costo de producción *m* (*AmL*); ~ **costs** *n pl* ACC costes básicos *m pl* (*Esp*), costos básicos *m pl* (*AmL*); ~ **entry** ACC entrada principal *f*, ingreso principal *m*, IMP/EXP entrada principal *f*; ~ **lending rate** BANK, FIN tasa de préstamo preferencial *f*, tipo preferencial para préstamos *m*; ~ **listening time** MEDIA *broadcast* tiempo de audiencia primaria *m*; ~ **location** PROP ubicación de primer orden *f*; ~ **paper** STOCK papel de primera línea *m*; ~ **position** S&M *in the market* posición de primera línea *f*; ~ **range audit** ACC auditoría de alcance primordial *f*, auditoría de largo alcance *f*; ~ **range file** TAX declaración preferente *f*; ~ **rate** BANK *BrE* (*cf prime AmE*) principal *m*, intereses preferenciales *m pl*, tasa de interés preferencial *f*; ~ **rate of interest** BANK tasa preferencial de interés *f*; ~-**rate loan** BANK, FIN préstamo a interés preferencial *m*; ~ **responsibility center** *AmE*, ~ **responsibility centre** *BrE* ACC centro de primera responsabilidad *m*, centro de responsabilidad directa *m*; ~ **site** PROP *retail property* emplazamiento de primer orden *m*; ~ **time** MEDIA *broadcast*, S&M horario selecto *m*, hora de máxima audiencia *f*; **~ unit** PROP unidad principal *f*; **~ viewing time** MEDIA, S&M *broadcast* horas de máxima audiencia *f pl*

Prime: **~ Minister** *n BrE* POL ≈ Presidente(-a) del Gobierno *m,f*

Prime-1 *n* BANK Prima-1 *f*

primitive: **~ economy** *n* ECON economía principal *f*

Prince: **~'s Youth Business Trust** *n BrE* GEN COMM fideicomiso del príncipe de Gales para empresas juveniles

principal *n* BANK capital de un préstamo *m*; **~ accounting system** ACC sistema de contabilidad principal *m*; **~ of accrual** ACC principal de la acumulación *m*; **~ asset** ACC activo principal *m*; **~ assets** *n pl* ACC activos de la explotación *m pl*; **~ business** GEN COMM negocio principal *m*; **~ business address** GEN COMM domicilio social *m*; **~ carrier** TRANSP transportista principal *mf*; **~ customer** GEN COMM cliente principal *mf*; **~ debtor** FIN, S&M deudor(a) principal *m,f*; **~ file** TAX *of taxpayer* declaración principal *f*; **~ place of business** GEN COMM domicilio social *m*; **~ residence** TAX residencia principal *f*; **~ shareholder** STOCK accionista principal *mf*; **~ stockholder** STOCK accionista principal *mf*; **~ sum** BANK, FIN principal *m*; **~ value** STOCK valor principal *m*; ◆ **on a ~-to-principal basis** STOCK *interbank money market* sobre una base de principal a principal

Principal: **~ Executive Committee** *n BrE* HRM Comisión Ejecutiva Principal *f*

principally *adv* GEN COMM fundamentalmente

principle *n* GEN COMM, MATH principio *m*; **~ of equalization** TAX principio de compensación *m*; **~ of voluntary compliance** TAX principio de cumplimiento voluntario *m*; ◆ **on ~** GEN COMM de principio

print[1]: **out of ~** *adj* (*o.p.*) MEDIA *print* agotado

print[2]: **~ bar** *n* COMP línea de linotipia *f*; **~ driver** *n* COMP unidad de impresión *f*; **~ line** *n* COMP línea de impresión *f*; **~ media** *n* MEDIA material impreso *m*; **~ out** *n* COMP salida impresa *f*; **~ preview** *n* COMP borrador de impresión *m*; **~ run** *n* MEDIA tirada *f*; **~ screen** *n* COMP impresión de pantalla *m*

print[3] *vt* COMP imprimir

print out *vt* ADMIN, COMP imprimir, sacar por impresora

printed[1]: **~ in bold type** *adj* MEDIA impreso en negrita

printed[2]: **~ form** *n* GEN COMM impreso *m*; **~ matter** *n* GEN COMM *postage*, MEDIA impresos *m pl*; **~ return** *n* TAX declaración impresa *f*

printer *n* COMP, GEN COMM *device* impresora *f*, *person* impresor(a) *m,f*; **~ port** COMP puerta de impresora *f*

printing *n* MEDIA tirada *f*, *in paper* impresión *f*; **~ press** MEDIA prensa de imprimir *f*; **~ speed** COMP velocidad de impresión *f*; **~ unit** GEN COMM unidad de impresión *f*; **~ work** MEDIA *print* trabajo de impresión *m*

printout *n* COMP, MEDIA *on paper* impresión *f*

prior[1]: **~ art** *n* PATENTS técnica anterior *f*; **~ charge** *n* ACC, BANK, FIN cargo previo *m*; **~ judicial authorization** *n* TAX autorización judicial previa *f*; **~-lien bond** *n* STOCK obligación con garantía preferente *f*, obligación con garantía privilegiada *f*; **~ period** *n* ACC ejercicio anterior *m*, periodo anterior *m*; **~ period adjustment** *n* ACC ajuste al ejercicio anterior *m*, ajuste por periodificación *m*; **~-preferred stock** *n* STOCK acciones preferidas a otras de igual clase *f pl*; **~ use** *n* PATENTS uso anterior *m*; **~ year adjustment** *n* ACC

ajuste del año anterior *m*, ajuste del ejercicio anterior *m*, ajuste por periodificación *m*

prior[2]: **~ to** *prep* GEN COMM previo a

priori[1]: **a ~ statement** *n* GEN COMM juicio a priori *m*

priori[2]: **a ~** *phr* GEN COMM a priori

prioritize *vt* GEN COMM, MGMNT *tasks* dar prioridad a, priorizar

priority[1] *adj* GEN COMM prioritario

priority[2] *n* GEN COMM, PATENTS prioridad *f*; **~ allocation** STOCK *of shares* adjudicación prioritaria *f*; **~ date** LAW, PATENTS *intellectual property* fecha prioritaria *f*, fecha de prioridad *f*; **~ mail** *AmE* (*cf priority post BrE*) COMMS correo de pronta expedición *m*; **~ payment instrument** BANK instrumento de pago prioritario *m*; **~ post** *BrE* (*cf priority mail AmE*) COMMS correo de pronta expedición *m*; **~ right** LAW, PATENTS, STOCK derecho de prioridad *m*; **~ share** FIN, HRM, STOCK acción de preferencia *f*; ◆ **take ~ over** GEN COMM preceder en prioridad a

prisoner: **~'s dilemma** *n* ECON *game theory* dilema del prisionero *m*

privacy: **~ law** *n* LAW ley de protección de la intimidad *f*

private[1] *adj* GEN COMM *proprietary* confidencial, privado; ◆ **by ~ contract** GEN COMM, LAW mediante acuerdo privado, según contrato privado

private[2]: **~ account** *n* ACC cuenta particular *f*; **~ agency** *n* GEN COMM agencia privada *f*; **~ arrangement** *n* GEN COMM acuerdo privado *m*, LAW contrato privado *m*; **~ attorney** *n* LAW apoderado(-a) *m,f*; **~ automatic branch exchange** *n BrE* (*PABX*) COMMS *telephone* centralita automática privada unida a la red pública *f*; **~ bank** *n* BANK banco privado *m*; **~ banking** *n* BANK banca privada *f*; **~ bonded warehouse** *n* IMP/EXP, TRANSP depósito aduanero privado *m*; **~ brand** *n* S&M marca privada *f*; **~ capital** *n* GEN COMM capital privado *m*; **~ carrier** *n* S&M transportista privado *mf*; **~ company** *n* GEN COMM compañía de un solo propietario *f*, empresa sin cotización en bolsa *f*, compañía privada *f*; **~ consumption** *n* ECON, GEN COMM consumo privado *m*; **~ contract** *n* GEN COMM, LAW escritura privada *f*; **~ contribution** *n* ECON *development assistance* contribución privada *f*; **~ cost** *n* ECON coste privado *m* (*Esp*), costo privado *m* (*AmL*); **~ enterprise** *n* ECON, GEN COMM empresa privada *f*; **~ enterprise system** *n* ECON sistema privado de empresa *m*; **~ foundation** *n* TAX fundación privada *f*; **~ fuel** *n BrE* TAX combustible de uso privado *m*; **~ good** *n* ECON bien privado *m*; **~ health fund** *n* HRM fondo de salud privado *m*; **~ health scheme** *n* HRM, WEL plan privado de seguro médico *m*; **~ health services plan** *n* INS, WEL plan de servicios médicos privados *m*; **~ hearing** *n* LAW vista a puerta cerrada *f*; **~ holding corporation** *n* STOCK empresa de titularidad privada *f*; **~ hospital treatment** *n* WEL tratamiento en hospital privado *m*; **~ household** *n* GEN COMM hogar privado *m*, vivienda privada *f*; **~ individual** *n* GEN COMM persona privada *f*; **~ institution** *n* GEN COMM, PROP institución privada *f*; **~ investment** *n* BANK, FIN inversión privada *f*; **~ investment client** *n* BANK, FIN cliente de inversión privado(-a) *m,f*; **~ investor** *n* STOCK inversor(a) privado(-a) *m,f*; **~ issue** *n* STOCK emisión privada *f*; **~ law** *n* LAW derecho privado *m*; **~ ledger** *n* ACC libro mayor privado *m*; **~ lender** *n* BANK, FIN prestamista privado(-a) *m,f*; **~ limited company** *n* GEN COMM ≈ sociedad limitada *f* (*S.L.*); **~ limited**

partnership n STOCK sociedad limitada sin cotización en bolsa f; **~ marginal benefit** n ECON beneficio marginal privado m; **~ means** n pl FIN fortuna personal f, rentas f pl; **~ mortgage insurance** n INS seguro privado sobre hipoteca m; **~ office** n HRM despacho privado m, oficina privada f; **~ patient** n WEL paciente privado(-a) m,f; **~ patients plan** n (PPP) WEL plan de pacientes privados m; **~ placement** n BANK colocación privada f; **~ placing** n FIN colocación privada f; **~ property** n LAW propiedad privada f; **~ purpose bond** n STOCK bono para fines privados m; **~ rate of discount** n BANK tasa privada de descuento f; **~ ruling** n TAX resolución privada f; **~ school** n GEN COMM colegio privado m, escuela privada f; **~ secretary** n ADMIN, HRM secretario(-a) particular m,f, secretario(-a) personal m,f; **~ sector** n ECON, IND sector privado m; **~ sector award** n HRM incentivo del sector privado m; **~ sector borrower** n BANK, FIN prestamista del sector privado mf; **~ sector company** n ECON, GEN COMM empresa del sector privado f, empresa privada f; **~ sector enterprise** n GEN COMM empresa del sector privado f; **~ sector investment** n ECON, FIN inversión del sector privado f; **~ sector liquidity** n (PSL) ECON liquidez del sector privado f; **~ siding** n BrE TRANSP apartadero particular m; **~ term** n (pt) GEN COMM término particular m; **~ treaty** n PROP documento privado m, tratado particular m; **~ tuition** n WEL clases particulares f pl

privatization n ECON, GEN COMM, POL privatización f; **~ proceeds** n pl ECON privatización de los resultados f; **~ program** AmE, **~ programme** BrE ECON, POL programa de privatización m

privatize vt ECON, GEN COMM, POL privatizar

privatized: ~ company n ECON compañía privatizada f

privilege n AmE STOCK contrato de opción m; **~ leave** HRM permiso privilegiado m

privileged adj GEN COMM privilegiado

privity n HRM, LAW relación contractual f

Privy: ~ Council n BrE GEN COMM, POL Consejo de la Corona m

prize n TAX premio m; **~ bond** FIN, STOCK bono de premio m, bono de recompensa m, bono de remuneración m

pro[1]: **~-communist** adj POL procomunista; **~ forma** adj ADMIN pro forma; **~ rata** adj GEN COMM, HRM a prorrata

pro[2]: **~ forma balance sheet** n ACC, BANK, GEN COMM balance proforma m; **~ forma invoice** n GEN COMM factura proforma f; **~ forma return** n TAX declaración proforma f; **~-rata freight** n TRANSP flete proporcional a la distancia m

PRO abbr (public relations officer) HRM, S&M funcionario(-a) de relaciones públicas m,f

proactive[1] adj GEN COMM, MGMNT proactivo, muy activo

proactive[2]: **~ strategy** n GEN COMM, MGMNT estrategia proactiva f

pro-American adj POL pro-americano

probability n MATH probabilidad f; **~ sample** MATH statistics muestra de probabilidad f; **~ theory** MATH, MGMNT teoría de la probabilidad f

probable[1] adj GEN COMM, MATH probable

probable[2]: **~ error** n MATH statistics error probable m

probate: ~ court n LAW tribunal de sucesiones m; **~ price** n STOCK precio de homologación m

probation: ~ period n GEN COMM, HRM periodo de prueba m

probationary: ~ employee n HRM empleado(-a) a prueba m,f; **~ period** n GEN COMM, HRM periodo de prueba m

problem n GEN COMM problema m; **~ analysis** HRM, MATH, MGMNT análisis del problema m; **~ area** GEN COMM región con problemas f; **~ assessment** GEN COMM, MGMNT valoración de un problema f, evaluación del problema f; **~ customer** GEN COMM cliente problema mf; **~ determination** COMP determinación del problema f; **~ loan** BANK, FIN problema de préstamo m; **~ solving** GEN COMM, MATH, MGMNT resolución del problema f, resolución de problemas f

PROBO abbr (product/oil/bulk/ore carrier) TRANSP shipping vehículo de transporte para minerales/graneles/petróleo/productos m

procedural[1] adj GEN COMM, LAW, MGMNT procesal

procedural[2]: **~ agreement** n HRM acuerdo de procedimiento m; **~ delays** n pl GEN COMM demoras de trámite f pl; **~ issue** n GEN COMM problema de procedimiento m

procedure: ~ agreement n HRM acuerdo de procedimiento m; **~ for the avoidance of disputes** n HRM procedimiento para evitar disputas m

proceeding n GEN COMM procedimiento m, LAW procedimiento m, diligencia f, procedimiento legal m, auto m

proceeds: ~ from resale n pl GEN COMM producto de la reventa m; **~ of a loan** n pl ACC, BANK importe de un préstamo m; **~ of sales** n pl GEN COMM producto de las ventas m

process[1] n COMP, GEN COMM, IND production proceso m; **~ analysis** GEN COMM análisis de procesos m; **~ chart** COMP diagrama de procedimientos m; **~ control** GEN COMM, IND control de procesos m; **~ costing** ACC, IND estimación del coste de proceso f (Esp), estimación del costo de proceso f (AmL), cálculo de costes de proceso m (Esp), cálculo de costos de proceso m (AmL), costeo de proceso m (AmL); **~ engineering** IND técnica de fabricación f; **~ equipment layout** IND distribución de equipo de disposición m, distribución de equipo de presentación f, distribución de equipo de procesado f; **~ industry** ECON, IND industria de procesado f; **~ stage** IND etapa del proceso f; **~ worker** HRM fotolitógrafo(-a) m,f; ◆ **be in ~** GEN COMM estar en proceso

process[2] vt COMP data procesar, GEN COMM tratar, IND goods for re-exportation procesar

processed: ~ food n GEN COMM, IND producto alimenticio elaborado m

processing n BANK of cheques procesamiento f, COMP elaboración f, PATENTS of application trámite m, TAX tramitación f, elaboración f; **~ fee** BANK gastos de procesamiento m pl; **~ industry** ECON, IND industria de transformación f; **~ plant** IND planta de procesado f; **~ profits** n pl ECON beneficios de fabricación m pl

processor n COMP equipment procesador m

procuration: ~ fee n FIN comisión de prestamista f

procurement n GEN COMM procuración f, S&M obtención f; **~ agent** GEN COMM agente de compras mf; **~ costs** n pl GEN COMM costes de abastecimiento m pl (Esp), costes de compras m pl (Esp), costes de proveeduría m pl (Esp), costos de abastecimiento m pl (AmL), costos de compras m pl (AmL), costos de proveeduría m pl (AmL); **~ department** GEN COMM departamento de compras m; **~ manager** HRM gerente de compras mf, jefe(-a) de compras *m,f*; ~ **officer** GEN COMM, HRM funcionario(-a) de compras *m,f*

procuring: ~ **cause** *n* LAW causa próxima *f*

produce[1] *n* ECON producto *m*; ~ **trade** S&M comercio de ultramarinos *m*

produce[2] *vt* GEN COMM producir, LEIS realizar

producer: ~ **advertising** *n* S&M publicidad del productor *f*; ~**'s brand** *n* S&M marca del productor *f*; ~ **buyer** *n* IND comprador(a) industrial *m,f*, comprador(a) productor(a) *m,f*; ~**'s goods** *n pl* ECON bienes de producción *m pl*; ~ **price** *n* ENVIR, S&M precio al productor *m*; ~ **price index** *n* (*PPI*) ECON índice de precios a la producción *m*; ~**'s profits** *n pl* LEIS beneficios del productor *m pl*; ~ **subsidy equivalent** *n* ECON subvención equivalente a la producción *f*; ~**'s surplus** *n* ECON superávit del productor *m*, IND excedente del productor *m*

product *n* GEN COMM producto *m*; ~ **acceptance** S&M aceptación del producto *f*; ~ **adaptation** GEN COMM adaptación del producto *f*; ~ **advertising** S&M publicidad del producto *f*; ~ **analysis** S&M análisis del producto *m*; ~ **awareness** S&M conocimiento del producto *m*; ~ **benefits** *n pl* S&M beneficios del producto *m pl*; ~ **classification** GEN COMM clasificación de productos *f*; ~ **compatibility** ECON compatibilidad de productos *f*; ~ **conception** S&M concepción del producto *f*; ~ **cost** S&M coste del producto *m* (*Esp*), costo del producto *m* (*AmL*); ~ **costing** ACC cálculo de costes del producto *m* (*Esp*), cálculo de costos del producto *m* (*AmL*), S&M *price setting* fijación del precio *f*; ~ **creation** S&M creación de producto *f*; ~ **cycle** ECON, IND ciclo del producto *m*; ~ **design** S&M diseño de producto *m*; ~ **development** IND, S&M desarrollo del producto *m*; ~ **development cycle** S&M ciclo de desarrollo del producto *m*; ~ **diversification** S&M diversificación de productos *f*; ~ **dynamics** *n pl* S&M dinámica de producto *f*; ~ **engineer** COMP, HRM, IND ingeniero(-a) de producto *m,f*; ~ **engineering** IND, S&M ingeniería de producto *f*; ~ **evaluation** S&M evaluación del producto *f*; ~ **family** IND, S&M familia de productos *f*; ~ **form** TRANSP formulario de producto *m*; ~ **generation** S&M generación de producto *f*; ~ **group** S&M grupo de productos *m*; ~ **image** S&M imagen del producto *f*; ~ **improvement** S&M mejora del producto *f*; ~ **initiation** S&M iniciación del producto *f*; ~ **introduction** S&M introducción del producto *f*; ~ **knowledge** S&M conocimiento del producto *m*; ~ **launch** S&M lanzamiento del producto *m*; ~ **liability** GEN COMM responsabilidad legal del producto *f*; ~ **life** S&M vida de un producto *f*; ~ **life cycle** S&M ciclo de vida de un producto *m*; ~ **life expectancy** S&M esperanza de vida del producto *f*; ~ **line** IND abanico *m*, S&M línea del producto *f*, abanico *m*; ~ **management** MGMNT, S&M dirección del producto *f*, gerencia del producto *f*; ~ **manager** HRM jefe(-a) del producto *m,f*; ~ **marketing** S&M marketing del producto *m*; ~ **mix** S&M combinación de estrategias de productos *f*, mezcla de estrategias de productos *f*; ~ **moment formula** MATH *statistics* fórmula del momento producto *f*; ~ **organization** MGMNT, S&M organización del producto *f*; ~ **performance** S&M rendimiento del producto *m*; ~ **planning** S&M planificación de los productos *f*; ~**-plus** S&M plus del producto *m*; ~ **portfolio** FIN, S&M, STOCK cartera de productos *f*; ~ **positioning** S&M posicionamiento del producto *m*;

~ **possibility curve** ECON, IND curva de posibilidades de producción *f*; ~ **profile** GEN COMM, S&M perfil del producto *m*; ~ **profitability** ACC, FIN, S&M rentabilidad del producto *f*; ~ **quality differentiation** S&M diferenciación de la calidad del producto *f*; ~ **range** GEN COMM, S&M gama de productos *f*; ~ **reliability** S&M fiabilidad del producto *f*; ~ **research** S&M investigación del producto *f*; ~ **research and development** IND *production* investigación y desarrollo del producto *f*; ~ **standard** LAW norma de fabricación *f*, S&M norma de producto *f*; ~ **strategy** GEN COMM, S&M estrategia de producto *f*; ~ **testing** S&M prueba del producto *f*; ◆ **this ~ is overpriced** GEN COMM este producto tiene un precio demasiado alto

Product: ~ **Co-operation Unit** *n* (*PCU*) IMP/EXP Unidad de Cooperación de Productos *f*

production *n* GEN COMM producción *f*, LEIS realización *f*; ~ **asymmetry** ECON asimetría de la producción *f*; ~ **bonus** IND prima de producción *f*; ~ **brigade** *jarg* ECON *socialist countries* brigada de producción *f*; ~ **capacity** IND, INS capacidad de producción *f*; ~ **coefficient** GEN COMM coeficiente de producción *m*; ~ **complex** IND complejo productivo *m*; ~ **control** IND control de producción *m*; ~ **cost** ACC, ECON, IND coste de producción *m* (*Esp*), costo de producción *m* (*AmL*); ~ **cut** FIN, IND disminución de la producción *f*, disminución en las cuotas de producción *f*; ~ **department** IND departamento de producción *m*; ~ **director** GEN COMM, HRM, IND, MGMNT director(a) de producción *m,f*; ~ **ecology** ENVIR ecología de la producción *f*; ~ **engineering** IND, MGMNT ingeniería de producción *f*; ~ **function** ECON función de producción *f*; ~ **goods** *n pl* ACC, PROP bienes de producción *m pl*; ~ **implement** GEN COMM herramienta de producción *f*, implemento de producción *m*; ~ **incentive** HRM incentivo a la producción *m*; ~ **line** GEN COMM cadena de producción *f*; ~ **loan** BANK, IND préstamo industrial *m*; ~ **management** IND administración de la producción *f*, gestión de la producción *f*; ~ **manager** GEN COMM, HRM, IND director(a) de producción *m,f*, gerente de fabricación *mf*, gerente de producción *mf*; ~ **manageress** GEN COMM, HRM, IND directora de producción *f* gerente de fabricación *f*, gerente de producción *f*; ~ **planning** GEN COMM, IND, MGMNT *production* planificación de la producción *f*; ~ **planning and control** GEN COMM planificación y control de producción *f*; ~ **possibility frontier** (*PPF*) ECON frontera de posibilidades de producción *f*; ~ **process** IND proceso de producción *m*; ~ **rate** STOCK índice de producción *m*; ~ **revenue** TAX ingresos por producción *m pl*; ~ **revenue tax** TAX impuesto sobre la producción *f*; ~ **run** IND corrida de producción *f* (*AmL*), fase de ejecución *f*; ~ **schedule** IND, MGMNT programa de producción *m*; ~ **scheduling** IND, MGMNT programación de la producción *f*; ~ **standard** GEN COMM, IND norma de producción *f*; ~ **surplus** IND excedente de producción *m*; ~ **technique** IND técnica de producción *f*; ~ **volume** IND volumen de producción *m*; ~ **worker** HRM, IND obrero(-a) manual *m,f*

productive[1] *adj* HRM, MGMNT *workforce* productivo

productive[2]: ~ **capital** *n* ECON capital productivo *m*; ~ **labor** *AmE*, ~ **labour** *BrE* *n* HRM mano de obra productiva *f*, *tasks* trabajo productivo *m*; ~ **maintenance** *n* IND mantenimiento productivo *m*;

~ potential *n* ECON *natural rate of growth* potencial productivo *m*

productivity *n* GEN COMM productividad *f*; **~ agreement** GEN COMM acuerdo de productividad *m*; **~ bargaining** ECON acuerdo de productividad *m*, HRM, IND, LAW acuerdo de productividad *m*, negociación sobre la productividad *f*; **~ campaign** IND, S&M campaña de productividad *f*; **~ drive** IND, S&M campaña de productividad *f*; **~ gains** *n pl* GEN COMM beneficios de productividad *m pl*; **~ measurement** IND medición de la productividad; **~ shock** ECON choque de productividad *m*

product/oil/bulk/ore: **~ carrier** *n* (*PROBO*) TRANSP *shipping* vehículo de transporte para minerales/graneles/petróleo/productos *m*

products: **~ and completed operations insurance** *n* INS seguro sobre productos y operaciones terminadas *m*

profession *n* HRM *job* oficio *m*

professional[1] *adj* GEN COMM, HRM profesional

professional[2] *n* GEN COMM, LEIS *sport* profesional *mf*; **~ achievement** GEN COMM *on CV* logro profesional *m*; **~ body** GEN COMM organismo profesional *m*; **~ ethics** *n pl* GEN COMM ética profesional *f*; **~ fees** *n pl* GEN COMM honorarios profesionales *m pl*; **~ income** ACC, TAX ingresos profesionales *m pl*; **~ liability** LAW responsabilidad profesional *f*; **~ qualifications** *n pl* HRM cualificaciones profesionales *f pl*; **~ secret** GEN COMM secreto profesional de los funcionarios *m*; **~ service** GEN COMM servicio profesional *m*; **~ speculator** STOCK especulador(a) profesional *m,f*; **~ status** HRM categoría profesional *f*; **~ trader** ECON comercial profesional *mf*

professionalism *n* GEN COMM profesionalismo *m*

professionalization *n* GEN COMM profesionalización *f*

professor *n* GEN COMM catedrático(-a) *m,f*

profile *n* GEN COMM, TRANSP *shipping* perfil *m*; **~ risk** FIN riesgo de perfil *m*

profit[1]: **~-making** *adj* GEN COMM con ánimo de lucro

profit[2] *n* GEN COMM beneficio *m*, ganancia *f*, lucro *m*; **~ before taxes** ACC, TAX beneficio antes de impuestos *m*; **~ breakdown** ACC distribución de los beneficios *f*; **~ carried forward** ACC beneficio a cuenta nueva *m*; **~ ceiling** ECON beneficio máximo *m*; **~ center** *AmE see profit centre BrE*; **~ center accounting** *AmE see profit centre accounting BrE*; **~ centre** *BrE* ECON, FIN, MGMNT beneficio central *m* centro de beneficios *m*; **~ centre accounting** *BrE* ACC, FIN contabilidad de un centro de beneficio *f*, contabilidad del beneficio obtenido por un departamento *f*; **~-factor analysis** FIN, GEN COMM análisis del factor de beneficio *m* análisis de factores de las utilidades *m*; **~ for the financial year** ACC beneficio del ejercicio *m*; **~ for the year after tax** BANK, ACC beneficio anual después de impuestos *m* (*BDI, BDT*), beneficio del ejercicio después de impuestos *m* (*BDI, BDT*); **~ goal** ACC, FIN meta de beneficios *f*; **~ graph** FIN gráfica de utilidad *f*; **~ impact** GEN COMM, FIN impacto del beneficio *m*, impacto en las utilidades *m*; **~ implication** FIN, GEN COMM implicación del beneficio *f*, implicación de las utilidades *f*; **~ improvement** FIN, GEN COMM mejora de beneficios *f*, aumento en las utilidades *m*; **~ and loss** *n pl* (*P&L*) ACC, FIN pérdidas y ganancias *f pl*; **~ and loss account** (*P&L account*) ACC cuenta de pérdidas y ganancias *f*, cuenta de resultados *f*; **~ and loss statement** (*P&L statement*) ACC cuenta de pérdidas y ganancias *f*, cuenta

de resultados *f*, estado de pérdidas y ganancias *m*; **~-making enterprise** GEN COMM empresa rentable *f*; **~ margin** GEN COMM margen de beneficio *m*, S&M margen de ganancia *m*; **~ maximization** GEN COMM, optimización de las ganancias *f*, maximización de beneficios *f*; **~ motive** GEN COMM motivo de ganancias *m*; **~ optimization** GEN COMM optimización de beneficios *f*; **~ outlook** ECON expectativa de beneficio *f*, GEN COMM perspectivas de beneficio *f pl*; **~ performance** FIN resultado de beneficios *m*, GEN COMM beneficios obtenidos *m pl*; **~ and performance planning** (*PPP*) FIN, MGMNT plan de beneficios y rendimientos *m*; **~ planning** FIN, GEN COMM, MGMNT planificación de utilidad *f*, planificación de beneficios *f*; **~ potential** STOCK potencial de beneficio *m*; **~ price benefit** ECON espiral de precios-beneficios *m*; **~ profile** STOCK *straddle* configuración del beneficio *f*; **~ projection** GEN COMM proyección de beneficios *f*; **~-related pay** (*PRP*) HRM remuneración vinculada a los beneficios *f*; **~ sensitivity analysis** ACC *project assessment* análisis de sensibilidad del beneficio *m*; **~ sharing** FIN, GEN COMM reparto de ganancias *m*, participación en las ganancias *f*, participación en los beneficios *f*, participación en las ganancias *f*, reparto de ganancias *m*, HRM, MGMNT participación de los trabajadores en los beneficios *f* (*PTU*); **~-sharing bond** FIN, STOCK bono con reparto de beneficios *m*; **~-sharing plan** GEN COMM plan de participación en beneficios *m*; **~-sharing scheme** GEN COMM *employee benefits* plan de participación en los beneficios *m*; **~ splitting** MGMNT determinación de los beneficios *f*; **~ squeeze** ECON reducción de las ganancias *f*, reducción de márgenes en los beneficios *f*; **~ strategy** FIN, GEN COMM estrategia de beneficios *f*; **~ taking** ECON realización de beneficios *f*, FIN retirada de dividendos *f*; **~-taking strategy** MGMNT estrategia de realización de beneficios *f*; **~ target** ACC, BANK, FIN objetivo de beneficios *m*; **~ test** ACC análisis de beneficios *m*, comprobación de beneficios *f*; **~-volume ratio** (*P/V*) FIN coeficiente de volumen de beneficios *m*, porcentaje del volumen de beneficios *m*, proporción beneficio-volumen *f*, relación del volumen de beneficios *f*; ◆ **at a ~ of** ACC con beneficio de

profitability *n* GEN COMM rentabilidad *f*; **~ analysis** ACC, FIN análisis de la rentabilidad *m*; **~ ratio** ACC, FIN proporción de rentabilidad *f*, relación de rentabilidad *f*; **~ requirement** FIN exigencia de rentabilidad *m*

profitable[1] *adj* GEN COMM lucrativo, productivo, provechoso, rentable

profitable[2]: **~ firm** *n* ACC empresa rentable *f*

profiteer *n* GEN COMM acaparador(a) *m,f*

profits[1]: **~ insurance** *n* INS seguro de utilidades *m*; **~ tax** *n* ACC, TAX impuesto sobre beneficios *m*

profits[2]: **~ surpassed forecasts in the first quarter** *phr* FIN los beneficios superaron las previsiones en el primer trimestre

program[1] *n* COMP programa *m*, GEN COMM *see programme BrE*; **~ analyst** COMP analista de programas *mf*; **~ bug** COMP error del programa *m*; **~ file** COMP archivo de programa *m*, fichero de programa *m*; **~ flow** COMP desarrollo del programa *m*; **~ language** COMP lenguaje de programación *m*; **~ library** COMP biblioteca de programas *f*; **~ package** COMP, FIN, MGMNT conjunto de programas *m*, paquete de programas *m*; **~ testing** COMP prueba del programa *f*; **~ trading** COMP contratación automática por ordenador *f* (*Esp*), contratación automática por computador *f* (*AmL*), contratación automática por computadora *f* (*AmL*),

program[2] *vt* COMP programar

Program: **~ for Provision of Operational Assistance** *AmE see* Programme for Provision of Operational Assistance *BrE*

programmable: **~ function** *n* COMP función programable *f*

programme *n* BrE ECON *m*, GEN COMM plan *m*, programa *m*; **~ adjustment loan** *BrE* (*PAL*) BANK, ECON préstamo de ajuste de programa *m*; **~ budgeting** *BrE* ACC, FIN elaboración de presupuestos por programa *f*, presupuestación de programas *f*; **~ deal** *BrE* ECON contratación automática *f*, programa comercial *m*; **~ evaluation plan** *BrE* GEN COMM plan de evaluación del programa *m*; **~ evaluation and review technique** *BrE* (*PERT*) MGMNT técnica de evaluación y revisión del programa *f*; **~ forecast** *BrE* GEN COMM predicción de programa *f*, previsión del programa *f*; **~ structure** *BrE* GEN COMM estructura del programa *f*; **~ trade** *BrE* GEN COMM intercambio de programa *m*, operación programada *f*

Programme: **~ for Provision of Operational Assistance** *n BrE* BANK *development* programa para la provisión de asistencia operativa

programmed *adj* COMP programado; **~ instruction** *n* GEN COMM instrucción programada *f*; **~ learning** *n* WEL aprendizaje programado *m*; **~ management** *n* MGMNT administración programada *f*, dirección programada *f*, gestión programada *f*

programming *n* COMP, GEN COMM programación *f*; **~ aid** COMP, GEN COMM ayuda a la programación *f*

progress *n* GEN COMM progreso *m*; **~ control** GEN COMM, IND, MGMNT control de avance, *m*, control de progreso *m*; **~ obsolescence** S&M obsolescencia progresiva *f*; **~ payment** BANK, FIN pago escalonado *m*; **~ report** GEN COMM informe sobre la labor realizada *m* (*Esp*), reporte sobre la labor realizada *m* (*AmL*)

progressive: **~ aliquot part** *n* MATH parte alícuota progresiva *f*; **~ part** *n* MATH parte alícuota *f*; **~ income tax system** *n* TAX sistema progresivo de impuesto sobre la renta *m*; **~ rates** *n pl* MATH alícuotas progresivas *f pl*; **~ scale** *n* TAX escala progresiva *f*; **~ tax** *n* TAX impuesto progresivo *m*; **~ tax system** *n* TAX sistema progresivo de tributación *m*

progressively *adv* GEN COMM progresivamente

prohibit *vt* COMP, LAW prohibir

prohibited: **~ goods** *n pl* GEN COMM mercancías prohibidas *f pl*

prohibition *n* GEN COMM, LAW prohibición *f*; **~ notice** HRM *health and safety* apercibimiento de prohibición *m*, notificación de prohibición *f*; **~ right** LAW, PATENTS derecho de prohibición *m*

project *n* GEN COMM proyecto *m*; **~ agent** HRM agente de proyecto *mf*; **~ aid** ECON ayuda al proyecto *f*; **~ analysis** ACC análisis de inversiones *m*, FIN, HRM, MGMNT análisis de proyectos *m*; **~ appraisal** ECON evaluación de proyectos *f*; **~ approval** GEN COMM aprobación del proyecto *f*; **~ assessment** GEN COMM avalúo del proyecto *m* (*AmL*), evaluación del proyecto *f*, valoración de proyecto *f* (*Esp*); **~ design** IND diseño de proyecto *m*; **~ engineer** GEN COMM, HRM ingeniero(-a) de proyectos *m,f*; **~ finance** FIN financiación de un proyecto *f*; **~ financing** FIN financiación de un

proyecto *f*; **~ forwarding** TRANSP avance de proyecto *m*; **~ leader** GEN COMM director(a) de proyecto *m,f*, jefe(-a) de proyecto *m,f*; **~ link** ECON modelo econométrico de vinculación y proyección *m*; **~ management** FIN, HRM, MGMNT administración de proyectos *f*, dirección de proyectos *f*, gestión de proyectos *f*; **~ manager** GEN COMM, HRM director(a) de proyecto *m,f*, jefe(-a) de proyecto *m,f*; **~ note** STOCK pagaré para financiar un proyecto *m*; **~ participants' insolvency cover** INS cobertura por insolvencia de participantes en el proyecto *f*; **~ planning** FIN, MGMNT organización de un proyecto *f*, planificación de un proyecto *f*; **~ sponsor** FIN patrocinador(a) de un proyecto *m,f*; **~ preparation facility** (*PPF*) FIN servicio de preparación de proyectos *m* (*SPP*); **~ study** GEN COMM estudio de un proyecto *m*

projected: **~ balance sheet** *n* ACC balance general previsto *m*; **~ benefit application** *n* HRM aplicación prevista de un beneficio *f*

projectile *n* TRANSP *dangerous classified cargo* proyectil *m*

projection *n* GEN COMM, MATH proyección *f*

projective: **~ test** *n* S&M prueba de proyección *f*

projects: **~ business** *n* ECON empresa de proyectos *f*

proletarian: **~ internationalism** *n* ECON, POL internacionalismo proletario *m*

proletarianization *n* ECON, POL proletarización *f*

proletariat *n* ECON, POL proletariado *m*

prolong *vt* GEN COMM prolongado

prolonged *adj* GEN COMM prolongado

prominent *adj* GEN COMM, S&M prominente

promise[1] *n* GEN COMM promesa *f*; **~ to pay** GEN COMM promesa de pago; **~ to sell** S&M promesa de vender

promise[2] *vt* GEN COMM prometer

promissory: **~ note** *n* BANK, FIN (*P/N, PN*) pagaré *m*

promo *abbr jarg* (*promotion*) GEN COMM, S&M *of product, service* promoción *f*

promotary: **~ company** *n AmE* FIN compañía promotora *f*

promote *vt* GEN COMM *encourage* fomentar, promover, *articles, goods* promocionar, HRM *employee* ascender, promover, S&M *articles, goods* promocionar; ◆ **~ efficiency** GEN COMM promover la eficiencia

promoted: **be ~** *phr* HRM ser ascendido

promoter *n* GEN COMM *of plans* promotor(a) *m,f*, TAX empresario(-a) *m,f*, fundador(a) *m,f*, promotor(a) *m,f*

promotion *n* (*promo*) GEN COMM, S&M promoción *f*, HRM *personnel* ascenso *m*; **~ cost** ACC, S&M costes de promoción *m pl* (*Esp*), costos de promoción *m pl* (*AmL*); **~ ladder** HRM escala de promoción *f*; **~ mix** S&M *advertising* combinación de estrategias de promoción *f*

promotional[1] *adj* GEN COMM, S&M promocional

promotional[2]: **~ allowance** *n* S&M *advertising* descuento promocional *m*; **~ budget** *n* S&M *advertising* presupuesto promocional *m*; **~ exercise** *n* S&M campaña promocional *f*; **~ mix** *n* S&M *advertising* combinación de estrategias promocionales *f*; **~ phase** *n* S&M fase de promoción *f*; **~ platform** *n* S&M plataforma promocional *f*; **~ policy** *n* GEN COMM, S&M política de promoción *f*

prompt[1] *adj* (*ppt*) GEN COMM pronto, TRANSP *loading* listo **prompt**[2] *n* COMP indicación *f*, GEN COMM incitación *f*; **~ note** FIN aviso inmediato *m*; **~ payment** ACC, FIN pago puntual *m*; ~ **payment of invoices** FIN pronto pago de las facturas *m*

prompt[3] *vt* GEN COMM *give rise to* incitar

pronounce: ~ **a judicial decree** *phr* LAW dictar un auto; ~ **an order** *phr* GEN COMM dictar un auto

proof *n* LAW, MEDIA *printing, photography* prueba *f*; ~ **of debt** (*POD*) FIN comprobante de deuda *m*; ~ **of delivery** (*POD*) TRANSP prueba de entrega *f*; ~ **of loss** INS prueba del siniestro *f*; ~ **of ownership** STOCK *of registered shares* prueba de pertenencia *f*; ~ **of posting** ACC comprobante de asientos contables *m*; ~ **of title** LAW prueba de propiedad *f*, PROP justificación de título *f*; ◆ **at** ~ **stage** MEDIA *before printing* en fase de pruebas

proofread *vt* MEDIA corregir pruebas de

proofreader *n* MEDIA corrector(a) de pruebas *m,f*

proofs *n pl* MEDIA *print* capillas *f pl*, hojas de prueba *f pl*

prop up *vt* ECON *the pound* entibar

propensity *n* GEN COMM propensión *f*; ~ **to consume** ECON propensión a consumir *f*; ~ **to invest** ECON, FIN propensión a invertir *f*; ~ **to save** ECON, FIN propensión a ahorrar *f*; ~ **to work** ECON propensión al trabajo *f*

propertied: ~ **class** *n* PROP los propietarios *m pl*

property *n* PROP propiedad *f*, *land* finca *f*, S&M *advertising* producto de gran aceptación *m*; ~ **acquired** PROP propiedad adquirida *f*; ~ **bond** FIN, PROP bono de propiedad *m*; ~ **capital** GEN COMM capital constituido por valores mobiliarios *m*; ~ **and casualty policy insuring agreement** INS convenio asegurador de daños a terceros *m*; ~ **company** GEN COMM, PROP sociedad inmobiliaria *f*; ~ **damage** INS, PROP daño material *m*; ~ **depreciation insurance** INS seguro sobre depreciación de una propiedad *m*; ~ **developer** GEN COMM, PROP promotor(a) inmobiliario(a) *m,f*; ~ **development** PROP ampliación de la propiedad *f*; ~ **development project** PROP proyecto de explotación de la propiedad *m*; ~ **held in joint names** LAW, PROP propiedad mancomunada *f*; ~ **income** PROP, TAX renta de la propiedad *f*; ~ **insurer** INS asegurador(a) de bienes *m,f*; ~ **insuring company** INS aseguradora de bienes *f*; ~ **line** PROP límite *m*, límite de propiedad *m*, linde *f*; ~ **management** PROP gestión inmobiliaria *f*; ~ **market** PROP, S&M mercado de propiedades *m*; ~ **owner** PROP propietario(-a), GEN COMM derechos de la propiedad *m pl*; ~ **speculator** PROP, S&M especulador(a) inmobiliario(-a) *m,f*; ~ **tax** TAX contribución territorial *f*; ~ **tax allowance** PROP, TAX desgravación fiscal de la propiedad *f*; ~ **tax credit** TAX desgravación fiscal de la propiedad *f*

proportion *n* GEN COMM proporción *f*; ◆ **in** ~ **to** MATH en proporción a; **as a** ~ **of** GEN COMM como proporción de

proportional: ~ **consolidation** *n* ACC consolidación proporcional *f*; ~ **income tax** *n* TAX impuesto proporcional sobre la renta *m*; ~ **rate** *n* TRANSP tarifa proporcional *f*; ~ **representation** *n* POL representación proporcional *f*; ~ **tax** *n* TAX impuesto de tipo fijo *m*, impuesto proporcional *m*

proportionality *n* GEN COMM proporcionalidad *f*

proportionate[1] *adj* GEN COMM adecuado, proporcionado

proportionate[2]: ~ **grant** *n* ECON subvención proporcionada *f*

proportionately *adv* GEN COMM proporcionalmente

proportions *n* GEN COMM proprciones *f pl*

proposal *n* GEN COMM propuesta *f*; **our** ~ **still stands** *phr* GEN COMM nuestra proposición sigue en pie

propose *vt* GEN COMM *motion* proponer

proposed *adj* GEN COMM propuesto

proposer *n* GEN COMM proponente *mf*

proposition *n* GEN COMM proposición *f*

proprietary[1] *adj* GEN COMM patrimonial

proprietary[2]: ~ **brand** *n* GEN COMM marca exclusiva *f*; ~ **company** *n* FIN, GEN COMM compañía de un solo propietario, empresa sin cotización en bolsa *f*, sociedad tenedora *f*; ~ **drug** *n pl* GEN COMM medicamento de marca registrada *m*; ~ **goods** *n pl* GEN COMM productos exclusivos *m pl*; ~ **insurance** *n* INS seguro patrimonial *m*; ~ **rights** *n pl* GEN COMM derechos de la propiedad *m pl*

proprietor *n* GEN COMM *of business*, HRM, LAW, PATENTS propietario(-a) *m,f*

proprietorship *n* GEN COMM *sole ownership* empresa de un solo propietario *f*, LAW, PROP derecho de propiedad *m*

propulsion: ~ **assistance** *n* TRANSP *shipping* ayuda a la propulsión *f*

prorate *n* GEN COMM, HRM prorrata *f*

proration *n* TRANSP prorrateo *m*; ~ **mileage** TRANSP recorrido prorrateado *m*; ~ **rate** TRANSP tasa prorrateada *f*

pros: ~ **and cons** *phr* GEN COMM pros y contras

prosecute *vt* LAW procesar, PATENTS *application* proseguir; ◆ ~ **sb for forgery** LAW procesar a alguien por falsificación

prosecution *n* LAW *act* acusación *f*, *case* proceso *m*, juicio *m*

prospect *n* GEN COMM perspectiva *f*, *potential buyer* cliente potencial *m*, *something preseen* expectativa *f*

prospecting *n* GEN COMM prospección *f*, prospectiva *f*

prospective[1] *adj* S&M *customer* anticipado, probable

prospective[2]: ~ **buyer** *n* S&M posible comprador(a) *m,f*; ~ **customer** *n* GEN COMM, S&M cliente futuro(-a) *m,f*, posible cliente(-a) *m,f*; ~ **rating** *n* INS fijación de precios prospectiva *f*, tarifación prospectiva *f*

prospector *n* GEN COMM explorador(a) *m,f*

prospectus *n* FIN folleto explicativo de una emisión *m*, GEN COMM prospecto *m*, STOCK folleto explicativo de una emisión *m*

prosperity *n* GEN COMM prosperidad *f*; ~ **indicator** ECON, POL indicador de prosperidad *m*

prosperous *adj* ECON próspero

protean: ~ **economy** *n* ECON economía variable *f*

protect *vt* ECON, ENVIR proteger, GEN COMM *national interests* tutelar; ◆ ~ **the interests of** GEN COMM *country, consumers* proteger los intereses de; ~ **oneself** GEN COMM protegerse

protected: ~ **by tariffs** *adj* TAX arancelario

protection *n* GEN COMM amparo *m*, protección *f*; ~ **and indemnity** (*P&I*) TRANSP protección e indemnización *f*; ~ **and indemnity club** TRANSP asociación para la protección e indemnización *f*

Protection: ~ **and Indemnity Association** *n* INS *marine* Asociación de Protección e Indemnización *f*; ~ **& Oil Pollution Indemnity Clause** *n* (*PIOPIC*) ENVIR cláusula de indemnización por contaminación petrolera

protectionism *n* ECON proteccionismo *m*

protectionist *n* ECON proteccionista *mf*

protective: ~ **award** *n* HRM fallo preventivo *m*;

~ covenant *n* FIN pacto de protección *m*; **~ duties** *n pl* TAX derechos proteccionistas *m pl*; **~ location** *n* (*PL*) TRANSP *oil tanker* posición de protección *f*; **~ safety screen** *n* GEN COMM pantalla protectora de seguridad *f*; **~ tariff** *n* ECON, IMP/EXP, TAX arancel proteccionista *m*

protest: **~ charges** *n pl* LAW gastos de protesto *m pl*; **~ strike** *n* HRM huelga de protesta *f*; **~ vote** *n* POL voto de protesta *m*

protocol *n* COMP, GEN COMM protocolo *m*

protoindustrialization *n* HRM protoindustrialización *f*

protoproletariat *n* ECON protoproletariado *m*

prototype *n* GEN COMM, S&M prototipo *m*

prove *vt* ACC *debt* justificar, GEN COMM probar, hacer público; ◆ **~ sb's identity** LAW verificar la identidad de alguien; **~ right** GEN COMM resultar acertado; **~ wrong** GEN COMM resultar equivocado

proven: **~ track record** *n* HRM historial probado *m*

provide *vt* BANK otorgar, FIN *funds* proveer, GEN COMM proveer, *assistance* proporcionar; ◆ **~ the base for** BANK estipular las bases para; **~ capital** BANK, GEN COMM aportar capital, aportar fondos; **~ a market for** STOCK *trading shares* proporcionar un mercado para

provide against *vt* GEN COMM proveer contra; ◆ **~ a risk** INS reservar contra un riesgo

provided: **not ~ for** *phr* BANK no condicionado para; **not specially ~ for** *phr* (*nspf*) GEN COMM no específicamente dispuesto; **~ that** *phr* GEN COMM en el entendido de que, siempre y cuando

provident: **~ fund** *n* FIN fondo de previsión *m*

provider *n* ECON proveedor(a) *m,f*

province *n* *BrE* GEN COMM, POL unidad administrativa equivalente a una provincia, ≈ Comunidad Autónoma *f* (*Esp*) (*CA*), provincia *f*, región *f*

provincial[1] *adj* GEN COMM provincial

provincial[2]: **~ Crown corporation** *n* ECON empresa pública provincial *f*; **~ press** *n* MEDIA, S&M prensa de provincia *f*

provision *n* GEN COMM provisión *f*, LAW *of act* disposición *f*, provisión *f*, TAX provisión *f*; **~ account** ACC cuenta de provisión *f*; **~ for bad debts** ACC, BANK, FIN provisión para pérdidas *f*; **~ for contingency** ACC, BANK, TAX provisión para riesgos y gastos *f*; **~ for loan loss** BANK provisión para pérdidas de préstamos *f*; **~ of services** GEN COMM prestación de servicios *f*

provisions: **~ allocation** *n pl* ACC dotación para provisiones *f*, GEN COMM asignación para provisiones *f*;

provisional[1] *adj* GEN COMM interino, provisional

provisional[2]: **~ acceptance** *n* GEN COMM aceptación provisional *f*; **~ account** *n* BANK, ACC, FIN cuenta provisional *f*; **~ collection of taxes** *n* TAX recaudación provisional de impuestos *f*; **~ invoice** *n* GEN COMM factura provisional *f*; **~ policy** *n* INS póliza provisional *f*; **~ protection** *n* PATENTS protección provisional *f*

provisionally *adv* GEN COMM provisionalmente

prox. *abbr* (*proximo*) GEN COMM pmo. (*próximo*)

proximo *adv* (*prox.*) GEN COMM próximo (*pmo.*)

proxy *n* BANK carta poder *f*, ECON delegación de poderes *f*, LAW carta poder *f*; **~ fight** STOCK lucha por la mayoría de votos *f*; **~ statement** LAW información que debe ser suministrada a los accionistas por quien solicita de éstos poderes para representarlos en la asamblea de accionistas; **~ vote** POL voto aproximado *m*; ◆ **by ~** LAW por poder

proxyholder *n* LAW *civil law* apoderado(-a) *m,f*, mandatario(-a) *m,f*

PRP *abbr* HRM (*profit-related pay*) remuneración vinculada a los beneficios *f*, (*performance-related pay*) pago según desempeño *m*, remuneración dependiente del rendimiento *f*

PRT *abbr* (*petroleum revenue tax*) TAX impuesto sobre explotaciones petrolíferas *m*

PRTO *abbr* (*Price Reporting Terminal Operator*) STOCK operador terminal de comunicación de precios *m*

prudent[1] *adj* GEN COMM prudente

prudent[2]: **~-man rule** *n* GEN COMM, STOCK norma de la prudencia *f* regla del hombre prudente *f*; **~ policy** *n* GEN COMM política prudente *f*; **~ portfolio approach** *n* GEN COMM orientación prudente de una cartera *f*

prudential: **~ committee** *n* AmE (*cf advisory committee BrE*) GEN COMM comisión asesora *f*, comité asesor *m*; **~ consideration** *n* BANK retribución prudencial *f*

prudently *adv* GEN COMM prudentemente

pruning *n* GEN COMM poda *f*

P.S. *abbr* COMMS, GEN COMM (*postscript*) P.D. (*posdata*), GEN COMM, HRM (*personal secretary*) secretario(-a) personal *m,f*

PSBR *abbr* (*public sector borrowing requirements*) ECON necesidades de préstamo del sector público *f pl*

PSE *abbr* HRM (*public service employment*) empleo en el servicio público *m*, (*public sector employment*) empleo en el sector público *m*, STOCK (*Pacific Stock Exchange*) bolsa de valores del Pacífico *f*

pseudo: **~ product testing** *n* S&M seudoprueba de producto *f*; **~-production function** *n* ECON función de pseudo-producción *f*

PSI *abbr* (*pounds per square inch*) TRANSP libras por pulgada cuadrada

PSL *abbr* (*private sector liquidity*) ECON liquidez del sector privado *f*

psychic: **~ income** *n* ECON renta psíquica *f*, HRM beneficio psíquico *m*

psychographics *n pl* S&M *advertising* psicográficos *m pl*

psychological: **~ economy** *n* ECON economía psicológica *f*; **~ hook** *n* S&M gancho psicológico *m*; **~ price** *n* S&M precio psicológico *m*; **~ pricing** *n* S&M fijación de precios psicológicos *f*; **~ test** *n* HRM, S&M prueba psicológica *f*

psychology *n* GEN COMM psicología *f*; **~ of selling** S&M psicología de la venta *f*

psychometric: **~ test** *n* HRM, MATH, S&M prueba psicométrica *f*; **~ testing** *n* HRM, MATH, S&M aplicación de pruebas psicométricas *f*

psychometrics *n pl* GEN COMM, HRM, S&M psicometría *f*

pt *abbr* GEN COMM (*pint*) pinta *f*, (*private term*) término particular *m*

PTA *abbr* (*prepaid ticket advice*) LEIS, TRANSP aviso de billete de pago anticipado *m*

public[1] *adj* GEN COMM público; ◆ **go ~** FIN, STOCK cotizar en bolsa, ofrecer acciones al público, entrar en la bolsa

public[2] *n* GEN COMM público *m*; **~ access** LAW *to information* acceso público *m*; **~ accounting** ACC, BANK contabilidad pública *f*; **~ address system** (*PA system*) COMMS, GEN COMM sistema altavoces *m*; **~ administration** LAW, POL administración pública *f*; **~ administration lawyer** BANK, GEN COMM, LAW ≈ abogado(-a) administrativista *m,f*; **~ affairs** *n pl*

POL asuntos públicos *m pl*; ~ **amenities** *n pl* WEL entretenimientos públicos *m pl*; ~ **authorities** *n pl* POL poderes públicos *m pl*; ~ **authority** POL, TAX organismo gubernamental *m*, autoridad pública *f*; ~ **body** GEN COMM organismo público *m*, POL entidad pública *f*, funcionariado *m*; ~ **bonded warehouse** IMP/EXP, TRANSP depósito aduanero público *m*; ~ **choice theory** ECON teoría de elección pública *f*; ~ **company** ECON, GEN COMM compañía pública *f*, empresa que cotiza en bolsa *f*; ~ **consumption** ECON consumo público *m*; ~ **contract** GEN COMM contrato público *m*; ~ **corporation** GEN COMM sociedad pública *f*; ~ **credit** BANK, FIN crédito al gobierno *m*; ~ **debt** ECON deuda pública *f*; ~ **debt charges** *n pl* FIN cargos de la deuda pública *m pl*; ~ **debt envelope** FIN, POL partida de la deuda pública *f*; ~ **debt management** *AmE* (*cf national debt management BrE*) LAW, POL administración de la deuda pública *f*, gestión de la deuda pública *f*; ~ **debt service** FIN servicio de la deuda pública *m*; ~ **development** ECON *of land* desarrollo público *m*; ~ **distribution of securities** STOCK distribución pública de valores *f*; ~ **domain software** COMP programas de dominio público *m pl*; ~ **economics** ECON economía pública *f*; ~ **engagement** GEN COMM contratación pública *f*; ~ **enterprise** ECON, GEN COMM empresa pública *f*; ~ **enterprise rationalization loan** (*PERL*) FIN préstamo de racionalización de la empresa pública *m*; ~ **enterprise reform loan** (*PERL*) FIN préstamo de reforma de la empresa pública *m*; ~ **enterprise rehabilitation loan** (*PERL*) BANK, FIN préstamo de rehabilitación de la empresa pública *m*; ~ **examination** WEL examen público *m*; ~ **expenditure** GEN COMM gasto público *m*; ~ **expenditure control** GEN COMM control del gasto público *m*; ~ **expenditure survey** GEN COMM supervisión del gasto público *f*; ~ **finance** ECON, FIN finanzas públicas *f pl*; ~ **finances** *n pl* ECON, FIN finanzas públicas *f pl*; ~ **foundation** TAX fundación pública *f*; ~ **funds** *n pl* ACC fondos públicos *m pl*; ~ **good** ECON bien público *m*; ~ **health** GEN COMM, WEL salud pública *f*; ~ **holiday** GEN COMM día no laborable *m*, día festivo *m*; ~ **hospital** WEL hospital público *m*; ~ **housing authority bond** FIN, STOCK bono de vivienda *m*; ~ **instrument** LAW escritura pública *f*; ~ **interest company** ECON compañía con intereses públicos *f*, compañía de interés público *f*; ~ **investor** STOCK inversor(a) público(-a) *m,f*; ~ **invitation to bid** GEN COMM invitación pública a ofertar *f*; ~ **issue** STOCK emisión pública *f*; ~ **law** LAW derecho público *m*; ~ **lending right** (*PLR*) BANK derecho a empréstito público *m*; ~ **limited company** *BrE* (*plc*) GEN COMM ≈ sociedad anónima *f* (*S.A.*), ≈ sociedad anónima por acciones *f* (*S.A.A.*); ~ **limited partnership** STOCK sociedad limitada con cotización en bolsa *f*; ~ **loan** FIN empréstito público *m*; ~ **monies** *n pl* ECON erario público *m*; ~ **offering** GEN COMM, STOCK oferta pública de enajenación *f*, oferta pública de venta *f* (*OPV*); ~ **opinion** GEN COMM opinión pública *f*; ~ **outcry** GEN COMM clamor público *m*; ~ **ownership** FIN propiedad pública *f*; ~ **pricing** ECON precio público *m*; ~ **procurement** ECON *EU* aprovisionamiento del Estado *m*; ~ **prosecutor** LAW acusador(a) público(-a) *m,f*, fiscal *mf*; ~ **purse** ECON, FIN tesoro público *m*; ~ **relations** *n pl* (*PR*) HRM, MEDIA, S&M relaciones públicas *f pl*; ~ **relations agency** MEDIA, S&M agencia de relaciones públicas *f*; ~ **relations consultancy** GEN COMM, MEDIA, S&M asesoría de relaciones públicas *f*;

~ **relations consultant** MEDIA, S&M asesor(a) de imagen *m,f* asesor(a) de relaciones públicas *m,f*; ~ **relations officer** (*PRO*) HRM, S&M funcionario(-a) de relaciones públicas *m,f*; ~ **resources** *n pl* GEN COMM recursos públicos *m pl*; ~ **school** *AmE* (*cf state school BrE*) GEN COMM escuela pública *f*, escuela del estado *f*; ~ **sector** ECON sector público *m*; ~ **sector balance sheet** ACC, ECON hoja de balance del sector público *f*; ~ **sector body** GEN COMM, TAX organismo del sector público *m*; ~ **sector borrowing requirements** (*PSBR*) ECON necesidades crediticias del sector público *f pl*, necesidades de préstamo del sector público *f pl*; ~ **sector company** ECON empresa pública *f*; ~ **sector debt repayment** ECON devolución de la deuda del sector público *f*; ~ **sector deficit** ECON déficit del sector público *m*; ~ **sector employment** (*PSE*) HRM empleo en el sector público *m*; ~ **sector pay** ECON sueldos del sector público *m pl*; ~ **securities association** STOCK asociación pública de valores *f*; ~ **service** POL servicio público *m*; ~ **service advertising** S&M publicidad de un servicio público *f*; ~ **service body** GEN COMM, TAX organismo de servicio público *m*; ~ **service borrowing requirement** (*PSBR*) BANK, FIN requisito de préstamo del servicio público *m*; ~ **service contract** GEN COMM contrato de servicio público *m*; ~ **service corporation** *AmE* ECON, GEN COMM empresa de servicios públicos *f*; ~ **service dormobile** GEN COMM, TRANSP combinación de servicio público *f*; ~ **service employment** (*PSE*) HRM empleo en el servicio público *m*; ~ **service vehicle** (*PSV*) TRANSP vehículo de servicio público *m*; ~ **services** *n pl* HRM servicios públicos *m pl*; ~ **spending** GEN COMM, ECON, FIN gasto público *m*; ~ **spending plans** *n pl* ECON previsiones de gasto público *f pl*; ~ **spending ratio** ECON proporción del gasto público *f*; ~ **transport** TRANSP transporte público *m*; ~ **transport system** TRANSP sistema de transporte público *m*; ~ **treasury** ECON erario público *m*; ~ **use** PATENTS uso público *m*; ~ **utility** GEN COMM empresa de servicios públicos *f*, servicio público *m*; ~ **utility company** ECON empresa de servicios públicos *f*, GEN COMM empresa de servicios públicos *f*, sociedad de servicios públicos *f*; ~ **warning** GEN COMM advertencia pública *f*; ~ **welfare** WEL asistencia pública *f*, beneficiencia pública *f*; ~ **work** ECON obra pública *f*; ~ **works program** *AmE*, ~ **works programme** *BrE* GEN COMM programa de obras públicas *m*; ♦ **the ~ at large** GEN COMM el público en general

Public: ~ **Accounts Committee** *n BrE* ACC, POL *parliamentary* comisión del gasto público *f*; ~ **Broadcasting Services** *n pl AmE* (*PBS*) MEDIA cadena pública estadounidense de radiodifusión; ~ **Expenditure Survey Committee** *n* ECON Comité de Investigación del Gasto Público *m*; ~ **Expenditure White Paper** *n BrE* (*PEWP*) ECON libro blanco del gasto público *m*; ~ **Order Act** *n BrE* HRM, POL *1986* Ley de Orden Público; ~ **Record Office** *n BrE* GEN COMM, POL ≈ Archivo Nacional *m* (*Esp*), ≈ Oficina de Registro *f* (*Esp*)

publication: ~ **date** *n* MEDIA, S&M fecha de publicación *f*

publicity *n* GEN COMM publicidad *f*; ~ **department** MEDIA, S&M departamento de publicidad *m*; ~ **expenses** *n pl* ACC, FIN, S&M gastos publicitarios *m pl*; ~ **man** HRM publicista *mf*; ~ **manager** HRM, S&M director(a) de publicidad *m,f*; ~ **material** S&M material publicitario *m*; ~ **stunt** S&M truco publicitario *m*

publicly[1]: **~-funded** *adj* FIN, GEN COMM financiado con dineros públicos

publicly[2]: **~-listed company** *n* ECON compañía de cotización oficial pública *f*, FIN empresa con cotización pública *f*, GEN COMM, STOCK compañía que cotiza en bolsa *f*; **~ traded company** *n* STOCK empresa de gestión pública *f*; **~-traded share** *n* FIN, STOCK acción negociada públicamente *f*

publish *vt* GEN COMM editar, publicar

published[1] *adj* GEN COMM editado, publicado; **~ monthly** MEDIA *print* de publicación mensual

published[2]: **~ accounts** *n pl* ACC cuentas publicadas *f pl*; **~ charge** *n* TRANSP coste anunciado *m* (*Esp*), costo anunciado *m* (*AmL*); **~ fare** *n* TRANSP tarifa anunciada *f*; **~ information** *n* GEN COMM información publicada *f*; **~ price** *n* GEN COMM, S&M precio publicado *m*; **~ rate** *n* TRANSP tasa anunciada *f*; **~ research** *n* MATH *statistics* encuesta publicada *f*

publisher *n* GEN COMM, MEDIA editor(a) *m,f*; **~'s statement** MEDIA, S&M declaración del editor *f*

publishing: **~ director** *n* HRM director(a) editorial *m,f*; **~ house** *n* MEDIA casa editorial *f*

PUD *abbr* (*planned unit development*) PROP desarrollo previsto de una unidad *m*

PUF *abbr* (*purchase underwriting facility*) FIN, STOCK servicio de compra de suscripciones *m*

pull[1] *n jarg* S&M *advertising* primera prueba *f*; **~ of prices** GEN COMM tirón de los precios *m*; **~-through box** TRANSP caja de tracción *f*

pull[2] *vt* GEN COMM *withdraw* retirar; ♦ **~ the plug** *jarg* STOCK chafar un plan (*jarg*), retirar el apoyo; **~ strings** BrE (*cf pull wires AmE*) GEN COMM tocar resortes; **~ wires for sb** AmE (*cf pull strings BrE*) GEN COMM tocar resortes

pull down *vt* ECON *inflation* frenar

pull off *vt* infrml GEN COMM *achieve* lograr; ♦ **~ a deal** GEN COMM llevar a cabo una negociación

pull out *vi* GEN COMM *withdraw from deal* sacar

Pullman *n* TRANSP *rail* pulman *m*

pulse *n* COMP impulso *m*

pump[1]: **~ priming** *n jarg*, GEN COMM reactivación de la economía *f*, reactivación estimulada *f*

pump[2] *vt* ENVIR bombear; ♦ **~ funds into** FIN bombear fondos hacia; **~ prime** ECON, GEN COMM, POL *the economy* reactivar

punch[1] *n* COMP *device* perforadora *f*; **~ card** COMP, GEN COMM tarjeta perforada *f*; **~ card check** AmE, **~ card cheque** BrE BANK, FIN cheque perforado *m*; **~ code** GEN COMM código de perforación *m*; **~ list** GEN COMM lista perforada *f*

punch[2] *vt* GEN COMM *card* fichar; ♦ **~ the time clock** HRM, IND fichar la hora (*Esp*)

punch in *vi* AmE (*cf clock on BrE*) HRM, IND checar la tarjeta (*AmL*), fichar la entrada (*Esp*)

punch out *vi* AmE (*cf clock off BrE*) HRM, IND checar la tarjeta (*AmL*), fichar la salida (*Esp*)

punched: **~ card** *n* COMP, GEN COMM tarjeta perforada *f*; **~ paper** *n* LEIS *theatre* entrada picada *f*, invitación *f*

punctuality *n* TRANSP puntualidad *f*; **~ analysis** TRANSP análisis de puntualidad *m*; **~ performance** TRANSP cumplimiento de la puntualidad *m*

puncture *n* TRANSP pinchazo *m*

punitive: **~ damages** *n pl* INS, LAW daños punitivos *m pl*

punt *n* GEN COMM libra irlandesa *f*, STOCK (*jarg*) inversión en bolsa de valores con muy poca probabilidad de dar beneficios

punt down *vt* MEDIA *print* componer en minúsculas

punter *n infrml* GEN COMM cliente *mf*

pupil *n* GEN COMM, LAW pasante *mf*

pupillage *n* BANK, GEN COMM, LAW ≈ pasantería *f*

purchase[1] *n* GEN COMM adquisición *f*, compra *f*; **~ acquisition** FIN adquisición por compra *f*; **~ of assets** GEN COMM compra de activos *f*; **~ book** S&M libro de compras *m*; **~ cost** GEN COMM *of assets* precio de compra *m*; **~ credit** GEN COMM crédito para comprar *m*; **~ decision** GEN COMM decisión de compra *f*; **~ denominated in foreign currency** ACC, FIN compras en divisas *f pl*; **~ for settlement** STOCK compra en liquidación *f*; **~ fund** GEN COMM fondo de compras *m*; **~ group** FIN grupo de compra *m*; **~ group agreement** FIN acuerdo de grupo comprador *m*; **~ invoice** GEN COMM factura de compra *f*; **~ issue facility** (*PIF*) FIN, STOCK servicio de compra de emisiones *m*; **~ method** ACC método de compra *m*; **~ money mortgage** BANK, FIN, PROP hipoteca de dinero de compra *f* hipoteca parcial del precio de compra *f*; **~ order** (*P.O.*) GEN COMM orden de compra *f* (*O/C*); **~ price** GEN COMM precio de compra *m*; **~ price method** STOCK método de precio de compra *m*; **~ and resale agreement** (*PRA*) STOCK compromiso de compra y reventa *m*; **~ returns** *n pl* S&M devolución de compras *f*; **~ returns and allowances** *n pl* S&M rendimientos y descuentos de las compras *m pl*; **~ and sale** (*P&S*) STOCK compra y venta *f*; **~ and sale statement** (*P&S statement*) STOCK declaración de compra y venta *f*; **~ tax** TAX impuesto sobre compras *m*; **~ underwriting facility** (*PUF*) FIN, STOCK servicio de compra de suscripciones *m*; ♦ **no ~ necessary** S&M *sales promotion* sin obligación de compra

purchase[2] *vt* GEN COMM adquirir, comprar

purchased: **~ company** *n* GEN COMM compañía adquirida *f*

purchases: **~ journal** *n* ACC diario de compras *m*

purchasing *n* GEN COMM, S&M compra *f*; **~ company** GEN COMM compañía adquirente *f*; **~ costs** *n pl* GEN COMM costes de compras *m pl* (*Esp*), costos de compras *m pl* (*AmL*); **~ department** GEN COMM departamento de compras *m*; **~ hedge** STOCK cobertura de compra *f*; **~ manager** HRM, MGMNT, S&M director(a) de compras *m,f*; **~ motivator** S&M motivador(a) de compras *m,f*; **~ officer** GEN COMM, HRM funcionario(-a) de compras *m,f*; **~ pattern** S&M modelo de compra *m*, tendencia de las compras *f*; **~ parity** ECON paridad adquisitiva *f*; **~ power** GEN COMM poder adquisitivo *m*

pure: **~ capitalism** *n* ECON, IND, POL capitalismo puro *m*; **~ competition** *n* ECON competencia perfecta *f*; **~ discretion** *n* ECON libertad de acción total en materia de política económica; **~ economic rent** *n* ECON renta económica pura *f*; **~ economy credit** *n* ECON crédito económico puro *m*; **~ holding company** *n* BANK sociedad principal *f*; **~ inflation** *n* ECON inflación pura *f*; **~ interest rate** *n* ECON, GEN COMM proporción de interés puro *f*, tasa de interés absoluta *f*; **~ market economy** *n* ECON, POL economía de mercado pura *f* pura economía de mercado *f*; **~ monopoly** *n* ECON monopolio puro *m*; **~ play** *n jarg* STOCK empresa especializada *f*; **~ profit** *n* ACC, FIN beneficio neto *m*, utilidad absoluta *f*

purification *n* ENVIR depuración *f*; ~ **plant** ENVIR, IND planta depuradora *f*

purify *vt* ENVIR depurar

purpose[1]: **~-built** *adj* PROP construido con propósitos específicos, TRANSP construido por encargo

purpose[2] *n* GEN COMM objeto *m*, propósito *m*, MGMNT objeto *m*; **~-built block** PROP *of flats* bloque de viviendas construido con propósitos específicos *m*; **~-built tonnage** TRANSP *shipping* tonelaje construido de encargo *m*; **~-built vehicle** TRANSP vehículo construido de encargo *m*; ~ **loan** BANK, STOCK préstamo específico respaldado *m*

purposes: ~ **statement** *n* MGMNT, STOCK declaración de objetivos *f*

pursuant: ~ **to article** *phr* LAW de conformidad con el artículo

pursue *vt* GEN COMM *policy* seguir

push[1]: **~-button telephone** *n* COMMS teléfono de botonera *m* (*AmL*), teléfono de teclado *m* (*Esp*); ~ **incentive** *n pl* S&M *advertising* incentivo de empuje *m*; ~ **money** *n* GEN COMM, S&M incentivo de ventas *m*; **~-tow barge** *n* TRANSP barcaza para remolque empujando *f*

push[2] *vt* GEN COMM, S&M *promote* promocionar; ◆ ~ **sb to the limit** GEN COMM llevar a alguien hasta el límite; ~ **sb to the wall** GEN COMM acorralar a alguien

pushback *n* TRANSP *aircraft* rechazo de un pasajero *m*

push/pull: ~ **strategy** *n* S&M estrategia de tira y afloja *f*

put[1] *n* STOCK opción de venta *f*; ~ **bond** FIN, STOCK bono con opción de venta *m*; ~ **buying hedge** STOCK cobertura de compra con posición larga *f*; ~ **and call** STOCK operación con dobles primas *f*; ~ **delta** STOCK delta de una opción de venta *f*; **~-in-use rule** TAX norma aplicada *f*; ~ **option** STOCK opción de venta *f*; ~ **premium** STOCK prima de venta *f*; ~ **purchase** STOCK adquisición de una opción de venta *f*; ~ **ratio backspread** STOCK *options* margen a ratio vendedor inverso *m*; ~ **spread** STOCK margen de venta *m*; ~**'s strike** STOCK ejercicio de una opción de venta *m*; ~ **through** STOCK colocación privada *f*; ~ **writer** STOCK *futures* vendedor(a) de una opción de venta *m,f*

put[2] **1.** *vt* GEN COMM poner; ◆ ~ **a damper on** *infrml* GEN COMM echar un jarro de agua fría sobre; ~ **the final touch to sth** GEN COMM dar el toque final a algo; ~ **a guard on sb** GEN COMM vigilar a alguien; ~ **in an application** HRM meter una solicitud (*AmL*) presentar una solicitud (*Esp*); ~ **in an application for a job** HRM presentar una solicitud de empleo; ~ **in a claim** LAW presentar una reclamación; ~ **in mailbox** COMMS poner en el buzón; ~ **in order** ADMIN poner en orden; ~ **in a plea** LAW presentar un alegato; ~ **in touch** COMMS *one party with another* poner en contacto; ~ **in a word for**

sb GEN COMM decir unas palabras en favor de alguien; ~ **into effect** GEN COMM *policies* poner en práctica; ~ **into force** LAW poner en vigor; ~ **into receivership** LAW poner en manos de la administración judicial; ~ **money down** FIN adelantar el dinero; ~ **on the back burner** GEN COMM dar carpetazo (*infrml*), dejar de lado; ~ **on the market** PROP poner en venta; ~ **on a spurt** *infrml* GEN COMM acelerar; ~ **one's affairs in order** GEN COMM poner sus asuntos en orden; ~ **one's seal to** GEN COMM sellar; ~ **out for tender** GEN COMM sacar a licitación; ~ **out a statement** MEDIA publicar unas declaraciones; ~ **a plan into action** GEN COMM poner un plan en acción; ~ **pressure on sb** GEN COMM presionar a alguien; ~ **sb in for a job** *infrml* HRM recomendar a alguien para un puesto; ~ **sth in the window** GEN COMM poner algo en el escaparate; ~ **sth into cold storage** *infrml* GEN COMM poner algo en un almacén frigorífico; ~ **sth into execution** GEN COMM poner algo en marcha; ~ **sth into order** GEN COMM ordenar algo; ~ **sth into production** IND poner algo en producción; ~ **sth on the agenda** GEN COMM poner algo al orden del día; ~ **sth on record** GEN COMM hacer constar algo; ~ **sth through the proper channels** GEN COMM canalizar algo debidamente; ~ **sth to the test** GEN COMM poner algo a prueba; ~ **a suggestion before a committee** GEN COMM exponer una sugerencia ante un comité; ~ **up for tender** GEN COMM sacar a licitación; ~ **a veto on** GEN COMM vetar

put away *vt* BANK *money in bank* guardar, ahorrar, LAW *imprison* encarcelar

put forward *vt* GEN COMM objetar, MGMNT *proposals* adelantar

put up *vt* FIN *capital* ofrecer

putty: **~-clay** *n* ACC, ECON, FIN, GEN COMM capital maleable *m*; **~-putty** *n infrml* ACC, ECON, GEN COMM, FIN capital maleable *m*

p.v. *abbr* (*par value*) STOCK valor a la par *m*

P/V *abbr* (*profit-volume ratio*) ACC proporción beneficio-volumen *f*, FIN coeficiente de volumen de beneficios *m*

pyramid[1]: ~ **hierarchy** *n* HRM jerarquía piramidal *f*; ~ **selling** *n* S&M venta piramidal *f*

pyramid[2] *vi* STOCK acumular

pyramidal *adj* GEN COMM piramidal

pyramiding *n* STOCK compra escalonada de acciones *f*, ahorro de capital social *m*, compra de acciones con sus dividendos *f*

pyrometer *n* GEN COMM pirómetro *m*

pyrotechnic: ~ **substance** *n* TRANSP *dangerous cargo* productos pirotécnicos *m pl*

PYT *abbr* (*payment*) GEN COMM pago *m*

Q

Q: ~ **sailing** n TRANSP navegación Q f

QC abbr HRM (Queen's Counsel BrE) consejero(-a) de la Reina m,f, IND (quality control) control de calidad m, (quality circle) círculo de calidad m, LAW (Queen's Counsel) consejero(-a) de la Reina m,f

qnty abbr (quantity) GEN COMM ctdad (cantidad)

QR abbr (quantitative restriction) ECON restricción cuantitativa f

qt abbr (quart) GEN COMM qt (cuarto)

qtr abbr (quarter) GEN COMM cuarto m, trimestre m

qty abbr (quantity) GEN COMM ctdad (cantidad)

quad: ~ **crown** n S&M anuncio de 75 x 100 cm m

quadrennial: ~ **survey** n TAX of vessels inspección cuatrienal f

quadripartite: ~ **agreement** n GEN COMM acuerdo cuadripartito m

quadruple: ~ **expansion** n TRANSP shipping cuádruple expansión f; ~ **stacker** n TRANSP fijador cuádruple m

quadruplicate: in ~ phr GEN COMM en cuadruplicado

qualification n ACC aptitud f, calificación f, capacidad f, GEN COMM modifying condition condición modificante f, suitability calificación f, HRM academic calificación f, requisito m, título m, WEL calificación f; ~ **of opinion** FIN capacidad de opinión f; ~ **period** WEL periodo de formación m; ~ **shares** n pl STOCK acciones entregadas en garantía f pl; ◆ **without** ~ ACC sin cualificación

qualifications n pl HRM titulación f; ◆ **have the right** ~ **for the job** HRM cumplir todos los requisitos para el puesto, estar debidamente calificado para el puesto

qualified[1] adj GEN COMM suitable competente, HRM cualificado; ◆ **be** ~ **to do** HRM estar cualificado para hacer, ser apto para hacer

qualified[2]: ~ **acceptance** n FIN, GEN COMM aceptación condicionada f, aceptación en firme f; ~ **accountant** n ACC contable autorizado(-a) m,f (Esp), contable cualificado(-a) m,f (Esp), contable diplomado(-a) m,f (Esp), contable habilitado(-a) m,f (Esp), contador(a) autorizado(-a) m,f (AmL), contador(a) cualificado(-a) m,f (AmL), contador(a) habilitado(-a) m,f (AmL); ~ **activities** n TAX manufacturing and processing actividades cualificadas f pl; ~ **approval** n GEN COMM aprobación con reservas f; ~ **borrowing** n GEN COMM empréstito calificado m; ~ **certificate** n GEN COMM certificado con salvedades m; ~ **endorsement** n BANK endoso calificado m; ~ **expenditure** n ECON, FIN, TAX gasto deducible m; ~ **insurance corporation** n INS compañía aseguradora cualificada f; ~ **investment** n STOCK inversión cualificada f, inversión de calidad f; ~ **majority** n POL mayoría cualificada f; ~ **majority vote** n GEN COMM voto mayoritario calificado m; ~ **opinion** n GEN COMM dictamen con salvedades m; ~ **pension income** n ACC, TAX ingresos procedentes de pensiones cualificadas m pl; ~ **plan** n HRM plan cualificado m; ~ **relation** n TAX relación cualificada f; ~ **report** n ACC informe con salvedades m (Esp), reporte con salvedades m (AmL); ~ **transportation equipment** n TRANSP equipo de transporte cualificado m; ~ **trust** n HRM consorcio cualificado m

qualify vt GEN COMM, HRM calificar; ◆ ~ **sb to do** HRM calificar a alguien para hacer

qualifying[1] adj GEN COMM, HRM calificatorio, eliminatorio

qualifying[2]: ~ **annuity** n FIN anualidad habilitante f; ~ **certificate** n GEN COMM certificado de aptitud m; ~ **debt obligation** n TAX obligación de deuda cualificada f; ~ **distribution** n ACC, GEN COMM distribución eliminatoria f, distribución selectiva f; ~ **items** n pl FIN artículos cualificados m pl; ~ **period** n TAX periodo de carencia m; ~ **share** n FIN, STOCK acción habilitante f; ~ **small business corporation** n GEN COMM, TAX pequeña empresa sujeta f; ~ **stock option** n STOCK opción privilegiada de compra de acciones f; ~ **taxable dividends paid** n TAX pago de dividendos deducibles m; ~ **utility** n STOCK empresa pública de régimen especial f

qualitative[1] adj GEN COMM cualitativo

qualitative[2]: ~ **analysis** n IND, S&M market research análisis cualitativo m; ~ **approach** n STOCK enfoque cualitativo m; ~ **controls** n pl BANK lending directives controles cualitativos m pl; ~ **methodology** n S&M market research metodología cualitativa f; ~ **research** n S&M of market investigación cualitativa f

qualitatively adv GEN COMM cualitativamente

quality n GEN COMM calidad f, ~ **assessment** GEN COMM valoración de la calidad f; ~ **asset** FIN activo de calidad m; ~ **of assets** FIN calidad de los activos f; ~ **assurance** GEN COMM aseguramiento de calidad m, garantía de calidad f; ~ **certificate** GEN COMM, IMP/EXP, TRANSP certificado de calidad m; ~ **circle** HRM, IND, MGMNT círculo de calidad m; ~ **control** (QC) IND control de calidad m, administración de la calidad f (AmL), gestión de la calidad f (Esp); ~ **of earnings** FIN calidad de los beneficios f; ~ **engineering** IND ingeniería de calidad f; ~ **good** GEN COMM producto de calidad m; ~ **label** GEN COMM etiqueta de calidad f; ~ **of the labor force** AmE, ~ **of the labour force** BrE ECON, HRM calidad de la mano de obra f; ~ **of life** ECON, WEL calidad de vida f; ~ **loan** BANK préstamo de calidad m; ~ **management** IND dirección de calidad f, MGMNT dirección de calidad f, gerencia de calidad f; ~ **market** S&M mercado de calidad m; ~ **newspaper** GEN COMM, MEDIA periódico de calidad m; ~**-price ratio** S&M relación calidad-precio f; ~ **standard** GEN COMM norma de calidad f; ~ **teams** n pl MGMNT equipos de calidad m pl; ~ **of working life** (QWL) ECON, HRM, WEL calidad de vida en el trabajo f

Quango abbr BrE (quasi-autonomous non-governmental-organization) POL organización no gubernamental que funciona como órgano consultivo

quantification n ACC, GEN COMM, MATH cuantificación f

quantify vt ACC, GEN COMM, MATH cuantificar

quantitative[1] adj ACC, GEN COMM, MATH cuantitativo

quantitative[2]: ~ **analysis** n IND, MGMNT, S&M market research análisis cuantitativo m; ~ **controls** n pl BANK lending directives controles cuantitativos m pl; ~ **methodology** n S&M market research metodología cuantitativa f; ~ **research** n S&M of market investigación cuantitativa *f*; ~ **restriction** *n* (*QR*) ECON restricción cuantitativa *f*; ~ **rule** *n* STOCK regla cuantitativa *f*

quantity *n* (*qty*) GEN COMM cantidad *f* (*ctdad*); ~ **buyer** GEN COMM comprador(a) de cantidad *m,f*; ~ **discount** ACC, GEN COMM, S&M descuento por cantidad *m*; **surveying** IND comprobación de cantidades *f*; ~ **surveyor** IND inspector(-a) de cantidades *m,f*; ~ **theory of money** ACC, BANK, ECON, FIN teoría cuantitativa del dinero *f*

quantum *n* GEN COMM cuanto *m*; ~ **merit** GEN COMM fijación de valor ante la falta de precio contractual *f*

quarantine *n* GEN COMM, IMP/EXP cuarentena *f*; ~ **due** GEN COMM, IMP/EXP tasa de cuarentena *f*

quart *n* (*qt*) GEN COMM cuarto *m* (*qt*)

quarter *n* (*qtr*) GEN COMM cuarto *m*, trimestre *m*; ~**-end** ACC, GEN COMM fin de trimestre *m*; ~ **page advertisement** MEDIA, S&M anuncio de un cuarto de página *m*; ~ **of a pound** GEN COMM cuarto de libra *m*; ~ **up price** *jarg* STOCK precio de $25 para arriba

quartering *n jarg* HRM *industrial relations* penalización por falta de puntualidad *f*

quarterly[1] *adj* GEN COMM trimestral

quarterly[2] *adv* GEN COMM trimestralmente

quarterly[3] *n* MEDIA *print* trimestral *m*; ~ **dividend** STOCK dividendo trimestral *m*; ~ **installment** *AmE*, ~ **instalment** *BrE* GEN COMM abono trimestral *m*, cuota trimestral *f*, pago trimestral *m*

quartile: ~ **deviation** *n* ECON rango semiintercuartílico *m*

quash *vt* LAW *writ, sentence, order* abolir, anular

quasi[1] *adv* GEN COMM cuasi

quasi[2]: ~**-autonomous non-governmental-organization** *n BrE* (*Quango*) POL organización no gubernamental que funciona como órgano consultivo; ~**-concavity** *n* ECON cuasi-concavidad *f*; ~ **contract** *n* LAW cuasi contrato *m*; ~ **fixed factor** *n* ECON factor casi fijo *m*; ~**-independence** *n* GEN COMM cuasi independencia *f*; ~**-manufacturer** *n* IND *retail chains* maquiladora *f* (*AmL*), semifabricante *m* (*Esp*); ~**-money** *n* ACC, FIN, GEN COMM activo casi líquido *m*, cuasi-dinero *m*; ~**-monopoly** *n* ECON cuasi monopolio *m*; ~**-performing loan** *n* BANK préstamo no totalmente ejecutado *m*; ~**-rent** *n* ECON cuasi-renta *f*

quay *n* IMP/EXP, TRANSP *port* amarradero *m*, muelle *m*; ~ **fitting** IMP/EXP, TRANSP amarrado al muelle *m*; ♦ ~ **to quay** IMP/EXP, TRANSP de muelle a muelle

quayage *n* IMP/EXP, TRANSP muelles *m pl*

Queen: ~**'s Award to Industry** *n BrE* IND premio de la Reina a la industria; ~**'s Counsel** *n BrE* (*QC*) HRM, LAW consejero(-a) de la Reina *m,f*

query[1] *n* GEN COMM consulta *f*, pregunta *f*; ~ **language** COMP lenguaje de consulta *m*, lenguaje de interrogación *m*

query[2] *vt* GEN COMM interrogar

question: ~ **of jurisdiction** *n* LAW cuestión jurisdiccional *f*; ~ **time** *n BrE* POL sesión de interpelaciones dirigidas al primer ministro

questionnaire *n* GEN COMM, S&M *market research* cuestionario *m*

queue *n* COMP, GEN COMM cola *f*

queue up *vi BrE* (*cf wait in line AmE*) GEN COMM hacer cola

queueing: ~ **system** *n* ECON sistema de colas *m*; ~ **theory** *n BrE* (*cf waiting line theory AmE*) ECON, MATH teoría de las colas *f*

quick: ~ **asset** *n* ACC, FIN, PROP activo líquido *m*, activo realizable *m*; ~ **assets ratio** *n* BANK, FIN relación de activos de rápida realización *f*; ~**-buck artist** *n* STOCK oportunista *mf*; ~**-disbursing loan** *n* BANK préstamo de rápido desembolso *m*; ~ **fix** *n* FIN, GEN COMM arreglo rápido *m*, fijo disponible *m*; ~ **flip** *n* TAX golpe rápido *m*; ~ **ratio** *n* ACC proporción de activo disponible a pasivo corriente *f*, proporción de liquidez inmediata *f*, ratio de activo disponible a pasivo corriente *m*, ratio de liquidez inmediata *m*; ~ **returns** *n pl* FIN, GEN COMM venta rápida *f*; ~ **sale** *n* GEN COMM, S&M venta fácil *f*; ~ **succession** *n* TAX sucesión rápida *f*; ~ **tite**® *n* TRANSP *containers* cierre rápido *m*

quid pro quo *n* ECON, GEN COMM, TAX compensación *f*

quiet[1] *adj* GEN COMM *market, business* tranquilo

quiet[2]: ~ **enjoyment** *n* PROP posesión pacífica *f*; ~ **market** *n* STOCK mercado inactivo *m*, mercado poco animado *m*; ~ **title suit** *n* LAW, PROP pleito sobre asuntos de propiedad

quintal *n* GEN COMM quintal métrico *m*

quit[1]: ~ **rate** *n* ECON, HRM tasa de abandono del empleo *f*, tasa de dimisión del empleo *f*, tasa de rotación de personal *f*

quit[2] *vt* COMP abandonar

quitclaim *n* LAW finiquito *m*; ~ **deed** LAW recibo de finiquito *m*, PROP escritura de cesión de un derecho *f*, escritura de renuncia de un derecho *f*

quo warranto *n* LAW acción por usurpación de funciones *f*

quod vide *n* (*qv*) GEN COMM que ve

quoin *n* TRANSP cuña *f*

quondam *adj* GEN COMM antiguo

quorum *n* GEN COMM, LAW, MGMNT quorum *m*

quota *n* GEN COMM cuota *f*; ~ **fixing** GEN COMM fijación de cuotas *f*; ~ **sampling** GEN COMM, S&M *market research* muestreo por cuotas *m*; ~ **system** GEN COMM sistema de cuotas *m*, IMP/EXP sistema de cupos *m*; ♦ **above** ~ GEN COMM por encima de la cuota

quotable *adj* STOCK cotizable

quotation *n* GEN COMM, STOCK cotización *f*; ~ **board** STOCK tablero de cotización *m*; ~ **marks** *n pl* GEN COMM comillas *f pl*; ~ **spread** STOCK margen de cotización *m*

quotations *n pl* ACC, ECON, FIN, STOCK cotizaciones *f pl*

quote[1] *n* ACC, ECON, FIN cotización *f*, GEN COMM comillas *f pl*, STOCK cotización *f*; ~ **value** STOCK valor de cotización *m*

quote[2] *vt* GEN COMM cotizar

quoted: ~ **company** *n* ECON, STOCK empresa cotizada en bolsa *f*; ~ **price** *n* STOCK precio de cotización *m*; ~ **securities** *n pl* STOCK valores cotizados *m pl*; ~ **security** *n* STOCK título cotizado *m*; ~ **shares** *n pl* STOCK valores cotizados *m pl*

quotient *n* GEN COMM cociente *m*

qv *abbr* (*quod vide*) GEN COMM que ve

QWERTY: ~ **keyboard** *n* COMP teclado QWERTY *m*

QWL *abbr* (*quality of working life*) ECON, HRM, WEL calidad de vida en el trabajo *f*

R

R *abbr* TRANSP (*refrigeration*) R (*refrigeración*), (*riveted*) remachado, (*reconditioned*) reacondicionado

R/A *abbr* (*refer to acceptor*) BANK referir al aceptante, remitir al aceptante

rabbi *n AmE jarg* POL rabino *m*

RAC *abbr BrE* (*Royal Automobile Club, cf AAA AmE*) TRANSP organización para el automovilista, ≈ ADA (*Esp*) (*Ayuda del Automovilista*), ≈ RAC (*AmL*) (*Real Automóvil Club*)

race: **~ discrimination** *n* HRM, LAW, WEL discriminación racial *f*

Race: **~ Relations Act** *n* (*RRA*) HRM, LAW, WEL ley de relaciones interraciales

racial: **~ discrimination** *n* HRM, LAW, WEL discriminación racial *f*

rack *n* COMP casillero *m*; **~ jobber** *jarg* MEDIA *print, broadcast* mayorista de estanterías *mf*

racket *n infrml* STOCK chanchullo *m*

racking *n* TRANSP traslación *f*

RAD *abbr* (*raised after-deck*) TRANSP cubierta de popa elevada *f*

radar *n* TRANSP radar *m*; **~ alert** STOCK vigilancia activa *f*; **~ beacon** COMMS, TRANSP baliza de radar *f*

Radcliffe: **~ Report** *n BrE* ECON *monetary system* informe Radcliffe *m* (*Esp*), reporte Radcliffe *m* (*AmL*)

radiation *n* ENVIR radiación *f*; **~ pollution** ENVIR contaminación por radiación *f*

radical[1] *adj* GEN COMM radical

radical[2]: **~ economics** *n* ECON economía radical *f*

radio: **~ advertising** *n* MEDIA, S&M publicidad en la radio *f*; **~ announcement** *n* MEDIA, S&M anuncio de radio *m*, comunicado radiofónico *m*; **~ announcer** *n* MEDIA comentarista de radio *mf*, locutor(a) de radio *m,f*; **~ audience** *n* MEDIA, S&M audiencia de radio *f*; **~ authority** *n* MEDIA, S&M autoridad de la emisora *f*; **~ broadcast** *n* MEDIA, S&M emisión de radio *f*; **~ commercial** *n* MEDIA, S&M anuncio comercial en la radio *m*; **~ officer** *n* HRM, TRANSP radiotelegrafista *mf*; **~ program** *AmE*, **~ programme** *BrE n* MEDIA, S&M programa de radio *m*; **~ set** *n* MEDIA equipo radioeléctrico *m*; **~ station** *n* MEDIA emisora de radio *f*

radiotelegram *n* COMMS radiotelegrama *m*

radiotelegraphy *n* COMMS radiotelegrafía *f*

radiotelephone *n* COMMS, MEDIA, TRANSP *shipping* radioteléfono *m*

radiotelephony *n* (*RT*) COMMS, MEDIA, TRANSP *shipping* radiotelefonía *f*

RAFT *abbr* (*revolving acceptance facility by tender*) FIN servicio de aceptación renovable por oferta

rag *n infrml* MEDIA *print* periodicucho *m* (*infrml*); **~ content** ADMIN, MEDIA contenido de trapo *m*

ragged *adj* GEN COMM, S&M desigual, desordenado, irregular

raid *vt* GEN COMM, atacar, absorber; ♦ **~ a company** STOCK absorber una compañía de manera hostil; **~ the market** *jarg* STOCK especular en el mercado

raider *n* GEN COMM, STOCK tiburón *m*

rail *n* TRANSP riel *m*, ferrocarril *m*; **~-air link** LEIS enlace rail-avión *m*; **~ freight** TRANSP flete ferroviario *m*; **~ guided tour** LEIS, TRANSP excursión con guía por ferrocarril *f*; **~ link** TRANSP conexión ferroviaria *f*; **~ network** TRANSP red ferroviaria *f*; **~ shares** *n pl* STOCK acciones de ferrocarril *f pl*; **~ shipment** TRANSP transporte por ferrocarril *m*; **~ strike** HRM, TRANSP huelga ferroviaria *f*; **~ terminal** LEIS, TRANSP terminal ferroviaria *f*; **~ tour** LEIS, TRANSP excursión en ferrocarril *f*; **~ traffic** TRANSP tráfico de ferrocarril *m*; **~ transport** TRANSP transporte por ferrocarril *m*; **~ traveler** *AmE*, **~ traveller** *BrE* LEIS, TRANSP viajero(-a) de ferrocarril *m,f*

railcar *n AmE* (*cf railway carriage BrE, railway coach BrE*) TRANSP vagón de ferrocarril *m*, vagón de tren *m*

railhead *n* TRANSP cabeza de carril *f*, cabeza de línea *f*, extremo de carril *m*

railman *n AmE* (*cf railwayman BrE*) HRM, TRANSP ferrocarrilero *m*, ferroviario *m*

railroad *n AmE* (*cf railway BrE*) TRANSP ferrocarril *m*; **~ bill of lading** *AmE* (*cf railway bill of lading BrE*) carta de porte por ferrocarril *f*, resguardo de transporte por tren *m*; **~ consignment note** *AmE* (*cf railway consignment note BrE*) declaración de expedición ferroviaria *f*; **~ network** *AmE* (*cf railway network BrE*) TRANSP red de ferrocarriles *f*; **~ retirement act** *AmE* HRM fondo de jubilación independiente de la seguridad social para los trabajadores ferroviarios; **~ securities** *n pl AmE* (*cf railway securities BrE*) STOCK valores ferroviarios *m pl*; **~ service** *AmE* (*cf railway service BrE*) TRANSP servicio de ferrocarril *m*; **~ station** *AmE* (*cf railway station BrE, train station BrE*) TRANSP estación de ferrocarril *f*; **~ system** (*cf railway system BrE*) TRANSP red de ferrocarriles *f*; **~ timetable** *AmE* (*cf railway timetable BrE*) TRANSP horario de trenes *m*

Railrover *n BrE* LEIS billete de duración limitada con kilometraje ilimitado

railway *n BrE* (*rly, cf railroad AmE*) TRANSP ferrocarril *m* (*FC*); **~ bill of lading** *BrE* (*cf railroad bill of lading AmE*) TRANSP carta de porte por ferrocarril *f*, resguardo de transporte por tren *m*; **~ carriage** *BrE* (*cf railcar AmE*) TRANSP vagón de ferrocarril *m*, vagón de tren *m*; **~ coach** *BrE* (*cf railcar AmE*) TRANSP vagón de ferrocarril *m* vagón de tren *m*; **~ consignment note** *BrE* (*cf railroad consignment note AmE*) TRANSP declaración de expedición ferroviaria *f*; **~ network** (*cf railroad network AmE*) TRANSP red de ferrocarriles *f*; **~ securities** *n pl BrE* (*cf railroad securities AmE*) STOCK valores ferroviarios *m pl*; **~ service** *BrE* (*cf railroad service AmE*) TRANSP servicio de ferrocarril *m*; **~ station** *BrE* (*cf railroad station AmE*) TRANSP estación de ferrocarril *f*; **~ system** (*cf railroad system AmE*) TRANSP red de ferrocarriles *f*; **~ timetable** *BrE* (*cf railroad timetable AmE*) LEIS, TRANSP horario de trenes *m*; **~ yard** *BrE* (*cf railyard AmE*) TRANSP estación de clasificación *f*

railwayman *n BrE* (*cf railman AmE*) HRM, TRANSP ferrocarrilero *m*, ferroviario *m*

railyard *n AmE* (*cf* **railway yard** *BrE*) TRANSP estación de clasificación *f*

rainbow: ~ **book** *n BrE jarg* HRM listado de las remuneraciones de los funcionarios del gobierno local

rainforest *n* ENVIR selva tropical *f*

rainmaker *n AmE jarg* LAW, POL abogado que atrae a nuevos clientes para su despacho

raise[1] *n* GEN COMM *in earnings* aumento *m*, elevación *f*

raise[2] *vt* GEN COMM tomar, *wages* aumentar, *embargo* levantar, plantear, *objection* objetar, STOCK *capital* reunir, TAX imponer; ◆ ~ **awareness** ENVIR tomar conciencia; ~ **a check** *AmE*, ~ **a cheque** *BrE* BANK extender un cheque; ~ **external funds** GEN COMM recaudar fondos externos; ~ **funds** GEN COMM recaudar fondos; ~ **a loan** BANK aumentar el préstamo; ~ **money** FIN, GEN COMM juntar dinero; ~ **money on sth** GEN COMM ganar dinero con algo

raised: ~ **after-deck** *n* (*RAD*) TRANSP cubierta de popa elevada *f*; ~ **deck** *n* (*Rdk*) TRANSP cubierta de castillo *f*, cubierta elevada *f*

raising: ~ **of funds** *n* ACC, FIN obtención de fondos *f*

rake in *vt infrml* GEN COMM recoger

rally[1] *n* GEN COMM, STOCK *of market* recuperación del mercado *f*, *of prices* recuperación *m*

rally[2] *vi* GEN COMM, STOCK *the market* reactivarse, recuperarse

rallying *n* GEN COMM, STOCK reunión *f*; ~ **point** GEN COMM, STOCK punto de reunión *m*

RAM[1] *abbr* (*random access memory*) COMP memoria de acceso aleatorio *f*

RAM[2]: ~ **disk** *n* COMP disco de RAM *m*

rambler *n jarg* LEIS, PROP bungalow *m*, chalet *m*

Rambouillet: ~ **summit** *n* ECON cumbre de Rambouillet *f*

ramp *n* GEN COMM, LAW, S&M *swindle* engaño *m*, estafa *f*, TRANSP rampa *f*; ~ **stillage** TRANSP plataforma de rampa *f*

ramped: ~ **cargo berth** *n* TRANSP muelle de carga en rampa *m*

Ramsey: ~ **price** *n* ECON precio de Ramsey *m*; ~ **saving rule** *n* ECON ley de ahorro de ramsey *f*; ~ **savings model** *n* ECON modelo de ahorro de Ramsey *m*

RAN *abbr* (*revenue anticipation note*) STOCK emisión de deuda municipal a corto plazo *f*

rancher *n AmE* (*cf* **stockbreeder** *BrE*) GEN COMM ganadero(-a) *m,f*

Randall: ~ **Commission** *n AmE* ECON comisión Randall *f*

R&CC *abbr* (*riots and civil commotions*) WEL tumultos y agitaciones sociales *m pl*

R&D[1] *abbr* (*research and development*) IND I&D (*investigación y desarrollo*)

R&D[2]: ~ **expenditure** *n* GEN COMM gastos de I&D *m pl*

random[1] *adj* GEN COMM aleatorio; ◆ **at** ~ GEN COMM aleatoriamente, al azar

random[2]: ~ **access** *n* COMP acceso aleatorio *m*; ~ **access memory** *n* (*RAM*) COMP memoria de acceso aleatorio *f*; ~ **channel** *n* COMP canal probabilístico *m*; ~ **check** *n* COMP, MATH *statistics* control aleatorio *m*; ~ **error** *n* COMP, MATH *statistics* error aleatorio *m*; ~ **factor** *n* ECON factor aleatorio *m*; ~ **number** *n* COMP, MATH número aleatorio *m*; ~ **number generator** *n* COMP, MATH *statistics* generador de números aleatorios *m*; ~ **observation method** *n* MATH, MGMNT, S&M método de observación aleatoria *m*; ~ **sample** *n* MATH, S&M

muestra aleatoria *f*; ~ **sampling** *n* MATH *statistics*, S&M muestreo al azar *m*; ~ **selection** *n* MATH selección al azar *f*; ~ **size** *n* GEN COMM tamaño aleatorio *m*; ~ **variable** *n* COMP, MATH *statistics* variable aleatoria *f*; ~ **variation** *n* ECON variación aleatoria *f*; ~ **walk** *n* ECON, STOCK paseo aleatorio *m*; ~ **walk theory** *n* ECON, STOCK teoría del camino aleatorio *f*

randomization *n* GEN COMM aleatorización *f*

randomly *adv* GEN COMM aleatoriamente

range *n* MATH intervalo *m*, STOCK *futures market* banda *f*, TAX abanico *m*; ~ **of options** GEN COMM gama de opciones *f*; ~ **of products** GEN COMM, S&M gama de productos *f*; ◆ **be out of** ~ GEN COMM estar fuera de alcance; **top end of the** ~ GEN COMM, S&M parte alta de la gama *f*

rank[1]: ~**-and-file** *n* ECON, HRM empleados sin cargo *m pl*, empleados y trabajadores del más bajo nivel *m pl*, personal del nivel más bajo *m*; ~ **correlation** *n* MATH *statistics* correlación por rangos *f*; ~ **order** *n* MATH jerarquía *f*

rank[2] **1.** *vt* ADMIN, ECON, GEN COMM clasificar, establecer un orden, figurar; **2.** *vi* GEN COMM clasificarse, figurar

rank above *vt* GEN COMM, STOCK figurar por encima de

rank after *vt* GEN COMM, STOCK figurar después de

rank below *vt* GEN COMM, STOCK figurar por debajo de

ranking *n* GEN COMM, HRM clasificación *f*, orden de importancia *m*, ordenación por importancia *f*; ~ **in order of seniority** GEN COMM clasificación por antigüedad *f*

rapid: ~ **growth** *n* ECON, IND crecimiento rápido *m*; ~ **premium decay** *n* STOCK rápida decadencia de la prima *f*; ~ **technological progress** *n* ECON, IND progreso tecnológico rápido *m*; ~ **transit system** *n* TRANSP sistema de tránsito rápido *m*

rappel *n* GEN COMM rappel *m*

raster *n* COMP trama *f*

rat: ~ **race** *n infrml* GEN COMM febril competitividad *f*

ratable[1] *adj* GEN COMM gravable

ratable[2]: ~ **value** *n BrE* (*cf* **assessed valuation** *AmE*) PROP, TAX valor imponible *m*

ratchet: ~ **effect** *n* ECON efecto de trinquete *m*, efecto palanca *m*

rate *n* COMP velocidad *f*, ECON rate *f*, *exchange* tipo *m*, *of prices* tarifa *f*; ~ **asked** STOCK coeficiente solicitado *m*; ~ **below cost** TRANSP tarifa bajo costes *f* (*Esp*), tarifa bajo costos *f* (*AmL*); ~ **card** S&M tarifa publicitaria *f*; ~ **ceiling** BANK, ECON, FIN *interest* tasa tope *f*; ~ **class** TRANSP clase de tarifa *f*; ~ **construction** TRANSP elaboración de tarifas *f*; ~ **cutting** HRM recorte de precios *m*, TRANSP disminución de la prima *f*; ~ **of decay** STOCK *options* índice de decadencia *m*; ~ **of depreciation** ACC tasa de depreciación *f*, tipo de depreciación *m*; ~ **differential** STOCK *of interest* diferencial de tipo *m*; ~ **dilution** TRANSP reducción de tarifas *f*; ~ **of discount** FIN, GEN COMM, STOCK tipo de descuento *m*; ~ **of exchange** ECON, GEN COMM tipo de cambio *m*; ~ **of exploitation** ECON proporción de explotación *f*; ~ **fixing** HRM fijación de tarifas *f*; ~ **flexibility** TRANSP flexibilidad de tarifas *f*; ~ **floor** GEN COMM *interest* tasa mínima *f*, tipo mínimo *m*; ~ **for the job** HRM precio según el trabajo *m*; ~ **of increase** ECON tasa de incremento *f*; ~ **of interest** GEN COMM tasa de interés *f*; ~ **not reported** (*RNR*) TRANSP tarifa no comunicada *f*; ~ **of relief** TAX tipo de la deducción *m*; ~ **resetter** (*RR*) STOCK mecanismo de puesta a cero del tipo *m*; ~ **of return** ACC índice de rendimiento *f*, tasa de rentabilidad *f*, BANK tasa de devolución *f*, tasa de rendimiento *f*, FIN porcentaje de devolución *m*, proporción de beneficios a capital invertido *f*; ~ **of return on capital employed** (*RORCE*) ACC, BANK, ECON, FIN tasa de rendimiento del capital invertido *f*; ~ **risk** ACC, BANK, FIN riesgo de tasa *m*; ~ **of rolling** STOCK tasa de renovación *f*; ~ **support grant** (*RSG*) ECON tipo mínimo garantizado *m*; ~ **of surplus value** BANK tasa de valor superávit *f*; ~ **of tax** TAX tipo impositivo *m*; ~ **of taxation** TAX tipo del impuesto *m*, tipo impositivo *m*; ~ **trend** TRANSP tendencia de tarifa *f*; ~ **war** GEN COMM guerra de tarifas *f*; ◆ **at an annual** ~ GEN COMM a una tasa anual; **at a current** ~ GEN COMM a un tipo actual; **at the top** ~ TAX al tipo más alto; **take the** ~ STOCK aceptar el porcentaje; ~ **to be agreed** (*RTBA*) TRANSP tasa a acordar

rated[1]: **not** ~ *adj* FIN *mercantile agencies* no clasificado

rated[2]: ~ **policy** *n* INS póliza tarificada *f*

ratepayer *n* POL, TAX contribuyente municipal *mf*

rates *n pl* GEN COMM cotizaciones *f pl*, TRANSP tarifas *f pl*; ~ **and classifications** COMMS tarifas y clasificaciones *f pl*; ~ **clerk** *n* HRM funcionario(-a) de tarifas *m,f*; ~ **formulation** *n* TRANSP formulación de tarifas *f*; ~ **officer** *n* HRM funcionario(-a) de tarifas *m,f*; ~ **review** *n* TRANSP revisión de tarifas *f*; ~ **strategy** *n* TRANSP estatregia de tarifas *f*; ~ **structure** *n* TRANSP estructura de tarifas *f*

ratification *n* GEN COMM *treaty* ratificación *f*

ratify *vt* GEN COMM *treaty* ratificar

rating *n* FIN tarifación *f*, S&M *of audience* índice *m*, STOCK clasificación *f*, tarifación *f*, TAX tarifación *f*; ~ **agency** FIN, STOCK organismo de clasificación de valores *m*, organismo de clasificación *m*; ~ **scale** GEN COMM escala de valoración *f*

ratio *n* GEN COMM cociente *m*, *coefficient* coeficiente *m*, *proportion* proporción *f*, ratio *m*, relación *f*; ~ **analysis** MATH *statistics* análisis de ratios *m*, análisis de razones *m*; ~ **call spread** STOCK *options* margen a ratio comprador *m*; ~ **chart** MATH gráfico de ratios *m*; ~ **of external debt to exports** ECON, IMP/EXP proporción de deuda externa por exportaciones *f*, relación de deuda externa a exportaciones *f*; ~ **scale** MATH escala porcentual *f*; ~ **spread** STOCK *options* compra o venta de opciones en proporciones diferentes; ~ **writer** STOCK emisor(a) de opciones en descubierto parcial *m,f*

ratio decendi *n* GEN COMM razón de la decisión *f*;

rational[1] *adj* GEN COMM racional

rational[2]: ~ **decision** *n* GEN COMM decisión racional *f*; ~ **economics** *n* ECON economía racional *f*; ~ **expectations** *n pl* (*RE*) ECON expectativas racionales *f pl*; ~ **management** *n* MGMNT administración racionalizada *f*, gestión racionalizada *f*

rationale *n* GEN COMM, HRM, MGMNT análisis *m*, exposición racional de principio *f*, exposición razonada *f*

rationalization *n* GEN COMM racionalización *f*; ~ **program** *AmE*, ~ **programme** *BrE* ECON, FIN, IND programa de racionalización *m*

rationalize *vt* GEN COMM racionalizar

rationing *n* BANK, ECON racionamiento *m*

RATs *abbr* (*ready assets trusts*) STOCK fondos a corto *m pl*

RATS *abbr* (*Restricted Articles Terminal System*) TRANSP Sistema Terminal de Artículos Restringidos *m*

ratten *vt AmE jarg* HRM *industrial relations* forzar una huelga mediante la inutilización de las herramientas de trabajo

raw[1] *adj* GEN COMM bruto

raw[2]: ~ **data** *n* COMP, MATH *statistics* datos brutos *m pl*, datos no procesados *m pl*; ~ **land** *n* PROP terreno no acondicionado *m*; ~ **materials** *n pl* ECON, IND materias primas *f pl*

Rawlsian: ~ **difference principle** *n* ECON principio de la diferencia rawlsiana *m*; ~ **justice** *n* ECON justicia rawlsiana *f*

RBT *abbr* (*rebuilt*) COMP, GEN COMM reconstruido

r/c *abbr* (*return cargo*) TRANSP carga de retorno *f*

RCCS *abbr* (*riots, civil commotions and strikes*) WEL motines, disturbios populares y huelgas *m pl*

RCH *abbr* (*Recognized Clearing House*) BANK Cámara de Compensación Autorizada *f*

rcvd *abbr* (*received*) GEN COMM recibido

Rd. *abbr* (*road*) TRANSP carretera *f*

RD *abbr* BANK (*refer to drawer*) RD (*dirigirse al librador, devuélvase al firmante*), ECON (*reserve deposit*) depósito de reserva *m*

RDB *abbr* (*relational database*) COMP BDR (*base de datos relacional*)

Rdk *abbr* (*raised deck*) TRANSP cubierta de castillo *f*, cubierta elevada *f*

re. *abbr* (*regarding*) COMMS acerca de, con referencia a, en cuanto a

RE *abbr* ECON (*rational expectations*) expectativas racionales *f pl*, STOCK (*Royal Exchange*) Bolsa de Valores de Londres

reach[1] *n* S&M alcance *m*; ~ **and frequency** S&M alcance y frecuencia *m*

reach[2] *vt* GEN COMM *agreement* lograr, alcanzar, llegar; ◆ ~ **an agreement** GEN COMM llegar a un acuerdo; ~ **an amicable settlement** GEN COMM llegar a un acuerdo amistoso; ~ **a compromise** GEN COMM llegar a un compromiso; ~ **a consensus on** GEN COMM consensuar; ~ **a joint agreement on** GEN COMM consensuar; ~ **saturation point** GEN COMM alcanzar el punto de saturación; ~ **a stalemate** GEN COMM llegar a un punto muerto; ~ **a total of** GEN COMM alcanzar un total de

reachback *n* TAX retroactividad *f*

react *vi* GEN COMM reaccionar; ◆ ~ **well under stress** GEN COMM, HRM reaccionar bien estando bajo tensión

reaction *n* GEN COMM reacción *f*; ~ **function** ECON función de reacción *f*; ~ **time** IND tiempo de reacción *m*

reactionary *n* POL reaccionario *m*

reactivate *vt* COMP *software* reactivar

reactivation *n* COMP reactivación

reactive[1] *adj* GEN COMM reactivo *m*

reactive[2]: ~ **strategy** *n* GEN COMM estrategia reactiva *f*

read[1]: **most** ~ *adj* S&M más leído

read[2] *n* COMP, GEN COMM lectura *f*; ~ **head** COMP cabeza de lectura *f*; ~ **only memory** (*ROM*) COMP memoria de sólo lectura *f*; ~ **-write head** COMP cabeza lectora-grabadora *f*

read[3] *vt* COMP leer, WEL *university degree* estudiar; ◆ ~ **the tape** STOCK leer la cinta

reader *n* COMP, MEDIA, S&M *advertising* lector(a) *m,f*;

~ **involvement** S&M implicación del lector *f*; ~ **service card** S&M tarjeta de servicio al lector *f*

readership *n* MEDIA *of newspaper, book,* S&M número de lectores *m*; ~ **profile** MEDIA, S&M *market research* perfil de los lectores *m*; ~ **replication** S&M réplica de los lectores *f*; ~ **survey** S&M *market research* estudio sobre el perfil de los lectores *m*

reading¹: ~ **notice** *n jarg* MEDIA *print* anuncio en forma de noticia *m*

reading²: **take a** ~ *phr* GEN COMM leer

readjustment *n* ECON, GEN COMM reajuste *m*

ReadMe: ~ **file** *n* COMP fichero de lectura *m*

read/write *n* COMP lector/escritor *m*

ready¹ *adj* GEN COMM listo

ready²: ~ **assets trusts** *n pl* (*RATs*) STOCK fondos a corto *m pl*; ~ **berth** *n* TRANSP amarradero disponible *m*; ~ **cash** *n* GEN COMM caja *f*, efectivo *m*; ~~**made meal** *n* GEN COMM, S&M comida preparada *f*; ~ **money** *n* GEN COMM dinero en efectivo *m*, dinero en metálico *m*; ~ **reckoner** *n* GEN COMM contador de dinero *m*

reaffirm *vt* GEN COMM reafirmar

reafforestation *n* ENVIR reforestación *f*, repoblación forestal *f*

Reaganomics *n* ECON, POL reaganomía *f*, reaganomics *m*

real¹ *adj* GEN COMM real

real²: ~ **address** *n* COMP dirección real *f*; ~ **agreement** *n* LAW acuerdo efectivo *m*; ~ **asset** *n* FIN, PROP activo inmobiliario *m*; ~ **bills doctrine** *n* ECON *law of reflux* doctrina de saldos reales *f*; ~ **cost** *n* ACC, TAX coste real *m* (*Esp*), costo real *m* (*AmL*); ~ **earnings** *n pl* ECON, HRM ingresos reales *m pl*; ~ **economy of scale** *n* ECON economía real de escala *f*; ~ **estate** *n* LAW, PROP bienes inmuebles *m pl*, bienes raíces *m pl*; ~ **estate agency** *n* AmE (*cf estate agency BrE*) PROP agencia inmobiliaria *f*; ~ **estate appraisal** *n* TAX tasación inmobiliaria *f*; ~ **estate closing** *n* PROP cierre de la venta de una propiedad *m*; ~ **estate commission** *n* PROP comisión inmobiliaria *f*; ~ **estate company** *n* GEN COMM, PROP empresa inmobiliaria *f*, sociedad inmobiliaria *f*; ~ **estate funds** *n pl* ACC fondos inmobiliarios *m pl*; ~ **estate gain** *n* TAX rendimiento de la propiedad inmobiliaria *m*; ~ **estate investment trust** *n* (*REIT*) BANK, PROP, STOCK compañía de inversiones en bienes muebles *f*, consorcio de inversiones inmobiliarias *m*, fideicomiso de inversión de bienes raíces *m*; ~ **estate market** *n* GEN COMM, PROP mercado de bienes raices *m*, mercado inmobiliario *m*; ~ **exchange rate** *n* GEN COMM tasa de cambio real *f*; ~ **GDP growth** *n* ECON crecimiento real del PIB *m*; ~ **growth** *n* ECON crecimiento real *m*; ~ **income** *n* ACC, HRM, TAX renta real *f*; ~ **interest rate** *n* GEN COMM tasa de interés real *f*; ~ **investment** *n* BANK, FIN inversión real *f*; ~ **money** *n jarg* ECON dinero auténtico *m*; ~ **number** *n* COMP número real *m*; ~ **pay** *n* HRM pago efectivo *m*; ~ **property tax** *n* TAX contribución territorial *f*, contribución territorial urbana *f*; ~ **rate of return** *n* (*RRR*) BANK, FIN tasa real de devolución *f*, tasa real de rendimiento *f*; ~ **state investment fund** *n* FIN, STOCK fondo de inversión mobiliario *m* (*FIM*); ~ **storage** *n* COMP memoria real *f*; ~ **time** *n* GEN COMM tiempo real *m*; ~~**wage hypothesis** *n* ECON, HRM hipótesis del salario real *f*; ~ **wages** *n pl* ECON, HRM salario real *m*

realism *n* GEN COMM, LAW, POL realismo *m*

realistic *adj* GEN COMM, LAW, POL realista

realizable *adj* GEN COMM realizable

realization *n* GEN COMM realización *f*; ~ **of assets** ACC realización de activos *f*

realize *vt* ACC *profit* realizar, GEN COMM *goal* conseguir, STOCK *profit* realizar

realized: ~ **cost of funds** *n* STOCK coste de fondos realizado *m* (*Esp*), costo de fondos realizado *m* (*AmL*); ~ **gains** *n pl* ACC, FIN beneficios realizados *m pl*, ganancias obtenidas *f pl*; ~ **losses** *n pl* ACC, FIN pérdidas realizadas *f pl*; ~ **minimum return** *n* STOCK rendimiento mínimo obtenido *m*

reallocate *vt* ACC redistribuir, FIN reasignar

reallocation *n* ACC redistribución *f*, FIN reasignación *f*

reallowance *n* STOCK doble bonificación *f*, doble compensación *f*

Realpolitik *n* POL política real *f*

realtor *n* AmE (*cf estate agent BrE*) GEN COMM, PROP agente inmobiliario(-a) *m,f*

reap: ~ **the benefits** *phr* STOCK disfrutar los beneficios; ~ **the rewards** *phr* STOCK disfrutar las gratificaciones

reason *n* GEN COMM razón *f*; ◆ **for no** ~ GEN COMM por ninguna razón

reasonable¹ *adj* GEN COMM, LAW razonable

reasonable²: ~ **expense** *n* GEN COMM gasto razonable *m*; ~ **price** *n* GEN COMM precio razonable *m*

reasonably *adv* GEN COMM razonablemente

reasoned: ~ **amendment** *n* POL enmienda razonada *f*

reassess *vt* TAX reevaluar

reassessment *n* TAX reevaluación fiscal *f*; ~ **of interests** TAX reevaluación de intereses *f*; ~ **of penalties** TAX reevaluación de recargos *f*; ~ **of tax** TAX reevaluación de impuestos *f*

reassign *vt* FIN *funds* reasignar

reassignment *n* FIN reasignación *f*

rebagging *n* TRANSP reensacado *m*

rebate *n* ECON, FIN *of money paid* rebaja *f*, reducción *f*, GEN COMM bonificación *f*, TAX exención parcial *f*

rebateable *adj* TRANSP bonificable, irrebatible

reboot *vt* COMP reinicializar

rebooting *n* COMP reiniciación *f*

rebuild *vt* COMP *hardware, software,* GEN COMM reconstruir

rebuilt *adj* (*RBT*) COMP, GEN COMM reconstruido

rebuy *vt* S&M recomprar

recalculate *vt* MATH recalcular

recall¹ *n* GEN COMM, STOCK *of option* recompra *f*; ~ **study** GEN COMM estudio retirado *m*

recall² *vt* STOCK *option* recomprar

recapitalization *n* FIN, STOCK recapitalización *f*

recapturable: ~ **depreciation** *n* ACC amortización recuperable *f*, depreciación recuperable *f*

recapture *vt* ACC recobrar, GEN COMM recuperar; ◆ ~ **a debt** FIN refundir una deuda

receipt *n* (*rept*) GEN COMM resguardo *m*, recibo *m*; ~ **acknowledgement** GEN COMM acuse de recibo *m*; ~ **book** GEN COMM talonario de recibos *m*; ~ **for documents** PATENTS recibo de los documentos *m*; ~ **for payment** GEN COMM resguardo de un pago *m*; ~ **of goods** (*ROG*) TRANSP *cargo* recepción de mercancías *f*; ~ **slip** GEN COMM justificante *m*; ~ **stamp** COMMS sello de recibo *m*; ◆ **on** ~ **of** GEN COMM a la recepción de; **be in ~ of** GEN COMM *letter, payment* estar en posesión de

receipts *n pl* STOCK *futures* ingresos *m pl*; **~ credited to the fund** FIN entradas acreditadas en el fondo *f pl*; **~ and payments account** *n* ACC cuenta de cobros y pagos *f*

receivable *n* ACC valor por cobrar *m*; **~ basis** ACC base de cuentas a cobrar *f*, base de liquidación *f*; **~ method** ACC método aceptable *m*, método válido *m*

receivables *n pl* ACC cuentas a cobrar *f pl*; **~ turnover** *n* FIN renovación del activo exigible *f*

receive *vt* GEN COMM recibir; ◆ **~ against payment** BANK, FIN recibir contra pago; **~ an answer** GEN COMM obtener una respuesta

received[1] *adj (rcvd)* GEN COMM recibido

received[2]: **~ for shipment bill of lading** *n* IMP/EXP, TRANSP conocimiento de mercancía recibida para embarque *m*

receiver *n* GEN COMM, LAW consignatario(-a) *m,f*, depositario(-a) judicial *m,f*, recaudador(a) *m,f*, síndico(-a) *m,f*, destinatario(-a) *m,f*; **~'s agent** HRM agente del consignatario *mf*; **~'s certificate** FIN certificado del síndico interventor *m*; **~ and manager** FIN *bankruptcy* depositario(-a) y administrador(a) *m,f*, GEN COMM *bankruptcy* síndico(-a) y administrador(a) *m,f*, LAW *bankruptcy* receptor(a) y administrador(a) *m,f*; **~ of wrecks** HRM *of customs* interventor(a) del naufragio *m,f (Esp)*, contralor(a) del naufragio *m,f (AmL)*; ◆ **at ~'s risk** GEN COMM por cuenta y riesgo del receptor

receivership *n* FIN, LAW administración judicial *f*; ◆ **go into ~** FIN, LAW pasar a administración judicial

receiving: **~ bank** *n* BANK banco receptor *m*; **~ carrier** *n* TRANSP *shipping* transportista receptor *m*; **~ date** *n* TRANSP *shipping* fecha de recepción *f*; **~ office** *n (RO)* GEN COMM, PATENTS oficina de recepción *f*; **~ order** *n (RO)* TRANSP albarán de entrada *m*; **~ station** *n* COMMS, TRANSP *rail* estación receptora *f*

recent: **in ~ years** *phr* GEN COMM en los últimos años

reception *n* ADMIN recibimiento *m*, GEN COMM recepción *f*; **~ area** ADMIN, LEIS área de recepción *f*; **~ depot** TRANSP depósito receptor *m*; **~ desk** GEN COMM recepción *f*; **~ point** LEIS punto de recepción *m*

receptionist *n* HRM recepcionista *mf*

recession *n* ECON, GEN COMM recesión *f*, periodo de recesión *f*, retroceso *m*

recessionary[1] *adj* GEN COMM recesionario

recessionary[2]: **~ gap** *n* ECON, GEN COMM periodo de recesión *m*; **~ phase** *n* ECON fase de recesión *f*

recipient *n* GEN COMM, destinatario(-a) *m,f*; **~ of an allowance** BrE *(cf welfare recipient AmE)* HRM, WEL beneficiario(-a) de un subsidio *m,f*; **~ bank** BANK banco receptor *m*

reciprocal[1] *adj* GEN COMM recíproco

reciprocal[2] *n* MATH recíproca *f*; **~ agreement** LAW acuerdo recíproco *m*; **~ buying** S&M compra bilateral *f*; **~ ratio** MATH razón recíproca *f*; **~ taxation agreement** TAX acuerdo de imposición recíproca *m*; **~ trading** ECON, GEN COMM comercio recíproco *m*, negocio recíproco *m*

reciprocally *adv* GEN COMM a título de reciprocidad

reciprocity *n* ECON reciprocidad *f*

reckoning *n* GEN COMM cálculo *m*, cómputo *m*, cuenta *f*

reclaim[1]: **~ area** *n* TRANSP área de recuperación *f*

reclaim[2] *vt* ENVIR *land* reclamar

reclamation *n* TRANSP *of cargo, luggage* recuperación *f*

reclassification *n* GEN COMM reclasificación *f*; **~ entry** ACC asiento de reclasificación *m*

reclassify *vt* GEN COMM reclasificar

recognition *n* GEN COMM reconocimiento *m*; **~ of loss** ACC reconocimiento de pérdidas *m*; **~-only clause** BrE HRM cláusula de reconocimiento exclusivo *f*; **~-only practice** HRM práctica de simple reconocimiento *f*; **~ test** S&M prueba de reconocimiento *f*

recognize *vt* GEN COMM, HRM *rights, union* reconocer

recognized[1] *adj* GEN COMM reconocido

recognized[2]: **~ gains** *n pl* TAX ganancias reconocidas *f pl*; **~ investment exchange** *n (RIE)* STOCK bolsa de inversión reconocida *f*; **~ political party** *n* POL, TAX partido político reconocido *m*; **~ professional body** *n (RPB)* ECON, FIN cuerpo profesional reconocido *m*; **~ third-world investment firms** *n* FIN empresas de inversión del tercer mundo reconocidas *f pl*; **~ labor union** *n AmE (cf recognized trade union BrE)* HRM, POL sindicato reconocido *m*; **~ trade union** *n BrE (cf recognized labor union AmE)* HRM, POL sindicato reconocido *m*

Recognized: **~ Clearing House** *n (RCH)* BANK Cámara de Compensación Autorizada *f*

recommend *vt* GEN COMM recomendar

recommendation *n* GEN COMM recomendación *f*

recommended: **~ retail price** *n (RRP)* GEN COMM precio de venta al público *m (P.V.P.)*

recommissioned *adj (recmd)* GEN COMM vuelto al servicio

recompilation *n* COMP recopilación *f*

recompile *vt* COMP recopilar

reconcile *vt* ACC, BANK, GEN COMM reconciliar

reconciliation *n* ACC *of statements* conciliación contable *f*, GEN COMM, HRM conciliación *f*; **~ account** ACC, BANK, FIN, STOCK cuenta de reconciliación *f*; **~ of accounts** ACC, BANK reconciliación de cuentas *f*; **~ bill** ECON letra de conciliación *f*, FIN factura de conciliación *f*, LAW acta de reconciliación *f*; **~ statement** ACC estado de conciliación *m*, estado de reconciliación *m*; **~ table** ACC cuadro de conciliación *m*

reconditioned *adj (R)* GEN COMM, TRANSP reacondicionado

reconfiguration *n* GEN COMM reconfiguración *f*

reconnaissance: **~ survey** *n* GEN COMM estudio preliminar *m*

reconsider *vt* GEN COMM reconsiderar; ◆ **~ an assessment** TAX reconsiderar una liquidación

reconsign *vt* TRANSP *freight* cambiar de destinatario

reconstruction *n* ECON, GEN COMM, IND *of company* reestructuración *f*, reconstrucción *f*

reconversion *n* GEN COMM reconversión *f*

reconvert *vt* COMP reconvertir

reconveyance *n* PROP restitución *f*

record[1]: **~-high** *adj* ECON, GEN COMM *profits, unemployment* sin precedentes

record[2] *n* GEN COMM *list* registro *m*, *written* expediente *m*; **~ breaker** HRM plusmarquista *mf*, recordman *m*; **~ date** GEN COMM, STOCK fecha de registro *f*; **~ format** COMP formato de registro *m*; **~ keeper** ADMIN, HRM archivador(a) *m,f (Esp)*, archivero(-a) *m,f (AmL)*, archivista *mf*; **~ key** COMP clave de registro *f*;

~ **locking** COMP matriz de registro *f*; ~ **result** GEN COMM resultado sin precedentes *m*; ~ **sale** S&M venta excelente *f*

record[3] *vt* STOCK *a low, a high* experimentar, registrar; ◆ ~ **in the register** PATENTS inscribir en el registro; ~ **a meeting** GEN COMM registrar una reunión

recorded: ~ **delivery** *n BrE* COMMS correo certificado con acuso de recibo *m*; ~ **market information** *n* STOCK información registrada del mercado *f*

records *n pl* ACC protocolos *m pl*, registros *m pl*; ~ **management** *n* MGMNT dirección de registros *f*, gerencia de registros *f*

recoup *vt* LAW deducir

recourse *n* LAW recurso *m*; ~ **loan** BANK, FIN préstamo con aval *m*

recover 1. *vt* ECON recobrar; **2.** *vi* ACC, GEN COMM recuperarse

recoverable: ~ **cost** *n* ACC coste recuperable *m* (*Esp*), costo recuperable *m* (*AmL*); ~ **date** *n* ACC fecha exigible *f*, vencimiento *m*; ~ **error** *n* COMP, MATH error recuperable *m*; ~ **material** *n* ENVIR *recycling* material recuperable *m*; ~ **reserve** *n* ENVIR *of minerals* reserva recuperable *f*

recovery *n* COMP *lost file, data*, ECON recuperación *f*, GEN COMM *reacquisition* reactivación *f*, *market* recuperación *f*; ~ **of expenses** ACC, FIN recuperación de gastos *f*; ~ **plan** ECON plan de rehabilitación *m*; ~ **scheme** GEN COMM programa de recuperación *m*; ~ **vehicle** TRANSP vehículo recuperador *m*

recreational: ~ **facility** *n* GEN COMM instalación recreativa *f*

recruit *vt* HRM reclutar

recruiting: ~ **office** *n* HRM oficina de reclutamiento *f*; ~ **officer** *n* HRM ejecutivo(-a) de reclutamiento *m,f*, jefe(-a) de reclutamiento *m,f*

recruitment *n* HRM *of staff* reclutamiento *m*; ~ **advertising** S&M publicidad de reclutamiento *f*; ~ **agency** GEN COMM, HRM agencia de colocaciones *f*, oficina de empleo *f*, oficina de trabajo *f*; ~ **bonus** HRM bonificación por contratación *f*; ~ **consultant** HRM asesor(a) de selección *m,f*; ~ **manager** HRM gerente de contratación *mf*; ~ **and selection** HRM contratación y selección *f*

rectification *n* GEN COMM, PATENTS, POL rectificación *f*

rectify *vt* GEN COMM rectificar

recto *n* MEDIA anverso *m*, recto *m*

recurrent: ~ **disability** *n* HRM incapacidad recurrente *f*

recursive: ~ **system** *n* ECON *econometrics* sistema recursivo *m*

recyclable *adj* ENVIR reciclable

recycle *vt* ENVIR reciclar

recycled: ~ **paper** *n* ENVIR papel reciclado *m*

recycling *n* ENVIR reciclaje *m*

red. *abbr* (*redeemable*) GEN COMM reembolsable

red[1]: ~ **clause** *n* BANK, FIN, IMP/EXP, TRANSP cláusula roja *f*; ~ **clause credit** *n* TRANSP *shipping* crédito con cláusula roja *m*; ~ **goods** *n pl jarg* S&M *advertising* bienes de rápido consumo y pronta reposición; ~ **and green system** *n* IMP/EXP *customs* sistema rojo y verde *m*; ~ **herring** *n* STOCK folleto informativo de una nueva emisión *m*; ~**-herring prospectus** *n* STOCK prospecto preliminar *m*; ~**-line clause** *n* INS cláusula de línea roja

f; ~ **tape** *n* GEN COMM, MGMNT, POL rutina administrativa *f*, trámites burocráticos *m pl*

red[2]: **be in the** ~ *phr* GEN COMM, BANK estar en números rojos

Red: ~ **Book** *n AmE infrml* FIN Libro Rojo *m*

redeem *vt* ACC, STOCK rescatar

redeemable[1] *adj* (*red.*) GEN COMM reembolsable

redeemable[2]: ~ **bond** *n* STOCK obligación amortizable *f*; ~ **preference share** *n* STOCK acción preferente amortizable *f*; ~ **retractable preferred share** *n* STOCK acción preferente retractable amortizable *f*; ~ **shares** *n pl* STOCK acciones amortizables *f pl*; ~ **stock** *n* STOCK acciones rescatables *f pl*

redeemed[1] *adj* ACC, STOCK *share* rescatado

redeemed[2]: ~ **debenture** *n* STOCK obligación rescatada *f*

redelivery *n* TRANSP devolución *f*, retorno *m*

redemption *n* ACC rescate *m*, FIN redención *f*, TAX exención de cuota variable *f*, rescate *m*; ~ **before due date** FIN reembolso anticipado *m*, amortización antes del vencimiento *f*; ~ **bond** FIN, STOCK bono de amortización *m*; ~ **call** STOCK aviso de amortización *m*; ~ **date** GEN COMM, STOCK fecha de amortización *f*, fecha de rescate *f*, vencimiento *m*; ~ **fee** STOCK tasa de amortización *f*; ~ **fund** ACC, FIN, STOCK fondo de rescate *m*; ~ **premium** ACC prima de amortización *f*, prima de cancelación *f*, prima de rescate *f*; ~ **price** STOCK precio de rescate *m*; ~ **of a promissory note** BANK cancelación de un pagaré *f*; ~ **table** ACC, BANK cuadro de amortización *m*; ~ **value** STOCK valor de rescate *m*; ~ **yield** ACC, ECON, FIN, STOCK rendimiento de una acción en la fecha de rescate

redeploy *vt* GEN COMM redistribuir, HRM dar un nuevo destino a, disponer de otro modo, reorganizar

redeployment *n* GEN COMM redistribución *f*, HRM reorganización *f*; ~ **premium** HRM prima por reconversión *f*

redeposit *vt* BANK redepositar

redesign *vt* GEN COMM rediseñar

redevelop *vt* ECON revelar de nuevo, PROP reorganizar

redevelopment *n* PROP reorganización *f*

rediscount: ~ **rate** *n* ACC, FIN tipo de redescuento *m*

rediscountable *adj* ACC, BANK, FIN redescontable

rediscounter *n* ACC, BANK, FIN redescontador *m*

rediscounting *n* ACC, BANK, FIN redescuento *m*

redistribute *vt* GEN COMM redistribuir

redistribution *n* GEN COMM redistribución *f*

redlining *n jarg* FIN negación de hipotecas sobre terrenos o propiedades

redraft *n* BANK giro renovado *m*

redress[1] *n* LAW reparación *f*

redress[2]: ~ **the balance** *vi* ACC cuadrar, equilibrar el balance, restablecer el equilibrio del balance

REDS *abbr* (*Registered Excise Dealers and Shippers*) IMP/EXP, TRANSP intermediarios y exportadores de derechos registrados *m pl*

reduce *vt* ECON, GEN COMM *prices, investment* reducir, *expenses* mermar, recortar

reduced[1] *adj* GEN COMM reducido

reduced[2]: ~ **class rate** *n* TRANSP *of air freight* tasa de reducción de clase *f*; ~ **fare** *n* LEIS, TRANSP tarifa reducida *f*; ~ **form equation** *n* ECON ecuación en forma reducida *f*; ~ **lead time** *n* IND tiempo de entrega reducido *m*; ~ **price** *n* S&M precio rebajado *m*; ~ **rate** *n* TAX tipo reducido *m*; ~ **tax** *n* TAX impuesto reducido *m*; ~ **weight** *n* (*RW*) TRANSP *shipping* peso reducido *m*

reduction *n* BANK, FIN *in interest rates* recorte *m*, GEN COMM reducción *f*; ~ **of capital** STOCK reducción de capital *f*; ~ **for senior citizens** TAX reducción para la tercera edad *f*; ~ **in force** (*RIF*) HRM reducción de los empleos secundarios *f*

redundancy *n* COMP, GEN COMM redundancia *f*, HRM despido *m*; ~ **benefit** HRM indemnización por despido *f*; ~ **check** COMP verificación por redundancia *f*; ~ **consultation** HRM consulta por despido colectivo *f*; ~ **letter** COMMS *notice in writing*, HRM boleta de despido *f* (*AmL*), carta de despido *f* (*Esp*); ~ **pay** HRM, WEL compensación por despido *f*; ~ **payment** GEN COMM subsidio sindical de paro *m*, HRM, WEL compensación por despido *f*; ~ **procedure** HRM procedimiento de despido *m*

Redundancy: ~ **Payments Act** *n* BrE HRM, LAW ley de compensaciones por despido colectivo

redundant[1] *adj* COMP, GEN COMM *unneeded, outdated* redundante, HRM despedido

redundant[2]: ~ **farmland** *n* ENVIR tierra de cultivo redundante *f*

re-educate *vt* GEN COMM, HRM reeducar

reefer *n* TRANSP *container* frigorífico *m*; ~ **container** TRANSP contenedor frigorífico *m*; ~ **ship** TRANSP buque frigorífico *m*; ~ **trade** ECON, TRANSP sector frigorífico *m*

reel[1]: ~**-fed** *adj* MEDIA, S&M *printing* con carrete colocado

reel[2] *n* COMP, MEDIA, S&M carrete *m*

re-election *n* GEN COMM, POL reelección *f*

re-embark *vi* GEN COMM reembarcarse

re-emphasize *vt* GEN COMM volver a insistir en

re-employment *n* HRM reempleo *m*

re-endorsement *n* BANK reendoso *m*

re-enter *vt* COMP *data, program* reintroducir por teclado

re-establishment *n* GEN COMM rehabilitación *f*

re-evaluation: ~ **of assets** *n* FIN reevaluación de activos *f*

re-examination *n* GEN COMM reexamen *m*

re-examine *vt* GEN COMM reexaminar

re-exportation *n* IMP/EXP reexportación *f*

re-exporter *n* IMP/EXP reexportador(a) *m,f*

ref. *abbr* (*reference*) GEN COMM, HRM referencia *f*; ◆ **your** ~ (*your reference*) COMMS su referencia

refer 1. *vt* PATENTS remitir; ◆ ~ **to acceptor** (*R/A*) BANK referir al aceptante, remitir al aceptante; ~ **sth back to sb** GEN COMM achacar algo a alguien; **2.** ~ **to drawer** BANK, GEN COMM dirigirse al librador (*RD*), devuélvase al firmante (*RD*)

referee: ~ **in case of need** *n* BANK interventor(a) en caso de necesidad *m,f* (*Esp*), contralor(a) en caso de necesidad *m,f* (*AmL*)

reference *n* (*ref.*) GEN COMM, HRM referencia *f*; ~ **currency** BANK, ECON divisa de referencia *f*; ~ **cycle** GEN COMM ciclo industrial *m*; ~ **file** COMP, GEN COMM fichero de referencias *m*; ~ **group** GEN COMM grupo de referencia *m*; ~ **level** FIN nivel de referencia *m*; ~ **line** PATENTS línea de referencia *f*; ~ **material** GEN COMM material de referencia *m*; ~ **sign** PATENTS signo de referencia *m*; ◆ **by** ~ **to** GEN COMM con respecto a; **in** ~ **to** PATENTS en lo que afecta a; **with** ~ **to** COMMS

acerca de, con referencia a, en cuanto a, en el caso de; **your** ~ (*your ref.*) COMMS su referencia

referendum *n* GEN COMM, POL referéndum *m*

referral: **by** ~ **to** *phr* GEN COMM referido a

referring: ~ **to** *phr* GEN COMM referido a

refinance[1]: ~ **credit** *n* BANK crédito de refinanciación *m*

refinance[2] *vt* BANK, FIN, GEN COMM refinanciar

refinancing *n* BANK, FIN, GEN COMM refinanciación *f*; ~ **risk** BANK, FIN riesgo relacionado con la refinanciación *m*

refined[1] *adj* IND refinado

refined[2]: ~ **metal** *n* ENVIR, INS metal refinado *m*

refinery *n* ENVIR, IND refinería *f*

refining *n* IND refinación *f*

reflate *vt* ECON reactivar

reflect *vt* GEN COMM reflejar

reflected: **be** ~ **in** *phr* GEN COMM reflejarse en

refloating *n* FIN, STOCK reflotamiento *m*

refocusing *AmE see* **refocussing** *BrE*

refocussing *n* BrE GEN COMM nuevo enfoque *m*

reform[1] *n* GEN COMM, LAW reform; ~ **package** POL paquete de reformas *m*; ~ **program** *AmE*, ~ **programme** *BrE* ECON programa de reforma *m*

reform[2] *vt* GEN COMM reformar

reformat *vt* COMP *disk* reformatear

reformism *n* POL *Marxism* reformismo *m*

reforwarding *n* TRANSP reexpedición *f*

refrain from *vt* GEN COMM desistir de

refresh *vt* COMP *update memory* refrescar

refresher *n* LAW recordatorio *m*

refrigerated[1] *adj* TRANSP refrigerado

refrigerated[2]: ~ **box van** *n* TRANSP furgón con caja frigorífica *m*, furgón con caja refrigerada *m*; ~ **capacity** *n* TRANSP *of container* capacidad de refrigeración *f*; ~ **container** *n* TRANSP contenedor frigorífico *m*; ~ **lorry** *n* BrE (*cf refrigerated truck AmE*) TRANSP camión refrigerado *m*; ~ **ship** *n* TRANSP buque refrigerado *m*; ~ **truck** *n* AmE (*cf refrigerated lorry BrE*) TRANSP camión refrigerado *m*; ~ **vessel** *n* TRANSP *shipping* buque refrigerado *m*; ~ **warehouse** *n* GEN COMM almacén refrigerado *m*

refrigeration *n* (*R*) TRANSP refrigeración *f* (*R*)

refueling *AmE see* **refuelling** *BrE*

refuelling *n* BrE TRANSP repostado de combustible *m*, repostaje *m*

refugee *n* GEN COMM refugiado(-a) *m,f*; ~ **capital** FIN capital errante *m*

refund *n* GEN COMM reembolso *m*, PATENTS, TAX devolución *f*; ~ **return** TAX declaración del reintegro *f*; ~ **slip** GEN COMM recibo de reintegro *m*; ~ **of tax** TAX desgravación fiscal *f*

refundable[1] *adj* GEN COMM, STOCK, TAX reembolsable

refundable[2]: ~ **deposit** *n* GEN COMM, PROP depósito reembolsable *m*; ~ **federal sales tax credit** *n* TAX desgravación federal reembolsable sobre ventas *f*; ~ **prepaid credit** *n* TAX abono a cuenta reembolsable *m*; ~ **tax credit** *n* TAX desgravación fiscal reembolsable *f*

refunding *n* STOCK consolidación *f*; ~ **bond** FIN, STOCK bono de conversión *m*; ~ **of a loan** BANK, FIN conversión de un préstamo *f*

refurbish *vt* PROP renovar

refurbished *adj* GEN COMM, TRANSP reacondicionado

refurbishment *n* GEN COMM reacondicionamiento *m*, PROP renovación *f*, reacondicionamiento *m*, TRANSP reacondicionamiento *m*

refusal *n* GEN COMM, PATENTS negativa *f*

refuse[1]: ~ **collection** *n* GEN COMM recogida de basuras *f*; ~ **disposal** *n* ENVIR evacuación de residuos *f*

refuse[2] *vt* GEN COMM rehusar, LAW denegar, TRANSP *pasenger* rechazar; ◆ ~ **acceptance of a draft** BANK rechazar la aceptación de una letra, rehusar la aceptación de una letra; ~ **bail** LAW denegar una fianza

regard: **have a high ~ for sb** *phr* GEN COMM tener a alguien en gran estima

regarding *prep* (*re.*) COMMS acerca de, con referencia a, en cuanto a

regd. *abbr* (*registered*) COMMS registrado

regime *n* GEN COMM régimen *m*

region *n* GEN COMM, POL provincia *f*, región *f*; ◆ **in the ~ of** GEN COMM *approximately* alrededor de

regional[1] *adj* GEN COMM regional

regional[2]: ~ **agreement** *n* ECON acuerdo regional *m*; ~ **bank** *n* BANK banco regional *m*; ~ **banking pact** *n* BANK pacto bancario regional *m*; ~ **center** *AmE*, ~ **centre** *BrE* *n* GEN COMM centro regional *m*; ~ **development** *n* ECON desarrollo regional *m*; ~ **distribution center** *AmE*, ~ **distribution centre** *BrE* *n* BANK centro de distribución del estado *m*, centro de distribución regional *m*; ~ **economics** *n* ECON economía regional *f*; ~ **employment premium** *n* (*REP*) HRM bonificación por empleo regional *f*; ~ **grouping** *n* ECON *NAFTA* agrupamiento regional *m*; ~ **manager** *n* HRM, MGMNT director(a) provincial *m,f*; ~ **market** *n* S&M mercado regional *m*; ~ **multiplier** *n* ECON multiplicador regional *m*; ~ **office** *n* GEN COMM oficina regional *f*; ~ **organization** *n* GEN COMM, MGMNT organización regional *f*; ~ **patent** *n* LAW, PATENTS patente regional *f*; ~ **policy** *n* ECON política regional *f*; ~ **press** *n* MEDIA, S&M prensa de provincia, prensa regional *f*; ~ **quota** *n* ECON cuota regional *f*; ~ **representation** *n* S&M representación regional *f*; ~ **selective assistance** *n* ECON ayuda regional selectiva *f*; ~ **stock exchange** *n* STOCK bolsa regional de valores *f*; ~ **tax effects** *n pl* ACC, TAX efectos fiscales regionales *m pl*; ~ **trend** *n* ECON, S&M tendencia regional *f*; ~ **wage bargaining** *n* HRM negociación regional de salarios *f*

regionally *adv* GEN COMM regionalmente

register[1] *n* GEN COMM *book* registro *m*, PATENTS libro registro *m*, STOCK registrador *m*; ~ **book** PATENTS libro registro *m*; ~ **of companies** IND registro mercantil *m*; ~ **of deeds** LAW registrador de la propiedad *m* (*Esp*), registro público de la propiedad y del comercio *m* (*AmL*); ~ **of mortgages** LAW, PROP registro de la propiedad *m*; ~ **tonnage** GEN COMM *maritime*, TRANSP tonelaje de registro *m*

register[2] *vt* GEN COMM *business name* registrar; ◆ ~ **a high** STOCK registrar un alza

Register: ~ **of Members** *n pl* GEN COMM registro de miembros *m*, registro de socios *m*, LAW registro de accionistas *m*

registered[1] *adj* (*regd.*) COMMS nominativo, registrado; ~ **unemployed** HRM, WEL registrado desempleado

registered[2]: ~ **address** *n* GEN COMM domicilio social *m*; ~ **applicants for work** *n pl infrml* GEN COMM aspirantes a un trabajo registrados *m pl*; ~ **baggage** *n* TRANSP equipaje registrado *m*; ~ **bond** *n* FIN, STOCK bono registrado *m*; ~ **broker** *n* STOCK corredor(a) titulado(-a) *m,f*; ~ **capital** *n* GEN COMM capital registrado *m*; ~ **charity** *n* GEN COMM, TAX institución benéfica registrada *f*; ~ **check** *AmE*, ~ **cheque** *BrE* *n* BANK cheque registrado *m*; ~ **company** *n* GEN COMM sociedad legalmente constituida *f*; ~ **competitive market maker** *n* STOCK creador(a) autorizado(-a) de mercado competitivo *m,f*; ~ **competitive trader** *n* STOCK operador(a) competitivo(-a) autorizado(-a) *m,f*; ~ **design** *n* LAW proyecto registrado *m*; ~ **equity market maker** *n* STOCK creador(a) autorizado(-a) de mercado de valores *m,f*; ~ **letter** *n* ACC, ADMIN, BANK carta certificada *f*; ~ **life insurance policy** *n* INS póliza registrada de seguro de vida *f*; ~ **luggage** *n* TRANSP equipaje facturado *m*; ~ **manager** *n* HRM *shipping*, MGMNT director(a) registrado(-a) *m,f*; ~ **office** *n* GEN COMM, LAW domicilio social *m*, sede social *f*; ~ **options broker** *n* STOCK broker de opciones registrado *mf*, intermediario(-a) de opciones registrado(-a) *m,f*; ~ **options trader** *n* STOCK operador(a) de opciones autorizado(-a) *m,f*; ~ **owner** *n* STOCK *of bond* propietario(-a) nominal *m,f*; ~ **political party** *n* POL, TAX partido político legalizado *m*; ~ **post** *n* *BrE* (*cf certified mail AmE*) COMMS correo certificado *m*; ~ **proprietor** *n* LAW, PROP propietario(-a) registrado(-a) *m,f*; ~ **representative** *n* GEN COMM, HRM, STOCK representante autorizado(-a) *m,f*; ~ **retirement savings plan** *n* (*RRSP*) GEN COMM plan nominativo de ahorro y pensión *m*; ~ **secondary offering** *n* STOCK oferta secundaria autorizada *f*; ~ **security** *n* STOCK título registrado *m*; ~ **share** *n* ACC, STOCK acción nominativa *f*; ~ **shareholder** *n* STOCK accionista nominativo(-a) *m,f*; ~ **ship** *n* TRANSP buque registrado *m*; ~ **stockholder** *n* STOCK accionista nominativo(-a) *m,f*; ~ **title** *n* MEDIA título nominativo *m*, título registrado *m*; ~ **ton** *n* GEN COMM, TRANSP tonelaje registrado *m*; ~ **trademark** *n* GEN COMM marca industrial registrada *f*, marca registrada *f*; ~ **unemployment** *n* ECON paro registrado *m*; ~ **user** *n* LAW, PATENTS usuario(-a) registrado(-a) *m,f*

Registered: ~ **Excise Dealers and Shippers** *n* (*REDS*) IMP/EXP, TRANSP intermediarios y exportadores de derechos registrados *m pl*; ~ **International Exchange** *n* (*RIE*) STOCK Bolsa Internacional Oficial de Valores *f*

registrant *n* STOCK *securities* registrador(a) *m,f*

registrar: ~**'s department** *n* BANK departamento del registrador *m*; ~ **of companies** *n* HRM encargado del Registro Mercantil *m*; ~ **fee** *n* TAX gastos de secretaría *m pl*; ~**'s office** *n* ADMIN oficina del Registro Civil *f*; ~ **of transfers** *n* FIN registrador(a) de transferencias *m,f*

registration *n* GEN COMM *of company name* registro *m*, PATENTS inscripción *f*, matriculación *f*; ~ **fee** STOCK derechos de certificación *m pl*; ~ **form** MEDIA boletín de suscripción *m*; ~ **number** GEN COMM, TRANSP número de matrícula *m*, número de registro *m*; ~ **office** ADMIN oficina de registro *f*; ~ **statement** STOCK declaración de registro *f*; ~ **threshold** TAX nivel de inscripción *m*

registry: ~ **of deeds** *n* LAW, PROP registro de escrituras *m*, registro de la propiedad *m*; ~ **office** *n* *BrE* ADMIN oficina del Registro Civil *f*; ~ **of shipping** *n* TRANSP registro de navegación *m*

regression *n* MATH *statistics* regresión *f*; ~ **analysis** ECON, FIN, MATH *statistics* análisis de regresión *m*; ~ **coefficient** GEN COMM coeficiente de regresión *m*; ~ **curve** MATH *statistics* curva de regresión *f*

regressive: ~ **scale** *n* MATH escala regresiva *f*; ~ **supply** *n*

ECON oferta regresiva *f*; ~ **taxation** *n* TAX imposición regresiva *f*

regroup *vt* GEN COMM reagrupar

regular: ~ **and continuous basis** *n* TAX base regular y continua *f*; ~ **customer** *n* GEN COMM cliente habitual *mf*; ~ **expenditure** *n* FIN gasto regular *m*; ~ **hours** *n pl* GEN COMM horarios regulares *m pl*; ~ **meeting** *n* GEN COMM, MGMNT junta ordinaria *f*; ~ **payment** *n* GEN COMM pago regular *m*; ~ **service** *n* LEIS servicio regular *m*; ~ **statement** *n* GEN COMM declaración ordinaria *f*; ~ **supplementary estimates** *n pl* FIN estimaciones complementarias regulares *f pl*; ~ **way delivery** *n* GEN COMM, STOCK operación normal de bolsa *f*, entrega por vía regular *f*

regulate *vt* GEN COMM regular

regulated: ~ **agreement** *n* FIN acuerdo regulado *m*; ~ **commodity** *n* STOCK producto básico controlado *m*; ~ **firm** *n* ECON empresa regulada *f*; ~ **industry** *n* ECON, IND industria regulada *f*; ~ **investment company** *n* ECON, FIN empresa de inversión regulada *f*; ~ **market** *n* ECON, FIN mercado regulado *m*

regulation *n* GEN COMM disposición *f*, norma *f*, reglamento *m*, MGMNT normativa *f*

Regulation: ~ **School** *n* ECON escuela de regulación *f*; ~ **Z** *n* ECON, FIN regulación Z *f*

regulator *n* LAW, TAX regulador *m*

regulatory[1] *adj* GEN COMM, LAW, POL reglamentario

regulatory[2]: ~ **agency** *n* GEN COMM organismo con potestad normativa *m*; ~ **authorities** *n pl* GEN COMM, LAW autoridades reguladoras *f pl*; ~ **authority** *n* GEN COMM, LAW poder regulador *m*; ~ **body** *n* GEN COMM, LAW organismo regulador *m*; ~ **capture** *n* ECON captura reguladora *f*; ~ **committee** *n* LAW, POL comisión reguladora *f*; ~ **measure** *n* LAW medida reguladora *f*; ~ **system** *n* LAW sistema regulador *m*; ~ **theory** *n* GEN COMM teoría reguladora *f*

Regulatory: ~ **News Service** *n* (*RNS*) MEDIA, STOCK servicio de control de la información

rehabilitate *vt* GEN COMM *reputation, company* rehabilitar

rehabilitation *n* ENVIR *of abandoned waste dumping sites*, GEN COMM rehabilitación *f*; ~ **import credit** (*RIC*) FIN crédito de rehabilitación de la importación *m*; ~ **import loan** (*RIL*) FIN, IMP/EXP préstamo de rehabilitación de la importación *m*

reheater *n* TRANSP *engine* recalentador intermedio *m*

rehypothecation *n* STOCK constitución de segundas hipotecas *f*

reign[1] *n* GEN COMM reinado *m*

reimburse *vt* GEN COMM reembolsar

reimbursing: ~ **bank** *n* BANK, FIN, GEN COMM banco reembolsador *m*

reimpose *vt* GEN COMM volver a imponer

reinforce *vt* GEN COMM *effect, impact* reforzar

reinforced *adj* ECON, GEN COMM reforzado

reinforcement *n* GEN COMM reforzamiento *m*, refuerzo *m*

reinfusion *n* FIN reintroducción *f*

reinitiate *vt* GEN COMM reiniciar

reinstatement *n* GEN COMM *employee, insurance* reposición *f*

reinsurance *n* INS, STOCK reaseguro *m*; ~ **company** INS compañía reaseguradora *f*; ~ **treaty** INS contrato de reaseguro *m*

reinvent: ~ **the wheel** *phr* GEN COMM volver a inventar la rueda

reinvest *vt* GEN COMM, STOCK reinvertir

reinvestment *n* GEN COMM, STOCK reinversión *f*; ~ **loss** ACC pérdida de reinversión *f*; ~ **privilege** STOCK privilegio de reinversión *m*; ~ **rate** GEN COMM, STOCK *of futures* tasa de reinversión *f*, tipo de reinversión *m*

reissue[1] *n* BANK *bill of exchange*, STOCK nueva emisión *f*

reissue[2] *vt* STOCK emitir de nuevo

REIT *abbr* (*real estate investment trust*) BANK, PROP, STOCK fideicomiso de inversión de bienes raíces *m*, compañía de inversiones en bienes muebles *f*, consorcio de inversiones inmobiliarias *m*

reiterate *vt* GEN COMM reiterar

reject[1]: ~ **bin** *n* GEN COMM almacén de rechazos *m*

reject[2] *vt* GEN COMM rechazar

rejection *n* GEN COMM rechazo *m*

related: ~ **business** *n* GEN COMM, TAX empresa relacionada *f*, empresa vinculada *f*; ~ **group** *n* GEN COMM grupo relacionado *m*; ~ **party** *n* GEN COMM parte interesada *f*; ~ **person** *n* TAX persona relacionada *f*

relation *n* GEN COMM relación *f*; ♦ **in ~ to** GEN COMM en relación con

relational: ~ **database** *n* (*RDB*) COMP base de datos relacional *f* (*BDR*)

relations: ~ **analysis** *n* HRM análisis de las relaciones *m*

relationship *n* GEN COMM relación *f*, TAX parentesco *m*; ~ **marketing** S&M marketing de relaciones *m*

relative[1] *adj* GEN COMM relativo; ♦ ~ **to** GEN COMM relativo a

relative[2]: ~ **concentration** *n* MATH *statistics* concentración relativa *f*; ~ **error** *n* COMP error relativo *m*; ~ **frequency** *n* MATH frecuencia relativa *f*; ~ **income hypothesis** *n* ECON hipótesis de la renta relativa *f*; ~ **market share** *n* S&M cuota de mercado relativa *f*; ~ **price** *n* ECON precio relativo *m*; ~ **price level** *n* ECON nivel de precios relativo *m*; ~ **surplus value** *n* ECON valor añadido relativo *m*

relatively *adv* GEN COMM relativamente

relativities *n pl* HRM proporciones relativas *f pl*

relaunch[1] *n* GEN COMM, S&M relanzamiento *m*

relaunch[2] *vt* GEN COMM, S&M relanzar

relax *vt* GEN COMM relajar, MGMNT *policy* suavizar

relaxation *n* GEN COMM relajación *f*

release[1] *n* COMP *software, product*, S&M lanzamiento *m*, TAX cesión *f*; ~ **date** STOCK *for shares allocated to employees* fecha de liberación *f*; ~ **for shipment** TRANSP autorización para embarcar *f*; ~ **note** (*RN*) TRANSP permiso de descarga *m*; ~ **on bail** LAW libertad bajo fianza *f*; ~ **of pay checks** *AmE*, ~ **of pay cheques** *BrE* BANK desbloqueo de los sueldos *m*, emisión de cheques de sueldos *f*, exención de los sueldos *f*; ~ **of recognizance** LAW renuncia al reconocimiento *f*

release[2] *vt* BANK desbloquear, COMP lanzar, *version of software, product* publicar, ECON liberar, GEN COMM *publish* autorizar; ♦ ~ **sb on bail** LAW liberar a alguien bajo fianza, poner en libertad a alguien bajo fianza

relevant: ~ **act** *n* HRM, LAW *trade unions* acción relevante *f*; ~ **authority** *n* GEN COMM autoridad pertinente *f*; ~ **cost approach** *n* MGMNT enfoque de costes aplicables *m* (*Esp*), enfoque de costos aplicables *m* (*AmL*); ~ **cost base** *n* ACC, TAX *of property* base de coste aplicable *f* (*Esp*), base de costo aplicable *f* (*AmL*); ~ **earnings** *n*

FIN *classification for pension purposes*, TAX rendimiento principal *m*; **~ period** *n* TAX periodo aplicable *m*

reliability *n* GEN COMM fiabilidad *f*; **~ test** GEN COMM prueba de fiabilidad *f*

reliable[1] *adj* GEN COMM confiable, fiable

reliable[2]: **~ source** *n* GEN COMM fuente autorizada *f*

reliance *n* GEN COMM confianza *f*

relief *n* INS deducción *f*; **~ goods** *n pl* IMP/EXP mercancías de auxilio *f*; **~ on business assets** TAX deducción sobre activos empresariales *f*; **~ sailing** TRANSP navegación de auxilio *f*; **~ shift** HRM cambio de turno *m*, turno de relevo *m*

relieve *vt* TAX suavizar

religious: **~ discrimination** *n* HRM, LAW, WEL discriminación por religión *f*; **~ monitoring** *n* HRM control religioso *m*; **~ organization** *n* TAX organización religiosa *f*

relinquish *vt* GEN COMM *power, freedom* renunciar a

reload *vt* COMP *software* recargar

relocatable[1] *adj* COMP *area of memory* relocalizable

relocatable[2]: **~ address** *n* COMP dirección reubicable *f*

relocation *n* COMP, GEN COMM, HRM relocalización *f*

reluctant *adj* GEN COMM reacio

rely on *vi* GEN COMM confiar en, *person* fiarse de

remain *vi* GEN COMM quedar; ◆ **~ in suspense** GEN COMM quedar pendiente; **~ on board** (*ROB*) TRANSP *cargo* quedar a bordo

remainder *n* MATH resto *m*

remainderman *n* FIN proprietario(-a) desnudo(-a) *m,f*

remake *n* LEIS, MEDIA nueva versión *f*

remand[1] *n* LAW remisión *f*; ◆ **be on ~** LAW estar detenido

remand[2]: **~ in custody** *phr* LAW dictar un auto de prisión preventiva

remapping *n* COMP remapeo *m*, reproyección *f*

remargining *n* FIN nueva colocación de fondos *f*

remarketing *n* S&M marketing de nuevo lanzamiento *m*

remarks *n pl* GEN COMM *section heading* observaciones *f pl*

remedy[1] *n* GEN COMM *legal, financial* solución *f*

remedy[2] *vt* GEN COMM solucionar

reminder: **~ advertising** *n* S&M publicidad recordatoria *f*

remise *n* GEN COMM entrega *f*

remission *n* TAX exoneración *f*; **~ of charges** TAX exoneración de gastos *f*; **~ of tax** TAX remisión de un impuesto *f*

remit: **~ rate** *n* MEDIA *print* tasa de devolución *f*

remittal *n* LAW *sentence, debt* renuncia *f*

remittance *n* GEN COMM remesa *f*; **~ account** BANK, GEN COMM, TAX cuenta de remesa *m*; **~ account number** BANK, TAX número de cuenta de remesa *m*; **~ advice** FIN notificación de envío *f*; **~ for collection** BANK remesa de cobro *f*; **~ policy** GEN COMM política de pagos *f*; **~ return** FIN, TAX declaración de remesas *f*; **~ seal** BANK sello de remesa *m*; **~ slip** GEN COMM aviso de remesa *m*; **~ of tax** TAX aplazamiento del impuesto *m*, remesa del impuesto *f*

remnants *n pl* GEN COMM remanentes *m pl*

remote[1] *adj* COMP a distancia, remoto; **~-controlled** COMP controlado a distancia

remote[2]: **~ access** *n* COMP acceso a distancia *m*; **~ batch processing** *n* COMP proceso por lotes a distancia *m*; **~ control** *n* COMMS telemando *m*; **~ maintenance** *n* COMP mantenimiento a distancia *m*; **~ possibility** *n* GEN COMM posibilidad remota *f*; **~ printing** *n* COMP, MEDIA teleimpresión *f*; **~ processing** *n* COMP procesamiento remoto *m*; **~ support** *n* COMP ayuda a distancia *f*

removal *n* COMP eliminación *f*, GEN COMM eliminación *f*, *of tariff barriers* remoción *f*; **~ allowance** HRM bonificación por traslado *f*; **~ bond** FIN fianza de traslado *f*; **~ note** IMP/EXP, TRANSP nota de mercancías sujetas a derechos *f*; **~ of tax distortions** TAX eliminación de las distorsiones fiscales *f*; **~ van** TRANSP camión de mudanza *m*

remove *vt* COMP, GEN COMM *restrictions* eliminar

removed: **not to be ~** *phr* GEN COMM no es para llevar

remuneration *n* GEN COMM, HRM remuneración *f*; **~ package** GEN COMM, HRM paquete de remuneración *m*

rename *vt* COMP renombrar

render *vt* GEN COMM rendir; ◆ **~ null and void** LAW anular

rendu *n* INS rendu *m*

renegociation *n* GEN COMM renegociación *f*

renegotiate *vt* GEN COMM renegociar

renegotiated: **~ rate mortgage** *n* BANK, PROP hipoteca con tipo renegociado *f*; **~ mortgage rate** *n* BANK tasa de hipoteca reestructurada *f*

renew *vt* GEN COMM, MEDIA renovar

renewable: **~ annual term insurance** *n* INS seguro a plazo renovable por anualidades *m*; **~ resources** *n pl* ECON, GEN COMM recursos renovables *m pl*

renewal *n* GEN COMM, MEDIA *of subscription* renovación *f*; **~ clause** INS cláusula sobre prórroga *f*; **~ fee** PATENTS tasa de renovación *f*; **~ fund** ACC fondo de reposición *m*; **~ of mortgage** BANK, PROP renovación de hipoteca *f*; **~ option** PROP *of leasehold contract* opción de renovación *f*

renewed *adj* GEN COMM renovado

renounce *vt* GEN COMM renunciar a

renounceable: **~ documents** *n pl* STOCK documentos temporales *m pl*

renovated *adj* GEN COMM renovado

renown *n* GEN COMM renombre *m*

renowned *adj* GEN COMM renombrado

rent[1]: **~-free** *adj* PROP, TAX sin pago de alquiler

rent[2] *n* PROP, WEL alquiler *m*, *price* renta *f*; **~ allowance** PROP, WEL subsidio para el pago de alquiler *m*; **~ collector** PROP cobrador(a) de alquileres *m,f*; **~-free period** PROP, WEL periodo de ocupación gratuita *m*; **~ freeze** PROP, WEL congelación de alquileres *f*; **~ pcm** BrE (*rent per calendar month*) PROP alquiler por mes de calendario *m*; **~ per calendar month** BrE (*rent pcm*) PROP alquiler por mes de calendario *m*; **~ rebate** PROP, WEL devolución del alquiler *f*; **~ receipt** PROP recibo del alquiler *m*; **~-up period** PROP entrega de llaves *f*; ◆ **for ~** AmE (*cf to let* BrE) PROP se alquila; **~ seeking** PROP en busca de alquiler

rent[3] *vt* PROP dar en arrendamiento, rentar, alquilar

Rent: **~-a-Container** *n* (*Rentcon*) TRANSP sociedad de alquiler de contenedores

rentable: **~ area** *n* PROP zona arrendable *f*

rental *n* ECON, PROP, TAX, WEL alquiler *m*; **~ agreement** GEN COMM acuerdo de arrendamiento *m*; **~ cost** PROP, TAX, WEL coste de arrendamiento *m* (*Esp*), costo de arrendamiento *m* (*AmL*), precio del alquiler *m*;

~ income TAX renta por arrendamiento *f*; **~ level** PROP nivel de arrendamiento *m*; **~ payment** PROP, WEL pago del alquiler *m*; **~ period** PROP, TAX periodo del alquiler *m*; **~ rate** PROP, WEL tarifa de arrendamiento *f*, tipo de alquiler *m*; **~ right** LAW *intellectual property*, PROP, WEL derecho de arrendamiento *m*; **~ term** PROP, TAX periodo del alquiler *m*; **~ value** PROP, TAX valor de arrendamiento *m*

rental/turnover: ~ ratio *n* ACC proporción renta/volumen de facturación *f*

Rentcon *abbr* (*Rent-a-Container*) TRANSP sociedad de alquiler de contenedores

renters': ~ tax credit *n* TAX desgravación fiscal de los inquilinos *f*

rentier *n* TAX rentista *mf*

reopener: ~ clause *n* HRM cláusula de reanudación *f*

reorder: ~ form *n* GEN COMM solicitud de un nuevo pedido *f*; **~ point** *n* ACC, GEN COMM punto de reaprovisionamiento *m*

reorganization *n* ECON, GEN COMM reordenación *f*, reorganización *f*; **~ plan** MGMNT plan de saneamiento *m*

rep *abbr* (*sales representative*) HRM, S&M corredor(a) de comercio *m,f*, representante comercial *mf*, representante de ventas *mf*, viajante de comercio *mf*

rep. *abbr* (*representative*) GEN COMM delegado(-a) *m,f*, representante *mf*, representativo(-a) *m,f*

REP *abbr infrml* (*regional employment premium*) HRM bonificación por empleo regional *f*

repack *vt* IMP/EXP reempaquetar

repackage *vt* S&M nuevo paquete *m*

repackaging *n* STOCK venta parcial de una emisión de bonos como si fuera un activo mismo

repair[1]: **~ kit** *n* GEN COMM equipo de reparación *m*; **~ man** *n* GEN COMM técnico *m*; **~ shop** *n* GEN COMM taller de reparación *m*

repair[2]: **in good ~** *phr* GEN COMM en buen estado

reparation: ~ for damage *n* INS indemnización por daños *f*

repatriate *vt* ECON, FIN repatriar

repatriation *n* ECON, FIN repatriación *f*; **~ of capital** ECON, FIN repatriación de capital *f*; **~ of funds** ECON, FIN repatriación de fondos *f*; **~ of overseas funds** ECON, FIN repatriación de fondos extranjeros *f*; **~ of profits** ECON, FIN repatriación de beneficios *f*

repay *vt* FIN reintegrar, GEN COMM repagar, *pay* resarcirse de; ◆ **~ a loan** BANK amortizar un empréstito, devolver un préstamo

repayable *adj* GEN COMM reembolsable; **~ on demand** GEN COMM exigible sin previo aviso

repayment *n* GEN COMM amortización *f*; **~ claim** TAX reclamación de devolución *f*; **~ of a loan** BANK, GEN COMM amortización de un préstamo *f*; **~ schedule** GEN COMM, FIN plan de amortización *m*; **~ term** GEN COMM periodo de pago *m*, periodo de reembolso *m*; **~ over 2 years** GEN COMM amortización a 2 años *f*

repeal[1] *n* LAW, TAX abrogación *f*

repeal[2] *vt* LAW, TAX abrogar

repeat[1]: **~ business** *n* GEN COMM, S&M negocio que se repite *m*; **~ buying** *n* S&M compra repetida *f*; **~ demand** *n* GEN COMM demanda persistente *f*; **~ purchase** *n* GEN COMM, S&M compra persistente *f*; **~ rate** *n* S&M índice de repetición *m*; **~ sales** *n pl* S&M ventas repetidas *f pl*

repeat[2] *vt* GEN COMM repetir

repeated: ~ warnings *n pl* GEN COMM advertencias repetidas *f pl*

repeater: ~ loan *n* BANK, FIN préstamo reincidente *m*

repercussion *n* GEN COMM repercusión *f*

repertoire *n* COMP *instructions* repertorio *m*

repetitive: ~ strain injury *n* (*RSI*) HRM, WEL lesión por fatiga crónica *f*

replace *vt* GEN COMM reemplazar

replaceable: ~ good *n* ECON bien fungible *m*

replacement *n* GEN COMM sustitución *f*; **~ bond** FIN, STOCK bono de renovación *m*; **~ capital** FIN capital de reemplazos *m*, capital de reposiciones *m*; **~ clause** INS cláusula de reposición *f*; **~ cost** ACC, ECON, FIN, INS, MGMNT coste de reemplazo *m* (*Esp*), costo de reemplazo *m* (*AmL*), coste corriente *m* (*Esp*), coste de reposición *m* (*Esp*), costo corriente *m* (*AmL*), costo de reposición *m* (*AmL*)coste de sustitución *m* (*Esp*), costo de sustitución *m* (*AmL*); **~ cost accounting** ACC contabilidad de coste de reposición *f* (*Esp*), contabilidad de costo de reposición *f* (*AmL*); **~ costing** ACC, ECON, FIN, INS coste de sustitución *m* (*Esp*), costo de sustitución *m* (*AmL*); **~ demand** ECON demanda de reposición *f*; **~ engine** GEN COMM, IND motor de repuesto *m*; **~ investment** ACC, FIN inversión de reposición *f*; **~ labor force** *AmE*, **~ labour force** *BrE* HRM fuerza de trabajo de reemplazo *f*; **~ market** GEN COMM mercado de intercambio *m*; **~ part** GEN COMM, IND pieza de repuesto *f*; **~ planning** ACC, FIN plan de reposición *m*; **~ price** S&M precio de sustitución *m*; **~ property** PROP, TAX propiedad de reemplazo *f*; **~ ratio** WEL tasa de reposición *f*; **~ tax** TAX impuesto sustitutivo *m*; **~ technology** GEN COMM tecnología sustituta *f*; **~ value** ACC valor de reposición *m*

replay *vt* COMP repetir; ◆ **~ one's stocks** GEN COMM reponer las existencias

replevin *n* LAW solicitud de levantamiento provisional de embargo a la espera del fallo

replica *n* MEDIA réplica *f*

reply[1] *n* LAW réplica *f*; **~ device** S&M *mail order merchandising* dispositivo de respuesta *m*; **~ paid** COMMS respuesta pagada *f*; **~-paid card** COMMS cupón de respuesta pagada *m*; **~ vehicle** S&M *mail order merchandising* medio de respuesta *m*; ◆ **there's no ~** GEN COMM no hay respuesta; **in ~ to your letter** COMMS en respuesta a su carta

reply[2] **1.** *vt* GEN COMM contestar; **2.** *vi* GEN COMM contestar; ◆ **~ by return mail** COMMS contestar a vuelta de correo

repo *abbr* (*repurchase agreement*) STOCK repo (*pacto de recompra*)

reponsibility *n* GEN COMM responsabilidad *f*; ◆ **take ~ for** GEN COMM asumir la responsabilidad de

report[1] *n* GEN COMM boletín, informe *m* (*Esp*), reporte *m* (*AmL*), memoria *f*, MEDIA *in newspaper* crónica *f*; **~ card** HRM libreta de calificaciones *f*; **~ file** COMP fichero de edición *m*; **~ form** GEN COMM formato de informe *m* (*Esp*), formato de reporte *m* (*AmL*); **~ generation** COMP generación de estados *f*; **~ terminal** COMP terminal de información *m*

report[2] **1.** *vt* GEN COMM declarar; ◆ **~ one's conclusions** GEN COMM informar de sus conclusiones; **~ one's findings to sb** GEN COMM informar a alguien de sus resultados; **2.** *vi* GEN COMM informar

reported: as ~ *phr* COMMS según se anuncia

reporting *n* ACC informe *m*, presentación *f*, FIN producción de estados *f*; **~ corporation** GEN COMM corporación informante *f*; **~ currency** FIN moneda en que se expresa un estado financiero; **~ day** TRANSP día de aviso *m*; **~ dealer** STOCK intermediario(-a) notificador(a) *m,f*; **~ of income** TAX declaración de los ingresos *f*; **~ object** GEN COMM objeto del informe *m*; **~ object code** ACC código objeto de la información *m*; **~ period** TAX periodo de declaración *m*; **~ policy** FIN política de presentación de informes *f*; **~ requirement** TAX requisito de la declaración *m*; **~ restriction** MEDIA restricción a la información *f*; **~ standard** GEN COMM norma para hacer los informes *f*; **~ system** FIN sistema de informes *m*; **~ treatment** ACC tratamiento de informes *m*

repositioning *n* GEN COMM, S&M reposicionamiento *m*

repository *n* GEN COMM depósito *m*

represent *vt* GEN COMM manifestar, representar

representation *n* GEN COMM representación *f*, LAW exposición *f*, representación *f*; **~ letter** ACC, ADMIN, BANK carta de declaración *f*, carta de manifestaciones *f*, carta de representación *f*

representative *n* (*rep.*) GEN COMM delegado(-a) *m,f*, representante *mf*, representativo(-a) *m,f*; **~ firm** ECON empresa representativa *f*, empresa tipo *f*; **~ sample** MATH *statistics* muestra representativa *f*

reprivatization *n* ECON, POL reprivatización *f*

reprivatize *vt* ECON, POL reprivatizar

repro: ~ pulls *n pl* S&M pruebas de imprenta para reproducción *f pl*

reproduction *n* GEN COMM reproducción *f*; **~ cost** GEN COMM coste de renovación *m* (*Esp*), coste de sustitución *m* (*Esp*), costo de renovación *m* (*AmL*), costo de sustitución *m* (*AmL*); **~ rate** GEN COMM tasa de reproducción *f*

reprogram *vt* COMP reprogramar

reprography *n* GEN COMM reprografía *f*

rept *abbr* (*receipt*) GEN COMM resguardo *m*, recibo *m*

republish *vt* MEDIA *print* reeditar

repudiate *vt* HRM *industrial action* repudiar

repurchase[1]: **~ agreement** *n* (*repo, RP*) STOCK pacto de recompra *m* (*repo*); **~ rate** *n* BANK tasa de recompra *f*

repurchase[2] *vt* GEN COMM *debt* recomprar

repurchased: ~ share *n* STOCK acción recomprada *f*

reputation *n* GEN COMM reputación *f*

request *n* COMP, PATENTS petición *f*; **~ for change** (*RFC*) GEN COMM petición de cambio *f*; **~ for proposals** FIN solicitud de ofertas *f*; **~ to off-load** TRANSP petición de descarga *f*; ♦ **at the ~ of** LAW a instancia de; **by popular ~** GEN COMM por demanda popular

require *vt* GEN COMM exigir, requerir; ♦ **~ sb to do sth** GEN COMM pedir a alguien que haga algo; **~ sth of sb** GEN COMM exigir algo de alguien

required: ~ action *n* GEN COMM acción necesaria *f*; **~ freight rate** *n* (*RFR*) IMP/EXP, TRANSP tarifa de carga requerida *f*; **~ rate of return** *n* FIN tasa de rendimiento requerida *f*; **~ rental on capital** *n* ECON rentabilidad exigida al capital *f*; **~ reserve** *n* BANK reserva obligatoria *f*; **~-reserve ratio** *n* BANK coeficiente de la reserva requerida *m*

requirement *n* GEN COMM necesidad *f*, requisito *m*

rerouting *n* TRANSP reencaminamiento *m*, cambio de consignatario *m*

rerun *vt* COMP, GEN COMM reprocesar

res communis *n* GEN COMM cooperativa *f*, copropiedad *f*

res gestae *n* LAW testimonio irrefutable *m*

res integra *n* LAW el objeto de un litigio respecto del cual no existen antecedentes jurisprudenciales aplicables

res ipsa loquitur *n* LAW presunción de que quien tiene el control y manejo de una cosa es culpable por los daños que sean causados por esa cosa

res judicata *n* LAW cosa juzgada *f*

res nullius *n* LAW, PROP cosa de nadie *f*

resale *n* GEN COMM reventa *f*; **~ price** GEN COMM precio de reventa *m*; **~ price maintenance** (*RPM*) GEN COMM, S&M mantenimiento de los precios al por menor *m*, mantenimiento del precio de reventa *m*; **~ value** GEN COMM valor de reventa *m*

reschedule *vt* BANK *loan*, GEN COMM reestructurar

rescheduled *adj* BANK *loan*, GEN COMM reestructurado

rescheduling *n* BANK *of loan*, GEN COMM reestructuración *f*; **~ of debt** BANK, FIN reajuste del calendario de la deuda *m*

rescind *vt* LAW rescindir

rescission *n* LAW rescisión *f*

rescription *n* STOCK *bills and money market paper* rescripción *f*

research[1]: **~-intensive** *adj* GEN COMM, IND con investigación intensiva; **~-oriented** *adj* GEN COMM, IND orientado a la investigación

research[2] *n* GEN COMM investigación *f*; **~ budget** GEN COMM presupuesto para la investigación *m*; **~ and development** (*R&D*) IND investigación y desarrollo *f* (*I&D*); **~ and development limited partnership** GEN COMM sociedad limitada de investigación y desarrollo *f*; **~ director** HRM, MGMNT director(a) de investigación *m,f*; **~ grant** GEN COMM beca de investigación *f*; **~ laboratory** IND laboratorio de investigación *m*; **~ objective** GEN COMM objetivo de investigación *m*; **~ program** *AmE*, **~ programme** *BrE* IND programa de investigación *m*; **~ student** IND, WEL becario(-a) de investigación *m,f*; **~ team** S&M *market research* equipo de investigación *m*

reseller: ~ market *n* S&M mercado de reventa *m*

reservable[1] *adj* BANK reservable

reservable[2]: **~ day** *n* BANK día reservable *m*

reservation *n* *AmE* (*cf booking BrE*) GEN COMM, LEIS, reserva *f*; **~ of cargo** TRANSP reserva de carga *f*; **~ counter** GEN COMM mostrador de reservas *m*; **~ form** LEIS formulario de reserva *m*; **~ price** *AmE* S&M *auction sales* precio mínimo *m*; **~ system** GEN COMM, LEIS, S&M sistema de reservas *m*; ♦ **on the ~** *AmE* *jarg* POL persona leal a la ideología de su partido político

reserve[1] *n* GEN COMM reserva *f*; **~ account** BANK cuenta de reserva *f*; **~ army of labor** *AmE*, **~ army of labour** *BrE* HRM fuerza de trabajo de reserva *f*; **~ assets** *n pl* BANK, FIN activos de reserva *m pl*; **~-assets ratio** BANK, FIN porcentaje de activos de reserva *m*, relación de activos de reserva *f*; **~ bank** BANK banco de reserva *m*; **~ base** BANK base de reserva *f*; **~ burden** BANK carga de reserva *f*; **~ capital** ACC, BANK, ECON, FIN, GEN COMM capital de reserva *m*; **~ currency** BANK moneda de reserva *f*; **~ deposit** (*RD*) ECON depósito de reserva *m*; **~ entry** ACC partida de reserva *f*; **~ for credit risk**

losses BANK reserva para pérdidas de créditos de riesgo *f*; **~ for deferred income tax** TAX reserva del impuesto aplazado sobre la renta *f*; **~ for fluctuation** BANK fondo de fluctuación *m*; **~ for unpaid claims** INS reserva para reclamaciones sin pagar *f*; **~ liability** INS reserva de garantía *f*; **~ price** GEN COMM cargo por reservación *m*; **~ rate** BANK tasa de reserva *f*; **~ ratio** BANK coeficiente de reserva *m*; **~ requirement** BANK encajes legales *m pl*, requisito de reserva *m*; **~-stock control** GEN COMM control de existencias de reserva *m*; **~ stringency** ACC, BANK, FIN escasez de reservas *m*

reserve[2] *vt* LEIS *seat, room* reservar; ◆ **~ judgment** LAW reservarse el fallo, reservarse la opinión; **~ the right to** BANK reservarse el derecho de

Reserve: ~ Bank of Australia *n* BANK banco de reserva de Australia

reset[1] *n* COMP restauración *f*

reset[2] *vt* COMP *clock, counter, data* poner a cero

resettlement *n* GEN COMM reasentamiento *m*

residence *n* GEN COMM residencia *f*; **~ permit** HRM, LAW, POL permiso de residencia *m*; **~ status** TAX situación de residencia *f*; **~ visa** *BrE* (*cf green card AmE*) HRM, LAW, POL visado de residencia *m*

residency *n* BANK *of depositor* residencia *f*

resident[1] *adj* COMP residente

resident[2] *n* GEN COMM, TAX residente *mf*; **~ alien** POL extranjero residente *m*; **~ bank** BANK banco residente *m*; **~ manager** PROP director(a) residente *m,f*; **~ population** ECON población residente *f*; **~ taxpayer** TAX contribuyente residente *mf*

residential[1] *adj* PROP *construction* residencial

residential[2]: **~ accommodation** *n* PROP, WEL alojamiento residencial *m*; **~ amount** *n* HRM cantidad para vivienda *f*; **~ course** *n* HRM curso a tiempo completo *m*; **~ energy credit** *n* ENVIR crédito de energía para usos domésticos *m*; **~ mortgage** *n* BANK, PROP hipoteca residencial *f*; **~ mortgage loan** *n* BANK, PROP préstamo residencial hipotecario *m*; **~ occupancy** *n* PROP ocupación residencial *f*; **~ service contract** *n* GEN COMM, PROP contrato de servicio residencial *m*; **~ tax rate** *n* TAX tipo impositivo para la vivienda *m*

residual: ~ cost *n* ACC coste residual *m* (*Esp*), costo residual *m* (*AmL*); **~ error** *n* ECON error residual *m*; **~ family** *n* WEL familia residual *f*; **~ financial instrument** *n* FIN instrumento financiero residual *m*; **~ lender** *n* BANK, FIN prestamista residual *mf*; **~ value** *n* TAX valor residual *m*

residualization *n* WEL residualización *f*

residuary: ~ estate *n* PROP propiedad residual *f*; **~ legatee** *n* LAW legatario(-a) residual *m,f*

residue *n* ENVIR *from industrial production* residuos *m pl*, FIN resto *m*

residuum *n* LAW bienes residuales *m pl*

resignation *n* HRM, MGMNT dimisión *f*

resigning: ~ addendum *n* INS apéndice de renuncia *m*

resilience *n* ECON elasticidad *f*

resistance *n* GEN COMM resistencia *f*; **~ level** STOCK nivel de resistencia *m*

resistant *adj* GEN COMM resistente

resizing *n* MGMNT redimensionamiento *m*

resolution *n* COMP, GEN COMM, LAW resolución *f*, MGMNT acuerdo *m*

Resolution: ~ Trust Corporation *n AmE* (*RTC*) ECON resolución de fusión corporativa *f*

resolve *vt* GEN COMM *differences* acordar

resolved *adj* GEN COMM resuelto

resort *n* GEN COMM recurso *m*; ◆ **as a last ~** GEN COMM en última instancia

resort to *vt* GEN COMM recurrir a

resource *n* GEN COMM, TAX recurso *m*; **~ aggregation** GEN COMM agregación de recursos *f*; **~ allocation** GEN COMM adjudicación de recursos *f*, asignación de recursos *f*, distribución de los recursos *f*; **~ appraisal** GEN COMM evaluación de recursos *f*, valoración de recursos *f*; **~ availability** FIN disponibilidad de recursos *f*; **~ economics** ECON economía de recursos *f*; **~ income** TAX entrada de recursos *f*; **~ industry** IND aplicación de recursos *f*; **~ management** GEN COMM, MGMNT dirección de recursos *f*, gerencia de recursos *f*, gestión de recursos *f*; **~ profile** GEN COMM, HRM perfil de recursos *m*; **~ time** GEN COMM tiempo de recurso *m*

resources *n pl* GEN COMM, ENVIR, HRM recursos *m pl*; **~ gap** *n* ECON déficit de recursos *m*

respect[1] *vt* LAW respetar

respect[2] *n* GEN COMM respecto; ◆ **in this ~** GEN COMM a este respecto

respectively *adv* GEN COMM respectivamente

respondant *n* MEDIA, S&M *to market research survey* entrevistado(-a) *m,f*

respondeat: ~ superior *n* GEN COMM, LAW responsabilidad subsidiaria del principal *f*, responsabilidad subsidiaria del superior *f*

response *n* GEN COMM respuesta *f*; **~ elasticity** S&M elasticidad de la respuesta *f*; **~ function** S&M función de respuesta *f*; **~ projection** S&M *advertising* proyección de la respuesta *f*; **~ rate** S&M porcentaje de respuesta *m*; ◆ **in ~ to** GEN COMM en contestación a

responsibility: ~ accounting *n* ACC, FIN contabilidad de responsabilidad *f*; **~ budgeting** *n* ACC presupuestación de obligaciones *f*, presupuestación de responsabilidad *f*; **~ center** *AmE see* responsibility centre *BrE*; **~ center manager** *AmE see* responsibility centre manager *BrE*; **~ centre** *BrE n* FIN, MGMNT centro de responsabilidad *m*; **~ centre manager** *n BrE* ACC, FIN, HRM, MGMNT director(a) de centro de responsabilidad *m,f*, gestor(a) de centro de responsabilidad *m,f*; **~ classification** *n* ACC clasificación de responsabilidad *f*

responsible *adj* GEN COMM responsable; **~ in law** LAW responsable ante la ley

responsive *adj* ECON correspondiente

rest[1]: **~ account** *n* STOCK cuenta de saldo *f*; **~ fund** *n* STOCK fondo sobrante *m*

rest[2]: **~ assured that** *phr* COMMS tenga la seguridad de que; **~ on** *phr* GEN COMM depender mucho de, depender de; **~ one's case** *phr* LAW terminar su alegato

Rest: ~ Of the World *n* (*ROW*) ECON resto del mundo *m*

restart[1] *n* COMP reanudación *f*, rearranque *m*; **~ program** COMP programa de rearranque *m*

restart[2] *vt* COMP *system, hardware* reanudar, rearrancar

restate *vt* ACC, ECON, MATH, STOCK ajustar al precio del mercado

restaurant *n* GEN COMM, LEIS restaurante *m*; **~ car** LEIS, TRANSP coche restaurante *m*; **~ proprietor** HRM dueño(-a) de restaurante *m,f*, propietario(-a) de restaurante *m,f*

restaurateur *n* GEN COMM, HRM dueño(-a) de restaurante *m,f*

restoration *n* GEN COMM restauración *f*

resting: ~ **order** *n* STOCK orden tope *f*

restitutio in integrum *n* GEN COMM beneficio de restitución *m*

restock *vt* S&M renovar existencias

restore *vt* COMP *file, directory* restaurar; ♦ ~ **an assessment** TAX restablecer un gravamen; ~ **law and order** LAW restablecer el orden público

restowage *n* TRANSP realmacenaje *m*

restrained *adj* LAW embargado

restraint: ~ **of alienation** *n* LAW restricción de la enajenación de bienes *f*, restricción de la transferencia de dominio *f*; ~ **of trade** *n* ECON limitación al libre comercio *f*

restrict *vt* GEN COMM *numbers* restringir

restricted[1] *adj* GEN COMM restringido

restricted[2]: ~ **account** *n* ACC, BANK, STOCK cuenta inactiva por falta de margen *f*, cuenta restringida *f*; ~ **area** *n* TRANSP zona restringida *f*, *aviation* área restringida *f*; ~ **article** *n* (*REART*) TRANSP artículo restringido *m*; ~ **credit** *n* BANK, FIN crédito restringido *m*; ~ **letter of credit** *n* BANK, FIN carta de crédito restringida *f*; ~ **market** *n* ECON, STOCK mercado restringido *m*; ~ **surplus** *n* AmE (*cf undistributable reserve BrE*) ACC excedente restringido *m*, fondos no repartidos *m pl*, plusvalía restringida *f*, reserva no distribuible *f*

Restricted: ~ **Articles Regulations** *n pl* (*RAR*) TRANSP Reglamento de Artículos Restringidos *m*; ~ **Articles Terminal System** *n* (*RATS*) TRANSP Sistema Terminal de Artículos Restringidos *m*

restriction *n* GEN COMM, LAW, TRANSP restricción *f*; ~ **of credit** FIN restricción crediticia *f*

restrictive[1] *adj* GEN COMM *policy* represivo

restrictive[2]: ~ **covenant** *n* GEN COMM convenio de restricción del comercio *m*; ~ **monetary policy** *n* ECON, POL política monetaria restrictiva *f*; ~ **practice** *n* GEN COMM práctica comercial restrictiva *f*, práctica restrictiva *f*

Restrictive: ~ **Practices Court** *n* BrE LAW tribunal de defensa de la competencia

restroom *n* AmE (*cf cloakroom BrE*) TRANSP guardarropa *m*

restructure *vt* GEN COMM reconvertir, reestructurar

restructured[1] *adj* GEN COMM reestructurado

restructured[2]: ~ **loan** *n* BANK préstamo reestructurado *m*

restructuring *n* GEN COMM reconversión *f*, reestructuración *f*; ~ **of industry** IND reestructuración industrial *f*

result *n* GEN COMM resultado *m*; ♦ **as a** ~ GEN COMM como consecuencia, como resultado; **with the** ~ **that** GEN COMM con el resultado de que

result in *vt* GEN COMM venir a parar en

results *n pl* ACC *trading figures* resultados *m pl*; ~ **account** *n* ACC cuenta de resultados *f*

resume *vt* COMP *start again* reanudar

résumé *n* AmE (*cf curriculum vitae BrE*) curriculum vitae *m*, datos biográficos *m pl*

resurgence *n* GEN COMM *in prices* resurgimiento *m*

resyndication: ~ **limited partnership** *n* PROP sociedad limitada de resindicación *f*

retail[1] *adj* S&M al por menor

retail[2]: ~ **audit** *n* S&M auditoría de minorista *f*; ~ **bank** *n* BANK banco de menudeo *m*, banco minorista *m*; ~ **banking** *n* BANK banca al menudeo *f*, banca al por menor *f*, banca minorista *f*; ~ **broker** *n* STOCK intermediario(-a) de bolsa minorista *m,f*; ~ **business** *n* GEN COMM, S&M comercio al por menor *m*; ~ **center** AmE, ~ **centre** BrE *n* PROP, S&M centro comercial *m*, centro de venta al por menor *m*; ~ **cooperative** *n* S&M cooperativa de minoristas *f*; ~ **deposit** *n* STOCK depósito al por menor *m*; ~ **deposits** *n pl* BANK depósitos de clientes particulares *m pl*; ~ **display allowance** *n* S&M concesión de representación minorista *f*; ~ **floorspace** *n* S&M superficie minorista *f*; ~ **food business** *n* S&M negocio de alimentación al por menor *m*; ~ **house** *n* FIN, S&M casa minorista *f*; ~ **investor** *n* STOCK inversor(a) minorista *m,f*; ~ **management** *n* IND, S&M administración de menudeo *f* (*AmL*), gestión al por menor *f* (*Esp*), gestión minorista *f* (*Esp*); ~ **margin** *n* S&M margen del minorista *m*; ~ **network** *n* S&M red de minoristas *f*; ~ **offer** *n* S&M, STOCK oferta minorista *f*; ~ **outlet** *n* GEN COMM, PROP, S&M mercado al por menor *m*; ~ **personal deposits** *n pl* BANK depósitos personales *m pl*; ~ **price maintenance** *n* GEN COMM mantenimiento al por menor *m*; ~ **price index** *n* ECON, STOCK índice de precios al por menor; ~ **property** *n* PROP propiedad de venta al detalle *f*; ~ **sale** *n* GEN COMM, S&M venta al por menor *f*; ~ **sales analysis** *n* S&M análisis de ventas al por menor *m*; ~ **sales tax** *n* TAX impuesto sobre las ventas al detalle *m*; ~ **trade** *n* GEN COMM, IND, S&M comercio al menudeo *m*, comercio al por menor *m*; ~ **trader** *n* GEN COMM, IND, S&M comerciante al por menor *mf*; ~ **warehouse** *n* S&M almacén para minoristas *m*

Retail: ~ **Price Index** *n* (*RPI*) ECON, FIN Índice de Precios al Detalle *m* (*IPD*)

retailer *n* S&M detallista *mf*

retailing *n* GEN COMM, IND, S&M venta al por menor *f*

retain *vt* STOCK *shares* retener; ♦ ~ **sb's services** GEN COMM contratar los servicios de alguien

retainage *n* PROP retención *f*

retained: ~ **earnings** *n pl* ACC, FIN autofinanciación de enriquecimiento *f*, beneficios no distribuidos *m pl*, beneficios retenidos *m pl*, ganancias no distribuidas *f pl*; ~ **income** *n* ACC renta acumulada *f*; ~ **profits** *n pl* ACC, FIN beneficios retenidos *m pl*

retainer *n* GEN COMM iguala *f*, acaparador *m*, S&M anticipo *m*; ♦ **on a** ~ GEN COMM sobre un acaparador

retake *vt* WEL *exams* presentarse segunda vez a

retaliation: **in** ~ *phr* GEN COMM como represalia

retaliatory[1] *adj* GEN COMM que toma represalias

retaliatory[2]: ~ **duty** *n* ENVIR arancel antidumping *m*; ~ **eviction** *n* PROP desahucio por represalia *m*, expulsión por represalia *f*; ~ **measure** *n* GEN COMM medida de represalia *f*

retendering *n* STOCK reoferta *f*

retention *n* GEN COMM retención *f*; ~ **bond** FIN, STOCK bono de retención *m*; ~ **date** GEN COMM fecha de conservación *f*; ~ **money** GEN COMM retención de garantía *f*; ~ **on wages** HRM retención sobre el sueldo *f*; ~ **period** STOCK *shares allocated to employees* periodo de conservación *m*; ~ **requirement** TAX exigencia de retención *f*, requisito de retención *m*

rethink *vt* GEN COMM reconsiderar

retire **1.** *vt* STOCK retirar; **2.** *vi* GEN COMM *withdraw* retirarse, HRM jubilarse; ◆ **~ from business** GEN COMM retirarse del negocio; **~ on a pension** HRM jubilarse con pensión

retired[1] *adj* GEN COMM, HRM jubilado

retired[2]: **~ person** *n* GEN COMM jubilado(-a) *m,f*, persona jubilada *f*

retiree *n frml* GEN COMM jubilado(-a) *m,f*

retirement *n* GEN COMM, HRM, IND jubilación *f*, retiro *m*; **~ age** HRM edad de jubilación *f*; **~ annuity policy** *BrE* FIN, TAX póliza de jubilación *f*; **~ of debt** FIN, TAX redención de la deuda *f*; **~ fund** FIN fondo de retiros *m*; **~ income** FIN, INS, TAX jubilación *f*; **~ income fund** (*RRIF*) HRM, INS fondo de jubilaciones *m*; **~ income security act** HRM, LAW ley de garantía de pensiones *f*; **~ on the job** HRM jubilación *f*; **~ pay** FIN, WEL pensión de jubilación *f*; **~ payment** FIN pago de la pensión *m*; **~ pension** FIN, WEL pensión de jubilación *f*; **~ pension rights** GEN COMM derechos de pensión de jubilación *m pl*; **~ plan** GEN COMM plan de jubilación *m*; **~ savings plan** BANK, FIN plan de ahorro para pensión *m*; **~ savings program** *AmE*, **~ savings programme** *BrE* GEN COMM programa de ahorro de jubilación *m*, programa de ahorro para pensión *m*; **~ scheme** GEN COMM plan de jubilaciones *m*

retiring: **~ allowance** *n* FIN, WEL pensión de jubilación *f*

retouch *vt* S&M retocar

retracement *n* GEN COMM reconstrucción *f*

retractable[1] *adj* FIN, STOCK *share, bond* retractable

retractable[2]: **~ bond** *n* FIN, STOCK bono amortizable antes del vencimiento *m*, bono retractable *m*; **~ share** *n* FIN, STOCK acción amortizable antes del vencimiento *f*

retraction *n* FIN, STOCK retractación *f*

retrain *vt* HRM reciclar

retraining *n* GEN COMM, HRM reciclaje profesional *m*, reeducación profesional *f*, reorientación profesional *f*; **~ course** HRM curso de reciclaje *m*

retranslation *n* ECON *of foreign currency* reconversión *f*

retrieval: **~ time** *n* COMP tiempo de recuperación *m*

retrieve *vt* COMP *data, file* recuperar

retroactive[1] *adj* GEN COMM retroactivo

retroactive[2]: **~ adjustment** *n* ECON ajuste retroactivo *m*; **~ classification** *n* POL clasificación retroactiva *f*; **~ financing** *n* FIN financiación retroactiva *f*

retrogress *vi* ECON retroceder

retrogression *n* ECON retrogresión *f*

retrospective: **~ claim** *n* INS reclamación retrospectiva *f*; **~ pay** *n* HRM paga retrospectiva *f*; **~ rebate** *n* TRANSP *on traffic already conveyed* descuento retrospectivo *m*

return[1] *n* GEN COMM beneficio *m*, ganancia *f*; **~ address** COMMS dirección de devolución *f*; **~ cargo** (*r/c*) TRANSP carga de retorno *f*; **~ fare** *BrE* (*cf round-trip fare AmE*) LEIS, TRANSP tarifa de ida y vuelta *f*; **~ flight** LEIS, TRANSP vuelo de vuelta *m*; **~ freight** TRANSP flete de vuelta *m*; **~ of guarantee** GEN COMM devolución de la fianza *f*; **~ of income** ACC, TAX declaración sobre la renta *f*; **~ journey time** *BrE* (*cf round-trip time AmE*) TRANSP tiempo del viaje de ida y vuelta *m*; **~ leg** LEIS, TRANSP trayecto de vuelta *m*; **~ load** TRANSP carga de retorno *f*; **~ on assets** (*ROA*) ACC, BANK, ECON, FIN rendimiento de los activos *m*, rentabilidad de los activos *f*; **~ on capital** (*ROC*) GEN COMM rendimiento del capital *m*, rendimiento sobre el capital *m*; **~ on capital**

employed (*ROCE*) GEN COMM rendimiento del capital invertido *m*; **~ on common shareholders' equity** ACC beneficio sobre el capital de acciones ordinarias *m*; **~ on equity** (*ROE*) ACC rentabilidad del capital *f*, FIN, STOCK rendimiento sobre el patrimonio *m*, remuneración por acción *f*, rendimiento sobre acción *m*; **~ on invested capital** (*ROIC*) GEN COMM rendimiento sobre capital invertido *m*; **~ on investment** (*ROI*) ACC, BANK, ECON, FIN rendimiento de la inversión *m*; **~ on net assets** ACC beneficio sobre activos netos *m*; **~ on net assets employed** ACC beneficio sobre activos netos empleados *m*; **~ on real estate** PROP rendimiento de los bienes inmuebles *m*; **~ on sales** ACC, FIN, S&M devoluciones de ventas *f pl*, rendimiento de ventas *m*; **~ rate** *BrE* (*cf round trip rate AmE*) LEIS, TRANSP tarifa de ida y vuelta *f*; **~ ticket** *BrE* (*cf round-trip ticket AmE*) LEIS billete de ida y vuelta *m*; **~ trip** TRANSP *BrE* (*cf round trip AmE*) viaje de ida y vuelta *m*; ◆ **in ~ for** GEN COMM a cambio de

return[2] **1.** *vt* COMMS *package*, S&M *goods* devolver; ◆ **~ amount overpaid** GEN COMM, TAX devolver una cantidad pagada de más; **~ a phone call** COMMS devolver una llamada telefónica; **~ a verdict** LAW pronunciar un veredicto; **2.** *vi* GEN COMM volver; ◆ **~ to port for orders** (*R/p*) TRANSP volver a puerto para recibir órdenes; **~ to sender** COMMS devolver al remitente

returnable[1] *adj* ENVIR, GEN COMM, S&M *bottles* retornable

returnable[2]: **~ goods** *n pl* GEN COMM, S&M mercancías restituibles *f pl*

returned: **~ book** *n* MEDIA libro devuelto *m*; **~ check** *AmE*, **~ cheque** *BrE* n BANK, FIN cheque devuelto *m*; **~ empty** *n* ENVIR, S&M envase vacío devuelto *m*; **~ goods** *n pl* GEN COMM artículos devueltos *m pl*

returns: **~ to scale** *n pl* ECON rendimiento de escala *m*

retype *vt* COMP reintroducir por teclado

reusable: **~ pack** *n* ENVIR, GEN COMM, S&M envase reutilizable *m*

reuse *vt* ENVIR, TRANSP reutilizar

REV *abbr* (*reversing*) GEN COMM marcha atrás *f*

revalorization *n* ECON revalorización *f*

revaluate *vt* GEN COMM ajustar al precio del mercado

revaluation *n* GEN COMM revalorización *f*, revaluación *f*; **~ of assets** ACC, FIN actualización de activos *f*, revalorización de activos *f*; **~ of exchange rate** BANK, ECON, FIN revaluación de la tasa de cambio *f*; **~ reserve** ACC reserva de revalorización *f*

revalue *vt* GEN COMM revalorar, revalorizar

revamp *vt* S&M *product image* modernizar, renovar

revealed: **~ preference** *n* ECON preferencia manifiesta *f*

revenge: **~ barter** *n jarg* ECON economía de trueque *f*

revenue *n* ECON entradas brutas *f pl*, entradas *f*, TAX *company, individual* ingresos *m pl*; **~ allocation** TAX destino de los impuestos *f*, TRANSP asignación de ingresos *f*; **~ anticipation note** (*RAN*) STOCK emisión de deuda municipal a corto plazo *f*; **~ budget** ACC presupuesto de ingresos *m*; **~ center** *AmE*, **~ centre** *BrE* GEN COMM, TAX centro de ingresos *m*; **~ claim** TAX demanda fiscal *f*; **~ curve** ECON, TAX curva de ingresos *f*; **~ department** TAX departamento fiscal *m*; **~ dependency** FIN dependencia de los ingresos *f*; **~ dilution** GEN COMM, TAX reducción de ingresos *f*; **~ earner** ECON receptor(a) de ingresos *m,f*; **~ economy** ECON economía de rentas *f*; **~ and expenses** *n pl* ACC,

TAX ingresos y gastos *m pl*; ~ **guarantee** TAX garantía fiscal *f*; ~ **loss** ACC, FIN pérdida de beneficios *m*; ~ **maximization** GEN COMM maximización de los ingresos *f*, maximización del beneficio *f*; ~ **office** TAX oficina de recaudación de impuestos *f*; ~ **production** GEN COMM producción de ingresos *f*; ~ **project** GEN COMM plan de ingresos *m*; ~ **ruling** TAX resolución fiscal *f*; ~ **sharing** *AmE* ECON coparticipación en los ingresos *f*; ~ **test** ACC, TAX examen de ingresos *m*, prueba de ingresos *f*; ◆ **apply** ~ ACC aplicar ingresos a un periodo

reversal *n* ACC *of entries* reposición *f*, retrocesión *f*, sustitución *f*

reverse[1] *n* MEDIA cara posterior *f*; ~ **annuity mortgage** BANK hipoteca inversa de pago anual *f*; ~ **causation hypothesis** ECON hipótesis de la inversión de causa *f*; ~ **channel** COMP canal de retorno *m*; ~~**charge call** *BrE* (*cf collect call AmE*) COMMS *telephone* comunicación de cobro revertido *f*, conferencia a cobro revertido *f*, llamada a cobro revertido *f*, llamada pagadera en destino *f* (*AmL*); ~ **conversion** STOCK conversión inversa *f*; ~ **engineering** GEN COMM ingeniería invertida *f*; ~ **gearing** *BrE* (*cf reverse leverage AmE*) ACC apalancamiento inverso *m*, apalancamiento negativo *m*; ~ **income tax** TAX impuesto negativo sobre la renta *m*; ~ **J-shaped frequency curve** ECON curva inversa de frecuencia en forma de J *f*; ~ **leverage** *AmE* (*cf reverse gearing BrE*) ACC apalancamiento inverso *m*, apalancamiento negativo *m*; ~ **printing** COMP impresión inversa *f*; ~ **repurchase** BANK, FIN recompra inversa *f*; ~ **repurchase agreement** FIN acuerdo de retroventa inversa *m*; ~ **split** FIN división inversa *f*; ~ **takeover** ECON fusión inversa *f*; ~ **triangular merger** GEN COMM fusión triangular inversa *f*; ~ **yield gap** STOCK exceso de rendimiento sobre la deuda *m*

reverse[2] *vt* ECON *trend* invertir; ◆ ~ **the charges** *BrE* COMMS llamar por teléfono, a cobro revertido; ~ **an entry** ACC anular un asiento, anular un registro contable, anular una anotación; ~ **a swop** STOCK revertir un pase

reversed: ~ **takeover** *n* FIN absorción invertida *f*

reversible[1] *adj* TRANSP *charter party* reversible

reversible[2]: ~ **annuity** *n* INS anualidad reversible *f*; ~ **laytime** *n* TRANSP *charter party* días de plancha *m pl*, estadía *f*; ~ **pallet** *n* TRANSP plataforma de carga reversible *f*

reversing *n* (*REV*) GEN COMM marcha atrás *f*; ~ **entry** ACC contraasiento *m*

reversion: ~ **clause on bargain and sale** *n* GEN COMM, LAW contrato de retroventa *m*

reversionary: ~ **annuity** *n* INS anualidad reversible *f*; ~ **bonus** *n* ECON bonificación diferida *f*, FIN bonos reversionarios *m pl*; ~ **factor** *n* MATH *statistics* factor de reversión *m*; ~ **value** *n* PROP valor reversible *m*

reversioner *n* HRM tenedor(a) de reversión *m,f*

review[1] *n* MGMT *examination* revisión *f*; ~ **board** HRM, S&M junta de revisión *f*; ~ **body** HRM, MGMNT, S&M organismo de revisión *m*; ◆ **under** ~ GEN COMM bajo revisión

review[2] *vt* GEN COMM, MGMNT analizar, estudiar, repasar, revisar

revise *vt* LAW revisar; ◆ ~ **downward** GEN COMM corregir a la baja

revised: ~ **edition** *n* MEDIA *print* edición revisada *f*;

~ **figures** *n pl* GEN COMM cifras revisadas *f pl*; ~ **net income** *n* ACC, BANK, FIN, TAX ingreso neto revisado *m*; ~ **version** *n* MEDIA *print* versión revisada *f*

revision *n* GEN COMM *of guidelines* reexamen *m*

revisionism *n* POL revisionismo *m*

revitalization *n* GEN COMM revitalización *f*

revival *n* LEIS *theatre* reposición *f*

revive *vt* GEN COMM renovar

revocable[1] *adj* GEN COMM revocable

revocable[2]: ~ **credit** *n* BANK, FIN crédito revocable *m*; ~ **letter of credit** *n* BANK, FIN carta de crédito revocable *f*; ~ **trust** *n* FIN fideicomiso revocable *m*

revocation *n* FIN *of pension plan*, PATENTS revocación *f*

revoke *vt* FIN, PATENTS revocar

revolving: ~ **acceptance facility by tender** *n* (*RAFT*) FIN servicio renovable de financiación por subasta mediante aceptaciones; ~ **charge account** *n* BANK cuenta de crédito revolvente *f*; ~ **credit** *n* BANK, FIN crédito rotativo *m*, crédito renovable *m*; ~ **fund** *n* ACC, FIN fondo renovable *m*, *governmental accounting* fondo rotatorio *m*; ~ **letter of credit** *n* BANK, FIN carta de crédito renovable *f*; ~ **line of credit** *n* BANK, FIN línea de crédito renovable *f*; ~ **underwriting facility** *n* (*RUF*) BANK, INS *investment banking* facilidad de crédito autorrenovable *f*, compromiso de aseguramiento continuado *m* (*CAC*)

reward *n* GEN COMM, S&M recompensa *f*; ◆ **as a** ~ **for** GEN COMM como recompensa *f*

rewarding[1] *adj* GEN COMM gratificante

rewarding[2]: ~ **job** *n* HRM trabajo que compensa *m*

rewind *vt* COMP, MEDIA *cassette, tape* rebobinar

rewrite[1] *n* GEN COMM reposición de información *f*

rewrite[2] *vt* COMP *software*, MEDIA *print* reescribir

RFC *abbr* (*request for change*) GEN COMM petición de cambio *f*

RFDS *abbr* (*rural free delivery service*) COMMS servicio rural de entrega gratuita *m*

RFR *abbr* (*required freight rate*) IMP/EXP, TRANSP tarifa de carga requerida *f*

RHA *abbr* *BrE* (*Road Haulage Association*) TRANSP asociación británica de transportes por carretera

rhetoric *n* ECON retórica *f*

Rhinelands: ~ **hourglass** *n* ECON países más prósperos de la UE

ribbon *n* COMP, GEN COMM, MEDIA *print* cinta *f*; ~ **cartridge** COMP, MEDIA *print* cartucho de cinta *m*

Ricardian: ~ **equivalence theorem** *n* ECON *labour theory of value* teorema de equivalencia ricardiana *m*; ~ **theory of value** *n* ECON teoría ricardiana del valor *f*

Ricardo: ~ **effect** *n* ECON efecto de Ricardo *m*; ~ **invariance principle** *n* ECON principio invariable de Ricardo *m*

rich *adj* GEN COMM rico

RIE *abbr* STOCK (*recognized investment exchange*) bolsa de inversión reconocida *f*, (*registered international exchange*) bolsa internacional de valores *f*

riff: ~ **money** *n jarg* HRM dinero extra *m*

rig[1] *n* ECON, LAW control monetario *m*

rig[2] *vt* FIN *prices*, HRM *industrial relations*, POL *votes*, STOCK manipular

rigged: ~ **market** *n* STOCK mercado manipulado *m*

rigging *n* ECON, LAW control ilegal del mercado *m*, FIN *prices*, HRM *industrial relations*, POL *votes*, STOCK manipulación *f*

right[1]: **~-justified** *adj* COMMS, MEDIA *word-processed document* justificado a la derecha; **~-wing** *adj* POL de derechas

right[2] *n* GEN COMM *permission* derecho *m*, STOCK *share issue* ampliación de capital *m*; **~ of appeal** LAW derecho de apelación *m*; **~ column** ACC, GEN COMM columna derecha *f*; **~ of combination** LAW derecho de combinación *m*; **~ of entry** LAW derecho de entrada *m*; **~ of establishment** LAW derecho de establecimiento *m*; **~-hand column** ACC, GEN COMM columna derecha *f*; **~ of interest in a share** STOCK derecho de participación en una acción *m*; **~ of offset** BANK derecho de cancelación *m*; **~-of-way** LAW servidumbre de paso *f*; **~ of recovery** LAW derecho de recuperación *m*; **~ of redemption** FIN derecho de redención *m*, derecho de retracto *m*; **~ of redress** LAW derecho de compensación *m*; **~ of reply** LAW derecho de réplica *m*; **~ of resale** LAW, S&M derecho de reventa *m*; **~ of rescission** LAW derecho de rescisión *m*; **~ of residence** POL derecho de residencia *m*; **~ of resumption** LAW derecho de reanudación *m*; **~ of return** GEN COMM derecho de devolución *m*; **~ shift** COMP desplazamiento a la derecha *m*; **~ of survivorship** LAW derecho de supervivencia *m*; **~ time** TRANSP *of departure, arrival* hora prevista *f*, tiempo previsto *m*; **~ to associate** HRM derecho de asociación *m*; **~ to convert** STOCK derecho a convertir *m*; **~ to dissociate** HRM derecho de disociación *m*; **~ to know** POL derecho a saber *m*; **~ to manage** HRM, MGMNT derecho a administrar *m*, derecho de gestión *m*; **~ to organize** HRM derecho a organizarse *m*, derecho sindical *m*; **~ to a patent** LAW, PATENTS derecho de la patente *m*; **~ to strike** HRM derecho a la huelga *m*; **~ to vote** GEN COMM *in elections* derecho de voto *m*; **~ to work** HRM, LAW derecho a trabajar *m*, derecho al trabajo *m*; **~ to work state** AmE HRM, LAW estado que prohíbe la filiación sindical obligatoria para acceder a un puesto de trabajo; ◆ **be in the ~** GEN COMM tener razón; **in its own ~** GEN COMM por derecho propio; **with no ~ of appeal** LAW sin derecho a apelar

right[3]: **~ justify** *vt* COMMS, MEDIA *document* justificar a la derecha

rightful: **~ heir** *n* LAW, PROP, TAX heredero(-a) legítimo(-a) *m,f*; **~ owner** *n* LAW, PROP propietario(-a) legítimo(-a) *m,f*

rightism *n* POL *Communist countries* derechismo *m*

rights *n pl* GEN COMM derechos *m pl*; **~ and actions** LAW *intellectual property*, PATENTS derechos y acciones *m pl*; **~ afforded** PATENTS derechos conferidos *m pl*; **~ of conversion** STOCK derechos de conversión *m pl*; **~ of exchange** STOCK derechos de negociación *m pl*; **~ holder** *n* STOCK titular *mf*, titular de derechos *mf*; **~ issue** *n* ACC, LAW, STOCK emisión con derechos para los accionistas *f*, emisión de derechos *f*, emisión con derecho preferente de suscripción *f*, emisión con derechos de suscripción *f*; ◆ **all ~ reserved** BrE LAW reservados todos los derechos

rightsize *vt* HRM tener el número de trabajadores ideal

rigid: **~ vehicle** *n* TRANSP vehículo rígido *m*

RIL *abbr* (*rehabilitation import loan*) FIN, IMP/EXP préstamo de rehabilitación de la importación *m*

RIN *abbr* (*Royal Institute of Navigation*) TRANSP real instituto marítimo

ring *n* STOCK corro *m*; **~-fence** ECON parqué *m*, TAX cerco *m*; **~ road** TRANSP carretera de circunvalación *f*, cinturón de ronda *m*, ronda *f*

ringfence *vi* ECON reservar fondos

ringfencing *n* ECON reserva de fondos *f*

ringing: **~ out** *n* AmE *jarg* STOCK *futures* liquidación de contratos antes del vencimiento *f*

riots: **~ and civil commotions** *n pl* (*R&CC*) HRM, IND, WEL tumultos y agitaciones sociales *m pl*; **~, civil commotions and strikes** *n pl* (*RCCS*) WEL motines, disturbios populares y huelgas *m pl*

riparian: **~ rights** *n pl* LAW derechos ribereños *m pl*

ripper: **~ bill** *n* AmE *jarg* POL ley presentada en el parlamento con el fin de destruir la base en la que se asienta el partido oponente

ripple: **~ effect** *n* ECON efecto residual *m*

rise[1] *n* ACC, FIN, GEN COMM alza *f*, aumento *m*, elevación *f*, subida *f*; **~ in exports** GEN COMM aumento de la exportación *m*; **~ in unemployment** ECON, HRM, WEL crecimiento del desempleo *m*; **~ in wages** HRM aumento salarial *m*

rise[2] **1.** *vt* ACC aumentar, GEN COMM ascender, subir, aumentar; **2.** *vi* GEN COMM aumentar; ◆ **~ in line with inflation** ECON *price, benefit* aumentar a tono con la inflación

rising[1] *adj* ECON en alza

rising[2] *n* GEN COMM levantamiento *m*; **~ bottom** *jarg* STOCK precio al alza *m*; **~ cost** ECON coste creciente *m* (*Esp*), costo creciente *m* (*AmL*); **~ inflation** BANK, ECON inflación creciente *f*; **~ interest rate** GEN COMM tipo de interés en aumento *m*; **~ trend** GEN COMM, STOCK tendencia al alza *f*, tendencia alcista *f*; **~ unemployment** ECON, HRM, WEL desempleo creciente *m*

risk[1]: **~-free** *adj* STOCK libre de riesgo; **~-minimizing** *adj* STOCK de riesgo mínimo; **~-oriented** *adj* GEN COMM con disposición al riesgo; **~-reward** *adj* ACC compensación del riesgo *f*

risk[2] *n* GEN COMM riesgo *m*; **~-adjusted discount rate** BANK, FIN tasa de descuento ajustado a riesgo *f*, tipo de descuento ajustado a riesgo *m*; **~ analysis** FIN, INS análisis de riesgos *m*; **~ arbitrage** STOCK arbitraje con riesgo *m*; **~ assessment** FIN, INS, MGMNT estimación de riesgos *f*; **~ asset system** BANK sistema de activos de riesgo *m*; **~ aversion** ECON, GEN COMM aversión al riesgo *f*; **~-avoiding capital** FIN capital libre de riesgo *m*; **~-based banking standards** *n pl* BANK estándares bancarios basados en riesgo *m pl*; **~-based premium** INS prima basada en riesgos *f*; **~-bearing capital** BANK, ECON, FIN, GEN COMM capital de riesgo *m*; **~ capital** BANK, ECON, FIN, GEN COMM capital de riesgo *m*; **~ evaluation** FIN, INS, STOCK evaluación de riesgos *f*; **~ exposure** ACC exposición al riesgo *f*; **~ factor** ECON factor de riesgo *m*; **~-free debt instrument** STOCK *Treasury bills* instrumento de deuda exento de riesgo *m*; **~ in the goods** LAW, TRANSP riesgo de las mercancías *m*; **all ~ insurance** INS seguro contra riesgos múltiples *m*; **~ lover** GEN COMM amante del riesgo *mf*; **~ management** FIN, MGMNT, STOCK administración del riesgo *f*, dirección de riesgos *f*; **~ manager** GEN COMM gestor(a) de riesgos *m,f*, gerente de riesgos *mf*; **~ monitoring** MGMNT control del riesgo *m*, supervisión del riesgo *f*; **~ of nonrepayment** BANK riesgo de no pago *m*; **~ package** FIN paquete de riesgo *m*; **~ pooling**

INS riesgo compartido *m*; ~ **position** STOCK posición de riesgo *f*; ~ **premium** INS prima del riesgo *f*; ~ **profile** INS perfil de riesgo *m*; ~**-related premium** INS prima vinculada al riesgo *f*; ~ **sharing** INS riesgo compartido *m*; ~**-taking acceptance** BANK, FIN aceptación del riesgo *f*; ~ **weighting** FIN subsidio del riesgo *m*; ◆ **at** ~ STOCK a riesgo; **no** ~ **after discharge** (*nrad*) INS sin riesgos después de la descarga; **no** ~ **until confirmed** (*nr*) INS sin riesgo hasta la confirmación; **at one's own** ~ GEN COMM por cuenta propia; **take a** ~ GEN COMM asumir un riesgo

riskless¹ *adj* GEN COMM seguro, exento de riesgo

riskless²: ~ **transaction** *n* STOCK transacción exenta de riesgo *f*

risks: **all** ~ *n pl* (*A/R*) INS todo riesgo; **all-~ cover** *n* INS cobertura contra todo riesgo *f*

risky¹ *adj* GEN COMM arriesgado

risky²: ~ **asset** *n* BANK activo de riesgo *m*

rival: ~ **brand** *n* S&M marca rival *f*

river: ~ **bus** *n* LEIS, TRANSP autobús fluvial *m*; ~ **navigation** *n* INS, TRANSP navegación fluvial *f*; ~ **pollution** *n* ENVIR contaminación de los ríos *f*; ~ **tonnage dues** *n pl* TRANSP *shipping* derechos de navegación fluvial *m pl*

riveted *adj* GEN COMM, TRANSP (*R*) remachado; ◆ ~ **and welded** (*RW*) TRANSP remachado y soldado

rly *abbr* (*railway*) TRANSP FC (*ferrocarril*)

RN *abbr* (*release note*) TRANSP *cargo* permiso de descarga *m*

RNR *abbr* (*rate not reported*) TRANSP tarifa no comunicada *f*

RNS *abbr* (*Regulatory News Service*) MEDIA, STOCK servicio de control de la información

R/O *abbr* (*routing order*) TRANSP *cargo* orden de ruta *f*

ROA *abbr* (*return on assets*) ACC, BANK, ECON, FIN rentabilidad de los activos *f*, rendimiento de los activos *m*

road *n* (*Rd.*) TRANSP carretera *f*; ~ **building** ECON, ENVIR, POL construcción de carreteras *f*; ~ **fatalities** *n pl* TRANSP víctimas de accidentes en carretera *f pl*; ~ **haulage company** TRANSP compañía de transporte por carretera *f*; ~ **haulage contractor** TRANSP contratista de transporte por carretera *mf*; ~ **haulage vehicle** (*RHV*) TRANSP vehículo de transporte por carretera *m*; ~ **network** TRANSP red de carreteras *f*; ~**-rail transport** TRANSP transporte combinado por carretera y ferrocarril *m*; ~ **safety** TRANSP seguridad en la carretera *f*; ~ **sector** ECON, TRANSP sector de carreteras *m*; ~ **tax** TAX, TRANSP impuesto por el uso de carreteras *m*; ~ **toll** GEN COMM, TRANSP peaje *m*; ~ **traffic** TRANSP circulación por carretera *f*, circulación vial *f*; ~ **train** TRANSP *haulage* tren de carretera *m*; ~ **transport** TRANSP transporte por carretera *m*; ◆ **on the** ~ LEIS *exhibition* de gira

Road: ~ **Haulage Association** *n BrE* (*RHA*) TRANSP asociación británica de transportes por carretera

roads *n pl* TRANSP *shipping* rutas *f pl*

roadshow *n jarg* MEDIA *cinema* película que se queda más tiempo en algunos de los cines mayores

roadsite: ~ **site** *n* S&M *for advertising poster* valla publicitaria en carretera *f*

roadworks *n pl* TRANSP obra en carretera *f*

rob: ~ **the till** *vt* GEN COMM robar la caja

ROB *abbr* (*remain on board*) TRANSP *cargo* restante a bordo

robot *n* IND robot *m*; ~ **salesperson** HRM, S&M vendedor(a) robotizado(-a) *m,f*

robotics *n* IND robótica *f*

robotize *vt* IND robotizar

robust *adj* GEN COMM fornido

ROC *abbr* (*return on capital*) GEN COMM rendimiento del capital *m*, rendimiento sobre el capital *m*

ROCE *abbr* (*return on capital employed*) GEN COMM rendimiento del capital invertido *m*

rock¹: ~**-bottom price** *n* GEN COMM, S&M precio más bajo posible *m*

rock²: ~ **the boat** *phr infrml* GEN COMM desestabilizar una situación

rocket: ~ **scientist** *n jarg* STOCK creador(a) de valores innovadores *m,f* (*jarg*)

rocks: **be on the** ~ *phr* GEN COMM estar sin blanca (*infrml*), estar sin un centavo

rodent: ~ **control certificate** *n* TRANSP certificado de control de roedores *m*

ROE *abbr* (*return on equity*) FIN, STOCK rendimiento sobre el patrimonio *m*, remuneración por acción *f*, rendimiento sobre acción *m*

ROG *abbr* (*receipt of goods*) TRANSP *cargo* recepción de mercancías *f*

ROI *abbr* (*return on investment*) ACC, BANK, ECON, FIN rendimiento de la inversión *m*

ROIC *abbr* (*return on invested capital*) GEN COMM rendimiento sobre capital invertido *m*

role *n* GEN COMM rol *m*; ~**-playing** MGMNT representación de un papel *f*, *of business* juegos de rol *m pl*; ~ **set** MGMNT asignación de tareas *f*

roll¹: ~**-back** *n jarg* ECON *price* bajada *f*; ~ **down** *n* STOCK renovación a la baja *f*; ~**-on container** *n* TRANSP contenedor rodante *m*; ~**-on/roll-off** *n* (*ro/ro*) TRANSP embarque y desembarque autopropulsado (*ro/ro*); ~**-out** *n* TRANSP *vehicle* rodamiento *m*; ~**-over credit** *n* BANK crédito refinanciable *m*; ~**-over credit facility** *n* BANK línea de crédito con interés variable *f*; ~**-over date** *n* BANK fecha de ampliación *f*; ~**-over loan** *n* BANK préstamo con tipo variable *m*, crédito rotatorio *m*; ~**-over order** *n* STOCK orden de renovar al vencimiento *f*; ~ **up** *n* GEN COMM subida *f*

roll² *vt* TRANSP rodar

roll out *vt* GEN COMM transferir a disco, S&M introducir un producto en un mercado de prueba antes del lanzamiento general

roll over *vt* BANK variar el tipo de interés, *interests* renovar, TAX refinanciar

rolled: ~**-up income** *n* TAX ingreso obtenido por un cambio de posición *m*

roller: ~ **bed lorry** *n BrE* (*cf roller bed truck AmE*) TRANSP camión de soporte de rodillos *m*; ~ **bed truck** *n AmE* (*cf roller bed lorry BrE*) TRANSP camión de soporte de rodillos *m*; ~ **swop** *n* FIN intercambio rotativo *m*

rolling: ~ **down** *n* STOCK *options* cambio a una posición más baja; ~ **in** *n* STOCK *options* cambio de una posición *m*; ~ **options positions** *n pl* STOCK *on Eurodollar futures* posiciones de las opciones renovables *f pl*; ~ **out** *n* STOCK *options* abandono de una posición *m*; ~ **plan** *n* GEN COMM plan renovable *m*; ~ **program**

AmE, ~ **programme** *BrE* *n* FIN programa de renovación *m*, programa de rotación *m*; ~ **rate** *n* FIN, STOCK tipo renovable *m*; ~**-rate note** *n* FIN, STOCK documento de tipo renovable *m*; ~ **settlement** *n* STOCK sistema por el cual un inversor puede efectuar el pago días después de la compra o venta de valores; ~ **stock** *n* TRANSP material rodante *m*; ~ **strikes** *n pl jarg* HRM *industrial relations* huelgas alternativas *f pl*; ~ **up** *n* STOCK *options* cambio a una posición más alta *m*

rollover *n* BANK crédito flotante *m*, TAX refinanciación *f*, renovación *f*; ~ **mortgage** BANK, PROP hipoteca a medio plazo *f*; ~ **relief** TAX deducción por refinanciación *f*

ROM *abbr* (*read only memory*) COMP memoria de sólo lectura *f*

Roman: ~ **law** *n* LAW derecho romano *m*

roof: ~ **load** *n* TRANSP *containers* carga admisible sobre techo *f*; ~ **rail** *n* TRANSP *container* largueros de techo *m pl*; ~ **tax** *n* TAX tope fiscal *m*

room *n* GEN COMM sala *f*; ~ **service** LEIS servicio de habitaciones *m*; ~ **temperature** GEN COMM temperatura ambiente *f*

root *n* COMP raíz *f*; ~ **directory** COMP directorio raíz *m*; ~ **segment** COMP segmento de base *m*

ROP *abbr* (*run-of-paper*) MEDIA *print*, S&M ubicación indeterminada *f*, lugar de inserción indeterminado *m*

RORCE *abbr* (*rate of return on capital employed*) ACC, BANK, ECON, FIN tasa de rendimiento del capital invertido *f*

ro/ro[1] *abbr* (*roll-on/roll-off*) TRANSP *shipping* ro/ro (*embarque y desembarque autopropulsado*)

ro/ro[2]: ~ **berth** *n* TRANSP muelle para transporte de cargas rodadas *m*; ~ **drivers' cabin** *n* TRANSP cabina de conductores de cargas rodadas *f*; ~ **rate** *n* IMP/EXP, TRANSP *shipping* tarifa de carga autopropulsada *f*; ~ **vessel** *n* TRANSP buque para transporte de cargas rodadas *m*

roster *n* HRM *personnel duty* lista *f*

rosy *adj* GEN COMM *prospects* halagüeño

rotating: ~ **shift** *n* HRM turno rotativo *m*

rotation *n* GEN COMM rotación; ~ **clause** BANK *underwriting* cláusula de rotación *f*; ◆ **in** ~ GEN COMM por turno

rotogravure *n* S&M huecograbado *m*

rough *n* S&M *advertising* borrador *m*; ~ **draft** LAW primer borrador *m*; ~ **estimate** GEN COMM estimación aproximativa *f*; ~ **guide** GEN COMM guía aproximada *f*

round[1]: ~**-the-clock** *adj* *BrE* (*cf around-the-clock AmE*) GEN COMM continuo

round[2]: ~**-the-clock** *adv* *BrE* (*cf around-the-clock AmE*) GEN COMM continuamente

round[3] *n* ECON *of discussions* ronda *f*, IMP/EXP ronda negociadora *f*; ~ **bottom** (*RDBTN*) TRANSP *of ship* fondo redondo *m*; ~ **brackets** *n pl* COMP, MEDIA *typography* paréntesis *m pl*; ~ **charter party** TRANSP fletamento de ida y vuelta *m*; ~ **chartering** TRANSP flete de ida y vuelta *m*; ~ **lot** *AmE jarg* STOCK unidad de contratación *f*; ~**-off error** MATH error por redondeo *m*; ~ **robin** ADMIN, COMMS *letter* circular *f*; ~ **sum allowance** TAX desgravación de suma redonda *f*; ~ **table** GEN COMM mesa redonda *f*; ~**-the-clock service** *BrE* (*cf around-the-clock service AmE*) GEN COMM servicio de 24 horas *m*; ~ **trip** STOCK compraventa a corto plazo *f*, TRANSP *AmE* (*cf return trip BrE*)

viaje de ida y vuelta *m*; ~ **trip cost** TRANSP coste de viaje de ida y vuelta *m* (*Esp*), costo de viaje de ida y vuelta *m* (*AmL*); ~**-trip fare** *AmE* (*cf return fare BrE*) LEIS, TRANSP tarifa de ida y vuelta *f*; ~ **trip rate** *AmE* (*cf return rate BrE*) TRANSP tarifa de viaje de ida y vuelta *f*; ~**-trip ticket** *AmE* (*cf return ticket BrE*) LEIS billete de ida y vuelta *m*; ~ **trip time** *AmE* (*cf return journey time BrE*) TRANSP tiempo del viaje de ida y vuelta *m*; ~ **trip trade** STOCK compra y venta muy próximas de un valor *f*; ~ **turn** STOCK compraventa a corto plazo *f*, *commission* transacción doble cerrada *f*; ~ **the world service** (*Rws*) TRANSP *shipping* servicio extendido a todo el mundo *m*; ◆ **in** ~ **numbering** GEN COMM en números redondos

round off *vt* ACC *number*, FIN *figures* redondear, GEN COMM *meeting* concluir

round up *vt* MATH redondear por exceso

roundabout *n* *BrE* (*cf traffic circle AmE*) GEN COMM glorieta *f*, rotonda *f*

roundhouse *n* PROP rotonda *f*

rounding: ~ **error** *n* MATH error de redondeo *m*

roundtripping *n* *infrml* BANK pelota *f*, peloteo *m*

route *n* GEN COMM ruta *f*; ~ **analysis** TRANSP análisis de la ruta *m*; ~ **capacity** TRANSP capacidad de la ruta *f*; ~ **capacity control airline** (*RCCA*) TRANSP línea de control de la capacidad de una vía *f*; ~ **diversion** TRANSP desvío de la ruta *m* (*Esp*), reencaminamiento de la ruta *m* (*AmL*); ~ **option** TRANSP opción de ruta *f*; ~ **order** TRANSP orden de ruta *f*; ~ **planning** TRANSP plan de ruta *m*; ◆ **en** ~ TRANSP en ruta

routeing *n* TRANSP ponerse en marcha; ~ **certificate** TRANSP certificado de ruta *m*

routes: ~ **section** *n* TRANSP sección de ruta *f*

routine[1] *adj* GEN COMM rutinario

routine[2] *n* COMP, GEN COMM rutina *f*; ~ **check** GEN COMM control de rutina *m*; ~ **control** TRANSP control rutinario *m*; ~ **duties** *n pl* GEN COMM deberes rutinarios *m pl*; ~ **maintenance** GEN COMM conservación ordinaria *f*; ◆ **as a matter of** ~ GEN COMM por rutina

routing *n* COMP *data*, GEN COMM, TRANSP determinación de itinerarios *f*; ~ **order** (*R/O*) TRANSP *cargo* orden de ruta *f*, orden de conducción del tráfico *f*; ~ **salesperson** S&M vendedor(a) itinerante *m,f*

row *n* GEN COMM *of figures* fila *f*

ROW *abbr* (*Rest Of the World*) ECON resto del mundo *m*

royal[1] *adj* GEN COMM real

royal[2]: ~ **decree** *n* GEN COMM real decreto *m*

Royal: ~ **Automobile Club** *n* *BrE* (*RAC, cf AAA AmE*) TRANSP organización para el automovilista, ≈ Ayuda del Automovilista *f* (*Esp*) (*ADA*), ≈ Real Automóvil Club *m* (*RAC*); ~ **Economic Society** *n* ECON real sociedad de economía; ~ **Exchange** *n* *BrE* (*RE*) STOCK bolsa de Londres; **Her** ~ **Highness** *n* *BrE* (*HRH*) GEN COMM ≈ Su Alteza Real *f* (*Esp*) (*S.A.R.*); **His** ~ **Highness** *n* *BrE* (*HRH*) GEN COMM ≈ Su Alteza Real *m* (*Esp*) (*S.A.R.*); ~ **Institute of Navigation** *n* (*RIN*) TRANSP real instituto marítimo; ~ **Mint** *n* *BrE* BANK, ECON ≈ Casa de la Moneda *f* (*Esp*); ~ **Society of Arts** *n* (*RSA*) GEN COMM, WEL sociedad británica que promueve las humanidades

royalties *n pl* GEN COMM, MEDIA, S&M *print* canon *m*, derechos de autor *m pl*, royalty *m*, derechos de patente *m pl*

royalty *n* GEN COMM *of author* derechos de patente *m pl*, *patentens* canon *m*; ~ **exemption limit** TAX límite de exención de derechos *m*; ~ **holder** TAX titular de los derechos *mf*; ~ **trust** ENVIR consorcio de explotación *m*

R/p *abbr* (*return to port for orders*) TRANSP volver a puerto para recibir órdenes

RP *abbr* (*repurchase agreement*) STOCK repo (*pacto de recompra*)

RPI *abbr* (*Retail Price Index*) ECON, STOCK, FIN IPD (*Índice de Precios al Detalle*)

RPM *abbr* (*resale price maintenance*) GEN COMM, S&M mantenimiento de los precios al por menor *m*, mantenimiento del precio de reventa *m*

RR *abbr* (*rate resetter*) STOCK mecanismo de puesta a cero del tipo *m*

RRA *abbr* (*Race Relations Act*) HRM, LAW ley de relaciones interraciales

RRP *abbr* (*recommended retail price*) GEN COMM, S&M P.V.P. *m* (*precio de venta al público*)

RRR *abbr* (*real rate of return*) GEN COMM, FIN tasa real de devolución *f*, tasa real de rendimiento *f*

RRSP *abbr* (*registered retirement savings plan*) GEN COMM plan nominativo de ahorro y pensión *m*

RSA *abbr* (*Royal Society of Arts*) GEN COMM, WEL sociedad británica que promueve las humanidades

RSG *abbr* (*rate support grant*) ECON tipo mínimo garantizado *m*

RSI *abbr* (*repetitive strain injury*) HRM, WEL lesión por fatiga crónica *f*

RSVP *abbr* (*please reply*) COMMS se ruega contestación

RT *abbr* (*radiotelephony*) COMMS, MEDIA, TRANSP radiotelefonía *m*

Rt Hon *abbr BrE* (*Right Honourable*) GEN COMM Su Excelencia *f*

RTh *abbr* (*high frequency radiotelephony*) COMMS, MEDIA, TRANSP radiotelefonía de alta frecuencia *f*

RTm *abbr* (*medium frequency radiotelephony*) COMMS, MEDIA, TRANSP radiotelefonía de frecuencia media *f*

rubber: ~ **band** *n* GEN COMM banda de goma *f*; ~ **bearing** *n* (*RB*) TRANSP apoyo de caucho *m*; ~ **check** *AmE infrml*, ~ **cheque** *BrE infrml n* BANK, FIN cheque sin fondos *m*; ~ **stamp** *n* GEN COMM sello de goma *m*; **~-tired traffic** *AmE*, **~-tyred traffic** *BrE n* TRANSP tráfico sobre neumáticos *m*

RUF *abbr* (*revolving underwriting facility*) BANK, INS CAC (*compromiso de aseguramiento continuado*)

rule *n* GEN COMM norma *f*, regla *f*, LAW fallo *m*, precepto *m*, MGMNT pauta *f*, precepto *m*, rutina *f*; **under the ~** *AmE jarg* STOCK operación de bolsa bajo cuerda *f*; ~ **book** GEN COMM, HRM libro de normas *m*, manual de procedimientos *m*; ~ **of law** LAW precepto legal *m*; ~ **of thumb** GEN COMM procedimiento empírico *m*, regla general *f*

rule out *vt* GEN COMM excluir

ruled: ~ **paper** *n* GEN COMM papel pautado *m*, papel reglado *m*

rules[1]: ~ **of fair practice** *n pl* GEN COMM, STOCK código de conducta *m*; ~ **and regulations** *n pl* GEN COMM, LAW normas y reglamentos *f pl*

rules[2]: ~ **versus discretion** *phr* ECON reglas sobre discreción *f pl*

ruling: ~ **class** *n* GEN COMM, WEL clase dominante *f*;

~ **price** *n* ECON, GEN COMM, S&M precio corriente *m*, precio que rige *m*

rummage: ~ **sale** *n AmE* (*cf jumble sale BrE*) S&M venta de objetos usados *f*, venta de prendas usadas *f*

rumor *AmE see rumour BrE*

rumour[1] *n BrE* GEN COMM rumor *m*

run[1]: **~-of-the-mill** *adj* GEN COMM corriente y moliente; **~-on** *adj* (*infrml*) text unido al párrafo anterior

run[2] *n* GEN COMM tendencia *f*, *series* serie *f*; **~-around** MEDIA *print* interespacio para intercalar una ilustración; **~-off** IND desagüe *m*; **~-off election** *AmE jarg* POL segunda vuelta *f*; **~-of-paper** (*ROP*) MEDIA, S&M ubicación indeterminada *f*, lugar de inserción indeterminado *m*; **~-of-week spot** S&M anuncio de frecuencia semanal *m*; ~ **on the banks** STOCK incursión por los bancos; ~ **on the dollar** GEN COMM movimiento especulativo contra el dólar *m*; ~ **of schedule** LAW, PROP marcha del calendario de trabajo *f*; ~ **of the ship** TRANSP finos de popa *m pl*; ~ **time** COMP *program* tiempo de proceso *m*, GEN COMM tiempo de pasada *m*; **~-up** STOCK alza de precios *f*; ♦ **in the long ~** GEN COMM a la larga; **in the ~-up to** POL *elections* en la carrera hacia *f*

run[3] **1.** *vt* ADMIN administrar, BANK *referring to interest* caer, GEN COMM, MGMNT administrar, ejecutar; ♦ ~ **an errand** GEN COMM hacer un recado; ~ **with the land** LAW transmitirse con la tierra; ~ **the risk of** GEN COMM correr el riesgo de; ~ **the show** GEN COMM llevar la voz cantante; **2.** *vi* POL *for public office* presentarse; ♦ ~ **aground** TRANSP *ship* encallar, varar; ~ **empty** TRANSP *bus, train* ir de vacío; ~ **foul of the authorities** TAX topar con las autoridades fiscales; ~ **into debt** GEN COMM entrar en pérdidas; ~ **low** STOCK escasear

run at *vt* GEN COMM lanzarse sobre

run back *vi* STOCK retroceder

run down *vt* ECON *liquid assets* disminuir

run off *vt* IND desaguar

run on *vi* FIN continuar

run out *vi* FIN expirar

run out of *vt* GEN COMM quedarse sin

run short of *vt* GEN COMM estar escaso de

run up *vt* BANK *overdraft, debt* dejar acumular; ♦ ~ **a debt** BANK, FIN acumular deudas; ~ **a deficit** ECON aumentar un déficit, manejar un déficit, FIN aumentar un déficit; ~ **a surplus** ECON manejar un superávit

runaway: ~ **industry** *n* ECON, IND industria oportunista *f*; ~ **inflation** *n* ECON inflación desenfrenada *f*; ~ **shop** *n jarg* HRM empresa itinerante *f*, IND taller oportunista *m*

runner *n jarg* GEN COMM corredor(a) *m,f*, mensajero(-a) *m,f*, HRM, mensajero(-a) *m,f*

running *n* GEN COMM marcha *f*; ~ **ahead** STOCK compra y venta ilegal de un valor por cuenta del propio intermediario antes de gestionarla para un cliente; ~ **broker** STOCK intermediario de efectos de descuento *m*; ~ **cable** COMP cable de suspensión *m*; ~ **costs** *n pl* GEN COMM costes de operación *m pl* (*Esp*), costos de operación *m pl* (*AmL*), gastos de mantenimiento *m pl*; ~ **days** *n pl* GEN COMM, LAW días corridos *m pl*, (*Rd*) TRANSP *ships* días de plancha *m pl*; ~ **down clause** (*RDC*) INS *marine* cláusula de colisión *f*; ~ **expenses** *n pl* GEN COMM gastos de mantenimiento *m pl*; ~ **hour** TRANSP *charter party* hora corriente *f*; **~-in period** GEN COMM periodo de rodaje *m*; ~ **interest** BANK interés corriente *m*;

~ **mate** *AmE* POL candidato(-a) a la vicepresidencia *m,f*; ~ **number** GEN COMM número consecutivo *m*; ~ **total** GEN COMM total actualizado *m*, total hasta la fecha *m*; ~ **working day** TRANSP *charter party* día laborable consecutivo *m*; ◆ **be in the ~ for** GEN COMM *promotion* tener posibilidades de; **be out of the ~** GEN COMM no tener ninguna posibilidad de ganar

runoff *n AmE* POL segunda vuelta *f*

runway *n* TRANSP pista de salida *f*

rural: ~ **area** *n* ECON, ENVIR área rural *f*; ~ **community** *n* ECON, ENVIR comunidad rural *f*; ~ **free delivery service** *n* (*RFDS*) COMMS servicio rural de entrega gratuita *m*; ~ **land** *n* PROP terreno rural *m*; ~ **sector** *n* IND sector rural *m*; ~ **tourism** *n* LEIS turismo rural *m*

Rural: ~ **Development Area** *n BrE* (*RDA*) ECON zona de desarrollo rural *f*

rush: ~ **hour** *n* TRANSP hora pico *f* (*AmL*), hora punta *f* (*Esp*); ~ **job** *n* GEN COMM trabajo urgente *m*; ~ **order** *n* GEN COMM, S&M pedido urgente *m*

rusty *adj* IND oxidado

Rybczynski: ~ **theorem** *n* ECON *terms of trade* teorema de Rybczynski *m*

S

S[1] *abbr* (*station*) TRANSP S (*estación*), (*starboard side*) estribor *m*

S[2]: **~ curve** *n* ECON curva S *f*

s/a *abbr* (*safe arrival*) TRANSP feliz arribo *m* (*AmL*), feliz llegada *f* (*Esp*)

s.a.a.r. *abbr* (*seasonally-adjusted annual rate*) ECON tipo anual con ajuste estacional *m*

sack *vt infrml* HRM *staff* cesar, despedir, echar; ◆ **~ sb** HRM poner a alguien de patitas en la calle (*infrml*)

sacked *adj infrml* HRM despedido

sacrifice[1]: **~ theory** *n* ECON teoría del sacrificio *f*

sacrifice[2] *vt* GEN COMM sacrificar

SAD *abbr* (*single administrative document*) ADMIN documento administrativo único *m*, documento administrativo simple *m*

saddle: **~ point** *n* ECON *game theory* punto de inflexión *m*

s.a.e. *abbr* COMMS (*self-addressed envelope*) sobre con la dirección del remitente, (*stamped-addressed envelope*) sobre con la dirección del remitente y sello

SAEF *abbr* (*SEAQ Automated Execution Facility*) STOCK instalación de operaciones automatizadas de la bolsa

SAF *abbr* (*structural adjustment facility*) FIN mecanismo de ajuste estructural *m*

safe *n* BANK caja de seguridad bancaria *f*, caja fuerte *f*; **~ arrival** (*s/a*) TRANSP feliz arribo *m* (*AmL*), feliz llegada *f* (*Esp*); **~ asset** FIN activo seguro *m*, posesión segura *f*; **~ berth** TRANSP *shipping* muelle seguro *m*; **~ custody department** BANK departamento de seguridad *m*; **~ deposit** BANK depósito en caja de seguridad *m*; **~-deposit box** BANK caja de seguridad *f*; **~-deposit vault** BANK bóveda de seguridad *f*; **~ estimate** GEN COMM cálculo exacto *m*; **~ harbor rule** *AmE*, **~ harbour rule** *BrE* TAX norma de seguridad portuaria *f*; **~ hedge** STOCK protección segura *f*; **~ investment** BANK, FIN colocación segura *f*; **~ port** TRANSP puerto seguro *m*; **~ working load** IND carga sin riesgo de trabajo *f*; ◆ **be on the ~ side** GEN COMM estar más seguro

safeguard 1. *vt* GEN COMM *assets* salvaguardar; **2.** *vi* GEN COMM salvaguardarse; ◆ **~ against inflation** ECON salvaguardarse contra la inflación

safekeeping *n* GEN COMM, LAW custodia *f*; **~ of assets** BANK custodia de activos *f*, custodia de haberes *f*

safety *n* GEN COMM seguridad *f*; **~ bank** GEN COMM banco de seguridad *m*; **~ belt** TRANSP cinturón de seguridad *m* (*Esp*), faja de seguridad *f* (*AmL*); **~ check** GEN COMM cheque de seguridad *m*, inspección de seguridad *f*; **~-deposit box** BANK caja para depósitos de seguridad *f*, caja de seguridad *f*; **~-deposit-box charges** BANK gastos de la caja de seguridad *m pl*; **~ engineer** HRM, IND ingeniero(-a) de seguridad *m,f*; **~ equipment certificate** TRANSP certificado de dispositivo de seguridad *m*; **~ hazard** GEN COMM riesgo de seguridad *m*; **~ management** HRM, INS, MGMNT dirección de seguridad *f*, gerencia de seguridad *f*; **~ margin** GEN COMM margen de seguridad *m*; **~ measure** ENVIR, GEN COMM medida de seguridad *f*; **~ officer** HRM empleado(-a) de seguridad *m,f*; **~ precaution** GEN COMM medida de seguridad *f*; **~ regulation** GEN COMM norma de seguridad *f*; **~ representative** HRM representante de seguridad *mf*; **~ requirement** GEN COMM, IND, S&M *for products* requisito de seguridad *m*; **~ share** STOCK acción segura *f*; **~ standard** GEN COMM norma de seguridad *f*; **~ stock** GEN COMM existencias de seguridad *f pl*, acción segura *f*, stock de seguridad *f pl*; **~ vault** BANK caja de seguridad *f*; **~ violation** LAW violación de la seguridad *f*

Safety: **~ Commission** *n AmE* WEL *governmental organization* comisión para la seguridad; **~ Committee** *n AmE* WEL *private sector organization* comisión para la seguridad

sagging *adj* GEN COMM hundido

sail: **~ close to the wind** *phr* GEN COMM navegar como el viento; **~ from** *phr* TRANSP zarpar desde

sailing: **~ date** *n* (*S/D*) TRANSP fecha de salida *f*; **~ schedule** *n* TRANSP horarios de salidas *m pl*

salariat *n* HRM asalariado(-a) *m,f*

salaried: **~ agent** *n* HRM agente asalariado(-a) *m,f*; **~ employee** *n* GEN COMM, HRM asalariado(-a) *m,f* empleado(-a) a sueldo *m,f*; **~ person** *n* HRM asalariado(-a) *m,f*; **~ staff** *n* HRM personal asalariado *m*

salaries: **~ and wages** *n pl* HRM sueldos y jornales *m pl*; **~, wages and fringe benefits** *n pl* HRM salarios, sueldos y beneficios complementarios

salary *n* GEN COMM, HRM salario *m*, sueldo *m*; **~-adjustment reserve allotment** (*SARA*) HRM cuota de reserva para ajustes salariales *f*; **~ base** HRM base salarial *f*; **~ deduction** HRM deducción salarial *f*; **~ deferral arrangement** HRM arreglo de aplazamiento de salario *m*; **~ earner** HRM asalariado(-a) *m,f*; **~ grade** HRM nivel de sueldo *m*; **~ increase** HRM incremento salarial *m*; **~ progression curve** HRM curva de progresión de sueldos *f*; **~ rate** HRM índice salarial *m*; **~ reduction plan** HRM plan de reducción salarial *m*; **~ review** HRM revisión del salario *f*, revisión salarial *f*; **~ sacrifice scheme** TAX plan de sacrificio salarial *m*; **~ scale** HRM escala de salarios *f*, escala de sueldos *f*; **~ scheme** HRM plan salarial *m*; **~ structure** ECON, HRM estructura salarial *f*; ◆ **~ to be negotiated** HRM sueldo negociable

sale *n* GEN COMM, S&M realización *f*, venta *f*, *at reduced prices* barata *f* (*AmL*), rebaja *f* (*Esp*); **~ by tender** S&M venta mediante licitación pública *f*; **~ charges** *n pl* ACC, GEN COMM, S&M gastos comerciales *m pl*; **~ commission** S&M comisión de venta *f*; **~ for delivery** STOCK venta con entrega aplazada *f*; **~ of goods** S&M venta de bienes *f*, venta de mercancías *f*; **~ and leaseback** ACC, GEN COMM venta con acuerdo de alquiler *f*, venta y arriendo al vendedor *f*; **~ on approval** S&M venta a prueba *f*; **~ on return** FIN, S&M, STOCK compra con derecho a devolución *f*; **~ price** GEN COMM precio de oferta *m*; **~ proceeds** *n pl* GEN COMM ingresos de venta *m pl*; **~ and purchase broker** HRM agente de compraventa *mf*; **~ value** S&M valor de venta *m*; **~ of vessel clause** INS cláusula de venta del buque *f*; ◆ **be on ~** GEN COMM estar a la venta; **~ or return** *BrE* S&M acuerdo de venta que permite al comprador devolver la mercancía que no vende; **~ subject to safe arrival** S&M venta condicionada a una llegada *f*

saleableness *n* S&M facilidad de venta *f*

sales *n pl* GEN COMM ventas *f pl*; **~ account** *n* (*a/s*) ACC, BANK, GEN COMM, S&M cuenta de ventas *f*; **~ activity** *n* GEN COMM, S&M actividad de ventas *f*; **~ agency** *n* S&M agencia de ventas *f*; **~ agent** *n* GEN COMM, HRM, S&M agente de ventas *mf*; **~ agreement** *n* BANK, LAW, S&M contrato de venta *m*; **~ aid** *n* S&M elemento auxiliar de la venta *m pl*; **~ analysis** *n* S&M análisis de ventas *m*; **~ analyst** *n* HRM, S&M analista de ventas *mf*; **~ appeal** *n* S&M atractivo de las ventas *m*; **~ approach** *n* S&M método de abordar las ventas *m*, propuesta comercial de venta *f*; **~ area** *n* S&M *in stores* zona de ventas *f*; **~ book** *n* S&M libro de ventas *m*; **~ budget** *n* S&M presupuesto de ventas *m*; **~ call** *n* S&M visita de venta *f*; **~ campaign** *n* S&M campaña de ventas *f*; **~ charge** *n* STOCK cargo por ventas *m*; **~ clerk** *n AmE* (*cf shop assistant BrE*) HRM, S&M dependiente(-a) de tienda *m,f*; **~ conference** *n* S&M conferencia de ventas *f*; **~ contest** *n* S&M concurso de ventas *m*; **~ contract** *n* BANK, LAW, S&M contrato de venta *m*; **~ control** *n* S&M control de ventas *m*; **~ costs** S&M costes de ventas *m pl* (*Esp*), costos de ventas *m pl* (*AmL*); **~ coverage** *n* S&M cobertura de ventas *f*; **~ data** *n* S&M cifras de ventas *f*; **~ department** *n* S&M departamento de ventas *m*; **~ director** *n* HRM, MGMNT, S&M director(a) de ventas *m,f*; **~ discount** *n* GEN COMM descuento a clientes *m*, S&M descuento de venta *m*; **~ effectiveness test** *n* S&M prueba de efectividad de las ventas *f*; **~ effort** *n* S&M esfuerzo de venta *m*; **~ engineer** *n* HRM, S&M ingeniero(-a) de ventas *m,f*; **~ estimate** *n* S&M estimación de ventas *f*, cálculo de ventas *m*; **~ executive** *n* HRM, S&M ejecutivo(-a) de ventas *m,f*; **~ feature** *n* S&M artículo de venta *m*; **~ figures** S&M cifras de ventas *f pl*; **~ folder** *n* S&M folleto publicitario *m*; **~ force** *n* S&M equipo de venta *m*, personal de ventas *m*; **~ forecast** *n* ECON, S&M previsión de ventas *f*; **~ goal** *n* FIN, S&M meta de ventas *f*; **~ goods** S&M productos a la venta *m pl*; **~ of goods law** *n* LAW, S&M ley de venta de mercancías *f*; **~ incentive** *n* GEN COMM, S&M incentivo a la venta *m*, incentivo de ventas *m*; **~ interview** *n* S&M entrevista de ventas *f*; **~ journal** *n* GEN COMM, S&M diario de ventas *m*; **~ kit** *n* S&M avíos de venta *m pl*; **~ lead** *n* S&M información que puede provocar una venta; **~ leaflet** *n* S&M folleto publicitario *m*; **~ ledger** *n* ACC, GEN COMM, S&M libro mayor de ventas *m*; **~ letter** *n* S&M carta de venta *f*; **~ literature** *n* S&M folleto publicitario *m*; **~ management** *n* MGMNT, S&M dirección de ventas *f*, gerencia de ventas *f*; **~ manager** *n* HRM, MGMNT, S&M director(a) de ventas *m,f*, gerente de ventas *mf*, jefe(-a) de ventas *m,f*; **~ manual** *n* S&M manual de ventas *m*; **~ maximization** *n* S&M maximización de las ventas *f*; **~ meeting** *n* S&M reunión de ventas *f*; **~ mix** *n* S&M mezcla de estrategias de ventas *f*; **~ network** *n* S&M red de ventas *f*; **~ offensive** *n* S&M ofensiva comercial *f*; **~ office** *n* S&M oficina de ventas *f*; **~ office manager** *n* S&M jefe(-a) de oficina de ventas *m,f*; **~ opportunity** *n* S&M oportunidad de ventas *f*; **~ organization** *n* S&M organización de ventas *f*; **~ organizer** *n* S&M organizador(a) de ventas *m,f*; **~ orientation** *n* S&M orientación de ventas *f*; **~ penetration** *n* S&M penetración de ventas *f*; **~ performance** *n* ACC, FIN, S&M rendimiento de ventas *m*; **~ personnel** *n* S&M personal de ventas *m*; **~ pitch** *n* S&M rollo publicitario *m*; **~ planning** *n* S&M planificación de las ventas *f*; **~ platform** *n* S&M plataforma de ventas *f*; **~ policy** *n* S&M política de ventas *f*; **~ portfolio** *n* S&M cartera de ventas *f*; **~ potential** *n* S&M potencial de ventas *m*; **~ presentation** *n* S&M presentación comercial *f*; **~ price** *n* GEN COMM, S&M precio de venta *m*; **~ price** *n* GEN COMM, S&M precio de venta *m*; **~ projection** *n* S&M proyección de ventas *f*; **~ promotion** *n* S&M promoción de ventas *f*; **~ prospects** S&M perspectivas de ventas *f pl*; **~ and purchase broker** HRM agente de compraventa *mf*; **~ push** *n* S&M empuje de ventas *m*; **~ quota** *n* S&M cupo de ventas *m*; **~ ratio** *n* S&M proporción de ventas *f*, relación de ventas *f*; **~ receipt** *n* S&M recibo de ventas *m*, resguardo de ventas *m*; **~ record** *n* S&M registro de ventas *m*; **~ representative** *n* (*rep*) HRM, S&M corredor(-a) de comercio *m,f*, representante de ventas *mf*, representante comercial *mf*, viajante de comercio *mf*; **~ research** *n* S&M investigación de ventas *f*; **~ resistance** *n* S&M resistencia a la venta *f*; **~ returns** *n* ACC, S&M devoluciones de ventas *f pl*; **~ revenue** *n* S&M ingresos por ventas *m pl*, facturación de ventas *f*; **~ service** *n* S&M servicio de ventas *m*; **~ slip** *n* GEN COMM, S&M recibo de caja *f*; **~ slump** *n* S&M bajada de las ventas *f*; **~ strategy** *n* S&M estrategia de ventas *f*; **~ talk** *n* S&M jerga de vendedor *f*; **~ target** *n* GEN COMM, S&M objetivo de ventas *m*; **~ tax** *n* TAX impuesto sobre las ventas *m*; **~ tax credit** *n* TAX desgravación de la venta *f*; **~ technique** *n* S&M técnica de ventas *f*; **~ territory** *n* S&M territorio de ventas *m*; **~ test** *n* S&M prueba de ventas *f*; **~ tool** *n* S&M herramienta de ventas *f*; **~ turnover** *n* S&M cifras de ventas *f*, facturación de ventas *f*; **~ type lease** *n* FIN alquiler tipo venta *m*; **~ value** ACC, S&M importe de las ventas *m*; **~ volume** *n* ACC, GEN COMM, S&M cifra de ventas *f*, volumen de ventas *m*

salesman *n* GEN COMM, HRM, S&M vendedor(a) *m,f*, viajante *mf*

salesmanship *n* S&M arte de vender *m*

saleswoman *n* GEN COMM, HRM, S&M vendedora *f*

salinity: **~ level** *n* ENVIR nivel de salinidad *m*

salt: **~ a memo** *phr jarg* ADMIN falsificar un memorandum

Salt: **~ Lake City Stock Exchange** *n* STOCK Bolsa de Valores de Salt Lake *f*

salvage[1] *n* GEN COMM, TRANSP *shipping* salvamento *m*; **~ agreement** TRANSP *shipping* contrato de salvamento *m*; **~ bond** STOCK emisión de rating dudoso *f*; **~ charges** *n pl* TRANSP gastos de salvamento *m pl*; **~ loss** INS pérdida de salvamento *f*; **~ value** ECON valor residual *m*

salvage[2] *vt* GEN COMM, TRANSP salvar

salvaged: **~ return** *n* TAX declaración recuperada *f*

salvor *n* TRANSP *shipping* buque de salvamento *m*

same[1]: **~~day** *adj* GEN COMM, TRANSP en el día

same[2]: **~~day delivery** *n* GEN COMM, TRANSP entrega en el día *f*; **~~day value** *n* BANK valor del mismo día *m*; **~ sea and coast** (*SS&C*) TRANSP transporte por el mismo mar y costa *m*; **~ sea and country** (*SS&C*) TRANSP transporte por el mismo mar y país *m*; **~ size** *n* S&M igual tamaño *m*

same[3]: **on the ~ footing** *phr* GEN COMM en pie de igualdad, en iguales condiciones

sample *n* GEN COMM muestra *f*; **~ audit** ACC auditoría de muestra *f*; **~ card** GEN COMM ficha para muestras *f*;

~ **case** S&M maleta de muestra *f*; ~ **census** S&M censo por muestras *m*; ~ **data** COMP datos de muestra *m pl*; ~ **drawing** MATH diseño de la muestra *m*, disposición de la muestra *f*; ~ **licence** *BrE*, ~ **license** *AmE* IMP/EXP licencia para muestras *f*, licencia patrón *f*; ~ **mailing** COMMS lista de direcciones de muestra *f*; ~ **mean** MATH media muestral *f*; ~ **policy** INS póliza en blanco *f*; ~ **rate** GEN COMM porcentaje de la muestra *m*; ~ **space** MATH espacio muestral *m*; ~ **study** S&M *market research* estudio de muestra *m*; ~ **survey** S&M *market research* encuesta por muestreo *f*; ♦ **take a** ~ MATH, S&M tomar una muestra

samples: ~ **fair** *n* GEN COMM, S&M feria de muestras *f*

sampling: ~ **deviation** *n* MATH desviación de la muestra *f*; ~ **distribution** *n* MATH distribución de muestra *f*; ~ **error** *n* MATH error de muestreo *m*; ~ **frame** *n* MATH marco del muestreo *m*; ~ **grid** *n* MATH cuadrícula de la muestra *f*; ~ **offer** *n* GEN COMM oferta de muestras *f*; ~ **point** *n* S&M punto de prueba *m*; ~ **variance** *n* MATH variación de muestreo *f*

samurai: ~ **bond** *n* FIN, STOCK *Japan* bono samurai *m*

sanction *n* GEN COMM sanción *f*

s&c *abbr* (*shipper and carrier*) TRANSP expedidor(a) y transportista *m,f*

S&FA *abbr* (*shipping and forwarding agent*) HRM, TRANSP agente de transportes marítimos *mf*

S&L *abbr AmE* (*savings and loan association*) BANK ≈ banco hipotecario *m*, ≈ banco de crédito hipotecario *m*, PROP cooperativa de ahorro y crédito a la construcción

S&P500 *abbr* (*Standard and Poor's 500 Stock Index*) STOCK índice bursátil de Standard and Poor *m*

sandwich: ~ **board** *n* S&M cartelón *m*; ~ **course** *n* WEL curso académico con periodo en prácticas; ~ **lease** *n infrml* PROP arrendamiento por un subarrendatario *m*

SANR *abbr* (*subject approval no risk*) INS sujeto a aprobación sin riesgo

sans: ~ **serif** *n* MEDIA *typography* grotesca *f*

Santiago: ~ **Stock Exchange** *n* STOCK Bolsa de Santiago *f*

SAR *abbr* (*Search and Rescue*) WEL Servicio de Rescate *m*

s.a.s.e. *abbr* (*self-addressed stamped envelope*) COMMS sobre con la dirección del remitente y sello

satellite *n* COMMS, MEDIA satélite *m*; ~ **broadcasting** GEN COMM, MEDIA transmisión por vía satélite *f*; ~ **communication** COMMS comunicación por vía satélite *f*; ~ **communications** *n pl* COMMS telecomunicaciones por satélite *f pl*; ~ **computer** COMP computador satélite *m* (*AmL*), computadora satélite *f* (*AmL*), ordenador auxiliar *m* (*Esp*); ~ **television** MEDIA televisión por satélite *f*; ~ **town** GEN COMM ciudad satélite *f*

satisfaction[1]: ~ **of a debt** *n* ACC, BANK, FIN pago de una deuda *m*; ~ **note** *n jarg* FIN, INS comprobante de pago *m*; ~ **piece** *n jarg* PROP notificación de liquidación *f*

satisfaction[2]: **in** ~ **of** *phr* ACC, BANK, FIN en pago de

satisfactory *adj* GEN COMM satisfactorio

satisfied[1] *adj* GEN COMM satisfecho

satisfied[2]: ~ **lien** *n* TAX gravamen liquidado *m*

satisfy *vt* GEN COMM satisfacer

saturate *vt* GEN COMM *economy, market* saturar

saturation *n* COMP, ECON, GEN COMM, S&M *of the market* saturación *f*; ~ **campaign** S&M *advertising* campaña de saturación *f*; ~ **point** GEN COMM punto de saturación *m*

Saturday: ~ **night special** *n jarg* FIN especial fin de semana *m*

saucer *n* MATH *statistics* platillo *m*

save[1]: ~ **as you earn** *n BrE* (*SAYE*) ECON plan de ahorro mediante descuentos en el sueldo

save[2] *vt* COMP *data* salvar, GEN COMM ahorrar, *data* salvar

saver: ~**'s surplus** *n* BANK excedente del ahorrador *m*

saving *n* GEN COMM ahorro *m*

savings[1]: ~**-linked** *adj* GEN COMM ligado al ahorro

savings[2] *n BrE* (*cf thrift AmE*) GEN COMM ahorros *m pl*; ~ **account** BANK cuenta de ahorros *f*; ~ **bank** BANK banco de ahorros *m*, caja de ahorros *f* (*Esp*); ~ **bank book** STOCK libreta de ahorros *f*; ~ **bond** FIN, STOCK bono de ahorro *m*; ~ **book** BANK cartilla de ahorros *f*; ~ **certificate** BANK, STOCK certificado de ahorro *m*; ~ **deposit** BANK depósito de ahorro *m*; ~ **function** ECON *of country* función de ahorro *f*; ~ **institution** *BrE* (*cf thrift institution AmE*) BANK entidad de ahorro y préstamo *f*, institución de ahorro y préstamo *f*; ~ **and loan association** *AmE* (*S&L*) (*cf building society BrE*) BANK banco hipotecario *m*, banco de crédito hipotecario *m*, PROP cooperativa de ahorro y crédito a la construcción *f*; ~ **passbook** BANK libreta de ahorro *f*; ~ **plan** BANK, FIN plan de ahorro *m*; ~ **ratio** ECON, FIN proporción del ahorro *f*; ~**-to-income ratio** FIN porcentaje de los ingresos que se ahorran *m*, relación de los ingresos que se ahorran *f*

sawbuck *n AmE infrml* FIN billete de diez dólares

say: ~ **a few words of welcome** *phr* GEN COMM decir unas palabras de bienvenida; **have a** ~ **in sth** *phr* GEN COMM tener voz y voto

SAYE *abbr BrE* (*save as you earn*) ECON plan de ahorro mediante descuentos en el sueldo

Say: ~**'s Law** *n* ECON, LAW Ley de Say *f*

SBA *abbr* (*small business administration*) GEN COMM, MGMNT administración de la pequeña empresa *f*, dirección general de la pequeña empresa *f*, gestión de la pequeña empresa *f*

SBAC *abbr* (*Society of British Aerospace Companies*) TRANSP ≈ AECA (*Asociación Española de Compañías Aéreas*)

SC *abbr* (*Sports Council*) LEIS organismo autónomo de promoción del deporte

scab *n infrml* HRM *strike-breaker* esquirol *mf* (*infrml*); ~ **union** *infrml* HRM *industrial relations* sindicato esquirol *m* (*infrml*)

scale[1] *n* GEN COMM escala *f*, *of problem* envergadura *f*; ~ **buying** GEN COMM compra a precios escalonados *f*; ~ **charge** TAX cobro escalonado; ~ **of charges** GEN COMM escala de cargos *f*; ~ **of commission** STOCK escala de la comisión *f*; ~ **fee** LAW honorarios según escala *m pl*; ~ **model** MEDIA maqueta *f*; ~ **of points value** HRM puntuación del personal *f*; ♦ **on an international** ~ GEN COMM a escala internacional; **on a large** ~ GEN COMM gran escala; **on a small** ~ GEN COMM a pequeña escala; **on a worldwide** ~ GEN COMM a escala mundial

scale[2] *vt* GEN COMM escalar; ♦ ~ **the ladder** HRM escalar posiciones

scale down *vt* S&M recoltar proporcionalmente, disminuir proporcionalmente, STOCK reducir

scale up *vt* GEN COMM escalar

scaler *n jarg* HRM *industrial relations* tasa salarial para un puesto de trabajo, negociada y determinada por un sindicato

scalp *n AmE infrml* STOCK *futures market* operación rápida de bolsa con idea de beneficio *f*

scalper *n AmE infrml* STOCK especulador(a) a muy corto plazo *m,f*

scalping *n AmE infrml* STOCK especulación a muy corto plazo *f*

scamp *n jarg* S&M *advertising* borrador *m*

scan[1]: **~ area** *n* COMP superficie de exploración *f*

scan[2] *vt* COMP *electronic* explorar, GEN COMM *statements, report* examinar

scandal *n* GEN COMM escándalo *m*

scanner *n* COMP escáner *m*, GEN COMM explorador *m*, interrogador *m*, lector *m*

scanning *n* COMP *electronic*, GEN COMM exploración *f*

scant: **~ coverage** *n* GEN COMM cobertura escasa *f*

scapegoat *n BrE infrml* (*cf fall guy AmE*) STOCK cabeza de turco *f* (*infrml*)

scarce[1] *adj* GEN COMM *resources* escaso; ◆ **in ~ supply** GEN COMM escaso

scarce[2]: **~ good** *n* GEN COMM bien escaso *m*

scarcity *n* GEN COMM escasez *f*; **~ index** ECON índice de escasez *m*; **~ value** ECON valor de escasez *m*

scatter: **~ diagram** *n* MATH *statistics*, MGMNT diagrama de dispersión *m*

scattered: **~ site housing** *n BrE* (*cf scattersite housing AmE*) WEL asentamientos de población dispersos *m pl*

scattergram *n* MATH *statistics*, MGMNT diagrama de dispersión *m*

scattershot *n* TRANSP carga dispersiva *f*

scattersite: **~ housing** *n AmE* (*cf scattered site housing BrE*) WEL asentamientos de población dispersos *m pl*

scavenger: **~ sale** *n infrml* PROP venta de embargo *f*

SCC *abbr* GEN COMM (*Spanish Chamber of Commerce*) Cámara de Comercio Española *f*, MEDIA (*single column centimeter AmE, single column centimetre BrE*) centímetro-columna *m*

scenario *n* GEN COMM, MEDIA guión *m*

scenic: **~ easement** *n* PROP servidumbre turística *f*

scepticism *n BrE* GEN COMM escepticismo *m*

schedular: **~ tax** *n* TAX impuesto cedular *m*

schedule[1] *n* GEN COMM *timetable* horario *m*, horario de trabajo *m*, inventario *m*, *of repayments* calendario *m*, cuadro *m*; **~ code** GEN COMM código inventarial *m*; **~ of repayments** BANK calendario de pagos *m*; ◆ **ahead of ~** GEN COMM antes del plazo previsto; **on ~** GEN COMM conforme al programa, *train, flight* puntual, a tiempo, a la hora prevista

schedule[2] *vt* GEN COMM programar

scheduled[1] *adj* GEN COMM programado; ◆ **as ~** GEN COMM según lo programado; **be ~ for** GEN COMM estar previsto para; **~ to begin in** GEN COMM cuyo comienzo está previsto para

scheduled[2]: **~ flight** *n* LEIS, TRANSP vuelo programado *m*; **~ price** *n* GEN COMM precio listado *m*; **~ service** *n* LEIS, TRANSP servicio programado *m*, servicio regular *m*

scheduling *n* IND *production*, MGMNT calendario de acciones *m*, calendario de ejecución *m*

schematic *adj* ECON, GEN COMM esquemático

scheme *n* ECON esquema *m*, GEN COMM esquema *m*, ardid *m*, S&M planes *m pl*, TAX *evasion* ardid *m*

Schengen: **~ Agreement** *n* IMP/EXP, POL *EU frontier control* Acuerdo de Schengen *m*

scholarship *n* WEL beca *f*

school *n* GEN COMM escuela *f*; **~ report** GEN COMM informe escolar *m* (*Esp*), reporte escolar *m* (*AmL*)

schooner *n* (*Sr*) TRANSP goleta *f*

SCI *abbr* (*single column inch*) MEDIA pulgada de columna de a uno *f*

science: **~ park** *n* IND parque científico *m*

Science: **~ and Technology for Environmental Protection Programme** *n* (*STEP*) ENVIR Programa de Ciencia y Tecnología para la Protección Medioambiental *m*

scientific: **~ management** *n* GEN COMM administración científica *f*, dirección científica *f*, gestión científica *f*; **~ programming** *n* COMP, MATH programación científica *f*; **~ research** *n* IND investigación científica *f*; **~ research expenditure** *n* TAX *capital allowances* gasto en investigación científica *m*; **~ research tax credit** *n* TAX desgravación de la investigación científica *f*

Scientific: **~ Instrument Manufacturers Association** *n* (*SIMA*) IND asociación de fabricantes de instrumentos científicos

scientist *n* HRM científico(-a) *m,f*

scissor: **~ lift** *n* TRANSP ascensor de tijera *m*

Scitovsky: **~ reversal test** *n* ECON test de inversión de Scitovsky *m*

scoop *n* FIN pelotazo *m*, MEDIA *print* primicia informativa *f*, MGMNT escope *m*

scope *n* GEN COMM alcance *m*, PATENTS *of claims* ámbito *m*, alcance *m*; **~ of agreement** HRM alcance del acuerdo *m*; **~ of coverage** INS ámbito de cobertura *m*, alcance de la cobertura *m*; **~ of employment** HRM alcance del empleo *m*, extensión del empleo *f*; ◆ **there is ~ for improvement** GEN COMM hay perspectivas de mejoría

scorched: **~-earth defence** *n BrE*, **-earth defense** *AmE n* FIN, MGMNT defensa de tierra abrasada *f*; **~-earth policy** *n* FIN, MGMNT política de la tierra quemada *f*

score: **on that ~** *phr* GEN COMM a ese respecto; **~ good viewer ratings** *phr* MEDIA conseguir un gran número de telespectadores; **~ a hit** *phr* GEN COMM marcar un hito

SCP[1] *abbr* BANK (*sterling commercial paper*) papel comercial en libras esterlinas *m*, IMP/EXP (*simplified clearance procedure*) procedimiento de certificación de aduanas simplificado *m*

SCP[2]: **~ market** *n* BANK mercado de papel comercial en libras esterlinas *m*

scrambled: **~ message** *n* COMMS *satellite communication* mensaje cifrado *m*

scrap[1]: **~ and build regulation** *n* TRANSP *shipping* reglamentación de desguace y construcción *f*; **~ dealer** *n* GEN COMM chatarrero(-a) *m,f*; **~ of evidence** *n* GEN COMM indicio de prueba *m*; **~ metal** *n* ENVIR chatarra *f*; **~ paper** *n* GEN COMM papel de borrador *m*; **~ yard** *n* GEN COMM parque de desguace *m*

scrap[2] *vt* GEN COMM *idea, project* descartar

scrape along *vi infrml* GEN COMM pasar rozando

scrape through *vi* GEN COMM pasar por los pelos

scratch *n* COMP tachadura *m*; **~ area** COMP zona de trabajo *f*; **~ disk** COMP disco de trabajo *m*; **~ file** COMP fichero transitorio *m*; **~ pad** COMP cuaderno de anotaciones *m*

scratching n GEN COMM *countersignature* visado m

screamline n *jarg* MEDIA *print* titular en grandes caracteres m, titular sensacionalista m

screen[1] n COMP pantalla f; ~ **advertising** S&M publicidad en los cines f; ~ **copy** COMP copia de la pantalla f; ~ **driver** COMP unidad de pantalla f; ~ **dump** COMP vaciado de pantalla m; ~ **editor** COMP editor de pantalla m; ~ **test** MEDIA prueba de imagen en pantalla f

screen[2] vt GEN COMM, HRM filtrar, seleccionar

screen out vt GEN COMM, HRM filtrar

screening n GEN COMM, HRM *of candidates* selección f, MATH screening m; ~ **board** HRM consejo de selección m; ~ **process** HRM proceso de selección m

screw n TRANSP tensor m; ~ **propulsion** TRANSP propulsión a hélice f

scrimp: ~ **and save** *phr* GEN COMM apretarse el cinturón, escatimar y ahorrar

scrip n *jarg* STOCK vale canjeable m; ~ **certificate** GEN COMM certificado de acción fraccionaria m; ~ **dividend** FIN certificado de dividendo diferido m; ~ **issue** (*cf bonus issue BrE, capitalization issue BrE, stock dividend AmE, stock split AmE*) ACC, STOCK dividendo en acciones m, emisión de acciones liberadas f

scripophily n STOCK cedulofilia f

script n MEDIA, S&M guión m; ~ **dividend** ACC, FIN, STOCK dividendo con pagarés m

scroll vt COMP desplazar línea a línea; ~ **up** COMP enrollar

scrolling n COMP desplazamiento en pantalla m; ~ **down** COMP desplazamiento hacia abajo m; ~ **up** COMP desplazamiento hacia arriba m

s/d *abbr* (*small damage*) INS avería menor f, daño menor m

SD *abbr* (*sea damage*) INS, TRANSP avería producida por el mar f

S/D *abbr* GEN COMM (*sight draft*) efecto a la vista m, giro m, letra f, TRANSP (*sailing date*) fecha de salida f

SDA *abbr* BrE (*Sex Discrimination Act*) GEN COMM ley de discriminación sexual

sea[1]: ~ **-damaged** *adj* TRANSP averiado por el agua del mar

sea[2]: ~ **anchor** n TRANSP ancla flotante f; ~ **carrier** n TRANSP empresa de transporte marítimo f; ~ **damage** n (*SD*) INS, TRANSP avería producida por el mar f; **~-going barge** n TRANSP gabarra de altamar f; ~ **insurance** n INS seguro marítimo m; ~ **letter** n TRANSP permiso de navegación m; ~ **risk** n TRANSP riesgo de mar m; ~ **route** n TRANSP ruta marítima f

sea[3]: **by** ~ *phr* TRANSP por mar

SEA *abbr* (*Single European Act*) LAW, POL AUE (*Acta Unica Europea*)

seaborne *adj* TRANSP transportado por mar

seafarming n ECON cultivos marinos m pl

seal[1] n ADMIN sello m; ~ **of approval** GEN COMM garantía de una aprobación f; ~ **of quality** GEN COMM, S&M sello de calidad m

seal[2] vt GEN COMM *deal* sellar

seal off vt GEN COMM cerrar

sealed[1]: **~-bid tendering** n S&M oferta de propuesta cerrada f; ~ **tender** n COMMS oferta en pliego cerrado f

sealed[2]: **in a** ~ **envelope** *phr* COMMS en sobre cerrado

sealing: ~ **wax** n COMMS lacre m

seaport n TRANSP puerto de mar m, puerto marítimo m

SEAQ[1] *abbr* (*Stock Exchange Automated Quotation System*) STOCK cotización automatizada del mercado de valores f

SEAQ[2]: ~ **Automated Execution Facility** n (*SAEF*) STOCK instalación de operaciones automatizadas de la bolsa; ~ **International** n (*Stock Exchange Automated Quotation International*) STOCK bolsa internacional de cotización automatizada

search[1] n GEN COMM búsqueda f, PATENTS investigación f, registro m; ~ **cycle** GEN COMM ciclo de búsqueda m; ~ **key** COMP clave de búsqueda f; ~ **and replace** COMP *word processor* busca y cambia; ~ **report** PATENTS informe sobre el estado de la técnica m (*Esp*), reporte sobre el estado de la técnica m (*AmL*); ~ **and seizure** GEN COMM búsqueda y captura m; ~ **warrant** LAW orden de registro f

search[2] vt COMP, GEN COMM buscar

Search: ~ **and Advisory Service** n BrE, PATENTS servicio de revisión y asistencia de la oficina británica de patentes; ~ **and Rescue** n (*SAR*) WEL Servicio de Rescate m

season[1]: **off** ~ n GEN COMM temporada baja f, temporada inactiva f; ~ **ticket** n BrE (*cf commutation ticket AmE*) GEN COMM, TRANSP abono m; ~ **ticket holder** n BrE GEN COMM, TRANSP poseedor(a) de un abono m,f

season[2]: **off** ~ *phr* GEN COMM fuera de temporada; **out of** ~ *phr* GEN COMM fuera de temporada

seasonal[1] *adj* GEN COMM estacional

seasonal[2]: ~ **adjustment** n GEN COMM ajuste estacional m; ~ **concentration** n S&M concentración de temporada f; ~ **demand** n ECON, S&M demanda estacional f; ~ **discount** n S&M descuento de temporada m; ~ **factor** n ECON, GEN COMM factor estacional m; ~ **fluctuation** n ECON, GEN COMM fluctuación estacional f; ~ **fluctuations** n pl ECON, GEN COMM oscilaciones estacionales f pl; ~ **rate** n S&M tarifa de temporada f; ~ **swing** n GEN COMM cambio estacional m; ~ **unemployment** n ECON, HRM, WEL desempleo estacional m; ~ **variation** n ECON variación estacional f; ~ **worker** n HRM jornalero(-a) m,f, temporero(-a) m,f

seasonality: ~ **of demand** n ECON estacionalidad de la demanda f

seasonally[1]: **~-adjusted** *adj* ECON, GEN COMM, HRM *unemployment figures* desestacionalizado, reajustado según la estación

seasonally[2]: **~-adjusted annual rate** n (*s.a.a.r.*) ECON tipo anual con ajuste estacional m; **~-adjusted figures** n pl FIN, GEN COMM cifras ajustadas estacionalmente f pl; **~-unadjusted employment figures** n pl HRM, POL, WEL cifras de empleo no ajustadas según los cambios estacionales f pl

seasoned[1] *adj* GEN COMM, HRM experimentado

seasoned[2]: ~ **CD** n STOCK certificados de depósito acreditados m pl; ~ **loan** n BANK, ECON préstamo acreditado m, préstamo periódico m, préstamo temporal m

seat n LEIS asiento m, plaza f, POL *in Parliament* escaño m; ~ **belt** TRANSP cinturón de seguridad m (*Esp*), faja de seguridad f (*AmL*); ~ **mile** LEIS, TRANSP asiento-milla m; ~ **pitch** TRANSP distancia eje a eje de los asientos f; ~ **reservation system** LEIS sistema de reserva de plazas m

SEATS *abbr* BrE (*Stock Exchange Alternative Trading Service*) STOCK sistema operativo de cotizaciones

seaworthiness n TRANSP navegabilidad f

SEB *abbr* (*specialist electronic book*) STOCK libro electrónico especializado *m*

sec. *abbr* (*secretary*) GEN COMM, HRM secretario(-a) *m,f*

SEC *abbr AmE* (*Securities and Exchange Commission*) STOCK comisión de vigilancia del mercado de valores, ≈ CNMV (*Esp*) (*Comisión Nacional del Mercado de Valores*), (*Stock Exchange Commission, cf SIB BrE*) STOCK consejo de inversiones de acciones, bonos y valores, ≈ CNMV (*Esp*) (*Comisión Nacional del Mercado de Valores*)

SECAL *abbr* (*sector adjustment loan*) BANK, FIN préstamo de ajuste del sector *m*

second[1]: **~-grade** *adj* GEN COMM de segundo grado; **~-hand** *adj* GEN COMM *goods* de segunda mano, seminuevo; **~ to none** *adj* GEN COMM no inferior a nadie

second[2]: **~ best** *n* GEN COMM mejor después del óptimo *f*; **~ carrier** *n* TRANSP segundo transportista *m*; **~-class citizen** *n* GEN COMM ciudadano(-a) de segunda clase *m,f*; **~-class mail** *n AmE* (*cf second-class post BrE*) COMMS correo ordinario *m*; **~-class paper** *n* FIN título de segunda categoría *m*; **~-class post** *n BrE* (*cf second-class mail AmE*) COMMS correo ordinario *m*; **~ debenture** *n* BANK, FIN segunda obligación *f*; **~-degree price discrimination** *n* GEN COMM, S&M discriminación de precios de segundo grado *f*; **~ economy** *n* ECON economía secundaria *f*; **~ generation** *n* GEN COMM segunda generación *f*; **~-generation product** *n* S&M producto de segunda generación *m*; **~-generation type** *n* PROP *of warehouse* tipo de segunda generación *m*; **~ half of the year** *n* GEN COMM segunda parte del año *f*; **~-hand case** *n* S&M envase de segunda mano *m*; **~-hand market** *n* GEN COMM mercado de segunda mano *m*; **~-hand shop** *n BrE* (*cf thrift shop AmE*) GEN COMM, S&M tienda de artículos de segunda mano *f*; **~-hand tonnage** *n* TRANSP tonelaje de segunda mano *m*; **~ home** *n* PROP, TAX segunda residencia *f*; **~ installment base** *AmE*, **~ instalment base** *BrE n* FIN, TAX base del segundo plazo *f*; **~ mortgage** *n BrE* (*cf junior mortgage AmE*) BANK, PROP hipoteca en segundo grado *f*, segunda hipoteca *f*; **~ mortgage lending** *n* BANK, FIN, PROP préstamo con segunda hipoteca *m*; **~ offence** *BrE*, **~ offense** *AmE n* LAW reincidencia *m*; **~ or further occurrence penalty** *n* TAX penalización por segunda o posteriores incidencias *f*, recargo por segunda o siguientes presentaciones *m*; **~ quarter** *n* GEN COMM segundo trimestre *m*; **~ rank consultant** *n* HRM consultor(a) de segundo nivel *m,f*; **~ reading** *n* LAW, POL *of bill, directive* segunda lectura *f*; **~ residence** *n* PROP, TAX segunda residencia *f*; **~-tier company** *n* GEN COMM empresa de segunda fila *f*; **~ trial balance** *n* ACC balance de inventario *m*

second[3] *vt* GEN COMM *motion* apoyar, secundar; **~-guess** GEN COMM anticiparse a

Second: **~ Generation Banks** *n pl* BANK bancos de la segunda generación; **~ World countries** *n* GEN COMM países de economía planificada *m pl*

secondary: **~ action** *n* HRM actuación subordinada *f*; **~ activities** *n pl* GEN COMM actividades secundarias *f pl*; **~ bank** *n* BANK banco secundario *m*; **~ banking crisis** *n* BANK crisis bancaria secundaria *f*; **~ claim** *n* ACC reclamación secundaria *f*; **~ coverage** *n* S&M cobertura secundaria *f*; **~ data** *n* GEN COMM, S&M datos secundarios *m pl*; **~ distribution** *n* STOCK *of shares* reventa fraccionada *f*; **~ education** *n* WEL educación secundaria

f; **~ employment** *n* HRM empleo secundario *m*; **~ explosive** *n* TRANSP explosivo secundario *m*; **~ income** *n* ACC, FIN ingresos secundarios *m pl*; **~ labor market** *AmE*, **~ labour market** *BrE n* HRM mercado de trabajo secundario *m*, *workers* mercado laboral secundario *m*; **~ legislation** *n* LAW, POL *EU* legislación secundaria *f*; **~ market** *n* ECON, STOCK mercado secundario *m*; **~ meaning** *n* S&M significado secundario *m*; **~ needs** *n pl* ECON, S&M necesidades secundarias *f pl*; **~ offering** *n* STOCK colocación en el mercado secundario *f*; **~ picketing** *n* HRM piquete secundario *m*; **~ premises** *n pl* GEN COMM, PROP local secundario *m*; **~-primary distribution** *n* STOCK distribución secundaria-primaria *f*; **~ product** *n* ECON, IND producto secundario *m*; **~ production industry** *n* ECON, IND sector secundario *m*; **~ readership** *n* MEDIA, S&M número secundario de lectores *m*; **~ sector** *n* ECON, IND sector secundario *m*; **~ standard** *n* ENVIR patrón secundario *m*

Secondary: **~ Market Association** *n* (*SMA*) STOCK Asociación de Mercados de Negociación *f*

secondly *adv* GEN COMM en segundo lugar

secondment *n* HRM, recolocación *f*, traslado temporal *m*

secrecy *n* GEN COMM secreto *m*

secret[1] *adj* GEN COMM secreto

secret[2] *n* GEN COMM secreto; **~ ballot** HRM *industrial action* votación secreta *f*; **~ clause** BANK, INS, LAW cláusula secreta *f*; **~ payment** HRM pago secreto *m*; **~ reserve** ACC, BANK fondos secretos *m pl*, reserva oculta *f*

secretarial: **~ skill** *n* ADMIN, HRM técnica de secretariado *f*; **~ staff** *n* HRM personal de secretaría *m*

secretariat *n* ADMIN, HRM secretaría *f*, POL *government* secretariado *m*

secretary *n* (*sec.*) GEN COMM, HRM secretario(-a) *m,f*

Secretary: **~ of State** *n* POL *BrE* Secretario(-a) de Estado *m,f*, ministro(-a) del gobierno *m,f*, *AmE* ministro(-a) de asuntos exteriores *m,f*; **~ of State for Transport** *n BrE* POL, TRANSP secretario(-a) de estado para el transporte *m,f*

section *n* GEN COMM sección *f*; **~ manager** GEN COMM gerente de área *m*

sectional: **~ rate** *n* TRANSP *aviation* tarifa regional *f*

sector[1] *n* GEN COMM sector *m*; **~ adjustment lending** ECON ajuste del sector crediticio *m*; **~ adjustment loan** (*SECAL*) BANK, FIN préstamo de ajuste del sector *m*; **~ analysis** GEN COMM análisis sectorial *m*; **~ investment and maintenance loan** (*SIM*) BANK, FIN préstamo sectorial de inversión y mantenimiento *m*; **~-specific aid** ECON, POL *development* ayuda a sectores específicos *f*, ayuda a un sector específico *f*; **~ study** GEN COMM estudio sectorial *m*

sector[2] *vt* COMP *disk* sectorizar

sectoral[1] *adj* ACC, ECON, MGMNT sectorial

sectoral[2]: **~ accounting plan** *n* ACC plan contable sectorial *m*; **~ strategy** *n* MGMNT estrategia sectorial *f*

sectorial: **~ manager** *n* HRM, MGMNT director(a) provincial *m,f*, director(a) regional *m,f*, director(a) sectorial *m,f*, gerente regional *mf*;

secular: **~ trend** *n* ECON tendencia secular *f*

secure[1] *adj* GEN COMM seguro, *financially* protegido

secure[2]: **~ investment** *n* BANK, FIN inversión segura *f*; **~ job** *n* HRM trabajo seguro *m*

secure³ *vt* BANK afianzar, GEN COMM obtener, FIN afianzar, STOCK *price* asegurar; ◆ **~ a debt by mortgage** BANK garantizar una deuda con una hipoteca; **~ a loan** BANK avalar un préstamo; **~ new orders** GEN COMM conseguir nuevos pedidos

secured: **~ advance** *n* BANK anticipo garantizado *m*; **~ bond** *n* BANK, FIN, STOCK bono con garantía *m*, bono hipotecario *m*; **~ credit** *n* ACC, BANK, FIN crédito cubierto *m*, crédito garantizado *m*; **~ creditor** *n* ACC, BANK, FIN acreedor(a) asegurado *m,f*; **~ debenture** *n* BANK, FIN obligación garantizada *f*; **~ debt** *n* BANK, FIN deuda garantizada *f*; **~ fixed-term loan** *n* BANK préstamo a término fijo garantizado *m*; **~ loan** *n* BANK empréstito con garantía *m*, préstamo con caución *m*, préstamo con garantía *m*, préstamo garantizado *m*; **~ personal loan** *n* BANK préstamo personal garantizado *m*

securities *n pl* BANK obligaciones *f pl*, GEN COMM títulos valores *m pl*, valores *m pl*, valores mobiliarios *m pl*; **~ account** *n* BANK cuenta de valores *f*; **~ administrator** *n* GEN COMM administrador(a) de valores *m,f*; **~ analysis** *n* FIN análisis de valores *m*; **~ borrowing** *n* BANK, FIN, STOCK préstamo en valores *m*; **~ business** *n* STOCK operaciones con valores *f pl*; **~ cancellation** *n* STOCK cancelación de títulos *f*; **~ dealing** *n* STOCK operaciones de valores *f pl*; **~ department** *n* STOCK departamento de valores *m*; **~ exchange** *n* FIN, STOCK Bolsa de Comercio *f*, Bolsa de Valores *f*; **~ held in trust** STOCK valores en un trust *m pl*; **~ house** *n* STOCK casa de valores *f*; **~ in hand** ACC, STOCK efectos en cartera *m pl*; **~ in portfolio** STOCK títulos en cartera *m pl*; **~ lending** *n* BANK, FIN, STOCK préstamo en valores *m*; **~ listing** *n* STOCK cotización de valores *f*; **~ loan** *n* BANK, FIN, STOCK préstamo de valores entre operadores *m*; **~ market** *n* STOCK Bolsa de Comercio *f*; **~ sold under repurchase agreement** *n* STOCK valores vendidos con acuerdo de recompra *m pl*; **~ tax** *n* TAX impuesto sobre valores *m*; **~ transaction** *n* STOCK transacción de títulos *f*; ◆ **~ wanted** STOCK se necesitan valores

Securities: **~ Act** *n* FIN, LAW Ley de Valores *f*; **~ Acts amendments** *n pl* STOCK enmiendas de1975 sobre las leyes de valores *f pl*; **~ Association** *n* STOCK sociedad de cartera; **~ and Exchange Commission** *n* (*SEC*) *AmE* STOCK comisión de vigilancia del mercado de valores, ≈ Comisión Nacional del Mercado de Valores (*CNMV*) (*Esp*); **~ and Futures Authority** *n* (*SFA*) STOCK autoridad en materia de valores y futuros; **~ and Investments Board** *n BrE* (*SIB, cf Stock Exchange Commission AmE*) FIN, STOCK consejo de inversiones de acciones, bonos y valores, ≈ Comisión Nacional del Mercado de Valores *f* (*CNMV*) (*Esp*); **~ Market** *n* FIN Bolsa de Valores *f*

securitization *n* BANK, FIN, STOCK titulización *f*, valorización *f*, aseguración *f*

securitize *vt* BANK, FIN, STOCK titulizar, asegurar

securitized: **~ note commitment facility** *n* (*SNCF*) STOCK sistema de compra de un pagaré garantizado *m*

security *n* BANK, FIN colateral *m*, documento de crédito *m*, prenda *f*, título *m*, GEN COMM *safety* seguridad *f*, colateral *m*, endoso *m*, LAW documento de crédito *m*; **~ backup** COMP copia de respaldo *f*; **~ bond for down payment** STOCK fianza por hacer un pago inicial *f*; **~ copy** COMP copia de seguridad *f*; **~ dealer** STOCK corredor(a) de valores *m,f*; **~ disposal** STOCK venta de

títulos *f*; **~ holder** STOCK tenedor(a) de títulos *m,f*; **~ holding** STOCK tenencia de valores *f*; **~ interest** STOCK interés de garantía *m*; **~ leak** GEN COMM falla de seguridad *f*, fuga de seguridad *f*; **~ margin** GEN COMM margen de seguridad *m*; **~ market line** STOCK línea del mercado de valores *f*; **~ measure** GEN COMM medida de seguridad *f*; **~ rating** STOCK clasificación de valores *f*, evaluación de valores *f*; **~ risk** GEN COMM riesgo de seguridad *m*; **~ service** WEL servicio de seguridad *m*; **~ of tenure** PROP seguridad de posesión *f*

see: **~ overleaf** *phr* MEDIA *print* véase a la vuelta

seed *n* S&M *of idea* germinación *f*; **~ capital** FIN capital generador *m*; **~ money** FIN dinero generador *m*

seek¹: **~ key** *n* COMP clave de búsqueda *f*

seek² *vt* GEN COMM *advice* pedir, *approval* solicitar, *help, employment* buscar; ◆ **~ expert advice** GEN COMM pedir la opinión de un experto; **~ legal advice** LAW solicitar asesoramiento jurídico, solicitar consejo jurídico; **~ a market** STOCK buscar un mercado; **~ redress** LAW exigir compensación

seepage *n* GEN COMM infiltración *f*

segment¹ *n* GEN COMM segmento *m*; **~ information** GEN COMM información segmentada *f*; **~ margin** ACC margen de segmento *m*; **~ profit** ACC beneficio de segmento *m*

segment² *vt* GEN COMM, MGMNT, S&M segmentar *the market* reducir

segmental: **~ reporting** *n* ACC informe segmentado *m* (*Esp*), reporte segmentado *m* (*AmL*)

segmentation *n* GEN COMM segmentación *f*; **~ strategy** S&M estrategia de segmentación *f*

segmented: **~ labor market theory** *AmE*, **~ labour market theory** *BrE* ECON teoría del mercado laboral segmentado *f*; **~ return** *n* TAX declaración segmentada *f*

segregated¹ *adj* GEN COMM segregado

segregated²: **~ free position** *n* STOCK posición libre segregada *f*

segregation *n* GEN COMM segregación racial *f*; **~ of duties** MGMNT separación de deberes *f*, separación de funciones *f*

seize *vt* LAW incautar

seizure *n* LAW incautación *f*

select¹: **~ committee** *n BrE* POL comisión especial *f*

select² *vt* GEN COMM seleccionar

select out *vt* ADMIN seleccionar en salida

selected: **~ dealer agreement** *n* STOCK acuerdo de intermediario seleccionado *m*

selection *n* GEN COMM selección *f*; **~ board** HRM *interview panel* consejo de selección *m*

selective: **~ attention** *n* S&M atención selectiva *f*; **~ distribution** *n* GEN COMM distribución selectiva *f*; **~ employment tax** *n* TAX impuesto selectivo sobre el empleo *m*; **~ hedge** *n* STOCK cobertura selectiva *f*; **~ perception** *n* S&M percepción selectiva *f*; **~ positioning** *n* S&M posicionamiento selectivo *m*; **~ selling** *n* S&M venta selectiva *f*

Selective: **~ Financial Assistance** *n BrE* ECON *regional development* Ayuda Financiera Selectiva *f*

selector: **~ channel** *n* COMP canal selector *m*

self¹: **~-catering** *adj* LEIS *apartment, holiday* sin servicio de comidas; **~-contained** *adj* GEN COMM autónomo; **~-generated** *adj* GEN COMM autogenerado; **~-governing** *adj* GEN COMM autorregulado; **~-loading**

adj GEN COMM autocargador; **~-styled** *adj* GEN COMM, HRM, POL *leader* a su manera; **~-sufficient** *adj* GEN COMM autosuficiente; **~-supporting** *adj* GEN COMM autoestable; **~-sustained** *adj* GEN COMM *growth* auto-sostenido

self[2]: **~-actualization** *n* HRM, MGMNT autoactualización *f*, realización personal *f* autoactualización *f*; **~-addressed envelope** *n* (*s.a.e.*) COMMS sobre con la dirección del remitente; **~-addressed stamped envelope** *n* (*s.a.s.e.*) COMMS sobre con la dirección del remitente y sello; **~-amortizing mortgage** *n* BANK, PROP hipoteca autoamortizable *f*; **~-appraisal** *n* HRM autoevaluación *f*; **~-assessing system** *n* TAX sistema de autoliquidación *m*; **~-assessment** *n* TAX autoliquidación tributaria *f*; **~-dealing** *n* FIN negociación por cuenta propia *f*, STOCK autocontrato *m*, préstamo vinculado *m*; **~-demounting pallet** *n* TRANSP plataforma de carga autodesmontable *f*; **~-drive hire** *n* LEIS, TRANSP alquiler de vehículo sin conductor *m*; **~-employed person** *n* HRM, TAX trabajador(a) autónomo(-a) *m,f*, trabajador(a) por cuenta propia *m,f*; **~-employed worker** *n* HRM, TAX trabajador(a) autónomo(-a) *m,f*, trabajador(a) por cuenta propia *m,f*; **~-employment** *n* HRM, TAX autoempleo *m*, trabajo por cuenta propia *m*; **~-employment income** *n* ACC, TAX ingresos del trabajo por cuenta propia *m pl*; **~-financing** *n* ACC, FIN autofinanciación *f*, autofinanciamiento *m*; **~-fulfilling prophecy** *n* GEN COMM profecía de cumplimiento inevitable *f*; **~-generated funds** *n pl* FIN fondos autogenerados *m pl*; **~-governing nation** *n* POL país autónomo *m*, país dotado de autogobierno *m*; **~-governing port** *n* TRANSP puerto autónomo *m*; **~-government** *n* POL autogobierno *m*; **~-help** *n* GEN COMM autoayuda *f*, esfuerzo personal *m*; **~-help passenger luggage trolley** *n* LEIS, TRANSP carro de equipajes para uso de los pasajeros *m*; **~-image** *n* HRM, S&M autoimagen *f*; **~-insurance** *n* INS autoseguro *m*; **~-liquidating offer** *n* S&M oferta de autoliquidación *f*; **~-liquidation** *n* GEN COMM autoliquidación tributaria *f*; **~-liquidator** *n* S&M *advertising* oferta que, a pesar de tener un precio muy atractivo, cubre los gastos publicitarios; **~-loading trailer** *n* TRANSP vehículo remolque auto-cargador *m*; **~-management** *n* HRM, MGMNT autodirección *f*, autogestión *f*; **~-motivation** *n* GEN COMM, HRM automotivación *f*; **~-propelled hyperbaric lifeboat** *n* (*SPHL*) TRANSP bote salvavidas hiperbárico de autopropulsión *m*; **~-regulating organization** *n* (*SRO*) GEN COMM organización autorregulada *f*; **~-regulation** *n* GEN COMM autorregulación *f*; **~-regulatory organization** *n* (*SRO*) GEN COMM organización autorreguladora *f*; **~-restraint** *n* GEN COMM autodominio *m*; **~-selection** *n* S&M autoselección *f*; **~-service** *n* GEN COMM autoservicio *m*; **~-service banking** *n* BANK, COMP banca automatizada *f*, banca de autoservicio *f*; **~-service shop** *n* BrE (*cf self service store AmE*) S&M tienda de autoservicio *f*; **~-service store** *n* AmE (*cf self service shop BrE*) S&M tienda de autoservicio *f*; **~-start** *n* COMP autoarranque *m*; **~-starter** *n* COMP arrancador automático *m*, HRM persona dinámica *f*, persona emprendedora *f*; **~-sufficiency** *n* ECON autosuficiencia *f*, autoabastecimiento *m*; **~-sufficient economy** *n* ECON economía autárquica *f*; **~-supporting debt** *n* FIN deuda rentable *f*; **~-taught person** *n* WEL autodidacta *mf*

self-finance *vt* FIN autofinanciar

sell[1]: **~-by date** *n* S&M *food* fecha de caducidad *f*; **~-in** *n* S&M venta inicial *f*; **~-off** *n* STOCK venta precipitada *f*; **~ and report agreement** *n* TRANSP acuerdo de venta e información *m*; **~ short** *n* STOCK venta al descubierto *f*; **~-stop order** *n* STOCK orden de venta al precio límite *f*

sell[2] **1.** *vt* GEN COMM vender, S&M vender, realizar; ◆ **~ at market price** STOCK vender a precio de mercado; **~ a bear** STOCK vender a plazo en firme; **~ for the account** STOCK vender a cuenta; **~ for the settlement** STOCK vender a término; **~ in bulk** S&M vender a granel; **~ on close** STOCK *futures* vender al cierre; **~ on commission** S&M vender a comisión; **~ on credit** S&M vender a crédito; **~ on special offer** S&M ofertar; **~ one's wares** GEN COMM vender las mercancías; **~ on trust** S&M vender a crédito; **~ one's wares** GEN COMM vender las mercancías; **~ short** STOCK vender al descubierto; **~ spot** STOCK vender al contado; **~ sth by auction** GEN COMM vender algo en subasta; **~ sth by private treaty** GEN COMM vender algo mediante acuerdo privado; **~ sth for scrap** GEN COMM vender algo como chatarra; **2.** *vi* GEN COMM, S&M *product, range* vender; ◆ **the product does not ~ well** GEN COMM, S&M el producto no tiene demanda; **~ directly to the public** GEN COMM, S&M vender directamente al público

sell back *vt* GEN COMM, STOCK revender

sell forward *vt* GEN COMM, STOCK vender a futuro

sell off *vt* GEN COMM liquidar, S&M saldar

sell out *vi* GEN COMM vender todas las existencias, STOCK *futures* vender

sell up *vi* GEN COMM, S&M *dispose of all stock* vender totalmente

seller *n* GEN COMM vendedor(a) *m,f*; **~'s option** (*s.o.*) STOCK prima de opción a vender *f*

sellers': **~ market** *n* ECON, STOCK mercado de vendedores *m*

selling *n* GEN COMM venta *f*; **~ agent** STOCK intermediario(-a) de ventas *m,f*; **~ climax** STOCK auge de ventas *m*; **~ concession** STOCK descuento de venta *m*; **~ expenses** *n pl* ACC, GEN COMM, S&M gastos comerciales *m pl*, gastos de comercialización *m pl*, gastos de venta *m pl*; **~ group** S&M grupo de ventas *m*; **~ hedge** STOCK cobertura de venta *f*; **~ point** S&M característica especial que se utiliza para la venta de un producto; **~ price** GEN COMM, S&M precio de venta *m*; **~ proposition** S&M propuesta de venta *f*; **~ rate** GEN COMM cambio de venta *m*; **~ short** STOCK venta en descubierto *f*; **~ space** S&M espacio de ventas *m*

sellout *n* infrml LEIS *theatre, cinema* agotamiento de localidades *m*

SEM *abbr* (*special employment measure*) HRM medida especial de empleo *f*

semantic: **~ differential** *n* S&M diferencial semántico *m*

semiannual[1] *adj* GEN COMM semianual

semiannual[2]: **~ dividend** *n* STOCK dividendo semianual *m*

semiblack: **~ market** *n* ECON mercado seminegro *m*

semicolon *n* GEN COMM punto y coma *m*

semiconductor *n* COMP, IND semiconductor *m*

semidetached: **~ house** *n* BrE (*cf duplex AmE*) PROP casa adosada *f*, casa semiseparada *f*

semidisplay: **~ advertising** *n* S&M publicidad semiintensiva *f*

semidurable: **~ goods** *n pl* GEN COMM, S&M bienes semiperecederos *m pl*

semifinished: ~ **goods** n pl GEN COMM productos semimanufacturados m pl, productos semiterminados m pl; ~ **product** n GEN COMM, IND, S&M producto semielaborado m, producto semimanufacturado m

semifixed: ~ **cost** n ACC, S&M coste semifijo m (Esp), costo semifijo m (AmL)

semi-industrialized adj ECON, IND, POL countries semiindustrializado

semi-interquartile: ~ **range** n MATH statistics recorrido semi-intercuartílico m

semi-knocked: ~ **down** adj (SKD) TRANSP packaging semidesarmado

seminar n GEN COMM, MGMNT seminario m

semiprivate: ~ **bank** n BANK banco semiprivado m

semiprocessed: ~ **products** n pl GEN COMM productos semielaborados m pl

semirigid: ~ **receptacle** n GEN COMM receptáculo semirrígido m

semiskilled[1] adj ECON, HRM semicualificado

semiskilled[2]: ~ **labor** AmE, ~ **labour** BrE n ECON task trabajo para persona semiexperta m, HRM mano de obra semicualificada f, task trabajo para persona semiexperta m; ~ **worker** n ECON, HRM trabajador(a) semiespecializado(-a) m,f

semistructured adj GEN COMM semiestructurado

semitrailer n TRANSP semirremolque m

semivariable: ~ **costs** n GEN COMM costes mixtos m pl (Esp), costes semifijos m pl (Esp), costes semivariables m pl (Esp), costos mixtos m pl (AmL) costos semifijos m pl (AmL), costos semivariables m pl (AmL); ~ **expense** n GEN COMM gasto semivariable m

Senate: The ~ n AmE POL Cámara Alta

send vt COMMS, COMP enviar; ♦ ~ **away for sth** COMMS escribir pidiendo algo; ~ **by fax** ADMIN, COMMS enviar por fax; ~ **by parcel post** COMMS enviar por paquete postal; ~ **by post** ADMIN, COMMS enviar por correo; ~ **off for sth** COMMS pedir algo; ~ **an order by wire** COMMS enviar una orden por telegrama; ~ **sb for sth** GEN COMM mandar a alguien a buscar algo; ~ **sth via an agent** GEN COMM mandar algo mediante un representante; ~ **under plain cover** COMMS enviar con la mayor discreción; ~ **a written request** GEN COMM enviar una petición por escrito

sender n COMMS on envelope remitente mf (rte.)

senior[1] adj (Snr) GEN COMM, HRM de categoría superior, más antiguo, veterano, position superior

senior[2] n BANK padre m, HRM jefe(-a) m,f, superior mf; ~ **auditor** ACC auditor(a) principal m,f; ~ **citizen** HRM, TAX, WEL persona de la tercera edad f; ~ **civil servant** HRM funcionario(-a) con antigüedad m,f; ~ **clerk** HRM administrativo(-a) superior m,f, contable principal mf Esp, contador principal mf AmL, LAW jefe(-a) administrativo(-a) m,f; ~ **debt** BANK deuda principal f; ~ **executive** GEN COMM, HRM, MGMNT alto(-a) ejecutivo(-a) m,f; ~ **export clerk** HRM, IMP/EXP funcionario(-a) principal de exportación m,f, jefe(-a) de exportación m,f; ~ **financial auditor** ACC auditor(a) financiero(-a) responsable m,f; ~ **financial officer** ACC técnico(-a) financiero(-a) principal m,f; ~ **import clerk** HRM, IMP/EXP funcionario(-a) principal de importación m,f, jefe(-a) de importación m,f; ~ **information officer** (SIO) HRM, MGMNT director(a) de información m,f; ~ **issue** STOCK emisión prioritaria f; ~ **loan** BANK préstamo principal m, préstamo prioritario m;

~ **management** HRM, MGMNT administración de más alto rango f, administración superior f, dirección superior f; ~ **manager** FIN director(a) principal m,f, HRM, MGMNT director(a) ejecutivo(-a) m,f, director(a) general m,f (DG), director(a) principal m,f; ~ **officer** (SO) HRM funcionario(-a) de rango superior m,f; ~ **refunding** STOCK conversión de la antigüedad f; ~ **security** STOCK título de garantía preferente m; ~ **systems analyst** COMP analista de sistemas superior mf; ~ **vice president** AmE HRM, MGMNT vicepresidente(-a) principal m,f, vicepresidente(-a) adjunto(-a) m,f

seniority n HRM antigüedad f; ~ **bonus** HRM prima por antigüedad f; ~ **premium** HRM prima por antigüedad f; ~ **principle** HRM principio de antigüedad m; ~ **system** HRM sistema por antigüedad m

sense: ~ **of responsibility** n GEN COMM sentido de responsabilidad m

sensitive[1] adj GEN COMM market sensible

sensitive[2]: ~ **form** n TAX formulario copiativo m; ~ **market** n GEN COMM mercado sensible m; ~ **zone** n ENVIR zona sensible f

sensitivity: ~ **analysis** n FIN, MATH statistics análisis de sensibilidad m; ~ **training** n GEN COMM, HRM, MGMNT capacitación de sensibilidad f (AmL), entrenamiento para el trabajo en equipo m, formación de sensibilidad f (Esp)

sensitize vt GEN COMM sensibilizar

sensory: ~ **deprivation** n MGMNT aislamiento sensorial m; ~ **overload** n MGMNT sobrecarga sensorial f

sentence[1] n LAW fallo m

sentence[2] vt LAW condenar

separate: ~ **customer** n STOCK cliente por derecho propio m; ~ **residence** n PROP, TAX residencia por separado f; ~ **tax return** n TAX declaración de la renta separada f

Separate: ~ **Trading of Registered Interest and Principal Securities** n (STRIPS) STOCK negociación por separado de los flujos que generan los valores registrados

separately adv GEN COMM separadamente

separation: ~ **agreement** n LAW acuerdo de separación m; ~ **allowance** n TAX deducción por separación f; ~ **allowance income** n TAX ingreso de pensión por separación m; ~ **allowance paid** n TAX pensión alimenticia f

separator n COMP separador m

SEPON abbr (Stock Exchange Pool Nominees) STOCK candidatos al fondo de la bolsa de valores

sequence n GEN COMM secuencia f; ~ **error** COMP error de secuencia m; ~ **number** COMP, MATH número de secuencia m

sequential[1] adj GEN COMM secuencial

sequential[2]: ~ **access** n COMP acceso secuencial m; ~ **analysis** n FIN, MATH, S&M análisis secuencial m; ~ **externality** n ECON externalidad secuencial f; ~ **number** n COMP, MATH número secuencial m; ~ **sampling** n MATH muestreo secuencial m

sequestration n FIN, LAW secuestro m

sequestrator n FIN, LAW confiscador(a) m,f, embargador(a) m,f,

serial[1] adj COMP en serie; ~-**parallel** COMP serial-paralelo

serial[2]: ~ **access** n COMP acceso en serie m; ~ **adaptor** n COMP adaptador en serie m; ~ **bond** n FIN, STOCK bono con vencimiento elegido al azar m, bono de vencimiento escalonado *m*; ~ **computer** *n* COMP computador en serie *m* (*AmL*), computadora en serie *f* (*AmL*), ordenador en serie *m* (*Esp*); ~ **correlation** *n* MATH *statistics* correlación serial *f*; ~ **number** *n* COMP, GEN COMM, PATENTS número de orden *m*; ~ **operation** *n* COMP operación en serie *f*; ~ **port** *n* COMP puerta en serie *f*; ~ **printer** *n* COMP impresora en serie *f*; ~ **processing** *n* COMP procesamiento en serie *m*; ~ **reader** *n* COMP lector en serie *m*

seriatim *adv* GEN COMM separadamente

series *n* GEN COMM serie *f*; ~ **discount** S&M descuento de series *m*; ~ **hh bond** STOCK bono de la serie hh *m*; ~ **of options** STOCK serie de opciones *f*

serif *n* COMP, MEDIA trazo terminal *m*

serious: ~ **crime** *n* BrE (*cf grand larceny AmE*) LAW hurto mayor *m*; ~ **misdeclaration penalty** *n* BrE TAX sanción por declaración incorrecta *f*

Serious: ~ **Fraud Office** *n* (*SFO*) LAW brigada anti-corrupción *f*, STOCK oficina de delitos monetarios graves

SERPS *abbr* BrE (*State Earnings Related Pension Scheme*) ECON, WEL plan estatal de pensiones

serve 1. *vt* GEN COMM *purpose* servir, *customer* atender, LAW *notice* entregar, dar traslado a, S&M *the market* abastecer, servir; ◆ ~ **the company** HRM trabajar para la compañía; ~ **counternotice** LAW, PROP *land compensation* presentar un contrainforme; ~ **the purpose** GEN COMM servir para el caso; ~ **sb with a warrant** LAW notificar a alguien una orden de detención, notificar a alguien una orden de registro; **2.** *vi* GEN COMM servir, *on committee* trabajar

server *n* COMP servidor *m*

service[1] *n* GEN COMM servicio *m*; ~ **abuse** GEN COMM mal uso del servicio *m*; ~ **agreement** COMP, GEN COMM contrato de mantenimiento *m*, acuerdo de servicio *m*; ~ **benefit** ACC beneficio por prestación de servicios *m*; ~ **boat** TRANSP bote de servicio *m*; ~ **bureau** COMP centro de servicios informáticos *m*; ~ **card** COMP tarjeta de servicio *f*; ~ **charge** BANK cargo por servicios *m*; ~ **company** COMP *manufacturer* compañía de servicios *f*; ~ **consultancy** ECON, WEL servicio de consulta *m*; ~ **contract** COMP, GEN COMM, HRM, LAW contrato de servicios *m*; ~ **delivery** GEN COMM prestación de servicios *f*; ~ **department** S&M departamento de servicios *m*; ~ **engineer** IND, HRM ingeniero(-a) de funcionamiento *m,f*, ingeniero(-a) de reparaciones *m,f*, ingeniero(-a) de servicio *m,f*; ~ **enterprise** GEN COMM empresa de servicios *f*; ~ **entrance** *AmE* (*cf trade entrance BrE*) GEN COMM puerta de servicio *f*; ~ **fee** GEN COMM tasa de servicio *f*; ~ **handbook** GEN COMM guía de servicios *f*; ~ **hours** *n pl* GEN COMM horas de servicio *f pl*; ~ **industry** ECON, IND industria de servicios *f*; ~ **manual** GEN COMM manual de mantenimiento *m*; ~ **mark** LAW marca de identificación de servicios *f*, PATENTS marca de servicios *f*; ~ **pick up** TRANSP recogida de servicio *f*; ~ **qualification** HRM calificación del servicio *f*, cualificación del servicio *f*; ~ **sector** ECON, HRM, IND sector de servicios *m*; ~ **sector job** HRM trabajo en el sector de servicios *m*; ~ **station** TRANSP estación de servicio *f*; ◆ **be out of** ~ COMMS, GEN COMM *telephone, machine* estar fuera de servicio; ~ **not included** GEN COMM, LEIS servicio no incluido

service[2] *vt* BANK, FIN *loan* entregar

services: **for** ~ **rendered** *phr* GEN COMM por servicios prestados

servicing *n* COMP mantenimiento y reparación *m*; ◆ ~ **of a debt** FIN pago de intereses de la deuda

session *n* COMP, GEN COMM sesión *f*

set[1] *adj* GEN COMM *resolved* resuelto; ~ **solid** S&M solidificado; ◆ ~ **on doing sth** GEN COMM resuelto a hacer algo

set[2] *n* COMP *data, values* conjunto matemático *m*; ~ **of accounts** ACC grupo de cuentas *m*; ~ **of bills** FIN juego de facturas *m*; ~ **of chattels** TAX conjunto de bienes muebles *m*; ~ **of claims** PATENTS expediente de reclamaciones *m*; ~ **of measures** GEN COMM conjunto de medidas *m*; ~**-off** BANK compensación *f*; ~ **of notes** FIN juego de facturas *m*; ~ **of options** STOCK conjunto de opciones *m*; ~ **of rules** GEN COMM conjunto de reglas *m*; ~**-up costs** *n pl* ACC costes de primer establecimiento *m pl* (*Esp*), costos de primer establecimiento *m pl* (*AmL*), BANK gastos de organización *m pl*, FIN costes de primer establecimiento *m pl* (*Esp*), costos de primer establecimiento *m pl* (*AmL*)

set[3] *vt* COMP colocar, *preset value* seleccionar, ECON *value* establecer, GEN COMM *rules* imponer, *record* establecer, determinar; ◆ ~ **about doing** GEN COMM empezar a hacer; ~ **a date** GEN COMM poner una fecha; ~ **a new high** ECON establecer un nuevo máximo; ~ **off a debit against a credit** ACC, BANK, FIN compensar un débito a cuenta de un crédito; ~ **the pace** GEN COMM dar la pauta; ~ **parameters** COMP, MATH fijar los parámetros; ~ **a price-point** ECON fijar un precio; ~ **the standards** MGMNT establecer las normas, establecer los estándares; ~ **down sth in writing** GEN COMM poner algo por escrito; ~ **sth in motion** GEN COMM poner algo en marcha; ~ **a trend** GEN COMM marcar la tónica; ~ **the trend** GEN COMM imponer la moda

set against *vt* ACC, FIN compensar

set forth *vt* GEN COMM poner de manifiesto; ◆ ~ **the spending authority** ADMIN consignar la autoridad que hace el gasto

set out *vt* GEN COMM *conditions* exponer

set up *vt* COMP *start* arrancar, *to install* montar, ECON establecer, GEN COMM fundar, *business* establecer, LAW *claim* presentar; ◆ ~ **an interview** HRM concertar una entrevista; ~ **on one's own account** GEN COMM establecerse por cuenta propia

setback *n* GEN COMM dificultad *f*, obstáculo *m*

sets: **in** ~ **of** *phr* GEN COMM en series de

setting *n* WEL agrupación por aptitud *f*; ~**-up costs** *n pl* ACC, FIN costes de primer establecimiento *m pl* (*Esp*), costos de primer establecimiento *m pl* (*AmL*)

settings *n pl* COMP posicionamientos *m pl*

settle 1. *vt* BANK *transactions* acordar, establecer, ECON, FIN fijar, liquidar, GEN COMM *dispute* entablar, *question* plantear, *account* ajustar, STOCK fijar; ◆ ~ **accounts** GEN COMM ajustar cuentas; ~ **the bill** GEN COMM arreglar cuentas; ~ **a dispute by arbitration** IND resolver una disputa mediante arbitraje; ~ **the figure** LAW *of compensation* fijar la cifra; ~ **in cash** STOCK liquidar en metálico; ~ **old scores** *infrml* GEN COMM ajustar cuentas pendientes; **2.** *vi* GEN COMM *in job, in country* establecerse

settlement *n* BANK, FIN, GEN COMM *compromise* arreglo *m*, INS liquidación *f*, pago *m*, POL colonización, STOCK *futures price* colonización *f*, *security, bond* liquidación *f*; ~ **account** BANK cuenta de liquidación *f*; ~ **of account** BANK pago de facturas *m*; ~ **bargaining** STOCK negociación del pago *f*; ~ **date** STOCK *security* fecha de liquidación *f*; ~ **day** STOCK día de liquidación en la bolsa *m*; ~ **of debts** BANK *with other banks or the government* liquidación de deudas *f*; ~ **discount** FIN descuento de liquidación *m*; ~ **of disputes** HRM arreglo de disputas *m*; ~ **draft** BANK letra de liquidación *f*; ~ **in full** ACC pago íntegro *m*; ~ **per contra** BANK compensación de deudas *f*; ~ **pattern** ECON *wage round* patrón de establecimiento *m*, GEN COMM asignación *f*; ~ **price** STOCK precio de liquidación *m*; ~ **of sum insured** INS liquidación de la suma asegurada *f*; ~ **to the market** STOCK liquidación a precios de mercado *f*; ~ **transaction** STOCK transacción de liquidación *f*; ◆ **in ~ of** BANK, FIN, GEN COMM *debt* en pago de

settlements: ~ **department** *n* BANK departamento de liquidaciones *m*

settling: ~ **of an annuity** *n* LAW determinación de una renta *f*

settlor *n BrE* LAW fideicomitente *m*

setup *n* COMP preparación *f*

Seventh: ~ **Company Law Directive** *n* GEN COMM, LAW, POL *EU* Séptima Directiva sobre el derecho de Sociedades *f*, Séptima Directiva sobre Sociedades *f*; ~ **EU Directive** *n* GEN COMM, LAW, POL Séptima Directiva de la UE *f*

sever *vt* GEN COMM cortar; ◆ ~ **links with** ECON *international*, POL romper relaciones con

severally: ~ **but not jointly** *adj* LAW, STOCK solidariamente pero no mancomunadamente; ~ **liable** *adj* LAW, STOCK responsable solidariamente

severance *n* PROP *from land* división *f*, separación *f*; ~ **pay** HRM, WEL compensación por despido *f*; ~ **wage** HRM remuneración por despido *f*

severely: ~ **indebted low-income country** *n* (*SILIC*) ECON, POL país de baja renta endeudado fuertemente

sewage: ~ **treatment** *n* ENVIR, IND depuración de aguas residuales *m*; ~ **treatment works** *n pl* ENVIR, IND planta depuradora de aguas cloacales *f*

Sex: ~ **Discrimination Act** *n BrE* (*SDA*) GEN COMM ley de discriminación sexual

sexual: ~ **discrimination** *n* GEN COMM discriminación sexual *f*, discriminación por sexo *f*; ~ **division of labor** *AmE*, ~ **division of labour** *BrE* ECON, HRM división del trabajo por sexos *f*; ~ **harassment** *n* HRM acoso sexual *m*; ~ **stereotyping** *n* HRM, WEL estereotipia de los sexos *f*

SFA *abbr* (*Securities and Futures Authority*) STOCK autoridad en materia de valores y futuros

SFO *abbr* (*Serious Fraud Office*) LAW brigada anticorrupción *f*, STOCK oficina de delitos monetarios graves

SG *abbr* (*specific gravity*) GEN COMM gravedad específica *f*

sgd *abbr* (*signed*) COMMS, GEN COMM firmado

sh *abbr* (*share*) GEN COMM acción *f*

shackle *n* TRANSP *cargo* grillete *m*

shade *vt* GEN COMM amparar

shading *n* COMP, MEDIA *illustration* sombreado *m*

shadow[1] *n* GEN COMM sombra *f*; ~ **economy** ECON economía sombría *f*; ~ **price** ACC coste de oportunidad *m* (*Esp*), costo de oportunidad *m* (*AmL*); ~ **prices** *n pl* ECON, FIN precios contables *m pl*, precios fantasmas *m pl*

shadow[2] *vt* STOCK *currency* proteger

Shadow: ~ **Cabinet** *n BrE* POL grupo de diputados de la oposición que vigila la política del partido en el gobierno; ~ **Chancellor** *n BrE* POL portavoz para asuntos económicos del partido de la oposición

shady[1] *adj* GEN COMM fuera de la ley

shady[2]: ~ **dealing** *n* FIN, STOCK actividad clandestina *f*

shaft: ~ **horsepower** *n* (*shp*) TRANSP *turbine* potencia en el eje *f*

shake: ~**-out** *n* GEN COMM, INS, STOCK sacudida *f*; ~**-up** *n* HRM, MGMNT reorganización *f*

shake up *vt* GEN COMM, HRM, MGMNT reorganizar, trastornar

shakedown *n AmE infrml* GEN COMM exacción de dinero *f*

shaky *adj* GEN COMM insolvente

shallow: ~ **market** *n* STOCK mercado superficial *m*

sham: ~ **dividend** *n* ACC, FIN, STOCK dividendo ficticio *m*; ~ **trading** *n* STOCK contratación de intangibles *f*

shape[1] *n* ECON modelo *m*, GEN COMM configuración *f*; ◆ **the ~ of the future** GEN COMM la configuración del futuro *f*; **the ~ of things to come** GEN COMM la forma de las cosas por venir *f*; ~ **of the world economy** ECON configuración de la economía mundial *f*

shape[2] *vt* STOCK *the options price* configurar

shape up *vi* GEN COMM, STOCK configurar

Shapley: ~ **value** *n* ECON valor de Shapley *m*

share[1] *n* (*sh, shr*) GEN COMM acción *f*; ~ **allotment** STOCK reparto de acciones *m*; ~ **bond** FIN, STOCK bono en acciones *m*; ~ **borrowing** STOCK préstamo de títulos *m*; ~ **buy back** STOCK compra de acciones propias *f*; ~ **capital** GEN COMM capital accionario *m*, capital en acciones *m*; ~ **certificate** *BrE* (*cf stock certificate AmE*) STOCK bono social *m*; ~ **classification** STOCK clasificación de acciones *f*; ~ **dividend** STOCK dividendo de una acción *m*; ~ **economy** ECON, STOCK economía participada *f*; ~ **index** STOCK índice de cotización de acciones en bolsa *m*, índice bursátil *m*; ~ **investments in other companies** ACC, STOCK inversión en acciones de otras compañías *f*; ~ **issue for cash** FIN, STOCK emisión de acciones al contado *f*; ~ **issued for cash** FIN, STOCK acción emitida al contado *f*; ~ **of market** S&M cuota de mercado *f*; ~ **option** GEN COMM opción de compra de acciones *f*, opción sobre acciones *f*; ~ **option scheme** GEN COMM *employee benefits* plan de opción de acciones *m*; ~ **ownership** STOCK titularidad de acciones *f*; ~ **participation scheme** HRM, STOCK, TAX *for employees* plan de participación de acciones *m*; ~ **premium** *BrE* (*cf capital surplus AmE*) GEN COMM prima de emisión *f*, excedente de capital *m*, plusvalía de capital *f*, superávit de capital *m*; ~ **price performance** STOCK rendimiento del precio de una acción *m*; ~ **of production plan** GEN COMM, IND participación del plan de producción *f*, cuota del plan de producción *f*; ~ **rating** STOCK clasificación de acciones *f*; ~ **redemption** STOCK rescate de una acción *m*; ~ **register** STOCK registro de acciones *m*; ~ **repurchase plan** STOCK plan de recompra de acciones *m*; ~ **scheme** HRM, STOCK *for company employees* plan de adquisición de acciones *m*; ~ **split** STOCK partición de acciones *f*; ~ **support operation** STOCK operación para mantener el precio *f*; ~ **transfer** STOCK transferencia de participación *f*; ~ **warrant to bearer** GEN COMM certificado de acciones al portador *m*

share[2] *vt* COMP *software, peripherals*, GEN COMM compartir

sharecropper *n AmE* ECON *agriculture* aparcero(-a) *m,f*

shared: ~ **accommodation** n PROP, TAX alojamiento compartido m; ~ **appreciation mortgage** n BANK, PROP hipoteca de plusvalía compartida f, hipoteca de revalorización compartida f; ~ **database** n COMP base de datos compartida f; ~ **monopoly** n ECON monopolio compartido m

shareholder n HRM, STOCK public accionista mf; ~ **of record** AmE HRM, STOCK accionista registrado(-a) m,f; ~'**s auditor** STOCK comisario(-a) m,f; ~'**s equity** GEN COMM capital contable m, capital de los accionistas m

shareholders': ~ **meeting** n HRM, STOCK asamblea de accionistas f (AmL) junta de accionistas f (Esp)

shareholding n STOCK participación accionaria f

shareownership n ACC, BANK, FIN cartera de acciones f

shares n pl (shs) GEN COMM acciones f pl, valores m pl, títulos valores m pl; ~ **authorized** n STOCK acciones autorizadas f pl; ~ **deposited in trust** FIN, STOCK acciones depositadas en fideicomiso f pl; ~ **moved ahead** STOCK acciones que se anticipan al mercado f pl; ~ **outstanding** n STOCK acciones en circulacion f pl

shareware n COMP equipos compartidos m pl

shark: ~ **watcher** n jarg STOCK empresa especializada en la pronta detección de intentos de absorción

sharp: ~ **call** n BANK exigencia de devolución inmediata de un préstamo f; ~ **dive** n ECON market, GEN COMM brusco descenso m, descenso en picado m; ~ **drop** n ECON market, GEN COMM caída pronunciada f, fuerte caída f; ~ **movement** n STOCK option price movimiento rápido m; ~ **protest** n GEN COMM protesta encarnizada f; ~ **rise** n ECON price aumento sostenido m

sharply adv ACC, ECON, GEN COMM fall fuertemente

shed vt GEN COMM, HRM workers, stock desprenderse de; ♦ ~ **light on** GEN COMM, MGMNT aclarar

sheet n GEN COMM hoja f; ~ **feeder** COMP alimentador de hojas m

shelf: ~ **display** n S&M exposición en estantes f; ~ **filler** n S&M persona que repone mercancía en los estantes de una tienda; ~ **life** n S&M of product duración de vida f, vida en estantería f; ~ **price** n S&M precio de un producto puesto en la estantería; ~ **registration** n STOCK registro automático m; ~ **space** n S&M espacio en estante m; ~~**talker** n jarg S&M advertising pequeño dispositivo para puntos de venta con mensaje publicitario; ~ **warmer** n GEN COMM, S&M artículo sin venta m

shell: ~ **company** n BrE jarg TAX empresa que funciona como tapadera f; ~ **corporation** n AmE GEN COMM corporación que existe para mantener acciones en otras compañías, empresa que funciona como tapadera f; ~ **operation** n STOCK adquisición de una empresa que aunque ha cesado actividades cotiza en bolsa

shelter vi TAX sustraerse

sheltered: ~ **employment** n HRM, WEL empleo protegido m; ~ **industries** n pl IND industrias protegidas f pl

shelve vt GEN COMM presentar

shield vt GEN COMM proteger

shift n ECON in demand or supply curve desviación f, GEN COMM in emphasis cambio m, HRM turno m; ~ **differential** HRM diferencial de turnos m, turno m; ~ **in consumption** S&M desplazamiento del consumo m; ~ **in demand** S&M desplazamiento de la demanda m; ~ **key** COMP tecla de mayúsculas f; ~ **work** HRM trabajo por turnos m; ~ **worker** HRM trabajador(a) por turnos m,f

shifting: ~ **berth** n TRANSP shipping muelle de trasvase m;

~ **board** n TRANSP tablones contra corrimiento de estiba m pl; ~ **of the tax burden** n TAX repercusión de la carga tributaria f; ~ **of taxes** n TAX repercusión de los impuestos f

ship[1] n TRANSP buque m; ~'**s agent** GEN COMM, TRANSP consignatario(-a) de buques m,f; ~'**s articles** n pl TRANSP contrato de enrolamiento m; ~'**s chandler** TRANSP purchasing proveedor(a) de efectos navales m,f; ~'**s clerk** TRANSP port vigilante de carga y descarga de buques mf; ~'**s cubic capacity** TRANSP capacidad cúbica del buque f; ~'**s deadweight** TRANSP peso muerto del buque m; ~'**s delivery order** TRANSP orden de entrega del buque f; ~'**s husband** TRANSP consignatario(-a) del buque m,f; ~'**s inward report** IMP/EXP, TRANSP informe de entrada de buque m (Esp), reporte de entrada de buque m (AmL); ~'**s log** TRANSP diario de navegación m; ~'**s manifest** TRANSP manifiesto del buque m; ~'**s papers** n pl LAW, TRANSP documentos del buque m pl; ~'**s protest** n LAW protesta de mar f; ~'**s rail** TRANSP batayola del buque f; ~'**s special survey** (SS) TRANSP revisión extraordinaria de un buque f; ~ **conversion** TRANSP conversión de un buque f; ~ **design strategy** TRANSP estrategia de diseño de un buque f; ~ **lease** GEN COMM arrendamiento de un buque m; ~ **plan** TRANSP plan de navegación m; ~ **planning** TRANSP design planificación de buque f; ~ **specification** TRANSP especificación del buque f; ~ **subsidy** TRANSP subvención del buque f; ~ **survey** TRANSP inspección del buque f; ~ **turnaround time** AmE, ~ **turnround time** BrE TRANSP tiempo de ida y vuelta del barco m, tiempo de viaje redondo m; ♦ **the** ~ **is in trim** TRANSP el buque está siendo reparado

ship[2] vt TRANSP freight embarcar

shipboard: ~ **facility** n LEIS, TRANSP servicio a bordo m; ~ **management** n TRANSP gestión a bordo f

shipborne: ~ **barge** n TRANSP barcaza de a bordo f

shipbroker n TRANSP agente marítimo(-a) m,f, consignatario(-a) m,f, corredor(a) marítimo(-a) m,f

shipbuilder n IND, TRANSP constructor(a) de naves m,f

Shipbuilders: ~ **and Repairers National Association** n BrE (SRNA) TRANSP asociación nacional de constructores y reparadores de buques

shipbuilding n IND, TRANSP construcción naval f

shipment n TRANSP carga f, embarque m, envío m; ~ **received** (SR) TRANSP recibo de embarque m; ♦ **ready for** ~ TRANSP listo para embarcar

shipowner n IMP/EXP, TRANSP fletante mf, armador(a) m,f; ~'**s liability** (SOL) LAW, TRANSP responsabilidad civil del armador(a) f

shipped[1]: ~ **aboard** adj GEN COMM, IMP/EXP, TRANSP embarcado a bordo; ~ **on board** adj GEN COMM, IMP/EXP, TRANSP embarcado a bordo

shipped[2]: ~ **bill** n IMP/EXP, TRANSP conocimiento a bordo m, conocimiento de embarque a bordo m, conocimiento embarcado m; ~ **bill of lading** n IMP/EXP, TRANSP conocimiento de embarque m

shipper n TRANSP cargador(a) m,f, expedidor(a) m,f, fletador(a) m,f; ~'**s letter of instruction** IMP/EXP, TRANSP carta de instrucciones del expedidor(a) f; ~'**s letter of instruction for issuing air waybills** IMP/EXP, TRANSP carta de instrucción del expedidor(a) para la emidión de cartas de rutas aéreas f, carta de instrucciones para emisión de conocimientos aéreos f; ~'**s load and count** TRANSP carga y valor declarados por el expedidor *m pl*; ~ **and carrier** (*s&c*) TRANSP expedidor(a) y transportista *m,f*; ~ **weight** (*SW*) TRANSP peso declarado por el expedidor *m*

shipping *n* TRANSP despacho *m*, embarque *m*, envío *m*, navegación *f*; ~ **address** TRANSP dirección marítima *f*; ~ **agency** TRANSP agencia de transporte marítimo *f*; ~ **agent** GEN COMM, TRANSP consignatario(-a) de buques *m,f*; ~ **bill** IMP/EXP, TRANSP certificado de embarque *m*, declaración de reexportación de almacén *f*, factura de embarque *f*; ~ **business** GEN COMM, TRANSP negocios marítimos *m pl*; ~ **clerk** TRANSP expedidor(a) *m,f*; ~ **documents** *n pl* IMP/EXP, TRANSP juego de documentos *m*, documentos de embarque *m pl*, lista de embarque *f*, manifiesto de carga *m*; ~ **exchange** FIN, STOCK, TRANSP bolsa de fletes *f*; ~ **and forwarding agent** (*S&FA*) HRM, TRANSP agente de transportes marítimos *mf*; ~ **instruction** TRANSP instrucción de embarque *f*; ~ **invoice** TRANSP factura de embarque *f*, factura de transporte *f*; ~ **lane** TRANSP ruta de navegación *f*; ~ **line** TRANSP compañía de navegación *f*, línea de navegación *f*; ~ **loan** BANK préstamo de embarque *m*; ~ **note** (*S/N*) IMP/EXP, TRANSP talón de embarque *m*; ~ **office** TRANSP agencia marítima *f*; ~ **officer** IMP/EXP, TRANSP expedidor(a) *m,f*, *customs* oficial(a) de embarque *m,f*; ~ **overcapacity** TRANSP saturación en el transporte *f*; ~ **ton** TRANSP tonelada marítima *f*; ~ **trade** GEN COMM comercio marítimo *m*

Shiprepairers: ~ **and Shipbuilders Independent Association** *n* (*SSIA*) TRANSP asociación independiente de reparadores y constructores de buques

shipyard: ~ **subsidy** *n* TRANSP *government* subsidio de astillero *m*

shirker *n infrml* GEN COMM persona que evade sus responsabilidades, flojo *m*

shoot[1] *n jarg* MEDIA, S&M *advertising, photo session* instantánea *f*

shoot[2] *vt* LEIS, MEDIA, S&M *advertising, films* rodar

shoot up *vi* GEN COMM espigar

shooting *n* LEIS, MEDIA, S&M *advertising, films* rodaje *m*; ~ **script** MEDIA, S&M guión de rodaje *m*

shop *n* GEN COMM *BrE* (*cf store AmE*) tienda *f*, S&M *advertising agency* taller *m*; ~**'s articles** *n pl* HRM artículos de una tienda *m pl*; ~ **assistant** *BrE* (*cf sales clerk AmE*) HRM, S&M dependiente(-a) de tienda *m,f*; ~ **audit** S&M auditoría de tienda *f*; ~ **factory** GEN COMM, HRM, IND fábrica *f*; ~ **floor** GEN COMM, HRM, IND fábrica *f*, piso de producción *m*; ~**-floor agreement** *BrE* HRM acuerdo de fábrica *m* (*Esp*), contrato de fábrica *m* (*AmL*); ~**-floor bargaining** GEN COMM, HRM, IND, LAW negociación en la fábrica *f*; ~**-floor participation** HRM participación de los obreros *f*; ~ **front** GEN COMM, S&M parte delantera de la tienda *f*; ~ **steward** HRM, IND delegado(-a) gremial *m,f*, enlace sindical *mf*, representante obrero(-a) *m,f*, representante del personal obrero *mf*, representante sindical *mf*, MGMNT dependiente(-a) *m,f*; ~ **traffic** S&M tráfico de tienda *m*; ~ **unit** S&M unidad de venta *f*; ~ **window** GEN COMM, S&M escaparate *m*

shopkeeper *n BrE* (*cf store owner AmE*) S&M tendero(-a) *m,f*

shoplifting *n* LAW, S&M hurto en tiendas *m*

shopper *n* GEN COMM comprador(a) *m,f*

shopping *n* GEN COMM compra *f*; ~ **center** *AmE*,

~ **centre** *BrE* GEN COMM centro comercial *m*; ~ **mall** *AmE* (*cf shopping precinct BrE*) GEN COMM centro comercial *m*, zona comercial peatonal *f*; ~ **precinct** *BrE* (*cf shopping mall AmE*) GEN COMM centro comercial *m*, zona comercial peatonal *f*; ~ **street** GEN COMM calle comercial *f*; ~ **trolley** GEN COMM carrito de la compra *m*

shore *n* TRANSP *of sea* orilla *f*, costa *f*, litoral *m*, *prop* escora *f*

short[1]: ~**-handed** *adj* HRM falto de mano de obra; ~**-haul** *adj* TRANSP de corto recorrido; ~**-range** *adj* GEN COMM de corto alcance; ~**-run** *adj* GEN COMM, STOCK a corto plazo, de corta duración; ~**-sighted** *adj* POL *decision* miope; ~**-staffed** *adj* HRM con poco personal, de plantilla escasa, falto de personal; ~**-term** *adj* ACC, GEN COMM, STOCK *bond, debt* a corto plazo, de corta duración

short[2] *n* STOCK *Government stocks, futures market* corto *m*, descubierto *m*, TRANSP *legal* corto *m*; ~ **account** BANK cuenta en descubierto *f*, STOCK posición de vendedor *f*; ~ **account position** STOCK posición en descubierto *f*; ~ **bill** (*SB*) TRANSP letra a corto plazo *f*; ~ **butterfly** STOCK *calls and puts* mariposa vendida *f*; ~ **call** STOCK *options* compra a corto *f*; ~ **call position** FIN, STOCK posición corta sobre opción de venta *f*; ~**-circuit** IND corto circuito *m*; ~ **closing** TRANSP cierre defectuoso *m*; ~ **coupon** STOCK cupón a corto plazo *m*; ~ **covering** STOCK cobertura de posición faltante *f*; ~ **date financing rate** STOCK *of futures* tasa de financiación a corto plazo *f*; ~ **delivery** GEN COMM entrega de mercancía incompleta *f*; ~ **form** IMP/EXP *bill of lading*, TRANSP formulario abreviado *m*; ~ **form bill of lading** IMP/EXP, TRANSP conocimiento de embarque abreviado *m*; ~ **futures position** FIN, STOCK posición corta sobre futuros *f*; ~ **hedge** STOCK cobertura de una posición corta *f*, operación de cobertura por venta a plazo *f*; ~ **in a currency** BANK déficit en una divisa *m*; ~ **interest** BANK, STOCK *of future, securities* interés reducido *m*; ~**-interest theory** BANK, STOCK teoría del interés reducido *f*; ~ **international voyage** GEN COMM, TRANSP viaje internacional corto *m*; ~ **market** STOCK mercado a corto plazo *m*; ~ **option position** FIN, STOCK posición corta *f*, posición corta sobre una opción *f*; ~ **put** STOCK opción de venta en descubierto *f*; ~ **put position** STOCK posición de venta en descubierto *f*; ~**-range maturity date** STOCK *Eurodollar deposits* fecha de vencimiento a corto plazo *f*; ~**-range planning** GEN COMM, FIN planificación de corto alcance *f*; ~ **rate** FIN, S&M tipo a corto plazo *m*; ~ **run** GEN COMM corto plazo *m*; ~**-run equilibrium** ECON equilibrio a corto plazo *m*; ~ **sale** STOCK venta al descubierto *f*; ~**-sale rule** STOCK regla de la venta al descubierto *f*; ~ **sea shipping** TRANSP transporte en travesías cortas *m*; ~ **sea trade** TRANSP comercio de navegación corta *m*; ~ **seller** STOCK vendedor(a) al descubierto *m,f*; ~ **selling** STOCK venta a corto *f*; ~ **shipment** TRANSP embarque parcial *m*, envío incompleto *m*; ~ **squeeze** STOCK vuelta rápida a corto *f*; ~ **straddle** STOCK *options* opción doble a corto *f*; ~ **straddle position** STOCK posición mixta corta *f*; ~ **strangle** STOCK *options* strangle corta *f*; ~ **tail** INS *risk* responsabilidad de corto plazo *f*; ~ **takeoff and landing** (*STOL*) TRANSP despegue y aterrizaje corto *m*; ~ **taxation year** TAX año de recaudación irregular *m*; ~ **term** GEN COMM corto plazo *m*; ~**-term advance** BANK anticipo a corto plazo *m*; ~**-term bond** FIN, STOCK bono a corto plazo *m*; ~**-term capital** GEN COMM capital a corto plazo *m*; **~-term contract** HRM contrato a corto plazo *m*; **~-term credit** BANK crédito a corto plazo *m*; **~-term debt** ACC, BANK, FIN deuda a corto plazo *f*; **~-term deposit** BANK depósito a corto plazo *m*; **~-term financing** FIN financiación a corto plazo *f*; **~-term fluctuations** *n pl* ECON fluctuaciones a corto plazo *f pl*; **~-term gain** ACC beneficio a corto plazo *m*, STOCK ganancia a corto plazo *f*; **~-term interest rate** BANK, GEN COMM tipo de interés a corto plazo *m*; **~-term interest rate futures contract** STOCK contrato de futuros de tipo de interés a corto plazo *m*; **~-term interest rate risk** STOCK *financial futures* riesgo sobre tipo de interés a corto plazo *m*; **~-term investment asset** STOCK activo líquido a corto plazo *m*; **~-term investment portfolio** FIN, STOCK cartera de inversiones a corto plazo *f*; **~-term liabilities** *n pl* ACC obligaciones a corto plazo *f pl*; **~-term loan** BANK préstamo a corto plazo *m*; **~-term loss** STOCK, TAX pérdida a corto plazo *f*; **~-term market** STOCK mercado a corto plazo *m*; **~-term money market** STOCK mercado monetario a corto plazo *m*; **~-term money market instrument** STOCK *balance sheet* instrumento del mercado de dinero a corto plazo *m*; **~-term note issuance facility** (*SNIF*) STOCK sistema de emisión de un pagaré a corto plazo *m*; **~-term objective** GEN COMM objetivo a corto plazo *m*; **~-term planning** FIN, GEN COMM planificación a corto plazo *f*; **~-term prepayments** *n pl* ACC anticipos a corto plazo *m pl*; **~-term securities** *n pl* STOCK obligaciones a corto plazo *f pl*; **~-term security** STOCK título a corto plazo *m*; **~-term vehicle park** (*STVP*) TRANSP aparcamiento de corta duración *m*, tiempo reducido de aparcamiento de vehículos *m*; **~-term worker** HRM trabajador(a) temporal *m,f*; **~ termism** STOCK tendencia a privilegiar el corto plazo *f*

short[3]: **~ change** *vt* GEN COMM *give too little money* dar muy poco dinero, *in shop* escamotear el cambio; **~-circuit** *vt* IND *involuntary* causar corto circuito en

short[4]: **in ~** *phr* GEN COMM en resumidas cuentas, en breve; **be in ~ supply** *phr* ECON, GEN COMM escasear

shortage *n* ECON, GEN COMM carestía *f*, escasez *f*, falta *f*; **~ economy** ECON economía de escasez *f*; **~ of manpower** HRM escasez de mano de obra *f*

shortages *n pl* GEN COMM *cash, stock* escasez *f*

shorten *vt* GEN COMM, STOCK acortar

shorter: **~-term liability** *n* STOCK pasivo a más corto plazo *m*; **~-term option** *n* STOCK opción a plazo más corto *f*, opción a menor plazo *f*

shortfall *n* ACC, GEN COMM déficit *m*, insuficiencia *f*, diferencia entre el resultado y lo previsto *f*, TRANSP insuficiencia *f*; **~ in earnings** GEN COMM lucro cesante *m*

shorthand *n* ADMIN, GEN COMM taquigrafía *f*; **~ typist** ADMIN, GEN COMM, HRM estenotipista *mf*, taquimecanógrafo(-a) *m,f*

shortlist[1] *n* GEN COMM lista de seleccionados *f*

shortlist[2] *vt* GEN COMM, HRM establecer la lista final, hacer la lista final

shortlived *adj* GEN COMM efímero

shorts *n pl* BrE *jarg* STOCK posiciones cortas *f pl*

shot *n* LEIS, MEDIA plano *m*; **~ in the dark** GEN COMM disparo a ciegas *m*

shoulder: **~ time** *n* S&M franja horaria previa o posterior a la de máxima audiencia *f*

show[1] *n* GEN COMM demostración *f*, S&M *exhibition* feria *f*, *of goods* demostración *f*; **~ business** GEN COMM, MEDIA mundo del espectáculo *m*; **~ card** GEN COMM colección de muestras *f*, rótulo *m*; **~ flat** PROP piso modelo *m*; **~ house** PROP casa modelo *f*

show[2] *vt* ACC *loss, surplus*, GEN COMM mostrar; ♦ **~ around** GEN COMM *visitor* llevar a visitar; **~ a balance of** ACC presentar un balance de; **~ one's hand** *infrml* GEN COMM poner las cartas sobre la mesa; **~ round** GEN COMM *visitor* llevar a visitar

showcase *n* GEN COMM *exhibition* vitrina *f*

showdown *n* GEN COMM confrontación *f*

showpiece *n* GEN COMM *of collection* obra maestra *f*

showthrough *n* MEDIA, S&M traspaso de la imagen de una página a otra

shr *abbr* (*share*) GEN COMM acción *f*

shredder *n* ADMIN máquina destructora de documentos *f*

shrink[1]: **~ packaging** *n* GEN COMM envases de plástico transparente *m pl*; **~ wrapping** *n* GEN COMM, IND, TRANSP embalaje por contracción *m*

shrink[2] *vi* ECON contraerse

shrinkage *n* GEN COMM pérdida por evaporación *f*, S&M contracción de la demanda *m*, disminución *f*

shrinking: **~ market** *n* GEN COMM, S&M mercado retraído *m*; **~ profits** *n pl* GEN COMM beneficios en disminución *m pl*

shs *abbr* (*shares*) GEN COMM acciones *f pl*, títulos valores *m pl*

shunter *n* STOCK derivador *m*

shunting *n* STOCK comercio triangular *m*

shut: **~-down of plants** *n* GEN COMM cierre de empresas *m*; **~ out cargo** *n* TRANSP cargamento no embarcado *m* cargamento que no se ha podido embarcar en su totalidad *m*

shut down *vi* GEN COMM interrumpir

shut off *vt* GEN COMM interceptar

shut up: **~ shop** *phr* GEN COMM liquidar un negocio

shutdown *n* GEN COMM interrupción *f*, *factory, computer* parada *f*, STOCK cierre patronal *m*; **~ price** GEN COMM precio de liquidación *m*

shuttle *n* TRANSP *flight* puente aéreo *m*; **~ service** TRANSP servicio de transbordadores *m*

shyster *n* *infrml* GEN COMM picapleitos *mf*

SIB *abbr* BrE (*Securities and Investments Board*) FIN, STOCK consejo de inversiones de acciones, bonos y valores, ≈ CNMV (*Comisión Nacional del Mercado de Valores*)

SIC *abbr* (*standard industrial classification*) IND clasificación industrial común *f*, clasificación industrial estándar *f*

SICA *abbr* (*Society of Industrial and Cost Accountants*) ACC asociación de contables industriales y de costes

sick[1]: **~ allowance** *n* HRM, WEL subsidio de enfermedad *m*; **~ building syndrome** *n* WEL síndrome del edificio enfermo *m*; **~ leave** *n* HRM ausencia por enfermedad *f*; **~-out** *n jarg* HRM *industrial relations* ausencia por enfermedad *f*; **~ pay scheme** *n* BrE HRM, WEL plan de compensaciones por enfermedad *m*

sick[2]: **off ~** *phr* *infrml* HRM ausente por enfermedad, incapacitado

sickness: **~ benefit** *n* HRM, WEL subsidio de enfermedad *m*; **~ insurance** *n* HRM, INS seguro de enfermedad *m*; **~ insurance premium** *n* HRM prima de seguro de enfermedad *f*

side[1]: **~-by-side trading** *n* STOCK negociación paralela *f*;

~ effect *n* GEN COMM efecto colateral *m*; **~ frame handling** *n* TRANSP *loading* bastidor lateral *m*; **~ issue** *n* GEN COMM cuestión secundaria *f*; **~ note** *n* GEN COMM anotación al margen *f*; **~ track** *n* AmE (*cf siding BrE*) TRANSP apartadero *m*, vía muerta *f*, vía secundaria *f*; **~ wheel** *n* (*SDW*) TRANSP rueda lateral *f*

side²: on the ~ *phr* GEN COMM por añadidura

sidehead *n* S&M subtítulo *m*

sideline: ~ job *n* HRM trabajo secundario *m*; **~ point** *n* TRANSP *cargo tariff* punto de vía secundaria *m*

sidestep *vt* GEN COMM esquivar

sideways: ~ market *n* STOCK mercado lateral *m*

siding *n* BrE (*cf side track AmE*) TRANSP apartadero *m*, vía muerta *f*, vía secundaria *f*

siege: ~ economy *n* ECON economía de asedio *f*, economía de sitio *f*

sifting: ~ sort *n* COMP clasificación por cribadura *f*

siftproof: ~ packaging *n* TRANSP envasado a prueba de posamiento *m*

sight *n* FIN *treaty* alcance *m*; **~ bill** ACC, BANK, FIN billete nuevo *m*, efecto a la vista *m*, letra a la vista *f*; **~ deposit** BANK depósito a la vista *m*; **~ deposit account** ACC, FIN cuenta corriente (*c/c*); **~ draft** (*S/D*) GEN COMM efecto a la vista *m*, giro *m*, letra *f*, giro a la vista *m*; **~ letter of credit** BANK, FIN carta de crédito a la vista *f*; ◆ **at ~** (*a/s*) GEN COMM a la vista; **at ~ draft** GEN COMM giro a la vista *m*

sighting: ~ bills of lading *phr* TRANSP *cargo* verificación de los conocimientos de embarque *f*

sign¹ *n* GEN COMM *indication*, MATH signo *m*

sign² *vt* GEN COMM firmar

sign in *vi* HRM firmar al entrar a la empresa

sign off *vi* MEDIA concluir la emisión

sign on *vi* BrE GEN COMM, HRM, WEL registrarse, firmar el paro; ◆ **~ the dotted line** ADMIN *on form* firmar sobre la línea de puntos

sign up *vi* GEN COMM alistarse

signal *n* GEN COMM *indication* señal *f*; **~ jamming** GEN COMM, MEDIA, TRANSP interferencias *f pl*; **~ light** COMP indicador luminoso *m*

signaling AmE *see* **signalling** BrE

signalling *n* BrE GEN COMM señalización *f*

signatory *n* GEN COMM, LAW firmante *mf*

signature *n* GEN COMM firma *f*; **~ card** BANK tarjeta de firma *f*; **~ tune** MEDIA *broadcast* indicativo *m*; ◆ **for ~** GEN COMM para firmar

signed *adj* (*sgd*) COMMS, GEN COMM firmado

significance: ~ level *n* MATH grado de significación *m* (*Esp*), grado de significancia *m* (*AmL*); **~ test** *n* MATH prueba de significación *f* (*Esp*), prueba de significancia *f* (*AmL*)

significant *adj* GEN COMM importante, significante, significativo

signify *vt* GEN COMM significar

signing: ~ officer *n* BANK director(a) con firma autorizada *m,f*; **~ slip** *n* ACC ficha de firmas *f*, hoja de firmas *f*

signpost *n* TRANSP hito *m*, mojón *m*, poste indicador de señales *m*

SIL *abbr* BANK, FIN (*specific investment loan*) préstamo de inversión específico *m*, IMP/EXP, TRANSP (*specific indivi-*

dual licence BrE, specific individual license AmE) licencia individual específica *f*

silent: the ~ majority *n* POL la mayoría silenciosa *f*; **~ salesperson** *n* HRM, S&M vendedor(a) silencioso(-a) *m,f*

SILIC *abbr* (*severely indebted low-income country*) ECON, POL país de baja renta endeudado fuertemente

silicon: ~ chip *n* COMP, IND chip de silicio *m*, microplaqueta de silicio *f*

silk: ~ screening *n* S&M serigrafía *m*

silver: ~ ore *n* ENVIR, IND mineral de plata *m*; **~ ring** *n* *jarg* FIN anillo de plata *m*; **~ standard** *n* ECON, FIN patrón plata *m*

SIM *abbr* (*sector investment and maintenance loan*) BANK, FIN préstamo sectorial de inversión y mantenimiento *m*

SIMA *abbr* (*Scientific Instrument Manufacturers Association*) IND asociación de fabricantes de instrumentos científicos

similar: on a ~ occasion *phr* GEN COMM en semejante ocasión

SIMO: ~ chart *n* ADMIN gráfico de SIMO *m*

simple: ~ contract *n* GEN COMM contrato simple *m*; **~ correlation** *n* MATH correlación simple *f*; **~ deferment** *n* ACC, FIN aplazamiento simple *m*; **~ fraction** *n* MATH fracción simple *f*; **~ interest** *n* BANK interés simple *m*; **~ labor** AmE, **~ labour** BrE *n* HRM mano de obra no cualificada *f*, *task* trabajo simple *m*; **~ linear regression** *n* ACC, MATH regresión lineal simple *f*; **~ majority** *n* POL mayoría simple *f*; **~ yield** *n* STOCK rendimiento simple *m*

simplex *adj* COMP *transmission* unidireccional

simplified: ~ clearance procedure *n* (*SCP*) IMP/EXP procedimiento de certificación de aduanas simplificado *m*; **~ employee pension plan** *n* HRM plan simplificado de jubilación para empleados *m*; **~ procedure for goods carried by rail** *n* (*SPGER*) TRANSP procedimiento simplificado de transporte de mercancías por ferrocarril *m*

simplify *vt* GEN COMM simplificar; ◆ **~ matters** GEN COMM simplificar cuestiones

simulate *vt* COMP, GEN COMM simular

simulation *n* COMP, GEN COMM simulación *f*; **~ model** ECON modelo de simulación *m*; **~ modeling** AmE, **~ modelling** BrE ECON modelo de simulación *m*

simulcast *abbr jarg* (*simultaneous broadcast*) MEDIA transmisión simultnána *f*

simultaneous¹ *adj* GEN COMM simultáneo

simultaneous²: ~ broadcast *n* (*simulcast*) MEDIA transmisión simultánea *f*; **~ payments clause** *n* FIN cláusula de pagos simultáneos *f*; **~ translation** *n* GEN COMM traducción simultánea *f*

sincerity *n* GEN COMM sinceridad *f*

sinecure *n* HRM prebenda *f*, sinecura *f*

sine die *phr* GEN COMM, LAW sin fijar fecha

single¹ *adj* LEIS *room* individual; **~-deck** TRANSP *ship* de una sola cubierta; **~-plane** TRANSP *engineering* de un solo nivel; **~-sided** COMP de una cara

single² *n* TRANSP *sleeping-car* compartimento individual *m*; **~ administrative document** (*SAD*) ADMIN documento administrativo simple *m*, documento administrativo único *m*; **~ arbitrator** BrE HRM árbitro(-a) exclusivo(-a) *m,f*; **~ back** TRANSP barco que vuelve de hacer su entrega; **~-berth cabin** TRANSP camarote para uno *m*; ~ **capacity** STOCK capacidad única *f*; ~ **capacity trading** STOCK restricción de actividades a los intermediarios; ~ **channel** *BrE* HRM canal único *m*; ~ **column centimeter** *AmE*, ~ **column centimetre** *BrE* (*SCC*) MEDIA centímetro-columna *m*; ~ **column inch** (*SCI*) MEDIA pulgada de columna de a uno *f*; ~ **commission** STOCK comisión única *f*; ~ **contract finance** FIN finanza de contrato simple *f*; ~ **country data capture** ADMIN captura de datos en un solo país *f*; ~ **currency** BANK, ECON, POL divisa única *f*, moneda única *f*; ~**-decker bus** TRANSP autobús de un solo piso *m*; ~ **density** COMP densidad simple *f*; ~**-employer bargaining** HRM negociación con un empresario individual *f*; ~**-entry book-keeping** ACC, ECON contabilidad por partida simple *f*; ~**-entry visa** LEIS, POL visado para una sola entrada *m*; ~ **European currency** GEN COMM moneda única europea *f*; ~**-family dwelling** PROP, TAX, WEL vivienda unifamiliar *f*; ~**-family home** *AmE* (*cf single-family house BrE*) PROP, TAX, WEL vivienda unifamiliar *f*; ~**-family house** *BrE* (*cf single-family home AmE*) PROP, TAX, WEL vivienda unifamiliar *f*; ~ **labor market** *AmE*, ~ **labour market** *BrE* ECON, HRM mercado único de trabajo *m*, mercado único laboral *m*; ~ **manning** TRANSP tripulación de un solo miembro *f*; ~ **parent** GEN COMM madre soltera *f*, padre soltero *m*; ~**-parent family** GEN COMM familia monoparental *f*; ~ **payment** BANK, FIN pago global *m*; ~ **person** GEN COMM, LAW soltero(-a) *m,f*; ~**-person household** GEN COMM vivienda unipersonal *f*; ~ **point mooring** TRANSP *oil tanker* único punto de amarre *m*; ~ **precision** COMP precisión simple *f*; ~ **premium** GEN COMM prima única *f*; ~**-premium deferred annuity** FIN anualidad diferida de prima única *f*; ~**-premium life insurance** INS seguro de vida de prima única *m*; ~ **room** LEIS habitación individual *f*; ~**-room supplement** LEIS suplemento por habitación individual *m*; ~**-sheet feeder** ADMIN, COMP alimentador de papel manual *m*; ~**-sided disk** (*SSD*) COMP disco de una cara *m*; ~**-sided double density** (*SSDD*) COMP doble densidad por una cara; ~**-sided single density** (*SSSD*) COMP baja densidad por una cara *f*; ~ **sourcing** GEN COMM fuente única *f*; ~ **spacing** COMP a un espacio *phr*; ~**-state municipal bond fund** FIN, STOCK fondo de bonos municipales de un solo estado *m*; ~ **status** HRM categoría única *f*; ~ **table bargaining** HRM negociación en un nivel único *f*; ~ **tax credit** TAX deducción única de impuestos *f*; ~ **tax movement** TAX movimiento de impuesto único *m*; ~ **ticket** LEIS, TRANSP billete sencillo *m*, billete de ida *m*; ~ **transport document** ADMIN, IMP/EXP, TRANSP documento único de embarque *m*; ~ **union agreement** *BrE* HRM acuerdo con un solo sindicato *m*; ~ **union deal** *BrE* HRM acuerdo de un solo sindicato *m*, arreglo con un solo sindicato *m*; ~ **union no-strike agreement** *BrE* HRM contrato de un solo sindicato de no ir a la huelga *m*; ~ **user port** TRANSP puerto para un único usuario *m*

single out *vt* GEN COMM seleccionar

Single: ~ **European Act** *n* (*SEA*) LAW, POL Acta Única Europea *f* (*AUE*); ~ **Market** *n* GEN COMM mercado único *m*

Single-Company: ~ **Personal Equity Plans** *n pl BrE* STOCK planes personales de compra de acciones de una empresa

singly *adv* GEN COMM individualmente

sink *vt* ACC, FIN *money, funds* amortizar, GEN COMM hacer desaparecer

sinking: ~ **fund** *n* ACC, FIN, STOCK fondo de amortización *m*, fondo de amortización de deudas *m*; ~ **fund loan** *n* ACC préstamo con fondo de amortización *m*

SIO *abbr* (*senior information officer*) HRM, MGMNT director(a) de información *m,f*

SIPROCOM *abbr* (*Committee for the Simplification of International Trade Procedures*) ECON, POL Comisión para la Simplificación del Comercio Internacional *f*

SIS *abbr* (*special intermediate survey*) TRANSP revisión extraordinaria intermedia *f*

sister: ~ **company** *n* GEN COMM sociedad hermana *f*; ~ **ship** *n* TRANSP buque gemelo *m*

sit. *abbr* (*situation*) HRM puesto *m*

sit[1]: ~**-down strike** *n* HRM huelga de brazos caídos *f*; ~**-in** *n* HRM *industrial action* sentada *f*, huelga de ocupación *f*

sit[2] *vi* POL *parliament* reunirse en sesión parlamentaria (*Esp*), sesionar (*AmL*); ◆ ~ **in judgment** LAW celebrar juicio; ~ **on the fence** *infrml* GEN COMM no comprometerse; ~ **tight** GEN COMM no moverse

SITC *abbr* (*Standard International Trade Classification*) GEN COMM Clasificación Normativa para el Comercio Internacional *f*

site *n* COMP emplazamiento *m*, GEN COMM, IND *of factory* emplazamiento *m*, lugar *m*, obra *f*, sitio *m*; ~ **audit** ACC, GEN COMM auditoría en la sede de la empresa *f*; ~ **development** ENVIR preparación del terreno *f*; ~ **engineer** HRM, IND ingeniero(-a) de obra *m,f*; ~ **foreman** HRM capataz(a) a pie de obra *m,f*; ~ **licence** *BrE*, ~ **license** *AmE* COMP licencia de instalación *f*, licencia de uso *f*; ~ **manager** HRM, IND jefe(-a) de obra *m,f*; ~ **operation** ENVIR operación de emplazamiento *f*; ~ **planning** COMP planificación de las instalaciones *f*; ~ **selection** ENVIR selección del emplazamiento *f*

Site: ~ **of Special Scientific Interest** *n* (*SSSI*) ENVIR lugar de especial interés científico *m*

siting *n* COMP, IND emplazamiento *m*

sits. vac. *abbr BrE* (*situations vacant*) HRM puestos vacantes *m pl*

sitting: ~ **tenant** *n* PROP inquilino(-a) en posesión *m,f*

situation *n* (*sit.*) HRM puesto *m*; ~ **report** GEN COMM informe de la situación *m* (*Esp*), reporte de la situación *m* (*AmL*); ◆ **have the** ~ **well in hand** GEN COMM tener la situación bajo control

situations: ~ **vacant** *n pl BrE* (*sits. vac.*) HRM puestos vacantes *m pl*

six: ~**-monthly periods** *n pl* GEN COMM periodos semestrales *m pl*

sixteen: ~ **sheet** *n* S&M anuncio de 2 x 3 metros *m*

size *n* ECON *of population* proporción *f*, GEN COMM tamaño *m*

size up *vt infrml* GEN COMM evaluar

sizeable *adj* ECON *budget* proporcionado; ~ **budget** *n* ACC, ECON, FIN presupuesto proporcionado *m*

SKD *abbr* (*semi-knocked down*) TRANSP semidesarmado

skeletal: ~ **trailer** *n* TRANSP chasis de remolque *m*

skeleton: ~ **case** *n* TRANSP *cargo packing* caja jaula para materiales frágiles *f*; ~ **contract** *n* GEN COMM contrato marco *m*; ~ **service** *n* TRANSP servicio mínimo *m*; ~ **staff** *n* HRM personal reducido *m*

skepticism *AmE see scepticism BrE*

sketch *n* GEN COMM bosquejo *m*

skewed: **~ frequency curve** *n* MATH curva de frecuencias asimétrica *f*

skewness *n* MATH asimetría *f*

skid *n* TRANSP *cargo handling* defensa *f*

skill[1]: **~-intensive** *adj* HRM con uso intensivo de personal cualificado

skill[2] *n* HRM habilidad *f*, especialidad *f*; **~ differential** HRM diferencial de habilidad *m*

skilled[1] *adj* HRM cualificado

skilled[2]: **~ labor** *AmE see skilled labour BrE*; **~ labor force** *AmE see skilled labour force BrE*; **~ labour** *BrE n* ECON *job* trabajo cualificado *m*, trabajo especializado *m*, HRM mano de obra especializada *f*, mano de obra cualificada *f*, *job* trabajo cualificado *m*, trabajo especializado *m*; **~ labour force** *n BrE* HRM fuerza de trabajo cualificada *f*; **~ union** *n* HRM sindicato cualificado *m*; **~ worker** *n* HRM, IND obrero(-a) cualificado(-a) *m,f*

skills: **~ analysis** *n* HRM análisis por aptitudes *m*

skimming *n* GEN COMM substracción de ganancias *f*; **~ policy** S&M política superficial *f*

skimp on *vt* GEN COMM escatimar

skin *n* TRANSP *shipping* forro *m*

skip[1] *n* COMP salto *m*; **~ account** BANK cuenta de un deudor moroso que ha desaparecido sin dejar rastro; **~-payment privilege** BANK, FIN privilegio de omisión de pago *m*

skip[2] *vt* COMP saltar; ♦ **~ the details** GEN COMM saltarse los detalles; **~ a payment** *infrml* BANK, FIN omitir un pago

skyrocket *vi infrml* GEN COMM subir rápidamente

SL *abbr* (*surveillance licence BrE, surveillance license AmE*) IMP/EXP licencia de vigilancia *f*

slack[1] *adj* GEN COMM *business* flojo, HRM negligente

slack[2] *n* ECON exceso de oferta agregada *m*, oferta desanimada *f*, GEN COMM *of business* paralización *f*; **~ fill** *jarg* S&M presentación engañosa de un producto *f*; **~ period** GEN COMM, IND, S&M periodo flojo *m*; **~ water** TRANSP marea muerta *f*

slack off *vi* GEN COMM *worker, business, demand* disminuir

slacken *vi* ECON *recovery* retardar; ♦ **~ the reins** ECON aflojar las riendas

slackening *n* ECON desánimo comercial *m*, desaliento mercantil *m*

slander: **~ action** *n* LAW demanda por calumnia *f*

slanderous *adj* LAW calumnioso

slant *vt* GEN COMM inclinación *f*

slash *n* COMP, MEDIA *typography* barra *f*, barra oblicua *f*

slate[1] *n* POL candidatura *f*, lista electoral *f*

slate[2] *vt* GEN COMM *criticize* poner por los suelos, *AmE* POL *post* designar

S/LC *abbr* (*sue and labor clause AmE, sue and labour clause BrE*) INS, LAW cláusula de medidas preventivas *f*, cláusula de gestión y trabajo *f*

sleeper *n* GEN COMM, S&M *success story* éxito inesperado *m*, *poor selling product* artículo sin venta *m*, TRANSP coche cama *m*, *BrE* (*cf crosstie AmE*) *on rail* traviesa *f*

sleeping: **~ beauty** *n jarg* STOCK empresas pequeñas que atraen la atención de las grandes corporaciones; **~ car** *n* TRANSP coche cama *m*; **~ economy** *n* ECON economía

dormida *f*; **~ partner** *n* GEN COMM socio(-a) comanditario(-a) inactivo(-a) *m,f*

slice: **~ of the market** *n* S&M cuota de mercado *f*

slick *n* ENVIR, GEN COMM *oil* mancha *f*, mancha oleosa *f*

slide: **~ projector** *n* MEDIA proyector de diapositivas *m*; **~ rule** *n* GEN COMM, MATH regla de cálculo *f*

sliding: **~ fifth wheel** *n* TRANSP *semitrailer* rueda de respeto deslizable *f*; **~ parity** *n* STOCK paridad móvil *f*; **~ scale** *n* ACC, GEN COMM escala móvil *f*; **~ wage scale** *n* HRM escala móvil de salarios *f*, escala salarial móvil *f*

slight *adj* GEN COMM leve

slim: **~-line** *adj* COMP *hardware design* de trazo fino

slim down *vt* ECON *workforce* reconvertir

sling *n* TRANSP cadena de suspensión *f*, eslinga *f*, *cargo* cabestrillo *m*

slip[1] *n* GEN COMM, INS borderó *m*; **~ sheet** TRANSP propuesta-borrador *f*; **~ system bookkeeping** ACC, ADMIN contabilidad simplificada *f*

slip[2] *vi* STOCK bajar

slip back *vi* GEN COMM volver sigilosamente

SLMA *abbr* (*student loan marketing association*) BANK, FIN asociación de comercialización de préstamos a estudiantes *f*

slog *n* HRM trabajo duro *m*

slogan *n* MEDIA, S&M *advertising* eslogan *m*, slogan *m*

slope *n* GEN COMM inclinación *f*, declive *m*

slot *n* COMP *for expansion card*, GEN COMM ranura *f*, MEDIA *print* espacio *m*, TRANSP *shipping* ranura *f*; **~ machine** GEN COMM *for tickets* expendedora automática *f*

slot in *vt* COMP insertar en su sitio

slow[1] *adj* ECON, GEN COMM lento

slow[2]: **~ decline** *n* STOCK *currency* lenta disminución *f*; **~ motion** *safe n* BANK cámara lenta *f*; **~-moving goods** *n pl* GEN COMM, S&M artículos de venta difícil *m pl*; **~ payer** *n* FIN, GEN COMM pagador(a) moroso(-a) *m,f*, moroso(-a) *m,f*; **~ rise** *n* STOCK *currency* lento aumento *m*; **~ steaming** *n* TRANSP navegación a vapor lenta *f*

slow[3]**1.** *vt* GEN COMM ralentizar; **2.** *vi* ECON ralentizarse

slow down *vi* ECON trabajar moderadamente, ralentizarse

slowdown *n* GEN COMM *of pace* moderación del ritmo *f*, *strike* huelga de brazos caídos *f*

sluggish *adj* ECON, GEN COMM, LAW débil, STOCK *market* lento

sluggishness *n* GEN COMM *of demand* debilidad *f*

sluice: **~-gate price** *n jarg* ECON *EC* precio de compuerta *m*

slump[1] *n* ECON baja repentina *f*, caída repentina *f*, *oil prices, world trade* desplome *m*, depresión económica *f*, crisis económica *f*, GEN COMM baja repentina *f*, caída repentina *f*, STOCK caída en picado *f*; **~ in sales** GEN COMM caída de ventas *f*

slump[2] *vi* STOCK caer en picado, sufrir una gran pérdida

slumpflation *n jarg* ECON depresión con inflación *f*

slush: **~ fund** *n* FIN, POL dinero para sobornos *m*, fondo para sobornos *m*

Slutsky: **~ effect** *n* ECON efecto de Slutsky *m*; **~ equation** *n* ECON ecuación de Slutsky *f*

SMA *abbr* STOCK (*special miscellaneous account*) cuenta miscelánea especial *f*, (*Secondary Market Association*) Asociación de Mercados de Negociación *f*

small: **~ ads** *n pl* MEDIA, S&M pequeños anuncios *m pl*; **~ business** *n* GEN COMM pequeña empresa *f*; **~ business administration** *n* (*SBA*) GEN COMM, MGMNT administración de la pequeña empresa *f*, dirección de la pequeña empresa *f*, gestión de la pequeña empresa *f*; **~ business bond** *n* FIN, STOCK bono de la pequeña empresa *m*; **~ business deduction** *n* TAX deducción de las pequeñas empresas *f*; **~ business development bond** *n* (*SBDB*) GEN COMM bono para el desarrollo de la pequeña empresa *m*; **~ business investment amount** *n* TAX volumen de inversión de la pequeña empresa *m*; **~ business lobby** *n jarg* POL grupo de presión de la pequeña empresa *m*; **~ business property** *n* TAX propiedad de la pequeña empresa *f*; **~ business venture capital tax credit** *n* TAX desgravación fiscal del capital de riesgo de las PYME *f*; **~ change** *n* GEN COMM calderilla *f*, cambio *m*, suelto *m*, POL moneda fraccionaria *f*; **~ claims** *n pl* LAW demandas de menor cuantía *f pl*; **~ damage** *n* (*s/d*) INS avería menor *f*, daño menor *m*; **~ denomination** *n* BANK, FIN *notes* baja denominación *f*; **~ earnings** *n pl* ACC, TAX ingresos de menor cuantía *m pl*; **~ employer** *n* HRM pequeño(-a) empresario(-a) *m,f*; **~ firm** *n* GEN COMM empresa pequeña *f*; **~ investor** *n* FIN pequeño(-a) inversionista *m,f*; **~ and medium-size enterprise** *n* (*SME*) ECON pequeña y mediana empresa *f* (*PYME*); **~ and medium-sized manufacturing companies** *n pl* ECON, GEN COMM pequeñas y medianas empresas industriales *f pl*; **~ print** *n* GEN COMM, LAW *in contract* cláusulas de un contrato de adhesión impresas en un tipo de letra pequeña; **~ producers' tax credit** *n* TAX reducción fiscal para los pequeños productores *f*; **~ savings** *n pl* BANK, FIN pequeños ahorros *m pl*; **~-scale company** *n* ECON, GEN COMM, IND empresa a pequeña escala *f*; **~ speculator** *n* STOCK pequeño(-a) especulador(a) *m,f*

smallholder *n* ECON pequeño(-a) agricultor(a) *m,f*

smalls *n pl* MEDIA, S&M *advertising* anuncios por palabras *m pl*, clasificados *m pl*

smart: **~ card** *n* GEN COMM tarjeta inteligente *f*; **~ money** *n* BANK, FIN dinero rápido *m*; **~ set** *n* GEN COMM gente selecta *f*; **~ terminal** *n* COMP terminal inteligente *m*

SME *abbr* (*small and medium-size enterprise*) ECON PYME (*pequeña y mediana empresa*)

smelt *vt* IND fundir

smelting: **~ works** *n pl* IND taller de fundición *m*

SMMT *abbr* (*Society of Motor Manufacturers and Traders*) IND, TRANSP sociedad de fabricantes y comerciantes de automóviles

smokeless: **~ powder** *n* ENVIR, TRANSP pólvora sin humo *f*

smokestack *n* IND, TRANSP chimenea *f*; **~ American stocks** *n pl* STOCK acciones de la industria pesada americana; **~ industry** IND industria de chimeneas *f*

smoking[1]: **~ room** *n* HRM, LEIS salón de fumar *m*

smoking[2]: **no ~** *phr* GEN COMM se prohíbe fumar, no fumar

smooth *vt* ECON *fluctuations* atenuar

smooth out *vt* GEN COMM suavizar

smoothly *adv* GEN COMM lisamente, suavemente

SMP *abbr* (*special multiperil insurance*) INS seguro especial multirriesgo *m*

smuggle *vt* IMP/EXP, TAX contrabandear, pasar de contrabando

smuggled: **~ goods** *n pl* IMP/EXP, TAX artículos de contrabando *m pl*

smuggler *n* IMP/EXP, TAX contrabandista *mf*

smuggling *n* IMP/EXP, TAX *activity* contrabando *m*

S/N *abbr* (*shipping note*) IMP/EXP, TRANSP talón de embarque *m*

snag *n infrml* GEN COMM dificultad imprevista *f*

snake *n* ECON *EC* serpiente *f*

snap: **~ strike** *n* HRM huelga rápida *f*

snatch *vt* GEN COMM arrebatar

sneak: **~ preview** *n* MEDIA *television, cinema* anticipo no oficial *m*, preestreno *m*

sneeze at *vt* GEN COMM despreciar

SNIF *abbr* (*short-term note issuance facility*) STOCK sistema de emisión de un pagaré a corto plazo *m*

SNIG *abbr* (*sustained noninflationary growth*) ECON, POL crecimiento sostenido no inflacionario *m*

snipe *n jarg* POL crítica sin posibilidad de réplica *f*

snowball *vi* GEN COMM aumentar con rapidez

snugging *n* ECON, GEN COMM ajuste *m*

s.o. *abbr* (*seller's option*) STOCK prima de opción a vender *f*

SO *abbr* (*senior officer*) HRM funcionario(-a) de rango superior *m,f*

soar *vi* GEN COMM *profits, prices* elevarse

soaring *adj* GEN COMM muy elevado

social[1] *adj* GEN COMM social

social[2]: **~ accounting** *n* ACC contabilidad social *f*; **~ adjustment cost** *n* HRM coste de ajuste social *m* (*Esp*), costo de ajuste social *m* (*AmL*); **~ analysis** *n* S&M, WEL análisis social *m*; **~ assistance payment** *n* HRM, WEL pago de la asistencia social *m*; **~ balance** *n* ACC, BANK, GEN COMM balance social *m*; **~ capital** *n* ECON capital social *m*; **~ category** *n* S&M *market research*, WEL categoría social *f*; **~ choice theory** *n* ECON teoría de la elección social *f*; **~ class** *n* GEN COMM, HRM, WEL clase social *f*; **~ conscience fund** *n* ECON *ethical unit trust* fundación social *f*; **~ consciousness mutual fund** *n* FIN fondo mutuo de interés social *m*; **~ contract** *n* HRM contrato social *m*; **~ cost** *n* ECON coste social *m* (*Esp*), costo social *m* (*AmL*); **~ cost of monopoly** *n* ECON coste social del monopolio *m* (*Esp*), costo social del monopolio *m* (*AmL*); **~ cost of unemployment** *n* ECON, HRM, WEL coste social del desempleo *m* (*Esp*), costo social del desempleo *m* (*AmL*); **~ credit** *n* GEN COMM crédito social *m*; **~ democracy** *n* ECON, POL democracia social *f*, socialdemocracia *f*; **~ development envelope** *n* POL partida de desarrollo social *f*; **~ development tax** *n* TAX impuesto para el desarrollo social *m*; **~ dividend scheme** *n* ECON, TAX esquema del dividendo social *m*; **~ expenditure** *n* ACC, HRM gastos de seguridad social *m pl*; **~ good** *n* GEN COMM bien social *m*; **~ grade** *n* GEN COMM, HRM, WEL clase social *f*; **~ insurance** *n* HRM, TAX, WEL seguro social *m*; **~ liberalism** *n* ECON, POL liberalismo social *m*; **~ market economy** *n* ECON economía social de mercado *f*; **~ opportunity cost of foreign exchange** *n* STOCK coste de oportunidad social de las divisas *f* (*Esp*), costo de oportunidad social de las divisas *f* (*AmL*); **~ organization** *n* POL organización social *f*; **~ overhead capital** *n* FIN capital para infraestructura social *m*; ~ **ownership** *n* GEN COMM cooperativa *f*; ~ **policy** *n* GEN COMM, POL política social *f*; ~ **product** *n* ECON producto social *m*; ~ **profit** *n* ECON beneficio social *m*; ~ **rate of discount** *n* FIN tasa social de descuento *f*; ~ **secretary** *n* HRM secretario(-a) de asuntos sociales *m,f*; ~ **security benefit** *n pl* HRM, WEL subsidio de la seguridad social *m*; ~ **security contribution** *n* TAX contribución a la seguridad social *f*, cuota de la seguridad social *f*; ~ **security creditor** *n* ACC acreedor(a) de la seguridad social *m,f*; ~**security recipient** *n BrE* (*cf welfare recipient AmE*) HRM, WEL beneficiario(-a) de asistencia social *m,f*; ~ **spending** *n* GEN COMM gastos de previsión social *m pl*; ~ **standing** *n* WEL posición social *f*; ~ **status** *n* WEL estatus social *m*; ~ **stratification** *n* WEL estratificación social *f*; ~ **studies** *n pl* WEL estudios sociales *m pl*; ~ **system** *n* WEL sistema de bienestar social *m*; ~ **wage** *n* HRM salario social *m*; ~ **wants** *n* WEL preferencias colectivas *f pl*; ~ **welfare** *n* WEL bienestar social *m*; ~ **welfare function** *n* ECON, HRM, WEL función del bienestar social *f*; ~ **worker** *n* HRM trabajador(a) social *m,f*

Social: ~ **Charter** *n* GEN COMM, POL *EC* Carta Social *f*; ~ **Contract** *n* POL Contrato Social *m*; ~ **Development Committee** *n* POL comisión del gobierno británico para el desarrollo social *m*; ~ **Security Administration** *n* POL, WEL Dirección de la Seguridad Social *f*; ~ **Security Act** *n BrE* LAW Ley de Seguridad Social *f*

socialism *n* POL socialismo *m*

socialist *n* POL socialista *mf*; ~ **economy** ECON, POL economía socialista *f*; ~ **market** ECON mercado socialista *m*

Socialist: ~ **Labour Party** *n* POL Partido Laborista Socialista *m*

socialite *n* POL persona mundana *f*

socialization *n* HRM, WEL socialización *f*

society *n* GEN COMM sociedad *f*

Society: ~ **of Automotive Engineers** *n* IND sociedad de ingenieros automotores; ~ **of British Aerospace Companies** *n* (*SBAC*) TRANSP sociedad de compañías aeroespaciales británicas, ≈ Asociación Española de Compañías Aéreas *f* (*AECA*); ~ **for Worldwide Interbank Financial Telecommunications** *n* (*SWIFT*) BANK, COMMS Sociedad para las Telecomunicaciones Financieras Interbancarias Internacionales *f* (*SITF*); ~ **of Industrial and Cost Accountants** *n* (*SICA*) ACC asociación de contables industriales y de costes; ~ **of Motor Manufacturers and Traders** *n* (*SMMT*) IND, TRANSP sociedad de fabricantes y comerciantes de automóviles

sociocultural *adj* S&M, WEL sociocultural

socioeconomic[1] *adj* ECON, S&M, WEL socioeconómico

socioeconomic[2]: ~ **climate** *n* ECON, WEL clima socioeconómico *m*; ~ **groups** *n pl* ECON, S&M, WEL grupo socioeconómico *m*; ~ **status** *n* ECON, WEL posición socioeconómica *f*

sociological: ~ **statistics** *n pl* HRM, MATH estadística sociológica *f*

sociometric *adj* MATH, S&M sociométrico

sociometry *n* MATH, S&M sociometría *f*

socioprofessional: ~ **class** *n* POL categoría socioprofesional *f*

sociotechnical: ~ **system** *n* GEN COMM sistema sociotécnico *m*

soft[1]: ~ **commission** *n* STOCK comisión inferior a lo habitual *f*; ~ **commodity** *n* STOCK mercancía blanda *f*; ~ **copy** *n* COMP imagen de pantalla *f*; ~ **cost** *n* GEN COMM coste suave *m* (*Esp*), costo suave *m* (*AmL*); ~ **cover book** *n* MEDIA libro encuadernado en rústica *m*; ~ **credit** *n* BANK, ECON, FIN crédito blando *m*; ~ **currency** *n* BANK, ECON divisa débil *f*; ~ **dollars** *n* ECON dólares falsos *m pl*; ~ **funding** *n jarg* FIN, POL financiación en condiciones favorables *f*; ~ **goods** *n pl* GEN COMM, S&M bienes de consumo perecederos *m pl*; ~ **keyboard** *n* COMP teclado en función programable *m*; ~ **landing** *n* TRANSP aterrizaje suave *m*; ~ **loan** *n* BANK, ECON, FIN crédito privilegiado *m*, crédito blando *m*; ~ **market** *n jarg* ECON, STOCK mercado débil *m*; ~ **marketing** *n* S&M marketing blando *m*; ~ **modeling** *AmE*, ~ **modelling** *BrE n* ECON modelo flexible *m*; ~ **money** *n* WEL *education* fondos de procedencia desconocida *m pl*; ~ **offer** *n* GEN COMM oferta sin presión *f*; ~ **sectoring** *n* COMP sectorización lógica *f*; ~ **sell** *n* S&M venta por convencimiento *f*, venta por persuasión *f*; ~ **technology** *n* ENVIR tecnología flexible *f*; ~ **top container** *n* TRANSP contenedor de techo abierto *m*

soft[2]: ~~**pedal** *vt infrml* GEN COMM moderar, POL quitar hierro a, restar importancia a

soften up *vt* GEN COMM debilitar

software[1]: ~~**driven** *adj* COMP gestionado por programa

software[2] *n* COMP aplicación informática *f*, programas *m pl*, software *m*, soporte lógico *m*; ~ **application** COMP aplicación de software *f*; ~ **company** COMP empresa de programación *f*; ~ **engineer** COMP, HRM ingeniero(-a) de programación *m,f*; ~ **engineering** COMP ingeniería de programas *f*; ~ **error** COMP error de programa *m*; ~ **house** COMP empresa productora de programas *f*; ~ **language** COMP lenguaje de programación *m*; ~ **package** COMP paquete de programas *m*; ~ **release** COMP versión de un programa *f*; ~ **rot** COMP corrupción de un programa *f*

soil: ~ **bank** *n* ENVIR *agricultural* banco rural *m*; ~ **degradation** *n* ENVIR degradación del suelo *f*

solar: ~ **energy** *n* ENVIR, IND energía solar *f*; ~ **power** *n* ENVIR, IND potencia solar *f*

sold: ~ **daybook** *n* GEN COMM, S&M diario de ventas *m*; ~ **message** *n* TRANSP nota de venta *f*

sole[1] *adj* GEN COMM solo, único; ◆ **with the ~ object of** GEN COMM con el único objeto de

sole[2]: ~ **agency** *n* GEN COMM representación exclusiva *f*; ~ **agent** *n* ECON, GEN COMM, S&M representante único(-a) *m,f*, representante exclusivo(-a) *m,f*; ~ **arbitrator** *n* INS árbitro(-a) único(-a) *m,f*; ~ **bargaining agent** *n* HRM agente exclusivo(-a) de negociación *m,f*; ~ **bargaining rights** *n pl* HRM derechos exclusivos de negociación *m pl*; ~ **director and C.E.O** *n* HRM, MGMNT administrador(a) único(-a) *m,f*; ~ **inventor** *n* PATENTS inventor(a) único(-a) *m,f*; ~ **legatee** *n* LAW legatario(-a) único(-a) *m,f*; ~ **owner** *n* PROP dueño(-a) único(-a) *m,f*; ~ **proprietor** *n* GEN COMM empresario(-a) individual *m,f*, propietario(-a) único *m,f*; ~ **proprietorship** *n* GEN COMM empresa individual *f*; ~ **trader** *n* GEN COMM comerciante individual *mf*

solicitation *n* S&M solicitación *f*

solicitor *n* LAW ≈ abogado(-a) *m,f*, ≈ notario(-a) *m,f*, *bureaucratic transactions* ≈ procurador(a) *m,f*

solid[1] *adj* GEN COMM *argument* sólido, *vote* unánime; ◆ **on ~ ground** GEN COMM sobre una base sólida

solid[2]: ~ **frame securing system** *n* TRANSP *containers* sistema de seguridad de la armadura sólida *m*; ~ **gold** *n* ENVIR oro puro *m*; ~ **line** *n* MATH *on graph* trazado total *m*; ~**-state** *n* GEN COMM estado sólido *m*

solidarism *n* ECON, POL solidarismo *m*

solidarity: ~ **action** *n* HRM acción solidaria *f*

Solow: ~ **residual** *n* ECON residuo de Solow *m*

solus: ~ **position** *n* S&M espacio aislado *m*

solution *n* GEN COMM solución *f*

solve *vt* GEN COMM resolver

solvency *n* ACC, BANK, FIN solvencia *f*; ~ **margin** ACC, FIN margen de solvencia *m*; ~ **ratio** ACC, FIN índice de solvencia *m*, coeficiente de solvencia *m*, proporción de solvencia *f*

solvent[1] *adj* ACC, BANK, FIN, GEN COMM solvente

solvent[2]: ~ **debt** *n* BANK, FIN deuda solvente *f*, deuda exigible *f*

sophisticated[1] *adj* GEN COMM complicado

sophisticated[2]: ~ **market** *n* STOCK mercado de gran complejidad *m*, mercado sofisticado *m*

sophistication *n* GEN COMM complejidad *f*, S&M *of the market* sofisticación *f*

sort *n* COMP clase *f*; ~ **file** COMP fichero de clasificación *m*; ~ **key** COMP clave de clasificación *f*

sort out *vt* GEN COMM seleccionar y ordenar

sorter *n* GEN COMM clasificador(a) *m,f*

sorting *n* COMP clasificación *f*

sought: ~**-after** *adj* GEN COMM solicitado

sound *n* COMP sonido *m*; ~ **check** COMMS prueba de sonido *f*; ~ **currency** ECON moneda solvente *f*; ~ **effects** *n pl* MEDIA efectos especiales sonoros *m pl*; ~ **insulation** COMMS, ENVIR aislamiento sonoro *m*; ~ **pick-up** MEDIA captación *f*, fonocaptor *m*; ~ **track** COMMS banda de sonido *f*; ♦ **on a** ~ **footing** GEN COMM sobre una base sólida

sound out *vt* GEN COMM sondear

soundness: ~ **certificate** *n* BANK, ECON, GEN COMM certificado de solvencia *m*

source *n* COMP, GEN COMM *of funds, information* fuente *f*, informante *mf*; ~ **address** COMMS, COMP dirección de origen *f*; ~ **and application of funds** ACC, FIN origen y aplicación de fondos; ~ **and application of funds statement** ACC, FIN declaración de origen y aplicación de fondos *f*; ~ **of capital** BANK, FIN fuente de capital *f*; ~ **code** COMP código fuente *m*; ~ **computer** COMP computador fuente *m* (*AmL*), computadora fuente *f* (*AmL*), ordenador fuente *m* (*Esp*); ~ **credibility** S&M credibilidad de la fuente *f*; ~ **data** COMP datos de fuente *m pl*; ~ **deduction** FIN deducción en origen *f*; ~ **disk** COMP disco de origen *m*; ~ **and disposition of funds** ACC, FIN origen y destino de los fondos, fuente y disposición de fondos *f*; ~ **document** ACC documento fuente *m*, documento original *m*; ~ **file** COMP archivo fuente *m*; ~ **of funds** ACC, FIN fuente de fondos *f*, fuente de recursos *f*; ~ **of income** TAX fuente de ingresos *f*; ~ **language** COMP, GEN COMM lenguaje fuente *m*; ~ **object** ACC objeto fuente *m*; ~ **program** COMP programa fuente *m*; ~ **tax** TAX impuesto a la fuente *m*

South: ~ **Atlantic rates** *n pl* TRANSP tarifas del Atlántico sur *f pl*; ~ **Pacific rates** *n pl* TRANSP tarifas del Pacífico sur *f pl*

southbound *adj* TRANSP de dirección sur

southern *adj* GEN COMM meridional

sovereign *n* GEN COMM *coin*, POL soberano *m*; ~ **borrower** BANK, FIN prestatario(-a) supremo(-a) *m,f*; ~ **loan** BANK, FIN préstamo supremo *m*; ~ **risk** FIN riesgo soberano *m*; ~ **risk loan** BANK préstamo de riesgo supremo *m*

space *n* COMP *in text*, MEDIA *print* espacio *m*; ~ **arbitrage** GEN COMM arbitraje espacial *m*; ~ **bar** COMP barra de espaciado *f*, barra espaciadora *f*; ~ **broker** S&M corredor(a) de espacio publicitario *m,f* ~ **buying** S&M compra de espacios publicitarios *f*; ~ **rates** *n pl* S&M tarifa por espacio publicitario *f*; ~ **shuttle** TRANSP transbordador espacial *m*; ~ **writer** MEDIA *print* escritor(a) pagado(-a) por líneas *m,f*

spaceman: ~ **economy** *n* ECON economía del despilfarro y la irresponsabilidad

spacer *n* TRANSP espaciador *m*

spacing: ~ **material** *n* MEDIA blanco de relleno *m*

span: ~ **of control** *n* GEN COMM área de control *f*

Spanish: ~ **Chamber of Commerce** *n* (*SCC*) GEN COMM Cámara de Comercio Española *f*; ~ **Register of Shipping** *n* GEN COMM, TRANSP Registro Español de Buques *m*; ~**-speaking world** *n* GEN COMM mundo hispanohablante *m*

SPAR *abbr* (*Standard Portfolio Analysis of Risk*) FIN análisis de riesgo de una cartera estándar *m*

spare: ~ **capacity** *n* ECON, IND capacidad excedente *f*, capacidad sobrante *f*, exceso de capacidad *m*, TRANSP espacio disponible *m*

spares *n pl* IND repuestos *m pl*

spark off *vt* *infrml* GEN COMM causar

sparsely: ~ **populated** *adj* ECON *area* escasamente poblado, de población poco densa

spate *n* GEN COMM aguacero *m*

spatial: ~ **benefit limitation** *n* ECON *Tiebout hypothesis* límite espacial del beneficio *m*; ~ **duopoly** *n* ECON duopolio espacial *m*; ~ **equalization** *n* ECON ecualización espacial *f*, IND igualación de espacios *f*; ~ **monopoly** *n* ECON monopolio espacial *m*; ~ **oligopoly** *n* ECON oligopolio espacial *m*

SPC *abbr* GEN COMM, PATENTS (*Supplementary Protection Certificate*) certificado de protección complementaria *m*

spd *abbr* (*steamer pays dues*) TRANSP derechos pagados de un barco de vapor *m pl*

speaker *n* GEN COMM conferenciante *mf* (*Esp*), conferencista *mf* (*AmL*), orador(a) *m,f*, ponente *mf*

spearhead *n* GEN COMM vanguardia *f*

spearman: ~**'s rank correlation formula** *n* MATH fórmula de correlación por rangos de spearman *f*

spec[1]: ~ **house** *n* PROP inmobiliaria de especulación *f*

spec[2]: **on** ~ *phr* (*on speculation*) GEN COMM por especulación, HRM *job application* en plan aleatorio

special: ~ **accounts** *n pl* ACC cuentas especiales *f pl*; ~ **arbitrage account** *n* STOCK cuenta de arbitraje especial *f*; ~ **arrangements** *n pl* GEN COMM gestiones especiales *f pl*; ~ **assessment** *n* TAX impuesto especial *m*; ~ **bracket firm** *n* BANK firma especializada *f*; ~ **case** *n* LAW juicio incidental *m*; ~ **circumstances** *n pl* GEN COMM circunstancias especiales *f pl*; ~ **clearing** *n* BANK compensación especial *f*; ~ **commercial exchange rate** *n* ECON tipo de cambio comercial especial *m*; ~ **commissioner** *n* BrE TAX *appeals* interventor(a) especial *m,f* (*Esp*), contralor(a) especial *m,f* (*AmL*);

~ **credit facility** *n* BANK línea de crédito especial *f*;
~ **deposit** *n* BANK depósito especial *m*; ~ **district bond**
n FIN, STOCK bono especial de distrito *m*; ~ **drawing**
rights *n pl* BANK, LAW derechos especiales de giro *m pl*
(*DEG*); ~ **economic zone** *n* ECON, POL zona económica
especial *f*; ~ **employment measure** *n* (*SEM*) HRM
medida especial de empleo *f*; ~ **endorsement** *n* BANK
endoso especial *m*; ~ **feature** *n* GEN COMM, S&M
particularidad *f*, característica especial *f*; ~ **fourth-**
class mail *n* COMMS correo de tarifa reducida *m*;
~ **intermediate survey** *n* (*SIS*) TRANSP revisión extraordinaria intermedia *f*; ~ **journal** *n* ACC libro diario
especial *m*; ~ **jury** *n* LAW jurado especial *m*; ~ **meeting**
n GEN COMM, MGMNT reunión extraordinaria *f*; ~ **mis-**
cellaneous account *n* (*SMA*) STOCK cuenta miscelánea
especial *f*; ~ **multiperil insurance** *n* (*SMP*) INS seguro
especial multirriesgo *m*; ~ **non-marketable bonds** *n*
(*SGAT*) STOCK *issued to the Canada Pension Plan*
Investment Fund bonos especiales no negociables *m pl*;
~ **offer** *n* S&M oferta especial *f*, oferta *f*; ~ **position** *n*
S&M posición especial *f*; ~ **provision for losses on**
transborder claims *n* ACC, BANK, FIN provisión especial
para pérdidas fuera del país *f*; ~ **provisions** *n pl* TAX
National Insurance contributions disposiciones especiales *f pl*; ~ **purchase** *n* S&M compra especial *f*;
~ **purpose allotment** *n* GEN COMM asignación para un
fin concreto *f*; ~ **reserve** *n* ACC reserva especial *f*;
~ **situation** *n* GEN COMM situación especial *f*; ~ **survey**
n (*SS*) TRANSP *shipping* inspección extraordinaria *f*,
revisión extraordinaria *f*; ~ **tax bond** *n* STOCK, TAX
bono con bonificación fiscal *m*; ~ **tax rate** *n* TAX tipo
impositivo especial *m*; ~ **terms for the trade** *n pl* GEN
COMM plazos especiales para el negocio *m pl*; ~ **traffic**
notice *n* (*STN*) TRANSP aviso especial de tráfico *m*,
notificación especial de tráfico *f*; ~ **warrant** *n* POL
garantía especial *f*

Special: ~ **Branch** *n* *BrE* LAW servicio policial británico
contra la subversión; ~ **Commissioners** *n pl* *BrE* TAX
interventores especiales *m pl*; ~ **Recovery Capital**
Projects Program *n* *AmE* (*SRCPP*) GEN COMM
programa especial de proyectos de recuperación de
capital *m*

specialist *n* GEN COMM especialista *mf*; ~ **block pur-**
chase and sale STOCK compra-venta en bloque por un
especialista *f*; ~ **electronic book** (*SEB*) STOCK libro
electrónico especializado *m*; ~ **information** GEN COMM
información especializada *f*; ~ **knowledge** GEN COMM,
HRM conocimiento especializado *m*; ~**'s short-sale**
ratio STOCK proporción de venta en descubierto de un
especialista *f*

speciality *n* *BrE* GEN COMM especialidad *f*; ~ **advertising**
BrE S&M publicidad especializada *f*; ~ **goods** *n pl* *BrE*
GEN COMM, S&M artículos de calidad *m pl*, artículos
especializados *m pl*; ~ **retailer** *BrE* S&M minorista
especializado(-a) *m,f*; ~ **salesperson** *BrE* HRM, S&M
vendedor(a) especializado(-a) *m,f*; ~ **selling** *BrE* S&M
venta especializada *f*; ~ **trade** *BrE* S&M comercio
especializado *m*

specialization *n* GEN COMM especialización *f*
specialized[1] *adj* GEN COMM especializado
specialized[2]: ~ **fair** *n* GEN COMM feria especializada *f*
specialize in *vt* GEN COMM especializarse en
specialty *AmE* see *speciality* *BrE*
specie *n* BANK dinero contante *m*; ~**-flow mechanism**
BANK mecanismo de flujo de especie *m*; ~ **point** GEN

COMM puntos numéricos *m pl*; ◆ **in** ~ GEN COMM
payment en especie
specific[1] *adj* GEN COMM específico
specific[2]: ~ **amount** *n* ACC importe específico *m*, GEN
COMM cantidad específica *f*; ~ **commitment** *n* GEN
COMM compromiso específico *m*; ~ **commodity rate** *n*
TRANSP *air freight* tarifa de impuesto específico *f*; ~ **cycle**
n GEN COMM ciclo específico *m*; ~ **duty** *n* IMP/EXP, TAX
derecho específico *m*; ~ **gravity** *n* (*SG*) GEN COMM
gravedad específica *f*; ~ **individual licence** *BrE*, ~ **indi-**
vidual license *AmE* *n* (*SIL*) IMP/EXP, TRANSP licencia
individual específica *f*; ~ **investment loan** *n* (*SIL*)
BANK, FIN préstamo de inversión específico *m*, préstamo específico para inversión *m*; ~ **offer** *n* S&M oferta
específica *f*; ~ **payment** *n* GEN COMM pago específico *m*;
~ **performance** *n* LAW ejecución forzosa *f*, cumplimiento forzado *m*; ~ **provision** *n* ACC, BANK, FIN provisión
específica *f*; ~ **tariff** *n* GEN COMM arancel específico *m*;
~ **tax** *n* IMP/EXP, TAX impuesto específico *m*; ~ **training**
n HRM capacitación específica *f* (*AmL*), entrenamiento
específico *m*, formación específica *f* (*Esp*)
specification *n* GEN COMM especificación *f*; ~ **change**
notice (*SCN*) TRANSP *aviation* aviso de cambio de
condiciones *m*; ~ **of goods** PATENTS descripción de los
productos *f*; ~ **of services** PATENTS descripción de los
servicios *f*; ~ **of total contents** TRANSP desglose del
contenido *m*, especificación del contenido *f*; ◆ **no** ~ **of**
the total contents TRANSP sin especificación del
contenido
specifics *n* BANK productos específicos *m pl*
specified[1] *adj* GEN COMM especificado; ◆ **not elsewhere**
~ (*NES*) GEN COMM no especificado en otro punto
specified[2]: ~ **employer** *n* TAX patrón(a) determinado(-a)
m,f; ~ **financial institution** *n* FIN institución financiera
especificada *f*; ~ **gift** *n* TAX donación determinada *f*;
~ **member** *n* TAX miembro especificado(-a) *m,f*;
~ **percentage** *n* TAX porcentaje especificado *m*;
~ **person** *n* TAX persona especificada *f*; ~ **property** *n*
TAX propiedad especificada *f*; ~ **purpose** *n* TAX
propósito especificado *m*; ~ **purpose accounts** *n pl*
ACC, POL cuentas para fines específicos *f pl*, cuentas
para propósitos específicos *f pl*; ~ **rate** *n* TRANSP tarifa
especificada *f*; ~ **right** *n* TAX derecho especificado *m*;
~ **shareholder** *n* STOCK accionista especificado(-a) *m,f*;
~ **stockholder** *n* STOCK accionista especificado(-a) *m,f*
specify *vt* GEN COMM, PATENTS especificar
specimen: ~ **copy** *n* GEN COMM espécimen *m*; ~ **invoice**
n GEN COMM factura de muestra *f*; ~ **signature** *n* BANK
muestra de firma *f*; ~ **signature card** *n* BANK tarjeta de
muestra de firma *f*
spectacular *n jarg* S&M *mail order merchandising* objeto
tridimensional que se forma al abrir un paquete
spectail *n* STOCK especulador(a)-minorista *m,f*
speculate *vi* GEN COMM especular
speculation *n* GEN COMM especulación *f*; ~ **motive** FIN
finalidad especulativa *f*; ◆ **on** ~ (*on spec*) GEN COMM
por especulación, HRM *job application* en plan aleatorio
speculative[1] *adj* GEN COMM especulativo
speculative[2]: ~ **application** *n* HRM solicitud de trabajo
especulativa *f*; ~ **buying** *n* GEN COMM compra especulativa *f*; ~ **cornering of goods** *n* FIN, GEN COMM
acaparamiento de bienes con fines especulativos *m*;
~ **demand** *n* ECON *for money* demanda monetaria
especulativa *f*; ~ **fund** *n* STOCK fondo especulativo *m*;

~ hoarding of goods *n* FIN, GEN COMM acaparamiento de bienes con fines especulativos *m*; **~ monopolization of goods** *n* FIN, GEN COMM acaparamiento de bienes con fines especulativos *m*; **~ securities** *n pl* STOCK valores especulativos *m pl*; **~ trading** *n* STOCK comercio especulativo *m*

speculator *n* GEN COMM especulador(a) *m,f*

speech: **~ processing** *n* COMP procesador de sonido *m*; **~ recognition** *n* COMP reconocimiento de la voz *m*; **~ recognition software** *n* COMP programa de reconocimiento de la voz *m*, software de reconocimiento de la voz *m*

speed *n* COMP velocidad *f*; **~-up** GEN COMM, HRM *production* aumento de la productividad *m*, aumento de la tasa de producción *m*

speed up *vt* GEN COMM acelerar

spell out *vt* GEN COMM estudiar

spellcheck *n* COMP verificador ortográfico *m*

spellchecker *n* COMP corrector ortográfico *m*

spend *vt* GEN COMM gastar

spending: **~ authority** *n* ECON, POL autoridad del control de gastos *f*, autoridad responsable de gasto *f*; **~ level** *n* GEN COMM nivel de gasto *m*; **~ money** *n* GEN COMM dinero para pequeños gastos *m*; **~ pattern** *n* GEN COMM pauta de gastos *f*; **~ power** *n* GEN COMM poder adquisitivo *m*; **~ spree** *n infrml* GEN COMM exhibición de despilfarro *f*, periodo de derroche *m*; **~ surge** *n* GEN COMM oleada de gastos *f*

spendthrift *adj* GEN COMM pródigo

SPGER *abbr* (*simplified procedure for goods carried by rail*) TRANSP procedimiento simplificado de transporte de mercancias por ferrocarril *m*

sphere *n* GEN COMM esfera *f*; **~ of activity** GEN COMM, HRM, IND campo de actividad *m*, esfera de actividad *f*; ◆ **in a limited ~** GEN COMM en un campo limitado

SPHL *abbr* (*self-propelled hyperbaric lifeboat*) TRANSP bote salvavidas hiperbárico de autopropulsión *m*

spiel *n infrml* GEN COMM, S&M charla *f*

spike[1] *n jarg* STOCK *futures market* clavo *m*

spike[2] *vt jarg* MEDIA *print* descartar

spill: **~-over effect** *n* GEN COMM efecto indirecto *m*, efecto de rebosamiento *m*

spill over *vi* GEN COMM desbordarse

spillage *n* ENVIR vertido *m*

spillover *n* GEN COMM desbordamiento *m*; **~ benefit** ACC beneficio de derramamiento *m*, beneficio de desbordamiento *m*, beneficio indirecto *m*; **~ effect** ACC, ECON, FIN efecto subsidiario *m*

spin[1]: **~-off** *n* ECON transferencia de activo *f*, FIN reparto de acciones *m*, GEN COMM cambio de acciones *m*, transferencia de activo *f*, S&M *effect* beneficios indirectos *m pl*, repercusión *f*; **~-off product** *n* GEN COMM producto secundario *m*

spin[2]: **~ red tape** *phr* ADMIN poner en marcha el papeleo

spin off *vt* ECON derivar

spiral *n* ECON *of prices* espiral *f*

spiralling: **~ inflation** *n* ECON espiral de inflación *f*

spirit: **~ of enterprise** *n* GEN COMM espíritu de empresa *m*

splash *n* MEDIA *print* salpicadura *f*

splinter: **~ group** *n* POL grupo disidente *m*, grupo escindido *m*; **~ union** *n* HRM sindicato fragmentado *m*

splintered: **~ authority** *n* MGMNT autoridad fraccionada *f*

split[1]: **~ charter** *n* TRANSP *air freight* fletamiento dividido *m*; **~ commission** *n* POL comisión dividida *f*; **~ credit sale** *n* S&M venta a crédito partido *f*; **~ dollar life insurance** *n* INS seguro de vida de pago compartido por empleador y empleado *m*; **~-off** *n* GEN COMM reparto de acciones *m*; **~ offering** *n* STOCK emisión escalonada de obligaciones *f*; **~ rating** *n* FIN desdoblamiento de precios *m*; **~ run** *n jarg* S&M *advertising* uso de anuncios ligeramente diferentes en distintas ediciones de un mismo periódico; **~ screen** *n* COMP pantalla dividida *f*; **~-second timing** *n* GEN COMM cronometraje muy exacto *m*; **~ shift** *n* HRM jornada laboral partida *f*; **~ ticket** *n AmE* POL candidatos divididos *m pl*

split[2] *vt* GEN COMM dividir; ◆ **~ the difference** GEN COMM partir la diferencia

split up *vi* GEN COMM *party, meeting* disolverse

splitting: **~ spread** *n* STOCK *option on Eurodollar futures* opción de compra o venta divisible *f*

spoil *vt* GEN COMM arruinar

spoilage *n* GEN COMM chatarra *f*

spoiler *n jarg* POL candidato sin posibilidades de ganar que se presenta para impedir la victoria de su rival

spoils: **~ system** *n AmE* POL sistema de recompensas *m*

spoilt: **~ ballot paper** *n* GEN COMM, HRM, POL papeleta anulada *f*; **~ voting paper** *n* GEN COMM, POL papeleta de voto defectuosa *f*

Spokane: **~ Stock Exchange** *n* STOCK Bolsa de Valores de Spokane *f*

spokesperson *n* GEN COMM portavoz *mf*

sponsor[1] *n* FIN fiador(a) *m,f*; **~ demand** ECON promotor(-a) de demanda *m,f*

sponsor[2] *vt* GEN COMM patrocinar

sponsored: **~ book** *n* S&M libro patrocinado *m*; **~ event** *n* S&M acontecimiento patrocinado *m*; **~ television** *n* MEDIA, S&M televisión patrocinada *f*

sponsorship *n* GEN COMM esponsorización *f*, patrocinio *m*

spontaneous: **~ combustion** *n* TRANSP combustión espontánea *f*; **~ ignition temperature** *n* GEN COMM temperatura de autoinflamación *f*; **~ recall** *n* S&M recuerdo espontáneo *m*

spool[1] *n* COMP bobina *f*; **~ file** COMP fichero de espera *m*

spool[2] *vt* COMP bobinar

spooling *n* COMP integración de E/S *f*, simultaneidad de periféricos *f*

spoon-feed *vt infrml* GEN COMM *information* dar de comer con cuchara

sporadic[1] *adj* GEN COMM, TRANSP esporádico

sporadic[2]: **~ maintenance** *n* GEN COMM mantenimiento esporádico *m*; **~ service** *n* TRANSP servicio de transporte esporádico *m*

sports: **~ event** *n* GEN COMM, LEIS acontecimiento deportivo *m*

Sports: **~ Council** *n* (*SC*) LEIS organismo autónomo de promoción del deporte, ≈ Consejería de Juventud y Deportes *f* (*Esp*)

spot[1] *adj* STOCK al contado

spot[2] *n jarg* MEDIA, S&M *advertising* espacio *m*; **~ business** GEN COMM, S&M venta inmediata *f*; **~ charter** TRANSP flete listo *m*; **~ check** GEN COMM comprobación al azar *f*, comprobación in situ *f*; **~ color** *AmE*, **~ colour** *BrE* S&M color del anuncio *m*; **~ commodity** STOCK producto al contado *m*;

~ **cotton** IND algodón en plaza *m*; ~ **coverage** MEDIA *TV* cobertura local *f*; ~ **credit** BANK, FIN crédito disponible de inmediato *m*, crédito disponible de spot *m*; ~ **currency market** ECON, STOCK mercado de divisas al contado *m*; ~ **delivery** STOCK *futures* entrega inmediata *f*; ~ **delivery month** STOCK mes de entrega más próximo *m*; ~ **exchange rate** ECON tipo de cambio al contado *m*; ~ **lengths** *n pl* MEDIA, S&M duraciones de los espacios publicitarios *f pl*; ~ **market** STOCK mercado al contado *m*; ~ **month** STOCK primer mes de cotización *m*; ~ **position** STOCK posición al contado *f*; ~ **price** GEN COMM cambio al contado *m*, STOCK cotización al contado *f*; ~ **quotation** STOCK cotización inmediata *f*; ~ **rate** STOCK tasa de cambio al contado *f*; ~ **rate spread** STOCK margen de cambio al contado *m*; ~ **recall** S&M recordatorio de anuncio *m*; ~ **trading** ACC, FIN, GEN COMM, STOCK operación de contado *f*; ~ **zoning** PROP división por zonas *f*, planificación localizada *f*; ◆ **on the** ~ GEN COMM en el acto

spotlight *n* GEN COMM proyector de luz concentrada *m*

spousal: ~ **IRA** *n* BANK cuenta de jubilación individual a nombre del cónyugue

spouse *n* TAX consorte *mf*, cónyugue *mf*; ~**'s allowance** TAX deducción por la esposa *f*

spout *n* TRANSP tubo de salida *m*

spread¹ *n* BANK margen bancario *m*, registro en detalle *m*, tipo diferencial *m*, GEN COMM comisión de suscripción *f*, S&M diferencia entre el precio de oferta y demanda *f*, *of stores* extensión *f*, STOCK margen de venta *m*; ~ **effect** ECON efecto de propagación *m*; ~ **order** STOCK orden de compraventa a crédito *f*; ~ **position** STOCK posición diferencial de compraventa *f*; ~ **risk** STOCK riesgo relacionado con el margen *m*; ~ **trading** STOCK *currency market* operación con margen *f*; ~ **traffic** S&M tráfico diseminado *m*

spread² *vt* FIN *repayments* espaciar, INS *risks* espaciar; ◆ ~ **the cost** ACC repartir el coste (*Esp*), repartir el costo (*AmL*); ~ **repayments** GEN COMM espaciar las devoluciones; ~ **the risk** INS repartir el riesgo

spreader *n* TRANSP transportador de contenedores *m*

spreading *n* STOCK difusión *f*; ~ **agreement** STOCK acuerdo sobre margen *m*

spreadover *n jarg* HRM *industrial relations* horario escalonado *m*; ~ **working** *jarg* HRM trabajo escalonado *m*

spreadsheet *n* GEN COMM hoja de cálculo *f*; ~ **program** COMP hoja electrónica *f*

spring: ~ **multi-year operational plan** *n* (*spring MYOP*) FIN, POL plan operativo plurianual de primavera *m*; ~ **multi-year operational plan submission** *n* FIN, POL presentación del plan operativo plurianual de primavera *f*; ~ **tide** *n* TRANSP marea viva *f*

squander *vt* GEN COMM malgastar

square¹ *adj* (*sq*) GEN COMM cuadrado

square²: ~ **brackets** *n pl* COMP, MEDIA *typography* corchetes *m pl*; ~ **foot** *n* GEN COMM pie cuadrado *m*; ~ **footage** *n* GEN COMM, PROP superficie en pies cuadrados *f*; ~ **measure** *n* GEN COMM medida de superficie *f*, medida cuadrada *f*; ~ **mile** *n* GEN COMM milla cuadrada *f*

Square: ~ **Mile** *n* ACC, BANK, FIN, STOCK centro financiero en Londres, la City *f*

squatter: ~**'s rights** *n pl* LAW, PROP derechos del ocupante ilegal *m pl*

squeegee: ~ **agreement** *n jarg* STOCK acuerdo por el cual se garantiza respaldar un valor en un periodo fijado con pérdidas

squeeze¹ *n* ECON *prices* restricción *f*; ~ **clamp** TRANSP *cargo handling* abrazadera a presión *f*

squeeze² *vt* ECON *prices* restringir; ◆ ~ **and freeze** *jarg* ECON presionar y congelar; ~ **the bears** *infrml* STOCK restringir a los bajistas; ~ **the shorts** *jarg* STOCK apretar a los cortos

Sr *abbr* (*schooner*) TRANSP goleta *f*

SR *abbr* (*shipment received*) TRANSP recibo de embarque *m*

SR&CC *abbr* (*strikes, riots and civil commotions*) LAW huelgas, tumultos y desórdenes *f pl*

SRCPP *abbr AmE* (*Special Recovery Capital Projects Program*) GEN COMM programa especial de proyectos de recuperación de capital *m*

SRNA *abbr BrE* (*Shipbuilders and Repairers National Association*) TRANSP asociación nacional de constructores y reparadores de buques

SRO *abbr* GEN COMM (*self-regulatory organization*) organización autorreguladora *f*, (*self-regulating organization*) organización autorregulada *f*

ss *abbr* (*steamship*) TRANSP barco de vapor *m*

SS *abbr* (*special survey*) TRANSP *shipping* revisión extraordinaria *f*, revisión extraordinaria de un buque *f*

SS&C *abbr* TRANSP *shipping* (*same sea and coast*) transporte por el mismo mar y costa *m*, (*same sea and country*) transporte por el mismo mar y país *m*

SSAP *abbr* (*Statement of Standard Accounting Practice*) ACC declaración sobre las normas de práctica contable *f*

SSD *abbr* (*single-sided disk*) COMP disco de una cara *m*

SSDD *abbr* (*single-sided double density*) COMP doble densidad por una cara

SSIA *abbr* (*Shiprepairers and Shipbuilders Independent Association*) TRANSP asociación independiente de reparadores y constructores de buques

SSP *abbr* (*statutory sick pay*) HRM, INS, WEL subsidio de enfermedad obligatorio *m*

SSSI *abbr* (*Site of Special Scientific Interest*) ENVIR lugar de especial interés científico *m*

SST *abbr* (*supplementary service tariff*) TRANSP tarifa adicional por servicio *f*

St. *abbr* (*street*) GEN COMM c/ (*calle*)

St Petersburg: ~ **paradox** *n* ECON paradoja de San Petersburgo *f*

stabex: ~ **system** *n* ECON *agricultural* sistema STABEX *m*

stability *n* GEN COMM estabilidad *f*; ~ **zone** WEL zona de estabilidad *f*

stabilization *n* GEN COMM estabilización *f*; ~ **fund** TAX fondo de estabilización *m*; ~ **policy** ECON *countercyclical* política de estabilización *f*

stabilize 1. *vt* GEN COMM estabilizar; **2.** *vi* GEN COMM estabilizarse

stabilized: ~ **price** *n* ECON precio estabilizado *m*

stabilizer *n* ECON, FIN, POL estabilizador *m*

stable¹ *adj* GEN COMM estable

stable² *n* LEIS cuadra *f*; ~ **equilibrium** ECON equilibrio estable *m*; ~ **market** S&M mercado estable *m*; ~ **rate** TRANSP tarifa de flete estable *f*; ~~**rate funds** *n pl* BANK fondos a interés estable *m pl*

stack[1] *n* COMP *data* pila *f*, IND, TRANSP chimenea *f*
stack[2] *vt* GEN COMM, TRANSP *merchandise* apilar
Stackelberg: **~ duopoly model** *n* ECON modelo duopolista de Stackelberg *m*
stacker *n* TRANSP *of containers* apiladora *f*, cono *m*
stacking *n* GEN COMM, TRANSP apilamiento *m*; **~ of cargo** TRANSP apilamiento de carga *m*; **~ fitting** TRANSP *containers* bastidor *m*
staff[1] *n* GEN COMM, HRM empleados *m pl*, personal *m*, planta *f*, plantilla *f*; **~ appraisal** HRM, MGMNT evaluación del personal *f*; **~ association** HRM asociación de empleados *f*; **~ audit** ACC, HRM auditoría de personal *f*; **~ canteen** HRM restaurante para los empleados *m*; **~ commitment** HRM compromiso del personal *m*; **~ costs** *n pl* ECON, HRM costes de personal *m* (*Esp*), costos de personal *m* (*AmL*); **~ cutback** HRM, MGMNT reducción de personal *f*; **~ department** GEN COMM, HRM departamento de personal *m*; **~ development** HRM, MGMNT desarrollo del personal *m*; **~ forecasting** HRM previsión de la fuerza de trabajo *f*, previsión de personal *f*; **~ incentive** HRM incentivo del personal *m*; **~ inspection** HRM inspección de personal *f*; **~ levy** TAX gravamen del personal *m*; **~ list** HRM relación del personal *f*; **~ management** HRM, MGMNT administración del personal *f*, dirección del personal *f*, gerencia del personal *f*, gestión del personal *f*; **~ manager** HRM, MGMNT gerente de personal *mf*; **~ meeting** GEN COMM claustro *m*; **~ member** HRM miembro en plantilla *mf*; **~ mobility** HRM movilidad del personal *f*; **~ organization** HRM, MGMNT organización del personal *f*; **~ planning** HRM, MGMNT planificación del personal *f*; **~ provident fund** HRM, STOCK fondo de previsión del personal *m*; **~ representative** HRM representante del personal *mf*; **~ resourcing** HRM contratación y gestión del personal *f*; **~ status** HRM situación del personal *f*; **~ strategy** HRM estrategia de personal *f*; **~ training** HRM, MGMNT capacitación de personal *f* (*AmL*), formación de personal *f* (*Esp*); **~ transfer** HRM transferencia de personal *f*; **~ turnover** HRM rotación de personal *f*, rotación de mano obra *f*; **~ welfare fund** HRM, WEL fondo de previsión del personal *m*
staff[2] *vt* HRM *office* dotar de personal
staff up *vt* HRM aumentar la plantilla
staffed *adj* HRM dotado de personal
staffer *n* HRM directivo(-a) de personal *m,f*
staffing *n* HRM dotación de personal *f*; **~ level** HRM dotación de personal *f*, nivel de empleo de personal *m*
stag *n* GEN COMM, STOCK especulador(a) *m,f*, ciervo *m*
stage[1] *n* GEN COMM *of negotiations* escenario *m*, etapa *f*, fase *f*; **~ of completion** IND fase de acabado *f*; **~ of economic growth** ECON fase de crecimiento económico *f*; **~ payment** BANK, FIN pago escalonado *m*; **~ of transition** ECON *of market* etapa de transición *f*; ♦ **at some ~** GEN COMM en determinada etapa
stage[2] *vt* GEN COMM, MGMNT *conference* organizar, preparar, presentar; ♦ **~ a go-slow** *jarg* HRM organizar una huelga de celo; **~ a strike** HRM organizar una huelga; **~ a walkout** HRM organizar una huelga
staged: **~ agreement** *n* HRM acuerdo organizado *m*, contrato por etapas *m*
stages[1]: **~ theory** *n* ECON teoría de etapas *f*
stages[2]: **in ~** *phr* GEN COMM por etapas
stagflation *n* ECON estanflación *f*, stagflación *f*

stagger[1] *n* GEN COMM escalonamiento *m*
stagger[2] *vt* GEN COMM *costs* escalonar
staggered: **~ board of directors** *n* HRM, MGMNT consejo de administración escalonado *m*; **~ election** *n* POL elección escalonada *f*; **~ holidays** *n pl BrE* (*cf staggered vacations AmE*) HRM, LEIS vacaciones escalonadas *f pl*; **~ vacations** *n pl AmE* (*cf staggered holidays BrE*) HRM, LEIS vacaciones escalonadas *f pl*
staggering *n infrml* GEN COMM bamboleo *m*; **~ budget deficit** GEN COMM déficit presupuestario creciente *m*; **~ of holidays** *BrE* (*cf staggering of vacations AmE*) HRM escalonamiento de las vacaciones *m*; **~ maturities** *n pl* STOCK vencimientos escalonados *m pl*; **~ of vacations** *AmE* (*cf staggering of holidays BrE*) HRM escalonamiento de las vacaciones *m*
staggism *n* STOCK suscripción inflada *f*
staging *n* HRM puesta en escena *f*
stagnant *adj* ECON, GEN COMM estancado
stagnate *vi* ECON, GEN COMM estancarse
stagnation *n* ECON, GEN COMM estagnación *f*, estancamiento *f*
STAGs *abbr BrE* (*sterling transferable accruing government securities*) STOCK bonos del Tesoro en libras esterlinas acumulables y transferibles
stainless: **~ steel** *n* IND acero inoxidable *m*
stake *n* FIN *in company* riesgo *m*; **~ in a bank** BANK interés en un banco *m*; **~ in a business** GEN COMM participación en una empresa *f*; **~ in property** *BrE* (*cf stake in real estate AmE*) PROP participación inmobiliaria *f*; **~ in real estate** *AmE* (*cf stake in property BrE*) PROP participación inmobiliaria *f*
stakeholder *n* GEN COMM depositario(-a) de una apuesta *m,f*
stakes: **the ~ are high** *phr* GEN COMM los riesgos son altos
stakrak: **~ cargo unit** *n* TRANSP unidad de carga stakrak *f*
stale: **~ bill of lading** *n* BANK factura de conocimiento no traspasable *f*, letra de cambio de conocimiento no traspasable *f*, IMP/EXP, TRANSP conocimiento de embarque tardío *m*, conocimiento de embarque caducado *m*; **~ bull** *n* STOCK alcista rezagado *m*; **~ check** *AmE*, **~ cheque** *BrE* BANK, FIN cheque no presentado a tiempo al cobro *m*, cheque prescrito *m*; **~-dated check** *AmE*, **~-dated cheque** *BrE* *n* BANK, FIN cheque de fecha atrasada *m*; **~ market** *n* GEN COMM mercado desanimado *m*
stalemate *n* GEN COMM paralización *f*
stalemated *adj* GEN COMM *talks* estancado
stalls *n pl* LEIS *cinema, theatre* butacas *f pl*
stamp[1] *n* ADMIN *seal* sello *m*, COMMS *postage* sello *m* (*Esp*), sello de correo *m* (*Esp*), estampilla *f* (*AmL*); **~ duty** *BrE* TAX sellado fiscal *m*; **~ pad** GEN COMM tampón para sellos *m*
stamp[2] *vt* GEN COMM estampar, imprimir; ♦ **~ the date** ADMIN *on form* estampar la fecha
stamp out *vt* ECON *inflation* eliminar
stamped: **~-addressed envelope** *n* (*s.a.e.*) COMMS sobre con la dirección del remitente y sello
stampede *n* STOCK pánico *m*
stamping: **~ machine** *n* ADMIN, COMMS máquina estampilladora *f*, máquina expendedora de sellos *f*
stance *n* GEN COMM *on issue* postura *f*

stand[1]: **~-alone** *adj* COMP *computer, system* autónomo; **~-by** *adj* HRM *duty* de reserva, sustitutivo, en alerta

stand[2] *n jarg* S&M *advertising* expositor *m*, *at exhibition* stand *m*; **~ alone cost** *BrE* (*cf constrained market pricing AmE*) ECON coste autónomo *m* (*Esp*), costo autónomo *m* (*AmL*), fijación restrictiva de precios de mercado *f*; **~-alone system** COMP sistema autónomo *m*; **~-in** HRM suplente *mf*, sustituto(-a) *m,f*

stand[3] **1.** *vt* GEN COMM estar vigente; **2.** *vi* GEN COMM *offer, price, bid* mantenerse; ◆ **~ the acid test of competition** GEN COMM pasar la prueba de fuego de la competencia; **~ as guarantor for sb** FIN servir como garante de alguien; **~ at a discount** STOCK mantenerse un descuento; **~ at a premium** STOCK mantenerse una prima de emisión; **~ the cost of** GEN COMM sufragar los gastos de; **~ firm** GEN COMM mantenerse firme, no retroceder; **~ firm in the belief that** GEN COMM mantenerse firme en la creencia de que; **~ for election** GEN COMM, POL presentarse para la elección; **~ for sthg** GEN COMM *initials* representar algo; **~ for the committee** GEN COMM representar al comité; **~ good** STOCK *sale* resultar aceptable; **~ a good chance of** GEN COMM tener muchas posibilidades de; **~ a loss** GEN COMM asumir una pérdida; **~ one's ground** GEN COMM mantenerse en sus trece; **~ surety** BANK mantener la seguridad; **~ surety for sb** BANK prestar una fianza a alguien

stand by *vi BrE* HRM *on alert* estar a la espectativa, estar presente

stand down *vi* POL retirarse, ceder

stand in: **~ for sb** *vi* HRM sustituir a alguien

stand off *vt* HRM dejar sin trabajo

stand out: **~ for** *vi* GEN COMM insistir en

stand over *vi* GEN COMM quedar pendiente

stand up *vi* GEN COMM *argument* convencer; ◆ **~ for** GEN COMM defender; **the case did not ~ in court** LAW la acusación no se mantuvo en el tribunal

standage: **~ area** *n* TRANSP área de depósito *f*

standard[1] *adj* COMP, GEN COMM estándar; **~-rated** TAX *VAT* gravado con la tarifa vigente; ◆ **of ~-size** COMP de talla estándar; **it is ~ practice to do so** GEN COMM es la práctica habitual

standard[2] *n* (*Std*) GEN COMM tipo *m*, norma *f*, estándar *m*, *of measurement* patrón *m*; **~ agreement** GEN COMM acuerdo estándar *m*; **~ allotment** POL asignación estándar *f*; **~ code** GEN COMM código estándar *m*; **~ commodity** STOCK mercancía estándar *f*; **~ cost** GEN COMM coste estándar *m* (*Esp*), coste normalizado *m* (*Esp*), costo estándar *m* (*AmL*), costo normalizado *m* (*AmL*); **~ cost accounting** ACC, GEN COMM contabilidad de costes normalizados *f* (*Esp*), contabilidad de costos normalizados *f* (*AmL*); **~-cost system** GEN COMM sistema de coste estándar *m* (*Esp*), sistema de costo estándar *m* (*AmL*); **~ costing** ACC, FIN determinación de costes estándar *f* (*Esp*), determinación de costos estándar *f* (*AmL*); **~ deduction** TAX deducción estándar *f*, deducción global *f*; **~ deviation** FIN, MATH desviación típica *f*; **~ directory of advertisers** S&M guía estándar de anunciantes; **~ of equalization** GEN COMM norma de compensación *f*; **~ error** MATH error típico *m*; **~ estimate error** MATH error típico de la estimación *m*; **~ fire policy** INS póliza de incendio *f*; **~ freight trade classification** (*SFTC*) TRANSP clasificación normalizada de mercancías de flete *f*; **~ grade** GEN COMM tipo

normalizado *m*; **~ individual income tax** TAX impuesto normalizado sobre la renta de las personas físicas *m*; **~ industrial classification** (*SIC*) IND clasificación industrial común *f*, clasificación industrial estándar *f*; **~ industrial classification system** IND sistema normalizado de clasificación industrial *m*; **~ letter** S&M carta estándar *f*; **~ of living** ECON, WEL nivel de vida *m*; **~ mean error** MATH error típico de la media *m*; **~ object** POL objeto normalizado *m*; **~ object code** POL código de objeto normalizado *m*; **~ object of expenditure** POL partida ordinaria de gasto *f*; **~ object of revenue** POL partida ordinaria de ingresos *f*; **~ operating procedure** (*s.o.p.*) GEN COMM reglas permanentes del servicio *f pl*; **~ performance** HRM rendimiento normal *m*; **~ and practice** *n pl* MEDIA norma y uso *f*; **~ price** ECON, GEN COMM, S&M precio estándar *m*, precio corriente *m*; **~ rate of interest** *BrE* TAX tipo de interés vigente *m*; **~-rate tax** TAX impuesto de tipo estándar *m*; **~ shipping note** IMP/EXP, TRANSP aviso de embarque normalizado *m*, talón de embarque normalizado *m*; **~ slip** TRANSP *shipping* borderó normalizado *m*; **~ specimen signature card** BANK tarjeta de muestra de firma normalizada *f*; **~ tax** TAX impuesto de tipo normal *m*; **~ time** GEN COMM, HRM hora legal *f*; **~ of value clause** INS, LAW cláusula de actualización de precio *f*; ◆ **be up to ~** GEN COMM, HRM ser del nivel requerido

Standard: **~ Interchange Facilities** *n pl* (*SIT*) TRANSP instalaciones de intercambio normalizadas *f pl*; **~ International Trade Classification** *n* (*SITC*) GEN COMM Clasificación Normativa para el Comercio Internacional *f*; **~ Metropolitan Statistical Area** *n* (*SMSA*) MATH zona estadística metropolitana normalizada *f*; **~ Portfolio Analysis of Risk** *n* (*SPAR*) FIN análisis de riesgo de una cartera estándar *m*; **~ Spending Assessment** *n* (*SSA*) FIN tasa de gastos estándar *f*

standardization *n* GEN COMM estandarización *f*, normalización *f*, tipificación *f*; **~ agreement** GEN COMM acuerdo de normalización *m*

standardize *vt* GEN COMM normalizar, estandarizar, uniformar, LAW uniformar

standardized[1] *adj* GEN COMM normalizado

standardized[2]: **~ sales presentation** *n* S&M presentación de ventas estandarizada *f*

standardizing *adj* GEN COMM estandarizante

standby[1]: **on ~** *adj* COMP en reposo

standby[2]: **~ agreement** *n* GEN COMM acuerdo contingente *m*; **~ charges** *n pl* BANK cargos por mantenimiento *m pl*; **~ control** *n* GEN COMM control provisional *m*; **~ credit** *n* BANK crédito de disposición inmediata *m*, crédito de reserva *m*; **~ facility** *n* BANK línea de disposición inmediata *f*; **~ line of credit** *n* BANK línea de crédito de contingencia *f*; **~ loan** *n* BANK, FIN préstamo contingente *m*; **~ power plant** *n* IND planta eléctrica de reserva *f*; **~ rate** *n BrE* HRM tasa de relevo *f*; **~ ticket** *n* TRANSP billete en lista de espera *m*; **~ underwriter** *n* FIN *securities, lending* suscriptor(a) supletorio(-a) *m,f*

standfirst *n jarg* MEDIA *print* prefacio *m*

standing *n* GEN COMM *reputation* crédito *m*; **~ advance** ACC, BANK anticipo fijo *m*; **~ authorization** IMP/EXP autorización permanente *f*; **~ committee** POL *European Parliament* comisión permanente *f*; **~ deposit** IMP/EXP depósito permanente *m*; **~ expenses** *n pl* ACC, GEN COMM gastos generales *m pl*; **~ order** *BrE* BANK orden permanente *f*; ~ **procedure** GEN COMM procedimiento vigente *m*; ~ **travel advance** GEN COMM anticipo fijo para viajes *m*

Standing: ~ **Committee on Miscellaneous Estimates** *n* POL comité permanente de estimación; ~ **Committee on Public Accounts** *n* POL comité permanente de cuentas públicas

standoff *n* HRM punto muerto *m*

stands *n pl jarg* STOCK tenderetes *m pl*

standstill: ~ **agreement** *n* FIN, GEN COMM moratoria *f*

staple: ~ **commodity** *n* ECON bien de primera necesidad *m*; ~ **export** *n* IMP/EXP exportación de materias primas *f*; ~ **matter** *n* HRM asunto principal *m*; ~ **product** *n* GEN COMM, S&M producto principal *m*; ~ **stock** *n* GEN COMM existencias de productos básicos *f pl*

stapler *n* GEN COMM grapadora *f*

star: ~ **network** *n* COMP red en estrella *f*; ~ **product** *n* S&M producto estrella *m*

starboard: ~ **side** *n* (*S*) TRANSP *shipping* estribor *m*

starch: ~ **ratings** *n pl* S&M método para evaluar la eficacia de la publicidad

start[1] *n* COMP *file* principio *m*, *machine, peripheral* arranque *m*, ECON, GEN COMM arranque *m*; ~ **bit** COMP bitio de inicio *m*; ~**-up** ECON, GEN COMM, STOCK arranque *m*, *venture capital* puesta en marcha *f*; ~**-up capital** FIN capital de arranque *m*; ~**-up costs** *n pl* ACC, ECON, FIN costes de puesta en marcha *m pl* (*Esp*), costos de puesta en marcha *m pl* (*AmL*)

start[2] **1.** *vt* ECON, GEN COMM *firm, company* arrancar; ~ **up** ECON, GEN COMM *firm, company* arrancar; ◆ ~ **an entry** ACC abrir un asiento contable, registrar una escritura; ~ **from scratch** GEN COMM empezar desde cero; ~ **proceedings** LAW abrir un expediente; ~ **sb off as** HRM iniciar a alguien en; **2.** *vi* GEN COMM empezar; ◆ ~ **in business** GEN COMM iniciarse en los negocios

starter: ~ **home** *n* PROP primera vivienda *f*

starting: ~ **point** *n* GEN COMM punto de partida *m*; ~ **price** *n* STOCK precio inicial *m*; ~ **salary** *n* IIRM salario inicial *m*, sueldo inicial *m*; ~ **wage** *n* HRM salario inicial *m*

state[1]: ~**-aided** *adj* POL, WEL subvencionado por el Estado; ~**-of-the-art** *adj* GEN COMM, IND de vanguardia, moderno, vanguardista, *technology* de punta (*AmL*), puntera (*Esp*); ~**-owned** *adj* IND estatal

state[2] *n* COMP, GEN COMM, POL estado *m*; ~ **of affairs** GEN COMM estado de cosas *m*; ~ **assistance** WEL ayuda estatal *f*; ~ **bonds** STOCK bonos del estado *m pl*; ~ **capitalism** ECON, IND, POL capitalismo de Estado *m*; ~ **control** ECON, POL control estatal *m*, control del Estado *m*; ~ **of the economy** ECON estado de la economía *m*; ~ **of emergency** POL estado de excepción *m*; ~ **enterprise** ECON empresa estatal *f*; ~ **government tribunal** HRM tribunal oficial del Estado *m*; ~ **intervention** ECON, POL intervención estatal *f*; ~ **monopoly capitalism** ECON monopolio capitalista del Estado *m*; ~**-owned bank** BANK banca estatal *f*; ~ **ownership** ECON, POL propiedad estatal *f*; ~ **pension** HRM, WEL pensión del Estado *f*; ~ **of registry** TRANSP país de registro *m*; ~ **school** *BrE* (*cf public school AmE*) GEN COMM escuela del estado *f*, escuela pública *f*; ~ **subsidy** ECON, POL, WEL subsidio estatal *m*; ~ **tax** TAX impuesto estatal *m*; ~ **theory** ECON teoría de estado *f*; ◆ **in a ~ of neglect** GEN COMM descuidado

state[3] *vt* GEN COMM declarar; ◆ ~ **categorically** GEN COMM exponer categóricamente; ~ **the obvious** GEN COMM exponer lo obvio

State: ~ **Earnings Related Pension Scheme** *n BrE* (*SERPS*) ECON, WEL plan estatal de pensiones

stated: ~ **capital** *n* GEN COMM capital declarado *m*, capital establecido *m*; ~ **value** *n* ACC valor declarado *m*

stateless: ~ **currency** *n* ECON moneda sin respaldo estatal *f*

statement *n* ACC balance *m*, estado contable *m*, informe *m*, memoria *f*, COMP instrucción *f*, FIN balance *m*, GEN COMM memoria *f*, LAW alegato *m*, declaración *f*; ~ **of account** GEN COMM estado de cuenta *m*; ~ **of affairs** BANK *in bankruptcy*, GEN COMM balance de liquidación *m*; ~ **analysis** ACC análisis de balances *m*, análisis de estados contables *m pl*; ~ **of assets and liabilities** ACC balance de ejercicio *m*, estado de activos y pasivos *m*; ~ **of claim** LAW cuerpo de la demanda *m*; ~ **of condition** BANK, FIN estado de situación *m*; ~ **of earnings** ACC estado de ganancias *m*; ~ **of financial position** ACC estado de posición financiera *m*; ~ **in lieu of prospectus** STOCK informe en lugar del folleto de emisión *m* (*Esp*), reporte crediticio *m* (*AmL*); ~ **of income** ACC cuenta de pérdidas y ganancias *f*, estado de resultados *m*; ~ **of income and expenditure** ACC balance de origen y aplicación de fondos *m*; ~ **of income and expenses** ACC estado de ingresos y gastos *m*; ~ **of instruments issued** BANK situación de los instrumentos emitidos *f*; ~ **of objectives** MGMNT, STOCK declaración de objetivos *f*; ~ **of prosecution** LAW declaración de la acusación *f*; ~ **of terms and conditions** HRM declaración de condiciones *f*; ~ **of witness** LAW declaración de un testigo *f*; ◆ **as per ~** BANK como está establecido

Statement: ~ **of Standard Accounting Practice** *n* (*SSAP*) ACC declaración sobre las normas de práctica contable *f*

static[1] *adj* ECON, GEN COMM *output, prices* estático

static[2]: ~ **method** *n* ACC método estático *m*; ~ **model** *n* ECON modelo estático *m*; ~ **risk** *n* MATH *statistics* riesgo estático *m*

station *n* (*S*) COMP, TRANSP estación *f* (*S*); ~ **break** *AmE* (*cf commercial break BrE*) MEDIA *advertising*, S&M espacio publicitario *m*, pausa para la publicidad *f*; ~ **price** GEN COMM precio según la categoría *m*; ~ **time** GEN COMM, MEDIA *broadcast* hora de salida *f*

stationary: ~ **state** *n* ECON estado estacionario *m*

stationer *n* GEN COMM papelero *m*

stationery *n* ADMIN, GEN COMM papelería *f*, artículos de escritorio *m pl*

stationmaster *n* TRANSP jefe(-a) de estación *m,f*

statistical[1] *adj* MATH estadístico

statistical[2]: ~ **control** *n* MATH control estadístico *m*; ~ **inference** *n* MATH inferencia estadística *f*; ~ **modeling** *AmE*, ~ **modelling** *BrE n* MATH modelación estadística *f*, representación con modelo estadístico *f*; ~ **population** *n* MATH población estadística *f*; ~ **process control** *n* MATH control del proceso estadístico *m*; ~ **quality control** *n* (*SQC*) MATH control estadístico de la calidad *m*; ~ **return** *n* TAX *VAT* declaración estadística *f*; ~ **returns** *n pl* MATH datos estadísticos *m pl*; ~ **sampling** *n* MATH, S&M muestreo estadístico *m*; ~ **significance** *n* MATH importancia estadística *f*; ~ **software** *n* COMP, MATH programa de estadística *m*, software de estadística *m*; ~ **spread** *n* MATH dispersión estadística *f*, margen estadístico *m*

statistically: ~ **significant** *adj* MATH estadísticamente significativo

statistician *n* MATH estadístico(-a) *m,f*

statistics[1] *n* MATH *as discipline* estadística *f*

statistics[2] *n pl* GEN COMM *figures* estadísticas *f pl*

status *n* COMP estado *m*, GEN COMM estatus *m*, LAW estado legal *m*; ~ **bar** COMP barra de estado *f*; ~ **information** GEN COMM información de prestigio *f*; ~ **inquiry** BANK, GEN COMM, S&M petición de informes sobre créditos *f*; ~ **line** COMP línea de condición *f*; ~ **offender** *AmE* (*cf young offender BrE*) LAW delincuente juvenil internado en un centro de protección de menores; ~ **quo clause** HRM cláusula de status quo *f*; ~ **report** GEN COMM informe sobre la labor realizada *m* (*Esp*), reporte sobre la labor realizada *m* (*AmL*), MGMNT informe de la situación *m* (*Esp*), reporte de la situación *m* (*AmL*), reporte de la condición *m* (*AmL*), reporte del estado *m* (*AmL*); ~ **seeker** GEN COMM persona que busca cierta posición social *f*; ~ **symbol** GEN COMM símbolo de prestigio *m*

statute *n* LAW ley parlamentaria *f*; ~ **book** LAW códigos legales *m pl*; ~ **of frauds** LAW requisito de hacer constar un acto jurídico por escrito; ~ **law** LAW derecho parlamentario *m*; ~ **of limitation of action** LAW ley de prescripción de acciones *f*; ~ **of limitations** LAW ley de exención de derechos *f*, ley de prescripción *f*

statutory[1] *adj* LAW estatutario, obligatorio; ◆ **have** ~ **effect** LAW tener efecto legal

statutory[2]: ~ **accounts** *n pl* ACC cuentas estatutarias *f pl*, cuentas obligatorias *f pl*, cuentas reglamentarias *f pl*; ~ **allocation** *n* POL asignación reglamentaria *f*; ~ **appropriation** *n* POL asignación reglamentaria *f*; ~ **appropriations** *n pl* LAW apropiaciones legales *f pl*; ~ **audit** *n* ACC auditoría de cuentas obligatoria *f*, auditoría legal *f*; ~ **authority** *n* POL autoridad competente *f*; ~ **body** *n* LAW organismo legal *m*; ~ **books** *n pl* LAW libros legales *m pl*; ~ **company** *n* GEN COMM, LAW empresa pública creada por ley *f*; ~ **exclusion** *n* INS exclusión estatutaria *f*, exclusión legal *f*; ~ **exemption** *n* LAW exención establecida por la ley *f*; ~ **expenditure** *n* ECON, POL gasto estatutario *m*, gastos reglamentarios *m pl*; ~ **foreclosure** *n* LAW ejecución hipotecaria estatutaria *f*; ~ **holidays** *n pl BrE* (*cf statutory vacations AmE*) GEN COMM, HRM vacaciones establecidas *f pl*; ~ **immunities** *n pl* HRM, LAW inmunidad legal *f*, *trade union* inmunidades sindicales *f pl*; ~ **incidence** *n* TAX incidencia reglamentaria *f*; ~ **instrument** *n* LAW instrumento legal *m*; ~ **investment** *n* FIN inversión reglamentaria *f*; ~ **item** *n* POL cuestión estatutaria *f*; ~ **lien** *n* TAX gravamen estatutario *m*; ~ **meeting** *n* LAW junta constitutiva *f*; ~ **merger** *n* LAW absorción de una compañía amparada por la ley *f*; ~ **minimum wage** *n* ECON, HRM, LAW salario mínimo legal *m*; ~ **notice** *n* LAW notificación legal *f*; ~ **obligation** *n* LAW obligación legal *f*; ~ **policy** *n* HRM, LAW política legal *f*; ~ **program** *AmE*, ~ **programme** *BrE* *n* POL programa estatutario *m*, programa legal *m*; ~ **rate** *n* TAX tipo legal *m*; ~ **report** *n* GEN COMM informe legal *m* (*Esp*), reporte legal *m* (*AmL*); ~ **requirement** *n* LAW, POL requisito legal *m*; ~ **right** *n* LAW derecho legal *m*; ~ **sick pay** *n* (*SSP*) HRM, INS, WEL subsidio de enfermedad obligatorio *m*; ~ **tax rate** *n* TAX tipo impositivo legal *m*; ~ **vacations** *n pl AmE* (*cf statutory holidays BrE*) GEN

COMM vacaciones establecidas *f pl*; ~ **vote** *n* POL capítulo presupuestario obligatorio *m*; ~ **voting** *n* LAW voto obligatorio *m*

stay[1]: ~ **of appeal** *n* LAW suspensión de la apelación *f*; **~-in strike** *n* ECON, HRM huelga de brazos caídos *f*; **~-out strike** *n* ECON, HRM huelga de ausencia en el puesto de trabajo *f*

stay[2]: ~ **in-the-money** *phr* STOCK mantenerse indiferente, permanecer en un valor

stay out *vi* HRM *on strike* estar en huelga

staying: ~ **power** *n* FIN resistencia *f*

stck *abbr* (*stock*) GEN COMM *shares* acción *f*, valor *m*, *supplies* existencias *f pl*, MGMNT estocaje *m*, estoraje *m*

stcks *abbr* (*stocks*) GEN COMM capital *m*, *shares* acciones *f pl*, *supplies* existencias *f pl*

Std *abbr* (*standard*) GEN COMM estándar *m*, norma *f*, tipo *m*, *measurement* patrón *m*, LAW tipo *m*

steadily *adv* GEN COMM constantemente

steady[1] *adj* GEN COMM estable

steady[2]: ~ **growth** *n* ECON crecimiento constante *m*, crecimiento sostenido *m*; **~-growth method** *n* ECON método de crecimiento sostenido *m*; ~ **state economy** *n* ECON economía constante *f*; ~ **state equilibrium** *n* ECON equilibrio sostenido *m*

steadying: ~ **factor** *n* ECON factor estabilizador *m*

steam *n* (*STM*) TRANSP vapor *m*, vapor de agua *m*

steamboat *n* TRANSP barco de vapor *m*

steamer: **any one** ~ *phr* (*AOS*) INS *marine*, TRANSP cualquier vapor *m*; ~ **pays dues** *phr* (*spd*) TRANSP *shipping* derechos pagados de un barco de vapor *m pl*

steamroller[1] *n* IND apisonadora *f* (*Esp*), aplanadora *f* (*AmL*)

steamroller[2] *vt* GEN COMM *project* imponer

steamship *n* (*ss*) TRANSP barco de vapor *m*

steel *n* ENVIR, IND acero *m*; **~-collar worker** HRM robot *m*; ~ **cover** TRANSP tapa de acero *f*; ~ **industry** ECON, IND industria del acero *f*; **~-intensive production** IND producción con utilización intensiva de acero *f*; ~ **securities** *n pl* STOCK valores seguros *m pl*; ~ **terminal** TRANSP estación de carga del acero *f*

steelworker *n* HRM, IND obrero(-a) de acería *m,f*

steelworks *n pl* IND acería *f*

steep *adj* ECON exorbitante, tenaz

steepen *vi* MATH *curve* pronunciar

steeple *n* TRANSP torre *f*

steeply *adv* GEN COMM vertiginosamente

steering *n* LAW gobierno *m*, PROP dirección *f*; ~ **committee** BANK, FIN *rescheduling of debt* comité directivo de cuerpo legislativo *m*; ~ **system** TRANSP sistema de dirección *m*; ~ **wheel** TRANSP volante *m*

stellage: ~ **straddle option** *n* STOCK opción sobre posición mixta stellage *f*

stem from *vt* GEN COMM provenir de

stencil *vt* ADMIN hacer un cliché, imprimir con plantilla

stenographer *n* ADMIN, HRM estenógrafo(-a) *m,f*, taquígrafo(-a) *m,f*

stenography *n* ADMIN, HRM estenografía *f*, taquigrafía *f*

step[1]: ~ **by step** *adj* COMP *program, operation*, GEN COMM paso a paso

step[2]: ~ **transaction** *n* TAX transacción en planos *f*; **~-up lease** *n* FIN alquiler progresivo *m*; **~-up loan** *n* BANK préstamo ampliado *m*

step[3]: **~ over the mark** *phr* HRM saltarse las normas

step back *vi* GEN COMM retroceder

step in *vi infrml* GEN COMM intervenir

step up *vt* GEN COMM *increase* elevar

STEP *abbr* (*Science and Technology for Environmental Protection Programme*) ENVIR programa ciencia y tecnología para la protección medioambiental *f*

stepped[1] *adj* GEN COMM escalonado

stepped[2]: **~ bond** *n* STOCK bono de interés por etapas *m*; **~-up basis** *n* TAX base gradual *f*

steps: **~ method** *n* COMP método de pasos *m*

sterilization *n* FIN esterilización *f*

sterling: **~ balance** *n* BANK, ECON, FIN reserva en libras esterlinas *f*; **~ commercial paper** *n* (*SCP*) BANK, STOCK papel comercial en esterlinas *m*; **~ commercial paper market** *n* (*SCP market*) BANK, STOCK mercado de papel comercial en libras esterlinas *m*; **~ transferable accruing government securities** *n* BrE (*STAGs*) STOCK bonos del Tesoro en esterlinas acumulables y transferibles; **~ warrant into gilt edged stock** *n* BrE (*SWING*) BANK, STOCK opción de compra o venta de un título de deuda pública

Sterling: **~ Area** *n* FIN zona de la libra esterlina *f*

stevedore *n* (*stvdr*) HRM, TRANSP alijador(a) *m,f* (*AmL*), estibador(a) *m,f* (*Esp*)

stevedoring: **~ department** *n* TRANSP departamento de estiba y desestiba *m*; **~ gang** *n* GEN COMM, HRM, TRANSP estibadores *m pl* (*Esp*), alijadores *m pl* (*AmL*)

steward *n* LEIS, TRANSP auxiliar de vuelo *mf*

stewardship *n* ADMIN administración *f* (*admón.*)

stick[1]: **~-on label** *n* COMMS etiqueta adhesiva *f*

stick[2]: **~ no bills** *phr* S&M *advertising* prohibido pegar carteles

sticking: **~ point** *n* GEN COMM punto de retención *m*

sticky[1] *adj jarg* GEN COMM pegajoso

sticky[2]: **~ deal** *n* STOCK operación difícil *f*; **~ price** *n* ECON *liquidity trap* precio rígido *m*

stiff: **~ competition** *n* ECON competencia dura *f*; **~ vessel** *n* TRANSP *with low centre of gravity* buque celoso *m*, buque duro *m*

still *adj* S&M fijo

stillage *n* TRANSP pequeña plataforma portátil *f*

stimulate *vt* GEN COMM *sales* estimular

stimulating *adj* GEN COMM estimulante

stimulative: **~ measure** *n* ECON medida estimulante *f*

stimulus *n* GEN COMM estímulo *m*; ◆ **be a ~ for exports** IMP/EXP ser un estímulo para las exportaciones

stint *n* GEN COMM periodo *m*

stipulate *vt* GEN COMM estipular

stk *abbr* (*stock*) GEN COMM *shares* acción *f*, valor *m*

stk. *abbr* (*stock exchange*) GEN COMM bolsa de comercio *f*, bolsa de valores *f*

stks *abbr* (*stocks*) GEN COMM capital *m*, *shares* acciones *f pl*

STM *abbr* (*steam*) TRANSP vapor *m*, vapor de agua *m*

STN *abbr* (*special traffic notice*) TRANSP aviso especial de tráfico *m*, notificación especial de tráfico *f*

stochastic[1] *adj* GEN COMM, MATH, MGMNT estocástico

stochastic[2]: **~ process** *n* GEN COMM proceso estocástico *m*; **~ simulation** *n* MGMNT simulación estocástica *f*; **~ term** *n* MATH *statistics* término estocástico *m*

stock[1]: **~-exchange** *adj* STOCK bursátil; **~-market** *adj* STOCK bursátil

stock[2] *n* GEN COMM *supplies* existencias *f pl*, (*stk*) *shares* acción *f*, valor *m*, MGMNT estocaje *m*, estoraje *m*; **~ adjustment principle** STOCK principio de ajuste del precio *m*; **~ analysis** ACC análisis de inventarios *m*; **~ arbitrage** STOCK arbitraje de acciones *m*; **~ borrowing** STOCK préstamo de títulos *m*; **~ brokerage firm** STOCK empresa mediadora en el mercado financiero *f*, sociedad de intermediación bursátil *f*; **~ of bullion** GEN COMM reserva de oro *f*; **~ card** ACC ficha de existencias *f*; **~ certificate** *AmE* (*cf share certificate BrE*) STOCK bono social *m*, póliza de compra *f*; **~ check** *AmE*, **~ cheque** *BrE* BANK, FIN cheque a la vista *m*, cheque de acciones *m*; **~ contract** STOCK contrato bursátil *m*; **~ control** ACC, ECON control de stocks *m*, control de existencias *m*; **~ control card** ACC ficha de almacén *f*; **~ controller** HRM controlador(a) de almacén *m,f*, controlador(a) de existencias *m,f*, responsable de almacén *mf*; **~ cycle** GEN COMM ciclo de existencias *m*; **~ discount** GEN COMM, STOCK descuento sobre acciones *m*; **~ dividend** *AmE* (*cf bonus issue BrE, capitalization issue BrE, scrip issue BrE, stock split AmE*) ACC, FIN, STOCK dividendo en acciones *m*, emisión de acciones liberadas *f*; **~ draft** GEN COMM giro a la vista *m*; **~ exchange clearing house** STOCK cámara de compensación de valores bursátiles *f*; **~ exchange hours** *n pl* STOCK horario de la bolsa *m*; **~ exchange list** STOCK lista de valores cotizados *f*; **~ exchange opacity** STOCK opacidad bursátil *f*; **~ exchange price index** STOCK índice de precios de la Bolsa de Valores *m*, índice de precios bursátiles *m*; **~ exchange quotation** STOCK cotización del mercado de valores *f*; **~ exchange ratio** BANK, ECON, FIN, STOCK coeficiente bursátil *m*; **~ exchange transaction** STOCK operación bursátil *f*, operación de bolsa *f*; **~ farming** GEN COMM crianza de animales *f*; **~ in** ACC, S&M existencias en almacén *f pl*; **~ in hand** ACC, GEN COMM inventario *m*, existencias *f pl*, existencias disponibles *f pl*; **~ index arbitrage** STOCK mercancía sobre el índice de arbitraje *m*; **~ index and average** STOCK indicador de la bolsa *m*; **~ index contract** STOCK contrato sobre el índice bursátil *m*; **~ index futures** *n pl* STOCK futuros sobre índices bursátiles *m pl*; **~ index futures market** STOCK mercado de futuros sobre acciones *m*; **~ index option** STOCK opción sobre el índice bursátil *f*; **~ indexes and averages** *n pl* STOCK índices de la bolsa *m pl*; **~ insurance company** STOCK sociedad anónima de seguros *f*; **~ inventory** GEN COMM inventario de existencias *m*, inventario de stock *m*; **~ issue** STOCK emisión de acciones *f*; **~ issue bonus** STOCK prima de emisión de acciones *f*; **~ jobbery** STOCK especulación bursátil *f*; **~ line** GEN COMM, S&M gama de productos *f*; **~ list** STOCK boletín de cotizaciones *f*; **~ management** GEN COMM, MGMNT, S&M gestión de almacén *f*; **~ market capitalization** STOCK capitalización del mercado de valores *f*; **~ market collapse** STOCK colapso del mercado de valores *m*; **~ market cycle** STOCK ciclo del mercado de valores *m*; **~ market index** STOCK índice del mercado de valores *m*, índice bursátil *m*; **~ market price index** STOCK índice de precios del mercado de valores *m*; **~ option** STOCK opción de compra de acciones *f*; **~ option plan** STOCK plan de opción de compra de acciones *m*; **~-output ratio** STOCK relación valores-productos *f*; **~ ownership** STOCK titularidad de acciones *f*; **~ portfolio** FIN, STOCK cartera de existencias *f*, cartera de valores *f*; ~ **power BANK**, **STOCK** carta de poder sobre acciones *f*, carta-poder para la venta de valores *f*, poder escrito para vender acciones *m*; ~ **price index STOCK** índice de cotización de valores *m*, índice bursátil *m*; ~ **purchase warrant STOCK** certificado para compra de valores *m*; ~ **quotation STOCK** cotización de acciones *f*; ~ **quoted officially STOCK** acciones cotizadas oficialmente *f pl*; ~ **ratio ACC** proporción de existencias *f*; ~ **receipt STOCK** recibo de almacén *m*; ~ **record STOCK** registro bursátil *m*; ~ **register STOCK** registro de acciones *m*; ~ **right STOCK** derecho de suscripción *m*; ~ **rotation GEN COMM** facturación *f*, rotación de existencias *f*; ~ **sheet GEN COMM** hoja de almacén *f*; ~ **shortage GEN COMM** mermas de las existencias *f pl*; ~ **split** *AmE* (*cf bonus issue BrE, capitalization issue BrE, scrip issue BrE, stock dividend AmE*) **ACC, STOCK** dividendo en acciones *m*, emisión de acciones liberadas *f*; ~ **split down GEN COMM** desdoble de acciones *m*; ~ **with subscription rights STOCK** acciones con derechos de suscripción *f pl*; ~ **symbol STOCK** código bursátil *m*; ~ **tips** *n pl* **STOCK** información confidencial bursátil *f*; ~**-transfer agent STOCK** intermediario(-a) de transferencias *m,f*; ~ **transfer form STOCK** formulario de transferencia de acciones *m*; ~ **turnover GEN COMM** facturación *f*, rotación de existencias *f*, **STOCK** rotación de títulos *f*; ~ **valuation ACC, GEN COMM** valoración de existencias *f*; ~ **watcher STOCK** control informatizado de operaciones bursátiles *m*; ~ **yield STOCK** rendimiento bursátil *m*; ◆ **in** ~ **GEN COMM** *trade* en existencia, en almacén; **on the** ~ **exchange STOCK** en la bolsa; **out of** ~ **GEN COMM** *trade* agotado, sin existencias; **take in** ~ **STOCK** comprar acciones; **the** ~ **market made solid ground STOCK** el mercado de valores se consolidó

Stock: ~ **Exchange** *n* **GEN COMM** Bolsa de Valores *f*; ~ **Exchange Alternative Trading Service** *n BrE* (*SEATS*) **STOCK** sistema operativo de cotizaciones; ~ **Exchange Automated Quotation** *n BrE* (*SEAQ*) **STOCK** sistema de cotización automatizada del mercado de valores; ~ **Exchange Automated Quotation International** *n BrE* **STOCK** bolsa internacional de cotización automatizada; ~ **Exchange Commission** *n AmE* (*SEC*) **FIN, STOCK** consejo de inversiones de acciones, bonos y valores, ≈ Comisión Nacional del Mercado de Valores *f* (*Esp*) (*CNMV*); ~ **Exchange Committee** *n* **ECON, GEN COMM, STOCK** Junta Sindical de Agentes de Cambio y Bolsa *f*, ≈ Cámara Sindical de Agentes de Comercio *f*; ~ **Exchange Daily Official List** *n BrE* **GEN COMM** boletín de la bolsa *m*; ~ **Exchange Pool Nominees** *n pl* (*SEPON*) **STOCK** candidatos al fondo de la bolsa de valores; ~ **Market** *n* **STOCK** Bolsa de Valores *f*

stockbreeder *n BrE* (*cf rancher AmE*) **GEN COMM** ganadero(-a) *m,f*

stockbroker *n* **STOCK** broker *mf*, intermediario(-a) financiero(-a) *m,f*

stockbroking *n* **STOCK** corretaje de bolsa *m*

stockholder *n* **STOCK** accionista *mf*; ~ **diffusion STOCK** dispersión del accionista *f*, dispersión de la accionista *f*; ~ **of record** *AmE* **STOCK** accionista registrado(-a) *m,f*

stockholders': ~ **equity** *n* **STOCK** valor neto *m*, capital social *m*

stockholding *n* **STOCK** accionariado *m*

Stockholm: ~ **School** *n* **ECON** escuela de Estocolmo *f*

stockist *n* **HRM** distribuidor(a) *m,f*; ~ **agent HRM** agente de almacén *mf*, agente de existencias *mf*

stockjobber *n* **STOCK** corredor(a) de bolsa *m,f*, intermediario(-a) de bolsa *m,f*

stockkeeping: ~ **unit** *n* **GEN COMM** unidad de almacenamiento *f*

stockman *n AmE* (*cf storeman BrE*) **HRM** almacenista *mf*, guarda de almacén *mf*, jefe(-a) de almacén *m,f*

stockpile[1] *n* **GEN COMM, TRANSP** apilamiento *m*, existencias para casos de emergencia *f pl*

stockpile[2] *vt* **TRANSP** almacenar, apilar, acaparar

stockpiling *n* **GEN COMM, TRANSP** acumulación de existencias *f*

stocks *n pl* (*stcks, stks*) **GEN COMM** capital *m*, *shares* acciones *f pl*; ◆ **while** ~ **last S&M** mientras duren las existencias

stocktaking *n* **GEN COMM** recuento de existencias *m*, inventario *m*; ~ **sale GEN COMM** venta posbalance *f*; ~ **value ACC** valor de inventario *m*

stockyard *n* **GEN COMM** corral de ganado *m*

STOL *abbr* (*short takeoff and landing*) **TRANSP** despegue y aterrizaje corto *m*

Stolper: ~ **Samuelson theorem** *n* **ECON** *free trade* teorema de Stolper-Samuelson *m*

stop[1]: ~ **bit** *n* **COMP** bitio de detención *m*; ~**-go** *n BrE* *jarg* **ECON** frenazo y expansión *m*; ~**-go cycle of inflation** *n* **ECON** ciclo de inflación de alternancias de recesión-expansión *m*; ~**-go policy** *n BrE* **ECON** política de frenazo y expansión *f*; ~**-limit order** *n AmE* **STOCK** orden stop con límite *f*; ~**-loss order** *n* **STOCK** orden de pérdida limitada *f*; ~**-loss reinsurance** *n* **INS** reaseguro limitador de pérdidas *m*; ~**-loss rules** *n* **BANK, STOCK** *investment* instrucción de pérdida limitada *f*; ~ **motion** *n* **MEDIA, S&M** filmación de imagen por imagen *f*; ~ **order** *n* **STOCK** orden de bloqueo *f*; ~**-out price** *n* **STOCK** precio mínimo en subasta *m*; ~ **payment order** *n* **BANK** orden de suspensión de pagos *f*; ~ **signal** *n* **COMP, TRANSP** señal de parada *f*; ~ **time** *n* **COMP** tiempo de parada *m*

stop[2] **1.** *vt* **COMP** parar, **GEN COMM** *bankruptcy proceedings* detener; ◆ ~ **a check** *AmE*, ~ **a cheque** *BrE* **BANK** bloquear el pago de un cheque, suspender el pago de un cheque; ~ **payment of a check** *AmE*, ~ **payment of a cheque** *BrE* **BANK** suspender el pago de un cheque; ~ **sb's allowance GEN COMM** interrumpir el subsidio de alguien; ~ **a stock** *jarg* **STOCK** suspender un capital en acciones; **2.** *vi* **COMP** pararse

stop over *vi* **TRANSP** hacer escala

stopover *n* **TRANSP** escala intermedia *f*

stoppage *n* **HRM** cese *m*; ~ **in transit COMMS, IMP/EXP** retención de mercancías *f*, **LAW** derecho de retención de mercancías en tránsito *m*, **S&M** interrupción de tránsito *f*, **TRANSP** retención de mercancías *f*; ~ **of trade GEN COMM** suspensión del negocio *f*; ~ **of work HRM** *due to industrial action* interrupción de los trabajos *m*

stopped: ~ **bonds** *n pl* **FIN** bonos bloqueados *m pl*; ~ **check** *AmE*, ~ **cheque** *BrE n* **BANK** cheque bloqueado *m*; ~ **payment** *n* **BANK** pago retenido *m*; ~ **stock** *n* **FIN, STOCK** acción congelada *f*

stopper *n* **S&M** *advertising* tope *m*

stopwatch: ~ **studies** *n pl* **MGMNT** estudios cronometrados *m pl*

storage *n* **GEN COMM** almacenaje *m*, almacenamiento *m*;

~ **allocation** COMP asignación de almacenamiento *f*; ~ **area** COMP, GEN COMM área de almacenamiento *f*; ~ **capacity** COMP capacidad de memoria *f*, GEN COMM capacidad de almacenamiento *f*; ~ **capacity information** COMP capacidad de almacenamiento de información; ~ **charges** *n pl* GEN COMM, TRANSP gastos de almacenaje *m pl*; ~ **device** COMP dispositivo de almacenamiento *m*; ~ **dump** COMP volcado de la memoria *m*; ~ **facility** ENVIR *for toxic waste*, GEN COMM instalación de almacenamiento *f*; ~ **field** COMP campo de almacenamiento *m*; ~ **map** COMP topograma de la memoria *m*; ~ **medium** COMP medio de almacenamiento *m*; ~ **requirements** COMP necesidades de memoria *f pl*

store¹: ~ **accounting** *n* ACC contabilidad de almacén *f*; ~ **audit** *n* ACC auditoría de almacén *f*, auditoría de existencias *f*; ~ **brand** *n* S&M marca comercial *f*; ~ **demonstration** *n* S&M demostración en tienda *f*; ~ **card** *n* BANK, FIN tarjeta de crédito de una tienda específica *f*; ~ **group** *n* S&M grupo de tiendas *m*; ~ **traffic** *n* S&M tráfico de almacén *m*; ~ **of value** *n* ECON reserva de valor *f*

store² *vt* COMP *data*, TRANSP *goods* almacenar

storehouse *n* GEN COMM, IMP/EXP, TRANSP almacén *m*

storekeeper: ~**'s liability insurance** *n* INS seguro de responsabilidad del almacenista *m*

storeman *n BrE* (*cf warehouseman AmE, stockman AmE*) HRM almacenista *mf*, guarda de almacén *mf*, jefe(-a) de almacén *m,f*

storeroom *n* GEN COMM depósito *m*

storeowner *n AmE* (*cf shopkeeper BrE*) S&M tendero(-a) *m,f*

storey *n BrE* PROP planta *f*

story *AmE see storey BrE*

storyboard *n* MEDIA, S&M *advertising* guión gráfico *m*

stow *vt* GEN COMM, HRM, TRANSP *cargo* estibar

stowage *n* TRANSP gastos de estiba *m pl*; ~ **area** TRANSP área de estiba *f*; ~ **factor** GEN COMM, TRANSP factor de estiba *m*; ~ **order** TRANSP orden de estiba *f*; ~ **plan** TRANSP plan de estiba *m*

straddle *n* ECON, FIN, GEN COMM especulación mixta *f*, STOCK cono *m*, especulación mixta *f*, straddle *f*; ~ **buyer** STOCK comprador(a) con opción de compra o venta *m,f*; ~ **carrier** TRANSP camión de trinquinal *m* (*Esp*), cargador de caballete *m* (*AmL*); ~ **combination** STOCK combinación de opción de compra y venta *f*; ~ **seller** STOCK vendedor(a) con opción de compra y venta *m,f*; ~ **writer** STOCK vendedor(a) de contratos de compra y venta *m,f*

straight¹: ~ **bill of lading** *n* IMP/EXP, TRANSP conocimiento de embarque no traspasable *m*, conocimiento de embarque nominativo *m*; ~ **bond** *n* STOCK bono ordinario *m*; ~ **choice arbitration** *n* BANK arbitraje de elección simple *m*; ~ **investment** *n* BANK inversión directa *f*; ~ **letter of credit** *n* BANK, FIN carta de crédito confirmada e irrevocable *f*; ~ **lift** *n* TRANSP *cargo* elevador de carrera vertical *m*; ~**-line depreciation** *n* ACC amortización anual uniforme *f*, amortización constante *f*, amortización de cuota fija *f*, amortización lineal *f*; ~**-line method** *n* ACC *depreciation* método de cuotas constantes *m*, método de la línea recta *m*, método lineal *m*; ~**-line method of depreciation** *n* ACC método de amortización anual uniforme *m*, método de

amortización lineal *m*; ~ **loan** *n* BANK préstamo directo *m*

straight²: **go** ~ **to** *phr* GEN COMM ir directo a

straighten: ~ **things out** *phr* GEN COMM arreglar las cosas

straightforward *adj* GEN COMM *simple* sencillo, HRM directo, sincero

straights: ~ **market** *n* FIN mercado nominativo *m*

strained *adj* GEN COMM *relations* tenso

stranded: ~ **goods** *n pl* INS artículos de naufragio *m pl*

strangle *n* STOCK posición de compraventa de opciones a distintos precios

stranglehold: **have a** ~ **on the market** *phr* GEN COMM, ECON, S&M dominar totalmente el mercado

strap *n* STOCK compra strap *f*; ~ **option** STOCK opción strap *f*

strapped: **be** ~ **for cash** *phr* ECON estar en apuros económicos

strapping *n* TRANSP enganche directo *m*

stratagem *n* GEN COMM, TAX ardid *m*

strategic¹ *adj* GEN COMM, MGMNT estratégico

strategic²: ~ **alliance** *n* GEN COMM, MGMNT alianza estratégica *f*; ~ **business unit** *n* ECON, GEN COMM, MGMNT unidad de negocio estratégico *f*, unidad estratégica de negocio *f*; ~ **innovation** *n* S&M innovación estratégica *f*; ~ **interdependence** *n* GEN COMM, MGMNT interdependencia estratégica *f*; ~ **issue** *n* MGMNT asunto estratégico *m*, cuestión estratégica *f*; ~ **management accounting** *n* ACC contabilidad de dirección estratégica *f*, contabilidad de gestión estratégica *f*; ~ **overview** *n* POL análisis estratégico *m*; ~ **plan** *n* GEN COMM, MGMNT plan estratégico *m*; ~ **planning** *n* GEN COMM, MGMNT planificación estratégica *f*; ~ **pricing** *n* S&M fijación estratégica de precios *f*; ~ **stockpiling** *n* GEN COMM acaparamiento con fines estratégicos *m*; ~ **tax planning** *n* ECON, TAX planificación fiscal estratégica *f*

strategy *n* GEN COMM, MGMNT estrategia *f*; ~ **formulation** ECON, GEN COMM formulación de una estrategia *f*, formulación estratégica *f*; ~ **implementation** GEN COMM, MGMNT implementación estratégica *f*, puesta en práctica de estrategias *f*

stratification *n* S&M estratificación *f*

stratified: ~ **random sampling** *n* MATH, S&M muestreo aleatorio estratificado *m*; ~ **sampling** *n* MATH, S&M muestreo estratificado *m*

stratifying: ~ **the market** *phr* S&M estratificando el mercado

straw: ~ **boss** *n AmE infrml* HRM jefe(-a) falso(-a) *m,f*; ~ **poll** *n* POL *unofficial vote* votación de tanteo *f*; ~ **vote** *n* POL *unofficial vote* votación de tanteo *f*

strawboard *n* GEN COMM cartón *m*, cel-o-tex *m*

streaker *n* BANK bono de cupón cero *m*

streamer *n* MEDIA *print* titular en bandera *m*

streamline *vt* ECON modernizar, MGMNT racionalizar

streamlining *n* ECON modernización *f*, MGMNT racionalización *f*

street *n* (*St.*) GEN COMM calle *f* (*c/*); ~ **book** *jarg* STOCK *futures* registro de valores gestionados *m*; ~ **dealing** STOCK venta de valores no oficial *f*; ~ **money** *AmE jarg* POL dinero entregado a los que van haciendo campaña electoral puerta a puerta; ~ **name** STOCK valores a nombre del propio operador *m pl*; ~ **price** STOCK cambios cotizados después de la sesión oficial *m pl*; **~ trader** *BrE* (*cf street vendor AmE*) GEN COMM, S&M comerciante callejero(-a) *m,f*, vendedor(a) callejero(-a) *m,f*; **~ vendor** *AmE* (*cf street trader BrE*) GEN COMM, S&M comerciante callejero(-a) *m,f*, vendedor(a) callejero(-a) *m,f*

strength *n* ECON *of currency* fuerza; ◆ **~ of the market** GEN COMM fuerza del mercado; **~ of materials** IND resistencia de materiales *f*

strengthen *vt* GEN COMM reforzar

strengthened *adj* GEN COMM reforzado

strengthening *n* ECON *of currency*, GEN COMM reforzamiento *m*

strengths: ~, weaknesses, opportunities and threats analysis *n* (*SWOT*) S&M análisis de las fuerzas, debilidades, oportunidades y amenazas *m*

stress *n* HRM estrés *m*, tensión *f*; **~ interview** HRM entrevista en profundidad *f*

strict: ~ adherence to the contract *n* LAW estricta adhesión al contrato *f*; **~ cost price** *n* ACC precio de coste estricto *m* (*Esp*), precio de coste obligatorio *m* (*Esp*), precio de costo estricto *m* (*AmL*), precio de costo obligatorio *m* (*AmL*); **~ foreclosure** *n* LAW ejecución hipotecaria forzosa *f*; **~ time limit** *n* GEN COMM plazo perentorio *m*

strife: ~-ridden period *n* HRM periodo conflictivo *m*

strike[1] *n* GEN COMM huelga *f*; **~ action** HRM medida de huelga *f*; **~ ballot** HRM votación de huelga *f*; **~ benefits** *n pl* HRM subsidio de huelga *m*; **~ call** HRM, IND emplazamiento de huelga *m*; **~ clause** HRM cláusula de huelga *f*; **~ committee** HRM comité de huelga *m*; **~-free agreement** HRM acuerdo sin necesidad de huelga *m*; **~ fund** HRM fondo de huelga *m*; **~ notice** GEN COMM, HRM, IND aviso de huelga *m*; **~ pay** HRM paga de huelga *f*; **~ picket** HRM piquete de huelga *m*; **~ price** STOCK precio de ejercicio *m*; **~ price interval** STOCK *options* intervalo en el precio de ejecución *m*; **~ rate** *jarg* S&M índice de eficacia *m*; **~ threat** HRM amenaza de huelga *f*; **~ vote** HRM votación de huelga *f*; **~ yield** STOCK *of futures* rendimiento del ejercicio *m*; ◆ **come out on ~** *BrE* HRM ir a la huelga; **go on ~** HRM ir a la huelga; **on ~** HRM estar en huelga; **turn out on ~** HRM ir a la huelga; **the ~ has been called off** GEN COMM, HRM se canceló la huelga

strike[2] *vi* GEN COMM hacer huelga; ◆ **~ a balance** ACC hacer balance; **~ a deal** GEN COMM hacer un trato, llegar a un acuerdo; **~ sb off the list** GEN COMM borrar a alguien de la lista; **~ it rich** *infrml* GEN COMM hacerse rico; **~ in sympathy** HRM hacer huelga por simpatía, hacer huelga por solidaridad

strikebound *adj* HRM paralizado por la huelga

strikebreaker *n* HRM esquirol *mf* (*infrml*)

strikebreaking *n* HRM esquirolismo *m* (*infrml*)

strikeover *n* COMP *on word processor* doble pulsación *f*

striker *n* GEN COMM, HRM, IND huelguista *mf*

strikes: ~, riots and civil commotions *n pl* (*SR&CC*) HRM, IND, WEL huelgas, tumultos y desórdenes *m pl*

string *n* COMP cadena *f*

stringent[1] *adj* GEN COMM *measures, programme* estricto

stringent[2]: **~ money market** *n* FIN mercado monetario restrictivo *m*

stringently *adv* GEN COMM estrictamente

stringer *n jarg* MEDIA *print* corresponsal accidental *m*

strings: no ~ attached *phr* GEN COMM sin condiciones, sin cortapisas

strip[1] *n* FIN, GEN COMM cupón *m*, PROP *of land* franja *f*, S&M cupón *m*, STOCK cupón *m*, compra strip *f*; **~ bond** STOCK strip *m*; **~ development** GEN COMM desarrollo por zonas *m*; **~ mining** *AmE* (*cf open cast mining BrE*) ENVIR, IND explotación a cielo abierto *f*, explotación minera a cielo abierto *f*

strip[2] *vt* ACC, BANK, GEN COMM desglosar, TRANSP desmontar

stripped: ~ bond *n* FIN, STOCK bono sin cupón *m*; **~ security** *n* STOCK seguridad sin cupón *f*

stripping *vi* TRANSP reachique *m*

STRIPS *abbr* (*Separate Trading of Registered Interest and Principal Securities*) STOCK negociación por separado de los flujos que generan los valores registrados

strong[1] *adj* GEN COMM *currency, indication* fuerte, *reputation* sólido

strong[2]: **~ bearish play** *n jarg* STOCK *options* juego marcadamente bajista *m*; **~ bullish play** *n jarg* STOCK *options* fuerte tendencia alcista *f*; **~ equilibrium** *n* ECON equilibrio firme *m*; **~ room** *n* BANK bóveda de seguridad *f*, cámara acorazada *f*

Strong: ~ Vocational Interest Blank *n* HRM Formulario de Interés Vocacional de Strong *m*

strongbox *n* BANK caja de seguridad bancaria *f*, caja fuerte *f*

Strong-Campbell: ~ Interest Inventory *n* HRM inventario de intereses de Strong y Campbell *m*

strongly *adv* GEN COMM fuertemente

structural: ~ adjustment *n* MGMNT ajuste estructural *m*; **~ adjustment facility** *n* (*SAF*) FIN mecanismo de ajuste estructural *m*; **~ adjustment loan** *n* BANK, ECON *international* préstamo de ajuste estructural *m*; **~ adjustment policy** *n* ECON política estructural de ajuste *f*; **~ change** *n* MGMNT cambio estructural *m*; **~ crisis** *n* MGMNT crisis estructural *f*; **~ deficit** *n* ECON déficit estructural *m*; **~ engineering** *n* IND ingeniería estructural *f*; **~ funds** *n pl* ECON *EU* fondos estructurales *m pl*; **~ inflation** *n* ECON inflación estructural *f*; **~ model** *n* ECON modelo estructural *m*; **~ unemployment** *n* ECON, HRM, WEL desempleo estructural *m*

structure[1] *n* GEN COMM estructura *f*; **~ of the market** ECON, S&M estructura del mercado *f*

structure[2] *vt* GEN COMM estructurar

structured[1] *adj* GEN COMM estructurado

structured[2]: **~ interview** *n* HRM entrevista estructurada *f*; **~ programming** *n* COMP programación estructurada *f*

structuring *n* GEN COMM estructuración *f*

struggle *n* GEN COMM lucha *f*

stub *n* BANK *of cheque* talón *m* (*AmL*), resguardo *m* (*Esp*), *in paying-in book* resguardo de ingreso *m*

student *n* HRM, WEL estudiante *m*; **~ loan** BANK, FIN préstamo de estudiante *m*, HRM crédito para estudios *m*; **~ loan marketing association** (*SLMA*) BANK, FIN asociación de comercialización de préstamos a estudiantes *f*

Student: ~'s t-distribution *n* MATH *statistics* distribución t de Student *f*

studio *n* GEN COMM estudio *m*

study[1] *n* GEN COMM estudio *m*; **~ day** WEL día de estudio *m*; ~ **group** GEN COMM grupo de estudios *m*; ~ **trip** WEL viaje de estudios *m*

study² *vt* GEN COMM estudiar

stuff *vt BrE* TRANSP *container* atestar, rellenar

stuffing *n* TRANSP relleno *m*; ~ **and stripping** GEN COMM empaquetado y desempaquetado *m*

stumbling: ~ **block** *n* GEN COMM atolladero *m*

stump: ~ **up** *vt jarg* GEN COMM aflojar

stunt: ~ **advertising** *n* S&M anuncio sensacionalista *m*

stvdr *abbr* (*stevedore*) HRM, TRANSP alijador(a) *m,f*, estibador(a) *m,f*

STVP *abbr* (*short-term vehicle park*) TRANSP aparcamiento de corta duración *m*

style *n* GEN COMM *of management* estilo *m*; ~ **sheet** COMP hoja de estilo *f*

stylist *n* GEN COMM estilista *mf*

stylize *vt* COMP, GEN COMM, MGMNT estilizar

stylized: ~ **fact** *n* ECON razón social *f*

stylus *n* COMP *pen-based device* estilete *m*, *video* aguja grabadora *f*

stymie *vt jarg* GEN COMM obstruir

sub *n* GEN COMM *jarg* (*subaltern*) subalterno(-a) *m,f*, HRM, MEDIA *BrE infrml* (*sub-editor*) *print* secretario(-a) de redacción *m,f*

subactivity *n* ECON, GEN COMM actividad secundaria *f*, subactividad *f*

subagent *n* GEN COMM subagente *mf*

suballotment *n* POL subasignación *f*

subaltern *n BrE* (*sub*) GEN COMM subalterno(-a) *m,f* (*infrml*)

subchapter *n* TAX apartado *m*, subcapítulo *m*

subcharter *vt* TRANSP subcontratar

subcompact *adj* GEN COMM subcompacto

subcontract¹ *n* GEN COMM subcontrato *m*

subcontract² *vt* GEN COMM subcontratar

subcontracting *n* GEN COMM subcontratación *f*

subcontractor *n* GEN COMM subcontratista *mf*

subcustody *n* FIN subcustodia *f*

subdirectory *n* COMP subdirectorio *m*

subdivided *adj* GEN COMM subdividido

subdivision *n* GEN COMM subdivisión *f*

subdued *adj* GEN COMM *prices* moderado

sub-editor *n BrE* (*sub*) HRM, MEDIA *print* secretario(-a) de redacción *m,f*

subemployment *n jarg* ECON subempleo *m*

sub-entry *n* COMP subentrada *f*

subfile *n* COMP subarchivo *m*

subgroup *n* GEN COMM subgrupo *m*

sub-head *n* MEDIA, S&M subtítulo *m*

subholding: ~ **company** *n* MGMNT subholding *m*

subject¹: ~ **to approval** *adj* GEN COMM, S&M sujeto a aprobación, pendiente de aprobación; ~ **to breakage** *adj* INS sujeto a indemnización por rotura; ~ **to CFTC approval** *adj* STOCK sujeto a la aprobación de CFTC; ~ **to change** *adj* GEN COMM sujeto al cambio; ~ **to mortgage** *adj* PROP sujeto a hipoteca; ~ **to particular average** *adj* (*SPA*) INS sujeto a avería simple; ~ **to price controls** *adj* ECON *products* sujeto a controles de precio; ~ **to quota** *adj* GEN COMM sometido a contingente; ~ **to taxation** *adj* TAX sujeto a impuesto

subject² *n* GEN COMM *negotiation* asunto *m*; ~ **filing**

ADMIN, GEN COMM archivo por materias *m*; ~ **index** ADMIN índice de materias *m*; ~ **matter** COMP, FIN contenido *m*, GEN COMM contenido *m*, materia en consideración *f*, PATENTS asunto *m*, contenido *m*; ~ **unsold** GEN COMM asunto sin resolver *m*; ♦ ~ **approval no risk** (*SANR*) INS sujeto a aprobación sin riesgo; **be ~ to** GEN COMM estar sujeto a, estar propenso a

subjective: ~ **perception** *n* S&M percepción subjetiva *f*

sub judice *adj* LAW pendiente de resolución judicial

sublease *n* GEN COMM, PROP subarriendo *m*

subletting *n* GEN COMM, PROP arrendamiento por un subarrendatario *m*

sublicence *n BrE* GEN COMM, PATENTS subconcesión *f*, sublicencia *f*

sublicense *AmE see* **sublicence** *BrE*

subliminal: ~ **advertising** *n* S&M publicidad subliminal *f*

submanager *n* BANK, HRM, MGMNT director(a) adjunto(-a) *m,f*

submarginal *n* ECON submarginal *m*

submission *n* GEN COMM propuesta *f*; ~ **of bids** GEN COMM presentación de ofertas *f*; ~ **for deletions of debts** BANK presentación para cancelaciones de deudas *f*

submit *vt* GEN COMM *proposal* presentar, *claim, application* someter; ♦ ~ **to arbitration** GEN COMM someter a arbitraje

submortgage *n* BANK, PROP hipoteca con garantía de otra hipoteca *f*

suboffice *n* ADMIN, GEN COMM suboficina *f*

suboptimization *n* ECON, FIN, GEN COMM suboptimización *f*

subordinate¹ *adj* HRM subalterno

subordinate² *vt* GEN COMM subordinar

subordinated: ~ **asset** *n* ACC activo subordinado *m*; ~ **bond issue** *n* STOCK emisión de bonos subordinados *f*; ~ **convertible bond issue** *n* STOCK emisión de bonos subordinados convertibles *f*; ~ **debenture** *n* STOCK obligación subordinada *f*; ~ **debt** *n* FIN, STOCK deuda subordinada *f*; ~ **interest** *n* FIN, STOCK interés subordinado *m*; ~ **liabilities** *n pl* ACC, BANK pasivo subordinado *m*; ~ **loan** *n* BANK, FIN préstamo subordinado *m*; ~ **mortgage** *n* BANK, PROP hipoteca subordinada *f*; ~ **perpetual bond** *n* FIN, STOCK bono perpetuo subordinado *m*; ~ **redeemable bond** *n* FIN, STOCK bono amortizable subordinado *m*; ~ **warrant issue** *n* STOCK emisión garantizada subordinada *f*

subordination: ~ **agreement** *n* GEN COMM acuerdo de subordinación *m*; ~ **interest** *n* BANK interés de subordinación *m*

subparagraph *n* ADMIN subinciso *m*

subpoena *n* LAW cédula de citación so pena de sanción *f*, requerimiento *m*

sub-post: ~ **office** *n* COMMS estafeta de correos *f*

subprogram *n* COMP subprograma *m*, subrutina *f*

subrogation: ~ **clause** *n* LAW cláusula de subrogación *f*

subroutine *n* GEN COMM subrutina *f*

subscribe 1. *vt* GEN COMM *donate* donar; **2.** *vi* GEN COMM *for a loan, shares* suscribir; ♦ ~ **to an issue** FIN aprobar una emisión, suscribir una emisión

subscribed: ~ **capital** *n* STOCK capital suscrito *m*; ~ **circulation** *n* S&M tirada suscrita *f*

subscriber *n* GEN COMM suscriptor(a) *m,f*; ~**'s insurance**

policy GEN COMM, INS seguro de abonado *m*, seguro de suscriptor *m*; ~ **trunk dialing** *AmE*, ~ **trunk dialling** *BrE* (*STD*) COMMS llamada interurbana de abonado *f*, selección automática a distancia del abonado *f*

subscribing: ~ **option** *n* LAW facultad de suscribir *f*

subscript *n* COMP subíndice *m*

subscription *n* GEN COMM suscripción *f*; ~ **club** STOCK club de suscripción *m*; ~ **for shares** STOCK suscripción de acciones *f*; ~ **form** GEN COMM, STOCK formulario de suscripción *m*; ~ **price** GEN COMM, STOCK precio de suscripción *m*; ~ **privilege** STOCK privilegio de suscripción *m*; ~ **ratio** STOCK proporción de suscripción *f*; ~ **receivable** STOCK valor por cobrar por suscripción *m*; ~ **right** STOCK derecho de suscripción *m*; ~ **warrant** STOCK certificado de suscripción *m*; ♦ **take out a** ~ GEN COMM suscribirse

subscriptions: ~ **to the International Monetary Fund** *n* POL suscripciones para el Fondo Monetario Internacional *f pl*

subsector *n* GEN COMM subsector *m*

subsequent: ~ **event** *n* GEN COMM hecho posterior *m*, suceso subsecuente *m*

subset *n* GEN COMM subconjunto *m*

subshare *n* STOCK acción subdividida *f*

subsidiarity *n* ECON, GEN COMM, POL subsidiaridad *f*

subsidiary[1] *adj* GEN COMM filial, subsidiario

subsidiary[2] *n* GEN COMM *company* compañía subsidiaria *f*; ~ **account** ACC, BANK cuenta auxiliar *f*, subcuenta *f*, cuenta subsidiaria *f*; ~ **accounting record** ACC libro auxiliar *m*, registro contable auxiliar *m*; ~ **accounting system** ACC sistema de contabilidad auxiliar *m*; ~ **bank** BANK banco filial *m*; ~ **company** *BrE* (*cf subsidiary corporation AmE*) GEN COMM compañía filial *f*, empresa subsidiaria *f*; ~ **corporation** *AmE* (*cf subsidiary company BrE*) GEN COMM compañía filial *f*, empresa subsidiaria *f*; ~ **dividends** *n pl* ACC, FIN, STOCK dividendos de una empresa subsidiaria *m pl*; ~ **firm** GEN COMM compañía filial *f*, empresa subsidiaria *f*; ~ **ledger** ACC libro mayor auxiliar *m*

subsidization *n* GEN COMM, FIN subvención *f*

subsidized[1] *adj* FIN, GEN COMM *prices* subsidiado, subvencionado

subsidized[2]: ~ **exports** *n pl* ECON, IMP/EXP exportaciones con subsidio *f pl*, exportaciones subvencionadas *f pl*; ~ **travel** *n* LEIS, TRANSP viaje subvencionado *m*

subsidy *n* FIN, GEN COMM subvención

subsistence *n* WEL subsistencia *f*; ~ **allowance** GEN COMM, HRM dieta *f* (*Esp*), viático *m* (*AmL*); ~ **crops** *n pl* ECON *agricultural* cultivos de subsistencia *m pl*; ~ **farming** ECON, ENVIR cultivo de subsistencia *m*; ~ **theory of wages** ECON teoría del salario de subsistencia *f*

substance *n* GEN COMM sustancia *f*; **in** ~ **defeasance** ACC anulación en sustancia *f*; ~ **explosive** TRANSP sustancia explosiva *f*; ~ **over form** ACC sustancia sobre forma *f*

substandard[1] *adj* GEN COMM inferior al nivel medio

substandard[2]: ~ **ship** *n* TRANSP barco inferior al promedio *m*

substantial[1] *adj* GEN COMM material

substantial[2]: ~ **interest** *n* BANK interés considerable *m*; ~ **risk** *n* STOCK riesgo sustancial *m*

substantiate: ~ **a claim** *phr* LAW probar una reclamación

substantive: ~ **agreement** *n* HRM acuerdo independiente *m*; ~ **law** *n* LAW derecho sustantivo *m*

substitute[1] *adj* HRM sustitutivo

substitute[2] *n* GEN COMM *BrE* (*cf alternate AmE*) *stand-in* alternativo(-a) *m,f*, IND sustituto(-a) *m,f*; ~ **goods** *n pl* S&M bienes de sustitución *m pl*

substituted: ~ **expenses** *n pl* INS gastos suplidos *m pl*; ~ **property** *n* PROP, TAX propiedad suplente *f*; ~ **share** *n* STOCK acción sustituida *f*

substitution *n* ECON, GEN COMM sustitución *f*, HRM *of job* cambio *m*; ~ **effect** ECON efecto de sustitución *m*; ~ **law** LAW ley de reemplazo *f*; ~ **slope** ECON pendiente de renovación *f*

substructure *n* ECON, GEN COMM infraestructura *f*

subtenant *n* PROP subarrendatario *m*

subtotal *n* ACC, MATH subtotal *m*

subtract *vt* ACC, MATH restar

suburb *n* GEN COMM barrio *m*

suburbs *n pl* GEN COMM barrios exteriores *m pl*

subway *n* *AmE* (*cf underground BrE, tube BrE*) TRANSP ferrocarril subterráneo *m*, metro *m*

succeed *vi* GEN COMM tener éxito, acertar, triunfar

succeeding: ~ **account** *n* FIN cuenta siguiente *f*

success *n* GEN COMM acierto *m*, éxito *m*, triunfo *m*; ~ **stories** *n pl* S&M *advertising* historias de éxito *f*

successful[1] *adj* GEN COMM exitoso, acertado

successful[2]: ~ **outcome** *n* GEN COMM *to negotiations* resultado óptimo *m*

succession: ~ **law** *n* TAX derecho de sucesión *m*, impuesto de sucesión *m*

successive[1] *adj* GEN COMM consecutivo, sucesivo

successive[2]: ~ **days** *n pl* GEN COMM días consecutivos *m pl*

successor *n* GEN COMM causahabiente *m*; ~ **in title** PATENTS sucesor en el título de propiedad *m*; ~ **rule** TAX, PROP norma del derechohabiente *f*

sue[1]: ~ **and labor charges** *AmE see* sue and labour charges *BrE*; ~ **and labor clause** *AmE see* sue and labour clause *BrE*; ~ **and labor insurance** *AmE see* sue and labour insurance *BrE*; ~ **and labour charges** *n pl* *BrE* INS, LAW gastos de pleito y trabajo *m pl*, cargos por seguro de medidas preventivas *m pl*; ~ **and labour clause** *n* *BrE* (*S/LC*) INS, LAW cláusula de medidas preventivas *f*, cláusula de gestión y trabajo *f*; ~ **and labour insurance** *n* *BrE* INS, LAW seguro de medidas preventivas *m*

sue[2] *vt* LAW demandar; ♦ ~ **for infringement of patent** LAW, PATENTS demandar a alguien por violar una patente; ~ **for libel** LAW demandar a alguien por libelo

suffer *vt* GEN COMM *consequences, damage* sufrir; ♦ ~ **a loss** GEN COMM, LAW sufrir una pérdida; ~ **a setback** GEN COMM sufrir un revés

sufficient: **not** ~ **funds** *n pl* (*N.S.F.*) BANK, GEN COMM fondos insuficientes *m pl*; **not-~-funds check** *AmE* (*N.S.F. check*), **not-~-funds cheque** *BrE* *n* (*N.S.F. cheque*) BANK, FIN cheque con fondos insuficientes *m*, cheque sin fondos suficientes *m*, cheque sin provisión suficiente de fondos *m*

sugar: ~ **production** *n* GEN COMM, IND producción azucarera *f*

suggested: ~ **retail price** *n* S&M precio al por menor sugerido *m*

suggestion *n* GEN COMM sugerencia *f*; ~ **box** GEN COMM buzón de sugerencias *m*; ~ **scheme** GEN COMM sistema de sugerencias *m*, MGMNT diagrama de sugerencias *m*, esquema de sugerencias *m*, programa de sugerencias *m*, proyecto de sugerencias *m*; ~ **selling** S&M venta por sugerencia *f*; ◆ **there is no ~ of corruption** LAW no hay sombra de corrupción

suit *n* GEN COMM demanda *f*

suitability *n* GEN COMM idoneidad *f*; ~ **rule** FIN regla de aptitud *f*

suitable *adj* GEN COMM adecuado, idóneo

suitcase *n* LEIS maleta *f*

sulfur *AmE see* sulphur *BrE*

sulfuryl *AmE see* sulphuryl *BrE*

sulphur: ~ **dioxide** *n* BrE ENVIR *acid rain* bióxido de azufre *m*; ~ **emission** *n* BrE ENVIR emisión de azufre *f*

sulphuryl: ~ **fluoride** *n* BrE TRANSP *container fumigation* fluoruro de azufre *m*, fluoruro sulfúrico *m*

sum[1]: ~ **advanced** *n* BANK, GEN COMM, STOCK anticipo *m*; ~ **assured** *n* BANK suma asegurada *f*; ~ **at length** *n* GEN COMM cantidad detallada *f*

sum[2]: **this ~ does not appear in the accounts** *phr* ACC esta cantidad no figura en las cuentas

sum up *vt* ACC, GEN COMM resumir

summarize *vt* GEN COMM resumir

summary *n* GEN COMM extracto *m*; ~ **application** LAW ejecución rápida *f*; ~ **dismissal** GEN COMM, HRM dimisión sumaria *f*, despido sumario *m*; ~ **of input factors** ECON *PEMS form* resumen de los factores de producción *m*; ~ **possession** LAW posesión sumaria *f*; ~ **of the proceedings** GEN COMM sumario del proceso *m*; ~ **report** GEN COMM informe resumido *m* (*Esp*), reporte resumido *m* (*AmL*); ~ **of the situation** GEN COMM recapitulación de la situación *f*; ~ **statement** GEN COMM estado resumido *m*; ~ **of tax and credits** TAX resumen de impuestos y deducciones *m*

summer: ~ **recess** *n* POL *Parliament* receso estival *m*

summit *n* ECON, POL *international* cumbre *f*; ~ **conference** GEN COMM conferencia de alto nivel *f*

summons: **take out a ~ against sb** *phr* HRM, LAW citar a uno, entablar demanda contra uno, mandar una citación a alguien

sumptuary: ~ **law** *n* LAW ley que prohibe o limita la comercialización o consumo de productos suntuarios

Sundays: ~ **and holidays excepted** *phr* GEN COMM, LEIS, TRANSP salvo domingos y días festivos

sundries *n pl* ACC varios *m pl*

sundry: ~ **accounts** *n pl* ACC cuentas de varios *f pl*, cuentas diversas *f pl*; ~ **articles** *n pl* ACC artículos varios *m pl*; ~ **expenses** *n pl* GEN COMM gastos varios *m pl*

sunk: ~ **capital** *n* GEN COMM capital amortizado *m*; ~ **cost** *n* FIN coste hundido *m* (*Esp*), costo hundido *m* (*AmL*); ~ **cost fallacy** *n* FIN falsedad de coste sumergido *f* (*Esp*), falsedad de costo sumergido *f* (*AmL*); ~ **costs** *n pl* ACC costes ocultos *m pl* (*Esp*), costes sumergidos *m pl* (*Esp*), costos ocultos *m pl* (*AmL*), costos sumergidos *m pl* (*AmL*)

sunrise: ~ **industry** *n AmE* ECON, IND industria en los albores *f*, industria incipiente *f*

sunset: ~ **act** *n* LAW, POL ley a punto de ser retirada *f*; ~ **industry** *n* ECON, IND industria consolidada *f*; ~ **law** *n AmE jarg* LAW ley que require que los entes administrativos justifiquen periódicamente ante la legislatura los motivos de su existencia; ~ **provision** *n* LAW disposición que especi-

fica una fecha de expiración; ~ **report** *n* POL informe a punto de caducar *m* (*Esp*), reporte a punto de caducar *m* (*AmL*)

sunshine: ~ **law** *n AmE* LAW ley de transparencia *f*

sunspot: ~ **theory** *n* ECON teoría de las manchas solares *f*

super[1] *abbr* (*superstructure*) GEN COMM superestructura *f*

super[2]: ~ **high cube** *n* (*SHC*) TRANSP depósito muy alto *m*; ~ **multiplier** *n* ECON super multiplicador *m*; ~ **NOW account** *n AmE* BANK cuenta sin límite de depósito y de reembolso *f*; ~ **saver** *n* GEN COMM superahorrador *m*; ~ **sinker bond** *n* FIN, STOCK bono con cupón a largo y vencimiento a corto *m*; ~ **video graphics array** *n* (*SVGA*) COMP conjunto de gráficos de supervídeo *m* (*Esp*) (*SVGA*), conjunto de gráficos de supervideo *m* (*AmL*) (*SVGA*)

superannuated *adj* HRM jubilado por edad

superannuation: ~ **accounts** *n pl* INS cuentas de jubilación *f pl*; ~ **contribution** *n* GEN COMM contribución por jubilación *f*; ~ **fund** *n* GEN COMM fondo de jubilación *m*, fondo de pensiones de vejez *m*; ~ **scheme** *n* GEN COMM fondo de pensiones *m*, pensión de retiro *f*, plan de jubilación *m*

supercomputer *n* COMP supercomputador *m* (*AmL*), supercomputadora *f* (*AmL*), superordenador *m* (*Esp*)

superficial: ~ **loss** *n* FIN, GEN COMM pérdida superficial *f*

superfund *n AmE* FIN, POL cuenta establecida por el gobierno federal para la limpieza de zonas contaminadas por desperdicios peligrosos

superheater: ~ **safety valve** *n* (*SHSV*) TRANSP válvula de seguridad del recalentador *f*

superhighway *n AmE* TRANSP autopista *f*

superimposed: ~ **tax** *n* TAX gravamen superpuesto *m*

Superintendent: ~ **of Bankruptcy** *n* GEN COMM, LAW *commercial* interventor(a) de quiebras *m,f* (*Esp*), contralor(a) de quiebras *m,f* (*AmL*), supervisor(a) de quiebras *m,f*; ~ **of Insurance** *n* HRM, INS superintendente de seguros *mf*

supermarket *n* S&M supermercado *m*

superneutrality *n* ECON *policies* superneutralidad *f*

supernormal: ~ **profit** *n* ACC, FIN utilidad superior a lo normal *f* (*AmL*), beneficio superior a lo normal *f* (*Esp*)

supernumerary *n* HRM supernumerario *m*

superposed: ~ **tax** *n* TAX impuesto superpuesto *m*

superpower *n* GEN COMM, POL superpotencia *f*

superscript *n* COMP, MEDIA *typography* índice superior *m*

supersede *vt* GEN COMM substituir, suplantar, suprimir

supersite *n* S&M espacio para carteles de gran tamaño

superstore *n* S&M hipermercado *m*

superstructure *n* (*super*) GEN COMM superestructura *f*

supertanker *n* ENVIR superpetrolero *m*

supervise *vt* GEN COMM, HRM, MGMNT inspeccionar, supervisar

supervision *n* GEN COMM control *m*, supervisión *f*; ~ **of credit institutions** FIN supervisión de las instituciones de crédito *f*

supervisor *n* COMP, GEN COMM, HRM supervisor(a) *m,f*, apoderado(-a) *m,f*

supervisory[1] *adj* COMP de supervisión

supervisory[2]: ~ **board** *n* GEN COMM comité de vigilancia *m*, consejo de supervisión *m*; ~ **management** *n* HRM, MGMNT dirección de supervisión *f*, gerencia de supervisión *f*; ~ **personnel** *n* HRM personal de supervisión *m*

supplement[1] *n* MEDIA *magazines, newspapers,* S&M suplemento *m*

supplement[2] *vt* GEN COMM complementar

supplementaries *n pl* POL suplementarios *m pl*

supplementary[1] *adj* GEN COMM complementario, suplementario

supplementary[2]: ~ **accounting system** *n* ACC sistema de contabilidad suplementario *m*; ~ **agreement** *n* GEN COMM acuerdo complementario *m*; ~ **assistance** *n* FIN apoyo suplementario *m*; ~ **benefit** *n* HRM beneficio suplementario *m*; ~ **budget** *n* ACC, ECON, FIN presupuesto suplementario *m*; ~ **company pension scheme** *n* FIN, HRM plan de pensiones suplementario de la compañía *m*; ~ **cost** *n* FIN coste suplementario *m* (*Esp*), costo suplementario *m* (*AmL*); ~ **entry** *n* ACC asiento contable suplementario *m*; ~ **estimates** *n pl* FIN cálculos adicionales *m pl*, POL previsiones presupuestarias suplementarias *f pl*; ~ **financing facility** *n* FIN cálculo financiero adicional *m*; ~ **intercompany pension scheme** *n* FIN plan de pensiones suplementario de empresas del grupo *m*; ~ **pension scheme** *n* FIN, HRM plan de pensiones suplementario *m*; ~ **period** *n* TAX periodo suplementario *m*; ~ **protection certificate** *n* (*SPC*) GEN COMM, PATENTS certificado de protección complementaria *m*; ~ **reserve** *n* BANK reserva complementaria *f*; ~ **service tariff** *n* (*SST*) TRANSP tarifa adicional por servicio *f*; ~ **special deposits scheme** *n* FIN cuadro de depósitos especiales suplementarios *m*, plan de depósitos especiales suplementarios *m*; ~ **stocks guarantee** *n* IMP/EXP garantía suplementaria de los stocks *f*

supplemented *adj* GEN COMM complementado

supplier *n* GEN COMM proveedor(a) *m,f*; ~ **credit** IMP/EXP crédito de suministrador *m*; ~ **evaluation** GEN COMM evaluación de proveedores *f*

supplies *n pl* GEN COMM consumibles *m pl*, S&M existencias *f pl*

supply[1] *n* GEN COMM abastecimiento *m*, suministro *m*, aprovisionamiento *m*; ~ **bill** POL *central government* borrador de presupuesto *m*; ~ **committee** POL comisión de presupuesto *f*; ~ **control** ECON control de la oferta *m*; ~ **curve** ECON curva de oferta *f*; ~ **function** ECON función de oferta *f*; ~ **network** *AmE* (*cf mains BrE*) COMP, IND red de alimentación *f*, línea principal *f*; ~ **price** ECON, HRM precio de abastecimiento *m*, precio de oferta *m*; ~ **revolving fund** ECON, FIN fondo renovable de provisión *m*; ~ **of services** ECON suministro de servicios *m*; ~ **shock** ECON choque de oferta *m*; ~ **side economics** ECON economía de oferta *f*; ~ **side shock** ECON choque del lado de la oferta *m*; ~ **work** HRM sustitución *f*, suplencia *f*; ◆ ~ **and demand** GEN COMM oferta y demanda

supply[2] *vt* GEN COMM abastecer, suministrar, aprovisionar; ◆ ~ **collateral** BANK aportar una garantía; ~ **goods on trust** GEN COMM suministrar bienes a crédito; ~ **references** GEN COMM dar referencias

support[1] *n* COMP, GEN COMM apoyo *m*, TAX *of dependant* sostén *m*; ~ **activities** *n pl* COMP, GEN COMM, MGMNT actividades de apoyo *f pl* actividad de apoyo *f*; ~ **hotline** COMP línea directa de consulta *f*; ~ **level** ECON nivel de apoyo *m*; ~ **price** ECON *agricultural* precio de garantía *m*; ~ **service** GEN COMM, POL *to government* servicio de apoyo *m*

support[2] *vt* ECON *currency,* GEN COMM apoyar, TAX *dependant* mantener

supported: ~ **by** *adj* FIN respaldado por

supporter *n* GEN COMM, POL partidario(-a) *m,f*

supporting: ~ **data** *n* MATH datos justificativos *m pl*; ~ **documents** *n pl* ACC, ADMIN, LAW documentos justificantes *m pl*; ~ **film** *n* LEIS película suplementaria *f*; ~ **individual** *n* TAX individuo que se hace cargo *m*; ~ **person** *n* TAX persona que se hace cargo *f*; ~ **purchases** *n pl* GEN COMM compras secundarias *f pl*; ~ **receipt** *n* GEN COMM recibo secundario *m*

suppress *vt* COMP suprimir

suppressed: ~ **inflation** *n* ECON inflación contenida *f*

supra *adv* GEN COMM supra

supranational *adj* GEN COMM supranacional

supraorganization *n* GEN COMM supraorganización *f*

Supreme: ~ **Court** *n* *AmE* (*cf High Court BrE*) LAW, POL Corte Suprema *f*, Tribunal Supremo *m*, ≈ Audiencia Nacional *f* (*Esp*)

surcharge *n* GEN COMM sobretasa *f*; ~ **letter** ACC, ADMIN, BANK carta con sobretasa *f*; ~ **value** TRANSP recargo *m*

surety *n* GEN COMM, FIN fiador *m*; ~ **in cash** LAW fianza en efectivo *f*

surf[1]: ~ **day** *n* TRANSP *shipping, charter party* día de oleaje *m*

surf[2] *vt* COMMS, COMP *internet* navegar, surfear

surface[1]: **by** ~ **mail** *adv* COMMS por correo marítimo o terrestre

surface[2] *n* GEN COMM superficie *f*; ~ **area** GEN COMM área de una superficie *f*

surpass *vt* ACC, ECON, GEN COMM exceder, superar

surplus *n* ACC, ECON excedente *m*, superávit *m*; ~ **approach** ECON estudio del excedente *m*; ~ **of assets over liabilities** GEN COMM excedente del activo sobre el pasivo *m*, plusvalía *f*, superávit *m*; ~ **capacity** ECON, IND capacidad excedente *f*; ~ **charge** ACC, BANK, FIN cargo al superávit *m*; ~ **dividend** FIN dividendo extraordinario *m*; ~ **reserve** FIN reserva del excedente *f*; ~ **stripping** TAX cesión del excedente *f*; ~ **value** ACC, ECON valor de la plusvalía *m*, valor del excedente *m*, valor del superávit *m*; ◆ **in** ~ ECON, FIN en excedente; **in financial** ~ ECON, FIN en situación de excedente financiero, en situación de superávit financiero

surprise: ~ **function** *n* ECON función sorpresa *f*

surrender *n* TAX dejación *f*; ~ **charge** INS coste de rescate *m* (*Esp*), costo de rescate *m* (*AmL*); ~ **of foreign exchange** BANK, ECON entrega de divisas *f*; ~ **of a patent** LAW, PATENTS cesión de una patente *f*; ~ **value** ACC valor de rescate *m*; ◆ **for** ~ STOCK *security* para rescate

surrogate *n* *AmE jarg* POL suplente *mf*, sustituto(-a) *m,f*

surtax *n* TAX impuesto adicional *m*, sobretasa *f*

surveillance *n* LAW vigilancia *f*; ~ **department of exchanges** STOCK departamento de vigilancia bursátil *m*; ~ **licence** *BrE*, ~ **license** *AmE* (*SL*) IMP/EXP licencia de vigilancia *f*

survey[1] *n* GEN COMM encuesta *f*, inspección *f*, sondeo *m*, PROP evaluación *f*, S&M sondeo *m*, TRANSP *vessels* revisión *f*; ~ **by contact** S&M encuesta por contacto *f*; ~ **certificate** GEN COMM certificado de un estudio *m*; ~ **fee** FIN *finance houses* honorarios de inspección *m pl*; ~ **fees** *n pl* GEN COMM gastos de peritación *m pl*; ~ **of observation** S&M encuesta por observación *f*; ~ **on**

investment FIN estudio de inversiones *m*; ~ **report** INS informe de averías *m* (*Esp*), reporte de averías *m* (*AmL*); ~ **research** S&M investigación por encuestas *f*

survey[2] *vt* PROP medir; ♦ ~ **the situation** GEN COMM inspeccionar la situación

surveyor *n* HRM *land* agrimensor(a) *m,f*, topógrafo(-a) *m,f*, PROP inspector(a) *m,f*

survival: ~ **process** *n* ECON *of firms*, GEN COMM proceso de supervivencia *m*; ~ **strategy** *n* ECON, GEN COMM estrategia de supervivencia *f*

survive *vi* ECON, GEN COMM sobrevivir

surviving: ~ **company** *n* GEN COMM compañía superviviente *f*; ~ **spouse** *n* TAX cónyuge superviviente *mf*

survivor: ~ **policy** *n* INS póliza para los beneficiarios *f*, póliza para los herederos *f*

survivorship *n* INS, LAW, PROP supervivencia *f*; ~ **account** BANK cuenta de supervivencia *f*; ~ **annuity** INS anualidad de supervivencia *f*, renta vitalicia *f*; ~ **clause** INS cláusula de supervivencia *f*; ~ **insurance** INS seguro de supervivencia *m*

susceptible: ~ **of industrial application** *adj* PATENTS susceptible de aplicación industrial

suspect: ~ **bill of health** *n* GEN COMM, WEL patente de sanidad poco fiable *f*

suspend *vt* GEN COMM, STOCK *trading, authorisation* suspender

suspended: ~ **sentence** *n* LAW condena condicional *f*; ~ **solid** *n* IND sólido suspendido *m*; ~ **trading** *n* STOCK negociación interrumpida *f*

suspense: ~ **account** *n* ACC, BANK, FIN cuenta de suspensión transitoria *f*, cuenta provisional *f*, cuenta transitoria *f*, partida en suspenso *f*; ~ **balance** *n* BANK saldo de incertidumbre *m*, saldo transitorio *m*; ~ **collator** *n* GEN COMM cotejador transitorio *m*; ~ **entry** *n* ACC, BANK, FIN asiento contable en suspenso *m*, partida en suspenso *f*; ~ **return** *n* TAX declaración en suspenso *f*

suspension *n* HRM suspensión *f*; ~ **seat** TRANSP asiento de suspensión *m*; ~ **of trading** STOCK suspensión de operaciones *f*

sustain *vt* ACC *losses* sostener, ECON *growth* afirmarse, LAW *loss, injury* soportar; ♦ ~ **one's claim** LAW considerar una demanda

sustainable: ~ **development** *n* ECON, ENVIR, POL desarrollo sostenible *m*; ~ **economic growth rate** *n* ECON, FIN, POL proporción de crecimiento económico sostenible *f*, tasa de crecimiento económico sostenible *f*; ~ **growth** *n* ECON, POL crecimiento sostenible *m*; ~ **level** *n* ECON *of demand* nivel sostenible *m*

sustained: ~ **noninflationary growth** *n* (*SNIG*) ECON, POL crecimiento sostenido no inflacionario *m*; ~ **resurgence** *n* ECON *of growth* resurgimiento sostenible *m*

sustaining: ~ **grant** *n* POL subsidio básico *m*, subsidio mínimo *m*

SVGA *abbr* COMP (*super video graphics array*) SVGA (*conjunto de gráficos de supervídeo Esp, conjunto de gráficos de supervideo AmL*)

SW *abbr* (*shipper weight*) TRANSP peso declarado por el expedidor *m*

swamp *vt* GEN COMM empantanar

swatch *n* GEN COMM muestrario *m*

sway *vt* GEN COMM *outcome* influir en

swear *vi* LAW prestar juramento; ♦ ~ **on affidavit** LAW declarar bajo juramento

sweated: ~ **goods** *n pl* GEN COMM bienes fabricados por mano de obra mal pagada; ~ **labor** *AmE*, ~ **labour** *BrE n* HRM, WEL mano de obra explotada *f*, *task* trabajo explotador *m*, trabajo muy mal pagado *m*

sweatshop *n* HRM, WEL empresa que explota al personal

Swedish: ~ **School** *n* ECON Escuela sueca *f*

sweeping *adj* GEN COMM *changes* radical

sweetener *n infrml* FIN, GEN COMM, POL *bribe* astilla *f* (*infrml*)

sweetheart: ~ **contract** *n* HRM *industrial relations* convenio colectivo favorable al empresario *m*

swell *vt* GEN COMM *accounts, coffers* inflar

SWIFT *abbr* (*Society for Worldwide Interbank Financial Telecommunications*) BANK, COMMS SITF (*Sociedad para las Telecomunicaciones Financieras Interbancarias Internacionales*)

swindle *n* GEN COMM estafa *f*

swindler *n* GEN COMM estafador(a) *m,f*

swing[1] *n* GEN COMM oscilaciones *f pl, of market* vaivenes *m pl*, POL *to the left/right* cambio *m*; ~ **clearance** TRANSP certificado de aduana para salir *m*; ~ **credits** *n pl jarg* ECON *international* créditos recíprocos al descubierto *m pl*; ~ **loan** BANK préstamo puente *m*, préstamo recíproco al descubierto *m*; ~ **producer** IND productor(a) complementario(-a) *m,f*; ~ **shift** HRM cambio de turno *m*, turno de relevo *m*; ~ **voter** *jarg* POL votante indeciso(-a) *m,f*

swing[2]: ~ **the deal** *phr jarg* GEN COMM conseguir un trato

SWING *abbr BrE* (*sterling warrant into gilt edged stock*) BANK, STOCK opción de compra o venta de un título de deuda pública

swinging: ~ **tariff** *n* IMP/EXP arancel recíproco *m*

Swiss: ~ **National Bank** *n* BANK, ECON, FIN banco nacional de Suiza *m*

switch[1] *n* COMP *device* interruptor *m, program* desvío *m*, GEN COMM intercambio *m*; ~ **dealing** *jarg* ECON transacción de arbitraje *f*; ~ **selling** S&M venta forzada de artículos más caros que los artículos en promoción, STOCK venta de un valor para comprar otro con mejor perspectiva; ~ **trading** GEN COMM comercio triangular *m*, comercio circular *m*, STOCK negociación rotativa *f*

switch[2] *vi* GEN COMM *from one thing to another* cambiar, pasarse; ♦ ~ **production** IND cambiar la producción

switch over *vt* GEN COMM cambiar; ♦ ~ **to** GEN COMM conmutar a

switchboard *n* COMP tablero de distribución *m*, GEN COMM cuadro repartidor *m*; ~ **operator** COMMS, HRM operador(a) de teléfonos *m,f*, telefonista *mf*

switching *n* FIN cambio de posición *m*, GEN COMM conmutación *f*, STOCK venta de títulos sin reinversión inmediata *f*; ~ **in rate** GEN COMM tipo más cercano *m*; ~ **out rate** GEN COMM tipo más alejado *m*

switchover *n* GEN COMM cambio *m*

swop *n* BANK, FIN crédito recíproco *m*, swap *m*, GEN COMM operación de dobles *f*, STOCK cambio *m*, operaciones de dobles *f pl*, permuta financiera *f*, *interest rates* crédito recíproco *m*, swap *m*; ~ **line** FIN línea de compraventa de divisas *f*; ~ **market** STOCK mercado de créditos recíprocos *m*, mercado de swaps *m*; ~ **network** STOCK red de créditos recíprocos *m*, red de swaps *f*; ~ **option** STOCK opción sobre permuta financiera *f*

swoption *n* FIN intercambio *m*

sworn: ~ **broker** *n* STOCK corredor(a) jurado *m,f*; ~ **statement** *n* LAW declaración jurada por escrito *f*

SWOT *abbr* (*strengths, weaknesses, opportunities and threats analysis*) S&M análisis de las fuerzas, debilidades, oportunidades y amenazas *m*

symbiotic: ~ **marketing** *n* S&M marketing simbiótico *m*

symbol *n* GEN COMM símbolo *m*; ~ **retailer** S&M minorista de marca *mf*

symbolic: ~ **association** *n* S&M asociación simbólica *f*

symmetrical: ~ **frequency curve** *n* MATH curva de frecuencias simétricas *f*

sympathiser *n* GEN COMM simpatizante *mf*

sympathy: ~ **action** *n* HRM acción por simpatía *f*, acción por solidaridad *f*; ~ **strike** *n* HRM, IND huelga de solidaridad *f*

symposium *n* GEN COMM simposio *m*

sync[1] *abbr* (*synchronization*) GEN COMM sincronización *f*

sync[2]: **out of** ~ *phr* GEN COMM no sincronizado

synchronization *n* (*sync*) GEN COMM sincronización *f*

sinchronized *adj* GEN COMM sincronizado

synchronous[1] *adj* COMP síncrono

synchronous[2]: ~ **system** *n* TRANSP sistema sincrónico *m*, sistema sincronizado *m*; ~ **transmitter receiver** *n* GEN COMM receptor transmisor síncrono *m*

syncro: ~ **marketing** *n* S&M marketing sincronizado *m*

syndicalism *n* HRM, POL sindicalismo *m*

syndicate[1] *n* BANK consorcio bancario *m*, sindicato bancario *m*, *AmE* (*cf union BrE, trade union BrE*) sindicato *m*; ~ **of investors** STOCK sindicato de inversores *m*; ~ **manager** BANK *corporate financing* gestor(a) del sindicato *m,f*

syndicate[2] *vt* BANK *loan* sindicar

syndicated[1] *adj* S&M sindicado

syndicated[2]: ~ **column** *n* MEDIA *print* columna sindicada *f*; ~ **loan** *n* BANK, FIN crédito sindicado *m*; ~ **swop** *n* FIN intercambio sindicado *m*

syndication *n* BANK formación de un consorcio *f*; ~ **official** BANK ejecutivo(-a) del sindicato *m,f*

synergism *n* ECON, GEN COMM sinergismo *m*

synergy *n* ECON, GEN COMM sinergia *f*

synetics *n pl* MGMNT método de resolver problemas recurriendo a la creatividad

synopsis *n* GEN COMM sinopsis *f*

syntax *n* COMP sintaxis *f*; ~ **error** COMP error de sintaxis *m*

synthesis *n* GEN COMM síntesis *f*

synthetic[1] *adj* GEN COMM sintético

synthetic[2]: ~ **bond** *n* STOCK bono sintético *m*; ~ **incentive** *n* ECON incentivo artificial *m*; ~ **long call** *n* STOCK *options* orden de compra a largo simulada *f*; ~ **long put** *n* STOCK *options* venta sintética a largo *f*

system *n* GEN COMM sistema *m*; ~ **of accounts** ACC sistema de cuentas *m*; ~ **administrator** COMP administrador(a) del sistema *m,f*; **~-based audit** ACC auditoría basada en un sistema *f*; ~ **development** COMP desarrollo del sistema *m*; ~ **disk** COMP disco de sistema *m*; ~ **failure** COMP *hardware* fallo del sistema *m*; **~-provider** FIN sistema-proveedor *m*; ~ **requirement** COMP requerimiento de sistema *m*; ~ **software** COMP programas de base *m pl*; ~ **of taxation** ECON, POL, TAX sistema impositivo *m*

System: ~ **of National Accounts** *n* (*SNA*) ACC Sistema de Cuentas Nacionales *m*

systematic[1] *adj* GEN COMM sistemático

systematic[2]: ~ **cost basis** *n* ACC base sistemática del coste *f* (*Esp*), base sistemática del costo *f* (*AmL*); ~ **risk** *n* STOCK riesgo sistemático *m*; ~ **sampling** *n* MATH, S&M muestreo sistemático *m*; ~ **withdrawal plan** *n* STOCK plan sistemático de reembolsos *m*

systematize *vt* GEN COMM sistematizar

systems: ~ **analysis** *n* COMP, GEN COMM análisis de sistemas *m*; ~ **analyst** *n* COMP analista de sistemas *mf*; **~ approach** *n* COMP enfoque de sistemas *m*; **~-based auditing** *n* ACC auditoría basada en sistemas *f*; ~ **design** *n* COMP diseño de sistemas *m*; ~ **engineering** *n* COMP ingeniería de sistemas *f*; ~ **management** *n* COMP, MGMNT dirección de sistemas *f*, gerencia de sistemas *f*, gestión de sistemas *f*; ~ **planning** *n* COMP, GEN COMM planificación de sistemas *f*; ~ **and procedures** *n pl* COMP, GEN COMM sistemas y procedimientos *m pl*; ~ **programmer** *n* COMP programador(a) de sistemas *m,f*; ~ **programming** *n* COMP programación de sistemas *f*; ~ **software** *n* COMP logical de sistemas *m*; ~ **theory** *n* MGMNT teoría de sistemas *f*

T

t. *abbr* (*tare*) GEN COMM T. (*tara*)

TA *abbr* COMMS (*telegraphic address*) domicilio telegráfico *m*, FIN, MGMNT (*transactional analysis*) análisis de transacción *m*, análisis transaccional *m*, HRM (*technical assistant*) asistente(-a) técnico(-a) *m,f*, (*training agency*) agencia de capacitación *f* (*AmL*), agencia de formación *f* (*Esp*)

TAAG *abbr* (*Tropical Africa Advisory Group*) ENVIR grupo consultor del Africa tropical

tab[1] *abbr* (*tabulation*) ADMIN, COMP tabulación *f*

tab[2]: **~ setting** *n* COMP posición de tabulación *f*

tab[3] *vt* ADMIN, COMP tabular

TAB *abbr AmE* (*tax anticipation bill*) TAX certificado de previo pago de impuestos *m*

table[1] *n* COMP listado *m*, GEN COMM *in document* cuadro *m*, tabla *f*; **~ of contents** GEN COMM índice de materias *m*; **~ of par values** STOCK tabla de valores nominales *f*; ◆ **on the ~** GEN COMM *proposal* sobre la mesa

table[2] *vt* GEN COMM catalogar, listar, POL *motion* presentar; ◆ **~ an amendment** LAW *BrE* someter a aprobación una enmienda, *AmE* aplazar la discusión de una enmienda

tabloid *n* MEDIA *print* tabloide *m*; **~ press** MEDIA *print* prensa amarilla *f*, prensa sensacionalista

tabular: **~ report** *n* GEN COMM informe tabular *m* (*Esp*), reporte tabular *m* (*AmL*)

tabulated: **in ~ form** *phr* ADMIN en forma de tabla

tabulating: **~ machine** *n* ADMIN maquina tabuladora *f*

tabulation *n* (*tab*) ADMIN, COMP tabulación *f*; **~ character** ADMIN, COMP carácter de tabulación *m*

T-account *n* ACC cuenta contable tipo T *f*, BANK Cuenta T *f*

tachograph *n* TRANSP tacógrafo *m*

tacit[1]: **~ acceptance** *n* BANK, FIN aceptación implícita *f*; **~ knowledge** *n* ECON, GEN COMM conocimiento tácito *m*; **~ renewal** *n* GEN COMM renovación tácita *f*

tacit[2]: **by ~ agreement** *phr* GEN COMM por acuerdo tácito

tackle[1] *n* TRANSP *cargo lifting* aparejo *m*

tackle[2] *vt* GEN COMM, MGMNT *problems* abordar, afrontar

TACs *abbr* (*total allowable catches*) ENVIR *fishing* captura total permitida *f*

tactical: **~ plan** *n* GEN COMM plan táctico *m*; **~ planning** *n* GEN COMM planificación táctica *f*; **~ pricing** *n* S&M fijación de precios táctica *f*

tactile: **~ keyboard** *n* COMP teclado táctil *m*

Taft-Hartley: **~ Act** *n AmE* ECON, LAW ley Taft-Hartley *f*

tag *n* COMP campo de identificación *m*, etiqueta *f*, S&M, TRANSP *identification of cargo* etiqueta *f*; **~ reader** COMP lector de etiquetas *m*

tagboard *n AmE* GEN COMM *electricity, telephony* cuadro repartidor *m*

tagline *n* MEDIA, S&M *advertising* eslogan *m*

tail[1] *n* GEN COMM *of list*, STOCK *insurance, treasury auctions, underwriting* cola *f*; **~ end of the season** GEN COMM final de la estación *m*; **~-lift** TRANSP plataforma de carga elevadora *f*

tail[2]: **~ away** *vi* GEN COMM ir disminuyendo

tailgating *n* STOCK oferta fraudulenta *f*

tailor[1]: **~-made** *adj* GEN COMM *package*, IND, S&M hecho a medida

tailor[2] *n* GEN COMM sastre *mf*; **~-made contract** LAW contrato a medida *m*

tailor[3] *vt* GEN COMM adaptar, configurar

tailored *adj* GEN COMM adaptado, configurado

tailoring *n* GEN COMM adaptación especial *f*

tailspin *n infrml* GEN COMM caída en picado *f*

taint *vt* TRANSP contaminar

take[1]: **~-home pay** *n* HRM sueldo neto *m*; **~-or-pay contract** *n* STOCK contrato de pago mínimo obligatorio *m*; **~-out loan** *n* BANK, PROP hipoteca de pago fijo *f*; **~-over bid** *n* (*TOB*) GEN COMM, STOCK oferta pública de compra *f* (*OPC*), oferta pública de adquisición *f* (*OPA*); **~-over merger** *n* STOCK adquisición mayoritaria de las acciones de una sociedad por otra *f*; **~-up** *n* WEL *social work* compensación *f*; **~-up rate** *n* FIN, WEL tasa de reclamación *f*

take[2] **1.** *vt* STOCK *one's profit* aceptar; ◆ **~ accommodation** FIN *loan, credit* aceptar una garantía; **~ account of** GEN COMM tomar nota de; **~ advantage of** GEN COMM aprovecharse de; **~ advantage of an opportunity to do sth** GEN COMM aprovecharse de una oportunidad para hacer algo; **~ a bill** FIN pagar una letra; **~ early retirement** HRM jubilarse anticipadamente; **~ effect** GEN COMM tener efectivo; LAW entrar en vigencia; **~ effect from** GEN COMM *date* entrar en vigor desde; **~ French leave** GEN COMM despedirse a la francesa; **~ a heavy toll of bankruptcies** FIN cobrarse muchas víctimas de la bancarrota; **~ a holiday** *BrE* (*cf take a vacation AmE*) LEIS ir de vacaciones; **~ in extra work** HRM aceptar trabajo extra; **~ into account** GEN COMM tomar en consideración; **~ a loan** BANK, FIN constituir un préstamo; **~ one's leave** HRM despedirse; **~ one's pick** *infrml* GEN COMM escoger; **~ an option** STOCK adquirir una opción; **~ possession** PROP tomar posesión; **~ from sb** GEN COMM sustituir a alguien; **~ sb to court** LAW llevar a alguien a los tribunales; **~ sb's debts** FIN, GEN COMM hacerse cargo de las deudas de alguien; **~ sb's references** HRM aceptar referencias de alguien; **~ sides with** GEN COMM tomar partido por; **~ steps** GEN COMM dar pasos; **~ sth aboard** GEN COMM, TRANSP izar algo a bordo; **~ sth at face value** GEN COMM adquirir algo a precio nominal; **~ stock** GEN COMM hacer inventario; **~ such steps as are considered necessary** LAW dar los pasos que se consideran necesarios; **~ legal residence** LAW adquirir la residencia legal; **~ the slack** *infrml* ECON rebajar el exceso de oferta agregada; **~ stocks** STOCK adquirir acciones; **~ a turn** GEN COMM dar un vuelco; **~ a vacation** *AmE* (*cf take a holiday BrE*) LEIS ir de vacaciones; **~ the wind out of sb's sails** HRM desanimar a alguien; **2.** *vi* GEN COMM *succeed* tener éxito; ◆ **~ part in** GEN COMM tomar parte en; **~ place** GEN COMM tener lugar; **~ shape** GEN COMM *idea* cobrar forma

take[3]: **be on the ~** *phr infrml* GEN COMM dejarse sobornar

take away *vt* GEN COMM llevar

take back *vt* GEN COMM *former employee, returned goods* retractar

take down *vt* GEN COMM bajar; ♦ **~ in shorthand** GEN COMM taquigrafiar

take in *vt infrml* GEN COMM abastecerse de

take off *vi* GEN COMM *business* despegar; ♦ **~ the market** GEN COMM quitar del mercado

take on *vt* GEN COMM *responsibility* asumir, HRM *staff* contratar

take out *vt* INS firmar, PATENTS obtener

take over *vt* ECON absorber, MGMNT asumir el control; ♦ **~ from sb** GEN COMM sustituir a alguien

take up *vt* GEN COMM *request, suggestion, wish* aceptar, *stand, stance* adoptar, STOCK *shares* tomar, WEL compensar

takeback: **~ bargaining** *n* HRM negociación revocable *f*

takeoff *n* ECON despegue *m*, GEN COMM, TRANSP despegue *m*; **~ point** ECON punto de conexión *m*

takeover *n* ECON absorción *f*, toma de control *f*, toma de mayoría *f*, FIN, STOCK toma de control *f*

taker *n* STOCK tomador, a *m,f*; **~ for a put and call** STOCK tomador de opción de venta y compra *m*; **~ of a rate** STOCK comprador(a) de una cuota *m,f*

takers: **~-in** *n pl* STOCK compradores *m pl*, suscriptores *m pl*

takeup: **~ rate** *n* GEN COMM, STOCK *shares* tarifa aceptada *f*; **~ reel** *n* IND bobina receptora *f*; **~ of shares** *n* STOCK adquisición de acciones *f*; **~ of Treasury bills** *n* FIN suscripción de bonos del Tesoro *f*

TAL *abbr* (*technical assistance loan*) BANK, FIN préstamo de asistencia técnica *m*

talisman *n* STOCK persona designada para completar un jurado

talk *vi* GEN COMM hablar; ♦ **~ business** GEN COMM hablar de negocios; **~ shop** *infrml* GEN COMM hablar del oficio, hablar del trabajo

talking: **~ heads** *n pl jarg* MEDIA *broadcast* bustos parlantes *m pl*

tally[1]: **~ clerk** *n* HRM, TRANSP *shipping* listero(-a) *m,f*; **~ register** *n* GEN COMM registro de cuentas *m*; **~-roll** *n* GEN COMM rollo de papel de máquina de calcular *m*; **~ sheet** *n* HRM hoja de registro *f*; **~ trade** *n* GEN COMM venta a plazos *f*

tally[2] *vt* TRANSP anotar mercancías

tallyman *n* S&M vendedor a crédito *m*

talon *n* STOCK talón *m*

tamper: **~-proof** *adj* GEN COMM a prueba de destrozos

TAN *abbr* (*tax anticipation note*) TAX certificado con intereses aplicables al pago de impuestos *m*

tandem *n* TRANSP tándem *m*; **~ account** BANK cuenta doble *f*

tangible[1] *adj* GEN COMM tangible

tangible[2]: **~ asset** *n* GEN COMM activo material *m*, activo tangible *m*, bien material *m*, bien tangible *m*; **~ assets** *n* ACC activos tangibles *m pl*, bienes tangibles *m pl*, ECON activos tangibles *m pl*, FIN activos tangibles *m pl*, bienes tangibles *m pl*, STOCK activos tangibles *m pl*; **~ capital property** *n* ACC bienes de capital tangibles *m pl*; **~ fixed assets** *n pl* ACC activos fijos tangibles *m pl*, inmovilizado material *m*, FIN inmovilizado material *m*; **~ good** *n* ECON bien tangible *m*; **~ personal property** *n* PROP

bienes tangibles personales *m pl*; **~ wealth** *n* ECON riqueza tangible *f*

tangibles *n pl* ACC, ECON, FIN, STOCK activos tangibles *m pl*

tank *n* (*TK*) TRANSP cisterna *f*, tanque *m*; **~ cleaning** TRANSP limpieza de cisterna *f*; **~ container** TRANSP contenedor cisterna *m*; **~ farm** TRANSP patio de tanques *m*; **~ pressure** TRANSP presión del tanque *f*; **~ top** (*TT*) TRANSP tapa de tanque *f*; **~ truck** *AmE* (*cf tanker lorry BrE*) TRANSP camión cisterna *m*, camión cuba *m*; **~-type stabilizer** (*TNK*) TRANSP estabilizador tipo tanques *m*

tanker *n* TRANSP buque cisterna *m*; **~ lorry** *BrE* (*cf tank truck AmE*) TRANSP camión cisterna *m*; **~ motor vessel** (*TMV*) TRANSP buque cisterna de motor *m*, petrolero *m*

Tanker: **~ Owners' Voluntary Agreement Concerning Liability for Oil Pollution** *n* (*TOVALOP*) ENVIR, TRANSP Acuerdo Voluntario de Armadores de Petroleros sobre la Responsabilidad por Contaminación de Crudos *m*

tanktainer *n* TRANSP tanque contenedor *m*

tap[1] *n jarg* STOCK tap *f*; **~ bills** *n pl* STOCK valores continuos *m pl*; **~ issue** STOCK emisión a goteo *f*; **~ stock** ECON, STOCK acciones disponibles *f pl*; **~ stocks** *n pl BrE* STOCK acciones estabilizadoras del mercado *f pl*

tap[2] *vt* GEN COMM *market* pulsar, *resources* desviar, *telephone call* derivar; ♦ **~ the market for** STOCK tantear el mercado en busca de

tap into *vt* COMP *telephone call* conectar, intervenir, GEN COMM *resources, market* extraer de, sacar de

tape *n* COMP, GEN COMM, MEDIA cinta *f*; **~ cartridge** COMP cargador de cinta magnética *m*; **~ drive** COMP unidad de cinta *f*; **~ feed** COMP alimentación de cinta *f*; **~ file** COMP fichero registrado en cinta *m*; **~ library** GEN COMM biblioteca de cintas *f*; **~ measure** GEN COMM cinta métrica *f*; **~ punch** COMP perforadora de cinta *f*; **~ recording** GEN COMM, MEDIA grabación en cinta *f*; **~ unit** GEN COMM unidad de cinta *f*

taper[1]: **~ relief** *n* TAX *inheritance, lifetime gifts* deducción progresiva *f*

taper[2] *vt* TAX *tax relief* segmentar

taper off *vi* ECON disminuir gradualmente

tapering *n* HRM variación gradual *f*

tapping: **~ of oil resources** *n* ENVIR explotación de recursos petrolíferos *f*

tare *n* (*t.*) GEN COMM, TRANSP *packaging* tara *f* (*T.*); **~ weight** GEN COMM, TRANSP peso de tara *f*, taraje *m*

target[1] *n* GEN COMM objetivo *m*, puntuación umbral *f*, meta *f*, IND, MGMNT, S&M meta *f*; **~ audience** S&M público objetivo *m*; **~ buyer** S&M comprador(a) objetivo(-a) *m,f*; **~ company** GEN COMM empresa objetivo *f*; **~ computer** COMP computador destinatario *m* (*AmL*), computadora destinataria *f* (*AmL*), ordenador destinatario *m* (*Esp*); **~ date** GEN COMM fecha propuesta *f*; **~ field** COMP campo de referencia *m*; **~ group** S&M *market research* grupo estratégico *m*; **~ group index** S&M indicación del grupo objetivo *f*; **~ language** COMP, GEN COMM lenguaje objeto *m*; **~ market** S&M mercado objetivo *m*; **~ marketing** S&M marketing de objetivos *m*; **~ price** GEN COMM precio indicativo *m*; **~ pricing** GEN COMM, S&M fijación de precios indicativos *f*; **~ range** ECON distancia al objetivo *f*; **~ rate** ACC, STOCK *interest rate futures* tipo objetivo *m*; **~ risk** INS riesgo meta *m*; **~ segment** S&M segmento objetivo *m*; **~ setting** GEN

COMM, S&M determinación de objetivos *f*, fijación de objetivos *f*, establecimiento de objetivos *m*; ~ **variable** ECON variable objetivo *f*; ~ **zone** ECON *exchange rates* zona meta *f*; ◆ **undershoot a ~** ECON no alcanzar un objetivo

target² *vt* GEN COMM dirigir, apuntar a

targeted¹ *adj* S&M dirigido

targeted²: ~ **campaign** *n* S&M campaña dirigida a un público concreto

targeting *n* ECON fijación *f*, S&M fijación de objetivos *f*

tariff² *n* ECON arancel *m*, tarifa aduanera *f*, GEN COMM *of prices* tarifa *f*, IMP/EXP, POL tarifa aduanera *f*, TAX arancel *m*; ~ **agreement** IMP/EXP, POL, TAX, TRANSP acuerdo aduanero *m*; ~ **barrier** ECON, GEN COMM, IMP/EXP, TAX barrera arancelaria *f*; ~ **concession** ECON, IMP/EXP, TAX, TRANSP concesión arancelaria *f*; ~ **cut** ECON, IMP/EXP, TAX rebaja arancelaria *f*; ~ **expenditures** ACC, ECON, IMP/EXP gastos aduaneros *m pl*; ~ **legislation** IMP/EXP, LAW, POL, TAX legislación arancelaria *f*, legislación de tarifas *f*; ~ **level** ECON, IMP/EXP, POL, TAX nivel arancelario *m*; ~ **policy** ECON, IMP/EXP, POL, TAX política arancelaria *f*; ~ **protection** ECON, IMP/EXP, TAX protección arancelaria *f*; ~ **quota** GEN COMM cuota de tarifa *f*, IMP/EXP contingente arancelario *m*, cuota de tarifa *f*; ~ **rate** ECON, IMP/EXP, POL, TAX tipo de arancel *f*; ~ **schedule** GEN COMM programa de tarifas *m*; ~ **system** ECON, IMP/EXP, POL, TAX sistema arancelario *m*; ~ **wall** ECON, GEN COMM, IMP/EXP, TAX barrera arancelaria *f*; ~ **war** GEN COMM guerra de tarifas *f*

taring *n* GEN COMM determinación de la tara *f*

task *n* GEN COMM tarea *f*, trabajo *m*, POL asunto *m*; ~ **analysis** IND evaluación de tareas *f*; ~ **closure** GEN COMM cancelación de tarea *f*; ~ **flexibility** HRM flexibilidad en la tarea *f*; ~ **initiation** COMP comienzo de una tarea *m*; ~ **management** COMP gestión de tareas *f*, MGMNT dirección de tarea *f*, gerencia de tarea *f*; ~ **method** S&M cálculo de adecuación de la publicidad *m*; ~ **scheduling** GEN COMM programación de tareas *f*; ~ **setting** GEN COMM determinación de tareas *f*; ~ **work** GEN COMM destajo *m*

taste *n* GEN COMM, S&M gusto *m*

TAT *abbr* (*transitional automated ticket*) TRANSP billete de transición automatizado *m*, billete mecanizado transitorio *m*

TAURUS *abbr* (*Transfer & Automated Registration of Uncertified Stock*) ECON, STOCK transferencia y registro automático de valores no certificados

TAWB *abbr* (*through air waybill*) IMP/EXP, TRANSP conocimiento de embarque aéreo directo *m*

tax¹ *adj* GEN COMM impositivo; ~**-deductible** TAX deducible a efectos impositivos; ~**-efficient** TAX eficiente desde el punto de vista fiscal; ~**-exempt** ECON, FIN, TAX exento de impuestos, libre de contribución; ~**-free** ECON, FIN, GEN COMM, TAX exento de impuestos, libre de impuestos

tax² *n* ACC, ECON contribución *f*, gravamen *m*, imposición *f*, impuesto *m*;

~ a ~ **abatement** TAX reducción del tipo impositivo *f*; ~ **accounting** ACC, BANK, TAX contabilidad fiscal *f*; ~ **accrual** TAX impuesto acumulado *m*; ~ **adjustment** GEN COMM, TAX ajuste impositivo *m*, reajuste impositivo *m*; ~ **administration** TAX administración tributaria *f*; ~ **advantage** TAX ventaja fiscal *f*; ~ **advisor** TAX

asesor(a) fiscal *m,f*, consejero(-a) fiscal *m,f*; ~ **agent** ECON, FIN, GEN COMM, TAX consejero(-a) impositivo(-a) *m,f*; ~ **agreement** ECON, POL acuerdo fiscal *m*, TAX acuerdo fiscal *m*, convenio fiscal *m*; ~ **allowance** TAX desgravación fiscal *f*; ~ **anticipation bill** AmE (*TAB*) TAX certificado de previo pago de impuestos *m*; ~ **anticipation certificate** TAX certificado con intereses aplicables al pago de impuestos *m*; ~ **anticipation note** (*TAN*) TAX certificado con intereses aplicables al pago de impuestos *m*; ~ **appeal** TAX recurso fiscal *m*; ~ **arrears** *n pl* ACC, TAX impuestos atrasados *m pl*, impuestos vencidos *m pl*; ~**-assessed accounts** *n pl* ACC, TAX cuentas tras liquidación de impuestos *f pl*; ~ **assessment** TAX determinación del impuesto *f*, estimación de la base imponible *f*, estimación de la base impositiva *f*, evaluación fiscal *f*; ~ **assessor** TAX tasador(a) de Hacienda *m,f*; ~ **assistance** TAX ayuda fiscal *f*; ~ **audit** TAX auditoría fiscal *f*, intervención fiscal *f*; ~ **avoidance** TAX elusión legal de impuestos *f*, evasión de impuestos *f*; ~ **awareness** TAX conciencia fiscal *f*, conciencia tributaria *f*;

~ b ~ **band** TAX banda fiscal *f*; ~ **barrier** TAX barrera fiscal *f*; ~ **base** ECON, TAX base del impuesto *f*, base imponible *f*, base impositiva *f*; ~ **base broadening** ECON, TAX ampliación de la base impositiva *f*; ~**-based depreciation** ACC, TAX amortización de la base impositiva *f*, depreciación de la base impositiva *f*; ~**-based incomes policy** (*TIP*) TAX política de rentas con base fiscal *f*; ~ **benefit** TAX beneficio fiscal *m*; ~ **bill** TAX cuota a pagar *f*, cuota tributaria final *f*; ~ **bracket** ECON, TAX categoría impositiva *f*; ~**-bracket creep** TAX tramo del impuesto progresivo *m*; ~ **break** TAX amnistía fiscal *f*; ~ **buoyancy** ECON, TAX elasticidad tributaria *f*; ~ **burden** ACC, ECON, TAX carga fiscal *f*;

~ c ~ **capitalization** ECON, TAX *fiscal mobility* capitalización del impuesto *f*; ~ **category** ECON, TAX categoría fiscal *f*; ~ **certificate** BANK, ECON, GEN COMM, TAX certificado impositivo *m*, certificado fiscal *m*; ~ **charge** ACC, ECON, TAX carga fiscal *f*; ~ **claim** TAX reclamación fiscal *f*; ~ **code** TAX código impositivo *m*, código fiscal *m*; ~ **collection** TAX recaudación de impuestos *f*; ~ **collector** HRM, TAX recaudador(a) de impuestos *m,f*; ~ **compliance** TAX cumplimiento de las obligaciones fiscales *m*, cumplimiento tributario *m*; ~ **component** TAX componente tributario *m*; ~ **concession** TAX concesión fiscal *f*; ~ **consequences** *n pl* ECON, TAX efectos económicos del impuesto *m pl*; ~ **consultant** TAX asesor(a) fiscal *m,f*; ~ **cost** TAX coste fiscal *m* (*Esp*), costo fiscal *m* (*AmL*); ~ **court** LAW, TAX tribunal fiscal *m*; ~ **credit** GEN COMM bonificación fiscal *f*, crédito tributario *m*; ~**-credit system** TAX sistema de bonificación fiscal *m*; ~ **cut** ECON, POL, TAX reducción de impuestos *f*;

~ d ~ **debtor** TAX deudor(a) fiscal *m,f*; ~ **deducted at source** TAX impuesto retenido en origen *f*; ~ **deductibility** TAX posibilidad de deducción fiscal *f*; ~ **deduction** TAX deducción impositiva *f*; ~ **deferral** TAX aplazamiento del pago de impuestos *m*; ~ **department** TAX departamento de impuestos *m*; ~ **disc** BrE TAX *automobile* pegatina del impuesto de circulación *f*; ~ **discounting** TAX descuento de impuestos *m*; ~ **district** BrE TAX distrito fiscal *m*; ~ **doctrine** TAX doctrina fiscal *f*; ~ **dodger** *infrml* TAX defraudador(a) de impuestos *m,f*; ~ **dodging** ECON, TAX evasión fiscal *f*; ~ **domicile** LAW, TAX domiciliación fiscal *f*, domicilio fiscal *m*;

~ e **~-efficient investment** ECON, FIN, TAX inversión que genera beneficios fiscales *f*; ~ **effort** ECON, TAX esfuerzo fiscal *m*; ~ **elasticity** ECON, TAX elasticidad tributaria *f*; ~ **environment** TAX ambiente fiscal *m*; ~ **equalization** TAX equiparación fiscal *f*; ~ **equalization account** TAX cuenta de liquidación de impuestos *f*, cuenta de compensación tributaria *f*; ~ **equalization scheme** TAX plan de compensación tributaria *m*, plan de liquidación fiscal *m*; ~ **equity** TAX equidad impositiva *f*; ~ **erosion** ECON erosión fiscal *f*, TAX disminución de ingresos tributarios *f*; ~ **evader** ECON, TAX evasor(a) de impuestos *m,f*; ~ **evasion** ECON, FIN, TAX evasión de impuestos *f*, evasión fiscal *f*; **~-exempt corporation** INS, TAX sociedad exenta de contribución *f*, sociedad exenta de tributación *f*; **~-exempt security** STOCK, TAX valor exento *m*; ~ **exemption** TAX exención fiscal *f*; ~ **exile** TAX exilio fiscal *m*; ~ **expenditure** ECON, TAX gasto fiscal *m*; ~ **expert** TAX experto(-a) fiscal *m,f*;

~ f ~ **fairness** TAX equidad fiscal *f*; ~ **farming** TAX cesión por el gobierno de la acción recaudatoria a un particular; ~ **field** TAX sector tributario *m*; ~ **foreclosure** TAX embargo fiscal *m*; ~ **form** TAX formulario de Hacienda *m*; ~ **fraud** TAX fraude fiscal *m*; **~-free allowance** TAX bonificación libre de impuestos *f*; **~-free benefit** ACC, TAX beneficio libre de impuestos *m*;

~ g ~ **gap** TAX diferencial fiscal *f*; ~ **gimmick** TAX trampa fiscal *m*, truco fiscal *m*; ~ **guidelines** *n pl* TAX directrices fiscales *f pl*;

~ h ~ **harmonization** ECON, TAX armonización fiscal *f*; ~ **haven** ECON, TAX paraíso fiscal *m*; ~ **holiday** TAX franquicia fiscal *f*, tregua tributaria *f*;

~ i ~ **immunity** TAX inmunidad fiscal *f*; ~ **incentive** TAX incentivo fiscal *m*; ~ **incidence** TAX incidencia fiscal *f*; ~ **increase** ECON, POL, TAX aumento de los impuestos *m*; ~ **influence** ACC, TAX influencia fiscal *f*; ~ **inspector** TAX inspector(a) de Hacienda *m,f*; ~ **installment** *AmE*, ~ **instalment** *BrE* TAX pago fraccionario del impuesto *m*;

~ j ~ **jurisdiction** TAX jurisdicción fiscal *f*;

~ l ~ **law** LAW, TAX derecho fiscal *m*; ~ **lawyer** GEN COMM, LAW, TAX ≈ abogado(-a) tributarista *m,f*; ~ **liability** TAX cuota líquida *f*, deuda fiscal *f*, deuda impositiva *f*; ~ **lien** TAX embargo fiscal *m*; ~ **and loan account** BANK, TAX cuenta de impuestos y préstamos *f*; ~ **loophole** TAX discriminación fiscal *f*, exención fiscal *f*; ~ **loss carryback** TAX compensación fiscal retroactiva *f*; ~ **loss carryforward** TAX compensación fiscal retardada *f*;

~ m ~ **measure** TAX medida fiscal *f*;

~ o ~ **offence** TAX infracción fiscal *f*; ~ **offset** TAX crédito por impuestos pagados *m*; ~ **otherwise payable** ACC, TAX impuestos pagaderos en especies *m pl*;

~ p ~ **package** TAX conjunto de medidas fiscales *m*; **~-paid guaranteed growth bond** FIN, STOCK bono de crecimiento garantizado con impuesto pagado *m*; **~-paid income** TAX ingresos después de impuestos *m pl*; ~ **payable** TAX deuda tributaria *f*; **~-payable basis** TAX base de la cuota a ingresar *f*; ~ **penalty** TAX sanción fiscal *f*; ~ **pool** TAX conjunto de impuestos *m*; ~ **position** TAX situación fiscal *f*; ~ **practitioner** TAX asesor(a) fiscal *m,f*, experto(-a) en impuestos *m,f*, experto(-a) fiscal *m,f*, gestor(a) fiscal *m,f*; ~ **preference**

item TAX partida de preferencia fiscal *f*; ~ **pressure** ECON, TAX presión fiscal *f*; ~ **privilege** TAX privilegio fiscal *m*; ~ **proceeds** *n pl* TAX rendimiento fiscal *m*; ~ **professional** TAX experto(-a) fiscal *m,f*; ~ **proposals** *n pl* ECON, TAX propuestas fiscales *f pl*; ~ **provision** ACC, TAX provisión fiscal *f*, provisión para impuestos *f*, reserva para impuestos *f*; ~ **purposes** *n pl* ACC, TAX fines fiscales *m pl*; ~ **pyramiding** TAX piramidación fiscal *f*, repercusión excesiva del impuesto *f*;

~ r ~ **rate** TAX tipo del impuesto *m*, tipo impositivo *m*; ~ **rate schedule** TAX tarifa del impuesto *f*; ~ **rate structure** TAX escala de tipos de impuesto *f*, tarifa del impuesto *f*; ~ **ratio** TAX coeficiente tributario *m*; ~ **rebate** TAX devolución de impuestos *f*; ~ **receipt** ACC, TAX recaudación impositiva *f*; ~ **receipts** *n pl* ACC, TAX ingresos fiscales *m pl*, ingresos tributarios *m pl*, recaudación tributaria *f*; ~ **record** TAX registro fiscal *m*; ~ **reduction** TAX reducción impositiva *f*; ~ **reform** ECON, TAX reforma fiscal *f*; ~ **refund** TAX devolución del impuesto *f*; ~ **relief** TAX desgravación *f*, desgravación fiscal *f*; ~ **relief at source** *BrE* TAX desgravación fiscal en origen *f*; ~ **relief for business cars** TAX desgravación fiscal para coches de empresa *f*; ~ **remission** TAX exoneración de impuestos *f*; ~ **restriction** TAX restricción fiscal *f*; ~ **return** ACC declaración sobre la renta *f*, declaración del impuesto sobre la renta *f*, TAX declaración a hacienda *f*, declaración del impuesto sobre la renta *f*, declaración sobre la renta *f*; ~ **return form** TAX formulario de declaración sobre la renta *m*, impreso de declaración sobre la renta *m*; ~ **revenue** ACC, TAX ingresos fiscales *m pl*, ingresos tributarios *m pl*, recaudación tributaria *f*; ~ **roll** TAX lista de contribuyentes *f*; ~ **rule** TAX norma fiscal *f*;

~ s ~ **sale** PROP, TAX venta de bienes embargados por el fisco; ~ **schedule** TAX calendario fiscal *m*; ~ **selling** TAX venta de acciones poseídas durante más de seis meses y que valen menos de su coste; ~ **shelter** TAX refugio fiscal *m*, amparo tributario *m*; ~ **shelter promoter** TAX promotor(a) de refugios fiscales *m,f*; **~-sheltered account** BANK, TAX cuenta protegida de impuestos *f*; ~ **shield** TAX desgravación fiscal *f*, amparo fiscal *m*; ~ **software** COMP, TAX programa para el tratamiento de datos fiscales *m*, software para el tratamiento de datos fiscales *m*; ~ **stimuli** TAX estímulos fiscales *m pl*; ~ **straddle** TAX arbitraje fiscal *m*; ~ **strategy** TAX estrategia fiscal *f*; ~ **structure** ECON, TAX estructura fiscal *f*, estructura impositiva *f*; ~ **system** ECON, POL, TAX sistema fiscal *m*, sistema impositivo *m*, sistema tributario *m*;

~ t ~ **take** ACC, TAX ingresos fiscales *m pl*; ~ **threshold** ECON, FIN, TAX nivel de tributación *m*, umbral impositivo *m*; ~ **transparency** TAX transparencia fiscal *f*; ~ **treatment** TAX tratamiento fiscal *m*; ~ **treaty** ECON, POL, TAX acuerdo fiscal *m*;

~ u ~ **umbrella** TAX cobertura fiscal *m*; ~ **unit** ECON tasa unitaria *f*, TAX unidad impositiva *f*;

~ v ~ **voucher** STOCK justificante fiscal *m*;

~ w **~-wedge** ECON, TAX acuñación del impuesto *f*; ~ **withholding** TAX retención fiscal *f*; ~ **write-off** TAX amortización fiscal *f*;

~ y ~ **year** TAX año fiscal *m*, ejercicio fiscal *m*; ~ **yield** TAX recaudación tributaria *f*, rendimiento fiscal *m*; ◆ **after ~** TAX después de deducidos los impuestos, después de deducir los impuestos; **before ~** TAX antes de deducidos los impuestos, antes de deducir los impuestos

tax[3] *vt* TAX gravar

Tax: ~ **Equity and Fiscal Responsibility Act** *n AmE* (*TEFRA*) TAX ley de equidad impositiva y responsabilidad fiscal de 1982; ~-**Exempt Special Savings Account** *n BrE* (*TESSA*) BANK, FIN, TAX cuenta de ahorros especial exenta de impuestos; ~ **Information Registry** *n* TAX Registro de Información Fiscal *m* (*RIF*); ~ **Reform Act** TAX Ley de Reforma Fiscal *f*

taxable[1] *adj* ACC, GEN COMM, TAX gravable, gravado, imponible, sujeto a impuesto; ◆ ~ **in the trust** TAX imponible en el consorcio; ~ **in the hands of** TAX imponible en poder de

taxable[2]: ~ **allowance** *n* TAX subsidio imponible *m*; ~ **allowances and benefits** *n pl* TAX retribuciones y beneficios gravables *m pl*, subsidios y prestaciones gravables *m pl*; ~ **article** *n* TAX artículo gravable *m*; ~ **beneficiary** *n* TAX beneficiario(-a) sujeto(-a) a impuesto *m,f*; ~ **benefit** *n* ACC, TAX beneficio imponible *m*; ~ **capacity** *n* ECON, TAX capacidad tributaria *f*; ~ **capital** *n* TAX capital imponible *m*; ~ **capital gains** *n* TAX ganancias imponibles del capital *f pl*; ~ **corporation** *n* TAX compañía sujeta a tributación *f*; ~ **dividend** *n* TAX dividendo imponible *m*; ~ **event** *n* TAX hecho imponible *m*; ~ **family allowance payment** *n* TAX pago imponible del subsidio familiar *m*; ~ **capital gain** *n* TAX ganancia imponible del capital *f*; ~ **income** *n* GEN COMM, TAX renta gravable *f* (*Esp*), utilidad gravable *f* (*AmL*); ~ **incremental oil revenue** *n* TAX ingresos petrolíferos progresivos imponibles *m pl*; ~ **item** *n* TAX artículo gravable *m*; ~ **municipal bond** *n* TAX bono municipal imponible *m*; ~ **net gain** *n* TAX ganancia neta imponible *f*; ~ **obligation** *n* TAX obligación imponible *f*; ~ **preferred share** *n* TAX acción preferente imponible *f*; ~ **profit** *n* ECON, GEN COMM, TAX beneficio gravable *m* (*Esp*), renta gravable *f* (*Esp*), utilidad gravable *f* (*AmL*); ~ **quota** *n* TAX parte imponible *f*; ~ **sale** *n* S&M, TAX venta sujeta a impuesto *f*; ~ **social security benefits** *n pl* TAX, WEL prestaciones imponibles de la seguridad social *f pl*; ~ **tax gain** *n* TAX ganancia imponible *f*; ~ **value** *n BrE* (*cf assessed valuation AmE*) PROP, TAX valor imponible *m*; ~ **year** *n* TAX ejercicio fiscal *m*

taxation *n* ACC, FIN imposición *f*, TAX fijación de impuestos *f*; ~ **authorities** *n pl* TAX autoridades fiscales *f pl*; ~ **capacity** TAX capacidad de tributación *f*; ~ **creditor** ACC acreedor(a) de impuestos *m,f*; ~ **period** GEN COMM periodo fiscal *m*; ~ **system** ECON, POL, TAX sistema fiscal *m*, sistema impositivo *m*, sistema tributario *m*; ~ **year** TAX ejercicio fiscal *m*

taxed *adj* TAX gravado; ~ **at source** TAX gravado en origen

taxes: ~ **actually paid** *n pl* ACC, TAX *balance sheet* impuestos ya pagados *m pl*; ~ **due** *n pl* ACC, TAX *balance sheet* impuestos debidos *m pl*; ~ **withheld** *n pl* ACC, TAX *balance sheet* impuestos retenidos *m pl*

taxfiler *n* TAX contribuyente que presenta la declaración

taxflation *n* ECON, TAX rémora fiscal *f*

taxi *n* TRANSP taxi *m*; ~ **rank** TRANSP parada de taxis *f*

taxing: ~ **capacity** *n* TAX capacidad fiscal *f*

taxiway *n* TRANSP pista de rodaje *f*

taxman *n* TAX recaudador(a) *m,f*

taxpayer *n* ECON, TAX contribuyente *mf*; ~ **number** TAX

número de identificación fiscal *m* (*NIF*), número de identificación tributaria *m* (*NIT*)

taxpayers': ~ **equity** *n* TAX equidad entre los contribuyentes *f*

taxpaying: ~ **ability** *n* BANK, ECON, GEN COMM, TAX capacidad contributiva *f*, capacidad impositiva *f*

Taylorism *n* ECON, HRM taylorismo *m*

T-bill *n AmE* (*treasury bill*) BANK, ECON letra del tesoro *f*, letra de tesorería *f*, STOCK pagaré del tesoro *m*; ~ **futures** *n pl* STOCK futuros sobre letras del tesoro *m pl*

TBN *abbr* (*total base number*) ENVIR número de base total *m*

T/C *abbr* (*time charter*) TRANSP fletamento por tiempo *m*

TCDC *abbr* (*Technical Cooperation amongst Developing Countries*) ECON, POL Cooperación Técnica entre Países en Desarrollo *f*

TDA *abbr* (*transport distribution analysis*) TRANSP análisis de la distribución del transporte *m*

TDB *abbr* (*Trade Development Board*) ECON *international* Junta de Desarrollo del Comercio *f*

TDC *abbr* (*top dead center AmE, top dead centre BrE*) TRANSP punta fija superior *f*

TDED *abbr* (*Trade Data Elements Directory*) ECON *international* anuario de datos comerciales *m*

TDI *abbr* (*trade data interchange*) ECON *international* intercambio de datos comerciales *m*

TDP *abbr* (*tradeable discharge permit*) ECON autorización de pago negociable *f*

TDW *abbr* (*tons deadweight, tonnes deadweight*) TRANSP toneladas de peso muerto *f pl*

TE *abbr* TRANSP (*triple expansion*) de triple expansión, (*turbo-electric*) turboeléctrico

teacher *n* HRM, WEL profesor(a) *m,f*

teaching: ~ **company** *n* WEL empresa de enseñanza *f*; ~ **machine** *n* WEL máquina de autoenseñanza *f*

team *n* HRM equipo *m*, equipo de trabajo *m*, equipo humano *m*; ~ **briefing** HRM, MGMNT análisis de situación en equipo *m*; ~ **building** COMP, HRM, MGMNT formación de equipo *f*; ~ **leader** HRM jefe(-a) de equipo *m,f*, líder del equipo *mf*; ~ **member** HRM miembro de un grupo de trabajo *m,f*, MGMNT componente de un equipo *m,f*; ~ **spirit** GEN COMM, HRM espíritu de equipo *m*; ~ **theory** ECON, HRM teoría de equipo *f*

teamster *n AmE* (*cf lorry driver BrE*) TRANSP camionero(-a) *m,f*, conductor(a) de camión *m,f*

Teamsters: ~ **Union** *n pl* HRM miembros de un sindicato americano de camioneros y trabajadores del sector automovilístico

teamwork *n* HRM trabajo en equipo *m*

tear[1]: ~-**proof** *adj* GEN COMM a prueba de desgarro

tear[2]: ~-**off calendar** *n* GEN COMM calendario de taco *m*; ~-**off coupon** *n* GEN COMM cupón para arrancar *m*; ~-**off portion** *n* BANK *of cheque book* parte recortable *f*; ~ **sheet** *n AmE jarg* STOCK página de comentarios de Bolsa publicada por S&P; ~ **strip** *n* GEN COMM tira de rasgado *f*

teaser: ~ **ad** *n* S&M publicidad de intriga *f*; ~ **campaign** *n* S&M campaña publicitaria de intriga *f*; ~ **rate** *n* FIN tarifa provocadora *f*, tasa provocadora *f*

TEC *abbr BrE* (*Training and Enterprise Council*) HRM agencia para programas de formación empresarial

TECH: ~ **cargo** *n* (*toxic, explosive, corrosive, hazardous*

cargo) TRANSP carga tóxica, explosiva, corrosiva, peligrosa *f*

technical¹ *adj* GEN COMM técnico

technical²: **~ advisor** *n* HRM consejero(-a) técnico(-a) *m,f*; **~ analysis** *n* STOCK análisis técnico *m*; **~ assistance** *n* ECON servicio técnico *m*, IND asistencia técnica *f*, POL ayuda técnica *f*; **~ assistance loan** *n* (*TAL*) BANK, FIN préstamo de asistencia técnica *m*; **~ assistant** *n* (*TA*) HRM asistente(-a) técnico(-a) *m,f*; **~ barrier to trade** *n* ECON, IND, POL barrera técnica al comercio *f*; **~ basis** *n* ACC, BANK base técnica *f*; **~ college** *n* WEL centro de educación técnica *m*; **~ consultant** *n* GEN COMM, HRM asesor(a) técnico(-a) *m,f*; **~ co-operation** *n* GEN COMM cooperación técnica *f*; **~ data** *n* GEN COMM datos técnicos *m pl*; **~ director** *n* COMP, HRM, MGMNT director(a) técnico(-a) *m,f*; **~ education institution** *n* WEL centro de educación técnica *m*; **~ efficiency** *n* ECON eficiencia técnica *f*; **~ field** *n* PATENTS campo técnico *m*; **~ help to exporters** *n* (*THE*) IMP/EXP ayuda técnica para exportadores *f*; **~ hitch** *n* GEN COMM dificultad técnica *f*; **~ manager** *n* COMP, HRM, MGMNT director(a) técnico(-a) *m,f*, gerente técnico(-a) *m,f*; **~ market** *n* STOCK mercado técnico *m*; **~ mastery** *n* GEN COMM dominio técnico *m*; **~ point** *n* LAW cuestión técnica *f*; **~ policy** *n* ECON, POL política técnica *f*; **~ press** *n* MEDIA, S&M prensa especializada *f*; **~ profile** *n* GEN COMM perfil técnico *m*; **~ progress** *n* ECON progreso técnico *m*; **~ rally** *n* STOCK recuperación técnica *f*; **~ salesperson** *n* HRM, MGMNT, S&M vendedor(a) técnico(-a) *m,f*; **~ sign** *n* STOCK signo técnico *m*; **~ standard** *n* IND *of product safety* norma técnica *f*; **~ support** *n* COMP apoyo técnico *m*, IND asistencia técnica *f*; **~ trespass** *n* *AmE jarg* POL infracción técnica *f*

Technical: **~ Advisory Sub-Committee** *n* (*TASC*) TRANSP Subcomité de Asesoría Técnica *m*; **~ Cooperation amongst Developing Countries** *n* (*TCDC*) ECON, POL *UN/ODA* Cooperación Técnica entre Países en Desarrollo *f*

technicality *n* GEN COMM, LAW tecnicidad *f*

technique *n* GEN COMM técnica *f*

technocracy *n* ECON, GEN COMM tecnocracia *f*

technocrat *n* ECON, GEN COMM tecnócrata *mf*

technocratic *adj* ECON, GEN COMM tecnocrático

technological: **~ change** *n* ECON, IND cambio tecnológico *m*; **~ edge** *n* GEN COMM vertiente tecnológica *f*; **~ forecast** *n* GEN COMM, IND pronóstico tecnológico *m*; **~ forecasting** *n* GEN COMM, IND predicción tecnológica *f*; **~ gap** *n* ECON brecha tecnológica *f*, IND vacío tecnológico *m*; **~ innovation** *n* GEN COMM innovación tecnológica *f*; **~ obsolescence** *n* IND obsolescencia tecnológica *f*; **~ park** *n* ECON, IND parque tecnológico *m*; **~ progress** *n* ECON, IND avance tecnológico *m*; **~ rent** *n* ECON arrendamiento tecnológico *m*; **~ transfer** *n* IND transmisión de tecnología *f*

technologically: **~ advanced** *adj* GEN COMM tecnológicamente avanzado

technology *n* GEN COMM tecnología *f*; **~-based industry** ECON, IND industria tecnológica *f*; **~ cooperation** GEN COMM cooperación tecnológica *f*; **~ and market interface** GEN COMM interacción tecnología-mercado *f*; **~ transfer** (*TT*) GEN COMM transferencia de tecnología *f*

Technology: **~ Education & Training Organization for Overseas Countries** *n* (*TETOC*) ECON *ODA* organización para la educación y formación para países extranjeros

technostructure *n* ECON tecnoestructura *f*

TED: **~ spread** *n* STOCK *futures* diferencial TED *m*

teenage: **~ market** *n* S&M mercado de los adolescentes *m*

TEFRA *abbr AmE* (*Tax Equity and Fiscal Responsibility Act*) TAX ley de equidad impositiva y responsabilidad fiscal de 1982

tel. *abbr* (*telephone*) COMMS teléfono *m* (*teléf.*)

tel. no. *abbr* (*telephone number*) COMMS número de teléfono *m* (*teléf.*)

telebanking *n* BANK telebanca *f*

telecommunicate *vt* COMMS transmitir por telecomunicaciones

telecommunication: **~ network** *n* COMMS red de telecomunicaciones *f*

telecommunications *n pl* COMMS telecomunicaciones *f pl*

telecommuting *n* COMMS trabajo a distancia *m*, trabajo a domicilio *m*

teleconference *n* COMMS, COMP, S&M teleconferencia *f*

telecottage *n* HRM trabajo desde casa a través de una red informática

telegraph: **~ pole** *n* COMMS poste de telégrafos *m*

telegraphic: **~ address** *n* (*TA*) COMMS dirección telegráfica *f*; **~ money order** *n* (*TMO*) COMMS, GEN COMM giro telegráfico *m*; **~ office** *n* (*TO*) COMMS oficina de telégrafos *f*; **~ transfer** *n* (*TT*) COMMS transferencia cablegráfica *f*, transferencia telegráfica *f*

telemarket *n* FIN, MGMNT, S&M telemarket *m*

telemarketing *n* FIN, MGMNT, S&M telemarketing *m*

telematics *n* COMMS, COMP, GEN COMM telemática *f*

teleordering *n* COMMS, COMP, S&M telepedido *m*

telephone *n* (*tel.*) COMMS teléfono *m* (*teléf.*); **~ answering service** COMMS, GEN COMM, S&M servicio de respuesta telefónica *m*; **~ bill** COMMS factura telefónica *f*; **~ book** COMMS agenda telefónica *f*; **~ booking** *BrE* (*cf telephone reservation AmE*) LEIS reserva por teléfono *f*; **~ box** *BrE* (*cf call box AmE*) COMMS cabina de teléfono *f* (*Esp*), locutorio *m* (*AmL*); **~ company** COMMS compañía telefónica *f*; **~ directory** COMMS guía de teléfonos *f*; **~ exchange** COMMS central telefónica *f*; **~ extension** (*X*) COMMS extensión telefónica *f* (*Esp*), interno telefónico *m* (*AmL*); **~ interviewing** S&M *market research* entrevistas telefónicas *f pl*; **~ message** COMMS mensaje telefónico *m*; **~ number** (*tel. no.*) COMMS número de teléfono *m*; **~ operator** COMMS, HRM telefonista *mf*; **~ receiver** COMMS receptor telefónico *m*; **~ reservation** *AmE* (*cf telephone booking BrE*) LEIS reserva por teléfono *f*; **~ sale** S&M venta por teléfono *f*; **~ selling** S&M venta telefónica *f*; **~ subscriber** COMMS abonado(-a) telefónico(-a) *m,f*; **~ tap** COMMS intervención telefónica *f*; **~ tapping** COMMS intervención de un teléfono *f*

telephonic *adj* ADMIN, COMMS telefónico

telephony *n* ADMIN, COMMS telefonía *f*

teleprinter *n* COMP, MEDIA teleimpresora *f*

teleprocessing *n* (*TP*) COMP, GEN COMM teleproceso *m*

telerecording *n* COMMS teleregistro *m*

telesales *n* FIN, S&M televentas *f pl*; **~ person** FIN, S&M vendedor(a) de televentas *m,f*

teleshopping *n* FIN, S&M compra telefónica *f*

Teletex: **~ Output Price Information by Computer** *n*

(*TOPIC*) STOCK información bursátil por videotexto de la Bolsa de Valores de Londres

teletext *n* COMMS, COMP, MEDIA teletexto *m*

teletypewriter *n* COMP terminal teleescritor *m*

television *n* (*TV*) MEDIA televisión *f* (*TV*); **~ advertising** MEDIA, S&M publicidad televisiva *f*; **~ announcer** MEDIA comentarista de televisión *mf*, locutor(a) de televisión *m,f*, presentador(a) de televisión *m,f*; **~ audience** MEDIA, S&M telespectadores *m pl*; **~ commercial** MEDIA, S&M anuncio comercial televisivo *m*; **~ consumer audit** S&M *market research* auditoría del consumo televisivo *f*; **~ coverage** MEDIA cobertura televisiva *f*; **~ networks** *n pl* MEDIA cadenas de televisión *f pl*; **~ rating** (*TVR*) MEDIA índice de audiencia televisiva *f*; **~ screen** COMMS pantalla de televisión *f*; **~ support** S&M *advertising* soporte televisivo *m*

televisual: **~ audience data** *n* MEDIA, S&M datos sobre la audiencia televisiva *m pl*

telework *n* COMMS, ECON, HRM teletrabajo *m*

teleworker *n* COMMS, ECON, HRM teletrabajador(a) *m,f*

teleworking *n* COMMS, ECON, HRM teletrabajo *m*

telewriter *n* ADMIN, COMMS telecopiadora *f*

telewriting *n* ADMIN, COMMS teletranscripción *f*

telex: **~ machine** *n* ADMIN, COMMS teletranscriptor *m*

teller: **~'s shortage** *n* BANK déficit de caja *m*

temp. *abbr* (*temporary*) HRM empleado(-a) eventual *m,f*, temporero(-a) *m,f*

temperature: **~-controlled transport** *n* TRANSP transporte a temperatura controlada *m*

temping: **~ agency** *n* GEN COMM, HRM agencia de trabajo temporal *f*

template *n* COMP *on keyboard*, IND plantilla *f*

temporal: **~ method** *n* ACC *currency translation* método temporal *m*

temporary[1] *adj* GEN COMM temporero

temporary[2] *n* (*temp.*) HRM empleado(-a) eventual *m,f*, temporero(-a) *m,f*, trabajador, a temporal; **~ difference** ACC *deferred tax* diferencia temporal *f*; **~ disability benefit** INS, WEL incapacidad laboral transitoria *f* (*ILT*); **~ employment** HRM empleo temporal *m*; **~ equilibrium** ECON equilibrio temporal *m*; **~ export** IMP/EXP exportación temporal *f*; **~ importation** IMP/EXP importaciones estacionales *f pl*; **~ residence** LAW *permit*, PROP, TAX residencia temporal *f*; **~ residence permit** HRM, LAW, POL permiso de residencia temporal *m*; **~ residence visa** HRM, LAW, POL, visado de residencia temporal *m*; **~ resident** LAW, PROP, TAX residente temporal *mf*; **~ secretary** ADMIN, HRM secretario(-a) temporal *m,f*, secretario(-a) interino(-a) *m,f*; **~ staff** HRM empleados eventuales *m pl*; **~ status** LAW estado temporal *m*, régimen temporal *m*; **~ work** HRM trabajo temporal *m*, trabajo eventual *m*, trabajo ocasional *m*

ten: **~ percent guideline** *n* TAX directriz del diez por ciento *f*

tenancy *n* PROP arriendo *m*, arrendamiento *m*, inquilinato *m*; **~ at will** LAW, PROP arrendamiento sin plazo fijo *m*; **~ for years** FIN, PROP arrendamiento por años *m*; **~ in severalty** LAW, PROP arrendamiento en posesión exclusiva *m*

tenant *n* GEN COMM, LAW, PROP, TAX arrendatario(-a) *m,f*, inquilino(-a) *m,f*; **~'s repair** LAW, PROP, WEL reparación del inquilino *f*; **~ right** LAW, PROP *land compensation* derecho del arrendatario *m*, derecho del inquilino *m*

tend *vi* GEN COMM *in direction* tender

tend toward *vt* GEN COMM tender a

tender[1] *n* GEN COMM licitación *f*, oferta *f*, *currency* moneda de curso legal *f*, oferta *f*; **~ documents** BANK documentos del precio que el comprador ofrece por pagar por el título; **~ offer** STOCK oferta pública de adquisición de una empresa *f* (*OPA*); **~ panel** (*TP*) FIN panel de ofertas *m*; **~ to contract** (*TTC*) GEN COMM licitación *f*, propuesta de contrato *f*, LAW concurso *m*; **~ vessel** TRANSP *shipping* buque blando *m*

tender[2] **1.** *vt* GEN COMM licitar, ofertar; ◆ **~ money in discharge of debt** LAW ofrecer dinero para saldar una deuda; **~ notice** STOCK *to exercise* proponer una convocatoria; **2.** *vi* GEN COMM *project* hacer una oferta; ◆ **~ by private contract** S&M ofrecer mediante contrato privado

tender for *vt* MGMNT *contract* licitar

tendered *adj* GEN COMM ofertado

tendering *n* GEN COMM licitación *f*

tenement *n* PROP vivienda *f*

Ten-Forty *n* *AmE* ECON título del estado rescatable a 10 años y pagadero a 40 años

tenor *n* COMP, FIN, GEN COMM, PATENTS contenido *m*; **~ bill** FIN letra de cambio *f*

tentative: **~ agenda** *n* GEN COMM agenda provisional *f*; **~ estimate** *n* GEN COMM cálculo provisional *m*; **~ plan** *n* GEN COMM plan provisional *m*

tenure *n* HRM ejercicio de un cargo *m*; **~ in land** PROP propiedad de tierras *f*; ◆ **have security of ~** HRM tener estabilidad en el cargo

tenured: **~ post** *n* HRM puesto permanente *m*; **~ staff** *n* HRM personal permanente *m*

term *n* BANK *of loan* vencimiento *m*, *time* plazo *m*, COMMS vencimiento *m*, GEN COMM term, POL *of government, of treaty* duración *f*; **~ bond** FIN, STOCK bono a plazo fijo *m*; **~ certificate** FIN, STOCK certificado a plazo *m*; **~ day** GEN COMM día de vencimiento *m*; **~ deposit** BANK depósito a plazo *m*; **~ draft** BANK, STOCK letra de cambio al vencimiento *f*; **~ insurance** INS seguro temporal *m*; **~ insurance policy** INS póliza de seguros a término *f*; **~ life insurance** INS seguro temporal de vida *m*; **~ of limitation** GEN COMM tiempo de prescripción *m*; **~ loan** BANK préstamo a plazo *m*; **~ of office** GEN COMM incumbencia *f*; **~ of patent** PATENTS duración de la patente *f*; **~ of payment** BANK plazo de devolución *m*; **~ policy** BANK, FIN periodo de la póliza *m*; **~ premium** ECON vencimiento de la prima *m*; **~ purchase** GEN COMM compra estacional *f*; **~ structure of interest rates** ECON estructura temporal de los tipos de interés *f*; **~ to maturity** STOCK plazo para el vencimiento *m*; ◆ **in the long ~** GEN COMM a largo plazo; **in the medium ~** GEN COMM por término medio; **in the short ~** GEN COMM a corto plazo

terminable *adj* GEN COMM rescindible

terminal *n* COMP, TRANSP terminal *m*; **~ account** BANK cuenta fiscal *f*; **~ bonus** ECON, FIN, INS bonificación final *f*, bonos de reversión *m pl*; **~ charges** *n pl* TRANSP gastos de estación de carga *m pl*; **~ computer** COMP computador terminal *m* (*AmL*), computadora terminal *f* (*AmL*), ordenador terminal *m* (*Esp*); **~ emulator** COMP emulador de terminal *m*; **~ loss** ACC pérdida al cierre *f*; **~ manager** TRANSP director(a) de terminal *m,f*;

~ **market** STOCK mercado a plazo *m*; ~ **operator** COMP operador(a) de terminal *m,f*; ~ **price** STOCK precio final *m*; ~ **screen** COMP pantalla terminal *f*; ~ **throughput** TRANSP tráfico total en una estación de carga *m*; ~ **traffic** TRANSP tráfico de la estación de carga *m*; ~ **user** COMP usuario(-a) de terminal *m,f*

terminate *vt* GEN COMM terminar; ♦ ~ **a fund** FIN agotar una provisión; ~ **sb's employment** HRM rescindir el contrato a alguien

termination *n* LAW *of contract* rescisión *f*; ~ **of appointment** GEN COMM final de una cita *m*; ~ **benefits** *n pl* HRM indemnización por despido *f*, indemnizaciones por cesantía *f pl*; ~ **clause** LAW cláusula de rescisión *f*, cláusula resolutoria *f*; ~ **of employment** HRM final del empleo *m*; ~ **with notice** *BrE* HRM cese con preaviso *m*, despido con notificación *m*; ~ **papers** *n pl* HRM documentos de rescisión *m pl*; ~ **payment** TAX *of retirement* finiquito *m*; ~ **of a policy** INS vencimiento de una póliza *m*; ~ **risk** FIN fin del riesgo *m*; ~ **of tenancy** PROP fin del contrato de arrendamiento *m*

terminology *n* GEN COMM terminología *f*

terms *n pl* GEN COMM condiciones *f pl*, términos *m pl*; ~ **of acceptance** FIN condiciones de aceptación *f pl*; ~ **and conditions** GEN COMM *of policy, arrangement*, INS plazos y condiciones *m pl*; ~ **and conditions of an issue** STOCK modalidades de una emisión *f pl*; ~ **of employment** HRM condiciones de empleo *f pl*; ~ **of export sale** IMP/EXP condiciones de las ventas de exportaciones *f pl*; ~ **of payment** BANK, GEN COMM condiciones de pago *f pl*; ~ **of reference** GEN COMM *of committee* objeto de la misión *m*; ~ **of sale** ECON, GEN COMM, IMP/EXP, S&M condiciones de venta *f pl*; ~ **of shipment** IMP/EXP, TRANSP condiciones de embarque *f pl*; ~ **of tender** GEN COMM condiciones de la oferta *f pl*; ~ **of trade** ECON, GEN COMM, IMP/EXP condiciones del intercambio *f pl*, términos del intercambio *m pl*; ♦ **in ~ of** GEN COMM *price* en cuanto a; **under the ~ of the contract** LAW según los términos del contrato; **not on any ~** GEN COMM bajo ningún concepto; **in real ~** ECON en cifras reales; **in relative ~** ECON en términos relativos; **in the same ~** GEN COMM en los mismos términos

terotechnology *n* ECON *theories* terotecnología *f*

terrestrial *adj* GEN COMM, MEDIA *broadcasting* terrestre

territorial: ~ **waters** *n pl* LAW, POL aguas jurisdiccionales *f pl*, aguas territoriales *f pl*

territory *n* GEN COMM, POL territorio *m*

terrorem: **in ~** *phr* GEN COMM bajo amenaza

terrorism *n* POL terrorismo *m*

tertiary: ~ **activities** *n pl* GEN COMM actividades terciarias *f pl*; ~ **education** *n* WEL educación superior *f*, educación terciaria *f*; ~ **product** *n* ECON *service industry* producto terciario *m*; ~ **readership** *n* MEDIA, S&M número terciario de lectores *m*; ~ **sector** *n* ECON, IND sector terciario *m*

TESSA *abbr BrE* (*Tax-Exempt Special Savings Account*) BANK, FIN, TAX cuenta de ahorros especial exenta de impuestos

test[1] *n* COMP, S&M prueba *f*; ~ **area** S&M zona de pruebas *f*; ~ **audit** ACC, GEN COMM auditoría de prueba *f*; ~ **bench** GEN COMM banco de ensayos *m*; ~ **close** S&M final de prueba *m*; ~ **drive** TRANSP prueba de carretera *f*; ~ **equipment** COMP equipo de prueba *m*; ~ **mailing** S&M *advertising* envío de folletos por correo a un grupo reducido de gente para hacer una prueba; ~ **problem** GEN COMM problema de ensayo *m*; ~ **rate of discount** ECON test de la tasa de descuento *m*; ~ **run** COMP, GEN COMM, IND, S&M *system, machine* ejecución de prueba *f*, prueba *f*; ~ **shot** MEDIA *film test* toma de prueba *f*; ~ **stage** GEN COMM etapa de prueba *f*; ~ **statistic** ECON, MATH estadística de contraste *f*, estadística de prueba *f*; ~ **town** GEN COMM ciudad de prueba *f*; ~ **transit** TRANSP *distribution* prueba en tránsito *f*

test[2] *vt* COMP, GEN COMM probar

test out *vt* GEN COMM *theory* poner en práctica

testamentary: ~ **debt** *n* TAX deuda testamentaria *f*; ~ **trust** *n* LAW fideicomiso testamentario *m*

testbed *n* GEN COMM zona de pruebas *f*

testdeck *n* COMP paquete de prueba *m*

testify *vi* LAW testificar, declarar

testimonial: ~ **advertisement** *n* S&M anuncio testimonial *m*

testimonials *n pl* HRM recomendaciones *f pl*

testimony *n* LAW testimonio *m*

testing *n* IND *of products* pruebas *f pl*; ~ **plant** IND planta de pruebas *f*; ~ **procedure** IND procedimiento de prueba *m*

tetrapak *n* S&M tetrapak *m*

text *n* MEDIA, S&M texto *m*; ~ **editing** COMP, MEDIA edición de texto *f*; ~ **editor** COMP, MEDIA editor(a) de textos *m,f*; ~ **in full** GEN COMM texto completo *m*; ~ **mode** COMP modalidad textual *f*, modo texto *m*

textbook: ~ **case** *n* GEN COMM, LAW caso modelo *m*; ~ **operation** *n* GEN COMM operación modelo *f*

textile: ~ **industry** *n* ECON, IND industria textil *f*, ~ **trade** *n* IND comercio textil *m*

textiles *n pl* GEN COMM, IND textiles *m pl*

Tf *abbr* (*triple screw*) TRANSP de tres helices

TF *abbr* (*tropical fresh water*) ENVIR, TRANSP agua dulce tropical *f*

thank[1]: ~**-you letter** *n* GEN COMM carta de agradecimiento *f*; ~**-you note** *n* GEN COMM breve misiva de agradecimiento *f*

thank[2] *vt* GEN COMM agradecer

thanking: ~ **you in advance** *phr* COMMS gracias anticipadas, gracias por anticipado; ~ **you in anticipation** *phr* COMMS gracias anticipadas, gracias por anticipado

Thatcherism *n* ECON, POL Thatcherismo *m*

THE *abbr* (*technical help to exporters*) IMP/EXP ayuda técnica para exportadores *f*

theft[1]: ~ **proof** *adj* GEN COMM a prueba de robo

theft[2]: ~ **risk** *n* INS riesgo de robo *m*

theme *n* GEN COMM *topic* objeto *m*; ~ **advertising** S&M publicidad temática *f*; ~ **park** LEIS parque de atracciones *m*; ~ **tune** MEDIA *broadcast* tema musical *m*

theonomy *n* ECON teonomía *f*

theoretical[1] *adj* GEN COMM teórico

theoretical[2]: ~ **capacity** *n* GEN COMM capacidad teórica *f*

theory[1]: ~ **of clubs** *n* ECON teoría de grupos *f*; ~ **of comparative costs** *n* ECON teoría de costes comparativos *f* (*Esp*), teoría de costos comparativos *f* (*AmL*); ~ **X** *n jarg* HRM teoría X *f*; ~ **Y** *n jarg* HRM teoría Y *f*

theory[2]: **in ~** *phr* GEN COMM en teoría

thermal: ~ **container** *n* TRANSP contenedor térmico *m*; ~ **energy** *n* ENVIR, IND energía térmica *f*; ~ **power station** *n* ENVIR, IND central termoeléctrica *f*

thermostatic: ~ **fan** *n* IND ventilador termostático *m*

thin: ~ **capitalization** *n* ACC *tax concept* capitalización escasa *f*; ~ **corporation** *n* GEN COMM empresa endeudada *f*; ~ **market** *n* STOCK mercado con escasez de operaciones *m*, mercado flojo *m*

think[1]: ~**-tank** *n* *infrml* GEN COMM grupo de expertos *m*

think[2] *vt* GEN COMM creer; ◆ ~ **the unthinkable** GEN COMM pensar lo impensable

thinking *n* GEN COMM pensamiento *m*

third[1] *adj* GEN COMM tercer; ~ **class** TRANSP de clase tercera; ~**-rate** GEN COMM de poca calidad

third[2]: ~ **age** *n* ECON tercera era *f*; ~ **carrier** *n* TRANSP *air distribution* tercer(a) transportista *m,f*; ~**-class mail** *n* *AmE* COMMS correo con tarifa económica *m*; ~**-class matter** *n* *AmE* GEN COMM asunto de tercera clase *m*; ~ **country cooperation** *n* ECON, IMP/EXP, POL *international trade* cooperación de un tercer país *f*; ~ **currency** *n* GEN COMM tercera moneda *f*; ~ **degree price discrimination** *n* GEN COMM, S&M discriminación de precios de tercer grado *f*; ~ **flag carrier** *n* TRANSP *shipping* transportista de tercera bandera *mf*; ~ **force** *n* *jarg* POL tercera potencia *f*; ~**-generation computer** *n* COMP computador de tercera generación *m* (*AmL*), computadora de tercera generación *f* (*AmL*), ordenador de tercera generación *m* (*Esp*); ~ **market** *n* *jarg* ECON, FIN, STOCK tercer mercado *m*; ~ **party** *n* GEN COMM terceros *m pl*, INS, LAW, PATENTS terceras personas *f pl*; ~**-party check** *AmE*, ~**-party cheque** *BrE* *n* BANK, FIN cheque endosado *m*; ~**-party claim** *n* LAW reclamación a terceros *f*; ~**-party credibility** *n* *jarg* GEN COMM *public relations* credibilidad de un tercero *f*; ~**-party currency** *n* IMP/EXP cuando la moneda con la que se acuerda pagar una exportación no es ni la del país exportador, ni la del país importador; ~**-party effect** *n* ECON *externality* efecto de un tercero *m*; ~**-party endorsement** *n* S&M endoso de un tercero *m*; ~**-party fire and theft insurance** *n* INS seguro de responsabilidad contra terceros, incendios y robos *m*; ~**-party insurance cover** *n* INS seguro con cobertura contra responsabilidad civil *m*; ~**-party insurance policy** *n* INS póliza de seguro contra responsabilidad civil *f*; ~**-party intervention** *n* HRM intervención de un tercero *f*; ~**-party liability** *n* LAW responsabilidad civil de terceros *f*; ~**-party risk** *n* INS riesgo de terceros *m*; ~**-party sale** *n* S&M venta de terceros *f*; ~ **person** *n* GEN COMM tercera persona *f*; ~ **quarter** *n* GEN COMM tercer trimestre *m*; ~ **world country** *n* GEN COMM país del tercer mundo *m*

thirty: ~**-day visible supply** *n* STOCK entrega visible a treinta días *f*

Thirty: ~**-Share index** *n* STOCK índice de cotización de Treinta Valores *m*

Thomson: ~ **Report** *n* ECON *regional policy in EU* informe Thomson *m* (*Esp*), reporte Thomson *m* (*AmL*)

thrash out *vt* GEN COMM *problem* discutir a fondo

threat: ~ **effect** *n* ECON efecto amenazador *m*

three[2]: ~ **axle vehicle** *n* TRANSP vehículo con tres ejes *m*; ~**-course rotation** *n* ECON *agricultural* rotación en tres ciclos *f*; ~**-digit industry** *n* ECON industria de tres dígitos *f*; ~**-martini lunch** *n* *AmE infrml* TAX despilfarro *m*; ~**-month add-on yield** *n* STOCK rendimiento positivo a tres meses *m*; ~**-month bond equivalent yield** *n* STOCK rendimiento equivalente de bonos a tres meses *m*; ~**-month Eurodollar Time Deposits** *n pl* STOCK depósitos a plazo fijo de tres meses en eurodólares *m pl*;

~**-month US Treasury bills** *n pl* STOCK letras del Tesoro de los Estados Unidos a tres meses; ~**-months' rate** *n* FIN tasa trimestral *f*, trimensualidad *f*; ~**-piece box** *n* TRANSP caja de tres piezas *f*; ~**-ply organization** *n jarg* GEN COMM organización en tres niveles *f*; ~**-stage least squares method** *n pl* ECON método de los cuadrados mínimos en tres etapas *m*; ~**-way call** *n* COMMS llamada tridireccional *f*; ~**-way split** *n* GEN COMM división en tercios *f*

threshold *n* GEN COMM umbral *m*, TAX nivel *m*; ~ **agreement** HRM acuerdo umbral *m*; ~ **amount** TAX cantidad mínima perceptible *f*; ~ **level** GEN COMM nivel de umbral *m*; ~ **point** STOCK punto de umbral *m*; ~ **population** ECON umbral de población *m*; ~ **price** GEN COMM precio umbral *m*; ~ **rate** HRM tarifa mínima *f*; ~ **value** COMP valor de umbral *m*; ~ **worker** *AmE jarg* HRM trabajador(a) no cualificado(-a) *m,f*

thrift *n* (*cf savings BrE*) BANK, ECON, FIN, GEN COMM, POL *austerity* economía *f*, ahorros *m pl*; ~ **institution** *AmE* (*cf savings institution BrE*) BANK entidad de ahorro y préstamo *f*, institución de ahorro y préstamo *f*; ~ **paradox** ECON paradoja de la frugalidad *f*; ~ **shop** *AmE* (*cf second-hand shop BrE*) GEN COMM, S&M tienda de artículos de segunda mano *f*

thriving *adj* GEN COMM próspero

through[1]: ~ **air waybill** *n* (*TAWB*) IMP/EXP, TRANSP conocimiento de embarque aéreo directo *m*; ~ **bill of lading** *n* IMP/EXP *shipping*, TRANSP conocimiento de embarque corrido *m*; ~ **charge** *n* IMP/EXP precio corrido *m*, TRANSP coste total *m* (*Esp*), costo total *m* (*AmL*); ~ **fare** *n* TRANSP tarifa total *f*; ~ **rate** *n* GEN COMM, IMP/EXP, TRANSP gastos directos *m pl*; ~ **shipment** *n* TRANSP embarque directo *m*; ~ **train** *n* TRANSP tren directo *m*; ~ **transport system** *n* TRANSP sistema de transporte total *m*

through[2]: ~ **the agency of** *phr* GEN COMM con los buenos oficios de; ~ **sb's agency** *phr* GEN COMM por intermedio de alguien

throughput *n* ACC contribución marginal bruta *f*, productividad *f*, COMP producción *f*, *capacity* caudal de proceso y transferencia *m*, FIN, IND rendimiento total *m*

throughway *n* *AmE* (*cf motorway BrE*) TRANSP autopista *f*

throw: ~ **the rule book at sb** *phr* GEN COMM arrojarle a alguien las normas a la cara; ~ **light on** *phr* GEN COMM esclarecer

thruput *n* *AmE* COMP caudal de proceso y transferencia

thruster *n* HRM impulsor(a) *m,f*

THS: ~ **transaction** *n* STOCK transacción THS *f*

thumb: ~ **index** *n* GEN COMM uñero *m*

Thw *abbr* (*thwartship*) TRANSP bancada de bote *f*

thwartship *adv* (*Thw*) TRANSP bancada de bote *f*

TIBOR *abbr* (*Tokyo Interbank Offered Rate*) BANK, ECON Tipo de Interés Interbancario de Tokio *m*

tick *n* STOCK punto básico *m*, valor mínimo de variación *m*; ~ **mark** ACC, GEN COMM punteo *m*; ~ **size** *infrml* STOCK magnitud del crédito *f*

tick off *vt* GEN COMM *on list* marcar

tick up *vt* BANK tildar

ticker *n* STOCK tablero automático de cotizaciones *m*; ~ **symbol** STOCK código valor para transmitir información *m*, signo del indicador electrónico *m*; ~ **tape** STOCK cinta de teletipo *f*

ticket *n* POL lista de candidatos *f*, STOCK resguardo *m*, TRANSP billete *m*; ~ **agency** GEN COMM, LEIS, TRANSP agencia de venta de localidades *f*, agencia de venta de billetes *f*; ~ **analysis** TRANSP análisis del billete *m*; ~ **collector** GEN COMM revisor(a) *m,f*; ~ **day** STOCK *London Stock Exchange* día anterior al de liquidación *m*; ~ **office** LEIS, TRANSP despacho de billetes *m*; ~ **tout** LEIS revendedor(a) *m,f*

tickler: ~ **file** *n* BANK archivo de vencimientos *m*

tidal: ~ **dock** *n* TRANSP dique de mareas *m*; ~ **fall** *n* TRANSP reflujo *m*; ~ **power** *n* ENVIR, IND energía maremotriz *f*; ~ **range** *n* TRANSP carrera de marea *f*; ~ **river estuary** *n* TRANSP estuario afectado por las mareas *m*; ~ **river navigation** *n* TRANSP navegación en río con corriente *f*

tie *n* GEN COMM *bond* atadura *f*; ~~**in advertising** S&M anuncio colectivo *m*; ~~**in display** S&M *advertising* promoción conjunta *f*; ~~**in promotion** MEDIA, S&M promoción combinada *f*; ~~**in sale** GEN COMM, S&M venta acoplada *f*

Tiebout: ~ **hypothesis** *n* ECON hipótesis de Tiebout *f*

tied[1]: ~ **aid** *n* BANK, ECON, MGMNT, POL ayuda condicionada *f*, ayuda vinculada *f*; ~ **house** *n* ECON, S&M tienda franquiciada *f*; ~ **loan** *n* BANK, FIN préstamo atado *m*; ~~**up capital** *n* ACC capital inmovilizado *m*

tied[2]: **be** ~ **to** *phr* GEN COMM estar vinculado a

tier *n* TRANSP andana *f*, tongada de cadena estibada *f*

Tier: ~ **One assets** *n pl* STOCK *sterling assets* activos de primera fila *m pl*; ~ **Two assets** *n pl* STOCK *sterling assets* activos de segunda fila *m pl*

tiger: ~ **team** *n AmE jarg* POL equipo de gran acometividad *m*

tight: ~ **budget** *n* ACC, ECON, FIN presupuesto ajustado *m*; ~ **controls** *n pl* LAW controles estrictos *m pl*; ~ **fiscal policy** *n* ECON, POL, TAX política fiscal restrictiva *f*; ~ **market** *n* S&M, STOCK mercado escaso *m*; ~ **monetary policy** *n* ECON, POL política monetaria restrictiva *f*; ~ **money** *n* FIN dinero caro *m*; ~ **money policy** *n* ECON, POL política de restricción de crédito *f*; ~ **ship** *n infrml* MGMNT organización estricta *f*

tighten *vt* ECON, GEN COMM, LAW *credit controls, rules* endurecer; ◆ ~ **the monetary reins** ECON intensificar las restricciones monetarias; ~ **one's belt** GEN COMM apretarse el cinturón

tighten up *vi* LAW poner condiciones más estrictas

tightening: ~~**up** *n* ECON, GEN COMM, LAW *of rules* endurecimiento *m*

tighter: ~ **controls** *n pl* LAW controles más estrictos *m pl*

till: ~ **money** *n* BANK dinero en caja *m*, efectivo disponible *m*, efectivo en caja *m*, ECON dinero en caja *m*, GEN COMM dinero en caja *m*, efectivo disponible *m*, efectivo en caja *m*; ~ **receipt** *n* GEN COMM, S&M recibo de caja *f*

tilt[1] *n* TRANSP lona *f*; ~ **trailer** (*Tt*) TRANSP *road* trailer basculante *m*

tilt[2]: ~ **the balance** *phr* GEN COMM inclinar la balanza

timber *n BrE* (*cf lumber AmE*) IND madera *f*; ~ **industry** *BrE* (*cf lumber industry AmE*) ECON, IND industria maderera *f*

time[1]: ~~**barred** *adj* LAW prescrito; ~~**consuming** *adj* GEN COMM que requiere mucho tiempo; ~~**saving** *adj* COMP, GEN COMM, MGMNT que ahorra tiempo

time[2] *n* GEN COMM tiempo *m*, TRANSP hora *f*; ~ **after sight** GEN COMM plazo después de la vista *m*;

~ **arbitrage** GEN COMM arbitraje en el tiempo *m*; ~ **band** TRANSP periodo de tiempo concreto *m*; ~ **bar** LAW prescripción *f*; ~ **bill** BANK, FIN letra a plazo *f*; ~ **book** HRM libreta de jornales *f*; ~ **budget** MGMNT tiempo estimado *m*; ~ **budget survey** ECON estudio del presupuesto temporal *m*; ~ **buyer** S&M comprador(a) de tiempo *m,f*, ~ **card** HRM ficha de control *f*, tarjeta de fichar *f*, tarjeta reloj *f*; ~ **charter** (*T/C*) TRANSP fletamento por tiempo y precio determinado *m*; ~ **charter party** TRANSP *shipping* póliza de fletamento por tiempo y precio determinado *f*; ~ **clock** IND reloj de control de asistencia *m*; ~ **component** GEN COMM componente tiempo *m*; ~ **constraint** HRM restricción de tiempo *f*; ~ **of delivery** GEN COMM plazo de entrega *m*; ~ **deposit** (*TD*) *AmE* (*cf fixed-term deposit BrE*) BANK depósito a plazo fijo *m*, ECON imposición a plazo *f*; ~ **discount** S&M *advertising* descuento según el tiempo comprado; ~ **for payment** BANK plazo de pago *m*; ~ **frame** GEN COMM, MGMNT marco temporal *m*, periodo de tiempo *m*; ~ **freight** TRANSP flete por tiempo *m*; ~ **horizon** MGMNT fecha límite *f*; ~~**keeping** COMMS, GEN COMM control de tiempo *m*, cronometración de tiempo *m*; ~ **lag** ECON, TAX desfase cronológico *m*; ~ **letter of credit** BANK, FIN carta de crédito a plazo *f*; ~ **limit** GEN COMM plazo *m*; ~ **management** MGMNT dirección de los horarios de trabajo *f*, gerencia de los horarios de trabajo *f*; ~ **and methods study** GEN COMM estudio de tiempo y métodos *m*; ~ **and motion study** ECON, GEN COMM, HRM, IND estudio de desplazamientos y tiempos *m*, estudio de tiempo y movimientos *m*; ~ **off** GEN COMM, HRM tiempo libre fuera del trabajo *m*; ~ **off work** GEN COMM, HRM tiempo libre *m*; ~ **on risk** INS tiempo en riesgo *m*; ~ **policy** INS póliza con vencimiento fijo *f*; ~ **premium** STOCK prima debida por el periodo corrido del seguro *f*; ~ **pressure** GEN COMM apremio *m*; ~ **rate** ECON tarifa por hora *f*, HRM pago por horas *m*, remuneración por unidad de tiempo *f*; ~ **risk** INS riesgo temporal *m*; ~ **segment** S&M *advertising* franja horaria *f*; ~ **series** *n pl* ECON, GEN COMM, MATH *statistics* serie cronológica *f*, serie temporal *f*; ~ **series analysis** ECON, GEN COMM, MATH análisis de series temporales *m*; ~ **served** HRM tiempo prestado de servicio *m*; ~~**sharing** (*TS*) COMP, HRM tiempo compartido *m*, PROP multipropiedad *f*; ~ **sheet** HRM hoja de jornales devengados *f* (*Esp*), hoja de tiempo *f* (*AmL*), parte de horas trabajadas *m*; ~ **slot** GEN COMM cuota de tiempo *f*; ~ **spantem** ECON tiempo máximo para realizar una tarea *m*, espacio temporal *m*, GEN COMM periodo *m*; ~ **spread** STOCK margen de tiempo *m*, diferencial horizontal *m*; ~ **study** GEN COMM, MATH *statistics* estudio de tiempos *m*; ~ **to market** GEN COMM hora de ir al mercado *f*; ~ **value** STOCK *options* valor tiempo *m*; ~ **value rate of decay** STOCK *options* índice de decadencia del factor tiempo *m*; ~ **work** HRM trabajo pagado por horas *m*; ~ **zone** GEN COMM uso horario *m*; ◆ **at the appointed** ~ GEN COMM a la hora fijada; **at a given** ~ GEN COMM en un tiempo determinado; **at the present** ~ GEN COMM en la actualidad; **at the specified** ~ GEN COMM dentro del plazo especificado; **be on short** ~ HRM tener jornada reducida; ~ **is money** GEN COMM el tiempo es oro; **at a given** ~ **in the future** GEN COMM en un tiempo futuro; **at some** ~ **in the future** GEN COMM en algún momento futuro; **be on** ~ **and a half** HRM cobrar la jornada y media; **this** ~ **next week** GEN COMM dentro de una semana; **all** ~ **saved** TRANSP *shipping* todo tiempo ahorrado; **on a** ~ **sharing basis**

PROP en multipropiedad; **with ~ to spare** GEN COMM con tiempo de sobra

timed: ~ **backup** *n* COMP copia de seguridad temporizada *f*

timekeeper *n* ADMIN, GEN COMM medidor(a) de intervalos de tiempo *m,f*

timely *adj* GEN COMM oportuno

timeout *n* COMP compás de espera *m* (*jarg*)

timer *n* COMP reloj *m*

times: ~ **fixed charges** *n pl* ACC gastos fijos proporcionales al tiempo *m pl*, gastos proporcionales al tiempo *m pl*; ~ **uncovered** *n* FIN fondos de deuda divididos *m pl*

timescale *n* GEN COMM calendario *m*, horario *m*

timeshare *n* ECON, PROP multipropiedad *f*; ~ **developer** *n pl* PROP promotor(a) de multipropiedades *m,f*; ~ **property** PROP multipropiedad *f*

timetable *n* (*TT*) GEN COMM, MGMNT, TRANSP horario *m*; ~ **analysis** TRANSP análisis del horario *m*; ~ **planning** TRANSP programación del horario *f*

timing *n* ACC cálculo de tiempo *m*, COMP duración *f*, FIN, GEN COMM, HRM cálculo de tiempo *m*, cronometraje *m*; ~ **difference** ACC *deferred tax*, TAX diferencia de periodos *f*

tin: ~ **ore** *n* ENVIR, IND mineral de estaño *m*; ~ **shares** *n pl* STOCK acciones de mala calidad *f pl*

TINA *abbr* (*there is no alternative*) GEN COMM no hay alternativa

tip[1] *n* BANK extratipo *m*, GEN COMM propina *f*, *advice* informe confidencial *m* (*Esp*), reporte confidencial *m* (*AmL*), LEIS propina *f*, TAX informe confidencial *m* (*Esp*), reporte confidencial *m* (*AmL*); ~**-in** MEDIA *newspapers, magazines* encarte *m*; ~**-off** GEN COMM informe confidencial *m* (*Esp*), reporte confidencial *m* (*AmL*); ◆ ~ **of the iceberg** GEN COMM punta del iceberg *f*

tip[2]: ~ **the scales** *phr* GEN COMM inclinar la balanza

TIP *abbr* (*tax-based incomes policy*) TAX política de rentas con base fiscal *f*

tipper *n* TRANSP camión basculante *m*, vagón basculante *m*

tipping *n* TRANSP basculamiento *m*, ladeo *m*, vuelco *m*

tire *AmE see* tyre *BrE*

title *n* GEN COMM *to goods* denominación *f*, MEDIA *magazines*, S&M título *m*; ~ **of an account** ACC, BANK título de una cuenta *m*; ~ **deed** LAW, PROP escritura de propiedad *f*, título de propiedad *m*; ~ **insurance** INS seguro de título *m*; ~ **of the invention** PATENTS licencia de pleno derecho del invento *m*; ~ **page** MEDIA *print* página de portada *f*; ~ **protection insurance** INS seguro de protección de título *m*; ~ **theory state** LAW situación de la teoría de la propiedad *f*; ~ **to the goods** GEN COMM, LAW título de propiedad de los bienes *m*, título sobre los bienes *m*

titular: ~ **head of an organization** *n* HRM titular de una organización *mf*

TK *abbr* (*tank*) TRANSP cisterna *f*, tanque *m*

TL *abbr* (*total loss*) GEN COMM, INS pérdida total *f*

TLF *abbr* (*transferable loan facilities*) BANK, FIN línea de préstamo transferible *m*

TLI *abbr* (*transferable loan instrument*) BANK, FIN instrumento de préstamo transferible *m*

TLO *abbr* (*total loss only*) GEN COMM, INS sólo pérdida total

TM *abbr* HRM, (*traffic manager*) gerente de tráfico *mf*, TRANSP (*ton mile*) tonelada-milla *f*

TML *abbr* (*transportable moisture limit*) TRANSP límite de humedad transportable *m*

TMO *abbr* (*telegraphic money order*) COMMS, GEN COMM giro telegráfico *m*

TMV *abbr* (*tanker motor vessel*) TRANSP buque cisterna de motor *m*, petrolero *m*

TNC *abbr* (*transnational corporation*) ECON, POL TNC *f* (*corporación transnacional*), multinacional *f*, empresa transnacional *f*

TNK *abbr* (*tank-type stabilizer*) TRANSP estabilizador tipo tanques *m*

TO *abbr* (*telegraphic office*) COMMS oficina de telégrafos *f*

TOB *abbr* (*take-over bid*) GEN COMM, STOCK OPA (*oferta pública de adquisición*), OPC (*oferta pública de compra*)

tobacco *n* GEN COMM tabaco *m*; ~ **products** *n pl* GEN COMM, TAX labores de tabaco *f pl*

Tobin: ~ **tax** *n* ECON, TAX tasa de Tobin *f*

Tobit: ~ **model** *n* ECON modelo de Tobit *m*

toehold: ~ **purchase** *n* STOCK toma de posición menor al 5 por ciento

TOFC *abbr* (*trailer on flat car*) TRANSP vagón plataforma plana *m*

toggle[1] *n* COMP interruptor *m*, palanca basculante *f*; ~ **switch** COMP interruptor basculante *m*, interruptor de palanca *m*

toggle[2] *vi* COMP bascular

toiletries *n pl* GEN COMM artículos de tocador *m pl*

token *n* COMP contraseña *f*; ~ **money** *BrE* (*cf fiat money AmE*) BANK, FIN moneda despreciada *f*, moneda fiduciaria *f*, moneda nominal *f*; ~ **stoppage** HRM suspensión simbólica *f*; ~ **strike** HRM huelga simbólica *f*

tokenism *n* LAW igualdad de oportunidades aparente *f*

Tokyo: ~**-based company** *n* GEN COMM empresa establecida en Tokio; ~ **Interbank Offered Rate** *n* (*TIBOR*) BANK, ECON Tipo de Interés Interbancario de Tokio *m*; ~ **Round** *n* ECON Ronda de Tokio *f*

tolerance *n* GEN COMM tolerancia *f*; ~ **level** FIN nivel de tolerancia *m*

toll[1]: ~**-free** *adj* TRANSP libre de gastos, libre de peaje

toll[2] *n* GEN COMM, TRANSP *motorways* peaje *m*; ~ **call** *AmE* (*cf trunk call BrE*) COMMS conferencia interurbana *f*, comunicación interurbana *f*, llamada de larga distancia *f*; ~**-free call** COMMS llamada libre de tasas *f*; ~**-free number** *AmE* COMMS número exento de pago *m*; ~ **model** ECON modelo de peaje *m*; ~ **motorway** *BrE* (*cf turnpike AmE*) TRANSP autopista de peaje *f*; ~ **revenue bond** FIN, STOCK bono municipal de respaldo fiscal *m*

tollbooth *n* TRANSP cabina de portazgo *f*

tollbridge *n* TRANSP puente de peaje *m*

tom *n* TRANSP *cargo securing equipment* cable tensor *m*

tombstone *n* ECON, STOCK anuncio de emisión sindicada *m*, tombstone *m*; ~ **ad** FIN esquela *f*, STOCK anuncio de emisión sindicada *m*, tombstone *m*

tom/next *abbr* (*from tomorrow to the next business day*) STOCK el próximo día hábil a partir de mañana

tomorrow[1]: ~ **week** *n* GEN COMM de aquí a una semana

tomorrow[2]: **from ~ to the next business day** *phr* (*tom/next*) STOCK el próximo día hábil a partir de mañana

ton *n* GEN COMM tonelada *f*; ~ **equivalent unit** TRANSP unidad equivalente a una tonelada *f*; ~ **kilometer** *AmE*,

~ **kilometre** *BrE* GEN COMM tonelada por kilómetro *f*; ~ **mile** GEN COMM, TRANSP tonelada por milla *f*; ~ **miles per vehicle hour** *n pl* TRANSP toneladas por milla y hora *f pl*; ~ **per centimeter** *AmE*, ~ **per centimetre** *BrE* GEN COMM tonelada por centímetro *f*

toner *n* COMP tonalizador *m*

tongs *n pl* TRANSP *cargo equipment* tenazas de elevación *f pl*

tonnage: ~ **calculation** *n* TRANSP *shipping* cálculo de tonelaje *m*; ~ **dues** *n pl* TRANSP derechos de tonelaje *m pl*; ~ **dues slip** *n* TRANSP recibo de derechos de tonelaje *m*; ~ **mark** *n* TRANSP marcos de tonelaje *m pl*; ~ **measurement** *n* TRANSP medición del tonelaje *f*; ~ **slip** *n* TRANSP error de tonelaje *m*

tonne *see* **ton**

tons: ~ **deadweight** *n pl* (*TDW*) TRANSP toneladas de peso muerto *f pl*

tontine *n* ECON, LAW tontina *f*

tool *n* COMP herramienta *f*, GEN COMM herramienta *f*, instrumento *m*; ~ **bar** COMP barra de trabajo *f*; ~ **of the trade** GEN COMM herramienta de trabajo *f*

tool up *vt* IND dotar de herramientas

toolmaker *n* GEN COMM, IND fabricante de herramientas *mf*

toolroom *n* IND taller *m*

tool *n pl* GEN COMM utillaje *m*

top¹: ~**-flight** *adj* GEN COMM sobresaliente, de primera categoría; ~**-heavy** *adj* GEN COMM sobredimensionado; ~**-level** *adj* COMP, HRM de alto nivel; ~**-of-the-range** *adj* GEN COMM, S&M de gama alta; ~**-ranking** *adj* GEN COMM de primera categoría, destacado; ~**-rated** *adj* BANK, GEN COMM escogido; ~**-secret** *adj* BANK, GEN COMM, LAW, POL, TAX confidencial, de alto secreto

top²: ~ **down** *adv* GEN COMM de forma jerárquica

top³ *n* HRM *of the organization* cúpula *f*; ~ **copy** GEN COMM copia original *f*; ~ **dead center** *AmE*, ~ **dead centre** *BrE* (*TDC*) TRANSP punto muerto superior *m*; ~**-down approach to investing** FIN enfoque descendente de la inversión *m*; ~**-down management** MGMNT gestión vertical *f*; ~ **end of the market** S&M gama superior del mercado *f*, gama alta del mercado *f*; ~ **executive** GEN COMM, HRM, MGMNT alto(-a) ejecutivo(-a) *m,f*; ~ **hand** *jarg* GEN COMM ganadera experimentada *f*, ganadera productiva *f*; ~**-hat pension** *infrml* FIN pensión de altos cargos *f*; ~**-level efficiency** ECON eficiencia de más alto nivel *f*; ~ **level talks** *n pl* MGMNT conversaciones de alto nivel *f pl*; ~ **loader container** TRANSP contenedor de carga superior *m*; ~ **management approach** HRM, MGMNT planteamiento de alta dirección *m*, propuesta de alta dirección *f*; ~ **management personnel** HRM, MGMNT personal de alta dirección *m*; ~ **price** ECON, GEN COMM, STOCK precio máximo *m*; ~ **quality** GEN COMM alta calidad *f*; ~**-rank product** GEN COMM, S&M producto de primera categoría *m*; ~**-ranking official** GEN COMM, HRM alto(-a) funcionario(-a) *m,f*; ~ **rate of tax** TAX tipo máximo del impuesto *m*; ~ **salaries review body** HRM, MGMNT organismo de revisión de los salarios más altos *m*; ~**-sided-federalism** POL, TAX federalismo fiscal *m*; ~**-up deduction** TAX deducción ampliada *f*; ◆ ~ **of the league** GEN COMM cabeza de la liga *f*; **be on ~ of one's work** HRM tener el trabajo al día; ~ **of the tree** *infrml* GEN COMM *status* máxima categoría jerárquica *f*; ~ **wages paid** HRM pagado con los más altos salarios

top⁴ *vt* GEN COMM *surpass* aventajar

top out *vi* GEN COMM *rate, price, cost* cotizar al máximo

top up *vt* GEN COMM equilibrar, *savings* reponer

TOPIC *abbr* (*Teletex Output of Price Information by Computer*) STOCK información bursátil por videotexto de la Bolsa de Valores de Londres

topping: ~ **out** *n* GEN COMM valor techo *m*; ~**-up clause** *n* BANK cláusula de relleno *f*

Toronto: ~ **Composite** *n* STOCK índice compuesto de la Bolsa de Toronto

tort *n* LAW *England and Wales* acto ilícito civil *m*; ~**-feasor** GEN COMM injuriador(a) *m,f*; ~ **liability** LAW responsabilidad por lesión jurídica *f*

total¹ *adj* MATH total

total² *n* GEN COMM total *m*; ~ **allowable catches** *n pl* (*TACs*) ENVIR *fishing* captura total permitida *f*; ~ **assets** *n pl* GEN COMM activos totales *m pl*; ~ **base number** (*TBN*) ENVIR número de base total *m*; ~ **capitalization** FIN capitalización total *f*; ~ **cost of credit to the consumer** FIN coste total de crédito del consumidor *m* (*Esp*), costo total de crédito del consumidor *m* (*AmL*); ~ **costs** *n pl* ECON costes totales *m pl* (*Esp*), costos totales *m pl* (*AmL*); ~ **current spending** ECON gasto corriente total *m*; ~ **to date** FIN total a la fecha *m*; ~ **effective exposure** S&M *advertising* exposición totalmente efectiva *f*; ~ **estimates** *n pl* FIN estimaciones totales *f pl*; ~ **fertility rate** (*TRF*) ECON tasa de fecundidad total *f*; ~ **funds applied** *n pl* FIN fondos totales solicitados *m pl*; ~ **funds provided** *n pl* FIN fondos totales asignados *m pl*; ~ **income** ACC, TAX ingresos totales *m pl*; ~ **liability** ACC, BANK pasivo total *m*; ~ **loss** (*TL*) GEN COMM, INS pérdida total *f*; ~ **loss only** (*TLO*) GEN COMM, INS sólo pérdida total; ~ **maintenance** GEN COMM, IND mantenimiento general *m*; ~ **net flow** ECON flujo neto total *m*; ~ **net redemptions** *n pl* BANK amortizaciones netas totales *f pl*; ~ **plant maintenance** GEN COMM mantenimiento total de la planta *m*; ~ **public debt** ECON deuda pública total *f*; ~ **public expenditure** ECON, POL gasto público total *m*; ~ **public spending** POL, ECON gasto público total *m*; ~ **quality** IND, MGMNT calidad total *f*; ~ **quality control** (*TQC*) IND, MGMNT control de calidad total *m*; ~ **quality management** MGMNT dirección de calidad total *f*, gerencia de calidad total *f*; ~ **quality marketing** S&M marketing de calidad total *m*; ~ **revenue** ACC, ECON, FIN, TAX ingreso total *m*; ~ **sales** *n pl* GEN COMM, S&M ventas totales *f pl*; ~ **social charges** *n pl* ACC, POL, WEL cargas sociales totales *f pl*, gastos sociales totales *m pl*; ~ **votes cast** *n pl* GEN COMM, HRM, POL total de votos emitidos *m*; ~ **wages and salaries** ACC, HRM sueldos y salarios totales *m pl*

totality *n* GEN COMM totalidad *f*

totalizator *n* GEN COMM totalizador *m*

totalize *vt* GEN COMM totalizar

tote: ~ **bin** *n* TRANSP compartimento de carga *m*

toto: in ~ *phr* GEN COMM totalmente

Totten: ~ **trust** *n* BANK fideicomiso de cuenta de ahorro *m*

touch¹: ~**-activated** *adj* COMP activado por el tacto; ~ **and go** *adj* ECON de suceso arriesgado; ~**-sensitive** *adj* COMP táctil

touch² *n* STOCK contacto *m*; ~ **key** COMP tecla de contacto *f*; ~**-sensitive screen** COMP pantalla sensible al tacto *f*; ~**-tone phone** COMMS teléfono con teclado *m*

touch off *vt* GEN COMM provocar

touch-type *vi* ADMIN, COMP, GEN COMM mecanografiar al tacto, mecanografiar sin mirar al teclado

tough[1] *adj* GEN COMM *conditions* duro

tough[2]: **~ competitor** *n* GEN COMM serio(-a) competidor(a) *m,f*; **~ stance** *n* GEN COMM posición dura *f*

tour *n* LEIS gira *f*, recorrido turístico *m*; **~ company** LEIS *theatre* compañía de gira *f*; **~ operator** LEIS, TRANSP tour operador(a) *m,f*; ◆ **on ~** LEIS *theatre* de gira

tourism *n* GEN COMM, LEIS turismo *m*

tourist *n* GEN COMM, LEIS turista *mf*; **~ attraction** LEIS atracción turística *f*; **~ class** LEIS, TRANSP clase turista *f*; **~ exchange rate** ECON *formerly in Russia* tipo de cambio para turistas *m*; **~ fare** LEIS tarifa turista *f*; **~ information office** LEIS oficina de información turística *f*; **~ season** ECON, LEIS estación turística *f*; **~ tax** LEIS, TAX impuesto para turistas *m*; **~ trade** ECON, LEIS industria turística *f*; **~ visa** LEIS visado turístico *m*

Tourist: **~ Board** *n BrE* LEIS Cámara de Turismo *f*

tout: **~ for custom** *phr* GEN COMM buscar clientes

TOVALOP *abbr* (*Tanker Owners' Voluntary Agreement Concerning Liability for Oil Pollution*) ENVIR, TRANSP TOVALOP (*Acuerdo Voluntario de Armadores de Petroleros sobre la Responsabilidad por Contaminación de Crudos*)

tow *n* TRANSP arrastre *m*; **~ truck** *AmE* (*cf breakdown van BrE*) TRANSP furgoneta de socorro *f*

towage: **~ charges** *n pl* TRANSP derechos de remolque *m pl*; **~ contractor** *n* TRANSP contratista de remolques *mf*; **~ dues** *n pl* TRANSP derechos de remolque *m pl*

towaway: **~ zone** *n AmE* TRANSP aparcamiento de donde se permite llevar a grúa los coches mal aparcados

towboat *n* TRANSP remolcador *m*

tower: **~ block** *n* WEL bloque de edificios *m*

towing: **~ dolly** *n jarg* TRANSP tractor para remolque *m*

town[1]: **out of ~** *adj* GEN COMM, IND, S&M del extrarradio, fuera del centro de la ciudad

town[2]: **~-center** *AmE see town centre BrE*; **~-center food store** *AmE see town-centre food store BrE*; **~ centre** *n BrE* GEN COMM centro de la ciudad *m*; **~-centre food store** *n BrE* S&M tienda de alimentación del centro *f*; **~ councillor** *n* GEN COMM, POL concejal *mf*; **~ hall** *n BrE* (*cf city hall AmE*) GEN COMM, POL Ayuntamiento *m*; **~ hall test** *n* S&M prueba municipal *f*; **~ house** *n* PROP residencia urbana *f*; **~ planner** *n* GEN COMM urbanista *mf*; **~ planning** *n* GEN COMM urbanismo *m*; **out of ~ shopping** *n* S&M compras fuera de la ciudad *f pl*

Town: **~ and Country Planning Act** *n BrE* LAW ley de planificación urbana y rural

toxic[1] *adj* ENVIR, GEN COMM, TRANSP tóxico

toxic[2]: **~, explosive, corrosive, hazardous cargo** *n* (*TECH cargo*) TRANSP carga tóxica, explosiva, corrosiva, peligrosa; **~ waste** *n* ENVIR, IND residuos tóxicos *m pl*

toxicity *n* ENVIR, GEN COMM, TRANSP toxicidad *f*

toxicological *adj* ENVIR, GEN COMM toxicológico

TP *abbr* FIN (*tender panel*) panel de ofertas *m*, COMP, GEN COMM (*teleprocessing*) teleproceso *m*

TPC *abbr* (*ton per centimetre, tonne per centimetre*) GEN COMM tonelada por centímetro *f*

tr. *abbr* (*transfer*) BANK transferencia *f*, GEN COMM traspaso *m*, TRANSP transbordo *m*, transferencia *f*

TR *abbr* (*triple reduction*) GEN COMM triple reducción *f*

trace *vt* BANK *payment*, COMMS *call*, GEN COMM, TRANSP localizar, rastrear

trace back *vt* GEN COMM remontarse a

traceable: **~ cost** *n* ACC coste identificable *m* (*Esp*), costo identificable *m* (*AmL*)

tracer *n* GEN COMM trazador *m*

track[1]: **on ~** *adj* (*ot*) TRANSP *rail* en la vía

track[2]: **~-price** *n* TRANSP precio del recorrido *m*; **~ record** *n* GEN COMM registro de trayectoria *m*, HRM experiencia comprobada *f*, historial *m*

track[3] *vt* GEN COMM *spending* seguir

track[4]: **be on the right ~** *phr* GEN COMM ir por buen camino; **be on the wrong ~** *phr* GEN COMM ir por mal camino

track down *vt* GEN COMM, TRANSP localizar, rastrear

trackball *n* COMP bola rodante *f*

tracking *n* GEN COMM *sales, costs, expenses* seguimiento *m*; **~ study** S&M *market research* estudio de seguimiento *m*; **~ system** GEN COMM sistema de seguimiento *m*

tract: **~ house** *n* PROP casa construida en serie *f*

tractive: **~ unit** *n* TRANSP unidad de tracción *f*

tractor[1]: **~-fed** *adj* COMP con arrastre de dientes

tractor[2]: **~ feed** *n* COMP alimentación por arrastre *f*

trade[1]: **~-related** *adj* ECON, GEN COMM, S&M relacionado con el comercio

trade[2] *n* ECON, GEN COMM negocio *m*, comercio *m*, intercambio comercial *m*, HRM *of job* negocio *m*, oficio *m*, S&M comercio *m*, industria *f*, negocio *m*; **~ acceptance** GEN COMM aceptación comercial *f*; **~ account** ECON cuenta comercial *f*; **~ account payable** ACC cuenta comercial a pagar *f*, cuenta de proveedores *f*; **~ account receivable** ACC cuenta comercial a cobrar *f*; **~ accounts payable** *n pl* ACC cuentas de clientes por pagar *f pl*; **~ accounts receivable** *n pl* ACC cuentas de clientes por cobrar *f pl*; **~ advertising** S&M publicidad comercial *f*; **~ agreement** ECON, POL acuerdo comercial *m*, convenio comercial *m*; **~ allowance** ACC, GEN COMM descuento comercial *m*; **~ association** GEN COMM asociación comercial *f*; **~ balance** ECON balanza comercial *f*, saldo comercial *m*; **~ barrier** ECON, GEN COMM, POL barrera comercial *f*; **~ bill** BANK letra comercial *f*; **~ book** MEDIA *print* libro comercial *m*; **~ brief** ECON *international* informe comercial *m* (*Esp*), reporte comercial *m* (*AmL*); **~ car** TRANSP vehículo comercial *m*; **~ channel** GEN COMM canal comercial *m*; **~ counter** GEN COMM *in shop* mostrador *m*; **~ creation** ECON, GEN COMM creación comercial *f*; **~ credit** ACC crédito comercial *m*; **~ creditor** ACC, GEN COMM acreedor(a) comercial *m,f*; **~ custom** GEN COMM costumbre del oficio *f*; **~ cycle** ECON, GEN COMM ciclo comercial *m*; **~ data interchange** (*TDI*) ECON *international* intercambio de datos comerciales *m*; **~ date** STOCK fecha de operación *f*; **~ debtor** ACC deudor(a) comercial *m,f*; **~ deficit** ECON, GEN COMM, POL déficit comercial *m*; **~ description** S&M *advertising* descripción comercial *f*; **~ directory** GEN COMM directorio comercial *m*; **~ discount** ACC, GEN COMM descuento comercial *m*; **~ dispute** ECON, HRM, POL conflicto laboral *m*, conflicto colectivo *m*; **~ distortion** ECON distorsión comercial *f*; **~ diversion** ECON, IMP/EXP, TRANSP desviación de corrientes comerciales *f*; **~ entrance** *BrE* (*cf service entrance AmE*) GEN COMM entrada comercial *f*; **~ exhibition** S&M exposición comercial *f*; **~ expert** S&M experto(-a) en comercio *m,f*; **~ facilitation** ECON *international* facilitación comercial *f*; **~ fair** GEN COMM, S&M feria comercial *f*, feria de muestras *f*; **~ figures** *n pl* GEN COMM cifras comerciales *f pl*; **~ financing** BANK, FIN financiación del comercio *f*; **~ fixture** PROP instalación comercial *f*; **~ flow** ECON flujo comercial *m*; **~ gap** GEN COMM déficit de la balanza comercial *m*; **~ imbalance** ECON desequilibrio comercial *m*; **~-in allowance** GEN COMM bonificación por entrega como parte de pago *f*; **~ in industrial goods** ECON, GEN COMM, IND negocio de bienes industriales *m*; **~ investment** STOCK inversión comercial *f*; **~ journal** GEN COMM, MEDIA diario comercial *m*; **~ liberalization** ECON liberalización comercial *f*; **~ magazine** GEN COMM revista comercial *f*; **~ mark agent** LAW agente de marcas registradas *mf*, PATENTS agente de la propiedad industrial *mf*; **~ name** GEN COMM razón social *f*, PATENTS marca comercial *f*; **~-off** ECON *unemployment, inflation*, GEN COMM compensación *f*; **~-off between growth and profitability** ECON compromiso entre el crecimiento y la rentabilidad *m*; **~ organization** GEN COMM organización comercial *f*; **~ paperback** *jarg* MEDIA *print* publicación comercial *f*; **~ practice** GEN COMM práctica comercial *f*; **~ press** MEDIA *print* prensa para comerciantes *f*; **~ price** STOCK precio al por mayor *m*; **~ promotion** S&M *advertising* fomento del comercio *m*; **~ protectionism** ECON *international* proteccionismo comercial *m*; **~ publication** MEDIA *print* publicación comercial *f*; **~ receivables** *n pl* ACC, GEN COMM cuentas comerciales por cobrar *f pl*, cuentas de clientes por cobrar *f pl*; **~ regime** ECON, POL régimen comercial *m*; **~ register** GEN COMM registro de comercio *m*; **~ regulation** ECON ordenanza comercial *f*; **~ report** STOCK boletín comercial *m*; **~ representative** HRM representante de comercio *mf*; **~ restraint** GEN COMM restricción comercial *f*; **~ restriction** GEN COMM restricción comercial *f*, POL *international* restricción al comercio *f*; **~ return** GEN COMM rendimiento comercial *m*; **~ route** ECON, TRANSP ruta comercial *f*; **~ sanction** ECON, POL sanción comercial *f*; **~ secret** GEN COMM secreto de fabricación *m*; **~ setting** S&M montaje del negocio *m*; **~ show** S&M exposición comercial *f*; **~ sign** GEN COMM rótulo comercial *m*; **~ strategy** ECON, GEN COMM estrategia comercial *f*; **~ surplus** ECON balanza comercial favorable *f*, superávit de la balanza comercial *m*; **~ talk** ECON, POL *international* reunión informal sobre intercambios *f*; **~ talks** *n pl* ECON, POL *international* conferencias comerciales *f pl*; **~ terms** *n pl* ECON, GEN COMM, IMP/EXP, S&M condiciones de venta *f pl*; **~ ticket** PATENTS, STOCK marca comercial *f*; **~ union** *BrE* (*cf syndicate AmE*) GEN COMM sindicato *m*; **~ union contributions** *n pl BrE* HRM aportaciones de los sindicatos *f pl*; **~ union dues** *n pl BrE* HRM cuotas sindicales *f pl*; **~ union immunities** *n pl BrE* HRM, LAW inmunidades sindicales *f pl*; **~ union liability** *BrE* HRM responsabilidad sindical *f*; **~ union membership** *BrE* HRM afiliación a un sindicato *f*, afiliación sindical *f*; **~ union recognition** *BrE* HRM reconocimiento de un sindicato *m*; **~ union representative** *BrE* HRM delegado(-a) sindical *m,f*; **~ union subscription** *BrE* HRM afiliación a un sindicato *f*, afiliación sindical *f*; **~ unionism** *BrE* HRM sindicalismo *m*, tradeunionismo *m*, POL sindicalismo *m*; **~ volume** ECON volumen comercial *m*; **~ war** ECON,

POL guerra comercial *f*; **~-weighted exchange rate** ECON, GEN COMM tipo de cambio medido según la importancia del comercio *m*; **~-weighted external value** ECON *of currency* valor externo ponderado según el comercio exterior *m*

trade³ **1.** *vt* GEN COMM comerciar, traficar, ECON comerciar; ◆ **~ as** GEN COMM trabajar como; **~ on one's account** STOCK comerciar por cuenta propia; **~ raw materials for manufactured goods** GEN COMM cambiar materias primas por bienes manufacturados; **~ under the name of** GEN COMM comerciar bajo nombre de; **~ within the European Union** GEN COMM negociar dentro de la Unión Europea; **2.** *vi* ECON comercializar, traficar, *with other countries* comerciar; ◆ **~ for one's account** STOCK comerciar por cuenta propia; **~ in stocks and bonds** STOCK negociar con valores y bonos

trade at *vt* STOCK negociarse

trade down *vi* GEN COMM comprar o vender bienes más baratos que nunca

trade in *vt* GEN COMM *old model for new* cambiar

trade off *vi* GEN COMM llegar a una solución de compromiso; ◆ **~ market share against profit margins** ECON compensar cuota de mercado con márgenes de beneficio; **~ one thing for another** ECON, GEN COMM cambiar una cosa por otra

Trade: ~ Data Elements Directory *n* (*TDED*) ECON *international* anuario de datos comerciales *m*; **~ Descriptions Act** *n BrE* LAW *advertising*, S&M decreto sobre la descripción de las marcas comerciales; **~ Development Board** *n* (*TDB*) ECON *international* Junta de Desarrollo del Comercio *f*; **~ Union** *n BrE* (*TU BrE*) HRM sindicato de trabajadores *m*, unión de trabajadores *f*

tradeability *n* GEN COMM comerciabilidad *f*

tradeable¹ *adj* GEN COMM comerciable

tradeable²: **~ discharge permit** *n* (*TDP*) ECON autorización de pago negociable *f*; **~ emission permit** *n* ENVIR, GEN COMM concesión transferible *f*; **~ promissory note** *n* STOCK pagaré negociable *m*

traded: ~ exchange option *n* STOCK opción de cambio negociada *f*; **~ option** *n* STOCK opción objeto de comercio *f*, opción negociada *f*

trademark *n* ACC, GEN COMM, PATENTS, S&M marca comercial *f*, marca de fábrica *f*, S&M marca de fábrica *f*

trader *n* BANK comerciante *mf*, GEN COMM, HRM, S&M *large-scale* almacenista *mf*, comerciante *mf*, vendedor(a) *m,f*, *shopkeeper* negociante *mf*, STOCK corredor(a) de bolsa *m,f*, intermediario(-a) *m,f*; **~ in securities** STOCK intermediario(-a) en títulos *m,f*

Trades: ~ Union Congress *n BrE* (*TUC*) HRM, POL confederación de los sindicatos británicos

tradesman: ~'s entrance *n* GEN COMM entrada de proveedores *f*, puerta de servicio *f*

tradespeople *n pl* GEN COMM gente de comercio *f*

trading *n* GEN COMM intercambio comercial *m*, registro de patentes *m*; **in and out ~** *jarg* STOCK compra seguida de venta de los mismos títulos *f*, compra y venta del mismo valor en un día *f*; **~ account** ACC, BANK cuenta de beneficios brutos *f*, cuenta de beneficios en bruto *f*; **~ activity** STOCK actividad de compraventa *f*; **~ area** GEN COMM área de comercio *f*, zona comercial *f*, S&M *shop* zona de comercio *f*, *territory* zona comercial *f*; **~ authorization** GEN COMM autorización de comercio *f*;

~ **block** ECON, POL bloque comercial *m*; ~ **book** FIN *of institution* libro de comercio *m*; ~ **company** GEN COMM, IMP/EXP sociedad comercial *f*; ~ **currencies** *n pl* ECON divisas comerciales *f pl*; ~ **debts** *n pl* ACC deudas comerciales *f pl*; ~ **desk** STOCK corro de contratación *m*; ~ **estate** PROP inmueble comercial *m*; ~ **floor** STOCK parqué de operaciones *m*; ~ **hours** *n pl* STOCK horario de contratación *m*; ~ **income** ACC, FIN beneficio bruto *m* (*Esp*), ganancia bruta *f*, renta bruta *f* (*Esp*), resultado bruto *m* (*Esp*), utilidad bruta *f* (*AmL*); ~ **life** STOCK *futures* vida de una transacción *f*; ~ **limit** TRANSP *shipping* precio límite *m*; ~ **losses** *n pl* ACC pérdidas del ejercicio *f pl*; ~ **member** STOCK *of exchange* socio activo *m*; ~ **name** GEN COMM, IND, PATENTS nombre comercial *m*; ~ **operation** BANK operación comercial *f*; ~ **partner** ECON, POL socio comercial *m*; ~ **party** STOCK *money market* parte de la negociación *f*; ~ **pattern** STOCK modelo de negociación *m*; ~ **pit** *jarg* STOCK mercado comercial *m*; ~ **port** TRANSP puerto comercial *m*; ~ **portfolio** BANK, FIN *of investments* cartera comercial *f*; ~ **post** *jarg* STOCK puesto de operaciones *m*; ~ **program** *AmE*, ~ **programme** *BrE* FIN, GEN COMM programa comercial *m*; ~ **range** STOCK *commodities, securities* banda de fluctuación de precios *f*; ~ **rights** STOCK derechos de negociación *m pl*; ~ **room** BANK cámara de comercio *f*; ~ **security** STOCK efecto negociable *m*; ~ **session** STOCK sesión de contratación *f*; ~ **stamp** GEN COMM cupón con prima *m* (*Esp*), sello de premio *m* (*AmL*); ~ **standard** GEN COMM norma comercial *f*; ~ **unit** STOCK *Eurodollar options* unidad de contratación *f*; ~ **up** S&M venta a precios superiores *f*; ~ **variation** STOCK variación de mercado *f*, variación mercantil *f*; ~ **vessel** TRANSP barco mercante *m*; ~ **volume** GEN COMM volumen de contratación *m*; ~ **year** GEN COMM año comercial *m*; ♦ **be** ~ **at** STOCK ser cliente de

Trading: ~ **Standards Office** *n AmE* ECON departamento de normas comerciales

tradition *n* GEN COMM tradición *f*

traditional *adj* GEN COMM tradicional

traffic *n* TRANSP tráfico *m*; ~ **analysis** TRANSP análisis de tráfico *m*; ~ **builder** *jarg* S&M *advertising* promoción destinada a estimular el flujo de personas en un establecimiento; ~ **circle** *AmE* (*cf roundabout BrE*) TRANSP glorieta *f*, rotonda *f*; ~ **congestion** TRANSP congestión del tráfico *f*; ~ **control** TRANSP control de tráfico *m*; ~ **control tower** TRANSP *airport, seaport* torre de control de tráfico *f*; ~ **count** S&M *advertising* recuento de circulación *m*; ~ **density** TRANSP densidad del tráfico *f*; ~ **department** S&M departamento de expedición *m*; ~ **executive** HRM directivo(-a) comercial *m,f*, ejecutivo(-a) de tráfico *m,f*; ~ **flow** TRANSP volumen de tráfico *m*; ~ **forecast** TRANSP parte de tráfico *m*; ~ **jam** ENVIR, TRANSP atasco *m*, embotellamiento de tráfico *m*; ~ **lane** TRANSP carril de tránsito *m*; ~ **manager** HRM gerente de tráfico *mf*, jefe(-a) de movimiento *m,f*; ~ **mixture** TRANSP composición de tráfico *f*; ~ **planning** S&M *advertising* gestión de los flujos de trabajo *f*, planificación de los anuncios según la audiencia *f*; ~ **potential** TRANSP potencial de tráfico *m*; ~ **rights** *n pl* TRANSP derechos de tráfico *m pl*; ~ **separation scheme** TRANSP sistema de separación del tráfico *m*; ~ **sign** TRANSP señal de tráfico *f*; ~ **superintendent** HRM superintendente de tráfico *mf*; ~ **supervisor** HRM supervisor(a) de tráfico *m,f*; ~ **trend** TRANSP tendencia del tráfico *f*; ~ **yield** TRANSP rendimiento del tráfico *m*

traffic in *vt* GEN COMM comerciar en, traficar en

trafficker *n* GEN COMM traficante *mf*

trail *vt* MEDIA *broadcast* arrastrar

trailblazing *adj* GEN COMM precursor

trailer *n* IMP/EXP, LEIS, TRANSP remolque *m*; ~ **on flat car** (*TOFC*) TRANSP vagón plataforma plana *m*; ~ **park** PROP *AmE* (*cf mobile-home park BrE*) parque de vivienda móvil *m*, TRANSP estacionamiento para remolques *m*; ~ **unladen weight** GEN COMM camión de tara *m*; ~ **utilization** TRANSP explotación del remolque *f*

train[1]: ~ **fare** *n* LEIS, TRANSP tarifa ferroviaria *f*; ~ **ferry** *n* TRANSP transbordador de trenes *m*; ~ **ferry deck** *n* TRANSP cubierta de trenes *f*; ~ **number** *n* TRANSP número de tren *m*; ~ **station** *n BrE* (*cf railroad station AmE*) TRANSP estación de ferrocarril *f*; ~ **timetable** *n* LEIS horario de trenes *m*

train[2] **1.** *vt* HRM capacitar (*AmL*), formar (*Esp*), entrenar; **2.** *vi* HRM entrenarse, formarse

trainee *n* GEN COMM aprendiz *mf*, persona en prácticas *f*, LAW pasante *mf*; ~ **civil servant** HRM funcionario(-a) en prácticas *m,f*; ~ **manager** HRM, MGMNT director(a) de prácticas *m,f*; ~ **programmer** COMP programador(a) aprendiz(a) *m,f*, programador(a) en prácticas *m,f*

traineeship *n* GEN COMM pasantería *f*, HRM periodo de entrenamiento *m*

trainer *n* HRM instructor(a) *m,f*

training *n* GEN COMM instrucción *f*, HRM adiestramiento *m*, capacitación *f* (*AmL*), formación *f* (*Esp*), entrenamiento *m*; ~ **agency** *BrE* (*TA*) HRM agencia de capacitación *f* (*AmL*), agencia de formación *f* (*Esp*); ~ **center** *AmE*, ~ **centre** *BrE* HRM centro de capacitación *m* (*AmL*), centro de formación *m* (*Esp*), centro de formación profesional *m* (*Esp*); ~ **contract** BANK, GEN COMM, LAW ≈ pasantería *f*; ~ **course** GEN COMM, HRM curso de capacitación *m* (*AmL*), curso de formación *m* (*Esp*); ~ **manager** HRM, MGMNT director(a) de formación *m,f* (*Esp*), gerente de capacitación *mf* (*AmL*), gerente de entrenamiento *mf* (*AmL*), gerente de formación *mf* (*Esp*); ~ **needs** *n pl* GEN COMM, HRM necesidades de capacitación *f pl* (*AmL*), necesidades de formación *f pl* (*Esp*); ~ **needs analysis** GEN COMM, HRM, S&M análisis de las necesidades de capacitación *m* (*AmL*), análisis de las necesidades de formación *m* (*Esp*); ~ **officer** GEN COMM capacitador(a) *m,f* (*AmL*), formador(a) *m,f* (*Esp*), jefe(-a) de capacitación *m,f* (*AmL*), oficial(a) de formación *m,f* (*Esp*), HRM capacitador(a) *m,f* (*AmL*), formador(a) *m,f* (*Esp*), funcionario(-a) de capacitación *m,f* (*AmL*), funcionario(-a) de formación *m,f* (*Esp*), jefe(-a) de capacitación *m,f* (*AmL*), oficial(a) de capacitación *m,f* (*AmL*), oficial(a) de formación *m,f* (*Esp*); ~ **program** *AmE*, ~ **programme** *BrE* HRM programa de capacitación *m* (*AmL*), programa de formación *m* (*Esp*); ~ **scheme** HRM plan de capacitación (*AmL*), *m*, plan de formación *m* (*Esp*); ~ **of trainers** HRM capacitación de capacitadores *f* (*AmL*), capacitación de entrenadores *f* (*AmL*), capacitación de instructores *f* (*AmL*), formación condicional *f* (*Esp*), formación de entrenadores *f* (*Esp*), formación de formadores *f* (*Esp*), formación de instructores *f* (*Esp*); ~ **within industry** (*TWI*) HRM, IND capacitación dentro de la empresa *f* (*AmL*), entrenamiento dentro de la industria *m*, formación dentro de la empresa *f* (*Esp*)

Training: ~ **Agency** *n BrE obs* HRM comisión de servicios laborales; ~ **and Enterprise Council** *n BrE* (*TEC*) HRM agencia para programas de formación empresarial

tramp *n* TRANSP *vessel* barco de ruta variable *m*

tramping *n* TRANSP navegación sin itinerario *f*

tranche: ~ **underwritten facility** *n* (*TUF*) STOCK servicio financiero de suscripción parcial *m*

transaction *n* GEN COMM transacción *f*; ~ **balance report** ACC informe de saldos para transacciones *m* (*Esp*), reporte de saldos para transacciones *m* (*AmL*); ~ **cost** BANK, ECON, STOCK coste de las transacciones *m* (*Esp*), costo de las transacciones *m* (*AmL*); ~ **with customers** BANK operación con los clientes *f*; ~ **date** STOCK fecha de operación *f*; ~ **fee** BANK gastos de transacción *m pl*; ~ **file** COMP fichero de movimientos *m*; ~ **loss** ECON pérdida en la transacción *f*; ~ **management** COMP gestión de transacciones *f*; ~ **management software** COMP programa de gestión de transacciones *m*, software de gestión de transacciones *m*; ~ **processing** COMP proceso de transacción *m*; ~ **profit** ACC beneficio en la transacción *m*; ~ **risk** STOCK riesgo de la transacción *m*; ~ **status** GEN COMM, IND, S&M situación de transacción *f*; ~ **tax** STOCK, TAX impuesto sobre transacciones *m*

transactional[1] *adj* GEN COMM transaccional

transactional[2]: ~ **analysis** *n* (*TA*) FIN, GEN COMM, MGMNT análisis de transacción *m*, análisis transaccional *m*

transcode *vt* COMMS transcodificar

transcoder *n* COMMS transcodificador *m*

transcribe *vt* COMMS, COMP, GEN COMM transcribir

transcriber *n* COMMS, COMP, GEN COMM aparato de transcripción *m*

transcription *n* COMMS, COMP, GEN COMM transcripción *f*

transducer *n* COMMS transductor *m*

transeuropean[1] *adj* GEN COMM transeuropeo

transeuropean[2]: ~ **network** *n* COMMS, GEN COMM, TRANSP red transeuropea *f*

transfer[1] *n* BANK (*tr.*) traducción *f*, transferencia *f*, GEN COMM cesión *f*, transferencia *f*, *of responsibilities* traspaso *m*, STOCK transferencia *f*, TRANSP (*trf.*) transferencia *f*, transbordo *m*; ~ **account** BANK cuenta de transferencia *f*; ~ **address** COMP dirección de transferencia *f*; ~ **of assets** ACC transferencia de activos *f*; ~ **by endorsement** BANK transferencia por endoso *f*; ~ **deed** GEN COMM escritura de transmisión *f*; ~ **development rights** *n pl* PROP derechos de desarrollo de un traspaso *m pl*, derechos de explotación de un traspaso *m pl*; ~ **earnings** *n pl* ACC, TAX ingresos de transferencia *m pl*; ~ **of engagement** *BrE* HRM transferencia de contrato *f*; ~ **fee** LEIS *sport* derechos de traspaso *m pl*, traspaso *m*; ~ **fees** *n pl* LAW derechos de transferencia *m pl*, PROP honorarios de traspaso *m pl*; ~ **of funds** ACC, BANK, FIN transferencia de fondos *f*; ~ **of funds voucher** BANK comprobante de transferencia de fondos *m*; ~ **income** ECON renta de transferencia *f*; ~ **manifest** IMP/EXP, TRANSP manifiesto del cargamento *m*; ~ **order** BANK, FIN orden de transferencia *f*; ~ **payment** BANK, FIN pago de transferencia *m*; ~ **price** GEN COMM precio de cesión *m*; ~ **pricing** ECON fijación del precio de transferencias *f*; ~ **problem** ECON problema de traspaso *m*; ~ **rate** COMP velocidad de transferencia *f*; ~ **register** STOCK registro de transferencias *m*; ~ **tax** ECON, GEN

COMM, TAX impuesto sobre transmisiones patrimoniales *m* (*ITP*); ~ **of technology** ECON transmisión de tecnología *f*; ~ **of technology method** ECON método de transferencia de tecnología *m*; ~ **to business** GEN COMM transferencia a la actividad comercial *f*; ~ **to reserve fund** ACC asignación al fondo de reserva *f*; ~ **of undertaking** *BrE* HRM transferencia de compromiso *f*

transfer[2] **1.** *vt* ACC traspasar, BANK transferir, traspasar, ECON *funds* transferir, PROP pasar, STOCK traspasar; ♦ ~ **by wire** BANK transferir por cable; ~ **the charges** COMMS poner una conferencia a cobro revertido; ~ **ownership of** PROP transferir la propiedad de; ~ **sb** HRM *to another branch* trasladar a alguien; **2.** *vi* TRANSP *from one train to another* trasladar

Transfer: ~ **& Automated Registration of Uncertified Stock** *n obs* (*TAURUS*) ECON, STOCK transferencia y registro automático de valores no certificados

transferability *n* STOCK *of registered shares* transmisibilidad *f*

transferable[1] *adj* STOCK *options* transferible; **not** ~ STOCK intransferible

transferable[2]: ~ **credit** *n* ACC, BANK crédito transferible *m*; ~ **discharge permit** *n* ENVIR, GEN COMM concesión transferible *f*; ~ **loan certificates** *n* BANK, FIN certificado de préstamo transferible *m*; ~ **loan facilities** *n* (*TLF*) BANK, FIN línea de préstamo transferible *f*; ~ **loan instrument** *n* (*TLI*) BANK, FIN instrumento de préstamo transferible *m*; ~ **revolving underwriting security** *n* (*TRUS*) STOCK valor transferible de suscripción renovable *m*; ~ **security** *n* FIN, STOCK valor mobiliario *m*

transferee *n* BANK beneficiario(-a) de una transferencia *m,f*; ~ **company** GEN COMM compañía cesionaria *f*

transferor *n BrE* BANK transferidor *m*, TAX *inheritance rights* cesionista *mf*; ~ **company** GEN COMM empresa cedente *f*

transferred: ~ **charge call** *n* COMMS conferencia a cobro revertido *f*; ~ **share** *n* STOCK acción transferida *f*

transform *vt* GEN COMM transformar

transformation: ~ **curve** *n* ECON curva de transformación *f*; ~ **industries** *n pl* ECON, IND industrias de transformación *f pl*; ~ **problem** *n* ECON problema de transformación *n*

tranship *vt* TRANSP transbordar

transhipment *n* TRANSP transbordo *m*; ~ **bill of lading** IMP/EXP, TRANSP conocimiento de embarque de transbordo *m*, conocimiento de carga de transbordo *m*; ~ **bond** IMP/EXP, TRANSP bono de transbordo *m*, declaración de tránsito *f*, obligación de transbordo *f*; ~ **delivery order** TRANSP orden de entrega del transbordo *f*; ~ **entry** IMP/EXP, TRANSP declaración de aduana en el transbordo *f*; ~ **freight** TRANSP flete del transbordo *m*

transient: ~ **medium** *n* S&M soporte transitorio *m*; ~ **worker** *n* HRM trabajador(a) transitorio(-a) *m,f*

transire *n* IMP/EXP permiso aduanero de retirada de mercancías

transit[1]: **in** ~ *adj* BANK, GEN COMM en tránsito

transit[2] *n* TRANSP tránsito *m*; ~ **bond note** IMP/EXP guía de tránsito *f*; ~ **card** LEIS *airline travel* tarjeta de tránsito *f*; ~ **clause** INS, TRANSP *cargo policy* cláusula de tránsito *f*; ~ **credit** BANK crédito en tránsito *m*; ~ **document** GEN COMM documento de tránsito *m*; ~ **lounge** LEIS sala de tránsito *f*; ~ **market** FIN, STOCK mercado de tránsito *m*; ~ **passenger** LEIS, TRANSP pasajero(-a) en tránsito *m,f*; ~ **rights** *n pl* TRANSP derechos de tránsito *m pl*; ~ **shed** IMP/EXP almacén de tránsito *m*; ~ **time** TRANSP hora de paso *f*, tiempo de tránsito *m*; ~ **trade** TRANSP comercio de tránsito *m*; ~ **traffic** TRANSP tráfico en tránsito *m*

transition: ~ **period** *n* GEN COMM periodo de transición *m*

transitional[1] *adj* GEN COMM transitorio

transitional[2]: ~ **automated ticket** *n* (*TAT*) TRANSP billete de transición automatizado *m*, billete mecanizado transitorio *m*; ~ **period** *n* GEN COMM periodo transitorio *m*; ~ **provision** *n* TAX medida transitoria *f*; ~ **relief** *n* TAX subsidio transitorio *m*

transitory: ~ **income** *n* ECON renta imprevista *f*

translate *vt* ECON *currency*, GEN COMM traducir

translation *n* COMMS, GEN COMM traducción *f*, ECON *of currency* traslación *f*; ~ **difference** ACC *from consolidation of foreign subsidiaries* diferencia de conversión *f*, diferencia en moneda extranjera *f*, diferencia de cambio *f*; ~ **differential** GEN COMM diferencial de traducción *m*; ~ **loss** ECON pérdida de traducción *f*; ~ **profit** ECON beneficio de translación *m*; ~ **program** COMP programa traductor *m*; ~ **rate** BANK, ECON tasa de conversión *f*

translator *n* GEN COMM traductor(a) *m,f*; ~**'s note** GEN COMM nota del traductor *f* (*N.T.*)

transmission *n* COMMS, GEN COMM transmisión *f*; ~ **expenses** *n pl* ACC *of loss, profit* gastos de transmisión *m pl*; ~ **mechanism** ECON *monetarism* mecanismo de transmisión *m*

transmit *vt* COMMS, COMP, GEN COMM transmitir

transmittal: ~ **letter** *n* COMMS carta de envío *f*

transmitter *n* COMMS emisor(a) *m,f*

transmitting[1] *adj* COMMS, COMP, GEN COMM transmisor

transmitting[2]: ~ **station** *n* COMMS estación emisora *f*

transnational[1] *adj* GEN COMM transnacional

transnational[2]: ~ **corporation** *n* (*TNC*) ECON, GEN COMM, POL corporación transnacional *f* (*TNC*), multinacional *f*, empresa transnacional *f*

Transpacific: ~ **Westbound Rate Agreement** *n* (*TWRA*) TRANSP acuerdo de tarifas del comercio interpacífico con rumbo al oeste

transparency *n* ACC claridad *f*, GEN COMM transparencia *f*; ~ **of information** *jarg* POL transparencia informativa *f*

transparent *adj* COMP *device, network*, GEN COMM transparente

transplant: ~ **factory** *n* ENVIR, IND fábrica de transplantes *f*

transponder *n* COMMS baliza de radar *f*

transport[1] *n* TRANSP transporte *m*; ~ **advertising** S&M publicidad en medios de transporte *f*; ~ **agent** TRANSP agente de transportes *mf*; ~ **company** BrE (*cf trucking company AmE*) TRANSP compañía de transportes *f*, empresa de transportes *f*; ~ **controller** HRM controlador(a) de transporte *m,f*; ~ **distribution analysis** (*TDA*) TRANSP análisis de la distribución del transporte *m*; ~ **document** TRANSP documento de transporte *m*; ~ **economics** ECON economía del transporte *f*; ~ **emergency card** TRANSP *road transport scheme* tarjeta de transporte de emergencia *f*; ~ **facilitation** TRANSP optimización del transporte *f*; ~ **facilities** *n pl* GEN COMM, TRANSP medios de transporte *m pl*; ~ **instruction** TRANSP instrucción de transporte *f*; ~ **instruction form** TRANSP formulario de instrucciones

de transporte *m*; ~ **insurance** INS, TRANSP seguro de transportes *m*; ~ **international routier** (*TIR*) IMP/EXP, TRANSP transporte internacional por carretera *m*; ~ **international routier carnet** (*TIR carnet*) IMP/EXP, TRANSP documento aduanero de tránsito internacional *m* (*TIR*), documento de transporte internacional en ruta *m*; ~ **link** TRANSP enlace de transporte *m*; ~ **mode** TRANSP tipo de transporte *m*; ~ **quota** TRANSP cuota de transporte *f*; ~ **system** TRANSP sistema de transporte *m*; ~ **unit** TRANSP unidad de arrastre *f*

transport[2] *vt* TRANSP transportar; ♦ ~ **by air** TRANSP transportar por avión

Transport: ~ **Act** *n* BrE LAW, TRANSP Ley de Transporte *f*

transportable[1] *adj* GEN COMM transportable

transportable[2]: ~ **moisture limit** *n* (*TML*) TRANSP límite de humedad transportable *m*

transportation: ~ **car** *n* TRANSP vehículo de transporte *m*; ~ **document** *n* TRANSP documento de transporte *m*; ~ **equipment** *n* TRANSP equipo de transporte *m*; ~ **expenses** *n pl* TRANSP gastos de transporte *m pl*

transposal *n* LAW trasposición *f*, POL adaptación *f*

transposition: ~ **error** *n* GEN COMM error de trasposición *m*

Trans-Siberian: ~ **landbridge** *n* (*TSR*) TRANSP puente de tierra transiberiano *m*; ~ **Railway** *n* (*TSR*) TRANSP *rail* ferrocarril transiberiano *m*

transverse *adj* GEN COMM transversal

trashy: ~ **goods** *n pl infrml* GEN COMM, S&M bienes de baja calidad *m pl*

travel[1]: ~ **advance** *n* ECON anticipo de viaje *m*; ~ **agency** *n* LEIS agencia de viajes *f*; ~ **agent** *n* HRM, LEIS, TRANSP agente de viajes *mf*; ~ **allocation** *n* GEN COMM asignación para viajes *f*; ~ **allowance** *n* GEN COMM asignación para transporte *f*; ~ **bureau** *n* LEIS agencia de viajes *f*; ~ **document** *n* LEIS documentación de viaje *f*; ~ **expense claim** *n* GEN COMM reclamación de gastos de viaje *f*; ~ **expenses** *n* HRM gastos de viaje *m pl*; ~ **incentive** *n* S&M *advertising* incentivo de viaje *m*; ~ **restriction** *n* TRANSP restricción de recorrido *f*; ~ **service** *n* ECON, LEIS servicio de viajes *m*; ~ **to work area** *n* GEN COMM viaje hasta la zona de trabajo *m*; ~ **voucher** *n* TRANSP bono de viaje *m*

travel[2] *vi* TRANSP viajar

travelator *n* AmE GEN COMM cinta transbordadora *f*, pasillo rodante *m*

traveler AmE *see* **traveller** BrE

traveling AmE *see* **travelling** BrE

traveller *n* BrE LEIS, TRANSP viajero(-a) *m,f*; ~**'s cheque** BrE BANK, FIN, LEIS cheque de viajero *m*

travelling: ~ **allowance** *n* BrE GEN COMM dietas de viaje *f pl* (*Esp*), viáticos *m pl* (*AmL*); ~ **exhibition** *n* BrE S&M exposición ambulante *f*; ~ **expenses** *n pl* BrE GEN COMM dietas de viaje *f pl* (*Esp*), viáticos *m pl* (*AmL*); ~ **fair** *n* BrE LEIS feria itinerante *f*; ~ **salesman** *n* BrE HRM, S&M corredor(a) de comercio *m,f*, viajante de comercio *mf*

traversable *adj* LAW contradictorio

traverse[1] *n* LAW contradicción *f*

traverse[2] *vt* LAW contradecir

trawler *n* TRANSP pesquero de arrastre *m*

tray: out-~ *n* ADMIN, GEN COMM bandeja de salida *f* (*Esp*), charola de salida *f* (*AmL*)

treasurer: ~ **check** AmE, ~ **cheque** BrE *n* BANK cheque de tesorería *m*; ~'**s report** *n* FIN informe del tesorero *m* (*Esp*), reporte del tesoro *m* (*AmL*)

treasury *n* FIN fisco *m*; ~ **bill** (*T-bill*) *AmE* BANK, ECON letra del Tesoro *f*, letra de tesorería *f*, STOCK letra del Tesoro *f*, pagaré del tesoro *m*; ~ **bill futures** *n pl* (*T-bill futures*) STOCK futuros sobre letras del tesoro *m pl*; ~ **bill futures contract** STOCK contrato de futuros en letras del tesoro *m*; ~ **bond** BANK, ECON, STOCK fontesoro *m*, letra del Tesoro *f*; ~ **note** STOCK pagaré del tesoro *m*; ~ **stock** *AmE* (*cf own shares BrE*) ACC, STOCK acciones propias readquiridas *f pl*, acciones rescatadas *f pl*; ~ **swop** FIN intercambio de la tesorería *m*

Treasury *n* ECON, FIN, POL el Tesoro *m*, Tesoro Público *m*, el erario *m*; **The ~** *BrE* (*cf Treasury Department AmE*) ECON, FIN, POL ministerio del gobierno británico para asuntos fiscales, ≈ Hacienda Pública *f*, ≈ Ministerio de Economía y Hacienda *m* (*Esp*); ~ **Bill Bond** ECON obligación del tesoro *f*; ~ **Bill Rate** (*TBR*) STOCK Cotización de las Letras del Tesoro *f*; ~ **bill tender** ECON oferta de letras del tesoro *f*; ~ **Board** POL Consejo Económico *m*; ~ **Board contingencies vote** POL capítulo presupuestario de gastos imprevistos del Consejo del Tesoro *m*; ~ **Board Secretariat** POL Secretariado del Consejo del Tesoro *m*; ~ **bond** *AmE* STOCK bono del tesoro *m*; ~ **Department** *AmE* (*cf The Treasury BrE*) ECON, POL, TAX ministerio del gobierno estadounidense para asuntos fiscales, ≈ Hacienda *f* (*Esp*), ≈ Ministerio de Economía y Hacienda *m* (*Esp*); ~ **and interbank operation** BANK *balance sheet* operación del Tesoro e interbancaria *m pl*; ~ **investment** *n pl BrE* ACC *annual accounts* inversión del Tesoro *f*, inversión estatal *f*; ~ **model** ECON modelo de tesorería *m*; ~'**s purse** *BrE* TAX las arcas del Tesoro *f pl*; ~ **stock** *BrE* STOCK autocartera *f*, bono del tesoro *m*

treat *vt* GEN COMM tratar; ♦ ~ **sewage** ENVIR, IND depurar las aguas residuales; ~ **wastewater** ENVIR, IND depurar las aguas residuales

treatment *n* GEN COMM tratamiento *m*

treaty *n* GEN COMM tratado *m*; ~ **port** *obs* TRANSP puerto convenido *m*; ~ **shopping** TAX aprovechamiento de las ventajas fiscales concedidas a terceros países, a través de filiales en estos

Treaty: ~ of Rome *n* ECON, POL Tratado de Roma *m*

tree: ~ structure *n* COMP estructura en árbol *f*

trend[1]: ~-**setting** *adj* GEN COMM que inicia una moda

trend[2] *n* ECON, GEN COMM *upward, yield* corriente *f*, tendencia *f*; ~ **analysis** ECON análisis de tendencias *m*; ~ **of events** GEN COMM orientación de los acontecimientos *f*; ~ **reversal** GEN COMM reversión de tendencia *f*

trendsetter *n* GEN COMM iniciador(a) de una moda *m,f*

trendy *adj BrE infrml* GEN COMM, S&M moderno

trespasser *n* LAW infractor(a) *m,f*

trespassers: ~ will be prosecuted *phr* LAW prohibido el paso

trespassing *n* LAW invasión *f*; ~ **on private property** LAW invasión de la propiedad privada *f*; ♦ **no ~** LAW prohibido el paso

tret *n* TRANSP deducción *f*, merma *f*

trf. *abbr* (*transfer*) BANK transferencia *f*, GEN COMM traspaso *m*, TRANSP transbordo *m*, transferencia *f*

TRF *abbr* (*total fertility rate*) ECON tasa de fecundidad total *f*

trial *n* LAW causa *f*, juicio oral *m*, IND, S&M, TRANSP

prueba de aceptación *f*; ~ **balance** ACC balance de comprobación *m*; ~ **court** LAW, POL tribunal de primera instancia *m*; ~-**and-error method** ECON, MATH método de tanteo *m*; ~ **examiner** LAW instructor(a) *m,f*; ~ **jury** LAW jurado ordinario *m*; ~ **offer** GEN COMM, S&M oferta de prueba *f*; ~ **order** GEN COMM, S&M pedido de prueba *m*; ~ **period** GEN COMM, HRM periodo de prueba *m*; ~ **purchase** S&M compra de prueba *f*; ~ **run** GEN COMM pasada de comprobación *f*; ~ **subscriber** MEDIA abonado(-a) a prueba *m,f*; ~ **subscription** (*TS*) MEDIA suscripción de prueba a una publicación *f*; ♦ **have a jury ~** LAW tener un juicio con jurado

triangle: ~ service *n* TRANSP servicio triangular *m*

triangular[1] *adj* GEN COMM triangular

triangular[2]: ~ **compensation** *n* ECON *with financial switch* compensación triangular *f*; ~ **merger** *n* GEN COMM fusión triangular *f*; ~ **operation** *n* ECON operación triangular *f*

triangulation *n* IMP/EXP triangulación *f*

tribunal: ~ of enquiry *n* LAW tribunal de consulta *m*

trick *vt* GEN COMM embaucar

trickle: ~ diversions *n pl jarg* GEN COMM escasas desviaciones *f pl*; ~ **down theory** *n* ECON teoría de la filtración *f*

tricks: ~ of the trade *n pl infrml* GEN COMM gajes del oficio *m pl*

trifling *adj* GEN COMM insignificante

trigger[1]: ~ **clause** *n* LAW cláusula de revisión *f*; ~ **mechanism** *n* GEN COMM mecanismo del disparador *m*; ~ **point** *n* GEN COMM punto de provocación *m*; ~ **price** *n* GEN COMM, IMP/EXP precio de intervención *m*; ~ **pricing** *n* GEN COMM fijar precios de intervención

trigger[2] *vt* GEN COMM *cost*, POL provocar

trim[1] *vt* TRANSP equilibrar los calados; ♦ ~ **the investment program** *AmE*, ~ **the investment programme** *BrE* FIN recortar el programa de inversión; ~ **the workforce** HRM reducir la mano de obra

trim[2]: **in good ~** *phr infrml* GEN COMM en buen estado

trip *n* GEN COMM, TRANSP viaje *m*; ~ **advance** ECON anticipo de viaje *m*; ~ **analysis** TRANSP análisis de la travesía *f*; ~ **charter** TRANSP *shipping* contrato mixto *m*

tripack *n* GEN COMM envasado triple *m*

tripartism *n* HRM tripartismo *m*

triple[1]: ~ **expansion** *adj* (*TE*) TRANSP de triple expansión; ~ **screw** *adj* (*Tr*) TRANSP de tres hélices

triple[2]: ~ **A bond** *n* FIN, STOCK *Standard & Poor's* bono clase AAA *m*; ~ **expansion engine** *n* TRANSP máquina de triple expansión *f*; ~ **reduction** *n* (*TR*) GEN COMM triple reducción *f*; ~ **tax exempt** *n* TAX triple exención fiscal *f*; ~ **witching hour** *n* GEN COMM triple hora bruja *f*

triple[3] *vt* MATH triplicar

triple-A: ~-rated borrower *n* STOCK prestatario con calificación triple A *m*; ~ **rating** *n* STOCK calificación triple A *f*

triplicate *adj* GEN COMM triplicado; ♦ **in ~** GEN COMM por triplicado

TRK *abbr* (*trunk*) TRANSP enlace común *m*, mamparo encerrador de escotilla *m*

troika *n jarg* POL troika *f*

trolley *n* TRANSP carrito *m*

tropical: ~ fresh water *n* (*TF*) ENVIR, TRANSP agua dulce tropical *f*

Tropical: **~ Africa Advisory Group** *n* (*TAAG*) ENVIR grupo consultor del Africa tropical

trouble[1]: **~-free** *adj* GEN COMM sin problemas

trouble[2] *n* COMP *problem* anomalía *f*; **~ spot** GEN COMM foco de perturbaciones *m*; ◆ **be in ~** GEN COMM estar en apuros

troubled *adj* HRM conflictivo

troubleshoot *vi* COMP buscar averías

troubleshooter *n* COMP *debugging*, GEN COMM localizador(a) de fallas *m,f* (*AmL*), localizador(a) de fallos *m,f* (*Esp*), HRM conciliador(a) *m,f*

troubleshooting *n* COMP localización de averías *f*, GEN COMM localización y corrección de fallas *f* (*AmL*), localización y corrección de fallos *f* (*Esp*)

trough *n* ECON *of graph, curve* depresión *f*

troy: **~ ounce** *n* ECON onza de oro fino *f*; **~ weight** *n* GEN COMM peso troy *m*

truck *n* *AmE* (*cf lorry BrE*) TRANSP camión *m*; **~ farmer** *AmE* (*cf market gardener BrE*) ECON hortelano(-a) *m,f*; **~ farming** *AmE* (*cf market gardening BrE*) ECON cultivo de huertos *m*, horticultura comercial *f*; **~ reception area** *AmE* (*cf lorry reception area BrE*) TRANSP área de recepción de camiones *f*; **~ service** *AmE* (*cf lorry service BrE*) TRANSP servicio de transporte en camión *m*

trucking *n* *AmE* TRANSP transporte por carretera *m*; **~ bill of lading** *AmE* TRANSP carta de porte en carretera *f*; **~ charges** *n pl* TRANSP gastos de transporte en camión *m pl*; **~ company** *AmE* (*cf transport company BrE*) TRANSP compañía de transportes *f*, empresa de transportes *f*; **~ contractor** TRANSP contratista de camiones *mf*

truck-mounted: **~ crane** *n* *AmE* (*cf lorry-mounted crane BrE*) TRANSP grúa sobre camión *f*

true[1]: **~ and fair** *adj* ACC *audit, view* verdadero y equitativo; **~ to sample** *adj* GEN COMM conforme a la muestra

true[2]: **~ copy** *n* ADMIN, LAW copia fiel *f*; **~ and fair view** *n* *BrE* (*cf fair representation AmE*) ACC imagen fiel *f*; **~ lease** *n* FIN arrendamiento real *m*; **~ owner** *n* LAW, PROP propietario(-a) legítimo(-a) *m,f*, titular verdadero(-a) *m,f*

truncate *vt* BANK, COMP, GEN COMM truncar

truncation *n* BANK, COMP, GEN COMM truncamiento *m*

trunk *n* (*TRK*) TRANSP enlace común *m*, mamparo encerrador de escotilla *m*; **~ call** *BrE obs* (*cf toll call AmE*) COMMS comunicación interurbana *f*, conferencia interurbana *f*, llamada de larga distancia *f*; **~ line** COMMS línea aérea principal *f*, TRANSP *rail* línea de enlace *f*; **~ road** *BrE* (*cf highway AmE*) TRANSP carretera principal *f*, carretera nacional *f*

TRUS *abbr* (*transferable underwriting security*) STOCK valor transferible de suscripción renovable *m*

trust *n* ADMIN comisión de confianza *f*, trust *m*, BANK, ECON consorcio monopolístico *m*, fideicomiso *m*, LAW administración por cuenta ajena *f*; **~ account** BANK cuenta de fideicomiso *f*; **~ agreement** GEN COMM acuerdo de fideicomiso *m*; **~ bank** BANK banco fiduciario *m*; **~ banking** BANK banco fiduciario *m*; **~ beneficiary** GEN COMM beneficiario de bienes a cargo de fiduciario *m*; **~ company** BANK, FIN, LAW banco fiduciario *m*, compañía fiduciaria *f*; **~-control dilemma** MGMNT dilema entre la confianza y el control *m*; **~ deal** GEN COMM, LAW contrato de fideicomiso *m*; **~ deed** LAW escritura fiduciaria *f*; **~ department** MGMNT departamento de administración de bienes *m*; **~ fund** GEN COMM fondo de fideicomiso *m*, fondo en custodia *m*, fondo fiduciario *m*; **~ indenture** GEN COMM, LAW contrato de fideicomiso *m*; **~ instrument** LAW *document* escritura fiduciaria *f*; **~ letter** ACC, BANK, LAW carta fiduciaria *f*; **~ mortgage** BANK hipoteca fiduciaria *f*; **~ receipt** GEN COMM justificante de depósito *m*; **~ unit** STOCK unidad fiduciaria *f*

trustbusting *n infrml* GEN COMM desmontaje de un trust *m*

trustee *n* BANK, LAW, PROP, STOCK administrador(a) del consorcio *m,f*, administrador(a) fiduciario(-a) *m,f*, fideicomisario(-a) *m,f*, fiduciario(-a) *m,f*, síndico(-a) *m,f*; **~ in bankruptcy** BANK síndico(-a) en quiebra *m,f*; **~ status** STOCK categoría de fideicomisario *m*

trusteeship *n* LAW administración fiduciaria *f*, condición de fideicomiso *f*, fideicomiso *m*, gestión fiduciaria *f*, STOCK fiduciaría *f*

trustification *n* GEN COMM, LAW trustificación *f*

trustify *vt* GEN COMM, LAW trustificar

trustworthiness *n* GEN COMM exactitud *f*, honradez *f*

trustworthy *adj* GEN COMM digno de confianza

truth: **~ in lending** *n* *AmE jarg* BANK, FIN, LAW *commercial* declaración veraz de los términos del préstamo *f*, veracidad en contratos de préstamo *f*; **~ in lending act** *n* BANK, ECON, FIN, LAW ley de verificación de las tasas de interés aplicadas a los préstamos; **~ in lending law** *n* BANK, FIN, LAW ley de veracidad en los préstamos *f*; **~ squad** *n infrml* POL escuadrón de la verdad *m*

truthfulness *n* ACC veracidad *f*

try out *vt* GEN COMM poner a prueba

tryout *n* GEN COMM prueba de aptitud *f*

TS *abbr* (*time-sharing*) HRM tiempo compartido *m*

TSL *abbr* (*Trans-Siberian landbridge*) TRANSP puente de tierra transiberiano *m*

TSR *abbr* (*Trans-Siberian Railway*) TRANSP *rail* ferrocarril transiberiano *m*

TT *abbr* COMMS (*telegraphic transfer*) transferencia cablegráfica *f*, transferencia telegráfica *f*, GEN COMM (*timetable*) horario *m*, (*technology transfer*) transferencia de tecnología *f*

Tt *abbr* (*tilt trailer*) TRANSP trailer basculante *m*

TTC *abbr* (*tender to contract*) GEN COMM licitación *f*, propuesta de contrato *f*, LAW concurso *m*

T-test *n* MATH *statistics* ensayo T *m*, prueba T *f*

TUA *abbr* *BrE* (*Trade Union Act*) HRM, LAW, POL ley sindical de 1984

tube *n* *BrE infrml* (*cf subway AmE*) TRANSP ferrocarril subterráneo *m*, metro *m*

TUC *abbr* *BrE* (*Trades Union Congress*) HRM, POL confederación de los sindicatos británicos

tug *n* TRANSP remolcador *m*; **~ boat** TRANSP remolcador *m*; **~-of-war** GEN COMM tira y afloja *m*

tugmaster *n* TRANSP *port* patrón de remolcador *m*

tuition: **~ fees** *n pl* WEL gastos de matrícula *m pl*

TULRA *abbr* *BrE* (*Trade Unions and Labour Relations Act*) HRM, LAW, POL ley de sindicatos y relaciones laborales

tuning *n* GEN COMM adaptación *f*

tunnel *n* ECON, TRANSP túnel *m*; **~ toll** TRANSP *tariffs* peaje de túnel *m*

turbine: ~ **steamship** *n* TRANSP buque de vapor a turbinas *m*

turbo: ~**-electric** *adj* (*TE*) TRANSP turboeléctrico

turn[1] *n* STOCK ganancia del intermediario *f;* ~ **time** TRANSP *port* tiempo del turno de atraque *m;* ◆ ~ **for the better** GEN COMM cambio para mejor; ~ **for the worse** GEN COMM cambio para peor

turn[2]: ~ **into cash** *phr* GEN COMM hacer dinero; ~ **one's attention to** *phr* GEN COMM dirigir la atención hacia; ~ **out to vote** *phr* POL acudir a votar

turn around 1. *vt* FIN cambiar a mejor; **2.** *vi* ECON, GEN COMM *trend* invertirse

turn away *vt* GEN COMM desviar

turn off *vt* COMP apagar

turn on *vt* COMP encender

turnabout *n* GEN COMM cambio completo *m*

turnaround *AmE see* turnround *BrE*

turncoat *n infrml* POL chaquetero *m* (*infrml*)

turning: ~ **basin** *n* TRANSP *port* dársena de giro *f;* ~ **circle** *n* TRANSP área de viraje *f,* curva de evolución del buque *f;* ~ **point** *n* ECON, GEN COMM punto de flexión *m*

turnkey[1] *adj* COMP *system, project* llave en mano *f*

turnkey[2] *n* GEN COMM, IMP/EXP llave en mano *f;* ~ **contract** ECON contrato de montaje llave en mano *m*

turnout *n* GEN COMM concurrencia *f,* IMP/EXP ciclo de ocupación *m,* POL concurrencia *f,* TRANSP *carriages, vessels* ciclo de ocupación *m*

turnover *n* GEN COMM cifra de negocios *f,* facturación *f,* rotación *f,* volumen de venta *m,* volumen de negocios *m,* HRM *of staff* movimiento de personal *m,* MGMNT cifra de negocios *f,* facturación *f;* ~ **rate** GEN COMM índice de rotación de existencias *m;* ~ **ratio** GEN COMM proporción de rotación *f;* ~ **tax** TAX impuesto sobre el volumen de ventas *m,* impuesto sobre el tráfico de empresas *m* (*ITE*)

turnpike *n AmE* (*cf toll motorway BrE*) TRANSP autopista de peaje *f;* ~ **theorem** ECON teorema de la autopista *m*

turnround *n BrE* FIN cambio de posición *m,* GEN COMM *in trend* vuelco *m,* TRANSP área de viraje *f, of ship* ciclo de carga *m;* ~ **period** *BrE* GEN COMM periodo de respuesta *m;* ~ **time** *BrE* GEN COMM tiempo de recorrido *m,* TRANSP tiempo de carga y descarga *m*

TV *abbr* (*television*) MEDIA TV (*televisión*)

TVR *abbr* (*television rating*) MEDIA índice de audiencia televisiva *f*

tweak *vt* COMP reajustar, retocar

twenty: ~**-four hour service** *n* GEN COMM servicio de 24 horas *m;* ~**-four hour trading** *n* GEN COMM negocio abierto las veinticuatro horas del día *m,* STOCK bolsa abierta las veinticuatro horas del día *f*

TWI *abbr* (*training within industry*) HRM, IND capacitación dentro de la empresa *f* (*AmL*), entrenamiento dentro de la industria *m,* formación dentro de la empresa *f* (*Esp*)

twice: ~ **a week** *adj* GEN COMM, MEDIA bisemanal

twilight: ~ **shift** *n* HRM turno vespertino *m*

twin: ~ **room** *n* LEIS habitación doble *f*

twisting *n jarg* FIN inducción a operaciones innecesarias *f*

twistlock *n* TRANSP tensor *m*

two[1]: ~**-color** *AmE,* ~**-colour** *BrE adj* MEDIA a dos colores; ~**-sided** *adj* COMP de dos caras; ~**-way** *adj* COMP de dos direcciones, TRANSP de dos vías

two[2]: ~**-axle vehicle** *n* TRANSP vehículo de dos ejes *m;* ~**-berth cabin** *n* TRANSP camarote de dos literas *m;* ~**-bits** *n pl AmE infrml* FIN moneda de 25 centavos; ~**-class vessel** *n* TRANSP buque de pasajeros con clases primera y turista *m;* ~**-digit inflation** *n* ECON, FIN inflación de dos dígitos *f;* ~**-dollar broker** *n* STOCK agente de contratación con un 2 por ciento de comisión; ~**-gap development model** *n* ECON modelo de desarrollo de dos brechas *m;* ~**-lane deck** *n* TRANSP cubierta de dos carriles *f;* ~**-part tariff** *n* ECON tarifa de dos elementos *f;* ~**-rate system** *n* TAX sistema de doble tarifa *m;* ~**-sided market** *n* STOCK mercado bilateral *m;* ~**-stage least squares method** *n pl* ECON método de los cuadrados mínimos en dos etapas *m;* ~**-tailed test** *n* MATH prueba de doble cola *f;* ~**-tier bargaining** *n jarg* HRM negociación en dos niveles *f;* ~**-tier system** *n* GEN COMM sistema de dos niveles *m;* ~**-tier wage structure** *n* HRM estructura salarial de dos niveles *f;* ~**-way analysis of variance** *n* MATH análisis bidireccional de varianza *m,* análisis de varianza de dos entradas *m;* ~**-way scheme** *n* TRANSP *shipping, port* sistema bidireccional *m;* ~**-way split** *n* GEN COMM ruptura en dos direcciones *f*

TWRA *abbr* (*Transpacific Westbound Rate Agreement*) TRANSP acuerdo de tarifas del comercio interpacífico con rumbo al oeste

tycoon *n* HRM magnate *mf*

tying: ~ **contract** *n* ECON *product compatibility* contrato de relación exclusiva *m,* LAW contrato vinculante *m*

type[1] *n* COMP tipo *m;* ~ **area** S&M zona tipo *f;* ~ **of costs** FIN tipo de costes *m* (*Esp*), tipo de costos *m* (*AmL*); ~ **font** COMP fuente de tipos *f*

type[2] *vt* ADMIN, COMP mecanografiar

typebar *n* ADMIN, COMP línea de linotipia *f*

typeface *n* ADMIN, COMP, MEDIA tipo de escritura *m*

typesetting *n* COMP, GEN COMM, MEDIA *printing* composición *f,* composición tipográfica *f,* fotocomposición *f*

typewrite *vt* ADMIN, COMP mecanografiar

typewriter *n* ADMIN, COMP máquina de escribir *f;* ~ **ball** ADMIN esfera de impresión de máquina de escribir *f*

typewritten *adj* ADMIN mecanografiado, escrito a máquina

typically *adv* GEN COMM típicamente

typify *vt* GEN COMM tipificar

typing: ~ **error** *n* (*typo*) COMP error de pulsación *m,* GEN COMM error mecanográfico *m;* ~ **service** *n* ADMIN servicio mecanográfico *m;* ~ **speed** *n* ADMIN, COMP, GEN COMM velocidad mecanográfica *f*

typist *n* ADMIN mecanógrafo(-a) *m,f*

typo *n infrml* COMP, GEN COMM, MEDIA *print* errata *f,* error tipográfico *m*

typographer *n* GEN COMM, S&M tipógrafo(-a) *m,f*

typographic: ~ **error** *n* COMP, GEN COMM, MEDIA errata *f,* error tipográfico *m*

typological: ~ **analysis** *n* S&M análisis tipológico *m*

typology *n* GEN COMM tipología *f*

tyre *n BrE* TRANSP neumático *m;* ~ **gauge** *BrE* TRANSP anchura de neumático *f,* medidor de neumático *m*

U

U *abbr* TRANSP (*universal container*) contenedor universal *m*, (*universal load*) carga unitaria *f*

U/a *abbr* (*underwriting account*) INS cuenta de subscripción de seguros *f*

UAW *abbr AmE* (*United Automobile Workers*) HRM ≈ Sindicato de Trabajadores de la Industria Automotriz *m*

UAWB *abbr* (*universal air waybill*) IMP/EXP, TRANSP conocimiento de embarque aéreo universal *m*

uberrimae fides *n* GEN COMM, LAW con absoluta buena fe, de total buena fe

ubi remedium ibi jus *phr* GEN COMM donde hay un recurso hay un derecho

UBR *abbr* (*Uniform Business Rate*) FIN tipo empresarial uniforme

UC&P *abbr* (*uniform customs and practice for documentary credits*) GEN COMM usos y prácticas normalizados de créditos documentarios *m pl*

UDEAC *abbr* (*Central African Customs and Economics Union*) ECON, IMP/EXP unión aduanera y económica de Africa Central

U-form *n* ECON forma U *f*

U-hypothesis *n* ECON *income distribution* hipótesis U *f*

UK[1]: **~-incorporated** *adj* LAW incorporado al R.U.

UK[2]: **~ gilts market** *n BrE* STOCK mercado británico de deuda pública; **~ government stocks** *n pl BrE* STOCK bonos del Estado del R.U. *m pl*; **~-South Africa Trade Association** *n* ECON asociación comercial del Reino Unido y el Sur de Africa; **~ taxation** *n* TAX sistema tributario británico

UKAEA *abbr* (*United Kingdom Atomic Energy Authority*) IND autoridad de energía atómica del Reino Unido

UKASTA *abbr* (*United Kingdom Agricultural Supply Trade Association*) ECON asociación comercial de suministros agrícolas del Reino Unido

UKIBIK *abbr* (*United Kingdom Insurance Brokers' European Committee*) INS comité europeo de agencias de seguros del Reino Unido

UKOOA *abbr* (*United Kingdom Offshore Operators' Association*) TRANSP asociación de operadores costeros del Reino Unido

UKREP *abbr* (*United Kingdom Permanent Representative to the European Union*) POL *international* representante permanente del Reino Unido en la Unión Europea *f*

UKTA *abbr* (*United Kingdom Trade Agency*) ECON *developing countries* agencia comercial del Reino Unido

ULCC *abbr* (*ultra large crude carrier*) TRANSP superpetrolero *m*

ULD *abbr* (*unit load device*) TRANSP dispositivo de carga unitaria *m*

ullage *n* TRANSP merma *f*

ult. *abbr* (*ultimo*) GEN COMM pdo. (*pasado*)

ultimate: **~ consumer** *n* S&M consumidor(a) final *m,f*; **~ risk** *n* BANK riesgo máximo *m*

ultimo *adj* (*ult.*) GEN COMM pasado (*pdo.*)

ultra: **~ large crude carrier** *n* (*ULCC*) TRANSP superpetrolero *m*

ultravires[1] *adj* LAW acto no comparado por un poder, antiestatutario

ultravires[2]: **~ borrowing** *n* BANK empréstito ultra vires *m*; **~ activities** *n pl* LAW actividades que sobrepasan sus atribuciones *f pl*

UMA *abbr* (*union membership agreement*) HRM acuerdo de las bases de un sindicato *m*

umbrella[1]: **~ agent** *n* TRANSP agente consignatario(-a) *m,f*; **~ fund** *n* FIN fondo de contingencia *m*; **~ group** *n* FIN grupo paraguas *m*; **~ liability insurance** *n* INS seguro de cobertura general *m*; **~ project** *n* GEN COMM proyecto que sirve de marco para otros *m*

umbrella[2]: **under the ~ of** *phr* GEN COMM bajo la protección de

UMLER *abbr* (*Universal Machine Language Equipment Register*) TRANSP Registro de Equipo para Lenguaje Universal de Máquina *m*

Un: **~ Dk** *abbr* (*under deck tank*) TRANSP tanque bajo cubierta *m*

UN: **~ number** *n* TRANSP número ONU *m*

UNA *abbr* (*United Nations Association*) POL ANU (*Asociación de las Naciones Unidas*)

unabridged *adj* GEN COMM íntegro, completo

unaccepted *adj* GEN COMM *bill* inaceptado

unaccompanied: **~ baggage** *n* TRANSP equipaje no acompañado *m*

unaccounted: **~ for** *adj* GEN COMM inexplicado

unacknowledged *adj* GEN COMM no reconocido

unadjusted *adj* GEN COMM *figures, statistics* desajustado; ♦ **in ~ figures** GEN COMM en cifras desajustadas

unadvertised *adj* GEN COMM no anunciado

unaffiliated[1] *adj* GEN COMM no afiliado, no asociado

unaffiliated[2]: **~ union** *n* HRM sindicato no afiliado *m*

unalienable *adj* LAW inalienable

unallocated *adj* COMP no asignado

unallotted *adj* STOCK *shares* no distribuido

unaltered *adj* GEN COMM, STOCK *share prices* inalterado

unamortized[1] *adj* ACC, FIN, STOCK no amortizado, pendiente de amortizar

unamortized[2]: **~ bond discount** *n* STOCK descuento sobre bonos no amortizados *m*; **~ discount on Treasury bills** *n* STOCK descuento no amortizado sobre Bonos del Tesoro *m*; **~ premiums on investments** *n pl* STOCK primas sobre inversiones no amortizadas *f pl*

unanimity *n* GEN COMM unanimidad *f*

unanimous *adj* GEN COMM *decision* unánime

unanimously *adv* GEN COMM por unanimidad; **~ accepted** GEN COMM aceptado unánimemente

unanticipated *adj* GEN COMM imprevisto

unappropriated[1] *adj* FIN, GEN COMM no aplicado, no asignado

unappropriated[2]: **~ profit** *n* FIN beneficio no asignado *m*; **~ retained earnings** *n pl* FIN beneficios retenidos no asignados *m pl*; **~ surplus** *n* FIN, GEN COMM superávit disponible *m*

unapproved: **~ funds** *n pl* FIN fondos desaprobados *m pl*

unassailable *adj* GEN COMM inatacable

unassessed *adj* GEN COMM no evaluado

unassignable *adj* LAW intransferible

unassured *adj* INS no asegurado

unattainable *adj* GEN COMM *objective* inalcanzable

unattended *adj* IND *production* desatendido

unaudited[1] *adj* ACC no auditado

unauthenticated[1] *adj* LAW, STOCK no autentificado

unauthenticated[2]: **~ signature** *n* BANK, LAW firma no autentificada *f*

unauthorized: **~ shares** *n pl* STOCK acciones no autorizadas *f pl*; **~ signature** *n* LAW firma no autorizada *f*

unavailability *n* COMP, GEN COMM inaccesibilidad *f*

unavailable *adj* COMP no disponible, GEN COMM indisponible

unavoidable[1] *adj* GEN COMM inevitable

unavoidable[2]: **~ costs** *n pl* ACC costes inevitables *m pl* (*Esp*), costos inevitables *m pl* (*AmL*)

unbacked *adj* BANK no respaldado

unbalanced: **~ growth** *n* ECON, FIN crecimiento desequilibrado *m*

unbiased: **~ estimator** *n* ECON estimador insesgado *m*

unblock *vt* COMP, GEN COMM desbloquear

unbounded: **~ risk** *n* STOCK *of futures* riesgo no vinculado *m*

unbranded: **~ goods** *n pl* GEN COMM artículos sin marca *m pl*

unbundle *vt* GEN COMM facturar separadamente

unbundling *n* ACC, BANK, GEN COMM desglose *m*

unbusinesslike *adj* GEN COMM anticomercial

uncallable[1] *adj* BANK, FIN no denunciable

uncallable[2]: **~ loan** *n* BANK, FIN préstamo no denunciable *m*

uncalled: **~ capital** *n* GEN COMM capital no desembolsado *m*, capital suscrito y no desembolsado *m*

uncanceled *AmE see uncancelled debt BrE*

uncancelled: **~ debt** *n BrE* ACC, BANK, FIN deuda activa *f*

uncashed[1] *adj* BANK, FIN, GEN COMM no cobrado

uncashed[2]: **~ check** *AmE*, **~ cheque** *BrE n* BANK, FIN cheque no cobrado *m*

UNCED *abbr* (*United Nations Conference on Environment and Development*) ENVIR, POL Conferencia de las Naciones Unidas sobre Medio Ambiente y Desarrollo *f*

unchanged *adj* GEN COMM inmodificado, sin modificar

unchecked[1] *adj* GEN COMM *figures*, S&M no cotejado

unchecked[2]: **~ baggage** *n* TRANSP equipaje no comprobado *m*; **~ inflationary economy** *n* ECON economía inflacionista no controlada *f*

UNCITRAL *abbr* (*United Nations Commission of International Trade Law*) ECON, LAW, POL Comisión de las Naciones Unidas para el Derecho Mercantil Internacional *f*

unclaimed: **~ balance** *n* BANK saldo no reclamado *m*; **~ deposit** *n* BANK depósito no reclamado *m*; **~ letter** *n* COMMS carta no reclamada *f*; **~ right** *n* LAW derecho no reclamado *m*

unclean: **~ bill of health** *n* GEN COMM, WEL patente de sanidad defectuosa *f*

uncollectable[1] *adj* ACC, TAX incobrable

uncollectable[2]: **~ account** *n* ACC cuenta incobrable *f*; **~ taxes** *n pl* ACC, TAX impuestos incobrables *m pl*

uncollected: **~ funds** *n pl* BANK fondos no cobrados *m pl*, fondos no recaudados *m pl*

uncommitted: **~ funds** *n* FIN fondos disponibles *m pl*

uncompromising *adj* GEN COMM inflexible

UNCON *abbr* (*uncontainerable goods*) TRANSP mercancías no contenerizables *f pl*

unconditional[1] *adj* GEN COMM incondicional

unconditional[2]: **~ acceptance** *n* GEN COMM aceptación incondicional *f*; **~ remission** *n* FIN *of debt* remisión incondicional *f*

unconfirmed: **~ credit** *n* BANK crédito no confirmado *m*; **~ irrevocable letter of credit** *n* BANK, FIN crédito documentario irrevocable no confirmado *m*; **~ letter of credit** *n* BANK, FIN carta de crédito no confirmada *f*

unconscionable: **~ bargain** *n* LAW transacción leonina *f*

unconsolidated: **on an ~ basis** *phr* ACC con carácter no consolidado

unconstitutional: **~ strike** *n* HRM, IND, LAW huelga ilegal *f*

uncontainerable: **~ goods** *n pl* (*UNCON*) TRANSP mercancías no contenerizables *f pl*

unconverted[1] *adj* GEN COMM no convertido

unconverted[2]: **~ share** *n* FIN, STOCK acción inconvertible *f*

uncorrected *adj* GEN COMM sin corregir

uncovered: **~ advance** *n* STOCK anticipo en descubierto *m*; **~ amount** *n* BANK cantidad en descubierto *f*; **~ balance** *n* FIN balance descubierto *m*; **~ bear** *n* STOCK especulador(a) a la baja sin provisión de fondos *m,f*; **~ call** *n* STOCK opción de compra sin cobertura *f*; **~ call option** *n* STOCK opción de compra sin cobertura *f*; **~ call writer** *n* STOCK emisor(a) de una opción de compra al descubierto *m,f*; **~ check** *AmE*, **~ cheque** *BrE n* BANK, FIN cheque sin fondos *m*, cheque sin provisión de fondos *m*; **~ hedge loss** *n* STOCK pérdida de cobertura al descubierto *f*; **~ loan** *n* BANK empréstito sin garantía *m*, préstamo fiduciario *m*, préstamo sin garantía *m*; **~ option** *n* STOCK opción sin cubrir *f*; **~ put** *n* STOCK opción de venta sin cobertura *f*; **~ writer** *n* STOCK emisor(a) de opciones abiertas *m,f*

uncrossed: **~ check** *AmE*, **~ cheque** *BrE n* BANK, FIN cheque no cruzado *m*, cheque sin cruzar *m*

UNCTAD *abbr* (*United Nations Conference on Trade and Development*) ECON, POL UNCTAD (*Conferencia de las Naciones Unidas sobre Comercio y Desarrollo*)

uncurbed *adj* GEN COMM *competition* libre

uncurtailed *adj* GEN COMM *competition, rights* sin restricciones

uncustomed *adj* IMP/EXP no pasado por la aduana

undamaged *adj* GEN COMM indemne

undamped *adj* ECON *demand* persistente

undated *adj* GEN COMM sin fecha

undecided *adj* GEN COMM indeciso

undelete *vt* COMP restituir

undeliverable: **~ check** *AmE*, **~ cheque** *BrE n* BANK, FIN cheque intransferible *m*, cheque no librable *m*

undelivered: **if ~ please return to sender** *phr* COMMS si no se entrega al destinatario, por favor devuélvase al remitente

undepreciated[1] *adj* GEN COMM no depreciado

undepreciated[2]: ~ **capital cost** n FIN gastos de instalación no amortizados m pl; ~ **cost** n ACC coste no depreciado m (*Esp*), costo no depreciado m (*AmL*)

undepressed adj STOCK no deprimido

underabsorb vt ACC absorber de forma insuficiente

underabsorbed: ~ **expenses** n pl ACC gastos no absorbidos o aplicados m pl

underabsorption: ~ **of costs** n ACC absorción insuficiente de costes f

under-achiever n jarg WEL persona de rendimiento inferior a lo esperado

underapplied: ~ **overheads** n pl ACC gastos generales subutilizados m pl

underassess vt ACC liquidar de forma insuficiente

underassessment n TAX infravaloración de la renta a efectos fiscales

underbid vi GEN COMM ofrecer a la baja

undercapacity n GEN COMM, IND subcapacidad f

undercapitalized adj FIN, GEN COMM, IND descapitalizado, infracapitalizado, subcapitalizado

undercharged: ~ **account** n BANK cuenta a la que se carga de menos f

underclass n ECON subclase f

underconsumption n ECON subconsumo m

undercover: ~ **audit** n ACC auditoría secreta f; ~ **payment** n GEN COMM pago secreto m

undercut vt ECON *competitor* socavar, GEN COMM ofrecer precios más bajos que

undercutting n GEN COMM oferta a bajo precio f

underdeclaration n TAX declaración incompleta f

underdeclared: ~ **tax** n TAX liquidación insuficiente del impuesto f

underdelivery: ~ **spread** n STOCK opción de compra o venta no entregada del todo f

underdeveloped: ~ **country** n GEN COMM país subdesarrollado m

underemployed[1] adj HRM infraocupado, subempleado

underemployed[2]: ~ **capacity** n BANK, ECON, GEN COMM, IND capacidad subutilizada f

underemployment n HRM subempleo m

underestimate vt GEN COMM menospreciar, subestimar

underestimation n ECON, GEN COMM infravaloración f

underevaluation n GEN COMM evaluación modesta f

underfunded adj FIN poco consolidado

undergo vt GEN COMM sufrir

undergraduate n WEL estudiante universitario(-a) m,f

underground n TRANSP *BrE* (*cf subway AmE*) ferrocarril subterráneo m, metro m; ~ **economy** ECON, FIN economía clandestina f, economía sumergida f; ~ **employment** ECON empleo sumergido m

underinvestment n BANK subinversión f

underlessee n PROP subarrendatario(-a) m,f

underling n HRM subordinado(-a) m,f

underlying[1] adj STOCK subsidiario, subyacente

underlying[2]: ~ **asset** n STOCK activo subyacente m; ~ **bond** n STOCK título prioritario m; ~ **company** n *infrml* GEN COMM compañía subsidiaria f; ~ **debt** n ACC, BANK, FIN *real estate, securities* deuda precedente f; ~ **futures** n pl STOCK futuros subyacentes m pl; ~ **futures contract** n STOCK contrato de futuros subyacente m; ~ **inflation** n ECON inflación subyacente f; ~ **inflation rate** n ECON proporción de inflación

subyacente f; ~ **mortgage** n BANK, PROP hipoteca fundamental f, hipoteca implícita f, hipoteca de prioridad f, hipoteca subyacente f; ~ **net assets** n pl FIN activos netos subsidiarios m pl; ~ **rate** n ECON proporción subyacente f; ~ **security** n STOCK título garantizado m; ~ **tendency** n GEN COMM tendencia oculta f; ~ **trend** n GEN COMM tendencia subyacente f

undermanned adj HRM falto de personal, con menos personal del necesario, TRANSP con tripulación incompleta; ♦ **be** ~ HRM estar falto de personal

undermargined: ~ **account** n STOCK cuenta submarginal f

undermentioned adj GEN COMM abajo mencionado

underperform vi ECON rendir menos de lo normal, GEN COMM tener bajo rendimiento

underperforming adj GEN COMM pobre

underpin vt ECON *currency* apuntalar

underpopulated adj GEN COMM poco poblado

underprice vt GEN COMM, S&M fijar un precio muy bajo, señalar a un precio más bajo

underpriced adj GEN COMM, S&M con un precio por debajo de lo normal, vendido a un precio demasiado bajo, señalado a un precio más bajo

underprivileged adj GEN COMM desfavorecido

underproduction n IND producción deficitaria f, subproducción f

under-proportionately adv MATH menos que proporcionalmente

underquote vt GEN COMM ofrecer a precio inferior

underreport vt GEN COMM dar pocos informes

under-represent vt GEN COMM representar insuficientemente

underrun n FIN *appropriation* diferencia entre dinero solicitado y obtenido f; ~ **costs** n pl ACC costes inferiores a los previstos m pl (*Esp*), costos inferiores a los previstos m pl (*AmL*)

underscore vt COMP *text*, GEN COMM subrayar

undersecretary n HRM, POL *government* subsecretario, -a mf, vicesecretario m

undersell: ~ **oneself** phr GEN COMM malvenderse

underselling n S&M *prices* venta a un precio más bajo f

undersigned: **I, the ~, declare that** phr COMMS el abajo firmante, declara que

underspend vt ACC, GEN COMM gastar de menos, *budget* gastar por debajo del presupuesto

underspending n ACC *budget*, GEN COMM gasto por debajo del presupuesto m, gasto menor de lo debido m

understaffed adj HRM escaso de personal, escaso de plantilla

understaffing n HRM escasez de personal f

understanding: **on the ~ that** phr GEN COMM a condición de que

understatement: ~ **of income** n TAX subestimación de la renta f

undersubscribed adj FIN suscrito de forma insuficiente

undertake vt GEN COMM tomar a su cargo, comprometerse a, *task* emprender, acometer

undertaking n GEN COMM *venture* empresa f, tarea f, *contract* compromiso m, LAW, POL compromiso m

undertax vt TAX gravar con un impuesto más bajo del establecido

under-the-counter: ~ **sale** n S&M venta bajo mano f

undertrade *vt* FIN, GEN COMM, STOCK abaratar

undertrading *n* FIN, STOCK abaratamiento *m*

underuse *vt* GEN COMM infrautilizar

underutilize *vt* GEN COMM *resources* infrautilizar

undervaluation *n* ECON, FIN, GEN COMM, STOCK infravaloración *f*, minusvaloración *f*, subvaloración *f*

undervalue[1] *n* STOCK *of shares* subestimación *f*

undervalue[2] *vt* ECON, FIN, GEN COMM, STOCK subvalorar

undervalued[1] *adj* ECON, FIN, GEN COMM, STOCK infravalorado

undervalued[2]: **~ currency** *n* ECON *international* moneda subvalorada *f*

underway *adj* GEN COMM en curso

underwriter *n* (*U/W*) INS *person* asegurador(a) *m,f*, *company* empresa aseguradora *f*

underwriting *n* INS, STOCK reaseguro *m*; **~ account** (*U/a*) INS cuenta de subscripción de seguros *f*; **~ agreement** STOCK acuerdo de suscripción *m*; **~ commission** FIN comisión de suscripción *f*; **~ fee** BANK, FIN comisión de garantía *f*; **~ spread** STOCK margen de suscripción *m*; **~ syndicate** INS consorcio de aseguradores *m*

underwritten *adj* BANK, FIN, INS, STOCK suscrito

undifferentiated: **~ marketing** *n* S&M marketing no diferenciado *m*; **~ products** *n pl* S&M productos indiferenciados *m pl*

undischarged[1] *adj* ACC, FIN, GEN COMM, LAW, TRANSP *shipping* no librado

undischarged[2]: **~ commitment** *n* ACC compromiso no librado *m*, compromiso no pagado *m*

undisclosed: **~ sum** *n* FIN suma no rehabilitada *f*

undiscovered: **~ loss clause** *n* FIN, INS, LAW, TRANSP cláusula de pérdida sin descubrir *f*

undisposed: **~ of** *adj* GEN COMM *stock* no vendido

undistributable: **~ capital** *n* FIN capital no distribuible *m*; **~ reserve** *n BrE* (*cf restricted surplus AmE*) ACC excedente restringido *m*, fondos no repartidos *m pl*, plusvalía restringida *f*, reserva no distribuible *f*, superávit restringido *m*

undistributed: **~ allotment** *n* GEN COMM asignación no distribuida *f*; **~ balance** *n* ACC saldo no distribuido *m*; **~ income** *n* ECON renta no distribuida *f*; **~ interest** *n* FIN interés sin repartir *m*; **~ profit** *n* ACC, FIN utilidad por distribuir *f* (*AmL*), beneficio por distribuir *f* (*Esp*); **~ profits** *n pl* ACC, FIN beneficios no distribuidos *m pl*, beneficios retenidos *m pl*; **~ profits tax** *n* TAX impuesto sobre beneficios no distribuidos *m*

undivided: **~ profits** *n pl* BANK, FIN beneficio sin repartir *m*; **~ property** *n* PROP propiedad no repartida *f*

undocumented: **~ worker** *n* HRM trabajador(a) indocumentado(-a) *m,f*, LAW trabajador(a) sin documentación *m,f*

UNDP *abbr* (*United Nations Development Programme*) ECON, POL PNUD (*Programa de las Naciones Unidas para el Desarrollo*)

undue: **~ hardship** *n* TAX apremio indebido *m*; **~ influence** *n* GEN COMM coacción *f*

unduly *adv* GEN COMM indebidamente

unearned: **~ dividend** *n* STOCK dividendo no devengado *m*; **~ income** *n* ACC ingresos diferidos *m pl*; **~ increment** *n* FIN, PROP incremento no ganado *m*; **~ increment of land** *n* FIN, PROP plusvalía de la tierra *f*; **~ interest** *n* ACC, BANK intereses no devengados *m pl*;

~ premium *n* FIN, TAX prima no cobrada *f*, prima no ganada *f*

UN-ECLA *abbr* (*United Nations Economic Commission for Latin America*) ECON, POL ≈ CEPAL (*Comisión Económica para América Latina*)

uneconomic *adj* ECON, GEN COMM, IND, S&M antieconómico

unemployed[1] *adj* ECON parado, GEN COMM desempleado, HRM, POL, WEL parado; ◆ **be ~** HRM estar en el paro

unemployed[2]: **the ~** *n pl* GEN COMM los desempleados *m pl*; **~ labor force** *AmE*, **~ labour force** *BrE* *n* ECON, HRM, POL, WEL población activa sin empleo *f*

unemployment *n* GEN COMM desempleo *m*, paro *m*; **~ benefit** *BrE* (*cf unemployment compensation AmE*) WEL indemnización por desempleo *f*, seguro de desempleo *m*, subsidio de desempleo *m*; **~ compensation** *AmE* (*cf unemployment benefit BrE*) WEL indemnización por desempleo *f*, seguro de desempleo *m*, subsidio de desempleo *m*; **~ figures** *n pl* HRM, POL, WEL cifras de desempleo *f pl*; **~ insurance** HRM, INS, POL, WEL seguro de paro *m*, seguro de desempleo *f*; **~ pay** HRM subsidio de paro *m*; **~ rate** GEN COMM índice de desempleo *m*, tasa de desempleo *f*; **~ statistics** ECON, HRM, POL estadística de desempleo *f*; **~ trap** HRM, WEL trampa del desempleo *f*

Unemployment: **~ Benefit Office** *n BrE* WEL oficina británica para cobrar el subsidio de desempleo, ≈ oficina del paro *f* (*infrml*) (*Esp*); **~ Insurance Account** *n* HRM, INS cuenta de seguro de desempleo *f*

unencumbered[1] *adj* PROP libre de gravamen

unencumbered[2]: **~ balance** *n* ACC *government* saldo sin cargas *m*; **~ estate property** *n* PROP propiedad sin gravamen *f*

unendorsed *adj* BANK, GEN COMM no endosado, no garantizado

unenforceable[1] *adj* LAW inexigible

unenforceable[2]: **~ contract** *n* LAW contrato no ejecutable *m*

unequal: **~ exchange** *n* GEN COMM intercambio desigual *m*; **~ trade** *n* ECON comercio desigual *m*

uneven[1] *adj* GEN COMM *trend* irregular

uneven[2]: **~ lot** *n* GEN COMM lote desigual *m*

unexchangeable *adj* GEN COMM incambiable

unexecuted *adj* GEN COMM no ejecutado

unexpended[1] *adj* GEN COMM no gastado

unexpended[2]: **~ balance** *n* FIN *of appropriation* saldo no gastado *m*

unexpired[1] *adj* LAW vigente

unexpired[2]: **~ cost** *n* ECON coste no vencido *m* (*Esp*), costo no vencido *m* (*AmL*)

unfailing *adj* GEN COMM infalible

unfair: **~ competition** *n* GEN COMM competencia desleal *f*; **~ dismissal** *n* HRM despido injustificado *m*; **~ house** *n jarg* HRM empresa desleal *f*; **~ labor practice** *AmE*, **~ labour practice** *BrE* *n* HRM práctica laboral injusta *f*; **~ shop** *n* HRM comercio desleal *m*; **~ trade** *n* GEN COMM negocio sucio *m*; **~ trading practice** *n* GEN COMM práctica de negocio sucio *f*

unfavorable *AmE see* unfavourable *BrE*

unfavorably *AmE see* unfavourably *BrE*

unfavourable[1] *adj BrE* GEN COMM desfavorable

unfavourable[2]: **~ balance of trade** *n BrE* ECON balanza comercial desfavorable *f*, GEN COMM déficit de la balanza comercial *m*; ~ **difference** *n BrE* ACC diferencia desfavorable *f*; ~ **exchange** *n BrE* GEN COMM cambio desfavorable *m*

unfavourably: **be ~ impressed** *phr BrE* GEN COMM recibir una impresión desfavorable, tener una impresión desfavorable

unfeasible *adj* GEN COMM irrealizable

unfilled: ~ **vacancy** *n* HRM vacante no cubierta *f*

unfit *adj* GEN COMM incapacitado, *incapable* incapaz; ♦ ~ **for consumption** GEN COMM no apto para el consumo

unforeseeable *adj* GEN COMM imprevisible

unforeseen[1] *adj* GEN COMM imprevisto

unforeseen[2]: ~ **problem** *n* GEN COMM dificultad imprevista *f*

unformatted *adj* COMP sin formatear

unfreeze *vt* ECON descongelar

unfriendly: ~ **takeover attempt** *n* FIN intento de absorción hostil *m*; ~ **takeover bid** *n* FIN intento de absorción hostil *m*

unfulfilled: ~ **order** *n* GEN COMM, S&M pedido no despachado *m*

unfunded: ~ **borrowing** *n* BANK empréstito no consolidado *m*; ~ **debt** *n* FIN deuda flotante *f*; ~ **pension** *n* FIN, HRM pensión no consolidada *f*; ~ **pension scheme** *n* FIN, HRM plan de pensiones no consolidado *m*

ungeared: ~ **balance sheet** *n* ACC balance de situación mal estructurado *m*

ungraded *adj* GEN COMM no clasificado

UNHCR *abbr* (*United Nations High Commission for Refugees*) POL, WEL ACNUR (*Oficina del Alto Comisionado de las Naciones Unidas para los Refugiados*)

unhedged *adj* STOCK sin cobertura

UNICEF *abbr* (*United Nations Children's Fund*) POL, WEL UNICEF (*Agencia de las Naciones Unidas para la Ayuda a la Infancia*)

unidimensional *adj* GEN COMM unidimensional

UNIDO *abbr* (*United Nations Industrial Development Organization*) ECON, IND, POL ONUDI (*Organización de las Naciones Unidas para el Desarrollo Industrial*)

unification *n* POL unificación *f*

unified: ~ **credit** *n* TAX crédito unificado *m*

uniform[1] *adj* GEN COMM uniforme

uniform[2]: ~ **accounting** *n* ACC contabilidad uniforme *f*; ~ **customs and practice for documentary credits** *n* (*UC&P*) GEN COMM usos y prácticas normalizados de créditos documentarios *m pl*; ~ **gifts to minors act** *n* LAW ley uniforme de legados a menores *f*; ~ **practice code** *n AmE* STOCK código de procedimiento uniforme *m*; ~ **price** *n* ECON, GEN COMM, S&M precio constante *m*, precio uniforme *m*; ~ **rules for collections** *n pl* BANK reglas uniformes de cobro *f pl*

Uniform: ~ **Business Rate** *n* (*UBR*) FIN tipo empresarial uniforme; ~ **Commercial Code** *n* LAW Código Uniforme de Comercio *m*; ~ **Securities Agent State Law Examination** *n* (*USASLE*) LAW ley uniforme del estado para el reconocimiento de los agentes de bolsa

uniformity *n* GEN COMM uniformidad *f*; ~ **assumption** ECON hipótesis de la uniformidad *f*

unify *vt* POL unificar

unilateral[1] *adj* ECON, GEN COMM, HRM unilateral

unilateral[2]: ~ **agreement** *n* ECON, LAW, POL acuerdo unilateral *m*; ~ **measure** *n* GEN COMM medida unilateral

f; ~ **reference** *n* HRM consulta unilateral *f*; ~ **regulation** *n* HRM reglamento unilateral *m*

unilaterally *adv* ECON, GEN COMM, HRM unilateralmente

unimodal: ~ **distribution** *n* MATH distribución unimodal *f*

unimpaired: ~ **capital** *n* ACC, ECON, FIN, GEN COMM capital libre de cargas *m*, capital libre de gravámenes *m*

unimpeachable *adj* GEN COMM *contract, evidence* irreprochable

unincorporated: ~ **business** *n* GEN COMM empresa no incorporada *f*; ~ **company** *n* GEN COMM compañía no incorporada *f*

uninfected *adj* COMP no infectado

uninsurable[1] *adj* INS inasegurable

uninsurable[2]: ~ **title** *n* INS título no asegurable *m*

uninsured *adj* INS no asegurado

unintended: ~ **investment** *n* BANK inversión no planificada *f*

uninterruptible: ~ **power supply** *n* (*UPS*) COMP alimentación eléctrica ininterrumpible *f*

union *n BrE* (*cf syndicate AmE*) GEN COMM sindicato *m*; ~ **affiliation** HRM afiliación a un sindicato *f*, afiliación sindical *f*; ~ **agent** INS delegado(-a) del gremio *m,f*; ~ **agreement** HRM acuerdo sindical *m*, contrato sindical *m*; ~ **bashing** *jarg* HRM golpe sindical *m*; ~ **certification** HRM inscripción de un sindicato *f*; ~ **contract** HRM convenio sindical *m*; ~ **density** HRM densidad sindical *f*; ~ **fees** *n pl* HRM cuotas sindicales *f pl*; ~ **government** HRM gobierno sindical *m*; ~ **label** HRM etiqueta sindical *f*; ~ **labor contract** *AmE*, ~ **labour contract** *BrE* HRM, IND contrato colectivo de trabajo *m*; ~ **leave** HRM permiso sindical *m*; ~ **member** HRM, POL sindicalista *mf*; ~ **membership** HRM afiliación a un sindicato *f*, afiliación sindical *f*; ~ **membership agreement** (*UMA*) HRM acuerdo de las bases de un sindicato *m*; ~ **movement** HRM movimiento sindical *m*; ~ **officer** HRM dirigente sindical *mf*; ~ **official** HRM empleado(-a) sindical *m,f*; **~-only clause** *BrE* HRM cláusula exclusivamente sindical *f*; **~-only practice** *BrE* HRM práctica de representación del personal por los sindicatos *f*; ~ **purchase** TRANSP *cargo handling* aparejo a la americana *m*; ~ **rate** HRM porcentaje de sindicalismo *m*; ~ **representative** HRM representante sindical *mf*; ~ **rights** *n pl* HRM derechos sindicales *m pl*; ~ **rule** HRM norma sindical *f*; ~ **rule book** HRM libro de normas de un sindicato *m*; ~ **security clause** BANK, INS, LAW cláusula sindical en contrato laboral *f*; ~ **shop** HRM taller agremiado *m*; ~ **structure** HRM estructura sindical *f*; ~ **wage effect** FIN efecto de salarios sindicales *m*; ~ **wage policy** HRM política salarial sindical *f*

unionized *adj* HRM sindicado

unionization *n* HRM, POL sindicalización *f*

Union: ~ **of Shop, Distributive & Allied Workers** *n* (*USDAW*) HRM sindicato del sector comercio, distribución y afines

unique[1] *adj* GEN COMM peculiar

unique[2]: ~ **impairment** *n* INS incapacidad peculiar *f*; ~ **reference number** *n* (*URN*) GEN COMM folio único de referencia *m*; ~ **selling proposition** *n* (*USP*) S&M proposición única de venta *f*

unissuable: ~ **note** *n* BANK nota no emisible *f*

unissued: ~ **capital** *n* STOCK capital no emitido *m*; ~ **capital stock** *n* STOCK acciones no emitidas *f pl*;

~ **stock** *n* STOCK acciones no emitidas *f pl*; ~ **Treasury share** *n* STOCK bono del Tesoro en cartera *m*

unit *n* GEN COMM unidad *f*; ~ **of account** ACC moneda de cuenta *f*; ~ **banking** BANK banca única *f*, banca sin sucursales *f*; ~ **of a collective investment undertaking** FIN unidad de una empresa de inversión colectiva *f*; ~ **cost** ACC coste unitario *m* (*Esp*), costo unitario *m* (*AmL*); ~ **holder** STOCK tenedor(a) unitario(-a) *m,f*; ~ **labor cost** *AmE see unit labour cost BrE*; ~ **labor costs** *AmE see unit labour costs BrE*; ~ **labour cost** *BrE* IND coste unitario del trabajo *m* (*Esp*), costo unitario del trabajo *m* (*AmL*); ~ **labour costs** *BrE n pl* ACC, ECON, HRM costes de unidad laboral *m pl* (*Esp*), costos de unidad laboral *m pl* (*AmL*), costes unitarios de la mano de obra *m pl* (*Esp*), costos unitarios de la mano de obra *m pl* (*AmL*), importe unitario de la mano de obra *m*; ~ **load** (*U*) TRANSP *distribution* carga unitaria *f*; ~ **load device** (*ULD*) TRANSP dispositivo de carga unitaria *m*; ~ **pack** S&M envase unitario *m*; ~ **price** GEN COMM, S&M precio por pieza *m*, precio unitario *m*; ~ **pricing** GEN COMM, S&M fijación de precios por unidad *f*; ~ **stocking plan** FIN, STOCK plan de compra de acciones unitarias *m*; ~ **of trading** STOCK unidad de negociación *f*; ~ **trust** FIN, STOCK sociedad de inversión de capital variable *f* (*SICAV*), sociedad inversora por obligaciones *f*; ~ **trust management** STOCK gestión de una sociedad inversora por obligaciones *f*; ~ **value** ECON, GEN COMM valor unitario *m*; ~ **value index** (*UVI*) ECON índice de valor unitario *m*

UNITAR *abbr* (*United Nations Institute for Training and Research*) HRM, POL, WEL UNITAR (*Instituto de las Naciones Unidas para la Formación Profesional y la Investigación*)

unitary: ~ **approach** *n* WEL *social work* enfoque unitario *m*; ~ **elasticity** *n* ECON elasticidad unitaria *f*; ~ **model** *n* WEL *social work* modelo unitario *m*

Unitas: ~ **all share index** *n* STOCK índice general de cotización de valores de la bolsa de Helsinki

United: ~ **Automobile Workers** *n pl AmE* (*UAW*) HRM ≈ Sindicato de Trabajadores de la Industria Automotriz *m*; ~ **Kingdom Agricultural Supply Trade Association** *n* (*UKASTA*) ECON asociación comercial de suministros agrícolas del Reino Unido; ~ **Kingdom Atomic Energy Authority** *n* (*UKAEA*) IND autoridad de energía atómica del Reino Unido; ~ **Kingdom Insurance Brokers' European Committee** *n* (*UKIBIK*) INS comité europeo de agencias de seguros del Reino Unido; ~ **Kingdom Offshore Operators' Association** *n* (*UKOOA*) TRANSP asociación de operadores costeros del Reino Unido; ~ **Kingdom Permanent Representative to the European Union** *n* (*UKREP*) POL representante permanente del Reino Unido en la Unión Europea *f*; ~ **Kingdom Stock Exchanges** *n* federación de bolsas del Reino Unido; ~ **Kingdom Trade Agency** *n* (*UKTA*) ECON *developing countries* agencia comercial del Reino Unido; ~ **Nations Association** *n* (*UNA*) POL Asociación de las Naciones Unidas *f* (*ANU*); ~ **Nations Children's Fund** *n* (*UNICEF*) POL, WEL Agencia de las Naciones Unidas para la Ayuda a la Infancia *f* (*UNICEF*); ~ **Nations Commission of International Trade Law** *n* (*UNCITRAL*) ECON, LAW, POL Comisión de las Naciones Unidas para el Derecho Mercantil Internacional *f*; ~ **Nations Conference on Environment and Development** *n* (*UNCED*) ENVIR, POL Conferencia de las Naciones Unidas sobre Medio Ambiente y Desa-

rrollo *f*; ~ **Nations Conference on Trade and Development** *n* (*UNCTAD*) ECON, POL Conferencia de las Naciones Unidas sobre Comercio y Desarrollo *f* (*UNCTAD*); ~ **Nations Development Programme** *n* (*UNDP*) ECON, POL Programa de las Naciones Unidas para el Desarrollo *m* (*PNUD*); ~ **Nations Economic Commission for Latin America** *n* (*UN-ECLA*) ECON, POL ≈ Comisión Económica para América Latina *f* (*CEPAL*); ~ **Nations High Commission for Refugees** *n* (*UNHCR*) POL, WEL Oficina del Alto Comisionado de las Naciones Unidas para los Refugiados *f* (*ACNUR*); ~ **Nations Industrial Development Organization** *n* (*UNIDO*) ECON, IND, POL Organización de las Naciones Unidas para el Desarrollo Industrial *f* (*ONUDI*); ~ **Nations Institute for Training and Research** *n* (*UNITAR*) HRM, POL, WEL Instituto de las Naciones Unidas para la Formación Profesional y la Investigación *m* (*UNITAR*); ~ **Nations layout key** *n* (*UNLK*) ECON, POL *internacional* plan clave de las Naciones Unidas *m*; ~ **Nations Organization** *n* (*UNO*) ECON, POL Organización de las Naciones Unidas *f* (*ONU*); ~ **Nations Relief and World Agency** *n* (*UNRWA*) POL, WEL Agencia de las Naciones Unidas para la Ayuda a los Refugiados *f*; ~ **Nations Research Institute for Social Development** *n* POL Agencia de Naciones Unidas para el Desarrollo Social *f* (*ANUDS*); ~ **States East Coast** *n* (*USEC*) TRANSP costa este de los Estados Unidos *f*; ~ **States Environmental Protection Agency** *n* ENVIR agencia de protección medioambiental de los Estados Unidos; ~ **States Information Agency** *n* (*USIA*) COMMS agencia de información de los Estados Unidos; ~ **States Maritime Commission** *n* (*USMC*) TRANSP comisión marítima de los Estados Unidos; ~ **States Mint** *n* (*USM*) BANK casa de la moneda de los Estados Unidos; ~ **States Postal Office** *n* (*USPO*) COMMS correos de los Estados Unidos; ~ **States Postal Service** *n* (*USPS*) COMMS servicio postal de los Estados Unidos; ~ **States West Coast** *n* (*USWC*) TRANSP costa oeste de los Estados Unidos *f*

units: ~**-of-production method** *n* ACC método de unidades de producción *m*

unity: ~ **of European patent** *n* PATENTS unidad de patentes europeas *f*; ~ **of invention** *n* PATENTS unidad de invento *f*

universal: ~ **agent** *n* LAW apoderado(-a) general *m,f*; ~ **air waybill** *n* (*UAWB*) IMP/EXP, TRANSP conocimiento de embarque aéreo universal *m*; ~ **bank** *n* BANK banco universal *m*; ~ **container** *n* (*U*) TRANSP contenedor universal *m*; ~ **life insurance** *n* INS seguro de vida universal *m*; ~ **life-policy** *n* INS póliza de seguro de vida universal *f*; ~ **suffrage** *n* POL sufragio universal *m*

Universal: ~ **Machine Language Equipment Register** *n* (*UMLER*) TRANSP Registro de Equipo para Lenguaje Universal de Máquina *m*; ~ **Postal Union** *n* (*UPU*) COMMS Unión Postal Universal *f* (*UPU*)

universalism *n* GEN COMM, WEL universalismo *m*

universe *n* S&M universo *m*

university *n* GEN COMM universidad *f*

unjustified: ~ **threat** *n* LAW amenaza injustificada *f*

unknown *adj* GEN COMM desconocido; ♦ ~ **at this address** COMMS desconocido en esta dirección

unladen: ~ **weight** *n* GEN COMM peso sin cargamento *m*, TRANSP peso descargado *m*

unlawful[1] *adj* LAW ilegal

unlawful²: ~ **act** *n* LAW acción ilegal *f*; ~ **picketing** *n* HRM formación de piquetes de huelga ilegales *f*; ~ **trespass** *n* LAW infracción *f*, traspaso ilegal *m*

unlawfully *adv* LAW ilegalmente

unless: ~ **caused by** *phr* INS *marine* excepto que esté causado por; ~ **general average** *phr* INS excepto avería gruesa; ~ **otherwise agreed** *phr* GEN COMM salvo convenio en contrario, salvo que se acuerde lo contrario; ~ **otherwise provided** *phr* LAW a menos que se disponga lo contrario; ~ **otherwise specified** *phr* GEN COMM si no se especifica lo contrario; ~ **used** *phr* TRANSP *shipping* salvo si se utilizó

unleveraged: ~ **program** *AmE*, ~ **programme** *BrE n* FIN programa no apalancado *m*

unlicensed: ~ **broker** *n* STOCK corredor(a) de bolsa sin licencia *m,f*

unlimited¹ *adj* GEN COMM ilimitado; ~ **on the upside** STOCK *options maximum return* creciente ilimitado; ~ **on upside** STOCK *options risk* sin límite al alza

unlimited²: ~ **accounts** *n pl* BANK cuentas sin límite *f pl*; ~ **checking** *AmE*, ~ **chequing** *BrE n* BANK emisión ilimitada de cheques *f*; ~ **company** *n* GEN COMM sociedad ilimitada *f*; ~ **fine** *n* LAW multa ilimitada *f*; ~ **liability** *n* GEN COMM, INS responsabilidad ilimitada *f*; ~ **securities** *n pl* STOCK valores sin límite *m pl*; ~ **tax bond** *n* STOCK bono garantizado mediante tasas sin límite de tipo de importe

unlisted¹ *adj* ECON, STOCK sin cotización

unlisted²: ~ **company** *n* GEN COMM compañía no bursátil *f*, STOCK sociedad que no cotiza en bolsa *f*; ~ **market** *n* STOCK mercado sin cotización oficial *m*; ~ **securities** *n pl* STOCK valores no inscritos en la bolsa *m pl*, valores no cotizables en bolsa *m pl*; ~ **security** *n* FIN, STOCK valor sin cotización *m*, valor no cotizado en la bolsa *m*; ~ **share** *n* FIN, STOCK acción sin cotización oficial *f*; ~ **trader** *n* STOCK intermediario(-a) de valores sin cotización *m,f*; ~ **trading** *n* STOCK operación con valores no cotizados *f*; ~ **warrant** *n* STOCK cédula sin cotización *f*

Unlisted: ~ **Securities Market** *n* (*USM*) STOCK mercado de valores no cotizados

UNLK *abbr* (*United Nations layout key*) ECON, POL *international* plan clave de las Naciones Unidas *m*

unload¹ *vt* TRANSP descargar

unload²: ~ **stocks on the market** *phr* STOCK vender títulos en el mercado

unloader: ~ **crane** *n* TRANSP grúa de descarga *f*

unloading *n* TRANSP descarga *f*; ~ **platform** TRANSP plataforma de descarga *f*; ~ **risk** GEN COMM riesgo de descarga *m*

unlock *vt* COMP *keyboard*, GEN COMM desbloquear; ◆ ~ **funds** FIN liberar fondos

unmanageable *adj* GEN COMM inmanejable

unmanifested: ~ **cargo** *n* TRANSP carga no declarada *f*

unmanned: ~ **machinery spaces** *n pl* IND maquinaria sin operador *f*

unmanufactured: ~ **materials** *n pl* IND materias primas *f pl*

unmarketable *adj* GEN COMM, S&M invendible

unmatched *adj* STOCK desequilibrado

unmatured¹ *adj* STOCK *coupon* no devengado

unmatured²: ~ **debt** *n* STOCK deuda no vencida *f*

unmoor *vt* TRANSP soltar amarras

unmortgaged *adj* GEN COMM no hipotecado, libre de hipotecas

unnamed *adj* COMP *disk, file* innominado

unnegotiable *adj* BANK, FIN, GEN COMM innegociable

UNO *abbr* (*United Nations Organization*) ECON, POL ONU (*Organización de las Naciones Unidas*)

unofficial¹ *adj* GEN COMM extraoficial; ◆ **in an** ~ **capacity** GEN COMM con carácter extraoficial

unofficial²: ~ **action** *n* HRM acción no oficial *f*; ~ **industrial action** *n* HRM acción empresarial no oficial *f*; ~ **strike** *n* HRM, IND, LAW huelga no oficial *f*

unpack *vt* GEN COMM desempaquetar

unpacked *adj* GEN COMM desempaquetado, no embalado

unpaid¹ *adj* GEN COMM impagado, no pagado

unpaid²: ~ **bill** *n* ACC factura impagada *f*; ~ **capital** *n* ACC, ECON, FIN, GEN COMM capital no desembolsado *m*; ~ **check** *AmE*, ~ **cheque** *BrE n* BANK, FIN cheque impagado *m*, cheque no pagado *m*; ~ **claim reserve** *n* INS reserva para reclamaciones pendientes *f*; ~ **dividend** *n* FIN dividendo no pagado *m*; ~ **tax** *n* TAX impuesto impagado *m*

unpatented *adj* GEN COMM, LAW, PATENTS no patentado

unpostable *adj* ACC no registrable

unprecedented *adj* GEN COMM sin precedentes

unpredictable *adj* GEN COMM imprevisible

unpresented: ~ **check** *AmE*, ~ **cheque** *BrE n* BANK, FIN cheque no presentado *m*, cheque sin cobrar *m*

unprocessable *adj* COMP no procesable

unprocessed *adj* COMP sin procesar

unproductive¹ *adj* GEN COMM improductivo

unproductive²: ~ **labor** *AmE*, ~ **labour** *BrE n* HRM mano de obra improductiva *f*, *task* trabajo no productivo *m*

unprofessional: ~ **conduct** *n* GEN COMM conducta poco profesional *f*

unprofitable *adj* FIN, GEN COMM infructuoso

unprogrammed *adj* GEN COMM no programado

unprompted: ~ **response** *n* S&M respuesta espontánea *f*

unprotested *adj* FIN no protestado

unpublished¹ *adj* GEN COMM, MEDIA no editado

unpublished²: ~ **band** *n* ECON *Bank of England* banda no publicada *f*

unqualified¹ *adj* HRM incompetente, no cualificado

unqualified²: ~ **acceptance** *n* FIN aceptación sin salvedades *f*; ~ **opinion** *n* ACC auditoría limpia *f*, opinión favorable *f*

unquestionable *adj* GEN COMM indiscutible

unquoted¹ *adj* ECON, STOCK sin cotización

unquoted²: ~ **securities** *n pl* STOCK valores no cotizados *m pl*; ~ **shares** *n pl* STOCK valores no cotizables en bolsa *m pl*; ~ **trading company** *n* ECON empresa comercial sin cotización oficial *f*

unrealized: ~ **gains** *n pl* TAX ganancias no realizadas *f pl*; ~ **losses** *n* ACC, FIN pérdidas no realizadas *f pl*; ~ **profit** *n* ACC, FIN beneficios no realizados *m pl*

unreceipted *adj* GEN COMM *invoices* sin acuse de recibo

unrecorded¹ *adj* GEN COMM inarchivado

unrecorded²: ~ **deed** *n* GEN COMM hecho sin precedentes *m*

unrecoverable *adj* COMP irrecuperable

unregistered¹ *adj* GEN COMM no registrado

unregistered²: ~ **labor** *AmE*, ~ **labour** *BrE n* HRM *task* trabajo no registrado *m*, *workforce* mano de obra no registrada *f*; ~ **person** *n* TAX persona sin registrar *f*; ~ **stock** *n* STOCK acciones no registradas *f pl*; ~ **trademark** *n* GEN COMM, LAW, PATENTS, S&M marca no registrada *f*

unremunerative *adj* GEN COMM poco remunerador

unrepealed *adj* GEN COMM, LAW no revocado

unrequired: ~ **dividend** *n* ACC dividendo no exigido *m*

unresponsive *adj* GEN COMM *market* insensible

unrest *n* GEN COMM agitación *f*

unrestricted: ~ **access** *n* GEN COMM acceso no restringido *m*; ~ **labor** *AmE*, ~ **labour** *BrE* *n* HRM *task* trabajo sin restricciones *m*, *workforce* mano de obra ilimitada *f*; ~ **letter of credit** *n* BANK, FIN carta de crédito ilimitada *f*, carta de crédito sin restricción *f*; ~ **quota** *n* GEN COMM cuota sin restricciones *f*

UNRWA *abbr* (*United Nations Relief and World Agency*) POL, WEL Agencia de las Naciones Unidas para la Ayuda a los Refugiados *f*

unsafe: ~ **paper** *n* FIN documento inseguro *m*

unsaleable *adj* GEN COMM, S&M invendible

unsatisfied: ~ **lien** *n* TAX gravamen no liquidado *m*

unscheduled *adj* GEN COMM no programado

unscramble *vt* COMMS, COMP, GEN COMM descifrar

unscreened *adj* GEN COMM no protegido

unseat: ~ **the board** *phr* MGMNT destituir al consejo

unseaworthiness *n* TRANSP innavegabilidad *f*

unsecured[1] *adj* GEN COMM sin garantía

unsecured[2]: ~ **bond** *n* STOCK obligación sin garantía *f*; ~ **credit** *n* ACC, BANK, FIN crédito descubierto *m*; ~ **creditor** *n* ACC acreedor(a) no asegurado(-a) *m,f*, acreedor(a) no garantizado(-a) *m,f*; ~ **debt** *n* BANK, FIN deuda quirografaria *f*; ~ **fixed-term loan** *n* BANK préstamo a plazo fijo no garantizado *m*; ~ **loan** *n* BANK empréstito sin garantía *m*, préstamo sin garantía *m*; ~ **overdraft** *n* BANK descubierto no garantizado *m*, sobregiro no garantizado *m*

unsigned *adj* GEN COMM sin firmar

unskilled[1] *adj* HRM no cualificado

unskilled[2]: ~ **labor** *AmE*, ~ **labour** *BrE* *n* HRM *task* trabajo no especializado *m*, *workforce* mano de obra no cualificada *f*

unsocial: ~ **hours** *n pl* HRM horario fuera de lo normal *m*

unsold[1] *adj* GEN COMM invendido

unsold[2]: ~ **goods** *n pl* GEN COMM mercancías no vendidas *f pl*

unsolicited[1] *adj* GEN COMM, HRM, LAW, S&M no solicitado

unsolicited[2]: ~ **application** *n* HRM solicitud no pedida *f*; ~ **goods and services** *n pl* GEN COMM bienes y servicios no solicitados *m pl*; ~ **testimonial** *n* LAW testigo no solicitado *m*

unsorted *adj* (*u/s*) GEN COMM sin clasificar

unsound: ~ **risk** *n* GEN COMM riesgo poco seguro *m*

unspent[1] *adj* GEN COMM no gastado

unspent[2]: ~ **cash balance** *n* ACC *governmental accounting* saldo de caja no utilizado *m*

unstable: ~ **equilibrium** *n* ECON equilibrio inestable *m*; ~ **government** *n* POL gobierno débil *m*, gobierno inestable *m*

unstamped: ~ **debenture** *n* STOCK obligación sin sellar *f*

unstocked *adj* GEN COMM no inventariado

unstructured[1] *adj* GEN COMM desestructurado

unstructured[2]: ~ **interview** *n* HRM entrevista no estructurada *f*

unsubsidized *adj* GEN COMM no subvencionado

unsubstantiated *adj* GEN COMM sin confirmar

unsystematic: ~ **risk** *n* GEN COMM riesgo no sistemático *m*

untapped *adj* GEN COMM *resources, market* sin explotar

untargeted *adj* S&M *consumer base* no dirigido

untenanted *adj* PROP no arrendado

untested *adj* GEN COMM no ensayado

untied: ~ **aid** *n* BANK, ECON, MGMNT ayuda desvinculada *f*, ayuda no condicionada *f*, POL ayuda no condicionada *f*

untimely *adj* GEN COMM extemporáneo, intempestivo

untrained *adj* WEL sin preparación

untransferable *adj* STOCK intransferible

unused[1] *adj* GEN COMM, TAX no utilizado

unused[2]: ~ **credit** *n* TAX crédito no utilizado *m*; ~ **part** *n* TAX parte no utilizada *f*; ~ **portion** *n* TAX porción sin utilizar *f*; ~ **relief** *n* TAX deducción no utilizada *f*; ~ **tax credit** *n* TAX reducción fiscal no utilizada *f*

unusual: ~ **item** *n* GEN COMM partida inusual *f*

unvalued: ~ **policy** *n* INS póliza en blanco *f*

unverified *adj* GEN COMM no verificado

unvouched: ~ **for** *adj* GEN COMM no garantizado

unweighted *adj* GEN COMM *index, figures* sin compensación

unwind: ~ **a tape** *phr* STOCK volver atrás una operación

unworkable *adj* GEN COMM improcesable

unwritten: ~ **agreement** *n* GEN COMM, LAW acuerdo no escrito *m*

up[1] *adj infrml* COMP *functioning* en funcionamiento; ~**-and-coming** GEN COMM joven y prometedor; ~**-market** GEN COMM de gama alta, *product* superior, S&M de gama alta; ~**-to-date** COMP, GEN COMM actualizado; ~**-to-sample** GEN COMM conforme a los resultados de la muestra; ~**-to-the-minute** GEN COMM *information* al instante; ◆ **be ~ to scratch** *infrml* GEN COMM, HRM ser del nivel requerido; **be ~ to one's neck in work** *infrml* HRM estar hasta la coronilla de trabajo (*infrml*)

up[2] *adv* GEN COMM arriba; ~ **front** GEN COMM *pay* por adelantado

up[3]: ~**-front cost** *n infrml* GEN COMM coste abierto *m* (*Esp*), costo abierto *m* (*AmL*); ~**-market product** *n* S&M producto de alta calidad *m*; ~**-market service** *n* S&M servicio de alta calidad *m*; ~**-to-date information** *n* GEN COMM información actualizada *f*

up[4] *vt* GEN COMM *bid* subir

update[1] *n* COMP, GEN COMM actualización *f*

update[2] *vt* COMP, FIN, GEN COMM actualizar, poner al día

updating *n* COMP, GEN COMM actualización *f*

upgrade *vt* COMP modernizar, *memory* aumentar, GEN COMM mejorar, HRM *employee* ascender, LEIS *aviation* poner en primera viajeros con billetes de segunda clase; ◆ ~ **a post** HRM ascender un puesto

upgradeable *adj* COMP ampliable

upgraded *adj* COMP modernizado, GEN COMM, S&M *quality of product* mejorado

upgrading *n* COMP evolución *f*, GEN COMM, S&M mejoramiento; ~ **of a loan** BANK aumento de la cuantía de un préstamo *m*

upload *vt* COMP *data* cargar

upmarket: **~ good** *n* S&M artículo de primera calidad *m*; **~ goods** *n pl* GEN COMM artículos de primera calidad *m pl*

upper: **~ cap** *n* TAX *relief* tope máximo *m*; **~ case letter** *n* COMP, MEDIA letra mayúscula *f*, mayúsculas *f pl*; **~ income** *n* ACC, TAX ingresos superiores *m pl*; **~ limit** *n* STOCK *on value of shares* límite superior *m*; **~ quartile** *n* MATH cuartil superior *m*

ups: **~ and downs** *n pl* STOCK *market* turbulencias *f pl*

UPS *abbr* (*uninterruptible power supply*) COMP alimentación eléctrica ininterrumpible *f*

upset: **~ price** *n* AmE GEN COMM *auction sale* precio mínimo *m*

upside: **~ break-even** *n* STOCK *options* punto neutro de ganancias o con pequeñas ganancias; **~ break-even point** *n* STOCK punto de equilibrio al alza *m*; **~ potential** *n* FIN potencial ascendente *m*; **~ profit potential** *n* STOCK *options* potencial de beneficios crecientes *m*; **~ risk** *n* STOCK *options* riesgo ascendente *m*

upstairs: **~ market** *n* AmE STOCK transacción al margen de la bolsa *f*

upstream: **~ float** *n* GEN COMM flotación contracorriente *f*; **~ loan** *n jarg* BANK, FIN préstamo de una subsidiaria a la empresa matriz *m*

upsurge *n* GEN COMM *in activity* fase de expansión *f*

upswing *n* ECON, GEN COMM alza *f*, fase ascendente *f*, fase de expansión *f*

uptick *n* STOCK operación a precio más alto que una anterior

uptrend *n* ECON tendencia al alza *f*

upturn *n* ECON, GEN COMM alza *f*, fase ascendente *f*, fase de expansión *f*

UPU *abbr* (*Universal Postal Union*) COMMS UPU (*Unión Postal Universal*)

upward[1] *adj* COMP, ECON ascendente, GEN COMM *trend* alcista

upward[2] *adv* GEN COMM *move* hacia arriba

upward[3]: **~ compatibility** *n* COMP compatibilidad ascendente *f*; **~ movement** *n* ECON, GEN COMM movimiento ascendente *m*; **~ pressure** *n* ECON *on budget* presión ascendente *f*; **~ price movement** *n* STOCK movimiento alcista de los precios *m*; **~ revision** *n* GEN COMM *prices* revisión al alza *f*; **~ spiral** *n* GEN COMM *in wages, prices* espiral ascendente *f*; **~ trend** *n* STOCK tendencia alcista *f*, tendencia al alza *f*

upwardly: **~ mobile** *adj* GEN COMM variable hacia arriba, HRM de movimiento social ascendente

upwards *adv* GEN COMM *move* hacia arriba

urban: **~ area** *n* GEN COMM área urbana *f*; **~ center** *AmE*, **~ centre** *BrE* *n* GEN COMM centro urbano *m*; **~ economics** *n* ECON economía urbana *f*; **~ planning** *n* GEN COMM urbanismo *m*; **~ planner** *n* GEN COMM urbanista *mf*; **~ renewal** *n* GEN COMM remodelación urbana *f*

Urban: **~ Development Corporation** *n BrE* ECON, POL corporación de desarrollo urbano, corporación municipal para el desarrollo urbano; **~ Programme Area** *n BrE* GEN COMM, POL Área Programática Urbana *f*

urbanization *n* GEN COMM urbanización *f*

urbanize *vt* GEN COMM urbanizar

URN *abbr* (*unique reference number*) GEN COMM folio único de referencia *m*

urge: **~ sb to do sth** *phr* GEN COMM exhortar a alguien a hacer algo

urgent *adj* GEN COMM, COMMS, TRANSP *service* urgente

Uruguay: **~ Round** *n* ECON Ronda Uruguay *f*

u/s *abbr* (*unsorted*) GEN COMM sin clasificar

US: **~ federal finance** *n* FIN finanzas federales de los Estados Unidos; **~ federal government paper** *n* STOCK papel del gobierno federal de los Estados Unidos; **~ Treasury bond market** *n AmE* STOCK mercado de bonos del Tesoro de los Estados Unidos; **~ Treasury market** *n AmE* FIN mercado de la tesorería de los Estados Unidos

usance *n* FIN costumbre *f*; **~ bill** BANK letra a plazo *f*, FIN letra a plazo *f*, letra de cambio al uso *f*; **~ credit** BANK, FIN crédito a plazos *m*; ◆ **at thirty days' ~** GEN COMM en un plazo de treinta días

USASLE *abbr* (*Uniform Securities Agent State Law Examination*) LAW ley uniforme del estado para el reconocimiento de los agentes de bolsa

USDAW *abbr* (*Union of Shop, Distributive & Allied Workers*) HRM sindicato del sector comercio, distribución y afines

use[1] *n* GEN COMM, PATENTS uso *m*, utilización *f*; **~-by date** S&M fecha de caducidad *f*; **~ of funds** ACC, BANK, FIN uso de los fondos *m*; **~ value** ECON valor en uso *m*; ◆ **have the ~ of sth** GEN COMM usar algo

use[2] *vt* GEN COMM utilizar; ◆ **~ strong-arm tactics** GEN COMM hacer uso de la fuerza; **~ a window of opportunity** GEN COMM aprovechar una oportunidad

USEC *abbr* (*United States East Coast*) TRANSP costa este de los Estados Unidos *f*

used: **~ assets** *n pl* TAX bienes de segunda mano *m pl*

useful: **~ economic life** *n* ACC, ECON vida económica útil *f*; **~ life** *n* ACC *of asset*, IND *of machine* vida útil *f*

user[1]: **~-friendly** *adj* COMP de fácil manejo, de uso fácil, GEN COMM de uso fácil; **~-oriented** *adj* COMP concebido para el usuario, orientado al usuario, personalizado, GEN COMM, S&M orientado al usuario; **~-unfriendly** *adj* COMP de difícil utilización, difícil de utilizar, S&M difícil de usar

user[2] *n* COMP, GEN COMM usuario(-a) *m,f*; **~ attitude** S&M actitud del usuario *f*; **~ charge** ACC aportación de tarifa *f*, aportación del usuario *f*, pago del usuario *m*; **~ cost** FIN coste de uso *m* (*Esp*), costo de uso *m* (*AmL*); **~ fee** BANK cuota del usuario *m*, pago del cliente *m*; **~ group** COMP grupo de usuarios *m*; **~ interface** COMP interfaz de usuario *m*; **~ profile** S&M perfil del usuario *m*; **~ strategy** GEN COMM, S&M estrategia de usuario *f*

uses: **~ of funds** *n pl* ACC aplicaciones de fondos *f pl*

USIA *abbr* (*United States Information Agency*) COMMS agencia de información de los Estados Unidos

USM *abbr* BANK (*United States Mint*) casa de la moneda de los Estados Unidos, STOCK (*Unlisted Securities Market*) mercado de valores no cotizados, segundo mercado

USMC *abbr* (*United States Maritime Commission*) TRANSP comisión marítima de los Estados Unidos

USP *abbr* (*unique selling proposition*) S&M proposición única de venta *f*

USPO *abbr* (*United States Postal Office*) COMMS correos de los Estados Unidos

USPS *abbr* (*United States Postal Service*) COMMS servicio postal de los Estados Unidos

usual[1]: ~ **first name** n HRM, LAW nombre habitual m

usual[2]: **with the ~ proviso** phr GEN COMM, LAW con los requisitos establecidos; **on ~ terms** phr GEN COMM en condiciones normales

usufruct n LAW usufructo m

usufructuary n LAW usufructuador(a) m,f, usufructuario(-a) m,f

usurer n BANK, FIN usurero(-a) m,f

usurious[1] adj BANK, FIN usurario

usurious[2]: ~ **capital** n ACC, ECON, FIN capital usurario m

usury n BANK, FIN usura f

USWC abbr (United States West Coast) TRANSP costa oeste de los Estados Unidos f

UTC abbr (coordinated universal time) GEN COMM HUC (hora universal coordinada)

utilitarianism n ECON utilitarismo m

utilities: ~ **sector** n IND sector de servicios públicos m

utility n COMP utilidad f, ECON, GEN COMM empresa de servicios públicos f, utilidad f, TAX servicio general m; ~ **average** STOCK promedio de utilidad m; ~ **certificate** PATENTS certificado de utilidad m; ~ **function** ECON función de utilidad f; ~ **model** PATENTS modelo de utilidad m; ~ **possibility frontier** ECON frontera de posibilidades de utilidad f; ~ **program** COMP programa de utilidades m; ~ **revenue bond** FIN bono municipal pagadero con los ingresos m

utilization n ENVIR of natural resources empleo m, GEN COMM utilización f; ~ **percent** GEN COMM porcentaje de utilización m

utilize vt ENVIR emplear, GEN COMM utilizar

utilized: ~ **capacity** n BANK, ECON, FIN, IND capacidad aprovechada f, capacidad utilizada f

utmost: ~ **good faith** n GEN COMM, INS, LAW principio de buena fe m

UVI abbr (unit value index) ECON índice de valor unitario m

U/W abbr (underwriter) INS person asegurador(a) m,f, company empresa aseguradora f

V

V *abbr* (*volt*) GEN COMM v *voltio*)

vacancy *n* BANK, HRM, IND vacante *f*; **~ notice** BANK, HRM, IND aviso de vacante *m*

vacant: **~ land** *n* PROP terreno inocupado *m*; **~ lot** *n* PROP solar desocupado *m*; **~ possession** *n* LAW derecho del comprador de encontrar libre la vivienda una vez escriturada

vacation *n* AmE (*cf holiday BrE*) GEN COMM, LEIS vacaciones *f pl*; **~ accommodation** AmE (*cf holiday accommodation BrE*) LEIS, PROP alojamiento de vacaciones *m*; **~ entitlement** AmE (*cf holiday entitlement BrE*) HRM derecho a vacaciones *m*; **~ leave** AmE (*cf holiday leave BrE*) HRM permiso de vacaciones *m*; **~ and leisure insurance** AmE (*cf holiday and leisure insurance BrE*) INS, LEIS seguro por vacaciones y ocio *m*; **~ pay** AmE (*cf holiday pay BrE*) HRM paga de vacaciones *f*; **~ period** AmE (*cf holiday period BrE*) HRM, LEIS periodo de vacaciones *m*; ◆ **go on ~** AmE (*cf go on holiday BrE*) LEIS ir de vacaciones; **take a ~** AmE (*cf take a holiday BrE*) HRM tomarse unas vacaciones

vacationer *n* AmE (*cf holiday-maker BrE*) LEIS veraneante *mf*

vacations *n pl* AmE (*cf holidays BrE*) HRM, LEIS vacaciones *f pl*

vaccination *n* IMP/EXP, WEL vacunación *f*

vacuum: **~ packaging** *n* GEN COMM envase vacío *m*; **~ relief valve** *n* (*PV*) TRANSP válvula de seguridad de vacío *f*

Valdez: **~ principle** *n* ENVIR principio de Valdez *m*

Valencia: **~ Stock Exchange** *n* STOCK Bolsa de Valencia *f*

valid *adj* COMP, GEN COMM *argument, excuse* válido, LAW, *document* vigente

validate *vt* COMP, GEN COMM *document, claim* validar, LAW legalizar

validation *n* COMP, GEN COMM validación *f*, LAW legalización *f*

validity *n* GEN COMM, PATENTS, TAX validez *f*; **~ check** TAX comprobación de validez *f*; **~ period** GEN COMM plazo de validez *m*

valorization *n* ECON, GEN COMM valorización *f*; **~ scheme** ECON esquema intervencionista en los mercados bursátiles *m*

valorize *vt* GEN COMM *goods* tasar

valuable: **~ consideration** *n* GEN COMM remuneración valiosa *f*; **~ papers insurance** *n* INS seguro sobre documentos de valor *m*

valuables *n pl* GEN COMM valores *m pl*, artículos de valor *m pl*, S&M artículos de valor *m pl*

valuation *n* PROP evaluación *f*, peritaje *m*, registro *m*, STOCK *shares* tasación *f*; **~ adjustment** ACC reajuste del valor de los activos *m*; **~ allowance** ACC bonificación *f*, GEN COMM descuento *m* (*dto.*); **~ at average cost** ACC evaluación al coste medio *f* (*Esp*), evaluación al costo medio (*AmL*) *f*; **~ at estimated cost** ACC evaluación al coste estimado *f* (*Esp*), evaluación al costo estimado (*AmL*) *f*; **~ at standard cost** ACC evaluación al coste estándar *f* (*Esp*), evaluación al costo estándar (*AmL*) *f*; **~ charge** TRANSP coste de tasación *m* (*Esp*), costo de tasación *m* (*AmL*); **~ clause** (*VC*) INS cláusula de valoración *f*; **~ criterion** ACC criterio de valoración *m*, criterio de evaluación *m*; **~ day** TAX fecha de valoración *f*; **~ price** STOCK precio de valoración *m*; **~ principle** ACC principio de valoración *m*; **~ report** GEN COMM tasación *f* (*Esp*), avalúo *f* (*AmL*); **~ restriction** ECON *of currency* restricción de valoración *f*; **~ of stocks** ACC evaluación de existencias *f*

value *n* ECON, GEN COMM valor *m*; **~-added** ACC, ECON, GEN COMM, S&M, TAX valor agregado *m* (*AmL*), valor añadido *m* (*Esp*); **~-added network** (*VAN*) COMP red de valor añadido *f*; **~ added network service** ECON servicio de cadena de valor añadido *m*; **~-added reseller** (*VAR*) COMP revendedor de valor añadido *m*; **~ added statement** ACC relación del valor añadido *f*; **~ analysis** (*VA*) FIN, S&M análisis del valor *m*; **~ as marine policy** (*VMP*) INS valor como póliza marina *m*; **~ at cost** ACC valor al coste *m* (*Esp*), valor al costo *m* (*AmL*); **~ broker** HRM, STOCK operador de descuento *m*; **~ chain** FIN cadena de valor *f*; **~ concept** FIN concepto de valor *m*; **~ date** FIN, STOCK fecha de valor *f*; **~ discrepancy hypothesis** ECON hipótesis de discrepancia del valor *f*; **~ engineering** ACC estudio de los componentes de un artículo *m*, FIN análisis del valor *m*, estudio de los componentes de un producto *m*; **~ for collection** ACC valor al cobro *m*; **~ in use** ECON valor de uso *m*; **~ judgment** GEN COMM juicio de valor *m*; **~-line composite index** STOCK índice compuesto de fecha valor *m*; **~-line investment survey** FIN encuesta de inversión de la línea de valor *f*, modelo proyectivo de investigación de inversiones *m*; **~ of money** ECON valor del dinero *m*; **~ of one point** STOCK valor de un punto *m*; **~ position** STOCK *short* posición de precio *f*; **~ proposal** ACC valor propuesto *m*, FIN propuesta de valor *f*; **~ share** STOCK acción de valor; **~ subtractor** ECON valor negativo *m*; **~ surcharge** TRANSP coste sobre el valor *m* (*Esp*), costo sobre el valor *m* (*AmL*); **~ test** TAX prueba de valor *f*; **~ to weight ratio** TRANSP *of conveyed goods* relación valor-peso *f*; ◆ **at face ~** FIN, STOCK a la par; **~ as in original policy** (*VOP*) INS valor de la póliza marina *m*; **no ~ declared** (*NVD*) IMP/EXP sin declaración de valor

Value: **~ Added Tax** *n* BrE (*VAT*) TAX impuesto sobre el valor añadido *m* (*IVA*); **~ Line Stock Index** *n* STOCK Índice de Valores Value Line *m*

valued[1]: **~ policy** *n* INS póliza de valor declarado *f*; **~ position** *n* BANK posición valorada *f*;

valued[2]: **be ~ at** *phr* STOCK estar valorado en

valueless *adj* GEN COMM sin valor

van *n* TRANSP furgón *m*

VAN *abbr* (*value-added network*) COMP red de valor añadido *f*

vandalism: **~ and malicious mischief insurance** *n* INS seguro contra hechos dolosos y vandálicos *m*

vanguard: **in the ~** *adj* GEN COMM a la vanguardia

VAR *abbr* COMP (*value-added reseller*) revendedor de valor añadido *m*, MATH (*vector autoregression*) autorregresión vectorial *f*

variability *n* MATH variabilidad *f*

variable *n* COMP, FIN, GEN COMM variable *f*; ~ **budget** ECON presupuesto flexible *m*; ~ **capital** FIN capital variable *m*; ~ **charge** (*VC*) GEN COMM cargo variable *m*; ~ **costs** *n pl* ACC, FIN costes variables *m pl* (*Esp*), costos variables *m pl* (*AmL*); ~ **expenses** *n pl* GEN COMM gastos variables *m pl*; ~ **interest rate** GEN COMM tasa de interés variable *f*; ~ **lending rate** (*VLR*) BANK, FIN tasa de préstamo variable *f*, tipo de préstamo variable *m*; ~ **life insurance** INS seguro de vida variable *m*; ~ **overhead cost** ACC coste de gastos indirectos variables *m* (*Esp*), costo de gastos indirectos variables *m* (*AmL*); ~ **rate** BANK, FIN tasa variable *f*; ~**-rate demand note** BANK, FIN pagaré a la vista de tipo variable *m*; ~ **rate mortgage** BANK, FIN hipoteca de tasa variable *f*; ~**-size font** MEDIA matriz de medida variable *f*; ~ **yield fund** STOCK fondo de inversión de renta variable *m*

variables: ~ **sampling** *n* MATH muestreo de variables *m*

variance *n* ACC desviación *f*, MATH *statistics* variación *f*; ~ **analysis** ACC análisis de desviaciones *m pl*, análisis de la varianza *m*

variation *n* FIN, GEN COMM, STOCK variación *f*; ~ **margin** STOCK margen de fluctuación *m*, margen de variación *m*

variety: ~ **reduction** *n* ECON, GEN COMM reducción de tipos *f*

variometer *n* IND variómetro *m*

vary *vt* GEN COMM variar, LAW *terms* modificar

vary with *vt* GEN COMM variar según

varying: **in ~ degrees** *phr* GEN COMM en diferentes proporciones

vast: ~ **sum** *n* FIN suma enorme *f*

VAT[1] *abbr BrE* (*Value Added Tax*) TAX IVA (*impuesto sobre el valor añadido*)

VAT[2]: ~ **payment** *n BrE* TAX pago del IVA *m*; ~ **registered trader** *n BrE* TAX comerciante que repercute IVA *mf*; ~ **registration number** *n BrE* TAX número de inscripción del IVA *m*; ~ **return** *n* TAX declaración del IVA *f*

vault *n* BANK bóveda *f*, caja *f*, GEN COMM caja *f*; ~ **cash** BANK efectivo en caja *m*; ~ **reserve** *AmE* BANK reserva en banco central *f*

V BLT *abbr AmE* (*vee built*) TRANSP *shipping* construido en V

V BTM *abbr AmE* (*vee bottom*) TRANSP fondo en V *m*

VC *abbr* GEN COMM (*variable charge*) cargo variable *m*, INS (*valuation clause*) cláusula de valoración *f*, TRANSP (*ventilated container*) contenedor ventilado *m*

VDT *abbr* (*visual display terminal*) COMP terminal con pantalla de visualización *m*

VDU *abbr* (*visual display unit*) COMP unidad de representación visual *f*

Veblen: ~ **good** *n* ECON *conspicuous consumption* bien Veblen *m*

Veblenian: ~ **school** *n* ECON escuela vebleniana *f*

vector *n* GEN COMM vector *m*; ~ **autoregression** (*VAR*) MATH autorregresión vectorial *f*

vee[1]: ~ **built** *adj AmE* (*V BLT*) TRANSP *shipping* construido en V

vee[2]: ~ **bottom** *n AmE* (*V BTM*) TRANSP fondo en V *m*

veep *abbr* (*vice president*) HRM, MGMNT, POL VP (*vicepresidente*)

veer *vi* GEN COMM arribar

vega *n* STOCK vega *m*

vegetative: ~ **control** *n* ECON control vegetativo *m*

vehicle *n* TRANSP vehículo *m*; ~ **hire** TRANSP alquiler de vehículos *m*; ~ **leasing** TRANSP alquiler de vehículos *m*; ~ **sling** TRANSP eslinga para automóviles *f*; ~ **transhipment** IMP/EXP, TRANSP transbordo a otro vehículo *m*; ~ **turnaround time** *AmE* TRANSP tiempo de carga y descarga de automóviles *m*, tiempo de retorno de un vehículo *m*; ~ **turnround time** *BrE* TRANSP tiempo de carga y descarga de automóviles *m*, tiempo de retorno de un vehículo *m*; ~ **unladen weight** TRANSP peso de descarga de automóviles *m*

vehicular: ~ **ferry** *n* TRANSP transporte de automóviles *m*

velocity *n* ECON, FIN, GEN COMM, TRANSP velocidad *f*; ~ **of circulation** FIN velocidad de circulación *f*; ~ **of circulation of money** FIN velocidad de circulación monetaria *f*; ~ **of money** ECON, FIN velocidad del dinero *f*

velvet *n* FIN ganancia especulativa *f*

vendee *n* GEN COMM cesionario *m*

vendible *adj* GEN COMM vendible

vending: ~ **machine** *n* GEN COMM máquina expendedora *f*

vendor *n* LAW, PROP vendedor(a) *m,f*; ~ **company** GEN COMM empresa vendedora *f*; ~ **finance** FIN financiado por el vendedor; ~ **rating** GEN COMM calificación de proveedores *f*

vent: ~ **for surplus** *n* ECON venta para obtener plusvalía *f*

ventilated: ~ **container** *n* (*VC*) TRANSP contenedor ventilado *m*

ventilation: ~ **industry** *n* ECON, IND industria de la ventilación *f*

venture *n* FIN especulación eventual *f*, INS riesgo *m*, GEN COMM actividad comercial arriesgada *f*, operación empresarial con riesgo *f*, STOCK especulación eventual *f*; ~ **capital** GEN COMM capital de riesgo *m*; ~ **capital company** FIN compañía de capitales de riesgo *f*; ~ **capital corporation** BANK compañía de capital de riesgo *f*, corporación de capital de riesgo *f*; ~ **capital limited partnership** FIN sociedad limitada de capital de riesgo *f*; ~ **capitalist** ECON empresa capitalista *f*, FIN capitalista de riesgo *mf*; ~ **management** FIN, MGMNT, STOCK administración del riesgo *f*; ~ **team** S&M equipo encargado de un nuevo producto *m*

venture on *vt* GEN COMM *project* aventurarse en

venue *n* GEN COMM *meeting, conference* punto de reunión *m*

VER *abbr* (*voluntary export restraint*) IMP/EXP contención voluntaria a la exportación *f*

verbal: ~ **agreement** *n* GEN COMM acuerdo verbal *m*; ~ **communication** *n* GEN COMM, MGMNT comunicación verbal *f*; ~ **offer** *n* GEN COMM oferta verbal *f*; ~ **warning** *n* HRM, MGMNT advertencia verbal *f*

verbatim *adv* GEN COMM al pie de la letra

Verdoorn: ~**'s Law** *n* LAW Ley de Verdoorn *f*

verge: **on the ~ of bankrupcy** *phr* GEN COMM al borde de la bancarrota

verifiable *adj* ACC, GEN COMM verificable

verification *n* ACC, GEN COMM verificación *f*; ~ **of accounts** ACC verificación de cuentas *f*; ~ **phase** ACC, GEN COMM etapa de verificación *f*, fase de verificación *f*

verify *vt* ACC, GEN COMM verificar

versatility *n* COMP versatilidad *f*

version *n* COMP, GEN COMM versión *f*

versus *prep* GEN COMM versus

vert *abbr* (*vertical*) GEN COMM vert (*vertical*)

vertical[1] *adj* (*vert*) GEN COMM vertical (*vert*)

vertical[2]: **~ access** *n* TRANSP acceso vertical *m*; **~ amalgamation** *n* GEN COMM fusión vertical *f*; **~ analysis** *n* ACC análisis vertical *m*; **~ balance sheet** *n* ACC balance en forma vertical *m*, balance escalonado *m*, hoja de balance vertical *f*; **~ business integration** *n* GEN COMM integración empresarial vertical *f*; **~ circulation** *n* S&M tirada vertical *f*; **~ combination** *n* ECON empresa vertical *f*; **~ communication** *n* COMMS comunicación vertical *f*; **~ discrimination** *n* ECON discriminación vertical *f*; **~ equity** *n* ECON capital accionario vertical *m*, TAX patrimonio vertical *m*; **~ expansion** *n* GEN COMM integración vertical *f*; **~ format profit and loss account** *n* ACC cuenta de pérdidas y ganancias en forma de lista *f*; **~ formation** *n* GEN COMM formación vertical *f*; **~ integration** *n* GEN COMM integración vertical *f*, ampliación vertical *f*; **~ line charting** *n* STOCK diagrama de líneas verticales *m*; **~ market** *n* S&M mercado vertical *m*; **~ merger** *n* GEN COMM fusión vertical *f*; **~ mobility** *n* HRM movilidad vertical *f*; **~ organization** *n* MGMNT organización vertical *f*; **~ planning** *n* GEN COMM planificación vertical *f*; **~ profit and loss account format** *n* ACC formato vertical de la cuenta de pérdidas y ganancias *m*; **~ promotion** *n* HRM promoción vertical *f*; **~ publication** *n* MEDIA *print* publicación vertical *f*; **~ specialization** *n* GEN COMM especialización vertical *f*; **~ spread** *n* STOCK diferencial vertical *m*; **~ union** *n* HRM sindicato vertical *m*

verticalized: **~ cargo space** *n* TRANSP espacio de carga vertical *m*

vessel *n* TRANSP buque *m*; **~ broker** TRANSP corredor(a) marítimo(-a) *m,f*; **~ crossing** TRANSP travesía de barco *f*; **~ traffic management system** (*VTMS*) TRANSP sistema de gestión del tráfico de buques *m*; **~ traffic service** TRANSP servicio de tráfico de buques *m*; ◆ **any one ~** (*AOV*) INS *marine* cualquier navío *m*

vest *vt* STOCK investir; ◆ **~ sb with sth** GEN COMM *authorithy* investir a alguien de algo

vested[1] *adj* TAX *trustee, beneficiary* adquirido

vested[2]: **~ benefits** *n pl* INS beneficios otorgados *m pl*; **~ interest** *n* GEN COMM derecho adquirido *m*; **~ rights** *n pl* LAW derechos inalienables *m pl*

Veterans': **~ Administration mortgage** *n* BANK, PROP hipoteca de la administración de veteranos *f*; **~ Land Act Fund advances** *n pl* POL avances sobre el Fondo de la Ley Agraria de los Veteranos *m pl*

veterinary: **~ certificate** *n* IMP/EXP certificado veterinario *m*; **~ controls** *n pl* IMP/EXP controles veterinarios *m pl*

veto[1] *n* GEN COMM veto *m*

veto[2] *vt* GEN COMM vetar

vetting *n* GEN COMM validación *f*

VGA[1] *abbr* (*video graphics adaptor*) COMP VGA (*adaptador de gráficos de vídeo Esp, adaptador de gráficos de video AmL, adaptador videográfico*)

VGA[2]: **~ card** *n* COMP tarjeta VGA *f*

VHF *abbr* (*very high frequency*) COMMS VHF (*frecuencia muy alta*)

via *prep* COMMS por medio de

viability *n* GEN COMM viabilidad *f*

viable *adj* GEN COMM viable

VIC *abbr* (*very important cargo*) TRANSP carga muy importante *f*

vicarious: **~ liability** *n* LAW responsabilidad civil subsidiaria *f*

vice versa *adv* GEN COMM viceversa

vice: **~ chairman** *n* HRM, MGMNT vicepresidente(-a) *m,f* (*VP*); **~ chancellor** *n* HRM *British universities* rector(a) *m,f*; **~ president** *n* (*VP*) HRM, MGMNT, POL vicepresidente(-a) *m,f* (*VP*); **~ secretary** *n* HRM, POL vicesecretario(-a) *m,f*

vicious: **~ cycle** *n jarg* ECON ciclo vicioso *m*

victim *n* GEN COMM víctima *f*

victimization *n* HRM persecución *f*, represalias *f pl*

victualling *n* ECON, GEN COMM abastecimiento *m*

video *n* MEDIA vídeo *m* (*Esp*), video *m* (*AmL*); **~ camera** MEDIA videocámara *f*; **~ card** COMP tarjeta de video *f* (*AmL*), tarjeta de vídeo *f* (*Esp*); **~ cassette recorder** COMP videograbadora de casete *f*; **~ conference** COMMS, MEDIA videoconferencia *f*; **~ conferencing** COMMS, MEDIA videoconferencia *f*; **~ disk** COMP videodisco *m*; **~ display** COMMS pantalla de vídeo *f* (*Esp*), pantalla de video *f* (*AmL*); **~ display unit** COMP unidad de visualización de vídeo *f* (*Esp*), unidad de visualización de video *f* (*AmL*); **~ graphics adaptor** (*VGA*) COMP adaptador de gráficos de vídeo *m* (*Esp*) (*VGA*), adaptador de gráficos de video *m* (*AmL*) (*VGA*), adaptador videográfico *m* (*VGA*); **~ graphics array** (*VGA*) COMP matriz de vídeo gráfico *f* (*Esp*), matriz de video gráfico *f* (*AmL*); **~ piracy** GEN COMM videopiratería *f*, MEDIA piratería de videos *f* (*AmL*), piratería de vídeos *f* (*Esp*); **~ tape recording** (*VTR*) COMMS grabación en vídeo *f* (*Esp*) (*VTR*), grabación en video *f* (*AmL*) (*VTR*); **~ terminal** COMP terminal de vídeo *m* (*Esp*), terminal de video *m* (*AmL*)

videocassette *n* COMMS, COMP, MEDIA cinta de vídeo *f* (*Esp*), cinta de video *f* (*AmL*); **~ recording** COMMS, S&M grabación en videocasete *f*

videophone *n* COMMS videoteléfono *m*

videotape[1] *n* COMMS, COMP, MEDIA cinta de vídeo *f* (*Esp*), cinta de video *f* (*AmL*); **~ recorder** COMMS, COMP, MEDIA registrador de vídeo *m* (*Esp*), registrador de video *m* (*AmL*)

videotape[2] *vt* COMMS, COMP, MEDIA grabar en vídeo (*Esp*), grabar en video (*AmL*); ◆ **~ an interview** COMMS, MEDIA grabar en vídeo una entrevista (*Esp*), grabar en video una entrevista (*AmL*)

view[1]: **~ screen** *n* COMP videopantalla *f*

view[2] *vt* COMP visionar

view[3]: **take a different ~** *phr* GEN COMM adoptar una postura diferente; **take a gloomy ~ of the situation** *phr* GEN COMM tener una opinión pesimista de la situación; **with a ~ to** *phr* GEN COMM con miras a

viewers *n pl* MEDIA, S&M telespectadores *m pl*

viewing: **~ habits** *n pl* MEDIA *broadcast* hábitos de selección de programas de los telespectadores *m pl*; **~ room** *n* MEDIA sala de visionado *f*

vignette *n* S&M *advertising* viñeta *f*

villa: **~ economy** *n* ECON comunidad económica *f*, WEL agricultura económica *f*

vindictive: **~ damages** *n pl* INS, LAW daños punitivos *m pl*

vine: **~-growing district** *n* GEN COMM región viticultora *f*; **~ harvest** *n* GEN COMM cosecha de vid *f*

vineyard *n* GEN COMM viña *f*

vintage *n* ECON cosecha de vino *f*; **~ effect** ECON efecto envejecimiento de los medios de producción *m*

vintner *n* GEN COMM, HRM vinatero(-a) *m,f*

vinyl: ~ **chloride monomer** *n* IND polímero de cloruro de vinilo *m*

violate *vt* GEN COMM violar, LAW infringir, violar

violation *n* GEN COMM violación *f*; ◆ **in ~ of** LAW en violación de

VIP *abbr* (*very important person*) GEN COMM persona muy destacada *f*

virtual *adj* COMP virtual

virtue: **by ~ of** *phr* GEN COMM en virtud de

virtute officii *phr* GEN COMM en virtud de su puesto

virus¹: ~**-free** *adj* COMP sin virus

virus² *n* COMP virus *m*

visa *n* LEIS visado *m*

vis-à-vis *adv* GEN COMM cara a cara

Visby: ~ **Rules** *n pl* TRANSP Reglas de Visby *f pl*

viscosity *n* ECON viscosidad *f*

viscous: ~ **demand** *n* ECON demanda viscosa *f*; ~ **supply** *n* ECON oferta viscosa *f*

visible: ~ **export** *n* IMP/EXP exportación visible *f*; ~ **hand** *n* ECON mano visible de la economía *f*; ~ **import** *n* IMP/EXP importación visible *f*; ~ **trade balance** *n* ECON balanza comercial visible *f*

visibles *n pl* ECON visibles *m pl*

vision *n* GEN COMM, MGMNT visión *f*

visit *n* GEN COMM visita *f*

visitation *n* GEN COMM inspección *f*

visiting¹ *adj* GEN COMM visitante

visiting²: ~ **card** *n* GEN COMM tarjeta de visita *f*

visitor *n* GEN COMM visitante *mf*; **'s tax** TAX impuesto de no residente *m*, impuesto de visitante *m*; ~ **with student authorization** TAX visitante con autorización de estudios *mf*

visual¹ *adj* COMMS, COMP, GEN COMM, MEDIA, S&M visual

visual²: ~ **appeal** *n* COMMS atractivo visual *m*; ~ **arts** *n pl* MEDIA artes visuales *m pl*; ~ **display terminal** *n* (*VDT*) COMP terminal con pantalla de visualización *m*; ~ **display unit** *n* (*VDU*) COMP unidad de representación visual *f*; ~ **impact** *n* GEN COMM impacto visual *m*; ~ **telephone** *n* COMMS teléfono visual *m*

visualizer *n* COMP, S&M visualizador(a) *m,f*

visuals *n pl* GEN COMM, MEDIA, S&M *for presentation* elementos visuales *m pl*

vital: ~ **records management** *n* MGMNT dirección del registro civil *f*; ~ **revolution** *n* ECON *demographic transition* revolución demográfica *f*

viz *abbr* (*namely*) GEN COMM v.gr. (*verbigracia*)

VLR *abbr* (*variable lending rate*) BANK, FIN tasa de préstamo variable *m*, tipo de préstamo variable *m*

VMP *abbr* (*value as marine policy*) INS valor como póliza marina *m*

vocation *n* HRM, WEL vocación *f*

vocational: ~ **guidance** *n* HRM orientación profesional *f*; ~ **guide** *n* WEL guía profesional *m*; ~ **rehabilitation** *n* HRM, WEL capacitación profesional *f* (*AmL*), formación profesional *f* (*Esp*); ~ **school** *n* WEL escuela de formación profesional *f*; ~ **training** *n* HRM, WEL capacitación profesional *f* (*AmL*), formación profesional *f* (*Esp*)

voice¹: ~**-activated** *adj* COMP activado por la voz; ~**-actuated** *adj* COMP activado por la voz; ~**-hand span** *n* ADMIN lapso ojo-voz *m*

voice² *n* COMMS, COMP, HRM, MEDIA voz *f*; ~ **mail** COMMS, COMP audiomensajería *f*; ~**-over** MEDIA, S&M voz en off *f*; ~ **recognition** COMP reconocimiento de la voz *m*

void¹: ~ **of** *adj* GEN COMM desprovisto de

void²: ~ **contract** *n* GEN COMM, LAW contrato nulo *m*; ~ **policy** *n* INS póliza nula *f*

voidable *adj* ACC, GEN COMM, HRM, INS, LAW anulable

voidance *n* HRM, LAW anulación *f*

vol. *abbr* (*volume*) GEN COMM volumen *m*

volatile¹ *adj* GEN COMM volátil, STOCK *market* inestable

volatile²: ~ **capital** *n* GEN COMM capital fugaz *m*, capital volátil *m*

volatility *n* GEN COMM volatilidad *f*

volcoa *abbr* (*volume contract of affreightment*) TRANSP volcoa (*contrato por volumen del flete*)

volt *n* (*V*) GEN COMM voltio *m* (*v*)

voltage: ~ **regulator** *n* ENVIR regulador de voltaje *m*

volume *n* (*vol.*) ACC cantidad *f*, GEN COMM volumen *m*; ~ **charge** TRANSP *tariff* coste por volumen *m* (*Esp*), costo por volumen *m* (*AmL*); ~ **contract of affreightment** (*volcoa*) TRANSP contrato por volumen del flete *m* (*volcoa*); ~ **deleted** STOCK volumen borrado *m*; ~ **discount** GEN COMM descuento por volumen *m*; ~ **of exports** ECON, IMP/EXP, TRANSP volumen de exportaciones *m*; ~ **index** GEN COMM índice de volumen *m*; ~ **merchandise allowance** S&M descuento por volumen de mercancía *m*; ~ **of orders** GEN COMM volumen de pedidos *m*; ~ **ratio** ECON proporción volumen de trabajo *f*; ~ **rebate** TRANSP *cargo* bonificación por volumen *f*; ~ **of retail sales** ECON, GEN COMM, S&M volumen de ventas al por menor *m*; ~ **shipping** IMP/EXP embarque volumétrico *m*, TRANSP transporte de volumen *m*; ~ **trading** STOCK contratación por volumen *f*; ~ **of wholesale** ECON, S&M volumen de ventas al por mayor *m*

voluntarism *n jarg* HRM voluntarismo *m*

voluntary: ~ **accumulation plan** *n* FIN plan de acumulación voluntaria *m*; ~ **agency** *n* WEL agencia de voluntariado *f*; ~ **arbitration** *n* HRM arbitraje voluntario *m*; ~ **bankruptcy** *n* FIN bancarrota voluntaria *f*; ~ **body** *n* WEL cuerpo de voluntarios *m*; ~ **chain** *n* GEN COMM cadena voluntaria *f*; ~ **compliance** *n* TAX cumplimiento voluntario *m*; ~ **contributions** *n pl BrE* TAX, WEL *National Insurance* aportaciones voluntarias *f pl*, cuotas voluntarias *f pl*; ~ **controls** *n pl* S&M controles voluntarios *m pl*; ~ **export restraint** *n* (*VER*) IMP/EXP contención voluntaria a la exportación *f*; ~ **group** *n* S&M grupo voluntario *m*; ~ **insurance** *n* INS seguro voluntario *m*; ~ **policy** *n* HRM póliza voluntaria *f*; ~ **redundancy** *n* HRM despido voluntario *m*; ~ **unemployment** *n* ECON, HRM paro voluntario *m*; ~ **winding-up** *n* GEN COMM liquidación voluntaria *f*; ~ **work** *n* HRM trabajo voluntario *m*

volunteer¹ *n* HRM voluntario(-a) *m,f*; ~ **development worker** GEN COMM cooperante para el desarrollo *mf*

volunteer² *vt* GEN COMM *information* ofrecer voluntariamente

von Neumann: ~ **Morgenstern stable set** *n* ECON juego estable de von Neumann Morgenstern *m*

VOP *abbr* (*value as in original policy*) INS valor de la póliza marina *m*

vote¹ *n* GEN COMM, POL votación *f*, voto *m*; ~ **against** POL voto en contra *m*; ~ **in favor** *AmE*, ~ **in favour** *BrE* POL voto a favor *m*; ~ **netting** FIN rendimiento en votos *m*;

~-**netting revenue** FIN, POL ingreso calculado por capítulo presupuestario *m*; ~ **structure** ACC *government* estructura de votos *f*, POL *government accounting* estructura del gasto *f*; ~ **title** POL título del capítulo presupuestario *m*; ~ **wording** POL justificación del capítulo presupuestario *f*

vote² *vi* ACC votar (*Esp*), GEN COMM dar el vencimiento; ♦ ~ **by show of hands** *BrE* HRM votar a mano alzada; ~ **full supply** POL votar un fondo total; ~ **interim supply** POL votar un fondo provisional

vote for *vt* POL votar

voter: ~ **turnout** *n* POL número de votantes *m*

voting *n* MGMNT *at board meetings*, POL votación *f*; ~ **booth** POL cabina electoral *f*, cabina para votar *f*; ~ **paper** HRM *union ballot*, POL papeleta *f*, papeleta de votación *f*, papeleta de voto *f*; ~ **paradox** ECON paradoja de la votación *f*; ~ **power** STOCK, TAX derecho de voto *m*; ~ **procedures** *n pl* POL mecanismos de votación *m pl*; ~ **right** GEN COMM derecho de voto *m*; ~ **security** STOCK valores con derecho de voto *m pl*; ~ **share** FIN, STOCK acción con derecho de voto *f*; ~ **stock** STOCK acciones con derecho de voto *f pl*; ~ **trust certificate** STOCK certificado de delegación de voto *m*

vouch: ~ **mark** *n* ACC prueba testimonial *f*

voucher *n* BANK *receipt* comprobante de pago *m*, GEN COMM comprobante *m*, vale *m*, bono *m*, STOCK comprobante *m*, boleta *f* (*AmL*), vale canjeable *m*; ~ **system** S&M sistema de vales *m*

vouchers *n pl* TAX *benefits* comprobantes *m pl*

voyage *n* TRANSP viaje *m*; ~ **account report** TRANSP informe de gastos del viaje *m* (*Esp*), reporte de gastos del viaje *m* (*AmL*); ~ **charter** TRANSP fletamento por viaje *m*; ~ **charter party** TRANSP póliza de fletamento por viaje *f*; ~ **estimate** TRANSP presupuesto del viaje *m*; ~ **fixture** TRANSP condiciones del viaje *f pl*; ~ **policy** INS póliza de viaje *f*; ~ **report** TRANSP informe del viaje *m* (*Esp*), reporte del viaje *m* (*AmL*)

VP *abbr* (*vice president*) HRM, MGMNT, POL VP (*vice-presidente*)

Vredeling: ~ **directive** *n* HRM directriz Vredeling *f*

VTMS *abbr* (*vessel traffic management system*) TRANSP sistema de gestión del tráfico de buques *m*

VTR *abbr* (*video tape recording*) COMMS VTR (*grabación en vídeo Esp, grabación en video AmL*)

vulgar: ~ **economists** *n pl* ECON economistas vulgares *m pl*

vulgarize *vt* GEN COMM vulgarizar

vulnerable *adj* GEN COMM vulnerable

vulture: ~ **fund** *n* FIN fondo buitre *m*

W

W: ~ **formation** *n* STOCK configuración en W *f*

W.A.[1] *abbr* (*with average*) INS *marine insurance* con avería

W.A.[2]: ~ **cover** *n* INS *marine* cobertura con averías *f*

WACCC *abbr* (*Worldwide Air Cargo Commodity Classification*) TRANSP clasificación del transporte aéreo internacional de mercancías

wad *n infrml* BANK *of notes* fajo *m*

wage *n* GEN COMM, HRM salario *m*, sueldo *m*; ~ **adjustment** GEN COMM, HRM ajuste salarial *m*; ~ **agreement** HRM convenio salarial *m*; ~**-and-price guidelines** *n pl* HRM directrices de salarios y precios *f pl*; ~ **arbitration** HRM arbitraje salarial *m*; ~ **assignment** HRM asignación salarial *f*; ~ **bonus** HRM prima salarial *f*; ~ **bracket** HRM categoría salarial *f*; ~ **ceiling** HRM límite superior de salario *m*; ~ **claim** HRM reclamación salarial *f*; ~ **contour** HRM configuración de salarios *f*; ~ **control** ECON regulación salarial *f*, HRM control de salarios *m*, regulación salarial *f*; ~ **cost** ECON coste salarial *m* (*Esp*), costo salarial *m* (*AmL*); ~ **demand** HRM demanda salarial *f*; ~ **differential** HRM diferencial de salarios *m*; ~ **differentials** ECON, HRM diferencias salariales *f pl*; ~ **diffusion** ECON difusión salarial *f*; ~ **drift** *jarg* HRM deriva salarial *f* (*jarg*), desviación salarial *f*; ~ **explosion** HRM explosión salarial *f*; ~ **flexibility** ECON, HRM flexibilidad salarial *f*; ~ **freeze** HRM congelación salarial *f*; ~ **gap** HRM diferencial de salarios *m*; ~ **incentive** HRM incentivo salarial *m*; ~ **increase** HRM aumento salarial *m*; ~ **indexation** HRM indización salarial *f*; ~ **inflation** ECON, HRM inflación de salarios *f*; ~ **lag** HRM desfase salarial *m* (*Esp*), rezago salarial *m* (*AmL*); ~ **level** HRM nivel de sueldo *m*; ~ **negotiation** HRM negociación salarial *f*; ~ **policy** HRM política salarial *f*; ~**-price inflation spiral** ECON espiral inflacionista de salarios y precios *f*; ~**-price spiral** ECON espiral precios-salarios *f*; ~**-push inflation** *jarg* ECON, HRM inflación de salarios *f*; ~ **rental ratio** ECON proporción salario-renta *f*; ~ **restraint** HRM moderación salarial *f*; ~ **rigidity** ECON rigidez salarial *f*; ~ **round** ECON negociación salarial *f*, HRM serie de negociaciones salariales *f*; ~ **and salary administration** HRM administración de sueldos y salarios *f*, gestión de sueldos y salarios *f*; ~ **and salary survey** HRM estudio de sueldos y salarios *m*; ~ **scale** HRM escala de salarios *f*, escala de sueldos *f*; ~ **settlement** HRM liquidación salarial *f*; ~ **spread** HRM escala de salarios *f*, escala de sueldos *f*; ~ **stabilization** HRM estabilización salarial *f*; ~ **standstill** HRM congelación de salarios *f*; ~ **structure** HRM estructura de los salarios *f*; ~ **subsidy** ECON subsidio salarial *m*; ~ **system** HRM sistema salarial *m*; ~**-tax spiral** ECON, TAX *taxflation* expiral del impuesto sobre los salarios *f*; ~ **theory** ECON, HRM teoría salarial *f*; ~ **unit** HRM unidad salarial *f*; ~ **withholding** HRM retención salarial *f*; ~ **zone** HRM zona salarial *f*

wager *n* GEN COMM cantidad apostada *f*

wages *n pl* GEN COMM, HRM salario *m*, HRM jornales *m pl*; ~ **fund theory** *n* ECON teoría del fondo de salarios *f*

Wages: ~ **Council** *n* BrE HRM consejo salarial;

~ **Inspectorate** *n* BrE HRM agencia de inspección salarial; ~ **Act** *n* HRM, LAW Ley Salarial *f*

Wagner: ~ **Act** *n* ECON, LAW Ley de Wagner *f*; ~**'s Law** *n* ECON, LAW Ley de Wagner *f*

wagonload: ~ **rate** *n* AmE (*cf carload rate BrE*) TRANSP *rail* tarifa por vagón completo *f*

wait[1]: ~**-and-see policy** *n* ECON política de seguir los acontecimientos *f*; ~ **days** *n pl* GEN COMM días de espera *m pl*; ~ **list** *n* GEN COMM, LEIS, TRANSP lista de espera *f*

wait[2] *vi* GEN COMM esperar; ◆ ~ **in line** AmE (*cf queue up BrE*) GEN COMM hacer cola

waiter *n* BrE STOCK camarero *m*, GEN COMM, HRM camarero *m*

waiting[1]: ~ **line theory** *n* AmE (*cf queueing theory BrE*) ECON, MATH teoría de las colas *f*; ~ **list** *n* GEN COMM, LEIS, TRANSP lista de espera *f*; ~ **period** *n* GEN COMM periodo de espera *m*, STOCK plazo de carencia *m*; ~ **time** *n* GEN COMM tiempo de espera *m*

waiting[2]: ~ **a berth** *phr* TRANSP *shipping* esperando atraque

waitress *n* GEN COMM, HRM camarera *f*

waive *vt* GEN COMM renunciar, TAX eximir

waiver *n* TAX exención *f*, exención de una obligación *f*; ~ **clause** INS cláusula de renuncia *f*

waiving *n* PATENTS renuncia *f*

walk: ~**-through assessment** *n* TAX cálculo aproximado del impuesto *m*

walkaway *n jarg* GEN COMM pan comido *m*

walkie: ~**-talkie** *n* COMMS, TRANSP radioteléfono portátil *m*

walkout *n* GEN COMM, HRM, IND huelga laboral *f*

walkover *n infrml* GEN COMM victoria fácil *f*

walk-up *n jarg* PROP edificio sin ascensor *m*

Wall: ~ **Street Crash** *n* STOCK colapso de la bolsa de Wall Street

wallflower *n jarg* STOCK acciones de escasa aceptación *f pl*

Wall-Streeter *n* STOCK persona que trabaja en Wall Street *f*

Walras': ~ **Law** *n* ECON, LAW Ley de Walras *f*

Walrasian: ~ **stability** *n* ECON estabilidad walrasiana *f*

Walsh: ~ **Healey Act** *n* ECON, LAW Ley de Walsh Healey *f*

WAN *abbr* (*wide area network*) COMP red de gran amplitud *f*

W&M: ~ **cover** *n* (*war and marine transportation cover*) INS cobertura de guerra y transporte marino *f*

wane *vi* ECON, GEN COMM decaer

want: ~ **of capital** *n* STOCK falta de capital *f*

war[1]: ~ **babies** *n pl jarg* STOCK bonos y valores de empresas relacionadas con la defensa; ~ **chest** *n* AmE GEN COMM fondos utilizados para financiar una campaña política; ~ **clause** *n* INS *marine* cláusula de guerra *f*; ~ **fever** *n* GEN COMM psicosis de guerra *f*; ~ **games** *n pl* GEN COMM juegos de guerra *m pl*; ~ **and marine transportation cover** *n* (*W&M cover*) INS cobertura de guerra y transporte marino *f*; ~ **risk** *n* INS *marine* riesgo de guerra *m*; ~ **tax** *n* TAX impuesto sobre las riquezas acumuladas durante la guerra; ~ **veteran's allowance** *n* TAX desgravación para los veteranos de guerra *f*

war² : ~ **risk only** *phr* (*wro*) INS sólo riesgo de guerra

War: ~ **Loan** *n* FIN empréstito de guerra *m*

ward *n* LAW protección *f*

warehouse¹ *n* (*whse*) GEN COMM, IMP/EXP, TRANSP *stock* almacén *m*; ~ **book** (*WB*) TRANSP *stock control* libro de almacén *m*; ~ **charges** *n pl* GEN COMM gastos de almacenaje *m pl*, IMP/EXP derechos de almacenaje *m pl*, TRANSP gastos de almacenaje *m pl*; ~ **economy** ECON economía de almacenaje *f*; ~ **entry** IMP/EXP, TRANSP *customs* entrada para almacén *f*; ~ **keeper** GEN COMM vigilante de almacén *mf*; ~ **officer** HRM, IMP/EXP, TRANSP oficial(a) de almacén *m,f*; ~ **receipt** (*WR*) IMP/EXP, TRANSP certificado de depósito *m*, S&M *document* recibo de almacén *m*, *cargo* recepción en almacén *f*, TRANSP certificado de depósito *m*, recibo de almacén *m*; ~ **supervisor** GEN COMM supervisor(a) de almacén *m,f*; ~ **warrant** (*WW*) GEN COMM comprobante de almacén *m*, LAW *commercial* duplicado del certificado de almacén *m*, garantía de almacén *f*

warehouse² *vt* IMP/EXP, TRANSP almacenar, guarder en bodega (*AmL*), guarder en depósito (*Esp*)

warehouseman *n AmE* (*cf storeman BrE*) HRM almacenista *mf*, guarda de almacén *mf*, jefe(-a) de almacén *m,f*

warehousing *n* IND, TRANSP almacenamiento *m*; ~ **entry** GEN COMM declaración de almacenaje *f*

warm: ~ **restart** *n* COMP arranque en caliente *m*; ~~**up session** *n* MGMNT sesión de calentamiento *f*

warn *vt* GEN COMM, HRM, MGMNT advertir

warning *n* HRM advertencia *f*; ~ **device** GEN COMM dispositivo de alerta *m*; ~ **indicator** GEN COMM indicador de aviso *m*; ~ **list** BANK lista de alerta *f*; ~ **sign** GEN COMM señal de peligro *f*

warrant¹ *n* FIN comprobante *m*, GEN COMM garantía *f*, INS comprobante *m*, POL autorización legal *f*, garantía *f*, STOCK comprobante *m*, warrant *m*; ~ **of attorney** LAW poder *m*; ~ **discounting** FIN descuento con certificado *m*; ~ **for payment** GEN COMM mandato de pago *m*; ~ **holder** STOCK *for buying shares* titular de un certificado *mf*; ~ **into government securities** (*WINGS*) STOCK garantía de los bonos del Estado *f*; ~ **issue** FIN emisión garantizada *f*

warrant² *vt* GEN COMM garantizar

warranted¹ *adj* GEN COMM (*wd.*) garantizado, INS (*W/d*) comprobado; ~ **existing class maintained** (*wecm*) TRANSP garantía de mantenimiento de la categoría *f*

warranted² : ~ **rate of growth** *n* ECON tasa de crecimiento garantizada *f*

warrantee *n* LAW beneficiario(-a) de un aval *m,f*

warranter *n* LAW garante *mf*

warrantless: ~ **investigation** *n jarg* POL investigación sin garantías *f*

warranty *n* GEN COMM garantía *f*; ~ **card** BANK tarjeta de garantía *f*; ~ **of merchantability** GEN COMM garantía de comerciabilidad *f*; ~ **of title** GEN COMM garantía de propiedad *f*

Warsaw: ~ **Convention** *n* TRANSP Convención de Varsovia *f*

wash: ~ **sale** *n* STOCK transacción ficticia *f*, venta aparente *f*

washed: ~ **overboard** *adj* (*wob*) TRANSP *shipping* arrastrado por un golpe de mar

WASP *abbr* (*wind assisted ship propulsion*) TRANSP propulsión del buque asistida por el viento *f*

wastage *n* GEN COMM pérdida *f*, HRM desperdicio *m*, despilfarro *m*

waste *n* ENVIR, IND desechos *m pl*; ~ **circulation** S&M difusión de publicación que no llega al público-objetivo *f*; ~ **disposal** ENVIR eliminación de desperdicios *f*; ~ **dumping** ENVIR vertido de desperdicios *m*; ~ **heat water tube boiler** TRANSP *shipping* caldera de tubos de agua de recuperación *f*; ~ **land** ENVIR, PROP tierra baldía *f*, yermo *m*; ~ **management** GEN COMM gestión de los residuos *f*; ~ **oils** *n pl* ENVIR aceites de desecho *m pl*; ~ **paper** ENVIR papelote *m*; ~ **prevention** ENVIR prevención del despilfarro *f*; ~ **product** ENVIR desperdicio *m*; ~ **recycling** ENVIR reciclado de residuos *m*; **the ~ society** GEN COMM la sociedad del despilfarro *f*; ~ **treatment** ENVIR tratamiento de los residuos *m*; ~~**water treatment** ENVIR, IND depuración de aguas residuales *m*

wasteful: ~ **expenditure** *n* FIN desembolso no rentable *m*

wasting: ~ **asset** *n* ACC activo consumible *m*, STOCK activo no renovable *m*; ~ **assets** *n pl* ACC haberes que pierden valor *m pl*, ECON activos para consumo *m pl*, ENVIR bienes consumibles *m pl*

watch¹ : ~ **list** *n* BANK lista de control *f*

watch² **1.** *vt* STOCK *the value* vigilar; ◆ ~ **one's back** GEN COMM estar alerta; **2.** *vi* GEN COMM vigilar

watchdog *n* GEN COMM censor *m*; ~ **committee** GEN COMM comité censor *m*, POL comité de control *m*

watchlist *n* STOCK lista de control *f*

watchman *n* HRM vigilante *mf*

watchword *n* GEN COMM frase publicitaria *f*

water¹ : ~~**generated** *adj* ENVIR *electricity*, IND hidrogenerado

water² : ~ **company** *n* IND compañía de agua *f*; ~ **damage** *n* GEN COMM, INS daño por agua *m*; ~ **monitor** *n* (*WM*) TRANSP *ship* monitor del agua *m*; ~ **pollution** *n* ENVIR contaminación del agua *f*; ~ **power** *n* ENVIR, IND energía hidráulica *f*; ~ **purification** *n* ENVIR depuración del agua *f*; ~ **supply** *n* ENVIR suministro de agua *m*; ~ **transportation** *n* TRANSP transporte por agua *m*; ~ **treatment** *n* ENVIR tratamiento del agua *m*

waterborne: ~ **agreement** *n* INS *marine* acuerdo de abordo *m*

watered: ~ **capital** *n* ACC, ECON, FIN, GEN COMM capital inflado *m*, capital desvalorizado *m*; ~ **stock** *n* STOCK acciones mojadas *f pl*

Waterguard: ~ **Service** *n BrE* IMP/EXP organización de la aduana británica

watermark *n* BANK, ECON *on bank note* filigrana *f*

watermarked *adj* BANK, ECON *bank note* filigranado

waterproof: ~ **packing** *n* S&M embalaje impermeable *m*; ~ **paper** *n* IND papel a prueba de humedad *m*

watertight *adj* (*WT*) GEN COMM *container, excuse, plan* sin fisuras, TRANSP estanco al agua

wave *n* GEN COMM onda *f*; ~ **power** ENVIR potencia de onda *f*; ~ **theory** GEN COMM teoría de la onda *f*

wavelength: **be on the same ~** *phr* GEN COMM estar en la misma onda

waybill *n* (*WB*) IMP/EXP *detailing route, cost,* TRANSP carta de porte *f*

ways: **~ and means** *n pl* ECON medios y arbitrios; **~ and means committee** *n* AmE POL *of the House of Representatives* comisión económica del congreso

WB *abbr* IMP/EXP (*waybill*) carta de porte *f*, TRANSP (*warehouse book*) libro de almacén *m*, (*waybill*) carta de porte *f*

wbs *abbr* (*without benefit of salvage*) INS *marine* sin beneficio de salvamento

w.c. *abbr* (*without charge*) GEN COMM gratis, sin cargo

wd. *abbr warranted*) GEN COMM garantizado

W/d *abbr* (*warranted*) INS comprobado

weak[1] *adj* ECON, GEN COMM, LAW débil

weak[2]: **~ market** *n* ECON, FIN, STOCK mercado débil *m*

weaken *vt* ECON *currency value* atenuar, GEN COMM debilitar

weakest: **~ link theory** *n* GEN COMM teoría de que el hilo se rompe por lo más delgado

weakness *n* GEN COMM debilidad *f*

wealth *n* ECON opulencia *f*, patrimonio *m*, GEN COMM abundancia *f*, riqueza *f*, HRM, INS, POL, WEL opulencia *f*; **~ distribution** ECON distribución de la riqueza *f*; **~ effect** ECON efecto riqueza *m*; **~ of opportunities** GEN COMM abundancia de oportunidades *f*; **~ tax** TAX impuesto sobre el patrimonio *m*

Wealth: **~ of Nations** *n* ECON riqueza de las naciones *f*

wear: **~ and tear** *phr* GEN COMM uso y desgaste

wearout: **~ factor** *n* S&M *advertising* factor de desgaste *m*

weather[1] *n* GEN COMM tiempo *m*; **~ permitting** (*WP*) GEN COMM, TRANSP si el tiempo lo permite; **~ report** GEN COMM informe meteorológico *m* (*Esp*), reporte meteorológico *m* (*AmL*); **~ working day of 24 hours** TRANSP *charter party* día de trabajo de 24 horas con tiempo favorable *m*; **~ working days** (*wwd*) *n pl* TRANSP *charter party* días de trabajo con tiempo favorable *m pl*; **~ working days, Friday and holidays excluded** *n pl* GEN COMM, TRANSP *shipping, chartering term* días de trabajo con tiempo favorable, salvo viernes y festivos *m pl*; **~ working days, Sundays and holidays excluded** *n pl* GEN COMM, TRANSP *shipping, chartering term* días de trabajo con tiempo favorable, salvo domingos y festivos *m pl*

weather[2]: **~ the recession** *phr* ECON capear la recesión

weaving: **~ loom** *n* IND telar *m*; **~ mill** *n* IND tejeduría *f*

web: **~-offset** *n* S&M máquina offset de bobinas *f*

Web: **the ~** *n* COMP Internet *m*, la Web *f*, la Telaraña *f*, la Web *f*; **~ page** *n* COMP página web *f*

webs *n pl* AmE MEDIA cadenas de televisión *f pl*

wecm *abbr* (*warranted existing class maintained*) TRANSP garantía de mantenimiento de la categoría *f*

wedge *n* TRANSP calzo *m*

weed: **~ out** *vt* GEN COMM suprimir

week[1]: **~ order** *n* STOCK orden para una semana *f*

week[2]: **a ~ in advance** *phr* GEN COMM una semana por adelantado

weekdays: **on ~** *adv* GEN COMM en días laborables

weekend[1]: **~ freight tariff** *n* TRANSP ro/ro tarifa de fletes para fines de semana *f*; **~ return fare** *n* BrE (*cf weekend round-trip fare AmE*) LEIS, TRANSP tarifa de ida y vuelta

para fin de semana *f*; **~ round-trip fare** *n* AmE (*cf weekend return fare BrE*) LEIS, TRANSP tarifa de ida y vuelta para fin de semana *f*; **~ travel home allowance** *n* GEN COMM viáticos para regreso a casa en fines de semana *m pl* (*AmL*)

weekend[2]: **have a long ~** *phr* GEN COMM, HRM hacer puente

weekly: **~ rent** *n* PROP alquiler semanal *m*; **~ return** *n* BANK, FIN rendimiento semanal *m*; **~ volume** *n* STOCK volumen total negociado *m*; **~ wage** *n* HRM salario semanal *m*

w.e.f. *abbr* (*with effect from*) GEN COMM efectivo desde el día

weigh: **~ up the pros and cons** *phr* GEN COMM sopesar los pros y los contras

weighbridge *n* TRANSP *cargo* puente-báscula *m*

weighing: **~ scale** *n* TRANSP báscula *f*

weight[1] *n* (*wt., wgt*) GEN COMM, TRANSP peso *m*; **~ allowed free** GEN COMM peso permitido sin cargas *m*; **~ ascertained** GEN COMM peso comprobado *m*; **~ of cargo** TRANSP peso de la carga *m*; **~ charge** TRANSP coste por peso *m* (*Esp*), costo por peso *m* (*AmL*); **~ coefficient** BANK, ECON, FIN, STOCK coeficiente de ponderación *m*; **~ guaranteed** (*wg*) TRANSP *stock control* peso garantizado *m*; **~ limit** GEN COMM, TRANSP peso máximo autorizado *m*; **~ note** GEN COMM nota de peso *f*; **~ ton** GEN COMM tonelada de peso *f*; **~ when empty** GEN COMM, TRANSP peso estando vacío *m*

weight[2] *vt* STOCK *option positions* ponderar

weighted[1] *adj* GEN COMM ponderado

weighted[2]: **~ average** *n* ECON, GEN COMM, MATH promedio ponderado *m*; **~ average cost** *n* ACC coste medio ponderado *m* (*Esp*), costo medio ponderado *m* (*AmL*); **~ distribution** *n* ECON distribución ponderada *f*; **~ index** *n* GEN COMM índice ponderado *m*

weighting *n* FIN, MATH, S&M ponderación *f*

weights: **~ and measures** *n* GEN COMM pesos y medidas

welcome[1]: **~ message** *n* COMP, S&M mensaje de bienvenida *m*

welcome[2] *vt* GEN COMM dar la bienvenida a

welfare *n* HRM bienestar *m*; **~ agency** HRM, WEL oficina de bienestar social *f*; **~ benefit** HRM, WEL subsidio de bienestar social *m*; **~ department** WEL departamento de bienestar social *m*; **~ economics** ECON economía del bienestar *f*; **~ fund** WEL fondo de bienestar *m*; **~ legislation** HRM, LAW, WEL legislación social *f*; **~ payment** HRM, WEL asistencia social *f*, pago de asistencia pública *m*, prestación social *f*; **~ recipient** AmE HRM (*cf recipient of an allowance, cf social-security recipient*), WEL (*cf social-security recipient*) beneficiario(-a) de asistencia social *m,f*, beneficiario(-a) de un subsidio *m,f*; **~ service** HRM, WEL servicio de bienestar social *m*; **~ state** ECON estado del bienestar *m*; **~ trap** WEL trampa del bienestar *f*; **~ worker** WEL trabajador(a) social *m,f*; ◆ **be on ~** AmE HRM, WEL (*cf be on benefits BrE, cf be on the dole BrE*) vivir de subsidios sociales

welfarist *n* POL defensor(a) del estado del bienestar *m,f*

well[1]: **~-balanced** *adj* ACC, GEN COMM equilibrado; **~-educated** *adj* HRM bien preparado, con una capacitación adecuada (*AmL*), con una formación adecuada (*Esp*); **~-established** *adj* GEN COMM consolidado; **~-grounded** *adj* GEN COMM bien fundado; **~-informed** *adj* GEN COMM, POL bien informado; **~-meaning** *adj*

GEN COMM bienintencionado; **~-motivated** *adj* HRM bien motivado; **~ off** *adj* GEN COMM en buena posición; **~-packaged** *adj* S&M bien embalado; **~-paid** *adj* HRM bien pagado; **~-placed** *adj* GEN COMM bien situado; **~-positioned** *adj* GEN COMM bien colocado; **~-stocked** *adj* GEN COMM bien surtido; **~-tried** *adj* GEN COMM *method* bien seguro

well[2]: **~-known mark** *n* GEN COMM marca conocida *f*

wellhead: **~ cost** *n* IND *oil industry* coste en pozo *m* (*Esp*), costo en pozo *m* (*AmL*); **~ price** *n* GEN COMM precio firme *m*

Weltanschauung *n jarg* GEN COMM, HRM, POL concepción global *f*

Werner: **~ Report** *n* ECON *economic and monetary union* informe de Werner *m* (*Esp*), reporte de Werner *m* (*AmL*)

West: **~ compass point** *n* TRANSP *navigation* cuarta de la rosa con rumbo al oeste *f*

western: **~-style** *adj* GEN COMM de estilo occidental

Western: **~ European Union** *n* (*WEU*) ECON, POL Unión Europea Occidental *f* (*UEO*)

westernized[1] *adj* GEN COMM occidentalizado

westernized[2]: **become ~** *vi* GEN COMM occidentalizarse

wet: **~ bulk cargo** *n* TRANSP carga de graneles líquidos *f*; **~ dock** *n* TRANSP *port* dársena *f*, dique flotante *m*; **~ goods** *n pl* GEN COMM mercancías líquidas *f pl*; **~ sell** *n jarg* GEN COMM venta de líquidos envasados *f*; **~ stock** *n* GEN COMM mercancías líquidas *f pl*; **~ textile waste** *n* ENVIR, IND desechos líquidos de materiales textiles *m pl*

wetback *n AmE infrml* GEN COMM *illegal Mexican immigrant* espalda mojada *f*

wets *n pl BrE infrml* POL políticos que apoyan medidas moderadas y se oponen a medidas extremas

WEU *abbr* (*Western European Union*) ECON, POL UEO (*Unión Europea Occidental*)

WFP *abbr* (*World Food Programme*) ECON, POL Programa de Alimentación Mundial *m*

WFSE *abbr* (*World Federation of Stock Exchanges*) STOCK federación mundial de bolsas

WFTU *abbr* (*World Federation of Trade Unions*) HRM federación mundial de sindicatos

WFUNA *abbr* (*World Federation of United Nations Associations*) POL FMANU (*Federación Mundial de Asociaciones de las Naciones Unidas*)

wg *abbr* (*weight guaranteed*) TRANSP peso garantizado *m*

wgt *abbr* (*weight*) GEN COMM peso *m*

WH *abbr* (*workable hatch*) TRANSP escotilla practicable *f*

wharf *n* IMP/EXP amarradero *m*, TRANSP *port* amarradero *m*, desembarcadero *m*; **~ apron** TRANSP *port* zona de descarga *f*; **~ charter** TRANSP póliza de muelle *f*; **~ dues** *n pl* TRANSP derechos de muelle *m pl*; **~ owner's liability** (*WOL*) LAW responsabilidad civil de la autoridad portuaria *f*

wharfage *n* TRANSP *tariff* derechos de muelle *m pl*; **~ charges** *n pl* TRANSP gastos de atraque *m pl*; **~ dues** *n pl* TRANSP derechos de muelle *m pl*

wharfinger *n* GEN COMM, HRM, TRANSP alijador(a) *m,f* (*AmL*), estibador(a) *m,f* (*Esp*)

Wharton: **~ model** *n* ECON modelo Wharton *m*

what: **~ you see is what you get** *phr* (*WYSIWYG*) COMP programa que muestra por pantalla el documento tal y como será impreso

wheeler-dealer *n infrml* GEN COMM trapichero(-a) *m,f* (*infrml*)

wheelhouse *n* TRANSP *of ship* caseta de gobierno *f*, caseta del timón *f*

wheeling: **~ and dealing** *phr infrml* GEN COMM comercio poco escrupuloso *m*

wheels: **~ of government** *n pl* POL maquinaria administrativa *f*

whereas: **the ~ clauses** *n pl* LAW los considerandos *m pl*

wherefores: **whys and ~** *n pl* GEN COMM los porqués *m pl*

whether: **~ in berth or not** *phr* (*WIBON*) TRANSP *charter party term* esté o no atracado

whiplash *n* STOCK latigazo *m*

whipsaw[1] *n AmE* (*cf double-edged sword BrE*) HRM *union bargaining process* arma de doble filo *m*, POL maniobra de enfrentamiento *f*

whipsaw[2] *vt AmE jarg* STOCK perder por partida doble

whipsawed *adj AmE jarg* STOCK con pérdidas por partida doble

whistle: **~-blower** *n infrml* GEN COMM, LAW empleado que informa sobre actividades ilícitas en su empresa; **~ blowing** *n infrml* GEN COMM, LAW revelación de actividades ilícitas en el organismo en el que se trabaja

whistle-stop[1]: **~ campaign** *n* POL campaña electoral en tren visitando brevemente las localidades de la circunscripción

whistle-stop[2] *vi* POL hacer campaña electoral en tren visitando brevemente las localidades de la circunscripción

white: **~ coal** *n* ENVIR hulla blanca *f*; **~ coat** *n jarg* HRM *police* examinador(a) de taxistas *m,f*; **~ coat rule** *n jarg* S&M *advertising* norma de la bata blanca *f*; **~-collar crime** *n* LAW delito de guante blanco *m*; **~-collar job** *n* HRM puesto de trabajo de oficina *m*; **~-collar union** *n* HRM sindicato de empleados *m*; **~-collar worker** *n* HRM administrativo(-a) *m,f*, empleado(-a) de oficina *m,f*, oficinista *mf*; **~ goods** *n pl* S&M electrodomésticos *m pl*; **~ knight** *n infrml* FIN *takeovers* persona respetuosa *f*; **~ land** *n jarg* PROP terreno sin calificar *m*; **~ market** *n* ECON mercado legalizado *m*; **~ noise** *n* MATH ruido blanco *m*; **~ revolution** *n* ECON *agricultural* revolución blanca *f*

White: **~ Paper** *n BrE* LAW, POL Libro Blanco *m*; **~'s rating** *n* STOCK clasificación de White *f*

whitewash *vt infrml* GEN COMM justificar

whittle down *vt* GEN COMM *costs, commissions* reducir poco a poco

whizz: **~ kid** *n infrml* GEN COMM chico(-a) prodigio *m,f*, joven promesa *mf*

WHO *abbr* (*World Health Organization*) POL, WEL OMS (*Organización Mundial de la Salud*)

whole: **~ cargo charter** *n* TRANSP fletamiento de carga completa *m*; **~ life insurance** *n* INS seguro de vida entera *m*; **~ life insurance policy** *n* INS póliza de vida entera *f*; **~ loan** *n* BANK, FIN, PROP primer préstamo hipotecario para la vivienda *m*; **~ years** *n pl* TAX años completos *m pl*

wholesale[1] *adj* GEN COMM al por mayor; ◆ **by ~** GEN COMM al por mayor

wholesale[2]: **~ bank** *n* BANK banco mayorista *m*; **~ banking** *n* BANK banca al mayoreo *f* (*AmL*), banca al por mayor *f* (*Esp*), banca mayorista *f* (*Esp*); **~ business** *n* GEN COMM, INS, S&M comercio al por mayor *m*; **~ cooperative** *n* HRM cooperativa de mayoristas *f*; ~ **dealer** *n* GEN COMM, INS, S&M comerciante mayorista *mf*; ~ **delivery** *n* S&M entrega al por mayor *f*; ~ **deposits** *n pl* BANK depósitos de clientes institucionales *m pl*; ~ **goods** *n pl* GEN COMM mercancías al por mayor *f pl*; ~ **manufacture** *n* IND confección al mayoreo *f* (*AmL*), confección al por mayor *f* (*Esp*); ~ **market** *n* GEN COMM mercado al por mayor *m*; ~ **merchant** *n* GEN COMM, INS, S&M comerciante(-a) al por mayor *m,f*; ~ **money market** *n* FIN mercado de venta de la moneda al por mayor *m*; ~ **price** *n* S&M precio al por mayor *m*; ~ **price index** *n* ECON, S&M *statistics* índice de precios al por mayor *m*; ~ **price inflation** *n* ECON inflación de los precios al por mayor *f*; ~ **purchasing** *n* S&M compra al por mayor *f*; ~ **trade** *n* GEN COMM, INS, S&M comercio al por mayor *m*; ~ **trader** *n* GEN COMM, S&M negociante(-a) al por mayor *mf*

wholesaler *n* GEN COMM *securities* mayorista *mf*

wholesaling *n* S&M venta al por mayor *f*

wholly[1]: ~ **dependent** *adj* GEN COMM totalmente dependiente

wholly[2]: ~ **and exclusively** *adv* LAW total y exclusivamente

wholly[3]: ~**owned corporation** *n* STOCK compañía en propiedad absoluta *f*; ~**owned subsidiary** *n* STOCK subsidiaria en propiedad absoluta *f*

whse *abbr* (*warehouse*) IMP/EXP, TRANSP almacén *m*

WIBON *abbr* (*whether in berth or not*) TRANSP *charter party term* esté o no atracado

wide[1]: ~**ranging** *adj* GEN COMM de amplia cobertura

wide[2]: ~ **area network** *n* (*WAN*) COMP red de área extendida *f*, red de gran amplitud *f*, MGMNT red de área extendida *f*; ~**body aircraft** *n* TRANSP avión de fuselaje ancho *m*; ~ **monetary base** *n* FIN base monetaria extendida *f*; ~ **opening** *n* STOCK *session* diferencial desusadamente amplio *m*; ~ **range** *n* S&M amplia gama *f*

widely: ~ **recognized** *adv* GEN COMM ampliamente reconocido

widen *vt* GEN COMM *gap*, TAX *tax base* ampliar

widening *n* GEN COMM ensanchamiento *m*

widespread *adj* GEN COMM muy difundido

widow *n* GEN COMM viuda *f*; ~**and-orphan stock** STOCK *reliable, high-dividend stock* acción defensiva *f*

widower *n* GEN COMM viudo *m*

widow: ~'s **bereavement allowance** *n* TAX deducción por viudedad *f*; ~ **pension** *n* FIN viudedad *f*

width *n* COMP anchura *f*

wild: ~ **card** *n* COMP comodín *m*

wildcat: ~ **drilling** *n* ENVIR, IND perforación exploratoria *f*; ~ **strike** *n* HRM, IND huelga salvaje *f*; ~ **venture** *n* GEN COMM aventura descabellada *f*

wilful: ~ **default** *n* BrE TAX incumplimiento voluntario *f*; ~ **misrepresentation of facts** *n* BrE LAW desfiguración voluntaria de los hechos

will *n* LAW testamento *m*

willfull *AmE see* wilful *BrE*

Williams: ~ **act** *n* LAW ley de Williams *f*

win *vt* GEN COMM *customers* ganar; ◆ ~ **one's spurs** GEN COMM dar pruebas de sus aptitudes; ~ **sb's favor** *AmE*, ~ **sb's favour** *BrE* GEN COMM ganarse el favor de alguien, obtener el favor de alguien

win over *vt* GEN COMM convencer

winches *n pl* TRANSP cabrestantes *m pl*

wind *n* GEN COMM viento *m*; ~ **assisted ship propulsion** (*WASP*) TRANSP propulsión del buque asistida por el viento *f*; ~ **power** ENVIR fuerza del viento *f*

wind down *vt* FIN *company*, GEN COMM terminar gradualmente

wind up *vt* GEN COMM *meeting* concluir, MGMNT finalizar

windfall: ~ **benefit** *n* ACC, ECON, FIN beneficio imprevisto *m*, beneficio inesperado *m*; ~ **gain** *n* ECON ganancias imprevistas *f pl*; ~ **loss** *n* ECON pérdida inesperada *f*; ~ **profit** *n* GEN COMM ganancia inesperada *f*; ~ **profits tax** *n* TAX impuesto sobre beneficios extraordinarios *m*; ~ **tax** *n* POL, TAX impuesto extraordinario *m*

winding: ~**up** *n* ACC *of corporation*, BANK liquidación *f*, conclusión *f*, GEN COMM conclusión *f*, FIN liquidación *f*, MGMNT *meeting* finalización *f*, STOCK liquidación *f*; ~**up arrangements** *n pl* LAW acuerdos de disolución *m pl*; ~**up order** *n* LAW orden de disolución *f*; ~**up sale** *n* GEN COMM venta de liquidación *f*

window *n* COMMS ventanilla *f*, COMP ventana *f*, GEN COMM *sales counter* ventanilla *f*; ~ **bill** GEN COMM letra de ventanilla *f*; ~ **display** GEN COMM, S&M escaparate *m*; ~**dressing** ACC *annual accounts* alteración falaz de un balance *f*, falseamiento *m*, manipulación de la contabilidad *f*, manipulación de la contabilidad mediante operaciones *f*, BANK manipulación de la contabilidad *f*, manipulación de la contabilidad mediante operaciones *f*, FIN *of accounts* falseamiento *m*, STOCK *statement of accounts* alteración falaz de un balance *f*; ~ **envelope** COMMS sobre con ventanilla *m*; ~**guidance** TRANSP ventana guía *f*; ~ **of opportunity** GEN COMM resquicio de oportunidad *m*, ventana de oportunidad *f*, hueco de oportunidad *m*, S&M espacio favorable *m*; ~ **sticker** GEN COMM cinta adhesiva para las ventanas *f*; ◆ **out the** ~ STOCK por la ventana

window[2]: ~**shop** *vi* GEN COMM mirar los escaparates

winds: ~ **of change** *n pl* GEN COMM vientos de cambio *m pl*

wine: ~**bottling** *n* ECON, IND embotellado de vino *m*; ~ **industry** *n* ECON, IND industria vinícola *f*; ~ **list** *n* GEN COMM carta de vinos *f*; ~ **merchant** *n* GEN COMM, HRM vinatero(-a) *m,f*; ~**producing area** *n* ECON, IND área vinícola *f*; ~ **trade** *n* IND negocio de vinos *m*; ~ **warehouse** *n* IMP/EXP *stock control* almacén de vino *m*

winged: ~ **pallet** *n* TRANSP bandeja de carga con alas *f*

winner *n* GEN COMM ganador(a) *m,f*; ◆ ~ **takes all** GEN COMM todo para el ganador

winning: ~ **streak** *n infrml* GEN COMM racha de triunfos *f*

wipe: ~ **the slate clean** *phr* GEN COMM hacer borrón y cuenta nueva; ~ **sth from a tape** *phr* GEN COMM borrar algo de una cinta

WIPO *abbr* (*World Intellectual Property Organization*) LAW Organización Mundial para la Propiedad Intelectual *f*

wire: ~**house** *n infrml* GEN COMM correduría en la que las sucursales están conectadas con la sed principal mediante cables telefónicos y telegráficos; ~ **lashing** *n* TRANSP amarre con cable *m*; ~ **service** *n* AmE (*cf news agency* BrE) COMMS, MEDIA agencia de noticias *f*; ~ **transfer** *n* BANK, FIN giro telegráfico *m*

wireless *adj* COMMS inalámbrico

wiretapping *n* COMMS escucha telefónica *f*

withdraw 1. *vt* BANK *funds* retirar, GEN COMM *from*

meeting retirar, *offer* rescindir, STOCK *funds* retirar; **2.** *vi* ECON *from business activity* retirarse

withdrawal *n* BANK retiro de fondos *m*, GEN COMM retirada *f*, STOCK *shares* retiro *m*; ~ **of appeal** TAX retirada de reclamación *f*; ~ **of capital** BANK retiro de capital *m*; ~ **from stocks** GEN COMM retirada de existencias *f*; ~ **notice** BANK, HRM, IND aviso de retirada de fondos *m*; ~ **of an objection** TAX retirada de una objeción *f*; ~ **slip** BANK comprobante de separación *m*; ~ **warrant** BANK autorización para retirar fondos *f*

withhold *vt* LAW denegar *f*, TAX retener; ♦ ~ **information** LAW denegar información

withholding *n* STOCK *securities, taxes* retención fraudulenta *f*; ~ **tax** TAX impuesto retenido *m*

within *prep* GEN COMM dentro de; ♦ ~ **the allotted time frame** GEN COMM dentro del tiempo permitido; ~ **a period of** GEN COMM en un periodo de; ~ **prescribed limits** LAW dentro de los límites prescritos; ~ **the prescribed time** GEN COMM dentro del plazo fijado; ~ **reach** GEN COMM al alcance de; ~ **a week** GEN COMM dentro de una semana

without *prep* (*w/o*) GEN COMM sin; ♦ ~ **any liability on our part** GEN COMM sin ninguna responsabilidad por nuestra parte; ~ **benefit of salvage** (*wbs*) INS *marine* sin beneficio de salvamento; ~ **charge** (*w.c.*) GEN COMM gratis, sin cargo; ~ **engagement** GEN COMM sin compromiso; ~ **a hitch** GEN COMM sin ningún tropiezo; ~ **obligation** S&M sin obligación; ~ **prejudice** (*wp*) INS sin prejuzgar; ~ **previous warning** GEN COMM sin advertencia previa; ~ **privileges** (*x pri*) GEN COMM sin privilegios; ~ **respite** COMMS *from work* sin respiro; ~ **warning** GEN COMM sin aviso

witness[1]: ~ **for the defence** *BrE*, ~ **for the defense** *AmE n* LAW testigo de descargo *m*, testigo de la defensa *m*; ~ **for the prosecution** *n* LAW testigo de cargo *m*

witness[2] *vt* GEN COMM, LAW atestiguar; ♦ ~ **sb's signature** GEN COMM, LAW atestiguar la firma de alguien

witness[3]: **in** ~ **whereof** *phr* LAW en fe de lo cual, en testimonio de lo cual

wizard *n* COMP experto(-a) *m,f*

WM *abbr* (*water monitor*) TRANSP monitor del agua *m*

wob *abbr* (*washed overboard*) TRANSP *shipping* arrastrado por un golpe de mar

wobbly *adj* GEN COMM *recovery* tambaleante

WOL *abbr* (*wharf owner's liability*) LAW responsabilidad civil de la autoridad portuaria *f*

wolf *n jarg* STOCK seductor *m*

wooden: ~ **pallet** *n* IMP/EXP, TRANSP *distribution* plataforma de carga de madera *f*; ~ **covers** *n pl* TRANSP cubiertas de madera *f pl*

woodland *n* GEN COMM zona forestal *f*

woods: **be out of the** ~ *phr* GEN COMM estar a salvo

wool *n* GEN COMM lana *f*; ~ **industry** ECON, IND industria de la lana *f*; ~ **merchant** ECON, IND comerciante(-a) en lana *m,f*; ~ **textiles manufacturer** ECON fabricante de lanas *mf*; ~ **trade** ECON, IND comercio de la lana *m*; ~ **yarn manufacturer** ECON, IND fabricante de lanas *mf*

woollen: ~ **manufacturer** *n* ECON, IND fabricante de lanas *mf*

word *n* COMP, GEN COMM palabra *f*; ~ **of advice** MGMNT advertencia *f*; ~ **count** COMP recuento de palabras *m*; ~ **and device mark** PATENTS marca de palabras e

imágenes, figuras, símbolos, gráficos, letras, cifras y formas tridimensionales; ~**-engineering** POL manipulación de la información *f*; ~ **length** COMP longitud de palabra *f*; ~**-of-mouth advertising** S&M publicidad boca a boca *f*; ~**-of-mouth marketing** S&M marketing boca a boca *m*; ~ **processing** ADMIN, COMP tratamiento de texto *m*; ~**-processing center** *AmE*, ~**-processing centre** *BrE* COMP centro de procesamiento de texto *m*, centro de tratamiento de textos *m*; ~**-processing software** COMP programa de procesamiento de textos *m*, software de procesamiento de texto *m*; ~**-processing system** COMP sistema de procesamiento de texto *m*; ~ **processor** (*WP*) ADMIN, COMP procesado de texto *m* (*AmL*) (*WP*), procesador de textos *m* (*Esp*) (*WP*); ~ **speller** COMP deletreador *m*; ~ **of warning** GEN COMM advertencia *f*; ~ **wrap** COMP salto de línea *m*; ♦ **have a** ~ **with sb about** GEN COMM hablar de algo con alguien

words: ~ **per minute** *phr* (*wpm*) ADMIN, HRM palabras por minuto (*ppm*)

wording *n* GEN COMM, LAW *of contract* redacción *f*; ~ **of a vote** BANK término de un voto *m*

work[1]: **out of** ~ *adj* GEN COMM desempleado, HRM parado

work[2] *n* GEN COMM trabajo *m*, *employment* empleo *m*, IND *machine* marcha *f*; ~ **backlog** GEN COMM, IND volumen de trabajo pendiente *m*; ~ **canteen** HRM cafetería para empleados *f*, cantina de la empresa *f*; ~ **classification** HRM clasificación laboral *f*; ~ **content** GEN COMM valor del trabajo *m*; ~ **cycle** GEN COMM, HRM ciclo de trabajo *m*; ~ **design** GEN COMM estilo de trabajo *m*; ~ **ethic** HRM ética del trabajo *f*; ~ **experience** GEN COMM, HRM experiencia laboral *f*; ~ **flow** COMP flujo de operaciones *m*, GEN COMM flujo de trabajo *m*; ~ **force** HRM *workers* fuerza de trabajo *f*, fuerza laboral *f*, personal obrero *m*, mano de obra *f*, IND personal obrero *m*; ~ **history** HRM historial laboral *m*; ~**-in** HRM *in EC regulations* huelga a la japonesa; ~**-in-process** *AmE* (*cf work-in-progress BrE*) GEN COMM trabajo en curso *m*, trabajo en curso de ejecución *m*, trabajo en desarrollo *m*, trabajo en proceso *m*; ~**-in-progress** (*cf work-in-process AmE*) GEN COMM trabajo en curso *m*, trabajo en curso de ejecución *m*, trabajo en desarrollo *m*, trabajo en proceso *m*; ~ **location** HRM *city, town* lugar de trabajo *m*; ~ **mark** PATENTS nombre comercial *m*; ~ **measurement** GEN COMM, IND, MGMNT medición del trabajo *f*; ~ **order** HRM, IND orden de trabajo *f*; ~ **organization** GEN COMM, HRM, MGMNT organización del trabajo *f*; ~ **permit** , HRM, LAW, WEL permiso de trabajo *m*; ~ **plan** HRM, MGMNT plan de trabajo *m*; ~ **prospects** *n pl* HRM perspectivas de trabajo *f pl*; ~ **rule** HRM norma de trabajo *f*, pauta de trabajo *f*; ~ **sampling** HRM muestreo del trabajo *m*; ~ **schedule** GEN COMM horario de trabajo *m*, MGMNT horario de trabajo *m*, plan de trabajo *m*, programa de trabajo *m*, TRANSP horario de trabajo *m*; ~ **sharing** HRM trabajo compartido *m*; ~ **sheet** COMP hoja de programación *f*; ~ **simplification** HRM, MGMNT simplificación del trabajo *f*; ~ **stoppage** HRM interrupción del trabajo *f*; ~ **stress** HRM, MGMNT estrés laboral *m*; ~ **structuring** GEN COMM estructuración del trabajo *f*, HRM estructura laboral *f*; ~ **study** GEN COMM, HRM, MGMNT estudio del trabajo *m*; ~**-to-rule** HRM, IND huelga de celo *f*; ♦ **at** ~ GEN COMM *process, machine* en marcha

work[3] **1.** *vt* GEN COMM funcionar, trabajar, HRM trabajar, PATENTS *patent* explotar; ♦ ~ **closely with** GEN COMM, HRM trabajar en estrecha colaboración con; ~ **in**

partnership with MGMNT trabajar en sociedad con; ~ **in tandem with** GEN COMM trabajar a medias con; **2.** *vi* GEN COMM funcionar, trabajar, HRM trabajar; ◆ ~ **alongside** HRM trabajar codo con codo; ~ **alternate weekends** GEN COMM trabajar fines de semana alternos; ~ **as part of a team** HRM trabajar como parte de un equipo; ~ **for a living** WEL trabajar para ganarse la vida; ~ **full time** HRM trabajar a tiempo completo; ~ **in the media** MEDIA trabajar en medios de comunicación; ~ **in shifts** HRM trabajar por turnos; ~ **like a beaver** *infrml* HRM trabajar incansablemente; ~ **overtime** HRM trabajar horas extras; ~ **to a very tight schedule** GEN COMM trabajar en un horario muy preciso; ~ **together** GEN COMM trabajar juntos, colaborar; ~ **unsocial hours** HRM trabajar en horarios insociables

work on *vt* GEN COMM trabajar en

work out *vt* GEN COMM *settlement* lograr, *terms, details* concretar

work share *vi* HRM compartir el trabajo

workable: ~ **competition** *n* ECON competencia viable *f*; ~ **hatch** *n* (*WH*) TRANSP *charter party* escotilla practicable *f*

workaholic *n* HRM adicto(-a) al trabajo *m,f*

workday *n* *AmE* (*cf working day BrE*) GEN COMM, HRM día de trabajo *m*, día laborable *m*, jornada laboral *f*

worker *n* GEN COMM operario(-a) *m,f*, obrero(-a) *m,f*, HRM trabajador(a) *m,f*; ~ **buy-out** FIN compra por los trabajadores *f*; **manual** ~ HRM, IND obrero(-a) manual *m,f*; ~ **compensation insurance** HRM, INS seguro de compensaciones laborales *m*; ~ **control** HRM control de los trabajadores *m*; ~ **director** HRM delegado(-a) de planta *m,f*; ~ **involvement** HRM *in organization's activities* implicación de los empleados *f*, implicación de los trabajadores *f*; ~ **representation** HRM representación de los trabajadores *f*

workers': ~ **collective** *n* HRM colectivo de trabajadores *m*; ~ **compensation** *n* HRM compensación a los trabajadores *f*; ~ **compensation act** *n* HRM, LAW ley de remuneración a los trabajadores *f*; ~ **compensation and employers' liability agreement** *n* INS acuerdo asegurador de responsabilidad civil y salarial del empresario *m*

workfare *n* ECON precio del trabajo *m*

workforce: ~ **rating** *n* HRM categoría de los trabajadores *f*

working *n* GEN COMM *functioning* funcionamiento *m*, *gainful employment* trabajo *m*; ~ **account** BANK cuenta de trabajo *f*; ~ **area** COMP, HRM *in office* zona de trabajo *f*; ~ **asset** ACC activo de explotación *m*; ~ **capital** ACC capital de explotación *m*, fondo de maniobra *m*, BANK capital circulante *m*, ECON, FIN, GEN COMM capital circulante *m*, capital de explotación *m*; ~ **capital advance** FIN, POL adelanto de capital circulante *m*; ~ **capital ratio** FIN proporción de fondo de maniobra *f*; **the** ~ **class** HRM la clase trabajadora *f*; ~ **conditions** *n pl* HRM condiciones de trabajo *f pl*; ~ **control** FIN, GEN COMM control efectivo *m*; ~ **copy** TAX *return* borrador *m*; ~ **day** *BrE* (*cf workday AmE*) GEN COMM, HRM día de trabajo *m*, día laborable *m*, jornada laboral *f*; ~ **environment** HRM ambiente laboral *m*; ~ **group** POL grupo de trabajo *m*; ~ **holiday** GEN COMM día feriado *m*; ~ **hypothesis** GEN COMM hipótesis de trabajo *f*; ~ **interest** FIN participación en la explotación *f*;

~ **meeting** ACC encuentro de trabajo *m*; ~ **paper** POL documento de trabajo *m*; ~ **papers** ACC *audit* documentación auxiliar contable *f*, papeles de trabajo *m pl*; ~ **party** (*WIP*) GEN COMM grupo de trabajo *m*, HRM, POL reunión de trabajo *f*; ~ **pattern** HRM norma de trabajo *f*, pauta de trabajo *f*; ~ **population** ECON, HRM población activa *f*; ~ **practice** GEN COMM práctica laboral *f*; ~ **pressure** TRANSP presión de trabajo *f*; ~ **ratio** ACC coeficiente de explotación *m*; ~ **session** ACC sesión de trabajo *f*; ~ **storage** COMP almacenamiento de trabajo *m*; ~ **time** GEN COMM, MGMNT, TRANSP horario de trabajo *m*; **all** ~ **time saved** TRANSP ahorrado todo el tiempo laborable; ~ **timetable** GEN COMM, MGMNT, TRANSP horario de trabajo *m*; ~ **visa** HRM, LAW, WEL permiso de trabajo *m*; ~ **week** *BrE* (*cf workweek AmE*) HRM semana laborable *f*

workless *adj* GEN COMM desempleado

workload *n* HRM carga de trabajo *f*, *task* cantidad de trabajo *f*, MGMNT cantidad de trabajo *f*

workmate *n* HRM compañero(-a) *m,f*, compañero(-a) de trabajo *m,f*

workplace *n* GEN COMM *company, organization, building* lugar de trabajo *m*; ~ **bargaining** HRM negociación en el lugar de trabajo *f*

works: ~ **committee** *n* *BrE* HRM comité de empresa *m*; ~ **contract** *n* GEN COMM contrato de obras *m*; ~ **council** *n* *BrE* HRM comité de trabajadores *m*; ~ **manager** *n* HRM, IND, MGMNT director de fábrica *m*, director de la planta *m*, gerente de fábrica *mf*; ~ **regulation** *n* HRM reglamento laboral *m*

Works: ~ **Council** *n* HRM *EU* comisión de operarios *f*

worksheet *n* ACC hoja de trabajo *f*

workshop *n* GEN COMM *training* taller *m*, IND taller *m*, taller artesanal *m*; ~ **bargaining** GEN COMM, HRM, IND, LAW negociación en la fábrica *f*

workspace *n* HRM área de trabajo *f*

workstation *n* ADMIN, COMP, HRM estación de trabajo *f*

workweek *n* *AmE* (*cf working week BrE*) HRM semana laborable *f*

world *n* GEN COMM mundo *m*; ~~**class** GEN COMM clase mundial *f*; ~ **consumption** ECON consumo mundial *m*; ~ **debt problem** ECON, POL problema de la deuda mundial *m*; ~ **economic groupings** *n pl* ECON agrupaciones económicas mundiales *f pl*; ~ **economy** ECON, POL economía mundial *f*; ~ **exports** *n pl* IMP/EXP exportaciones mundiales *f pl*; ~ **fair** GEN COMM feria mundial *f*; ~ **of finance** FIN mundo de las finanzas *m*; ~ **inflation** ECON inflación mundial *f*; ~ **leader** S&M líder mundial *mf*; ~ **market** ECON, POL, S&M mercado mundial *m*; ~ **monetary reserve assets** FIN activos de la reserva monetaria mundial *m pl*; ~ **monetary system** ECON, FIN sistema monetario mundial *m*; ~ **money order** BANK giro postal internacional *m*; ~ **price** ECON precio mundial *m*; ~ **systems perspective** ECON perspectiva de los sistemas mundiales *f*; ~ **trade** ECON, POL comercio mundial *m*; ~ **trade route** TRANSP *shipping* ruta comercial internacional *f*; ~ **welfare** ECON, POL bienestar mundial *m*; ◆ **all over the** ~ GEN COMM en todo el mundo

World: ~ **Bank** *n* BANK Banco Mundial *m*; ~ **Bank Capital Markets System** *n* (*CMS*) BANK, STOCK Sistema de Mercados de Capital del Banco Mundial *m*; ~ **Bank classification of countries** *n* BANK clasificación de países del Banco Mundial *f*; ~ **Bank Group** *n*

BANK, ECON, FIN Grupo del Banco Mundial *m*; ~ **Federation of Stock Exchanges** *n* (*WFSE*) STOCK Federación Mundial de Bolsas; ~ **Federation of Trade Unions** *n* (*WFTU*) HRM federación mundial de sindicatos; ~ **Federation of United Nations Associations** *n* (*WFUNA*) POL Federación Mundial de Asociaciones de las Naciones Unidas *f* (*FMANU*); ~ **Food Programme** *n* (*WFP*) ECON, POL Programa Mundial de Alimentación *m*; ~ **Health Organization** *n* (*WHO*) POL, WEL Organización Mundial de la Salud *f* (*OMS*); ~ **Intellectual Property Organization** *n* (*WIPO*) LAW Organización Mundial para la Propiedad Intelectual *f*; ~ **Power Conference** *n* ENVIR Conferencia Mundial de la Energía *f*; ~ **Trade Center** *n* *AmE* ECON centro del comercio mundial *m*; ~ **Trade Centre** *n* *BrE* ECON, S&M centro del comercio mundial *m*; ~ **Trade Centre** *n* (*WTC*) ECON, S&M centro del comercio mundial *m*; ~ **University Service** *n* (*WUS*) WEL servicio universitario mundial *m*; ~ **Wide Web** *n* (*WWW*) COMP Telaraña mundial *f*

worldscale *adj* TRANSP *shipping* a escala mundial

worldwide[1] *adj* GEN COMM universal, mundial

worldwide[2] *adv* GEN COMM universalmente

Worldwide: ~ **Air Cargo Commodity Classification** *n* (*WACCC*) TRANSP clasificación del transporte aéreo internacional de mercancías

worse: ~ **off** *adj* GEN COMM más pobre

worsen *vi* GEN COMM empeorar

worst: ~**-case projection** *n* ECON proyección del peor caso posible *f*; ~**-case scenario** *n* GEN COMM argumento de supuesto pésimo *m*, escenario para el peor de los casos *m*

worth[1] *n* GEN COMM *monetary* valor *m*, HRM *merit* mérito *m*, valía *f*

worth[2]: **be** ~ *vt* GEN COMM valer

worth[3]: **not** ~ **a bean** *phr infrml* GEN COMM no valer un duro (*infrml*) (*Esp*); ~ **a mint** GEN COMM valer un potosí; **not** ~ **a penny** *phr* GEN COMM no valer un duro (*infrml*) (*Esp*)

worthless[1] *adj* GEN COMM sin valor

worthless[2]: ~ **check** *AmE*, ~ **cheque** *BrE* *n* BANK, FIN cheque sin valor *m*

worthwhile *adj* GEN COMM que vale la pena

wove: ~ **paper** *n* ADMIN papel avitelado *m*

wp *abbr* (*without prejudice*) INS sin prejuicio

WP *abbr* ADMIN, COMP (*word processor*) WP (*procesado de texto AmL, procesador de textos Esp*), GEN COMM, TRANSP (*weather permitting*) si el tiempo lo permite

W/P *abbr* (*working party*) GEN COMM grupo de trabajo *m*

W.P.A *abbr* (*with particular average*) INS con avería particular

wpm *abbr* (*words per minute*) ADMIN, HRM ppm (*palabras por minuto*)

WR *abbr* (*warehouse receipt*) IMP/EXP, TRANSP certificado de depósito *m* (*CD*) recibo de almacén *m*

wrap: ~**-up** *n* *AmE* MGMNT resumen *m*

wrap up *vt* GEN COMM envolver

wraparound *n* COMP *memory* renovación *f*, *text* retorno de cursor *m*; ~ **annuity** FIN anualidad cruzada *f*, anualidad protegida *f*; ~ **mortgage** BANK, PROP hipoteca refinanciada *f*

wrapped *adj* GEN COMM recubierto

wrapper *n* GEN COMM cubierta *f*

wreck *vt* GEN COMM arruinar

wrecked: ~ **ship** *n* TRANSP resto de un naufragio *m*

wrinkle *n* *infrml* STOCK característica nueva *f*

writ: ~ **of attachment** *n* LAW mandamiento de embargo *m*; ~ **of error** *n* LAW auto de casación *m*; ~ **of sequestration** *n* LAW auto de embargo *m*; ~ **of subpoena** *n* LAW auto de requerimiento *m*

write[1]: ~**-down** *n* ACC, STOCK depreciación de un activo *f*; ~**-down of the value of assets** *n* ACC amortización de activos *f*, depreciación de los activos *f*, STOCK depreciación de los activos *f*; ~**-in candidate** *n* POL candidato(-a) añadido(-a) a la lista oficial *m,f*; ~**-in vote** *n* *AmE* POL voto en el que se escribe el nombre del candidato ya que no figura en la lista; ~**-off** *n* FIN cancelación total *f*, pérdida total *f*, siniestro total *m*, GEN COMM amortización *f*, anulación *f*, cancelación *f*; ~**-up** *n* GEN COMM revaluación *f*

write[2] **1.** *vt* COMP *in memory* escribir, GEN COMM redactar, STOCK *option* emitir; ♦ ~ **a check** *AmE*, ~ **a cheque** *BrE* BANK extender un cheque; ~ **a fair copy** GEN COMM pasar a limpio; ~ **an option against** STOCK vender una opción sobre; ~ **a stock option** STOCK suscribir una opción de compra de acciones; **2.** *vi* GEN COMM escribir

write against *vi* STOCK reajustar con referencia a

write back *vi* GEN COMM contestar por carta

write down *vt* ACC amortizar un activo, amortizar, reducir el valor contable de, GEN COMM depreciar

write off 1. *vt* ACC *entry* anular, cancelar, cancelar en libros, dar de baja, eliminar, BANK condonar; **2.** *vi* ACC amortizar

write-protect *vt* COMP proteger de escritura

write up *vt* ACC actualizar, poner al corriente, revalorizar

writer *n* FIN, GEN COMM, STOCK emisor(a) *m,f*

writing[1]: ~**-back** *n* ACC carta de respuesta *f*; ~ **cash-secured puts** *n pl* STOCK suscripción de opciones de venta con depósito en dinero *f*; ~ **down allowance** *n* TAX descuento con rebaja de valor *m*; ~ **naked** *n* STOCK suscripción sin garantía *f*; ~**-off** *n* ACC baja *f*, minoración de valor *f*

writing[2]: **in** ~ *phr* COMMS, GEN COMM por escrito; ~ **put to acquire stock** *phr* STOCK opción de venta suscrita para adquisición de acciones *f*

written: ~ **agreement** *n* LAW acuerdo por escrito *m*; ~ **call** *n* STOCK opción de compra emitida *f*; ~**-down value** *n* ACC valor amortizado *m*; ~ **evidence** *n* LAW prueba escrita *f*; ~ **line** *n* INS pleno de suscripción *m*; ~ **notice** *n* HRM aviso escrito *m*; ~ **offer** *n* GEN COMM oferta por escrito *f*; ~ **option** *n* STOCK opción emitida *f*; ~ **order to pay** *n* ACC orden escrita de pago *f*; ~ **put** *n* STOCK opción de venta emitida *f*; ~ **statement** *n* LAW declaración por escrito *f*; ~ **warning** *n* HRM, MGMNT advertencia escrita *f*

wro *abbr* (*war risk only*) INS sólo riesgo de guerra

wrong[1] *adj* GEN COMM falso, incorrecto; ♦ **be in the** ~ **job** HRM haberse equivocado de profesión

wrong[2]: ~ **connection** *n* COMMS *telephone* falsa llamada *f*

wrong[3]: ~**-foot** *vt* *infrml* GEN COMM desequilibrar

wrongdoing *n* LAW comisión de un delito *f*, comisión de una falta *f*

wrongful: ~ **dismissal** *n* HRM despido improcedente *m*

wrongly *adv* GEN COMM sin razón

wrongshipped *adj* GEN COMM mal transportado

wt. *abbr* (*weight*) GEN COMM peso *m*

WT *abbr* (*watertight*) TRANSP estanco al agua

WTC *abbr* (*World Trade Centre*) ECON centro del comercio mundial *m*

WUS *abbr* (*World University Service*) WEL servicio universitario mundial *m*

WW *abbr* (*warehouse warrant*) GEN COMM comprobante de almacén *m*, LAW duplicado del certificado de almacén *m*, garantía de almacén *f*

wwd *abbr* (*weather working days*) TRANSP días de trabajo con tiempo favorable *m pl*

WWW *abbr* (*World Wide Web*) COMP Telaraña mundial *f*

WYSIWYG *abbr jarg* (*what you see is what you get*) COMP programa que muestra por pantalla el documento tal y como será impreso

X Y Z

X[1] *abbr* (*telephone extension*) COMMS extensión telefónica *f* (*Esp*), interno telefónico *m* (*AmL*)

X[2]: **~ efficiency** *n* ECON eficiencia X *f*

xc. *abbr* (*ex cp., ex-coupon*) STOCK sin cupón

x-d. *abbr* (*ex-dividend*) FIN ex dividendo

xerographic *adj* ADMIN xerográfico

Xerox® *vt* ADMIN fotocopiar, xerografiar®

X-form *n* ECON *business organization division* forma X *f*

x-interest *n* FIN interés x *m*

xl&ul *abbr* (*exclusive of loading and unloading*) IMP/EXP, TRANSP exceptuando la carga y descarga, exclusivo de carga y descarga

x-pri *abbr* (*without privileges*) GEN COMM sin privilegios

x-quay *abbr* (*ex-quay*) IMP/EXP, TRANSP en el muelle, franco muelle

x-ship *abbr* (*ex-ship*) IMP/EXP, TRANSP *shipping* al costado del buque, sobre buque

x-wharf *abbr* (*ex-wharf*) GEN COMM, IMP/EXP, TRANSP sobre embarcadero, en el embarcadero

X-Y: **~ plotter** *n* ADMIN trazador de curvas X-Y *m*

yankee: **~ bond** *n* *AmE* FIN, STOCK bono yanqui *m*; **~ bond market** *n* *AmE* STOCK mercado de los bonos yanquis *m*

yankees *n pl jarg* STOCK *bonds* títulos estadounidenses *m pl*, yanquis *m pl*

YAR *abbr* (*York Antwerp Rules*) INS Reglas de York Amberes *f pl*

yard *n* (*yd*) ECON, GEN COMM yarda *f*, PROP *construction* patio *m*; **~ dolly** TRANSP plataforma móvil *f*

yardage *n* GEN COMM metraje *m*

yardstick *n* GEN COMM *to measure performance* criterio *f*

year[1]: **~-end** *adj* ECON de fin de ejercicio; **~-on-year** *adj* GEN COMM *decline* anual; **~-to-year** *adj* GEN COMM anual

year[2] *n* (*yr*) GEN COMM año *m*; **~ of acquisition** ACC año de adquisición *m*, año de la compra *m*, ejercicio de adquisición *m*; **~ of assessment** TAX año fiscal *m*; **~ of averaging** TAX año del promedio *m*; **~ end** ACC, GEN COMM fin de año *m*; **~-end adjustment** ACC ajuste de cierre de ejercicio *m*, regularización *f*; **~-end adjustments for accrued expenses** *n pl* FIN ajustes de fin de año por gastos acumulados *m pl*; **~-end audit** ACC auditoría de cierre de ejercicio *f*; **~-end closing** ACC cierre de ejercicio *m*; **~-end closing entry** ACC asiento de cierre de ejercicio *m*; **~-end dividend** ACC dividendo complementario *m*, dividendo complementario de fin de año *m*; **~-end procedures** *n pl* GEN COMM trámites de cierre de ejercicio *m pl*; **~ of grace survey** (*YGS*) TRANSP revisión del año de gracia *f*; **~ of issue** STOCK año de emisión *m*; **~ then ended** TAX año que acaba de finalizar *m*; ♦ **~ to date** ACC, TAX año hasta la fecha, ejercicio hasta la fecha; **in the ~ of** GEN COMM en el año de; **the ~ under review** GEN COMM el año a examen

yearbook *n* MEDIA anuario *m*

yearling *n* *BrE* (*cf government bond AmE*) ECON, STOCK bono del Estado *m*

yearly[1] *adj* GEN COMM anual

yearly[2] *adv* GEN COMM anualmente

yearly[3]: **~ allowance** *n* TAX anualidad *f*; **~ dividend** *n* GEN COMM dividendo anual *m*; **~ installment** *AmE*, **~ instalment** *BrE* *n* ACC, FIN, GEN COMM, INS cuota anual *f*; **~ payment** *n* GEN COMM pago anual *m*; **~ settlement** *n* ACC liquidación anual *f*, liquidación de fin de año *f*

yellow: **~-dog contract** *n* *AmE* HRM, LAW contrato con renuncia a la afiliación sindical; **~-dog fund** *n* *AmE* HRM previsión para los obreros sin filiación sindical; **~ goods** *n pl jarg* GEN COMM productos de la línea amarilla *m pl*; **~ sheets** *n pl* STOCK publicación diaria de la oficina nacional de cotizaciones; **strip** *n* STOCK cobertura amarilla *f*; **~ unions** *n pl jarg* HRM sindicatos con más lealtad a los empresarios que a los propios trabajadores

Yellow: **~ Book** *n* *BrE* STOCK libro amarillo *m*; **~ Pages**® *n pl* COMMS, S&M Páginas Amarillas® *f pl*

YGS *abbr* (*year of grace survey*) TRANSP *shipping* revisión del año de gracia *f*

yield[1] *n* ACC, FIN rendimiento financiero *m*, GEN COMM beneficio *m*, STOCK rendimiento financiero *m*; **~ adjustment** ACC ajuste de intereses *m*, ajuste de rendimientos *m*; **~ advantage** STOCK interés remunerativo *m*, ventaja remuneratoria *f*; **~ book** GEN COMM libro de rendimiento *m*; **~ comparison** STOCK *Treasury bonds* comparación de rendimiento *f*; **~ curve** BANK, ECON curva de rendimiento *f*; **~ equivalence** STOCK equivalencia de rendimiento *f*, equivalencia remunerativa *f*; **~ gap** ECON diferencial de rendimiento *m*, STOCK diferencia de rendimiento *f*; **~ load** TRANSP carga límite de rotura *f*; **~ maintenance** STOCK mantenimiento de rendimientos *m*; **~ per acre** ECON *agricultural* producción por acre *f*; **~ of a tax** TAX producto de un impuesto *m*; **~ to average life** STOCK rentabilidad a vida media *f*; **~ to call** GEN COMM rendimiento sobre pedido *m*; **~ to maturity** (*YTM*) BANK, FIN, STOCK rendimiento al vencimiento *m*; **~ to redemption** STOCK rentabilidad hasta el rescate *f*; **~ to worst** GEN COMM rendimiento a la baja *m*; **~ variance** GEN COMM variación de rendimiento *f*

yield[2] *vt* GEN COMM *profit* rendir, INS *negotiations*, LAW, PATENTS ceder; ♦ **~ a loss** STOCK producir una pérdida; **~ a profit** STOCK producir un beneficio

York: **~ Antwerp Rules** *n pl* (*YAR*) INS Reglas de York Amberes *f pl*

young: **~ offender** *n* *BrE* (*cf status offender AmE*) LAW delincuente juvenil internado en un centro de protección de menores; **~ upwardly mobile professional** *n* (*yumpie, yuppie*) GEN COMM joven profesional con ambiciones *mf*; **~ worker** *n* HRM trabajador(a) joven *m,f*

Yours: **~ faithfully** *phr* COMMS *letter-ending* le saluda atentamente; **~ sincerely** *phr* COMMS *letter-ending* le saluda atentamente

youth: **~ training** *n* *BrE* (*YT*) HRM aprendizaje juvenil *m*

yo-yo[1]: **~ stock** *n jarg* STOCK acciones de fluctuación volátil *f pl*

yo-yo[2] *vi jarg* GEN COMM fluctuar

yr *abbr* (*year*) GEN COMM año *m*

YT *abbr BrE* (*youth training*) HRM aprendizaje juvenil *m*

YTM *abbr* (*yield to maturity*) BANK, FIN, STOCK rendimiento al vencimiento *m*

yumpie *n infrml* (*young upwardly mobile professional*) GEN COMM joven profesional con ambiciones *mf*

yuppie *n infrml* (*young upwardly mobile professional*) GEN COMM joven profesional con ambiciones *mf*

zero: **be ~ rated for VAT** *phr* TAX ser tipo cero para el IVA

zip: **~ code** *n AmE* (*cf postcode BrE*) COMMS, GEN COMM código postal *m*

zonal: **~ distribution** *n* S&M distribución por zonas *f*

English–Spanish appendix/
Apéndice inglés–español

Contents/Índice de contenidos

Business correspondence and documents/ Correspondencia y documentos del mundo de los negocios

Job application/Carta de solicitud de empleo

Dear Ms Jones,

Application for the post of Technical Translator

I am writing in response to your advertisement in the August issue of the *ITI Bulletin* for the post of Technical Translator with Spanish.

I am an English native speaker and I am fluent in both French and Spanish. I took my first degree at the University of the West of England in 1992 and have been in continuous employment ever since. At present, I am working for British Telecom in the sales and export department as a translator, which requires a good command of business and technical Spanish.

While working as an editorial assistant and clerical assistant I gained general administrative skills in addition to the organizational skills needed to work as a translator. The use of IT systems was an integral part of my work, and I am also familiar with technical and scientific dictionaries as tools for translation.

I hope my application will be of interest to you and I would appreciate the chance to discuss it further.

I look forward to hearing from you.

Yours sincerely,

Anne Drummond

Curriculum vitae

NAME:	**Anne Drummond**
ADDRESS:	10 Keswick Road London SW10 3BA
TELEPHONE:	0171 772 2890
NATIONALITY:	British
DATE OF BIRTH:	12th September, 1969

EDUCATION

1993–1994   **University of Westminster**
Postgraduate diploma in Technical
and Specialized Translation
(part-time course) in French and Spanish

1992–1993   **INSEAD (European Institute of Business Administration),**
Fontainbleau, France
MBA course in French and Spanish

1988–1992   **University of the West of England**
BA (Hons) MODERN LANGUAGES
AND EUROPEAN STUDIES
(French and Spanish)

1982–1987   **South Hampstead High School, London**
9 'O' levels: English Language, English Literature,
Mathematics, French, German, Biology, Physics,
Geography, Home Economics

3 'A' levels: English, French, Spanish

WORK EXPERIENCE

May 1995–present   **British Telecom (BT), London**
Translator from Spanish into English. Duties include
coordinating and supervising the work of other translators
and undertaking technical and commercial translations for
the sales and exports department

January 1995–
May 1995   **European Parliament, Strasbourg, France**
Translator and ad hoc interpreter for the Department of the
Environment

February 1994–
November 1994   **Routledge Publishers, London**
Editorial Assistant on the Language and Linguistics book
list

August 1993 – December 1993	**Johnathan Allbright's Ltd, London** Clerical Assistant in Managing Director's office. Duties included general office administration and organizing hotels and travel for Managing Director
1987–1988	**Thomson Holidays** Tour representative on the Costa del Sol, Spain. The position involved greeting guests at the airport and directing them to their respective hotels, offering support and advice during their stay and coordinating excursions
OTHER SKILLS:	Word processing experience (WordPerfect 5.1, 6.1 & Word for Windows 6.0) Lotus 123, Microsoft Excel 5.0 Database experience including Foxpro Full, clean British driving licence
HOBBIES:	I enjoy travelling, skiing, aerobics, reading, singing and visiting the cinema, the theatre and art exhibitions
REFERENCES:	available on request

Offer of employment/Contrato de trabajo

Dear Ms Drummond,

I have pleasure in formally offering you the position of Technical Translator. The position is based at our offices in central London.

Salary
Your salary will be at the rate of £25,000 per annum, and your appointment will be subject to a probationary period which will not exceed twenty-four weeks. You will be informed by your Head of Department when your probationary period has ended. Luncheon vouchers are paid at the rate of £36.50 per month.

Hours of work
Your hours of work will be 9am to 5pm Monday to Friday, with one hour for lunch.

Holidays
The holiday year runs with the calendar year, and holiday entitlement is calculated on the basis of 22 working days in the first calendar year after joining, with one extra day per full year of service up to a maximum of 28 days. Holidays for the actual year of joining are calculated pro rata of 22 days. Holiday dates must be agreed with your line manager two weeks prior to the start of the leave period.

Notice Period
The period of notice of termination of employment will be one month on either side.

I would like you to take up your appointment on 15th November 1997. If there are any aspects of this proposal that you would like to discuss with me, please do not hesitate to telephone.

Will you please be good enough to let me have your acceptance of the appointment on the terms and conditions set out above by signing the attached copy of this letter and returning this to me as soon as possible.

Yours sincerely,

P Jones
Personnel Manager

I accept the above position in accordance with the terms and conditions set out above.

Signed .... Date ....

Balance sheet/Hoja de balance

	(millions of £)	
December 31	1996	1995
Assets		
Current assets:		
Cash and short-term investments, at cost which approximates market	37.2	50.1
Receivable from sale of property	46.7	-
Accounts receivable	91.9	84.4
Inventories	35.0	31.3
Prepaid expenses and other current assets	32.7	34.6
	243.5	200.4
Property	160.3	155.8
Equipment	76.2	72.8
Goodwill	196.9	156.5
Other assets	34.0	34.7
	710.9	620.2
Liabilities and shareholders' equity		
Current liabilities:		
Short-term indebtedness	1.6	22.4
Accounts payable	136.3	119.8
Deferred revenue	65.1	63.1
Current portion of long-term debt	7.7	2.6
Finance leases	11.0	0.5
	221.7	208.4
Long-term debt	281.6	317.4
Finance leases	31.5	36.2
Other liabilities	46.1	42.9
Deferred income taxes	38.8	34.3
	398.0	430.8
Shareholders' equity:		
Share capital	97.8	85.8
Cumulative translation adjustment	(27.4)	(35.4)
Retained earnings	242.5	139.0
	312.9	189.4
	710.9	620.2

Approved by the Board

Ken Knight, *Director*   Barry Brown, *Director*

Job titles used in commerce/Profesiones dentro del mundo de los negocios

in the UK and US *en el R.U. y los EE.UU.*	in Spain and Latin America *en España y América Latina*
account executive	*in finance* director,a de cuentas *m,f*, *in PR company, advertising* ejecutivo,-a de cuentas *m,f*
account manager	*in advertising* gerente de cuentas *mf*, jefe,-a de cuentas *m,f*, *in finance* director,a de cuentas *m,f*, gestor,a de cuentas *m,f*
accountant general	jefe,-a de contabilidad *m,f*
adjunct professor *AmE*	catedrático,-a adjunto(-a) *m,f*
administration officer	jefe,-a administrativo(-a) *m,f*
administrative agent	gestor,a administrativo(-a) *m,f*
administrative assistant	auxiliar administrativo(-a) *m,f*, administrativo,-a *m,f*
administrator	administrador,a *m,f*, gestor,a *m,f*, administrativo,-a *m,f*
advertising director	director,a de publicidad *m,f*
advertising manager	gerente de publicidad *mf AmL*, jefe,-a de publicidad *m,f*
advisor	consejero,-a *m,f*
after-sales manager	director,a de posventa *m,f*
agency representative	representante de agencia *mf*
area manager	gerente de área *mf*, gerente de zona *mf*
artistic director	director,a artístico(-a) *m,f*
asset manager	administrador,a de activos *m,f*
assistant controller	interventor,a adjunto(-a) *m,f Esp*
assistant director	director,a adjunto(-a) *m,f*, subdirector,a *m,f*
assistant director general	director,a general adjunto(-a) *m,f*
assistant general manager	subdirector,a general *m,f*, director,a general adjunto(-a) *m,f*
assistant head of section	jefe,-a auxiliar de sección *m,f*
assistant manager	director,a adjunto(-a) *m,f*, subdirector,a *m,f*, subgerente *mf*
associate director	director,a adjunto(-a) *m,f*
associate lecturer	profesor,a asociado(-a) *m,f*
associate manager	director,a adjunto(-a) *m,f*
associate professor *BrE*	catedrático,-a adjunto(-a) *m,f*
attorney-in-fact *AmE*	apoderado,-a *m,f*
auditor	auditor,a *m,f*, interventor,a de cuentas *m,f Esp*
authorized representative	representante autorizado(-a) *m,f*
bailiff	*property* administrador,a *m,f*
blue collar worker	obrero,-a *m,f*, trabajador,a de cuello azul
broker	*stock exchange* broker *mf*, corredor,a de bolsa *m,f*, comisionista *mf*
business manager	directivo,-a comercial *m,f*, director,a comercial *m,f*
businessman	comerciante *mf*, empresario,-a *m,f*, hombre de negocios *m*

in the UK and US *en el R.U. y los EE.UU.*	in Spain and Latin America *en España y América Latina*
careers advisor	orientador,a vocacional *m,f*, consejero,-a vocacional *m,f*
cargo inspector	inspector,a de carga *m,f*
cargo superintendent	inspector,a de carga *m,f*
cargo surveyor	supervisor,a de carga *m,f*
cash manager	jefe,-a de caja *m,f*
certified accountant	contable colegiado(-a) *m,f Esp*, contador,a colegiado(-a) *m,f AmL*
chairman	*of meeting, conference, company* presidente,-a *m,f*
chairman of the administrative board	presidente,-a del consejo de administración *m,f*
chairman of the board	presidente,-a del consejo *m,f*
chairman of the board of directors	presidente,-a de la junta directiva *m,f*, presidente,-a del consejo de administración *m,f*
chairman of the board of management	presidente,-a de la junta directiva *m,f*
chairman and chief executive *AmE*	presidente,-a y director,a general *m,f*, presidente,-a y director,a ejecutivo(-a) *m,f*, presidente,-a y director,a gerente *m,f*
chairman of the executive board	presidente,-a de la junta directiva *m,f*, presidente,-a del consejo de administración *m,f*
chairman of the executive committee	presidente,-a de la junta directiva *m,f*, presidente,-a del consejo de administración *m,f*
chairman and general manager	presidente,-a y director,a general *m,f*, presidente,-a y director,a ejecutivo(-a) *m,f*, presidente,-a y director,a gerente *m,f*
chairman and managing director *BrE*	presidente,-a y director,a ejecutivo(-a) *m,f*, presidente,-a y director,a gerente *m,f*, presidente,-a y director,a general *m,f*
chairman of the supervisory board	presidente,-a de la junta supervisora *m,f*
charge hand	capataz,a *m,f*
chartered accountant	contable colegiado(-a) *mf Esp*, contador,a colegiado(-a) *m,f AmL*
checker	*quality control* verificador,a *m,f*, revisor,a *m,f*
chief	jefe,-a *m,f*
chief accountant	jefe,-a de cuentas *m,f*
chief buyer	jefe,-a de compras *m,f*
chief clerk	contable principal *mf Esp*, contador,a principal *m,f AmL*
chief executive	director,a ejecutivo(-a) *m,f*, gerente general *mf*
chief executive officer *AmE*	director,a general *m,f*, gerente general *mf*, jefe,-a ejecutivo(-a) *m,f*, presidente,-a ejecutivo(-a) *m,f*
chief financial officer	director,a de finanzas *m,f*
chief immigration officer	jefe,-a de inmigración *m,f*
chief information officer	director,a de información *m,f*
chief inspector	inspector,a jefe(-a) *m,f*
Chief of Staff	*military* jefe,-a de Estado Mayor *m,f*
chief operating officer	director,a general *m,f*, director,a general de operaciones *m,f*
chief supervisor	supervisor,a en jefe *m,f*
civil servant	funcionario,-a *m,f*, funcionario,-a público(-a) *m,f*, funcionario,-a de la Administración *m,f*
claims manager	director,a de reclamaciones *m,f*, jefe,-a de reclamaciones *m,f*
clearance agent	*customs* agente de despacho de aduanas *mf*

in the UK and US *en el R.U. y los EE.UU.*	in Spain and Latin America *en España y América Latina*
co-director	codirector,a *m,f*
collector	*customs* cobrador,a *m,f*
co-manager	codirector,a *m,f*
commercial agent	representante de comercio *mf*
commercial and development manager	director,a comercial y de desarrollo *m,f*
commercial director	director,a comercial *m,f*, jefe,-a comercial *m,f*, directivo,-a comercial *m,f*
commercial manager	director,a comercial *m,f*, jefe,-a comercial *m,f*, directivo,-a comercial *m,f*
commercial traveler *AmE*	viajante de comercio *mf*
commercial traveller *BrE*	viajante de comercio *mf*
commission agent	comisionista *mf*
commission broker	comisionista *mf*
commission merchant	comisionista *mf*
commission salesman	vendedor,a a comisión *m,f*
commissionnaire	comisionario,-a *m,f*
company secretary	secretario,-a general *m,f*, secretario,-a de la empresa *m,f*
compliance accountant	interventor,a *m,f*
comptroller	contralor,a *m,f AmL*, director,a administrativo,-a *m,f*, inspector,a *m,f*, interventor,a *m,f Esp*
confidential secretary	secretario,-a de confianza *m,f*
consignor	expedidor,a *m,f*
consultant	consejero,-a *m,f*
consumer relations manager	director,a de atención al cliente *m,f*
contractor	contratista *mf*
contracts manager	director,a de contratos *m,f*, jefe,-a de contratos *m,f*
contracts officer	contratista *mf*, *works* listero,-a *m,f*
controller	contralor,a *m,f AmL*, director,a administrativo,-a *m,f*, inspector,a *m,f*, interventor,a *m,f Esp*
co-owner	codueño,-a *m,f*, condómino,-a *m,f*, copropietario,-a *m,f*
convenor	*in the workplace* representante sindical *mf*, *committee* presidente,-a *m,f*, organizador,a de una reunión *m,f*
corporate executive	ejecutivo,-a de empresa *m,f*, ejecutivo,-a de una corporación *m,f*
courier	*transport* mensajero,-a *m,f*
credit controller	supervisor,a de cobro *m,f*, supervisor,a de crédito *m,f*
cultural attaché	agregado,-a cultural *m,f*
customer relations manager	director,a de atención al cliente *m,f*
customs broker	agente de aduanas *mf*, oficial,a de aduanas *m,f*
customs clearance agent	agente de despacho de aduanas *mf*
customs officer	agente de aduanas *mf*, oficial,a de aduanas *m,f*
dealer	comerciante *mf*
defence advisor *BrE*	consejero,-a de defensa *m,f*
defence attaché *BrE*	agregado,-a de defensa *m,f*, agregado,-a militar *m,f*
defense advisor *AmE*	consejero,-a de defensa *m,f*
defense attaché *AmE*	agregado,-a de defensa *m,f*, agregado,-a militar *m,f*
department head	*company* director,a de departamento *m,f*, jefe,-a de departamento *m,f*
departmental manager	gerente de departamento *mf*, jefe,-a de servicio *m,f*
deputy	suplente *mf*
deputy chairman	vicepresidente,-a *m,f*

in the UK and US *en el R.U. y los EE.UU.*	in Spain and Latin America *en España y América Latina*
deputy chairman of the supervisory board	vicepresidente,-a del consejo *m,f*
deputy chairman of the board of management	vicepresidente,-a del consejo *m,f*
deputy chief executive	director,a ejecutivo(-a) adjunto(-a) *m,f*
deputy director	director,a adjunto(-a) *m,f*, subgerente *mf*
deputy manager	director,a adjunto(-a) *m,f*, gerente adjunto(-a) *m,f*, subdirector,a *m,f*, subgerente *mf*
deputy managing director	subdirector,a gerente *m,f*, director,a ejecutivo(-a) adjunto(-a) *m,f*
deputy member of the board of management	suplente de la junta directiva *mf*
deputy receiver general	interventor,a general adjunto(-a) *m,f Esp*
development director	director,a de desarrollo *m,f*
development manager	director,a de desarrollo *m,f*
director	consejero,-a *m,f*, presidente,-a *m,f*, consejero,-a de administración *m,f*, director,a *m,f*
director-general	director,a general *m,f*
director of labor relations *AmE*	director,a de relaciones laborales *m,f*
director of labour relations *BrE*	director,a de relaciones laborales *m,f*
director of public relations	director,a de relaciones públicas *m,f*
disburser	pagador,a *m,f*
dispatcher	expedidor,a *m,f*
district manager	gerente regional *mf*, director,a provincial *m,f*, gerente de territorio *mf*, jefe,-a de distrito *m,f*
district officer	oficial,a de distrito *m,f*
district traffic superintendent	superintendente de tráfico *mf*
district training officer	oficial,a de formación de distrito *m,f*
division head	jefe,-a de división *m,f*, jefe,-a de sección *m,f*, director,a de división *m,f*, gerente de división *mf*
division manager	jefe,-a de división *m,f*, jefe,-a de sección *m,f*, director,a de división *m,f*, gerente de división *mf*
door-to-door salesman	vendedor,a a domicilio *m,f*
duty officer	oficial,a de guardia *m,f*
employer	empresario,-a *m,f*, patrón,-ona *m,f*
engineering manager	director,a técnico(-a) *m,f*
entrepreneur	empresario,-a *m,f*
estate manager	administrador,a de fincas *m,f*, administrador,a de bienes *m,f*, administrador,a de herencias *m,f*, administrador,a de propiedades *m,f*
executive director	director,a ejecutivo(-a) *m,f*
executive manager	director,a ejecutivo(-a) *m,f*, gerente ejecutivo(-a) *m,f*
executive officer	oficial,a ejecutivo(-a) *m,f*
executive vice president	vicepresidente,-a ejecutivo(-a) *m,f*
exchange control officer	oficial,a de control de divisas *m,f*
export agent	comisionista de exportación *mf*, agente de exportación *mf*
export clerk	empleado,-a de exportación *m,f*, oficial,a de exportación *m,f*
export coordinator	coordinador,a de exportación *m,f*
export manager	director,a de exportación *m,f*, jefe,-a de exportación *m,f*
export marketing manager	director,a de marketing para la exportación *m,f*
export merchant	exportador,a *m,f*
exporter	exportador,a *m,f*

in the UK and US *en el R.U. y los EE.UU.*	in Spain and Latin America *en España y América Latina*
external director	director,a externo(-a) *m,f*
ferry line manager	director,a de línea de transbordadores *m,f*
field sales manager	director,a de ventas de campo *m,f*
financial accountant	interventor,a *m,f*, contable financiero(-a) *m,f Esp*, contador,a financiero(-a) *m,f AmL*
financial manager	gerente financiero(-a) *m,f*
first-line manager	gerente de primera línea *mf*, supervisor,a de primera línea *m,f*, encargado,-a *m,f*, supervisor,a *m,f*
first-line supervisor	supervisor,a de primera línea *m,f*
first vice president	vicepresidente,-a primero(-a) *m,f*
floor manager *BrE*	jefe,-a de sección *m,f*, jefe,-a de planta *m,f*
floorwalker *AmE*	jefe,-a de sección *m,f*, jefe,-a de planta *m,f*
foreman	capataz,a *m,f*, sobrestante *mf*
forwarder	expedidor,a *m,f*
forwarding clerk	expedidor,a *m,f*
full-time lecturer	profesor,a a tiempo completo *m,f*
general counsel *AmE*	director,a jurídico(-a) *m,f*
general executive manager	director,a general ejecutivo(-a) *m,f*, gerente general ejecutivo(-a) *m,f*
general manager *AmE*	director,a general *m,f*
general partner	socio,-a colectivo(-a) *m,f*
general secretary	secretario,-a general *m,f*
group leader	jefe,-a de grupo *m,f*, líder de grupo *mf*
head	jefe,-a *m,f*
head buyer	director,a de compras *m,f*, jefe,-a de compras *m,f*, responsable de compras *mf*
head clerk	jefe,-a de oficina *m,f*
head of department	jefe,-a de departamento *m,f*, jefe,-a de sección *m,f*
head foreman	jefe,-a de taller *m,f*, supervisor,a en jefe *m,f*
head of legal department *BrE*	director,a jurídico(-a) *m,f*
head of personnel	director,a de personal *m,f*, jefe,-a de negociado *m,f*
head of section	director,a de división *m,f*, director,a de planta *m,f*, gerente de división *m,f*, jefe,-a de sección *m,f*
head of unit	jefe,-a de unidad *m,f*
health officer	inspector,a de sanidad *m,f*
honorary chairman	presidente,-a honorario(-a) *m,f*
honorary chairman of the board of directors	presidente,-a honorario(-a) de la junta de directores *m,f*
honorary president	presidente,-a honorario(-a) *m,f*
human resources director	director,a de recursos humanos *m,f*
human resources manager	jefe,-a de negociado *m,f*, jefe,-a de personal *m,f*
immigration officer	funcionario,-a de inmigración *m,f*
import clerk	funcionario,-a de importación *m,f*
import documentation supervisor	supervisor,a de documentación de importación *m,f*
import groupage operator	agente de agrupamiento de importaciones *mf*
import manager	director,a de importación *m,f*
import sales executive	ejecutivo,-a de ventas de importación *m,f*
industrial relations director	director,a de relaciones industriales *m,f*
industrial relations manager	gerente de relaciones industriales *mf*, jefe,-a de relaciones industriales *m,f*

in the UK and US *en el R.U. y los EE.UU.*	in Spain and Latin America *en España y América Latina*
information officer	responsable de información *mf*
inspector	inspector,a *m,f*
inspector general of banks	inspector,a general de banca *m,f*
inspector of taxes	inspector,a de Hacienda *m,f*
joint auditor	coauditor,a *m,f*
joint director	codirector,a *m,f*
joint manager	cogerente *mf*
joint owner	codueño,-a *m,f*, cogerente *m,f*, condómino,-a *m,f*, copropietario,-a *m,f*
land agent	administrador,a de fincas *m,f*, corredor,a de fincas *m,f*
landing officer *BrE*	oficial,a de desembarque *m,f*, *shipping* oficial,a de descarga *m,f*
leader	jefe,-a *m,f*, líder *mf*
lecturer	*teaching* profesor,a *m,f*, *visitor* conferenciante *mf*, conferencista *mf*
limited liability partner	socio,-a comanditario(-a) *m,f*
limited owner	socio,-a comanditario(-a) *m,f*
limited partner	socio,-a comanditario(-a) *m,f*, comanditario,-a *m,f*, socio,-a limitado(-a) *m,f*
line assistant	asistente,-a de línea *m,f*, ayudante,-a de línea *m,f*
line executive	ejecutivo,-a de línea *m,f*
line manager	gerente de línea *mf*
line supervisor	supervisor,a de línea *m,f*
liner broker	consignatario,-a de línea marítima *m,f*
loading agent	agente de carga *mf*
loss adjuster	tasador,a de pérdidas *m,f*
machine operator	maquinista *mf*
mail clerk *AmE*	empleado,-a postal *m,f*
main owner	propietario,-a principal *m,f*
manager	director,a *m,f*, gerente *mf*, jefe,-a *m,f*, apoderado,-a *m,f*, manager *mf*
managing director	director,a gerente *m,f*
managing partner	socio,-a administrador(a) *m,f*, socio,-a director(a) *m,f*
market analyst	analista de mercados *mf*
marketeer	experto,-a en marketing *m,f Esp*, experto,-a en mercadotecnia *m,f AmL*
marketing director	director,a de marketing *m,f Esp*, director,a de mercadotecnia *m,f AmL*
marketing executive	ejecutivo,-a de marketing *m,f Esp*, ejecutivo,-a de mercadotecnia *m,f AmL*
marketing manager	director,a de marketing *m,f Esp*, director,a de mercadotecnia *m,f AmL*
marketing officer	administrador,a de marketing *m,f Esp*, administrador,a de mercadotecnia *m,f AmL*
master owner	propietario,-a principal *m,f*
member	socio,-a *m,f*
member of the board of management	miembro del consejo de administración *mf*
member of the supervisory board	miembro del consejo de supervisión *mf*
merchandising director	director,a comercial *m,f*
merchandiser	comerciante *mf*
merchant	comerciante *mf*
messenger	mensajero,-a *m,f*

in the UK and US *en el R.U. y los EE.UU.*	in Spain and Latin America *en España y América Latina*
middle manager	directivo,-a medio(-a) *m,f*, gerente intermediario,-a *m,f*, gerente medio *mf*
motor transport officer	oficial,a de transporte motorizado *m,f*
multimodal transport operator	agente de transporte multimodal *mf*
national accounts manager	director,a de cuentas nacionales *m,f*
non-executive director	director,a sin funciones ejecutivas *m,f*
office manager	jefe,-a de oficina *m,f*, director,a de oficina *m,f*
officer	funcionario,-a *m,f*
official	*bank* apoderado,-a *m,f*, funcionario,-a *m,f*
operational manager	gerente de operaciones *mf*, director,a de operaciones *m,f*
operations director	director,a de operaciones *m,f*
operations manager	director,a de operaciones *m,f*, gerente de operaciones *mf*
organizer	*of conference, meeting* organizador,-a *m,f*
outside director	director,a externo(-a) *m,f*
overseer	capataz *mf*
owner-manager	gerente propietario,-a *m,f*
partner	socio,-a *m,f*
part-time lecturer	profesor,a a tiempo parcial *m,f*
payer *BrE*	pagador,a *m,f*
payor *AmE*	pagador,a *m,f*
paymaster	pagador,a *m,f*
personal assistant	secretario,-a particular *m,f*, secretario,-a personal *m,f*
personal secretary	secretario,-a personal *m,f*
personnel director	director,a de personal *m,f*
personnel officer	jefe,-a de personal *m,f*
personnel manager	director,a de personal *m,f*, gerente de personal *mf*, jefe,-a de negociado(-a) *m,f*, jefe,-a de personal *m,f*
plant manager	director,a de fábrica *m,f*
port director	director,a de puerto *m,f*
port manager	director,a de puerto *m,f*
post operations officer	encargado,-a de posoperaciones *m,f*
postal clerk *BrE*	empleado,-a postal *m,f*
postmaster general *BrE*	director,a general de correos y telégrafos *m,f*
president	presidente,-a *m,f*
President of the Government *AmE*	presidente,-a del gobierno *m,f*
president of the group executive board *AmE*	presidente,-a del consejo de administración *m,f*, presidente,-a de la junta directiva *m,f*
President of the Treasury *AmE*	presidente,-a del consejo del tesoro *m,f*
press officer	agregado,-a de prensa *m,f*, oficial,a de prensa *m,f*
Prime Minister *BrE*	primer(a) ministro,-a *m,f*
private attorney	apoderado,-a *m,f*
private secretary	secretario,-a particular *m,f*
procurement manager	jefe,-a de compras *m,f*
product manager	jefe,-a de producto *m,f*
production director	director,a de producción *m,f*
production manager	director,a de producción *m,f*, gerente de producción *mf*
production worker	obrero,-a manual *m,f*
professor	catedrático,-a *m,f*

in the UK and US *en el R.U. y los EE.UU.*	in Spain and Latin America *en España y América Latina*
project agent	agente de proyecto *mf*
project leader	director,a de proyecto *m,f*, jefe,-a de proyecto *m,f*
project manager	director,a de proyecto *m,f*, jefe,-a de proyecto *m,f*
property owner	propietario,-a *m,f*
proprietor	*of a business, patent* propietario,-a *m,f*
proxy holder	apoderado,-a *m,f*
publicity manager	director,a de publicidad *m,f*
public relations officer	funcionario,-a de relaciones públicas *m,f*
purchasing manager	director,a de compras *m,f*
rates clerk	funcionario,-a de tarifas *m,f*
rates officer	funcionario,-a de tarifas *m,f*
realtor *AmE*	corredor,a de fincas *m,f*, agente inmobiliario(-a) *m,f*, administrador,a de fincas *m,f*
receiver agent	agente consignatario(-a) *m,f*
recruiting officer	ejecutivo,-a de reclutamiento *m,f*, responsable de selección *mf*, responsable de contratación *mf*
recruitment consultant	asesor,a de selección *m,f*, asesor,a de contratación *m,f*
recruitment manager	gerente de contratación *mf*, jefe,-a de contratación *m,f*, ejecutivo,-a de reclutamiento *m,f*, jefe,-a de reclutamiento *m,f*
recruitment officer	ejecutivo,-a de reclutamiento *m,f*, jefe,-a de reclutamiento *m,f*, jefe,-a de contratación *m,f*
regional manager	director,a provincial *m,f*, jefe,-a provincial *m,f*
registered representative	representante autorizado(-a) *m,f*
research director	director,a de investigación *m,f*
restaurant proprietor	dueño,-a de restaurante *m,f*, propietario,a de restaurante *m,f*
restaurateur	dueño,-a de restaurante *m,f*, propietario,-a de resaurante *m,f*
runner	mensajero,-a *m,f*, corredor,a *m,f*
salaried agent	agente asalariado(-a) *m,f*
sales agent	agente de ventas *mf*
sales analyst	analista de ventas *mf*
sales director	director,a de ventas *m,f*
sales engineer	ingeniero,-a de ventas *m,f*
sales executive	ejecutivo,-a de ventas *m,f*, ingeniero,-a de ventas *m,f*
salesman	vendedor,a *m,f*, viajante *mf*
sales manager	director,a de ventas *m,f*, gerente de ventas *mf*, jefe,-a de ventas *m,f*
sales office manager	jefe,-a de oficina de ventas *m,f*
sales and purchase broker	agente de compraventa *mf*
sales representative	viajante de comercio *mf*, representante de ventas *mf*
section manager	gerente de área *mf*
sectorial manager	director,a provincial *m,f*, director,a regional *m,f*, director,a sectorial *m,f*, gerente regional *mf*
senior civil servant	funcionario,-a con antigüedad *m,f*
senior clerk	administrativo,-a superior *m,f*, jefe,-a administrativo(-a) *m,f*, contable principal *mf Esp*, contador,a principal *m,f*
senior executive	alto(-a) ejecutivo,-a *m,f*
senior export clerk	funcionario,-a principal de exportación *m,f*
senior import clerk	funcionario,-a principal de importación *m,f*
senior information officer	director,a de información *m,f*

in the UK and US *en el R.U. y los EE.UU.*	in Spain and Latin America *en España y América Latina*
senior manager	director,a ejecutivo(-a) *m,f*, director,a general *m,f*
senior officer	funcionario,-a superior *m,f*, funcionario,-a de rango superior *m,f*
senior vice president	vicepresidente,-a principal *m,f*, vicepresidente,-a adjunto(-a) *m,f*
service engineer	ingeniero,-a de funcionamiento *m,f*, ingenierio,-a de reparaciones *m,f*, ingenierio,-a de servicio *m,f*
shareholder *BrE*	accionista *mf*
shipper	expedidor,a *m,f*
shipping clerk	expedidor,a *m,f*
shipping and fowarding agent	agente de transportes marítimos *mf*, transportista *mf*
shipping officer	expedidor,a *m,f*
shop steward	enlace sindical *mf*, delegado,-a gremial *m,f*, representante obrero(-a) *m,f*, representante del personal *mf*
staff manager	gerente de personal *mf*, jefe,-a de personal *m,f*
stockbroker	broker *mf*
stock controller	controlador,a de existencias *m,f*, controlador,a de almacén *m,f*, jefe,-a de almacén *m,f*
stockholder *AmE*	accionista *mf*
stockjobber *AmE*	corredor,a de bolsa *m,f*
stockist agent	agente de existencias *mf*, agente de almacén *mf*
stockman *AmE*	almacenista *mf*, jefe,-a de almacén *m,f*, guarda de almacén *mf*
storeman *BrE*	almacenista *mf*, jefe,-a de almacén *m,f*, guarda de almacén *mf*
supervisor	supervisor,a *m,f*, apoderado,-a *m,f*
surveyor	*of land* agrimensor,a *m,f*, topógrafo,-a *m,f*, *of property* inspector,a *m,f*
switchboard operator	operador,a de teléfonos *m,f*
teacher	profesor,a *m,f*
team leader	jefe,-a de equipo *m,f*, líder del equipo *mf*
technical assistant	asistente,-a técnico(-a) *m,f*, ayudante técnico(-a) *m,f*
technical director	director,a técnico(-a) *m,f*
technical manager	director,a técnico(-a) *m,f*, gerente técnico(-a) *m,f*
temporary secretary	secretario,-a interino(-a) *m,f*, secretario,-a temporal *m,f*
top executive	alto(-a) ejecutivo,-a *m,f*
town planner	urbanista *mf*
trade representative	representante de comercio *mf*
trader	comerciante *mf*, corredor,a de bolsa *m,f*
traffic manager	gerente de tráfico *mf*, jefe,-a de movimiento *m,f*
traffic superintendent	superintente de tráfico *mf*
traffic supervisor	supervisor,a de tráfico *m,f*
trainee manager	aprendiz,a de administración *m,f*
training manager	director,a de prácticas *m,f*, jefe,-a de formación *m,f Esp*, jefe,-a de capacitación *m,f AmL*, formador,a *m,f Esp*, capacitador,a *m,f AmL*, oficial,a de formación *m,f Esp*, oficial,a de capacitación *m,f AmL*
training officer	responsable de prácticas *mf*, jefe,-a de formación *m,f Esp*, jefe,-a de capacitación *m,f AmL*, formador,a *m,f Esp*, capacitador,a *m,f AmL*, oficial,a de formación *m,f Esp*, oficial,a de capacitación *m,f AmL*

in the UK and US	in Spain and Latin America
en el R.U. y los EE.UU.	*en España y América Latina*

transport controller	controlador,a de transporte *m,f*
trade representative	representante de comercio *mf*
travel agent	agente de viajes *mf*
traveling salesman *AmE*	viajante de comercio *mf*
travelling salesman *BrE*	viajante de comercio *mf*
trustee	administrador,a fiducidiario(-a) *m,f*
undersecretary	vicesecretario,a *m,f,* subsecretario,-a *m,f*
urban planner	urbanista *mf*
vice-chairman	vicepresidente,-a *m,f*
vice chancellor	*British Universities* rector,a *m,f*
vice president	vicepresidente,-a *m,f*
vice secretary	vicesecretario,-a *m,f*
warehouse keeper *AmE*	almacenista *mf,* guarda de almacén *mf*
warehouseman *AmE*	almacenista *mf,* guarda de almacén *mf*
watchman	vigilante *mf*
white-collar worker	administrativo,-a *m,f,* trabajador,a de cuello blanco
works manager	director,a de fábrica *m,f,* director,a de la planta *m,f,* gerente de fábrica *mf*

Stock exchanges/Bolsas

English name	Country, city	Spanish name
Nombre inglés	País, ciudad	Nombre español
	UK	
	R.U.	
Association of International Bond Dealers	London	organismo autorregulador del mercado de eurobonos
Baltic Futures Exchange	London	Mercado de Futuros Báltico m
Baltic International Freight Futures Exchange	London	Bolsa Internacional Báltica de Futuros de Fletes f
Belfast Stock Exchange	Belfast	Bolsa de Valores de Belfast f
Birmingham Stock Exchange	Birmingham	Bolsa de Valores de Birmingham f
Glasgow Stock Exchange	Glasgow	Bolsa de Valores de Glasgow f
International Petroleum Exchange	London	Mercado Internacional del Petróleo m
International Primary Market Association	London	Asociación Internacional de Entidades del Mercado Primario de Bonos f
Liverpool Commodity Exchange	Liverpool	Mercado de Mercaderías de Liverpool m
Liverpool Stock Exchange	Liverpool	Bolsa de Valores de Liverpool f
London Commodity Exchange	London	Bolsa de Contratación de Materias Primas de Londres f
London Foreign Exchange Market	London	Mercado Londinense de Valores Extranjeros m
London Futures and Options Exchange	London	Mercado de Opciones y Futuros de Londres m
London International Financial Futures Exchange	London	Mercado de Futuros Financieros de Londres m
London Metal Exchange	London	Bolsa de Contratos Futuros sobre Metales f
London Stock Exchange	London	Bolsa de Valores de Londres f
London Stock Exchange Board	London	Junta Directiva de la Bolsa de Valores de Londres f
London Traded Options Market	London	Mercado de Londres de Opciones Negociadas m
Manchester Commodity Exchange	Manchester	Mercado de Mercaderías de Manchester m
Stock Exchange Alternative Trading Service	London	Sistema Operativo de Cotizaciones m

English name *Nombre inglés*	Country, city *País, ciudad*	Spanish name *Nombre español*
Stock Exchange Automated Quotation	London	Cotización automatizada del Mercado de Valores *f*
United Kingdom Stock Exchanges	London	Federación de Bolsas del Reino Unido *f*
Unlisted Securities Market	London	Mercado de Valores no Cotizados *m*
	US **EE.UU.**	
American Stock Exchange	New York	Bolsa Americana de Valores *f*
Amex Commodity Exchange	New York	Bolsa de Productos Amex *f*, Bolsa de Contratación Amex *f*
Boston Stock Exchange	Boston	Bolsa de Valores de Boston *f*
Chicago Board of Trade	Chicago	Mercado de Futuros de Chicago *m*
Chicago Board Options Exchange	Chicago	Mercado de Opciones de Chicago *m*
Chicago Mercantile Exchange	Chicago	Bolsa Mercantil de Chicago *f*
Chicago Rice and Cotton Exchange	Chicago	Bolsa de Arroz y Algodón de Chicago *f*
Chicago Stock Exchange	Chicago	Bolsa de Valores de Chicago *f*
Cincinnatti Stock Exchange	Cincinnatti	Bolsa de Valores de Cincinnatti *f*
Clearing House Interbank Payment System	New York	sistema de compensación y liquidación en el que intervienen más de 130 bancos, trabajando con divisas y eurodólares
Commodity Exchange Inc. of New York	New York	Mercado de Contratación de Derivados de Nueva York *m*
Commodities Futures Trading Commission	Washington	organismo estadounidense que regula los mercados de futuros
International Monetary Market	Chicago	Mercado Monetario Internacional *m*
Mid-America Commodity Exchange	Chicago	Bolsa de Productos Básicos de Medio América *f*
Midwest Stock Exchange	Chicago	Bolsa de Valores del Medio Oeste *f*
Minneapolis Grain Exchange	Minneapolis	Mercado del Cereal de Minneapolis *m*
New Orleans Commodity Exchange	New Orleans	Mercado de Mercaderías de Nueva Orleans *m*
New York Coffee, Sugar and Cocoa Exchange	New York	Bolsa de Café, Azúcar y Cacao de Nueva York *f*
New York Cotton Exchange	New York	Mercado de Algodón de Nueva York *m*

English name *Nombre inglés*	Country, city *País, ciudad*	Spanish name *Nombre español*
New York Cotton Exchange and Petroleum and Citrus Associates	New York	Mercado de Algodón, Petróleo y Asociados de Cítricos *m*
New York Curb Exchange	New York	Bolsa Secundaria de Nueva York *f*
New York Futures Exchange	New York	Mercado de Futuros de Nueva York *m*
New York Mercantile Exchange	New York	Bolsa Mercantil de Nueva York *f*
New York Stock Exchange	New York	Bolsa de Nueva York *f*
Pacific Stock Exchange (Los Angeles Stock Exchange *and* San Francisco Stock Exchange)	Los Angeles & San Francisco	Bolsa de Valores del Pacífico *f*
Philadelphia Stock Exchange	Philadelphia	Bolsa de Valores de Filadelfia *f*
Salt Lake City Stock Exchange	Salt Lake City	Bolsa de Valores de Salt Lake *f*
Spokane Stock Exchange	Spokane	Bolsa de Valores de Spokane *f*
	Belgium ***Bélgica***	
Euroclear	Brussels	Cámara de Compensación de Eurobonos *f*
	Latin America ***América Latina***	
Lima Stock Exchange	Lima	Bolsa de Lima *f*
Merval Stock Exchange	Buenos Aires	Bolsa de Argentina *f*
Mexico City Stock Exchange	Mexico City	Bolsa de Méjico *f*
Montevideo Stock Exchange	Montevideo	Bolsa de Montevideo *f*
Santiago Stock Exchange	Santiago	Bolsa de Santiago *f*
	Netherlands ***Países Bajos***	
European Options Exchange	Amsterdam	Mercado Europeo de Opciones *m*
	Spain ***España***	
Barcelona Stock Exchange	Barcelona	Bolsa de Barcelona *f*
Bilbao Stock Exchange	Bilbao	Bolsa de Bilbao *f*
Madrid Stock Exchange	Madrid	Bolsa de Madrid *f*
Valencia Stock Exchange	Valencia	Bolsa de Valencia *f*

Financial and economic indexes/
Índices financieros y económicos

English name	Spanish name
Nombre inglés	*Nombre español*

General coverage
Cobertura general

English name	Spanish name
bond index	cotización de bonos *f*
commodities index	índice de mercaderías *m*
composite index	índice mixto *m*
composite leading index	índice adelantado compuesto *m*
construction cost index	índice del coste de la construcción *m*
consumer price index	índice de precios al consumo *m*
cost-of-living index	índice del coste de la vida *m*
diffusion index	índice de difusión *m*
discomfort index	índice de malestar *m*
golds index	índice de acciones de las minas *m*
growth index	índice de crecimiento *m*
Herfindahl-Hirschman Index	índice Herfindahl-Hirschman *m*
implied price index	índice de precios implícitos *m*
index of coincident indicators	índice de indicadores coincidentes *m*
index of lagging indicators	índice de indicadores retardados *m*
index of leading indicators	índice de indicadores anticipados *m*, índice de indicadores adelantados *m*
index of longer leading indicators	índice de indicadores muy adelantados *m*
index of shorter leading indicators	índice de indicadores poco adelantados *m*
Laspeyre's Index	índice de Laspeyres *m*
Lerner Index	índice de Lerner *m*
market capitalization index	índice de capitalización bursátil *m*
market index	índice del mercado *m*
market value-weighted index	índice de valores estimados del mercado *m*
Paasche Index	índice de Paasche *m*
physical quality of life index	índice de calidad física de vida *m*
price index	índice de precios *m*
price-weighted index	índice de precios ponderados *m*
producer price index	índice de precios a la producción *m*
retail price index	índice de precios al por menor *m*
scarcity index	índice de la escasez *m*
share index	índice de cotización de acciones en bolsa *m*
stock exchange price index	índice de precios de la bolsa de valores *m*, índice de precios bursátiles *m*
stock indexes and averages	índices de la bolsa *m pl*, índices bursátiles *m pl*
stock market index	índice del mercado de valores *m*, índice bursátil *m*
stock market price index	índice de precios del mercado de valores *m*, índice de precios bursátiles *m*
stock price index	índice de cotización bursátil *m*
unit value index	índice de valor unitario *m*

English name	Spanish name
Nombre inglés	*Nombre español*

weighted index	índice ponderado *m*
wholesale price index	índice de precios al por mayor *m*

Australia
Australia

All Ordinaries Index	índice All Ordinaries *m*

Belgium
Bélgica

Eurodollar Index	índice del Eurodollar *m*

Finland
Finlandia

Unitas All Share Index	índice general de cotización de valores de la Bolsa de Helsinki

Hong Kong
Hong Kong

Hang Seng Index	índice Hang Seng *m*

International
Internacional

Capital International World Index	índice Mundial del Capital Internacional *m*
Forex index	índice de divisas *m*
Donoghue's Money Fund Average	promedio del fondo monetario Donoghue *m*
international monetary market certificate of deposit index	índice de certificados de depósito del mercado monetario internacional *m*
international monetary market three-month add-on index	índice de compra a plazo a tres meses del mercado monetario internacional *m*
international monetary market three-month discount index	índice de descuento a tres meses del mercado monetario internacional *m*
international monetary market treasury-bill index	índice de letras del tesoro del mercado monetario *m*

Italy
Italia

Comit Index	índice de las principales acciones de la Bolsa de Milán

Japan
Japón

Nikkei average	promedio Nikkei *m*, índice Nikkei *m*
Nikkei index	promedio Nikkei *m*, índice Nikkei *m*

Netherlands
Países Bajos

CBS Tendency Index	índice de valores CBS *m*

Spain
España

IBEX 35 Index	índice IBEX 35 *m*

English name	Spanish name
Nombre inglés	*Nombre español*

Switzerland
Suiza

Credit Suisse Index	índice del Crédito Suizo *m*

UK
R.U.

Financial Times Actuaries All Share Index, All Share Index	índice de precios de valores de los actuarios del Financial Times *m*
Financial Times Index, FT Index	índice del Financial Times *m*, índice del FT *m*
Financial Times Industrial Ordinary Share Index	índice bursátil de valores industriales del Financial Times *m*
Financial Times Stock Exchange 100 Share Index, FT-SE 100, Footsie	índice Footsie *m*
Financial Times Stock Exchange Eurotrack 100 Index, FT-SE Eurotrack 100 Index	índice Footsie Eurotrack 100 *m*
Financial Times Stock Exchange Eurotrack 200 Index, FT-SE Eurotrack 200 Index	índice Footsie Eurotrack 200 *m*
index of industrial production	índice de producción industrial *m*
Thirty-Share Index	índice de cotización de Treinta Valores *m*

US
EE.UU.

Barron's Confidence Index	índice de Confianza de Barron *m*
Dow Jones Index	índice Dow Jones *m*
Morgan Stanley Capital International World Index, MSCI Index	parámetros internacionales para la comparación de índices de futuros financieros
New York Stock Exchange Composite Index	índice compuesto de la Bolsa de Nueva York *m*
value line composite index	índice compuesto de fecha valor *m*
value line stock index	índice bursátil de fecha valor *m*

Countries and principal dependencies/
Países y dependencias principales

Countries and principal dependencies	Capital	Inhabitant	Official language(s)	Currency
Países y dependencias principales *	*Capital*	*Habitante ***	*Lengua(s) oficial(es) ****	*Moneda*
Afghanistan	Kabul	Afghan	Pashto/Pushtu, Dari	afghani
Afganistán	*Kabul*	*afgano,-a m,f*	*pashtu, dari*	*afganí m*
Albania	Tirana	Albanian	Albanian	lek
Albania	*Tirana*	*albano,-a m,f/ albanés,-esa m,f*	*albanés*	*lek m*
Algeria	Algiers	Algerian	Arabic	dinar
Argelia	*Argel*	*argelino,-a m,f*	*árabe*	*dinar argelino m*
American Samoa (US)	Fagatogo	Samoan	English, Samoan	US dollar
Samoa Estadounidense (EE.UU.)	*Fagatogo*	*samoano,-a m,f*	*inglés, samoano*	*dólar americano m*
Andorra	Andorra la Vella	Andorran	Catalan, French, Spanish	French franc, peseta
Andorra	*Andorra la Vella*	*andorrano,-a m,f*	*catalán, francés, español*	*franco francés m, peseta f*
Angola	Luanda	Angolan	Portuguese	kwanza
Angola	*Luanda*	*angoleño,-a m,f*	*portugués*	*kwanza f*
Anguilla (UK)	The Valley	Anguillan	English, Creole	East Caribbean dollar
Anguila/Anguila (R.U.)	*The Valley*	*de Anguila*	*inglés, criollo*	*dólar del Caribe Oriental m*
Antigua and Barbuda	St. John's	Antiguan/Barbudan	English	East Caribbean dollar
Antigua y Barbuda	*St. Johns*	*de Antigua y Barbuda*	*inglés*	*dólar del Caribe Oriental m*
Argentina	Buenos Aires	Argentinian/ Argentine	Spanish	peso
Argentina	*Buenos Aires*	*argentino,-a m,f*	*español*	*peso m*
Armenia	Yerevan	Armenian	Armenian	dram
Armenia	*Yereván*	*armenio,-a m,f*	*armenio*	*dram m*
Aruba (Netherlands)	Oranjestad	Aruban	Dutch	guilder
Aruba (Países Bajos)	*Oranjestad*	*arubeño,-a m,f*	*holandés*	*florín m*
Australia	Canberra	Australian	English	Australian dollar
Australia	*Canberra*	*australiano,-a m,f*	*inglés*	*dólar australiano m*
Austria	Vienna	Austrian	German	schilling
Austria	*Viena*	*austriaco,-a m,f*	*alemán*	*chelín m*
Azerbaijan	Baku	Azeri/Azerbaijani	Azeri, Russian	manat
Azerbaiyán	*Bakú*	*azerbaiyano,-a m,f*	*azerí, ruso*	*manat m*

Countries and principal dependencies	Capital	Inhabitant	Official language(s)	Currency
Países y dependencias principales *	*Capital*	*Habitante* **	*Lengua(s) oficial(es)* ***	*Moneda*
Bahamas	Nassau	Bahamian	English	Bahamian dollar
Bahamas	*Nassau*	*bahamense mf/ bahamés,-esa m,f/ bahameño,-a m,f*	*inglés*	*dólar de Bahamas m*
Bahrain/Bahrein	Manama	Bahraini	Arabic	Bahrain dinar
Bahrein	*Manama*	*bahreiní mf*	*árabe*	*dinar de Bahrein m*
Bangladesh	Dhaka	Bangladeshi	Bengali, English	taka
Bangladesh	*Dacca/Dhaka*	*bangladesí mf*	*bengalí, inglés*	*taka m*
Barbados	Bridgetown	Barbadian	English	Barbados dollar
Barbados	*Bridgetown*	*barbadense mf*	*inglés*	*dólar de Barbados m*
Belarus	Minsk	Belarussian	Belarussian	Belarussian rouble
Bielorrusia	*Minsk*	*bielorruso,-a m,f*	*bielorruso*	*rublo bielorruso m*
Belgium	Brussels	Belgian	French, Flemish, German	Belgian franc
Bélgica	*Bruselas*	*belga mf*	*francés, flamenco, alemán*	*franco belga m*
Belize	Belmopan	Belizean	English, Spanish	Belize dollar
Belice	*Belmopán*	*beliceño,-a m,f*	*inglés, español*	*dólar de Belice m*
Benin	Porto Novo	Beninese	French	CFA franc
Benín	*Porto Novo*	*beninés,-esa m,f/ aboense mf*	*francés*	*franco CFA m*
Bermuda (UK)	Hamilton	Bermudan/ Bermudian	English	Bermudian dollar
Bermudas (R.U.)	*Hamilton*	*de Bermudas*	*inglés*	*dólar de Bermudas m*
Bhutan	Thimphu	Bhutanese	Dzongka	ngultrum, Indian rupee
Bután	*Thimbu*	*butanés,-esa m,f*	*dzong-kha*	*ngultrum m, rupia india f*
Bolivia	La Paz (seat of government), Sucre (legal and judicial seat)	Bolivian	Spanish, Quechua, Aymara	boliviano
Bolivia	*La Paz (sede del gobierno), Sucre (sede legal y judicial)*	*boliviano,-a m,f*	*español, quechua, aimará*	*boliviano m*
Bosnia-Herzegovina	Sarajevo	Bosnian	Bosnian	Bosnian dinar
Bosnia-Herzegovina	*Sarajevo*	*bosnio,-a m,f*	*bosnio*	*dinar bosnio m*
Botswana	Gaborone	Botswanan	English, Setswana	pula
Botswana	*Gaborone*	*botsuano,-a m,f/ botsuanés,-esa m,f*	*inglés, setswana*	*pula m*
Brazil	Brasilia	Brazilian	Portuguese	cruzeiro
Brasil	*Brasilia*	*brasileño,-a m,f*	*portugués*	*cruzeiro m*
Brunei	Bandar Seri Begawan	Bruneian	Malay, English	Brunei dollar
Brunei	*Bandar Seri Begawan*	*de Brunei*	*malayo, inglés*	*dólar de Brunei m*

Countries and principal dependencies	Capital	Inhabitant	Official language(s)	Currency
Países y dependencias principales *	*Capital*	*Habitante* **	*Lengua(s) oficial(es)* ***	*Moneda*
Bulgaria	Sofia	Bulgarian	Bulgarian	lev
Bulgaria	*Sofía*	*búlgaro,-a m,f*	*búlgaro*	*lev m*
Burkina Faso	Ouagadougou	Burkinabe	French, Mossi	CFA franc
Burkina Faso	*Uagadugú*	*voltense mf*	*francés, mossi*	*franco CFA m*
Burundi	Bujumbura	Burundian	Kirundi, French	Burundi franc
Burundi	*Bujumbura*	*burundés,-esa m,f*	*kirundi, francés*	*franco Burundés m*
Cambodia	Phnom Penh	Cambodian	Khmer	riel
Camboya	*Phnom Penh*	*camboyano,-a m,f*	*khmer*	*riel m*
Cameroon	Yaoundé	Cameroonian	French, English	CFA franc
Camerún	*Yaoundé*	*camerunés,-esa m,f*	*francés, inglés*	*franco CFA m*
Canada	Ottawa	Canadian	English, French	Canadian dollar
Canadá	*Ottawa*	*canadiense mf*	*inglés, francés*	*dólar canadiense m*
Cape Verde Islands	Praia	Cape Verdean	Portuguese	Cape Verdean escudo
Cabo Verde	*Praia*	*caboverdiano,-a m,f*	*portugués*	*escudo Caboverdianos m*
Cayman Islands (UK)	George Town	Caymanian	English	US dollar
Islas Caimán (R.U.)	*George Town*	*de Caimán*	*inglés*	*dólar americano m*
Central African Republic	Bangui	from the Central African Republic	French, Sango	CFA franc
República Centroafricana	*Bangui*	*centroafricano,-a m,f/de la República Centroafricana*	*francés, sango*	*franco CFA m*
Chad	N'Djamena	Chadian	Arabic, French	CFA franc
Chad	*N'Djamena*	*chadí mf/chadiano,-a m,f*	*árabe, francés*	*franco CFA m*
Chile	Santiago	Chilean	Spanish	peso
Chile	*Santiago*	*chileno,-a m,f*	*español*	*peso m*
China	Beijing	Chinese	Chinese, Mandarin	yuan
China	*Pekín*	*chino,-a m,f*	*chino, mandarín*	*yuan m*
Christmas Island (Australia)	politically dependent on Canberra	Christmas Islander	English	Australian dollar
Christmas (Australia)	*depende políticamente de Canberra*	*de Christmas*	*inglés*	*dólar australiano m*
Cocos Islands/ Keeling Islands (Australia)	politically dependent on Canberra	Cocos Malay/Cocos Islander	English	Australian dollar
Islas Cocos/Islas Keeling (Australia)	*dependen políticamente de Canberra*	*de Cocos*	*inglés*	*dólar australiano m*
Colombia	Bogotá	Colombian	Spanish	Colombian peso
Colombia	*Bogotá*	*colombiano,-a m,f*	*español*	*peso colombiano m*
Comoros	Moroni	Comorian	French, Arabic	CFA franc
Comoras	*Moroni*	*comorano,-a m,f*	*francés, árabe*	*franco CFA m*

Countries and principal dependencies	Capital	Inhabitant	Official language(s)	Currency
Países y dependencias principales *	*Capital*	*Habitante* **	*Lengua(s) oficial(es)* ***	*Moneda*
Congo	Brazzaville	Congolese	French	CFA franc
Congo	*Brazzaville*	*congoleño,-a m,f/ congolés,-esa m,f*	*francés*	*franco CFA m*
Cook Islands (New Zealand)	Avarua	Cook islander	English, Rarotongan	New Zealand dollar
Islas Cook (Nueva Zelanda)	*Avarua*	*de Cook*	*inglés, rarotongano*	*dólar neozelandés m*
Costa Rica	San José	Costa Rican	Spanish	colón
Costa Rica	*San José*	*costarricense mf*	*español*	*colón m*
Croatia, Republic of	Zagreb	Croat/Croatian	Croatian	kuna
Croacia, República de	*Zagreb*	*croata mf*	*croata*	*kuna f*
Cuba	Havana	Cuban	Spanish	Cuban peso
Cuba	*La Habana*	*cubano,-a m,f*	*español*	*peso cubano m*
Cyprus	Nicosia	Cypriot	Greek, Turkish	Cyprus pound
Chipre	*Nicosia*	*chipriota mf*	*griego, turco*	*libra chipriota f*
Czech Republic	Prague	Czech	Czech	czech koruna
República Checa	*Praga*	*checo,-a m,f*	*checo*	*corona checa f*
Denmark	Copenhagen	Dane	Danish	Danish krone
Dinamarca	*Copenhague*	*danés,-esa m,f*	*danés*	*corona danesa f*
Djibouti	Djibouti	Djibuti/Djibutian	Arabic, French	Djibouti franc
Yibuti	*Yibuti*	*de Yibut*	*árabe, francés*	*franco de Yibuti m*
Dominica	Roseau	Dominican	English	East Caribbean dollar
Dominica	*Roseau*	*dominicano,-a m,f*	*inglés*	*dólar del Caribe Oriental m*
Dominican Republic	Santo Domingo	Dominican	Spanish	Dominican peso
República Dominicana	*Santo Domingo*	*dominicano,-a m,f*	*español*	*peso dominicano m*
Ecuador	Quito	Ecuadorian/ Ecuadoran	Spanish	sucre
Ecuador	*Quito*	*ecuatoriano,-a m,f*	*español*	*sucre m*
Egypt	Cairo	Egyptian	Arabic	Egyptian pound
Egipto	*El Cairo*	*egipcio,-a m,f*	*árabe*	*libra egipcia f*
El Salvador	San Salvador	Salvadoran	Spanish	colón
El Salvador	*San Salvador*	*salvadoreño,-a m,f*	*español*	*colón m*
England	London	Englishman, Englishwoman	English	Sterling pound
Inglaterra	*Londres*	*inglés,-esa m,f*	*inglés*	*libra esterlina f*
Equatorial Guinea	Malabo	Equatorial Guinean	Spanish	CFA franc
Guinea Ecuatorial	*Malabo*	*ecuatoguineano,-a m,f*	*español*	*franco CFA m*
Eritrea	Asmara	Eritrean	Arabic, English	birr
Eritrea	*Asmara*	*de Eritrea*	*árabe, inglés*	*birr m*
Estonia	Tallinn	Estonian	Estonian	kroon
Estonia	*Tallin*	*estoniano,-a m,f*	*estonio*	*corona f*

Countries and principal dependencies	Capital	Inhabitant	Official language(s)	Currency
Países y dependencias principales *	*Capital*	*Habitante* **	*Lengua(s) oficial(es)* ***	*Moneda*
Ethiopia	Addis Ababa	Ethiopian	Amharic	birr
Etiopía	*Addis Abeba*	*etíope mf/etiope mf/ abisinio,-a m,f*	*amárico/amhárico*	*birr m*
Faeroe Islands/ Faeroes (Denmark)	Tórshavn	Faeroese	Faeroese, Danish	Danish krone
Islas Feroe (Dinamarca)	*Thorshavn*	*de Islas Feroe*	*feroés, danés*	*corona danesa f*
Falkland Islands (UK)	Stanley	Falklander	English	Sterling pound
Islas Malvinas (R.U.)	*Stanley*	*malvinense mf*	*inglés*	*libra esterlina f*
Fiji	Suva	Fijian	English	Fiji dollar
Fiji	*Suva*	*fijiano,-a m,f*	*inglés*	*dólar de Fiji m*
Finland	Helsinki	Finn	Finnish, Swedish	markka
Finlandia	*Helsinki*	*finlandés,-esa m,f/ finés,-esa m,f*	*finlandés, sueco*	*marco m*
France	Paris	Frenchman, Frenchwoman	French	French franc
Francia	*París*	*francés,-esa m,f*	*francés*	*franco francés m*
French Guiana (France)	Cayenne	French Guianese/ Guianan	French	French franc
Guayana Francesa (Francia)	*Cayena*	*de la Guayana Francesa*	*francés*	*franco francés m*
French Polynesia (France)	Papeete	French Polynesian	French	Pacific franc
Polinesia Francesa (Francia)	*Papeete*	*de la Polinesia Francesa*	*francés*	*franco del Pacífico m*
Gabon	Libreville	Gabonese	French	CFA franc
Gabón	*Libreville*	*gabonés,-esa m,f*	*francés*	*franco CFA m*
Gambia	Banjul	Gambian	English	dalasi
Gambia	*Banjul*	*gambiano,-a m,f*	*inglés*	*dalasi m*
Georgia	Tbilisi	Georgian	Georgian	lari
Georgia	*Tiflis*	*georgiano,-a m,f*	*georgiano*	*lari m*
Germany	Berlin	German	German	German Mark
Alemania	*Berlín*	*alemán,-ana m,f*	*alemán*	*marco alemán m*
Ghana	Accra	Ghanaian	English	cedi
Ghana	*Acra*	*ghanés,-esa m,f*	*inglés*	*cedi m*
Gibraltar (UK)	Gibraltar	Gibraltarian	English	Sterling pound
Gibraltar (R.U.)	*Gibraltar*	*gibraltareño,-a m,f*	*inglés*	*libra esterlina f*
Greece	Athens	Greek	Greek	drachma
Grecia	*Atenas*	*griego,-a m,f/ heleno,-a m,f*	*griego*	*dracma m*
Greenland (Denmark)	Nuuk	Greenlander	Danish, Eskimo	Danish krone
Groenlandia (Dinamarca)	*Nuuk*	*groenlandés,-esa m,f*	*danés, esquimal*	*corona danesa f*

Countries and principal dependencies	Capital	Inhabitant	Official language(s)	Currency
*Países y dependencias principales**	*Capital*	*Habitante***	*Lengua(s) oficial(es)****	*Moneda*
Grenada	St. George's	Grenadian	English	East Caribbean dollar
Granada	*St. Georges*	*granadino,-a m,f*	*inglés*	*dólar del Caribe Oriental m*
Guadeloupe (France)	Basse-Terre	from Guadeloupe	French	French franc
Guadalupe (Francia)	*Basse-Terre*	*guadalupeño,-a m,f*	*francés*	*franco francés m*
Guam (US)	Agaña	Guamanian	English, Chamorro	US dollar
Guam (EE.UU.)	*Agaña*	*de Guam*	*inglés, chamorro*	*dólar americano m*
Guatemala	Guatemala City	Guatemalan	Spanish	quetzal
Guatemala	*Ciudad de Guatemala*	*guatemalteco,-a m,f*	*español*	*quetzal m*
Guinea	Conakry	Guinean	French	Guinean franc
Guinea	*Konakry*	*guineo,-a m,f/ guineano,-a m,f*	*francés*	*franco guineano m*
Guinea-Bissau	Bissau	from Guinea-Bissau	Portuguese	Guinea-Bissau peso
Guinea-Bissau	*Bissau*	*de Guinea-Bissau*	*portugués*	*peso de Guinea-Bissau m*
Guyana	Georgetown	Guyanese	English	Guyana dollar
Guyana	*Georgetown*	*guyanés,-esa m,f*	*inglés*	*dólar guyanés m*
Haiti	Port-au-Prince	Haitian	French	gourde
Haití	*Port-au-Prince*	*haitiano,-a m,f*	*francés*	*gourde m*
Holland/ Netherlands, the	Amsterdam, The Hague (*seat of government*)	Dutchman, Dutchwoman/ Netherlander	Dutch	guilder
Holanda/Países Bajos	*Amsterdam, La Haya (sede del gobierno)*	*holandés,-esa m,f/ neerlandés,-esa m,f*	*holandés*	*florín m*
Honduras	Tegucigalpa	Honduran	Spanish	lempira
Honduras	*Tegucigalpa*	*hondureño,-a m,f*	*español*	*lempira f*
Hong Kong (China)	Victoria	from Hong Kong	English, Chinese	Hong Kong dollar
Hong Kong (China)	*Victoria*	*de Hong Kong*	*inglés, chino*	*dólar de Hong Kong m*
Hungary	Budapest	Hungarian	Magyar, Hungarian	forint
Hungría	*Budapest*	*húngaro,-a m,f*	*magyar, húngaro*	*florín m*
Iceland	Reykjavik	Icelander	Icelandic	Icelandic krona
Islandia	*Reykiavik*	*islandés,-esa m,f*	*islandés*	*corona f*
Ireland, Republic of	Dublin	Irishman, Irishwoman	Irish Gaelic, English	Irish pound/punt
Irlanda, República de	*Dublín*	*irlandés,-esa m,f*	*gaélico irlandés, inglés*	*libra irlandesa f*
India	New Delhi	Indian	Hindi, English	Indian rupee
India	*Nueva Delhi*	*indio,-a m,f*	*hindi, inglés*	*rupia india f*
Indonesia	Jakarta	Indonesian	Bahasa Indonesia	Indonesian rupiah
Indonesia	*Yakarta*	*indonesio,-a m,f*	*bahasa indonesio*	*rupia indonesia f*
Iran	Tehran/Teheran	Iranian	Farsi	rial
Irán	*Teherán*	*iraní mf*	*farsi*	*rial m*

Countries and principal dependencies	Capital	Inhabitant	Official language(s)	Currency
Países y dependencias principales *	*Capital*	*Habitante* **	*Lengua(s) oficial(es)* ***	*Moneda*
Iraq/Irak	Baghdad	Iraqi/Iraki	Arabic	Iraqi dinar/Iraki dinar
Iraq/Irak	*Bagdad*	*iraquí mf*	*árabe*	*dinar iraquí m*
Israel	Jerusalem	Israeli/Israelite	Hebrew, Arabic	New shekel
Israel	*Jerusalén*	*israelí mf/israelita mf*	*hebreo, árabe*	*shekel m/siclo m*
Italy	Rome	Italian	Italian	lira
Italia	*Roma*	*italiano,-a m,f*	*italiano*	*lira f*
Ivory Coast	Yamoussoukro	Ivoirian	French	CFA franc
Costa de Marfil	*Yamaussoukro*	*marfileño,-a m,f*	*francés*	*franco CFA m*
Jamaica	Kingston	Jamaican	English	Jamaican dollar
Jamaica	*Kingston*	*jamaicano,-a m,f/ jamaiquino,-a m,f*	*inglés*	*dólar jamaicano m*
Japan	Tokyo	Japanese	Japanese	yen
Japón	*Tokio*	*japonés,-esa m,f*	*japonés*	*yen m*
Jordan	Amman	Jordanian	Arabic	Jordanian dinar
Jordania	*Ammán*	*jordano,-a m,f*	*árabe*	*dinar jordano m*
Kazakhstan	Alma-Ata	Kazakh/Kazak	Kazakh, Russian	tenge
Kazajstán	*Alma-Ata*	*kazajo,-a m,f*	*kazajo, ruso*	*tenge m*
Keeling Islands/ Cocos Islands (Australia)	politically dependent on Canberra	Cocos Malay/Cocos Islander	English	Australian dollar
Islas Keeling/Islas Cocos (Australia)	*dependen políticamente de Canberra*	*de Cocos*	*inglés*	*dólar australiano m*
Kenya	Nairobi	Kenyan	Swahili, English	Kenyan shilling
Kenia/Kenya	*Nairobi*	*keniata mf/ kenyano,-a m,f*	*suahili, inglés*	*chelín de Kenya m*
Kiribati	Bairiki	Kiribatian	English, Gilbertese	Australian dollar
Kiribati	*Bairiki*	*kiribatiano,-a m,f*	*inglés, gilbertés*	*dólar australiano m*
Kuwait	Kuwait City	Kuwaiti	Arabic	Kuwaiti dinar
Kuwait/Koweit	*Al-Kuwait*	*kuwaití mf*	*árabe*	*dinar kuwaití m*
Kyrgyzstan	Bishkek	Kyrgyzstani	Kyrgyz	som
Kirgüizistán	*Pishpek*	*kirguiz mf*	*kirguiz*	*som m*
Laos	Vientiane	Laotian	Lao	kip
Laos	*Vientiane*	*lao,-a m,f/ laosiano,-a m,f*	*laosiano*	*kip m*
Latvia	Riga	Latvian	Latvian/Lettish	lat
Letonia	*Riga*	*letón,-ona m,f*	*letón*	*lat m*
Lebanon	Beirut	Lebanese	Arabic	Lebanese pound
Líbano	*Beirut*	*libanés,-esa m,f*	*árabe*	*libra libanesa f*
Lesotho	Maseru	Basotho	Sesotho, English	loti
Lesoto	*Maseru*	*basoto,-a m,f*	*sesotho, inglés*	*loti m*
Liberia	Monrovia	Liberian	English	Liberian dollar
Liberia	*Monrovia*	*liberiano,-a m,f*	*inglés*	*dólar liberiano m*

Countries and principal dependencies	Capital	Inhabitant	Official language(s)	Currency
Países y dependencias principales *	*Capital*	*Habitante* **	*Lengua(s) oficial(es)* ***	*Moneda*
Libya	Tripoli	Libyan	Arabic	Libyan dinar
Libia	*Trípoli*	*libio,-a m,f*	*árabe*	*dinar libio m*
Liechtenstein	Vaduz	Liechtensteiner	German	Swiss franc
Liechtenstein	*Vaduz*	*liechtenstiense mf*	*alemán*	*franco suizo m*
Lithuania	Vilnius	Lithuanian	Lithuanian	Lithuanian lita
Lituania	*Vilna*	*lituano,-a m,f*	*lituano*	*lita lituana f*
Luxembourg	Luxembourg	Luxemburger	French, German	Belgian franc
Luxemburgo	*Luxemburgo*	*luxemburgués,-esa m,f*	*francés, alemán*	*franco belga m*
Macao (Portugal)	Macao City	Macanese	Portugese, Cantonese	pataca
Macao (Portugal)	*Ciudad de Macao*	*de Macao*	*portugués, cantonés*	*pataca f*
Macedonia, Republic of	Skopje	Macedonian	Macedonian	dinar
Macedonia, República de	*Skopje*	*macedonio,-a m,f*	*macedonio*	*dinar m*
Madagascar	Antananarivo	Malagasy	Malagasy, French	Malagasy franc
Madagascar	*Antananarivo*	*malgache mf*	*malgache, francés*	*franco malgache m*
Malawi	Lilongwe	Malawian	English, Chichewa	kwacha
Malawi	*Lilongwe*	*malawiano,-a m,fl malawí mf*	*inglés, chichewa*	*kwacha m*
Malaysia	Kuala Lumpur	Malaysian/Malay	Malay	Malaysian ringgit
Malasia	*Kuala Lumpur*	*malasio,-a m,fl malayo,-a m,f*	*malayo*	*ringgit de Malasia m*
Maldives	Malé	Maldivian	Divehi	Maldivian rupee
Maldivas	*Male*	*maldivo,-a m,f*	*maldivo*	*rupia maldiva f*
Mali	Bamako	Malian	French	CFA franc
Malí	*Bamako*	*maliense mf*	*francés*	*franco CFA m*
Malta	Valletta	Maltese	Maltese, English	Maltese pound
Malta	*La Valetta*	*maltense mfl maltés,-esa m,f*	*maltés, inglés*	*libra maltesa f*
Marshall Islands	Dalap-Uliga-Darrit	Marshallese	Marshallese	US dollar
Islas Marshall	*Dalap-Uliga-Darrit*	*de las Islas Marshall*	*marshalés*	*dólar americano m*
Martinique (France)	Fort-de-France	Martinican	French	French franc
Martinica (Francia)	*Fort-de-France*	*de Martinical martiniqueño,-a m,f*	*francés*	*franco francés m*
Mauritania	Nouakchott	Mauritanian	Arabic	ouguiya
Mauritania	*Nouakchott*	*mauritano,-a m,f*	*árabe*	*ouguiya m*
Mauritius	Port Louis	Mauritian	English, French	Mauritian rupee
Mauricio	*Port Louis*	*mauriciano,-a m,f*	*inglés, francés*	*rupia de Mauricio f*
Mayotte (France)	Mamoutzu	from Mayotte	French, Mahorian	French franc
Mayotte (Francia)	*Mamoutzu*	*de Mayotte*	*francés, mahoriano*	*franco francés m*
Mexico	Mexico City	Mexican	Spanish	Mexican peso
Méjico/México	*Ciudad de México*	*mejicano,-a m,fl mexicano,-a m,f*	*español*	*peso m*

Countries and principal dependencies	Capital	Inhabitant	Official language(s)	Currency
Países y dependencias principales *	*Capital*	*Habitante* **	*Lengua(s) oficial(es)* ***	*Moneda*
Micronesia, Federated States of	Palikir	from the Federated States of Micronesia	English	US dollar
Micronesia, Estados Federados de	*Palikir*	*de los Estados Federados de Micronesia*	*inglés*	*dólar americano m*
Moldova/Moldavia	Kishinev	Moldovan	Moldovan	Moldovan leu
Moldavia/Moldova	*Chisinau*	*moldavo,-a m,f*	*moldavo*	*leu moldavo m*
Monaco	Monaco	Monegasque	French	French franc
Mónaco	*Mónaco*	*monegasco,-a m,f*	*francés*	*franco francés m*
Mongolia	Ulaanbaatar/ Ulan Bator	Mongolian	Khalkha Mongol	tugrik
Mongolia	*Ulan Bator*	*mongol,a m,f*	*mongol khalkha*	*tugrik m*
Montserrat (UK)	Plymouth	Montserratian	English	East Caribbean dollar
Montserrat (R.U.)	*Plymouth*	*de Montserrat*	*inglés*	*dólar del Caribe Oriental m*
Morocco	Rabat	Moroccan	Arabic	dirham
Marruecos	*Rabat*	*marroquí mf*	*árabe*	*dirham marroquí m*
Mozambique	Maputo	Mozambican	Portuguese	metical
Mozambique	*Maputo*	*mozambiqueño,-a m,f/ mozambiqués,-esa m,f*	*portugués*	*metical m*
Myanmar	Yangon	Burmese	Burmese	kyat
Mianmar	*Yangón*	*burmano,-a m,f*	*burmés*	*kyat m*
Namibia	Windhoek	Namibian	English, Afrikaans	Namibian dollar
Namibia	*Windhoek*	*namibio,-a m,f*	*inglés, africaans*	*dólar namibio m*
Nauru	Yaren District	Nauruan	English, Naurian	Australian dollar
Nauru	*Yaren*	*nauruano,-a m,f*	*inglés, nauruano*	*dólar austral m*
Nepal	Kathmandu	Nepalese/Nepali	Nepali	Nepali rupee
Nepal	*Katmandú*	*nepalés,-esa m,f/ nepalí mf*	*nepalí*	*rupia nepalí f*
Netherlands, the/ Holland	Amsterdam, The Hague (*seat of government*)	Dutchman, Dutchwoman/ Netherlander	Dutch	guilder
Países Bajos/ Holanda	*Amsterdam, La Haya (sede del gobierno)*	*holandés,-esa m,f/ neerlandés,-esa m,f*	*holandés*	*florín m*
Netherlands Antilles (Netherlands)	Willemstad	from Netherlands Antilles	Dutch	guilder
Antillas Holandesas (Holanda)	*Willemstad*	*de las Antillas Holandesas*	*holandés*	*florín m*
New Caledonia (France)	Nouméa	from New Caledonia	French	Pacific franc
Nueva Caledonia (Francia)	*Nouméa*	*de Nueva Caledonia*	*francés*	*franco del Pacífico m*

Countries and principal dependencies	Capital	Inhabitant	Official language(s)	Currency
Países y dependencias principales *	*Capital*	*Habitante* **	*Lengua(s) oficial(es)* ***	*Moneda*
New Zealand	Wellington	New Zealander	English, Maori	New Zealand dollar
Nueva Zelanda	*Wellington*	*neozelandés,-esa m,f*	*inglés, maorí*	*dólar neozelandés m*
Nicaragua	Managua	Nicaraguan	Spanish	córdoba
Nicaragua	*Managua*	*nicaragüense mf*	*español*	*córdoba m*
Niger	Niamey	Nigerien	French	CFA franc
Níger	*Niamey*	*nigerino,-a m,f*	*francés*	*franco CFA m*
Nigeria	Abuja	Nigerian	English	naira
Nigeria	*Abuja*	*nigerino,a m,f*	*inglés*	*naira nigeriana f*
Niue (New Zealand)	Alofi	from Niue	English	New Zealand dollar
Niue (Nueva Zelanda)	*Alofi*	*de Niue*	*inglés*	*dólar neozelandés m*
Norfolk Island (Australia)	Kingston	Norfolk Islander	English	Australian dollar
Norfolk (Australia)	*Kingston*	*de Norfolk*	*inglés*	*dólar australiano m*
North Korea/ Democratic People's Republic of Korea	Pyongyang	North Korean	Korean	won
Corea del Norte/ República Democrática Popular de Corea	*Piongyang*	*norcoreano,-a m,f*	*coreano*	*won m*
Northern Ireland	Belfast	from Northern Ireland	English	Sterling pound
Irlanda del Norte	*Belfast*	*de Irlanda del Norte*	*inglés*	*libra esterlina f*
Northern Marianas (US)	Chalan Kanoa	from Northern Marianas	English	US dollar
Islas Marianas (EE.UU.)	*Garapan*	*de las Islas Marianas*	*inglés*	*dólar americano m*
Norway	Oslo	Norse/Norwegian	Norwegian	Norwegian krone
Noruega	*Oslo*	*noruego,-a m,f*	*noruego*	*corona noruega f*
Oman	Muscat	Omani	Arabic	Omani rial
Omán	*Mascate*	*omaní mf*	*árabe*	*rial omaní m*
Pakistan	Islamabad	Pakistani	Urdu, English	Pakistan rupee
Paquistán/Pakistán	*Islamabad*	*paquistaní mf*	*urdu, inglés*	*rupia paquistaní f*
Palau (US)	Koror	Palavan	English, Sonsorolese-Tobian	US dollar
Palaos (EE.UU.)	*Koror*	*de Palaos*	*inglés, sonsorolese-tobiano*	*dólar americano m*
Panama	Panama City	Panamanian	Spanish	balboa
Panamá	*Panamá*	*panameño,-a m,f*	*español*	*balboa m*
Papua New Guinea	Port Moresby	Papua New Guinean, Papuan	English	kina
Papua Nueva Guinea	*Port Moresby*	*papuano,-a m,f/ papú mf*	*inglés*	*kina f*
Paraguay	Asunción	Paraguayan	Spanish	guaraní
Paraguay	*Asunción*	*paraguayo,-a m,f*	*español*	*guaraní paraguayo m*

Countries and principal dependencies	Capital	Inhabitant	Official language(s)	Currency
Países y dependencias principales *	*Capital*	*Habitante* **	*Lengua(s) oficial(es)* ***	*Moneda*
Peru	Lima	Peruvian	Spanish, Quechua	nuevo sol
Perú	*Lima*	*peruano,-a m,f*	*español, quechua*	*sol m*
Philippines	Manila	Filipino	Filipino, English	Philippine peso
Filipinas	*Manila*	*filipino,-a m,f*	*filipino, inglés*	*peso filipino m*
Pitcairn Islands (UK)	Adamstown	from Pitcairn	English	New Zealand dollar
Pitcairn (R.U.)	*Adamstown*	*de Pitcairn*	*inglés*	*dólar neozelandés m*
Poland	Warsaw	Pole	Polish	zloty
Polonia	*Varsovia*	*polonés,-esa m,f| polaco,-a m,f*	*polaco*	*zloty m*
Portugal	Lisbon	Portuguese	portuguese	escudo
Portugal	*Lisboa*	*portugués,-esa m,f*	*portugués*	*escudo m*
Puerto Rico (US)	San Juan	Puerto Rican	Spanish, English	US dollar
Puerto Rico (EE.UU.)	*San Juan*	*puertorriqueño,-a m,f*	*español, inglés*	*dólar americano m*
Qatar	Doha	Qatari	Arabic	Qatari riyal
Qatar/Katar	*Doha*	*qatarí/katarí mf*	*árabe*	*rial de Qatar m*
Réunion (France)	Saint-Denis	from Réunion	French, Creole	French franc
Reunión (Francia)	*Saint Denis*	*de Reunión*	*francés, criollo*	*franco francés m*
Romania/Rumania	Bucharest	Romanian/ Rumanian	Romanian	Romanian leu
Rumanía	*Bucarest*	*rumano,-a m,f*	*rumano*	*leu m*
Russia	Moscow	Russian	Russian	rouble
Rusia	*Moscú*	*ruso,-a m,f*	*ruso*	*rublo m*
Rwanda	Kigali	Rwandese/Rwandan	French, Kinyarwanda	Rwanda franc
Ruanda	*Kigali*	*ruandés,-esa m,f*	*francés, kinyaruanda*	*franco ruandés m*
St. Helena and dependencies (UK)	Jamestown	from St. Helena	English	Sterling pound
Santa Helena y dependencias (R.U.)	*Jamestown*	*de Santa Helena*	*inglés*	*libra esterlina f*
Saint Kitts and Nevis	Basseterre	Kittsian and Nevisian	English	East Caribbean dollar
Saint Kitts y Nevis	*Basseterre*	*de Saint Kitts y Nevis*	*inglés*	*dólar del Caribe Oriental m*
Saint Lucia	Castries	Saint Lucian	English	East Caribbean dollar
Santa Lucía	*Castries*	*santalucense mf*	*inglés*	*dólar del Caribe Oriental m*
St. Pierre and Miquelon (France)	St. Pierre	from St. Pierre	French	French franc
St. Pierre y Miquelon (Francia)	*St. Pierre*	*de St. Pierre*	*francés*	*franco francés m*

Countries and principal dependencies	Capital	Inhabitant	Official language(s)	Currency
Países y dependencias principales *	*Capital*	*Habitante ***	*Lengua(s) oficial(es) ****	*Moneda*
Saint Vincent and the Grenadines	Kingstown	St. Vincentian	English	East Caribbean dollar
San Vicente y Granadinas	*Kingstown*	*de San Vicente*	*inglés*	*dólar del Caribe Oriental m*
San Marino	San Marino	San Marinese	Italian	Italian lira, San Marino lira
San Marino	*San Marino*	*sanmarinense mfl sanmarinés,-esa m,f*	*italiano*	*lira italiana f, lira de San Marino f*
São Tomé and Principe	São Tomé	São Toméan	Portuguese	dobra
Santo Tomé y Principe	*Santo Tomé*	*santomense mf*	*portugués*	*dobra f*
Saudi Arabia	Riyadh	Saudi/Saudi Arabian	Arabic	Saudi riyal
Arabia Saudí	*Riyadh*	*saudí/árabe saudita mf*	*árabe*	*rial saudí m*
Scotland	Edinburgh	Scot/Scotsman, Scotswoman	English	Sterling pound
Escocia	*Edimburgo*	*escocés,-esa m,f*	*inglés*	*libra esterlina f*
Senegal	Dakar	Senegalese	French	CFA franc
Senegal	*Dakar*	*senegalés,-esa m,f*	*francés*	*franco CFA m*
Seychelles	Victoria	Seychellois	English, French, Creole	Seychelles rupee
Seychelles	*Victoria*	*de Seychelles*	*inglés, francés, criollo*	*rupia de Seychelles f*
Sierra Leone	Freetown	Sierra Leonean	English	leone
Sierra Leona	*Freetown*	*sierraleonense mfl sierraleonés,-esa m,f*	*inglés*	*leone m*
Singapore	Singapore	Singaporean	Chinese, Malay, English, Tamil	Singapore dollar
Singapore/Singapur	*Singapur*	*singapurense mf*	*chino, malayo, inglés, tamil*	*dólar de Singapur m*
Slovakia	Bratislava	Slovak	Slovak	Slovak koruna
Eslovaquia	*Bratislava*	*eslovaco,-a m,f*	*eslovaco*	*corona eslovaca f*
Slovenia	Ljubljana	Slovenian/Slovene	Slovenian	tolar
Eslovenia	*Lubliana*	*esloveno,-a m,f*	*esloveno*	*tólar m*
Solomon Islands	Honiara	Solomon islander	English	Solomon Islands dollar
Islas Salomón	*Honiara*	*de Islas Salomón*	*inglés*	*dólar de Salomón m*
Somalia	Mogadishu	Somali	Somali	Somali shilling
Somalia	*Mogadiscio*	*somalí mf*	*somalí*	*chelín somalí m*
South Africa	Pretoria (*administrative*), Cape Town (*legislative*)	South African	Afrikaans, English	South African rand
Sudáfrica/República Sudafricana	*Pretoria (administrativa), Ciudad del Cabo (legislativa)*	*sudafricano,-a m,f*	*afrikaans, inglés*	*rand sudafricano m*

Countries and principal dependencies	Capital	Inhabitant	Official language(s)	Currency
Países y dependencias principales *	*Capital*	*Habitante* **	*Lengua(s) oficial(es)* ***	*Moneda*
South Korea/ Republic of Korea/Korea	Seoul	South Korean	Korean	won
Corea del Sur/ República de Corea/Corea	*Seúl*	*surcoreano,-a m,f*	*coreano*	*won m*
Spain	Madrid	Spaniard	Spanish	peseta
España	*Madrid*	*español,a m,f*	*español*	*peseta f*
Sri Lanka	Colombo	Sri Lankan	Singhala, Tamil	Sri Lanka rupee
Sri Lanka	*Colombo*	*srilanqués,-esa m,f/ cingalés,-esa m,f*	*cingalés, tamil*	*rupia de Sri Lanka f*
Sudan	Khartoum	Sudanese	Arabic	Sudanese pound
Sudán	*Jartum*	*sudanés,-esa m,f*	*árabe*	*libra sudanesa f*
Suriname	Paramaribo	Surinamese	Dutch	Suriname guilder
Surinam	*Paramaribo*	*surinamés,-esa m,f/ surinamita mf*	*holandés*	*florín de Surinam m*
Svalbard (Norway)	Longyearbyen	from Svalbard	Norwegian, Russian	Norwegian krone
Svalbard (Noruega)	*Longyearbyen*	*de Svalbard*	*noruego, ruso*	*corona noruega f*
Swaziland	Mbabane	Swazi	Siswati, English	lilangeni
Swazilandia	*Mbabane*	*suazi mf/ swazilandés,-esa m,f*	*siswati, inglés*	*lilangeni m*
Sweden	Stockholm	Swede	Swedish	Swedish krona
Suecia	*Estocolmo*	*sueco,-a m,f*	*sueco*	*corona sueca f*
Switzerland	Bern	Swiss	French, German, Italian, Romansch	Swiss franc
Suiza	*Berna*	*suizo,-a m,f*	*francés, alemán, italiano, romanche*	*franco suizo m*
Syria	Damascus	Syrian	Arabic	Syrian pound
Siria	*Damasco*	*sirio,-a m,f*	*árabe*	*libra siria f*
Taiwan	Taipei	Taiwanese	Mandarin Chinese	New Taiwan dollar
Taiwán	*Taipei/Taipeh*	*taiwanés,-esa m,f*	*chino mandarín*	*nuevo dolár de Taiwán m*
Tajikistan	Dushanbe	Tajikistani	Tajik	rouble
Tayikistán	*Dushanbe*	*tayiko,-a m,f*	*tayiko*	*rublo m*
Tanzania	Dodoma	Tanzanian	Swahili, English	Tanzanian shilling
Tanzania	*Dodoma*	*tanzanés,-esa m,f/ tanzano,-a m,f*	*suahili, inglés*	*chelín de Tanzania m*
Thailand	Bangkok	Thai	Thai	baht
Tailandia	*Bangkok*	*tailandés,-esa m,f*	*tai*	*baht m*
Togo	Lomé	Togolese	French	CFA franc
Togo	*Lomé*	*togolés,-esa m,f*	*francés*	*franco CFA m*
Tonga	Nuku'alofa	Tongan	English, Tongan	pa'anga
Tonga	*Nuku'alofa*	*tongano,-a m,f*	*inglés, tongano*	*pa'anga m*

Countries and principal dependencies	Capital	Inhabitant	Official language(s)	Currency
Países y dependencias principales *	*Capital*	*Habitante* **	*Lengua(s) oficial(es)* ***	*Moneda*
Trinidad and Tobago	Port of Spain	Trinidadian/ Tobagoan/ Tobagodian	English	Trinidad and Tobago dollar
Trinidad y Tobago	*Puerto España*	*trinidense mf/de Trinidad y Tobago/ trinitario,-a m,f*	*inglés*	*dólar de Trinidad y Tobago m*
Tunisia	Tunis	Tunisian	Arabic	Tunisian dinar
Tunicia	*Túnez*	*tunecino,-a m,f*	*árabe*	*dinar tunecino m*
Turkey	Ankara	Turk	Turkish	Turkish lira
Turquía	*Ankara*	*turco,-a m,f*	*turco*	*lira turca f*
Turkmenistan	Ashkhabad	Turkmenistani	Turkmen, Russian	Turkmenian manat
Turkmenistán	*Asjabad*	*turkmeno,-a m,f*	*turkmeno, ruso*	*manat m*
Turks and Caicos Islands (UK)	Cockburn Town	from the Turks and Caicos Islands	English	US dollar
Turcas y Caicos (R.U.)	*Cockburn Town*	*de las Islas Turcas*	*inglés*	*dólar americano m*
Tuvalu	Funafuti	Tuvaluan	English, Tuvaluan	Australian dollar
Tuvalu	*Vaiaku*	*de Tuvalu*	*inglés, tuvalu*	*dólar australiano m*
Uganda	Kampala	Ugandan	English	New Uganda shilling
Uganda	*Kampala*	*ugandés,-esa m,f*	*inglés*	*nuevo chelín ugandés m*
Ukraine	Kiev	Ukrainian	Ukrainian, Russian	hryvnia
Ucrania	*Kiev*	*ucranio,-a m,f/ ucraniano,-a m,f*	*ucraniano, ruso*	*hryvnia m*
United Arab Emirates	Abu Dhabi	Emirian	Arabic	dirham
Emiratos Árabes Unidos/Unión de Emiratos Árabes	*Abu Dhabi*	*de los Emiratos Árabes Unidos*	*árabe*	*dirham m*
United Kingdom	London	Briton	English	Sterling pound
Reino Unido	*Londres*	*británico,-a m,f*	*inglés*	*libra esterlina f*
United States of America	Washington, D.C.	from the United States	English	US dollar
Estados Unidos de América	*Washington, D.C.*	*estadounidense mf*	*inglés*	*dólar americano m*
Uruguay	Montevideo	Uruguayan	Spanish	Uruguayan peso
Uruguay	*Montevideo*	*uruguayo,-a m,f*	*español*	*nuevo peso uruguayo m*
Uzbekistan	Tashkent	Uzbekistani	Uzbek	som
Uzbekistán	*Tashkent*	*uzbeko,-a m,f*	*uzbeko*	*som m*
Vanuatu	Port Vila	Vanuatuan	English, French, Bislama	vatu
Vanuatu	*Port Vila*	*de Vanuatu*	*inglés, francés, bislama*	*vatu m*
Venezuela	Caracas	Venezuelan	Spanish	bolívar
Venezuela	*Caracas*	*venezolano,-a m,f*	*español*	*bolívar m*

Countries and principal dependencies	Capital	Inhabitant	Official language(s)	Currency
Países y dependencias principales *	*Capital*	*Habitante* **	*Lengua(s) oficial(es)* ***	*Moneda*
Vietnam	Hanoi	Vietnamese	Vietnamese	dong
Vietnam	*Hanoi*	*vietnamita mf*	*vietnamita*	*dong m*
Virgin Islands (US)	Charlotte Amalie	from the Virgin Islands	English	US dollar
Islas Vírgenes (EE.UU.)	*Charlotte Amalie*	*de las Islas Vírgenes*	*inglés*	*dólar americano m*
Virgin Islands, British (UK)	Road Town	from the Virgin Islands	English	US dollar
Islas Vírgenes (R.U.)	*Road Town*	*de las Islas Vírgenes*	*inglés*	*dólar americano m*
Wales	Cardiff	Welshman, Welshwoman	English, Welsh	Sterling pound
País de Gales	*Cardiff*	*galés,-esa m,f*	*inglés, galés*	*libra esterlina f*
Wallis and Futuna Islands (France)	Mata-Utu	from Wallis and Fortuna	French, Uvean	French franc
Wallis y Futuna (Francia)	*Mata-Utu*	*de Wallis y Futuna*	*francés, uveano*	*franco francés m*
Western Sahara (Morocco)	Al-Aioun	Saharaui	Arabic	dirham
Sáhara Occidental (Marruecos)	*El Aaiún*	*saharaui mf*	*árabe*	*dirham m*
Western Samoa	Apia	Western Samoan	English, Samoan	tala
Samoa Occidental	*Apia*	*samoano,-a m,f*	*inglés, samoano*	*tala m*
Yemen	Sana'a (*administrative*), Aden (*commercial*)	Yemeni	Arabic	Yemeni riyal, dinar
Yemen, República del	*Sana'a (administrativa), Adén (comercial)*	*yemení mf*	*árabe*	*rial del Yemen m, dinar yemení m*
Yugoslavia, Federal Republic of	Belgrade	Yugoslavian	Serbian	dinar
Yugoslavia, República Federal de	*Belgrado*	*yugoslavo,-a m,f*	*serbio*	*dinar m*
Zaïre	Kinshasa	Zaïrese/Zairean	French	zaïre
Zaire	*Kinshasa*	*zairense mfl zaireño,-a m,f*	*francés*	*zaïre m*
Zambia	Lusaka	Zambian	English	kwacha
Zambia	*Lusaka*	*zambiano,-a m,f*	*inglés*	*kwacha de Zambia m*
Zimbabwe	Harare	Zimbabwean	English	Zimbabwe dollar
Zimbabwe/ Zimbabue	*Harare*	*zimbabuense mfl zimbabuo,-a m,f*	*inglés*	*dólar de Zimbabwe m*

*Controlling countries of dependencies and colonies are shown in brackets/Las dependencias y colonias llevan en paréntesis el país del que dependen

**Where no name exists for the inhabitant of a country, the form '(to be) from + country/dependency' is used in place of the noun/Cuando no existe un gentilicio, se utiliza la forma '(ser) de + nombre del país o dependencia'

***All official languages listed in this table are given in the masculine form/Todas las lenguas oficiales de este listado aparecen en masculino

Time zones/Husos horarios

English name	Spanish name
Nombre inglés	*Nombre español*
British Standard Time	hora británica *f*
British Summer Time	horario de verano británico *m*
Central European Time	hora centroeuropea *f*
Central Standard Time	hora central establecida *f*
coordinated universal time	hora universal coordinada *f*
Eastern European Time	horario de Europa Oriental *m*
Eastern Standard Time	hora del meridiano 75 al oeste de Greenwich *f*
Greenwich Mean Time	hora media de Greenwich *f,* hora del meridiano de Greenwich *f*
international time differences	diferencias horarias internacionales *f pl*
international time zone	huso horario internacional *m*
local time	hora local *f*
Mountain Standard Time	hora de las Montañas Rocosas *f*
Pacific Standard Time	hora de la Costa Oeste *f*